Collins

Collins
Italian
Dictionary

William Collins' dream of knowledge
for all began with the publication of
his first book in 1819. A self-educated
mill worker, he not only enriched
millions of lives, but also founded a
flourishing publishing house. Today,
staying true to this spirit, Collins books
are packed with inspiration, innovation,
and practical expertise.
They place you at the centre of a world
of possibility and give you exactly what
you need to explore it.

Language is the key to this exploration,
and at the heart of Collins Dictionaries
is language as it is really used. New
words, phrases, and meanings spring
up every day, and all of them are
captured and analysed by the Collins
Word Web. Constantly updated, and
with over 2.5 billion entries, this living
language resource is unique to our
dictionaries.

Words are tools for life. And a Collins
Dictionary makes them work for you.

Collins. Do more.

Collins

Collins
Italian
Dictionary

HarperCollins Publishers
Westerhill Road
Bishopbriggs
Glasgow
G64 2QT
Great Britain

Third Edition 2006

Reprint 10 9 8 7 6 5 4

© HarperCollins Publishers 2000, 2005, 2006

ISBN-13 978-0-00-722390-9
ISBN-10 0-00-722390-0

www.collins.co.uk

A catalogue record for this book is available from the British Library

HarperCollins Publishers, 10 East 53rd Street, New York, NY 10022

COLLINS ITALIAN CONCISE DICTIONARY.
Fourth US Edition 2005

ISBN-13 978-0-06-078732-5
ISBN-10 0-06-078732-5

Library of Congress Cataloging-in-Publication Data has been applied for

www.harpercollins.com

HarperCollins books may be purchased for educational, business, or sales promotional use. For information, please write to: Special Markets Department, HarperCollins Publishers, 10 East 53rd Street, New York, NY 10022

Typeset by Morton Word Processing Ltd, Scarborough

Printed in Italy by Legoprint S.p.A

Acknowledgements
We would like to thank those authors and publishers who kindly gave permission for copyright material to be used in the Collins Word Web. We would also like to thank Times Newspapers Ltd for providing valuable data.

INDICE

CONTENTS

Catherine E. Love • Michela Clari

with/hanno collaborato
Gabriella Bacchelli • Elizabeth Potter • Donatella Boi
Angela Jack • Daphne Day

editorial staff/segreteria di redazione
Joyce Littlejohn • Megan Thomson • Isobel Gordon
Elspeth Anderson • Anne Convery • Anne Marie Banks

series editor/collana a cura di
Lorna Sinclair Knight

editorial management/coordinamento redazionale
Vivian Marr

I marchi registrati

I termini che a nostro parere
costituiscono un marchio registrato
sono stati designati come tali. In ogni
caso, né la presenza né l'assenza di tale
designazione implicano alcuna
valutazione del loro reale stato
giuridico.

Note on trademarks

Words which we have reason to believe
constitute trademarks have been
designated as such. However, neither
the presence nor the absence of such
designation should be regarded as
affecting the legal status of any
trademark.

INTRODUZIONE

Se desiderate imparare l'inglese o approfondire le conoscenze già acquisite, se volete leggere o redigere dei testi in inglese, oppure conversare con interlocutori di madrelingua inglese, se siete studenti, turisti, uomini o donne d'affari avete scelto il compagno di viaggio ideale per esprimervi e comunicare in inglese sia a voce che per iscritto. Strumento pratico e moderno, il vostro dizionario dà largo spazio al linguaggio quotidiano in campi quali l'attualità, gli affari, la gestione d'ufficio, l'informatica e il turismo. Come in tutti i nostri dizionari, grande importanza è stata data alla lingua contemporanea e alle espressioni idiomatiche.

COME USARE IL DIZIONARIO

Troverete qui di seguito alcune spiegazioni sul modo in cui le informazioni sono state presentate nel testo. L'obiettivo del dizionario è quello di darvi il maggior numero possibile di informazioni senza tuttavia sacrificare la chiarezza all'interno delle voci.

Le voci

Qui di seguito verranno descritti i vari elementi di cui si compone una voce tipo del vostro dizionario.

La trascrizione fonetica

Come regola generale è stata data la pronuncia di tutte le parole inglesi e quella delle parole italiane che potevano presentare qualche difficoltà per il parlante inglese. Nella parte inglese-italiano, tuttavia, per la pronuncia di nomi composti formati da due parole non unite dal trattino si dovrà cercare la trascrizione di ciascuna di queste parole alla rispettiva posizione alfabetica. La pronuncia si trova tra parentesi quadra, subito dopo il lemma. Come nella maggior parte dei dizionari moderni è stato adottato il sistema noto come "alfabeto fonetico internazionale". Troverete qui di seguito, a pagina xiii e xiv, un elenco completo dei caratteri utilizzati in questo sistema.

La categorie grammaticali

Tutte le parole appartengono ad una categoria grammaticale, cioè possono essere sostantivi, verbi, aggettivi, avverbi, pronomi, articoli, congiunzioni o abbreviazioni. I sostantivi possono essere singolari o plurali, sia in italiano che in inglese, e maschili o femminili in italiano. I verbi possono essere transitivi o intransitivi in entrambe le lingue, ma anche riflessivi o impersonali in italiano. La categoria grammaticale è stata introdotta in *corsivo* subito dopo la pronuncia ed eventuali informazioni di tipo morfologico (plurali irregolari ecc.).

Numerose voci sono state suddivise in varie categorie grammaticali. Per esempio la parola italiana **bene** può essere sia un avverbio che un aggettivo o un sostantivo, e la parola inglese **sneeze** può essere sia un sostantivo (starnuto) che un verbo intransitivo (starnutire). Analogamente il verbo italiano **correre** può essere usato sia come verbo intransitivo ("correre alla stazione") che come transitivo ("correre un rischio"). Per presentare la voce con maggiore chiarezza e permettervi di trovare rapidamente la traduzione che cercate, è stato introdotto il simbolo ♦ per contrassegnare il passaggio da una categoria grammaticale ad un'altra.

Suddivisioni semantiche

La maggior parte delle parole ha più di un significato. Per esempio, la parola **fiocco** può essere sia un'annodatura di un nastro che una falda di neve. Molte parole si traducono in modo diverso a seconda del contesto in cui sono usate: per esempio **scala** si tradurrà in inglese con "staircase" o "stairs" se si tratta di una scala con gradini, con "ladder" se è una scala a pioli. Per permettervi di scegliere la traduzione giusta per ciascuno dei contesti in cui la parola si può trovare, le voci sono state suddivise in categorie di significato. Ciascuna suddivisione è introdotta da un "indicatore d'uso" tra parentesi in *corsivo*. Le voci **fiocco** e **scala** compariranno quindi nel testo nel modo seguente:

fiocco, chi *sm (di nastro)* bow; *(di stoffa, lana)* flock; *(di neve)* flake
scala *sf (a gradini etc)* staircase, stairs pl; *(a pioli, di corda)* ladder

Per segnalare la traduzione appropriata sono stati introdotti anche degli indicatori d'ambito d'uso in CORSIVO MAIUSCOLO tra parentesi, spesso in forma abbreviata, come per esempio nel caso della voce **tromba**:

tromba *sf (MUS)* trumpet; *(AUT)* horn

Troverete un elenco completo delle abbreviazioni adottate all'interno del dizionario alle pp x, xi, xii.

Le traduzioni

Per la maggior parte delle parole inglesi ed italiane ci sono traduzioni precise a seconda del significato o del contesto, come risulta dagli esempi riportati fin qui. A volte, tuttavia, le parole non hanno un preciso equivalente nella lingua d'arrivo: in questi casi è stato fornito un equivalente approssimativo, preceduto dal segno ≈, come ad esempio per l'abbreviazione **RAC**, per cui è stato dato l'equivalente italiano "A.C.I.", dato che le due associazioni svolgono nei due paesi funzioni analoghe:

RAC *n abbr (BRIT.* = *Royal Automobile Club)* ≈ *A.C.I.* m (= *Automobile Club d' Italia)*

A volte è persino impossibile trovare un equivalente approssimativo. Questo è il caso, per esempio, di piatti tipici di un certo paese, come ad esempio **pandoro**:

pandoro *sm type of sponge cake eaten at Christmas*

In questi casi, al posto della traduzione, che non esiste, comparirà una spiegazione: per maggiore chiarezza questa spiegazione o glossa è stata messa in *corsivo*.

Molto spesso la traduzione di una parola può non funzionare all'interno di una data locuzione. Ad esempio alla voce **dare**, verbo spesso tradotto con "to give" in inglese, troviamo varie locuzioni per alcune delle quali la traduzione fornita all'inizio della voce non si può utilizzare: **quanti anni mi dai?** "how old do you think I am?" **danno ancora quel film?** "is that film still showing?", **dare per certo qc** "to consider sth certain", e così via. Ed è proprio in questi casi che potrete verificare l'utilità e la completezza del dizionario, che contiene una ricca gamma di composti, locuzioni e frasi idiomatiche.

Il registro linguistico

In italiano sapete istintivamente scegliere l'espressione corretta da usare a seconda del contesto in cui vi esprimete. Per esempio saprete quando dire **Non me ne importa!** e quando invece potete dire **Chi se ne frega?** Più difficile sarà farlo in inglese, dove avete minore consapevolezza delle sfumature di registro linguistico. Per questo motivo nella parte inglese-italiano le parole ed espressioni inglesi di uso più familiare sono segnalate dall'abbreviazione *(col)*, mentre *(col!)* segnala le parole ed espressioni volgari. Nella parte italiano-inglese (*!*) dopo una traduzione segnala che si tratta di una parola od espressione volgare.

Parole chiave

Come vedrete, ad alcune voci è stato riservato un trattamento particolare sia dal punto di vista grafico che da quello linguistico. Si tratta di voci come **essere** o **fare**, o dei loro equivalenti inglesi **be** e **do**, che per la loro importanza e complessità meritano una strutturazione più articolata ed un maggior numero di locuzioni illustrative. Queste voci sono strutturate in diverse categorie di significato contrassegnate da numeri, e le costruzioni sintattiche e locuzioni che illustrano quel particolare significato sono riportate all'interno della relativa categoria.

Informazioni culturali

Le voci che compaiono nel testo delimitate da due linee approfondiscono aspetti della cultura italiana o di quella dei paesi di lingua inglese in argomenti quali la politica, la scuola, i mass media e le festività nazionali.

INTRODUCTION

You may be starting to learn Italian, or you may wish to extend your knowledge of the language. Perhaps you want to read and study Italian books, newspapers and magazines, or perhaps simply have a conversation with Italian speakers. Whatever the reason, whether you're a student, a tourist or want to use Italian for business, this is the ideal book to help you understand and communicate. This modern, user-friendly dictionary gives priority to everyday vocabulary and the language of current affairs, business and tourism. As in all Collins dictionaries, the emphasis is firmly placed on contemporary language and expressions.

HOW TO USE THE DICTIONARY

Below you will find an outline of how information is presented in your dictionary. Our aim is to give you the maximum amount of detail in the clearest and most helpful way.

Entries

A typical entry in your dictionary will be made up of the following elements:

Phonetic transcription

Phonetics appear in square brackets immediately after the headword. They are shown using the International Phonetic Alphabet (IPA), and a complete list of the symbols used in this system can be found on pages xiii and xiv.

Grammatical information

All words belong to one of the following parts of speech: noun, verb, adjective, adverb, pronoun, article, conjunction, preposition, abbreviation. Nouns can be singular or plural and, in Italian, masculine or feminine. Verbs can be transitive, intransitive, reflexive or impersonal. Parts of speech appear in *italics* immediately after the phonetic spelling of the headword.

Often a word can have more than one part of speech. Just as the English word **chemical** can be an adjective or a noun, the Italian word **fondo** can be an adjective ("deep") or a masculine noun ("bottom"). In the same way the verb **to walk** is sometimes transitive, ie it takes an object ("to walk the dog") and sometimes intransitive, ie it doesn't take an object ("to walk to school"). To help you find the meaning you are looking for quickly and for clarity of presentation, the different part of speech categories are separated by a black lozenge ♦.

Meaning divisions

Most words have more than one meaning. Take, for example, **punch** which can be, amongst other things, a blow with the fist or an object used for making holes. Other words are translated differently depending on the context in which they are used. The transitive verb **to roll up**, for example, can be translated by "arrotolare" or "rimboccare" depending on *what* it is you are rolling up. To help you select the most appropriate translation in every context, entries are divided according to meaning. Each different meaning is introduced by an "indicator" in *italics* and in brackets. Thus, the examples given above will be shown as follows:

> **punch** n (*blow*) pugno; (*tool*) punzone m
> **roll up** vt (*carpet, cloth, map*) arrotolare; (*sleeves*) rimboccare

Likewise, some words can have a different meaning when used to talk about a specific subject area or field. For example, **bishop**, which is generally used to mean a high-ranking clergyman, is also the name of a chess piece. To show English speakers which translation to use, we have added "subject field labels" in capitals and in brackets, in this case (*CHESS*):

bishop *n* vescovo; (*CHESS*) alfiere *m*

Field labels are often shortened to save space. You will find a complete list of abbreviations used in the dictionary on pages x, xi, xii.

Translations

Most English words have a direct translation in Italian and vice versa, as shown in the examples given above. Sometimes, however, no exact equivalent exists in the target language. In such cases we have given an approximate equivalent, indicated by the sign ≈. Such is the case of **National Insurance**, the Italian equivalent of which is "Previdenza Sociale". This is not an exact translation since the systems of the two countries in question are quite different:

National Insurance *n* (*BRIT*) ≈ Previdenza Sociale

On occasion it is impossible to find even an approximate equivalent. This may be the case, for example, with the names of types of food:

cottage pie *n piatto a base di carne macinata in sugo e purè di patate*

Here the translation (which doesn't exist) is replaced by an explanation. For increased clarity the explanation, or "gloss", is shown in *italics*.

It is often the case that a word, or a particular meaning of a word, cannot be translated in isolation. The translation of **Dutch**, for example, is "olandese". However, the phrase **to go Dutch** is rendered by "fare alla romana". Even an expression as simple as **washing powder** needs a separate translation since it translates as "detersivo (in polvere)", not "polvere per lavare". This is where your dictionary will prove to be particularly informative and useful since it contains an abundance of compounds, phrases and idiomatic expressions.

Levels of formality and familiarity

In English you instinctively know when to say **I'm broke** *or* **I'm a bit short of cash** and when to say **I don't have any money**. When you are trying to understand someone who is speaking Italian, however, or when you yourself try to speak Italian, it is important to know what is polite and what is less so, and what you can say in a relaxed situation but not in a formal context. To help you with this, on the Italian-English side we have added the label (*fam*) to show that an Italian word or expression is colloquial, while those word or expressions which are vulgar are given an exclamation mark (*fam!*), warning you they can cause serious offence. Note also that on the English-Italian side, translations which are vulgar are followed by an exclamation mark in brackets.

Keywords

Words labelled in the text as *KEYWORDS*, such as **be** and **do** or their Italian equivalents **essere** and **fare**, have been given special treatment because they form the basic elements of the language. This extra help will ensure that you know how to use these complex words with confidence.

Cultural information

Entries which appear separated from the main text by a line above and below them explain aspects of culture in Italy and English-speaking countries. Subject areas covered include politics, education, media and national festivals.

ABBREVIAZIONI

ABBREVIATIONS

abbreviazione	**abbr**	abbreviation
aggettivo	**adj**	adjective
amministrazione	**ADMIN**	administration
avverbio	**adv**	adverb
aeronautica, viaggi aerei	**AER**	flying, air travel
aggettivo	**ag**	adjective
agricoltura	**AGR**	agriculture
amministrazione	**AMM**	administration
anatomia	**ANAT**	anatomy
architettura	**ARCHIT**	architecture
astronomia, astrologia	**ASTR**	astronomy, astrology
l'automobile	**AUT**	the motor car and motoring
verbo ausiliare	**aux vb**	auxiliary verb
avverbio	**av**	adverb
aeronautica, viaggi aerei	**AVIAT**	flying, air travel
biologia	**BIOL**	biology
botanica	**BOT**	botany
inglese della Gran Bretagna	**BRIT**	British English
consonante	**C**	consonant
chimica	**CHIM, CHEM**	chemistry
familiare (! da evitare)	**col(!)**	colloquial usage (! particularly offensive)
commercio, finanza, banca	**COMM**	commerce, finance, banking
informatica	**COMPUT**	computing
congiunzione	**cong**	conjunction
congiunzione	**conj**	conjunction
edilizia	**CONSTR**	building
sostantivo usato come aggettivo, non può essere usato né come attributo, né dopo il sostantivo qualificato	**cpd**	compound element: noun used as adjective and which cannot follow the noun it qualifies
cucina	**CUC, CULIN**	cookery
davanti a	**dav**	before
determinante: articolo, aggettivo dimostrativo o indefinito etc	**det**	determiner: article, demonstrative etc
diritto	**DIR**	law
economia	**ECON**	economics
edilizia	**EDIL**	building
elettricità, elettronica	**ELETTR, ELEC**	electricity, electronics
esclamazione, interiezione	**escl, excl**	exclamation, interjection
specialmente	**esp**	especially
femminile	**f**	feminine
familiare (! da evitare)	**fam(!)**	colloquial usage (! particularly offensive)
ferrovia	**FERR**	railways
figurato	**fig**	figurative use
fisiologia	**FISIOL**	physiology
fotografia	**FOT**	photography
(verbo inglese) la cui particella è inseparabile dal verbo	**fus**	(phrasal verb) where the particle cannot be separated from main verb
nella maggior parte dei sensi; generalmente	**gen**	in most or all senses; generally
geografia, geologia	**GEO**	geography, geology
geometria	**GEOM**	geometry
impersonale	**impers**	impersonal

xi

informatica	INFORM	computing
insegnamento, sistema scolastico e universitario	INS	schooling, schools and universities
invariabile	inv	invariable
irregolare	irreg	irregular
grammatica, linguistica	LING	grammar, linguistics
maschile	m	masculine
matematica	MAT(H)	mathematics
termine medico, medicina	MED	medical term, medicine
il tempo, meteorologia	METEOR	the weather, meteorology
maschile o femminile	m/f	either masculine or feminine depending on sex
esercito, linguaggio militare	MIL	military matters
musica	MUS	music
sostantivo	n	noun
nautica	NAUT	sailing, navigation
sostantivo che non si usa al plurale	no pl	uncountable noun: not used in the plural
numerale (aggettivo, sostantivo)	num	numeral adjective or noun
	o.s.	oneself
peggiorativo	peg, pej	derogatory, pejorative
fotografia	PHOT	photography
fisiologia	PHYSIOL	physiology
plurale	pl	plural
politica	POL	politics
participio passato	pp	past participle
preposizione	prep	preposition
pronome	pron	pronoun
psicologia, psichiatria	PSIC, PSYCH	psychology, psychiatry
tempo passato	pt	past tense
qualcosa	qc	
qualcuno	qn	
religione, liturgia	REL	religions, church service
sostantivo	s	noun
	sb	somebody
insegnamento, sistema scolastico e universitario	SCOL	schooling, schools and universities
singolare	sg	singular
soggetto (grammaticale)	sog	(grammatical) subject
	sth	something
congiuntivo	sub	subjunctive
soggetto (grammaticale)	subj	(grammatical) subject
termine tecnico, tecnologia	TECN, TECH	technical term, technology
telecomunicazioni	TEL	telecommunications
tipografia	TIP	typography, printing
televisione	TV	television
tipografia	TYP	typography, printing
inglese degli Stati Uniti	US	American English
vocale	V	vowel
verbo (ausiliare)	vb (aus)	(auxiliary) verb
verbo o gruppo verbale con funzione intransitiva	vi	verb or phrasal verb used intransitively
verbo riflessivo	vr	reflexive verb
verbo o gruppo verbale con funzione transitiva	vt	verb or phrasal verb used transitively
zoologia	ZOOL	zoology
marchio registrato	®	registered trademark
introduce un'equivalenza culturale	≈	introduces a cultural equivalent

TRASCRIZIONE FONETICA

Consonanti		Consonants

NB. **p, b, t, d, k, g** sono seguite da un'aspirazione in inglese.

NB. **p, b, t, d, k, g** are not aspirated in Italian.

Italiano	IPA	English
<u>p</u>adre	p	<u>p</u>u<u>pp</u>y
<u>b</u>am<u>b</u>ino	b	<u>b</u>a<u>b</u>y
<u>tutt</u>o	t	<u>t</u>en<u>t</u>
<u>d</u>a<u>d</u>o	d	<u>d</u>a<u>dd</u>y
<u>c</u>ane <u>ch</u>e	k	<u>c</u>or<u>k</u> <u>k</u>iss <u>ch</u>ord
gola <u>gh</u>iro	g	<u>g</u>ag <u>g</u>uess
<u>s</u>ano	s	<u>s</u>o ri<u>c</u>e ki<u>ss</u>
<u>s</u>vago e<u>s</u>ame	z	cou<u>s</u>in bu<u>zz</u>
<u>sc</u>ena	ʃ	<u>sh</u>eep <u>s</u>ugar
	ʒ	plea<u>s</u>ure bei<u>g</u>e
pe<u>c</u>e lan<u>c</u>iare	tʃ	<u>ch</u>ur<u>ch</u>
giro <u>g</u>ioco	dʒ	<u>j</u>ud<u>g</u>e general
a<u>f</u>a <u>f</u>aro	f	<u>f</u>arm ra<u>ff</u>le
<u>v</u>ero bra<u>v</u>o	v	<u>v</u>ery re<u>v</u>
	θ	<u>th</u>in ma<u>th</u>s
	ð	<u>th</u>at o<u>th</u>er
<u>l</u>etto a<u>l</u>a	l	<u>l</u>itt<u>l</u>e ba<u>ll</u>
<u>gl</u>i	ʎ	
<u>r</u>ete a<u>r</u>co	r	<u>r</u>at b<u>r</u>at
ra<u>m</u>o <u>m</u>adre	m	<u>m</u>u<u>mm</u>y co<u>mb</u>
<u>n</u>o fuma<u>n</u>te	n	<u>n</u>o ra<u>n</u>
<u>gn</u>omo	ɲ	
	ŋ	si<u>ng</u>ing ba<u>n</u>k
	h	<u>h</u>at re<u>h</u>eat
bu<u>i</u>o p<u>i</u>acere	j	<u>y</u>et
<u>u</u>omo g<u>u</u>aio	w	<u>w</u>all be<u>w</u>ail
	x	lo<u>ch</u>

Varie		Miscellaneous

per l'inglese: la "r" finale viene pronunciata se seguita da una vocale | * |

precede la sillaba accentata | ' | precedes the stressed syllable

Come regola generale, in tutte le voci la trascrizione fonetica in parentesi quadra segue il termine cui si riferisce. Tuttavia, dalla parte inglese-italiano del dizionario, per la pronuncia di composti che sono formati da più parole non unite da trattino che appaiono comunque nel dizionario, si veda la trascrizione fonetica di ciascuna di queste parole alla rispettiva posizione alfabetica.

PHONETIC TRANSCRIPTION

Vocali

NB. La messa in equivalenza di certi suoni indica solo una rassomiglianza approssimativa.

Vowels

NB. The pairing of some vowel sounds only indicates approximate equivalence.

vino idea	i iː	heel bead
	ɪ	hit pity
stella edera	e	
epoca eccetto	ɛ	set tent
mamma amore	a æ	apple bat
	ɑː	after car calm
	ʌ	fun cousin
	ə	over above
	əː	urn fern work
rosa occhio	ɔ	wash pot
	ɔː	born cork
ponte ognuno	o	
utile zucca	u	full soot
	uː	boon lewd

Dittonghi

Diphthongs

	ɪə	beer tier
	ɛə	tear fair there
	eɪ	date plaice day
	aɪ	life buy cry
	au	owl foul now
	əu	low no
	ɔɪ	boil boy oily
	uə	poor tour

In general, we give the pronunciation of each entry in square brackets after the word in question. However, on the English-Italian side, where the entry is composed of two or more unhyphenated words, each of which is given elsewhere in this dictionary, you will find the pronunciation of each word in its alphabetical position.

ITALIAN PRONUNCIATION

Vowels

Where the vowel **e** or the vowel **o** appears in a stressed syllable it can be either open [ɛ], [ɔ] or closed [e], [o]. As the open or closed pronunciation of these vowels is subject to regional variation, the distinction is of little importance to the user of this dictionary. Phonetic transcription for headwords containing these vowels will therefore only appear where other pronunciation difficulties are present.

Consonants

c before "e" or "i" is pronounced *tch*.

ch is pronounced like the "k" in "kit".

g before "e" or "i" is pronounced like the "j" in "jet".

gh is pronounced like the "g" in "get".

gl before "e" or "i" is normally pronounced like the "lli" in "million", and in a few cases only like the "gl" in "glove".

gn is pronounced like the "ny" in "canyon".

sc before "e" or "i" is pronounced *sh*.

z is pronounced like the "ts" in "stetson", or like the "d's" in "bird's-eye".

Headwords containing the above consonants and consonantal groups have been given full phonetic transcription in this dictionary.

NB. All double written consonants in Italian are fully sounded: e.g. the *tt* in "tutto" is pronounced as in "ha*t t*rick".

ITALIAN VERBS

1 Gerundio *2* Participio passato *3* Presente *4* Imperfetto *5* Passato remoto *6* Futuro
7 Condizionale *8* Congiuntivo presente *9* Congiuntivo passato *10* Imperativo

accadere *like* **cadere**
accedere *like* **concedere**
accendere *2* acceso *5* accesi, accendesti
accludere *like* **alludere**
accogliere *like* **cogliere**
accondiscendere *like* **scendere**
accorgersi *like* **scorgere**
accorrere *like* **correre**
accrescere *like* **crescere**
addirsi *like* **dire**
addurre *like* **ridurre**
affiggere *2* affisso *5* affissi, affiggesti
affliggere *2* afflitto *5* afflissi, affliggesti
aggiungere *like* **giungere**
alludere *2* alluso *5* allusi, alludesti
ammettere *like* **mettere**
andare *3* vado, vai, va, andiamo, andate, vanno *6* andrò *etc* *8* vada *10* va'!, vada!, andate!, vadano!
annettere *2* annesso *5* annessi *o* annettei, annettesti
apparire *2* apparso *3* appaio, appari *o* apparisci, appare *o* apparisce, appaiono *o* appariscono *5* apparvi *o* apparsi, appa-risti, apparve *o* apparì *o* apparse, appar-vero *o* apparirono *o* apparsero *8* appaia *o* apparisca
appartenere *like* **tenere**
appendere *2* appeso *5* appesi, appendesti
apporre *like* **porre**
apprendere *like* **prendere**
aprire *2* aperto *3* apro *5* aprii *o* apersi, apristi *8* apra
ardere *2* arso *5* arsi, ardesti
ascendere *like* **scendere**
aspergere *2* asperso *5* aspersi, aspergesti
assalire *like* **salire**
assistere *2* assistito
assolvere *2* assolto *5* assolsi *o* assolvei *o* assolvetti, assolvesti
assumere *2* assunto *5* assunsi, assumesti
astenersi *like* **tenere**
attendere *like* **tendere**
attingere *like* **tingere**
AVERE *3* ho, hai, ha, abbiamo, avete, han-no *5* ebbi, avesti, ebbe, avemmo, aveste, ebbero *6* avrò *etc* *8* abbia *etc* *10* abbi!, ab-bia!, abbiate!, abbiano!
avvedersi *like* **vedere**
avvenire *like* **venire**
avvincere *like* **vincere**
avvolgere *like* **volgere**
benedire *like* **dire**
bere *1* bevendo *2* bevuto *3* bevo *etc* *4* beve-vo *etc* *5* bevvi *o* bevetti, bevesti *6* berrò *etc* *8* beva *etc* *9* bevessi *etc*

cadere *5* caddi, cadesti *6* cadrò *etc*
chiedere *2* chiesto *5* chiesi, chiedesti
chiudere *2* chiuso *5* chiusi, chiudesti
cingere *2* cinto *5* cinsi, cingesti
cogliere *2* colto *3* colgo, colgono *5* colsi, cogliesti *8* colga
coincidere *2* coinciso *5* coincisi, coincide-sti
coinvolgere *like* **volgere**
commettere *like* **mettere**
commuovere *like* **muovere**
comparire *like* **apparire**
compiacere *like* **piacere**
compiangere *like* **piangere**
comporre *like* **porre**
comprendere *like* **prendere**
comprimere *2* compresso *5* compressi, comprimesti
compromettere *like* **mettere**
concedere *2* concesso *o* conceduto *5* con-cessi *o* concedei *o* concedetti, concedesti
concludere *like* **alludere**
concorrere *like* **correre**
condurre *like* **ridurre**
confondere *like* **fondere**
congiungere *like* **giungere**
connettere *like* **annettere**
conoscere *2* conosciuto *5* conobbi, cono-scesti
consistere *like* **assistere**
contendere *like* **tendere**
contenere *like* **tenere**
contorcere *like* **torcere**
contraddire *like* **dire**
contraffare *like* **fare**
contrarre *like* **trarre**
convenire *like* **venire**
convincere *like* **vincere**
coprire *like* **aprire**
correggere *like* **reggere**
correre *2* corso *5* corsi, corresti
corrispondere *like* **rispondere**
corrompere *like* **rompere**
costringere *like* **stringere**
costruire *5* costrussi, costruisti
crescere *2* cresciuto *5* crebbi, crescesti
cuocere *2* cotto *3* cuocio, cociamo, cuocio-no *5* cossi, cocesti
dare *3* do, dai, dà, diamo, date, danno *5* diedi *o* detti, desti *6* darò *etc* *8* dia *etc* *9* dessi *etc* *10* da'!, dai!, date!, diano!
decidere *2* deciso *5* decisi, decidesti
decrescere *like* **crescere**
dedurre *like* **ridurre**

deludere *like* alludere
deporre *like* porre
deprimere *like* comprimere
deridere *like* ridere
descrivere *like* scrivere
desumere *like* assumere
detergere *like* tergere
devolvere 2 devoluto
difendere 2 difeso 5 difesi, difendesti
diffondere *like* fondere
dipendere *like* appendere
dipingere *like* tingere
dire *1* dicendo *2* detto *3* dico, dici, dice, diciamo, dite, dicono *4* dicevo *etc 5* dissi, dicesti *6* dirò *etc 8* dica, diciamo, diciate, dicano *9* dicessi *etc 10* di'!, dica!, dite!, dicano!
dirigere 2 diretto 5 diressi, dirigesti
discendere *like* scendere
dischiudere *like* chiudere
disciogliere *like* sciogliere
discorrere *like* correre
discutere 2 discusso 5 discussi, discutesti
disfare *like* fare
disilludere *like* alludere
disperdere *like* perdere
dispiacere *like* piacere
disporre *like* porre
dissolvere 2 dissolto *o* dissoluto 5 dissolsi *o* dissolvetti *o* dissolvei, dissolvesti
dissuadere *like* persuadere
distendere *like* tendere
distinguere 2 distinto 5 distinsi, distinguesti
distogliere *like* togliere
distrarre *like* trarre
distruggere *like* struggere
divenire *like* venire
dividere 2 diviso 5 divisi, dividesti
dolere *3* dolgo, duoli, duole, dolgono *5* dolsi, dolesti *6* dorrò *etc 8* dolga
DORMIRE *1* GERUNDIO dormendo
2 PARTICIPIO PASSATO dormito
3 PRESENTE dormo, dormi, dorme, dormiamo, dormite, dormono
4 IMPERFETTO dormivo, dormivi, dormiva, dormivamo, dormivate, dormivano
5 PASSATO REMOTO dormii, dormisti, dormì, dormimmo, dormiste, dormirono
6 FUTURO dormirò, dormirai, dormirà, dormiremo, dormirete, dormiranno
7 CONDIZIONALE dormirei, dormiresti, dormirebbe, dormiremmo, dormireste, dormirebbero
8 CONGIUNTIVO PRESENTE dorma, dorma, dorma, dormiamo, dormiate, dormano
9 CONGIUNTIVO PASSATO dormissi, dormissi, dormisse, dormissimo, dormiste, dormissero
10 IMPERATIVO dormi!, dorma!, dormite!, dormano!
dovere *3* devo *o* debbo, devi, deve, dobbiamo, dovete, devono *o* debbono *6* dovrò *etc*

8 debba, dobbiamo, dobbiate, devano *o* debbano
eccellere 2 eccelso 5 eccelsi, eccellesti
eludere *like* alludere
emergere 2 emerso 5 emersi, emergesti
emettere *like* mettere
erigere *like* dirigere
escludere *like* alludere
esigere 2 esatto
esistere 2 esistito
espellere 2 espulso 5 espulsi, espellesti
esplodere 2 esploso 5 esplosi, esplodesti
esporre *like* porre
esprimere *like* comprimere
ESSERE 2 stato 3 sono, sei, è, siamo, siete, sono 4 ero, eri, era, eravamo, eravate, erano 5 fui, fosti, fu, fummo, foste, furono 6 sarò *etc 8* sia *etc 9* fossi, fossi, fosse, fossimo, foste, fossero *10* sii!, sia!, siate!, siano!
estendere *like* tendere
estinguere *like* distinguere
estrarre *like* trarre
evadere 2 evaso 5 evasi, evadesti
evolvere 2 evoluto
fare *1* facendo *2* fatto *3* faccio, fai, fa, facciamo, fate, fanno *4* facevo *etc 5* feci, facesti *6* farò *etc 8* faccia *etc 9* facessi *etc 10* fa'!, faccia!, fate!, facciano!
fingere *like* cingere
FINIRE *1* GERUNDIO finendo
2 PARTICIPIO PASSATO finito
3 PRESENTE finisco, finisci, finisce, finiamo, finite, finiscono
4 IMPERFETTO finivo, finivi, finiva, finivamo, finivate, finivano
5 PASSATO REMOTO finii, finisti, finì, finimmo, finiste, finirono
6 FUTURO finirò, finirai, finirà, finiremo, finirete, finiranno
7 CONDIZIONALE finirei, finiresti, finirebbe, finiremmo, finireste, finirebbero
8 CONGIUNTIVO PRESENTE finisca, finisca, finisca, finiamo, finiate, finiscano
9 CONGIUNTIVO PASSATO finissi, finissi, finisse, finissimo, finiste, finissero
10 IMPERATIVO finisci!, finisca!, finite!, finiscano!
flettere 2 flesso
fondere 2 fuso 5 fusi, fondesti
friggere 2 fritto 5 frissi, friggesti
fungere 2 funto 5 funsi, fungesti
giacere 2 giaccio, giaci, giace, giac(c)iamo, giacete, giacciono 5 giacqui, giacesti *8* giaccia *etc 10* giaci!, giaccia!, giac(c)iamo!, giacete!, giacciano!
giungere 2 giunto 5 giunsi, giungesti
godere *6* godrò *etc*
illudere *like* alludere
immergere *like* emergere
immettere *like* mettere
imporre *like* porre
imprimere *like* comprimere

incidere *like* decidere
includere *like* alludere
incorrere *like* correre
incutere *like* discutere
indulgere 2 indulto 5 indulsi, indulgesti
indurre *like* ridurre
inferire[1] 2 inferto 5 infersi, inferisti
inferire[2] 2 inferito 5 inferii, inferisti
infliggere *like* affliggere
infrangere 2 infranto 5 infransi, infrangesti
infondere *like* fondere
insistere *like* assistere
intendere *like* tendere
interdire *like* dire
interporre *like* porre
interrompere *like* rompere
intervenire *like* venire
intraprendere *like* prendere
introdurre *like* ridurre
invadere *like* evadere
irrompere *like* rompere
iscrivere *like* scrivere
istruire *like* costruire
ledere 2 leso 5 lesi, ledesti
leggere 2 letto 5 lessi, leggesti
maledire *like* dire
mantenere *like* tenere
mettere 2 messo 5 misi, mettesti
mordere 2 morso 5 morsi, mordesti
morire 2 morto 3 muoio, muori, muore, moriamo, morite, muoiono 6 morirò *o* morrò *etc* 8 muoia
mungere 2 munto 5 munsi, mungesti
muovere 2 mosso 5 mossi, movesti
nascere 2 nato 5 nacqui, nascesti
nascondere 2 nascosto 5 nascosi, nascondesti
nuocere 2 nuociuto 3 nuoccio, nuoci, nuoce, nociamo *o* nuociamo, nuocete, nuocciono 4 nuocevo *etc* 5 nocqui, nuocesti 6 nuocerò *etc* 7 nuoccia
occorrere *like* correre
offendere *like* difendere
offrire 2 offerto 3 offro 5 offersi *o* offrii, offristi 8 offra
omettere *like* mettere
opporre *like* porre
opprimere *like* comprimere
ottenere *like* tenere
parere 2 parso 3 paio, paiamo, paiono 5 parvi *o* parsi, paresti 6 parrò *etc* 8 paia, paiamo, paiate, paiano
PARLARE 1 GERUNDIO parlando
2 PARTICIPIO PASSATO parlato
3 PRESENTE parlo, parli, parla, parliamo, parlate, parlano
4 IMPERFETTO parlavo, parlavi, parlava, parlavamo, parlavate, parlavano
5 PASSATO REMOTO parlai, parlasti, parlò, parlammo, parlaste, parlarono
6 FUTURO parlerò, parlerai, parlerà, parleremo, parlerete, parleranno
7 CONDIZIONALE parlerei, parleresti, parlerebbe, parleremmo, parlereste, parlerebbero
8 CONGIUNTIVO PRESENTE parli, parli, parli, parliamo, parliate, parlino
9 CONGIUNTIVO PASSATO parlassi, parlassi, parlasse, parlassimo, parlaste, parlassero
10 IMPERATIVO parla!, parli!, parlate!, parlino!
percorrere *like* correre
percuotere 2 percosso 5 percossi, percotesti
perdere 2 perso *o* perduto 5 persi *o* perdei *o* perdetti, perdesti
permettere *like* mettere
persuadere 2 persuaso 5 persuasi, persuadesti
pervenire *like* venire
piacere 2 piaciuto 3 piaccio, piacciamo, piacciono 5 piacqui, piacesti 8 piaccia *etc*
piangere 2 pianto 5 piansi, piangesti
piovere 5 piovve
porgere 2 porto 5 porsi, porgesti
porre 1 ponendo 2 posto 3 pongo, poni, pone, poniamo, ponete, pongono 4 ponevo *etc* 5 posi, ponesti 6 porrò *etc* 8 ponga, poniamo, poniate, pongano 9 ponessi *etc*
posporre *like* porre
possedere *like* sedere
potere 3 posso, puoi, può, possiamo, potete, possono 6 potrò *etc* 8 possa, possiamo, possiate, possano
prediligere 2 prediletto 5 predilessi, prediligesti
predire *like* dire
prefiggersi *like* affiggere
preludere *like* alludere
prendere 2 preso 5 presi, prendesti
preporre *like* porre
prescrivere *like* scrivere
presiedere *like* sedere
presumere *like* assumere
pretendere *like* tendere
prevalere *like* valere
prevedere *like* vedere
prevenire *like* venire
produrre *like* ridurre
proferire *like* inferire[2]
profondere *like* fondere
promettere *like* mettere
promuovere *like* muovere
proporre *like* porre
prorompere *like* rompere
proscrivere *like* scrivere
proteggere 2 protetto 5 protessi, proteggesti
provenire *like* venire
provvedere *like* vedere
pungere 2 punto 5 punsi, pungesti
racchiudere *like* chiudere
raccogliere *like* cogliere
radere 2 raso 5 rasi, radesti

raggiungere *like* giungere
rapprendere *like* prendere
ravvedersi *like* vedere
recidere *like* decidere
redigere 2 redatto
redimere 2 redento 5 redensi, redimesti
reggere 2 retto 5 ressi, reggesti
rendere 2 reso 5 resi, rendesti
reprimere *like* comprimere
rescindere *like* scindere
respingere *like* spingere
restringere *like* stringere
ricadere *like* cadere
richiedere *like* chiedere
riconoscere *like* conoscere
ricoprire *like* coprire
ricorrere *like* correre
ridere 2 riso 5 risi, ridesti
ridire *like* dire
ridurre 1 riducendo 2 ridotto 3 riduco *etc* 4 riducevo *etc* 5 ridussi, riducesti 6 ridurrò *etc* 8 riduca *etc* 9 riducessi *etc*
riempire 1 riempiendo 3 riempio, riempi, riempie, riempiono
rifare *like* fare
riflettere 2 riflettuto *o* riflesso
rifrangere *like* infrangere
rimanere 2 rimasto 3 rimango, rimangono 5 rimasi, rimanesti 6 rimarrò *etc* 8 rimanga
rimettere *like* mettere
rimpiangere *like* piangere
rinchiudere *like* chiudere
rincrescere *like* crescere
rinvenire *like* venire
ripercuotere *like* percuotere
riporre *like* porre
riprendere *like* prendere
riprodurre *like* ridurre
riscuotere *like* scuotere
risolvere *like* assolvere
risorgere *like* sorgere
rispondere 2 risposto 5 risposi, rispondesti
ritenere *like* tenere
ritrarre *like* trarre
riuscire *like* uscire
rivedere *like* vedere
rivivere *like* vivere
rivolgere *like* volgere
rodere 2 roso 5 rosi, rodesti
rompere 2 rotto 5 ruppi, rompesti
salire 3 salgo, sali, salgono 8 salga
sapere 3 so, sai, sa, sappiamo, sapete, sanno 5 seppi, sapesti 6 saprò *etc* 8 sappia *etc* 10 sappi!, sappia!, sappiate!, sappiano!
scadere *like* cadere
scegliere 2 scelto 3 scelgo, scegli, sceglie, scegliamo, scegliete, scelgono 5 scelsi, scegliesti 8 scelga, scegliamo, scegliate, scelgano 10 scegli!, scelga!, scegliamo!, scegliete!, scelgano!
scendere 2 sceso 5 scesi, scendesti

schiudere *like* chiudere
scindere 2 scisso 5 scissi, scindesti
sciogliere 2 sciolto 3 sciolgo, sciolgi, scioglie, sciogliamo, sciogliete, sciolgono 5 sciolsi, sciogliesti 8 sciolga, sciogliamo, sciogliate, sciolgano 10 sciogli!, sciolga!, sciogliamo!, sciogliete!, sciolgano!
scommettere *like* mettere
scomparire *like* apparire
scomporre *like* porre
sconfiggere 2 sconfitto 5 sconfissi, sconfiggesti
sconvolgere *like* volgere
scoprire *like* aprire
scorgere 2 scorto 5 scorsi, scorgesti
scorrere *like* correre
scrivere 2 scritto 5 scrissi, scrivesti
scuotere 2 scosso 3 scuoto, scuoti, scuote, scotiamo, scotete, scuotono 5 scossi, scotesti 6 scoterò *etc* 8 scuota, scotiamo, scotiate, scuotano 10 scuoti!, scuota!, scotiamo!, scotete!, scuotano!
sedere 3 siedo, siedi, siede, siedono 8 sieda
seppellire 2 sepolto
smettere *like* mettere
smuovere *like* muovere
socchiudere *like* chiudere
soccorrere *like* correre
soddisfare *like* fare
soffriggere *like* friggere
soffrire 2 sofferto 5 soffersi *o* soffrii, soffristi
soggiungere *like* giungere
solere 2 solito 3 soglio, suoli, suole, sogliamo, solete, sogliono 8 soglia, sogliamo, sogliate, sogliano
sommergere *like* emergere
sopprimere *like* comprimere
sorgere 2 sorto 3 sorsi, sorgesti
sorprendere *like* prendere
sorreggere *like* reggere
sorridere *like* ridere
sospendere *like* appendere
sospingere *like* spingere
sostenere *like* tenere
sottintendere *like* tendere
spandere 2 spanto
spargere 2 sparso 5 sparsi, spargesti
sparire 5 sparii *o* sparvi, sparisti
spegnere 2 spento 3 spengo, spengono 5 spensi, spegnesti 8 spenga
spendere 2 speso 5 spesi, spendesti
spingere 2 spinto 5 spinsi, spingesti
sporgere *like* porgere
stare 2 stato 3 sto, stai, sta, stiamo, state, stanno 5 stetti, stesti 6 starò *etc* 8 stia *etc* 9 stessi *etc* 10 sta'!, stia!, state!, stiano!
stendere *like* tendere
storcere *like* torcere
stringere 2 stretto 5 strinsi, stringesti
struggere 2 strutto 5 strussi, struggesti
succedere *like* concedere

supporre *like* **porre**
svenire *like* **venire**
svolgere *like* **volgere**
tacere *2* taciuto *3* taccio, taccion0 *5* tacqui, tacesti *8* taccia
tendere *2* teso *5* tesi, tendesti *etc*
tenere *3* tengo, tieni, tiene, tengono *5* tenni, tenesti *6* terrò *etc* *8* tenga
tingere *2* tinto *5* tinsi, tingesti
togliere *2* tolto *3* tolgo, togli, toglie, togliamo, togliete, tolgono *5* tolsi, togliesti *8* tolga, togliamo, togliate, tolgano *10* togli!, tolga!, togliamo!, togliete!, tolgano!
torcere *2* torto *5* torsi, torcesti
tradurre *like* **ridurre**
trafiggere *like* **sconfiggere**
transigere *like* **esigere**
trarre *1* traendo *2* tratto *3* traggo, trai, trae, traiamo, traete, traggono *4* traevo *etc* *5* trassi, traesti *6* trarrò *etc* *8* tragga *9* traessi *etc*
trascorrere *like* **correre**
trascrivere *like* **scrivere**
trasmettere *like* **mettere**
trasparire *like* **apparire**
trattenere *like* **tenere**
uccidere *2* ucciso *5* uccisi, uccidesti
udire *3* odo, odi, ode, odono *8* oda
ungere *2* unto *5* unsi, ungesti
uscire *3* esco, esci, esce, escono *8* esca
valere *2* valso *3* valgo, valgono *5* valsi, valesti *6* varrò *etc* *8* valga

vedere *2* visto *o* veduto *5* vidi, vedesti *6* vedrò *etc*
VENDERE *1* GERUNDIO vendendo
2 PARTICIPIO PASSATO venduto
3 PRESENTE vendo, vendi, vende, vendiamo, vendete, vendono
4 IMPERFETTO vendevo, vendevi, vendeva, vendevamo, vendevate, vendevano
5 PASSATO REMOTO vendei *o* vendetti, vendesti, vendé *o* vendette, vendemmo, vendeste, venderono *o* vendettero
6 FUTURO venderò, venderai, venderà, venderemo, venderete, venderanno
7 CONDIZIONALE venderei, venderesti, venderebbe, venderemmo, vendereste, venderebbero
8 CONGIUNTIVO PRESENTE venda, venda, venda, vendiamo, vendiate, vendano
9 CONGIUNTIVO PASSATO vendessi, vendessi, vendesse, vendessimo, vendeste, vendessero
10 IMPERATIVO vendi!, venda!, vendete!, vendano!
venire *2* venuto *3* vengo, vieni, viene, vengono *5* venni, venisti *6* verrò *etc* *8* venga
vincere *2* vinto *5* vinsi, vincesti
vivere *2* vissuto *5* vissi, vivesti
volere *3* voglio, vuoi, vuole, vogliamo, volete, vogliono *5* volli, volesti *6* vorrò *etc* *8* voglia *etc* *10* vogli!, voglia!, vogliate!, vogliano!
volgere *2* volto *5* volsi, volgesti

VERBI INGLESI

present	pt	pp
arise	arose	arisen
awake	awoke	awoken
be (am, is, are; being)	was, were	been
bear	bore	born(e)
beat	beat	beaten
become	became	become
befall	befell	befallen
begin	began	begun
behold	beheld	beheld
bend	bent	bent
beset	beset	beset
bet	bet, betted	bet, betted
bid (at auction, cards)	bid	bid
bid (say)	bade	bidden
bind	bound	bound
bite	bit	bitten
bleed	bled	bled
blow	blew	blown
break	broke	broken
breed	bred	bred
bring	brought	brought
build	built	built
burn	burnt, burned	burnt, burned
burst	burst	burst
buy	bought	bought
can	could	(been able)
cast	cast	cast
catch	caught	caught
choose	chose	chosen
cling	clung	clung
come	came	come
cost	cost	cost
cost (work out price of)	costed	costed
creep	crept	crept
cut	cut	cut
deal	dealt	dealt
dig	dug	dug
do (3rd person: he/she/it does)	did	done
draw	drew	drawn
dream	dreamed, dreamt	dreamed, dreamt
drink	drank	drunk

present	pt	pp
drive	drove	driven
dwell	dwelt	dwelt
eat	ate	eaten
fall	fell	fallen
feed	fed	fed
feel	felt	felt
fight	fought	fought
find	found	found
flee	fled	fled
fling	flung	flung
fly	flew	flown
forbid	forbad(e)	forbidden
forecast	forecast	forecast
forget	forgot	forgotten
forgive	forgave	forgiven
forsake	forsook	forsaken
freeze	froze	frozen
get	got	got, (US) gotten
give	gave	given
go (goes)	went	gone
grind	ground	ground
grow	grew	grown
hang	hung	hung
hang (execute)	hanged	hanged
have	had	had
hear	heard	heard
hide	hid	hidden
hit	hit	hit
hold	held	held
hurt	hurt	hurt
keep	kept	kept
kneel	knelt, kneeled	knelt, kneeled
know	knew	known
lay	laid	laid
lead	led	led
lean	leant, leaned	leant, leaned
leap	leapt, leaped	leapt, leaped
learn	learnt, learned	learnt, learned
leave	left	left
lend	lent	lent
let	let	let
lie (lying)	lay	lain
light	lit, lighted	lit, lighted
lose	lost	lost
make	made	made
may	might	—

present	pt	pp	present	pt	pp
mean	meant	meant	speed	sped,	sped,
meet	met	met		speeded	speeded
mistake	mistook	mistaken	spell	spelt,	spelt,
mow	mowed	mown,		spelled	spelled
		mowed	spend	spent	spent
must	(had to)	(had to)	spill	spilt,	spilt,
pay	paid	paid		spilled	spilled
put	put	put	spin	spun	spun
quit	quit,	quit,	spit	spat	spat
	quitted	quitted	spoil	spoiled,	spoiled,
read	read	read		spoilt	spoilt
rid	rid	rid	spread	spread	spread
ride	rode	ridden	spring	sprang	sprung
ring	rang	rung	stand	stood	stood
rise	rose	risen	steal	stole	stolen
run	ran	run	stick	stuck	stuck
saw	sawed	sawed,	sting	stung	stung
		sawn	stink	stank	stunk
say	said	said	stride	strode	stridden
see	saw	seen	strike	struck	struck
seek	sought	sought	strive	strove	striven
sell	sold	sold	swear	swore	sworn
send	sent	sent	sweep	swept	swept
set	set	set	swell	swelled	swollen,
sew	sewed	sewn			swelled
shake	shook	shaken	swim	swam	swum
shear	sheared	shorn,	swing	swung	swung
		sheared	take	took	taken
shed	shed	shed	teach	taught	taught
shine	shone	shone	tear	tore	torn
shoot	shot	shot	tell	told	told
show	showed	shown	think	thought	thought
shrink	shrank	shrunk	throw	threw	thrown
shut	shut	shut	thrust	thrust	thrust
sing	sang	sung	tread	trod	trodden
sink	sank	sunk	wake	woke,	woken,
sit	sat	sat		waked	waked
slay	slew	slain	wear	wore	worn
sleep	slept	slept	weave	wove	woven
slide	slid	slid	weave	weaved	weaved
sling	slung	slung	*(wind)*		
slit	slit	slit	wed	wedded,	wedded,
smell	smelt,	smelt,		wed	wed
	smelled	smelled	weep	wept	wept
sow	sowed	sown,	win	won	won
		sowed	wind	wound	wound
speak	spoke	spoken	wring	wrung	wrung
			write	wrote	written

I NUMERI   NUMBERS

uno(a)	1	one
due	2	two
tre	3	three
quattro	4	four
cinque	5	five
sei	6	six
sette	7	seven
otto	8	eight
nove	9	nine
dieci	10	ten
undici	11	eleven
dodici	12	twelve
tredici	13	thirteen
quattordici	14	fourteen
quindici	15	fifteen
sedici	16	sixteen
diciassette	17	seventeen
diciotto	18	eighteen
diciannove	19	nineteen
venti	20	twenty
ventuno	21	twenty-one
ventidue	22	twenty-two
ventitré	23	twenty-three
ventotto	28	twenty-eight
trenta	30	thirty
quaranta	40	forty
cinquanta	50	fifty
sessanta	60	sixty
settanta	70	seventy
ottanta	80	eighty
novanta	90	ninety
cento	100	a hundred, one hundred
centouno	101	a hundred and one
duecento	200	two hundred
mille	1 000	a thousand, one thousand
milleduecentodue	1 202	one thousand two hundred and two
cinquemila	5 000	five thousand
un milione	1 000 000	a million, one million

I NUMERI

NUMBERS

primo(a), 1°	first, 1st
secondo(a), 2°	second, 2nd
terzo(a), 3°	third, 3rd
quarto(a)	fourth, 4th
quinto(a)	fifth, 5th
sesto(a)	sixth, 6th
settimo(a)	seventh
ottavo(a)	eighth
nono(a)	ninth
decimo(a)	tenth
undicesimo(a)	eleventh
dodicesimo(a)	twelfth
tredicesimo(a)	thirteenth
quattordicesimo(a)	fourteenth
quindicesimo(a)	fifteenth
sedicesimo(a)	sixteenth
diciassettesimo(a)	seventeenth
diciottesimo(a)	eighteenth
diciannovesimo(a)	nineteenth
ventesimo(a)	twentieth
ventunesimo(a)	twenty-first
ventiduesimo(a)	twenty-second
ventitreesimo(a)	twenty-third
ventottesimo(a)	twenty-eighth
trentesimo(a)	thirtieth
centesimo(a)	hundredth
centunesimo(a)	hundred-and-first
millesimo(a)	thousandth
milionesimo(a)	millionth

L'ORA

THE TIME

che ora è?, che ore sono?
è ..., sono ...

what time is it?
it's ...

mezzanotte	midnight
l'una (del mattino)	one o'clock (in the morning) , one (am)
l'una e cinque	five past one
l'una e dieci	ten past one
l'una e un quarto, l'una e quindici	a quarter past one, one fifteen
l'una e venticinque	twenty-five past one, one twenty-five
l'una e mezzo *o* mezza, l'una e trenta	half past one, one thirty
l'una e trentacinque	twenty-five to two, one thirty-five
le due meno venti, l'una e quaranta	twenty to two, one forty
le due meno un quarto, l'una e quarantacinque	a quarter to two, one forty-five
le due meno dieci, l'una e cinquanta	ten to two, one fifty
mezzogiorno	twelve o'clock, midday, noon
le tre, le quindici	three o'clock (in the afternoon), three (pm)
le sette (di sera), le diciannove	seven o'clock (in the evening), seven (pm)

a che ora?

at what time?

a mezzanotte	at midnight
alle sette	at seven o'clock
fra venti minuti	in twenty minutes
venti minuti fa	twenty minutes ago

LA DATA

THE DATE

oggi	today
domani	tomorrow
dopodomani	the day after tomorrow
ieri	yesterday
l'altro ieri	the day before yesterday
il giorno prima	the day before, the previous day
il giorno dopo	the next *or* following day

la mattina	morning
la sera	evening
stamattina	this morning
stasera	this evening
questo pomeriggio	this afternoon
ieri mattina	yesterday morning
ieri sera	yesterday evening
domani mattina	tomorrow morning
domani sera	tomorrow evening
nella notte tra sabato e domenica	during Saturday night, during the night of Saturday to Sunday
viene sabato	he's coming on Saturday
il sabato	on Saturdays
tutti i sabati	every Saturday
sabato scorso, lo scorso sabato	last Saturday
il prossimo sabato	next Saturday
fra due sabati	a week on Saturday
fra tre sabati	a fortnight or two weeks on Saturday
da lunedì a sabato	from Monday to Saturday
tutti i giorni	every day
una volta alla settimana	once a week
una volta al mese	once a month
due volte alla settimana	twice a week
una settimana fa	a week ago
quindici giorni fa	a fortnight or two weeks ago
l'anno scorso or passato	last year
fra due giorni	in two days
fra una settimana	in a week
fra quindici giorni	in a fortnight or two weeks
il mese prossimo	next month
l'anno prossimo	next year

che giorno è oggi?	*what day is it?*
il primo/24 ottobre 1996	the 1st/24th of October 1996, October 1st/24th 1996
nel 1996	in 1996
il millenovecentonovantacinque	nineteen ninety-five
44 a.C.	44 BC
14 d.C.	14 AD
nel diciannovesimo secolo, nel XIX secolo, nell'Ottocento	in the nineteenth century
negli anni trenta	in the thirties
c'era una volta ...	once upon a time ...

Italiano-Inglese
Italian-English

A a

A, a [a] *sf o m inv* (*lettera*) A, a; **A come Ancona** ≈ A for Andrew (*BRIT*), A for Able (*US*); **dalla a alla z** from a to z. **A** *abbr* (= *altezza*) h; (= *area*) A; (= *autostrada*) ≈ M (*BRIT*).

═══════════════════ PAROLA CHIAVE

a (*a + il* = **al**, *a + lo* = **allo**, *a + l'* = **all'**, *a + la* = **alla**, *a + i* = **ai**, *a + gli* = **agli**, *a + le* = **alle**) *prep* **1** (*stato in luogo*) at; (: *in*) in; **essere alla stazione** to be at the station; **essere ~ casa/~ scuola/~ Roma** to be at home/at school/in Rome; **è ~ 10 km da qui** it's 10 km from here, it's 10 km away; **restare ~ cena** to stay for dinner

2 (*moto a luogo*) to; **andare ~ casa/~ scuola/alla stazione** to go home/to school/to the station; **andare ~ Roma/al mare** to go to Rome/to the seaside

3 (*tempo*) at; (*epoca, stagione*) in; **alle cinque** at five (o'clock); **~ mezzanotte/Natale** at midnight/Christmas; **al mattino** in the morning; **~ maggio/primavera** in May/spring; **~ cinquant'anni** at fifty (years of age); **~ domani!** see you tomorrow!; **~ lunedì!** see you on Monday!; **~ giorni** within (a few) days

4 (*complemento di termine*) to; **dare qc ~ qn** to give sb sth, give sth to sb; **l'ho chiesto ~ lui** I asked him

5 (*mezzo, modo*) with, by; **~ piedi/cavallo** on foot/horseback; **viaggiare ~ 100 km all'ora** to travel at 100 km an *o* per hour; **alla televisione/radio** on television/the radio; **fatto ~ mano** made by hand, handmade; **una barca ~ motore** a motorboat; **una stufa ~ gas** a gas heater;

~ uno ~ uno one by one; **~ fatica** with difficulty; **all'italiana** the Italian way, in the Italian fashion

6 (*rapporto*) a, per; (: *con prezzi*) at; **due volte al giorno/mese** twice a day/month; **prendo 2000 euro al mese** I get 2000 euros a *o* per month; **pagato ~ ore** paid by the hour; **vendere qc ~ 2 euro il chilo** to sell sth at 2 euros a *o* per kilo; **cinque ~ zero** (*punteggio*) five nil.

AA *sigla* = *Alto Adige*.

AAST *sigla f* = **Azienda Autonoma di Soggiorno e turismo**.

AA.VV. *abbr* = *autori vari*.

ab. *abbr* = *abitante*.

a'bate *sm* abbot.

abbacchi'ato, a [abbak'kjato] *ag* downhearted, in low spirits.

abbacin'are [abbatʃi'nare] *vt* to dazzle.

abbagli'ante [abbaʎ'ʎante] *ag* dazzling; **~i** *smpl* (*AUT*): **accendere gli ~i** to put one's headlights on full (*BRIT*) *o* high (*US*) beam.

abbagli'are [abbaʎ'ʎare] *vt* to dazzle; (*illudere*) to delude.

ab'baglio [ab'baʎʎo] *sm* blunder; **prendere un ~** to blunder, make a blunder.

abbai'are *vi* to bark.

abba'ino *sm* dormer window; (*soffitta*) attic room.

abbando'nare *vt* to leave, abandon, desert; (*trascurare*) to neglect; (*rinunciare a*) to abandon, give up; **~rsi** *vr* to let o.s. go; **~ il campo** (*MIL*) to retreat; **~ la presa** to let go; **~rsi a** (*ricordi, vizio*) to give o.s. up to.

abbando'nato, a *ag* (*casa*) deserted; (*miniera*) disused; (*trascurato: terreno*, *podere*) neglected; (*bambino*) abandoned.

abban'dono *sm* abandoning; neglecting; (*stato*) abandonment; neglect; (*SPORT*) withdrawal; (*fig*) abandon; **in** ~ (*edificio, giardino*) neglected.

abbarbi'carsi *vr:* ~ **(a)** (*anche fig*) to cling (to).

abbassa'mento *sm* lowering; (*di pressione, livello dell'acqua*) fall; (*di prezzi*) reduction; ~ **di temperatura** drop in temperature.

abbas'sare *vt* to lower; (*radio*) to turn down; ~**rsi** *vr* (*chinarsi*) to stoop; (*livello, sole*) to go down; (*fig: umiliarsi*) to demean o.s.; ~ **i fari** (*AUT*) to dip (*BRIT*) o dim (*US*) one's lights; ~ **le armi** (*MIL*) to lay down one's arms.

ab'basso *escl:* ~ **il re!** down with the king!

abbas'tanza [abbas'tantsa] *av* (*a sufficienza*) enough; (*alquanto*) quite, rather, fairly; **non è** ~ **furbo** he's not shrewd enough; **un vino** ~ **dolce** quite a sweet wine, a fairly sweet wine; **averne** ~ **di qn/qc** to have had enough of sb/sth.

ab'battere *vt* (*muro, casa, ostacolo*) to knock down; (*albero*) to fell; (: *sog: vento*) to bring down; (*bestie da macello*) to slaughter; (*cane, cavallo*) to destroy, put down; (*selvaggina, aereo*) to shoot down; (*fig: sog: malattia, disgrazia*) to lay low; ~**rsi** *vr* (*avvilirsi*) to lose heart; ~**rsi a terra** o **al suolo** to fall to the ground; ~**rsi su** (*sog: maltempo*) to beat down on; (: *disgrazia*) to hit, strike.

abbatti'mento *sm* knocking down; felling; (*di casa*) demolition; (*prostrazione: fisica*) exhaustion; (: *morale*) despondency.

abbat'tuto, a *ag* despondent, depressed.

abba'zia [abbat'tsia] *sf* abbey.

abbece'dario [abbetʃe'darjo] *sm* primer.

abbelli'mento *sm* embellishment.

abbel'lire *vt* to make beautiful; (*ornare*) to embellish.

abbeve'rare *vt* to water; ~**rsi** *vr* to drink.

abbevera'toio *sm* drinking trough.

'abbi, 'abbia, abbi'amo, 'abbiano, abbi'ate *vb vedi* **avere**.

abbiccì [abbit'tʃi] *sm inv* alphabet; (*sillabario*) primer; (*fig*) rudiments *pl*.

abbi'ente *ag* well-to-do, well-off.

abbi'etto, a *ag* = **abietto**.

abbiezi'one [abbjet'tsjone] *sf* = **abiezione**.

abbiglia'mento [abbiʎʎa'mento] *sm* dress *no pl*; (*indumenti*) clothes *pl*; (*industria*) clothing industry.

abbigli'are [abbiʎ'ʎare] *vt* to dress up.

abbina'mento *sm* combination; linking; matching.

abbi'nare *vt:* ~ **(con** o **a)** (*gen*) to combine

(with); (*nomi*) to link (with); ~ **qc a qc** (*colori etc*) to match sth with sth.

abbindo'lare *vt* (*fig*) to cheat, trick.

abbocca'mento *sm* (*colloquio*) talks *pl*, meeting; (*TECN: di tubi*) connection.

abboc'care *vt* (*tubi, canali*) to connect, join up ♦ *vi* (*pesce*) to bite; (*tubi*) to join; ~ (**all'amo**) (*fig*) to swallow the bait.

abboc'cato, a *ag* (*vino*) sweetish.

abbona'mento *sm* subscription; (*alle ferrovie etc*) season ticket; **in** ~ for subscribers only; for season ticket holders only; **fare l'**~ **(a)** to take out a subscription (to); to buy a season ticket (for).

abbo'nare *vt* (*cifra*) to deduct; (*fig: perdonare*) to forgive; ~**rsi** *vr:* ~**rsi a un giornale** to take out a subscription to a newspaper; ~**rsi al teatro/alle ferrovie** to take out a season ticket for the theatre/the train.

abbo'nato, a *sm/f* subscriber; season-ticket holder; **elenco degli** ~**i** telephone directory.

abbon'dante *ag* abundant, plentiful; (*giacca*) roomy.

abbon'danza [abbon'dantsa] *sf* abundance; plenty.

abbon'dare *vi* to abound, be plentiful; ~ **in** o **di** to be full of, abound in.

abbor'dabile *ag* (*persona*) approachable; (*prezzo*) reasonable.

abbor'dare *vt* (*nave*) to board; (*persona*) to approach; (*argomento*) to tackle; ~ **una curva** to take a bend.

abbotto'nare *vt* to button up, do up; ~**rsi** *vr* to button (up).

abbotto'nato, a *ag* (*camicia etc*) buttoned (up); (*fig*) reserved.

abbottona'tura *sf* buttons *pl*; **questo cappotto ha l'**~ **da uomo/da donna** this coat buttons on the man's/woman's side.

abboz'zare [abbot'tsare] *vt* to sketch, outline; (*SCULTURA*) to rough-hew; ~ **un sorriso** to give a hint of a smile.

ab'bozzo [ab'bɔttso] *sm* sketch, outline; (*DIR*) draft.

abbracci'are [abbrat'tʃare] *vt* to embrace; (*persona*) to hug, embrace; (*professione*) to take up; (*contenere*) to include; ~**rsi** *vr* to hug o embrace (one another).

ab'braccio [ab'brattʃo] *sm* hug, embrace.

abbrevi'are *vt* to shorten; (*parola*) to abbreviate, shorten.

abbreviazi'one [abbrevjat'tsjone] *sf* abbreviation.

abbron'zante [abbron'dzante] *ag* tanning, sun *cpd*.

abbron'zare [abbron'dzare] vt (pelle) to tan; (metalli) to bronze; ~**rsi** vr to tan, get a tan.

abbron'zato, a [abbron'dzato] ag (sun)tanned.

abbronza'tura [abbrondza'tura] sf tan, suntan.

abbrusto'lire vt (pane) to toast; (caffè) to roast.

abbruti'mento sm exhaustion; degradation.

abbru'tire vt (snervare, stancare) to exhaust; (degradare) to degrade; **essere abbrutito dall'alcool** to be ruined by drink.

abbuf'farsi vr (fam): ~ **(di qc)** to stuff o.s. (with sth).

abbuf'fata sf (fam) nosh-up; (fig) binge; **farsi un'**~ to stuff o.s.

abbuo'nare vt = **abbonare**.

abbu'ono sm (COMM) allowance, discount; (SPORT) handicap.

abdi'care vi to abdicate; ~ **a** to give up.

abdicazi'one [abdikat'tsjone] sf abdication.

aberrazi'one [aberrat'tsjone] sf aberration.

abe'taia sf fir wood.

a'bete sm fir (tree); ~ **bianco** silver fir; ~ **rosso** spruce.

abi'etto, a ag despicable, abject.

abiezi'one [abjet'tsjone] sf abjection.

'abile ag (idoneo): ~ **(a qc/a fare qc)** fit (for sth/to do sth); (capace) able; (astuto) clever; (accorto) skilful; ~ **al servizio militare** fit for military service.

abilità sf inv ability; cleverness; skill.

abili'tante ag qualifying; **corsi** ~**i** (INS) ≈ teacher training sg.

abili'tare vt: ~ **qn a qc/a fare qc** to qualify sb for sth/to do sth; **è stato abilitato all'insegnamento** he has qualified as a teacher.

abili'tato, a ag qualified; (TEL) which has an outside line.

abilitazi'one [abilitat'tsjone] sf qualification.

abis'sale ag abysmal; (fig: senza limiti) profound.

abis'sino, a ag, sm/f Abyssinian.

a'bisso sm abyss, gulf.

abitabilità sf: **licenza di** ~ document stating that a property is fit for habitation.

abi'tacolo sm (AER) cockpit; (AUT) inside; (di camion) (driver's) cab.

abi'tante sm/f inhabitant.

abi'tare vt to live in, dwell in ♦ vi: ~ **in campagna/a Roma** to live in the country/in Rome.

abi'tato, a ag inhabited; lived in ♦ sm

(anche: **centro** ~) built-up area.

abitazi'one [abitat'tsjone] sf residence; house.

'abito sm dress no pl; (da uomo) suit; (da donna) dress; (abitudine, disposizione, REL) habit; ~**i** smpl (vestiti) clothes; **in** ~ **da cerimonia** in formal dress; **in** ~ **da sera** in evening dress; **"è gradito l'**~ **scuro"** "dress formal"; ~ **mentale** way of thinking.

abitu'ale ag usual, habitual; (cliente) regular.

abitual'mente av usually, normally.

abitu'are vt: ~ **qn a** to get sb used o accustomed to; ~**rsi a** to get used to, accustom o.s. to.

abitudi'nario, a ag of fixed habits ♦ sm/f creature of habit.

abi'tudine sf habit; **aver l'**~ **di fare qc** to be in the habit of doing sth; **d'**~ usually; **per** ~ from o out of habit.

abiu'rare vt to renounce.

abla'tivo sm ablative.

abnegazi'one [abnegat'tsjone] sf (self-) abnegation, self-denial.

ab'norme ag (enorme) extraordinary; (anormale) abnormal.

abo'lire vt to abolish; (DIR) to repeal.

abolizi'one [abolit'tsjone] sf abolition; repeal.

abomi'nevole ag abominable.

abo'rigeno [abo'ridʒeno] sm aborigine.

abor'rire vt to abhor, detest.

abor'tire vi (MED: accidentalmente) to miscarry, have a miscarriage; (: deliberatamente) to have an abortion; (fig) to miscarry, fail.

abor'tista, i, e ag pro-choice, pro-abortion ♦ sm/f pro-choicer.

a'borto sm miscarriage; abortion; (fig) freak; ~ **clandestino** backstreet abortion.

abrasi'one sf abrasion.

abra'sivo, a ag, sm abrasive.

abro'gare vt to repeal, abrogate.

abrogazi'one [abrogat'tsjone] sf repeal.

abruz'zese [abrut'tsese] ag of (o from) the Abruzzi.

A'bruzzo [a'bruttso] sm: **l'**~, **gli** ~**i** the Abruzzi.

ABS [abi'ɛsse] sigla m ABS (= anti-lock braking system).

'abside sf apse.

'Abu 'Dhabi sf Abu Dhabi.

a'bulico, a, ci, che ag lacking in willpower.

abu'sare vi: ~ **di** to abuse, misuse; (approfittare, violare) to take advantage of; ~ **dell'alcool/dei cibi** to drink/eat to excess.

abusi'vismo *sm* (*anche*: ~ **edilizio**) unlawful building, building without planning permission (*BRIT*).

abu'sivo, a *ag* unauthorized, unlawful; (**occupante**) ~ (*di una casa*) squatter.

a'buso *sm* abuse, misuse; excessive use; **fare** ~ **di** (*stupefacenti, medicine*) to abuse.

a.C. *abbr av* (= *avanti Cristo*) BC.

a'cacia, cie [a'katʃa] *sf* acacia.

'acca *sf* letter H; **non capire un'**~ not to understand a thing.

ac'cadde *vb vedi* **accadere**.

acca'demia *sf* (*società*) learned society; (*scuola: d'arte, militare*) academy; ~ **di Belle Arti** art school.

acca'demico, a, ci, che *ag* academic ♦ *sm* academician.

acca'dere *vi* to happen, occur.

acca'duto *sm* event; **raccontare l'**~ to describe what has happened.

accalappia'cani *sm inv* dog-catcher.

accalappi'are *vt* to catch; (*fig*) to trick, dupe.

accal'care *vt*, **~rsi** *vr* to crowd, throng.

accal'darsi *vr* to grow hot.

accalo'rarsi *vr* (*fig*) to get excited.

accampa'mento *sm* camp.

accam'pare *vt* to encamp; (*fig*) to put forward, advance; **~rsi** *vr* to camp; ~ **scuse** to make excuses.

accani'mento *sm* fury; (*tenacia*) tenacity, perseverance.

acca'nirsi *vr* (*infierire*) to rage; (*ostinarsi*) to persist.

accanita'mente *av* fiercely; assiduously.

acca'nito, a *ag* (*odio, gelosia*) fierce, bitter; (*lavoratore*) assiduous; (*giocatore*) inveterate; (*tifoso, sostenitore*) keen; **fumatore** ~ chain smoker.

ac'canto *av* near, nearby; ~ **a** *prep* near, beside, close to; **la casa** ~ the house next door.

accanto'nare *vt* (*problema*) to shelve; (*somma*) to set aside.

accaparra'mento *sm* (*COMM*) cornering, buying up.

accapar'rare *vt* (*COMM*) to corner, buy up; (*versare una caparra*) to pay a deposit on; **~rsi** *vr*: **~rsi qc** (*fig: simpatia, voti*) to secure sth (for o.s.).

accapigli'arsi [akkapiʎ'ʎarsi] *vr* to come to blows; (*fig*) to quarrel.

accappa'toio *sm* bathrobe.

accappo'nare *vi*: **far** ~ **la pelle a qn** (*fig*) to bring sb out in goosepimples.

accarez'zare [akkaret'tsare] *vt* to caress,

stroke, fondle; (*fig*) to toy with.

accartocci'are [akkartot'tʃare] *vt* (*carta*) to roll up, screw up; **~rsi** *vr* (*foglie*) to curl up.

acca'sarsi *vr* to set up house; to get married.

accasci'arsi [akkaʃ'ʃarsi] *vr* to collapse; (*fig*) to lose heart.

accatas'tare *vt* to stack, pile.

accatto'naggio [akkatto'naddʒo] *sm* begging.

accat'tone, a *sm/f* beggar.

accaval'lare *vt* (*gambe*) to cross; **~rsi** *vr* (*sovrapporsi*) to overlap; (*addensarsi*) to gather.

acce'care [attʃe'kare] *vt* to blind ♦ *vi* to go blind.

ac'cedere [at'tʃɛdere] *vi*: ~ **a** to enter; (*richiesta*) to grant, accede to; (*fonte*) to gain access to.

accele'rare [attʃele'rare] *vt* to speed up ♦ *vi* (*AUT*) to accelerate; ~ **il passo** to quicken one's pace.

accele'rato, a [attʃele'rato] *ag* quick, rapid ♦ *sm* (*FERR*) local train, stopping train.

accelera'tore [attʃelera'tore] *sm* (*AUT*) accelerator.

accelerazi'one [attʃelerat'tsjone] *sf* acceleration.

ac'cendere [at'tʃɛndere] *vt* (*fuoco, sigaretta*) to light; (*luce, televisione*) to put o switch o turn on; (*AUT: motore*) to switch on; (*COMM: conto*) to open; (: *debito*) to contract; (: *ipoteca*) to raise; (*fig: suscitare*) to inflame, stir up; **~rsi** *vr* (*luce*) to come o go on; (*legna*) to catch fire, ignite; (*fig: lotta, conflitto*) to break out.

accen'dino [attʃen'dino], **accendi'sigaro** [attʃendi'sigaro] *sm* (*cigarette*) lighter.

accen'nare [attʃen'nare] *vt* to indicate, point out; (*MUS*) to pick out the notes of; to hum ♦ *vi*: ~ **a** (*fig: alludere a*) to hint at; (: *far atto di*) to make as if; ~ **un saluto** (*con la mano*) to make as if to wave; (*col capo*) to half nod; ~ **un sorriso** to half smile; **accenna a piovere** it looks as if it's going to rain.

ac'cenno [at'tʃenno] *sm* (*cenno*) sign; nod; (*allusione*) hint.

accensi'one [attʃen'sjone] *sf* (*vedi accendere*) lighting; switching on; opening; (*AUT*) ignition.

accen'tare [attʃen'tare] *vt* (*parlando*) to stress; (*scrivendo*) to accent.

accentazi'one [attʃentat'tsjone] *sf* accentuation; stressing.

ac'cento [at'tʃento] *sm* accent; (*FONETICA, fig*) stress; (*inflessione*) tone (of voice).

accentra'mento [attʃentra'mento] sm centralization.

accen'trare [attʃen'trare] vt to centralize.

accentra'tore, 'trice [attʃentra'tore] ag (persona) unwilling to delegate; **politica** ~**trice** policy of centralization.

accentu'are [attʃentu'are] vt to stress, emphasize; ~**rsi** vr to become more noticeable.

accerchi'are [attʃer'kjare] vt to surround, encircle.

accerta'mento [attʃerta'mento] sm check; assessment.

accer'tare [attʃer'tare] vt to ascertain; (verificare) to check; (reddito) to assess; ~**rsi** vr: ~**rsi (di qc/che)** to make sure (of sth/that).

ac'ceso, a [at'tʃeso] pp di **accendere ♦** ag lit; on; open; (colore) bright; ~ **di** (ira, entusiasmo etc) burning with.

acces'sibile [attʃes'sibile] ag (luogo) accessible; (persona) approachable; (prezzo) reasonable; (idea): ~ **a qn** within the reach of sb.

ac'cesso [at'tʃɛsso] sm (anche INFORM) access; (MED) attack, fit; (impulso violento) fit, outburst; **programmi dell'**~ (TV) educational programmes; **tempo di** ~ (INFORM) access time; ~ **casuale/seriale/ sequenziale** (INFORM) random/serial/ sequential access.

accessori'ato, a [attʃesso'rjato] ag with accessories.

acces'sorio, a [attʃes'sɔrjo] ag secondary, of secondary importance; ~**i** smpl accessories.

ac'cetta [at'tʃetta] sf hatchet.

accet'tabile [attʃet'tabile] ag acceptable.

accet'tare [attʃet'tare] vt to accept; ~ **di fare qc** to agree to do sth.

accettazi'one [attʃettat'tsjone] sf acceptance; (locale di servizio pubblico) reception; ~ **bagagli** (AER) check-in (desk); ~ **con riserva** qualified acceptance.

ac'cetto, a [at'tʃetto] ag (persona) welcome; **(ben)** ~ **a tutti** well-liked by everybody.

accezi'one [attʃet'tsjone] sf meaning.

acchiap'pare [akkjap'pare] vt to catch; (afferrare) to seize.

ac'chito [ak'kito] sm: **a primo** ~ at first sight.

acciac'cato, a [attʃak'kato] ag (persona) full of aches and pains; (abito) crushed.

acci'acco, chi [at'tʃakko] sm ailment; ~**chi** smpl aches and pains.

acciaie'ria [attʃaje'ria] sf steelworks sg.

acci'aio [at'tʃajo] sm steel; ~ **inossidabile** stainless steel.

acciden'tale [attʃiden'tale] ag accidental.

accidental'mente [attʃidental'mente] av (per caso) by chance; (non deliberatamente) accidentally, by accident.

acciden'tato, a [attʃiden'tato] ag (terreno etc) uneven.

acci'dente [attʃi'dente] sm (caso imprevisto) accident; (disgrazia) mishap; ~**i!** (fam: per rabbia) damn (it)!; (: per meraviglia) good heavens!; ~**i a lui!** damn him!; **non vale un** ~ it's not worth a damn; **non capisco un** ~ it's as clear as mud to me; **mandare un** ~ **a qn** to curse sb.

ac'cidia [at'tʃidja] sf (REL) sloth.

accigli'ato, a [attʃiʎ'ʎato] ag frowning.

ac'cingersi [at'tʃindʒersi] vr: ~ **a fare** to be about to do.

acciotto'lato [attʃotto'lato] sm cobbles pl.

acciuf'fare [attʃuf'fare] vt to seize, catch.

acci'uga, ghe [at'tʃuga] sf anchovy; **magro come un'**~ as thin as a rake.

accla'mare vt (applaudire) to applaud; (eleggere) to acclaim.

acclamazi'one [akklamat'tsjone] sf applause; acclamation.

acclima'tare vt to acclimatize; ~**rsi** vr to become acclimatized.

acclimatazi'one [akklimatat'tsjone] sf acclimatization.

ac'cludere vt to enclose.

ac'cluso, a pp di **accludere ♦** ag enclosed.

accocco'larsi vr to crouch.

acco'darsi vr to follow, tag on (behind).

accogli'ente [akkoʎ'ʎɛnte] ag welcoming, friendly.

accogli'enza [akkoʎ'ʎɛntsa] sf reception; welcome; **fare una buona** ~ **a qn** to welcome sb.

ac'cogliere [ak'kɔʎʎere] vt (ricevere) to receive; (dare il benvenuto) to welcome; (approvare) to agree to, accept; (contenere) to hold, accommodate.

ac'colgo etc vb vedi **accogliere**.

accol'lare vt (fig): ~ **qc a qn** to force sth on sb; ~**rsi** vr: ~**rsi qc** to take sth upon o.s., shoulder sth.

accol'lato, a ag (vestito) high-necked.

ac'colsi etc vb vedi **accogliere**.

accoltel'lare vt to knife, stab.

ac'colto, a pp di **accogliere**.

accoman'dita sf (DIR) limited partnership.

accomia'tare vt to dismiss; ~**rsi** vr: ~**rsi (da)** to take one's leave (of).

accomoda'mento sm agreement, settlement.

accomo'dante ag accommodating.

accomo'dare vt (aggiustare) to repair, mend; (riordinare) to tidy; (sistemare: questione, lite) to settle; ~rsi vr (sedersi) to sit down; (fig: risolversi: situazione) to work out; **si accomodi!** (venga avanti) come in!; (si sieda) take a seat!

accompagna'mento [akkompaɲɲa'mento] sm (MUS) accompaniment; (COMM): **lettera di** ~ accompanying letter.

accompa'gnare [akkompaɲ'ɲare] vt to accompany, come o go with; (MUS) to accompany; (unire) to couple; ~**rsi** vr (armonizzarsi) to go well together; ~ **qn a casa** to see sb home; ~ **qn alla porta** to show sb out; ~ **un regalo con un biglietto** to put in o send a card with a present; ~ **qn con lo sguardo** to follow sb with one's eyes; ~ **la porta** to close the door gently; ~**rsi a** (frequentare) to frequent; (colori) to go with, match; (cibi) to go with.

accompagna'tore, 'trice [akkompaɲɲa 'tore] sm/f companion, escort; (MUS) accompanist; (SPORT) team manager; ~ **turistico** courier; tour guide.

accomu'nare vt to pool, share; (avvicinare) to unite.

acconcia'tura [akkontʃa'tura] sf hairstyle.

accondiscen'dente [akkondiʃʃen'dɛnte] ag affable.

accondi'scendere [akkondiʃ'ʃendere] vi: ~ **a** to agree o consent to.

accondi'sceso, a [akkondiʃ'ʃeso] pp di **accondiscendere**.

acconsen'tire vi: ~ **(a)** to agree o consent (to); **chi tace acconsente** silence means consent.

acconten'tare vt to satisfy; ~**rsi** vr: ~**rsi di** to be satisfied with, content o.s. with; **chi si accontenta gode** there's no point in complaining.

ac'conto sm part payment; **pagare una somma in** ~ to pay a sum of money as a deposit; ~ **di dividendo** interim dividend.

accoppia'mento sm pairing off; mating; (ELETTR, INFORM) coupling.

accoppi'are vt to couple, pair off; (BIOL) to mate; ~**rsi** vr to pair off; to mate.

accoppia'tore sm (TECN) coupler; ~ **acustico** (INFORM) acoustic coupler.

acco'rato, a ag heartfelt.

accorci'are [akkor'tʃare] vt to shorten; ~**rsi** vr to become shorter; (vestiti: nel lavaggio) to shrink.

accor'dare vt to reconcile; (colori) to match; (MUS) to tune; (LING): ~ **qc con qc** to make sth agree with sth; (DIR) to grant; ~**rsi** vr to agree, come to an agreement; (colori) to match.

ac'cordo sm agreement; (armonia) harmony; (MUS) chord; **essere d'**~ to agree; **andare d'**~ to get on well together; **d'**~! all right!, agreed!; **mettersi d'**~ **(con qn)** to agree o come to an agreement with sb; **prendere** ~**i con** to reach an agreement with; ~ **commerciale** trade agreement; **A**~ **generale sulle tariffe ed il commercio** General Agreement on Tariffs and Trade, GATT.

ac'corgersi [ak'kɔrdʒersi] vr: ~ **di** to notice; (fig) to realize.

accorgi'mento [akkordʒi'mento] sm shrewdness no pl; (espediente) trick, device.

ac'correre vi to run up.

ac'corsi vb vedi **accorgersi**; **accorrere**.

ac'corso, a pp di **accorrere**.

accor'tezza [akkor'tettsa] sf (avvedutezza) good sense; (astuzia) shrewdness.

ac'corto, a pp di **accorgersi** ♦ ag shrewd; **stare** ~ to be on one's guard.

accosta'mento sm (di colori etc) combination.

accos'tare vt (avvicinarsi a) to approach; (socchiudere: imposte) to half-close; (: porta) to leave ajar ♦ vi: ~ **(a)** (NAUT) to come alongside; (AUT) to draw up (at); ~**rsi** vr: ~**rsi a** to draw near, approach; (somigliare) to be like, resemble; (fede, religione) to turn to; (idee politiche) to come to agree with; ~ **qc a** (avvicinare) to bring sth near to, put sth near to; (colori, stili) to match sth with; (appoggiare: scala etc) to lean sth against.

accovacci'arsi [akkovat'tʃarsi] vr to crouch.

accoz'zaglia [akkot'tsaʎʎa] sf (peg: di idee, oggetti) jumble, hotchpotch; (: di persone) odd assortment.

ac'crebbi etc vb vedi **accrescere**.

accredi'tare vt (notizia) to confirm the truth of; (COMM) to credit; (diplomatico) to accredit; ~**rsi** vr (fig) to gain credit.

ac'credito sm (COMM: atto) crediting; (: effetto) credit.

ac'crescere [ak'kreʃʃere] vt to increase; ~**rsi** vr to increase, grow.

accresci'mento [akkreʃʃi'mento] sm increase, growth.

accresci'tivo, a [akkreʃʃi'tivo] ag, sm (LING) augmentative.

accresci'uto, a [akkreʃ'ʃuto] pp di **accrescere**.

accucci'arsi [akkut'tʃarsi] vr (cane) to lie down; (persona) to crouch down.

accu'dire vi: ~ **a** vt to attend to; to look after.

acculturazi'one [akkulturat'tsjone] sf

(*SOCIOLOGIA*) integration.
accumu'lare *vt* to accumulate; ~**rsi** *vr* to accumulate; (*FINANZA*) to accrue.
accumula'tore *sm* (*ELETTR*) accumulator.
accumulazi'one [akkumulat'tsjone] *sf* accumulation.
ac'cumulo *sm* accumulation.
accurata'mente *av* carefully.
accura'tezza [akkura'tettsa] *sf* care; accuracy.
accu'rato, a *ag* (*diligente*) careful; (*preciso*) accurate.
ac'cusa *sf* accusation; (*DIR*) charge; **l'~, la pubblica** ~ (*DIR*) the prosecution; **mettere qn sotto** ~ to indict sb; **in stato di** ~ committed for trial.
accu'sare *vt* (*sentire*: *dolore*) to feel; ~ **qn di qc** to accuse sb of sth; (*DIR*) to charge sb with sth; ~ **ricevuta di** (*COMM*) to acknowledge receipt of; ~ **la fatica** to show signs of exhaustion; **ha accusato il colpo** (*anche fig*) you could see that he had felt the blow.
accusa'tivo *sm* accusative.
accu'sato, a *sm/f* accused.
accusa'tore, 'trice *ag* accusing ♦ *sm/f* accuser ♦ *sm* (*DIR*) prosecutor.
a'cerbo, a [a'tʃɛrbo] *ag* bitter; (*frutta*) sour, unripe; (*persona*) immature.
'acero ['atʃero] *sm* maple.
a'cerrimo, a [a'tʃɛrrimo] *ag* very fierce.
ace'tato [atʃe'tato] *sm* acetate.
a'ceto [a'tʃeto] *sm* vinegar; **mettere sotto** ~ to pickle.
ace'tone [atʃe'tone] *sm* nail varnish remover.
'A.C.I. ['atʃi] *sigla m* (= *Automobile Club d'Italia*) ≈ AA (*BRIT*), AAA (*US*).
acidità [atʃidi'ta] *sf* acidity; sourness; ~ **(di stomaco)** heartburn.
'acido, a ['atʃido] *ag* (*sapore*) acid, sour; (*CHIM, colore*) acid ♦ *sm* (*CHIM*) acid.
a'cidulo, a [a'tʃidulo] *ag* slightly sour, slightly acid.
'acino ['atʃino] *sm* berry; ~ **d'uva** grape.
'ACLI *sigla fpl* (= *Associazioni Cristiane dei Lavoratori Italiani*) Christian Trade Union Association.
'acme *sf* (*fig*) acme, peak; (*MED*) crisis.
'acne *sf* acne.
ACNUR *sigla m* (= *Alto Commissariato delle Nazioni Unite per i Rifugiati*) UNHCR.
'acqua *sf* water; (*pioggia*) rain; ~**e** *sfpl* waters; **fare** ~ (*NAUT*) to leak, take in water; **essere con** *o* **avere l'** ~ **alla gola** to be in great difficulty; **tirare** ~ **al proprio mulino** to feather one's own nest; **navigare in cattive** ~**e** (*fig*) to be in deep

water; ~ **in bocca!** mum's the word!; ~ **corrente** running water; ~ **dolce** fresh water; ~ **di mare** sea water; ~ **minerale** mineral water; ~ **ossigenata** hydrogen peroxide; ~ **piovana** rain water; ~ **potabile** drinking water; ~ **salata** *o* **salmastra** salt water; ~ **tonica** tonic water.
acqua'forte, *pl* acque'forti *sf* etching.
a'cquaio *sm* sink.
acqua'ragia [akkwa'radʒa] *sf* turpentine.
a'cquario *sm* aquarium; (*dello zodiaco*): **A**~ Aquarius; **essere dell'A**~ to be Aquarius.
acquartie'rare *vt* (*MIL*) to quarter.
acqua'santa *sf* holy water.
acquas'cooter [akkwas'cuter] *sm inv* Jet Ski ®.
a'cquatico, a, ci, che *ag* aquatic; (*sport, sci*) water *cpd*.
acquat'tarsi *vr* to crouch (down).
acqua'vite *sf* brandy.
acquaz'zone [akkwat'tsone] *sm* cloudburst, heavy shower.
acque'dotto *sm* aqueduct; waterworks *pl*, water system.
'acqueo, a *ag*: **vapore** ~ water vapour (*BRIT*) *o* vapor (*US*); **umore** ~ aqueous humour (*BRIT*) *o* humor (*US*).
acque'rello *sm* watercolour (*BRIT*), watercolor (*US*).
acque'rugiola [akkwe'rudʒola] *sf* drizzle.
acquie'tare *vt* to appease; (*dolore*) to ease; ~**rsi** *vr* to calm down.
acqui'rente *sm/f* purchaser, buyer.
acqui'sire *vt* to acquire.
acquisizi'one [akkwizit'tsjone] *sf* acquisition.
acquis'tare *vt* to purchase, buy; (*fig*) to gain ♦ *vt* to improve; ~ **in bellezza** to become more beautiful; **ha acquistato in salute** his health has improved.
a'cquisto *sm* purchase; **fare** ~**i** to go shopping; **ufficio** ~**i** (*COMM*) purchasing department; ~ **rateale** instalment purchase, hire purchase (*BRIT*).
acqui'trino *sm* bog, marsh.
acquo'lina *sf*: **far venire l'**~ **in bocca a qn** to make sb's mouth water.
a'cquoso, a *ag* watery.
'acre *ag* acrid, pungent; (*fig*) harsh, biting.
a'credine *sf* (*fig*) bitterness.
a'crilico, a, ci, che *ag*, *sm* acrylic.
a'critico, a, ci, che *ag* uncritical.
a'crobata, i, e *sm/f* acrobat.
acro'batico, a, ci, che *ag* (*ginnastica*) acrobatic; (*AER*) aerobatic ♦ *sf* acrobatics *sg*.
acroba'zia [akrobat'tsia] *sf* acrobatic feat;

~e aeree aerobatics.
a'cronimo *sm* acronym.
a'cropoli *sf inv:* **l'A~** the Acropolis.
acu'ire *vt* to sharpen; **~rsi** *vr* (*gen*) to increase; (*crisi*) to worsen.
a'culeo *sm* (*ZOOL*) sting; (*BOT*) prickle.
a'cume *sm* acumen, perspicacity.
acumi'nato, a *ag* sharp.
a'custico, a, ci, che *ag* acoustic ♦ *sf* (*scienza*) acoustics *sg*; (*di una sala*) acoustics *pl*; **apparecchio** ~ hearing aid; **cornetto** ~ ear trumpet.
acu'tezza [aku'tettsa] *sf* sharpness; shrillness; acuteness; high pitch; intensity; keenness.
acutiz'zare [akutid'dzare] *vt* (*fig*) to intensify; **~rsi** *vr* (*fig: crisi, malattia*) to become worse, worsen.
a'cuto, a *ag* (*appuntito*) sharp, pointed; (*suono, voce*) shrill, piercing; (*MAT, LING, MED*) acute; (*MUS*) high-pitched; (*fig: dolore, desiderio*) intense; (*: perspicace*) acute, keen ♦ *sm* (*MUS*) high note.
ad *prep* (*dav V*) = **a**.
adagi'are [ada'dʒare] *vt* to lay *o* set down carefully; **~rsi** *vr* to lie down, stretch out.
a'dagio [a'dadʒo] *av* slowly ♦ *sm* (*MUS*) adagio; (*proverbio*) adage, saying.
ada'mitico, a, ci, che *ag:* **in costume** ~ in one's birthday suit.
adat'tabile *ag* adaptable.
adattabilità *sf* adaptability.
adatta'mento *sm* adaptation; **avere spirito di** ~ to be adaptable.
adat'tare *vt* to adapt; (*sistemare*) to fit; **~rsi** *vr:* **~rsi (a)** (*ambiente, tempi*) to adapt (to); (*essere adatto*) to be suitable (for); (*accontentarsi*): **~rsi a qc/a fare qc** to make the best of sth/of doing sth.
adatta'tore *sm* (*ELETTR*) adapter, adaptor.
a'datto, a *ag:* ~ **(a)** suitable (for), right (for).
addebi'tare *vt:* ~ **qc a qn** to debit sb with sth; (*fig: incolpare*) to blame sb for sth.
ad'debito *sm* (*COMM*) debit.
addensa'mento *sm* thickening; gathering.
adden'sare *vt* to thicken; **~rsi** *vr* to thicken; (*nuvole*) to gather.
adden'tare *vt* to bite into.
adden'trarsi *vr:* ~ **in** to penetrate, go into.
ad'dentro *av* (*fig*): **essere molto** ~ **in qc** to be well-versed in sth.
addestra'mento *sm* training; ~ **aziendale** company training.
addes'trare *vt*, **~rsi** *vr* to train; **~rsi in qc** to practise (*BRIT*) *o* practice (*US*) sth.
ad'detto, a *ag:* ~ **a** (*persona*) assigned to; (*oggetto*) intended for ♦ *sm* employee;

(*funzionario*) attaché; ~ **commerciale/ stampa** commercial/press attaché; ~ **al telex** telex operator; **gli ~i ai lavori** authorized personnel; (*fig*) those in the know; **"vietato l'ingresso ai non ~i ai lavori"** "authorized personnel only".
addì *av* (*AMM*): ~ **3 luglio 1989** on the 3rd of July 1989 (*BRIT*), on July 3rd 1989 (*US*).
addi'accio [ad'djattʃo] *sm* (*MIL*) bivouac; **dormire all'**~ to sleep in the open.
addi'etro *av* (*indietro*) behind; (*nel passato, prima*) before, ago.
ad'dio *sm*, *escl* goodbye, farewell.
addirit'tura *av* (*veramente*) really, absolutely; (*perfino*) even; (*direttamente*) directly, right away.
ad'dirsi *vr:* ~ **a** to suit, be suitable for.
'Addis A'beba *sf* Addis Ababa.
addi'tare *vt* to point out; (*fig*) to expose.
addi'tivo *sm* additive.
addizio'nale [addittsjo'nale] *ag* additional ♦ *sf* (*anche:* **imposta** ~) surtax.
addizio'nare [addittsjo'nare] *vt* (*MAT*) to add (up).
addizi'one [addit'tsjone] *sf* addition.
addob'bare *vt* to decorate.
ad'dobbo *sm* decoration.
addol'cire [addol'tʃire] *vt* (*caffè etc*) to sweeten; (*acqua, fig: carattere*) to soften; **~rsi** *vr* (*fig*) to mellow, soften; ~ **la pillola** (*fig*) to sugar the pill.
addolo'rare *vt* to pain, grieve; **~rsi** *vr:* **~rsi (per)** to be distressed (by).
addolo'rato, a *ag* distressed, upset; **l'A~a** (*REL*) Our Lady of Sorrows.
ad'dome *sm* abdomen.
addomesti'care *vt* to tame.
addomi'nale *ag* abdominal; **(muscoli** *mpl*) **~i** stomach muscles.
addormen'tare *vt* to put to sleep; **~rsi** *vr* to fall asleep, go to sleep.
addormen'tato, a *ag* sleeping, asleep; (*fig: tardo*) stupid, dopey.
addos'sare *vt* (*appoggiare*): ~ **qc a qc** to lean sth against sth; (*fig*): ~ **la colpa a qn** to lay the blame on sb; **~rsi** *vr:* **~rsi qc** (*responsabilità etc*) to shoulder sth.
ad'dosso *av* (*sulla persona*) on; ~ **a** *prep* (*sopra*) on; (*molto vicino*) right next to; **mettersi** ~ **il cappotto** to put one's coat on; **andare** (*o* **venire**) ~ **a** (*AUT: altra macchina*) to run into; (*: pedone*) to run over; **non ho soldi** ~ I don't have any money on me; **stare** ~ **a qn** (*fig*) to breathe down sb's neck; **dare** ~ **a qn** (*fig*) to attack sb; **mettere gli occhi** ~ **a qn/qc** to take quite a fancy to sb/sth; **mettere le mani** ~ **a qn** (*picchiare*) to hit sb;

(*catturare*) to seize sb; (*molestare*: *donna*) to touch sb up.
ad'dotto, a *pp di* **addurre**.
ad'duco *etc vb vedi* **addurre**.
ad'durre *vt* (*DIR*) to produce; (*citare*) to cite.
ad'dussi *etc vb vedi* **addurre**.
adegu'are *vt*: ~ **qc a** to adjust sth to; ~**rsi** *vr* to adapt.
adegua'tezza [adegwa'tettsa] *sf* adequacy; suitability; fairness.
adegu'ato, a *ag* adequate; (*conveniente*) suitable; (*equo*) fair.
a'dempiere *vt* to fulfil (*BRIT*), fulfill (*US*), carry out; (*comando*) to carry out.
adempi'mento *sm* fulfilment (*BRIT*), fulfillment (*US*); carrying out; **nell'**~ **del proprio dovere** in the performance of one's duty.
adem'pire *vt* = **adempiere**.
'Aden: il golfo di ~ *sm* the Gulf of Aden.
ade'noidi *sfpl* adenoids.
a'depto *sm* disciple, follower.
ade'rente *ag* adhesive; (*vestito*) close-fitting ◊ *smlf* follower.
ade'renza [ade'rɛntsa] *sf* adhesion; ~**e** *sfpl* (*fig*) connections, contacts.
ade'rire *vi* (*stare attaccato*) to adhere, stick; ~ **a** to adhere to, stick to; (*fig*: *società*, *partito*) to join; (: *opinione*) to support; (*richiesta*) to agree to.
ades'care *vt* (*attirare*) to lure, entice; (*TECN*: *pompa*) to prime.
adesi'one *sf* adhesion; (*fig*: *assenso*) agreement, acceptance; (*appoggio*) support.
ade'sivo, a *ag, sm* adhesive.
a'desso *av* (*ora*) now; (*or ora, poco fa*) just now; (*tra poco*) any moment now; **da** ~ **in poi** from now on; **per** ~ for the moment, for now.
adia'cente [adja'tʃɛnte] *ag* adjacent.
adi'bire *vt* (*usare*): ~ **qc a** to turn sth into.
'Adige ['adidʒe] *sm*: **l'**~ the Adige.
'adipe *sm* fat.
adi'poso, a *ag* (*tessuto, zona*) adipose.
adi'rarsi *vr*: ~ (**con** *o* **contro qn per qc**) to get angry (with sb over sth).
adi'rato, a *ag* angry.
a'dire *vt* (*DIR*): ~ **le vie legali** to take legal proceedings; ~ **un'eredità** to take legal possession of an inheritance.
'adito *sm*: **dare** ~ **a** (*sospetti*) to give rise to.
adocchi'are [adok'kjare] *vt* (*scorgere*) to catch sight of; (*occhieggiare*) to eye.
adole'scente [adoleʃ'ʃɛnte] *ag, smlf* adolescent.
adole'scenza [adoleʃ'ʃɛntsa] *sf* adolescence.

adolescenzi'ale [adoleʃʃen'tsjale] *ag* adolescent.
adom'brarsi *vr* (*cavallo*) to shy; (*persona*) to grow suspicious; (: *aversene a male*) to be offended.
adope'rare *vt* to use; ~**rsi** *vr* to strive; ~**rsi per qn/qc** to do one's best for sb/sth.
ado'rabile *ag* adorable.
ado'rare *vt* to adore; (*REL*) to adore, worship.
adorazi'one [adorat'tsjone] *sf* adoration; worship.
ador'nare *vt* to adorn.
a'dorno, a *ag*: ~ (**di**) adorned (with).
adot'tare *vt* to adopt; (*decisione, provvedimenti*) to pass.
adot'tivo, a *ag* (*genitori*) adoptive; (*figlio, patria*) adopted.
adozi'one [adot'tsjone] *sf* adoption; ~ **a distanza** child sponsorship.
adrena'linico, a, ci, che *ag* (*fig*: *vivace, eccitato*) charged-up.
adri'atico, a, ci, che *ag* Adriatic ◊ *sm*: **l'A**~, **il mare A**~ the Adriatic, the Adriatic Sea.
adu'lare *vt* to flatter.
adula'tore, 'trice *smlf* flatterer.
adula'torio, a *ag* flattering.
adulazi'one [adulat'tsjone] *sf* flattery.
adulte'rare *vt* to adulterate.
adul'terio *sm* adultery.
a'dultero, a *ag* adulterous ◊ *smlf* adulterer/adulteress.
a'dulto, a *ag* adult; (*fig*) mature ◊ *sm* adult, grown-up.
adu'nanza [adu'nantsa] *sf* assembly, meeting.
adu'nare *vt*, ~**rsi** *vr* to assemble, gather.
adu'nata *sf* (*MIL*) parade, muster.
a'dunco, a, chi, che *ag* hooked.
aerazi'one [aerat'tsjone] *sf* ventilation; (*TECN*) aeration.
a'ereo, a *ag* air *cpd*; (*radice*) aerial ◊ *sm* aerial; (*aeroplano*) plane; ~ **da caccia** fighter (plane); ~ **di linea** airliner; ~ **a reazione** jet (plane).
ae'robica *sf* aerobics *sg*.
aerodi'namico, a, ci, che *ag* aerodynamic; (*affusolato*) streamlined ◊ *sf* aerodynamics *sg*.
aeromo'dello *sm* model aircraft.
aero'nautica *sf* (*scienza*) aeronautics *sg*; ~ **militare** air force.
aerona'vale *ag* (*forze, manovre*) air and sea *cpd*.
aero'plano *sm* (aero)plane (*BRIT*), (air)plane (*US*).
aero'porto *sm* airport.

aeroportu'ale *ag* airport *cpd.*
aeros'calo *sm* airstrip.
aero'sol *sm inv* aerosol.
aerospazi'ale [aerospat'tsjale] *ag* aerospace.
aeros'tatico, a, ci, che *ag* aerostatic; **pallone** ~ air balloon.
ae'rostato *sm* aerostat.
A.F. *abbr* (= *alta frequenza*) HF; (*AMM*) = **assegni familiari.**
'afa *sf* sultriness.
af'fabile *ag* affable.
affabilità *sf* affability.
affaccen'darsi [affattʃen'darsi] *vr:* ~ **intorno a qc** to busy o.s. with sth.
affaccen'dato, a [affattʃen'dato] *ag* busy.
affacci'arsi [affat'tʃarsi] *vr:* ~ **(a)** to appear (at); ~ **alla vita** to come into the world.
affa'mato, a *ag* starving; (*fig*): ~ **(di)** eager (for).
affan'nare *vt* to leave breathless; (*fig*) to worry; ~**rsi** *vr:* ~**rsi per qn/qc** to worry about sb/sth.
af'fanno *sm* breathlessness; (*fig*) anxiety, worry.
affannosa'mente *av* with difficulty; anxiously.
affan'noso, a *ag* (*respiro*) difficult; (*fig*) troubled, anxious.
af'fare *sm* (*faccenda*) matter, affair; (*COMM*) piece of business, (business) deal; (*occasione*) bargain; (*DIR*) case; (*fam: cosa*) thing; ~**i** *smpl* (*COMM*) business *sg*; ~ **fatto!** done!, it's a deal!; **sono** ~**i miei** that's my business; **bada agli** ~**i tuoi!** mind your own business!; **uomo d'**~**i** businessman; **ministro degli A**~**i Esteri** Foreign Secretary (*BRIT*), Secretary of State (*US*).
affa'rista, i *sm* profiteer, unscrupulous businessman.
affasci'nante [affaʃʃi'nante] *ag* fascinating.
affasci'nare [affaʃʃi'nare] *vt* to bewitch; (*fig*) to charm, fascinate.
affatica'mento *sm* tiredness.
affati'care *vt* to tire; ~**rsi** *vr* (*durar fatica*) to tire o.s. out.
af'fatto *av* completely; **non** ... ~ not ... at all; **niente** ~ not at all.
affer'mare *vi* (*dire di si*) to say yes ♦ *vt* (*dichiarare*) to maintain, affirm; ~**rsi** *vr* to assert o.s., make one's name known.
affermativa'mente *av* in the affirmative, affirmatively.
afferma'tivo, a *ag* affirmative.
affer'mato, a *ag* established, well-known.
affermazi'one [affermat'tsjone] *sf* affirmation, assertion; (*successo*) achievement.

affer'rare *vt* to seize, grasp; (*fig: idea*) to grasp; ~**rsi** *vr:* ~**rsi a** to cling to.
Aff. Est. *abbr* = *Affari Esteri.*
affet'tare *vt* (*tagliare a fette*) to slice; (*ostentare*) to affect.
affet'tato, a *ag* sliced; affected ♦ *sm* sliced cold meat.
affetta'trice [affetta'tritʃe] *sf* meat slicer.
affettazi'one [affettat'tsjone] *sf* affectation.
affet'tivo, a *ag* emotional, affective.
af'fetto, a *ag:* ~ **da** to suffer from ♦ *sm* affection; **gli** ~**i familiari** one's nearest and dearest.
affettuosa'mente *av* affectionately; (*nelle lettere*): **(ti saluto)** ~, **Maria** love, Maria.
affettuosità *sf inv* affection; ~ *sfpl* (*manifestazioni*) demonstrations of affection.
affettu'oso, a *ag* affectionate.
affezio'narsi [affettsjo'narsi] *vr:* ~ **a** to grow fond of.
affezio'nato, a [affettsjo'nato] *ag:* ~ **a qn/qc** fond of sb/sth; (*attaccato*) attached to sb/sth.
affezi'one [affet'tsjone] *sf* (*affetto*) affection; (*MED*) ailment, disorder.
affian'care *vt* to place side by side; (*MIL*) to flank; (*fig*) to support; ~ **qc a qc** to place sth next to *o* beside sth; ~**rsi** *vr:* ~**rsi a qn** to stand beside sb.
affiata'mento *sm* understanding.
affia'tato, a *ag:* **essere** ~**i** to work well together *o* get on; **formano una squadra** ~**a** they make a good team.
affibbi'are *vt* to buckle, do up; (*fig: dare*) to give.
affi'dabile *ag* reliable.
affidabilità *sf* reliability.
affida'mento *sm* (*DIR: di bambino*) custody; (*fiducia*): **fare** ~ **su qn** to rely on sb; **non dà nessun** ~ he's not to be trusted.
affi'dare *vt:* ~ **qc** *o* **qn a qn** to entrust sth *o* sb to sb; ~**rsi** *vr:* ~**rsi a** to place one's trust in.
affievo'lirsi *vr* to grow weak.
af'figgere [af'fiddʒere] *vt* to stick up, post up.
affi'lare *vt* to sharpen.
affi'lato, a *ag* (*gen*) sharp; (*volto, naso*) thin.
affili'are *vt* to affiliate; ~**rsi** *vr:* ~**rsi a** to become affiliated to.
affi'nare *vt* to sharpen.
affinché [affin'ke] *cong* in order that, so that.
af'fine *ag* similar.
affinità *sf inv* affinity.

affio'rare vi to emerge.

af'fissi etc vb vedi **affiggere**.

affissi'one sf billposting.

af'fisso, a pp di **affiggere** ◊ sm bill, poster; (LING) affix.

affitta'camere sm/f inv landlord/landlady.

affit'tare vt (dare in affitto) to let, rent (out); (prendere in affitto) to rent.

af'fitto sm rent; (contratto) lease; **dare in** ~ to rent (out), let; **prendere in** ~ to rent.

affittu'ario sm lessee.

af'fliggere [af'fliddʒere] vt to torment; ~**rsi** vr to grieve.

af'flissi etc vb vedi **affliggere**.

af'flitto, a pp di **affliggere**.

afflizi'one [afflit'tsjone] sf distress, torment.

afflosci'arsi [affloʃ'ʃarsi] vr to go limp; (frutta) to go soft.

afflu'ente sm tributary.

afflu'enza [afflu'ɛntsa] sf flow; (di persone) crowd.

afflu'ire vi to flow; (fig: merci, persone) to pour in.

af'flusso sm influx.

affo'gare vt, vi to drown; ~**rsi** vr to drown; (deliberatamente) to drown o.s.

affo'gato, a ag drowned; (CUC: uova) poached.

affolla'mento sm crowding; (folla) crowd.

affol'lare vt, ~**rsi** vr to crowd.

affol'lato, a ag crowded.

affonda'mento sm (di nave) sinking.

affon'dare vt to sink.

affran'care vt to free, liberate; (AMM) to redeem; (lettera) to stamp; (: meccanicamente) to frank (BRIT), meter (US); ~**rsi** vr to free o.s.

affranca'trice [affranka'tritʃe] sf franking machine (BRIT), postage meter (US).

affranca'tura sf (di francobollo) stamping; franking (BRIT), metering (US); (tassa di spedizione) postage; ~ **a carico del destinatario** postage paid.

af'franto, a ag (esausto) worn out; (abbattuto) overcome.

af'fresco, schi sm fresco.

affret'tare vt to quicken, speed up; ~**rsi** vr to hurry; ~**rsi a fare qc** to hurry o hasten to do sth.

affret'tato, a ag (veloce: passo, ritmo) quick, fast; (frettoloso: decisione) hurried, hasty; (: lavoro) rushed.

affron'tare vt (pericolo etc) to face; (assalire: nemico) to confront; ~**rsi** vr (reciproco) to confront each other.

af'fronto sm affront, insult; **fare un** ~ **a qn** to insult sb.

affumi'care vt to fill with smoke; to blacken with smoke; (alimenti) to smoke.

affuso'lato, a ag tapering.

af'gano, a ag, sm/f Afghan.

Af'ghanistan [af'ganistan] sm: l'~ Afghanistan.

af'ghano, a ag, sm/f = **afgano**.

afo'risma, i sm aphorism.

a'foso, a ag sultry, close.

'Africa sf: l'~ Africa.

afri'cano, a ag, sm/f African.

afroasi'atico a, ci, che ag Afro-Asian.

afrodi'siaco, a, ci, che ag, sm aphrodisiac.

AG sigla = Agrigento.

a'genda [a'dʒɛnda] sf diary; ~ **tascabile/da tavolo** pocket/desk diary.

a'gente [a'dʒɛnte] sm agent; ~ **di cambio** stockbroker; ~ **di custodia** prison officer; ~ **marittimo** shipping agent; ~ **di polizia** police officer; ~ **provocatore** agent provocateur; ~ **delle tasse** tax inspector; ~ **di vendita** sales agent; **resistente agli** ~**i atmosferici** weather-resistant.

agen'zia [adʒen'tsia] sf agency; (succursale) branch; ~ **di collocamento** employment agency; ~ **immobiliare** estate agent's (office) (BRIT), real estate office (US); **A**~ **Internazionale per l'Energia Atomica (AIEA)** International Atomic Energy Agency (IAEA); ~ **matrimoniale** marriage bureau; ~ **pubblicitaria** advertising agency; ~ **di stampa** press agency; ~ **viaggi** travel agency.

agevo'lare [adʒevo'lare] vt to facilitate, make easy.

agevolazi'one [adʒevolat'tsjone] sf (facilitazione economica) facility; ~ **di pagamento** payment on easy terms; ~**i creditizie** credit facilities; ~**i fiscali** tax concessions.

a'gevole [a'dʒevole] ag easy; (strada) smooth.

agganci'are [aggan'tʃare] vt to hook up; (FERR) to couple; ~**rsi** vr: ~**rsi a** to hook up to; (fig: pretesto) to seize on.

ag'gancio [ag'gantʃo] sm (TECN) coupling; (fig: conoscenza) contact.

ag'geggio [ad'dʒeddʒo] sm gadget, contraption.

agget'tivo [add'ʒet'tivo] sm adjective.

agghiacci'ante [aggjat'tʃante] ag (fig) chilling.

agghiacci'are [aggjat'tʃare] vt to freeze; (fig) to make one's blood run cold; ~**rsi** vr to freeze.

agghin'darsi [aggin'darsi] vr to deck o.s. out.

aggiorna'mento [addʒorna'mento] sm

updating; revision; postponement; **corso di** ~ refresher course.

aggior'nare [addʒor'nare] *vt* (*opera, manuale*) to bring up-to-date; (: *rivedere*) to revise; (*listino*) to maintain, up-date; (*seduta etc*) to postpone; ~**rsi** *vr* to bring (*o keep*) o.s. up-to-date.

aggior'nato, a [addʒor'nato] *ag* up-to-date.

aggio'taggio [addʒo'taddʒo] *sm* (*ECON*) rigging the market.

aggi'rare [addʒi'rare] *vt* to go round; (*fig: ingannare*) to trick; ~**rsi** *vr* to wander about; **il prezzo s'aggira sul milione** the price is around the million mark.

aggiudi'care [addʒudi'kare] *vt* to award; (*all'asta*) to knock down; ~**rsi qc** to win sth.

aggi'ungere [ad'dʒundʒere] *vt* to add.

aggi'unsi [ad'dʒunsi] *etc vb vedi* **aggiungere**.

aggi'unto, a [ad'dʒunto] *pp di* **aggiungere** ♦ *ag* assistant *cpd* ♦ *sm* assistant ♦ *sf* addition; **sindaco** ~ deputy mayor; **in** ~**a** ... what's more ....

aggius'tare [addʒus'tare] *vt* (*accomodare*) to mend, repair; (*riassettare*) to adjust; (*fig: lite*) to settle; ~**rsi** *vr* (*arrangiarsi*) to make do; (*con senso reciproco*) to come to an agreement; **ti aggiusto io!** I'll fix you!

agglome'rato *sm* (*di rocce*) conglomerate; (*di legno*) chipboard; ~ **urbano** built-up area.

aggrap'parsi *vr*: ~ **a** to cling to.

aggrava'mento *sm* worsening.

aggra'vante *ag* (*DIR*) aggravating ♦ *sf* aggravation.

aggra'vare *vt* (*aumentare*) to increase; (*appesantire: anche fig*) to weigh down, make heavy; (*fig: pena*) to make worse; ~**rsi** *vr* (*fig*) to worsen, become worse.

ag'gravio *sm*: ~ **di costi** increase in costs.

aggrazi'ato, a [aggrat'tsjato] *ag* graceful.

aggre'dire *vt* to attack, assault.

aggre'gare *vt*: ~ **qn a qc** to admit sb to sth; ~**rsi** *vr* to join; ~**rsi a** to join, become a member of.

aggre'gato, a *ag* associated ♦ *sm* aggregate; ~ **urbano** built-up area.

aggressi'one *sf* aggression; (*atto*) attack; ~ **a mano armata** armed assault.

aggressività *sf* aggressiveness.

aggres'sivo, a *ag* aggressive.

aggres'sore *sm* aggressor, attacker.

aggrot'tare *vt*: ~ **le sopracciglia** to frown.

aggrovigli'are [aggroviʎ'ʎare] *vt* to tangle; ~**rsi** *vr* (*fig*) to become complicated.

agguan'tare *vt* to catch, seize.

aggu'ato *sm* trap; (*imboscata*) ambush; **tendere un** ~ **a qn** to set a trap for sb.

agguer'rito, a *ag* (*sostenitore, nemico*) fierce.

agia'tezza [adʒa'tettsa] *sf* prosperity.

agi'ato, a [a'dʒato] *ag* (*vita*) easy; (*persona*) well-off, well-to-do.

'agile ['adʒile] *ag* agile, nimble.

agilità [adʒili'ta] *sf* agility, nimbleness.

'agio ['adʒo] *sm* ease, comfort; ~**i** *smpl* comforts; **mettersi a proprio** ~ to make o.s. at home *o* comfortable; **dare** ~ **a qn di fare qc** to give sb the chance of doing sth.

a'gire [a'dʒire] *vi* to act; (*esercitare un'azione*) to take effect; (*TECN*) to work, function; ~ **contro qn** (*DIR*) to take action against sb.

agi'tare [adʒi'tare] *vt* (*bottiglia*) to shake; (*mano, fazzoletto*) to wave; (*fig: turbare*) to disturb; (: *incitare*) to stir (up); ~**rsi** *vr* (*mare*) to be rough; (*malato, dormitore*) to toss and turn; (*bambino*) to fidget; (*emozionarsi*) to get upset; (*POL*) to agitate.

agi'tato, a [adʒi'tato] *ag* rough; restless; fidgety; upset, perturbed.

agita'tore, 'trice [adʒita'tore] *sm/f* (*POL*) agitator.

agitazi'one [adʒitat'tsjone] *sf* agitation; (*POL*) unrest, agitation; **mettere in** ~ **qn** to upset *o* distress sb.

'agli ['aʎʎi] *prep + det vedi* **a**.

'aglio ['aʎʎo] *sm* garlic.

a'gnello [aɲ'ɲɛllo] *sm* lamb.

a'gnostico, a, ci, che [aɲ'ɲɔstiko] *ag, sm/f* agnostic.

'ago, *pl* **'aghi** *sm* needle; ~ **da calza** knitting needle.

ago. *abbr* (= *agosto*) Aug.

ago'nia *sf* agony.

ago'nistico, a, ci, che *ag* athletic; (*fig*) competitive.

agoniz'zante [agonid'dzante] *ag* dying.

agoniz'zare [agonid'dzare] *vi* to be dying.

agopun'tura *sf* acupuncture.

agorafo'bia *sf* agoraphobia.

a'gosto *sm* August; *per fraseologia vedi* **luglio**.

a'grario, a *ag* agrarian, agricultural; (*riforma*) land *cpd* ♦ *sm* landowner ♦ *sf* agriculture.

a'gricolo, a *ag* agricultural, farm *cpd*.

agricol'tore *sm* farmer.

agricol'tura *sf* agriculture, farming.

agri'foglio [agri'fɔʎʎo] *sm* holly.

agrimen'sore *sm* land surveyor.

agritu'rismo *sm* farm holidays *pl*.

agritu'ristico, a, ci, che *ag* farm holiday *cpd*.

'agro, a *ag* sour, sharp.

agro'dolce [agro'doltʃe] *ag* bittersweet;

(*salsa*) sweet and sour.
agrono'mia *sf* agronomy.
a'gronomo *sm* agronomist.
a'grume *sm* (*spesso al pl: pianta*) citrus;
(*: frutto*) citrus fruit.
agru'meto *sm* citrus grove.
aguz'zare [agut'tsare] *vt* to sharpen; ~ **gli
orecchi** to prick up one's ears; ~
l'ingegno to use one's wits.
aguz'zino, a [agud'dzino] *sm/f* jailer; (*fig*)
tyrant.
a'guzzo, a [a'guttso] *ag* sharp.
'ahi *escl* (*dolore*) ouch!
ahimè *escl* alas!
'ai *prep* + *det vedi* **a**.
'Aia *sf*: **L'**~ The Hague.
'aia *sf* threshing floor.
AIDDA *sigla f* (= *Associazione Imprenditrici
Donne Dirigenti d'Azienda*) *association of
women entrepreneurs and managers*.
AIDS ['aids] *abbr m o f* AIDS.
AIE *sigla f* (= *Associazione Italiana degli
Editori*) *publishers' association*.
AIEA *sigla f vedi* **Agenzia Internazionale per
l'Energia Atomica**.
AIED *sigla f* (= *Associazione Italiana
Educazione Demografica*) ≈ FPA (= *Family
Planning Association*).
AIG *sigla f* (= *Associazione Italiana Alberghi
per la Gioventù*) ≈ YHA (*BRIT*).
ai'ola *sf* = **aiuola**.
airbag *sm inv* air bag.
AIRC *abbr f* = *associazione italiana per la
ricerca sul cancro*.
ai'rone *sm* heron.
ai'tante *ag* robust.
aiu'ola *sf* flower bed.
aiu'tante *sm/f* assistant ♦ *sm* (*MIL*) adjutant;
(*NAUT*) master-at-arms; ~ **di campo** aide-
de-camp.
aiu'tare *vt* to help; ~ **qn (a fare)** to help sb
(to do).
ai'uto *sm* help, assistance, aid; (*aiutante*)
assistant; **venire in** ~ **di qn** to come to sb's
aid; ~ **chirurgo** assistant surgeon.
aiz'zare [ait'tsare] *vt* to incite; ~ **i cani
contro qn** to set the dogs on sb.
al *prep* + *det vedi* **a**.
a.l. *abbr* = **anno luce**.
'ala, *pl* **'ali** *sf* wing; **fare** ~ to fall back,
make way; ~ **destra/sinistra** (*SPORT*)
right/left wing.
ala'bastro *sm* alabaster.
'alacre *ag* quick, brisk.
alacrità *sf* promptness, speed.
alam'bicco, chi *sm* still (*CHIM*).
a'lano *sm* Great Dane.
a'lare *ag* wing *cpd*; ~**i** *smpl* firedogs.

A'laska *sf*: **l'**~ Alaska.
a'lato, a *ag* winged.
'alba *sf* dawn; **all'**~ at dawn.
alba'nese *ag, sm/f, sm* Albanian.
Alba'nia *sf*: **l'**~ Albania.
'albatro *sm* albatross.
albeggi'are [albed'dʒare] *vi, vb impers* to
dawn.
albe'rato, a *ag* (*viale, piazza*) lined with
trees, tree-lined.
albera'tura *sf* (*NAUT*) masts *pl*.
alber'gare *vt* (*dare albergo*) to
accommodate ♦ *vi* (*poetico*) to dwell.
alberga'tore, 'trice *sm/f* hotelier, hotel
owner.
alberghi'ero, a [alber'gjɛro] *ag* hotel *cpd*.
al'bergo, ghi *sm* hotel; ~ **diurno** *public
toilets with washing and shaving
facilities etc*; ~ **della gioventù** youth
hostel.
'albero *sm* tree; (*NAUT*) mast; (*TECN*) shaft;
~ **a camme** camshaft; ~ **genealogico**
family tree; ~ **a gomiti** crankshaft; ~
maestro mainmast; ~ **di Natale**
Christmas tree; ~ **di trasmissione**
transmission shaft.
albi'cocca, che *sf* apricot.
albi'cocco, chi *sm* apricot tree.
al'bino, a *ag, sm/f* albino.
'albo *sm* (*registro*) register, roll; (*AMM*)
notice board.
'album *sm* album; ~ **da disegno** sketch
book.
al'bume *sm* albumen; (*bianco d'uovo*) egg
white.
albu'mina *sf* albumin.
'alce ['altʃe] *sm* elk.
al'chimia [al'kimja] *sf* alchemy.
alchi'mista, i [alki'mista] *sm* alchemist.
'alcol *sm inv* = **alcool**.
alcolicità [alkolitʃi'ta] *sf* alcohol(ic)
content.
al'colico, a, ci, che *ag* alcoholic ♦ *sm*
alcoholic drink.
alco'lismo *sm* alcoholism.
alco'lista, i, e *sm/f* alcoholic.
alcoliz'zato, a [alkolid'dzato] *sm/f* alcoholic.
'alcool *sm inv* alcohol; ~ **denaturato**
methylated spirits *pl* (*BRIT*), wood alcohol
(*US*); ~ **etilico** ethyl alcohol; ~ **metilico**
methyl alcohol.
alco'olico *etc vedi* **alcolico** *etc*.
alco'test *sm inv* Breathalyser ® (*BRIT*),
Breathalyzer ® (*US*).
al'cova *sf* alcove.
al'cuno, a *det* (*dav sm*: **alcun** + *C, V,* **alcuno**
+ *s impura, gn, pn, ps, x, z; dav sf*: **alcuna** +
C, **alcun'** +*V*) (*nessuno*): **non ...** ~ no, not

any; ~i(e) det pl, pron pl some, a few; non
c'è ~a fretta there's no hurry, there isn't
any hurry; senza alcun riguardo without
any consideration.
aldilà sm inv: l'~ the next life, the after-life.
alea'torio, a ag (incerto) uncertain.
aleggi'are [aled'dʒare] vi (fig: profumo,
sospetto) to be in the air.
Ales'sandria sf (anche: ~ d'Egitto)
Alexandria.
a'letta sf (TECN) fin; tab.
alet'tone sm (AER) aileron.
Aleu'tine sfpl: le isole ~ the Aleutian
Islands.
alfa'betico, a, ci, che ag alphabetical.
alfa'beto sm alphabet.
alfanu'merico, a, ci, che ag
alphanumeric.
alfi'ere sm standard-bearer; (SCACCHI)
bishop.
al'fine av finally, in the end.
'alga, ghe sf seaweed no pl, alga.
'algebra ['aldʒebra] sf algebra.
Al'geri [al'dʒeri] sf Algiers.
Alge'ria [aldʒe'ria] sf: l'~ Algeria.
alge'rino, a [aldʒe'rino] ag, sm/f Algerian.
algo'ritmo sm algorithm.
ALI sigla f (= Associazione Librai Italiani)
booksellers' association.
ali'ante sm (AER) glider.
'alibi sm inv alibi.
a'lice [a'litʃe] sf anchovy.
alie'nare vt (DIR) to transfer; (rendere
ostile) to alienate; ~rsi qn to alienate sb.
alie'nato, a ag alienated; transferred; (fuor
di senno) insane ♦ sm lunatic, insane
person.
alienazi'one [aljenat'tsjone] sf alienation;
transfer; insanity.
ali'eno, a ag (avverso): ~ (da) opposed (to),
averse (to) ♦ sm/f alien.
alimen'tare vt to feed; (TECN) to feed,
supply; (fig) to sustain ♦ ag food cpd; ~i
smpl foodstuffs; (anche: negozio di ~i)
grocer's shop; regime ~ diet.
alimenta'tore sm (ELETTR) feeder.
alimentazi'one [alimentat'tsjone] sf
feeding; (cibi) diet; ~ di fogli (INFORM)
sheet feed.
ali'mento sm food; ~i smpl food sg; (DIR)
alimony.
a'liquota sf share; ~ d'imposta tax rate; ~
minima (FISCO) basic rate.
alis'cafo sm hydrofoil.
'alito sm breath.
all. abbr (= allegato) enc., encl.
'alla prep + det vedi a.
allaccia'mento [allattʃa'mento] sm (TECN)

connection.
allacci'are [allat'tʃare] vt (scarpe) to tie,
lace (up); (cintura) to do up, fasten; (due
località) to link; (luce, gas) to connect;
(amicizia) to form; ~rsi vr (vestito) to
fasten; ~ o ~rsi la cintura to fasten one's
belt.
allaccia'tura [allattʃa'tura] sf fastening.
allaga'mento sm flooding no pl; flood.
alla'gare vt, ~rsi vr to flood.
allampa'nato, a ag lanky.
allar'gare vt to widen; (vestito) to let out;
(aprire) to open; (fig: dilatare) to extend;
~rsi vr (gen) to widen; (scarpe, pantaloni) to
stretch; (fig: problema, fenomeno) to
spread.
allar'mare vt to alarm; ~rsi vr to become
alarmed.
al'larme sm alarm; mettere qn in ~ to
alarm sb; ~ aereo air-raid warning.
allar'mismo sm scaremongering.
allar'mista, i, e sm/f scaremonger,
alarmist.
allat'tare vt (sog: donna) to (breast-)feed;
(: animale) to suckle; ~ artificialmente to
bottle-feed.
'alle prep + det vedi a.
alle'anza [alle'antsa] sf alliance; A~
Democratica (POL) moderate centre-left
party; A~ Nazionale (POL) party on the far
right.
alle'arsi vr to form an alliance.
alle'ato, a ag allied ♦ sm/f ally.
alleg. abbr = all.
alle'gare vt (accludere) to enclose; (DIR:
citare) to cite, adduce; (denti) to set on
edge.
alle'gato, a ag enclosed ♦ sm enclosure; (di
e-mail) attachment; in ~ enclosed; in ~ Vi
inviamo ... please find enclosed ....
allegge'rire [alleddʒe'rire] vt to lighten,
make lighter; (fig: sofferenza) to alleviate,
lessen; (: lavoro, tasse) to reduce.
allego'ria sf allegory.
alle'gorico, a, ci, che ag allegorical.
alle'gria sf gaiety, cheerfulness.
al'legro, a ag cheerful, merry; (un po'
brillo) merry, tipsy; (vivace: colore) bright
♦ sm (MUS) allegro.
allena'mento sm training.
alle'nare vt, ~rsi vr to train.
allena'tore sm (SPORT) trainer, coach.
allen'tare vt to slacken; (disciplina) to
relax; ~rsi vr to become slack;
(ingranaggio) to work loose.
aller'gia, 'gie [aller'dʒia] sf allergy.
al'lergico, a, ci, che [al'lɛrdʒiko] ag
allergic.

allesti'mento sm preparation, setting up; **in** ~ in preparation.
alles'tire vt (cena) to prepare; (esercito, nave) to equip, fit out; (spettacolo) to stage.
allet'tante ag attractive, alluring.
allet'tare vt to lure, entice.
alleva'mento sm breeding, rearing; (luogo) stock farm; **pollo d'**~ battery hen.
alle'vare vt (animale) to breed, rear; (bambino) to bring up.
alleva'tore sm breeder.
allevi'are vt to alleviate.
alli'bire vi to turn pale; (essere turbato) to be disconcerted.
alli'bito, a ag pale; disconcerted.
allibra'tore sm bookmaker.
allie'tare vt to cheer up, gladden.
alli'evo sm pupil; (apprendista) apprentice; ~ **ufficiale** cadet.
alliga'tore sm alligator.
allinea'mento sm alignment.
alline'are vt (persone, cose) to line up; (TIP) to align; (fig: economia, salari) to adjust, align; ~**rsi** vr to line up; (fig: a idee): ~**rsi a** to come into line with.
alline'ato, a ag aligned, in line; **paesi non** ~**i** (POL) non-aligned countries.
'allo prep + det vedi **a**.
allo'care vt to allocate.
al'locco, a, chi, che sm tawny owl ♦ smlf oaf.
allocuzi'one [allokut'tsjone] sf address, solemn speech.
al'lodola sf (sky)lark.
alloggi'are [allod'dʒare] vt to accommodate ♦ vi to live.
al'loggio [al'lɔddʒo] sm lodging, accommodation (BRIT), accommodations (US); (appartamento) flat (BRIT), apartment (US).
allontana'mento sm removal; dismissal; estrangement.
allonta'nare vt to send away, send off; (impiegato) to dismiss; (pericolo) to avert, remove; (estraniare) to alienate; ~**rsi** vr: ~**rsi (da)** to go away (from); (estraniarsi) to become estranged (from).
al'lora av (in quel momento) then ♦ cong (in questo caso) well then; (dunque) well then, so; **la gente d'**~ people then o in those days; **da** ~ **in poi** from then on; **e** ~**?** (che fare?) what now?; (e con ciò?) so what?
allor'ché [allor'ke] cong (formale) when, as soon as.
al'loro sm laurel; **riposare** o **dormire sugli** ~**i** to rest on one's laurels.
'alluce ['allutʃe] sm big toe.

alluci'nante [allutʃi'nante] ag (scena, spettacolo) awful, terrifying; (fam: incredibile) amazing.
alluci'nato, a [allutʃi'nato] ag terrified; (fuori di sé) bewildered, confused.
allucinazi'one [allutʃinat'tsjone] sf hallucination.
al'ludere vi: ~ **a** to allude to, hint at.
allu'minio sm aluminium (BRIT), aluminum (US).
allu'naggio [allu'naddʒo] sm moon landing.
allu'nare vi to land on the moon.
allun'gare vt to lengthen; (distendere) to prolong, extend; (diluire) to water down; ~**rsi** vr to lengthen; (ragazzo) to stretch, grow taller; (sdraiarsi) to lie down, stretch out; ~ **le mani** (rubare) to pick pockets; **gli allungò uno schiaffo** he took a swipe at him.
al'lusi etc vb vedi **alludere**.
allusi'one sf hint, allusion.
al'luso, a pp di **alludere**.
alluvi'one sf flood.
alma'nacco, chi sm almanac.
al'meno av at least ♦ cong: **(se)** ~ if only; **(se)** ~ **piovesse!** if only it would rain!
a'logeno a [a'lɔdʒeno] ag: **lampada** ~**a** halogen lamp.
a'lone sm halo.
al'pestre ag (delle alpi) alpine; (montuoso) mountainous.
'Alpi sfpl: **le** ~ the Alps.
alpi'nismo sm mountaineering, climbing.
alpi'nista, i, e smlf mountaineer, climber.
al'pino, a ag Alpine; mountain cpd; ~**i** smpl (MIL) Italian Alpine troops.
al'quanto av rather, a little; ~, **a** det a certain amount of, some ♦ pron a certain amount, some; ~**i(e)** det pl, pron pl several, quite a few.
Al'sazia [al'sattsja] sf Alsace.
alt escl halt!, stop! ♦ sm: **dare l'**~ to call a halt.
alta'lena sf (a funi) swing; (in bilico, anche fig) seesaw.
alta'mente av extremely, highly.
al'tare sm altar.
alte'rare vt to alter, change; (cibo) to adulterate; (registro) to falsify; (persona) to irritate; ~**rsi** vr to alter; (cibo) to go bad; (persona) to lose one's temper.
alterazi'one [alterat'tsjone] sf alteration, change; adulteration; falsification; annoyance.
al'terco, chi sm altercation, wrangle.
alter'nanza [alter'nantsa] sf alternation; (AGR) rotation.
alter'nare vt, ~**rsi** vr to alternate.

alterna'tivo, a *ag* alternative ♦ *sf* alternative; **non abbiamo** ~**e** we have no alternative.

alter'nato, a *ag* alternate; (*ELETTR*) alternating.

alterna'tore *sm* alternator.

al'terno, a *ag* alternate; **a giorni** ~**i** on alternate days, every other day; **circolazione a targhe** ~**e** (*AUT*) *system of restricting vehicle use to odd/even registrations on alternate days.*

al'tero, a *ag* proud.

al'tezza [al'tettsa] *sf* (*di edificio, persona*) height; (*di tessuto*) width, breadth; (*di acqua, pozzo*) depth; (*di suono*) pitch; (*GEO*) latitude; (*titolo*) highness; (*fig: nobiltà*) greatness; **essere all'**~ **di** to be on a level with; (*fig*) to be up to *o* equal to; **all'**~ **della farmacia** near the chemist's.

altez'zoso, a [altet'tsoso] *ag* haughty.

al'ticcio, a, ci, ce [al'tittʃo] *ag* tipsy.

altipi'ano *sm* = **altopiano**.

altiso'nante *ag* (*fig*) high-sounding, pompous.

alti'tudine *sf* altitude.

'alto, a *ag* high; (*persona*) tall; (*tessuto*) wide, broad; (*sonno, acque*) deep; (*suono*) high(-pitched); (*GEO*) upper; (: *settentrionale*) northern ♦ *sm* top (part) ♦ *av* high; (*parlare*) aloud, loudly; **il palazzo è** ~ **20 metri** the building is 20 metres high; **il tessuto è** ~ **70 cm** the material is 70 cm wide; **ad** ~**a voce** aloud; **a notte** ~**a** in the dead of night; **in** ~ up, upwards; at the top; **mani in** ~! hands up!; **dall'**~ **in** *o* **al basso** up and down; **degli** ~**i e bassi** (*fig*) ups and downs; **andare a testa** ~**a** (*fig*) to carry one's head high; **essere in** ~ **mare** (*fig*) to be far from a solution; ~**a fedeltà** high fidelity, hi-fi; ~**a moda** haute couture; **l'A**~ **Medioevo** the Early Middle Ages; **l'**~ **Po** the upper reaches of the Po.

altoate'sino, a *ag* of (*o* from) the Alto Adige.

alto'forno *sm* blast furnace.

altolo'cato, a *ag* of high rank, highly placed.

altopar'lante *sm* loudspeaker.

altopi'ano, *pl* **alti'piani** *sm* upland plain, plateau.

'Alto 'Volta *sm*: **l'**~ Upper Volta.

altret'tanto, a *ag, pron* as much; (*pl*) as many ♦ *av* equally; **tanti auguri!** — **grazie,** ~ all the best! — thank you, the same to you.

'altri *pron inv* (*qualcuno*) somebody; (: *in espressioni negative*) anybody; (*un'altra persona*) another (person).

altri'menti *av* otherwise.

══════════════════ **PAROLA CHIAVE**

'altro, a *det* **1** (*diverso*) other, different; **questa è un'**~**a cosa** that's another *o* a different thing; **passami l'**~**a penna** give me the other pen

2 (*supplementare*) other; **prendi un** ~ **cioccolatino** have another chocolate; **hai avuto** ~**e notizie?** have you had any more *o* any other news?; **hai** ~ **pane?** have you got any more bread?

3 (*nel tempo*): **l'**~ **giorno** the other day; **l'altr'anno** last year; **l'**~ **ieri** the day before yesterday; **domani l'**~ the day after tomorrow; **quest'**~ **mese** next month

4: **d'**~**a parte** on the other hand
♦ *pron* **1** (*persona, cosa diversa o supplementare*): **un** ~, **un'**~**a** another (one); **lo farà un** ~ someone else will do it; ~**i, e** others; **gli** ~**i** (*la gente*) others, other people; **l'uno e l'**~ both (of them); **aiutarsi l'un l'**~ to help one another; **prendine un** ~ have another (one); **da un giorno all'**~ from day to day; (*nel giro di 24 ore*) from one day to the next; (*da un momento all'altro*) any day now

2 (*sostantivato: solo maschile*) something else; (: *in espressioni interrogative*) anything else; **non ho** ~ **da dire** I have nothing else *o* I don't have anything else to say; **desidera** ~? do you want anything else?; **più che** ~ above all; **se non** ~ if nothing else, at least; **tra l'**~ among other things; **ci mancherebbe** ~! that's all we need!; **non faccio** ~ **che lavorare** I do nothing but work; **contento?** — ~ **che!** are you pleased? — I certainly am!; *vedi anche* **senza; noialtri; voialtri; tutto.**

altroché [altro'ke] *escl* certainly!, and how!

al'tronde *av*: **d'**~ on the other hand.

al'trove *av* elsewhere, somewhere else.

al'trui *ag inv* other people's ♦ *sm*: **l'**~ other people's belongings *pl*.

altru'ismo *sm* altruism.

altru'ista, i, e *ag* altruistic ♦ *sm/f* altruist.

al'tura *sf* (*rialto*) height, high ground; (*alto mare*) open sea; **pesca d'**~ deep-sea fishing.

a'lunno, a *sm/f* pupil.

alve'are *sm* hive.

'alveo *sm* riverbed.

alzabandi'era [altsaban'djera] *sm inv* (*MIL*): **l'**~ the raising of the flag.

al'zare [al'tsare] *vt* to raise, lift; (*issare*) to hoist; (*costruire*) to build, erect; ~**rsi** *vr* to rise; (*dal letto*) to get up; (*crescere*) to grow tall (*o* taller); ~ **le spalle** to shrug one's shoulders; ~ **le carte** to cut the cards; ~ **il gomito** to drink too much; ~ **le mani su qn** to raise one's hand to sb; ~ **i tacchi** to take to one's heels; ~**rsi in piedi** to stand up, get to one's feet; ~**rsi col piede sbagliato** to get out of bed on the wrong side.

al'zata [al'tsata] *sf* lifting, raising; **un'**~ **di spalle** a shrug.

A.M. *abbr* = **aeronautica militare.**

a'mabile *ag* lovable; (*vino*) sweet.

'**AMAC** *sigla f* = *Aeronautica Militare-Aviazione Civile.*

a'maca, che *sf* hammock.

amalga'mare *vt*, ~**rsi** *vr* to amalgamate.

a'mante *ag*: ~ **di** (*musica etc*) fond of ♦ *sm/f* lover/mistress.

amara'mente *av* bitterly.

ama'ranto *sm* (*BOT*) love-lies-bleeding ♦ *ag inv*: **color** ~ reddish purple.

a'mare *vt* to love; (*amico, musica, sport*) to like.

amareggi'are [amared'dʒare] *vt* to sadden, upset; ~**rsi** *vr* to get upset; ~**rsi la vita** to make one's life a misery.

amareggi'ato, a [amared'dʒato] *ag* upset, saddened.

ama'rena *sf* sour black cherry.

ama'retto *sm* (*dolce*) macaroon; (*liquore*) *bitter liqueur made with almonds.*

ama'rezza [ama'rettsa] *sf* bitterness.

a'maro, a *ag* bitter ♦ *sm* bitterness; (*liquore*) bitters *pl.*

ama'rognolo, a [ama'roɲɲolo] *ag* slightly bitter.

a'mato, a *ag* beloved, loved, dear ♦ *sm/f* loved one.

ama'tore, 'trice *sm/f* (*amante*) lover; (*intenditore: di vini etc*) connoisseur; (*dilettante*) amateur.

a'mazzone [a'maddzone] *sf* (*MITOLOGIA*) Amazon; (*cavallerizza*) horsewoman; (*abito*) riding habit; **cavalcare all'**~ to ride sidesaddle; **il Rio delle A**~**i** the (river) Amazon.

Amaz'zonia [amad'dzonja] *sf* Amazonia.

amaz'zonico, a, ci, che [amad'dzɔniko] *ag* Amazonian; Amazon *cpd.*

ambasce'ria [ambaʃʃe'ria] *sf* embassy.

ambasci'ata [ambaʃ'ʃata] *sf* embassy; (*messaggio*) message.

ambascia'tore, 'trice [ambaʃʃa'tore] *sm/f* ambassador/ambassadress.

ambe'due *ag inv*: ~ **i ragazzi** both boys ♦ *pron inv* both.

ambi'destro, a *ag* ambidextrous.

ambien'tale *ag* (*temperatura*) ambient *cpd*; (*problemi, tutela*) environmental.

ambienta'lismo *sm* environmentalism.

ambienta'lista, i, e *ag* environmental ♦ *sm/f* environmentalist.

ambien'tare *vt* to acclimatize; (*romanzo, film*) to set; ~**rsi** *vr* to get used to one's surroundings.

ambientazi'one [ambjentat'tsjone] *sf* setting.

ambi'ente *sm* environment; (*fig: insieme di persone*) milieu; (*stanza*) room.

ambiguità *sf inv* ambiguity.

am'biguo, a *ag* ambiguous; (*persona*) shady.

am'bire *vt* (*anche: vi*: ~ **a**) to aspire to; **un premio molto ambito** a much sought-after prize.

'**ambito** *sm* sphere, field.

ambiva'lente *ag* ambivalent; **questo apparecchio è** ~ this is a dual-purpose device.

ambizi'one [ambit'tsjone] *sf* ambition.

ambizi'oso, a [ambit'tsjoso] *ag* ambitious.

'**ambo** *ag inv* both.

'**ambra** *sf* amber; ~ **grigia** ambergris.

ambu'lante *ag* travelling, itinerant.

ambu'lanza [ambu'lantsa] *sf* ambulance.

ambulatori'ale *ag* (*MED*) outpatients *cpd*; **operazione** ~ operation as an outpatient; **visita** ~ visit to the doctor's surgery (*BRIT*) *o* office (*US*).

ambula'torio *sm* (*studio medico*) surgery (*BRIT*), doctor's office (*US*).

'**AMDI** *sigla f* = *Associazione Medici Dentisti Italiani.*

a'meba *sf* amoeba (*BRIT*), ameba (*US*).

amenità *sf inv* pleasantness *no pl*; (*facezia*) pleasantry.

a'meno, a *ag* pleasant; (*strano*) funny, strange; (*spiritoso*) amusing.

A'merica *sf*: **l'**~ America; **l'**~ **latina** Latin America; **l'**~ **del sud** South America.

america'nata *sf* (*peg*): **le Olimpiadi sono state una vera** ~ the Olympics were a typically vulgar American extravaganza.

america'nismo *sm* Americanism; (*ammirazione*) love of America.

ameri'cano, a *ag*, *sm/f* American.

ame'tista *sf* amethyst.

ami'anto *sm* asbestos.

a'mica *sf vedi* **amico.**

ami'chevole [ami'kevole] *ag* friendly.

ami'cizia [ami'tʃittsja] *sf* friendship; ~**e** *sfpl* (*amici*) friends; **fare** ~ **con qn** to make friends with sb.

a'mico, a, ci, che *sm/f* friend; (*amante*) boyfriend/girlfriend; ~ **del cuore** *o* **intimo**

bosom friend; ~ **d'infanzia** childhood friend.

'amido sm starch.

ammac'care vt (pentola) to dent; (persona) to bruise; ~**rsi** vr to bruise.

ammacca'tura sf dent; bruise.

ammaes'trare vt (animale) to train; (persona) to teach.

ammai'nare vt to lower, haul down.

amma'larsi vr to fall ill.

amma'lato, a ag ill, sick ♦ sm/f sick person; (paziente) patient.

ammali'are vt (fig) to enchant, charm.

ammalia'tore, 'trice sm/f enchanter/enchantress.

am'manco, chi sm (ECON) deficit.

ammanet'tare vt to handcuff.

ammani'cato, a, ammanigli'ato, a [ammaniʎ'ʎato] ag (fig) with friends in high places.

amman'sire vt (animale) to tame; (fig: persona) to calm down, placate.

amman'tarsi vr: ~ **di** (persona) to wrap o.s. in; (fig: prato etc) to be covered in.

amma'raggio [amma'raddʒo] sm (sea) landing; splashdown.

amma'rare vi (AER) to make a sea landing; (astronave) to splash down.

ammas'sare vt (ammucchiare) to amass; (raccogliere) to gather together; ~**rsi** vr to pile up; to gather.

am'masso sm mass; (mucchio) pile, heap; (ECON) stockpile.

ammat'tire vi to go mad.

ammaz'zare [ammat'tsare] vt to kill; ~**rsi** vr (uccidersi) to kill o.s.; (rimanere ucciso) to be killed; ~**rsi di lavoro** to work o.s. to death.

am'menda sf amends pl; (DIR, SPORT) fine; **fare** ~ **di qc** to make amends for sth.

am'messo, a pp di **ammettere** ♦ cong: ~ **che** supposing that.

am'mettere vt to admit; (riconoscere: fatto) to acknowledge, admit; (permettere) to allow, accept; (supporre) to suppose; **ammettiamo che** ... let us suppose that ....

ammez'zato [ammed'dzato] sm (anche: **piano** ~) entresol, mezzanine.

ammic'care vi: ~ **(a)** to wink (at).

amminis'trare vt to run, manage; (REL, DIR) to administer.

amministra'tivo, a ag administrative.

amministra'tore sm administrator; (COMM) director; ~ **aggiunto** associate director; ~ **delegato** managing director; ~ **fiduciario** trustee; ~ **unico** sole director.

amministrazi'one [amministrat'tsjone] sf management; administration; **consiglio d'**~ board of directors; **l'**~ **comunale** local government; ~ **fiduciaria** trust.

ammi'raglia [ammi'raʎʎa] sf flagship.

ammiragli'ato [ammiraʎ'ʎato] sm admiralty.

ammi'raglio [ammi'raʎʎo] sm admiral.

ammi'rare vt to admire.

ammira'tore, 'trice sm/f admirer.

ammirazi'one [ammirat'tsjone] sf admiration.

am'misi etc vb vedi **ammettere**.

ammis'sibile ag admissible, acceptable.

ammissi'one sf admission; (approvazione) acknowledgment.

Amm.ne abbr = **amministrazione**.

ammobili'are vt to furnish.

ammobili'ato, a ag (camera, appartamento) furnished.

ammoder'nare vt to modernize.

am'modo, a 'modo av properly ♦ ag inv respectable, nice.

ammogli'are [ammoʎ'ʎare] vt to find a wife for; ~**rsi** vr to marry, take a wife.

am'mollo sm: **lasciare in** ~ to leave to soak.

ammo'niaca sf ammonia.

ammoni'mento sm warning; admonishment.

ammo'nire vt (avvertire) to warn; (rimproverare) to admonish; (DIR) to caution.

ammonizi'one [ammonit'tsjone] sf (monito: anche SPORT) warning; (rimprovero) reprimand; (DIR) caution.

ammon'tare vi: ~ **a** to amount to ♦ sm (total) amount.

ammonticchi'are [ammontik'kjare] vt to pile up, heap up.

ammor'bare vt (diffondere malattia) to infect; (sog: odore) to taint, foul.

ammorbi'dente sm fabric softener.

ammorbi'dire vt to soften.

ammorta'mento sm redemption; amortization; ~ **fiscale** capital allowance.

ammor'tare vt (FINANZA: debito) to pay off, redeem; (: spese d'impianto) to write off.

ammortiz'zare [ammortid'dzare] vt (FINANZA) to pay off, redeem; (: spese d'impianto) to write off; (AUT, TECN) to absorb, deaden.

ammortizza'tore [ammortiddza'tore] sm (AUT, TECN) shock absorber.

ammucchi'are [ammuk'kjare] vt, ~**rsi** vr to pile up, accumulate.

ammuf'fire vi to go mouldy (BRIT) o moldy (US).

ammutina'mento *sm* mutiny.

ammuti'narsi *vr* to mutiny.

ammuti'nato, a *ag* mutinous ♦ *sm* mutineer.

ammuto'lire *vi* to be struck dumb.

amne'sia *sf* amnesia.

amnis'tia *sf* amnesty.

'amo *sm* (PESCA) hook; (fig) bait.

amo'rale *ag* amoral.

a'more *sm* love; ~i *smpl* love affairs; **il tuo bambino è un** ~ your baby's a darling; **fare l'**~ *o* **all'**~ to make love; **andare d'**~ **e d'accordo con qn** to get on like a house on fire with sb; **per** ~ *o* **per forza** by hook or by crook; **amor proprio** self-esteem, pride.

amoreggi'are [amored'dʒare] *vi* to flirt.

amo'revole *ag* loving, affectionate.

a'morfo, a *ag* amorphous; (fig: persona) lifeless.

amo'rino *sm* cupid.

amo'roso, a *ag* (affettuoso) loving, affectionate; (d'amore: sguardo) amorous; (: poesia, relazione) love *cpd*.

am'pere [ã'pɛr] *sm inv* amp(ère).

ampi'ezza [am'pjɛttsa] *sf* width, breadth; spaciousness; (fig: importanza) scale, size; ~ **di vedute** broad-mindedness.

'ampio, a *ag* wide, broad; (spazioso) spacious; (abbondante: vestito) loose; (: gonna) full; (: spiegazione) ample, full.

am'plesso *sm* (sessuale) intercourse.

amplia'mento *sm* (di strada) widening; (di aeroporto) expansion; (fig) broadening.

ampli'are *vt* (allargare) to widen; (fig: discorso) to enlarge on; ~**rsi** *vr* to grow, increase; ~ **la propria cultura** to broaden one's mind.

amplifi'care *vt* to amplify; (magnificare) to extol.

amplifica'tore *sm* (TECN, MUS) amplifier.

amplificazi'one [amplifikat'tsjone] *sf* amplification.

am'polla *sf* (vasetto) cruet.

ampol'loso, a *ag* bombastic, pompous.

ampu'tare *vt* (MED) to amputate.

amputazi'one [amputat'tsjone] *sf* amputation.

'Amsterdam *sf* Amsterdam.

amu'leto *sm* lucky charm.

AN *sigla* = Ancona.

A.N. *sigla f* (POL) = **Alleanza Nazionale**.

anabbagli'ante [anabbaʎ'ʎante] *ag* (AUT) dipped (BRIT), dimmed (US); ~**i** *smpl* dipped *o* dimmed headlights.

anaboliz'zante [anabolid'dzante] *sm* anabolic steroid ♦ *ag* (sostanza) anabolic.

anacro'nismo *sm* anachronism.

a'nagrafe *sf* (registro) register of births, marriages and deaths; (ufficio) registry office (BRIT), office of vital statistics (US).

ana'grafico, a, ci, che *ag* (AMM): **dati** ~**ci** personal data; **comune di residenza** ~**a** district where resident.

ana'gramma, i *sm* anagram.

anal'colico, a, ci, che *ag* non-alcoholic ♦ *sm* soft drink; **bevanda** ~**a** soft drink.

a'nale *ag* anal.

analfa'beta, i, e *ag*, *smf* illiterate.

analfabe'tismo *sm* illiteracy.

anal'gesico, a, ci, che [anal'dʒɛziko] *ag*, *sm* analgesic.

a'nalisi *sf inv* analysis; (MED: esame) test; **in ultima** ~ in conclusion, in the final analysis; ~ **grammaticale** parsing; ~ **del sangue** blood test; ~ **dei sistemi/costi** systems/cost analysis.

ana'lista, i, e *smf* analyst; (PSIC) (psycho)analyst; ~ **finanziario** financial analyst; ~ **di sistemi** systems analyst.

ana'litico, a, ci, che *ag* analytic(al).

analiz'zare [analid'dzare] *vt* to analyse (BRIT), analyze (US); (MED) to test.

analo'gia, 'gie [analo'dʒia] *sf* analogy.

ana'logico, a, ci, che [ana'lɔdʒiko] *ag* analogical; (calcolatore, orologio) analog(ue).

a'nalogo, a, ghi, ghe *ag* analogous.

'ananas *sm inv* pineapple.

anar'chia [anar'kia] *sf* anarchy.

a'narchico, a, ci, che [a'narkiko] *ag* anarchic(al) ♦ *smf* anarchist.

anarco-insurreziona'lista [anarko,insurrettsjona'lista] *ag* anarcho-revolutionary.

'A.N.A.S. *sigla f* (= Azienda Nazionale Autonoma delle Strade) national roads department.

ana'tema, i *sm* anathema.

anato'mia *sf* anatomy.

ana'tomico, a, ci, che *ag* anatomical; (sedile) contoured.

'anatra *sf* duck; ~ **selvatica** mallard.

ana'troccolo *sm* duckling.

'ANCA *sigla f* = Associazione Nazionale Cooperative Agricole.

'anca, che *sf* (ANAT) hip; (ZOOL) haunch.

ANCC *sigla f* = Associazione Nazionale Carabinieri.

'anche ['anke] *cong* also; (perfino) even; **vengo anch'io!** I'm coming too!; ~ **se** even if; ~ **volendo, non finiremmo in tempo** even if we wanted to, we wouldn't finish in time.

ancheggi'are [anked'dʒare] *vi* to wiggle (one's hips).

anchilo'sato, a [ankilo'zato] *ag* stiff.
'ANCI ['antʃi] *sigla f* (= *Associazione
Nazionale dei Comuni Italiani*) *national
confederation of local authorities.*
ancone'tano, a *ag* of (*o* from) Ancona.
an'cora *av* still; (*di nuovo*) again; (*di più*)
some more; (*persino*): ~ **più forte** even
stronger; **non** ~ not yet; ~ **una volta** once
more, once again; ~ **un po'** a little more;
(*di tempo*) a little longer.
'ancora *sf* anchor; **gettare/levare l'**~ to
cast/weigh anchor; ~ **di salvezza** (*fig*) last
hope.
anco'raggio [anko'raddʒo] *sm* anchorage.
anco'rare *vt*, **~rsi** *vr* to anchor.
ANCR *sigla f* (= *Associazione Nazionale
Combattenti e Reduci*) *servicemen's and
ex-servicemen's association.*
Andalu'sia *sf*: **l'**~ Andalusia.
anda'luso, a *ag*, *sm/f* Andalusian.
anda'mento *sm* (*di strada, malattia*) course;
(*del mercato*) state.
an'dante *ag* (*corrente*) current; (*di poco
pregio*) cheap, second-rate ♦ *sm* (*MUS*)
andante.
an'dare *sm*: **a lungo** ~ in the long run; **con
l'andar del tempo** with the passing of
time; **racconta storie a tutto** ~ she's
forever talking rubbish ♦ *vi* (*gen*) to go;
(*essere adatto*): ~ **a** to suit; (*piacere*): **il suo
comportamento non mi va** I don't like the
way he behaves; **ti va di** ~ **al cinema?** do
you feel like going to the cinema?; ~ **a
cavallo** to ride; ~ **in macchina/aereo** to go
by car/plane; ~ **a fare qc** to go and do sth;
~ **a pescare/sciare** to go fishing/skiing;
andarsene to go away; **vado e vengo** I'll
be back in a minute; ~ **per i 50** (*età*) to be
getting on for 50; ~ **a male** to go bad; ~
fiero di qc/qn to be proud of sth/sb; ~
perduto to be lost; **come va?** (*lavoro,
progetto*) how are things?; **come va?** —
bene, grazie! how are you? — fine,
thanks!; **va fatto entro oggi** it's got to be
done today; **ne va della nostra vita** our
lives are at stake; **se non vado errato** if
I'm not mistaken; **le mele vanno molto**
apples are selling well; **va da sé** (*è
naturale*) it goes without saying; **per
questa volta vada** let's say no more about
it this time.
an'data *sf* (*viaggio*) outward journey;
biglietto di sola ~ single (*BRIT*) *o* one-way
ticket; **biglietto di** ~ **e ritorno** return
(*BRIT*) *o* round-trip (*US*) ticket.
anda'tura *sf* (*modo di andare*) walk, gait;
(*SPORT*) pace; (*NAUT*) tack.
an'dazzo [an'dattso] *sm* (*peg*): **prendere un**

brutto ~ to take a turn for the worse.
'Ande *sfpl*: **le** ~ the Andes.
an'dino, a *ag* Andean.
andirivi'eni *sm inv* coming and going.
'andito *sm* corridor, passage.
An'dorra *sf* Andorra.
andrò *etc vb vedi* **andare**.
an'drone *sm* entrance hall.
a'neddoto *sm* anecdote.
ane'lare *vi*: ~ **a** (*fig*) to long for, yearn for.
a'nelito *sm* (*fig*): ~ **di** longing *o* yearning
for.
a'nello *sm* ring; (*di catena*) link.
ane'mia *sf* anaemia (*BRIT*), anemia (*US*).
a'nemico, a, ci, che *ag* anaemic (*BRIT*),
anemic (*US*).
a'nemone *sm* anemone.
aneste'sia *sf* anaesthesia (*BRIT*),
anesthesia (*US*).
aneste'sista, i, e *sm/f* anaesthetist (*BRIT*),
anesthetist (*US*).
anes'tetico, a, ci, che *ag*, *sm* anaesthetic
(*BRIT*), anesthetic (*US*).
anestetiz'zare [anestetid'dzare] *vt* to
anaesthetize (*BRIT*), anesthetize (*US*).
anfeta'mina *sf* amphetamine.
anfeta'minico, a, ci, che *ag* (*fig*) hyper.
an'fibio, a *ag* amphibious ♦ *sm* amphibian;
(*AUT*) amphibious vehicle.
anfite'atro *sm* amphitheatre (*BRIT*),
amphitheater (*US*).
anfitri'one *sm* host.
'anfora *sf* amphora.
an'fratto *sm* ravine.
an'gelico, a, ci, che [an'dʒɛliko] *ag*
angelic(al).
'angelo ['andʒelo] *sm* angel; ~ **custode**
guardian angel; **l'**~ **del focolare** (*fig*) the
perfect housewife.
anghe'ria [ange'ria] *sf* vexation.
an'gina [an'dʒina] *sf* tonsillitis; ~ **pectoris**
angina.
angli'cano, a *ag* Anglican.
angli'cismo [angli'tʃizmo] *sm* anglicism.
an'glofilo, a *ag* anglophilic ♦ *sm/f*
anglophile.
anglo'sassone *ag* Anglo-Saxon.
An'gola *sf*: **l'**~ Angola.
ango'lano, a *ag*, *sm/f* Angolan.
ango'lare *ag* angular.
angola'tura *sf* angle.
angolazi'one [angolat'tsjone] *sf* (*di angolo*)
angulation; (*FOT, CINE, TV, fig*) angle.
'angolo *sm* corner; (*MAT*) angle; ~ **cottura**
(*di appartamento etc*) cooking area; **fare** ~
con (*strada*) to run into; **dietro l'**~ (*anche
fig*) round the corner.
ango'loso, a *ag* (*oggetto*) angular; (*volto*,

corpo) angular, bony.
'angora *sf*: **lana d'~** angora.
an'goscia, sce [an'gɔʃʃa] *sf* deep anxiety, anguish *no pl*.
angosci'are [angoʃ'ʃare] *vt* to cause anguish to; **~rsi** *vr*: **~rsi (per)** (*preoccuparsi*) to become anxious (about); (*provare angoscia*) to get upset (about *o* over).
angosci'oso, a [angoʃ'ʃoso] *ag* (*d'angoscia*) anguished; (*che dà angoscia*) distressing, painful.
angu'illa *sf* eel.
an'guria *sf* watermelon.
an'gustia *sf* (*ansia*) anguish, distress; (*povertà*) poverty, want.
angusti'are *vt* to distress; **~rsi** *vr*: **~rsi (per)** to worry (about).
an'gusto, a *ag* (*stretto*) narrow; (*fig*) mean, petty.
'anice ['anitʃe] *sm* (*CUC*) aniseed; (*BOT*) anise; (*liquore*) anisette.
ani'dride *sf* (*CHIM*): **~ carbonica/solforosa** carbon/sulphur dioxide.
'anima *sf* soul; (*abitante*) inhabitant; **~ gemella** soul mate; **un'~ in pena** (*anche* fig) a tormented soul; **non c'era ~ viva** there wasn't a living soul; **volere un bene dell'~** a qn to be extremely fond of sb; **rompere l'~** a qn to drive sb mad; **il nonno buon'~** ... Grandfather, God rest his soul ....
ani'male *sm, ag* animal.
anima'lesco, a, schi, sche *ag* (*gesto, atteggiamento*) animal-like.
anima'lista, i, e *ag* animal rights *cpd* ♦ *sm/f* animal rights activist.
ani'mare *vt* to give life to, liven up; (*incoraggiare*) to encourage; **~rsi** *vr* to become animated, come to life.
ani'mato, a *ag* animate; (*vivace*) lively, animated; (*: strada*) busy.
anima'tore, 'trice *sm/f* guiding spirit; (*CINE*) animator; (*di festa*) life and soul.
animazi'one [animat'tsjone] *sf* liveliness; (*di strada*) bustle; (*CINE*) animation; **~ teatrale** amateur dramatics.
'animo *sm* (*mente*) mind; (*cuore*) heart; (*coraggio*) courage; (*disposizione*) character, disposition; **avere in ~ di fare qc** to intend *o* have a mind to do sth; **farsi ~** to pluck up courage; **fare qc di buon/mal ~** to do sth willingly/unwillingly; **perdersi d'~** to lose heart.
animosità *sf* animosity.
A'NITA *sigla f* = *Associazione Naturista Italiana*.
'anitra *sf* = **anatra**.

'Ankara *sf* Ankara.
ANM *sigla f* (= *Associazione Nazionale dei Magistrati*) *national association of magistrates*.
ANMI *sigla f* (= *Associazione Nazionale Marinai d'Italia*) *national association of seamen*.
ANMIG *sigla f* (= *Associazione Nazionale fra Mutilati e Invalidi di Guerra*) *national association for disabled ex-servicemen*.
anna'cquare *vt* to water down, dilute.
annaffi'are *vt* to water.
annaffia'toio *sm* watering can.
an'nali *smpl* annals.
annas'pare *vi* (*nell'acqua*) to flounder; (*fig*: *nel buio, nell'incertezza*) to grope.
an'nata *sf* year; (*importo annuo*) annual amount; **vino di ~** vintage wine.
annebbi'are *vt* (*fig*) to cloud; **~rsi** *vr* to become foggy; (*vista*) to become dim.
annega'mento *sm* drowning.
anne'gare *vt, vi* to drown; **~rsi** *vr* (*accidentalmente*) to drown; (*deliberatamente*) to drown o.s.
anne'rire *vt* to blacken ♦ *vi* to become black.
annessi'one *sf* (*POL*) annexation.
an'nesso, a *pp di* **annettere** ♦ *ag* attached; (*POL*) annexed; **... e tutti gli ~i e connessi** ... and so on and so forth.
an'nettere *vt* (*POL*) to annex; (*accludere*) to attach.
annichi'lire [anniki'lire] *vt* to annihilate.
anni'darsi *vr* to nest.
annienta'mento *sm* annihilation, destruction.
annien'tare *vt* to annihilate, destroy.
anniver'sario *sm* anniversary.
'anno *sm* year; **quanti ~i hai? — ho 40 ~i** how old are you? — I'm 40 (years old); **gli ~i 20** the 20s; **porta bene gli ~i** she doesn't look her age; **porta male gli ~i** she looks older than she is; **~ commerciale** business year; **~ giudiziario** legal year; **~ luce** light year; **gli ~i di piombo** *the Seventies in Italy, characterized by terrorist attacks and killings*.
anno'dare *vt* to knot, tie; (*fig*: *rapporto*) to form.
annoi'are *vt* to bore; (*seccare*) to annoy; **~rsi** *vr* to be bored; to be annoyed.
an'noso, a *ag* (*albero*) old; (*fig*: *problema etc*) age-old.
anno'tare *vt* (*registrare*) to note, note down (*BRIT*); (*commentare*) to annotate.
annotazi'one [annotat'tsjone] *sf* note; annotation.
annove'rare *vt* to number.

annu'ale *ag* annual.

annual'mente *av* annually, yearly.

annu'ario *sm* yearbook.

annu'ire *vi* to nod; (*acconsentire*) to agree.

annulla'mento *sm* annihilation, destruction; cancellation; annulment; quashing.

annul'lare *vt* to annihilate, destroy; (*contratto, francobollo*) to cancel; (*matrimonio*) to annul; (*sentenza*) to quash; (*risultati*) to declare void.

annunci'are [annun'tʃare] *vt* to announce; (*dar segni rivelatori*) to herald.

annuncia'tore, 'trice [annuntʃa'tore] *sm/f* (*RADIO, TV*) announcer.

Annunciazi'one [annuntʃat'tsjone] *sf* (*REL*): **l'~** the Annunciation.

an'nuncio [an'nuntʃo] *sm* announcement; (*fig*) sign; **~ pubblicitario** advertisement; **~i economici** classified advertisements, small ads; **piccoli ~i** small ads, classified ads; **~i mortuari** (*colonna*) obituary column.

'annuo, a *ag* annual, yearly.

annu'sare *vt* to sniff, smell; **~ tabacco** to take snuff.

annuvola'mento *sm* clouding (over).

annuvo'lare *vt* to cloud; **~rsi** *vr* to become cloudy, cloud over.

'ano *sm* anus.

'anodo *sm* anode.

anoma'lia *sf* anomaly.

a'nomalo, a *ag* anomalous.

anoni'mato *sm* anonymity; **conservare l'~** to remain anonymous.

a'nonimo, a *ag* anonymous ♦ *sm* (*autore*) anonymous writer (*o* painter *etc*); **un tipo ~** (*peg*) a colourless (*BRIT*) *o* colorless (*US*) character.

anores'sia *sf* anorexia; **~ nervosa** anorexia nervosa.

ano'ressico, a, ci, che *ag* anorexic.

anor'male *ag* abnormal ♦ *sm/f* subnormal person; (*eufemismo*) homosexual.

anormalità *sf inv* abnormality.

'ANSA *sigla f* (= *Agenzia Nazionale Stampa Associata*) national press agency.

'ansa *sf* (*manico*) handle; (*di fiume*) bend.

an'sante *ag* out of breath, panting.

'ANSEA *sigla f* (= *Associazione delle Nazioni del Sud-Est asiatico*) ASEAN.

'ansia *sf* anxiety; **stare in ~ (per qn/qc)** to be anxious (about sb/sth).

ansietà *sf* anxiety.

ansi'mare *vi* to pant.

ansi'oso, a *ag* anxious.

'anta *sf* (*di finestra*) shutter; (*di armadio*) door.

antago'nismo *sm* antagonism.

antago'nista, i, e *sm/f* antagonist.

an'tartico, a, ci, che *ag* Antarctic ♦ *sm*: **l'A~** the Antarctic.

An'tartide *sf*: **l'~** Antarctica.

ante'bellico, a, ci, che *ag* prewar *cpd*.

antece'dente [antetʃe'dɛnte] *ag* preceding, previous.

ante'fatto *sm* previous events *pl*; previous history.

antegu'erra *sm* pre-war period.

ante'nato *sm* ancestor, forefather.

an'tenna *sf* (*RADIO, TV*) aerial; (*ZOOL*) antenna, feeler; **rizzare le ~e** (*fig*) to prick up one's ears; **~ parabolica** (*TV*) satellite dish.

ante'porre *vt*: **~ qc a qc** to place *o* put sth before sth.

ante'posto, a *pp di* **anteporre**.

ante'prima *sf* preview; **~ di stampa** (*INFORM*) print preview.

anteri'ore *ag* (*ruota, zampa*) front *cpd*; (*fatti*) previous, preceding.

antesi'gnano [antesiɲ'ɲano] *sm* (*STORIA*) standard-bearer; (*fig*) forerunner.

antiade'rente *ag* non-stick.

antia'ereo, a *ag* anti-aircraft *cpd*.

antial'lergico, a [antial'lɛrdʒiko] *ag, sm* hypoallergenic.

antia'tomico, a, ci, che *ag* anti-nuclear; **rifugio ~** fallout shelter.

antibi'otico, a, ci, che *ag, sm* antibiotic.

anti'caglia [anti'kaʎʎa] *sf* junk *no pl*.

antical'care *ag* (*prodotto, detersivo*) anti-limescale.

anti'camera *sf* anteroom; **fare ~** to be kept waiting; **non mi passerebbe neanche per l'~ del cervello** it wouldn't even cross my mind.

anti'carie *ag inv* which fights tooth decay.

antichità [antiki'ta] *sf inv* antiquity; (*oggetto*) antique.

antici'clone [antitʃi'klone] *sm* anticyclone.

antici'pare [antitʃi'pare] *vt* (*consegna, visita*) to bring forward, anticipate; (*somma di denaro*) to pay in advance; (*notizia*) to disclose ♦ *vi* to be ahead of time.

antici'pato, a [antitʃi'pato] *ag* (*prima del previsto*) early; **pagamento ~** payment in advance.

anticipazi'one [antitʃipat'tsjone] *sf* anticipation; (*di notizia*) advance information; (*somma di denaro*) advance.

an'ticipo [an'titʃipo] *sm* anticipation; (*di denaro*) advance; **in ~** early, in advance; **con un sensibile ~** well in advance.

antic'lan *ag inv* (*magistrato, processo*) anti-Mafia.

an'tico, a, chi, che ag (*quadro, mobili*) antique; (*dell'antichità*) ancient; **all'~a** old-fashioned.

anticoncezio'nale [antikontʃettsjo'nale] sm contraceptive.

anticonfor'mista, i, e ag, sm/f nonconformist.

anticonge'lante [antikondʒe'lante] ag, sm antifreeze.

anticongiuntu'rale [antikondʒuntu'rale] ag (*ECON*): **misure ~i** measures to remedy the economic situation.

anti'corpo sm antibody.

anticostituzio'nale [antikostituttsjo'nale] ag unconstitutional.

antidepres'sivo, a ag, sm antidepressant.

antidiluvi'ano, a ag (*fig*: *antiquato*) ancient.

antidolo'rifico, ci sm painkiller.

anti'doping sm, ag inv drug testing; **test ~** drugs (*BRIT*) o drug (*US*) test.

an'tidoto sm antidote.

anti'droga ag inv anti-drugs cpd.

antie'stetico, a, ci, che ag unsightly.

an'tifona sf (*MUS, REL*) antiphon; **capire l'~** (*fig*) to take the hint.

anti'forfora ag inv anti-dandruff.

anti'furto sm anti-theft device.

anti'gelo [anti'dʒɛlo] ag inv antifreeze cpd ♦ sm (*per motore*) antifreeze; (*per cristalli*) de-icer.

an'tigene [an'tidʒene] sm antigen.

antigi'enico, a, ci, che [anti'dʒɛniko] ag unhygienic.

antiglobalizza'zione [antiglobalizza'tsjone] ag anti-globalization cpd.

An'tille sfpl: **le ~** the West Indies.

an'tilope sf antelope.

anti'mafia ag inv anti-mafia cpd.

antin'cendio [antin'tʃendjo] ag inv fire cpd; **bombola ~** fire extinguisher.

anti'nebbia sm inv (*anche*: **faro ~**: *AUT*) fog lamp.

antine'vralgico, a, ci, che [antine'vraldʒiko] ag painkilling ♦ sm painkiller.

antin'fiammatorio, a ag, sm anti-inflammatory.

antio'rario ag: **in senso ~** in an anticlockwise (*BRIT*) o counterclockwise (*US*) direction, anticlockwise, counterclockwise.

anti'pasto sm hors d'œuvre.

antipa'tia sf antipathy, dislike.

anti'patico, a, ci, che ag unpleasant, disagreeable.

anti'placca ag inv (*dentifricio*) anti-plaque.

an'tipodi smpl: **essere agli ~** (*fig*: *di idee*

opposte) to be poles apart.

antipro'iettile ag inv bulletproof.

antiquari'ato sm antique trade; **un pezzo d'~** an antique.

anti'quario sm antique dealer.

anti'quato, a ag antiquated, old-fashioned.

antirici'claggio [antiritʃi'kladdʒo] ag (*attività, operazioni*) anti-laundering.

antiri'flesso ag inv (*schermo*) non-glare cpd.

anti'ruggine [anti'ruddʒine] ag anti-rust cpd ♦ sm inv rust-preventer.

anti'rughe [anti'ruge] ag inv anti-wrinkle.

antise'mita, i, e ag anti-semitic.

antisemi'tismo sm anti-semitism.

anti'settico, a, ci, che ag, sm antiseptic.

antista'minico, a, ci, che ag, sm antihistamine.

anti'stante ag opposite.

anti'tartaro ag inv anti-tartar.

antiterro'rismo sm anti-terrorist measures pl.

an'titesi sf antithesis.

antitraspi'rante ag antiperspirant.

anti'vipera ag inv: **siero ~** remedy for snake bites.

anti'virus [anti'virus] sm inv antivirus software no pl.

antolo'gia, 'gie [antolo'dʒia] sf anthology.

antono'masia sf antonomasia; **per ~** par excellence.

antra'cite [antra'tʃite] sf anthracite.

'antro sm cavern.

antro'pofago, gi sm cannibal.

antropolo'gia [antropolo'dʒia] sf anthropology.

antropo'logico, a, ci, che [antropo'lɔdʒiko] ag anthropological.

antro'pologo, a, gi, ghe sm/f anthropologist.

anu'lare ag ring cpd ♦ sm ring finger.

An'versa sf Antwerp.

'anzi ['antsi] av (*invece*) on the contrary; (*o meglio*) or rather, or better still.

anzianità [antsjani'ta] sf old age; (*AMM*) seniority.

anzi'ano, a [an'tsjano] ag old; (*AMM*) senior ♦ sm/f old person; senior member.

anziché [antsi'ke] cong rather than.

anzi'tempo [antsi'tɛmpo] av (*in anticipo*) early.

anzi'tutto [antsi'tutto] av first of all.

AO sigla = Aosta.

a'orta sf aorta.

aos'tano, a ag of (*o* from) Aosta.

AP sigla = Ascoli Piceno.

apar'titico, a, ci, che ag (*POL*) non-party cpd.

apa'tia sf apathy, indifference.

a'patico, a, ci, che *ag* apathetic, indifferent.

a.p.c. *abbr* = a pronta cassa.

'ape *sf* bee.

aperi'tivo *sm* apéritif.

aperta'mente *av* openly.

a'perto, a *pp di* aprire ♦ *ag* open ♦ *sm:* all'~ in the open (air); rimanere a bocca ~a (*fig*) to be taken aback.

aper'tura *sf* opening; (*ampiezza*) width, spread; (*POL*) approach; (*FOT*) aperture; ~ alare wing span; ~ mentale openmindedness; ~ di credito (*COMM*) granting of credit.

API *sigla f* = Associazione Piccole e Medie Industrie.

'apice ['apitʃe] *sm* apex; (*fig*) height.

apicol'tore *sm* beekeeper.

apicol'tura *sf* beekeeping.

ap'nea *sf:* immergersi in ~ to dive without breathing apparatus.

apoca'lisse *sf* apocalypse.

apo'geo [apo'dʒεo] *sm* (*ASTR*) apogee; (*fig:* culmine) zenith.

a'polide *ag* stateless.

apo'litico, a, ci, che *ag* (*neutrale*) nonpolitical; (*indifferente*) apolitical.

apolo'gia, gie [apolo'dʒia] *sf* (*difesa*) apologia; (*esaltazione*) praise; ~ di reato attempt to defend criminal acts.

apoples'sia *sf* (*MED*) apoplexy.

apop'lettico, a, ci, che *ag* apoplectic; colpo ~ apoplectic fit.

a'postolo *sm* apostle.

apostro'fare *vt* (*parola*) to write with an apostrophe; (*persona*) to address.

a'postrofo *sm* apostrophe.

app. *abbr* (= appendice) app.

appaga'mento *sm* satisfaction; fulfilment.

appa'gare *vt* to satisfy; (*desiderio*) to fulfil; ~rsi *vr:* ~rsi di to be satisfied with.

appa'gato, a *ag* satisfied.

appai'are *vt* to couple, pair.

ap'paio *etc vb vedi* apparire.

appallotto'lare *vt* (*carta, foglio*) to screw into a ball; ~rsi *vr* (*gatto*) to roll up into a ball.

appalta'tore *sm* contractor.

ap'palto *sm* (*COMM*) contract; dare/prendere in ~ un lavoro to let out/undertake a job on contract.

appan'naggio [appan'naddʒo] *sm* (*compenso*) annuity; (*fig*) privilege, prerogative.

appan'nare *vt* (*vetro*) to mist; (*metallo*) to tarnish; (*vista*) to dim; ~rsi *vr* to mist over; to tarnish; to grow dim.

appa'rato *sm* equipment, machinery;

(*ANAT*) apparatus; ~ scenico (*TEAT*) props *pl.*

apparecchi'are [apparek'kjare] *vt* to prepare; (*tavola*) to set ♦ *vi* to set the table.

apparecchia'tura [apparekkja'tura] *sf* equipment; (*macchina*) machine, device.

appa'recchio [appa'rekkjo] *sm* piece of apparatus, device; (*aeroplano*) aircraft *inv*; ~i sanitari bathroom *o* sanitary appliances; ~ televisivo/telefonico television set/telephone.

appa'rente *ag* apparent.

apparente'mente *av* apparently.

appa'renza [appa'rεntsa] *sf* appearance; in *o* all'~ apparently, to all appearances.

appa'rire *vi* to appear; (*sembrare*) to seem, appear.

appari'scente [appariʃ'ʃεnte] *ag* (*colore*) garish, gaudy; (*bellezza*) striking.

apparizi'one [apparit'tsjone] *sf* apparition.

ap'parso, a *pp di* apparire.

apparta'mento *sm* flat (*BRIT*), apartment (*US*).

appar'tarsi *vr* to withdraw.

appar'tato, a *ag* (*luogo*) secluded.

appar'tenenza [apparte'nεntsa] *sf:* ~ (a) (*gen*) belonging (to); (*a un partito, club*) membership (of).

appar'tenere *vi:* ~ a to belong to.

ap'parvi *etc vb vedi* apparire.

appassio'nante *ag* thrilling, exciting.

appassio'nare *vt* to thrill; (*commuovere*) to move; ~rsi *vr:* ~rsi a qc to take a great interest in sth; to be deeply moved by sth.

appassio'nato, a *ag* passionate; (*entusiasta*): ~ (di) keen (on).

appas'sire *vi* to wither.

appel'larsi *vr* (*ricorrere*): ~ a to appeal to; (*DIR*): ~ contro to appeal against.

ap'pello *sm* roll-call; (*implorazione, DIR*) appeal; (*sessione d'esame*) exam session; fare ~ a to appeal to; fare l'~ (*INS*) to call the register *o* roll; (*MIL*) to call the roll.

ap'pena *av* (*a stento*) hardly, scarcely; (*solamente, da poco*) just ♦ *cong* as soon as; (non) ~ furono arrivati ... as soon as they had arrived ...; basta ~ a sfamarli it's scarcely enough to feed them; ho ~ finito I have just finished.

ap'pendere *vt* to hang (up).

appendi'abiti *sm inv* hook, peg; (*mobile*) hall stand (*BRIT*), hall tree (*US*).

appen'dice [appen'ditʃe] *sf* appendix; romanzo d'~ popular serial.

appendi'cite [appendi'tʃite] *sf* appendicitis.

appen'dino *sm* (coat) hook.

Appen'nini *smpl:* gli ~ the Apennines.

appesan'tire *vt* to make heavy; ~**rsi** *vr* to grow stout.

ap'peso, a *pp di* **appendere**.

appe'tito *sm* appetite.

appeti'toso, a *ag* appetising; (*fig*) attractive, desirable.

appezza'mento [appettsa'mento] *sm* (*anche*: ~ **di terreno**) plot, piece of ground.

appia'nare *vt* to level; (*fig*) to smooth away, iron out; ~**rsi** *vr* (*divergenze*) to be ironed out.

appiat'tire *vt* to flatten; ~**rsi** *vr* to become flatter; (*farsi piatto*) to flatten o.s.; ~**rsi al suolo** to lie flat on the ground.

appic'care *vt*: ~ **il fuoco a** to set fire to, set on fire.

appicci'care [appittʃi'kare] *vt* to stick; (*fig*): ~ **qc a qn** to palm sth off on sb; ~**rsi** *vr* to stick; (*fig: persona*) to cling.

appiccica'ticcio, a, ci, ce [appittʃika'tittʃo] *ag*, **appicci'coso, a** [appittʃi'koso] *ag* sticky; (*fig: persona*): **essere** ~ to cling like a leech.

appie'dato, a *ag*: **rimanere** ~ to be left without means of transport.

appi'eno *av* fully.

appigli'arsi [appiʎ'ʎarsi] *vr*: ~ **a** (*afferrarsi*) to take hold of; (*fig*) to cling to.

ap'piglio [ap'piʎʎo] *sm* hold; (*fig*) pretext.

appiop'pare *vt*: ~ **qc a qn** (*nomignolo*) to pin sth on sb; (*compito difficile*) to saddle sb with sth; **gli ha appioppato un pugno sul muso** he punched him in the face.

appiso'larsi *vr* to doze off.

applau'dire *vt, vi* to applaud.

ap'plauso *sm* applause *no pl*.

appli'cabile *ag*: ~ **(a)** applicable (to).

appli'care *vt* to apply; (*regolamento*) to enforce; ~**rsi** *vr* to apply o.s.

appli'cato, a *ag* (*arte, scienze*) applied ♦ *sm* (*AMM*) clerk.

applica'tore *sm* applicator.

applicazi'one [applikat'tsjone] *sf* application; enforcement; ~**i tecniche** (*INS*) practical subjects.

appoggi'are [appod'dʒare] *vt* (*mettere contro*): ~ **qc a qc** to lean *o* rest sth against sth; (*fig: sostenere*) to support; ~**rsi** *vr*: ~**rsi a** to lean against; (*fig*) to rely upon.

ap'poggio [ap'pɔddʒo] *sm* support.

appollai'arsi *vr* (*anche fig*) to perch.

ap'pongo, ap'poni *etc vb vedi* **apporre**.

ap'porre *vt* to affix.

appor'tare *vt* to bring.

ap'porto *sm* (*gen, FINANZA*) contribution.

ap'posi *etc vb vedi* **apporre**.

apposita'mente *av* (*apposta*) on purpose; (*specialmente*) specially.

ap'posito, a *ag* appropriate.

ap'posta *av* on purpose, deliberately; **neanche a farlo** ~, ... by sheer coincidence, ...

appos'tarsi *vr* to lie in wait.

ap'posto, a *pp di* **apporre**.

ap'prendere *vt* (*imparare*) to learn; (*comprendere*) to grasp.

apprendi'mento *sm* learning.

appren'dista, i, e *smf* apprentice.

apprendi'stato *sm* apprenticeship.

apprensi'one *sf* apprehension.

appren'sivo, a *ag* apprehensive.

ap'preso, a *pp di* **apprendere**.

ap'presso *av* (*accanto, vicino*) close by, near; (*dietro*) behind; (*dopo, più tardi*) after, later ♦ *ag inv* (*dopo*): **il giorno** ~ the next day; ~ **a** *prep* (*vicino a*) near, close to.

appres'tare *vt* to prepare, get ready; ~**rsi** *vr*: ~**rsi a fare qc** to prepare *o* get ready to do sth.

ap'pretto *sm* starch.

apprez'zabile [appret'tsabile] *ag* (*notevole*) noteworthy, significant; (*percepibile*) appreciable.

apprezza'mento [apprettsa'mento] *sm* appreciation; (*giudizio*) opinion; (*commento*) comment.

apprez'zare [appret'tsare] *vt* to appreciate.

ap'proccio [ap'prɔttʃo] *sm* approach.

appro'dare *vi* (*NAUT*) to land; (*fig*): **non** ~ **a nulla** to come to nothing.

ap'prodo *sm* landing; (*luogo*) landing place.

approfit'tare *vi*: ~ **di** (*persona, situazione*) to take advantage of; (*occasione, opportunità*) to make the most of, profit by.

approfon'dire *vt* to deepen; (*fig*) to study in depth; ~**rsi** *vr* (*gen, fig*) to deepen; (*peggiorare*) to get worse.

appron'tare *vt* to prepare, get ready.

appropri'arsi *vr*: ~ **di qc** to appropriate sth, take possession of sth; ~ **indebitamente di** to embezzle.

appropri'ato, a *ag* appropriate.

appropriazi'one [approprjat'tsjone] *sf* appropriation; ~ **indebita** (*DIR*) embezzlement.

approssi'mare *vt* (*cifra*): ~ **per eccesso/per difetto** to round up/down; ~**rsi** *vr*: ~**rsi a** to approach, draw near.

approssima'tivo, a *ag* approximate, rough; (*impreciso*) inexact, imprecise.

approssimazi'one [approssimat'tsjone] *sf* approximation; **per** ~ approximately, roughly.

appro'vare vt (condotta, azione) to approve of; (candidato) to pass; (progetto di legge) to approve.

approvazi'one [approvat'tsjone] sf approval.

approvvigiona'mento [approvvidʒona 'mento] sm supplying; stocking up; ~i smpl (MIL) supplies.

approvvigio'nare [approvvidʒo'nare] vt to supply; ~rsi vr to lay in provisions, stock up; ~ qn di qc to supply sb with sth.

appunta'mento sm appointment; (amoroso) date; **darsi** ~ to arrange to meet (one another).

appun'tare vt (rendere aguzzo) to sharpen; (fissare) to pin, fix; (annotare) to note down.

appun'tato sm (CARABINIERI) corporal.

appun'tire vt to sharpen.

ap'punto sm note; (rimprovero) reproach ♦ av (proprio) exactly, just; **per l'**~!, ~! exactly!

appu'rare vt to check, verify.

apr. abbr (= aprile) Apr.

apribot'tiglie [apribot'tiʎʎe] sm inv bottleopener.

a'prile sm April; **pesce d'**~! April Fool!; per fraseologia vedi **luglio.**

a'prire vt to open; (via, cadavere) to open up; (gas, luce, acqua) to turn on ♦ vi to open; ~rsi vr to open; ~ **le ostilità** (MIL) to start up o begin hostilities; ~ **una sessione** (INFORM) to log on; ~rsi **a qn** to confide in sb, open one's heart to sb; **mi si è aperto lo stomaco** I feel rather peckish; **apriti cielo!** heaven forbid!

apris'catole sm inv tin (BRIT) o can opener.

APT sigla f (= Azienda di Promozione Turistica) ≈ tourist board.

AQ sigla = L'Aquila.

aquagym [akwa'dʒim] sf aquarobics.

a'quario sm = **acquario.**

'aquila sf (ZOOL) eagle; (fig) genius.

aqui'lino, a ag aquiline.

aqui'lone sm (giocattolo) kite; (vento) North wind.

AR sigla = Arezzo.

A/R abbr (= andata e ritorno) return.

ara'besco sm (decorazione) arabesque.

A'rabia Sau'dita sf: **l'**~ Saudi Arabia.

a'rabico, a, ci, che ag: **il Deserto** ~ the Arabian Desert.

a'rabile ag arable.

'arabo, a ag, sm/f Arab ♦ sm (LING) Arabic; **parlare** ~ (fig) to speak double Dutch (BRIT).

a'rachide [a'rakide] sf peanut.

ara'gosta sf spiny lobster.

a'raldica sf heraldry.

a'raldo sm herald.

aran'ceto [aran'tʃeto] sm orange grove.

a'rancia, ce [a'rantʃa] sf orange.

aranci'ata [aran'tʃata] sf orangeade.

a'rancio [a'rantʃo] sm (BOT) orange tree; (colore) orange ♦ ag inv (colore) orange; **fiori di** ~ orange blossom sg.

aranci'one [aran'tʃone] ag inv: **(color)** ~ bright orange.

a'rare vt to plough (BRIT), plow (US).

ara'tore sm ploughman (BRIT), plowman (US).

a'ratro sm plough (BRIT), plow (US).

ara'tura sf ploughing (BRIT), plowing (US).

a'razzo [a'rattso] sm tapestry.

arbi'traggio [arbi'traddʒo] sm (SPORT) refereeing; umpiring; (DIR) arbitration; (COMM) arbitrage.

arbi'trare vt (SPORT) to referee; to umpire; (DIR) to arbitrate.

arbi'trario, a ag arbitrary.

arbi'trato sm arbitration.

ar'bitrio sm will; (abuso, soprusi) arbitrary act.

'arbitro sm arbiter, judge; (DIR) arbitrator; (SPORT) referee; (: TENNIS, CRICKET) umpire.

ar'busto sm shrub.

'arca, che sf (sarcofago) sarcophagus; **l'**~ **di Noè** Noah's ark.

ar'caico, a, ci, che ag archaic.

arca'ismo sm (LING) archaism.

ar'cangelo [ar'kandʒelo] sm archangel.

ar'cano, a ag arcane, mysterious ♦ sm mystery.

ar'cata sf (ARCHIT, ANAT) arch; (ordine di archi) arcade.

archeolo'gia [arkeolo'dʒia] sf arch(a)eology.

archeo'logico, a, ci, che [arkeo'lɔdʒiko] ag arch(a)eological.

arche'ologo, a, gi, ghe [arke'ɔlogo] sm/f arch(a)eologist.

ar'chetipo [ar'kɛtipo] sm archetype.

ar'chetto [ar'ketto] sm (MUS) bow.

architet'tare [arkitet'tare] vt (fig: ideare) to devise; (: macchinare) to plan, concoct.

archi'tetto [arki'tetto] sm architect.

architet'tonico, a, ci, che [arkitet'tɔniko] ag architectural.

architet'tura [arkitet'tura] sf architecture.

archivi'are [arki'vjare] vt (documenti) to file; (DIR) to dismiss.

archiviazi'one [arkivjat'tsjone] sf filing; dismissal.

ar'chivio [ar'kivjo] sm archives pl; (INFORM)

file; ~ **principale** (*INFORM*) master file.
archi'vista, i, e [arki'vista] *sm/f* (*AMM*)
archivist; (*in ufficio*) filing clerk.
'ARCI ['artʃi] *sigla f* (= *Associazione Ricreativa
Culturale Italiana*) *cultural society.*
arci'duca, chi [artʃi'duka] *sm* archduke.
arci'ere [ar'tʃɛre] *sm* archer.
ar'cigno, a [ar'tʃiɲɲo] *ag* grim, severe.
arci'pelago, ghi [artʃi'pɛlago] *sm*
archipelago.
arci'vescovo [artʃi'veskovo] *sm*
archbishop.
'arco, chi *sm* (*arma, MUS*) bow; (*ARCHIT*)
arch; (*MAT*) arc; **nell'**~ **di 3 settimane**
within the space of 3 weeks; ~
costituzionale *political parties involved
in formulating Italy's post-war
constitution.*
arcoba'leno *sm* rainbow.
arcu'ato, a *ag* curved, bent; **dalle gambe**
~**e** bow-legged.
ar'dente *ag* burning; (*fig*) burning, ardent.
'ardere *vt, vi* to burn; **legna da** ~ firewood.
ar'desia *sf* slate.
ardi'mento *sm* daring.
ar'dire *vi* to dare ♦ *sm* daring.
ar'dito, a *ag* brave, daring, bold; (*sfacciato*)
bold.
ar'dore *sm* blazing heat; (*fig*) ardour,
fervour.
'arduo, a *ag* arduous, difficult.
'area *sf* area; (*EDIL*) land, ground; **nell'**~ **dei
partiti di sinistra** among the parties of the
left; ~ **fabbricabile** building land; ~ **di
rigore** (*SPORT*) penalty area; ~ **di servizio**
(*AUT*) service area.
a'rena *sf* arena; (*per corride*) bullring;
(*sabbia*) sand.
are'naria *sf* sandstone.
are'narsi *vr* to run aground; (*fig: trattative*)
to come to a standstill.
areo'plano *sm* = **aeroplano**.
are'tino, a *ag* of (*o from*) Arezzo.
'argano *sm* winch.
argen'tato, a [ardʒen'tato] *ag* silver-
plated; (*colore*) silver, silvery; (*capelli*)
silver(-grey).
ar'genteo, a [ar'dʒɛnteo] *ag* silver, silvery.
argente'ria [ardʒente'ria] *sf* silverware,
silver.
Argen'tina [ardʒen'tina] *sf*: **l'**~ Argentina.
argen'tino, a [ardʒen'tino] *ag, sm/f*
(*dell'Argentina*) Argentinian ♦ *sf* crewneck
sweater.
ar'gento [ar'dʒɛnto] *sm* silver; ~ **vivo**
quicksilver; **avere l'**~ (**vivo**) **addosso** (*fig*)
to be fidgety.
ar'gilla [ar'dʒilla] *sf* clay.

argil'loso, a [ardʒil'loso] *ag* (*contenente
argilla*) clayey; (*simile ad argilla*) clay-like.
argi'nare [ardʒi'nare] *vt* (*fiume, acque*) to
embank; (: *con diga*) to dyke up; (*fig:
inflazione, corruzione*) to check; (: *spese*) to
limit.
'argine ['ardʒine] *sm* embankment, bank;
(*diga*) dyke, dike; **far** ~ **a, porre un** ~ **a**
(*fig*) to check, hold back.
argomen'tare *vi* to argue.
argo'mento *sm* argument; (*materia, tema*)
subject; **tornare sull'**~ to bring the
matter up again.
argu'ire *vt* to deduce.
ar'guto, a *ag* sharp, quick-witted;
(*spiritoso*) witty.
ar'guzia [ar'guttsja] *sf* wit; (*battuta*) witty
remark.
'aria *sf* air; (*espressione, aspetto*) air, look;
(*MUS: melodia*) tune; (: *di opera*) aria; **all'**~
aperta in the open (air); **manca l'**~ it's
stuffy; **andare all'**~ (*piano, progetto*) to
come to nothing; **mandare all'**~ **qc** to ruin
o upset sth; **darsi delle** ~**e** to put on airs
and graces; **ha la testa per** ~ his head is
in the clouds; **che** ~ **tira?** (*fig: atmosfera*)
what's the atmosphere like?
aridità *sf* aridity, dryness; (*fig*) lack of
feeling.
'arido, a *ag* arid.
arieggi'are [arjed'dʒare] *vt* (*cambiare aria*)
to air; (*imitare*) to imitate.
ari'ete *sm* ram; (*MIL*) battering ram; (*dello
zodiaco*): **A**~ Aries; **essere dell'A**~ to be
Aries.
a'ringa, ghe *sf* herring *inv*; ~ **affumicata**
smoked herring, kipper; ~ **marinata**
pickled herring.
ari'oso, a *ag* (*ambiente, stanza*) airy; (*MUS*)
ariose.
'arista *sf* (*CUC*) chine of pork.
aristo'cratico, a, ci, che *ag* aristocratic.
aristocra'zia [aristokrat'tsia] *sf* aristocracy.
arit'metica *sf* arithmetic.
arit'metico, a, ci, che *ag* arithmetical.
arlec'chino [arlek'kino] *sm* harlequin.
'arma, i *sf* weapon, arm; (*parte dell'esercito*)
arm; **alle** ~**i!** to arms!; **chiamare alle** ~**i** to
call up (*BRIT*), draft (*US*); **sotto le** ~**i** in the
army (*o* forces); **combattere ad** ~**i pari**
(*anche fig*) to fight on equal terms; **essere
alle prime** ~**i** (*fig*) to be a novice; **passare
qn per le** ~**i** to execute sb; ~ **a doppio
taglio** (*anche fig*) double-edged weapon; ~
da fuoco firearm; ~**i convenzionali/non
convenzionali** conventional/
unconventional weapons; ~**i di
distruzione di massa** weapons of mass

destruction.
arma'dietto sm (*dei medicinali*) medicine
cabinet o cupboard; (*in cucina*) (kitchen)
cupboard; (*per riporre abiti*) locker.
ar'madio sm cupboard; (*per abiti*)
wardrobe; ~ **a muro** built-in cupboard.
armamen'tario sm equipment,
instruments pl.
arma'mento sm (*MIL*) armament;
(: *materiale*) arms pl, weapons pl; (*NAUT*)
fitting out; manning; **la corsa agli** ~**i** the
arms race.
ar'mare vt to arm; (*arma da fuoco*) to cock;
(*NAUT: nave*) to rig, fit out; to man; (*EDIL:
volta, galleria*) to prop up, shore up; ~**rsi** vr
to arm o.s.; (*MIL*) to take up arms.
ar'mato, a ag: ~ (**di**) (*anche fig*) armed
(with) ♦ sf (*MIL*) army; (*NAUT*) fleet; **rapina
a mano** ~**a** armed robbery.
arma'tore sm shipowner.
arma'tura sf (*struttura di sostegno*)
framework; (*impalcatura*) scaffolding;
(*STORIA*) armour no pl (*BRIT*), armor no pl
(*US*).
armeggi'are [armed'dʒare] vi
(*affaccendarsi*): ~ (**intorno a qc**) to mess
about (with sth).
ar'meno, a ag, sm/f, sm Armenian.
arme'ria sf (*deposito*) armoury (*BRIT*),
armory (*US*); (*collezione*) collection of
arms.
armis'tizio [armis'tittsjo] sm armistice.
armo'nia sf harmony.
ar'monico, a, ci, che ag harmonic; (*fig*)
harmonious ♦ sf (*MUS*) harmonica; ~**a a
bocca** mouth organ.
armoni'oso, a ag harmonious.
armoniz'zare [armonid'dzare] vt to
harmonize; (*colori, abiti*) to match ♦ vi to
be in harmony; to match.
ar'nese sm tool, implement; (*oggetto
indeterminato*) thing, contraption; **male in**
~ (*malvestito*) badly dressed; (*di salute
malferma*) in poor health; (*di condizioni
economiche*) down-at-heel.
'arnia sf hive.
a'roma, i sm aroma; fragrance; ~**i** smpl
herbs and spices; ~**i naturali/artificiali**
natural/artificial flavouring sg (*BRIT*) o
flavoring sg (*US*).
aromatera'pia sf aromatherapy.
aro'matico, a, ci, che ag aromatic; (*cibo*)
spicy.
aromatiz'zare [aromatid'dzare] vt to
season, flavour (*BRIT*), flavor (*US*).
'arpa sf (*MUS*) harp.
ar'peggio [ar'peddʒo] sm (*MUS*) arpeggio.
ar'pia sf (*anche fig*) harpy.

arpi'one sm (*gancio*) hook; (*cardine*) hinge;
(*PESCA*) harpoon.
arrabat'tarsi vr to do all one can, strive.
arrabbi'are vi (*cane*) to be affected with
rabies; ~**rsi** vr (*essere preso dall'ira*) to get
angry, fly into a rage.
arrabbi'ato, a ag (*cane*) rabid, with rabies;
(*persona*) furious, angry.
arrabbia'tura sf: **prendersi un'**~ (**per qc**) to
become furious (over sth).
arraf'fare vt to snatch, seize; (*sottrarre*) to
pinch.
arrampi'carsi vr to climb (up); ~ **sui vetri**
o **sugli specchi** (*fig*) to clutch at straws.
arrampi'cata sf climb.
arrampica'tore, 'trice sm/f (*gen, SPORT*)
climber; ~ **sociale** (*fig*) social climber.
arran'care vi to limp, hobble; (*fig*) to
struggle along.
arrangia'mento [arrandʒa'mento] sm (*MUS*)
arrangement.
arran'giare [arran'dʒare] vt to arrange; ~**rsi**
vr to manage, do the best one can.
arre'care vt to bring; (*causare*) to cause.
arreda'mento sm (*studio*) interior design;
(*mobili etc*) furnishings pl.
arre'dare vt to furnish.
arreda'tore, 'trice sm/f interior designer.
ar'redo sm fittings pl, furnishings pl; ~ **per
uffici** office furnishings.
arrem'baggio [arrem'baddʒo] sm (*NAUT*)
boarding.
ar'rendersi vr to surrender; ~ **all'evidenza
(dei fatti)** to face (the) facts.
arren'devole ag (*persona*) yielding,
compliant.
arrendevo'lezza [arrendevo'lettsa] sf
compliancy.
ar'reso, a pp di **arrendersi**.
arres'tare vt (*fermare*) to stop, halt;
(*catturare*) to arrest; ~**rsi** vr (*fermarsi*) to
stop.
arres'tato, a sm/f person under arrest.
ar'resto sm (*cessazione*) stopping; (*fermata*)
stop; (*cattura, MED*) arrest; (*COMM*: ~ **in
produzione**) stoppage; **subire un** ~ to come
to a stop o standstill; **mettere agli** ~**i** to
place under arrest; ~**i domiciliari** (*DIR*)
house arrest.
arre'trare vt, vi to withdraw.
arre'trato, a ag (*lavoro*) behind schedule;
(*paese, bambino*) backward; (*numero di
giornale*) back cpd; ~**i** smpl arrears; **gli** ~**i
dello stipendio** back pay sg.
arricchi'mento [arrikki'mento] sm
enrichment.
arric'chire [arrik'kire] vt to enrich; ~**rsi** vr to
become rich.

arric'chito, a [arrik'kito] *sm/f* nouveau riche.

arricci'are [arrit't∫are] *vt* to curl; ~ **il naso** to turn up one's nose.

ar'ridere *vi*: ~ **a qn** (*fortuna, successo*) to smile on sb.

ar'ringa, ghe *sf* harangue; (*DIR*) address by counsel.

arrischi'are [arris'kjare] *vt* to risk; ~**rsi** *vr* to venture, dare.

arrischi'ato, a [arris'kjato] *ag* risky; (*temerario*) reckless, rash.

ar'riso, a *pp di* **arridere.**

arri'vare *vi* to arrive; (*avvicinarsi*) to come; (*accadere*) to happen, occur; ~ **a** (*livello, grado etc*) to reach; **lui arriva a Roma alle 7** he gets to *o* arrives at Rome at 7; ~ **a fare qc** to manage to do sth, succeed in doing sth; **non ci arrivo** I can't reach it; (*fig: non capisco*) I can't understand it.

arri'vato, a *ag* (*persona*: *di successo*) successful ♦ *sm/f*: **essere un** ~ to have made it; **nuovo** ~ newcomer; **ben** ~! welcome!; **non sono l'ultimo** ~! (*fig*) I'm no fool!

arrive'derci [arrive'dert∫i] *escl* goodbye!

arrive'derla *escl* (*forma di cortesia*) goodbye!

arri'vismo *sm* (*ambizione*) ambitiousness; (*sociale*) social climbing.

arri'vista, i *sm/f* go-getter.

ar'rivo *sm* arrival; (*SPORT*) finish, finishing line.

arro'gante *ag* arrogant.

arro'ganza [arro'gantsa] *sf* arrogance.

arro'gare *vt*: ~**rsi il diritto di fare qc** to assume the right to do sth; ~**rsi il merito di qc** to claim credit for sth.

arrossa'mento *sm* reddening.

arros'sare *vt* (*occhi, pelle*) to redden, make red; ~**rsi** *vr* to go *o* become red.

arros'sire *vi* (*per vergogna, timidezza*) to blush; (*per gioia*) to flush, blush.

arros'tire *vt* to roast; (*pane*) to toast; (*ai ferri*) to grill.

ar'rosto *sm, ag inv* roast; ~ **di manzo** roast beef.

arro'tare *vt* to sharpen; (*investire con un veicolo*) to run over.

arro'tino *sm* knife-grinder.

arroto'lare *vt* to roll up.

arroton'dare *vt* (*forma, oggetto*) to round; (*stipendio*) to add to; (*somma*) to round off.

arrovel'larsi *vr* (*anche*: ~ **il cervello**) to rack one's brains.

arroven'tato, a *ag* red-hot.

arruf'fare *vt* to ruffle; (*fili*) to tangle; (*fig*:

questione) to confuse.

arruggi'nire [arruddʒi'nire] *vt* to rust; ~**rsi** *vr* to rust; (*fig*) to become rusty.

arruola'mento *sm* (*MIL*) enlistment.

arruo'lare *vt* (*MIL*) to enlist; ~**rsi** *vr* to enlist, join up.

arse'nale *sm* (*MIL*) arsenal; (*cantiere navale*) dockyard.

ar'senico *sm* arsenic.

'arsi *vb vedi* **ardere.**

'arso, a *pp di* **ardere** ♦ *ag* (*bruciato*) burnt; (*arido*) dry.

ar'sura *sf* (*calore opprimente*) burning heat; (*siccità*) drought.

art. *abbr* (= *articolo*) art.

'arte *sf* art; (*abilità*) skill; **a regola d'**~ (*fig*) perfectly; **senz'**~ **né parte** penniless and out of a job; ~**i figurative** visual arts.

arte'fatto, a *ag* (*stile, modi*) affected; (*cibo*) adulterated.

ar'tefice [ar'tefit∫e] *sm/f* craftsman/woman; (*autore*) author.

ar'teria *sf* artery.

arterioscle'rosi *sf* arteriosclerosis, hardening of the arteries.

arteri'oso, a *ag* arterial.

'artico, a, ci, che *ag* Arctic ♦ *sm*: **l'A**~ the Arctic; **il Circolo polare** ~ the Arctic Circle; **l'Oceano** ~ the Arctic Ocean.

artico'lare *ag* (*ANAT*) of the joints, articular ♦ *vt* to articulate; (*suddividere*) to divide, split up; ~**rsi** *vr*: ~**rsi in** (*discorso, progetto*) to be divided into.

artico'lato, a *ag* (*linguaggio*) articulate; (*AUT*) articulated.

articolazi'one [artikolat'tsjone] *sf* (*ANAT, TECN*) joint; (*di voce, concetto*) articulation.

ar'ticolo *sm* article; ~ **di fondo** (*STAMPA*) leader, leading article; ~**i di marca** branded goods; **un bell'**~ (*fig*) a real character.

'Artide *sm*: **l'**~ the Arctic.

artifici'ale [artifi't∫ale] *ag* artificial.

artifici'ere [artifi't∫ɛre] *sm* (*MIL*) artificer; (: *per disinnescare bombe*) bomb-disposal expert.

arti'ficio [arti'fit∫o] *sm* (*espediente*) trick, artifice; (*ricerca di effetto*) artificiality.

artifici'oso, a [artifi't∫oso] *ag* cunning; (*non spontaneo*) affected.

artigia'nale [artidʒa'nale] *ag* craft *cpd*.

artigia'nato [artidʒa'nato] *sm* craftsmanship; craftsmen *pl.*

artigi'ano, a [arti'dʒano] *sm/f* craftsman/woman.

artigli'ere [artiʎ'ʎere] *sm* artilleryman.

artiglie'ria [artiʎʎe'ria] *sf* artillery.

ar'tiglio [ar'tiʎʎo] *sm* claw; (*di rapaci*) talon;

sfoderare gli ~**i** (*fig*) to show one's claws.
ar'tista, i, e *sm/f* artist; **un lavoro da** ~ (*fig*) a professional piece of work.
ar'tistico, a, ci, che *ag* artistic.
'arto *sm* (*ANAT*) limb.
ar'trite *sf* (*MED*) arthritis.
ar'trosi *sf* osteoarthritis.
arzigogo'lato, a [ardzigogo'lato] *ag* tortuous.
ar'zillo, a [ar'dzillo] *ag* lively, sprightly.
a'scella [aʃ'ʃɛlla] *sf* (*ANAT*) armpit.
ascen'dente [aʃʃen'dɛnte] *sm* ancestor; (*fig*) ascendancy; (*ASTR*) ascendant.
a'scendere [aʃ'ʃendere] *vi*: ~ **al trono** to ascend the throne.
ascensi'one [aʃʃen'sjone] *sf* (*ALPINISMO*) ascent; (*REL*): **l'A**~ the Ascension; **isola dell'A**~ Ascension Island.
ascen'sore [aʃʃen'sore] *sm* lift.
a'scesa [aʃ'ʃesa] *sf* ascent; (*al trono*) accession; (*al potere*) rise.
a'scesi [aʃ'ʃɛzi] *sf* asceticism.
a'sceso, a [aʃ'ʃeso] *pp di* **ascendere**.
a'scesso [aʃ'ʃɛsso] *sm* (*MED*) abscess.
a'sceta, i [aʃ'ʃɛta] *sm* ascetic.
'ascia, pl 'asce ['aʃʃa] *sf* axe.
asciugaca'pelli [aʃʃugaka'pelli] *sm* hair dryer.
asciuga'mano [aʃʃuga'mano] *sm* towel.
asciu'gare [aʃʃu'gare] *vt* to dry; ~**rsi** *vr* to dry o.s.; (*diventare asciutto*) to dry.
asciuga'trice [aʃʃuga'tritʃe] *sf* spin-dryer.
asciut'tezza [aʃʃut'tettsa] *sf* dryness; leanness; curtness.
asci'utto, a [aʃ'ʃutto] *ag* dry; (*fig: magro*) lean; (: *burbero*) curt ♦ *sm*: **restare all'**~ (*fig*) to be left penniless; **restare a bocca** ~**a** (*fig*) to be disappointed.
asco'lano, a *ag* of (*o* from) Ascoli.
ascol'tare *vt* to listen to; ~ **il consiglio di qn** to listen to *o* heed sb's advice.
ascolta'tore, 'trice *sm/f* listener.
as'colto *sm*: **essere** *o* **stare in** ~ to be listening; **dare** *o* **prestare** ~ **(a)** to pay attention (to); **indice di** ~ (*TV, RADIO*) audience rating.
AS. COM. *sigla f* = *Associazione Commercianti*.
as'critto, a *pp di* **ascrivere**.
as'crivere *vt* (*attribuire*): ~ **qc a qn** to attribute sth to sb; ~ **qc a merito di qn** to give sb credit for sth.
a'settico, a, ci, che *ag* aseptic.
asfal'tare *vt* to asphalt.
as'falto *sm* asphalt.
asfis'sia *sf* asphyxia, asphyxiation.
asfissi'ante *ag* (*gas*) asphyxiating; (*fig: calore, ambiente*) stifling, suffocating;

(: *persona*) tiresome.
asfissi'are *vt* to asphyxiate, suffocate; (*fig: opprimere*) to stifle; (: *infastidire*) to get on sb's nerves ♦ *vi* to suffocate, asphyxiate.
'Asia *sf*: **l'**~ Asia.
asi'atico, a, ci, che *ag, sm/f* Asiatic, Asian.
a'silo *sm* refuge, sanctuary; ~ **(d'infanzia)** nursery(-school); ~ **nido** day nursery, crèche (*for children aged 0 to 3*); ~ **politico** political asylum.
asim'metrico, a, ci, che *ag* asymmetric(al).
'asino *sm* donkey, ass; **la bellezza dell'**~ (*fig: di ragazza*) the beauty of youth; **qui casca l'**~! there's the rub!
ASL [azl] *sigla f* (= *Azienda Sanitaria Locale*) local health centre.
'asma *sf* asthma.
as'matico, a, ci, che *ag, sm/f* asthmatic.
asoci'ale [aso'tʃale] *ag* antisocial.
'asola *sf* buttonhole.
as'parago, gi *sm* asparagus *no pl*.
as'pergere [as'pɛrdʒere] *vt*: ~ **(di** *o* **con)** to sprinkle (with).
asperità *sf inv* roughness *no pl*; (*fig*) harshness *no pl*.
as'persi *etc vb vedi* **aspergere**.
as'perso, a *pp di* **aspergere**.
aspet'tare *vt* to wait for; (*anche COMM*) to await; (*aspettarsi*) to expect; (*essere in serbo: notizia, evento etc*) to be in store for, lie ahead of ♦ *vi* to wait; ~**rsi qc** to expect sth; ~ **un bambino** to be expecting (a baby); **questo non me l'aspettavo** I wasn't expecting this; **me l'aspettavo!** I thought as much!
aspetta'tiva *sf* expectation; **inferiore all'**~ worse than expected; **essere/mettersi in** ~ (*AMM*) to be on/take leave of absence.
as'petto *sm* (*apparenza*) aspect, appearance, look; (*punto di vista*) point of view; **di bell'**~ good-looking.
aspi'rante *ag* (*attore etc*) aspiring ♦ *sm/f* candidate, applicant.
aspira'polvere *sm inv* vacuum cleaner.
aspi'rare *vt* (*respirare*) to breathe in, inhale; (*sog: apparecchi*) to suck (up) ♦ *vi*: ~ **a** to aspire to.
aspira'tore *sm* extractor fan.
aspirazi'one [aspirat'tsjone] *sf* (*TECN*) suction; (*anelito*) aspiration.
aspi'rina *sf* aspirin.
aspor'tare *vt* (*anche MED*) to remove, take away.
as'prezza [as'prettsa] *sf* sourness, tartness; pungency; harshness; roughness; rugged nature.
'aspro, a *ag* (*sapore*) sour, tart; (*odore*)

acrid, pungent; (*voce, clima, fig*) harsh;
(*superficie*) rough; (*paesaggio*) rugged.
Ass. *abbr* = **assicurazione; assicurata;
assegno.**
assaggi'are [assad'dʒare] *vt* to taste.
assag'gini [assad'dʒini] *smpl* (*CUC*) *selection
of first courses.*
as'saggio [as'saddʒo] *sm* tasting; (*piccola
quantità*) taste; (*campione*) sample.
as'sai *av* (*molto*) a lot, much; (: *con ag*)
very; (*a sufficienza*) enough ♦ *ag inv*
(*quantità*) a lot of, much; (*numero*) a lot of,
many; ~ **contento** very pleased.
as'salgo *etc vb vedi* **assalire.**
assa'lire *vt* to attack, assail.
assali'tore, 'trice *sm/f* attacker, assailant.
assal'tare *vt* (*MIL*) to storm; (*banca*) to raid;
(*treno, diligenza*) to hold up.
as'salto *sm* attack, assault; **prendere d'**~
(*fig: negozio, treno*) to storm; (: *personalità*)
to besiege; **d'**~ (*editoria, giornalista etc*)
aggressive.
assapo'rare *vt* to savour (*BRIT*), savor (*US*).
assassi'nare *vt* to murder; (*POL*) to
assassinate; (*fig*) to ruin.
assas'sinio *sm* murder; assassination.
assas'sino, a *ag* murderous ♦ *sm/f*
murderer; assassin.
'asse *sm* (*TECN*) axle; (*MAT*) axis ♦ *sf* board;
~ **da stiro** ironing board.
assecon'dare *vt*: ~ **qn (in qc)** to go along
with sb (in sth); ~ **i desideri di qn** to go
along with sb's wishes; ~ **i capricci di qn**
to give in to sb's whims.
assedi'are *vt* to besiege.
as'sedio *sm* siege.
asse'gnare [assep'ɲare] *vt* to assign, allot;
(*premio*) to award.
assegna'tario [assepɲa'tarjo] *sm* (*DIR*)
assignee; (*COMM*) recipient; **l'**~ **del
premio** the person awarded the prize.
assegnazi'one [assepɲat'tsjone] *sf* (*di casa,
somma*) allocation; (*di carica*) assignment;
(*di premio, borsa di studio*) awarding.
as'segno [as'seɲɲo] *sm* allowance; (*anche*:
~ **bancario**) cheque (*BRIT*), check (*US*);
contro ~ cash on delivery; ~ **circolare**
bank draft; ~ **di invalidità** *o* **di malattia**
injury *o* sickness benefit; ~ **post-datato**
post-dated cheque; ~ **sbarrato** crossed
cheque; ~ **non sbarrato** uncrossed
cheque; ~ **di studio** study grant; "~ **non
trasferibile**" "account payee only"; ~ **di
viaggio** travel(l)er's cheque; ~ **a vuoto**
dud cheque; ~**i alimentari** alimony *sg*; ~**i
familiari** ≈ child benefit *sg*.
assem'blaggio [assem'bladdʒo] *sm*
(*INDUSTRIA*) assembly.

assem'blare *vt* to assemble.
assem'blea *sf* assembly; (*raduno,
adunanza*) meeting.
assembra'mento *sm* public gathering;
divieto di ~ ban on public meetings.
assen'nato, a *ag* sensible.
as'senso *sm* assent, consent.
assen'tarsi *vr* to go out.
as'sente *ag* absent; (*fig*) faraway, vacant
♦ *sm/f* absentee.
assente'ismo *sm* absenteeism.
assente'ista, i, e *sm/f* (*dal lavoro*) absentee.
assen'tire *vi*: ~ **(a)** to agree (to), assent
(to).
as'senza [as'sɛntsa] *sf* absence.
asse'rire *vt* to maintain, assert.
asserragli'arsi [asserraʎ'ʎarsi] *vr*: ~ **(in)** to
barricade o.s. (in).
asser'vire *vt* to enslave; (*fig: animo,
passioni*) to subdue; ~**rsi** *vr*: ~**rsi (a)** to
submit (to).
asserzi'one [asser'tsjone] *sf* assertion.
assesso'rato *sm* councillorship.
asses'sore *sm* councillor.
assesta'mento *sm* (*sistemazione*)
arrangement; (*EDIL, GEO*) settlement.
asses'tare *vt* (*mettere in ordine*) to put in
order, arrange; ~**rsi** *vr* to settle in; (*GEO*)
to settle; ~ **un colpo a qn** to deal sb a
blow.
asse'tato, a *ag* thirsty, parched.
as'setto *sm* order, arrangement; (*NAUT,
AER*) trim; **in** ~ **di guerra** on a war footing;
~ **territoriale** country planning.
assicu'rare *vt* (*accertare*) to ensure;
(*infondere certezza*) to assure; (*fermare,
legare*) to make fast, secure; (*fare un
contratto di assicurazione*) to insure; ~**rsi** *vr*
(*accertarsi*): ~**rsi (di)** to make sure (of);
(*contro il furto etc*): ~**rsi (contro)** to insure
o.s. (against).
assicu'rato, a *ag* insured ♦ *sf* (*anche*:
lettera ~**a**) registered letter.
assicura'tore, 'trice *ag* insurance *cpd*
♦ *sm/f* insurance agent; **società** ~**trice**
insurance company.
assicurazi'one [assikurat'tsjone] *sf*
assurance; insurance; ~ **multi-rischio**
comprehensive insurance.
assidera'mento *sm* exposure.
asside'rare *vt* to freeze; ~**rsi** *vr* to freeze;
morire assiderato to die of exposure.
as'siduo, a *ag* (*costante*) assiduous;
(*regolare*) regular.
assi'eme *av* (*insieme*) together ♦ *prep*: ~ **a**
(together) with.
assil'lante *ag* (*dubbio, pensiero*) nagging;
(*creditore*) pestering.

assil'lare *vt* to pester, torment.

as'sillo *sm (fig)* worrying thought.

assimi'lare *vt* to assimilate.

assimilazi'one [assimilat'tsjone] *sf* assimilation.

assi'oma, i *sm* axiom.

assio'matico, a, ci, che *ag* axiomatic.

as'sise *sfpl (DIR)* assizes *(BRIT)*; **corte** *f* **d'**~ court of assizes, ≈ crown court *(BRIT)*; *vedi anche* **Corte d'Assise.**

assis'tente *sm/f* assistant; ~ **sociale** social worker; ~ **universitario** (assistant) lecturer; ~ **di volo** *(AER)* steward/ stewardess.

assis'tenza [assis'tɛntsa] *sf* assistance; ~ **legale** legal aid; ~ **ospedaliera** free hospital treatment; ~ **sanitaria** health service; ~ **sociale** welfare services *pl.*

assistenzi'ale [assisten'tsjale] *ag (ente, organizzazione)* welfare *cpd*; *(opera)* charitable.

assistenzia'lismo [assistentsja'lizmo] *sm (peg)* excessive state aid.

as'sistere *vt (aiutare)* to assist, help; *(curare)* to treat ♦ *vi*: ~ **(a qc)** *(essere presente)* to be present (at sth), attend (sth).

assis'tito, a *pp di* **assistere.**

'asso *sm* ace; **piantare qn in** ~ to leave sb in the lurch.

associ'are [asso't ʃare] *vt* to associate; *(rendere partecipe)*: ~ **qn a** *(affari)* to take sb into partnership in; *(partito)* to make sb a member of; ~**rsi** *vr* to enter into partnership; ~**rsi a** to become a member of, join; *(dolori, gioie)* to share in; ~ **qn alle carceri** to take sb to prison.

associazi'one [assot ʃat'tsjone] *sf* association; ~ **di categoria** trade association; ~ **a** *o* **per delinquere** *(DIR)* criminal association; **A**~ **Europea di Libero Scambio** European Free Trade Association, EFTA; ~ **in partecipazione** *(COMM)* joint venture.

asso'dare *vt (muro, posizione)* to strengthen; *(fatti, verità)* to ascertain.

asso'dato, a *ag* well-founded.

assogget'tare [assoddʒet'tare] *vt* to subject, subjugate; ~**rsi** *vr*: ~**rsi a** to submit to.

asso'lato, a *ag* sunny.

assol'dare *vt* to recruit.

as'solsi *etc vb vedi* **assolvere.**

as'solto, a *pp di* **assolvere.**

assoluta'mente *av* absolutely.

asso'luto, a *ag* absolute.

assoluzi'one [assolut'tsjone] *sf (DIR)* acquittal; *(REL)* absolution.

as'solvere *vt (DIR)* to acquit; *(REL)* to

absolve; *(adempiere)* to carry out, perform.

assomigli'are [assomiʎ'ʎare] *vi*: ~ **a** to resemble, look like.

asson'nato, a *ag* sleepy.

asso'pirsi *vr* to doze off.

assor'bente *ag* absorbent ♦ *sm*: ~ **igienico** sanitary towel; ~ **interno** tampon.

assor'bire *vt* to absorb; *(fig: far proprio)* to assimilate.

assor'dante *ag (rumore, musica)* deafening.

assor'dare *vt* to deafen.

assorti'mento *sm* assortment.

assor'tire *vt (disporre)* to arrange.

assor'tito, a *ag* assorted; *(colori)* matched, matching.

as'sorto, a *ag* absorbed, engrossed.

assottigli'are [assottiʎ'ʎare] *vt* to make thin, thin; *(aguzzare)* to sharpen; *(ridurre)* to reduce; ~**rsi** *vr* to grow thin; *(fig: ridursi)* to be reduced.

assue'fare *vt* to accustom; ~**rsi** *vr*: ~**rsi a** to get used to, accustom o.s. to.

assue'fatto, a *pp di* **assuefare.**

assuefazi'one [assuefat'tsjone] *sf (MED)* addiction.

as'sumere *vt (impiegato)* to take on, engage; *(responsabilità)* to assume, take upon o.s.; *(contegno, espressione)* to assume, put on; *(droga)* to consume.

as'sunsi *etc vb vedi* **assumere.**

as'sunto, a *pp di* **assumere** ♦ *sm (tesi)* proposition.

assunzi'one [assun'tsjone] *sf (di impiegati)* employment, engagement; *(REL)*: **l'A**~ the Assumption.

assurdità *sf inv* absurdity; **dire delle** ~ to talk nonsense.

as'surdo, a *ag* absurd.

'asta *sf* pole; *(modo di vendita)* auction.

as'tante *sm* bystander.

astante'ria *sf* casualty department.

as'temio, a *ag* teetotal ♦ *sm/f* teetotaller.

aste'nersi *vr*: ~ **(da)** to abstain (from), refrain (from); *(POL)* to abstain (from).

astensi'one *sf* abstention.

astensio'nista, i, e *sm/f (POL)* abstentionist.

aste'risco, schi *sm* asterisk.

aste'roide *sm* asteroid.

'astice ['astit ʃe] *sm* lobster.

astigi'ano, a [asti'dʒano] *ag* of (*o* from) Asti.

astig'matico, a, ci, che *ag* astigmatic.

asti'nenza [asti'nɛntsa] *sf* abstinence; **essere in crisi di** ~ to suffer from withdrawal symptoms.

'astio *sm* rancour, resentment.

asti'oso, a *ag* resentful.
astrat'tismo *sm* (*ARTE*) abstract art.
as'tratto, a *ag* abstract.
astrin'gente [astrin'dʒɛnte] *ag, sm*
astringent.
'astro *sm* star.
astrolo'gia [astrolo'dʒia] *sf* astrology.
astro'logico, a, ci, che [astro'lɔdʒiko] *ag*
astrological.
as'trologo, a, ghi, ghe *sm/f* astrologer.
astro'nauta, i, e *sm/f* astronaut.
astro'nautica *sf* astronautics *sg*.
astro'nave *sf* space ship.
astrono'mia *sf* astronomy.
astro'nomico, a, ci, che *ag*
astronomic(al).
as'tronomo *sm* astronomer.
as'truso, a *ag* (*discorso, ragionamento*)
abstruse.
as'tuccio [as'tuttʃo] *sm* case, box, holder.
as'tuto, a *ag* astute, cunning, shrewd.
as'tuzia [as'tuttsja] *sf* astuteness,
shrewdness; (*azione*) trick.
AT *sigla* = Asti.
a'tavico, a, ci, che *ag* atavistic.
ate'ismo *sm* atheism.
atelier [atə'lje] *sm inv* (*laboratorio*)
workshop; (*studio*) studio; (*sartoria*)
fashion house.
A'tene *sf* Athens.
ate'neo *sm* university.
ateni'ese *ag, sm/f* Athenian.
'ateo, a *ag, sm/f* atheist.
a'tipico, a, ci, che *ag* atypical.
at'lante *sm* atlas; i Monti dell'A~ the Atlas
Mountains.
at'lantico, a, ci, che *ag* Atlantic ♦ *sm*: l'A~,
l'Oceano A~ the Atlantic, the Atlantic
Ocean.
at'leta, i, e *sm/f* athlete.
at'letica *sf* athletics *sg*; ~ leggera track and
field events *pl*; ~ pesante weightlifting
and wrestling.
ATM *sigla f* = Azienda Tranviaria Municipale.
atmos'fera *sf* atmosphere.
atmos'ferico, a, ci, che *ag* atmospheric.
a'tollo *sm* atoll.
a'tomico, a, ci, che *ag* atomic; (*nucleare*)
atomic, atom *cpd*, nuclear.
atomizza'tore [atomiddza'tore] *sm* (*di
acqua, lacca*) spray; (*di profumo*) atomizer.
'atomo *sm* atom.
'atono, a *ag* (*FONETICA*) unstressed.
'atrio *sm* entrance hall, lobby.
a'troce [a'trotʃe] *ag* (*che provoca orrore*)
dreadful; (*terribile*) atrocious.
atrocità [atrotʃi'ta] *sf inv* atrocity.
atro'fia *sf* atrophy.

attacca'brighe [attakka'brige] *sm/f inv*
quarrelsome person.
attacca'mento *sm* (*fig*) attachment,
affection.
attacca'panni *sm* hook, peg; (*mobile*) hall
stand.
attac'care *vt* (*unire*) to attach; (*cucendo*) to
sew on; (*far aderire*) to stick (on);
(*appendere*) to hang (up); (*assalire: anche
fig*) to attack; (*iniziare*) to begin, start; (*fig:
contagiare*) to pass on ♦ *vi* to stick, adhere;
~rsi *vr* to stick, adhere; (*trasmettersi per
contagio*) to be contagious; (*afferrarsi*): ~rsi
(a) to cling (to); (*fig: affezionarsi*): ~rsi (a)
to become attached (to); ~ discorso to
start a conversation; con me non attacca!
that won't work with me!
attacca'ticcio, a, ci, ce [attakka'tittʃo] *ag*
sticky.
attacca'tura *sf* (*di manica*) join; ~ (dei
capelli) hairline.
at'tacco, chi *sm* (*azione offensiva: anche fig*)
attack; (*MED*) attack, fit; (*SCI*) binding;
(*ELETTR*) socket.
attanagli'are [attanaʎ'ʎare] *vt* (*anche fig*) to
grip.
attar'darsi *vr*: ~ a fare qc (*fermarsi*) to stop
to do sth; (*stare più a lungo*) to stay behind
to do sth.
attec'chire [attek'kire] *vi* (*pianta*) to take
root; (*fig*) to catch on.
atteggia'mento [atteddʒa'mento] *sm*
attitude.
atteggi'arsi [atted'dʒarsi] *vr*: ~ a to pose as.
attem'pato, a *ag* elderly.
atten'dente *sm* (*MIL*) orderly, batman.
at'tendere *vt* to wait for, await ♦ *vi*: ~ a to
attend to.
atten'dibile *ag* (*scusa, storia*) credible;
(*fonte, testimone, notizia*) reliable; (*persona*)
trustworthy.
atte'nersi *vr*: ~ a to keep o stick to.
atten'tare *vi*: ~ a to make an attempt on.
atten'tato *sm* attack; ~ alla vita di qn
attempt on sb's life.
at'tento, a *ag* attentive; (*accurato*) careful,
thorough ♦ *escl* be careful!; stare ~ a qc to
pay attention to sth; ~i! (*MIL*) attention!;
~i al cane beware of the dog.
attenu'ante *sf* (*DIR*) extenuating
circumstance.
attenu'are *vt* to alleviate, ease; (*diminuire*)
to reduce; ~rsi *vr* to ease, abate.
attenuazi'one [attenuat'tsjone] *sf*
alleviation; easing; reduction.
attenzi'one [atten'tsjone] *sf* attention
♦ *escl* watch out!, be careful!; coprire qn di
~i to lavish attention on sb.

atter'raggio [atter'raddʒo] *sm* landing; ~ **di fortuna** emergency landing.
atter'rare *vt* to bring down ♦ *vi* to land.
atter'rire *vt* to terrify.
at'tesa *sf vedi* **atteso**.
at'tesi *etc vb vedi* **attendere**.
at'teso, a *pp di* **attendere** ♦ *sf* waiting; (*tempo trascorso aspettando*) wait; **essere in** ~**a di qc** to be waiting for sth; **in** ~**a di una vostra risposta** (*COMM*) awaiting your reply; **restiamo in** ~**a di Vostre ulteriori notizie** (*COMM*) we look forward to hearing (further) from you.
attes'tare *vt*: ~ **qc/che** to testify to sth/(to the fact) that.
attes'tato *sm* certificate.
attestazi'one [attestat'tsjone] *sf* (*certificato*) certificate; (*dichiarazione*) statement.
'attico, ci *sm* attic.
at'tiguo, a *ag* adjacent, adjoining.
attil'lato, a *ag* (*vestito*) close-fitting, tight; (*persona*) dressed up.
'attimo *sm* moment; **in un** ~ in a moment.
atti'nente *ag*: ~ **a** relating to, concerning.
atti'nenza [atti'nɛntsa] *sf* connection.
at'tingere [at'tindʒere] *vt*: ~ **a** *o* **da** (*acqua*) to draw from; (*denaro, notizie*) to obtain from.
at'tinto, a *pp di* **attingere**.
atti'rare *vt* to attract; ~**rsi delle critiche** to incur criticism.
atti'tudine *sf* (*disposizione*) aptitude; (*atteggiamento*) attitude.
atti'vare *vt* to activate; (*far funzionare*) to set going, start.
atti'vista, i, e *sm/f* activist.
attività *sf inv* activity; (*COMM*) assets *pl*; ~ **liquide** (*COMM*) liquid assets.
at'tivo, a *ag* active; (*COMM*) profit-making ♦ *sm* (*COMM*) assets *pl*; **in** ~ in credit; **chiudere in** ~ to show a profit; **avere qc al proprio** ~ (*fig*) to have sth to one's credit.
attiz'zare [attit'tsare] *vt* (*fuoco*) to poke; (*fig*) to stir up.
attizza'toio [attittsa'tojo] *sm* poker.
'atto, a *ag*: ~ **a** fit for, capable of ♦ *sm* act; (*azione, gesto*) action, act, deed; (*DIR: documento*) deed, document; ~**i** *smpl* (*di congressi etc*) proceedings; **essere in** ~ to be under way; **mettere in** ~ to put into action; **fare** ~ **di fare qc** to make as if to do sth; **all'**~ **pratico** in practice; **dare** ~ **a qn di qc** to give sb credit for sth; ~ **di nascita/morte** birth/death certificate; ~ **di proprietà** title deed; ~ **pubblico** official document; ~ **di vendita** bill of sale; ~**i osceni (in luogo pubblico)** (*DIR*) indecent exposure; ~**i verbali** transactions.

at'tonito, a *ag* dumbfounded, astonished.
attorcigli'are [attortʃiʎ'ʎare] *vt*, ~**rsi** *vr* to twist.
at'tore, 'trice *smlf* actor/actress.
attorni'are *vt* (*circondare*) to surround; ~**rsi** *vr*: ~**rsi di** to surround o.s. with.
at'torno *av*, ~ **a** *prep* round, around, about.
attrac'care *vt, vi* (*NAUT*) to dock, berth.
at'tracco, chi *sm* (*NAUT: manovra*) docking, berthing; (*luogo*) berth.
at'trae *etc vb vedi* **attrarre**.
attra'ente *ag* attractive.
at'traggo *etc vb vedi* **attrarre**.
at'trarre *vt* to attract.
at'trassi *etc vb vedi* **attrarre**.
attrat'tiva *sf* attraction, charm.
at'tratto, a *pp di* **attrarre**.
attraversa'mento *sm* crossing; ~ **pedonale** pedestrian crossing.
attraver'sare *vt* to cross; (*città, bosco, fig: periodo*) to go through; (*sog: fiume*) to run through.
attra'verso *prep* through; (*da una parte all'altra*) across.
attrazi'one [attrat'tsjone] *sf* attraction.
attrez'zare [attret'tsare] *vt* to equip; (*NAUT*) to rig.
attrezza'tura [attrettsa'tura] *sf* equipment *no pl*; rigging; ~**e per uffici** office equipment.
at'trezzo [at'trettso] *sm* tool, instrument; (*SPORT*) piece of equipment.
attribu'ire *vt*: ~ **qc a qn** (*assegnare*) to give *o* award sth to sb; (*quadro etc*) to attribute sth to sb.
attri'buto *sm* attribute.
at'trice [at'tritʃe] *sf vedi* **attore**.
at'trito *sm* (*anche fig*) friction.
attu'abile *ag* feasible.
attuabilità *sf* feasibility.
attu'ale *ag* (*presente*) present; (*di attualità*) topical; (*che è in atto*) actual.
attualità *sf inv* topicality; (*avvenimento*) current event; **notizie d'**~ (*TV*) the news *sg*.
attualiz'zare [attualid'dzare] *vt* to update, bring up to date.
attual'mente *av* at the moment.
attu'are *vt* to carry out; ~**rsi** *vr* to be realized.
attuazi'one [attuat'tsjone] *sf* carrying out.
attu'tire *vt* to deaden, reduce; ~**rsi** *vr* to die down.
au'dace [au'datʃe] *ag* audacious, daring; (*provocante*) provocative; (*sfacciato*) impudent.
au'dacia [au'datʃa] *sf* audacity, daring; boldness; provocativeness; impudence.

'**audio** *sm* (*TV, RADIO, CINE*) sound.
audiocas'setta *sf* (audio) cassette.
audio'leso, a *sm/f* person who is hard of hearing.
audiovi'sivo, a *ag* audiovisual.
audi'torio *sm*, **audi'torium** *sm inv* auditorium.
audizi'one [audit'tsjone] *sf* hearing; (*MUS*) audition.
'**auge** ['audʒe] *sf* (*della gloria, carriera*) height, peak; **essere in** ~ to be at the top.
augu'rale *ag*: **messaggio** ~ greeting; **biglietto** ~ greetings card.
augu'rare *vt* to wish; ~**rsi qc** to hope for sth.
au'gurio *sm* (*presagio*) omen; (*voto di benessere etc*) (good) wish; **essere di buon/cattivo** ~ to be of good omen/be ominous; **fare gli** ~**i a qn** to give sb one's best wishes; **tanti** ~**i!** all the best!
'**aula** *sf* (*scolastica*) classroom; (*universitaria*) lecture theatre; (*di edificio pubblico*) hall; ~ **magna** main hall; ~ **del tribunale** courtroom.
aumen'tare *vt*, *vi* to increase; ~ **di peso** (*persona*) to put on weight; **la produzione è aumentata del 50%** production has increased by 50%.
au'mento *sm* increase.
'**aureo**, a *ag* (*di oro*) gold *cpd*; (*fig: colore, periodo*) golden.
au'reola *sf* halo.
au'rora *sf* dawn.
ausili'are *ag*, *sm*, *sm/f* auxiliary.
au'silio *sm* aid.
auspi'cabile *ag* desirable.
auspi'care *vt* to call for.
aus'picio [aus'pitʃo] *sm* omen; (*protezione*) patronage; **sotto gli** ~**i di** under the auspices of; **è di buon** ~ it augurs well.
austerità *sf inv* austerity.
aus'tero, a *ag* austere.
aus'trale *ag* southern.
Aus'tralia *sf*: **l'**~ Australia.
australi'ano, a *ag*, *sm/f* Australian.
'**Austria** *sf*: **l'**~ Austria.
aus'triaco, a, ci, che *ag*, *sm/f* Austrian.
au'tarchico, a, ci, che [au'tarkiko] *ag* (*sistema*) self-sufficient, autarkic; (*prodotto*) home *cpd*, home-produced.
'**aut 'aut** *sm inv* ultimatum.
autenti'care *vt* to authenticate.
autenticità [autentitʃi'ta] *sf* authenticity.
au'tentico, a, ci, che *ag* (*quadro, firma*) authentic, genuine; (*fatto*) true, genuine.
au'tista, i *sm* driver; (*personale*) chauffeur.
'**auto** *sf inv* car; ~ **blu** official car.
autoabbron'zante [autoabbron'dzante] *ag*

self-tanning.
autoade'sivo, a *ag* self-adhesive ♦ *sm* sticker.
autoartico'lato *sm* articulated lorry (*BRIT*), semi (trailer) (*US*).
autobiogra'fia *sf* autobiography.
autobio'grafico, a, ci, che *ag* autobiographic(al).
auto'blinda *sf* armoured (*BRIT*) o armored (*US*) car.
auto'bomba *sf inv* car carrying a bomb; **l'**~ **si trovava a pochi metri** the car bomb was a few metres away.
auto'botte *sf* tanker.
'**autobus** *sm inv* bus.
autocari'cabile *ag*: **scheda** ~ top-up card.
auto'carro *sm* lorry (*BRIT*), truck.
autocertificazi'one [autotʃertifikat'tsjone] *sf* self-declaration.
autocis'terna [autotʃis'tɛrna] *sf* tanker.
autoco'lonna *sf* convoy.
autocon'trollo *sm* self-control.
autocopia'tivo, a *ag*: **carta** ~**a** carbonless paper.
autocorri'era *sf* coach, bus.
auto'cratico, a, ci, che *ag* autocratic.
auto'critica, **che** *sf* self-criticism.
au'toctono, a *ag*, *sm/f* native.
autodemolizi'one [autodemolit'tsjone] *sf* breaker's yard (*BRIT*).
autodi'datta, i, e *sm/f* autodidact, self-taught person.
autodi'fesa *sf* self-defence.
autoferrotranvi'ario, a *ag* public transport *cpd*.
autogesti'one [autodʒes'tjone] *sf* worker management.
autoges'tito, a [autodʒes'tito] *ag* under worker management.
au'tografo, a *ag*, *sm* autograph.
auto'grill *sm inv* motorway café (*BRIT*), roadside restaurant (*US*).
autoim'mune *ag* autoimmune.
autolesio'nismo *sm* (*fig*) self-destruction.
auto'linea *sf* bus route.
au'toma, i *sm* automaton.
auto'matico, a, ci, che *ag* automatic ♦ *sm* (*bottone*) snap fastener; (*fucile*) automatic; **selezione** ~**a** (*TEL*) direct dialling.
automazi'one [automat'tsjone] *sf*: ~ **delle procedure d'ufficio** office automation.
automedicazi'one [automedikat'tsjone] *sf* (*medicine, farmaci*): **medicinale di** ~ self-medication.
auto'mezzo [auto'mɛddzo] *sm* motor vehicle.
auto'mobile *sf* (motor) car; ~ **da corsa** racing car (*BRIT*), race car (*US*).

automobi'lismo *sm* (*gen*) motoring; (*SPORT*) motor racing.

automobi'lista, i, e *smf* motorist.

automobi'listico, a, ci, che *ag* car *cpd* (*BRIT*), automobile *cpd* (*US*); (*sport*) motor *cpd*.

autono'leggio [autono'leddʒo] *sm* car hire (*BRIT*), car rental.

autono'mia *sf* autonomy; (*di volo*) range.

au'tonomo, a *ag* autonomous; (*sindacato, pensiero*) independent.

auto'parco, chi *sm* (*parcheggio*) car park (*BRIT*), parking lot (*US*); (*insieme di automezzi*) transport fleet.

auto'pompa *sf* fire engine.

autop'sia *sf* post-mortem (examination), autopsy.

auto'radio *sf inv* (*apparecchio*) car radio; (*autoveicolo*) radio car.

au'tore, 'trice *smlf* author; **l'~ del furto** the person who committed the robbery; **diritti d'~** copyright *sg*; (*compenso*) royalties.

autoregolamentazi'one [autoregolamentat'tsjone] *sf* self-regulation.

auto'revole *ag* authoritative; (*persona*) influential.

autori'messa *sf* garage.

autorità *sf inv* authority.

autori'tratto *sm* self-portrait.

autoriz'zare [autorid'dzare] *vt* to authorize, give permission for.

autorizzazi'one [autoriddzat'tsjone] *sf* authorization; **~ a procedere** (*DIR*) authorization to proceed.

autos'catto *sm* (*FOT*) timer.

autos'contro *sm* dodgem car (*BRIT*), bumper car (*US*).

autoscu'ola *sf* driving school.

autosno'dato *sm* articulated vehicle.

autos'top *sm* hitchhiking.

autostop'pista, i, e *smlf* hitchhiker.

autos'trada *sf* motorway (*BRIT*), highway (*US*); **~ informatica** information superhighway.

autosuffici'ente [autosuffi'tʃɛnte] *ag* self-sufficient.

autosuffici'enza [autosuffi'tʃɛntsa] *sf* self-sufficiency.

auto'treno *sm* articulated lorry (*BRIT*), semi (trailer) (*US*).

autove'icolo *sm* motor vehicle.

auto'velox ® *sm inv* (police) speed camera.

autovet'tura *sf* (motor) car.

autun'nale *ag* (*di autunno*) autumn *cpd*; (*da autunno*) autumnal.

au'tunno *sm* autumn.

AV *sigla* = *Avellino*.

aval'lare *vt* (*FINANZA*) to guarantee; (*fig: sostenere*) to back; (: *confermare*) to confirm.

a'vallo *sm* (*FINANZA*) guarantee.

avam'braccio, *pl(f)* **-cia** [avam'brattʃo] *sm* forearm.

avam'posto *sm* (*MIL*) outpost.

A'vana *sf*: **l'~** Havana.

a'vana *sm inv* (*sigaro*) Havana (cigar); (*colore*) Havana brown.

avangu'ardia *sf* vanguard; (*ARTE*) avant-garde.

avansco'perta *sf* (*MIL*) reconnaissance; **andare in ~** to reconnoitre.

a'vanti *av* (*stato in luogo*) in front; (*moto: andare, venire*) forward; (*tempo: prima*) before ♦ *prep* (*luogo*): **~ a** before, in front of; (*tempo*): **~ Cristo** before Christ ♦ *escl* (*entrate*) come (*o* go) in!; (*MIL*) forward!; (*coraggio*) come on! ♦ *sm inv* (*SPORT*) forward; **il giorno ~** the day before; **~ e indietro** backwards and forwards; **andare ~** to go forward; (*continuare*) to go on; (*precedere*) to go (on) ahead; (*orologio*) to be fast; **essere ~ negli studi** to be well advanced with one's studies; **mandare ~ la famiglia** to provide for one's family; **mandare ~ un'azienda** to run a business; **~ il prossimo!** next please!

avan'treno *sm* (*AUT*) front chassis.

avanza'mento [avantsa'mento] *sm* (*gen*) advance; (*fig*) progress; promotion.

avan'zare [avan'tsare] *vt* (*spostare in avanti*) to move forward, advance; (*domanda*) to put forward; (*promuovere*) to promote; (*essere creditore*): **~ qc da qn** to be owed sth by sb ♦ *vi* (*andare avanti*) to move forward, advance; (*fig: progredire*) to make progress; (*essere d'avanzo*) to be left, remain; **basta e avanza** that's more than enough.

avan'zato, a [avan'tsato] *ag* (*teoria, tecnica*) advanced ♦ *sf* (*MIL*) advance; **in età ~a** advanced in years, up in years.

a'vanzo [a'vantso] *sm* (*residuo*) remains *pl*, left-overs *pl*; (*MAT*) remainder; (*COMM*) surplus; (*eccedenza di bilancio*) profit carried forward; **averne d'~ di qc** to have more than enough of sth; **~ di cassa** cash in hand; **~ di galera** (*fig*) jailbird.

ava'ria *sf* (*guasto*) damage; (: *meccanico*) breakdown.

avari'ato, a *ag* (*merce*) damaged; (*cibo*) off.

ava'rizia [ava'rittsja] *sf* avarice; **crepi l'~!** to hang with the expense!

a'varo, a *ag* avaricious, miserly ♦ *sm* miser.

a'vena *sf* oats *pl*.

PAROLA CHIAVE

a'vere sm (COMM) credit; **gli ~i** (ricchezze) wealth sg, possessions
♦ vt **1** (possedere) to have; **ha due bambini/ una bella casa** she has (got) two children/ a lovely house; **ha i capelli lunghi** he has (got) long hair; **non ho da mangiare/bere** I've (got) nothing to eat/drink, I don't have anything to eat/drink
2 (indossare) to wear, have on; **aveva una maglietta rossa** he was wearing o he had on a red T-shirt; **ha gli occhiali** he wears o has glasses
3 (ricevere) to get; **hai avuto l'assegno?** did you get o have you had the cheque?
4 (età, dimensione) to be; **ha 9 anni** he is 9 (years old); **la stanza ha 3 metri di lunghezza** the room is 3 metres in length; vedi **fame; paura; sonno** etc
5 (tempo): **quanti ne abbiamo oggi?** what's the date today?; **ne hai per molto?** will you be long?
6 (fraseologia): **avercela con qn** to be angry with sb; **cos'hai?** what's wrong o what's the matter (with you)?; **non ha niente a che vedere o fare con me** it's got nothing to do with me
♦ vb aus **1** to have; **aver bevuto/mangiato** to have drunk/eaten; **l'ho già visto** I have seen it already; **l'ho visto ieri** I saw it yesterday; **ci ha creduto?** did he believe it?
2 (+ da + infinito): **~ da fare qc** to have to do sth; **non ho niente da dire** I have nothing to say; **non hai che da chiederlo** you only have to ask him.

avia'tore, 'trice sm/f aviator, pilot.
aviazi'one [avjat'tsjone] sf aviation; (MIL) air force; **~ civile** civil aviation.
avicol'tura sf bird breeding; (di pollame) poultry farming.
avidità sf eagerness; greed.
'avido, a ag eager; (peg) greedy.
avi'ere sm (MIL) airman.
avitami'nosi sf vitamin deficiency.
'avo sm (antenato) ancestor; **i nostri ~i** our ancestors.
avo'cado sm avocado.
a'vorio sm ivory.
a'vulso, a ag: **parole ~e dal contesto** words out of context; **~ dalla società** (fig) cut off from society.
Avv. abbr = **avvocato**.
avva'lersi vr: **~ di** to avail o.s. of.
avvalla'mento sm sinking no pl; (effetto) depression.

avvalo'rare vt to confirm.
avvantaggi'are [avvantad'dʒare] vt to favour (BRIT), favor (US); **~rsi** vr (trarre vantaggio): **~rsi di** to take advantage of; (prevalere): **~rsi negli affari/sui concorrenti** to get ahead in business/of one's competitors.
avve'dersi vr: **~ di qn/qc** to notice sb/sth.
avve'duto, a ag (accorto) prudent; (scaltro) astute.
avvelena'mento sm poisoning.
avvele'nare vt to poison.
avve'nente ag attractive, charming.
avve'nenza [avve'nɛntsa] sf good looks pl.
av'vengo etc vb vedi **avvenire**.
avveni'mento sm event.
avve'nire vi, vb impers to happen, occur ♦ sm future.
av'venni etc vb vedi **avvenire**.
avven'tarsi vr: **~ su** o **contro qn/qc** to hurl o.s. o rush at sb/sth.
avven'tato, a ag rash, reckless.
avven'tizio, a [avven'tittsjo] ag (impiegato) temporary; (guadagno) casual.
av'vento sm advent, coming; (REL): **l'A~** Advent.
avven'tore sm customer.
avven'tura sf adventure; (amorosa) affair; **avere spirito d'~** to be adventurous.
avventu'rarsi vr to venture.
avventuri'ero, a sm/f adventurer/ adventuress.
avventu'roso, a ag adventurous.
avve'nuto, a pp di **avvenire**.
avve'rarsi vr to come true.
av'verbio sm adverb.
avver'rò etc vb vedi **avvenire**.
avver'sare vt to oppose.
avver'sario, a ag opposing ♦ sm opponent, adversary.
avversi'one sf aversion.
avversità sf inv adversity, misfortune.
av'verso, a ag (contrario) contrary; (sfavorevole) unfavourable (BRIT), unfavorable (US).
avver'tenza [avver'tɛntsa] sf (ammonimento) warning; (cautela) care; (premessa) foreword; **~e** sfpl (istruzioni per l'uso) instructions.
avverti'mento sm warning.
avver'tire vt (avvisare) to warn; (rendere consapevole) to inform, notify; (percepire) to feel.
av'vezzo, a [av'vettso] ag: **~ a** used to.
avvia'mento sm (atto) starting; (effetto) start; (AUT) starting; (: dispositivo) starter; (COMM) goodwill.
avvi'are vt (mettere sul cammino) to direct;

(*impresa*, *trattative*) to begin, start; (*motore*) to start; ~**rsi** *vr* to set off, set out.

avvicenda'mento [avvitʃenda'mento] *sm* alternation; (*AGR*) rotation; **c'è molto** ~ **di personale** there is a high turnover of staff.

avvicen'dare [avvitʃen'dare] *vt*, ~**rsi** *vr* to alternate.

avvicina'mento [avvitʃina'mento] *sm* approach.

avvici'nare [avvitʃi'nare] *vt* to bring near; (*trattare con: persona*) to approach; ~**rsi** *vr*: ~**rsi (a qn/qc)** to approach (sb/sth), draw near (to sb/sth); (*somigliare*) to be similar (to sb/sth), be close (to sb/sth).

avvi'lente *ag* (*umiliante*) humiliating; (*scoraggiante*) discouraging, disheartening.

avvili'mento *sm* humiliation; disgrace; discouragement.

avvi'lire *vt* (*umiliare*) to humiliate; (*degradare*) to disgrace; (*scoraggiare*) to dishearten, discourage; ~**rsi** *vr* (*abbattersi*) to lose heart.

avvilup'pare *vt* (*avvolgere*) to wrap up; (*ingarbugliare*) to entangle.

avvinaz'zato, a [avvinat'tsato] *ag* drunk.

avvin'cente [avvin'tʃɛnte] *ag* (*film, racconto*) enthralling.

av'vincere [av'vintʃere] *vt* to charm, enthral.

avvinghi'are [avvin'gjare] *vt* to clasp; ~**rsi** *vr*: ~**rsi a** to cling to.

av'vinsi *etc vb vedi* **avvincere.**

av'vinto, a *pp di* **avvincere.**

av'vio *sm* start, beginning; **dare l'**~ **a qc** to start sth off; **prendere l'**~ to get going, get under way.

avvi'saglia [avvi'zaʎʎa] *sf* (*sintomo: di temporale etc*) sign; (*di malattia*) manifestation, sign, symptom; (*scaramuccia*) skirmish.

avvi'sare *vt* (*far sapere*) to inform; (*mettere in guardia*) to warn.

avvisa'tore *sm* (*apparecchio d'allarme*) alarm; ~ **acustico** horn; ~ **d'incendio** fire alarm.

av'viso *sm* warning; (*annuncio*) announcement; (*affisso*) notice; (*inserzione pubblicitaria*) advertisement; **a mio** ~ **in my opinion; mettere qn sull'**~ to put sb on their guard; **fino a nuovo** ~ until further notice; ~ **di chiamata** (*servizio*) call waiting; (*segnale*) call waiting signal; ~ **di consegna/spedizione** (*COMM*) delivery/ consignment note; ~ **di garanzia** (*DIR*) notification (*of impending investigation and of the right to name a defence laywer*); ~ **di pagamento** (*COMM*) payment advice.

avvista'mento *sm* sighting.

avvis'tare *vt* to sight.

avvi'tare *vt* to screw down (*o* in).

avviz'zire [avvit'tsire] *vi* to wither.

avvo'cato, 'essa *sm/f* (*DIR*) barrister (*BRIT*), lawyer; (*fig*) defender, advocate; ~ **del diavolo: fare l'**~ **del diavolo** to play devil's advocate; ~ **difensore** counsel for the defence; ~ **di parte civile** counsel for the plaintiff.

av'volgere [av'vɔldʒere] *vt* to roll up; (*bobina*) to wind up; (*avviluppare*) to wrap up; ~**rsi** *vr* (*avvilupparsi*) to wrap o.s. up.

avvol'gibile [avvol'dʒibile] *sm* roller blind (*BRIT*), blind.

avvolgi'mento [avvoldʒi'mento] *sm* winding.

av'volsi *etc vb vedi* **avvolgere.**

av'volto, a *pp di* **avvolgere.**

avvol'toio *sm* vulture.

aza'lea [addza'lɛa] *sf* azalea.

Azerbaigi'an [addzɛrbai'dʒan] *sm* Azerbaijan.

azerbaig'iano, a [addzɛrbai'dʒano] *ag* Azerbaijani ♦ *sm/f* (*abitante*) Azerbaijani ♦ *sm* (*LING*) Azerbaijani.

a'zero, a [ad'dzɛro] *sm/f* Azeri.

azi'enda [ad'dzjɛnda] *sf* business, firm, concern; ~ **agricola** farm; ~ (**autonoma**) **di soggiorno** tourist board; ~ **a partecipazione statale** *business in which the State has a financial interest*; ~**e pubbliche** public corporations.

azien'dale [addzjen'dale] *ag* company *cpd*; **organizzazione** ~ business administration.

azio'nare [attsjo'nare] *vt* to activate.

azio'nario, a [attsjo'narjo] *ag* share *cpd*; **capitale** ~ share capital; **mercato** ~ stock market.

azi'one [at'tsjone] *sf* action; (*COMM*) share; ~ **sindacale** industrial action; ~**i preferenziali** preference shares (*BRIT*), preferred stock *sg* (*US*).

azio'nista, i, e [attsjo'nista] *sm/f* (*COMM*) shareholder.

a'zoto [ad'dzɔto] *sm* nitrogen.

az'teco, a, ci, che [as'tɛko] *ag, sm/f* Aztec.

azzan'nare [attsan'nare] *vt* to sink one's teeth into.

azzar'dare [addzar'dare] *vt* (*soldi, vita*) to risk, hazard; (*domanda, ipotesi*) to hazard, venture; ~**rsi** *vr*: ~**rsi a fare** to dare (to) do.

azzar'dato, a [addzar'dato] *ag* (*impresa*) risky; (*risposta*) rash.

az'zardo [ad'dzardo] *sm* risk; **gioco d'**~ game of chance.

azzec'care [attsek'kare] vt (bersaglio) to hit, strike; (risposta, pronostico) to get right; (fig: indovinare) to guess.

azzera'mento [addzera'mento] sm (INFORM) reset.

azze'rare [addze'rare] vt (MAT, FISICA) to make equal to zero, reduce to zero; (TECN: strumento) to (re)set to zero.

'azzimo, a ['addzimo] ag unleavened ♦ sm unleavened bread.

azzop'pare [attsop'pare] vt to lame, make lame.

Az'zorre [ad'dzorre] sfpl: **le** ~ the Azores.

azzuf'farsi [attsuf'farsi] vr to come to blows.

az'zurro, a [ad'dzurro] ag blue ♦ sm (colore) blue; **gli** ~**i** (SPORT) the Italian national team.

azzur'rognolo, a [addzur'roɲɲolo] ag bluish.

B b

B, b [bi] sf o m inv (lettera) B, b; ~ **come Bologna** ≈ B for Benjamin (BRIT), B for Baker (US).

BA sigla = Bari.

ba'bau sm inv ogre, bogey man.

bab'beo sm simpleton.

'babbo sm (fam) dad, daddy; **B~ Natale** Father Christmas.

bab'buccia, ce [bab'buttʃa] sf slipper; (per neonati) bootee.

babbu'ino sm baboon.

babilo'nese ag, sm/f Babylonian.

Babi'lonia sf Babylonia.

ba'bordo sm (NAUT) port side.

baby'sitter ['beɪbɪsitə*] sm/f inv baby-sitter.

ba'cato, a ag worm-eaten, rotten; (fig: mente) diseased; (: persona) corrupt.

'bacca, che sf berry.

baccalà sm dried salted cod; (fig: peg) dummy.

bac'cano sm din, clamour (BRIT), clamor (US).

bac'cello [bat'tʃɛllo] sm pod.

bac'chetta [bak'ketta] sf (verga) stick, rod; (di direttore d'orchestra) baton; (di tamburo) drumstick; **comandare a** ~ to rule with a rod of iron; ~ **magica** magic wand.

ba'checa, che [ba'kɛka] sf (mobile) showcase, display case; (UNIVERSITÀ, in ufficio) notice board (BRIT), bulletin board (US).

bacia'mano [batʃa'mano] sm: **fare il** ~ **a qn** to kiss sb's hand.

baci'are [ba'tʃare] vt to kiss; ~**rsi** vr to kiss (one another).

ba'cillo [ba'tʃillo] sm bacillus, germ.

baci'nella [batʃi'nɛlla] sf basin.

ba'cino [ba'tʃino] sm basin; (MINERALOGIA) field, bed; (ANAT) pelvis; (NAUT) dock; ~ **carbonifero** coalfield; ~ **di carenaggio** dry dock; ~ **petrolifero** oilfield.

'bacio ['batʃo] sm kiss.

'baco, chi sm worm; ~ **da seta** silkworm.

'bada sf: **tenere qn a** ~ (tener d'occhio) to keep an eye on sb; (tenere a distanza) to hold sb at bay.

ba'dare vi (fare attenzione) to take care, be careful; ~ **a** (occuparsi di) to look after, take care of; (dar ascolto) to pay attention to; **è un tipo che non bada a spese** money is no object to him; **bada ai fatti tuoi!** mind your own business!

ba'dia sf abbey.

ba'dile sm shovel.

'baffi smpl moustache sg, mustache sg (US); (di animale) whiskers; **leccarsi i** ~ to lick one's lips; **ridere sotto i** ~ to laugh up one's sleeve.

bagagli'aio [bagaʎ'ʎajo] sm luggage van (BRIT) o car (US); (AUT) boot (BRIT), trunk (US).

ba'gaglio [ba'gaʎʎo] sm luggage no pl, baggage no pl; **fare/disfare i** ~**i** to pack/ unpack; ~ **a mano** hand luggage.

bagat'tella sf trifle, trifling matter.

Bag'dad sf Baghdad.

baggia'nata [baddʒa'nata] sf foolish action; **dire** ~**e** to talk nonsense.

bagli'ore [baʎ'ʎore] sm flash, dazzling light; **un** ~ **di speranza** a sudden ray of hope.

ba'gnante [baɲ'ɲante] sm/f bather.

ba'gnare [baɲ'ɲare] vt to wet; (inzuppare) to soak; (innaffiare) to water; (sog: fiume) to flow through; (: mare) to wash, bathe; (brindare) to drink to, toast; ~**rsi** vr (al mare) to go swimming o bathing; (in vasca) to have a bath.

ba'gnato, a [baɲ'ɲato] ag wet; **era come un pulcino** ~ he looked like a drowned rat.

ba'gnino [baɲ'ɲino] sm lifeguard.

'bagno ['baɲɲo] sm bath; (locale) bathroom; ~**i** smpl (stabilimento) baths; **fare il** ~ to have a bath; (nel mare) to go swimming o bathing; **fare il** ~ **a qn** to give sb a bath; **mettere a** ~ to soak.

bagnoma'ria [baɲɲoma'ria] sm: **cuocere a**

~ to cook in a double saucepan (*BRIT*) *o* double boiler (*US*).

bagnoschi'uma [baɲɲoskj'uma] *sm inv* bubble bath.

Ba'hama [ba'ama] *sfpl*: **le** ~ the Bahamas.

Bah'rein [ba'rein] *sm*: **il** ~ Bahrain *o* Bahrein.

'**baia** *sf* bay.

baio'netta *sf* bayonet.

'**baita** *sf* mountain hut.

balaus'trata *sf* balustrade.

balbet'tare *vi* to stutter, stammer; (*bimbo*) to babble ♦ *vt* to stammer out.

bal'buzie [bal'buttsje] *sf* stammer.

balbuzi'ente [balbut'tsjɛnte] *ag* stuttering, stammering.

Bal'cani *smpl*: **i** ~ the Balkans.

bal'canico, a, ci, che *ag* Balkan.

bal'cone *sm* balcony.

baldac'chino [baldak'kino] *sm* canopy; **letto a** ~ four-poster (bed).

bal'danza [bal'dantsa] *sf* self-confidence; boldness.

'**baldo, a** *ag* bold, daring.

bal'doria *sf*: **fare** ~ to have a riotous time.

Bale'ari *sfpl*: **le isole** ~ the Balearic Islands.

ba'lena *sf* whale.

bale'nare *vb impers*: **balena** there's lightning ♦ *vi* to flash; **mi balenò un'idea** an idea flashed through my mind.

ba'leno *sm* flash of lightning; **in un** ~ in a flash.

ba'lera *sf* (*locale*) dance hall; (*pista*) dance floor.

ba'lestra *sf* crossbow.

'**balia** *sf* wet-nurse; ~ **asciutta** nanny.

ba'lia *sf*: **in** ~ **di** at the mercy of; **essere lasciato in** ~ **di se stesso** to be left to one's own devices.

ba'lilla *sm inv* (*STORIA*) *member of Fascist youth group*.

ba'listico, a, ci, che *ag* ballistic ♦ *sf* ballistics *sg*; **perito** ~ ballistics expert.

'**balla** *sf* (*di merci*) bale; (*fandonia*) (tall) story.

bal'labile *sm* dance number, dance tune.

bal'lare *vt*, *vi* to dance.

bal'lata *sf* ballad.

balla'toio *sm* (*terrazzina*) gallery.

balle'rina *sf* dancer; ballet dancer; (*scarpa*) pump; ~ **di rivista** chorus girl.

balle'rino *sm* dancer; ballet dancer.

bal'letto *sm* ballet.

'**ballo** *sm* dance; (*azione*) dancing *no pl*; ~ **in maschera** *o* **mascherato** fancy-dress ball;

essere in ~ (*fig: persona*) to be involved; (: *cosa*) to be at stake; **tirare in** ~ **qc** to bring sth up, raise sth.

ballot'taggio [ballot'taddʒo] *sm* (*POL*) second ballot.

balne'are *ag* seaside *cpd*; (*stagione*) bathing.

ba'locco, chi *sm* toy.

ba'lordo, a *ag* stupid, senseless.

bal'samico, a, ci, che *ag* (*aria, brezza*) balmy; **pomata** ~**a** balsam.

'**balsamo** *sm* (*aroma*) balsam; (*lenimento, fig*) balm; (*per capelli*) (hair) conditioner.

'**baltico, a, ci, che** *ag* Baltic; **il (mar) B**~ the Baltic (Sea).

balu'ardo *sm* bulwark.

'**balza** ['baltsa] *sf* (*dirupo*) crag; (*di stoffa*) frill.

bal'zano, a [bal'tsano] *ag* (*persona, idea*) queer, odd.

bal'zare [bal'tsare] *vi* to bounce; (*lanciarsi*) to jump, leap; **la verità balza agli occhi** the truth of the matter is obvious.

'**balzo** ['baltso] *sm* bounce; jump, leap; (*del terreno*) crag; **prendere la palla al** ~ (*fig*) to seize one's opportunity.

bam'bagia [bam'badʒa] *sf* (*ovatta*) cotton wool (*BRIT*), absorbent cotton (*US*); (*cascame*) cotton waste; **tenere qn nella** ~ (*fig*) to mollycoddle sb.

bam'bina *sf vedi* **bambino**.

bambi'naia *sf* nanny, nurse(maid).

bam'bino, a *sm/f* child; **fare il** ~ to behave childishly.

bam'boccio [bam'bɔttʃo] *sm* plump child; (*pupazzo*) rag doll.

'**bambola** *sf* doll.

bambo'lotto *sm* male doll.

bambù *sm* bamboo.

ba'nale *ag* banal, commonplace.

banalità *sf inv* banality.

ba'nana *sf* banana.

ba'nano *sm* banana tree.

'**banca, che** *sf* bank; ~ **d'affari** merchant bank; ~ **(di) dati** data bank.

banca'rella *sf* stall.

ban'cario, a *ag* banking, bank *cpd* ♦ *sm* bank clerk.

banca'rotta *sf* bankruptcy; **fare** ~ to go bankrupt.

bancarotti'ere *sm* bankrupt.

ban'chetto [ban'ketto] *sm* banquet.

banchi'ere [ban'kjɛre] *sm* banker.

ban'china [ban'kina] *sf* (*di porto*) quay; (*per pedoni, ciclisti*) path; (*di stazione*) platform; ~ **cedevole** (*AUT*) soft verge (*BRIT*) *o* shoulder (*US*); ~ **spartitraffico** (*AUT*) central reservation (*BRIT*), median (strip)

(US).

ban'chisa [ban'kiza] sf pack ice.

'banco, chi sm bench; (di negozio) counter; (di mercato) stall; (di officina) (work)bench; (GEO, banca) bank; sotto ~ (fig) under the counter; tenere il ~ (nei giochi) to be (the) banker; tener ~ (fig) to monopolize the conversation; medicinali da ~ over-the-counter medicines; ~ di chiesa pew; ~ di corallo coral reef; ~ degli imputati dock; ~ del Lotto lottery-ticket office;~ di prova (fig) testing ground; ~ dei testimoni witness box (BRIT) o stand (US).

banco'giro [banko'dʒiro] sm credit transfer.

'Bancomat ® sm inv automated banking; (tessera) cash card.

banco'nota sf banknote.

'banda sf band; (di stoffa) band, stripe; (lato, parte) side; (di calcolatore) tape; ~ perforata punch tape.

banderu'ola sf (METEOR) weathercock, weathervane; essere una ~ (fig) to be fickle.

bandi'era sf flag, banner; battere ~ italiana (nave etc) to fly the Italian flag; cambiare ~ (fig) to change sides; ~ di comodo flag of convenience.

ban'dire vt to proclaim; (esiliare) to exile; (fig) to dispense with.

ban'dito sm outlaw, bandit.

bandi'tore sm (di aste) auctioneer.

'bando sm proclamation; (esilio) exile, banishment; mettere al ~ qn to exile sb; (fig) to freeze sb out; ~ alle ciance! that's enough talk!

'bandolo sm (di matassa) end; trovare il ~ della matassa (fig) to find the key to the problem.

Bang'kok [ban'kɔk] sf Bangkok.

Bangla'desh [bangla'dɛʃ] sm: il ~ Bangladesh.

bar sm inv bar.

'bara sf coffin.

ba'racca, che sf shed, hut; (peg) hovel; mandare avanti la ~ to keep things going; piantare ~ e burattini to throw everything up.

barac'cato, a sm/f person living in temporary camp.

barac'chino [barak'kino] sm (chiosco) stall; (apparecchio) CB radio.

barac'cone sm booth, stall; ~i smpl (luna park) funfair sg (BRIT), amusement park; fenomeno da ~ circus freak.

barac'copoli sf inv shanty town.

bara'onda sf hubbub, bustle.

ba'rare vi to cheat.

'baratro sm abyss.

barat'tare vt: ~ qc con to barter sth for, swap sth for.

ba'ratto sm barter.

ba'rattolo sm (di latta) tin; (di vetro) jar; (di coccio) pot.

'barba sf beard; farsi la ~ to shave; farla in ~ a qn (fig) to fool sb; servire qn di ~ e capelli (fig) to teach sb a lesson; che ~! what a bore!

barbabi'etola sf beetroot (BRIT), beet (US); ~ da zucchero sugar beet.

Bar'bados sfsg Barbados.

bar'barico, a, ci, che ag (invasione) barbarian; (usanze, metodi) barbaric.

bar'barie sf barbarity.

'barbaro, a ag barbarous ♦ sm barbarian; i B~i the Barbarians.

'barbecue ['baːbikjuː] sm inv barbecue.

barbi'ere sm barber.

barbi'turico, a, ci, che ag barbituric ♦ sm barbiturate.

bar'bone sm (cane) poodle; (vagabondo) tramp.

bar'buto, a ag bearded.

'barca, che sf boat; una ~ di (fig) heaps of, tons of; mandare avanti la ~ (fig) to keep things going; ~ a remi rowing boat (BRIT), rowboat (US); ~ a vela sailing boat (BRIT), sailboat (US).

barcai'olo sm boatman.

barcame'narsi vr (nel lavoro) to get by; (a parole) to beat about the bush.

Barcel'lona [bartʃel'lona] sf Barcelona.

barcol'lare vi to stagger.

bar'cone sm (per ponti di barche) pontoon.

ba'rella sf (lettiga) stretcher.

'Barents: il mar di ~ sm the Barents Sea.

ba'rese ag of (o from) Bari.

bari'centro [bari'tʃentro] sm centre (BRIT) o center (US) of gravity.

ba'rile sm barrel, cask.

ba'rista, i, e sm/f barman/barmaid; bar owner.

ba'ritono sm baritone.

bar'lume sm glimmer, gleam.

'baro sm (CARTE) cardsharp.

ba'rocco, a, chi, che ag, sm baroque.

ba'rometro sm barometer.

ba'rone sm baron; i ~i della medicina (fig peg) the top brass in the medical faculty.

baro'nessa sf baroness.

'barra sf bar; (NAUT) helm; (segno grafico) stroke.

bar'rare vt to bar.

barri'care vt to barricade.

barri'cata sf barricade; essere dall'altra parte della ~ (fig) to be on the other side of the fence.

barri'era *sf* barrier; (*GEO*) reef; **la Grande B~ Corallina** the Great Barrier Reef.

bar'roccio [bar'rɔttʃo] *sm* cart.

ba'ruffa *sf* scuffle; **fare ~** to squabble.

barzel'letta [bardzel'letta] *sf* joke, funny story.

basa'mento *sm* (*parte inferiore, piedestallo*) base; (*TECN*) bed, base plate.

ba'sare *vt* to base, found; **~rsi** *vr*: **~rsi su** (*sog: fatti, prove*) to be based *o* founded on; (: *persona*) to base one's arguments on.

'basco, a, schi, sche *ag* Basque ♦ *sm/f* Basque ♦ *sm* (*lingua*) Basque; (*copricapo*) beret.

bas'culla *sf* weighing machine, weighbridge.

'base *sf* base; (*fig: fondamento*) basis; (*POL*) rank and file; **di ~** basic; **in ~ a** on the basis of, according to; **in ~ a ciò ...** on that basis ...; **a ~ di caffè** coffee-based; **essere alla ~ di qc** to be at the root of sth; **gettare le ~i per qc** to lay the basis *o* foundations for sth; **avere buone ~i** (*INS*) to have a sound educational background.

'baseball ['beisbɔːl] *sm* baseball.

ba'setta *sf* sideburn.

basi'lare *ag* basic, fundamental.

Basi'lea *sf* Basle.

ba'silica, che *sf* basilica.

ba'silico *sm* basil.

bas'sezza [bas'settsa] *sf* (*d'animo, di sentimenti*) baseness; (*azione*) base action.

bas'sista, i, e *sm/f* bass player.

'basso, a *ag* low; (*di statura*) short; (*meridionale*) southern ♦ *sm* bottom, lower part; (*MUS*) bass; **a occhi ~i** with eyes lowered; **a ~ prezzo** cheap; **scendere da ~** to go downstairs; **cadere in ~** (*fig*) to come down in the world; **la ~a Italia** southern Italy; **il ~ Medioevo** the late Middle Ages.

basso'fondo, *pl* **bassi'fondi** *sm* (*GEO*) shallows *pl*; **i bassifondi (della città)** the seediest parts of the town.

bassorili'evo *sm* bas-relief.

bas'sotto, a *ag* squat ♦ *sm* (*cane*) dachshund.

bas'tardo, a *ag* (*animale, pianta*) hybrid, crossbreed; (*persona*) illegitimate, bastard (*peg*) ♦ *sm/f* illegitimate child, bastard (*peg*); (*cane*) mongrel.

bas'tare *vi, vb impers* to be enough, be sufficient; **~ a qn** to be enough for sb; **~ a se stesso** to be self-sufficient; **basta chiedere** *o* **che chieda a un vigile** you have only to *o* need only ask a policeman; **basti dire che ...** suffice it to say that ...; **basta!**

that's enough!, that will do!; **basta così?** (*al bar etc*) will that be all?; **punto e basta!** and that's that!

basti'an *sm*: **~ contrario** awkward customer.

basti'mento *sm* ship, vessel.

basti'one *sm* bastion.

basto'nare *vt* to beat, thrash; **avere l'aria di un cane bastonato** to look crestfallen.

basto'nata *sf* blow (with a stick); **prendere qn a ~e** to give sb a good beating.

baston'cino [baston'tʃino] *sm* (*piccolo bastone*) small stick; (*TECN*) rod; (*SCI*) ski pole; **~i di pesce** (*CUC*) fish fingers (*BRIT*), fish sticks (*US*).

bas'tone *sm* stick; **~i** *smpl* (*CARTE*) *suit in Neapolitan pack of cards*; **~ da passeggio** walking stick; **mettere i ~i fra le ruote a qn** to put a spoke in sb's wheel.

bat'tage [ba'taʒ] *sm inv*: **~ promozionale** *o* **pubblicitario** publicity campaign.

bat'taglia [bat'taʎʎa] *sf* battle.

bat'taglio [bat'taʎʎo] *sm* (*di campana*) clapper; (*di porta*) knocker.

battagli'one [battaʎ'ʎone] *sm* battalion.

bat'tello *sm* boat.

bat'tente *sm* (*imposta: di porta*) wing, flap; (: *di finestra*) shutter; (*per bussare*) knocker; (*di orologio*) hammer; **chiudere i ~i** (*fig*) to shut up shop.

'battere *vt* to beat; (*grano*) to thresh; (*percorrere*) to scour; (*rintoccare: le ore*) to strike ♦ *vi* (*bussare*) to knock; (*urtare*): **~ contro** to hit *o* strike against; (*pioggia, sole*) to beat down; (*cuore*) to beat; (*TENNIS*) to serve; **~rsi** *vr* to fight; **~ le mani** to clap; **~ i piedi** to stamp one's feet; **~ su un argomento** to hammer home an argument; **~ a macchina** to type; **~ il marciapiede** (*peg*) to walk the streets, be on the game; **~ un rigore** (*CALCIO*) to take a penalty; **~ in testa** (*AUT*) to knock; **in un batter d'occhio** in the twinkling of an eye; **senza ~ ciglio** without batting an eyelid; **battersela** to run off.

batte'ria *sf* battery; (*MUS*) drums *pl*; **~ da cucina** pots and pans *pl*.

bat'terio *sm* bacterium; **~i** *smpl* bacteria.

batteriolo'gia [batterjolo'dʒia] *sf* bacteriology.

bat'tesimo *sm* (*sacramento*) baptism; (*rito*) baptism, christening; **tenere qn a ~** to be godfather (*o* godmother) to sb.

battez'zare [batted'dzare] *vt* to baptize; to christen.

battiba'leno *sm*: **in un ~** in a flash.

batti'becco, chi *sm* squabble.

batticu'ore *sm* palpitations *pl*; **avere il ~ to**

be frightened to death.

bat'tigia [bat'tidʒa] *sf* water's edge.

batti'mano *sm* applause.

batti'panni *sm inv* carpet-beater.

battis'tero *sm* baptistry.

battis'trada *sm inv* (*di pneumatico*) tread; (*di gara*) pacemaker.

battitap'peto *sm inv* upright vacuum cleaner.

'**battito** *sm* beat, throb; ~ **cardiaco** heartbeat; ~ **della pioggia/dell'orologio** beating of the rain/ticking of the clock.

batti'tore *sm* (*CRICKET*) batsman; (*BASEBALL*) batter; (*CACCIA*) beater.

batti'tura *sf* (*anche:* ~ **a macchina**) typing; (*del grano*) threshing.

bat'tuta *sf* blow; (*di macchina da scrivere*) stroke; (*MUS*) bar; beat; (*TEAT*) cue; (*di caccia*) beating; (*POLIZIA*) combing, scouring; (*TENNIS*) service; **fare una** ~ **to crack a joke, make a witty remark; aver la** ~ **pronta** (*fig*) to have a ready answer; **è ancora alle prime** ~**e** it's just started.

ba'tuffolo *sm* wad.

ba'ule *sm* trunk; (*AUT*) boot (*BRIT*), trunk (*US*).

bau'xite [bauk'site] *sf* bauxite.

'**bava** *sf* (*di animale*) slaver, slobber; (*di lumaca*) slime; (*di vento*) breath.

bava'glino [bavaʎ'ʎino] *sm* bib.

ba'vaglio [ba'vaʎʎo] *sm* gag.

bava'rese *ag, sm/f* Bavarian.

'**bavero** *sm* collar.

Bavi'era *sf* Bavaria.

ba'zar [bad'dzar] *sm inv* bazaar.

baz'zecola [bad'dzekola] *sf* trifle.

bazzi'care [battsi'kare] *vt* (*persona*) to hang about with; (*posto*) to hang about ♦ *vi:* ~ **in/con** to hang about/hang about with.

BCE *sigla f* (= *Banca centrale europea*) ECB.

be'arsi *vr:* ~ **di qc/a fare qc** to delight in sth/in doing sth; ~ **alla vista di** to enjoy looking at.

beati'tudine *sf* bliss.

be'ato, a *ag* blessed; (*fig*) happy; ~ **te!** lucky you!

bebè *sm inv* baby.

bec'care *vt* to peck; (*fig: raffreddore*) to pick up, catch; ~**rsi** *vr* (*fig*) to squabble.

bec'cata *sf* peck.

beccheggi'are [bekked'dʒare] *vi* to pitch.

beccherò *etc* [bekke'rɔ] *vb vedi* **beccare**.

bec'chime [bek'kime] *sm* birdseed.

bec'chino [bek'kino] *sm* gravedigger.

'**becco, chi** *sm* beak, bill; (*di caffettiera etc*) spout; lip; **mettere** ~ (*fam*) to butt in; **chiudi il** ~**!** (*fam*) shut your mouth!; **non**

ho il ~ **di un quattrino** (*fam*) I'm broke.

Be'fana *sf old woman who, according to legend, brings children their presents at the Epiphany;* (*Epifania*) Epiphany; (*donna brutta*): **b**~ hag, witch; *vedi nota nel riquadro.*

BEFANA

Marking the end of the traditional 12 days of Christmas on 6 January, the **Befana**, *or the feast of the Epiphany, is a national holiday in Italy. It is named after the old woman who, legend has it, comes down the chimney the night before, bringing gifts to children who have been good during the year and leaving lumps of coal for those who have not.*

'**beffa** *sf* practical joke; **farsi** ~ *o* ~**e di qn** to make a fool of sb.

bef'fardo, a *ag* scornful, mocking.

bef'fare *vt* (*anche:* ~**rsi di**) to make a fool of, mock.

'**bega, ghe** *sf* quarrel.

'**begli** ['beʎʎi], '**bei** *ag vedi* **bello**.

beige [bɛʒ] *ag inv* beige.

Bei'rut *sf* Beirut.

bel *ag vedi* **bello**.

be'lare *vi* to bleat.

'**belga, gi, ghe** *ag, sm/f* Belgian.

'**Belgio** ['bɛldʒo] *sm:* **il** ~ Belgium.

Bel'grado *sf* Belgrade.

'**bella** *sf vedi* **bello**.

bel'lezza [bel'lettsa] *sf* beauty; **chiudere** *o* **finire qc in** ~ to finish sth with a flourish; **che** ~**!** fantastic!; **ho pagato la** ~ **di 300 euro** I paid 300 euros, no less.

belli'coso, a *ag* warlike.

bellige'rante [bellidʒe'rante] *ag* belligerent.

bellim'busto *sm* dandy.

PAROLA CHIAVE

'**bello, a** (*ag: dav sm* **bel** + *C*, **bell'** + *V*, **bello** + *s impura, gn, pn, ps, x, z, pl* **bei** + *C*, **begli** ∣ *s impura etc o V*) *ag* **1** (*oggetto, donna, paesaggio*) beautiful; (*uomo*) handsome; (*tempo*) beautiful, fine, lovely; **farsi** ~ **di qc** to show off about sth; **fare la** ~**a vita** to have an easy life; **le** ~**e arti** fine arts

2 (*quantità*): **una** ~**a cifra** a considerable sum of money; **un bel niente** absolutely nothing

3 (*rafforzativo*): **è una truffa** ~**a e buona!** it's a real fraud!; **oh** ~**a!**, **anche questa è** ~**a!** (*ironico*) that's nice!; **è bell'e finito** it's already finished

♦ *sm/f* (*innamorato*) sweetheart

♦ *sm* **1** (*bellezza*) beauty; (*tempo*) fine

weather
2: **adesso viene il** ~ now comes the best bit;
sul più ~ at the crucial point; **cosa fai di** ~?
are you doing anything interesting?
♦ *sf* (*anche*: ~**a copia**) fair copy; (*SPORT*,
CARTE) decider
♦ *av*: **fa** ~ the weather is fine, it's fine; **alla bell'e meglio** somehow or other.

bellu'nese *ag* of (*o* from) Belluno.
'belva *sf* wild animal.
belve'dere *sm inv* panoramic viewpoint.
benché [ben'ke] *cong* although.
'benda *sf* bandage; (*per gli occhi*) blindfold.
ben'dare *vt* to bandage; to blindfold.
bendis'posto, a *ag*: ~ **a qn/qc** well disposed towards sb/sth.
'bene *av* well; (*completamente, affatto*): **è ben difficile** it's very difficult ♦ *ag inv*: **gente** ~ well-to-do people ♦ *sm* good; (*COMM*) asset; ~**i** *smpl* (*averi*) property *sg*, estate *sg*; **io sto** ~/**poco** ~ I'm well/not very well; **va** ~ all right; **ben più lungo/caro** much longer/more expensive; **lo spero** ~ I certainly hope so; **volere un** ~ **dell'anima a qn** to love sb very much; **un uomo per** ~ a respectable man; **fare** ~ **to** do the right thing; **fare del** ~ **a qn** to do sb a good turn; **di** ~ **in meglio** better and better; ~**i ambientali** environmental assets; ~**i di consumo** consumer goods; ~**i di consumo durevole** consumer durables; ~**i culturali** cultural heritage; ~**i immateriali** immaterial *o* intangible assets; ~**i patrimoniali** fixed assets; ~**i privati** private property *sg*; ~**i pubblici** public property *sg*; ~**i reali** tangible assets.
bene'detto, a *pp di* **benedire** ♦ *ag* blessed, holy.
bene'dire *vt* to bless; to consecrate; **l'ho mandato a farsi** ~ (*fig*) I told him to go to hell.
benedizi'one [benedit'tsjone] *sf* blessing.
benedu'cato, a *ag* well-mannered.
benefat'tore, 'trice *sm/f* benefactor/benefactress.
benefi'cenza [benefi'tʃɛntsa] *sf* charity.
benefici'are [benefi'tʃare] *vi*: ~ **di** to benefit by, benefit from.
benefici'ario, a [benefi'tʃarjo] *ag, sm/f* beneficiary.
bene'ficio [bene'fitʃo] *sm* benefit; **con** ~ **d'inventario** (*fig*) with reservations.
be'nefico, a, ci, che *ag* beneficial; charitable.
'Benelux *sm*: **il** ~ Benelux, the Benelux countries.

beneme'renza [beneme'rɛntsa] *sf* merit.
bene'merito, a *ag* meritorious.
bene'placito [bene'platʃito] *sm* (*approvazione*) approval; (*permesso*) permission.
be'nessere *sm* well-being.
benes'tante *ag* well-to-do.
benes'tare *sm* consent, approval.
benevo'lenza [benevo'lɛntsa] *sf* benevolence.
be'nevolo, a *ag* benevolent.
ben'godi *sm* land of plenty.
benia'mino, a *sm/f* favourite (*BRIT*), favorite (*US*).
be'nigno, a [be'niɲɲo] *ag* kind, kindly; (*critica etc*) favourable (*BRIT*), favorable (*US*); (*MED*) benign.
benintenzio'nato, a [benintentsjo'nato] *ag* well-meaning.
benin'teso *av* of course; ~ **che** *cong* provided that.
benpen'sante *sm/f* conformist.
benser'vito *sm*: **dare il** ~ **a qn** (*sul lavoro*) to give sb the sack, fire sb; (*fig*) to send sb packing.
bensì *cong* but (rather).
benve'nuto, a *ag, sm* welcome; **dare il** ~ **a qn** to welcome sb.
ben'visto, a *ag*: **essere** ~ (**da**) to be well thought of (by).
benvo'lere *vt*: **farsi** ~ **da tutti** to win everybody's affection; **prendere a** ~ **qn/qc** to take a liking to sb/sth.
ben'zina [ben'dzina] *sf* petrol (*BRIT*), gas (*US*); **fare** ~ to get petrol *o* gas; **rimanere senza** ~ to run out of petrol *o* gas; ~ **verde** unleaded petrol, lead-free petrol.
benzi'naio [bendzi'najo] *sm* petrol (*BRIT*) *o* gas (*US*) pump attendant.
be'one *sm* heavy drinker.
'bere *vt* to drink; (*assorbire*) to soak up; **questa volta non me la dai a** ~! I won't be taken in this time!
berga'masco, a, schi, sche *ag* of (*o* from) Bergamo.
'Bering ['beriŋ]: **il mar di** ~ *sm* the Bering Sea.
ber'lina *sf* (*AUT*) saloon (car) (*BRIT*), sedan (*US*); **mettere alla** ~ (*fig*) to hold up to ridicule.
Ber'lino *sf* Berlin; ~ **est/ovest** East/West Berlin.
Ber'muda *sfpl*: **le** ~ Bermuda *sg*.
ber'muda *smpl* (*calzoncini*) Bermuda shorts.
'Berna *sf* Bern.
ber'noccolo *sm* bump; (*inclinazione*) flair.
ber'retto *sm* cap.

berrò etc vb vedi **bere.**

bersagli'are [bersaʎ'ʎare] vt to shoot at; (colpire ripetutamente, fig) to bombard; **bersagliato dalla sfortuna** dogged by ill fortune.

bersagli'ere [bersaʎ'ʎɛre] sm member of rifle regiment in Italian army.

ber'saglio [ber'saʎʎo] sm target.

bes'temmia sf curse; (REL) blasphemy.

bestemmi'are vi to curse, swear; to blaspheme ♦ vt to curse, swear at; to blaspheme; ~ **come un turco** to swear like a trooper.

'bestia sf animal; **lavorare come una** ~ to work like a dog; **andare in** ~ (fig) to fly into a rage; **una** ~ **rara** (fig: persona) an oddball; ~ **da soma** beast of burden.

besti'ale ag bestial, brutish; (fam): **fa un caldo** ~ it's terribly hot; **fa un freddo** ~ it's bitterly cold.

besti'ame sm livestock; (bovino) cattle pl.

Bet'lemme sf Bethlehem.

betoni'era sf cement mixer.

'bettola sf (peg) dive.

be'tulla sf birch.

be'vanda sf drink, beverage.

bevi'tore, 'trice sm/f drinker.

'bevo etc vb vedi **bere.**

be'vuto, a pp di **bere** ♦ sf drink.

'bevvi etc vb vedi **bere.**

BG sigla = Bergamo.

BI sigla f = Banca d'Italia ♦ sigla = Biella.

bi'ada sf fodder.

bianche'ria [bjanke'ria] sf linen; ~ **intima** underwear; ~ **da donna** ladies' underwear, lingerie.

bi'anco, a, chi, che ag white; (non scritto) blank ♦ sm white; (intonaco) whitewash ♦ sm/f white, white man/woman; **in** ~ (foglio, assegno) blank; **in** ~ **e nero** (TV, FOT) black and white; **mangiare in** ~ to follow a bland diet; **pesce in** ~ boiled fish; **andare in** ~ (non riuscire) to fail; (in amore) to be rejected; **notte** ~**a** o **in** ~ sleepless night; **voce** ~**a** (MUS) treble (voice); ~ **dell'uovo** egg-white.

bianco'segno [bjanko'seɲɲo] sm signature to a blank document.

biancos'pino sm hawthorn.

biasci'care [bjaʃʃi'kare] vt to mumble.

biasi'mare vt to disapprove of, censure.

'bibbia sf bible.

bibe'ron sm inv feeding bottle.

'bibita sf (soft) drink.

bibliogra'fia sf bibliography.

biblio'teca, che sf library; (mobile) bookcase.

bibliote'cario, a sm/f librarian.

bicame'rale ag (POL) two-chamber cpd.

bicarbo'nato sm: ~ **(di sodio)** bicarbonate (of soda).

bicchi'ere [bik'kjɛre] sm glass; **è (facile) come bere un bicchier d'acqua** it's as easy as pie.

bici'cletta [bitʃi'kletta] sf bicycle; **andare in** ~ to cycle.

bi'cipite [bi'tʃipite] sm bicep.

bidè sm inv bidet.

bi'dello, a sm/f (INS) janitor.

bi'det sm inv = **bidè.**

bido'nare vt (fam: piantare in asso) to let down; (: imbrogliare) to cheat, swindle.

bido'nata sf (fam) swindle.

bi'done sm drum, can; (anche: ~ **dell'immondizia**) (dust)bin; (fam: truffa) swindle; **fare un** ~ **a qn** (fam) to let sb down; to cheat sb.

bidon'ville [bidɔ'vil] sf inv shanty town.

bi'eco, a, chi, che ag sinister.

Bielo'russia sf Belarus.

bielo'russo, a ag, sm/f Belarussian.

bien'nale ag biennial ♦ sf: **la B~ di Venezia** the Venice Arts Festival; vedi nota nel riquadro.

BIENNALE DI VENEZIA

Dating back to 1895, the **Biennale di Venezia** is an international festival of the contemporary arts. It takes place every two years in the "Giardini Pubblici". The various countries taking part each put on exhibitions in their own pavilions. There is a section dedicated to the work of young artists, as well as a special exhibition organized around a specific theme for that year.

---

bi'ennio sm period of two years.

bi'erre sm/f member of the Red Brigades.

bi'etola sf beet.

bifami'liare ag (villa, casetta) semi-detached.

bifo'cale ag bifocal.

bi'folco, a, chi, che sm/f (peg) bumpkin.

'bifora sf (ARCHIT) mullioned window.

bifor'carsi vr to fork.

biforcazi'one [biforkat'tsjone] sf fork.

bifor'cuto, a ag (anche fig) forked.

biga'mia sf bigamy.

'bigamo, a ag bigamous ♦ sm/f bigamist.

bighello'nare [bigello'nare] vi to loaf (about).

bighel'lone, a [bigel'lone] sm/f loafer.

bigiotte'ria [bidʒotte'ria] sf costume jewellery (BRIT) o jewelry (US); (negozio) jeweller's (shop) (BRIT) o jewelry store (US) (selling only costume jewellery).

bigli'ardo [biʎ'ʎardo] sm = **biliardo**.

bigliet'taio, a [biʎʎet'tajo] sm/f (nei treni) ticket inspector; (in autobus etc) conductor/conductress; (CINE, TEAT) box-office attendant.

bigliette'ria [biʎʎette'ria] sf (di stazione) ticket office; booking office; (di teatro) box office.

bigli'etto [biʎ'ʎetto] sm (per viaggi, spettacoli etc) ticket; (cartoncino) card; (anche: ~ **di banca**) (bank)note; ~ **d'auguri/da visita** greetings/visiting card; ~ **d'andata e ritorno** return (BRIT) o round-trip (US) ticket; ~ **omaggio** complimentary ticket.

bignè [biɲ'ɲɛ] sm inv cream puff.

bigo'dino sm roller, curler.

bi'gotto, a ag over-pious ♦ sm/f church fiend.

bi'kini sm inv bikini.

bi'lancia, ce [bi'lantʃa] sf (pesa) scales pl; (: di precisione) balance; (dello zodiaco): **B~** Libra; **essere della B~** to be Libra; ~ **commerciale/dei pagamenti** balance of trade/payments.

bilanci'are [bilan'tʃare] vt (pesare) to weigh; (: fig) to weigh up; ~ **le uscite e le entrate** (COMM) to balance expenditure and revenue.

bi'lancio [bi'lantʃo] sm (COMM) balance (sheet); (statale) budget; **far quadrare il** ~ to balance the books; **chiudere il** ~ **in attivo/passivo** to make a profit/loss; **fare il** ~ **di** (fig) to assess; ~ **consolidato** consolidated balance; ~ **consuntivo** (final) balance; ~ **preventivo** budget; ~ **pubblico** national budget; ~ **di verifica** trial balance.

bilate'rale ag bilateral.

'bile sf bile; (fig) rage, anger.

bili'ardo sm billiards sg; (tavolo) billiard table.

'bilico, chi sm: **essere in** ~ to be balanced; (fig) to be undecided; **tenere qn in** ~ to keep sb in suspense.

bi'lingue ag bilingual.

bili'one sm (mille milioni) thousand million, billion (US); (milione di milioni) billion (BRIT), trillion (US).

bilo'cale sm two-room flat (BRIT) o apartment (US).

'bimbo, a sm/f little boy/girl.

bimen'sile ag fortnightly.

bimes'trale ag two-monthly, bimonthly.

bi'mestre sm two-month period; **ogni** ~ every two months.

bi'nario, a ag binary ♦ sm (railway) track o line; (piattaforma) platform; ~ **morto** dead-end track.

bi'nocolo sm binoculars pl.

bio'chimica [bio'kimika] sf biochemistry.

biodegra'dabile ag biodegradable.

biodiversità sf biodiversity.

bio'etica sf bioethics sg.

bio'etico, a, ci, che ag bioethical.

bio'fabbrica sf factory producing biological control agents.

bio'fisica sf biophysics sg.

biogra'fia sf biography.

bio'grafico, a, ci, che ag biographical.

bi'ografo, a sm/f biographer.

biolo'gia [biolo'dʒia] sf biology.

bio'logico, a, ci, che [bio'lɔdʒiko] ag (scienze, fenomeni etc) biological; (agricoltura, prodotti) organic.

bi'ologo, a, ghi, ghe sm/f biologist.

bi'ondo, a ag blond, fair.

bi'onico, a, ci, che ag bionic.

biop'sia sf biopsy.

bio'ritmo sm biorhythm.

bios'fera sf biosphere.

biotecnolo'gia [bioteknolo'dʒia] sf biotechnology.

bipar'tito, a ag (POL) two-party cpd ♦ sm (POL) two-party alliance.

'birba sf rascal, rogue.

bir'bante sm rascal, rogue.

birbo'nata sf naughty trick.

bir'bone, a ag (bambino) naughty ♦ sm/f little rascal.

biri'chino, a [biri'kino] ag mischievous ♦ sm/f scamp, little rascal.

bi'rillo sm skittle (BRIT), pin (US); ~**i** smpl (gioco) skittles sg (BRIT), bowling no pl (US).

Bir'mania sf: **la** ~ Burma.

bir'mano, a ag, sm/f Burmese (inv).

'biro ® sf inv biro ®.

'birra sf beer; ~ **scura** stout; **a tutta** ~ (fig) at top speed.

birre'ria sf (locale) ≈ bierkeller; (fabbrica) brewery.

bis escl, sm inv encore ♦ ag inv (treno, autobus) relief cpd (BRIT), additional; (numero): **12** ~ 12a.

bi'saccia, ce [bi'zattʃa] sf knapsack.

Bi'sanzio [bi'zantsjo] sf Byzantium.

bis'betico, a, ci, che ag ill-tempered, crabby.

bisbigli'are [bizbiʎ'ʎare] vt, vi to whisper.

bis'biglio [biz'biʎʎo] sm whisper; (notizia) rumour (BRIT), rumor (US).

bisbi'glio [bizbiʎ'ʎio] sm whispering.

bis'boccia, ce [biz'bɔttʃa] sf binge, spree;

fare ~ to have a binge.

'bisca, sche *sf* gambling house.

Bis'caglia [bis'kaʎʎa] *sf*: il golfo di ~ the Bay of Biscay.

'bischero ['biskero] *sm* (*MUS*) peg; (*fam*: *toscano*) fool, idiot.

'biscia, sce ['biʃʃa] *sf* snake; ~ d'acqua water snake.

biscot'tato, a *ag* crisp; fette ~e rusks.

bis'cotto *sm* biscuit.

bisessu'ale *ag*, *sm/f* bisexual.

bises'tile *ag*: anno ~ leap year.

bisezi'one [biset'tsjone] *sf* dichotomy.

bis'lacco, a, chi, che *ag* odd, weird.

bis'lungo, a, ghi, ghe *ag* oblong.

biso'gnare [bizoɲ'ɲare] *vb impers*: bisogna che tu parta/lo faccia you'll have to go/do it; bisogna parlargli we'll (*o* I'll) have to talk to him ♦ *vi* (*esser utile*) to be necessary.

bi'sogno [bi'zoɲɲo] *sm* need; ~i *smpl* (*necessità corporali*): fare i propri ~i to relieve o.s.; avere ~ di qc/di fare qc to need sth/to do sth; al ~, in caso di ~ if need be.

biso'gnoso, a [bizoɲ'ɲoso] *ag* needy, poor; ~ di in need of, needing.

bi'sonte *sm* (*ZOOL*) bison.

bis'tecca, che *sf* steak, beefsteak; ~ al sangue/ai ferri rare/grilled steak.

bisticci'are [bistit'tʃare] *vi*, ~rsi *vr* to quarrel, bicker.

bis'ticcio [bis'tittʃo] *sm* quarrel, squabble; (*gioco di parole*) pun.

bistrat'tare *vt* to maltreat.

'bisturi *sm inv* scalpel.

bi'sunto, a *ag* very greasy.

bi'torzolo [bi'tortsolo] *sm* (*sulla testa*) bump; (*sul corpo*) lump.

'bitter *sm inv* bitters *pl*.

bi'tume *sm* bitumen.

bivac'care *vi* (*MIL*) to bivouac; (*fig*) to bed down.

bi'vacco, chi *sm* bivouac.

'bivio *sm* fork; (*fig*) dilemma.

bizan'tino, a [biddzan'tino] *ag* Byzantine.

'bizza ['biddza] *sf* tantrum; fare le ~e to throw a tantrum.

biz'zarro, a [bid'dzarro] *ag* bizarre, strange.

biz'zeffe [bid'dzɛffe]: a ~ *av* in plenty, galore.

BL *sigla* = Belluno.

blan'dire *vt* to soothe; to flatter.

'blando, a *ag* mild, gentle.

blas'femo, a *ag* blasphemous ♦ *sm/f* blasphemer.

bla'sone *sm* coat of arms.

blate'rare *vi* to chatter.

'blatta *sf* cockroach.

blin'dare *vt* to armour (*BRIT*), armor (*US*).

blin'data *sf* (*macchina*) armoured car *o* limousine.

blin'dato, a *ag* armoured (*BRIT*), armored (*US*); camera ~a strongroom; mezzo ~ armoured vehicle; porta ~a reinforced door; vita ~a life amid maximum security; vetro ~ bulletproof glass.

bloc'care *vt* to block; (*isolare*) to isolate, cut off; (*porto*) to blockade; (*prezzi, beni*) to freeze; (*meccanismo*) to jam; ~rsi *vr* (*motore*) to stall; (*freni, porta*) to jam, stick; (*ascensore*) to get stuck, stop; ha bloccato la macchina (*AUT*) he jammed on the brakes.

bloccas'terzo [blokkas'tɛrtso] *sm* (*AUT*) steering lock.

bloccherò *etc* [blokke'rɔ] *vb vedi* bloccare.

bloc'chetto [blok'ketto] *sm* notebook; (*di biglietti*) book.

'blocco, chi *sm* block; (*MIL*) blockade; (*dei fitti*) restriction; (*quadernetto*) pad; (*fig*: *unione*) coalition; (*il bloccare*) blocking; isolating, cutting-off; blockading; freezing; jamming; in ~ (*nell'insieme*) as a whole; (*COMM*) in bulk; ~ cardiaco cardiac arrest.

bloc-'notes [blɔk'nɔt] *sm inv* notebook, notepad.

blu *ag inv*, *sm inv* dark blue.

bluff [blɛf] *sm inv* bluff.

bluf'fare *vt* (*anche fig*) to bluff.

'blusa *sf* (*camiciotto*) smock; (*camicetta*) blouse.

BN *sigla* = Benevento.

BO *sigla* = Bologna.

'boa *sm inv* (*ZOOL*) boa constrictor; (*sciarpa*) feather boa ♦ *sf* buoy.

bo'ato *sm* rumble, roar.

bob [bɔb] *sm inv* bobsleigh.

bo'bina *sf* reel, spool; (*di pellicola*) spool; (*di film*) reel; (*ELETTR*) coil.

'bocca, che *sf* mouth; essere di buona ~ to be a hearty eater; (*fig*) to be easily satisfied; essere sulla ~ di tutti (*persona, notizia*) to be the talk of the town; rimanere a ~ asciutta to have nothing to eat; (*fig*) to be disappointed; in ~ al lupo! good luck!; ~ di leone (*BOT*) snapdragon.

boc'caccia, ce [bok'kattʃa] *sf* (*malalingua*) gossip; (*smorfia*): fare le ~ce to pull faces.

boc'caglio [bok'kaʎʎo] *sm* (*TECN*) nozzle; (*di respiratore*) mouthpiece.

boc'cale *sm* jug; ~ da birra tankard.

bocca'scena [bokkaʃ'ʃɛna] *sm inv* proscenium.

boc'cata *sf* mouthful; (*di fumo*) puff; **prendere una ~ d'aria** to go out for a breath of (fresh) air.

boc'cetta [bot'tʃetta] *sf* small bottle.

boccheggi'are [bokked'dʒare] *vi* to gasp.

boc'chino [bok'kino] *sm* (*di sigaretta, sigaro: cannella*) cigarette-holder; cigar-holder; (*di pipa, strumenti musicali*) mouthpiece.

'boccia, ce ['bottʃa] *sf* bottle; (*da vino*) decanter, carafe; (*palla di legno, metallo*) bowl; **gioco delle ~ce** bowls *sg*.

bocci'are [bot'tʃare] *vt* (*proposta, progetto*) to reject; (*INS*) to fail; (*BOCCE*) to hit.

boccia'tura [bottʃa'tura] *sf* failure.

bocci'olo [bot'tʃɔlo] *sm* bud.

'boccolo *sm* curl.

boccon'cino [bokkon'tʃino] *sm* (*pietanza deliziosa*) delicacy.

boc'cone *sm* mouthful, morsel; **mangiare un ~** to have a bite to eat.

boc'coni *av* face downwards.

Bo'emia *sf* Bohemia.

bo'emo, a *ag, sm/f* Bohemian.

bofonchi'are [bofon'kjare] *vi* to grumble.

Bogotá *sf* Bogotá.

'boia *sm inv* executioner; hangman; **fa un freddo ~** (*fam*) it's cold as hell; **mondo ~!**, **~ d'un mondo ladro!** (*fam*) damn!, blast!

boi'ata *sf* botch.

boicot'taggio [boikot'taddʒo] *sm* boycott.

boicot'tare *vt* to boycott.

'bolgia, ge ['bɔldʒa] *sf* (*fig*): **c'era una tale ~ al cinema** the cinema was absolutely mobbed.

'bolide *sm* (*ASTR*) meteor; (*macchina: da corsa*) racing car (*BRIT*), race car (*US*); (: *elaborata*) performance car; **come un ~** like a flash, at top speed; **entrare/uscire come un ~** to charge in/out.

Bo'livia *sf*: **la ~** Bolivia.

bolivi'ano, a *ag, sm/f* Bolivian.

'bolla *sf* bubble; (*MED*) blister; (*COMM*) bill, receipt; **finire in una ~ di sapone** (*fig*) to come to nothing; **~ di accompagnamento** waybill; **~ di consegna** delivery note; **~ papale** papal bull.

bol'lare *vt* to stamp; (*fig*) to brand.

bol'lente *ag* boiling; boiling hot; **calmare i ~i spiriti** to sober up, calm down.

bol'letta *sf* bill; (*ricevuta*) receipt; **essere in ~** to be hard up; **~ di consegna** delivery note; **~ doganale** clearance certificate; **~ di trasporto aereo** air waybill.

bollet'tino *sm* bulletin; (*COMM*) note; **~ meteorologico** weather forecast; **~ di ordinazione** order form; **~ di spedizione** consignment note.

bolli'cina [bolli'tʃina] *sf* bubble; **acqua con le ~** fizzy water.

bol'lire *vt, vi* to boil; **qualcosa bolle in pentola** (*fig*) there's something brewing.

bol'lito *sm* (*CUC*) boiled meat.

bolli'tore *sm* (*TECN*) boiler; (*CUC: per acqua*) kettle; (: *per latte*) milk pan.

bolli'tura *sf* boiling.

'bollo *sm* stamp; **imposta di ~** stamp duty; **~ auto** road tax; **~ per patente** driving licence tax; **~ postale** postmark.

bol'lore *sm*: **dare un ~ a qc** to bring sth to the boil (*BRIT*) o a boil (*US*); **i ~i della gioventù** youthful enthusiasm *sg*.

Bo'logna [bo'lɔɲɲa] *sf* Bologna.

bolo'gnese [bolɔɲ'ɲese] *ag* Bolognese; **spaghetti alla ~** spaghetti bolognese.

'bomba *sf* bomb; **tornare a ~** (*fig*) to get back to the point; **sei stato una ~!** you were tremendous!; **~ atomica** atom bomb; **~ a mano** hand grenade; **~ ad orologeria** time bomb.

bombarda'mento *sm* bombardment; bombing.

bombar'dare *vt* to bombard; (*da aereo*) to bomb.

bombardi'ere *sm* bomber.

bom'betta *sf* bowler (hat) (*BRIT*), derby (*US*).

'bombola *sf* cylinder; **~ del gas** gas cylinder.

bombo'letta *sf*: **~ f spray** *inv* spray can.

bomboni'era *sf* box of sweets (*as souvenir at weddings, first communions etc*).

bo'naccia, ce [bo'nattʃa] *sf* dead calm.

bonacci'one, a [bonat'tʃone] *ag* good-natured ♦ *sm/f* good-natured sort.

bo'nario, a *ag* good-natured, kind.

bo'nifica, che *sf* reclamation; reclaimed land.

bo'nifico, ci *sm* (*riduzione, abbuono*) discount; (*versamento a terzi*) credit transfer.

Bonn *sf* Bonn.

bontà *sf* goodness; (*cortesia*) kindness; **aver la ~ di fare qc** to be good o kind enough to do sth.

'bonus-'malus *sm inv* ≈ no-claims bonus.

bor'bonico, a, ci, che *ag* Bourbon; (*fig*) backward, out of date.

borbot'tare *vi* to mumble; (*stomaco*) to rumble.

borbot'tio, ii *sm* mumbling; rumbling.

'borchia ['borkja] *sf* stud.

borda'tura *sf* (*SARTORIA*) border, trim.

bor'deaux [bor'dɔ] *sm inv* (*colore*) burgundy, maroon; (*vino*) Bordeaux.

bor'dello *sm* brothel.

'bordo *sm* (*NAUT*) ship's side; (*orlo*) edge;

(*striscia di guarnizione*) border, trim; **a ~ di**
(*nave, aereo*) aboard, on board; (*macchina*)
in; **sul ~ della strada** at the roadside;
persona d'alto ~ VIP.

bor'dura *sf* border.

bor'gata *sf* hamlet; (*a Roma*) working-class
suburb.

bor'ghese [bor'geze] *ag* (*spesso peg*)
middle-class; bourgeois; **abito ~** civilian
dress; **poliziotto in ~** plainclothes
policeman.

borghe'sia [borge'zia] *sf* middle classes *pl*;
bourgeoisie.

'borgo, ghi *sm* (*paesino*) village; (*quartiere*)
district; (*sobborgo*) suburb.

'boria *sf* self-conceit, arrogance.

bori'oso, a *ag* arrogant.

bor'lotto *sm* kidney bean.

'Borneo *sm*: **il ~** Borneo.

boro'talco *sm* talcum powder.

bor'raccia, ce [bor'rattʃa] *sf* canteen,
water-bottle.

'borsa *sf* bag; (*anche:* **~ da signora**)
handbag; (*ECON*): **la B~ (valori)** the Stock
Exchange; **~ dell'acqua calda** hot-water
bottle; **B~ merci** commodity exchange; **~
nera** black market; **~ della spesa**
shopping bag; **~ di studio** grant.

borsai'olo *sm* pickpocket.

bor'seggio [bor'seddʒo] *sm* pickpocketing.

borsel'lino *sm* purse.

bor'sello *sm* gent's handbag.

bor'setta *sf* handbag.

bor'sista, i, e *smlf* (*ECON*) speculator; (*INS*)
grant-holder.

bos'caglia [bos'kaʎʎa] *sf* woodlands *pl*.

boscai'olo, boscaiu'olo *sm* woodcutter;
forester.

bos'chetto [bos'ketto] *sm* copse, grove.

'bosco, schi *sm* wood.

bos'coso, a *ag* wooded.

bos'niaco, a, ci, che *ag*, *smlf* Bosnian.

'Bosnia-Erze'govina ['bɔsnja erdze'govina]
sf: **la ~** Bosnia-Herzegovina.

'bossolo *sm* cartridge case.

Bot, bot *sigla m inv vedi* **buono ordinario del
Tesoro**.

bo'tanico, a, ci, che *ag* botanical ♦ *sm*
botanist ♦ *sf* botany.

'botola *sf* trap door.

Bots'wana [bots'vana] *sm*: **il ~** Botswana.

'botta *sf* blow; (*rumore*) bang; **dare (un
sacco di) ~e a qn** to give sb a good
thrashing; **~ e risposta** (*fig*) cut and
thrust.

'botte *sf* barrel, cask; **essere in una ~ di
ferro** (*fig*) to be as safe as houses; **volere
la ~ piena e la moglie ubriaca** to want to

have one's cake and eat it.

bot'tega, ghe *sf* shop; (*officina*) workshop;
stare a ~ (da qn) to serve one's
apprenticeship (with sb); **le B~ghe
Oscure** *headquarters of the DS, Italian
left-wing party*.

botte'gaio, a *smlf* shopkeeper.

botte'ghino [botte'gino] *sm* ticket office;
(*del lotto*) public lottery office.

bot'tiglia [bot'tiʎʎa] *sf* bottle.

bottiglie'ria [bottiʎʎe'ria] *sf* wine shop.

bot'tino *sm* (*di guerra*) booty; (*di rapina,
furto*) loot; **fare ~ di qc** (*anche fig*) to make
off with sth.

'botto *sm* bang; crash; **di ~** suddenly; **d'un
~** (*fam*) in a flash.

bot'tone *sm* button; (*BOT*) bud; **stanza dei
~i** control room; (*fig*) nerve centre;
attaccare (un) ~ a qn to buttonhole sb.

bo'vino, a *ag* bovine; **~i** *smpl* cattle.

box [bɔks] *sm inv* (*per cavalli*) horsebox; (*per
macchina*) lock-up; (*per macchina da corsa*)
pit; (*per bambini*) playpen.

boxe [bɔks] *sf* boxing.

'boxer ['bɔksɛr] *sm inv* (*cane*) boxer ♦ *smpl*
(*mutande*): **un paio di ~** a pair of boxer
shorts.

'bozza ['bɔttsa] *sf* draft; (*TIP*) proof; **~ di
stampa/impaginata** galley/page proof.

boz'zetto [bot'tsetto] *sm* sketch.

'bozzolo ['bɔttsolo] *sm* cocoon.

BR *sigla fpl* = **Brigate Rosse** ♦ *sigla* = **Brindisi**.

'braca, che *sf* (*gamba di pantalone*) trouser
leg; **~che** *sfpl* (*fam*) trousers, pants (*US*);
(*mutandoni*) drawers; **calare le ~che** (*fig*
fam) to chicken out.

brac'care *vt* to hunt.

brac'cetto [brat'tʃetto] *sm*: **a ~** arm in arm.

braccherò *etc* [brakke'rɔ] *vb vedi* **braccare**.

bracci'ale [brat'tʃale] *sm* bracelet; (*per
nuotare, anche distintivo*) armband.

braccia'letto [brattʃa'letto] *sm* bracelet,
bangle.

bracci'ante [brat'tʃante] *sm* (*AGR*) day
labourer.

bracci'ata [brat'tʃata] *sf* armful; (*nel nuoto*)
stroke.

'braccio ['brattʃo] *sm* (*pl(f)* **braccia**: *ANAT*)
arm; (*pl(m)* **bracci**: *di gru, fiume*) arm;
(*: di edificio*) wing; **camminare sotto ~** to
walk arm in arm; **è il suo ~ destro** he's
his right-hand man; **~ di ferro** (*anche fig*)
trial of strength; **~ di mare** sound.

bracci'olo [brat'tʃolo] *sm* (*appoggio*) arm.

'bracco, chi *sm* hound.

bracconi'ere *sm* poacher.

'brace ['bratʃe] *sf* embers *pl*.

braci'ere [bra'tʃɛre] *sm* brazier.

braci'ola [bra'tʃɔla] *sf* (*CUC*) chop.
'bradipo *sm* (*ZOOL*) sloth.
'brado, a *ag*: **allo stato** ~ in the wild *o* natural state.
'brama *sf*: ~ (**di/di fare**) longing (for/to do), yearning (for/to do).
bra'mare *vt*: ~ (**qc/di fare qc**) to long (for sth/to do sth), yearn (for sth/to do sth).
bramo'sia *sf*: ~ (**di**) longing (for), yearning (for).
'branca, che *sf* branch.
'branchia ['brankja] *sf* (*ZOOL*) gill.
'branco, chi *sm* (*di cani, lupi*) pack; (*di uccelli, pecore*) flock; (*peg: di persone*) gang, pack.
branco'lare *vi* to grope, feel one's way.
'branda *sf* camp bed.
bran'dello *sm* scrap, shred; **a** ~**i** in tatters, in rags; **fare a** ~**i** to tear to shreds.
bran'dina *sf* camp bed (*BRIT*), cot (*US*).
bran'dire *vt* to brandish.
'brano *sm* piece; (*di libro*) passage.
bra'sare *vt* to braise.
bra'sato *sm* braised beef.
Bra'sile *sm*: **il** ~ Brazil.
Bra'silia *sf* Brasilia.
brasili'ano, a *ag*, *sm/f* Brazilian.
bra'vata *sf* (*azione spavalda*) act of bravado.
'bravo, a *ag* (*abile*) clever, capable, skilful; (*buono*) good, honest; (*: bambino*) good; (*coraggioso*) brave; ~! well done!; (*al teatro*) bravo!; **su da** ~! (*fam*) there's a good boy!; **mi sono fatto le mie** ~**e 8 ore di lavoro** I put in a full 8 hours' work.
bra'vura *sf* cleverness, skill.
'breccia, ce ['brettʃa] *sf* breach; **essere sulla** ~ (*fig*) to be going strong; **fare** ~ **nell'animo** *o* **nel cuore di qn** to find the way to sb's heart.
'Brema *sf* Bremen.
bre'saola *sf* kind of dried salted beef.
bresci'ano, a [breʃ'ʃano] *ag* of (*o* from) Brescia.
Bre'tagna [bre'taɲɲa] *sf*: **la** ~ Brittany.
bre'tella *sf* (*AUT*) link; ~**e** *sfpl* braces.
'bret(t)one *ag*, *sm/f* Breton.
'breve *ag* brief, short; **in** ~ in short; **per farla** ~ to cut a long story short; **a** ~ (*COMM*) short-term.
brevet'tare *vt* to patent.
bre'vetto *sm* patent; ~ **di pilotaggio** pilot's licence (*BRIT*) *o* license (*US*).
brevità *sf* brevity.
'brezza ['breddza] *sf* breeze.
'bricco, chi *sm* jug; ~ **del caffè** coffeepot.
bricco'nata *sf* mischievous trick.
bric'cone, a *sm/f* rogue, rascal.

'briciola ['britʃola] *sf* crumb.
'briciolo ['britʃolo] *sm* (*specie fig*) bit.
bridge [bridʒ] *sm* bridge.
'briga, ghe *sf* (*fastidio*) trouble, bother; **attaccar** ~ to start a quarrel; **pigliarsi la** ~ **di fare qc** to take the trouble to do sth.
brigadi'ere *sm* (*dei carabinieri etc*) ≈ sergeant.
bri'gante *sm* bandit.
bri'gata *sf* (*MIL*) brigade; (*gruppo*) group, party; **le B**~**e Rosse** (*POL*) the Red Brigades.
briga'tismo *sm* phenomenon of the Red Brigades.
briga'tista, i, e *sm/f* (*POL*) member of the Red Brigades.
'briglia ['briʎʎa] *sf* rein; **a** ~ **sciolta** at full gallop; (*fig*) at full speed.
bril'lante *ag* bright; (*anche fig*) brilliant; (*che luccica*) shining ♦ *sm* diamond.
brillan'tina *sf* brilliantine.
bril'lare *vi* to shine; (*mina*) to blow up ♦ *vt* (*mina*) to set off.
'brillo, a *ag* merry, tipsy.
'brina *sf* hoarfrost.
brin'dare *vi*: ~ **a qn/qc** to drink to *o* toast sb/sth.
'brindisi *sm inv* toast.
'brio *sm* liveliness, go.
bri'oche [bri'ɔʃ] *sf inv* brioche (bun).
bri'oso, a *ag* lively.
'briscola *sf* type of card game; (*seme vincente*) trump(s); (*carta*) trump card.
bri'tannico, a, ci, che *ag* British ♦ *sm/f* Briton; **i B**~**ci** the British *pl*.
'brivido *sm* shiver; (*di ribrezzo*) shudder; (*fig*) thrill; **racconti del** ~ suspense stories.
brizzo'lato, a [brittso'lato] *ag* (*persona*) going grey; (*barba, capelli*) greying.
'brocca, che *sf* jug.
broc'cato *sm* brocade.
'broccolo *sm* broccoli *no pl*.
bro'daglia [bro'daʎʎa] *sf* (*peg*) dishwater.
'brodo *sm* broth; (*per cucinare*) stock; ~ **ristretto** consommé; **lasciare (cuocere) qn nel suo** ~ to let sb stew (in his own juice); **tutto fa** ~ every little bit helps.
'broglio ['brɔʎʎo] *sm*: ~ **elettorale** gerrymandering; ~**i** *smpl* (*DIR*) malpractices.
'bromo *sm* (*CHIM*) bromine.
bron'chite [bron'kite] *sf* (*MED*) bronchitis.
'broncio ['brontʃo] *sm* sulky expression; **tenere il** ~ to sulk.
'bronco, chi *sm* bronchial tube.
bronto'lare *vi* to grumble; (*tuono, stomaco*) to rumble.
bronto'lio *sm* grumbling, mumbling.

bronto'lone, a *ag* grumbling ♦ *sm/f* grumbler.

bron'zina [bron'dzina] *sf* (*TECN*) bush.

'bronzo ['brondzo] *sm* bronze; **che faccia di ~!** what a brass neck!

bross. *abbr* = **in brossura**.

bros'sura *sf*: **in ~** (*libro*) limpback.

'browser ['brauzer] *sm inv* (*INFORM*) browser.

bru'care *vt* to browse on, nibble at.

brucherà *etc* [bruke'ra] *vb vedi* **brucare**.

bruciacchi'are [brut∫ak'kjare] *vt* to singe, scorch; **~rsi** *vr* to become singed *o* scorched.

brucia'pelo [brut∫a'pelo]: **a ~** *av* pointblank.

bruci'are [bru't∫are] *vt* to burn; (*scottare*) to scald ♦ *vi* to burn; **~ gli avversari** (*SPORT, fig*) to leave the rest of the field behind; **~ le tappe** *o* **i tempi** (*SPORT, fig*) to shoot ahead; **~rsi la carriera** to put an end to one's career.

brucia'tore [brut∫a'tore] *sm* burner.

brucia'tura [brut∫a'tura] *sf* (*atto*) burning *no pl*; (*segno*) burn; (*scottatura*) scald.

bruci'ore [bru't∫ore] *sm* burning *o* smarting sensation.

'bruco, chi *sm* grub; (*di farfalla*) caterpillar.

'brufolo *sm* pimple, spot.

brughi'era [bru'gjɛra] *sf* heath, moor.

bruli'care *vi* to swarm.

bruli'chio, ii [bruli'kio] *sm* swarming.

'brullo, a *ag* bare, bleak.

'bruma *sf* mist.

'bruno, a *ag* brown, dark; (*persona*) dark(-haired).

brusca'mente *av* (*frenare, fermarsi*) suddenly; (*rispondere, reagire*) sharply.

'brusco, a, schi, sche *ag* (*sapore*) sharp; (*modi, persona*) brusque, abrupt; (*movimento*) abrupt, sudden.

bru'sio *sm* buzz, buzzing.

bru'tale *ag* brutal.

brutalità *sf inv* brutality.

'bruto, a *ag* (*forza*) brute *cpd* ♦ *sm* brute.

'brutta *sf vedi* **brutto**.

brut'tezza [brut'tettsa] *sf* ugliness.

'brutto, a *ag* ugly; (*cattivo*) bad; (*malattia, strada, affare*) nasty, bad ♦ *sm*: **guardare qn di ~** to give sb a nasty look ♦ *sf* rough copy, first draft; **~ tempo** bad weather; **passare un ~ quarto d'ora** to have a nasty time of it; **vedersela ~a** (*per un attimo*) to have a nasty moment; (*per un periodo*) to have a bad time of it.

brut'tura *sf* (*cosa brutta*) ugly thing; (*sudiciume*) filth; (*azione meschina*) mean action.

Bru'xelles [bry'sɛl] *sf* Brussels.

BS *sigla* = *Brescia*.

BSE [bi'ɛsse'ɛ] *sigla f* BSE (= *bovine*

spongiform encephalopathy).

B.T. *abbr* (= *bassa tensione*) LT ♦ *sigla m inv* = **buono del Tesoro**.

btg *abbr* = **battaglione**.

Btp *sigla m* (= *buono del Tesoro poliennale, vedi* **buono**.

bub'bone *sm* swelling.

'buca, che *sf* hole; (*avvallamento*) hollow; **~ delle lettere** letterbox.

buca'neve *sm inv* snowdrop.

bu'care *vt* (*forare*) to make a hole (*o* holes) in; (*pungere*) to pierce; (*biglietto*) to punch; **~rsi** *vr* (*con eroina*) to mainline; **~ una gomma** to have a puncture; **avere le mani bucate** (*fig*) to be a spendthrift.

'Bucarest *sf* Bucharest.

bu'cato *sm* (*operazione*) washing; (*panni*) wash, washing.

'buccia, ce ['butt∫a] *sf* skin, peel; (*corteccia*) bark.

bucherel'lare [bukerel'lare] *vt* to riddle with holes.

bucherò *etc* [buke'rɔ] *vb vedi* **bucare**.

'buco, chi *sm* hole; **fare un ~ nell'acqua** to fail, draw a blank; **farsi un ~** (*fam*: *drogarsi*) to have a fix; **~ nero** (*anche fig*) black hole.

'Budapest *sf* Budapest.

'Budda *sm inv* Buddha.

bud'dismo *sm* Buddhism.

bu'dello *sm* intestine; (*fig*: *tubo*) tube; (*vicolo*) alley; **~a** *sfpl* bowels, guts.

bu'dino *sm* pudding.

'bue, *pl* **bu'oi** *sm* ox; (*anche*: **carne di ~**) beef; **uovo all'occhio di ~** fried egg.

Bu'enos 'Aires *sf* Buenos Aires.

'bufalo *sm* buffalo.

bu'fera *sf* storm.

buf'fetto *sm* flick.

'buffo, a *ag* funny; (*TEAT*) comic.

buffo'nata *sf* (*azione*) prank, jest; (*parola*) jest.

buf'fone *sm* buffoon.

bugge'rare [budd3e'rare] *vt* to swindle, cheat.

bu'gia, 'gie [bu'd3ia] *sf* lie; (*candeliere*) candleholder.

bugi'ardo, a [bu'd3ardo] *ag* lying, deceitful ♦ *sm/f* liar.

bugi'gattolo [bud3i'gattolo] *sm* poky little room.

'buio, a *ag* dark ♦ *sm* dark, darkness; **fa ~ pesto** it's pitch-dark.

'bulbo *sm* (*BOT*) bulb; **~ oculare** eyeball.

Bulga'ria *sf*: **la ~** Bulgaria.

'bulgaro, a *ag, sm/f, sm* Bulgarian.

buli'mia *sf* bulimia.

'bullo *sm* (*persona*) tough.

bul'lone *sm* bolt.
bu'oi *smpl di* **bue.**
buona'fede *sf* good faith.
buon'anima *sf* = **buon'anima**; *vedi* **anima.**
buona'notte *escl* good night! ◆ *sf*: **dare la ~ a** to say good night to.
buona'sera *escl* good evening!
buoncos'tume *sm* public morality; **la (squadra del) ~** (*POLIZIA*) the vice squad.
buondì *escl* hello!
buongi'orno [bwon'dʒorno] *escl* good morning (*o* afternoon)!
buon'grado *av*: **di ~** willingly.
buongus'taio, a *sm/f* gourmet.
buon'gusto *sm* good taste.

=============== PAROLA CHIAVE

bu'ono, a (*ag: dav sm* **buon** + *C o V*, **buono** + *s impura, gn, pn, ps, x, z; dav sf* **buon'** + *V*) *ag* **1** (*gen*) good; **un buon pranzo/ ristorante** a good lunch/restaurant; **(stai) ~! behave!; che ~!** (*cibo*) this is nice!
2 (*benevolo*): **~ (con)** good (to), kind (to)
3 (*giusto, valido*) right; **al momento ~** at the right moment
4 (*adatto*): **~ a/da** fit for/to; **essere ~ a nulla** to be no good *o* use at anything
5 (*auguri*): **buon compleanno!** happy birthday!; **buon divertimento!** have a nice time!; **~a fortuna!** good luck!; **buon riposo!** sleep well!; **buon viaggio!** have a good trip!
6: ad ogni buon conto in any case; **tante ~e cose!** all the best!; **di buon cuore** (*persona*) goodhearted; **di buon grado** willingly; **le ~e maniere** good manners; **di buon mattino** early in the morning; **a buon mercato** cheap; **di buon'ora** early; **mettere una ~a parola** to put in a good word; **di buon passo** at a good pace; **buon pro ti faccia!** much good may it do you!; **buon senso** common sense; **la ~a società** the upper classes; **una ~a volta** once and for all; **alla ~a** *ag* simple ◆ *av* in a simple way, without any fuss; **un tipo alla ~a** an easy-going sort ◆ *sm/f*: **essere un ~/una ~a** to be a good person; **~ a nulla** good for nothing; **i ~i e i cattivi** (*in storia, film*) the goodies and the baddies; **accetterà con le ~e o con le cattive** one way or another he's going to agree to it ◆ *sm* **1** (*bontà*) goodness, good
2 (*COMM*) voucher, coupon; **~ d'acquisto** credit note; **~ di cassa** cash voucher; **~ di consegna** delivery note; **~ fruttifero** interest-bearing bond; **~ ordinario del Tesoro** short-term Treasury bond; **~**

postale fruttifero interest-bearing bond (*issued by Italian Post Office*); **~ del Tesoro** Treasury bill.

buon'senso *sm* = **buon senso.**
buontem'pone, a *sm/f* jovial person.
buonu'scita [bwonuʃ'ʃita] *sf* (*INDUSTRIA*) golden handshake; (*di affitti*) *sum paid for the relinquishing of tenancy rights.*
buratti'naio *sm* puppeteer, puppet master.
burat'tino *sm* puppet.
'burbero, a *ag* surly, gruff.
'burla *sf* prank, trick.
bur'lare *vt*: **~ qc/qn, ~rsi di qc/qn** to make fun of sth/sb.
bu'rocrate *sm* bureaucrat.
buro'cratico, a, ci, che *ag* bureaucratic.
burocra'zia [burokrat'tsia] *sf* bureaucracy.
bur'rasca, sche *sf* storm.
burras'coso, a *ag* stormy.
'burro *sm* butter.
bur'rone *sm* ravine.
bus'care *vt* (*anche: ~rsi: raffreddore*) to get, catch; **buscarle** (*fam*) to get a hiding.
buscherò *etc* [buske'rɔ] *vb vedi* **buscare.**
bus'sare *vi* to knock; **~ a quattrini** (*fig*) to ask for money.
'bussola *sf* compass; **perdere la ~** (*fig*) to lose one's bearings.
'busta *sf* (*da lettera*) envelope; (*astuccio*) case; **in ~ aperta/chiusa** in an unsealed/ sealed envelope; **~ paga** pay packet.
busta'rella *sf* bribe, backhander.
bus'tina *sf* (*piccola busta*) envelope; (*di cibi, farmaci*) sachet; (*MIL*) forage cap; **~ di tè** tea bag.
'busto *sm* bust; (*indumento*) corset, girdle; **a mezzo ~** (*fotografia, ritratto*) half-length.
bu'tano *sm* butane.
but'tare *vt* to throw; (*anche: ~ via*) to throw away; **~rsi** *vr* (*saltare*) to jump; **~ giù** (*scritto*) to scribble down, dash off; (*cibo*) to gulp down; (*edificio*) to pull down, demolish; (*pasta, verdura*) to put into boiling water; **ho buttato là una frase** I mentioned it in passing; **buttiamoci!** (*saltiamo*) let's jump!; (*rischiamo*) let's have a go!; **~rsi dalla finestra** to jump out of the window.
'buzzo ['buddzo] *sm* (*fam: pancia*) belly, paunch; **di ~ buono** (*con impegno*) with a will.

Cc

C, c [t∫i] *sf o m inv* (*lettera*) C, c ♦ *abbr* (*GEO*)
= **capo**; (= *Celsius, centigrado*) C;
(= *conto*) a/c; ~ **come Como** ≈ C for
Charlie.
CA *sigla* = *Cagliari.*
c.a. *abbr* (*ELETTR*) *vedi* **corrente alternata**;
(*COMM*) = *corrente anno.*
caba'ret [kaba're] *sm inv* cabaret.
ca'bina *sf* (*di nave*) cabin; (*da spiaggia*)
beach hut; (*di autocarro, treno*) cab; (*di
aereo*) cockpit; (*di ascensore*) cage; ~ **di
proiezione** (*CINE*) projection booth; ~ **di
registrazione** recording booth; ~
telefonica callbox, (tele)phone box *o*
booth.
cabi'nato *sm* cabin cruiser.
ca'blaggio [ka'bladdʒo] *sm* wiring.
cablo'gramma *sm* cable(gram).
ca'cao *sm* cocoa.
'cacca *sf* (*fam: anche fig*) shit (*!*).
'caccia ['katt∫a] *sf* hunting; (*con fucile*)
shooting; (*inseguimento*) chase;
(*cacciagione*) game ♦ *sm inv* (*aereo*) fighter;
(*nave*) destroyer; **andare a** ~ to go
hunting; **andare a** ~ **di guai** to be asking
for trouble; ~ **grossa** big-game hunting;
~ **all'uomo** manhunt.
cacciabombardi'ere [katt∫abombar'djɛre]
sm fighter-bomber.
cacciagi'one [katt∫a'dʒone] *sf* game.
cacci'are [kat't∫are] *vt* to hunt; (*mandar via*)
to chase away; (*ficcare*) to shove, stick
♦ *vi* to hunt; ~**rsi** *vr* (*fam: mettersi*): ~**rsi tra
la folla** to plunge into the crowd; **dove s'è
cacciata la mia borsa?** where has my bag
got to?; ~**rsi nei guai** to get into trouble;
~ **fuori qc** to whip *o* pull sth out; ~ **un urlo**
to let out a yell.
caccia'tora [katt∫a'tora] *sf* (*giacca*) hunting
jacket; (*CUC*): **pollo** *etc* **alla** ~ chicken *etc*
chasseur.
caccia'tore [katt∫a'tore] *sm* hunter; ~ **di
frodo** poacher; ~ **di dote** fortune-hunter.
cacciatorpedini'ere [katt∫atorpedi'njɛre]
sm destroyer.
caccia'vite [katt∫a'vite] *sm inv* screwdriver.
cache'mire [ka∫'mir] *sm inv* cashmere.
ca'chet [ka'∫ɛ] *sm* (*MED*) capsule;

(*: compressa*) tablet; (*compenso*) fee;
(*colorante per capelli*) rinse.
'cachi ['kaki] *sm inv* (*albero, frutto*)
persimmon; (*colore*) khaki ♦ *ag inv* khaki.
'cacio ['kat∫o] *sm* cheese; **essere come il** ~
sui maccheroni (*fig*) to turn up at the right
moment.
'cactus *sm inv* cactus.
ca'davere *sm* (dead) body, corpse.
cada'verico, a, ci, che *ag* (*fig*) deathly pale.
'caddi *etc vb vedi* **cadere**.
ca'dente *ag* falling; (*casa*) tumbledown;
(*persona*) decrepit.
ca'denza [ka'dɛntsa] *sf* cadence;
(*andamento ritmico*) rhythm; (*MUS*)
cadenza.
ca'dere *vi* to fall; (*denti, capelli*) to fall out;
(*tetto*) to fall in; **questa gonna cade bene**
this skirt hangs well; **lasciar** ~ (*anche fig*)
to drop; ~ **dal sonno** to be falling asleep
on one's feet; ~ **ammalato** to fall ill; ~
dalle nuvole (*fig*) to be taken aback.
ca'detto *sm* cadet.
cadrò *etc vb vedi* **cadere**.
ca'duto, a *ag* (*morto*) dead ♦ *sm* dead
soldier ♦ *sf* fall; **monumento ai** ~**i** war
memorial; ~**a di temperatura** drop in
temperature; **la** ~**a dei capelli** hair loss;
~**a del sistema** (*INFORM*) system failure.
caffè *sm inv* coffee; (*locale*) café; ~ **corretto**
coffee with liqueur; ~ **in grani** coffee
beans; ~ **macchiato** coffee with a dash of
milk; ~ **macinato** ground coffee.
caffe'ina *sf* caffeine.
caffel'latte *sm inv* white coffee.
caffette'ria *sf* coffee shop.
caffetti'era *sf* coffeepot.
ca'fone *sm* (*contadino*) peasant; (*peg*) boor.
cagio'nare [kadʒo'nare] *vt* to cause, be the
cause of.
cagio'nevole [kadʒo'nevole] *ag* delicate,
weak.
cagli'are [kaʎ'ʎare] *vi* to curdle.
cagliari'tano, a [kaʎʎari'tano] *ag* of (*o*
from) Cagliari.
'cagna ['kaɲɲa] *sf* (*ZOOL, peg*) bitch.
ca'gnara [kaɲ'ɲara] *sf* (*fig*) uproar.
ca'gnesco, a, schi, sche [kaɲ'ɲesko] *ag*
(*fig*): **guardare qn in** ~ to scowl at sb.
CAI *sigla m* = *Club Alpino Italiano.*
'Cairo *sm*: **il** ~ Cairo.
cala'brese *ag, sm/f* Calabrian.
cala'brone *sm* hornet.
Cala'hari [kala'ari]: **il Deserto di** ~ *sm* the
Kalahari Desert.
cala'maio *sm* inkpot; inkwell.
cala'maro *sm* squid.
cala'mita *sf* magnet.

calamità *sf inv* calamity, disaster; ~ **naturale** natural disaster.

ca'lare *vt* (*far discendere*) to lower; (*MAGLIA*) to decrease ♦ *vi* (*discendere*) to go (*o* come) down; (*tramontare*) to set, go down; ~ **di peso** to lose weight.

ca'lata *sf* (*invasione*) invasion.

'calca *sf* throng, press.

cal'cagno [kal'kaɲɲo] *sm* heel.

cal'care *sm* limestone; (*incrostazione*) (lime)scale ♦ *vt* (*premere coi piedi*) to tread, press down; (*premere con forza*) to press down; (*mettere in rilievo*) to stress; ~ **la mano** to overdo it, exaggerate; ~ **le scene** (*fig*) to be on the stage; ~ **le orme di qn** (*fig*) to follow in sb's footsteps.

'calce ['kaltʃe] *sm*: **in** ~ at the foot of the page ♦ *sf* lime; ~ **viva** quicklime.

calces'truzzo [kaltʃes'truttso] *sm* concrete.

calcherò *etc* [kalke'rɔ] *vb vedi* **calcare**.

calci'are [kal'tʃare] *vt, vi* to kick.

calcia'tore [kaltʃa'tore] *sm* footballer (*BRIT*), (football) player.

cal'cina [kal'tʃina] *sf* (lime) mortar.

calci'naccio [kaltʃi'nattʃo] *sm* flake of plaster.

'calcio ['kaltʃo] *sm* (*pedata*) kick; (*sport*) football, soccer; (*di pistola, fucile*) butt; (*CHIM*) calcium; ~ **d'angolo** (*SPORT*) corner (kick); ~ **di punizione** (*SPORT*) free kick.

'calco, chi *sm* (*ARTE*) casting, moulding (*BRIT*), molding (*US*); cast, mo(u)ld.

calco'lare *vt* to calculate, work out, reckon; (*ponderare*) to weigh (up).

calcola'tore, 'trice *ag* calculating ♦ *sm* calculator; (*fig*) calculating person ♦ *sf* (*anche*: **macchina calcolatrice**) calculator; ~ **digitale** digital computer; ~ **elettronico** computer; ~ **da tavolo** desktop computer.

'calcolo *sm* (*anche MAT*) calculation; (*infinitesimale etc*) calculus; (*MED*) stone; **fare il** ~ **di qc** to work sth out; **fare i propri** ~**i** (*fig*) to weigh the pros and cons; **per** ~ out of self-interest.

cal'daia *sf* boiler.

caldar'rosta *sf* roast chestnut.

caldeggi'are [kalded'dʒare] *vt* to support.

'caldo, a *ag* warm; (*molto* ~) hot; (*fig: appassionato*) keen ♦ *sm* heat; **ho** ~ I'm warm; I'm hot; **fa** ~ it's warm; it's hot; **non mi fa né** ~ **né freddo** I couldn't care less; **a** ~ (*fig*) in the heat of the moment.

caleidos'copio *sm* kaleidoscope.

calen'dario *sm* calendar.

ca'lende *sfpl* calends; **rimandare qc alle** ~ **greche** to put sth off indefinitely.

ca'lesse *sm* gig.

'calibro *sm* (*di arma*) calibre, bore; (*TECN*) callipers *pl*; (*fig*) calibre; **di grosso** ~ (*fig*) prominent.

'calice ['kalitʃe] *sm* goblet; (*REL*) chalice.

Cali'fornia *sf* California.

californi'ano, a *ag* Californian.

ca'ligine [ka'lidʒine] *sf* fog; (*mista con fumo*) smog.

calligra'fia *sf* (*scrittura*) handwriting; (*arte*) calligraphy.

'callo *sm* callus; (*ai piedi*) corn; **fare il** ~ **a qc** to get used to sth.

'calma *sf* calm; **faccia con** ~ take your time.

cal'mante *sm* sedative, tranquillizer.

cal'mare *vt* to calm; (*lenire*) to soothe; ~**rsi** *vr* to grow calm, calm down; (*vento*) to abate; (*dolori*) to ease.

calmi'ere *sm* controlled price.

'calmo, a *ag* calm, quiet.

'calo *sm* (*COMM: di prezzi*) fall; (*: di volume*) shrinkage; (*: di peso*) loss.

ca'lore *sm* warmth; (*intenso, FISICA*) heat; **essere in** ~ (*ZOOL*) to be on heat.

calo'ria *sf* calorie.

calo'rifero *sm* radiator.

calo'roso, a *ag* warm; **essere** ~ not to feel the cold.

calpes'tare *vt* to tread on, trample on; **"è vietato** ~ **l'erba"** "keep off the grass".

ca'lunnia *sf* slander; (*scritta*) libel.

calunni'are *vt* to slander.

cal'vario *sm* (*fig*) affliction, cross.

cal'vizie [kal'vittsje] *sf* baldness.

'calvo, a *ag* bald.

'calza ['kaltsa] *sf* (*da donna*) stocking; (*da uomo*) sock; **fare la** ~ to knit; ~**e di nailon** nylons, (nylon) stockings.

calza'maglia [kaltsa'maʎʎa] *sf* tights *pl*; (*per danza, ginnastica*) leotard.

cal'zare [kal'tsare] *vt* (*scarpe, guanti: mettersi*) to put on; (*: portare*) to wear ♦ *vi* to fit; ~ **a pennello** to fit like a glove.

calza'tura [kaltsa'tura] *sf* footwear.

calzaturi'ficio [kaltsaturi'fitʃo] *sm* shoe *o* footwear factory.

cal'zetta [kal'tsetta] *sf* ankle sock; **una mezza** ~ (*fig*) a nobody.

calzet'tone [kaltset'tone] *sm* heavy knee-length sock.

cal'zino [kal'tsino] *sm* sock.

calzo'laio [kaltso'lajo] *sm* shoemaker; (*che ripara scarpe*) cobbler.

calzole'ria [kaltsole'ria] *sf* (*negozio*) shoe shop; (*arte*) shoemaking.

calzon'cini [kaltson'tʃini] *smpl* shorts; ~ **da bagno** (swimming) trunks.

cal'zone [kal'tsone] *sm* trouser leg; (*CUC*)

savoury turnover made with pizza dough; ~i *smpl* trousers (*BRIT*), pants (*US*).

camale'onte *sm* chameleon.

cambi'ale *sf* bill (of exchange); (*pagherò cambiario*) promissory note; ~ **di comodo** *o* **di favore** accommodation bill.

cambia'mento *sm* change.

cambi'are *vt* to change; (*modificare*) to alter, change; (*barattare*): ~ **(qc con qn/qc)** to exchange (sth with sb/for sth) ♦ *vi* to change, alter; ~**rsi** *vr* (*variare abito*) to change; ~ **casa** to move (house); ~ **idea** to change one's mind; ~ **treno** to change trains; ~ **le carte in tavola** (*fig*) to change one's tune; ~ **(l')aria in una stanza** to air a room; **è ora di** ~ **aria** (*andarsene*) it's time to move on.

cambiava'lute *sm inv* exchange office.

'cambio *sm* change; (*modifica*) alteration, change; (*scambio, COMM*) exchange; (*corso dei cambi*) rate (of exchange); (*TECN, AUT*) gears *pl*; **in** ~ **di** in exchange for; **dare il** ~ **a qn** to take over from sb; **fare il** *o* **un** ~ to change (over); ~ **a termine** (*COMM*) forward exchange.

'Cambital *sigla m* = *Ufficio Italiano dei Cambi*.

Cam'bogia [kam'bɔdʒa] *sf:* **la** ~ Cambodia.

cambogi'ano, a [kambo'dʒano] *ag, smlf* Cambodian.

cam'busa *sf* storeroom.

'camera *sf* room; (*anche:* ~ **da letto**) bedroom; (*POL*) chamber, house; ~ **ardente** mortuary chapel; ~ **d'aria** inner tube; (*di pallone*) bladder; ~ **blindata** strongroom; **C**~ **di Commercio** Chamber of Commerce; **C**~ **dei Deputati** Chamber of Deputies, ≈ House of Commons (*BRIT*), ~ House of Representatives (*US*); *vedi nota nel riquadro;* ~ **a gas** gas chamber; ~ **del lavoro** trades union centre (*BRIT*), labor union center (*US*); ~ **a un letto/a due letti/matrimoniale** single/twin-bedded/double room; ~ **oscura** (*FOT*) dark room; ~ **da pranzo** dining room.

CAMERA DEI DEPUTATI

The **Camera dei deputati** *is the lower house of the Italian Parliament and is presided over by the "Presidente della Camera", who is chosen by the "deputati". Elections to the Chamber are normally held every five years. Since the electoral reform of 1993 members have been voted in via a system which combines a first-past-the-post element with proportional representation. See also* **Parlamento***.*

---

came'rata, i, e *smlf* companion, mate ♦ *sf* dormitory.

camera'tismo *sm* comradeship.

cameri'era *sf* (*domestica*) maid; (*che serve a tavola*) waitress; (*che fa le camere*) chambermaid.

cameri'ere *sm* (man)servant; (*di ristorante*) waiter.

came'rino *sm* (*TEAT*) dressing room.

'Camerun *sm:* **il** ~ Cameroon.

'camice ['kamitʃe] *sm* (*REL*) alb; (*per medici etc*) white coat.

cami'cetta [kami'tʃetta] *sf* blouse.

ca'micia, cie [ka'mitʃa] *sf* (*da uomo*) shirt; (*da donna*) blouse; **nascere con la** ~ (*fig*) to be born lucky; **sudare sette** ~**cie** (*fig*) to have a hell of a time; ~ **di forza** straitjacket; ~ **da notte** (*da donna*) nightdress; (*da uomo*) nightshirt; **C**~ **nera** (*fascista*) Blackshirt.

camici'ola [kami'tʃɔla] *sf* vest.

camici'otto [kami'tʃɔtto] *sm* casual shirt; (*per operai*) smock.

cami'netto *sm* hearth, fireplace.

ca'mino *sm* chimney; (*focolare*) fireplace, hearth.

'camion *sm inv* lorry (*BRIT*), truck (*US*).

camion'cino [kamjon'tʃino] *sm* van.

camio'netta *sf* jeep.

camio'nista, i *sm* lorry driver (*BRIT*), truck driver (*US*).

'camma *sf* cam; **albero a** ~**e** camshaft.

cam'mello *sm* (*ZOOL*) camel; (*tessuto*) camel hair.

cam'meo *sm* cameo.

cammi'nare *vi* to walk; (*funzionare*) to work, go; ~ **a carponi** *o* **a quattro zampe** to go on all fours.

cammi'nata *sf* walk; **fare una** ~ to go for a walk.

cam'mino *sm* walk; (*sentiero*) path; (*itinerario, direzione, tragitto*) way; **mettersi in** ~ to set *o* start off; **cammin facendo** on the way; **riprendere il** ~ to continue on one's way.

camo'milla *sf* camomile; (*infuso*) camomile tea.

ca'morra *sf* Camorra; (*fig*) racket.

camor'rista, i, e *smlf* member of the Camorra; (*fig*) racketeer.

ca'moscio [ka'mɔʃʃo] *sm* chamois.

cam'pagna [kam'paɲɲa] *sf* country, countryside; (*POL, COMM, MIL*) campaign; **in** ~ in the country; **andare in** ~ to go to the country; **fare una** ~ to campaign; ~ **promozionale vendite** sales campaign.

campa'gnolo, a [kampaɲ'ɲɔlo] *ag* country *cpd* ♦ *sf* (*AUT*) cross-country vehicle.
cam'pale *ag* field *cpd*; (*fig*): **una giornata** ~ a hard day.
cam'pana *sf* bell; (*anche:* ~ **di vetro**) bell jar; **sordo come una** ~ as deaf as a doorpost; **sentire l'altra** ~ (*fig*) to hear the other side of the story.
campa'nella *sf* small bell; (*di tenda*) curtain ring.
campa'nello *sm* (*all'uscio, da tavola*) bell.
campa'nile *sm* bell tower, belfry.
campani'lismo *sm* parochialism.
cam'pano, a *ag* of (*o* from) Campania.
cam'pare *vi* to live; (*tirare avanti*) to get by, manage; ~ **alla giornata** to live from day to day.
cam'pato, a *ag*: ~ **in aria** unsound, unfounded.
campeggi'are [kamped'dʒare] *vi* to camp; (*risaltare*) to stand out.
campeggia'tore, 'trice [kampeddʒa'tore] *sm/f* camper.
cam'peggio [kam'peddʒo] *sm* camping; (*terreno*) camp site; **fare (del)** ~ to go camping.
cam'pestre *ag* country *cpd*, rural; **corsa** ~ cross-country race.
Campi'doglio [kampi'dɔʎʎo] *sm*: **il** ~ the Capitol; *vedi nota nel riquadro*.

CAMPIDOGLIO

The **Campidoglio**, one of the Seven Hills of Rome, is the home of the "Comune di Roma".

'camping ['kæmpiŋ] *sm inv* camp site.
campiona'mento *sm* sampling.
campio'nario, a *ag*: **fiera** ~**a** a trade fair ♦ *sm* collection of samples.
campio'nato *sm* championship.
campiona'tura *sf* (*COMM*) production of samples; (*STATISTICA*) sampling.
campi'one, 'essa *sm/f* (*SPORT*) champion ♦ *sm* (*COMM*) sample; ~ **gratuito** free sample; **prelievi di** ~ product samples.
'campo *sm* (*gen*) field; (*MIL*) field; (*: accampamento*) camp; (*spazio delimitato: sportivo etc*) ground; field; (*di quadro*) background; **i** ~**i** (*campagna*) the countryside; **padrone del** ~ (*fig*) victor; ~ **da aviazione** airfield; ~ **di concentramento** concentration camp; ~ **di golf** golf course; ~ **lungo** (*CINE, TV, FOT*) long shot; ~ **nomadi** travellers' camp; ~ **da tennis** tennis court; ~ **visivo** field of vision.
campobas'sano, a *ag* of (*o* from)

Campobasso.
campo'santo, pl campi'santi *sm* cemetery.
camuf'fare *vt* to disguise; ~**rsi** *vr*: ~**rsi (da)** to disguise o.s. (as); (*per ballo in maschera*) to dress up (as).
CAN *abbr* (= *Costo, Assicurazione e Nolo*) CIF.
Can. *abbr* (*GEO*) = **canale**.
'Canada *sm*: **il** ~ Canada.
cana'dese *ag, sm/f* Canadian ♦ *sf* (*anche:* **tenda** ~) ridge tent.
ca'naglia [ka'naʎʎa] *sf* rabble, mob; (*persona*) scoundrel, rogue.
ca'nale *sm* (*anche fig*) channel; (*artificiale*) canal.
'canapa *sf* hemp; ~ **indiana** cannabis.
Ca'narie *sfpl*: **le (isole)** ~ the Canary Islands, the Canaries.
cana'rino *sm* canary.
Can'berra *sf* Canberra.
cancel'lare [kantʃel'lare] *vt* (*con la gomma*) to rub out, erase; (*con la penna*) to strike out; (*annullare, disdire*) to cancel.
cancel'lata [kantʃel'lata] *sf* railing(s) (*pl*).
cancelle'ria [kantʃelle'ria] *sf* chancery; (*quanto necessario per scrivere*) stationery.
cancelli'ere [kantʃel'ljere] *sm* chancellor; (*di tribunale*) clerk of the court.
can'cello [kan'tʃello] *sm* gate.
cance'rogeno, a [kantʃe'rɔdʒeno] *ag* carcinogenic ♦ *sm* carcinogen.
cance'rologo, a, gi, ghe [kantʃe'rɔlogo] *sm/f* cancer specialist.
cance'roso, a [kantʃe'roso] *ag* cancerous ♦ *sm/f* cancer patient.
can'crena *sf* gangrene.
'cancro *sm* (*MED*) cancer; (*dello zodiaco*): **C**~ Cancer; **essere del C**~ to be Cancer.
candeggi'are [kanded'dʒare] *vt* to bleach.
candeg'gina [kanded'dʒina] *sf* bleach.
can'dela *sf* candle; ~ **(di accensione)** (*AUT*) spark(ing) plug; **una lampadina da 100** ~**e** (*ELETTR*) a 100 watt bulb; **a lume di** ~ by candlelight; **tenere la** ~ (*fig*) to play gooseberry (*BRIT*), act as chaperone.
cande'labro *sm* candelabra.
candeli'ere *sm* candlestick.
cande'lotto *sm* candle; ~ **di dinamite** stick of dynamite; ~ **lacrimogeno** tear gas grenade.
candi'dare *vt* to present as candidate; ~**rsi** *vr* to present o.s. as candidate.
candi'dato, a *sm/f* candidate; (*aspirante a una carica*) applicant.
candida'tura *sf* candidature; application.
'candido, a *ag* white as snow; (*puro*) pure; (*sincero*) sincere, candid.

can'dito, a *ag* candied.

can'dore *sm* brilliant white; purity; sincerity, candour (*BRIT*); candor (*US*).

'cane *sm* dog; (*di pistola, fucile*) cock; **fa un freddo** ~ it's bitterly cold; **non c'era un** ~ there wasn't a soul; **quell'attore è un** ~ he's a rotten actor; ~ **da caccia** hunting dog; ~ **da guardia** guard dog; ~ **lupo** alsatian; ~ **da salotto** lap dog; ~ **da slitta** husky.

ca'nestro *sm* basket; **fare un** ~ (*SPORT*) to shoot a basket.

'canfora *sf* camphor.

cangi'ante [kan'dʒante] *ag* iridescent; **seta** ~ shot silk.

can'guro *sm* kangaroo.

ca'nicola *sf* scorching heat.

ca'nile *sm* kennel; (*di allevamento*) kennels *pl*; ~ **municipale** dog pound.

ca'nino, a *ag, sm* canine.

'canna *sf* (*pianta*) reed; (*: indica, da zucchero*) cane; (*bastone*) stick, cane; (*di fucile*) barrel; (*di organo*) pipe; (*DROGA: gergo*) joint; ~ **fumaria** chimney flue; ~ **da pesca** (fishing) rod; ~ **da zucchero** sugar cane.

can'nella *sf* (*CUC*) cinnamon; (*di conduttura, botte*) tap.

cannel'loni *smpl pasta tubes stuffed with sauce and baked.*

can'neto *sm* bed of reeds.

can'nibale *sm* cannibal.

cannocchi'ale [kannok'kjale] *sm* telescope.

canno'nata *sf*: **è una vera** ~! (*fig*) it's (*o* he's *etc*) fantastic!

can'none *sm* (*MIL*) gun; (*: STORIA*) cannon; (*tubo*) pipe, tube; (*piega*) box pleat; (*fig*) ace; **donna** ~ fat woman.

cannoni'ere *sm* (*NAUT*) gunner; (*CALCIO*) goal scorer.

can'nuccia, ce [kan'nuttʃa] *sf* (drinking) straw.

'canone *sm* canon, criterion; (*mensile, annuo*) rent; fee; **legge dell'equo** ~ fair rent act.

ca'nonica, che *sf* presbytery.

ca'nonico, ci *sm* (*REL*) canon.

canoniz'zare [kanonid'dzare] *vt* to canonize.

ca'noro, a *ag* (*uccello*) singing, song *cpd.*

ca'notta *sf* vest.

canot'taggio [kanot'taddʒo] *sm* rowing.

canotti'era *sf* vest (*BRIT*), undershirt (*US*).

ca'notto *sm* small boat, dinghy; canoe.

cano'vaccio [kano'vattʃo] *sm* (*tela*) canvas; (*strofinaccio*) duster; (*trama*) plot.

can'tante *sm/f* singer.

can'tare *vt, vi* to sing; ~ **vittoria** to crow;

fare ~ **qn** (*fig*) to make sb talk.

cantas'torie *sm/f inv* storyteller.

cantau'tore, 'trice *sm/f* singer-composer.

canterel'lare *vt, vi* to hum, sing to o.s.

canticchi'are [kantik'kjare] *vt, vi* to hum, sing to o.s.

canti'ere *sm* (*EDIL*) (building) site; (*anche:* ~ **navale**) shipyard.

canti'lena *sf* (*filastrocca*) lullaby; (*fig*) singsong voice.

can'tina *sf* (*locale*) cellar; (*bottega*) wine shop.

'canto *sm* song; (*arte*) singing; (*REL*) chant; chanting; (*POESIA*) poem, lyric; (*parte di una poesia*) canto; (*parte, lato*): **da un** ~ on the one hand; **d'altro** ~ on the other hand.

canto'nata *sf* (*di edificio*) corner; **prendere una** ~ (*fig*) to blunder.

can'tone *sm* (*in Svizzera*) canton.

cantoni'era *ag*: (**casa**) ~ road inspector's house.

can'tuccio [kan'tuttʃo] *sm* corner, nook.

ca'nuto, a *ag* white, whitehaired.

canzo'nare [kantso'nare] *vt* to tease.

canzona'tura [kantsona'tura] *sf* teasing; (*beffa*) joke.

can'zone [kan'tsone] *sf* song; (*POESIA*) canzone.

canzoni'ere [kantso'njɛre] *sm* (*MUS*) songbook; (*LETTERATURA*) collection of poems.

'caos *sm inv* chaos.

ca'otico, a, ci, che *ag* chaotic.

CAP *sigla m vedi* **codice di avviamento postale**.

cap. *abbr* (= *capitolo*) ch.

ca'pace [ka'patʃe] *ag* able, capable; (*ampio, vasto*) large, capacious; **sei** ~ **di farlo?** can you *o* are you able to do it?; ~ **d'intendere e di volere** (*DIR*) in full possession of one's faculties.

capacità [kapatʃi'ta] *sf inv* ability; (*DIR, di recipiente*) capacity; ~ **produttiva** production capacity.

capaci'tarsi [kapatʃi'tarsi] *vr*: ~ **di** to make out, understand.

ca'panna *sf* hut.

capan'nello *sm* knot (of people).

ca'panno *sm* (*di cacciatori*) hide; (*da spiaggia*) bathing hut.

capan'none *sm* (*AGR*) barn; (*fabbricato industriale*) (factory) shed.

caparbietà *sf* stubbornness.

ca'parbio, a *ag* stubborn.

ca'parra *sf* deposit, down payment.

capa'tina *sf*: **fare una** ~ **da qn/in centro** to pop in on sb/into town.

capeggi'are [kaped'dʒare] *vt* (*rivolta etc*) to

head, lead.

ca'pello *sm* hair; ~i *smpl* (*capigliatura*) hair *sg*; **averne fin sopra i** ~i **di qc/qn** to be fed up to the (back) teeth with sth/sb; **mi ci hanno tirato per i** ~i (*fig*) they dragged me into it; **tirato per i** ~i (*spiegazione*) far-fetched.

capel'lone, a *sm/f* hippie.

capel'luto, a *ag*: **cuoio** ~ scalp.

capez'zale [kapet'tsale] *sm* bolster; (*fig*) bedside.

ca'pezzolo [ka'pettsolo] *sm* nipple.

capi'ente *ag* capacious.

capi'enza [ka'pjɛntsa] *sf* capacity.

capiglia'tura [kapiʎʎa'tura] *sf* hair.

capil'lare *ag* (*fig*) detailed ♦ *sm* (*ANAT*: *anche*: **vaso** ~) capillary.

ca'pire *vt* to understand; ~ **al volo** to catch on straight away; **si capisce!** (*certamente!*) of course!, certainly!

capi'tale *ag* (*mortale*) capital; (*fondamentale*) main *cpd*, chief *cpd* ♦ *sf* (*città*) capital ♦ *sm* (*ECON*) capital; ~ **azionario** equity capital, share capital; ~ **d'esercizio** working capital; ~ **fisso** capital assets, fixed capital; ~ **immobile** real estate; ~ **liquido** cash assets *pl*; ~ **mobile** movables *pl*; ~ **di rischio** risk capital; ~ **sociale** (*di società*) authorized capital; (*di club*) funds *pl*; ~ **di ventura** venture capital, risk capital.

capita'lismo *sm* capitalism.

capita'lista, i, e *ag*, *sm/f* capitalist.

capitaliz'zare [kapitalid'dzare] *vt* to capitalize.

capitalizzazi'one [kapitaliddzat'tsjone] *sf* capitalization.

capita'nare *vt* to lead; (*CALCIO*) to captain.

capitane'ria *sf*: ~ (*di porto*) port authorities *pl*.

capi'tano *sm* captain; ~ **di lungo corso** master mariner; ~ **di ventura** (*STORIA*) mercenary leader.

capi'tare *vi* (*giungere casualmente*) to happen to go, find o.s.; (*accadere*) to happen; (*presentarsi: cosa*) to turn up, present itself ♦ *vb impers* to happen; ~ **a proposito/bene/male** to turn up at the right moment/at a good time/at a bad time; **mi è capitato un guaio** I've had a spot of trouble.

capi'tello *sm* (*ARCHIT*) capital.

capito'lare *vi* to capitulate.

capitolazi'one [kapitolat'tsjone] *sf* capitulation.

ca'pitolo *sm* chapter; ~**i** *smpl* (*COMM*) items; **non ho voce in** ~ (*fig*) I have no say in the matter.

capi'tombolo *sm* headlong fall, tumble.

'capo *sm* (*ANAT*) head; (*persona*) head, leader; (: *in ufficio*) head, boss; (: *in tribù*) chief; (*estremità*: *di tavolo, scale*) head, top; (: *di filo*) end; (*GEO*) cape; **andare a** ~ **to** start a new paragraph; **"punto a** ~**"** "full stop — new paragraph"; **da** ~ over again; **in** ~ **a** (*tempo*) within; **da un** ~ **all'altro** from one end to the other; **fra** ~ **e collo** (*all'improvviso*) out of the blue; **un discorso senza né** ~ **né coda** a senseless o meaningless speech; ~ **d'accusa** (*DIR*) charge; ~ **di bestiame** head *inv* of cattle; **C**~ **di Buona Speranza** Cape of Good Hope; ~ **di vestiario** item of clothing.

capo'banda, *pl* capi'banda *sm* (*MUS*) bandmaster; (*di malviventi, fig*) gang leader.

ca'poccia [ka'pɔttʃa] *sm inv* (*di lavoranti*) overseer; (*peg*: *capobanda*) boss.

capo'classe, *pl(m)* capi'classe, *pl(f) inv sm/f* (*INS*) ≈ form captain (*BRIT*), class president (*US*).

capocu'oco, chi *sm* head cook.

Capo'danno *sm* New Year.

capofa'miglia, *pl(m)* capifa'miglia, *pl(f) inv* [kapofa'miʎʎa] *sm/f* head of the family.

capo'fitto: **a** ~ *av* headfirst, headlong.

capo'giro [kapo'dʒiro] *sm* dizziness *no pl*; **da** ~ (*fig*) astonishing, staggering.

capo'gruppo, *pl(m)* capi'gruppo, *pl(f) inv sm/f* group leader.

capola'voro, i *sm* masterpiece.

capo'linea, *pl* capi'linea *sm* terminus; (*fig*) end of the line.

capo'lino *sm*: **far** ~ to peep out (*o in etc*).

capo'lista, *pl(m)* capi'lista, *pl(f) inv sm/f* (*POL*) top candidate on electoral list.

capolu'ogo, *pl* ghi *o* capilu'oghi *sm* chief town, administrative centre (*BRIT*) *o* center (*US*).

capo'mastro, *pl* i *o* capi'mastri *sm* master builder.

capo'rale *sm* (*MIL*) lance corporal (*BRIT*), private first class (*US*).

capore'parto, *pl(m)* capire'parto, *pl(f) inv sm/f* (*di operai*) foreman; (*di ufficio, negozio*) head of department.

capo'sala *sf inv* (*MED*) ward sister.

capo'saldo, *pl* capi'saldi *sm* stronghold; (*fig: fondamento*) basis, cornerstone.

capo'squadra, *pl* capi'squadra *sm* (*di operai*) foreman, ganger; (*MIL*) squad leader; (*SPORT*) team captain.

capostazi'one, *pl* capistazi'one [kapostat'tsjone] *sm* station master.

capos'tipite *sm* progenitor; (*fig*) earliest example.

capo'tavola, pl(m) **capi'tavola,** pl(f) inv smlf (persona) head of the table; **sedere a** ~ to sit at the head of the table.

ca'pote [ka'pɔt] sf inv (AUT) hood (BRIT), soft top.

capo'treno, pl **capi'treno** o **capo'treni** sm guard.

capouf'ficio, pl(m) **capiuf'ficio,** pl(f) inv [kapouf'fitʃo] smlf head clerk.

capo'verso sm (di verso, periodo) first line; (TIP) indent; (paragrafo) paragraph; (DIR: comma) section.

capo'volgere [kapo'voldʒere] vt to overturn; (fig) to reverse; ~**rsi** vr to overturn; (barca) to capsize; (fig) to be reversed.

capovolgi'mento [kapovoldʒi'mento] sm (fig) reversal, complete change.

capo'volto, a pp di **capovolgere** ♦ ag upside down; (barca) capsized.

'cappa sf (mantello) cape, cloak; (del camino) hood.

cap'pella sf (REL) chapel.

cappel'lano sm chaplain.

cap'pello sm hat; **Tanto di** ~**!** (flg) I take my hat off to you!; ~ **a bombetta** bowler (hat), derby (US); ~ **a cilindro** top hat; ~ **di paglia** straw hat.

'cappero sm caper.

cap'pone sm capon.

cappot'tare vi (AUT) to overturn.

cap'potto sm (over)coat.

cappuc'cino [kapput'tʃino] sm (frate) Capuchin monk; (bevanda) cappuccino.

cap'puccio [kap'puttʃo] sm (copricapo) hood; (della biro) cap.

'capra sf (she-)goat.

ca'prese ag from (o of) Capri.

ca'pretto sm kid.

ca'priccio [ka'prittʃo] sm caprice, whim; (bizza) tantrum; **fare i** ~**i** to be very naughty; ~ **della sorte** quirk of fate.

capricci'oso, a [kaprit'tʃoso] ag capricious, whimsical; naughty.

Capri'corno sm Capricorn; **essere del** ~ (dello zodiaco) to be Capricorn.

capri'foglio [kapri'fɔʎʎo] sm honeysuckle.

capri'ola sf somersault.

capri'olo sm roe deer.

'capro sm billy-goat; **espiatorio** (fig) scapegoat.

ca'prone sm billy-goat.

'capsula sf capsule; (di arma, per bottiglie) cap.

cap'tare vt (RADIO, TV) to pick up; (cattivarsi) to gain, win.

CAR sigla m = Centro Addestramento Reclute.

cara'bina sf rifle.

carabini'ere sm member of Italian military police force; vedi nota nel riquadro.

CARABINIERI

Originally part of the armed forces, the **Carabinieri** are police who now have civil as well as military duties, such as maintaining public order. They include paratroop units and mounted divisions and report to either the Minister of the Interior or the Minister of Defence, depending on the function they are performing.

Ca'racas sf Caracas.

ca'raffa sf carafe.

Ca'raibi smpl: **il mar dei** ~ the Caribbean (Sea).

cara'ibico, a, ci, che ag Caribbean.

cara'mella sf sweet.

cara'mello sm caramel.

ca'rato sm (di oro, diamante etc) carat.

ca'rattere sm character; (caratteristica) characteristic, trait; **avere un buon** ~ to be good-natured; **informazione di** ~ **tecnico/confidenziale** information of a technical/confidential nature; **essere in** ~ **con qc** (intonarsi) to be in harmony with sth; ~ **jolly** wild card.

caratte'rino sm difficult nature o character.

caratte'ristico, a, ci, che ag characteristic ♦ sf characteristic, feature; **segni** ~**ci** (su passaporto etc) distinguishing marks.

caratteriz'zare [karatterid'dzare] vt to characterize, distinguish.

carboi'drato sm carbohydrate.

carbo'naio sm (chi fa carbone) charcoal-burner; (commerciante) coalman, coal merchant.

car'bone sm coal; ~ **fossile** (pit) coal; **essere** o **stare sui** ~**i ardenti** to be like a cat on hot bricks.

car'bonio sm (CHIM) carbon.

carboniz'zare [karbonid'dzare] vt (legna) to carbonize; (: parzialmente) to char; **morire carbonizzato** to be burned to death.

carbu'rante sm (motor) fuel.

carbura'tore sm carburettor.

car'cassa sf carcass; (fig: peg: macchina etc) (old) wreck.

carce'rato, a [kartʃe'rato] smlf prisoner.

'carcere ['kartʃere] sm prison; (pena) imprisonment; ~ **di massima sicurezza** top-security prison.

carceri'ere, a [kartʃe'rjɛre] smlf (anche fig)

jailer.

carci'ofo [kar'tʃɔfo] *sm* artichoke.

cardel'lino *sm* goldfinch.

car'diaco, a, ci, che *ag* cardiac, heart *cpd.*

cardi'nale *ag, sm* cardinal.

'cardine *sm* hinge.

cardiolo'gia [kardjolo'dʒia] *sf* cardiology.

cardi'ologo, gi *sm* heart specialist, cardiologist.

'cardo *sm* thistle.

ca'rente *ag:* ~ **di** lacking in.

ca'renza [ka'rɛntsa] *sf* lack, scarcity; (*vitaminica*) deficiency.

cares'tia *sf* famine; (*penuria*) scarcity, dearth.

ca'rezza [ka'rettsa] *sf* caress; **dare** *o* **fare una** ~ **a** (*persona*) to caress; (*animale*) to stroke, pat.

carez'zare [karet'tsare] *vt* to caress, stroke, fondle.

carez'zevole [karet'tsevole] *ag* sweet, endearing.

cari'are *vt,* **~rsi** *vr* (*denti*) to decay.

'carica *sf vedi* **carico.**

caricabatte'rie *sm inv* (*ELETTR*) battery charger.

cari'care *vt* to load; (*aggravare: anche fig*) to weigh down; (*orologio*) to wind up; (*batteria, MIL*) to charge; (*INFORM*) to load; **~rsi** *vr:* **~rsi di** to burden *o* load o.s. with; (*fig: di responsabilità, impegni*) to burden o.s. with.

carica'tura *sf* caricature.

'carico, a, chi, che *ag* (*che porta un peso*): ~ **di** loaded *o* laden with; (*fucile*) loaded; (*orologio*) wound up; (*batteria*) charged; (*colore*) deep; (*caffè, tè*) strong ♦ *sm* (*il caricare*) loading; (*ciò che si carica*) load; (*COMM*) shipment; (*fig: peso*) burden, weight ♦ *sf* (*mansione ufficiale*) office, position; (*MIL, TECN, ELETTR*) charge; ~ **di debiti** up to one's ears in debt; **persona a** ~ dependent; **essere a** ~ **di qn** (*spese etc*) to be charged to sb; (*accusa, prova*) to be against sb; **testimone a** ~ witness for the prosecution; **farsi** ~ **di** (*problema, responsabilità*) to take on; **a** ~ **del cliente** at the customer's expense; ~ **di lavoro** (*di ditta, reparto*) workload; ~ **utile** payload; **capacità di** ~ cargo capacity; **entrare/essere in** ~a to come into/be in office; **ricoprire** *o* **rivestire una** ~a to hold a position; **uscire di** ~a to leave office; **dare la** ~a a (*orologio*) to wind up; (*fig: persona*) to back up; **tornare alla** ~a (*fig*) to insist, persist; **ha una forte** ~a **di simpatia** he's very likeable.

'carie *sf* (*dentaria*) decay.

ca'rino, a *ag* lovely, pretty, nice; (*simpatico*) nice.

ca'risma [ka'rizma] *sm* charisma.

caris'matico, a, ci, che *ag* charismatic.

carità *sf* charity; **per** ~! (*escl di rifiuto*) good heavens, no!

carita'tevole *ag* charitable.

carnagi'one [karna'dʒone] *sf* complexion.

car'nale *ag* (*amore*) carnal; (*fratello*) blood *cpd.*

'carne *sf* flesh; (*bovina, ovina etc*) meat; **in** ~ **e ossa** in the flesh, in person; **essere (bene) in** ~ to be well padded, be plump; **non essere né** ~ **né pesce** (*fig*) to be neither fish nor fowl; ~ **di manzo/maiale/pecora** beef/pork/mutton; ~ **in scatola** tinned *o* canned meat; ~ **tritata** mince (*BRIT*), hamburger meat (*US*), minced (*BRIT*) *o* ground (*US*) meat.

car'nefice [kar'nefitʃe] *sm* executioner; hangman.

carnefi'cina [karnefi'tʃina] *sf* carnage; (*fig*) disaster.

carne'vale *sm* carnival; **C**~ *vedi nota nel riquadro.*

CARNEVALE

Carnevale *is the name given to the period between Epiphany (6 January) and the beginning of Lent, when people throw parties, put on processions with spectacular floats, build bonfires in the "piazze" and dress up in fabulous costumes and masks. Building to a peak just before Lent,* **Carnevale** *culminates in the festivities of "Martedì grasso" (Shrove Tuesday).*

---

car'nivoro, a *ag* carnivorous.

car'noso, a *ag* fleshy; (*pianta, frutto, radice*) pulpy; (*labbra*) full.

'caro, a *ag* (*amato*) dear; (*costoso*) dear, expensive.

ca'rogna [ka'roɲɲa] *sf* carrion; (*fig fam*) swine.

caro'sello *sm* merry-go-round.

ca'rota *sf* carrot.

caro'vana *sf* caravan.

caro'vita *sm* high cost of living.

'carpa *sf* carp.

Car'pazi [kar'patsi] *smpl:* **i** ~ the Carpathian Mountains.

carpente'ria *sf* carpentry.

carpenti'ere *sm* carpenter.

car'pire *vt:* ~ **qc a qn** (*segreto etc*) to get sth out of sb.

car'poni *av* on all fours.

car'rabile *ag* suitable for vehicles; **"passo**

~" "keep clear". **car'raio, a** *ag*: **passo** ~ vehicle entrance. **carré** *sm* (*acconciatura*) bob. **carreggi'ata** [karred'dʒata] *sf* carriageway (*BRIT*), roadway; **rimettersi in** ~ (*fig*: *recuperare*) to catch up; **tenersi in** ~ (*fig*) to keep to the right path.

carrel'lata *sf* (*CINE, TV*: *tecnica*) tracking; (: *scena*) running shot; ~ **di successi** medley of hit tunes.

car'rello *sm* trolley; (*AER*) undercarriage; (*CINE*) dolly; (*di macchina da scrivere*) carriage.

car'retta *sf*: **tirare la** ~ (*fig*) to plod along.

car'retto *sm* handcart.

carri'era *sf* career; **fare** ~ to get on; **ufficiale di** ~ (*MIL*) regular officer; **a gran** ~ at full speed.

carri'ola *sf* wheelbarrow.

'**carro** *sm* cart, wagon; **il Gran/Piccolo C~** (*ASTR*) the Great/Little Bear; **mettere il** ~ **avanti ai buoi** (*fig*) to put the cart before the horse; ~ **armato** tank; ~ **attrezzi** (*AUT*) breakdown van (*BRIT*), tow truck (*US*); ~ **funebre** hearse; ~ **merci/bestiame** (*FERR*) goods/animal wagon.

car'roccio [kar'rɔtʃo] *sm* (*POL*): **il C~** *symbol of Lega Nord*.

car'rozza [kar'rɔttsa] *sf* carriage, coach; ~ **letto** (*FERR*) sleeper; ~ **ristorante** (*FERR*) dining car.

carroz'zella [karrot'tsɛlla] *sf* (*per bambini*) pram (*BRIT*), baby carriage (*US*); (*per invalidi*) wheelchair.

carrozze'ria [karrottse'ria] *sf* body, coachwork (*BRIT*); (*officina*) coachbuilder's workshop (*BRIT*), body shop.

carrozzi'ere [karrot'tsjɛre] *sm* (*AUT*: *progettista*) car designer; (: *meccanico*) coachbuilder.

carroz'zina [karrot'tsina] *sf* pram (*BRIT*), baby carriage (*US*).

carroz'zone [karrot'tsone] *sm* (*da circo, di zingari*) caravan.

car'rucola *sf* pulley.

'**carta** *sf* paper; (*al ristorante*) menu; (*GEO*) map; plan; (*documento, da gioco*) card; (*costituzione*) charter; ~**e** *sfpl* (*documenti*) papers, documents; **alla** ~ (*al ristorante*) à la carte; **cambiare le** ~**e in tavola** (*fig*) to shift one's ground; **fare** ~**e false** (*fig*) to go to great lengths; ~ **assegni** bank card; ~ **assorbente** blotting paper; ~ **bollata** *o* **da bollo** (*AMM*) official stamped paper; ~ **di credito** credit card; ~ **di debito** cash card; ~ (**geografica**) map; ~ **d'identità** identity card; ~ **igienica** toilet paper; ~ **d'imbarco**

(*AER, NAUT*) boarding card, boarding pass; ~ **da lettere** writing paper; ~ **libera** (*AMM*) unstamped paper; ~ **millimetrata** graph paper; ~ **oleata** waxed paper; ~ **da pacchi**, ~ **da imballo** wrapping paper, brown paper; ~ **da parati** wallpaper; ~ **verde** (*AUT*) green card; ~ **vetrata** sandpaper; ~ **da visita** visiting card.

cartacar'bone, *pl* **cartecar'bone** *sf* carbon paper.

car'taccia [kar'tattʃa] *sf* waste paper.

cartamo'dello *sm* (*CUCITO*) paper pattern.

cartamo'neta *sf* paper money.

carta'pecora *sf* parchment.

carta'pesta *sf* papier-mâché.

cartas'traccia [kartas'trattʃa] *sf* waste paper.

car'teggio [kar'teddʒo] *sm* correspondence.

car'tella *sf* (*scheda*) card; (*custodia: di cartone, INFORM*) folder; (: *di uomo d'affari etc*) briefcase; (: *di scolaro*) schoolbag, satchel; ~ **clinica** (*MED*) case sheet.

cartel'lino *sm* (*etichetta*) label; (*su porta*) notice; (*scheda*) card; **timbrare il** ~ (*all'entrata*) to clock in; (*all'uscita*) to clock out; ~ **di presenza** clock card, timecard.

car'tello *sm* sign; (*pubblicitario*) poster; (*stradale*) sign, signpost; (*in dimostrazioni*) placard; (*ECON*) cartel.

cartel'lone *sm* (*pubblicitario*) advertising poster; (*della tombola*) scoring frame; (*TEAT*) playbill; **tenere il** ~ (*spettacolo*) to have a long run.

carti'era *sf* paper mill.

carti'lagine [karti'ladʒine] *sf* cartilage.

car'tina *sf* (*AUT, GEO*) map.

car'toccio [kar'tɔttʃo] *sm* paper bag; **cuocere al** ~ (*CUC*) to bake in tinfoil.

cartogra'fia *sf* cartography.

carto'laio, a *sm/f* stationer.

cartole'ria *sf* stationer's (shop) (*BRIT*).

carto'lina *sf* postcard; ~ **di auguri** greetings card; ~ **precetto** *o* **rosa** (*MIL*) call-up card.

carto'mante *sm/f* fortune-teller (*using cards*).

carton'cino [karton'tʃino] *sm* (*materiale*) thin cardboard; (*biglietto*) card; ~ **della società** compliments slip.

car'tone *sm* cardboard; (*del latte, dell'aranciata*) carton; (*ARTE*) cartoon; ~**i animati** (*CINE*) cartoons.

car'tuccia, ce [kar'tuttʃa] *sf* cartridge; ~ **a salve** blank cartridge; **mezza** ~ (*fig*: *persona*) good-for-nothing.

'**casa** *sf* house; (*specialmente la propria* ~) home; (*COMM*) firm, house; **essere a** ~ to be at home; **vado a** ~ **mia/tua** I'm going home/to your house; ~ **di correzione** ≈ community home (*BRIT*), reformatory (*US*); ~ **di cura** nursing home; ~ **editrice** publishing house; **C~ delle Libertà** House of Liberties, *centre-right coalition*; ~ **di riposo** (old people's) home, care home; ~ **dello studente** student hostel; ~ **di tolleranza,** ~ **d'appuntamenti** brothel; **~e popolari** ≈ council houses (*o* flats) (*BRIT*), ≈ public housing units (*US*).

ca'sacca, che *sf* military coat; (*di fantino*) blouse.

ca'sale *sm* (*gruppo di case*) hamlet; (*casa di campagna*) farmhouse.

casa'lingo, a, ghi, ghe *ag* household, domestic; (*fatto a casa*) home-made; (*semplice*) homely; (*amante della casa*) home-loving ♦ *sf* housewife; ~**ghi** *smpl* (*oggetti*) household articles; **cucina** ~**a** plain home cooking.

ca'sata *sf* family lineage.

ca'sato *sm* family name.

casca'morto *sm* woman-chaser; **fare il** ~ **to** chase women.

cas'care *vi* to fall; ~ **bene/male** (*fig*) to land lucky/unlucky; ~ **dalle nuvole** (*fig*) to be taken aback; ~ **dal sonno** to be falling asleep on one's feet; **caschi il mondo** no matter what; **non cascherà il mondo se ...** it won't be the end of the world if ....

cas'cata *sf* fall; (*d'acqua*) cascade, waterfall.

cascherò *etc* [kaske'rɔ] *vb vedi* **cascare**.

ca'scina [kaʃ'ʃina] *sf* farmstead.

casci'nale [kaʃʃi'nale] *sm* (*casolare*) farmhouse; (*cascina*) farmstead.

'casco, schi *sm* helmet; (*del parrucchiere*) hair-dryer; (*di banane*) bunch; ~ **blu** (*MIL*) blue helmet (*UN soldier*).

caseggi'ato [kased'dʒato] *sm* (*edificio*) large block of flats (*BRIT*) *o* apartment building (*US*); (*gruppo di case*) group of houses.

casei'ficio [kazei'fitʃo] *sm* creamery.

ca'sella *sf* pigeonhole; ~ **postale (C.P.)** post office box (P.O. box).

casel'lario *sm* (*mobile*) filing cabinet; (*raccolta di pratiche*) files *pl*; ~ **giudiziale** court records *pl*; ~ **penale** police files *pl*.

ca'sello *sm* (*di autostrada*) tollgate.

case'reccio, a, ci, ce [kase'rettʃo] *ag* home-made.

ca'serma *sf* barracks *pl*.

caser'tano, a *ag* of (*o* from) Caserta.

ca'sino *sm* (*confusione*) row, racket; (*casa di prostituzione*) brothel.

casinò *sm inv* casino.

ca'sistica *sf* (*MED*) record of cases; **secondo la** ~ **degli incidenti stradali**

according to road accident data.

'caso *sm* chance; (*fatto, vicenda*) event, incident; (*possibilità*) possibility; (*MED, LING*) case; **a** ~ at random; **per** ~ by chance, by accident; **in ogni** ~, **in tutti i** ~**i** in any case, at any rate; **in** ~ **contrario** otherwise; **al** ~ should the opportunity arise; **nel** ~ **che** in case; ~ **mai** if by chance; **far** ~ **a qc/qn** to pay attention to sth/sb; **fare** *o* **porre** *o* **mettere il** ~ **che** to suppose that; **fa proprio al** ~ **nostro** it's just what we need; **guarda** ~ ... strangely enough ...; **è il** ~ **che ce ne andiamo** we'd better go; ~ **limite** borderline case.

caso'lare *sm* cottage.

'Caspio *sm*: **il mar** ~ the Caspian Sea.

'caspita *escl* (*di sorpresa*) good heavens!; (*di impazienza*) for goodness' sake!

'cassa *sf* case, crate, box; (*bara*) coffin; (*mobile*) chest; (*involucro: di orologio etc*) case; (*macchina*) cash register; (*luogo di pagamento*) cash desk, checkout (counter); (*fondo*) fund; (*istituto bancario*) bank; **battere** ~ (*fig*) to come looking for money; ~ **automatica prelievi** automatic telling machine, cash dispenser; ~ **continua** night safe; **mettere in** ~ **integrazione** ≈ to lay off; **C~ del Mezzogiorno** *development fund for the South of Italy*; ~ **mutua** *o* **malattia** health insurance scheme; ~ **di risonanza** (*MUS*) soundbox; (*fig*) platform; ~ **di risparmio** savings bank; ~ **rurale e artigiana** credit institution (*serving farmers and craftsmen*); ~ **toracica** (*ANAT*) chest.

cassa'forte, *pl* **casse'forti** *sf* safe.

cassa'panca, *pl* **cassa'panche** *o* **casse'panche** *sf* settle.

casseru'ola, casse'rola *sf* saucepan.

cas'setta *sf* box; (*per registratore*) cassette; (*CINE, TEAT*) box-office takings *pl*; **pane a** *o* **in** ~ toasting loaf; **film di** ~ (*commerciale*) box-office draw; **far** ~ to be a box-office success; ~ **delle lettere** letterbox; ~ **di sicurezza** strongbox.

cas'setto *sm* drawer.

casset'tone *sm* chest of drawers.

cassi'ere, a *sm/f* cashier; (*di banca*) teller.

cassinte'grato, a *sm/f* person who has been laid off.

cas'sone *sm* (*cassa*) large case, large chest.

'casta *sf* caste.

cas'tagna [kas'tapɲa] *sf* chestnut; **prendere qn in** ~ (*fig*) to catch sb in the act.

cas'tagno [kas'tapɲo] *sm* chestnut (tree).

cas'tano, a *ag* chestnut (brown).

cas'tello *sm* castle; (*TECN*) scaffolding.

casti'gare *vt* to punish.

casti'gato, a *ag* (*casto, modesto*) pure, chaste; (*emendato: prosa, versione*) expurgated, amended.

cas'tigo, ghi *sm* punishment.

castità *sf* chastity.

'casto, a *ag* chaste, pure.

cas'toro *sm* beaver.

cas'trante *ag* frustrating.

cas'trare *vt* to castrate; to geld; to doctor (*BRIT*), fix (*US*); (*fig: iniziativa*) to frustrate.

castrone'ria *sf* (*fam*): **dire ~e** to talk rubbish.

casu'ale *ag* chance *cpd*.

ca'supola *sf* simple little cottage.

catac'lisma, i *sm* (*fig*) catastrophe.

cata'comba *sf* catacomb.

cata'fascio [kata'faʃʃo] *sm*: **andare a ~** to collapse; **mandare a ~** to wreck.

cata'litico, a, ci, che *ag*: **marmitta ~a** (*AUT*) catalytic converter.

cataliz'zare [katalid'dzare] *vt* (*fig*) to act as a catalyst (up)on.

cataliz'zato, a [katalid'dzato] *ag* (*AUT*) with catalytic converter.

catalizza'tore [kataliddza'tore] *sm* (*anche* *fig*) catalyst; (*AUT*) catalytic converter.

Cata'logna [kata'loɲɲa] *sf*: **la ~** Catalonia.

ca'talogo, ghi *sm* catalogue; **~ dei prezzi** price list.

cata'nese *ag* of (*o* from) Catania.

catanza'rese [katandza'rese] *ag* of (*o* from) Catanzaro.

cata'pecchia [kata'pekkja] *sf* hovel.

cata'pulta *sf* catapult.

catarifran'gente [katarifran'dʒɛnte] *sm* (*AUT*) reflector.

ca'tarro *sm* catarrh.

ca'tarsi *sf inv* catharsis.

ca'tasta *sf* stack, pile.

ca'tasto *sm* land register; land registry office.

ca'tastrofe *sf* catastrophe, disaster.

catas'trofico, a, ci, che *ag* (*evento*) catastrophic; (*persona, previsione*) pessimistic.

cate'chismo [kate'kizmo] *sm* catechism.

catego'ria *sf* category; (*di albergo*) class.

cate'gorico, a, ci, che *ag* categorical.

ca'tena *sf* chain; **reazione a ~** chain reaction; **susseguirsi a ~** to happen in quick succession; **~ alimentare** food chain; **~ di montaggio** assembly line; **~ montuosa** mountain range; **~e da neve** (*AUT*) snow chains.

cate'naccio [kate'nattʃo] *sm* bolt.

cate'nella *sf* (*ornamento*) chain; (*di orologio*) watch chain; (*di porta*) door chain.

cate'ratta *sf* cataract; (*chiusa*) sluice gate.

ca'terva *sf* (*di cose*) loads *pl*, heaps *pl*; (*di persone*) horde.

cate'tere *sm* (*MED*) catheter.

cati'nella *sf*: **piovere a ~e** to pour, rain cats and dogs.

ca'tino *sm* basin.

ca'todico, a, ci, che *ag*: **tubo a raggi ~ci** cathode-ray tube.

ca'torcio [ka'tɔrtʃo] *sm* (*peg*) old wreck.

ca'trame *sm* tar.

'cattedra *sf* teacher's desk; (*di università*) chair; **salire** *o* **montare in ~** (*fig*) to pontificate.

catte'drale *sf* cathedral.

catte'dratico, a, ci, che *ag* (*insegnamento*) university *cpd*; (*ironico*) pedantic ♦ *sm/f* professor.

catti'veria *sf* (*qualità*) wickedness; (*di bambino*) naughtiness; (*azione*) wicked action; **fare una ~** to do something wicked; to be naughty.

cattività *sf* captivity.

cat'tivo, a *ag* bad; (*malvagio*) bad, wicked; (*turbolento: bambino*) bad, naughty; (*: mare*) rough; (*odore, sapore*) nasty, bad ♦ *sm/f* bad *o* wicked person; **farsi ~ sangue** to worry, get in a state; **farsi un ~ nome** to earn o.s. a bad reputation; **i ~i** (*nei film*) the baddies (*BRIT*), the bad guys (*US*).

cattocomu'nista, i, e *ag combining* Catholic and communist ideas.

cattoli'cesimo [kattoli'tʃezimo] *sm* Catholicism.

cat'tolico, a, ci, che *ag*, *sm/f* (Roman) Catholic.

cat'tura *sf* capture.

cattu'rare *vt* to capture.

cau'casico, a, ci, che *ag*, *sm/f* Caucasian.

'Caucaso *sm*: **il ~** the Caucasus.

caucciù [kaut'tʃu] *sm* rubber.

'causa *sf* cause; (*DIR*) lawsuit, case, action; **a ~ di** because of; **per ~ sua** because of him; **fare** *o* **muovere ~ a qn** to take legal action against sb; **parte in ~** litigant.

cau'sale *ag* (*LING*) causal ♦ *sf* cause, reason.

cau'sare *vt* to cause.

'caustico, a, ci, che *ag* caustic.

cau'tela *sf* caution, prudence.

caute'lare *vt* to protect; **~rsi** *vr*: **~rsi (da** *o* **contro)** to take precautions (against).

'cauto, a *ag* cautious, prudent.

cauzio'nare [kauttsjo'nare] *vt* to guarantee.

cauzi'one [kaut'tsjone] *sf* security; (*DIR*) bail; **rilasciare dietro ~** to release on bail.

cav. *abbr* = **cavaliere**.

'cava *sf* quarry.

caval'care *vt* (*cavallo*) to ride; (*muro*) to sit astride; (*sog: ponte*) to span.
caval'cata *sf* ride; (*gruppo di persone*) riding party.
cavalca'via *sm inv* flyover.
cavalci'oni [kaval'tʃoni]: **a ~ di** *prep* astride.
cavali'ere *sm* rider; (*feudale, titolo*) knight; (*soldato*) cavalryman; (*al ballo*) partner.
cavalleg'gero [kavalled'dʒɛro] *sm* (*MIL*) light cavalryman.
cavalle'resco, a, schi, sche *ag* chivalrous.
cavalle'ria *sf* chivalry; (*milizia a cavallo*) cavalry.
cavalle'rizzo, a [kavalle'rittso] *sm/f* riding instructor; circus rider.
caval'letta *sf* grasshopper; (*dannosa*) locust.
caval'letto *sm* (*FOT*) tripod; (*da pittore*) easel.
caval'lina *sf* (*GINNASTICA*) horse; (*gioco*) leap-frog; **correre la ~** (*fig*) to sow one's wild oats.
ca'vallo *sm* horse; (*SCACCHI*) knight; (*AUT: anche:* **~ vapore**) horsepower; (*dei pantaloni*) crotch; **a ~** on horseback; **a ~ di** astride, straddling; **siamo a ~** (*fig*) we've made it; **da ~** (*fig: dose*) drastic; (*: febbre*) raging; **vivere a ~ tra due periodi** to straddle two periods; **~ di battaglia** (*TEAT*) tour de force; (*fig*) hobbyhorse; **~ da corsa** racehorse; **~ a dondolo** rocking horse; **~ da sella** saddle horse; **~ da soma** packhorse.
ca'vare *vt* (*togliere*) to draw out, extract, take out; (*: giacca, scarpe*) to take off; (*: fame, sete, voglia*) to satisfy; **~rsi** *vr*: **~rsi da** (*guai, problemi*) to get out of; **cavarsela** to get away with it; to manage, get on all right; **non ci caverà un bel nulla** you'll get nothing out of it (*o him etc*).
cava'tappi *sm inv* corkscrew.
ca'verna *sf* cave.
caver'noso, a *ag* (*luogo*) cavernous; (*fig: voce*) deep; (*: tosse*) raucous.
ca'vezza [ka'vettsa] *sf* halter.
'cavia *sf* guinea pig.
cavi'ale *sm* caviar.
ca'viglia [ka'viʎʎa] *sf* ankle.
cavil'lare *vi* to quibble.
ca'villo *sm* quibble.
cavil'loso, a *ag* quibbling, hair-splitting.
cavità *sf inv* cavity.
'cavo, a *ag* hollow ♦ *sm* (*ANAT*) cavity; (*grossa corda*) rope, cable; (*ELETTR, TEL*) cable.
cavo'lata *sf* (*fam*) stupid thing.
cavolfi'ore *sm* cauliflower.

'cavolo *sm* cabbage; **non m'importa un ~** (*fam*) I don't give a hoot; **che ~ vuoi?** (*fam*) what the heck do you want?; **~ di** **Bruxelles** Brussels sprout.
caz'zata [kat'tsata] *sf* (*fam!: stupidaggine*) stupid thing, something stupid.
'cazzo ['kattso] *sm* (*fam!: pene*) prick (*!*); **non gliene importa un ~** (*fig fam!*) he doesn't give a damn about it; **fatti i ~i tuoi** (*fig fam!*) mind your own damn business.
caz'zotto [kat'tsotto] *sm* punch; **fare a ~i to** have a punch-up.
cazzu'ola [kat'tswɔla] *sf* trowel.
CB *sigla* = *Campobasso*.
CC *abbr* = *Carabinieri*.
cc *abbr* (= *centimetro cubico*) cc.
C.C. *abbr* = **codice civile**.
c.c. *abbr* (= *conto corrente*) c/a, a/c; (*ELETTR*) *vedi* **corrente continua**.
c/c *abbr* (= *conto corrente*) c/a, a/c.
C.C.D. *sigla m* (*POL* = *Centro Cristiano Democratico*) *party originating from Democrazia Cristiana*.
CCI *sigla f* (= *Camera di Commercio Internazionale*) ICC (= *International Chamber of Commerce*).
CCIAA *abbr* = *Camera di Commercio Industria, Agricoltura e Artigianato*.
CCT *sigla m vedi* **certificato di credito del** **Tesoro**.
C.D. *abbr* (= *Corpo Diplomatico*) CD ♦ *sm inv* (= *compact disc*) CD.
c.d. *abbr* = **cosiddetto**.
C.d.A. *abbr* = **Consiglio di Amministrazione**.
c.d.d. *abbr* (= *come dovevasi dimostrare*) QED (= *quod erat demonstrandum*).
C.d.M. *abbr* = **Cassa del Mezzogiorno**.
CD-Rom [tʃidi'rɔm] *sigla m inv* (= *Compact Disc Read Only Memory*) CD-Rom.
C.d.U. [tʃidi'u] *sigla m* (= *Cristiano Democratici Uniti*) United Christian Democrats (*Italian centre-right political party*).
CE *sigla* = *Caserta*.
ce [tʃe] *pron, av vedi* **ci**.
C.E. *sigla* = **Consiglio d'Europa**.
cec'chino [tʃek'kino] *sm* sniper; (*POL*) *member of parliament who votes against his own party*.
'cece ['tʃetʃe] *sm* chickpea, garbanzo (*US*).
Ce'cenia [tʃe'tʃenja] *sf* Chechnya.
ce'ceno, a [tʃe'tʃeno] *ag, sm/f* Chechen.
cecità [tʃetʃi'ta] *sf* blindness.
'ceco, a, chi, che ['tʃɛko] *ag, sm/f, sm* Czech; **la Repubblica C~a** the Czech Republic.
Cecoslo'vacchia [tʃekozlo'vakkja] *sf*: **la ~** Czechoslovakia.

cecoslo'vacco, a, chi, che [tʃekozlo'vakko] ag, sm/f Czechoslovakian.
CED [tʃɛd] sigla m = centro elaborazione dati.
'cedere ['tʃɛdere] vt (concedere: posto) to give up; (DIR) to transfer, make over ♦ vi (cadere) to give way, subside; ~ (a) to surrender (to), yield (to), give in (to); ~ il passo (a qn) to let (sb) pass in front; ~ il passo a qc (fig) to give way to sth; ~ la parola (a qn) to hand over (to sb).
ce'devole [tʃe'devole] ag (terreno) soft; (fig) yielding.
'cedola ['tʃɛdola] sf (COMM) coupon; voucher.
ce'drata [tʃe'drata] sf citron juice.
'cedro ['tʃɛdro] sm cedar; (albero da frutto, frutto) citron.
'CEE ['tʃee] sigla f vedi Comunità Economica Europea.
'ceffo ['tʃɛffo] sm (peg) ugly mug.
cef'fone [tʃef'fone] sm slap, smack.
'ceko, a ['tʃɛko] ag, sm/f, sm = ceco.
ce'lare [tʃe'lare] vt to conceal; ~rsi vr to hide.
cele'brare [tʃele'brare] vt to celebrate; (cerimonia) to hold; ~ le lodi di qc/qn to sing the praises of sth/sb.
celebrazi'one [tʃelebrat'tsjone] sf celebration.
'celebre ['tʃɛlebre] ag famous, celebrated.
celebrità [tʃelebri'ta] sf inv fame; (persona) celebrity.
'celere ['tʃɛlere] ag fast, swift; (corso) crash cpd ♦ sf (POLIZIA) riot police.
ce'leste [tʃe'lɛste] ag celestial; heavenly; (colore) sky-blue.
'celia [tʃɛlja] sf joke; per ~ for a joke.
celi'bato [tʃeli'bato] sm celibacy.
'celibe ['tʃɛlibe] ag single, unmarried ♦ sm bachelor.
'cella ['tʃɛlla] sf cell; ~ di rigore punishment cell.
cello'phane ® [sɛlo'fan] sm cellophane ®.
'cellula ['tʃɛllula] sf (BIOL, ELETTR, POL) cell.
cellu'lare [tʃellu'lare] ag cellular ♦ sm (furgone) police van; (telefono) cellphone; segregazione ~ (DIR) solitary confinement.
cellu'lite [tʃellu'lite] sf cellulitis.
'celta ['tʃelta] sm/f Celt.
'celtico, a, ci, che ['tʃeltiko] ag, sm Celtic.
'cembalo ['tʃembalo] sm (MUS) harpsichord.
cemen'tare [tʃemen'tare] vt (anche fig) to cement.
ce'mento [tʃe'mento] sm cement; ~ armato reinforced concrete.

'cena ['tʃena] sf dinner; (leggera) supper.
ce'nacolo [tʃe'nakolo] sm (circolo) coterie, circle; (REL, dipinto) Last Supper.
ce'nare [tʃe'nare] vi to dine, have dinner.
'cencio ['tʃentʃo] sm piece of cloth, rag; (per spolverare) duster; essere bianco come un ~ to be as white as a sheet.
'cenere ['tʃenere] sf ash.
Cene'rentola [tʃene'rɛntola] sf (anche fig) Cinderella.
'cenno ['tʃenno] sm (segno) sign, signal; (gesto) gesture; (col capo) nod; (con la mano) wave; (allusione) hint, mention; (breve esposizione) short account; far ~ di sì/no to nod (one's head)/shake one's head; ~ d'intesa sign of agreement; ~i di storia dell'arte an outline of the history of art.
censi'mento [tʃensi'mento] sm census.
cen'sire [tʃen'sire] vt to take a census of.
'CENSIS ['tʃensis] sigla m (= Centro Studi Investimenti Sociali) independent institute carrying out research on Italy's social and cultural welfare.
cen'sore [tʃen'sore] sm censor.
cen'sura [tʃen'sura] sf censorship; censor's office; (fig) censure.
censu'rare [tʃensu'rare] vt to censor; to censure.
cent. abbr = centesimo.
centelli'nare [tʃentelli'nare] vt to sip; (fig) to savour (BRIT), savor (US).
cente'nario, a [tʃente'narjo] ag (che ha cento anni) hundred-year-old; (che ricorre ogni cento anni) centennial, centenary cpd ♦ sm/f centenarian ♦ sm centenary.
cen'tesimo, a [tʃen'tɛzimo] ag, sm hundredth; (di euro, dollaro) cent; essere senza un ~ to be penniless.
cen'tigrado, a [tʃen'tigrado] ag centigrade; 20 gradi ~i 20 degrees centigrade.
cen'tilitro [tʃen'tilitro] sm centilitre.
cen'timetro [tʃen'timetro] sm centimetre (BRIT), centimeter (US); (nastro) measuring tape (in centimetres).
centi'naio, pl(f) -aia [tʃenti'najo] sm: un ~ (di) a hundred; about a hundred.
'cento ['tʃento] num a hundred, one hundred; per ~ per cent; al ~ per ~ a hundred per cent; ~ di questi giorni! many happy returns (of the day)!
centodi'eci [tʃento'djetʃi] num one hundred and ten; ~ e lode (UNIVERSITÀ) ≈ first-class honours.
cento'mila [tʃento'mila] num a o one hundred thousand; te l'ho detto ~ volte (fig) I've told you a thousand times.
Cen'trafrica [tʃen'trafrika] sm: il ~ the

Central African Republic.

cen'trale [tʃen'trale] ag central ♦ sf: ~
elettrica electric power station; ~ del
latte dairy; ~ di polizia police
headquarters pl; ~ telefonica (telephone)
exchange; sede ~ head office.

centrali'nista [tʃentrali'nista] sm/f operator.

centra'lino [tʃentra'lino] sm (telephone)
exchange; (di albergo etc) switchboard.

centraliz'zare [tʃentralid'dzare] vt to
centralize.

cen'trare [tʃen'trare] vt to hit the centre
(BRIT) o center (US) of; (TECN) to centre; ~
una risposta to get the right answer; ha
centrato il problema you've hit the nail on
the head.

centra'vanti [tʃentra'vanti] sm inv centre
forward.

cen'trifuga [tʃen'trifuga] sf spin-dryer.

centrifu'gare [tʃentrifu'gare] vt (TECN) to
centrifuge; (biancheria) to spin-dry.

'centro ['tʃentro] sm centre (BRIT), center
(US); fare ~ to hit the bull's eye; (CALCIO)
to score; (fig) to hit the nail on the head;
~ balneare seaside resort; ~ commerciale
shopping centre; (città) commercial
centre; ~ di costo cost centre; ~
elaborazione dati data-processing unit; ~
ospedaliero hospital complex; ~ sociale
community centre; ~i vitali (anche fig)
vital organs.

centromedi'ano [tʃentrome'djano] sm
(CALCIO) centre half.

'ceppo ['tʃeppo] sm (di albero) stump; (pezzo
di legno) log.

'cera ['tʃera] sf wax; (aspetto) appearance,
look; ~ per pavimenti floor polish.

cera'lacca [tʃera'lakka] sf sealing wax.

ce'ramica, che [tʃe'ramika] sf ceramic;
(ARTE) ceramics sg.

cerbi'atto [tʃer'bjatto] sm fawn.

'cerca ['tʃerka] sf: in o alla ~ di in search of.

cercaper'sone [tʃerkaper'sone] sm inv
bleeper.

cer'care [tʃer'kare] vt to look for, search
for ♦ vi: ~ di fare qc to try to do sth.

cercherò etc [tʃerke'rɔ] vb vedi cercare.

'cerchia ['tʃerkja] sf circle.

cerchi'ato, a [tʃer'kjato] ag: occhiali ~i
d'osso horn-rimmed spectacles; avere gli
occhi ~i to have dark rings under one's
eyes.

'cerchio ['tʃerkjo] sm circle; (giocattolo, di
botte) hoop; dare un colpo al ~ e uno alla
botte (fig) to keep two things going at the
same time.

cerchi'one [tʃer'kjone] sm (wheel)rim.

cere'ale [tʃere'ale] sm cereal.

cere'brale [tʃere'brale] ag cerebral.

ceri'monia [tʃeri'mɔnja] sf ceremony;
senza tante ~e (senza formalità)
informally; (bruscamente)
unceremoniously, without so much as a
by-your-leave.

cerimoni'ale [tʃerimo'njale] sm etiquette;
ceremonial.

cerimoni'ere [tʃerimo'njɛre] sm master of
ceremonies.

cerimoni'oso, a [tʃerimo'njoso] ag formal,
ceremonious.

ce'rino [tʃe'rino] sm wax match.

CERN [tʃern] sigla m (= Comitato Europeo di
Ricerche Nucleari) CERN.

'cernia ['tʃernja] sf (ZOOL) stone bass.

cerni'era [tʃer'njɛra] sf hinge; ~ lampo zip
(fastener) (BRIT), zipper (US).

'cernita ['tʃernita] sf selection; fare una ~
di to select.

'cero ['tʃero] sm (church) candle.

ce'rone [tʃe'rone] sm (trucco) greasepaint.

ce'rotto [tʃe'rɔtto] sm sticking plaster.

certa'mente [tʃerta'mente] av certainly,
surely.

cer'tezza [tʃer'tettsa] sf certainty.

certifi'care [tʃertifi'kare] vt to certify.

certifi'cato [tʃertifi'kato] sm certificate; ~
medico/di nascita medical/birth
certificate; ~ di credito del Tesoro (CCT)
treasury bill.

certificazi'one [tʃertifikat'tsjone] sf
certification; ~ di bilancio (COMM)
external audit.

═══════════════ PAROLA CHIAVE

'certo, a ['tʃerto] ag (sicuro): ~ (di/che)
certain o sure (of/that)
♦ det 1 (tale) certain; un ~ signor Smith a
(certain) Mr Smith
2 (qualche; con valore intensivo) some;
dopo un ~ tempo after some time; un
fatto di una ~a importanza a matter of
some importance; di una ~a età past
one's prime, not so young
♦ pron: ~i, e pl some
♦ av (certamente) certainly; (senz'altro) of
course; di ~ certainly; no (di) ~!, ~ che
no! certainly not!; sì ~ yes indeed,
certainly.

certo'sino [tʃerto'zino] sm Carthusian
monk; (liquore) chartreuse; è un lavoro da
~ it's a pernickety job.

cer'tuni [tʃer'tuni] pron pl some (people).

ce'rume [tʃe'rume] sm (ear) wax.

'cerva ['tʃɛrva] sf (female) deer, doe.

cer'vello, pl i (anche: pl(f) a o e) [tʃer'vɛllo]

sm brain; ~ **elettronico** computer; **avere il**
o **essere un** ~ **fino** to be sharp-witted; **è**
uscito di ~, **gli è dato di volta il** ~ he's
gone off his head.
cervi'cale [tʃervi'kale] *ag* cervical.
'cervo, a ['tʃɛrvo] *sm/f* stag/hind ♦ *sm* deer;
~ **volante** stag beetle.
cesel'lare [tʃezel'lare] *vt* to chisel; (*incidere*)
to engrave.
ce'sello [tʃe'zɛllo] *sm* chisel.
ce'soie [tʃe'zoje] *sfpl* shears.
ces'puglio [tʃes'puʎʎo] *sm* bush.
ces'sare [tʃes'sare] *vi, vt* to stop, cease; ~ **di
fare qc** to stop doing sth; **"cessato
allarme"** "all clear".
ces'sate il fu'oco [tʃes'sate-] *sm*
ceasefire.
cessazi'one [tʃessat'tsjone] *sf* cessation;
(*interruzione*) suspension.
cessi'one [tʃes'sjone] *sf* transfer.
'cesso ['tʃɛsso] *sm* (*fam: gabinetto*) bog.
'cesta ['tʃesta] *sf* (large) basket.
ces'tello [tʃes'tɛllo] *sm* (*per bottiglie*) crate;
(*di lavatrice*) drum.
cesti'nare [tʃesti'nare] *vt* to throw away;
(*fig: proposta*) to turn down; (: *romanzo*) to
reject.
ces'tino [tʃes'tino] *sm* basket; (*per la carta
straccia*) wastepaper basket; ~ **da viaggio**
(*FERR*) packed lunch (*o* dinner).
'cesto ['tʃesto] *sm* basket.
ce'sura [tʃe'zura] *sf* caesura.
ce'taceo [tʃe'tatʃeo] *sm* sea mammal.
'ceto ['tʃeto] *sm* (social) class.
'cetra ['tʃetra] *sf* (*MUS*) zither; (*fig: di poeta*)
lyre.
cetrio'lino [tʃetrio'lino] *sm* gherkin.
cetri'olo [tʃetri'ɔlo] *sm* cucumber.
Cf., Cfr. *abbr* (= *confronta*) cf.
CFC [tʃiɛffe'tʃi] *abbr mpl*
(= *clorofluorocarburi*) CFC.
CFS *sigla m* (= *Corpo Forestale dello Stato*)
*body responsible for the planting and
management of forests.*
cg *abbr* (= *centigrammo*) cg.
C.G.I.L. [tʃidʒi'elle] *sigla f* (= *Confederazione
Generale Italiana del Lavoro*) *trades union
organization.*
CH *sigla* = *Chieti*.
cha'let [ʃa'lɛ] *sm inv* chalet.
cham'pagne [ʃã'paɲ] *sm inv* champagne.
chance [ʃãs] *sf inv* chance.
charme [ʃarm] *sm* charm.
'charter ['tʃaːtər] *ag inv* (*volo*) charter *cpd*;
(*aereo*) chartered ♦ *sm inv* chartered
plane.
chat'tare [tʃat'tare] *vi* to chat; (*online*) to
chat.

─────── **PAROLA CHIAVE**

che [ke] *pron* **1** (*relativo: persona: soggetto*)
who; (: *oggetto*) whom, that; (: *cosa,
animale*) which, that; **il ragazzo** ~ **è venuto**
the boy who came; **l'uomo** ~ **io vedo** the
man (whom) I see; **il libro** ~ **è sul tavolo**
the book which *o* that is on the table; **il
libro** ~ **vedi** the book (which *o* that) you
see; **la sera** ~ **ti ho visto** the evening I
saw you
2 (*interrogativo, esclamativo*) what; ~
(cosa) fai? what are you doing?; **a** ~ **(cosa)
pensi?** what are you thinking about?; **non
sa** ~ **(cosa) fare** he doesn't know what to
do; **sai di** ~ **si tratta?** do you know what
it's about?; ~ **(cosa) succede?** what's
happening?; **ma** ~ **dici!** what are you
saying!
3 (*indefinito*): **quell'uomo ha un** ~ **di losco**
there's something suspicious about that
man; **un certo non so** ~ an indefinable
something; **non è un gran** ~ it's nothing
much
♦ *det* **1** (*interrogativo: tra tanti*) what; (: *tra
pochi*) which; ~ **tipo di film preferisci?**
what sort of film do you prefer?; ~
vestito ti vuoi mettere? what (*o* which)
dress do you want to put on?
2 (*esclamativo: seguito da aggettivo*) how;
(: *seguito da sostantivo*) what; ~ **buono!**
how delicious!; ~ **bel vestito!** what a
lovely dress!; ~ **macchina!** what a car!
♦ *cong* **1** (*con proposizioni subordinate*) that;
credo ~ **verrà** I think he'll come; **voglio** ~
tu studi I want you to study; **so** ~ **tu c'eri**
I know (that) you were there; **non** ~ **sia
sbagliato, ma** ... not that it's wrong, but ...
2 (*finale*) so that; **vieni qua,** ~ **ti veda** come
here, so (that) I can see you; **stai attento** ~
non cada mind it doesn't fall
3 (*temporale*): **arrivai** ~ **eri già partito** you
had already left when I arrived; **sono
anni** ~ **non lo vedo** I haven't seen him for
years
4 (*in frasi imperative, concessive*): ~ **venga
pure!** let him come by all means!; ~ **tu sia
benedetto!** may God bless you!; ~ **tu venga
o no partiamo lo stesso** we're going
whether you come or not
5 (*comparativo: con più, meno*) than; **è più
lungo** ~ **largo** it's longer than it's wide; **più
bella** ~ **mai** more beautiful than ever; *vedi
anche* **più; meno; così** *etc*.

'checca, che ['kekka] *sf* (*fam: omosessuale*)
fairy.
chef [ʃɛf] *sm inv* chef.

chemiotera'pia [kemjotera'pia] *sf*
chemotherapy.

chero'sene [kero'zɛne] *sm* kerosene.

cheru'bino [keru'bino] *sm* cherub.

che'tare [ke'tare] *vt* to hush, silence; ~**rsi** *vr*
to quieten down, fall silent.

cheti'chella [keti'kɛlla]: **alla** ~ *av* stealthily,
unobtrusively; **andarsene alla** ~ to slip
away.

'cheto, a ['keto] *ag* quiet, silent.

=============== PAROLA CHIAVE

chi [ki] *pron* **1** (*interrogativo: soggetto*) who;
(: *oggetto*) who, whom; ~ **è?** who is it?; **di**
~ **è questo libro?** whose book is this?,
whose is this book?; **con** ~ **parli?** who are
you talking to?; **a** ~ **pensi?** who are you
thinking about?; ~ **di voi?** which of you?;
non so a ~ **rivolgermi** I don't know who to
ask
2 (*relativo*) whoever, anyone who; **dillo a**
~ **vuoi** tell whoever you like; **portate** ~
volete bring anyone you like; **so io di** ~
parlo I know who I'm talking about; **lo**
riferirò a ~ **di dovere** I'll pass it on to the
relevant person
3 (*indefinito*): ~ ... ~ ... some ... others ...;
~ **dice una cosa,** ~ **dice un'altra** some say
one thing, others say another.

chiacchie'rare [kjakkje'rare] *vi* to chat;
(*discorrere futilmente*) to chatter; (*far*
pettegolezzi) to gossip.

chiacchie'rata [kjakkje'rata] *sf* chat; **farsi**
una ~ to have a chat.

chi'acchiere ['kjakkjere] *sfpl* chatter *no pl*;
gossip *no pl*; **fare due o quattro** ~ to have a
chat; **perdersi in** ~ to waste time
talking.

chiacchie'rone, a [kjakkje'rone] *ag*
talkative, chatty; gossipy ♦ *sm/f*
chatterbox; gossip.

chia'mare [kja'mare] *vt* to call; (*rivolgersi a*
qn) to call (in), send for; ~**rsi** *vr* (*aver*
nome) to be called; **mi chiamo Paolo** my
name is Paolo, I'm called Paolo; **mandare**
a ~ **qn** to send for sb, call sb in; ~ **alle**
armi to call up; ~ **in giudizio** to summon;
~ **qn da parte** to take sb aside.

chia'mata [kja'mata] *sf* (*TEL*) call; (*MIL*)
call-up; ~ **interurbana** long-distance call;
~ **con preavviso** person-to-person call; ~
alle urne (*POL*) election.

chi'appa ['kjappa] *sf* (*fam: natica*) cheek; ~**e**
sfpl bottom *sg*.

chi'ara ['kjara] *sf* egg white.

chia'rezza [kja'rettsa] *sf* clearness; clarity.

chiarifi'care [kjarifi'kare] *vt* (*anche fig*) to

clarify.

chiarificazi'one [kjarifikat'tsjone] *sf*
clarification.

chiari'mento [kjari'mento] *sm* clarification
no pl, explanation.

chia'rire [kja'rire] *vt* to make clear; (*fig:*
spiegare) to clear up, explain; ~**rsi** *vr* to
become clear; **si sono chiariti** they've
sorted things out.

chi'aro, a ['kjaro] *ag* clear; (*luminoso*)
clear, bright; (*colore*) pale, light ♦ *av*
(*parlare, vedere*) clearly; **si sta facendo** ~
the day is dawning; **sia** ~**a una cosa** let's
get one thing straight; **mettere in** ~ **qc**
(*fig*) to clear sth up; **parliamoci** ~ let's be
frank; **trasmissione in** ~ (*TV*) uncoded
broadcast.

chia'rore [kja'rore] *sm* (diffuse) light.

chiaroveg'gente [kjaroved'dʒɛnte] *sm/f*
clairvoyant.

chi'asso ['kjasso] *sm* uproar, row; **far** ~ to
make a din; (*fig*) to make a fuss;
(: *scalpore*) to cause a stir.

chias'soso, a [kjas'soso] *ag* noisy, rowdy;
(*vistoso*) showy, gaudy.

'chiatta ['kjatta] *sf* barge.

chi'ave ['kjave] *sf* key ♦ *ag inv* key *cpd*;
chiudere a ~ to lock; ~ **d'accensione**
(*AUT*) ignition key; ~ **a forcella** fork
spanner; ~ **inglese** monkey wrench; **in** ~
politica in political terms; ~ **di volta**
(*anche fig*) keystone; ~**i in mano**
(*contratto*) turn-key *cpd*; **prezzo** ~**i in mano**
(*di macchina*) on-the-road price.

chiavis'tello [kjavis'tɛllo] *sm* bolt.

chi'azza ['kjattsa] *sf* stain, splash.

chiaz'zare [kjat'tsare] *vt* to stain, splash.

chic [ʃik] *ag inv* chic, elegant.

chicches'sia [kikkes'sia] *pron* anyone,
anybody.

'chicco, chi ['kikko] *sm* (*di cereale, riso*)
grain; (*di caffè*) bean; ~ **di grandine**
hailstone; ~ **d'uva** grape.

chi'edere ['kjɛdere] *vt* (*per sapere*) to ask;
(*per avere*) to ask for ♦ *vi*: ~ **di qn** to ask
after sb; (*al telefono*) to ask for *o* want sb;
~**rsi** *vr*: ~**rsi (se)** to wonder (whether); ~
qc a qn to ask sb sth; to ask sb for sth; ~
scusa a qn to apologize to sb; ~
l'elemosina to beg; **non chiedo altro** that's
all I want.

chieri'chetto [kjeri'ketto] *sm* altar boy.

chi'erico, ci ['kjeriko] *sm* cleric; altar boy.

chi'esa ['kjɛza] *sf* church.

chi'esi *etc* ['kjɛzi] *vb vedi* **chiedere**.

chi'esto, a ['kjɛsto] *pp di* **chiedere**.

'Chigi ['kidʒi]: **palazzo** ~ *sm* (*POL*) *offices of*
the Italian Prime Minister.

'chiglia ['kiʎʎa] sf keel.
'chilo ['kilo] sm kilo.
chilo'grammo [kilo'grammo] sm
kilogram(me).
chilome'traggio [kilome'traddʒo] sm (AUT)
≈ mileage.
chilo'metrico, a, ci, che [kilo'mεtriko] ag
kilometric; (fig) endless.
chi'lometro [ki'lɔmetro] sm kilometre
(BRIT), kilometer (US).
'chimico, a, ci, che ['kimiko] ag chemical
♦ sm/f chemist ♦ sf chemistry.
chi'mono [ki'mɔno] sm inv kimono.
'china ['kina] sf (pendio) slope, descent;
(BOT) cinchona; (inchiostro di) ~ Indian
ink; risalire la ~ (fig) to be on the road to
recovery.
chi'nare [ki'nare] vt to lower, bend; ~rsi vr
to stoop, bend.
chincaglie'ria [kinkaʎʎe'ria] sf fancy-goods
shop; ~e sfpl fancy goods, knick-knacks.
chi'nino [ki'nino] sm quinine.
'chino, a ['kino] ag: a capo ~, a testa ~a
head bent o bowed.
chi'occia, ce ['kjɔttʃa] sf brooding
hen.
chi'occio, a, ci, ce ['kjɔttʃo] ag (voce)
clucking.
chi'occiola ['kjɔttʃola] sf snail; (di indirizzo
e-mail) at; scala a ~ spiral staircase.
chi'odo ['kjɔdo] sm nail; (fig) obsession; ~
scaccia ~ (proverbio) one problem drives
away another; roba da ~i! it's
unbelievable!; ~ di garofano (CUC)
clove.
chi'oma ['kjɔma] sf (capelli) head of hair;
(di albero) foliage.
chi'osco, schi ['kjɔsko] sm kiosk,
stall.
chi'ostro ['kjɔstro] sm cloister.
chiro'mante [kiro'mante] sm/f palmist;
(indovino) fortune-teller.
chirur'gia [kirur'dʒia] sf surgery.
chi'rurgico, a, ci, che [ki'rurdʒiko] ag
(anche fig) surgical.
chi'rurgo, ghi o gi [ki'rurgo] sm surgeon.
chissà [kis'sa] av who knows, I wonder.
chi'tarra [ki'tarra] sf guitar.
chitar'rista, i, e [kitar'rista] sm/f guitarist,
guitar player.
chi'udere ['kjudere] vt to close, shut;
(luce, acqua) to put off, turn off;
(definitivamente: fabbrica) to close down,
shut down; (strada) to close; (recingere) to
enclose; (porre termine) to end ♦ vi to
close, shut; to close down, shut down; to
end; ~rsi vr to shut, close; (ritirarsi: anche
fig) to shut o.s. away; (ferita) to close up;

~ un occhio su (fig) to turn a blind eye
to; chiudi la bocca! o il becco! (fam) shut
up!
chi'unque [ki'unkwe] pron (relativo)
whoever; (indefinito) anyone, anybody; ~
sia whoever it is.
'chiusi etc ['kjusi] vb vedi chiudere.
chi'uso, a ['kjuso] pp di chiudere ♦ ag (porta)
shut, closed; (: a chiave) locked; (senza
uscita: strada etc) blocked off; (rubinetto)
off; (persona) uncommunicative;
(ambiente, club) exclusive ♦ sm: stare al ~
(fig) to be shut up ♦ sf (di corso d'acqua)
sluice, lock; (recinto) enclosure; (di
discorso etc) conclusion, ending; "~"
(negozio etc) "closed"; "~ al pubblico" "no
admittance to the public".
chiu'sura [kju'sura] sf closing; shutting;
closing o shutting down; enclosing;
putting o turning off; ending; (dispositivo)
catch; fastening; fastener; orario di ~
closing time; ~ lampo ® zip (fastener)
(BRIT), zipper (US).

========= PAROLA CHIAVE

ci [tʃi] (dav lo, la, li, le, ne diventa ce) pron 1
(personale: complemento oggetto) us; (: a
noi: complemento di termine) (to) us;
(: riflessivo) ourselves; (: reciproco) each
other, one another; (impersonale): ~ si
veste we get dressed; ~ ha visti he's seen
us; non ~ ha dato niente he gave us
nothing; ~ vestiamo we get dressed; ~
amiamo we love one another o each
other; ~ siamo divertiti we had a good
time
2 (dimostrativo: di ciò, su ciò, in ciò etc)
about (o on o of) it; non ~ capisco nulla I
can't make head nor tail of it; non so cosa
far~ I don't know what to do about it; che
~ posso fare? what can I do about it?; che
c'entro io? what have I got to do with it?;
~ puoi giurare you can bet on it; ~ puoi
contare you can depend on it; ~ sei? (sei
pronto?) are you ready?; (hai capito?) are
you with me?
♦ av (qui) here; (lì) there; (moto attraverso
luogo): ~ passa sopra un ponte a
bridge passes over it; non ~ passa più
nessuno nobody comes this way any
more; qui ~ abito da un anno I've been
living here for a year; esser~ vedi
essere.

C.I. abbr = carta d'identità.
CIA ['tʃia] sigla f (= Central Intelligence
Agency) CIA.
C.ia abbr (= compagnia) Co.

cia'batta [tʃa'batta] *sf* mule, slipper.
ciabat'tino [tʃabat'tino] *sm* cobbler.
ciac [tʃak] *sm* (*CINE*) clapper board; ~, **si gira!** action!
Ci'ad [tʃad] *sm*: **il** ~ Chad.
ci'alda ['tʃalda] *sf* (*CUC*) wafer.
cial'trone [tʃal'trone] *sm* good-for-nothing.
ciam'bella [tʃam'bella] *sf* (*CUC*) ring-shaped cake; (*salvagente*) rubber ring.
ci'ancia, ce ['tʃantʃa] *sf* gossip *no pl*, tittle-tattle *no pl*.
cianfru'saglie [tʃanfru'zaʎʎe] *sfpl* bits and pieces.
cia'nuro [tʃa'nuro] *sm* cyanide.
ci'ao ['tʃao] *escl* (*all'arrivo*) hello!; (*alla partenza*) cheerio! (*BRIT*), bye!
ciar'lare [tʃar'lare] *vi* to chatter; (*peg*) to gossip.
ciarla'tano [tʃarla'tano] *sm* charlatan.
cias'cuno, a [tʃas'kuno] (*dav sm*: **ciascun** +*C, V*, **ciascuno** +*s impura, gn, pn, ps, x, z*; *dav sf*: **ciascuna** +*C*, **ciascun'** +*V*) *det, pron* each.
ci'bare [tʃi'bare] *vt* to feed; ~**rsi** *vr*: ~**rsi di** to eat.
ci'barie [tʃi'barje] *sfpl* foodstuffs.
ciber'netica [tʃiber'nɛtika] *sf* cybernetics *sg*.
'cibo ['tʃibo] *sm* food.
ci'cala [tʃi'kala] *sf* cicada.
cica'trice [tʃika'tritʃe] *sf* scar.
cicatriz'zarsi [tʃikatrid'dzarsi] *vr* to form a scar, heal (up).
'cicca, che ['tʃikka] *sf* cigarette end; (*fam*: *sigaretta*) fag; **non vale una** ~ (*fig*) it's worthless.
'ciccia ['tʃittʃa] *sf* (*fam*: *carne*) meat; (: *grasso umano*) fat, flesh.
cicci'one, a [tʃit'tʃone] *sm/f* (*fam*) fatty.
cice'rone [tʃitʃe'rone] *sm* guide.
cicla'mino [tʃikla'mino] *sm* cyclamen.
ci'clismo [tʃi'klizmo] *sm* cycling.
ci'clista, i, e [tʃi'klista] *sm/f* cyclist.
'ciclo ['tʃiklo] *sm* cycle; (*di malattia*) course.
ciclomo'tore [tʃiklomo'tore] *sm* moped.
ci'clone [tʃi'klone] *sm* cyclone.
ciclos'tile [tʃiklos'tile] *sm* cyclostyle (*BRIT*).
ci'cogna [tʃi'koɲɲa] *sf* stork.
ci'coria [tʃi'kɔrja] *sf* chicory.
ci'eco, a, chi, che ['tʃɛko] *ag* blind ♦ *sm/f* blind man/woman; **alla** ~**a** (*anche fig*) blindly.
ciel'lino, a [tʃiel'lino] *sm/f* (*POL*) member of CL movement.
ci'elo ['tʃɛlo] *sm* sky; (*REL*) heaven; **toccare il** ~ **con un dito** (*fig*) to walk on air; **per amor del** ~! for heavens' sake!

'cifra ['tʃifra] *sf* (*numero*) figure, numeral; (*somma di denaro*) sum, figure; (*monogramma*) monogram, initials *pl*; (*codice*) code, cipher.
ci'frare [tʃi'frare] *vt* (*messaggio*) to code; (*lenzuola etc*) to embroider with a monogram.
'ciglio ['tʃiʎʎo] *sm* (*margine*) edge, verge; (*pl*(*f*) **ciglia**: *delle palpebre*) (eye)lash; (*sopracciglio*) eyebrow; **non ha battuto** ~ (*fig*) he didn't bat an eyelid.
'cigno ['tʃiɲɲo] *sm* swan.
cigo'lante [tʃigo'lante] *ag* squeaking, creaking.
cigo'lare [tʃigo'lare] *vi* to squeak, creak.
'Cile ['tʃile] *sm*: **il** ~ Chile.
ci'lecca [tʃi'lekka] *sf*: **far** ~ to fail.
ci'leno, a [tʃi'lɛno] *ag, sm/f* Chilean.
cili'egia, gie *o* **ge** [tʃi'ljɛdʒa] *sf* cherry.
cilie'gina [tʃiljɛ'dʒina] *sf* glacé cherry; **la** ~ **sulla torta** (*fig*) the icing *o* cherry on the cake.
cili'egio [tʃi'ljɛdʒo] *sm* cherry tree.
cilin'drata [tʃilin'drata] *sf* (*AUT*) (cubic) capacity; **una macchina di grossa** ~ a big-engined car.
ci'lindro [tʃi'lindro] *sm* cylinder; (*cappello*) top hat.
CIM [tʃim] *sigla m* = *centro d'igiene mentale*.
'cima ['tʃima] *sf* (*sommità*) top; (*di monte*) top, summit; (*estremità*) end; (*fig*: *persona*) genius; **in** ~ **a** at the top of; **da** ~ **a fondo** from top to bottom; (*fig*) from beginning to end.
ci'melio [tʃi'mɛljo] *sm* relic.
cimen'tarsi [tʃimen'tarsi] *vr*: ~**rsi in** (*atleta*, *concorrente*) to try one's hand at.
'cimice ['tʃimitʃe] *sf* (*ZOOL*) bug; (*puntina*) drawing pin (*BRIT*), thumbtack (*US*).
cimini'era [tʃimi'njɛra] *sf* chimney; (*di nave*) funnel.
cimi'tero [tʃimi'tɛro] *sm* cemetery.
ci'murro [tʃi'murro] *sm* (*di cani*) distemper.
'Cina ['tʃina] *sf*: **la** ~ China.
cin'cin, cin cin [tʃin'tʃin] *escl* cheers!
cincischi'are [tʃintʃis'kjare] *vi* to mess about.
'cine ['tʃine] *sm inv* (*fam*) cinema.
cine'asta, i, e [tʃine'asta] *sm/f* person in the film industry; film-maker.
cinegior'nale [tʃinedʒor'nale] *sm* newsreel.
'cinema ['tʃinema] *sm inv* cinema; ~ **muto** silent films; ~ **d'essai** (*locale*) avant-garde cinema, experimental cinema.
cinemato'grafico, a, ci, che [tʃinemato'grafiko] *ag* (*attore, critica*) movie *cpd*, film *cpd*; (*festival*) film *cpd*; **sala** ~**a** cinema; **successo** ~ box-office success.

cinema'tografo [tʃinema'tɔgrafo] sm cinema.

cine'presa [tʃine'presa] sf cine-camera.

ci'nese [tʃi'nese] ag, sm/f, sm Chinese inv.

cine'teca, che [tʃine'tɛka] sf (collezione) film collection; (locale) film library.

ci'netico, a, ci, che [tʃi'nɛtiko] ag kinetic.

'cingere ['tʃindʒere] vt (attorniare) to surround, encircle; ~ **la vita con una cintura** to put a belt round one's waist; ~ **d'assedio** to besiege, lay siege to.

'cinghia ['tʃingja] sf strap; (cintura, TECN) belt; **tirare la** ~ (fig) to tighten one's belt.

cinghi'ale [tʃin'gjale] sm wild boar.

cinguet'tare [tʃingwet'tare] vi to twitter.

'cinico, a, ci, che ['tʃiniko] ag cynical ♦ sm/f cynic.

ci'nismo [tʃi'nizmo] sm cynicism.

cin'quanta [tʃin'kwanta] num fifty.

cinquante'nario [tʃinkwante'narjo] sm fiftieth anniversary.

cinquan'tenne [tʃinkwan'tɛnne] sm/f fifty-year-old man/woman.

cinquan'tesimo, a [tʃinkwan'tɛzimo] num fiftieth.

cinquan'tina [tʃinkwan'tina] sf (serie): **una** ~ **(di)** about fifty; (età): **essere sulla** ~ to be about fifty.

'cinque ['tʃinkwe] num five; **avere** ~ **anni** to be five (years old); **il** ~ **dicembre 1988** the fifth of December 1988; **alle** ~ (ora) at five (o'clock); **siamo in** ~ there are five of us.

cinquecen'tesco, a, schi, sche [tʃinkwetʃen'tesko] ag sixteenth-century.

cinque'cento [tʃinkwe'tʃento] num five hundred ♦ sm: **il C**~ the sixteenth century.

cinque'mila [tʃinkwe'mila] num five thousand.

'cinsi etc ['tʃinsi] vb vedi **cingere**.

'cinta ['tʃinta] sf (anche: ~ **muraria**) city walls pl; **muro di** ~ (di giardino etc) surrounding wall.

cin'tare [tʃin'tare] vt to enclose.

'cinto, a ['tʃinto] pp di **cingere**.

'cintola ['tʃintola] sf (cintura) belt; (vita) waist.

cin'tura [tʃin'tura] sf belt; ~ **di salvataggio** lifebelt (BRIT), life preserver (US); ~ **di sicurezza** (AUT, AER) safety o seat belt.

cintu'rino [tʃintu'rino] sm strap; ~ **dell'orologio** watch strap.

CIO sigla m (= Comitato Internazionale Olimpico) IOC (= International Olympic Committee).

ciò [tʃɔ] pron this; that; ~ **che** what; ~ **nonostante** o **nondimeno** nevertheless, in spite of that; **con tutto** ~ for all that, in spite of everything.

ci'occa, che ['tʃɔkka] sf (di capelli) lock.

ciocco'lata [tʃokko'lata] sf chocolate; (bevanda) (hot) chocolate; ~ **al latte/fondente** milk/plain chocolate.

cioccola'tino [tʃokkola'tino] sm chocolate.

ciocco'lato [tʃokko'lato] sm chocolate.

cio'è [tʃo'ɛ] av that is (to say).

ciondo'lare [tʃondo'lare] vt (far dondolare) to dangle, swing ♦ vi to dangle; (fig) to loaf (about).

ci'ondolo ['tʃondolo] sm pendant; ~ **portafortuna** charm.

ciondo'loni [tʃondo'loni] av: **con le braccia/gambe** ~ with arms/legs dangling.

ciononos'tante [tʃononos'tante] av nonetheless, nevertheless.

ci'otola ['tʃɔtola] sf bowl.

ci'ottolo ['tʃɔttolo] sm pebble; (di strada) cobble(stone).

C.I.P. [tʃip] sigla m (= comitato interministeriale prezzi) vedi **comitato**.

Cipe ['tʃipe] sigla m (= comitato interministeriale per la programmazione economica) vedi **comitato**.

'Cipi ['tʃipi] sigla m (= comitato interministeriale per lo sviluppo industriale) vedi **comitato**.

ci'piglio [tʃi'piʎʎo] sm frown.

ci'polla [tʃi'polla] sf onion; (di tulipano etc) bulb.

cipol'lina [tʃipol'lina] sf onion; ~ **e sottaceto** pickled onions; ~ **e sottolio** baby onions in oil.

ci'presso [tʃi'prɛsso] sm cypress (tree).

'cipria ['tʃiprja] sf (face) powder.

cipri'ota, i, e [tʃipri'ɔta] ag, sm/f Cypriot.

'Cipro ['tʃipro] sm Cyprus.

'circa ['tʃirka] av about, roughly ♦ prep about, concerning; **a mezzogiorno** ~ about midday.

'circo, chi ['tʃirko] sm circus.

circo'lare [tʃirko'lare] vi to circulate; (AUT) to drive (along), move (along) ♦ ag circular ♦ sf (AMM) circular; (di autobus) circle (line); **circola voce che ...** there is a rumour going about that ...; **assegno** ~ banker's draft.

circolazi'one [tʃirkolat'tsjone] sf circulation; (AUT): **la** ~ (the) traffic; **libretto di** ~ log book, registration book; **tassa di** ~ road tax; ~ **a targhe alterne** vedi nota nel riquadro.

CIRCOLAZIONE A TARGHE ALTERNE

Circolazione a targhe alterne was introduced by some town councils to combat the increase in traffic and pollution in town centres. _It stipulates that on days with an even date, only cars whose number plate ends in an even number or a zero may be on the road; on days with an odd date, only cars with odd registration numbers may be used. Public holidays are generally, but not always, exempt._

'circolo ['tʃirkolo] sm circle; **entrare in** ~ (ANAT) to enter the bloodstream.

circoncisi'one [tʃirkontʃi'zjone] sf circumcision.

circon'dare [tʃirkon'dare] vt to surround.

circondari'ale [tʃirkonda'rjale] ag: **casa di pena** ~ district prison.

circon'dario [tʃirkon'darjo] sm (DIR) administrative district; (zona circostante) neighbourhood (BRIT), neighborhood (US).

circonfe'renza [tʃirkonfe'rentsa] sf circumference.

circonvallazi'one [tʃirkonvallat'tsjone] sf ring road (BRIT), beltway (US); (per evitare una città) by-pass.

circos'critto, a [tʃirkos'kritto] pp di **circoscrivere**.

circos'crivere [tʃirkos'krivere] vt to circumscribe; (fig) to limit, restrict.

circoscrizi'one [tʃirkoskrit'tsjone] sf (AMM) district, area; ~ **elettorale** constituency.

circos'petto, a [tʃirkos'pɛtto] ag circumspect, cautious.

circos'tante [tʃirkos'tante] ag surrounding, neighbouring (BRIT), neighboring (US).

circos'tanza [tʃirkos'tantsa] sf circumstance; (occasione) occasion; **parole di** ~ words suited to the occasion.

circu'ire [tʃirku'ire] vt (fig) to fool, take in.

cir'cuito [tʃir'kuito] sm circuit; **andare in o fare corto** ~ to short-circuit; ~ **integrato** integrated circuit.

ci'rillico, a, ci, che [tʃi'rilliko] ag Cyrillic.

cir'rosi [tʃir'rɔzi] sf: ~ **epatica** cirrhosis (of the liver).

'C.I.S.A.L. ['tʃizal] sigla f (= Confederazione Italiana Sindacati Autonomi dei Lavoratori) trades union organization.

C.I.S.L. [tʃizl] sigla f (= Confederazione Italiana Sindacati Lavoratori) trades union organization.

'C.I.S.N.A.L. ['tʃiznal] sigla f (= Confederazione Italiana Sindacati Nazionali dei Lavoratori) trades union organization.

'ciste ['tʃiste] sf = **cisti**.

cis'terna [tʃis'tɛrna] sf tank, cistern.

'cisti ['tʃisti] sf inv cyst.

cis'tite [tʃis'tite] sf cystitis.

'C.I.T. [tʃit] sigla f = Compagnia Italiana Turismo.

cit. abbr (= citato, citata) cit.

ci'tare [tʃi'tare] vt (DIR) to summon; (autore) to quote; (a esempio, modello) to cite; ~ **qn per danni** to sue sb.

citazi'one [tʃitat'tsjone] sf summons sg; quotation; (di persona) mention.

ci'tofono [tʃi'tɔfono] sm entry phone; (in uffici) intercom.

cito'logico, a, ci, che [tʃito'lɔdʒiko] ag: **esame** ~ test for detection of cancerous cells.

'citrico, a, ci, che ['tʃitriko] ag citric.

città [tʃit'ta] sf inv town; (importante) city; ~ **giardino** garden city; ~ **mercato** shopping centre, mall; ~ **universitaria** university campus; **C**~ **del Capo** Cape Town.

citta'della [tʃitta'dɛlla] sf citadel, stronghold.

cittadi'nanza [tʃittadi'nantsa] sf citizens pl, inhabitants pl of a town (o city); (DIR) citizenship.

citta'dino, a [tʃitta'dino] ag town cpd; city cpd ♦ sm/f (di uno Stato) citizen; (abitante di città) town dweller, city dweller.

ci'uccio ['tʃuttʃo] sm (fam) comforter, dummy (BRIT), pacifier (US).

ci'uco, a, chi, che ['tʃuko] sm/f ass.

ci'uffo ['tʃuffo] sm tuft.

ci'urma ['tʃurma] sf (di nave) crew.

ci'vetta [tʃi'vetta] sf (ZOOL) owl; (fig: donna) coquette, flirt ♦ ag inv: **auto/nave** ~ decoy car/ship; **fare la** ~ **con qn** to flirt with sb.

civet'tare [tʃivet'tare] vi to flirt.

civette'ria [tʃivette'ria] sf coquetry, coquettishness.

civettu'olo, a [tʃivet'twɔlo] ag flirtatious.

'civico, a, ci, che ['tʃiviko] ag civic; (museo) municipal, town cpd; **guardia** ~**a** town policeman; **senso** ~ public spirit.

ci'vile [tʃi'vile] ag civil; (non militare) civilian; (nazione) civilized ♦ sm civilian; **stato** ~ marital status; **abiti** ~**i** civvies.

civi'lista, i, e [tʃivi'lista] sm/f (avvocato) civil lawyer; (studioso) expert in civil law.

civiliz'zare [tʃivilid'dzare] vt to civilize.

civilizzazi'one [tʃiviliddzat'tsjone] sf civilization.

civiltà [tʃivil'ta] sf civilization; (cortesia) civility.

ci'vismo [tʃi'vizmo] sm public spirit.

CL [tʃi'elle] sigla f (POL: = Comunione e Liberazione) Catholic youth movement ♦ sigla = Caltanissetta.

cl abbr (= centilitro) cl.

'clacson sm inv (AUT) horn.

cla'more sm (frastuono) din, uproar, clamour (BRIT), clamor (US); (fig) outcry.

clamo'roso, a *ag* noisy; (*fig*) sensational.

clan *sm inv* clan.

clandestinità *sf* (*di attività*) secret nature; **vivere nella** ~ to live in hiding; (*ricercato politico*) to live underground.

clandes'tino, a *ag* clandestine; (*POL*) underground, clandestine ♦ *sm/f* stowaway; (*anche*: **immigrato** ~) illegal immigrant.

clari'netto *sm* clarinet.

'classe *sf* class; **di** ~ (*fig*) with class; of excellent quality; ~ **turistica** (*AER*) economy class.

classi'cismo [klassi'tʃizmo] *sm* classicism.

'classico, a, ci, che *ag* classical; (*tradizionale: moda*) classic(al) ♦ *sm* classic; classical author; (*anche*: **liceo** ~) secondary school with emphasis on humanities.

clas'sifica, che *sf* classification; (*SPORT*) placings *pl*; (*di dischi*) charts *pl*.

classifi'care *vt* to classify; (*candidato, compito*) to grade; ~**rsi** *vr* to be placed.

classifica'tore *sm* filing cabinet.

classificazi'one [klassifikat'tsjone] *sf* classification; grading.

clas'sista, i, e *ag* class-conscious ♦ *sm/f* class-conscious person.

claudi'cante *ag* (*zoppo*) lame; (*fig: prosa*) halting.

'clausola *sf* (*DIR*) clause.

claustro'fobico, a, ci, che *ag* claustrophobic.

clau'sura *sf* (*REL*): **monaca di** ~ nun belonging to an enclosed order; **fare una vita di** ~ (*fig*) to lead a cloistered life.

'clava *sf* club.

clavi'cembalo [klavi'tʃembalo] *sm* harpsichord.

cla'vicola *sf* (*ANAT*) collarbone.

cle'mente *ag* merciful; (*clima*) mild.

cle'menza [kle'mɛntsa] *sf* mercy, clemency; mildness.

clep'tomane *sm/f* kleptomaniac.

cleri'cale *ag* clerical.

'clero *sm* clergy.

cles'sidra *sf* (*a sabbia*) hourglass; (*ad acqua*) water clock.

clic'care *vi* (*INFORM*): ~ **su** to click on.

cliché [kli'ʃe] *sm inv* (*TIP*) plate; (*fig*) cliché.

cli'ente *sm/f* customer, client.

clien'tela *sf* customers *pl*, clientèle.

cliente'lismo *sm*: ~ **politico** political nepotism.

'clima, i *sm* climate.

cli'matico, a, ci, che *ag* climatic; **stazione** ~**a** health resort.

climatizza'tore [klimatiddza'tore] *sm* air

conditioner.

climatizzazi'one [klimatiddzat'tsjone] *sf* air conditioning.

'clinico, a, ci, che *ag* clinical ♦ *sm* (*medico*) clinician ♦ *sf* (*scienza*) clinical medicine; (*casa di cura*) clinic, nursing home; (*settore d'ospedale*) clinic; **quadro** ~ anamnesis; **avere l'occhio** ~ (*fig*) to have an expert eye.

clis'tere *sm* (*MED*) enema; (: *apparecchio*) device used to give an enema.

clo'aca, che *sf* sewer.

cloche [klɔʃ] *sf inv* control stick, joystick; **cambio a** ~ (*AUT*) floor-mounted gear lever.

clo'nare *vt* to clone.

clona'zione [clonat'tsjone] *sf* (*BIOL, fig*) cloning.

'cloro *sm* chlorine.

cloro'filla *sf* chlorophyll.

cloro'formio *sm* chloroform.

club *sm inv* club.

cm *abbr* (= *centimetro*) cm.

c.m. *abbr* (= *corrente mese*) inst.

CN *sigla* = *Cuneo*.

c/n *abbr* = *conto nuovo*.

CNEN *sigla m* (= *Comitato Nazionale per l'Energia Nucleare*) ~ ΛΕΑ (*BRIT*), ΛEC (*US*).

CNR *sigla m* (= *Consiglio Nazionale delle Ricerche*) *science research council*.

CNRN *sigla m* = *Comitato Nazionale Ricerche Nucleari*.

CO *sigla* = *Como*.

Co. *abbr* (= *compagnia*) Co.

c/o *abbr* (= *care of*) c/o.

coabi'tare *vi* to live together.

coagu'lare *vt* to coagulate ♦ *vi*, ~**rsi** *vr* to coagulate; (*latte*) to curdle.

coalizi'one [koalit'tsjone] *sf* coalition.

co'atto, a *ag* (*DIR*) compulsory, forced; **condannare al domicilio** ~ to place under house arrest.

'COBAS *sigla mpl* (= *Comitati di base*) independent trades unions.

'cobra *sm inv* cobra.

'coca 'cola ® *sf* coca cola ®.

coca'ina *sf* cocaine.

coc'carda *sf* cockade.

cocchi'ere [kok'kjɛre] *sm* coachman.

'cocchio ['kɔkkjo] *sm* (*carrozza*) coach; (*biga*) chariot.

cocci'nella [kottʃi'nɛlla] *sf* ladybird (*BRIT*), ladybug (*US*).

'coccio ['kɔttʃo] *sm* earthenware; (*vaso*) earthenware pot; ~**i** *smpl* fragments (of pottery).

cocciu'taggine [kottʃu'taddʒine] *sf*

stubbornness, pig-headedness.
cocci'uto, a [kot'tʃuto] *ag* stubborn, pigheaded.
'**cocco, chi** *sm* (*pianta*) coconut palm; (*frutto*): **noce di** ~ coconut ◊ *sm/f* (*fam*) darling; **è il** ~ **della mamma** he's mummy's darling.
cocco'drillo *sm* crocodile.
cocco'lare *vt* to cuddle, fondle.
co'cente [ko'tʃɛnte] *ag* (*anche fig*) burning.
cocerò *etc* [kotʃe'rɔ] *vb vedi* **cuocere**.
co'comero *sm* watermelon.
co'cuzzolo [ko'kuttsolo] *sm* top; (*di capo, cappello*) crown.
cod. *abbr* = **codice**.
'**coda** *sf* tail; (*fila di persone, auto*) queue (*BRIT*), line (*US*); (*di abiti*) train; **con la** ~ **dell'occhio** out of the corner of one's eye; **mettersi in** ~ to queue (up) (*BRIT*), line up (*US*); to join the queue *o* line; ~ **di cavallo** (*acconciatura*) ponytail; **avere la** ~ **di paglia** (*fig*) to have a guilty conscience; ~ **di rospo** (*CUC*) frogfish tail.
codar'dia *sf* cowardice.
co'dardo, a *ag* cowardly ◊ *sm/f* coward.
co'desto, a *ag, pron* (*poetico*) this; that.
'**codice** ['kɔditʃe] *sm* code; (*manoscritto antico*) codex; ~ **di avviamento postale** (**CAP**) postcode (*BRIT*), zip code (*US*); ~ **a barre** bar code; ~ **civile** civil code; ~ **fiscale** tax code; ~ **penale** penal code; ~ **segreto** (*di tessera magnetica*) PIN (number); ~ **della strada** highway code.
co'difica *sf* codification; (*INFORM: di programma*) coding.
codifi'care *vt* (*DIR*) to codify; (*cifrare*) to code.
codificazi'one [kodifikat'tsjone] *sf* coding.
coercizi'one [koertʃit'tsjone] *sf* coercion.
coe'rente *ag* coherent.
coe'renza [koe'rentsa] *sf* coherence.
coesi'one *sf* cohesion.
coe'sistere *vi* to coexist.
coe'taneo, a *ag, sm/f* contemporary; **essere** ~ **di qn** to be the same age as sb.
cofa'netto *sm* casket; ~ **dei gioielli** jewel case.
'**cofano** *sm* (*AUT*) bonnet (*BRIT*), hood (*US*); (*forziere*) chest.
'**coffa** *sf* (*NAUT*) top.
'**cogli** ['koʎʎi] *prep* + *det vedi* **con**.
'**cogliere** ['kɔʎʎere] *vt* (*fiore, frutto*) to pick, gather; (*sorprendere*) to catch, surprise; (*bersaglio*) to hit; (*fig: momento opportuno etc*) to grasp, seize, take; (: *capire*) to grasp; ~ **l'occasione** (**per fare**) to take the opportunity (to do); ~ **sul fatto** *o* **in flagrante/alla sprovvista** to catch red-

handed/unprepared; ~ **nel segno** (*fig*) to hit the nail on the head.
cogli'one [koʎ'ʎone] *sm* (*fam!: testicolo*): ~**i** balls (*!*); (: *fig: persona sciocca*) jerk; **rompere i** ~**i a qn** to get on sb's tits (*!*).
co'gnac [kɔ'ɲak] *sm inv* cognac.
co'gnato, a [koɲ'ɲato] *sm/f* brother-/sister-in-law.
cognizi'one [koɲɲit'tsjone] *sf* knowledge; **con** ~ **di causa** with full knowledge of the facts.
co'gnome [koɲ'ɲome] *sm* surname.
'**coi** *prep* + *det vedi* **con**.
coi'bente *ag* insulating.
coinci'denza [kointʃi'dɛntsa] *sf* coincidence; (*FERR, AER, di autobus*) connection.
coin'cidere [koin'tʃidere] *vi* to coincide.
coin'ciso, a [koin'tʃizo] *pp di* **coincidere**.
coinqui'lino *sm* fellow tenant.
cointeres'senza [kointeres'sɛntsa] *sf* (*COMM*): **avere una** ~ **in qc** to own shares in sth; ~ **dei lavoratori** profit-sharing.
coin'volgere [koin'vɔldʒere] *vt*: ~ **in** to involve in.
coinvolgi'mento [koinvoldʒi'mento] *sm* involvement.
coin'volto, a *pp di* **coinvolgere**.
col *prep* + *det vedi* **con**.
Col. *abbr* (= *colonnello*) Col.
colà *av* there.
cola'brodo *sm inv* strainer.
cola'pasta *sm inv* colander.
co'lare *vt* (*liquido*) to strain; (*pasta*) to drain; (*oro fuso*) to pour ◊ *vi* (*sudore*) to drip; (*botte*) to leak; (*cera*) to melt; ~ **a picco** *vt, vi* (*nave*) to sink.
co'lata *sf* (*di lava*) flow; (*FONDERIA*) casting.
colazi'one [kolat'tsjone] *sf* (*anche: prima* ~) breakfast; (*anche: seconda* ~) lunch; **fare** ~ to have breakfast (*o* lunch); ~ **di lavoro** working lunch.
Coldi'retti *abbr f* (= *Confederazione nazionale coltivatori diretti*) *federation of Italian farmers*.
co'lei *pron vedi* **colui**.
co'lera *sm* (*MED*) cholera.
coleste'rolo *sm* cholesterol.
colf *abbr f* = **collaboratrice familiare**.
'**colgo** *etc vb vedi* **cogliere**.
colibrì *sm* hummingbird.
'**colica** *sf* (*MED*) colic.
co'lino *sm* strainer.
'**colla** *prep* + *det vedi* **con** ◊ *sf* glue; (*di farina*) paste.
collabo'rare *vi* to collaborate; (*con la polizia*) to co-operate; ~ **a** to collaborate on; (*giornale*) to contribute to.

collabora'tore, 'trice *sm/f* collaborator; (*di giornale, rivista*) contributor; ~ **esterno** freelance; ~**trice familiare** home help; ~ **di giustizia** = **pentito, a.**

collaborazi'one [kollaborat'tsjone] *sf* collaboration; contribution.

col'lana *sf* necklace; (*collezione*) collection, series.

col'lant [kɔ'lã] *sm inv* tights *pl.*

col'lare *sm* collar.

col'lasso *sm* (*MED*) collapse.

collate'rale *ag* collateral; **effetti** ~**i** side effects.

col'laudo *sm* testing *no pl;* test.

'colle *prep* + *det vedi* **con** ♦ *sm* hill.

col'lega, ghi, ghe *sm/f* colleague.

collega'mento *sm* connection; (*MIL*) liaison; (*RADIO*) link(-up); (*INFORM*) link; **ufficiale di** ~ liaison officer; ~ **ipertestuale** hyperlink.

colle'gare *vt* to connect, join, link; ~**rsi** *vr* (*RADIO, TV*) to link up; ~**rsi con** (*TEL*) to get through to.

collegi'ale [kolle'dʒale] *ag* (*riunione, decisione*) collective; (*INS*) boarding school *cpd* ♦ *sm/f* boarder; (*fig: persona timida e inesperta*) schoolboy/girl.

col'legio [kol'lɛdʒo] *sm* college; (*convitto*) boarding school; ~ **elettorale** (*POL*) constituency.

'collera *sf* anger; **andare in** ~ to get angry.

col'lerico, a, ci, che *ag* quick-tempered, irascible.

col'letta *sf* collection.

collettività *sf* community.

collet'tivo, a *ag* collective; (*interesse*) general, everybody's; (*biglietto, visita etc*) group *cpd* ♦ *sm* (*POL*) (political) group; **società in nome** ~ (*COMM*) partnership.

col'letto *sm* collar; ~**i bianchi** (*fig*) white-collar workers.

collezio'nare [kollettsjo'nare] *vt* to collect.

collezi'one [kollet'tsjone] *sf* collection.

collezio'nista [kollettsjo'nista] *sm/f* collector.

colli'mare *vi* to correspond, coincide.

col'lina *sf* hill.

colli'nare *ag* hill *cpd.*

col'lirio *sm* eyewash.

collisi'one *sf* collision.

'collo *prep* + *det vedi* **con** ♦ *sm* neck; (*di abito*) neck, collar; (*pacco*) parcel; ~ **del piede** instep.

colloca'mento *sm* (*impiego*) employment; (*disposizione*) placing, arrangement; **ufficio di** ~ ≈ Jobcentre (*BRIT*), state (*o federal*) employment agency (*US*); ~ **a riposo** retirement.

collo'care *vt* (*libri, mobili*) to place; (*persona: trovare un lavoro per*) to find a job for, place; (*COMM: merce*) to find a market for; ~ **qn a riposo** to retire sb.

collocazi'one [kollokat'tsjone] *sf* placing; (*di libro*) classification.

colloqui'ale *ag* (*termine etc*) colloquial; (*tono*) informal.

col'loquio *sm* conversation, talk; (*ufficiale, per un lavoro*) interview; (*INS*) preliminary oral exam; **avviare un** ~ **con qn** (*POL etc*) to start talks with sb.

col'loso, a *ag* sticky.

col'lottola *sf* nape *o* scruff of the neck; **afferrare qn per la** ~ to grab sb by the scruff of the neck.

collusi'one *sf* (*DIR*) collusion.

colluttazi'one [kolluttat'tsjone] *sf* scuffle.

col'mare *vt*: ~ **di** (*anche fig*) to fill with; (*dare in abbondanza*) to load *o* overwhelm with; ~ **un divario** (*fig*) to bridge a gap.

'colmo, a *ag*: ~ (**di**) full (of) ♦ *sm* summit, top; (*fig*) height; **al** ~ **della disperazione** in the depths of despair; **è il** ~**!** it's the last straw!; **e per** ~ **di sfortuna** ... and to cap it all ....

co'lomba *sf vedi* **colombo.**

Co'lombia *sf.* **la** ~ Colombia.

colombi'ano, a *ag, sm/f* Colombian.

co'lombo, a *sm/f* dove; pigeon; ~**i** (*fig fam*) lovebirds.

Co'lonia *sf* Cologne.

co'lonia *sf* colony; (*per bambini*) holiday camp; (**acqua di**) ~ (eau de) cologne.

coloni'ale *ag* colonial ♦ *sm/f* colonist, settler.

co'lonico, a, ci, che *ag*: **casa** ~**a** farmhouse.

coloniz'zare [kolonid'dzare] *vt* to colonize.

co'lonna *sf* column; ~ **sonora** (*CINE*) sound track; ~ **vertebrale** spine, spinal column.

colon'nello *sm* colonel.

co'lono *sm* (*coltivatore*) tenant farmer.

colo'rante *sm* colouring (*BRIT*), coloring (*US*).

colo'rare *vt* to colour (*BRIT*), color (*US*); (*disegno*) to colo(u)r in.

co'lore *sm* colour (*BRIT*), color (*US*); (*CARTE*) suit; **a** ~**i** in colo(u)r, colo(u)r *cpd*; **la gente di** ~ colo(u)red people; **diventare di tutti i** ~**i** to turn scarlet; **farne di tutti i** ~**i** to get up to all sorts of mischief; **passarne di tutti i** ~**i** to go through all sorts of problems.

colo'rito, a *ag* coloured (*BRIT*), colored (*US*); (*viso*) rosy, pink; (*linguaggio*) colourful (*BRIT*), colorful (*US*) ♦ *sm* (*tinta*) colour (*BRIT*), color (*US*); (*carnagione*) complexion.

co'loro *pron pl vedi* **colui.**

çolos'sale *ag* colossal, enormous.

co'losso *sm* colossus.

'colpa *sf* fault; (*biasimo*) blame; (*colpevolezza*) guilt; (*azione colpevole*) offence; (*peccato*) sin; **di chi è la ~?** whose fault is it?; **è ~ sua** it's his fault; **per ~ di** through, owing to; **senso di ~** sense of guilt; **dare la ~ a qn di qc** to blame sb for sth.

col'pevole *ag* guilty.

colpevoliz'zare [kolpevolid'dzare] *vt*: **~ qn** to make sb feel guilty.

col'pire *vt* to hit, strike; (*fig*) to strike; **rimanere colpito da qc** to be amazed *o* struck by sth; **è stato colpito da ordine di cattura** there is a warrant out for his arrest; **~ nel segno** (*fig*) to hit the nail on the head, be spot on (*BRIT*).

'colpo *sm* (*urto*) knock; (*fig: affettivo*) blow, shock; (*: aggressivo*) blow; (*di pistola*) shot; (*MED*) stroke; (*furto*) raid; **di ~, tutto d'un ~** suddenly; **fare ~** to make a strong impression; **il motore perde ~i** (*AUT*) the engine is misfiring; **è morto sul ~** he died instantly; **mi hai fatto venire un ~!** what a fright you gave me!; **ti venisse un ~!** (*fam*) drop dead!; **~ d'aria** chill; **~ in banca** bank job *o* raid; **~ basso** (*PUGILATO, fig*) punch below the belt; **~ di fulmine** love at first sight; **~ di grazia** coup de grâce; (*fig*) finishing blow; **a ~ d'occhio** at a glance; **~ di scena** (*TEAT*) coup de théâtre; (*fig*) dramatic turn of events; **~ di sole** sunstroke; **~i di sole** (*nei capelli*) highlights; **~ di Stato** coup d'état; **~ di telefono** phone call; **~ di testa** (sudden) impulse *o* whim; **~ di vento** gust (of wind).

col'poso, a *ag*: **omicidio ~** manslaughter.

'colsi *etc vb vedi* **cogliere.**

coltel'lata *sf* stab.

col'tello *sm* knife; **avere il ~ dalla parte del manico** (*fig*) to have the whip hand; **~ a serramanico** clasp knife.

colti'vare *vt* to cultivate; (*verdura*) to grow, cultivate.

coltiva'tore *sm* farmer; **~ diretto** small independent farmer.

coltivazi'one [koltivat'tsjone] *sf* cultivation; growing; **~ intensiva** intensive farming.

'colto, a *pp di* **cogliere ♦** *ag* (*istruito*) cultured, educated.

'coltre *sf* blanket.

col'tura *sf* cultivation; **~ alternata** crop rotation.

co'lui, co'lei, *pl* **co'loro** *pron* the one; **~ che parla** the one *o* the man *o* the person who is speaking; **colei che amo** the one *o* the woman *o* the person (whom) I love.

com. *abbr* = **comunale; commissione.**

'coma *sm inv* coma.

comanda'mento *sm* (*REL*) commandment.

coman'dante *sm* (*MIL*) commander, commandant; (*di reggimento*) commanding officer; (*NAUT, AER*) captain.

coman'dare *vi* to be in command **♦** *vt* to command; (*imporre*) to order, command; **~ a qn di fare** to order sb to do.

co'mando *sm* (*ingiunzione*) order, command; (*autorità*) command; (*TECN*) control; **~ generale** general headquarters *pl*; **~ a distanza** remote control.

co'mare *sf* (*madrina*) godmother; (*donna pettegola*) gossip.

co'masco, a, schi, sche *ag* of (*o* from) Como.

combaci'are [komba'tʃare] *vi* to meet; (*fig: coincidere*) to coincide, correspond.

combat'tente *ag* fighting **♦** *sm* combatant; **ex-~** ex-serviceman.

com'battere *vt* to fight; (*fig*) to combat, fight against **♦** *vi* to fight.

combatti'mento *sm* fight; fighting *no pl*; (*di pugilato*) match; **mettere fuori ~** to knock out.

combat'tivo, a *ag* pugnacious.

combat'tuto, a *ag* (*incerto: persona*) uncertain, undecided; (*gara, partita*) hard fought.

combi'nare *vt* to combine; (*organizzare*) to arrange; (*fam: fare*) to make, cause **♦** *vi* (*corrispondere*): **~ (con)** to correspond (with).

combinazi'one [kombinat'tsjone] *sf* combination; (*caso fortuito*) coincidence; **per ~** by chance.

com'briccola *sf* (*gruppo*) party; (*banda*) gang.

combus'tibile *ag* combustible **♦** *sm* fuel.

combusti'one *sf* combustion.

com'butta *sf* (*peg*) gang; **in ~** in league.

=============== *PAROLA CHIAVE*

'come *av* **1** (*alla maniera di*) like; **ti comporti ~ lui** you behave like him *o* like he does; **bianco ~ la neve** (as) white as snow; **~ se** as if, as though; **com'è vero Dio!** as God is my witness!

2 (*in qualità di*) as a; **lavora ~ autista** he works as a driver

3 (*interrogativo*) how; ~ **ti chiami?** what's your name?; ~ **sta?** how are you?; **com'è il tuo amico?** what is your friend like?; ~? (*prego?*) pardon?, sorry?; ~ **mai?** how come?; ~ **mai non ci hai avvertiti?** how come you didn't warn us?
4 (*esclamativo*): ~ **sei bravo!** how clever you are!; ~ **mi dispiace!** I'm terribly sorry!

♦ *cong* 1 (*in che modo*) how; **mi ha spiegato** ~ **l'ha conosciuto** he told me how he met him; **non so** ~ **sia successo** I don't know how it happened; **attento a** ~ **parli!** watch your mouth!
2 (*correlativo*) as; (*con comparativi di maggioranza*) than; **non è bravo** ~ **pensavo** he isn't as clever as I thought; **è meglio di** ~ **pensassi** it's better than I thought
3 (*quasi se*) as; **è** ~ **se fosse ancora qui** it's as if he was still here; ~ **se niente fosse** as if nothing had happened; ~ **non detto!** let's forget it!
4 (*appena che, quando*) as soon as; ~ **arrivò, iniziò a lavorare** as soon as he arrived, he set to work; *vedi anche* **così;** **oggi; ora.**

'**COMECON** *abbr m* (= *Consiglio di Mutua Assistenza Economica*) COMECON.
come'done *sm* blackhead.
co'meta *sf* comet.
'**comico, a, ci, che** *ag* (*TEAT*) comic; (*buffo*) comical ♦ *sm* (*attore*) comedian, comic actor; (*comicità*) comic spirit, comedy.
co'mignolo [ko'miɲɲolo] *sm* chimney top.
cominci'are [komin't ʃare] *vt, vi* to begin, start; ~ **a fare/col fare** to begin to do/by doing; **cominciamo bene!** (*ironico*) we're off to a fine start!
comi'tato *sm* committee; ~ **direttivo** steering committee; ~ **di gestione** works council; ~ **interministeriale prezzi** interdepartmental committee on prices; ~ **interministeriale per la programmazione economica** interdepartmental committee for economic planning; ~ **interministeriale per lo sviluppo industriale** interdepartmental committee for industrial development.
comi'tiva *sf* party, group.
co'mizio [ko'mittsjo] *sm* (*POL*) meeting, assembly; ~ **elettorale** election rally.
'**comma, i** *sm* (*DIR*) subsection.
com'mando *sm inv* commando (squad).
com'media *sf* comedy; (*opera teatrale*) play; (: *che fa ridere*) comedy; (*fig*) playacting *no pl*.

commedi'ante *sm/f* (*peg*) third-rate actor/actress; (: *fig*) sham.
commedi'ografo, a *sm/f* (*autore*) comedy writer.
commemo'rare *vt* to commemorate.
commemorazi'one [kommemorat'tsjone] *sf* commemoration.
commenda'tore *sm official title awarded for services to one's country.*
commen'sale *sm/f* table companion.
commen'tare *vt* to comment on; (*testo*) to annotate; (*RADIO, TV*) to give a commentary on.
commenta'tore, 'trice *sm/f* commentator.
com'mento *sm* comment; (*a un testo, RADIO, TV*) commentary; ~ **musicale** (*CINE*) background music.
commerci'ale [kommer't ʃale] *ag* commercial, trading; (*peg*) commercial.
commercia'lista, i, e [kommertʃa'lista] *sm/f* (*laureato*) graduate in economics and commerce; (*consulente*) business consultant.
commercializ'zare [kommertʃalid'dzare] *vt* to market.
commercializzazi'one [kommertʃaliddzat 'tsjone] *sf* marketing.
commerci'ante [kommer't ʃante] *sm/f* trader, dealer; (*negoziante*) shopkeeper; ~ **all'ingrosso** wholesaler; ~ **in proprio** sole trader.
commerci'are [kommer't ʃare] *vi:* ~ **in** *vt* to deal *o* trade in.
com'mercio [kom'mertʃo] *sm* trade, commerce; **essere in** ~ (*prodotto*) to be on the market *o* on sale; **essere nel** ~ (*persona*) to be in business; ~ **all'ingrosso/al minuto** wholesale/retail trade.
com'messo, a *pp di* **commettere** ♦ *sm/f* shop assistant (*BRIT*), sales clerk (*US*) ♦ *sm* (*impiegato*) clerk ♦ *sf* (*COMM*) order; ~ **viaggiatore** commercial traveller.
commes'tibile *ag* edible; ~**i** *smpl* foodstuffs.
com'mettere *vt* to commit; (*ordinare*) to commission, order.
commi'ato *sm* leave-taking; **prendere** ~ **da qn** to take one's leave of sb.
commi'nare *vt* (*DIR*) to make provision for.
commise'rare *vt* to sympathize with, commiserate with.
commiserazi'one [kommizerat'tsjone] *sf* commiseration.
com'misi *etc vb vedi* **commettere.**
commissaria'mento *sm* temporary receivership.

commissari'are *vt* to put under temporary receivership.

commissari'ato *sm* (*AMM*) commissionership; (: *sede*) commissioner's office; (: *di polizia*) police station.

commis'sario *sm* commissioner; (*di pubblica sicurezza*) ≈ (police) superintendent (*BRIT*), (police) captain (*US*); (*SPORT*) steward; (*membro di commissione*) member of a committee *o* board; **alto** ~ high commissioner; ~ **di bordo** (*NAUT*) purser; ~ **d'esame** member of an examining board; ~ **di gara** race official; ~ **tecnico** (*SPORT*) national coach.

commissio'nare *vt* to order, place an order for.

commissio'nario *sm* (*COMM*) agent, broker.

commissi'one *sf* (*incarico*) errand; (*comitato, percentuale*) commission; (*COMM*: *ordinazione*) order; ~**i** *sfpl* (*acquisti*) shopping *sg*; ~ **d'esame** examining board; ~ **d'inchiesta** committee of enquiry; ~ **permanente** standing committee; ~**i bancarie** bank charges.

commit'tente *sm/f* (*COMM*) purchaser, customer.

com'mosso, a *pp di* **commuovere**.

commo'vente *ag* moving.

commozi'one [kommot'tsjone] *sf* emotion, deep feeling; ~ **cerebrale** (*MED*) concussion.

commu'overe *vt* to move, affect; ~**rsi** *vr* to be moved.

commu'tare *vt* (*pena*) to commute; (*ELETTR*) to change *o* switch over.

commutazi'one [kommutat'tsjone] *sf* (*DIR, ELETTR*) commutation.

comò *sm inv* chest of drawers.

como'dino *sm* bedside table.

comodità *sf inv* comfort; convenience.

'comodo, a *ag* comfortable; (*facile*) easy; (*conveniente*) convenient; (*utile*) useful, handy ♦ *sm* comfort; convenience; con ~ at one's convenience *o* leisure; **fare il proprio** ~ to do as one pleases; **far** ~ to be useful *o* handy; **stia** ~! don't bother to get up!

'compact disc *sm inv* compact disc.

compae'sano, a *sm/f* fellow-countryman/woman; person from the same town.

com'pagine [kom'padʒine] *sf* (*squadra*) team.

compa'gnia [kompaɲ'ɲia] *sf* company; (*gruppo*) gathering; **fare** ~ **a qn** to keep sb company; **essere di** ~ to be sociable.

com'pagno, a [kom'paɲɲo] *sm/f* (*di classe*, gioco) companion; (*POL*) comrade; ~ **di lavoro** workmate; ~ **di scuola** schoolfriend; ~ **di viaggio** fellow traveller.

com'paio *etc vb vedi* **comparire**.

compa'rare *vt* to compare.

compara'tivo, a *ag, sm* comparative.

comparazi'one [komparat'tsjone] *sf* comparison.

com'pare *sm* (*padrino*) godfather; (*complice*) accomplice; (*fam: amico*) old pal, old mate.

compa'rire *vi* to appear; ~ **in giudizio** (*DIR*) to appear before the court.

comparizi'one [komparit'tsjone] *sf* (*DIR*) appearance; **mandato di** ~ summons *sg*.

com'parso, a *pp di* **comparire** ♦ *sf* appearance; (*TEAT*) walk-on; (*CINE*) extra.

comparteci'pare [kompartetʃi'pare] *vi* (*COMM*): ~ **a** to have a share in.

compartecipazi'one [kompartetʃipat'tsjone] *sf* sharing; (*quota*) share; ~ **agli utili** profit- sharing; **in** ~ jointly.

comparti'mento *sm* compartment; (*AMM*) district.

com'parvi *etc vb vedi* **comparire**.

compas'sato, a *ag* (*persona*) composed; **freddo e** ~ cool and collected.

compassi'one *sf* compassion, pity; **avere** ~ **di qn** to feel sorry for sb, pity sb; **fare** ~ to arouse pity.

compassio'nevole *ag* compassionate.

com'passo *sm* (pair of) compasses *pl*; callipers *pl*.

compa'tibile *ag* (*scusabile*) excusable; (*conciliabile, INFORM*) compatible.

compati'mento *sm* compassion; indulgence; **con aria di** ~ with a condescending air.

compa'tire *vt* (*aver compassione di*) to sympathize with, feel sorry for; (*scusare*) to make allowances for.

compatri'ota, i, e *sm/f* compatriot.

compat'tezza [kompat'tettsa] *sf* (*solidità*) compactness; (*fig: unità*) solidarity.

com'patto, a *ag* compact; (*roccia*) solid; (*folla*) dense; (*fig: gruppo, partito*) united, close-knit.

com'pendio *sm* summary; (*libro*) compendium.

compen'sare *vt* (*equilibrare*) to compensate for, make up for; ~**rsi** *vr* (*reciproco*) to balance each other out; ~ **qn di** (*rimunerare*) to pay *o* remunerate sb for; (*risarcire*) to pay compensation to sb for; (*fig: fatiche, dolori*) to reward sb for.

compen'sato *sm* (*anche*: **legno** ~)

plywood.

com'penso *sm* compensation; payment, remuneration; reward; **in** ~ (*d'altra parte*) on the other hand.

'compera *sf* purchase; **fare le** ~**e** to do the shopping.

compe'rare *vt* = **comprare**.

compe'tente *ag* competent; (*mancia*) apt, suitable; (*capace*) qualified; **rivolgersi all'ufficio** ~ to apply to the office concerned.

compe'tenza [kompe'tɛntsa] *sf* competence; (*DIR*: *autorità*) jurisdiction; (*TECN, COMM*) expertise; ~**e** *sfpl* (*onorari*) fees; **definire le** ~**e** to establish responsibilities.

com'petere *vi* to compete, vie; (*DIR*: *spettare*): ~ **a** to lie within the competence of.

competitività *sf inv* competitiveness.

competi'tivo, a *ag* competitive.

competi'tore, 'trice *sm/f* competitor.

competizi'one [kompetit'tsjone] *sf* competition; **spirito di** ~ competitive spirit.

compia'cente [kompja'tʃɛnte] *ag* courteous, obliging.

compia'cenza [kompja'tʃɛntsa] *sf* courtesy.

compia'cere [kompja'tʃere] *vi*: ~ **a** to gratify, please ♦ *vt* to please; ~**rsi** *vr* (*provare soddisfazione*): ~**rsi di** *o* **per qc** to be delighted at sth; (*rallegrarsi*): ~**rsi con qn** to congratulate sb; (*degnarsi*): ~**rsi di fare** to be so good as to do.

compiaci'mento [kompjatʃi'mento] *sm* satisfaction.

compiaci'uto, a [kompja'tʃuto] *pp di* **compiacere**.

compi'angere [kom'pjandʒere] *vt* to sympathize with, feel sorry for.

compi'anto, a *pp di* **compiangere** ♦ *ag*: **il** ~ **presidente** the late lamented president ♦ *sm* mourning, grief.

'compiere *vt* (*concludere*) to finish, complete; (*adempiere*) to carry out, fulfil; ~**rsi** *vr* (*avverarsi*) to be fulfilled, come true; ~ **gli anni** to have one's birthday.

compi'lare *vt* to compile; (*modulo*) to complete, fill in (*BRIT*), fill out (*US*).

compila'tore, 'trice *sm/f* compiler.

compilazi'one [kompilat'tsjone] *sf* compilation; completion.

compi'mento *sm* (*termine, conclusione*) completion, fulfilment; **portare a** ~ **qc** to conclude sth, bring sth to a conclusion.

com'pire *vb* = **compiere**.

'compito *sm* (*incarico*) task, duty; (*dovere*) duty; (*INS*) exercise; (: *a casa*) piece of

homework; **fare i** ~**i** to do one's homework.

com'pito, a *ag* well-mannered, polite.

compiu'tezza [kompju'tettsa] *sf* (*completezza*) completeness; (*perfezione*) perfection.

compi'uto, a *pp di* **compiere** ♦ *ag*: **a 20 anni** ~**i** at 20 years of age, at age 20; **un fatto** ~ a fait accompli.

comple'anno *sm* birthday.

complemen'tare *ag* complementary; (*INS*: *materia*) subsidiary.

comple'mento *sm* complement; (*MIL*) reserve (troops); ~ **oggetto** (*LING*) direct object.

comples'sato, a *ag, sm/f*: **essere (un)** ~ to be full of complexes *o* hang-ups (*fam*).

complessità *sf* complexity.

complessiva'mente *av* (*nell'insieme*) on the whole; (*in tutto*) altogether.

comples'sivo, a *ag* (*globale*) comprehensive, overall; (*totale: cifra*) total; **visione** ~**a** overview.

com'plesso, a *ag* complex ♦ *sm* (*PSIC, EDIL*) complex; (*MUS*: *corale*) ensemble; (: *orchestrina*) band; (: *di musica pop*) group; **in** *o* **nel** ~ on the whole.

completa'mento *sm* completion.

comple'tare *vt* to complete.

com'pleto, a *ag* complete; (*teatro, autobus*) full ♦ *sm* suit; **al** ~ full; (*tutti presenti*) all present; **essere al** ~ (*teatro*) to be sold out; ~ **da sci** ski suit.

compli'care *vt* to complicate; ~**rsi** *vr* to become complicated.

complicazi'one [komplikat'tsjone] *sf* complication; **salvo** ~**i** unless any difficulties arise.

'complice ['kɔmplitʃe] *sm/f* accomplice.

complicità [komplitʃi'ta] *sf inv* complicity; **un sorriso/uno sguardo di** ~ a knowing smile/look.

complimen'tarsi *vr*: ~ **con** to congratulate.

compli'mento *sm* compliment; ~**i** *smpl* (*cortesia eccessiva*) ceremony *sg*; ~**i!** congratulations!; **senza** ~**i!** don't stand on ceremony!; make yourself at home!; help yourself!

complot'tare *vi* to plot, conspire.

com'plotto *sm* plot, conspiracy.

com'pone *etc vb vedi* **comporre**.

compo'nente *sm/f* member ♦ *sm* component.

com'pongo *etc vb vedi* **comporre**.

compo'nibile *ag* (*mobili, cucina*) fitted.

componi'mento *sm* (*DIR*) settlement; (*INS*) composition; (*poetico, teatrale*) work.

com'porre vt (musica, testo) to compose; (mettere in ordine) to arrange; (DIR: lite) to settle; (TIP) to set; (TEL) to dial; **comporsi** vr: **comporsi di** to consist of, be composed of.

comportamen'tale ag behavioural (BRIT), behavioral (US).

comporta'mento sm behaviour (BRIT), behavior (US); (di prodotto) performance.

compor'tare vt (implicare) to involve, entail; (consentire) to permit, allow (of); ~rsi vr (condursi) to behave.

com'posi etc vb vedi comporre.

composi'tore, 'trice sm/f composer; (TIP) compositor, typesetter.

composizi'one [kompozit'tsjone] sf composition; (DIR) settlement.

com'posta sf vedi composto.

compos'tezza [kompos'tettsa] sf composure; decorum.

com'posto, a pp di comporre ♦ ag (persona) composed, self-possessed; (: decoroso) dignified; (formato da più elementi) compound cpd ♦ sm compound; (CUC etc) mixture ♦ sf (CUC) stewed fruit no pl; (AGR) compost.

com'prare vt to buy; (corrompere) to bribe.

compra'tore, 'trice sm/f buyer, purchaser.

compra'vendita sf (COMM) (contract of) sale; **un atto di** ~ a deed of sale.

com'prendere vt (contenere) to comprise, consist of; (capire) to understand.

compren'donio sm: **essere duro di** ~ to be slow on the uptake.

compren'sibile ag understandable.

comprensi'one sf understanding.

compren'sivo, a ag (prezzo): ~ **di** inclusive of; (indulgente) understanding.

compren'sorio sm area, territory; (AMM) district.

com'preso, a pp di comprendere ♦ ag (incluso) included; **tutto** ~ all included, all-in (BRIT).

com'pressa sf vedi compresso.

compressi'one sf compression.

com'presso, a pp di comprimere ♦ ag (vedi comprimere) pressed; compressed; repressed ♦ sf (MED: garza) compress; (: pastiglia) tablet.

compres'sore sm compressor; (anche: **rullo** ~) steamroller.

compri'mario, a sm/f (TEAT) supporting actor/actress.

com'primere vt (premere) to press; (FISICA) to compress; (fig) to repress.

compro'messo, a pp di compromettere ♦ sm compromise.

compro'mettere vt to compromise; ~rsi vr

to compromise o.s.

comproprietà sf (DIR) joint ownership.

compro'vare vt to confirm.

com'punto, a ag contrite; **con fare** ~ with a solemn air.

compunzi'one [kompun'tsjone] sf contrition; solemnity.

compu'tare vt to calculate; (addebitare): ~ **qc a qn** to debit sb with sth.

com'puter [kəm'pju:tər] sm inv computer.

computeriz'zato, a [komputerid'dzato] ag computerized.

computerizzazi'one [komputeriddzat 'tsjone] sf computerization.

computiste'ria sf accounting, bookkeeping.

'computo sm calculation; **fare il** ~ **di** to count.

comu'nale ag municipal, town cpd; **consiglio/palazzo** ~ town council/hall; **è un impiegato** ~ he works for the local council.

Co'mune (AMM) town council; (sede) town hall; vedi nota nel riquadro.

COMUNE

The **Comune** is the smallest autonomous political and administrative unit. It keeps records of births, marriages and deaths and has the power to levy taxes and vet proposals for public works and town planning. It is run by a "Giunta comunale", which is elected by the "Consiglio comunale". The **Comune** is headed by the "sindaco" (mayor) who since 1993 has been elected directly by the citizens.

---

co'mune ag common; (consueto) common, everyday; (di livello medio) average; (ordinario) ordinary ♦ sf (di persone) commune; **fuori del** ~ out of the ordinary; **avere in** ~ to have in common, share; **mettere in** ~ to share; **un nostro** ~ **amico** a mutual friend of ours; **fare cassa** ~ to pool one's money.

comuni'care vt (notizia) to pass on, convey; (malattia) to pass on; (ansia etc) to communicate; (trasmettere: calore etc) to transmit, communicate; (REL) to administer communion to ♦ vi to communicate; ~rsi vr (propagarsi): ~rsi a to spread to; (REL) to receive communion.

comunica'tivo, a ag (sentimento) infectious; (persona) communicative ♦ sf communicativeness.

comuni'cato sm communiqué; ~ **stampa** press release.

comunicazi'one [komunikat'tsjone] sf communication; (annuncio) announcement; (*TEL*): ~ **(telefonica)** (telephone) call; **dare la ~ a qn** to put sb through; **ottenere la ~** to get through; **salvo ~i contrarie da parte Vostra** unless we hear from you to the contrary.

comuni'one *sf* communion; ~ **dei beni** (*DIR*: *tra coniugi*) joint ownership of property.

comu'nismo *sm* communism.

comu'nista, i, e *ag*, *sm/f* communist.

comunità *sf inv* community; **C~ Economica Europea (CEE)** European Economic Community (EEC); ~ **terapeutica** *rehabilitation centre run by voluntary organizations for people with drug, alcohol etc dependency.*

comuni'tario, a *ag* community *cpd*.

co'munque *cong* however, no matter how ♦ *av* (*in ogni modo*) in any case; (*tuttavia*) however, nevertheless.

con *prep* (*nei seguenti casi* **con** *può fondersi con l'articolo definito:* **con** + *il* = **col**, **con** + *la* = **colla**, **con** + *gli* = **cogli**, **con** + *i* = **coi**, **con** + *le* = **colle**) with; **partire col treno** to leave by train; **~ mio grande stupore** to my great astonishment; **~ la forza** by force; **~ questo freddo** in this cold weather; **~ il 1° di ottobre** as of October 1st; **~ tutto ciò** in spite of that, for all that; **~ tutto che era arrabbiato** even though he was angry, in spite of the fact that he was angry; **e ~ questo?** so what?

co'nato *sm*: **~ di vomito** retching.

'conca, che *sf* (*GEO*) valley.

concate'nare *vt* to link up, connect; ~**rsi** *vr* to be connected.

'concavo, a *ag* concave.

con'cedere [kon'tʃɛdere] *vt* (*accordare*) to grant; (*ammettere*) to admit, concede; ~**rsi qc** to treat o.s. to sth, allow o.s. sth.

concentra'mento [kontʃentra'mento] *sm* concentration.

concen'trare [kontʃen'trare] *vt*, ~**rsi** *vr* to concentrate.

concen'trato [kontʃen'trato] *sm* concentrate; ~ **di pomodoro** tomato purée.

concentrazi'one [kontʃentrat'tsjone] *sf* concentration; ~ **orizzontale/verticale** (*ECON*) horizontal/vertical integration.

con'centrico, a, ci, che [kon'tʃɛntriko] *ag* concentric.

conce'pibile [kontʃe'pibile] *ag* conceivable.

concepi'mento [kontʃepi'mento] *sm* conception.

conce'pire [kontʃe'pire] *vt* (*bambino*) to conceive; (*progetto, idea*) to conceive (of);

(*metodo, piano*) to devise; (*situazione*) to imagine, understand.

con'cernere [kon'tʃɛrnere] *vt* to concern; **per quanto mi concerne** as far as I'm concerned.

concer'tare [kontʃer'tare] *vt* (*MUS*) to harmonize; (*ordire*) to devise, plan; ~**rsi** *vr* to agree.

concer'tista, i, e [kontʃer'tista] *sm/f* (*MUS*) concert performer.

con'certo [kon'tʃɛrto] *sm* (*MUS*) concert; (: *componimento*) concerto.

con'cessi *etc* [kon'tʃɛssi] *vb vedi* **concedere**.

concessio'nario [kontʃessjo'narjo] *sm* (*COMM*) agent, dealer; ~ **esclusivo (di)** sole agent (for).

concessi'one [kontʃes'sjone] *sf* concession.

con'cesso, a [kon'tʃɛsso] *pp di* **concedere**.

con'cetto [kon'tʃɛtto] *sm* (*pensiero, idea*) concept; (*opinione*) opinion; **è un impiegato di ~ ≈** he's a white-collar worker.

concezi'one [kontʃet'tsjone] *sf* conception; (*idea*) view, idea.

con'chiglia [kon'kiʎʎa] *sf* shell.

'concia ['kontʃa] *sf* (*di pelli*) tanning; (*di tabacco*) curing; (*sostanza*) tannin.

conci'are [kon'tʃare] *vt* (*pelli*) to tan; (*tabacco*) to cure; (*fig: ridurre in cattivo stato*) to beat up; ~**rsi** *vr* (*sporcarsi*) to get in a mess; (*vestirsi male*) to dress badly; **ti hanno conciato male o per le feste!** they've really beaten you up!

concili'abile [kontʃi'ljabile] *ag* compatible.

concili'abolo [kontʃi'ljabolo] *sm* secret meeting.

concili'ante [kontʃi'ljante] *ag* conciliatory.

concili'are [kontʃi'ljare] *vt* to reconcile; (*contravvenzione*) to pay on the spot; (*favorire: sonno*) to be conducive to, induce; (*procurare: simpatia*) to gain; ~**rsi qc** to gain *o* win sth (for o.s.); ~**rsi qn** to win sb over; ~**rsi con** to be reconciled with.

conciliazi'one [kontʃiljat'tsjone] *sf* reconciliation; (*DIR*) settlement; **la C~** (*STORIA*) the Lateran Pact.

con'cilio [kon'tʃiljo] *sm* (*REL*) council.

conci'mare [kontʃi'mare] *vt* to fertilize; (*con letame*) to manure.

con'cime [kon'tʃime] *sm* manure; (*chimico*) fertilizer.

concisi'one [kontʃi'zjone] *sf* concision, conciseness.

con'ciso, a [kon'tʃizo] *ag* concise, succinct.

conci'tato, a [kontʃi'tato] *ag* excited, emotional.

concitta'dino, a [kontʃitta'dino] *sm/f* fellow

citizen.

con'clave *sm* conclave.

con'cludere *vt* to conclude; (*portare a compimento*) to conclude, finish, bring to an end; (*operare positivamente*) to achieve ♦ *vi* (*essere convincente*) to be conclusive; ~**rsi** *vr* to come to an end, close.

conclusi'one *sf* conclusion; (*risultato*) result.

conclu'sivo, a *ag* conclusive; (*finale*) final.

con'cluso, a *pp di* **concludere**.

concomi'tanza [konkomi'tantsa] *sf* (*di circostanze, fatti*) combination.

concor'danza [konkor'dantsa] *sf* (*anche LING*) agreement.

concor'dare *vt* (*prezzo*) to agree on; (*LING*) to make agree ♦ *vi* to agree; ~ **una tregua** to agree to a truce.

concor'dato *sm* agreement; (*REL*) concordat.

con'corde *ag* (*d'accordo*) in agreement; (*simultaneo*) simultaneous.

con'cordia *sf* harmony, concord.

concor'rente *ag* competing; (*MAT*) concurrent ♦ *sm/f* (*SPORT, COMM*) competitor; (*a un concorso di bellezza*) contestant.

concor'renza [konkor'rɛntsa] *sf* competition; ~ **sleale** unfair competition; **a prezzi di** ~ at competitive prices.

concorrenzi'ale [konkorren'tsjale] *ag* competitive.

con'correre *vi*: ~ (**in**) (*MAT*) to converge *o* meet (in); ~ (**a**) (*competere*) to compete (for); (: *INS: a una cattedra*) to apply (for); (*partecipare: a un'impresa*) to take part (in), contribute (to).

con'corso, a *pp di* **concorrere** ♦ *sm* competition; (*esame*) competitive examination; ~ **di bellezza** beauty contest; ~ **di circostanze** combination of circumstances; ~ **di colpa** (*DIR*) contributory negligence; **un** ~ **ippico** a showjumping event; ~ **in reato** (*DIR*) complicity in a crime; ~ **per titoli** competitive examination for qualified candidates.

con'creto, a *ag* concrete ♦ *sm*: **in** ~ **in** reality.

concu'bina *sf* concubine ♦ *sm*: **sono** ~**i** they are living together.

concussi'one *sf* (*DIR*) extortion.

con'danna *sf* condemnation; sentence; conviction; ~ **a morte** death sentence.

condan'nare *vt* (*disapprovare*) to condemn; (*DIR*): ~ **a** to sentence to; ~ **per** to convict of.

condan'nato, a *sm/f* convict.

con'densa *sf* condensation.

conden'sare *vt*, ~**rsi** *vr* to condense.

condensa'tore *sm* capacitor.

condensazi'one [kondensat'tsjone] *sf* condensation.

condi'mento *sm* seasoning; dressing.

con'dire *vt* to season; (*insalata*) to dress.

condiscen'dente [kondiʃʃen'dɛnte] *ag* obliging; compliant.

condiscen'denza [kondiʃʃen'dɛntsa] *sf* (*disponibilità*) obligingness; (*arrendevolezza*) compliance.

condi'scendere [kondiʃ'ʃendere] *vi*: ~ **a** to agree to.

condi'sceso, a [kondiʃ'ʃeso] *pp di* **condiscendere**.

condi'videre *vt* to share.

condi'viso, a *pp di* **condividere**.

condizio'nale [kondittsjo'nale] *ag* conditional ♦ *sm* (*LING*) conditional ♦ *sf* (*DIR*) suspended sentence.

condiziona'mento [kondittsjona'mento] *sm* conditioning; ~ **d'aria** air conditioning.

condizio'nare [kondittsjo'nare] *vt* to condition; **ad aria condizionata** air-conditioned.

condiziona'tore [kondittsjona'tore] *sm* air conditioner.

condizi'one [kondit'tsjone] *sf* condition; ~**i** *sfpl* (*di pagamento etc*) terms, conditions; **a** ~ **che** on condition that, provided that; **a nessuna** ~ on no account; ~**i di convenirsi** terms to be arranged; ~**i di lavoro** working conditions; ~**i di vendita** sales terms.

condogli'anze [kondoʎ'ʎantse] *sfpl* condolences.

condomini'ale *ag*: **riunione** ~ residents' meeting; **spese** ~**i** common charges.

condo'minio *sm* joint ownership; (*edificio*) jointly-owned building.

con'domino *sm* joint owner.

condo'nare *vt* (*DIR*) to remit.

con'dono *sm* remission; ~ **fiscale** conditional amnesty for people evading tax.

con'dotta *sf vedi* **condotto**.

con'dotto, a *pp di* **condurre** ♦ *ag*: **medico** ~ local authority doctor (*in country district*) ♦ *sm* (*canale, tubo*) pipe, conduit; (*ANAT*) duct ♦ *sf* (*modo di comportarsi*) conduct, behaviour (*BRIT*), behavior (*US*); (*di un affare etc*) handling; (*di acqua*) piping; (*incarico sanitario*) country medical practice controlled by a local authority.

condu'cente [kondu'tʃɛnte] *sm* driver.

con'duco *etc vb vedi* **condurre**.

con'durre *vt* to conduct; (*azienda*) to

manage; (*accompagnare: bambino*) to take; (*automobile*) to drive; (*trasportare: acqua, gas*) to convey, conduct; (*fig*) to lead ♦ *vi* to lead; **condursi** *vr* to behave, conduct o.s.; ~ **a termine** to conclude.
con'dussi *etc vb vedi* **condurre.**
condut'tore, 'trice *ag*: **filo** ~ (*fig*) thread; **motivo** ~ leitmotiv ♦ *sm* (*di mezzi pubblici*) driver; (*FISICA*) conductor.
condut'tura *sf* (*gen*) pipe; (*di acqua, gas*) main.
conduzi'one [kondut'tsjone] *sf* (*di affari, ditta*) management; (*DIR: locazione*) lease; (*FISICA*) conduction.
confabu'lare *vi* to confab.
confa'cente [konfa'tʃɛnte] *ag*: ~ **a qn/qc** suitable for sb/sth; **clima** ~ **alla salute** healthy climate.
CONFAGRICOL'TURA *abbr f* (= *Confederazione generale dell'Agricoltura Italiana*) *confederation of Italian farmers.*
CON'FAPI *sigla f* = *Confederazione Nazionale della Piccola Industria.*
con'farsi *vr*: ~ **a** to suit, agree with.
CONFARTIGIA'NATO [konfartidʒa'nato] *abbr f* = *Confederazione Generale dell'Artigianato Italiano.*
con'fatto, a *pp di* **confarsi.**
CONFCOM'MERCIO [konfkom'mɛrtʃo] *abbr f* = *Confederazione Generale del Commercio.*
confederazi'one [konfederat'tsjone] *sf* confederation; ~ **imprenditoriale** employers' association.
confe'renza [konfe'rɛntsa] *sf* (*discorso*) lecture; (*riunione*) conference; ~ **stampa** press conference.
conferenzi'ere, a [konferen'tsjɛre] *sm/f* lecturer.
conferi'mento *sm* conferring, awarding.
confe'rire *vt*: ~ **qc a qn** to give sth to sb, confer sth on sb ♦ *vi* to confer.
con'ferma *sf* confirmation.
confer'mare *vt* to confirm.
confes'sare *vt*, ~**rsi** *vr* to confess; **andare a** ~**rsi** (*REL*) to go to confession.
confessio'nale *ag, sm* confessional.
confessi'one *sf* confession; (*setta religiosa*) denomination.
con'fesso, a *ag*: **essere reo** ~ to have pleaded guilty.
confes'sore *sm* confessor.
con'fetto *sm* sugared almond; (*MED*) pill.
confet'tura *sf* (*gen*) jam; (*di arance*) marmalade.
confezio'nare [konfettsjo'nare] *vt* (*vestito*) to make (up); (*merci, pacchi*) to package.
confezi'one [konfet'tsjone] *sf* (*di abiti: da*

uomo) tailoring; (: *da donna*) dressmaking; (*imballaggio*) packaging; ~ **regalo** gift pack; ~ **risparmio** economy size; ~ **da viaggio** travel pack; ~**i per signora** ladies' wear *no pl*; ~**i da uomo** menswear *no pl*.
confic'care *vt*: ~ **qc in** to hammer *o* drive sth into; ~**rsi** *vr* to stick.
confi'dare *vi*: ~ **in** to confide in, rely on ♦ *vt* to confide; ~**rsi con qn** to confide in sb.
confi'dente *sm/f* (*persona amica*) confidant/ confidante; (*informatore*) informer.
confi'denza [konfi'dɛntsa] *sf* (*familiarità*) intimacy, familiarity; (*fiducia*) trust, confidence; (*rivelazione*) confidence; **prendersi (troppe)** ~**e** to take liberties; **fare una** ~ **a qn** to confide something to sb.
confidenzi'ale [konfiden'tsjale] *ag* familiar, friendly; (*segreto*) confidential; **in via** ~ confidentially.
configu'rare *vt* (*INFORM*) to set; ~**rsi** *vr*: ~ **a** to assume the shape *o* form of.
configurazi'one [konfigurat'tsjone] *sf* configuration; (*INFORM*) setting.
confi'nante *ag* neighbouring (*BRIT*), neighboring (*US*).
confi'nare *vi*: ~ **con** to border on ♦ *vt* (*POL*) to intern; (*fig*) to confine; ~**rsi** *vr* (*isolarsi*): ~**rsi in** to shut o.s. up in.
confi'nato, a *ag* interned ♦ *sm/f* internee.
CONFIN'DUSTRIA *sigla f* (= *Confederazione Generale dell'Industria Italiana*) *employers' association*, ≈ CBI (*BRIT*).
con'fine *sm* boundary; (*di paese*) border, frontier; **territorio di** ~ border zone.
con'fino *sm* internment.
con'fisca *sf* confiscation.
confis'care *vt* to confiscate.
conflagrazi'one [konflagrat'tsjone] *sf* conflagration.
con'flitto *sm* conflict; **essere in** ~ **con qc** to clash with sth; **essere in** ~ **con qn** to be at loggerheads with sb.
conflittu'ale *ag*: **rapporto** ~ relationship based on conflict.
conflittualità *sf* conflicts *pl*.
conflu'enza [konflu'ɛntsa] *sf* (*di fiumi*) confluence; (*di strade*) junction.
conflu'ire *vi* (*fiumi*) to flow into each other, meet; (*strade*) to meet.
con'fondere *vt* to mix up, confuse; (*imbarazzare*) to embarrass; ~**rsi** *vr* (*mescolarsi*) to mingle; (*turbarsi*) to be confused; (*sbagliare*) to get mixed up; ~ **le idee a qn** to mix sb up, confuse sb.
confor'mare *vt* (*adeguare*): ~ **a** to adapt *o*

conform to; ~rsi vr: ~rsi (a) to conform (to).

con'forme ag: ~ a (simile) similar to; (corrispondente) in keeping with.

conforme'mente av accordingly; ~ a in accordance with.

confor'mismo sm conformity.

confor'mista, i, e sm/f conformist.

conformità sf conformity; in ~ a in conformity with.

confor'tare vt to comfort, console.

confor'tevole ag (consolante) comforting; (comodo) comfortable.

con'forto sm (consolazione, sollievo) comfort, consolation; (conferma) support; a ~ di qc in support of sth; i ~i (religiosi) the last sacraments.

confra'ternita sf brotherhood.

confron'tare vt to compare; ~rsi vr (scontrarsi) to have a confrontation.

con'fronto sm comparison; (DIR, MIL, POL) confrontation; in o a ~ di in comparison with, compared to; nei miei (o tuoi etc) ~i towards me (o you etc).

con'fusi etc vb vedi confondere.

confusi'one sf confusion; (imbarazzo) embarrassment; far ~ (disordine) to make a mess; (chiasso) to make a racket; (confondere) to confuse things.

con'fuso, a pp di confondere ♦ ag (vedi confondere) confused; embarrassed.

confu'tare vt to refute.

conge'dare [kondʒe'dare] vt to dismiss; (MIL) to demobilize; ~rsi vr to take one's leave.

con'gedo [kon'dʒedo] sm (anche MIL) leave; prendere ~ da qn to take one's leave of sb; ~ assoluto (MIL) discharge.

conge'gnare [kondʒeɲ'ɲare] vt to construct, put together.

con'gegno [kon'dʒeɲɲo] sm device, mechanism.

congela'mento [kondʒela'mento] sm (gen) freezing; (MED) frostbite; ~ salariale wage freeze.

conge'lare [kondʒe'lare] vt, ~rsi vr to freeze.

congela'tore [kondʒela'tore] sm freezer.

con'genito, a [kon'dʒɛnito] ag congenital.

con'gerie [kon'dʒɛrje] sf inv (di oggetti) heap; (di idee) muddle, jumble.

congestio'nare [kondʒestjo'nare] vt to congest; essere congestionato (persona, viso) to be flushed; (zona: per traffico) to be congested.

congesti'one [kondʒes'tjone] sf congestion.

conget'tura [kondʒet'tura] sf conjecture, supposition.

con'giungere [kon'dʒundʒere] vt, ~rsi vr to join (together).

congiunti'vite [kondʒunti'vite] sf conjunctivitis.

congiun'tivo [kondʒun'tivo] sm (LING) subjunctive.

congi'unto, a [kon'dʒunto] pp di congiungere ♦ ag (unito) joined ♦ sm/f (parente) relative.

congiun'tura [kondʒun'tura] sf (giuntura) junction, join; (ANAT) joint; (circostanza) juncture; (ECON) economic situation.

congiuntu'rale [kondʒuntu'rale] ag of the economic situation; crisi ~ economic crisis.

congiunzi'one [kondʒun'tsjone] sf (LING) conjunction.

congi'ura [kon'dʒura] sf conspiracy.

congiu'rare [kondʒu'rare] vi to conspire.

conglome'rato sm (GEO) conglomerate; (fig) conglomeration; (EDIL) concrete.

'Congo sm: il ~ the Congo.

congo'lese ag, sm/f Congolese inv.

congratu'larsi vr: ~ con qn per qc to congratulate sb on sth.

congratulazi'oni [kongratulat'tsjoni] sfpl congratulations.

con'grega, ghe sf band, bunch.

congregazi'one [kongregat'tsjone] sf congregation.

congres'sista, i, e sm/f participant at a congress.

con'gresso sm congress.

'congruo, a ag (prezzo, compenso) adequate, fair; (ragionamento) coherent, consistent.

conguagli'are [kongwaʎ'ʎare] vt to balance; (stipendio) to adjust.

congu'aglio [kon'gwaʎʎo] sm balancing; adjusting; (somma di denaro) balance; fare il ~ di to balance; to adjust.

coni'are vt to mint, coin; (fig) to coin.

coniazi'one [konjat'tsjone] sf mintage.

'conico, a, ci, che ag conical.

co'nifere sfpl conifers.

conigli'era [koniʎ'ʎera] sf (gabbia) rabbit hutch; (più grande) rabbit run.

conigli'etta [koniʎ'ʎetta] sf bunny girl.

conigli'etto [koniʎ'ʎetto] sm bunny.

co'niglio [ko'niʎʎo] sm rabbit; sei un ~! (fig) you're chicken!

coniu'gale ag (amore, diritti) conjugal; (vita) married, conjugal.

coniu'gare vt to combine; (LING) to conjugate; ~rsi vr to get married.

coniu'gato, a ag (AMM) married.

coniugazi'one [konjugat'tsjone] sf (LING)

conjugation.
'coniuge ['kɔnjudʒe] sm/f spouse.
connatu'rato, a ag inborn.
connazio'nale [konnattsjo'nale] sm/f
fellow-countryman/woman.
connessi'one sf connection.
con'nesso, a pp di connettere.
con'nettere vt to connect, join ♦ vi (fig) to
think straight.
connet'tore sm (ELETTR) connector.
conni'vente ag conniving.
conno'tati smpl distinguishing marks;
rispondere ai ~i to fit the description;
cambiare i ~i a qn (fam) to beat sb up.
con'nubio sm (matrimonio) marriage; (fig)
union.
'cono sm cone; ~ gelato ice-cream cone.
co'nobbi etc vb vedi conoscere.
cono'scente [konoʃ'ʃɛnte] sm/f
acquaintance.
cono'scenza [konoʃ'ʃɛntsa] sf (il sapere)
knowledge no pl; (persona) acquaintance;
(facoltà sensoriale) consciousness no pl;
essere a ~ di qc to know sth; portare qn a
~ di qc to inform sb of sth; per vostra ~
for your information; fare la ~ di qn to
make sb's acquaintance; perdere ~ to
lose consciousness; ~ tecnica know-how.
co'noscere [ko'noʃʃere] vt to know; ci
siamo conosciuti a Firenze we (first) met
in Florence; ~ qn di vista to know sb by
sight; farsi ~ (fig) to make a name for o.s.
conosci'tore, 'trice [konoʃʃi'tore] sm/f
connoisseur.
conosci'uto, a [konoʃ'ʃuto] pp di conoscere
♦ ag well-known.
con'quista sf conquest.
conquis'tare vt to conquer; (fig) to gain,
win.
conquista'tore, 'trice sm/f (in guerra)
conqueror ♦ sm (seduttore) lady-killer.
cons. abbr = consiglio.
consa'crare vt (REL) to consecrate;
(: sacerdote) to ordain; (dedicare) to
dedicate; (fig: uso etc) to sanction; ~rsi a
to dedicate o.s. to.
consangu'ineo, a sm/f blood relation.
consa'pevole ag: ~ di aware of.
consapevo'lezza [konsapevo'lettsa] sf
awareness, consciousness.
conscia'mente [konʃa'mente] av
consciously.
'conscio, a, sci, sce ['kɔnʃo] ag: ~ di
aware o conscious of.
consecu'tivo, a ag consecutive;
(successivo: giorno) following, next.
con'segna [kon'seɲɲa] sf delivery; (merce
consegnata) consignment; (custodia) care,

custody; (MIL: ordine) orders pl;
(: punizione) confinement to barracks; alla
~ on delivery; dare qc in ~ a qn to
entrust sth to sb; passare le ~e a qn to
hand over to sb; ~ a domicilio home
delivery; ~ in contrassegno, pagamento
alla ~ cash on delivery; ~ sollecita
prompt delivery.
conse'gnare [konseɲ'ɲare] vt to deliver;
(affidare) to entrust, hand over; (MIL) to
confine to barracks.
consegna'tario [konseɲɲa'tarjo] sm
consignee.
consegu'ente ag consequent.
conseguente'mente av consequently.
consegu'enza [konse'gwɛntsa] sf
consequence; per o di ~ consequently.
consegui'mento sm (di scopo, risultato etc)
achievement, attainment; al ~ della
laurea on graduation.
consegu'ire vt to achieve ♦ vi to follow,
result; ~ la laurea to graduate, obtain
one's degree.
con'senso sm approval, consent.
consensu'ale ag (DIR) by mutual consent.
consen'tire vi: ~ a to consent o agree to
♦ vt to allow, permit; mi si consenta di
ringraziare ... I would like to thank ....
consenzi'ente [konsen'tsjɛnte] ag (gen, DIR)
consenting.
con'serto, a ag: a braccia ~e with one's
arms folded.
con'serva sf (CUC) preserve; ~ di frutta
jam; ~ di pomodoro tomato purée; ~e
alimentari tinned (o canned o bottled)
foods.
conser'vante sm (per alimenti)
preservative.
conser'vare vt (CUC) to preserve;
(custodire) to keep; (: dalla distruzione etc)
to preserve, conserve; ~rsi vr to keep.
conserva'tore, 'trice ag, sm/f (POL)
conservative.
conserva'torio sm (di musica)
conservatory.
conservato'rismo sm (POL) conservatism.
conservazi'one [konservat'tsjone] sf
preservation; conservation; istinto di ~
instinct for self-preservation; a lunga ~
(latte, panna) long-life cpd.
con'sesso sm (assemblea) assembly;
(riunione) meeting.
conside'rabile ag worthy of consideration.
conside'rare vt to consider; (reputare) to
consider, regard; ~ molto qn to think
highly of sb.
conside'rato, a ag (prudente) cautious,

careful; (*stimato*) highly thought of, esteemed.

considerazi'one [konsiderat'tsjone] *sf* (*esame, riflessione*) consideration; (*stima*) regard, esteem; (*pensiero, osservazione*) observation; **prendere in** ~ to take into consideration.

conside'revole *ag* considerable.

consigli'abile [konsiʎ'ʎabile] *ag* advisable.

consigli'are [konsiʎ'ʎare] *vt* (*persona*) to advise; (*metodo, azione*) to recommend, advise, suggest; ~**rsi** *vr*: ~**rsi con qn** to ask sb for advice.

consigli'ere, a [konsiʎ'ʎɛre] *sm/f* adviser ♦ *sm*: ~ **d'amministrazione** board member; ~ **comunale** town councillor; ~ **delegato** (*COMM*) managing director.

con'siglio [kon'siʎʎo] *sm* (*suggerimento*) advice *no pl*, piece of advice; (*assemblea*) council; ~ **d'amministrazione** board; **C**~ **d'Europa** Council of Europe; ~ **di fabbrica** works council; **il C**~ **dei Ministri** (*POL*) ≈ the Cabinet; **C**~ **di stato** *advisory body to the Italian government on administrative matters and their legal implications*; **C**~ **superiore della magistratura** *state body responsible for judicial appointments and regulations*; *vedi nota nel riquadro.*

CONSIGLI

The **Consiglio dei Ministri***, the Italian Cabinet, is headed by the "Presidente del Consiglio", the Prime Minister, who is the leader of the Government.*

The **Consiglio superiore della Magistratura***, the magistrates' governing body, ensures their autonomy and independence as enshrined in the Constitution. Chaired by the "Presidente della Repubblica", it mainly deals with appointments and transfers, and can take disciplinary action as required. Of the 30 magistrates elected to the* **Consiglio** *for a period of four years, 20 are chosen by their fellow magistrates and 10 by Parliament. The "Presidente della Repubblica" and the "Vicepresidente" are ex officio members.*

---

con'simile *ag* similar.

consis'tente *ag* solid; (*fig*) sound, valid.

consis'tenza [konsis'tɛntsa] *sf* (*di impasto*) consistency; (*di stoffa*) texture; **senza** ~ (*sospetti, voci*) ill-founded, groundless; ~ **di cassa/di magazzino** cash/stock in hand; ~ **patrimoniale** financial solidity.

con'sistere *vi*: ~ **in** to consist of.

consis'tito, a *pp di* **consistere**.

'CONSOB *sigla f* (= *Commissione nazionale per le società e la borsa*) *regulatory body for the Italian Stock Exchange.*

consoci'arsi [konso't∫arsi] *vr* to go into partnership.

consociati'vismo [konsot∫ati'vizmo] *sm* (*POL*) pact-building.

consocia'tivo, a [konsot∫a'tivo] *ag* (*POL*: *democrazia*) based on pacts.

consoci'ato, a [konso't∫ato] *ag* associated ♦ *sm/f* associate.

conso'lante *ag* consoling, comforting.

conso'lare *ag* consular ♦ *vt* (*confortare*) to console, comfort; (*rallegrare*) to cheer up; ~**rsi** *vr* to be comforted; to cheer up.

conso'lato *sm* consulate.

consolazi'one [konsolat'tsjone] *sf* consolation, comfort.

'console *sm* consul ♦ *sf* [kõ'sɔl] (*quadro di comando*) console.

consolida'mento *sm* strengthening; consolidation.

consoli'dare *vt* to strengthen, reinforce; (*MIL, terreno*) to consolidate; ~**rsi** *vr* to consolidate.

consolidazi'one [konsolidat'tsjone] *sf* strengthening; consolidation.

consommé [kõsɔ'me] *sm inv* consommé.

conso'nante *sf* consonant.

conso'nanza [konso'nantsa] *sf* consonance.

'consono, a *ag*: ~ **a** consistent with, consonant with.

con'sorte *sm/f* consort.

con'sorzio [kon'sɔrtsjo] *sm* consortium; ~ **agrario** farmers' cooperative; ~ **di garanzia** (*COMM*) underwriting syndicate.

con'stare *vi*: ~ **di** to consist of ♦ *vb impers*: **mi consta che** it has come to my knowledge that, it appears that; **a quanto mi consta** as far as I know.

consta'tare *vt* to establish, verify; (*notare*) to notice, observe.

constatazi'one [konstatat'tsjone] *sf* observation; ~ **amichevole** (*in incidenti*) jointly-agreed statement for insurance purposes.

consu'eto, a *ag* habitual, usual ♦ *sm*: **come di** ~ as usual.

consuetudi'nario, a *ag*: **diritto** ~ (*DIR*) common law.

consue'tudine *sf* habit; (*usanza*) custom.

consu'lente *sm/f* consultant; ~ **aziendale/tecnico** management/technical consultant.

consu'lenza [konsu'lɛntsa] *sf* consultancy;

~ **medica/legale** medical/legal advice;
ufficio di ~ **fiscale** tax consultancy office;
~ **tecnica** technical consultancy o advice.
consul'tare vt to consult; ~**rsi** vr: ~**rsi con
qn** to seek the advice of sb.
consultazi'one [konsultat'tsjone] sf
consultation; ~**i** sfpl (POL) talks,
consultations; **libro di** ~ reference book.
consul'tivo, a ag consultative.
consul'torio sm: ~ **familiare** o
matrimoniale marriage guidance centre;
~ **pediatrico** children's clinic.
consu'mare vt (logorare: abiti, scarpe) to
wear out; (usare) to consume, use up;
(mangiare, bere) to consume; (DIR) to
consummate; ~**rsi** vr to wear out; to be
used up; (anche fig) to be consumed;
(combustibile) to burn out.
consu'mato, a ag (vestiti, scarpe, tappeto)
worn; (persona: esperto) accomplished.
consuma'tore sm consumer.
consumazi'one [konsumat'tsjone] sf
(bibita) drink; (spuntino) snack; (DIR)
consummation.
consu'mismo sm consumerism.
con'sumo sm consumption; wear; use;
generi o **beni di** ~ consumer goods; **beni
di largo** -- basic commodities; **imposta sui**
~**i** tax on consumer goods.
consun'tivo sm (ECON) final balance.
con'sunto, a ag worn-out; (viso) wasted.
'conta sf (nei giochi): **fare la** ~ to see who is
going to be "it".
con'tabile ag accounts cpd, accounting
♦ smlf accountant.
contabilità sf (attività, tecnica) accounting,
accountancy; (insieme dei libri etc) books
pl, accounts pl; (ufficio) ~ accounts
department; ~ **finanziaria** financial
accounting; ~ **di gestione** management
accounting.
contachi'lometri [kontaki'lɔmetri] sm inv
≈ mileometer.
conta'dino, a smlf countryman/woman;
farm worker; (peg) peasant.
contagi'are [konta'dʒare] vt to infect.
con'tagio [kon'tadʒo] sm infection; (per
contatto diretto) contagion; (epidemia)
epidemic.
contagi'oso, a [konta'dʒoso] ag infectious;
contagious.
conta'giri [konta'dʒiri] sm inv (AUT) rev
counter.
conta'gocce [konta'gottʃe] sm inv dropper.
contami'nare vt to contaminate.
contaminazi'one [kontaminat'tsjone] sf
contamination.
con'tante sm cash; **pagare in** ~**i** to pay

cash.
con'tare vt to count; (considerare) to
consider ♦ vi to count, be of importance;
~ **su qn** to count o rely on sb; ~ **di fare qc**
to intend to do sth; **ha i giorni contati, ha
le ore contate** his days are numbered; **la
gente che conta** people who matter.
contas'catti sm inv telephone meter.
conta'tore sm meter.
contat'tare vt to contact.
con'tatto sm contact; **essere in** ~ **con qn** to
be in touch with sb; **fare** ~ (ELETTR: fili) to
touch.
'conte sm count.
con'tea sf (STORIA) earldom; (AMM) county.
conteggi'are [konted'dʒare] vt to charge,
put on the bill.
con'teggio [kon'tedd3o] sm calculation.
con'tegno [kon'teɲɲo] sm (comportamento)
behaviour (BRIT), behavior (US);
(atteggiamento) attitude; **darsi un** ~
(ostentare disinvoltura) to act nonchalant;
(ricomporsi) to pull o.s. together.
conte'gnoso, a [konteɲ'ɲoso] ag reserved,
dignified.
contem'plare vt to contemplate, gaze at;
(DIR) to make provision for.
contempla'tivo, a ag contemplative.
contemplazi'one [kontemplat'tsjone] sf
contemplation.
con'tempo sm: **nel** ~ meanwhile, in the
meantime.
contemporanea'mente av
simultaneously; at the same time.
contempo'raneo, a ag, smlf
contemporary.
conten'dente smlf opponent, adversary.
con'tendere vi (competere) to compete;
(litigare) to quarrel ♦ vt: ~ **qc a qn** to
contend with o be in competition with sb
for sth.
conte'nere vt to contain; ~**rsi** vr to contain
o.s.
conteni'tore sm container.
conten'tabile ag: **difficilmente** ~ difficult
to please.
conten'tare vt to please, satisfy; ~**rsi** vr:
~**rsi di** to be satisfied with, content o.s.
with; **si contenta di poco** he is easily
satisfied.
conten'tezza [konten'tettsa] sf
contentment.
conten'tino sm sop.
con'tento, a ag pleased, glad; ~ **di** pleased
with.
conte'nuto ag (ira, entusiasmo) restrained,
suppressed; (forza) contained ♦ sm
contents pl; (argomento) content.

contenzi'oso, a [kɔnten'tsjɔso] *ag* (*DIR*) contentious ♦ *sm* (*AMM*: *ufficio*) legal department.

con'teso, a *pp di* **contendere** ♦ *sf* dispute, argument.

con'tessa *sf* countess.

contes'tare *vt* (*DIR*) to notify; (*fig*) to dispute; ~ **il sistema** to protest against the system.

contesta'tore, 'trice *ag* anti-establishment ♦ *sm/f* protester.

contestazi'one [kontestat'tsjone] *sf* (*DIR*: *disputa*) dispute; (: *notifica*) notification; (*POL*) anti-establishment activity; **in caso di** ~ if there are any objections.

con'testo *sm* context.

con'tiguo, a *ag*: ~ (**a**) adjacent (to).

continen'tale *ag* continental.

conti'nente *ag* continent ♦ *sm* (*GEO*) continent; (: *terra ferma*) mainland.

conti'nenza [konti'nɛntsa] *sf* continence.

contin'gente [kontin'dʒɛnte] *ag* contingent ♦ *sm* (*COMM*) quota; (*MIL*) contingent.

contin'genza [kontin'dʒɛntsa] *sf* circumstance; (**indennità di**) ~ cost-of-living allowance.

continua'mente *av* (*senza interruzione*) continuously, nonstop; (*ripetutamente*) continually.

continu'are *vt* to continue (with), go on with ♦ *vi* to continue, go on; ~ **a fare qc** to go on *o* continue doing sth; **continua a nevicare/a fare freddo** it's still snowing/cold.

continua'tivo, a *ag* (*occupazione*) permanent; (*periodo*) consecutive.

continuazi'one [kontinuat'tsjone] *sf* continuation.

continuità *sf* continuity.

con'tinuo, a *ag* (*numerazione*) continuous; (*pioggia*) continual, constant; (*ELETTR*: *corrente*) direct; **di** ~ continually.

'conto *sm* (*calcolo*) calculation; (*COMM*, *ECON*) account; (*di ristorante*, *albergo*) bill; (*fig*: *stima*) consideration, esteem; **avere un** ~ **in sospeso** (**con qn**) to have an outstanding account (with sb); (*fig*) to have a score to settle (with sb); **fare i** ~**i con qn** to settle one's account with sb; **fare** ~ **su qn** to count *o* rely on sb; **fare** ~ **che** (*supporre*) to suppose that; **rendere** ~ **a qn di qc** to be accountable to sb for sth; **rendersi** ~ **di qc/che** to realize sth/that; **tener** ~ **di qn/qc** to take sb/sth into account; **tenere qc da** ~ to take great care of sth; **ad ogni buon** ~ in any case; **di poco/nessun** ~ of little/no importance; **per** ~ **di** on behalf of; **per** ~ **mio** as far as

I'm concerned; (*da solo*) on my own; **a** ~**i fatti, in fin dei** ~**i** all things considered; **mi hanno detto strane cose sul suo** ~ I've heard some strange things about him; ~ **capitale** capital account; ~ **cifrato** numbered account; ~ **corrente** current account (*BRIT*), checking account (*US*); ~ **corrente postale** Post Office account; ~ **economico** profit and loss account; ~ **in partecipazione** joint account; ~ **passivo** account payable; ~ **profitti e perdite** profit and loss account; ~ **alla rovescia** countdown; ~ **valutario** foreign currency account.

con'torcere [kon'tɔrtʃere] *vt* to twist; (*panni*) to wring (out); ~**rsi** *vr* to twist, writhe.

contor'nare *vt* to surround; ~**rsi** *vr*: ~**rsi di** to surround o.s. with.

con'torno *sm* (*linea*) outline, contour; (*ornamento*) border; (*CUC*) vegetables *pl*; **fare da** ~ **a** to surround.

contorsi'one *sf* contortion.

con'torto, a *pp di* **contorcere**.

contrabban'dare *vt* to smuggle.

contrabbandi'ere, a *sm/f* smuggler.

contrab'bando *sm* smuggling, contraband; **merce di** ~ contraband, smuggled goods *pl*.

contrab'basso *sm* (*MUS*) (double) bass.

contraccambi'are *vt* (*favore etc*) to return; **vorrei** ~ **I'd** like to show my appreciation.

contraccet'tivo, a [kontrattʃet'tivo] *ag, sm* contraceptive.

contrac'colpo *sm* rebound; (*di arma da fuoco*) recoil; (*fig*) repercussion.

con'trada *sf* street; district; *vedi anche* **Palio**.

contrad'detto, a *pp di* **contraddire**.

contrad'dire *vt* to contradict; ~**rsi** *vr* to contradict o.s.; (*uso reciproco*: *persone*) to contradict each other *o* one another; (: *testimonianze etc*) to be contradictory.

contraddis'tinguere *vt* (*merce*) to mark; (*fig*: *atteggiamento*, *persona*) to distinguish.

contraddis'tinto, a *pp di* **contraddistinguere**.

contraddit'torio, a *ag* contradictory; (*sentimenti*) conflicting ♦ *sm* (*DIR*) cross-examination.

contraddizi'one [kontraddit'tsjone] *sf* contradiction; **cadere in** ~ to contradict o.s.; **essere in** ~ (*tesi*, *affermazioni*) to contradict one another; **spirito di** ~ argumentativeness.

con'trae *etc vb vedi* **contrarre**.

contra'ente *sm* contractor.

contra'erea *sf* (*MIL*) anti-aircraft artillery.

contra'ereo, a *ag* anti-aircraft.

contraf'fare vt (persona) to mimic; (voce) to disguise; (firma) to forge, counterfeit. **contraf'fatto, a** pp di **contraffare ♦** ag counterfeit.

contraffazi'one [kontraffat'tsjone] sf mimicking no pl; disguising no pl; forging no pl; (cosa contraffatta) forgery.

contraf'forte sm (ARCHIT) buttress; (GEO) spur.

con'traggo etc vb vedi **contrarre.**

con'tralto sm (MUS) contralto.

contrap'pello sm (MIL) second roll call.

contrappe'sare vt to counterbalance; (fig: decisione) to weigh up.

contrap'peso sm counterbalance, counterweight.

contrap'porre vt: ~ **qc a qc** to counter sth with sth; (paragonare) to compare sth with sth; **contrapporsi** vr: **contrapporsi a qc** to contrast with sth, be opposed to sth.

contrap'posto, a pp di **contrapporre.**

contraria'mente av: ~ **a** contrary to.

contrari'are vt (contrastare) to thwart, oppose; (irritare) to annoy, bother; ~**rsi** vr to get annoyed.

contrari'ato, a ag annoyed.

contrarietà sf adversity; (fig) aversion.

con'trario, a ag opposite; (sfavorevole) unfavourable (BRIT), unfavorable (US) ♦ sm opposite; **essere** ~ **a qc** (persona) to be against sth; **al** ~ on the contrary; **in caso** ~ otherwise; **avere qualcosa in** ~ to have some objection; **non ho niente in** ~ I have no objection.

con'trarre vt (malattia, debito) to contract; (muscoli) to tense; (abitudine, vizio) to pick up; (accordo, patto) to enter into; **contrarsi** vr to contract; ~ **matrimonio** to marry.

contrasse'gnare [kontrasseɲ'ɲare] vt to mark.

contras'segno [kontras'seɲɲo] sm (distintivo) distinguishing mark; **spedire in** ~ (COMM) to send COD.

con'trassi etc vb vedi **contrarre.**

contras'tante ag contrasting.

contras'tare vt (avversare) to oppose; (impedire) to bar; (negare: diritto) to contest, dispute ♦ vi: ~ **(con)** (essere in disaccordo) to contrast (with); (lottare) to struggle (with).

con'trasto sm contrast; (conflitto) conflict; (litigio) dispute.

contrat'tacco sm counterattack; **passare al** ~ (fig) to fight back.

contrat'tare vt, vi to negotiate.

contrat'tempo sm hitch.

con'tratto, a pp di **contrarre ♦** sm contract; ~ **di acquisto** purchase agreement; ~ **di**

affitto, ~ **di locazione** lease; ~ **collettivo di lavoro** collective agreement; ~ **di lavoro** contract of employment; ~ **a termine** forward contract.

contrattu'ale ag contractual; **forza** ~ (di sindacato) bargaining power.

contravve'nire vi: ~ **a** (legge) to contravene; (obbligo) to fail to meet.

contravven'tore, 'trice sm/f offender.

contravve'nuto, a pp di **contravvenire.**

contravvenzi'one [kontravven'tsjone] sf contravention; (ammenda) fine.

contrazi'one [kontrat'tsjone] sf contraction; (di prezzi etc) reduction.

contribu'ente sm/f taxpayer; ratepayer (BRIT), property tax payer (US).

contribu'ire vi to contribute.

contribu'tivo, a ag contributory.

contri'buto sm contribution; (sovvenzione) subsidy, contribution; (tassa) tax; ~**i previdenziali** ≈ national insurance (BRIT) o welfare (US) contributions; ~**i sindacali** trade union dues.

con'trito, a ag contrite, penitent.

'contro prep against; ~ **di me/lui** against me/him; **pastiglie** ~ **la tosse** throat lozenges; (ammenda) ~ (COMM) on payment; ~ **ogni mia aspettativa** contrary to my expectations; **per** ~ on the other hand.

contro'battere vt (fig: a parole) to answer back; (: confutare) to refute.

controbilanci'are [kontrobilan'tʃare] vt to counterbalance.

controcor'rente av: **andare** ~ (anche fig) to swim against the tide.

controcul'tura sf counterculture.

contro'esodo sm return from holiday.

contro'fax sm inv reply to a fax.

controffen'siva sf counteroffensive.

controfi'gura sf (CINE) double.

controfir'mare vt to countersign.

control'lare vt (accertare) to check; (sorvegliare) to watch, control; (tenere nel proprio potere, fig: dominare) to control; ~**rsi** vr to control o.s.

control'lato, a ag (persona) self-possessed; (reazioni) controlled ♦ sf (COMM: società) associated company.

con'trollo sm check; watch; control; **base di** ~ (AER) ground control; **telefono sotto** ~ tapped telephone; **visita di** ~ (MED) checkup; ~ **doganale** customs inspection; ~ **di gestione** management control; ~ **delle nascite** birth control; ~ **di qualità** quality control.

control'lore sm (FERR, AUTOBUS) (ticket) inspector; ~ **di volo** o **del traffico aereo**

air traffic controller.

contro'luce [kontro'lutʃe] *sf inv* (*FOT*) backlit shot ♦ *av*: **(in)** ~ against the light; (*fotografare*) into the light.

contro'mano *av*: **guidare** ~ to drive on the wrong side of the road; (*in un senso unico*) to drive the wrong way up a one-way street.

contropar'tita *sf* (*fig*: *compenso*): **come** ~ in return.

contropi'ede *sm* (*SPORT*): **azione di** ~ sudden counter-attack; **prendere qn in** ~ (*fig*) to catch sb off his (*o* her) guard.

controprodu'cente [kontroprodu'tʃɛnte] *ag* counterproductive.

con'trordine *sm* counter-order; **salvo** ~ unless I (*o* you *etc*) hear to the contrary.

contro'senso *sm* (*contraddizione*) contradiction in terms; (*assurdità*) nonsense.

controspio'naggio [kontrospio'naddʒo] *sm* counterespionage.

controva'lore *sm* equivalent (value).

contro'vento *av* against the wind; **navigare** ~ (*NAUT*) to sail to windward.

contro'versia *sf* controversy; (*DIR*) dispute; ~ **sindacale** industrial dispute.

contro'verso, a *ag* controversial.

contro'voglia [kontro'vɔʎʎa] *av* unwillingly.

contu'mace [kontu'matʃe] *ag* (*DIR*): **rendersi** ~ to default, fail to appear in court ♦ *sm/f* (*DIR*) defaulter.

contu'macia [kontu'matʃa] *sf* (*DIR*) default.

contun'dente *ag*: **corpo** ~ blunt instrument.

contur'bante *ag* (*sguardo, bellezza*) disturbing.

contur'bare *vt* to disturb, upset.

contusi'one *sf* (*MED*) bruise.

convale'scente [konvaleʃ'ʃɛnte] *ag*, *sm/f* convalescent.

convale'scenza [konvaleʃ'ʃɛntsa] *sf* convalescence.

con'valida *sf* (*DIR*) confirmation; (*di biglietto*) stamping.

convali'dare *vt* (*AMM*) to validate; (*fig*: *sospetto, dubbio*) to confirm.

con'vegno [kon'veɲɲo] *sm* (*incontro*) meeting; (*congresso*) convention, congress; (*luogo*) meeting place.

conve'nevoli *smpl* civilities.

conveni'ente *ag* suitable; (*vantaggioso*) profitable; (: *prezzo*) cheap.

conveni'enza [konve'njɛntsa] *sf* suitability; advantage; cheapness; ~**e** *sfpl* social conventions.

conve'nire *vt* to agree upon ♦ *vi* (*riunirsi*) to

gather, assemble; (*concordare*) to agree; (*tornare utile*) to be worthwhile ♦ *vb impers*: **conviene fare questo** it is advisable to do this; **conviene andarsene** we should go; **ne convengo** I agree; **come convenuto** as agreed; **in data da** ~ on a date to be agreed; **come (si) conviene ad una signorina** as befits a young lady.

conven'ticola *sf* (*cricca*) clique; (*riunione*) secret meeting.

con'vento *sm* (*di frati*) monastery; (*di suore*) convent.

conve'nuto, a *pp di* **convenire** ♦ *sm* (*cosa pattuita*) agreement ♦ *sm/f* (*DIR*) defendant; **i** ~**i** (*i presenti*) those present.

convenzio'nale [konventsjo'nale] *ag* conventional.

convenzio'nato, a [konventsjo'nato] *ag* (*ospedale, clinica*) providing free health care, ≈ National Health Service *cpd* (*BRIT*).

convenzi'one [konven'tsjone] *sf* (*DIR*) agreement; (*nella società*) convention; **le** ~**i** (*sociali*) social conventions.

conver'gente [konver'dʒɛnte] *ag* convergent.

conver'genza [konver'dʒɛntsa] *sf* convergence.

con'vergere [kon'vɛrdʒere] *vi* to converge.

con'versa *sf* (*REL*) lay sister.

conver'sare *vi* to have a conversation, converse.

conversazi'one [konversat'tsjone] *sf* conversation; **fare** ~ (*chiacchierare*) to chat, have a chat.

conversi'one *sf* conversion; ~ **ad U** (*AUT*) U-turn.

con'verso, a *pp di* **convergere**; **per** ~ *av* conversely.

conver'tire *vt* (*trasformare*) to change; (*INFORM, POL, REL*) to convert; ~**rsi** *vr*: ~**rsi (a)** to be converted (to).

conver'tito, a *sm/f* convert.

converti'tore *sm* (*ELETTR*) converter.

con'vesso, a *ag* convex.

convin'cente [konvin'tʃɛnte] *ag* convincing.

con'vincere [kon'vintʃere] *vt* to convince; ~ **qn di qc** to convince sb of sth; (*DIR*) to prove sb guilty of sth; ~ **qn a fare qc** to persuade sb to do sth.

con'vinto, a *pp di* **convincere** ♦ *ag*: **reo** ~ (*DIR*) convicted criminal.

convinzi'one [konvin'tsjone] *sf* conviction, firm belief.

convis'suto, a *pp di* **convivere**.

convi'tato, a *sm/f* guest.

con'vitto *sm* (*INS*) boarding school.

convi'venza [konvi'vɛntsa] *sf* living together; (*DIR*) cohabitation.

con'vivere *vi* to live together.

convivi'ale *ag* convivial.

convo'care *vt* to call, convene; (*DIR*) to summon.

convocazi'one [konvokat'tsjone] *sf* meeting; summons *sg*; **lettera di** ~ (letter of) notification to appear *o* attend.

convogli'are [konvoʎ'ʎare] *vt* to convey; (*dirigere*) to direct, send.

con'voglio [kon'vɔʎʎo] *sm* (*di veicoli*) convoy; (*FERR*) train; ~ **funebre** funeral procession.

convo'lare *vi*: ~ **a (giuste) nozze** (*scherzoso*) to tie the knot.

convulsi'one *sf* convulsion.

con'vulso, a *ag* (*pianto*) violent, convulsive; (*attività*) feverish.

COOP *abbr f* = **cooperativa**.

coope'rare *vi*: ~ **(a)** to cooperate (in).

coopera'tiva *sf* cooperative.

cooperazi'one [kooperat'tsjone] *sf* cooperation.

coordina'mento *sm* coordination.

coordi'nare *vt* to coordinate.

coordi'nato, a *ag* (*movimenti*) coordinated ♦ *sf* (*LING, GEO, MAT*) coordinate ♦ *smpl*: ~i (*MODA*) coordinates.

coordinazi'one [koordinat'tsjone] *sf* coordination.

co'perchio [ko'perkjo] *sm* cover; (*di pentola*) lid.

co'perta *sf* cover; (*di lana*) blanket; (*da viaggio*) rug; (*NAUT*) deck.

coper'tina *sf* (*STAMPA*) cover, jacket.

co'perto, a *pp di* **coprire** ♦ *ag* covered; (*cielo*) overcast ♦ *sm* place setting; (*posto a tavola*) place; (*al ristorante*) cover charge; ~ **di** covered in *o* with.

coper'tone *sm* (*telo impermeabile*) tarpaulin; (*AUT*) rubber tyre.

coper'tura *sf* (*anche ECON, MIL*) cover; (*di edificio*) roofing; **fare un gioco di** ~ (*SPORT*) to play a defensive game; ~ **assicurativa** insurance cover.

'copia *sf* copy; (*FOT*) print; **brutta/bella** ~ rough/final copy; ~ **conforme** (*DIR*) certified copy; ~ **omaggio** presentation copy.

copi'are *vt* to copy.

copia'trice [kopja'tritʃe] *sf* copier, copying machine.

copi'one *sm* (*CINE, TEAT*) script.

'coppa *sf* (*bicchiere*) goblet; (*per frutta, gelato*) dish; (*trofeo*) cup, trophy; ~**e** *sfpl* (*CARTE*) suit in Neapolitan pack of cards; ~ **dell'olio** oil sump (*BRIT*) *o* pan (*US*).

'coppia *sf* (*di persone*) couple; (*di animali, SPORT*) pair.

cop'rente *ag* (*colore, cosmetico*) covering; (*calze*) opaque.

copri'capo *sm* headgear; (*cappello*) hat.

coprifu'oco, chi *sm* curfew.

copri'letto *sm* bedspread.

copripiu'mino *sm inv* duvet cover.

co'prire *vt* to cover; (*occupare: carica, posto*) to hold; ~**rsi** *vr* (*cielo*) to cloud over; (*vestirsi*) to wrap up, cover up; (*ECON*) to cover o.s.; ~**rsi di** (*macchie, muffa*) to become covered in; ~ **qn di baci** to smother sb with kisses; ~ **le spese** to break even; ~**rsi le spalle** (*fig*) to cover o.s.

coque [kɔk] *sf*: **uovo alla** ~ boiled egg.

co'raggio [ko'raddʒo] *sm* courage, bravery; ~**!** (*forza!*) come on!; (*animo!*) cheer up!; **farsi** ~ to pluck up courage; **hai un bel** ~**!** (*sfacciataggine*) you've got a nerve *o* a cheek!

coraggi'oso, a [korad'dʒoso] *ag* courageous, brave.

co'rale *ag* choral; (*approvazione*) unanimous.

co'rallo *sm* coral; **il mar dei C**~**i** the Coral Sea.

co'rano *sm* (*REL*) Koran.

co'razza [ko'rattsa] *sf* armour (*BRIT*), armor (*US*); (*di animali*) carapace, shell; (*MIL*) armo(u)r(-plating).

coraz'zato, a [korat'tsato] *ag* (*MIL*) armoured (*BRIT*), armored (*US*) ♦ *sf* battleship.

corazzi'ere [korat'tsjɛre] *sm* (*STORIA*) cuirassier; (*guardia presidenziale*) carabiniere of the President's guard.

corbelle'ria *sf* stupid remark, ~**e** *sfpl* (*sciocchezze*) nonsense *no pl*.

'corda *sf* cord; (*fune*) rope; (*spago, MUS*) string; **dare** ~ **a qn** (*fig*) to let sb have his (*o* her) way; **tenere sulla** ~ **qn** (*fig*) to keep sb on tenterhooks; **tagliare la** ~ (*fig*) to slip away, sneak off; **essere giù di** ~ to feel down; ~**e vocali** vocal cords.

cor'data *sf* (*ALPINISMO*) roped party; (*fig*) alliance system in financial and business world.

cordi'ale *ag* cordial, warm ♦ *sm* (*bevanda*) cordial.

cordialità *sf inv* warmth, cordiality; ~ *sfpl* (*saluti*) best wishes.

cor'doglio [kor'dɔʎʎo] *sm* grief; (*lutto*) mourning.

cor'done *sm* cord, string; (*linea: di polizia*) cordon; ~ **ombelicale** umbilical cord; ~ **sanitario** quarantine line.

Co'rea sf: **la** ~ Korea; **la** ~ **del Nord/Sud** North/South Korea.
core'ano, a ag, sm/f Korean.
coreogra'fia sf choreography.
core'ografo, a sm/f choreographer.
cori'aceo, a [ko'rjatʃeo] ag (BOT, ZOOL) coriaceous; (fig) tough.
cori'andolo sm (BOT) coriander; ~**i** smpl (per carnevale etc) confetti no pl.
cori'care vt to put to bed; ~**rsi** vr to go to bed.
coricherò etc [korike'rɔ] vb vedi **coricare.**
Co'rinto sf Corinth.
co'rista, i, e sm/f (REL) choir member, chorister; (TEAT) member of the chorus.
'corna sfpl vedi **corno.**
cor'nacchia [kor'nakkja] sf crow.
corna'musa sf bagpipes pl.
'cornea sf (ANAT) cornea.
'corner sm inv (CALCIO) corner (kick); **salvarsi in** ~ (fig: in gara, esame etc) to get through by the skin of one's teeth.
cor'netta sf (MUS) cornet; (TEL) receiver.
cor'netto sm (CUC) croissant; ~ **acustico** ear trumpet.
cor'nice [kor'nitʃe] sf frame; (fig) background, setting.
cornici'one [korni'tʃone] sm (di edificio) ledge; (ARCHIT) cornice.
'corno sm (ZOOL: pl(f) ~**a**, MUS) horn; (fam): **fare le** ~**a a qn** to be unfaithful to sb; **dire peste e** ~**a di qn** to call sb every name under the sun; **un** ~**!** not on your life!
Corno'vaglia [korno'vaʎʎa] sf: **la** ~ Cornwall.
cor'nuto, a ag (con corna) horned; (fam!: marito) cuckolded ♦ sm (fam!) cuckold; (: insulto) bastard (!).
'coro sm chorus; (REL) choir.
corol'lario sm corollary.
co'rona sf crown; (di fiori) wreath.
corona'mento sm (di impresa) completion; (di carriera) crowning achievement; **il** ~ **dei propri sogni** the fulfilment of one's dreams.
coro'nare vt to crown.
coro'naria sf coronary artery.
'corpo sm body; (cadavere) (dead) body; (militare, diplomatico) corps inv; (di opere) corpus; **prendere** ~ to take shape; **darsi anima e** ~ **a** to give o.s. heart and soul to; **a** ~ **a** ~ hand-to-hand; ~ **d'armata** army corps; ~ **di ballo** corps de ballet; ~ **dei carabinieri** ≈ police force; ~ **celeste** heavenly body; ~ **di guardia** (soldati) guard; (locale) guardroom; ~ **insegnante** teaching staff; ~ **del reato** material evidence.

corpo'rale ag bodily; (punizione) corporal.
corpora'tura sf build, physique.
corporazi'one [korporat'tsjone] sf corporation.
cor'poreo, a ag bodily, physical.
cor'poso, a ag (vino) full-bodied.
corpu'lento, a ag stout, corpulent.
corpu'lenza [korpu'lɛntsa] sf stoutness, corpulence.
cor'puscolo sm corpuscle.
corre'dare vt: ~ **di** to provide o furnish with; **domanda corredata dai seguenti documenti** application accompanied by the following documents.
cor'redo sm equipment; (di sposa) trousseau.
cor'reggere [kor'rɛddʒere] vt to correct; (compiti) to correct, mark.
cor'rente ag (fiume) flowing; (acqua del rubinetto) running; (moneta, prezzo) current; (comune) everyday ♦ sm: **essere al** ~ **(di)** to be well-informed (about) ♦ sf (movimento di liquido) current, stream; (spiffero) draught; (ELETTR, METEOR) current; (fig) trend, tendency; **mettere al** ~ **(di)** to inform (of); **la vostra lettera del 5** ~ **mese** (in lettere commerciali) in your letter of the 5th inst.; **articoli di qualità** ~ average-quality products; ~ **alternata** (c.a.) alternating current (AC); ~ **continua (c.c.)** direct current (DC).
corrente'mente av (comunemente) commonly; **parlare una lingua** ~ to speak a language fluently.
corren'tista, i, e sm/f (current (BRIT) o checking (US)) account holder.
cor'reo, a sm/f (DIR) accomplice.
'correre vi to run; (precipitarsi) to rush; (partecipare a una gara) to race, run; (fig: diffondersi) to go round ♦ vt (SPORT: gara) to compete in; (rischio) to run; (pericolo) to face; ~ **dietro a qn** to run after sb; **corre voce che ...** it is rumoured that ....
corresponsabilità sf joint responsibility; (DIR) joint liability.
corresponsi'one sf payment.
cor'ressi etc vb vedi **correggere.**
corret'tezza [korret'tettsa] sf (di comportamento) correctness; (SPORT) fair play.
cor'retto, a pp di **correggere** ♦ ag (comportamento) correct, proper; **caffè** ~ **al cognac** coffee laced with brandy.
corret'tore, 'trice sm/f: ~ **di bozze** proofreader ♦ sm: (liquido) ~ **correction fluid.**
correzi'one [korret'tsjone] sf correction; marking; ~ **di bozze** proofreading.

cor'rida *sf* bullfight.
corri'doio *sm* corridor; **manovre di** ~ (*POL*) lobbying *sg*.
corri'dore *sm* (*SPORT*) runner; (: *su veicolo*) racer.
corri'era *sf* coach (*BRIT*), bus.
corri'ere *sm* (*diplomatico, di guerra*) courier; (*posta*) mail, post; (*spedizioniere*) carrier.
corri'mano *sm* handrail.
corrispet'tivo *sm* amount due; **versare a qn il** ~ **di una prestazione** to pay sb the amount due for his (*o* her) services.
corrispon'dente *ag* corresponding ♦ *sm/f* correspondent.
corrispon'denza [korrispon'dɛntsa] *sf* correspondence; ~ **in arrivo/partenza** incoming/outgoing mail.
corris'pondere *vi* (*equivalere*): ~ (a) to correspond (to); (*per lettera*): ~ **con** to correspond with ♦ *vt* (*stipendio*) to pay; (*fig: amore*) to return.
corris'posto, a *pp di* **corrispondere**.
corrobo'rare *vt* to strengthen, fortify; (*fig*) to corroborate, bear out.
cor'rodere *vt*, ~**rsi** *vr* to corrode.
cor'rompere *vt* to corrupt; (*comprare*) to bribe.
corrosi'one *sf* corrosion.
corro'sivo, a *ag* corrosive.
cor'roso, a *pp di* **corrodere**.
corrotta'mente *av* corruptly.
cor'rotto, a *pp di* **corrompere** ♦ *ag* corrupt.
corrucci'arsi [korrut'tʃarsi] *vr* to grow angry *o* vexed.
corru'gare *vt* to wrinkle; ~ **la fronte** to knit one's brows.
cor'ruppi *etc vb vedi* **corrompere**.
corrut'tela *sf* corruption, depravity.
corruzi'one [korrut'tsjone] *sf* corruption; bribery; ~ **di minorenne** (*DIR*) corruption of a minor.
'corsa *sf* running *no pl*; (*gara*) race; (*di autobus, taxi*) journey, trip; **fare una** ~ to run, dash; (*SPORT*) to run a race; **andare** *o* **essere di** ~ to be in a hurry; ~ **automobilistica/ciclistica** motor/cycle racing; ~ **campestre** cross-country racing; ~ **ad ostacoli** (*IPPICA*) steeplechase; (*ATLETICA*) hurdles race.
cor'saro, a *ag*: **nave** ~**a** privateer ♦ *sm* privateer.
'corsi *etc vb vedi* **correre**.
cor'sia *sf* (*AUT, SPORT*) lane; (*di ospedale*) ward; ~ **di emergenza** (*AUT*) hard shoulder; ~ **preferenziale** ≈ bus lane; (*fig*)

fast track; ~ **di sorpasso** (*AUT*) overtaking lane.
'Corsica *sf*: **la** ~ Corsica.
cor'sivo *sm* cursive (writing); (*TIP*) italics *pl*.
'corso, a *pp di* **correre** ♦ *ag*, *sm/f* Corsican ♦ *sm* course; (*strada cittadina*) main street; (*di unità monetaria*) circulation; (*di titoli, valori*) rate, price; **dar libero** ~ **a** to give free expression to; **in** ~ in progress, under way; (*annata*) current; ~ **d'acqua** river; stream; (*artificiale*) waterway; ~ **serale** evening class; **aver** ~ **legale** to be legal tender.
'corte *sf* (court)yard; (*DIR, regale*) court; **fare la** ~ **a qn** to court sb; ~ **d'appello** court of appeal; ~ **di cassazione** final court of appeal; **C**~ **dei Conti** *State audit court*; **C**~ **Costituzionale** *special court dealing with constitutional and ministerial matters*; ~ **marziale** court-martial; *vedi nota nel riquadro*.

CORTI

The **Corte d'Appello** *hears appeals against sentences passed by courts in both civil and criminal cases and can modify sentences where necessary. The* **Corte d'Assise** *tries serious crimes such as manslaughter and murder; its judges include both legal professionals and members of the public. Similar in structure, the* **Corte d'Assise d'Appello** *hears appeals imposed by these two courts. The* **Corte di Cassazione** *is the highest judicial authority and ensures that the law is correctly applied by the other courts; it may call for a retrial if required. The politically independent* **Corte Costituzionale** *decides whether laws comply with the principles of the Constitution, and has the power to impeach the "Presidente della Repubblica". The* **Corte dei Conti** *ensures the Government's compliance with the law and the Constitution. Reporting directly to Parliament, it oversees the financial aspects of the state budget.*

---

cor'teccia, ce [kor'tettʃa] *sf* bark.
corteggia'mento [korteddʒa'mento] *sm* courtship.
corteggi'are [korted'dʒare] *vt* to court.
corteggia'tore [korteddʒa'tore] *sm* suitor.
cor'teo *sm* procession; ~ **funebre** funeral cortège.
cor'tese *ag* courteous.
corte'sia *sf* courtesy; **fare una** ~ **a qn** to do sb a favour; **per** ~, **dov'è ...?** excuse me, please, where is ...?

cortigi'ano, a [korti'dʒano] *smlf* courtier
♦ *sf* courtesan.
cor'tile *sm* (court)yard.
cor'tina *sf* curtain; (*anche fig*) screen.
corti'sone *sm* cortisone.
'corto, a *ag* short ♦ *av*: **tagliare** ~ to come
straight to the point; **essere a** ~ **di qc** to
be short of sth; **essere a** ~ **di parole** to be
at a loss for words; **la settimana** ~**a** the
5-day week; ~ **circuito** short-circuit.
cortocir'cuito [kortotʃir'kuito] *sm* = **corto**
circuito.
cortome'traggio [kortome'traddʒo] *sm*
short (feature film).
cor'vino, a *ag* (*capelli*) jet-black.
'corvo *sm* raven.
'cosa *sf* thing; (*faccenda*) affair, matter,
business *no pl*; **(che)** ~**?** what?; **(che) cos'è?**
what is it?; **a** ~ **pensi?** what are you
thinking about?; **tante belle** ~**e!** all the
best!; **ormai è** ~ **fatta!** (*positivo*) it's in the
bag!; (*negativo*) it's done now!; **a** ~**e fatte**
when it's all over.
'Cosa 'Nostra *sf* Cosa Nostra.
'cosca, sche *sf* (*di mafiosi*) clan.
'coscia, sce ['kɔʃʃa] *sf* thigh; ~ **di pollo**
(*CUC*) chicken leg.
cosci'ente [koʃ'ʃɛnte] *ag* conscious; ~ **di**
conscious *o* aware of.
cosci'enza [koʃ'ʃɛntsa] *sf* conscience;
(*consapevolezza*) consciousness; ~ **politica**
political awareness.
coscienzi'oso, a [koʃʃen'tsjoso] *ag*
conscientious.
cosci'otto [koʃ'ʃɔtto] *sm* (*CUC*) leg.
cos'critto *sm* (*MIL*) conscript.
coscrizi'one [koskrit'tsjone] *sf*
conscription.

================= *PAROLA CHIAVE*

così *av* **1** (*in questo modo*) like this, (in) this
way; (*in tal modo*) so; **le cose stanno** ~ this
is the way things stand; **non ho detto** ~**!** I
didn't say that!; **come stai?** — **(e)** ~ **how**
are you? — so-so; **e** ~ **via** and so on; **per** ~
dire so to speak; ~ **sia** amen
2 (*tanto*) so; ~ **lontano** so far away; **un**
ragazzo ~ **intelligente** such an intelligent
boy
♦ *ag inv* (*tale*): **non ho mai visto un film** ~
I've never seen such a film
♦ *cong* **1** (*perciò*) so, therefore; **e** ~ **ho**
deciso di lasciarlo so I decided to leave
him
2: ~ ... **come** as ... as; **non è** ~ **bravo**
come te he's not as good as you; ~ ... **che**
so ... that.

cosicché [kosik'ke] *cong* so (that).
cosid'detto, a *ag* so-called.
cos'mesi *sf* (*scienza*) cosmetics *sg*;
(*prodotti*) cosmetics *pl*; (*trattamento*)
beauty treatment.
cos'metico, a, ci, che *ag, sm* cosmetic.
'cosmico, a, ci, che *ag* cosmic.
'cosmo *sm* cosmos.
cosmo'nauta, i, e *smlf* cosmonaut.
cosmopo'lita, i, e *ag* cosmopolitan.
'coso *sm* (*fam*: *oggetto*) thing, thingumajig;
(: *aggeggio*) contraption; (: *persona*) what's
his name, thingumajig.
cos'pargere [kos'pardʒere] *vt*: ~ **di** to
sprinkle with.
cos'parso, a *pp di* **cospargere.**
cos'petto *sm*: **al** ~ **di** in front of; in the
presence of.
cospicuità *sf* vast quantity.
cos'picuo, a *ag* considerable, large.
cospi'rare *vi* to conspire.
cospira'tore, 'trice *smlf* conspirator.
cospirazi'one [kospirat'tsjone] *sf*
conspiracy.
'cossi *etc vb vedi* **cuocere.**
Cost. *abbr* = **costituzione.**
'costa *sf* (*tra terra e mare*) coast(line);
(*litorale*) shore; (*pendio*) slope; (*ANAT*) rib;
navigare sotto ~ to hug the coast; **la C**~
Azzurra the French Riviera; **la C**~
d'Avorio the Ivory Coast; **velluto a** ~**e**
corduroy.
costà *av* there.
cos'tante *ag* constant; (*persona*) steadfast
♦ *sf* constant.
cos'tanza [kos'tantsa] *sf* (*gen*) constancy;
(*fermezza*) constancy, steadfastness; **il**
Lago di C~ Lake Constance.
cos'tare *vi, vt* to cost; ~ **caro** to be
expensive, cost a lot; ~ **un occhio della**
testa to cost a fortune; **costi quel che**
costi no matter what.
'Costa 'Rica *sf*: **la** ~ Costa Rica.
cos'tata *sf* (*CUC*: *di manzo*) large chop.
cos'tato *sm* (*ANAT*) ribs *pl*.
costeggi'are [kosted'dʒare] *vt* to be close
to; to run alongside.
cos'tei *pron vedi* **costui.**
costellazi'one [kostellat'tsjone] *sf*
constellation.
coster'nare *vt* to dismay.
coster'nato, a *ag* dismayed.
costernazi'one [kosternat'tsjone] *sf*
dismay, consternation.
costi'ero, a *ag* coastal, coast *cpd* ♦ *sf*
stretch of coast.
costi'pato, a *ag* (*stitico*) constipated.
costitu'ire *vt* (*comitato, gruppo*) to set up,

form; (*collezione*) to put together, build up; (*sog: elementi, parti: comporre*) to make up, constitute; (*rappresentare*) to constitute; (*DIR*) to appoint; ~**rsi** *vr:* ~**rsi (alla polizia)** to give o.s. up (to the police); ~**rsi parte civile** (*DIR*) *to associate in an action with the public prosecutor for damages*; **il fatto non costituisce reato** this is not a crime.

costitu'tivo, a *ag* constituent, component; **atto** ~ (*DIR: di società*) memorandum of association.

costituzio'nale [kostituttsjo'nale] *ag* constitutional.

costituzi'one [kostitut'tsjone] *sf* setting up; building up; constitution.

'costo *sm* cost; **sotto** ~ for less than cost price; **a ogni o qualunque** ~, **a tutti i** ~**i** at all costs; ~**i di esercizio** running costs; ~**i fissi** fixed costs; ~**i di gestione** operating costs; ~**i di produzione** production costs.

'costola *sf* (*ANAT*) rib; **ha la polizia alle** ~**e** the police are hard on his heels.

costo'letta *sf* (*CUC*) cutlet.

cos'toro *pron pl vedi* **costui.**

cos'toso, a *ag* expensive, costly.

cos'tretto, a *pp di* **costringere.**

cos'tringere [kos'trindʒere] *vt:* ~ **qn a faro qc** to force sb to do sth.

costrit'tivo, a *ag* coercive.

costrizi'one [kostrit'tsjone] *sf* coercion.

costru'ire *vt* to construct, build.

costrut'tivo, a *ag* (*EDIL*) building *cpd*; (*fig*) constructive.

costruzi'one [kostrut'tsjone] *sf* construction, building; **di** ~ **inglese** British-made.

cos'tui, cos'tei, *pl* **cos'toro** *pron* (*soggetto*) he/she; *pl* they; (*complemento*) him/her; *pl* them; **si può sapere chi è** ~? (*peg*) just who is that fellow?

cos'tume *sm* (*uso*) custom; (*foggia di vestire, indumento*) costume; **il buon** ~ public morality; **donna di facili** ~**i** woman of easy morals; ~ **da bagno** bathing o swimming costume (*BRIT*), swimsuit; (*da uomo*) bathing o swimming trunks *pl.*

costu'mista, i, e *sm/f* costume maker, costume designer.

co'tenna *sf* bacon rind.

co'togna [ko'toɲɲa] *sf* quince.

coto'letta *sf* (*di maiale, montone*) chop; (*di vitello, agnello*) cutlet.

coto'nare *vt* (*capelli*) to backcomb.

co'tone *sm* cotton; ~ **idrofilo** cotton wool (*BRIT*), absorbent cotton (*US*).

cotoni'ficio [kotoni'fitʃo] *sm* cotton mill.

'cotta *sf* (*REL*) surplice; (*fam:*

innamoramento) crush.

'cottimo *sm:* **lavorare a** ~ to do piecework.

'cotto, a *pp di* **cuocere** ♦ *ag* cooked; (*fam: innamorato*) head-over-heels in love ♦ *sm* brickwork; ~ **a puntino** cooked to perfection; **dirne di** ~**e e di crude a qn** to call sb every name under the sun; **farne di** ~**e e di crude** to get up to all kinds of mischief; **mattone di** ~ fired brick; **pavimento in** ~ tile floor.

cot'tura *sf* cooking; (*in forno*) baking; (*in umido*) stewing; ~ **a fuoco lento** simmering; **angolo (di)** ~ cooking area.

co'vare *vt* to hatch; (*fig: malattia*) to be sickening for; (*: odio, rancore*) to nurse ♦ *vi* (*fuoco, fig*) to smoulder (*BRIT*), smolder (*US*).

co'vata *sf* (*anche fig*) brood.

'covo *sm* den; ~ **di terroristi** terrorist base.

co'vone *sm* sheaf.

'cozza ['kɔttsa] *sf* mussel.

coz'zare [kot'tsare] *vi:* ~ **contro** to bang into, collide with.

'cozzo ['kɔttso] *sm* collision.

C.P. *abbr* (= *cartolina postale*) pc; (*POSTA*) *vedi* **casella postale**; (*NAUT*) = **capitaneria (di porto)**; (*DIR*) = **codice penale.**

crack *sm inv* (*droga*) crack.

Cra'covia *sf* Cracow.

'crampo *sm* cramp.

'cranio *sm* skull.

cra'tere *sm* crater.

cra'vatta *sf* tie; ~ **a farfalla** bow tie.

cravat'tino *sm* bow tie.

cre'anza [kre'antsa] *sf* manners *pl*; **per buona** ~ out of politeness.

cre'are *vt* to create.

creatività *sf* creativity.

cre'ato *sm* creation.

crea'tore, 'trice *ag* creative ♦ *sm/f* creator; **un** ~ **di alta moda** fashion designer; **andare al C**~ to go to meet one's maker.

crea'tura *sf* creature; (*bimbo*) baby, infant.

creazi'one [kreat'tsjone] *sf* creation; (*fondazione*) foundation, establishment.

'crebbi *etc vb vedi* **crescere.**

cre'dente *sm/f* (*REL*) believer.

cre'denza [kre'dentsa] *sf* belief; (*armadio*) sideboard.

credenzi'ali [kreden'tsjali] *sfpl* credentials.

'credere *vt* to believe ♦ *vi:* ~ **in**, ~ **a** to believe in; ~ **qn onesto** to believe sb (to be) honest; ~ **che** to believe o think that; ~**rsi furbo** to think one is clever; **lo credo bene!** I can well believe it!; **fai quello che credi** o **come credi** do as you please.

cre'dibile *ag* credible, believable.

credibilità *sf* credibility.

credi'tizio, a [kredi'tittsjo] *ag* credit.
'credito *sm* (*anche* COMM) credit; (*reputazione*) esteem, repute; **comprare a** ~ to buy on credit; ~ **agevolato** easy credit terms; ~ **d'imposta** tax credit.
credi'tore, 'trice *sm/f* creditor.
'credo *sm inv* creed.
'credulo, a *ag* credulous.
credu'lone, a *sm/f* simpleton, sucker (*fam*).
'crema *sf* cream; (*con uova, zucchero etc*) custard; ~ **idratante** moisturizing cream; ~ **pasticciera** confectioner's custard; ~ **solare** sun cream.
cre'mare *vt* to cremate.
crema'torio *sm* crematorium.
cremazi'one [kremat'tsjone] *sf* cremation.
'cremisi *ag inv, sm inv* crimson.
Crem'lino *sm*: **il** ~ the Kremlin.
cremo'nese *ag* of (*o* from) Cremona.
cre'moso, a *ag* creamy.
'crepa *sf* crack.
cre'paccio [kre'pattʃo] *sm* large crack, fissure; (*di ghiacciaio*) crevasse.
crepacu'ore *sm* broken heart.
crepa'pelle *av*: **ridere a** ~ to split one's sides laughing.
cre'pare *vi* (*fam: morire*) to snuff it (BRIT), kick the bucket; ~ **dalle risa** to split one's sides laughing; ~ **dall'invidia** to be green with envy.
crepi'tare *vi* (*fuoco*) to crackle; (*pioggia*) to patter.
crepi'tio, ii *sm* crackling; pattering.
cre'puscolo *sm* twilight, dusk.
cre'scendo [kreʃ'ʃendo] *sm* (MUS) crescendo.
cre'scente [kreʃ'ʃente] *ag* (*gen*) growing, increasing; (*luna*) waxing.
'crescere ['kreʃʃere] *vi* to grow ♦ *vt* (*figli*) to raise.
cre'scione [kreʃ'ʃone] *sm* watercress.
'crescita ['kreʃʃita] *sf* growth.
cresci'uto, a [kreʃ'ʃuto] *pp di* **crescere**.
'cresima *sf* (REL) confirmation.
cresi'mare *vt* to confirm.
'crespo, a *ag* (*capelli*) frizzy; (*tessuto*) puckered ♦ *sm* crêpe.
'cresta *sf* crest; (*di polli, uccelli*) crest, comb; **alzare la** ~ (*fig*) to become cocky; **abbassare la** ~ (*fig*) to climb down; **essere sulla** ~ **dell'onda** (*fig*) to be riding high.
'Creta *sf* Crete.
'creta *sf* (*gesso*) chalk; (*argilla*) clay.
cre'tese *ag, sm/f* Cretan.
creti'nata *sf* (*fam*): **dire/fare una** ~ to say/ do a stupid thing.
cre'tino, a *ag* stupid ♦ *sm/f* idiot, fool.
CRI *sigla f* = *Croce Rossa Italiana*.

cric *sm inv* (TECN) jack.
'cricca, che *sf* clique.
'cricco, chi *sm* = **cric**.
cri'ceto [kri'tʃeto] *sm* hamster.
crimi'nale *ag, sm/f* criminal.
criminalità *sf* crime; ~ **organizzata** organized crime.
'Criminalpol *abbr* = **polizia criminale**.
'crimine *sm* (DIR) crime.
criminolo'gia [kriminolo'dʒia] *sf* criminology.
crimi'noso, a *ag* criminal.
cri'nale *sm* ridge.
'crine *sm* horsehair.
crini'era *sf* mane.
'cripta *sf* crypt.
crip'tare *vt* (TV: *programma*) to encrypt.
crip'tato, a *ag* (*programma, messaggio*) encrypted.
crisan'temo *sm* chrysanthemum; *vedi anche* **Giorno dei Morti**.
'crisi *sf inv* crisis; (MED) attack, fit; **essere in** ~ (*partito, impresa etc*) to be in a state of crisis; ~ **energetica** energy crisis; ~ **di nervi** attack *o* fit of nerves.
cristalle'ria *sf* (*fabbrica*) crystal glassworks *sg*; (*oggetti*) crystalware.
cristal'lino, a *ag* (MINERALOGIA) crystalline; (*fig: suono, acque*) crystal clear ♦ *sm* (ANAT) crystalline lens.
cristalliz'zare [kristallid'dzare] *vi*, ~**rsi** *vr* to crystallize; (*fig*) to become fossilized.
cris'tallo *sm* crystal.
cristia'nesimo *sm* Christianity.
cristianità *sf* Christianity; (*i cristiani*) Christendom.
cristi'ano, a *ag, sm/f* Christian; **un povero** ~ (*fig*) a poor soul *o* beggar; **comportarsi da** ~ (*fig*) to behave in a civilized manner.
'cristo *sm*: **C**~ Christ; (**un**) **povero** ~ (a) poor beggar.
cri'terio *sm* criterion; (*buon senso*) (common) sense.
'critica, che *sf vedi* **critico**.
criti'care *vt* to criticize.
'critico, a, ci, che *ag* critical ♦ *sm* critic ♦ *sf* criticism; **la** ~**a** (*attività*) criticism; (*persone*) the critics *pl*.
criti'cone, a *sm/f* faultfinder.
crivel'lare *vt*: ~ (**di**) to riddle (with).
cri'vello *sm* riddle.
cro'ato, a *ag, sm/f* Croatian, Croat.
Cro'azia [kro'attsja] *sf*: **la** ~ Croatia.
croc'cante *ag* crisp, crunchy ♦ *sm* (CUC) almond crunch.
'crocchia ['krɔkkja] *sf* chignon, bun.
'crocchio ['krɔkkjo] *sm* (*di persone*) small

group, cluster.

'croce ['krɔtʃe] *sf* cross; **in** ~ (*di traverso*) crosswise; (*fig*) on tenterhooks; **mettere in** ~ (*anche fig: criticare*) to crucify; (: *tormentare*) to nag to death; **la C**~ **Rossa** the Red Cross; ~ **uncinata** swastika.

croce'figgere *etc* [krotʃe'fiddʒere] = **crocifiggere** *etc*.

croceros'sina [krotʃeros'sina] *sf* Red Cross nurse.

croce'via [krotʃe'via] *sm inv* crossroads *sg*.

croci'ato, a [kro'tʃato] *ag* cross-shaped ♦ *sm* (*anche fig*) crusader ♦ *sf* crusade.

cro'cicchio [kro'tʃikkjo] *sm* crossroads *sg*.

croci'era [kro'tʃɛra] *sf* (*viaggio*) cruise; (*ARCHIT*) transept; **altezza di** ~ (*AER*) cruising height; **velocità di** ~ (*AER, NAUT*) cruising speed.

croci'figgere [krotʃi'fiddʒere] *vt* to crucify.

crocifissi'one [krotʃifis'sjone] *sf* crucifixion.

croci'fisso, a [krotʃi'fisso] *pp di* **crocifiggere** ♦ *sm* crucifix.

crogio'larsi [krodʒo'larsi] *vr*: ~ **al sole** to bask in the sun.

crogi'olo [kro'dʒɔlo], **crogiu'olo** [kro'dʒwɔlo] *sm* crucible; (*fig*) melting pot.

crol'lare *vi* to collapse.

'crollo *sm* collapse; (*di prezzi*) slump, sudden fall.

'croma *sf* (*MUS*) quaver (*BRIT*), eighth note (*US*).

cro'mato, a *ag* chromium-plated.

'cromo *sm* chrome, chromium.

cromo'soma, i *sm* chromosome.

'cronaca, che *sf* chronicle; (*STAMPA*) news *sg*; (: *rubrica*) column; (*TV, RADIO*) commentary; **fatto** *o* **episodio di** ~ news item; ~ **nera** crime news *sg*; crime column.

'cronico, a, ci, che *ag* chronic.

cro'nista, i *sm* (*STAMPA*) reporter, columnist.

cronis'toria *sf* chronicle; (*fig: ironico*) blow-by-blow account.

cro'nografo *sm* (*strumento*) chronograph.

cronolo'gia [kronolo'dʒia] *sf* chronology.

cronome'trare *vt* to time.

cro'nometro *sm* chronometer; (*a scatto*) stopwatch.

'crosta *sf* crust; (*MED*) scab; (*ZOOL*) shell; (*di ghiaccio*) layer; (*fig peg: quadro*) daub.

cros'tacei [kros'tatʃei] *smpl* shellfish.

cros'tata *sf* (*CUC*) tart.

cros'tino *sm* (*CUC*) croûton; (: *da antipasto*) canapé.

crucci'are [krut'tʃare] *vt* to torment, worry; ~**rsi** *vr*: ~**rsi per** to torment o.s. over.

'cruccio ['kruttʃo] *sm* worry, torment.

cruci'ale [kru'tʃale] *ag* crucial.

cruci'verba [krutʃi'vɛrba] *sm inv* crossword (puzzle).

cru'dele *ag* cruel.

crudeltà *sf* cruelty.

'crudo, a *ag* (*non cotto*) raw; (*aspro*) harsh, severe.

cru'ento, a *ag* bloody.

cru'miro *sm* (*peg*) blackleg (*BRIT*), scab.

'cruna *sf* eye (of a needle).

'crusca *sf* bran.

crus'cotto *sm* (*AUT*) dashboard.

CS *sigla* = *Cosenza*.

c.s. *abbr* = *come sopra*.

CSI [tʃi'ɛsse'i] *sigla f* (= *Comunità di Stati Indipendenti*) CIS.

CSM [tʃiɛsse'ɛmme] *sigla m* (= *consiglio superiore della magistratura*) Magistrates' Board of Supervisors.

CT *sigla* = *Catania*.

c.t. *abbr* = **commissario tecnico**.

'Cuba *sf* Cuba.

cu'bano, a *ag*, *sm/f* Cuban.

cu'betto *sm* (small) cube; ~ **di ghiaccio** ice cube.

'cubico, a, ci, che *ag* cubic.

cu'bista *sf* podium dancer, *dancer who performs on stage in a club*.

'cubo, a *ag* cubic ♦ *sm* cube; **elevare al** ~ (*MAT*) to cube.

cuc'cagna [kuk'kaɲɲa] *sf*: **paese della** ~ land of plenty; **albero della** ~ greasy pole (*fig*).

cuc'cetta [kut'tʃetta] *sf* (*FERR*) couchette; (*NAUT*) berth.

cucchiai'ata [kukkja'jata] *sf* spoonful; tablespoonful.

cucchia'ino [kukkja'ino] *sm* teaspoon; coffee spoon.

cucchi'aio [kuk'kjajo] *sm* spoon; (*da tavola*) tablespoon; (*cucchiaiata*) spoonful; tablespoonful.

'cuccia, ce ['kuttʃa] *sf* dog's bed; **a** ~! down!

cuccio'lata [kuttʃo'lata] *sf* litter.

'cucciolo ['kuttʃolo] *sm* cub; (*di cane*) puppy.

cu'cina [ku'tʃina] *sf* (*locale*) kitchen; (*arte culinaria*) cooking, cookery; (*le vivande*) food, cooking; (*apparecchio*) cooker; **di** ~ (*libro, lezione*) cookery *cpd*; ~ **componibile** fitted kitchen; ~ **economica** kitchen range.

cuci'nare [kutʃi'nare] *vt* to cook.

cuci'nino [kutʃi'nino] *sm* kitchenette.

cu'cire [ku'tʃire] *vt* to sew, stitch; ~ **la bocca a qn** (*fig*) to shut sb up.

cu'cito, a [ku'tʃito] *sm* sewing; (*INS*) sewing, needlework.
cuci'trice [kutʃi'tritʃe] *sf* (*TIP*: *per libri*) stitching machine; (*per fogli*) stapler.
cuci'tura [kutʃi'tura] *sf* sewing, stitching; (*costura*) seam.
cucù *sm inv*, **cu'culo** *sm* cuckoo.
'cuffia *sf* bonnet, cap; (*da infermiera*) cap; (*da bagno*) (bathing) cap; (*per ascoltare*) headphones *pl*, headset.
cu'gino, a [ku'dʒino] *sm/f* cousin.

━━━━━━━━━━━━━ PAROLA CHIAVE

'cui *pron* **1** (*nei complementi indiretti: persona*) whom; (*: oggetto, animale*) which; **la persona/le persone a ~ accennavi** the person/people you were referring to *o* to whom you were referring; **la penna con ~ scrivo** the pen I'm writing with; **il paese da ~ viene** the country he comes from; **i libri di ~ parlavo** the books I was talking about *o* about which I was talking; **parla varie lingue, fra ~ l'inglese** he speaks several languages, including English; **il quartiere in ~ abito** the district where I live; **visto il modo in ~ ti ha trattato** ... considering how he treated you ...; **la ragione per ~** the reason why; **per ~ non so più che fare** that's why I don't know what to do
2 (*inserito tra articolo e sostantivo*) whose; **la donna i ~ figli sono scomparsi** the woman whose children have disappeared; **il signore, dal ~ figlio ho avuto il libro** the man from whose son I got the book.

culi'naria *sf* cookery.
culi'nario, a *ag* culinary.
'culla *sf* cradle.
cul'lare *vt* to rock; (*fig: idea, speranza*) to cherish; **~rsi** *vr* (*gen*) to sway; **~rsi in vane speranze** (*fig*) to cherish fond hopes; **~rsi nel dolce far niente** (*fig*) to sit back and relax.
culmi'nante *ag*: **posizione ~** (*ASTR*) highest point; **punto** *o* **momento ~** (*fig*) climax.
culmi'nare *vi*: **~ in** *o* **con** to culminate in.
'culmine *sm* top, summit.
'culo *sm* (*fam!*) arse (*BRIT!*), ass (*US!*); (*: fig: fortuna*): **aver ~** to have the luck of the devil; **prendere qn per il ~** to take the piss out of sb (*!*).
'culto *sm* (*religione*) religion; (*adorazione*) worship, adoration; (*venerazione: anche fig*) cult.
cul'tura *sf* (*gen*) culture; (*conoscenza*)

education, learning; **di ~** (*persona*) cultured; (*istituto*) cultural, of culture; **~ generale** general knowledge; **~ di massa** mass culture.
cultu'rale *ag* cultural.
cultu'rismo *sm* body-building.
cumu'lare *vt* to accumulate, amass.
cumula'tivo, a *ag* cumulative; (*prezzo*) inclusive; (*biglietto*) group *cpd*.
'cumulo *sm* (*mucchio*) pile, heap; (*METEOR*) cumulus; **~ dei redditi** (*FISCO*) combined incomes; **~ delle pene** (*DIR*) consecutive sentences.
'cuneo *sm* wedge.
cu'netta *sf* (*di strada etc*) bump; (*scolo: nelle strade di città*) gutter; (*: di campagna*) ditch.
cu'nicolo *sm* (*galleria*) tunnel; (*di miniera*) pit, shaft; (*di talpa*) hole.
cu'oca *sf vedi* **cuoco**.
cu'ocere ['kwɔtʃere] *vt* (*alimenti*) to cook; (*mattoni etc*) to fire ♦ *vi* to cook; **~ in umido/a vapore/in padella** to stew/steam/fry; **~ al forno** (*pane*) to bake; (*arrosto*) to roast.
cu'oco, a, chi, che *sm/f* cook; (*di ristorante*) chef.
cuoi'ame *sm* leather goods *pl*.
cu'oio *sm* leather; **~ capelluto** scalp; **tirare le ~a** (*fam*) to kick the bucket.
cu'ore *sm* heart; **~i** *smpl* (*CARTE*) hearts; **avere buon ~** to be kind-hearted; **stare a ~ a qn** to be important to sb; **un grazie di ~** heartfelt thanks; **ringraziare di ~** to thank sincerely; **nel profondo del ~** in one's heart of hearts; **avere la morte nel ~** to be sick at heart; **club dei ~i solitari** lonely hearts club.
cupi'digia [kupi'didʒa] *sf* greed, covetousness.
'cupo, a *ag* dark; (*suono*) dull; (*fig*) gloomy, dismal.
'cupola *sf* dome; (*più piccola*) cupola; (*fig*) Mafia high command.
'cura *sf* care; (*MED: trattamento*) (course of) treatment; **aver ~ di** (*occuparsi di*) to look after; **a ~ di** (*libro*) edited by; **fare una ~** to follow a course of treatment; **~ dimagrante** diet.
cu'rabile *ag* curable.
cu'rante *ag*: **medico ~** doctor (in charge of a patient).
cu'rare *vt* (*malato, malattia*) to treat; (*: guarire*) to cure; (*aver cura di*) to take care of; (*testo*) to edit; **~rsi** *vr* to take care of o.s.; (*MED*) to follow a course of treatment; **~rsi di** to pay attention to; (*occuparsi di*) to look after.
cu'rato *sm* parish priest; (*protestante*)

vicar, minister.
cura'tore, 'trice *sm/f* (*DIR*) trustee; (*di antologia etc*) editor; ~ **fallimentare** (official) receiver.
'curdo, a *ag* Kurdish ♦ *sm/f* Kurd.
'curia *sf* (*REL*): **la** ~ **romana** the Roman curia; ~ **notarile** notaries' association *o* guild.
curio'saggine [kurjo'saddʒine] *sf* nosiness.
curio'sare *vi* to look round, wander round; (*tra libri*) to browse; ~ **nei negozi** to look *o* wander round the shops; ~ **nelle faccende altrui** to poke one's nose into other people's affairs.
curiosità *sf inv* curiosity; (*cosa rara*) curio, curiosity.
curi'oso, a *ag* (*che vuol sapere*) curious, inquiring; (*ficcanaso*) curious, inquisitive; (*bizzarro*) strange, curious ♦ *sm/f* busybody, nosy parker; **essere** ~ **di** to be curious about; **una folla di** ~**i** a crowd of onlookers.
cur'riculum *sm inv*: ~ (**vitae**) curriculum vitae.
cur'sore *sm* (*INFORM*) cursor.
'curva *sf* curve; (*stradale*) bend, curve.
cur'vare *vt* to bend ♦ *vi* (*veicolo*) to take a bend; (*strada*) to bend, curve; ~**rsi** *vr* to bend; (*legno*) to warp.
'curvo, a *ag* curved; (*piegato*) bent.
CUS *sigla m* = *Centro Universitario Sportivo.*
cusci'netto [kuʃʃi'netto] *sm* pad; (*TECN*) bearing ♦ *ag inv*: **stato** ~ buffer state; ~ **a sfere** ball bearing.
cu'scino [kuʃ'ʃino] *sm* cushion; (*guanciale*) pillow.
'cuspide *sf* (*ARCHIT*) spire.
cus'tode *sm/f* (*di museo*) keeper, custodian; (*di parco*) warden; (*di casa*) concierge; (*di fabbrica, carcere*) guard.
cus'todia *sf* care; (*DIR*) custody; (*astuccio*) case, holder; **avere qc in** ~ to look after sth; **dare qc in** ~ **a qn** to entrust sth to sb's care; **agente di** ~ prison warder; ~ **delle carceri** prison security; ~ **cautelare** (*DIR*) remand.
custo'dire *vt* (*conservare*) to keep; (*assistere*) to look after, take care of; (*fare la guardia*) to guard.
'cute *sf* (*ANAT*) skin.
cu'ticola *sf* cuticle.
C.V. *abbr* = **cavallo vapore.**
c.v.d. *abbr* (= *come volevasi dimostrare*) QED (= *quod erat demonstrandum*).
c.vo *abbr* = **corsivo.**
cy'clette ® [si'klɛt] *sf inv* exercise bike.
CZ *sigla* = *Catanzaro.*

D d

D, d [di] *sf o m inv* (*lettera*) D, d; **D come Domodossola** ≈ D for David (*BRIT*), D for Dog (*US*).
D *abbr* (= *destra*) R; (*FERR*) = **diretto.**

═══════════════ *PAROLA CHIAVE*

da (*da* + *il* = **dal**, *da* + *lo* = **dallo**, *da* + *l'* = **dall'**, *da* + *la* = **dalla**, *da* + *i* = **dai**, *da* + *gli* = **dagli**, *da* + *le* = **dalle**) *prep* **1** (*agente*) by; **dipinto** ~ **un grande artista** painted by a great artist
2 (*causa*) with; **tremare dalla paura** to tremble with fear
3 (*stato in luogo*) at; **abito** ~ **lui** I'm living at his house *o* with him; **sono dal giornalaio** I'm at the newsagent's; **era** ~ **Francesco** she was at Francesco's (house)
4 (*moto a luogo*) to; (*moto per luogo*) through; **vado** ~ **Pietro/dal giornalaio** I'm going to Pietro's (house)/to the newsagent's; **sono passati dalla finestra** they came in through the window
5 (*provenienza, allontanamento*) from; ~ ... **a** from ... to; **arrivare/partire** ~ **Milano** to arrive/depart from Milan; **scendere dal treno/dalla macchina** to get off the train/ out of the car; **viene** ~ **una famiglia povera** he comes from a poor background; **viene dalla Scozia** he comes from Scotland; **ti chiamo** ~ **una cabina** I'm phoning from a call box; **si trova a 5 km** ~ **qui** it's 5 km from here
6 (*tempo: durata*) for; (: *a partire da: nel passato*) since; (: *nel futuro*) from; **vivo qui** ~ **un anno** I've been living here for a year; **è dalle 3 che ti aspetto** I've been waiting for you since 3 (o'clock); ~ **mattina a sera** from morning till night; ~ **oggi in poi** from today onwards; ~ **bambino** as a child, when I (*o* he *etc*) was a child
7 (*modo, maniera*) like; **comportarsi** ~ **uomo** to behave like a man; **l'ho fatto** ~ **me** I did it (by) myself; **non è** ~ **lui** it's not like him
8 (*descrittivo*): **una macchina** ~ **corsa** a racing car; **è una cosa** ~ **poco** it's nothing special; **una ragazza dai capelli biondi** a

girl with blonde hair; **sordo ~ un orecchio** deaf in one ear; **abbigliamento ~ uomo** menswear; **un vestito ~ 100 euro** a 100 euro dress; **qualcosa ~ bere/mangiare** something to drink/eat.

dà *vb vedi* **dare.**

dab'bene *ag inv* honest, decent.

'Dacca *sf* Dacca.

dac'capo, da 'capo *av* (*di nuovo*) (once) again; (*dal principio*) all over again, from the beginning.

dacché [dak'ke] *cong* since.

'dado *sm* (*da gioco*) dice *o* die (*pl* dice); (*CUC*) stock cube (*BRIT*), bouillon cube (*US*); (*TECN*) (screw) nut; **~i** *smpl* (game of) dice.

daf'fare, da 'fare *sm* work, toil; **avere un gran ~** to be very busy.

'dagli ['daʎʎi], **'dai** *prep* + *det vedi* **da.**

'daino *sm* (fallow) deer *inv*; (*pelle*) buckskin.

Da'kar *sf* Dakar.

dal *prep* + *det vedi* **da.**

dal *abbr* (= *decalitro*) dal.

dall', 'dalla, 'dalle, 'dallo *prep* + *det vedi* **da.**

dal'tonico, a, ci, che *ag* colour-blind (*BRIT*), colorblind (*US*).

dam *abbr* (= *decametro*) dam.

'dama *sf* lady; (*nei balli*) partner; (*gioco*) draughts *sg* (*BRIT*), checkers *sg* (*US*); **far ~** (*nel gioco*) to make a crown; **~ di compagnia** lady's companion; **~ di corte** lady-in-waiting.

Da'masco *sf* Damascus.

dami'gella [dami'dʒɛlla] *sf* (*STORIA*) damsel; (: *titolo*) mistress; **~ d'onore** (*di sposa*) bridesmaid.

damigi'ana [dami'dʒana] *sf* demijohn.

dam'meno *ag inv*: **per non essere ~ di qn** so as not to be outdone by sb.

DAMS *sigla m* (= *Disciplina delle Arti, della Musica, dello Spettacolo*) *study of the performing arts.*

da'naro *sm* = denaro.

dana'roso, a *ag* wealthy.

da'nese *ag* Danish ♦ *sm/f* Dane ♦ *sm* (*LING*) Danish.

Dani'marca *sf*: **la ~** Denmark.

dan'nare *vt* (*REL*) to damn; **~rsi** *vr*: **~rsi** (**per**) (*fig: tormentarsi*) to be worried to death (by); **far ~ qn** to drive sb mad; **~rsi l'anima per qc** (*affannarsi*) to work o.s. to death for sth; (*tormentarsi*) to worry o.s. to death over sth.

dan'nato, a *ag* damned.

dannazi'one [dannat'tsjone] *sf* damnation.

danneggi'are [danned'dʒare] *vt* to damage; (*rovinare*) to spoil; (*nuocere*) to harm; **la parte danneggiata** (*DIR*) the injured party.

'danno *vb vedi* **dare** ♦ *sm* damage; (*a persona*) harm, injury; **~i** *smpl* (*DIR*) damages; **a ~ di qn** to sb's detriment; **chiedere/risarcire i ~i** to sue for/pay damages.

dan'noso, a *ag*: **~ (a *o* per)** harmful (to), bad (for).

dan'tesco, a schi, sche *ag* Dantesque; **l'opera ~a** Dante's work.

Da'nubio *sm*: **il ~** the Danube.

'danza ['dantsa] *sf*: **la ~** dancing; **una ~ a** dance.

dan'zante [dan'tsante] *ag* dancing; **serata ~** dance.

dan'zare [dan'tsare] *vt, vi* to dance.

danza'tore, 'trice [dantsa'tore] *sm/f* dancer.

dapper'tutto *av* everywhere.

dap'poco *ag inv* inept; worthless.

dap'prima *av* at first.

Darda'nelli *smpl*: **i ~** the Dardanelles.

'dardo *sm* dart.

'dare *sm* (*COMM*) debit ♦ *vt* to give; (*produrre: frutti, suono*) to produce ♦ *vi* (*guardare*): **~ su** to look (out) onto; **~rsi** *vr*: **~rsi a** to dedicate o.s. to; **quanti anni mi dai?** how old do you think I am?; **danno ancora quel film?** is that film still showing?; **~ da mangiare a qn** to give sb something to eat; **~ per certo qc** to consider sth certain; **~ ad intendere a qn che ...** to lead sb to believe that ...; **~ per morto qn** to give sb up for dead; **~ qc per scontato** to take sth for granted; **~rsi ammalato** to report sick; **~rsi alla bella vita** to have a good time; **~rsi al bere** to take to drink; **~rsi al commercio** to go into business; **~rsi da fare per fare qc** to go to a lot of bother to do sth; **~rsi per vinto** to give in; **può ~rsi** maybe, perhaps; **si dà il caso che ...** it so happens that ...; **darsela a gambe** to take to one's heels; **il ~ e l'avere** (*ECON*) debits and credits *pl*.

Dar-es-Sa'laam *sf* Dar-es-Salaam.

'darsena *sf* dock.

'data *sf* date; **in ~ da destinarsi** on a date still to be announced; **in ~ odierna** as of today; **amicizia di lunga *o* vecchia ~** long-standing friendship; **~ di emissione** date of issue; **~ di nascita** date of birth; **~ di scadenza** expiry date; **~ limite d'utilizzo *o* di consumo** (*COMM*) best-before date.

da'tare *vt* to date ♦ *vi*: **~ da** to date from.

da'tato, a *ag* dated.

da'tivo *sm* dative.

'dato, a *ag* (*stabilito*) given ♦ *sm* datum; ~i *smpl* data *pl*; ~ che given that; in ~i casi in certain cases; è un ~ di fatto it's a fact.
da'tore, 'trice *sm/f*: ~ di lavoro employer.
'dattero *sm* date (*BOT*).
dattilogra'fare *vt* to type.
dattilogra'fia *sf* typing.
datti'lografo, a *sm/f* typist.
dattilos'critto *sm* typescript.
da'vanti *av* in front; (*dirimpetto*) opposite ♦ *ag inv* front ♦ *sm* front; ~ a *prep* in front of; (*dirimpetto a*) facing, opposite; (*in presenza di*) before, in front of.
davan'zale [davan'tsale] *sm* windowsill.
da'vanzo, d'a'vanzo [da'vantso] *av* more than enough.
dav'vero *av* really, indeed; dico ~ I mean it.
dazi'ario, a [dat'tsjarjo] *ag* excise *cpd*.
'dazio ['dattsjo] *sm* (*somma*) duty; (*luogo*) customs *pl*; ~ d'importazione import duty.
db *abbr* (= *decibel*) dB.
DC *sigla f* = Democrazia Cristiana (*former political party*).
d.C. *av abbr* (= *dopo Cristo*) A.D.
D.D.T. *abbr m* (= *dicloro-difenil-tricloroetano*) D.D.T.
'dea *sf* goddess.
'debbo *etc vb vedi* dovere.
debel'lare *vt* to overcome, conquer.
debili'tare *vt* to debilitate.
debita'mente *av* duly, properly.
'debito, a *ag* due, proper ♦ *sm* debt; (*COMM*: *dare*) debit; a tempo ~ at the right time; portare a ~ di qn to debit sb with; ~ consolidato consolidated debt; ~ d'imposta tax liability; ~ pubblico national debt.
debi'tore, 'trice *sm/f* debtor.
'debole *ag* weak, feeble; (*suono*) faint; (*luce*) dim ♦ *sm* weakness.
debo'lezza [debo'lettsa] *sf* weakness.
debut'tante *sm/f* (*gen*) beginner, novice; (*TEAT*) actor/actress at the beginning of his (*o* her) career.
debut'tare *vi* to make one's début.
de'butto *sm* début.
'decade *sf* period of ten days.
deca'dente *ag* decadent.
deca'denza [deka'dentsa] *sf* decline; (*DIR*) loss, forfeiture.
deca'dere *vi* to decline.
deca'duto, a *ag* (*persona*) impoverished; (*norma*) lapsed.
decaffei'nato, a *ag* decaffeinated.
de'calogo *sm* (*fig*) rulebook.
de'cano *sm* (*REL*) dean.
decan'tare *vt* (*virtù, bravura etc*) to praise;

(*persona*) to sing the praises of.
decapi'tare *vt* to decapitate, behead.
decappot'tabile *ag, sf* convertible.
dece'duto, a [detʃe'duto] *ag* deceased.
decele'rare [detʃele'rare] *vt, vi* to decelerate, slow down.
decen'nale [detʃen'nale] *ag* (*che dura 10 anni*) ten-year *cpd*; (*che ricorre ogni 10 anni*) ten-yearly, every ten years ♦ *sm* (*ricorrenza*) tenth anniversary.
de'cenne [de'tʃenne] *ag*: un bambino ~ a ten-year-old child, a child of ten.
de'cennio [de'tʃennjo] *sm* decade.
de'cente [de'tʃente] *ag* decent, respectable, proper; (*accettabile*) satisfactory, decent.
decentraliz'zare [detʃentralid'dzare] *vt* (*AMM*) to decentralize.
decentra'mento [detʃentra'mento] *sm* decentralization.
decen'trare [detʃen'trare] *vt* to decentralize, move out of the centre.
de'cenza [de'tʃentsa] *sf* decency, propriety.
de'cesso [de'tʃesso] *sm* death; atto di ~ death certificate.
de'cidere [de'tʃidere] *vi* to decide, make up one's mind ♦ *vt*: ~ qc to decide on sth; (*questione, lite*) to settle sth; ~rsi *vr*: ~rsi (a fare) to decide (to do), make up one's mind (to do); ~ di fare/che to decide to do/that; ~ di qc (*sog: cosa*) to determine sth.
deci'frare [detʃi'frare] *vt* to decode; (*fig*) to decipher, make out.
de'cilitro [de'tʃilitro] *sm* decilitre (*BRIT*), deciliter (*US*).
deci'male [detʃi'male] *ag* decimal.
deci'mare [detʃi'mare] *vt* to decimate.
de'cimetro [de'tʃimetro] *sm* decimetre.
'decimo, a [de'tʃimo] *num* tenth.
de'cina [de'tʃina] *sf* ten; (*circa dieci*): una ~ (di) about ten.
de'cisi [de'tʃizi] *etc vb vedi* decidere.
decisio'nale [detʃizjo'nale] *ag* decision-making *cpd*.
decisi'one [detʃi'zjone] *sf* decision; prendere una ~ to make a decision; con ~ decisively, resolutely.
deci'sivo, a [detʃi'zivo] *ag* (*gen*) decisive; (*fattore*) deciding.
de'ciso, a [de'tʃizo] *pp di* decidere ♦ *ag* (*persona, carattere*) determined; (*tono*) firm, resolute.
declas'sare *vt* to downgrade; to lower in status; 1ª declassata (*FERR*) first-class carriage which may be used by second-class passengers.
decli'nare *vi* (*pendio*) to slope down; (*fig*:

diminuire) to decline; (*tramontare*) to set, go down ♦ *vt* to decline; ~ **le proprie generalità** (*fig*) to give one's particulars; ~ **ogni responsabilità** to disclaim all responsibility.

declinazi'one [deklinat'tsjone] *sf* (*LING*) declension.

de'clino *sm* decline.

de'clivio *sm* (downward) slope.

decodifi'care *vt* to decode.

decodifica'tore *sm* decoder.

decol'lare *vi* (*AER*) to take off.

décolleté [dekol'te] *ag inv* (*abito*) low-necked, low-cut ♦ *sm* (*di abito*) low neckline; (*di donna*) cleavage.

de'collo *sm* take-off.

decolo'rare *vt* to bleach.

decom'porre *vt*, **decomporsi** *vr* to decompose.

decomposizi'one [dekompozit'tsjone] *sf* decomposition.

decom'posto, a *pp di* **decomporre**.

decompressi'one *sf* decompression.

deconge'lare [dekondʒe'lare] *vt* to defrost.

decongestio'nare [dekondʒestjo'nare] *vt* (*MED*, *traffico*) to relieve congestion in.

deco'rare *vt* to decorate.

decora'tivo, a *ag* decorative.

decora'tore, 'trice *sm/f* (interior) decorator.

decorazi'one [dekorat'tsjone] *sf* decoration.

de'coro *sm* decorum.

deco'roso, a *ag* decorous, dignified.

decor'renza [dekor'rɛntsa] *sf*: **con ~ da** (as) from.

de'correre *vi* to pass, elapse; (*avere effetto*) to run, have effect.

de'corso, a *pp di* **decorrere** ♦ *sm* (*evoluzione: anche MED*) course.

de'crebbi *etc vb vedi* **decrescere**.

de'crepito, a *ag* decrepit.

de'crescere [de'kreʃʃere] *vi* (*diminuire*) to decrease, diminish; (*acque*) to subside, go down; (*prezzi*) to go down.

decresci'uto, a [dekreʃ'ʃuto] *pp di* **decrescere**.

decre'tare *vt* (*norma*) to decree; (*mobilitazione*) to order; ~ **lo stato d'emergenza** to declare a state of emergency; ~ **la nomina di qn** to decide on the appointment of sb.

de'creto *sm* decree; ~ **legge** *decree with the force of law*; ~ **di sfratto** eviction order.

decur'tare *vt* (*debito, somma*) to reduce.

decurtazi'one [dekurtat'tsjone] *sf* reduction.

'dedalo *sm* maze, labyrinth.

'dedica, che *sf* dedication.

dedi'care *vt* to dedicate; ~**rsi** *vr*: ~**rsi a** (*votarsi*) to devote o.s. to.

dedicherò *etc* [dedike'rɔ] *vb vedi* **dedicare**.

'dedito, a *ag*: ~ **a** (*studio etc*) dedicated *o* devoted to; (*vizio*) addicted to.

de'dotto, a *pp di* **dedurre**.

de'duco *etc vb vedi* **dedurre**.

de'durre *vt* (*concludere*) to deduce; (*defalcare*) to deduct.

de'dussi *etc vb vedi* **dedurre**.

deduzi'one [dedut'tsjone] *sf* deduction.

defal'care *vt* to deduct.

defenes'trare *vt* to throw out of the window; (*fig*) to remove from office.

defe'rente *ag* respectful, deferential.

defe'rire *vt* (*DIR*): ~ **a** to refer to.

defezi'one [defet'tsjone] *sf* defection, desertion.

defici'ente [defi'tʃɛnte] *ag* (*mancante*): ~ **di** deficient in; (*insufficiente*) insufficient ♦ *sm/f* mental defective; (*peg: cretino*) idiot.

defici'enza [defi'tʃɛntsa] *sf* deficiency; (*carenza*) shortage; (*fig: lacuna*) weakness.

'deficit ['dɛfitʃit] *sm inv* (*ECON*) deficit.

defi'nire *vt* to define; (*risolvere*) to settle; (*questione*) to finalize.

defini'tivo, a *ag* definitive, final ♦ *sf*: **in ~a** (*dopotutto*) when all is said and done; (*dunque*) well then.

defi'nito, a *ag* definite; **ben ~** clear, clear cut.

definizi'one [definit'tsjone] *sf* (*gen*) definition; (*di disputa, vertenza*) settlement; (*di tempi, obiettivi*) establishment.

deflagrazi'one [deflagrat'tsjone] *sf* explosion.

deflazi'one [deflat'tsjone] *sf* (*ECON*) deflation.

deflet'tore *sm* (*AUT*) quarterlight (*BRIT*), deflector (*US*).

deflu'ire *vi*: ~ **da** (*liquido*) to flow away from; (*fig: capitali*) to flow out of.

de'flusso *sm* (*della marea*) ebb.

defor'mare *vt* (*alterare*) to put out of shape; (*corpo*) to deform; (*pensiero, fatto*) to distort; ~**rsi** *vr* to lose its shape.

deformazi'one [deformat'tsjone] *sf* (*MED*) deformation; **questa è ~ professionale!** that's force of habit because of your (*o* his *etc*) job!

de'forme *ag* deformed; disfigured.

deformità *sf inv* deformity.

defrau'dare *vt*: ~ **qn di qc** to defraud sb of sth, cheat sb out of sth.

de'funto, a *ag* late *cpd* ♦ *smlf* deceased.
degene'rare [dedʒene'rare] *vi* to degenerate.
degenerazi'one [dedʒenerat'tsjone] *sf* degeneration.
de'genere [de'dʒɛnere] *ag* degenerate.
de'gente [de'dʒɛnte] *smlf* bedridden person; (*ricoverato in ospedale*) in-patient.
de'genza [de'dʒɛntsa] *sf* confinement to bed; ~ **ospedaliera** period in hospital.
'degli ['deʎʎi] *prep* + *det vedi* **di**.
deglu'tire *vt* to swallow.
de'gnare [deɲ'ɲare] *vt*: ~ **qn della propria presenza** to honour sb with one's presence; ~**rsi** *vr*: ~**rsi di fare qc** to deign *o* condescend to do sth; **non mi ha degnato di uno sguardo** he wouldn't even look at me.
'degno, a ['deɲɲo] *ag* dignified; ~ **di** worthy of; ~ **di lode** praiseworthy.
degra'dare *vt* (*MIL*) to demote; (*privare della dignità*) to degrade; ~**rsi** *vr* to demean o.s.
de'grado *sm*: ~ **urbano** urban decline.
degus'tare *vt* to sample, taste.
degustazi'one [degustat'tsjone] *sf* sampling, tasting; ~ **di vini** (*locale*) specialist wine bar; ~ **di caffè** (*locale*) specialist coffee shop.
'dei *smpl di* **dio** ♦ *prep* + *det vedi* **di**.
del *prep* + *det vedi* **di**.
dela'tore, 'trice *smlf* police informer.
delazi'one [delat'tsjone] *sf* informing.
'delega, ghe *sf* (*procura*) proxy; **per** ~ **notarile** ≈ through a solicitor (*BRIT*) *o* lawyer.
dele'gare *vt* to delegate.
dele'gato *sm* delegate.
delegazi'one [delegat'tsjone] *sf* delegation.
delegherò *etc* [delegɛ'rɔ] *vb vedi* **delegare**.
dele'terio, a *ag* deleterious, noxious.
del'fino *sm* (*ZOOL*) dolphin; (*STORIA*) dauphin; (*fig*) probable successor.
'Delhi ['dɛli] *sf* Delhi.
de'libera *sf* decision.
delibe'rare *vt* to come to a decision on ♦ *vi* (*DIR*): ~ (**su qc**) to rule (on sth).
delica'tezza [delika'tettsa] *sf* delicacy; frailty; thoughtfulness; tactfulness.
deli'cato, a *ag* delicate; (*salute*) delicate, frail; (*fig: gentile*) thoughtful, considerate; (*: che dimostra tatto*) tactful.
delimi'tare *vt* (*anche fig*) to delimit.
deline'are *vt* to outline; ~**rsi** *vr* to be outlined; (*fig*) to emerge.
delin'quente *smlf* criminal, delinquent.
delin'quenza [delin'kwɛntsa] *sf* criminality, delinquency; ~ **minorile** juvenile delinquency.

de'liquio *sm* (*MED*) swoon; **cadere in** ~ to swoon.
deli'rante *ag* (*MED*) delirious; (*fig: folla*) frenzied; (*: discorso, mente*) insane.
deli'rare *vi* to be delirious, rave; (*fig*) to rave.
de'lirio *sm* delirium; (*ragionamento insensato*) raving; (*fig*): **andare/mandare in** ~ to go/send into a frenzy.
de'litto *sm* crime; ~ **d'onore** *crime committed to avenge one's honour.*
delittu'oso, a *ag* criminal.
de'lizia [de'littsja] *sf* delight.
delizi'are [delit'tsjare] *vt* to delight; ~**rsi** *vr*: ~**rsi di qc/a fare qc** to take delight in sth/ in doing sth.
delizi'oso, a [delit'tsjoso] *ag* delightful; (*cibi*) delicious.
dell', 'della, 'delle, 'dello *prep* + *det vedi* **di**.
'delta *sm inv* delta.
delta'plano *sm* hang-glider; **volo col** ~ hang-gliding.
delucidazi'one [delutʃidat'tsjone] *sf* clarification *no pl*.
delu'dente *ag* disappointing.
de'ludere *vt* to disappoint.
delusi'one *sf* disappointment.
de'luso, a *pp di* **deludere** ♦ *ag* disappointed.
dema'gogico, a, ci, che [dema'gɔdʒiko] *ag* popularity-seeking, demagogic.
dema'gogo, ghi *sm* demagogue.
de'manio *sm* state property.
de'mente *ag* (*MED*) demented, mentally deranged; (*fig*) crazy, mad.
de'menza [de'mɛntsa] *sf* dementia; madness; ~ **senile** senile dementia.
demenzi'ale [demen'tsjale] *ag* (*fig*) off-the-wall.
'demmo *vb vedi* **dare**.
demo'cratico, a, ci, che *ag* democratic.
democra'zia [demokrat'tsia] *sf* democracy; **la D**~ **Cristiana** the Christian Democrat Party.
democristi'ano, a *ag, smlf* Christian Democrat.
demogra'fia *sf* demography.
demo'grafico, a, ci, che *ag* demographic; **incremento** ~ increase in population.
demo'lire *vt* to demolish.
demolizi'one [demolit'tsjone] *sf* demolition.
'demone *sm* demon.
de'monio *sm* demon, devil; **il D**~ the Devil.
demoniz'zare [demonid'dzare] *vt* to make a monster of.
demonizzazi'one [demoniddzat'tsjone] *sf* demonizing, demonization.

demoraliz'zare [demoralid'dzare] *vt* to demoralize; **~rsi** *vr* to become demoralized.

de'mordere *vi*: **non ~ (da)** to refuse to give up.

demoti'vare *vt*: **~ qn** to take away sb's motivation.

demoti'vato, a *ag* unmotivated, lacking motivation.

de'naro *sm* money; **~i** *smpl* (*CARTE*) *suit in Neapolitan pack of cards*.

denatu'rato, a *ag vedi* **alcool**.

deni'grare *vt* to denigrate, run down.

denomi'nare *vt* to name; **~rsi** *vr* to be named *o* called.

denomina'tore *sm* (*MAT*) denominator.

denominazi'one [denominat'tsjone] *sf* name; denomination; **~ di origine controllata (D.O.C.)** *label guaranteeing the quality and origin of a wine*.

deno'tare *vt* to denote, indicate.

densità *sf inv* density; (*di nebbia*) thickness, denseness; **ad alta/bassa ~ di popolazione** densely/sparsely populated.

'denso, a *ag* thick, dense.

den'tale *ag* dental.

den'tario, a *ag* dental.

denta'tura *sf* set of teeth, teeth *pl*; (*TECN*: *di ruota*) serration.

'dente *sm* tooth; (*di forchetta*) prong; (*GEO*: *cima*) jagged peak; **al ~** (*CUC*: *pasta*) *cooked so as to be firm when eaten*; **mettere i ~i** to teethe; **mettere qc sotto i ~i** to have a bite to eat; **avere il ~ avvelenato contro** *o* **con qn** to bear sb a grudge; **~ di leone** (*BOT*) dandelion; **~i del giudizio** wisdom teeth.

'dentice ['dɛntitʃe] *sm* (*ZOOL*) sea bream.

denti'era *sf* (set of) false teeth *pl*.

denti'fricio [denti'fritʃo] *sm* toothpaste.

den'tista, i, e *sm/f* dentist.

'dentro *av* inside; (*in casa*) indoors; (*fig*: *nell'intimo*) inwardly ♦ *prep*: **~ (a)** in; **piegato in ~** folded over; **qui/là ~** in here/there; **~ di sé** (*pensare, brontolare*) to oneself; **tenere tutto ~** to keep everything bottled up (inside o.s.); **darci ~** (*fig fam*) to slog away, work hard.

denucleariz'zato, a [denuklearid'dzato] *ag* denuclearized, nuclear-free.

denu'dare *vt* (*persona*) to strip; (*parte del corpo*) to bare; **~rsi** *vr* to strip.

de'nuncia, ce *o* **cie** [de'nuntʃa], **de'nunzia** [de'nuntsja] *sf* denunciation; declaration; **fare una ~** *o* **sporgere ~ contro qn** (*DIR*) to report sb to the police; **~ del reddito** (income) tax return.

denunci'are [denun'tʃare], **denunzi'are** [denun'tsjare] *vt* to denounce; (*dichiarare*) to declare; **~ qn/qc (alla polizia)** to report sb/sth to the police.

denu'trito, a *ag* undernourished.

denutrizi'one [denutrit'tsjone] *sf* malnutrition.

deodo'rante *sm* deodorant.

deontolo'gia [deontolo'dʒia] *sf* (*professionale*) professional code of conduct.

depenalizzazi'one [depenaliddzat'tsjone] *sf* decriminalization.

dépen'dance [depã'dãs] *sf inv* outbuilding.

depe'ribile *ag* perishable; **merce ~** perishables *pl*, perishable goods *pl*.

deperi'mento *sm* (*di persona*) wasting away; (*di merci*) deterioration.

depe'rire *vi* to waste away.

depi'lare *vt* to depilate.

depila'torio, a *ag* hair-removing, depilatory ♦ *sm* hair remover, depilatory.

depilazi'one [depilat'tsjone] *sf* hair removal, depilation.

depis'taggio [depis'taddʒo] *sm* diversion.

depis'tare *vt* to set on the wrong track.

dépli'ant [depli'ã] *sm inv* leaflet; (*opuscolo*) brochure.

deplo'rare *vt* to deplore; to lament.

deplo'revole *ag* deplorable.

de'pone, de'pongo *etc vb vedi* **deporre**.

de'porre *vt* (*depositare*) to put down; (*rimuovere: da una carica*) to remove; (*: re*) to depose; (*DIR*) to testify; **~ le armi** (*MIL*) to lay down arms; **~ le uova** to lay eggs.

depor'tare *vt* to deport.

depor'tato, a *sm/f* deportee.

deportazi'one [deportat'tsjone] *sf* deportation.

de'posi *etc vb vedi* **deporre**.

deposi'tante *sm* (*COMM*) depositor.

deposi'tare *vt* (*gen, GEO, ECON*) to deposit; (*lasciare*) to leave; (*merci*) to store; **~rsi** *vr* (*sabbia, polvere*) to settle.

deposi'tario *sm* (*COMM*) depository.

de'posito *sm* deposit; (*luogo*) warehouse; depot; (*: MIL*) depot; **~ bagagli** left-luggage office; **~ di munizioni** ammunition dump.

deposizi'one [depozit'tsjone] *sf* deposition; (*da una carica*) removal; **rendere una falsa ~** to perjure o.s.

de'posto, a *pp di* **deporre**.

depra'vare *vt* to corrupt, pervert.

depra'vato, a *ag* depraved ♦ *sm/f* degenerate.

depre'care *vt* to deprecate, deplore.

depre'dare *vt* to rob, plunder.

depressi'one *sf* depression; **area** *o* **zona di**

~ (*METEOR*) area of low pressure; (*ECON*) depressed area.

de'presso, a *pp di* deprimere ♦ *ag* depressed.

deprezza'mento [deprettsa'mento] *sm* depreciation.

deprez'zare [depret'tsare] *vt* (*ECON*) to depreciate.

depri'mente *ag* depressing.

de'primere *vt* to depress.

depu'rare *vt* to purify.

depura'tore *sm*: ~ d'acqua water purifier; ~ di gas scrubber.

depu'tato, a *sm/f* (*POL*) deputy, ≈ Member of Parliament (*BRIT*), ≈ Congressman/ woman (*US*); *vedi anche* Camera dei Deputati.

deputazi'one [deputat'tsjone] *sf* deputation; (*POL*) position of deputy, ≈ parliamentary seat (*BRIT*), ≈ seat in Congress (*US*).

deraglia'mento [deraʎʎa'mento] *sm* derailment.

deragli'are [deraʎ'ʎare] *vi* to be derailed; far ~ to derail.

dera'pare *vi* (*veicolo*) to skid; (*SCI*) to sideslip.

derattizzazi'one [dcrattiddzat'tsjonc] *sf* rodent control.

deregolamen'tare *vt* to deregulate.

deregolamentazi'one [deregolamentat'tsjone] *sf* deregulation.

dere'litto, a *ag* derelict.

dere'tano *sm* (*fam*) bottom, buttocks *pl*.

de'ridere *vt* to mock, deride.

de'risi *etc vb vedi* deridere.

derisi'one *sf* derision, mockery.

de'riso, a *pp di* deridere.

deri'sorio, a *ag* (*gesto, tono*) mocking.

de'riva *sf* (*NAUT, AER*) drift; (*dispositivo*: *AER*) fin; (: *NAUT*) centre-board (*BRIT*), centerboard (*US*); andare alla ~ (*anche fig*) to drift.

deri'vare *vi*: ~ da to derive from ♦ *vt* to derive; (*corso d'acqua*) to divert.

deri'vato, a *ag* derived ♦ *sm* (*CHIM, LING*) derivative; (*prodotto*) by-product.

derivazi'one [derivat'tsjone] *sf* derivation; diversion.

derma'tite *sf* dermatitis.

dermatolo'gia [dermatolo'dʒia] *sf* dermatology.

derma'tologo, a, gi, ghe *sm/f* dermatologist.

dermoprotet'tivo, a *ag* (*crema, azione*) protecting the skin.

'deroga, ghe *sf* (special) dispensation; in ~ a as a (special) dispensation to.

dero'gare *vi*: ~ a (*DIR*) to repeal in part.

der'rate *sfpl* commodities; ~ alimentari foodstuffs.

deru'bare *vt* to rob.

des'critto, a *pp di* descrivere.

des'crivere *vt* to describe.

descrizi'one [deskrit'tsjone] *sf* description.

de'serto, a *ag* deserted ♦ *sm* (*GEO*) desert; isola ~a desert island.

deside'rabile *ag* desirable.

deside'rare *vt* to want, wish for; (*sessualmente*) to desire; ~ fare/che qn faccia to want *o* wish to do/sb to do; desidera fare una passeggiata? would you like to go for a walk?; farsi ~ (*fare il prezioso*) to play hard to get; (*farsi aspettare*) to take one's time; lascia molto a ~ it leaves a lot to be desired.

desi'derio *sm* wish; (*più intenso, carnale*) desire.

deside'roso, a *ag*: ~ di longing *o* eager for.

desi'gnare [desiɲ'ɲare] *vt* to designate, appoint; (*data*) to fix; la vittima designata the intended victim.

designazi'one [desiɲɲat'tsjone] *sf* designation, appointment.

desi'nare *vi* to dine, have dinner ♦ *sm* dinner.

desi'nenza [dezi'nɛntsa] *sf* (*LING*) ending, inflexion.

de'sistere *vi*: ~ da to give up, desist from.

desis'tito, a *pp di* desistere.

deso'lante *ag* distressing.

deso'lato, a *ag* (*paesaggio*) desolate; (*persona: spiacente*) sorry.

desolazi'one [dezolat'tsjone] *sf* desolation.

'despota, i *sm* despot.

'dessi *etc vb vedi* dare.

destabiliz'zare [destabilid'dzare] *vt* to destabilize.

des'tare *vt* to wake (up); (*fig*) to awaken, arouse; ~rsi *vr* to wake (up).

'deste *etc vb vedi* dare.

desti'nare *vt* to destine; (*assegnare*) to appoint, assign; (*indirizzare*) to address; ~ qc a qn to intend to give sth to sb, intend sb to have sth.

destina'tario, a *sm/f* (*di lettera*) addressee; (*di merce*) consignee; (*di mandato*) payee.

destinazi'one [destinat'tsjone] *sf* destination; (*uso*) purpose.

des'tino *sm* destiny, fate.

destitu'ire *vt* to dismiss, remove.

destituzi'one [destitut'tsjone] *sf* dismissal, removal.

'desto, a *ag* (wide) awake.

'destra *sf vedi* destro.

destreggi'arsi [destred'dʒarsi] *vr* to manoeuvre (*BRIT*), maneuver (*US*).

des'trezza [des'trettsa] *sf* skill, dexterity.

'destro, a *ag* right, right-hand; (*abile*) skilful (*BRIT*), skillful (*US*), adroit ♦ *sf* (*mano*) right hand; (*parte*) right (side); (*POL*): **la** ~**a** the right ♦ *sm* (*BOXE*) right; **a** ~**a** (*essere*) on the right; (*andare*) to the right; **tenere la** ~**a** to keep to the right.

de'sumere *vt* (*dedurre*) to infer, deduce; (*trarre: informazioni*) to obtain.

de'sunto, a *pp di* **desumere.**

detas'sare *vt* to remove the duty (*o* tax) from.

dete'nere *vt* (*incarico, primato*) to hold; (*proprietà*) to have, possess; (*in prigione*) to detain, hold.

de'tengo, de'tenni *etc vb vedi* **detenere.**

deten'tivo, a *ag*: **mandato** ~ imprisonment order; **pena** ~**a** prison sentence.

deten'tore, 'trice *sm/f* (*di titolo, primato etc*) holder.

dete'nuto, a *sm/f* prisoner.

detenzi'one [deten'tsjone] *sf* holding; possession; detention.

deter'gente [deter'dʒɛnte] *ag* detergent; (*crema, latte*) cleansing ♦ *sm* detergent.

de'tergere [de'tɛrdʒere] *vt* (*gen*) to clean; (*pelle, viso*) to cleanse; (*sudore*) to wipe (away).

deteriora'mento *sm*: ~ (**di**) deterioration (in).

deterio'rare *vt* to damage; ~**rsi** *vr* to deteriorate.

deteri'ore *ag* (*merce*) second-rate; (*significato*) pejorative; (*tradizione letteraria*) lesser, minor.

determi'nante *ag* decisive, determining.

determi'nare *vt* to determine.

determina'tivo, a *ag* determining; **articolo** ~ (*LING*) definite article.

determi'nato, a *ag* (*gen*) certain; (*particolare*) specific; (*risoluto*) determined, resolute.

determinazi'one [determinat'tsjone] *sf* determination; (*decisione*) decision.

deter'rente *ag, sm* deterrent.

deterrò *etc vb vedi* **detenere.**

deter'sivo *sm* detergent; (*per bucato: in polvere*) washing powder (*BRIT*), soap powder.

de'terso, a *pp di* **detergere.**

detes'tare *vt* to detest, hate.

deti'ene *etc vb vedi* **detenere.**

deto'nare *vi* to detonate.

detona'tore *sm* detonator.

detonazi'one [detonat'tsjone] *sf* (*di*

esplosivo) detonation, explosion; (*di arma*) bang; (*di motore*) pinking (*BRIT*), knocking.

de'trae, de'traggo *etc vb vedi* **detrarre.**

de'trarre *vt*: ~ (**da**) to deduct (from), take away (from).

de'trassi *etc vb vedi* **detrarre.**

de'tratto, a *pp di* **detrarre.**

detrazi'one [detrat'tsjone] *sf* deduction; ~ **d'imposta** tax allowance.

detri'mento *sm* detriment, harm; **a** ~ **di** to the detriment of.

de'trito *sm* (*GEO*) detritus.

detroniz'zare [detronid'dzare] *vt* to dethrone.

'detta *sf*: **a** ~ **di** according to.

dettagli'ante [dettaʎ'ʎante] *sm/f* (*COMM*) retailer.

dettagli'are [dettaʎ'ʎare] *vt* to detail, give full details of.

dettagliata'mente [dettaʎʎata'mente] *av* in detail.

det'taglio [det'taʎʎo] *sm* detail; (*COMM*): **il** ~ retail; **al** ~ (*COMM*) retail; separately.

det'tame *sm* dictate, precept.

det'tare *vt* to dictate; ~ **legge** (*fig*) to lay down the law.

det'tato *sm* dictation.

detta'tura *sf* dictation.

'detto, a *pp di* **dire** ♦ *ag* (*soprannominato*) called, known as; (*già nominato*) above-mentioned ♦ *sm* saying; ~ **fatto** no sooner said than done; **presto** ~! it's easier said than done!

detur'pare *vt* to disfigure; (*moralmente*) to sully.

devas'tante *ag* (*anche fig*) devastating.

devas'tare *vt* to devastate; (*fig*) to ravage.

devastazi'one [devastat'tsjone] *sf* devastation, destruction.

devi'are *vi*: ~ (**da**) to turn off (from) ♦ *vt* to divert.

devi'ato, a *ag* (*fig: persona, organizzazione*) corrupt, bent (*col*).

deviazi'one [devjat'tsjone] *sf* (*anche AUT*) diversion; **fare una** ~ to make a detour.

'devo *etc vb vedi* **dovere.**

devo'luto, a *pp di* **devolvere.**

devoluzi'one [devolut'tsjone] *sf* (*DIR*) devolution, transfer.

de'volvere *vt* (*DIR*) to transfer, devolve; ~ **qc in beneficenza** to give sth to charity.

de'voto, a *ag* (*REL*) devout, pious; (*affezionato*) devoted.

devozi'one [devot'tsjone] *sf* devoutness; (*anche REL*) devotion.

dg *abbr* (= *decigrammo*) dg.

========== PAROLA CHIAVE

di (*di* + *il* = **del,** *di* + *lo* = **dello,** *di* + *l'*
= **dell',** *di* + *la* = **della,** *di* + *i* = **dei,** *di* + *gli*
= **degli,** *di* + *le* = **delle**) *prep* **1** (*possesso,*
specificazione) of; (*composto da, scritto da*)
by; **la macchina ~ Paolo/~ mio fratello**
Paolo's/my brother's car; **un amico ~ mio**
fratello a friend of my brother's, one of
my brother's friends; **la grandezza della**
casa the size of the house; **le foto delle**
vacanze the holiday photos; **la città ~**
Firenze the city of Florence; **il nome ~**
Maria the name Mary; **un quadro ~**
Botticelli a painting by Botticelli
2 (*caratterizzazione, misura*) of; **una casa ~**
mattoni a brick house, a house made of
bricks; **un orologio d'oro** a gold watch; **un**
bimbo ~ 3 anni a child of 3, a 3-year-old
child; **una trota ~ un chilo** a trout
weighing a kilo; **una strada ~ 10 km** a
road 10 km long; **un quadro ~ valore** a
valuable picture
3 (*causa, mezzo, modo*) with; **tremare ~**
paura to tremble with fear; **morire ~**
cancro to die of cancer; **spalmare ~ burro**
to spread with butter
4 (*argomento*) about, of; **discutere ~ sport**
to talk about sport; **parlare ~ politica/**
lavoro to talk about politics/work
5 (*luogo: provenienza*) from; out of; **essere**
~ Roma to be from Rome; **uscire ~ casa**
to come out of *o* leave the house
6 (*tempo*) in; **d'estate/d'inverno** in (the)
summer/winter; **~ notte** by night, at
night; **~ mattina/sera** in the morning/
evening; **~ lunedì** on Mondays; **~ ora in**
ora by the hour
7 (*partitivo*) of; **alcuni ~ voi/noi** some of
you/us; **il più bravo ~ tutti** the best of all;
il migliore del mondo the best in the
world; **non c'è niente ~ peggio** there's
nothing worse
8 (*paragone*) than; **più veloce ~ me** faster
than me; **guadagna meno ~ me** he earns
less than me
♦ *det* (*una certa quantità di*) some;
(: *negativo*) any; (: *interrogativo*) any, some;
del pane (some) bread; **delle caramelle**
(some) sweets; **degli amici miei** some
friends of mine; **vuoi del vino?** do you
want some *o* any wine?

dì *sm* day; **buon ~!** hallo!; **a ~ =** **addì.**
DIA *sigla f* = *Direzione investigativa antimafia.*
dia'bete *sm* diabetes *sg.*
dia'betico, a, ci, che *ag, sm/f* diabetic.
dia'bolico, a, ci, che *ag* diabolical.

di'acono *sm* (*REL*) deacon.
dia'dema, i *sm* diadem; (*di donna*) tiara.
di'afano, a *ag* (*trasparente*) diaphanous;
(*pelle*) transparent.
dia'framma, i *sm* (*divisione*) screen; (*ANAT,*
FOT, contraccettivo) diaphragm.
di'agnosi [di'aɲɲozi] *sf* diagnosis *sg.*
diagnosti'care [diaɲɲosti'kare] *vt* to
diagnose.
dia'gnostico, a, ci, che [diaɲ'ɲɔstiko] *ag*
diagnostic; **aiuti ~ci** (*INFORM*) debugging
aids.
diago'nale *ag, sf* diagonal.
dia'gramma, i *sm* diagram; **~ a barre** bar
chart; **~ di flusso** flow chart.
dialet'tale *ag* dialectal; **poesia ~** poetry in
dialect.
dia'letto *sm* dialect.
di'alisi *sf* dialysis.
dialo'gante *ag:* **unità ~** (*INFORM*)
interactive terminal.
dialo'gare *vi:* **~ (con)** to have a dialogue
(with); (*conversare*) to converse (with)
♦ *vt* (*scena*) to write the dialogue for.
di'alogo, ghi *sm* dialogue.
dia'mante *sm* diamond.
di'ametro *sm* diameter.
di'amine *escl:* **che ~ ...?** what on
earth ...?
diaposi'tiva *sf* transparency, slide.
di'aria *sf* daily (expense) allowance.
di'ario *sm* diary; **~ di bordo** (*NAUT*)
log(book); **~ di classe** (*INS*) class register;
~ degli esami (*INS*) exam timetable.
diar'rea *sf* diarrhoea.
dia'triba *sf* diatribe.
diavole'ria *sf* (*azione*) act of mischief;
(*aggeggio*) weird contraption.
di'avolo *sm* devil; **è un buon ~** he's a good
sort; **avere un ~ per capello** to be in a foul
temper; **avere una fame/un freddo del ~**
to be ravenously hungry/frozen stiff;
mandare qn al ~ (*fam*) to tell sb to go to
hell; **fare il ~ a quattro** to kick up a fuss.
di'battere *vt* to debate, discuss; **~rsi** *vr* to
struggle.
dibatti'mento *sm* (*dibattito*) debate,
discussion; (*DIR*) hearing.
di'battito *sm* debate, discussion.
dic. *abbr* (= *dicembre*) Dec.
dicas'tero *sm* ministry.
'dice ['ditʃe] *vb vedi* **dire.**
di'cembre [di'tʃembre] *sm* December; *per*
fraseologia vedi **luglio.**
dice'ria [ditʃe'ria] *sf* rumour (*BRIT*), rumor
(*US*), piece of gossip.
dichia'rare [dikja'rare] *vt* to declare; **~rsi** *vr*
to declare o.s.; (*innamorato*) to declare

one's love; **si dichiara che** ... it is hereby declared that ...; **~rsi vinto** to admit defeat.

dichia'rato, a [dikja'rato] *ag* (*nemico, ateo*) avowed.

dichiarazi'one [dikjarat'tsjone] *sf* declaration; **~ dei redditi** statement of income; (*modulo*) tax return.

dician'nove [ditʃan'nɔve] *num* nineteen.

dicianno've nne [ditʃanno'vɛnne] *ag, smf* nineteen-year-old.

dicias'sette [ditʃas'sɛtte] *num* seventeen.

diciasset'tenne [ditʃasset'tɛnne] *ag, smf* seventeen-year-old.

diciot'tenne [ditʃot'tɛnne] *ag, smf* eighteen-year-old.

dici'otto [di'tʃɔtto] *num* eighteen ♦ *sm inv* (*INS*) *minimum satisfactory mark awarded in Italian universities.*

dici'tura [ditʃi'tura] *sf* words *pl*, wording.

'dico *etc vb vedi* **dire.**

didasca'lia *sf* (*di illustrazione*) caption; (*CINE*) subtitle; (*TEAT*) stage directions *pl*.

di'dattico, a, ci, che *ag* didactic; (*metodo, programma*) teaching; (*libro*) educational ♦ *sf* didactics *sg*; teaching methodology.

di'dentro *av* inside, indoors.

didi'etro *av* behind ♦ *ag inv* (*ruota, giardino*) back, rear *cpd* ♦ *sm* (*di casa*) rear; (*fam: sedere*) backside.

di'eci ['djɛtʃi] *num* ten.

dieci'mila [djetʃi'mila] *num* ten thousand.

die'cina [dje'tʃina] *sf* = **decina.**

di'edi *etc vb vedi* **dare.**

di'eresi *sf* dieresis *sg*.

'diesel ['diːzəl] *sm inv* diesel engine.

dies'sino, a *ag* (*POL*) of o belonging to the Democrats of the Left (*Italian left-wing party*).

di'eta *sf* diet; **essere a ~** to be on a diet.

die'tetica *sf* dietetics *sg*.

die'tologo, a, gi, ghe *smf* dietician.

di'etro *av* behind; (*in fondo*) at the back ♦ *prep* behind; (*tempo: dopo*) after ♦ *sm* (*di foglio, giacca*) back; (*di casa*) back, rear ♦ *ag inv* back *cpd*; **le zampe di ~** the hind legs; **~ ricevuta** against receipt; **~ richiesta** on demand; (*scritta*) on application; **andare ~ a** (*anche fig*) to follow; **stare ~ a qn** (*sorvegliare*) to keep an eye on sb; (*corteggiare*) to hang around sb; **portarsi ~ qn/qc** to bring sb/sth with one, bring sb/sth along; **gli hanno riso/parlato ~** they laughed at/talked about him behind his back.

di'etro 'front *escl* about turn! (*BRIT*), about face! (*US*) ♦ *sm* (*MIL*) about-turn, about-face; (*fig*) volte-face, about-turn, about-

face; **fare ~** (*MIL, fig*) to about-turn, about-face; (*tornare indietro*) to turn round.

di'fatti *cong* in fact, as a matter of fact.

di'fendere *vt* to defend; **~rsi** *vr* (*cavarsela*) to get by; **~rsi da/contro** to defend o.s. from/against; **~rsi dal freddo** to protect o.s. from the cold; **sapersi ~** to know how to look after o.s.

difen'sivo, a *ag* defensive ♦ *sf*: **stare sulla ~a** (*anche fig*) to be on the defensive.

difen'sore, a *smf* defender; **avvocato ~** counsel for the defence (*BRIT*) o defense (*US*).

di'fesa *sf vedi* **difeso.**

di'fesi *etc vb vedi* **difendere.**

di'feso, a *pp di* **difendere** ♦ *sf* defence (*BRIT*), defense (*US*); **prendere le ~e di qn** to defend sb, take sb's part.

difet'tare *vi* to be defective; **~ di** to be lacking in, lack.

difet'tivo, a *ag* defective.

di'fetto *sm* (*mancanza*): **~ di** lack of; (*di fabbricazione*) fault, flaw, defect; (*morale*) fault, failing, defect; (*fisico*) defect; **far ~** to be lacking; **in ~** at fault; in the wrong.

difet'toso, a *ag* defective, faulty.

diffa'mare *vt* (*a parole*) to slander; (*per iscritto*) to libel.

diffama'torio, a *ag* slanderous; libellous.

diffamazi'one [diffamat'tsjone] *sf* slander; libel.

diffe'rente *ag* different.

diffe'renza [diffe'rɛntsa] *sf* difference; **a ~ di** unlike; **non fare ~ (tra)** to make no distinction (between).

differenzi'ale [differen'tsjale] *ag, sm* differential; **classi ~i** (*INS*) special classes (*for backward children*).

differenzi'are [differen'tsjare] *vt* to differentiate; **~rsi da** to differentiate o.s. from; to differ from.

diffe'rire *vt* to postpone, defer ♦ *vi* to be different.

diffe'rita *sf*: **in ~** (*trasmettere*) prerecorded.

dif'ficile [dif'fitʃile] *ag* difficult; (*persona*) hard to please, difficult (to please); (*poco probabile*): **è ~ che sia libero** it is unlikely that he'll be free ♦ *smf*: **fare il(la) ~** to be difficult, be awkward ♦ *sm* difficult part; difficulty; **essere ~ nel mangiare** to be fussy about one's food.

difficil'mente [diffitʃil'mente] *av* (*con difficoltà*) with difficulty; **~ verrà** he's unlikely to come.

difficoltà *sf inv* difficulty.

difficol'toso, a *ag* (*compito*) difficult, hard; (*persona*) difficult, hard to please;

digestione ~a poor digestion.

dif'fida *sf* (*DIR*) warning, notice.

diffi'dare *vi*: ~ **di** to be suspicious *o* distrustful of ♦ *vt* (*DIR*) to warn; ~ **qn dal fare qc** to warn sb not to do sth, caution sb against doing sth.

diffi'dente *ag* suspicious, distrustful.

diffi'denza [diffi'dɛntsa] *sf* suspicion, distrust.

dif'fondere *vt* (*luce, calore*) to diffuse; (*notizie*) to spread, circulate; ~**rsi** *vr* to spread.

dif'fusi *etc vb vedi* **diffondere**.

diffusi'one *sf* diffusion; spread; (*anche di giornale*) circulation; (*FISICA*) scattering.

dif'fuso, a *pp di* **diffondere** ♦ *ag* (*FISICA*) diffuse; (*notizia, malattia etc*) widespread; **è opinione** ~**a che** ... it's widely held that ....

difi'lato *av* (*direttamente*) straight, directly; (*subito*) straight away.

difte'rite *sf* diphtheria.

'diga, ghe *sf* dam; (*portuale*) breakwater.

dige'rente [didʒe'rɛnte] *ag* (*apparato*) digestive.

dige'rire [didʒe'rire] *vt* to digest.

digesti'one [didʒes'tjone] *sf* digestion.

diges'tivo, a [didʒes'tivo] *ag* digestive ♦ *sm* (*after-dinner*) liqueur.

Digi'one [di'dʒone] *sf* Dijon.

digi'tale [didʒi'tale] *ag* digital; (*delle dita*) finger *cpd*, digital ♦ *sf* (*BOT*) foxglove.

digi'tare [didʒi'tare] *vt* (*dati*) to key (in); (*tasto*) to press.

digiu'nare [didʒu'nare] *vi* to starve o.s.; (*REL*) to fast.

digi'uno, a [di'dʒuno] *ag*: **essere** ~ not to have eaten ♦ *sm* fast; **a** ~ on an empty stomach.

dignità [diɲɲi'ta] *sf inv* dignity.

digni'tario [diɲɲi'tarjo] *sm* dignitary.

digni'toso, a [diɲɲi'toso] *ag* dignified.

'DIGOS *sigla f* (= *Divisione Investigazioni Generali e Operazioni Speciali*) *police department dealing with political security.*

digressi'one *sf* digression.

digri'gnare [digriɲ'ɲare] *vt*: ~ **i denti** to grind one's teeth.

dila'gare *vi* to flood; (*fig*) to spread.

dilani'are *vt* to tear to pieces.

dilapi'dare *vt* to squander, waste.

dila'tare *vt* to dilate; (*gas*) to cause to expand; (*passaggio, cavità*) to open (up); ~**rsi** *vr* to dilate; (*FISICA*) to expand.

dilatazi'one [dilatat'tsjone] *sf* (*ANAT*) dilation; (*di gas, metallo*) expansion.

dilazio'nare [dilattsjo'nare] *vt* to delay, defer.

dilazi'one [dilat'tsjone] *sf* deferment.

dileggi'are [diled'dʒare] *vt* to mock, deride.

dilegu'are *vi*, ~**rsi** *vr* to vanish, disappear.

di'lemma, i *sm* dilemma.

dilet'tante *sm/f* dilettante; (*anche SPORT*) amateur.

dilet'tare *vt* to give pleasure to, delight; ~**rsi** *vr*: ~**rsi di** to take pleasure in, enjoy.

dilet'tevole *ag* delightful.

di'letto, a *ag* dear, beloved ♦ *sm* pleasure, delight.

dili'gente [dili'dʒɛnte] *ag* (*scrupoloso*) diligent; (*accurato*) careful, accurate.

dili'genza [dili'dʒɛntsa] *sf* diligence; care; (*carrozza*) stagecoach.

dilu'ire *vt* to dilute.

dilun'garsi *vr* (*fig*): ~ **su** to talk at length on *o* about.

diluvi'are *vb impers* to pour (down).

di'luvio *sm* downpour; (*inondazione, fig*) flood; **il** ~ **universale** the Flood.

dima'grante *ag* slimming *cpd*.

dima'grire *vi* to get thinner, lose weight.

dime'nare *vt* to wave, shake; ~**rsi** *vr* to toss and turn; (*fig*) to struggle; ~ **la coda** (*sog: cane*) to wag its tail.

dimensi'one *sf* dimension; (*grandezza*) size; **considerare un discorso nella sua** ~ **politica** to look at a speech in terms of its political significance.

dimenti'canza [dimenti'kantsa] *sf* forgetfulness; (*errore*) oversight, slip; **per** ~ inadvertently.

dimenti'care *vt* to forget; ~**rsi** *vr*: ~**rsi di qc** to forget sth.

dimentica'toio *sm* (*scherzoso*): **cadere/ mettere nel** ~ to sink into/consign to oblivion.

di'mentico, a, chi, che *ag*: ~ **di** (*che non ricorda*) forgetful of; (*incurante*) oblivious of, unmindful of.

di'messo, a *pp di* **dimettere** ♦ *ag* (*voce*) subdued; (*uomo, abito*) modest, humble.

dimesti'chezza [dimesti'kettsa] *sf* familiarity.

di'mettere *vt*: ~ **qn da** to dismiss sb from; (*dall'ospedale*) to discharge sb from; ~**rsi** *vr*: ~**rsi (da)** to resign (from).

dimez'zare [dimed'dzare] *vt* to halve.

diminu'ire *vt* to reduce, diminish; (*prezzi*) to bring down, reduce ♦ *vi* to decrease, diminish; (*rumore*) to die down, die away; (*prezzi*) to fall, go down.

diminu'tivo, a *ag, sm* diminutive.

diminuzi'one [diminut'tsjone] *sf* decreasing, diminishing; **in** ~ on the decrease; ~ **della produttività** fall in productivity.

di'misi etc vb vedi **dimettere**.

dimissio'nario, a ag outgoing, resigning.

dimissi'oni sfpl resignation sg; **dare o presentare le** ~ to resign, hand in one's resignation.

di'mora sf residence; **senza fissa** ~ of no fixed address o abode.

dimo'rare vi to reside.

dimos'trante sm/f (POL) demonstrator.

dimos'trare vt to demonstrate, show; (provare) to prove, demonstrate; ~**rsi** vr: ~**rsi molto abile** to show o.s. o prove to be very clever; **non dimostra la sua età** he doesn't look his age; **dimostra 30 anni** he looks about 30 (years old).

dimostra'tivo, a ag (anche LING) demonstrative.

dimostrazi'one [dimostrat'tsjone] sf demonstration; proof.

di'namico, a, ci, che ag dynamic ♦ sf dynamics sg.

dina'mismo sm dynamism.

dinami'tardo, a ag: **attentato** ~ dynamite attack ♦ sm/f dynamiter.

dina'mite sf dynamite.

'dinamo sf inv dynamo.

di'nanzi [di'nantsi]: ~ **a** prep in front of.

dinas'tia sf dynasty.

dini'ego, ghi sm (rifiuto) refusal; (negazione) denial.

dinocco'lato, a ag lanky; **camminare** ~ to walk with a slouch.

dino'sauro sm dinosaur.

din'torno av round, (round) about; ~**i** smpl outskirts; **nei** ~**i di** in the vicinity o neighbourhood of.

'dio, pl **'dei** sm god; **D**~ God; **gli dei** the gods; **si crede un** ~ he thinks he's wonderful; **D**~ **mio!** my God!; **D**~ **ce la mandi buona** let's hope for the best; **D**~ **ce ne scampi e liberi!** God forbid!

di'ocesi [di'ɔtʃezi] sf inv diocese.

dios'sina sf dioxin.

dipa'nare vt (lana) to wind into a ball; (fig) to disentangle, sort out.

diparti'mento sm department.

dipen'dente ag dependent ♦ sm/f employee.

dipen'denza [dipen'dɛntsa] sf dependence; **essere alle** ~**e di qn** to be employed by sb o in sb's employ.

di'pendere vi: ~ **da** to depend on; (finanziariamente) to be dependent on; (derivare) to come from, be due to.

di'pesi etc vb vedi **dipendere**.

di'peso, a pp di **dipendere**.

di'pingere [di'pindʒere] vt to paint.

di'pinsi etc vb vedi **dipingere**.

di'pinto, a pp di **dipingere** ♦ sm painting.

di'ploma, i sm diploma.

diplo'mare vt to award a diploma to, graduate (US) ♦ vi to obtain a diploma, graduate (US).

diplo'matico, a, ci, che ag diplomatic ♦ sm diplomat.

diplo'mato, a ag qualified ♦ sm/f qualified person, holder of a diploma.

diploma'zia [diplomat'tsia] sf diplomacy.

di'porto sm: **imbarcazione** f **da** ~ pleasure craft.

dira'dare vt to thin (out); (visite) to reduce, make less frequent; ~**rsi** vr to disperse; (nebbia) to clear (up).

dira'mare vt to issue ♦ vi, ~**rsi** vr (strade) to branch.

'dire vt to say; (segreto, fatto) to tell; ~ **qc a qn** to tell sb sth; ~ **a qn di fare qc** to tell sb to do sth; ~ **di sì/no** to say yes/no; **si dice che ...** they say that ...; **mi si dice che ...** I am told that ...; **si direbbe che ...** it looks (o sounds) as though ...; **dica, signora?** (in un negozio) yes, Madam, can I help you?; **sì quello che dice** he knows what he's talking about; **lascialo** ~ (esprimersi) let him have his say; (ignoralo) just ignore him; **come sarebbe a** ~**?** what do you mean?; **che ne diresti di andarcene?** how about leaving?; **chi l'avrebbe mai detto!** who would have thought it!; **si dicono esperti** they say they are experts; **per così** ~ so to speak; **a dir poco** to say the least; **non c'è che** ~ there's no doubt about it; **non dico di no** I can't deny it; **il che è tutto** ~ need I say more?

di'ressi etc vb vedi **dirigere**.

di'retta sf vedi **diretto**.

diretta'mente av (immediatamente) directly, straight; (personalmente) directly; (senza intermediari) direct, straight.

diret'tissima sf (tragitto) most direct route; (DIR): **processo per** ~ summary trial.

diret'tissimo sm (FERR) fast (through) train.

diret'tivo, a ag (POL, AMM) executive; (COMM) managerial, executive ♦ sm leadership, leaders pl ♦ sf directive, instruction.

di'retto, a pp di **dirigere** ♦ ag direct ♦ sm (FERR) through train ♦ sf: **in (linea)** ~**a** (RADIO, TV) live; **il mio** ~ **superiore** my immediate superior.

diret'tore, 'trice sm/f (di azienda) director;

manager/ess; (*di scuola elementare*) head (teacher) (*BRIT*), principal (*US*); ~ **amministrativo** company secretary (*BRIT*), corporate executive secretary (*US*); ~ **del carcere** prison governor (*BRIT*) *o* warden (*US*); ~ **di filiale** branch manager; ~ **d'orchestra** conductor; ~ **di produzione** (*CINE*) producer; ~ **sportivo** team manager; ~ **tecnico** (*SPORT*) trainer, coach.

direzi'one [diret'tsjone] *sf* (*senso: anche fig*) direction; (*conduzione*: *gen*) running; (: *di partito*) leadership; (: *di società*) management; (: *di giornale*) editorship; (*direttori*) management; **in** ~ **di** in the direction of, towards.

diri'gente [diri'dʒɛnte] *ag* managerial ♦ *smlf* executive; (*POL*) leader; **classe** ~ ruling class.

diri'genza [diri'dʒɛntsa] *sf* management; (*POL*) leadership.

dirigenzi'ale [diridʒen'tsjale] *ag* managerial.

di'rigere [di'ridʒere] *vt* to direct; (*impresa*) to run, manage; (*MUS*) to conduct; **~rsi** *vr*: **~rsi verso** *o* **a** to make *o* head for; ~ **i propri passi verso** to make one's way towards; **il treno era diretto a Pavia** the train was heading for Pavia.

diri'gibile [diri'dʒibile] *sm* airship.

dirim'petto *av* opposite; ~ **a** *prep* opposite, facing.

di'ritto, a *ag* straight; (*onesto*) straight, upright ♦ *av* straight, directly ♦ *sm* right side; (*TENNIS*) forehand; (*MAGLIA*) plain stitch, knit stitch; (*prerogativa*) right; (*leggi, scienza*): **il** ~ law; **stare** ~ to stand up straight; **aver** ~ **a qc** to be entitled to sth; **punto** ~ plain (stitch); **andare** ~ to go straight on; **a buon** ~ quite rightly; **~i (d'autore)** royalties; ~ **di successione** right of succession.

dirit'tura *sf* (*SPORT*) straight; (*fig*) rectitude.

diroc'cato, a *ag* tumbledown, in ruins.

dirom'pente *ag* (*anche fig*) explosive.

dirotta'mento *sm*: ~ **(aereo)** hijack.

dirot'tare *vt* (*nave, aereo*) to change the course of; (*aereo: sotto minaccia*) to hijack; (*traffico*) to divert ♦ *vi* (*nave, aereo*) to change course.

dirotta'tore, 'trice *smlf* hijacker.

di'rotto, a *ag* (*pioggia*) torrential; (*pianto*) unrestrained; **piovere a** ~ to pour, rain cats and dogs; **piangere a** ~ to cry one's heart out.

di'rupo *sm* crag, precipice.

di'sabile *smlf* disabled person.

disabi'tato, a *ag* uninhabited.

disabitu'arsi *vr*: ~ **a** to get out of the habit of.

disac'cordo *sm* disagreement.

disadat'tato, a *ag* (*PSIC*) maladjusted.

disa'dorno, a *ag* plain, unadorned.

disaffezi'one [dizaffet'tsjone] *sf* disaffection.

disa'gevole [disa'dʒevole] *ag* (*scomodo*) uncomfortable; (*difficile*) difficult.

disagi'ato, a [diza'dʒato] *ag* poor, needy; (*vita*) hard.

di'sagio [di'zadʒo] *sm* discomfort; (*disturbo*) inconvenience; (*fig: imbarazzo*) embarrassment; **~i** *smpl* hardship *sg*, poverty *sg*; **essere a** ~ to be ill at ease.

di'samina *sf* close examination.

disappro'vare *vt* to disapprove of.

disapprovazi'one [dizapprovat'tsjone] *sf* disapproval.

disap'punto *sm* disappointment.

disarcio'nare [dizartʃo'nare] *vt* to unhorse.

disar'mante *ag* (*fig*) disarming.

disar'mare *vt*, *vi* to disarm.

di'sarmo *sm* (*MIL*) disarmament.

di'sastro *sm* disaster.

disas'troso, a *ag* disastrous.

disat'tento, a *ag* inattentive.

disattenzi'one [dizatten'tsjone] *sf* carelessness, lack of attention.

disatti'vare *vt* (*bomba*) to de-activate, defuse.

disa'vanzo [diza'vantso] *sm* (*ECON*) deficit.

disavven'tura *sf* misadventure, mishap.

dis'brigo, ghi *sm* (*prompt*) clearing up *o* settlement.

dis'capito *sm*: **a** ~ **di** to the detriment of.

dis'carica, che *sf* (*di rifiuti*) rubbish tip *o* dump.

discen'dente [diʃʃen'dɛnte] *ag* descending ♦ *smlf* descendant.

di'scendere [diʃ'ʃɛndere] *vt* to go (*o* come) down ♦ *vi* to go (*o* come) down; (*smontare*) to get off; ~ **da** (*famiglia*) to be descended from; ~ **dalla macchina/dal treno** to get out of the car/out of *o* off the train; ~ **da cavallo** to dismount, get off one's horse.

di'scepolo, a [diʃ'ʃepolo] *smlf* disciple.

di'scernere [diʃ'ʃɛrnere] *vt* to discern.

discerni'mento [diʃʃerni'mento] *sm* discernment.

disce'sista [diʃʃe'sista] *smlf* downhill skier.

di'sceso, a [diʃ'ʃeso] *pp di* **discendere** ♦ *sf* descent; (*pendio*) slope; **in** ~ **a** (*strada*) downhill *cpd*, sloping; **~a libera** (*SCI*) downhill race.

dischi'udere [dis'kjudere] *vt* (*aprire*) to open; (*fig: rivelare*) to disclose, reveal.

dischi'usi etc [dis'kjusi] vb vedi **dischiudere**.
dischi'uso, a [dis'kjuso] pp di **dischiudere**.
di'scinto, a [diʃ'ʃinto] ag (anche: **in abiti ~i**)
half-undressed.
disci'ogliere [diʃ'ʃɔʎʎere] vt, **~rsi** vr to
dissolve; (fondere) to melt.
disci'plina [diʃʃi'plina] sf discipline.
discipli'nare [diʃʃipli'nare] ag disciplinary
♦ vt to discipline.
'disco, schi sm disc, disk; (SPORT) discus;
(fonografico) record; (INFORM) disk; **~
magnetico** (INFORM) magnetic disk; **~
orario** (AUT) parking disc; **~ rigido**
(INFORM) hard disk; **~ volante** flying
saucer.
discogra'fia sf (tecnica) recording, record-
making; (industria) record industry.
disco'grafico, a, ci, che ag record cpd,
recording cpd ♦ sm record producer; **casa
~a** record(ing) company.
'discolo, a ag (bambino) undisciplined,
unruly ♦ sm/f rascal.
discol'pare vt to clear of blame; **~rsi** vr to
clear o.s., prove one's innocence;
(giustificarsi) to excuse o.s.
disco'noscere [disko'noʃʃere] vt (figlio) to
disown; (meriti) to ignore, disregard.
disconosci'uto, a [diskonoʃ'ʃuto] pp di
disconoscere.
discon'tinuo, a ag (linea) broken;
(rendimento, stile) irregular; (interesse)
sporadic.
dis'corde ag conflicting, clashing.
dis'cordia sf discord; (dissidio)
disagreement, clash.
dis'correre vi: **~ (di)** to talk (about).
dis'corso, a pp di **discorrere** ♦ sm speech;
(conversazione) conversation, talk.
dis'costo, a ag faraway, distant ♦ av far
away; **~ da** prep far from.
disco'teca, che sf (raccolta) record library;
(luogo di ballo) disco(theque).
discre'panza [diskre'pantsa] sf
discrepancy.
dis'creto, a ag discreet; (abbastanza buono)
reasonable, fair.
discrezi'one [diskret'tsjone] sf discretion;
(giudizio) judgment, discernment; **a ~ di**
at the discretion of.
discrimi'nante ag (fattore, elemento)
decisive ♦ sf (DIR) extenuating
circumstance.
discrimi'nare vt to discrimate.
discriminazi'one [diskriminat'tsjone] sf
discrimination.
dis'cussi etc vb vedi **discutere**.
discussi'one sf discussion; (litigio)
argument; **mettere in ~** to bring into

question; **fuori ~** out of the question.
dis'cusso, a pp di **discutere**.
dis'cutere vt to discuss, debate;
(contestare) to question, dispute ♦ vi
(conversare): **~ (di)** to discuss; (litigare) to
argue.
discu'tibile ag questionable.
disde'gnare [dizdeɲ'ɲare] vt to scorn.
dis'degno [diz'deɲɲo] sm scorn, disdain.
disde'gnoso, a [dizdeɲ'ɲoso] ag
disdainful, scornful.
dis'detto, a pp di **disdire** ♦ sf cancellation;
(sfortuna) bad luck.
disdi'cevole [dizdi'tʃevole] ag improper,
unseemly.
dis'dire vt (prenotazione) to cancel; **~ un
contratto d'affitto** (DIR) to give notice (to
quit).
dise'gnare [diseɲ'ɲare] vt to draw;
(progettare) to design; (fig) to outline.
disegna'tore, 'trice [diseɲɲa'tore] sm/f
designer.
di'segno [di'zeɲɲo] sm drawing; (su stoffa
etc) design; (fig: schema) outline; **~
industriale** industriale design; **~ di legge**
(DIR) bill.
diser'bante sm weedkiller.
disere'dare vt to disinherit.
diser'tare vt, vi to desert.
diser'tore sm (MIL) deserter.
diserzi'one [dizer'tsjone] sf (MIL) desertion.
disfaci'mento [disfatʃi'mento] sm (di
cadavere) decay; (fig: di istituzione, impero,
società) decline, decay; **in ~** in decay.
dis'fare vt to undo; (valigie) to unpack;
(meccanismo) to take to pieces; (lavoro,
paese) to destroy; (neve) to melt; **~rsi** vr to
come undone; (neve) to melt; **~ il letto** to
strip the bed; **~rsi di qn** (liberarsi) to get
rid of sb.
dis'fatta sf vedi **disfatto**.
disfat'tista, i, e sm/f defeatist.
dis'fatto, a pp di **disfare** ♦ ag (gen) undone,
untied; (letto) unmade; (persona: sfinito)
exhausted, worn-out; (: addolorato) grief-
stricken ♦ sf (sconfitta) rout.
disfunzi'one [disfun'tsjone] sf (MED)
dysfunction; **~ cardiaca** heart trouble.
disge'lare [dizdʒe'lare] vt, vi, **~rsi** vr to
thaw.
dis'gelo [diz'dʒɛlo] sm thaw.
dis'grazia [diz'grattsja] sf (sventura)
misfortune; (incidente) accident, mishap.
disgrazi'ato, a [dizgrat'tsjato] ag
unfortunate ♦ sm/f wretch.
disgre'gare vt, **~rsi** vr to break up.
disgu'ido sm hitch; **~ postale** error in
postal delivery.

disgus'tare vt to disgust; ~**rsi** vr: ~**rsi di** to be disgusted by.

dis'gusto sm disgust.

disgus'toso, a ag disgusting.

disidra'tare vt to dehydrate.

disidra'tato, a ag dehydrated.

disil'ludere vt to disillusion, disenchant.

disillusi'one sf disillusion, disenchantment.

disimpa'rare vt to forget.

disimpe'gnare [dizimpeɲ'ɲare] vt (persona: da obblighi): ~ **da** to release from; (oggetto dato in pegno) to redeem, get out of pawn; ~**rsi** vr: ~**rsi da** (obblighi) to release o.s. from, free o.s. from.

disincagli'are [dizinkaʎ'ʎare] vt (barca) to refloat; ~**rsi** vr to get afloat again.

disincan'tato, a ag disenchanted, disillusioned.

disincenti'vare [dizintʃenti'vare] vt to discourage.

disinfes'tare vt to disinfest.

disinfestazi'one [dizinfestat'tsjone] sf disinfestation.

disinfet'tante ag, sm disinfectant.

disinfet'tare vt to disinfect.

disinfezi'one [dizinfet'tsjone] sf disinfection.

disingan'nare vt to disillusion.

disin'ganno sm disillusion.

disini'bito, a ag uninhibited.

disinnes'care vt to defuse.

disinnes'tare vt (marcia) to disengage.

disinqui'nare vt to free from pollution.

disinte'grare vt, vi to disintegrate.

disinteres'sarsi vr: ~ **di** to take no interest in.

disinte'resse sm indifference; (generosità) unselfishness.

disintossi'care vt (alcolizzato, drogato) to treat for alcoholism (o drug addiction); ~**rsi** vr to clear out one's system; (alcolizzato, drogato) to be treated for alcoholism (o drug addiction).

disintossicazi'one [dizintossikat'tsjone] sf treatment for alcoholism (o drug addiction).

disin'volto, a ag casual, free and easy.

disinvol'tura sf casualness, ease.

disles'sia sf dyslexia.

disli'vello sm difference in height; (fig) gap.

dislo'care vt to station, position.

dismi'sura sf excess; **a** ~ to excess, excessively.

disobbe'dire etc = **disubbidire** etc.

disoccu'pato, a ag unemployed ♦ sm/f unemployed person.

disoccupazi'one [dizokkupat'tsjone] sf unemployment.

disonestà sf dishonesty.

diso'nesto, a ag dishonest.

disono'rare vt to dishonour (BRIT), dishonor (US), bring disgrace upon.

diso'nore sm dishonour (BRIT), dishonor (US), disgrace.

di'sopra av (con contatto) on top; (senza contatto) above; (al piano superiore) upstairs ♦ ag inv (superiore) upper ♦ sm inv top, upper part; **la gente** ~ the people upstairs; **il piano** ~ the floor above.

disordi'nare vt to mess up, disarrange; (MIL) to throw into disorder.

disordi'nato, a ag untidy; (privo di misura) irregular, wild.

di'sordine sm (confusione) disorder, confusion; (sregolatezza) debauchery; ~**i** smpl (POL etc) disorder sg; (tumulti) riots.

disor'ganico, a, ci, che ag incoherent, disorganized.

disorganiz'zato, a [dizorganid'dzato] ag disorganized.

disorienta'mento sm (fig) confusion, bewilderment.

disorien'tare vt to disorientate; ~**rsi** vr (fig) to get confused, lose one's bearings.

disorien'tato, a ag disorientated.

disos'sare vt (CUC) to bone.

di'sotto av below, underneath; (in fondo) at the bottom; (al piano inferiore) downstairs ♦ ag inv (inferiore) lower; bottom cpd ♦ sm inv (parte inferiore) lower part; bottom; **la gente** ~ the people downstairs; **il piano** ~ the floor below.

dis'paccio [dis'pattʃo] sm dispatch.

dispa'rato, a ag disparate.

'dispari ag inv odd, uneven.

disparità sf inv disparity.

dis'parte: **in** ~ av (da lato) aside, apart; **tenersi o starsene in** ~ to keep to o.s., hold aloof.

dis'pendio sm (di denaro, energie) expenditure; (: spreco) waste.

dispendi'oso, a ag expensive.

dis'pensa sf pantry, larder; (mobile) sideboard; (DIR) exemption; (REL) dispensation; (fascicolo) number, issue.

dispen'sare vt (elemosine, favori) to distribute; (esonerare) to exempt.

dispe'rare vi: ~ **(di)** to despair (of); ~**rsi** vr to despair.

dispe'rato, a ag (persona) in despair; (caso, tentativo) desperate.

disperazi'one [disperat'tsjone] sf despair.

dis'perdere vt (disseminare) to disperse; (MIL) to scatter, rout; (fig: consumare) to waste, squander; ~rsi *vr* to disperse; to scatter.

dispersi'one *sf* dispersion, dispersal; (*FISICA, CHIM*) dispersion.

disper'sivo, a *ag* (*lavoro etc*) disorganized.

dis'perso, a *pp di* disperdere ♦ *sm/f* missing person; (*MIL*) missing soldier.

dis'petto *sm* spite *no pl*, spitefulness *no pl*; fare un ~ a qn to play a (nasty) trick on sb; a ~ di in spite of; con suo grande ~ much to his annoyance.

dispet'toso, a *ag* spiteful.

dispia'cere [dispja'tʃere] *sm* (*rammarico*) regret, sorrow; (*dolore*) grief ♦ *vi*: ~ a to displease ♦ *vb impers*: mi dispiace (che) I am sorry (that); ~i *smpl* (*preoccupazioni*) troubles, worries; se non le dispiace, me ne vado adesso if you don't mind, I'll go now.

dispiaci'uto, a [dispja'tʃuto] *pp di* dispiacere ♦ *ag* sorry.

dis'pone, dis'pongo *etc vb vedi* disporre.

dispo'nibile *ag* available; (*persona: solerte, gentile*) helpful.

disponibilità *sf inv* availability; (*solerzia, gentilezza*) helpfulness; disponibilità *sfpl* (*economiche*) resources.

dis'porre *vt* (*sistemare*) to arrange; (*preparare*) to prepare; (*DIR*) to order; (*persuadere*): ~ qn a to incline o dispose sb towards ♦ *vi* (*decidere*) to decide; (*usufruire*): ~ di to use, have at one's disposal; (*essere dotato*): ~ di to have; disporsi *vr* (*ordinarsi*) to place o.s., arrange o.s.; disporsi a fare to get ready to do; disporsi all'attacco to prepare for an attack; disporsi in cerchio to form a circle.

dis'posi *etc vb vedi* disporre.

disposi'tivo *sm* (*meccanismo*) device; (*DIR*) pronouncement; ~ di controllo o di comando control device; ~ di sicurezza (*gen*) safety device; (*di arma da fuoco*) safety catch.

disposizi'one [dispozit'tsjone] *sf* arrangement, layout; (*stato d'animo*) mood; (*tendenza*) bent, inclination; (*comando*) order; (*DIR*) provision, regulation; a ~ di qn at sb's disposal; per ~ di legge by law; ~ testamentaria provisions of a will.

dis'posto, a *pp di* disporre ♦ *ag* (*incline*): ~ a fare disposed o prepared to do.

dis'potico, a, ci, che *ag* despotic.

dispo'tismo *sm* despotism.

disprez'zare [dispret'tsare] *vt* to despise.

dis'prezzo [dis'prettso] *sm* contempt; con ~ del pericolo with a total disregard for the danger involved.

'disputa *sf* dispute, quarrel.

dispu'tare *vt* (*contendere*) to dispute, contest; (*SPORT: partita*) to play; (: *gara*) to take part in ♦ *vi* to quarrel; ~ di to discuss; ~rsi qc to fight for sth.

disqui'sire *vi* to discourse on.

disquisizi'one [diskwizit'tsjone] *sf* detailed analysis.

dissa'crare *vt* to desecrate.

dissangua'mento *sm* loss of blood.

dissangua're *vt* (*fig: persona*) to bleed white; (: *patrimonio*) to suck dry; ~rsi *vr* (*MED*) to lose blood; (*fig*) to ruin o.s.; morire dissanguato to bleed to death.

dissa'pore *sm* slight disagreement.

'disse *vb vedi* dire.

disse'care *vt* to dissect.

dissec'care *vt*, ~rsi *vr* to dry up.

dissemi'nare *vt* to scatter; (*fig: notizie*) to spread.

dissenna'tezza [dissenna'tettsa] *sf* foolishness.

dis'senso *sm* dissent; (*disapprovazione*) disapproval.

dissente'ria *sf* dysentery.

dissen'tire *vi*: ~ (da) to disagree (with).

disseppel'lire *vt* (*esumare: cadavere*) to disinter, exhume; (*dissotterrare: anche fig*) to dig up, unearth; (: *rancori*) to resurrect.

dissertazi'one [dissertat'tsjone] *sf* dissertation.

disser'vizio [disser'vittsjo] *sm* inefficiency.

disses'tare *vt* (*ECON*) to ruin.

disses'tato, a *ag* (*fondo stradale*) uneven; (*economia, finanze*) shaky; "strada ~a" (*per lavori in corso*) "road up" (*BRIT*), "road out" (*US*).

dis'sesto *sm* (financial) ruin.

disse'tante *ag* refreshing.

disse'tare *vt* to quench the thirst of; ~rsi *vr* to quench one's thirst.

dissezi'one [disset'tsjone] *sf* dissection.

'dissi *vb vedi* dire.

dissi'dente *ag, sm/f* dissident.

dis'sidio *sm* disagreement.

dis'simile *ag* different, dissimilar.

dissimu'lare *vt* (*fingere*) to dissemble; (*nascondere*) to conceal.

dissimula'tore, 'trice *sm/f* dissembler.

dissimulazi'one [dissimulat'tsjone] *sf* dissembling; concealment.

dissi'pare *vt* to dissipate; (*scialacquare*) to squander, waste.

dissipa'tezza [dissipa'tettsa] *sf* dissipation.

dissi'pato, a *ag* dissolute, dissipated.

dissipazi'one [dissipat'tsjone] *sf* squandering.

dissoci'are [disso't∫are] vt to dissociate.
dis'solto, a pp di **dissolvere**.
disso'lubile ag soluble.
dissolu'tezza [dissolu'tettsa] sf dissoluteness.
dissolu'tivo, a ag (forza) divisive; **processo** ~ (anche fig) process of dissolution.
disso'luto, a pp di **dissolvere ♦** ag dissolute, licentious.
dissol'venza [dissol'vɛntsa] sf (CINE) fading.
dis'solvere vt to dissolve; (neve) to melt; (fumo) to disperse; ~**rsi** vr to dissolve; to melt; to disperse.
disso'nante ag discordant.
disso'nanza [disso'nantsa] sf (fig: di opinioni) clash.
dissotter'rare vt (cadavere) to disinter, exhume; (tesori, rovine) to dig up, unearth; (fig: sentimenti, odio) to bring up again, resurrect.
dissu'adere vt: ~ **qn da** to dissuade sb from.
dissuasi'one sf dissuasion.
dissu'aso, a pp di **dissuadere**.
distacca'mento sm (MIL) detachment.
distac'care vt to detach, separate; (SPORT) to leave behind; ~**rsi** vr to be detached; (fig) to stand out; ~**rsi da** (fig: allontanarsi) to grow away from.
dis'tacco, chi sm (separazione) separation; (fig: indifferenza) detachment; (SPORT): **vincere con un** ~ **di** ... to win by a distance of ....
dis'tante av far away ♦ ag distant, far away; **essere** ~ **(da)** to be a long way (from); **è** ~ **da qui?** is it far from here?; **essere** ~ **nel tempo** to be in the distant past.
dis'tanza [dis'tantsa] sf distance; **comando a** ~ remote control; **a** ~ **di 2 giorni** 2 days later; **tener qn a** ~ to keep sb at arm's length; **prendere le** ~**e da qc/qn** to dissociate o.s. from sth/sb; **tenere o mantenere le** ~**e** to keep one's distance; ~ **focale** focal length; ~ **di sicurezza** safe distance; (AUT) braking distance; ~ **di tiro** range; ~ **di visibilità** visibility.
distanzi'are [distan'tsjare] vt to space out, place at intervals; (SPORT) to outdistance; (fig: superare) to outstrip, surpass.
dis'tare vi: **distiamo pochi chilometri da Roma** we are only a few kilometres (away) from Rome; **dista molto da qui?** is it far (away) from here?; **non dista molto** it's not far (away).
dis'tendere vt (coperta) to spread out; (gambe) to stretch (out); (mettere a

giacere) to lay; (rilassare: muscoli, nervi) to relax; ~**rsi** vr (rilassarsi) to relax; (sdraiarsi) to lie down.
distensi'one sf stretching; relaxation; (POL) détente.
disten'sivo, a ag (gen) relaxing, restful; (farmaco) tranquillizing; (POL) conciliatory.
dis'teso, a pp di **distendere ♦** ag (allungato: persona, gamba) stretched out; (rilassato: persona, atmosfera) relaxed ♦ sf expanse, stretch; **avere un volto** ~ to look relaxed.
distil'lare vt to distil.
distil'lato sm distillate.
distillazi'one [distillat'tsjone] sf distillation.
distille'ria sf distillery.
dis'tinguere vt to distinguish; ~**rsi** vr (essere riconoscibile) to be distinguished; (emergere) to stand out, be conspicuous; distinguish o.s.; **un vino che si distingue per il suo aroma** a wine with a distinctive bouquet.
dis'tinguo sm inv distinction.
dis'tinta sf (nota) note; (elenco) list; ~ **di pagamento** receipt; ~ **di versamento** pay-in slip.
distin'tivo, a ag distinctive; distinguishing ♦ sm badge.
dis'tinto, a pp di **distinguere ♦** ag (dignitoso ed elegante) distinguished; ~**i saluti** (in lettera) yours faithfully.
distinzi'one [distin'tsjone] sf distinction; **non faccio** ~**i** (tra persone) I don't discriminate; (tra cose) it's all one to me; **senza** ~ **di razza/religione** ... no matter what one's race/creed ....
dis'togliere [dis'tɔʎʎere] vt: ~ **da** to take away from; (fig) to dissuade from.
dis'tolto, a pp di **distogliere**.
dis'torcere [dis'tɔrt∫ere] vt to twist; (fig) to twist, distort; ~**rsi** vr (contorcersi) to twist.
distorsi'one sf (MED) sprain; (FISICA, OTTICA) distortion.
dis'torto, a pp di **distorcere**.
dis'trarre vt to distract; (divertire) to entertain, amuse; **distrarsi** vr (non fare attenzione) to be distracted, let one's mind wander; (svagarsi) to amuse o enjoy o.s.; ~ **lo sguardo** to look away; **non distrarti!** pay attention!
distratta'mente av absent-mindedly, without thinking.
dis'tratto, a pp di **distrarre ♦** ag absent-minded; (disattento) inattentive.
distrazi'one [distrat'tsjone] sf absent-mindedness; inattention; (svago) distraction, entertainment; **errori di** ~

careless mistakes.

dis'tretto *sm* district.

distribu'ire *vt* to distribute; (*CARTE*) to deal (out); (*consegnare: posta*) to deliver; (*lavoro*) to allocate, assign; (*ripartire*) to share out.

distribu'tore *sm* (*di benzina*) petrol (*BRIT*) *o* gas (*US*) pump; (*AUT, ELETTR*) distributor; (*automatico*) vending machine.

distribuzi'one [distribut'tsjone] *sf* distribution; delivery; allocation; assignment; sharing out.

distri'care *vt* to disentangle, unravel; **~rsi** *vr* (*tirarsi fuori*): **~rsi da** to get out of, disentangle o.s. from; (*fig: cavarsela*) to manage, get by.

dis'truggere [dis'truddʒere] *vt* to destroy.

distrut'tivo, a *ag* destructive.

dis'trutto, a *pp di* **distruggere**.

distruzi'one [distrut'tsjone] *sf* destruction.

distur'bare *vt* to disturb, trouble; (*sonno, lezioni*) to disturb, interrupt; **~rsi** *vr* to put o.s. out; **non si disturbi** please don't bother.

dis'turbo *sm* trouble, bother, inconvenience; (*indisposizione*) (slight) disorder, ailment; **~i** *smpl* (*RADIO, TV*) static *sg*; **~ della quiete pubblica** (*DIR*) disturbance of the peace; **~i di stomaco** stomach trouble *sg*.

disubbidi'ente *ag* disobedient.

disubbidi'enza [dizubbi'djɛntsa] *sf* disobedience; **~ civile** civil disobedience.

disubbi'dire *vi*: **~ (a qn)** to disobey (sb).

disuguagli'anza [dizugwaʎ'ʎantsa] *sf* inequality.

disugu'ale *ag* unequal; (*diverso*) different; (*irregolare*) uneven.

disumanità *sf* inhumanity.

disu'mano, a *ag* inhuman; **un grido ~ a** terrible cry.

disuni'one *sf* disunity.

disu'nire *vt* to divide, disunite.

di'suso *sm*: **andare** *o* **cadere in ~** to fall into disuse.

'dita *sfpl di* **dito**.

di'tale *sm* thimble.

di'tata *sf* (*colpo*) jab (with one's finger); (*segno*) fingermark.

'dito, pl(f) 'dita *sm* finger; (*misura*) finger, finger's breadth; **~ (del piede)** toe; **mettersi le ~a nel naso** to pick one's nose; **mettere il ~ sulla piaga** (*fig*) to touch a sore spot; **non ha mosso un ~ (per aiutarmi)** he didn't lift a finger (to help me); **ormai è segnato a ~** everyone knows about him now.

'ditta *sf* firm, business; **macchina della ~**

company car.

dit'tafono *sm* Dictaphone ®.

ditta'tore *sm* dictator.

ditta'tura *sf* dictatorship.

dit'tongo, ghi *sm* diphthong.

di'urno, a *ag* day *cpd*, daytime *cpd*; **ore ~e** daytime *sg*; **spettacolo ~** matinee; **turno ~** day shift; *vedi anche* **albergo**.

'diva *sf vedi* **divo**.

diva'gare *vi* to digress.

divagazi'one [divagat'tsjone] *sf* digression; **~i sul tema** variations on a theme.

divam'pare *vi* to flare up, blaze up.

di'vano *sm* sofa; (*senza schienale*) divan; **~ letto** bed settee, sofa bed.

divari'care *vt* to open wide.

di'vario *sm* difference.

di'vengo *etc vb vedi* **divenire**.

dive'nire *vi* = **diventare**.

di'venni *etc vb vedi* **divenire**.

diven'tare *vi* to become; **~ famoso/ professore** to become famous/a teacher; **~ vecchio** to grow old; **c'è da ~ matti** it's enough to drive you mad.

dive'nuto, a *pp di* **divenire**.

di'verbio *sm* altercation.

diver'gente [diver'dʒɛnte] *ag* divergent.

diver'genza [diver'dʒɛntsa] *sf* divergence; **~ d'opinioni** difference of opinion.

di'vergere [di'vɛrdʒere] *vi* to diverge.

diverrò *etc vb vedi* **divenire**.

diversa'mente *av* (*in modo differente*) differently; (*altrimenti*) otherwise; **~ da** **quanto stabilito** contrary to what had been decided.

diversifi'care *vt* to diversify, vary; **~rsi** *vr*: **~rsi (per)** to differ (in).

diversificazi'one [diversifikat'tsjone] *sf* diversification; difference.

diversi'one *sf* diversion.

diversità *sf inv* difference, diversity; (*varietà*) variety.

diver'sivo, a *ag* diversionary ♦ *sm* diversion, distraction; **fare un'azione ~a** to create a diversion.

di'verso, a *ag* (*differente*): **~ (da)** different (from) ♦ *sm* (*omosessuale*) homosexual; **~i, e** *det pl* several, various; (*COMM*) sundry ♦ *pron pl* several (people), many (people).

diver'tente *ag* amusing.

diverti'mento *sm* amusement, pleasure; (*passatempo*) pastime, recreation; **buon ~!** enjoy yourself!, have a nice time!

diver'tire *vt* to amuse, entertain; **~rsi** *vr* to amuse *o* enjoy o.s.; **divertiti!** enjoy yourself, have a good time!; **~rsi alle spalle di qn** to have a laugh at sb's

expense.
diver'tito, a *ag* amused.
divi'dendo *sm* dividend.
di'videre *vt* (*anche MAT*) to divide;
(*distribuire, ripartire*) to divide (up), split
(up); ~**rsi** *vr* (*persone*) to separate, part;
(*coppia*) to separate; ~**rsi** (**in**) (*scindersi*) to
divide (into), split up (into); (*ramificarsi*)
to fork; **è diviso dalla moglie** he's
separated from his wife; **si divide tra casa
e lavoro** he divides his time between
home and work.
divi'eto *sm* prohibition; "~ **di accesso**" "no
entry"; "~ **di caccia**" "no hunting"; "~ **di
parcheggio**" "no parking"; "~ **di sosta**"
(*AUT*) "no waiting".
divinco'larsi *vr* to wriggle, writhe.
divinità *sf inv* divinity.
di'vino, a *ag* divine.
di'visa *sf* (*MIL etc*) uniform; (*COMM*) foreign
currency.
di'visi *etc vb vedi* **dividere**.
divisi'one *sf* division; ~ **in sillabe** syllable
division; (*a fine riga*) hyphenation.
di'vismo *sm* (*esibizionismo*) playing to the
crowd.
di'viso, a *pp di* **dividere**.
divi'sorio, a *ag* (*siepe, muro esterno*)
dividing; (*muro interno*) dividing,
partition *cpd* ♦ *sm* (*in una stanza*) partition.
'divo, a *sm/f* star; **come una** ~**a** like a
prima donna.
divo'rare *vt* to devour; ~ **qc con gli occhi** to
eye sth greedily.
divorzi'are [divor'tsjare] *vi*: ~ (**da qn**) to
divorce (sb).
divorzi'ato, a [divor'tsjato] *ag* divorced
♦ *sm/f* divorcee.
di'vorzio [di'vɔrtsjo] *sm* divorce.
divul'gare *vt* to divulge, disclose; (*rendere
comprensibile*) to popularize; ~**rsi** *vr* to
spread.
divulgazi'one [divulgat'tsjone] *sf* (*vedi vb*)
disclosure; popularization; spread.
dizio'nario [dittsjo'narjo] *sm* dictionary.
dizi'one [dit'tsjone] *sf* diction;
pronunciation.
Dja'karta [dʒa'karta] *sf* Djakarta.
dl *abbr* (= *decilitro*) dl.
dm *abbr* (= *decimetro*) dm.
DNA [di'ennɛa] *sigla m* (*BIOL*: = *acido
deossiribonucleico*) DNA ♦ *sigla f*
= *direzione nazionale antimafia*.
do *sm* (*MUS*) C; (: *solfeggiando la scala*)
do(h).
dobbi'amo *vb vedi* **dovere**.
D.O.C. [dɔk] *sigla vedi* **denominazione di
origine controllata**.

doc. *abbr* = **documento**.
'doccia, ce ['dottʃa] *sf* (*bagno*) shower;
(*condotto*) pipe; **fare la** ~ to have a
shower; ~ **fredda** (*fig*) slap in the face.
do'cente [do'tʃɛnte] *ag* teaching ♦ *sm/f*
teacher; (*di università*) lecturer; **personale
non** ~ non-teaching staff.
do'cenza [do'tʃɛntsa] *sf* university
teaching *o* lecturing; **ottenere la libera** ~
to become a lecturer.
D.O.C.G. *sigla* (= *denominazione di origine
controllata e garantita*) label guaranteeing
the quality and origin of a wine.
'docile ['dɔtʃile] *ag* docile.
docilità [dotʃili'ta] *sf* docility.
documen'tare *vt* to document; ~**rsi** *vr*: ~**rsi
(su)** to gather information *o* material
(about).
documen'tario, a *ag, sm* documentary.
documentazi'one [dokumentat'tsjone] *sf*
documentation.
docu'mento *sm* document; ~**i** *smpl*
(*d'identità etc*) papers.
Dodecan'neso *sm*: **le Isole del** ~ the
Dodecanese Islands.
dodi'cenne [dodi'tʃɛnne] *ag, sm/f* twelve-
year-old.
dodi'cesimo, a [dodi'tʃɛzimo] *num* twelfth.
'dodici ['doditʃi] *num* twelve.
do'gana *sf* (*ufficio*) customs *pl*; (*tassa*)
(customs) duty; **passare la** ~ to go
through customs.
doga'nale *ag* customs *cpd*.
dogani'ere *sm* customs officer.
'doglie ['dɔʎʎe] *sfpl* (*MED*) labour *sg* (*BRIT*),
labor *sg* (*US*), labo(u)r pains.
'dogma, i *sm* dogma.
dog'matico, a, ci, che *ag* dogmatic.
'dolce ['doltʃe] *ag* sweet; (*colore*) soft;
(*carattere, persona*) gentle, mild; (*fig: mite:
clima*) mild; (*non ripido: pendio*) gentle
♦ *sm* (*sapore* ~) sweetness, sweet taste;
(*CUC: portata*) sweet, dessert; (: *torta*) cake;
il ~ **far niente** sweet idleness.
dolcemente *av* (*baciare, trattare*) gently;
(*sorridere, cantare*) sweetly; (*parlare*) softly.
dol'cezza [dol'tʃettsa] *sf* sweetness;
softness; mildness; gentleness.
dolci'ario, a [dol'tʃarjo] *ag* confectionery
cpd.
dolci'astro, a [dol'tʃastro] *ag* (*sapore*)
sweetish.
dolcifi'cante [doltʃifi'kante] *ag* sweetening
♦ *sm* sweetener.
dolci'umi [dol'tʃumi] *smpl* sweets.
do'lente *ag* sorrowful, sad.
do'lere *vi* to be sore, hurt, ache; ~**rsi** *vr* to
complain; (*essere spiacente*): ~**rsi di** to be

sorry for; **mi duole la testa** my head aches, I've got a headache.
'dolgo etc vb vedi **dolere.**
'dollaro sm dollar.
'dolo sm (DIR) malice; (frode) fraud, deceit.
Dolo'miti sfpl: **le ~** the Dolomites.
dolo'rante ag aching, sore.
do'lore sm (fisico) pain; (morale) sorrow, grief; **se lo scoprono sono ~i!** if they find out there'll be trouble!
dolo'roso, a ag painful; sorrowful, sad.
do'loso, a ag (DIR) malicious; **incendio ~** arson.
'dolsi etc vb vedi **dolere.**
dom. abbr (= domenica) Sun.
do'manda sf (interrogazione) question; (richiesta) demand; (: cortese) request; (DIR: richiesta scritta) application; (ECON): **la ~** demand; **fare una ~ a qn** to ask sb a question; **fare ~ (per un lavoro)** to apply (for a job); **far regolare ~ (di qc)** to apply through the proper channels (for sth); **fare ~ all'autorità giudiziaria** to apply to the courts; **~ di divorzio** divorce petition; **~ di matrimonio** proposal.
doman'dare vt (per avere) to ask for; (per sapere) to ask; (esigere) to demand; **~rsi** vr to wonder, ask o.s.; **~ qc a qn** to ask sb for sth; to ask sb sth.
do'mani av tomorrow ♦ sm (l'indomani) next day, following day; **il ~** (il futuro) the future; (il giorno successivo) the next day; **un ~** some day; **~ l'altro** the day after tomorrow; **~ (a) otto** tomorrow week, a week tomorrow; **a ~!** see you tomorrow!
do'mare vt to tame.
doma'tore, 'trice sm/f (gen) tamer; **~ di cavalli** horsebreaker; **~ di leoni** lion tamer.
domat'tina av tomorrow morning.
do'menica, che sf Sunday; per fraseologia vedi **martedì.**
domeni'cale ag Sunday cpd.
domeni'cano, a ag, sm/f Dominican.
do'mestica, che sf vedi **domestico.**
do'mestico, a, ci, che ag domestic ♦ sm/f servant, domestic; **le pareti ~che** one's own four walls; **animale** m **~** pet; **una ~a a ore** a daily (woman).
domicili'are [domitʃi'ljare] ag vedi **arresto.**
domicili'arsi [domitʃi'ljarsi] vr to take up residence.
domi'cilio [domi'tʃiljo] sm (DIR) domicile, place of residence; **visita a ~** (MED) house call; **"recapito a ~"** "deliveries"; **violazione di ~** (DIR) breaking and entering.
domi'nante ag (colore, nota) dominant;

(opinione) prevailing; (idea) main cpd, chief cpd; (posizione) dominating cpd; (classe, partito) ruling cpd.
domi'nare vt to dominate; (fig: sentimenti) to control, master ♦ vi to be in the dominant position; **~rsi** vr (controllarsi) to control o.s.; **~ su** (fig) to surpass, outclass.
domina'tore, 'trice ag ruling cpd ♦ sm/f ruler.
dominazi'one [dominat'tsjone] sf domination.
domini'cano, a ag: **la Repubblica D~a** the Dominican Republic.
do'minio sm dominion; (fig: campo) field, domain; **~i coloniali** colonies; **essere di ~ pubblico** (notizia etc) to be common knowledge.
don sm (REL) Father.
do'nare vt to give, present; (per beneficenza etc) to donate ♦ vi (fig): **~ a** to suit, become; **~ sangue** to give blood.
dona'tore, 'trice sm/f donor; **~ di sangue/ di organi** blood/organ donor.
donazi'one [donat'tsjone] sf donation; **atto di ~** (DIR) deed of gift.
'donde av (poetico) whence.
dondo'lare vt (cullare) to rock; **~rsi** vr to swing, sway.
'dondolo sm: **sedia/cavallo a ~** rocking chair/horse.
dongio'vanni [dondʒo'vanni] sm Don Juan, ladies' man.
'donna sf woman; (titolo) Donna; (CARTE) queen; **figlio di buona ~!** (fam) son of a bitch!; **~ di casa** housewife; **~ a ore** daily (help o woman); **~ delle pulizie** cleaning lady, cleaner; **~ di servizio** maid; **~ di vita** o **di strada** prostitute, streetwalker.
donnai'olo sm ladykiller.
'donnola sf weasel.
'dono sm gift.
'doping sm doping.
'dopo av (tempo) afterwards; (: più tardi) later; (luogo) after, next ♦ prep after ♦ cong (temporale): **~ aver studiato** after having studied ♦ ag inv: **il giorno ~** the following day; **~ mangiato va a dormire** after having eaten o after a meal he goes for a sleep; **un anno ~** a year later; **~ di me/lui** after me/him; **~ che** = dopoché.
dopo'barba sm inv after-shave.
dopoché [dopo'ke] cong after, when.
dopodiché [dopodi'ke] av after which.
dopodo'mani av the day after tomorrow.
dopogu'erra sm postwar years pl.
dopola'voro sm recreational club.
dopo'pranzo [dopo'prandzo] av after lunch

(o dinner).

doposcì [dopoʃ'ʃi] *sm inv* après-ski outfit.

doposcu'ola *sm inv* school club *offering extra tuition and recreational facilities.*

dopo'sole *sm inv, ag inv*: **(lozione/crema)** ~ aftersun (lotion/cream).

dopo'tutto *av* after all.

doppi'aggio [dop'pjaddʒo] *sm* (*CINE*) dubbing.

doppi'are *vt* (*NAUT*) to round; (*SPORT*) to lap; (*CINE*) to dub.

doppia'tore, 'trice *sm/f* dubber.

doppi'etta *sf* (*fucile*) double-barrelled (*BRIT*) *o* double-barreled (*US*) shotgun; (*sparo*) shot from both barrels; (*CALCIO*) double; (*PUGILATO*) one-two; (*AUT*) double-declutch (*BRIT*), double-clutch (*US*).

doppi'ezza [dop'pjettsa] *sf* (*fig: di persona*) duplicity, double-dealing.

'doppio, a *ag* double; (*fig: falso*) double-dealing, deceitful ♦ *sm* (*quantità*): **il ~ (di)** twice as much (o many), double the amount (o number) of; (*SPORT*) doubles *pl* ♦ *av* double; **battere una lettera in ~a copia** to type a letter with a carbon copy; **fare il ~ gioco** (*fig*) to play a double game; **chiudere a ~a mandata** to double-lock; **~ senso** double entendre; **frase a ~ senso** sentence with a double meaning; **un utensile a ~ uso** a dual-purpose utensil.

doppio'fondo *sm* (*di valigia*) false bottom; (*NAUT*) double hull.

doppi'one *sm* duplicate (copy).

doppio'petto *sm* double-breasted jacket.

dop'pista *sm/f* (*TENNIS*) doubles player.

do'rare *vt* to gild; (*CUC*) to brown; **~ la pillola** (*fig*) to sugar the pill.

do'rato, a *ag* golden; (*ricoperto d'oro*) gilt, gilded.

dora'tura *sf* gilding.

dormicchi'are [dormik'kjare] *vi* to doze.

dormi'ente *ag* sleeping ♦ *sm/f* sleeper.

dormigli'one, a [dormiʎ'ʎone] *sm/f* sleepyhead.

dor'mire *vi* to sleep; (*essere addormentato*) to be asleep, be sleeping; **il caffè non mi fa** ~ coffee keeps me awake; **~ come un ghiro** to sleep like a log; **~ della grossa** to sleep soundly; **~ in piedi** (*essere stanco*) to be asleep on one's feet.

dor'mita *sf*: **farsi una** ~ to have a good sleep.

dormi'torio *sm* dormitory; **~ pubblico** doss house (*BRIT*) *o* flophouse (*US*) (*run by local authority*).

dormi'veglia [dormi've ʎʎa] *sm* drowsiness.

dorrò *etc vb vedi* **dolere**.

dor'sale *ag*: **spina** ~ backbone, spine.

'dorso *sm* back; (*di montagna*) ridge, crest; (*di libro*) spine; (*NUOTO*) backstroke; **a ~ di cavallo** on horseback.

do'saggio [do'zaddʒo] *sm* (*atto*) measuring out; **sbagliare il** ~ to get the proportions wrong.

do'sare *vt* to measure out; (*MED*) to dose.

'dose *sf* quantity, amount; (*MED*) dose.

dossi'er [do'sje] *sm inv* dossier, file.

'dosso *sm* (*rilievo*) rise; (: *di strada*) bump; (*dorso*): **levarsi di** ~ **i vestiti** to take one's clothes off; **levarsi un peso di** ~ (*fig*) to take a weight off one's mind.

do'tare *vt*: **~ di** to provide *o* supply with; (*fig*) to endow with.

do'tato, a *ag*: **~ di** (*attrezzature*) equipped with; (*bellezza, intelligenza*) endowed with; **un uomo** ~ a gifted man.

dotazi'one [dotat'tsjone] *sf* (*insieme di beni*) endowment; (*di macchine etc*) equipment; **dare qc in** ~ **a** qn to issue sb with sth; **i macchinari in** ~ **alla fabbrica** the machinery in use in the factory.

'dote *sf* (*di sposa*) dowry; (*assegnata a un ente*) endowment; (*fig*) gift, talent.

Dott. *abbr* (= *dottore*) Dr.

'dotto, a *ag* (*colto*) learned ♦ *sm* (*sapiente*) scholar; (*ANAT*) duct.

dotto'rato *sm* degree; **~ di ricerca** doctorate, doctor's degree.

dot'tore, 'essa *sm/f* doctor.

dot'trina *sf* doctrine.

Dott.ssa *abbr* (= *dottoressa*) Dr.

double-'face [dubl'fas] *ag inv* reversible.

'dove *av* where; (*in cui*) where, in which; (*dovunque*) wherever ♦ *sm*: **per ogni** ~ everywhere; **di dov'è?** where are you from?; **da** ~ **abito vedo tutta la città** I can see the whole city from where I live; **per** ~ **si passa?** which way should we go?; **le dò una mano fin** ~ **posso** I'll help you as much as I can.

do'vere *sm* (*obbligo*) duty ♦ *vt* (*essere debitore*): **~ qc (a qn)** to owe (sb) sth ♦ *vi* (*seguito dall'infinito: obbligo*) to have to; **lui deve farlo** he has to do it, he must do it; **è dovuto partire** he had to leave; **ha dovuto pagare** he had to pay; (: *intenzione*): **devo partire domani** I'm (due) to leave tomorrow; (: *probabilità*): **dev'essere tardi** it must be late; **doveva accadere** it was bound to happen; **avere il senso del** ~ to have a sense of duty; **rivolgersi a chi di** ~ to apply to the appropriate authority *o* person; **a** ~ (*bene*) properly; (*debitamente*) as he (*o* she *etc*) deserves; **come si deve** (*bene*) properly; (*merita-*

tamente) properly, as he (*o* she *etc*) deserves; **una persona come si deve** a respectable person.

dove'roso, a *ag* (right and) proper.

do'vizia [do'vittsja] *sf* abundance.

dovrò *etc vb vedi* **dovere.**

do'vunque *av* (*in qualunque luogo*) wherever; (*dappertutto*) everywhere; ~ **io vada** wherever I go.

dovuta'mente *av* (*debitamente*: *redigere, compilare*) correctly; (: *rimproverare*) as he (*o* she *etc*) deserves.

do'vuto, a *ag* (*causato*): ~ **a** due to ♦ *sm* due; **nel modo** ~ in the proper way; **ho lavorato più del** ~ I worked more than was necessary.

doz'zina [dod'dzina] *sf* dozen; **una** ~ **di uova** a dozen eggs; **di** *o* **da** ~ (*scrittore, spettacolo*) second-rate.

dozzi'nale [doddzi'nale] *ag* cheap, second-rate.

DP *sigla f* (= *Democrazia Proletaria*) *political party.*

'draga, ghe *sf* dredger.

dra'gare *vt* to dredge.

dragherò *etc* [drage'rɔ] *vb vedi* **dragare.**

'drago, ghi *sm* dragon; (*fig fam*) genius.

'dramma, i *sm* drama; **fare un** ~ **di qc** to make a drama out of sth.

dram'matico, a, ci, che *ag* dramatic.

drammatiz'zare [drammatid'dzare] *vt* to dramatize.

dramma'turgo, ghi *sm* playwright.

drappeggi'are [drapped'dʒare] *vt* to drape.

drap'peggio [drap'peddʒo] *sm* (*tessuto*) drapery; (*di abito*) folds.

drap'pello *sm* (*MIL*) squad; (*gruppo*) band, group.

'drappo *sm* cloth.

'drastico, a, ci, che *ag* drastic.

dre'naggio [dre'naddʒo] *sm* drainage.

dre'nare *vt* to drain.

'Dresda *sf* Dresden.

drib'blare *vi* (*CALCIO*) to dribble ♦ *vt* (*avversario*) to dodge, avoid.

'dritto, a *ag, av* = **diritto** ♦ *sm/f* (*fam*: *furbo*): **è un** ~ he's a crafty *o* sly one ♦ *sf* (*destra*) right, right hand; (*NAUT*) starboard; **a** ~**a e a manca** (*fig*) on all sides, right, left and centre.

driz'zare [drit'tsare] *vt* (*far tornare diritto*) to straighten; (*volgere: sguardo, occhi*) to turn, direct; (*innalzare: antenna, muro*) to erect; ~**rsi** *vr* to stand up; ~ **le orecchie** to prick up one's ears; ~**rsi in piedi** to rise to one's feet; ~**rsi a sedere** to sit up.

'droga, ghe *sf* (*sostanza aromatica*) spice; (*stupefacente*) drug; ~**ghe pesanti/leggere**

hard/soft drugs.

dro'gare *vt* to drug, dope; ~**rsi** *vr* to take drugs.

dro'gato, a *sm/f* drug addict.

droghe'ria [droge'ria] *sf* grocer's (shop) (*BRIT*), grocery (store) (*US*).

drogherò *etc* [droge'rɔ] *vb vedi* **drogare.**

droghi'ere, a [dro'gjɛre] *sm/f* grocer.

drome'dario *sm* dromedary.

DS [di'ɛsse] *smpl* (= *Democratici di Sinistra*) Democrats of the Left (*Italian left-wing party*).

'dubbio, a *ag* (*incerto*) doubtful, dubious; (*ambiguo*) dubious ♦ *sm* (*incertezza*) doubt; **avere il** ~ **che** to be afraid that, suspect that; **essere in** ~ **fra** to hesitate between; **mettere in** ~ **qc** to question sth; **nutrire seri** ~**i su qc** to have grave doubts about sth; **senza** ~ doubtless, no doubt.

dubbi'oso, a *ag* doubtful, dubious.

dubi'tare *vi*: ~ **di** (*onestà*) to doubt; (*risultato*) to be doubtful of; ~ **di qn** to mistrust sb; ~ **di sé** to be unsure of o.s.

Du'blino *sf* Dublin.

'duca, chi *sm* duke.

'duce ['dutʃe] *sm* (*STORIA*) captain; (: *del fascismo*) duce.

du'chessa [du'kessa] *sf* duchess.

'due *num* two; **a** ~ **a** ~ two at a time, two by two; **dire** ~ **parole** to say a few words; **ci metto** ~ **minuti** I'll have it done in a jiffy.

duecen'tesco, a, schi, sche [duetʃen'tesko] *ag* thirteenth-century.

due'cento [due'tʃɛnto] *num* two hundred ♦ *sm*: **il D**~ the thirteenth century.

duel'lare *vi* to fight a duel.

du'ello *sm* duel.

due'mila *num* two thousand ♦ *sm inv*: **il** ~ the year two thousand.

due'pezzi [due'pɛttsi] *sm* (*costume da bagno*) two-piece swimsuit; (*abito femminile*) two-piece suit.

du'etto *sm* duet.

'dulcis in 'fundo ['dultʃisin'fundo] *av* to cap it all.

'duna *sf* dune.

'dunque *cong* (*perciò*) so, therefore; (*riprendendo il discorso*) well (then) ♦ *sm inv*: **venire al** ~ to come to the point.

'duo *sm inv* (*MUS*) duet; (*TEAT, CINE, fig*) duo.

du'ole *etc vb vedi* **dolere.**

du'omo *sm* cathedral.

'duplex *sm inv* (*TEL*) party line.

dupli'cato *sm* duplicate.

'duplice ['duplitʃe] *ag* double, twofold; **in** ~ **copia** in duplicate.

duplicità [duplitʃi'ta] *sf* (*fig*) duplicity.

du'rante *prep* during; **vita natural** ~ for

life.
du'rare *vi* to last; **non può** ~! this can't go
on any longer!; ~ **fatica a** to have
difficulty in; ~ **in carica** to remain in
office.
du'rata *sf* length (of time); duration; **per
tutta la** ~ **di** throughout; ~ **media della
vita** life expectancy.
dura'turo, a *ag,* du'revole *ag* (*ricordo*)
lasting; (*materiale*) durable.
du'rezza [du'rettsa] *sf* hardness;
stubbornness; harshness; toughness.
'duro, a *ag* (*pietra, lavoro, materasso,
problema*) hard; (*persona: ostinato*)
stubborn, obstinate; (: *severo*) harsh,
hard; (*voce*) harsh; (*carne*) tough ♦ *sm/f*
(*persona*) tough one ♦ *av*: **tener** ~ (*resistere*)
to stand firm, hold out; **avere la pelle** ~**a**
(*fig: persona*) to be tough; **fare il** ~ to act
tough; ~ **di comprendonio** slow-witted; ~
d'orecchi hard of hearing.
du'rone *sm* hard skin.
'duttile *ag* (*sostanza*) malleable; (*fig:
carattere*) docile, biddable; (: *stile*)
adaptable.
DVD [divu'di] *sm inv* DVD; (*lettore*) DVD
player.

E e

E, e [e] *sf o m inv* (*lettera*) E, e; **E come Empoli**
≈ E for Edward (*BRIT*), E for Easy (*US*).
E *abbr* (= *est*) E; (*AUT*) = **itinerario europeo.**
e, *dav V spesso* **ed** *cong* and; (*avversativo*) but;
(*eppure*) and yet; ~ **lui?** what about him?;
~ **compralo!** well buy it then!
è *vb vedi* **essere.**
E.A.D. *sigla f vedi* **elaborazione automatica
dei dati.**
ebaniste'ria *sf* cabinet-making; (*negozio*)
cabinet-maker's shop.
'ebano *sm* ebony.
eb'bene *cong* well (then).
'ebbi *etc vb vedi* **avere.**
eb'brezza [eb'brettsa] *sf* intoxication.
'ebbro, a *ag* drunk; ~ **di** (*gioia etc*) beside
o.s. *o* wild with.
'ebete *ag* stupid, idiotic.
ebe'tismo *sm* stupidity.
ebollizi'one [ebollit'tsjone] *sf* boiling;
punto di ~ boiling point.

e'braico, a, ci, che *ag* Hebrew, Hebraic
♦ *sm* (*LING*) Hebrew.
e'breo, a *ag* Jewish ♦ *sm/f* Jew/Jewess.
'Ebridi *sfpl*: **le (isole)** ~ the Hebrides.
e'burneo, a *ag* ivory *cpd.*
E/C *abbr* = **estratto conto.**
eca'tombe *sf* (*strage*) slaughter, massacre.
ecc. *abbr av* (= *eccetera*) etc.
ecce'dente [ett∫e'dɛnte] *sm* surplus.
ecce'denza [ett∫e'dɛntsa] *sf* excess,
surplus; (*INFORM*) overflow.
ec'cedere [et't∫ɛdere] *vt* to exceed ♦ *vi* to go
too far; ~ **nel bere/mangiare** to indulge in
drink/food to excess.
eccel'lente [ett∫el'lɛnte] *ag* excellent;
(*cadavere, arresto*) of a prominent person.
eccel'lenza [ett∫e'lɛntsa] *sf* excellence;
(*titolo*): **Sua E**~ His Excellency.
ec'cellere [et't∫ɛllere] *vi*: ~ **(in)** to excel
(at); ~ **su tutti** to surpass everyone.
ec'celso, a [et't∫ɛlso] *pp di* **eccellere** ♦ *ag*
(*cima, montagna*) high; (*fig: ingegno*) great,
exceptional.
ec'centrico, a, ci, che [et't∫ɛntriko] *ag*
eccentric.
ecces'sivo, a [ett∫es'sivo] *ag* excessive.
ec'cesso [et't∫ɛsso] *sm* excess; **all'**~
(*gentile, generoso*) to excess, excessively;
dare in ~**i** to fly into a rage; ~ **di velocità**
(*AUT*) speeding; ~ **di zelo**
overzealousness.
ec'cetera [et't∫etera] *av* et cetera, and so
on.
ec'cetto [et't∫etto] *prep* except, with the
exception of; ~ **che** *cong* except, other
than; ~ **che (non)** unless.
eccettu'are [ett∫ettu'are] *vt* to except;
eccettuati i presenti present company
excepted.
eccezio'nale [ett∫ettsjo'nale] *ag*
exceptional; **in via del tutto** ~ in this
instance, exceptionally.
eccezi'one [ett∫et'tsjone] *sf* exception;
(*DIR*) objection; **a** ~ **di** with the exception
of, except for; **d'**~ exceptional; **fare un'**~
alla regola to make an exception to the
rule.
ec'chimosi [ek'kimozi] *sf inv* bruise.
ec'cidio [et't∫idjo] *sm* massacre.
ecci'tante [ett∫i'tante] *ag* (*gen*) exciting;
(*sostanza*) stimulating ♦ *sm* stimulant.
ecci'tare [ett∫i'tare] *vt* (*curiosità, interesse*)
to excite, arouse; (*folla*) to incite; ~**rsi** *vr*
to get excited; (*sessualmente*) to become
aroused.
eccitazi'one [ett∫itat'tsjone] *sf* excitement.
ecclesi'astico, a, ci, che *ag* ecclesiastical,
church *cpd*; clerical ♦ *sm* ecclesiastic.

'ecco *av* (*per dimostrare*): ~ **il treno!** here's o here comes the train!; (*dav pronome*): ~**mi!** here I am!; ~**ne uno!** here's one (of them)!; (*dav pp*): ~ **fatto!** there, that's it done!

ec'come *av* rather; **ti piace?** — ~! do you like it? — I'll say! o and how! o rather! (*BRIT*).

ECG *sigla m* = **elettrocardiogramma**.

echeggi'are [eked'dʒare] *vi* to echo.

e'clettico, a, ci, che *ag, sm/f* eclectic.

eclet'tismo *sm* eclecticism.

eclis'sare *vt* to eclipse; (*fig*) to eclipse, overshadow; ~**rsi** *vr* (*persona*: *scherzoso*) to slip away.

e'clissi *sf* eclipse.

'eco, *pl*(*m*) **'echi** *sm o f* echo; **suscitò** o **ebbe una profonda** ~ it caused quite a stir.

ecogra'fia *sf* (*MED*) ultrasound.

ecolo'gia [ekolo'dʒia] *sf* ecology.

eco'logico, a, ci, che [eko'lɔdʒiko] *ag* ecological.

ecolo'gista, i, e [ekolo'dʒista] *ag* ecological ♦ *sm/f* ecologist, environmentalist.

e'cologo, a, gi, ghe *sm/f* ecologist.

econo'mato *sm* (*INS*) bursar's office.

econo'mia *sf* economy; (*scienza*) economics *sg*; (*risparmio*: *azione*) saving; **fare** ~ to economize, make economies; **l'**~ **sommersa** the black (*BRIT*) o underground (*US*) economy; ~ **di mercato** market economy; ~ **pianificata** planned economy.

eco'nomico, a, ci, che *ag* economic; (*poco costoso*) economical; **edizione** ~**a** economy edition.

econo'mista, i *sm* economist.

economiz'zare [ekonomid'dzare] *vt, vi* to save.

e'conomo, a *ag* thrifty ♦ *sm/f* (*INS*) bursar.

ecosis'tema, i *sm* ecosystem.

'ecstasy ['ekstasi] *sf inv* ecstasy.

'Ecuador *sm*: **l'**~ Ecuador.

ecu'menico, a, ci, che *ag* ecumenical.

ec'zema [ek'dzɛma] *sm* eczema.

ed *cong vedi* **e**.

Ed. *abbr* = **editore**.

ed. *abbr* = **edizione**.

'edera *sf* ivy.

e'dicola *sf* newspaper kiosk o stand (*US*).

edico'lante *sm/f* news vendor (*in kiosk*).

edifi'cante *ag* edifying.

edifi'care *vt* to build; (*fig*: *teoria, azienda*) to establish; (*indurre al bene*) to edify.

edi'ficio [edi'fitʃo] *sm* building; (*fig*) structure.

e'dile *ag* building *cpd*.

edi'lizio, a [edi'littsjo] *ag* building *cpd* ♦ *sf* building, building trade.

Edim'burgo *sf* Edinburgh.

'edito, a *ag* published.

edi'tore, 'trice *ag* publishing *cpd* ♦ *sm/f* publisher; (*curatore*) editor.

edito'ria *sf* publishing.

editori'ale *ag* publishing *cpd* ♦ *sm* (*articolo di fondo*) editorial, leader.

e'ditto *sm* edict.

edizi'one [edit'tsjone] *sf* edition; (*tiratura*) printing; ~ **a tiratura limitata** limited edition.

edo'nismo *sm* hedonism.

e'dotto, a *ag* informed; **rendere qn** ~ **su qc** to inform sb about sth.

edu'canda *sf* boarder.

edu'care *vt* to educate; (*gusto, mente*) to train; ~ **qn a fare** to train sb to do.

educa'tivo, a *ag* educational.

edu'cato, a *ag* polite, well-mannered.

educazi'one [edukat'tsjone] *sf* education; (*familiare*) upbringing; (*comportamento*) (good) manners *pl*; **per** ~ out of politeness; **questa è pura mancanza d'**~! this is sheer bad manners!; ~ **fisica** (*INS*) physical training o education.

educherò *etc* [eduke'rɔ] *vb vedi* **educare**.

E.E.D. *sigla f vedi* **elaborazione elettronica dei dati**.

EEG *sigla m* = **elettroencefalogramma**.

e'felide *sf* freckle.

effemi'nato, a *ag* effeminate.

effe'rato, a *ag* brutal, savage.

efferve'scente [efferveʃ'ʃɛnte] *ag* effervescent.

effettiva'mente *av* (*in effetti*) in fact; (*a dire il vero*) really, actually.

effet'tivo, a *ag* (*reale*) real, actual; (*impiegato, professore*) permanent; (*MIL*) regular ♦ *sm* (*MIL*) strength; (*di patrimonio etc*) sum total.

ef'fetto *sm* effect; (*COMM*: *cambiale*) bill; (*fig*: *impressione*) impression; **far** ~ (*medicina*) to take effect, (*start to*) work; **cercare l'**~ to seek attention; **in** ~**i** in fact; ~**i attivi** (*COMM*) bills receivable; ~**i passivi** (*COMM*) bills payable; ~**i personali** personal effects, personal belongings; ~ **serra** greenhouse effect; ~**i speciali** (*CINE*) special effects.

effettu'are *vt* to effect, carry out.

effi'cace [effi'katʃe] *ag* effective.

effi'cacia [effi'katʃa] *sf* effectiveness.

effici'ente [effi'tʃɛnte] *ag* efficient.

efficien'tismo [effitʃen'tizmo] *sm* maximum efficiency.

effici'enza [effi'tʃɛntsa] *sf* efficiency.

effigi'are [effi'dʒare] *vt* to represent, portray.

ef'figie [ef'fidʒe] *sf inv* effigy.
ef'fimero, a *ag* ephemeral.
ef'fluvio *sm (anche peg, ironico)* scent, perfume.
effusi'one *sf* effusion.
e.g. *abbr* (= *exempli gratia*) e.g.
egemo'nia [edʒemo'nia] *sf* hegemony.
E'geo [e'dʒɛo] *sm*: **l'~, il mare ~** the Aegean (Sea).
'egida ['ɛdʒida] *sf*: **sotto l'~ di** under the aegis of.
E'gitto [e'dʒitto] *sm*: **l'~** Egypt.
egizi'ano, a [edʒit'tsjano] *ag, sm/f* Egyptian.
e'gizio, a [e'dʒittsjo] *ag, sm/f* (ancient) Egyptian.
'egli ['eʎʎi] *pron* he; **~ stesso** he himself.
'ego *sm inv* (*PSIC*) ego.
ego'centrico, a, ci, che [ego'tʃɛntriko] *ag* egocentric(al) ♦ *sm/f* self-centred (*BRIT*) *o* self-centered (*US*) person.
egocen'trismo [egotʃen'trizmo] *sm* egocentricity.
ego'ismo *sm* selfishness, egoism.
ego'ista, i, e *ag* selfish, egoistic ♦ *sm/f* egoist.
ego'istico, a, ci, che *ag* egoistic, selfish.
ego'tismo *sm* egotism.
ego'tista, i, e *ag* egotistic ♦ *sm/f* egotist.
Egr. *abbr* = **Egregio.**
e'gregio, a, gi, gie [e'grɛdʒo] *ag* distinguished; (*nelle lettere*): **E~ Signore** Dear Sir.
eguagli'anza *etc* [egwaʎ'ʎantsa] *vedi* **uguaglianza** *etc*.
eguali'tario, a *ag, sm/f* egalitarian.
E.I. *abbr* = *Esercito Italiano.*
eiaculazi'one [ejakulat'tsjone] *sf* ejaculation; **~ precoce** premature ejaculation.
elabo'rare *vt* (*progetto*) to work out, elaborate; (*dati*) to process; (*digerire*) to digest.
elabora'tore *sm* (*INFORM*): **~ elettronico** computer.
elaborazi'one [elaborat'tsjone] *sf* elaboration; processing; digestion; **~ automatica dei dati (E.A.D.)** (*INFORM*) automatic data processing (A.D.P.); **~ elettronica dei dati (E.E.D.)** (*INFORM*) electronic data processing (E.D.P.); **~ testi** (*INFORM*) text processing.
elar'gire [elar'dʒire] *vt* to hand out.
elargizi'one [elardʒit'tsjone] *sf* donation.
elasticiz'zato, a [elastitʃid'dzato] *ag* (*tessuto*) stretch *cpd*.
e'lastico, a, ci, che *ag* elastic; (*fig: andatura*) springy; (: *decisione, vedute*) flexible ♦ *sm* (*gommino*) rubber band; (*per*

il cucito) elastic *no pl*.
ele'fante *sm* elephant.
ele'gante *ag* elegant.
ele'ganza [ele'gantsa] *sf* elegance.
e'leggere [e'lɛddʒere] *vt* to elect.
elemen'tare *ag* elementary; **le (scuole) ~i** *vedi* **scuola elementare**; **prima ~** first year of primary school, ≈ infants' class (*BRIT*), ≈ 1st grade (*US*).
ele'mento *sm* element; (*parte componente*) element, component, part; **~i** *smpl* (*della scienza etc*) elements, rudiments.
ele'mosina *sf* charity, alms *pl*; **chiedere l'~** to beg.
elemosi'nare *vt* to beg for, ask for ♦ *vi* to beg.
elen'care *vt* to list.
elencherò *etc* [elenke'rɔ] *vb vedi* **elencare**.
e'lenco, chi *sm* list; **~ nominativo** list of names; **~ telefonico** telephone directory.
e'lessi *etc vb vedi* **eleggere**.
elet'tivo, a *ag* (*carica etc*) elected.
e'letto, a *pp di* **eleggere** ♦ *sm/f* (*nominato*) elected member.
eletto'rale *ag* electoral, election *cpd*.
eletto'rato *sm* electorate.
elet'tore, 'trice *sm/f* voter, elector.
elet'trauto *sm inv* workshop for car electrical repairs; (*tecnico*) car electrician.
elettri'cista, i [elettri'tʃista] *sm* electrician.
elettricità [elettritʃi'ta] *sf* electricity.
e'lettrico, a, ci, che *ag* electric(al).
elettrifi'care *vt* to electrify.
elettriz'zante [elettrid'dzante] *ag* (*fig*) electrifying, thrilling.
elettriz'zare [elettrid'dzare] *vt* to electrify; **~rsi** *vr* to become charged with electricity; (*fig: persona*) to be thrilled.
e'lettro... *prefisso* electro....
elettrocardio'gramma, i *sm* electrocardiogram.
e'lettrodo *sm* electrode.
elettrodo'mestico, a, ci, che *ag*: **apparecchi ~ci** domestic (electrical) appliances.
elettroencefalo'gramma, i [elettroentʃefalo'gramma] *sm* electroencephalogram.
elet'trogeno, a [elet'trɔdʒeno] *ag*: **gruppo ~** generator.
elet'trolisi *sf* electrolysis.
elettroma'gnetico, a, ci, che [elettroman'ɲɛtiko] *ag* electromagnetic.
elettromo'trice [elettromo'tritʃe] *sf* electric train.
elet'trone *sm* electron.
elet'tronico, a, ci, che *ag* electronic ♦ *sf*

electronics *sg*.
elettro'shock [elettroʃ'ʃɔk] *sm inv*
(electro)shock treatment.
elettro'tecnico, a, ci, che *ag*
electrotechnical ♦ *sm* electrical engineer.
ele'vare *vt* to raise; (*edificio*) to erect;
(*multa*) to impose; ~ **un numero al**
quadrato to square a number.
eleva'tezza [eleva'tettsa] *sf* (*altezza*)
elevation; (*di animo, pensiero*) loftiness.
ele'vato, a *ag* (*gen*) high; (*cime*) high, lofty;
(*fig*: *stile, sentimenti*) lofty.
elevazi'one [elevat'tsjone] *sf* elevation;
(*l'elevare*) raising.
elezi'one [elet'tsjone] *sf* election; ~**i** *sfpl*
(*POL*) election(s); **patria d'**~ chosen
country.
'elica, che *sf* propeller.
eli'cottero *sm* helicopter.
e'lidere *vt* (*FONETICA*) to elide; ~**rsi** *vr* (*forze*)
to cancel each other out.
elimi'nare *vt* to eliminate.
elimina'toria *sf* eliminating round.
eliminazi'one [eliminat'tsjone] *sf*
elimination.
'elio *sm* helium.
eli'porto *sm* heliport.
elisabetti'ano, a *ag* Elizabethan.
eli'sir *sm inv* elixir.
e'liso, a *pp di* **elidere**.
elisoc'corso *sm* helicopter ambulance.
eli'tario, a *ag* elitist.
é'lite [e'lit] *sf inv* élite.
'ella *pron* she; (*forma di cortesia*) you; ~
stessa she herself; you yourself.
el'lisse *sf* ellipse.
el'littico, a, ci, che *ag* elliptic(al).
el'metto *sm* helmet.
'elmo *sm* helmet.
elogi'are [elo'dʒare] *vt* to praise.
elogia'tivo, a [elodʒa'tivo] *ag* laudatory.
e'logio [e'lɔdʒo] *sm* (*discorso, scritto*)
eulogy; (*lode*) praise; ~ **funebre** funeral
oration.
elo'quente *ag* eloquent; **questi dati sono**
~**i** these facts speak for themselves.
elo'quenza [elo'kwɛntsa] *sf* eloquence.
e'loquio *sm* speech, language.
elucu'brare *vt* to ponder about *o* over.
elucubrazi'oni [elukubrat'tsjoni] *sfpl* (*anche*
ironico) cogitations, ponderings.
e'ludere *vt* to evade.
e'lusi *etc vb vedi* **eludere**.
elusi'one *sf*: ~ **d'imposta** tax evasion.
elu'sivo, a *ag* evasive.
e'luso, a *pp di* **eludere**.
el'vetico, a, ci, che *ag* Swiss.
emaci'ato, a [ema'tʃato] *ag* emaciated.

e-'mail, e'mail [e'mail] *sf inv, ag inv* email;
indirizzo ~ e-mail address.
ema'nare *vt* to send out, give off; (*fig*:
leggi) to promulgate; (: *decreti*) to issue
♦ *vi*: ~ **da** to come from.
emanazi'one [emanat'tsjone] *sf* (*di raggi*,
calore) emanation; (*di odori*) exhalation;
(*di legge*) promulgation; (*di ordine,*
circolare) issuing.
emanci'pare [emant ʃi'pare] *vt* to
emancipate; ~**rsi** *vr* (*fig*) to become
liberated *o* emancipated.
emancipazi'one [emant ʃipat'tsjone] *sf*
emancipation.
emargi'nare [emardʒi'nare] *vt* (*fig*:
socialmente) to cast out.
emargi'nato, a [emardʒi'nato] *sm/f* outcast.
ematolo'gia [ematolo'dʒia] *sf* haematology
(*BRIT*), hematology (*US*).
ema'toma, i *sm* haematoma (*BRIT*),
hematoma (*US*).
em'blema, i *sm* emblem.
emble'matico, a, ci, che *ag* emblematic;
(*fig*: *atteggiamento, parole*) symbolic.
embo'lia *sf* embolism.
embrio'nale, i, e *ag* embryonic, embryo
cpd; **allo stadio** ~ at the embryo stage.
embri'one *sm* embryo.
emenda'mento *sm* amendment.
emen'dare *vt* to amend.
emer'gente [emer'dʒɛnte] *ag* emerging.
emer'genza [emer'dʒɛntsa] *sf* emergency;
in caso di ~ in an emergency.
e'mergere [e'mɛrdʒere] *vi* to emerge;
(*sommergibile*) to surface; (*fig*:
distinguersi) to stand out.
e'merito, a *ag* (*insigne*) distinguished; **è un**
~ **cretino!** he's a complete idiot!
e'mersi *etc vb vedi* **emergere**.
e'merso, a *pp di* **emergere** ♦ *ag* (*GEO*): **terre**
~**e** lands above sea level.
e'messo, a *pp di* **emettere**.
e'mettere *vt* (*suono, luce*) to give out, emit;
(*onde radio*) to send out; (*assegno,*
francobollo, ordine) to issue; (*fig*: *giudizio*)
to express, voice; ~ **la sentenza** (*DIR*) to
pass sentence.
emi'crania *sf* migraine.
emi'grante *ag, sm/f* emigrant.
emi'grare *vi* to emigrate.
emi'grato, a *ag* emigrant ♦ *sm/f* emigrant;
(*STORIA*) émigré.
emigrazi'one [emigrat'tsjone] *sf*
emigration.
emili'ano, a *ag* of (*o* from) Emilia.
emi'nente *ag* eminent, distinguished.
emi'nenza [emi'nɛntsa] *sf* eminence; ~
grigia (*fig*) éminence grise.

emi'rato *sm* emirate; **gli E~i Arabi Uniti** the United Arab Emirates.

e'miro *sm* emir.

emis'fero *sm* hemisphere; ~ **boreale/ australe** northern/southern hemisphere.

e'misi *etc vb vedi* **emettere.**

emis'sario *sm* (*GEO*) outlet, effluent; (*inviato*) emissary.

emissi'one *sf* (*vedi emettere*) emission; sending out; issue; (*RADIO*) broadcast.

emit'tente *ag* (*banca*) issuing; (*RADIO*) broadcasting, transmitting ♦ *sf* (*RADIO*) transmitter.

emofi'lia *sf* haemophilia (*BRIT*), hemophilia (*US*).

emofi'liaco, a, ci, che *ag, sm/f* haemophiliac (*BRIT*), hemophiliac (*US*).

emoglo'bina *sf* haemoglobin (*BRIT*), hemoglobin (*US*).

emolli'ente *ag* soothing.

emorra'gia, 'gie [emorra'dʒia] *sf* haemorrhage (*BRIT*), hemorrhage (*US*).

emor'roidi *sfpl* haemorrhoids (*BRIT*), hemorrhoids (*US*).

emos'tatico, a, ci, che *ag* haemostatic (*BRIT*), hemostatic (*US*); **laccio ~** tourniquet; **matita ~a** styptic pencil.

emotività *sf* emotionalism.

emo'tivo, a *ag* emotional.

emozio'nante [emottsjo'nante] *ag* exciting, thrilling.

emozio'nare [emottsjo'nare] *vt* (*appassionare*) to thrill, excite; (*commuovere*) to move; (*innervosire*) to upset; **~rsi** *vr* to be excited; to be moved; to be upset.

emozi'one [emot'tsjone] *sf* emotion; (*agitazione*) excitement.

'empio, a *ag* (*sacrilego*) impious; (*spietato*) cruel, pitiless; (*malvagio*) wicked, evil.

em'pirico, a, ci, che *ag* empirical.

em'porio *sm* general store.

emu'lare *vt* to emulate.

'emulo, a *sm/f* imitator.

emulsi'one *sf* emulsion.

EN *sigla* = *Enna.*

en'ciclica, che [en'tʃiklika] *sf* (*REL*) encyclical.

enciclope'dia [entʃiklope'dia] *sf* encyclop(a)edia.

encomi'abile *ag* commendable, praiseworthy.

encomi'are *vt* to commend, praise.

en'comio *sm* commendation; ~ **solenne** (*MIL*) mention in dispatches.

endove'noso, a *ag* (*MED*) intravenous ♦ *sf* intravenous injection.

E'NEA *sigla f* = *Comitato nazionale per la ricerca e lo sviluppo dell'Energia Nucleare e delle Energie Alternative.*

'E.N.E.L. *sigla m* (= *Ente Nazionale per l'Energia Elettrica*) national electricity company.

ener'getico, a, ci, che [ener'dʒɛtiko] *ag* (*risorse, crisi*) energy *cpd*; (*sostanza, alimento*) energy-giving.

ener'gia, 'gie [ener'dʒia] *sf* (*FISICA*) energy; (*fig*) energy, strength, vigour (*BRIT*), vigor (*US*).

e'nergico, a, ci, che [e'nɛrdʒiko] *ag* energetic, vigorous.

'enfasi *sf* emphasis; (*peg*) bombast, pomposity.

en'fatico, a, ci, che *ag* emphatic; pompous.

enfatiz'zare [enfatid'dzare] *vt* to emphasize, stress.

enfi'sema *sm* emphysema.

'ENI *sigla m* = *Ente Nazionale Idrocarburi.*

e'nigma, i *sm* enigma.

enig'matico, a, ci, che *ag* enigmatic.

'ENIT *sigla m* (= *Ente Nazionale Italiano per il Turismo*) Italian tourist authority.

en'nesimo, a *ag* (*MAT, fig*) nth; **per l'~a volta** for the umpteenth time.

enolo'gia [enolo'dʒia] *sf* oenology (*BRIT*), enology (*US*).

e'nologo, gi *sm* wine expert.

e'norme *ag* enormous, huge.

enormità *sf inv* enormity, huge size; (*assurdità*) absurdity; **non dire ~!** I don't talk nonsense!

eno'teca, che *sf* (*negozio*) wine bar.

'E.N.P.A. *sigla m* (= *Ente Nazionale Protezione Animali*) ≈ RSPCA (*BRIT*), ≈ SPCA (*US*).

'E.N.P.A.S. *sigla m* (= *Ente Nazionale di Previdenza e Assistenza per i Dipendenti Statali*) welfare organization for State employees.

'ente *sm* (*istituzione*) body, board, corporation; (*FILOSOFIA*) being; ~ **locale** local authority (*BRIT*), local government (*US*); ~ **pubblico** public body; ~ **di ricerca** research organization.

ente'rite *sf* enteritis.

entità *sf* (*FILOSOFIA*) entity; (*di perdita, danni, investimenti*) extent; (*di popolazione*) size; **di molta/poca ~** (*avvenimento, incidente*) of great/little importance.

en'trambi, e *pron pl* both (of them) ♦ *ag pl*: **~ i ragazzi** both boys, both of the boys.

en'trante *ag* (*prossimo: mese, anno*) next, coming.

en'trare *vi* to enter, go (*o* come) in; ~ **in** (*luogo*) to enter, go (*o* come) into; (*trovar* *posto, poter stare*) to fit into; (*essere ammesso a: club etc*) to join, become a member of; ~ **in automobile** to get into the car; **far** ~ **qn** (*visitatore etc*) to show sb in; ~ **in società/in commercio con qn** to go into partnership/business with sb; **questo non c'entra** (*fig*) that's got nothing to do with it.

en'trata *sf* entrance, entry; ~**e** *sfpl* (*COMM*) receipts, takings; (*ECON*) income *sg*; "~ **libera**" "admission free"; **con l'~ in vigore dei nuovi provvedimenti ...** once the new measures come into effect ...; ~**e tributarie** tax revenue *sg*.

'entro *prep* (*temporale*) within; ~ **domani** by tomorrow; ~ **e non oltre il 25 aprile** no later than 25th April.

entro'terra *sm inv* hinterland.

entusias'mante *ag* exciting.

entusias'mare *vt* to excite, fill with enthusiasm; ~**rsi** *vr*: ~**rsi (per qc/qn)** to become enthusiastic (about sth/sb).

entusi'asmo *sm* enthusiasm.

entusi'asta, i, e *ag* enthusiastic ♦ *sm/f* enthusiast.

entusi'astico, a, ci, che *ag* enthusiastic.

enucle'are *vt* (*formale: chiarire*) to explain.

enume'rare *vt* to enumerate, list.

enunci'are [enun'tʃare] *vt* (*teoria*) to enunciate, set out.

en'zima, i *sm* enzyme.

e'patico, a, ci, che *ag* hepatic; **cirrosi** ~**a** cirrhosis of the liver.

epa'tite *sf* hepatitis.

'epico, a, ci, che *ag* epic.

epide'mia *sf* epidemic.

epi'dermico, a, ci, che *ag* (*ANAT*) skin *cpd*; (*fig: interesse, impressioni*) superficial.

epi'dermide *sf* skin, epidermis.

Epifa'nia *sf* Epiphany.

e'pigono *sm* imitator.

e'pigrafe *sf* epigraph; (*su libro*) dedication.

epiles'sia *sf* epilepsy.

epi'lettico, a, ci, che *ag, sm/f* epileptic.

e'pilogo, ghi *sm* conclusion.

epi'sodico, a, ci, che *ag* (*romanzo, narrazione*) episodic; (*fig: occasionale*) occasional.

epi'sodio *sm* episode; **sceneggiato a** ~**i** serial.

e'pistola *sf* epistle.

episto'lare *ag* epistolary; **essere in rapporto** *o* **relazione** ~ **con qn** to correspond *o* be in correspondence with sb.

e'piteto *sm* epithet.

'epoca, che *sf* (*periodo storico*) age, era; (*tempo*) time; (*GEO*) age; **mobili d'**~ period

furniture; **fare** ~ (*scandalo*) to cause a stir; (*cantante, moda*) to mark a new era.

epo'pea *sf* (*anche fig*) epic.

ep'pure *cong* and yet, nevertheless.

EPT *sigla m* (= *Ente Provinciale per il Turismo*) *district tourist bureau*.

epu'rare *vt* (*POL*) to purge.

equ'anime *ag* (*imparziale*) fair, impartial.

equa'tore *sm* equator.

equazi'one [ekwat'tsjone] *sf* (*MAT*) equation.

e'questre *ag* equestrian.

equi'latero, a *ag* equilateral.

equili'brare *vt* to balance.

equili'brato, a *ag* (*carico, fig: giudizio*) balanced; (*vita*) well-regulated; (*persona*) stable, well-balanced.

equi'librio *sm* balance, equilibrium; **perdere l'**~ to lose one's balance; **stare in** ~ **su** (*persona*) to balance on; (*oggetto*) to be balanced on.

equili'brismo *sm* tightrope walking; (*fig*) juggling.

e'quino, a *ag* horse *cpd*, equine.

equi'nozio [ekwi'nɔttsjo] *sm* equinox.

equipaggia'mento [ekwipaddʒa'mento] *sm* (*operazione: di nave*) equipping, fitting out; (: *di spedizione, esercito*) equipping, kitting out; (*attrezzatura*) equipment.

equipaggi'are [ekwipad'dʒare] *vt* to equip; ~**rsi** *vr* to equip o.s.

equi'paggio [ekwi'paddʒo] *sm* crew.

equipa'rare *vt* to make equal.

é'quipe [e'kip] *sf* (*SPORT, gen*) team.

equità *sf* equity, fairness.

equitazi'one [ekwitat'tsjone] *sf* (horse-) riding.

equiva'lente *ag, sm* equivalent.

equiva'lenza [ekwiva'lɛntsa] *sf* equivalence.

equiva'lere *vi*: ~ **a** to be equivalent to; ~**rsi** *vr* (*forze etc*) to counterbalance each other; (*soluzioni*) to amount to the same thing; **equivale a dire che ...** that is the same as saying that ....

equi'valso, a *pp di* **equivalere**.

equivo'care *vi* to misunderstand.

e'quivoco, a, ci, che *ag* equivocal, ambiguous; (*sospetto*) dubious ♦ *sm* misunderstanding; **a scanso di** ~**ci** to avoid any misunderstanding; **giocare sull'**~ to equivocate.

'equo, a *ag* fair, just.

'era *sf* era.

'era *etc vb vedi* **essere**.

erari'ale *ag*: **ufficio** ~ ≈ tax office; **imposte** ~**i** revenue taxes; **spese** ~**i** public expenditure *sg*.

e'rario *sm*: l'~ ≈ the Treasury.
'erba *sf* grass; (*aromatica, medicinale*) herb;
in ~ (*fig*) budding; fare di ogni ~ un fascio
(*fig*) to lump everything (*o* everybody)
together.
er'baccia, ce [er'battʃa] *sf* weed.
er'bivoro, a *ag* herbivorous ♦ *sm/f*
herbivore.
erbo'rista, i, e *sm/f* herbalist.
erboriste'ria *sf* (*scienza*) study of
medicinal herbs; (*negozio*) herbalist's
(shop).
er'boso, a *ag* grassy.
e'rede *sm/f* heir; ~ legittimo heir-at-law.
eredità *sf* (*DIR*) inheritance; (*BIOL*)
heredity; lasciare qc in ~ a qn to leave *o*
bequeath sth to sb.
eredi'tare *vt* to inherit.
eredi'tario, a *ag* hereditary.
erediti'era *sf* heiress.
ere'mita, i *sm* hermit.
eremi'taggio [eremi'taddʒo] *sm* hermitage.
'eremo *sm* hermitage; (*fig*) retreat.
ere'sia *sf* heresy.
e'ressi *etc vb vedi* erigere.
e'retico, a, ci, che *ag* heretical ♦ *sm/f*
heretic.
e'retto, a *pp di* erigere ♦ *ag* erect, upright.
erezi'one [eret'tsjone] *sf* (*FISIOL*) erection.
ergasto'lano, a *sm/f* prisoner serving a
life sentence, lifer (*fam*).
er'gastolo *sm* (*DIR*: *pena*) life
imprisonment; (: *luogo di pena*) prison (*for
those serving life sentences*).
ergono'mia *sf* ergonomics *sg*.
ergo'nomico, a, ci, che *ag* ergonomic(al).
'erica *sf* heather.
e'rigere [e'ridʒere] *vt* to erect, raise; (*fig*:
fondare) to found.
eri'tema *sm* (*MED*) inflammation,
erythema; ~ solare sunburn.
Eri'trea *sf* Eritrea.
ermel'lino *sm* ermine.
er'metico, a, ci, che *ag* hermetic.
'ernia *sf* (*MED*) hernia; ~ del disco slipped
disc.
'ero *vb vedi* essere.
e'rodere *vt* to erode.
e'roe *sm* hero.
ero'gare *vt* (*somme*) to distribute; (*gas,
servizi*) to supply.
erogazi'one [erogat'tsjone] *sf* distribution;
supply.
e'roico, a, ci, che *ag* heroic.
ero'ina *sf* heroine; (*droga*) heroin.
ero'ismo *sm* heroism.
'eros *sm* Eros.
erosi'one *sf* erosion.

e'roso, a *pp di* erodere.
e'rotico, a, ci, che *ag* erotic.
ero'tismo *sm* eroticism.
'erpete *sm* herpes *sg*.
'erpice ['erpitʃe] *sm* (*AGR*) harrow.
er'rare *vi* (*vagare*) to wander, roam;
(*sbagliare*) to be mistaken.
er'roneo, a *ag* erroneous, wrong.
er'rore *sm* error, mistake; (*morale*) error;
per ~ by mistake; ~ giudiziario
miscarriage of justice.
'erto, a *ag* (very) steep ♦ *sf* steep slope;
stare all'~a to be on the alert.
eru'dire *vt* to teach, educate.
eru'dito, a *ag* learned, erudite.
erut'tare *vt* (*sog*: *vulcano*) to throw out,
belch.
eruzi'one [erut'tsjone] *sf* eruption; (*MED*)
rash.
es. *abbr* (= *esempio*) e.g.
E.S. *sigla m* (= *elettroshock*) ECT.
E.S.A. ['eza] *sigla m* (= *European Space
Agency*) ESA.
esacer'bare [ezatʃer'bare] *vt* to exacerbate.
esage'rare [ezadʒe'rare] *vt* to exaggerate
♦ *vi* to exaggerate; (*eccedere*) to go too far;
senza ~ without exaggeration.
esage'rato, a [ezadʒe'rato] *ag* (*notizia,
proporzioni*) exaggerated; (*curiosità,
pignoleria*) excessive; (*prezzo*) exorbitant
♦ *sm/f*: sei il solito ~ you are exaggerating
as usual.
esagerazi'one [ezadʒerat'tsjone] *sf*
exaggeration.
esago'nale *ag* hexagonal.
e'sagono *sm* hexagon.
esa'lare *vt* (*odori*) to give off ♦ *vi*: ~ (da) to
emanate (from); ~ l'ultimo respiro (*fig*) to
breathe one's last.
esalazi'one [ezalat'tsjone] *sf* (*emissione*)
exhalation; (*odore*) fumes *pl*.
esal'tante *ag* exciting.
esal'tare *vt* to exalt; (*entusiasmare*) to
excite, stir; ~rsi *vr*: ~rsi (per qc) to grow
excited (about sth).
esal'tato, a *sm/f* fanatic.
esaltazi'one [ezaltat'tsjone] *sf* (*elogio*)
extolling, exalting; (*nervosa*) intense
excitement; (*mistica*) exaltation.
e'same *sm* examination, (*INS*) exam,
examination; fare *o* dare un ~ to sit *o* take
an exam; fare un ~ di coscienza to search
one's conscience; ~ di guida driving test;
~ del sangue blood test.
esami'nare *vt* to examine.
e'sangue *ag* bloodless; (*fig*: *pallido*) pale,
wan; (: *privo di vigore*) lifeless.
e'sanime *ag* lifeless.

esaspe'rare *vt* to exasperate; (*situazione*) to exacerbate; ~**rsi** *vr* to become annoyed *o* exasperated.

esasperazi'one [ezasperat'tsjone] *sf* exasperation.

esatta'mente *av* exactly; accurately, precisely.

esat'tezza [ezat'tettsa] *sf* exactitude, accuracy, precision; **per l'**~ to be precise.

e'satto, a *pp di* **esigere** ♦ *ag* (*calcolo, ora*) correct, right, exact; (*preciso*) accurate, precise; (*puntuale*) punctual.

esat'tore *sm* (*di imposte etc*) collector.

esatto'ria *sf*: ~ **comunale** district rates office (*BRIT*) *o* assessor's office (*US*).

esau'dire *vt* to grant, fulfil (*BRIT*), fulfill (*US*).

esauri'ente *ag* exhaustive.

esauri'mento *sm* exhaustion; ~ **nervoso** nervous breakdown; **svendita (fino) ad** ~ **della merce** clearance sale.

esau'rire *vt* (*stancare*) to exhaust, wear out; (*provviste, miniera*) to exhaust; ~**rsi** *vr* to exhaust o.s., wear o.s. out; (*provviste*) to run out.

esau'rito, a *ag* exhausted; (*merci*) sold out; (*libri*) out of print; **essere** ~ (*persona*) to be run down; **registrare il tutto** ~ (*TEAT*) to have a full house.

e'sausto, a *ag* exhausted.

esauto'rare *vt* (*dirigente, funzionario*) to deprive of authority.

esazi'one [ezat'tsjone] *sf* collection (of taxes).

'esca, pl 'esche *sf* bait.

escamo'tage [ɛskamɔ'taʒ] *sm* subterfuge.

escande'scenza [ɛskandeʃ'ʃɛntsa] *sf*: **dare in** ~**e** to lose one's temper, fly into a rage.

'esce [ˈɛʃʃe] *vb vedi* **uscire**.

eschi'mese [eski'mese] *ag, sm/f, sm* Eskimo.

'esci [ˈɛʃʃi] *vb vedi* **uscire**.

escl. *abbr* (= *escluso*) excl.

escla'mare *vi* to exclaim, cry out.

esclama'tivo, a *ag*: **punto** ~ exclamation mark.

esclamazi'one [esklamat'tsjone] *sf* exclamation.

es'cludere *vt* to exclude.

es'clusi *etc vb vedi* **escludere**.

esclusi'one *sf* exclusion; **a** ~ **di, fatta** ~ **per** except (for), apart from; **senza** ~ (**alcuna**) without exception; **procedere per** ~ to follow a process of elimination; **senza** ~ **di colpi** (*fig*) with no holds barred.

esclu'siva *sf vedi* **esclusivo**.

esclusiva'mente *av* exclusively, solely.

esclu'sivo, a *ag* exclusive ♦ *sf* (*DIR, COMM*) exclusive *o* sole rights *pl*.

es'cluso, a *pp di* **escludere** ♦ *ag*: **nessuno** ~ without exception; **IVA** ~**a** excluding VAT, exclusive of VAT.

'esco *vb vedi* **uscire**.

escogi'tare [eskodʒi'tare] *vt* to devise, think up.

'escono *vb vedi* **uscire**.

escoriazi'one [eskorjat'tsjone] *sf* abrasion, graze.

escre'menti *smpl* excrement *sg*, faeces.

es'cudo *sm* (*pl* ~**s**) escudo.

escursi'one *sf* (*gita*) excursion, trip; (: *a piedi*) hike, walk; (*METEOR*): ~ **termica** temperature range.

escursio'nista, i, e *sm/f* (*gitante*) (day) tripper; (: *a piedi*) hiker, walker.

ese'crare *vt* to loathe, abhor.

esecu'tivo, a *ag, sm* executive.

esecu'tore, 'trice *sm/f* (*MUS*) performer; (*DIR*) executor.

esecuzi'one [ezekut'tsjone] *sf* execution, carrying out; (*MUS*) performance; ~ **capitale** execution.

ese'geta, i [eze'dʒɛta] *sm* commentator.

esegu'ire *vt* to carry out, execute; (*MUS*) to perform, execute.

e'sempio *sm* example; **per** ~ for example, for instance; **fare un** ~ to give an example.

esem'plare *ag* exemplary ♦ *sm* example; (*copia*) copy; (*BOT, ZOOL, GEO*) specimen.

esemplifi'care *vt* to exemplify.

esen'tare *vt*: ~ **qn/qc da** to exempt sb/sth from.

esen'tasse *ag inv* tax-free.

e'sente *ag*: ~ **da** (*dispensato da*) exempt from; (*privo di*) free from.

esenzi'one [ezen'tsjone] *sf* exemption.

e'sequie *sfpl* funeral rites; funeral service *sg*.

eser'cente [ezer'tʃɛnte] *sm/f* trader, dealer; shopkeeper.

eserci'tare [ezertʃi'tare] *vt* (*professione*) to practise (*BRIT*), practice (*US*); (*allenare: corpo, mente*) to exercise, train; (*diritto*) to exercise; (*influenza, pressione*) to exert; ~**rsi** *vr* to practise; ~**rsi nella guida** to practise one's driving.

esercitazi'one [ezertʃitat'tsjone] *sf* (*scolastica, militare*) exercise; ~**i di tiro** target practice *sg*.

e'sercito [e'zɛrtʃito] *sm* army.

eser'cizio [ezer'tʃittsjo] *sm* practice; (*compito, movimento*) exercise; (*azienda*) business, concern; (*ECON*): ~ **finanziario** financial year; **in** ~ (*medico etc*) practising (*BRIT*), practicing (*US*); **nell'**~ **delle proprie funzioni** in the execution of one's duties.

esfoli'ante *sm* exfoliator.

esi'bire *vt* to exhibit, display; (*documenti*) to produce, present; ~**rsi** *vr* (*attore*) to perform; (*fig*) to show off.

esibizi'one [ezibit'tsjone] *sf* exhibition; (*di documento*) presentation; (*spettacolo*) show, performance.

esibizio'nista, i, e [ezibittsjo'nista] *sm/f* exhibitionist.

esi'gente [ezi'dʒɛnte] *ag* demanding.

esi'genza [ezi'dʒɛntsa] *sf* demand, requirement.

e'sigere [e'zidʒere] *vt* (*pretendere*) to demand; (*richiedere*) to demand, require; (*imposte*) to collect.

esi'gibile [ezi'dʒibile] *ag* payable.

e'siguo, a *ag* small, slight.

esila'rante *ag* hilarious; **gas** ~ laughing gas.

'esile *ag* (*persona*) slender, slim; (*stelo*) thin; (*voce*) faint.

esili'are *vt* to exile.

esili'ato, a *ag* exiled ♦ *sm/f* exile.

e'silio *sm* exile.

e'simere *vt*: ~ **qn/qc da** to exempt sb/sth from; ~**rsi** *vr*: ~**rsi da** to get out of.

esis'tente *ag* existing; (*attuale*) present, current.

esis'tenza [ezis'tɛntsa] *sf* existence.

esistenzia'lismo [ezistentsja'lizmo] *sm* existentialism.

e'sistere *vi* to exist; **esiste più di una versione dell'opera** there is more than one version of the work; **non esiste!** (*fam*) no way!

esis'tito, a *pp di* **esistere**.

esi'tante *ag* hesitant; (*voce*) faltering.

esi'tare *vi* to hesitate.

esitazi'one [ezitat'tsjone] *sf* hesitation.

'esito *sm* result, outcome.

'eskimo *sm* (*giaccone*) parka.

'esodo *sm* exodus.

e'sofago, gi *sm* oesophagus (*BRIT*), esophagus (*US*).

esone'rare *vt*: ~ **qn da** to exempt sb from.

esorbi'tante *ag* exorbitant, excessive.

esor'cismo [ezor'tʃizmo] *sm* exorcism.

esor'cista, i [ezor'tʃista] *sm* exorcist.

esorciz'zare [ezortʃid'dzare] *vt* to exorcize.

esordi'ente *sm/f* beginner.

e'sordio *sm* debut.

esor'dire *vi* (*nel teatro*) to make one's debut; (*fig*) to start out, begin (one's career); **esordì dicendo che ...** he began by saying (that) ....

esor'tare *vt*: ~ **qn a fare** to urge sb to do.

esortazi'one [ezortat'tsjone] *sf* exhortation.

e'soso, a *ag* (*prezzo*) exorbitant; (*persona*: *avido*) grasping.

eso'terico, a, ci, che *ag* esoteric.

e'sotico, a, ci, che *ag* exotic.

es'pandere *vt* to expand; (*confini*) to extend; (*influenza*) to extend, spread; ~**rsi** *vr* to expand.

espansi'one *sf* expansion.

espansività *sf* expansiveness.

espan'sivo, a *ag* expansive, communicative.

es'panso, a *pp di* **espandere**.

espatri'are *vi* to leave one's country.

es'patrio *sm* expatriation; **permesso di** ~ authorization to leave the country.

espedi'ente *sm* expedient; **vivere di** ~**i** to live by one's wits.

es'pellere *vt* to expel.

esperi'enza [espe'rjɛntsa] *sf* experience; (*SCIENZA: prova*) experiment; **parlare per** ~ to speak from experience.

esperi'mento *sm* experiment; **fare un** ~ to carry out *o* do an experiment.

es'perto, a *ag*, *sm/f* expert.

espi'anto *sm* (*MED*) removal.

espi'are *vt* to atone for.

espiazi'one [espiat'tsjone] *sf*: ~ (**di**) expiation (of), atonement (for).

espi'rare *vt*, *vi* to breathe out.

esple'tamento *sm* (*AMM*) carrying out.

esple'tare *vt* (*AMM*) to carry out.

espli'care *vt* (*attività*) to carry out, perform.

esplica'tivo, a *ag* explanatory.

es'plicito, a [es'plitʃito] *ag* explicit.

es'plodere *vi* (*anche fig*) to explode ♦ *vt* to fire.

esplo'rare *vt* to explore.

esplora'tore, 'trice *sm/f* explorer; (*anche*: **giovane** ~) (boy) scout/(girl) guide (*BRIT*) *o* scout (*US*) ♦ *sm* (*NAUT*) scout (ship).

esplorazi'one [esplorat'tsjone] *sf* exploration; **mandare qn in** ~ (*MIL*) to send sb to scout ahead.

esplosi'one *sf* (*anche fig*) explosion.

esplo'sivo, a *ag*, *sm* explosive.

es'ploso, a *pp di* **esplodere**.

es'pone *etc vb vedi* **esporre**.

espo'nente *sm/f* (*rappresentante*) representative.

esponenzi'ale [esponen'tsjale] *ag* (*MAT*) exponential.

es'pongo, es'poni *etc vb vedi* **esporre**.

es'porre *vt* (*merci*) to display; (*quadro*) to exhibit, show; (*fatti, idee*) to explain, set out; (*porre in pericolo, FOT*) to expose;

esporsi *vr*: **esporsi a** (*sole, pericolo*) to expose o.s. to; (*critiche*) to lay o.s. open to.

espor'tare *vt* to export.

esporta'tore, 'trice *ag* exporting ♦ *sm* exporter.

esportazi'one [esportat'tsjone] *sf* (*azione*) exportation, export; (*insieme di prodotti*) exports *pl*.

es'pose *etc vb vedi* **esporre**.

espo'simetro *sm* exposure meter.

esposizi'one [espozit'tsjone] *sf* displaying; exhibiting; setting out; (*anche FOT*) exposure; (*mostra*) exhibition; (*narrazione*) explanation, exposition.

es'posto, a *pp di* **esporre** ♦ *ag*: ~ **a nord** facing north, north-facing ♦ *sm* (*AMM*) statement, account; (: *petizione*) petition.

espressi'one *sf* expression.

espres'sivo, a *ag* expressive.

es'presso, a *pp di* **esprimere** ♦ *ag* express ♦ *sm* (*lettera*) express letter; (*anche*: **treno** ~) express train; (*anche*: **caffè** ~) espresso.

es'primere *vt* to express; ~**rsi** *vr* to express o.s.

espropri'are *vt* (*terreni, edifici*) to place a compulsory purchase order on; (*persona*) to dispossess.

espropriazi'one [esproprjat'tsjone] *sf*, **es'proprio** *sm* expropriation; ~ **per pubblica utilità** compulsory purchase.

espu'gnare [espuɲ'ɲare] *vt* to take by force, storm.

es'pulsi *etc vb vedi* **espellere**.

espulsi'one *sf* expulsion.

es'pulso, a *pp di* **espellere**.

'essa *pron f*, **'esse** *pron fpl vedi* **esso**.

es'senza [es'sɛntsa] *sf* essence.

essenzi'ale [essen'tsjale] *ag* essential; (*stile, linea*) simple ♦ *sm*: **l'**~ the main o most important thing.

=========== *PAROLA CHIAVE* ===========

'essere *sm* being; ~ **umano** human being ♦ *vb copulativo* **1** (*con attributo, sostantivo*) to be; **sei giovane/simpatico** you are o you're young/nice; **è medico** he is o he's a doctor

2 (+ *di: appartenere*) to be; **di chi è la penna?** whose pen is it?; **è di Carla** it is o it's Carla's, it belongs to Carla

3 (+ *di: provenire*) to be; **è di Venezia** he is o he's from Venice

4 (*data, ora*): **è il 15 agosto** it is o it's the 15th of August; **è lunedì** it is o it's

Monday; **che ora è?, che ore sono?** what time is it?; **è l'una** it is o it's one o'clock; **sono le due** it is o it's two o'clock

5 (*costare*): **quant'è?** how much is it?; **sono 20 euro** it's 20 euros

♦ *vb aus* **1** (*attivo*): ~ **arrivato/venuto** to have arrived/come; **è già partita** she has already left

2 (*passivo*) to be; ~ **fatto da** to be made by; **è stata uccisa** she has been killed

3 (*riflessivo*): **si sono lavati** they washed, they got washed

4 (+ *da* + *infinito*): **è da farsi subito** it must be done o is to be done immediately

♦ *vi* **1** (*esistere, trovarsi*) to be; **sono a casa** I'm at home; ~ **in piedi/seduto** to be standing/sitting

2 (*succedere*): **sarà quel che sarà** what will be will be; **sia quel che sia, io me ne vado** come what may, I'm going now

3: **esserci**: **c'è** there is; **ci sono** there are; **che c'è?** what's the matter?, what is it?; **non c'è niente da fare** there's nothing we can do; **c'è da sperare che ...** one can only hope that ...; **ci sono!** (*sono pronto*) I'm ready; (*ho capito*) I get it!; *vedi anche* **ci**

♦ *vb impers*: **è tardi/Pasqua** it's late/Easter; **è mezzanotte** it's midnight; **è bello/ caldo/freddo** it's nice/hot/cold; **è possibile che venga** he may come; **è così** that's the way it is.

'essi *pron mpl vedi* **esso**.

essic'care *vt* (*gen*) to dry; (*legname*) to season; (*cibi*) to desiccate; (*bacino, palude*) to drain; ~**rsi** *vr* (*fiume, pozzo*) to dry up; (*vernice*) to dry (out).

'esso, a *pron* it; (*riferito a persona: soggetto*) he/she; (: *complemento*) him/her; ~**i, e** *pron pl* they; (*complemento*) them.

est *sm* east; **i paesi dell'E**~ the Eastern bloc *sg*.

'estasi *sf* ecstasy.

estasi'are *vt* to send into raptures; ~**rsi** *vr*: ~**rsi (davanti a)** to go into ecstasies (over), go into raptures (over).

es'tate *sf* summer.

es'tatico, a, ci, che *ag* ecstatic.

estempo'raneo, a *ag* (*discorso*) extempore, impromptu; (*brano musicale*) impromptu.

es'tendere *vt* to extend; ~**rsi** *vr* (*diffondersi*) to spread; (*territorio, confini*) to extend.

estensi'one *sf* extension; (*di superficie*) expanse; (*di voce*) range.

estenu'ante *ag* wearing, tiring.

estenu'are *vt* (*stancare*) to wear out, tire

out.

esteri'ore *ag* outward, external.

esteriorità *sf inv* outward appearance.

esterioriz'zare [esterjorid'dzare] *vt* (*gioia etc*) to show.

ester'nare *vt* to express; ~ **un sospetto** to voice a suspicion.

es'terno, a *ag* (*porta, muro*) outer, outside; (*scala*) outside; (*alunno, impressione*) external ♦ *sm* outside, exterior ♦ *sm/f* (*allievo*) day pupil; **"per uso** ~**"** "for external use only"; **gli** ~**i sono stati girati a Glasgow** (*CINE*) the location shots were taken in Glasgow.

'estero, a *ag* foreign ♦ *sm*: **all'**~ abroad; **Ministero degli E**~**i, gli E**~**i** Ministry for Foreign Affairs, ≈ Foreign Office (*BRIT*), ≈ State Department (*US*).

esterofi'lia *sf* excessive love of foreign things.

esterre'fatto, a *ag* (*costernato*) horrified; (*sbalordito*) astounded.

es'tesi *etc vb vedi* **estendere**.

es'teso, a *pp di* **estendere** ♦ *ag* extensive, large; **scrivere per** ~ to write in full.

estetica'mente *av* aesthetically.

es'tetico, a, ci, che *ag* aesthetic ♦ *sf* (*disciplina*) aesthetics *sg*; (*bellezza*) attractiveness; **chirurgia** ~**a** cosmetic surgery; **cura** ~**a** beauty treatment.

este'tista, i, e *sm/f* beautician.

'estimo *sm* valuation; (*disciplina*) surveying.

es'tinguere *vt* to extinguish, put out; (*debito*) to pay off; (*conto*) to close; ~**rsi** *vr* to go out; (*specie*) to become extinct.

es'tinsi *etc vb vedi* **estinguere**.

es'tinto, a *pp di* **estinguere**.

estin'tore *sm* (fire) extinguisher.

estinzi'one [estin'tsjone] *sf* putting out; (*di specie*) extinction; (*di debito*) payment; (*di conto*) closing.

estir'pare *vt* (*pianta*) to uproot, pull up; (*dente*) to extract; (*tumore*) to remove; (*fig: vizio*) to eradicate.

es'tivo, a *ag* summer *cpd*.

'estone *ag, sm/f, sm* Estonian.

Es'tonia *sf*: **l'**~ Estonia.

es'torcere [es'tɔrtʃere] *vt*: ~ **qc (a qn)** to extort sth (from sb).

estorsi'one *sf* extortion.

es'torto, a *pp di* **estorcere**.

estra'dare *vt* to extradite.

estradizi'one [estradit'tsjone] *sf* extradition.

es'trae, es'traggo *etc vb vedi* **estrarre**.

es'traneo, a *ag* foreign; (*discorso*) extraneous, unrelated ♦ *sm/f* stranger;

rimanere ~ **a qc** to take no part in sth; **sentirsi** ~ **a** (*famiglia, società*) to feel alienated from; **"ingresso vietato agli** ~**i"** "no admittance to unauthorized personnel".

estrani'arsi *vr*: ~ (**da**) to cut o.s. off (from).

es'trarre *vt* to extract; (*minerali*) to mine; (*sorteggiare*) to draw; ~ **a sorte** to draw lots.

es'trassi *etc vb vedi* **estrarre**.

es'tratto, a *pp di* **estrarre** ♦ *sm* extract; (*di documento*) abstract; ~ **conto** (bank) statement; ~ **di nascita** birth certificate.

estrazi'one [estrat'tsjone] *sf* extraction; mining; drawing *no pl*; draw.

estrema'mente *av* extremely.

estre'mismo *sm* extremism.

estre'mista, i, e *sm/f* extremist.

estremità *sf inv* extremity, end ♦ *sfpl* (*ANAT*) extremities.

es'tremo, a *ag* extreme; (*ultimo: ora, tentativo*) final, last ♦ *sm* extreme; (*di pazienza, forza*) limit, end; ~**i** *smpl* (*DIR*) essential elements; (*AMM: dati essenziali*) details, particulars; **l'E**~ **Oriente** the Far East.

estrinse'care *vt* to express, show.

'estro *sm* (*capriccio*) whim, fancy; (*ispirazione creativa*) inspiration.

estro'messo, a *pp di* **estromettere**.

estro'mettere *vt*: ~ (**da**) (*partito, club etc*) to expel (from); (*discussione*) to exclude (from).

estromissi'one *sf* expulsion.

es'troso, a *ag* whimsical, capricious; inspired.

estro'verso, a *ag, sm* extrovert.

estu'ario *sm* estuary.

esube'rante *ag* exuberant; (*COMM*) redundant (*BRIT*).

esube'ranza [ezube'rantsa] *sf* (*di persona*) exuberance; ~ **di personale** (*COMM*) overmanning (*BRIT*), over-staffing (*US*).

e'subero *sm*: ~ **di personale** surplus staff; **in** ~ redundant, due to be laid off.

esu'lare *vi*: ~ **da** (*competenza*) to be beyond; (*compiti*) not to be part of.

'esule *sm/f* exile.

esul'tanza [ezul'tantsa] *sf* exultation.

esul'tare *vi* to exult.

esu'mare *vt* (*salma*) to exhume, disinter; (*fig*) to unearth.

età *sf inv* age; **all'**~ **di 8 anni** at the age of 8, at 8 years of age; **ha la mia** ~ he (*o* she) is the same age as me *o* as I am; **di mezza** ~ middle-aged; **raggiungere la maggiore** ~ to come of age; **essere in** ~ **minore** to be

under age.
eta'nolo _sm_ ethanol.
etc. _abbr_ etc.
'etere _sm_ ether; **via** ~ on the airwaves.
e'tereo, a _ag_ ethereal.
eternità _sf_ eternity.
e'terno, a _ag_ eternal; (_interminabile_: _lamenti, attesa_) never-ending; **in** ~ for ever.
etero'geneo, a [etero'dʒɛneo] _ag_ heterogeneous.
eterosessu'ale _ag, sm/f_ heterosexual.
'etica _sf vedi_ **etico**.
eti'chetta [eti'ketta] _sf_ label; (_cerimoniale_): **l'**~ etiquette.
'etico, a, ci, che _ag_ ethical ♦ _sf_ ethics _sg_.
eti'lometro _sm_ Breathalyzer ®.
etimolo'gia, 'gie [etimolo'dʒia] _sf_ etymology.
etimo'logico, a, ci, che [etimo'lɔdʒiko] _ag_ etymological.
e'tiope _ag, sm/f_ Ethiopian.
Eti'opia _sf_: **l'**~ Ethiopia.
eti'opico, a, ci, che _ag, sm_ (_LING_) Ethiopian.
'Etna _sm_: **l'**~ Etna.
'etnico, a, ci, che _ag_ ethnic.
e'trusco, a, schi, sche _ag, sm/f_ Etruscan.
'ettaro _sm_ hectare (= _10,000 m²_).
'etto _sm abbr_ = **ettogrammo**.
etto'grammo _sm_ hectogram(me) (= _100 grams_).
et'tolitro _sm_ hectolitre (_BRIT_), hectoliter (_US_).
et'tometro _sm_ hectometre.
EU _abbr_ = **Europa**.
euca'lipto _sm_ eucalyptus.
Eucaris'tia _sf_: **l'**~ the Eucharist.
eufe'mismo _sm_ euphemism.
eufe'mistico, a, ci, che _ag_ euphemistic.
eufo'ria _sf_ euphoria.
eu'forico, a, ci, che _ag_ euphoric.
Eu'rasia _sf_ Eurasia.
eurasi'atico, a, ci, che _ag, sm/f_ Eurasian.
Eura'tom _sigla f_ (= _Comunità Europea dell'Energia Atomica_) Euratom.
'euro _sm inv_ (_divisa_) euro.
euro'corpo _sm_ European force.
eurodepu'tato _sm_ Euro MP.
eurodi'visa _sf_ Eurocurrency.
euro'dollaro _sm_ Eurodollar.
Euro'landia _sf_ Euroland.
euromer'cato _sm_ Euromarket.
euro'missile _sm_ Euro-missile.
Eu'ropa _sf_: **l'**~ Europe.
europarlamen'tare _sm/f_ Member of the European Parliament, MEP.
euro'peo, a _ag, sm/f_ European.
euro'scettico, a, ci, che [euroʃ'ʃɛttiko]

_sm/f_ Euro-sceptic.
eutana'sia _sf_ euthanasia.
E.V. _abbr_ = _Eccellenza Vostra_.
evacu'are _vt_ to evacuate.
evacuazi'one [evakuat'tsjone] _sf_ evacuation.
e'vadere _vi_ (_fuggire_): ~ **da** to escape from ♦ _vt_ (_sbrigare_) to deal with, dispatch; (_tasse_) to evade.
evan'gelico, a, ci, che [evan'dʒɛliko] _ag_ evangelical.
evange'lista, i [evandʒe'lista] _sm_ evangelist.
evapo'rare _vi_ to evaporate.
evaporazi'one [evaporat'tsjone] _sf_ evaporation.
e'vasi _etc vb vedi_ **evadere**.
evasi'one _sf_ (_vedi evadere_) escape; dispatch; **dare** ~ **ad un ordine** to carry out _o_ execute an order; **letteratura d'**~ escapist literature; ~ **fiscale** tax evasion.
eva'sivo, a _ag_ evasive.
e'vaso, a _pp di_ **evadere** ♦ _sm_ escapee.
eva'sore _sm_: ~ (**fiscale**) tax evader.
eveni'enza [eve'njɛntsa] _sf_: **nell'**~ **che ciò succeda** should that happen; **essere pronto ad ogni** ~ to be ready for anything _o_ any eventuality.
e'vento _sm_ event.
eventu'ale _ag_ possible.
eventualità _sf inv_ eventuality, possibility; **nell'**~ **di** in the event of.
eventual'mente _av_ if need be, if necessary.
'Everest _sm_: **l'**~, **il Monte** ~ (Mount) Everest.
eversi'one _sf_ subversion.
ever'sivo, a _ag_ subversive.
evi'dente _ag_ evident, obvious.
evidente'mente _av_ evidently; (_palesemente_) obviously, evidently.
evi'denza [evi'dɛntsa] _sf_ obviousness; **mettere in** ~ to point out, highlight; **tenere in** ~ **qc** to bear sth in mind.
evidenzi'are [eviden'tsjare] _vt_ (_sottolineare_) to emphasize, highlight; (_con evidenziatore_) to highlight.
evidenzia'tore [evidentsja'tore] _sm_ (_penna_) highlighter.
evi'rare _vt_ to castrate.
evi'tabile _ag_ avoidable.
evi'tare _vt_ to avoid; ~ **di fare** to avoid doing; ~ **qc a qn** to spare sb sth.
'evo _sm_ age, epoch.
evo'care _vt_ to evoke.
evoca'tivo, a _ag_ evocative.
evocherò _etc_ [evoke'rɔ] _vb vedi_ **evocare**.
evolu'tivo, a _ag_ (_gen, BIOL_) evolutionary;

(*MED*) progressive.

evo'luto, a *pp di* **evolversi** ♦ *ag* (*popolo, civiltà*) (highly) developed, advanced; (*persona: emancipato*) independent; (: *senza pregiudizi*) broad-minded.

evoluzi'one [evolut'tsjone] *sf* evolution.

e'volversi *vr* to evolve; **con l'~ della situazione** as the situation develops.

ev'viva *escl* hurrah!; ~ **il re!** long live the king!, hurrah for the king!

ex *prefisso* ex-, former ♦ *sm/f inv* ex-boyfriend/girlfriend.

ex 'aequo [εg'zεkwo] *av*: **classificarsi primo** ~ to come joint first, come equal first.

'extra *ag inv, sm inv* extra.

extracomuni'tario, a *ag* non-EEC ♦ *sm/f* non-EEC national (*often referring to non-European immigrant*).

extraconiu'gale *ag* extramarital.

extraparlamen'tare *ag* extraparliamentary.

extrasensori'ale *ag*: **percezione** *f* ~ extrasensory perception.

extrater'restre *ag, sm/f* extraterrestrial.

extraur'bano, a *ag* suburban.

Ff

F, f ['effe] *sf o m inv* (*lettera*) F, f; **F come Firenze** ≈ F for Frederick (*BRIT*), F for Fox (*US*).

F *abbr* (= *Fahrenheit*) F.

F. *abbr* (= *fiume*) R.

fa *vb vedi* **fare** ♦ *sm inv* (*MUS*) F; (: *solfeggiando la scala*) fa ♦ *av*: **10 anni** ~ 10 years ago.

fabbi'sogno [fabbi'zoɲɲo] *sm* needs *pl*, requirements *pl*; **il** ~ **nazionale di petrolio** the country's oil requirements; ~ **del settore pubblico** public sector borrowing requirement (*BRIT*), government debt borrowing (*US*).

'fabbrica *sf* factory.

fabbri'cante *sm* manufacturer, maker.

fabbri'care *vt* to build; (*produrre*) to manufacture, make; (*fig*) to fabricate, invent.

fabbri'cato *sm* building.

fabbricazi'one [fabbrikat'tsjone] *sf* building, fabrication; making, manufacture, manufacturing.

'fabbro *sm* (black)smith.

fac'cenda [fat't∫εnda] *sf* matter, affair; (*cosa da fare*) task, chore; **le** ~**e domestiche** the housework *sg*.

faccendi'ere [fatt∫en'djεre] *sm* wheeler-dealer, (shady) operator.

fac'cetta [fat't∫etta] *sf* (*di pietra preziosa*) facet.

fac'chino [fak'kino] *sm* porter.

'faccia, ce ['fatt∫a] *sf* face; (*di moneta, medaglia*) side; ~ **a** ~ face to face; **di** ~ **a** opposite, facing; **avere la** ~ (**tosta**) **di dire/fare qc** to have the cheek *o* nerve to say/do sth; **fare qc alla** ~ **di qn** to do sth to spite sb; **leggere qc in** ~ **a qn** to see sth written all over sb's face.

facci'ata [fat't∫ata] *sf* façade; (*di pagina*) side.

'faccio *etc* ['fatt∫o] *vb vedi* **fare**.

fa'cente [fa't∫ente]: ~ **funzione** *sm* (*AMM*) deputy.

fa'cessi *etc* [fa't∫essi] *vb vedi* **fare**.

fa'ceto, a [fa't∫eto] *ag* witty, humorous.

fa'cevo *etc* [fa't∫evo] *vb vedi* **fare**.

fa'cezia [fa't∫εttsja] *sf* witticism, witty remark.

fa'chiro [fa'kiro] *sm* fakir.

'facile ['fat∫ile] *ag* easy; (*affabile*) easy-going; (*disposto*): ~ **a** inclined to, prone to; (*probabile*): **è** ~ **che piova** it's likely to rain; **donna di** ~**i costumi** woman of easy virtue, loose woman.

facilità [fat∫ili'ta] *sf* easiness; (*disposizione, dono*) aptitude.

facili'tare [fat∫ili'tare] *vt* to make easier.

facilitazi'one [fat∫ilitat'tsjone] *sf* (*gen*) facilities *pl*; ~**i di pagamento** easy terms, credit facilities.

facil'mente [fat∫il'mente] *av* (*gen*) easily; (*probabilmente*) probably.

faci'lone, a [fat∫i'lone] *sm/f* (*peg*) happy-go-lucky person.

facino'roso, a [fat∫ino'roso] *ag* violent.

facoltà *sf inv* faculty; (*CHIM*) property; (*autorità*) power.

facolta'tivo, a *ag* optional; (*fermata d'autobus*) request *cpd*.

facol'toso, a *ag* wealthy, rich.

fac'simile *sm* facsimile.

'faggio ['fadd3o] *sm* beech.

fagi'ano [fa'd3ano] *sm* pheasant.

fagio'lino [fad3o'lino] *sm* French (*BRIT*) *o* string bean.

fagi'olo [fa'd3ɔlo] *sm* bean; **capitare a** ~ to come at the right time.

fagoci'tare [fagot∫i'tare] *vt* (*fig: industria etc*) to absorb, swallow up; (*scherzoso: cibo*) to devour.

fa'gotto *sm* bundle; (*MUS*) bassoon; **far ~** (*fig*) to pack up and go.

'fai *vb vedi* **fare.**

'faida *sf* feud.

'fai-da-'te *sm inv* DIY, do-it-yourself.

fa'ina *sf* (*ZOOL*) stone marten.

'Fahrenheit ['faːrənheit] *sm* Fahrenheit.

fa'lange [fa'landʒe] *sf* (*ANAT, MIL*) phalanx.

fal'cata *sf* stride.

'falce ['faltʃe] *sf* scythe; **~ e martello** (*POL*) hammer and sickle.

fal'cetto [fal'tʃetto] *sm* sickle.

falci'are [fal'tʃare] *vt* to cut; (*fig*) to mow down.

falcia'trice [faltʃa'tritʃe] *sf* (*per fieno*) reaping machine; (*per erba*) mowing machine.

'falco, chi *sm* (*anche fig*) hawk.

fal'cone *sm* falcon.

'falda *sf* (*GEO*) layer, stratum; (*di cappello*) brim; (*di cappotto*) tails *pl*; (*di monte*) lower slope; (*di tetto*) pitch; (*di neve*) flake; **abito a ~e** tails *pl*.

fale'gname [faleɲ'ɲame] *sm* joiner.

fa'lena *sf* (*ZOOL*) moth.

'Falkland ['fɔːlklənd] *sfpl*: **le isole ~** the Falkland Islands.

fal'lace [fal'latʃe] *ag* misleading, deceptive.

'fallico, a, ci, che *ag* phallic.

fallimen'tare *ag* (*COMM*) bankruptcy *cpd*; **bilancio ~** negative balance, deficit; **diritto ~** bankruptcy law.

falli'mento *sm* failure; bankruptcy.

fal'lire *vi* (*non riuscire*): **~ (in)** to fail (in); (*DIR*) to go bankrupt ♦ *vt* (*colpo, bersaglio*) to miss.

fal'lito, a *ag* unsuccessful; bankrupt ♦ *sm/f* bankrupt.

'fallo *sm* error, mistake; (*imperfezione*) defect, flaw; (*SPORT*) foul; fault; (*ANAT*) phallus; **senza ~** without fail; **cogliere qn in ~** to catch sb out; **mettere il piede in ~** to slip.

fal'locrate *sm* male chauvinist.

falò *sm inv* bonfire.

fal'sare *vt* to distort, misrepresent.

falsa'riga, ghe *sf* lined page, ruled page; **sulla ~ di ...** (*fig*) along the lines of ....

fal'sario *sm* forger; counterfeiter.

falsifi'care *vt* to forge; (*monete*) to forge, counterfeit.

falsità *sf inv* (*di persona, notizia*) falseness; (*bugia*) falsehood, lie.

'falso, a *ag* false; (*errato*) wrong; (*falsificato*) forged; fake; (: *oro, gioielli*) imitation *cpd* ♦ *sm* forgery; **essere un ~ magro** to be heavier than one looks; **giurare il ~** to commit perjury; **~ in atto pubblico**

forgery (of a legal document).

'fama *sf* fame; (*reputazione*) reputation, name.

'fame *sf* hunger; **aver ~** to be hungry; **fare la ~** (*fig*) to starve, exist at subsistence level.

fa'melico, a, ci, che *ag* ravenous.

famige'rato, a [famidʒe'rato] *ag* notorious, ill-famed.

fa'miglia [fa'miʎʎa] *sf* family.

famili'are *ag* (*della famiglia*) family *cpd*; (*ben noto*) familiar; (*rapporti, atmosfera*) friendly; (*LING*) informal, colloquial ♦ *sm/f* relative, relation; **una vettura ~** a family car.

familiarità *sf* familiarity; friendliness; informality.

familiariz'zare [familjarid'dzare] *vi*: **~ con qn** to get to know sb; **abbiamo familiarizzato subito** we got on well together from the start.

fa'moso, a *ag* famous, well-known.

fa'nale *sm* (*AUT*) light, lamp (*BRIT*); (*luce stradale, NAUT*) light; (*di faro*) beacon.

fa'natico, a, ci, che *ag* fanatical; (*del teatro, calcio etc*): **~ di o per** mad o crazy about ♦ *sm/f* fanatic; (*tifoso*) fan.

fana'tismo *sm* fanaticism.

fanciul'lezza [fantʃul'lettsa] *sf* childhood.

fanci'ullo, a [fan'tʃullo] *sm/f* child.

fan'donia *sf* tall story; **~e** *sfpl* nonsense *sg*.

fan'fara *sf* brass band; (*musica*) fanfare.

fanfa'rone *sm* braggart.

fan'ghiglia [fan'giʎʎa] *sf* mire, mud.

'fango, ghi *sm* mud; **fare i ~ghi** (*MED*) to take a course of mud baths.

fan'goso, a *ag* muddy.

'fanno *vb vedi* **fare.**

fannul'lone, a *sm/f* idler, loafer.

fantasci'enza [fantaʃ'ʃɛntsa] *sf* science fiction.

fanta'sia *sf* fantasy, imagination; (*capriccio*) whim, caprice ♦ *ag inv*: **vestito ~** patterned dress.

fantasi'oso, a *ag* (*dotato di fantasia*) imaginative; (*bizzarro*) fanciful, strange.

fan'tasma, i *sm* ghost, phantom.

fantasti'care *vi* to daydream.

fantastiche'ria [fantastike'ria] *sf* daydream.

fan'tastico, a, ci, che *ag* fantastic; (*potenza, ingegno*) imaginative.

'fante *sm* infantryman; (*CARTE*) jack, knave (*BRIT*).

fante'ria *sf* infantry.

fan'tino *sm* jockey.

fan'toccio [fan'tɔttʃo] *sm* puppet.

fanto'matico, a, ci, che *ag* (*nave, esercito*)

phantom cpd; (personaggio) mysterious.
FAO sigla f FAO (= *Food and Agriculture Organization*).
fara'butto sm crook.
fara'ona sf guinea fowl.
fara'one sm (*STORIA*) Pharaoh.
fara'onico, a, ci, che ag of the Pharaohs; (*fig*) enormous, huge.
far'cire [far'tʃire] vt (*carni, peperoni etc*) to stuff; (*torte*) to fill.
fard [far] sm inv blusher.
far'dello sm bundle; (*fig*) burden.

═══════════════════ *PAROLA CHIAVE*

'fare sm 1 (*modo di fare*): **con ~ distratto** absent-mindedly; **ha un ~ simpatico** he has a pleasant manner
2: **sul far del giorno/della notte** at daybreak/nightfall
♦ vt 1 (*fabbricare, creare*) to make; (: *casa*) to build; (: *assegno*) to make out; **~ una promessa/un film** to make a promise/a film; **~ rumore** to make a noise
2 (*effettuare: lavoro, attività, studi*) to do; (: *sport*) to play; **cosa fa?** (*adesso*) what are you doing?; (*di professione*) what do you do?; **~ psicologia/italiano** to do psychology/Italian; **~ tennis** to play tennis; **~ un viaggio** to go on a trip o journey; **~ una passeggiata** to go for a walk; **~ la spesa** to do the shopping
3 (*funzione*) to be; (*TEAT*) to play; **~ il medico** to be a doctor; **~ il malato** (*fingere*) to act the invalid
4 (*suscitare: sentimenti*): **~ paura a qn** to frighten sb; **mi fa rabbia** it makes me angry; **(non) fa niente** (*non importa*) it doesn't matter
5 (*ammontare*): **3 più 3 fa 6** 3 and 3 are o make 6; **fanno 6 euro** that's 6 euros; **Roma fa oltre 2.000.000 di abitanti** Rome has over 2,000,000 inhabitants; **che ora fai?** what time do you make it?
6 (+ *infinito*): **far ~ qc a qn** (*obbligare*) to make sb do sth; (*permettere*) to let sb do sth; **~ piangere/ridere qn** to make sb cry/laugh; **~ venire qn** to send for sb; **fammi vedere** let me see; **far partire il motore** to start (up) the engine; **far riparare la macchina/costruire una casa** to get o have the car repaired/a house built
7: **~rsi: ~rsi una gonna** to make o.s. a skirt; **~rsi un nome** to make a name for o.s.; **~rsi la permanente** to get a perm; **~rsi notare** to get o.s. noticed; **~rsi tagliare i capelli** to get one's hair cut; **~rsi operare** to have an operation
8 (*fraseologia*): **farcela** to succeed,

manage; **non ce la faccio più** I can't go on; **ce la faremo** we'll make it; **me l'hanno fatta!** I've been done!; **lo facevo più giovane** I thought he was younger; **fare si/no con la testa** to nod/shake one's head
♦ vi 1 (*agire*) to act, do; **fate come volete** do as you like; **~ presto** to be quick; **~ da** to act as; **non c'è niente da ~** it's no use; **saperci ~ con qn/qc** to know how to deal with sb/sth; **ci sa ~** she's very good at it; **faccia pure!** go ahead!
2 (*dire*) to say; **"davvero?" fece** "really?" he said
3: **~ per** (*essere adatto*) to be suitable for; **~ per ~ qc** to be about to do sth; **fece per andarsene** he made as if to leave
4: **~rsi: si fa così** you do it like this, this is the way it's done; **non si fa così!** (*rimprovero*) that's no way to behave!; **la festa non si fa** the party is off
5: **~ a gara con qn** to compete with sb; **~ a pugni** to come to blows; **~ in tempo a ~** to be in time to do
♦ vb impers: **fa bel tempo** the weather is fine; **fa caldo/freddo** it's hot/cold; **fa notte** it's getting dark
♦ vr: **~rsi 1** (*diventare*) to become; **~rsi prete** to become a priest; **~rsi grande/vecchio** to grow tall/old
2 (*spostarsi*): **~rsi avanti/indietro** to move forward/back; **fatti più in là** move along a bit
3 (*fam: drogarsi*) to be a junkie.
└────────────────────────────┘

fa'retra sf quiver.
far'falla sf butterfly.
farfugli'are [farfuʎ'ʎare] vt, vi to mumble, mutter.
fa'rina sf flour; **~ gialla** maize (*BRIT*) o corn (*US*) flour; **~ integrale** wholemeal (*BRIT*) o whole-wheat (*US*) flour; **questa non è ~ del tuo sacco** (*fig*) this isn't your own idea (o work).
fari'nacei [fari'natʃei] smpl starches.
fa'ringe [fa'rindʒe] sf (*ANAT*) pharynx.
farin'gite [farin'dʒite] sf pharyngitis.
fari'noso, a ag (*patate*) floury; (*neve, mela*) powdery.
farma'ceutico, a, ci, che [farma'tʃeutiko] ag pharmaceutical.
farma'cia, 'cie [farma'tʃia] sf pharmacy; (*negozio*) chemist's (shop) (*BRIT*), pharmacy.
farma'cista, i, e [farma'tʃista] sm/f chemist (*BRIT*), pharmacist.
'farmaco, ci o **chi** sm drug, medicine.
farneti'care vi to rave, be delirious.
'faro sm (*NAUT*) lighthouse; (*AER*) beacon;

(*AUT*) headlight, headlamp (*BRIT*).

farragi'noso, a [farradʒi'noso] *ag* (*stile*) muddled, confused.

'farsa *sf* farce.

far'sesco, a, schi, sche *ag* farcical.

fasc. *abbr* = **fascicolo.**

'fascia, sce ['faʃʃa] *sf* band, strip; (*MED*) bandage; (*di sindaco, ufficiale*) sash; (*parte di territorio*) strip, belt; (*di contribuenti etc*) group, band; **essere in ~sce** (*anche fig*) to be in one's infancy; ~ **oraria** time band.

fasci'are [faʃ'ʃare] *vt* to bind; (*MED*) to bandage; (*bambino*) to put a nappy (*BRIT*) *o* diaper (*US*) on.

fascia'tura [faʃʃa'tura] *sf* (*azione*) bandaging; (*fascia*) bandage.

fa'scicolo [faʃ'ʃikolo] *sm* (*di documenti*) file, dossier; (*di rivista*) issue, number; (*opuscolo*) booklet, pamphlet.

'fascino ['faʃʃino] *sm* charm, fascination.

'fascio ['faʃʃo] *sm* bundle, sheaf; (*di fiori*) bunch; (*di luce*) beam; (*POL*): **il F~** the Fascist Party.

fa'scismo [faʃ'ʃizmo] *sm* fascism.

fa'scista, i, e [faʃ'ʃista] *ag, sm/f* fascist.

'fase *sf* phase; (*TECN*) stroke; **in ~ di espansione** in a period of expansion; **essere fuori ~** (*motore*) to be rough (*BRIT*), run roughly; (*fig*) to feel rough (*BRIT*) *o* rotten.

fas'tidio *sm* bother, trouble; **dare ~ a qn** to bother *o* annoy sb; **sento ~ allo stomaco** my stomach's upset; **avere ~i con la polizia** to have trouble *o* bother with the police.

fastidi'oso, a *ag* annoying, tiresome; (*schifiltoso*) fastidious.

'fasto *sm* pomp, splendour (*BRIT*), splendor (*US*).

fas'toso, a *ag* sumptuous, lavish.

fa'sullo, a *ag* (*gen*) fake; (*dichiarazione, persona*) false; (*pretesto*) bogus.

'fata *sf* fairy.

fa'tale *ag* fatal; (*inevitabile*) inevitable; (*fig*) irresistible.

fata'lismo *sm* fatalism.

fatalità *sf inv* inevitability; (*avversità*) misfortune; (*fato*) fate, destiny.

fa'tato, a *ag* (*spada, chiave*) magic; (*castello*) enchanted.

fa'tica, che *sf* hard work, toil; (*sforzo*) effort; (*di metalli*) fatigue; **a ~ with** difficulty; **respirare a ~** to have difficulty (in) breathing; **fare ~ a fare qc** to find it difficult to do sth; **animale da ~** beast of burden.

fati'caccia, ce [fati'kattʃa] *sf*: **fu una ~** it was hard work, it was a hell of a job (*fam*).

fati'care *vi* to toil; ~ **a fare qc** to have difficulty doing sth.

fati'cata *sf* hard work.

fa'tichi *etc* [fa'tiki] *vb vedi* **faticare.**

fati'coso, a *ag* (*viaggio, camminata*) tiring, exhausting; (*lavoro*) laborious.

fa'tidico, a, ci, che *ag* fateful.

'fato *sm* fate, destiny.

Fatt. *abbr* (= *fattura*) inv.

fat'taccio [fat'tattʃo] *sm* foul deed.

fat'tezze [fat'tettse] *sfpl* features.

fat'tibile *ag* feasible, possible.

fattis'pecie [fattis'pɛtʃe] *sf*: **nella** *o* **in ~ in** this case *o* instance.

'fatto, a *pp di* **fare ♦** *ag*: **un uomo ~ a** grown man **♦** *sm* fact; (*azione*) deed; (*avvenimento*) event, occurrence; (*di romanzo, film*) action, story; ~ **a mano/in casa** hand-/home-made; **è ben ~a** she has a nice figure; **cogliere qn sul ~** to catch sb red-handed; **il ~ sta** *o* **è che** the fact remains *o* is that; **in ~ di** as for, as far as ... is concerned; **fare i ~i propri** to mind one's own business; **è uno che sa il ~ suo** he knows what he's about; **gli ho detto il ~ suo** I told him what I thought of him; **porre qn di fronte al ~ compiuto** to present sb with a fait accompli.

fat'tore *sm* (*AGR*) farm manager; (*MAT*: *elemento costitutivo*) factor.

fatto'ria *sf* farm; (*casa*) farmhouse.

fatto'rino *sm* errand boy; (*di ufficio*) office boy; (*d'albergo*) porter.

fattucchi'era [fattuk'kjera] *sf* witch.

fat'tura *sf* (*COMM*) invoice; (*di abito*) tailoring; (*malia*) spell; **pagamento contro presentazione ~** payment on invoice.

fattu'rare *vt* (*COMM*) to invoice; (*prodotto*) to produce; (*vino*) to adulterate.

fattu'rato *sm* (*COMM*) turnover.

fatturazi'one [fatturat'tsjone] *sf* billing, invoicing.

'fatuo, a *ag* vain, fatuous; **fuoco ~** (*anche fig*) will-o'-the-wisp.

'fauci ['fautʃi] *sfpl* (*di leone etc*) jaws; (*di vulcano*) mouth *sg.*

'fauna *sf* fauna.

'fausto, a *ag* (*formale*) happy; **un ~ presagio** a good omen.

fau'tore, 'trice *sm/f* advocate, supporter.

'fava *sf* broad bean.

fa'vella *sf* speech.

fa'villa *sf* spark.

'favo *sm* (*di api*) honeycomb.

'favola *sf* (*fiaba*) fairy tale; (*d'intento morale*) fable; (*fandonia*) yarn; **essere la ~ del paese** (*oggetto di critica*) to be the talk of the town; (*zimbello*) to be a

laughing stock.
favo'loso, a *ag* fabulous; (*incredibile*)
incredible.
fa'vore *sm* favour (*BRIT*), favor (*US*); **per** ~
please; **prezzo/trattamento di** ~
preferential price/treatment; **condizioni
di** ~ (*COMM*) favo(u)rable terms; **fare un**
~ **a qn** to do sb a favo(u)r; **col** ~ **delle
tenebre** under cover of darkness.
favoreggia'mento [favoreddʒa'mento] *sm*
(*DIR*) aiding and abetting.
favo'revole *ag* favourable (*BRIT*),
favorable (*US*).
favo'rire *vt* to favour (*BRIT*), favor (*US*); (*il
commercio, l'industria, le arti*) to promote,
encourage; **vuole** ~**?** won't you help
yourself?; **favorisca in salotto** please
come into the sitting room; **mi favorisca i
documenti** please may I see your papers?
favori'tismo *sm* favouritism (*BRIT*),
favoritism (*US*).
favo'rito, a *ag*, *sm/f* favourite (*BRIT*),
favorite (*US*).
fax *sm inv* fax; **mandare qc via** ~ to fax sth.
fa'xare *vt* to fax.
fazi'one [fat'tsjone] *sf* faction.
faziosità [fattsjosi'ta] *sf* sectarianism.
fazzo'letto [fattso'letto] *sm* handkerchief;
(*per la testa*) (head)scarf.
F.B.I. *sigla f* (= *Federal Bureau of
Investigation*) FBI.
F.C. *abbr* = **fuoricorso.**
f.co *abbr* = **franco.**
FE *sigla* – *Ferrara.*
febb. *abbr* (= *febbraio*) Feb.
feb'braio *sm* February; *per fraseologia vedi*
luglio.
'febbre *sf* fever; **aver la** ~ to have a high
temperature; ~ **da fieno** hay fever.
feb'brile *ag* (*anche fig*) feverish.
'feccia, ce ['fettʃa] *sf* dregs *pl*.
'feci ['fɛtʃi] *sfpl* faeces, excrement *sg*.
'feci *etc* ['fɛtʃi] *vb vedi* **fare.**
'fecola *sf* potato flour.
fecon'dare *vt* to fertilize.
fecondazi'one [fekondat'tsjone] *sf*
fertilization; ~ **artificiale** artificial
insemination.
fecondità *sf* fertility.
fe'condo, a *ag* fertile.
'Fedcom *sigla m* = *Fondo Europeo di
Cooperazione Monetaria.*
'fede *sf* (*credenza*) belief, faith; (*REL*) faith;
(*fiducia*) faith, trust; (*fedeltà*) loyalty;
(*anello*) wedding ring; (*attestato*)
certificate; **aver** ~ **in qn** to have faith in
sb; **tener** ~ **a** (*ideale*) to remain loyal to;
(*giuramento, promessa*) to keep; **in buona/**

cattiva ~ in good/bad faith; **"in** ~**"** (*DIR*)
"in witness whereof".
fe'dele *ag* (*leale*): ~ **(a)** faithful (to);
(*veritiero*) true, accurate ♦ *sm/f* follower;
i ~**i** (*REL*) the faithful.
fedeltà *sf* faithfulness; (*coniugale*) fidelity;
(*esattezza: di copia, traduzione*) accuracy;
alta ~ (*RADIO*) high fidelity.
'federa *sf* pillowslip, pillowcase.
fede'rale *ag* federal.
federa'lismo *sm* (*POL*) federalism.
federa'lista, i, e *ag*, *sm/f* (*POL*) federalist.
federazi'one [federat'tsjone] *sf* federation.
Feder'caccia [feder'kattʃa] *abbr f*
(= *Federazione Italiana della Caccia*) *hunting
federation.*
Feder'calcio [feder'kaltʃo] *abbr m*
(= *Federazione Italiana Gioco Calcio*) *Italian
football association.*
Federcon'sorzi [federkon'sɔrtsi] *abbr f*
(= *Federazione Italiana dei Consorzi Agrari*)
federation of farmers' cooperatives.
fe'difrago, a, ghi, ghe *ag* faithless,
perfidious.
fe'dina *sf* (*DIR*): ~ **(penale)** record; **avere la**
~ **penale sporca** to have a police record.
'fegato *sm* liver; (*fig*) guts *pl*, nerve;
mangiarsi *o* **rodersi il** ~ to be consumed
with rage.
'felce ['feltʃe] *sf* fern.
fe'lice [fe'litʃe] *ag* happy; (*fortunato*) lucky.
felicità [felitʃi'ta] *sf* happiness.
felici'tarsi [felitʃi'tarsi] *vr* (*congratularsi*): ~
con qn per qc to congratulate sb on sth.
felicitazi'oni [felitʃitat'tsjoni] *sfpl*
congratulations.
fe'lino, a *ag*, *sm* feline.
'felpa *sf* sweatshirt.
fel'pato, a *ag* (*tessuto*) brushed; (*passo*)
stealthy; **con passo** ~ stealthily.
'feltro *sm* felt.
'femmina *sf* (*ZOOL, TECN*) female; (*figlia*)
girl, daughter; (*spesso peg*) woman.
femmi'nile *ag* feminine; (*sesso*) female;
(*lavoro, giornale*) woman's, women's;
(*moda*) women's ♦ *sm* (*LING*) feminine.
femminilità *sf* femininity.
femmi'nismo *sm* feminism.
femmi'nista, i, e *ag*, *sm/f* feminist.
'femore *sm* thighbone, femur.
'fendere *vt* to cut through.
fendi'nebbia *sm* (*AUT*) fog lamp.
fendi'tura *sf* (*gen*) crack; (*di roccia*) cleft,
crack.
fe'nomeno *sm* phenomenon.
'feretro *sm* coffin.
feri'ale *ag*: **giorno** ~ weekday, working
day.

'**ferie** *sfpl* holidays (*BRIT*), vacation *sg* (*US*); **andare in** ~ to go on holiday *o* vacation; **25 giorni** ~ **pagate** 25 days' holiday *o* vacation with pay.

feri'mento *sm* wounding.

fe'rire *vt* to injure; (*deliberatamente*: *MIL etc*) to wound; (*colpire*) to hurt; ~**rsi** *vr* to hurt o.s., injure o.s.

fe'rito, a *sm/f* wounded *o* injured man/woman ♦ *sf* injury; wound.

feri'toia *sf* slit.

'**ferma** *sf* (*MIL*) (period of) service; (*CACCIA*): **cane da** ~ pointer.

ferma'carte *sm inv* paperweight.

fermacra'vatta *sm inv* tiepin (*BRIT*), tie tack (*US*).

fer'maglio [fer'maʎʎo] *sm* clasp; (*gioiello*) brooch; (*per documenti*) clip.

ferma'mente *av* firmly.

fer'mare *vt* to stop, halt; (*POLIZIA*) to detain, hold; (*bottone etc*) to fasten, fix ♦ *vi* to stop; ~**rsi** *vr* to stop, halt; ~**rsi a fare qc** to stop to do sth.

fer'mata *sf* stop; ~ **dell'autobus** bus stop.

fermen'tare *vi* to ferment; (*fig*) to be in a ferment.

fermentazi'one [fermentat'tsjone] *sf* fermentation.

fer'mento *sm* (*anche fig*) ferment; (*lievito*) yeast; ~**i lattici** probiotics, probiotic bacteria.

fer'mezza [fer'mettsa] *sf* (*fig*) firmness, steadfastness.

'**fermo, a** *ag* still, motionless; (*veicolo*) stationary; (*orologio*) not working; (*saldo*: *anche fig*) firm; (*voce, mano*) steady ♦ *escl* stop!; keep still! ♦ *sm* (*chiusura*) catch, lock; (*DIR*): ~ **di polizia** police detention; ~ **restando che** ... it being understood that ....

'**fermo 'posta** *av, sm inv* poste restante (*BRIT*), general delivery (*US*).

fe'roce [fe'rɔtʃe] *ag* (*animale*) wild, fierce, ferocious; (*persona*) cruel, fierce; (*fame, dolore*) raging.

fe'rocia, cie [fe'rɔtʃa] *sf* ferocity.

Ferr. *abbr* = **ferrovia**.

fer'raglia [fer'raʎʎa] *sf* scrap iron.

ferra'gosto *sm* (*festa*) feast of the Assumption; (*periodo*) August holidays *pl* (*BRIT*) *o* vacation (*US*); *vedi nota nel riquadro*.

FERRAGOSTO

Ferragosto, *15 August, is a national holiday. Marking the feast of the Assumption, its origins are religious but in recent years it has simply become the most important public holiday of the summer season. Most people take some extra time off work and head out of town to the holiday resorts. Consequently, most of industry and commerce grind to a standstill.*

ferra'menta *sfpl* ironmongery *sg* (*BRIT*), hardware *sg*; **negozio di** ~ ironmonger's (*BRIT*), hardware shop *o* store (*US*).

fer'rare *vt* (*cavallo*) to shoe.

fer'rato, a *ag* (*FERR*): **strada** ~**a** railway line (*BRIT*), railroad line (*US*); (*fig*): **essere** ~ **in** (*materia*) to be well up in.

ferra'vecchio [ferra'vɛkkjo] *sm* scrap merchant.

'**ferreo, a** *ag* iron *cpd*.

ferri'era *sf* ironworks *sg o pl*.

'**ferro** *sm* iron; **una bistecca ai** ~**i** a grilled steak; **mettere a** ~ **e fuoco** to put to the sword; **essere ai** ~**i corti** (*fig*) to be at daggers drawn; **tocca** ~! touch wood!; ~ **battuto** wrought iron; ~ **di cavallo** horseshoe; ~ **da stiro** iron; ~**i da calza** knitting needles; **i** ~**i del mestiere** the tools of the trade.

ferrotranvi'ario, a *ag* public transport *cpd*.

Ferrotranvi'eri *abbr f* (= *Federazione Nazionale Lavoratori Autoferrotranvieri e Internavigatori*) *transport workers' union*.

ferro'vecchio [ferro'vɛkkjo] *sm* = **ferravecchio**.

ferro'via *sf* railway (*BRIT*), railroad (*US*).

ferrovi'ario, a *ag* railway *cpd* (*BRIT*), railroad *cpd* (*US*).

ferrovi'ere *sm* railwayman (*BRIT*), railroad man (*US*).

'**fertile** *ag* fertile.

fertilità *sf* fertility.

fertiliz'zante [fertilid'dzante] *sm* fertilizer.

fertiliz'zare [fertilid'dzare] *vt* to fertilize.

fer'vente *ag* fervent, ardent.

'**fervere** *vi*: **fervono i preparativi per** ... they are making feverish preparations for ....

'**fervido, a** *ag* fervent, ardent.

fer'vore *sm* fervour (*BRIT*), fervor (*US*), ardour (*BRIT*), ardor (*US*); (*punto culminante*) height.

'**fesa** *sf* (*CUC*) rump of veal.

fesse'ria *sf* stupidity; **dire** ~**e** to talk nonsense.

'**fesso, a** *pp di* **fendere** ♦ *ag* (*fam*: *sciocco*) crazy, cracked.

fes'sura *sf* crack, split; (*per gettone, moneta*) slot.

'**festa** *sf* (*religiosa*) feast; (*pubblica*) holiday; (*compleanno*) birthday; (*onomastico*) name day; (*ricevimento*) celebration, party; **far** ~ to have a holiday; (*far baldoria*) to live it

up; **far ~ a qn** to give sb a warm
welcome; **essere vestito a ~** to be dressed
up to the nines; **~ comandata** (*REL*)
holiday of obligation; **la ~ della mamma/
del papà** Mother's/Father's Day; **la F~
della Repubblica** *vedi nota nel riquadro*.

FESTA DELLA REPUBBLICA

The **Festa della Repubblica**, *2 June,
celebrates the founding of the Italian Republic
after the fall of the monarchy and the
subsequent referendum in 1946. It is marked by
military parades and political speeches.*

---

festeggia'menti [festeddʒa'menti] *smpl*
celebrations.
festeggi'are [fested'dʒare] *vt* to celebrate;
(*persona*) to have a celebration for.
fes'tino *sm* party; (*con balli*) ball.
fes'tivo, a *ag* (*atmosfera*) festive; **giorno ~**
holiday.
fes'toso, a *ag* merry, joyful.
fe'tente *ag* (*puzzolente*) fetid;
(*comportamento*) disgusting.
fe'ticcio [fe'tittʃo] *sm* fetish.
'feto *sm* foetus (*BRIT*), fetus (*US*).
fe'tore *sm* stench, stink.
'fetta *sf* slice.
fet'tuccia, ce [fet'tuttʃa] *sf* tape, ribbon.
fettuc'cine [fettut'tʃine] *sfpl* (*CUC*) ribbon-
shaped pasta.
feu'dale *ag* feudal.
'feudo *sm* (*STORIA*) fief; (*fig*) stronghold.
ff *abbr* (*AMM*) = **facente funzione**; (= *fogli*)
pp.
FF.AA *abbr* = **forze armate**.
FG *sigla* = *Foggia*.
FI *sigla* = *Firenze* ♦ *abbr* = **Forza Italia**.
fi'aba *sf* fairy tale.
fia'besco, a, schi, sche *ag* fairy-tale *cpd*.
fi'acca *sf* weariness; (*svogliatezza*)
listlessness; **battere la ~** to shirk.
fiac'care *vt* to weaken.
fiaccherò *etc* [fjakke'rɔ] *vb vedi* **fiaccare**.
fi'acco, a, chi, che *ag* (*stanco*) tired,
weary; (*svogliato*) listless; (*debole*) weak;
(*mercato*) slack.
fi'accola *sf* torch.
fiacco'lata *sf* torchlight procession.
fi'ala *sf* phial.
fi'amma *sf* flame; (*NAUT*) pennant.
fiam'mante *ag* (*colore*) flaming; **nuovo ~**
brand new.
fiam'mata *sf* blaze.
fiammeggi'are [fjammed'dʒare] *vi* to blaze.
fiam'mifero *sm* match.
fiam'mingo, a, ghi, ghe *ag* Flemish ♦ *sm/f*

Fleming ♦ *sm* (*LING*) Flemish; (*ZOOL*)
flamingo; **i F~ghi** the Flemish.
fian'cata *sf* (*di nave etc*) side; (*NAUT*)
broadside.
fiancheggi'are [fjanked'dʒare] *vt* to border;
(*fig*) to support, back (up); (*MIL*) to flank.
fi'anco, chi *sm* side; (*di persona*) hip; (*MIL*)
flank; **di ~** sideways, from the side; **a ~ a
~** side by side; **prestare il proprio ~ alle
critiche** to leave o.s. open to criticism; **~
destr/sinistr!** (*MIL*) right/left turn!
Fi'andre *sfpl*: **le ~** Flanders *sg*.
fiaschette'ria [fjaskette'ria] *sf* wine shop.
fi'asco, schi *sm* flask; (*fig*) fiasco; **fare ~** to
be a fiasco.
fia'tare *vi* (*fig: parlare*): **senza ~** without
saying a word.
fi'ato *sm* breath; (*resistenza*) stamina; **~i**
smpl (*MUS*) wind instruments; **avere il ~
grosso** to be out of breath; **prendere ~** to
catch one's breath; **bere qc tutto d'un ~**
to drink sth in one go *o* gulp.
'fibbia *sf* buckle.
'fibra *sf* fibre, fiber (*US*); (*fig*) constitution;
~ ottica optical fibre; **~ di vetro**
fibreglass (*BRIT*), fiberglass (*US*).
ficca'naso, *pl(m)* **~i,** *pl(f) inv sm/f* busybody,
nos(e)y parker.
fic'care *vt* to push, thrust, drive; **~rsi** *vr*
(*andare a finire*) to get to; **~ il naso negli
affari altrui** (*fig*) to poke *o* stick one's nose
into other people's business; **~rsi nei
pasticci** *o* **nei guai** to get into a fix.
ficcherò *etc* [fikke'rɔ] *vb vedi* **ficcare**.
fiche [fiʃ] *sf inv* (*nei giochi d'azzardo*) chip.
'fico, chi *sm* (*pianta*) fig tree; (*frutto*) fig; **~
d'India** prickly pear; **~ secco** dried fig.
fidanza'mento [fidantsa'mento] *sm*
engagement.
fidan'zarsi [fidan'tsarsi] *vr* to get engaged.
fidan'zato, a [fidan'tsato] *sm/f* fiancé/
fiancée.
fi'darsi *vr*: **~ di** to trust; **~rsi è bene non
~rsi è meglio** (*proverbio*) better safe than
sorry.
fi'dato, a *ag* reliable, trustworthy.
fide'ismo *sm* unquestioning belief.
fide'istico, a, ci, che *ag* (*atteggiamento,
posizione*) totally uncritical.
fidelus'sore *sm* (*DIR*) guarantor.
'fido, a *ag* faithful, loyal ♦ *sm* (*COMM*)
credit.
fi'ducia [fi'dutʃa] *sf* confidence, trust;
incarico di ~ position of trust,
responsible position; **persona di ~**
reliable person; **è il mio uomo di ~** he is
my right-hand man; **porre la questione di
~** (*POL*) to ask for a vote of confidence.

fiduci'oso, a [fidu'tʃoso] *ag* trusting.

fi'ele *sm* (*MED*) bile; (*fig*) bitterness.

fie'nile *sm* hayloft.

fi'eno *sm* hay.

fi'era *sf* fair; (*animale*) wild beast; ~ **di beneficenza** charity bazaar; ~ **campionaria** trade fair.

fie'rezza [fje'rettsa] *sf* pride.

fi'ero, a *ag* proud; (*crudele*) fierce, cruel; (*audace*) bold.

fi'evole *ag* (*luce*) dim; (*suono*) weak.

F.I.F.A. *sigla f* (= *Fédération Internationale de Football Association*) FIFA.

'fifa *sf* (*fam*): **aver** ~ to have the jitters.

fi'fone, a *sm/f* (*fam, scherzoso*) coward.

fig. *abbr* (= *figura*) fig.

FIGC *sigla f* (= *Federazione Italiana Gioco Calcio*) *Italian football association*.

'Figi ['fidʒi] *sfpl*: **le isole** ~ Fiji, the Fiji Islands.

'figlia ['fiʎʎa] *sf* daughter; (*COMM*) counterfoil (*BRIT*), stub.

figli'are [fiʎ'ʎare] *vi* to give birth.

figli'astro, a [fiʎ'ʎastro] *sm/f* stepson/daughter.

'figlio ['fiʎʎo] *sm* son; (*senza distinzione di sesso*) child; ~ **d'arte: essere** ~ **d'arte** to come from a theatrical (*o* musical *etc*) family; ~ **di puttana** (*fam!*) son of a bitch (*!*); ~ **unico** only child.

figli'occio, a, ci, ce [fiʎ'ʎɔttʃo] *sm/f* godchild, godson/daughter.

figli'ola [fiʎ'ʎɔla] *sf* daughter; (*fig: ragazza*) girl.

figli'olo [fiʎ'ʎɔlo] *sm* (*anche fig: ragazzo*) son.

fi'gura *sf* figure; (*forma, aspetto esterno*) form, shape; (*illustrazione*) picture, illustration; **far** ~ to look smart; **fare una brutta** ~ to make a bad impression; **che** ~! how embarrassing!

figu'raccia, ce [figu'rattʃa] *sf*: **fare una** ~ to create a bad impression.

figu'rare *vi* to appear ♦ *vt*: ~**rsi qc** to imagine sth; ~**rsi** *vr*: **figurati!** imagine that!; **ti do noia?** — **ma figurati!** am I disturbing you? — not at all!

figura'tivo, a *ag* figurative.

figu'rina *sf* (*statuetta*) figurine; (*cartoncino*) picture card.

figuri'nista, e *sm/f* dress designer.

figu'rino *sm* fashion sketch.

fi'guro *sm*: **un losco** ~ a suspicious character.

figu'rone *sm*: **fare un** ~ (*persona, oggetto*) to look terrific; (*persona: con un discorso etc*) to make an excellent impression.

'fila *sf* row, line; (*coda*) queue; (*serie*) series, string; **di** ~ in succession; **fare la**

~ to queue; **in** ~ **indiana** in single file.

fila'mento *sm* filament.

fi'lanca ® *sf* stretch material.

fi'landa *sf* spinning mill.

fi'lante *ag*: **stella** ~ (*stella cadente*) shooting star; (*striscia di carta*) streamer.

filantro'pia *sf* philanthropy.

filan'tropico, a, ci, che *ag* philanthropic(al).

fi'lantropo *sm* philanthropist.

fi'lare *vt* to spin; (*NAUT*) to pay out ♦ *vi* (*baco, ragno*) to spin; (*formaggio fuso*) to go stringy; (*liquido*) to trickle; (*discorso*) to hang together; (*fam: amoreggiare*) to go steady; (*muoversi a forte velocità*) to go at full speed; (*andarsene lestamente*) to make o.s. scarce ♦ *sm* (*di alberi etc*) row, line; ~ **diritto** (*fig*) to toe the line.

filar'monico, a, ci, che *ag* philharmonic.

filas'trocca, che *sf* nursery rhyme.

filate'lia *sf* philately, stamp collecting.

fi'lato, a *ag* spun ♦ *sm* yarn ♦ *av*: **vai dritto** ~ **a casa** go straight home; **3 giorni** ~**i** 3 days running *o* on end.

fila'tura *sf* spinning; (*luogo*) spinning mill.

fi'letto *sm* (*ornamento*) braid, trimming; (*di vite*) thread; (*di carne*) fillet.

fili'ale *ag* filial ♦ *sf* (*di impresa*) branch.

filibusti'ere *sm* pirate; (*fig*) adventurer.

fili'grana *sf* (*in oreficeria*) filigree; (*su carta*) watermark.

fi'lippica *sf* invective.

Filip'pine *sfpl*: **le** ~ the Philippines.

filip'pino, a *ag, sm/f* Filipino.

film *sm inv* film.

fil'mare *vt* to film.

fil'mato *sm* short film.

fil'mina *sf* film strip.

'filo *sm* (*anche fig*) thread; (*filato*) yarn; (*metallico*) wire; (*di lama, rasoio*) edge; **con un** ~ **di voce** in a whisper; **un** ~ **d'aria** (*fig*) a breath of air; **dare del** ~ **da torcere a qn** to create difficulties for sb, make life difficult for sb; **fare il** ~ **a qn** (*corteggiare*) to be after sb, chase sb; **per** ~ **e per segno** in detail; ~ **d'erba** blade of grass; ~ **interdentale** dental floss; ~ **di perle** string of pearls; ~ **di Scozia** fine cotton yarn; ~ **spinato** barbed wire.

filoameri'cano, a *ag* pro-American.

'filobus *sm inv* trolley bus.

filodiffusi'one *sf* rediffusion.

filodram'matico, a, ci, che *ag*: (**compagnia**) ~**a** amateur dramatic society ♦ *sm/f* amateur actor/actress.

filon'cino [filon'tʃino] *sm* ≈ French stick.

fi'lone *sm* (*di minerali*) seam, vein; (*pane*) ≈ Vienna loaf; (*fig*) trend.

filoso'fia *sf* philosophy.
filo'sofico, a, ci, che *ag* philosophical.
fi'losofo, a *smlf* philosopher.
filosovi'etico, a, ci, che *ag* pro-Soviet.
filo'via *sf* (*linea*) trolley line; (*bus*) trolley bus.
fil'trare *vt, vi* to filter.
'filtro *sm* filter; (*pozione*) potion; ~ **dell'olio** (*AUT*) oil filter.
'filza ['filtsa] *sf* (*anche fig*) string.
FIN *sigla f* = *Federazione Italiana Nuoto.*
fin *av, prep* = **fino.**
fi'nale *ag* final ♦ *sm* (*di libro, film*) end, ending; (*MUS*) finale ♦ *sf* (*SPORT*) final.
fina'lista, i, e *smlf* finalist.
finalità *sf* (*scopo*) aim, purpose.
finaliz'zare [finalid'dzare] *vt*: ~ **a** to direct towards.
final'mente *av* finally, at last.
fi'nanza [fi'nantsa] *sf* finance; ~**e** *sfpl* (*di individuo, Stato*) finances; **(Guardia di)** ~ (*di frontiera*) ≈ Customs and Excise (*BRIT*), ≈ Customs Service (*US*); **(Intendenza di)** ~ ≈ Inland Revenue (*BRIT*), ≈ Internal Revenue Service (*US*); **Ministro delle** ~**e** Minister of Finance, ≈ Chancellor of the Exchequer (*BRIT*), ≈ Secretary of the Treasury (*US*).
finanzia'mento [finantsja'mento] *sm* (*azione*) financing; (*denaro fornito*) funds *pl.*
finanzi'are [finan'tsjare] *vt* to finance, fund.
finanzi'ario, a [finan'tsjarjo] *ag* financial ♦ *sf* (*anche:* **società** ~**a**) investment company; (*anche:* **legge** ~**a**) finance act, ≈ budget (*BRIT*).
finanzia'tore, 'trice *ag*: **ente** ~, **società** ~**trice** backer ♦ *smlf* backer.
finanzi'ere [finan'tsjɛre] *sm* financier; (*guardia di finanza: doganale*) customs officer; (: *tributaria*) Inland Revenue official (*BRIT*), Internal Revenue official (*US*).
finché [fin'ke] *cong* (*per tutto il tempo che*) as long as; (*fino al momento in cui*) until; ~ **vorrai** as long as you like; **aspetta** ~ **non esca** wait until he goes (*o* comes) out.
'fine *ag* (*lamina, carta*) thin; (*capelli, polvere*) fine; (*vista, udito*) keen, sharp; (*persona:* raffinata) refined, distinguished; (*osservazione*) subtle ♦ *sf* end ♦ *sm* aim, purpose; (*esito*) result, outcome; **in** *o* **alla** ~ in the end, finally; **alla fin** ~ at the end of the day, in the end; **che** ~ **ha fatto?** what became of him?; **buona** ~ **e buon principio!** (*augurio*) happy New Year!; **a fin di bene** with the best of intentions; **al** ~ **di fare qc** (in order) to do sth; **condurre**

qc a buon ~ to bring sth to a successful conclusion; **secondo** ~ ulterior motive.
'fine setti'mana *sm o f inv* weekend.
fi'nestra *sf* window.
fines'trino *sm* (*di treno, auto*) window.
fi'nezza [fi'nettsa] *sf* thinness; fineness; keenness, sharpness; refinement; subtlety.
'fingere ['findʒere] *vt* to feign; (*supporre*) to imagine, suppose; ~**rsi** *vr*: ~**rsi ubriaco/ pazzo** to pretend to be drunk/crazy; ~ **di fare** to pretend to do.
fini'menti *smpl* (*di cavallo etc*) harness *sg.*
fini'mondo *sm* pandemonium.
fi'nire *vt* to finish ♦ *vi* to finish, end ♦ *sm*: **sul** ~ **della festa** towards the end of the party; ~ **di fare** (*compiere*) to finish doing; (*smettere*) to stop doing; ~ **in galera** to end up *o* finish up in prison; **farla finita** (*con la vita*) to put an end to one's life; **farla finita con qc** to have done with sth; **com'è andata a** ~? what happened in the end?; **finiscila!** stop it!
fini'tura *sf* finish.
finlan'dese *ag* Finnish ♦ *smlf* Finn ♦ *sm* (*LING*) Finnish.
Fin'landia *sf*: **la** ~ Finland.
'fino, a *ag* (*capelli, seta*) fine; (*oro*) pure; (*fig: acuto*) shrewd ♦ *av* (*spesso troncato in* **fin**: *pure, anche*) even ♦ *prep* (*spesso troncato in* **fin**: *tempo*): till when?; (: *luogo*): **fin qui** as far as here; ~ **a** (*tempo*) until, till; (*luogo*) as far as, (up) to; **fin da domani** from tomorrow onwards; **fin da ieri** since yesterday; **fin dalla nascita** from *o* since birth.
fi'nocchio [fi'nɔkkjo] *sm* fennel; (*fam peg: pederasta*) queer.
fi'nora *av* up till now.
'finsi *etc vb vedi* **fingere.**
'finto, a *pp di* **fingere** ♦ *ag* (*capelli, dente*) false; (*fiori*) artificial; (*cuoio, pelle*) imitation *cpd*; (*fig: simulato: pazzia etc*) feigned, sham ♦ *sf* pretence (*BRIT*), pretense (*US*), sham; (*SPORT*) feint; **far** ~**a** (**di fare**) to pretend (to do); **l'ho detto per** ~**a** I was only pretending; (*per scherzo*) I was only kidding.
finzi'one [fin'tsjone] *sf* pretence (*BRIT*), pretense (*US*), sham.
fioc'care *vi* (*neve*) to fall; (*fig: insulti etc*) to fall thick and fast.
fi'occo, chi *sm* (*di nastro*) bow; (*di stoffa, lana*) flock; (*di neve*) flake; (*NAUT*) jib; **coi** ~**chi** (*fig*) first-rate; ~**chi di granoturco** cornflakes.
fi'ocina ['fjɔtʃina] *sf* harpoon.
fi'oco, a, chi, che *ag* faint, dim.

fi'onda *sf* catapult.
fio'raio, a *smf* florist.
fiorda'liso *sm* (*BOT*) cornflower.
fi'ordo *sm* fjord.
fi'ore *sm* flower; ~i *smpl* (*CARTE*) clubs; **nel** ~ **degli anni** in one's prime; **a fior d'acqua** on the surface of the water; **a fior di labbra** in a whisper; **aver i nervi a fior di pelle** to be on edge; **fior di latte** cream; **è costato fior di soldi** it cost a pretty penny; **il fior** ~ **della società** the cream of society; ~ **all'occhiello** feather in the cap; ~**i di campo** wild flowers.
fio'rente *ag* (*industria, paese*) flourishing; (*salute*) blooming; (*petto*) ample.
fioren'tino, a *ag, smf* Florentine ♦ *sf* (*CUC*) T-bone steak.
fio'retto *sm* (*SCHERMA*) foil.
fio'rino *sm* florin.
fio'rire *vi* (*rosa*) to flower; (*albero*) to blossom; (*fig*) to flourish.
fio'rista, i, e *smf* florist.
fiori'tura *sf* (*di pianta*) flowering, blooming; (*di albero*) blossoming; (*fig: di commercio, arte*) flourishing; (*insieme dei fiori*) flowers *pl*; (*MUS*) fioritura.
fi'otto *sm* (*di lacrime*) flow, flood; (*di sangue*) gush, spurt.
'FIPE *sigla f* = *Federazione Italiana Pubblici Esercizi*.
Fi'renze [fi'rɛntse] *sf* Florence.
'firma *sf* signature; (*reputazione*) name.
firma'mento *sm* firmament.
fir'mare *vt* to sign.
firma'tario, a *smf* signatory.
fisar'monica, che *sf* accordion.
fis'cale *ag* fiscal, tax *cpd*; (*meticoloso*) punctilious; **medico** ~ *doctor employed by Social Security to verify cases of sick leave*.
fisca'lista, i, e *smf* tax consultant.
fiscaliz'zare [fiskalid'dzare] *vt* to exempt from taxes.
fischi'are [fis'kjare] *vi* to whistle ♦ *vt* to whistle; (*attore*) to boo, hiss; **mi fischian le orecchie** my ears are singing; (*fig*) my ears are burning.
fischiet'tare [fiskjet'tare] *vi, vt* to whistle.
fischi'etto [fis'kjetto] *sm* (*strumento*) whistle.
'fischio ['fiskjo] *sm* whistle; **prendere** ~**i per fiaschi** to get hold of the wrong end of the stick.
'fisco *sm* tax authorities *pl*, ≈ Inland Revenue (*BRIT*), ≈ Internal Revenue Service (*US*).
'fisica *sf vedi* **fisico**.
fisica'mente *av* physically.

'fisico, a, ci, che *ag* physical ♦ *smf* physicist ♦ *sm* physique ♦ *sf* physics *sg*.
'fisima *sf* fixation.
fisiolo'gia [fizjolo'dʒia] *sf* physiology.
fisiono'mia *sf* face, physiognomy.
fisiotera'pia *sf* physiotherapy.
fisiotera'pista *smf* physiotherapist.
fis'saggio [fis'saddʒo] *sm* (*FOT*) fixing.
fis'sante *ag* (*spray, lozione*) holding.
fis'sare *vt* to fix, fasten; (*guardare intensamente*) to stare at; (*data, condizioni*) to fix, establish, set; (*prenotare*) to book; ~**rsi** *vr*: ~**rsi su** (*sog: sguardo, attenzione*) to focus on; (*fig: idea*) to become obsessed with.
fissazi'one [fissat'tsjone] *sf* (*PSIC*) fixation.
fissi'one *sf* fission.
'fisso, a *ag* fixed; (*stipendio, impiego*) regular ♦ *av*: **guardar** ~ **qn/qc** to stare at sb/sth; **avere un ragazzo** ~ to have a steady boyfriend; **senza** ~**a dimora** of no fixed abode.
fitoterma'lismo *sm* herbal hydrotherapy.
'fitta *sf vedi* **fitto**.
fit'tavolo *sm* tenant.
fit'tizio, a [fit'tittsjo] *ag* fictitious, imaginary.
'fitto, a *ag* thick, dense; (*pioggia*) heavy ♦ *sm* (*affitto, pigione*) rent ♦ *sf* sharp pain; **una** ~**a al cuore** (*fig*) a pang of grief; **nel** ~ **del bosco** in the heart *o* depths of the wood.
fiu'mana *sf* torrent; (*fig*) stream, flood.
fi'ume *sm* river ♦ *ag inv*: **processo** ~ long-running trial; **scorrere a** ~**i** (*acqua, sangue*) to flow in torrents.
fiu'tare *vt* to smell, sniff; (*sog: animale*) to scent; (*fig: inganno*) to get wind of, smell; ~ **tabacco** to take snuff; ~ **cocaina** to snort cocaine.
fi'uto *sm* (sense of) smell; (*fig*) nose.
'flaccido, a ['flattʃido] *ag* flabby.
fla'cone *sm* bottle.
flagel'lare [fladʒel'lare] *vt* to flog, scourge; (*sog: onde*) to beat against.
fla'gello [fla'dʒello] *sm* scourge.
fla'grante *ag* flagrant; **cogliere qn in** ~ to catch sb red-handed.
fla'nella *sf* flannel.
flash [flaʃ] *sm inv* (*FOT*) flash; (*giornalistico*) newsflash.
flau'tista, i *smf* flautist.
'flauto *sm* flute.
'flebile *ag* faint, feeble.
fle'bite *sf* phlebitis.
'flemma *sf* (*calma*) coolness, phlegm; (*MED*) phlegm.
flem'matico, a, ci, che *ag* phlegmatic,

cool.

fles'sibile *ag* pliable; (*fig: che si adatta*) flexible.

flessi'one *sf* (*gen*) bending; (*GINNASTICA: a terra*) sit-up; (: *in piedi*) forward bend; (: *sulle gambe*) knee-bend; (*diminuzione*) slight drop, slight fall; (*LING*) inflection; **fare una** ~ to bend; **una** ~ **economica** a downward trend in the economy.

'flesso, a *pp di* **flettere.**

flessu'oso, a *ag* supple, lithe; (*andatura*) flowing, graceful.

'flettere *vt* to bend.

'flipper ['flipper] *sm inv* pinball machine.

flirt [flɔːt] *sm inv* brief romance, flirtation.

flir'tare *vi* to flirt.

F.lli *abbr* (= *fratelli*) Bros.

'flora *sf* flora.

'florido, a *ag* flourishing; (*fig*) glowing with health.

'floscio, a, sci, sce ['flɔʃʃo] *ag* (*cappello*) floppy, soft; (*muscoli*) flabby.

'flotta *sf* fleet.

flot'tante *sm* (*ECON*): **titoli a largo** ~ **blue chips,** stocks on the market.

'fluido, a *ag, sm* fluid.

flu'ire *vi* to flow.

fluore'scente [fluoreʃˈʃɛnte] *ag* fluorescent.

flu'oro *sm* fluorine.

fluo'ruro *sm* fluoride.

'flusso *sm* flow; (*FISICA, MED*) flux; ~ **e riflusso** ebb and flow; ~ **di cassa** (*COMM*) cash flow.

'flutti *smpl* waves.

fluttu'are *vi* to rise and fall; (*ECON*) to fluctuate.

fluvi'ale *ag* river *cpd*, fluvial.

FM *abbr vedi* **modulazione di frequenza.**

FMI *sigla m vedi* **Fondo Monetario Internazionale.**

FO *sigla* = **Forlì.**

fo'bia *sf* phobia.

'foca, che *sf* (*ZOOL*) seal.

fo'caccia, ce [foˈkattʃa] *sf kind of pizza;* (*dolce*) bun; **rendere pan per** ~ to get one's own back, give tit for tat.

fo'cale *ag* focal.

focaliz'zare [fokalidˈdzare] *vt* (*FOT: immagine*) to get into focus; (*fig: situazione*) to get into perspective; ~ **l'attenzione su** to focus one's attention on.

'foce ['fotʃe] *sf* (*GEO*) mouth.

fo'chista, i [foˈkista] *sm* (*FERR*) stoker, fireman.

foco'laio *sm* (*MED*) centre (*BRIT*) o center (*US*) of infection; (*fig*) hotbed.

foco'lare *sm* hearth, fireside; (*TECN*) furnace.

fo'coso, a *ag* fiery; (*cavallo*) mettlesome, fiery.

'fodera *sf* (*di vestito*) lining; (*di libro, poltrona*) cover.

fode'rare *vt* to line; to cover.

'fodero *sm* (*di spada*) scabbard; (*di pugnale*) sheath; (*di pistola*) holster.

'foga *sf* enthusiasm, ardour (*BRIT*), ardor (*US*).

'foggia, ge ['fɔddʒa] *sf* (*maniera*) style; (*aspetto*) form, shape; (*moda*) fashion, style.

foggi'are [fodˈdʒare] *vt* to shape; to style.

'foglia ['fɔʎʎa] *sf* leaf; **ha mangiato la** ~ (*fig*) he's caught on; ~ **d'argento/d'oro** silver/gold leaf.

fogli'ame [foʎˈʎame] *sm* foliage, leaves *pl*.

fogli'etto [foʎˈʎetto] *sm* (*piccolo foglio*) slip of paper, piece of paper; (*manifestino*) leaflet, handout.

'foglio ['fɔʎʎo] *sm* (*di carta*) sheet (of paper); (*di metallo*) sheet; (*documento*) document; (*banconota*) (bank)note; ~ **di calcolo** spreadsheet; ~ **rosa** (*AUT*) provisional licence; ~ **di via** (*DIR*) expulsion order; ~ **volante** pamphlet.

'fogna ['foɲɲa] *sf* drain, sewer.

fogna'tura [foɲɲa'tura] *sf* drainage, sewerage.

föhn [føːn] *sm inv* hair-dryer.

fo'lata *sf* gust.

fol'clore *sm* folklore.

folclo'ristico, a, ci, che *ag* folk *cpd*.

folgo'rare *vt* (*sog: fulmine*) to strike down; (: *alta tensione*) to electrocute.

folgorazi'one [folgorat'tsjone] *sf* electrocution; **ebbe una** ~ (*fig: idea*) he had a brainwave.

'folgore *sf* thunderbolt.

'folla *sf* crowd, throng.

'folle *ag* mad, insane; (*TECN*) idle; **in** ~ (*AUT*) in neutral.

folleggi'are [folledˈdʒare] *vi* (*divertirsi*) to paint the town red.

fol'letto *sm* elf.

fol'lia *sf* folly, foolishness; foolish act; (*pazzia*) madness, lunacy; **amare qn alla** ~ to love sb to distraction; **costare una** ~ to cost the earth.

'folto, a *ag* thick.

fomen'tare *vt* to stir up, foment.

fon *sm inv* = **föhn.**

fon'dale *sm* (*del mare*) bottom; (*TEAT*) backdrop; **il** ~ **marino** the sea bed.

fondamen'tale *ag* fundamental, basic.

fondamenta'lista, i, e *ag, sm/f* (*REL*) fundamentalist.

fonda'mento *sm* foundation; ~**a** *sfpl* (*EDIL*) foundations.
fon'dare *vt* to found; (*fig: dar base*): ~ **qc su** to base sth on; ~**rsi** *vr* (*teorie*): ~**rsi (su)** to be based (on).
fonda'tezza [fonda'tettsa] *sf* (*di ragioni*) soundness; (*di dubbio, sospetto*) basis in fact.
fon'dato, a *ag* (*ragioni*) sound; (*dubbio, sospetto*) well-founded.
fondazi'one [fondat'tsjone] *sf* foundation.
fon'dente *ag*: **cioccolato** ~ plain *o* dark chocolate.
'fondere *vt* (*neve*) to melt; (*metallo*) to fuse, melt; (*fig: colori*) to merge, blend; (: *imprese, gruppi*) to merge ♦ *vi* to melt; ~**rsi** *vr* to melt; (*fig: partiti, correnti*) to unite, merge.
fonde'ria *sf* foundry.
fondi'ario, a *ag* land *cpd*.
fon'dina *sf* (*piatto fondo*) soup plate; (*portapistola*) holster.
'fondo, a *ag* deep ♦ *sm* (*di recipiente, pozzo*) bottom; (*di stanza*) back; (*quantità di liquido che resta, deposito*) dregs *pl*; (*sfondo*) background; (*unità immobiliare*) property, estate; (*somma di denaro*) fund; (*SPORT*) long-distance race; ~**i** *smpl* (*denaro*) funds; **a notte** ~**a** at dead of night; **in** ~ **a** at the bottom of; at the back of; (*strada*) at the end of; **laggiù in** ~ (*lontano*) over there; (*in profondità*) down there; **in** ~ (*fig*) after all, all things considered; **andare fino in** ~ **a** (*fig*) to examine thoroughly; **andare a** ~ (*nave*) to sink; **conoscere a** ~ to know inside out; **dar** ~ **a** (*fig: provvisti, soldi*) to use up; **toccare il** ~ (*fig*) to plumb the depths; **a** ~ **perduto** (*COMM*) without security; ~ **comune di investimento** investment trust; **F**~ **Monetario Internazionale (FMI)** International Monetary Fund (IMF); ~ **di previdenza** social insurance fund; ~ **di riserva** reserve fund; ~ **urbano** town property; ~**i di caffè** coffee grounds; ~**i d'esercizio** working capital *sg*; ~**i liquidi** ready money *sg*, liquid assets; ~**i di magazzino** old *o* unsold stock *sg*; ~**i neri** slush fund *sg*.
fondo'tinta *sm inv* (*cosmetico*) foundation.
fo'nema *sm* phoneme.
fo'netica *sf* phonetics *sg*.
fo'netico, a, ci, che *ag* phonetic.
fon'tana *sf* fountain.
fonta'nella *sf* drinking fountain.
'fonte *sf* spring, source; (*fig*) source ♦ *sm*: ~ **battesimale** (*REL*) font.
fon'tina *sm full fat hard, sweet cheese*.

'footing ['futiŋ] *sm* jogging.
forag'giare [forad'dʒare] *vt* (*cavalli*) to fodder; (*fig: partito etc*) to bankroll.
fo'raggio [fo'raddʒo] *sm* fodder, forage.
fo'rare *vt* to pierce, make a hole in; (*pallone*) to burst; (*pneumatico*) to puncture; (*biglietto*) to punch; ~**rsi** *vr* (*gen*) to develop a hole; (*AUT, pallone, timpano*) to burst; ~ **una gomma** to burst a tyre (*BRIT*) *o* tire (*US*).
fora'tura *sf* piercing; bursting; puncturing; punching.
'forbici ['fɔrbitʃi] *sfpl* scissors.
forbi'cina [forbi'tʃina] *sf* earwig.
for'bito, a *ag* (*stile, modi*) polished.
'forca, che *sf* (*AGR*) fork, pitchfork; (*patibolo*) gallows *sg*.
for'cella [for'tʃɛlla] *sf* (*TECN*) fork; (*di monte*) pass.
for'chetta [for'ketta] *sf* fork; **essere una buona** ~ to enjoy one's food.
for'cina [for'tʃina] *sf* hairpin.
'forcipe ['fɔrtʃipe] *sm* forceps *pl*.
for'cone *sm* pitchfork.
fo'rense *ag* (*linguaggio*) legal; **avvocato** ~ barrister (*BRIT*), lawyer.
fo'resta *sf* forest; **la F**~ **Nera** the Black Forest.
fores'tale *ag* forest *cpd*; **guardia** ~ forester.
foreste'ria *sf* (*di convento, palazzo etc*) guest rooms *pl*, guest quarters *pl*.
foresti'ero, a *ag* foreign ♦ *sm/f* foreigner.
for'fait [fɔr'fɛ] *sm inv*: (**prezzo a**) ~ fixed price, set price; **dichiarare** ~ (*SPORT*) to withdraw; (*fig*) to give up.
forfe'tario, a *ag*: **prezzo** ~ (*da pagare*) fixed *o* set price; (*da ricevere*) lump sum.
'forfora *sf* dandruff.
'forgia, ge ['fɔrdʒa] *sf* forge.
forgi'are [for'dʒare] *vt* to forge.
'forma *sf* form; (*aspetto esteriore*) form, shape; (*DIR: procedura*) procedure; (*per calzature*) last; (*stampo da cucina*) mould (*BRIT*), mold (*US*); ~**e** *sfpl* (*del corpo*) figure, shape; **le** ~**e** (*convenzioni*) appearances; **errori di** ~ stylistic errors; **essere in** ~ to be in good shape; **tenersi in** ~ to keep fit; **in** ~ **ufficiale/privata** officially/privately; **una** ~ **di formaggio** a (whole) cheese.
formag'gino [formad'dʒino] *sm* processed cheese.
for'maggio [for'maddʒo] *sm* cheese.
for'male *ag* formal.
formalità *sf inv* formality.
formaliz'zare [formalid'dzare] *vt* to formalize.
for'mare *vt* to form, shape, make; (*numero*

formato–fossa

di telefono) to dial; (*fig: carattere*) to form, mould (*BRIT*), mold (*US*); ~**rsi** *vr* to form, take shape; **il treno si forma a Milano** the train starts from Milan.

for'mato *sm* format, size.

format'tare *vt* (*INFORM*) to format.

formattazi'one [formattat'tsjone] *sf* (*INFORM*) formatting.

formazi'one [format'tsjone] *sf* formation; (*fig: educazione*) training; ~ **professionale** vocational training.

for'mica, che *sf* ant.

formi'caio *sm* anthill.

formico'lare *vi* (*gamba, braccio*) to tingle; (*brulicare: anche fig*): ~ **di** to be swarming with; **mi formicola la gamba** I've got pins and needles in my leg, my leg's tingling.

formico'lio *sm* pins and needles *pl*; swarming.

formi'dabile *ag* powerful, formidable; (*straordinario*) remarkable.

for'moso, a *ag* shapely.

'formula *sf* formula; ~ **di cortesia** (*nelle lettere*) letter ending.

formu'lare *vt* to formulate.

for'nace [for'natʃe] *sf* (*per laterizi etc*) kiln; (*per metalli*) furnace.

for'naio *sm* baker.

for'nello *sm* (*elettrico, a gas*) ring; (*di pipa*) bowl.

for'nire *vt*: ~ **qn di qc,** ~ **qc a qn** to provide *o* supply sb with sth, supply sth to sb; ~**rsi** *vr*: ~**rsi di** (*procurarsi*) to provide o.s. with.

for'nito, a *ag*: **ben** ~ (*negozio*) well-stocked.

forni'tore, 'trice *ag*: **ditta** ~**trice di** ... company supplying ... ♦ *smf* supplier.

forni'tura *sf* supply.

'forno *sm* (*di cucina*) oven; (*panetteria*) bakery; (*TECN: per calce etc*) kiln; (: *per metalli*) furnace; **fare i** ~**i** (*MED*) to undergo heat treatment.

'foro *sm* (*buco*) hole; (*STORIA*) forum; (*tribunale*) (law) court.

'forse *av* perhaps, maybe; (*circa*) about; **essere in** ~ to be in doubt.

forsen'nato, a *ag* mad, crazy, insane.

'forte *ag* strong; (*suono*) loud; (*spesa*) considerable, great ♦ *av* strongly; (*velocemente*) fast; (*a voce alta*) loud(ly); (*violentemente*) hard ♦ *sm* (*edificio*) fort; (*specialità*) forte, strong point; **piatto** ~ (*CUC*) main dish; **avere un** ~ **mal di testa/ raffreddore** to have a bad headache/cold; **essere** ~ **in qc** to be good at sth; **farsi** ~ **di qc** to make use of sth; **dare man** ~ **a qn** to back sb up, support sb; **usare le maniere**

~**i** to use strong-arm tactics.

for'tezza [for'tettsa] *sf* (*morale*) strength; (*luogo fortificato*) fortress.

fortifi'care *vt* to fortify, strengthen.

for'tuito, a *ag* fortuitous, chance *cpd*.

for'tuna *sf* (*destino*) fortune, luck; (*buona sorte*) success, fortune; (*eredità, averi*) fortune; **per** ~ luckily, fortunately; **di** ~ makeshift, improvised; **atterraggio di** ~ emergency landing.

fortu'nale *sm* storm.

fortunata'mente *av* luckily, fortunately.

fortu'nato, a *ag* lucky, fortunate; (*coronato da successo*) successful.

fortu'noso, a *ag* (*vita*) eventful; (*avvenimento*) unlucky.

fo'runcolo *sm* (*MED*) boil.

forvi'are *vt, vi* = **fuorviare**.

'forza ['fortsa] *sf* strength; (*potere*) power; (*FISICA*) force ♦ *escl* come on!; ~**e** *sfpl* (*fisiche*) strength *sg*; (*MIL*) forces; **per** ~ against one's will; (*naturalmente*) of course; **per** ~ **di cose** by force of circumstances; **a viva** ~ by force; **a** ~ **di** by dint of; **farsi** ~ (*coraggio*) to pluck up one's courage; **bella** ~! (*ironico*) how clever of you (*o* him *etc*)!; ~ **lavoro** work force, manpower; **per causa di** ~ **maggiore** (*DIR*) by reason of an act of God; (*per estensione*) due to circumstances beyond one's control; **la** ~ **pubblica** the police *pl*; ~ **di pace** peacekeeping force; ~ **di vendita** (*COMM*) sales force; ~ **di volontà** willpower; **le** ~**e armate** the armed forces; **F**~ **Italia** (*POL*) moderate right-wing party.

for'zare [for'tsare] *vt* to force; (*cassaforte, porta*) to force (open); (*voce*) to strain; ~ **qn a fare** to force sb to do.

for'zato, a [for'tsato] *ag* forced ♦ *sm* (*DIR*) prisoner sentenced to hard labour (*BRIT*) *o* labor (*US*).

forzi'ere [for'tsjɛre] *sm* strongbox; (*di pirati*) treasure chest.

for'zista, i, e [for'tsista] *ag* of Forza Italia ♦ *smf* member (*o* supporter) of Forza Italia.

for'zuto, a [for'tsuto] *ag* big and strong.

fos'chia [fos'kia] *sf* mist, haze.

'fosco, a, schi, sche *ag* dark, gloomy; **dipingere qc a tinte** ~**sche** (*fig*) to paint a gloomy picture of sth.

fos'fato *sm* phosphate.

fosfore'scente [fosforeʃ'ʃɛnte] *ag* phosphorescent; (*lancetta dell'orologio etc*) luminous.

'fosforo *sm* phosphorous.

'fossa *sf* pit; (*di cimitero*) grave; ~ **comune**

mass grave.

fos'sato *sm* ditch; (*di fortezza*) moat.

fos'setta *sf* dimple.

'fossi *etc vb vedi* **essere**.

'fossile *ag, sm* fossil (*cpd*).

'fosso *sm* ditch; (*MIL*) trench.

'foste *etc vb vedi* **essere**.

'foto *sf inv* photo; ~ **ricordo** souvenir photo; ~ **tessera** passport(-type) photo.

foto... *prefisso* photo....

foto'camera *sf*: ~ **digitale** digital camera.

fotocomposi'tore *sm* filmsetter.

fotocomposizi'one [fotokompozit'tsjone] *sf* film setting.

foto'copia *sf* photocopy.

fotocopi'are *vt* to photocopy.

fotocopiste'ria *sf* photocopy shop.

foto'genico, a, ci, che [foto'dʒɛniko] *ag* photogenic.

fotogra'fare *vt* to photograph.

fotogra'fia *sf* (*procedimento*) photography; (*immagine*) photograph; **fare una** ~ to take a photograph; **una** ~ **a colori/in bianco e nero** a colour/black and white photograph.

foto'grafico, a, ci, che *ag* photographic; **macchina** ~**a** camera.

fo'tografo, a *sm/f* photographer.

foto'gramma, i *sm* (*CINE*) frame.

fotomo'dello, a *sm/f* fashion model.

fotomon'taggio [fotomon'taddʒo] *sm* photomontage.

fotore'porter *sm/f inv* newspaper (*o* magazine) photographer.

fotoro'manzo [fotoro'mandzo] *sm* romantic picture story.

foto'sintesi *sf* photosynthesis.

'fottere *vt* (*fam!: avere rapporti sessuali*) to fuck (*!*), screw (*!*); (: *rubare*) to pinch, swipe; (: *fregare*): **mi hanno fottuto** they played a dirty trick on me; **vai a farti** ~**!** fuck off! (*!*).

fot'tuto, a *ag* (*fam!*) bloody, fucking (*!*).

fou'lard [fu'lar] *sm inv* scarf.

FR *sigla* = Frosinone.

fra *prep* = **tra**.

fracas'sare *vt* to shatter, smash; ~**rsi** *vr* to shatter, smash; (*veicolo*) to crash.

fra'casso *sm* smash; crash; (*baccano*) din, racket.

'fradicio, a, ci, ce ['fraditʃo] *ag* (*guasto*) rotten; (*molto bagnato*) soaking (wet); **ubriaco** ~ blind drunk.

'fragile ['fradʒile] *ag* fragile; (*salute*) delicate; (*nervi, vetro*) brittle.

fragilità [fradʒili'ta] *sf* (*vedi ag*) fragility; delicacy; brittleness.

'fragola *sf* strawberry.

fra'gore *sm* (*di cascate, carro armato*) roar; (*di tuono*) rumble.

frago'roso, a *ag* deafening; **ridere in modo** ~ to roar with laughter.

fra'grante *ag* fragrant.

fraintendi'mento *sm* misunderstanding.

frain'tendere *vt* to misunderstand.

frain'teso, a *pp di* **fraintendere**.

fram'mento *sm* fragment.

fram'misto, a *ag*: ~ **a** interspersed with.

'frana *sf* landslide; (*fig: persona*): **essere una** ~ to be useless, be a walking disaster area.

fra'nare *vi* to slip, slide down.

franca'mente *av* frankly.

fran'cese [fran'tʃeze] *ag* French ♦ *sm/f* Frenchman/woman ♦ *sm* (*LING*) French; **i F~i** the French.

fran'chezza [fran'kettsa] *sf* frankness, openness.

fran'chigia, gie [fran'kidʒa] *sf* (*AMM*) exemption; (*DIR*) franchise; (*NAUT*) shore leave; ~ **doganale** exemption from customs duty.

'Francia ['frantʃa] *sf*: **la** ~ France.

'franco, a, chi, che *ag* (*COMM*) free; (*sincero*) frank, open, sincere ♦ *sm* (*moneta*) franc; **farla** ~**a** (*fig*) to get off scot-free; ~ **a bordo** free on board; ~ **di dogana** duty-free; ~ **a domicilio** delivered free of charge; ~ **fabbrica** ex factory, ex works; **prezzo** ~ **fabbrica** ex-works price; ~ **magazzino** ex warehouse; ~ **di porto** carriage free; ~ **vagone** free on rail; ~ **tiratore** *sm* sniper; (*POL*) *member of parliament who votes against his own party*.

franco'bollo *sm* (postage) stamp.

franco-cana'dese *ag, sm/f* French Canadian.

Franco'forte *sf* Frankfurt.

fran'gente [fran'dʒɛnte] *sm* (*onda*) breaker; (*scoglio emergente*) reef; (*circostanza*) situation, circumstance.

'frangia, ge ['frandʒa] *sf* fringe.

frangi'flutti [frandʒi'flutti] *sm inv* breakwater.

frangi'vento [frandʒi'vɛnto] *sm* windbreak.

fran'toio *sm* (*AGR*) olive press; (*TECN*) crusher.

frantu'mare *vt*, ~**rsi** *vr* to break into pieces, shatter.

fran'tumi *smpl* pieces, bits; (*schegge*) splinters; **andare in** ~, **mandare in** ~ to shatter, smash to pieces *o* smithereens.

frappé *sm* (*CUC*) milk shake.

fra'sario *sm* (*gergo*) vocabulary, language.

'frasca, sche *sf* (leafy) branch; **saltare di**

palo in ~ to jump from one subject to another.

'frase *sf* (*LING*) sentence; (*locuzione, espressione, MUS*) phrase; ~ **fatta** set phrase.

fraseolo'gia [frazeolo'dʒia] *sf* phraseology.

'frassino *sm* ash (tree).

frastagli'ato, a [frastaʎ'ʎato] *ag* (*costa*) indented, jagged.

frastor'nare *vt* (*intontire*) to daze; (*confondere*) to bewilder, befuddle.

frastor'nato, a *ag* dazed; bewildered.

frastu'ono *sm* hubbub, din.

'frate *sm* friar, monk.

fratel'lanza [fratel'lantsa] *sf* brotherhood; (*associazione*) fraternity.

fratel'lastro *sm* stepbrother; (*con genitore in comune*) half brother.

fra'tello *sm* brother; ~**i** *smpl* brothers; (*nel senso di fratelli e sorelle*) brothers and sisters.

fra'terno, a *ag* fraternal, brotherly.

fratri'cida, i, e [fratri'tʃida] *ag* fratricidal ♦ *sm/f* fratricide; **guerra** ~ civil war.

frat'taglie [frat'taʎʎe] *sfpl* (*CUC: gen*) offal *sg*; (: *di pollo*) giblets.

frat'tanto *av* in the meantime, meanwhile.

frat'tempo *sm*: **nel** ~ in the meantime, meanwhile.

frat'tura *sf* fracture; (*fig*) split, break.

frattu'rare *vt* to fracture.

fraudo'lento, a *ag* fraudulent.

fraziona'mento [frattsjona'mento] *sm* division, splitting up.

frazio'nare [frattsjo'nare] *vt* to divide, split up.

frazi'one [frat'tsjone] *sf* fraction; (*borgata*): ~ **di comune** hamlet.

'freccia, ce ['frettʃa] *sf* arrow; ~ **di direzione** (*AUT*) indicator.

frec'ciata [fret'tʃata] *sf*: **lanciare una** ~ to make a cutting remark.

fred'dare *vt* to shoot dead.

fred'dezza [fred'dettsa] *sf* coldness.

'freddo, a *ag, sm* cold; **fa** ~ it's cold; **aver** ~ to be cold; **soffrire il** ~ to feel the cold; **a** ~ (*fig*) deliberately.

freddo'loso, a *ag* sensitive to the cold.

fred'dura *sf* pun.

'freezer ['frizer] *sm inv* fridge-freezer.

fre'gare *vt* to rub; (*fam: truffare*) to take in, cheat; (: *rubare*) to swipe, pinch; **fregarsene** (*fam!*): **chi se ne frega?** who gives a damn (about it)?

fre'gata *sf* rub; (*fam*) swindle; (*NAUT*) frigate.

frega'tura *sf* (*fam: imbroglio*) rip-off; (: *delusione*) let-down.

fregherò *etc* [frege'rɔ] *vb vedi* **fregare**.

'fregio ['fredʒo] *sm* (*ARCHIT*) frieze; (*ornamento*) decoration.

'fremere *vi*: ~ **di** to tremble o quiver with; ~ **d'impazienza** to be champing at the bit.

'fremito *sm* tremor, quiver.

fre'nare *vt* (*veicolo*) to slow down; (*cavallo*) to rein in; (*lacrime*) to restrain, hold back ♦ *vi* to brake; ~**rsi** *vr* (*fig*) to restrain o.s., control o.s.

fre'nata *sf*: **fare una** ~ to brake.

frene'sia *sf* frenzy.

fre'netico, a, ci, che *ag* frenetic.

'freno *sm* brake; (*morso*) bit; **tenere a** ~ (*passioni etc*) to restrain; **tenere a** ~ **la lingua** to hold one's tongue; ~ **a disco** disc brake; ~ **a mano** handbrake.

'freon ® *sm inv* (*CHIM*) Freon ®.

frequen'tare *vt* (*scuola, corso*) to attend; (*locale, bar*) to go to, frequent; (*persone*) to see (often).

frequen'tato, a *ag* (*locale*) busy.

fre'quente *ag* frequent; **di** ~ frequently.

fre'quenza [fre'kwɛntsa] *sf* frequency; (*INS*) attendance.

fre'sare *vt* (*TECN*) to mill.

fres'chezza [fres'kettsa] *sf* freshness.

'fresco, a, schi, sche *ag* fresh; (*temperatura*) cool; (*notizia*) recent, fresh ♦ *sm*: **godere il** ~ to enjoy the cool air; ~ **di bucato** straight from the wash, newly washed; **stare** ~ (*fig*) to be in for it; **mettere al** ~ to put in a cool place; (*fig: in prigione*) to put inside o in the cooler.

fres'cura *sf* cool.

'fresia *sf* freesia.

'fretta *sf* hurry, haste; **in** ~ in a hurry; **in** ~ **e furia** in a mad rush; **aver** ~ to be in a hurry; **far** ~ **a qn** to hurry sb.

frettolosa'mente *av* hurriedly, in a rush.

fretto'loso, a *ag* (*persona*) in a hurry; (*lavoro etc*) hurried, rushed.

fri'abile *ag* (*terreno*) friable; (*pasta*) crumbly.

'friggere ['friddʒere] *vt* to fry ♦ *vi* (*olio etc*) to sizzle; **vai a farti** ~! (*fam*) get lost!

frigidità [fridʒidi'ta] *sf* frigidity.

'frigido, a ['fridʒido] *ag* (*MED*) frigid.

fri'gnare [friɲ'ɲare] *vi* to whine, snivel.

fri'gnone, a [friɲ'ɲone] *sm/f* whiner, sniveller.

'frigo, ghi *sm* fridge.

frigo'bar *sm inv* minibar.

frigo'rifero, a *ag* refrigerating ♦ *sm* refrigerator; **cella** ~ a cold store.

fringu'ello *sm* chaffinch.

'frissi *etc vb vedi* **friggere**.

frit'tata *sf* omelet(te); **fare una** ~ (*fig*) to

make a mess of things.
frit'tella *sf* (*CUC*) pancake; (: *ripiena*) fritter.
'fritto, a *pp di* **friggere** ♦ *ag* fried ♦ *sm* fried food; **ormai siamo ~i!** (*fig fam*) now we've had it!; **è un argomento ~ e rifritto** that's old hat; **~ misto** mixed fry.
frit'tura *sf* (*cibo*) fried food; **~ di pesce** mixed fried fish.
friu'lano, a *ag* of (*o* from) Friuli.
frivo'lezza [frivo'lettsa] *sf* frivolity.
'frivolo, a *ag* frivolous.
frizi'one [frit'tsjone] *sf* friction; (*di pelle*) rub, rub-down; (*AUT*) clutch.
friz'zante [frid'dzante] *ag* (*anche fig*) sparkling.
'frizzo ['friddzo] *sm* witticism.
fro'dare *vt* to defraud, cheat.
'frode *sf* fraud; **~ fiscale** tax evasion.
'frodo *sm*: **di ~** illegal, contraband; **pescatore di ~, cacciatore di ~** poacher.
'frogia, gie ['frɔdʒa] *sf* (*di cavallo etc*) nostril.
'frollo, a *ag* (*carne*) tender; (: *di selvaggina*) high; (*fig: persona*) soft; **pasta ~a** short(crust) pastry.
'fronda *sf* (leafy) branch; (*di partito politico*) internal opposition; **~e** *sfpl* (*di albero*) foliage *sg*.
fron'tale *ag* frontal; (*scontro*) head-on.
'fronte *sf* (*ANAT*) forehead; (*di edificio*) front, façade ♦ *sm* (*MIL, POL, METEOR*) front; **a ~, di ~** facing, opposite; **di ~ a** (*posizione*) opposite, facing, in front of; (*a paragone di*) compared with; **far ~ a** (*nemico, problema*) to confront; (*responsabilità*) to face up to; (*spese*) to cope with.
fronteggi'are [fronted'dʒare] *vt* (*avversari, difficoltà*) to face, stand up to; (*spese*) to cope with.
frontes'pizio [frontes'pittsjo] *sm* (*ARCHIT*) frontispiece; (*di libro*) title page.
fronti'era *sf* border, frontier.
fron'tone *sm* pediment.
'fronzolo ['frondzolo] *sm* frill.
'frotta *sf* crowd; **in ~, a ~e** in their hundreds, in droves.
'frottola *sf* fib; **raccontare un sacco di ~e** to tell a pack of lies.
fru'gale *ag* frugal.
fru'gare *vi* to rummage ♦ *vt* to search.
frugherò *etc* [fruge'rɔ] *vb vedi* **frugare**.
frui'tore *sm* user.
fruizi'one [fruit'tsjone] *sf* use.
frul'lare *vt* (*CUC*) to whisk ♦ *vi* (*uccelli*) to flutter; **cosa ti frulla in mente?** what is going on in that mind of yours?
frul'lato *sm* (*CUC*) milk shake; (: *con solo frutta*) fruit drink.
frulla'tore *sm* electric mixer.
frul'lino *sm* whisk.
fru'mento *sm* wheat.
frusci'are [fruʃ'ʃare] *vi* to rustle.
fru'scio [fruʃ'ʃio] *sm* rustle; rustling.
'frusta *sf* whip; (*CUC*) whisk.
frus'tare *vt* to whip.
frus'tata *sf* lash.
frus'tino *sm* riding crop.
frus'trare *vt* to frustrate.
frus'trato, a *ag* frustrated.
frustrazi'one [frustrat'tsjone] *sf* frustration.
'frutta *sf* fruit; (*portata*) dessert; **~ candita/secca** candied/dried fruit.
frut'tare *vi* (*investimenti, deposito*) to bear dividends, give a return; **il mio deposito in banca (mi) frutta il 10%** my bank deposits bring (me) in 10%; **quella gara gli fruttò la medaglia d'oro** he won the gold medal in that competition.
frut'teto *sm* orchard.
frutticol'tura *sf* fruit growing.
frut'tifero, a *ag* (*albero etc*) fruit-bearing; (*fig: che frutta*) fruitful, profitable; **deposito ~** interest-bearing deposit.
frutti'vendolo, a *sm/f* greengrocer (*BRIT*), produce dealer (*US*).
'frutto *sm* fruit; (*fig: risultato*) result(s); (*ECON: interesse*) interest; (: *reddito*) income; **è ~ della tua immaginazione** it's a figment of your imagination; **~i di mare** seafood *sg*.
fruttu'oso, a *ag* fruitful, profitable.
FS *abbr* (= *Ferrovie dello Stato*) *Italian railways*.
f.t. *abbr* = **fuori testo**.
f.to *abbr* (= *firmato*) signed.
fu *vb vedi* **essere** ♦ *ag inv*: **il ~ Paolo Bianchi** the late Paolo Bianchi.
fuci'lare [futʃi'lare] *vt* to shoot.
fuci'lata [futʃi'lata] *sf* rifle shot.
fucilazi'one [futʃilat'tsjone] *sf* execution (by firing squad).
fu'cile [fu'tʃile] *sm* rifle, gun; (*da caccia*) shotgun, gun; **~ a canne mozze** sawn-off shotgun.
fu'cina [fu'tʃina] *sf* forge.
'fuco, chi *sm* drone.
'fucsia *sf* fuchsia.
'fuga, ghe *sf* escape, flight; (*di gas, liquidi*) leak; (*MUS*) fugue; **mettere qn in ~** to put sb to flight; **~ di cervelli** brain drain.
fu'gace [fu'gatʃe] *ag* fleeting, transient.
fu'gare *vt* (*dubbi, incertezze*) to dispel, drive out.
fug'gevole [fud'dʒevole] *ag* fleeting.

fuggi'asco, a, schi, sche [fud'dʒasko] *ag, sm/f* fugitive.

fuggi'fuggi [fuddʒi'fuddʒi] *sm* scramble, stampede.

fug'gire [fud'dʒire] *vi* to flee, run away; (*fig: passar veloce*) to fly ♦ *vt* to avoid.

fuggi'tivo, a [fuddʒi'tivo] *sm/f* fugitive, runaway.

'fui *vb vedi* **essere.**

'fulcro *sm* (*FISICA*) fulcrum; (*fig: di teoria, questione*) central *o* key point.

ful'gore *sm* brilliance, splendour (*BRIT*), splendor (*US*).

fu'liggine [fu'liddʒine] *sf* soot.

fulmi'nare *vt* (*sog: elettricità*) to electrocute; (*con arma da fuoco*) to shoot dead; **~rsi** *vr* (*lampadina*) to go, blow; (*fig: con lo sguardo*): **mi fulminò (con uno sguardo)** he looked daggers at me.

'fulmine *sm* bolt of lightning; **~i** *smpl* lightning *sg*; **~ a ciel sereno** bolt from the blue.

ful'mineo, a *ag* (*fig: scatto*) rapid; (: *minaccioso*) threatening.

'fulvo, a *ag* tawny.

fumai'olo *sm* (*di nave*) funnel; (*di fabbrica*) chimney.

fu'mante *ag* (*piatto etc*) steaming.

fu'mare *vi* to smoke; (*emettere vapore*) to steam ♦ *vt* to smoke.

fu'mario, a *ag*: **canna ~a** flue.

fu'mata *sf* (*segnale*) smoke signal; **farsi una ~** to have a smoke; **~ bianca/nera** (*in Vaticano*) signal that a new pope has/has not been elected.

fuma'tore, 'trice *sm/f* smoker.

fu'metto *sm* comic strip; **giornale** *m* **a ~i** comic.

'fummo *vb vedi* **essere.**

'fumo *sm* smoke; (*vapore*) steam; (*il fumare tabacco*) smoking; **~i** *smpl* (*industriali etc*) fumes; **vendere ~** to deceive, cheat; **è tutto ~ e niente arrosto** it has no substance to it; **i ~i dell'alcool** (*fig*) the after-effects of drink; **~ passivo** passive smoking.

fu'mogeno, a [fu'mɔdʒeno] *ag* (*candelotto*) smoke *cpd* ♦ *sm* smoke bomb; **cortina ~a** smoke screen.

fu'moso, a *ag* smoky; (*fig*) muddled.

fu'nambolo, a *sm/f* tightrope walker.

'fune *sf* rope, cord; (*più grossa*) cable.

'funebre *ag* (*rito*) funeral; (*aspetto*) gloomy, funereal.

fune'rale *sm* funeral.

fu'nesto, a *ag* (*incidente*) fatal; (*errore, decisione*) fatal, disastrous; (*atmosfera*) gloomy, dismal.

'fungere ['fundʒere] *vi:* **~ da** to act as.

'fungo, ghi *sm* fungus; (*commestibile*) mushroom; **~ velenoso** toadstool; **crescere come i ~ghi** (*fig*) to spring up overnight.

funico'lare *sf* funicular railway.

funi'via *sf* cable railway.

'funsi *etc vb vedi* **fungere.**

'funto, a *pp di* **fungere.**

funzio'nare [funtsjo'nare] *vi* to work, function; (*fungere*): **~ da** to act as.

funzio'nario [funtsjo'narjo] *sm* official; **~ statale** civil servant.

funzi'one [fun'tsjone] *sf* function; (*carica*) post, position; (*REL*) service; **in ~** (*meccanismo*) in operation; **in ~ di** (*come*) as; **vive in ~ dei figli** he lives for his children; **far ~ di** to act as; **fare la ~ di qn** (*farne le veci*) to take sb's place.

fu'oco, chi *sm* fire; (*fornello*) ring; (*FOT, FISICA*) focus; **dare ~ a qc** to set fire to sth; **far ~** (*sparare*) to fire; **prendere ~** to catch fire; **~ d'artificio** firework; **~ di paglia** flash in the pan; **~ sacro** *o* **di Sant'Antonio** (*MED fam*) shingles *sg*.

fuorché [fwor'ke] *cong, prep* except.

FU'ORI *sigla m* (= *Fronte Unitario Omosessuale Rivoluzionario Italiano*) gay liberation movement.

fu'ori *av* outside; (*all'aperto*) outdoors, outside; (~ *di casa, SPORT*) out; (*esclamativo*) get out! ♦ *prep:* **~ (di)** out of, outside ♦ *sm* outside; **essere in ~** (*sporgere*) to stick out; **lasciar ~ qc/qn** to leave sth/sb out; **far ~** (*fam: soldi*) to spend; (: *cioccolatini*) to eat up; (: *rubare*) to nick; **far ~ qn** (*fam*) to kill sb, do sb in; **essere tagliato ~** (*da un gruppo, ambiente*) to be excluded; **essere ~ di sé** to be beside oneself; **~ luogo** (*inopportuno*) out of place, uncalled for; **~ mano** out of the way, remote; **~ pasto** between meals; **~ pericolo** out of danger; **~ dai piedi!** get out of the way!; **~ servizio** out of order; **~ stagione** out of season; **illustrazione ~ testo** (*STAMPA*) plate; **~ uso** out of use.

fuori'bordo *sm inv* speedboat (with outboard motor); outboard motor.

fuori'busta *sm inv* unofficial payment.

fuori'classe *sm/f inv* (undisputed) champion.

fuori'corso *ag inv* (*moneta*) no longer in circulation; (*INS*): (**studente**) **~** *undergraduate who has not completed a course in due time.*

fuorigi'oco [fwori'dʒɔko] *sm* offside.

fuori'legge [fwori'leddʒe] *sm/f inv* outlaw.

fuoriprog'ramma *sm inv* (*TV, RADIO*)

unscheduled programme; (*fig*) change of plan *o* programme.

fuori'serie *ag inv* (*auto etc*) custom-built ♦ *sf* custom-built car.

fuoris'trada *sm* (*AUT*) cross-country vehicle.

fuoru'scito, a, fuoriu'scito, a [fwor(i)uʃ'ʃito] *sm/f* exile ♦ *sf* (*di gas*) leakage, escape; (*di sangue, linfa*) seepage.

fuorvi'are *vt* to mislead; (*fig*) to lead astray ♦ *vi* to go astray.

furbacchi'one, a [furbak'kjone] *sm/f* cunning old devil.

fur'bizia [fur'bittsja] *sf* (*vedi ag*) cleverness; cunning; **una** ~ a cunning trick.

'furbo, a *ag* clever, smart; (*peg*) cunning ♦ *sm/f*: **fare il** ~ to (try to) be clever *o* smart; **fatti** ~! show a bit of sense!

fu'rente *ag*: ~ (**contro**) furious (with).

fure'ria *sf* (*MIL*) orderly room.

fu'retto *sm* ferret.

fur'fante *sm* rascal, scoundrel.

furgon'cino [furgon'tʃino] *sm* small van.

fur'gone *sm* van.

'furia *sf* (*ira*) fury, rage; (*fig: impeto*) fury, violence; (*fretta*) rush; **a** ~ **di** by dint of; **andare su tutte le** ~**e** to fly into a rage.

furi'bondo, a *ag* furious.

furi'ere *sm* quartermaster.

furi'oso, a *ag* furious; (*mare, vento*) raging.

'furono *vb vedi* **essere**.

fu'rore *sm* fury; (*esaltazione*) frenzy; **far** ~ to be all the rage.

furtiva'mente *av* furtively.

fur'tivo, a *ag* furtive.

'furto *sm* theft; ~ **con scasso** burglary.

'fusa *sfpl*: **fare le** ~ to purr.

fu'scello [fuʃ'ʃello] *sm* twig.

fu'seaux *smpl inv* leggings.

'fusi *etc vb vedi* **fondere**.

fu'sibile *sm* (*ELETTR*) fuse.

fusi'one *sf* (*di metalli*) fusion, melting; (*colata*) casting; (*COMM*) merger; (*fig*) merging.

'fuso, a *pp di* **fondere** ♦ *sm* (*FILATURA*) spindle; **diritto come un** ~ as stiff as a ramrod; ~ **orario** time zone.

fusoli'era *sf* (*AER*) fusillage.

fus'tagno [fus'taɲɲo] *sm* corduroy.

fus'tella *sf* (*su scatola di medicinali*) tear-off tab.

fusti'gare *vt* (*frustare*) to flog; (*fig: costumi*) to censure, denounce.

fus'tino *sm* (*di detersivo*) tub.

'fusto *sm* stem; (*ANAT, di albero*) trunk; (*recipiente*) drum, can; (*fam*) he-man.

'futile *ag* vain, futile.

futilità *sf inv* futility.

futu'rismo *sm* futurism.

G, g [dʒi] *sf o m inv* (*lettera*) G, g; **G come Genova** ≈ G for George.

g *abbr* (= *grammo*) g.

G7 [dʒi'sɛtte] *smpl* G7 (*Group of Seven*).

gabar'dine [gabar'din] *sm* (*tessuto*) gabardine; (*soprabito*) gabardine raincoat.

gab'bare *vt* to take in, dupe; ~**rsi** *vr*: ~**rsi di qn** to make fun of sb.

'gabbia *sf* cage; (*DIR*) dock; (*da imballaggio*) crate; **la** ~ **degli accusati** (*DIR*) the dock; ~ **dell'ascensore** lift (*BRIT*) *o* elevator (*US*) shaft; ~ **toracica** (*ANAT*) rib cage.

gabbi'ano *sm* (sea)gull.

gabi'netto *sm* (*MED etc*) consulting room; (*POL*) ministry; (*di decenza*) toilet, lavatory; (*INS: di fisica etc*) laboratory.

Ga'bon *sm*: **il** ~ Gabon.

ga'elico, a, ci, che *ag, sm* Gaelic.

gaffe [gaf] *sf inv* blunder, boob (*fam*).

gagli'ardo, a [gaʎ'ʎardo] *ag* strong, vigorous.

gai'ezza [ga'jettsa] *sf* gaiety, cheerfulness.

'gaio, a *ag* cheerful.

'gala *sf* (*sfarzo*) pomp; (*festa*) gala.

ga'lante *ag* gallant, courteous; (*avventura, poesia*) amorous.

galante'ria *sf* gallantry.

galantu'omo, pl galantu'omini *sm* gentleman.

Ga'lapagos *sfpl*: **le (isole)** ~ the Galapagos Islands.

ga'lassia *sf* galaxy.

gala'teo *sm* (good) manners *pl*, etiquette.

gale'otto *sm* (*rematore*) galley slave; (*carcerato*) convict.

ga'lera *sf* (*NAUT*) galley; (*prigione*) prison.

'galla *sf*: **a** ~ afloat; **venire a** ~ to surface, come to the surface; (*fig: verità*) to come out.

galleggia'mento [galleddʒa'mento] *sm* floating; **linea di** ~ (*di nave*) waterline.

galleggi'ante [galled'dʒante] *ag* floating ♦ *sm* (*natante*) barge; (*di pescatore, lenza, TECN*) float.

galleggi'are [galled'dʒare] *vi* to float.

galle'ria *sf* (*traforo*) tunnel; (*ARCHIT, d'arte*) gallery; (*TEAT*) circle; (*strada coperta con*

negozi) arcade; ~ **del vento** *o*
aerodinamica (*AER*) wind tunnel.
'**Galles** *sm*: **il** ~ Wales.
gal'lese *ag* Welsh ♦ *sm/f* Welshman/woman
♦ *sm* (*LING*) Welsh; **i G~i** the Welsh.
gal'letta *sf* cracker; (*NAUT*) ship's biscuit.
gal'letto *sm* young cock, cockerel; (*fig*)
cocky young man; **fare il** ~ to play the
gallant.
'**Gallia** *sf*: **la** ~ Gaul.
gal'lina *sf* hen; **andare a letto con le** ~**e** to
go to bed early.
gal'lismo *sm* machismo.
'**gallo** *sm* cock; **al canto del** ~ at daybreak,
at cockcrow; **fare il** ~ to play the gallant.
gal'lone *sm* piece of braid; (*MIL*) stripe;
(*unità di misura*) gallon.
galop'pare *vi* to gallop.
galop'pino *sm* errand boy; (*POL*)
canvasser.
ga'loppo *sm* gallop; **al** *o* **di** ~ at a gallop.
galvaniz'zare [galvanid'dzare] *vt* to
galvanize.
'**gamba** *sf* leg; (*asta: di lettera*) stem; **in** ~ (*in
buona salute*) well; (*bravo, sveglio*) bright,
smart; **prendere qc sotto** ~ (*fig*) to treat
sth too lightly; **scappare a** ~**e levate** to
take to one's heels; ~**e!** scatter!
gam'bale *sm* legging.
gambe'retto *sm* shrimp.
'**gambero** *sm* (*di acqua dolce*) crayfish; (*di
mare*) prawn.
'**Gambia** *sf*: **la** ~ the Gambia.
gambiz'zare [gambid'dzare] *vt* to kneecap.
'**gambo** *sm* stem; (*di frutta*) stalk.
ga'mella *sf* mess tin.
'**gamma** *sf* (*MUS*) scale; (*di colori, fig*)
range; ~ **di prodotti** product range.
ga'nascia, sce [ga'naʃʃa] *sf* jaw; ~**sce del
freno** (*AUT*) brake shoes.
'**gancio** ['gantʃo] *sm* hook.
'**Gange** ['gandʒe] *sm*: **il** ~ the Ganges.
'**gangheri** ['gangeri] *smpl*: **uscire dai** ~ (*fig*)
to fly into a temper.
gan'grena *sf* = **cancrena**.
'**gara** *sf* competition; (*SPORT*) competition;
contest; match; (: *corsa*) race; **fare a** ~ to
compete, vie; ~ **d'appalto** (*COMM*) tender.
ga'rage [ga'raʒ] *sm inv* garage.
ga'rante *sm/f* guarantor.
garan'tire *vt* to guarantee; (*debito*) to stand
surety for; (*dare per certo*) to assure.
garan'tismo *sm* protection of civil
liberties.
garan'tista, i, e *ag* concerned with civil
liberties.
garan'zia [garan'tsia] *sf* guarantee; (*pegno*)
security; **in** ~ under guarantee.

gar'bare *vi*: **non mi garba** I don't like it (*o*
him *etc*).
garba'tezza [garba'tettsa] *sf* courtesy,
politeness.
gar'bato, a *ag* courteous, polite.
'**garbo** *sm* (*buone maniere*) politeness,
courtesy; (*di vestito etc*) grace, style.
gar'buglio [gar'buʎʎo] *sm* tangle; (*fig*)
muddle, mess.
gareggi'are [gared'dʒare] *vi* to compete.
garga'nella *sf*: **a** ~ from the bottle.
garga'rismo *sm* gargle; **fare i** ~**i** to gargle.
ga'ritta *sf* (*di caserma*) sentry box.
ga'rofano *sm* carnation; **chiodo di** ~ clove.
gar'retto *sm* hock.
gar'rire *vi* to chirp.
'**garrulo, a** *ag* (*uccello*) chirping; (*persona:
loquace*) garrulous, talkative.
'**garza** ['gardza] *sf* (*per bende*) gauze.
gar'zone [gar'dzone] *sm* (*di negozio*) boy.
gas *sm inv* gas; **a tutto** ~ at full speed; **dare**
~ (*AUT*) to accelerate; ~ **lacrimogeno** tear
gas; ~ **naturale** natural gas.
ga'sare *etc* = **gassare** *etc*.
ga'sato, a *sm/f* (*fam: persona*) freak.
gas'dotto *sm* gas pipeline.
ga'solio *sm* diesel (oil).
ga's(s)are *vt* to aerate, carbonate;
(*asfissiare*) to gas; ~**rsi** *vr* (*fam*) to get
excited.
ga's(s)ato, a *ag* (*bibita*) aerated, fizzy.
gas'soso, a *ag* gaseous; gassy ♦ *sf* fizzy
drink.
'**gastrico, a, ci, che** *ag* gastric.
gast'rite *sf* gastritis.
gastroente'rite *sf* gastroenteritis.
gastrono'mia *sf* gastronomy.
gas'tronomo, a *sm/f* gourmet,
gastronome.
G.A.T.T. *sigla m* (= *General Agreement on
Tariffs and Trade*) GATT.
'**gatta** *sf* cat, she-cat; **una** ~ **da pelare** (*fam*)
a thankless task; **qui** ~ **ci cova!** I smell a
rat!, there's something fishy going on
here!
gatta'buia *sf* (*fam scherzoso: prigione*)
clink.
gat'tino *sm* kitten.
'**gatto** *sm* cat, tomcat; ~ **delle nevi** (*AUT,
SCI*) snowcat; ~ **a nove code** cat-o'-nine-
tails; ~ **selvatico** wildcat.
gatto'pardo *sm*: ~ **africano** serval; ~
americano ocelot.
gat'tuccio [gat'tuttʃo] *sm* dogfish.
gau'dente *sm/f* pleasure-seeker.
'**gaudio** *sm* joy, happiness.
ga'vetta *sf* (*MIL*) mess tin; **venire dalla** ~
(*MIL, fig*) to rise from the ranks.

'gazza ['gaddza] sf magpie.

gaz'zarra [gad'dzarra] sf racket, din.

gaz'zella [gad'dzɛlla] sf gazelle; (dei carabinieri) (high-speed) police car.

gaz'zetta [gad'dzetta] sf news sheet; G~ Ufficiale official publication containing details of new laws.

gaz'zoso, a [gad'dzoso] ag = gassoso.

Gazz. Uff. abbr = Gazzetta Ufficiale.

GB sigla (= Gran Bretagna) GB.

G.C. abbr = genio civile.

G.d.F. abbr = guardia di finanza.

GE sigla = Genova.

gel [dʒɛl] sm inv gel.

ge'lare [dʒe'lare] vt, vi, vb impers to freeze; mi ha gelato il sangue (fig) it made my blood run cold.

ge'lata [dʒe'lata] sf frost.

gela'taio, a [dʒela'tajo] sm/f ice-cream vendor.

gelate'ria [dʒelate'ria] sf ice-cream shop.

gela'tina [dʒela'tina] sf gelatine; ~ esplosiva gelignite; ~ di frutta fruit jelly.

gelati'noso, a [dʒelati'noso] ag gelatinous, jelly-like.

ge'lato, a [dʒe'lato] ag frozen ♦ sm ice cream.

'gelido, a ['dʒɛlido] ag icy, ice-cold.

'gelo ['dʒɛlo] sm (temperatura) intense cold; (brina) frost; (fig) chill.

ge'lone [dʒe'lone] sm chilblain.

gelo'sia [dʒelo'sia] sf jealousy.

ge'loso, a [dʒe'loso] ag jealous.

'gelso ['dʒɛlso] sm mulberry (tree).

gelso'mino [dʒelso'mino] sm jasmine.

gemel'laggio [dʒemel'laddʒo] sm twinning.

gemel'lare [dʒemel'lare] ag twin cpd ♦ vt (città) to twin.

ge'mello, a [dʒe'mɛllo] ag, sm/f twin; ~i smpl (di camicia) cufflinks; (dello zodiaco): G~i Gemini sg; essere dei G~i to be Gemini.

'gemere ['dʒɛmere] vi to moan, groan; (cigolare) to creak; (gocciolare) to drip, ooze.

'gemito ['dʒɛmito] sm moan, groan.

'gemma ['dʒɛmma] sf (BOT) bud; (pietra preziosa) gem.

Gen. abbr (MIL: = generale) Gen.

gen. abbr (= generale, generalmente) gen.

gen'darme [dʒen'darme] sm policeman; (fig) martinet.

'gene ['dʒɛne] sm gene.

genealo'gia, 'gie [dʒenealo'dʒia] sf genealogy.

genea'logico, a, ci, che [dʒenea'lɔdʒiko] ag genealogical; albero ~ family tree.

gene'rale [dʒene'rale] ag, sm general; in ~ (per sommi capi) in general terms; (di

solito) usually, in general; a ~ richiesta by popular request.

generalità [dʒenerali'ta] sfpl (dati d'identità) particulars.

generaliz'zare [dʒeneralid'dzare] vt, vi to generalize.

generalizzazi'one [dʒeneraliddzat'tsjone] sf generalization.

general'mente [dʒeneral'mente] av generally.

gene'rare [dʒene'rare] vt (dar vita) to give birth to; (produrre) to produce; (causare) to arouse; (TECN) to produce, generate.

genera'tore [dʒenera'tore] sm (TECN) generator.

generazi'one [dʒenerat'tsjone] sf generation.

'genere ['dʒɛnere] sm kind, type, sort; (BIOL) genus; (merce) article, product; (LING) gender; (ARTE, LETTERATURA) genre; in ~ generally, as a rule; cose del o di questo ~ such things; il ~ umano mankind; ~i alimentari foodstuffs; ~i di consumo consumer goods; ~i di prima necessità basic essentials.

ge'nerico, a, ci, che [dʒe'nɛriko] ag generic; (vago) vague, imprecise; medico ~ general practitioner.

'genero ['dʒɛnero] sm son-in-law.

generosità [dʒenerosi'ta] sf generosity.

gene'roso, a [dʒene'roso] ag generous.

'genesi ['dʒɛnezi] sf genesis.

ge'netico, a, ci, che [dʒe'nɛtiko] ag genetic ♦ sf genetics sg.

gen'giva [dʒen'dʒiva] sf (ANAT) gum.

ge'nia [dʒe'nia] sf (peg) mob, gang.

geni'ale [dʒe'njale] ag (persona) of genius; (idea) ingenious, brilliant.

'genio ['dʒɛnjo] sm genius; (attitudine, talento) talent, flair, genius; andare a ~ a qn to be to sb's liking, appeal to sb; ~ civile civil engineers pl; il ~ (militare) the Engineers.

geni'tale [dʒeni'tale] ag genital; ~i smpl genitals.

geni'tore [dʒeni'tore] sm parent, father o mother; ~i smpl parents.

genn. abbr (= gennaio) Jan.

gen'naio [dʒen'najo] sm January; per fraseologia vedi luglio.

geno'cidio [dʒeno't ʃidjo] sm genocide.

'Genova ['dʒɛnova] sf Genoa.

geno'vese [dʒeno'vese] ag, sm/f Genoese (pl inv).

gen'taglia [dʒen'taʎʎa] sf (peg) rabble.

'gente ['dʒɛnte] sf people pl.

gentil'donna [dʒentil'dɔnna] sf lady.

gen'tile [dʒen'tile] ag (persona, atto) kind;

(: *garbato*) courteous, polite; (*nelle lettere*):
G~ **Signore** Dear Sir; (: *sulla busta*): **G**~
Signor Fernando Villa Mr Fernando Villa.

genti'lezza [dʒenti'lettsa] *sf* kindness;
courtesy, politeness; **per** ~ (*per favore*)
please.

gentilu'omo, *pl* **gentilu'omini**
[dʒenti'lwɔmo] *sm* gentleman.

genuflessi'one [dʒenufles'sjone] *sf*
genuflection.

genu'ino, a [dʒenu'ino] *ag* (*prodotto*)
natural; (*persona, sentimento*)
genuine, sincere.

geogra'fia [dʒeogra'fia] *sf* geography.

geo'grafico, a, ci, che [dʒeo'grafiko] *ag*
geographical.

ge'ografo, a [dʒe'ɔgrafo] *sm/f* geographer.

geolo'gia [dʒeolo'dʒia] *sf* geology.

geo'logico, a, ci, che [dʒeo'lɔdʒiko] *ag*
geological.

ge'ometra, i, e [dʒe'ɔmetra] *sm/f*
(*professionista*) surveyor.

geome'tria [dʒeome'tria] *sf* geometry.

geo'metrico, a, ci, che [dʒeo'mɛtriko] *ag*
geometric(al).

geopo'litico, a, ci, che [dʒeopo'litiko] *ag*
geopolitical.

Ge'orgia [dʒe'ɔrdʒa] *sf* Georgia.

geor'giano, a [dʒeor'dʒano] *ag, sm/f*
Georgian.

ge'ranio [dʒe'ranjo] *sm* geranium.

ge'rarca, chi [dʒe'rarka] *sm* (*STORIA: nel
fascismo*) party official.

gerar'chia [dʒerar'kia] *sf* hierarchy.

ge'rarchico, a, ci, che [dʒe'rarkiko] *ag*
hierarchical.

ge'rente [dʒe'rɛnte] *sm/f* manager/
manageress.

ge'renza [dʒe'rɛntsa] *sf* management.

ger'gale [dʒer'gale] *ag* slang *cpd*.

'gergo, ghi ['dʒergo] *sm* jargon; slang.

geria'tria [dʒerja'tria] *sf* geriatrics *sg*.

geri'atrico, a, ci, che [dʒe'rjatriko] *ag*
geriatric.

'gerla ['dʒɛrla] *sf* conical wicker basket.

Ger'mania [dʒer'manja] *sf*: **la** ~ Germany;
la ~ **occidentale/orientale** West/East
Germany.

'germe ['dʒɛrme] *sm* germ; (*fig*) seed.

germinazi'one [dʒerminat'tsjone] *sf*
germination.

germogli'are [dʒermoʎ'ʎare] *vi* (*emettere
germogli*) to sprout; (*germinare*) to
germinate.

ger'moglio [dʒer'moʎʎo] *sm* shoot;
(*gemma*) bud.

gero'glifico, ci [dʒero'glifiko] *sm*
hieroglyphic.

geron'tologo, a, gi, ghe [dʒeron'tɔlogo]
sm/f specialist in geriatrics.

ge'rundio [dʒe'rundjo] *sm* gerund.

Gerusa'lemme [dʒeruza'lɛmme] *sf*
Jerusalem.

'gesso ['dʒɛsso] *sm* chalk; (*SCULTURA, MED,
EDIL*) plaster; (*statua*) plaster figure;
(*minerale*) gypsum.

'gesta ['dʒɛsta] *sfpl* (*letterario*) deeds, feats.

ges'tante [dʒes'tante] *sf* expectant mother.

gestazi'one [dʒestat'tsjone] *sf* gestation.

gestico'lare [dʒestiko'lare] *vi* to
gesticulate.

gestio'nale [dʒestjo'nale] *ag*
administrative, management *cpd*.

gesti'one [dʒes'tjone] *sf* management; ~ **di
magazzino** stock control; ~ **patrimoniale**
investment management.

ges'tire [dʒes'tire] *vt* to run, manage.

'gesto ['dʒɛsto] *sm* gesture.

ges'tore [dʒes'tore] *sm* manager.

Gesù [dʒe'zu] *sm* Jesus; ~ **bambino** the
Christ Child.

gesu'ita, i [dʒezu'ita] *sm* Jesuit.

get'tare [dʒet'tare] *vt* to throw; (*anche*: ~
via) to throw away *o* out; (*SCULTURA*) to
cast; (*EDIL*) to lay; (*acqua*) to spout; (*grido*)
to utter; **~rsi** *vr*: **~rsi in** (*impresa*) to throw
o.s. into; (*mischia*) to hurl o.s. into; (*sog:
fiume*) to flow into; ~ **uno sguardo su** to
take a quick look at.

get'tata [dʒet'tata] *sf* (*di cemento, gesso,
metalli*) cast; (*diga*) jetty.

'gettito ['dʒettito] *sm* revenue.

'getto ['dʒetto] *sm* (*di gas, liquido, AER*) jet;
(*BOT*) shoot; **a** ~ **continuo**
uninterruptedly; **di** ~ (*fig*) straight off, in
one go.

get'tone [dʒet'tone] *sm* token; (*per giochi*)
counter; (: *roulette etc*) chip; ~ **di presenza**
attendance fee; ~ **telefonico** telephone
token.

gettoni'era [dʒetto'njɛra] *sf* telephone-
token dispenser.

'geyser ['gaizə] *sm inv* geyser.

'Ghana ['gana] *sm*: **il** ~ Ghana.

'ghenga, ghe ['gɛnga] *sf* (*fam*) gang,
crowd.

ghe'pardo [ge'pardo] *sm* cheetah.

gher'mire [ger'mire] *vt* to grasp, clasp,
clutch.

'ghetta ['getta] *sf* (*gambale*) gaiter.

ghettiz'zare [gettid'dzare] *vt* to segregate.

'ghetto ['getto] *sm* ghetto.

ghiacci'aia [gjat'tʃaja] *sf* (*anche fig*) icebox.

ghiacci'aio [gjat'tʃajo] *sm* glacier.

ghiacci'are [gjat'tʃare] *vt* to freeze; (*fig*): ~
qn to make sb's blood run cold ♦ *vi* to

freeze, ice over.
ghiacci'ato, a [gjat'tʃato] *ag* frozen; (*bevanda*) ice-cold.
ghi'accio ['gjattʃo] *sm* ice.
ghiacci'olo [gjat'tʃɔlo] *sm* icicle; (*tipo di gelato*) ice lolly (*BRIT*), popsicle (*US*).
ghi'aia ['gjaja] *sf* gravel.
ghi'anda ['gjanda] *sf* (*BOT*) acorn.
ghi'andola ['gjandola] *sf* gland.
ghiando'lare [gjando'lare] *ag* glandular.
ghigliot'tina [giʎʎot'tina] *sf* guillotine.
ghi'gnare [giɲ'ɲare] *vi* to sneer.
'ghigno ['giɲɲo] *sm* (*espressione*) sneer; (*risata*) mocking laugh.
'ghingheri ['gingeri] *smpl*: **in** ~ all dolled up; **mettersi in** ~ to put on one's Sunday best.
ghi'otto, a ['gjotto] *ag* greedy; (*cibo*) delicious, appetizing.
ghiot'tone, a [gjot'tone] *smf* glutton.
ghiottone'ria [gjottone'ria] *sf* greed, gluttony; (*cibo*) delicacy, titbit (*BRIT*), tidbit (*US*).
ghiri'goro [giri'gɔro] *sm* scribble, squiggle.
ghir'landa [gir'landa] *sf* garland, wreath.
'ghiro ['giro] *sm* dormouse.
'ghisa ['giza] *sf* cast iron.
G.I. *abbr* = **giudice istruttore**.
già [dʒa] *av* already; (*ex, in precedenza*) formerly ♦ *escl* of course!, yes indeed!; ~ **che ci sei** ... while you are at it ....
gi'acca, che ['dʒakka] *sf* jacket; ~ **a vento** windcheater (*BRIT*), windbreaker (*US*).
giacché [dʒak'ke] *cong* since, as.
giac'chetta [dʒak'ketta] *sf* (light) jacket.
'giaccio *etc* ['dʒattʃo] *vb vedi* **giacere**.
giac'cone [dʒak'kone] *sm* heavy jacket.
gia'cenza [dʒa'tʃɛntsa] *sf*: **merce in** ~ goods in stock; **capitale in** ~ uninvested capital; ~**e di magazzino** unsold stock.
gia'cere [dʒa'tʃere] *vi* to lie.
giaci'mento [dʒatʃi'mento] *sm* deposit.
gia'cinto [dʒa'tʃinto] *sm* hyacinth.
giaci'uto, a [dʒa'tʃuto] *pp di* **giacere**.
gi'acqui *etc* ['dʒakkwi] *vb vedi* **giacere**.
gi'ada ['dʒada] *sf* jade.
giaggi'olo [dʒad'dʒɔlo] *sm* iris.
giagu'aro [dʒa'gwaro] *sm* jaguar.
gial'lastro, a [dʒal'lastro] *ag* yellowish; (*carnagione*) sallow.
gi'allo ['dʒallo] *ag* yellow; (*carnagione*) sallow ♦ *sm* yellow; (*anche:* **romanzo** ~) detective novel; (*anche:* **film** ~) detective film; ~ **dell'uovo** yolk; **il mar G**~ the Yellow Sea.
gial'lognolo, a [dʒal'loɲɲolo] *ag* yellowish, dirty yellow.
Gia'maica [dʒa'maika] *sf*: **la** ~ Jamaica.

giamai'cano, a [dʒamai'kano] *ag, smf* Jamaican.
giam'mai [dʒam'mai] *av* never.
Giap'pone [dʒap'pone] *sm*: **il** ~ Japan.
giappo'nese [dʒappo'nese] *ag, smf, sm* Japanese *inv*.
gi'ara ['dʒara] *sf* jar.
giardi'naggio [dʒardi'nadd3o] *sm* gardening.
giardi'netta [dʒardi'netta] *sf* estate car (*BRIT*), station wagon (*US*).
giardini'ere, a [dʒardi'njɛre] *smf* gardener ♦ *sf* (*misto di sottaceti*) mixed pickles *pl*; (*automobile*) = **giardinetta**.
giar'dino [dʒar'dino] *sm* garden; ~ **d'infanzia** nursery school; ~ **pubblico** public gardens *pl*, (public) park; ~ **zoologico** zoo.
giarretti'era [dʒarret'tjɛra] *sf* garter.
Gi'ava ['dʒava] *sf* Java.
giavel'lotto [dʒavel'lɔtto] *sm* javelin.
gib'boso, a [dʒib'boso] *ag* (*superficie*) bumpy; (*naso*) crooked.
Gibil'terra [dʒibil'tɛrra] *sf* Gibraltar.
gi'gante [dʒi'gante] *smf* giant ♦ *ag* giant, gigantic; (*COMM*) giant-size.
gigan'tesco, a, schi, sche [dʒigan'tesko] *ag* gigantic.
gigantogra'fia [dʒigantogra'fia] *sf* (*FOT*) blow-up.
'giglio ['dʒiʎʎo] *sm* lily.
gilè [dʒi'lɛ] *sm inv* waistcoat.
gin [dʒin] *sm inv* gin.
gin'cana [dʒin'kana] *sf* gymkhana.
ginecolo'gia [dʒinekolo'dʒia] *sf* gynaecology (*BRIT*), gynecology (*US*).
gine'cologo, a, gi, ghe [dʒine'kɔlogo] *smf* gynaecologist (*BRIT*), gynecologist (*US*).
gi'nepro [dʒi'nepro] *sm* juniper.
gi'nestra [dʒi'nɛstra] *sf* (*BOT*) broom.
Gi'nevra [dʒi'nevra] *sf* Geneva; **il Lago di** ~ Lake Geneva.
gingil'larsi [dʒindʒil'larsi] *vr* to fritter away one's time; (*giocare*): ~ **con** to fiddle with.
gin'gillo [dʒin'dʒillo] *sm* plaything.
gin'nasio [dʒin'nazjo] *sm* the 4th and 5th year of secondary school in Italy.
gin'nasta, i, e [dʒin'nasta] *smf* gymnast.
gin'nastica [dʒin'nastika] *sf* gymnastics *sg*; (*esercizio fisico*) keep-fit exercises *pl*; (*INS*) physical education.
'ginnico, a, ci, che ['dʒinniko] *ag* gymnastic.
gi'nocchio [dʒi'nɔkkjo], *pl(m)* **gi'nocchi** *o pl(f)* **gi'nocchia** *sm* knee; **stare in** ~ to kneel, be on one's knees; **mettersi in** ~ to kneel (down).
ginocchi'oni [dʒinok'kjoni] *av* on one's

knees.

gio'care [dʒo'kare] *vt* to play; (*scommettere*) to stake, wager, bet; (*ingannare*) to take in ♦ *vi* to play; (*a roulette etc*) to gamble; (*fig*) to play a part, be important; (*TECN: meccanismo*) to be loose; ~ **a** (*gioco, sport*) to play; (*cavalli*) to bet on; ~ **d'astuzia** to be crafty; ~**rsi la carriera** to put one's career at risk; ~**rsi tutto** to risk everything; **a che gioco giochiamo?** what are you playing at?

gioca'tore, 'trice [dʒoka'tore] *sm/f* player; gambler.

gio'cattolo [dʒo'kattolo] *sm* toy.

giocherel'lare [dʒokerel'lare] *vi*: ~ **con** to play with.

giocherò *etc* [dʒoke'rɔ] *vb vedi* **giocare.**

gio'chetto [dʒo'ketto] *sm* (*gioco*) game; (*tranello*) trick; (*fig*): **è un** ~ it's child's play.

gi'oco, chi ['dʒɔko] *sm* game; (*divertimento, TECN*) play; (*al casinò*) gambling; (*CARTE*) hand; (*insieme di pezzi etc necessari per un gioco*) set; **per** ~ for fun; **fare il doppio** ~ **con qn** to double-cross sb; **prendersi** ~ **di qn** to pull sb's leg; **stare al** ~ **di qn** to play along with sb; **è in** ~ **la mia reputazione** my reputation is at stake; ~ **d'azzardo** game of chance; ~ **della palla** ball game; ~ **degli scacchi** chess set; **i G**~**chi Olimpici** the Olympic Games.

gioco'forza [dʒoko'fɔrtsa] *sm*: **essere** ~ to be inevitable.

giocoli'ere [dʒoko'ljɛre] *sm* juggler.

gio'coso, a [dʒo'koso] *ag* playful, jesting.

gio'gaia [dʒo'gaja] *sf* (*GEO*) range of mountains.

gi'ogo, ghi ['dʒogo] *sm* yoke.

gi'oia ['dʒɔja] *sf* joy, delight; (*pietra preziosa*) jewel, precious stone.

gioiel'leria [dʒojelle'ria] *sf* jeweller's (*BRIT*) *o* jeweler's (*US*) craft; (*negozio*) jewel(l)er's (shop).

gioiel'liere, a [dʒojel'ljɛre] *sm/f* jeweller (*BRIT*), jeweler (*US*).

gioi'ello [dʒo'jɛllo] *sm* jewel, piece of jewellery (*BRIT*) *o* jewelry (*US*); ~**i** *smpl* (*gioie*) jewel(l)ery *sg*.

gioi'oso, a [dʒo'joso] *ag* joyful.

Gior'dania [dʒor'danja] *sf*: **la** ~ Jordan.

Gior'dano [dʒor'dano] *sm*: **il** ~ the Jordan.

gior'dano, a [dʒor'dano] *ag, sm/f* Jordanian.

giorna'laio, a [dʒorna'lajo] *sm/f* newsagent (*BRIT*), newsdealer (*US*).

gior'nale [dʒor'nale] *sm* (*news*)paper; (*diario*) journal, diary; (*COMM*) journal; ~ **di bordo** (*NAUT*) ship's log; ~ **radio** radio news *sg*.

giorna'letto [dʒorna'letto] *sm* (children's) comic.

giornali'ero, a [dʒorna'ljero] *ag* daily.

giorna'lino [dʒorna'lino] *sm* children's comic.

giorna'lismo [dʒorna'lizmo] *sm* journalism.

giorna'lista, i, e [dʒorna'lista] *sm/f* journalist.

giorna'listico, a, ci, che [dʒorna'listiko] *ag* journalistic; **stile** ~ journalese.

gior'nalmente [dʒornal'mente] *av* daily.

gior'nata [dʒor'nata] *sf* day; (*paga*) day's wages, day's pay; **durante la** ~ **di ieri** yesterday; **fresco di** ~ (*uovo*) freshly laid; **vivere alla** ~ to live from day to day; ~ **lavorativa** working day.

gi'orno ['dʒorno] *sm* day; (*opposto alla notte*) day, daytime; (*luce del* ~) daylight; **al** ~ per day; **di** ~ by day; ~ **per** ~ day by day; **al** ~ **d'oggi** nowadays; **tutto il santo** ~ all day long; **il G**~ **dei Morti** *vedi nota nel riquadro.*

IL GIORNO DEI MORTI

Il Giorno dei Morti, *All Souls' Day, falls on 2 November. At this time of year people visit cemeteries to lay flowers on the graves of their loved ones.*

---

gi'ostra ['dʒɔstra] *sf* (*per bimbi*) merry-go-round; (*torneo storico*) joust.

gios'trare [dʒos'trare] *vi* (*STORIA*) to joust, tilt; ~**rsi** *vr* to manage.

giov. *abbr* (= *giovedì*) Thur(s).

giova'mento [dʒova'mento] *sm* benefit, help.

gi'ovane ['dʒovane] *ag* young; (*aspetto*) youthful ♦ *sm/f* youth/girl, young man/woman; **i** ~**i** young people; **è** ~ **del mestiere** he's new to the job.

giova'netto, a [dʒova'netto] *sm/f* young man/woman.

giova'nile [dʒova'nile] *ag* youthful; (*scritti*) early; (*errore*) of youth.

giova'notto [dʒova'nɔtto] *sm* young man.

gio'vare [dʒo'vare] *vi*: ~ **a** (*essere utile*) to be useful to; (*far bene*) to be good for ♦ *vb impers* (*essere bene, utile*) to be useful; ~**rsi** *vr*: ~ **rsi di qc** to make use of sth; **a che giova prendersela?** what's the point of getting upset?

Gi'ove ['dʒove] *sm* (*MITOLOGIA*) Jove; (*ASTR*) Jupiter.

giovedì [dʒove'di] *sm inv* Thursday; *per fraseologia vedi* **martedì.**

gio'venca, che [dʒo'vɛnka] *sf* heifer.

gioventù [dʒoven'tu] *sf* (*periodo*) youth; (*i*

giovani) young people *pl*, youth.

giovi'ale [dʒo'vjale] *ag* jovial, jolly.

giovi'nastro [dʒovi'nastro] *sm* young thug.

giovin'cello [dʒovin'tʃɛllo] *sm* young lad.

giovi'nezza [dʒovi'nettsa] *sf* youth.

gip [dʒip] *sigla m inv* (= *giudice per le indagini preliminari*) judge for preliminary enquiries.

gira'dischi [dʒira'diski] *sm inv* record player.

gi'raffa [dʒi'raffa] *sf* giraffe; (*TV, CINE, RADIO*) boom.

gira'mento [dʒira'mento] *sm*: ~ **di testa** fit of dizziness.

gira'mondo [dʒira'mondo] *sm/f inv* globetrotter.

gi'randola [dʒi'randola] *sf* (*fuoco d'artificio*) Catherine wheel; (*giocattolo*) toy windmill; (*banderuola*) weather vane, weathercock.

gi'rante [dʒi'rante] *sm/f* (*di assegno*) endorser.

gi'rare [dʒi'rare] *vt* (*far ruotare*) to turn; (*percorrere, visitare*) to go round; (*CINE*) to shoot; (: *film: come regista*) to make; (*COMM*) to endorse ♦ *vi* to turn; (*più veloce*) to spin; (*andare in giro*) to wander, go around; ~**rsi** *vr* to turn; ~ **attorno a** to go round; to revolve round; **si girava e rigirava nel letto** he tossed and turned in bed; **far** ~ **la testa a qn** to make sb dizzy; (*fig*) to turn sb's head; **gira al largo** keep your distance; **girala come ti pare** (*fig*) look at it whichever way you like; **gira e rigira** ... after a lot of driving (*o* walking) about ...; (*fig*) whichever way you look at it; **cosa ti gira?** (*fam*) what's got into you?; **mi ha fatto** ~ **le scatole** (*fam*) he drove me crazy.

girar'rosto [dʒirar'rɔsto] *sm* (*CUC*) spit.

gira'sole [dʒira'sole] *sm* sunflower.

gi'rata [dʒi'rata] *sf* (*passeggiata*) stroll; (*con veicolo*) drive; (*COMM*) endorsement.

gira'tario, a [dʒira'tarjo] *sm/f* endorsee.

gira'volta [dʒira'vɔlta] *sf* twirl, turn; (*curva*) sharp bend; (*fig*) about-turn.

gi'rello [dʒi'rɛllo] *sm* (*di bambino*) Babywalker ® (*BRIT*), go-cart (*US*); (*taglio di carne*) topside (*BRIT*), top round (*US*).

gi'retto [dʒi'retto] *sm* (*passeggiata*) walk, stroll; (: *in macchina*) drive, spin; (: *in bicicletta*) ride.

gi'revole [dʒi'revole] *ag* revolving, turning.

gi'rino [dʒi'rino] *sm* tadpole.

'giro ['dʒiro] *sm* (*circuito, cerchio*) circle; (*di chiave, manovella*) turn; (*viaggio*) tour, excursion; (*passeggiata*) stroll, walk; (*in macchina*) drive; (*in bicicletta*) ride; (*SPORT*:

della pista) lap; (*di denaro*) circulation; (*CARTE*) hand; (*TECN*) revolution; **fare un** ~ to go for a walk (*o* a drive *o* a ride); **fare il** ~ **di** (*parco, città*) to go round; **andare in** ~ (*a piedi*) to go about, walk around; **guardarsi in** ~ to look around; **prendere in** ~ **qn** (*fig*) to take sb for a ride; **a stretto** ~ **di posta** by return of post; **nel** ~ **di un mese** in a month's time; **essere nel** ~ (*fig*) to belong to a circle (of friends); ~ **d'affari** (*viaggio*) business tour; (*COMM*) turnover; ~ **di parole** circumlocution; ~ **di prova** (*AUT*) test drive; ~ **turistico** sightseeing tour; ~ **vita** waist measurement.

giro'collo [dʒiro'kɔllo] *sm*: **a** ~ crewneck *cpd*.

giro'conto [dʒiro'konto] *sm* (*ECON*) credit transfer.

gi'rone [dʒi'rone] *sm* (*SPORT*) series of games; ~ **di andata/ritorno** (*CALCIO*) first/second half of the season.

gironzo'lare [dʒirondzo'lare] *vi* to stroll about.

giro'tondo [dʒiro'tondo] *sm* ring-a-ring-o'roses (*BRIT*), ring-around-the-rosey (*US*); **in** ~ in a circle.

girova'gare [dʒirova'gare] *vi* to wander about.

gi'rovago, a, ghi, ghe [dʒi'rɔvago] *sm/f* (*vagabondo*) tramp; (*venditore*) peddler; **una compagnia di** ~**ghi** (*attori*) a company of strolling actors.

'gita ['dʒita] *sf* excursion, trip; **fare una** ~ to go for a trip, go on an outing.

gi'tano, a [dʒi'tano] *sm/f* gipsy.

gi'tante [dʒi'tante] *sm/f* member of a tour.

giù [dʒu] *av* down; (*dabbasso*) downstairs; **in** ~ downwards, down; **la mia casa è un po'** **più in** ~ my house is a bit further on; ~ **di** **lì** (*pressappoco*) thereabouts; **bambini dai** **6 anni in** ~ children aged 6 and under; **cadere** ~ **per le scale** to fall down the stairs; ~ **le mani!** hands off!; **essere** ~ (*fig: di salute*) to be run down; (: *di spirito*) to be depressed; **quel tipo non** **mi va** ~ I can't stand that guy.

gi'ubba ['dʒubba] *sf* jacket.

giub'botto [dʒub'bɔtto] *sm* jerkin; ~ **antiproiettile** bulletproof vest.

giubi'lare [dʒubi'lare] *vi* to rejoice.

gi'ubilo ['dʒubilo] *sm* rejoicing.

giudi'care [dʒudi'kare] *vt* to judge; (*accusato*) to try; (*lite*) to arbitrate in; ~ **qn/qc bello** to consider sb/sth (to be) beautiful.

giudi'cato [dʒudi'kato] *sm* (*DIR*): **passare in** ~ to pass final judgment.

gi'udice ['dʒuditʃe] *sm* judge; ~ **collegiale** member of the court; ~ **conciliatore** justice of the peace; ~ **istruttore** examining (*BRIT*) *o* committing (*US*) magistrate; ~ **popolare** member of a jury.

giudizi'ale [dʒudit'tsjale] *ag* judicial.

giudizi'ario, a [dʒudit'tsjarjo] *ag* legal, judicial.

giu'dizio [dʒu'dittsjo] *sm* judgment; (*opinione*) opinion; (*DIR*) judgment, sentence; (: *processo*) trial; (: *verdetto*) verdict; **aver** ~ to be wise *o* prudent; **essere in attesa di** ~ to be awaiting trial; **citare in** ~ to summons; **l'imputato è stato rinviato a** ~ the accused has been committed for trial.

giudizi'oso, a [dʒudit'tsjoso] *ag* prudent, judicious.

gi'uggiola ['dʒuddʒola] *sf*: **andare in brodo di** ~**e** (*fam*) to be over the moon.

gi'ugno ['dʒuɲɲo] *sm* June; *per fraseologia vedi* **luglio.**

giu'livo, a [dʒu'livo] *ag* merry.

giul'lare [dʒul'lare] *sm* jester.

giu'menta [dʒu'menta] *sf* mare.

gi'unco, chi ['dʒunko] *sm* (*BOT*) rush.

gi'ungere ['dʒundʒere] *vi* to arrive ♦ *vt* (*mani etc*) to join; ~ **a** to arrive at, reach; ~ **nuovo a qn** to come as news to sb; ~ **in porto** to reach harbour; (*fig*) to be brought to a successful outcome.

gi'ungla ['dʒungla] *sf* jungle.

gi'unsi *etc* ['dʒunsi] *vb vedi* **giungere.**

gi'unto, a ['dʒunto] *pp di* **giungere** ♦ *sm* (*TECN*) coupling, joint ♦ *sf* addition; (*organo esecutivo, amministrativo*) council, board; **per** ~**a** into the bargain, in addition; ~**a militare** military junta; *vedi anche* **Comune; Provincia; Regione.**

giun'tura [dʒun'tura] *sf* joint.

giuo'care [dʒwo'kare] *vt, vi* = **giocare.**

giu'oco ['dʒwɔko] *sm* = **gioco.**

giura'mento [dʒura'mento] *sm* oath; ~ **falso** perjury.

giu'rare [dʒu'rare] *vt* to swear ♦ *vi* to swear, take an oath; **gliel'ho giurata** I swore I would get even with him.

giu'rato, a [dʒu'rato] *ag*: **nemico** ~ sworn enemy ♦ *sm/f* juror, juryman/woman.

giu'ria [dʒu'ria] *sf* jury.

giu'ridico, a, ci, che [dʒu'ridiko] *ag* legal.

giurisdizi'one [dʒurizdit'tsjone] *sf* jurisdiction.

giurispru'denza [dʒurispru'dɛntsa] *sf* jurisprudence.

giu'rista, i, e [dʒu'rista] *sm/f* jurist.

giustap'porre [dʒustap'porre] *vt* to juxtapose.

giustapposizi'one [dʒustappozit'tsjone] *sf* juxtaposition.

giustap'posto, a [dʒustap'posto] *pp di* **giustapporre.**

giustifi'care [dʒustifi'kare] *vt* to justify; ~**rsi** *vr*: ~**rsi di** *o* **per qc** to justify *o* excuse o.s. for sth.

giustifica'tivo, a [dʒustifika'tivo] *ag* (*AMM*): **nota** *o* **pezza** ~**a** receipt.

giustificazi'one [dʒustifikat'tsjone] *sf* justification; (*INS*) (note of) excuse.

gius'tizia [dʒus'tittsja] *sf* justice; **farsi** ~ (**da sé**) (*vendicarsi*) to take the law into one's own hands.

giustizi'are [dʒustit'tsjare] *vt* to execute, put to death.

giustizi'ere [dʒustit'tsjɛre] *sm* executioner.

gi'usto, a ['dʒusto] *ag* (*equo*) fair, just; (*vero*) true, correct; (*adatto*) right, suitable; (*preciso*) exact, correct ♦ *av* (*esattamente*) exactly, precisely; (*per l'appunto, appena*) just; **arrivare** ~ to arrive just in time; **ho** ~ **bisogno di te** you're just the person I need.

'glabro, a *ag* hairless.

glaci'ale [gla'tʃale] *ag* glacial.

gla'diolo *sm* gladiolus.

'glandola *sf* = **ghiandola.**

'glassa *sf* (*CUC*) icing.

glau'coma *sm* glaucoma.

gli [ʎi] *det mpl* (*dav V, s impura, gn, pn, ps, x, z*) the ♦ *pron* (*a lui*) to him; (*a esso*) to it; (*in coppia con lo, la, li, le, ne: a lui, a lei, a loro etc*): **gliele do** I'm giving them to him (*o* her *o* them); **gliene ho parlato** I spoke to him (*o* her *o* them) about it; *vedi anche* **il.**

glice'mia [glitʃe'mia] *sf* glycaemia.

glice'rina [glitʃe'rina] *sf* glycerine.

'glicine ['glitʃine] *sm* wistaria.

gli'ela *etc* ['ʎela] *vedi* **gli.**

glo'bale *ag* overall; (*vista*) global.

'globo *sm* globe.

'globulo *sm* (*ANAT*): ~ **rosso/bianco** red/white corpuscle.

'gloria *sf* glory; **farsi** ~ **di qc** to pride o.s. on sth, take pride in sth.

glori'arsi *vr*: ~ **di qc** to pride o.s. on sth, glory *o* take pride in sth.

glorifi'care *vt* to glorify.

glori'oso, a *ag* glorious.

glos'sario *sm* glossary.

glu'cosio *sm* glucose.

'gluteo *sm* gluteus; ~**i** *smpl* buttocks.

GM *abbr* = **genio militare.**

'gnocchi ['ɲɔkki] *smpl* (*CUC*) *small dumplings made of semolina pasta or potato.*

'gnomo ['ɲɔmo] *sm* gnome.

'gnorri ['ɲɔrri] *sm/f inv*: non fare lo ~! stop acting as if you didn't know anything about it!

GO *sigla* = *Gorizia*.

'goal ['goul] *sm inv* (*SPORT*) goal.

'gobba *sf* (*ANAT*) hump; (*protuberanza*) bump.

'gobbo, a *ag* hunchbacked; (*ricurvo*) round-shouldered ♦ *sm/f* hunchback.

'Gobi *smpl*: il Deserto dei ~ the Gobi Desert.

'goccia, ce ['gottʃa] *sf* drop; ~ di rugiada dewdrop; somigliarsi come due ~ce d'acqua to be as like as two peas in a pod; è la ~ che fa traboccare il vaso! it's the last straw!

'goccio ['gottʃo] *sm* drop, spot.

goccio'lare [gottʃo'lare] *vi, vt* to drip.

goccio'lio [gottʃo'lio] *sm* dripping.

go'dere *vi* (*compiacersi*): ~ (di) to be delighted (at), rejoice (at); (*trarre vantaggio*): ~ di to enjoy, benefit from ♦ *vt* to enjoy; ~rsi la vita to enjoy life; godersela to have a good time, enjoy o.s.

godi'mento *sm* enjoyment.

godrò *etc vb vedi* godere.

gof'faggine [gof'faddʒine] *sf* clumsiness.

'goffo, a *ag* clumsy, awkward.

'gogna ['goɲɲa] *sf* pillory.

gol *sm inv* = goal.

'gola *sf* (*ANAT*) throat; (*golosità*) gluttony, greed; (*di camino*) flue; (*di monte*) gorge; fare ~ (*anche fig*) to tempt; ricacciare il pianto *o* le lacrime in ~ to swallow one's tears.

go'letta *sf* (*NAUT*) schooner.

golf *sm inv* (*SPORT*) golf; (*maglia*) cardigan.

'golfo *sm* gulf.

goli'ardico, a, ci, che *ag* (*canto, vita*) student *cpd*.

go'loso, a *ag* greedy.

'golpe *sm inv* (*POL*) coup.

gomi'tata *sf*: dare una ~ a qn to elbow sb; farsi avanti a (forza *o* furia di) ~e to elbow one's way through; fare a ~e per qc to fight to get sth.

'gomito *sm* elbow; (*di strada etc*) sharp bend.

go'mitolo *sm* ball.

'gomma *sf* rubber; (*colla*) gum; (*per cancellare*) rubber, eraser; (*di veicolo*) tyre (*BRIT*), tire (*US*); ~ da masticare chewing gum; ~ a terra flat tyre.

gommapi'uma ® *sf* foam rubber.

gom'mino *sm* rubber tip; (*rondella*) rubber washer.

gom'mista, i, e *sm/f* tyre (*BRIT*) *o* tire (*US*)

specialist; (*rivenditore*) tyre *o* tire merchant.

gom'mone *sm* rubber dinghy.

gom'moso, a *ag* rubbery.

'gondola *sf* gondola.

gondoli'ere *sm* gondolier.

gonfa'lone *sm* banner.

gonfi'are *vt* (*pallone*) to blow up, inflate; (*dilatare, ingrossare*) to swell; (*fig: notizia*) to exaggerate; ~rsi *vr* to swell; (*fiume*) to rise.

'gonfio, a *ag* swollen; (*stomaco*) bloated; (*palloncino, gomme*) inflated, blown up; (*con pompa*) pumped up; (*vela*) full; occhi ~i di pianto eyes swollen with tears; ~ di orgoglio (*persona*) puffed up (with pride); avere il portafoglio ~ to have a bulging wallet.

gonfi'ore *sm* swelling.

gongo'lare *vi* to look pleased with o.s.; ~ di gioia to be overjoyed.

'gonna *sf* skirt; ~ pantalone culottes *pl*.

'gonzo ['gondzo] *sm* simpleton, fool.

gorgheggi'are [gorged'dʒare] *vi* to warble; to trill.

gor'gheggio [gor'geddʒo] *sm* (*MUS, di uccello*) trill.

'gorgo, ghi *sm* whirlpool.

gorgogli'are [gorgoʎ'ʎare] *vi* to gurgle.

gorgo'glio [gorgoʎ'ʎio] *sm* gurgling.

go'rilla *sm inv* gorilla; (*guardia del corpo*) bodyguard.

'Gotha *sm inv* (*del cinema, letteratura, industria*) leading lights *pl*.

'gotico, a, ci, che *ag, sm* Gothic.

'gotta *sf* gout.

gover'nante *sm/f* ruler ♦ *sf* (*di bambini*) governess; (*donna di servizio*) housekeeper.

gover'nare *vt* (*stato*) to govern, rule; (*pilotare, guidare*) to steer; (*bestiame*) to tend, look after.

governa'tivo, a *ag* (*politica, decreto*) government *cpd*, governmental; (*stampa*) pro-government.

governa'tore *sm* governor.

go'verno *sm* government; ~ ombra shadow cabinet.

'gozzo ['gottso] *sm* (*ZOOL*) crop; (*MED*) goitre; (*fig fam*) throat.

gozzovigli'are [gottsoviʎ'ʎare] *vi* to make merry, carouse.

GPL [dʒipi'ɛlle] *sigla m* (= *Gas di Petrolio Liquefatto*) LPG (= *Liquefied Petroleum Gas*).

GPS [dʒipi'esse] *sigla m* GPS = (*Global Positioning System*).

gpm *abbr* (= *giri per minuto*) rpm.

GR [dzi'erre] sigla = Grosseto ♦ sigla m (= **giornale radio**) radio news.
gracchi'are [grak'kjare] vi to caw.
graci'dare [gratʃi'dare] vi to croak.
graci'dio, ii [gratʃi'dio] sm croaking.
'gracile ['gratʃile] ag frail, delicate.
gra'dasso sm boaster.
gradata'mente av gradually, by degrees.
gradazi'one [gradat'tsjone] sf (sfumatura) gradation; ~ **alcolica** alcoholic content.
gra'devole ag pleasant, agreeable.
gradi'mento sm pleasure, satisfaction; **essere di mio** (o **tuo** etc) ~ to be to my (o your etc) liking.
gradi'nata sf flight of steps; (in teatro, stadio) tiers pl.
gra'dino sm step, (ALPINISMO) foothold.
gra'dire vt (accettare con piacere) to accept; (desiderare) to wish, like; **gradisce una tazza di tè?** would you like a cup of tea?
gra'dito, a ag welcome.
'grado sm (MAT, FISICA etc) degree; (stadio) degree, level; (MIL, sociale) rank; **essere in** ~ **di fare** to be in a position to do; **di buon** ~ willingly; **per** ~**i** by degrees; **un cugino di primo/secondo** ~ a first/second cousin; **subire il terzo** ~ (anche fig) to be given the third degree.
gradu'ale ag gradual.
gradu'are vt to grade.
gradu'ato, a ag (esercizi) graded; (scala, termometro) graduated ♦ sm (MIL) non-commissioned officer.
gradua'toria sf (di concorso) list; (per la promozione) order of seniority.
'graffa sf (gancio) clip; (segno grafico) brace.
graf'fetta sf paper clip.
graffi'are vt to scratch.
graffia'tura sf scratch.
'graffio sm scratch.
graf'fiti smpl graffiti.
gra'fia sf spelling; (scrittura) handwriting.
'grafico, a, ci, che ag graphic ♦ sm graph; (persona) graphic designer ♦ sf graphic arts pl; ~ **a torta** pie chart.
gra'migna [gra'minɲa] sf weed; couch grass.
gram'matica, che sf grammar.
grammati'cale ag grammatical.
'grammo sm gram(me).
gram'mofono sm gramophone.
'gramo, a ag (vita) wretched.
gran ag vedi **grande**.
'grana sf (granello, di minerali, corpi spezzati) grain; (fam: seccatura) trouble; (: soldi) cash ♦ sm inv cheese similar to Parmesan.
gra'naglie [gra'naʎʎe] sfpl corn sg, seed sg.

gra'naio sm granary, barn.
gra'nata sf (frutto) pomegranate; (pietra preziosa) garnet; (proiettile) grenade.
granati'ere sm (MIL) grenadier; (fig) fine figure of a man.
Gran Bre'tagna [granbre'taɲɲa] sf: **la** ~ Great Britain.
gran'cassa sf (MUS) bass drum.
'granchio ['grankjo] sm crab; (fig) blunder; **prendere un** ~ (fig) to blunder.
grandango'lare sm wide-angle lens sg.
gran'dangolo sm (FOT) wide-angle lens sg.
'grande ag (qualche volta **gran** +C, **grand'** + V) (grosso, largo, vasto) big, large; (alto) tall; (lungo) long; (in sensi astratti) great ♦ smf (persona adulta) adult, grown-up; (chi ha ingegno e potenza) great man/woman; **mio fratello più** ~ my big o older brother; **il gran pubblico** the general public; **di gran classe** (prodotto) high-class; **cosa farai da** ~? what will you be o do when you grow up?; **fare le cose in** ~ to do things in style; **fare il** ~ (strafare) to act big; **una gran bella donna** a very beautiful woman; **non è una gran cosa** o **un gran che** it's nothing special; **non ne so gran che** I don't know very much about it.
grandeggi'are [granded'dʒare] vi (emergere per grandezza): ~ **su** to tower over; (darsi arie) to put on airs.
gran'dezza [gran'dettsa] sf (dimensione) size; (fig) greatness; **in** ~ **naturale** lifesize; **manie di** ~ delusions of grandeur.
grandi'nare vb impers to hail.
'grandine sf hail.
grandi'oso, a ag grand, grandiose.
gran'duca, chi sm grand duke.
grandu'cato sm grand duchy.
grandu'chessa [grandu'kessa] sf grand duchess.
gra'nello sm (di cereali, uva) seed; (di frutta) pip; (di sabbia, sale etc) grain.
gra'nita sf kind of water ice.
gra'nito sm granite.
'grano sm (in quasi tutti i sensi) grain; (frumento) wheat; (di rosario, collana) bead; ~ **di pepe** peppercorn.
gran'turco sm maize.
'granulo sm granule; (MED) pellet.
'grappa sf rough, strong brandy.
'grappolo sm bunch, cluster.
'graspo sm bunch (of grapes).
gras'setto sm (TIP) bold (type) (BRIT), bold face.
'grasso, a ag fat; (cibo) fatty; (pelle) greasy; (terreno) rich; (fig: guadagno, annata) plentiful; (: volgare) coarse, lewd ♦ sm (di persona, animale) fat; (sostanza che

unge) grease.
gras'soccio, a, ci, ce [gras'sɔttʃo] *ag* plump.
gras'sone, a *sm/f (fam: persona)* dumpling.
'grata *sf* grating.
gra'ticcio [gra'tittʃo] *sm* trellis; (*stuoia*) mat.
gra'ticola *sf* grill.
gra'tifica, che *sf* bonus; ~ **natalizia** Christmas bonus.
gratificazi'one [gratifikat'tsjone] *sf* (*soddisfazione*) satisfaction, reward.
grati'nare *vt (CUC)* to cook au gratin.
'gratis *av* free, for nothing.
grati'tudine *sf* gratitude.
'grato, a *ag* grateful.
gratta'capo *sm* worry, headache.
grattaci'elo [gratta'tʃɛlo] *sm* skyscraper.
gratta e 'vinci [grattae'vintʃi] *sm (lotteria)* lottery; (*biglietto*) scratchcard.
grat'tare *vt (pelle)* to scratch; (*raschiare*) to scrape; (*pane, formaggio, carote*) to grate; (*fam: rubare*) to pinch ♦ *vi (stridere)* to grate; (*AUT*) to grind; ~**rsi** *vr* to scratch o.s.; ~**rsi la pancia** (*fig*) to twiddle one's thumbs.
grat'tata *sf* scratch; **fare una** ~ (*AUT: fam*) to grind the gears.
grat'tugia, gie [grat'tudʒa] *sf* grater.
grattugi'are [grattu'dʒare] *vt* to grate; **pane** *m* **grattugiato** breadcrumbs *pl.*
gratuità *sf (fig)* gratuitousness.
gra'tuito, a *ag* free; (*fig*) gratuitous.
gra'vame *sm* tax; (*fig*) burden, weight.
gra'vare *vt* to burden ♦ *vi:* ~ **su** to weigh on.
'grave *ag (danno, pericolo, peccato etc)* grave, serious; (*responsabilità*) heavy, grave; (*contegno*) grave, solemn; (*voce, suono*) deep, low-pitched; (*LING*): **accento** ~ grave accent ♦ *sm (FISICA)* (heavy) body; **un malato** ~ a person who is seriously ill.
grave'mente *av (ammalato, ferito)* seriously.
gravi'danza [gravi'dantsa] *sf* pregnancy.
'gravido, a *ag* pregnant.
gravità *sf* seriousness; (*anche FISICA*) gravity.
gravi'tare *vi (FISICA):* ~ **intorno a** to gravitate round.
gra'voso, a *ag* heavy, onerous.
'grazia ['grattsja] *sf* grace; (*favore*) favour (*BRIT*), favor (*US*); (*DIR*) pardon; **di** ~ (*ironico*) if you please; **troppa** ~**!** (*ironico*) you're too generous!; **quanta** ~ **di Dio!** what abundance!; **entrare nelle** ~**e di qn** to win sb's favour; **Ministero di G**~ **e**

Giustizia Ministry of Justice, ≈ Lord Chancellor's Office (*BRIT*), ≈ Department of Justice (*US*).
grazi'are [grat'tsjare] *vt (DIR)* to pardon.
'grazie ['grattsje] *escl* thank you!; ~ **mille!** *o* **tante!** *o* **infinite!** thank you very much!; ~ **a thanks to**.
grazi'oso, a [grat'tsjoso] *ag* charming, delightful; (*gentile*) gracious.
'Grecia ['grɛtʃa] *sf:* **la** ~ Greece.
'greco, a, ci, che *ag, sm/f, sm* Greek.
gre'gario *sm (CICLISMO)* supporting rider.
'gregge, *pl(f)* **i** ['greddʒe] *sm* flock.
'greggio, a, gi, ge ['greddʒo] *ag* raw, unrefined; (*diamante*) rough, uncut; (*tessuto*) unbleached ♦ *sm (anche:* **petrolio** ~) crude (oil).
grembi'ule *sm* apron; (*sopravveste*) overall.
'grembo *sm* lap; (*ventre della madre*) womb.
gre'mito, a *ag:* ~ **(di)** packed *o* crowded (with).
'greto *sm* (exposed) gravel bed of a river.
'gretto, a *ag* mean, stingy; (*fig*) narrow-minded.
'greve *ag* heavy.
'grezzo, a ['greddzo] *ag* = **greggio.**
gri'dare *vi (per chiamare)* to shout, cry (out); (*strillare*) to scream, yell ♦ *vt* to shout (out), yell (out); ~ **aiuto** to cry *o* shout for help.
'grido, *pl(m)* **i** *o pl(f)* **a** *sm* shout, cry; scream, yell; (*di animale*) cry; **di** ~ famous; **all'ultimo** ~ in the latest style.
'grigio, a, gi, gie ['gridʒo] *ag, sm* grey (*BRIT*), gray (*US*).
'griglia ['griʎʎa] *sf (per arrostire)* grill; (*ELETTR*) grid; (*inferriata*) grating; **alla** ~ (*CUC*) grilled.
grigli'ata [griʎ'ʎata] *sf (CUC)* grill.
gril'letto *sm* trigger.
'grillo *sm (ZOOL)* cricket; (*fig*) whim; **ha dei** ~**i per la testa** his head is full of nonsense.
grimal'dello *sm* picklock.
'grinfia *sf:* **cadere nelle** ~**e di qn** (*fig*) to fall into sb's clutches.
'grinta *sf* grim expression; (*SPORT*) fighting spirit; **avere molta** ~ to be very determined.
grintoso, a *ag* forceful.
'grinza ['grintsa] *sf* crease, wrinkle; (*ruga*) wrinkle; **il tuo ragionamento non fa una** ~ your argument is faultless.
grin'zoso, a [grin'tsoso] *ag* wrinkled; creased.
grip'pare *vi (TECN)* to seize.
gris'sino *sm* bread-stick.
groenlan'dese *ag* Greenland *cpd* ♦ *sm/f*

Greenlander.
Groen'landia *sf*: **la** ~ Greenland.
'gronda *sf* eaves *pl*.
gron'daia *sf* gutter.
gron'dante *ag* dripping.
gron'dare *vi* to pour; (*essere bagnato*): ~ **di** to be dripping with ♦ *vt* to drip with.
'groppa *sf* (*di animale*) back, rump; (*fam*: *dell'uomo*) back, shoulders *pl*.
'groppo *sm* tangle; **avere un** ~ **alla gola** (*fig*) to have a lump in one's throat.
'grossa *sf* (*unità di misura*) gross.
gros'sezza [gros'settsa] *sf* size; thickness.
gros'sista, i, e *sm/f* (*COMM*) wholesaler.
'grosso, a *ag* big, large; (*di spessore*) thick; (*grossolano*: *anche fig*) coarse; (*grave, insopportabile*) serious, great; (*tempo, mare*) rough ♦ *sm*: **il** ~ **di** the bulk of; **un pezzo** ~ (*fig*) a VIP, a bigwig; **farla** ~**a** to do something very stupid; **dirle** ~**e** to tell tall stories (*BRIT*) *o* tales (*US*); **questa è** ~**a**! that's a good one!; **sbagliarsi di** ~ to be completely wrong; **dormire della** ~**a** to sleep like a log.
grossolanità *sf* coarseness.
grosso'lano, a *ag* rough, coarse; (*fig*) coarse, crude; (: *errore*) stupid.
grosso'modo *av* roughly.
'grotta *sf* cave; grotto.
grot'tesco, a, schi, sche *ag* grotesque.
grovi'era *sm o f* gruyère (cheese).
gro'viglio [gro'viʎʎo] *sm* tangle; (*fig*) muddle.
gru *sf inv* crane.
'gruccia, ce ['gruttʃa] *sf* (*per camminare*) crutch; (*per abiti*) coat-hanger.
gru'gnire [gruɲ'ɲire] *vi* to grunt.
gru'gnito [gruɲ'ɲito] *sm* grunt.
'grugno ['gruɲɲo] *sm* snout; (*fam*: *faccia*) mug.
'grullo, a *ag* silly, stupid.
'grumo *sm* (*di sangue*) clot; (*di farina etc*) lump.
gru'moso, a *ag* lumpy.
'gruppo *sm* group; ~ **sanguigno** blood group.
gruvi'era *sm o f* = **groviera**.
'gruzzolo ['gruttsolo] *sm* (*di denaro*) hoard.
GT *abbr* (*AUT*: = *gran turismo*) GT.
G.U. *abbr* = **Gazzetta Ufficiale**.
guada'gnare [gwadaɲ'ɲare] *vt* (*ottenere*) to gain; (*soldi, stipendio*) to earn; (*vincere*) to win; (*raggiungere*) to reach; **tanto di guadagnato!** so much the better!
gua'dagno [gwa'daɲɲo] *sm* earnings *pl*; (*COMM*) profit; (*vantaggio, utile*) advantage, gain; ~ **di capitale** capital gains *pl*; ~ **lordo/netto** gross/net earnings

pl.
gu'ado *sm* ford; **passare a** ~ to ford.
gu'ai *escl*: ~ **a te** (*o* **lui** *etc*)! woe betide you (*o* him *etc*)!
gua'ina *sf* (*fodero*) sheath; (*indumento per donna*) girdle.
gu'aio *sm* trouble, mishap; (*inconveniente*) trouble, snag.
gua'ire *vi* to whine, yelp.
gua'ito *sm* (*di cane*) yelp, whine; (*il guaire*) yelping, whining.
gu'ancia, ce ['gwantʃa] *sf* cheek.
guanci'ale [gwan'tʃale] *sm* pillow; **dormire fra due** ~**i** (*fig*) to sleep easy, have no worries.
gu'anto *sm* glove; **trattare qn con i** ~**i** (*fig*) to handle sb with kid gloves; **gettare/raccogliere il** ~ (*fig*) to throw down/take up the gauntlet.
guan'tone *sm* boxing glove.
guarda'boschi [gwarda'bɔski] *sm inv* forester.
guarda'caccia [gwarda'kattʃa] *sm inv* gamekeeper.
guarda'coste *sm inv* coastguard; (*nave*) coastguard patrol vessel.
guarda'linee *sm inv* (*SPORT*) linesman.
guarda'macchine [gwarda'makkine] *sm/f inv* car-park (*BRIT*) *o* parking lot (*US*) attendant.
guar'dare *vt* (*con lo sguardo: osservare*) to look at; (*film, televisione*) to watch; (*custodire*) to look after, take care of ♦ *vi* to look; (*badare*): ~ **a** to pay attention to; (*luoghi: esser orientato*): ~ **a** to face; ~**rsi** *vr* to look at o.s; ~ **di** to try to; ~**rsi da** (*astenersi*) to refrain from; (*stare in guardia*) to beware of; ~**rsi dal fare** to take care not to do; **ma guarda un po'!** good heavens!; **e guarda caso** ... as if by coincidence ...; ~ **qn dall'alto in basso** to look down on sb; **non** ~ **in faccia a nessuno** (*fig*) to have no regard for anybody; ~ **di traverso** to scowl *o* frown at; ~ **a vista qn** to keep a close watch on sb.
guarda'roba *sm inv* wardrobe; (*locale*) cloakroom.
guardarobi'ere, a *sm/f* cloakroom attendant.
guardasi'gilli [gwardasi'dʒilli] *sm inv* ≈ Lord Chancellor (*BRIT*), ≈ Attorney General (*US*).
gu'ardia *sf* (*individuo, corpo*) guard; (*sorveglianza*) watch; **fare la** ~ **a qc/qn** to guard sth/sb; **stare in** ~ (*fig*) to be on one's guard; **il medico di** ~ the doctor on call; **il fiume ha raggiunto il livello di** ~

the river has reached the high-water mark; ~ **carceraria** (prison) warder (*BRIT*) *o* guard (*US*); ~ **del corpo** bodyguard; ~ **di finanza** (*corpo*) customs *pl*; (*persona*) customs officer; ~ **forestale** forest ranger; ~ **giurata** security guard; ~ **medica** emergency doctor service; ~ **municipale** town policeman; ~ **notturna** night security guard; ~ **di pubblica sicurezza** policeman; *vedi nota nel riquadro*.

GUARDIA DI FINANZA

The **Guardia di Finanza** *is a military body which deals with infringements of the laws governing income tax and monopolies. It reports to the Ministers of Finance, Justice or Agriculture, depending on the function it is performing.*

---

guardia'caccia [gwardja'kattʃa] *sm inv* = **guardacaccia**.

guardi'ano, a *sm/f* (*di carcere*) warder (*BRIT*), guard (*US*); (*di villa etc*) caretaker; (*di museo*) custodian; (*di zoo*) keeper; ~ **notturno** night watchman.

guar'dina *sf* cell.

guar'dingo, a, ghi, ghe *ag* wary, cautious.

guardi'ola *sf* porter's lodge; (*MIL*) look-out tower.

guarigi'one [gwari'dʒone] *sf* recovery.

gua'rire *vt* (*persona, malattia*) to cure; (*ferita*) to heal ♦ *vi* to recover, be cured; to heal (up).

guarnigi'one [gwarni'dʒone] *sf* garrison.

guar'nire *vt* (*ornare: abiti*) to trim; (*CUC*) to garnish.

guarnizi'one [gwarnit'tsjone] *sf* trimming; garnish; (*TECN*) gasket.

guasta'feste *sm/f inv* spoilsport.

guas'tare *vt* to spoil, ruin; (*meccanismo*) to break; ~**rsi** *vr* (*cibo*) to go bad; (*meccanismo*) to break down; (*tempo*) to change for the worse; (*amici*) to quarrel.

gu'asto, a *ag* (*non funzionante*) broken; (: *telefono etc*) out of order; (*andato a male*) bad, rotten; (: *dente*) decayed, bad; (*fig: corrotto*) depraved ♦ *sm* breakdown; (*avaria*) failure; ~ **al motore** engine failure.

Guate'mala *sm*: **il** ~ Guatemala.

guatemal'teco, a, ci, che *ag, sm/f* Guatemalan.

gu'ercio, a, ci, ce ['gwertʃo] *ag* cross-eyed.

gu'erra *sf* war; (*tecnica: atomica, chimica etc*) warfare; **fare la** ~ **(a)** to wage war (against); **la** ~ **fredda** the Cold War; ~ **mondiale** world war; ~ **preventiva**

preventative war; **la prima/seconda** ~ **mondiale** the First/Second World War.

guerrafon'daio *sm* warmonger.

guerreggi'are [gwerred'dʒare] *vi* to wage war.

guerri'ero, a *ag* warlike ♦ *sm* warrior.

guer'riglia [gwer'riʎʎa] *sf* guerrilla warfare.

guerrigli'ero [gwerriʎ'ʎɛro] *sm* guerrilla.

'gufo *sm* owl.

'guglia ['guʎʎa] *sf* (*ARCHIT*) spire; (*di roccia*) needle.

Gui'ana *sf*: **la** ~ **francese** French Guiana.

gu'ida *sf* (*persona*) guide; (*libro*) guide(book); (*comando, direzione*) guidance, direction; (*AUT*) driving; (: *sterzo*) steering; (*tappeto, di tenda, cassetto*) runner; ~ **a destra/sinistra** (*AUT*) right-/left-hand drive; **essere alla** ~ **di** (*governo*) to head; (*spedizione, paese*) to lead; **far da** ~ **a qn** (*mostrare la strada*) to show sb the way; (*in una città*) to show sb (a)round; ~ **telefonica** telephone directory.

gui'dare *vt* to guide; (*condurre a capo*) to lead; (*auto*) to drive; (*aereo, nave*) to pilot; **sa** ~? can you drive?

guida'tore, 'trice *sm/f* (*conducente*) driver.

Gui'nea *sf*: **la Repubblica di** ~ the Republic of Guinea; **la** ~ **Equatoriale** Equatorial Guinea.

guin'zaglio [gwin'tsaʎʎo] *sm* leash, lead.

gu'isa *sf*: **a** ~ **di** like, in the manner of.

guiz'zare [gwit'tsare] *vi* to dart; to flicker; to leap; ~ **via** (*fuggire*) to slip away.

gu'izzo ['gwittso] *sm* (*di animali*) dart; (*di fulmine*) flash.

'guru *sm inv* (*REL, anche fig*) guru.

'guscio ['guʃʃo] *sm* shell.

gus'tare *vt* (*cibi*) to taste; (: *assaporare con piacere*) to enjoy, savour (*BRIT*), savor (*US*); (*fig*) to enjoy, appreciate ♦ *vi*: ~ **a** to please; **non mi gusta affatto** I don't like it at all.

gusta'tivo, a *ag*: **papille** *fpl* ~**e** taste buds.

'gusto *sm* (*senso*) taste; (*sapore*) taste, flavour (*BRIT*), flavor (*US*); (*godimento*) enjoyment; **al** ~ **di fragola** strawberry-flavo(u)red; **di** ~ **barocco** in the baroque style; **mangiare di** ~ to eat heartily; **prenderci** ~: **ci ha preso** ~ he's acquired a taste for it, he's got to like it.

gus'toso, a *ag* tasty; (*fig*) agreeable.

guttu'rale *ag* guttural.

Gu'yana [gu'jana] *sf*: **la** ~ Guyana.

Hh

H, h ['akka] *sf o m inv* (*lettera*) H, h ♦ *abbr*
(= *ora*) hr; (= *etto, altezza*) h; **H come hotel**
≈ H for Harry (*BRIT*), H for How (*US*).
ha¹, 'hai [a, ai] *vb vedi* **avere.**
ha² *abbr* (= *ettaro*) ha.
Ha'iti [a'iti] *sf* Haiti.
haiti'ano, a [ai'tjano] *ag, sm/f* Haitian.
hall [hɔːl] *sf inv* hall, foyer.
'handicap ['handikap] *sm inv* handicap.
handicap'pato, a [andikap'pato] *ag*
handicapped ♦ *sm/f* handicapped person,
disabled person.
'hanno ['anno] *vb vedi* **avere.**
ha'scisc [aʃ'ʃiʃ] *sm* hashish.
hawai'ano, a [ava'jano] *ag, sm/f* Hawaiian.
Ha'waii [a'vai] *sfpl:* **le ~ Hawaii** *sg.*
'Helsinki ['ɛlsinki] *sf* Helsinki.
'herpes ['ɛrpes] *sm* (*MED*) herpes *sg;* ~
zoster shingles *sg.*
hg *abbr* (= *ettogrammo*) hg.
'hi-fi ['haifai] *sm inv, ag inv* hi-fi.
Hima'laia [ima'laja] *sm:* **l'~** the Himalayas
pl.
hl *abbr* (= *ettolitro*) hl.
ho [ɔ] *vb vedi* **avere.**
'hobby ['hɔbi] *sm inv* hobby.
'hockey ['hɔki] *sm* hockey; ~ **su ghiaccio**
ice hockey.
'holding ['houldiŋ] *sf inv* holding company.
Hon'duras [on'duras] *sm* Honduras.
'Hong Kong ['ɔkɔg] *sf* Hong Kong.
Hono'lulu [ono'lulu] *sf* Honolulu.
'hostess ['houstis] *sf inv* air hostess (*BRIT*) *o*
stewardess.
ho'tel [o'tɛl] *sm inv* hotel.
Hz *abbr* (= *hertz*) Hz.

Ii

I, i [i] *sf o m inv* (*lettera*) I, i; **I come Imola** ≈ I
for Isaac (*BRIT*), I for Item (*US*).
i *det mpl* the; *vedi anche* **il.**
IACP *sigla m* (= *Istituto Autonomo per le Case*
Popolari) *public housing association.*
i'ato *sm* hiatus.
i'berico, a, ci, che *ag* Iberian; **la Penisola**
I~a the Iberian Peninsula.
iber'nare *vi* to hibernate ♦ *vt* (*MED*) to
induce hypothermia in.
ibernazi'one [ibernat'tsjone] *sf*
hibernation.
ibid. *abbr* (= *ibidem*) ib(id).
'ibrido, a *ag, sm* hybrid.
IC *abbr* = **intercity.**
'ICE ['itʃe] *sigla m* (= *Istituto nazionale per il*
Commercio Estero) *overseas trade board.*
i'cona *sf* icon.
id *abbr* (= *idem*) do.
Id'dio *sm* God.
i'dea *sf* idea; (*opinione*) opinion, view;
(*ideale*) ideal; **avere le ~e chiare** to know
one's mind; **cambiare** ~ to change one's
mind; **dare l'~ di** to seem, look like;
neanche *o* **neppure per** ~! certainly not!,
no way!; ~ **fissa** obsession.
ide'ale *ag, sm* ideal.
idea'lismo *sm* idealism.
idea'lista, i, e *sm/f* idealist.
idea'listico, a, ci, che *ag* idealistic.
idealiz'zare [idealid'dzare] *vt* to idealize.
ide'are *vt* (*immaginare*) to think up,
conceive; (*progettare*) to plan.
idea'tore, 'trice *sm/f* author.
i'dentico, a, ci, che *ag* identical.
identifi'care *vt* to identify.
identificazi'one [identifikat'tsjone] *sf*
identification.
identità *sf inv* identity.
ideolo'gia, 'gie [ideolo'dʒia] *sf* ideology.
ideo'logico, a, ci, che [ideo'lɔdʒiko] *ag*
ideological.
idil'liaco, a, ci, che *ag* = **idillico.**
i'dillico, a, ci, che *ag* idyllic.
i'dillio *sm* idyll; **tra di loro è nato un** ~ they
have fallen in love.
idi'oma, i *sm* idiom, language.
idio'matico, a, ci, che *ag* idiomatic; **frase** *f*

~a idiom.
idiosincra'sia *sf* idiosyncrasy.
idi'ota, i, e *ag* idiotic ♦ *sm/f* idiot.
idio'zia [idjot'tsia] *sf* idiocy; (*atto, discorso*) idiotic thing to do (*o* say).
ido'latra, i, e *ag* idolatrous ♦ *sm/f* idolater.
idola'trare *vt* to worship; (*fig*) to idolize.
idola'tria *sf* idolatry.
'idolo *sm* idol.
idoneità *sf* suitability; **esame** *m* **di** ~ qualifying examination.
i'doneo, a *ag*: ~ **a** suitable for, fit for; (*MIL*) fit for; (*qualificato*) qualified for.
i'drante *sm* hydrant.
idra'tante *ag* (*crema*) moisturizing ♦ *sm* moisturizer.
idra'tare *vt* (*pelle*) to moisturize.
idratazi'one [idratat'tsjone] *sf* moisturizing.
i'draulico, a, ci, che *ag* hydraulic ♦ *sm* plumber ♦ *sf* hydraulics *sg*.
'idrico, a, ci, che *ag* water *cpd*.
idrocar'buro *sm* hydrocarbon.
idroe'lettrico, a, ci, che *ag* hydroelectric.
i'drofilo, a *ag*: **cotone** *m* ~ cotton wool (*BRIT*), absorbent cotton (*US*).
idrofo'bia *sf* rabies *sg*.
i'drofobo, a *ag* rabid; (*fig*) furious.
i'drogeno [i'drɔdʒeno] *sm* hydrogen.
idroli'pidico, a, ci, che *ag* hydrolipid.
idro'porto *sm* (*AER*) seaplane base.
idrorepel'lente *ag* water-repellent.
idros'calo *sm* = **idroporto**.
idrovo'lante *sm* seaplane.
i'ella *sf* bad luck.
iel'lato, a *ag* plagued by bad luck.
i'ena *sf* hyena.
ie'ratico, a, ci, che *ag* (*REL: scrittura*) hieratic; (*fig: atteggiamento*) solemn.
i'eri *av, sm* yesterday; **il giornale di** ~ yesterday's paper; ~ **l'altro** the day before yesterday; ~ **sera** yesterday evening.
ietta'tore, 'trice *sm/f* jinx.
igi'ene [i'dʒɛne] *sf* hygiene; **norme d'**~ sanitary regulations; **ufficio d'**~ public health office; ~ **mentale** mental health; ~ **pubblica** public health.
igi'enico, a, ci, che [i'dʒɛniko] *ag* hygienic; (*salubre*) healthy.
igloo [i'glu] *sm inv* igloo; (*tenda*) dome tent.
IGM *sigla m* (= *Ispettorato Generale della Motorizzazione*) road traffic inspectorate.
i'gnaro, a [iɲ'ɲaro] *ag*: ~ **di** unaware of, ignorant of.
i'gnifugo, a, ghi, ghe [iɲ'ɲifugo] *ag* flame-resistant, fireproof.
i'gnobile [iɲ'ɲɔbile] *ag* despicable, vile.

igno'minia [iɲɲo'minja] *sf* ignominy.
igno'rante [iɲɲo'rante] *ag* ignorant.
igno'ranza [iɲɲo'rantsa] *sf* ignorance.
igno'rare [iɲɲo'rare] *vt* (*non sapere, conoscere*) to be ignorant *o* unaware of, not to know; (*fingere di non vedere, sentire*) to ignore.
i'gnoto, a [iɲ'ɲɔto] *ag* unknown ♦ *sm/f*: **figlio di** ~**i** child of unknown parentage; **il Milite I**~ the Unknown Soldier.

══════════════════ *PAROLA CHIAVE*

il (*pl* (*m*) **i**; *diventa* **lo** (*pl* **gli**) *davanti a s impura, gn, pn, ps, x, z; f* **la** (*pl* **le**)) *det m* **1** the; ~ **libro/lo studente/l'acqua** the book/ the student/the water; **gli scolari** the pupils
2 (*astrazione*): ~ **coraggio/l'amore/la giovinezza** courage/love/youth
3 (*tempo*): ~ **mattino/la sera** in the morning/evening; ~ **venerdì** (*abitualmente*) on Fridays; (*quel giorno*) on (the) Friday; **la settimana prossima** next week
4 (*distributivo*) a, an; **2 euro** ~ **chilo/paio** 2 euros a *o* per kilo/pair
5 (*partitivo*) some, any; **hai messo lo zucchero?** have you added sugar?; **hai comprato** ~ **latte?** did you buy (some *o* any) milk?
6 (*possesso*): **aprire gli occhi** to open one's eyes; **rompersi la gamba** to break one's leg; **avere i capelli neri/**~ **naso rosso** to have dark hair/a red nose; **mettiti le scarpe** put your shoes on
7 (*con nomi propri*): ~ **Petrarca** Petrarch; ~ **Presidente Bush** President Bush; **dov'è la Francesca?** where's Francesca?
8 (*con nomi geografici*): ~ **Tevere** the Tiber; **l'Italia** Italy; ~ **Regno Unito** the United Kingdom; **l'Everest** Everest.

─────────────────────────────

'ilare *ag* cheerful.
ilarità *sf* hilarity, mirth.
ill. *abbr* (= *illustrazione; illustrato*) ill.
illangui'dire *vi* to grow weak *o* feeble.
illazi'one [illat'tsjone] *sf* inference, deduction.
il'lecito, a [il'letʃito] *ag* illicit.
ille'gale *ag* illegal.
illegalità *sf* illegality.
illeg'gibile [illed'dʒibile] *ag* illegible.
illegittimità [illedʒittimi'ta] *sf* illegitimacy.
ille'gittimo, a [ille'dʒittimo] *ag* illegitimate.
il'leso, a *ag* unhurt, unharmed.
illette'rato, a *ag* illiterate.
illiba'tezza [illiba'tettsa] *sf* (*di donna*) virginity.

illi 'bato, a *ag:* **donna** ~**a** virgin.
illimi 'tato, a *ag* boundless; unlimited.
illivi 'dire *vi* (*volto, mani*) to turn livid;
(*cielo*) to grow leaden.
ill.mo *abbr* = **illustrissimo**.
il 'logico, a, ci, che [il'lɔdʒiko] *ag* illogical.
il 'ludere *vt* to deceive, delude; ~**rsi** *vr* to
deceive o.s., delude o.s.
illumi 'nare *vt* to light up, illuminate; (*fig*)
to enlighten; ~**rsi** *vr* to light up; ~ **a giorno**
(*con riflettori*) to floodlight.
illumi 'nato, a *ag* (*fig: sovrano, spirito*)
enlightened.
illuminazi 'one [illuminat'tsjone] *sf* lighting;
illumination; floodlighting; (*fig*) flash of
inspiration.
illumi 'nismo *sm* (*STORIA*): **l'l**~ the
Enlightenment.
il 'lusi *etc vb vedi* **illudere**.
illusi 'one *sf* illusion; **farsi delle** ~**i** to delude
o.s.
illusio 'nismo *sm* conjuring.
illusio 'nista, i, e *sm/f* conjurer.
il 'luso, a *pp di* **illudere**.
illu 'sorio, a *ag* illusory.
illus 'trare *vt* to illustrate.
illustra 'tivo, a *ag* illustrative.
illustrazi 'one [illustrat'tsjone] *sf*
illustration.
il 'lustre *ag* eminent, renowned.
illus 'trissimo, a *ag* (*negli indirizzi*) very
revered.
'ILOR *sigla f vedi* **imposta locale sui redditi**.
IM *sigla* = *Imperia*.
imbacuc 'care *vt*, ~**rsi** *vr* to wrap up.
imbaldan 'zire [imbaldan'tsire] *vt* to give
confidence to; ~**rsi** *vr* to grow bold.
imbal 'laggio [imbal'laddʒo] *sm* packing
no pl.
imbal 'lare *vt* to pack; (*AUT*) to race; ~**rsi** *vr*
(*AUT*) to race.
imbalsa 'mare *vt* to embalm.
imbalsa 'mato, a *ag* embalmed.
imbambo 'lato, a *ag* (*sguardo, espressione*)
vacant, blank.
imban 'dire *vt*: ~ **un banchetto** to prepare
a lavish feast.
imban 'dito, a *ag*: **tavola** ~**a** lavishly *o*
sumptuously decked table.
imbaraz 'zante [imbarat'tsante] *ag*
embarrassing, awkward.
imbaraz 'zare [imbarat'tsare] *vt* (*mettere a
disagio*) to embarrass; (*ostacolare:
movimenti*) to hamper; (: *stomaco*) to lie
heavily on; ~**rsi** *vr* to become
embarrassed.
imbaraz 'zato, a [imbarat'tsato] *ag*
embarrassed; **avere lo stomaco** ~ to have

an upset stomach.
imba 'razzo [imba'rattso] *sm* (*disagio*)
embarrassment; (*perplessità*) puzzlement,
bewilderment; **essere** *o* **trovarsi in** ~ to be
in an awkward situation *o* predicament;
mettere in ~ to embarrass; ~ **di stomaco**
indigestion.
imbarbari 'mento *sm* (*di civiltà, costumi*)
barbarization.
imbarca 'dero *sm* landing stage.
imbar 'care *vt* (*passeggeri*) to embark;
(*merci*) to load; ~**rsi** *vr*: ~**rsi su** to board;
~**rsi per l'America** to sail for America;
~**rsi in** (*fig: affare*) to embark on.
imbarcazi 'one [imbarkat'tsjone] *sf* (small)
boat, (small) craft *inv*; ~ **di salvataggio**
lifeboat.
im 'barco, chi *sm* embarkation; loading;
boarding; (*banchina*) landing stage; **carta
d'**~ boarding pass (*BRIT*), boarding card.
imbastar 'dire *vt* to bastardize, debase;
~**rsi** *vr* to degenerate, become debased.
imbas 'tire *vt* (*cucire*) to tack; (*fig:
abbozzare*) to sketch, outline.
im 'battersi *vr*: ~ **in** (*incontrare*) to bump *o*
run into.
imbat 'tibile *ag* unbeatable, invincible.
imbavagli 'are [imbavaʎ'ʎare] *vt* to gag.
imbec 'care *vt* (*uccelli*) to feed; (*fig*) to
prompt, put words into sb's mouth.
imbec 'cata *sf* (*TEAT*) prompt; **dare l'**~ **a qn**
to prompt sb; (*fig*) to give sb their cue.
imbe 'cille [imbe't ʃille] *ag* idiotic ♦ *sm/f* idiot;
(*MED*) imbecile.
imbecillità [imbet ʃilli'ta] *sf inv* (*MED, fig*)
imbecility, idiocy; **dire** ~ to talk
nonsense.
imbellet 'tare *vt* (*viso*) to make up, put
make-up on; ~**rsi** *vr* to make o.s. up, put
on one's make-up.
imbel 'lire *vt* to adorn, embellish ♦ *vi* to
grow more beautiful.
im 'berbe *ag* beardless; **un giovanotto** ~ a
callow youth.
imbestia 'lire *vt* to infuriate; ~**rsi** *vr* to
become infuriated, fly into a rage.
im 'bevere *vt* to soak; ~**rsi** *vr*: ~**rsi di** to
soak up, absorb.
imbe 'vuto, a *ag*: ~ (**di**) soaked (in).
imbian 'care *vt* to whiten; (*muro*) to
whitewash ♦ *vi* to become *o* turn white.
imbianca 'tura *sf* (*di muro: con bianco di
calce*) whitewashing; (: *con altre pitture*)
painting.
imbian 'chino [imbjan'kino] *sm* (*house*)
painter, painter and decorator.
imbion 'dire *vt* (*capelli*) to lighten; (*CUC:
cipolla*) to brown; ~**rsi** *vr* (*capelli*) to

lighten, go blonde, go fair; (*messi*) to turn golden, ripen.

imbizzar'rirsi [imbiddzar'rirsi] *vr* (*cavallo*) to become frisky.

imboc'care *vt* (*bambino*) to feed; (*entrare*: *strada*) to enter, turn into ♦ *vi*: ~ **in** (*sog*: *strada*) to lead into; (: *fiume*) to flow into.

imbocca'tura *sf* mouth; (*di strada, porto*) entrance; (*MUS, del morso*) mouthpiece.

im'bocco, chi *sm* entrance.

imboni'tore *sm* (*di spettacolo, circo*) barker.

imborghe'sire [imborge'zire] *vi*, ~**rsi** *vr* to become bourgeois.

imbos'care *vt* to hide; ~**rsi** *vr* (*MIL*) to evade military service.

imbos'cata *sf* ambush.

imbos'cato *sm* draft dodger (*US*).

imboschi'mento [imboski'mento] *sm* afforestation.

imbottigli'are [imbottiʎ'ʎare] *vt* to bottle; (*NAUT*) to blockade; (*MIL*) to hem in; ~**rsi** *vr* to be stuck in a traffic jam.

imbot'tire *vt* to stuff; (*giacca*) to pad; ~**rsi** *vr*: ~**rsi di** (*rimpinzarsi*) to stuff o.s. with.

imbot'tito, a *ag* (*sedia*) upholstered; (*giacca*) padded ♦ *sf* quilt.

imbotti'tura *sf* stuffing; padding.

imbracci'are [imbrat'tʃare] *vt* (*fucile*) to shoulder; (*scudo*) to grasp.

imbra'nato, a *ag* clumsy, awkward ♦ *sm/f* clumsy person.

imbratta'carte *sm/f* (*peg*) scribbler.

imbrat'tare *vt* to dirty, smear, daub; ~**rsi** *vr*: ~**rsi (di)** to dirty o.s. (with).

imbratta'tele *sm/f* (*peg*) dauber.

imbrigli'are [imbriʎ'ʎare] *vt* to bridle.

imbroc'care *vt* (*fig*) to guess correctly.

imbrogli'are [imbroʎ'ʎare] *vt* to mix up; (*fig*: *raggirare*) to deceive, cheat; (: *confondere*) to confuse, mix up; ~**rsi** *vr* to get tangled; (*fig*) to become confused.

im'broglio [im'brɔʎʎo] *sm* (*groviglio*) tangle; (*situazione confusa*) mess; (*truffa*) swindle, trick.

imbrogli'one, a [imbroʎ'ʎone] *sm/f* cheat, swindler.

imbronci'ato, a [imbron'tʃato] *ag* (*persona*) sulky; (*cielo*) cloudy, threatening.

imbru'nire *vi*, *vb impers* to grow dark; **all'**~ at dusk.

imbrut'tire *vt* to make ugly ♦ *vi* to become ugly.

imbu'care *vt* to post.

imbur'rare *vt* to butter.

imbuti'forme *ag* funnel-shaped.

im'buto *sm* funnel.

I.M.C.T.C. *sigla* (= *Ispettorato Generale della Motorizzazione Civile e dei Trasporti in*

Concessione) ≈ DVLA.

i'mene *sm* hymen.

imi'tare *vt* to imitate; (*riprodurre*) to copy; (*assomigliare*) to look like.

imita'tore, 'trice *sm/f* (*gen*) imitator; (*TEAT*) impersonator, impressionist.

imitazi'one [imitat'tsjone] *sf* imitation.

immaco'lato, a *ag* spotless; immaculate.

immagazzi'nare [immagaddzi'nare] *vt* to store.

immagi'nabile [immadʒi'nabile] *ag* imaginable.

immagi'nare [immadʒi'nare] *vt* to imagine; (*supporre*) to suppose; (*inventare*) to invent; **s'immagini!** don't mention it!, not at all!

immagi'nario, a [immadʒi'narjo] *ag* imaginary.

immagina'tiva [immadʒina'tiva] *sf* imagination.

immaginazi'one [immadʒinat'tsjone] *sf* imagination; (*cosa immaginata*) fancy.

im'magine [im'madʒine] *sf* image; (*rappresentazione grafica, mentale*) picture.

immagi'noso, a [immadʒi'noso] *ag* (*linguaggio, stile*) fantastic.

immalinco'nire *vt* to sadden, depress; ~**rsi** *vr* to become depressed, become melancholy.

imman'cabile *ag* unfailing.

immancabil'mente *av* without fail, unfailingly.

im'mane *ag* (*smisurato*) huge; (*spaventoso, inumano*) terrible.

imma'nente *ag* (*FILOSOFIA*) inherent, immanent.

immangi'abile [imman'dʒabile] *ag* inedible.

immatrico'lare *vt* to register; ~**rsi** *vr* (*INS*) to matriculate, enrol.

immatricolazi'one [immatrikolat'tsjone] *sf* registration; matriculation, enrolment.

immaturità *sf* immaturity.

imma'turo, a *ag* (*frutto*) unripe; (*persona*) immature; (*prematuro*) premature.

immedesi'marsi *vr*: ~ **in** to identify with.

immediata'mente *av* immediately, at once.

immedia'tezza [immedja'tettsa] *sf* immediacy.

immedi'ato, a *ag* immediate.

immemo'rabile *ag* immemorial; **da tempo** ~ from time immemorial.

im'memore *ag*: ~ **di** forgetful of.

immensità *sf* immensity.

im'menso, a *ag* immense.

im'mergere [im'merdʒere] *vt* to immerse, plunge; ~**rsi** *vr* to plunge; (*sommergibile*) to dive, submerge; (*dedicarsi a*): ~**rsi in** to

immerse o.s. in.
immeri'tato, a ag undeserved.
immeri'tevole ag undeserving, unworthy.
immersi'one sf immersion; (di sommergibile) submersion, dive; (di palombaro) dive; linea di ~ (NAUT) water line.
im'merso, a pp di immergere.
im'messo, a pp di immettere.
im'mettere vt: ~ (in) to introduce (into); ~ dati in un computer to enter data on a computer.
immi'grante ag, sm/f immigrant.
immi'grare vi to immigrate.
immi'grato, a sm/f immigrant.
immigrazi'one [immigrat'tsjone] sf immigration.
immi'nente ag imminent.
immi'nenza [immi'nɛntsa] sf imminence.
immischi'are [immis'kjare] vt: ~ qn in to involve sb in; ~rsi vr: ~rsi in to interfere o meddle in.
immiseri'mento sm impoverishment.
immise'rire vt to impoverish.
immis'sario sm (GEO) affluent, tributary.
immissi'one sf (gen) introduction; (di aria, gas) intake; ~ di dati (INFORM) data entry.
im'mobile ag motionless, still; (beni) ~i smpl real estate sg.
immobili'are ag (DIR) property cpd; patrimonio ~ real estate; società ~ property company.
immobi'lismo sm inertia.
immobilità sf immobility.
immobiliz'zare [immobilid'dzare] vt to immobilize; (ECON) to lock up.
immobi'lizzo [immobi'liddzo] sm: spese d'~ capital expenditure.
immo'destia sf immodesty.
immo'desto, a ag immodest.
immo'lare vt to sacrifice.
immondez'zaio [immondet'tsajo] sm rubbish dump.
immon'dizia [immon'dittsja] sf dirt, filth; (spesso al pl: spazzatura, rifiuti) rubbish no pl, refuse no pl.
immo'rale ag immoral.
immoralità sf immorality.
immorta'lare vt to immortalize.
immor'tale ag immortal.
immortalità sf immortality.
im'mune ag (esente) exempt; (MED, DIR) immune.
immunità sf immunity; ~ diplomatica diplomatic immunity; ~ parlamentare parliamentary privilege.
immuniz'zare [immunid'dzare] vt (MED) to immunize.

immunizzazi'one [immuniddzat'tsjone] sf immunization.
immunodefi'cienza [immunodefi'tʃɛntsa] sf: ~ acquisita acquired immunodeficiency.
immuno'logico, a, ci, che [immuno'lɔdʒiko] ag immunological.
immu'tabile ag immutable; unchanging.
impac'care vt to pack.
impacchet'tare [impakket'tare] vt to pack up.
impacci'are [impat'tʃare] vt to hinder, hamper.
impacci'ato, a [impat'tʃato] ag awkward, clumsy; (imbarazzato) embarrassed.
im'paccio [im'pattʃo] sm obstacle; (imbarazzo) embarrassment; (situazione imbarazzante) awkward situation.
im'pacco, chi sm (MED) compress.
impadro'nirsi vr: ~ di to seize, take possession of; (fig: apprendere a fondo) to master.
impa'gabile ag priceless.
impagi'nare [impadʒi'nare] vt (TIP) to paginate, page (up).
impaginazi'one [impadʒinat'tsjone] sf pagination.
impagli'are [impaʎ'ʎare] vt to stuff (with straw).
impa'lato, a ag (fig) stiff as a board.
impalca'tura sf scaffolding; (anche fig) framework.
impalli'dire vi to turn pale; (fig) to fade.
impalli'nare vt to riddle with shot.
impal'pabile ag impalpable.
impa'nare vt (CUC) to dip (o roll) in breadcrumbs, bread (US).
impanta'narsi vr to sink (in the mud); (fig) to get bogged down.
impape'rarsi vr to stumble over a word.
impappi'narsi vr to stammer, falter.
impa'rare vt to learn; così impari! that'll teach you!
impara'ticcio [impara'tittʃo] sm half-baked notions pl.
impareggi'abile [impared'dʒabile] ag incomparable.
imparen'tarsi vr: ~ con (famiglia) to marry into.
'impari ag inv (disuguale) unequal; (dispari) odd.
impar'tire vt to bestow, give.
imparzi'ale [impar'tsjale] ag impartial, unbiased.
imparzialità [impartsjali'ta] sf impartiality.
impas'sibile ag impassive.
impas'tare vt (pasta) to knead; (colori) to mix.

impastic 'carsi vr to pop pills.

im 'pasto sm (l'impastare: di pane) kneading; (: di cemento) mixing; (pasta) dough; (anche fig) mixture.

im 'patto sm impact; ~ ambientale impact on the environment.

impau 'rire vt to scare, frighten ♦ vi (anche: ~rsi) to become scared o frightened.

im 'pavido, a ag intrepid, fearless.

impazi 'ente [impat'tsjɛnte] ag impatient.

impazi 'enza [impat'tsjɛntsa] sf impatience.

impaz 'zata [impat'tsata] sf: all'~ (precipitosamente) at breakneck speed; (colpire) wildly.

impaz 'zire [impat'tsire] vi to go mad; ~ per qn/qc to be crazy about sb/sth.

impec 'cabile ag impeccable.

impedi 'mento sm obstacle, hindrance.

impe 'dire vt (vietare): ~ a qn di fare to prevent sb from doing; (ostruire) to obstruct; (impacciare) to hamper, hinder.

impe 'gnare [impeɲ'ɲare] vt (dare in pegno) to pawn; (onore etc) to pledge; (prenotare) to book, reserve; (obbligare) to oblige; (occupare) to keep busy; (MIL: nemico) to engage; ~rsi vr (vincolarsi): ~rsi a fare to undertake to do; (mettersi risolutamente): ~rsi in qc to devote o.s. to sth; ~rsi con qn (accordarsi) to come to an agreement with sb.

impegna 'tivo, a [impeɲɲa'tivo] ag binding; (lavoro) demanding, exacting.

impe 'gnato, a [impeɲ'nato] ag (occupato) busy; (fig: romanzo, autore) committed, engagé.

im 'pegno [im'peɲɲo] sm (obbligo) obligation; (promessa) promise, pledge; (zelo) diligence, zeal; (compito, d'autore) commitment; ~i di lavoro business commitments.

impego 'larsi vr (fig): ~ in to get heavily involved in.

impela 'garsi vr = impegolarsi.

impel 'lente ag pressing, urgent.

impene 'trabile ag impenetrable.

impen 'narsi vr (cavallo) to rear up; (AER) to go into a climb; (fig) to bridle.

impen 'nata sf (di cavallo) rearing up; (di aereo) climb, nose-up; (fig: scatto d'ira) burst of anger; (: di prezzi etc) sudden increase.

impen 'sabile ag (inaccettabile) unthinkable; (difficile da concepire) inconceivable.

impen 'sato, a ag unforeseen, unexpected.

impensie 'rire vt, ~rsi vr to worry.

impe 'rante ag prevailing.

impe 'rare vi (anche fig) to reign, rule.

impera 'tivo, a ag, sm imperative.

impera 'tore, 'trice sm/f emperor/empress.

impercet 'tibile [impertʃet'tibile] ag imperceptible.

imperdo 'nabile ag unforgivable, unpardonable.

imper 'fetto, a ag imperfect ♦ sm (LING) imperfect (tense).

imperfezi 'one [imperfet'tsjone] sf imperfection.

imperi 'ale ag imperial.

imperia 'lismo sm imperialism.

imperia 'lista, i, e ag imperialist.

imperi 'oso, a ag (persona) imperious; (motivo, esigenza) urgent, pressing.

imperi 'turo, a ag everlasting.

impe 'rizia [impe'rittsja] sf lack of experience.

imperma 'lirsi vr to take offence.

imperme 'abile ag waterproof ♦ sm raincoat.

imperni 'are vt: ~ qc su to hinge sth on; (fig: discorso, relazione etc) to base sth on; ~rsi vr (fig): ~rsi su to be based on.

im 'pero sm empire; (forza, autorità) rule, control.

imperscru 'tabile ag inscrutable.

imperso 'nale ag impersonal.

imperso 'nare vt to personify; (TEAT) to play, act (the part of); ~rsi vr: ~rsi in un ruolo to get into a part, live a part.

imper 'territo, a ag unperturbed.

imperti 'nente ag impertinent.

imperti 'nenza [imperti'nɛntsa] sf impertinence.

impertur 'babile ag imperturbable.

imperver 'sare vi to rage.

im 'pervio, a ag (luogo) inaccessible; (strada) impassable.

'impeto sm (moto, forza) force, impetus; (assalto) onslaught; (fig: impulso) impulse; (: slancio) transport; con ~ (parlare) forcefully, energetically.

impet 'tito, a ag stiff, erect; camminare ~ to strut.

impetu 'oso, a ag (vento) strong, raging; (persona) impetuous.

impian 'tare vt (motore) to install; (azienda, discussione) to establish, start.

impian 'tistica sf plant design and installation.

impi 'anto sm (installazione) installation; (apparecchiature) plant; (sistema) system; ~ elettrico wiring; ~ sportivo sports complex; ~i di risalita (SCI) ski lifts.

impias 'trare, impiastricci 'are [impjastrit'tʃare] vt to smear, dirty.

impi 'astro sm poultice; (fig fam: persona)

nuisance.

impiccagi 'one [impikka'dʒone] *sf* hanging.

impic 'care *vt* to hang; ~**rsi** *vr* to hang o.s.

impicci 'are [impit'tʃare] *vt* to hinder, hamper; ~**rsi** *vr* to meddle, interfere; **impicciati degli affari tuoi!** mind your own business!

im 'piccio [im'pittʃo] *sm* (*ostacolo*) hindrance; (*seccatura*) trouble, bother; (*affare imbrogliato*) mess; **essere d'** ~ to be in the way; **cavare** *o* **togliere qn dagli** ~**i** to get sb out of trouble.

impicci 'one, a [impit'tʃone] *sm/f* busybody.

impie 'gare *vt* (*usare*) to use, employ; (*assumere*) to employ, take on; (*spendere*: *denaro, tempo*) to spend; (*investire*) to invest; ~**rsi** *vr* to get a job, obtain employment; **impiego un quarto d'ora per andare a casa** it takes me *o* I take a quarter of an hour to get home.

impiega 'tizio, a [impjega'tittsjo] *ag* clerical, white-collar *cpd*; **lavoro/ceto** ~ clerical *o* white-collar work/workers *pl*.

impie 'gato, a *sm/f* employee; ~ **statale** state employee.

impi 'ego, ghi *sm* (*uso*) use; (*occupazione*) employment; (*posto di lavoro*) (regular) job, post; (*ECON*) investment; ~ **pubblico** job in the public sector.

impieto 'sire *vt* to move to pity; ~**rsi** *vr* to be moved to pity.

impie 'toso, a *ag* pitiless, cruel.

impie 'trire *vt* (*anche fig*) to petrify.

impigli 'are [impiʎ'ʎare] *vt* to catch, entangle; ~**rsi** *vr* to get caught up *o* entangled.

impi 'grire *vt* to make lazy ♦ *vi* (*anche*: ~**rsi**) to grow lazy.

impingu 'are *vt* (*maiale etc*) to fatten; (*fig*: *tasche, casse dello Stato*) to stuff with money.

impiom 'bare *vt* (*pacco*) to seal (with lead); (*dente*) to fill.

impla 'cabile *ag* implacable.

implemen 'tare *vt* to implement.

impli 'care *vt* to imply; (*coinvolgere*) to involve; ~**rsi** *vr*: ~**rsi (in)** to become involved (in).

implicazi 'one [implikat'tsjone] *sf* implication.

im 'plicito, a [im'plitʃito] *ag* implicit.

implo 'rare *vt* to implore.

implorazi 'one [implorat'tsjone] *sf* plea, entreaty.

impolli 'nare *vt* to pollinate.

impollinazi 'one [impollinat'tsjone] *sf* pollination.

impolve 'rare *vt* to cover with dust; ~**rsi** *vr* to get dusty.

impoma 'tare *vt* (*pelle*) to put ointment on; (*capelli*) to pomade; (*baffi*) to wax; ~**rsi** *vr* (*fam*) to get spruced up.

imponde 'rabile *ag* imponderable.

im 'pone *etc vb vedi* **imporre**.

impo 'nente *ag* imposing, impressive.

im 'pongo *etc vb vedi* **imporre**.

impo 'nibile *ag* taxable ♦ *sm* taxable income.

impopo 'lare *ag* unpopular.

impopolarità *sf* unpopularity.

im 'porre *vt* to impose; (*costringere*) to force, make; (*far valere*) to impose, enforce; **imporsi** *vr* (*persona*) to assert o.s.; (*cosa*: *rendersi necessario*) to become necessary; (*aver successo*: *moda, attore*) to become popular; ~ **a qn di fare** to force sb to do, make sb do.

impor 'tante *ag* important.

impor 'tanza [impor'tantsa] *sf* importance; **dare** ~ **a qc** to attach importance to sth; **darsi** ~ to give o.s. airs.

impor 'tare *vt* (*introdurre dall'estero*) to import ♦ *vi* to matter, be important ♦ *vb impers* (*essere necessario*) to be necessary; (*interessare*) to matter; **non importa!** it doesn't matter!; **non me ne importa!** I don't care!

importa 'tore, 'trice *ag* importing ♦ *sm/f* importer.

importazi 'one [importat'tsjone] *sf* importation; (*merci importate*) imports *pl*.

im 'porto *sm* (*total*) amount.

importu 'nare *vt* to bother.

impor 'tuno, a *ag* irksome, annoying.

im 'posi *etc vb vedi* **imporre**.

imposizi 'one [impozit'tsjone] *sf* imposition; (*ordine*) order, command; (*onere, imposta*) tax.

imposses 'sarsi *vr*: ~ **di** to seize, take possession of.

impos 'sibile *ag* impossible; **fare l'**~ to do one's utmost, do all one can.

impossibilità *sf* impossibility; **essere nell'**~ **di fare qc** to be unable to do sth.

impossibili 'tato, a *ag*: **essere** ~ **a fare qc** to be unable to do sth.

im 'posta *sf* (*di finestra*) shutter; (*tassa*) tax; ~ **indiretta sui consumi** excise duty *o* tax; ~ **locale sui redditi (ILOR)** tax on unearned income; ~ **patrimoniale** property tax; ~ **sul reddito** income tax; ~ **sul reddito delle persone fisiche (IRPEF)** personal income tax; ~ **di successione** capital transfer tax (*BRIT*), inheritance tax (*US*); ~ **sugli utili** tax on profits; ~ **sul valore aggiunto (I.V.A.)** value added tax

(VAT) (*BRIT*), sales tax (*US*).
impos'tare *vt* (*imbucare*) to post; (*servizio, organizzazione*) to set up; (*lavoro*) to organize, plan; (*resoconto, rapporto*) to plan; (*problema*) to set out, formulate; (*TIP: pagina*) to lay out; ~ **la voce** (*MUS*) to pitch one's voice.
impostazi'one [impostat'tsjone] *sf* (*di lettera*) posting (*BRIT*), mailing (*US*); (*di problema, questione*) formulation, statement; (*di lavoro*) organization, planning; (*di attività*) setting up; (*MUS*: *di voce*) pitch.
im'posto, a *pp di* **imporre**.
impos'tore, a *sm/f* impostor.
impo'tente *ag* weak, powerless; (*anche MED*) impotent.
impo'tenza [impo'tɛntsa] *sf* weakness, powerlessness; impotence.
impove'rire *vt* to impoverish ♦ *vi* (*anche*: ~**rsi**) to become poor.
imprati'cabile *ag* (*strada*) impassable; (*campo da gioco*) unplayable.
imprati'chire [imprati'kire] *vt* to train; ~**rsi** *vr*: ~**rsi in qc** to practise (*BRIT*) *o* practice (*US*) sth.
impre'care *vi* to curse, swear; ~ **contro** to hurl abuse at.
imprecazi'one [imprekat'tsjone] *sf* abuse, curse.
impreci'sato, a [impretʃi'zato] *ag* (*non preciso*: *quantità, numero*) indeterminate.
imprecisi'one [impretʃi'zjone] *sf* imprecision; inaccuracy.
impre'ciso, a [impre'tʃizo] *ag* imprecise, vague; (*calcolo*) inaccurate.
impre'gnare [impreɲ'ɲare] *vt*: ~ **(di)** (*imbevere*) to soak *o* impregnate (with); (*riempire*: *anche fig*) to fill (with).
imprendi'tore *sm* (*industriale*) entrepreneur; (*appaltatore*) contractor; **piccolo** ~ small businessman.
imprendito'ria *sf* enterprise; (*imprenditori*) entrepreneurs *pl*.
imprenditori'ale *ag* (*ceto, classe*) entrepreneurial.
imprepa'rato, a *ag*: ~ **(a)** (*gen*) unprepared (for); (*lavoratore*) untrained (for); **cogliere qn** ~ to catch sb unawares.
impreparazi'one [impreparat'tsjone] *sf* lack of preparation.
im'presa *sf* (*iniziativa*) enterprise; (*azione*) exploit; (*azienda*) firm, concern; ~ **familiare** family firm; ~ **pubblica** state-owned enterprise.
impre'sario *sm* (*TEAT*) manager, impresario; ~ **di pompe funebri** funeral director.

imprescin'dibile [impreʃʃin'dibile] *ag* not to be ignored.
im'pressi *etc vb vedi* **imprimere**.
impressio'nante *ag* impressive; upsetting.
impressio'nare *vt* to impress; (*turbare*) to upset; (*FOT*) to expose; ~**rsi** *vr* to be easily upset.
impressi'one *sf* impression; (*fig*: *sensazione*) sensation, feeling; (*stampa*) printing; **fare** ~ (*colpire*) to impress; (*turbare*) to frighten, upset; **fare buona/cattiva** ~ **a** to make a good/bad impression on.
im'presso, a *pp di* **imprimere**.
impres'tare *vt*: ~ **qc a qn** to lend sth to sb.
impreve'dibile *ag* unforeseeable; (*persona*) unpredictable.
imprevi'dente *ag* lacking in foresight.
imprevi'denza [imprevi'dɛntsa] *sf* lack of foresight.
impre'visto, a *ag* unexpected, unforeseen ♦ *sm* unforeseen event; **salvo** ~**i** unless anything unexpected happens.
imprezio'sire [imprettsjo'sire] *vt*: ~ **di** to embellish with.
imprigiona'mento [impridʒona'mento] *sm* imprisonment.
imprigio'nare [impridʒo'nare] *vt* to imprison.
im'primere *vt* (*anche fig*) to impress, stamp; (*comunicare*: *movimento*) to transmit, give.
impro'babile *ag* improbable, unlikely.
'improbo, a *ag* (*fatica, lavoro*) hard, laborious.
improdut'tivo, a *ag* (*investimento*) unprofitable; (*terreno*) unfruitful; (*fig*: *sforzo*) fruitless.
im'pronta *sf* imprint, impression, sign; (*di piede, mano*) print; (*fig*) mark, stamp; ~ **digitale** fingerprint; **rilevamento delle** ~**e genetiche** genetic fingerprinting.
impro'perio *sm* insult.
impropo'nibile *ag* which cannot be proposed *o* suggested.
im'proprio, a *ag* improper; **arma** ~**a** offensive weapon.
improro'gabile *ag* (*termine*) that cannot be extended.
improvvisa'mente *av* suddenly; unexpectedly.
improvvi'sare *vt* to improvise; ~**rsi** *vr*: ~**rsi cuoco** to (decide to) act as cook.
improvvi'sata *sf* (pleasant) surprise.
improvvisazi'one [improvvizat'tsjone] *sf* improvisation; **spirito d'**~ spirit of

invention.
improv'viso, a *ag* (*imprevisto*) unexpected; (*subitaneo*) sudden; **all'~** unexpectedly; suddenly.
impru'dente *ag* foolish, imprudent; (*osservazione*) unwise.
impru'denza [impru'dɛntsa] *sf* foolishness, imprudence; **è stata un'~** that was a foolish *o* an imprudent thing to do.
impu'dente *ag* impudent.
impu'denza [impu'dɛntsa] *sf* impudence.
impudi'cizia [impudi'tʃittsja] *sf* immodesty.
impu'dico, a, chi, che *ag* immodest.
impu'gnare [impuɲ'ɲare] *vt* to grasp, grip; (*DIR*) to contest.
impugna'tura [impuɲɲa'tura] *sf* grip, grasp; (*manico*) handle; (: *di spada*) hilt.
impulsività *sf* impulsiveness.
impul'sivo, a *ag* impulsive.
im'pulso *sm* impulse; **dare un ~ alle vendite** to boost sales.
impune'mente *av* with impunity.
impunità *sf* impunity.
impun'tarsi *vr* to stop dead, refuse to budge; (*fig*) to be obstinate.
impun'tura *sf* stitching.
impurità *sf inv* impurity.
im'puro, a *ag* impure.
impu'tare *vt* (*ascrivere*): **~ qc a** to attribute sth to; (*DIR: accusare*): **~ qn di** to charge sb with, accuse sb of.
impu'tato, a *sm/f* (*DIR*) accused, defendant.
imputazi'one [imputat'tsjone] *sf* (*DIR*) charge; (*di spese*) allocation.
imputri'dire *vi* to rot.

========== *PAROLA CHIAVE* ==========

in (*in* + *il* = **nel**, *in* + *lo* = **nello**, *in* + *l'* = **nell'**, *in* + *la* = **nella**, *in* + *i* = **nei**, *in* + *gli* = **negli**, *in* + *le* = **nelle**) *prep* **1** (*stato in luogo*) in; **vivere ~ Italia/città** to live in Italy/town; **essere ~ casa/ufficio** to be at home/the office; **è nel cassetto/~ salotto** it's in the drawer/in the sitting room; **se fossi ~ te** if I were you
2 (*moto a luogo*) to; (: *dentro*) into; **andare ~ Germania/città** to go to Germany/town; **andare ~ ufficio** to go to the office; **entrare ~ macchina/casa** to get into the car/go into the house
3 (*tempo*) in; **nel 1989** in 1989; **~ giugno/estate** in June/summer; **l'ha fatto ~ sei mesi** he did it in six months; **~ gioventù, io ... when I was young, I ...
4 (*modo, maniera*) in; **~ silenzio** in silence; **parlare ~ tedesco** to speak (in) German; **~ abito da sera** in evening

dress; **~ guerra** at war; **~ vacanza** on holiday; **Maria Bianchi ~ Rossi** Maria Rossi née Bianchi
5 (*mezzo*) by; **viaggiare ~ autobus/treno** to travel by bus/train
6 (*materia*) made of; **~ marmo** made of marble, marble *cpd*; **una collana ~ oro** a gold necklace
7 (*misura*) in; **siamo ~ quattro** there are four of us; **~ tutto** in all
8 (*fine*): **dare ~ dono** to give as a gift; **spende tutto ~ alcool** he spends all his money on drink; **~ onore di** in honour of.

i'nabile *ag*: **~ a** incapable of; (*fisicamente, MIL*) unfit for.
inabilità *sf*: **~ (a)** unfitness (for).
inabis'sare *vt* (*nave*) to sink; **~rsi** *vr* to go down.
inabi'tabile *ag* uninhabitable.
inabi'tato, a *ag* uninhabited.
inacces'sibile [inattʃes'sibile] *ag* (*luogo*) inaccessible; (*persona*) unapproachable; (*mistero*) unfathomable.
inaccet'tabile [inattʃet'tabile] *ag* unacceptable.
inacer'bire [inatʃer'bire] *vt* to exacerbate; **~rsi** *vr* (*persona*) to become embittered.
inaci'dire [inatʃi'dire] *vt* (*persona, carattere*) to embitter; **~rsi** *vr* (*latte*) to go sour; (*fig: persona, carattere*) to become sour, become embittered.
ina'datto, a *ag*: **~ (a)** unsuitable *o* unfit (for).
inadegu'ato, a *ag* inadequate.
inadempi'ente *ag* defaulting ♦ *sm/f* defaulter.
inadempi'enza [inadem'pjɛntsa] *sf*: **~ a un contratto** non-fulfilment of a contract; **dovuto alle ~e dei funzionari** due to negligence on the part of the officials.
inadempi'mento *sm* non-fulfilment.
inaffer'rabile *ag* elusive; (*concetto, senso*) difficult to grasp.
'INAIL *sigla m* (= *Istituto Nazionale per l'Assicurazione contro gli Infortuni sul Lavoro*) *state body providing sickness benefit in the event of accidents at work.*
ina'lare *vt* to inhale.
inala'tore *sm* inhaler.
inalazi'one [inalat'tsjone] *sf* inhalation.
inalbe'rare *vt* (*NAUT*) to hoist, raise; **~rsi** *vr* (*fig*) to flare up, fly off the handle.
inalte'rabile *ag* unchangeable; (*colore*) fast, permanent; (*affetto*) constant.
inalte'rato, a *ag* unchanged.
inami'dare *vt* to starch.
inami'dato, a *ag* starched.

inammis'sibile *ag* inadmissible.

inani'mato, a *ag* inanimate; (*senza vita*: *corpo*) lifeless.

inappa'gabile *ag* insatiable.

inappel'labile *ag* (*decisione*) final, irrevocable; (*DIR*) final, not open to appeal.

inappe'tenza [inappe'tɛntsa] *sf* (*MED*) lack of appetite.

inappun'tabile *ag* irreproachable, flawless.

inar'care *vt* (*schiena*) to arch; (*sopracciglia*) to raise; ~**rsi** *vr* to arch.

inaridi'mento *sm* (*anche fig*) drying up.

inari'dire *vt* to make arid, dry up ♦ *vi* (*anche*: ~**rsi**) to dry up, become arid.

inarres'tabile *ag* (*processo*) irreversible; (*emorragia*) that cannot be stemmed; (*corsa del tempo*) relentless.

inascol'tato, a *ag* unheeded, unheard.

inaspettata'mente *av* unexpectedly.

inaspet'tato, a *ag* unexpected.

inas'prire *vt* (*disciplina*) to tighten up, make harsher; (*carattere*) to embitter; (*rapporti*) to make worse; ~**rsi** *vr* to become harsher; to become bitter; to become worse.

inattac'cabile *ag* (*anche fig*) unassailable; (*alibi*) cast-iron.

inatten'dibile *ag* unreliable.

inat'teso, a *ag* unexpected.

inat'tivo, a *ag* inactive, idle; (*CHIM*) inactive.

inattu'abile *ag* impracticable.

inau'dito, a *ag* unheard of.

inaugu'rale *ag* inaugural.

inaugu'rare *vt* to inaugurate, open; (*monumento*) to unveil.

inaugurazi'one [inaugurat'tsjone] *sf* inauguration; unveiling.

inavve'duto, a *ag* careless, inadvertent.

inavver'tenza [inavver'tɛntsa] *sf* carelessness, inadvertence.

inavvertita'mente *av* inadvertently, unintentionally.

inavvici'nabile [inavvitʃi'nabile] *ag* unapproachable.

'Inca *ag inv, smf inv* Inca.

incagli'are [inkaʎ'ʎare] *vi* (*NAUT: anche:* ~**rsi**) to run aground.

incalco'labile *ag* incalculable.

incal'lito, a *ag* calloused; (*fig*) hardened, inveterate; (: *insensibile*) hard.

incal'zante [inkal'tsante] *ag* urgent, insistent; (*crisi*) imminent.

incal'zare [inkal'tsare] *vt* to follow *o* pursue closely; (*fig*) to press ♦ *vi* (*urgere*) to be pressing; (*essere imminente*) to be imminent.

incame'rare *vt* (*DIR*) to expropriate.

incammi'nare *vt* (*fig: avviare*) to start up; ~**rsi** *vr* to set off.

incana'lare *vt* (*anche fig*) to channel; ~**rsi** *vr* (*folla*): ~**rsi verso** to converge on.

incancre'nire *vi*, **incancre'nirsi** *vi* to become gangrenous.

incande'scente [inkandeʃ'ʃɛnte] *ag* incandescent, white-hot.

incan'tare *vt* to enchant, bewitch; ~**rsi** *vr* (*rimanere intontito*) to be spellbound; to be in a daze; (*meccanismo: bloccarsi*) to jam.

incanta'tore, 'trice *ag* enchanting, bewitching ♦ *sm/f* enchanter/enchantress.

incan'tesimo *sm* spell, charm.

incan'tevole *ag* charming, enchanting.

in'canto *sm* spell, charm, enchantment; (*asta*) auction; **come per** ~ as if by magic; **ti sta d'**~! (*vestito etc*) it really suits you!; **mettere all'**~ to put up for auction.

incanu'tire *vi* to go white.

inca'pace [inka'patʃe] *ag* incapable.

incapacità [inkapatʃi'ta] *sf* inability; (*DIR*) incapacity; ~ **d'intendere e di volere** diminished responsibility.

incapo'nirsi *vr* to be stubborn, be determined.

incap'pare *vi*: ~ **in qc/qn** (*anche fig*) to run into sth/sb.

incappucci'are [inkapput'tʃare] *vt* to put a hood on; ~**rsi** *vr* (*persona*) to put on a hood.

incapricci'arsi [inkaprit'tʃarsi] *vr*: ~ **di** to take a fancy to *o* for.

incapsu'lare *vt* (*dente*) to crown.

incarce'rare [inkartʃe'rare] *vt* to imprison.

incari'care *vt*: ~ **qn di fare** to give sb the responsibility of doing; ~**rsi** *vr*: ~**rsi di** to take care *o* charge of.

incari'cato, a *ag*: ~ (**di**) in charge (of), responsible (for) ♦ *sm/f* delegate, representative; **docente** ~ (*di università*) lecturer without tenure; ~ **d'affari** (*POL*) chargé d'affaires.

in'carico, chi *sm* task, job; (*INS*) temporary post.

incar'nare *vt* to embody; ~**rsi** *vr* to be embodied; (*REL*) to become incarnate.

incarnazi'one [inkarnat'tsjone] *sf* incarnation; (*fig*) embodiment.

incarta'mento *sm* dossier, file.

incartapeco'rito, a *ag* (*pelle*) wizened, shrivelled (*BRIT*), shriveled (*US*).

incar'tare *vt* to wrap (in paper).

incasel'lare *vt* (*posta*) to sort; (*fig: nozioni*) to pigeonhole.

incas'sare *vt* (*merce*) to pack (in cases); (*gemma: incastonare*) to set; (*ECON:*

riscuotere) to collect; (*PUGILATO: colpi*) to take, stand up to.

in 'casso *sm* cashing, encashment; (*introito*) takings *pl.*

incasto 'nare *vt* to set.

incastona 'tura *sf* setting.

incas 'trare *vt* to fit in, insert; (*fig:* *intrappolare*) to catch; ~**rsi** *vr* (*combaciare*) to fit together; (*restare bloccato*) to become stuck.

in 'castro *sm* slot, groove; (*punto di unione*) joint; **gioco a** ~ interlocking puzzle.

incate 'nare *vt* to chain up.

incatra 'mare *vt* to tar.

incatti 'vire *vt* to make wicked; ~**rsi** *vr* to turn nasty.

in 'cauto, a *ag* imprudent, rash.

inca 'vare *vt* to hollow out.

inca 'vato, a *ag* hollow; (*occhi*) sunken.

in 'cavo *sm* hollow; (*solco*) groove.

incavo 'larsi *vr* (*fam*) to lose one's temper, get annoyed.

incaz 'zarsi [inkat'tsarsi] *vr* (*fam!*) to get steamed up.

in 'cedere [in't ʃɛdere] *vi* (*poetico*) to advance solemnly ♦ *sm* solemn gait.

incendi 'are [intʃen'djare] *vt* to set fire to; ~**rsi** *vr* to catch fire, burst into flames.

incendi 'ario, a [intʃen'djarjo] *ag* incendiary ♦ *sm/f* arsonist.

in 'cendio [in'tʃendjo] *sm* fire.

incene 'rire [intʃene'rire] *vt* to burn to ashes, incinerate; (*cadavere*) to cremate; ~**rsi** *vr* to be burnt to ashes.

inceneri 'tore [intʃeneri'tore] *sm* incinerator.

in 'censo [in'tʃɛnso] *sm* incense.

incensu 'rato, a [intʃensu'rato] *ag* (*DIR*): **essere** ~ to have a clean record.

incenti 'vare [intʃenti'vare] *vt* (*produzione, vendite*) to boost; (*persona*) to motivate.

incen 'tivo [intʃen'tivo] *sm* incentive.

incen 'trarsi [intʃen'trarsi] *vr*: ~ **su** (*fig*) to centre (*BRIT*) *o* center (*US*) on.

incep 'pare [intʃep'pare] *vt* to obstruct, hamper; ~**rsi** *vr* to jam.

ince 'rata [intʃe'rata] *sf* (*tela*) tarpaulin; (*impermeabile*) oilskins *pl.*

incer 'tezza [intʃer'tettsa] *sf* uncertainty.

in 'certo, a [in'tʃɛrto] *ag* uncertain; (*irresoluto*) undecided, hesitating ♦ *sm* uncertainty; **gli** ~**i del mestiere** the risks of the job.

incespi 'care [intʃespi'kare] *vi*: ~ (**in qc**) to trip (over sth).

inces 'sante [intʃes'sante] *ag* incessant.

in 'cesto [in'tʃɛsto] *sm* incest.

incestu 'oso, a [intʃestu'oso] *ag* incestuous.

in 'cetta [in'tʃɛtta] *sf* buying up; **fare** ~ **di qc** to buy up sth.

inchi 'esta [in'kjɛsta] *sf* investigation, inquiry.

inchi 'nare [inki'nare] *vt* to bow; ~**rsi** *vr* to bend down; (*per riverenza*) to bow; (*: donna*) to curtsy.

in 'chino [in'kino] *sm* bow; curtsy.

inchio 'dare [inkjo'dare] *vt* to nail (down); ~ **la macchina** (*AUT*) to jam on the brakes.

inchi 'ostro [in'kjɔstro] *sm* ink; ~ **simpatico** invisible ink.

inciam 'pare [intʃam'pare] *vi* to trip, stumble.

inci 'ampo [in'tʃampo] *sm* obstacle; **essere d'**~ **a qn** (*fig*) to be in sb's way.

inciden 'tale [intʃiden'tale] *ag* incidental.

incidental 'mente [intʃidental'mente] *av* (*per caso*) by chance; (*per inciso*) incidentally, by the way.

inci 'dente [intʃi'dɛnte] *sm* accident; (*episodio*) incident; **e con questo l'**~ **è chiuso** and that is the end of the matter; ~ **d'auto** car accident; ~ **diplomatico** diplomatic incident.

inci 'denza [intʃi'dɛntsa] *sf* incidence; **avere una forte** ~ **su qc** to affect sth greatly.

in 'cidere [in'tʃidere] *vi*: ~ **su** to bear upon, affect ♦ *vt* (*tagliare incavando*) to cut into; (*ARTE*) to engrave; to etch; (*canzone*) to record.

in 'cinta [in'tʃinta] *ag f* pregnant.

incipi 'ente [intʃi'pjɛnte] *ag* incipient.

incipri 'are [intʃi'prjare] *vt* to powder.

in 'circa [in'tʃirka] *av*: **all'**~ more or less, very nearly.

in 'cisi *etc* [in'tʃizi] *vb vedi* **incidere**.

incisi 'one [intʃi'zjone] *sf* cut; (*disegno*) engraving; etching; (*registrazione*) recording; (*MED*) incision.

inci 'sivo, a [intʃi'zivo] *ag* incisive; (*ANAT*): (**dente**) ~ incisor.

in 'ciso, a [in'tʃizo] *pp di* **incidere** ♦ *sm*: **per** ~ incidentally, by the way.

inci 'sore [intʃi'zore] *sm* (*ARTE*) engraver.

incita 'mento [intʃita'mento] *sm* incitement.

inci 'tare [intʃi'tare] *vt* to incite.

inci 'vile [intʃi'vile] *ag* uncivilized; (*villano*) impolite.

incivi 'lire [intʃivi'lire] *vt* to civilize.

inciviltà [intʃivil'ta] *sf* (*di popolazione*) barbarism; (*fig: di trattamento*) barbarity; (*: maleducazione*) incivility, rudeness.

incl. *abbr* (= *incluso*) encl.

incle 'mente *ag* (*giudice, sentenza*) severe, harsh; (*fig: clima*) harsh; (*: tempo*) inclement.

incle 'menza [inkle'mɛntsa] *sf* severity;

harshness; inclemency.

incli'nabile *ag* (*schienale*) reclinable.

incli'nare *vt* to tilt ♦ *vi* (*fig*): ~ **a qc/a fare** to incline towards sth/doing; to tend towards sth/to do; ~**rsi** *vr* (*barca*) to list; (*aereo*) to bank.

incli'nato, a *ag* sloping.

inclinazi'one [inklinat'tsjone] *sf* slope; (*fig*) inclination, tendency.

in'cline *ag*: ~ **a** inclined to.

in'cludere *vt* to include; (*accludere*) to enclose.

inclusi'one *sf* inclusion.

inclu'sivo, a *ag*: ~ **di** inclusive of.

in'cluso, a *pp di* **includere** ♦ *ag* included; enclosed.

incoe'rente *ag* incoherent; (*contraddittorio*) inconsistent.

incoe'renza [inkoe'rɛntsa] *sf* incoherence; inconsistency.

in'cognito, a [in'kɔɲɲito] *ag* unknown ♦ *sm*: **in** ~ incognito ♦ *sf* (*MAT, fig*) unknown quantity.

incol'lare *vt* to glue, gum; (*unire con colla*) to stick together; ~ **gli occhi addosso a qn** (*fig*) to fix one's eyes on sb.

incolla'tura *sf* (*IPPICA*): **vincere/perdere di un'**~ to win/lose by a head.

incolon'nare *vt* to draw up in columns.

inco'lore *ag* colourless (*BRIT*), colorless (*US*).

incol'pare *vt*: ~ **qn di** to charge sb with.

in'colto, a *ag* (*terreno*) uncultivated; (*trascurato: capelli*) neglected; (*persona*) uneducated.

in'colume *ag* safe and sound, unhurt.

incolumità *sf* safety.

incom'bente *ag* (*pericolo*) imminent, impending.

incom'benza [inkom'bɛntsa] *sf* duty, task.

in'combere *vi* (*sovrastare minacciando*): ~ **su** to threaten, hang over.

incominci'are [inkomin'tʃare] *vi*, *vt* to begin, start.

incomo'dare *vt* to trouble, inconvenience; ~**rsi** *vr* to put o.s. out.

in'comodo, a *ag* uncomfortable; (*inopportuno*) inconvenient ♦ *sm* inconvenience, bother.

incompa'rabile *ag* incomparable.

incompa'tibile *ag* incompatible.

incompatibilità *sf* incompatibility; ~ **di carattere** (mutual) incompatibility.

incompe'tente *ag* incompetent.

incompe'tenza [inkompe'tɛntsa] *sf* incompetence.

incompi'uto, a *ag* unfinished, incomplete.

incom'pleto, a *ag* incomplete.

incompren'sibile *ag* incomprehensible.

incomprensi'one *sf* incomprehension.

incom'preso, a *ag* not understood; misunderstood.

inconce'pibile [inkontʃe'pibile] *ag* inconceivable.

inconcili'abile [inkontʃi'ljabile] *ag* irreconcilable.

inconclu'dente *ag* inconclusive; (*persona*) ineffectual.

incondizio'nato, a [inkondittsjo'nato] *ag* unconditional.

inconfes'sabile *ag* (*pensiero, peccato*) unmentionable.

inconfon'dibile *ag* unmistakable.

inconfu'tabile *ag* irrefutable.

incongru'ente *ag* inconsistent.

incongru'enza [inkongru'ɛntsa] *sf* inconsistency.

in'congruo, a *ag* incongruous.

inconsa'pevole *ag*: ~ **di** unaware of, ignorant of.

inconsapevo'lezza [inkonsapevo'lettsa] *sf* ignorance, lack of awareness.

in'conscio, a, sci, sce [in'kɔnʃo] *ag* unconscious ♦ *sm* (*PSIC*): **l'**~ the unconscious.

inconsis'tente *ag* (*patrimonio*) insubstantial; (*dubbio*) unfounded; (*ragionamento, prove*) tenuous, flimsy.

inconsis'tenza [inkonsis'tɛntsa] *sf* insubstantial nature; lack of foundation; flimsiness.

inconso'labile *ag* inconsolable.

inconsu'eto, a *ag* unusual.

incon'sulto, a *ag* rash.

inconte'nibile *ag* (*rabbia*) uncontrollable; (*entusiasmo*) irrepressible.

inconten'tabile *ag* (*desiderio, avidità*) insatiable; (*persona: capriccioso*) hard to please, very demanding.

incontes'tabile *ag* incontrovertible, indisputable.

incontes'tato, a *ag* undisputed.

inconti'nenza [inkonti'nɛntsa] *sf* incontinence.

incon'trare *vt* to meet; (*difficoltà*) to meet with; ~**rsi** *vr* to meet.

incon'trario *av*: **all'**~ (*sottosopra*) upside down; (*alla rovescia*) back to front; (*all'indietro*) backwards; (*nel senso contrario*) the other way round.

incontras'tabile *ag* incontrovertible, indisputable.

incontras'tato, a *ag* (*successo, vittoria, verità*) uncontested, undisputed.

in'contro *av*: ~ **a** (*verso*) towards ♦ *sm* meeting; (*SPORT*) match; meeting;

(*fortuito*) encounter; **venire** ~ **a** (*richieste, esigenze*) to comply with; ~ **di calcio** football match (*BRIT*), soccer game (*US*).

incontrol'labile *ag* uncontrollable.

inconveni'ente *sm* drawback, snag.

incoraggia'mento [inkoraddʒa'mento] *sm* encouragement; **premio d'**~ consolation prize.

incoraggi'are [inkorad'dʒare] *vt* to encourage.

incor'nare *vt* to gore.

incornici'are [inkorni'tʃare] *vt* to frame.

incoro'nare *vt* to crown.

incoronazi'one [inkoronat'tsjone] *sf* coronation.

incorpo'rare *vt* to incorporate; (*fig: annettere*) to annex.

incorreg'gibile [inkorred'dʒibile] *ag* incorrigible.

in'correre *vi*: ~ **in** to meet with, run into.

incorrut'tibile *ag* incorruptible.

in'corso, a *pp di* **incorrere**.

incosci'ente [inkoʃ'ʃɛnte] *ag* (*inconscio*) unconscious; (*irresponsabile*) reckless, thoughtless.

incosci'enza [inkoʃ'ʃɛntsa] *sf* unconsciousness; recklessness, thoughtlessness.

incos'tante *ag* (*studente, impiegato*) inconsistent; (*carattere*) fickle, inconstant; (*rendimento*) sporadic.

incos'tanza [inkos'tantsa] *sf* inconstancy, fickleness.

incostituzio'nale [inkostituttsjo'nale] *ag* unconstitutional.

incre'dibile *ag* incredible, unbelievable.

incredulità *sf* incredulity.

in'credulo, a *ag* incredulous, disbelieving.

incremen'tare *vt* to increase; (*dar sviluppo a*) to promote.

incre'mento *sm* (*sviluppo*) development; (*aumento numerico*) increase, growth.

incresci'oso, a [inkreʃ'ʃoso] *ag* (*spiacevole*) unpleasant; regrettable.

incres'pare *vt* (*capelli*) to curl; (*acque*) to ripple; ~**rsi** *vr* (*vedi vt*) to curl; to ripple.

incrimi'nare *vt* (*DIR*) to charge.

incriminazi'one [inkriminat'tsjone] *sf* (*atto d'accusa*) indictment, charge.

incri'nare *vt* to crack; (*fig: rapporti, amicizia*) to cause to deteriorate; ~**rsi** *vr* to crack; to deteriorate.

incrina'tura *sf* crack; (*fig*) rift.

incroci'are [inkro'tʃare] *vt* to cross; (*incontrare*) to meet ♦ *vi* (*NAUT, AER*) to cruise; ~**rsi** *vr* (*strade*) to cross, intersect; (*persone, veicoli*) to pass each other; ~ **le braccia/le gambe** to fold one's arms/cross

one's legs.

incrocia'tore [inkrotʃa'tore] *sm* cruiser.

in'crocio [in'krotʃo] *sm* (*anche FERR*) crossing; (*di strade*) crossroads.

incrol'labile *ag* (*fede*) unshakeable, firm.

incros'tare *vt* to encrust; ~**rsi** *vr*: ~**rsi di** to become encrusted with.

incrostazi'one [inkrostat'tsjone] *sf* encrustation; (*di calcare*) scale; (*nelle tubature*) fur (*BRIT*), scale.

incru'ento, a *ag* (*battaglia*) without bloodshed, bloodless.

incuba'trice [inkuba'tritʃe] *sf* incubator.

incubazi'one [inkubat'tsjone] *sf* incubation.

'incubo *sm* nightmare.

in'cudine *sf* anvil; **trovarsi** *o* **essere tra l'**~ **e il martello** (*fig*) to be between the devil and the deep blue sea.

incul'care *vt*: ~ **qc in** to inculcate sth into, instill sth into.

incune'are *vt* to wedge.

incu'pire *vt* (*rendere scuro*) to darken; (*fig: intristire*) to fill with gloom ♦ *vi* (*vedi vt*) to darken; to become gloomy.

incu'rabile *ag* incurable.

incu'rante *ag*: ~ **(di)** heedless (of), careless (of).

in'curia *sf* negligence.

incurio'sire *vt* to make curious; ~**rsi** *vr* to become curious.

incursi'one *sf* raid.

incur'vare *vt*, ~**rsi** *vr* to bend, curve.

in'cusso, a *pp di* **incutere**.

incusto'dito, a *ag* unguarded, unattended; **passaggio a livello** ~ unmanned level crossing.

in'cutere *vt* to arouse; ~ **timore/rispetto a qn** to strike fear into sb/command sb's respect.

'indaco *sm* indigo.

indaffa'rato, a *ag* busy.

inda'gare *vt* to investigate.

indaga'tore, 'trice *ag* (*sguardo, domanda*) searching; (*mente*) inquiring.

in'dagine [in'dadʒine] *sf* investigation, inquiry; (*ricerca*) research, study; ~ **di mercato** market survey.

indebita'mente *av* (*immeritatamente*) undeservedly; (*erroneamente*) wrongfully.

indebi'tare *vt*: ~ **qn** to get sb into debt; ~**rsi** *vr* to run *o* get into debt.

in'debito, a *ag* undeserved; wrongful.

indeboli'mento *sm* weakening; (*debolezza*) weakness.

indebo'lire *vt*, *vi* (*anche*: ~**rsi**) to weaken.

inde'cente [inde'tʃɛnte] *ag* indecent.

inde'cenza [inde'tʃɛntsa] *sf* indecency; **è un'**~! (*vergogna*) it's scandalous!, it's a disgracc!

indeci'frabile [indetʃi'frabile] *ag* indecipherable.

indecisi'one [indetʃi'zjone] *sf* indecisiveness; indecision.

inde 'ciso, a [inde'tʃizo] *ag* indecisive; (*irresoluto*) undecided.

indeco 'roso, a *ag* (*comportamento*) indecorous, unseemly.

inde 'fesso, a *ag* untiring, indefatigable.

indefi 'nibile *ag* indefinable.

indefi 'nito, a *ag* (*anche LING*) indefinite; (*impreciso, non determinato*) undefined.

indefor 'mabile *ag* crushproof.

in 'degno, a [in'deɲɲo] *ag* (*atto*) shameful; (*persona*) unworthy.

inde 'lebile *ag* indelible.

indelica 'tezza [indelika'tettsa] *sf* tactlessness.

indeli 'cato, a *ag* (*domanda*) indiscreet, tactless.

indemoni 'ato, a *ag* possessed (by the devil).

in 'denne *ag* unhurt, uninjured.

indennità *sf inv* (*rimborso: di spese*) allowance; (*: di perdita*) compensation, indemnity; ~ **di contingenza** cost-of-living allowance; ~ **di fine rapporto** severance payment (*on retirement, redundancy or when taking up other employment*); ~ **di trasferta** travel expenses *pl.*

indenniz 'zare [indennid'dzare] *vt* to compensate.

inden 'nizzo [inden'niddzo] *sm* (*somma*) compensation, indemnity.

indero 'gabile *ag* binding.

indescri 'vibile *ag* indescribable.

indeside 'rabile *ag* undesirable.

indeside 'rato, a *ag* unwanted.

indetermina 'tezza [indetermina'tettsa] *sf* vagueness.

indetermina 'tivo, a *ag* (*LING*) indefinite.

indetermi 'nato, a *ag* indefinite, indeterminate.

in 'detto, a *pp di* **indire.**

India *sf*: l'~ India; **le** ~**e occidentali** the West Indies.

indi 'ano, a *ag* Indian ♦ *sm/f* (*d'India*) Indian; (*d'America*) Red Indian; **l'Oceano I**~ the Indian Ocean.

indiavo 'lato, a *ag* possessed (by the devil); (*vivace, violento*) wild.

indi 'care *vt* (*mostrare*) to show, indicate; (*: col dito*) to point to, point out; (*consigliare*) to suggest, recommend.

indica 'tivo, a *ag* indicative ♦ *sm* (*LING*) indicative (mood).

indi 'cato, a *ag* (*consigliato*) advisable; (*adatto*): ~ **per** suitable for, appropriate for.

indica 'tore, 'trice *ag* indicating ♦ *sm* (*elenco*) guide; directory; (*TECN*) gauge; indicator; **cartello** ~ sign; ~ **della benzina** petrol (*BRIT*) *o* gas (*US*) gauge, fuel gauge; ~ **di velocità** (*AUT*) speedometer; (*AER*) airspeed indicator.

indicazi 'one [indikat'tsjone] *sf* indication; (*informazione*) piece of information; ~**i per l'uso** instructions for use.

'indice ['inditʃe] *sm* (*ANAT: dito*) index finger, forefinger; (*lancetta*) needle, pointer; (*fig: indizio*) sign; (*TECN, MAT, nei libri*) index; ~ **azionario** share index; ~ **di gradimento** (*RADIO, TV*) popularity rating; ~ **dei prezzi al consumo** ≈ retail price index.

indicherò *etc* [indike'rɔ] *vb vedi* **indicare.**

indi 'cibile [indi'tʃibile] *ag* inexpressible.

indiciz 'zare [inditʃid'dzare] *vt*: ~ **al costo della vita** to index-link (*BRIT*), index (*US*).

indiciz 'zato, a [inditʃid'dzato] *ag* (*polizza, salario etc*) index-linked (*BRIT*), indexed (*US*).

indicizzazi 'one [inditʃiddzat'tsjone] *sf* indexing.

indietreggi 'are [indjetred'dʒare] *vi* to draw back, retreat.

indi 'etro *av* back; (*guardare*) behind, back; (*andare, cadere: anche*: **all'**~) backwards; **rimanere** ~ to be left behind; **essere** ~ (*col lavoro*) to be behind; (*orologio*) to be slow; **rimandare qc** ~ to send sth back; **non vado né avanti né** ~ (*fig*) I'm not getting anywhere, I'm getting nowhere.

indi 'feso, a *ag* (*città, confine*) undefended; (*persona*) defenceless (*BRIT*), defenseless (*US*), helpless.

indiffe 'rente *ag* indifferent ♦ *sm*: **fare l'**~ to pretend to be indifferent, be *o* act casual; (*fingere di non vedere o sentire*) to pretend not to notice.

indiffe 'renza [indiffe'rɛntsa] *sf* indifference.

in 'digeno, a [in'didʒeno] *ag* indigenous, native ♦ *sm/f* native.

indi 'gente [indi'dʒɛnte] *ag* poverty-stricken, destitute.

indi 'genza [indi'dʒɛntsa] *sf* extreme poverty.

indigesti 'one [indidʒes'tjone] *sf* indigestion.

indi 'gesto, a [indi'dʒɛsto] *ag* indigestible.

indi 'gnare [indiɲ'ɲare] *vt* to fill with indignation; ~**rsi** *vr* to be (*o* get) indignant.

indignazi'one [indiɲɲat'tsjone] sf indignation.

indimenti'cabile ag unforgettable.

'indio, a ag, sm/f (South American) Indian.

indipen'dente ag independent.

indipendente'mente av independently; ~ **dal fatto che gli piaccia o meno, verrà!** he's coming, whether he likes it or not!

indipen'denza [indipen'dɛntsa] sf independence.

in 'dire vt (concorso) to announce; (elezioni) to call.

indi'retto, a ag indirect.

indiriz'zare [indirit'tsare] vt (dirigere) to direct; (mandare) to send; (lettera) to address; ~ **la parola a qn** to address sb.

indiriz'zario [indirit'tsarjo] sm mailing list.

indi'rizzo [indi'rittso] sm address; (direzione) direction; (avvio) trend, course; ~ **assoluto** (INFORM) absolute address.

indisci'plina [indiʃʃi'plina] sf indiscipline.

indiscipli'nato, a [indiʃʃipli'nato] ag undisciplined, unruly.

indis'creto, a ag indiscreet.

indiscrezi'one [indiskret'tsjone] sf indiscretion.

indiscrimi'nato, a ag indiscriminate.

indis'cusso, a ag unquestioned.

indiscu'tibile ag indisputable, unquestionable.

indispen'sabile ag indispensable, essential.

indispet'tire vt to irritate, annoy ♦ vi (anche: ~**rsi**) to get irritated o annoyed.

indispo'nente ag irritating, annoying.

indis'porre vt to antagonize.

indisposizi'one [indispozit'tsjone] sf (slight) indisposition.

indis'posto, a pp di **indisporre** ♦ ag indisposed, unwell.

indisso'lubile ag indissoluble.

indissolubil'mente av indissolubly.

indis'tinta'mente av (senza distinzioni) indiscriminately, without exception; (in modo indefinito: vedere, sentire) vaguely, faintly.

indis'tinto, a ag indistinct.

indistrut'tibile ag indestructible.

in 'divia sf endive.

individu'ale ag individual.

individua'lismo sm individualism.

individua'lista, i, e sm/f individualist.

individualità sf individuality.

individual'mente av individually.

individu'are vt (da forma distinta a) to characterize; (determinare) to locate; (riconoscere) to single out.

indi'viduo sm individual.

indivi'sibile ag indivisible; **quei due sono** ~**i** (fig) those two are inseparable.

indizi'are [indit'tsjare] vt: ~ **qn di qc** to cast suspicion on sb for sth.

indizi'ato, a [indit'tsjato] ag suspected ♦ sm/f suspect.

in 'dizio [in'dittsjo] sm (segno) sign, indication; (POLIZIA) clue; (DIR) piece of evidence.

Indo'cina [indo'tʃina] sf: l'~ Indochina.

'indole sf nature, character.

indo'lente ag indolent.

indo'lenza [indo'lɛntsa] sf indolence.

indolen'zire [indolen'tsire] vt (gambe, braccia etc) to make stiff, cause to ache; (: intorpidire) to numb; ~**rsi** vr to become stiff; to go numb.

indolen'zito, a [indolen'tsito] ag stiff, aching; (intorpidito) numb.

indo'lore ag (anche fig) painless.

indo'mani sm: l'~ the next day, the following day.

Indo'nesia sf: l'~ Indonesia.

indonesi'ano, a ag, sm/f, sm Indonesian.

indo'rare vt (rivestire in oro) to gild; (CUC) to dip in egg yolk; ~ **la pillola** (fig) to sugar the pill.

indos'sare vt (mettere indosso) to put on; (avere indosso) to have on.

indossa'tore, 'trice sm/f model.

in 'dotto, a pp di **indurre**.

indottri'nare vt to indoctrinate.

indovi'nare vt (scoprire) to guess; (immaginare) to imagine, guess; (il futuro) to foretell; **tirare a** ~ to make a shot in the dark.

indovi'nato, a ag successful; (scelta) inspired.

indovi'nello sm riddle.

indo'vino, a sm/f fortuneteller.

indù ag, sm/f Hindu.

indubbia'mente av undoubtedly.

in 'dubbio, a ag certain, undoubted.

in 'duco etc vb vedi **indurre**.

indugi'are [indu'dʒare] vi to take one's time, delay.

in 'dugio [in'dudʒo] sm (ritardo) delay; **senza** ~ without delay.

indul'gente [indul'dʒɛnte] ag indulgent; (giudice) lenient.

indul'genza [indul'dʒɛntsa] sf indulgence; leniency.

in 'dulgere [in'duldʒere] vi: ~ **a** (accondiscendere) to comply with; (abbandonarsi) to indulge in.

in 'dulto, a pp di **indulgere** ♦ sm (DIR) pardon.

indu'mento sm article of clothing,

garment; ~i smpl (vestiti) clothes; ~i intimi underwear sg.
induri'mento sm hardening.
indu'rire vt to harden ♦ vi (anche: ~rsi) to harden, become hard.
in'durre vt: ~ qn a fare qc to induce o persuade sb to do sth; ~ qn in errore to mislead sb; ~ in tentazione to lead into temptation.
in'dussi etc vb vedi indurre.
in'dustria sf industry; la piccola/grande ~ small/big business.
industri'ale ag industrial ♦ sm industrialist.
industrializ'zare [industrjalid'dzare] vt to industrialize.
industrializzazi'one [industrjaliddzat'tsjone] sf industrialization.
industri'arsi vr to do one's best, try hard.
industri'oso, a ag industrious, hardworking.
induzi'one [indut'tsjone] sf induction.
inebe'tito, a ag dazed, stunned.
inebri'are vt (anche fig) to intoxicate; ~rsi vr to become intoxicated.
inecce'pibile [inettʃe'pibile] ag unexceptionable.
i'nedia sf starvation.
i'nedito, a ag unpublished.
inef'fabile ag ineffable.
ineffi'cace [ineffi'katʃe] ag ineffective.
ineffi'cacia [ineffi'katʃa] sf inefficacy, ineffectiveness.
ineffici'ente [ineffi'tʃɛnte] ag inefficient.
ineffici'enza [ineffi'tʃɛntsa] sf inefficiency.
ineguagli'abile [inegwaʎ'ʎabile] ag incomparable, matchless.
ineguagli'anza [inegwaʎ'ʎantsa] sf (sociale) inequality; (di superficie, livello) unevenness.
inegu'ale ag unequal; (irregolare) uneven.
inelut'tabile ag inescapable.
ineluttabilità sf inescapability.
inenar'rabile ag unutterable.
inequivo'cabile ag unequivocal.
ine'rente ag: ~ a concerning, regarding.
i'nerme ag unarmed, defenceless (BRIT), defenseless (US).
inerpi'carsi vr: ~ (su) to clamber (up).
i'nerte ag inert; (inattivo) indolent, sluggish.
i'nerzia [i'nɛrtsja] sf inertia; indolence, sluggishness.
inesat'tezza [inezat'tettsa] sf inaccuracy.
ine'satto, a ag (impreciso) inaccurate, inexact; (erroneo) incorrect; (AMM: non riscosso) uncollected.

inesau'ribile ag inexhaustible.
inesis'tente ag non-existent.
ineso'rabile ag inexorable, relentless.
inesorabil'mente av inexorably.
inesperi'enza [inespe'rjɛntsa] sf inexperience.
ines'perto, a ag inexperienced.
inespli'cabile ag inexplicable.
inesplo'rato, a ag unexplored.
ines'ploso, a ag unexploded.
inespres'sivo, a ag (viso) expressionless, inexpressive.
ines'presso, a ag unexpressed.
inespri'mibile ag inexpressible.
inespu'gnabile [inespuɲ'ɲabile] ag (fortezza, torre etc) impregnable.
ineste'tismo sm beauty problem.
inesti'mabile ag inestimable; (valore) incalculable.
inestir'pabile ag ineradicable.
inestri'cabile ag (anche fig) impenetrable.
inetti'tudine sf ineptitude.
i'netto, a ag (incapace) inept; (che non ha attitudine): ~ (a) unsuited (to).
ine'vaso, a ag (ordine, corrispondenza) outstanding.
inevi'tabile ag inevitable.
inevitabil'mente av inevitably.
i'nezia [i'nɛttsja] sf trifle, thing of no importance.
infagot'tare vt to bundle up, wrap up; ~rsi vr to wrap up.
infal'libile ag infallible.
infallibilità sf infallibility.
infa'mante ag (accusa) defamatory, slanderous.
infa'mare vt to defame.
in'fame ag infamous; (fig: cosa, compito) awful, dreadful.
in'famia sf infamy.
infan'gare vt (sporcare) to cover with mud; (nome, reputazione) to sully; ~rsi vr to get covered in mud; to be sullied.
infan'tile ag child cpd; childlike; (adulto, azione) childish; letteratura ~ children's books pl.
in'fanzia [in'fantsja] sf childhood; (bambini) children pl; prima ~ babyhood, infancy.
infari'nare vt to cover with (o sprinkle with o dip in) flour; ~ di zucchero to sprinkle with sugar.
infarina'tura sf (fig) smattering.
in'farto sm (MED): ~ (cardiaco) coronary.
infasti'dire vt to annoy, irritate; ~rsi vr to get annoyed o irritated.
infati'cabile ag tireless, untiring.
in'fatti cong as a matter of fact, in fact, actually.

infatu'arsi vr: ~ **di** o **per** to become infatuated with, fall for.

infatuazi'one [infatuat'tsjone] sf infatuation.

in'fausto, a ag unpropitious, unfavourable (BRIT), unfavorable (US).

infecondità sf infertility.

infe'condo, a ag infertile.

infe'dele ag unfaithful.

infedeltà sf infidelity.

infe'lice [infe'litʃe] ag unhappy; (sfortunato) unlucky, unfortunate; (inopportuno) inopportune, ill-timed; (mal riuscito: lavoro) bad, poor.

infelicità [infelitʃi'ta] sf unhappiness.

infel'trire vi, ~**rsi** vr (lana) to become matted.

infe'renza [infe'rɛntsa] sf inference.

inferi'ore ag lower; (per intelligenza, qualità) inferior ♦ sm/f inferior; ~ **a** (numero, quantità) less o smaller than; (meno buono) inferior to; ~ **alla media** below average.

inferiorità sf inferiority.

infe'rire vt (dedurre) to infer, deduce.

inferme'ria sf infirmary; (di scuola, nave) sick bay.

infermi'ere, a sm/f nurse.

infermità sf inv illness; infirmity; ~ **di mente** mental illness.

in'fermo, a ag (ammalato) ill; (debole) infirm; ~ **di mente** mentally ill.

infer'nale ag infernal; (proposito, complotto) diabolical; **un tempo** ~ (fam) hellish weather.

in'ferno sm hell; **soffrire le pene dell'**~ (fig) to go through hell.

infero'cire [infero'tʃire] vt to make fierce ♦ vi, ~**rsi** vr to become fierce.

inferri'ata sf grating.

infervo'rare vt to arouse enthusiasm in; ~**rsi** vr to get excited, get carried away.

infes'tare vt to infest.

infet'tare vt to infect; ~**rsi** vr to become infected.

infet'tivo, a ag infectious.

in'fetto, a ag infected; (acque) polluted, contaminated.

infezi'one [infet'tsjone] sf infection.

infiac'chire [infjak'kire] vt to weaken ♦ vi (anche: ~**rsi**) to grow weak.

infiam'mabile ag inflammable.

infiam'mare vt to set alight; (fig, MED) to inflame; ~**rsi** vr to catch fire; (MED) to become inflamed; (fig): ~**rsi di** to be fired with.

infiammazi'one [infjammat'tsjone] sf (MED) inflammation.

infias'care vt to bottle.

infici'are [infi'tʃare] vt (DIR: atto, dichiarazione) to challenge.

in'fido, a ag unreliable, treacherous.

infie'rire vi: ~ **su** (fisicamente) to attack furiously; (verbalmente) to rage at; (epidemia) to rage over.

in'figgere [in'fiddʒere] vt: ~ **qc in** to thrust o drive sth into.

infi'lare vt (ago) to thread; (mettere: chiave) to insert; (: vestito) to slip o put on; (strada) to turn into, take; ~**rsi** vr: ~**rsi in** to slip into; (indossare) to slip on; ~ **un anello al dito** to slip a ring on one's finger; ~ **l'uscio** to slip in; to slip out; ~**rsi la giacca** to put on one's jacket.

infil'trarsi vr to penetrate, seep through; (MIL) to infiltrate.

infil'trato, a sm/f infiltrator.

infiltrazi'one [infiltrat'tsjone] sf infiltration.

infil'zare [infil'tsare] vt (infilare) to string together; (trafiggere) to pierce.

'infimo, a ag lowest; **un albergo di** ~ **ordine** a third-rate hotel.

in'fine av finally; (insomma) in short.

infin'gardo, a ag lazy ♦ sm/f slacker.

infinità sf infinity; (in quantità): **un'**~ **di** an infinite number of.

infinitesi'male ag infinitesimal.

infi'nito, a ag infinite; (LING) infinitive ♦ sm infinity; (LING) infinitive; **all'**~ (senza fine) endlessly; (LING) in the infinitive.

infinocchi'are [infinok'kjare] vt (fam) to hoodwink.

infiore'scenza [infjoreʃ'ʃɛntsa] sf inflorescence.

infir'mare vt (DIR) to invalidate.

infischi'arsi [infis'kjarsi] vr: ~ **di** not to care about.

in'fisso, a pp di **infiggere** ♦ sm fixture; (di porta, finestra) frame.

infit'tire vt, vi (anche: ~**rsi**) to thicken.

inflazio'nare [inflattsjo'nare] vt to inflate.

inflazi'one [inflat'tsjone] sf inflation.

inflazio'nistico, a, ci, che [inflattsjo'nistiko] ag inflationary.

infles'sibile ag inflexible; (ferreo) unyielding.

inflessi'one sf inflexion.

in'fliggere [in'fliddʒere] vt to inflict.

in'flissi etc vb vedi **infliggere**.

in'flitto, a pp di **infliggere**.

influ'ente ag influential.

influ'enza [influ'ɛntsa] sf influence; (MED) influenza, flu.

influen'zare [influen'tsare] vt to influence, have an influence on.

influ'ire vi: ~ **su** to influence.

in 'flusso sm influence.
INFN sigla m = Istituto Nazionale di Fisica
Nucleare.
info 'cato, a ag = infuocato.
info 'gnarsi [infoɲ'ɲarsi] vr (fam) to get into
a mess; ~ in un mare di debiti to be up to
one's o the eyes in debt.
infol 'tire vt, vi to thicken.
infon 'dato, a ag unfounded, groundless.
in 'fondere vt: ~ qc in qn to instill sth in sb;
~ fiducia in qn to inspire sb with
confidence.
infor 'care vt to fork (up); (bicicletta, cavallo)
to get on; (occhiali) to put on.
infor 'male ag informal.
infor 'mare vt to inform, tell; ~rsi vr: ~rsi
(di o su) to inquire (about); tenere
informato qn to keep sb informed.
infor 'matico, a, ci, che ag (settore)
computer cpd ♦ sf computer science.
informa 'tivo, a ag informative; a titolo ~
for information only.
informatiz 'zare [informatid'dzare] vt to
computerize.
infor 'mato, a ag informed; tenersi ~ to
keep o.s. (well-)informed.
informa 'tore sm informer.
informazi 'one [informat'tsjone] sf piece of
information; ~i sfpl information sg;
chiedere un'~ to ask for (some)
information; ~ di garanzia (DIR) = avviso
di garanzia.
in 'forme ag shapeless.
informico 'larsi vr, informico 'lirsi vr: mi si
è informicolata una gamba I've got pins
and needles in my leg.
infor 'nare vt to put in the oven.
infor 'nata sf (anche fig) batch.
infortu 'narsi vr to injure o.s., have an
accident.
infortu 'nato, a ag injured, hurt ♦ sm/f
injured person.
infor 'tunio sm accident; ~ sul lavoro
industrial accident, accident at work.
infortu 'nistica sf study of (industrial)
accidents.
infos 'sarsi vr (terreno) to sink; (guance) to
become hollow.
infos 'sato, a ag hollow; (occhi) deep-set;
(: per malattia) sunken.
infradici 'are [infradi'tʃare] vt (inzuppare) to
soak, drench; (marcire) to rot; ~rsi vr to
get soaked, get drenched; to rot.
infra 'dito sm inv (calzatura) flip flop (BRIT),
thong (US).
in 'frangere [in'frandʒere] vt to smash; (fig:
legge, patti) to break; ~rsi vr to smash,
break.

infran 'gibile [infran'dʒibile] ag
unbreakable.
in 'franto, a pp di infrangere ♦ ag broken.
infra 'rosso, a ag, sm infrared.
infrasettima 'nale ag midweek cpd.
infrastrut 'tura sf infrastructure.
infrazi 'one [infrat'tsjone] sf: ~ a breaking
of, violation of.
infredda 'tura sf slight cold.
infreddo 'lito, a ag cold, chilled.
infre 'quente ag infrequent, rare.
infrol 'lire vi, ~rsi vr (selvaggina) to become
high.
infruttu 'oso, a ag fruitless.
infuo 'cato, a ag (metallo) red-hot; (sabbia)
burning; (fig: discorso) heated, passionate.
infu 'ori av ou; all'~ outwards; all'~ di
(eccetto) except, with the exception of.
infuri 'are vi to rage; ~rsi vr to fly into a
rage.
infusi 'one sf infusion.
in 'fuso, a pp di infondere ♦ ag: scienza ~a
(anche ironico) innate knowledge ♦ sm
infusion; ~ di camomilla camomile tea.
Ing. abbr = ingegnere.
ingabbi 'are vt to (put in a) cage.
ingaggi 'are [ingad'dʒare] vt (assumere con
compenso) to take on, hire; (SPORT) to
sign on; (MIL) to engage.
in 'gaggio [in'gaddʒo] sm hiring; signing on.
ingagliar 'dire [ingaʎʎar'dire] vt to
strengthen, invigorate ♦ vi (anche: ~rsi) to
grow stronger.
ingan 'nare vt to deceive; (coniuge) to be
unfaithful to; (fisco) to cheat; (eludere) to
dodge, elude; (fig: tempo) to while away
♦ vi (apparenza) to be deceptive; ~rsi vr to
be mistaken, be wrong.
inganna 'tore, 'trice ag deceptive;
(persona) deceitful.
ingan 'nevole ag deceptive.
in 'ganno sm deceit, deception; (azione)
trick; (menzogna, frode) cheat, swindle;
(illusione) illusion.
ingarbugli 'are [ingarbuʎ'ʎare] vt to tangle;
(fig) to confuse, muddle; ~rsi vr to become
confused o muddled.
ingarbu 'gliato, a [ingarbuʎ'ʎato] ag
tangled; confused, muddled.
inge 'gnarsi [indʒeɲ'ɲarsi] vr to do one's
best, try hard; ~ per vivere to live by
one's wits; basta ~ un po' you just need a
bit of ingenuity.
inge 'gnere [indʒeɲ'ɲɛre] sm engineer; ~
civile/navale civil/naval engineer.
ingegne 'ria [indʒeɲɲe'ria] sf engineering.
in 'gegno [in'dʒeɲɲo] sm (intelligenza)
intelligence, brains pl; (capacità creativa)

ingenuity; (*disposizione*) talent.
ingegnosità [indʒeɲɲosi'ta] *sf* ingenuity.
inge 'gnoso, a [indʒeɲ'ɲoso] *ag* ingenious,
clever.
ingelo 'sire [indʒelo'sire] *vt* to make jealous
♦ *vi* (*anche*: ~rsi) to become jealous.
in 'gente [in'dʒɛnte] *ag* huge, enormous.
ingenti 'lire [indʒenti'lire] *vt* to refine,
civilize; ~rsi *vr* to become more refined,
become more civilized.
ingenuità [indʒenui'ta] *sf* ingenuousness.
in 'genuo, a [in'dʒɛnuo] *ag* ingenuous,
naïve.
inge 'renza [indʒe'rentsa] *sf* interference.
inge 'rire [indʒe'rire] *vt* to ingest.
inges 'sare [indʒes'sare] *vt* (*MED*) to put in
plaster.
ingessa 'tura [indʒessa'tura] *sf* plaster.
Inghil 'terra [ingil'tɛrra] *sf*: l'~ England.
inghiot 'tire [ingjot'tire] *vt* to swallow.
in 'ghippo [in'gippo] *sm* trick.
ingial 'lire [indʒal'lire] *vi* to go yellow.
ingigan 'tire [indʒigan'tire] *vt* to enlarge,
magnify ♦ *vi* to become gigantic *o*
enormous.
inginocchi 'arsi [indʒinok'kjarsi] *vr* to kneel
(down).
inginocchia 'toio [indʒinokkja'tojo] *sm*
prie-dieu.
ingioiel 'lare [indʒojel'lare] *vt* to bejewel,
adorn with jewels.
ingiù [in'dʒu] *av* down, downwards.
ingi 'ungere [in'dʒundʒere] *vt*: ~ a qn di fare
qc to enjoin *o* order sb to do sth.
ingi 'unto, a [in'dʒunto] *pp* di ingiungere.
ingiunzi 'one [indʒun'tsjone] *sf* injunction,
command; ~ di pagamento final demand.
ingi 'uria [in'dʒurja] *sf* insult; (*fig: danno*)
damage.
ingiuri 'are [indʒu'rjare] *vt* to insult, abuse.
ingiuri 'oso, a [indʒu'rjoso] *ag* insulting,
abusive.
ingiusta 'mente [indʒusta'mente] *av*
unjustly.
ingiustifi 'cabile [indʒustifi'kabile] *ag*
unjustifiable.
ingiustifi 'cato, a [indʒustifi'kato] *ag*
unjustified.
ingius 'tizia [indʒus'tittsja] *sf* injustice.
ingi 'usto, a [in'dʒusto] *ag* unjust, unfair.
in 'glese *ag* English ♦ *sm/f* Englishman/
woman ♦ *sm* (*LING*) English; gli I~ the
English; andarsene *o* filare all'~ to take
French leave.
inglori 'oso, a *ag* inglorious.
ingob 'bire *vi*, ~rsi *vr* to become stooped.
ingoi 'are *vt* to gulp (down); (*fig*) to swallow
(up); ha dovuto ~ il rospo (*fig*) he had to

accept the situation.
ingol 'fare *vt*, ~rsi *vr* (*motore*) to flood.
ingolo 'sire *vt*: ~ qn to make sb's mouth
water; (*fig*) to attract sb ♦ *vi* (*anche*: ~rsi):
~ (di) (*anche fig*) to become greedy (for).
ingom 'brante *ag* cumbersome.
ingom 'brare *vt* (*strada*) to block; (*stanza*) to
clutter up.
in 'gombro, a *ag*: ~ di (*strada*) blocked by;
(*stanza*) cluttered up with ♦ *sm* obstacle;
essere d'~ to be in the way; per ragioni di
~ for reasons of space.
ingor 'digia [ingor'didʒa] *sf*: ~ (di) greed
(for); avidity (for).
in 'gordo, a *ag*: ~ di greedy for; (*fig*)
greedy *o* avid for ♦ *sm/f* glutton.
ingor 'gare *vt* to block; ~rsi *vr* to be
blocked up, be choked up.
in 'gorgo, ghi *sm* blockage, obstruction;
(*anche*: ~ stradale) traffic jam.
ingoz 'zare [ingot'tsare] *vt* (*animali*) to
fatten; (*fig: persona*) to stuff; ~rsi *vr*: ~rsi
(di) to stuff o.s. (with).
ingra 'naggio [ingra'naddʒo] *sm* (*TECN*)
gear; (*di orologio*) mechanism; gli ~i della
burocrazia the bureaucratic machinery.
ingra 'nare *vi* to mesh, engage ♦ *vt* to
engage; ~ la marcia to get into gear.
ingrandi 'mento *sm* enlargement;
extension; magnification; growth;
expansion.
ingran 'dire *vt* (*anche FOT*) to enlarge;
(*estendere*) to extend; (*OTTICA, fig*) to
magnify ♦ *vi* (*anche*: ~rsi) to become
larger *o* bigger; (*aumentare*) to grow,
increase; (*espandersi*) to expand.
ingrandi 'tore *sm* (*FOT*) enlarger.
ingras 'saggio [ingras'saddʒo] *sm* greasing.
ingras 'sare *vt* to make fat; (*animali*) to
fatten; (*AGR: terreno*) to manure;
(*lubrificare*) to grease ♦ *vi* (*anche*: ~rsi) to
get fat, put on weight.
ingrati 'tudine *sf* ingratitude.
in 'grato, a *ag* ungrateful; (*lavoro*)
thankless, unrewarding.
ingrazi 'are [ingrat'tsjare] *vt*: ~rsi qn to
ingratiate o.s. with sb.
ingredi 'ente *sm* ingredient.
in 'gresso *sm* (*porta*) entrance; (*atrio*) hall;
(*l'entrare*) entrance, entry; (*facoltà di
entrare*) admission; "~ libero" "admission
free"; ~ principale main entrance; ~ di
servizio tradesmen's entrance.
ingros 'sare *vt* to increase; (*folla, livello*) to
swell ♦ *vi* (*anche*: ~rsi) to increase; to
swell.
in 'grosso *av*: all'~ (*COMM*) wholesale;
(*all'incirca*) roughly, about.

ingru'gnato, a [ingruɲ'ɲato] *ag* grumpy.
inguai'arsi *vr* to get into trouble.
inguai'nare *vt* to sheathe.
ingual'cibile [ingwal'tʃibile] *ag* crease-resistant.
ingua'ribile *ag* incurable.
'inguine *sm* (*ANAT*) groin.
ingurgi'tare [ingurdʒi'tare] *vt* to gulp down.
ini'bire *vt* to forbid, prohibit; (*PSIC*) to inhibit.
ini'bito, a *ag* inhibited ♦ *sm/f* inhibited person.
inibi'torio, a *ag* (*PSIC*) inhibitory, inhibitive; (*provvedimento, misure*) restrictive.
inibizi'one [inibit'tsjone] *sf* prohibition; inhibition.
iniet'tare *vt* to inject; ~**rsi** *vr*: ~**rsi di sangue** (*occhi*) to become bloodshot.
iniet'tore *sm* injector.
iniezi'one [injet'tsjone] *sf* injection.
inimi'care *vt* to alienate, make hostile; ~**rsi** *vr*: ~**rsi con qn** to fall out with sb; **si è inimicato gli amici di un tempo** he has alienated his old friends.
inimi'cizia [inimi'tʃittsja] *sf* animosity.
inimi'tabile *ag* inimitable.
inimmagi'nabile [inimmadʒi'nabile] *ag* unimaginable.
ininfiam'mabile *ag* non-flammable.
inintelli'gibile [inintelli'dʒibile] *ag* unintelligible.
ininterrotta'mente *av* non-stop, continuously.
ininter'rotto, a *ag* (*fila*) unbroken; (*rumore*) uninterrupted.
iniquità *sf inv* iniquity; (*atto*) wicked action.
i'niquo, a *ag* iniquitous.
inizi'ale [init'tsjale] *ag, sf* initial.
inizializ'zare [inittsjalid'dzare] *vt* (*INFORM*) to boot.
inizial'mente [inittsjal'mente] *av* initially, at first.
inizi'are [init'tsjare] *vi, vt* to begin, start; ~ **qn a** to initiate sb into; (*pittura etc*) to introduce sb to; ~ **a fare qc** to start doing sth.
inizia'tiva [inittsja'tiva] *sf* initiative; ~ **privata** private enterprise.
inizia'tore, 'trice [inittsja'tore] *sm/f* initiator.
i'nizio [i'nittsjo] *sm* beginning; **all'**~ at the beginning, at the start; **dare** ~ **a qc** to start sth, get sth going; **essere agli** ~**i** (*progetto, lavoro etc*) to be in the initial stages.
innaffi'are *etc* = **annaffiare** *etc*.
innal'zare [innal'tsare] *vt* (*sollevare, alzare*)

to raise; (*rizzare*) to erect; ~**rsi** *vr* to rise.
innamora'mento *sm* falling in love.
innamo'rare *vt* to enchant, charm; ~**rsi** *vr*: ~**rsi (di qn)** to fall in love (with sb).
innamo'rato, a *ag* (*che nutre amore*): ~ **(di)** in love (with); (*appassionato*): ~ **di** very fond of ♦ *sm/f* lover; (*anche scherzoso*) sweetheart.
in'nanzi [in'nantsi] *av* (*stato in luogo*) in front, ahead; (*moto a luogo*) forward, on; (*tempo: prima*) before ♦ *prep* (*prima*) before; ~ **a** in front of; **d'ora** ~ from now on; **farsi** ~ to step forward; ~ **tempo** ahead of time.
innanzi'tutto [innantsi'tutto] *av* above all; (*per prima cosa*) first of all.
in'nato, a *ag* innate.
innatu'rale *ag* unnatural.
inne'gabile *ag* undeniable.
inneggi'are [inned'dʒare] *vi*: ~ **a** to sing hymns to; (*fig*) to sing the praises of.
innervo'sire *vt*: ~ **qn** to get on sb's nerves; ~**rsi** *vr* to get irritated *o* upset.
innes'care *vt* to prime.
in'nesco, schi *sm* primer.
innes'tare *vt* (*BOT, MED*) to graft; (*TECN*) to engage; (*inserire: presa*) to insert.
in'nesto *sm* graft; grafting *no pl*; (*TECN*) clutch; (*ELETTR*) connection.
'inno *sm* hymn; ~ **nazionale** national anthem.
inno'cente [inno'tʃente] *ag* innocent.
inno'cenza [inno'tʃentsa] *sf* innocence.
in'nocuo, a *ag* innocuous, harmless.
innomi'nato, a *ag* unnamed.
inno'vare *vt* to change, make innovations in.
innova'tivo, a *ag* innovative.
innovazi'one [innovat'tsjone] *sf* innovation.
innume'revole *ag* innumerable.
inocu'lare *vt* (*MED*) to inoculate.
ino'doro, a *ag* odourless (*BRIT*), odorless (*US*).
inoffen'sivo, a *ag* harmless.
inol'trare *vt* (*AMM*) to pass on, forward; ~**rsi** *vr* (*addentrarsi*) to advance, go forward.
inol'trato, a *ag*: **a notte** ~**a** late at night; **a primavera** ~**a** late in the spring.
i'noltre *av* besides, moreover.
i'noltro *sm* (*AMM*) forwarding.
inon'dare *vt* to flood.
inondazi'one [inondat'tsjone] *sf* flooding *no pl*; flood.
inope'roso, a *ag* inactive, idle.
inopi'nato, a *ag* unexpected.
inoppor'tuno, a *ag* untimely, ill-timed; (*poco adatto*) inappropriate; (*momento*)

inopportune.

inoppu'gnabile [inoppuɲ'ɲabile] *ag* incontrovertible.

inor'ganico, a, ci, che *ag* inorganic.

inorgo'glire [inorgoʎ'ʎire] *vt* to make proud ♦ *vi* (*anche:* ~rsi) to become proud; ~rsi di qc to pride o.s. on sth.

inorri'dire *vt* to horrify ♦ *vi* to be horrified.

inospi'tale *ag* inhospitable.

inosser'vante *ag:* essere ~ di to fail to comply with.

inosser'vato, a *ag* (*non notato*) unobserved; (*non rispettato*) not observed, not kept; passare ~ to go unobserved, escape notice.

inossi'dabile *ag* stainless.

INPS *sigla m* (= *Istituto Nazionale Previdenza Sociale*) social security service.

inqua'drare *vt* (*foto, immagine*) to frame; (*fig*) to situate, set.

inquadra'tura *sf* (*CINE, FOT: atto*) framing; (: *immagine*) shot; (: *sequenza*) sequence.

inqualifi'cabile *ag* unspeakable.

inquie'tante *ag* disturbing, worrying.

inquie'tare *vt* (*turbare*) to disturb, worry; ~rsi *vr* to worry, become anxious; (*impazientirsi*) to get upset.

inqui'eto, a *ag* restless; (*preoccupato*) worried, anxious.

inquie'tudine *sf* anxiety, worry.

inqui'lino, a *sm/f* tenant.

inquina'mento *sm* pollution.

inqui'nare *vt* to pollute.

inqui'rente *ag* (*DIR*): magistrato ~ examining (*BRIT*) o committing (*US*) magistrate; commissione ~ commission of inquiry.

inqui'sire *vt, vi* to investigate.

inqui'sito, a *ag* (*persona*) under investigation.

inquisi'tore, 'trice *ag* (*sguardo*) inquiring.

inquisizi'one [inkwizit'tsjone] *sf* inquisition.

insabbia'mento *sm* (*fig*) shelving.

insabbi'are *vt* (*fig: pratica*) to shelve; ~rsi *vr* (*barca*) to run aground; (*fig: pratica*) to be shelved.

insac'care *vt* (*grano, farina etc*) to bag, put into sacks; (*carne*) to put into sausage skins.

insac'cati *smpl* (*CUC*) sausages.

insa'lata *sf* salad; (*pianta*) lettuce; ~ mista mixed salad.

insalati'era *sf* salad bowl.

insa'lubre *ag* unhealthy.

insa'nabile *ag* (*piaga*) which cannot be healed; (*situazione*) irremediable; (*odio*) implacable.

insangui'nare *vt* to stain with blood.

in'sania *sf* insanity.

in'sano, a *ag* (*pazzo, folle*) insane.

insapo'nare *vt* to soap; ~rsi le mani to soap one's hands.

insapo'nata *sf:* dare un'~ a qc to give sth a (quick) soaping.

insapo'rire *vt* to flavour (*BRIT*), flavor (*US*); (*con spezie*) to season; ~rsi *vr* to acquire flavo(u)r.

insa'poro, a *ag* tasteless, insipid.

insa'puta *sf:* all'~ di qn without sb knowing.

insazi'abile [insat'tsjabile] *ag* insatiable.

inscato'lare *vt* (*frutta, carne*) to can.

insce'nare [inʃe'nare] *vt* (*TEAT*) to stage, put on; (*fig*) to stage.

inscin'dibile [inʃin'dibile] *ag* (*fattori*) inseparable; (*legame*) indissoluble.

insec'chire [insek'kire] *vt* (*seccare*) to dry up; (: *piante*) to wither ♦ *vi* to dry up, become dry; to wither.

insedia'mento *sm* (*AMM: in carica, ufficio*) installation; (*villaggio, colonia*) settlement.

insedi'are *vt* (*AMM*) to install; ~rsi *vr* (*AMM*) to take up office; (*colonia, profughi etc*) to settle; (*MIL*) to take up positions.

in'segna [in'seɲɲa] *sf* sign; (*emblema*) sign, emblem; (*bandiera*) flag, banner; ~e *sfpl* (*decorazioni*) insignia *pl*.

insegna'mento [inseɲɲa'mento] *sm* teaching; trarre ~ da un'esperienza to learn from an experience, draw a lesson from an experience; che ti serva da ~ let this be a lesson to you.

inse'gnante [inseɲ'ɲante] *ag* teaching ♦ *sm/f* teacher.

inse'gnare [inseɲ'ɲare] *vt, vi* to teach; ~ a qn qc to teach sb sth; ~ a qn a fare qc to teach sb (how) to do sth; come lei ben m'insegna ... (*ironico*) as you will doubtless be aware ....

insegui'mento *sm* pursuit, chase; darsi all'~ di qn to give chase to sb.

insegui're *vt* to pursue, chase.

insegui'tore, 'trice *sm/f* pursuer.

insel'lare *vt* to saddle.

inselvati'chire [inselvati'kire] *vt* (*persona*) to make unsociable ♦ *vi* (*anche:* ~rsi) to grow wild; (*persona*) to become unsociable.

inseminazi'one [inseminat'tsjone] *sf* insemination.

insena'tura *sf* inlet, creek.

insen'sato, a *ag* senseless, stupid.

insen'sibile *ag* (*anche fig*) insensitive.

insensibilità *sf* insensitivity, insensibility.

insepa'rabile *ag* inseparable.

inse 'polto, a *ag* unburied.

inseri 'mento *sm* (*gen*) insertion; **problemi di** ~ (*di persona*) adjustment problems.

inse 'rire *vt* to insert; (*ELETTR*) to connect; (*allegare*) to enclose; ~**rsi** *vr* (*fig*): ~**rsi in** to become part of; ~ **un annuncio sul giornale** to put *o* place an advertisement in the newspaper.

in 'serto *sm* (*pubblicazione*) insert; ~ **filmato** (film) clip.

inser 'vibile *ag* useless.

inservi 'ente *sm/f* attendant.

inserzi 'one [inser'tsjone] *sf* insertion; (*avviso*) advertisement; **fare un'**~ **sul giornale** to put an advertisement in the newspaper.

inserzio 'nista, i, e [insertsjo'nista] *sm/f* advertiser.

insetti 'cida, i [insetti'tʃida] *sm* insecticide.

in 'setto *sm* insect.

insicu 'rezza [insiku'rettsa] *sf* insecurity.

insi 'curo, a *ag* insecure.

in 'sidia *sf* snare, trap; (*pericolo*) hidden danger; **tendere un'**~ **a qn** to lay *o* set a trap for sb.

insidi 'are *vt* (*MIL*) to harass; ~ **la vita di qn** to make an attempt on sb's life.

insidi 'oso, a *ag* insidious.

insi 'eme *av* together; (*contemporaneamente*) at the same time ♦ *prep*: ~ **a** *o* **con** together with ♦ *sm* whole; (*MAT, servizio, assortimento*) set; (*MODA*) ensemble, outfit; **tutti** ~ all together; **tutto** ~ all together; (*in una volta*) at one go; **nell'**~ on the whole; **d'**~ (*veduta etc*) overall.

in 'signe [in'siɲɲe] *ag* (*persona*) famous, distinguished, eminent; (*città, monumento*) notable.

insignifi 'cante [insiɲɲifi'kante] *ag* insignificant.

insi 'gnire [insiɲ'ɲire] *vt*: ~ **qn di** to honour (*BRIT*) *o* honor (*US*) sb with, decorate sb with.

insin 'cero, a [insin'tʃero] *ag* insincere.

insinda 'cabile *ag* unquestionable.

insinu 'ante *ag* (*osservazione, sguardo*) insinuating; (*maniere*) ingratiating.

insinu 'are *vt* (*introdurre*): ~ **qc in** to slip *o* slide sth into; (*fig*) to insinuate, imply; ~**rsi** *vr*: ~**rsi in** to seep into; (*fig*) to creep into; to worm one's way into.

insinuazi 'one [insinuat'tsjone] *sf* (*fig*) insinuation.

in 'sipido, a *ag* insipid.

insis 'tente *ag* insistent; (*pioggia, dolore*) persistent.

insistente 'mente *av* repeatedly.

insis 'tenza [insis'tɛntsa] *sf* insistence; persistence.

in 'sistere *vi*: ~ **su qc** to insist on sth; ~ **in qc/a fare** (*perseverare*) to persist in sth/in doing.

insis 'tito, a *pp di* **insistere**.

'insito, a *ag*: ~ (**in**) inherent (in).

insoddis 'fatto, a *ag* dissatisfied.

insoddisfazi 'one [insoddisfat'tsjone] *sf* dissatisfaction.

insoffe 'rente *ag* intolerant.

insoffe 'renza [insoffe'rɛntsa] *sf* impatience.

insolazi 'one [insolat'tsjone] *sf* (*MED*) sunstroke.

inso 'lente *ag* insolent.

insolen 'tire *vi* to grow insolent ♦ *vt* to insult, be rude to.

inso 'lenza [inso'lɛntsa] *sf* insolence.

in 'solito, a *ag* unusual, out of the ordinary.

inso 'lubile *ag* insoluble.

inso 'luto, a *ag* (*non risolto*) unsolved; (*non pagato*) unpaid, outstanding.

insol 'vente *ag* (*DIR*) insolvent.

insol 'venza [insol'vɛntsa] *sf* (*DIR*) insolvency.

insol 'vibile *ag* insolvent.

in 'somma *av* (*in breve, in conclusione*) in short; (*dunque*) well ♦ *escl* for heaven's sake!

inson 'dabile *ag* unfathomable.

in 'sonne *ag* sleepless.

in 'sonnia *sf* insomnia, sleeplessness.

insonno 'lito, a *ag* sleepy, drowsy.

insonorizzazi 'one [insonoriddzat'tsjone] *sf* soundproofing.

insoppor 'tabile *ag* unbearable.

insoppri 'mibile *ag* insuppressible.

insor 'genza [insor'dʒɛntsa] *sf* (*di malattia*) onset.

in 'sorgere [in'sordʒere] *vi* (*ribellarsi*) to rise up, rebel; (*apparire*) to come up, arise.

insormon 'tabile *ag* (*ostacolo*) insurmountable, insuperable.

in 'sorsi *etc vb vedi* **insorgere**.

in 'sorto, a *pp di* **insorgere** ♦ *sm/f* rebel, insurgent.

insospet 'tabile *ag* (*al di sopra di ogni sospetto*) above suspicion; (*inatteso*) unsuspected.

insospet 'tire *vt* to make suspicious ♦ *vi* (*anche*: ~**rsi**) to become suspicious.

insoste 'nibile *ag* (*posizione, teoria*) untenable; (*dolore, situazione*) intolerable, unbearable; **le spese di manutenzione sono** ~**i** the maintenance costs are excessive.

insostitu 'ibile *ag* (*persona*) irreplaceable; (*aiuto, presenza*) invaluable.

insoz'zare [insot'tsare] vt (pavimento) to make dirty; (fig: reputazione, memoria) to tarnish, sully; ~**rsi** vr to get dirty.

inspe'rabile ag: **la guarigione/salvezza era** ~ there was no hope of a cure/of rescue; **abbiamo ottenuto risultati** ~**i** the results we achieved were far better than we had hoped.

inspe'rato, a ag unhoped-for.

inspie'gabile ag inexplicable.

inspi'rare vt to breathe in, inhale.

in'stabile ag (carico, indole) unstable; (tempo) unsettled; (equilibrio) unsteady.

instabilità sf instability; (di tempo) changeability.

instal'lare vt to install; ~**rsi** vr (sistemarsi): ~**rsi in** to settle in.

installazi'one [installat'tsjone] sf installation.

instan'cabile ag untiring, indefatigable.

instau'rare vt to establish.

instaurazi'one [instaurat'tsjone] sf establishment.

instil'lare vt to instil.

instra'dare vt = istradare.

insù av up, upwards; **guardare all'**~ to look up o upwards; **naso all'**~ turned-up nose.

insubordinazi'one [insubordinat'tsjone] sf insubordination.

insuc'cesso [insut'tʃɛsso] sm failure, flop.

insudici'are [insudi'tʃare] vt to dirty; ~**rsi** vr to get dirty.

insuffici'ente [insuffi'tʃɛnte] ag insufficient; (compito, allievo) inadequate.

insuffici'enza [insuffi'tʃɛntsa] sf insufficiency; inadequacy; (INS) fail; ~ **di prove** (DIR) lack of evidence.

insu'lare ag insular.

insu'lina sf insulin.

in'sulso, a ag (sciocco) inane, silly; (persona) dull, insipid.

insul'tare vt to insult, affront.

in'sulto sm insult, affront.

insupe'rabile ag (ostacolo, difficoltà) insuperable, insurmountable; (eccellente: qualità, prodotto) unbeatable; (: persona, interpretazione) unequalled.

insuper'bire vt to make proud, make arrogant; ~**rsi** vr to become arrogant.

insurrezi'one [insurret'tsjone] sf revolt, insurrection.

insussis'tente ag non-existent.

intac'care vt (fare tacche) to cut into; (corrodere) to corrode; (fig: cominciare ad usare: risparmi) to break into; (: ledere) to damage.

intagli'are [intaʎ'ʎare] vt to carve.

intaglia'tore, 'trice [intaʎʎa'tore] sm/f engraver.

in'taglio [in'taʎʎo] sm carving.

intan'gibile [intan'dʒibile] ag (bene, patrimonio) untouchable; (fig: diritto) inviolable.

in'tanto av (nel frattempo) meanwhile, in the meantime; (per cominciare) just to begin with; ~ **che** cong while.

intarsi'are vt to inlay.

in'tarsio sm inlaying no pl, marquetry no pl; inlay.

intasa'mento sm (ostruzione) blockage, obstruction; (AUT: ingorgo) traffic jam.

inta'sare vt to choke (up), block (up); (AUT) to obstruct, block; ~**rsi** vr to become choked o blocked.

intas'care vt to pocket.

in'tatto, a ag intact; (puro) unsullied.

intavo'lare vt to start, enter into.

inte'gerrimo, a [inte'dʒɛrrimo] ag honest, upright.

inte'grale ag complete; (pane, farina) wholemeal (BRIT), wholewheat (US); **film in versione** ~ uncut version of a film; **calcolo** ~ (MAT) integral calculus; **edizione** ~ unabridged edition.

inte'grante ag: **parte** f ~ integral part.

inte'grare vt to complete; (MAT) to integrate; ~**rsi** vr (persona) to become integrated.

integra'tivo, a ag (assegno) supplementary; (INS): **esame** ~ assessment test sat when changing schools.

integra'tore sm: ~**i alimentari** nutritional supplements.

integrazi'one [integrat'tsjone] sf integration.

integrità sf integrity.

'integro, a ag (intatto, intero) complete, whole; (retto) upright.

intelaia'tura sf frame; (fig) structure, framework.

intel'letto sm intellect.

intellettu'ale ag, sm/f intellectual.

intellettu'aloide (peg) ag pseudo-intellectual ♦ sm/f pseudo-intellectual, would-be intellectual.

intelli'gente [intelli'dʒɛnte] ag intelligent.

intelli'genza [intelli'dʒɛntsa] sf intelligence.

intelli'ghenzia [intelli'gɛntsja] sf intelligentsia.

intelli'gibile [intelli'dʒibile] ag intelligible.

inteme'rato, a ag (persona, vita) blameless, irreproachable; (coscienza) clear; (fama) unblemished.

intempe'rante ag intemperate,

immoderate.
intempe'ranza [intempe'rantsa] *sf*
intemperance; ~**e** *sfpl* (*eccessi*) excesses.
intem'perie *sfpl* bad weather *sg.*
intempes'tivo, a *ag* untimely.
inten'dente *sm*: ~ **di Finanza** inland (*BRIT*)
o internal (*US*) revenue officer.
inten'denza [inten'dɛntsa] *sf*: ~ **di Finanza**
inland (*BRIT*) *o* internal (*US*) revenue
office.
in'tendere *vt* (*avere intenzione*): ~ **fare qc** to
intend *o* mean to do sth; (*comprendere*) to
understand; (*udire*) to hear; (*significare*) to
mean; ~**rsi** *vr* (*conoscere*): ~**rsi di** to know
a lot about, be a connoisseur of;
(*accordarsi*) to get on (well); ~**rsi con qn**
su qc to come to an agreement with sb
about sth; **intendersela con qn** (*avere una
relazione amorosa*) to have an affair with
sb; **mi ha dato a ~ che ...** he led me to
believe that ...; **non vuole ~ ragione** he
won't listen to reason; **s'intende!**
naturally!, of course!; **intendiamoci** let's
get it quite clear; **ci siamo intesi?** is that
clear?, is that understood?
intendi'mento *sm* (*intelligenza*)
understanding; (*proposito*) intention.
intendi'tore, 'trice *sm/f* connoisseur,
expert; **a buon intenditor poche parole**
(*proverbio*) a word is enough to the wise.
intene'rire *vt* (*fig*) to move (to pity); ~**rsi** *vr*
(*fig*) to be moved.
intensifi'care *vt*, ~**rsi** *vr* to intensify.
intensità *sf* intensity; (*del vento*) force,
strength.
inten'sivo, a *ag* intensive.
in'tenso, a *ag* (*luce, profumo*) strong;
(*colore*) intense, deep.
inten'tare *vt* (*DIR*): ~ **causa contro qn** to
start *o* institute proceedings against sb.
inten'tato, a *ag*: **non lasciare nulla d'~** to
leave no stone unturned, try everything.
in'tento, a *ag* (*teso, assorto*): ~ **(a)** intent
(on), absorbed (in) ♦ *sm* aim, purpose; **fare
qc con l'~ di** to do sth with the intention
of; **riuscire nell'~** to achieve one's aim.
intenzio'nale [intentsjo'nale] *ag*
intentional; (*DIR*: *omicidio*) premeditated;
fallo ~ (*SPORT*) deliberate foul.
intenzio'nato, a [intentsjo'nato] *ag*: **essere
~ a fare qc** to intend to do sth, have the
intention of doing sth; **ben** ~ well-
meaning, well-intentioned; **mal** ~ ill-
intentioned.
intenzi'one [inten'tsjone] *sf* intention; (*DIR*)
intent; **avere ~ di fare qc** to intend to do
sth, have the intention of doing sth.
intera'gire [intera'dʒire] *vi* to interact.

intera'mente *av* entirely, completely.
interat'tivo, a *ag* interactive.
interazi'one [interat'tsjone] *sf* interaction.
interca'lare *sm* pet phrase, stock phrase
♦ *vt* to insert.
interca'pedine *sf* gap, cavity.
inter'cedere [inter'tʃɛdere] *vi* to intercede.
intercessi'one [intertʃes'sjone] *sf*
intercession.
intercetta'mento [intertʃetta'mento] *sm*
= **intercettazione**.
intercet'tare [intertʃet'tare] *vt* to intercept.
intercettazi'one [intertʃettat'tsjone] *sf*: ~
telefonica telephone tapping.
intercity [inter'siti] *sm inv* (*FERR*) ≈ intercity
(train).
intercon'nettere *vt* to interconnect.
inter'correre *vi* (*esserci*) to exist; (*passare:
tempo*) to elapse.
inter'corso, a *pp di* **intercorrere**.
inter'detto, a *pp di* **interdire** ♦ *ag* forbidden,
prohibited; (*sconcertato*) dumbfounded
♦ *sm* (*REL*) interdict; **rimanere** ~ to be
taken aback.
inter'dire *vt* to forbid, prohibit, ban; (*REL*)
to interdict; (*DIR*) to deprive of civil
rights.
interdizi'one [interdit'tsjone] *sf*
prohibition, ban.
interessa'mento *sm* interest; (*intervento*)
intervention, good offices *pl*.
interes'sante *ag* interesting; **essere in
stato** ~ to be expecting (a baby).
interes'sare *vt* to interest; (*concernere*) to
concern, be of interest to; (*far intervenire*):
~ **qn a** to draw sb's attention to ♦ *vi*: ~ **a**
to interest, matter to; ~**rsi** *vr* (*mostrare
interesse*): ~**rsi a** to take an interest in, be
interested in; (*occuparsi*): ~**rsi di** to take
care of; **precipitazioni che interessano le
regioni settentrionali** rainfall affecting
the north; **si è interessato di farmi avere
quei biglietti** he took the trouble to get
me those tickets.
interes'sato, a *ag* (*coinvolto*) interested,
involved; (*peg*): **essere** ~ to act out of
pure self-interest ♦ *sm/f* (*coinvolto*) person
concerned; **a tutti gli** ~**i** to all those
concerned, to all interested parties.
inte'resse *sm* (*anche COMM*) interest;
(*tornaconto*): **fare qc per** ~ to do sth out of
self-interest; ~ **maturato** (*ECON*) accrued
interest; ~ **privato in atti di ufficio** (*AMM*)
abuse of public office.
interes'senza [interes'sɛntsa] *sf* (*ECON*)
profit-sharing.
inter'faccia, ce [inter'fattʃa] *sf* (*INFORM*)
interface; ~ **utente** user interface.

interfacci'are [interfat't∫are] vt (INFORM) to interface.
interfe'renza [interfe'rɛntsa] sf interference.
interfe'rire vi to interfere.
inter'fono sm intercom; (apparecchio) internal phone.
interiezi'one [interjet'tsjone] sf exclamation, interjection.
'interim sm inv (periodo) interim, interval; **ministro ad** ~ acting o interim minister; (incarico) temporary appointment.
interi'ora sfpl entrails.
interi'ore ag inner cpd; **parte** f ~ inside.
interiorità sf inner being.
interioriz'zare [interjorid'dzare] vt to internalize.
inter'linea sf (DATTILOGRAFIA) spacing; (TIP) leading; **doppia** ~ double spacing.
interlocu'tore, 'trice sm/f speaker.
interlocu'torio, a ag interlocutory.
inter'ludio sm (MUS) interlude.
intermedi'ario, a ag, sm/f intermediary.
intermediazi'one [intermedjat'tsjone] sf mediation.
inter'medio, a ag intermediate.
inter'mezzo [inter'mɛddzo] sm (intervallo) interval; (breve spettacolo) intermezzo.
intermi'nabile ag interminable, endless.
intermit'tente ag intermittent.
intermit'tenza [intermit'tentsa] sf: **ad** ~ intermittent.
interna'mento sm internment; confinement (to a mental hospital).
inter'nare vt (arrestare) to intern; (MED) to confine to a mental hospital.
inter'nato, a ag interned; confined (to a mental hospital) ♦ sm/f internee; inmate (of a mental hospital) ♦ sm (collegio) boarding school; (MED) period as a houseman (BRIT) o an intern (US).
internazio'nale [internattsjo'nale] ag international.
'Internet ['internet] sf Internet; **in** ~ on the Internet.
inter'nista, i, e sm/f specialist in internal medicine.
in'terno, a ag (di dentro) internal, interior, inner; (: mare) inland; (nazionale) domestic; (allievo) boarding ♦ sm inside, interior; (di paese) interior; (fodera) lining; (di appartamento) flat (BRIT) o apartment (US) (number); (TEL) extension ♦ sm/f (INS) boarder; ~**i** smpl (CINE) interior shots; **commissione** ~**a** (INS) internal examination board; **"per uso** ~**"** (MED) "to be taken internally"; **all'**~ inside; **Ministero degli I~i** Ministry of the

Interior, ≈ Home Office (BRIT), ≈ Department of the Interior (US); **notizie dall'**~ (STAMPA) home news.
in'tero, a ag (integro, intatto) whole, entire; (completo, totale) complete; (numero) whole; (non ridotto: biglietto) full.
interpel'lanza [interpel'lantsa] sf: **presentare un'**~ (POL) to ask a (parliamentary) question; ~ **parlamentare** interpellation.
interpel'lare vt to consult; (POL) to question.
INTER'POL sigla f (= International Criminal Police Organization) INTERPOL.
inter'porre vt (ostacolo): ~ **qc a qc** to put sth in the way of sth; (influenza) to use; **interporsi** vr to intervene; ~ **appello** (DIR) to appeal; **interporsi fra** (mettersi in mezzo) to come between.
inter'posto, a pp di **interporre**.
interpre'tare vt (spiegare, tradurre) to interpret; (MUS, TEAT) to perform; (personaggio, sonata) to play; (canzone) to sing.
interpretari'ato sm interpreting.
interpretazi'one [interpretat'tsjone] sf interpretation.
in'terprete sm/f interpreter; (TEAT) actor/ actress, performer; (MUS) performer; **farsi** ~ **di** to act as a spokesman for.
interpunzi'one [interpun'tsjone] sf punctuation; **segni di** ~ punctuation marks.
inter'rare vt (seme, pianta) to plant; (tubature etc) to lay underground; (MIL: pezzo d'artiglieria) to dig in; (riempire di terra: canale) to fill in.
interregio'nale [interred3o'nale] sm train that travels between two or more regions of Italy.
interro'gare vt to question; (INS) to test.
interroga'tivo, a ag (occhi, sguardo) questioning, inquiring; (LING) interrogative ♦ sm question; (fig) mystery.
interroga'torio, a ag interrogatory, questioning ♦ sm (DIR) questioning no pl.
interrogazi'one [interrogat'tsjone] sf questioning no pl; (INS) oral test; (POL): ~ **(parlamentare)** question.
inter'rompere vt to interrupt; (studi, trattative) to break off, interrupt; **-rsi** vi to break off, stop.
inter'rotto, a pp di **interrompere**.
interrut'tore sm switch.
interruzi'one [interrut'tsjone] sf (vedi interrompere) interruption; break; ~ **di gravidanza** termination of pregnancy.
interse'care vt, ~**rsi** vr to intersect.
inter'stizio [inter'stittsjo] sm interstice,

crack.

interur bano, a *ag* inter-city; (*TEL:
chiamata*) trunk *cpd* (*BRIT*), long-distance; (*:
telefono*) long-distance ♦ *sf* trunk call
(*BRIT*), long-distance call.

inter Vallo *sm* interval; (*spazio*) space, gap;
~ **pubblicitario** (*TV*) commercial break.

interve hire *vi* (*partecipare*): ~ **a** to take
part in; (*intromettersi: anche POL*) to
intervene; (*MED: operare*) to operate.

interven tista, i, e *ag*, *sm/f* interventionist.

inter Vento *sm* participation; (*intromissio-
ne*) intervention; (*MED*) operation; (*breve
discorso*) speech; **fare un** ~ **nel corso di**
(*dibattito, programma*) to take part in.

interve huto, a *pp di* **intervenire** ♦ *sm*: **gli** ~**i**
those present.

inter Vista *sf* interview.

intervis tare *vt* to interview.

intervista tore, trice *sm/f* interviewer.

in teso, a *pp di* **intendere** ♦ *ag* agreed ♦ *sf*
understanding; (*accordo*) agreement,
understanding; **resta** ~ **che** ... it is
understood that ...; **non darsi per** ~ **di qc**
to take no notice of sth; **uno sguardo d'**~**a**
a knowing look.

in tessere *vt* to weave together; (*fig: trama,
storia*) to weave.

intes tare *vt* (*lettera*) to address; (*proprietà*):
~ **a** to register in the name of; ~ **un
assegno a qn** to make out a cheque to sb.

intesta tario, a *sm/f* holder.

intestato, a *ag* (*proprietà, casa, conto*) in the
name of; (*assegno*) made out to; **carta** ~**a**
headed paper.

intestazi one [intestat'tsjone] *sf* heading;
(*su carta da lettere*) letterhead;
(*registrazione*) registration.

intesti nale *ag* intestinal.

intes tino, a *ag* (*lotte*) internal, civil ♦ *sm*
(*ANAT*) intestine.

intiepi dire *vt* (*riscaldare*) to warm (up);
(*raffreddare*) to cool (down); (*fig: amicizia
etc*) to cool; ~**rsi** *vr* to warm (up); to cool
(down); to cool.

Inti fada *sf* Intifada.

intima mente *av* intimately; **sono** ~
convinto che ... I'm firmly *o* deeply
convinced that ...; **i due fatti sono** ~
connessi the two events are closely
connected.

inti mare *vt* to order, command; ~ **la resa
a qn** (*MIL*) to call upon sb to surrender.

intimazi one [intimat'tsjone] *sf* order,
command.

intimida torio, a *ag* threatening.

intimidazi one [intimidat'tsjone] *sf*
intimidation.

intimi dire *vt* to intimidate ♦ *vi* (*anche:
~rsi*) to grow shy.

intimità *sf* intimacy; privacy; (*familiarità*)
familiarity.

intimo, a *ag* intimate; (*affetti, vita*) private;
(*fig: profondo*) inmost ♦ *sm* (*persona*)
intimate *o* close friend; (*dell'animo*)
bottom, depths *pl*; **parti** ~**e** (*ANAT*) private
parts; **rapporti** ~**i** (*sessuali*) intimate
relations.

intimo rire *vt* to frighten; ~**rsi** *vr* to
become frightened.

in tingere [in'tindʒere] *vt* to dip.

in tingolo *sm* sauce; (*pietanza*) stew.

in tinto, a *pp di* **intingere**.

intiriz zire [intirid'dzire] *vt* to numb ♦ *vi*
(*anche*: ~**rsi**) to go numb.

intiriz zito, a [intirid'dzito] *ag* numb (with
cold).

intito lare *vt* to give a title to; (*dedicare*) to
dedicate; ~**rsi** *vr* (*libro, film*) to be called.

intolle rabile *ag* intolerable.

intolle rante *ag* intolerant.

intolle ranza [intolle'rantsa] *sf* intolerance.

intona care *vt* to plaster.

in tonaco, ci *o* **chi** *sm* plaster.

into nare *vt* (*canto*) to start to sing;
(*armonizzare*) to match; ~**rsi** *vr* (*colori*) to
go together; ~**rsi a** (*carnagione*) to suit;
(*abito*) to go with, match.

intonazi one [intonat'tsjone] *sf* intonation.

inton tire *vt* to stun, daze ♦ *vi*, ~**rsi** *vr* to be
stunned *o* dazed.

inton tito, a *ag* stunned, dazed; ~ **dal
sonno** stupid with sleep.

in toppo *sm* stumbling block, obstacle.

intorbi dire *vt* (*liquido*) to make turbid;
(*mente*) to cloud; ~ **le acque** (*fig*) to
muddy the waters.

in torno *av* around; ~ **a** *prep* (*attorno a*)
around; (*riguardo, circa*) about.

intorpi dire *vt* to numb; (*fig*) to make
sluggish ♦ *vi* (*anche*: ~**rsi**) to grow numb;
(*fig*) to become sluggish.

intossi care *vt* to poison.

intossicazi one [intossikat'tsjone] *sf*
poisoning.

intradu cibile [intradu'tʃibile] *ag*
untranslatable.

intralci are [intral'tʃare] *vt* to hamper, hold
up.

in tralcio [in'traltʃo] *sm* hitch.

intrallaz zare [intrallat'tsare] *vi* to intrigue,
scheme.

intral lazzo [intral'lattso] *sm* (*POL*) intrigue,
manoeuvre (*BRIT*), maneuver (*US*); (*traffico
losco*) racket.

intramon tabile *ag* timeless.

intramusco 'lare ag intramuscular.
'Intranet ['intranet] sf intranet.
intransi 'gente [intransi'dʒɛnte] ag
intransigent, uncompromising.
intransi 'genza [intransi'dʒɛntsa] sf
intransigence.
intransi 'tivo, a ag, sm intransitive.
intrappo 'lare vt to trap; rimanere
intrappolato to be trapped; farsi ~ to get
caught.
intrapren 'dente ag enterprising, go-
ahead; (con le donne) forward, bold.
intrapren 'denza [intrapren'dɛntsa] sf
audacity, initiative; (con le donne)
boldness.
intra 'prendere vt to undertake; (carriera)
to embark (up)on.
intra 'preso, a pp di intraprendere.
intrat 'tabile ag intractable.
intratte 'nere vt (divertire) to entertain;
(chiacchierando) to engage in
conversation; (rapporti) to have, maintain;
~rsi vr to linger; ~rsi su qc to dwell on
sth.
intratteni 'mento sm entertainment.
intrave 'dere vt to catch a glimpse of; (fig)
to foresee.
intrecci 'are [intret'tʃare] vt (capelli) to plait,
braid; (intessere: anche fig) to weave,
interweave, intertwine; ~rsi vr to
intertwine, become interwoven; ~ le
mani to clasp one's hands; ~ una
relazione amorosa (fig) to begin an affair.
In 'treccio [in'trettʃo] sm (fig: trama) plot,
story.
in 'trepido, a ag fearless, intrepid.
intri 'care vt (fili) to tangle; (fig: faccenda) to
complicate; ~rsi vr to become tangled; to
become complicated.
in 'trico, chi sm (anche fig) tangle.
intri 'gante ag scheming ♦ sm/f schemer,
intriguer.
intri 'gare vi to manoeuvre (BRIT),
maneuver (US), scheme.
in 'trigo, ghi sm plot, intrigue.
in 'trinseco, a, ci, che ag intrinsic.
in 'triso, a ag: ~ (di) soaked (in).
intris 'tire vi (persona: diventare triste) to
grow sad; (pianta) to wilt.
intro 'dotto, a pp di introdurre.
intro 'durre vt to introduce; (chiave etc): ~
qc in to insert sth into; (persona: far
entrare) to show in; introdursi vr (moda,
tecniche) to be introduced; introdursi in
(persona: penetrare) to enter; (: entrare
furtivamente) to steal o slip into.
in 'troito sm income, revenue.
intro 'messo, a pp di intromettersi.

intro 'mettersi vr to interfere, meddle;
(interporsi) to intervene.
intromissi 'one sf interference, meddling;
intervention.
introspezi 'one [introspet'tsjone] sf
introspection.
intro 'vabile ag (persona, oggetto) who (o
which) cannot be found; (libro etc)
unobtainable.
intro 'verso, a ag introverted ♦ sm/f
introvert.
intrufo 'larsi vr: ~ (in) (stanza) to sneak
in(to), slip in(to); (conversazione) to butt in
(on).
in 'truglio [in'truʎʎo] sm concoction.
intrusi 'one sf intrusion; interference.
in 'truso, a sm/f intruder.
intu 'ire vt to perceive by intuition;
(rendersi conto) to realize.
in 'tuito sm intuition; (perspicacia)
perspicacity.
intuizi 'one [intuit'tsjone] sf intuition.
inturgi 'dire [inturdʒi'dire] vi, ~rsi vr to
swell.
Inumanità sf inv inhumanity.
inu 'mano, a ag inhuman.
inu 'mare vt (seppellire) to bury, inter.
inumazi 'one [inumat'tsjone] sf burial,
interment.
inumi 'dire vt to dampen, moisten; ~rsi vr
to become damp o wet.
inurba 'mento sm urbanization.
inusi 'tato, a ag unusual.
i 'nutile ag useless; (superfluo) pointless,
unnecessary; è stato tutto ~! it was all in
vain!
inutilità sf uselessness; pointlessness.
inutiliz 'zabile [inutilid'dzabile] ag unusable.
inutil 'mente av (senza risultato) fruitlessly;
(senza utilità, scopo) unnecessarily,
needlessly; l'ho cercato ~ I looked for
him in vain; ti preoccupi ~ there's
nothing for you to worry about, there's
no need for you to worry.
inva 'dente ag (fig) intrusive.
inva 'denza [inva'dɛntsa] sf intrusiveness.
in 'vadere vt to invade; (affollare) to swarm
into, overrun; (sog: acque) to flood.
invadi 'trice [invadi'tritʃe] ag f vedi invasore.
inva 'ghirsi [inva'girsi] vr: ~ di to take a
fancy to.
invali 'cabile ag (montagna) impassable.
invali 'dare vt to invalidate.
invalidità sf infirmity; disability; (DIR)
invalidity.
in 'valido, a ag (infermo) infirm; (al lavoro)
disabled; (DIR: nullo) invalid ♦ sm/f invalid;
disabled person; ~ di guerra disabled ex-

serviceman; ~ **del lavoro** industrially disabled person.

in'valso, a *ag* (*diffuso*) established.

in'vano *av* in vain.

invari'abile *ag* invariable.

invari'ato, a *ag* unchanged.

inva'sare *vt* (*pianta*) to pot.

inva'sato, a *ag* possessed (by the devil) ♦ *sm/f* person possessed by the devil; **urlare come un** ~ to shout like a madman.

invasi'one *sf* invasion.

in'vaso, a *pp di* **invadere**.

inva'sore, invadi'trice [invadi'tritʃe] *ag* invading ♦ *sm* invader.

invecchia'mento [invekkja'mento] *sm* growing old; ageing; **questo whisky ha un** ~ **di 12 anni** this whisky has been matured for 12 years.

invecchi'are [invek'kjare] *vi* (*persona*) to grow old; (*vino, popolazione*) to age; (*moda*) to become dated ♦ *vt* to age; (*far apparire più vecchio*) to make look older; **lo trovo invecchiato** I find he has aged.

in'vece [in'vetʃe] *av* instead; (*al contrario*) on the contrary; ~ **di** *prep* instead of.

inve'ire *vi*: ~ **contro** to rail against.

invele'nire *vt* to embitter; ~**rsi** *vr* to become bitter.

inven'duto, a *ag* unsold.

inven'tare *vt* to invent; (*pericoli, pettegolezzi*) to make up, invent.

inventari'are *vt* to make an inventory of, inventory.

inven'tario *sm* inventory; (*COMM*) stocktaking *no pl*.

inven'tivo, a *ag* inventive ♦ *sf* inventiveness.

inven'tore, 'trice *sm/f* inventor.

invenzi'one [inven'tsjone] *sf* invention; (*bugia*) lie, story.

invere'condia *sf* shamelessness, immodesty.

inver'nale *ag* winter *cpd*; (*simile all'inverno*) wintry.

in'verno *sm* winter; **d'**~ in (the) winter.

invero'simile *ag* unlikely ♦ *sm*: **ha dell'**~ it's hard to believe, it's incredible.

inversi'one *sf* inversion; "**divieto d'**~" (*AUT*) "no U-turns".

in'verso, a *ag* opposite; (*MAT*) inverse ♦ *sm* contrary, opposite; **in senso** ~ in the opposite direction; **in ordine** ~ in reverse order.

inverte'brato, a *ag, sm* invertebrate.

inver'tire *vt* to invert; (*disposizione, posti*) to change; (*ruoli*) to exchange; ~ **la marcia** (*AUT*) to do a U-turn; ~ **la rotta** (*NAUT*) to go about; (*fig*) to do a U-turn.

inver'tito, a *sm/f* homosexual.

investi'gare *vt, vi* to investigate.

investiga'tivo, a *ag*: **squadra** ~**a** detective squad.

investiga'tore, 'trice *sm/f* investigator, detective.

investigazi'one [investigat'tsjone] *sf* investigation, inquiry.

investi'mento *sm* (*ECON*) investment; (*di veicolo*) crash, collision; (*di pedone*) knocking down.

inves'tire *vt* (*denaro*) to invest; (*sog: veicolo: pedone*) to knock down; (: *altro veicolo*) to crash into; (*apostrofare*) to assail; (*incaricare*): ~ **qn di** to invest sb with; ~**rsi** *vr* (*fig*): ~**rsi di una parte** to enter thoroughly into a role.

investi'tore, 'trice *sm/f* driver responsible for an accident.

investi'tura *sf* investiture.

invete'rato, a *ag* inveterate.

invet'tiva *sf* invective.

invi'are *vt* to send.

invi'ato, a *sm/f* envoy; (*STAMPA*) correspondent.

in'vidia *sf* envy; **fare** ~ **a qn** to make sb envious.

invidi'abile *ag* enviable.

invidi'are *vt*: ~ **qn (per qc)** to envy sb (for sth); ~ **qc a qn** to envy sb sth; **non aver nulla da** ~ **a nessuno** to be as good as the next one.

invidi'oso, a *ag* envious.

invin'cibile [invin'tʃibile] *ag* invincible.

in'vio, 'vii *sm* sending; (*insieme di merci*) consignment; (*tasto*) Return (key), Enter (key).

invio'labile *ag* inviolable.

invio'lato, a *ag* (*diritto, segreto*) inviolate; (*foresta*) virgin *cpd*; (*montagna, vetta*) unscaled.

invipe'rire *vi*, ~**rsi** *vr* to become furious, fly into a temper.

invipe'rito, a *ag* furious.

invis'chiare [invis'kjare] *vt* (*fig*): ~ **qn in qc** to involve sb in sth, mix sb up in sth; ~**rsi** *vr*: ~**rsi (con qn/in qc)** to get mixed up *o* involved (with sb/in sth).

invi'sibile *ag* invisible.

in'viso, a *ag*: ~ **a** unpopular with.

invi'tante *ag* (*proposta, odorino*) inviting; (*sorriso*) appealing, attractive.

invi'tare *vt* to invite; ~ **qn a fare** to invite sb to do.

invi'tato, a *sm/f* guest.

in'vito *sm* invitation; **dietro** ~ **del sig. Rossi** at Mr Rossi's invitation.

invo'care *vt* (*chiedere: aiuto, pace*) to cry

out for; (appellarsi: la legge, Dio) to appeal
to, invoke.
invogli'are [invoʎ'ʎare] vt: ~ **qn a fare** to
tempt sb to do, induce sb to do.
involon'tario, a ag (errore) unintentional;
(gesto) involuntary.
invol'tino sm (CUC) roulade.
in'volto sm (pacco) parcel; (fagotto) bundle.
in'volucro sm cover, wrapping.
involu'tivo, a ag: **subire un processo** ~ to
regress.
invo'luto, a ag involved, intricate.
involuzi'one [involut'tsjone] sf (di stile)
convolutedness; (regresso): **subire un'**~ to
regress.
invulne'rabile ag invulnerable.
inzacche'rare [intsakke'rare] vt to spatter
with mud; ~**rsi** vr to get muddy.
inzup'pare [intsup'pare] vt to soak; ~**rsi** vr
to get soaked; **inzuppò i biscotti nel latte**
he dipped the biscuits in the milk.
'io pron I ◆ sm inv: **l'**~ the ego, the self; ~
stesso(a) I myself; **sono** ~ it's me.
i'odio sm iodine.
i'ogurt sm inv = **yoghurt**.
i'one sm ion.
l'onio sm: **lo** ~, **il mar** ~ the Ionian (Sea).
ionizza'tore [joniddza'tore] sm ioniser.
'iosa: a ~ av in abundance.
'IPAB sigla fpl (= Istituzioni pubbliche di
Assistenza e Beneficenza) charitable
institutions.
i'perbole sf (LETTERATURA) hyperbole;
(MAT) hyperbola.
iper'bolico, a, ci, che ag (LETTERATURA,
MAT) hyperbolic(al); (fig: esagerato)
exaggerated.
ipermer'cato sm hypermarket.
ipersen'sibile ag (persona) hypersensitive;
(FOT: lastra, pellicola) hypersensitized.
ipertecno'logico, a, ci, che
[ipertekno'lɔdʒiko] ag hi-tech.
ipertensi'one sf high blood pressure,
hypertension.
iper'testo sm hypertext.
ip'nosi sf hypnosis.
ip'notico, a, ci, che ag hypnotic.
ipno'tismo sm hypnotism.
ipnotiz'zare [ipnotid'dzare] vt to hypnotize.
ipoaller'genico, a, ci, che
[ipoaller'dʒɛniko] ag hypoallergenic.
ipocon'dria sf hypochondria.
ipocon'driaco, a, ci, che ag, sm/f
hypochondriac.
ipocri'sia sf hypocrisy.
i'pocrita, i, e ag hypocritical ◆ sm/f
hypocrite.
ipo'sodico, a, ci, che ag low sodium cpd.

ipo'teca, che sf mortgage.
ipote'care vt to mortgage.
ipote'nusa sf hypotenuse.
i'potesi sf inv hypothesis; **facciamo l'**~ **che**
..., ammettiamo per ~ **che...** let's suppose
o assume that...; **nella peggiore/migliore**
delle ~**i** at worst/best; **nell'**~ **che venga**
should he come, if he comes; **se per** ~ **io**
partissi... just supposing I were to
leave....
ipo'tetico, a, ci, che ag hypothetical.
ipotiz'zare [ipotid'dzare] vt: ~ **che** to form
the hypothesis that.
'ippico, a, ci, che ag horse cpd ◆ sf horse-
racing.
ippocas'tano sm horse chestnut.
ip'podromo sm racecourse.
ippo'potamo sm hippopotamus.
'ipsilon sf o m inv (lettera) Y, y; (: dell'alfabeto
greco) epsilon.
IP'SOA sigla m (= Istituto Post-Universitario
per lo Studio dell'Organizzazione Aziendale)
postgraduate institute of business
administration.
IR abbr (FERR) = **interregionale**.
IRA sigla f (= Irish Republican Army) IRA.
'ira sf anger, wrath.
ira'cheno, a [ira'kɛno] ag, sm/f Iraqi.
l'ran sm: **l'**~ Iran.
irani'ano, a ag, sm/f Iranian.
l'raq sm: **l'**~ Iraq.
iras'cibile [iraʃ'ʃibile] ag quick-
tempered.
'IRCE ['irtʃe] sigla m = Istituto per le relazioni
culturali con l'Estero.
'IRI sigla m (= Istituto per la Ricostruzione
Industriale) state-controlled industrial
investment office.
'iride sf (arcobaleno) rainbow; (ANAT, BOT)
iris.
'iris sm inv iris.
Ir'landa sf: **l'**~ Ireland; **l'**~ **del Nord**
Northern Ireland, Ulster; **la Repubblica**
d'~ Eire, the Republic of Ireland; **il mar**
d'~ the Irish Sea.
irlan'dese ag Irish ◆ sm/f Irishman/woman;
gli l~**i** the Irish.
iro'nia sf irony.
i'ronico, a, ci, che ag ironic(al).
ironiz'zare [ironid'dzare] vi, vi: ~ **su** to be
ironical about.
i'roso, a ag (sguardo, tono) angry, wrathful;
(persona) irascible.
'IRPEF sigla f vedi **imposta sul reddito delle**
persone fisiche.
ir'pino, a ag of (o from) Irpinia.
irradi'are vt to radiate; (sog: raggi di luce:
illuminare) to shine on ◆ vi (diffondersi:

anche: ~**rsi**) to radiate.
irradiazi 'one [irradjat'tsjone] *sf* radiation.
irraggiun 'gibile [irraddʒun'dʒibile] *ag*
unreachable; (*fig: meta*) unattainable.
irragio 'nevole [irradʒo'nevole] *ag* (*privo di
ragione*) irrational; (*fig: persona, pretese,
prezzo*) unreasonable.
irrazio 'nale [irrattsjo'nale] *ag* irrational.
irre 'ale *ag* unreal.
irrealiz 'zabile [irrealid'dzabile] *ag* (*sogno,
desiderio*) unattainable, unrealizable; (*progetto*) unworkable, impracticable.
irrealtà *sf* unreality.
irrecupe 'rabile *ag* (*gen*) irretrievable; (*fig:
persona*) irredeemable.
irrecu 'sabile *ag* (*offerta*) not to be refused;
(*prova*) irrefutable.
irreden 'tista, i, e *ag, smlf* (*STORIA*)
Irredentist.
irrefre 'nabile *ag* uncontrollable.
irrefu 'tabile *ag* irrefutable.
irrego 'lare *ag* irregular; (*terreno*) uneven.
irregolarità *sf inv* irregularity; unevenness
no pl.
irremo 'vibile *ag* (*fig*) unshakeable,
unyielding.
irrepa 'rabile *ag* irreparable; (*fig*)
inevitable.
irrepe 'ribile *ag* nowhere to be found.
irrepren 'sibile *ag* irreproachable.
irrequi 'eto, a *ag* restless.
irresis 'tibile *ag* irresistible.
irreso 'luto, a *ag* irresolute.
irrespi 'rabile *ag* (*aria*) unbreathable; (*fig:
opprimente*) stifling, oppressive;
(: *malsano*) unhealthy.
irrespon 'sabile *ag* irresponsible.
irrestrin 'gibile [irrestrin'dʒibile] *ag*
unshrinkable, non-shrink (*BRIT*).
irre 'tire *vt* to seduce.
irrever 'sibile *ag* irreversible.
irrevo 'cabile *ag* irrevocable.
irricono 'scibile [irrikonoʃ'ʃibile] *ag*
unrecognizable.
irridu 'cibile [irridu'tʃibile] *ag* irreducible;
(*fig*) unshakeable.
irrifles 'sivo, a *ag* thoughtless.
irri 'gare *vt* (*annaffiare*) to irrigate; (*sog:
fiume etc*) to flow through.
irrigazi 'one [irrigat'tsjone] *sf* irrigation.
irrigidi 'mento [irridʒidi'mento] *sm*
stiffening; hardening; tightening.
irrigi 'dire [irridʒi'dire] *vt* to stiffen;
(*disciplina*) to tighten; ~**rsi** *vr* to stiffen;
(*posizione, atteggiamento*) to harden.
irriguar 'doso, a *ag* disrespectful.
irrile 'vante *ag* (*trascurabile*) insignificant.
irrimedi 'abile *ag*: **un errore** ~ a mistake

which cannot be rectified; **non è** ~! we
can do something about it!
irrinunci 'abile [irrinun'tʃabile] *ag* vital;
which cannot be abandoned.
irripe 'tibile *ag* unrepeatable.
irri 'solto, a *ag* (*problema*) unresolved.
irri 'sorio, a *ag* derisory.
irrispet 'toso, a *ag* disrespectful.
irri 'tabile *ag* irritable.
irri 'tante *ag* (*atteggiamento*) irritating,
annoying; (*MED*) irritant.
irri 'tare *vt* (*mettere di malumore*) to irritate,
annoy; (*MED*) to irritate; ~**rsi** *vr* (*stizzirsi*)
to become irritated *o* annoyed; (*MED*) to
become irritated.
irritazi 'one [irritat'tsjone] *sf* irritation;
annoyance.
irrive 'rente *ag* irreverent.
irrobus 'tire *vt* (*persona*) to make stronger,
make more robust; (*muscoli*) to
strengthen; ~**rsi** *vr* to become stronger.
ir 'rompere *vi*: ~ **in** to burst into.
irro 'rare *vt* to sprinkle; (*AGR*) to spray.
ir 'rotto, a *pp di* **irrompere.**
irru 'ente *ag* (*fig*) impetuous, violent.
irru 'enza [irru'entsa] *sf* impetuousness; **con**
~ impetuously.
ir 'ruppi *etc vb vedi* **irrompere.**
irruvi 'dire *vt* to roughen ♦ *vi* (*anche:* ~**rsi**)
to become rough.
irruzi 'one [irrut'tsjone] *sf*: **fare** ~ **in** to burst
into; (*sog: polizia*) to raid.
ir 'suto, a *ag* (*petto*) hairy; (*barba*) bristly.
'irto, a *ag* bristly; ~ **di** bristling with.
Is. *abbr* (= *isola*) I.
ISBN *abbr* (= *International Standard Book
Number*) ISBN.
is 'crissi *etc vb vedi* **iscrivere.**
is 'critto, a *pp di* **iscrivere** ♦ *smlf* member; **gli**
~**i alla gara** the competitors; **per** *o* **in** ~ in
writing.
is 'crivere *vt* to register, enter; (*persona*): ~
(**a**) to register (in), enrol (in); ~**rsi** *vr*: ~**rsi**
(**a**) (*club, partito*) to join; (*università*) to
register *o* enrol (at); (*esame, concorso*) to
register *o* enter (for).
iscrizi 'one [iskrit'tsjone] *sf* (*epigrafe etc*)
inscription; (*a scuola, società etc*)
enrolment; registration.
'ISEF *sigla m* = *Istituto Superiore di
Educazione Fisica.*
Is 'lam *sm*: **l'**~ Islam.
is 'lamico, a, ci, che *ag* Islamic.
Is 'landa *sf*: **l'**~ Iceland.
islan 'dese *ag* Icelandic ♦ *smlf* Icelander
♦ *sm* (*LING*) Icelandic.
'isola *sf* island; ~ **pedonale** (*AUT*)
pedestrian precinct.

isola'mento sm isolation; (TECN) insulation; **essere in cella di** ~ to be in solitary confinement; ~ **acustico** soundproofing; ~ **termico** thermal insulation.

iso'lano, a ag island cpd ♦ sm/f islander.

iso'lante ag insulating ♦ sm insulator.

iso'lare vt to isolate; (TECN) to insulate; (: acusticamente) to soundproof.

iso'lato, a ag isolated; insulated ♦ sm (edificio) block.

isolazio'nismo [isolattsjo'nismo] sm isolationism.

i'sotopo sm isotope.

ispessi'mento sm thickening.

ispes'sire vt to thicken; ~**rsi** vr to get thicker, thicken.

ispetto'rato sm inspectorate.

ispet'tore, 'trice sm/f inspector; (COMM) supervisor; ~ **di zona** (COMM) area supervisor o manager; ~ **di reparto** shop walker (BRIT), floor walker (US).

ispezio'nare [ispettsjo'nare] vt to inspect.

ispezi'one [ispet'tsjone] sf inspection.

'ispido, a ag bristly, shaggy.

ispi'rare vt to inspire; ~**rsi** vr: ~**rsi a** to draw one's inspiration from; (conformarsi) to be based on; **l'idea m'ispira** the idea appeals to me.

ispira'tore, 'trice ag inspiring ♦ sm/f inspirer; (di ribellione) instigator.

ispirazi'one [ispirat'tsjone] sf inspiration; **secondo l'**~ **del momento** according to the mood of the moment.

israeli'ano, a ag, sm/f Israeli.

israe'lita, i, e sm/f Jew/Jewess; (STORIA) Israelite.

israe'litico, a, ci, che ag Jewish.

is'sare vt to hoist; ~ **l'ancora** to weigh anchor.

'Istanbul sf Istanbul.

istan'taneo, a ag instantaneous ♦ sf (FOT) snapshot.

is'tante sm instant, moment; **all'**~, **sull'**~ instantly, immediately.

is'tanza [is'tantsa] sf petition, request; **giudice di prima** ~ (DIR) judge of the court of first instance; **giudizio di seconda** ~ judgment on appeal; **in ultima** ~ (fig) finally; ~ **di divorzio** petition for divorce.

'ISTAT sigla m = Istituto Centrale di Statistica.

'ISTEL sigla f = Indagine sull'ascolto delle televisioni in Italia.

is'terico, a, ci, che ag hysterical.

isteri'lire vt (terreno) to render infertile; (fig: fantasia) to dry up; ~**rsi** vr to become infertile; to dry up.

iste'rismo sm hysteria.

isti'gare vt to incite.

istigazi'one [istigat'tsjone] sf instigation; ~ **a delinquere** (DIR) incitement to crime.

istin'tivo, a ag instinctive.

is'tinto sm instinct.

istitu'ire vt (fondare) to institute, found; (porre: confronto) to establish; (intraprendere: inchiesta) to set up.

isti'tuto sm institute; (di università) department; (ente, DIR) institution; ~ **di bellezza** beauty salon; ~ **di credito** bank, banking institution; ~ **tecnico commerciale** ≈ commercial college; ~ **tecnico industriale statale** ≈ technical college.

istitu'tore, 'trice sm/f (fondatore) founder; (precettore) tutor/governess.

istituzi'one [istitut'tsjone] sf institution; ~**i** sfpl (DIR) institutes; **lotta alle** ~**i** struggle against the Establishment.

'istmo sm (GEO) isthmus.

isto'gramma, i sm histogram.

istra'dare vt (fig: persona): ~ (**a/verso**) to direct (to/towards).

istri'ano, a ag, sm/f Istrian.

'istrice ['istritʃe] sm porcupine.

istri'one sm (peg) ham (actor).

istru'ire vt (insegnare) to teach; (ammaestrare) to train; (informare) to instruct, inform; (DIR) to prepare.

istru'ito, a ag educated.

istrut'tivo, a ag instructive.

istrut'tore, 'trice sm/f instructor ♦ ag: **giudice** ~ examining (BRIT) o committing (US) magistrate.

istrut'toria sf (DIR) (preliminary) investigation and hearing; **formalizzare un'**~ to proceed to a formal hearing.

istruzi'one [istrut'tsjone] sf (gen) training; (INS, cultura) education; (direttiva) instruction; (DIR) = **istruttoria**; **Ministero della Pubblica I**~ Ministry of Education; ~**i di spedizione** forwarding instructions; ~**i per l'uso** instructions (for use).

istupi'dire vt (sog: colpo) to stun, daze; (: droga, stanchezza) to stupefy; ~**rsi** vr to become stupid.

'ISVE sigla m (= Istituto di Studi per lo Sviluppo Economico) institute for research into economic development.

I'talia sf: **l'**~ Italy.

itali'ano, a ag Italian ♦ sm/f Italian ♦ sm (LING) Italian; **gli I**~**i** the Italians.

ITC sigla m = istituto tecnico commerciale.

'iter sm passage, course; **l'**~ **burocratico** the bureaucratic process.

itine'rante ag wandering, itinerant; **mostra** ~ touring exhibition; **spettacolo** ~

travelling (*BRIT*) *o* traveling (*US*) show, touring show.

itine'rario *sm* itinerary.

'ITIS *sigla m* = **istituto tecnico industriale statale**.

itte'rizia [itte'rittsja] *sf* (*MED*) jaundice.

'ittico, a, ci, che *ag* fish *cpd*; fishing *cpd*.

IUD *sigla m inv* (= *intra-uterine device*) IUD.

Iugos'lavia *sf* = **Jugoslavia**.

iugos'lavo, a *ag, sm/f* = **jugoslavo, a**.

i'uta *sf* jute.

'I.V.A. *sigla f vedi* **imposta sul valore aggiunto**.

'ivi *av* (*formale, poetico*) therein; (*nelle citazioni*) ibid.

J j

J, j [i'lunga] *sm o f inv* (*lettera*) J, j; ~ **come Jersey** ≈ J for Jack (*BRIT*), J for Jig (*US*).

jazz [dʒaz] *sm* jazz.

jaz'zista, i [dʒad'dzista] *sm* jazz player.

jeans [dʒinz] *smpl* jeans.

jeep [dʒip] *sm inv* jeep.

'jersey ['dʒɛrzi] *sm inv* jersey (cloth).

'jockey ['dʒɔki] *sm inv* (*CARTE*) jack; (*fantino*) jockey.

'jogging ['dʒɔgiŋ] *sm* jogging; **fare** ~ to go jogging.

'jolly ['dʒɔli] *sm inv* joker.

jr. *abbr* (= *junior*) Jr., jr.

ju'do [dʒu'dɔ] *sm* judo.

Jugos'lavia [jugoz'lavja] *sf*: **la** ~ Yugoslavia.

jugos'lavo, a *ag, sm/f* Yugoslav(ian).

'juke 'box ['dʒuk'bɔks] *sm inv* jukebox.

K k

K, k ['kappa] *sf o m inv* (*lettera*) K, k ♦ *abbr* (= *kilo-, chilo-*) k; (*INFORM*) K; **K come Kursaal** ≈ K for King.

Kam'pala *sf* Kampala.

kara'oke [kara'oke] *sm inv* karaoke.

karatè [kara'tɛ] *sm* karate.

'Kashmir ['kaʃmir] *sm*: **il** ~ Kashmir.

ka'yak [ka'jak] *sm inv* kayak.

Ka'zakistan [ka'dzakistan] *sm* Kazakhstan.

ka'zako, a [ka'dzako] *ag, sm/f* Kazakh.

'Kenia ['kenja] *sm*: **il** ~ Kenya.

keni'ano, a, keni'ota, i, e *ag, sm/f* Kenyan.

'Kenya ['kenja] *sm*: **il** ~ Kenya.

kero'sene [kero'zɛne] *sm* = **cherosene**.

kg *abbr* (= *chilogrammo*) kg.

kib'butz [kib'buts] *sm inv* kibbutz.

Kilimangi'aro [kiliman'dʒaro] *sm*: **il** ~ Kilimanjaro.

'killer ['killer] *sm inv* gunman, hired gun.

'kilo *etc* = **chilo** *etc*.

kilt [kilt] *sm inv* kilt.

ki'mono [ki'mɔno] *sm* = **chimono**.

Kir'ghizistan [kir'gidzistan] *sm* Kyrgyzstan.

kir'ghiso, a [kir'gizo] *ag, sm/f* Kyrgyz.

kitsch [kitʃ] *sm* kitsch.

'kiwi ['kiwi] *sm inv* kiwi (fruit).

km *abbr* (= *chilometro*) km.

kmq *abbr* (= *chilometro quadrato*) km^2.

ko'ala [ko'ala] *sm inv* koala (bear).

koso'varo, a *ag, sm/f* Kosovan.

'Kosovo *sm* Kosovo.

KR *sigla* = Crotone.

'krapfen ['krapfən] *sm inv* doughnut.

Ku'ala Lum'par *sf* Kuala Lumpur.

Ku'wait [ku'vait] *sm*: **il** ~ Kuwait.

kW *abbr* (= *kilowatt, chilowatt*) kW.

kWh *abbr* (= *kilowattora*) kW/h.

L l

L, l ['ɛlle] *sf o m inv* (*lettera*) L, l ♦ *abbr* (= *lira*) L; **L come Livorno** ≈ L for Lucy (*BRIT*), L for Love (*US*).

l *abbr* (= *litro*) l.

l' *det vedi* **la, lo.**

la *dot f* (*dav V l'*) the ♦ *pron* (*dav V l'*) (*oggetto*: *persona*) her; (: *cosa*) it; (: *forma di cortesia*) you ♦ *sm inv* (*MUS*) A; (: *solfeggiando la scala*) la; *vedi anche* **il.**

là *av* there; **di** ~ (*da quel luogo*) from there; (*in quel luogo*) in there; (*dall'altra parte*) over there; **di** ~ **di** beyond; **per di** ~ that way; **più in** ~ further on; (*tempo*) later on; ~ **dentro/sopra/sotto** in/up (*o* on)/under there; ~ **per** ~ (*sul momento*) there and then; **essere in** ~ **con gli anni** to be getting on (in years); **essere più di** ~ **che di qua** to be more dead than alive; **va'** ~! come off it!; **stavolta è andato troppo in** ~ this time he's gone too far; *vedi anche* **quello.**

'labbro *sm* (*pl*(*f*): **labbra**: *solo nel senso ANAT*) lip.

'labile *ag* fleeting, ephemeral.

labi'rinto *sm* labyrinth, maze.

labora'torio *sm* (*di ricerca*) laboratory; (*di arti, mestieri*) workshop; ~ **linguistico** language laboratory.

labori'oso, a *ag* (*faticoso*) laborious; (*attivo*) hard-working.

labu'rista, i, e *ag* Labour *cpd* (*BRIT*) ♦ *sm/f* Labour Party member (*BRIT*).

'lacca, che *sf* lacquer; (*per unghie*) nail varnish (*BRIT*), nail polish.

lac'care *vt* (*mobili*) to varnish, lacquer.

'laccio ['lattʃo] *sm* noose; (*legaccio, tirante*) lasso; (*di scarpa*) lace; ~ **emostatico** (*MED*) tourniquet.

lace'rante [latʃe'rante] *ag* (*suono*) piercing, shrill.

lace'rare [latʃe'rare] *vt* to tear to shreds, lacerate; ~**rsi** *vr* to tear.

lacerazi'one [latʃerat'tsjone] *sf* (*anche MED*) tear.

'lacero, a ['latʃero] *ag* (*logoro*) torn, tattered; (*MED*) lacerated; **ferita** ~-**contusa** injury with lacerations and bruising.

la'conico, a, ci, che *ag* laconic, brief.

'lacrima *sf* tear; (*goccia*) drop; **in** ~**e** in tears.

lacri'mare *vi* to water.

lacri'mevole *ag* heartrending, pitiful.

lacri'mogeno, a [lakri'mɔdʒeno] *ag*: **gas** ~ tear gas.

lacri'moso, a *ag* tearful.

la'cuna *sf* (*fig*) gap.

la'custre *ag* lake *cpd*.

lad'dove *cong* whereas.

'ladro *sm* thief; **al** ~! stop thief!

ladro'cinio [ladro'tʃinjo] *sm* theft, robbery.

la'druncolo, a *sm/f* petty thief.

laggiù [lad'dʒu] *av* down there; (*di là*) over there.

'lagna ['laɲɲa] *sf* (*fam*: *persona, cosa*) drag, bore; **fare la** ~ to whine, moan.

la'gnanza [laɲ'ɲantsa] *sf* complaint.

la'gnarsi [laɲ'ɲarsi] *vr*: ~ (**di**) to complain (about).

'lago, ghi *sm* lake.

'Lagos ['lagos] *sf* Lagos.

'lagrima *etc* = **lacrima** *etc*.

la'guna *sf* lagoon.

lagu'nare *ag* lagoon *cpd*.

'laico, a, ci, che *ag* (*apostolato*) lay; (*vita*) secular; (*scuola*) non-denominational ♦ *sm/f* layman/woman ♦ *sm* lay brother.

'laido, a *ag* filthy, foul; (*fig*: *osceno*) obscene, filthy.

'lama *sf* blade ♦ *sm inv* (*ZOOL*) llama; (*REL*) lama.

lambic'care *vt* to distil; ~**rsi il cervello** to rack one's brains.

lam'bire *vt* (*fig*: *sog*: *fiamme*) to lick; (: *acqua*) to lap.

lam'bretta ® *sf* scooter.

la'mella *sf* (*di metallo etc*) thin sheet, thin strip; (*di fungo*) gill.

lamen'tare *vt* to lament; ~**rsi** *vr* (*emettere lamenti*) to moan, groan; (*rammaricarsi*): ~**rsi** (**di**) to complain (about).

lamen'tela *sf* complaining *no pl*.

lamen'tevole *ag* (*voce*) complaining, plaintive; (*stato*) lamentable, pitiful.

la'mento *sm* moan, groan; (*per la morte di qn*) lament.

lamen'toso, a *ag* plaintive.

la'metta *sf* razor blade.

laml'era *sf* sheet metal.

'lamina *sf* (*lastra sottile*) thin sheet (*o* layer *o* plate); ~ **d'oro** gold leaf; gold foil.

lami'nare *vt* to laminate.

lami'nato, a *ag* laminated; (*tessuto*) lamé ♦ *sm* laminate.

'lampada *sf* lamp; ~ **a petrolio/a gas** oil/gas lamp; ~ **a spirito** blowlamp (*BRIT*), blowtorch; ~ **a stelo** standard lamp

(*BRIT*), floor lamp; ~ **da tavolo** table lamp.
lampa 'dario *sm* chandelier.
lampa 'dina *sf* light bulb; ~ **tascabile** pocket torch (*BRIT*), flashlight (*US*).
lam 'pante *ag* (*fig: evidente*) crystal clear, evident.
lam 'para *sf* fishing lamp; (*barca*) boat for fishing by lamplight (*in Mediterranean*).
lampeggi 'are [lamped'dʒare] *vi* (*luce, fari*) to flash ♦ *vb impers*: **lampeggia** there's lightning.
lampeggia 'tore [lampeddʒa'tore] *sm* (*AUT*) indicator.
lampi 'one *sm* street light *o* lamp (*BRIT*).
lampo *sm* (*METEOR*) flash of lightning; (*di luce, fig*) flash ♦ *ag inv*: **cerniera** ~ **zip** (fastener) (*BRIT*), zipper (*US*); **guerra** ~ blitzkrieg; ~**i** *smpl* (*METEOR*) lightning *no pl*; **passare come un** ~ to flash past *o* by.
lam 'pone *sm* raspberry.
lana *sf* wool; ~ **d'acciaio** steel wool; **pura** ~ **vergine** pure new wool; ~ **di vetro** glass wool.
lan 'cetta [lan'tʃetta] *sf* (*indice*) pointer, needle; (*di orologio*) hand.
lancia, ce ['lantʃa] *sf* (*arma*) lance; (: *picca*) spear; (*di pompa antincendio*) nozzle; (*imbarcazione*) launch; **partire** ~ **in resta** (*fig*) to set off ready for battle; **spezzare una** ~ **in favore di qn** (*fig*) to come to sb's defence; ~ **di salvataggio** lifeboat.
lancia bombe [lantʃa'bombe] *sm inv* (*MIL*) mortar.
lanciafi 'amme [lantʃa'fjamme] *sm inv* flamethrower.
lancia 'missili [lantʃa'missili] *ag inv* missile-launching ♦ *sm inv* missile launcher.
lancia 'razzi [lantʃa'raddzi] *ag inv* rocket-launching ♦ *sm inv* rocket launcher.
lanci 'are [lan'tʃare] *vt* to throw, hurl, fling; (*SPORT*) to throw; (*far partire: automobile*) to get up to full speed; (*bombe*) to drop; (*razzo, prodotto, moda*) to launch; (*emettere: grido*) to give out; ~**rsi** *vr*: ~**rsi contro/su** to throw *o* hurl *o* fling o.s. against/on; ~**rsi in** (*fig*) to embark on; ~ **un cavallo** to give a horse his head; ~ **il disco** (*SPORT*) to throw the discus; ~ **il peso** (*SPORT*) to put the shot; ~**rsi all'inseguimento di qn** to set off in pursuit of sb; ~**rsi col paracadute** to parachute.
lanci 'ato, a [lan'tʃato] *ag* (*affermato: attore, prodotto*) well-known, famous; (*veicolo*) speeding along, racing along.
lanci 'nante [lantʃi'nante] *ag* (*dolore*) shooting, throbbing; (*grido*) piercing.
lancio ['lantʃo] *sm* throwing *no pl*; throw;

dropping *no pl*; drop; launching *no pl*; launch; ~ **del disco** (*SPORT*) throwing the discus; ~ **del peso** (*SPORT*) putting the shot.
landa *sf* (*GEO*) moor.
languido, a *ag* (*fiacco*) languid, weak; (*tenero, malinconico*) languishing.
langu 'ire *vi* to languish; (*conversazione*) to flag.
langu 'ore *sm* weakness, languor.
lani 'ero, a *ag* wool *cpd*, woollen (*BRIT*), woolen (*US*).
lani 'ficio [lani'fitʃo] *sm* woollen (*BRIT*) *o* woolen (*US*) mill.
lano 'lina *sf* lanolin(e).
la 'noso, a *ag* woolly.
lan 'terna *sf* lantern; (*faro*) lighthouse.
lanter 'nino *sm*: **cercarsele col** ~ to be asking for trouble.
la 'hugine [la'nudʒine] *sf* down.
Laos *sm* Laos.
lapalissi 'ano, a *ag* self-evident.
La Paz [la'pas] *sf* La Paz.
lapi 'dare *vt* to stone.
lapi 'dario, a *ag* (*fig*) terse.
lapide *sf* (*di sepolcro*) tombstone; (*commemorativa*) plaque.
la 'pin [la'pɛ̃] *sm inv* coney.
lapis *sm inv* pencil.
lappone *ag, sm/f, sm* Lapp.
Lap 'ponia *sf*: **la** ~ Lapland.
lapsus *sm inv* slip.
laptop ['læp tɔp] *sm inv* laptop (computer).
lardo *sm* bacon fat, lard.
lar 'ghezza [lar'gettsa] *sf* width; breadth; looseness; generosity; ~ **di vedute** broad-mindedness.
lar 'gire [lar'dʒire] *vt* to give generously.
largo, a, ghi, ghe *ag* wide, broad; (*maniche*) wide; (*abito: troppo ampio*) loose; (*fig*) generous ♦ *sm* width; breadth; (*mare aperto*): **il** ~ the open sea ♦ *sf*: **stare** *o* **tenersi alla** ~**a** (**da qn/qc**) to keep one's distance (from sb/sth), keep away (from sb/sth); ~ **due metri** two metres wide; ~ **di spalle** broad-shouldered; **di** ~**ghe vedute** broad-minded; **in** ~**a misura** to a great *o* large extent; **su** ~**a scala** on a large scale; **di manica** ~**a** generous, open-handed; **al** ~ **di Genova** off (the coast of) Genoa; **farsi** ~ **tra la folla** to push one's way through the crowd.
larice ['laritʃe] *sm* (*BOT*) larch.
la 'ringe [la'rindʒe] *sf* larynx.
larin 'gite [larin'dʒite] *sf* laryngitis.
laringoi 'atra, i, e *sm/f* (*medico*) throat specialist.
larva *sf* larva; (*fig*) shadow.

la **'sagne** [la'zaɲɲe] *sfpl* lasagna *sg.*

lasciapas 'sare [laʃʃapas'sare] *sm inv* pass, permit.

lasci 'are [laʃ'ʃare] *vt* to leave; (*abbandonare*) to leave, abandon, give up; (*cessare di tenere*) to let go of ♦ *vb aux*: ~ **qn fare qc** to let sb do sth ♦ *vi*: ~ **di fare** (*smettere*) to stop doing; ~**rsi andare/truffare** to let o.s. go/be cheated; ~ **andare** *o* **correre** *o* **perdere** to let things go their own way; ~ **stare qc/qn** to leave sth/sb alone; ~ **qn erede** to make sb one's heir; ~ **la presa** to lose one's grip; ~ **il segno (su qc)** to leave a mark (on sth); (*fig*) to leave one's mark (on sth); ~ **(molto) a desiderare** to leave much to be desired; **ci ha lasciato la vita** it cost him his life.

'lascito ['laʃʃito] *sm* (*DIR*) legacy.

la **'scivia** [laʃ'ʃivja] *sf* lust, lasciviousness.

la **'scivo, a** [laʃ'ʃivo] *ag* lascivious.

'laser ['lazer] *ag, sm inv*: **(raggio)** ~ laser (beam).

lassa 'tivo, a *ag, sm* laxative.

las 'sismo *sm* laxity.

'lasso *sm*: ~ **di tempo** interval.

lassù *av* up there.

'lastra *sf* (*di pietra*) slab; (*di metallo, FOT*) plate; (*di ghiaccio, vetro*) sheet; (*radiografica*) X-ray (plate).

lastri 'care *vt* to pave.

lastri 'cato *sm* paving.

'lastrico, ci *o* **chi** *sm* paving; **essere sul** ~ (*fig*) to be penniless; **gettare qn sul** ~ (*fig*) to leave sb destitute.

las 'trone *sm* (*ALPINISMO*) sheer rock face.

la **'tente** *ag* latent.

late 'rale *ag* lateral, side *cpd*; (*uscita, ingresso etc*) side *cpd* ♦ *sm* (*CALCIO*) half-back.

lateral 'mente *av* sideways.

late 'rizio [late'rittsjo] *sm* (perforated) brick.

latifon 'dista, i, e *sm/f* large agricultural landowner.

lati 'fondo *sm* large estate.

la **'tino, a** *ag, sm* Latin.

la **'tinoameri 'cano, a** *ag, sm/f* Latin-American.

lati 'tante *ag*: **essere** ~ to be on the run ♦ *sm/f* fugitive (from justice).

lati 'tanza [lati'tantsa] *sf*: **darsi alla** ~ to go into hiding.

lati 'tudine *sf* latitude.

'lato, a *ag*: **in senso** ~ broadly speaking ♦ *sm* side; (*fig*) aspect, point of view; **d'altro** ~ (*d'altra parte*) on the other hand.

la **'trare** *vi* to bark.

lat 'rato *sm* howling.

la **'trina** *sf* public lavatory.

latro 'cinio [latro'tʃinjo] *sm* = **ladrocinio.**

'latta *sf* tin (plate); (*recipiente*) tin, can.

lat 'taio, a *sm/f* (*distributore*) milkman/woman; (*commerciante*) dairyman/woman.

lat 'tante *ag* unweaned ♦ *sm/f* breast-fed baby.

'latte *sm* milk; **fratello di** ~ foster brother; **avere ancora il** ~ **alla bocca** (*fig*) to be still wet behind the ears; **tutto** ~ **e miele** (*fig*) all smiles; ~ **detergente** cleansing milk *o* lotion; ~ **intero** full-cream milk; ~ **a lunga conservazione** UHT milk; ~ **magro** *o* **scremato** skimmed milk; ~ **secco** *o* **in polvere** dried *o* powdered milk.

'latteo, a *ag* milky; (*dieta, prodotto*) milk *cpd.*

latte 'ria *sf* dairy.

latti 'cini [latti'tʃini] *smpl* dairy *o* milk products.

lat 'tina *sf* (*di birra etc*) can.

lat 'tuga, ghe *sf* lettuce.

'laurea *sf* ≈ degree; ~ **breve** *university degree awarded at the end of a three-year course;* **avere una** ~ **in chimica** to have a degree in chemistry *o* a chemistry degree; *vedi nota nel riquadro.*

LAUREA

The **Laurea** *is awarded to students who successfully complete their degree courses. Traditionally, this takes between four and six years; a major element of the final examinations is the presentation and discussion of a dissertation. A shorter, more vocational course of study, taking from two to three years, is also available; at the end of this time students receive a diploma called the* **Laurea breve**.

---

laure 'ando, a *sm/f* final-year student.

laure 'are *vt* to confer a degree on; ~**rsi** *vr* to graduate.

laure 'ato, a *ag, sm/f* graduate.

'lauro *sm* laurel.

'lauto, a *ag* (*pranzo, mancia*) lavish.

'lava *sf* lava.

la **'vabo** *sm* washbasin.

la **'vaggio** [la'vaddʒo] *sm* washing *no pl*; ~ **del cervello** brainwashing *no pl.*

la **'vagna** [la'vaɲɲa] *sf* (*GEO*) slate; (*di scuola*) blackboard; ~ **luminosa** overhead projector.

la **'vanda** *sf* (*anche MED*) wash; (*BOT*) lavender; **fare una** ~ **gastrica a qn** to pump sb's stomach.

lavande'ria *sf* (*di ospedale, caserma etc*) laundry; ~ **automatica** launderette; ~ **a secco** dry-cleaner's.

lavan'dino *sm* sink; (*del bagno*) washbasin.

lavapi'atti *sm/f* dishwasher.

la'vare *vt* to wash; ~**rsi** *vr* to wash, have a wash; ~ **a secco** to dry-clean; ~**rsi le mani/i denti** to wash one's hands/clean one's teeth.

lava'secco *sm o f inv* dry-cleaner's.

lavasto'viglie [lavasto'viλλe] *sm o f inv* (*macchina*) dishwasher.

la'vata *sf* wash; (*fig*): **dare una** ~ **di capo a qn** to give sb a good telling-off.

lava'tivo *sm* (*clistere*) enema; (*buono a nulla*) good-for-nothing, idler.

lava'trice [lava'tritʃe] *sf* washing machine.

lava'tura *sf* washing *no pl*; ~ **di piatti** dishwater.

la'vello *sm* (kitchen) sink.

la'vina *sf* snowslide.

lavo'rare *vi* to work; (*fig: bar, studio etc*) to do good business ♦ *vt* to work; ~ **a** to work on; ~ **a maglia** to knit; ~ **di fantasia** (*suggestionarsi*) to imagine things; (*fantasticare*) to let one's imagination run free; ~**rsi qn** (*convincere*) to work on sb.

lavora'tivo, a *ag* working.

lavora'tore, 'trice *sm/f* worker ♦ *ag* working.

lavorazi'one [lavorat'tsjone] *sf* (*gen*) working; (*di legno, pietra*) carving; (*di film*) making; (*di prodotto*) manufacture; (*modo di esecuzione*) workmanship.

lavo'rio *sm* intense activity.

la'voro *sm* work; (*occupazione*) job, work *no pl*; (*opera*) piece of work, job; (*ECON*) labour (*BRIT*), labor (*US*); **Ministero del L~** Department of Employment (*BRIT*), Department of Labor (*US*); **(fare) i ~i di casa** (to do) the housework *sg*; ~**i forzati** hard labour *sg*; **i ~i del parlamento** the parliamentary session *sg*; ~**i pubblici** public works.

lazi'ale [lat'tsjale] *ag* of (*o* from) Lazio.

lazza'retto [laddza'retto] *sm* leper hospital.

lazza'rone [laddza'rone] *sm* scoundrel.

'lazzo ['laddzo] *sm* jest.

LC *sigla* = *Lecco.*

LE *sigla* = *Lecce.*

le *det fpl* the ♦ *pron* (*oggetto*) them; (: *a lei, a essa*) (to) her; (: *forma di cortesia*) (to) you; *vedi anche* **il.**

le'ale *ag* loyal; (*sincero*) sincere; (*onesto*) fair.

lea'lista, i, e *sm/f* loyalist.

lealtà *sf* loyalty; sincerity; fairness.

'leasing ['li:ziŋ] *sm* leasing; lease.

'lebbra *sf* leprosy.

'lecca 'lecca *sm inv* lollipop.

leccapi'edi *sm/f inv* (*peg*) toady, bootlicker.

lec'care *vt* to lick; (*sog: gatto: latte etc*) to lick *o* lap up; (*fig*) to flatter; ~**rsi** *vr* (*fig*) to preen o.s.; ~**rsi i baffi** to lick one's lips.

lec'cato, a *ag* affected ♦ *sf* lick.

leccherò *etc* [lekke'rɔ] *vb vedi* **leccare.**

'leccio ['lettʃo] *sm* holm oak, ilex.

leccor'nia *sf* titbit, delicacy.

'lecito, a ['letʃito] *ag* permitted, allowed; **se mi è** ~ if I may; **mi sia** ~ **far presente che** ... may I point out that ....

'ledere *vt* to damage, injure; ~ **gli interessi di qn** to be prejudicial to sb's interests.

'lega, ghe *sf* (*anche POL*) league; (*di metalli*) alloy; **metallo di bassa** ~ base metal; **gente di bassa** ~ common *o* vulgar people; **L~ Nord** (*POL*) *federalist party.*

le'gaccio [le'gattʃo] *sm* string, lace.

le'gale *ag* legal ♦ *sm* lawyer; **corso** ~ **delle monete** official exchange rate; **medicina** ~ forensic medicine; **studio** ~ lawyer's office.

legalità *sf* legality, lawfulness.

legaliz'zare [legalid'dzare] *vt* to legalize; (*documento*) to authenticate.

legalizzazi'one [legaliddzat'tsjone] *sf* (*vedi vt*) legalization; authentication.

le'game *sm* (*corda, fig: affettivo*) tie, bond; (*nesso logico*) link, connection; ~ **di sangue** *o* **di parentela** family tie.

lega'mento *sm* (*ANAT*) ligament.

le'gare *vt* (*prigioniero, capelli, cane*) to tie (up); (*libro*) to bind; (*CHIM*) to alloy; (*fig: collegare*) to bind, join ♦ *vi* (*far lega*) to unite; (*fig*) to get on well; **è pazzo da** ~ (*fam*) he should be locked up.

lega'tario, a *sm/f* (*DIR*) legatee.

le'gato *sm* (*REL*) legate; (*DIR*) legacy, bequest.

lega'toria *sf* (*attività*) bookbinding; (*negozio*) bookbinder's.

lega'tura *sf* (*di libro*) binding; (*MUS*) ligature.

legazi'one [legat'tsjone] *sf* legation.

le'genda [le'dʒɛnda] *sf* (*di carta geografica etc*) = **leggenda.**

'legge ['leddʒe] *sf* law; ~ **procedurale** procedural law.

leg'genda [led'dʒɛnda] *sf* (*narrazione*) legend; (*di carta geografica etc*) key, legend.

leggen'dario, a [leddʒen'darjo] *ag* legendary.

'leggere ['lɛddʒere] *vt, vi* to read; ~ **il pensiero di qn** to read sb's mind *o* thoughts.

legge'rezza [ledd3e'rettsa] sf lightness; thoughtlessness; fickleness.

leg'gero, a [led'd3ero] ag light; (agile, snello) nimble, agile, light; (tè, caffè) weak; (fig: non grave, piccolo) slight; (: spensierato) thoughtless; (: incostante) fickle; free and easy; una ragazza ~a (fig) a flighty girl; alla ~a thoughtlessly.

leggi'adro, a [led'd3adro] ag pretty, lovely; (movimenti) graceful.

leg'gibile [led'd3ibile] ag legible; (libro) readable, worth reading.

leg'gio, 'gii [led'd3io] sm lectern; (MUS) music stand.

legherò etc [lege'rɔ] vb vedi legare.

le'ghismo [le'gismo] sm political movement with federalist tendencies.

le'ghista, i, e [le'gista] (POL) ag of a "lega" (especially Lega Nord) ♦ sm/f member (o supporter) of a "lega" (especially Lega Nord).

legife'rare [ledʒife'rare] vi to legislate.

legio'nario [ledʒo'narjo] sm (romano) legionary; (volontario) legionnaire.

legi'one [le'dʒone] sf legion; ~ straniera foreign legion.

legisla'tivo, a [ledʒizla'tivo] ag legislative.

legisla'tore [ledʒizla'tore] sm legislator.

legisla'tura [ledʒizla'tura] sf legislature.

legislazi'one [ledʒizlat'tsjone] sf legislation.

legitti'mare [ledʒitti'mare] vt (figlio) to legitimize; (comportamento etc) to justify.

legittimità [ledʒittimi'ta] sf legitimacy.

le'gittimo, a [le'dʒittimo] ag legitimate; (fig: giustificato, lecito) justified, legitimate; ~a difesa (DIR) self-defence (BRIT), self-defense (US).

'legna ['leɲɲa] sf firewood.

le'gnaia [leɲ'ɲaja] sf woodshed.

legnai'olo [leɲɲa'jɔlo] sm woodcutter.

le'gname [leɲ'ɲame] sm wood, timber.

le'gnata [leɲ'ɲata] sf blow with a stick; dare a qn un sacco di ~e to give sb a good hiding.

'legno ['leɲɲo] sm wood; (pezzo di ~) piece of wood; di ~ wooden; ~ compensato plywood.

le'gnoso, a [leɲ'ɲoso] ag (di legno) wooden; (come il legno) woody; (carne) tough.

le'gume sm (BOT) pulse; ~i smpl (fagioli, piselli etc) pulses.

'lei pron (soggetto) she; (oggetto: per dare rilievo, con preposizione) her; (forma di cortesia: anche: L~) you ♦ sf inv: la mia ~ my beloved ♦ sm: dare del ~ a qn to address sb as "lei"; ~ stessa she herself; you yourself; è ~ it's her.

'lembo sm (di abito, strada) edge; (striscia sottile: di terra) strip.

'lemma, i sm headword.

'lemme 'lemme av (very) very slowly.

'lena sf (fig) energy, stamina; di buona ~ (lavorare, camminare) at a good pace.

Lenin'grado sf Leningrad.

le'nire vt to soothe.

lenta'mente av slowly.

'lente sf (OTTICA) lens sg; ~ d'ingrandimento magnifying glass; ~i a contatto, ~i corneali contact lenses; ~i (a contatto) morbide soft lenses; ~i (a contatto) rigide hard lenses.

len'tezza [len'tettsa] sf slowness.

len'ticchia [len'tikkja] sf (BOT) lentil.

len'tiggine [len'tiddʒine] sf freckle.

'lento, a ag slow; (molle: fune) slack; (non stretto: vite, abito) loose ♦ sm (ballo) slow dance.

'lenza ['lentsa] sf fishing line.

lenzu'olo [len'tswɔlo] sm sheet; ~a sfpl pair of sheets; ~ funebre shroud.

leon'cino [leon'tʃino] sm lion cub.

le'one sm lion; (dello zodiaco): L~ Leo; essere del L~ to be Leo.

leo'pardo sm leopard.

lepo'rino, a ag: labbro ~ harelip.

'lepre sf hare.

'lercio, a, ci, ce ['lertʃo] ag filthy.

lerci'ume [ler'tʃume] sm filth.

'lesbico, a, ci, che ag, sf lesbian.

'lesi etc vb vedi ledere.

lesi'nare vt to be stingy with ♦ vi: ~ (su) to skimp (on), be stingy (with).

lesi'one sf (MED) lesion; (DIR) injury, damage; (EDIL) crack.

le'sivo, a ag: ~ (di) damaging (to), detrimental (to).

'leso, a pp di ledere ♦ ag (offeso) injured; parte ~a (DIR) injured party; ~a maestà lese-majesty.

les'sare vt (CUC) to boil.

'lessi etc vb vedi leggere.

lessi'cale ag lexical.

'lessico, ci sm vocabulary; (dizionario) lexicon.

lessicogra'fia sf lexicography.

lessi'cografo, a sm/f lexicographer.

'lesso, a ag boiled ♦ sm boiled meat.

'lesto, a ag quick; (agile) nimble; ~ di mano (per rubare) light-fingered; (per picchiare) free with one's fists.

lesto'fante sm swindler, con man.

le'tale ag lethal, deadly.

leta'maio sm dunghill.

le'tame sm manure, dung.

le'targo, ghi sm lethargy; (ZOOL)

hibernation.

le **'tizia** [le'tittsja] *sf* joy, happiness.

'letta *sf*: **dare una ~ a qc** to glance *o* look through sth.

'lettera *sf* letter; **~e** *sfpl* (*letteratura*) literature *sg*; (*studi umanistici*) arts (subjects); **alla ~** literally; **in ~e** in words, in full; **diventar ~ morta** (*legge*) to become a dead letter; **restar ~ morta** (*consiglio, invito*) to go unheeded; **~ di accompagnamento** accompanying letter; **~ assicurata** registered letter; **~ di cambio** (*COMM*) bill of exchange; **~ di credito** (*COMM*) letter of credit; **~ di intenti** letter of intent; **~ di presentazione** *o* **raccomandazione** letter of introduction; **~ raccomandata** recorded delivery (*BRIT*) *o* certified (*US*) letter; **~ di trasporto aereo** (*COMM*) air waybill.

lette 'rale *ag* literal.

letteral 'mente *av* literally.

lette 'rario, a *ag* literary.

lette 'rato, a *ag* well-read, scholarly.

lettera 'tura *sf* literature.

let 'tiga, ghe *sf* (*portantina*) litter; (*barella*) stretcher.

let 'tino *sm* cot (*BRIT*), crib (*US*).

'letto, a *pp di* **leggere** ♦ *sm* bed; **andare a ~** to go to bed; **~ a castello** bunk beds *pl*; **~ a una piazza/a due piazze** *o* **matrimoniale** single/double bed.

'lettone *ag, sm/f* Latvian ♦ *sm* (*LING*) Latvian, Lettish.

Let 'tonia *sf*: **la ~** Latvia.

lettorato *sm* (*INS*) lectorship, assistantship; (*REL*) lectorate.

let 'tore, 'trice *sm/f* reader; (*INS*) (foreign language) assistant (*BRIT*), (foreign) teaching assistant (*US*) ♦ *sm*: **~ ottico (di caratteri)** optical character reader; **~ CD** CD player; **~ DVD** DVD player.

let 'tura *sf* reading.

leuce 'mia [leutʃe'mia] *sf* leukaemia.

'leva *sf* lever; (*MIL*) conscription; **far ~ su qn** to work on sb; **essere di ~** to be due for call-up; **~ del cambio** (*AUT*) gear lever.

le **'vante** *sm* east; (*vento*) East wind; **il L~** the Levant.

le **'vare** *vt* (*occhi, braccio*) to raise; (*sollevare, togliere: tassa, divieto*) to lift; (: *indumenti*) to take off, remove; (*rimuovere*) to take away; (: *dal di sopra*) to take off; (: *dal di dentro*) to take out; **~rsi** *vr* to get up; (*sole*) to rise; **~ le tende** (*fig*) to pack up and leave; **~rsi il pensiero** to put one's mind at rest; **levati di mezzo** *o* **di lì** *o* **di torno!** get out of my way!

le **'vata** *sf* (*di posta*) collection.

leva 'taccia, ce [leva'tattʃa] *sf* early rise.

leva 'toio, a *ag*: **ponte ~** drawbridge.

leva 'trice [leva'tritʃe] *sf* midwife.

leva 'tura *sf* intelligence, mental capacity.

levi 'gare *vt* to smooth; (*con carta vetrata*) to sand.

levi 'gato, a *ag* (*superficie*) smooth; (*fig: stile*) polished; (: *viso*) flawless.

levità *sf* lightness.

levri 'ere *sm* greyhound.

lezi 'one [let'tsjone] *sf* lesson; (*all'università, sgridata*) lecture; **fare ~** to teach; to lecture.

lezi 'oso, a [let'tsjoso] *ag* affected; simpering.

'lezzo ['leddzo] *sm* stench, stink.

LI *sigla* = Livorno.

li *pron pl* (*oggetto*) them.

lì *av* there; **di** *o* **da ~** from there; **per di ~** that way; **di ~ a pochi giorni** a few days later; **~ per ~** there and then; at first; **essere ~ (~) per fare** to be on the point of doing, be about to do; **~ dentro** in there; **~ sotto** under there; **~ sopra** on there; up there; **tutto ~** that's all; *vedi anche* **quello**.

libagi 'one [liba'dʒone] *sf* libation.

liba 'nese *ag, sm/f* Lebanese *inv*.

Li 'bano *sm*: **il ~** the Lebanon.

'libbra *sf* (*peso*) pound.

li 'beccio [li'bettʃo] *sm* south-west wind.

li 'bello *sm* libel.

li 'bellula *sf* dragonfly.

libe 'rale *ag, sm/f* liberal.

liberaliz 'zare [liberalid'dzare] *vt* to liberalize.

libe 'rare *vt* (*rendere libero: prigioniero*) to release; (: *popolo*) to free, liberate; (*sgombrare: passaggio*) to clear; (: *stanza*) to vacate; (*produrre: energia*) to release; **~rsi** *vr*: **~rsi di qc/qn** to get rid of sth/sb.

libera 'tore, 'trice *ag* liberating ♦ *sm/f* liberator.

liberazi 'one [liberat'tsjone] *sf* (*di prigioniero*) release; (*di popolo*) liberation; **che ~!** what a relief!; **la L~** *vedi nota nel riquadro.*

┌───┐
│ **LIBERAZIONE** │
│ │
│ *The **Liberazione** is a national holiday which* │
│ *falls on 25 April. It commemorates the* │
│ *liberation of Italy in 1945 from German forces* │
│ *and Mussolini's government and marks the end* │
│ *of the war on Italian soil.* │
└───┘

Li 'beria *sf*: **la ~** Liberia.

liberi 'ano, a *ag, sm/f* Liberian.

libe'rismo sm (ECON) laissez-faire.

'libero, a ag free; (strada) clear; (non occupato: posto etc) vacant, free; (TEL) not engaged; ~ **di fare qc** free to do sth; ~ **da** free from; **una donna dai** ~**i costumi** a woman of loose morals; **avere via** ~**a** to have a free hand; **dare via** ~**a a qn** to give sb the go-ahead; **via** ~**a!** all clear!; ~ **arbitrio** free will; ~ **professionista** self-employed professional person; ~ **scambio** free trade; ~**a uscita** (MIL) leave.

liberoscam'bismo sm (ECON) free trade.

libertà sf inv freedom; (tempo disponibile) free time ♦ sfpl (licenza) liberties; **essere in** ~ **provvisoria/vigilata** to be released without bail/be on probation; ~ **di riunione** right to hold meetings.

'liberty ['liberti] ag inv, sm art nouveau.

'Libia sf: **la** ~ Libya.

'libico, a, ci, che ag, sm/f Libyan.

li'bidine sf lust.

libidi'noso, a ag lustful, libidinous.

li'bido sf libido.

li'braio sm bookseller.

li'brario, a ag book cpd.

li'brarsi vr to hover.

libre'ria sf (bottega) bookshop; (stanza) library; (mobile) bookcase.

li'bretto sm booklet; (taccuino) notebook; (MUS) libretto; ~ **degli assegni** chequebook (BRIT), checkbook (US); ~ **di circolazione** (AUT) logbook; ~ **di deposito** (bank) deposit book; ~ **di risparmio** (savings) bankbook, passbook; ~ **universitario** student's report book.

'libro sm book; ~ **bianco** (POL) white paper; ~ **di cassa** cash book; ~ **di consultazione** reference book; ~ **mastro** ledger; ~ **paga** payroll; ~ **tascabile** paperback; ~ **di testo** textbook; ~**i contabili** (account) books; ~**i sociali** company records.

li'cantropo sm werewolf.

lice'ale [litʃe'ale] ag secondary school cpd (BRIT), high school cpd (US) ♦ sm/f secondary school o high school pupil.

li'cenza [li'tʃɛntsa] sf (permesso) permission, leave; (di pesca, caccia, circolazione) permit, licence (BRIT), license (US); (MIL) leave; (INS) school-leaving certificate; (libertà) liberty; (sfrenatezza) licentiousness; **andare in** ~ (MIL) to go on leave; **su** ~ **di** ... (COMM) under licence from ...; ~ **di esportazione** export licence; ~ **di fabbricazione** manufacturer's licence; ~ **poetica** poetic licence.

licenzia'mento [litʃentsja'mento] sm dismissal.

licenzi'are [litʃen'tsjare] vt (impiegato) to dismiss; (INS) to award a certificate to; ~**rsi** vr (impiegato) to resign, hand in one's notice; (INS) to obtain one's school-leaving certificate.

licenziosità [litʃentsjosi'ta] sf licentiousness.

licenzi'oso, a [litʃen'tsjoso] ag licentious.

li'ceo [li'tʃɛo] sm (INS) secondary (BRIT) o high (US) school (for 14 to 19-year-olds); ~ **classico/scientifico** secondary or high school specializing in classics/scientific subjects.

li'chene [li'kɛne] sm (BOT) lichen.

'lido sm beach, shore.

'Liechtenstein ['liktənstain] sm: **il** ~ Liechtenstein.

li'eto, a ag happy, glad; **"molto** ~**"** (nelle presentazioni) "pleased to meet you"; **a** ~ **fine** with a happy ending.

li'eve ag light; (di poco conto) slight; (sommesso: voce) faint, soft.

lievi'tare vi (anche fig) to rise ♦ vt to leaven.

li'evito sm yeast; ~ **di birra** brewer's yeast.

'ligio, a, gi, gie ['lidʒo] ag faithful, loyal.

li'gnaggio [liɲ'naddʒo] sm descent, lineage.

'ligure ag Ligurian; **la Riviera L**~ the Italian Riviera.

Li'kud [li'kud] sm Likud.

'lilla, lillà sm inv lilac.

'Lima sf Lima.

'lima sf file; ~ **da unghie** nail file.

limacci'oso, a [limat'tʃoso] ag muddy.

li'mare vt to file (down); (fig) to polish.

'limbo sm (REL) limbo.

li'metta sf nail file.

limi'tare vt to limit, restrict; (circoscrivere) to bound, surround.

limitata'mente av to a limited extent; ~ **alle mie possibilità** in so far as I am able.

limi'tato, a ag limited, restricted.

limitazi'one [limitat'tsjone] sf limitation, restriction.

'limite sm limit; (confine) border, boundary ♦ ag inv: **caso** ~ extreme case; **al** ~ if the worst comes to the worst (BRIT), if worst comes to worst (US); ~ **di velocità** speed limit.

li'mitrofo, a ag neighbouring (BRIT), neighboring (US).

'limo sm mud, slime; (GEO) silt.

limo'nata sf lemonade (BRIT), (lemon) soda (US); (spremuta) lemon squash (BRIT), lemonade (US).

li'mone sm (pianta) lemon tree; (frutto) lemon.

limpi'dezza [limpi'dettsa] sf clearness; (di discorso) clarity.

'limpido, a *ag* (*acqua*) limpid, clear; (*cielo*) clear; (*fig*: *discorso*) clear, lucid.

'lince ['lintʃe] *sf* lynx.

linci'aggio [lin'tʃaddʒo] *sm* lynching.

linci'are [lin'tʃare] *vt* to lynch.

'lindo, a *ag* tidy, spick and span; (*biancheria*) clean.

'linea *sf* (*gen*) line; (*di mezzi pubblici di trasporto: itinerario*) route; (: *servizio*) service; (*di prodotto: collezione*) collection; (: *stile*) style; **a grandi ~e** in outline; **mantenere la ~** to look after one's figure; **è caduta la ~** (*TEL*) I (*o* you *etc*) have been cut off; **di ~: aereo di ~** airliner; **nave di ~** liner; **volo di ~** scheduled flight; **in ~ diretta da** (*TV, RADIO*) coming to you direct from; **~ aerea** airline; **~ continua** solid line; **~ di partenza/d'arrivo** (*SPORT*) starting/finishing line; **~ punteggiata** dotted line; **~ di tiro** line of fire.

linea'menti *smpl* features; (*fig*) outlines.

line'are *ag* linear; (*fig*) coherent, logical.

line'etta *sf* (*trattino*) dash; (*d'unione*) hyphen.

'linfa *sf* (*BOT*) sap; (*ANAT*) lymph; **~ vitale** (*fig*) lifeblood.

lin'gotto *sm* ingot, bar.

'lingua *sf* (*ANAT, CUC*) tongue; (*idioma*) language; **mostrare la ~** to stick out one's tongue; **di ~ italiana** Italian-speaking; **~ madre** mother tongue; **una ~ di terra** a spit of land.

lingu'accia [lin'gwattʃa] *sf* (*fig*) spiteful gossip.

linguacci'uto, a [lingwat'tʃuto] *ag* gossipy.

lingu'aggio [lin'gwaddʒo] *sm* language; **~ giuridico** legal language; **~ macchina** (*INFORM*) machine language; **~ di programmazione** (*INFORM*) programming language.

lingu'etta *sf* (*di strumento*) reed; (*di scarpa, TECN*) tongue; (*di busta*) flap.

lingu'ista, i, e *sm/f* linguist.

lingu'istico, a, ci, che *ag* linguistic ♦ *sf* linguistics *sg*.

lini'mento *sm* liniment.

'lino *sm* (*pianta*) flax; (*tessuto*) linen.

li'noleum *sm inv* linoleum, lino.

liofiliz'zare [liofilid'dzare] *vt* to freeze-dry.

liofiliz'zati [liofilid'dzati] *smpl* freeze-dried foods.

Li'one *sf* Lyons.

liposuzi'one [liposut'tsjone] *sf* liposuction.

'LIPU *sigla f* (= *Lega Italiana Protezione Uccelli*) *society for the protection of birds*.

liqu'ame *sm* liquid sewage.

lique'fare *vt* (*render liquido*) to liquefy;

(*fondere*) to melt; **~rsi** *vr* to liquefy; to melt.

lique'fatto, a *pp di* **liquefare**.

liqui'dare *vt* (*società, beni, persona*: *uccidere*) to liquidate; (*persona*: *sbarazzarsene*) to get rid of; (*conto, problema*) to settle; (*COMM: merce*) to sell off, clear.

liquidazi'one [likwidat'tsjone] *sf* (*di società, persona*) liquidation; (*di conto*) settlement; (*di problema*) settling; (*COMM: di merce*) clearance sale; (*AMM*) severance pay (*on retirement, redundancy, or when taking up other employment*).

liquidità *sf* liquidity.

'liquido, a *ag, sm* liquid; **denaro ~** cash, ready money; **~ per freni** brake fluid.

liqui'gas ® *sm inv* Calor gas ® (*BRIT*), butane.

liqui'rizia [likwi'rittsja] *sf* liquorice.

li'quore *sm* liqueur.

liquo'roso, a *ag*: **vino ~** dessert wine.

'lira *sf* (*unità monetaria*) lira; (*MUS*) lyre; **~ sterlina** pound sterling.

'lirico, a, ci, che *ag* lyric(al); (*MUS*) lyric ♦ *sf* (*poesia*) lyric poetry; (*componimento poetico*) lyric; (*MUS*) opera; **cantante/teatro ~** opera singer/house.

li'rismo *sm* lyricism.

Lis'bona *sf* Lisbon.

'lisca, sche *sf* (*di pesce*) fishbone.

lisci'are [liʃ'ʃare] *vt* to smooth; (*fig*) to flatter; **~rsi i capelli** to straighten one's hair.

'liscio, a, sci, sce ['liʃʃo] *ag* smooth; (*capelli*) straight; (*mobile*) plain; (*bevanda alcolica*) neat; (*fig*) straightforward, simple ♦ *av*: **andare ~** to go smoothly; **passarla ~a** to get away with it.

'liso, a *ag* worn out, threadbare.

'lista *sf* (*striscia*) strip; (*elenco*) list; **~ elettorale** electoral roll; **~ delle vivande** menu.

lis'tare *vt*: **~ (di)** to edge (with), border (with).

lis'tato *sm* (*INFORM*) list, listing.

lis'tino *sm* list; **~ di borsa** the Stock Exchange list; **~ dei cambi** (foreign) exchange rate; **~ dei prezzi** price list.

lita'nia *sf* litany.

'lite *sf* quarrel, argument; (*DIR*) lawsuit.

liti'gare *vi* to quarrel; (*DIR*) to litigate.

li'tigio [li'tidʒo] *sm* quarrel.

litigi'oso, a [liti'dʒoso] *ag* quarrelsome; (*DIR*) litigious.

litogra'fia *sf* (*sistema*) lithography; (*stampa*) lithograph.

lito'grafico, a, ci, che *ag* lithographic.

lito'rale *ag* coastal, coast *cpd* ♦ *sm* coast.
lito'raneo, a *ag* coastal.
'litro *sm* litre (*BRIT*), liter (*US*).
lit'torio, a *ag* (*STORIA*) lictorial; **fascio** ~
  fasces *pl*.
Litu'ania *sf*: **la** ~ Lithuania.
litu'ano, a *ag*, *sm/f*, *sm* Lithuanian.
litur'gia, 'gie [litur'dʒia] *sf* liturgy.
li'uto *sm* lute.
li'vella *sf* level; ~ **a bolla d'aria** spirit level.
livel'lare *vt* to level, make level; ~**rsi** *vr* to
  become level; (*fig*) to level out, balance
  out.
livella'trice [livella'tritʃe] *sf* steamroller.
li'vello *sm* level; (*fig*) level, standard; **ad
  alto** ~ (*fig*) high-level; **a** ~ **mondiale**
  world-wide; **a** ~ **di confidenza**
  confidentially; ~ **di magazzino** stock
  level; ~ **del mare** sea level; **sul** ~ **del mare**
  above sea level; ~ **occupazionale** level of
  employment; ~ **retributivo** salary level.
'livido, a *ag* livid; (*per percosse*) bruised,
  black and blue; (*cielo*) leaden ♦ *sm* bruise.
li'vore *sm* malice, spite.
Li'vorno *sf* Livorno, Leghorn.
li'vrea *sf* livery.
'lizza ['littsa] *sf* lists *pl*; **essere in** ~ **per** (*fig*)
  to compete for; **scendere in** ~ (*anche fig*)
  to enter the lists.
LO *sigla* = Lodi.
lo *det m* (*dav s impura, gn, pn, ps, x, z*; *dav* **V l'**)
  the ♦ *pron* (*dav* **V l'**) (*oggetto: persona*) him;
  (: *cosa*) it; ~ **sapevo** I knew it; ~ **so** I
  know; **sii buono, anche se lui non** ~ **è** be
  good, even if he isn't; *vedi anche* **il**.
lob'bista, i, e *sm/f* lobbyist.
'lobby *sf inv* lobby.
'lobo *sm* lobe; ~ **dell'orecchio** ear lobe.
lo'cale *ag* local ♦ *sm* room; (*luogo pubblico*)
  premises *pl*; ~ **notturno** nightclub.
località *sf inv* locality.
localiz'zare [lokalid'dzare] *vt* (*circoscrivere*)
  to confine, localize; (*accertare*) to locate,
  place.
lo'canda *sf* inn.
locandi'ere, a *sm/f* innkeeper.
locan'dina *sf* (*TEAT*) poster.
lo'care *vt* (*casa*) to rent out, let; (*macchina*)
  to hire out (*BRIT*), rent (out).
loca'tario, a *sm/f* tenant.
loca'tivo, a *ag* (*DIR*) rentable.
loca'tore, 'trice *sm/f* landlord/lady.
locazi'one [lokat'tsjone] *sf* (*da parte del
  locatario*) renting *no pl*; (*da parte del
  locatore*) renting out *no pl*, letting *no pl*;
  (**contratto di**) ~ lease; (**canone di**) ~ rent;
  dare in ~ to rent out, let.
locomo'tiva *sf* locomotive.

locomo'tore *sm* electric locomotive.
locomot'rice [lokomo'tritʃe] *sf*
  = **locomotore**.
locomozi'one [lokomot'tsjone] *sf*
  locomotion; **mezzi di** ~ vehicles, means
  of transport.
'loculo *sm* burial recess.
lo'custa *sf* locust.
locuzi'one [lokut'tsjone] *sf* phrase,
  expression.
lo'dare *vt* to praise.
'lode *sf* praise; (*INS*): **laurearsi con 110 e** ~
  ≈ to graduate with first-class honours
  (*BRIT*), ≈ to graduate summa cum laude
  (*US*).
'loden *sm inv* (*stoffa*) loden; (*cappotto*) loden
  overcoat.
lo'devole *ag* praiseworthy.
loga'ritmo *sm* logarithm.
'loggia, ge ['lɔddʒa] *sf* (*ARCHIT*) loggia;
  (*circolo massonico*) lodge.
loggi'one [lod'dʒone] *sm* (*di teatro*): **il** ~ the
  Gods *sg*.
logica'mente [lodʒika'mente] *av* naturally,
  obviously.
logicità [lodʒitʃi'ta] *sf* logicality.
'logico, a, ci, che ['lɔdʒiko] *ag* logical ♦ *sf*
  logic.
lo'gistica [lo'dʒistika] *sf* logistics *sg*.
'logo *sm inv* logo.
logora'mento *sm* (*di vestiti etc*) wear.
logo'rante *ag* exhausting.
logo'rare *vt* to wear out; (*sciupare*) to
  waste; ~**rsi** *vr* to wear out; (*fig*) to wear
  o.s. out.
logo'rio *sm* wear and tear; (*fig*) strain.
'logoro, a *ag* (*stoffa*) worn out, threadbare;
  (*persona*) worn out.
'Loira *sf*: **la** ~ the Loire.
lom'baggine [lom'baddʒine] *sf* lumbago.
Lombar'dia *sf*: **la** ~ Lombardy.
lom'bardo, a *ag*, *sm/f* Lombard.
lom'bare *ag* (*ANAT, MED*) lumbar.
lom'bata *sf* (*taglio di carne*) loin.
'lombo *sm* (*ANAT*) loin.
lom'brico, chi *sm* earthworm.
londi'nese *ag* London *cpd* ♦ *sm/f* Londoner.
'Londra *sf* London.
lon'ganime *ag* forbearing.
longevità [londʒevi'ta] *sf* longevity.
lon'gevo, a [lon'dʒevo] *ag* long-lived.
longi'lineo, a [londʒi'lineo] *ag* long-limbed.
longi'tudine [londʒi'tudine] *sf* longitude.
lonta'namente *av* remotely; **non ci
  pensavo neppure** ~ it didn't even occur
  to me.
lonta'nanza [lonta'nantsa] *sf* distance;
  absence.

lon tano, a *ag (distante)* distant, faraway; *(assente)* absent; *(vago: sospetto)* slight, remote; *(tempo: remoto)* far-off, distant; *(parente)* distant, remote ♦ *av* far; **è ~a la casa?** is it far to the house?, is the house far from here?; **è ~ un chilometro** it's a kilometre away *o* a kilometre from here; **più ~** farther; **da** *o* **di ~** from a distance; **~ da** a long way from; **alla ~a** slightly, vaguely.

lontra *sf* otter.

lo quace [lo'kwatʃe] *ag* talkative, loquacious; *(fig: gesto etc)* eloquent.

loquacità [lokwatʃi'ta] *sf* talkativeness, loquacity.

lordo, a *ag* dirty, filthy; *(peso, stipendio)* gross; **~ d'imposta** pre-tax.

Lo rena *sf (GEO)* Lorraine.

loro *pron pl (oggetto, con preposizione)* them; *(complemento di termine)* to them; *(soggetto)* they; *(forma di cortesia: anche:* **L~)** you; to you; **il(la) ~, i(le) ~** *det* their; *(forma di cortesia: anche:* **L~)** your ♦ *pron* theirs; *(forma di cortesia: anche:* **L~)** yours ♦ *sm inv:* **il ~** their *(o your)* money ♦ *sf inv:* **la ~** *(opinione)* their *(o your)* view; **i ~** *(famiglia)* their *(o your)* family; *(amici etc)* their *(o your)* own people; **un ~ amico** a friend of theirs; **è dalla ~** he's on their *(o your)* side; **ne hanno fatto un'altra delle ~** they've *(o you've)* done it again; **~ stessi(e)** they themselves; you yourselves.

lo sanga, ghe *sf* diamond, lozenge.

Lo sanna *sf* Lausanne.

losco, a, schi, sche *ag (fig)* shady, suspicious.

lotta *sf* struggle, fight; *(SPORT)* wrestling; **essere in ~ (con)** to be in conflict (with); **fare la ~ (con)** to wrestle (with); **~ armata** armed struggle; **~ di classe** *(POL)* class struggle; **~ libera** *(SPORT)* all-in wrestling *(BRIT)*, freestyle.

lot tare *vi* to fight, struggle; to wrestle.

lotta tore, trice *sm/f* wrestler.

lotte ria *sf* lottery; *(di gara ippica)* sweepstake.

lottiz zare [lottid'dzare] *vt* to divide into plots; *(fig)* to share out.

lottizzazi one [lottiddzat'tsjone] *sf* division into plots; *(fig)* share-out.

lotto *sm (gioco)* (state) lottery; *(parte)* lot; *(EDIL)* site; **vincere un terno al ~** *(anche fig)* to hit the jackpot.

lozi one [lot'tsjone] *sf* lotion.

LT *sigla* = *Latina.*

LU *sigla* = *Lucca.*

lubrifi cante *sm* lubricant.

lubrifi care *vt* to lubricate.

lu cano, a *ag* of *(o* from) Lucania.

luc chetto [luk'ketto] *sm* padlock.

lucci care [luttʃi'kare] *vi* to sparkle; *(oro)* to glitter; *(stella)* to twinkle; *(occhi)* to glisten.

lucci chio [luttʃi'kio] *sm* sparkling; glittering; twinkling; glistening.

lucci cone [luttʃi'kone] *sm:* **avere i ~i agli occhi** to have tears in one's eyes.

luccio ['luttʃo] *sm (ZOOL)* pike.

lucciola ['luttʃola] *sf (ZOOL)* firefly; glow-worm; *(fam, fig: prostituta)* girl *(o* woman) on the game.

luce ['lutʃe] *sf* light; *(finestra)* window; **alla ~ di** by the light of; **fare qc alla ~ del sole** *(fig)* to do sth in the open; **dare alla ~** *(bambino)* to give birth to; **fare ~ su qc** *(fig)* to shed *o* throw light on sth; **~ del sole/della luna** sun/moonlight.

lu cente [lu'tʃente] *ag* shining.

lucen tezza [lutʃen'tettsa] *sf* shine.

lu cerna [lu'tʃerna] *sf* oil lamp.

lucer nario [lutʃer'narjo] *sm* skylight.

lu certola [lu'tʃertola] *sf* lizard.

luci dare [lutʃi'dare] *vt* to polish; *(ricalcare)* to trace.

lucida trice [lutʃida'tritʃe] *sf* floor polisher.

lucidità [lutʃidi'ta] *sf* lucidity.

lucido, a ['lutʃido] *ag* shining, bright; *(lucidato)* polished; *(fig)* lucid ♦ *sm* shine, lustre *(BRIT)*, luster *(US)*; *(per scarpe etc)* polish; *(disegno)* tracing.

lu cignolo [lu'tʃiɲɲolo] *sm* wick.

luc rare *vt* to make money out of.

lucra tivo, a *ag* lucrative; **a scopo ~** for gain.

lucro *sm* profit, gain; **a scopo di ~** for gain; **organizzazione senza scopo di ~** non-profit-making *(BRIT) o* non-profit *(US)* organization.

lu croso, a *ag* lucrative, profitable.

luculli ano, a *ag (pasto)* sumptuous.

lu dibrio *sm* mockery *no pl; (oggetto di scherno)* laughing stock.

lue *sf* syphilis.

luglio ['luʎʎo] *sm* July; **nel mese di ~** in July, in the month of July; **il primo ~** the first of July; **arrivare il 2 ~** to arrive on the 2nd of July; **all'inizio/alla fine di ~** at the beginning/at the end of July; **durante il mese di ~** during July; **a ~ del prossimo anno** in July of next year; **ogni anno a ~** every July; **che fai a ~?** what are you doing in July?; **ha piovuto molto a ~ quest'anno** July was very wet this year.

lugubre *ag* gloomy.

lui *pron (soggetto)* he; *(oggetto: per dare*

rilievo, con preposizione) him ♦ *sm inv*: **il mio** ~ my beloved; ~ **stesso** he himself; **è** ~ it's him.

lu 'maca, che *sf* slug; (*chiocciola*) snail.

luma 'cone *sm* (large) slug; (*fig*) slowcoach (*BRIT*), slowpoke (*US*).

lume *sm* light; (*lampada*) lamp; ~ **a olio** oil lamp; **chiedere** ~**i a qn** (*fig*) to ask sb for advice; **a** ~ **di naso** (*fig*) by rule of thumb.

lumi 'cino [lumi'tʃino] *sm* small *o* faint light; **essere (ridotto) al** ~ (*fig*) to be at death's door.

lumi 'era *sf* chandelier.

lumi 'nare *sm* luminary.

lumi 'naria *sf* (*per feste*) illuminations *pl*.

lumine 'scente [lumineʃ'ʃɛnte] *ag* luminescent.

lu 'mino *sm* small light; ~ **da notte** nightlight; ~ **per i morti** candle for the dead.

luminosità *sf* brightness; (*fig*: *di sorriso, volto*) radiance.

lumi 'noso, a *ag* (*che emette luce*) luminous; (*cielo, colore, stanza*) bright; (*sorgente*) of light, light *cpd*; (*fig*: *sorriso*) bright, radiant; **insegna** ~**a** neon sign.

lun. *abbr* (= *lunedì*) Mon.

luna *sf* moon; ~ **nuova/piena** new/full moon; **avere la** ~ to be in a bad mood; ~ **di miele** honeymoon.

luna park *sm inv* amusement park, funfair.

lu 'nare *ag* lunar, moon *cpd*.

lu 'nario *sm* almanac; **sbarcare il** ~ to make ends meet.

lu 'natico, a, ci, che *ag* whimsical, temperamental.

lunedì *sm inv* Monday; *per fraseologia vedi* **martedì**.

lun 'gaggine [lun'gaddʒine] *sf* slowness; ~**i della burocrazia** red tape.

lunga 'mente *av* (*a lungo*) for a long time; (*estesamente*) at length.

lun 'garno *sm* embankment along the Arno.

lun 'ghezza [lun'gettsa] *sf* length; ~ **d'onda** (*FISICA*) wavelength.

lungi ['lundʒi] *av*: ~ **da** *prep* far from.

lungimi 'rante [lundʒimi'rante] *ag* farsighted.

lungo, a, ghi, ghe *ag* long; (*lento: persona*) slow; (*diluito: caffè, brodo*) weak, watery, thin ♦ *sm* length ♦ *prep* along; ~ **3 metri** 3 metres long; **avere la barba** ~**a** to be unshaven; **a** ~ for a long time; **a** ~ **andare** in the long run; **di gran** ~**a** (*molto*) by far; **andare in** ~ *o* **per le lunghe** to drag on; **saperla** ~**a** to know what's what; **in** ~ **e in largo** far and wide, all over; ~ **il corso dei**

secoli throughout the centuries; **navigazione di** ~ **corso** ocean-going navigation.

lungofi 'ume *sm* embankment.

lungo 'lago *sm* road round a lake.

lungo 'mare *sm* promenade.

lungome 'traggio [lungome'traddʒo] *sm* (*CINE*) feature film.

lungo 'tevere *sm* embankment along the Tiber.

lu 'notto *sm* (*AUT*) rear *o* back window; ~ **termico** heated rear window.

lu 'ogo, ghi *sm* place; (*posto: di incidente etc*) scene, site; (*punto, passo di libro*) passage; **in** ~ **di** instead of; **in primo** ~ in the first place; **aver** ~ to take place; **dar** ~ **a** to give rise to; ~ **comune** commonplace; ~ **del delitto** scene of the crime; ~ **geometrico** locus; ~ **di nascita** birthplace; (*AMM*) place of birth; ~ **di pena** prison, penitentiary; ~ **di provenienza** place of origin.

luogote 'nente *sm* (*MIL*) lieutenant.

lupacchi 'otto [lupak'kjɔtto] *sm* (*ZOOL*) (wolf) cub.

lu 'para *sf* sawn-off shotgun.

iu 'petto *sm* (*ZOOL*) (wolf) cub; (*negli scouts*) cub scout.

lupo, a *sm/f* wolf/she-wolf; **cane** ~ alsatian (dog) (*BRIT*), German shepherd (dog); **tempo da** ~**i** filthy weather.

luppolo *sm* (*BOT*) hop.

lurido, a *ag* filthy.

luri 'dume *sm* filth.

lu 'singa, ghe *sf* (*spesso al pl*) flattery *no pl*.

lusin 'gare *vt* to flatter.

lusinghi 'ero, a [luzin'gjɛro] *ag* flattering, gratifying.

lus 'sare *vt* (*MED*) to dislocate.

lussazi 'one [lussat'tsjone] *sf* (*MED*) dislocation.

lussembur 'ghese [lussembur'gese] *ag* of (*o* from) Luxembourg ♦ *sm/f* native (*o* inhabitant) of Luxembourg.

Lussem 'burgo *sm* (*stato*): **il** ~ Luxembourg ♦ *sf* (*città*) Luxembourg.

lusso *sm* luxury; **di** ~ luxury *cpd*.

lussu 'oso, a *ag* luxurious.

lussureggi 'are [lussured'dʒare] *vi* to be luxuriant.

lus 'suria *sf* lust.

lussuri 'oso, a *ag* lascivious, lustful.

lus 'trare *vt* to polish, shine.

lustras 'carpe *sm/f inv* shoeshine.

lus 'trino *sm* sequin.

lustro, a *ag* shiny; (*pelliccia*) glossy ♦ *sm* shine, gloss; (*fig*) prestige, glory; (*quinquennio*) five-year period.

lute'rano, a *ag, sm/f,* Lutheran.
'lutto *sm* mourning; **essere in/portare il** ~ to be in/wear mourning.

M m

M, m ['ɛmme] *sf o m inv* (*lettera*) M, m; **M come Milano** ≈ M for Mary (*BRIT*), M for Mike (*US*).
m. *abbr* = **mese; metro; miglia; monte.**
ma *cong* but; ~ **insomma!** for goodness sake!; ~ **no!** of course not!
'macabro, a *ag* gruesome, macabre.
ma'caco, chi *sm* (*ZOOL*) macaque.
macché [mak'ke] *escl* not at all!, certainly not!
macche'roni [makke'roni] *smpl* macaroni *sg.*
'macchia ['makkja] *sf* stain, spot; (*chiazza di diverso colore*) spot; splash, patch; (*tipo di boscaglia*) scrub; ~ **d'inchiostro** ink stain; **estendersi a** ~ **d'olio** (*fig*) to spread rapidly; **darsi/vivere alla** ~ (*fig*) to go into/live in hiding.
macchi'are [mak'kjare] *vt* (*sporcare*) to stain, mark; ~**rsi** *vr* (*persona*) to get o.s. dirty; (*stoffa*) to stain; to get stained *o* marked; ~**rsi di un delitto** to be guilty of a crime.
macchi'ato, a [mak'kjato] *ag* (*pelle, pelo*) spotted; ~ **di** stained with; **caffè** ~ coffee with a dash of milk.
macchi'etta [mak'kjetta] *sf* (*disegno*) sketch, caricature; (*TEAT*) caricature; (*fig*: *persona*) character.
'macchina ['makkina] *sf* machine; (*motore, locomotiva*) engine; (*automobile*) car; (*fig*: *meccanismo*) machinery; **andare in** ~ (*AUT*) to go by car; (*STAMPA*) to go to press; **salire in** ~ to get into the car; **venire in** ~ to come by car; **sala** ~**e** (*NAUT*) engine room; ~ **da cucire** sewing machine; ~ **fotografica** camera; ~ **da presa** cine *o* movie camera; ~ **da scrivere** typewriter; ~ **utensile** machine tool; ~ **a vapore** steam engine.
macchinal'mente [makkinal'mente] *av* mechanically.
macchi'nare [makki'nare] *vt* to plot.
macchi'nario [makki'narjo] *sm* machinery.
macchinazi'one [makkinat'tsjone] *sf* plot, machination.

macchi'netta [makki'netta] *sf* (*fam*: *caffettiera*) percolator; (: *accendino*) lighter.
macchi'nista, i [makki'nista] *sm* (*di treno*) engine-driver; (*di nave*) engineer; (*TEAT, TV*) stagehand.
macchi'noso, a [makki'noso] *ag* complex, complicated.
ma'cedone [ma'tʃedone] *ag, sm/f* Macedonian.
Mace'donia [matʃe'dɔnja] *sm* Macedonia.
mace'donia [matʃe'dɔnja] *sf* fruit salad.
macel'laio [matʃel'lajo] *sm* butcher.
macel'lare [matʃel'lare] *vt* to slaughter, butcher.
macellazi'one [matʃellat'tsjone] *sf* slaughtering, butchering.
macelle'ria [matʃelle'ria] *sf* butcher's (shop).
ma'cello [ma'tʃello] *sm* (*mattatoio*) slaughterhouse, abattoir (*BRIT*); (*fig*) slaughter, massacre; (: *disastro*) shambles *sg.*
mace'rare [matʃe'rare] *vt* to macerate; (*CUC*) to marinate; ~**rsi** *vr* to waste away; (*fig*): ~**rsi in** to be consumed with.
macerazi'one [matʃerat'tsjone] *sf* maceration.
ma'cerie [ma'tʃerje] *sfpl* rubble *sg*, debris *sg.*
'macero ['matʃero] *sm* (*operazione*) pulping; (*stabilimento*) pulping mill; **carta da** ~ paper for pulping.
machia'vellico, a, ci, che [makja'vɛlliko] *ag* (*anche fig*) Machiavellian.
ma'cigno [ma'tʃiɲɲo] *sm* (*masso*) rock, boulder.
maci'lento, a [matʃi'lɛnto] *ag* emaciated.
'macina ['matʃina] *sf* (*pietra*) millstone; (*macchina*) grinder.
macinacaffè [matʃinakaf'fɛ] *sm inv* coffee grinder.
macina'pepe [matʃina'pepe] *sm inv* peppermill.
maci'nare [matʃi'nare] *vt* to grind; (*carne*) to mince (*BRIT*), grind (*US*).
maci'nato [matʃi'nato] *sm* meal, flour; (*carne*) minced (*BRIT*) *o* ground (*US*) meat.
maci'nino [matʃi'nino] *sm* (*per caffè*) coffee grinder; (*per pepe*) peppermill; (*scherzoso: macchina*) old banger (*BRIT*), clunker (*US*).
maciul'lare [matʃul'lare] *vt* (*canapa, lino*) to brake; (*fig*: *braccio etc*) to crush.
'macro ... *prefisso* macro....
macrobi'otico, a *ag* macrobiotic ♦ *sf* macrobiotics *sg.*
macu'lato, a *ag* (*pelo*) spotted.
Ma'dama: palazzo ~ *sm* (*POL*) seat of the

Italian Chamber of Senators.

made in Italy [meɪdɪ'nɪtəlɪ] *sm*: **il ~** Italian exports *pl* (*especially fashion goods*).

Ma'dera *sf* (*GEO*) Madeira ♦ *sm inv* (*vino*) Madeira.

'madido, a *ag*: **~ (di)** wet *o* moist (with).

Ma'donna *sf* (*REL*) Our Lady.

mador'nale *ag* enormous, huge.

'madre *sf* mother; (*matrice di bolletta*) counterfoil ♦ *ag inv* mother *cpd*; **ragazza ~** unmarried mother; **scena ~** (*TEAT*) principal scene; (*fig*) terrible scene.

madre'lingua *sf* mother tongue, native language.

madre'patria *sf* mother country, native land.

madre'perla *sf* mother-of-pearl.

Ma'drid *sf* Madrid.

madri'gale *sm* madrigal.

madri'leno, a *ag* of (*o* from) Madrid ♦ *sm/f* person from Madrid.

ma'drina *sf* godmother.

maestà *sf inv* majesty; **Sua M~ la Regina** Her Majesty the Queen.

maestosità *sf* majesty.

maes'toso, a *ag* majestic.

ma'estra *sf vedi* **maestro**.

maes'trale *sm* north-west wind.

maes'tranze [maes'trantse] *sfpl* workforce *sg*.

maes'tria *sf* mastery, skill.

ma'estro, a *sm/f* (*INS*: *anche*: **~ di scuola** *o* **elementare**) primary (*BRIT*) *o* grade school (*US*) teacher; (*esperto*) expert ♦ *sm* (*artigiano*, *fig*: *guida*) master; (*MUS*) maestro ♦ *ag* (*principale*) main; (*di grande abilità*) masterly, skilful (*BRIT*), skillful (*US*); **un colpo da ~** (*fig*) a masterly move; **muro ~** main wall; **strada ~a** main road; **~a d'asilo** nursery teacher; **~ di ballo** dancing master; **~ di cerimonie** master of ceremonies; **~ d'orchestra** conductor, director (*US*); **~ di scherma** fencing master; **~ di sci** ski instructor.

'mafia *sf* Mafia.

mafi'oso *sm* member of the Mafia.

'maga, ghe *sf* sorceress.

ma'gagna [ma'gaɲɲa] *sf* defect, flaw, blemish; (*noia, guaio*) problem.

ma'garl *escl* (*esprime desiderio*): **~ fosse vero!** if only it were true!; **ti piacerebbe andare in Scozia? — ~!** would you like to go to Scotland? — I certainly would! ♦ *av* (*anche*) even; (*forse*) perhaps.

magazzi'naggio [magaddzi'naddʒo] *sm*: **(spese di) ~** storage charges *pl*, warehousing charges *pl*.

magazzini'ere [magaddzi'njɛre] *sm*

warehouseman.

magaz'zino [magad'dzino] *sm* warehouse; **grande ~** department store; **~ doganale** bonded warehouse.

'maggio ['maddʒo] *sm* May; *per fraseologia vedi* **luglio**.

maggio'rana [maddʒo'rana] *sf* (*BOT*) (sweet) marjoram.

maggio'ranza [maddʒo'rantsa] *sf* majority; **nella ~ dei casi** in most cases.

maggio'rare [maddʒo'rare] *vt* to increase, raise.

maggiorazi'one [maddʒorat'tsjone] *sf* (*COMM*) rise, increase.

maggior'domo [maddʒor'dɔmo] *sm* butler.

maggi'ore [mad'dʒore] *ag* (*comparativo*: *più grande*) bigger, larger; taller; greater; (: *più vecchio*: *sorella, fratello*) older, elder; (: *di grado superiore*) senior; (: *più importante*, *MIL, MUS*) major; (*superlativo*) biggest, largest; tallest; greatest; oldest, eldest ♦ *sm/f* (*di grado*) superior; (*di età*) elder; (*MIL*) major; (: *AER*) squadron leader; **la maggior parte** the majority; **andare per la ~** (*cantante, attore etc*) to be very popular, be "in".

maggio'renne [maddʒo'rɛnne] *ag* of age ♦ *sm/f* person who has come of age.

maggiori'tario, a [maddʒori'tarjo] *ag* majority *cpd* ♦ (*POL*: *anche*: **sistema ~**) first-past-the-post system.

maggior'mente [maddʒor'mente] *av* much more; (*con senso superlativo*) most.

maghre'bino, a *ag*, *sm/f* Maghrebi.

ma'gia [ma'dʒia] *sf* magic.

'magico, a, ci, che ['madʒiko] *ag* magic; (*fig*) fascinating, charming, magical.

'magio ['madʒo] *sm* (*REL*): **i re Magi** the Magi, the Three Wise Men.

magis'tero [madʒis'tɛro] *sm* teaching; (*fig*: *maestria*) skill; (*INS*): **Facoltà di M~** ≈ teachers' training college.

magis'trale [madʒis'trale] *ag* primary (*BRIT*) *o* grade school (*US*) teachers', primary *o* grade school teaching *cpd*; (*abile*) skilful (*BRIT*), skillful (*US*); **istituto ~** secondary school for the training of primary teachers.

magis'trato [madʒis'trato] *sm* magistrate.

magistra'tura [madʒistra'tura] *sf* magistrature; (*magistrati*): **la ~** the Bench.

'maglia ['maʎʎa] *sf* stitch; (*lavoro ai ferri*) knitting *no pl*; (*tessuto, SPORT*) jersey; (*maglione*) jersey, sweater; (*di catena*) link; (*di rete*) mesh; **avviare/diminuire le ~e** to cast on/cast off; **lavorare a ~, fare la ~** to knit; **~ diritta/rovescia** plain/purl.

magli'aia [maʎ'ʎaja] *sf* knitter.

maglie'ria [maʎʎe'ria] *sf* knitwear;

(*negozio*) knitwear shop; **macchina per** ~ knitting machine.

magli 'etta [maʎ'ʎetta] *sf* (*canottiera*) vest; (*tipo camicia*) T-shirt.

magli 'ficio [maʎʎi'fitʃo] *sm* knitwear factory.

ma 'glina [maʎ'ʎina] *sf* (*tessuto*) jersey.

'maglio ['maʎʎo] *sm* mallet; (*macchina*) power hammer.

magli 'one [maʎ'ʎone] *sm* jersey, sweater.

'magma *sm* magma; (*fig*) mass.

ma 'gnaccia [maɲ'nattʃa] *sm inv* (*peg*) pimp.

magnanimità [maɲɲanimi'ta] *sf* magnanimity.

ma 'gnanimo, a [maɲ'ɲanimo] *ag* magnanimous.

ma 'gnate [maɲ'ɲate] *sm* tycoon, magnate.

ma 'gnesia [maɲ'ɲezja] *sf* (*CHIM*) magnesia.

ma 'gnesio [maɲ'ɲezjo] *sm* (*CHIM*) magnesium; **al** ~ (*lampada, flash*) magnesium *cpd*.

ma 'gnete [maɲ'ɲete] *sm* magnet.

ma 'gnetico, a, ci, che [maɲ'ɲetiko] *ag* magnetic.

magne 'tismo [maɲɲe'tizmo] *sm* magnetism.

magnetiz 'zare [maɲɲetid'dzare] *vt* (*FISICA*) to magnetize; (*fig*) to mesmerize.

magne 'tofono [maɲɲe'tɔfono] *sm* tape recorder.

magnifica 'mente [maɲɲifika'mente] *av* magnificently, extremely well.

magnifi 'cenza [maɲɲifi'tʃɛntsa] *sf* magnificence, splendour (*BRIT*), splendor (*US*).

ma 'gnifico, a, ci, che [maɲ'ɲifiko] *ag* magnificent, splendid; (*ospite*) generous.

'magno, a ['maɲɲo] *ag*: **aula** ~**a** main hall.

ma 'gnolia [maɲ'ɲɔlja] *sf* magnolia.

'mago, ghi *sm* (*stregone*) magician, wizard; (*illusionista*) magician.

ma 'grezza [ma'grettsa] *sf* thinness.

'magro, a *ag* (very) thin, skinny; (*carne*) lean; (*formaggio*) low-fat; (*fig: scarso, misero*) meagre (*BRIT*), meager (*US*), poor; (: *meschino: scusa*) poor, lame; **mangiare di** ~ not to eat meat.

'mai *av* (*nessuna volta*) never; (*talvolta*) ever; **non ...** ~ never; ~ **più** never again; **come** ~**?** why (*o* how) on earth?; **chi/ dove/quando** ~**?** whoever/wherever/ whenever?

mai 'ale *sm* (*ZOOL*) pig; (*carne*) pork.

mai 'olica *sf* majolica.

maio 'nese *sf* mayonnaise.

Mai 'orca *sf* Majorca.

'mais *sm* maize (*BRIT*), corn (*US*).

mai 'uscolo, a *ag* (*lettera*) capital ♦ *sf*

capital letter ♦ *sm* capital letters *pl*; (*TIP*) upper case; **scrivere tutto (in)** ~ to write everything in capitals *o* in capital letters.

mal *av*, *sm vedi* **male.**

'mala *sf* (*gergo*) underworld.

malac 'corto, a *ag* rash, careless.

mala 'fede *sf* bad faith.

malaf 'fare: di ~ *ag* (*gente*) shady, dishonest; **donna di** ~ prostitute.

mala 'gevole [mala'dʒevole] *ag* difficult, hard.

mala 'grazia [mala'grattsja] *sf*: **con** ~ with bad grace, impolitely.

mala 'lingua, *pl* **male 'lingue** *sf* gossip (*person*).

mala 'mente *av* badly; (*sgarbatamente*) rudely.

malan 'dato, a *ag* (*persona: di salute*) in poor health; (: *di condizioni finanziarie*) badly off; (*trascurato*) shabby.

ma 'lanimo *sm* ill will, malevolence; **di** ~ unwillingly.

ma 'lanno *sm* (*disgrazia*) misfortune; (*malattia*) ailment.

mala 'pena *sf*: **a** ~ hardly, scarcely.

ma 'laria *sf* malaria.

ma 'larico, a, ci, che *ag* malarial.

mala 'sorte *sf* bad luck.

mala 'ticcio, a [mala'tittʃo] *ag* sickly.

ma 'lato, a *ag* ill, sick; (*gamba*) bad; (*pianta*) diseased ♦ *sm/f* sick person; (*in ospedale*) patient; **darsi** ~ (*sul lavoro etc*) to go sick.

malat 'tia *sf* (*infettiva etc*) illness, disease; (*cattiva salute*) illness, sickness; (*di pianta*) disease; **mettersi in** ~ to go on sick leave; **fare una** ~ **di qc** (*fig: disperarsi*) to get in a state about sth.

malaugu 'rato, a *ag* ill-fated, unlucky.

malau 'gurio *sm* bad *o* ill omen; **uccello del** ~ bird of ill omen.

mala 'vita *sf* underworld.

malavi 'toso, a *sm/f* gangster.

mala 'voglia [mala'vɔʎʎa]: **di** ~ *av* unwillingly, reluctantly.

Ma 'lawi [ma'lavi] *sm*: **il** ~ Malawi.

Mala 'ysia *sf* Malaysia.

malaysi 'ano, a *ag, sm/f* Malaysian.

malcapi 'tato, a *ag* unlucky, unfortunate ♦ *sm/f* unfortunate person.

mal 'concio, a, ci, ce [mal'kontʃo] *ag* in a sorry state.

malcon 'tento *sm* discontent.

malcos 'tume *sm* immorality.

mal 'destro, a *ag* (*inabile*) inexpert, inexperienced; (*goffo*) awkward.

maldi 'cente [maldi'tʃɛnte] *ag* slanderous.

maldi 'cenza [maldi'tʃɛntsa] *sf* malicious gossip.

maldis'posto, a *ag*: ~ **(verso)** ill-disposed (towards).

Mal'dive *sfpl*: **le** ~ the Maldives.

'male *av* badly ♦ *sm* (*ciò che è ingiusto, disonesto*) evil; (*danno, svantaggio*) harm; (*sventura*) misfortune; (*dolore fisico, morale*) pain, ache; **sentirsi** ~ to feel ill; **aver mal di cuore/fegato** to have a heart/ liver complaint; **aver mal di denti/ d'orecchi/di testa** to have toothache/ earache/a headache; **aver mal di gola** to have a sore throat; **aver** ~ **ai piedi** to have sore feet; **far** ~ (*dolere*) to hurt; **far** ~ **alla salute** to be bad for one's health; **far del** ~ **a qn** to hurt *o* harm sb; **parlar** ~ **di qn** to speak ill of sb; **restare** *o* **rimanere** ~ to be sorry; to be disappointed; to be hurt; **trattar** ~ **qn** to ill-treat sb; **andare a** ~ to go off *o* bad; **come va?** — **non c'è** ~ how are you? — not bad; **di** ~ **in peggio** from bad to worse; **per** ~ **che vada** however badly things go; **non avertene a** ~, **non prendertela a** ~ don't take it to heart; **mal comune mezzo gaudio** (*proverbio*) a trouble shared is a trouble halved; **mal d'auto** carsickness; **mal di mare** seasickness.

male'detto, a *pp di* **maledire** ♦ *ag* cursed, damned; (*fig fam*) damned, blasted.

male'dire *vt* to curse.

maledizi'one [maledit'tsjone] *sf* curse; ~! damn it!

maledu'cato, a *ag* rude, ill-mannered.

maleducazi'one [maledukat'tsjone] *sf* rudeness.

male'fatta *sf* misdeed.

male'ficio [male'fitʃo] *sm* witchcraft.

ma'lefico, a, ci, che *ag* (*aria, cibo*) harmful, bad; (*influsso, azione*) evil.

ma'lese *ag, sm/f* Malay(an) ♦ *sm* (*LING*) Malay.

Ma'lesia *sf* Malaya.

ma'lessere *sm* indisposition, slight illness; (*fig*) uneasiness.

malevo'lenza [malevo'lɛntsa] *sf* malevolence.

ma'levolo, a *ag* malevolent.

malfa'mato, a *ag* notorious.

mal'fatto, a *ag* (*persona*) deformed; (*oggetto*) badly made; (*lavoro*) badly done.

malfat'tore, 'trice *sm/f* wrongdoer.

mal'fermo, a *ag* unsteady, shaky; (*salute*) poor, delicate.

malformazi'one [malformat'tsjone] *sf* malformation.

'malga, ghe *sf* Alpine hut.

malgo'verno *sm* maladministration.

mal'grado *prep* in spite of, despite ♦ *cong*

although; **mio** (*o* **tuo** *etc*) ~ against my (*o* your *etc*) will.

ma'lia *sf* spell; (*fig: fascino*) charm.

mali'ardo, a *ag* (*occhi, sorriso*) bewitching ♦ *sf* enchantress.

maligna'mente [maliɲɲa'mente] *av* maliciously.

mali'gnare [malin'ɲare] *vi*: ~ **su** to malign, speak ill of.

malignità [maliɲɲi'ta] *sf inv* (*qualità*) malice, spite; (*osservazione*) spiteful remark; **con** ~ spitefully, maliciously.

ma'ligno, a [ma'liɲɲo] *ag* (*malvagio*) malicious, malignant; (*MED*) malignant.

malinco'nia *sf* melancholy, gloom.

malin'conico, a, ci, che *ag* melancholy.

malincu'ore : **a** ~ *av* reluctantly, unwillingly.

malinfor'mato, a *ag* misinformed.

malintenzio'nato, a [malintentsjo'nato] *ag* ill-intentioned.

malin'teso, a *ag* misunderstood; (*riguardo, senso del dovere*) mistaken, wrong ♦ *sm* misunderstanding.

ma'lizia [ma'littsja] *sf* (*malignità*) malice; (*furbizia*) cunning; (*espediente*) trick.

malizi'oso, a [malit'tsjoso] *ag* malicious; cunning; (*vivace, birichino*) mischievous.

malle'abile *ag* malleable.

mal'loppo *sm* (*fam: refurtiva*) loot.

malme'nare *vt* to beat up; (*fig*) to ill-treat.

mal'messo, a *ag* shabby.

malnu'trito, a *ag* undernourished.

malnutrizi'one [malnutrit'tsjone] *sf* malnutrition.

'malo, a *ag*: **in** ~ **modo** badly.

ma'locchio [ma'lɔkkjo] *sm* evil eye.

ma'lora *sf* (*fam*): **andare in** ~ to go to the dogs; **va in** ~! go to hell!

ma'lore *sm* (sudden) illness.

malri'dotto, a *ag* (*abiti, scarpe, persona*) in a sorry state; (*casa, macchina*) dilapidated, in a poor state of repair.

mal'sano, a *ag* unhealthy.

malsi'curo, a *ag* unsafe.

'Malta *sf* Malta.

'malta *sf* (*EDIL*) mortar.

mal'tempo *sm* bad weather.

'malto *sm* malt.

mal'tolto *sm* ill-gotten gains *pl*.

maltratta'mento *sm* ill treatment.

maltrat'tare *vt* to ill-treat.

malu'more *sm* bad mood; (*irritabilità*) bad temper; (*discordia*) ill feeling; **di** ~ in a bad mood.

'malva *sf* (*BOT*) mallow ♦ *ag, sm inv* mauve.

mal'vagio, a, gi, gie [mal'vadʒo] *ag* wicked, evil.

malvagità [malvadʒi'ta] *sf inv* (*qualità*) wickedness; (*azione*) wicked deed.

malva 'sia *sf Italian dessert wine.*

malversazi 'one [malversat'tsjone] *sf* (*DIR*) embezzlement.

malves 'tito, a *ag* badly dressed, ill-clad.

mal 'visto, a *ag*: ~ (**da**) disliked (by), unpopular (with).

malvi 'vente *sm* criminal.

malvolenti 'eri *av* unwillingly, reluctantly.

malvo 'lere *vt*: **farsi ~ da qn** to make o.s. unpopular with sb ♦ *sm*: **prendere qn a ~** to take a dislike to sb.

'mamma *sf* mum(my) (*BRIT*), mom (*US*); ~ **mia!** my goodness!

mam 'mario, a *ag* (*ANAT*) mammary.

mam 'mella *sf* (*ANAT*) breast; (*di vacca, capra etc*) udder.

mam 'mifero *sm* mammal.

mam 'mismo *sm* excessive attachment to one's mother.

'mammola *sf* (*BOT*) violet.

'manager ['mænidʒə] *sm inv* manager.

manageri 'ale [manadʒe'rjale] *ag* managerial.

ma 'nata *sf* (*colpo*) slap; (*quantità*) handful.

'manca *sf* left (hand); **a destra e a** ~ left, right and centre, on all sides.

manca 'mento *sm* (*di forze*) (feeling of) faintness, weakness.

man 'canza [man'kantsa] *sf* lack; (*carenza*) shortage, scarcity; (*fallo*) fault; (*imperfezione*) failing, shortcoming; **per** ~ **di tempo** through lack of time; **in ~ di meglio** for lack of anything better; **sentire la ~ di qc/qn** to miss sth/sb.

man 'care *vi* (*essere insufficiente*) to be lacking; (*venir meno*) to fail; (*sbagliare*) to be wrong, make a mistake; (*non esserci*) to be missing, not to be there; (*essere lontano*): ~ (**da**) to be away (from) ♦ *vt* to miss; ~ **di** to lack; ~ **a** (*promessa*) to fail to keep; **tu mi manchi** I miss you; **mancò poco che morisse** he very nearly died; **mancano ancora 10 sterline** we're still £10 short; **manca un quarto alle 6** it's a quarter to 6; **non mancherò** I won't forget, I'll make sure I do; **ci mancherebbe altro!** of course I (*o you etc*) will!; ~ **da casa** to be away from home; ~ **di rispetto a** *o* **verso qn** to be lacking in respect towards sb, be disrespectful towards sb; ~ **di parola** not to keep one's word, go back on one's word; **sentirsi** ~ to feel faint.

man 'cato, a *ag* (*tentativo*) unsuccessful; (*artista*) failed.

manche [mãʃ] *sf inv* (*SPORT*) heat.

mancherò *etc* [manke'rɔ] *vb vedi* **mancare.**

man 'chevole [man'kevole] *ag* (*insufficiente*) inadequate, insufficient.

manchevo 'lezza [mankevo'lettsa] *sf* (*scorrettezza*) fault, shortcoming.

'mancia, ce ['mantʃa] *sf* tip; ~ **competente** reward.

manci 'ata [man'tʃata] *sf* handful.

man 'cino, a [man'tʃino] *ag* (*braccio*) left; (*persona*) left-handed; (*fig*) underhand.

'manco *av* (*nemmeno*): ~ **per sogno** *o* **per idea!** not on your life!

man 'dante *sm/f* (*DIR*) principal; (*istigatore*) instigator.

manda 'rancio [manda'rantʃo] *sm* clementine.

man 'dare *vt* to send; (*far funzionare: macchina*) to drive; (*emettere*) to send out; (*: grido*) to give, utter, let out; ~ **avanti** (*persona*) to send ahead; (*fig: famiglia*) to provide for; (*: ditta*) to look after, run; (*: pratica*) to attend to; ~ **a chiamare qn** to send for sb; ~ **giù** to send down; (*anche fig*) to swallow; ~ **in onda** (*RADIO, TV*) to broadcast; ~ **in rovina** to ruin; ~ **via** to send away; (*licenziare*) to fire.

manda 'rino *sm* mandarin (orange); (*cinese*) mandarin.

man 'data *sf* (*quantità*) lot, batch; (*di chiave*) turn; **chiudere a doppia** ~ to double-lock.

manda 'tario *sm* (*DIR*) representative, agent.

man 'dato *sm* (*incarico*) commission; (*DIR: provvedimento*) warrant; (*di deputato etc*) mandate; (*ordine di pagamento*) postal *o* money order; ~ **d'arresto,** ~ **di cattura** warrant for arrest; ~ **di comparizione** summons *sg*; ~ **di perquisizione** search warrant.

man 'dibola *sf* mandible, jaw.

mando 'lino *sm* mandolin(e).

'mandorla *sf* almond.

mandor 'lato *sm* nut brittle.

'mandorlo *sm* almond tree.

'mandria *sf* herd.

mandri 'ano *sm* cowherd, herdsman.

man 'drino *sm* (*TECN*) mandrel.

maneg 'gevole [maned'dʒevole] *ag* easy to handle.

maneggi 'are [maned'dʒare] *vt* (*creta, cera*) to mould (*BRIT*), mold (*US*), work, fashion; (*arnesi, utensili*) to handle; (*: adoperare*) to use; (*fig: persone, denaro*) to handle, deal with.

ma 'neggio [ma'neddʒo] *sm* moulding (*BRIT*), molding (*US*); handling; use; (*intrigo*) plot, scheme; (*per cavalli*) riding school.

ma'nesco, a, schi, sche *ag* free with one's fists.

ma'nette *sfpl* handcuffs.

manga'nello *sm* club.

manga'nese *sm* manganese.

mange'reccio, a, ci, ce [mandʒe'rettʃo] *ag* edible.

mangi'abile [man'dʒabile] *ag* edible, eatable.

mangia'dischi [mandʒa'diski] *sm inv* record player.

mangia'nastri [mandʒa'nastri] *sm inv* cassette-recorder.

mangi'are [man'dʒare] *vt* to eat; (*intaccare*) to eat into *o* away; (*CARTE, SCACCHI etc*) to take ♦ *vi* to eat ♦ *sm* eating; (*cibo*) food; (*cucina*) cooking; **fare da** ~ to do the cooking; ~**rsi le parole** to mumble; ~**rsi le unghie** to bite one's nails.

mangia'soldi [mandʒa'sɔldi] *ag inv* (*fam*): **macchinetta** ~ one-armed bandit.

mangia'toia [mandʒa'toja] *sf* feeding-trough.

man'gime [man'dʒime] *sm* fodder.

mangiucchi'are [mandʒuk'kjare] *vt* to nibble.

'mango, ghi *sm* mango.

ma'nia *sf* (*PSIC*) mania; (*fig*) obsession, craze; **avere la** ~ **di fare qc** to have a habit of doing sth; ~ **di persecuzione** persecution complex *o* mania.

mania'cale *ag* (*PSIC*) maniacal; (*fanatico*) fanatical.

ma'niaco, a, ci, che *ag* suffering from a mania; ~ (**di**) obsessed (by), crazy (about).

'manica, che *sf* sleeve; (*fig: gruppo*) gang, bunch; (*GEO*): **la M~, il Canale della M~** the (English) Channel; **senza** ~**che** sleeveless; **essere in** ~**che di camicia** to be in one's shirt sleeves; **essere di** ~ **larga/ stretta** to be easy-going/strict; ~ **a vento** (*AER*) wind sock.

manica'retto *sm* titbit (*BRIT*), tidbit (*US*).

mani'chino [mani'kino] *sm* (*di sarto, vetrina*) dummy.

'manico, ci *sm* handle; (*MUS*) neck; ~ **di scopa** broomstick.

mani'comio *sm* mental hospital; (*fig*) madhouse.

mani'cotto *sm* muff; (*TECN*) coupling; sleeve.

mani'cure *sm o f inv* manicure ♦ *sf inv* manicurist.

mani'era *sf* way, manner; (*stile*) style, manner; ~**e** *sfpl* manners; **in** ~ **da** so as to; **alla** ~ **di** in *o* after the style of; **in una** ~ **o nell'altra** one way or another; **in tutte le** ~**e** at all costs; **usare**

buone ~**e con qn** to be polite to sb; **usare le** ~**e forti** to use strong-arm tactics.

manie'rato, a *ag* affected.

mani'ero *sm* manor.

manifat'tura *sf* (*lavorazione*) manufacture; (*stabilimento*) factory.

manifatturi'ero, a *ag* manufacturing.

manifes'tante *sm/f* demonstrator.

manifes'tare *vt* to show, display; (*esprimere*) to express; (*rivelare*) to reveal, disclose ♦ *vi* to demonstrate; ~**rsi** *vr* to show *o.s.*; ~**rsi amico** to prove o.s. (to be) a friend.

manifestazi'one [manifestat'tsjone] *sf* show, display; expression; (*sintomo*) sign, symptom; (*dimostrazione pubblica*) demonstration; (*cerimonia*) event.

manifes'tino *sm* leaflet.

mani'festo, a *ag* obvious, evident ♦ *sm* poster, bill; (*scritto ideologico*) manifesto.

ma'niglia [ma'niʎʎa] *sf* handle; (*sostegno: negli autobus etc*) strap.

Ma'nila *sf* Manila.

manipo'lare *vt* to manipulate; (*alterare: vino*) to adulterate.

manipolazi'one [manipolat'tsjone] *sf* manipulation; adulteration.

ma'nipolo *sm* (*drappello*) handful.

manis'calco, chi *sm* blacksmith, farrier (*BRIT*).

'manna *sf* (*REL*) manna.

man'naia *sf* (*del boia*) (executioner's) axe *o* ax (*US*); (*per carni*) cleaver.

man'naro, a *ag*: **lupo** ~ werewolf.

'mano, i *sf* hand; (*strato: di vernice etc*) coat; **a** ~ by hand; **cucito a** ~ hand-sewn; **fatto a** ~ handmade; **alla** ~ (*persona*) easy-going; **fuori** ~ out of the way; **di prima** ~ (*notizia*) first-hand; **di seconda** ~ second-hand; **man** ~ little by little, gradually; **man** ~ **che** as; **a piene** ~**i** (*fig*) generously; **avere le** ~**i bucate** to spend money like water; **aver le** ~**i in pasta** to be in the know; **avere qc per le** ~**i** (*progetto, lavoro*) to have sth in hand; **dare una** ~ **a qn** to lend sb a hand; **dare una** ~ **di vernice a qc** to give sth a coat of paint; **darsi** *o* **stringersi la** ~ to shake hands; **forzare la** ~ to go too far; **mettere** ~ **a qc** to have a hand in sth; **mettere le** ~ **avanti** (*fig*) to safeguard o.s.; **restare a** ~**i vuote** to be left empty-handed; **venire alle** ~**i** to come to blows; ~**i in alto!** hands up!; ~**i pulite** *vedi nota nel riquadro*.

MANI PULITE

Mani pulite (*"clean hands"*) is the term used

to describe the judicial operation of the early 1990s to gather evidence against politicians and industrialists who were implicated in bribery and corruption scandals.

mano 'dopera *sf* labour (*BRIT*), labor (*US*).

mano 'messo, a *pp di* **manomettere.**

ma 'nometro *sm* gauge, manometer.

mano 'mettere *vt* (*alterare*) to tamper with; (*aprire indebitamente*) to break open illegally.

manomissi 'one *sf* (*di prove etc*) tampering; (*di lettera*) opening.

ma 'nopola *sf* (*dell'armatura*) gauntlet; (*guanto*) mitt; (*di impugnatura*) hand-grip; (*pomello*) knob.

manos 'critto, a *ag* handwritten ♦ *sm* manuscript.

mano 'vale *sm* labourer (*BRIT*), laborer (*US*).

mano 'vella *sf* handle; (*TECN*) crank.

ma 'novra *sf* manoeuvre (*BRIT*), maneuver (*US*); (*FERR*) shunting; ~**e di corridoio** palace intrigues.

mano 'vrare *vt* (*veicolo*) to manoeuvre (*BRIT*), maneuver (*US*); (*macchina, congegno*) to operate; (*fig: persona*) to manipulate ♦ *vi* to manoeuvre.

manro 'vescio [manro'vɛʃʃo] *sm* slap (*with back of hand*).

man 'sarda *sf* attic.

mansi 'one *sf* task, duty, job.

mansu 'eto, a *ag* (*animale*) tame; (*persona*) gentle, docile.

mansue 'tudine *sf* tameness; gentleness, docility.

man 'tello *sm* cloak; (*fig: di neve etc*) blanket, mantle; (*TECN: involucro*) casing, shell; (*ZOOL*) coat.

mante 'nere *vt* to maintain; (*adempiere: promesse*) to keep, abide by; (*provvedere a*) to support, maintain; ~**rsi** *vr:* ~**rsi calmo/giovane** to stay calm/young; ~ **i contatti con qn** to keep in touch with sb.

manteni 'mento *sm* maintenance.

mante 'nuto, a *sm/f* gigolo/kept woman.

'mantice ['mantitʃe] *sm* bellows *pl*; (*di carrozza, automobile*) hood.

'manto *sm* cloak; ~ **stradale** road surface.

'Mantova *sf* Mantua.

manto 'vano, a *ag* of (*o* from) Mantua.

manu 'ale *ag* manual ♦ *sm* (*testo*) manual, handbook.

manua 'listico, a, ci, che *ag* textbook *cpd*.

manual 'mente *av* manually, by hand.

ma 'nubrio *sm* handle; (*di bicicletta etc*)

handlebars *pl*; (*SPORT*) dumbbell.

manu 'fatto *sm* manufactured article; ~**i** *smpl* manufactured goods.

manutenzi 'one [manuten'tsjone] *sf* maintenance, upkeep; (*d'impianti*) maintenance, servicing.

'manzo ['mandzo] *sm* (*ZOOL*) steer; (*carne*) beef.

Mao 'metto *sm* Mohammed.

'mappa *sf* (*GEO*) map.

mappa 'mondo *sm* map of the world; (*globo girevole*) globe.

ma 'rasma, i *sm* (*fig*) decay, decline.

mara 'tona *sf* marathon.

'marca, che *sf* mark; (*bollo*) stamp; (*COMM: di prodotti*) brand; (*contrassegno, scontrino*) ticket, check; **prodotti di (gran)** ~ high-class products; ~ **da bollo** official stamp.

mar 'care *vt* (*munire di contrassegno*) to mark; (*a fuoco*) to brand; (*SPORT: gol*) to score; (*: avversario*) to mark; (*accentuare*) to stress; ~ **visita** (*MIL*) to report sick.

mar 'cato, a *ag* (*lineamenti, accento etc*) pronounced.

'Marche ['marke] *sfpl:* **le** ~ the Marches (*region of central Italy*).

marcherò *etc* [marke'rɔ] *vb vedi* **marcare.**

mar 'chese, a [mar'keze] *sm/f* marquis *o* marquess/marchioness.

marchi 'ano, a [mar'kjano] *ag* (*errore*) glaring, gross.

marchi 'are [mar'kjare] *vt* to brand.

marchigi 'ano, a [marki'dʒano] *ag* of (*o* from) the Marches.

'marchio ['markjo] *sm* (*di bestiame, COMM, fig*) brand; ~ **depositato** registered trademark; ~ **di fabbrica** trademark.

'marcia, ce ['martʃa] *sf* (*anche MUS, MIL*) march; (*funzionamento*) running; (*il camminare*) walking; (*AUT*) gear; **mettere in** ~ to start; **mettersi in** ~ to get moving; **far** ~ **indietro** (*AUT*) to reverse; (*fig*) to back-pedal; ~ **forzata** forced march; ~ **funebre** funeral march.

marciapi 'ede [martʃa'pjɛde] *sm* (*di strada*) pavement (*BRIT*), sidewalk (*US*); (*FERR*) platform.

marci 'are [mar'tʃare] *vi* to march; (*andare: treno, macchina*) to go; (*funzionare*) to run, work.

'marcio, a, ci, ce ['martʃo] *ag* (*frutta, legno*) rotten, bad; (*MED*) festering; (*fig*) corrupt, rotten ♦ *sm:* **c'è del** ~ **in questa storia** (*fig*) there's something fishy about this business; **avere torto** ~ to be utterly wrong.

mar 'cire [mar'tʃire] *vi* (*andare a male*) to go bad, rot; (*suppurare*) to fester; (*fig*) to rot.

marci 'ume [mar't∫ume] *sm* (*parte guasta*: *di cibi etc*) rotten part, bad part; (*di radice, pianta*) rot; (*fig*: *corruzione*) rottenness, corruption.

'marco, chi *sm* (*unità monetaria*) mark.

'mare *sm* sea; **di** ~ (*brezza, acqua, uccelli, pesce*) sea *cpd*; **in** ~ at sea; **per** ~ by sea; **sul** ~ (*barca*) on the sea; (*villaggio, località*) by *o* beside the sea; **andare al** ~ (*in vacanza etc*) to go to the seaside; **il mar Caspio** the Caspian Sea; **il mar Morto** the Dead Sea; **il mar Nero** the Black Sea; **il** ~ **del Nord** the North Sea; **il mar Rosso** the Red Sea; **il mar dei Sargassi** the Sargasso Sea; **i** ~**i del Sud** the South Seas.

ma 'rea *sf* tide; **alta/bassa** ~ high/low tide.

mareggi 'ata [mared'dʒata] *sf* heavy sea.

ma 'remma *sf* (*GEO*) maremma, swampy coastal area.

marem 'mano, a *ag* (*zona, macchia*) swampy; (*della Maremma*) of (*o* from) the Maremma.

mare 'moto *sm* seaquake.

maresci 'allo [mare∫'∫allo] *sm* (*MIL*) marshal; (: *sottufficiale*) warrant officer.

marez 'zato, a [mared'dzato] *ag* (*seta etc*) watered, moiré; (*legno*) veined; (*carta*) marbled.

marga 'rina *sf* margarine.

marghe 'rita [marge'rita] *sf* (ox-eye) daisy, marguerite; (*di stampante*) daisy wheel.

margheri 'tina [margeri'tina] *sf* daisy.

margi 'nale [mardʒi'nale] *ag* marginal.

'margine ['mardʒine] *sm* margin; (*di bosco, via*) edge, border; **avere un buon** ~ **di tempo/denaro** to have plenty of time/ money; ~ **di guadagno** *o* **di utile** profit margin; ~ **di sicurezza** safety margin.

mariju 'ana [mæri'waːnə] *sf* marijuana.

ma 'rina *sf* navy; (*costa*) coast; (*quadro*) seascape; ~ **mercantile** merchant navy (*BRIT*) *o* marine (*US*); ~ **militare (M.M.)** ≈ Royal Navy (RN) (*BRIT*), Navy (*US*).

mari 'naio *sm* sailor.

mari 'nare *vt* (*CUC*) to marinate; ~ **la scuola** to play truant.

mari 'naro, a *ag* (*tradizione, popolo*) seafaring; (*CUC*) with seafood; **alla** ~**a** (*vestito, cappello*) sailor *cpd*; **borgo** ~ district where fishing folk live.

mari 'nata *sf* marinade.

ma 'rino, a *ag* sea *cpd*, marine.

mario 'netta *sf* puppet.

mari 'tare *vt* to marry; ~**rsi** *vr*: ~**rsi a** *o* **con qn** to marry sb, get married to sb.

mari 'tato, a *ag* married.

ma 'rito *sm* husband; **prendere** ~ to get married; **ragazza (in età) da** ~ girl of

marriageable age.

ma 'rittimo, a *ag* maritime, sea *cpd*.

mar 'maglia [mar'maʎʎa] *sf* mob, riff-raff.

marmel 'lata *sf* jam; (*di agrumi*) marmalade.

mar 'mitta *sf* (*recipiente*) pot; (*AUT*) silencer; ~ **catalitica** catalytic converter.

'marmo *sm* marble.

mar 'mocchio [mar'mɔkkjo] *sm* (*fam*) (little) kid.

mar 'motta *sf* (*ZOOL*) marmot.

maroc 'chino, a [marok'kino] *ag, sm/f* Moroccan.

Ma 'rocco *sm*: **il** ~ Morocco.

ma 'roso *sm* breaker.

'marra *sf* hoe.

Marra 'kesh [marra'ke∫] *sf* Marrakesh.

mar 'rone *ag inv* brown ♦ *sm* (*BOT*) chestnut.

mar 'sala *sm inv* (*vino*) Marsala (wine).

Mar 'siglia [mar'siʎʎa] *sf* Marseilles.

mar 'sina *sf* tails *pl*, tail coat.

mar 'supio *sm* (*ZOOL*) pouch, marsupium.

mart. *abbr* (= *martedì*) Tue(s).

'Marte *sm* (*ASTR, MITOLOGIA*) Mars.

martedì *sm inv* Tuesday; **dì** *o* **ll** ~ on Tuesdays; **oggi è** ~ **3 aprile** (the date) today is Tuesday 3rd April; ~ **stavo male** I wasn't well on Tuesday; **il giornale di** ~ Tuesday's newspaper; ~ **grasso** Shrove Tuesday.

martel 'lante *ag* (*fig*: *dolore*) throbbing.

martel 'lare *vt* to hammer ♦ *vi* (*pulsare*) to throb; (: *cuore*) to thump.

martel 'letto *sm* (*di pianoforte*) hammer; (*di macchina da scrivere*) typebar; (*di giudice, nelle vendite all'asta*) gavel; (*MED*) percussion hammer.

mar 'tello *sm* hammer; (*di uscio*) knocker; **suonare a** ~ (*fig*: *campane*) to sound the tocsin; ~ **pneumatico** pneumatic drill.

marti 'netto *sm* (*TECN*) jack.

martin 'gala *sf* (*di giacca*) half-belt; (*di cavallo*) martingale.

'martire *sm/f* martyr.

mar 'tirio *sm* martyrdom; (*fig*) agony, torture.

martori 'are *vt* to torment, torture.

mar 'xismo *sm* Marxism.

mar 'xista, i, e *ag, sm/f* Marxist.

marza 'pane [martsa'pane] *sm* marzipan.

marzi 'ale [mar'tsjale] *ag* martial.

'marzo ['martso] *sm* March; *per fraseologia vedi* **luglio**.

marzo 'lino, a [martso'lino] *ag* March *cpd*.

mascalzo 'nata [maskaltso'nata] *sf* dirty trick.

mascal 'zone [maskal'tsone] *sm* rascal, scoundrel.

mas'cara *sm inv* mascara.

mascar'pone *sm soft cream cheese often used in desserts.*

ma'scella [maʃ'ʃella] *sf (ANAT)* jaw.

'maschera ['maskera] *sf* mask; (*travestimento*) disguise; (: *per un ballo etc*) fancy dress; (*TEAT, CINE*) usher/usherette; (*personaggio del teatro*) stock character; **in** ~ (*mascherato*) masked; **ballo in** ~ fancy-dress ball; **gettare la** ~ (*fig*) to reveal o.s.; ~ **antigas/subacquea** gas/diving mask; ~ **di bellezza** face pack.

masche'rare [maske'rare] *vt* to mask; (*travestire*) to disguise; to dress up; (*fig: celare*) to hide, conceal; (*MIL*) to camouflage; ~**rsi** *vr*: ~**rsi da** to disguise o.s. as; to dress up as; (*fig*) to masquerade as.

masche'rina [maske'rina] *sf* (*piccola maschera*) mask; (*di animale*) patch; (*di scarpe*) toe-cap; (*AUT*) radiator grill.

mas'chile [mas'kile] *ag* masculine; (*sesso, popolazione*) male; (*abiti*) men's; (*per ragazzi: scuola*) boys'.

'maschio, a ['maskjo] *ag* (*BIOL*) male; (*virile*) manly ♦ *sm* (*anche ZOOL, TECN*) male; (*uomo*) man; (*ragazzo*) boy; (*figlio*) son.

masco'lino, a *ag* masculine.

mas'cotte [mas'kɔt] *sf inv* mascot.

maso'chismo [mazo'kizmo] *sm* masochism.

maso'chista, i, e [mazo'kista] *ag* masochistic ♦ *sm/f* masochist.

'massa *sf* mass; (*di errori etc*): **una** ~ **di** heaps of, masses of; (*di gente*) mass, multitude; (*ELETTR*) earth; **in** ~ (*COMM*) in bulk; (*tutti insieme*) en masse; **adunata in** ~ mass meeting; **manifestazione/cultura di** ~ mass demonstration/culture; **produrre in** ~ to mass-produce; **la** ~ (**del popolo**) the masses *pl*.

massa'crante *ag* exhausting, gruelling.

massa'crare *vt* to massacre, slaughter.

mas'sacro *sm* massacre, slaughter; (*fig*) mess, disaster.

massaggi'are [massad'dʒare] *vt* to massage.

massaggia'tore, 'trice [massadd'ʒa'tore] *sm/f* masseur/masseuse.

mas'saggio [mas'saddʒo] *sm* massage.

mas'saia *sf* housewife.

masse'ria *sf* large farm.

masse'rizie [masse'rittsje] *sfpl* (household) furnishings.

massicci'ata [massit'tʃata] *sf* (*di strada, ferrovia*) ballast.

mas'siccio, a, ci, ce [mas'sittʃo] *ag* (*oro, legno*) solid; (*palazzo*) massive;

(*corporatura*) stout ♦ *sm* (*GEO*) massif.

'massima *sf vedi* **massimo**.

massi'male *sm* maximum; (*COMM*) ceiling, limit.

'massimo, a *ag, sm* maximum ♦ *sf* (*sentenza, regola*) maxim; (*METEOR*) maximum temperature; **in linea di** ~**a** generally speaking; **arrivare entro il tempo** ~ to arrive within the time limit; **al** ~ at (the) most; **sfruttare qc al** ~ to make full use of sth; **arriverò al** ~ **alle 5** I'll arrive at 5 at the latest; **erano presenti le** ~**e autorità** all the most important dignitaries were there; **il** ~ **della pena** (*DIR*) the maximum penalty.

mas'sivo, a *ag* (*intervento*) en masse; (*emigrazione*) mass; (*emorragia*) massive.

'masso *sm* rock, boulder.

mas'sone *sm* freemason.

massone'ria *sf* freemasonry.

mas'sonico, a, ci, che *ag* masonic.

mas'tello *sm* tub.

masteriz'zare [masterid'dzare] *vt* to burn.

masterizza'tore [masteriddza'tore] *sm* CD burner *o* writer.

masti'care *vt* to chew.

'mastice ['mastitʃe] *sm* mastic; (*per vetri*) putty.

mas'tino *sm* mastiff.

masto'dontico, a, ci, che *ag* gigantic, colossal.

mastur'barsi *vr* to masturbate.

masturbazi'one [masturbat'tsjone] *sf* masturbation.

ma'tassa *sf* skein.

mate'matico, a, ci, che *ag* mathematical ♦ *sm/f* mathematician ♦ *sf* mathematics *sg*.

materas'sino *sm* mat; ~ **gonfiabile** air bed.

mate'rasso *sm* mattress; ~ **a molle** spring *o* interior-sprung mattress.

ma'teria *sf* (*FISICA*) matter; (*TECN, COMM*) material, matter *no pl*; (*disciplina*) subject; (*argomento*) subject matter, material; **prima di entrare in** ~ ... before discussing the matter in hand ...; **un esperto in** ~ (**di musica** *etc*) an expert on the subject (of music *etc*); **sono ignorante in** ~ I know nothing about it; ~ **cerebrale** cerebral matter; ~ **grassa** fat; ~ **grigia** (*anche fig*) grey matter; ~**e plastiche** plastics; ~**e prime** raw materials.

materi'ale *ag* material; (*fig: grossolano*) rough, rude ♦ *sm* material; (*insieme di strumenti etc*) equipment *no pl*, materials *pl*; ~ **da costruzione** building materials *pl*.

materia'lista, i, e *ag* materialistic ♦ *sm/f* materialist.

materializ'zarsi [materjalid'dzarsi] *vr* to

materialize.

material'mente *av* (*fisicamente*)
materially; (*economicamente*) financially.

maternità *sf* motherhood, maternity;
(*clinica*) maternity hospital; **in (congedo
di)** ~ on maternity leave.

ma'terno, a *ag* (*amore, cura etc*) maternal,
motherly; (*nonno*) maternal; (*lingua, terra*)
mother *cpd*; *vedi anche* **scuola.**

ma'tita *sf* pencil; ~**e colorate** crayons; ~
per gli occhi eyeliner (pencil).

ma'trice [ma'tritʃe] *sf* matrix; (*COMM*)
counterfoil; (*fig*: *origine*) background.

ma'tricola *sf* (*registro*) register; (*numero*)
registration number; (*nell'università*)
freshman, fresher (*BRIT fam*).

ma'trigna [ma'triɲɲa] *sf* stepmother.

matrimoni'ale *ag* matrimonial, marriage
cpd; **camera/letto** ~ double room/bed.

matri'monio *sm* marriage, matrimony;
(*durata*) marriage, married life;
(*cerimonia*) wedding.

ma'trona *sf* (*fig*) matronly woman.

matta'toio *sm* abattoir (*BRIT*),
slaughterhouse.

mat'tina *sf* morning; **la** *o* **alla** *o* **di** ~ in the
morning; **di prima** ~, **la** ~ **presto** early in
the morning; **dalla** ~ **alla sera**
(*continuamente*) from morning to night;
(*improvvisamente*: *cambiare*) overnight.

matti'nata *sf* morning; (*spettacolo*)
matinée, afternoon performance; **in** ~ in
the course of the morning; **nella** ~ in the
morning; **nella tarda** ~ at the end of the
morning; **nella tarda** ~ **di sabato** late on
Saturday morning.

mattini'ero, a *ag*: **essere** ~ to be an early
riser.

mat'tino *sm* morning; **di buon** ~ early in
the morning.

'matto, a *ag* mad, crazy; (*fig*: *falso*) false,
imitation; (: *opaco*) matt, dull ♦ *sm/f*
madman/woman; **avere una voglia** ~**a di
qc** to be dying for sth; **far diventare** ~ **qn**
to drive sb mad *o* crazy; **una gabbia di** ~**i**
(*fig*) a madhouse.

mat'tone *sm* brick; (*fig*): **questo libro/
film è un** ~ this book/film is heavy going.

matto'nella *sf* tile.

mattu'tino, a *ag* morning *cpd*.

matu'rare *vi* (*anche*: ~**rsi**) (*frutta, grano*) to
ripen; (*ascesso*) to come to a head; (*fig*:
persona, idea, ECON) to mature ♦ *vt* to
ripen; to (make) mature; ~ **una decisione**
to come to a decision.

maturità *sf* maturity; (*di frutta*) ripeness,
maturity; (*INS*) school-leaving
examination, ≈ GCE A-levels (*BRIT*).

ma'turo, a *ag* mature; (*frutto*) ripe,
mature.

ma'tusa *sm/f inv* (*scherzoso*) old fogey.

Mauri'tania *sf*: **la** ~ Mauritania.

Mau'rizio [mau'rittsjo] *sf*: **(l'isola di)** ~
Mauritius.

mauso'leo *sm* mausoleum.

max. *abbr* (= *massimo*) max.

'maxi... *prefisso* maxi....

maxipro'cesso [maksipro'tʃɛsso] *sm vedi
nota nel riquadro.*

MAXIPROCESSO

A **maxiprocesso** is a criminal trial which is
characterized by a large number of co-
defendants. These people are usually members
of terrorist or criminal organizations. The trials
are often lengthy and many witnesses may be
called to give evidence.

---

maxis'chermo [maksis'kermo] *sm* giant
screen.

'mazza ['mattsa] *sf* (*bastone*) club; (*martello*)
sledge-hammer; (*SPORT*: *da golf*) club;
(: *da baseball, cricket*) bat.

maz'zata [mat'tsata] *sf* (*anche fig*) heavy
blow.

maz'zetta [mat'tsetta] *sf* (*di banconote etc*)
bundle; (*fig*) rake-off.

'mazzo ['mattso] *sm* (*di fiori, chiavi etc*)
bunch; (*di carte da gioco*) pack.

MC *sigla* = Macerata.

m.c.d. *abbr* (= *minimo comune
denominatore*) lcd.

m.c.m. *abbr* (= *minimo comune multiplo*)
lcm.

ME *sigla* = Messina.

me *pron* me; **sei bravo quanto** ~ you are as
clever as I (am) *o* as me.

me'andro *sm* meander.

M.E.C. [mɛk] *abbr m* = Mercato Comune
Europeo.

'Mecca *sf* (*anche fig*): **La** ~ Mecca.

meccanica'mente *av* mechanically.

mec'canico, a, ci, che *ag* mechanical ♦ *sm*
mechanic ♦ *sf* mechanics *sg*; (*attività
tecnologica*) mechanical engineering;
(*meccanismo*) mechanism; **officina** ~**a**
garage.

mecca'nismo *sm* mechanism.

meccaniz'zare [mekkanid'dzare] *vt* to
mechanize.

meccanizzazi'one [mekkaniddzat'tsjone] *sf*
mechanization.

mece'nate [metʃe'nate] *sm* patron.

mèche [mɛʃ] *sf inv* streak; **farsi le** ~ to have
one's hair streaked.

me 'daglia [me'daʎʎa] *sf* medal; ~ **d'oro**
(*oggetto*) gold medal; (*persona*) gold
medallist (*BRIT*) *o* medalist (*US*).
medagli 'one [medaʎ'ʎone] *sm* (*ARCHIT*)
medallion; (*gioiello*) locket.
me 'desimo, a *ag* same; (*in persona*): io ~ I
myself.
'media *sf vedi* medio.
media 'mente *av* on average.
medi 'ano, a *ag* median; (*valore*) mean ♦ *sm*
(*CALCIO*) half-back.
medi 'ante *prep* by means of.
medi 'are *vt* (*fare da mediatore*) to act as
mediator in; (*MAT*) to average.
medi 'ato, a *ag* indirect.
media 'tore, 'trice *sm/f* mediator; (*COMM*)
middle man, agent; **fare da ~ fra** to
mediate between.
mediazi 'one [medjat'tsjone] *sf* mediation;
(*COMM*: *azione, compenso*) brokerage.
medica 'mento *sm* medicine, drug.
medi 'care *vt* to treat; (*ferita*) to dress.
medi 'cato, a *ag* (*garza, shampoo*)
medicated.
medicazi 'one [medikat'tsjone] *sf*
treatment, medication; dressing; **fare una
~ a qn** to dress sb's wounds.
medi 'cina [medi't ʃina] *sf* medicine; ~ **legale**
forensic medicine.
medici 'nale [medit ʃi'nale] *ag* medicinal
♦ *sm* drug, medicine.
'medico, a, ci, che *ag* medical ♦ *sm* doctor;
~ **di bordo** ship's doctor; ~ **di famiglia**
family doctor; ~ **fiscale** *doctor who*
examines patients signed off sick for a
lengthy period by their private doctor; ~
generico general practitioner, GP.
medie 'vale *ag* medieval.
'medio, a *ag* average; (*punto, ceto*) middle;
(*altezza, statura*) medium ♦ *sm* (*dito*) middle
finger ♦ *sf* average; (*MAT*) mean; (*INS*:
voto) end-of-term average; ~**e** *sfpl vedi*
scuola media inferiore; **licenza** ~**a** *leaving*
certificate awarded at the end of 3 years
of secondary education; **in** ~**a** on
average; **al di sopra/sotto della** ~**a**
above/below average; **viaggiare ad una**
~**a di** ... to travel at an average speed of
...; **il M**~ **Oriente** the Middle East.
medi 'ocre *ag* (*gen*) mediocre; (*qualità,*
stipendio) poor.
mediocrità *sf* mediocrity; poorness.
medioe 'vale *ag* = **medievale**.
Medio 'evo *sm* Middle Ages *pl*.
medita 'bondo, a *ag* thoughtful.
medi 'tare *vt* to ponder over, meditate on;
(*progettare*) to plan, think out ♦ *vi* to
meditate.

medi 'tato, a *ag* (*gen*) meditated; (*parole*)
carefully-weighed; (*vendetta*)
premeditated; **ben ~** (*piano*) well
worked-out, neat.
meditazi 'one [meditat'tsjone] *sf*
meditation.
mediter 'raneo, a *ag* Mediterranean; **il**
(*mare*) **M**~ the Mediterranean (Sea).
'medium *sm/f inv* medium.
me 'dusa *sf* (*ZOOL*) jellyfish.
me 'gafono *sm* megaphone.
mega 'lomane *ag*, *sm/f* megalomaniac.
me 'gera [me'dʒɛra] *sf* (*peg: donna*) shrew.
'meglio ['meʎʎo] *av*, *ag inv* better; (*con senso*
superlativo) best ♦ *sm* (*la cosa migliore*): **il** ~
the best (thing); **faresti ~ ad andartene**
you had better leave; **alla ~** as best one
can; **andar di bene in** ~ to get better and
better; **fare del proprio** ~ to do one's best;
per il ~ for the best; **aver la ~ su qn** to get
the better of sb.
'mela *sf* apple; ~ **cotogna** quince.
mela 'grana *sf* pomegranate.
melan 'zana [melan'dzana] *sf* aubergine
(*BRIT*), eggplant (*US*).
me 'lassa *sf* molasses *sg*, treacle.
me 'lenso, a *ag* dull, stupid.
me 'lissa *sf* (*BOT*) balm.
mel 'lifluo, a *ag* (*peg*) sugary, honeyed.
'melma *sf* mud, mire.
'melo *sm* apple tree.
melo 'dia *sf* melody.
me 'lodico, a, ci, che *ag* melodic.
melodi 'oso, a *ag* melodious.
melo 'dramma, i *sm* melodrama.
me 'lone *sm* (*musk*) melon.
'membra *sfpl vedi* **membro**.
mem 'brana *sf* membrane.
'membro *sm* member; (*pl(f)* ~**a**: *arto*)
limb.
memo 'rabile *ag* memorable.
memo 'randum *sm inv* memorandum.
'memore *ag*: ~ **di** (*ricordando*) mindful of;
(*riconoscente*) grateful for.
me 'moria *sf* (*anche INFORM*) memory; ~**e**
sfpl (*opera autobiografica*) memoirs; **a** ~
(*imparare, sapere*) by heart; **a** ~ **d'uomo**
within living memory; ~ **di sola lettura**
(*INFORM*) read-only memory; ~ **tampone**
(*INFORM*) buffer.
memori 'ale *sm* (*raccolta di memorie*)
memoirs *pl*; (*DIR*) memorial.
memoriz 'zare [memorid'dzare] *vt* (*gen*) to
memorize; (*INFORM*) to store.
memorizzazi 'one [memoriddzat'tsjone] *sf*
memorization; storage.
'mena *sf* scheme.
mena 'dito: **a** ~ *av* perfectly, thoroughly;

sapere qc a ~ to have sth at one's fingertips.

mena 'gramo *sm/f inv* jinx, Jonah.

me 'nare *vt* to lead; (*picchiare*) to hit, beat; (*dare: colpi*) to deal; ~ **la coda** (*cane*) to wag its tail; ~ **qc per le lunghe** to drag sth out; ~ **il can per l'aia** (*fig*) to beat about (*BRIT*) o around (*US*) the bush.

mendi 'cante *sm/f* beggar.

mendi 'care *vt* to beg for ♦ *vi* to beg.

menefre 'ghismo [menefre'gizmo] *sm* (*fam*) couldn't-care-less attitude.

me 'hinge [me'nindʒe] *sf* (*MED*) meninx; **spremersi le ~i** to rack one's brains.

menin 'gite [menin'dʒite] *sf* meningitis.

me 'hisco *sm* (*ANAT, MAT, FISICA*) meniscus.

PAROLA CHIAVE

'meno *av* **1** (*in minore misura*) less; **dovresti mangiare** ~ you should eat less, you shouldn't eat so much; **è sempre** ~ **facile** it's getting less and less easy; **ne voglio di** ~ I don't want so much

2 (*comparativo*): ~ ... **di** not as ... as, less ... than; **sono** ~ **alto di te** I'm not as tall as you (are), I'm less tall than you (are); ~ ... **che** not as ... as, less ... than; ~ **che mai** less than ever; **è** ~ **intelligente che ricco** he's more rich than intelligent; ~ **fumo più mangio** the less I smoke the more I eat; ~ **di quanto pensassi** less than I thought

3 (*superlativo*) least; **il** ~ **dotato degli studenti** the least gifted of the students; **è quello che compro** ~ **spesso** it's the one I buy least often

4 (*MAT*) minus; **8** ~ **5** 8 minus 5, 8 take away 5; **sono le 8** ~ **un quarto** it's a quarter to 8; ~ **5 gradi** 5 degrees below zero, minus 5 degrees; **mille euro in** ~ a thousand euros less; **ha preso 6** ~ (*a scuola*) he scraped a pass; **cento euro** ~ **le spese** a hundred euros minus o less expenses

5 (*fraseologia*): **quanto** ~ **poteva telefonare** he could at least have phoned; **non so se accettare o** ~ I don't know whether to accept or not; **non essere da** ~ **di** not to be outdone by; **fare a** ~ **di qc/qn** to do without sth/sb; **non potevo fare a** ~ **di ridere** I couldn't help laughing; ~ **male!** thank goodness!; ~ **male che sei arrivato** it's a good job that you've come

♦ *ag inv* (*tempo, denaro*) less; (*errori, persone*) fewer; **ha fatto** ~ **errori di tutti** he made fewer mistakes than anyone, he made the fewest mistakes of all

♦ *sm inv* **1** : **il** ~ (*il minimo*) the least; **parlare**

del più e del ~ to talk about this and that; **era il** ~ **che ti potesse succedere** it was the least you could have expected

2 (*MAT*) minus

♦ *prep* (*eccetto*) except (for), apart from; **tutti** ~ **lui** everybody apart from o except him; **a** ~ **che, a** ~ **di** unless; **a** ~ **che non piova** unless it rains; **non posso, a** ~ **di prendere ferie** I can't, unless I take some leave; *vedi anche* **più.**

meno 'mare *vt* (*danneggiare*) to maim, disable.

meno 'mato, a *ag* (*persona*) disabled ♦ *sm/f* disabled person.

menomazi 'one [menomat'tsjone] *sf* disablement.

meno 'pausa *sf* menopause.

'mensa *sf* (*locale*) canteen; (: *MIL*) mess; (: *nelle università*) refectory.

men 'sile *ag* monthly ♦ *sm* (*periodico*) monthly (magazine); (*stipendio*) monthly salary.

mensil 'mente *av* (*ogni mese*) every month; (*una volta al mese*) monthly.

'mensola *sf* bracket; (*ripiano*) shelf; (*ARCHIT*) corbel.

'menta *sf* mint; (*anche*: ~ **piperita**) peppermint; (*bibita*) peppermint cordial; (*caramella*) mint, peppermint.

men 'tale *ag* mental.

mentalità *sf inv* mentality.

mental 'mente *av* mentally.

'mente *sf* mind; **imparare/sapere qc a** ~ to learn/know sth by heart; **avere in** ~ **qc** to have sth in mind; **avere in** ~ **di fare qc** to intend to do sth; **fare venire in** ~ **qc a qn** to remind sb of sth; **mettersi in** ~ **di fare qc** to make up one's mind to do sth; **passare di** ~ **a qn** to slip sb's mind; **tenere a** ~ **qc** to bear sth in mind; **a** ~ **fredda** objectively; **lasciami fare** ~ **locale** let me think.

mente 'catto, a *ag* half-witted ♦ *sm/f* halfwit, imbecile.

men 'tire *vi* to lie.

men 'tito, a *ag*: **sotto** ~**e spoglie** under false pretences (*BRIT*) o pretenses (*US*).

'mento *sm* chin; **doppio** ~ double chin.

'mento *sm* menthol.

'mentre *cong* (*temporale*) while; (*avversativo*) whereas ♦ *sm*: **in quel** ~ at that very moment.

menù *sm inv* (set) menu; ~ **turistico** standard o tourists' menu.

menzio 'nare [mentsjo'nare] *vt* to mention.

menzi 'one [men'tsjone] *sf* mention; **fare** ~ **di** to mention.

men'zogna [mɛn'tsɔɲɲa] *sf* lie.
menzo'gnero, a [mentsoɲ'ɲɛro] *ag* false, untrue.
mera'viglia [mera'viʎʎa] *sf* amazement, wonder; (*persona, cosa*) marvel, wonder; a ~ perfectly, wonderfully.
meravigli'are [meraviʎ'ʎare] *vt* to amaze, astonish; ~**rsi** *vr*: ~**rsi (di)** to marvel (at); (*stupirsi*) to be amazed (at), be astonished (at); **mi meraviglio di te!** I'm surprised at you!; **non c'è da** ~**rsi** it's not surprising.
meravigli'oso [meraviʎ'ʎoso] *ag* wonderful, marvellous (*BRIT*), marvelous (*US*).
merc. *abbr* (= *mercoledì*) Wed.
mer'cante *sm* merchant; ~ **d'arte** art dealer; ~ **di cavalli** horse dealer.
mercanteggi'are [merkanted'dʒare] *vt* (*onore, voto*) to sell ♦ *vi* to bargain, haggle.
mercan'tile *ag* commercial, mercantile; (*nave, marina*) merchant *cpd* ♦ *sm* (*nave*) merchantman.
mercan'zia [merkan'tsia] *sf* merchandise, goods *pl.*
merca'tino *sm* (*rionale*) local street market; (*ECON*) unofficial stock market.
mer'cato *sm* market; **di** ~ (*economia, prezzo, ricerche*) market *cpd*; **mettere o lanciare qc sul** ~ to launch sth on the market; **a buon** ~ *ag, av* cheap; ~ **dei cambi** exchange market; **M**~ **Comune (Europeo)** (European) Common Market; ~ **del lavoro** labour market, job market; ~ **nero** black market; ~ **al rialzo/al ribasso** (*BORSA*) sellers'/buyers' market.
'merce ['mɛrtʃe] *sf* goods *pl*, merchandise; ~ **deperibile** perishable goods *pl.*
mercé [mer'tʃe] *sf* mercy; **essere alla** ~ **di qn** to be at sb's mercy.
merce'nario, a [mertʃe'narjo] *ag, sm* mercenary.
merce'ria [mertʃe'ria] *sf* (*articoli*) haberdashery (*BRIT*), notions *pl* (*US*); (*bottega*) haberdasher's shop (*BRIT*), notions store (*US*).
mercoledì *sm inv* Wednesday; ~ **delle Ceneri** Ash Wednesday; *vedi nota nel riquadro*; *per fraseologia vedi* **martedì**.

┌─────────────────────────────────────┐
│ MERCOLEDÌ DELLE CENERI   │
│   │
│ *In the Catholic church,* **Mercoledì delle** │
│ **Ceneri** *signals the beginning of Lent.* │
│ *Churchgoers are marked on the forehead with* │
│ *ash from the burning of an olive branch. Ash* │
│ *Wednesday is traditionally a day of fasting,* │
│ *abstinence and repentance.* │
└─────────────────────────────────────┘

mer'curio *sm* mercury.
'merda *sf* (*fam!*) shit (*!*).
me'renda *sf* afternoon snack.
meren'dina *sf* snack.
meridi'ano, a *ag* (*di mezzogiorno*) midday *cpd*, noonday ♦ *sm* meridian ♦ *sf* (*orologio*) sundial.
meridio'nale *ag* southern ♦ *sm/f* southerner.
meridi'one *sm* south.
me'ringa, ghe *sf* (*CUC*) meringue.
meri'tare *vt* to deserve, merit ♦ *vb impers* (*valere la pena*): **merita andare** it is worth going; **non merita neanche parlarne** it's not worth talking about; **per quel che merita** for what it's worth.
meri'tevole *ag* worthy.
'merito *sm* merit; (*valore*) worth; **dare** ~ **a qn di** to give sb credit for; **finire a pari** ~ to finish joint first (*o* second *etc*); to tie; **in** ~ **a** as regards, with regard to; **entrare nel** ~ **di una questione** to go into a matter; **non so niente in** ~ I don't know anything about it.
meritocra'zia [meritokrat'tsia] *sf* meritocracy.
meri'torio, a *ag* praiseworthy.
mer'letto *sm* lace.
'merlo *sm* (*ZOOL*) blackbird; (*ARCHIT*) battlement.
mer'luzzo [mer'luttso] *sm* (*ZOOL*) cod.
'mescere ['meʃʃere] *vt* to pour (out).
meschinità [meskini'ta] *sf* wretchedness; meagreness; meanness; narrow-mindedness.
mes'chino, a [mes'kino] *ag* wretched; (*scarso*) meagre (*BRIT*), meager (*US*); (*persona: gretta*) mean; (: *limitata*) narrow-minded, petty; **fare una figura** ~**a** to cut a poor figure.
'mescita ['meʃʃita] *sf* wine shop.
mesci'uto, a [meʃ'ʃuto] *pp di* **mescere**.
mesco'lanza [mesko'lantsa] *sf* mixture.
mesco'lare *vt* to mix; (*vini, colori*) to blend; (*mettere in disordine*) to mix up, muddle up; (*carte*) to shuffle; ~**rsi** *vr* to mix; to blend; to get mixed up; (*fig*): ~**rsi in** to get mixed up in, meddle in.
'mese *sm* month; **il** ~ **scorso** last month; **il** ~ **corrente** ~ this month.
'messa *sf* (*REL*) mass; (*il mettere*): ~ **a fuoco** focusing; ~ **in moto** starting; ~ **in piega** (*acconciatura*) set; ~ **a punto** (*TECN*) adjustment; (*AUT*) tuning; (*fig*) clarification; ~ **in scena** = **messinscena**.
messagge'rie [messaddʒe'rie] *sfpl* (*ditta: di distribuzione*) distributors; (: *di trasporto*) freight company.

messag'gero [messad'dʒɛro] *sm* messenger.

messag'gino [messad'dʒino] *sm* (*di telefonino*) text (message).

mes'saggio [mes'saddʒo] *sm* message.

messag'gistica [messad'dʒistica] *sf*: ~ **immediata** (*COMPUT*) instant messaging; **programma di** ~ **immediata** instant messenger.

mes'sale *sm* (*REL*) missal.

'messe *sf* harvest.

Mes'sia *sm inv* (*REL*): **il** ~ the Messiah.

messi'cano, a *ag, sm/f* Mexican.

'Messico *sm*: **il** ~ Mexico; **Città del** ~ Mexico City.

messin'scena [messin'ʃɛna] *sf* (*TEAT*) production.

'messo, a *pp di* **mettere** ♦ *sm* messenger.

mestie'rante *sm/f* (*peg*) money-grubber; (: *scrittore*) hack.

mesti'ere *sm* (*professione*) job; (: *manuale*) trade; (: *artigianale*) craft; (*fig: abilità nel lavoro*) skill, technique; **di** ~ by *o* to trade; **essere del** ~ to know the tricks of the trade.

mes'tizia [mes'tittsja] *sf* sadness, melancholy.

'mesto, a *ag* sad, melancholy.

'mestolo *sm* (*CUC*) ladle.

mestru'ale *ag* menstrual.

mestruazi'one [mestruat'tsjone] *sf* menstruation; **avere le** ~**i** to have one's period.

'meta *sf* destination; (*fig*) aim, goal.

metà *sf inv* half; (*punto di mezzo*) middle; **dividere qc a** *o* **per** ~ to divide sth in half, halve sth; **fare a** ~ (**di qc con qn**) to go halves (with sb in sth); **a** ~ **prezzo** at half price; **a** ~ **settimana** midweek; **a** ~ **strada** halfway; **verso la** ~ **del mese** halfway through the month, towards the middle of the month; **dire le cose a** ~ to leave some things unsaid; **fare le cose a** ~ to leave things half-done; **la mia dolce** ~ (*fam scherzoso*) my better half.

metabo'lismo *sm* metabolism.

meta'done *sm* methadone.

meta'fisica *sf* metaphysics *sg*.

me'tafora *sf* metaphor.

meta'forico, a, ci, che *ag* metaphorical.

me'tallico, a, ci, che *ag* (*di metallo*) metal *cpd*; (*splendore, rumore etc*) metallic.

metalliz'zato, a [metallid'dzato] *ag* (*verniciatura*) metallic.

me'tallo *sm* metal; **di** ~ metal *cpd*.

metallur'gia [metallur'dʒia] *sf* metallurgy.

metalmec'canico, a, ci, che *ag* engineering *cpd* ♦ *sm* engineering worker.

meta'morfosi *sf* metamorphosis.

me'tano *sm* methane.

me'teora *sf* meteor.

meteo'rite *sm* meteorite.

meteorolo'gia [meteorolo'dʒia] *sf* meteorology.

meteoro'logico, a, ci, che [meteoro'lɔdʒiko] *ag* meteorological, weather *cpd*.

meteo'rologo, a, ghi, ghe *sm/f* meteorologist.

me'ticcio, a, ci, ce [me'tittʃo] *sm/f* half-caste, half-breed.

meticolosità *sf* meticulousness.

metico'loso, a *ag* meticulous.

me'todico, a, ci, che *ag* methodical.

'metodo *sm* method; (*manuale*) tutor (*BRIT*), manual; **far qc con/senza** ~ to do sth methodically/unmethodically.

me'traggio [me'traddʒo] *sm* (*SARTORIA*) length; (*CINE*) footage; **film a lungo** ~ feature film; **film a corto** ~ short film.

metra'tura *sf* length.

'metrico, a, ci, che *ag* metric; (*POESIA*) metrical ♦ *sf* metrics *sg*.

'metro *sm* metre (*BRIT*), meter (*US*); (*nastro*) tape measure; (*asta*) (metre) rule.

metrò *sm inv* underground (*BRIT*), subway (*US*).

metro'notte *sm inv* night security guard.

me'tropoli *sf inv* metropolis.

metropoli'tano, a *ag* metropolitan ♦ *sf* underground (*BRIT*), subway (*US*); ~**a leggera** metro (*mainly on the surface*).

'mettere *vt* to put; (*abito*) to put on; (: *portare*) to wear; (*installare: telefono*) to put in; (*fig: provocare*): ~ **fame/allegria a qn** to make sb hungry/happy; (*supporre*): **mettiamo che** ... let's suppose *o* say that ...; ~**rsi** *vr* (*persona*) to put o.s.; (*oggetto*) to go; (*disporsi: faccenda*) to turn out; ~**rsi a piangere/ridere** to start crying/laughing, start *o* begin to cry/laugh; ~**rsi a sedere** to sit down; ~**rsi al lavoro** to set to work; ~**rsi a letto** to get into bed; (*per malattia*) to take to one's bed; ~**rsi il cappello** to put on one's hat; ~**rsi sotto** to get down to things; ~**rsi in società** to set up in business; **si sono messi insieme** (*coppia*) they've started going out together (*BRIT*) *o* dating (*US*); ~**rci:** ~**rci molta cura/molto tempo** to take a lot of care/a lot of time; **mettercela tutta** to do one's best; **ci ho messo 3 ore per venire** it's taken me 3 hours to get here; ~ **un annuncio sul giornale** to place an advertisement in the paper; ~ **a confronto** to compare; ~ **in conto** (*somma etc*) to put on account; ~ **in**

luce (*problemi, errori*) to stress, highlight; ~ **a tacere qn/qc** to keep sb/sth quiet; ~ **su casa** to set up house; ~ **su un negozio** to start a shop; ~ **su peso** to put on weight; ~ **via** to put away.
mez'zadro [med'dzadro] *sm* (*AGR*) sharecropper.
mezza'luna [meddza'luna], *pl* **mezze'lune** *sf* half-moon; (*dell'islamismo*) crescent; (*coltello*) (semicircular) chopping knife.
mezza'nino [meddza'nino] *sm* mezzanine (floor).
mez'zano, a [med'dzano] *ag* (*medio*) average, medium; (*figlio*) middle *cpd* ♦ *sm/f* (*intermediario*) go-between; (*ruffiano*) pimp.
mezza'notte [meddza'nɔtte] *sf* midnight.
'mezzo, a ['mɛddzo] *ag* half; **un** ~ **litro/panino** half a litre/roll ♦ *av* half-; ~ **morto** half-dead ♦ *sm* (*metà*) half; (*parte centrale: di strada etc*) middle; (*per raggiungere un fine*) means *sg*; (*veicolo*) vehicle; (*nell'indicare l'ora*): **le nove e** ~ half past nine; **mezzogiorno e** ~ half past twelve ♦ *sf*: **la** ~**a** half-past twelve (in the afternoon); ~**i** *smpl* (*possibilità economiche*) means; **di** ~**a età** middle-aged; **aver una** ~**a idea di fare qc** to have half a mind to do sth; **è stato un** ~ **scandalo** it almost caused a scandal; **un soprabito di** ~**a stagione** a spring (*o* autumn) coat; **a** ~**a voce** in an undertone; **una volta e** ~ **più grande** one and a half times bigger; **di** ~ middle, in the middle; **andarci di** ~ (*patir danno*) to suffer; **esserci di** ~ (*ostacolo*) to be in the way; **levarsi** *o* **togliersi di** ~ to get out of the way; **mettersi di** ~ to interfere; **togliere di** ~ (*persona, cosa*) to get rid of; (*fam: uccidere*) to bump off; **non c'è una via di** ~ there's no middle course; **in** ~ **a** in the middle of; **nel bel** ~ (**di**) right in the middle (of); **per** *o* **a** ~ **di** by means of; **a** ~ **corriere** by carrier; ~**i di comunicazione di massa** mass media *pl*; ~**i pubblici** public transport *sg*; ~**i di trasporto** means of transport.
mezzogi'orno [meddzo'dʒorno] *sm* midday, noon; (*GEO*) south; **a** ~ **at 12 (o'clock)** *o* midday *o* noon; **il** ~ **d'Italia** southern Italy.
mez'z'ora, mez'zora [med'dzora] *sf* half-hour, half an hour.
MI *sigla* = *Milano*.
mi *pron* (*dav lo, la, li, le, ne diventa* **me**) (*oggetto*) me; (*complemento di termine*) (to) me; (*riflessivo*) myself ♦ *sm* (*MUS*) E; (*: solfeggiando la scala*) mi; ~ **aiuti?** will you help me?; **me ne ha parlato** he spoke

to me about it, he told me about it; ~ **servo da solo** I'll help myself.
'mia *vedi* **mio**.
miago'lare *vi* to miaow, mew.
Mib *sigla m, ag* (= *indice borsa Milano*) Milan Stock Exchange Index.
'mica *sf* (*CHIM*) mica ♦ *av* (*fam*): **non** ... ~ not ... at all; **non sono** ~ **stanco** I'm not a bit tired; **non sarà** ~ **partito?** he wouldn't have left, would he?; ~ **male** not bad.
'miccia, ce ['mittʃa] *sf* fuse.
micidi'ale [mitʃi'djale] *ag* fatal; (*dannosissimo*) deadly.
'micio, a, ci, cie ['mitʃo] *sm/f* pussy (cat).
microbiolo'gia [mikrobiolo'dʒia] *sf* microbiology.
'microbo *sm* microbe.
microcir'cuito [mikrotʃir'kuito] *sm* microcircuit.
micro'fibra *sf* microfibre.
micro'film *sm inv* microfilm.
mi'crofono *sm* microphone.
microinfor'matica *sf* microcomputing.
micro'onda *sf* microwave.
microproces'sore [mikroprotʃes'sore] *sm* microprocessor.
micros'copico, a, ci, che *ag* microscopic.
micros'copio *sm* microscope.
micro'solco, chi *sm* (*solco*) microgroove; (*disco: a 33 giri*) long-playing record, LP; (*: a 45 giri*) extended-play record, EP.
micros'pia *sf* hidden microphone, bug (*fam*).
mi'dollo, ** *pl(f)* ~a** *sm* (*ANAT*) marrow; ~ **spinale** spinal cord.
'mie, mi'ei *vedi* **mio**.
mi'ele *sm* honey.
mi'etere *vt* (*AGR*) to reap, harvest; (*fig: vite*) to take, claim.
mietitrebbia'trice [mjetitrebbja'tritʃe] *sf* combine harvester.
mieti'trice [mjeti'tritʃe] *sf* (*macchina*) harvester.
mieti'tura *sf* (*raccolto*) harvest; (*lavoro*) harvesting; (*tempo*) harvest-time.
'miglia ['miʎʎa] *sfpl di* **miglio**.
migli'aio [miʎ'ʎajo], *pl(f)* ~**a** *sm* thousand; **un** ~ **(di)** about a thousand; **a** ~**a** by the thousand, in thousands.
'miglio ['miʎʎo] *sm* (*BOT*) millet; (*pl(f)* ~**a**: *unità di misura*) mile; ~ **marino** *o* **nautico** nautical mile.
migliora'mento [miʎʎora'mento] *sm* improvement.
miglio'rare [miʎʎo'rare] *vt, vi* to improve.
migli'ore [miʎ'ʎore] *ag* (*comparativo*) better; (*superlativo*) best ♦ *sm*: **il** ~ **the best** (thing) ♦ *sm/f*: **il(la)** ~ **the best** (person); **il**

miglior vino di questa regione the best wine in this area; **i ~i auguri** best wishes.

miglio 'ria [miʎʎo'ria] sf improvement.

'mignolo ['miɲɲolo] sm (ANAT) little finger, pinkie; (: dito del piede) little toe.

mi 'grare vi to migrate.

migrazi 'one [migrat'tsjone] sf migration.

'mila pl di **mille.**

mila 'nese ag Milanese ♦ sm/f person from Milan; **i ~i** the Milanese; **cotoletta alla ~** (CUC) Wiener schnitzel; **risotto alla ~** (CUC) risotto with saffron.

Mi 'lano sf Milan.

miliar 'dario, a ag, sm/f millionaire.

mili 'ardo sm thousand million (BRIT), billion (US).

mili 'are ag: **pietra ~** milestone.

milio 'nario, a ag, sm/f millionaire.

mili 'one sm million; **un ~ di euro** a million euros.

mili 'tante ag, sm/f militant.

mili 'tanza [mili'tantsa] sf militancy.

mili 'tare vi (MIL) to be a soldier, serve; (fig: in un partito) to be a militant ♦ ag military ♦ sm serviceman; **fare il ~** to do one's military service; **~ di carriera** regular (soldier).

milita 'resco, a, schi, sche ag (portamento) military cpd.

'milite sm soldier.

mi 'lizia [mi'littsja] sf (corpo armato) militia.

milizi 'ano [milit'tsjano] sm militiaman.

millanta 'tore, 'trice sm/f boaster.

millante 'ria sf (qualità) boastfulness.

'mille num (pl **mila**) a o one thousand; **diecimila** ten thousand.

mille 'foglie [mille'fɔʎʎe] sm inv (CUC) cream o vanilla slice.

mil 'lennio sm millennium.

millepi 'edi sm inv centipede.

mil 'lesimo, a ag, sm thousandth.

milli 'grammo sm milligram(me).

mil 'lilitro sm millilitre (BRIT), milliliter (US).

mil 'limetro sm millimetre (BRIT), millimeter (US).

'milza ['miltsa] sf (ANAT) spleen.

mi 'metico, a, ci, che ag (arte) mimetic; **tuta ~a** (MIL) camouflage.

mime 'tismo sm camouflage.

mimetiz 'zare [mimetid'dzare] vt to camouflage; **~rsi** vr to camouflage o.s.

'mimica sf (arte) mime.

'mimo sm (attore, componimento) mime.

mi 'mosa sf mimosa.

min. abbr (= minuto, minimo) min.

'mina sf (esplosiva) mine; (di matita) lead.

mi 'naccia, ce [mi'nattʃa] sf threat; **sotto la**

~ di under threat of.

minacci 'are [minat'tʃare] vt to threaten; **~ qn di morte** to threaten to kill sb; **~ di fare qc** to threaten to do sth; **minaccia di piovere** it looks like rain.

minacci 'oso, a [minat'tʃoso] ag threatening.

mi 'nare vt (MIL) to mine; (fig) to undermine.

mina 'tore sm miner.

mina 'torio, a ag threatening.

minchi 'one, a [min'kjone] (fam) ag idiotic ♦ sm/f idiot.

mine 'rale ag, sm mineral.

mineralo 'gia [mineralo'dʒia] sf mineralogy.

mine 'rario, a ag (delle miniere) mining; (dei minerali) ore cpd.

mi 'nestra sf soup; **~ in brodo** noodle soup; **~ di verdura** vegetable soup.

mines 'trone sm thick vegetable and pasta soup.

mingher 'lino, a [minger'lino] ag thin, slender.

'mini ag inv mini ♦ sf inv miniskirt.

minia 'tura sf miniature.

mini 'bar sm inv minibar.

minielabora 'tore sm minicomputer.

mini 'era sf mine; **~ di carbone** coalmine; (impresa) colliery (BRIT), coalmine.

mini 'gonna sf miniskirt.

minima 'lista, i, e ag, sm/f minimalist.

minimiz 'zare [minimid'dzare] vt to minimize.

'minimo, a ag minimum, least, slightest; (piccolissimo) very small, slight; (il più basso) lowest, minimum ♦ sm minimum; **al ~** at least; **girare al ~** (AUT) to idle; **il ~ indispensabile** the bare minimum; **il ~ della pena** the minimum sentence.

minis 'tero sm (POL, REL) ministry; (governo) government; (DIR): **Pubblico M~** State Prosecutor; **M~ delle Finanze** Ministry of Finance, ≈ Treasury.

mi 'nistro sm (POL, REL) minister; **M~ delle Finanze** Minister of Finance, ≈ Chancellor of the Exchequer (BRIT).

mino 'ranza [mino'rantsa] sf minority; **essere in ~** to be in the minority.

mino 'rato, a ag handicapped ♦ sm/f physically (o mentally) handicapped person.

minorazi 'one [minorat'tsjone] sf handicap.

Mi 'norca sf Minorca.

mi 'nore ag (comparativo) less; (: più piccolo) smaller; (: numero) lower; (: inferiore) lower, inferior; (: meno importante) minor; (: più giovane) younger; (superlativo) least; smallest; lowest; least important; youngest ♦ sm/f (minorenne) minor, person under age; **in misura** ~ to a lesser extent; **questo è il male** ~ this is the lesser evil.

mino'renne *ag* under age ♦ *sm/f* minor, person under age.

mino'rile *ag* juvenile; **carcere** ~ young offenders' institution; **delinquenza** ~ juvenile delinquency.

minori'tario, a *ag* minority *cpd*.

mi'nuscolo, a *ag* (*scrittura, carattere*) small; (*piccolissimo*) tiny ♦ *sf* small letter ♦ *sm* small letters *pl*; (*TIP*) lower case; **scrivere tutto (in)** ~ to write everything in small letters.

mi'nuta *sf* rough copy, draft.

mi'nuto, a *ag* tiny, minute; (*pioggia*) fine; (*corporatura*) delicate, fine; (*lavoro*) detailed ♦ *sm* (*unità di misura*) minute; **al** ~ (*COMM*) retail; **avere i** ~**i contati** to have very little time.

mi'nuzia [mi'nuttsja] *sf* (*cura*) meticulousness; (*particolare*) detail.

minuziosa'mente [minuttsjosa'mente] *av* meticulously; in minute detail.

minuzi'oso, a [minut'tsjoso] *ag* (*persona, descrizione*) meticulous; (*esame*) minute.

'mio, 'mia, mi'ei, 'mie *det*: **il** ~, **la mia** *etc* my ♦ *pronome*: **il** ~, **la mia** *etc* mine ♦ *sm*: **ho speso del** ~ I spent my own money ♦ *sf*: **la mia** (*opinione*) my view; **i miei** my family; **un** ~ **amico** a friend of mine; **per amor** ~ for my sake; **è dalla mia** he is on my side; **anch'io ho avuto le mie** (*disavventure*) I've had my problems too; **ne ho fatta una delle mie!** (*sciocchezze*) I've done it again!; **cerco di stare sulle mie** I try to keep myself to myself.

'miope *ag* short-sighted.

mio'pia *sf* short-sightedness, myopia; (*fig*) short-sightedness.

'mira *sf* (*anche fig*) aim; **avere una buona/ cattiva** ~ to be a good/bad shot; **prendere la** ~ to take aim; **prendere di** ~ **qn** (*fig*) to pick on sb.

mi'rabile *ag* admirable, wonderful.

mi'racolo *sm* miracle.

miraco'loso, a *ag* miraculous.

mi'raggio [mi'radd3o] *sm* mirage.

mi'rare *vi*: ~ **a** to aim at.

mi'riade *sf* myriad.

mi'rino *sm* (*TECN*) sight; (*FOT*) viewer, viewfinder.

mir'tillo *sm* bilberry (*BRIT*), blueberry (*US*), whortleberry.

'mirto *sm* myrtle.

mi'santropo, a *sm/f* misanthropist.

mi'scela [miʃ'ʃɛla] *sf* mixture; (*di caffè*) blend.

miscel'lanea [miʃʃel'lanea] *sf* miscellany.

'mischia ['miskja] *sf* scuffle; (*RUGBY*) scrum, scrummage.

mischi'are [mis'kjare] *vt*, ~**rsi** *vr* to mix, blend.

misco'noscere [misko'noʃʃere] *vt* (*qualità, coraggio etc*) to fail to appreciate.

miscre'dente *ag* (*REL*) misbelieving; (: *incredulo*) unbelieving ♦ *sm/f* misbeliever; unbeliever.

mis'cuglio [mis'kuʎʎo] *sm* mixture, hotchpotch, jumble.

'mise *vb vedi* **mettere**.

mise'rabile *ag* (*infelice*) miserable, wretched; (*povero*) poverty-stricken; (*di scarso valore*) miserable.

mi'seria *sf* extreme poverty; (*infelicità*) misery; ~**e** *sfpl* (*del mondo etc*) misfortunes, troubles; **costare una** ~ to cost next to nothing; **piangere** ~ to plead poverty; **ridursi in** ~ to be reduced to poverty; **porca** ~! (*fam*) (bloody) hell!

miseri'cordia *sf* mercy, pity.

misericordi'oso, a *ag* merciful.

'misero, a *ag* miserable, wretched; (*povero*) poverty-stricken; (*insufficiente*) miserable.

mis'fatto *sm* misdeed, crime.

'misi *vb vedi* **mettere**.

mi'sogino [mi'zɔdʒino] *sm* misogynist.

'missile *sm* missile; ~ **cruise** *o* **di crociera** cruise missile; ~ **terra-aria** surface-to-air missile.

missio'nario, a *ag, sm/f* missionary.

missi'one *sf* mission.

misteri'oso, a *ag* mysterious.

mis'tero *sm* mystery; **fare** ~ **di qc** to make a mystery out of sth; **quanti** ~**i!** why all the mystery?

'mistico, a, ci, che *ag* mystic(al) ♦ *sm* mystic.

mistifi'care *vt* to fool, bamboozle.

'misto, a *ag* mixed; (*scuola*) mixed, coeducational ♦ *sm* mixture; **un tessuto in** ~ **lino** a linen mix.

mis'tura *sf* mixture.

mi'sura *sf* measure; (*misurazione, dimensione*) measurement; (*taglia*) size; (*provvedimento*) measure, step; (*moderazione*) moderation; (*MUS*) time; (: *divisione*) bar; (*fig: limite*) bounds *pl*, limit; **in** ~ **di** in accordance with, according to; **nella** ~ **in cui** inasmuch as, insofar as; **in giusta** ~ moderately; **oltre** ~ beyond measure; **su** ~ made to measure; **in ugual** ~ equally, in the same way; **a** ~ **d'uomo** on a human scale; **passare la** ~ to overstep the mark, go too far; **prendere le** ~**e a qn** to take sb's measurements, measure sb; **prendere le ~e di qc** to measure sth; **ho preso le mie ~e** I've taken the necessary steps; **non ha il senso della ~** he doesn't know when to stop; **~ di lunghezza/capacità** measure of length/capacity; **~e di sicurezza/ prevenzione** safety/precautionary measures.

misu'rare *vt* (*ambiente, stoffa*) to measure; (*terreno*) to survey; (*abito*) to try on; (*pesare*) to weigh; (*fig: parole etc*) to weigh up; (: *spese, cibo*) to limit ♦ *vi* to measure; **~rsi** *vr*: **~rsi con qn** to have a confrontation with sb; (*competere*) to compete with sb.

misu'rato, a *ag* (*ponderato*) measured; (*prudente*) cautious; (*moderato*) moderate.

misurazi'one [mizurat'tsjone] *sf* measuring; (*di terreni*) surveying.

'mite *ag* mild; (*prezzo*) moderate, reasonable.

'mitico, a, ci, che *ag* mythical.

miti'gare *vt* to mitigate, lessen; (*lenire*) to soothe, relieve; **~rsi** *vr* (*odio*) to subside; (*tempo*) to become milder.

'mitilo *sm* mussel.

'mito *sm* myth.

mitolo'gia, 'gie [mitolo'dʒia] *sf* mythology.

mito'logico, a, ci, che [mito'lɔdʒiko] *ag* mythological.

'mitra *sf* (*REL*) mitre (*BRIT*), miter (*US*) ♦ *sm inv* (*arma*) sub-machine gun.

mitragli'are [mitraʎ'ʎare] *vt* to machine-gun.

mitraglia'tore, 'trice [mitraʎʎa'tore] *ag*: **fucile** *m* **~** sub-machine gun ♦ *sf* machine gun.

mitteleuro'peo, a *ag* Central European.

mit'tente *sm/f* sender.

ml *abbr* (= *millilitro*) ml.

MLD *sigla m vedi* **Movimento per la Liberazione della Donna**.

MM *abbr* = **Metropolitana Milanese**.

mm *abbr* (= *millimetro*) mm.

M.M. *abbr vedi* **marina militare**.

mms ['ɛmme'ɛmme'ɛsse] *sigla m inv* (= *Multimedia Messaging Service*) MMS.

MN *sigla* = **Mantova**.

M/N, m/n *abbr* (= *motonave*) MV.

MO *sigla* = **Modena**.

M.O. *abbr* = **Medio Oriente**.

mo' *sm*: **a ~ di** *prep* like; **a ~ di esempio** by way of example.

'mobile *ag* mobile; (*parte di macchina*) moving; (*DIR: bene*) movable, personal ♦ *sm* (*arredamento*) piece of furniture; **~i** *smpl* furniture *sg*.

mo'bilia *sf* furniture.

mobili'are *ag* (*DIR*) personal, movable.

mo'bilio *sm* = **mobilia**.

mobilità *sf* mobility.

mobili'tare *vt* to mobilize; **~ l'opinione pubblica** to rouse public opinion.

mobilitazi'one [mobilitat'tsjone] *sf* mobilization.

mocas'sino *sm* moccasin.

mocci'oso, a [mot'tʃoso] *sm/f* (*bambino piccolo*) little kid; (*peg*) snotty-nosed kid.

'moccolo *sm* (*di candela*) candle end; (*fam: bestemmia*) oath; (: *moccio*) snot; **reggere il ~** to play gooseberry (*BRIT*), act as chaperon(e).

'moda *sf* fashion; **alla ~, di ~** fashionable, in fashion.

modalità *sf inv* formality; **seguire attentamente le ~ d'uso** to follow the instructions carefully; **~ giuridiche** legal procedures; **~ di pagamento** method of payment.

mo'della *sf* model.

model'lare *vt* (*creta*) to model, shape; **~rsi** *vr*: **~rsi su** to model o.s. on.

mo'dello *sm* model; (*stampo*) mould (*BRIT*), mold (*US*) ♦ *ag inv* model *cpd*.

'modem *sm inv* modem.

mode'nese *ag* of (*o* from) Modena.

mode'rare *vt* to moderate; **~rsi** *vr* to restrain o.s.; **~ la velocità** to reduce speed; **~ i termini** to weigh one's words.

mode'rato, a *ag* moderate.

modera'tore, 'trice *sm/f* moderator.

moderazi'one [moderat'tsjone] *sf* moderation.

moderniz'zare [modernid'dzare] *vt* to bring up to date, modernize; **~rsi** *vr* to get up to date.

mo'derno, a *ag* modern.

mo'destia *sf* modesty; **~ a parte ...** in all modesty ..., though I say it myself ....

mo'desto, a *ag* modest.

'modico, a, ci, che *ag* reasonable, moderate.

mo'difica, che *sf* modification; **subire delle ~che** to undergo some modifications.

modifi'cabile *ag* modifiable.

modifi'care *vt* to modify, alter; **~rsi** *vr* to alter, change.

mo'dista *sf* milliner.

'modo *sm* way, manner; (*mezzo*) means, way; (*occasione*) opportunity; (*LING*) mood; (*MUS*) mode; **~i** *smpl* (*maniere*) manners; **a suo ~, a ~ suo** in his own way; **ad o in ogni ~** anyway; **di o in ~ che** so that; **in ~ da** so as to; **in tutti i ~i** at all costs; (*comunque sia*) anyway; (*in ogni caso*) in any case; **in un certo qual ~** in a way, in some ways; **in qualche** ~ somehow or other; **oltre** ~ extremely; ~ **di dire** turn of phrase; **per** ~ **di dire** so to speak; **fare a** ~ **proprio** to do as one likes; **fare le cose a** ~ to do things properly; **una persona a** ~ a well-mannered person; **c'è** ~ **e** ~ **di farlo** there's a right way and a wrong way of doing it.

modu 'lare *vt* to modulate ♦ *ag* modular.

modulazi 'one [modulat'tsjone] *sf* modulation; ~ **di frequenza (FM)** frequency modulation (FM).

'modulo *sm* (*modello*) form; (*ARCHIT, lunare, di comando*) module; ~ **di domanda** application form; ~ **d'iscrizione** enrolment form; ~ **di versamento** deposit slip.

Moga 'discio [moga'diʃʃo] *sm* Mogadishu.

'mogano *sm* mahogany.

'mogio, a, gi, gie ['mɔdʒo] *ag* down in the dumps, dejected.

'moglie ['moʎʎe] *sf* wife.

mo 'hair [mɔ'ɛr] *sm* mohair.

mo 'ine *sfpl* cajolery *sg*; (*leziosità*) affectation *sg*; **fare le** ~ **a qn** to cajole sb.

'mola *sf* millstone; (*utensile abrasivo*) grindstone.

mo 'lare *vt* to grind ♦ *ag* (*pietra*) mill *cpd* ♦ *sm* (*dente*) molar.

'mole *sf* mass; (*dimensioni*) size; (*edificio grandioso*) massive structure; **una** ~ **di lavoro** masses (*BRIT*) *o* loads of work.

mo 'lecola *sf* molecule.

moles 'tare *vt* to bother, annoy.

mo 'lestia *sf* annoyance, bother; **recar** ~ **a qn** to bother sb; ~**e sessuali** sexual harassment *sg*.

mo 'lesto, a *ag* annoying.

moli 'sano, a *ag* of (*o* from) Molise.

'molla *sf* spring; ~**e** *sfpl* (*per camino*) tongs; **prendere qn con le** ~**e** to treat sb with kid gloves.

mol 'lare *vt* to release, let go; (*NAUT*) to ease; (*fig: ceffone*) to give ♦ *vi* (*cedere*) to give in; ~ **gli ormeggi** (*NAUT*) to cast off; ~ **la presa** to let go.

'molle *ag* soft; (*muscoli*) flabby; (*fig: debole*) weak, feeble.

molleggi 'ato, a [molled'dʒato] *ag* (*letto*) sprung; (*auto*) with good suspension.

mol 'leggio [mol'leddʒo] *sm* (*per veicoli*) suspension; (*elasticità*) springiness; (*GINNASTICA*) knee-bends *pl*.

mol 'letta *sf* (*per capelli*) hairgrip; (*per panni stesi*) clothes peg (*BRIT*) *o* pin (*US*); ~**e** *sfpl* (*per zucchero*) tongs.

mol 'lezza [mol'lettsa] *sf* softness; flabbiness; weakness, feebleness; ~**e** *sfpl*:

vivere nelle ~**e** to live in the lap of luxury.

mol 'lica, che *sf* crumb, soft part.

mol 'liccio, a, ci, ce [mol'littʃo] *ag* (*terreno, impasto*) soggy; (*frutta*) soft; (*floscio: mano*) limp; (: *muscolo*) flabby.

mol 'lusco, schi *sm* mollusc.

'molo *sm* jetty, pier.

mol 'teplice [mol'teplitʃe] *ag* (*formato di più elementi*) complex; ~**i** *pl* (*svariati: interessi, attività*) numerous, various.

molteplicità [molteplitʃi'ta] *sf* multiplicity.

moltipli 'care *vt* to multiply; ~**rsi** *vr* to multiply; (*richieste*) to increase in number.

moltiplicazi 'one [moltiplikat'tsjone] *sf* multiplication.

molti 'tudine *sf* multitude; **una** ~ **di** a vast number *o* a multitude of.

══════════════ *PAROLA CHIAVE*

'molto, a *det* (*quantità*) a lot of, much; (*numero*) a lot of, many; ~ **pane/carbone** a lot of bread/coal; ~**a gente** a lot of people, many people; ~**i libri** a lot of books, many books; **non ho** ~ **tempo** I haven't got much time; **per** ~ **(tempo)** for a long time; **ci vuole** ~ **(tempo)?** will it take long?; **arriverà fra non** ~ he'll arrive soon; **ne hai per** ~? will you be long?

♦ *av* **1** a lot, (very) much; **viaggia** ~ he travels a lot; **non viaggia** ~ he doesn't travel much *o* a lot

2 (*intensivo: con aggettivi, avverbi*) very; (: con participio passato) (very) much; ~ **buono** very good; ~ **migliore**, ~ **meglio** much *o* a lot better

♦ *pron* much, a lot; ~**i, e** *pron pl* many, a lot; ~**i pensano che ...** many (people) think that ...; ~**e sono rimaste a casa** a lot of them stayed at home; **c'era gente, ma non** ~**a** there were people there, but not many.

──────────────────────────

momentanea 'mente *av* at the moment, at present.

momen 'taneo, a *ag* momentary, fleeting.

mo 'mento *sm* moment; **da un** ~ **all'altro** at any moment; (*all'improvviso*) suddenly; **al** ~ **di fare** just as I was *o* am going; ~ **he was** *etc*) doing; **a** ~**i** (*da un* ~ *all'altro*) any time *o* moment now; (*quasi*) nearly; **per il** ~ for the time being; **dal** ~ **che** ever since; (*dato che*) since; ~ **culminante** climax.

'monaca, che *sf* nun.

'Monaco *sf* Monaco; ~ **(di Baviera)** Munich.

'monaco, ci *sm* monk.

mo 'narca, chi *sm* monarch.

monar 'chia [monar'kia] *sf* monarchy.

mo 'narchico, a, ci, che [mo'narkiko] *ag* (*stato, autorità*) monarchic; (*partito, fede*) monarchist ♦ *sm/f* monarchist.

monas 'tero *sm* (*di monaci*) monastery; (*di monache*) convent.

mo 'nastico, a, ci, che *ag* monastic.

'monco, a, chi, che *ag* maimed; (*fig*) incomplete; ~ d'un braccio one-armed.

mon 'cone *sm* stump.

mon 'dana *sf* prostitute.

mondanità *sf* (*frivolezza*) worldliness; le ~ (*piaceri*) the pleasures of the world.

mon 'dano, a *ag* (*anche fig*) worldly; (*dell'alta società*) society *cpd*; fashionable.

mon 'dare *vt* (*frutta, patate*) to peel; (*piselli*) to shell; (*pulire*) to clean.

mondez 'zaio [mondet'tsajo] *sm* rubbish (*BRIT*) *o* garbage (*US*) dump.

mondi 'ale *ag* (*campionato, popolazione*) world *cpd*; (*influenza*) world-wide; di fama ~ world famous.

'mondo *sm* world; (*grande quantità*): un ~ di lots of, a host of; il gran *o* bel ~ high society; per niente al ~, per nessuna cosa al ~ not for all the world; da che ~ è ~ since time *o* the world began; mandare qn all'altro ~ to kill sb; mettere/venire al ~ to bring/come into the world; vivere fuori dal ~ to be out of touch with the real world; (sono) cose dell'altro ~! it's incredible!; com'è piccolo il ~! it's a small world!

mone 'gasco, a, schi, sche *ag, sm/f* Monegasque.

monelle 'ria *sf* prank, naughty trick.

mo 'nello, a *sm/f* street urchin; (*ragazzo vivace*) scamp, imp.

mo 'neta *sf* coin; (*ECON: valuta*) currency; (*denaro spicciolo*) (small) change; ~ estera foreign currency; ~ legale legal tender.

mone 'tario, a *ag* monetary.

Mon 'golia *sf*: la ~ Mongolia.

mon 'golico, a, ci, che *ag* Mongolian.

mongo 'lismo *sm* Down's syndrome.

'mongolo, a *ag* Mongolian ♦ *sm/f, sm* Mongol, Mongolian.

mongo 'loide *ag, sm/f* (*MED*) mongol.

'monito *sm* warning.

'monitor *sm inv* (*TECN, TV*) monitor.

monito 'raggio [monito'raddʒo] *sm* monitoring.

monito 'rare *vt* to monitor.

mo 'nocolo *sm* (*lente*) monocle, eyeglass.

monoco 'lore *ag* (*POL*): governo ~ one-party government.

monoga 'mia *sf* monogamy.

mo 'nogamo, a *ag* monogamous ♦ *sm* monogamist.

monogra 'fia *sf* monograph.

mono 'gramma, i *sm* monogram.

mono 'lingue *ag* monolingual.

monolo 'cale *sm* ≈ studio flat.

mo 'nologo, ghi *sm* monologue.

mono 'pattino *sm* scooter.

mono 'polio *sm* monopoly; ~ di stato government monopoly.

monopoliz 'zare [monopolid'dzare] *vt* to monopolize.

mono 'sillabo, a *ag* monosyllabic ♦ *sm* monosyllable.

monoto 'nia *sf* monotony.

mo 'notono, a *ag* monotonous.

mono 'uso *ag inv* disposable.

monovo 'lume *sf inv* people carrier, people mover.

Mons. *abbr* (= Monsignore) Mgr.

monsi 'gnore [monsiɲ'ɲore] *sm* (*REL: titolo*) Your (*o* His) Grace.

mon 'sone *sm* monsoon.

monta 'carichi [monta'kariki] *sm inv* hoist, goods lift.

mon 'taggio [mon'taddʒo] *sm* (*TECN*) assembly; (*CINE*) editing.

mon 'tagna [mon'taɲɲa] *sf* mountain; (*zona montuosa*): la ~ the mountains *pl*; andare in ~ to go to the mountains; aria/strada di ~ mountain air/road; casa di ~ house in the mountains; ~e russe roller coaster *sg*.

monta 'gnoso, a [montaɲ'ɲoso] *ag* mountainous.

monta 'naro, a *ag* mountain *cpd* ♦ *sm/f* mountain dweller.

mon 'tano, a *ag* mountain *cpd*.

mon 'tante *sm* (*di porta*) jamb; (*di finestra*) upright; (*CALCIO: palo*) post; (*PUGILATO*) upper cut; (*COMM*) total amount.

mon 'tare *vt* to go (*o* come) up; (*cavallo*) to ride; (*apparecchiatura*) to set up, assemble; (*CUC*) to whip; (*ZOOL*) to cover; (*incastonare*) to mount, set; (*CINE*) to edit; (*FOT*) to mount ♦ *vi* to go (*o* come) up; (*a cavallo*): ~ bene/male to ride well/badly; (*aumentare di livello, volume*) to rise; ~rsi *vr* to become big-headed; ~ qc to exaggerate sth; ~ qn *o* la testa a qn to turn sb's head; ~rsi la testa to become big-headed; ~ in bicicletta/macchina/treno to get on a bicycle/ into a car/on a train; ~ a cavallo to get on *o* mount a horse; ~ la guardia (*MIL*) to mount guard.

monta 'tura *sf* assembling *no pl*; (*di occhiali*) frames *pl*; (*di gioiello*) mounting, setting; (*fig*): ~ pubblicitaria publicity stunt.

montavi'vande *sm inv* dumbwaiter.
'monte *sm* mountain; **a** ~ upstream;
andare a ~ (*fig*) to come to nothing;
mandare a ~ **qc** (*fig*) to upset sth, cause
sth to fail; **il M**~ **Bianco** Mont Blanc; **il
M**~ **Everest** Mount Everest; ~ **di pietà**
pawnshop; ~ **premi** prize.
Monteci'torio [montet∫i'torjo] *sm*: **palazzo**
~ (*POL*) seat of the Italian Chamber of
Deputies.
montene'grino, a *ag, sm/f* Montenegrin.
Monte'negro *sm* Montenegro.
mont'gomery [mɔnt'gʌmɔri] *sm inv* duffel
coat.
mon'tone *sm* (*ZOOL*) ram; (*anche*: **giacca di**
~) sheepskin (jacket); **carne di** ~ mutton.
montuosità *sf* mountainous nature.
montu'oso, a *ag* mountainous.
monu'mento *sm* monument.
mo'quette [mɔ'kɛt] *sf* fitted carpet.
'mora *sf* (*del rovo*) blackberry; (*del gelso*)
mulberry; (*DIR*) delay; (: *somma*) arrears
pl.
mo'rale *ag* moral ♦ *sf* (*scienza*) ethics *sg*,
moral philosophy; (*complesso di norme*)
moral standards *pl*, morality; (*condotta*)
morals *pl*; (*insegnamento morale*) moral
♦ *sm* morale; **la** ~ **della favola** the moral of
the tale; **essere giù di** ~ to be feeling
down; **aver il** ~ **alto/a terra** to be in good/
low spirits.
mora'lista, i, e *ag* moralistic ♦ *sm/f*
moralist.
moralità *sf* morality; (*condotta*) morals *pl.*
moraliz'zare [moralid'dzare] *vt* (*costumi,
vita pubblica*) to set moral standards for.
moralizzazi'one [moraliddzat'tsjone] *sf*
setting of moral standards.
mora'toria *sf* (*DIR*) moratorium.
morbi'dezza [morbi'dettsa] *sf* softness;
smoothness; tenderness.
'morbido, a *ag* soft; (*pelle*) soft, smooth;
(*carne*) tender.
mor'billo *sm* (*MED*) measles *sg.*
'morbo *sm* disease.
mor'boso, a *ag* (*fig*) morbid.
'morchia ['mɔrkja] *sf* (*residuo grasso*) dregs
pl; oily deposit.
mor'dente *sm* (*fig*: *di satira, critica*) bite; (: *di
persona*) drive.
'mordere *vt* to bite; (*addentare*) to bite into;
(*corrodere*) to eat into.
mordicchi'are [mordik'kjare] *vt* (*gen*) to
chew at.
mo'rente *ag* dying ♦ *sm/f* dying man/
woman.
mor'fina *sf* morphine.
mo'ria *sf* high mortality.

mori'bondo, a *ag* dying, moribund.
morige'rato, a [moridʒe'rato] *ag* of good
morals.
mo'rire *vi* to die; (*abitudine, civiltà*) to die
out; ~ **di dolore** to die of a broken heart;
~ **di fame** to die of hunger; (*fig*) to be
starving; ~ **di freddo** to freeze to death;
(*fig*) to be frozen; ~ **d'invidia** to be green
with envy; ~ **di noia/paura** to be bored/
scared to death; ~ **dalla voglia di fare qc**
to be dying to do sth; **fa un caldo da** ~ it's
terribly hot.
mormo'rare *vi* to murmur; (*brontolare*) to
grumble; **si mormora che ...** it's
rumoured (*BRIT*) *o* rumored (*US*) that ...;
la gente mormora people are talking.
mormo'rio *sm* murmuring; grumbling.
'moro, a *ag* dark(-haired);
dark(-complexioned); **i M**~**i** *smpl*
(*STORIA*) the Moors.
mo'roso, a *ag* in arrears ♦ *sm/f* (*fam*:
innamorato) sweetheart.
'morsa *sf* (*TECN*) vice (*BRIT*), vise (*US*); (*fig*:
stretta) grip.
mor'setto *sm* (*TECN*) clamp; (*ELETTR*)
terminal.
morsi'care *vt* to nibble (at), gnaw (at);
(*sog*: *insetto*) to bite.
'morso, a *pp di* **mordere** ♦ *sm* bite; (*di
insetto*) sting; (*parte della briglia*) bit; **dare
un** ~ **a qc/qn** to bite sth/sb; **i** ~**i della fame**
pangs of hunger.
morta'della *sf* (*CUC*) mortadella (*type of
salted pork meat*).
mor'taio *sm* mortar.
mor'tale *ag, sm* mortal.
mortalità *sf* mortality; (*STATISTICA*)
mortality, death rate.
'morte *sf* death; **in punto di** ~ at death's
door; **ferito a** ~ (*soldato*) mortally
wounded; (*in incidente*) fatally injured;
essere annoiato a ~ to be bored to death
o to tears; **avercela a** ~ **con qn** to be
bitterly resentful of sb; **avere la** ~ **nel
cuore** to have a heavy heart.
mortifi'care *vt* to mortify.
'morto, a *pp di* **morire** ♦ *ag* dead ♦ *sm/f* dead
man/woman; **i** ~**i** the dead; **fare il** ~
(*nell'acqua*) to float on one's back; **un** ~ **di
fame** (*fig peg*) a down-and-out; **le campane
suonavano a** ~ the funeral bells were
tolling; *vedi anche* **Giorno dei Morti.**
mor'torio *sm* (*anche fig*) funeral.
mo'saico, ci *sm* mosaic; **l'ultimo tassello
del** ~ (*fig*) the last piece of the puzzle.
'Mosca *sf* Moscow.
'mosca, sche *sf* fly; **rimanere** *o* **restare con
un pugno di** ~**sche** (*fig*) to be left empty-

handed; **non si sentiva volare una** ~ (*fig*)
you could have heard a pin drop; ~ **cieca**
blind-man's buff.

mos'cato *sm* muscatel (wine).

mosce'rino [moʃʃe'rino] *sm* midge, gnat.

mos'chea [mos'kɛa] *sf* mosque.

mos'chetto [mos'ketto] *sm* musket.

moschet'tone [mosket'tone] *sm* (*gancio*)
spring clip; (*ALPINISMO*) karabiner,
snaplink.

moschi'cida, i, e [moski'tʃida] *ag* fly *cpd*;
carta ~ flypaper.

'moscio, a, sci, sce ['moʃʃo] *ag* (*fig*)
lifeless; **ha la "r"** ~**a** he can't roll his
"r"s.

mos'cone *sm* (*ZOOL*) bluebottle; (*barca*)
pedalo; (: *a remi*) *kind of pedalo with oars.*

mosco'vita, i, e *ag*, *sm/f* Muscovite.

'mossa *sf* movement; (*nel gioco*) move;
darsi una ~ (*fig*) to give o.s. a shake;
prendere le ~**e da qc** to come about as the
result of sth.

'mossi *etc vb vedi* **muovere.**

'mosso, a *pp di* **muovere ♦** *ag* (*mare*) rough;
(*capelli*) wavy; (*FOT*) blurred; (*ritmo, prosa*)
animated.

mos'tarda *sf* mustard.

'mosto *sm* must.

'mostra *sf* exhibition, show; (*ostentazione*)
show; **in** ~ on show; **far** ~ **di** (*fingere*) to
pretend; **far** ~ **di sé** to show off; **mettersi**
in ~ to draw attention to o.s.

mos'trare *vt* to show ♦ *vi*: ~ **di fare** to
pretend to do; ~**rsi** *vr* to appear; ~ **la**
lingua to stick out one's tongue.

'mostro *sm* monster.

mostru'oso, a *ag* monstrous.

mo'tel *sm inv* motel.

moti'vare *vt* (*causare*) to cause;
(*giustificare*) to justify, account for.

motivazi'one [motivat'tsjone] *sf*
justification; (*PSIC*) motivation.

mo'tivo *sm* (*causa*) reason, cause;
(*movente*) motive; (*letterario*) (central)
theme; (*disegno*) motif, design; (*MUS*)
motif; **per quale** ~**?** why?, for what
reason?; **per** ~**i di salute** for health
reasons; ~**i personali** personal reasons.

'moto *sm* (*anche FISICA*) motion;
(*movimento, gesto*) movement; (*esercizio*
fisico) exercise; (*sommossa*) rising, revolt;
(*commozione*) feeling, impulse ♦ *sf inv*
(*motocicletta*) motorbike; **fare del** ~ to
take some exercise; **un** ~ **d'impazienza** an
impatient gesture; **mettere in** ~ to set in
motion; (*AUT*) to start up; ~ **d'acqua** Jet
Ski®.

moto'carro *sm* three-wheeler van.

motoci'cletta [mototʃi'kletta] *sf*
motorcycle.

motoci'clismo [mototʃi'klizmo] *sm*
motorcycling, motorcycle racing.

motoci'clista, i, e [mototʃi'klista] *sm/f*
motorcyclist.

moto'nave *sf* motor vessel.

motopesche'reccio [motopeske'rettʃo] *sm*
motor fishing vessel.

mo'tore, 'trice *ag* motor; (*TECN*) driving
♦ *sm* engine, motor ♦ *sf* (*TECN*) engine,
motor; **albero** ~ drive shaft; **forza** ~**trice**
driving force; **a** ~ motor *cpd*, power-
driven; ~ **a combustione interna/a**
reazione internal combustion/jet engine;
~ **di ricerca** (*INFORM*) search engine.

moto'rino *sm* moped; ~ **di avviamento**
(*AUT*) starter.

motoriz'zato, a [motorid'dzato] *ag* (*truppe*)
motorized; (*persona*) having a car *o*
transport.

motorizzazi'one [motoriddzat'tsjone] *sf*
(*ufficio tecnico e organizzativo*): (**ufficio**
della) ~ road traffic office.

motos'cafo *sm* motorboat.

motove'detta *sf* motor patrol vessel.

mo'trice [mo'tritʃe] *sf vedi* **motore.**

mot'teggio [mot'teddʒo] *sm* banter.

'motto *sm* (*battuta scherzosa*) witty remark;
(*frase emblematica*) motto, maxim.

mountain bike *sf inv* mountain bike.

'mouse ['maus] *sm inv* (*INFORM*) mouse.

mo'vente *sm* motive.

mo'venza [mo'vɛntsa] *sf* movement.

movimen'tare *vt* to liven up.

movimen'tato, a *ag* (*festa, partita*) lively;
(*riunione*) animated; (*strada, vita*) busy;
(*soggiorno*) eventful.

movi'mento *sm* movement; (*fig*) activity,
hustle and bustle; (*MUS*) tempo,
movement; **essere sempre in** ~ to be
always on the go; **fare un po' di** ~
(*esercizio fisico*) to take some exercise; **c'è**
molto ~ **in città** the town is very busy; ~
di capitali movement of capital; **M**~ **per la**
Liberazione della Donna (MLD) Women's
Movement.

movi'ola *sf* moviola; **rivedere qc alla** ~ to
see an action (*BRIT*) *o* instant (*US*) replay
of sth.

Mozam'bico [moddzam'biko] *sm*: **il** ~
Mozambique.

mozi'one [mot'tsjone] *sf* (*POL*) motion; ~
d'ordine (*POL*) point of order.

mozzafi'ato [mottsa'fjato] *ag inv*
breathtaking.

moz'zare [mot'tsare] *vt* to cut off; (*coda*) to
dock; ~ **il fiato** *o* **il respiro a qn** (*fig*) to

take sb's breath away.

mozza'rella [mottsa'rɛlla] *sf* mozzarella.

mozzi'cone [mottsi'kone] *sm* stub, butt, end; (*anche*: ~ **di sigaretta**) cigarette end.

'mozzo *sm* ['mɔddzo] (*MECCANICA*) hub; ['mottso] (*NAUT*) ship's boy; ~ **di stalla** stable boy.

mq *abbr* (= *metro quadro*) sq.m.

MS *sigla* = *Massa Carrara*.

M.S.I. *sigla m* (= *Movimento Sociale Italiano*) *former right-wing political party.*

Mti *abbr* = *monti*.

'mucca, che *sf* cow; ~ **pazza** BSE; (**morbo della**) ~ **pazza** mad cow disease, BSE; **l'emergenza** ~ **pazza** the mad cow crisis.

'mucchio ['mukkjo] *sm* pile, heap; (*fig*): **un** ~ **di** lots of, heaps of.

mucil'lagine [mutʃil'ladʒine] *sf* (*BOT*) mucilage (*green slime produced by plants growing in water*).

'muco, chi *sm* mucus.

mu'cosa *sf* mucous membrane.

'muesli [mjusli] *sm* muesli.

'muffa *sf* mould (*BRIT*), mold (*US*), mildew; **fare la** ~ to go mouldy (*BRIT*) o moldy (*US*).

mugghi'are [mug'gjare] *vi* (*fig*: *mare, tuono*) to roar; (: *vento*) to howl.

mug'gire [mud'dʒire] *vi* (*vacca*) to low, moo; (*toro*) to bellow; (*fig*) to roar.

mug'gito [mud'dʒito] *sm* moo; bellow; roar.

mu'ghetto [mu'getto] *sm* lily of the valley.

mu'gnaio, a [muɲ'ɲajo] *sm/f* miller.

mugo'lare *vi* (*cane*) to whimper, whine; (*fig*: *persona*) to moan.

mugu'gnare [muguɲ'ɲare] *vi* (*fam*) to mutter, mumble.

mulatti'era *sf* mule track.

mu'latto, a *ag, sm/f* mulatto.

muli'nare *vi* to whirl, spin (round and round).

muli'nello *sm* (*moto vorticoso*) eddy, whirl; (*di canna da pesca*) reel; (*NAUT*) windlass.

mu'lino *sm* mill; ~ **a vento** windmill.

'mulo *sm* mule.

'multa *sf* fine.

mul'tare *vt* to fine.

multico'lore *ag* multicoloured (*BRIT*), multicolored (*US*).

multi'etnico, a, ci, che *ag* multiethnic.

multi'forme *ag* (*paesaggio, attività, interessi*) varied; (*ingegno*) versatile.

multimedi'ale *ag* multimedia *cpd*.

multinazio'nale [multinattsjo'nale] *ag, sf* multinational; **forza** ~ **di pace** multinational peace-keeping force.

'multiplo, a *ag, sm* multiple.

multiu'tenza [multiu'tɛntsa] *sf* (*INFORM*) time sharing.

'mummia *sf* mummy.

'mungere ['mundʒere] *vt* (*anche fig*) to milk.

mungi'tura [mundʒi'tura] *sf* milking.

munici'pale [munitʃi'pale] *ag* (*gen*) municipal; **palazzo** ~ town hall; **autorità** ~i local authorities (*BRIT*), local government *sg*.

muni'cipio [muni'tʃipjo] *sm* town council; (*edificio*) town hall; **sposarsi in** ~ ≈ to get married in a registry office (*BRIT*), have a civil marriage.

munifi'cenza [munifi'tʃɛntsa] *sf* munificence.

mu'nifico, a, ci, che *ag* munificent, generous.

mu'nire *vt*: ~ **qc/qn di** to equip sth/sb with; ~ **di firma** (*documento*) to sign.

munizi'oni [munit'tsjoni] *sfpl* (*MIL*) ammunition *sg*.

'munsi *etc vb vedi* **mungere**.

'munto, a *pp di* **mungere**.

mu'oio *etc vb vedi* **morire**.

mu'overe *vt* to move; (*ruota, macchina*) to drive; (*sollevare*: *questione, obiezione*) to raise, bring up; (: *accusa*) to make, bring forward; ~**rsi** *vr* to move; ~ **causa a qn** (*DIR*) to take legal action against sb; ~ a **compassione** to move to pity; ~ **guerra a** *o* **contro qn** to wage war against sb; ~ **mari e monti** to move heaven and earth; ~ **al pianto** to move to tears; ~ **i primi passi** to take one's first steps; (*fig*) to be starting out; **muoviti!** hurry up!, get a move on!

'mura *sfpl vedi* **muro**.

mu'raglia [mu'raʎʎa] *sf* (high) wall.

mu'rale *ag* wall *cpd*; mural.

mu'rare *vt* (*persona, porta*) to wall up.

mu'rario, a *ag* building *cpd*; **arte** ~**a** masonry.

mura'tore *sm* (*con pietre*) mason; (*con mattoni*) bricklayer.

mura'tura *sf* (*lavoro murario*) masonry; **casa in** ~ (*di pietra*) stonebuilt house; (*di mattoni*) brick house.

'muro *sm* wall; ~**a** *sfpl* (*cinta cittadina*) walls; **a** ~ wall *cpd*; (*armadio etc*) built-in; **mettere al** ~ (*fucilare*) to shoot *o* execute (by firing squad); ~ **di cinta** surrounding wall; ~ **divisorio** dividing wall; ~ **del suono** sound barrier.

'musa *sf* muse.

'muschio ['muskjo] *sm* (*ZOOL*) musk; (*BOT*) moss.

musco'lare *ag* muscular, muscle *cpd*.

muscola'tura *sf* muscle structure.

'muscolo *sm* (*ANAT*) muscle.

musco'loso, a *ag* muscular.

mu'seo *sm* museum.
museru'ola *sf* muzzle.
'musica *sf* music; ~ **da ballo/camera**
dance/chamber music.
musi'cale *ag* musical.
musicas'setta *sf* (pre-recorded) cassette.
musi'cista, i, e [muzi'tʃista] *sm/f* musician.
musi'comane *sm/f* music lover.
'muso *sm* muzzle; (*di auto, aereo*) nose;
tenere il ~ to sulk.
mu'sone, a *sm/f* sulky person.
'mussola *sf* muslin.
mus(s)ul'mano, a *ag, sm/f* Muslim,
Moslem.
'muta *sf* (*di animali*) moulting (*BRIT*),
molting (*US*); (*di serpenti*) sloughing; (*per
immersioni subacquee*) diving suit; (*gruppo
di cani*) pack.
mu'tabile *ag* changeable.
muta'mento *sm* change.
mu'tande *sfpl* (*da uomo*) (under)pants.
mutan'dine *sfpl* (*da donna, bambino*) pants
(*BRIT*), briefs; ~ **di plastica** plastic pants.
mu'tare *vt, vi* to change, alter.
mutazi'one [mutat'tsjone] *sf* change,
alteration; (*BIOL*) mutation.
mu'tevole *ag* changeable.
muti'lare *vt* to mutilate, maim; (*fig*) to
mutilate, deface.
muti'lato, a *sm/f* disabled person (*through
loss of limbs*); ~ **di guerra** disabled ex-
serviceman (*BRIT*) o war veteran (*US*).
mutilazi'one [mutilat'tsjone] *sf* mutilation.
mu'tismo *sm* (*MED*) mutism;
(*atteggiamento*) (stubborn) silence.
'muto, a *ag* (*MED*) dumb; (*emozione, dolore,
CINE*) silent; (*LING*) silent, mute; (*carta
geografica*) blank; ~ **per lo stupore** *etc*
speechless with amazement *etc*; **ha fatto
scena ~a** he didn't utter a word.
'mutua *sf* (*anche*: **cassa** ~) health
insurance scheme; **medico della** ~
≈ National Health Service doctor (*BRIT*).
mutu'are *vt* (*fig*) to borrow.
mutu'ato, a *sm/f* member of a health
insurance scheme.
'mutuo, a *ag* (*reciproco*) mutual ♦ *sm* (*ECON*)
(long-term) loan; ~ **ipotecario** mortgage.

N n

N, n ['ɛnne] *sf o m* (*lettera*) N, n; **N come
Napoli** ≈ N for Nellie (*BRIT*), N for Nan
(*US*).
N *abbr* (= *nord*) N.
n *abbr* (= *numero*) no.
NA *sigla* = *Napoli*.
na'babbo *sm* (*anche fig*) nabob.
'nacchere ['nakkere] *sfpl* castanets.
NAD *sigla m* = **nucleo anti-droga**.
na'dir *sm* (*ASTR*) nadir.
'nafta *sf* naphtha; (*per motori diesel*) diesel
oil.
nafta'lina *sf* (*CHIM*) naphthalene; (*tarmicida*)
mothballs *pl*.
'naia *sf* (*ZOOL*) cobra; (*MIL*) slang term for
national service.
na'if [na'if] *ag inv* naïve.
'nailon *sm* – nylon.
Nai'robi *sf* Nairobi.
'nanna *sf* (*linguaggio infantile*): **andare a** ~
to go to beddy-byes.
'nano, a *ag, sm/f* dwarf.
napole'tano, a *ag, sm/f* Neapolitan ♦ *sf*
(*macchinetta da caffè*) Neapolitan coffee
pot.
'Napoli *sf* Naples.
'nappa *sf* tassel.
nar'ciso [nar'tʃizo] *sm* narcissus.
'narcos *sm inv* (*colombiano*) Colombian
drug trafficker.
narco'dollari *smpl* drug money *sg*.
nar'cosi *sf* general anaesthesia, narcosis.
nar'cotico, ci *sm* narcotic.
narcotraffi'cante *sm/f* drug trafficker.
narco'traffico *sm* drug trade.
na'rice [na'ritʃe] *sf* nostril.
nar'rare *vt* to tell the story of, recount.
narra'tivo, a *ag* narrative ♦ *sf* (*branca
letteraria*) fiction.
narra'tore, 'trice *sm/f* narrator.
narrazi'one [narrat'tsjone] *sf* narration;
(*racconto*) story, tale.
N.A.S.A. ['naza] *sigla f* (= *National
Aeronautics and Space Administration*)
NASA.
na'sale *ag* nasal.
na'scente [naʃ'ʃɛnte] *ag* (*sole, luna*) rising.
'nascere ['naʃʃere] *vi* (*bambino*) to be born;

(*pianta*) to come o spring up; (*fiume*) to
rise, have its source; (*sole*) to rise; (*dente*)
to come through; (*fig: derivare, conseguire*):
~ **da** to arise from, be born out of; **è nata
nel 1952** she was born in 1952; **da cosa
nasce cosa** one thing leads to another.
'**nascita** ['naʃʃita] *sf* birth.
nasci'turo, a [naʃʃi'turo] *sm/f* future child;
come si chiamerà il ~? what's the baby
going to be called?
nas'condere *vt* to hide, conceal; ~**rsi** *vr* to
hide.
nascon'diglio [naskon'diʎʎo] *sm* hiding
place.
nascon'dino *sm* (*gioco*) hide-and-seek.
nas'cosi *etc vb vedi* **nascondere.**
nas'costo, a *pp di* **nascondere ♦** *ag* hidden;
di ~ secretly.
na'sello *sm* (*ZOOL*) hake.
'**naso** *sm* nose.
Nas'sau *sf* Nassau.
'**nastro** *sm* ribbon; (*magnetico, isolante,
SPORT*) tape; ~ **adesivo** adhesive tape; ~
trasportatore conveyor belt.
nas'turzio [nas'turtsjo] *sm* nasturtium.
na'tale *ag* of one's birth ♦ *sm* (*REL*): **N**~
Christmas; (*giorno della nascita*) birthday;
~**i** *smpl*: **di illustri/umili** ~**i** of noble/
humble birth.
natalità *sf* birth rate.
nata'lizio, a [nata'littsjo] *ag* (*del Natale*)
Christmas *cpd*.
na'tante *sm* craft *inv*, boat.
'**natica, che** *sf* (*ANAT*) buttock.
na'tio, a, 'tii, 'tie *ag* native.
Natività *sf* (*REL*) Nativity.
na'tivo, a *ag*, *sm/f* native.
'**nato, a** *pp di* **nascere** ♦ *ag*: **un attore** ~ a
born actor; ~**a Pieri** née Pieri.
'**N.A.T.O.** *sigla f* NATO (= *North Atlantic
Treaty Organization*).
na'tura *sf* nature; **pagare in** ~ to pay in
kind; ~ **morta** still life.
natu'rale *ag* natural ♦ *sm*: **al** ~ (*alimenti*)
served plain; (*ritratto*) life-size; (**ma**) **è** ~!
(*in risposte*) of course!; **a grandezza** ~
life-size; **acqua** ~ spring water.
natura'lezza [natura'lettsa] *sf* naturalness.
natura'lista, i, e *sm/f* naturalist.
naturaliz'zare [naturalid'dzare] *vt* to
naturalize.
natural'mente *av* naturally; (*certamente,
si*) of course.
natu'rismo *sm* naturism, nudism.
natu'rista, i, e *ag*, *sm/f* naturist, nudist.
naufra'gare *vi* (*nave*) to be wrecked;
(*persona*) to be shipwrecked; (*fig*) to fall
through.

nau'fragio [nau'fradʒo] *sm* shipwreck; (*fig*)
ruin, failure.
'**naufrago, ghi** *sm* castaway, shipwreck
victim.
'**nausea** *sf* nausea; **avere la** ~ to feel sick
(*BRIT*) o ill (*US*); **fino alla** ~ ad nauseam.
nausea'bondo, a *ag*, **nause'ante** *ag*
nauseating, sickening.
nause'are *vt* to nauseate, make (feel) sick
(*BRIT*) o ill (*US*).
'**nautico, a, ci, che** *ag* nautical ♦ *sf* (art of)
navigation; **salone** ~ (*mostra*) boat show.
na'vale *ag* naval; **battaglia** ~ naval battle;
(*gioco*) battleships *pl*.
na'vata *sf* (*anche:* ~ **centrale**) nave; (*anche:*
~ **laterale**) aisle.
'**nave** *sf* ship, vessel; ~ **da carico** cargo
ship, freighter; ~ **cisterna** tanker; ~ **da
guerra** warship; ~ **di linea** liner; ~
passeggeri passenger ship; ~ **portaerei**
aircraft carrier; ~ **spaziale** spaceship.
na'vetta *sf* shuttle; (*servizio di
collegamento*) shuttle (service).
navi'cella [navi'tʃɛlla] *sf* (*di aerostato*)
gondola; ~ **spaziale** spaceship.
navi'gabile *ag* navigable.
navi'gante *sm* sailor, seaman.
navi'gare *vi* to sail; ~ **in cattive acque** (*fig*)
to be in deep water; ~ **in Internet** to surf
the Net.
navi'gato, a *ag* (*fig: esperto*) experienced.
naviga'tore, 'trice *sm/f* (*gen*) navigator; ~
solitario single-handed sailor; ~
satellitare satellite navigator.
navigazi'one [navigat'sjone] *sf* navigation;
dopo una settimana di ~ after a week at
sea.
na'viglio [na'viʎʎo] *sm* fleet, ships *pl*;
(*canale artificiale*) canal; ~ **da pesca** fishing
fleet.
nazio'nale [nattsjo'nale] *ag* national ♦ *sf*
(*SPORT*) national team.
naziona'lismo [nattsjona'lizmo] *sm*
nationalism.
naziona'lista, i, e [nattsjona'lista] *ag*, *sm/f*
nationalist.
nazionalità [nattsjonali'ta] *sf inv*
nationality.
nazionaliz'zare [nattsjonalid'dzare] *vt* to
nationalize.
nazionalizzazi'one [nattsjonalid-
dzat'tsjone] *sf* nationalization.
nazi'one [nat'tsjone] *sf* nation.
naziskin ['nɑːtsiskin] *sm inv* Nazi skinhead.
na'zismo [nat'tsizmo] *sm* Nazism.
na'zista, i, e [nat'tsista] *ag*, *sm/f* Nazi.
NB *abbr* (= *nota bene*) NB.
N.d.A. *abbr* (= *nota dell'autore*) author's

note.

N.d.D. *abbr* = *nota della direzione*.

N.d.E. *abbr* (= *nota dell'editore*) publisher's note.

N.d.R. *abbr* (= *nota della redazione*) editor's note.

'nd'rangheta [nd'rangeta] *sf* Calabrian Mafia.

N.d.T. *abbr* (= *nota del traduttore*) translator's note.

================ PAROLA CHIAVE

ne *pron* **1** (*di lui, lei, loro*) of him/her/them; about him/her/them; ~ **riconosco la voce** I recognize his (*o* her) voice
2 (*di questa, quella cosa*) of it; about it; ~ **voglio ancora** I want some more (of it *o* them); **non parliamone più!** let's not talk about it any more!
3 (*da ciò*) from this; ~ **deduco che l'avete trovato** I gather you've found it; ~ **consegue che** … it follows therefore that …
4 (*con valore partitivo*): **hai dei libri? — sì,** ~ **ho** have you any books? — yes, I have (some); **hai del pane? — no, non** ~ **ho** have you any bread? — no, I haven't any; **quanti anni hai?** — ~ **ho 17** how old are you? — I'm 17
♦ *av* (*moto da luogo: da lì*) from there; ~ **vengo ora** I've just come from there.

né *cong*: ~ … ~ neither … nor; ~ **l'uno** ~ **l'altro lo vuole** neither of them wants it; ~ **più** ~ **meno** no more no less; **non parla** ~ **l'italiano** ~ **il tedesco** he speaks neither Italian nor German, he doesn't speak either Italian or German; **non piove** ~ **nevica** it isn't raining or snowing.

N.E. *abbr* (= *nordest*) NE.

ne'anche [ne'anke] *av, cong* not even; **non** … ~ not even; ~ **se volesse potrebbe venire** he couldn't even come even if he wanted to; **non l'ho visto — neanch'io** I didn't see him — neither did I *o* I didn't either; ~ **per idea** *o* **sogno!** not on your life!; **non ci penso** ~! I wouldn't dream of it!; ~ **a pagarlo lo farebbe** he wouldn't do it even if you paid him.

'nebbia *sf* fog; (*foschia*) mist.

nebbi'oso, a *ag* foggy; misty.

nebulizza'tore [nebuliddza'tore] *sm* atomizer.

nebu'losa *sf* nebula.

nebulosità *sf* haziness.

nebu'loso, a *ag* (*atmosfera, cielo*) hazy; (*fig*) hazy, vague.

néces'saire [nesɛ'sɛr] *sm inv*: ~ **da viaggio** overnight case *o* bag.

necessaria'mente [netʃessarja'mente] *av* necessarily.

neces'sario, a [netʃes'sarjo] *ag* necessary; ♦ *sm*: **fare il** ~ to do what is necessary; **lo stretto** ~ the bare essentials *pl*.

necessità [netʃessi'ta] *sf inv* necessity; (*povertà*) need, poverty; **trovarsi nella** ~ **di fare qc** to be forced *o* obliged to do sth, have to do sth.

necessi'tare [netʃessi'tare] *vt* to require ♦ *vi* (*aver bisogno*): ~ **di** to need.

necro'logio [nekro'lɔdʒo] *sm* obituary notice; (*registro*) register of deaths.

ne'fando, a *ag* infamous, wicked.

ne'fasto, a *ag* inauspicious, ill-omened.

ne'gare *vt* to deny; (*rifiutare*) to deny, refuse; ~ **di aver fatto/che** to deny having done/that.

negativa'mente *av* negatively; **rispondere** ~ to give a negative response.

nega'tivo, a *ag, sf, sm* negative.

negazi'one [negat'tsjone] *sf* negation.

negherò *etc* [nege'rɔ] *vb vedi* **negare**.

ne'gletto, a [ne'glɛtto] *ag* (*trascurato*) neglected.

'negli ['neʎʎi] *prep* + *det vedi* **in**.

négli'gé [negli'ʒe] *sm inv* negligee.

negli'gente [negli'dʒɛnte] *ag* negligent, careless.

negli'genza [negli'dʒɛntsa] *sf* negligence, carelessness.

negozi'abile [negot'tsjabile] *ag* negotiable.

negozi'ante [negot'tsjante] *sm/f* trader, dealer; (*bottegaio*) shopkeeper (*BRIT*), storekeeper (*US*).

negozi'are [negot'tsjare] *vt* to negotiate ♦ *vi*: ~ **in** to trade *o* deal in.

negozi'ato [negot'tsjato] *sm* negotiation.

negozia'tore, 'trice [negottsja'tore] *sm/f* negotiator.

ne'gozio [ne'gɔttsjo] *sm* (*locale*) shop (*BRIT*), store (*US*); (*affare*) (piece of) business *no pl*; (*DIR*): ~ **giuridico** legal transaction.

negri'ere, a, negri'ero, a *sm* slave trader ♦ *sm/f* (*fig*) slave driver.

'negro, a *ag, sm/f* Negro.

negro'mante *sm/f* necromancer.

negroman'zia [negroman'tsia] *sf* necromancy.

'nei, nel, nell', 'nella, 'nelle, 'nello *prep* +*det vedi* **in**.

'nembo *sm* (*METEOR*) nimbus.

ne'mico, a, ci, che *ag* hostile; (*MIL*) enemy *cpd* ♦ *sm/f* enemy; **essere** ~ **di** to be strongly averse *o* opposed to.

nem 'meno *av, cong* = **neanche.**
'nenia *sf* dirge; (*motivo monotono*) monotonous tune.
'neo *sm* mole; (*fig*) (slight) flaw.
'neo... *prefisso* neo....
neofa 'scista, i, e [neofaʃ'ʃista] *sm/f* neofascist.
neolo 'gismo [neolo'dʒizmo] *sm* neologism.
'neon *sm* (*CHIM*) neon.
neo 'nato, a *ag* newborn ♦ *sm/f* newborn baby.
neozelan 'dese [neoddzelan'dese] *ag* New Zealand *cpd* ♦ *sm/f* New Zealander.
Ne 'pal *sm*: **il** ~ Nepal.
nepo 'tismo *sm* nepotism.
nep 'pure *av, cong* = **neanche.**
ner 'bata *sf* (*colpo*) blow; (*sferzata*) whiplash.
'nerbo *sm* lash; (*fig*) strength, backbone.
nerbo 'ruto, a *ag* muscular; robust.
ne 'retto *sm* (*TIP*) bold type.
'nero, a *ag* black; (*scuro*) dark ♦ *sm* black; **nella miseria più** ~**a** in utter *o* abject poverty; **essere di umore** ~, **essere** ~ to be in a filthy mood; **mettere qc** ~ **su bianco** to put sth down in black and white; **vedere tutto** ~ to look on the black side (of things).
nero 'fumo *sm* lampblack.
nerva 'tura *sf* (*ANAT*) nervous system; (*BOT*) veining; (*ARCHIT, TECN*) rib.
'nervo *sm* (*ANAT*) nerve; (*BOT*) vein; **avere i** ~**i** to be on edge; **dare sui** ~**i a qn** to get on sb's nerves; **tenere/avere i** ~**i saldi** to keep/be calm; **che** ~**i!** damn (it)!
nervo 'sismo *sm* (*PSIC*) nervousness; (*irritazione*) irritability.
ner 'voso, a *ag* nervous; (*irritabile*) irritable ♦ *sm* (*fam*): **far venire il** ~ **a qn** to get on sb's nerves; **farsi prendere dal** ~ to let o.s. get irritated.
'nespola *sf* (*BOT*) medlar; (*fig*) blow, punch.
'nespolo *sm* medlar tree.
'nesso *sm* connection, link.

================= *PAROLA CHIAVE*

nes 'suno, a (*det: dav sm* **nessun** + *C*, *V*, **nessuno** + *s impura, gn, pn, ps, x, z*; *dav sf* **nessuna** + *C*, **nessun'** + *V*) *det* **1** (*non uno*) no, *espressione negativa* + any; **non c'è nessun libro** there isn't any book, there is no book; **nessun altro** no one else, nobody else; **nessun'altra cosa** nothing else; **in nessun luogo** nowhere **2** (*qualche*) any; **hai** ~**a obiezione?** do you have any objections?
♦ *pron* **1** (*non uno*) no one, nobody,

espressione negativa + any(one); (: *cosa*) none, *espressione negativa* + any; ~ **è venuto,** **non è venuto** ~ nobody came **2** (*qualcuno*) anyone, anybody; **ha telefonato** ~**?** did anyone phone?

netta 'mente *av* clearly.
net 'tare *vt* to clean ♦ *sm* ['nɛttare] nectar.
net 'tezza [net'tettsa] *sf* cleanness, cleanliness; ~ **urbana** cleansing department (*BRIT*), department of sanitation (*US*).
'netto, a *ag* (*pulito*) clean; (*chiaro*) clear, clear-cut; (*deciso*) definite; (*ECON*) net; **tagliare qc di** ~ to cut sth clean off; **taglio** ~ **col passato** (*fig*) clean break with the past.
nettur 'bino *sm* dustman (*BRIT*), garbage collector (*US*).
'neuro... *prefisso* neuro....
neurochirur 'gia [neurokirur'dʒia] *sf* neurosurgery.
neurolo 'gia [neurolo'dʒia] *sf* neurology.
neuro 'logico, a, ci, che [neuro'lɔdʒiko] *ag* neurological.
neu 'rologo a, gi, ghe *sm/f* neurologist.
neu 'rosi *sf inv* = **nevrosi.**
neu 'trale *ag* neutral.
neutralità *sf* neutrality.
neutraliz 'zare [neutralid'dzare] *vt* to neutralize.
'neutro, a *ag* neutral; (*LING*) neuter ♦ *sm* (*LING*) neuter.
neu 'trone *sm* neutron.
ne 'vaio *sm* snowfield.
'neve *sf* snow; **montare a** ~ (*CUC*) to whip up; ~ **carbonica** dry ice.
nevi 'care *vb impers* to snow.
nevi 'cata *sf* snowfall.
ne 'vischio [ne'viskjo] *sm* sleet.
ne 'voso, a *ag* snowy; snow-covered.
nevral 'gia [nevral'dʒia] *sf* neuralgia.
ne 'vralgico, a, ci, che [ne'vraldʒiko] *ag*: **punto** ~ (*MED*) nerve centre; (*fig*) crucial point.
nevras 'tenico, a, ci, che *ag* (*MED*) neurasthenic; (*fig*) hot-tempered ♦ *sm/f* neurasthenic; hot-tempered person.
ne 'vrosi *sf inv* neurosis.
ne 'vrotico, a, ci, che *ag, sm/f* (*anche fig*) neurotic.
Nia 'gara *sm*: **le cascate del** ~ the Niagara Falls.
'nibbio *sm* (*ZOOL*) kite.
Nica 'ragua *sm*: **il** ~ Nicaragua.
nicaragu 'ense *ag, sm/f* Nicaraguan.
'nicchia ['nikkja] *sf* niche; (*naturale*) cavity, hollow; ~ **di mercato** (*COMM*) niche

nicchi 'are [nik'kjare] *vi* to shilly-shally, hesitate.

'nichel ['nikel] *sm* nickel.

nichi 'lismo [niki'lizmo] *sm* nihilism.

Nico 'sia *sf* Nicosia.

nico 'tina *sf* nicotine.

nidi 'ata *sf* (*di uccelli, fig: di bambini*) brood; (*di altri animali*) litter.

nidifi 'care *vi* to nest.

'nido *sm* nest ♦ *ag inv*: **asilo** ~ day nursery, crèche (*for children aged 0 to 3*); **a** ~ **d'ape** (*tessuto etc*) honeycomb *cpd*.

=================== **PAROLA CHIAVE**

ni 'ente *pron* **1** (*nessuna cosa*) nothing; ~ **può fermarlo** nothing can stop him; ~ **di** ~ absolutely nothing; **grazie!** — **di** ~**!** thank you! — not at all!; **nient'altro** nothing else; **nient'altro che** nothing but; ~ **affatto** not at all, not in the least; **come se** ~ **fosse** as if nothing had happened; **cose da** ~ trivial matters; **per** ~ (*gratis, invano*) for nothing; **non per** ~, **ma ... not** for any particular reason, but ...; **poco o** ~ next to nothing; **un uomo da** ~ a man of no consequence

2 (*qualcosa*): **hai bisogno di** ~**?** do you need anything?

3 : **non ...** ~ nothing, *espressione negativa* + anything; **non ho visto** ~ I saw nothing, I didn't see anything; **non può farci** ~ he can't do anything about it; **(non) fa** ~ (*non importa*) it doesn't matter; **non ho** ~ **da dire** I have nothing o haven't anything to say

♦ *ag inv*: ~ **paura!** never fear!; **e** ~ **scuse!** and I don't want to hear excuses!

♦ *sm* nothing; **un bel** ~ absolutely nothing; **basta un** ~ **per farla piangere** the slightest thing is enough to make her cry; **finire in** ~ to come to nothing

♦ *av* (*in nessuna misura*): **non ...** ~ not ... at all; **non è (per)** ~ **buono** it isn't good at all; **non ci penso per** ~ (*non ne ho nessuna intenzione*) I wouldn't think of it; ~ **male!** not bad at all!

===

nientedi 'meno, niente 'meno *av* actually, even ♦ *escl* really!, I say!

'Niger ['nidʒer] *sm*: **il** ~ Niger; (*fiume*) the Niger.

Ni 'geria [ni'dʒerja] *sf* Nigeria.

nigeri 'ano, a [nidʒe'rjano] *ag, sm/f* Nigerian.

'Nilo *sm*: **il** ~ the Nile.

'nimbo *sm* halo.

'ninfa *sf* nymph.

nin 'fea *sf* water lily.

nin 'fomane *sf* nymphomaniac.

ninna 'nanna *sf* lullaby.

'ninnolo *sm* (*balocco*) plaything; (*gingillo*) knick-knack.

ni 'pote *sm/f* (*di zii*) nephew/niece; (*di nonni*) grandson/daughter, grandchild.

nip 'ponico, a, ci, che *ag* Japanese.

niti 'dezza [niti'dettsa] *sf* (*gen*) clearness; (*di stile*) clarity; (*FOT, TV*) sharpness.

'nitido, a *ag* clear; (*immagine*) sharp.

ni 'trato *sm* nitrate.

'nitrico, a, ci, che *ag* nitric.

ni 'trire *vi* to neigh.

ni 'trito *sm* (*di cavallo*) neighing *no pl*; neigh; (*CHIM*) nitrite.

nitroglice 'rina [nitroglitʃe'rina] *sf* nitroglycerine.

'niveo, a *ag* snow-white.

'Nizza ['nittsa] *sf* Nice.

nn *abbr* (= *numeri*) nos.

NO *sigla* = Novara.

no *av* (*risposta*) no; **vieni o** ~**?** are you coming or not?; **come** ~**!** of course!, certainly!; **perché** ~**?** why not?

N.O. *abbr* (= *nordovest*) NW.

nobil 'donna *sf* noblewoman.

'nobile *ag* noble ♦ *sm/f* noble, nobleman/woman.

nobili 'are *ag* noble.

nobili 'tare *vt* (*anche fig*) to ennoble; ~**rsi** *vr* (*rendersi insigne*) to distinguish o.s.

nobiltà *sf* nobility; (*di azione etc*) nobleness.

nobilu 'omo *sm, pl* **-u'omini** nobleman.

'nocca, che *sf* (*ANAT*) knuckle.

'noccio *etc* ['nɔttʃo] *vb vedi* **nuocere.**

nocci 'ola [not'tʃɔla] *sf* hazelnut ♦ *ag inv* (*anche: **color** ~*) hazel, light brown.

noccio 'lina [nottʃo'lina] *sf* (*anche:* ~ **americana**) peanut.

'nocciolo ['nɔttʃolo] *sm* (*di frutto*) stone; (*fig*) heart, core; [not'tʃɔlo] (*albero*) hazel.

'noce ['notʃe] *sm* (*albero*) walnut tree ♦ *sf* (*frutto*) walnut; **una** ~ **di burro** (*CUC*) a knob of butter (*BRIT*), a dab of butter (*US*); ~ **di cocco** coconut; ~ **moscata** nutmeg.

noce 'pesca, sche [notʃe'pɛska] *sf* nectarine.

no 'cevo *etc* [no'tʃevo] *vb vedi* **nuocere.**

noci 'uto [no'tʃuto] *pp di* **nuocere.**

no 'civo, a [no'tʃivo] *ag* harmful, noxious.

'nocqui *etc vb vedi* **nuocere.**

'nodo *sm* (*di cravatta, legname, NAUT*) knot; (*AUT, FERR*) junction; (*MED, ASTR, BOT*) node; (*fig: legame*) bond, tie; (: *punto centrale*) heart, crux; **avere un** ~ **alla gola** to have a lump in one's throat; **tutti i** ~**i vengono al pettine** (*proverbio*) your sins will find you out.

no'doso, a *ag* (*tronco*) gnarled.

'nodulo *sm* (*ANAT, BOT*) nodule.

no-'global [no'global] *ag inv* anti-globalization *cpd*.

'noi *pron* (*soggetto*) we; (*oggetto: per dare rilievo, con preposizione*) us; ~ **stessi(e)** we ourselves; (*oggetto*) ourselves; **da** ~ (*nel nostro paese*) in our country, where we come from; (*a casa nostra*) at our house.

'noia *sf* boredom; (*disturbo, impaccio*) bother *no pl*, trouble *no pl*; **avere qn/qc a** ~ not to like sb/sth; **mi è venuto a** ~ I'm tired of it; **dare** ~ **a** to annoy; **avere delle** ~**e con qn** to have trouble with sb.

noi'altri *pron* we.

noi'oso, a *ag* boring; (*fastidioso*) annoying, troublesome.

noleggi'are [noled'dʒare] *vt* (*prendere a noleggio*) to hire (*BRIT*), rent; (*dare a noleggio*) to hire out (*BRIT*), rent out; (*aereo, nave*) to charter.

noleggia'tore, 'trice [noleddʒa'tore] *sm/f* hirer (*BRIT*), renter; charterer.

no'leggio [no'leddʒo] *sm* hire (*BRIT*), rental; charter.

no'lente *ag*: **volente o** ~ whether one likes it or not, willy-nilly.

'nolo *sm* hire (*BRIT*), rental; charter; (*per trasporto merci*) freight; **prendere/dare a** ~ **qc** to hire/hire out sth (*BRIT*), rent/rent out sth.

'nomade *ag* nomadic ♦ *sm/f* nomad.

noma'dismo *sm* nomadism.

'nome *sm* name; (*LING*) noun; **in** *o* **a** ~ **di** in the name of; **di** *o* **per** ~ (*chiamato*) called, named; **conoscere qn di** ~ to know sb by name; **fare il** ~ **di qn** to name sb; **faccia pure il mio** ~ feel free to mention my name; ~ **d'arte** stage name; ~ **di battesimo** Christian name; ~ **depositato** trade name; ~ **di famiglia** surname; ~ **da ragazza** maiden name; ~ **da sposata** married name.

no'mea *sf* notoriety.

nomencla'tura *sf* nomenclature.

nomenkla'tura *sf* (*di partito, stato*) nomenklatura.

no'mignolo [no'miɲɲolo] *sm* nickname.

'nomina *sf* appointment.

nomi'nale *ag* nominal; (*LING*) noun *cpd*.

nomi'nare *vt* to name; (*eleggere*) to appoint; (*citare*) to mention; **non l'ho mai sentito** ~ I've never heard of it (*o* him).

nomina'tivo, a *ag* (*intestato: titolo*) registered; (: *libretto*) personal; (*LING*) nominative ♦ *sm* (*nome*) name; (*LING*) nominative; **elenco** ~ list of names.

non *av* not ♦ *prefisso* non-; **grazie —** ~ **c'è di**

che thank you — don't mention it; **i** ~ **credenti** the unbelievers; *vedi anche* **affatto, appena** *etc.*

nonché [non'ke] *cong* (*tanto più, tanto meno*) let alone; (*e inoltre*) as well as.

nonconfor'mista, i, e *ag, sm/f* nonconformist.

noncu'rante *ag*: ~ (**di**) careless (of), indifferent (to); **con fare** ~ with a nonchalant air.

noncu'ranza [nonku'rantsa] *sf* carelessness, indifference; **un'aria di** ~ a nonchalant air.

nondi'meno *cong* (*tuttavia*) however; (*nonostante*) nevertheless.

'nonno, a *sm/f* grandfather/mother; (*in senso più familiare*) grandma/grandpa; ~**i** *smpl* grandparents.

non'nulla *sm inv*: **un** ~ nothing, a trifle.

'nono, a *num* ninth.

nonos'tante *prep* in spite of, notwithstanding ♦ *cong* although, even though.

non plus 'ultra *sm inv*: **il** ~ (**di**) the last word (in).

nontiscordardimé *sm inv* (*BOT*) forget-me-not.

nord *sm* north ♦ *ag inv* north; (*regione*) northern; **verso** ~ north, northwards; **l'America del N**~ North America.

nor'dest *sm* north-east.

'nordico, a, ci, che *ag* nordic, northern European.

nor'dista, i, e *ag, sm/f* Yankee.

nor'dovest *sm* north-west.

Norim'berga *sf* Nuremberg.

'norma *sf* (*principio*) norm; (*regola*) regulation, rule; (*consuetudine*) custom, rule; **di** ~ normally; **a** ~ **di legge** according to law, as laid down by law; **al di sopra della** ~ above average, above the norm; **per sua** ~ **e regola** for your information; **proporsi una** ~ **di vita** to set o.s. rules to live by; ~**e di sicurezza** safety regulations; ~**e per l'uso** instructions for use.

nor'male *ag* normal.

normalità *sf* normality.

normaliz'zare [normalid'dzare] *vt* to normalize, bring back to normal.

normal'mente *av* normally.

Norman'dia *sf*: **la** ~ Normandy.

nor'manno, a *ag, sm/f* Norman.

norma'tivo, a *ag* normative ♦ *sf* regulations *pl*.

norve'gese [norve'dʒese] *ag, sm/f, sm* Norwegian.

Nor'vegia [nor'vɛdʒa] *sf*: **la** ~ Norway.

noso'comio *sm* hospital.

nostal'gia [nostal'dʒia] *sf* (*di casa, paese*) homesickness; (*del passato*) nostalgia.

nos'talgico, a, ci, che [nos'taldʒiko] *ag* homesick; nostalgic ♦ *sm/f* (*POL*) *person who hopes for the return of Fascism.*

nos'trano, a *ag* local; (*pianta, frutta*) home-produced.

'nostro, a *det*: **il(la)** ~**(a)** *etc* our ♦ *pron*: **il(la)** ~**(a)** *etc* ours ♦ *sm*: **abbiamo speso del** ~ we spent our own money ♦ *sf*: **la** ~**a** (*opinione*) our view; **i** ~**i** our family; our own people; **è dei** ~**i** he's one of us; **è dalla** ~**a** (*parte*) he's on our side; **anche noi abbiamo avuto le** ~**e** (*disavventure*) we've had our problems too; **alla** ~**a!** (*brindisi*) to us!

nos'tromo *sm* boatswain.

'nota *sf* (*segno*) mark; (*comunicazione scritta, MUS*) note; (*fattura*) bill; (*elenco*) list; **prendere** ~ **di qc** to note sth, make a note of sth, write sth down; (*fig: fare attenzione*) to note sth, take note of sth; **degno di** ~ noteworthy, worthy of note; ~**e caratteristiche** distinguishing marks *o* features; ~**e a piè di pagina** footnotes.

no'tabile *ag* notable; (*persona*) important ♦ *sm* prominent citizen.

no'taio *sm* notary.

no'tare *vt* (*segnare: errori*) to mark; (*registrare*) to note (down), write down; (*rilevare, osservare*) to note, notice; **farsi** ~ to get o.s. noticed.

nota'rile *ag*: **atto** ~ legal document (*authorized by a notary*); **studio** ~ notary's office.

notazi'one [notat'tsjone] *sf* (*MUS*) notation.

no'tevole *ag* (*talento*) notable, remarkable; (*peso*) considerable.

no'tifica, che *sf* notification.

notifi'care *vt* (*DIR*): ~ **qc a qn** to notify sb of sth, give sb notice of sth.

notificazi'one [notifikat'tsjone] *sf* notification.

no'tizia [no'tittsja] *sf* (*piece of*) news *sg*; (*informazione*) piece of information; ~**e** *sfpl* news *sg*; information *sg*.

notizi'ario [notit'tsjarjo] *sm* (*RADIO, TV, STAMPA*) news *sg*.

'noto, a *ag* (well-)known.

notorietà *sf* fame; notoriety.

no'torio, a *ag* well-known; (*peg*) notorious.

not'tambulo, a *sm/f* night-bird (*fig*).

not'tata *sf* night.

'notte *sf* night; **di** ~ at night; (*durante la* ~) in the night, during the night; **questa** ~ (*passata*) last night; (*che viene*) tonight; **nella** ~ **dei tempi** in the mists of time;

come va? — **peggio che andar di** ~ how are things? — worse than ever; ~ **bianca** sleepless night.

notte'tempo *av* at night; during the night.

'nottola *sf* (*ZOOL*) noctule.

not'turno, a *ag* nocturnal; (*servizio, guardiano*) night *cpd* ♦ *sf* (*SPORT*) evening fixture (*BRIT*) *o* match.

nov. *abbr* (= *novembre*) Nov.

no'vanta *num* ninety.

novan'tenne *ag, sm/f* ninety-year-old.

novan'tesimo, a *num* ninetieth.

novan'tina *sf*: **una** ~ (**di**) about ninety.

'nove *num* nine.

novecen'tesco, a, schi, sche [novetʃen'tesko] *ag* twentieth-century.

nove'cento [nove'tʃɛnto] *num* nine hundred ♦ *sm*: **il N**~ the twentieth century.

no'vella *sf* (*LETTERATURA*) short story.

novel'lino, a *ag* (*pivello*) green, inexperienced.

novel'lista, i, e *sm/f* short-story writer.

novel'listica *sf* (*arte*) short-story writing; (*insieme di racconti*) short stories *pl*.

no'vello, a *ag* (*piante, patate*) new; (*insalata, verdura*) early; (*sposo*) newly-married.

no'vembre *sm* November; *per fraseologia vedi* **luglio**.

novem'brino, a *ag* November *cpd*.

nove'mila *num* nine thousand.

noven'nale *ag* (*che dura 9 anni*) nine-year *cpd*; (*ogni 9 anni*) nine-yearly.

novi'lunio *sm* (*ASTR*) new moon.

novità *sf inv* novelty; (*innovazione*) innovation; (*cosa originale, insolita*) something new; (*notizia*) (piece of) news *sg*; **le** ~ **della moda** the latest fashions.

novizi'ato [novit'tsjato] *sm* (*REL*) novitiate; (*tirocinio*) apprenticeship.

no'vizio, a [no'vittsjo] *sm/f* (*REL*) novice; (*tirocinante*) beginner, apprentice.

nozi'one [not'tsjone] *sf* notion, idea; ~**i** *sfpl* (*rudimenti*) basic knowledge *sg*, rudiments.

nozio'nismo [nottsjo'nizmo] *sm* superficial knowledge.

nozio'nistico, a, ci, che [nottsjo'nistiko] *ag* superficial.

'nozze ['nɔttse] *sfpl* wedding *sg*, marriage *sg*; ~ **d'argento/d'oro** silver/golden wedding *sg*.

ns. *abbr* (*COMM*) = **nostro**.

NU *sigla* = *Nuoro*.

N.U. *sigla* (= *Nazioni Unite*) UN.

'nube *sf* cloud.

nubi'fragio [nubi'fradʒo] *sm* cloudburst.

'nubile *ag* (*donna*) unmarried, single.

'nuca, che *sf* nape of the neck.

nucle 'are *ag* nuclear ♦ *sm*: **il** ~ nuclear energy.

'nucleo *sm* nucleus; (*gruppo*) team, unit, group; (*MIL, POLIZIA*) squad; ~ **antidroga** anti-drugs squad; **il** ~ **familiare** the family unit.

nu 'dismo *sm* nudism.

nu 'dista, i, e *sm/f* nudist.

nudità *sf inv* nudity, nakedness; (*di paesaggio*) bareness ♦ *sfpl* (*parti nude del corpo*) nakedness *sg*.

'nudo, a *ag* (*persona*) bare, naked, nude; (*membra*) bare, naked; (*montagna*) bare ♦ *sm* (*ARTE*) nude; **a occhio** ~ to the naked eye; **a piedi** ~**i** barefoot; **mettere a** ~ (*cuore, verità*) to lay bare; **gli ha detto** ~ **e crudo che** ... he told him bluntly that ....

'nugolo *sm*: **un** ~ **di** a whole host of.

'nulla *pron, av* = **niente** ♦ *sm*: **il** ~ nothing; **svanire nel** ~ to vanish into thin air; **basta un** ~ **per farlo arrabbiare** he gets annoyed over the slightest thing.

nulla 'osta *sm inv* authorization.

nullate 'nente *ag*: **essere** ~ to own nothing ♦ *sm/f* person with no property.

nullità *sf inv* nullity; (*persona*) nonentity.

'nullo, a *ag* useless, worthless; (*DIR*) null (and void); (*SPORT*): **incontro** ~ draw.

nume 'rale *ag, sm* numeral.

nume 'rare *vt* to number.

numera 'tore *sm* (*MAT*) numerator; (*macchina*) numbering device.

numerazi 'one [numerat'tsjone] *sf* numbering; (*araba, decimale*) notation.

nu 'merico, a, ci, che *ag* numerical.

'numero *sm* number; (*romano, arabo*) numeral; (*di spettacolo*) act, turn; **dare i** ~**i** (*farneticare*) not to be all there; **tanto per fare** ~ **invitiamo anche lui** why don't we invite him to make up the numbers?; **ha tutti i** ~**i per riuscire** he's got what it takes to succeed; **che** ~ **tuo fratello!** your brother is a real character!; ~ **civico** house number; ~ **chiuso** (*UNIVERSITÀ*) selective entry system; ~ **doppio** (*di rivista*) issue with supplement; ~ **di scarpe** size of shoe; ~ **verde** (*TEL*) ≈ Freephone ®.

nume 'roso, a *ag* numerous, many; (*folla, famiglia*) large.

numis 'matica *sf* numismatics *sg*, coin collecting.

'nunzio ['nuntsjo] *sm* (*REL*) nuncio.

nu 'occio *etc* ['nwɔttʃo] *vb vedi* **nuocere**.

nu 'ocere ['nwɔtʃere] *vi*: ~ **a** to harm, damage; **il tentar non nuoce** (*proverbio*) there's no harm in trying.

nuoci 'uto, a [nwo'tʃuto] *pp di* **nuocere**.

nu 'ora *sf* daughter-in-law.

nuo 'tare *vi* to swim; (*galleggiare: oggetti*) to float; ~ **a rana/sul dorso** to do the breast stroke/backstroke.

nuo 'tata *sf* swim.

nuota 'tore, 'trice *sm/f* swimmer.

nu 'oto *sm* swimming.

nu 'ova *sf vedi* **nuovo**.

nuova 'mente *av* again.

Nu 'ova York *sf* New York.

Nu 'ova Ze 'landa [-dze'landa] *sf*: **la** ~ New Zealand.

nu 'ovo, a *ag* new ♦ *sf* (*notizia*) (piece of) news *sg*; **come** ~ as good as new; **di** ~ again; **fino a** ~ **ordine** until further notice; **il suo volto non mi è** ~ I know his face; **rimettere a** ~ (*cosa, macchina*) to do up like new; **anno** ~, **vita** ~**a**! it's time to turn over a new leaf!; ~ **fiammante** *o* **di zecca** brand-new; **la N**~**a Guinea** New Guinea; **la N**~**a Inghilterra** New England; **la N**~**a Scozia** Nova Scotia.

nu 'trice [nu'tritʃe] *sf* wet nurse.

nutri 'ente *ag* nutritious, nourishing; (*crema, balsamo*) nourishing.

nutri 'mento *sm* food, nourishment.

nu 'trire *vt* to feed; (*fig: sentimenti*) to harbour (*BRIT*), harbor (*US*), nurse.

nutri 'tivo, a *ag* nutritional; (*alimento*) nutritious.

nu 'trito, a *ag* (*numeroso*) large; (*fitto*) heavy; **ben/mal** ~ well/poorly fed.

nutrizi 'one [nutrit'tsjone] *sf* nutrition.

'nuvolo, a *ag* cloudy ♦ *sf* cloud.

nuvolosità *sf* cloudiness.

nuvo 'loso, a *ag* cloudy.

nuzi 'ale [nut'tsjale] *ag* nuptial; wedding *cpd*.

'nylon ['nailən] *sm* nylon.

O o

O, o [ɔ] *sf o m inv* (*lettera*) O, o; ~ **come Otranto** ≈ O for Oliver (*BRIT*), O for Oboe (*US*).

o *cong* (*dav V spesso* **od**) or; ~ ... ~ either ... or; ~ **l'uno** ~ **l'altro** either (of them); ~ **meglio** or rather.

O. *abbr* (= *ovest*) W.

'oasi *sf inv* oasis.

obbedi 'ente *etc vedi* **ubbidiente** *etc*.

obbiet 'tare *etc vedi* **obiettare** *etc*.

obbli'gare *vt* (*costringere*): ~ qn a fare to force *o* oblige sb to do; (*DIR*) to bind; ~rsi *vr*: ~rsi a fare to undertake to do; ~rsi per qn (*DIR*) to stand surety for sb, act as guarantor for sb.

obbliga'tissimo, a *ag* (*ringraziamento*): ~! much obliged!

obbli'gato, a *ag* (*costretto, grato*) obliged; (*percorso, tappa*) set, fixed; passaggio ~ (*fig*) essential requirement.

obbliga'torio, a *ag* compulsory, obligatory.

obbligazi'one [obbligat'tsjone] *sf* obligation; (*COMM*) bond, debenture; ~ dello Stato government bond; ~i convertibili convertible loan stock, convertible debentures.

obbligazio'nista, i, e [obbligattsjo'nista] *smf* bond-holder.

'obbligo, ghi *sm* obligation; (*dovere*) duty; avere l'~ di fare, essere nell'~ di fare to be obliged to do; essere d'~ (*discorso, applauso*) to be called for; avere degli ~ghi con *o* verso qn to be under an obligation to sb, be indebted to sb; le formalità d'~ the necessary formalities.

obb.mo *abbr* = obbligatissimo.

ob'brobrio *sm* disgrace; (*fig*) mess, eyesore.

obe'lisco, schi *sm* obelisk.

obe'rato, a *ag*: ~ di (*lavoro*) overloaded *o* overburdened with; (*debiti*) crippled with.

obesità *sf* obesity.

o'beso, a *ag* obese.

obiet'tare *vt*: ~ che to object that; ~ su qc to object to sth, raise objections concerning sth.

obiettiva'mente *av* objectively.

obiettività *sf* objectivity.

obiet'tivo, a *ag* objective ♦ *sm* (*OTTICA, FOT*) lens *sg*, objective; (*MIL, fig*) objective.

obiet'tore *sm* objector; ~ di coscienza conscientious objector.

obiezi'one [objet'tsjone] *sf* objection.

obi'torio *sm* morgue.

o'bliquo, a *ag* oblique; (*inclinato*) slanting; (*fig*) devious, underhand; sguardo ~ sidelong glance.

oblite'rare *vt* (*francobollo*) to cancel; (*biglietto*) to stamp.

oblitera'trice [oblitera'tritʃe] *sf* (*anche*: macchina ~) cancelling machine; stamping machine.

oblò *sm inv* porthole.

o'blungo, a, ghi, ghe *ag* oblong.

'oboe *sm* oboe.

'obolo *sm* (*elemosina*) (small) offering, mite.

obsole'scenza [obsoleʃ'ʃentsa] *sf* (*ECON*) obsolescence.

obso'leto, a *ag* obsolete.

OC *abbr* (= onde corte) SW.

'oca, *pl* 'oche *sf* goose.

o'caggine [o'kaddʒine] *sf* silliness, stupidity.

occasio'nale *ag* (*incontro*) chance; (*cliente, guadagni*) casual, occasional.

occasi'one *sf* (*caso favorevole*) opportunity; (*causa, motivo, circostanza*) occasion; (*COMM*) bargain; all'~ should the need arise; alla prima ~ at the first opportunity; d'~ (*a buon prezzo*) bargain *cpd*; (*usato*) secondhand.

occhi'aia [ok'kjaja] *sf* eye socket; ~e *sfpl* (*sotto gli occhi*) shadows (under the eyes).

occhi'ali [ok'kjali] *smpl* glasses, spectacles; ~ da sole sunglasses.

occhi'ata [ok'kjata] *sf* look, glance; dare un'~ a to have a look at.

occhieggi'are [okkjed'dʒare] *vi* (*apparire qua e là*) to peep (out).

occhi'ello [ok'kjɛllo] *sm* buttonhole; (*asola*) eyelet.

'occhio ['ɔkkjo] *sm* eye; ~! careful!, watch out!; a ~ nudo with the naked eye; a quattr'~i privately, in private; avere ~ to have a good eye; chiudere un ~ (su) (*fig*) to turn a blind eye (to), shut one's eyes (to); costare un ~ della testa to cost a fortune; dare all'~ *o* nell'~ a qn to catch sb's eye; fare l'~ a qc to get used to sth; tenere d'~ qn to keep an eye on sb; vedere di buon/mal ~ qc to look favourably/unfavourably on sth.

occhio'lino [okkjo'lino] *sm*: fare l'~ a qn to wink at sb.

occiden'tale [ottʃiden'tale] *ag* western ♦ *smf* Westerner.

occi'dente [ottʃi'dente] *sm* west; (*POL*): l'O~ the West; a ~ in the west.

oc'cipite [ot'tʃipite] *sm* back of the head, occiput (*ANAT*).

oc'cludere *vt* to block.

occlusi'one *sf* blockage, obstruction.

oc'cluso, a *pp di* occludere.

occor'rente *ag* necessary ♦ *sm* all that is necessary.

occor'renza [okkor'rentsa] *sf* necessity, need; all'~ in case of need.

oc'correre *vi* to be needed, be required ♦ *vb impers*: occorre farlo it must be done; occorre che tu parta you must leave, you'll have to leave; mi occorrono i soldi I need the money.

oc'corso, a *pp di* occorrere.

occulta'mento *sm* concealment.

occul'tare *vt* to hide, conceal.

oc'culto, a *ag* hidden, concealed; (*scienze, forze*) occult.

occu'pante *sm/f* (*di casa*) occupier, occupant; ~ **abusivo** squatter.

occu'pare *vt* to occupy; (*manodopera*) to employ; (*ingombrare*) to occupy, take up; ~**rsi** *vr* to occupy o.s., keep o.s. busy; (*impiegarsi*) to get a job; ~**rsi di** (*interessarsi*) to take an interest in; (*prendersi cura di*) to look after, take care of.

occu'pato, a *ag* (*MIL, POL*) occupied; (*persona: affaccendato*) busy; (*posto, sedia*) taken; (*toilette, TEL*) engaged.

occupazio'nale [okkupattsjo'nale] *ag* employment *cpd*, of employment.

occupazi'one [okkupat'tsjone] *sf* occupation; (*impiego, lavoro*) job; (*ECON*) employment.

Oce'ania [otʃe'anja] *sf*: **l'**~ Oceania.

o'ceano [o'tʃɛano] *sm* ocean.

'ocra *sf* ochre.

'OCSE *sigla f* (= *Organizzazione per la Cooperazione e lo Sviluppo Economico*) OECD (= *Organization for Economic Cooperation and Development*).

ocu'lare *ag* ocular, eye *cpd*; **testimone** ~ eye witness.

ocula'tezza [okula'tettsa] *sf* caution; shrewdness.

ocu'lato, a *ag* (*attento*) cautious, prudent; (*accorto*) shrewd.

ocu'lista, i, e *sm/f* eye specialist, oculist.

od *cong vedi* **o**.

'ode *sf* ode.

'ode *etc vb vedi* **udire**.

odi'are *vt* to hate, detest.

odi'erno, a *ag* today's, of today; (*attuale*) present; **in data** ~**a** (*formale*) today.

'odio *sm* hatred; **avere in** ~ **qc/qn** to hate *o* detest sth/sb.

odi'oso, a *ag* hateful, odious; **rendersi** ~ **(a)** to make o.s. unpopular (with).

'odo *etc vb vedi* **udire**.

odontoi'atra, i, e *sm/f* dentist, dental surgeon.

odontoia'tria *sf* dentistry.

odo'rare *vt* (*annusare*) to smell; (*profumare*) to perfume, scent ♦ *vi*: ~ **(di)** to smell (of).

odo'rato *sm* sense of smell.

o'dore *sm* smell; **gli** ~**i** *smpl* (*CUC*) (aromatic) herbs; **sentire** ~ **di qc** to smell sth; **morire in** ~ **di santità** (*REL*) to die in the odour (*BRIT*) *o* odor (*US*) of sanctity.

odo'roso, a *ag* sweet-smelling.

of'fendere *vt* to offend; (*violare*) to break, violate; (*insultare*) to insult; (*ferire*) to hurt;

~**rsi** *vr* (*con senso reciproco*) to insult one another; (*risentirsi*): ~**rsi (di)** to take offence (at), be offended (by).

offen'sivo, a *ag, sf* offensive.

offen'sore *sm* offender; (*MIL*) aggressor.

offe'rente *sm* (*in aste*): **al migliore** ~ to the highest bidder.

of'ferto, a *pp di* **offrire** ♦ *sf* offer; (*donazione, anche REL*) offering; (*in gara d'appalto*) tender; (*in aste*) bid; (*ECON*) supply; **fare un'**~**a** to make an offer; (*per appalto*) to tender; (*ad un'asta*) to bid; ~**a pubblica d'acquisto (OPA)** takeover bid; ~**a pubblica di vendita (OPV)** public offer for sale; ~**a reale** tender; "~**e d'impiego**" (*STAMPA*) "situations vacant" (*BRIT*), "help wanted" (*US*).

of'feso, a *pp di* **offendere** ♦ *ag* offended; (*fisicamente*) hurt, injured ♦ *sm/f* offended party ♦ *sf* insult, affront; (*MIL*) attack; (*DIR*) offence (*BRIT*), offense (*US*); **essere** ~ **con qn** to be annoyed with sb; **parte** ~**a** (*DIR*) plaintiff.

offi'ciare [offi'tʃare] *vi* (*REL*) to officiate.

offi'cina [offi'tʃina] *sf* workshop.

of'frire *vt* to offer; ~**rsi** *vr* (*proporsi*) to offer (o.s.), volunteer; (*occasione*) to present itself; (*esporsi*): ~**rsi a** to expose o.s. to; **ti offro da bere** I'll buy you a drink; "**offresi posto di segretaria**" "secretarial vacancy", "vacancy for secretary"; "**segretaria offresi**" "secretary seeks post".

offus'care *vt* to obscure, darken; (*fig: intelletto*) to dim, cloud; (: *fama*) to obscure, overshadow; ~**rsi** *vr* to grow dark; to cloud, grow dim; to be obscured.

of'talmico, a, ci, che *ag* ophthalmic.

oggettività [oddʒettivi'ta] *sf* objectivity.

ogget'tivo, a [oddʒet'tivo] *ag* objective.

og'getto [od'dʒɛtto] *sm* object; (*materia, argomento*) subject (matter); (*in lettere commerciali*): ~ **...** re **...**; **essere** ~ **di** (*critiche, controversia*) to be the subject of; (*odio, pietà etc*) to be the object of; **essere** ~ **di scherno** to be a laughing stock; **in** ~ **a quanto detto** (*in lettere*) as regards the matter mentioned above; ~**i preziosi** valuables, articles of value; ~**i smarriti** lost property *sg* (*BRIT*), lost and found *sg* (*US*).

'oggi ['ɔddʒi] *av, sm* today; ~ **stesso** today, this very day; ~ **come** ~ at present, as things stand; **dall'** ~ **al domani** from one day to the next; **a tutt'**~ up till now, till today; **le spese a tutt'**~ **sono ...** expenses to date are ...; ~ **a otto** a week today.

oggigi'orno [oddʒi'dʒorno] *av* nowadays.

o'giva [o'dʒiva] *sf* ogive, pointed arch.

OGM [ɔdʒi'ɛmme] *sigla mpl* (= *organismi geneticamente modificati*) GMO (= *genetically modified organisms*).

'ogni ['oɲɲi] *det* every, each; (*tutti*) all; (*con valore distributivo*) every; ~ **uomo è mortale** all men are mortal; **viene** ~ **due giorni** he comes every two days; ~ **cosa** everything; **ad** ~ **costo** at all costs, at any price; **in** ~ **luogo** everywhere; ~ **tanto** every so often; ~ **volta che** every time that.

Ognis'santi [oɲɲis'santi] *sm* All Saints' Day.

o'gnuno [oɲ'ɲuno] *pron* everyone, everybody.

'ohi *escl* oh!; (*esprimente dolore*) ow!

ohimè *escl* oh dear!

'OIL *sigla f* (= *Organizzazione Internazionale del Lavoro*) ILO.

OL *abbr* (= *onde lunghe*) LW.

O'landa *sf*: **l'**~ Holland.

olan'dese *ag* Dutch ♦ *sm* (*LING*) Dutch ♦ *sm/f* Dutchman/woman; **gli O**~**i** the Dutch.

ole'andro *sm* oleander.

ole'ato, a *ag*: **carta** ~**a** greaseproof paper (*BRIT*), wax paper (*US*).

oleo'dotto *sm* oil pipeline.

ole'oso, a *ag* oily; (*che contiene olio*) oil *cpd*.

o'lezzo [o'leddzo] *sm* fragrance.

ol'fatto *sm* sense of smell.

oli'are *vt* to oil.

olia'tore *sm* oil can, oiler.

oli'era *sf* oil cruet.

oligar'chia [oligar'kia] *sf* oligarchy.

olim'piadi *sfpl* Olympic Games.

o'limpico, a, ci, che *ag* Olympic.

'olio *sm* oil; (*PITTURA*): **un (quadro a)** ~ **an** oil painting; **sott'**~ (*CUC*) in oil; ~ **di fegato di merluzzo** cod liver oil; ~ **d'oliva** olive oil; ~ **santo** holy oil; ~ **di semi** vegetable oil; ~ **solare** suntan oil.

o'liva *sf* olive.

oli'vastro, a *ag* olive(-coloured) (*BRIT*), olive(-colored) (*US*); (*carnagione*) sallow.

oli'veto *sm* olive grove.

o'livo *sm* olive tree.

'olmo *sm* elm.

olo'causto *sm* holocaust.

OLP *sigla f* (= *Organizzazione per la Liberazione della Palestina*) PLO.

oltraggi'are [oltrad'dʒare] *vt* to offend, insult.

ol'traggio [ol'traddʒo] *sm* offence (*BRIT*), offense (*US*), insult; (*DIR*): ~ **al pudore** indecent behaviour (*BRIT*) *o* behavior (*US*); ~ **alla corte** contempt of court.

oltraggi'oso, a [oltrad'dʒoso] *ag* offensive.

ol'tralpe *av* beyond the Alps.

ol'tranza [ol'trantsa] *sf*: **a** ~ to the last, to the bitter end; **sciopero ad** ~ all-out strike.

oltran'zismo [oltran'tsizmo] *sm* (*POL*) extremism.

oltran'zista, i, e [oltran'tsista] *sm/f* (*POL*) extremist.

'oltre *av* (*più in là*) further; (*di più: aspettare*) longer, more ♦ *prep* (*di là da*) beyond, over, on the other side of; (*più di*) more than, over; (*in aggiunta a*) besides; (*eccetto*): ~ **a** except, apart from; ~ **a tutto** on top of all that.

oltrecor'tina *av* behind the Iron Curtain; **paesi d'**~ Iron Curtain countries.

oltre'manica *av* across the Channel.

oltre'mare *av* overseas.

oltre'modo *av* extremely, greatly.

oltreo'ceano [oltreo'tʃeano] *av* overseas ♦ *sm*: **paesi d'**~ overseas countries.

oltrepas'sare *vt* to go beyond, exceed.

oltre'tomba *sm inv*: **l'**~ the hereafter.

OM *abbr* (= *onde medie*) MW; (*MIL*) – *ospedale militare*.

o'maggio [o'maddʒo] *sm* (*dono*) gift; (*segno di rispetto*) homage, tribute; ~**i** *smpl* (*complimenti*) respects; **in** ~ (*copia, biglietto*) complimentary; **rendere** ~ **a** to pay homage *o* tribute to; **presentare i propri** ~**i a qn** (*formale*) to pay one's respects to sb.

'Oman *sm*: **l'**~ Oman.

ombeli'cale *ag* umbilical.

ombe'lico, chi *sm* navel.

'ombra *sf* (*zona non assolata, fantasma*) shade; (*sagoma scura*) shadow ♦ *ag inv*: **bandiera** ~ flag of convenience; **governo** ~ (*POL*) shadow cabinet; **sedere all'**~ to sit in the shade; **nell'**~ (*tramare, agire*) secretly; **restare nell'**~ (*fig: persona*) to remain in obscurity; **senza** ~ **di dubbio** without the shadow of a doubt.

ombreggi'are [ombred'dʒare] *vt* to shade.

om'brello *sm* umbrella; ~ **da sole** parasol, sunshade.

ombrel'lone *sm* beach umbrella.

om'bretto *sm* eyeshadow.

om'broso, a *ag* shady, shaded; (*cavallo*) nervous, skittish; (*persona*) touchy, easily offended.

ome'lette [ɔmə'lɛt] *sf inv* omelet(te).

ome'lia *sf* (*REL*) homily, sermon.

ome'opata *sm/f* hom(o)eopath.

omeopa'tia *sf* hom(o)eopathy.

omeo'patico, a, ci, che *ag* hom(o)eopathic ♦ *sm* hom(o)eopath.

omertà *sf* conspiracy of silence.

o'messo, a pp di omettere.

o'mettere vt to omit, leave out; ~ di fare to omit o fail to do.

omi'cida, i, e [omi'tʃida] ag homicidal, murderous ♦ sm/f murderer/murderess.

omi'cidio [omi'tʃidjo] sm murder; ~ colposo (DIR) culpable homicide; ~ premeditato (DIR) murder.

o'misi etc vb vedi omettere.

omissi'one sf omission; reato d'~ criminal negligence; ~ di atti d'ufficio negligence (by a public employee); ~ di denuncia failure to report a crime; ~ di soccorso (DIR) failure to stop and give assistance.

omogeneiz'zato [omodʒeneid'dzato] sm baby food.

omo'geneo, a [omo'dʒɛneo] ag homogeneous.

omolo'gare vt (DIR) to approve, recognize; (ratificare) to ratify.

omologazi'one [omologat'tsjone] sf approval; ratification.

o'mologo, a, ghi, ghe ag homologous, corresponding ♦ sm/f opposite number.

o'monimo, a sm/f namesake ♦ sm (LING) homonym.

omosessu'ale ag, sm/f homosexual.

O.M.S. sigla f vedi Organizzazione Mondiale della Sanità.

On. abbr (POL) = onorevole.

'oncia, ce ['ontʃa] sf ounce.

'onda sf wave; mettere o mandare in ~ (RADIO, TV) to broadcast; andare in ~ (RADIO, TV) to go on the air; ~e corte/ medie/lunghe short/medium/long wave sg; l'~ verde (AUT) synchronized traffic lights pl.

on'data sf wave, billow; (fig) wave, surge; a ~e in waves; ~ di caldo heatwave; ~ di freddo cold spell o snap.

'onde cong (affinché: con il congiuntivo) so that, in order that; (: con l'infinito) so as to, in order to.

ondeggi'are [onded'dʒare] vi (acqua) to ripple; (muoversi sulle onde: barca) to rock, roll; (fig: muoversi come le onde, barcollare) to sway; (: essere incerto) to waver.

on'doso, a ag (moto) of the waves.

ondu'lato, a ag (capelli) wavy; (terreno) undulating; cartone ~ corrugated paper; lamiera ~a sheet of corrugated iron.

ondula'torio, a ag undulating; (FISICA) undulatory, wave cpd.

ondulazi'one [ondulat'tsjone] sf undulation; (acconciatura) wave.

one'rato, a ag: ~ di burdened with, loaded with.

'onere sm burden; ~ finanziario financial

charge; ~i fiscali taxes.

one'roso, a ag (fig) heavy, onerous.

onestà sf honesty.

onesta'mente av honestly; fairly; virtuously; (in verità) honestly, frankly.

o'nesto, a ag (probo, retto) honest; (giusto) fair; (casto) chaste, virtuous.

'onice ['ɔnitʃe] sf onyx.

o'nirico, a, ci, che ag dreamlike, dream cpd.

onnipo'tente ag omnipotent.

onnipre'sente ag omnipresent; (scherzoso) ubiquitous.

onnisci'ente [onniʃ'ʃɛnte] ag omniscient.

onniveg'gente [onnived'dʒɛnte] ag all-seeing.

ono'mastico, ci sm name day.

onomato'pea sf onomatopoeia.

onomato'peico, a, ci, che ag onomatopoeic.

ono'ranze [ono'rantse] sfpl honours (BRIT), honors (US).

ono'rare vt to honour (BRIT), honor (US); (far onore a) to do credit to; ~rsi vr: ~rsi di qc/di fare to feel hono(u)red by sth/to do.

ono'rario, a ag honorary ♦ sm fee.

onora'tissimo, a ag (in presentazioni): ~! delighted to meet you!

ono'rato, a ag (reputazione, famiglia, carriera) distinguished; essere ~ di fare qc to have the honour to do sth o of doing sth; ~ di conoscerla! (it is) a pleasure to meet you!

o'nore sm honour (BRIT), honor (US); in ~ di in hono(u)r of; fare gli ~i di casa to play host (o hostess); fare ~ a to hono(u)r; (pranzo) to do justice to; (famiglia) to be a credit to; farsi ~ to distinguish o.s.; posto d'~ place of hono(u)r; a onor del vero ... to tell the truth ....

ono'revole ag honourable (BRIT), honorable (US) ♦ sm/f (POL) ≈ Member of Parliament (BRIT), ≈ Congressman/ woman (US).

onorifi'cenza [onorifi'tʃentsa] sf honour (BRIT), honor (US); decoration.

ono'rifico, a, ci, che ag honorary.

'onta sf shame, disgrace; ad ~ di despite, notwithstanding.

on'tano sm alder.

'O.N.U. sigla f (= Organizzazione delle Nazioni Unite) UN, UNO.

'OPA sigla f vedi offerta pubblica d'acquisto.

o'paco, a, chi, che ag (vetro) opaque; (metallo) dull, matt.

o'pale sm o f opal.

'O.P.E.C. sigla f (= Organization of Petroleum Exporting Countries) OPEC.

'**opera** sf (gen) work; (azione rilevante) action, deed, work; (MUS) work; opus; (: melodramma) opera; (: teatro) opera house; (ente) institution, organization; **per ~ sua** thanks to him; **fare ~ di persuasione presso qn** to try to convince sb; **mettersi/essere all'~** to get down to/be at work; **~ d'arte** work of art; **~ buffa** comic opera; **~ lirica** (grand) opera; **~ pia** religious charity; **~e pubbliche (OO.PP.)** public works; **~e di restauro/di scavo** restoration/excavation work sg.

ope'raio, a ag working-class; workers'; (ZOOL: ape, formica) worker cpd ♦ sm/f worker; **classe ~a** working class; **~ di fabbrica** factory worker; **~ a giornata** day labourer (BRIT) o laborer (US); **~ specializzato** o **qualificato** skilled worker; **~ non specializzato** semi-skilled worker.

ope'rare vt to carry out, make; (MED) to operate on ♦ vi to operate, work; (rimedio) to act, work; (MED) to operate; **~rsi** vr to occur, take place; (MED) to have an operation; **~rsi d'appendicite** to have one's appendix out; **~ qn d'urgenza** to perform an emergency operation on sb.

opera'tivo, a ag operative, operating; **piano ~** (MIL) plan of operations.

ope'rato sm (comportamento) actions pl.

opera'tore, 'trice sm/f operator; (TV, CINE) cameraman; **aperto solo agli ~i** (COMM) open to the trade only; **~ di borsa** dealer on the stock exchange; **~ ecologico** refuse collector; **~ economico** agent, broker; **~ del suono** sound recordist; **~ turistico** tour operator.

opera'torio, a ag (MED) operating.

operazi'one [operat'tsjone] sf operation.

ope'retta sf (MUS) operetta, light opera.

operosità sf industry.

ope'roso, a ag industrious, hard-working.

opi'ficio [opi'fitʃo] sm factory, works pl.

opi'nabile ag (discutibile) debatable, questionable; **è ~** it is a matter of opinion.

opini'one sf opinion; **avere il coraggio delle proprie ~i** to have the courage of one's convictions; **l'~ pubblica** public opinion.

opinio'nista, i, e sm/f (political) columnist.

op là escl (per far saltare) hup!; (a bimbo che è caduto) upsy-daisy!

'**oppio** sm opium.

oppi'omane sm/f opium addict.

oppo'nente ag opposing ♦ sm/f opponent.

op'pongo etc vb vedi **opporre**.

op'porre vt to oppose; **opporsi** vr: **opporsi (a qc)** to oppose (sth); to object (to sth); **~ resistenza/un rifiuto** to offer resistance/to

refuse.

opportu'nista, i, e sm/f opportunist.

opportunità sf inv opportunity; (convenienza) opportuneness, timeliness.

oppor'tuno, a ag timely, opportune; (giusto) right, appropriate; **a tempo ~** at the right o the appropriate time.

op'posi etc vb vedi **opporre**.

opposi'tore, 'trice sm/f opposer, opponent.

opposi'zione [oppozit'tsjone] sf opposition; (DIR) objection; **essere in netta ~** (idee, opinioni) to clash, be in complete opposition; **fare ~ a qn/qc** to oppose sb/sth.

op'posto, a pp di **opporre** ♦ ag opposite; (opinioni) conflicting ♦ sm opposite, contrary; **all'~** on the contrary.

oppressi'one sf oppression.

oppres'sivo, a ag oppressive.

op'presso, a pp di **opprimere**.

oppres'sore sm oppressor.

oppri'mente ag (caldo, noia) oppressive; (persona) tiresome; (: deprimente) depressing.

op'primere vt (premere, gravare) to weigh down; (estenuare: sog: caldo) to suffocate, oppress; (tiranneggiare: popolo) to oppress.

oppu'gnare [oppuɲ'ɲare] vt (fig) to refute.

op'pure cong or (else).

op'tare vi: **~ per** (scegliere) to opt for, decide upon; (BORSA) to take (out) an option on.

'**optimum** sm inv optimum.

opu'lento, a ag (ricco) rich, wealthy, affluent; (: arredamento etc) opulent.

opu'lenza [opu'lɛntsa] sf (vedi ag) richness, wealth, affluence; opulence.

o'puscolo sm booklet, pamphlet.

OPV sigla f vedi **offerta pubblica di vendita**.

opzio'nale [optsjo'nale] ag optional.

opzi'one [op'tsjone] sf option.

OR sigla = Oristano.

'**ora** sf (60 minuti) hour; (momento) time ♦ av (adesso) now; (poco fa): **è uscito proprio ~** he's just gone out; (tra poco) presently, in a minute; (correlativo): **~ ... ~ ...** now ... now; **che ~ è?, che ~e sono?** what time is it?; **domani a quest'~** this time tomorrow; **non veder l'~ di fare** to long to do, look forward to doing; **fare le ~e piccole** to stay up till the early hours (of the morning) o the small hours; **è ~ di partire** it's time to go; **di buon' ~** early; **alla buon'~!** at last!; **~ legale** o **estiva** summer time (BRIT), daylight saving time (US); **~ locale** local time; **~ di pranzo** lunchtime; **~ di punta** (AUT) rush hour; **d'~ in avanti** o **poi** from now on; **or**

~ just now, a moment ago; ~ **come** ~ right now, at present; **10 anni or sono** 10 years ago.

o 'racolo sm oracle.

'orafo sm goldsmith.

o 'rale ag, sm oral.

oral 'mente av orally.

ora 'mai av = **ormai**.

o 'rario, a ag hourly; (fuso, segnale) time cpd; (velocità) per hour ♦ sm timetable, schedule; (di visite etc) hours pl, time(s pl); ~ **di apertura/chiusura** opening/closing time; ~ **di apertura degli sportelli** bank opening hours; ~ **elastico** o **flessibile** (INDUSTRIA) flexitime; ~ **ferroviario** railway timetable; ~ **di lavoro/d'ufficio** working/office hours.

o 'rata sf sea bream.

ora 'tore, 'trice sm/f speaker; orator.

ora 'torio, a ag oratorical ♦ sm (REL) oratory; (MUS) oratorio ♦ sf (arte) oratory.

orazi 'one [orat'tsjone] sf (REL) prayer; (discorso) speech, oration.

or 'bene cong so, well (then).

'orbita sf (ASTR, FISICA) orbit; (ANAT) (eye-) socket.

orbi 'tare vi to orbit.

'orbo, a ag blind.

'Orcadi sfpl: **le (isole)** ~ the Orkney Islands, the Orkneys.

or 'chestra [or'kɛstra] sf orchestra.

orches 'trale [orkes'trale] ag orchestral ♦ sm/f orchestra player.

orches 'trare [orkes'trare] vt to orchestrate; (fig) to stage-manage.

orchi 'dea [orki'dɛa] sf orchid.

'orcio ['ortʃo] sm jar.

'orco, chi sm ogre.

'orda sf horde.

or 'digno [or'diɲɲo] sm: ~ **esplosivo** explosive device.

ordi 'nale ag, sm ordinal.

ordina 'mento sm order, arrangement; (regolamento) regulations pl, rules pl; ~ **scolastico/giuridico** education/legal system.

ordi 'nanza [ordi'nantsa] sf (DIR, MIL) order; (AMM: decreto) decree; (persona: MIL) orderly, batman; **d'**~ (MIL) regulation cpd; **ufficiale d'**~ orderly; ~ **municipale** by(e)-law.

ordi 'nare vt (mettere in ordine) to arrange, organize; (COMM) to order; (prescrivere: medicina) to prescribe; (comandare): ~ **a qn di fare qc** to order o command sb to do sth; (REL) to ordain.

ordi 'nario, a ag (comune) ordinary; (grossolano) coarse, common ♦ sm

ordinary; (di università) full professor.

ordina 'tivo, a ag regulating, governing ♦ sm (COMM) order.

ordi 'nato, a ag tidy, orderly.

ordinazi 'one [ordinat'tsjone] sf (COMM) order; (REL) ordination; **fare un'**~ **di qc** to put in an order for sth, order sth; **eseguire qc su** ~ to make sth to order.

'ordine sm order; (carattere): **d'**~ **pratico** of a practical nature; **all'**~ (COMM: assegno) to order; **di prim'**~ first-class; **fino a nuovo** ~ until further notice; **essere in** ~ (documenti) to be in order; (persona, stanza) to be tidy; **mettere in** ~ to put in order, tidy (up); **richiamare all'**~ to call to order; **le forze dell'**~ the forces of law and order; ~ **d'acquisto** purchase order; **l'**~ **degli avvocati** ≈ the Bar; ~ **del giorno** (di seduta) agenda; (MIL) order of the day; **l'**~ **dei medici** ≈ the Medical Association; ~ **di pagamento** standing order (BRIT), automatic payment (US); **l'**~ **pubblico** law and order; ~**i (sacri)** (REL) holy orders.

or 'dire vt (fig) to plot, scheme.

or 'dito sm (di tessuto) warp.

orecchi 'abile [orek'kjabile] ag (canzone) catchy.

orec 'chino [orek'kino] sm earring.

o 'recchio [o'rekkjo], pl(f) **o 'recchie** sm (ANAT) ear; **avere** ~ to have a good ear (for music); **venire all'**~ **di qn** to come to sb's attention; **fare** ~**e da mercante (a)** to turn a deaf ear (to).

orecchi 'oni [orek'kjoni] smpl (MED) mumps sg.

o 'refice [o'refitʃe] sm goldsmith; jeweller (BRIT), jeweler (US).

orefice 'ria [orefitʃe'ria] sf (arte) goldsmith's art; (negozio) jeweller's (shop) (BRIT), jewelry store (US).

'orfano, a ag orphan(ed) ♦ sm/f orphan; ~ **di padre/madre** fatherless/motherless.

orfano 'trofio sm orphanage.

orga 'netto sm barrel organ; (fam: armonica a bocca) mouth organ; (: fisarmonica) accordion.

or 'ganico, a, ci, che ag organic ♦ sm personnel, staff.

organi 'gramma, i sm organization chart; (INFORM) computer flow chart.

orga 'nismo sm (BIOL) organism; (ANAT, AMM) body, organism.

orga 'nista, i, e sm/f organist.

organiz 'zare [organid'dzare] vt to organize; ~**rsi** vr to get organized.

organizza 'tivo, a [organiddza'tivo] ag organizational.

organizza 'tore, 'trice [organiddza'tore] ag

organizing ♦ sm/f organizer.
organizzazi'one [organiddzat'tsjone] sf (azione) organizing, arranging; (risultato) organization; **O~ Mondiale della Sanità (O.M.S.)** World Health Organization (WHO).
'organo sm organ; (di congegno) part; (portavoce) spokesman/woman, mouthpiece; **~i di trasmissione** (TECN) transmission (unit) sg.
or'gasmo sm (FISIOL) orgasm; (fig) agitation, anxiety.
'orgia, ge ['ɔrdʒa] sf orgy.
or'goglio [or'ɡoʎʎo] sm pride.
orgogli'oso, a [orɡoʎ'ʎoso] ag proud.
orien'tabile ag adjustable.
orien'tale ag (paese, regione) eastern; (tappeti, lingua, civiltà) oriental.
orienta'mento sm positioning; orientation; direction; **senso di ~** sense of direction; **perdere l'~** to lose one's bearings; **~ professionale** careers guidance.
orien'tare vt (situare) to position; (carta, bussola) to orientate; (fig) to direct; **~rsi** vr to find one's bearings; (fig: tendere) to tend, lean; (: indirizzarsi): **~rsi verso** to take up, go in for.
orienta'tivo, a ag indicative, for guidance; **a scopo ~** for guidance.
ori'ente sm east; **l'O~** the East, the Orient; **il Medio/l'Estremo O~** the Middle/Far East; **a ~** in the east.
ori'ficio [ori'fitʃo], **ori'fizio** [ori'fittsjo] sm (apertura) opening; (: di tubo) mouth; (ANAT) orifice.
o'rigano sm oregano.
origi'nale [oridʒi'nale] ag original; (bizzarro) eccentric ♦ sm original.
originalità [oridʒinali'ta] sf originality; eccentricity.
origi'nare [oridʒi'nare] vt to bring about, produce ♦ vi: **~ da** to arise o spring from.
origi'nario, a [oridʒi'narjo] ag original; **essere ~ di** to be a native of; (animale, pianta) to be indigenous to, be native to.
o'rigine [o'ridʒine] sf origin; **all'~** originally; **d'~ inglese** of English origin; **avere ~ da** to originate from; **dare ~ a** to give rise to.
origli'are [oriʎ'ʎare] vi: **~ (a)** to eavesdrop (on).
o'rina sf urine.
ori'nale sm chamberpot.
ori'nare vi to urinate ♦ vt to pass.
orina'toio sm (public) urinal.
ori'undo, a ag: **essere ~ di Milano** etc to be of Milanese etc extraction o origin

♦ sm/f person of foreign extraction o origin.
orizzon'tale [oriddzon'tale] ag horizontal.
oriz'zonte [orid'dzonte] sm horizon.
ORL sigla f (MED: = otorinolaringoiatria) ENT.
or'lare vt to hem.
orla'tura sf (azione) hemming no pl; (orlo) hem.
'orlo sm edge, border; (di recipiente) rim, brim; (di vestito etc) hem; **pieno fino all'~** full to the brim, brimful; **sull'~ della pazzia/della rovina** on the brink o verge of madness/ruin; **~ a giorno** hemstitch.
'orma sf (di persona) footprint; (di animale) track; (impronta, traccia) mark, trace; **seguire o calcare le ~e di qn** to follow in sb's footsteps.
or'mai av by now, by this time; (adesso) now; (quasi) almost, nearly.
ormeggi'are [ormed'dʒare] vt, **~rsi** vr (NAUT) to moor.
or'meggio [or'meddʒo] sm (atto) mooring no pl; (luogo) moorings pl; **posto d'~** berth.
ormo'nale ag hormonal; (disfunzione, cura) hormone cpd; **terapia ~** hormone therapy.
or'mone sm hormone.
ornamen'tale ag ornamental, decorative.
orna'mento sm ornament, decoration.
or'nare vt to adorn, decorate; **~rsi** vr: **~rsi (di)** to deck o.s. (out) (with).
or'nato, a ag ornate.
ornito'logia [ornitolo'dʒia] sf ornithology.
orni'tologo, a, gi, ghe sm/f ornithologist.
'oro sm gold; **d'~, in ~** gold cpd; **d'~** (colore, occasione) golden; (persona) marvellous (BRIT), marvelous (US); **un affare d'~** a real bargain; **prendere qc per ~ colato** to take sth as gospel (truth); **~ nero** black gold; **~ zecchino** pure gold.
orologe'ria [orolodʒe'ria] sf watchmaking no pl; watchmaker's (shop); clockmaker's (shop); **bomba a ~** time bomb.
orologi'aio [orolo'dʒajo] sm watchmaker; clockmaker.
oro'logio [oro'lodʒo] sm clock; (da tasca, da polso) watch; **~ biologico** biological clock; **~ da polso** wristwatch; **~ al quarzo** quartz watch; **~ a sveglia** alarm clock.
o'roscopo sm horoscope.
or'rendo, a ag (spaventoso) horrible, awful; (bruttissimo) hideous.
or'ribile ag horrible.
'orrido, a ag fearful, horrid.
orripi'lante ag hair-raising, horrifying.
or'rore sm horror; **avere in ~ qn/qc** to loathe o detest sb/sth; **mi fanno ~** I loathe o detest them.
orsacchi'otto [orsak'kjɔtto] sm teddy bear.
'orso sm bear; **~ bruno/bianco** brown/polar

bear.

orsù *escl* come now!

or 'taggio [or'taddʒo] *sm* vegetable.

or 'tensia *sf* hydrangea.

or 'tica, che *sf* (stinging) nettle.

orti 'caria *sf* nettle rash.

orticol 'tura *sf* horticulture.

'orto *sm* vegetable garden, kitchen garden; (*AGR*) market garden (*BRIT*), truck farm (*US*); ~ botanico botanical garden(s *pl*).

orto 'dosso, a *ag* orthodox.

ortofrut 'ticolo, a *ag* fruit and vegetable *cpd*.

ortogo 'nale *ag* perpendicular.

ortogra 'fia *sf* spelling.

orto 'lano, a *sm/f* (*venditore*) greengrocer (*BRIT*), produce dealer (*US*).

ortope 'dia *sf* orthopaedics *sg* (*BRIT*), orthopedics *sg* (*US*).

orto 'pedico, a, ci, che *ag* orthopaedic (*BRIT*), orthopedic (*US*) ♦ *sm* orthopaedic specialist (*BRIT*), orthopedist (*US*).

orzai 'olo [ordza'jɔlo], orzaiu 'olo [ordza'jwɔlo] *sm* (*MED*) stye.

or 'zata [or'dzata] *sf* barley water.

'orzo ['ɔrdzo] *sm* barley.

'OSA *sigla f* (= *Organizzazione degli Stati Americani*) OAS (= *Organization of American States*).

o 'sare *vt*, *vi* to dare; ~ fare to dare (to) do; come osi? how dare you?

oscenità [oʃʃeni'ta] *sf inv* obscenity.

o 'sceno, a [oʃ'ʃɛno] *ag* obscene; (*ripugnante*) ghastly.

oscil 'lare [oʃʃil'lare] *vi* (*pendolo*) to swing; (*dondolare: al vento etc*) to rock; (*variare*) to fluctuate; (*TECN*) to oscillate; (*fig*): ~ fra to waver between.

oscillazi 'one [oʃʃillat'tsjone] *sf* oscillation; (*di prezzi, temperatura*) fluctuation.

oscura 'mento *sm* darkening; obscuring; (*in tempo di guerra*) blackout.

oscu 'rare *vt* to darken, obscure; (*fig*) to obscure; ~rsi *vr* (*cielo*) to darken, cloud over; (*persona*): si oscurò in volto his face clouded over.

oscurità *sf* (*vedi ag*) darkness; obscurity; gloominess.

os 'curo, a *ag* dark; (*fig: incomprensibile*) obscure; (: *umile: vita, natali*) humble, obscure; (: *triste: pensiero*) gloomy, sombre ♦ *sm*: all'~ in the dark; tenere qn all'~ di qc to keep sb in the dark about sth.

'Oslo *sf* Oslo.

ospe 'dale *sm* hospital.

ospedali 'ero, a *ag* hospital *cpd*.

ospi 'tale *ag* hospitable.

ospitalità *sf* hospitality.

ospi 'tare *vt* to give hospitality to; (*sog: albergo*) to accommodate.

'ospite *sm/f* (*persona che ospita*) host/ hostess; (*persona ospitata*) guest.

os 'pizio [os'pittsjo] *sm* (*per vecchi etc*) home.

'ossa *sfpl vedi* osso.

os 'sario *sm* (*MIL*) war memorial (*with burial place*).

ossa 'tura *sf* (*ANAT*) skeletal structure, frame; (*TECN, fig*) framework.

'osseo, a *ag* bony; (*tessuto etc*) bone *cpd*.

osse 'quente *ag*: ~ alla legge law-abiding.

os 'sequio *sm* deference, respect; ~i *smpl* (*saluto*) respects, regards; porgere i propri ~i a qn (*formale*) to pay one's respects to sb; ~i alla signora! (give my) regards to your wife!

ossequi 'oso, a *ag* obsequious.

osser 'vanza [osser'vantsa] *sf* observance.

osser 'vare *vt* to observe, watch; (*esaminare*) to examine; (*notare, rilevare*) to notice, observe; (*DIR: la legge*) to observe, respect; (*mantenere: silenzio*) to keep, observe; far ~ qc a qn to point sth out to sb.

osserva 'tore, 'trice *ag* observant, perceptive ♦ *sm/f* observer.

osserva 'torio *sm* (*ASTR*) observatory; (*MIL*) observation post.

osservazi 'one [osservat'tsjone] *sf* observation; (*di legge etc*) observance; (*considerazione critica*) observation, remark; (*rimprovero*) reproof; in ~ under observation; fare un'~ to make a remark; to raise an objection; fare un'~ a qn to criticize sb.

ossessio 'nare *vt* to obsess, haunt; (*tormentare*) to torment, harass.

ossessi 'one *sf* obsession; (*seccatura*) nuisance.

osses 'sivo, a *ag* obsessive, haunting; troublesome.

os 'sesso, a *ag* (*spiritato*) possessed.

os 'sia *cong* that is, to be precise.

ossi 'buchi [ossi'buki] *smpl di* ossobuco.

ossi 'dare *vt*, ~rsi *vr* to oxidize.

ossidazi 'one [ossidat'tsjone] *sf* oxidization, oxidation.

'ossido *sm* oxide; ~ di carbonio carbon monoxide.

ossige 'nare [ossidʒe'nare] *vt* to oxygenate; (*decolorare*) to bleach; acqua ossigenata hydrogen peroxide.

os 'sigeno [os'sidʒeno] *sm* oxygen.

'osso *sm* (*pl(f)* ossa *nel senso ANAT*) bone; d'~ (*bottone etc*) of bone, bone *cpd*; avere le ~a rotte to be dead o dog tired; bagnato fino all'~ soaked to the skin; essere ridotto all'~ (fig: magro) to be just skin and bone; (: senza soldi) to be in dire straits; rompersi l'~ del collo to break one's neck; rimetterci l'~ del collo (fig) to ruin o.s., lose everything; un ~ duro (persona, impresa) a tough number; ~ di seppia cuttlebone.

osso 'buco, pl ossi 'buchi sm (CUC) marrowbone; (: piatto) stew made with knuckle of veal in tomato sauce.

os 'suto, a ag bony.

ostaco 'lare vt to block, obstruct.

os 'tacolo sm obstacle; (EQUITAZIONE) hurdle, jump; essere di ~ a qn/qc (fig) to stand in the way of sb/sth.

os 'taggio [os'taddʒo] sm hostage.

'oste, os 'tessa sm/f innkeeper.

osteggi 'are [osted'dʒare] vt to oppose, be opposed to.

os 'tello sm hostel; ~ della gioventù youth hostel.

osten 'sorio sm (REL) monstrance.

osten 'tare vt to make a show of, flaunt.

ostentazi 'one [ostentat'tsjone] sf ostentation, show.

oste 'ria sf inn.

os 'tessa sf vedi oste.

os 'tetrico, a, ci, che ag obstetric ♦ sm obstetrician ♦ sf midwife.

'ostia sf (REL) host; (per medicinali) wafer.

'ostico, a, ci, che ag difficult, tough.

os 'tile ag hostile.

ostilità sf hostility ♦ sfpl (MIL) hostilities.

osti 'narsi vr to insist, dig one's heels in; ~ a fare to persist (obstinately) in doing.

osti 'nato, a ag (caparbio) obstinate; (tenace) persistent, determined.

ostinazi 'one [ostinat'tsjone] sf obstinacy; persistence.

ostra 'cismo [ostra'tʃizmo] sm ostracism.

'ostrica, che sf oyster.

ostru 'ire vt to obstruct, block.

ostruzi 'one [ostrut'tsjone] sf obstruction, blockage.

ostruzio 'nismo [ostruttsjo'nizmo] sm (POL) obstructionism; (SPORT) obstruction; fare dell'~ a (progetto, legge) to obstruct; ~ sindacale work-to-rule (BRIT), slowdown (US).

o 'tite sf ear infection.

oto 'rino(laringoi 'atra), i, e sm/f ear, nose and throat specialist.

'otre sm (recipiente) goatskin.

ott. abbr (= ottobre) Oct.

ottago 'nale ag octagonal.

ot 'tagono sm octagon.

ot 'tano sm octane; numero di ~i octane rating.

ot 'tanta num eighty.

ottan 'tenne ag eighty-year-old ♦ sm/f octogenarian.

ottan 'tesimo, a num eightieth.

ottan 'tina sf: una ~ (di) about eighty.

ot 'tavo, a num eighth ♦ sf octave.

ottempe 'ranza [ottempe'rantsa] sf: in ~ a (AMM) in accordance with, in compliance with.

ottempe 'rare vi: ~ a to comply with, obey.

ottene 'brare vt to darken; (fig) to cloud.

otte 'nere vt to obtain, get; (risultato) to achieve, obtain.

'ottico, a, ci, che ag (della vista: nervo) optic; (dell'ottica) optical ♦ sm optician ♦ sf (scienza) optics sg; (FOT: lenti, prismi etc) optics pl.

otti 'male ag optimal, optimum.

ottima 'mente av excellently, very well.

otti 'mismo sm optimism.

otti 'mista, i, e sm/f optimist.

ottimiz 'zare [ottimid'dzare] vt to optimize.

ottimizzazi 'one [ottimiddzat'tsjone] sf optimization.

'ottimo, a ag excellent, very good.

'otto num eight.

ot 'tobre sm October; per fraseologia vedi luglio.

otto 'brino, a ag October cpd.

ottocen 'tesco, a, schi, sche [ottotʃen'tesko] ag nineteenth-century.

otto 'cento [otto'tʃɛnto] num eight hundred ♦ sm: l'O~ the nineteenth century.

otto 'mila num eight thousand.

ot 'tone sm brass; gli ~i (MUS) the brass.

ottuage 'nario, a [ottuadʒe'narjo] ag, sm/f octogenarian.

ot 'tundere vt (fig) to dull.

ottu 'rare vt to close (up); (dente) to fill.

ottura 'tore sm (FOT) shutter; (nelle armi) breechblock.

otturazi 'one [otturat'tsjone] sf closing (up); (dentaria) filling.

ottusità sf (vedi ag) obtuseness; dullness.

ot 'tuso, a pp di ottundere ♦ ag (MAT, fig) obtuse; (suono) dull.

o 'vaia sf, o 'vaio sm (ANAT) ovary.

o 'vale ag, sm oval.

o 'varico, a ag ovarian.

o 'vatta sf cotton wool; (per imbottire) padding, wadding.

ovat 'tare vt (imbottire) to pad; (fig: smorzare) to muffle.

ovazi 'one [ovat'tsjone] sf ovation.

'ovest sm west; a ~ (di) west (of); verso ~ westward(s).

o'vile *sm* pen, enclosure; **tornare all'**~ (*fig*) to return to the fold.

o'vino, a *ag* sheep *cpd*, ovine.

'O.V.N.I. *sigla m* (= *oggetto volante non identificato*) UFO.

ovulazi'one [ovulat'tsjone] *sf* ovulation.

'ovulo *sm* (*FISIOL*) ovum.

o'vunque *av* = **dovunque**.

ov'vero *cong* (*ossia*) that is, to be precise; (*oppure*) or (else).

ovvi'are *vi*: ~ **a** to obviate.

'ovvio, a *ag* obvious.

ozi'are [ot'tsjare] *vi* to laze around.

'ozio ['ɔttsjo] *sm* idleness; (*tempo libero*) leisure; **ore d'**~ leisure time; **stare in** ~ to be idle.

ozi'oso, a [ot'tsjoso] *ag* idle.

o'zono [od'dzɔno] *sm* ozone; **lo strato d'**~ the ozone layer.

ozonos'fera [oddzonos'fɛra] *sf* ozone layer.

Pp

P, p [pi] *sf o m inv* (*lettera*) P, p; **P come Padova** ≈ P for Peter.

P *abbr* (= *peso*) wt; (= *parcheggio*) P.

p. *abbr* (= *pagina*) p.

P2 *abbr f*: **la (loggia)** ~ the P2 masonic lodge.

PA *sigla* = *Palermo*.

P.A. *abbr* = **pubblica amministrazione**.

pa'care *vt* to calm; ~**rsi** *vr* (*tempesta, disordini*) to subside.

paca'tezza [paka'tettsa] *sf* quietness, calmness.

pa'cato, a *ag* quiet, calm.

'pacca, che *sf* slap.

pac'chetto [pak'ketto] *sm* packet; ~ **applicativo** (*INFORM*) applications package; ~ **azionario** (*FINANZA*) shareholding; ~ **software** (*INFORM*) software package; ~ **turistico** package holiday (*BRIT*) *o* tour.

pacchi'ano, a [pak'kjano] *ag* (*colori*) garish; (*abiti, arredamento*) vulgar, garish.

'pacco, chi *sm* parcel; (*involto*) bundle; ~ **postale** parcel.

paccot'tiglia [pakkot'tiʎʎa] *sf* trash, junk.

'pace ['patʃe] *sf* peace; **darsi** ~ to resign o.s.; **fare (la)** ~ **con qn** to make it up with sb.

pachis'tano, a [pakis'tano] *ag, sm/f* Pakistani.

pacifi'care [patʃifi'kare] *vt* (*riconciliare*) to reconcile, make peace between; (*mettere in pace*) to pacify.

pacificazi'one [patʃifikat'tsjone] *sf* (*vedi vt*) reconciliation; pacification.

pa'cifico, a, ci, che [pa'tʃifiko] *ag* (*persona*) peaceable; (*vita*) peaceful; (*fig*: *indiscusso*) indisputable; (: *ovvio*) obvious, clear ♦ *sm*: **il P**~, **l'Oceano P**~ the Pacific (Ocean).

paci'fismo [patʃi'fizmo] *sm* pacifism.

paci'fista, i, e [patʃi'fista] *sm/f* pacifist.

pa'dano, a *ag* of the Po; **la pianura** ~**a** the Lombardy plain.

pa'della *sf* frying pan; (*per infermi*) bedpan.

padigli'one [padiʎ'ʎone] *sm* pavilion.

'Padova *sf* Padua.

pado'vano, a *ag* of (*o* from) Padua.

'padre *sm* father; ~**i** *smpl* (*antenati*) forefathers.

Padre'terno *sm*: **il** ~ God the Father.

pa'drino *sm* godfather.

padro'nale *ag* (*scala, entrata*) main, principal; **casa** ~ country house.

padro'nanza [padro'nantsa] *sf* command, mastery.

padro'nato *sm*: **il** ~ the ruling class.

pa'drone, a *sm/f* master/mistress; (*proprietario*) owner; (*datore di lavoro*) employer; **essere** ~ **di sé** to be in control of o.s.; ~**/a di casa** master/mistress of the house; (*per gli inquilini*) landlord/lady.

padroneggi'are [padroned'dʒare] *vt* (*fig*: *sentimenti*) to master, control; (: *materia*) to master, know thoroughly; ~**rsi** *vr* to control o.s.

pae'saggio [pae'zaddʒo] *sm* landscape.

paesag'gista, i, e [paezad'dʒista] *sm/f* (*pittore*) landscape painter.

pae'sano, a *ag* country *cpd* ♦ *sm/f* villager; countryman/woman.

pa'ese *sm* (*nazione*) country, nation; (*terra*) country, land; (*villaggio*) village; ~ **di provenienza** country of origin; **i P**~**i Bassi** the Netherlands.

paf'futo, a *ag* chubby, plump.

'paga, ghe *sf* pay, wages *pl*; **giorno di** ~ pay day.

pa'gabile *ag* payable; ~ **alla consegna/a vista** payable on delivery/on demand.

pa'gaia *sf* paddle.

paga'mento *sm* payment; ~ **anticipato** payment in advance; ~ **alla consegna** payment on delivery; ~ **all'ordine** cash with order; **la TV a** ~ pay TV.

pa'gano, a *ag, sm/f* pagan.

pa'gare *vt* to pay; (*acquisto, fig*: *colpa*) to

pay for; (contraccambiare) to repay, pay back ♦ vi to pay; **quanto l'ha pagato?** how much did you pay for it?; ~ **con carta di credito** to pay by credit card; ~ **in contanti** to pay cash; ~ **di persona** (fig) to suffer the consequences; **l'ho pagata cara** (fig) I paid dearly for it.

pa'gella [pa'dʒɛlla] sf (INS) school report (BRIT), report card (US).

'paggio ['paddʒo] sm page(boy).

pagherò [page'rɔ] vb vedi **pagare** ♦ sm inv IOU; ~ **cambiario** promissory note.

'pagina ['padʒina] sf page; **P~e bianche** phone book, telephone directory; **P~e Gialle** ® Yellow Pages ®.

'paglia ['paʎʎa] sf straw; **avere la coda di** ~ (fig) to have a guilty conscience; **fuoco di** ~ (fig) flash in the pan.

pagliac'cetto [paʎʎat'tʃetto] sm (per bambini) rompers pl.

pagliac'ciata [paʎʎat'tʃata] sf farce.

pagli'accio [paʎ'ʎattʃo] sm clown.

pagli'aio [paʎ'ʎajo] sm haystack.

paglie'riccio [paʎʎe'rittʃo] sm straw mattress.

paglie'rino, a [paʎʎe'rino] ag: **giallo** ~ pale yellow.

pagli'etta [paʎ'ʎetta] sf (cappello per uomo) (straw) boater; (per tegami etc) steel wool.

pagli'uzza [paʎ'ʎuttsa] sf (blade of) straw; (d'oro etc) tiny particle, speck.

pa'gnotta [paɲ'ɲɔtta] sf round loaf.

'pago, a, ghi, ghe ag: ~ **(di)** satisfied (with).

pa'goda sf pagoda.

pail'lette [pa'jɛt] sf inv sequin.

'paio, pl(f) 'paia sm pair; **un** ~ **di occhiali** a pair of glasses; **un** ~ **di** (alcuni) a couple of; **è un altro** ~ **di maniche** (fig) that's another kettle of fish.

'paio etc vb vedi **parere**.

pai'olo, paiu'olo sm (copper) pot.

'Pakistan sm: **il** ~ Pakistan.

pakis'tano, a ag, sm/f = **pachistano**.

pal. abbr = **palude**.

'pala sf shovel; (di remo, ventilatore, elica) blade; (di ruota) paddle.

palan'drana sf (scherzoso: abito lungo e largo) tent.

pa'lata sf shovelful; **fare soldi a** ~**e** to make a mint.

pala'tale ag (ANAT, LING) palatal.

pa'lato sm palate.

pa'lazzo [pa'lattso] sm (reggia) palace; (edificio) building; ~ **di giustizia** courthouse; ~ **dello sport** sports stadium; vedi nota nel riquadro.

pal'chetto [pal'ketto] sm shelf.

'palco, chi sm (TEAT) box; (tavolato) platform, stand; (ripiano) layer.

palco'scenico, ci [palkoʃ'ʃeniko] sm (TEAT) stage.

palermi'tano, a ag of (o from) Palermo ♦ sm/f person from Palermo.

Pa'lermo sf Palermo.

pale'sare vt to reveal, disclose; ~**rsi** vr to reveal o show o.s.

pa'lese ag clear, evident.

Pales'tina sf: **la** ~ Palestine.

palesti'nese ag, sm/f Palestinian.

pa'lestra sf gymnasium; (esercizio atletico) exercise, training; (fig) training ground, school.

paletot [pal'to] sm inv overcoat.

pa'letta sf spade; (per il focolare) shovel; (del capostazione) signalling disc.

pa'letto sm stake, peg; (spranga) bolt.

palin'sesto sm (STORIA) palimpsest; (TV, RADIO) programme (BRIT) o program (US) schedule.

'palio sm (gara): **il P~** horserace run at Siena; **mettere qc in** ~ to offer sth as a prize; vedi nota nel riquadro.

palis'sandro *sm* rosewood.

paliz'zata [palit'tsata] *sf* palisade.

'palla *sf* ball; (*pallottola*) bullet; prendere la ~ al balzo (*fig*) to seize one's opportunity.

pallaca'nestro *sf* basketball.

pallanu'oto *sf* water polo.

palla'volo *sf* volleyball.

palleggi'are [palled'dʒare] *vi* (*CALCIO*) to practise (*BRIT*) *o* practice (*US*) with the ball; (*TENNIS*) to knock up.

pallia'tivo *sm* palliative; (*fig*) stopgap measure.

'pallido, a *ag* pale.

pal'lina *sf* (*bilia*) marble.

pal'lino *sm* (*BILIARDO*) cue ball; (*BOCCE*) jack; (*proiettile*) pellet; (*pois*) dot; bianco a ~i blu white with blue dots; avere il ~ di (*fig*) to be crazy about.

pallon'cino [pallon'tʃino] *sm* balloon; (*lampioncino*) Chinese lantern.

pal'lone *sm* (*palla*) ball; (*CALCIO*) football; (*aerostato*) balloon; gioco del ~ ball game.

pal'lore *sm* pallor, paleness.

pal'lottola *sf* pellet; (*proiettile*) bullet.

'palma *sf* (*ANAT*) = palmo; (*BOT*) palm; ~ da datteri date palm.

pal'mato, a *ag* (*ZOOL*: *piede*) webbed; (*BOT*) palmate.

pal'mipede *ag* web-footed.

pal'mizio [pal'mittsjo] *sm* (*palma*) palm tree; (*ramo*) palm.

'palmo *sm* (*ANAT*) palm; essere alto un ~ (*fig*) to be tiny; restare con un ~ di naso (*fig*) to be badly disappointed.

'palo *sm* (*legno appuntito*) stake; (*sostegno*) pole; fare da *o* il ~ (*fig*) to act as look-out; saltare di ~ in frasca (*fig*) to jump from one topic to another.

palom'baro *sm* diver.

pa'lombo *sm* (*pesce*) dogfish.

pal'pare *vt* to feel, finger.

'palpebra *sf* eyelid.

palpi'tare *vi* (*cuore, polso*) to beat; (: *più forte*) to pound, throb; (*fremere*) to quiver.

palpitazi'one [palpitat'tsjone] *sf* palpitation.

'palpito *sm* (*del cuore*) beat; (*fig*: *d'amore etc*) throb.

paltò *sm inv* overcoat.

pa'lude *sf* marsh, swamp.

palu'doso, a *ag* marshy, swampy.

pa'lustre *ag* marsh *cpd*, swamp *cpd*.

'pampino *sm* vine leaf.

pana'cea [pana'tʃɛa] *sf* panacea.

'Panama *sf* Panama; il canale di ~ the Panama Canal.

pana'mense *ag*, *sm/f* Panamanian.

'panca, che *sf* bench.

pancarrè *sm* sliced bread.

pan'cetta [pan'tʃetta] *sf* (*CUC*) bacon.

pan'chetto [pan'ketto] *sm* stool; footstool.

pan'china [pan'kina] *sf* garden seat; (*di giardino pubblico*) (park) bench.

'pancia, ce ['pantʃa] *sf* belly, stomach; mettere *o* fare ~ to be getting a paunch; avere mal di ~ to have stomach ache *o* a sore stomach.

panci'era [pan'tʃɛra] *sf* corset.

panci'olle [pan'tʃɔlle] *av*: stare in ~ to lounge about (*BRIT*) *o* around.

panci'otto [pan'tʃɔtto] *sm* waistcoat.

panci'uto, a [pan'tʃuto] *ag* (*persona*) potbellied; (*vaso, bottiglia*) rounded.

'pancreas *sm inv* pancreas.

'panda *sm inv* panda.

pande'monio *sm* pandemonium.

pan'doro *sm type of sponge cake eaten at Christmas*.

'pane *sm* bread; (*pagnotta*) loaf (of bread); (*forma*): un ~ di burro/cera *etc* a pat of butter/bar of wax *etc*; guadagnarsi il ~ to earn one's living; dire ~ al ~, vino al vino (*fig*) to call a spade a spade; rendere pan per focaccia (*fig*) to give tit for tat; ~ casereccio homemade bread; ~ a cassetta sliced bread; ~ integrale wholemeal bread; ~ di segale rye bread; pan di Spagna sponge cake; ~ tostato toast.

pane'girico [pane'dʒiriko] *sm* (*fig*) panegyric.

panette'ria *sf* (*forno*) bakery; (*negozio*) baker's (shop), bakery.

panetti'ere, a *sm/f* baker.

panet'tone *sm a kind of spiced brioche with sultanas, eaten at Christmas*.

'panfilo *sm* yacht.

pan'forte *sm Sienese nougat-type delicacy*.

pangrat'tato *sm* breadcrumbs *pl*.

'panico, a, ci, che *ag*, *sm* panic; essere in preda al ~ to be panic-stricken; lasciarsi prendere dal ~ to panic.

pani'ere *sm* basket.

panifica'tore, trice *sm/f* bread-maker, baker.

pani'ficio [pani'fitʃo] *sm* (*forno*) bakery; (*negozio*) baker's (shop), bakery.

pa'nino *sm* roll; ~ imbottito filled roll; sandwich.

panino'teca, che *sf* sandwich bar.

'panna *sf* (*CUC*) cream; (*AUT*) = panne; ~ di cucina cooking cream; ~ montata whipped cream.

'panne [pan] *sf inv* (*AUT*) breakdown; essere in ~ to have broken down.

pan'nello *sm* panel; ~ **di controllo** control panel; ~ **solare** solar panel.

'panno *sm* cloth; ~**i** *smpl* (*abiti*) clothes; **mettiti nei miei** ~**i** (*fig*) put yourself in my shoes.

pan'nocchia [pan'nɔkkja] *sf* (*di mais etc*) ear.

panno'lino *sm* (*per bambini*) nappy (*BRIT*), diaper (*US*).

pano'rama, i *sm* panorama.

pano'ramico, a, ci, che *ag* panoramic; **strada** ~**a** scenic route.

pantacol'lant *smpl* leggings.

panta'loni *smpl* trousers (*BRIT*), pants (*US*), pair *sg* of trousers *o* pants.

pan'tano *sm* bog.

pan'tera *sf* panther.

'pantheon ['panteon] *sm inv* pantheon.

pan'tofola *sf* slipper.

panto'mima *sf* pantomime.

pan'zana [pan'tsana] *sf* fib, tall story.

pao'nazzo, a [pao'nattso] *ag* purple.

'papa, i *sm* pope.

papà *sm inv* dad(dy); **figlio di** ~ spoilt young man.

pa'pale *ag* papal.

pa'pato *sm* papacy.

pa'pavero *sm* poppy.

'papero, a *smlf* (*ZOOL*) gosling ♦ *sf* (*fig*) slip of the tongue, blunder.

papi'llon [papi'jɔ̃] *sm inv* bow tie.

pa'piro *sm* papyrus.

'pappa *sf* baby cereal.

pappa'gallo *sm* parrot; (*fig*: *uomo*) Romeo.

pappa'gorgia, ge [pappa'gɔrdʒa] *sf* double chin.

pappar'della *sf* (*fig*) rigmarole.

pap'pare *vt* (*fam*: *anche*: ~**rsi**) to gobble up.

par. *abbr* (= *paragrafo*) par.

'para *sf*: **suole di** ~ crepe soles.

parà *abbr m inv* (= *paracadutista*) para.

pa'rabola *sf* (*MAT*) parabola; (*REL*) parable.

para'bolico, a, ci, che *ag* (*MAT*) parabolic; *vedi anche* **antenna**.

para'brezza [para'breddza] *sm inv* (*AUT*) windscreen (*BRIT*), windshield (*US*).

paracadu'tare *vt*, ~**rsi** *vr* to parachute.

paraca'dute *sm inv* parachute.

paracadu'tismo *sm* parachuting.

paracadu'tista, i, e *smlf* parachutist; (*MIL*) paratrooper.

para'carro *sm* kerbstone (*BRIT*), curbstone (*US*).

paradi'siaco, a, ci, che *ag* heavenly.

para'diso *sm* paradise; ~ **fiscale** tax haven.

parados'sale *ag* paradoxical.

para'dosso *sm* paradox.

para'fango, ghi *sm* mudguard.

paraf'fina *sf* paraffin, paraffin wax.

parafra'sare *vt* to paraphrase.

pa'rafrasi *sf inv* paraphrase.

para'fulmine *sm* lightning conductor.

pa'raggi [pa'raddʒi] *smpl*: **nei** ~ in the vicinity, in the neighbourhood (*BRIT*) *o* neighborhood (*US*).

parago'nare *vt*: ~ **con/a** to compare with/ to.

para'gone *sm* comparison; (*esempio analogo*) analogy, parallel; **reggere al** ~ to stand comparison.

pa'ragrafo *sm* paragraph.

paraguai'ano, a *ag*, *smlf* Paraguayan.

Paragu'ay [para'gwai] *sm*: **il** ~ Paraguay.

pa'ralisi *sf inv* paralysis.

para'litico, a, ci, che *ag*, *smlf* paralytic.

paraliz'zare [paralid'dzare] *vt* to paralyze.

parallela'mente *av* in parallel.

paralle'pipedo *sm* parallelepiped.

paralle'lismo *sm* (*MAT*) parallelism; (*fig*: *corrispondenza*) similarities *pl*.

paral'lelo, a *ag* parallel ♦ *sm* (*GEO*) parallel; (*comparazione*): **fare un** ~ **tra** to draw a parallel between ♦ *sf* parallel (line); ~**e** *sfpl* (*attrezzo ginnico*) parallel bars.

para'lume *sm* lampshade.

para'medico, a, ci, che *ag* paramedical.

para'menti *smpl* (*REL*) vestments.

pa'rametro *sm* parameter.

paramili'tare *ag* paramilitary.

pa'ranco, chi *sm* hoist.

para'noia *sf* paranoia; **andare/mandare in** ~ (*fam*) to freak/be freaked out.

para'noico, a, ci, che *ag*, *smlf* paranoid; (*fam*: *angosciato*) freaked (out).

paranor'male *ag* paranormal.

para'occhi [para'ɔkki] *smpl* blinkers (*BRIT*), blinders (*US*).

para'petto *sm* parapet.

para'piglia [para'piʎʎa] *sm* commotion.

parapsicolo'gia [parapsikolo'dʒia] *sf* parapsychology.

pa'rare *vt* (*addobbare*) to adorn, deck; (*proteggere*) to shield, protect; (*scansare*: *colpo*) to parry; (*CALCIO*) to save ♦ *vi*: **dove vuole andare a** ~**?** what are you driving at?; ~**rsi** *vr* (*presentarsi*) to appear, present o.s.

parasco'lastico, a, ci, che *ag* (*attività*) extracurricular.

para'sole *sm inv* parasol, sunshade.

paras'sita, i *sm* parasite.

parassi'tario, a *ag* parasitic.

parasta'tale *ag* state-controlled.

paras'tato *sm* *employees in the state-controlled sector*.

pa'rata *sf* (*SPORT*) save; (*MIL*) review,

parade.

pa'rati *smpl* hangings *pl*; **carta da** ~ wallpaper.

para'tia *sf* (*di nave*) bulkhead.

para'urti *sm inv* (*AUT*) bumper.

para'vento *sm* folding screen; **fare da** ~ **a qn** (*fig*) to shield sb.

par'cella [par'tʃɛlla] *sf* fee.

parcheggi'are [parked'dʒare] *vt* to park.

parcheggia'tore, trice [parkeddʒa'tore] *sm/f* parking attendant.

par'cheggio [par'keddʒo] *sm* parking *no pl*; (*luogo*) car park (*BRIT*), parking lot (*US*); (*singolo posto*) parking space.

par'chimetro [par'kimetro] *sm* parking meter.

'parco, chi *sm* park; (*spazio per deposito*) depot; (*complesso di veicoli*) fleet.

'parco, a, chi, che *ag*: ~ (**in**) (*sobrio*) moderate (in); (*avaro*) sparing (with).

par'cometro *sm* (*AUTO*) (Pay and Display) ticket machine.

pa'recchio, a [pa'rekkjo] *det* quite a lot of; (*tempo*) quite a lot of, a long ♦ *pron* quite a lot, quite a bit; (*tempo*) quite a while, a long time ♦ *av* (*con ag*) quite, rather; (*con vb*) quite a lot, quite a bit; ~**i(e)** *det pl* quite a lot of, several ♦ *pron pl* quite a lot, several.

pareggi'are [pared'dʒare] *vt* to make equal; (*terreno*) to level, make level; (*bilancio, conti*) to balance ♦ *vi* (*SPORT*) to draw.

pa'reggio [pa'reddʒo] *sm* (*ECON*) balance; (*SPORT*) draw.

paren'tado *sm* relatives *pl*, relations *pl*.

pa'rente *sm/f* relative, relation.

paren'tela *sf* (*vincolo di sangue, fig*) relationship; (*insieme dei parenti*) relations *pl*, relatives *pl*.

pa'rentesi *sf* (*segno grafico*) bracket, parenthesis; (*frase incisa*) parenthesis; (*digressione*) parenthesis, digression; **tra** ~ in brackets; (*fig*) incidentally.

pa'rere *sm* (*opinione*) opinion; (*consiglio*) advice, opinion; **a mio** ~ in my opinion ♦ *vi* to seem, appear ♦ *vb impers*: **pare che** it seems o appears that, they say that; **mi pare che** it seems to me that; **mi pare di sì/no** I think so/don't think so; **fai come ti pare** do as you like; **che ti pare del mio libro?** what do you think of my book?

pa'rete *sf* wall.

'pari *ag inv* (*uguale*) equal, same; (*in giochi*) equal; drawn, tied; (*MAT*) even ♦ *sm inv* (*POL: di Gran Bretagna*) peer ♦ *sm/f inv* peer, equal; **copiato** ~ ~ copied word for word; **siamo** ~ (*fig*) we are quits o even; **alla** ~ on the same level; (*BORSA*) at par; **ragazza**

alla ~ au pair (girl); **mettersi alla** ~ **con** to place o.s. on the same level as; **mettersi in** ~ **con** to catch up with; **andare di** ~ **passo con qn** to keep pace with sb.

parifi'care *vt* (*scuola*) to recognize officially.

parifi'cato, a *ag*: **scuola** ~**a** *officially recognized private school.*

Pa'rigi [pa'ridʒi] *sf* Paris.

pari'gino, a [pari'dʒino] *ag, sm/f* Parisian.

pa'riglia [pa'riʎʎa] *sf* pair; **rendere la** ~ to give tit for tat.

parità *sf* parity, equality; (*SPORT*) draw, tie.

pari'tetico, a, ci, che *ag*: **commissione** ~**a** joint committee; **rapporto** ~ equal relationship.

parlamen'tare *ag* parliamentary ♦ *sm/f* ≈ Member of Parliament (*BRIT*), ≈ Congressman/woman (*US*) ♦ *vi* to negotiate, parley.

parla'mento *sm* parliament; *vedi nota nel riquadro.*

PARLAMENTO

The Italian Constitution, which came into force on 1 January 1948, states that the **Parlamento** *has legislative power. It is made up of two chambers, the "Camera dei deputati" and the "Senato". Parliamentary elections are held every five years.*

---

parlan'tina *sf* (*fam*) talkativeness; **avere una buona** ~ to have the gift of the gab.

par'lare *vi* to speak, talk; (*confidare cose segrete*) to talk ♦ *vt* to speak; ~ (**a qn**) **di** to speak o talk (to sb) about; ~ **chiaro** to speak one's mind; ~ **male di** to speak ill of; ~ **del più e del meno** to talk of this and that; **ne ho sentito** ~ I have heard it mentioned; **non parliamone più** let's just forget about it; **i dati parlano** (*fig*) the facts speak for themselves.

par'lata *sf* (*dialetto*) dialect.

parla'tore, trice *sm/f* speaker.

parla'torio *sm* (*di carcere etc*) visiting room; (*REL*) parlour (*BRIT*), parlor (*US*).

parlot'tare *vi* to mutter.

parmigi'ano, a [parmi'dʒano] *ag* Parma *cpd*, of (*o* from) Parma ♦ *sm* (*grana*) Parmesan (cheese); **alla** ~**a** (*CUC*) with Parmesan cheese.

paro'dia *sf* parody.

pa'rola *sf* word; (*facoltà*) speech; ~**e** *sfpl* (*chiacchiere*) talk *sg*; **chiedere la** ~ to ask permission to speak; **dare la** ~ **a qn** to call on sb to speak; **dare la propria** ~ **a qn** to give sb one's word; **mantenere la** ~ **to keep** one's word; **mettere una buona** ~ **per qn** to put in a good word for sb; **passare dalle** ~**e ai fatti** to get down to business; **prendere la** ~ to take the floor; **rimanere senza** ~**e** to be speechless; **rimangiarsi la** ~ to go back on one's word; **non ho** ~**e per ringraziarla** I don't know how to thank you; **rivolgere la** ~ **a qn** to speak to sb; **non è detta l'ultima** ~ that's not the end of the matter; **è una persona di** ~ he is a man of his word; **in** ~**e povere** in plain English; ~ **d'onore** word of honour; ~ **d'ordine** (*MIL*) password; ~**e incrociate** crossword (puzzle) *sg*.

paro'laccia, ce [paro'lattʃa] *sf* bad word, swearword.

paros'sismo *sm* paroxysm.

par'quet [par'kɛ] *sm* parquet (flooring).

parrò *etc vb vedi* **parere**.

par'rocchia [par'rɔkkja] *sf* parish; (*chiesa*) parish church.

parrocchi'ano, a [parrok'kjano] *sm/f* parishioner.

'parroco, ci *sm* parish priest.

par'rucca, che *sf* wig.

parrucchi'ere, a [parruk'kjɛre] *sm/f* hairdresser ♦ *sm* barber.

parruc'cone *sm* (*peg*) old fogey.

parsi'monia *sf* frugality, thrift.

parsimoni'oso, a *ag* frugal, thrifty.

'parso, a *pp di* **parere**.

'parte *sf* part; (*lato*) side; (*quota spettante a ciascuno*) share; (*direzione*) direction; (*POL*) party; faction; (*DIR*) party; **a** ~ *ag* separate ♦ *av* separately; **scherzi a** ~ joking aside; **a** ~ **ciò** apart from that; **inviare a** ~ (*campioni etc*) to send under separate cover; **da** ~ (*in disparte*) to one side, aside; **mettere/prendere da** ~ to put/take aside; **d'altra** ~ on the other hand; **da** ~ **di** (*per conto di*) on behalf of; **da** ~ **mia** as far as I'm concerned, as for me; **da** ~ **di madre** on his (*o her etc*) mother's side; **essere dalla** ~ **della ragione** to be in the right; **da** ~ **a** ~ right through; **da qualche** ~ somewhere; **da nessuna** ~ nowhere; **da questa** ~ (*in questa direzione*) this way; **da ogni** ~ on all sides, everywhere; (*moto da luogo*) from all sides; **fare** ~ **di qc** to belong to sth; **prendere** ~ **a qc** to take part in sth; **prendere le** ~**i di qn** to take sb's side; **mettere qn a** ~ **di** qc to inform sb of sth; **costituirsi** ~ **civile contro qn** (*DIR*) to associate in an action with the public prosecutor against sb; **la** ~ **lesa** (*DIR*) the injured party; **le** ~**i in causa** the parties

concerned; ~**i sociali** *representatives of workers and employers.*

parteci'pante [partetʃi'pante] *sm/f*: ~ (**a**) (*a riunione, dibattito*) participant (in); (*a gara sportiva*) competitor (in); (*a concorso*) entrant (to).

parteci'pare [partetʃi'pare] *vi*: ~ **a** to take part in, participate in; (*utili etc*) to share in; (*spese etc*) to contribute to; (*dolore, successo di qn*) to share (in) ♦ *vt*: ~ **le nozze** (**a**) to announce one's wedding (to).

partecipazi'one [partetʃipat'tsjone] *sf* participation; sharing; (*ECON*) interest; ~ **a banda armata** (*DIR*) belonging to an armed gang; ~ **di maggioranza/ minoranza** controlling/minority interest; ~ **agli utili** profit-sharing; ~**i di nozze** *wedding announcement card*; **ministro delle P**~**i statali** *minister responsible for companies in which the state has a financial interest.*

par'tecipe [par'tetʃipe] *ag* participating; **essere** ~ **di** to take part in, participate in; (*gioia, dolore*) to share (in); (*consapevole*) to be aware of.

parteggi'are [parted'dʒare] *vi*: ~ **per** to side with, be on the side of.

par'tenza [par'tɛntsa] *sf* departure; (*SPORT*) start; **essere in** ~ to be about to leave, be leaving; **passeggeri in** ~ **per** passengers travelling (*BRIT*) *o* traveling (*US*) to; **siamo tornati al punto di** ~ (*fig*) we are back where we started; **falsa** ~ (*anche fig*) false start.

parti'cella [parti'tʃɛlla] *sf* particle.

parti'cipio [parti'tʃipjo] *sm* participle.

partico'lare *ag* (*specifico*) particular; (*proprio*) personal, private; (*speciale*) special, particular; (*caratteristico*) distinctive; (*fuori dal comune*) peculiar ♦ *sm* detail, particular; **in** ~ in particular, particularly; **entrare nei** ~**i** to go into details.

particolareggi'ato, a [partikolared'dʒato] *ag* (*extremely*) detailed.

particolarità *sf inv* (*carattere eccezionale*) peculiarity; (*dettaglio*) particularity, detail; (*caratteristica*) characteristic, feature.

partigi'ano, a [parti'dʒano] *ag* partisan ♦ *sm* (*fautore*) supporter, champion; (*MIL*) partisan.

par'tire *vi* to go, leave; (*allontanarsi*) to go (*o drive etc*) away *o* off; (*petardo, colpo*) to go off; (*fig: avere inizio, SPORT*) to start; **sono partita da Roma alle 7** I left Rome at 7; **il volo parte da Ciampino** the flight leaves from Ciampino; **a** ~ **da** from; **la**

seconda a ~ **da destra** the second from the right; ~ **in quarta** to drive off at top speed; (*fig*) to be very enthusiastic.

par 'tita *sf* (*COMM*) lot, consignment; (*ECON: registrazione*) entry, item; (*CARTE, SPORT: gioco*) game; (: *competizione*) match, game; ~ **di caccia** hunting party; ~ **IVA** VAT account; ~ **semplice/doppia** (*COMM*) single-/double-entry book-keeping.

par 'tito *sm* (*POL*) party; (*decisione*) decision, resolution; (*persona da maritare*) match; **per** ~ **preso** on principle; **mettere la testa a** ~ to settle down.

partitocra 'zia [partitokrat'tsia] *sf* hijacking *of institutions by the party system.*

parti 'tura *sf* (*MUS*) score.

'parto *sm* (*MED*) labour (*BRIT*), labor (*US*); **sala** ~ labo(u)r room; **morire di** ~ to die in childbirth.

partori 'ente *sf* woman in labour (*BRIT*) *o* labor (*US*).

parto 'rire *vt* to give birth to; (*fig*) to produce.

par 'venza [par'vɛntsa] *sf* semblance.

'parvi *etc vb vedi* **parere.**

parzi 'ale [par'tsjale] *ag* (*limitato*) partial; (*non obiettivo*) biased, partial.

parzialità [partsjali'ta] *sf*: ~ (**a favore di**) partiality (for), bias (towards); ~ (**contro**) bias (against).

'pascere ['paʃʃere] *vi* to graze ♦ *vt* (*brucare*) to graze on; (*far pascolare*) to graze, pasture.

pasci 'uto, a [paʃ'ʃuto] *pp di* **pascere** ♦ *ag*: **ben** ~ plump.

pasco 'lare *vt, vi* to graze.

'pascolo *sm* pasture.

'Pasqua *sf* Easter; **isola di** ~ Easter Island.

pas 'quale *ag* Easter *cpd*.

pasqu 'etta *sf* Easter Monday.

pas 'sabile *ag* fairly good, passable.

pas 'saggio [pas'saddʒo] *sm* passing *no pl*, passage; (*traversata*) crossing *no pl*, passage; (*luogo, prezzo della traversata, brano di libro etc*) passage; (*su veicolo altrui*) lift (*BRIT*), ride; (*SPORT*) pass; **di** ~ (*persona*) passing through; ~ **pedonale/a livello** pedestrian/level (*BRIT*) *o* grade (*US*) crossing; ~ **di proprietà** transfer of ownership.

passamane 'ria *sf* braid, trimming.

passamon 'tagna [passamon'taɲɲa] *sm inv* balaclava.

pas 'sante *sm/f* passer-by ♦ *sm* loop.

passa 'porto *sm* passport.

pas 'sare *vi* (*andare*) to go; (*veicolo, pedone*) to pass (by), go by; (*fare una breve sosta: postino etc*) to come, call; (: *amico: per fare*

una visita) to call *o* drop in; (*sole, aria, luce*) to get through; (*trascorrere: giorni, tempo*) to pass, go by; (*fig: proposta di legge*) to be passed; (: *dolore*) to pass, go away; (*CARTE*) to pass ♦ *vt* (*attraversare*) to cross; (*trasmettere: messaggio*): ~ **qc a qn** to pass sth on to sb; (*dare*): ~ **qc a qn** to pass sth to sb, give sb sth; (*trascorrere: tempo*) to spend; (*superare: esame*) to pass; (*triturare: verdura*) to strain; (*approvare*) to pass, approve; (*oltrepassare, sorpassare: anche fig*) to go beyond, pass; (*fig: subire*) to go through; ~ **da ... a** to pass from ... to; ~ **di padre in figlio** to be handed down *o* to pass from father to son; ~ **per** (*anche fig*) to go through; ~ **per stupido/un genio** to be taken for a fool/a genius; ~ **sopra** (*anche fig*) to pass over; ~ **attraverso** (*anche fig*) to go through; ~ **ad altro** to change the subject; (*in una riunione*) to discuss the next item; ~ **in banca/ufficio** to call (in) at the bank/office; ~ **alla storia** to pass into history; ~ **a un esame** to go up (to the next class) after an exam; ~ **di moda** to go out of fashion; ~ **a prendere qc/qn** to call and pick sth/sb up; **le passo il Signor X** (*al telefono*) here is Mr X, I'm putting you through to Mr X; **farsi** ~ **per qn/qc** to pass o.s. off as, pretend to be; **lasciar** ~ **qn/qc** to let sb/sth through; **col** ~ **degli anni** (*riferito al presente*) as time goes by; (*riferito al passato*) as time passed *o* went by; **il peggio è passato** the worst is over; **30 anni e passa** well over 30 years ago; ~ **una mano di vernice su qc** to give sth a coat of paint; **passarsela: come te la passi?** how are you getting on *o* along?

pas 'sata *sf*: **dare una** ~ **di vernice a qc** to give sth a coat of paint; **dare una** ~ **al giornale** to have a look at the paper, skim through the paper.

passa 'tempo *sm* pastime, hobby.

pas 'sato, a *ag* (*scorso*) last; (*finito: gloria, generazioni*) past; (*usanze*) out of date; (*sfiorito*) faded ♦ *sm* past; (*LING*) past (tense); **l'anno** ~ last year; **nel corso degli anni** ~i over the past years; **nei tempi** ~i in the past; **sono le 8** ~**e** it's past *o* after 8 o'clock; **è acqua** ~**a** (*fig*) it's over and done with; ~ **prossimo** (*LING*) present perfect; ~ **remoto** (*LING*) past historic; ~ **di verdura** (*CUC*) vegetable purée.

passa 'tutto *sm inv*, **passaver 'dura** *sm inv* vegetable mill.

passeg 'gero, a [passed'dʒɛro] *ag* passing ♦ *sm/f* passenger.

passeggi 'are [passed'dʒare] *vi* to go for a walk; (*in veicolo*) to go for a drive.

passeggi'ata [passed'dʒata] *sf* walk; drive; (*luogo*) promenade; **fare una** ~ to go for a walk (*o* drive).

passeg'gino [passed'dʒino] *sm* pushchair (*BRIT*), stroller (*US*).

pas'seggio [pas'seddʒo] *sm* walk, stroll; (*luogo*) promenade; **andare a** ~ to go for a walk *o* a stroll.

passe'rella *sf* footbridge; (*di nave, aereo*) gangway; (*pedana*) catwalk.

'passero *sm* sparrow.

pas'sibile *ag*: ~ **di** liable to.

passio'nale *ag* (*temperamento*) passionate; **delitto** ~ crime of passion.

passi'one *sf* passion.

passività *sf* (*qualità*) passivity, passiveness; (*COMM*) liability.

pas'sivo, a *ag* passive ♦ *sm* (*LING*) passive; (*ECON*) debit; (: *complesso dei debiti*) liabilities *pl*.

'passo *sm* step; (*andatura*) pace; (*rumore*) (foot)step; (*orma*) footprint; (*passaggio, fig: brano*) passage; (*valico*) pass; **a** ~ **d'uomo** at walking pace; (*AUT*) dead slow; ~ **(a)** ~ step by step; **fare due** *o* **quattro** ~**i** to go for a walk *o* a stroll; **andare al** ~ **coi tempi** to keep up with the times; **di questo** ~ (*fig*) at this rate; **fare i primi** ~**i** (*anche fig*) to take one's first steps; **fare il gran** ~ (*fig*) to take the plunge; **fare un** ~ **falso** (*fig*) to make the wrong move; **tornare sui propri** ~**i** to retrace one's steps; "~ **carraio**" "vehicle entrance — keep clear".

'pasta *sf* (*CUC*) dough; (: *impasto per dolce*) pastry; (: *anche*: ~ **alimentare**) pasta; (*massa molle di materia*) paste; (*fig: indole*) nature; ~**e** *sfpl* (*pasticcini*) pastries; ~ **in brodo** noodle soup; ~ **sfoglia** puff pastry *o* paste (*US*).

pastasci'utta [pastaʃ'ʃutta] *sf* pasta.

pasteggi'are [pasted'dʒare] *vi*: ~ **a vino/ champagne** to have wine/champagne with one's meal.

pas'tella *sf* batter.

pas'tello *sm* pastel.

pas'tetta *sf* (*CUC*) = **pastella**.

pas'ticca, che *sf* = **pastiglia**.

pasticce'ria [pastittʃe'ria] *sf* (*pasticcini*) pastries *pl*, cakes *pl*; (*negozio*) cake shop; (*arte*) confectionery.

pasticci'are [pastit'tʃare] *vt* to mess up, make a mess of ♦ *vi* to make a mess.

pasticci'ere, a [pastit'tʃɛre] *sm/f* pastrycook; confectioner.

pastic'cino [pastit'tʃino] *sm* petit four.

pas'ticcio [pas'tittʃo] *sm* (*CUC*) pie; (*lavoro disordinato, imbroglio*) mess; **trovarsi nei** ~**i** to get into trouble.

pasti'ficio [pasti'fitʃo] *sm* pasta factory.

pas'tiglia [pas'tiʎʎa] *sf* pastille, lozenge.

pas'tina *sf* small pasta shapes used in soup.

pasti'naca, che *sf* parsnip.

'pasto *sm* meal; **vino da** ~ table wine.

pas'toia *sf* (*fig*): ~ **burocratica** red tape.

pas'tone *sm* (*per animali*) mash; (*peg*) overcooked stodge.

pasto'rale *ag* pastoral.

pas'tore *sm* shepherd; (*REL*) pastor, minister; (*anche*: **cane** ~) sheepdog; ~ **scozzese** (*ZOOL*) collie; ~ **tedesco** (*ZOOL*) Alsatian (dog) (*BRIT*), German shepherd (dog).

pasto'rizia [pasto'rittsja] *sf* sheep-rearing, sheep farming.

pastoriz'zare [pastorid'dzare] *vt* to pasteurize.

pas'toso, a *ag* doughy; pasty; (*fig: voce, colore*) mellow, soft.

pas'trano *sm* greatcoat.

pa'tacca, che *sf* (*distintivo*) medal, decoration; (*fig: macchia*) grease spot, grease mark; (: *articolo scadente*) bit of rubbish.

pa'tata *sf* potato; ~**e fritte** chips (*BRIT*), French fries.

pata'tine *sfpl* (*potato*) crisps (*BRIT*) *o* chips (*US*).

pata'trac *sm* (*crollo: anche fig*) crash.

pâté [pa'te] *sm inv* pâté; ~ **di fegato d'oca** pâté de foie gras.

pa'tella *sf* (*ZOOL*) limpet.

pa'tema, i *sm* anxiety, worry.

paten'tato, a *ag* (*munito di patente*) licensed, certified; (*fig scherzoso: qualificato*) utter, thorough.

pa'tente *sf* licence (*BRIT*), license (*US*); (*anche*: ~ **di guida**) driving licence (*BRIT*), driver's license (*US*); ~ **a punti** *driving licence with penalty points*.

paten'tino *sm* temporary licence (*BRIT*) *o* license (*US*).

paterna'lismo *sm* paternalism.

paterna'lista *sm* paternalist.

paterna'listico, a, ci, che *ag* paternalistic.

paternità *sf* paternity, fatherhood.

pa'terno, a *ag* (*affetto, consigli*) fatherly; (*casa, autorità*) paternal.

pa'tetico, a, ci, che *ag* pathetic; (*commovente*) moving, touching.

'pathos ['patos] *sm* pathos.

pa'tibolo *sm* gallows *sg*, scaffold.

pati'mento *sm* suffering.

'patina *sf* (*su rame etc*) patina; (*sulla lingua*)

fur, coating.

pa'tire *vt, vi* to suffer.

pa'tito, a *sm/f* enthusiast, fan, lover.

patolo'gia [patolo'dʒia] *sf* pathology.

pato'logico, a, ci, che [pato'lɔdʒiko] *ag* pathological.

pa'tologo, a, gi, ghe *sm/f* pathologist.

'patria *sf* homeland; **amor di** ~ patriotism.

patri'arca, chi *sm* patriarch.

pa'trigno [pa'triɲɲo] *sm* stepfather.

patrimoni'ale *ag* (*rendita*) from property ♦ *sf* (*anche*: **imposta** ~) property tax.

patri'monio *sm* estate, property; (*fig*) heritage; **mi è costato un** ~ (*fig*) it cost me a fortune, I paid a fortune for it; ~ **spirituale/culturale** spiritual/cultural heritage; ~ **ereditario** (*fig*) hereditary characteristics *pl*; ~ **pubblico** public property.

'patrio, a, ii, ie *ag* (*di patria*) native *cpd*, of one's country; (*DIR*): ~**a potestà** parental authority; **amor** ~ love of one's country.

patri'ota, i, e *sm/f* patriot.

patri'ottico, a, ci, che *ag* patriotic.

patriot'tismo *sm* patriotism.

patroci'nare [patrotʃi'nare] *vt* (*DIR*: *difendere*) to defend; (*sostenere*) to sponsor, support.

patro'cinio [patro'tʃinjo] *sm* defence (*BRIT*), defense (*US*); support, sponsorship.

patro'nato *sm* patronage; (*istituzione benefica*) charitable institution *o* society.

pa'trono *sm* (*REL*) patron saint; (*socio di patronato*) patron; (*DIR*) counsel.

'patta *sf* flap; (*dei pantaloni*) fly.

patteggia'mento [patteddʒa'mento] *sm* (*DIR*) plea bargaining.

patteggi'are [patted'dʒare] *vt, vi* to negotiate.

patti'naggio [patti'naddʒo] *sm* skating.

patti'nare *vi* to skate; ~ **sul ghiaccio** to ice-skate.

pattina'tore, 'trice *sm/f* skater.

'pattino *sm* skate; (*di slitta*) runner; (*AER*) skid; (*TECN*) sliding block; ~**i (da ghiaccio)** (ice) skates; ~**i in linea** rollerblades; ~**i a rotelle** roller skates.

pat'tino *sm* (*barca*) kind of pedalo with oars.

pat'tista, i, e *ag* (*POL*) of Patto per l'Italia ♦ *sm/f* (*POL*) member (*o* supporter) of Patto per l'Italia.

'patto *sm* (*accordo*) pact, agreement; (*condizione*) term, condition; **a** ~ **che** on condition that; **a nessun** ~ under no circumstances; **venire** *o* **scendere a** ~**i (con)** to come to an agreement (with); **P~ per l'Italia** (*POL*) *centrist party.*

pat'tuglia [pat'tuʎʎa] *sf* (*MIL*) patrol.

pattugli'are [pattuʎ'ʎare] *vt* to patrol.

pattu'ire *vt* to reach an agreement on.

pattumi'era *sf* (dust)bin (*BRIT*), ashcan (*US*).

pa'ura *sf* fear; **aver** ~ **di/di fare/che** to be frightened *o* afraid of/of doing/that; **far** ~ **a** to frighten; **per** ~ **di/che** for fear of/ that; **ho** ~ **di sì/no** I am afraid so/not.

pau'roso, a *ag* (*che fa paura*) frightening; (*che ha paura*) fearful, timorous.

'pausa *sf* (*sosta*) break; (*nel parlare*, *MUS*) pause.

paven'tato, a *ag* much-feared.

pa'vese *ag* of (*o* from) Pavia.

'pavido, a *ag* (*letterario*) fearful.

pavimen'tare *vt* (*stanza*) to floor; (*strada*) to pave.

pavimentazi'one [pavimentat'tsjone] *sf* flooring; paving.

pavi'mento *sm* floor.

pa'vone *sm* peacock.

pavoneggi'arsi [pavoned'dʒarsi] *vr* to strut about, show off.

pazien'tare [pattsjen'tare] *vi* to be patient.

pazi'ente [pat'tsjɛnte] *ag*, *sm/f* patient.

pazi'enza [pat'tsjɛntsa] *sf* patience; **perdere la** ~ to lose (one's) patience.

pazza'mente [pattsa'mente] *av* madly; **essere** ~ **innamorato** to be madly in love.

paz'zesco, a, schi, sche [pat'tsesko] *ag* mad, crazy.

paz'zia [pat'tsia] *sf* (*MED*) madness, insanity; (*di azione, decisione*) madness, folly; **è stata una** ~! it was sheer madness!

'pazzo, a ['pattso] *ag* (*MED*) mad, insane; (*strano*) wild, mad ♦ *sm/f* madman/woman; ~ **di** (*gioia, amore etc*) mad *o* crazy with; ~ **per qc/qn** mad *o* crazy about sth/sb; **essere** ~ **da legare** to be raving mad *o* a raving lunatic.

PC *sigla* = Piacenza ♦ [pi't ʃi] *sigla m inv* (= *personal computer*) PC.

p.c. *abbr* = per condoglianze; per conoscenza.

p.c.c. *abbr* (= *per copia conforme*) cc.

P.C.I. *sigla m* (= *Partito Comunista Italiano*) *former political party.*

PCUS *sigla m* = Partito Comunista dell'Unione Sovietica.

PD *sigla* = Padova.

P.D. *abbr* = partita doppia.

PE *sigla* = Pescara.

'pecca, che *sf* defect, flaw, fault.

peccami'noso, a *ag* sinful.

pec'care *vi* to sin; (*fig*) to err.

pec'cato *sm* sin; **è un** ~ **che** it's a pity that; **che** ~! what a shame *o* pity!; **un** ~ **di**

gioventù (*fig*) a youthful error *o* indiscretion.

pecca'tore, 'trice *sm/f* sinner.

peccherò *etc* [pekke'rɔ] *vb vedi* **peccare**.

'pece ['petʃe] *sf* pitch.

pechi'nese [peki'nese] *ag*, *sm/f* Pekin(g)ese (*inv*) ♦ *sm* (*anche:* **cane** ~) Pekin(g)ese *inv*, Peke.

Pe'chino [pe'kino] *sf* Beijing, Peking.

'pecora *sf* sheep; ~ **nera** (*fig*) black sheep.

peco'raio *sm* shepherd.

peco'rella *sf* lamb; **la** ~ **smarrita** the lost sheep; **cielo a** ~**e** (*fig: nuvole*) mackerel sky.

peco'rino *sm* sheep's milk cheese.

pecu'lato *sm* (*DIR*) embezzlement.

peculi'are *ag*: ~ **di** peculiar to.

peculiarità *sf* peculiarity.

pecuni'ario, a *ag* financial, money *cpd*.

pe'daggio [pe'daddʒo] *sm* toll.

pedago'gia [pedago'dʒia] *sf* pedagogy, educational methods *pl*.

peda'gogico, a, ci, che [peda'gɔdʒiko] *ag* pedagogic(al).

peda'gogo, a, ghi, ghe *sm/f* pedagogue.

peda'lare *vi* to pedal; (*andare in bicicletta*) to cycle.

pe'dale *sm* pedal.

pe'dana *sf* footboard; (*SPORT: nel salto*) springboard; (: *nella scherma*) piste.

pe'dante *ag* pedantic ♦ *sm/f* pedant.

pedante'ria *sf* pedantry.

pe'data *sf* (*impronta*) footprint; (*colpo*) kick; **prendere a** ~**e qn/qc** to kick sb/sth.

pede'rasta, i *sm* pederast.

pe'destre *ag* prosaic, pedestrian.

pedi'atra, i, e *sm/f* paediatrician (*BRIT*), pediatrician (*US*).

pedia'tria *sf* paediatrics *sg* (*BRIT*), pediatrics *sg* (*US*).

pedi'atrico, a, ci, che *ag* pediatric.

pedi'cure *sm/f inv* chiropodist (*BRIT*), podiatrist (*US*).

pedigree *sm inv* pedigree.

pedi'luvio *sm* footbath.

pe'dina *sf* (*della dama*) draughtsman (*BRIT*), draftsman (*US*); (*fig*) pawn.

pedi'nare *vt* to shadow, tail.

pe'dofilo, a *ag*, *sm/f* paedophile.

pedo'nale *ag* pedestrian.

pe'done, a *sm/f* pedestrian ♦ *sm* (*SCACCHI*) pawn.

peeling ['piling] *sm inv* (*COSMESI*) facial scrub.

'peggio ['pɛddʒo] *av*, *ag inv* worse ♦ *sm o f*: **il** *o* **la** ~ the worst; **cambiare in** ~ to get *o* become worse; **alla** ~ at worst, if the worst comes to the worst; **tirare avanti**

alla meno ~ to get along as best one can; **avere la** ~ to come off worse, get the worst of it.

peggiora'mento [peddʒora'mento] *sm* worsening.

peggio'rare [peddʒo'rare] *vt* to make worse, worsen ♦ *vi* to grow worse, worsen.

peggiora'tivo, a [peddʒora'tivo] *ag* pejorative.

peggi'ore [ped'dʒore] *ag* (*comparativo*) worse; (*superlativo*) worst ♦ *sm/f*: **il(la)** ~ the worst (person); **nel** ~ **dei casi** if the worst comes to the worst.

'pegno ['peɲɲo] *sm* (*DIR*) security, pledge; (*nei giochi di società*) forfeit; (*fig*) pledge, token; **dare in** ~ **qc** to pawn sth, in ~ **d'amicizia** as a token of friendship; **banco dei** ~**i** pawnshop.

pelapa'tate *sm inv* potato peeler.

pe'lare *vt* (*spennare*) to pluck; (*spellare*) to skin; (*sbucciare*) to peel; (*fig*) to make pay through the nose; ~**rsi** *vr* to go bald.

pe'lato, a *ag* (*sbucciato*) peeled; (*calvo*) bald; (**pomodori**) ~**i** peeled tomatoes.

pel'lame *sm* skins *pl*, hides *pl*.

'pelle *sf* skin; (*di animale*) skin, hide; (*cuoio*) leather; **essere** ~ **ed ossa** to be skin and bone; **avere la** ~ **d'oca** to have goose pimples *o* goose flesh; **avere i nervi a fior di** ~ to be edgy; **non stare più nella** ~ **dalla gioia** to be beside o.s. with delight; **lasciarci la** ~ to lose one's life; **amici per la** ~ firm *o* close friends.

pellegri'naggio [pellegri'naddʒo] *sm* pilgrimage.

pelle'grino, a *sm/f* pilgrim.

pelle'rossa, pelli'rossa, *pl* **pelli'rosse** *sm/f* Red Indian.

pellette'ria *sf* (*articoli*) leather goods *pl*; (*negozio*) leather goods shop.

pelli'cano *sm* pelican.

pellicce'ria [pellittʃe'ria] *sf* (*negozio*) furrier's (shop); (*quantità di pellicce*) furs *pl*.

pel'liccia, ce [pel'littʃa] *sf* (*mantello di animale*) coat, fur; (*indumento*) fur coat; ~ **ecologica** fake fur.

pellicci'aio [pellit'tʃajo] *sm* furrier.

pel'licola *sf* (*membrana sottile*) film, layer; (*FOT, CINE*) film.

pelli'rossa *sm/f* = **pellerossa**.

'pelo *sm* hair; (*pelame*) coat, hair; (*pelliccia*) fur; (*di tappeto*) pile; (*di liquido*) surface; **per un** ~: **per un** ~ **non ho perduto il treno** I very nearly missed the train; **c'è mancato un** ~ **che affogasse** he narrowly escaped drowning; **cercare il** ~ **nell'uovo**

(*fig*) to pick holes, split hairs; **non aver ~i sulla lingua** (*fig*) to speak one's mind.
pe'loso, a *ag* hairy.
'peltro *sm* pewter.
pe'luche [pə'lyʃ] *sm* plush; **giocattoli di ~** soft toys.
pe'luria *sf* down.
'pelvi *sf inv* pelvis.
'pelvico, a, ci, che *ag* pelvic.
'pena *sf* (*DIR*) sentence; (*punizione*) punishment; (*sofferenza*) sadness *no pl*, sorrow; (*fatica*) trouble *no pl*, effort; (*difficoltà*) difficulty; **far ~** to be pitiful; **mi fai ~** I feel sorry for you; **essere** *o* **stare in ~ (per qc/qn)** to worry *o* be anxious (about sth/sb); **prendersi** *o* **darsi la ~ di fare** to go to the trouble of doing; **vale la ~ farlo** it's worth doing, it's worth it; **non ne vale la ~** it's not worth the effort, it's not worth it; **~ di morte** death sentence; **~ pecuniaria** fine.
pe'nale *ag* penal ♦ *sf* (*anche:* **clausola ~**) penalty clause; **causa ~** criminal trial; **diritto ~** criminal law; **pagare la ~** to pay the penalty.
pena'lista, i, e *smf* (*avvocato*) criminal lawyer.
penalità *sf inv* penalty.
penaliz'zare [penalid'dzare] *vt* (*SPORT*) to penalize.
penalizzazi'one [penaliddzat'tsjone] *sf* (*SPORT*) penalty.
pe'nare *vi* (*patire*) to suffer; (*faticare*) to struggle.
pen'dente *ag* hanging; leaning ♦ *sm* (*ciondolo*) pendant; (*orecchino*) drop earring.
pen'denza [pen'dɛntsa] *sf* slope, slant; (*grado d'inclinazione*) gradient; (*ECON*) outstanding account.
'pendere *vi* (*essere appeso*): **~ da** to hang from; (*essere inclinato*) to lean; (*fig: incombere*): **~ su** to hang over.
pen'dice [pen'ditʃe] *sf* (*di monte*) slope.
pen'dio, ii *sm* slope, slant; (*luogo in pendenza*) slope.
'pendola *sf* pendulum clock.
pendo'lare *ag* pendulum *cpd*, pendular ♦ *smf* commuter.
pendola'rismo *sm* commuting.
pendo'lino *sm* (*FERR*) high-speed tilting train.
'pendolo *sm* (*peso*) pendulum; (*anche:* **orologio a ~**) pendulum clock.
'pene *sm* penis.
pene'trante *ag* piercing, penetrating.
pene'trare *vi* to come *o* get in ♦ *vt* to penetrate; **~ in** to enter; (*sog: proiettile*) to

penetrate; (: *acqua, aria*) to go *o* come into.
penetrazi'one [penetrat'tsjone] *sf* penetration.
penicil'lina [penitʃil'lina] *sf* penicillin.
peninsu'lare *ag* peninsular; **l'Italia ~** mainland Italy.
pe'nisola *sf* peninsula.
peni'tente *sm/f* penitent.
peni'tenza [peni'tɛntsa] *sf* penitence; (*punizione*) penance.
peniten'ziario [peniten'tsjarjo] *sm* prison.
'penna *sf* (*di uccello*) feather; (*per scrivere*) pen; **~e** *sfpl* (*CUC*) quills (*type of pasta*); **~ a feltro/stilografica/a sfera** felt-tip/ fountain/ballpoint pen.
pen'nacchio [pen'nakkjo] *sm* (*ornamento*) plume.
penna'rello *sm* felt(-tip) pen.
pennel'lare *vi* to paint.
pennel'lata *sf* brushstroke.
pen'nello *sm* brush; (*per dipingere*) (paint)brush; **a ~** (*perfettamente*) to perfection, perfectly; **~ per la barba** shaving brush.
Pen'nini *smpl:* **i ~** the Pennines.
pen'nino *sm* nib.
pen'none *sm* (*NAUT*) yard; (*stendardo*) banner, standard.
pen'nuto *sm* bird.
pe'nombra *sf* half-light, dim light.
pe'noso, a *ag* painful, distressing; (*faticoso*) tiring, laborious.
pen'sare *vi* to think ♦ *vt* to think; (*inventare, escogitare*) to think out; **~ a** to think of; (*amico, vacanze*) to think of *o* about; (*problema*) to think about; **~ di fare qc** to think of doing sth; **~ bene/male di qn** to think well/badly of sb, have a good/bad opinion of sb; **penso di sì** I think so; **penso di no** I don't think so; **a pensarci bene ...** on second thoughts (*BRIT*) *o* thought (*US*) ...; **non voglio nemmeno pensarci** I don't even want to think about it; **ci penso io** I'll see to *o* take care of it.
pen'sata *sf* (*trovata*) idea, thought.
pensa'tore, 'trice *sm/f* thinker.
pensie'rino *sm* (*dono*) little gift; (*pensiero*): **ci farò un ~** I'll think about it.
pensi'ero *sm* thought; (*modo di pensare, dottrina*) thinking *no pl*; (*preoccupazione*) worry, care, trouble; **darsi ~ per qc** to worry about sth; **stare in ~ per qn** to be worried about sb; **un ~ gentile** (*anche fig: dono etc*) a kind thought.
pensie'roso, a *ag* thoughtful.
'pensile *ag* hanging.
pensi'lina *sf* (*in stazione*) platform roof.
pensiona'mento *sm* retirement; **~**

anticipato early retirement.
pensio'nante *sm/f* (*presso una famiglia*) lodger; (*di albergo*) guest.
pensio'nato, a *sm/f* pensioner ♦ *sm* (*istituto*) hostel.
pensi'one *sf* (*al prestatore di lavoro*) pension; (*vitto e alloggio*) board and lodging; (*albergo*) boarding house; **andare in** ~ to retire; **mezza** ~ half board; ~ **completa** full board; ~ **d'invalidità** disablement pension; ~ **di anzianità** old-age pension.
pensio'nistico, a, ci, che *ag* pension *cpd.*
pen'soso, a *ag* thoughtful, pensive, lost in thought.
pen'tagono *sm* pentagon; **il P~** the Pentagon.
pentag'ramma, i *sm* (*MUS*) staff, stave.
pentapar'tito *sm* (*POL*) five-party coalition government.
'pentathlon ['pentatlon] *sm* (*SPORT*) pentathlon.
Pente'coste *sf* Pentecost, Whit Sunday (*BRIT*).
penti'mento *sm* repentance, contrition.
pen'tirsi *vr*: ~ **di** to repent of; (*rammaricarsi*) to regret, be sorry for.
penti'tismo *sm confessions from terrorists and members of organized crime rackets; vedi nota nel riquadro.*

PENTITISMO

The practice of **pentitismo** *first emerged in Italy during the 1970s, a period marked by major terrorist activity. Once arrested, some members of terrorist groups would collaborate with the authorities by providing information in return for a reduced sentence, or indeed for their own reasons. In recent years it has become common practice for members of Mafia organizations to become "pentiti", and special legislation has had to be introduced to provide for the sentencing and personal protection of these informants.*

---

pen'tito, a *sm/f* ≈ supergrass (*BRIT*), *terrorist/criminal who turns police informer.*
'pentola *sf* pot; ~ **a pressione** pressure cooker.
pe'nultimo, a *ag* last but one (*BRIT*), next to last, penultimate.
pe'nuria *sf* shortage.
penzo'lare [pendzo'lare] *vi* to dangle, hang loosely.
penzo'loni [pendzo'loni] *av* dangling, hanging down; **stare** ~ to dangle, hang

down.
pe'pato, a *ag* (*condito con pepe*) peppery, hot; (*fig: pungente*) sharp.
'pepe *sm* pepper; ~ **macinato/in grani/nero** ground/whole/black pepper.
pepero'nata *sf stewed peppers, tomatoes and onions.*
peperon'cino [peperon'tʃino] *sm* chilli pepper.
pepe'rone *sm*: ~ (**rosso**) red pepper, capsicum; ~ (**verde**) green pepper, capsicum; **rosso come un** ~ as red as a beetroot (*BRIT*), fire-engine red (*US*); ~i **ripieni** stuffed peppers.
pe'pita *sf* nugget.

================= PAROLA CHIAVE

per *prep* **1** (*moto attraverso luogo*) through; **i ladri sono passati** ~ **la finestra** the thieves got in (*o* out) through the window; **l'ho cercato** ~ **tutta la casa** I've searched the whole house *o* all over the house for it
2 (*moto a luogo*) for, to; **partire** ~ **la Germania/il mare** to leave for Germany/ the sea; **il treno** ~ **Roma** the Rome train, the train for *o* to Rome; **proseguire** ~ **Londra** to go on to London
3 (*stato in luogo*): **seduto/sdraiato** ~ **terra** sitting/lying on the ground
4 (*tempo*) for; ~ **anni/tanto tempo** for years/a long time; ~ **tutta l'estate** throughout the summer, all summer long; **lo rividi** ~ **Natale** I saw him again at Christmas; **lo faccio** ~ **lunedì** I'll do it for Monday
5 (*mezzo, maniera*) by; ~ **lettera/ferrovia/ via aerea** by letter/rail/airmail; **prendere qn** ~ **un braccio** to take sb by the arm
6 (*causa, scopo*) for; **assente** ~ **malattia** absent because of *o* through *o* owing to illness; **ottimo** ~ **il mal di gola** excellent for sore throats; ~ **abitudine** out of habit, from habit
7 (*limitazione*) for; **è troppo difficile** ~ **lui** it's too difficult for him; ~ **quel che mi riguarda** as far as I'm concerned; ~ **poco che sia** however little it may be; ~ **questa volta ti perdono** I'll forgive you this time
8 (*prezzo, misura*) for; (*distributivo*) a, per; **venduto** ~ **3 milioni** sold for 3 million; **la strada continua** ~ **3 km** the street goes on for 3 km; **15 euro** ~ **persona** 15 euros a *o* per person; **uno** ~ **volta** one at a time; **uno** ~ **uno** one by one; **due** ~ **parte** two either side; **5** ~ **cento** 5 per cent; **3** ~ **4 fa 12** 3 times 4 equals 12; **dividere/moltipli-care 12** ~ **4** to divide/multiply 12 by 4
9 (*in qualità di*) as; (*al posto di*) for; **avere**

qn ~ **professore** to have sb as a teacher; **ti ho preso** ~ **Mario** I mistook you for Mario; **dare** ~ **morto qn** to give sb up for dead; **lo prenderanno** ~ **pazzo** they'll think he's crazy
10 (*seguito da vb*: *finale*): ~ **fare qc** (so as) to do sth, in order to do sth; (: *causale*): ~ **aver fatto qc** for having done sth; **studia** ~ **passare l'esame** he's studying in order to *o* (so as) to pass his exam; **l'hanno punito** ~ **aver rubato i soldi** he was punished for having stolen the money; **è abbastanza grande** ~ **andarci da solo** he's big enough to go on his own.

'**pera** *sf* pear.
pe'raltro *av* moreover, what's more.
per'bacco *escl* by Jove!
per'bene *ag inv* respectable, decent ♦ *av* (*con cura*) properly, well.
perbe'nismo *sm* (so-called) respectability.
percentu'ale [pertʃentu'ale] *sf* percentage; (*commissione*) commission.
perce'pire [pertʃe'pire] *vt* (*sentire*) to perceive; (*ricevere*) to receive.
percet'tibile [pertʃet'tibile] *ag* perceptible.
percezi'one [pertʃet'tsjone] *sf* perception.

========= *PAROLA CHIAVE*

perché [per'ke] *av* why; ~ **no?** why not?; ~ **non vuoi andarci?** why don't you want to go?; **spiegami** ~ **l'hai fatto** tell me why you did it
♦ *cong* **1** (*causale*) because; **non posso uscire** ~ **ho da fare** I can't go out because *o* as I've a lot to do
2 (*finale*) in order that, so that; **te lo do** ~ **tu lo legga** I'm giving it to you so (that) you can read it
3 (*consecutivo*): **è troppo forte** ~ **si possa batterlo** he's too strong to be beaten
♦ *sm inv* reason; **il** ~ **di** the reason for; **non c'è un vero** ~ there's no real reason for it.

perciò [per'tʃɔ] *cong* so, for this (*o* that) reason.
per'correre *vt* (*luogo*) to go all over; (: *paese*) to travel up and down, go all over; (*distanza*) to cover.
percor'ribile *ag* (*strada*) which can be followed.
per'corso, a *pp di* **percorrere** ♦ *sm* (*tragitto*) journey; (*tratto*) route.
per'cosso, a *pp di* **percuotere** ♦ *sf* blow.
percu'otere *vt* to hit, strike.
percussi'one *sf* percussion; **strumenti a** ~ (*MUS*) percussion instruments.
per'dente *ag* losing ♦ *sm/f* loser.

'**perdere** *vt* to lose; (*lasciarsi sfuggire*) to miss; (*sprecare*: *tempo*, *denaro*) to waste; (*mandare in rovina*: *persona*) to ruin ♦ *vi* to lose; (*serbatoio etc*) to leak; ~**rsi** *vr* (*smarrirsi*) to get lost; (*svanire*) to disappear, vanish; **saper** ~ to be a good loser; **lascia** ~! forget it!, never mind!; **non ho niente da** ~ (*fig*) I've got nothing to lose; **è un'occasione da non** ~ it's a marvellous opportunity; (*affare*) it's a great bargain; **è fatica persa** it's a waste of effort; ~ **al gioco** to lose money gambling; ~ **di vista qn** (*anche fig*) to lose sight of sb; ~**rsi di vista** to lose sight of each other; (*fig*) to lose touch; ~**rsi alla vista** to disappear from sight; ~**rsi in chiacchiere** to waste time talking.
perdifi'ato : **a** ~ *av* (*correre*) at breathtaking speed; (*gridare*) at the top of one's voice.
perdigi'orno [perdi'dʒorno] *sm/f inv* idler, waster.
'**perdita** *sf* loss; (*spreco*) waste; (*fuoriuscita*) leak; **siamo in** ~ (*COMM*) we are running at a loss; **a** ~ **d'occhio** as far as the eye can see.
perdi'tempo *sm/f inv* waster, idler.
perdizi'one [perdit'tsjone] *sf* (*REL*) perdition, damnation; **luogo di** ~ place of ill repute.
perdo'nare *vt* to pardon, forgive; (*scusare*) to excuse, pardon; **per farsi** ~ in order to be forgiven; **perdona la domanda** ... if you don't mind my asking ...; **vogliate** ~ **il (mio) ritardo** my apologies for being late; **un male che non perdona** an incurable disease.
per'dono *sm* forgiveness; (*DIR*) pardon; **chiedere** ~ **a qn (per)** to ask for sb's forgiveness (for); (*scusarsi*) to apologize to sb (for).
perdu'rare *vi* to go on, last; (*perseverare*) to persist.
perduta'mente *av* desperately, passionately.
per'duto, a *pp di* **perdere** ♦ *ag* (*gen*) lost; **sentirsi** *o* **vedersi** ~ (*fig*) to realize the hopelessness of one's position; **una donna** ~**a** (*fig*) a fallen woman.
peregri'nare *vi* to wander, roam.
pe'renne *ag* eternal, perpetual, perennial; (*BOT*) perennial.
peren'torio, a *ag* peremptory; (*definitivo*) final.
perfetta'mente *av* perfectly; **sai** ~ **che** ... you know perfectly well that ....
per'fetto, a *ag* perfect ♦ *sm* (*LING*) perfect (tense).

perfeziona'mento [perfettsjona'mento] *sm*: ~ **(di)** improvement (in), perfection (of); **corso di** ~ proficiency course.

perfezio'nare [perfettsjo'nare] *vt* to improve, perfect; ~**rsi** *vr* to improve.

perfezi'one [perfet'tsjone] *sf* perfection.

perfezio'nismo [perfettsjo'nizmo] *sm* perfectionism.

perfezio'nista, i, e [perfettsjo'nista] *sm/f* perfectionist.

per'fidia *sf* perfidy.

'perfido, a *ag* perfidious, treacherous.

per'fino *av* even.

perfo'rare *vt* to pierce; (*MED*) to perforate; (*banda, schede*) to punch; (*trivellare*) to drill.

perfora'tore, 'trice *sm/f* punch-card operator ♦ *sm* (*utensile*) punch; (*INFORM*): ~ **di schede** card punch ♦ *sf* (*TECN*) boring *o* drilling machine; (*INFORM*) card punch.

perforazi'one [perforat'tsjone] *sf* piercing; perforation; punching; drilling.

perga'mena *sf* parchment.

'pergola *sf* pergola.

pergo'lato *sm* pergola.

perico'lante *ag* precarious.

pe'ricolo *sm* danger; **essere fuori** ~ to be out of danger; (*MED*) to be off the danger list; **mettere in** ~ to endanger, put in danger.

perico'loso, a *ag* dangerous.

perife'ria *sf* (*anche fig*) periphery; (*di città*) outskirts *pl*.

peri'ferico, a, ci, che *ag* (*ANAT, INFORM*) peripheral; (*zona*) outlying.

pe'rifrasi *sf inv* circumlocution.

pe'rimetro *sm* perimeter.

peri'odico, a, ci, che *ag* periodic(al); (*MAT*) recurring ♦ *sm* periodical.

pe'riodo *sm* period; ~ **contabile** accounting period; ~ **di prova** trial period.

peripe'zie [peripet'tsie] *sfpl* ups and downs, vicissitudes.

'periplo *sm* circumnavigation.

pe'rire *vi* to perish, die.

peris'copio *sm* periscope.

pe'rito, a *ag* expert, skilled ♦ *sm/f* expert; (*agronomo, navale*) surveyor; **un** ~ **chimico** a qualified chemist.

perito'nite *sf* peritonitis.

pe'rizia [pe'rittsja] *sf* (*abilità*) ability; (*giudizio tecnico*) expert opinion; expert's report; ~ **psichiatrica** psychiatrist's report.

peri'zoma, i [peri'dʒoma] *sm* G-string.

'perla *sf* pearl.

per'lina *sf* bead.

perli'nato *sm* matchboarding.

perlo'meno *av* (*almeno*) at least.

perlopiù *av* (*quasi sempre*) in most cases, usually.

perlus'trare *vt* to patrol.

perlustrazi'one [perlustrat'tsjone] *sf* patrol, reconnaissance; **andare in** ~ to go on patrol.

perma'loso, a *ag* touchy.

perma'nente *ag* permanent ♦ *sf* permanent wave, perm.

perma'nenza [perma'nentsa] *sf* permanence; (*soggiorno*) stay; **buona** ~! enjoy your stay!

perma'nere *vi* to remain.

per'mango, per'masi *etc vb vedi* **permanere**.

perme'abile *ag* permeable.

perme'are *vt* to permeate.

per'messo, a *pp di* **permettere** ♦ *sm* (*autorizzazione*) permission, leave; (*dato a militare, impiegato*) leave; (*licenza*) licence (*BRIT*), license (*US*), permit; (*MIL: foglio*) pass; ~**?, è** ~**?** (*posso entrare?*) may I come in?; (*posso passare?*) excuse me; ~ **di lavoro/pesca** work/fishing permit.

per'mettere *vt* to allow, permit; ~ **a qn qc/di fare qc** to allow sb sth/to do sth; ~**rsi** *vr*: ~**rsi qc/di fare qc** (*concedersi*) to allow o.s. sth/to do sth; **permettete che mi presenti** let me introduce myself, may I introduce myself?; **mi sia permesso di sottolineare che** ... may I take the liberty of pointing out that ....

per'misi *etc vb vedi* **permettere**.

permis'sivo, a *ag* permissive.

'permuta *sf* (*DIR*) transfer; (*COMM*) trade-in; **accettare qc in** ~ to take sth as a trade-in; **valore di** ~ (*di macchina etc*) trade-in value.

permu'tare *vt* to exchange; (*MAT*) to permute.

per'nacchia [per'nakkja] *sf* (*fam*): **fare una** ~ to blow a raspberry.

per'nice [per'nitʃe] *sf* partridge.

'perno *sm* pivot.

pernotta'mento *sm* overnight stay.

pernot'tare *vi* to spend the night, stay overnight.

'pero *sm* pear tree.

però *cong* (*ma*) but; (*tuttavia*) however, nevertheless.

pero'rare *vt* (*DIR, fig*): ~ **la causa di qn** to plead sb's case.

perpendico'lare *ag, sf* perpendicular.

perpen'dicolo *sm*: **a** ~ perpendicularly.

perpe'trare *vt* to perpetrate.

perpetu'are *vt* to perpetuate.
per'petuo, a *ag* perpetual.
perplessità *sf inv* perplexity.
per'plesso, a *ag* perplexed, puzzled.
perqui'sire *vt* to search.
perquisizi'one [perkwizit'tsjone] *sf* (police) search; **mandato di** ~ search warrant.
'perse *etc vb vedi* **perdere**.
persecu'tore *sm* persecutor.
persecuzi'one [persekut'tsjone] *sf* persecution.
persegu'ibile *ag* (*DIR*): **essere ~ per legge** to be liable to prosecution.
persegu'ire *vt* to pursue; (*DIR*) to prosecute.
persegui'tare *vt* to persecute.
perseve'rante *ag* persevering.
perseve'ranza [perseve'rantsa] *sf* perseverance.
perseve'rare *vi* to persevere.
'persi *etc vb vedi* **perdere**.
'Persia *sf*: **la** ~ Persia.
persi'ano, a *ag*, *sm/f* Persian ♦ *sf* shutter; ~**a avvolgibile** roller blind.
'persico, a, ci, che *ag*: **il golfo P**~ the Persian Gulf; **pesce** ~ perch.
per'sino *av* = **perfino**.
persis'tente *ag* persistent.
persis'tenza [persis'tentsa] *sf* persistence.
per'sistere *vi* to persist; ~ **a fare** to persist in doing.
persis'tito, a *pp di* **persistere**.
'perso, a *pp di* **perdere** ♦ *ag* (*smarrito: anche fig*) lost; (*sprecato*) wasted; **fare qc a tempo** ~ to do sth in one's spare time; ~ **per** ~ I've (*o* we've *etc*) got nothing further to lose.
per'sona *sf* person; (*qualcuno*): **una** ~ someone, somebody, *espressione interrogativa* + anyone *o* anybody; ~**e** *sfpl* people *pl*; **non c'è** ~ **che ...** there's nobody who ..., there isn't anybody who ...; **in** ~, **di** ~ in person; **per interposta** ~ through an intermediary *o* a third party; ~ **giuridica** (*DIR*) legal person.
perso'naggio [perso'naddʒo] *sm* (*persona ragguardevole*) personality, figure; (*tipo*) character, individual; (*LETTERATURA*) character.
perso'nale *ag* personal ♦ *sm* staff, personnel; (*figura fisica*) build ♦ *sf* (*mostra*) one-man (*o* one-woman) exhibition.
personalità *sf inv* personality.
personaliz'zare [personalid'dzare] *vt* (*arredamento, stile*) to personalize; (*adattare*) to customize.
personaliz'zato, a [personalid'dzato] *ag* personalized.

personal'mente *av* personally.
personifi'care *vt* to personify; (*simboleggiare*) to embody.
personificazi'one [personifikat'tsjone] *sf* (*vedi vb*) personification; embodiment.
perspi'cace [perspi'katʃe] *ag* shrewd, discerning.
perspi'cacia [perspi'katʃa] *sf* perspicacity, shrewdness.
persu'adere *vt*: ~ **qn (di qc/a fare)** to persuade sb (of sth/to do).
persuasi'one *sf* persuasion.
persua'sivo, a *ag* persuasive.
persu'aso, a *pp di* **persuadere**.
per'tanto *cong* (*quindi*) so, therefore.
'pertica, che *sf* pole.
perti'nace [perti'natʃe] *ag* determined; persistent.
perti'nente *ag*: ~ **(a)** relevant (to), pertinent (to).
perti'nenza [perti'nɛntsa] *sf* (*attinenza*) pertinence, relevance; (*competenza*): **essere di** ~ **di qn** to be sb's business.
per'tosse *sf* whooping cough.
per'tugio [per'tudʒo] *sm* hole, opening.
pertur'bare *vt* to disrupt; (*persona*) to disturb, perturb.
perturbazi'one [perturbat'tsjone] *sf* disruption; disturbance.
Perù *sm*: **il** ~ Peru.
peru'gino, a [peru'dʒino] *ag* of (*o* from) Perugia.
peruvi'ano, a *ag*, *sm/f* Peruvian.
per'vadere *vt* to pervade.
per'vaso, a *pp di* **pervadere**.
perve'nire *vi*: ~ **a** to reach, arrive at, come to; (*venire in possesso*): **gli pervenne una fortuna** he inherited a fortune; **far** ~ **qc a** to have sth sent to.
perve'nuto, a *pp di* **pervenire**.
perversi'one *sf* perversion.
perversità *sf* perversity.
per'verso, a *ag* perverted.
perver'tire *vt* to pervert.
perver'tito, a *sm/f* pervert.
pervi'cace [pervi'katʃe] *ag* stubborn, obstinate.
pervi'cacia [pervi'katʃa] *sf* stubbornness, obstinacy.
per'vinca, che *sf* periwinkle ♦ *sm inv* (*colore*) periwinkle (blue).
p.es. *abbr* (= *per esempio*) e.g.
'pesa *sf* weighing *no pl*; weighbridge.
pe'sante *ag* heavy; (*fig: noioso*) dull, boring.
pesan'tezza [pesan'tettsa] *sf* (*anche fig*) heaviness; **avere** ~ **di stomaco** to feel bloated.

pesaper 'sone *ag inv*: (**bilancia**) ~ (weighing) scales *pl*; (*automatica*) weighing machine.

pe 'sare *vt* to weigh ♦ *vi* (*avere un peso*) to weigh, (*essere pesante*) to be heavy; (*fig*) to carry weight; ~ **su** (*fig*) to lie heavy on; to influence; to hang over; **mi pesa sgridarlo** I find it hard to scold him; **tutta la responsabilità pesa su di lui** all the responsibility rests on his shoulders; **è una situazione che mi pesa** it's a difficult situation for me; **il suo parere pesa molto** his opinion counts for a lot; ~ **le parole** to weigh one's words.

'pesca *sf* (*pl* **pesche**: *frutto*) peach; (*il pescare*) fishing; **andare a** ~ to go fishing; ~ **di beneficenza** (*lotteria*) lucky dip; ~ **con la lenza** angling; ~ **subacquea** underwater fishing.

pes 'caggio [pes'kaddʒo] *sm* (*NAUT*) draught (*BRIT*), draft (*US*).

pes 'care *vt* (*pesce*) to fish for; to catch; (*qc nell'acqua*) to fish out; (*fig*: *trovare*) to get hold of, find.

pesca 'tore *sm* fisherman; (*con lenza*) angler.

'pesce ['peʃʃe] *sm* fish *gen inv*; **P~i** (*dello zodiaco*) Pisces; **essere dei P~i** to be Pisces; **non saper che ~i prendere** (*fig*) not to know which way to turn; ~ **d'aprile!** April Fool! *vedi nota nel riquadro*; ~ **martello** hammerhead; ~ **rosso** goldfish; ~ **spada** swordfish.

IL PESCE D'APRILE

Il pesce d'aprile *is a sort of April Fool's joke, played on 1 April. Originally it took its name from a paper fish which was secretly attached to a person's back but nowadays all sorts of practical jokes are popular.*

---

pesce 'cane [peʃʃe'kane] *sm* shark.
pesche 'reccio [peske'rettʃo] *sm* fishing boat.
pesche 'ria [peske'ria] *sf* fishmonger's (shop) (*BRIT*), fish store (*US*).
pescherò *etc* [peske'rɔ] *vb vedi* **pescare**.
peschi 'era [pes'kjera] *sf* fishpond.
pesci 'vendolo, a [peʃʃi'vendolo] *sm/f* fishmonger (*BRIT*), fish merchant (*US*).
'pesco, schi *sm* peach tree.
pes 'coso, a *ag* teeming with fish.
pe 'seta *sf* peseta.
'peso *sm* weight; (*SPORT*) shot; **dar** ~ **a qc** to attach importance to sth; **essere di** ~ **a qn** (*fig*) to be a burden to sb; **rubare sul** ~ to give short weight; **lo portarono via di** ~

they carried him away bodily; **avere due** ~**i e due misure** (*fig*) to have double standards; ~ **lordo/netto** gross/net weight; ~ **piuma/mosca/gallo/medio/massimo** (*PUGILATO*) feather/fly/bantam/middle/heavyweight.

pessi 'mismo *sm* pessimism.
pessi 'mista, i, e *ag* pessimistic ♦ *sm/f* pessimist.
'pessimo, a *ag* very bad, awful; **di** ~**a qualità** of very poor quality.
pes 'tare *vt* to tread on, trample on; (*sale, pepe*) to grind; (*uva, aglio*) to crush; (*fig*: *picchiare*): ~ **qn** to beat sb up; ~ **i piedi** to stamp one's feet; ~ **i piedi a qn** (*anche fig*) to tread on sb's toes.
'peste *sf* plague; (*persona*) nuisance, pest.
pes 'tello *sm* pestle.
pesti 'cida, i [pesti'tʃida] *sm* pesticide.
pes 'tifero, a *ag* (*anche fig*) pestilential, pestiferous; (*odore*) noxious.
pesti 'lenza [pesti'lɛntsa] *sf* pestilence; (*fetore*) stench.
'pesto, a *ag*: **c'è buio** ~ it's pitch dark ♦ *sm* (*CUC*) *sauce made with basil, garlic, cheese and oil*; **occhio** ~ black eye.
'petalo *sm* (*BOT*) petal.
pe 'tardo *sm* firecracker, banger (*BRIT*).
petizi 'one [petit'tsjone] *sf* petition; **fare una** ~ **a** to petition.
'peto *sm* (*fam!*) fart (*!*).
petro 'dollaro *sm* petrodollar.
petrol 'chimica [petrol'kimika] *sf* petrochemical industry.
petroli 'era *sf* (*nave*) oil tanker.
petroli 'ere *sm* (*industriale*) oilman; (*tecnico*) worker in the oil industry.
petroli 'ero, a *ag* oil *cpd*.
petro 'lifero, a *ag* oil *cpd*.
pe 'trolio *sm* oil, petroleum; (*per lampada, fornello*) paraffin (*BRIT*), kerosene (*US*); **lume a** ~ oil *o* paraffin *o* kerosene lamp; ~ **grezzo** crude oil.
pettego 'lare *vi* to gossip.
pettego 'lezzo [pettego'leddzo] *sm* gossip *no pl*; **fare** ~**i** to gossip.
pet 'tegolo, a *ag* gossipy ♦ *sm/f* gossip.
petti 'nare *vt* to comb (the hair of); ~**rsi** *vr* to comb one's hair.
pettina 'tura *sf* (*acconciatura*) hairstyle.
'pettine *sm* comb; (*ZOOL*) scallop.
petti 'rosso *sm* robin.
'petto *sm* chest; (*seno*) breast, bust; (*CUC*: *di carne bovina*) brisket; (: *di pollo etc*) breast; **prendere qn/qc di** ~ to face up to sb/sth; **a doppio** ~ (*abito*) double-breasted.
petto 'rina *sf* (*di grembiule*) bib.

petto'ruto, a *ag* broad-chested; full-breasted.

petu'lante *ag* insolent.

pe'tunia *sf* petunia.

'pezza ['pɛttsa] *sf* piece of cloth; (*toppa*) patch; (*cencio*) rag, cloth; (*AMM*): ~ **d'appoggio** *o* **giustificativa** voucher; **trattare qn come una** ~ **da piedi** to treat sb like a doormat.

pez'zato, a [pet'tsato] *ag* piebald.

pez'zente [pet'tsɛnte] *smf* beggar.

'pezzo ['pɛttso] *sm* (*gen*) piece; (*brandello, frammento*) piece, bit; (*di macchina, arnese etc*) part; (*STAMPA*) article; (*di tempo*): **aspettare un** ~ to wait quite a while *o* some time; **andare a** ~**i** to break into pieces; **essere a** ~**i** (*oggetto*) to be in pieces *o* bits; (*fig: persona*) to be shattered; **un bel** ~ **d'uomo** a fine figure of a man; **abito a due** ~**i** two-piece suit; **essere tutto d'un** ~ (*fig*) to be a man (*o* woman) of integrity; ~ **di cronaca** (*STAMPA*) report; ~ **grosso** (*fig*) bigwig; ~ **di ricambio** spare part.

PG *sigla* = *Perugia*.

P.G. *abbr* = **procuratore generale.**

pH [pi'akka] *sm inv* (*CHIM*) pH.

PI *sigla* = *Pisa*.

P.I. *abbr* = **Pubblica Istruzione.**

pi'accio *etc* ['pjattʃo] *vb vedi* **piacere.**

pia'cente [pja'tʃɛnte] *ag* attractive, pleasant.

pia'cere [pja'tʃere] *vi* to please; ♦ *sm* pleasure; (*favore*) favour (*BRIT*), favor (*US*); **una ragazza che piace** (*piacevole*) a likeable girl; (*attraente*) an attractive girl; ~ **a: mi piace** I like it; **quei ragazzi non mi piacciono** I don't like those boys; **gli piacerebbe andare al cinema** he would like to go to the cinema; **il suo discorso è piaciuto molto** his speech was well received; "~!" (*nelle presentazioni*) "pleased to meet you!"; **con** ~ certainly, with pleasure; **per** ~ please; **fare un** ~ **a qn** to do sb a favour; **mi fa** ~ **per lui** I am pleased for him; **mi farebbe** ~ **rivederlo** I would like to see him again.

pia'cevole [pja'tʃevole] *ag* pleasant, agreeable.

piaci'mento [pjatʃi'mento] *sm*: **a** ~ (*a volontà*) as much as one likes, at will; **lo farà a suo** ~ he'll do it when it suits him.

piaci'uto, a [pja'tʃuto] *pp di* **piacere.**

pi'acqui *etc vb vedi* **piacere.**

pi'aga, ghe *sf* (*lesione*) sore; (*ferita: anche fig*) wound; (*fig: flagello*) scourge, curse; (: *persona*) pest, nuisance.

piagnis'teo [pjaɲɲis'tɛo] *sm* whining,

whimpering.

piagnuco'lare [pjaɲɲuko'lare] *vi* to whimper.

piagnuco'lio, ii [pjaɲɲuko'lio] *sm* whimpering.

piagnuco'loso, a [pjaɲɲuko'loso] *ag* whiny, whimpering, moaning.

pi'alla *sf* (*arnese*) plane.

pial'lare *vt* to plane.

pialla'trice [pjalla'tritʃe] *sf* planing machine.

pi'ana *sf* stretch of level ground; (*più esteso*) plain.

pianeggi'ante [pjaned'dʒante] *ag* flat, level.

piane'rottolo *sm* landing.

pia'neta *sm* (*ASTR*) planet.

pi'angere ['pjandʒere] *vi* to cry, weep; (*occhi*) to water ♦ *vt* to cry, weep; (*lamentare*) to bewail, lament; ~ **la morte di qn** to mourn sb's death.

pianifi'care *vt* to plan.

pianificazi'one [pjanifikat'tsjone] *sf* (*ECON*) planning; ~ **aziendale** corporate planning.

pia'nista, i, e *smf* pianist.

pi'ano, a *ag* (*piatto*) flat, level; (*MAT*) plane; (*facile*) straightforward, simple; (*chiaro*) clear, plain ♦ *av* (*adagio*) slowly; (*a bassa voce*) softly; (*con cautela*) slowly, carefully ♦ *sm* (*MAT*) plane; (*GEO*) plain; (*livello*) level, plane; (*di edificio*) floor; (*programma*) plan; (*MUS*) piano; **pian** ~ very slowly; (*poco a poco*) little by little; **una casa di 3** ~**i** a 3-storey (*BRIT*) *o* 3-storied (*US*) house; **al** ~ **di sopra/di sotto** on the floor above/below; **all'ultimo** ~ on the top floor; **al** ~ **terra** on the ground floor; **in primo/secondo** ~ (*FOT, CINE etc*) in the foreground/background; **fare un primo** ~ (*FOT, CINE*) to take a close-up; **di primo** ~ (*fig*) prominent, high-ranking; **un fattore di secondo** ~ a secondary *o* minor factor; **passare in secondo** ~ to become less important; **mettere tutto sullo stesso** ~ to lump everything together, give equal importance to everything; **tutto secondo i** ~**i** all according to plan; ~ **di lavoro** (*superficie*) worktop; (*programma*) work plan; ~ **regolatore** (*URBANISTICA*) town-planning scheme; ~ **stradale** road surface.

piano'forte *sm* piano, pianoforte.

piano'terra *sm inv* = **piano terra.**

pi'ansi *etc vb vedi* **piangere.**

pi'anta *sf* (*BOT*) plant; (*ANAT: anche:* ~ **del piede**) sole (of the foot); (*grafico*) plan; (*cartina topografica*) map; **ufficio a** ~ **aperta** open-plan office; **in** ~ **stabile** on the permanent staff; ~ **stradale** street map, street plan.

piantagi'one [pjanta'dʒone] *sf* plantation.

pianta'grane *smf inv* troublemaker.

pian'tare *vt* to plant; (*conficcare*) to drive *o* hammer in; (*tenda*) to put up, pitch; (*fig: lasciare*) to leave, desert; ~**rsi** *vr:* ~**rsi davanti a qn** to plant o.s. in front of sb; ~ **qn in asso** to leave sb in the lurch; ~ **grane** (*fig*) to cause trouble; **piantala!** (*fam*) cut it out!

pian'tato, a *ag:* **ben** ~ (*persona*) well-built.

pianta'tore *sm* planter.

pianter'reno *sm* ground floor.

pi'anto, a *pp di* **piangere** ♦ *sm* tears *pl*, crying.

pianto'nare *vt* to guard, watch over.

pian'tone *sm* (*vigilante*) sentry, guard; (*soldato*) orderly; (*AUT*) steering column.

pia'nura *sf* plain.

pi'astra *sf* plate; (*di pietra*) slab; (*di fornello*) hotplate; **panino alla** ~ ≈ toasted sandwich; ~ **di registrazione** tape deck.

pias'trella *sf* tile.

piastrel'lare *vt* to tile.

pias'trina *sf* (*ANAT*) platelet; (*MIL*) identity disc (*BRIT*) *o* tag (*US*).

piatta'forma *sf* (*anche fig*) platform; ~ **continentale** (*GEO*) continental shelf; ~ **girevole** (*TECN*) turntable; ~ **di lancio** (*MIL*) launching pad *o* platform; ~ **rivendicativa** *document prepared by the unions in an industry, setting out their claims*.

piat'tello *sm* clay pigeon; **tiro al** ~ clay-pigeon shooting (*BRIT*), trapshooting.

piat'tino *sm* (*di tazza*) saucer.

pi'atto, a *ag* flat; (*fig: scialbo*) dull ♦ *sm* (*recipiente, vivanda*) dish; (*portata*) course; (*parte piana*) flat (part); ~**i** *smpl* (*MUS*) cymbals; **un** ~ **di minestra** a plate of soup; ~ **fondo** soup dish; ~ **forte** main course; ~ **del giorno** dish of the day, plat du jour; ~ **del giradischi** turntable; ~**i già pronti** (*CUC*) ready-cooked dishes.

pi'azza ['pjattsa] *sf* square; (*COMM*) market; (*letto, lenzuolo*): **a una** ~ single; **a due** ~**e** double; **far** ~ **pulita** to make a clean sweep; **mettere in** ~ (*fig: rendere pubblico*) to make public; **scendere in** ~ (*fig*) to take to the streets, demonstrate; ~ **d'armi** (*MIL*) parade ground.

piazza'forte [pjattsa'forte], *pl* **piazze'forti** *sf* (*MIL*) stronghold.

piaz'zale [pjat'tsale] *sm* (large) square.

piazza'mento [pjattsa'mento] *sm* (*SPORT*) place, placing.

piaz'zare [pjat'tsare] *vt* to place; (*COMM*) to market, sell; ~**rsi** *vr* (*SPORT*) to be placed;

~**rsi bene** to finish with the leaders *o* in a good position.

piaz'zista, i [pjat'tsista] *sm* (*COMM*) commercial traveller.

piaz'zola [pjat'tsɔla] *sf* (*AUT*) lay-by (*BRIT*), (roadside) stopping place; (*di tenda*) pitch.

'picca, che *sf* pike; ~**che** *sfpl* (*CARTE*) spades; **rispondere** ~**che a qn** (*fig*) to give sb a flat refusal.

pic'cante *ag* hot, pungent; (*fig*) racy.

pic'carsi *vr:* ~ **di fare** to pride o.s. on one's ability to do; ~ **per qc** to take offence (*BRIT*) *o* offense (*US*) at sth.

picchet'taggio [pikket'taddʒo] *sm* picketing.

picchet'tare [pikket'tare] *vt* to picket.

pic'chetto [pik'ketto] *sm* (*MIL, di scioperanti*) picket.

picchi'are [pik'kjare] *vt* (*persona: colpire*) to hit, strike; (: *prendere a botte*) to beat (up); (*battere*) to beat; (*sbattere*) to bang ♦ *vi* (*bussare*) to knock; (: *con forza*) to bang; (*colpire*) to hit, strike; (*sole*) to beat down.

picchi'ata [pik'kjata] *sf* knock; bang; blow; (*percosse*) beating, thrashing; (*AER*) dive; **scendere in** ~ to (nose-)dive.

picchiet'tare [pikkjet'tare] *vt* (*punteggiare*) to spot, dot; (*colpire*) to tap.

'picchio ['pikkjo] *sm* woodpecker.

pic'cino, a [pit'tʃino] *ag* tiny, very small.

picci'olo [pit'tʃɔlo] *sm* (*BOT*) stalk.

piccio'naia [pittʃo'naja] *sf* pigeon-loft; (*TEAT*): **la** ~ the gods *sg* (*BRIT*), the gallery.

picci'one [pit'tʃone] *sm* pigeon; **pigliare due** ~**i con una fava** (*fig*) to kill two birds with one stone.

'picco, chi *sm* peak; **a** ~ vertically; **colare a** ~ (*NAUT, fig*) to sink.

picco'lezza [pikko'lettsa] *sf* (*dimensione*) smallness; (*fig: grettezza*) meanness, pettiness; (: *inezia*) trifle.

'piccolo, a *ag* small; (*oggetto, mano, di età: bambino*) small, little (*dav sostantivo*); (*di breve durata: viaggio*) short; (*fig*) mean, petty ♦ *smlf* child, little one ♦ *sm:* **nel mio** ~ in my own small way; ~**i** *smpl* (*di animale*) young *pl*; **in** ~ in miniature; **la** ~**a borghesia** the lower middle classes; (*peg*) the petty bourgeoisie.

pic'cone *sm* pick(-axe).

pic'cozza [pik'kɔttsa] *sf* ice-axe.

pic'nic *sm inv* picnic; **fare un** ~ to have a picnic.

pidies'sino, a *ag* (*POL*) of P.D.S. ♦ *smlf* member (*o* supporter) of P.D.S.

pi'docchio [pi'dɔkkjo] *sm* louse.

pidocchi'oso, a [pidok'kjoso] *ag* (*infestato*)

lousy; (*fig: taccagno*) mean, stingy, tight.

pidu 'ista, i, e *ag* P2 *cpd* (*masonic lodge*) ♦ *sm* member of the P2 masonic lodge.

piè *sm inv:* **a ogni ~ sospinto** (*fig*) at every step; **saltare a ~ pari** (*omettere*) to skip; **a ~ di pagina** at the foot of the page; **note a ~ di pagina** footnotes.

pi 'ede *sm* foot; (*di mobile*) leg; **in ~i** standing; **a ~i** on foot; **a ~i nudi** barefoot; **su due ~i** (*fig*) at once; **mettere qc in ~i** (*azienda etc*) to set sth up; **prendere ~** (*fig*) to gain ground, catch on; **puntare i ~i** (*fig*) to dig one's heels in; **sentirsi mancare la terra sotto i ~i** to feel lost; **non sta in ~i** (*persona*) he can't stand; (*fig: scusa etc*) it doesn't hold water; **tenere in ~i** (*persona*) to keep on his (*o* her) feet; (*fig: ditta etc*) to keep going; **a ~ libero** (*DIR*) on bail; **sul ~ di guerra** (*MIL*) ready for action; **~ di porco** crowbar.

piedipi 'atti *sm inv* (*peg: poliziotto*) cop.

piedis 'tallo, piedes 'tallo *sm* pedestal.

pi 'ega, ghe *sf* (*piegatura, GEO*) fold; (*di gonna*) pleat; (*di pantaloni*) crease; (*grinza*) wrinkle, crease; **prendere una brutta** *o* **cattiva ~** (*fig: persona*) to get into bad ways; (: *situazione*) to take a turn for the worse; **non fa una ~** (*fig: ragionamento*) it's faultless; **non ha fatto una ~** (*fig: persona*) he didn't bat an eye(lid) (*BRIT*) *o* an eye(lash) (*US*).

piega 'mento *sm* folding; bending; **~ sulle gambe** (*GINNASTICA*) kneebend.

pie 'gare *vt* to fold; (*braccia, gambe, testa*) to bend ♦ *vi* to bend; **~rsi** *vr* to bend; (*fig*): **~rsi (a)** to yield (to), submit (to).

piega 'tura *sf* folding *no pl*; bending *no pl*; fold; bend.

piegherò *etc* [pjege'rɔ] *vb vedi* **piegare**.

pieghet 'tare [pjeget'tare] *vt* to pleat.

pie 'ghevole [pje'gevole] *ag* pliable, flexible; (*porta*) folding; (*fig*) yielding.

Pie 'monte *sm:* **il ~** Piedmont.

piemon 'tese *ag, sm/f* Piedmontese.

pi 'ena *sf vedi* **pieno**.

pie 'nezza [pje'nettsa] *sf* fullness.

pi 'eno, a *ag* full; (*muro, mattone*) solid ♦ *sm* (*colmo*) height, peak; (*carico*) full load ♦ *sf* (*di fiume*) flood, spate; (*gran folla*) crowd, throng; **~ di** full of; **a ~e mani** abundantly; **a tempo ~** full-time; **a ~i voti** (*eleggere*) unanimously; **laurearsi a ~i voti** to graduate with full marks; **in ~ giorno** in broad daylight; **in ~ inverno** in the depths of winter; **in ~a notte** in the middle of the night; **in ~a stagione** at the height of the season; **in ~** (*completamente*: *sbagliare*) completely; (*colpire, centrare*)

bang *o* right in the middle; **avere ~i poteri** to have full powers; **nel ~ possesso delle sue facoltà** in full possession of his faculties; **fare il ~ (di benzina)** to fill up (with petrol).

pie 'none *sm:* **c'era il ~ al cinema/al teatro** the cinema/the theatre was packed.

piercing ['pirsing] *sm:* **farsi il ~ all'ombelico** to have one's navel pierced.

pietà *sf* pity; (*REL*) piety; **senza ~** (*agire*) ruthlessly; (*persona*) pitiless, ruthless; **avere ~ di** (*compassione*) to pity, feel sorry for; (*misericordia*) to have pity *o* mercy on; **far ~** to arouse pity; (*peg*) to be terrible.

pie 'tanza [pje'tantsa] *sf* dish, course.

pie 'toso, a *ag* (*compassionevole*) pitying, compassionate; (*che desta pietà*) pitiful.

pi 'etra *sf* stone; **mettiamoci una ~ sopra** (*fig*) let bygones be bygones; **~ preziosa** precious stone, gem; **~ dello scandalo** (*fig*) cause of scandal.

pie 'traia *sf* (*terreno*) stony ground.

pietrifi 'care *vt* to petrify; (*fig*) to transfix, paralyze.

piet 'rina *sf* (*per accendino*) flint.

pie 'trisco, schi *sm* crushed stone, road metal.

pi 'eve *sf* parish church.

'piffero *sm* (*MUS*) pipe.

pigi 'ama [pi'dʒama] *sm* pyjamas *pl*.

'pigia 'pigia ['pidʒa'pidʒa] *sm* crowd, press.

pigi 'are [pi'dʒare] *vt* to press.

pigia 'trice [pidʒa'tritʃe] *sf* (*macchina*) wine press.

pigi 'one [pi'dʒone] *sf* rent.

pigli 'are [piʎ'ʎare] *vt* to take, grab; (*afferrare*) to catch.

'piglio ['piʎʎo] *sm* look, expression.

pig 'mento *sm* pigment.

pig 'meo, a *sm/f* pygmy.

'pigna ['piɲɲa] *sf* pine cone.

pignole 'ria [piɲɲole'ria] *sf* fastidiousness, fussiness.

pi 'gnolo, a [piɲ'ɲɔlo] *ag* pernickety.

pigno 'rare [piɲɲo'rare] *vt* (*DIR*) to distrain.

pigo 'lare *vi* to cheep, chirp.

pigo 'lio *sm* cheeping, chirping.

pigra 'mente *av* lazily.

pi 'grizia [pi'grittsja] *sf* laziness.

'pigro, a *ag* lazy; (*fig: ottuso*) slow, dull.

PIL *sigla m vedi* **prodotto interno lordo**.

'pila *sf* (*catasta, di ponte*) pile; (*ELETTR*) battery; (*fam: torcia*) torch (*BRIT*), flashlight; **a ~, a ~e** battery-operated.

pi 'lastro *sm* pillar.

'pile ['pail] *sm inv* fleece.

'pillola *sf* pill; **prendere la ~** (*contraccettivo*) to be on the pill; ~ **del giorno dopo** morning-after pill.

pi lone sm (di ponte) pier; (di linea elettrica) pylon.

pi lota, i, e sm/f pilot; (AUT) driver ♦ ag inv pilot cpd; ~ **automatico** automatic pilot.

pilo taggio [pilo'taddʒo] sm: **cabina di** ~ flight deck.

pilo tare vt to pilot; to drive.

piluc care vt to nibble at.

pi mento sm pimento, allspice.

pim pante ag lively, full of beans.

pinaco teca, che sf art gallery.

pi neta sf pinewood.

ping- pong [piŋ'pɔŋ] sm table tennis.

pingue ag fat, corpulent.

pingu edine sf corpulence.

pingu ino sm (ZOOL) penguin.

pinna sf fin; (di pinguino, spatola di gomma) flipper.

pin nacolo sm pinnacle.

pino sm pine (tree).

pi nolo sm pine kernel.

pinta sf pint.

pinza ['pintsa] sf pliers pl; (MED) forceps pl; (ZOOL) pincer.

pinzette [pin'tsette] sfpl tweezers.

pio, a, pii, pie ag pious; (opere, istituzione) charitable, charity cpd.

piogge rella [pjoddʒe'rɛlla] sf drizzle.

pi oggia, ge ['pjɔddʒa] sf rain; (fig: di regali, fiori) shower; (di insulti) hail; **sotto la** ~ in the rain; ~ **acida** acid rain.

pi olo sm peg; (di scala) rung.

piom bare vi to fall heavily; (gettarsi con impeto): ~ **su** to fall upon, assail ♦ vt (dente) to fill.

piomba tura sf (di dente) filling.

piom bino sm (sigillo) (lead) seal; (del filo a piombo) plummet; (PESCA) sinker.

pi ombo sm (CHIM) lead; (sigillo) (lead) seal; (proiettile) (lead) shot; **a** ~ (cadere) straight down; (muro etc) plumb; **andare con i piedi di** ~ (fig) to tread carefully; **senza** ~ (benzina) unleaded, lead-free; **anni di** ~ (fig) era of terrorist outrages.

pioni ere, a sm/f pioneer.

pi oppo sm poplar.

pio vano, a ag: **acqua** ~a rainwater.

pi overe vb impers to rain ♦ vi (fig: scendere dall'alto) to rain down; (: affluire in gran numero): ~ **in** to pour into; **non ci piove sopra** (fig) there's no doubt about it.

pioviggi nare [pjoviddʒi'nare] vb impers to drizzle.

piovosità sf rainfall.

pio voso, a ag rainy.

pi ovra sf octopus.

pi ovve etc vb vedi **piovere**.

pipa sf pipe.

pipì sf (fam): **fare** ~ to have a wee (wee).

pipis trello sm (ZOOL) bat.

pi ramide sf pyramid.

pi ranha sm inv piranha.

pi rata, i sm pirate; ~ **informatico** hacker; ~ **della strada** hit-and-run driver.

Pire nei smpl: **i** ~ the Pyrenees.

pi retro sm pyrethrum.

pirico, a, ci, che ag: **polvere** ~a gunpowder.

pi rite sf pyrite.

piro etta sf pirouette.

pi rofilo, a ag heat-resistant ♦ sf heat-resistant glass; (tegame) heat-resistant dish.

pi roga, ghe sf dug-out canoe.

pi romane sm/f arsonist.

pi roscafo sm steamer, steamship.

Pisa sf Pisa.

pi sano, a ag Pisan.

pisci are [piʃ'ʃare] vi (fam!) to piss (!), pee (!).

pi scina [piʃ'ʃina] sf (swimming) pool.

pi sello sm pea.

piso lino sm nap; **fare un** ~ to have a nap.

pista sf (traccia) track, trail; (di stadio) track; (di pattinaggio) rink; (da sci) run; (AER) runway; (di circo) ring; ~ **da ballo** dance floor; ~ **ciclabile** cycle lane; ~ **di lancio** launch(ing) pad; ~ **di rullaggio** (AER) taxiway; ~ **di volo** (AER) runway.

pis tacchio [pis'takkjo] sm pistachio (tree); pistachio (nut).

pis tillo sm (BOT) pistil.

pis tola sf pistol, gun; ~ **a spruzzo** spray gun; ~ **a tamburo** revolver.

pis tone sm piston.

pi tocco, chi sm skinflint, miser.

pi tone sm python.

pittima sf (fig) bore.

pit tore, trice sm/f painter.

pitto resco, a, schi, sche ag picturesque.

pit torico, a, ci, che ag of painting, pictorial.

pit tura sf painting; ~ **fresca** wet paint.

pittu rare vt to paint.

=============== *PAROLA CHIAVE*

più av 1 (in maggiore quantità) more; ~ **del solito** more than usual; **in** ~, **di** ~ more; **ne voglio di** ~ I want some more; **ci sono 3 persone in** o **di** ~ there are 3 more o extra people; **costa di** ~ it's more expensive; **una volta di** ~ once more; ~ o **meno** more or less; **né** ~ **né meno** no more, no less; **per di** ~ (inoltre) what's more, moreover; **è sempre ~ difficile** it is getting more and more difficult; **chi ~ chi meno hanno tutti contribuito** everybody made a contribution of some sort; **~ dormo e ~ dormirei** the more I sleep the more I want to sleep **2** (*comparativo*) more; (*se monosillabo, spesso*): **+ ...er; ~ ... di/che** more ... than; **~ intelligente di lui** more intelligent than him; **~ furbo di te** smarter than you; **~ tardi di ...** later than ...; **lavoro ~ di te/di Paola** I work harder than you/than Paola; **è ~ fortunato che bravo** he is lucky rather than skilled; **~ di quanto pensassi** more than I thought; **~ che altro** mainly; **~ che mai** more than ever **3** (*superlativo*) most; (*se monosillabico, spesso*): **+ ...est; il ~ grande/intelligente** the biggest/most intelligent; **è quello che compro ~ spesso** that's the one I buy most often; **al ~ presto** as soon as possible; **al ~ tardi** at the latest **4** (*negazione*): **non ... ~** no more, no longer; **non ho ~ soldi** I've got no more money, I don't have any more money; **non lavoro ~** I'm no longer working, I don't work any more; **non ce n'è ~** there isn't any left; **non c'è ~ nessuno** there's no one left; **non c'è ~ niente da fare** there's nothing more to be done; **a ~ non posso** (*gridare*) at the top of one's voice; (*correre*) as fast as one can **5** (*MAT*) plus; **4 ~ 5 fa 9** 4 plus 5 equals 9; **~ 5 gradi** 5 degrees above freezing, plus 5; **6 ~** (*a scuola*) just above a pass ♦ *prep* plus; **500.000 ~ le spese** 500,000 plus expenses; **siamo in quattro ~ il nonno** there are four of us, plus grandpa ♦ *ag inv* **1:** **~ ... (di)** more ... (than); **~ denaro/tempo** more money/time; **~ persone di quante ci aspettassimo** more people than we expected **2** (*numerosi, diversi*) several; **l'aspettai per ~ giorni** I waited for it for several days ♦ *sm* **1** (*la maggior parte*): **il ~ è fatto** most of it is done; **il ~ delle volte** more often than not, generally; **parlare del ~ e del meno** to talk about this and that **2** (*MAT*) plus (sign) **3: i ~** the majority.

piuccheper'fetto [pjukkeper'fɛtto] *sm* (*LING*) pluperfect, past perfect.

pi'uma *sf* feather; **~e** *sfpl* down *sg*; (*piumaggio*) plumage *sg*, feathers.

piu'maggio [pju'maddʒo] *sm* plumage, feathers *pl*.

piu'mino *sm* (eider)down; (*per letto*) eiderdown; (: *tipo danese*) duvet, continental quilt; (*giacca*) quilted jacket (*with goose-feather padding*); (*per cipria*) powder puff; (*per spolverare*) feather duster.

piut'tosto *av* rather; **~ che** (*anziché*) rather than.

'piva *sf*: **con le ~e nel sacco** (*fig*) empty-handed.

pi'vello, a *smf* greenhorn.

'pizza ['pittsa] *sf* (*CUC*) pizza; (*CINE*) reel.

pizze'ria [pittse'ria] *sf* place where pizzas are made, sold or eaten.

pizzi'cagnolo, a [pittsi'kaɲɲolo] *smf* specialist grocer.

pizzi'care [pittsi'kare] *vt* (*stringere*) to nip, pinch; (*pungere*) to sting; to bite; (*MUS*) to pluck ♦ *vi* (*prudere*) to itch, be itchy; (*cibo*) to be hot *o* spicy.

pizziche'ria [pittsike'ria] *sf* delicatessen (shop).

'pizzico, chi ['pittsiko] *sm* (*pizzicotto*) pinch, nip; (*piccola quantità*) pinch, dash; (*d'insetto*) sting; bite.

pizzi'cotto [pittsi'kɔtto] *sm* pinch, nip.

'pizzo ['pittso] *sm* (*merletto*) lace; (*barbetta*) goatee beard; (*tangente*) protection money.

pla'care *vt* to placate, soothe; **~rsi** *vr* to calm down.

'placca, che *sf* plate; (*con iscrizione*) plaque; (*anche:* **~ dentaria**) (dental) plaque.

plac'care *vt* to plate; **placcato in oro/argento** gold-/silver-plated.

pla'centa [pla'tʃɛnta] *sf* placenta.

placidità [platʃidi'ta] *sf* calm, peacefulness.

'placido, a ['platʃido] *ag* placid, calm.

plafoni'era *sf* ceiling light.

plagi'are [pla'dʒare] *vt* (*copiare*) to plagiarize; (*DIR: influenzare*) to coerce.

'plagio ['pladʒo] *sm* plagiarism; (*DIR*) duress.

plaid [plɛd] *sm inv* (travelling) rug (*BRIT*), lap robe (*US*).

pla'nare *vi* (*AER*) to glide.

'plancia, ce ['plantʃa] *sf* (*NAUT*) bridge; (*AUT: cruscotto*) dashboard.

'plancton *sm inv* plankton.

plane'tario, a *ag* planetary ♦ *sm* (*locale*) planetarium.

planis'fero *sm* planisphere.

plan'tare *sm* arch support.

'plasma *sm* plasma.

plas'mare *vt* to mould (*BRIT*), mold (*US*), shape.

'plastico, a, ci, che *ag* plastic ♦ *sm* (*rappresentazione*) relief model;

(*esplosivo*): **bomba al** ~ plastic bomb ♦ *sf* (*arte*) plastic arts *pl*; (*MED*) plastic surgery; (*sostanza*) plastic; **in materiale** ~ plastic.

plasti'lina ® *sf* plasticine ®.

'platano *sm* plane tree.

pla'tea *sf* (*TEAT*) stalls *pl* (*BRIT*), orchestra (*US*).

plate'ale *ag* (*gesto, atteggiamento*) theatrical.

plateal'mente *av* theatrically.

'platino *sm* platinum.

pla'tonico, a, ci, che *ag* platonic.

plau'dire *vi*: ~ **a** to applaud.

plau'sibile *ag* plausible.

'plauso *sm* (*fig*) approval.

'playback ['plei bæk] *sm*: **cantare in** ~ to mime.

'playboy ['pleibɔi] *sm inv* playboy.

'playmaker ['pleimeikə*] *sm/f inv* (*SPORT*) playmaker.

'play-off ['pleiɔf] *sm inv* (*SPORT*) play-off.

ple'baglia [ple'baʎʎa] *sf* (*peg*) rabble, mob.

'plebe *sf* common people.

ple'beo, a *ag* plebeian; (*volgare*) coarse, common.

plebi'scito [plebiʃ'ʃito] *sm* plebiscite.

ple'nario, a *ag* plenary.

pleni'lunio *sm* full moon.

plenipotenzi'ario, a [plenipoten'tsjarjo] *ag* plenipotentiary.

'plenum *sm inv* plenum.

'plettro *sm* plectrum.

'pleura *sf* (*ANAT*) pleura.

pleu'rite *sf* pleurisy.

P.L.I. *sigla m* (= *Partito Liberale Italiano*) *former political party*.

'plico, chi *sm* (*pacco*) parcel; **in** ~ **a parte** (*COMM*) under separate cover.

plissé [pli'se] *ag inv* plissé *cpd* ♦ *sm inv* (*anche*: **tessuto** ~) plissé.

plisset'tato, a *ag* plissé *cpd*.

plo'tone *sm* (*MIL*) platoon; ~ **d'esecuzione** firing squad.

'plumbeo, a *ag* leaden.

plu'rale *ag*, *sm* plural.

plura'lismo *sm* pluralism.

pluralità *sf* plurality; (*maggioranza*) majority.

plusva'lenza [pluzva'lɛntsa] *sf* capital gain.

plusva'lore *sm* (*ECON*) surplus.

plu'tonio *sm* plutonium.

pluvi'ale *ag* rain *cpd*.

pluvi'ometro *sm* rain gauge.

P.M. *abbr* (*POL*) = **Pubblico Ministero**; (= *Polizia Militare*) MP (= *Military Police*).

pm *abbr* = *peso molecolare*.

PN *sigla* = *Pordenone*.

pneu'matico, a, ci, che *ag* inflatable; (*TECN*) pneumatic ♦ *sm* (*AUT*) tyre (*BRIT*), tire (*US*).

PNL *sigla m vedi* **prodotto nazionale lordo**.

PO *sigla* = *Prato*.

Po *sm*: **il** ~ the Po.

po' *av*, *sm vedi* **poco**.

P.O. *abbr* = **posta ordinaria**.

po'chezza [po'kettsa] *sf* insufficiency, shortage; (*fig*: *meschinità*) meanness, smallness.

=================== *PAROLA CHIAVE*

'poco, a, chi, che *ag* (*quantità*) little, not much; (*numero*) few, not many; ~ **pane/denaro/spazio** little *o* not much bread/money/space; **con** ~**a spesa** without spending much; **a** ~ **prezzo** at a low price, cheap; ~ (**tempo) fa** a short time ago; ~**che persone/idee** few *o* not many people/ideas; **è un tipo di** ~**che parole** he's a man of few words

♦ *av* **1** (*in piccola quantità*) little, not much; (*numero limitato*) few, not many; **guadagna** ~ he doesn't earn much, he earns little

2 (*con ag, av*) (a) little, not very; **è** ~ **più vecchia di lui** she's a little *o* slightly older than him; **è** ~ **socievole** he's not very sociable; **sta** ~ **bene** he isn't very well

3 (*tempo*): ~ **dopo/prima** shortly afterwards/before; **il film dura** ~ the film doesn't last very long; **ci vediamo molto** ~ we don't see each other very often, we hardly ever see each other

4: **un po'** a little, a bit; **è un po' corto** it's a little *o* a bit short; **arriverà fra un po'** he'll arrive shortly *o* in a little while

5: **a dir** ~ to say the least; **a** ~ **a** ~ little by little; **per** ~ **non cadevo** I nearly fell; **è una cosa da** ~ it's nothing, it's of no importance; **una persona da** ~ a worthless person

♦ *pron* (a) little; ~**chi**, ~**che** *pron pl* (*persone*) few (people); (*cose*) few; **ci vediamo tra** ~ see you soon; ~**chi lo sanno** not many people know it; **ci vuole tempo ed io ne ho** ~ it takes time, and I haven't got much to spare

♦ *sm* **1** little; **vive del** ~ **che ha** he lives on the little he has

2: **un po'** a little; **un po' di zucchero** a little sugar; **un bel po' di denaro** quite a lot of money; **un po' per ciascuno** a bit each.

po'dere *sm* (*AGR*) farm.

pode'roso, a *ag* powerful.

podestà *sm inv* (*nel fascismo*) podestà, mayor.

'podio *sm* dais, platform; (*MUS*) podium.

po'dismo *sm* (*SPORT*: *marcia*) walking; (: *corsa*) running.

po'dista, i, e *sm/f* walker; runner.

po'ema, i *sm* poem.

poe'sia *sf* (*arte*) poetry; (*componimento*) poem.

po'eta, 'essa *sm/f* poet/poetess.

poe'tare *vi* to write poetry.

po'etico, a, ci, che *ag* poetic(al).

poggi'are [pod'dʒare] *vt* to lean, rest; (*posare*) to lay, place.

poggia'testa [poddʒa'tɛsta] *sm inv* (*AUT*) headrest.

'poggio ['pɔddʒo] *sm* hillock, knoll.

poggi'olo [pod'dʒɔlo] *sm* balcony.

'poi *av* then; (*alla fine*) finally, at last ♦ *sm*: **pensare al** ~ to think of the future; **e** ~ (*inoltre*) and besides; **questa** ~ (**è bella**) (*ironico*) that's a good one!; **d'ora in** ~ from now on; **da domani in** ~ from tomorrow onwards.

poi'ana *sf* buzzard.

poiché [poi'ke] *cong* since, as.

pois [pwa] *sm inv* spot, (polka) dot; **a** ~ spotted, polka-dot *cpd*.

'poker *sm* poker.

po'lacco, a, chi, che *ag* Polish ♦ *sm/f* Pole.

po'lare *ag* polar.

polariz'zare [polarid'dzare] *vt* (*anche fig*) to polarize.

'polca, che *sf* polka.

po'lemico, a, ci, che *ag* polemic(al), controversial ♦ *sf* controversy; **fare ~che** to be contentious.

polemiz'zare [polemid'dzare] *vi*: ~ (**su qc**) to argue (about sth).

po'lenta *sf* (*CUC*) sort of thick porridge *made with maize flour*.

polen'tone, a *sm/f* slowcoach (*BRIT*), slowpoke (*US*).

pole'sano, a *ag* of (*o* from) Polesine (*area between the Po and the Adige*).

POL'FER *abbr f* = *Polizia Ferroviaria*.

'poli... *prefisso* poly....

poliambula'torio *sm* (*MED*) health clinic.

poli'clinico, ci *sm* general hospital.

poli'edro *sm* polyhedron.

poli'estere *sm* polyester.

poliga'mia *sf* polygamy.

po'ligono *sm* polygon; ~ **di tiro** rifle range.

Poli'nesia *sf*: **la** ~ Polynesia.

polinesi'ano, a *ag, sm/f* Polynesian.

'polio(mie'lite) *sf* polio(myelitis).

'polipo *sm* polyp.

polisti'rolo *sm* polystyrene.

poli'tecnico, ci *sm* postgraduate technical college.

po'litica, che *sf vedi* **politico**.

politi'cante *sm/f* (*peg*) petty politician.

politiciz'zare [polititʃid'dzare] *vt* to politicize.

po'litico, a, ci, che *ag* political ♦ *sm/f* politician ♦ *sf* politics *sg*; (*linea di condotta*) policy; **elezioni ~che** parliamentary (*BRIT*) *o* congressional (*US*) election(s); **uomo ~** politician; **darsi alla ~a** to go into politics; **fare ~a** (*militante*) to be a political activist; (*come professione*) to be in politics; **la ~a del governo** the government's policies; **~a aziendale** company policy; **~a estera** foreign policy; **~a dei prezzi** prices policy; **~a dei redditi** incomes policy.

poliva'lente *ag* multi-purpose.

poli'zia [polit'tsia] *sf* police; ~ **giudiziaria** ≈ Criminal Investigation Department (CID) (*BRIT*), Federal Bureau of Investigation (FBI) (*US*); ~ **sanitaria/tributaria** health/tax inspectorate; ~ **stradale** traffic police; ~ **di stato** *vedi nota nel riquadro*.

POLIZIA DI STATO

The remit of the **polizia di stato** *is to maintain public order, to uphold the law, and to prevent and investigate crime. This is a civilian branch of the police force; male and female officers perform similar duties. The* **polizia di stato** *reports to the Minister of the Interior.*

---

polizi'esco, a, schi, sche [polit'tsjesko] *ag* police *cpd*; (*film, romanzo*) detective *cpd*.

polizi'otto [polit'tsjɔtto] *sm* policeman; **cane ~** police dog; **donna ~** policewoman; ~ **di quartiere** local police officer.

'polizza ['pɔlittsa] *sf* (*COMM*) bill; ~ **di assicurazione** insurance policy; ~ **di carico** bill of lading.

pol'laio *sm* henhouse.

pollai'olo, a *sm/f* poulterer (*BRIT*), poultryman.

pol'lame *sm* poultry.

pol'lastra *sf* pullet; (*fig*: *ragazza*) chick.

pol'lastro *sm* (*ZOOL*) cockerel.

'pollice ['pɔllitʃe] *sm* thumb; (*unità di misura*) inch.

'polline *sm* pollen.

'pollo *sm* chicken; **far ridere i ~i** (*situazione, persona*) to be utterly ridiculous.

polmo'nare *ag* lung *cpd*, pulmonary.

pol'mone *sm* lung.

polmo 'nite *sf* pneumonia; ~ **atipica** SARS.
'Polo *sm* (*POL*) *centre-right coalition.*
'polo *sm* (*GEO, FISICA*) pole; (*gioco*) polo ♦ *sf inv* (*maglia*) polo shirt; **il P~ sud/nord** the South/North Pole.
Po 'Ionia *sf*: **la** ~ Poland.
'polpa *sf* flesh, pulp; (*carne*) lean meat.
pol 'paccio [pol'pattʃo] *sm* (*ANAT*) calf.
polpas 'trello *sm* fingertip.
pol 'petta *sf* (*CUC*) meatball.
polpet 'tone *sm* (*CUC*) meatloaf.
'polpo *sm* octopus.
pol 'poso, a *ag* fleshy.
pol 'sino *sm* cuff.
'polso *sm* (*ANAT*) wrist; (*pulsazione*) pulse; (*fig: forza*) drive, vigour (*BRIT*), vigor (*US*); **avere** ~ (*fig*) to be strong; **un uomo di** ~ a man of nerve.
pol 'tiglia [pol'tiʎʎa] *sf* (*composto*) mash, mush; (*di fango e neve*) slush.
pol 'trire *vi* to laze about.
pol 'trona *sf* armchair; (*TEAT: posto*) seat in the front stalls (*BRIT*) *o* the orchestra (*US*).
poltron 'cina [poltron'tʃina] *sf* (*TEAT*) seat in the back stalls (*BRIT*) *o* the orchestra (*US*).
pol 'trone *ag* lazy, slothful.
'polvere *sf* dust; (*anche*: ~ **da sparo**) (gun)powder; (*sostanza ridotta minutissima*) powder, dust; **caffè in** ~ instant coffee; **latte in** ~ dried *o* powdered milk; **sapone in** ~ soap powder; ~ **d'oro** gold dust; ~ **pirica** *o* **da sparo** gunpowder; ~**i sottili** particulates.
polveri 'era *sf* powder magazine.
polve 'rina *sf* (*gen, MED*) powder; (*gergo: cocaina*) snow.
polveriz 'zare [polverid'dzare] *vt* to pulverize; (*nebulizzare*) to atomize; (*fig*) to crush, pulverize; (: *record*) to smash.
polve 'rone *sm* thick cloud of dust.
polve 'roso, a *ag* dusty.
po 'mata *sf* ointment, cream.
po 'mello *sm* knob.
pomeridi 'ano, a *ag* afternoon *cpd*; **nelle ore** ~**e** in the afternoon.
pome 'riggio [pome'riddʒo] *sm* afternoon; **nel primo/tardo** ~ in the early/late afternoon.
'pomice ['pomitʃe] *sf* pumice.
pomici 'are [pomi'tʃare] *vi* (*fam: sbaciucchiarsi*) to neck.
'pomo *sm* (*mela*) apple; (*ornamentale*) knob; (*di sella*) pommel; ~ **d'Adamo** (*ANAT*) Adam's apple.
pomo 'doro *sm* tomato.
'pompa *sf* pump; (*sfarzo*) pomp (and ceremony); ~ **antincendio** fire hose; ~ **di**

benzina petrol (*BRIT*) *o* gas (*US*) pump; (*distributore*) filling *o* gas (*US*) station; (**impresa di**) ~**e funebri** funeral parlour *sg* (*BRIT*), undertaker's *sg*, mortician's (*US*).
pom 'pare *vt* to pump; (*trarre*) to pump out; (*gonfiare d'aria*) to pump up.
pompei 'ano, a *ag* of (*o* from) Pompei.
pom 'pelmo *sm* grapefruit.
pompi 'ere *sm* fireman.
pom 'pon [pom'pɔn] *sm inv* pompom, pompon.
pom 'poso, a *ag* pompous.
ponde 'rare *vt* to ponder over, consider carefully.
ponde 'roso, a *ag* (*anche fig*) weighty.
po 'nente *sm* west.
'pongo, 'poni *etc vb vedi* **porre.**
'ponte *sm* bridge; (*di nave*) deck; (: *anche*: ~ **di comando**) bridge; (*impalcatura*) scaffold; **vivere sotto i** ~**i** to be a tramp; **fare il** ~ (*fig*) to take the extra day off (*between 2 public holidays*); **governo** ~ interim government; ~ **aereo** airlift; ~ **di barche** (*MIL*) pontoon bridge; ~ **di coperta** (*NAUT*) upper deck; ~ **levatoio** drawbridge; ~ **radio** radio link; ~ **sospeso** suspension bridge.
pon 'tefice [pon'tefitʃe] *sm* (*REL*) pontiff.
ponti 'cello [ponti'tʃello] *sm* (*di occhiali, MUS*) bridge.
pontifi 'care *vi* (*anche fig*) to pontificate.
pontifi 'cato *sm* pontificate.
ponti 'ficio, a, ci, cie [ponti'fitʃo] *ag* papal; **Stato P**~ Papal State.
pon 'tile *sm* jetty.
'pony ['pɔni] *sm inv* pony.
pool [puːl] *sm inv* (*consorzio*) consortium; (*organismo internazionale*) pool; (*di esperti, ricercatori*) team; (*antimafia, antidroga*) working party.
pop [pɔp] *ag inv* pop *cpd*.
'popcorn ['pɔpkɔːn] *sm inv* popcorn.
'popeline ['pɔpelin] *sm* poplin.
popò *sm inv* (*sedere*) botty.
popo 'lano, a *ag* popular, of the people ♦ *sm/f* man/woman of the people.
popo 'lare *ag* popular; (*quartiere, clientela*) working-class; (*POL*) of P.P.I. ♦ *sm/f* (*POL*) member (*o* supporter) of P.P.I. ♦ *vt* (*rendere abitato*) to populate; **manifestarsi** with people, get crowded; **manifestazione** ~ mass demonstration; **repubblica** ~ people's republic.
popolarità *sf* popularity.
popolazi 'one [popolat'tsjone] *sf* population.
'popolo *sm* people.
popo 'loso, a *ag* densely populated.

po'pone *sm* melon.

'poppa *sf* (*di nave*) stern; (*fam*: *mammella*) breast; **a** ~ aft, astern.

pop'pante *sm/f* unweaned infant; (*fig*: *inesperto*) whippersnapper.

pop'pare *vt* to suck.

pop'pata *sf* (*allattamento*) feed.

poppa'toio *sm* (feeding) bottle.

popu'lista, i, e *ag* populist.

por'caio *sm* (*anche fig*) pigsty.

por'cata *sf* (*libro, film etc*) load of rubbish; **fare una** ~ **a qn** to play a dirty trick on sb.

porcel'lana [portʃel'lana] *sf* porcelain, china; (*oggetto*) piece of porcelain.

porcel'lino, a [portʃel'lino] *sm/f* piglet; ~ **d'India** guinea pig.

porche'ria [porke'ria] *sf* filth, muck; (*fig*: *oscenità*) obscenity; (: *azione disonesta*) dirty trick; (: *cosa mal fatta*) rubbish.

por'chetta [por'ketta] *sf* roast sucking pig.

por'cile [por'tʃile] *sm* pigsty.

por'cino, a [por'tʃino] *ag* of pigs, pork *cpd* ♦ *sm* (*fungo*) type of edible mushroom.

'porco, ci *sm* pig; (*carne*) pork.

porcos'pino *sm* porcupine.

'porfido *sm* porphyry.

'porgere ['pɔrdʒere] *vt* to hand, give; (*tendere*) to hold out.

'porno *ag inv* porn, porno.

pornogra'fia *sf* pornography.

porno'grafico, a, ci, che *ag* pornographic.

'poro *sm* pore.

po'roso, a *ag* porous.

'porpora *sf* purple.

'porre *vt* (*mettere*) to put; (*collocare*) to place; (*posare*) to lay (down), put (down); (*fig*: *supporre*): **poniamo (il caso) che ...** let's suppose that ...; **porsi** *vr* (*mettersi*): **porsi a sedere/in cammino** to sit down/ set off; ~ **le basi di** (*fig*) to lay the foundations of, establish; ~ **una domanda a qn** to ask sb a question, put a question to sb; ~ **la propria fiducia in qn** to place one's trust in sb; ~ **fine** *o* **termine a qc** to put an end *o* a stop to sth; **posto che ...** supposing that ..., on the assumption that ...; **porsi in salvo** to save o.s.

'porro *sm* (*BOT*) leek; (*MED*) wart.

'porsi *etc vb vedi* porgere.

'porta *sf* door; (*SPORT*) goal; (*INFORM*) port; ~**e** *sfpl* (*di città*) gates; **mettere qn alla** ~ to throw sb out; **sbattere** *o* **chiudere la** ~ **in faccia a qn** (*anche fig*) to slam the door in sb's face; **trovare tutte le** ~**e chiuse** (*fig*) to find the way barred; **a** ~**e chiuse** (*DIR*) in camera; **l'inverno è alle** ~**e** (*fig*) winter is upon us; **vendita** ~ **a** ~ door-to-door

selling; ~ **di servizio** tradesmen's entrance; ~ **di sicurezza** emergency exit; ~ **stagna** watertight door.

portaba'gagli [portaba'gaʎʎi] *sm inv* (*facchino*) porter; (*AUT, FERR*) luggage rack.

portabandi'era *sm inv* standard bearer.

porta'borse *sm inv* (*peg*) lackey.

portabot'tiglie [portabot'tiʎʎe] *sm inv* bottle rack.

porta-CD [portatʃi'di] *sm inv* CD rack; (*astuccio*) CD holder.

porta'cenere [porta'tʃenere] *sm inv* ashtray.

portachi'avi [porta'kjavi] *sm inv* keyring.

porta'cipria [porta'tʃiprja] *sm inv* powder compact.

porta'erei *sf inv* (*nave*) aircraft carrier ♦ *sm inv* (*aereo*) aircraft transporter.

portafi'nestra, *pl* portefi'nestre *sf* French window.

porta'foglio [porta'fɔʎʎo] *sm* (*busta*) wallet; (*cartella*) briefcase; (*POL, BORSA*) portfolio; ~ **titoli** investment portfolio.

portagi'oie [porta'dʒɔje] *sm inv*, portagioi'elli [portadʒo'jelli] *sm inv* jewellery (*BRIT*) *o* jewelry (*US*) box.

por'tale *sm* portal.

porta'lettere *sm/f inv* postman/woman (*BRIT*), mailman/woman (*US*).

porta'mento *sm* carriage, bearing.

portamo'nete *sm inv* purse.

por'tante *ag* (*muro etc*) supporting, load-bearing.

portan'tina *sf* sedan chair; (*per ammalati*) stretcher.

portaog'getti [portaod'dʒetti] *ag inv*: **vano** ~ (*in macchina*) glove compartment.

portaom'brelli *sm inv* umbrella stand.

porta'pacchi [porta'pakki] *sm inv* (*di moto, bicicletta*) luggage rack.

por'tare *vt* (*sostenere, sorreggere*: *peso, bambino, pacco*) to carry; (*indossare*: *abito, occhiali*) to wear; (: *capelli lunghi*) to have; (*avere*: *nome, titolo*) to have, bear; (*recare*): ~ **qc a qn** to take (*o* bring) sth to sb; (*fig*: *sentimenti*) to bear; ~**rsi** *vr* (*recarsi*) to go; ~ **avanti** (*discorso, idea*) to pursue; ~ **via** to take away; (*rubare*) to take; ~ **i bambini a spasso** to take the children for a walk; ~ **fortuna** to bring good luck; ~ **qc alla bocca** to lift *o* put sth to one's lips; **porta bene i suoi anni** he's wearing well; **dove porta questa strada?** where does this road lead?, where does this road take you?; **il documento porta la tua firma** the document has *o* bears your signature; **non gli porto rancore** I don't bear him a grudge; **la polizia si è portata sul luogo**

del disastro the police went to the scene of the disaster.
portarit'ratti *sm inv* photo(graph) frame.
portari'viste *sm inv* magazine rack.
portasa'pone *sm inv* soap dish.
portasiga'rette *sm inv* cigarette case.
portas'pilli *sm inv* pincushion.
por'tata *sf* (*vivanda*) course; (*AUT*) carrying (*o* loading) capacity; (*di arma*) range; (*volume d'acqua*) (rate of) flow; (*fig: limite*) scope, capability; (: *importanza*) impact, import; **alla ~ di tutti** (*conoscenza*) within everybody's capabilities; (*prezzo*) within everybody's means; **a/fuori ~ (di)** within/ out of reach (of); **a ~ di mano** within (arm's) reach; **di grande ~** of great importance.
por'tatile *ag* portable.
por'tato, a *ag* (*incline*): **~ a** inclined *o* apt to.
porta'tore, 'trice *sm/f* (*anche COMM*) bearer; (*MED*) carrier; **pagabile al ~** payable to the bearer; **~ di handicap** disabled person.
portatovagli'olo [portatovaʎ'ɔlo] *sm* napkin ring.
portau'ovo *sm inv* eggcup.
porta'voce [porta'votʃe] *sm/f inv* spokesman/woman.
por'tello *sm* (*di portone*) door; (*NAUT*) hatch.
portel'lone *sm* (*NAUT, AER*) hold door.
por'tento *sm* wonder, marvel.
porten'toso, a *ag* wonderful, marvellous (*BRIT*), marvelous (*US*).
porti'cato *sm* portico.
'portico, ci *sm* portico; (*riparo*) lean-to.
porti'era *sf* (*AUT*) door.
porti'ere *sm* (*portinaio*) concierge, caretaker; (*di hotel*) porter; (*nel calcio*) goalkeeper.
porti'naio, a *sm/f* concierge, caretaker.
portine'ria *sf* caretaker's lodge.
'porto, a *pp di* **porgere ♦** *sm* (*NAUT*) harbour (*BRIT*), harbor (*US*), port; (*spesa di trasporto*) carriage ♦ *sm inv* port (wine); **andare** *o* **giungere in ~** (*fig*) to come to a successful conclusion; **condurre qc in ~** to bring sth to a successful conclusion; **~ d'armi** gun licence (*BRIT*) *o* license (*US*); **~ fluviale** river port; **~ franco** free port; **~ marittimo** seaport; **~ militare** naval base; **~ pagato** carriage paid, post free *o* paid; **~ di scalo** port of call.
Porto'gallo *sm*: **il ~** Portugal.
porto'ghese [porto'gese] *ag, sm/f, sm* Portuguese *inv*.
por'tone *sm* main entrance, main door.

portori'cano, a *ag, sm/f* Puerto Rican.
Porto'rico *sf* Puerto Rico.
portu'ale *ag* harbour *cpd* (*BRIT*), harbor *cpd* (*US*), port *cpd* ♦ *sm* dock worker.
porzi'one [por'tsjone] *sf* portion, share; (*di cibo*) portion, helping.
'posa *sf* (*FOT*) exposure; (*atteggiamento, di modello*) pose; (*riposo*): **lavorare senza ~** to work without a break; **mettersi in ~** to pose; **teatro di ~** photographic studio.
posa'cenere [posa'tʃenere] *sm inv* ashtray.
po'sare *vt* to put (down), lay (down) ♦ *vi* (*ponte, edificio, teoria*): **~ su** to rest on; (*FOT, atteggiarsi*) to pose; **~rsi** *vr* (*ape, aereo*) to land; (*uccello*) to alight; (*sguardo*) to settle.
po'sata *sf* piece of cutlery; **~e** *sfpl* cutlery *sg*.
posa'tezza [posa'tettsa] *sf* (*di persona*) composure; (*di discorso*) balanced nature.
po'sato, a *ag* steady; (*discorso*) balanced.
pos'critto *sm* postscript.
'posi *etc vb vedi* **porre.**
positiva'mente *av* positively; (*rispondere*) in the affirmative, affirmatively.
posi'tivo, a *ag* positive.
posizi'one [pozit'tsjone] *sf* position; **farsi una ~** to make one's way in the world; **prendere ~** (*fig*) to take a stand; **luci di ~** (*AUT*) sidelights.
posolo'gia, 'gie [pozolo'dʒia] *sf* dosage, directions *pl* for use.
pos'porre *vt* to place after; (*differire*) to postpone, defer.
pos'posto, a *pp di* **posporre.**
posse'dere *vt* to own, possess; (*qualità, virtù*) to have, possess; (*conoscere a fondo: lingua etc*) to have a thorough knowledge of; (*sog: ira etc*) to possess.
possedi'mento *sm* possession.
pos'sente *ag* strong, powerful.
posses'sivo, a *ag* possessive.
pos'sesso *sm* possession; **essere in ~ di qc** to be in possession of sth; **prendere ~ di qc** to take possession of sth; **entrare in ~ dell'eredità** to come into one's inheritance.
posses'sore *sm* owner.
pos'sibile *ag* possible ♦ *sm*: **fare tutto il ~** to do everything possible; **nei limiti del ~** as far as possible; **al più tardi ~** as late as possible; **vieni prima ~** come as soon as possible.
possibi'lista, i, e *ag*: **essere ~** to keep an open mind.
possibilità *sf inv* possibility ♦ *sfpl* (*mezzi*) means; **aver la ~ di fare** to be in a position to do; to have the opportunity to do; **nei**

limiti delle nostre ~ in so far as we can.

possibil 'mente *av* if possible.

possi 'dente *sm/f* landowner.

possi 'edo *etc vb vedi* **possedere.**

'posso *etc vb vedi* **potere.**

post... *prefisso* post....

'posta *sf* (*servizio*) post, postal service; (*corrispondenza*) post, mail; (*ufficio postale*) post office; (*nei giochi d'azzardo*) stake; (*CACCIA*) hide (*BRIT*), blind (*US*); ~**e** *sfpl* (*amministrazione*) post office; **fare la** ~ **a qn** (*fig*) to lie in wait for sb; **la** ~ **in gioco è troppo alta** (*fig*) there's too much at stake; **a bella** ~ (*apposta*) on purpose; **piccola** ~ (*su giornale*) letters to the editor, letters page; ~ **aerea** airmail; ~ **elettronica** electronic mail; ~ **ordinaria** ≈ second-class mail; ~ **prioritaria** first class (post); **P~e e Telecomunicazioni (PP.TT.)** *postal and telecommunications service*; **ministro delle P~e e Telecomunicazioni** Postmaster General.

posta 'giro [posta'dʒiro] *sm* post office cheque (*BRIT*) *o* check (*US*), postal giro (*BRIT*).

pos 'tale *ag* postal, post office *cpd* ♦ *sm* (*treno*) mail train; (*nave*) mail boat; (*furgone*) mail van; **timbro** ~ postmark.

postazi 'one [postat'tsjone] *sf* (*MIL*) emplacement.

post 'bellico, a, ci, che *ag* postwar.

postda 'tare *vt* to postdate.

posteggi 'are [posted'dʒare] *vt, vi* to park.

posteggia 'tore, 'trice [posteddʒa'tore] *sm/f* car-park attendant (*BRIT*), parking-lot attendant (*US*).

pos 'teggio [pos'teddʒo] *sm* car park (*BRIT*), parking lot (*US*); (*di taxi*) rank (*BRIT*), stand (*US*).

postelegra 'fonico, a, ci, che *ag* postal and telecommunications *cpd*.

'poster *sm inv* poster.

'posteri *smpl* posterity *sg*; **i nostri** ~ our descendants.

posteri 'ore *ag* (*dietro*) back; (*dopo*) later ♦ *sm* (*fam*: *sedere*) behind.

posteri 'ori: a ~ *ag inv* after the event (*dopo sostantivo*) ♦ *av* looking back.

posterità *sf* posterity.

pos 'ticcio, a, ci, ce [pos'tittʃo] *ag* false ♦ *sm* hairpiece.

postici 'pare [postitʃi'pare] *vt* to defer, postpone.

pos 'tilla *sf* marginal note.

pos 'tino *sm* postman (*BRIT*), mailman (*US*).

'posto, a *pp di* **porre** ♦ *sm* (*sito, posizione*) place; (*impiego*) job; (*spazio libero*) room, space; (*di parcheggio*) space; (*sedile*: *al*

teatro, in treno etc) seat; (*MIL*) post; **a** ~ (*in ordine*) in place, tidy; (*fig*) settled; (: *persona*) reliable; **mettere a** ~ (*riordinare*) to tidy (up), put in order; (*faccende*: *sistemare*) to straighten out; **prender** ~ to take a seat; **al** ~ **di** in place of; **sul** ~ on the spot; ~ **di blocco** roadblock; ~ **di lavoro** job; ~ **di polizia** police station; ~ **telefonico pubblico (P.T.P.)** public telephone; ~ **di villeggiatura** holiday (*BRIT*) *o* tourist spot; **~i in piedi** (*TEAT, in autobus*) standing room.

postopera 'torio, a *ag* (*MED*) postoperative.

pos 'tribolo *sm* brothel.

post 'scriptum *sm inv* postscript.

'postumo, a *ag* posthumous; (*tardivo*) belated; **~i** *smpl* (*conseguenze*) aftereffects, consequences.

po 'tabile *ag* drinkable; **acqua** ~ drinking water.

po 'tare *vt* to prune.

po 'tassio *sm* potassium.

pota 'tura *sf* pruning.

po 'tente *ag* (*nazione*) strong, powerful; (*veleno, farmaco*) potent, strong.

poten 'tino, a *ag* of (*o* from) Potenza.

Po 'tenza [po'tɛntsa] *sf* Potenza.

po 'tenza [po'tɛntsa] *sf* power; (*forza*) strength; **all'ennesima** ~ to the nth degree; **le Grandi P~e** the Great Powers; ~ **militare** military might *o* strength.

potenzi 'ale [poten'tsjale] *ag, sm* potential.

potenzia 'mento [potentsja'mento] *sm* development.

potenzi 'are [poten'tsjare] *vt* to develop.

============ **PAROLA CHIAVE**

po 'tere *sm* power; **al** ~ (*partito etc*) in power; ~ **d'acquisto** purchasing power; ~ **esecutivo** executive power; ~ **giudiziario** legal power; ~ **legislativo** legislative power

♦ *vb aus* **1** (*essere in grado di*) can, be able to; **non ha potuto ripararlo** he couldn't *o* he wasn't able to repair it; **non è potuto venire** he couldn't *o* he wasn't able to come; **spiacente di non poter aiutare** sorry not to be able to help

2 (*avere il permesso*) can, may, be allowed to; **posso entrare?** can *o* may I come in?; **posso chiederti dove sei stato?** where, may I ask, have you been?

3 (*eventualità*) may, might, could; **potrebbe essere vero** it might *o* could be true; **può aver avuto un incidente** he may *o* might *o* could have had an accident;

può darsi perhaps; **può darsi** o **può essere che non venga** he may o might not come 4 (augurio): **potessi almeno parlargli!** if only I could speak to him! 5 (suggerimento): **potresti almeno scusarti!** you could at least apologize! ♦ vt can, be able to; **può molto per noi** he can do a lot for us; **non ne posso più** (per stanchezza) I'm exhausted; (per rabbia) I can't take any more.

potestà sf (potere) power; (DIR) authority.
potrò etc vb vedi **potere**.
pove raccio, a, ci, ce [pove'rattʃo] sm/f poor devil.
povero, a ag poor; (disadorno) plain, bare ♦ sm/f poor man/woman; **i** ~**i** the poor; ~ **di** lacking in, having little; **minerale** ~ **di ferro** ore with a low iron content; **paese** ~ **di risorse** country short of o lacking in resources.
povertà sf poverty.
pozi one [pot'tsjone] sf potion.
pozza ['pottsa] sf pool.
poz zanghera [pot'tsangera] sf puddle.
pozzo ['pottso] sm well; (cava: di carbone) pit; (di miniera) shaft; ~ **nero** cesspit; ~ **petrolifero** oil well.
pp. abbr (= pagine) pp.
p.p. abbr (= per procura) pp.
P.P.I. sigla m (POL) (= Partito Popolare Italiano) party originating from D.C.
PP.TT. abbr = **Poste e Telecomunicazioni**; vedi **posta**.
PR sigla = Parma ♦ sigla m (POL) = Partito Radicale.
P.R. abbr = **piano regolatore; procuratore della Repubblica**.
Praga sf Prague.
prag matico, a, ci, che ag pragmatic.
pram matica sf custom; **essere di** ~ to be customary.
pranotera pia sf pranotherapy.
pran zare [pran'dzare] vi to dine, have dinner; to lunch, have lunch.
pranzo ['prandzo] sm dinner; (a mezzogiorno) lunch.
prassi sf usual procedure.
pratica, che sf practice; (esperienza) experience; (conoscenza) knowledge, familiarity; (tirocinio) training, practice; (AMM: affare) matter, case; (: incartamento) file, dossier; **in** ~ (praticamente) in practice; **mettere in** ~ to put into practice; **fare le** ~**che per** (AMM) to do the paperwork for; ~ **restrittiva** restrictive practice; ~**che illecite** dishonest practices.

prati cabile ag (progetto) practicable, feasible; (luogo) passable, practicable.
pratica mente av (in modo pratico) in a practical way, practically; (quasi) practically, almost.
prati cante sm/f apprentice, trainee; (REL) (regular) churchgoer.
prati care vt to practise (BRIT), practice (US); (SPORT: tennis etc) to play; (: nuoto, scherma etc) to go in for; (eseguire: apertura, buco) to make; ~ **uno sconto** to give a discount.
praticità [pratitʃi'ta] sf practicality, practicalness; **per** ~ for practicality's sake.
pratico, a, ci, che ag practical; ~ **di** (esperto) experienced o skilled in; (familiare) familiar with; **all'atto** ~ in practice; **è** ~ **del mestiere** he knows his trade; **mi è più** ~ **venire di pomeriggio** it's more convenient for me to come in the afternoon.
prato sm meadow; (di giardino) lawn.
preal larme sm warning (signal).
Pre alpi sfpl: **le** ~ (the) Pre-Alps.
preal pino, a ag of the Pre-Alps.
pre ambolo sm preamble; **senza tanti** ~**i** without beating about (BRIT) o around (US) the bush.
preannunci are [preannun'tʃare], **preannunzi are** [preannun'tsjare] vt to give advance notice of.
preavvi sare vt to give advance notice of.
preav viso sm notice; **telefonata con** ~ personal o person to person call.
pre bellico, a, ci, che ag prewar cpd.
precari ato sm temporary employment.
precarietà sf precariousness.
pre cario, a ag precarious; (INS) temporary, without tenure.
precauzio nale [prekauttsjo'nale] ag precautionary.
precauzi one [prekaut'tsjone] sf caution, care; (misura) precaution; **prendere** ~**i** to take precautions.
prece dente [pretʃe'dente] ag previous ♦ sm precedent; **il discorso/film** ~ the previous o preceding speech/film; **senza** ~**i** unprecedented; ~**i penali** (DIR) criminal record sg.
precedente mente [pretʃedente'mente] av previously.
prece denza [pretʃe'dentsa] sf priority, precedence; (AUT) right of way; **dare** ~ **assoluta a qc** to give sth top priority.
pre cedere [pre'tʃedere] vt to precede, go (o come) before.
precet tare [pretʃet'tare] vt (lavoratori) to

order back to work (*via an injunction*).

precettazi'one [pretʃettat'tsjone] *sf* (*di lavoratori*) order to resume work.

pre'cetto [pre'tʃɛtto] *sm* precept; (*MIL*) call-up notice.

precet'tore [pretʃet'tore] *sm* (*private*) tutor.

precipi'tare [pretʃipi'tare] *vi* (*cadere*) to fall headlong; (*fig: situazione*) to get out of control ♦ *vt* (*gettare dall'alto in basso*) to hurl, fling; (*fig: affrettare*) to rush; ~**rsi** *vr* (*gettarsi*) to hurl *o* fling o.s.; (*affrettarsi*) to rush.

precipi'tato, a [pretʃipi'tato] *ag* hasty ♦ *sm* (*CHIM*) precipitate.

precipitazi'one [pretʃipitat'tsjone] *sf* (*METEOR*) precipitation; (*fig*) haste.

precipi'toso, a [pretʃipi'toso] *ag* (*caduta, fuga*) headlong; (*fig: avventato*) rash, reckless; (: *affrettato*) hasty, rushed.

preci'pizio [pretʃi'pittsjo] *sm* precipice; **a** ~ (*fig: correre*) headlong.

pre'cipuo, a [pre'tʃipuo] *ag* principal, main.

precisa'mente [pretʃiza'mente] *av* (*gen*) precisely; (*con esattezza*) exactly.

preci'sare [pretʃi'zare] *vt* to state, specify; (*spiegare*) to explain (in detail); **vi preciseremo la data in seguito** we'll let you know the exact date later; **tengo a** ~ **che** ... I must point out that ....

precisazi'one [pretʃizat'tsjone] *sf* clarification.

precisi'one [pretʃi'zjone] *sf* precision; accuracy; **strumenti di** ~ precision instruments.

pre'ciso, a [pre'tʃizo] *ag* (*esatto*) precise; (*accurato*) accurate, precise; (*deciso: idea*) precise, definite; (*uguale*): **2 vestiti** ~**i** 2 dresses exactly the same; **sono le 9** ~**e** it's exactly 9 o'clock.

pre'cludere *vt* to block, obstruct.

pre'cluso, a *pp di* **precludere**.

pre'coce [pre'kɔtʃe] *ag* early; (*bambino*) precocious; (*vecchiaia*) premature.

precocità [prekotʃi'ta] *sf* (*di morte*) untimeliness; (*di bambino*) precociousness.

precon'cetto, a [prekon'tʃɛtto] *ag* preconceived ♦ *sm* preconceived idea, prejudice.

pre'correre *vt* to anticipate; ~ **i tempi** to be ahead of one's time.

precorri'tore, 'trice *sm/f* precursor, forerunner.

pre'corso, a *pp di* **precorrere**.

precur'sore *sm* forerunner, precursor.

'preda *sf* (*bottino*) booty; (*animale, fig*) prey; **essere** ~ **di** to fall prey to; **essere in** ~ **a** to

be prey to.

pre'dare *vt* to plunder.

preda'tore *sm* predator.

predeces'sore, a [predetʃes'sore] *sm/f* predecessor.

pre'della *sf* platform, dais; altar-step.

predesti'nare *vt* to predestine.

predestinazi'one [predestinat'tsjone] *sf* predestination.

pre'detto, a *pp di* **predire** ♦ *ag* aforesaid, aforementioned.

'predica, che *sf* sermon; (*fig*) lecture, talking-to.

predi'care *vt, vi* to preach.

predica'tivo, a *ag* predicative.

predi'cato *sm* (*LING*) predicate.

predi'letto, a *pp di* **prediligere** ♦ *ag, sm/f* favourite (*BRIT*), favorite (*US*).

predilezi'one [predilet'tsjone] *sf* fondness, partiality; **avere una** ~ **per qc/qn** to be partial to sth/fond of sb.

predi'ligere [predi'lidʒere] *vt* to prefer, have a preference for.

pre'dire *vt* to foretell, predict.

predis'porre *vt* to get ready, prepare; ~ **qn a qc** to predispose sb to sth.

predisposizi'one [predispozit'tsjone] *sf* (*MED*) predisposition; (*attitudine*) bent, aptitude; **avere** ~ **alla musica** to have a bent for music.

predis'posto, a *pp di* **predisporre**.

predizi'one [predit'tsjone] *sf* prediction.

predomi'nante *ag* predominant.

predomi'nare *vi* (*prevalere*) to predominate; (*eccellere*) to excel.

predo'minio *sm* predominance; supremacy.

preesis'tente *ag* pre-existent.

pree'sistere *vi* to pre-exist.

preesis'tito, a *pp di* **preesistere**.

prefabbri'cato, a *ag* (*EDIL*) prefabricated.

prefazi'one [prefat'tsjone] *sf* preface, foreword.

prefe'renza [prefe'rɛntsa] *sf* preference; **a** ~ **di** rather than; **di** ~ preferably, by preference; **non ho** ~**e** I have no preferences either way, I don't mind.

preferenzi'ale [preferen'tsjale] *ag* preferential; **corsia** ~ (*AUT*) bus and taxi lane.

prefe'ribile *ag*: ~ (**a**) preferable (to), better (than); **sarebbe** ~ **andarsene** it would be better to go.

preferibil'mente *av* preferably.

prefe'rire *vt* to prefer, like better; ~ **il caffè al tè** to prefer coffee to tea, like coffee better than tea.

pre'fetto *sm* prefect.

prefet'tura *sf* prefecture.

pre'figgersi [pre'fidd3ersi] *vr:* ~ **uno scopo**
to set o.s. a goal.

prefigu'rare *vt* (*simboleggiare*) to
foreshadow; (*prevedere*) to foresee.

pre'fisso, a *pp di* **prefiggersi ♦** *sm* (*LING*)
prefix; (*TEL*) dialling (*BRIT*) o dial (*US*)
code.

Preg. *abbr* = **pregiatissimo.**

pre'gare *vi* to pray ♦ *vt* (*REL*) to pray to;
(*implorare*) to beg; (*chiedere*): ~ **qn di fare**
to ask sb to do; **farsi** ~ to need coaxing *o*
persuading.

pre'gevole [pre'd3evole] *ag* valuable.

pregherò *etc* [prege'rɔ] *vb vedi* **pregare.**

preghi'era [pre'gjɛra] *sf* (*REL*) prayer;
(*domanda*) request.

pregi'arsi [pre'd3arsi] *vr:* **mi pregio di farle**
sapere che ... I am pleased to inform you
that ....

pregia'tissimo, a [pred3a'tissimo] *ag* (*in*
lettere): ~ **Signor G. Agnelli** G. Agnelli
Esquire.

pregi'ato, a [pre'd3ato] *ag* (*opera*) valuable;
(*tessuto*) fine; (*valuta*) strong; **vino** ~
vintage wine.

'pregio ['prɛd3o] *sm* (*stima*) esteem, regard;
(*qualità*) (good) quality, merit; (*valore*)
value, worth; **il** ~ **di questo sistema è ...**
the merit of this system is ...; **oggetto di**
~ valuable object.

pregiudi'care [pred3udi'kare] *vt* to
prejudice, harm, be detrimental to.

pregiudi'cato, a [pred3udi'kato] *sm/f* (*DIR*)
previous offender.

pregiu'dizio [pred3u'dittsjo] *sm* (*idea errata*)
prejudice; (*danno*) harm *no pl.*

preg'nante [preɲ'ɲante] *ag* (*fig*) pregnant,
meaningful.

'pregno, a ['preɲɲo] *ag* (*saturo*): ~ **di** full
of, saturated with.

'prego *escl* (*a chi ringrazia*) don't mention
it!; (*invitando qn ad accomodarsi*) please sit
down!; (*invitando qn ad andare prima*) after
you!

pregus'tare *vt* to look forward to.

preis'toria *sf* prehistory.

preis'torico, a, ci, che *ag* prehistoric.

pre'lato *sm* prelate.

prela'vaggio [prela'vadd3o] *sm* pre-wash.

prelazi'one [prelat'tsjone] *sf* (*DIR*) pre-
emption; **avere il diritto di** ~ **su qc** to have
the first option on sth.

preleva'mento *sm* (*BANCA*) withdrawal; (*di*
merce) picking up, collection.

prele'vare *vt* (*denaro*) to withdraw;
(*campione*) to take; (*merce*) to pick up,
collect; (*sog: polizia*) to take, capture.

preli'evo *sm* (*BANCA*) withdrawal; (*MED*):
fare un ~ **(di)** to take a sample (of).

prelimi'nare *ag* preliminary; ~**i** *smpl*
preliminary talks; preliminaries.

pre'ludere *vi:* ~ **a** (*preannunciare: crisi,*
guerra, temporale) to herald, be a sign of;
(*introdurre: dibattito etc*) to introduce, be a
prelude to.

pre'ludio *sm* prelude.

pre'luso, a *pp di* **preludere.**

pre-ma'man [prema'mã] *sm inv* maternity
dress.

prematrimoni'ale *ag* premarital.

prema'turo, a *ag* premature.

premedi'tare *vt* to premeditate, plan.

premeditazi'one [premeditat'tsjone] *sf*
(*DIR*) premeditation; **con** ~ *ag*
premeditated ♦ *av* with intent.

'premere *vt* to press ♦ *vi:* ~ **su** to press
down on; (*fig*) to put pressure on; ~ **a** (*fig:*
importare) to matter to; ~ **il grilletto** to
pull the trigger.

pre'messo, a *pp di* **premettere ♦** *sf*
introductory statement, introduction;
mancano le ~**e per una buona riuscita** we
lack the basis for a successful outcome.

pre'mettere *vt* to put before; (*dire prima*)
to start by saying, state first; **premetto**
che ... I must say first of all that ...;
premesso che ... given that ...; **ciò**
premesso ... that having been said ....

premi'are *vt* to give a prize to; (*fig: merito,*
onestà) to reward.

premiazi'one [premjat'tsjone] *sf* prize
giving.

'premier ['prɛmjer] *sm inv* premier.

premi'nente *ag* pre-eminent.

'premio *sm* prize; (*ricompensa*) reward;
(*COMM*) premium; (*AMM: indennità*) bonus;
in ~ **per** as a prize (*o reward*) for; ~
d'ingaggio (*SPORT*) signing-on fee; ~ **di**
produzione productivity bonus.

pre'misi *etc vb vedi* **premettere.**

premoni'tore, 'trice *ag* premonitory.

premonizi'one [premonit'tsjone] *sf*
premonition.

premu'nirsi *vr:* ~ **di** to provide o.s. with; ~
contro to protect o.s. from, guard o.s.
against.

pre'mura *sf* (*fretta*) haste, hurry; (*riguardo*)
attention, care; **aver** ~ to be in a hurry;
far ~ **a qn** to hurry sb; **usare ogni** ~ **nei**
riguardi di qn, circondare qn di ~**e** to be
very attentive to sb.

premu'roso, a *ag* thoughtful, considerate.

prena'tale *ag* antenatal.

'prendere *vt* to take; (*andare a prendere*) to
get, fetch; (*ottenere*) to get; (*guadagnare*)

to get, earn; (*catturare*: *ladro, pesce*) to catch; (*collaboratore, dipendente*) to take on; (*passeggero*) to pick up; (*chiedere*: *somma, prezzo*) to charge, ask; (*trattare*: *persona*) to handle ◊ *vi* (*colla, cemento*) to set; (*pianta*) to take; (*fuoco: nel camino*) to catch; (*voltare*): ~ **a destra** to turn (to the) right; ~**rsi** *vr* (*azzuffarsi*): ~**rsi a pugni** to come to blows; **prende qualcosa?** (*da bere, da mangiare*) would you like something to eat (*o* drink)?; **prendo un caffè** I'll have a coffee; ~ **a fare qc** to start doing sth; ~ **qn/qc per** (*scambiare*) to take sb/sth for; ~ **l'abitudine di** to get into the habit of; ~ **fuoco** to catch fire; ~ **le generalità di qn** to take down sb's particulars; ~ **nota di** to take note of; ~ **parte a** to take part in; ~**rsi cura di qn/qc** to look after sb/sth; ~**rsi un impegno** to take on a commitment; **prendersela** (*adirarsi*) to get annoyed; (*preoccuparsi*) to get upset, worry.

prendi'sole *sm inv* sundress.

preno'tare *vt* to book, reserve.

prenotazi'one [prenotat'tsjone] *sf* booking, reservation.

'prensile *ag* prehensile.

preoccu'pante *ag* worrying.

preoccu'pare *vt* to worry; ~**rsi** *vr*: ~**rsi di qn/qc** to worry about sb/sth; ~**rsi per qn** to be anxious for sb.

preoccupazi'one [preokkupat'tsjone] *sf* worry, anxiety.

preordi'nato, a *ag* preordained.

prepa'rare *vt* to prepare; (*esame, concorso*) to prepare for; ~**rsi** *vr* (*vestirsi*) to get ready; ~**rsi a qc/a fare** to get ready *o* prepare (o.s.) for sth/to do; ~ **da mangiare** to prepare a meal.

prepara'tivi *smpl* preparations.

prepa'rato, a *ag* (*gen*) prepared; (*pronto*) ready ◊ *sm* (*prodotto*) preparation.

prepara'torio, a *ag* preparatory.

preparazi'one [preparat'tsjone] *sf* preparation; **non ha la necessaria** ~ **per svolgere questo lavoro** he lacks the qualifications necessary for the job.

prepensiona'mento *sm* early retirement.

preponde'rante *ag* predominant.

pre'porre *vt* to place before; (*fig*) to prefer.

preposizi'one [prepozit'tsjone] *sf* (*LING*) preposition.

pre'posto, a *pp di* **preporre**.

prepo'tente *ag* (*persona*) domineering, arrogant; (*bisogno, desiderio*) overwhelming, pressing ◊ *sm/f* bully.

prepo'tenza [prepo'tɛntsa] *sf* arrogance;

(*comportamento*) arrogant behaviour (*BRIT*) *o* behavior (*US*).

pre'puzio [pre'puttsjo] *sm* (*ANAT*) foreskin.

preroga'tiva *sf* prerogative.

'presa *sf* taking *no pl*; catching *no pl*; (*di città*) capture; (*indurimento: di cemento*) setting; (*appiglio, SPORT*) hold; (*di acqua, gas*) (supply) point; (*ELETTR*): ~ **(di corrente)** socket; (: *al muro*) point; (*piccola quantità*: *di sale etc*) pinch; (*CARTE*) trick; **far** ~ (*colla*) to set; **ha fatto** ~ **sul pubblico** (*fig*) it caught the public's imagination; **a** ~ **rapida** (*cemento*) quick-setting; **di forte** ~ (*fig*) with wide appeal; **essere alle** ~**e con qc** (*fig*) to be struggling with sth; **macchina da** ~ (*CINE*) cine camera (*BRIT*), movie camera (*US*); ~ **d'aria** air inlet; ~ **diretta** (*AUT*) direct drive; ~ **in giro** leg-pull (*BRIT*), joke; ~ **di posizione** stand.

pre'sagio [pre'zadʒo] *sm* omen.

presa'gire [preza'dʒire] *vt* to foresee.

presa'lario *sm* (*INS*) grant.

'presbite *ag* long-sighted.

presbiteri'ano, a *ag, sm/f* Presbyterian.

presbi'terio *sm* presbytery.

pre'scindere [preʃ'ʃindere] *vi*: ~ **da** to leave out of consideration; **a** ~ **da** apart from.

pre'scisso, a [preʃ'ʃisso] *pp di* **prescindere**.

presco'lastico, a, ci, che *ag* pre-school *cpd*.

pres'critto, a *pp di* **prescrivere**.

pres'crivere *vt* to prescribe.

prescrizi'one [preskrit'tsjone] *sf* (*MED, DIR*) prescription; (*norma*) rule, regulation; **cadere in** ~ (*DIR*) to become statute-barred.

'prese *etc vb vedi* **prendere**.

presen'tare *vt* to present; (*far conoscere*): ~ **qn (a)** to introduce sb (to); (*AMM: inoltrare*) to submit; ~**rsi** *vr* (*recarsi, farsi vedere*) to present o.s., appear; (*farsi conoscere*) to introduce o.s.; (*occasione*) to arise; ~ **qc in un'esposizione** to show *o* display sth at an exhibition; ~ **qn in società** to introduce sb into society; ~**rsi come candidato** (*POL*) to stand (*BRIT*) *o* run (*US*) as a candidate; ~**rsi bene/male** to have a good/poor appearance; **la situazione si presenta difficile** things aren't looking too good, things look a bit tricky.

presentazi'one [prezentat'tsjone] *sf* presentation; introduction.

pre'sente *ag* present; (*questo*) this ◊ *sm* present ◊ *sf* (*lettera*): **con la** ~ **vi comunico ... this** is to inform you that ... ◊ *sm/f* person present; **i** ~**i** those present; **aver** ~ **qc/qn** to remember sth/sb; **essere** ~ **a una**

riunione to be present at *o* attend a meeting; **tener** ~ **qn/qc** to keep sb/sth in mind; **esclusi i** ~**i** present company excepted.

presenti 'mento *sm* premonition.

pre 'senza [pre'zɛntsa] *sf* presence; (*aspetto esteriore*) appearance; **in** ~ **di** in (the) presence of; **di bella** ~ of good appearance; ~ **di spirito** presence of mind.

presenzi 'are [prezen'tsjare] *vi*: ~ **a** to be present at, attend.

pre 'sepio, pre 'sepe *sm* crib.

preser 'vare *vt* to protect.

preserva 'tivo *sm* sheath, condom.

'presi *etc vb vedi* **prendere**.

'preside *sm/f* (*INS*) head (teacher) (*BRIT*), principal (*US*); (*di facoltà universitaria*) dean.

presi 'dente *sm* (*POL*) president; (*di assemblea, COMM*) chairman; **il P**~ **della Camera** (*POL*) ≈ the Speaker; **P**~ **del Consiglio (dei Ministri)** ≈ Prime Minister; **P**~ **della Repubblica** President of the Republic; *vedi nota nel riquadro.*

PRESIDENTE

The **Presidente del Consiglio**, *the Italian Prime Minister, is the leader of the Government. He or she submits nominations for ministerial posts to the "Presidente della Repubblica", who then appoints them if approved. The* **Presidente del Consiglio** *is appointed by the "Presidente della Repubblica", in consultation with the leaders of the parliamentary parties, former heads of state, the "Presidente della Camera" and the "Presidente del Senato". The* **Presidente della Repubblica** *is the head of state. He or she must be an Italian citizen of at least 50 years of age, and is elected by Parliament and by three delegates from each of the Italian regions. He has the power to suspend the implementation of legislation and to dissolve one or both chambers of Parliament, and he presides over the magistrates' governing body (the "Consiglio Superiore della Magistratura").*

---

presiden 'tessa *sf* president; (*moglie*) president's wife; (*di assemblea, COMM*) chairwoman.

presi 'denza [presi'dɛntsa] *sf* presidency; office of president; chairmanship; **assumere la** ~ to become president; to take the chair; **essere alla** ~ to be president (*o* chairman); **candidato alla** ~ presidential candidate; candidate for the

chairmanship.

presidenzi 'ale [presidɛn'tsjale] *ag* presidential.

presidi 'are *vt* to garrison.

pre 'sidio *sm* garrison.

presi 'edere *vt* to preside over ♦ *vi*: ~ **a** to direct, be in charge of.

'preso, a *pp di* **prendere**.

'pressa *sf* (*TECN*) press.

pres 'sante *ag* (*bisogno, richiesta*) urgent, pressing.

pressap 'poco *av* about, roughly, approximately.

pres 'sare *vt* (*anche fig*) to press; ~ **qn con richieste** to pursue sb with demands.

pressi 'one *sf* pressure; **far** ~ **su qn** to put pressure on sb; **subire forti** ~**i** to be under strong pressure; ~ **sanguigna** blood pressure.

'presso *av* (*vicino*) nearby, close at hand ♦ *prep* (*vicino a*) near; (*accanto a*) beside, next to; (*in casa di*): ~ **qn** at sb's home; (*nelle lettere*) care of (*abbr* c/o); (*alle dipendenze di*): **lavora** ~ **di noi** he works for *o* with us ♦ *smpl*: **nei** ~**i di** near, in the vicinity of; **ha avuto grande successo** ~ **i giovani** it has been a hit with young people.

pressoché [presso'ke] *av* nearly, almost.

pressuriz 'zare [pressurid'dzare] *vt* to pressurize.

prestabi 'lire *vt* to arrange beforehand, arrange in advance.

presta 'nome *sm/f inv* (*peg*) figurehead.

pres 'tante *ag* good-looking.

pres 'tanza [pres'tantsa] *sf* (*robust*) good looks *pl*.

pres 'tare *vt*: ~ **(qc a qn)** to lend (sb sth *o* sth to sb); ~**rsi** *vr* (*offrirsi*): ~**rsi a** **fare** to offer to do; (*essere adatto*): ~**rsi a** to lend itself to, be suitable for; ~ **aiuto** to lend a hand; ~ **ascolto** *o* **orecchio** to listen; ~ **attenzione** to pay attention; ~ **fede a qc/ qn** to give credence to sth/sb; ~ **giuramento** to take an oath; **la frase si presta a molteplici interpretazioni** the phrase lends itself to numerous interpretations.

prestazi 'one [prestat'tsjone] *sf* (*TECN, SPORT*) performance, ~**i** *sfpl* (*di persona: servizi*) services.

prestigia 'tore, 'trice [prestidʒa'tore] *sm/f* conjurer.

pres 'tigio [pres'tidʒo] *sm* (*potere*) prestige; (*illusione*): **gioco di** ~ conjuring trick.

prestigi 'oso, a [presti'dʒoso] *ag* prestigious.

'prestito *sm* lending *no pl*; loan; dar in ~ to lend; prendere in ~ to borrow; ~ bancario bank loan; ~ pubblico public borrowing.

'presto *av* (*tra poco*) soon; (*in fretta*) quickly; (*di buon'ora*) early; a ~ see you soon; ~ o tardi sooner or later; fare ~ a fare qc to hurry up and do sth; (*non costare fatica*) to have no trouble doing sth; si fa ~ a criticare it's easy to criticize; è ancora ~ per decidere it's still too early *o* too soon to decide.

pre'sumere *vt* to presume, assume.

presu'mibile *ag* (*dati, risultati*) likely.

pre'sunsi *etc vb vedi* presumere.

pre'sunto, a *pp di* presumere ♦ *ag*: il ~ colpevole the alleged culprit.

presuntu'oso, a *ag* presumptuous.

presunzi'one [prezun'tsjone] *sf* presumption.

presup'porre *vt* to suppose; to presuppose.

presup'posto, a *pp di* presupporre ♦ *sm* (*premessa*) supposition, premise; partendo dal ~ che ... assuming that ...; mancano i ~i necessari the necessary conditions are lacking.

'prete *sm* priest.

preten'dente *sm/f* pretender ♦ *sm* (*corteggiatore*) suitor.

pre'tendere *vt* (*esigere*) to demand, require; (*sostenere*): ~ che to claim that; pretende di aver sempre ragione he thinks he's always right.

pretenzi'oso, a [preten'tsjoso] *ag* pretentious.

preterintenzio'nale [preterintentsjo'nale] *ag* (*DIR*): omicidio ~ manslaughter.

pre'teso, a *pp di* pretendere ♦ *sf* (*esigenza*) claim, demand; (*presunzione, sfarzo*) pretentiousness; avanzare una ~a to put forward a claim *o* demand; senza ~e *ag* unpretentious ♦ *av* unpretentiously.

pre'testo *sm* pretext, excuse; con il ~ di on the pretext of.

pretestu'oso, a *ag* (*data, motivo*) used as an excuse.

pre'tore *sm* magistrate.

pre'tura *sf* (*DIR: sede*) magistrate's court (*BRIT*), circuit *o* superior court (*US*); (: *magistratura*) magistracy.

preva'lente *ag* prevailing.

prevalente'mente *av* mainly, for the most part.

preva'lenza [preva'lɛntsa] *sf* predominance.

preva'lere *vi* to prevail.

pre'valso, a *pp di* prevalere.

prevari'care *vi* (*abusare del potere*) to abuse one's power.

prevaricazi'one [prevarikat'tsjone] *sf* (*abuso di potere*) abuse of power.

preve'dere *vt* (*indovinare*) to foresee; (*presagire*) to foretell; (*considerare*) to make provision for; nulla lasciava ~ che ... there was nothing to suggest *o* to make one think that ...; come previsto as expected; spese previste anticipated expenditure; previsto per martedì scheduled for Tuesday.

prev'edibile *ag* predictable; non era assolutamente ~ che ... no one could have foreseen that ....

prevedibil'mente *av* as one would expect.

preve'nire *vt* (*anticipare: obiezione*) to forestall; (: *domanda*) to anticipate; (*evitare*) to avoid, prevent; (*avvertire*): ~ qn (di) to warn sb (of); to inform sb (of).

preventi'vare *vt* (*COMM*) to estimate.

preven'tivo, a *ag* preventive ♦ *sm* (*COMM*) estimate; fare un ~ to give an estimate; bilancio ~ budget; carcere ~ custody (*pending trial*).

preve'nuto, a *ag* (*mal disposto*): ~ (contro qc/qn) prejudiced (against sth/sb).

prevenzi'one [preven'tsjone] *sf* prevention; (*preconcetto*) prejudice.

previ'dente *ag* showing foresight; prudent.

previ'denza [previ'dɛntsa] *sf* foresight; istituto di ~ provident institution; ~ sociale social security (*BRIT*), welfare (*US*).

pre'vidi *etc vb vedi* prevedere.

'previo, a *ag* (*COMM*): ~ avviso upon notice; ~ pagamento upon payment.

previsi'one *sf* forecast, prediction; ~i meteorologiche *o* del tempo weather forecast *sg*.

pre'visto, a *pp di* prevedere ♦ *sm*: piú/meno del ~ more/less than expected; prima del ~ earlier than expected.

prezi'oso, a [pret'tsjoso] *ag* precious; (*aiuto, consiglio*) invaluable ♦ *sm* jewel; valuable.

prez'zemolo [pret'tsemolo] *sm* parsley.

'prezzo ['prɛttso] *sm* price; a ~ di costo at cost, at cost price (*BRIT*); tirare sul ~ to bargain, haggle; il ~ pattuito è 1000 di euro the agreed price is 1000 euros; ~ d'acquisto/di vendita buying/selling price; ~ di fabbrica factory price; ~ di mercato market price; ~ scontato reduced price; ~ unitario unit price.

P.R.I. *sigla m* (= *Partito Repubblicano Italiano*) *former political party*.

prigi'one [pri'dʒone] *sf* prison.

prigio'nia [pridʒo'nia] *sf* imprisonment.

prigioni'ero, a [pridʒo'njɛro] *ag* captive ♦ *sm/f* prisoner.

'prima *sf vedi* **primo** ♦ *av* before; (*in anticipo*) in advance, beforehand; (*per l'addietro*) at one time, formerly; (*più presto*) sooner, earlier; (*in primo luogo*) first ♦ *cong*: ~ **di fare/che parta** before doing/he leaves; ~ **di** *prep* before; ~ **o poi** sooner or later; **due giorni** ~ two days before *o* earlier; ~ **d'ora** before now.

pri'mario, a *ag* primary; (*principale*) chief, leading, primary ♦ *sm/f* (*medico*) head physician, chief physician.

pri'mate *sm* (*REL, ZOOL*) primate.

prima'tista, i, e *sm/f* (*SPORT*) record holder.

pri'mato *sm* supremacy; (*SPORT*) record.

prima'vera *sf* spring.

primave'rile *ag* spring *cpd.*

primeggi'are [primed'dʒare] *vi* to excel, be one of the best.

primi'tivo, a *ag* (*gen*) primitive; (*significato*) original.

pri'mizie [pri'mittsje] *sfpl* early produce *sg.*

'primo, a *ag* first; (*fig*) initial; basic; prime ♦ *sm/f* first (one) ♦ *sm* (*CUC*) first course; (*in date*): **il** ~ **luglio** the first of July ♦ *sf* (*TEAT*) first night; (*CINE*) première; (*AUT*) first (gear); **le** ~**e ore del mattino** the early hours of the morning; **di** ~**a mattina** early in the morning; **in** ~**a pagina** (*STAMPA*) on the front page; **ai** ~**i freddi** at the first sign of cold weather; **ai** ~**i di maggio** at the beginning of May; **i** ~**i del Novecento** the early twentieth century; **viaggiare in** ~**a** to travel first-class; **per** ~**a cosa** firstly; **in** ~ **luogo** first of all, in the first place; **di prim'ordine** *o* ~**a qualità** first-class, first-rate; **in un** ~ **tempo** *o* **momento** at first; ~**a donna** leading lady; (*di opera lirica*) prima donna.

primo'genito, a [primo'dʒɛnito] *ag, sm/f* firstborn.

pri'mordi *smpl* beginnings.

primordi'ale *ag* primordial.

'primula *sf* primrose.

princi'pale [printʃi'pale] *ag* main, principal ♦ *sm* manager, boss; **sede** ~ head office.

principal'mente [printʃipal'mente] *av* mainly, principally.

princi'pato [printʃi'pato] *sm* principality.

'principe ['printʃipe] *sm* prince; ~ **ereditario** crown prince.

princi'pesco, a, schi, sche [printʃi'pesko] *ag* (*anche fig*) princely.

princi'pessa [printʃi'pessa] *sf* princess.

principi'ante [printʃi'pjante] *sm/f* beginner.

principi'are [printʃi'pjare] *vt, vi* to start, begin.

prin'cipio [prin'tʃipjo] *sm* (*inizio*) beginning, start; (*origine*) origin, cause; (*concetto, norma*) principle; **al** *o* **in** ~ at first; **fin dal** ~ right from the start; **per** ~ on principle; **una questione di** ~ a matter of principle; **una persona di sani** ~**i morali** a person of sound moral principles; ~ **attivo** active ingredient.

pri'ore *sm* (*REL*) prior.

pri'ori: a ~ *ag inv* prior; **a priori** ♦ *av* at first glance; initially; a priori.

priorità *sf* priority; **avere la** ~ **(su)** to have priority (over).

priori'tario, a *ag* (*scelta*) first; (*interesse*) overriding; **posta** ~ first class (post).

'prisma, i *sm* prism.

pri'vare *vt*: ~ **qn di** to deprive sb of; ~**rsi** *vr*: ~**rsi di** to go *o* do without.

priva'tiva *sf* (*ECON*) monopoly.

privatiz'zare [privatid'dzare] *vt* to privatize.

privatizzazi'one [privatiddzat'tsjone] *sf* privatization.

pri'vato, a *ag* private ♦ *sm/f* (*anche: ~ cittadino*) private citizen; **in** ~ in private; **diritto** ~ (*DIR*) civil law; **ritirarsi a vita** ~**a** to withdraw from public life; **"non vendiamo a** ~**i"** "wholesale only".

privazi'one [privat'tsjone] *sf* privation, hardship.

privilegi'are [privile'dʒare] *vt* to favour (*BRIT*), favor (*US*).

privilegi'ato, a [privile'dʒato] *ag* (*individuo, classe*) privileged; (*trattamento, COMM: credito*) preferential; **azioni** ~**e** preference shares (*BRIT*), preferred stock (*US*).

privi'legio [privi'lɛdʒo] *sm* privilege; **avere il** ~ **di fare** to have the privilege of doing, be privileged to do.

'privo, a *ag*: ~ **di** without, lacking.

pro *prep* for, on behalf of ♦ *sm inv* (*utilità*) advantage, benefit; **a che** ~**?** what's the use?; **il** ~ **e il contro** the pros and cons.

pro'babile *ag* probable, likely.

probabilità *sf inv* probability; **con molta** ~ very probably, in all probability.

probabil'mente *av* probably.

pro'bante *ag* convincing.

pro'blema, i *sm* problem.

proble'matico, a, ci, che *ag* problematic; (*incerto*) doubtful ♦ *sf* problems *pl.*

pro'boscide [pro'bɔʃʃide] *sf* (*di elefante*) trunk.

procacci'are [prokat'tʃare] *vt* to get, obtain.

procaccia'tore [prokattʃa'tore] *sm*: ~

d'affari sales executive.
pro 'cace [pro'katʃe] *ag* (*donna, aspetto*) provocative.
pro 'cedere [pro'tʃedere] *vi* to proceed; (*comportarsi*) to behave; (*iniziare*): ~ **a** to start; ~ **contro** (*DIR*) to start legal proceedings against; ~ **oltre** to go on ahead; **prima di** ~ **oltre** before going any further; **gli affari procedono bene** business is going well; **bisogna** ~ **con cautela** we have to proceed cautiously; **non luogo a** ~ (*DIR*) nonsuit.
procedi 'mento [protʃedi'mento] *sm* (*modo di condurre*) procedure; (*di avvenimenti*) course; (*TECN*) process; ~ **penale** (*DIR*) criminal proceedings *pl.*
proce 'dura [protʃe'dura] *sf* (*DIR*) procedure.
proces 'sare [protʃes'sare] *vt* (*DIR*) to try.
processi 'one [protʃes'sjone] *sf* procession.
pro 'cesso [pro'tʃɛsso] *sm* (*DIR*) trial; proceedings *pl*; (*metodo*) process; **essere sotto** ~ to be on trial; **mettere sotto** ~ (*anche fig*) to put on trial; ~ **di fabbricazione** manufacturing process; ~ **di pace** peace process.
processu 'ale [protʃessu'ale] *ag* (*DIR*): **atti** ~**i** records of a trial; **spese** ~**i** legal costs.
Proc. Gen. *abbr* = **procuratore generale.**
pro 'cinto [pro'tʃinto] *sm*: **in** ~ **di fare** about to do, on the point of doing.
pro 'clama, i *sm* proclamation.
procla 'mare *vt* to proclaim.
proclamazi 'one [proklamat'tsjone] *sf* proclamation, declaration.
procrasti 'nare *vt* (*data*) to postpone; (*pagamento*) to defer.
procre 'are *vt* to procreate.
pro 'cura *sf* (*DIR*) proxy, power of attorney; (*ufficio*) attorney's office; **per** ~ by proxy; **la P**~ **della Repubblica** the Public Prosecutor's Office.
procu 'rare *vt*: ~ **qc a qn** (*fornire*) to get *o* obtain sth for sb; (*causare: noie etc*) to bring *o* give sb sth.
procura 'tore, 'trice *smlf* (*DIR*) ≈ solicitor; (*: chi ha la procura*) holder of power of attorney; ~ **generale** (*in corte d'appello*) public prosecutor; (*in corte di cassazione*) Attorney General; ~ **legale** ≈ solicitor (*BRIT*), lawyer; ~ **della Repubblica** (*in corte d'assise, tribunale*) public prosecutor.
prodi 'gare *vt* to be lavish with; ~**rsi** *vr*: ~**rsi per qn** to do all one can for sb.
pro 'digio [pro'didʒo] *sm* marvel, wonder; (*persona*) prodigy.
prodigi 'oso, a [prodi'dʒoso] *ag* prodigious; phenomenal.
'prodigo, a, ghi, ghe *ag* lavish,

extravagant.
pro 'dotto, a *pp di* **produrre** ♦ *sm* product; ~ **di base** primary product; ~ **finale** end product; ~ **interno lordo (PIL)** gross domestic product (GDP); ~ **nazionale lordo (PNL)** gross national product (GNP); ~**i agricoli** farm produce *sg*; ~**i di bellezza** cosmetics; ~**i chimici** chemicals.
pro 'duco *etc vb vedi* **produrre.**
pro 'durre *vt* to produce.
pro 'dussi *etc vb vedi* **produrre.**
produttività *sf* productivity.
produt 'tivo, a *ag* productive.
produt 'tore, 'trice *ag* producing *cpd* ♦ *smlf* producer; **paese** ~ **di petrolio** oil-producing country.
produzi 'one [produt'tsjone] *sf* production; (*rendimento*) output; ~ **in serie** mass production.
pro 'emio *sm* introduction, preface.
Prof. *abbr* (= *professore*) Prof.
profa 'nare *vt* to desecrate.
pro 'fano, a *ag* (*mondano*) secular, profane; (*sacrilego*) profane.
profe 'rire *vt* to utter.
profes 'sare *vt* to profess; (*medicina etc*) to practise (*BRIT*), practice (*US*).
professio 'nale *ag* professional; **scuola** ~ training college.
professi 'one *sf* profession; **di** ~ professional, by profession; **libera** ~ profession.
professio 'nista, i, e *smlf* professional.
profes 'sore, 'essa *smlf* (*INS*) teacher; (*: di università*) lecturer; (*: titolare di cattedra*) professor; ~ **d'orchestra** member of an orchestra.
pro 'feta, i *sm* prophet.
pro 'fetico, a, ci, che *ag* prophetic.
profetiz 'zare [profetid'dzare] *vt* to prophesy.
profe 'zia [profet'tsia] *sf* prophecy.
pro 'ficuo, a *ag* useful, profitable.
profi 'lare *vt* to outline; (*ornare: vestito*) to edge; ~**rsi** *vr* to stand out, be silhouetted; to loom up.
profi 'lassi *sf* (*MED*) preventive treatment, prophylaxis.
profi 'lattico, a, ci, che *ag* prophylactic ♦ *sm* (*anticoncezionale*) sheath, condom.
pro 'filo *sm* profile; (*breve descrizione*) sketch, outline; **di** ~ in profile.
profit 'tare *vi*: ~ **di** (*trarre profitto*) to profit by; (*approfittare*) to take advantage of.
pro 'fitto *sm* advantage, profit, benefit; (*fig: progresso*) progress; (*COMM*) profit; **ricavare un** ~ **da** to make a profit from *o* out of; **vendere con** ~ to sell at a profit;

conto ~**i e perdite** profit and loss account.
pro 'fondere vt (lodi) to lavish; (denaro) to
squander; ~**rsi** vr: ~**rsi in** to be profuse in.
profondità sf inv depth.
pro 'fondo, a ag deep; (rancore, meditazione)
profound ♦ sm depth(s pl), bottom; ~ **8
metri** 8 metres deep.
pro 'forma ag routine cpd ♦ sm inv formality
♦ av: **fare qc** ~ to do sth as a formality.
'profugo, a, ghi, ghe sm/f refugee.
profu 'mare vt to perfume ♦ vi to be
fragrant; ~**rsi** vr to put on perfume o
scent.
profumata 'mente av: **pagare qc** ~ to pay
through the nose for sth.
profu 'mato, a ag (fiore, aria) fragrant;
(fazzoletto, saponetta) scented; (pelle)
sweet-smelling; (persona) with perfume
on.
profume 'ria sf perfumery; (negozio)
perfume shop.
pro 'fumo sm (prodotto) perfume, scent;
(fragranza) scent, fragrance.
profusi 'one sf profusion; **a** ~ in plenty.
pro 'fuso, a pp di **profondere**.
progeni 'tore, 'trice [prodʒeni'tore] sm/f
ancestor.
proget 'tare [prodʒet'tare] vt to plan; (TECN:
edificio) to plan, design; ~ **di fare qc** to
plan to do sth.
progettazi 'one [prodʒettat'tsjone] sf
planning; **in corso di** ~ at the planning
stage.
proget 'tista, i, e [prodʒet'tista] sm/f
designer.
pro 'getto [pro'dʒetto] sm plan; (idea) plan,
project; **avere in** ~ **di fare qc** to be
planning to do sth; ~ **di legge** (POL) bill.
'prognosi ['proɲɲozi] sf (MED) prognosis;
essere in ~ **riservata** to be on the danger
list.
pro 'gramma, i sm programme (BRIT),
program (US); (TV, RADIO) program(me)s
pl; (INS) syllabus, curriculum; (INFORM)
program; **avere in** ~ **di fare qc** to be
planning to do sth; ~ **applicativo** (INFORM)
application program.
program 'mare vt (TV, RADIO) to put on;
(INFORM) to program; (ECON) to plan.
programma 'tore, 'trice sm/f (INFORM)
computer programmer (BRIT) o
programer (US).
programmazi 'one [programmat'tsjone] sf
programming (BRIT), programing (US);
planning.
progre 'dire vi to progress, make progress.
progressi 'one sf progression.
progres 'sista, i, e ag, sm/f progressive.

progressiva 'mente av progressively.
progres 'sivo, a ag progressive.
pro 'gresso sm progress no pl; **fare** ~**i** to
make progress.
proi 'bire vt to forbid, prohibit; ~ **a qn di
fare qc** (vietare) to forbid sb to do sth;
(impedire) to prevent sb from doing sth.
proibi 'tivo, a ag prohibitive.
proi 'bito, a ag forbidden; **"è** ~ **l'accesso"**
"no admittance"; **"è** ~ **fumare"** "no
smoking".
proibizi 'one [proibit'tsjone] sf prohibition.
proibizio 'nismo [proibittsjo'nizmo] sm
prohibition.
proiet 'tare vt (gen, GEOM, CINE) to project;
(: presentare) to show, screen; (luce,
ombra) to throw, cast, project.
proi 'ettile sm projectile, bullet (o shell
etc).
proiet 'tore sm (CINE) projector; (AUT)
headlamp; (MIL) searchlight.
proiezi 'one [projet'tsjone] sf (CINE)
projection; showing.
'prole sf children pl, offspring.
proletari 'ato sm proletariat.
prole 'tario, a ag, sm/f proletarian.
prolife 'rare vi (fig) to proliferate.
pro 'lifico, a, ci, che ag prolific.
pro 'lisso, a ag verbose.
'prologo, ghi sm prologue.
pro 'lunga, ghe sf (di cavo elettrico etc)
extension.
prolunga 'mento sm (gen) extension; (di
strada) continuation.
prolun 'gare vt (discorso, attesa) to prolong;
(linea, termine) to extend.
prome 'moria sm inv memorandum.
pro 'messa sf promise; **fare/mantenere una**
~ to make/keep a promise.
pro 'messo, a pp di **promettere**.
promet 'tente ag promising.
pro 'mettere vt to promise ♦ vi to be o look
promising; ~ **a qn di fare** to promise sb
that one will do.
promi 'nente ag prominent.
promi 'nenza [promi'nɛntsa] sf prominence.
promiscuità sf promiscuousness.
pro 'miscuo, a ag: **matrimonio** ~ mixed
marriage; **nome** ~ (LING) common-gender
noun.
pro 'misi etc vb vedi **promettere**.
promon 'torio sm promontory, headland.
pro 'mosso, a pp di **promuovere**.
promo 'tore, 'trice sm/f promoter,
organizer.
promozio 'nale [promottsjo'nale] ag
promotional; **"vendita** ~**"** "special offer".
promozi 'one [promot'tsjone] sf promotion;

~ **delle vendite** sales promotion.
promul'gare *vt* to promulgate.
promulgazi'one [promulgat'tsjone] *sf* promulgation.
promu'overe *vt* to promote.
proni'pote *sm/f* (*di nonni*) great-grandchild, great-grandson/granddaughter; (*di zii*) great-nephew/niece; ~**i** *smpl* (*discendenti*) descendants.
pro'nome *sm* (*LING*) pronoun.
pronomi'nale *ag* pronominal.
pronosti'care *vt* to foretell, predict.
pro'nostico, ci *sm* forecast.
pron'tezza [pron'tettsa] *sf* readiness; quickness, promptness; ~ **di riflessi** quick reflexes; ~ **di spirito/mente** readiness of wit/mind.
'pronto, a *ag* ready; (*rapido*) fast, quick, prompt; ~! (*TEL*) hello!; **essere** ~ **a fare qc** to be ready to do sth; ~ **all'ira** quick-tempered; **a** ~**a cassa** (*COMM*) cash (*BRIT*) *o* collect (*US*) on delivery; ~**a consegna** (*COMM*) prompt delivery; ~ **soccorso** (*trattamento*) first aid; (*reparto*) A&E (*BRIT*) ER (*US*).
prontu'ario *sm* manual, handbook.
pro'nuncia [pro'nuntʃa] *sf* pronunciation.
pronunci'are [pronun'tʃare] *vt* (*parola, sentenza*) to pronounce; (*dire*) to utter; (*discorso*) to deliver; ~**rsi** *vr* to declare one's opinion; ~**rsi a favore di/contro** to pronounce o.s. in favour of/against; **non mi pronuncio** I'm not prepared to comment.
pronunci'ato, a [pronun'tʃato] *ag* (*spiccato*) pronounced, marked; (*sporgente*) prominent.
pro'nunzia *etc* [pro'nuntsja] = **pronuncia** *etc*.
propa'ganda *sf* propaganda.
propagan'dare *vt* (*idea*) to propagandize; (*prodotto, invenzione*) to push, plug (*fam*).
propa'gare *vt* (*FISICA, BIOL*) to propagate; (*notizia, idea, malattia*) to spread; ~**rsi** *vr* to propagate; to spread.
propagaz'ione [propagat'tsjone] *sf* (*vedi vb*) propagation; spreading.
prope'deutico, a, ci, che *ag* (*corso, trattato*) introductory.
pro'pendere *vi:* ~ **per** to favour (*BRIT*), favor (*US*), lean towards.
propensi'one *sf* inclination, propensity; **avere** ~ **a credere che** ... to be inclined to think that ....
pro'penso, a *pp di* **propendere** ♦ *ag:* **essere** ~ **a qc** to be in favour (*BRIT*) *o* favor (*US*) of sth; **essere** ~ **a fare qc** to be inclined to do sth.

propi'nare *vt* to administer.
pro'pizio, a [pro'pittsjo] *ag* favourable (*BRIT*), favorable (*US*).
pro'porre *vt* (*suggerire*): ~ **qc (a qn)** to suggest sth (to sb); (*candidato*) to put forward; (*legge, brindisi*) to propose; ~ **di fare** to suggest *o* propose doing; **proporsi di fare** to propose *o* intend to do; **proporsi una meta** to set o.s. a goal.
proporzio'nale [proportsjo'nale] *ag* proportional; (*sistema*) ~ (*POL*) proportional representation system.
proporzio'nato, a [proportsjo'nato] *ag:* ~ **a** proportionate to, proportional to; **ben** ~ well-proportioned.
proporzi'one [propor'tsjone] *sf* proportion; **in** ~ **a** in proportion to.
pro'posito *sm* (*intenzione*) intention, aim; (*argomento*) subject, matter; **a** ~ **di** regarding, with regard to; **a questo** ~ on this subject; **di** ~ (*apposta*) deliberately, on purpose; **a** ~ by the way; **capitare a** ~ (*cosa, persona*) to turn up at the right time.
proposizi'one [propozit'tsjone] *sf* (*LING*) clause; (: *periodo*) sentence.
pro'posto, a *pp di* **proporre** ♦ *sf* proposal; (*suggerimento*) suggestion; **fare una** ~**a** to put forward a proposal; to make a suggestion; ~**a di legge** (*POL*) bill.
propria'mente *av* (*correttamente*) properly, correctly; (*in modo specifico*) specifically; ~ **detto** in the strict sense of the word.
proprietà *sf inv* (*ciò che si possiede*) property *gen no pl*, estate; (*caratteristica*) property; (*correttezza*) correctness; **essere di** ~ **di qn** to belong to sb; ~ **edilizia** (*developed*) property; ~ **privata** private property.
proprie'tario, a *sm/f* owner; (*di albergo etc*) proprietor, owner; (*per l'inquilino*) landlord/lady; ~ **terriero** landowner.
'proprio, a *ag* (*possessivo*) own; (: *impersonale*) one's; (*esatto*) exact, correct, proper; (*senso, significato*) literal; (*LING: nome*) proper; (*particolare*): ~ **di** characteristic of, peculiar to ♦ *av* (*precisamente*) just, exactly; (*davvero*) really; (*affatto*): **non** ... ~ not ... at all ♦ *sm* (*COMM*): **mettersi in** ~ to set up on one's own; **l'ha visto con i (suoi)** ~**i occhi** he saw it with his own eyes.
propu'gnare [propuɲ'ɲare] *vt* to support.
propulsi'one *sf* propulsion; **a** ~ **atomica** atomic-powered.
propul'sore *sm* (*TECN*) propeller.
'prora *sf* (*NAUT*) bow(s *pl*), prow.
'proroga, ghe *sf* extension; postponement.

proro'gare vt to extend; (differire) to postpone, defer.

pro'rompere vi to burst out.

pro'rotto, a pp di **prorompere**.

pro'ruppi etc vb vedi **prorompere**.

'prosa sf prose; (TEAT): **la stagione della** ~ the theatre season; **attore di** ~ theatre actor; **compagnia di** ~ theatrical company.

pro'saico, a, ci, che ag (fig) prosaic, mundane.

pro'sciogliere [proʃ'ʃɔʎʎere] vt to release; (DIR) to acquit.

prosciogli'mento [proʃʃoʎʎi'mento] sm acquittal.

prosci'olto, a [proʃ'ʃɔlto] pp di **prosciogliere**.

prosciu'gare [proʃʃu'gare] vt (terreni) to drain, reclaim; **~rsi** vr to dry up.

prosci'utto [proʃ'ʃutto] sm ham.

pros'critto, a pp di **proscrivere** ♦ sm/f exile; outlaw.

pros'crivere vt to exile, banish.

proscrizi'one [proskrit'tsjone] sf (esilio) banishment, exile.

prosecuzi'one [prosekut'tsjone] sf continuation.

prosegui'mento sm continuation; **buon** ~! all the best!

prosegu'ire vt to carry on with, continue ♦ vi to carry on, go on.

pro'selito sm (REL, POL) convert.

prospe'rare vi to thrive.

prosperità sf prosperity.

'prospero, a ag (fiorente) flourishing, thriving, prosperous.

prospe'roso, a ag (robusto) hale and hearty; (: ragazza) buxom.

prospet'tare vt (esporre) to point out, show; (ipotesi) to advance; (affare) to outline; **~rsi** vr to look, appear.

prospet'tiva sf (ARTE) perspective; (veduta) view; (fig: previsione, possibilità) prospect.

pros'petto sm (DISEGNO) elevation; (veduta) view, prospect; (facciata) façade, front; (tabella) table; (sommario) summary.

prospici'ente [prospi'tʃɛnte] ag: ~ qc facing o overlooking sth.

prossima'mente av soon.

prossimità sf nearness, proximity; **in** ~ **di** near (to), close to; **in** ~ **delle feste natalizie** as Christmas approaches.

'prossimo, a ag (vicino): ~ **a** near (to), close to; (che viene subito dopo) next; (parente) close ♦ sm neighbour (BRIT), neighbor (US), fellow man; **nei** ~**i giorni**

in the next few days; **in un** ~ **futuro** in the near future; ~ **venturo (pv)** (AMM): **venerdì** ~ **venturo** next Friday.

'prostata sf prostate (gland).

prostitu'irsi vr to prostitute o.s.

prosti'tuta sf prostitute.

prostituzi'one [prostitut'tsjone] sf prostitution.

pros'trare vt (fig) to exhaust, wear out; **~rsi** vr (fig) to humble o.s.; **prostrato dal dolore** overcome o prostrate with grief.

prostrazi'one [prostrat'tsjone] sf prostration.

protago'nista, i, e sm/f protagonist.

pro'teggere [pro'tɛddʒere] vt to protect.

proteggi'slip [protɛddʒi'slip] sm inv panty liner.

pro'teico, a, ci, che ag protein cpd; **altamente** ~ high in protein.

prote'ina sf protein.

pro'tendere vt to stretch out.

'protesi sf inv (MED) prosthesis.

pro'teso, a pp di **protendere**.

pro'testa sf protest.

protes'tante ag, sm/f Protestant.

protes'tare vt, vi to protest; **~rsi** vr: **~rsi innocente** to protest one's innocence.

pro'testo sm (DIR) protest; **mandare una cambiale in** ~ to dishonour (BRIT) o dishonor (US) a bill.

protet'tivo, a ag protective.

pro'tetto, a pp di **proteggere**.

protetto'rato sm protectorate.

protet'tore, 'trice sm/f protector; (sostenitore) patron ♦ ag (REL): **santo** ~ patron saint; **società ~trice dei consumatori** consumer protection society.

protezi'one [protet'tsjone] sf protection; (patrocinio) patronage; **misure di** ~ protective measures; ~ **civile** civil defence (BRIT) o defense (US).

protezio'nismo [protettsjo'nizmo] sm protectionism.

protocol'lare vt to register ♦ ag formal; of protocol.

proto'collo sm protocol; (registro) register of documents ♦ ag inv: **foglio** ~ foolscap; **numero di** ~ reference number.

pro'tone sm proton.

pro'totipo sm prototype.

pro'trarre vt (prolungare) to prolong; **protrarsi** vr to go on, continue.

pro'tratto, a pp di **protrarre**.

protube'ranza [protube'rantsa] sf protuberance, bulge.

Prov. abbr (= provincia) Prov.

'prova sf (esperimento, cimento) test,

trial; (*tentativo*) attempt, try; (*MAT,
testimonianza etc*) proof *no pl*; (*DIR*)
evidence *no pl*, proof *no pl*; (*INS*) exam,
test; (*TEAT*) rehearsal; (*di abito*) fitting; **a
~ di** (*in testimonianza di*) as proof of; **a ~ di
fuoco** fireproof; **assumere in ~** (*per lavoro*)
to employ on a trial basis; **essere in ~**
(*persona*: *per lavoro*) to be on trial; **mettere
alla ~** to put to the test; **giro di ~** test *o*
trial run; **fino a ~ contraria** until (it's)
proved otherwise; **~ a carico/a discarico**
(*DIR*) evidence for the prosecution/for the
defence; **~ documentale** (*DIR*)
documentary evidence; **~ generale** (*TEAT*)
dress rehearsal.

pro '**vare** *vt* (*sperimentare*) to test; (*tentare*)
to try, attempt; (*assaggiare*) to try, taste;
(*sperimentare in sé*) to experience; (*sentire*)
to feel; (*cimentare*) to put to the test;
(*dimostrare*) to prove; (*abito*) to try on;
~rsi *vr*: **~rsi (a fare)** to try *o* attempt (to
do); **~ a fare** to try *o* attempt to do.

proveni '**enza** [prove'njɛntsa] *sf* origin,
source.

prove '**nire** *vi*: **~ da** to come from.

pro '**venti** *smpl* revenue *sg*.

prove '**nuto, a** *pp di* **provenire**.

Pro '**venza** [pro'vɛntsa] *sf*: **la ~** Provence.

proven '**zale** [proven'tsale] *ag* Provençal.

pro '**verbio** *sm* proverb.

pro '**vetta** *sf* test tube; **bambino in ~** test-
tube baby.

pro '**vetto, a** *ag* skilled, experienced.

pro '**vider** [pro'vaider] *sm inv* (*INFORM*)
service provider.

pro '**vincia, ce** *o* **cie** [pro'vintʃa] *sf*
province; *vedi nota nel riquadro*.

PROVINCIA

A **Provincia** is the autonomous political and
administrative unit which is on a level between
a "Comune" and a "Regione"; there are 103 in
the whole of Italy. The **Provincia** is
responsible for public health and sanitation, for
the maintenance of major roads and public
buildings such as schools, and for agriculture
and fisheries. Situated in the "capoluogo", or
chief town, each **Provincia** is run by a "Giunta
provinciale", which is elected by the "Consiglio
provinciale"; both of these bodies are presided
over by a "Presidente".

---

provinci '**ale** [provin'tʃale] *ag* provincial;
(**strada**) **~** main road (*BRIT*), highway (*US*).

pro '**vino** *sm* (*CINE*) screen test; (*campione*)
specimen.

provo '**cante** *ag* (*attraente*) provocative.

provo '**care** *vt* (*causare*) to cause, bring
about; (*eccitare*: *riso, pietà*) to arouse;
(*irritare, sfidare*) to provoke.

provoca '**tore, 'trice** *sm/f* agitator ♦ *ag*:
agente ~ agent provocateur.

provoca '**torio, a** *ag* provocative.

provocazi '**one** [provokat'tsjone] *sf*
provocation.

provve '**dere** *vi* (*disporre*): **~ (a)** to provide
(for); (*prendere un provvedimento*) to take
steps, act ♦ *vt*: **~ qc a qn** to supply sth to
sb; **~rsi** *vr*: **~rsi di** to provide o.s. with.

provvedi '**mento** *sm* measure; (*di
previdenza*) precaution; **~ disciplinare**
disciplinary measure.

provvedito '**rato** *sm* (*AMM*): **~ agli studi**
divisional education offices *pl*.

provvedi '**tore** *sm* (*AMM*): **~ agli studi**
divisional director of education.

provvi '**denza** [provvi'dɛntsa] *sf*: **la ~**
providence.

provvidenzi '**ale** [provviden'tsjale] *ag*
providential.

provvigi '**one** [provvi'dʒone] *sf* (*COMM*)
commission; **lavoro/stipendio a ~** job/
salary on a commission basis.

provvi '**sorio, a** *ag* temporary; (*governo*)
temporary, provisional.

prov '**vista** *sf* (*riserva*) supply, stock; **fare ~
di** to stock up with.

prov '**visto, a** *pp di* **provvedere** ♦ *sf*
provision, supply.

pro '**zia** [prot'tsia] *sf* great-aunt.

pro '**zio, zii** [prot'tsio] *sm* great-uncle.

'**prua** *sf* (*NAUT*) = **prora**.

pru '**dente** *ag* cautious, prudent;
(*assennato*) sensible, wise.

pru '**denza** [pru'dɛntsa] *sf* prudence,
caution; wisdom; **per ~** as a precaution,
to be on the safe side.

'**prudere** *vi* to itch, be itchy.

'**prugna** ['pruɲɲa] *sf* plum; **~ secca** prune.

prurigi '**noso, a** [pruridʒi'noso] *ag* itchy.

pru '**rito** *sm* itchiness *no pl*; itch.

PS *sigla* = **Pesaro**.

P.S. *abbr* (= *postscriptum*) P.S.; (*COMM*)
= **partita semplice** ♦ *sigla f vedi* **Pubblica
Sicurezza**.

P.S.D.I. *sigla m* (= *Partito Socialista
Democratico Italiano*) *former political
party*.

pseu '**donimo** *sm* pseudonym.

PSI *sigla m* (*POL*) = **Partito Socialista Italiano**.

psica '**nalisi** *sf* psychoanalysis.

psicana '**lista, i, e** *sm/f* psychoanalyst.

psicanaliz '**zare** [psikanalid'dzare] *vt* to
psychoanalyse.

'**psiche** ['psike] *sf* psyche.

psiche 'delico, a, ci, che [psike'dɛliko] *ag* psychedelic.

psichi 'atra, i, e [psi'kjatra] *sm/f* psychiatrist.

psichia 'tria [psikja'tria] *sf* psychiatry.

psichi 'atrico, a, ci, che [psi'kjatriko] *ag* (*caso*) psychiatric; (*reparto, ospedale*) psychiatric, mental.

'psichico, a, ci, che ['psikiko] *ag* psychological.

psico 'farmaco, ci *sm* (*MED*) drug used in treatment of mental conditions.

psicolo 'gia [psikolo'dʒia] *sf* psychology.

psico 'logico, a, ci, che [psiko'lɔdʒiko] *ag* psychological.

psi 'cologo, a, gi, ghe *sm/f* psychologist.

psico 'patico, a, ci, che *ag* psychopathic ♦ *sm/f* psychopath.

psi 'cosi *sf inv* (*MED*) psychosis; (*fig*) obsessive fear.

psicoso 'matico, a, ci, che *ag* psychosomatic.

PT *sigla* = Pistoia.

Pt. *abbr* (*GEO*: = *punta*) Pt.

P.T. *abbr* (= *Posta e Telegrafi*) ≈ PO (= *Post Office*); (*FISCO*) = **polizia tributaria.**

P.ta *abbr* = **porta.**

pubbli 'care *vt* to publish.

pubblicazi 'one [pubblikat'tsjone] *sf* publication; ~ **periodica** periodical; ~**i** (**matrimoniali**) *sfpl* (marriage) banns.

pubbli 'cista, i, e [pubbli'tʃista] *sm/f* (*STAMPA*) freelance journalist.

pubblicità [pubblitʃi'ta] *sf* (*diffusione*) publicity; (*attività*) advertising; (*annunci nei giornali*) advertisements *pl*; **fare ~ a qc** to advertise sth.

pubblici 'tario, a [pubblitʃi'tarjo] *ag* advertising *cpd*; (*trovata, film*) publicity *cpd* ♦ *sm* advertising agent; **annuncio** *o* **avviso** ~ advertisement.

'pubblico, a, ci, che *ag* public; (*statale*: *scuola etc*) state *cpd* ♦ *sm* public; (*spettatori*) audience; **in** ~ in public; **la** ~**a amministrazione** public administration; **un** ~ **esercizio** a catering (*o* hotel *o* entertainment) business; ~ **funzionario** civil servant; **Ministero della P~a Istruzione** ≈ Department of Education and Science (*BRIT*), ~ Department of Health, Education and Welfare (*US*); **P~ Ministero** Public Prosecutor's Office; **la P~a Sicurezza (P.S.)** the police.

'pube *sm* (*ANAT*) pubis.

pubertà *sf* puberty.

'pudico, a, ci, che *ag* modest.

pu 'dore *sm* modesty.

puericul 'tura *sf* infant care.

pue 'rile *ag* childish.

pu 'erpera *sf woman who has just given birth.*

pugi 'lato [pudʒi'lato] *sm* boxing.

'pugile ['pudʒile] *sm* boxer.

pugli 'ese [puʎ'ʎese] *ag* of (*o* from) Puglia.

pugna 'lare [puɲɲa'lare] *vt* to stab.

pu 'gnale [puɲ'ɲale] *sm* dagger.

'pugno ['puɲɲo] *sm* fist; (*colpo*) punch; (*quantità*) fistful; **avere qn in** ~ to have sb in the palm of one's hand; **tenere la situazione in** ~ to have control of the situation; **scrivere qc di proprio** ~ to write sth in one's own hand.

'pulce ['pultʃe] *sf* flea.

pul 'cino [pul'tʃino] *sm* chick.

pu 'ledro, a *sm/f* colt/filly.

pu 'leggia, ge [pu'leddʒa] *sf* pulley.

pu 'lire *vt* to clean; (*lucidare*) to polish; **far ~ qc** to have sth cleaned; ~ **a secco** to dry-clean.

pu 'lito, a *ag* (*anche fig*) clean; (*ordinato*) neat, tidy ♦ *sf* quick clean; **avere la coscienza** ~**a** to have a clear conscience.

puli 'tura *sf* cleaning; ~ **a secco** dry-cleaning.

puli 'zia [pulit'tsia] *sf* (*atto*) cleaning; (*condizione*) cleanness; **fare le** ~**e** to do the cleaning, do the housework; ~ **etnica** ethnic cleansing.

'pullman *sm inv* coach (*BRIT*), bus.

pul 'lover *sm inv* pullover, jumper.

pullu 'lare *vi* to swarm, teem.

pul 'mino *sm* minibus.

'pulpito *sm* pulpit.

pul 'sante *sm* (push-)button.

pul 'sare *vi* to pulsate, beat.

pulsazi 'one [pulsat'tsjone] *sf* beat.

pul 'viscolo *sm* fine dust.

'puma *sm inv* puma.

pun 'gente [pun'dʒɛnte] *ag* prickly; stinging; (*anche fig*) biting.

'pungere ['pundʒere] *vt* to prick; (*sog*: *insetto, ortica*) to sting; (: *freddo*) to bite; ~ **qn sul vivo** (*fig*) to cut sb to the quick.

pungigli 'one [pundʒiʎ'ʎone] *sm* sting.

pungo 'lare *vt* to goad.

pu 'nire *vt* to punish.

puni 'tivo, a *ag* punitive.

punizi 'one [punit'tsjone] *sf* punishment; (*SPORT*) penalty.

'punsi *etc vb vedi* **pungere.**

'punta *sf* point; (*parte terminale*) tip, end; (*di monte*) peak; (*di costa*) promontory; (*minima parte*) touch, trace; **in** ~ **di piedi** on tiptoe; **ore di** ~ peak hours; **uomo di** ~ (*SPORT, POL*) front-rank *o* leading man; **doppie** ~**e** split ends.

pun'tare *vt* (*piedi a terra, gomiti sul tavolo*) to plant; (*dirigere: pistola*) to point; (*scommettere*): ~ **su** to bet on ♦ *vi* (*mirare*): ~ **a** to aim at; (*avviarsi*): ~ **su** to head *o* make for; (*fig: contare*): ~ **su** to count *o* rely on.

puntas'pilli *sm inv* = **portaspilli.**

pun'tata *sf* (*gita*) short trip; (*scommessa*) bet; (*parte di opera*) instalment (*BRIT*), installment (*US*); **farò una** ~ **a Parigi** I'll pay a flying visit to Paris; **romanzo a** ~**e** serial.

punteggi'are [punted'dʒare] *vt* to punctuate.

punteggia'tura [punteddʒa'tura] *sf* punctuation.

pun'teggio [pun'teddʒo] *sm* score.

puntel'lare *vt* to support.

pun'tello *sm* prop, support.

punteru'olo *sm* (*TECN*) punch; (: *per stoffa*) bodkin.

pun'tiglio [pun'tiʎʎo] *sm* obstinacy, stubbornness.

puntigli'oso, a [puntiʎ'ʎoso] *ag* punctilious.

pun'tina *sf*: ~ **da disegno** drawing pin (*BRIT*), thumb tack (*US*); ~**e** *sfpl* (*AUT*) points.

pun'tino *sm* dot; **fare qc a** ~ to do sth properly; **arrivare a** ~ to arrive just at the right moment; **cotto a** ~ cooked to perfection; **mettere i** ~**i sulle "i"** (*fig*) to dot the i's and cross the t's.

'punto, a *pp di* **pungere** ♦ *sm* (*segno, macchiolina*) dot; (*LING*) full stop; (*MAT, momento, di punteggio, fig: argomento*) point; (*di indirizzo e-mail*) dot; (*posto*) spot; (*a scuola*) mark; (*nel cucire, nella maglia, MED*) stitch ♦ *av*: **non ...** ~ not ... at all; **due** ~**i** *sm inv* (*LING*) colon; **ad un certo** ~ at a certain point; **fino ad un certo** ~ (*fig*) to a certain extent; **sul** ~ **di fare** (just) about to do; **fare il** ~ (*NAUT*) to take a bearing; **fare il** ~ **della situazione** (*analisi*) to take stock of the situation; (*riassunto*) to sum up the situation; **alle 6 in** ~ at 6 o'clock sharp *o* on the dot; **essere a buon** ~ to have reached a satisfactory stage; **mettere a** ~ to adjust; (*motore*) to tune; (*cannocchiale*) to focus; (*fig*) to settle; **venire al** ~ to come to the point; **vestito di tutto** ~ all dressed up; **di** ~ **in bianco** point-blank; ~ **d'arrivo** arrival point; ~ **cardinale** point of the compass, cardinal point; ~ **debole** weak point; ~ **esclamativo/interrogativo** exclamation/question mark; ~ **d'incontro** meeting place, meeting point; ~ **morto** standstill;

~ **nero** (*comedone*) blackhead; ~ **nevralgico** (*anche fig*) nerve centre (*BRIT*) *o* center (*US*); ~ **di partenza** (*anche fig*) starting point; ~ **di riferimento** landmark; (*fig*) point of reference; ~ **di vendita** retail outlet; ~ **e virgola** semicolon; ~ **di vista** (*fig*) point of view; ~**i di sospensione** suspension points.

puntu'ale *ag* punctual.

puntualità *sf* punctuality.

puntualiz'zare [puntualid'dzare] *vt* to make clear.

puntual'mente *av* (*gen*) on time; (*ironico*: *al solito*) as usual.

pun'tura *sf* (*di ago*) prick; (*di insetto*) sting, bite; (*MED*) puncture; (: *iniezione*) injection; (*dolore*) sharp pain.

punzecchi'are [puntsek'kjare] *vt* to prick; (*fig*) to tease.

punzo'nare [puntso'nare] *vt* (*TECN*) to stamp.

pun'zone [pun'tsone] *sm* (*per metalli*) stamp, die.

può, pu'oi *vb vedi* **potere.**

'pupa *sf* doll.

pu'pazzo [pu'pattso] *sm* puppet.

pu'pillo, a *sm/f* (*DIR*) ward; (*prediletto*) favourite (*BRIT*), favorite (*US*), pet ♦ *sf* (*ANAT*) pupil.

purché [pur'ke] *cong* provided that, on condition that.

'pure *cong* (*tuttavia*) and yet, nevertheless; (*anche se*) even if ♦ *av* (*anche*) too, also; **pur di** (*al fine di*) just to; **faccia** ~! go ahead!, please do!

purè *sm*, **pu'rea** *sf* (*CUC*) purée; (: *di patate*) mashed potatoes.

pu'rezza [pu'rettsa] *sf* purity.

'purga, ghe *sf* purging *no pl*; purge.

pur'gante *sm* (*MED*) purgative, purge.

pur'gare *vt* (*MED, POL*) to purge; (*pulire*) to clean.

purga'torio *sm* purgatory.

purifi'care *vt* to purify; (*metallo*) to refine.

purificazi'one [purifikat'tsjone] *sf* purification; refinement.

puri'tano, a *ag*, *sm/f* puritan.

'puro, a *ag* pure; (*acqua*) clear, limpid; (*vino*) undiluted; **di razza** ~**a** thoroughbred; **per** ~ **caso** by sheer chance, purely by chance.

puro'sangue *sm/f inv* thoroughbred.

pur'troppo *av* unfortunately.

pus *sm* pus.

pusil'lanime *ag* cowardly.

'pustola *sf* pimple.

puta'caso *av* just supposing, suppose.

puti'ferio *sm* rumpus, row.

putre'fare *vi* to putrefy, rot.
putre'fatto, a *pp di* **putrefare.**
putrefazi'one [putrefat'tsjone] *sf*
  putrefaction.
'putrido, a *ag* putrid, rotten.
put'tana *sf (fam!)* whore *(!)*.
'putto *sm* cupid.
'puzza ['puttsa] *sf* = **puzzo.**
puz'zare [put'tsare] *vi* to stink; **la faccenda**
  puzza (d'imbroglio) the whole business
  stinks.
'puzzo ['puttso] *sm* stink, foul smell.
'puzzola ['puttsola] *sf* polecat.
puzzo'lente [puttso'lente] *ag* stinking.
PV *sigla = Pavia.*
pv *abbr* vedi **prossimo venturo.**
P.V.C. [pivi'tʃi] *sigla m* (= *polyvinyl chloride*)
  PVC.
PZ *sigla = Potenza.*
p. **zza** *abbr* = **piazza.**

$$Q\,q$$

Q, q [ku] *sf o m inv* (*lettera*) Q, q; **Q come**
  Quarto ≈ Q for Queen.
q *abbr* (= *quintale*) q.
Qa'tar [ka'tar] *sm*: **il** ~ Qatar.
q.b. *abbr* (= *quanto basta*) as needed;
  zucchero ~ sugar to taste.
Q.G. *abbr* = **quartier generale.**
Q.I. *abbr vedi* **quoziente d'intelligenza.**
qua *av* here; **in** ~ (*verso questa parte*) this
  way; ~ **dentro/sotto** *etc* in/under here
  etc; **da un anno in** ~ for a year now; **da**
  quando in ~? since when?; **per di** ~
  (*passare*) this way; **al di** ~ **di** (*fiume, strada*)
  on this side of; *vedi* **questo.**
'quacchero, a ['kwakkero] *sm/f* Quaker.
qua'derno *sm* notebook; (*per scuola*)
  exercise book.
qua'drangolo *sm* quadrangle.
qua'drante *sm* quadrant; (*di orologio*) face.
qua'drare *vi* (*bilancio*) to balance, tally;
  (*fig: corrispondere*): ~ **(con)** to correspond
  (with) ♦ *vt* (*MAT*) to square; **far** ~ **il**
  bilancio to balance the books; **non mi**
  quadra I don't like it.
qua'drato, a *ag* square; (*fig: equilibrato*)
  level-headed, sensible; (: *peg*) square
  ♦ *sm* (*MAT*) square; (*PUGILATO*) ring; **5 al** ~

5 squared.
quadret'tato, a *ag* (*foglio*) squared;
  (*tessuto*) checked.
qua'dretto *sm*: **a** ~**i** (*tessuto*) checked;
  (*foglio*) squared.
quadrien'nale *ag* (*che dura 4 anni*) four-
  year *cpd*; (*che avviene ogni 4 anni*) four-
  yearly.
quadri'foglio [kwadri'fɔʎʎo] *sm* four-leaf
  clover.
quadri'mestre *sm* (*periodo*) four-month
  period; (*INS*) term.
'quadro *sm* (*pittura*) painting, picture;
  (*quadrato*) square; (*tabella*) table, chart;
  (*TECN*) board, panel; (*TEAT*) scene; (*fig:*
  scena, spettacolo) sight; (: *descrizione*)
  outline, description; ~**i** (*smpl* (*POL*) party
  organizers; (*COMM*) managerial staff;
  (*MIL*) cadres; (*CARTE*) diamonds; **a** ~**i**
  (*disegno*) checked; **fare un** ~ **della**
  situazione to outline the situation; ~
  clinico (*MED*) case history; ~ **di comando**
  control panel; ~**i intermedi** middle
  management *sg.*
qua'drupede *sm* quadruped.
quadrupli'care *vt* to quadruple.
'quadruplo, a *ag, sm* quadruple.
quaggiù [kwad'dʒu] *av* down here.
'quaglia ['kwaʎʎa] *sf* quail.

PAROLA CHIAVE

'qualche ['kwalke] *det* **1** some, a few; (*in*
  interrogative) any; **ho comprato** ~ **libro**
  I've bought some *o* a few books; ~ **volta**
  sometimes; **hai** ~ **sigaretta?** have you any
  cigarettes?
  2 (*uno*): **c'è** ~ **medico?** is there a doctor?;
  in ~ **modo** somehow
  3 (*un certo, parecchio*) some; **un**
  personaggio di ~ **rilievo** a figure of some
  importance
  4: ~ **cosa = qualcosa.**

qualche'duno [kwalke'duno] *pron*
  = **qualcuno.**
qual'cosa *pron* something; (*in espressioni*
  interrogative) anything; **qualcos'altro**
  something else; anything else; ~ **di nuovo**
  something new; anything new; ~ **da**
  mangiare something to eat; anything to
  eat; **c'è** ~ **che non va?** is there something
  o anything wrong?
qual'cuno *pron* (*persona*) someone,
  somebody; (: *in espressioni interrogative*)
  anyone, anybody; (*alcuni*) some; ~ **è**
  favorevole a noi some are on our side;
  qualcun altro someone *o* somebody else;
  anyone *o* anybody else.

PAROLA CHIAVE

'**quale** (*spesso troncato in* **qual**) *det* **1**
(*interrogativo*) what; (: *scegliendo tra due o
più cose o persone*) which; ~ **uomo/
denaro?** what man/money?; which man/
money?; ~**i sono i tuoi programmi?** what
are your plans?; ~ **stanza preferisci?**
which room do you prefer?

2 (*relativo*: *come*): **il risultato fu** ~ **ci si
aspettava** the result was as expected
3 (*in elenchi*) such as, like; **piante** ~**i
l'edera** plants such as *o* like ivy
4 (*esclamativo*) what; ~ **disgrazia!** what
bad luck!
5: **in un certo qual modo** in a way, in
some ways; **per la qual cosa** for which
reason
♦ *pron* **1** (*interrogativo*) which; ~ **dei due
scegli?** which of the two do you want?
2 (*relativo*): **il(la)** ~ (*persona*: *soggetto*)
who; (: *oggetto, con preposizione*) whom;
(*cosa*) which; (*possessivo*) whose; **suo
padre, il** ~ **è avvocato,** ... his father, who
is a lawyer, ...; **a tutti coloro i** ~**i fossero
interessati** ... to whom it may concern ...;
il signore con il ~ **parlavo** the gentleman
to whom I was speaking; **l'albergo al** ~ **ci
siamo fermati** the hotel where we stayed
ọ which we stayed at; **la signora della** ~
ammiriamo la bellezza the lady whose
beauty we admire
♦ *av* (*in qualità di, come*) as; ~ **sindaco di
questa città** as mayor of this town.

qua 'lifica, che *sf* qualification; (*titolo*) title.
qualifi 'care *vt* to qualify; (*definire*): ~ **qn/
qc come** to describe sb/sth as; ~**rsi** *vr*
(*anche SPORT*) to qualify; ~**rsi a un
concorso** to pass a competitive exam.
qualifica 'tivo, a *ag* qualifying.
qualifi 'cato, a *ag* (*dotato di qualifica*)
qualified; (*esperto, abile*) skilled; **non mi
ritengo** ~ **per questo lavoro** I don't think
I'm qualified for this job; **è un medico
molto** ~ he is a very distinguished
doctor.
qualificazi 'one [kwalifikat'tsjone] *sf*
qualification; **gara di** ~ (*SPORT*) qualifying
event.
qualità *sf inv* quality; **di ottima** *o* **prima** ~
top quality; **in** ~ **di** in one's capacity as; **in**
~ **di amica** as a friend; **articoli di ogni** ~
all sorts of goods; **controllo (di)** ~ quality
control; **prodotto di** ~ quality product.
qualita 'tivo, a *ag* qualitative.
qua 'lora *cong* in case, if.
qual 'siasi, qua 'lunque *det inv* any; (*quale

che sia*) whatever; (*discriminativo*)
whichever; (*posposto*: *mediocre*) poor,
indifferent; ordinary; **mettiti un vestito** ~
put on any old dress; ~ **cosa** anything; ~
cosa accada whatever happens; a ~ **costo**
at any cost, whatever the cost; **l'uomo** ~
the man in the street; ~ **persona** anyone,
anybody.
qualunqu 'ista, i, e *sm/f person indifferent
to politics.*
'**qualo** *cong, av* when; ~ **sarò ricco** when
I'm rich; **da** ~ (*dacché*) since;
(*interrogativo*): **da** ~ **sei qui?** how long
have you been here?; **di** ~ **in** ~ from time
to time; **quand'anche** even if.
quantifi 'care *vt* to quantify.
quantità *sf inv* quantity; (*gran numero*): **una**
~ **di** a great deal of; a lot of; **in grande** ~
in large quantities.
quanta 'tivo, a *ag* quantitative ♦ *sm*
(*COMM*: *di merce*) amount, quantity.

PAROLA CHIAVE

'**quanto, a** *det* **1** (*interrogativo*: *quantità*) how
much; (: *numero*) how many; ~ **pane/
denaro?** how much bread/money?; ~**i
libri/ragazzi?** how many books/boys?; ~
tempo? how long?; ~**i anni hai?** how old
are you?
2 (*esclamativo*): ~**e storie!** what a lot of
nonsense!; ~ **tempo sprecato!** what a
waste of time!
3 (*relativo*: *quantità*) as much ... as;
(: *numero*) as many ... as; **ho** ~ **denaro mi
occorre** I have as much money as I need;
prendi ~**i libri vuoi** take as many books as
you like
♦ *pron* **1** (*interrogativo*: *quantità*) how much;
(: *numero*) how many; (: *tempo*) how long;
~ **mi dai?** how much will you give me?;
~**i me ne hai portati?** how many did you
bring me?; ~ **starai via?** how long will you
be away (for)?; **da** ~ **sei qui?** how long
have you been here?; ~**i ne abbiamo
oggi?** what's the date today?
2 (*relativo*: *quantità*) as much as;
(: *numero*) as many as; **farò** ~ **posso** I'll do
as much as I can; **a** ~ **dice lui** according
to him; **in risposta a** ~ **esposto nella sua
lettera** ... in answer to the points raised
in your letter; **possono venire
~i sono stati invitati** all those who have
been invited can come
♦ *av* **1** (*interrogativo*: *con ag, av*) how; (: *con
vb*) how much; ~ **stanco ti sembrava?** how
tired did he seem to you?; ~ **corre la tua
moto?** how fast can your motorbike go?;
~ **costa?** how much does it cost?;

quant'è? how much is it?
2 (*esclamativo: con ag, av*) how; (: *con vb*) how much; ~ **sono felice!** how happy I am!; **sapessi** ~ **abbiamo camminato!** if you knew how far we've walked!; **studierò** ~ **posso** I'll study as much as *o* all I can; ~ **prima** as soon as possible; ~ **più ... tanto meno** the more ... the less; ~ **più ... tanto più** the more ... the more **3**: **in** ~ (*in qualità di*) as; (*perché, per il fatto che*) as, since; **in** ~ **legale della signora** as the lady's lawyer; **non è possibile in** ~ **non possiamo permettercelo** it isn't possible, since we can't afford it; **(in)** ~ **a** (*per ciò che riguarda*) as for, as regards; **(in)** ~ **a lui** as far as he's concerned **4**: **per** ~ (*nonostante, anche se*) however; **per** ~ **si sforzi, non ce la farà** try as he may, he won't manage it; **per** ~ **sia brava, fa degli errori** however good she may be, she makes mistakes; **per** ~ **io sappia** as far as I know.

quan'tunque *cong* although, though.
qua'ranta *num* forty.
quaran'tena *sf* quarantine.
quaran'tenne *ag, sm/f* forty-year-old.
quaran'tennio *sm* (period of) forty years.
quaran'tesimo, a *num* fortieth.
quaran'tina *sf*: **una** ~ **(di)** about forty.
quaran'totto *sm inv* forty-eight; **fare un** ~ (*fam*) to raise hell.
Qua'resima *sf*: **la** ~ Lent.
'quarta *sf vedi* **quarto**.
quar'tetto *sm* quartet(te).
quarti'ere *sm* district, area; (*MIL*) quarters *pl*; ~ **generale (Q.G.)** headquarters *pl* (HQ); ~ **residenziale** residential area *o* district; **i** ~**i alti** the smart districts.
'quarto, a *ag* fourth ♦ *sm* fourth; (*quarta parte*) quarter ♦ *sf* (*AUT*) fourth (gear); (*INS: elementare*) *fourth year of primary school*; (: *superiore*) *seventh year of secondary school*; **un** ~ **di vino** a quarter-litre (*BRIT*) *o* quarter-liter (*US*) bottle of wine; **le 6 e un** ~ a quarter past (*BRIT*) *o* after (*US*) 6; ~ **d'ora** quarter of an hour; **tre** ~**i d'ora** three quarters of an hour; **le otto e tre** ~**i, le nove meno un** ~ **(a)** quarter to (*BRIT*) *o* of (*US*) nine; **passare un brutto** ~ **d'ora** (*fig*) to have a bad *o* nasty time of it; ~**i di finale** (*SPORT*) quarter finals.
'quarzo ['kwartso] *sm* quartz.
'quasi *av* almost, nearly ♦ *cong* (*anche*: ~ **che**) as if; **(non) ... ~ mai** hardly ever; ~ ~ **me ne andrei** I've half a mind to

leave.
quassù *av* up here.
'quatto, a *ag* crouched, squatting; (*silenzioso*) silent; ~ ~ very quietly; stealthily.
quattordi'cenne [kwattordi'tʃɛnne] *ag, sm/f* fourteen-year-old.
quat'tordici [kwat'torditʃi] *num* fourteen.
quat'trini *smpl* money *sg*, cash *sg*.
'quattro *num* four; **in** ~ **e quattr'otto** in less than no time; **dirne** ~ **a qn** to give sb a piece of one's mind; **fare il diavolo a** ~ to kick up a rumpus; **fare** ~ **chiacchiere** to have a chat; **farsi in** ~ **per qn** to go out of one's way for sb, put o.s. out for sb.
quat'trocchi [kwat'trɔkki] *sm inv* (*fig fam*: *persona con occhiali*) four-eyes; **a** ~ *av* (*tra 2 persone*) face to face; (*privatamente*) in private.
quattrocen'tesco, a, schi, sche [kwattrotʃen'tesko] *ag* fifteenth-century.
quattro'cento [kwattro'tʃɛnto] *num* four hundred ♦ *sm*: **il Q**~ the fifteenth century.
quattro'mila *num* four thousand.

=============== *PAROLA CHIAVE*

'quello, a (*dav sm* **quel** + *C*, **quell'** + *V*, **quello** + *s impura, gn, pn, ps, x, z; pl* **quei** + *C*, **quegli** + *V o s impura, gn, pn, ps, x, z; dav sf* **quella** + *C*, **quell'** + *V; pl* **quelle**) *det* that; those *pl*; ~**a casa** that house; **quegli uomini** those men; **voglio** ~**a camicia (lì** *o* **là)** I want that shirt; ~ **è mio fratello** that's my brother
♦ *pron* **1** (*dimostrativo*) that (one); those (ones) *pl*; (*ciò*) that; **conosci** ~**a?** do you know her?; **prendo** ~ **bianco** I'll take the white one; **chi è** ~**?** who's that?; **prendiamo** ~ **(lì** *o* **là)** let's take that one (there); **in quel di Milano** in the Milan area *o* region
2 (*relativo*): ~**(a) che** (*persona*) the one (who); (*cosa*) the one (which), the one (that); ~**i(e) che** (*persone*) those who; (*cose*) those which; **è lui** ~ **che non voleva venire** he's the one who didn't want to come; **ho fatto** ~ **che potevo** I did what I could; **è** ~**a che ti ho prestato** that's the one I lent you; **è proprio** ~ **che gli ho detto** that's exactly what I told him; **da** ~ **che ho sentito** from what I've heard.

'quercia, ce ['kwɛrtʃa] *sf* oak (tree); (*legno*) oak; **la Q**~(*POL*) symbol of *P.D.S.*
que'rela *sf* (*DIR*) (legal) action.
quere'lare *vt* to bring an action against.

que'sito *sm* question, query; problem.

'questi *pron* (*poetico*) this person.

questio'nario *sm* questionnaire.

questi'one *sf* problem, question; (*controversia*) issue; (*litigio*) quarrel; **in** ~ in question; **il caso in** ~ the matter at hand; **la persona in** ~ the person involved; **non voglio essere chiamato in** ~ I don't want to be dragged into the argument; **fuor di** ~ out of the question; **è** ~ **di tempo** it's a matter *o* question of time.

════════ *PAROLA CHIAVE*

'questo, a *det* **1** (*dimostrativo*) this; these *pl*; ~ **libro (qui** *o* **qua)** this book; **io prendo** ~ **cappotto, tu quello** I'll take this coat, you take that one; **quest'oggi** today; ~**a sera** this evening

2 (*enfatico*): **non fatemi più prendere di** ~**e paure** don't frighten me like that again

♦ *pron* (*dimostrativo*) this (one); these (ones) *pl*; (*ciò*) this; **prendo** ~ **(qui** *o* **qua)** I'll take this one; **preferisci** ~**i** *o* **quelli?** do you prefer these (ones) or those (ones)?; ~ **intendevo io** this is what I meant; ~ **non dovevi dirlo** you shouldn't have said that; **e con** ~**?** so what?; **e con** ~ **se n'è andato** and with that he left; **con tutto** ~ in spite of this, despite all this; ~ **è quanto** that's all.

ques'tore *sm* public official in charge of the police in the provincial capital, reporting to the *prefetto*; ≈ chief constable (*BRIT*), ≈ police commissioner (*US*).

'questua *sf* collection (of alms).

ques'tura *sf* police headquarters *pl*.

questu'rino *sm* (*fam: poliziotto*) cop.

qui *av* here; **da** *o* **di** ~ from here; **di** ~ **in avanti** from now on; **di** ~ **a poco/una settimana** in a little while/a week's time; ~ **dentro/sopra/vicino** in/up/near here; *vedi* **questo**.

quie'tanza [kwje'tantsa] *sf* receipt.

qui'ete *sf* quiet, quietness; calmness; stillness; peace; **turbare la** ~ **pubblica** (*DIR*) to disturb the peace.

qui'eto, a *ag* quiet; (*notte*) calm, still; (*mare*) calm; **l'ho fatto per il** ~ **vivere** I did it for a quiet life.

'quindi *av* then ♦ *cong* therefore, so.

quindi'cenne [kwindi'tʃɛnne] *ag, sm/f* fifteen-year-old.

'quindici ['kwinditʃi] *num* fifteen; ~ **giorni** a fortnight (*BRIT*), two weeks.

quindi'cina [kwindi'tʃina] *sf* (*serie*): **una** ~ **(di)** about fifteen; **fra una** ~ **di giorni** in a fortnight (*BRIT*) *o* two weeks.

quindici'nale [kwinditʃi'nale] *ag* fortnightly (*BRIT*), semimonthly (*US*) ♦ *sm* (*rivista*) fortnightly magazine (*BRIT*), semimonthly (*US*).

quinquen'nale *ag* (*che dura 5 anni*) five-year *cpd*; (*che avviene ogni 5 anni*) five-yearly.

quin'quennio *sm* period of five years.

quinta *sf vedi* **quinto**.

quin'tale *sm* quintal (*100 kg*).

quin'tetto *sm* quintet(te).

'quinto, a *num* fifth ♦ *sf* (*AUT*) fifth (gear); (*INS: elementare*) *fifth year of primary school*; (*: superiore*) *final year of secondary school*; (*TEAT*) wing; **un** ~ **della popolazione** a fifth of the population; **tre** ~**i** three fifths; **in** ~**a pagina** on the fifth page, on page five.

qui pro quo *sm inv* misunderstanding.

Quiri'nale *sm vedi nota nel riquadro.*

┌─────────────────────────────────────┐
│ QUIRINALE   │
│   │
│ The **Quirinale** *takes its name from one of the* │
│ *Seven Hills of Rome on which it stands. It is the* │
│ *official residence of the "Presidente della* │
│ *Repubblica".*   │
└─────────────────────────────────────┘

'Quito *sf* Quito.

quiz [kwidz] *sm inv* (*domanda*) question; (*anche:* **gioco a** ~) quiz game.

'quorum *sm* quorum.

'quota *sf* (*parte*) quota, share; (*AER*) height, altitude; (*IPPICA*) odds *pl*; **prendere/perdere** ~ (*AER*) to gain/lose height *o* altitude; ~ **imponibile** taxable income; ~ **d'iscrizione** (*INS*) enrolment fee; (*ad una gara*) entry fee; (*ad un club*) membership fee; ~ **di mercato** market share.

quo'tare *vt* (*BORSA*) to quote; (*valutare: anche fig*) to value; **è un pittore molto quotato** he is rated highly as a painter.

quotazi'one [kwotat'tsjone] *sf* quotation.

quotidiana'mente *av* daily, every day.

quotidi'ano, a *ag* daily; (*banale*) everyday ♦ *sm* (*giornale*) daily (paper).

quozi'ente [kwot'tsjɛnte] *sm* (*MAT*) quotient; ~ **di crescita zero** zero growth rate; ~ **d'intelligenza (Q.I.)** intelligence quotient (IQ).

R r

R, r ['ɛrre] *sf o m* (*lettera*) R, r; **R come Roma**
≈ R for Robert (*BRIT*), R for Roger (*US*).
R *abbr* (*POSTA*) = **raccomandata;** (*FERR*)
= **rapido.**
RA *sigla* = Ravenna.
ra'barbaro *sm* rhubarb.
Ra'bat *sf* Rabat.
rabberci'are [rabber'tʃare] *vt* (*anche fig*) to
patch up.
'rabbia *sf* (*ira*) anger, rage; (*accanimento*,
furia) fury; (*MED: idrofobia*) rabies *sg*.
rab'bino *sm* rabbi.
rabbi'oso, a *ag* angry, furious; (*facile
all'ira*) quick-tempered; (*forze, acqua etc*)
furious, raging; (*MED*) rabid, mad.
rabbo'nire *vt*, **~rsi** *vr* to calm down.
rabbrivi'dire *vi* to shudder, shiver.
rabbui'arsi *vr* to grow dark.
rabdo'mante *sm* water diviner.
racc. *abbr* (*POSTA*) = **raccomandata.**
raccapez'zarsi [rakkapet'tsarsi] *vr*: **non ~** to
be at a loss.
raccapricci'ante [rakkaprit'tʃante] *ag*
horrifying.
racca'priccio [rakka'prittʃo] *sm* horror.
raccatta'palle *sm inv* (*SPORT*) ballboy.
raccat'tare *vt* to pick up.
rac'chetta [rak'ketta] *sf* (*per tennis*) racket;
(*per ping-pong*) bat; **~ da neve** snowshoe;
~ da sci ski stick.
'racchio, a ['rakkjo] *ag* (*fam*) ugly.
racchi'udere [rak'kjudere] *vt* to contain.
racchi'uso, a [rak'kjuso] *pp di* **racchiudere.**
rac'cogliere [rak'kɔʎʎere] *vt* to collect;
(*raccattare*) to pick up; (*frutti, fiori*) to pick,
pluck; (*AGR*) to harvest; (*approvazione,
voti*) to win; (*profughi*) to take in; (*vele*) to
furl; (*capelli*) to put up; **~rsi** *vr* to gather;
(*fig*) to gather one's thoughts; to
meditate; **non ha raccolto** (*allusione*) he
didn't take the hint; (*frecciata*) he took no
notice of it; **~ i frutti del proprio lavoro**
(*fig*) to reap the benefits of one's work; **~
le idee** (*fig*) to gather one's thoughts.
raccogli'mento [rakkoʎʎi'mento] *sm*
meditation.
raccogli'tore [rakkoʎʎi'tore] *sm* (*cartella*)
folder, binder; **~ a fogli mobili** loose-leaf

binder.
rac'colto, a *pp di* **raccogliere** ♦ *ag* (*persona*:
pensoso) thoughtful; (*luogo*: *appartato*)
secluded, quiet ♦ *sm* (*AGR*) crop, harvest ♦
sf collecting *no pl*; collection; (*AGR*)
harvesting *no pl*, gathering *no pl*; harvest,
crop; **fare la ~a di qc** to collect sth;
chiamare a ~a to gather together; **~a
differenziata** (*dei rifiuti*) separate collection
of different kinds of household waste.
raccoman'dabile *ag* (highly)
commendable; **è un tipo poco ~**
he is not to be trusted.
raccoman'dare *vt* to recommend;
(*affidare*) to entrust; **~rsi** *vr*: **~rsi a qn** to
commend o.s. to sb; **~ a qn di fare qc** to
recommend that sb does sth; **~ a qn di
non fare qc** to tell *o* warn sb not to do sth;
~ qn a qn/alle cure di qn to entrust sb to
sb/to sb's care; **mi raccomando!** don't
forget!
raccoman'dato, a *ag* (*lettera, pacco*)
recorded-delivery (*BRIT*), certified (*US*);
(*candidato*) recommended ♦ *sm/f*: **essere
un(a) ~ (a) di ferro** to have friends in high
places ♦ *sf* (*anche*: **lettera ~a**) recorded-
delivery letter; **~a con ricevuta di ritorno**
(**Rrr**) recorded-delivery letter with advice
of receipt.
raccomandazi'one [rakkomandat'tsjone] *sf*
recommendation; **lettera di ~** letter of
introduction.
raccomo'dare *vt* (*riparare*) to repair,
mend.
raccon'tare *vt*: **~ (a qn)** (*dire*) to tell (sb);
(*narrare*) to relate (to sb), tell (sb) about; **a
me non la racconti** don't try and kid me;
cosa mi racconti di nuovo? what's new?
rac'conto *sm* telling *no pl*, relating *no pl*;
(*fatto raccontato*) story, tale; (*genere
letterario*) short story; **~i per bambini**
children's stories.
raccorci'are [rakkor'tʃare] *vt* to shorten.
raccor'dare *vt* to link up, join.
rac'cordo *sm* (*TECN: giunzione*) connection,
joint; (*AUT: di autostrada*) slip road (*BRIT*),
entrance (*o* exit) ramp (*US*); **~ anulare**
(*AUT*) ring road (*BRIT*), beltway (*US*).
ra'chitico, a, ci, che [ra'kitiko] *ag*
suffering from rickets; (*fig*) scraggy,
scrawny.
rachi'tismo [raki'tizmo] *sm* (*MED*) rickets
sg.
racimo'lare [ratʃimo'lare] *vt* (*fig*) to scrape
together, glean.
'rada *sf* (natural) harbour (*BRIT*) *o* harbor
(*US*).
'radar *sm inv* radar.

raddol 'cire [raddol'tʃire] *vt* (*persona*, *carattere*) to soften; ~**rsi** *vr* (*tempo*) to grow milder; (*persona*) to soften, mellow.

raddoppia 'mento *sm* doubling.

raddoppi 'are *vt*, *vi* to double.

rad 'doppio *sm* (*gen*) doubling; (*BILIARDO*) double; (*EQUITAZIONE*) gallop.

raddriz 'zare [raddrit'tsare] *vt* to straighten; (*fig*: *correggere*) to put straight, correct.

'radere *vt* (*barba*) to shave off; (*mento*) to shave; (*fig*: *rasentare*) to graze; to skim; ~**rsi** *vr* to shave (o.s.); ~ **al suolo** to raze to the ground.

radi 'ale *ag* radial.

radi 'ante *ag* (*calore*, *energia*) radiant.

radi 'are *vt* to strike off.

radia 'tore *sm* radiator.

radiazi 'one [radjat'tsjone] *sf* (*FISICA*) radiation; (*cancellazione*) striking off.

'radica *sf* (*BOT*): ~ **di noce** walnut (wood).

radi 'cale *ag* radical ♦ *sm* (*LING*) root; (*MAT, POL*) radical.

radi 'cato, a *ag* (*pregiudizio, credenza*) deep-seated, deeply-rooted.

ra 'dicchio [ra'dikkjo] *sm variety of chicory*.

ra 'dice [ra'ditʃe] *sf* root; **segno di** ~ (*MAT*) radical sign; **colpire alla** ~ (*fig*) to strike at the root; **mettere** ~**i** (*idee, odio etc*) to take root; (*persona*) to put down roots; ~ **quadrata** (*MAT*) square root.

'radio *sf inv* radio ♦ *sm* (*CHIM*) radium; **trasmettere per** ~ to broadcast; **stazione/ponte** ~ radio station/link; ~ **ricevente/trasmittente** receiver/transmitter.

radioabbo 'nato, a *sm/f* radio subscriber.

radioama 'tore, 'trice *sm/f* amateur radio operator, ham (*fam*).

radioascolta 'tore, 'trice *sm/f* (*radio*) listener.

radioattività *sf* radioactivity.

radioat 'tivo, a *ag* radioactive.

radiocoman 'dare *vt* to operate by remote control.

radiocoman 'dato, a *ag* remote-controlled.

radioco 'mando *sm* remote control.

radiocomunicazi 'one [radjokomunikat'tsjone] *sf* radio message.

radio 'cronaca, che *sf* radio commentary.

radiocro 'nista, i, e *sm/f* radio commentator.

radiodiffusi 'one *sf* (*radio*) broadcasting.

radio 'fonico, a, ci, che *ag* radio *cpd*.

radiogra 'fare *vt* to X-ray.

radiogra 'fia *sf* radiography; (*foto*) X-ray photograph.

radio 'lina *sf* portable radio, transistor (radio).

radiolo 'gia [radjolo'dʒia] *sf* radiology.

radi 'ologo, a, gi, ghe *sm/f* radiologist.

radiorice 'vente [radjoritʃe'vɛnte] *sf* (*anche*: **apparecchio** ~) receiver.

radi 'oso, a *ag* radiant.

radiostazi 'one [radjostat'tsjone] *sf* radio station.

radios 'veglia [radjoz'veʎʎa] *sf* radio alarm.

radio 'taxi *sm inv* radio taxi.

radio 'tecnico, a, ci, che *ag* radio engineering *cpd* ♦ *sm* radio engineer.

radiotelegra 'fista, i, e *sm/f* radiotelegrapher.

radiotera 'pia *sf* radiotherapy.

radiotrasmit 'tente *ag* (*radio*) broadcasting *cpd* ♦ *sf* (*radio*) broadcasting station.

'rado, a *ag* (*capelli*) sparse, thin; (*visite*) infrequent; **di** ~ rarely; **non di** ~ not uncommonly.

radu 'nare *vt*, ~**rsi** *vr* to gather, assemble.

radu 'nata *sf* (*MIL*) muster.

ra 'duno *sm* gathering, meeting.

ra 'dura *sf* clearing.

'rafano *sm* horseradish.

raffazzo 'nare [raffattso'nare] *vt* to patch up.

raf 'fermo, a *ag* stale.

'raffica, che *sf* (*METEOR*) gust (of wind); ~ **di colpi** (*di fucile*) burst of gunfire.

raffigu 'rare *vt* to represent.

raffigurazi 'one [raffigurat'tsjone] *sf* representation, depiction.

raffi 'nare *vt* to refine.

raffina 'tezza [raffina'tettsa] *sf* refinement.

raffi 'nato, a *ag* refined.

raffinazi 'one [raffinat'tsjone] *sf* (*di sostanza*) refining; ~ **del petrolio** oil refining.

raffine 'ria *sf* refinery.

raffor 'zare [raffor'tsare] *vt* to reinforce.

rafforza 'tivo, a [raffortsa'tivo] *ag* (*LING*) intensifying ♦ *sm* (*LING*) intensifier.

raffredda 'mento *sm* cooling.

raffred 'dare *vt* to cool; (*fig*) to dampen, have a cooling effect on; ~**rsi** *vr* to grow cool *o* cold; (*prendere un raffreddore*) to catch a cold; (*fig*) to cool (off).

raffred 'dato, a *ag* (*MED*): **essere** ~ to have a cold.

raffred 'dore *sm* (*MED*) cold.

raffron 'tare *vt* to compare.

raf 'fronto *sm* comparison.

'rafia *sf* (*fibra*) raffia.

raga 'nella *sf* (*ZOOL*) tree frog.

ra 'gazzo, a [ra'gattso] *sm/f* boy/girl; (*fam*: *fidanzato*) boyfriend/girlfriend; **nome da** ~**a** maiden name; ~**a madre** unmarried

mother; ~**a squillo** call girl.
ragge 'lare [radd3e'lare] *vt*, *vi*, **~rsi** *vr* to freeze.
raggi 'ante [rad'd3ante] *ag* radiant, shining; ~ **di gioia** beaming *o* radiant with joy.
raggi 'era [rad'd3era] *sf* (*di ruota*) spokes *pl*; **a** ~ with a sunburst pattern.
'raggio ['radd3o] *sm* (*di sole etc*) ray; (*MAT*, *distanza*) radius; (*di ruota etc*) spoke; **nel** ~ **di 20 km** within a radius of 20 km *o* a 20-km radius; **a largo** ~ (*esplorazione*, *incursione*) wide-ranging; ~ **d'azione** range; ~ **laser** laser beam; **~i X** X-rays.
raggi 'rare [radd3i'rare] *vt* to take in, trick.
rag 'giro [rad'd3iro] *sm* trick.
raggi 'ungere [rad'd3und3ere] *vt* to reach; (*persona*: *riprendere*) to catch up (with); (*bersaglio*) to hit; (*fig*: *meta*) to achieve; ~ **il proprio scopo** to reach one's goal, achieve one's aim; ~ **un accordo** to come to *o* reach an agreement.
raggi 'unto, a [rad'd3unto] *pp di* **raggiungere**.
raggomito 'larsi *vr* to curl up.
raggranel 'lare *vt* to scrape together.
raggrin 'zare [raggrin'tsare] *vt*, *vi* (*anche*: **~rsi**) to wrinkle.
raggrin 'zire [raggrin'tsire] *vt* = **raggrinzare**.
raggru 'mare *vt*, **~rsi** *vr* (*sangue*, *latte*) to clot.
raggruppa 'mento *sm* (*azione*) grouping; (*gruppo*) group; (: *MIL*) unit.
raggrup 'pare *vt* to group (together).
ragguagli 'are [raggwaʎ'ʎare] *vt* (*paragonare*) to compare; (*informare*) to inform.
raggu 'aglio [rag'gwaʎʎo] *sm* comparison; (*informazione*, *relazione*) piece of information.
ragguar 'devole *ag* (*degno di riguardo*) distinguished, notable; (*notevole*: *somma*) considerable.
'ragia ['radʒa] *sf*: **acqua** ~ turpentine.
ragiona 'mento [radʒona'mento] *sm* reasoning *no pl*; argument.
ragio 'nare [radʒo'nare] *vi* (*usare la ragione*) to reason; (*discorrere*): ~ **(di)** to argue (about); **cerca di** ~ try and be reasonable.
ragi 'one [ra'dʒone] *sf* reason; (*dimostrazione*, *prova*) argument, reason; (*diritto*) right; **aver** ~ to be right; **aver** ~ **di qn** to get the better of sb; **dare** ~ **a qn** (*sog*: *persona*) to side with sb; (: *fatto*) to prove sb right; **farsi una** ~ **di qc** to accept sth, come to terms with sth; **in** ~ **di** at the rate of; **a o con** ~ rightly, justly; **perdere la** ~ to become insane; (*fig*) to take leave of one's senses; **a ragion veduta** after due

consideration; **per ~i di famiglia** for family reasons; ~ **di scambio** terms of trade; ~ **sociale** (*COMM*) corporate name; **ragion di stato** reason of State.
ragione 'ria [radʒone'ria] *sf* accountancy; (*ufficio*) accounts department.
ragio 'nevole [radʒo'nevole] *ag* reasonable.
ragioni 'ere, a [radʒo'njɛre] *sm/f* accountant.
ragli 'are [raʎ'ʎare] *vi* to bray.
ragna 'tela [raɲɲa'tela] *sf* cobweb, spider's web.
'ragno ['raɲɲo] *sm* spider; **non cavare un** ~ **dal buco** (*fig*) to draw a blank.
ragù *sm inv* (*CUC*) meat sauce (*for pasta*).
RAI-TV [raiti'vu] *sigla f* (= *Radio televisione italiana*) *Italian Broadcasting Company*.
rallegra 'menti *smpl* congratulations.
ralle 'grare *vt* to cheer up; **~rsi** *vr* to cheer up; (*provare allegrezza*) to rejoice; **~rsi con qn** to congratulate sb.
rallenta 'mento *sm* slowing down; slackening.
rallen 'tare *vt*, *vi* to slow down; ~ **il passo** to slacken one's pace.
rallenta 'tore *sm* (*CINE*) slow-motion camera; **al** ~ (*anche fig*) in slow motion.
raman 'zina [raman'dzina] *sf* lecture, telling-off.
ra 'mare *vt* (*superficie*) to copper, coat with copper; (*AGR*: *vite*) to spray with copper sulphate.
ra 'marro *sm* green lizard.
ra 'mato, a *ag* (*oggetto*: *rivestito di rame*) copper-coated, coppered; (*capelli*, *barba*) coppery, copper-coloured (*BRIT*), copper-colored (*US*).
'rame *sm* (*CHIM*) copper; **di** ~ copper *cpd*; **incisione su** ~ copperplate.
ramifi 'care *vi* (*BOT*) to put out branches; **~rsi** *vr* (*diramarsi*) to branch out; (*MED*: *tumore*, *vene*) to ramify; **~rsi in** (*biforcarsi*) to branch into.
ramificazi 'one [ramifikat'tsjone] *sf* ramification.
ra 'mingo, a, ghi, ghe *ag* (*poetico*): **andare** ~ to go wandering, wander.
ra 'mino *sm* (*CARTE*) rummy.
rammari 'carsi *vr*: ~ **(di)** (*rincrescersi*) to be sorry (about), regret; (*lamentarsi*) to complain (about).
ram 'marico, chi *sm* regret.
rammen 'dare *vt* to mend; (*calza*) to darn.
ram 'mendo *sm* mending *no pl*; darning *no pl*; mend; darn.
rammen 'tare *vt* to remember, recall; **~rsi** *vr*: **~rsi (di qc)** to remember (sth); ~ **qc a qn** to remind sb of sth.

rammol'lire *vt* to soften ♦ *vi* (*anche:* ~**rsi**) to go soft.

rammol'lito, a *ag* weak ♦ *sm/f* weakling.

'ramo *sm* branch; (*di commercio*) field; **non è il mio** ~ it's not my field o line.

ramo'scello [ramoʃ'ʃɛllo] *sm* twig.

'rampa *sf* flight (of stairs); ~ **di lancio** launching pad.

rampi'cante *ag* (*BOT*) climbing.

ram'pino *sm* (*gancio*) hook; (*NAUT*) grapnel.

ram'pollo *sm* (*di acqua*) spring; (*BOT*: *germoglio*) shoot; (*fig*: *discendente*) descendant.

ram'pone *sm* harpoon; (*ALPINISMO*) crampon.

'rana *sf* frog; ~ **pescatrice** angler fish.

'rancido, a ['rantʃido] *ag* rancid.

'rancio ['rantʃo] *sm* (*MIL*) mess; **ora del** ~ mess time.

ran'core *sm* rancour (*BRIT*), rancor (*US*), resentment; **portare** ~ **a qn, provare** ~ **per** o **verso qn** to bear sb a grudge.

ran'dagio, a, gi, gie o **ge** [ran'dadʒo] *ag* (*gatto, cane*) stray.

ran'dello *sm* club, cudgel.

'rango, ghi *sm* (*grado*) rank; (*condizione sociale*) station, social standing; **persone di** ~ **inferiore** people of lower standing; **uscire dai** ~**ghi** to fall out; (*fig*) to step out of line.

Ran'gun *sf* Rangoon.

rannicchi'arsi [rannik'kjarsi] *vr* to crouch, huddle.

rannuvo'larsi *vr* to cloud over, become overcast.

ra'nocchio [ra'nɔkkjo] *sm* (edible) frog.

ranto'lare *vi* to wheeze.

ranto'lio *sm* (*il respirare affannoso*) wheezing; (: *di agonizzante*) death rattle.

'rantolo *sm* wheeze; death rattle.

ra'nuncolo *sm* (*BOT*) buttercup.

'rapa *sf* (*BOT*) turnip.

ra'pace [ra'patʃe] *ag* (*animale*) predatory; (*fig*) rapacious, grasping ♦ *sm* bird of prey.

ra'pare *vt* (*capelli*) to crop, cut very short.

'rapida *sf* vedi **rapido**.

rapida'mente *av* quickly, rapidly.

rapidità *sf* speed.

'rapido, a *ag* fast; (*esame, occhiata*) quick, rapid ♦ *sm* (*FERR*) express (train) ♦ *sf* (*di fiume*) rapid.

rapi'mento *sm* kidnapping; (*fig*) rapture.

ra'pina *sf* robbery; ~ **in banca** bank robbery; ~ **a mano armata** armed robbery.

rapi'nare *vt* to rob.

rapina'tore, 'trice *sm/f* robber.

ra'pire *vt* (*cose*) to steal; (*persone*) to kidnap; (*fig*) to enrapture, delight.

ra'pito, a *ag* (*persona*) kidnapped; (*fig*: *in estasi*): **ascoltare** ~ **qn** to be captivated by sb's words ♦ *sm/f* kidnapped person.

rapi'tore, 'trice *sm/f* kidnapper.

rappacifi'care [rappatʃifi'kare] *vt* (*riconciliare*) to reconcile; ~**rsi** *vr* (*uso reciproco*) to be reconciled, make it up (*fam*).

rappacificazi'one [rappatʃifikat'tsjone] *sf* reconciliation.

rappez'zare [rappet'tsare] *vt* to patch.

rappor'tare *vt* (*confrontare*) to compare; (*riprodurre*) to reproduce.

rap'porto *sm* (*resoconto*) report; (*legame*) relationship; (*MAT, TECN*) ratio; ~**i** *smpl* (*fra persone, paesi*) relations; **in** ~ **a quanto è successo** with regard to o in relation to what happened; **fare** ~ **a qn su qc** to report sth to sb; **andare a** ~ **da qn** to report to sb; **chiamare qn a** ~ (*MIL*) to summon sb; **essere in buoni/cattivi** ~**i con qn** to be on good/bad terms with sb; ~ **d'affari,** ~ **di lavoro** business relations; ~ **di compressione** (*TECN*) pressure ratio; ~ **coniugale** marital relationship; ~ **di trasmissione** (*TECN*) gear; ~**i sessuali** sexual intercourse *sg*.

rap'prendersi *vr* to coagulate, clot; (*latte*) to curdle.

rappre'saglia [rappre'saʎʎa] *sf* reprisal, retaliation.

rappresen'tante *sm/f* representative; ~ **di commercio** sales representative, sales rep (*fam*); ~ **sindacale** union delegate o representative.

rappresen'tanza [rapprezen'tantsa] *sf* delegation, deputation; (*COMM*: *ufficio, sede*) agency; **in** ~ **di qn** on behalf of sb; **spese di** ~ entertainment expenses; **macchina di** ~ official car; **avere la** ~ **di** to be the agent for; ~ **esclusiva** sole agency; **avere la** ~ **esclusiva** to be sole agent.

rappresen'tare *vt* to represent; (*TEAT*) to perform; **farsi** ~ **dal proprio legale** to be represented by one's lawyer.

rappresenta'tivo, a *ag* representative ♦ *sf* (*di partito, sindacale*) representative group; (*SPORT*: *squadra*) representative (team).

rappresentazi'one [rapprezentat'tsjone] *sf* representation; performing *no pl*; (*spettacolo*) performance; **prima** ~ **assoluta** world première.

rap'preso, a *pp di* **rapprendere**.

rapso'dia *sf* rhapsody.

'raptus *sm inv*: ~ di follia fit of madness.

rara'mente *av* seldom, rarely.

rare'fare *vt*, ~rsi *vr* to rarefy.

rare'fatto, a *pp di* rarefare ♦ *ag* rarefied.

rarefazi'one [rarefat'tsjone] *sf* rarefaction.

rarità *sf inv* rarity.

'raro, a *ag* rare.

ra'sare *vt* (*barba etc*) to shave off; (*siepi, erba*) to trim, cut; ~rsi *vr* to shave (o.s.).

ra'sato, a *ag* (*erba*) trimmed, cut; (*tessuto*) smooth; avere la barba ~a to be clean-shaven.

rasa'tura *sf* shave.

raschia'mento [raskja'mento] *sm* (*MED*) curettage; ~ uterino D and C.

raschi'are [ras'kjare] *vt* to scrape; (*macchia, fango*) to scrape off ♦ *vi* to clear one's throat.

rasen'tare *vt* (*andar rasente*) to keep close to; (*sfiorare*) to skim along (*o* over); (*fig*) to border on.

ra'sente *prep*: ~ (a) close to, very near.

'raso, a *pp di* radere ♦ *ag* (*barba*) shaved; (*capelli*) cropped; (*con misure di capacità*) level; (*pieno: bicchiere*) full to the brim ♦ *sm* (*tessuto*) satin; ~ terra close to the ground; volare ~ terra to hedgehop; un cucchiaio ~ a level spoonful.

ra'soio *sm* razor; ~ elettrico electric shaver *o* razor.

ras'pare *vt* (*levigare*) to rasp; (*grattare*) to scratch.

'raspo *sm* (*di uva*) grape stalk.

ras'segna [ras'seɲɲa] *sf* (*MIL*) inspection, review; (*esame*) inspection; (*resoconto*) review, survey; (*pubblicazione letteraria etc*) review; (*mostra*) exhibition, show; passare in ~ (*MIL, fig*) to review.

rasse'gnare [rasseɲ'ɲare] *vt*: ~ le dimissioni to resign, hand in one's resignation; ~rsi *vr* (*accettare*): ~rsi (a qc/a fare) to resign o.s. (to sth/to doing).

rassegnazi'one [rasseɲɲat'tsjone] *sf* resignation.

rassere'nare *vt* (*persona*) to cheer up; ~rsi *vr* (*tempo*) to clear up.

rasset'tare *vt* to tidy, put in order; (*aggiustare*) to repair, mend.

rassicu'rante *ag* reassuring.

rassicu'rare *vt* to reassure; ~rsi *vr* to take heart, recover one's confidence.

rassicurazi'one [rassikurat'tsjone] *sf* reassurance.

rasso'dare *vt* to harden, stiffen; (*fig*) to strengthen, consolidate.

rassomigli'anza [rassomiʎ'ʎantsa] *sf* resemblance.

rassomigli'are [rassomiʎ'ʎare] *vi*: ~ a to resemble, look like.

rastrella'mento *sm* (*MIL, di polizia*) (thorough) search.

rastrel'lare *vt* to rake; (*fig: perlustrare*) to comb.

rastrelli'era *sf* rack; (*per piatti*) dish rack.

ras'trello *sm* rake.

'rata *sf* (*quota*) instalment, installment (*US*); pagare a ~e to pay by instal(l)ments *o* on hire purchase (*BRIT*); comprare/vendere a ~e to buy/sell on hire purchase (*BRIT*) *o* on the installment plan (*US*).

rate'ale *ag*: pagamento ~ payment by instal(l)ments; vendita ~ hire purchase (*BRIT*), installment plan (*US*).

rate'are, rateiz'zare [rateid'dzare] *vt* to divide into instal(l)ments.

rateazi'one [rateat'tsjone] *sf* division into instal(l)ments.

'rateo *sm* (*COMM*) accrual.

ra'tifica, che *sf* ratification.

ratifi'care *vt* (*DIR*) to ratify.

'ratto *sm* (*DIR*) abduction; (*ZOOL*) rat.

rattop'pare *vt* to patch.

rat'toppo *sm* patching *no pl*; patch.

rattrap'pire *vt* to make stiff; ~rsi *vr* to be stiff.

rattris'tare *vt* to sadden; ~rsi *vr* to become sad.

rau'cedine [rau't ʃɛdine] *sf* hoarseness.

'rauco, a, chi, che *ag* hoarse.

rava'nello *sm* radish.

raven'nate *ag* of (*o* from) Ravenna.

ravi'oli *smpl* ravioli *sg*.

ravve'dersi *vr* to mend one's ways.

ravvi'are *vt* (*capelli*) to tidy; ~rsi i capelli to tidy one's hair.

ravvicina'mento [ravvit ʃina'mento] *sm* (*tra persone*) reconciliation; (*POL: tra paesi etc*) rapprochement.

ravvici'nare [ravvit ʃi'nare] *vt* (*avvicinare*): ~ qc a to bring sth nearer to; (*oggetti*) to bring closer together; (*fig: persone*) to reconcile, bring together; ~rsi *vr* to be reconciled.

ravvi'sare *vt* to recognize.

ravvi'vare *vt* to revive; (*fig*) to brighten up, enliven; ~rsi *vr* to revive; to brighten up.

Rawal'pindi [raval'pindi] *sf* Rawalpindi.

razio'cinio [rattsjo'tʃinjo] *sm* reasoning *no pl*; reason; (*buon senso*) common sense.

razio'nale [rattsjo'nale] *ag* rational.

razionalità [rattsjonali'ta] *sf* rationality; (*buon senso*) common sense.

razionaliz'zare [rattsjonalid'dzare] *vt* (*metodo, lavoro, programma*) to rationalize; (*problema, situazione*) to approach rationally.

raziona'mento [rattsjona'mento] *sm* rationing.

razio'nare [rattsjo'nare] *vt* to ration.

razi'one [rat'tsjone] *sf* ration; (*porzione*) portion, share.

'razza ['rattsa] *sf* race; (*ZOOL*) breed; (*discendenza, stirpe*) stock, race; (*sorta*) sort, kind.

raz'zia [rat'tsia] *sf* raid, foray.

razzi'ale [rat'tsjale] *ag* racial.

raz'zismo [rat'tsizmo] *sm* racism, racialism.

raz'zista, i, e [rat'tsista] *ag, sm/f* racist, racialist.

'razzo ['raddzo] *sm* rocket; ~ di segnalazione flare; ~ vettore vector rocket.

razzo'lare [rattso'lare] *vi* (*galline*) to scratch about.

RC *sigla* = *Reggio Calabria.*

RDT *sigla f vedi* Repubblica Democratica Tedesca.

RE *sigla* = *Reggio Emilia.*

re *sm inv* (*sovrano*) king; (*MUS*) D; (*: solfeggiando la scala*) re.

rea'gente [rea'dʒɛnte] *sm* reagent.

rea'gire [rea'dʒire] *vi* to react.

re'ale *ag* real; (*di, da re*) royal ♦ *sm*: il ~ reality; i R~i the Royal family.

rea'lismo *sm* realism.

rea'lista, i, e *sm/f* realist; (*POL*) royalist.

rea'listico, a, ci, che *ag* realistic.

realiz'zare [realid'dzare] *vt* (*progetto etc*) to realize, carry out; (*sogno, desiderio*) to realize, fulfil; (*scopo*) to achieve; (*COMM: titoli etc*) to realize; (*CALCIO etc*) to score; ~rsi *vr* to be realized.

realizzazi'one [realiddzat'tsjone] *sf* realization; fulfilment; achievement; ~ scenica stage production.

rea'lizzo [rea'liddzo] *sm* (*conversione in denaro*) conversion into cash; (*vendita forzata*) clearance sale.

real'mente *av* really, actually.

realtà *sf inv* reality; in ~ (*in effetti*) in fact; (*a dire il vero*) really.

re'ame *sm* kingdom, realm; (*fig*) realm.

re'ato *sm* offence (*BRIT*), offense (*US*).

reat'tore *sm* (*FISICA*) reactor; (*AER: aereo*) jet; (*: motore*) jet engine.

reazio'nario, a [reattsjo'narjo] *ag, sm/f* (*POL*) reactionary.

reazi'one [reat'tsjone] *sf* reaction; motore/aereo a ~ jet engine/plane; forze della ~ reactionary forces; ~ a catena (*anche fig*) chain reaction.

'rebbio *sm* prong.

'rebus *sm inv* rebus; (*fig*) puzzle; enigma.

recapi'tare *vt* to deliver.

re'capito *sm* (*indirizzo*) address; (*consegna*) delivery; ha un ~ telefonico? do you have a telephone number where you can be reached?; ~ a domicilio home delivery (service).

re'care *vt* (*portare*) to bring; (*avere su di sé*) to carry, bear; (*cagionare*) to cause, bring; ~rsi *vr* to go; ~ danno a qn to harm sb, cause harm to sb.

re'cedere [re'tʃedere] *vi* to withdraw.

recensi'one [retʃen'sjone] *sf* review.

recen'sire [retʃen'sire] *vt* to review.

recen'sore, a [retʃen'sore] *sm/f* reviewer.

re'cente [re'tʃɛnte] *ag* recent; di ~ recently; più ~ latest, most recent.

recente'mente [retʃente'mente] *av* recently.

rece'pire [retʃe'pire] *vt* to understand, take in.

recessi'one [retʃes'sjone] *sf* (*ECON*) recession.

re'cesso [re'tʃɛsso] *sm* (*azione*) recession, receding; (*DIR*) withdrawal; (*luogo*) recess.

recherò *etc* [reke'rɔ] *vb vedi* recare.

re'cidere [re'tʃidere] *vt* to cut off, chop off.

reci'divo, a [retʃi'divo] *sm/f* (*DIR*) second (*o* habitual) offender, recidivist ♦ *sf* recidivism.

recin'tare [retʃin'tare] *vt* to enclose, fence off.

re'cinto [re'tʃinto] *sm* enclosure; (*ciò che recinge*) fence; surrounding wall.

recinzi'one [retʃin'tsjone] *sf* (*azione*) enclosure, fencing-off; (*recinto: di legno*) fence; (*: di mattoni*) wall; (*: reticolato*) wire fencing; (*: a sbarre*) railings *pl.*

recipi'ente [retʃi'pjɛnte] *sm* container.

re'ciproco, a, ci, che [re'tʃiproko] *ag* reciprocal.

re'ciso, a [re'tʃizo] *pp di* recidere.

'recita ['rɛtʃita] *sf* performance.

'recital ['rɛtʃital] *sm inv* recital.

reci'tare [retʃi'tare] *vt* (*poesia, lezione*) to recite; (*dramma*) to perform; (*ruolo*) to play *o* act (the part of).

recitazi'one [retʃitat'tsjone] *sf* recitation; (*di attore*) acting; scuola di ~ drama school.

recla'mare *vi* to complain ♦ *vt* (*richiedere*) to demand.

ré'clame [re'klam] *sf inv* advertising *no pl*; (*avviso*) advertisement, advert (*BRIT*), ad (*fam*).

reclamiz'zare [reklamid'dzare] *vt* to advertise.

re'clamo *sm* complaint; sporgere ~ a to complain to, make a complaint to.

recli'nabile *ag* (*sedile*) reclining.
recli'nare *vt* (*capo*) to bow, lower; (*sedile*) to tilt.
reclusi'one *sf* (*DIR*) imprisonment.
re'cluso, a *sm/f* prisoner.
'recluta *sf* recruit.
recluta'mento *sm* recruitment.
reclu'tare *vt* to recruit.
re'condito, a *ag* secluded; (*fig*) secret, hidden.
'record *ag inv* record *cpd* ♦ *sm inv* record; in tempo ~, a tempo di ~ in record time; detenere il ~ di to hold the record for; ~ mondiale world record.
recrimi'nare *vi*: ~ (su qc) to complain (about sth).
recriminazi'one [rekriminat'tsjone] *sf* recrimination.
recrude'scenza [rekrudeʃ'ʃɛntsa] *sf* fresh outbreak.
recupe'rare *etc* = ricuperare *etc*.
re'dassi *etc vb vedi* redigere.
re'datto, a *pp di* redigere.
redat'tore, 'trice *sm/f* (*STAMPA*) editor; (*: di articolo*) writer; (*di dizionario etc*) compiler; ~ capo chief editor.
redazi'one [redat'tsjone] *sf* editing; writing; (*sede*) editorial office(s); (*personale*) editorial staff; (*versione*) version.
reddi'tizio, a [reddi'tittsjo] *ag* profitable.
'reddito *sm* income; (*dello Stato*) revenue; (*di un capitale*) yield; ~ complessivo gross income; ~ disponibile disposable income; ~ fisso fixed income; ~ imponibile/non imponibile taxable/non-taxable income; ~ da lavoro earned income; ~ nazionale national income; ~ pubblico public revenue.
re'densi *etc vb vedi* redimere.
re'dento, a *pp di* redimere.
reden'tore *sm*: il R~ the Redeemer.
redenzi'one [reden'tsjone] *sf* redemption.
re'digere [re'didʒere] *vt* to write; (*contratto*) to draw up.
re'dimere *vt* to deliver; (*REL*) to redeem.
'redini *sfpl* reins.
redi'vivo, a *ag* returned to life, reborn.
'reduce ['rɛdutʃe] *ag* (*gen*): ~ da returning from, back from ♦ *sm/f* survivor; (*veterano*) veteran; essere ~ da (*esame, colloquio*) to have been through; (*malattia*) to be just over.
'refe *sm* thread.
refe'rendum *sm inv* referendum.
refe'renza [refe'rɛntsa] *sf* reference.
re'ferto *sm* medical report.
refezi'one [refet'tsjone] *sf* (*INS*) school meal.

refrat'tario, a *ag* refractory; (*fig*): essere ~ alla matematica to have no aptitude for mathematics.
refrige'rare [refridʒe'rare] *vt* to refrigerate; (*rinfrescare*) to cool, refresh.
refrigerazi'one [refridʒerat'tsjone] *sf* refrigeration; (*TECN*) cooling; ~ ad acqua (*AUT*) water-cooling.
refri'gerio [refri'dʒɛrjo] *sm*: trovare ~ to find somewhere cool.
refur'tiva *sf* stolen goods *pl*.
Reg. *abbr* (= *reggimento*) Regt; (*AMM*) = regolamento.
rega'lare *vt* to give (as a present).
re'gale *ag* regal.
re'galo *sm* gift, present ♦ *ag inv*: confezione ~ gift pack; fare un ~ a qn to give sb a present; "articoli da ~" "gifts".
re'gata *sf* regatta.
reg'gente [red'dʒɛnte] *ag* (*proposizione*) main; (*sovrano*) reigning ♦ *sm/f* regent; principe ~ prince regent.
reg'genza [red'dʒɛntsa] *sf* regency.
'reggere ['rɛddʒere] *vt* (*tenere*) to hold; (*sostenere*) to support, bear, hold up; (*portare*) to carry, bear; (*resistere*) to withstand; (*dirigere: impresa*) to manage, run; (*governare*) to rule, govern; (*LING*) to take, be followed by ♦ *vi* (*resistere*): ~ a to stand up to, hold out against; (*sopportare*): ~ a to stand; (*durare*) to last; (*fig: teoria etc*) to hold water; ~rsi *vr* (*stare ritto*) to stand; (*fig: dominarsi*) to control o.s.; ~rsi sulle gambe *o* in piedi to stand up.
'reggia, ge ['rɛddʒa] *sf* royal palace.
reggi'calze [reddʒi'kaltse] *sm inv* suspender belt.
reggi'mento [reddʒi'mento] *sm* (*MIL*) regiment.
reggi'petto [reddʒi'pɛtto] *sm*, reggi'seno [reddʒi'seno] *sm* bra.
re'gia, 'gie [re'dʒia] *sf* (*TV, CINE etc*) direction.
re'gime [re'dʒime] *sm* (*POL*) regime; (*DIR: aureo, patrimoniale etc*) system; (*MED*) diet; (*TECN*) (engine) speed; ~ di giri (*di motore*) revs *pl* per minute; ~ vegetariano vegetarian diet.
re'gina [re'dʒina] *sf* queen.
'regio, a, gi, gie ['rɛdʒo] *ag* royal.
regio'nale [redʒo'nale] *ag* regional.
regi'one [re'dʒone] *sf* (*gen*) region; (*territorio*) region, area; *vedi nota nel riquadro*.

REGIONE

*The **Regione** is the biggest administrative unit in Italy. Each of the 20 **Regioni** consists of a* *variable number of "Province", which in turn are subdivided into "Comuni". Each of the regions has a "capoluogo", its chief province (for example, Florence is the chief province of the region of Tuscany). Five regions have special status and wider powers: Val d'Aosta, Friuli-Venezia Giulia, Trentino-Alto Adige, Sicily and Sardinia. A* **Regione** *is run by the "Giunta regionale", which is elected by the "Consiglio regionale"; both are presided over by a "Presidente". The "Giunta" has legislative powers within the region over the police, public health, schools, town planning and agriculture.*

re'gista, i, e [re'dʒista] *sm/f* (*TV, CINE etc*) director.

regis'trare [redʒis'trare] *vt* (*AMM*) to register; (*COMM*) to enter; (*notare*) to report, note; (*canzone, conversazione, sog: strumento di misura*) to record; (*mettere a punto*) to adjust, regulate; ~ **i bagagli** (*AER*) to check in one's luggage; ~ **i freni** (*TECN*) to adjust the brakes.

registra'tore [redʒistra'tore] *sm* (*strumento*) recorder, register; (*magnetofono*) tape recorder; ~ **di cassa** cash register; ~ **a cassette** cassette recorder; ~ **di volo** (*AER*) flight recorder, black box (*fam*).

registrazi'one [redʒistrat'tsjone] *sf* registration; entry; reporting; recording; adjustment; ~ **bagagli** (*AER*) check-in.

re'gistro [re'dʒistro] *sm* (*libro, MUS, TECN, LING*) register; (*DIR*) registry; (*COMM*): ~ (**di cassa**) ledger; **ufficio del** ~ registrar's office; ~ **di bordo** logbook; ~**i contabili** (*account*) books.

re'gnante [reɲ'ɲante] *ag* reigning, ruling ♦ *sm/f* ruler.

re'gnare [reɲ'ɲare] *vi* to reign, rule; (*fig*) to reign.

'regno ['reɲɲo] *sm* kingdom; (*periodo*) reign; (*fig*) realm; **il** ~ **animale/ vegetale** the animal/vegetable kingdom; **il R~ Unito** the United Kingdom.

'regola *sf* rule; **a** ~ **d'arte** duly; perfectly; **essere in** ~ (*dipendente*) to be a registered employee; (*fig: essere pulito*) to be clean; **fare le cose in** ~ to do things properly; **avere le carte in** ~ (*gen*) to have one's papers in order; (*fig: essere adatto*) to be the right person; **per tua (norma e)** ~ for your information; **un'eccezione alla** ~ an exception to the rule.

rego'labile *ag* adjustable.

regolamen'tare *ag* (*distanza, velocità*) regulation *cpd*, proper; (*disposizione*) statutory ♦ *vt* (*gen*) to control; **entro il tempo** ~ within the time allowed, within the prescribed time.

regola'mento *sm* (*complesso di norme*) regulations *pl*; (*di debito*) settlement; ~ **di conti** (*fig*) settling of scores.

rego'lare *ag* regular; (*velocità*) steady; (*superficie*) even; (*passo*) steady, even; (*in regola: documento*) in order ♦ *vt* to regulate, control; (*apparecchio*) to adjust, regulate; (*questione, conto, debito*) to settle; ~**rsi** *vr* (*moderarsi*): ~**rsi nel bere/ nello spendere** to control one's drinking/ spending; (*comportarsi*) to behave, act; **presentare** ~ **domanda** to apply through the proper channels; ~ **i conti** (*fig*) to settle old scores.

regolarità *sf inv* regularity; steadiness; evenness; (*nel pagare*) punctuality.

regolariz'zare [regolarid'dzare] *vt* (*posizione*) to regularize; (*debito*) to settle.

rego'lata *sf:* **darsi una** ~ to pull o.s. together.

regola'tezza [regola'tettsa] *sf* (*ordine*) orderliness; (*moderazione*) moderation.

rego'lato, a *ag* (*ordinato*) orderly; (*moderato*) moderate.

regola'tore *sm* (*TECN*) regulator; ~ **di frequenza/di volume** frequency/volume control.

'regolo *sm* ruler; ~ **calcolatore** slide rule.

regre'dire *vi* to regress.

regressi'one *sf* regression.

re'gresso *sm* (*fig: declino*) decline.

rei'etto, a *sm/f* outcast.

reincarnazi'one [reinkarnat'tsjone] *sf* reincarnation.

reinte'grare *vt* (*produzione*) to restore; (*energie*) to recover; (*dipendente*) to reinstate.

reintegrazi'one [reintegrat'tsjone] *sf* (*di produzione*) restoration; (*di dipendente*) reinstatement.

relativa'mente *av* relatively.

relatività *sf* relativity.

rela'tivo, a *ag* relative; (*attinente*) relevant; (*rispettivo*) respective; ~ **a** (*che concerne*) relating to, concerning; (*proporzionato*) in proportion to.

rela'tore, 'trice *sm/f* (*gen*) spokesman/ woman; (*INS: di tesi*) supervisor.

re'lax [re'laks] *sm* relaxation.

relazi'one [relat'tsjone] *sf* (*fra cose,*

persone) relation(ship); (*resoconto*) report, account; ~i *sfpl* (*conoscenze*) connections; **essere in** ~ to be connected; **mettere in** ~ (*fatti, elementi*) to make the connection between; **in** ~ **a quanto detto prima** with regard to what has already been said; **essere in buone** ~**i con qn** to be on good terms with sb; **fare una** ~ to make a report, give an account; ~**i pubbliche (RP)** public relations (PR).

rele'gare *vt* to banish; (*fig*) to relegate.

religi'one [reli'dʒone] *sf* religion.

religi'oso, a [reli'dʒoso] *ag* religious ♦ *sm/f* monk/nun.

re'liquia *sf* relic.

re'litto *sm* wreck; (*fig*) down-and-out.

re'mainder [ri'meɪndə*] *sm inv* (*libro*) remainder.

're'make ['riː'meɪk] *sm inv* (*CINE*) remake.

re'mare *vi* to row.

remini'scenze [reminiʃ'ʃentse] *sfpl* reminiscences.

remissi'one *sf* remission; (*deferenza*) submissiveness, compliance; ~ **del debito** remission of debt; ~ **di querela** (*DIR*) withdrawal of an action.

remissività *sf* submissiveness.

remis'sivo, a *ag* submissive, compliant.

'remo *sm* oar.

'remora *sf* (*poetico*: *indugio*) hesitation.

re'moto, a *ag* remote.

remune'rare *etc* = **rimunerare** *etc*.

'rena *sf* sand.

re'nale *ag* kidney *cpd*.

'rendere *vt* (*ridare*) to return, give back; (: *saluto etc*) to return; (*produrre*) to yield, bring in; (*esprimere, tradurre*) to render; (*far diventare*): ~ **qc possibile** to make sth possible ♦ *vi* (*fruttare*: *ditta*) to be profitable; (: *investimento, campo*) to yield, be productive; ~ **grazie a qn** to thank sb; ~ **omaggio a qn** to honour sb; ~ **un servizio a qn** to do sb a service; ~ **una testimonianza** to give evidence; ~ **la visita** to pay a return visit; **non so se rendo l'idea** I don't know whether I'm making myself clear; ~ **rsi utile** to make o.s. useful; ~**rsi conto di qc** to realize sth.

rendi'conto *sm* (*rapporto*) report, account; (*AMM, COMM*) statement of account.

rendi'mento *sm* (*reddito*) yield; (*di manodopera, TECN*) efficiency; (*capacità di produrre*) output; (*di studenti*) performance.

'rendita *sf* (*di individuo*) private *o* unearned

income; (*COMM*) revenue; ~ **annua** annuity; ~ **vitalizia** life annuity.

'rene *sm* kidney.

'reni *sfpl* back *sg*.

reni'tente *ag* reluctant, unwilling; ~ **ai consigli di qn** unwilling to follow sb's advice; **essere** ~ **alla leva** (*MIL*) to fail to report for military service.

'renna *sf* reindeer *inv*.

'Reno *sm*: **il** ~ the Rhine.

'reo, a *sm/f* (*DIR*) offender.

re'parto *sm* department, section; (*MIL*) detachment; ~ **acquisti** purchasing office.

repel'lente *ag* repulsive; (*CHIM*: *insettifugo*): **liquido** ~ (liquid) repellent.

repen'taglio [repen'taʎʎo] *sm*: **mettere a** ~ to jeopardize, risk.

repen'tino, a *ag* sudden, unexpected.

repe'ribile *ag* available.

repe'rire *vt* to find, trace.

re'perto *sm* (*ARCHEOLOGIA*) find; (*MED*) report; (*anche*: ~ **giudiziario**) exhibit.

reper'torio *sm* (*TEAT*) repertory; (*elenco*) index, (alphabetical) list.

'replica, che *sf* repetition; reply, answer; (*obiezione*) objection; (*TEAT, CINE*) repeat performance; (*copia*) replica.

repli'care *vt* (*ripetere*) to repeat; (*rispondere*) to answer, reply.

repor'tage [rəpɔr'taʒ] *sm inv* (*STAMPA*) report.

repressi'one *sf* repression.

repres'sivo, a *ag* repressive.

re'presso, a *pp di* **reprimere**.

re'primere *vt* to suppress, repress.

re'pubblica, che *sf* republic; **la R**~ **Democratica Tedesca (RDT)** the German Democratic Republic (GDR); **la R**~ **Federale Tedesca (RFT)** the Federal Republic of Germany (FRG); **la Prima/la Seconda R**~ *terms used to refer to Italy before and after the political changes resulting from the 1994 elections; vedi anche* **Festa della Repubblica; Seconda Repubblica.**

repubbli'cano, a *ag, sm/f* republican.

repu'tare *vt* to consider, judge.

reputazi'one [reputat'tsjone] *sf* reputation; **farsi una cattiva** ~ to get o.s. a bad name.

'requie *sf* rest; **dare** ~ **a qn** to give sb some peace; **senza** ~ unceasingly.

'requiem *sm inv* (*preghiera*) requiem, prayer for the dead; (*fig*: *ufficio funebre*) requiem.

requi'sire *vt* to requisition.

requi'sito *sm* requirement; **avere i** ~**i necessari per un lavoro** to have the necessary qualifications for a job.

requisi toria *sf* (*DIR*) closing speech (for the prosecution).

requisizi one [rekwizit'tsjone] *sf* requisition.

resa *sf* (*l'arrendersi*) surrender; (*restituzione, rendimento*) return; ~ **dei conti** rendering of accounts; (*fig*) day of reckoning.

re scindere [reʃ'ʃindere] *vt* (*DIR*) to rescind, annul.

re scisso, a [reʃ'ʃisso] *pp di* **rescindere**.

reset tare *vt* (*INFORM*) to reset.

resi *etc vb vedi* **rendere**.

resi dente *ag* resident.

resi denza [resi'dɛntsa] *sf* residence.

residenzi ale [residen'tsjale] *ag* residential.

re siduo, a *ag* residual, remaining ♦ *sm* remainder; (*CHIM*) residue; ~**i industriali** industrial waste *sg*.

resina *sf* resin.

resis tente *ag* (*che resiste*): ~ **a** resistant to; (*forte*) strong; (*duraturo*) long-lasting, durable; ~ **all'acqua** waterproof; ~ **al caldo** heat-resistant; ~ **al fuoco** fireproof; ~ **al gelo** frost-resistant.

resis tenza [resis'tɛntsa] *sf* (*gen, ELETTR*) resistance; (*di persona: fisica*) stamina, endurance; (*: mentale*) endurance, resistance; **opporre** ~ (**a**) to offer *o* put up resistance (to); (*decisione, scelta*) to show opposition (to); **la R**~ *vedi nota nel riquadro*.

RESISTENZA

The Italian **Resistenza** fought against both the Nazis and the Fascists during the Second World War. It was particularly active after the fall of the Fascist Government on 25 July 1943, throughout the German occupation and during the period of Mussolini's Republic of Salò in northern Italy. Resistance members spanned the whole political spectrum and played a vital role in the Liberation and the formation of the new democratic government.

---

re sistere *vi* to resist; ~ **a** to resist; (*dolore, sog: pianta*) to withstand; (*non patir danno*) to be resistant to.

resis tito, a *pp di* **resistere**.

reso, a *pp di* **rendere**.

reso conto *sm* report, account.

respin gente [respin'dʒɛnte] *sm* (*FERR*) buffer.

res pingere [res'pindʒere] *vt* to drive back, repel; (*rifiutare: pacco, lettera*) to return; (*: invito*) to refuse; (*: proposta*) to reject, turn down; (*INS: bocciare*) to fail.

res pinto, a *pp di* **respingere**.

respi rare *vi* to breathe; (*fig*) to get one's breath; to breathe again ♦ *vt* to breathe (in), inhale.

respira tore *sm* respirator.

respira torio, a *ag* respiratory.

respirazi one [respirat'tsjone] *sf* breathing; ~ **artificiale** artificial respiration; ~ **bocca a bocca** mouth-to-mouth resuscitation, kiss of life (*fam*).

res piro *sm* breathing *no pl*; (*singolo atto*) breath; (*fig*) respite, rest; **mandare un** ~ **di sollievo** to give a sigh of relief; **trattenere il** ~ to hold one's breath; **lavorare senza** ~ to work non-stop; **di ampio** ~ (*opera, lavoro*) far-reaching.

respon sabile *ag* responsible ♦ *smf* person responsible; (*capo*) person in charge; ~ **di** responsible for; (*DIR*) liable for.

responsabilità *sf inv* responsibility; (*legale*) liability; **assumere la** ~ **di** to take on the responsibility for; **affidare a qn la** ~ **di qc** to make sb responsible for sth; ~ **patrimoniale** debt liability; ~ **penale** criminal liability.

responsabiliz zare [responsabilid'dzare] *vt*: ~ **qn** to make sb feel responsible.

res ponso *sm* answer; (*DIR*) verdict.

ressa *sf* crowd, throng.

ressi *etc vb vedi* **reggere**.

res tare *vi* (*rimanere*) to remain, stay; (*diventare*): ~ **orfano/cieco** to become *o* be left an orphan/become blind; (*trovarsi*): ~ **sorpreso** to be surprised; (*avanzare*) to be left, remain; ~ **d'accordo** to agree; **non resta più niente** there's nothing left; **restano pochi giorni** there are only a few days left; **che resti tra di noi** this is just between ourselves; ~ **in buoni rapporti** to remain on good terms; ~ **senza parole** to be left speechless.

restau rare *vt* to restore.

restaura tore, trice *smf* restorer.

restaurazi one [restaurat'tsjone] *sf* (*POL*) restoration.

res tauro *sm* (*di edifici etc*) restoration; **in** ~ under repair; **sotto** ~ (*dipinto*) being restored; **chiuso per** ~**i** closed for repairs.

res tio, a, tii, tie *ag* restive; (*persona*): ~ **a** reluctant to.

restitu ire *vt* to return, give back; (*energie, forze*) to restore.

restituzi one [restitut'tsjone] *sf* return; (*di soldi*) repayment.

resto *sm* remainder, rest; (*denaro*) change; (*MAT*) remainder; ~**i** *smpl* leftovers; (*di città*) remains; **del** ~ moreover, besides; ~**i mortali** (mortal) remains.

res 'tringere [res'trindʒere] *vt* to reduce; (*vestito*) to take in; (*stoffa*) to shrink; (*fig*) to restrict, limit; ~**rsi** *vr* (*strada*) to narrow; (*stoffa*) to shrink.

restrit 'tivo, a *ag* restrictive.

restrizi 'one [restrit'tsjone] *sf* restriction.

resurrezi 'one [resurret'tsjone] *sf* = **risurrezione**.

resusci 'tare [resuʃʃi'tare] *vt, vi* = **risuscitare**.

re 'tata *sf* (*PESCA*) haul, catch; **fare una** ~ **di** (*fig: persone*) to round up.

'rete *sf* net; (*di recinzione*) wire netting; (*AUT, FERR, di spionaggio etc*) network; (*fig*) trap, snare; **segnare una** ~ (*CALCIO*) to score a goal; ~ **ferroviaria/stradale/di distribuzione** railway/road/distribution network; ~ **del letto** (sprung) bed base; ~ **da pesca** fishing net; ~ (**televisiva**) (*sistema*) network; (*canale*) channel; **la R**~ the Web; **calze a** ~ fishnet tights *o* stockings.

reti 'cente [reti'tʃɛnte] *ag* reticent.

reti 'cenza [reti'tʃɛntsa] *sf* reticence.

retico 'lato *sm* grid; (*rete metallica*) wire netting; (*di filo spinato*) barbed wire fence.

'retina *sf* (*ANAT*) retina.

re 'torico, a, ci, che *ag* rhetorical ♦ *sf* rhetoric.

retribu 'ire *vt* to pay; (*premiare*) to reward; **un lavoro mal retribuito** a poorly-paid job.

retribu 'tivo, a *ag* pay *cpd*.

retribuzi 'one [retribut'tsjone] *sf* payment; reward.

re 'trivo, a *ag* (*fig*) reactionary.

'retro *sm inv* back ♦ *av* (*dietro*): **vedi** ~ see over(leaf).

retroattività *sf* retroactivity.

retroat 'tivo, a *ag* (*DIR: legge*) retroactive; (*AMM: salario*) backdated.

retrobot 'tega, ghe *sf* back shop.

retro 'cedere [retro'tʃedere] *vi* to withdraw ♦ *vt* (*CALCIO*) to relegate; (*MIL*) to degrade; (*AMM*) to demote.

retrocessi 'one [retrotʃes'sjone] *sf* (*di impiegato*) demotion.

retro 'cesso, a [retro'tʃɛsso] *pp di* **retrocedere**.

retroda 'tare *vt* (*AMM*) to backdate.

re 'trogrado, a *ag* (*fig*) reactionary, backward-looking.

retrogu 'ardia *sf* (*anche fig*) rearguard.

retro 'marcia [retro'martʃa] *sf* (*AUT*) reverse; (: *dispositivo*) reverse gear.

retro 'scena [retroʃ'ʃena] *sf inv* (*TEAT*) backstage ♦ *sm inv* (*fig*) behind-the-scenes activity.

retrospet 'tivo, a *ag* retrospective ♦ *sf* (*ARTE*) retrospective (exhibition).

retros 'tante *ag*: ~ (**a**) at the back (of).

retro 'terra *sm* hinterland.

retro 'via *sf* (*MIL*) zone behind the front; **mandare nelle** ~**e** to send to the rear.

retrovi 'sore *sm* (*AUT*) (rear-view) mirror.

'retta *sf* (*MAT*) straight line; (*di convitto*) charge for bed and board; (*fig: ascolto*): **dar** ~ **a** to listen to, pay attention to.

rettango 'lare *ag* rectangular.

ret 'tangolo, a *ag* right-angled ♦ *sm* rectangle.

ret 'tifica, che *sf* rectification, correction.

rettifi 'care *vt* (*curva*) to straighten; (*fig*) to rectify, correct.

'rettile *sm* reptile.

retti 'lineo, a *ag* rectilinear.

retti 'tudine *sf* rectitude, uprightness.

'retto, a *pp di* **reggere** ♦ *ag* straight; (*MAT*): **angolo** ~ right angle; (*onesto*) honest, upright; (*giusto, esatto*) correct, proper, right.

ret 'tore *sm* (*REL*) rector; (*di università*) ≈ chancellor.

reuma 'tismo *sm* rheumatism.

Rev. *abbr* (= *Reverendo*) Rev(d).

reve 'rendo, a *ag*: **il** ~ **padre Belli** the Reverend Father Belli.

reve 'rente *ag* = **riverente**.

reve 'renza [reve'rɛntsa] *sf* = **riverenza**.

rever 'sibile *ag* reversible.

revisio 'nare *vt* (*conti*) to audit; (*TECN*) to overhaul, service; (*DIR: processo*) to review; (*componimento*) to revise.

revisi 'one *sf* auditing *no pl*; audit; servicing *no pl*; overhaul; review; revision; ~ **di bilancio** audit; ~ **di bozze** proofreading; ~ **contabile interna** internal audit.

revi 'sore *sm*: ~ **di conti/bozze** auditor/proofreader.

'revoca *sf* revocation.

revo 'care *vt* to revoke.

re 'volver *sm inv* revolver.

revolve 'rata *sf* revolver shot.

Reykjavik ['reikjavik] *sf* Reykjavik.

RFT *sigla f vedi* **Repubblica Federale Tedesca**.

ri 'abbia *etc vb vedi* **riavere**.

riabili 'tare *vt* to rehabilitate; (*fig*) to restore to favour (*BRIT*) *o* favor (*US*).

riabilitazi 'one [riabilitat'tsjone] *sf* rehabilitation.

riac 'cendere [riat'tʃɛndere] *vt* (*sigaretta, fuoco, gas*) to light again; (*luce, radio, TV*) to switch on again; (*fig: sentimenti, interesse*) to rekindle, revive; ~**rsi** *vr* (*fuoco*) to catch again; (*luce, radio, TV*) to come back on again; (*fig: sentimenti*) to revive, be rekindled.

riac'ceso, a [riat'tʃeso] *pp di* **riaccendere.**

riacqui'stare *vt* (*gen*) to buy again; (*ciò che si era venduto*) to buy back; (*fig*: *buonumore, sangue freddo, libertà*) to regain; ~ **la salute** to recover (one's health); ~ **le forze** to regain one's strength.

Ri'ad *sf* Riyadh.

riaddormen'tare *vt* to put to sleep again; ~**rsi** *vr* to fall asleep again.

riallac'ciare [riallat'tʃare] *vt* (*cintura, cavo etc*) to refasten, tie up *o* fasten again; (*fig*: *rapporti, amicizia*) to resume, renew; ~**rsi** *vr*: ~**rsi a** (*fig*: *a discorso, tema*) to resume, take up again.

rial'zare [rial'tsare] *vt* to raise, lift; (*alzare di più*) to heighten, raise; (*aumentare*: *prezzi*) to increase, raise ♦ *vi* (*prezzi*) to rise, increase.

rial'zato, a [rial'tsato] *ag*: **piano ~** mezzanine, entresol.

rial'zista, i [rial'tsista] *sm* (*BORSA*) bull.

ri'alzo [ri'altso] *sm* (*di prezzi*) increase, rise; (*sporgenza*) rise; **giocare al ~** (*BORSA*) to bull.

rian'dare *vi*: ~ **(in)**, ~ **(a)** to go back (to), return (to).

riani'mare *vt* (*MED*) to resuscitate; (*fig*: *rallegrare*) to cheer up; (: *dar coraggio*) to give heart to; ~**rsi** *vr* to recover consciousness; to cheer up; to take heart.

rianimazi'one [rianimat'tsjone] *sf* (*MED*) resuscitation; **centro di ~** intensive care unit.

ria'perto, a *pp di* **riaprire.**

riaper'tura *sf* reopening.

riappa'rire *vi* to reappear.

riap'parso, a *pp di* **riapparire.**

riap'pendere *vt* to rehang; (*TEL*) to hang up.

ria'prire *vt*, ~**rsi** *vr* to reopen, open again.

ri'armo *sm* (*MIL*) rearmament.

ri'arso, a *ag* (*terreno*) arid; (*gola*) parched; (*labbra*) dry.

riasset'tare *vt* (*vedi sm*) to rearrange; to reorganize.

rias'setto *sm* (*di stanza etc*) rearrangement; (*ordinamento*) reorganization.

rias'sumere *vt* (*riprendere*) to resume; (*impiegare di nuovo*) to re-employ; (*sintetizzare*) to summarize.

rias'sunto, a *pp di* **riassumere** ♦ *sm* summary.

riattac'care *vt* (*attaccare di nuovo*): ~ **(a)** (*manifesto, francobollo*) to stick back (on); (*bottone*) to sew back (on); (*quadro, chiavi*) to hang back up (on); ~ **(il telefono** *o* **il**

ricevitore) to hang up (the receiver).

riatti'vare *vt* to reactivate.

ria'vere *vt* to have again; (*avere indietro*) to get back; (*riacquistare*) to recover; ~**rsi** *vr* to recover; (*da svenimento, stordimento*) to come round.

riba'dire *vt* (*fig*) to confirm.

ri'balta *sf* (*sportello*) flap; (*TEAT*: *proscenio*) front of the stage; (: *apparecchio d'illuminazione*) footlights *pl*; (*fig*) limelight; **tornare alla ~** (*personaggio*) to make a comeback; (*problema*) to come up again.

ribal'tabile *ag* (*sedile*) tip-up.

ribal'tare *vt*, *vi* (*anche*: ~**rsi**) to turn over, tip over.

ribas'sare *vt* to lower, bring down ♦ *vi* to come down, fall.

ribas'sista, i *sm* (*BORSA*) bear.

ri'basso *sm* reduction, fall; (*azioni, prezzi*) to be down; (*fig*: *popolarità*) to be on the decline; **giocare al ~** (*BORSA*) to bear.

ri'battere *vt* (*battere di nuovo*) to beat again; (*con macchina da scrivere*) to type again; (*palla*) to return; (*confutare*) to refute; ~ **che** to retort that.

ribattez'zare [ribatted'dzare] *vt* to rename.

ribel'larsi *vr*: ~ **(a)** to rebel (against).

ri'belle *ag* (*soldati*) rebel; (*ragazzo*) rebellious ♦ *sm/f* rebel.

ribelli'one *sf* rebellion.

'ribes *sm inv* currant; ~ **nero** blackcurrant; ~ **rosso** redcurrant.

ribol'lire *vi* (*fermentare*) to ferment; (*fare bolle*) to bubble, boil; (*fig*) to seethe.

ri'brezzo [ri'breddzo] *sm* disgust, loathing; **far ~ a** to disgust.

ribut'tante *ag* disgusting, revolting.

ricacci'are [rikat'tʃare] *vt* (*respingere*) to drive back; ~ **qn fuori** to throw sb out.

rica'dere *vi* to fall again; (*scendere a terra, fig*: *nel peccato etc*) to fall back; (*vestiti, capelli etc*) to hang (down); (*riversarsi*: *fatiche, colpe*): ~ **su** to fall on.

rica'duta *sf* (*MED*) relapse.

rical'care *vt* (*disegni*) to trace; (*fig*) to follow faithfully.

ricalci'trare [rikaltʃi'trare] *vi* (*cavalli, asini, muli*) to kick.

rica'mare *vt* to embroider.

ricambi'are *vt* to change again; (*contraccambiare*) to return.

ri'cambio *sm* exchange, return; (*FISIOL*) metabolism; ~**i** *smpl*, **pezzi di ~** spare parts; ~ **della manodopera** labour turnover.

ri'camo *sm* embroidery; **senza ~i** (*fig*)

without frills.

ricapito'lare vt to recapitulate, sum up.

ricapitolazi'one [rikapitolat'tsjone] sf recapitulation, summary.

ricari'care vt (arma, macchina fotografica) to reload; (penna) to refill; (orologio, giocattolo) to rewind; (ELETTR) to recharge.

ricat'tare vt to blackmail.

ricatta'tore, 'trice sm/f blackmailer.

ri'catto sm blackmail; **fare un ~ a qn** to blackmail sb; **subire un ~** to be blackmailed.

rica'vare vt (estrarre) to draw out, extract; (ottenere) to obtain, gain.

rica'vato sm (di vendite) proceeds pl.

ri'cavo sm proceeds pl; (CONTABILITÀ) revenue.

ric'chezza [rik'kettsa] sf wealth; (fig) richness; **~e** sfpl (beni) wealth sg, riches; **~e naturali** natural resources.

'riccio, a, ci, ce ['rittʃo] ag curly ♦ sm (ZOOL) hedgehog; (: anche: **~ di mare**) sea urchin.

'ricciolo ['rittʃolo] sm curl.

ricci'uto, a [rit'tʃuto] ag curly.

'ricco, a, chi, che ag rich; (persona, paese) rich, wealthy ♦ sm/f rich man/woman; **i ~chi** the rich; **~ di** (idee, illustrazioni etc) full of; (risorse, fauna etc) rich in.

ri'cerca, che [ri'tʃerka] sf search; (indagine) investigation, inquiry; (studio): **la ~** research; **una ~** piece of research; **mettersi alla ~ di** to go in search of, look o search o hunt for; **essere alla ~ di** to be searching for, be looking for; **~ di mercato** market research; **~ operativa** operational research.

ricer'care [ritʃer'kare] vt (motivi, cause) to look for, try to determine; (successo, piacere) to pursue; (onore, gloria) to seek.

ricerca'tezza [ritʃerka'tettsa] sf (raffinatezza) refinement; (: peg) affectation.

ricer'cato, a [ritʃer'kato] ag (apprezzato) much sought-after; (affettato) studied, affected ♦ sm/f (POLIZIA) wanted man/woman.

ricerca'tore, 'trice [ritʃerka'tore] sm/f (INS) researcher.

ricetrasmit'tente [ritʃetrazmit'tɛnte] sf two-way radio, transceiver.

ri'cetta [ri'tʃetta] sf (MED) prescription; (CUC) recipe; (fig: antidoto): **~ contro** remedy for.

ricet'tacolo [ritʃet'takolo] sm (peg: luogo malfamato) den.

ricet'tario [ritʃet'tarjo] sm (MED)

prescription pad; (CULIN) recipe book.

ricetta'tore, 'trice [ritʃetta'tore] sm/f (DIR) receiver (of stolen goods).

ricettazi'one [ritʃettat'tsjone] sf (DIR) receiving (stolen goods).

ricet'tivo, a [ritʃet'tivo] ag receptive.

rice'vente [ritʃe'vɛnte] ag (RADIO, TV) receiving ♦ sm/f (COMM) receiver.

ri'cevere [ri'tʃevere] vt to receive; (stipendio, lettera) to get, receive; (accogliere: ospite) to welcome; (vedere: cliente, rappresentante etc) to see; **"confermiamo di aver ricevuto tale merce"** (COMM) "we acknowledge receipt of these goods".

ricevi'mento [ritʃevi'mento] sm receiving no pl; (trattenimento) reception; **al ~ della merce** on receipt of the goods.

ricevi'tore [ritʃevi'tore] sm (TECN) receiver; **~ delle imposte** tax collector.

ricevito'ria [ritʃevito'ria] sf (FISCO): **~ (delle imposte)** Inland Revenue (BRIT) o Internal Revenue (US) Office; **~ del lotto** lottery office.

rice'vuta [ritʃe'vuta] sf receipt; **accusare ~ di qc** (COMM) to acknowledge receipt of sth; **~ fiscale** official receipt (for tax purposes); **~ di ritorno** (POSTA) advice of receipt; **~ di versamento** receipt of payment.

ricezi'one [ritʃet'tsjone] sf (RADIO, TV) reception.

richia'mare [rikja'mare] vt (chiamare indietro, ritelefonare) to call back; (ambasciatore, truppe) to recall; (rimproverare) to reprimand; (attirare) to attract, draw; **~rsi** vr: **~rsi a** (riferirsi a) to refer to; **~ qn all'ordine** to call sb to order; **desidero ~ la vostra attenzione su ... I** would like to draw your attention to ....

richi'amo [ri'kjamo] sm call; recall; reprimand; attraction.

richie'dente [rikje'dɛnte] sm/f applicant.

richi'edere [ri'kjɛdere] vt to ask again for; (chiedere indietro): **~ qc** to ask for sth back; (chiedere: per sapere) to ask; (: per avere) to ask for; (AMM: documenti) to apply for; (esigere) to need, require; **essere molto richiesto** to be in great demand.

richi'esto, a [ri'kjɛsto] pp di **richiedere** ♦ sf (domanda) request; (AMM) application, request; (esigenza) demand, request; **a ~a** on request.

rici'claggio [ritʃi'kladdʒo] sm (fig) laundering; **~ di materiale** recycling; **~ di denaro sporco** money laundering.

rici'clare [rit∫i'klare] vt (vetro, carta, bottiglie) to recycle; (fig: personale) to retrain.

'ricino ['rit∫ino] sm: **olio di** ~ castor oil.

ricogni'tore [rikoɲɲi'tore] sm (AER) reconnaissance aircraft.

ricogni'zione [rikoɲɲit'tsjone] sf (MIL) reconnaissance; (DIR) recognition, acknowledgement.

ricolle'gare vt (collegare nuovamente: gen) to join again, link again; (connettere: fatti): ~ **(a, con)** to connect (with); ~**rsi** vr: ~**rsi a** (sog: fatti: connettersi) to be connected to; (: persona: riferirsi) to refer to.

ri'colmo, a ag: ~ **(di)** (bicchiere) full to the brim (with); (stanza) full (of).

ricomin'are [rikomin't∫are] vt, vi to start again, begin again; ~ **a fare qc** to begin doing o to do sth again, start doing o to do sth again.

ricom'pensa sf reward.

ricompen'sare vt to reward.

ricom'porsi vr to compose o.s., regain one's composure.

ricom'posto, a pp di **ricomporsi**.

riconcili'are [rikont∫i'ljare] vt to reconcile; ~**rsi** vr to be reconciled.

riconciliazi'one [rikont∫iliat'tsjone] sf reconciliation.

ricon'dotto, a pp di **ricondurre**.

ricon'durre vt to bring (o take) back.

ricon'ferma sf reconfirmation.

riconfer'mare vt to reconfirm.

ricono'scente [rikono∫'∫ɛnte] ag grateful.

ricono'scenza [rikono∫'∫ɛntsa] sf gratitude.

rico'noscere [riko'no∫∫ere] vt to recognize; (DIR: figlio, debito) to acknowledge; (ammettere: errore) to admit, acknowledge; ~ **qn colpevole** to find sb guilty.

riconosci'mento [rikono∫∫i'mento] sm recognition; acknowledgement; (identificazione) identification; **come** ~ **dei servizi resi** in recognition of services rendered; **documento di** ~ means of identification; **segno di** ~ distinguishing mark.

riconosci'uto, a [rikono∫'∫uto] pp di **riconoscere**.

riconquis'tare vt (MIL) to reconquer; (libertà, stima) to win back.

rico'perto, a pp di **ricoprire**.

ricopi'are vt to copy.

rico'prire vt to re-cover; (coprire) to cover; (occupare: carica) to hold.

ricor'dare vt to remember, recall; (richiamare alla memoria): ~ **qc a qn** to remind sb of sth; ~**rsi** vr: ~**rsi (di)** to remember; ~**rsi di qc/di aver fatto** to remember sth/having done.

ri'cordo sm memory; (regalo) keepsake, souvenir; (di viaggio) souvenir; ~**i** smpl (memorie) memoirs.

ricor'rente ag recurrent, recurring.

ricor'renza [rikor'rɛntsa] sf recurrence; (festività) anniversary.

ri'correre vi (ripetersi) to recur; ~ **a** (rivolgersi) to turn to; (: DIR) to appeal to; (servirsi di) to have recourse to; ~ **in appello** to lodge an appeal.

ri'corso, a pp di **ricorrere** ♦ sm recurrence; (DIR) appeal; **far** ~ **a** = **ricorrere a**.

ricostitu'ente ag (MED): **cura** ~ tonic treatment ♦ sm (MED) tonic.

ricostitu'ire vt (società) to build up again; (governo, partito) to re-form; ~**rsi** vr (gruppo etc) to re-form.

ricostru'ire vt (casa) to rebuild; (fatti) to reconstruct.

ricostruzi'one [rikostrut'tsjone] sf rebuilding no pl; reconstruction.

ri'cotta sf soft white unsalted cheese made from sheep's milk.

ricove'rare vt to give shelter to; ~ **qn in ospedale** to admit sb to hospital.

ricove'rato, a sm/f patient.

ri'covero sm shelter, refuge; (MIL) shelter; (MED) admission (to hospital); ~ **antiaereo** air-raid shelter.

ricre'are vt to recreate; (rinvigorire) to restore; (fig: distrarre) to amuse.

ricrea'tivo, a ag recreational.

ricreazi'one [rikreat'tsjone] sf recreation, entertainment; (INS) break.

ri'credersi vr to change one's mind.

ricupe'rare vt (rientrare in possesso di) to recover, get back; (tempo perduto) to make up for; (NAUT) to salvage; (: naufraghi) to rescue; (delinquente) to rehabilitate; ~ **lo svantaggio** (SPORT) to close the gap.

ri'cupero sm (gen) recovery; (di relitto etc) salvaging; **capacità di** ~ resilience.

ricu'sare vt to refuse.

ridacchi'are [ridak'kjare] vi to snigger.

ri'dare vt to return, give back.

'ridda sf (di ammiratori etc) swarm; (di pensieri) jumble.

ri'dente ag (occhi, volto) smiling; (paesaggio) delightful.

'ridere vi to laugh; (deridere, beffare): ~ **di** to laugh at, make fun of; **non c'è niente da** ~, **c'è poco da** ~ it's not a laughing matter.

rides'tare vt (fig: ricordi, passioni) to reawaken.

ri'detto, a pp di **ridire**.

ridico'laggine [ridiko'laddʒine] sf (di

situazione) absurdity; (*cosa detta o fatta*) nonsense *no pl.*

ridicoliz'zare [ridikolid'dzare] *vt* to ridicule.

ri'dicolo, a *ag* ridiculous, absurd ♦ *sm:* **cadere nel** ~ to become ridiculous; **rendersi** ~ to make a fool of o.s.

ridimensiona'mento *sm* reorganization; (*di fatto storico*) reappraisal.

ridimensio'nare *vt* to reorganize; (*fig*) to see in the right perspective.

ri'dire *vt* to repeat; (*criticare*) to find fault with; to object to; **trova sempre qualcosa da** ~ he always manages to find fault.

ridon'dante *ag* redundant.

ri'dosso *sm:* **a** ~ **di** (*dietro*) behind; (*contro*) against.

ri'dotto, a *pp di* **ridurre**.

ri'duco *etc vb vedi* **ridurre**.

ri'durre *vt* (*anche CHIM, MAT*) to reduce; (*prezzo, spese*) to cut, reduce; (*accorciare: opera letteraria*) to abridge; (: *RADIO, TV*) to adapt; **ridursi** *vr* (*diminuirsi*) to be reduced, shrink; **ridursi a** to be reduced to; **ridursi a pelle e ossa** to be reduced to skin and bone.

ri'dussi *etc vb vedi* **ridurre**.

ridut'tore *sm* (*TECN, CHIM, ELETTR*) reducer.

riduzi'one [ridut'tsjone] *sf* reduction; abridgement; adaptation.

ri'ebbi *etc vb vedi* **riavere**.

riecheg'giare [rieked'dʒare] *vi* to re-echo.

riedu'care *vt* (*persona, arto*) to re-educate; (*malato*) to rehabilitate.

rieducazi'one [riedukat'tsjone] *sf* re-education; rehabilitation; **centro di** ~ rehabilitation centre.

rie'leggere [rie'lɛddʒere] *vt* to re-elect.

rie'letto, a *pp di* **rieleggere**.

riempi'mento *sm* filling (up).

riem'pire *vt* to fill (up); (*modulo*) to fill in *o* out; ~**rsi** *vr* to fill (up); (*mangiare troppo*) to stuff o.s.; ~ **qc di** to fill sth (up) with.

riempi'tivo, a *ag* filling ♦ *sm* (*anche fig*) filler.

rien'tranza [rien'trantsa] *sf* recess; indentation.

rien'trare *vi* (*entrare di nuovo*) to go (*o* come) back in; (*tornare*) to return; (*fare una rientranza*) to go in, curve inwards; to be indented; (*riguardare*): ~ **in** to be included among, form part of; ~ **(a casa)** to get back home; **non rientriamo nelle spese** we are not within our budget.

ri'entro *sm* (*ritorno*) return; (*di astronave*) re-entry; **è iniziato il grande** ~ (*estivo*) people are coming back from their (summer) holidays.

riepilo'gare *vt* to summarize ♦ *vi* to

recapitulate.

rie'pilogo, ghi *sm* recapitulation; **fare un** ~ **di qc** to summarize sth.

rie'same *sm* re-examination.

riesami'nare *vt* to re-examine.

ri'esco *etc vb vedi* **riuscire**.

ri'essere *vi:* **ci risiamo!** (*fam*) we're back to this again!

rievo'care *vt* (*passato*) to recall; (*commemorare: figura, meriti*) to commemorate.

rievocazi'one [rievokat'tsjone] *sf* (*vedi vt*) recalling; commemoration.

rifaci'mento [rifatʃi'mento] *sm* (*di film*) remake; (*di opera letteraria*) rehashing.

ri'fare *vt* to do again; (*ricostruire*) to make again; (*nodo*) to tie again, do up again; (*imitare*) to imitate, copy; ~**rsi** *vr* (*risarcirsi*): ~**rsi di** to make up for; (*vendicarsi*): ~**rsi di qc su qn** to get one's own back on sb for sth; (*riferirsi*): ~**rsi a** (*periodo, fenomeno storico*) to go back to; ~ **il letto** to make the bed; ~**rsi una vita** to make a new life for o.s.

ri'fatto, a *pp di* **rifare**.

riferi'mento *sm* reference; **in** *o* **con** ~ **a** with reference to; **far** ~ **a** to refer to.

rife'rire *vt* (*riportare*) to report; (*ascrivere*): ~ **qc a** to attribute sth to ♦ *vi* to do a report; ~**rsi** *vr:* ~**rsi a** to refer to; **riferirò** I'll pass on the message.

rifi'lare *vt* (*tagliare a filo*) to trim; (*fam: affibbiare*): ~ **qc a qn** to palm sth off on sb.

rifi'nire *vt* to finish off, put the finishing touches to.

rifini'tura *sf* finishing touch; ~**e** *sfpl* (*di mobile, auto*) finish *sg*.

rifiu'tare *vt* to refuse; ~ **di fare** to refuse to do.

rifi'uto *sm* refusal; ~**i** *smpl* (*spazzatura*) rubbish *sg*, refuse *sg*; ~**i solidi urbani** solid urban waste *sg*.

riflessi'one *sf* (*FISICA*) reflection; (*il pensare*) thought, reflection; (*osservazione*) remark.

rifles'sivo, a *ag* (*persona*) thoughtful, reflective; (*LING*) reflexive.

ri'flesso, a *pp di* **riflettere** ♦ *sm* (*di luce, su specchio*) reflection; (*FISIOL*) reflex; (*su capelli*) light; (*fig*) effect; **di** *o* **per** ~ indirectly; **avere i** ~**i pronti** to have quick reflexes.

riflessolo'gia [riflessolo'dʒia] *sf:* ~ **(plantare)** reflexology.

ri'flettere *vt* to reflect ♦ *vi* to think; ~**rsi** *vr* to be reflected; (*ripercuotersi*): ~**rsi su** to have repercussions on; ~ **su** to think over.

riflet'tore *sm* reflector; (*proiettore*) floodlight; (: *MIL*) searchlight.

ri'flusso *sm* flowing back; (*della marea*) ebb; **un'epoca di** ~ an era of nostalgia.

rifocil'larsi [rifotʃil'larsi] *vr* (*poetico*) to take refreshment.

rifondazi'one [rifondat'tsjone] *sf* (*POL*): **R**~ **Comunista** *hard left party, originating from former P.C.I.*

ri'fondere *vt* (*rimborsare*) to refund, repay; ~ **le spese a qn** to refund sb's expenses; ~ **i danni a qn** to compensate sb for damages.

ri'forma *sf* reform; (*MIL*) declaration of unfitness for service; discharge (*on health grounds*); **la R**~ (*REL*) the Reformation.

rifor'mare *vt* to re-form; (*cambiare, innovare*) to reform; (*MIL*: *recluta*) to declare unfit for service; (: *soldato*) to invalid out, discharge.

riforma'tore, 'trice *ag* reforming ♦ *sm/f* reformer.

riforma'torio *sm* (*DIR*) community home (*BRIT*), reformatory (*US*).

rifor'mista, i, e *ag, sm/f* reformist.

riforni'mento *sm* supplying, providing; restocking; (*di carburante*) refuelling; ~**i** *smpl* supplies, provisions; **fare** ~ **di** (*viveri*) to stock up with; (*benzina*) to fill up with; **posto di** ~ filling *o* gas (*US*) station.

rifor'nire *vt* (*provvedere*): ~ **di** to supply *o* provide with; (*fornire di nuovo: casa etc*) to restock.

ri'frangere [ri'frandʒere] *vt* to refract.

ri'fratto, a *pp di* **rifrangere**.

rifrazi'one [rifrat'tsjone] *sf* refraction.

rifug'gire [rifud'dʒire] *vi* to escape again; (*fig*): ~ **da** to shun.

rifugi'arsi [rifu'dʒarsi] *vr* to take refuge.

rifugi'ato, a [rifu'dʒato] *sm/f* refugee.

ri'fugio [ri'fudʒo] *sm* refuge, shelter; (*in montagna*) shelter; ~ **antiaereo** air-raid shelter.

ri'fuso, a *pp di* **rifondere**.

'riga, ghe *sf* line; (*striscia*) stripe; (*di persone, cose*) line, row; (*regolo*) ruler; (*scriminatura*) parting; **mettersi in** ~ to line up; **a** ~**ghe** (*foglio*) lined; (*vestito*) striped; **buttare giù due** ~**ghe** (*note*) to jot down a few notes; **mandami due** ~**ghe appena arrivi** drop me a line as soon as you arrive.

ri'gagnolo [ri'gaɲɲolo] *sm* rivulet.

ri'gare *vt* (*foglio*) to rule ♦ *vi*: ~ **diritto** (*fig*) to toe the line.

riga'toni *smpl* (*CUC*) short, ridged pasta shapes.

rigatti'ere *sm* junk dealer.

riga'tura *sf* (*di pagina, quaderno*) lining, ruling; (*di fucile*) rifling.

rigene'rare [ridʒene'rare] *vt* (*gen, TECN*) to regenerate; (*forze*) to restore; (*gomma*) to retread; ~**rsi** *vr* (*gen*) to regenerate; (*ramo, tumore*) to regenerate, grow again; **gomma rigenerata** retread.

rigenerazi'one [ridʒenerat'tsjone] *sf* regeneration.

riget'tare [ridʒet'tare] *vt* (*gettare indietro*) to throw back; (*fig: respingere*) to reject; (*vomitare*) to bring *o* throw up.

ri'getto [ri'dʒɛtto] *sm* (*anche MED*) rejection.

ri'ghello [ri'gɛllo] *sm* ruler.

righerò *etc* [rige'rɔ] *vb vedi* **rigare**.

rigi'dezza [ridʒi'dettsa], **rigidità** [ridʒidi'ta] *sf* rigidity; stiffness; severity, rigours *pl* (*BRIT*), rigors *pl* (*US*); strictness.

'rigido, a [ʼridʒido] *ag* rigid, stiff; (*membra etc*: *indurite*) stiff; (*METEOR*) harsh, severe; (*fig*) strict.

rigi'rare [ridʒi'rare] *vt* to turn; ~**rsi** *vr* to turn round; (*nel letto*) to turn over; ~ **qc tra le mani** to turn sth over in one's hands; ~ **il discorso** to change the subject.

'rigo, ghi *sm* line; (*MUS*) staff, stave.

rigogli'oso, a [rigoʎ'ʎoso] *ag* (*pianta*) luxuriant; (*fig: commercio, sviluppo*) thriving.

rigonfia'mento *sm* (*ANAT*) swelling; (*su legno, intonaco etc*) bulge.

ri'gonfio, a *ag* swollen; (*grembiule, sporta*): ~ **di** bulging with.

ri'gore *sm* (*METEOR*) harshness, rigours *pl* (*BRIT*), rigors *pl* (*US*); (*fig*) severity, strictness; (*anche*: **calcio di** ~) penalty; **di** ~ compulsory; "**è di** ~ **l'abito da sera**" "evening dress"; **area di** ~ (*CALCIO*) penalty box (*BRIT*); **a rigor di termini** strictly speaking.

rigorosità *sf* strictness; rigour (*BRIT*), rigor (*US*).

rigo'roso, a *ag* (*severo: persona, ordine*) strict; (*preciso*) rigorous.

rigover'nare *vt* to wash (up).

riguar'dare *vt* to look at again; (*considerare*) to regard, consider; (*concernere*) to regard, concern; ~**rsi** *vr* (*aver cura di sé*) to look after o.s.; **per quel che mi riguarda** as far as I'm concerned; **sono affari che non ti riguardano** it's none of your business.

rigu'ardo *sm* (*attenzione*) care; (*considerazione*) regard, respect; ~ **a** concerning, with regard to; **per** ~ **a** out of respect for; **ospite/persona di** ~ very important guest/person; **non aver ~i nell'agire/nel parlare** to act/speak freely.

riguar'doso, a *ag* (*rispettoso*) respectful; (*premuroso*) considerate, thoughtful.

rigurgi'tare [rigurdʒi'tare] *vi* (*liquido*): ~ **da** to gush out from; (*recipiente*: *traboccare*): ~ **di** to overflow with.

ri'gurgito [ri'gurdʒito] *sm* (*MED*) regurgitation; (*fig*: *ritorno, risveglio*) revival.

rilanci'are [rilan't∫are] *vt* (*lanciare di nuovo*: *gen*) to throw again; (: *moda*) to bring back; (: *prodotto*) to re-launch; ~ **un'offerta** (*asta*) to make a higher bid.

ri'lancio [ri'lant∫o] *sm* (*CARTE, di offerta*) raising.

rilasci'are [rilaʃ'ʃare] *vt* (*rimettere in libertà*) to release; (*AMM*: *documenti*) to issue; (*intervista*) to give; ~ **delle dichiarazioni** to make a statement.

ri'lascio [ri'laʃʃo] *sm* release; issue.

rilassa'mento *sm* (*gen, MED*) relaxation.

rilas'sare *vt* to relax; ~**rsi** *vr* to relax; (*fig*: *disciplina*) to become slack.

rilassa'tezza [rilassa'tettsa] *sf* (*fig*: *di costumi, disciplina*) laxity.

rilas'sato, a *ag* (*persona, muscoli*) relaxed; (*disciplina, costumi*) lax.

rile'gare *vt* (*libro*) to bind.

rilega'tura *sf* binding.

ri'leggere [ri'leddʒere] *vt* to reread, read again; (*rivedere*) to read over.

ri'lento: a ~ *av* slowly.

ri'letto, a *pp di* **rileggere.**

rilet'tura *sf* (*vedi vt*) rereading; reading over.

rileva'mento *sm* (*topografico, statistico*) survey; (*NAUT*) bearing.

rile'vante *ag* considerable; important.

rile'vanza [rile'vantsa] *sf* importance.

rile'vare *vt* (*ricavare*) to find; (*notare*) to notice; (*mettere in evidenza*) to point out; (*venire a conoscere*: *notizia*) to learn; (*raccogliere*: *dati*) to gather, collect; (*TOPOGRAFIA*) to survey; (*MIL*) to relieve; (*COMM*) to take over.

rilevazi'one [rilevat'tsjone] *sf* survey.

rili'evo *sm* (*ARTE, GEO*) relief; (*fig*: *rilevanza*) importance; (*osservazione*) point, remark; (*TOPOGRAFIA*) survey; **dar ~ a o mettere in ~ qc** (*fig*) to bring sth out, highlight sth; **di poco/nessun ~** (*fig*) of little/no importance; **un personaggio di ~** an important person.

rilut'tante *ag* reluctant.

rilut'tanza [rilut'tantsa] *sf* reluctance.

'rima *sf* rhyme; (*verso*) verse; **far ~ con** to rhyme with; **rispondere a qn per le ~e** to

give sb tit for tat.

riman'dare *vt* to send again; (*restituire, rinviare*) to send back, return; (*differire*): ~ **qc (a)** to postpone sth *o* put sth off (till); (*fare riferimento*): ~ **qn a** to refer sb to; **essere rimandato** (*INS*) to have to resit one's exams.

ri'mando *sm* (*rinvio*) return; (*dilazione*) postponement; (*riferimento*) cross-reference.

rimaneggi'are [rimaned'dʒare] *vt* (*testo*) to reshape, recast; (*POL*) to reshuffle.

rima'nente *ag* remaining ♦ *sm* rest, remainder; **i ~i** (*persone*) the rest of them, the others.

rima'nenza [rima'nɛntsa] *sf* rest, remainder; ~**e** *sfpl* (*COMM*) unsold stock *sg*.

rima'nere *vi* (*restare*) to remain, stay; (*avanzare*) to be left, remain; (*restare stupito*) to be amazed; (*restare, mancare*): **rimangono poche settimane a Pasqua** there are only a few weeks left till Easter; (*diventare*): ~ **vedovo** to be left a widower; (*trovarsi*): ~ **confuso/sorpreso** to be confused/surprised; **rimane da vedere se** it remains to be seen whether.

rimangi'are [riman'dʒare] *vt* to eat again; ~**rsi la parola/una promessa** (*fig*) to go back on one's word/one's promise.

ri'mango *etc vb vedi* **rimanere.**

ri'mare *vt, vi* to rhyme.

rimargi'nare [rimardʒi'nare] *vt, vi* (*anche*: ~**rsi**) to heal.

ri'masto, a *pp di* **rimanere.**

rima'sugli [rima'suʎʎi] *smpl* leftovers.

rimbal'zare [rimbal'tsare] *vi* to bounce back, rebound; (*proiettile*) to ricochet.

rim'balzo [rim'baltso] *sm* rebound; ricochet.

rimbam'bire *vi* to be in one's dotage; (*rincretinire*) to grow foolish.

rimbam'bito, a *ag* senile, gaga (*fam*); **un vecchio ~** a doddering old man.

rimbec'care *vt* (*persona*) to answer back; (*offesa*) to return.

rimbecil'lire [rimbet∫il'lire] *vi*, ~**rsi** *vr* to become stupid.

rimboc'care *vt* (*orlo*) to turn up; (*coperta*) to tuck in; (*maniche, pantaloni*) to turn *o* roll up.

rimbom'bare *vi* to resound; (*artiglieria*) to boom; (*tuono*) to rumble.

rim'bombo *sm* (*vedi vi*) boom; rumble.

rimbor'sare *vt* to pay back, repay; ~ **qc a qn** to reimburse sb for sth.

rim'borso *sm* repayment; (*di spese, biglietto*) refund; ~ **d'imposta** tax rebate.

rimboschi'mento [rimboski'mento] *sm* reafforestation.

rimbos'chire [rimbos'kire] *vt* to reafforest.

rimbrot'tare *vt* to reproach.

rim'brotto *sm* reproach.

rimedi'are *vi*: ~ **a** to remedy ♦ *vt* (*fam*: *procurarsi*) to get *o* scrape together; ~ **da vivere** to scrape a living.

ri'medio *sm* (*medicina*) medicine; (*cura*, *fig*) remedy, cure; **porre ~ a qc** to remedy sth; **non c'è ~** there's no way out, there's nothing to be done about it.

rimesco'lare *vt* to mix well, stir well; (*carte*) to shuffle; **sentirsi ~ il sangue** (*per rabbia*) to feel one's blood boil.

ri'messa *sf* (*locale*: *per veicoli*) garage; (: *per aerei*) hangar; (*COMM*: *di merce*) consignment; (: *di denaro*) remittance; (*TENNIS*) return; (*CALCIO*: *anche*: ~ **in gioco**) throw-in.

ri'messo, a *pp di* **rimettere**.

rimes'tare *vt* (*mescolare*) to mix well, stir well; (*fig*: *passato*) to drag up again.

ri'mettere *vt* (*mettere di nuovo*) to put back; (*indossare di nuovo*): ~ **qc** to put sth back on, put sth on again; (*restituire*) to return, give back; (*affidare*) to entrust; (: *decisione*) to refer; (*condonare*) to remit; (*COMM*: *merci*) to deliver; (: *denaro*) to remit; (*vomitare*) to bring up; (*perdere*: *anche*: **rimetterci**) to lose; ~**rsi** *vr*: ~**rsi a** (*affidarsi*) to trust; ~ **a nuovo** (*casa etc*) to do up (*BRIT*) *o* over (*US*); **rimetterci di tasca propria** to be out of pocket; ~**rsi al bello** (*tempo*) to clear up; ~**rsi in cammino** to set off again; ~**rsi al lavoro** to start working again; ~**rsi in salute** to get better, recover one's health.

rimi'nese *ag* of (*o* from) Rimini.

ri'misi *etc vb vedi* **rimettere**.

'rimmel ® *sm inv* mascara.

rimoderna'mento *sm* modernization.

rimoder'nare *vt* to modernize.

ri'monta *sf* (*SPORT*, *gen*) recovery.

rimon'tare *vt* (*meccanismo*) to reassemble; (*tenda*) to put up again ♦ *vi* (*salire di nuovo*): ~ **in** (*macchina*, *treno*) to get back into; (*SPORT*) to close the gap.

rimorchi'are [rimor'kjare] *vt* to tow; (*fig*: *ragazza*) to pick up.

rimorchia'tore [rimorkja'tore] *sm* (*NAUT*) tug(boat).

ri'morchio [ri'mɔrkjo] *sm* tow; (*veicolo*) trailer; **andare a ~** to be towed; **prendere a ~** to tow; **cavo da ~** towrope; **autocarro con ~** articulated lorry (*BRIT*), semi(trailer) (*US*).

ri'morso *sm* remorse; **avere il ~ di aver**

fatto qc to deeply regret having done sth.

ri'mosso, a *pp di* **rimuovere**.

rimos'tranza [rimos'trantsa] *sf* protest, complaint; **fare le proprie ~e a qn** to remonstrate with sb.

rimozi'one [rimot'tsjone] *sf* removal; (*da un impiego*) dismissal; (*PSIC*) repression; "~ forzata"** "illegally parked vehicles will be removed at owner's expense".

rimpas'tare *vt* (*POL*: *ministero*) to reshuffle.

rim'pasto *sm* (*POL*) reshuffle; ~ **ministeriale** cabinet reshuffle.

rimpatri'are *vi* to return home ♦ *vt* to repatriate.

rim'patrio *sm* repatriation.

rimpi'angere [rim'pjandʒere] *vt* to regret; (*persona*) to miss; ~ **di (non) aver fatto qc** to regret (not) having done sth.

rimpi'anto, a *pp di* **rimpiangere** ♦ *sm* regret.

rimpiat'tino *sm* hide-and-seek.

rimpiaz'zare [rimpjat'tsare] *vt* to replace.

rimpiccio'lire [rimpittʃo'lire] *vt* to make smaller ♦ *vi* (*anche*: ~**rsi**) to become smaller.

rimpin'zare [rimpin'tsare] *vt*: ~ **di** to cram *o* stuff with.

rimprove'rare *vt* to rebuke, reprimand.

rim'provero *sm* rebuke, reprimand; **di ~** (*tono*, *occhiata*) reproachful; (*parole*) of reproach.

rimugi'nare [rimudʒi'nare] *vt* (*fig*) to turn over in one's mind.

rimune'rare *vt* (*retribuire*) to remunerate; (*ricompensare*: *sacrificio etc*) to reward; **un lavoro ben rimunerato** a well-paid job.

rimunera'tivo, a *ag* (*lavoro*, *attività*) remunerative, profitable.

rimunerazi'one [rimunerat'tsjone] *sf* remuneration; (*premio*) reward.

rimu'overe *vt* to remove; (*destituire*) to dismiss; (*fig*: *distogliere*) to dissuade.

rinascimen'tale [rinaʃʃimen'tale] *ag* Renaissance *cpd*, of the Renaissance.

Rinasci'mento [rinaʃʃi'mento] *sm*: **il ~** the Renaissance.

ri'nascita [ri'naʃʃita] *sf* rebirth, revival.

rincal'zare [rinkal'tsare] *vt* (*palo*, *albero*) to support, prop up; (*lenzuola*) to tuck in.

rin'calzo [rin'kaltso] *sm* support, prop; (*rinforzo*) reinforcement; (*SPORT*) reserve (*player*); ~**i** *smpl* (*MIL*) reserves.

rinca'rare *vt* to increase the price of ♦ *vi* to go up, become more expensive; ~ **la dose** (*fig*) to pile it on.

rin'caro *sm*: ~ **(di)** (*prezzi*, *costo della vita*) increase (in); (*prodotto*) increase in the price (of).

rinca'sare *vi* to go home.
rinchi'udere [rin'kjudere] *vt* to shut (*o* lock) up; ~**rsi** *vr*: ~**rsi in** to shut o.s. up in; ~**rsi in se stesso** to withdraw into o.s.
rinchi'uso, a [rin'kjuso] *pp di* **rinchiudere**.
rincitrul'lirsi [rintʃitrul'lirsi] *vr* to grow foolish.
rin'correre *vt* to chase, run after.
rin'corso, a *pp di* **rincorrere** ♦ *sf* short run.
rin'crescere [rin'kreʃʃere] *vb impers*: **mi rincresce che/di non poter fare** I'm sorry that/I can't do, I regret that/being unable to do.
rincresci'mento [rinkreʃʃi'mento] *sm* regret.
rincresci'uto, a [rinkreʃ'ʃuto] *pp di* **rincrescere**.
rincu'lare *vi* to draw back; (*arma*) to recoil.
rinfacci'are [rinfat'tʃare] *vt* (*fig*): ~ **qc a qn** to throw sth in sb's face.
rinfoco'lare *vt* (*fig*: *odio, passioni*) to rekindle; (: *risentimento, rabbia*) to stir up.
rinfor'zare [rinfor'tsare] *vt* to reinforce, strengthen ♦ *vi* (*anche*: ~**rsi**) to grow stronger.
rin'forzo [rin'fortso] *sm*: **mettere un ~ a** to strengthen; ~**i** *smpl* (*MIL*) reinforcements; **di** ~ (*asse, sbarra*) strengthening; (*esercito*) supporting; (*personale*) extra, additional.
rinfran'care *vt* to encourage, reassure.
rinfres'cante *ag* (*bibita*) refreshing.
rinfres'care *vt* (*atmosfera, temperatura*) to cool (down); (*abito, pareti*) to freshen up ♦ *vi* (*tempo*) to grow cooler; ~**rsi** *vr* (*ristorarsi*) to refresh o.s.; (*lavarsi*) to freshen up; ~ **la memoria a qn** to refresh sb's memory.
rin'fresco, schi *sm* (*festa*) party; ~**schi** *smpl* (*cibi e bevande*) refreshments.
rin'fusa *sf*: **alla** ~ in confusion, higgledy-piggledy.
ringhi'are [rin'gjare] *vi* to growl, snarl.
ringhi'era [rin'gjɛra] *sf* railing; (*delle scale*) banister(s *pl*).
'ringhio ['ringjo] *sm* growl, snarl.
ringhi'oso, a [rin'gjoso] *ag* growling, snarling.
ringiova'nire [rindʒova'nire] *vt* (*sog: vestito, acconciatura etc*): ~ **qn** to make sb look younger; (: *vacanze etc*) to rejuvenate ♦ *vi* (*anche*: ~**rsi**) to become (*o* look) younger.
ringrazia'mento [ringrattsja'mento] *sm* thanks *pl*; **lettera/biglietto di** ~ thank you letter/card.
ringrazi'are [ringrat'tsjare] *vt* to thank; ~ **qn di qc** to thank sb for sth; ~ **qn per aver fatto qc** to thank sb for doing sth.

rinne'gare *vt* (*fede*) to renounce; (*figlio*) to disown, repudiate.
rinne'gato, a *sm/f* renegade.
rinnova'mento *sm* renewal; (*economico*) revival.
rinno'vare *vt* to renew; (*ripetere*) to repeat, renew; ~**rsi** *vr* (*fenomeno*) to be repeated, recur.
rin'novo *sm* (*di contratto*) renewal; "**chiuso per** ~ (**dei**) **locali**" (*negozio*) "closed for alterations".
rinoce'ronte [rinotʃe'ronte] *sm* rhinoceros.
rino'mato, a *ag* renowned, celebrated.
rinsal'dare *vt* to strengthen.
rinsa'vire *vi* to come to one's senses.
rinsec'chito, a [rinsek'kito] *ag* (*vecchio, albero*) thin, gaunt.
rinta'narsi *vr* (*animale*) to go into its den; (*persona: nascondersi*) to hide.
rintoc'care *vi* (*campana*) to toll; (*orologio*) to strike.
rin'tocco, chi *sm* toll.
rintracci'are [rintrat'tʃare] *vt* to track down; (*persona scomparsa, documento*) to trace.
rintro'nare *vi* to boom, roar ♦ *vt* (*assordare*) to deafen; (*stordire*) to stun.
rintuz'zare [rintut'tsare] *vt* (*fig: sentimento*) to check, repress; (: *accusa*) to refute.
ri'nuncia [ri'nuntʃa] *sf* renunciation; ~ **a** (*carica*) resignation from; (*eredità*) relinquishment of; ~ **agli atti del giudizio** (*DIR*) abandonment of a claim.
rinunci'are [rinun'tʃare] *vi*: ~ **a** to give up, renounce; ~ **a fare qc** to give up doing sth.
rinuncia'tario, a [rinuntʃa'tarjo] *ag* defeatist.
ri'nunzia *etc* [ri'nuntsja] = **rinuncia** *etc*.
rinveni'mento *sm* (*ritrovamento*) recovery; (*scoperta*) discovery; (*METALLURGIA*) tempering.
rinve'nire *vt* to find, recover; (*scoprire*) to discover, find out ♦ *vi* (*riprendere i sensi*) to come round; (*riprendere l'aspetto naturale*) to revive.
rinve'nuto, a *pp di* **rinvenire**.
rinver'dire *vi* (*bosco, ramo*) to become green again.
rinvi'are *vt* (*rimandare indietro*) to send back, return; (*differire*): ~ **qc (a)** to postpone sth *o* put sth off (till); (: *seduta*) to adjourn sth (till); (*fare un rimando*): ~ **qn a** to refer sb to; ~ **a giudizio** (*DIR*) to commit for trial.
rinvigo'rire *vt* to strengthen.
rin'vio, 'vii *sm* (*rimando*) return; (*differimento*) postponement; (: *di seduta*)

adjournment; (*in un testo*) cross-reference; ~ **a giudizio** (*DIR*) indictment.
riò *etc vb vedi* **riavere.**
'Rio de Ja'neiro ['riodedʒa'neiro] *sf* Rio de Janeiro.
rio'nale *ag* (*mercato, cinema*) local, district *cpd.*
ri'one *sm* district, quarter.
riordina'mento *sm* (*di ente, azienda*) reorganization.
riordi'nare *vt* (*rimettere in ordine*) to tidy; (*riorganizzare*) to reorganize.
riorganiz'zare [riorganid'dzare] *vt* to reorganize.
riorganizzazi'one [riorganiddzat'tsjone] *sf* reorganization.
ripa'gare *vt* to repay.
ripa'rare *vt* (*proteggere*) to protect, defend; (*correggere: male, torto*) to make up for; (: *errore*) to put right; (*aggiustare*) to repair ♦ *vi* (*mettere rimedio*): ~ **a** to make up for; ~**rsi** *vr* (*rifugiarsi*) to take refuge *o* shelter.
ripa'rato, a *ag* (*posto*) sheltered.
riparazi'one [riparat'tsjone] *sf* (*di un torto*) reparation; (*di guasto, scarpe*) repairing *no pl*; repair; (*risarcimento*) compensation; (*INS*): **esame di** ~ resit (*BRIT*), test retake (*US*).
ri'paro *sm* (*protezione*) shelter, protection; (*rimedio*) remedy; **al** ~ **da** (*sole, vento*) sheltered from; **mettersi al** ~ to take shelter; **correre ai** ~**i** (*fig*) to take remedial action.
ripar'tire *vt* (*dividere*) to divide up; (*distribuire*) to share out, distribute ♦ *vi* to leave again; (*motore*) to start again.
ripartizi'one [ripartit'tsjone] *sf* division; sharing out, distribution; (*AMM: dipartimento*) department.
ripas'sare *vi* to come (*o* go) back ♦ *vt* (*scritto, lezione*) to go over (again).
ri'passo *sm* (*di lezione*) revision (*BRIT*), review (*US*).
ripensa'mento *sm* second thoughts *pl* (*BRIT*), change of mind; **avere un** ~ to have second thoughts, change one's mind.
ripen'sare *vi* to think; (*cambiare idea*) to change one's mind; (*tornare col pensiero*): ~ **a** to recall; **a ripensarci** ... on thinking it over ....
riper'correre *vt* (*itinerario*) to travel over again; (*strada*) to go along again; (*fig: ricordi, passato*) to go back over.
riper'corso, a *pp di* **ripercorrere.**
riper'cosso, a *pp di* **ripercuotersi.**
ripercu'otersi *vr*: ~ **su** (*fig*) to have

repercussions on.
ripercussi'one *sf* (*fig*): **avere una** ~ *o* **delle** ~**i su** to have repercussions on.
ripes'care *vt* (*pesce*) to catch again; (*persona, cosa*) to fish out; (*fig: ritrovare*) to dig out.
ripe'tente *sm/f* student repeating the year, repeater (*US*).
ri'petere *vt* to repeat; (*ripassare*) to go over.
ripeti'tore *sm* (*RADIO, TV*) relay.
ripetizi'one [ripetit'tsjone] *sf* repetition; (*di lezione*) revision; ~**i** *sfpl* (*INS*) private tutoring *o* coaching *sg*; **fucile a** ~ repeating rifle.
ripetuta'mente *av* repeatedly, again and again.
ripi'ano *sm* (*GEO*) terrace; (*di mobile*) shelf.
ri'picca *sf*: **per** ~ out of spite.
'ripido, a *ag* steep.
ripiega'mento *sm* (*MIL*) retreat.
ripie'gare *vt* to refold; (*piegare più volte*) to fold (up) ♦ *vi* (*MIL*) to retreat, fall back; (*fig: accontentarsi*): ~ **su** to make do with; ~**rsi** *vr* to bend.
ripi'ego, ghi *sm* expedient; **una soluzione di** ~ a makeshift solution.
ripi'eno, a *ag* full; (*CUC*) stuffed; (: *panino*) filled ♦ *sm* (*CUC*) stuffing.
ri'pone, ri'pongo *etc vb vedi* **riporre.**
ri'porre *vt* (*porre al suo posto*) to put back, replace; (*mettere via*) to put away; (*fiducia, speranza*): ~ **qc in qn** to place *o* put sth in sb.
ripor'tare *vt* (*portare indietro*) to bring (*o* take) back; (*riferire*) to report; (*citare*) to quote; (*ricevere*) to receive, get; (*vittoria*) to gain; (*successo*) to have; (*MAT*) to carry; (*COMM*) to carry forward; ~**rsi** *vr*: ~**rsi a** (*anche fig*) to go back to; (*riferirsi a*) to refer to; ~ **danni** to suffer damage; **ha riportato gravi ferite** he was seriously injured.
ri'porto *sm* amount carried over; amount carried forward.
ripo'sante *ag* (*gen*) restful; (*musica, colore*) soothing.
ripo'sare *vt* (*bicchiere, valigia*) to put down; (*dare sollievo*) to rest ♦ *vi* to rest; ~**rsi** *vr* to rest; **qui riposa** ... (*su tomba*) here lies ....
ripo'sato, a *ag* (*viso, aspetto*) rested; (*mente*) fresh.
ri'posi *etc vb vedi* **riporre.**
ri'poso *sm* rest; (*MIL*): ~! at ease!; **a** ~ (*in pensione*) retired; **giorno di** ~ day off; **"oggi** ~**"** (*CINE, TEAT*) "no performance today"; (*ristorante*) "closed today".
ripos'tiglio [ripos'tiʎʎo] *sm* lumber room

(*BRIT*), storage room (*US*).

ri'posto, a *pp di* **riporre ♦** *ag* (*fig: senso, significato*) hidden.

ri'prendere *vt* (*prigioniero, fortezza*) to recapture; (*prendere indietro*) to take back; (*ricominciare: lavoro*) to resume; (*andare a prendere*) to fetch, come back for; (*assumere di nuovo: impiegati*) to take on again, re-employ; (*rimproverare*) to tell off; (*restringere: abito*) to take in; (*CINE*) to shoot; **~rsi** *vr* to recover; (*correggersi*) to correct o.s.; **~ a fare qc** to start doing sth again; **~ il cammino** to set off again; **~ i sensi** to recover consciousness; **~ sonno** to go back to sleep.

ripresen'tare *vt* (*certificato*) to submit again; (*domanda*) to put forward again; (*persona*) to introduce again; **~rsi** *vr* (*ritornare: persona*) to come back; (*: occasione*) to arise again; **~rsi a** (*esame*) to sit (*BRIT*) *o* take (*US*) again; (*concorso*) to enter again; **~rsi come candidato** (*POL*) to stand (*BRIT*) *o* run (*US*) again (as a candidate).

ri'preso, a *pp di* **riprendere ♦** *sf* recapture; resumption; (*economica, da malattia, emozione*) recovery; (*AUT*) acceleration *no pl*; (*TEAT, CINE*) rerun; (*CINE: presa*) shooting *no pl*; shot; (*SPORT*) second half; (*: PUGILATO*) round; **a più ~e** on several occasions, several times.

ripristi'nare *vt* to restore.

ri'pristino *sm* (*gen*) restoration; (*di tradizioni*) revival.

ripro'dotto, a *pp di* **riprodurre**.

ripro'durre *vt* to reproduce; **riprodursi** *vr* (*BIOL*) to reproduce; (*riformarsi*) to form again.

riprodut'tivo, a *ag* reproductive.

riprodut'tore, 'trice *ag* (*organo*) reproductive **♦** *sm*: **~ acustico** pick-up; **~ a cassetta** cassette player.

riproduzi'one [riprodut'tsjone] *sf* reproduction; **~ vietata** all rights reserved.

ripro'messo, a *pp di* **ripromettersi**.

ripro'mettersi *vt* (*aspettarsi*): **~ qc da** to expect sth from; (*intendere*): **~ di fare qc** to intend to do sth.

ripro'porre *vt*: **riproporsi di fare qc** to intend to do sth.

ripro'posto, a *pp di* **riproporre**.

ri'prova *sf* confirmation; **a ~ di** as confirmation of.

ripro'vare *vt* (*provare di nuovo: gen*) to try again; (*: vestito*) to try on again; (*: sensazione*) to experience again **♦** *vi* (*tentare*): **~ (a fare qc)** to try (to do sth)

again; **riproverò più tardi** I'll try again later.

ripro'vevole *ag* reprehensible.

ripudi'are *vt* to repudiate, disown.

ri'pudio *sm* repudiation, disowning.

ripu'gnante [ripuɲ'ɲante] *ag* disgusting, repulsive.

ripu'gnanza [ripuɲ'ɲantsa] *sf* repugnance, disgust.

ripu'gnare [ripuɲ'ɲare] *vi*: **~ a qn** to repel *o* disgust sb.

ripu'lire *vt* to clean up; (*sog: ladri*) to clean out; (*perfezionare*) to polish, refine.

ripulsi'one *sf* (*FISICA, fig*) repulsion.

ri'quadro *sm* square; (*ARCHIT*) panel.

ri'sacca, che *sf* backwash.

ri'saia *sf* paddy field.

risa'lire *vi* (*ritornare in su*) to go back up; **~ a** (*ritornare con la mente*) to go back to; (*datare da*) to date back to, go back to.

risa'lita *sf*: **mezzi di ~** (*SCI*) ski lifts.

risal'tare *vi* (*fig: distinguersi*) to stand out; (*ARCHIT*) to project, jut out.

ri'salto *sm* prominence; (*sporgenza*) projection; **mettere** *o* **porre in ~ qc** to make sth stand out.

risana'mento *sm* (*economico*) improvement; (*bonifica*) reclamation; **~ del bilancio** reorganization of the budget; **~ edilizio** building improvement.

risa'nare *vt* (*guarire*) to heal, cure; (*palude*) to reclaim; (*economia*) to improve; (*bilancio*) to reorganize.

risa'pere *vt*: **~ qc** to come to know of sth.

risa'puto, a *ag*: **è ~ che ...** everyone knows that ..., it's common knowledge that ....

risarci'mento [risartʃi'mento] *sm*: **~ (di)** compensation (for); **aver diritto al ~ dei danni** to be entitled to damages.

risar'cire [risar'tʃire] *vt* (*cose*) to pay compensation for; (*persona*): **~ qn di qc** to compensate sb for sth; **~ i danni a qn** to pay sb damages.

ri'sata *sf* laugh.

riscalda'mento *sm* heating; **~ centrale** central heating.

riscal'dare *vt* (*scaldare*) to heat; (*: mani, persona*) to warm; (*minestra*) to reheat; **~rsi** *vr* to warm up.

ris'caldo *sm* (*fam*) (slight) inflammation.

riscat'tare *vt* (*prigioniero*) to ransom, pay a ransom for; (*DIR*) to redeem; **~rsi** *vr* (*da disonore*) to redeem o.s.

ris'catto *sm* ransom; redemption.

rischia'rare [riskja'rare] *vt* (*illuminare*) to light up; (*colore*) to make lighter; **~rsi** *vr* (*tempo*) to clear up; (*cielo*) to clear; (*fig: volto*) to brighten up; **~rsi la voce** to clear one's throat.

rischi'are [ris'kjare] *vt* to risk ♦ *vi*: ~ **di fare qc** to risk *o* run the risk of doing sth.

'rischio ['riskjo] *sm* risk; **a** ~ (*zona, situazione*) at risk, vulnerable; **a proprio** ~ **e pericolo** at one's own risk; **correre il** ~ **di fare qc** to run the risk of doing sth; ~ **del mestiere** occupational hazard.

rischi'oso, a [ris'kjoso] *ag* risky, dangerous.

risciac'quare [riʃʃak'kware] *vt* to rinse.

risci'acquo [riʃ'ʃakkwo] *sm* rinse.

riscon'trare *vt* (*confrontare: due cose*) to compare; (*esaminare*) to check, verify; (*rilevare*) to find.

ris'contro *sm* comparison; check, verification; (*AMM*: *lettera di risposta*) reply; **mettere a** ~ to compare; **in attesa di un vostro cortese** ~ we look forward to your reply.

risco'perto, a *pp di* **riscoprire.**

risco'prire *vt* to rediscover.

riscossi'one *sf* collection.

ris'cosso, a *pp di* **riscuotere** ♦ *sf* (*riconquista*) recovery, reconquest.

riscu'otere *vt* (*ritirare una somma dovuta*) to collect; (: *stipendio*) to draw, collect; (*fig: successo etc*) to win, earn; ~**rsi** *vr*: ~**rsi (da)** to shake o.s. (out of), rouse o.s. (from); ~ **un assegno** to cash a cheque.

'rise *etc vb vedi* **ridere.**

risenti'mento *sm* resentment.

risen'tire *vt* to hear again; (*provare*) to feel ♦ *vi*: ~ **di** to feel (*o* show) the effects of; ~**rsi** *vr*: ~**rsi di** *o* **per** to take offence (*BRIT*) *o* offense (*US*) at, resent.

risen'tito, a *ag* resentful.

ri'serbo *sm* reserve.

ri'serva *sf* reserve; (*di caccia, pesca*) preserve; (*restrizione, di indigeni*) reservation; (*CALCIO*) substitute; **fare** ~ **di** (*cibo*) to get in a supply of; **tenere di** ~ to keep in reserve; **con le dovute** ~**e** with certain reservations; **ha accettato con la** ~ **di potersi ritirare** he accepted with the proviso that he could pull out.

riser'vare *vt* (*tenere in serbo*) to keep, put aside; (*prenotare*) to book, reserve; ~**rsi** *vr*: ~**rsi di fare qc** to intend to do sth; ~**rsi il diritto di fare qc** to reserve the right to do sth.

riserva'tezza [riserva'tettsa] *sf* reserve.

riser'vato, a *ag* (*prenotato, fig: persona*) reserved; (*confidenziale*) confidential.

'risi *etc vb vedi* **ridere.**

ri'sibile *ag* laughable.

risi'cato, a *ag* (*vittoria etc*) very narrow.

risi'edere *vi*: ~ **a** *o* **in** to reside in.

'risma *sf* (*di carta*) ream; (*fig*) kind, sort.

'riso, a *pp di* **ridere** ♦ *sm* (*pianta*) rice; (*pl*(*f*) ~**a**: *il ridere*): **un** ~ a laugh; **il** ~ laughter; **uno scoppio di** ~**a** a burst of laughter.

riso'lino *sm* snigger.

risolle'vare *vt* (*sollevare di nuovo: testa*) to raise again, lift up again; (*fig: questione*) to raise again, bring up again; (: *morale*) to raise; ~**rsi** *vr* (*da terra*) to rise again; (*fig: da malattia*) to recover; ~ **le sorti di qc** to improve the chances of sth.

ri'solsi *etc vb vedi* **risolvere.**

ri'solto, a *pp di* **risolvere.**

risolu'tezza [risolu'tettsa] *sf* determination.

risolu'tivo, a *ag* (*determinante*) decisive; (*che risolve*): **arrivare ad una formula** ~**a** to come up with a formula to resolve a situation.

riso'luto, a *ag* determined, resolute.

risoluzi'one [risolut'tsjone] *sf* solving *no pl*; (*MAT*) solution; (*decisione, di immagine*) resolution.

ri'solvere *vt* (*difficoltà, controversia*) to resolve; (*problema*) to solve; (*decidere*): ~ **di fare** to resolve to do; ~**rsi** *vr* (*decidersi*): ~**rsi a fare** to make up one's mind to do; (*andare a finire*): ~**rsi in** to end up, turn out; ~**rsi in nulla** to come to nothing.

risol'vibile *ag* solvable.

riso'nanza [riso'nantsa] *sf* resonance; **aver vasta** ~ (*fig: fatto etc*) to be known far and wide; ~ **magnetica** magnetic resonance.

riso'nare *vt, vi* = **risuonare.**

ri'sorgere [ri'sordʒere] *vi* to rise again.

risorgi'mentale [risordʒimen'tale] *ag* of the Risorgimento.

risorgi'mento [risordʒi'mento] *sm* revival; **il R~** (*STORIA*) the Risorgimento; *vedi nota nel riquadro.*

RISORGIMENTO

The **Risorgimento**, *the period stretching from the early nineteenth century to 1861 and the proclamation of the Kingdom of Italy, saw considerable upheaval and change. Political and personal freedom took on new importance as the events of the French Revolution unfolded. The* **Risorgimento** *paved the way for the unification of Italy in 1871.*

---

ri'sorsa *sf* expedient, resort; ~**e** *sfpl* (*naturali, finanziarie etc*) resources; **persona piena di** ~**e** resourceful person.

ri'sorsi *etc vb vedi* **risorgere.**

ri'sorto, a *pp di* **risorgere.**

ri'sotto *sm* (*CUC*) risotto.

risparmi 'are *vt* to save; (*non uccidere*) to spare ♦ *vi* to save; ~ **qc a qn** to spare sb sth; ~ **fatica/fiato** to save one's energy/ breath; **risparmiati il disturbo** *o* **la fatica** (*anche ironico*) save yourself the trouble.

risparmia 'tore, 'trice *sm/f* saver.

ris 'parmio *sm* saving *no pl*; (*denaro*) savings *pl*.

rispecchi 'are [rispek'kjare] *vt* to reflect; ~**rsi** *vr* to be reflected.

rispe 'dire *vt* to send back; ~ **qc a qn** to send sth back to sb.

rispet 'tabile *ag* respectable; (*considerevole*: *somma*) sizeable, considerable.

rispet 'tare *vt* to respect; (*legge*) to obey, comply with, abide by; (*promessa*) to keep; **farsi** ~ to command respect; ~ **le distanze** to keep one's distance; ~ **i tempi** to keep to schedule; **ogni medico che si rispetti** every self-respecting doctor.

rispettiva 'mente *av* respectively.

rispet 'tivo, a *ag* respective.

ris 'petto *sm* respect; ~**i** *smpl* (*saluti*) respects, regards; ~ **a** (*in paragone a*) compared to; (*in relazione a*) as regards, as for; ~ **(di** *o* **per)** (*norme, leggi*) observance (of), compliance (with); **portare** ~ **a qn/qc** to have *o* feel respect for sb/sth; **mancare di** ~ **a qn** to be disrespectful to sb; **con** ~ **parlando** with respect, if you will excuse my saying so; **(porga) i miei** ~**i alla signora** (give) my regards to your wife.

rispet 'toso, a *ag* respectful.

risplen 'dente *ag* (*giornata, sole*) bright, shining; (*occhi*) sparkling.

ris 'plendere *vi* to shine.

rispon 'dente *ag*: ~ **a** in keeping *o* conformity with.

rispon 'denza [rispon'dɛntsa] *sf* correspondence.

ris 'pondere *vi* to answer, reply; (*freni*) to respond; ~ **a** (*domanda*) to answer, reply to; (*persona*) to answer; (*invito*) to reply to; (*provocazione, sog: veicolo, apparecchio*) to respond to; (*corrispondere a*) to correspond to; (: *speranze, bisogno*) to answer; ~ **a qn di qc** (*essere responsabile*) to be answerable to sb for sth.

rispo 'sarsi *vr* to get married again, remarry.

ris 'posto, a *pp di* **rispondere** ♦ *sf* answer, reply; **in** ~**a a** in reply to; **dare una** ~**a** to give an answer; **diamo** ~**a alla vostra lettera del** ... in reply to your letter of ....

'rissa *sf* brawl.

ris 'soso, a *ag* quarrelsome.

rist. *abbr* = **ristampa.**

ristabi 'lire *vt* to re-establish, restore; (*persona: sog: riposo etc*) to restore to health; ~**rsi** *vr* to recover.

rista 'gnare [ristaɲ'ɲare] *vi* (*acqua*) to become stagnant; (*sangue*) to cease flowing; (*fig: industria*) to stagnate.

ris 'tagno [ris'taɲɲo] *sm* stagnation; **c'è un** ~ **delle vendite** business is slack.

ris 'tampa *sf* reprinting *no pl*; reprint.

ristam 'pare *vt* to reprint.

risto 'rante *sm* restaurant.

risto 'rare *vt* (*persona, forze*) to revive, refresh; ~**rsi** *vr* (*rifocillarsi*) to have something to eat and drink; (*riposarsi*) to rest, have a rest.

ristora 'tore, 'trice *ag* refreshing, reviving ♦ *sm* (*gestore di ristorante*) restaurateur.

ris 'toro *sm* (*bevanda, cibo*) refreshment; **posto di** ~ (*FERR*) buffet, snack bar; **servizio di** ~ (*FERR*) refreshments *pl*.

ristret 'tezza [ristret'tettsa] *sf* (*strettezza*) narrowness; (*fig: scarsezza*) scarcity, lack; (: *meschinità*) meanness; ~**e** *sfpl* (*povertà*) poverty *sg*.

ris 'tretto, a *pp di* **restringere** ♦ *ag* (*racchiuso*) enclosed, hemmed in; (*angusto*) narrow; (*limitato*): ~ **(a)** restricted *o* limited (to); (*CUC: brodo*) thick; (: *caffè*) extra strong.

ristruttu 'rare *vt* (*azienda*) to reorganize; (*edificio*) to restore; (*appartamento*) to alter; (*sog: crema, balsamo*) to repair.

ristrutturazi 'one [ristrutturat'tsjone] *sf* reorganization; restoration; alteration.

risucchi 'are [risuk'kjare] *vt* to suck in.

ri 'succhio [ri'sukkjo] *sm* (*di acqua*) undertow, pull; (*di aria*) suction.

risul 'tare *vi* (*dimostrarsi*) to prove (to be), turn out (to be); (*riuscire*): ~ **vincitore** to emerge as the winner; ~ **da** (*provenire*) to result from, be the result of; **mi risulta che** ... I understand that ..., as far as I know ...; **(ne) risulta che** ... it follows that ...; **non mi risulta** not as far as I know.

risul 'tato *sm* result.

risuo 'nare *vi* (*rimbombare*) to resound.

risurrezi 'one [risurret'tsjone] *sf* (*REL*) resurrection.

risusci 'tare [risuʃʃi'tare] *vt* to resuscitate, restore to life; (*fig*) to revive, bring back ♦ *vi* to rise (from the dead).

risvegli 'are [rizveʎ'ʎare] *vt* (*gen*) to wake up, waken; (*fig: interesse*) to stir up, arouse; (: *curiosità*) to arouse; (*fig: dall'inerzia etc*): ~ **qn (da)** to rouse sb (from); ~**rsi** *vr* to wake up, awaken; (*fig: interesse, curiosità*) to be aroused.

ris'veglio [riz'veʎʎo] *sm* waking up; (*fig*) revival.

ris'volto *sm* (*di giacca*) lapel; (*di pantaloni*) turn-up (*BRIT*), cuff (*US*); (*di manica*) cuff; (*di tasca*) flap; (*di libro*) inside flap; (*fig*) implication.

ritagli'are [ritaʎ'ʎare] *vt* (*tagliar via*) to cut out.

ri'taglio [ri'taʎʎo] *sm* (*di giornale*) cutting, clipping; (*di stoffa etc*) scrap; **nei ~i di tempo** in one's spare time.

ritar'dare *vi* (*persona, treno*) to be late; (*orologio*) to be slow ♦ *vt* (*rallentare*) to slow down; (*impedire*) to delay, hold up; (*differire*) to postpone, delay; **~ il pagamento** to defer payment.

ritarda'tario, a *sm/f* latecomer.

ritar'dato, a *ag* (*PSIC*) retarded.

ri'tardo *sm* delay; (*di persona aspettata*) lateness *no pl*; (*fig: mentale*) backwardness; **in ~** late.

ri'tegno [ri'teɲɲo] *sm* restraint.

ritem'prare *vt* (*forze, spirito*) to restore.

rite'nere *vt* (*trattenere*) to hold back; (: *somma*) to deduct; (*giudicare*) to consider, believe.

ri'tengo, ri'tenni *etc vb vedi* **ritenere.**

riten'tare *vt* to try again, make another attempt at.

rite'nuta *sf* (*sul salario*) deduction; **~ d'acconto** advance deduction of tax; **~ alla fonte** (*FISCO*) taxation at source.

riterrò, riti'ene *etc vb vedi* **ritenere.**

riti'rare *vt* to withdraw; (*POL: richiamare*) to recall; (*andare a prendere: pacco etc*) to collect, pick up; **~rsi** *vr* to withdraw; (*da un'attività*) to retire; (*stoffa*) to shrink; (*marea*) to recede; **gli hanno ritirato la patente** they disqualified him from driving (*BRIT*), they took away his licence (*BRIT*) *o* license (*US*); **~rsi a vita privata** to withdraw from public life.

riti'rata *sf* (*MIL*) retreat; (*latrina*) lavatory.

riti'rato, a *ag* secluded; **fare vita ~a** to live in seclusion.

ri'tiro *sm* (*di truppe, candidati, soldi*) withdrawal; (*di pacchi*) collection; (*di passaporto*) confiscation; (*da attività*) retirement; (*luogo appartato*) retreat.

rit'mato, a *ag* rhythmic(al).

'ritmico, a, ci, che *ag* rhythmic(al).

'ritmo *sm* rhythm; (*fig*) rate; (: *della vita*) pace, tempo; **al ~ di** at a speed *o* rate of; **ballare al ~ di** to waltz.

'rito *sm* rite; **di ~** usual, customary.

ritoc'care *vt* (*disegno, fotografia*) to touch up; (*testo*) to alter.

ri'tocco, chi *sm* touching up *no pl*;

alteration.

ri'torcere [ri'tɔrtʃere] *vt* (*filato*) to twist; (*fig: accusa, insulto*) to throw back; **~rsi** *vr* (*tornare a danno di*): **~rsi contro** to turn against.

ritor'nare *vi* to return, go (*o* come) back; (*ripresentarsi*) to recur; (*ridiventare*): **~ ricco** to become rich again ♦ *vt* (*restituire*) to return, give back.

ritor'nello *sm* refrain.

ri'torno *sm* return; **durante il (viaggio di) ~** on the return trip, on the way back; **al ~** (*tornando*) on the way back; **essere di ~** to be back; **far ~** to return; **avere un ~ di fiamma** (*AUT*) to backfire; (*fig: persona*) to be back in love again.

ritorsi'one *sf* (*rappresaglia*) retaliation.

ri'torto, a *pp di* **ritorcere** ♦ *ag* (*cotone, corda*) twisted.

ri'trarre *vt* (*trarre indietro, via*) to withdraw; (*distogliere: sguardo*) to turn away; (*rappresentare*) to portray, depict; (*ricavare*) to get, obtain; **ritrarsi** *vr* to move back.

ritrat'tare *vt* (*disdire*) to retract, take back; (*trattare nuovamente*) to deal with again.

ritrattazi'one [ritrattat'tsjone] *sf* withdrawal.

ritrat'tista, i, e *sm/f* portrait painter.

ri'tratto, a *pp di* **ritrarre** ♦ *sm* portrait.

ri'trosia *sf* (*riluttanza*) reluctance, unwillingness; (*timidezza*) shyness.

ri'troso, a *ag* (*restio*): **~ (a)** reluctant (to); (*schivo*) shy; **andare a ~** to go backwards.

ritrova'mento *sm* (*di cadavere, oggetto smarrito etc*) finding; (*oggetto ritrovato*) find.

ritro'vare *vt* to find; (*salute*) to regain; (*persona*) to find; to meet again; **~rsi** *vr* (*essere, capitare*) to find o.s.; (*raccapezzarsi*) to find one's way; (*con senso reciproco*) to meet (again).

ritro'vato *sm* discovery.

ri'trovo *sm* meeting place; **~ notturno** night club.

'ritto, a *ag* (*in piedi*) standing, on one's feet; (*levato in alto*) erect, raised; (: *capelli*) standing on end; (*posto verticalmente*) upright.

ritu'ale *ag, sm* ritual.

riuni'one *sf* (*adunanza*) meeting; (*riconciliazione*) reunion; **essere in ~** to be at a meeting.

riu'nire *vt* (*ricongiungere*) to join (together); (*riconciliare*) to reunite, bring together (again); **~rsi** *vr* (*adunarsi*) to meet; (*tornare a stare insieme*) to be reunited; **siamo qui riuniti per festeggiare il vostro**

anniversario we are gathered here to celebrate your anniversary.

riu'scire [riuʃ'ʃire] vi (*uscire di nuovo*) to go out again, go back out; (*aver esito: fatti, azioni*) to go, turn out; (*aver successo*) to succeed, be successful; (*essere, apparire*) to be, prove; (*raggiungere il fine*) to manage, succeed; ~ **a fare qc** to manage o be able to do sth; **questo mi riesce nuovo** this is new to me.

riu'scita [riuʃ'ʃita] sf (*esito*) result, outcome; (*buon esito*) success.

riutiliz'zare [riutilid'dzare] vt to use again, re-use.

'riva sf (*di fiume*) bank; (*di lago, mare*) shore; **in** ~ **al mare** on the (sea) shore.

ri'vale ag rival cpd ♦ sm/f rival; **non avere** ~**i** (*anche fig*) to be unrivalled.

rivaleggi'are [rivaled'dʒare] vi to compete, vie.

rivalità sf rivalry.

ri'valsa sf (*rivincita*) revenge; (*risarcimento*) compensation; **prendersi una** ~ **su qn** to take revenge on sb.

rivalu'tare vt (ECON) to revalue.

rivalutazi'one [rivalutat'tsjone] sf (ECON) revaluation; (*fig*) re-evaluation.

rivan'gare vt (*ricordi etc*) to dig up (again).

rive'dere vt to see again; (*ripassare*) to revise; (*verificare*) to check.

rivedrò etc vb vedi **rivedere**.

rive'lare vt to reveal; (*divulgare*) to reveal, disclose; (*dare indizio*) to reveal, show; ~**rsi** vr (*manifestarsi*) to be revealed; ~**rsi onesto** etc to prove to be honest etc.

rivela'tore, 'trice ag revealing ♦ sm (TECN) detector; (FOT) developer.

rivelazi'one [rivelat'tsjone] sf revelation.

ri'vendere vt (*vendere: di nuovo*) to resell, sell again; (: *al dettaglio*) to retail, sell retail.

rivendi'care vt to claim, demand.

rivendicazi'one [rivendikat'tsjone] sf claim; ~**i salariali** wage claims.

ri'vendita sf (*bottega*) retailer's (shop); ~ **di tabacchi** tobacconist's (shop).

rivendi'tore, 'trice sm/f retailer; ~ **autorizzato** authorized dealer.

riverbe'rare vt to reflect.

ri'verbero vt (*di luce, calore*) reflection; (*di suono*) reverberation.

rive'rente ag reverent, respectful.

rive'renza [rive'rɛntsa] sf reverence; (*inchino*) bow; curtsey.

rive'rire vt (*rispettare*) to revere; (*salutare*) to pay one's respects to.

river'sare vt (*anche fig*) to pour; ~**rsi** vr (*fig: persone*) to pour out.

rivesti'mento sm covering; coating.

rives'tire vt to dress again; (*ricoprire*) to cover; (: *con vernice*) to coat; (*fig: carica*) to hold; ~**rsi** vr to get dressed again; to change (one's clothes); ~ **di piastrelle** to tile.

ri'vidi etc vb vedi **rivedere**.

rivi'era sf coast; **la** ~ **italiana** the Italian Riviera.

ri'vincita [ri'vintʃita] sf (SPORT) return match; (*fig*) revenge; **prendersi la** ~ (**su qn**) to take o get one's revenge (on sb).

rivis'suto, a pp di **rivivere**.

ri'vista sf review; (*periodico*) magazine, review; (TEAT) revue; variety show.

ri'visto, a pp di **rivedere**.

rivitaliz'zante [rivitalid'dzante] ag revitalizing.

rivitaliz'zare [rivitalid'dzare] vt to revitalize.

ri'vivere vi (*riacquistare forza*) to come alive again; (*tornare in uso*) to be revived ♦ vt to relive.

'rivo sm stream.

ri'volgere [ri'vɔldʒere] vt (*attenzione, sguardo*) to turn, direct; (*parole*) to address; ~**rsi** vr to turn round; (*fig: dirigersi per informazioni*): ~**rsi a** to go and see, go and speak to; ~ **un'accusa/una critica a qn** to accuse/criticize sb; ~**rsi all'ufficio competente** to apply to the office concerned.

rivolgi'mento [rivoldʒi'mento] sm upheaval.

ri'volsi etc vb vedi **rivolgere**.

ri'volta sf revolt, rebellion.

rivol'tante ag revolting, disgusting.

rivol'tare vt to turn over; (*con l'interno all'esterno*) to turn inside out; (*disgustare: stomaco*) to upset, turn; (: *fig*) to revolt, disgust; ~**rsi** vr (*ribellarsi*): ~**rsi (a)** to rebel (against).

rivol'tella sf revolver.

ri'volto, a pp di **rivolgere**.

rivol'toso, a ag rebellious ♦ sm/f rebel.

rivoluzio'nare [rivoluttsjo'nare] vt to revolutionize.

rivoluzio'nario, a [rivoluttsjo'narjo] ag, sm/f revolutionary.

rivoluzi'one [rivolut'tsjone] sf revolution.

riz'zare [rit'tsare] vt to raise, erect; ~**rsi** vr to stand up; (*capelli*) to stand on end; ~**rsi in piedi** to stand up, get to one's feet.

RN sigla = Rimini.

RNA sigla m RNA (= ribonucleic acid).

RO sigla = Rovigo.

'roba sf stuff, things pl; (*possessi, beni*) belongings pl, things pl, possessions pl; ~

da mangiare things to eat, food; ~ **da matti!** it's sheer madness *o* lunacy!

robi'vecchi [robi'vɛkki] *sm/f inv* junk dealer.

'robot *sm inv* robot.

ro'botica *sf* robotics *sg*.

robus'tezza [robus'tettsa] *sf* (*di persona, pianta*) robustness, sturdiness; (*di edificio, ponte*) soundness.

ro'busto, a *ag* robust, sturdy; (*solido: catena*) strong; (: *edificio, ponte*) sound, solid; (*vino*) full-bodied.

'rocca, che *sf* fortress.

rocca'forte *sf* stronghold.

roc'chetto [rok'ketto] *sm* reel, spool.

'roccia, ce ['rɔttʃa] *sf* rock; **fare** ~ (*SPORT*) to go rock climbing.

roccia'tore, 'trice [rottʃa'tore] *sm/f* rock climber.

rocci'oso, a [rot'tʃoso] *ag* rocky; **le Montagne R~e** the Rocky Mountains.

'roco, a, chi, che *ag* hoarse.

ro'daggio [ro'daddʒo] *sm* running (*BRIT*) *o* breaking (*US*) in; **in** ~ running *o* breaking in; **periodo di** ~ (*fig*) period of adjustment.

'Rodano *sm*: **il** ~ the Rhone.

ro'dare *vt* (*AUT, TECN*) to run (*BRIT*) *o* break (*US*) in.

ro'deo *sm* rodeo.

'rodere *vt* to gnaw (at); (*distruggere poco a poco*) to eat into.

'Rodi *sf* Rhodes.

rodi'tore *sm* (*ZOOL*) rodent.

rodo'dendro *sm* rhododendron.

'rogito ['rɔdʒito] *sm* (*DIR*) (notary's) deed.

'rogna ['rɔɲɲa] *sf* (*MED*) scabies *sg*; (*di animale*) mange; (*fig*) bother, nuisance.

ro'gnone [roɲ'ɲone] *sm* (*CUC*) kidney.

ro'gnoso, a [roɲ'ɲoso] *ag* (*persona*) scabby; (*animale*) mangy; (*fig*) troublesome.

'rogo, ghi *sm* (*per cadaveri*) (funeral) pyre; (*supplizio*): **il** ~ the stake.

rol'lare *vi* (*NAUT, AER*) to roll.

rol'lino *sm* = **rullino**.

rol'lio *sm* roll(ing).

'Roma *sf* Rome.

roma'gnolo, a [romaɲ'ɲɔlo] *ag* of (*o* from) Romagna.

roma'nesco, a, schi, sche *ag* Roman ♦ *sm* Roman dialect.

Roma'nia *sf*: **la** ~ Romania.

ro'manico, a, ci, che *ag* Romanesque.

ro'mano, a *ag, sm/f* Roman; **fare alla ~a** to go Dutch.

romantiche'ria [romantike'ria] *sf* sentimentality.

romanti'cismo [romanti'tʃizmo] *sm* romanticism.

ro'mantico, a, ci, che *ag* romantic.

ro'manza [ro'mandza] *sf* (*MUS, LETTERATURA*) romance.

roman'zare [roman'dzare] *vt* to romanticize.

roman'zesco, a, schi, sche [roman'dzesko] *ag* (*stile, personaggi*) fictional; (*fig*) storybook *cpd*.

romanzi'ere [roman'dzjɛre] *sm* novelist.

ro'manzo, a [ro'mandzo] *ag* (*LING*) romance *cpd* ♦ *sm* (*medievale*) romance; (*moderno*) novel; ~ **d'amore** love story; ~ **d'appendice** serial (story); ~ **cavalleresco** tale of chivalry; ~ **poliziesco**, ~ **giallo** detective story; ~ **rosa** romantic novel.

rom'bare *vi* to rumble, thunder, roar.

'rombo *sm* rumble, thunder, roar; (*MAT*) rhombus; (*ZOOL*) turbot.

ro'meno, a *ag, sm/f, sm* = **rumeno**.

'rompere *vt* to break; (*conversazione, fidanzamento*) to break off ♦ *vi* to break; ~**rsi** *vr* to break; **mi rompe le scatole** (*fam*) he (*o* she) is a pain in the neck; ~**rsi un braccio** to break an arm.

rompi'capo *sm* worry, headache; (*indovinello*) puzzle; (*in enigmistica*) brain-teaser.

rompi'collo *sm* daredevil.

rompighi'accio [rompi'gjattʃo] *sm* (*NAUT*) icebreaker.

rompis'catole *sm/f inv* (*fam*) pest, pain in the neck.

'ronda *sf* (*MIL*) rounds *pl*, patrol.

ron'della *sf* (*TECN*) washer.

'rondine *sf* (*ZOOL*) swallow.

ron'done *sm* (*ZOOL*) swift.

ron'fare *vi* (*russare*) to snore.

ron'zare [ron'dzare] *vi* to buzz, hum.

ron'zino [ron'dzino] *sm* (*peg: cavallo*) nag.

ron'zio, ii [ron'dzio] *sm* buzzing, humming; ~ **auricolare** (*MED*) tinnitus *sg*.

'rosa *sf* rose; (*fig: gruppo*): ~ **dei candidati** list of candidates ♦ *ag inv, sm* pink.

ro'saio *sm* (*pianta*) rosebush, rose tree; (*giardino*) rose garden.

ro'sario *sm* (*REL*) rosary.

ro'sato, a *ag* pink, rosy ♦ *sm* (*vino*) rosé (wine).

ro'seo, a *ag* (*anche fig*) rosy.

ro'seto *sm* rose garden.

ro'setta *sf* (*diamante*) rose-cut diamond; (*rondella*) washer.

'rosi *vb vedi* **rodere**.

rosicchi'are [rosik'kjare] *vt* to gnaw (at); (*mangiucchiare*) to nibble (at).

rosma'rino *sm* rosemary.

'roso, a *pp di* **rodere**.

roso'lare *vt* (*CUC*) to brown.

roso'lia *sf* (*MED*) German measles *sg*,
rubella.

'rospo *sm* (*ZOOL*) toad; **mandar giù** *o*
ingoiare un *o* **il** ~ (*fig*) to swallow a bitter
pill; **sputa il** ~! out with it!

ros'setto *sm* (*per labbra*) lipstick; (*per
guance*) rouge.

ros'siccio, a, ci, ce [ros'sittʃo] *ag* reddish.

'rosso, a *ag, sm, sm/f* red; **diventare** ~ **(per la
vergogna)** to blush *o* go red (with *o* for
shame); **il mar R**~ the Red Sea; ~ **d'uovo**
egg yolk.

ros'sore *sm* flush, blush.

rosticce'ria [rostittʃe'ria] *sf shop selling
roast meat and other cooked food.*

'rostro *sm* rostrum; (*becco*) beak.

ro'tabile *ag* (*percorribile*): **strada** ~
roadway; (*FERR*): **materiale** ~ rolling
stock.

ro'taia *sf* rut, track; (*FERR*) rail.

ro'tare *vt, vi* to rotate.

rota'tivo, a *ag* rotating, rotation *cpd.*

rotazi'one [rotat'tsjone] *sf* rotation.

rote'are *vt, vi* to whirl; ~ **gli occhi** to roll
one's eyes.

ro'tella *sf* small wheel; (*di mobile*) castor.

roto'calco, chi *sm* (*TIP*) rotogravure;
(*rivista*) illustrated magazine.

roto'lare *vt, vi* to roll; ~**rsi** *vr* to roll (about).

roto'lio *sm* rolling.

'rotolo *sm* (*di carta, stoffa*) roll; (*di corda*)
coil; **andare a** ~**i** (*fig*) to go to rack and
ruin; **mandare a** ~**i** (*fig*) to ruin.

ro'tondo, a *ag* round ♦ *sf* rotunda.

ro'tore *sm* rotor.

'rotta *sf* (*AER, NAUT*) course, route; (*MIL*)
rout; **a** ~ **di collo** at breakneck speed;
essere in ~ **con qn** to be on bad terms
with sb; **fare** ~ **su** *o* **per** *o* **verso** to head
for *o* towards; **cambiare** ~ (*anche fig*) to
change course; **in** ~ **di collisione** on a
collision course; **ufficiale di** ~ navigator,
navigating officer.

rotta'mare *vt to scrap old vehicles in return
for incentives.*

rottama'zione [rottamat'tsjone] *sf the
scrapping of old vehicles in return for
incentives.*

rot'tame *sm* fragment, scrap, broken bit;
~**i** *smpl* (*di nave, aereo etc*) wreckage *sg*; ~**i
di ferro** scrap iron *sg.*

'rotto, a *pp di* **rompere** ♦ *ag* broken; (*calzoni*)
torn, split; (*persona: pratico, resistente*): ~
a accustomed *o* inured to ♦ *sm*: **per il** ~
della cuffia by the skin of one's teeth; ~**i**
smpl: **20 euro e** ~**i** 20-odd euros.

rot'tura *sf* (*azione*) breaking *no pl*; (*di
rapporti*) breaking off; (*MED*) fracture,

break.

rou'lotte [ru'lɔt] *sf inv* caravan.

ro'vente *ag* red-hot.

'rovere *sm* oak.

ro'vescia [ro'veʃʃa] *sf*: **alla** ~ upside-down;
inside-out; **oggi mi va tutto alla** ~
everything is going wrong (for me)
today.

rovesci'are [roveʃ'ʃare] *vt* (*versare in giù*) to
pour; (: *accidentalmente*) to spill;
(*capovolgere*) to turn upside down; (*gettare
a terra*) to knock down; (: *fig: governo*) to
overthrow; (*piegare all'indietro: testa*) to
throw back; ~**rsi** *vr* (*sedia, macchina*) to
overturn; (*barca*) to capsize; (*liquido*) to
spill; (*fig: situazione*) to be reversed.

ro'vescio, sci [ro'veʃʃo] *sm* other side,
wrong side; (*della mano*) back; (*di moneta*)
reverse; (*pioggia*) sudden downpour; (*fig*)
setback; (*MAGLIA: anche: punto* ~) purl
(stitch); (*TENNIS*) backhand (stroke); **a** ~
(*sottosopra*) upside-down; (*con l'esterno
all'interno*) inside-out; **capire qc a** ~ to
misunderstand sth; ~ **di fortuna** setback.

ro'vina *sf* ruin; ~**e** *sfpl* ruins; **andare in** ~
(*andare a pezzi*) to collapse; (*fig*) to go to
rack and ruin; **mandare qc/qn in** ~ to ruin
sth/sb.

rovi'nare *vi* to collapse, fall down ♦ *vt* (*far
cadere giù: casa*) to demolish; (*danneggiare,
fig*) to ruin.

rovi'nato, a *ag* ruined, damaged; (*fig:
persona*) ruined.

rovi'noso, a *ag* ruinous.

rovis'tare *vt* (*casa*) to ransack; (*tasche*) to
rummage in (*o* through).

'rovo *sm* (*BOT*) blackberry *o* bramble bush.

roz'zezza [rod'dzettsa] *sf* roughness,
coarseness.

'rozzo, a ['roddzo] *ag* rough, coarse.

RP *sigla fpl vedi* **relazioni pubbliche**.

R.R. *abbr* (*POSTA*) = **ricevuta di ritorno**.

Rrr *abbr* (*POSTA*) = **raccomandata con
ricevuta di ritorno**.

RSVP *abbr* (= *répondez s'il vous plaît*) RSVP.

'ruba *sf*: **andare a** ~ to sell like hot cakes.

rubacu'ori *sm inv* ladykiller.

ru'bare *vt* to steal; ~ **qc a qn** to steal sth
from sb.

rubi'condo, a *ag* ruddy.

rubi'netto *sm* tap, faucet (*US*).

ru'bino *sm* ruby.

ru'bizzo, a [ru'bittso] *ag* lively, sprightly.

'rublo *sm* rouble.

ru'brica, che *sf* (*di giornale: colonna*)
column; (: *pagina*) page; (*quadernetto*)
index book; (: *per indirizzi*) address book.

'rude *ag* tough, rough.

'rudere *sm* (*rovina*) ruins *pl.*
rudimen'tale *ag* rudimentary, basic.
rudi'menti *smpl* rudiments; basic
principles.
ruffi'ano *sm* pimp.
'ruga, ghe *sf* wrinkle.
'ruggine ['ruddʒine] *sf* rust.
rug'gire [rud'dʒire] *vi* to roar.
rug'gito [rud'dʒito] *sm* roar.
rugi'ada [ru'dʒada] *sf* dew.
ru'goso, a *ag* wrinkled; (*scabro*: *superficie*
etc) rough.
rul'lare *vi* (*tamburo, nave*) to roll; (*aereo*) to
taxi.
rul'lino *sm* (*FOT*) roll of film, spool.
rul'lio, ii *sm* (*di tamburi*) roll.
'rullo *sm* (*di tamburi*) roll; (*arnese cilindrico,*
TIP) roller; ~ **compressore** steam roller; ~
di pellicola roll of film.
rum *sm* rum.
ru'meno, a *ag, sm/f, sm* Romanian.
rumi'nante *sm* (*ZOOL*) ruminant.
rumi'nare *vt* (*ZOOL*) to ruminate; (*fig*) to
ruminate on *o* over, chew over.
ru'more *sm*: **un** ~ a noise, a sound; **il** ~
noise; **fare** ~ to make a noise; **un** ~ **di**
passi the sound of footsteps; **la notizia ha**
fatto molto ~ (*fig*) the news aroused
great interest.
rumoreggi'are [rumored'dʒare] *vi* (*tuono*
etc) to rumble; (*fig*: *folla*) to clamour
(*BRIT*), clamor (*US*).
rumo'roso, a *ag* noisy.
ru'olo *sm* (*TEAT, fig*) role, part; (*elenco*) roll,
register, list; **di** ~ permanent, on the
permanent staff; **professore di** ~ (*INS*)
≈ lecturer with tenure; **fuori** ~ (*personale,*
insegnante) temporary.
ru'ota *sf* wheel; **a** ~ (*forma*) circular; ~
anteriore/posteriore front/back wheel; **an-**
dare a ~ **libera** to freewheel; **parlare a** ~
libera (*fig*) to speak freely; ~ **di scorta**
spare wheel.
ruo'tare *vt, vi* = **rotare**.
'rupe *sf* cliff, rock.
ru'pestre *ag* rocky.
ru'pia *sf* rupee.
'ruppi *etc vb vedi* **rompere**.
ru'rale *ag* rural, country *cpd.*
ru'scello [ruʃ'ʃello] *sm* stream.
'ruspa *sf* excavator.
rus'pante *ag* (*pollo*) free-range.
rus'sare *vi* to snore.
'Russia *sf*: **la** ~ Russia.
'russo, a *ag, sm/f, sm* Russian.
'rustico, a, ci, che *ag* country *cpd*, rural;
(*arredamento*) rustic; (*fig*) rough,
unrefined ♦ *sm* (*fabbricato*: *per attrezzi*)

shed; (*per abitazione*) farm labourer's
(*BRIT*) *o* farmhand's cottage.
'ruta *sf* (*BOT*) rue.
rut'tare *vi* to belch.
'rutto *sm* belch.
'ruvido, a *ag* rough, coarse.
ruzzo'lare [ruttso'lare] *vi* to tumble down.
ruzzo'lone [ruttso'lone] *sm* tumble, fall.
ruzzo'loni [ruttso'loni] *av*: **cadere** ~ to
tumble down; **fare le scale** ~ to tumble
down the stairs.

S s

S, s ['ɛsse] *sf o m* (*lettera*) S, s; **S come**
Savona ≈ S for Sugar.
s *abbr* (= *secondo*) sec.
S. *abbr* (= *sud*) S; (= *santo*) St.
SA *sigla* = *Salerno* ♦ *abbr vedi* **società**
anonima.
sa *vb vedi* **sapere**.
sab. *abbr* (= *sabato*) Sat.
'sabato *sm* Saturday; *per fraseologia vedi*
martedì.
'sabbia *sf* sand; ~**e mobili** quicksand(s *pl*).
sabbia'tura *sf* (*MED*) sand bath; (*TECN*)
sand-blasting; **fare le** ~**e** to take sand
baths.
sabbi'oso, a *ag* sandy.
sabo'taggio [sabo'taddʒo] *sm* sabotage.
sabo'tare *vt* to sabotage.
sabota'tore, 'trice *sm/f* saboteur.
'sacca, che *sf* bag; (*bisaccia*) haversack;
(*insenatura*) inlet; ~ **d'aria** air pocket; ~
da viaggio travelling bag.
sacca'rina *sf* saccharin(e).
sac'cente [sat'tʃɛnte] *sm/f* know-all (*BRIT*),
know-it-all (*US*).
saccheggi'are [sakked'dʒare] *vt* to sack,
plunder.
sac'cheggio [sak'keddʒo] *sm* sack(ing).
sac'chetto [sak'ketto] *sm* (*small*) bag;
(*small*) sack; ~ **di carta/di plastica** paper/
plastic bag.
'sacco, chi *sm* bag; (*per carbone etc*) sack;
(*ANAT, BIOL*) sac; (*tela*) sacking;
(*saccheggio*) sack(ing); (*fig*: *grande*
quantità): **un** ~ **di** lots of, heaps of;
cogliere *o* **prendere qn con le mani nel** ~
to catch sb red-handed; **vuotare il** ~ to
confess, spill the beans; **mettere qn nel** ~

to cheat sb; **colazione** f **al** ~ packed lunch; ~ **a pelo** sleeping bag; ~ **per i rifiuti** bin bag (*BRIT*), garbage bag (*US*).

sacer'dote [satʃer'dɔte] *sm* priest.

sacer'dozio [satʃer'dɔttsjo] *sm* priesthood.

'Sacra Co'rona U'nita *sf* the *mafia in Puglia*.

sacra'mento *sm* sacrament.

sa'crario *sm* memorial chapel.

sacres'tano *sm* = **sagrestano**.

sacres'tia *sf* = **sagrestia**.

sacrifi'care *vt* to sacrifice; ~**rsi** *vr* to sacrifice o.s.; (*privarsi di qc*) to make sacrifices.

sacrifi'cato, a *ag* sacrificed; (*non valorizzato*) wasted; **una vita** ~**a** a life of sacrifice.

sacri'ficio [sakri'fitʃo] *sm* sacrifice.

sacri'legio [sacri'lɛdʒo] *sm* sacrilege.

sa'crilego, a, ghi, ghe *ag* (*REL*) sacrilegious.

'sacro, a *ag* sacred.

sacro'santo, a *ag* sacrosanct.

'sadico, a, ci, che *ag* sadistic ♦ *sm/f* sadist.

sa'dismo *sm* sadism.

sadomaso'chismo [sadomazo'kismo] *sm* sadomasochism.

sa'etta *sf* arrow; (*fulmine: anche fig*) thunderbolt.

sa'fari *sm inv* safari.

sa'gace [sa'gatʃe] *ag* shrewd, sagacious.

sa'gacia [sa'gatʃa] *sf* sagacity, shrewdness.

sag'gezza [sad'dʒettsa] *sf* wisdom.

saggi'are [sad'dʒare] *vt* (*metalli*) to assay; (*fig*) to test.

'saggio, a, gi, ge ['saddʒo] *ag* wise ♦ *sm* (*persona*) sage; (*operazione sperimentale*) test; (: *dell'oro*) assay; (*fig: prova*) proof; (*campione indicativo*) sample; (*scritto: letterario*) essay; (: *INS*) written test; **dare** ~ **di** to give proof of; **in** ~ as a sample.

sag'gistica [sad'dʒistika] *sf* ≈ non-fiction.

Sagit'tario [sadʒit'tarjo] *sm* Sagittarius; **essere del** ~ to be Sagittarius.

'sagoma *sf* (*profilo*) outline, profile; (*forma*) form, shape; (*TECN*) template; (*bersaglio*) target; (*fig: persona*) character.

'sagra *sf* festival.

sa'grato *sm* churchyard.

sagres'tano *sm* sacristan; sexton.

sagres'tia *sf* sacristy; (*culto protestante*) vestry.

Sa'hara [sa'ara] *sm*: **il (Deserto del)** ~ the Sahara (Desert).

sahari'ana [saa'rjana] *sf* bush jacket.

'sai *vb vedi* **sapere**.

'saio *sm* (*REL*) habit.

'sala *sf* hall; (*stanza*) room; (*CINE: di proiezione*) screen; ~ **d'aspetto** waiting room; ~ **da ballo** ballroom; ~ (**dei**) **comandi** control room; ~ **per concerti** concert hall; ~ **per conferenze** (*INS*) lecture hall; (*in aziende*) conference room; ~ **corse** betting shop; ~ **giochi** amusement arcade; ~ **da gioco** gaming room; ~ **macchine** (*NAUT*) engine room; ~ **operatoria** (*MED*) operating theatre (*BRIT*) *o* room (*US*); ~ **da pranzo** dining room; ~ **per ricevimenti** banqueting hall; ~ **delle udienze** (*DIR*) courtroom.

sa'lace [sa'latʃe] *ag* (*spinto, piccante*) salacious, saucy; (*mordace*) cutting, biting.

sala'mandra *sf* salamander.

sa'lame *sm* salami *no pl*, salami sausage.

sala'moia *sf* (*CUC*) brine.

sa'lare *vt* to salt.

salari'ale *ag* wage *cpd*, pay *cpd*; **aumento** ~ wage *o* pay increase (*BRIT*) *o* raise (*US*).

salari'ato *sm/f* wage-earner.

sa'lario *sm* pay, wages *pl*; ~ **base** basic wage; ~ **minimo garantito** guaranteed minimum wage.

salas'sare *vt* (*MED*) to bleed.

sa'lasso *sm* (*MED*) bleeding, bloodletting; (*fig: forte spesa*) drain.

sala'tino *sm* cracker, salted biscuit.

sa'lato, a *ag* (*sapore*) salty; (*CUC*) salted, salt *cpd*; (*fig: discorso etc*) biting, sharp; (: *prezzi*) steep, stiff.

sal'dare *vt* (*congiungere*) to join, bind; (*parti metalliche*) to solder; (: *con saldatura autogena*) to weld; (*conto*) to settle, pay.

salda'tore *sm* (*operaio*) solderer; welder; (*utensile*) soldering iron.

salda'trice [salda'tritʃe] *sf* (*macchina*) welder, welding machine; ~ **ad arco** arc welder.

salda'tura *sf* soldering; welding; (*punto saldato*) soldered joint; weld; ~ **autogena** welding; ~ **dolce** soft soldering.

sal'dezza [sal'dettsa] *sf* firmness, strength.

'saldo, a *ag* (*resistente, forte*) strong, firm; (*fermo*) firm, steady, stable; (*fig*) firm, steadfast ♦ *sm* (*svendita*) sale; (*di conto*) settlement; (*ECON*) balance; **pagare a** ~ to pay in full; ~ **attivo** credit; ~ **passivo** deficit; ~ **da riportare** balance carried forward.

'sale *sm* salt; (*fig*) wit; ~**i** *smpl* (*MED: da annusare*) smelling salts; **sotto** ~ salted; **restare di** ~ (*fig*) to be dumbfounded; **ha poco** ~ **in zucca** he doesn't have much sense; ~ **da cucina**, ~ **grosso** cooking salt; ~ **da tavola**, ~ **fino** table salt; ~**i da bagno** bath salts; ~**i minerali** mineral salts; ~**i e**

tabacchi tobacconist's (shop).

sal'gemma [sal'dʒɛmma] *sm* rock salt.

'salgo *etc vb vedi* **salire**.

'salice ['salitʃe] *sm* willow; ~ **piangente** weeping willow.

sali'ente *ag (fig)* salient, main.

sali'era *sf* salt cellar.

sa'lino, a *ag* saline ♦ *sf* saltworks *sg*.

sa'lire *vi* to go (*o* come) up; (*aereo etc*) to climb, go up; (*passeggero*) to get on; (*sentiero, prezzi, livello*) to go up, rise ♦ *vt* (*scale, gradini*) to go (*o* come) up; ~ **su** to climb (up); ~ **sul treno/sull'autobus** to board the train/the bus; ~ **in macchina** to get into the car; ~ **a cavallo** to mount; ~ **al potere** to rise to power; ~ **al trono** to ascend the throne; ~ **alle stelle** (*prezzi*) to rocket.

sali'scendi [saliʃ'ʃendi] *sm inv* latch.

sa'lita *sf* climb, ascent; (*erta*) hill, slope; **in** ~ *ag, av* uphill.

sa'liva *sf* saliva.

'salma *sf* corpse.

sal'mastro, a *ag (acqua)* salt *cpd*; (*sapore*) salty ♦ *sm (sapore)* salty taste; (*odore*) salty smell.

salmì *sm (CUC)* salmi; **lepre in** ~ salmi of hare.

'salmo *sm* psalm.

sal'mone *sm* salmon.

salmo'nella *sf* salmonella.

Salo'mone: le isole ~ *sfpl* the Solomon Islands.

sa'lone *sm (stanza)* sitting room, lounge; (*in albergo*) lounge; (*di ricevimento*) reception room; (*su nave*) lounge, saloon; (*mostra*) show, exhibition; (*negozio: di parrucchiere*) hairdresser's (salon); ~ **dell'automobile** motor show; ~ **di bellezza** beauty salon.

salo'pette [salɔ'pɛt] *sf inv* dungarees *pl*.

salotti'ero, a *ag* mundane.

sa'lotto *sm* lounge, sitting room; (*mobilio*) lounge suite.

sal'pare *vi (NAUT)* to set sail; (*anche:* ~ **l'ancora**) to weigh anchor.

'salsa *sf (CUC)* sauce; **in tutte le** ~**e** (*fig*) in all kinds of ways; ~ **di pomodoro** tomato sauce.

sal'sedine *sf (del mare, vento)* saltiness; (*incrostazione*) (dried) salt.

sal'siccia, ce [sal'sittʃa] *sf* pork sausage.

salsi'era *sf* sauceboat (*BRIT*), gravy boat.

'salso *sm* saltiness.

sal'tare *vi* to jump, leap; (*esplodere*) to blow up, explode; (*: valvola*) to blow; (*venir via*) to pop off; (*non aver luogo: corso etc*) to be cancelled ♦ *vt* to jump (over), leap (over); (*fig: pranzo, capitolo*) to skip, miss

(out); (*CUC*) to sauté; **far** ~ to blow up; (*serratura: forzare*) to break; **far** ~ **il banco** (*GIOCO*) to break the bank; **farsi** ~ **le cervella** to blow one's brains out; **ma che ti salta in mente?** what are you thinking of?; ~ **da un argomento all'altro** to jump from one subject to another; ~ **addosso a qn** (*aggredire*) to attack sb; ~ **fuori** to jump out, leap out; (*venire trovato*) to turn up; ~ **fuori con** (*frase, commento*) to come out with; ~ **giù da qc** to jump off sth, jump down from sth.

saltel'lare *vi* to skip; to hop.

sal'tello *sm* hop, little jump.

saltim'banco, chi *sm* acrobat.

'salto *sm* jump; (*SPORT*) jumping; (*dislivello*) drop; **fare un** ~ to jump, leap; **fare un** ~ **da qn** to pop over to sb's (place); ~ **in alto/lungo** high/long jump; ~ **con l'asta** pole vaulting; ~ **mortale** somersault; **un** ~ **di qualità** (*miglioramento*) significant improvement.

saltu'ario, a *ag* occasional, irregular.

sa'lubre *ag* healthy, salubrious.

sa'lume *sm (CUC)* cured pork; ~**i** *smpl* (*insaccati*) cured pork meats.

salume'ria *sf* delicatessen.

salumi'ere, a *sm/f* ≈ delicatessen owner.

salumi'ficio [salumi'fitʃo] *sm* cured pork meat factory.

salu'tare *ag* healthy; (*fig*) salutary, beneficial ♦ *vt (per dire buon giorno, fig)* to greet; (*per dire addio*) to say goodbye to; (*MIL*) to salute; **mi saluti sua moglie** my regards to your wife.

sa'lute *sf* health; ~**!** (*a chi starnutisce*) bless you!; (*nei brindisi*) cheers!; **bere alla** ~ **di qn** to drink (to) sb's health; **la** ~ **pubblica** public welfare; **godere di buona** ~ to be healthy, enjoy good health.

sa'luto *sm (gesto)* wave; (*parola*) greeting; (*MIL*) salute; **gli ha tolto il** ~ he no longer says hello to him; **cari** ~**i, tanti** ~**i** best regards; **vogliate gradire i nostri più distinti** ~**i** yours faithfully; **i miei** ~**i alla sua signora** my regards to your wife.

'salva *sf* salvo.

salvacon'dotto *sm (MIL)* safe-conduct.

salva'naio *sm* moneybox, piggy bank.

salvado'regno, a [salvado'reɲɲo] *ag, sm/f* Salvadorean.

salva'gente [salva'dʒɛnte] *sm (NAUT)* lifebuoy; (*pl inv: stradale*) traffic island; ~ **a ciambella** lifebelt; ~ **a giubbotto** lifejacket (*BRIT*), life preserver (*US*).

salvaguar'dare *vt* to safeguard.

salvagu'ardia *sf* safeguard; **a** ~ **di** for the safeguard of.

sal 'vare *vt* to save; (*trarre da un pericolo*) to rescue; (*proteggere*) to protect; ~**rsi** *vr* to save. o.s.; to escape; ~ **la vita a qn** to save sb's life; ~ **le apparenze** to keep up appearances; **si salvi chi può!** every man for himself!

salvas 'chermo [salvas'kermo] *sm* (*INFORM*) screen saver.

salva 'slip ® *sm inv* pantyliner.

salva 'taggio [salva'taddʒo] *sm* rescue.

salva 'tore, 'trice *sm/f* saviour (*BRIT*), savior (*US*).

salvazi 'one [salvat'tsjone] *sf* (*REL*) salvation.

'salve *escl* (*fam*) hi!

sal 'vezza [sal'vettsa] *sf* salvation; (*sicurezza*) safety.

'salvia *sf* (*BOT*) sage.

salvi 'etta *sf* napkin, serviette.

'salvo, a *ag* safe, unhurt, unharmed; (*fuori pericolo*) safe, out of danger ◆ *sm*: **in** ~ safe ◆ *prep* (*eccetto*) except; ~ **che** *cong* (*a meno che*) unless; (*eccetto che*) except (that); **mettere qc in** ~ to put sth in a safe place; **mettersi in** ~ to reach safety; **portare qn in** ~ to lead sb to safety; ~ **contrordini** barring instructions to the contrary; - **errori e omissioni** errors and omissions excepted; ~ **imprevisti** barring accidents.

sam 'buca *sf* (*liquore*) sambuca (*type of anisette*).

sam 'buco *sm* elder (tree).

sa 'nare *vt* to heal, cure; (*economia*) to put right.

sana 'toria *sf* (*DIR*) act of indemnity.

sana 'torio *sm* sanatorium (*BRIT*), sanitarium (*US*).

san 'cire [san'tʃire] *vt* to sanction.

'sandalo *sm* (*BOT*) sandalwood; (*calzatura*) sandal.

sang 'ria [san'gria] *sf* (*bibita*) sangria.

'sangue *sm* blood; **farsi cattivo** ~ to fret, get worked up; **all'ultimo** ~ (*duello, lotta*) to the death; **non corre buon** ~ **tra di loro** there's bad blood between them; **buon** ~ **non mente!** blood will out!; ~ **freddo** (*fig*) sang-froid, calm; **a** ~ **freddo** in cold blood.

sangu 'igno, a [san'gwiɲɲo] *ag* blood *cpd*; (*colore*) blood-red.

sangui 'nante *ag* bleeding.

sangui 'nare *vi* to bleed.

sangui 'nario, a *ag* bloodthirsty.

sangui 'noso, a *ag* bloody.

sangui 'suga, ghe *sf* leech.

sanità *sf* health; (*salubrità*) healthiness; **Ministero della S~** Department of Health;

~ **mentale** sanity; ~ **pubblica** public health.

sani 'tario, a *ag* health *cpd*; (*condizioni*) sanitary ◆ *sm* (*AMM*) doctor; **Ufficiale S~** Health Officer; (**impianti**) ~**i** *smpl* bathroom *o* sanitary fittings.

San Ma 'rino *sf*: **la Repubblica di** ~ the Republic of San Marino.

'sanno *vb vedi* **sapere**.

'sano, a *ag* healthy; (*denti, costituzione*) healthy, sound; (*integro*) whole, unbroken; (*fig: politica, consigli*) sound; ~ **di mente** sane; **di** ~**a pianta** completely, entirely; ~ **e salvo** safe and sound.

Santi 'ago *sf*: ~ (**del Cile**) Santiago (de Chile).

santifi 'care *vt* to sanctify; (*feste*) to observe.

san 'tino *sm* holy picture.

san 'tissimo, a *ag*: **il S~ Sacramento** the Holy Sacrament; **il Padre S~** (*papa*) the Holy Father.

santità *sf* sanctity; holiness; **Sua/Vostra** ~ (*titolo di papa*) His/Your Holiness.

'santo, a *ag* holy; (*fig*) saintly; (*seguito da nome proprio: dav sm* **san** + *C,* **sant'** + *V,* **santo** + *s impura, gn, pn, ps, x, z; dav sf* **santa** + *C,* **sant'** + *V*) saint ◆ *sm/f* saint; **parole** ~**e!** very true!; **tutto il** ~ **giorno** the whole blessed day, all day long; **non c'è** ~ **che tenga!** that's no excuse!; **la S~a Sede** the Holy See.

san 'tone *sm* holy man.

santu 'ario *sm* sanctuary.

sanzio 'nare [santsjo'nare] *vt* to sanction.

sanzi 'one [san'tsjone] *sf* sanction; (*penale, civile*) sanction, penalty; ~**i economiche** economic sanctions.

sa 'pere *vt* to know; (*essere capace di*): **so nuotare** I know how to swim, I can swim ◆ *vi*: ~ **di** (*aver sapore*) to taste of; (*aver odore*) to smell of ◆ *sm* knowledge; **far** ~ **qc a qn** to inform sb about sth, let sb know sth; **venire a** ~ **qc (da qn)** to find out *o* hear about sth (from sb); **non ne vuole più** ~ **di lei** he doesn't want to have anything more to do with her; **mi sa che non sia vero** I don't think that's true.

sapi 'ente *ag* (*dotto*) learned; (*che rivela abilità*) masterly ◆ *sm/f* scholar.

sapien 'tone, a *sm/f* (*peg*) know-all (*BRIT*), know-it-all (*US*).

sapi 'enza [sa'pjentsa] *sf* wisdom.

sa 'pone *sm* soap; ~ **da barba** shaving soap; ~ **da bucato** washing soap; ~ **liquido** liquid soap; ~ **in scaglie** soapflakes *pl*.

sapo 'netta *sf* cake *o* bar *o* tablet of soap.

sa 'pore *sm* taste, flavour (*BRIT*), flavor (*US*).

sapo'rito, a *ag* tasty; (*fig*: *arguto*) witty; (: *piccante*) racy.

sappi'amo *vb vedi* **sapere.**

saprò *etc vb vedi* **sapere.**

sapu'tello, a *sm/f* know-all (*BRIT*), know-it-all (*US*).

sarà *etc vb vedi* **essere.**

sara'banda *sf* (*fig*) uproar.

saraci'nesca, sche [saratʃi'neska] *sf* (*serranda*) rolling shutter.

sar'casmo *sm* sarcasm *no pl*; sarcastic remark.

sar'castico, a, ci, che *ag* sarcastic.

sarchi'are [sar'kjare] *vt* (*AGR*) to hoe.

sar'cofago, gi *o* **ghi** *sm* sarcophagus.

Sar'degna [sar'deɲɲa] *sf*: **la** ~ Sardinia.

sar'dina *sf* sardine.

'sardo, a *ag, sm/f* Sardinian.

sar'donico, a, ci, che *ag* sardonic.

sa'rei *etc vb vedi* **essere.**

SARS *sf* SARS (= *severe acute respiratory syndrome*).

'sarta *sf vedi* **sarto.**

'sartia *sf* (*NAUT*) stay.

'sarto, a *sm/f* tailor/dressmaker; ~ **d'alta moda** couturier.

sarto'ria *sf* tailor's (shop); dressmaker's (shop); (*casa di moda*) fashion house; (*arte*) couture.

sassai'ola *sf* hail of stones.

sas'sata *sf* blow with a stone; **tirare una** ~ **contro** *o* **a qc/qn** to throw a stone at sth/sb.

'sasso *sm* stone; (*ciottolo*) pebble; (*masso*) rock; **restare** *o* **rimanere di** ~ to be dumbfounded.

sassofo'nista, i, e *sm/f* saxophonist.

sas'sofono *sm* saxophone.

sas'sone *ag, sm/f, sm* Saxon.

sas'soso, a *ag* stony; pebbly.

'Satana *sm* Satan.

sa'tanico, a, ci, che *ag* satanic, fiendish.

sa'tellite *sm, ag* satellite.

'satira *sf* satire.

satireggi'are [satired'dʒare] *vt* to satirize ♦ *vi* (*fare della satira*) to be satirical; (*scrivere satire*) to write satires.

sa'tirico, a, ci, che *ag* satiric(al).

sa'tollo, a *ag* full, replete.

satu'rare *vt* to saturate.

saturazi'one [saturat'tsjone] *sf* saturation.

'saturo, a *ag* saturated; (*fig*): ~ **di** full of; ~ **d'acqua** (*terreno*) waterlogged.

'SAUB *sigla f* (= *Struttura Amministrativa Unificata di Base*) *state welfare system.*

'sauna *sf* sauna; **fare la** ~ to have *o* take a sauna.

sa'vana *sf* savannah.

'savio, a *ag* wise, sensible ♦ *sm* wise man.

Sa'voia *sf*: **la** ~ Savoy.

savoi'ardo, a *ag* of Savoy, Savoyard ♦ *sm* (*biscotto*) sponge finger.

sazi'are [sat'tsjare] *vt* to satisfy, satiate; ~**rsi** *vr* (*riempirsi di cibo*): ~**rsi (di)** to eat one's fill (of); (*fig*): ~**rsi di** to grow tired *o* weary of.

sazietà [sattsje'ta] *sf* satiety, satiation.

'sazio, a ['sattsjo] *ag*: ~ **(di)** sated (with), full (of); (*fig*: *stufo*) fed up (with), sick (of).

sbada'taggine [zbada'taddʒine] *sf* (*sventatezza*) carelessness; (*azione*) oversight.

sba'dato, a *ag* careless, inattentive.

sbadigli'are [zbadiʎ'ʎare] *vi* to yawn.

sba'diglio [zba'diʎʎo] *sm* yawn; **fare uno** ~ to yawn.

'sbafo *sm*: **a** ~ at somebody else's expense.

sbagli'are [zbaʎ'ʎare] *vt* to make a mistake in, get wrong ♦ *vi* (*fare errori*) to make a mistake (*o* mistakes), be mistaken; (*ingannarsi*) to be wrong; (*operare in modo non giusto*) to err; ~**rsi** *vr* to make a mistake, be mistaken, be wrong; ~ **la mira/strada** to miss one's aim/take the wrong road; **scusi, ho sbagliato numero** (*TEL*) sorry, I've got the wrong number; **non c'è da** ~**rsi** there can be no mistake.

sbagli'ato, a [zbaʎ'ʎato] *ag* (*gen*) wrong; (*compito*) full of mistakes; (*conclusione*) erroneous.

'sbaglio ['zbaʎʎo] *sm* mistake, error; (*morale*) error; **fare uno** ~ to make a mistake.

sbales'trato, a *ag* (*persona*: *scombussolato*) unsettled.

sbal'lare *vt* (*merce*) to unpack ♦ *vi* (*nel fare un conto*) to overestimate; (*DROGA*: *gergo*) to get high.

sbal'lato, a *ag* (*calcolo*) wrong; (*fam*: *ragionamento, persona*) screwy.

'sballo *sm* (*DROGA*: *gergo*) trip.

sballot'tare *vt* to toss (about).

sbalor'dire *vt* to stun, amaze ♦ *vi* to be stunned, be amazed.

sbalordi'tivo, a *ag* amazing; (*prezzo*) incredible, absurd.

sbal'zare [zbal'tsare] *vt* to throw, hurl; (*fig*: *da una carica*) to remove, dismiss ♦ *vi* (*balzare*) to bounce; (*saltare*) to leap, bound.

'sbalzo ['zbaltso] *sm* (*spostamento improvviso*) jolt, jerk; **a** ~**i** jerkily; (*fig*) in fits and starts; **uno** ~ **di temperatura** a sudden change in temperature.

sban'care *vt* (*nei giochi*) to break the bank

at (o of); (fig) to ruin, bankrupt.

sbanda'mento sm (NAUT) list; (AUT) skid; (fig: di persona) confusion; ha avuto un periodo di ~ he went off the rails for a bit.

sban'dare vi (NAUT) to list; (AUT) to skid; ~rsi vr (folla) to disperse; (truppe) to scatter; (fig: famiglia) to break up.

sban'data sf (AUT) skid; (NAUT) list; prendere una ~ per qn (fig) to fall for sb.

sban'dato, a sm/f mixed-up person.

sbandie'rare vt (bandiera) to wave; (fig) to parade, show off.

'sbando sm: essere allo ~ to drift.

sbarac'care vt (libri, piatti etc) to clear (up).

sbaragli'are [zbaraʎ'ʎare] vt (MIL) to rout; (in gare sportive etc) to beat, defeat.

sba'raglio [zba'raʎʎo] sm: gettarsi allo ~ (soldato) to throw o.s. into the fray; (fig) to risk everything.

sbaraz'zarsi [zbarat'tsarsi] vr: ~ di to get rid of, rid o.s. of.

sbaraz'zino, a [zbarat'tsino] ag impish, cheeky.

sbar'bare vt, ~rsi vr to shave.

sbarba'tello sm novice, greenhorn.

sbar'care vt (passeggeri) to disembark; (merci) to unload ♦ vi to disembark.

'sbarco sm disembarkation; unloading; (MIL) landing.

'sbarra sf bar; (di passaggio a livello) barrier; (DIR): mettere/presentarsi alla ~ to bring/appear before the court.

sbarra'mento sm (stradale) barrier; (diga) dam, barrage; (MIL) barrage; (POL) cut-off point (level of support below which a political party is excluded from representation in Parliament).

sbar'rare vt (bloccare) to block, bar; (cancellare: assegno) to cross (BRIT); ~ il passo to bar the way; ~ gli occhi to open one's eyes wide.

sbar'rato, a ag (porta) barred; (passaggio) blocked, barred; (strada) blocked, obstructed; (occhi) staring; (assegno) crossed (BRIT).

'sbattere vt (porta) to bang; (tappeti, ali, CUC) to beat; (urtare) to knock, hit ♦ vi (porta, finestra) to bang; (agitarsi: ali, vele etc) to flap; ~ qn fuori/in galera to throw sb out/into prison; me ne sbatto! (fam) I don't give a damn!

sbat'tuto, a ag (viso, aria) dejected, worn out; (uovo) beaten.

sba'vare vi to dribble; (colore) to smear, smudge.

sbava'tura sf (di persone) dribbling; (di lumache) slime; (di rossetto, vernice) smear.

sbelli'carsi vr: ~ dalle risa to split one's sides laughing.

'sberla sf slap.

sber'leffo sm: fare uno ~ a qn to make a face at sb.

sbia'dire vi (anche: ~rsi), vt to fade.

sbia'dito, a ag faded; (fig) colourless (BRIT), colorless (US), dull.

sbian'care vt to whiten; (tessuto) to bleach ♦ vi (impallidire) to grow pale o white.

sbi'eco, a, chi, che ag (storto) squint, askew; di ~: guardare qn di ~ (fig) to look askance at sb; tagliare una stoffa di ~ to cut material on the bias.

sbigot'tire vt to dismay, stun ♦ vi (anche: ~rsi) to be dismayed.

sbilanci'are [zbilan'tʃare] vt to throw off balance; ~rsi vr (perdere l'equilibrio) to overbalance, lose one's balance; (fig: compromettersi) to compromise o.s.

sbi'lenco, a, chi, che ag (persona) crooked, misshapen; (fig: idea, ragionamento) twisted.

sbirci'are [zbir'tʃare] vt to cast sidelong glances at, eye.

sbirci'ata [zbir'tʃata] sf: dare una ~ a qc to glance at sth, have a look at sth.

'sbirro sm (peg) cop.

sbizzar'rirsi [zbiddzar'rirsi] vr to indulge one's whims.

sbloc'care vt to unblock, free; (freno) to release; (prezzi, affitti) to free from controls; ~rsi vr (gen) to become unblocked; (passaggio, strada) to clear, become unblocked; la situazione si è sbloccata things are moving again.

'sblocco, chi sm (vedi vt) unblocking, freeing; release.

sboc'care vi: ~ in (fiume) to flow into; (strada) to lead into; (persona) to come (out) into; (fig: concludersi) to end (up) in.

sboc'cato, a ag (persona) foul-mouthed; (linguaggio) foul.

sbocci'are [zbot'tʃare] vi (fiore ~ (MIL) to bloom, open (out).

'sbocco, chi sm (di fiume) mouth; (di strada) end; (di tubazione, COMM) outlet; (uscita: anche fig) way out; una strada senza ~ a dead end; siamo in una situazione senza ~chi there's no way out of this for us.

sbocconcel'lare [zbokkontʃel'lare] vt: ~ (qc) to nibble (at sth).

sbollen'tare vt (CUC) to parboil.

sbol'lire vi (fig) to cool down, calm down.

'sbornia sf (fam): prendersi una ~ to get plastered.

sbor'sare vt (denaro) to pay out.

sbot'tare *vi*: ~ **in una risata/per la collera** to burst out laughing/explode with anger.

sbotto'nare *vt* to unbutton, undo.

sbra'cato, a *ag* slovenly.

sbracci'arsi [zbrat'tʃarsi] *vr* to wave (one's arms about).

sbracci'ato, a [zbrat'tʃato] *ag* (*camicia*) sleeveless; (*persona*) bare-armed.

sbrai'tare *vi* to yell, bawl.

sbra'nare *vt* to tear to pieces.

sbricio'lare [zbritʃo'lare] *vt*, ~**rsi** *vr* to crumble.

sbri'gare *vt* to deal with, get through; (*cliente*) to attend to, deal with; ~**rsi** *vr* to hurry (up).

sbriga'tivo, a *ag* (*persona, modo*) quick, expeditious; (*giudizio*) hasty.

sbrina'mento *sm* defrosting.

sbri'nare *vt* to defrost.

sbrindel'lato, a *ag* tattered, in tatters.

sbrodo'lare *vt* to stain, dirty.

sbron'zarsi [zbron'tsarsi] *vr* (*fam*) to get sozzled.

'sbronzo, a ['zbrontso] (*fam*) *ag* sozzled ♦ *sf*: **prendersi una** ~**a** to get sozzled.

sbruf'fone, a *sm/f* boaster, braggart.

sbu'care *vi* (*apparire*) to pop out (*o* up).

sbucci'are [zbut'tʃare] *vt* (*arancia, patata*) to peel; (*piselli*) to shell; ~**rsi un ginocchio** to graze one's knee.

sbucherò *etc* [zbuke'rɔ] *vb vedi* **sbucare**.

sbudel'larsi *vr*: ~ **dalle risa** to split one's sides laughing.

sbuf'fare *vi* (*persona, cavallo*) to snort; (*: ansimare*) to puff, pant; (*treno*) to puff.

'sbuffo *sm* (*di aria, fumo, vapore*) puff; **maniche a** ~ puff(ed) sleeves.

sc. *abbr* (*TEAT*: = *scena*) sc.

'scabbia *sf* (*MED*) scabies *sg*.

'scabro, a *ag* rough, harsh; (*fig*) concise, terse.

sca'broso, a *ag* (*fig*: *difficile*) difficult, thorny; (*: imbarazzante*) embarrassing; (*: sconcio*) indecent.

scacchi'era [skak'kjɛra] *sf* chessboard.

scacchiere [skak'kjɛre] *sm* (*MIL*) sector; **S**~ (*in Gran Bretagna*) Exchequer.

scaccia'cani [skattʃa'kani] *sm o f inv* pistol with blanks.

scacciapensi'eri [skattʃapen'sjɛri] *sm inv* (*MUS*) jew's-harp.

scacci'are [skat'tʃare] *vt* to chase away *o* out, drive away *o* out; ~ **qn di casa** to turn sb out of the house.

'scacco, chi *sm* (*pezzo del gioco*) chessman; (*quadretto di scacchiera*) square; (*fig*)

setback, reverse; ~**chi** *smpl* (*gioco*) chess *sg*; **a** ~**chi** (*tessuto*) check(ed); **subire uno** ~ (*fig*: *sconfitta*) to suffer a setback.

scacco'matto *sm* checkmate; **dare** ~ **a qn** (*anche fig*) to checkmate sb.

'scaddi *etc vb vedi* **scadere**.

sca'dente *ag* shoddy, of poor quality.

sca'denza [ska'dɛntsa] *sf* (*di cambiale, contratto*) maturity; (*di passaporto*) expiry date; **a breve/lunga** ~ short-/long-term; **data di** ~ expiry date; ~ **a termine** fixed deadline.

sca'dere *vi* (*contratto etc*) to expire; (*debito*) to fall due; (*valore, forze, peso*) to decline, go down.

sca'fandro *sm* (*di palombaro*) diving suit; (*di astronauta*) spacesuit.

scaffala'tura *sf* shelving, shelves *pl*.

scaf'fale *sm* shelf; (*mobile*) set of shelves.

sca'fista *sm* (*di immigrati*) people smuggler (*by boat*).

'scafo *sm* (*NAUT, AER*) hull.

scagio'nare [skadʒo'nare] *vt* to exonerate, free from blame.

'scaglia ['skaʎʎa] *sf* (*ZOOL*) scale; (*scheggia*) chip, flake.

scagli'are [skaʎ'ʎare] *vt* (*lanciare: anche fig*) to hurl, fling; ~**rsi** *vr*: ~**rsi su** *o* **contro** to hurl *o* fling o.s. at; (*fig*) to rail at.

scagliona'mento [skaʎʎona'mento] *sm* (*MIL*) arrangement in echelons.

scaglio'nare [skaʎʎo'nare] *vt* (*pagamenti*) to space out, spread out; (*MIL*) to echelon.

scagli'one [skaʎ'ʎone] *sm* (*MIL*) echelon; (*GEO*) terrace; **a** ~**i** in groups.

sca'gnozzo [skaɲ'ɲɔttso] *sm* (*peg*) lackey.

'Scala *sf*: **la** ~ *vedi nota nel riquadro*.

LA SCALA

Milan's **la Scala** first opened its doors in 1778 with a performance of Salieri's opera, "L'Europa riconosciuta". Built on the site of the church of Santa Maria della Scala, the theatre suffered serious damage in the bombing campaigns of 1943 but reopened in 1946 with a concert conducted by Toscanini. Enjoying world-wide renown for its opera, **la Scala** also has a famous school of classical dance.

'scala *sf* (*a gradini etc*) staircase, stairs *pl*; (*a pioli, di corda*) ladder; (*MUS, GEO, di colori, valori, fig*) scale; ~**e** *sfpl* (*scalinata*) stairs; **su larga** *o* **vasta** ~ on a large scale; **su piccola** ~, **su** ~ **ridotta** on a small scale; **su** ~ **nazionale/mondiale** on a national/worldwide scale; **in** ~ **di 1 a 100.000** on a scale of 1 cm to 1 km; **riproduzione in** ~

reproduction to scale; ~ **a chiocciola** spiral staircase; ~ **a libretto** stepladder; ~ **di misure** system of weights and measures; ~ **mobile** escalator; (*ECON*) sliding scale; ~ **mobile (dei salari)** index-linked pay scale; ~ **di sicurezza** (*antincendio*) fire escape.

sca'lare *vt* (*ALPINISMO, muro*) to climb, scale; (*debito*) to scale down, reduce.

sca'lata *sf* scaling *no pl*, climbing *no pl*; (*arrampicata, fig*) climb; **dare la** ~ **a** (*fig*) to make a bid for.

scala'tore, 'trice *sm/f* climber.

scalca'gnato, a [skalkaɲ'ɲato] *ag* (*logoro*) worn; (*persona*) shabby.

scalci'are [skal'tʃare] *vi* to kick.

scalci'nato, a [skaltʃi'nato] *ag* (*fig peg*) shabby.

scalda'bagno [skalda'baɲɲo] *sm* water heater.

scal'dare *vt* to heat; ~**rsi** *vr* to warm up, heat up; (*al fuoco, al sole*) to warm o.s.; (*fig*) to get excited; ~ **la sedia** (*fig*) to twiddle one's thumbs.

scaldavi'vande *sm inv* dish warmer.

scal'dino *sm* (*per mani*) hand-warmer; (*per piedi*) foot-warmer; (*per letto*) bedwarmer.

scal'fire *vt* to scratch.

scalfit'tura *sf* scratch.

scali'nata *sf* staircase.

sca'lino *sm* (*anche fig*) step; (*di scala a pioli*) rung.

scal'mana *sf* (hot) flush.

scalma'narsi *vr* (*affaticarsi*) to rush about, rush around; (*agitarsi, darsi da fare*) to get all hot and bothered; (*arrabbiarsi*) to get excited, get steamed up.

scalma'nato, a *sm/f* hothead.

'scalo *sm* (*NAUT*) slipway; (: *porto d'approdo*) port of call; (*AER*) stopover; **fare** ~ **(a)** (*NAUT*) to call (at), put in (at); (*AER*) to land (at), make a stop (at); **volo senza** ~ non-stop flight; ~ **merci** (*FERR*) goods (*BRIT*) *o* freight yard.

sca'logna [ska'loɲɲa] *sf* (*fam*) bad luck.

scalo'gnato, a [skaloɲ'ɲato] *ag* (*fam*) unlucky.

scalop'pina *sf* (*CUC*) escalope.

scal'pello *sm* chisel.

scalpi'tare *vi* (*cavallo*) to paw the ground; (*persona*) to stamp one's feet.

scal'pore *sm* noise, row; **far** ~ (*notizia*) to cause a sensation *o* a stir.

'scaltro, a *ag* cunning, shrewd.

scal'zare [skal'tsare] *vt* (*albero*) to bare the roots of; (*muro, fig: autorità*) to undermine.

'scalzo, a ['skaltso] *ag* barefoot.

scambi'are *vt* to exchange; (*confondere*): ~ **qn/qc per** to take *o* mistake sb/sth for; **mi hanno scambiato il cappello** they've given me the wrong hat.

scambi'evole *ag* mutual, reciprocal.

'scambio *sm* exchange; (*COMM*) trade; (*FERR*) points *pl*; **fare (uno)** ~ to make a swap; **libero** ~ free trade; ~**i con l'estero** foreign trade.

scamosci'ato, a [skamoʃ'ʃato] *ag* suede.

scampa'gnata [skampaɲ'ɲata] *sf* trip to the country.

scampa'nare *vi* to peal.

scam'pare *vt* (*salvare*) to rescue, save; (*evitare: morte, prigione*) to escape ♦ *vi*: ~ **(a qc)** to survive (sth), escape (sth); **scamparla bella** to have a narrow escape.

'scampo *sm* (*salvezza*) escape; (*ZOOL*) prawn; **cercare** ~ **nella fuga** to seek safety in flight; **non c'è (via di)** ~ there's no way out.

'scampolo *sm* remnant.

scanala'tura *sf* (*incavo*) channel, groove.

scandagli'are [skandaʎ'ʎare] *vt* (*NAUT*) to sound; (*fig*) to sound out; to probe.

scanda'listico, a, ci, che *ag* (*settimanale etc*) sensational.

scandaliz'zare [skandalid'dzare] *vt* to shock, scandalize; ~**rsi** *vr* to be shocked.

'scandalo *sm* scandal; **dare** ~ to cause a scandal.

scanda'loso, a *ag* scandalous, shocking.

Scandi'navia *sf*: **la** ~ Scandinavia.

scandi'navo, a *ag, sm/f* Scandinavian.

scan'dire *vt* (*versi*) to scan; (*parole*) to articulate, pronounce distinctly; ~ **il tempo** (*MUS*) to beat time.

scan'nare *vt* (*animale*) to butcher, slaughter; (*persona*) to cut *o* slit the throat of.

'scanner ['skanner] *sm inv* scanner.

scanneriz'zare [skannerid'dzare] *vt* to scan.

'scanno *sm* seat, bench.

scansafa'tiche [skansafa'tike] *sm/f inv* idler, loafer.

scan'sare *vt* (*rimuovere*) to move (aside), shift; (*schivare: schiaffo*) to dodge; (*sfuggire*) to avoid; ~**rsi** *vr* to move aside.

scan'sia *sf* shelves *pl*; (*per libri*) bookcase.

'scanso *sm*: **a** ~ **di** in order to avoid, as a precaution against; **a** ~ **di equivoci** to avoid (any) misunderstanding.

scanti'nato *sm* basement.

scanto'nare *vi* to turn the corner; (*svignarsela*) to sneak off.

scanzo'nato, a [skantso'nato] *ag* easygoing.

scapacci'one [skapat'tʃone] *sm* clout, slap.

scapes'trato, a *ag* dissolute.

'scapito *sm* (*perdita*) loss; (*danno*) damage, detriment; **a ~ di** to the detriment of.

'scapola *sf* shoulder blade.

'scapolo *sm* bachelor.

scappa'mento *sm* (*AUT*) exhaust.

scap'pare *vi* (*fuggire*) to escape; (*andare via in fretta*) to rush off; **~ di prigione** to escape from prison; **~ di mano** (*oggetto*) to slip out of one's hands; **~ di mente a qn** to slip sb's mind; **lasciarsi ~** (*occasione, affare*) to miss, let go by; (*dettaglio*) to overlook; (*parola*) to let slip; (*prigioniero*) to let escape; **mi scappò detto** I let it slip.

scap'pata *sf* quick visit *o* call.

scappa'tella *sf* escapade.

scappa'toia *sf* way out.

scara'beo *sm* beetle.

scarabocchi'are [skarabok'kjare] *vt* to scribble, scrawl.

scara'bocchio [skara'bɔkkjo] *sm* scribble, scrawl.

scara'faggio [skara'faddʒo] *sm* cockroach.

scaraman'zia [skaraman'tsia] *sf*: **per ~ for** luck.

scara'muccia, ce [skara'muttʃa] *sf* skirmish.

scaraven'tare *vt* to fling, hurl.

scarce'rare [skartʃe'rare] *vt* to release (from prison).

scarcerazi'one [skartʃerat'tsjone] *sf* release (from prison).

scardi'nare *vt* to take off its hinges.

'scarica, che *sf* (*di più armi*) volley of shots; (*di sassi, pugni*) hail, shower; (*ELETTR*) discharge; **~ di mitra** burst of machine-gun fire.

scari'care *vt* (*merci, camion etc*) to unload; (*passeggeri*) to set down; (*da Internet*) to download; (*arma*) to unload; (: *sparare, ELETTR*) to discharge; (*sog: corso d'acqua*) to empty, pour; (*fig: liberare da un peso*) to unburden, relieve; **~rsi** *vr* (*orologio*) to run *o* wind down; (*batteria, accumulatore*) to go flat (*BRIT*) *o* dead; (*fig: rilassarsi*) to unwind; (: *sfogarsi*) to let off steam; **~ le proprie responsabilità su qn** to off-load one's responsibilities onto sb; **~ la colpa addosso a qn** to blame sb; **il fulmine si scaricò su un albero** the lightning struck a tree.

scarica'tore *sm* loader; (*di porto*) docker.

'scarico, a, chi, che *ag* unloaded; (*orologio*) run down; (*batteria, accumulatore*) dead, flat (*BRIT*) ♦ *sm* (*di merci, materiali*) unloading; (*di immondizie*) dumping, tipping (*BRIT*); (: *luogo*) rubbish dump; (*TECN: deflusso*) draining; (: *dispositivo*) drain; (*AUT*) exhaust; **~ del**

lavandino waste outlet.

scarlat'tina *sf* scarlet fever.

scar'latto, a *ag* scarlet.

'scarno, a *ag* thin, bony.

'scarpa *sf* shoe; **fare le ~e a qn** (*fig*) to double-cross sb; **~e da ginnastica** gym shoes; **~e coi tacchi (alti)** high-heeled shoes; **~e col tacco basso** low-heeled shoes; **~e senza tacco** flat shoes; **~e da tennis** tennis shoes.

scar'pata *sf* escarpment.

scarpi'era *sf* shoe rack.

scar'pone *sm* boot; **~i da montagna** climbing boots; **~i da sci** ski-boots.

scarroz'zare [skarrot'tsare] *vt* to drive around.

scarseggi'are [skarsed'dʒare] *vi* to be scarce; **~ di** to be short of, lack.

scar'sezza [skar'settsa] *sf* scarcity, lack.

'scarso, a *ag* (*insufficiente*) insufficient, meagre (*BRIT*), meager (*US*); (*povero: annata*) poor, lean; (*INS: voto*) poor; **~ di** lacking in; **3 chili ~i** just under 3 kilos.

scartabel'lare *vt* to skim through, glance through.

scarta'faccio [skarta'fattʃo] *sm* notebook.

scarta'mento *sm* (*FERR*) gauge; **~ normale/ridotto** standard/narrow gauge.

scar'tare *vt* (*pacco*) to unwrap; (*idea*) to reject; (*MIL*) to declare unfit for military service; (*carte da gioco*) to discard; (*CALCIO*) to dodge (past) ♦ *vi* to swerve.

'scarto *sm* (*cosa scartata, anche COMM*) reject; (*di veicolo*) swerve; (*differenza*) gap, difference; **~ salariale** wage differential.

scar'toffie *sfpl* (*peg*) papers *pl*.

scas'sare *vt* (*fam: rompere*) to wreck.

scassi'nare *vt* to break, force.

'scasso *sm vedi* **furto**.

scate'nare *vt* (*fig*) to incite, stir up; **~rsi** *vr* (*temporale*) to break; (*rivolta*) to break out; (*persona: infuriarsi*) to rage.

scate'nato, a *ag* wild.

'scatola *sf* box; (*di latta*) tin (*BRIT*), can; **cibi in ~** tinned (*BRIT*) *o* canned foods; **una ~ di cioccolatini** a box of chocolates; **comprare qc a ~ chiusa** to buy sth sight unseen; **~ cranica** cranium.

scato'lone *sm* box.

scat'tante *ag* quick off the mark; (*agile*) agile.

scat'tare *vt* (*fotografia*) to take ♦ *vi* (*congegno, molla etc*) to be released; (*balzare*) to spring up; (*SPORT*) to put on a spurt; (*fig: per l'ira*) to fly into a rage; (*legge, provvedimento*) to come into effect; **~ in piedi** to spring to one's feet; **far ~ to**

release.

'scatto sm (dispositivo) release; (: di arma da fuoco) trigger mechanism; (rumore) click; (balzo) jump, start; (SPORT) spurt; (fig: di ira etc) fit; (: di stipendio) increment; di ~ suddenly; serratura a ~ spring lock.
scatu'rire vi to gush, spring.
scaval'care vt (ostacolo) to pass (o climb) over; (fig) to get ahead of, overtake.
sca'vare vt (terreno) to dig; (legno) to hollow out; (pozzo, galleria) to bore; (città sepolta etc) to excavate.
scava'trice [skava'tritʃe] sf (macchina) excavator.
scavezza'collo [skavettsa'kɔllo] sm daredevil.
'scavo sm excavating no pl; excavation.
scazzot'tare [skattsot'tare] vt (fam) to beat up, give a thrashing to.
'scegliere ['ʃeʎʎere] vt (gen) to choose; (candidato, prodotto) to choose, select; ~ di fare to choose to do.
sce'icco, chi [ʃe'ikko] sm sheik.
'scelgo etc ['ʃelgo] vb vedi scegliere.
scelle'rato, a [ʃelle'rato] ag wicked, evil.
scel'lino [ʃel'lino] sm shilling.
'scelto, a ['ʃelto] pp di scegliere ♦ ag (gruppo) carefully selected; (frutta, verdura) choice, top quality; (MIL: specializzato) crack cpd, highly skilled ♦ sf choice; (selezione) selection, choice; frutta o formaggi a ~a choice of fruit or cheese; fare una ~a to make a choice, choose; non avere ~a to have no choice o option; di prima ~a top grade o quality.
sce'mare [ʃe'mare] vt, vi to diminish.
sce'menza [ʃe'mɛntsa] sf stupidity no pl; stupid thing (to do o say).
'scemo, a ['ʃemo] ag stupid, silly.
'scempio ['ʃempjo] sm slaughter, massacre; (fig) ruin; far ~ di (fig) to play havoc with, ruin.
'scena ['ʃena] sf (gen) scene; (palcoscenico) stage; le ~e (fig: teatro) the stage; andare in ~ to be staged o put on o performed; mettere in ~ to stage; uscire di ~ to leave the stage; (fig) to leave the scene; fare una ~ (fig) to make a scene; ha fatto ~ muta (fig) he didn't open his mouth.
sce'nario [ʃe'narjo] sm scenery; (di film) scenario.
sce'nata [ʃe'nata] sf row, scene.
'scendere ['ʃendere] vi to go (o come) down; (strada, sole) to go down; (notte) to fall; (passeggero: fermarsi) to get out, alight; (fig: temperatura, prezzi) to fall, drop ♦ vt (scale, pendio) to go (o come) down; ~ dalle scale to go (o come) down the stairs;

~ dal treno to get off o out of the train; ~ dalla macchina to get out of the car; ~ da cavallo to dismount, get off one's horse; ~ ad un albergo to put up o stay at a hotel.
sceneggi'ato [ʃened'dʒato] sm television drama.
sceneggia'tore, 'trice [ʃeneddʒa'tore] sm/f script-writer.
sceneggia'tura [ʃeneddʒa'tura] sf (TEAT) scenario; (CINE) screenplay, scenario.
'scenico, a, ci, che ['ʃeniko] ag stage cpd.
scenogra'fia [ʃenogra'fia] sf (TEAT) stage design; (CINE) set design; (elementi scenici) scenery.
sce'nografo, a [ʃe'nɔgrafo] sm/f set designer.
sce'riffo [ʃe'riffo] sm sheriff.
scervel'larsi [ʃervel'larsi] vr: ~ (su qc) to rack one's brains (over sth).
scervel'lato, a [ʃervel'lato] ag featherbrained.
'sceso, a ['ʃeso] pp di scendere.
scetti'cismo [ʃetti'tʃizmo] sm scepticism (BRIT), skepticism (US).
'scettico, a, ci, che ['ʃɛttiko] ag sceptical (BRIT), skeptical (US).
'scettro ['ʃettro] sm sceptre (BRIT), scepter (US).
'scheda ['skɛda] sf (index) card; (TV, RADIO) (brief) report; ~ audio (INFORM) sound card; ~ bianca/nulla (POL) unmarked/spoiled ballot paper; ~ a circuito stampato printed-circuit board; ~ elettorale ballot paper; ~ madre (INFORM) motherboard; ~ perforata punch card; ~ ricaricabile (TEL) top-up card; ~ telefonica phone card; ~ video (INFORM) video card.
sche'dare [ske'dare] vt (dati) to file; (libri) to catalogue; (registrare: anche POLIZIA) to put on one's files.
sche'dario [ske'darjo] sm file; (mobile) filing cabinet.
sche'dato, a [ske'dato] ag with a (police) record ♦ sm/f person with a (police) record.
sche'dina [ske'dina] sf ≈ pools coupon (BRIT).
'scheggia, ge ['skeddʒa] sf splinter, sliver; ~ impazzita (fig) maverick.
sche'letrico, a, ci, che [ske'lɛtriko] ag (anche ANAT) skeletal; (fig: essenziale) skeleton cpd.
'scheletro ['skɛletro] sm skeleton; avere uno ~ nell'armadio (fig) to have a skeleton in the cupboard.
'schema, i ['skɛma] sm (diagramma) diagram, sketch; (progetto, abbozzo)

outline, plan; **ribellarsi agli** ~**i** to rebel against traditional values; **secondo gli** ~**i tradizionali** in accordance with traditional values.

sche'matico, a, ci, che [ske'matiko] *ag* schematic.

schematiz'zare [skematid'dzare] *vt* to schematize.

'scherma ['skerma] *sf* fencing.

scher'maglia [sker'maʎʎa] *sf* (*fig*) skirmish.

scher'mirsi [sker'mirsi] *vr* to defend o.s.

'schermo ['skermo] *sm* shield, screen; (*CINE, TV*) screen.

schermogra'fia [skermogra'fia] *sf* X-rays *pl*.

scher'nire [sker'nire] *vt* to mock, sneer at.

'scherno ['skerno] *sm* mockery, derision; **farsi** ~ **di** to sneer at; **essere oggetto di** ~ to be a laughing stock.

scher'zare [sker'tsare] *vi* to joke.

'scherzo ['skertso] *sm* joke; (*tiro*) trick; (*MUS*) scherzo; **è uno** ~**!** (*una cosa facile*) it's child's play!, it's easy!; **per** ~ **for a** joke *o* a laugh; **fare un brutto** ~ **a qn** to play a nasty trick on sb; ~**i a parte** seriously, joking apart.

scher'zoso, a [sker'tsoso] *ag* (*tono, gesto*) playful; (*osservazione*) facetious; **è un tipo** ~ he likes a joke.

schiaccia'noci [skjattʃa'notʃi] *sm inv* nutcracker.

schiacci'ante [skjat'tʃante] *ag* overwhelming.

schiacci'are [skjat'tʃare] *vt* (*dito*) to crush; (*noci*) to crack; ~ **un pisolino** to have a nap.

schiaffeggi'are [skjaffed'dʒare] *vt* to slap.

schi'affo ['skjaffo] *sm* slap; **prendere qn a** ~**i** to slap sb's face; **uno** ~ **morale** a slap in the face, a rebuff.

schiamaz'zare [skjamat'tsare] *vi* to squawk, cackle.

schia'mazzo [skja'mattso] *sm* (*fig: chiasso*) din, racket.

schian'tare [skjan'tare] *vt* to break, tear apart; ~**rsi** *vr* to break (up), shatter; ~**rsi al suolo** (*aereo*) to crash (to the ground).

schi'anto ['skjanto] *sm* (*rumore*) crash; tearing sound; **è uno** ~**!** (*fam*) it's (*o* he's *o* she's) terrific!; **di** ~ all of a sudden.

schia'rire [skja'rire] *vt* to lighten, make lighter ♦ *vi* (*anche:* ~**rsi**) to grow lighter; (*tornar sereno*) to clear, brighten up; ~**rsi la voce** to clear one's throat.

schia'rita [skja'rita] *sf* (*METEOR*) bright spell; (*fig*) improvement, turn for the better.

schiat'tare [skjat'tare] *vi* to burst; ~

d'invidia to be green with envy; ~ **di rabbia** to be beside o.s. with rage.

schiavitù [skjavi'tu] *sf* slavery.

schiaviz'zare [skjavid'dzare] *vt* to enslave.

schi'avo, a ['skjavo] *sm/f* slave.

schi'ena ['skjɛna] *sf* (*ANAT*) back.

schie'nale [skje'nale] *sm* (*di sedia*) back.

schi'era ['skjɛra] *sf* (*MIL*) rank; (*gruppo*) group, band; **villette a** ~ ≈ terraced houses.

schiera'mento [skjera'mento] *sm* (*MIL, SPORT*) formation; (*fig*) alliance.

schie'rare [skje'rare] *vt* (*esercito*) to line up, draw up, marshal; ~**rsi** *vr* to line up; (*fig*): ~**rsi con** *o* **dalla parte di/contro qn** to side with/oppose sb.

schi'etto, a ['skjɛtto] *ag* (*puro*) pure; (*fig*) frank, straightforward.

schi'fare [ski'fare] *vt* to disgust.

schi'fezza [ski'fettsa] *sf*: **essere una** ~ (*cibo, bibita etc*) to be disgusting; (*film, libro*) to be dreadful.

schifil'toso, a [skifil'toso] *ag* fussy, difficult.

'schifo ['skifo] *sm* disgust; **fare** ~ (*essere fatto male, dare pessimi risultati*) to be awful; **mi fa** ~ it makes me sick, it's disgusting; **quel libro è uno** ~ that book's rotten.

schi'foso, a [ski'foso] *ag* disgusting, revolting; (*molto scadente*) rotten, lousy.

schioc'care [skjok'kare] *vt* (*frusta*) to crack; (*dita*) to snap; (*lingua*) to click; ~ **le labbra** to smack one's lips.

schioppet'tata [skjoppet'tata] *sf* gunshot.

schi'oppo ['skjɔppo] *sm* rifle, gun.

schi'udere ['skjudere] *vt*, ~**rsi** *vr* to open.

schi'uma ['skjuma] *sf* foam; (*di sapone*) lather; (*di latte*) froth.

schiu'mare [skju'mare] *vt* to skim ♦ *vi* to foam.

schi'uso, a ['skjuso] *pp di* **schiudere**.

schi'vare [ski'vare] *vt* to dodge, avoid.

'schivo, a ['skivo] *ag* (*ritroso*) stand-offish, reserved; (*timido*) shy.

schizofre'nia [skiddzofre'nia] *sf* schizophrenia.

schizo'frenico, a, ci, che [skiddzo'frɛniko] *ag* schizophrenic.

schiz'zare [skit'tsare] *vt* (*spruzzare*) to spurt, squirt; (*sporcare*) to splash, spatter; (*fig: abbozzare*) to sketch ♦ *vi* to spurt, squirt; (*saltar fuori*) to dart up (*o* off *etc*); ~ **via** (*animale, persona*) to dart away; (*macchina, moto*) to accelerate away.

schizzi'noso, a [skittsi'noso] *ag* fussy, finicky.

'schizzo ['skittso] *sm* (*di liquido*) spurt;

splash, spatter; (*abbozzo*) sketch.
sci [ʃi] *sm inv* (*attrezzo*) ski; (*attività*) skiing; ~ **di fondo** cross-country skiing, ski touring (*US*); ~ **nautico** water-skiing.
'scia, *pl* **'scie** ['ʃia] *sf* (*di imbarcazione*) wake; (*di profumo*) trail.
scià [ʃa] *sm inv* shah.
sci'abola ['ʃabola] *sf* sabre (*BRIT*), saber (*US*).
scia'callo [ʃa'kallo] *sm* jackal; (*fig peg*: *profittatore*) shark, profiteer; (: *ladro*) looter.
sciac'quare [ʃak'kware] *vt* to rinse.
scia'gura [ʃa'gura] *sf* disaster, calamity.
sciagu'rato, a [ʃagu'rato] *ag* unfortunate; (*malvagio*) wicked.
scialac'quare [ʃalak'kware] *vt* to squander.
scia'lare [ʃa'lare] *vi* to throw one's money around.
sci'albo, a ['ʃalbo] *ag* pale, dull; (*fig*) dull, colourless (*BRIT*), colorless (*US*).
sci'alle ['ʃalle] *sm* shawl.
sci'alo ['ʃalo] *sm* squandering, waste.
scia'luppa [ʃa'luppa] *sf* (*NAUT*) sloop; (*anche*: ~ **di salvataggio**) lifeboat.
scia'mare [ʃa'mare] *vi* to swarm.
sci'ame ['ʃame] *sm* swarm.
scian'cato, a [ʃan'kato] *ag* lame; (*mobile*) rickety.
sci'are [ʃi'are] *vi* to ski; **andare a** ~ to go skiing.
sci'arpa ['ʃarpa] *sf* scarf; (*fascia*) sash.
scia'tore, 'trice [ʃia'tore] *sm/f* skier.
sciat'tezza [ʃat'tettsa] *sf* slovenliness.
sci'atto, a ['ʃatto] *ag* (*persona*: *nell'aspetto*) slovenly, unkempt; (: *nel lavoro*) sloppy, careless.
'scibile ['ʃibile] *sm* knowledge.
scien'tifico, a, ci, che [ʃen'tifiko] *ag* scientific; **la (polizia)** ~**a** the forensic department.
sci'enza ['ʃɛntsa] *sf* science; (*sapere*) knowledge; ~**e** *sfpl* (*INS*) science *sg*; ~**e naturali** natural sciences; ~**e politiche** political science *sg*.
scienzi'ato, a [ʃen'tsjato] *sm/f* scientist.
'Scilly ['ʃilli]: **le isole** ~ *sfpl* the Scilly Isles.
'scimmia ['ʃimmja] *sf* monkey.
scimmiot'tare [ʃimmjot'tare] *vt* to ape, mimic.
scimpanzé [ʃimpan'tse] *sm inv* chimpanzee.
scimu'nito, a [ʃimu'nito] *ag* silly, idiotic.
'scindere ['ʃindere] *vt*, ~**rsi** *vr* to split (up).
scin'tilla [ʃin'tilla] *sf* spark.
scintil'lare [ʃintil'lare] *vi* to spark; (*acqua, occhi*) to sparkle.
scintil'lio [ʃintil'lio] *sm* sparkling.
scioc'care [ʃok'kare] *vt* to shock.

scioc'chezza [ʃok'kettsa] *sf* stupidity *no pl*; stupid *o* foolish thing; **dire** ~**e** to talk nonsense.
sci'occo, a, chi, che ['ʃokko] *ag* stupid, foolish.
sci'ogliere ['ʃɔʎʎere] *vt* (*nodo*) to untie; (*capelli*) to loosen; (*persona, animale*) to untie, release; (*fig*: *persona*): ~ **da** to release from; (*neve*) to melt; (*nell'acqua*: *zucchero etc*) to dissolve; (*fig*: *mistero*) to solve; (*porre fine a*: *contratto*) to cancel; (: *società, matrimonio*) to dissolve; (: *riunione*) to bring to an end; ~**rsi** *vr* to loosen, come untied; to melt; to dissolve; (*assemblea, corteo, duo*) to break up; ~ **i muscoli** to limber up; ~ **il ghiaccio** (*fig*) to break the ice; ~ **le vele** (*NAUT*) to set sail; ~**rsi dai legami** (*fig*) to free o.s. from all ties.
sci'olgo *etc* ['ʃɔlgo] *vb vedi* **sciogliere.**
sciol'tezza [ʃol'tettsa] *sf* agility; suppleness; ease.
sci'olto, a ['ʃɔlto] *pp di* **sciogliere ♦** *ag* loose; (*agile*) agile, nimble; (*disinvolto*) free and easy; **essere** ~ **nei movimenti** to be supple; **versi** ~**i** (*POESIA*) blank verse.
sciope'rante [ʃope'rante] *sm/f* striker.
sciope'rare [ʃope'rare] *vi* to strike, go on strike.
sci'opero ['ʃopero] *sm* strike; **fare** ~ to strike; **entrare in** ~ to go on *o* come out on strike; ~ **bianco** work-to-rule (*BRIT*), slowdown (*US*); ~ **della fame** hunger strike; ~ **selvaggio** wildcat strike; ~ **a singhiozzo** on-off strike; ~ **di solidarietà** sympathy strike.
sciori'nare [ʃori'nare] *vt* (*ostentare*) to show off, display.
scio'via [ʃio'via] *sf* ski lift.
sciovi'nismo [ʃovi'nizmo] *sm* chauvinism.
sciovi'nista, i, e [ʃovi'nista] *sm/f* chauvinist.
sci'pito, a [ʃi'pito] *ag* insipid.
scip'pare [ʃip'pare] *vt*: ~ **qn** to snatch sb's bag.
scippa'tore [ʃippa'tore] *sm* bag-snatcher.
'scippo ['ʃippo] *sm* bag-snatching.
sci'rocco [ʃi'rɔkko] *sm* sirocco.
sci'roppo [ʃi'rɔppo] *sm* syrup; ~ **per la tosse** cough syrup, cough mixture.
'scisma, i ['ʃizma] *sm* (*REL*) schism.
scissi'one [ʃis'sjone] *sf* (*anche fig*) split, division; (*FISICA*) fission.
'scisso, a ['ʃisso] *pp di* **scindere.**
sciu'pare [ʃu'pare] *vt* (*abito, libro, appetito*) to spoil, ruin; (*tempo, denaro*) to waste; ~**rsi** *vr* to get spoilt *o* ruined; (*rovinarsi la salute*) to ruin one's health.

scivo'lare [ʃivo'lare] *vi* to slide *o* glide along; (*involontariamente*) to slip, slide.

'scivolo ['ʃivolo] *sm* slide; (*TECN*) chute.

scivo'loso, a [ʃivo'loso] *ag* slippery.

scle'rosi *sf* sclerosis.

scoc'care *vt* (*freccia*) to shoot ♦ *vi* (*guizzare*) to shoot up; (*battere*: *ora*) to strike.

scoccherò *etc* [skokke'rɔ] *vb vedi* **scoccare**.

scocci'are [skot'tʃare] *vt* to bother, annoy; **~rsi** *vr* to be bothered *o* annoyed.

scoccia'tore, 'trice [skottʃa'tore] *sm/f* nuisance, pest (*fam*).

scoccia'tura [skottʃa'tura] *sf* nuisance, bore.

sco'della *sf* bowl.

scodinzo'lare [skodintso'lare] *vi* to wag its tail.

scogli'era [skoʎ'ʎɛra] *sf* reef; (*rupe*) cliff.

'scoglio ['skɔʎʎo] *sm* (*al mare*) rock; (*fig*: *ostacolo*) difficulty, stumbling block.

scogli'oso, a [skoʎ'ʎoso] *ag* rocky.

scoi'attolo *sm* squirrel.

scola'pasta *sm inv* colander.

sco'lare *ag*: **età ~** school age ♦ *vt* to drain ♦ *vi* to drip.

scola'resca *sf* schoolchildren *pl*, pupils *pl*.

sco'laro, a *sm/f* pupil, schoolboy/girl.

sco'lastico, a, ci, che *ag* (*gen*) scholastic; (*libro, anno, divisa*) school *cpd*.

scol'lare *vt* (*staccare*) to unstick; **~rsi** *vr* to come unstuck.

scol'lato, a *ag* (*vestito*) low-cut, low-necked; (*donna*) wearing a low-cut dress (*o* blouse *etc*).

scolla'tura *sf* neckline.

'scolo *sm* drainage; (*sbocco*) drain; (*acqua*) waste water; **canale di ~** drain; **tubo di ~** drainpipe.

scolo'rire *vt* to fade; to discolour (*BRIT*), discolor (*US*) ♦ *vi* (*anche*: **~rsi**) to fade; to become discolo(u)red; (*impallidire*) to turn pale.

scol'pire *vt* to carve, sculpt.

scombi'nare *vt* to mess up, upset.

scombi'nato, a *ag* confused, muddled.

scombusso'lare *vt* to upset.

scom'messo, a *pp di* **scommettere** ♦ *sf* bet, wager; **fare una ~a** to bet.

scom'mettere *vt, vi* to bet.

scomo'dare *vt* to trouble, bother, disturb; (*fig*: *nome famoso*) to involve, drag in; **~rsi** *vr* to put o.s. out; **~rsi a fare** to go to the bother *o* trouble of doing.

scomodità *sf inv* (*di sedia, letto etc*) discomfort; (*di orario, sistemazione etc*) inconvenience.

'scomodo, a *ag* uncomfortable; (*sistemazione, posto*) awkward,

inconvenient.

scompagi'nare [skompadʒi'nare] *vt* to upset, throw into disorder.

scompag'nato, a [skompaɲ'ɲato] *ag* (*calzini, guanti*) odd.

scompa'rire *vi* (*sparire*) to disappear, vanish; (*fig*) to be insignificant.

scom'parso, a *pp di* **scomparire** ♦ *sf* disappearance; (*fig*: *morte*) passing away, death.

scomparti'mento *sm* (*FERR*) compartment; (*sezione*) division.

scom'parto *sm* compartment, division.

scom'penso *sm* imbalance, lack of balance.

scompigli'are [skompiʎ'ʎare] *vt* (*cassetto, capelli*) to mess up, disarrange; (*fig*: *piani*) to upset.

scom'piglio [skom'piʎʎo] *sm* mess, confusion.

scom'porre *vt* (*parola, numero*) to break up; (*CHIM*) to decompose; **scomporsi** *vr* (*CHIM*) to decompose; (*fig*) to get upset, lose one's composure; **senza scomporsi** unperturbed.

scom'posto, a *pp di* **scomporre** ♦ *ag* (*gesto*) unseemly; (*capelli*) ruffled, dishevelled.

sco'munica, che *sf* excommunication.

scomuni'care *vt* to excommunicate.

sconcer'tante [skontʃer'tante] *ag* disconcerting.

sconcer'tare [skontʃer'tare] *vt* to disconcert, bewilder.

'sconcio, a, ci, ce ['skontʃo] *ag* (*osceno*) indecent, obscene ♦ *sm* (*cosa riprovevole, mal fatta*) disgrace.

sconclusio'nato, a *ag* incoherent, illogical.

sconfes'sare *vt* to renounce, disavow; to repudiate.

scon'figgere [skon'fiddʒere] *vt* to defeat, overcome.

sconfi'nare *vi* to cross the border; (*in proprietà privata*) to trespass; (*fig*): **~ da** to stray *o* digress from.

sconfi'nato, a *ag* boundless, unlimited.

scon'fitto, a *pp di* **sconfiggere** ♦ *sf* defeat.

sconfor'tante, a *ag* discouraging, disheartening.

sconfor'tare *vt* to discourage, dishearten; **~rsi** *vr* to become discouraged, become disheartened, lose heart.

scon'forto *sm* despondency.

sconge'lare [skondʒe'lare] *vt* to defrost.

scongiu'rare [skondʒu'rare] *vt* (*implorare*) to beseech, implore; (*eludere*: *pericolo*) to ward off, avert.

scongi'uro [skon'dʒuro] *sm* (*esorcismo*)

exorcism; **fare gli ~i** to touch wood (BRIT), knock on wood (US).

scon'nesso, a ag (fig: discorso) incoherent, rambling.

sconosci'uto, a [skonoʃ'ʃuto] ag unknown; new, strange ♦ sm/f stranger, unknown person.

sconquas'sare vt to shatter, smash.

scon'quasso sm (danno) damage; (fig) confusion.

sconside'rato, a ag thoughtless, rash.

sconsigli'are [skonsiʎ'ʎare] vt: ~ **qc a qn** to advise sb against sth; ~ **qn dal fare qc** to advise sb not to do o against doing sth.

sconso'lato, a ag disconsolate.

scon'tare vt (COMM: detrarre) to deduct; (: debito) to pay off; (: cambiale) to discount; (pena) to serve; (colpa, errori) to pay for, suffer for.

scon'tato, a ag (previsto) foreseen, taken for granted; (prezzo, merce) discounted, at a discount; **dare per ~ che** to take it for granted that.

sconten'tare vt to displease, dissatisfy.

sconten'tezza [skonten'tettsa] sf displeasure, dissatisfaction.

scon'tento, a ag: ~ **(di)** discontented o dissatisfied (with) ♦ sm discontent, dissatisfaction.

'sconto sm discount; **fare** o **concedere uno ~** to give a discount; **uno ~ del 10%** a 10% discount.

scon'trarsi vr (treni etc) to crash, collide; (venire ad uno scontro, fig) to clash; ~ **con** to crash into, collide with.

scon'trino sm ticket.

'scontro sm (MIL, fig) clash; (di veicoli) crash, collision; ~ **a fuoco** shoot-out.

scon'troso, a ag sullen, surly; (permaloso) touchy.

sconveni'ente ag unseemly, improper.

sconvol'gente [skonvol'dʒɛnte] ag (notizia, brutta esperienza) upsetting, disturbing; (bellezza) amazing; (passione) overwhelming.

scon'volgere [skon'vɔldʒere] vt to throw into confusion, upset; (turbare) to shake, disturb, upset.

scon'volto, a pp di **sconvolgere** ♦ ag (persona) distraught, very upset.

'scopa sf broom; (CARTE) Italian card game.

sco'pare vt to sweep; (fam!) to bonk (!).

sco'pata sf (fam!) bonk (!).

scoperchi'are [skoper'kjare] vt (pentola, vaso) to take the lid off, uncover; (casa) to take the roof off.

sco'perto, a pp di **scoprire** ♦ ag uncovered;

(capo) uncovered, bare; (macchina) open; (MIL) exposed, without cover; (conto) overdrawn ♦ sf discovery ♦ sm: **allo ~** (dormire etc) out in the open; **assegno ~** uncovered cheque; **avere un conto ~** to be overdrawn.

'scopo sm aim, purpose; **a che ~?** what for?; **adatto allo ~** fit for its purpose; **allo ~ di fare qc** in order to do sth; **a ~ di lucro** for gain o money; **senza ~** (fare, cercare) pointlessly.

scoppi'are vi (spaccarsi) to burst; (esplodere) to explode; (fig) to break out; ~ **in pianto** o **a piangere** to burst out crying; ~ **dalle risa** o **dal ridere** to split one's sides laughing; ~ **dal caldo** to be boiling; ~ **di salute** to be the picture of health.

scoppiet'tare vi to crackle.

'scoppio sm explosion; (di tuono, arma etc) crash, bang; (di pneumatico) bang; (fig: di guerra) outbreak; **a ~ ritardato** delayed-action; **reazione a ~ ritardato** delayed o slow reaction; **uno ~ di risa** a burst of laughter; **uno ~ di collera** an explosion of anger.

sco'prire vt to discover; (liberare da ciò che copre) to uncover; (: monumento) to unveil; ~**rsi** vr to put on lighter clothes; (fig) to give o.s. away.

scopri'tore, 'trice sm/f discoverer.

scoraggi'are [skorad'dʒare] vt to discourage; ~**rsi** vr to become discouraged, lose heart.

scor'butico, a, ci, che ag (fig) cantankerous.

scorcia'toia [skortʃa'toja] sf short cut.

'scorcio ['skortʃo] sm (ARTE) foreshortening; (di secolo, periodo) end, close; ~ **panoramico** vista.

scor'dare vt to forget; ~**rsi** vr: ~**rsi di qc/di fare** to forget sth/to do.

sco'reggia [sko'reddʒa] (fam!) sf fart (!).

scoreggi'are [skored'dʒare] (fam!) vi to fart (!).

'scorgere ['skɔrdʒere] vt to make out, distinguish, see.

sco'ria sf (di metalli) slag; (vulcanica) scoria; ~**e radioattive** (FISICA) radioactive waste sg.

'scorno sm ignominy, disgrace.

scorpacci'ata [skorpat'tʃata] sf: **fare una ~ (di)** to stuff o.s. (with), eat one's fill (of).

scorpi'one sm scorpion; (dello zodiaco): **S~** Scorpio; **essere dello S~** to be Scorpio.

'scorporo sm (POL) transfer of votes aimed at increasing the chances of representation for minority parties.

scorraz'zare [skorrat'tsare] *vi* to run about.
'scorrere *vt* (*giornale, lettera*) to run o skim through ♦ *vi* (*liquido, fiume*) to run, flow; (*fune*) to run; (*cassetto, porta*) to slide easily; (*tempo*) to pass (by).
scorre'ria *sf* raid, incursion.
scorret'tezza [skorret'tettsa] *sf* incorrectness; lack of politeness, rudeness; unfairness; **commettere una ~** (*essere sleale*) to be unfair.
scor'retto, a *ag* (*sbagliato*) incorrect; (*sgarbato*) impolite; (*sconveniente*) improper; (*sleale*) unfair; (*gioco*) foul.
scor'revole *ag* (*porta*) sliding; (*fig: stile*) fluent, flowing.
scorri'banda *sf* (*MIL*) raid; (*escursione*) trip, excursion.
'scorsi *etc vb vedi* **scorgere**.
'scorso, a *pp di* **scorrere** ♦ *ag* last ♦ *sf* quick look, glance; **lo ~ mese** last month.
scor'soio, a *ag:* **nodo ~** noose.
'scorta *sf* (*di personalità, convoglio*) escort; (*provvista*) supply, stock; **sotto la ~ di due agenti** escorted by two policemen; **fare ~ di** to stock up with, get in a supply of; **di ~** (*materiali*) spare; **ruota di ~** spare wheel.
scor'tare *vt* to escort.
scor'tese *ag* discourteous, rude.
scorte'sia *sf* discourtesy, rudeness; (*azione*) discourtesy.
scorti'care *vt* to skin.
'scorto, a *pp di* **scorgere**.
'scorza ['skɔrdza] *sf* (*di albero*) bark; (*di agrumi*) peel, skin.
sco'sceso, a [skoʃ'ʃeso] *ag* steep.
'scosso, a *pp di* **scuotere** ♦ *ag* (*turbato*) shaken, upset ♦ *sf* jerk, jolt, shake; (*ELETTR, fig*) shock; **prendere la ~a** to get an electric shock; **~a di terremoto** earth tremor.
scos'sone *sm:* **dare uno ~ a qn** to give sb a shake; **procedere a ~i** to jolt o jerk along.
scos'tante *ag* (*fig*) off-putting (*BRIT*), unpleasant.
scos'tare *vt* to move (away), shift; **~rsi** *vr* to move away.
scostu'mato, a *ag* immoral, dissolute.
scotch [skɔtʃ] *sm inv* (*whisky*) Scotch; ® (*nastro adesivo*) Scotch tape ®, Sellotape ®.
scot'tante *ag* (*fig: urgente*) pressing; (*: delicato*) delicate.
scot'tare *vt* (*ustionare*) to burn; (*: con liquido bollente*) to scald ♦ *vi* to burn; (*caffè*) to be too hot.
scotta'tura *sf* burn; scald.
'scotto, a *ag* overcooked ♦ *sm* (*fig*): **pagare lo ~ (di)** to pay the penalty (for).
sco'vare *vt* to drive out, flush out; (*fig*) to discover.

'Scozia ['skɔttsja] *sf:* **la ~** Scotland.
scoz'zese [skot'tsese] *ag* Scottish ♦ *sm/f* Scot.
screan'zato, a [skrean'tsato] *ag* ill-mannered ♦ *sm/f* boor.
scredi'tare *vt* to discredit.
scre'mare *vt* to skim.
scre'mato, a *ag* skimmed; **parzialmente ~** semi-skimmed.
screpo'lare *vt,* **~rsi** *vr* to crack.
screpola'tura *sf* cracking *no pl*; crack.
screzi'ato, a [skret'tsjato] *ag* streaked.
'screzio ['skrɛttsjo] *sm* disagreement.
scribac'chino [skribak'kino] *sm* (*peg: impiegato*) penpusher; (*: scrittore*) hack.
scricchio'lare [skrikkjo'lare] *vi* to creak, squeak.
scricchio'lio [skrikkjo'lio] *sm* creaking.
'scricciolo ['skrittʃolo] *sm* wren.
'scrigno ['skriɲɲo] *sm* casket.
scrimina'tura *sf* parting.
'scrissi *etc vb vedi* **scrivere**.
'scritto, a *pp di* **scrivere** ♦ *ag* written ♦ *sm* writing; (*lettera*) letter, note ♦ *sf* inscription; **~i** *smpl* (*letterari etc*) work(s), writings; **per o in ~** in writing.
scrit'toio *sm* writing desk.
scrit'tore, 'trice *sm/f* writer.
scrit'tura *sf* writing; (*COMM*) entry; (*contratto*) contract; (*REL*): **la Sacra S~** the Scriptures *pl*; **~e** *sfpl* (*COMM*) accounts, books.
scrittu'rare *vt* (*TEAT, CINE*) to sign up, engage; (*COMM*) to enter.
scriva'nia *sf* desk.
scri'vano *sm* (*amanuense*) scribe; (*impiegato*) clerk.
scri'vente *sm/f* writer.
'scrivere *vt* to write; **come si scrive?** how is it spelt?, how do you write it?; **~ qc a qn** to write sth to sb; **~ qc a macchina** to type sth; **~ a penna/matita** to write in pen/pencil; **~ qc maiuscolo/minuscolo** to write sth in capital/small letters.
scroc'care *vt* (*fam*) to scrounge, cadge.
scroc'cone, a *sm/f* scrounger.
'scrofa *sf* (*ZOOL*) sow.
scrol'lare *vt* to shake; **~rsi** *vr* (*anche fig*) to give o.s. a shake; **~ le spalle/il capo** to shrug one's shoulders/shake one's head; **~rsi qc di dosso** (*ache fig*) to shake sth off.
scrol'lata *sf* shake; **~ di spalle** shrug (of one's shoulders).
scrosci'ante [skroʃ'ʃante] *ag* (*pioggia*) pouring; (*fig: applausi*) thunderous.
scrosci'are [skroʃ'ʃare] *vi* (*pioggia*) to pour down, pelt down; (*torrente, fig: applausi*) to

thunder, roar.

'scroscio ['skrɔʃʃo] *sm* pelting; thunder, roar; (*di applausi*) burst.

scros'tare *vt* (*intonaco*) to scrape off, strip; ~**rsi** *vr* to peel off, flake off.

'scrupolo *sm* scruple; (*meticolosità*) care, conscientiousness; **essere senza** ~**i** to be unscrupulous.

scrupo'loso, a *ag* scrupulous; conscientious.

scru'tare *vt* to scrutinize; (*intenzioni, causa*) to examine, scrutinize.

scruta'tore, trice *sm/f* (*POL*) scrutineer.

scruti'nare *vt* (*voti*) to count.

scru'tinio *sm* (*votazione*) ballot; (*insieme delle operazioni*) poll; (*INS*) (*meeting for*) assignment *of marks at end of a term or year.*

scu'cire [sku'tʃire] *vt* (*orlo etc*) to unpick, undo; ~**rsi** *vr* to come unstitched.

scude'ria *sf* stable.

scu'detto *sm* (*SPORT*) (championship) shield; (*distintivo*) badge.

scu'discio [sku'diʃʃo] *sm* (riding) crop, (riding) whip.

'scudo *sm* shield; **farsi** ~ **di** *o* **con qc** to shield o.s. with sth; ~ **aereo/missilistico** air/missile defence (*BRIT*) *o* defense (*US*); ~ **termico** heat shield.

sculacci'are [skulat'tʃare] *vt* to spank.

sculacci'one [skulat'tʃone] *sm* spanking.

scul'tore, 'trice *sm/f* sculptor.

scul'tura *sf* sculpture.

scu'ola *sf* school; ~ **elementare** *o* **primaria** primary (*BRIT*) *o* grade (*US*) school (*for children from 6 to 11 years of age*); ~ **guida** driving school; ~ **materna** *o* **dell'infanzia** nursery school (*for children aged 3 to 6*); ~ *first 3 years of secondary school, for children from 11 to 14 years of age;* ~ **secondaria di secondo grado** secondary school (*for children aged 14 to 18*) ~ **dell' obbligo** compulsory education; ~ **privata/pubblica** private/state school; ~**e serali** evening classes, night school *sg*; ~ **tecnica** technical college; *vedi nota nel riquadro.*

SCUOLA

Italian children first go to school at the age of three. They remain at the "scuola materna" until they are six, when they move on to the "scuola primaria" for another five years. After this come three years of "scuola secondaria di primo grado". Students who wish to continue their schooling attend "scuola secondaria di secondo grado", choosing between several types of institution which specialize in different subject areas.

---

scu'otere *vt* to shake; ~**rsi** *vr* to jump, be startled; (*fig: muoversi*) to rouse o.s., stir o.s.; (: *turbarsi*) to be shaken.

'scure *sf* axe, ax (*US*).

scu'rire *vt* to darken, make darker.

'scuro, a *ag* dark; (*fig: espressione*) grim ♦ *sm* darkness; dark colour (*BRIT*) *o* color (*US*); (*imposta*) (window) shutter; **verde/rosso** *etc* ~ dark green/red *etc*.

scur'rile *ag* scurrilous.

'scusa *sf* excuse; ~**e** *sfpl* apology *sg*, apologies; **chiedere** ~ **a qn (per)** to apologize to sb (for); **chiedo** ~ I'm sorry; (*disturbando etc*) excuse me; **vi prego di accettare le mie** ~**e** please accept my apologies.

scu'sare *vt* to excuse; ~**rsi** *vr*: ~**rsi (di)** to apologize (for); **(mi) scusi** I'm sorry; (*per richiamare l'attenzione*) excuse me.

S.C.V. *sigla* = Stato della Città del Vaticano.

sdebi'tarsi *vt*: ~**rsi (con qn di** *o* **per qc)** (*anche fig*) to repay (sb for sth).

sde'gnare [zdeɲ'ɲare] *vt* to scorn, despise; ~**rsi** *vr* (*adirarsi*) to get angry.

sde'gnato, a [zdeɲ'ɲato] *ag* indignant, angry.

'sdegno ['zdeɲɲo] *sm* scorn, disdain.

sdegnosa'mente [zdeɲɲosa'mente] *av* scornfully, disdainfully.

sde'gnoso, a [zdeɲ'ɲoso] *ag* scornful, disdainful.

sdilin'quirsi *vr* (*illanguidirsi*) to become sentimental.

sdoga'nare *vt* (*COMM*) to clear through customs.

sdolci'nato, a [zdoltʃi'nato] *ag* mawkish, oversentimental.

sdoppia'mento *sm* (*CHIM: di composto*) splitting; (*PSIC*) ~ **della personalità** split personality.

sdoppi'are *vt* (*dividere*) to divide *o* split in two.

sdrai'arsi *vr* to stretch out, lie down.

'sdraio *sm*: **sedia a** ~ deck chair.

sdrammatiz'zare [zdrammatid'dzare] *vt* to play down, minimize.

sdruccio'lare [zdruttʃo'lare] *vi* to slip, slide.

sdruccio'levole [zdruttʃo'levole] *ag* slippery.

sdru'cito, a [zdru'tʃito] *ag* (*strappato*) torn; (*logoro*) threadbare.

━━━━━━━━━━━━ *PAROLA CHIAVE*

se *pron vedi* **si**
♦ *cong* **1** (*condizionale, ipotetica*) if; ~ **nevica non vengo** I won't come if it

snows; ~ **fossi in te** if I were you; **sarei rimasto** ~ **me l'avessero chiesto** I would have stayed if they'd asked me; **non puoi fare altro** ~ **non telefonare** all you can do is phone; ~ **mai** if, if ever; **siamo noi** ~ **mai che le siamo grati** it is we who should be grateful to you; ~ **no** (*altrimenti*) or (else), otherwise; ~ **non** (*anzi*) if not; (*tranne*) except; ~ **non altro** if nothing else, at least; ~ **solo** *o* **solamente** if only **2** (*in frasi dubitative, interrogative indirette*) if, whether; **non so** ~ **scrivere o telefonare** I don't know whether *o* if I should write or phone.

S.E. *abbr* (= *sud-est*) SE; (= *Sua Eccellenza*) HE.

sé *pron* (*gen*) oneself; (*esso, essa, lui, lei, loro*) itself; himself; herself; themselves; ~ **stesso(a)** *pron* oneself; itself; himself; herself; ~ **stessi(e)** *pron pl* themselves; **di per** ~ **non è un problema** it's no problem in itself; **parlare tra** ~ **e** ~ to talk to oneself; **va da** ~ **che** ... it goes without saying that ..., it's obvious that ..., it stands to reason that ...; **è un caso a** ~ *o* **a** ~ **stante** it's a special case; **un uomo che s'è fatto da** ~ a self-made man.

S.E.A.T.O. *sigla f* (= *Southeast Asia Treaty Organization*) SEATO.

seb'bene *cong* although, though.

'sebo *sm* sebum.

sec. *abbr* (= *secolo*) c.

'SECAM *sigla m* (= *séquentiel couleur à mémoire*) SECAM.

'secca *sf vedi* **secco**.

secca'mente *av* (*rispondere, rifiutare*) sharply, curtly.

sec'care *vt* to dry; (*prosciugare*) to dry up; (*fig: importunare*) to annoy, bother ♦ *vi* to dry; to dry up; ~**rsi** *vr* to dry; to dry up; (*fig*) to grow annoyed; **si è seccato molto** he was very annoyed.

sec'cato, a *ag* (*fig: infastidito*) bothered, annoyed; (: *stufo*) fed up.

secca'tore, 'trice *sm/f* nuisance, bother.

secca'tura *sf* (*fig*) bother *no pl*, trouble *no pl*.

seccherò *etc* [sekke'rɔ] *vb vedi* **seccare**.

'secchia ['sekkja] *sf* bucket, pail.

secchi'ello [sek'kjɛllo] *sm* (*per bambini*) bucket, pail.

'secchio ['sekkjo] *sm* bucket, pail; ~ **della spazzatura** *o* **delle immondizie** dustbin

(*BRIT*), garbage can (*US*).

'secco, a, chi, che *ag* dry; (*fichi, pesce*) dried; (*foglie, ramo*) withered; (*magro: persona*) thin, skinny; (*fig: risposta, modo di fare*) curt, abrupt; (: *colpo*) clean, sharp ♦ *sm* (*siccità*) drought ♦ *sf* (*del mare*) shallows *pl*; **restarci** ~ (*fig: morire sul colpo*) to drop dead; **avere la gola** ~**a** to feel dry, be parched; **lavare a** ~ to dry-clean; **tirare a** ~ (*barca*) to beach.

secen'tesco, a, schi, sche [setʃen'tesko] *ag* = **seicentesco**.

se'cernere [se'tʃɛrnere] *vt* to secrete.

seco'lare *ag* age-old, centuries-old; (*laico, mondano*) secular.

'secolo *sm* century; (*epoca*) age.

se'conda *sf vedi* **secondo**; S~ **Repubblica** *vedi nota nel riquadro*.

SECONDA REPUBBLICA

Seconda Repubblica *is the term used, especially by the Italian media, to refer to the Government and the country in general since the 1994 elections. This is when the old party system collapsed, following the "Tangentopoli" scandals. New political parties were set up and the electoral system was reformed, a first-past-the-post element being introduced side by side with proportional representation.*

---

secondaria'mente *av* secondly.

secon'dario, a *ag* secondary; **scuola/istruzione** ~**a** secondary school/education.

secon'dino *sm* prison officer, warder (*BRIT*).

se'condo, a *ag* second ♦ *sm* second; (*di pranzo*) main course ♦ *sf* (*AUT*) second (gear); (*FERR*) second class ♦ *prep* according to; (*nel modo prescritto*) in accordance with; ~ **me** in my opinion, to my mind; ~ **la legge/ quanto si era deciso** in accordance with the law/the decision taken; **di** ~**a classe** second-class; **di** ~**a mano** second-hand; **viaggiare in** ~**a** to travel second-class; **comandante** *m* **in** ~**a** second-in-command; ~ **a di** *prep* according to; in accordance with.

'sedano *sm* celery.

se'dare *vt* (*dolore*) to soothe; (*rivolta*) to put down, suppress.

seda'tivo, a *ag, sm* sedative.

'sede *sf* (*luogo di residenza*) (place of) residence; (*di ditta: principale*) head office; (: *secondaria*) branch (office); (*di* *organizzazione*) headquarters *pl*; (*di governo, parlamento*) seat; (*REL*) see; **in** ~ **di** (*in occasione di*) during; **in altra** ~ on another occasion; **in** ~ **legislativa** in legislative sitting; **prendere** ~ to take up residence; ~ **centrale** head office; ~ **sociale** registered office.

seden'tario, a *ag* sedentary.

se'dere *vi* to sit, be seated; ~**rsi** *vr* to sit down ♦ *sm* (*deretano*) bottom; **posto a** ~ seat.

'sedia *sf* chair; ~ **elettrica** electric chair; ~ **a rotelle** wheelchair.

sedi'cenne [sedi'tʃɛnne] *ag, smf* sixteen-year-old.

sedi'cente [sedi'tʃɛnte] *ag* self-styled.

sedi'cesimo, a [sedi'tʃɛzimo] *num* sixteenth.

'sedici ['seditʃi] *num* sixteen.

se'dile *sm* seat; (*panchina*) bench.

sedimen'tare *vi* to leave a sediment.

sedi'mento *sm* sediment.

sedizi'one [sedit'tsjone] *sf* revolt, rebellion.

sedizi'oso, a [sedit'tsjoso] *ag* seditious.

se'dotto, a *pp di* **sedurre**.

sedu'cente [sedu'tʃɛnte] *ag* seductive; (*proposta*) very attractive.

se'durre *vt* to seduce.

se'duta *sf* session, sitting; (*riunione*) meeting; **essere in** ~ to be in session, be sitting; ~ **stante** (*fig*) immediately; ~ **spiritica** seance.

sedut'tore, 'trice *smf* seducer/seductress.

seduzi'one [sedut'tsjone] *sf* seduction; (*fascino*) charm, appeal.

SEeO *abbr* (= *salvo errori e omissioni*) E & OE.

'sega, ghe *sf* saw; ~ **circolare** circular saw; ~ **a mano** handsaw.

'segale *sf* rye.

se'gare *vt* to saw; (*recidere*) to saw off.

sega'tura *sf* (*residuo*) sawdust.

'seggio ['sɛddʒo] *sm* seat; ~ **elettorale** polling station.

'seggiola ['sɛddʒola] *sf* chair.

seggio'lino [sɛddʒo'lino] *sm* seat; (*per bambini*) child's chair; ~ **di sicurezza** (*AUT*) child safety seat.

seggio'lone [sɛddʒo'lone] *sm* (*per bambini*) highchair.

seggio'via [sɛddʒo'via] *sf* chairlift.

seghe'ria [sege'ria] *sf* sawmill.

segherò *etc* [sege'rɔ] *vb vedi* **segare**.

seghet'tato, a [seget'tato] *ag* serrated.

se'ghetto [se'getto] *sm* hacksaw.

seg'mento *sm* segment.

segna'lare [seɲɲa'lare] *vt* (*essere segno di*) to indicate, be a sign of; (*avvertire*) to signal; (*menzionare*) to indicate; (: *fatto, risultato, aumento*) to report; (: *errore, dettaglio*) to point out; (*AUT*) to signal, indicate; ~**rsi** *vr* (*distinguersi*) to distinguish o.s.; ~ **qn a qn** (*per lavoro etc*) to bring sb to sb's attention.

segnalazi'one [seɲɲalat'tsjone] *sf* (*azione*) signalling; (*segnale*) signal; (*annuncio*) report; (*raccomandazione*) recommendation.

se'gnale [seɲ'ɲale] *sm* signal; (*cartello*): ~ **stradale** road sign; ~ **acustico** acoustic o sound signal; (*di segreteria telefonica*) tone; ~ **d'allarme** alarm; (*FERR*) communication cord; ~ **di linea libera** (*TEL*) dialling (*BRIT*) o dial (*US*) tone; ~ **luminoso** light signal; ~ **di occupato** (*TEL*) engaged tone (*BRIT*), busy signal (*US*); ~ **orario** (*RADIO*) time signal.

segna'letica [seɲɲa'lɛtika] *sf* signalling, signposting; ~ **stradale** road signs *pl*.

segna'libro [seɲɲa'libro] *sm* (*anche INFORM*) bookmark.

segna'punti [seɲɲa'punti] *smf inv* scorer, scorekeeper.

se'gnare [seɲ'ɲare] *vt* to mark, (*prendere nota*) to note; (*indicare*) to indicate, mark; (*SPORT: goal*) to score; ~**rsi** *vr* (*REL*) to make the sign of the cross, cross o.s.

'segno ['seɲɲo] *sm* sign; (*impronta, contrassegno*) mark; (*bersaglio*) target; **fare** ~ **di sì/no** to nod (one's head)/shake one's head; **fare** ~ **a qn di fermarsi** to motion (to) sb to stop; **cogliere** o **colpire nel** ~ (*fig*) to hit the mark; **in** o **come** ~ **d'amicizia** as a mark o token of friendship; "~**i particolari**" (*su documento etc*) "distinguishing marks".

segre'gare *vt* to segregate, isolate.

segregazi'one [segregat'tsjone] *sf* segregation.

se'greta *sf vedi* **segreto**.

segre'tario, a *smf* secretary; ~ **comunale** town clerk; ~ **del partito** party leader; **S**~ **di Stato** Secretary of State.

segrete'ria *sf* (*di ditta, scuola*) (secretary's) office; (*d'organizzazione internazionale*) secretariat; (*POL etc: carica*) office of Secretary; ~ **telefonica** answering service.

segre'tezza [segre'tettsa] *sf* secrecy; **notizie della massima** ~ confidential information; **in tutta** ~ in secret; (*confidenzialmente*) in confidence.

se'greto, a *ag* secret ♦ *sm* secret ♦ *sf*

dungeon; **in ~** in secret, secretly; **il ~ professionale** professional secrecy; **un ~ professionale** a professional secret.

segu'ace [se'gwatʃe] *sm/f* follower, disciple.

segu'ente *ag* following, next; **nel modo ~** as follows, in the following way.

se'gugio [se'gudʒo] *sm* hound, hunting dog; (*fig*) private eye, sleuth.

segu'ire *vt* to follow; (*frequentare*: *corso*) to attend ♦ *vi* to follow; (*continuare*: *testo*) to continue; **~ i consigli di qn** to follow *o* to take sb's advice; **~ gli avvenimenti di attualità** to follow *o* keep up with current events; **come segue** as follows; **"segue"** "to be continued".

segui'tare *vt* to continue, carry on with ♦ *vi* to continue, carry on.

'seguito *sm* (*scorta*) suite, retinue; (*discepoli*) followers *pl*; (*serie*) sequence, series *sg*; (*continuazione*) continuation; (*conseguenza*) result; **di ~** at a stretch, on end; **in ~** later on; **in ~ a, a ~ di** following; (*a causa di*) as a result of, owing to; **essere al ~ di qn** to be among sb's suite, be one of sb's retinue; **non aver ~** (*conseguenze*) to have no repercussions; **facciamo ~ alla lettera del** ... further to *o* in answer to your letter of ....

'sei *vb vedi* **essere** ♦ *num* six.

Sei'celle [sei'tʃɛlle] *sfpl*: **le ~** the Seychelles.

seicen'tesco, a, schi, sche [seitʃen'tesko] *ag* seventeenth-century.

sei'cento [sei'tʃɛnto] *num* six hundred ♦ *sm*: **il S~** the seventeenth century.

sei'mila *num* six thousand.

'selce ['seltʃe] *sf* flint, flintstone.

selci'ato [sel'tʃato] *sm* cobbled surface.

selet'tivo, a *ag* selective.

selet'tore *sm* (*TECN*) selector.

selezio'nare [selettsjo'nare] *vt* to select.

selezi'one [selet'tsjone] *sf* selection; **fare una ~** to make a selection *o* choice.

'sella *sf* saddle.

sel'lare *vt* to saddle.

sel'lino *sm* saddle.

seltz *sm inv* soda (water).

'selva *sf* (*bosco*) wood; (*foresta*) forest.

selvag'gina [selvad'dʒina] *sf* (*animali*) game.

sel'vaggio, a, gi, ge [sel'vaddʒo] *ag* wild; (*tribù*) savage, uncivilized; (*fig*: *brutale*) savage, brutal; (: *incontrollato*: *fenomeno, aumento etc*) uncontrolled ♦ *sm/f* savage; **inflazione ~a** runaway inflation.

sel'vatico, a, ci, che *ag* wild.

S.Em. *abbr* (= *Sua Eminenza*) HE.

se'maforo *sm* (*AUT*) traffic lights *pl*.

se'mantico, a *ag* semantic ♦ *sf* semantics *sg*.

sembi'anza [sem'bjantsa] *sf* (*poetico*: *aspetto*) appearance; **~e** *sfpl* (*lineamenti*) features; (*fig*: *falsa apparenza*) semblance *sg*.

sem'brare *vi* to seem ♦ *vb impers*: **sembra che** it seems that; **mi sembra che** it seems to me that; (*penso che*) I think (that); **~ di essere** to seem to be; **non mi sembra vero!** I can't believe it!

'seme *sm* seed; (*sperma*) semen; (*CARTE*) suit.

se'mente *sf* seed.

semes'trale *ag* (*che dura 6 mesi*) six-month *cpd*; (*che avviene ogni 6 mesi*) six-monthly.

se'mestre *sm* half-year, six-month period.

'semi ... *prefisso* semi ....

semi'cerchio [semi'tʃerkjo] *sm* semicircle.

semicondut'tore *sm* semiconductor.

semidetenzi'one [semideten'tsjone] *sf* custodial sentence whereby individual must spend a minimum of 10 hours per day in prison.

semifi'nale *sf* semifinal.

semi'freddo, a *ag* (*CUC*) chilled ♦ *sm* ice-cream cake.

semilibertà *sf* custodial sentence which allows prisoner to study or work outside prison for part of the day.

'semina *sf* (*AGR*) sowing.

semi'nare *vt* to sow.

semi'nario *sm* seminar; (*REL*) seminary.

semi'nato *sm*: **uscire dal ~** (*fig*) to wander off the point.

seminter'rato *sm* basement; (*appartamento*) basement flat (*BRIT*) *o* apartment (*US*).

semi'ologo, a, gi, ghe *sm/f* semiologist.

semi'otica *sf* semiotics *sg*.

se'mitico, a, ci, che *ag* semitic.

semivu'oto, a *ag* half-empty.

sem'mai = **se mai**.

'semola *sf* bran; **~ di grano duro** durum wheat.

semo'lato *ag*: **zucchero ~** caster sugar.

semo'lino *sm* semolina.

'semplice ['semplitʃe] *ag* simple; (*di un solo elemento*) single; **è una ~ formalità** it's a mere formality.

semplice'mente [semplitʃe'mente] *av* simply.

sempli'cistico, a, ci, che [sempli'tʃistiko] *ag* simplistic.

semplicità [semplitʃi'ta] *sf* simplicity.

semplifi'care *vt* to simplify.
semplificazi'one [semplifikat'tsjone] *sf* simplification; **fare una ~ di** to simplify.
'sempre *av* always; (*ancora*) still; **posso ~ tentare** I can always *o* still try; **da ~** always; **per ~** forever; **una volta per ~** once and for all; **~ che** *cong* as long as, provided (that); **~ più** more and more; **~ meno** less and less; **va ~ meglio** things are getting better and better; **è ~ più giovane** she gets younger and younger; **è ~ meglio che niente** it's better than nothing; **è (pur) ~ tuo fratello** he is still your brother (however); **c'è ~ la possibilità che ...** there's still a chance that ..., there's always the possibility that ....
sempre'verde *ag, sm o f* (*BOT*) evergreen.
Sen. *abbr* (= *senatore*) Sen.
'senape *sf* (*CUC*) mustard.
se'nato *sm* senate; **il S~** *vedi nota nel riquadro*.

SENATO

The **Senato** *is the upper house of the Italian Parliament, with similar functions to the "Camera dei deputati". Candidates must be at least 40 years of age and electors must be 25 or over. Elections are held every five years. Former heads of state become senators for life, as do five distinguished members of the public who are chosen by the head of state for their scientific, social, artistic or literary achievements. The Chamber is presided over by the "Presidente del Senato", who is elected by the senators.*

sena'tore, 'trice *sm/f* senator.
'Senegal *sm*: **il ~** Senegal.
senega'lese *ag, sm/f* Senegalese *inv*.
se'nese *ag* of (*o* from) Siena.
se'nile *ag* senile.
'Senna *sf*: **la ~** the Seine.
'senno *sm* judgment, (common) sense; **col ~ di poi** with hindsight.
sennò *av* = **se no**.
'seno *sm* (*ANAT*: *petto, mammella*) breast; (: *grembo, fig*) womb; (: *cavità*) sinus; (*GEO*) inlet, creek; (*MAT*) sine; **in ~ al partito** within the party.
sen'sale *sm* (*COMM*) agent.
sensa'tezza [sensa'tettsa] *sf* good sense, good judgment.
sen'sato, a *ag* sensible.
sensazio'nale [sensattsjo'nale] *ag* sensational.
sensazi'one [sensat'tsjone] *sf* feeling,

sensation; **fare ~** to cause a sensation, create a stir; **avere la ~ che** to have a feeling that.
sen'sibile *ag* sensitive; (*ai sensi*) perceptible; (*rilevante, notevole*) appreciable, noticeable; **~ a** sensitive to.
sensibilità *sf* sensitivity.
sensibiliz'zare [sensibilid'dzare] *vt* (*fig*) to make aware, awaken.
'senso *sm* (*FISIOL, istinto*) sense; (*impressione, sensazione*) feeling, sensation; (*significato*) meaning, sense; (*direzione*) direction; **~i** *smpl* (*coscienza*) consciousness *sg*; (*sensualità*) senses; **perdere/riprendere i ~i** to lose/regain consciousness; **avere ~ pratico** to be practical; **avere un sesto ~** to have a sixth sense; **fare ~ a** (*ripugnare*) to disgust, repel; **ciò non ha ~** that doesn't make sense; **senza** *o* **privo di ~** meaningless; **nel ~ che** in the sense that; **nel vero ~ della parola** in the true sense of the word; **nel ~ della lunghezza** lengthwise, lengthways; **nel ~ della larghezza** widthwise; **ho dato disposizioni in quel ~** I've given instructions to that end *o* effect; **~ comune** common sense; **~ del dovere** sense of duty; **in ~ opposto** in the opposite direction; **in ~ orario/antiorario** clockwise/anticlockwise; **~ dell'umorismo** sense of humour; **a ~ unico** one-way.
sensu'ale *ag* sensual; sensuous.
sensualità *sf* sensuality; sensuousness.
sen'tenza [sen'tentsa] *sf* (*DIR*) sentence; (*massima*) maxim.
sentenzi'are [senten'tsjare] *vi* (*DIR*) to pass judgment.
senti'ero *sm* path.
sentimen'tale *ag* sentimental; (*vita, avventura*) love *cpd*.
senti'mento *sm* feeling.
senti'nella *sf* sentry.
sen'tire *vt* (*percepire al tatto, fig*) to feel; (*udire*) to hear; (*ascoltare*) to listen to; (*odore*) to smell; (*avvertire con il gusto, assaggiare*) to taste ♦ *vi*: **~ di** (*avere sapore*) to taste of; (*avere odore*) to smell of; **~rsi** *vr* (*uso reciproco*) to be in touch; **~rsi bene/male** to feel well/unwell *o* ill; **~rsi di fare qc** (*essere disposto*) to feel like doing sth; **~ la mancanza di qn** to miss sb; **ho sentito dire che ...** I have heard that ...; **a ~ lui ...** to hear him talk ...; **fatti ~** keep in touch; **intendo ~ il mio legale** I'm going to consult my lawyer.
sentita'mente *av* sincerely; **ringraziare ~** to thank sincerely.

sen'tito, a *ag* (*sincero*) sincere, warm; **per ~ dire** by hearsay.

sen'tore *sm* rumour (*BRIT*), rumor (*US*), talk; **aver ~ di qc** to hear about sth.

'senza ['sɛntsa] *prep, cong* without; **~ dir nulla** without saying a word; **~ dire che …** not to mention the fact that …; **~ contare che …** without considering that …; **~; fare ~ qc** to do without sth; **~ di me** without me; **~ che io lo sapessi** without me *o* my knowing; **~ amici** friendless; **senz'altro** of course, certainly; **~ dubbio** no doubt; **~ scrupoli** unscrupulous; **i ~ lavoro** the jobless, the unemployed.

senza'tetto [sentsa'tetto] *sm/f inv* homeless person; **i ~** the homeless.

sepa'rare *vt* to separate; (*dividere*) to divide; (*tenere distinto*) to distinguish; **~rsi** *vr* (*coniugi*) to separate, part; (*amici*) to part; **~rsi da** (*coniuge*) to separate *o* part from; (*amico, socio*) to part company with; (*oggetto*) to part with.

separata'mente *av* separately.

sepa'rato, a *ag* (*letti, conto etc*) separate; (*coniugi*) separated.

separazi'one [separat'tsjone] *sf* separation; **~ dei beni** division of property.

séparé [sepa're] *sm inv* screen.

se'polcro *sm* sepulchre (*BRIT*), sepulcher (*US*).

se'polto, a *pp di* **seppellire**.

sepol'tura *sf* burial; **dare ~ a qn** to bury sb.

seppel'lire *vt* to bury.

'seppi *etc vb vedi* **sapere**.

'seppia *sf* cuttlefish ♦ *ag inv* sepia.

sep'pure *cong* even if.

se'quela *sf* (*di avvenimenti*) series, sequence; (*di offese, ingiurie*) string.

se'quenza [se'kwentsa] *sf* sequence.

sequenzi'ale [sekwen'tsjale] *ag* sequential.

seques'trare *vt* (*DIR*) to impound; (*rapire*) to kidnap; (*costringere in un luogo*) to keep, confine.

se'questro *sm* (*DIR*) impoundment; **~ di persona** kidnapping.

se'quoia *sf* sequoia.

'sera *sf* evening; **di ~** in the evening; **domani ~** tomorrow evening, tomorrow night; **questa ~** this evening, tonight.

se'rale *ag* evening *cpd*; **scuola ~** evening classes *pl*, night school.

se'rata *sf* evening; (*ricevimento*) party.

ser'bare *vt* to keep; (*mettere da parte*) to put aside; **~ rancore/odio verso qn** to bear sb a grudge/hate sb.

serba'toio *sm* tank; (*cisterna*) cistern.

'serbo *ag* Serbian ♦ *sm/f* Serbian, Serb ♦ *sm*

(*LING*) Serbian; (*il serbare*): **mettere/tenere *o* avere in ~ qc** to put/keep sth aside.

serbocro'ato, a *ag, sm* Serbo-Croat.

serena'mente *av* serenely, calmly.

sere'nata *sf* (*MUS*) serenade.

serenità *sf* serenity.

se'reno, a *ag* (*tempo, cielo*) clear; (*fig*) serene, calm ♦ *sm* (*tempo*) good weather; **un fulmine a ciel ~** (*fig*) a bolt from the blue.

serg. *abbr* (= *sergente*) Sgt.

ser'gente [ser'dʒɛnte] *sm* (*MIL*) sergeant.

seri'ale *ag* (*INFORM*) serial.

seria'mente *av* (*con serietà, in modo grave*) seriously; **lavorare ~** to take one's job seriously.

'serie *sf inv* (*successione*) series *inv*; (*gruppo, collezione*: *di chiavi etc*) set; (*SPORT*) division; league; (*COMM*): **modello di ~/ fuori ~** standard/custom-built model; **in ~** in quick succession; (*COMM*) mass *cpd*; **tutta una ~ di problemi** a whole string *o* series of problems.

serietà *sf* seriousness; reliability.

'serio, a *ag* serious; (*impiegato*) responsible, reliable; (*ditta, cliente*) reliable, dependable; **sul ~** (*davvero*) really, truly; (*seriamente*) seriously, in earnest; **dico sul ~** I'm serious; **faccio sul ~** I mean it; **prendere qc/qn sul ~** to take sth/sb seriously.

seri'oso, a *ag* (*persona, modi*): **un po' ~** a bit too serious.

ser'mone *sm* sermon.

'serpe *sf* snake; (*fig peg*) viper.

serpeggi'are [serped'dʒare] *vi* to wind; (*fig*) to spread.

ser'pente *sm* snake; **~ a sonagli** rattlesnake.

'serra *sf* greenhouse; hothouse; (*GEO*) sierra.

serra'manico *sm*: **coltello a ~** jack-knife.

ser'randa *sf* roller shutter.

ser'rare *vt* to close, shut; (*a chiave*) to lock; (*stringere*) to tighten; (*premere*: *nemico*) to close in on; **~ i pugni/i denti** to clench one's fists/teeth; **~ le file** to close ranks.

ser'rata *sf* (*INDUSTRIA*) lockout.

ser'rato, a *ag* (*veloce*): **a ritmo ~** quickly, fast.

serra'tura *sf* lock.

'serva *sf vedi* **servo**.

'server ['server] *sm inv* (*INFORM*) server.

ser'vigio [ser'vidʒo] *sm* favour (*BRIT*), favor (*US*), service.

ser'vire *vt* to serve; (*clienti: al ristorante*) to wait on; (: *al negozio*) to serve, attend to; (*fig: giovare*) to aid, help; (*CARTE*) to deal

◆ *vi* (*TENNIS*) to serve; (*essere utile*): ~ **a qn** to be of use to sb; ~ **a qc/a fare** (*utensile etc*) to be used for sth/for doing; ~ **(a qn)** **da** to serve as (for sb); ~**rsi** *vr* (*usare*): ~**rsi di** to use; (*prendere: cibo*): ~**rsi (di)** to help o.s. (to); (*essere cliente abituale*): ~**rsi da** to be a regular customer at, go to; **non mi serve più** I don't need it any more; **non serve che lei vada** you don't need to go.

servitù *sf* servitude; slavery; (*personale di servizio*) servants *pl*, domestic staff.

servizi'evole [servit'tsjevole] *ag* obliging, willing to help.

ser'vizio [ser'vittsjo] *sm* service; (*al ristorante: sul conto*) service (charge); (*STAMPA, TV, RADIO*) report; (*da tè, caffè etc*) set, service; ~**i** *smpl* (*di casa*) kitchen and bathroom; (*ECON*) services; **essere di** ~ to be on duty; **fuori** ~ (*telefono etc*) out of order; ~ **compreso/escluso** service included/not included; **entrata di** ~ service *o* tradesman's (*BRIT*) entrance; **casa con doppi** ~**i** house with two bathrooms; ~ **assistenza clienti** after-sales service; ~ **civile** ≈ community service; ~ **in diretta** (*TV, RADIO*) live coverage; ~ **fotografico** (*STAMPA*) photo feature; ~ **militare** military service; ~ **d'ordine** (*POLIZIA*) police patrol; (*di manifestanti*) team of stewards (*responsible for crowd control*); ~**i segreti** secret service *sg*; ~**i di sicurezza** security forces.

'servo, a *sm/f* servant.

servo'freno *sm* (*AUT*) servo brake.

servos'terzo [servos'tɛrtso] *sm* (*AUT*) power steering.

'sesamo *sm* (*BOT*) sesame.

ses'santa *num* sixty.

sessan'tenne *ag, sm/f* sixty-year-old.

sessan'tesimo, a *num* sixtieth.

sessan'tina *sf*: **una** ~ **(di)** about sixty.

sessantot'tino, a *sm/f a person who took part in the events of 1968*.

sessan'totto *sm vedi nota nel riquadro*.

SESSANTOTTO

Sessantotto *refers to the year 1968, the year of the student protests. Originating in France, unrest soon spread to other industrialized countries including Italy. What began as a purely student concern gradually came to include other parts of society and led to major political and social change. Among the changes that resulted from the protests were reform of schools and universities and a referendum on divorce.*

---

sessi'one *sf* session.

'sesso *sm* sex; **il** ~ **debole/forte** the weaker/stronger sex.

sessu'ale *ag* sexual, sex *cpd*.

sessualità *sf* sexuality.

sessu'ologo, a, gi, ghe *sm/f* sexologist, sex specialist.

ses'tante *sm* sextant.

'sesto, a *num* sixth ◆ *sm*: **rimettere in** ~ (*aggiustare*) to put back in order; (*fig: persona*) to put back on his (*o* her) feet; **rimettersi in** ~ (*riprendersi*) to recover, get well; (*riassettarsi*) to tidy o.s. up.

'seta *sf* silk.

setacci'are [setat't fare] *vt* (*farina etc*) to sift, sieve; (*fig: zona*) to search, comb.

se'taccio [se'tatt fo] *sm* sieve; **passare al** ~ (*fig*) to search, comb.

'sete *sf* thirst; **avere** ~ to be thirsty; ~ **di potere** thirst for power.

seti'ficio [seti'fit fo] *sm* silk factory.

'setola *sf* bristle.

sett. *abbr* (= *settembre*) Sept.

'setta *sf* sect.

set'tanta *num* seventy.

settan'tenne *ag, sm/f* seventy-year-old.

settan'tesimo, a *num* seventieth.

settan'tina *sf*: **una** ~ **(di)** about seventy.

'sette *num* seven.

settecen'tesco, a, schi, sche [settet fen'tesko] *ag* eighteenth-century.

sette'cento [sette't fɛnto] *num* seven hundred ◆ *sm*: **il S**~ the eighteenth century.

set'tembre *sm* September; *per fraseologia vedi* **luglio**.

sette'mila *num* seven thousand.

settentrio'nale *ag* northern ◆ *sm/f* northerner.

settentri'one *sm* north.

'settico, a, ci, che *ag* (*MED*) septic.

setti'mana *sf* week; **la** ~ **scorsa/prossima** last/next week; **a metà** ~ in the middle of the week; ~ **bianca** winter-sports holiday.

settima'nale *ag, sm* weekly.

'settimo, a *num* seventh.

set'tore *sm* sector; ~ **privato/pubblico** private/public sector; ~ **terziario** service industries *pl*.

Se'ul *sf* Seoul.

severità *sf* severity.

se'vero, a *ag* severe.

sevizi'are [sevit'tsjare] *vt* to torture.

se'vizie [se'vittsje] *sfpl* torture *sg*.

'sexy ['seksi] *ag inv* sexy.

sez. *abbr* = **sezione**.

sezio'nare [settsjo'nare] vt to divide into sections; (MED) to dissect.

sezi'one [set'tsjone] sf section; (MED) dissection.

sfaccen'dato, a [sfattʃen'dato] ag idle.

sfaccetta'tura [sfattʃetta'tura] sf (azione) faceting; (parte sfaccettata, fig) facet.

sfacchi'nare [sfakki'nare] vi (fam) to toil, drudge.

sfacchi'nata [sfakki'nata] sf (fam) chore, drudgery no pl.

sfaccia'taggine [sfattʃa'taddʒine] sf insolence, cheek.

sfacci'ato, a [sfat'tʃato] ag (maleducato) cheeky, impudent; (vistoso) gaudy.

sfa'celo [sfa'tʃɛlo] sm (fig) ruin, collapse.

sfal'darsi vr to flake (off).

sfal'sare vt to offset.

sfa'mare vt (nutrire) to feed; (soddisfare la fame): ~ qn to satisfy sb's hunger; ~rsi vr to satisfy one's hunger, fill o.s. up.

sfarfal'lio sm (CINE, TV) flickering.

'sfarzo ['sfartso] sm pomp, splendour (BRIT), splendor (US).

sfar'zoso, a [sfar'tsoso] ag splendid, magnificent.

sfasa'mento sm (ELETTR) phase displacement; (fig) confusion, bewilderment.

sfa'sato, a ag (ELETTR, motore) out of phase; (fig: persona) confused, bewildered.

sfasci'are [sfaʃ'ʃare] vt (ferita) to unbandage; (distruggere: porta) to smash, shatter; ~rsi vr (rompersi) to smash, shatter.

sfa'tare vt (leggenda) to explode.

sfati'cato, a sm/f idler, loafer.

'sfatto, a ag (letto) unmade; (orlo etc) undone; (gelato, neve) melted; (frutta) overripe; (riso, pasta etc) overdone, overcooked; (fam: persona, corpo) flabby.

sfavil'lare vi to spark, send out sparks; (risplendere) to sparkle.

sfa'vore sm disfavour (BRIT), disfavor (US), disapproval.

sfavo'revole ag unfavourable (BRIT), unfavorable (US).

sfega'tato, a ag fanatical.

'sfera sf sphere.

'sferico, a, ci, che ag spherical.

sfer'rare vt (fig: colpo) to land, deal; (: attacco) to launch.

sfer'zante [sfer'tsante] ag (critiche, parole) stinging.

sfer'zare [sfer'tsare] vt to whip; (fig) to lash out at.

sfian'care vt to wear out, exhaust; ~rsi vr to exhaust o.s., wear o.s. out.

sfia'tare vi to allow air (o gas etc) to escape.

sfiata'toio sm blowhole; (TECN) vent.

sfi'brante ag exhausting, energy-sapping.

sfi'brare vt (indebolire) to exhaust, enervate.

sfi'brato, a ag exhausted, worn out.

'sfida sf challenge.

sfi'dante ag challenging ♦ sm/f challenger.

sfi'dare vt to challenge; (fig) to defy, brave; ~ qn a fare qc to challenge sb to do sth; ~ un pericolo to brave a danger; **sfido che** ... I dare say (that) ....

sfi'ducia [sfi'dutʃa] sf distrust, mistrust; **avere** ~ **in qn/qc** to distrust sb/sth.

sfiduci'ato, a [sfidu'tʃato] ag lacking confidence.

sfi'gato, a (fam) ag: **essere** ~ (sfortunato) to be unlucky ♦ sm/f (fallito, sfortunato) loser; (fuori moda) dork.

sfigu'rare vt (persona) to disfigure; (quadro, statua) to deface ♦ vi (far cattiva figura) to make a bad impression.

sfilacci'are [sfilat'tʃare] vt, vi, ~rsi vr to fray.

sfi'lare vt (ago) to unthread; (abito, scarpe) to slip off ♦ vi (truppe) to march past, parade; (manifestanti) to march; ~rsi vr (perle etc) to come unstrung; (orlo, tessuto) to fray; (calza) to run, ladder.

sfi'lata sf (MIL) parade; (di manifestanti) march; ~ **di moda** fashion show.

'sfilza ['sfiltsa] sf (di case) row; (di errori) series inv.

'sfinge ['sfindʒe] sf sphinx.

sfini'mento sm exhaustion.

sfi'nito, a ag exhausted.

sfio'rare vt to brush (against); (argomento) to touch upon; ~ **la velocità di 150 km/h** to touch 150 km/h.

sfio'rire vi to wither, fade.

'sfitto, a ag vacant, empty.

sfo'cato, a ag (FOT) out of focus.

sfoci'are [sfo'tʃare] vi: ~ **in** to flow into; (fig: malcontento) to develop into.

sfode'rato, a ag (vestito) unlined.

sfo'gare vt to vent, pour out; ~rsi vr (sfogare la propria rabbia) to give vent to one's anger; (confidarsi): ~rsi **(con)** to pour out one's feelings (to); **non sfogarti su di me!** don't take your bad temper out on me!

sfoggi'are [sfod'dʒare] vt, vi to show off.

'sfoggio ['sfɔddʒo] sm show, display; **fare** ~ **di** to show off, display.

sfoggherò etc [sfoge'rɔ] vb vedi **sfogare**.

'sfoglia ['sfɔʎʎa] sf sheet of pasta dough;

pasta ~ (*CUC*) puff pastry.

sfogli'are [sfoʎ'ʎare] *vt* (*libro*) to leaf through.

'sfogo, ghi *sm* outlet; (*eruzione cutanea*) rash; (*fig*) outburst; **dare** ~ **a** (*fig*) to give vent to.

sfolgo'rante *ag* (*luce*) blazing; (*fig*: *vittoria*) brilliant.

sfolgo'rare *vi* to blaze.

sfolla'gente [sfolla'dʒɛnte] *sm inv* truncheon (*BRIT*), billy (*US*).

sfol'lare *vt* to empty, clear ♦ *vi* to disperse; ~ **da** (*città*) to evacuate.

sfol'lato, a *ag* evacuated ♦ *sm/f* evacuee.

sfol'tire *vt*, ~**rsi** *vr* to thin (out).

sfon'dare *vt* (*porta*) to break down; (*scarpe*) to wear a hole in; (*cesto, scatola*) to burst, knock the bottom out of; (*MIL*) to break through ♦ *vi* (*riuscire*) to make a name for o.s.

sfon'dato, a *ag* (*scarpe*) worn out; (*scatola*) burst; (*sedia*) broken, damaged; **essere ricco** ~ to be rolling in it.

'sfondo *sm* background.

sfo'rare *vi* to overrun.

sfor'mare *vt* to put out of shape, knock out of shape; ~**rsi** *vr* to lose shape, get out of shape.

sfor'mato, a *ag* (*che ha perso forma*) shapeless ♦ *sm* (*CUC*) type of soufflé.

sfor'nare *vt* (*pane*) to take out of the oven; (*fig*) to churn out.

sfor'nito, a *ag*: ~ **di** lacking in, without; (*negozio*) out of.

sfor'tuna *sf* misfortune, ill luck *no pl*; **avere** ~ to be unlucky; **che** ~! how unfortunate!

sfortu'nato, a *ag* unlucky; (*impresa, film*) unsuccessful.

sfor'zare [sfor'tsare] *vt* to force; (*voce, occhi*) to strain; ~**rsi** *vr*: ~**rsi di** *o* **a** *o* **per fare** to try hard to do.

'sforzo ['sfɔrtso] *sm* effort; (*tensione eccessiva, TECN*) strain; **fare uno** ~ to make an effort; **essere sotto** ~ (*motore, macchina, fig*: *persona*) to be under stress.

'sfottere *vt* (*fam*) to tease.

sfracel'lare [sfratʃel'lare] *vt*, ~**rsi** *vr* to smash.

sfrat'tare *vt* to evict.

'sfratto *sm* eviction; **dare lo** ~ **a qn** to give sb notice to quit.

sfrecci'are [sfret'tʃare] *vi* to shoot *o* flash past.

sfre'gare *vt* (*strofinare*) to rub; (*graffiare*) to scratch; ~**rsi le mani** to rub one's hands; ~ **un fiammifero** to strike a match.

sfregi'are [sfre'dʒare] *vt* to slash, gash; (*persona*) to disfigure; (*quadro*) to deface.

'sfregio ['sfredʒo] *sm* gash; scar; (*fig*) insult.

sfre'nato, a *ag* (*fig*) unrestrained, unbridled.

sfron'dare *vt* (*albero*) to prune, thin out; (*fig*: *discorso, scritto*) to prune (down).

sfronta'tezza [sfronta'tettsa] *sf* impudence, cheek.

sfron'tato, a *ag* impudent, cheeky.

sfrutta'mento *sm* exploitation.

sfrut'tare *vt* (*terreno*) to overwork, exhaust; (*miniera*) to exploit, work; (*fig*: *operai, occasione, potere*) to exploit.

sfrutta'tore, 'trice *sm/f* exploiter.

sfug'gente [sfud'dʒɛnte] *ag* (*fig*: *sguardo*) elusive; (*mento*) receding.

sfug'gire [sfud'dʒire] *vi* to escape; ~ **a** (*custode*) to escape (from); (*morte*) to escape; ~ **a qn** (*dettaglio, nome*) to escape sb; ~ **di mano a qn** to slip out of sb's hand (*o* hands); **lasciarsi** ~ **un'occasione** to let an opportunity go by; ~ **al controllo** (*macchina*) to go out of control; (*situazione*) to be no longer under control.

sfug'gita [sfud'dʒita] *sf*: **di** ~ (*rapidamente, in fretta*) in passing.

sfu'mare *vt* (*colori, contorni*) to soften, shade off ♦ *vi* to shade (off), fade; (*fig*: *svanire*) to vanish, disappear; (: *speranze*) to come to nothing.

sfuma'tura *sf* shading off *no pl*; (*tonalità*) shade, tone; (*fig*) touch, hint.

sfuo'cato, a *ag* = **sfocato**.

sfuri'ata *sf* (*scatto di collera*) fit of anger; (*rimprovero*) sharp rebuke.

'sfuso, a *ag* (*caramelle etc*) loose, unpacked; (*vino*) unbottled; (*birra*) draught (*BRIT*), draft (*US*).

sg. *abbr* = **seguente**.

sga'bello *sm* stool.

sgabuz'zino [zgabud'dzino] *sm* lumber room.

sgambet'tare *vi* to kick one's legs about.

sgam'betto *sm*: **far lo** ~ **a qn** to trip sb up; (*fig*) to oust sb.

sganasci'arsi [zganaʃ'ʃarsi] *vr*: ~ **dalle risa** to roar with laughter.

sganci'are [zgan'tʃare] *vt* to unhook; (*chiusura*) to unfasten, undo; (*FERR*) to uncouple; (*bombe: da aereo*) to release, drop; (*fig*: *fam: soldi*) to fork out; ~**rsi** *vr* to come unhooked; to come unfastened, come undone; to uncouple; (*fig*): ~**rsi (da)** to get away (from).

sganghe'rato, a *ag* (*porta*) off its hinges; (*auto*) ramshackle; (*riso*) wild, boisterous.

sgar'bato, a *ag* rude, impolite.

'sgarbo *sm*: **fare uno** ~ **a qn** to be rude to sb.

sgargi'ante [zgar'dʒante] *ag* gaudy, showy.

sgar'rare *vi* (*persona*) to step out of line; (*orologio*: *essere avanti*) to gain; (: *essere indietro*) to lose.

'sgarro *sm* inaccuracy.

sgattaio'lare *vi* to sneak away *o* off.

sge'lare [zdʒe'lare] *vi*, *vt* to thaw.

'sghembo, a ['zgembo] *ag* (*obliquo*) slanting; (*storto*) crooked.

sghignaz'zare [zgiɲɲat'tsare] *vi* to laugh scornfully.

sghignaz'zata [zgiɲɲat'tsata] *sf* scornful laugh.

sgob'bare *vi* (*fam*: *scolaro*) to swot; (: *operaio*) to slog.

sgoccio'lare [zgottʃo'lare] *vt* (*vuotare*) to drain (to the last drop) ♦ *vi* (*acqua*) to drip; (*recipiente*) to drain.

'sgoccioli ['zgottʃoli] *smpl*: **essere agli** ~ (*lavoro, provviste etc*) to be nearly finished; (*periodo*) to be nearly over; **siamo agli** ~ we've nearly finished, the end is in sight.

sgo'larsi *vr* to talk (*o* shout *o* sing) o.s. hoarse.

sgomb(e)'rare *vt* to clear; (*andarsene da*: *stanza*) to vacate; (*evacuare*) to evacuate.

'sgombero *sm vedi* **sgombro**.

'sgombro, a *ag*: ~ **(di)** clear (of), free (from) ♦ *sm* (*ZOOL*) mackerel; (*anche*: **sgombero**) clearing; vacating; evacuation; (: *trasloco*) removal.

sgomen'tare *vt* to dismay; ~**rsi** *vr* to be dismayed.

sgo'mento, a *ag* dismayed ♦ *sm* dismay, consternation.

sgomi'nare *vt* (*nemico*) to rout; (*avversario*) to defeat; (*fig*: *epidemia*) to overcome.

sgonfi'are *vt* to let down, deflate; ~**rsi** *vr* to go down.

'sgonfio, a *ag* (*pneumatico, pallone*) flat.

'sgorbio *sm* blot; scribble.

sgor'gare *vi* to gush (out).

sgoz'zare [zgot'tsare] *vt* to cut the throat of.

sgra'devole *ag* unpleasant, disagreeable.

sgra'dito, a *ag* unpleasant, unwelcome.

sgraffi'gnare [zgraffiɲ'ɲare] *vt* (*fam*) to pinch, swipe.

sgrammati'cato, a *ag* ungrammatical.

sgra'nare *vt* (*piselli*) to shell; ~ **gli occhi** to open one's eyes wide.

sgran'chirsi [zgran'kirsi] *vr* to stretch; ~ **le gambe** to stretch one's legs.

sgranocchi'are [zgranok'kjare] *vt* to munch.

sgras'sare *vt* to remove the grease from.

'sgravio *sm*: ~ **fiscale** *o* **contributivo** tax relief.

sgrazi'ato, a [zgrat'tsjato] *ag* clumsy, ungainly.

sgreto'lare *vt* to cause to crumble; ~**rsi** *vr* to crumble.

sgri'dare *vt* to scold.

sgri'data *sf* scolding.

sguai'ato, a *ag* coarse, vulgar.

sguai'nare *vt* to draw, unsheathe.

sgual'cire [zgwal'tʃire] *vt* to crumple (up), crease.

sgual'drina *sf* (*peg*) slut.

sgu'ardo *sm* (*occhiata*) look, glance; (*espressione*) look (in one's eye); **dare uno** ~ **a qc** to glance at sth, cast a glance *o* an eye over sth; **alzare** *o* **sollevare lo** ~ to raise one's eyes, look up; **cercare qc/qn con lo** ~ to look (a)round for sth/sb.

'sguattero, a *sm/f* scullery boy/maid.

sguaz'zare [zgwat'tsare] *vi* (*nell'acqua*) to splash about; (*nella melma*) to wallow; ~ **nell'oro** to be rolling in money.

sguinzagli'are [zgwintsaʎ'ʎare] *vt* to let off the leash; (*fig*: *persona*): ~ **qn dietro a qn** to set sb on sb.

sgusci'are [zguʃ'ʃare] *vt* to shell ♦ *vi* (*sfuggire di mano*) to slip; ~ **via** to slip *o* slink away.

'shaker ['ʃeikə*] *sm inv* (cocktail) shaker.

'shampoo ['ʃampo] *sm inv* shampoo.

'shiatzu ['tʃjatsu] *sm*, *ag inv* shiatsu.

shoc'care [ʃok'kare] *vt* = **shockare**.

shock [ʃɔk] *sm inv* shock.

shoc'kare [ʃok'kare] *vt* to shock.

SI *sigla* = Siena.

═══════════ *PAROLA CHIAVE*

si (*dav lo, la, li, le, ne diventa* **se**) *pron* **1** (*riflessivo*: *maschile*) himself; (: *femminile*) herself; (: *neutro*) itself; (: *impersonale*) oneself; (: *pl*) themselves; **lavarsi** to wash (oneself); ~ **è tagliato** he has cut himself; ~ **credono importanti** they think a lot of themselves

2 (*con complemento oggetto*): **lavarsi le mani** to wash one's hands; **sporcarsi i pantaloni** to get one's trousers dirty; ~ **sta lavando i capelli** he (*o* she) is washing his (*o* her) hair

3 (*reciproco*) one another, each other; **si amano** they love one another *o* each other

4 (*passivo*): ~ **ripara facilmente** it is easily repaired; **affittasi camera** room to let

5 (*impersonale*): ~ **dice che ...** they *o* people say that ...; ~ **vede che è vecchio** one *o* you can see that it's old; **non** ~ **fa**

credito we do not give credit; **ci ~ sbaglia facilmente** it's easy to make a mistake 6 (*noi*) we; **tra poco ~ parte** we're leaving soon.

sì *av* yes ♦ *sm*: **non mi aspettavo un ~** I didn't expect him (*o her etc*) to say yes; **per me è ~** I should think so, I expect so; **saranno stati ~ e no in 20** there must have been about 20 of them; **uno ~ e uno no** every other one; **un giorno ~ e uno no** every other day; **dire di ~** to say yes; **spero/penso di ~** I hope/think so; **fece di ~ col capo** he nodded (his head); **e ~ che** ... and to think that ....

'sia *cong*: **~ ... ~** (*o ... o*): **~ che lavori, ~ che non lavori** whether he works or not; (*tanto ... quanto*): **verranno ~ Luigi ~ suo fratello** both Luigi and his brother will be coming.

'sia *etc vb vedi* **essere.**

SIAE *sigla f* = *Società Italiana Autori ed Editori*.

Si'am *sm*: **il ~** Siam.

sia'mese *ag, sm/f* siamese *inv*.

si'amo *vb vedi* **essere.**

Si'beria *sf*: **la ~** Siberia.

siberi'ano, a *ag, sm/f* Siberian.

sibi'lare *vi* to hiss; (*fischiare*) to whistle.

'sibilo *sm* hiss; whistle.

si'cario *sm* hired killer.

sicché [sik'ke] *cong* (*perciò*) so (that), therefore; (*e quindi*) (and) so.

siccità [sittʃi'ta] *sf* drought.

sic'come *cong* since, as.

Si'cilia [si'tʃilja] *sf*: **la ~** Sicily.

sicili'ano, a [sitʃi'ljano] *ag, sm/f* Sicilian.

sico'moro *sm* sycamore.

'siculo, a *ag, sm/f* Sicilian.

si'cura *sf* (*di arma, spilla*) safety catch; (*di portiera*) safety lock.

sicura'mente *av* certainly.

sicu'rezza [siku'rettsa] *sf* safety; security; confidence; certainty; **di ~** safety *cpd*; **la ~ stradale** road safety; **avere la ~ di qc** to be sure *o* certain of sth; **lo so con ~** I am quite certain; **ha risposto con molta ~** he answered very confidently.

si'curo, a *ag* safe; (*ben difeso*) secure; (*fiducioso*) confident; (*certo*) sure, certain; (*notizia, amico*) reliable; (*esperto*) skilled ♦ *av* (*anche*: **di ~**) certainly ♦ *sm*: **andare sul ~** to play safe; **essere/mettere al ~** to be safe/put in a safe place; **~ di sé** self-confident, sure of o.s.; **sentirsi ~** to feel safe *o* secure; **essere ~ di/che** to be sure of/that; **da fonte ~a** from reliable sources.

siderur'gia [siderur'dʒia] *sf* iron and steel industry.

side'rurgico, a, ci, che [side'rurdʒiko] *ag* iron and steel *cpd*.

'sidro *sm* cider.

si'edo *etc vb vedi* **sedere.**

si'epe *sf* hedge.

si'ero *sm* (*MED*) serum; **~ antivipera** snake bite serum; **~ del latte** whey.

sieronegatività *sf inv* HIV-negative status.

sieronega'tivo, a *ag* HIV-negative ♦ *sm/f* HIV-negative person.

sieropositività *sf inv* HIV-positive status.

sieroposi'tivo, a *ag* HIV-positive ♦ *sm/f* HIV-positive person.

si'erra *sf* (*GEO*) sierra.

Si'erra Le'one *sf*: **la ~** Sierra Leone.

si'esta *sf* siesta, (afternoon) nap.

si'ete *vb vedi* **essere.**

si'filide *sf* syphilis.

si'fone *sm* siphon.

Sig. *abbr* (= *signore*) Mr.

siga'retta *sf* cigarette.

'sigaro *sm* cigar.

Sigg. *abbr* (= *signori*) Messrs.

sigil'lare [sidʒil'lare] *vt* to seal.

si'gillo [si'dʒillo] *sm* seal.

'sigla *sf* (*iniziali*) initials *pl*; (*abbreviazione*) acronym, abbreviation; **~ automobilistica** *abbreviation of province on vehicle number plate*; **~ musicale** signature tune.

si'glare *vt* to initial.

Sig.na *abbr* (= *signorina*) Miss.

signifi'care [siɲɲifi'kare] *vt* to mean; **cosa significa?** what does this mean?

significa'tivo, a [siɲɲifika'tivo] *ag* significant.

signifi'cato [siɲɲifi'kato] *sm* meaning.

si'gnora [siɲ'ɲora] *sf* lady; **la ~ X** Mrs ['mɪsɪz] X; **buon giorno S~/Signore/Signorina** good morning; (*deferente*) good morning Madam/Sir/Madam; (*quando si conosce il nome*) good morning Mrs/Mr/Miss X; **Gentile S~/Signore/Signorina** (*in una lettera*) Dear Madam/Sir/Madam; **Gentile** (*o* **Cara**) **S~ Rossi** Dear Mrs Rossi; **Gentile S~ Anna Rossi** (*sulle buste*) Mrs Anna Rossi; **il signor Rossi e ~ Mr** Rossi and his wife; **~e e signori** ladies and gentlemen; **le presento la mia ~** may I introduce my wife?

si'gnore [siɲ'ɲore] *sm* gentleman; (*padrone*) lord, master; (*REL*): **il S~** the Lord; **il signor X** Mr ['mɪstə*] X; **signor Presidente** Mr Chairman; **Gentile** (*o* **Caro**) **Signor Rossi** (*in lettere*) Dear Mr Rossi; **Gentile Signor Paolo Rossi** (*sulle buste*) Mr Paolo Rossi; **i ~i Bianchi** (*coniugi*) Mr and Mrs

Bianchi; *vedi anche* **signora.**

signo'ria [sip̮p̮o'ria] *sf (STORIA)* seignory, signoria; **S~ Vostra (S.V.)** *(AMM)* you.

signo'rile [sip̮p̮o'rile] *ag* refined.

signorilità [sip̮p̮orili'ta] *sf (raffinatezza)* refinement; *(eleganza)* elegance.

signo'rina [sip̮p̮o'rina] *sf* young lady; **la ~ X** Miss X; **Gentile** *(o Cara)* **S~ Rossi** *(in lettere)* Dear Miss Rossi; **Gentile S~ Anna Rossi** *(sulle buste)* Miss Anna Rossi; *vedi anche* **signora.**

signo'rino [sip̮p̮o'rino] *sm* young master.

Sig.ra *abbr* (= *signora*) Mrs.

silenzia'tore [silentsja'tore] *sm* silencer.

si'lenzio [si'lɛntsjo] *sm* silence; **fare ~** to be quiet, stop talking; **far passare qc sotto ~** to keep quiet about sth, hush sth up.

silenzi'oso, a [silen'tsjoso] *ag* silent, quiet.

'silice ['silitʃe] *sf* silica.

si'licio [si'litʃo] *sm* silicon; **piastrina di ~** silicon chip.

sili'cone *sm* silicone.

'sillaba *sf* syllable.

silu'rare *vt* to torpedo; *(fig: privare del comando)* to oust.

si'luro *sm* torpedo.

simbi'osi *sf (BIOL, fig)* symbiosis.

simboleggi'are [simboled'dʒare] *vt* to symbolize.

sim'bolico, a, ci, che *ag* symbolic(al).

simbo'lismo *sm* symbolism.

'simbolo *sm* symbol.

simi'lare *ag* similar.

'simile *ag (analogo)* similar; *(di questo tipo)*: **un uomo ~** such a man, a man like this ♦ *sm (persona)* fellow man; **libri ~i** such books; **~ a** similar to; **non ho mai visto niente di ~** I've never seen anything like that; **è insegnante o qualcosa di ~** he's a teacher or something like that; **vendono vasi e ~i** they sell vases and things like that; **i suoi ~i** one's fellow men; one's peers.

simili'tudine *sf (LING)* simile.

simme'tria *sf* symmetry.

sim'metrico, a, ci, che *ag* symmetric(al).

simpa'tia *sf (qualità)* pleasantness; *(inclinazione)* liking; **avere ~ per qn** to like sb, have a liking for sb; **con ~** *(su lettera etc)* with much affection.

sim'patico, a, ci, che *ag (persona)* nice, pleasant, likeable; *(casa, albergo etc)* nice, pleasant.

simpatiz'zante [simpatid'dzante] *sm/f* sympathizer.

simpatiz'zare [simpatid'dzare] *vi*: **~ con** to take a liking to.

sim'posio *sm* symposium.

simu'lacro *sm (monumento, statua)* image; *(fig)* semblance.

simu'lare *vt* to sham, simulate; *(TECN)* to simulate.

simulazi'one [simulat'tsjone] *sf* shamming; simulation.

simul'taneo, a *ag* simultaneous.

sin. *abbr* (= *sinistra*) L.

sina'goga, ghe *sf* synagogue.

sincera'mente [sintʃera'mente] *av (gen)* sincerely; *(francamente)* honestly, sincerely.

since'rarsi [sintʃe'rarsi] *vr*: **~ (di qc)** to make sure (of sth).

sincerità [sintʃeri'ta] *sf* sincerity.

sin'cero, a [sin'tʃero] *ag (genuino)* sincere; *(onesto)* genuine.

'sincope *sf* syncopation; *(MED)* blackout.

sincro'nia *sf (di movimento)* synchronism.

sin'cronico, a, ci, che *ag* synchronic.

sincroniz'zare [sinkronid'dzare] *vt* to synchronize.

sinda'cale *ag* (trade-)union *cpd*.

sindaca'lista, i, e *sm/f* trade unionist.

sinda'care *vt (controllare)* to inspect; *(fig: criticare)* to criticize.

sinda'cato *sm (di lavoratori)* (trade) union; **~ dei datori di lavoro** employers' association.

'sindaco, ci *sm* mayor.

'sindrome *sf (MED)* syndrome.

siner'gia, gie [siner'dʒia] *sf (anche fig)* synergy.

sinfo'nia *sf (MUS)* symphony.

sin'fonico, a, ci, che *ag* symphonic; *(orchestra)* symphony *cpd*.

singa'lese *ag, sm/f, sm* Sin(g)halese *inv*.

Singa'pore *sf* Singapore.

singhioz'zare [singjot'tsare] *vi* to sob; to hiccup.

singhi'ozzo [sin'gjottso] *sm (di pianto)* sob; *(MED)* hiccup; **avere il ~** to have the hiccups; **a ~** *(fig)* by fits and starts.

singo'lare *ag (insolito)* remarkable, singular; *(LING)* singular ♦ *sm (LING)* singular; *(TENNIS)*: **~ maschile/femminile** men's/women's singles.

singolar'mente *av (separatamente)* individually, one at a time; *(in modo strano)* strangely, peculiarly, oddly.

'singolo, a *ag* single, individual ♦ *sm (persona)* individual; *(TENNIS)* = **singolare**; **ogni ~ individuo** each individual; **camera ~a** single room.

sinis'trato, a *ag* damaged ♦ *sm/f* disaster victim; **zona ~a** disaster area.

si'nistro, a *ag* left, left-hand; *(fig)* sinister ♦ *sm (incidente)* accident ♦ *sf (POL)* left (wing); **a** ~**a** on the left; (*direzione*) to the left; **a** ~**a di** to the left of; **di** ~**a** left-wing; **tenere la** ~**a** to keep to the left; **guida a** ~**a** left-hand drive.

'sino *prep* = **fino**.

si'nonimo, a *ag* synonymous ♦ *sm* synonym; ~ **di** synonymous with.

sin'tassi *sf* syntax.

sin'tattico, a, ci, che *ag* syntactic.

'sintesi *sf* synthesis; (*riassunto*) summary, résumé; **in** ~ in brief, in short.

sin'tetico, a, ci, che *ag* synthetic; (*conciso*) brief, concise.

sintetiz'zare [sintetid'dzare] *vt* to synthesize; (*riassumere*) to summarize.

sintetizza'tore [sintetiddza'tore] *sm* (*MUS*) synthesizer; ~ **di voce** voice synthesizer.

sinto'matico, a, ci, che *ag* symptomatic.

'sintomo *sm* symptom.

sinto'nia *sf* (*RADIO*) tuning; **essere in** ~ **con qn** (*fig*) to be on the same wavelength as sb.

sintoniz'zare [sintonid'dzare] *vt* to tune (in); ~**rsi** *vr*: ~**rsi su** to tune in to.

sintonizza'tore [sintoniddza'tore] *sm* tuner.

sinu'oso, a *ag* (*strada*) winding.

sinu'site *sf* sinusitis.

SIP *sigla f* (– *Società Italiana per l'esercizio telefonico*) *former name of Italian telephone company*.

si'pario *sm* (*TEAT*) curtain.

si'rena *sf* (*apparecchio*) siren; (*nella mitologia, fig*) siren, mermaid; ~ **d'allarme** (*per incendio*) fire alarm; (*per furto*) burglar alarm.

'Siria *sf*: **la** ~ Syria.

siri'ano, a *ag, sm/f* Syrian.

si'ringa, ghe *sf* syringe.

'sisma, i *sm* earthquake.

'SISMI *sigla m* (= *Servizio per l'Informazione e la Sicurezza Militari*) *military security service*.

'sismico, a, ci, che *ag* seismic; (*zona*) earthquake *cpd*.

sis'mografo *sm* seismograph.

sissi'gnore [sissiɲ'ɲore] *av* (*a un superiore*) yes, sir; (*enfatico*) yes indeed, of course.

sis'tema, i *sm* system; (*metodo*) method, way; **trovare il** ~ **per fare qc** to find a way to do sth; ~ **decimale/metrico** decimal/metric system; ~ **operativo** (*INFORM*) operating system; ~ **solare** solar system; ~ **di vita** way of life.

siste'mare *vt* (*mettere a posto*) to tidy, put in order; (*risolvere: questione*) to sort out, settle; (*procurare un lavoro a*) to find a job for; (*dare un alloggio a*) to settle, find accommodation (*BRIT*) *o* accommodations

(*US*) for; ~**rsi** *vr* (*problema*) to be settled; (*persona*: trovare alloggio) to find accommodation(s); (: *trovarsi un lavoro*) to get fixed up with a job; **ti sistemo io!** I'll soon sort you out!; ~ **qn in un albergo** to fix sb up with a hotel.

sistematica'mente *av* systematically.

siste'matico, a, ci, che *ag* systematic.

sistemazi'one [sistemat'tsjone] *sf* arrangement, order; settlement; employment; accommodation (*BRIT*), accommodations (*US*).

'sito, a *ag* (*AMM*) situated ♦ *sm* (*letterario*) place; ~ **Internet** website.

situ'are *vt* to site, situate.

situ'ato, a *ag*: ~ **a/su** situated at/on.

situazi'one [situat'tsjone] *sf* situation; **vista la sua** ~ **familiare** given your family situation *o* circumstances; **nella sua** ~ in your present *o* situation; **mi trovo in una** ~ **critica** I'm in a very difficult position.

'skai ® *sm* Leatherette ®.

ski-lift [ski'lift] *sm inv* ski lift.

ski pass [ski'paːs] *sm inv* ski pass.

slacci'are [zlat'tʃare] *vt* to undo, unfasten.

slanci'arsi [zlan'tʃarsi] *vr* to dash, fling o.s.

slanci'ato, a [zlan'tʃato] *ag* slender.

'slancio ['zlantʃo] *sm* dash, leap; (*fig*) surge; **in uno** ~ **d'affetto** in a burst *o* rush of affection; **di** ~ impetuously.

sla'vato, a *ag* faded, washed out; (*fig: viso, occhi*) pale, colourless (*BRIT*), colorless (*US*).

sla'vina *sf* snowslide.

'slavo, a *ag* Slav(onic), Slavic.

sle'ale *ag* disloyal; (*concorrenza etc*) unfair.

slealtà *sf* disloyalty; unfairness.

sle'gare *vt* to untie.

slip *sm inv* (*mutandine*) briefs *pl*; (*da bagno*: *per uomo*) (swimming) trunks *pl*; (: *per donna*) bikini bottoms *pl*.

'slitta *sf* sledge; (*trainata*) sleigh.

slitta'mento *sm* slipping; skidding; postponement; ~ **salariale** wage drift.

slit'tare *vi* to slip, slide; (*AUT*) to skid; (*incontro, conferenza*) to be put off, be postponed.

s.l.m. *abbr* (= *sul livello del mare*) a.s.l.

slo'gare *vt* (*MED*) to dislocate; (: *caviglia, polso*) to sprain.

sloga'tura *sf* dislocation; sprain.

sloggi'are [zlod'dʒare] *vt* (*inquilino*) to turn out; (*nemico*) to drive out, dislodge ♦ *vi* to move out.

Slo'vacchia [zlo'vakkja] *sf* Slovakia.

slo'vacco, a, ci, che *ag, sm/f* Slovak, Slovakian; **la Repubblica S~a** the Slovak Republic.

Slo'venia sf Slovenia.

slo'veno, a ag, sm/f Slovene, Slovenian ♦ sm (LING) Slovene.

S.M. abbr (MIL) = **Stato Maggiore**; (= Sua Maestà) HM.

smac'cato, a ag (fig) excessive.

smacchi'are [zmak'kjare] vt to remove stains from.

smacchia'tore [zmakkja'tore] sm stain remover.

'smacco, chi sm humiliating defeat.

smagli'ante [zmaʎ'ʎante] ag brilliant, dazzling.

smagli'are [zmaʎ'ʎare] vt, ~rsi vr (calza) to ladder.

smaglia'tura [zmaʎʎa'tura] sf (su maglia, calza) ladder (BRIT), run; (MED: sulla pelle) stretch mark.

sma'grire vt to make thin ♦ vi to get o grow thin, lose weight.

sma'grito, a ag: **essere** ~ to have lost a lot of weight.

smalizi'ato, a [smalit'tsjato] ag shrewd, cunning.

smal'tare vt to enamel; (ceramica) to glaze; (unghie) to varnish.

smalti'mento sm (di rifiuti) disposal.

smal'tire vt (merce) to sell off; (rifiuti) to dispose of; (cibo) to digest; (peso) to lose; (rabbia) to get over; ~ **la sbornia** to sober up.

'smalto sm (anche di denti) enamel; (per ceramica) glaze; ~ **per unghie** nail varnish.

smance'rie [zmantʃe'rie] sfpl mawkishness sg.

'smania sf agitation, restlessness; (fig): ~ **di** thirst for, craving for; **avere la** ~ **addosso** to have the fidgets; **avere la** ~ **di fare** to long o yearn to do.

smani'are vi (agitarsi) to be restless o agitated; (fig): ~ **di fare** to long o yearn to do.

smantella'mento sm dismantling.

smantel'lare vt to dismantle.

smar'carsi vr (SPORT) to get free of marking.

smargi'asso [zmar'dʒasso] sm show-off.

smarri'mento sm loss; (fig) bewilderment; dismay.

smar'rire vt to lose; (non riuscire a trovare) to mislay; ~rsi vr (perdersi) to lose one's way, get lost; (: oggetto) to go astray.

smar'rito, a ag (oggetto) lost; (fig: confuso: persona) bewildered, nonplussed; (: sguardo) bewildered; **ufficio oggetti** ~**i** lost property office (BRIT), lost and found (US).

smasche'rare [zmaske'rare] vt to unmask.

SME abbr = **Stato Maggiore Esercito** ♦ sigla m (= Sistema Monetario Europeo) EMS (= European Monetary System).

smem'brare vt (gruppo, partito etc) to split; ~**rsi** vr to split up.

smemo'rato, a ag forgetful.

smen'tire vt (negare) to deny; (testimonianza) to refute; (reputazione) to give the lie to; ~**rsi** vr to be inconsistent.

smen'tita sf denial; refutation.

sme'raldo sm, ag inv emerald.

smerci'are [zmer'tʃare] vt (COMM) to sell; (: svendere) to sell off.

'smercio ['zmɛrtʃo] sm sale; **avere poco/ molto** ~ to have poor/good sales.

smerigli'ato, a [zmeriʎ'ʎato] ag: **carta** ~**a** emery paper; **vetro** ~ frosted glass.

sme'riglio [zme'riʎʎo] sm emery.

'smesso, a pp di **smettere** ♦ ag: **abiti** mpl ~**i** cast-offs.

'smettere vt to stop; (vestiti) to stop wearing ♦ vi to stop, cease; ~ **di fare** to stop doing.

smidol'lato, a ag spineless ♦ sm/f spineless person.

smilitarizzazi'one [zmilitariddzat'tsjone] sf demilitarization.

'smilzo, a ['zmiltso] ag thin, lean.

sminu'ire vt to diminish, lessen; (fig) to belittle; ~ **l'importanza di qc** to play sth down.

sminuz'zare [zminut'tsare] vt to break into small pieces; to crumble.

'smisi etc vb vedi **smettere**.

smista'mento sm (di posta) sorting; (FERR) shunting.

smis'tare vt (pacchi etc) to sort; (FERR) to shunt.

smisu'rato, a ag boundless, immeasurable; (grandissimo) immense, enormous.

smitiz'zare [zmitid'dzare] vt to debunk.

smobili'tare vt to demobilize.

smobilitazi'one [zmobilitat'tsjone] sf demobilization.

smobi'lizzo [zmobi'liddzo] sm (COMM) disinvestment.

smo'dato, a ag excessive, unrestrained.

smode'rato, a ag immoderate.

smog [zmɔg] sm inv smog.

'smoking ['smoukiŋ] sm inv dinner jacket (BRIT), tuxedo (US).

smon'tare vt (mobile, macchina etc) to take to pieces, dismantle; (fig: scoraggiare) to dishearten ♦ vi (scendere: da cavallo) to dismount; (: da treno) to get off; (terminare il lavoro) to stop (work); ~**rsi** vr to lose heart; to lose one's enthusiasm.

'**smorfia** *sf* grimace; (*atteggiamento lezioso*) simpering; **fare** ~**e** to make faces; to simper.

smorfi'oso, a *ag* simpering.

'**smorto, a** *ag* (*viso*) pale, wan; (*colore*) dull.

smor'zare [zmor'tsare] *vt* (*suoni*) to deaden; (*colori*) to tone down; (*luce*) to dim; (*sete*) to quench; (*entusiasmo*) to dampen; ~**rsi** *vr* (*suono, luce*) to fade; (*entusiasmo*) to dampen.

'**smosso, a** *pp di* **smuovere**.

smotta'mento *sm* landslide.

sms *sm inv* text (message).

'**smunto, a** *ag* haggard, pinched.

smu'overe *vt* to move, shift; (*fig: commuovere*) to move; (: *dall'inerzia*) to rouse, stir; ~**rsi** *vr* to move, shift.

smus'sare *vt* (*angolo*) to round off, smooth; (*lama etc*) to blunt; ~**rsi** *vr* to become blunt.

s.n. *abbr* = *senza numero*.

snatu'rato, a *ag* inhuman, heartless.

snazionaliz'zare [znattsjonalid'dzare] *vt* to denationalize.

snelli'mento *sm* (*di traffico*) speeding up; (*di procedura*) streamlining.

snel'lire *vt* (*persona*) to make slim; (*traffico*) to speed up; (*procedura*) to streamline; ~**rsi** *vr* (*persona*) to (get) slim; (*traffico*) to speed up.

'**snello, a** *ag* (*agile*) agile; (*svelto*) slender, slim.

sner'vante *ag* (*attesa, lavoro*) exasperating.

sner'vare *vt* to enervate, wear out; ~**rsi** *vr* to become enervated.

sni'dare *vt* to drive out, flush out.

snob'bare *vt* to snub.

sno'bismo *sm* snobbery.

snoccio'lare [znott∫o'lare] *vt* (*frutta*) to stone; (*fig: orazioni*) to rattle off; (: *verità*) to blab; (: *fam: soldi*) to shell out.

sno'dabile *ag* (*lampada*) adjustable; (*tubo, braccio*) hinged; **rasoio con testina** ~ swivel-head razor.

sno'dare *vt* to untie, undo; (*rendere agile, mobile*) to loosen; ~**rsi** *vr* to come loose; (*articolarsi*) to bend; (*strada, fiume*) to wind.

SO *sigla* = *Sondrio*.

so *vb vedi* **sapere**.

S.O. *abbr* (= *sudovest*) SW.

so'ave *ag* (*voce, maniera*) gentle; (*volto*) delicate, sweet; (*musica*) soft, sweet; (*profumo*) delicate.

soavità *sf* gentleness; delicacy; sweetness; softness.

sobbal'zare [sobbal'tsare] *vi* to jolt, jerk; (*trasalire*) to jump, start.

sob'balzo [sob'baltso] *sm* jerk, jolt; jump; start.

sobbar'carsi *vr*: ~ **a** to take on, undertake.

sob'borgo, ghi *sm* suburb.

sobil'lare *vt* to stir up, incite.

'**sobrio, a** *ag* sober.

Soc. *abbr* (= *società*) Soc.

socchi'udere [sok'kjudere] *vt* (*porta*) to leave ajar; (*occhi*) to half-close.

socchi'uso, a [sok'kjuso] *pp di* **socchiudere** ♦ *ag* (*porta, finestra*) ajar; (*occhi*) half-closed.

soc'combere *vi* to succumb, give way.

soc'correre *vt* to help, assist.

soccorri'tore, 'trice *sm/f* rescuer.

soc'corso, a *pp di* **soccorrere** ♦ *sm* help, aid, assistance; ~**i** *smpl* relief *sg*, aid *sg*; **prestare** ~ **a qn** to help *o* assist sb; **venire in** ~ **di qn** to help sb, come to sb's aid; **operazioni di** ~ rescue operations; ~ **stradale** breakdown service.

socialdemo'cratico, a, ci, che [sot∫aldemo'kratiko] *sm/f* Social Democrat.

soci'ale [so't∫ale] *ag* social; (*di associazione*) club *cpd*, association *cpd*.

socia'lismo [sot∫a'lizmo] *sm* socialism.

socia'lista, i, e [sot∫a'lista] *ag, sm/f* socialist.

socializ'zare [sot∫alid'dzare] *vi* to socialize.

società [sot∫e'ta] *sf inv* society; (*sportiva*) club; (*COMM*) company; **in** ~ **con qn** in partnership with sb; **mettersi in** ~ **con qn** to go into business with sb; **l'alta** ~ high society; ~ **anonima (SA)** ≈ limited (*BRIT*) *o* incorporated (*US*) company; ~ **per azioni (S.p.A.)** joint-stock company; ~ **di comodo** shell company; ~ **fiduciaria** trust company; ~ **di mutuo soccorso** friendly society (*BRIT*), benefit society (*US*); ~ **a responsabilità limitata (S.r.l.)** *type of* limited liability company.

soci'evole [so't∫evole] *ag* sociable.

socievo'lezza [sot∫evo'lettsa] *sf* sociableness.

'**socio** ['sɔt∫o] *sm* (*DIR, COMM*) partner; (*membro di associazione*) member.

sociolo'gia [sot∫olo'dʒia] *sf* sociology.

soci'ologo, a, gi, ghe [so't∫ɔlogo] *sm/f* sociologist.

'**soda** *sf* (*CHIM*) soda; (*acqua gassata*) soda (water).

soda'lizio [soda'littsjo] *sm* association, society.

soddisfa'cente [soddisfa't∫ɛnte] *ag* satisfactory.

soddis'fare *vt, vi*: ~ **a** to satisfy; (*impegno*) to fulfil; (*debito*) to pay off; (*richiesta*) to meet, comply with; (*offesa*) to make amends for.

soddis'fatto, a *pp di* soddisfare ♦ *ag*
satisfied, pleased; essere ~ di to be
satisfied *o* pleased with.

soddisfazi'one [soddisfat'tsjone] *sf*
satisfaction.

'sodio *sm* (*CHIM*) sodium.

'sodo, a *ag* firm, hard ♦ *sm*: venire al ~ to
come to the point ♦ *av* (*picchiare, lavorare*)
hard; dormire ~ to sleep soundly.

sofà *sm inv* sofa.

soffe'renza [soffe'rɛntsa] *sf* suffering;
(*COMM*): in ~ unpaid.

sof'ferto, a *pp di* soffrire ♦ *ag* (*vittoria*)
hard-fought; (*distacco, decisione*) painful.

soffi'are *vt* to blow; (*notizia, segreto*) to
whisper ♦ *vi* to blow; (*sbuffare*) to puff
(and blow); ~rsi il naso to blow one's
nose; ~ qc/qn a qn (*fig*) to pinch *o* steal
sth/sb from sb; ~ via qc to blow sth away.

soffi'ata *sf* (*fam*) tip-off; fare una ~ alla
polizia to tip off the police.

'soffice ['sɔffitʃe] *ag* soft.

soffi'etto *sm* (*MUS, per fuoco*) bellows *pl*;
porta a ~ folding door.

'soffio *sm* (*di vento*) breath; (*di fumo*) puff;
(*MED*) murmur.

soffi'one *sm* (*BOT*) dandelion.

sof'fitta *sf* attic.

sof'fitto *sm* ceiling.

soffo'cante *ag* suffocating, stifling.

soffo'care *vi* (*anche*: ~rsi) to suffocate,
choke ♦ *vt* to suffocate, choke; (*fig*) to
stifle, suppress.

soffocazi'one [soffokat'tsjone] *sf*
suffocation.

sof'friggere [sof'friddʒere] *vt* to fry lightly.

sof'frire *vt* to suffer, endure; (*sopportare*)
to bear, stand ♦ *vi* to suffer; to be in pain;
~ (di) qc (*MED*) to suffer from sth.

sof'fritto, a *pp di* soffriggere ♦ *sm* (*CUC*)
fried mixture of herbs, bacon and onions.

sof'fuso, a *ag* (*di luce*) suffused.

So'fia *sf* (*GEO*) Sofia.

sofisti'care *vt* (*vino, cibo*) to adulterate.

sofisti'cato, a *ag* sophisticated; (*vino*)
adulterated.

sofisticazi'one [sofistikat'tsjone] *sf*
adulteration.

'software ['sɔftwɛə] *sm*: ~ applicativo
applications package.

sogget'tivo, a [soddʒet'tivo] *ag* subjective.

sog'getto, a [sod'dʒɛtto] *ag*: ~ a
(*sottomesso*) subject to; (*esposto: a
variazioni, danni etc*) subject *o* liable to
♦ *sm* subject; ~ a tassa taxable; recitare
a ~ (*TEAT*) to improvise.

soggezi'one [soddʒet'tsjone] *sf* subjection;
(*timidezza*) awe; avere ~ di qn to be ill at

ease in sb's presence.

sogghi'gnare [soggiɲ'ɲare] *vi* to sneer.

sog'ghigno [sog'giɲɲo] *sm* sneer.

soggia'cere [soddʒa'tʃere] *vi*: ~ a to be
subjected to.

soggio'gare [soddʒo'gare] *vt* to subdue,
subjugate.

soggior'nare [soddʒor'nare] *vi* to stay.

soggi'orno [sod'dʒorno] *sm* (*invernale,
marino*) stay; (*stanza*) living room.

soggi'ungere [sod'dʒundʒere] *vt* to add.

soggi'unto, a [sod'dʒunto] *pp di*
soggiungere.

'soglia ['sɔʎʎa] *sf* doorstep; (*anche fig*)
threshold.

'sogliola ['sɔʎʎola] *sf* (*ZOOL*) sole.

so'gnante [soɲ'ɲante] *ag* dreamy.

so'gnare [soɲ'ɲare] *vt, vi* to dream; ~ a
occhi aperti to daydream.

sogna'tore, 'trice [soɲɲa'tore] *sm/f*
dreamer.

'sogno ['soɲɲo] *sm* dream.

'soia *sf* (*BOT*) soya.

sol *sm* (*MUS*) G; (: *solfeggiando la scala*)
so(h).

so'laio *sm* (*soffitta*) attic.

sola'mente *av* only, just.

so'lare *ag* solar, sun *cpd*.

sol'care *vt* (*terreno, fig: mari*) to plough
(*BRIT*), plow (*US*).

'solco, chi *sm* (*scavo, fig: ruga*) furrow;
(*incavo*) rut, track; (*di disco*) groove; (*scia*)
wake.

sol'dato *sm* soldier; ~ di leva conscript; ~
semplice private.

'soldo *sm* (*fig*): non avere un ~ to be
penniless; non vale un ~ it's not worth a
penny; ~i *smpl* (*denaro*) money *sg*.

'sole *sm* sun; (*luce*) sun(light); (*tempo
assolato*) sun(shine); prendere il ~ to
sunbathe; il S~ che ride (*POL*) symbol of
the Italian Green party.

soleggi'ato, a [soled'dʒato] *ag* sunny.

so'lenne *ag* solemn.

solennità *sf* solemnity; (*festività*) holiday,
feast day.

so'lere *vt*: ~ fare qc to be in the habit of
doing sth ♦ *vb impers*: come suole accadere
as is usually the case, as usually
happens; come si suol dire as they say.

so'lerte *ag* diligent.

so'lerzia [so'lɛrtsja] *sf* diligence.

so'letta *sf* (*per scarpe*) insole.

sol'fato *sm* sulphate (*BRIT*), sulfate (*US*).

sol'forico, a, ci, che *ag* sulphuric (*BRIT*),
sulfuric (*US*); acido ~ sulphuric *o*
sulfuric acid.

sol'furo *sm* sulphur (*BRIT*), sulfur (*US*).

soli'dale *ag* in agreement; essere ~ con qn (*essere d'accordo*) to be in agreement with sb; (*appoggiare*) to be behind sb.
solidarietà *sf* solidarity.
solidifi'care *vt, vi* (*anche:* ~rsi) to solidify.
solidità *sf* solidity.
'solido, a *ag* solid; (*forte, robusto*) sturdy, solid; (*fig: ditta*) sound, solid ♦ *sm* (*MAT*) solid.
soli'loquio *sm* soliloquy.
so'lista, i, e *ag* solo ♦ *sm/f* soloist.
solita'mente *av* usually, as a rule.
soli'tario, a *ag* (*senza compagnia*) solitary, lonely; (*solo, isolato*) solitary, lone; (*deserto*) lonely ♦ *sm* (*gioiello, gioco*) solitaire.
'solito, a *ag* usual; essere ~ fare to be in the habit of doing; di ~ usually; più tardi del ~ later than usual; come al ~ as usual; siamo alle ~e! (*fam*) here we go again!
soli'tudine *sf* solitude.
sollaz'zare [sollat'tsare] *vt* to entertain; ~rsi *vr* to amuse o.s.
sol'lazzo [sol'lattso] *sm* amusement.
solleci'tare [solletʃi'tare] *vt* (*lavoro*) to speed up; (*persona*) to urge on; (*chiedere con insistenza*) to press for, request urgently; (*stimolare*): ~ qn a fare to urge sb to do; (*TECN*) to stress.
sollecitazi'one [solletʃitat'tsjone] *sf* entreaty, request; (*fig*) incentive; (*TECN*) stress; lettera di ~ (*COMM*) reminder.
sol'lecito, a [sol'letʃito] *ag* prompt, quick ♦ *sm* (*COMM*) reminder; ~ di pagamento payment reminder.
solleci'tudine [solletʃi'tudine] *sf* promptness, speed.
solleti'care *vt* to tickle.
sol'letico *sm* tickling; soffrire il ~ to be ticklish.
solleva'mento *sm* raising; lifting; (*ribellione*) revolt; ~ pesi (*sport*) weight-lifting.
solle'vare *vt* to lift, raise; (*fig: persona: alleggerire*): ~ (da) to relieve (of); (*: dar conforto*) to comfort, relieve; (*: questione*) to raise; (*: far insorgere*) to stir (to revolt); ~rsi *vr* to rise; (*fig: riprendersi*) to recover; (*: ribellarsi*) to rise up; ~rsi da terra (*persona*) to get up from the ground; (*aereo*) to take off; sentirsi sollevato to feel relieved.
solli'evo *sm* relief; (*conforto*) comfort; con mio grande ~ to my great relief.
'solo, a *ag* alone; (*in senso spirituale: isolato*) lonely; (*unico*): un ~ libro only one book, a single book; (*con ag numerale*): veniamo

noi tre ~i just *o* only the three of us are coming ♦ *av* (*soltanto*) only, just; ~ che *cong* but; è il ~ proprietario he's the sole proprietor; l'incontrò due ~e volte he only met him twice; non ~ ... ma anche not only ... but also; fare qc ~ to do sth (all) by oneself; vive (da) ~ he lives on his own; possiamo vederci da ~i? can I see you in private?
sol'stizio [sol'stittsjo] *sm* solstice.
sol'tanto *av* only.
so'lubile *ag* (*sostanza*) soluble; caffè ~ instant coffee.
soluzi'one [solut'tsjone] *sf* solution; senza ~ di continuità uninterruptedly.
sol'vente *ag, sm* solvent; ~ per unghie nail polish remover; ~ per vernici paint remover.
sol'venza [sol'ventsa] *sf* (*COMM*) solvency.
'soma *sf* load, burden; bestia da ~ beast of burden.
So'malia *sf*: la ~ Somalia.
'somalo, a *ag, sm/f, sm* Somali.
so'maro *sm* ass, donkey.
so'matico, a, ci, che *ag* somatic.
somigli'anza [somiʎ'ʎantsa] *sf* resemblance.
somigli'are [somiʎ'ʎare] *vi*: ~ a to be like, resemble; (*nell'aspetto fisico*) to look like; ~rsi *vr* to be (*o* look) alike.
'somma *sf* (*MAT*) sum; (*di denaro*) sum (of money); (*complesso di varie cose*) whole amount, sum total; tirare le ~e (*fig*) to sum up; tirate le ~e (*fig*) all things considered.
som'mare *vt* to add up; (*aggiungere*) to add; tutto sommato all things considered.
som'mario, a *ag* (*racconto, indagine*) brief; (*giustizia*) summary ♦ *sm* summary.
som'mergere [som'mɛrdʒere] *vt* to submerge.
sommer'gibile [sommer'dʒibile] *sm* submarine.
som'merso, a *pp di* sommergere.
som'messo, a *ag* (*voce*) soft, subdued.
somminis'trare *vt* to give, administer.
sommità *sf inv* summit, top; (*fig*) height.
'sommo, a *ag* highest; (*rispetto*) highest, greatest; (*poeta, artista*) great, outstanding ♦ *sm* (*fig*) height; per ~i capi in short, in brief.
som'mossa *sf* uprising.
sommozza'tore [sommottsa'tore] *sm* (*deep-sea*) diver; (*MIL*) frogman.
so'naglio [so'naʎʎo] *sm* (*di mucche etc*) bell; (*per bambini*) rattle.
so'nante *ag*: denaro *o* moneta ~ (ready)

cash.

so'nare etc = **suonare** etc.

'sonda sf (MED, METEOR, AER) probe; (MINERALOGIA) drill ♦ ag inv: **pallone** m ~ weather balloon.

son'daggio [son'daddʒo] sm sounding; probe; boring, drilling; (indagine) survey; ~ **d'opinioni** opinion poll.

son'dare vt (NAUT) to sound; (atmosfera, piaga) to probe; (MINERALOGIA) to bore, drill; (fig: opinione etc) to survey, poll.

so'netto sm sonnet.

son'nambulo, a sm/f sleepwalker.

sonnecchi'are [sonnek'kjare] vi to doze, nod.

sonnel'lino sm nap.

son'nifero sm sleeping drug (o pill).

'sonno sm sleep; **aver** ~ to be sleepy; **prendere** ~ to fall asleep.

sonno'lento, a ag sleepy, drowsy; (movimenti) sluggish.

sonno'lenza [sonno'lɛntsa] sf sleepiness, drowsiness.

'sono vb vedi **essere**.

sonoriz'zare [sonorid'dzare] vt (LING) to voice; (CINE) to add a sound-track to.

so'noro, a ag (ambiente) resonant; (voce) sonorous, ringing; (onde, film) sound cpd ♦ sm: **il** ~ (CINE) the talkies pl.

sontu'oso, a ag sumptuous.

so'pire vt (fig: dolore, tensione) to soothe.

so'pore sm drowsiness.

sopo'rifero, a ag soporific.

soppe'rire vi: ~ **a** to provide for; ~ **alla mancanza di** qc to make up for the lack of sth.

soppe'sare vt to weigh in one's hand(s), feel the weight of; (fig) to weigh up.

soppian'tare vt to supplant.

soppi'atto av: **di** ~ secretly; furtively.

soppor'tabile ag tolerable, bearable.

soppor'tare vt (reggere) to support; (subire: perdita, spese) to bear, sustain; (soffrire: dolore) to bear, endure; (sog: cosa: freddo) to withstand; (: persona: freddo, vino) to take; (tollerare) to put up with, tolerate.

sopportazi'one [sopportat'tsjone] sf patience; **avere spirito di** ~, **avere capacità di** ~ to be long-suffering.

soppressi'one sf abolition; withdrawal; suppression; deletion; elimination, liquidation.

sop'presso, a pp di **sopprimere**.

sop'primere vt (carica, privilegi etc) to abolish, do away with; (servizio) to withdraw; (pubblicazione) to suppress; (parola, frase) to delete; (uccidere) to eliminate, liquidate.

'sopra prep (gen) on; (al di sopra di, più in alto di) above; over; (riguardo a) on, about ♦ av on top; (attaccato, scritto) on it; (al di sopra) above; (al piano superiore) upstairs; **donne** ~ **i 30 anni** women over 30 (years of age); **100 metri** ~ **il livello del mare** 100 metres above sea level; **5 gradi** ~ **lo zero** 5 degrees above zero; **abito di** ~ I live upstairs; **essere al di** ~ **di** ogni sospetto to be above suspicion; **per i motivi** ~ **illustrati** for the above-mentioned reasons, for the reasons shown above; **dormirci** ~ (fig) to sleep on it; **passar** ~ **a** qc (anche fig) to pass over sth.

so'prabito sm overcoat.

sopraccen'nato, a [soprattʃen'nato] ag above-mentioned.

soprac'ciglio [soprat'tʃiʎʎo], pl(f) **soprac'ciglia** sm eyebrow.

sopracco'perta sf (di letto) bedspread; (di libro) jacket.

soprad'detto, a ag aforesaid.

sopraf'fare vt to overcome, overwhelm.

sopraf'fatto, a pp di **sopraffare**.

sopraffazi'one [sopraffat'tsjone] sf overwhelming, overpowering.

sopraf'fino, a ag (pranzo, vino) excellent; (fig) masterly.

sopraggi'ungere [soprad'dʒundʒere] vi (giungere all'improvviso) to arrive (unexpectedly); (accadere) to occur (unexpectedly).

sopraggi'unto, a [soprad'dʒunto] pp di **sopraggiungere**.

soprallu'ogo, ghi sm (di esperti) inspection; (di polizia) on-the-spot investigation.

sopram'mobile sm ornament.

soprannatu'rale ag supernatural.

sopran'nome sm nickname.

soprannomi'nare vt to nickname.

sopran'numero av: **in** ~ in excess.

so'prano, a sm/f (persona) soprano ♦ sm (voce) soprano.

soprappensi'ero av lost in thought.

soprappiù sm surplus, extra; **in** ~ extra, surplus; (per giunta) besides, in addition.

sopras'salto sm: **di** ~ with a start, with a jump.

soprasse'dere vi: ~ **a** to delay, put off.

soprat'tassa sf surtax.

soprat'tutto av (anzitutto) above all; (specialmente) especially.

sopravvalu'tare vt (persona, capacità) to overestimate.

sopravve'nire vi to arrive, appear; (fatto) to occur.

soprav'vento sm: **avere/prendere il** ~ **su**

qn to have/get the upper hand over sb.
sopravvis'suto, a *pp di* **sopravvivere ♦** *sm/f*
survivor.
sopravvi'venza [sopravvi'vɛntsa] *sf*
survival.
soprav'vivere *vi* to survive; (*continuare a
vivere*): ~ **(in)** to live on (in); ~ **a** (*incidente
etc*) to survive; (*persona*) to outlive.
soprele'vata *sf* (*di strada, ferrovia*) elevated
section.
soprinten'dente *sm/f* supervisor; (*statale:
di belle arti etc*) keeper.
soprinten'denza [soprinten'dɛntsa] *sf*
supervision; (*ente*): ~ **alle Belle Arti**
*government department responsible for
monuments and artistic treasures.*
soprin'tendere *vi*: ~ **a** to superintend,
supervise.
soprin'teso, a *pp di* **soprintendere.**
so'pruso *sm* abuse of power; **subire un** ~
to be abused.
soq'quadro *sm*: **mettere a** ~ to turn
upside-down.
sor'betto *sm* sorbet, water ice (*BRIT*).
sor'bire *vt* to sip; (*fig*) to put up with.
'sorcio ['sortʃo] *sm* mouse.
'sordido, a *ag* sordid; (*fig: gretto*) stingy.
sor'dina *sf*: **in** ~ softly; (*fig*) on the sly.
sordità *sf* deafness.
'sordo, a *ag* deaf; (*rumore*) muffled;
(*dolore*) dull; (*lotta*) silent, hidden; (*odio,
rancore*) veiled ♦ *sm/f* deaf person.
sordo'muto, a *ag* deaf-and-dumb ♦ *sm/f*
deaf-mute.
so'rella *sf* sister.
sorel'lastra *sf* stepsister; (*con genitore in
comune*) half sister.
sor'gente [sor'dʒɛnte] *sf* (*acqua che sgorga*)
spring; (*di fiume, FISICA, fig*) source; **acqua
di** ~ spring water; ~ **di calore** source of
heat; ~ **termale** thermal spring.
'sorgere ['sordʒere] *vi* to rise; (*scaturire*) to
spring, rise; (*fig: difficoltà*) to arise ♦ *sm*: **al**
~ **del sole** at sunrise.
sori'ano, a *ag, sm/f* tabby.
sormon'tare *vt* (*fig*) to overcome,
surmount.
sorni'one, a *ag* sly.
sorpas'sare *vt* (*AUT*) to overtake; (*fig*) to
surpass; (: *eccedere*) to exceed, go
beyond; ~ **in altezza** to be higher than;
(*persona*) to be taller than.
sorpas'sato, a *ag* (*metodo, moda*)
outmoded, old-fashioned; (*macchina*)
obsolete.
sor'passo *sm* (*AUT*) overtaking.
sorpren'dente *ag* surprising; (*eccezionale,
inaspettato*) astonishing, amazing.

sor'prendere *vt* (*cogliere: in flagrante etc*) to
catch; (*stupire*) to surprise; ~**rsi** *vr*: ~**rsi
(di)** to be surprised (at).
sor'preso, a *pp di* **sorprendere ♦** *sf* surprise;
fare una ~**a a qn** to give sb a surprise;
prendere qn di ~**a** to take sb by surprise
o unawares.
sor'reggere [sor'reddʒere] *vt* to support,
hold up; (*fig*) to sustain.
sor'retto, a *pp di* **sorreggere.**
sor'ridere *vi* to smile.
sor'riso, a *pp di* **sorridere ♦** *sm* smile.
sor'sata *sf* gulp; **bere a** ~**e** to gulp.
sorseggi'are [sorsed'dʒare] *vt* to sip.
'sorsi *etc vb vedi* **sorgere.**
'sorso *sm* sip; **d'un** ~, **in un** ~ **solo** at one
gulp.
'sorta *sf* sort, kind; **di** ~ whatever, of any
kind at all; **ogni** ~ **di** all sorts of; **di ogni** ~
of every kind.
'sorte *sf* (*fato*) fate, destiny; (*evento fortuito*)
chance; **tirare a** ~ to draw lots; **tentare la**
~ to try one's luck.
sorteggi'are [sorted'dʒare] *vt* to draw for.
sor'teggio [sor'teddʒo] *sm* draw.
sorti'legio [sorti'lɛdʒo] *sm* witchcraft *no pl*;
(*incantesimo*) spell; **fare un** ~ **a qn** to cast
a spell on sb.
sor'tire *vt* (*ottenere*) to produce.
sor'tita *sf* (*MIL*) sortie.
'sorto, a *pp di* **sorgere.**
sorvegli'ante [sorveʎ'ʎante] *sm/f* (*di carcere*)
guard, warder (*BRIT*); (*di fabbrica etc*)
supervisor.
sorvegli'anza [sorveʎ'ʎantsa] *sf* watch;
supervision; (*POLIZIA, MIL*) surveillance.
sorvegli'are [sorveʎ'ʎare] *vt* (*bambino,
bagagli, prigioniero*) to watch, keep an eye
on; (*malato*) to watch over; (*territorio, casa*)
to watch *o* keep watch over; (*lavori*) to
supervise.
sorvo'lare *vt* (*territorio*) to fly over ♦ *vi*: ~
su (*fig*) to skim over.
S.O.S. *sigla m* mayday, SOS.
'sosia *sm inv* double.
sos'pendere *vt* (*appendere*) to hang (up);
(*interrompere, privare di una carica*) to
suspend; (*rimandare*) to defer; ~ **un
quadro al muro/un lampadario al soffitto**
to hang a picture on the wall/a chandelier
from the ceiling; ~ **qn dal suo incarico** to
suspend sb from office.
sospensi'one *sf* (*anche CHIM, AUT*)
suspension; deferment; ~ **condizionale
della pena** (*DIR*) suspended sentence.
sos'peso, a *pp di* **sospendere ♦** *ag* (*appeso*):
~ **a** hanging on (*o* from); (*treno, autobus*)
cancelled; **in** ~ in abeyance; (*conto*)

outstanding; **tenere in** ~ (*fig*) to keep in suspense; **col fiato** ~ with bated breath.

sospet'tare *vt* to suspect ♦ *vi*: ~ **di** to suspect; (*diffidare*) to be suspicious of.

sos'petto, a *ag* suspicious ♦ *sm* suspicion; **destare** ~**i** to arouse suspicion.

sospet'toso, a *ag* suspicious.

sos'pingere [sos'pindʒere] *vt* to drive, push.

sos'pinto, a *pp di* **sospingere**.

sospi'rare *vi* to sigh ♦ *vt* to long for, yearn for.

sos'piro *sm* sigh; ~ **di sollievo** sigh of relief.

'sosta *sf* (*fermata*) stop, halt; (*pausa*) pause, break; **senza** ~ non-stop, without a break.

sostanti'vato, a *ag* (*LING*): **aggettivo** ~ adjective used as a noun.

sostan'tivo *sm* noun, substantive.

sos'tanza [sos'tantsa] *sf* substance; ~**e** *sfpl* (*ricchezze*) wealth *sg*, possessions; **in** ~ in short, to sum up; **la** ~ **del discorso** the essence of the speech.

sostanzi'ale [sostan'tsjale] *ag* substantial.

sostanzi'oso, a [sostan'tsjoso] *ag* (*cibo*) nourishing, substantial.

sos'tare *vi* (*fermarsi*) to stop (for a while), stay; (*fare una pausa*) to take a break.

sos'tegno [sos'teɲɲo] *sm* support; **a** ~ **di** in support of; **muro di** ~ supporting wall.

soste'nere *vt* to support; (*prendere su di sé*) to take on, bear; (*resistere*) to withstand, stand up to; (*affermare*): ~ **che** to maintain that; ~**rsi** *vr* to hold o.s. up, support o.s.; (*fig*) to keep up one's strength; ~ **qn** (*moralmente*) to be a support to sb; (*difendere*) to stand up for sb, take sb's part; ~ **gli esami** to sit exams; ~ **il confronto** to bear *o* stand comparison.

soste'nibile *ag* (*tesi*) tenable; (*spese*) bearable; (*sviluppo*) sustainable.

sosteni'tore, 'trice *sm/f* supporter.

sostenta'mento *sm* maintenance, support; **mezzi di** ~ means of support.

soste'nuto, a *ag* (*stile*) elevated; (*velocità, ritmo*) sustained; (*prezzo*) high ♦ *sm/f*: **fare il(la)** ~**(a)** to be standoffish, keep one's distance.

sostitu'ire *vt* (*mettere al posto di*): ~ **qn/qc a** to substitute sb/sth for; (*prendere il posto di*) to replace, take the place of.

sostitu'tivo, a *ag* (*AMM*: *documento, certificato*) equivalent.

sosti'tuto, a *sm/f* substitute; ~ **procuratore della Repubblica** (*DIR*) deputy public prosecutor.

sostituzi'one [sostitut'tsjone] *sf* substitution; **in** ~ **di** as a substitute for, in

place of.

sotta'ceti [sotta't ʃeti] *smpl* pickles.

sot'tana *sf* (*sottoveste*) underskirt; (*gonna*) skirt; (*REL*) soutane, cassock.

sot'tecchi [sot'tekki] *av*: **guardare di** ~ to steal a glance at.

sotter'fugio [sotter'fudʒo] *sm* subterfuge.

sotter'raneo, a *ag* underground ♦ *sm* cellar.

sotter'rare *vt* to bury.

sottigli'ezza [sottiʎ'ʎettsa] *sf* thinness; slimness; (*fig*: *acutezza*) subtlety; shrewdness; ~**e** *sfpl* (*pedanteria*) quibbles.

sot'tile *ag* thin; (*figura, caviglia*) thin, slim, slender; (*fine*: *polvere, capelli*) fine; (*fig*: *leggero*) light; (: *vista*) sharp, keen; (: *olfatto*) fine, discriminating; (: *mente*) subtle; shrewd ♦ *sm*: **non andare per il** ~ not to mince matters.

sottiliz'zare [sottilid'dzare] *vi* to split hairs.

sottin'tendere *vt* (*intendere qc non espresso*) to understand; (*implicare*) to imply; **lasciare** ~ **che** to let it be understood that.

sottin'teso, a *pp di* **sottintendere** ♦ *sm* allusion; **parlare senza** ~**i** to speak plainly.

'sotto *prep* (*gen*) under; (*più in basso di*) below ♦ *av* underneath, beneath; below; (*al piano inferiore*): (**al piano**) **di** ~ downstairs; ~ **il monte** at the foot of the mountain; ~ **la pioggia/il sole** in the rain/sun(shine); **tutti quelli** ~ **i 18 anni** all those under 18 (years of age) (*BRIT*) *o* under age 18 (*US*); ~ **il livello del mare** below sea level; ~ **il chilo** under *o* less than a kilo; **ha 5 impiegati** ~ **di sé** he has 5 clerks under him; **siamo** ~ **Natale/Pasqua** it's nearly Christmas/Easter; ~ **un certo punto di vista** in a sense; ~ **forma di** in the form of; ~ **falso nome** under a false name; ~ **terra** underground; ~ **voce** in a low voice; **chiuso** ~ **vuoto** vacuum packed.

sotto'banco *av* (*di nascosto*: *vendere, comprare*) under the counter; (*agire*) in an underhand way.

sottobicchi'ere [sottobik'kjɛre] *sm* mat, coaster.

sotto'bosco, schi *sm* undergrowth *no pl*.

sotto'braccio [sotto'brattʃo] *av* by the arm; **prendere qn** ~ to take sb by the arm; **camminare** ~ **a qn** to walk arm in arm with sb.

sottochi'ave [sotto'kjave] *av* under lock and key.

sottoco'perta *av* (*NAUT*) below deck.

sotto'costo *av* below cost (price).

sottocu'taneo, a *ag* subcutaneous.
sottoes'posto, a *ag* (*fotografia, pellicola*) underexposed.
sotto'fondo *sm* background; ~ **musicale** background music.
sotto'gamba *av*: **prendere qc** ~ not to take sth seriously.
sotto'gonna *sf* underskirt.
sottogo'verno *sm* political patronage.
sotto'gruppo *sm* subgroup; (*di partito*) faction.
sottoline'are *vt* to underline; (*fig*) to emphasize, stress.
sot't'olio *av, ag inv* in oil.
sotto'mano *av* (*a portata di mano*) within reach, to hand; (*di nascosto*) secretly.
sottoma'rino, a *ag* (*flora*) submarine; (*cavo, navigazione*) underwater ♦ *sm* (*NAUT*) submarine.
sotto'messo, a *pp di* **sottomettere** ♦ *ag* submissive.
sotto'mettere *vt* to subdue, subjugate; ~**rsi** *vr* to submit.
sottomissi'one *sf* submission.
sottopas'saggio [sottopas'saddʒo] *sm* (*AUT*) underpass; (*pedonale*) subway, underpass.
sotto'porre *vt* (*costringere*) to subject; (*fig*: *presentare*) to submit; **sottoporsi** *vr* to submit; **sottoporsi a** (*subire*) to undergo.
sotto'posto, a *pp di* **sottoporre**.
sottopro'dotto *sm* by-product.
sottoproduzi'one [sottoprodut'tsjone] *sf* underproduction.
sottoproletari'ato *sm*: **il** ~ **the** underprivileged class.
sot'tordine *av*: **passare in** ~ to become of minor importance.
sottos'cala *sm inv* (*ripostiglio*) cupboard (*BRIT*) *o* closet (*US*) under the stairs; (*stanza*) room under the stairs.
sottos'critto, a *pp di* **sottoscrivere** ♦ *sm/f*: **io** ~, **il** ~ the undersigned.
sottos'crivere *vt* to sign ♦ *vi*: ~ **a** to subscribe to.
sottoscrizi'one [sottoskrit'tsjone] *sf* signing; subscription.
sottosegre'tario *sm*: **S**~ **di Stato** undersecretary of state (*BRIT*), assistant secretary of state (*US*).
sotto'sopra *av* upside-down.
sottos'tante *ag* (*piani*) lower; **nella valle** ~ in the valley below.
sottos'tare *vi*: ~ **a** (*assoggettarsi a*) to submit to; (: *richieste*) to give in to; (*subire*: *prova*) to undergo.
sottosu'olo *sm* subsoil.
sottosvilup'pato, a *ag* underdeveloped.

sottosvi'luppo *sm* underdevelopment.
sottote'nente *sm* (*MIL*) second lieutenant.
sotto'terra *av* underground.
sotto'tetto *sm* attic.
sotto'titolo *sm* subtitle.
sottovalu'tare *vt* (*persona, prova*) to underestimate, underrate.
sotto'vento *av* (*NAUT*) leeward(s) ♦ *ag inv* (*lato*) leeward, lee.
sotto'veste *sf* underskirt.
sotto'voce [sotto'votʃe] *av* in a low voice.
sottovu'oto *av*: **confezionare** ~ to vacuum-pack ♦ *ag*: **confezione** *f* ~ vacuum pack.
sot'trarre *vt* (*MAT*) to subtract, take away; **sottrarsi** *vr*: **sottrarsi a** (*sfuggire*) to escape; (*evitare*) to avoid; ~ **qn/qc a** (*togliere*) to remove sb/sth from; (*salvare*) to save *o* rescue sb/sth from; ~ **qc a qn** (*rubare*) to steal sth from sb; **sottratte le spese** once expenses have been deducted.
sot'tratto, a *pp di* **sottrarre**.
sottrazi'one [sottrat'tsjone] *sf* (*MAT*) subtraction; (*furto*) removal.
sottuffici'ale [sottuffi'tʃale] *sm* (*MIL*) non-commissioned officer; (*NAUT*) petty officer.
soufflé [su'flε] *sm inv* (*CUC*) soufflé.
souve'nir [suv(ə)'nir] *sm inv* souvenir.
so'vente *av* often.
soverchi'are [sover'kjare] *vt* to overpower, overwhelm.
soverchie'ria [soverkje'ria] *sf* (*prepotenza*) abuse (of power).
sovi'etico, a, ci, che *ag* Soviet ♦ *sm/f* Soviet citizen.
sovrabbon'dante *ag* overabundant.
sovrabbon'danza [sovrabbon'dantsa] *sf* overabundance; **in** ~ in excess.
sovraccari'care *vt* to overload.
sovrac'carico, a, chi, che *ag*: ~ **(di)** overloaded (with) ♦ *sm* excess load; ~ **di lavoro** extra work.
sovraesposizi'one [sovraespozit'tsjone] *sf* (*FOT*) overexposure.
sovraffol'lato, a *ag* overcrowded.
sovraimmagazzi'nare [sovraimmagaddzi'nare] *vt* to overstock.
sovranità *sf* sovereignty; (*fig*: *superiorità*) supremacy.
sovrannatu'rale *ag* = **soprannaturale**.
so'vrano, a *ag* sovereign; (*fig*: *sommo*) supreme ♦ *sm/f* sovereign, monarch.
sovrappopolazi'one [sovrappopolat'tsjone] *sf* overpopulation.
sovrap'porre *vt* to place on top of, put on top of; (*FOT, GEOM*) to superimpose; **sovrapporsi** *vr* (*fig*: *aggiungersi*) to be

added; (FOT) to be superimposed.

sovrapposizi'one [sovrapposit'tsjone] sf superimposition.

sovrap'posto, a pp di **sovrapporre.**

sovrapproduzi'one [sovrapprodut'tsjone] sf overproduction.

sovras'tante ag overhanging; (fig) imminent.

sovras'tare vi: ~ **a** vt (vallata, fiume) to overhang; (fig) to hang over, threaten.

sovrastrut'tura sf superstructure.

sovrecci'tare [sovrettʃi'tare] vt to overexcite.

sovrimpressi'one sf (FOT, CINE) double exposure; **immagini in** ~ superimposed images.

sovrinten'dente etc = **soprintendente** etc.

sovru'mano, a ag superhuman.

sovve'nire vi (venire in mente): ~ **a** to occur to.

sovvenzio'nare [sovventsjo'nare] vt to subsidize.

sovvenzi'one [sovven'tsjone] sf subsidy, grant.

sovver'sivo, a ag subversive.

sovverti'mento sm subversion, undermining.

sovver'tire vt (POL: ordine, stato) to subvert, undermine.

'sozzo, a ['sottso] ag filthy, dirty.

SP sigla = **La Spezia.**

S.P. abbr = **strada provinciale;** vedi **provinciale.**

S.p.A. abbr vedi **società per azioni.**

spac'care vt to split, break; (legna) to chop; (fig) to divide; ~**rsi** vr to split, break.

spacca'tura sf split.

spaccherò [spakke'rɔ] etc vb vedi **spaccare.**

spacci'are [spat'tʃare] vt (vendere) to sell (off); (mettere in circolazione) to circulate; (droga) to peddle, push; ~**rsi** vr: ~**rsi per** (farsi credere) to pass o.s. off as, pretend to be.

spacci'ato, a [spat'tʃato] ag (fam: malato, fuggiasco): **essere** ~ to be done for.

spaccia'tore, 'trice [spattʃa'tore] smf (di droga) pusher; (di denaro falso) dealer.

'spaccio ['spattʃo] sm (di merce rubata, droga): ~ **(di)** trafficking (in); (di denaro falso): ~ **(di)** passing (of); (vendita) sale; (bottega) shop.

'spacco, chi sm (fenditura) split, crack; (strappo) tear; (di gonna) slit.

spac'cone smf boaster, braggart.

'spada sf sword.

spadroneggi'are [spadroned'dʒare] vi to swagger.

spae'sato, a ag disorientated, lost.

spaghet'tata [spaget'tata] sf spaghetti meal.

spa'ghetti [spa'getti] smpl (CUC) spaghetti sg.

'Spagna ['spaɲɲa] sf: **la** ~ Spain.

spa'gnolo, a [spaɲ'ɲɔlo] ag Spanish ♦ smf Spaniard ♦ sm (LING) Spanish; **gli S~i** the Spanish.

'spago, ghi sm string, twine; **dare** ~ **a qn** (fig) to let sb have his (o her) way.

spai'ato, a ag (calza, guanto) odd.

spalan'care vt, ~**rsi** vr to open wide.

spa'lare vt to shovel.

'spalla sf shoulder; (fig: TEAT) stooge; ~**e** sfpl (dorso) back; **di** ~**e** from behind; **seduto alle mie** ~**e** sitting behind me; **prendere/colpire qn alle** ~**e** to take/hit sb from behind; **mettere qn con le** ~**e al muro** (fig) to put sb with his (o her) back to the wall; **vivere alle** ~**e di qn** (fig) to live off sb.

spal'lata sf (urto) shove o push with the shoulder; **dare una** ~ **a qc** to give sth a push o shove with one's shoulder.

spalleggi'are [spalled'dʒare] vt to back up, support.

spal'letta sf (parapetto) parapet.

spalli'era sf (di sedia etc) back; (di letto: da capo) head(board); (: da piedi) foot(board); (GINNASTICA) wall bars pl.

spal'lina sf (MIL) epaulette; (di sottoveste, maglietta) strap; **senza** ~**e** strapless.

spal'mare vt to spread.

'spalti smpl (di stadio) terraces (BRIT), ≈ bleachers (US).

'spandere vt to spread; (versare) to pour (out); ~**rsi** vr to spread; ~ **lacrime** to shed tears.

'spanto, a pp di **spandere.**

spa'rare vt to fire ♦ vi (far fuoco) to fire; (tirare) to shoot; ~ **a qn/qc** to shoot sb/sth, fire at sb/sth.

spa'rato sm (di camicia) dicky.

spara'tore sm gunman.

spara'toria sf exchange of shots.

sparecchi'are [sparek'kjare] vt: ~ **(la tavola)** to clear the table.

spa'reggio [spa'reddʒo] sm (SPORT) play-off.

'spargere ['spardʒere] vt (sparpagliare) to scatter; (versare: vino) to spill; (: lacrime, sangue) to shed; (diffondere) to spread; (emanare) to give off (o out); ~**rsi** vr (voce, notizia) to spread; (persone) to scatter; **si è sparsa una voce sul suo conto** there is a rumour going round about him.

spargi'mento [spardʒi'mento] sm

scattering; spilling; shedding; ~ **di sangue** bloodshed.

spa'rire *vi* to disappear, vanish; ~ **dalla circolazione** (*fig fam*) to lie low, keep a low profile.

sparizi'one [sparit'tsjone] *sf* disappearance.

spar'lare *vi*: ~ **di** to run down, speak ill of.

'sparo *sm* shot.

sparpagli'are [sparpaʎ'ʎare] *vt*, ~**rsi** *vr* to scatter.

'sparso, a *pp di* **spargere ♦** *ag* scattered; (*sciolto*) loose; **in ordine** ~ (*MIL*) in open order.

sparti'acque *sm* (*GEO*) watershed.

sparti'neve *sm inv* snowplough (*BRIT*), snowplow (*US*).

spar'tire *vt* (*eredità, bottino*) to share out; (*avversari*) to separate.

spar'tito *sm* (*MUS*) score.

sparti'traffico *sm inv* (*AUT*) central reservation (*BRIT*), median (strip) (*US*).

spartizi'one [spartit'tsjone] *sf* division.

spa'ruto, a *ag* (*viso etc*) haggard.

sparvi'ero *sm* (*ZOOL*) sparrowhawk.

spasi'mante *sm* suitor.

spasi'mare *vi* to be in agony; ~ **di fare** (*fig*) to yearn to do; ~ **per qn** to be madly in love with sb.

'spasimo *sm* pang.

'spasmo *sm* (*MED*) spasm.

spas'modico, a, ci, che *ag* (*angoscioso*) agonizing; (*MED*) spasmodic.

spas'sarsela *vi* to enjoy o.s., have a good time.

spassio'nato, a *ag* dispassionate, impartial.

'spasso *sm* (*divertimento*) amusement, enjoyment; **andare a** ~ to go out for a walk; **essere a** ~ (*fig*) to be out of work; **mandare qn a** ~ (*fig*) to give sb the sack.

spas'soso, a *ag* amusing, entertaining.

'spastico, a, ci, che *ag, sm/f* spastic.

'spatola *sf* spatula.

spau'racchio [spau'rakkjo] *sm* scarecrow.

spau'rire *vt* to frighten, terrify.

spavalde'ria *sf* boldness, arrogance.

spa'valdo, a *ag* arrogant, bold.

spaventa'passeri *sm inv* scarecrow.

spaven'tare *vt* to frighten, scare; ~**rsi** *vr* to become frightened, become scared.

spa'vento *sm* fear, fright; **far** ~ **a qn** to give sb a fright.

spaven'toso, a *ag* frightening, terrible; (*fig fam*) tremendous, fantastic.

spazi'ale [spat'tsjale] *ag* (*volo, nave, tuta*) space *cpd*; (*ARCHIT, GEOM*) spatial.

spazia'tura [spattsja'tura] *sf* (*TIP*) spacing.

spazien'tire [spattsjen'tire] *vi* (*anche:* ~**rsi**) to lose one's patience.

'spazio ['spattsjo] *sm* space; (*posto*) room, space; **fare** ~ **per qc/qn** to make room for sth/sb; **nello** ~ **di un'ora** within an hour, in the space of an hour; **dare** ~ **a** (*fig*) to make room for; ~ **aereo** airspace.

spazi'oso, a [spat'tsjoso] *ag* spacious.

spazzaca'mino [spattsaka'mino] *sm* chimney sweep.

spazza'neve [spattsa'neve] *sm inv* (*spartineve, SCI*) snowplough (*BRIT*), snowplow (*US*).

spaz'zare [spat'tsare] *vt* to sweep; (*foglie etc*) to sweep up; (*cacciare*) to sweep away.

spazza'tura [spattsa'tura] *sf* sweepings *pl*; (*immondizia*) rubbish.

spaz'zino [spat'tsino] *sm* street sweeper.

'spazzola ['spattsola] *sf* brush; **capelli a** ~ crew cut *sg*; ~ **per abiti** clothesbrush; ~ **da capelli** hairbrush.

spazzo'lare [spattso'lare] *vt* to brush.

spazzo'lino [spattso'lino] *sm* (small) brush; ~ **da denti** toothbrush.

specchi'arsi [spek'kjarsi] *vr* to look at o.s. in a mirror; (*riflettersi*) to be mirrored, be reflected.

specchi'era [spek'kjera] *sf* large mirror; (*mobile*) dressing table.

specchi'etto [spek'kjetto] *sm* (*tabella*) table, chart; ~ **da borsetta** pocket mirror; ~ **retrovisore** (*AUT*) rear-view mirror.

'specchio ['spekkjo] *sm* mirror; (*tabella*) table, chart; **uno** ~ **d'acqua** a sheet of water.

speci'ale [spe't∫ale] *ag* special; **in special modo** especially; **inviato** ~ (*RADIO, TV, STAMPA*) special correspondent; **offerta** ~ special offer; **poteri/leggi** ~**i** (*POL*) emergency powers/legislation.

specia'lista, i, e [spet∫a'lista] *sm/f* specialist.

specia'listico, a, ci, che [spet∫a'listiko] *ag* (*conoscenza, preparazione*) specialized.

specialità [spet∫ali'ta] *sf inv* speciality; (*branca di studio*) special field, speciality.

specializ'zare [spet∫alid'dzare] *vt* (*industria*) to make more specialized; ~**rsi** *vr*: ~**rsi (in)** to specialize (in).

specializ'zato, a [spet∫alid'dzato] *ag* (*manodopera*) skilled; **operaio non** ~ semiskilled worker; **essere** ~ **in** to be a specialist in.

specializzazi'one [spet∫aliddzat'tsjone] *sf* specialization; **prendere la** ~ **in** to specialize in.

special'mente [spet∫al'mente] *av* especially, particularly.

'specie ['spɛtʃe] *sf inv* (*BIOL, BOT, ZOOL*) species *inv*; (*tipo*) kind, sort ♦ *av* especially, particularly; **una ~ di** a kind of; **fare ~ a qn** to surprise sb; **la ~ umana** mankind.

spe'cifica, che [spe'tʃifika] *sf* specification.

specifi'care [spetʃifi'kare] *vt* to specify, state.

specificata'mente [spetʃifikata'mente] *av* in detail.

spe'cifico, a, ci, che [spe'tʃifiko] *ag* specific.

speck [ʃpɛk] *sm inv* kind of smoked ham.

specu'lare *vi*: **~ su** (*COMM*) to speculate in; (*sfruttare*) to exploit; (*meditare*) to speculate on.

specula'tore, 'trice *sm/f* (*COMM*) speculator.

speculazi'one [spekulat'tsjone] *sf* speculation.

spe'dire *vt* to send; (*COMM*) to dispatch, forward; **~ per posta** to post (*BRIT*), mail (*US*); **~ per mare** to ship.

spedita'mente *av* quickly; **camminare ~** to walk at a brisk pace.

spe'dito, a *ag* (*gen*) quick; **con passo ~** at a brisk pace.

spedizi'one [spedit'tsjone] *sf* sending; (*collo*) consignment; (*scientifica etc*) expedition; (*COMM*) forwarding; shipping; **fare una ~** to send a consignment; **agenzia di ~** forwarding agency; **spese di ~** postal charges; (*COMM*) forwarding charges.

spedizioni'ere [spedittsjo'njɛre] *sm* forwarding agent, shipping agent.

'spegnere ['spɛɲɲere] *vt* (*fuoco, sigaretta*) to put out, extinguish; (*apparecchio elettrico*) to turn *o* switch off; (*gas*) to turn off; (*fig: suoni, passioni*) to stifle; (*debito*) to extinguish; **~rsi** *vr* to go out; to go off; (*morire*) to pass away.

speleolo'gia [speleolo'dʒia] *sf* (*studio*) speleology; (*pratica*) potholing (*BRIT*), speleology.

spele'ologo, a, gi, ghe *sm/f* speleologist; potholer.

spel'lare *vt* (*scuoiare*) to skin; (*scorticare*) to graze; **~rsi** *vr* to peel.

spendacci'one, a [spendat'tʃone] *sm/f* spendthrift.

'spendere *vt* to spend; **~ una buona parola per qn** (*fig*) to put in a good word for sb.

'spengo *etc vb vedi* **spegnere**.

spen'nare *vt* to pluck.

'spensi *etc vb vedi* **spegnere**.

spensiera'tezza [spensjera'tettsa] *sf* carefreeness, lightheartedness.

spensie'rato, a *ag* carefree.

'spento, a *pp di* **spegnere** ♦ *ag* (*suono*) muffled; (*colore*) dull; (*sigaretta*) out; (*civiltà, vulcano*) extinct.

spe'ranza [spe'rantsa] *sf* hope; **nella ~ di rivederti** hoping to see *o* in the hope of seeing you again; **pieno di ~e** hopeful; **senza ~** (*situazione*) hopeless; (*amare*) without hope.

speran'zoso, a [speran'tsoso] *ag* hopeful.

spe'rare *vt* to hope for ♦ *vi*: **~ in** to trust in; **~ che/di fare** to hope that/to do; **lo spero, spero di sì** I hope so; **tutto fa ~ per il meglio** everything leads one to hope for the best.

sper'duto, a *ag* (*isolato*) out-of-the-way; (*persona: smarrita, a disagio*) lost.

spergi'uro, a [sper'dʒuro] *sm/f* perjurer ♦ *sm* perjury.

sperico'lato, a *ag* fearless, daring; (*guidatore*) reckless.

sperimen'tale *ag* experimental; **fare qc in via ~** to try sth out.

sperimen'tare *vt* to experiment with, test; (*fig*) to test, put to the test.

sperimentazi'one [sperimentat'tsjone] *sf* experimentation.

'sperma, i *sm* (*BIOL*) sperm.

spermato'zoo, i [spermatod'dzɔo] *sm* spermatozoon.

spe'rone *sm* spur.

sperpe'rare *vt* to squander.

'sperpero *sm* (*di denaro*) squandering, waste; (*di cibo, materiali*) waste.

'spesa *sf* (*soldi spesi*) expense; (*costo*) cost; (*acquisto*) purchase; (*fam: acquisto del cibo quotidiano*) shopping; **~e** *sfpl* expenses; (*COMM*) costs; charges; **ridurre le ~e** (*gen*) to cut down; (*COMM*) to reduce expenditure; **fare la ~** to do the shopping; **fare le ~e di qc** (*fig*) to pay the price for sth; **a ~e di** (*a carico di*) at the expense of; **con la modica ~ di 200 euro** for the modest sum *o* outlay of 200 euros; **~ pubblica** public expenditure; **~e accessorie** incidental expenses; **~e generali** overheads; **~e di gestione** operating expenses; **~e d'impianto** initial outlay; **~e legali** legal costs; **~e di manutenzione, ~e di mantenimento** maintenance costs; **~e postali** postage *sg*; **~e di sbarco e sdoganamento** landing charges; **~e di trasporto** handling charge; **~e di viaggio** travelling (*BRIT*) *o* traveling (*US*) expenses.

spe'sare *vt*: **viaggio tutto spesato** all-expenses-paid trip.

'speso, a *pp di* **spendere**.

'spesso, a *ag (fitto)* thick; *(frequente)* frequent ♦ *av* often; **~e volte** frequently, often.

spes'sore *sm* thickness; **ha uno ~ di 20 cm** it is 20 cm thick.

Spett. *abbr vedi* **spettabile.**

spet'tabile *ag (abbr:* **Spett.**): *in lettere):* **~ ditta X** Messrs X and Co; **avvertiamo la ~ clientela** ... we inform our customers ....

spettaco'lare *ag* spectacular.

spet'tacolo *sm (rappresentazione)* performance, show; *(vista, scena)* sight; **dare ~ di sé** to make an exhibition *o* a spectacle of o.s.

spettaco'loso, a *ag* spectacular.

spet'tanza [spet'tantsa] *sf (competenza)* concern; **non è di mia ~** it's no concern of mine.

spet'tare *vi*: **~ a** *(decisione)* to be up to; *(stipendio)* to be due to; **spetta a lei decidere** it's up to you to decide.

spetta'tore, 'trice *sm/f (CINE, TEAT)* member of the audience; *(di avvenimento)* onlooker, witness.

spettego'lare *vi* to gossip.

spetti'nare *vt*: **~ qn** to ruffle sb's hair; **~rsi** *vr* to get one's hair in a mess.

spet'trale *ag* spectral, ghostly.

'spettro *sm (fantasma)* spectre *(BRIT),* specter *(US); (FISICA)* spectrum.

'spezie ['spɛttsje] *sfpl (CUC)* spices.

spez'zare [spet'tsare] *vt (rompere)* to break; *(fig: interrompere)* to break up; **~rsi** *vr* to break.

spezza'tino [spettsa'tino] *sm (CUC)* stew.

spez'zato, a [spet'tsato] *ag (unghia, ramo, braccio)* broken ♦ *sm (abito maschile)* coordinated jacket and trousers *(BRIT) o* pants *(US);* **fare orario ~** to work a split shift.

spezzet'tare [spettset'tare] *vt* to break up *(o* chop) into small pieces.

spez'zino, a [spet'tsino] *ag* of *(o* from) La Spezia.

spez'zone [spet'tsone] *sm (CINE)* clip.

'spia *sf* spy; *(confidente della polizia)* informer; *(ELETTR)* indicating light; warning light; *(fessura)* peephole; *(fig: sintomo)* sign, indication; **~ dell'olio** *(AUT)* oil warning light.

spiacci'care [spjattʃi'kare] *vt* to squash, crush.

spia'cente [spja'tʃɛnte] *ag* sorry; **essere ~ di qc/di fare qc** to be sorry about sth/for doing sth; **siamo ~i di dovervi annunciare che** ... we regret to announce that ....

spia'cevole [spja'tʃevole] *ag* unpleasant, disagreeable.

spi'aggia, ge ['spjaddʒa] *sf* beach.

spia'nare *vt (terreno)* to level, make level; *(edificio)* to raze to the ground; *(pasta)* to roll out; *(rendere liscio)* to smooth (out).

spi'ano *sm*: **a tutto ~** *(lavorare)* non-stop, without a break; *(spendere)* lavishly.

spian'tato, a *ag* penniless, ruined.

spi'are *vt* to spy on; *(occasione etc)* to watch *o* wait for.

spi'ata *sf* tip-off.

spiattel'lare *vt (fam: verità, segreto)* to blurt out.

spi'azzo ['spjattso] *sm* open space; *(radura)* clearing.

spic'care *vt (assegno, mandato di cattura)* to issue ♦ *vi (risaltare)* to stand out; **~ il volo** to fly off; *(fig)* to spread one's wings; **~ un balzo** to jump, leap.

spic'cato, a *ag (marcato)* marked, strong; *(notevole)* remarkable.

spiccherò *etc* [spikke'rɔ] *vb vedi* **spiccare.**

'spicchio ['spikkjo] *sm (di agrumi)* segment; *(di aglio)* clove; *(parte)* piece, slice.

spicci'are [spit'tʃare] *vt (faccenda, impegno)* to finish off; **~rsi** *vr (fare in fretta)* to hurry up, get a move on.

'spiccio, a, ci, ce ['spittʃo] *ag (modi, mezzi)* quick; **andare per le ~ce** to be quick off the mark, waste no time.

spiccio'lata [spittʃo'lata] *av*: **alla ~** in dribs and drabs, a few at a time.

'spicciolo, a ['spittʃolo] *ag*: **moneta ~a, ~i** *smpl* (small) change.

'spicco, chi *sm*: **fare ~** to stand out; **di ~** outstanding, prominent; *(tema)* main, principal.

spie'dino *sm (utensile)* skewer; *(cibo)* kebab.

spi'edo *sm (CUC)* spit; **pollo allo ~** spit-roasted chicken.

spiega'mento *sm (MIL)*: **~ di forze** deployment of forces.

spie'gare *vt (far capire)* to explain; *(tovaglia)* to unfold; *(vele)* to unfurl; **~rsi** *vr* to explain o.s., make o.s. clear; **~ qc a qn** to explain sth to sb; **il problema si spiega** one can understand the problem; **non mi spiego come** ... I can't understand how ....

spiegazi'one [spjegat'tsjone] *sf* explanation; **avere una ~ con qn** to have it out with sb.

spiegaz'zare [spjegat'tsare] *vt* to crease, crumple.

spiegherò *etc* [spjege'rɔ] *vb vedi* **spiegare.**

spie'tato, a *ag* ruthless, pitiless.

spiffe'rare *vt (fam)* to blurt out, blab.

'spiffero *sm* draught *(BRIT),* draft *(US).*

'spiga, ghe *sf* (*BOT*) ear.
spigli'ato, a [spiʎ'ʎato] *ag* self-possessed, self-confident.
spigo'lare *vt* (*anche fig*) to glean.
'spigolo *sm* corner; (*GEOM*) edge.
spigo'loso, a *ag* (*mobile*) angular; (*persona, carattere*) difficult.
'spilla *sf* brooch; (*da cravatta, cappello*) pin.
spil'lare *vt* (*vino, fig*) to tap; ~ **denaro/ notizie a qn** to tap sb for money/ information.
'spillo *sm* pin; (*spilla*) brooch; **tacco a** ~ stiletto heel (*BRIT*), spike heel (*US*); ~ **di sicurezza** *o* **da balia** safety pin; ~ **di sicurezza** (*MIL*) (safety) pin.
spilorce'ria [spilortʃe'ria] *sf* meanness, stinginess.
spi'lorcio, a, ci, ce [spi'lortʃo] *ag* mean, stingy.
spilun'gone *sm/f* beanpole.
'spina *sf* (*BOT*) thorn; (*ZOOL*) spine, prickle; (*di pesce*) bone; (*ELETTR*) plug; (*di botte*) bunghole; **birra alla** ~ draught beer; **stare sulle** ~**e** (*fig*) to be on tenterhooks; ~ **dorsale** (*ANAT*) backbone.
spi'nacio [spi'natʃo] *sm* spinach *no pl*; (*CUC*): ~**i** spinach *sg*.
spi'nale *ag* (*ANAT*) spinal.
spi'nato, a *ag* (*fornito di spine*): **filo** ~ barbed wire; (*tessuto*) herringbone *cpd*.
spi'nello *sm* (*DROGA*: *gergo*) joint.
'spingere ['spindʒere] *vt* to push; (*condurre: anche fig*) to drive; (*stimolare*): ~ **qn a fare** to urge *o* press sb to do; ~**rsi** *vr* (*inoltrarsi*) to push on, carry on; ~**rsi troppo lontano** (*anche fig*) to go too far.
'spino *sm* (*BOT*) thorn bush.
spi'noso, a *ag* thorny, prickly.
'spinsi *etc vb vedi* **spingere**.
spinte'rogeno [spinte'rodʒeno] *sm* (*AUT*) coil ignition.
'spinto, a *pp di* **spingere** ♦ *sf* (*urto*) push; (*FISICA*) thrust; (*fig: stimolo*) incentive, spur; (: *appoggio*) string-pulling *no pl*; **dare una** ~ **a a qn** (*fig*) to pull strings for sb.
spinto'nare *vt* to shove, push.
spin'tone *sm* push, shove.
spio'naggio [spio'naddʒo] *sm* espionage, spying.
spion'cino [spion'tʃino] *sm* peephole.
spi'one, a *sm/f* (*spia*) informer; (*ragazzino, collega*) telltale, sneak.
spio'nistico, a, ci, che *ag* (*organizzazione*) spy *cpd*; **rete** ~**a** spy ring.
spi'overe *vi* (*scorrere*) to flow down; (*ricadere*) to hang down, fall.
'spira *sf* coil.
spi'raglio [spi'raʎʎo] *sm* (*fessura*) chink,

narrow opening; (*raggio di luce, fig*) glimmer, gleam.
spi'rale *sf* spiral; (*contraccettivo*) coil; **a** ~ spiral(-shaped); ~ **inflazionistica** inflationary spiral.
spi'rare *vi* (*vento*) to blow; (*morire*) to expire, pass away.
spiri'tato, a *ag* possessed; (*fig: persona, espressione*) wild.
spiri'tismo *sm* spiritualism.
'spirito *sm* (*REL, CHIM, disposizione d'animo, di legge etc, fantasma*) spirit; (*pensieri, intelletto*) mind; (*arguzia*) wit; (*umorismo*) humour, wit; **in buone condizioni di** ~ in the right frame of mind; **è una persona di** ~ he has a sense of humour (*BRIT*) *o* humor (*US*); **battuta di** ~ joke; ~ **di classe** class consciousness; **non ha** ~ **di parte** he never takes sides; **lo S**~ **Santo** the Holy Spirit *o* Ghost.
spirito'saggine [spirito'saddʒine] *sf* witticism; (*peg*) wisecrack.
spiri'toso, a *ag* witty.
spiritu'ale *ag* spiritual.
splen'dente *ag* (*giornata*) bright, sunny; (*occhi*) shining; (*pavimento*) shining, gleaming.
'splendere *vi* to shine.
'splendido, a *ag* splendid; (*splendente*) shining; (*sfarzoso*) magnificent, splendid.
splen'dore *sm* splendour (*BRIT*), splendor (*US*); (*luce intensa*) brilliance, brightness.
spodes'tare *vt* to deprive of power; (*sovrano*) to depose.
'spoglia ['spoʎʎa] *sf vedi* **spoglio**.
spogli'are [spoʎ'ʎare] *vt* (*svestire*) to undress; (*privare, fig: depredare*): ~ **qn di qc** to deprive sb of sth; (*togliere ornamenti: anche fig*): ~ **qn/qc di** to strip sb/sth of; ~**rsi** *vr* to undress, strip; ~**rsi di** (*ricchezze etc*) to deprive o.s. of, give up; (*pregiudizi*) to rid o.s. of.
spoglia'rello [spoʎʎa'rɛllo] *sm* striptease.
spoglia'toio [spoʎʎa'tojo] *sm* dressing room; (*di scuola etc*) cloakroom; (*SPORT*) changing room.
'spoglio, a ['spoʎʎo] *ag* (*pianta, terreno*) bare; (*privo*): ~ **di** stripped of; lacking in, without ♦ *sm* (*di voti*) counting ♦ *sf* (*ZOOL*) skin, hide; (: *di rettile*) slough; ~**e** *sfpl* (*salma*) remains; (*preda*) spoils, booty *sg*.
'spola *sf* shuttle; (*bobina*) spool; **fare la** ~ (*fra*) to go to and fro *o* shuttle (between).
spo'letta *sf* (*CUCITO: bobina*) spool; (*di bomba*) fuse.
spol'pare *vt* to strip the flesh off.
spolve'rare *vt* (*anche CUC*) to dust; (*con spazzola*) to brush; (*con battipanni*) to beat;

spolverino – sproposito

(*fig: mangiare*) to polish off ♦ *vi* to dust.

spolve'rino *sm* (*soprabito*) dust coat.

'sponda *sf* (*di fiume*) bank; (*di mare, lago*) shore; (*bordo*) edge.

sponsoriz'zare [sponsorid'dzare] *vt* to sponsor.

sponsorizzazi'one [sponsoriddzat'tsjone] *sf* sponsorship.

spontanea'mente *av* (*comportarsi*) naturally; (*agire*) spontaneously; (*reagire*) instinctively, spontaneously.

spon'taneo, a *ag* spontaneous; (*persona*) unaffected, natural; **di sua ~a volontà** of his own free will.

spopo'lare *vt* to depopulate ♦ *vi* (*attirare folla*) to draw the crowds; **~rsi** *vr* to become depopulated.

spo'radico, a, ci, che *ag* sporadic.

sporcacci'one, a [sporkat'tʃone] *sm/f* (*peg*) pig, filthy person.

spor'care *vt* to dirty, make dirty; (*fig*) to sully, soil; **~rsi** *vr* to get dirty.

spor'cizia [spor'tʃittsja] *sf* (*stato*) dirtiness; (*sudiciume*) dirt, filth; (*fig: cosa oscena*) obscenity.

'sporco, a, chi, che *ag* dirty, filthy; **avere la coscienza ~a** to have a guilty conscience.

spor'genza [spor'dʒentsa] *sf* projection.

'sporgere ['spordʒere] *vt* to put out, stretch out ♦ *vi* (*venire in fuori*) to stick out; **~rsi** *vr* to lean out; **~ querela contro qn** (*DIR*) to take legal action against sb.

'sporsi *etc vb vedi* **sporgere**.

sport *sm inv* sport.

'sporta *sf* shopping bag.

spor'tello *sm* (*di treno, auto etc*) door; (*di banca, ufficio*) window, counter; **~ automatico** (*BANCA*) cash dispenser, automated telling machine.

spor'tivo, a *ag* (*gara, giornale*) sports *cpd*; (*persona*) sporty; (*abito*) casual; (*spirito, atteggiamento*) sporting ♦ *sm/f* sportsman/ woman; **campo ~** playing field; **giacca ~a** sports (*BRIT*) *o* sport (*US*) jacket.

'sporto, a *pp di* **sporgere**.

'sposa *sf* bride; (*moglie*) wife; **abito** *o* **vestito da ~** wedding dress.

sposa'lizio [spoza'littsjo] *sm* wedding.

spo'sare *vt* to marry; (*fig: idea, fede*) to espouse; **~rsi** *vr* to get married, marry; **~rsi con qn** to marry sb, get married to sb.

spo'sato, a *ag* married.

'sposo *sm* (bride)groom; (*marito*) husband; **gli ~i** the newlyweds.

spos'sante *ag* exhausting.

spossa'tezza [spossa'tettsa] *sf* exhaustion.

spos'sato, a *ag* exhausted, weary.

sposta'mento *sm* movement, change of position.

spos'tare *vt* to move, shift; (*cambiare: orario*) to change; **~rsi** *vr* to move; **hanno spostato la partenza di qualche giorno** they postponed *o* put off their departure by a few days.

spot [spɔt] *sm inv* (*faretto*) spotlight, spot; (*TV*) advert, commercial, ad.

'spranga, ghe *sf* (*sbarra*) bar; (*catenaccio*) bolt.

spran'gare *vt* to bar; to bolt.

spray ['spraɪ] *sm inv* (*dispositivo, sostanza*) spray ♦ *ag inv* (*bombola, confezione*) spray *cpd*.

'sprazzo ['sprattso] *sm* (*di sole etc*) flash; (*fig: di gioia etc*) burst.

spre'care *vt* to waste; **~rsi** *vr* (*persona*) to waste one's energy.

'spreco, chi *sm* waste.

spre'gevole [spre'dʒevole] *ag* contemptible, despicable.

'spregio ['spredʒo] *sm* scorn, disdain.

spregiudi'cato, a [spredʒudi'kato] *ag* unprejudiced, unbiased; (*peg*) unscrupulous.

'spremere *vt* to squeeze; **~rsi le meningi** (*fig*) to rack one's brains.

spre'muta *sf* fresh fruit juice; **~ d'arancia** fresh orange juice.

sprez'zante [spret'tsante] *ag* scornful, contemptuous.

'sprezzo ['sprettso] *sm* contempt, scorn, disdain.

sprigio'nare [spridʒo'nare] *vt* to give off, emit; **~rsi** *vr* to emanate; (*uscire con impeto*) to burst out.

spriz'zare [sprit'tsare] *vt, vi* to spurt; **~ gioia/salute** to be bursting with joy/ health.

sprofon'dare *vi* to sink; (*casa*) to collapse; (*suolo*) to give way, subside; **~rsi** *vr*: **~rsi in** (*poltrona*) to sink into; (*fig*) to become immersed *o* absorbed in.

sproloqui'are *vi* to ramble on.

spro'loquio *sm* rambling speech.

spro'nare *vt* to spur (on).

'sprone *sm* (*sperone, fig*) spur.

sproporzio'nato, a [sproportsjo'nato] *ag* disproportionate, out of all proportion.

sproporzi'one [sproportsjone] *sf* disproportion.

spropositato, a *ag* (*lettera, discorso*) full of mistakes; (*fig: costo*) excessive, enormous.

spro'posito *sm* blunder; **a ~** at the wrong time; (*rispondere, parlare*) irrelevantly.

sprovve'duto, a *ag* inexperienced, naïve.

sprov'visto, a *ag* (*mancante*): ~ **di** lacking in, without; **ne siamo ~i** (*negozio*) we are out of it (*o* them); **alla ~a** unawares.

spruz'zare [sprut'tsare] *vt* (*a nebulizzazione*) to spray; (*aspergere*) to sprinkle; (*inzaccherare*) to splash.

spruzza'tore [spruttsa'tore] *sm* (*per profumi*) spray, atomizer; (*per biancheria*) sprinkler, spray.

'spruzzo ['spruttso] *sm* spray; splash; **verniciatura a** ~ spray painting.

spudora'tezza [spudora'tettsa] *sf* shamelessness.

spudo'rato, a *ag* shameless.

'spugna ['spuɲɲa] *sf* (*ZOOL*) sponge; (*tessuto*) towelling.

spu'gnoso, a [spuɲ'ɲoso] *ag* spongy.

spulci'are [spul't∫are] *vt* (*animali*) to rid of fleas; (*fig: testo, compito*) to examine thoroughly.

'spuma *sf* (*schiuma*) foam; (*bibita*) fizzy drink.

spu'mante *sm* sparkling wine.

spumeggi'ante [spumed'dʒante] *ag* (*vino, fig*) sparkling; (*birra, mare*) foaming.

spu'mone *sm* (*CUC*) mousse.

spun'tare *sm*: **allo** ~ **del sole** at sunrise; **allo** ~ **del giorno** at daybreak ♦ *vt* (*coltello*) to break the point of; (*capelli*) to trim; (*elenco*) to tick off (*BRIT*), check off (*US*) ♦ *vi* (*uscire: germogli*) to sprout; (: *capelli*) to begin to grow; (: *denti*) to come through; (*apparire*) to appear (suddenly); ~**rsi** *vr* to become blunt, lose its point; **spuntarla** (*fig*) to make it, win through.

spun'tino *sm* snack.

'spunto *sm* (*TEAT, MUS*) cue; (*fig*) starting point; **dare lo** ~ **a** to give rise to; **prendere** ~ **da qc** to take sth as one's starting point.

spur'gare *vt* (*fogna*) to clean, clear; ~**rsi** *vr* (*MED*) to expectorate.

spu'tare *vt* to spit out; (*fig*) to belch (out) ♦ *vi* to spit.

'sputo *sm* spittle *no pl*, spit *no pl*.

sputta'nare *vt* (*fam*) to bad-mouth.

'squadra *sf* (*strumento*) (set) square; (*gruppo*) team, squad; (*di operai*) gang, squad; (*MIL*) squad; (: *AER, NAUT*) squadron; (*SPORT*) team; **lavoro a ~e** teamwork; ~ **mobile/del buon costume** (*POLIZIA*) flying/vice squad.

squa'drare *vt* to square, make square; (*osservare*) to look at closely.

squa'driglia [skwa'driʎʎa] *sf* (*AER*) flight; (*NAUT*) squadron.

squa'drone *sm* squadron.

squagli'arsi [skwaʎ'ʎarsi] *vr* to melt; (*fig*) to sneak off.

squa'lifica, che *sf* disqualification.

squalifi'care *vt* to disqualify.

'squallido, a *ag* wretched, bleak.

squal'lore *sm* wretchedness, bleakness.

'squalo *sm* shark.

'squama *sf* scale.

squa'mare *vt* to scale; ~**rsi** *vr* to flake *o* peel (off).

squarcia'gola [skwart∫a'gola]: **a** ~ *av* at the top of one's voice.

squarci'are [skwar't∫are] *vt* (*muro, corpo*) to rip open; (*tessuto*) to rip; (*fig: tenebre, silenzio*) to split; (: *nuvole*) to pierce.

'squarcio ['skwart∫o] *sm* (*ferita*) gash; (*in lenzuolo, abito*) rip; (*in un muro*) breach; (*in una nave*) hole; (*brano*) passage, excerpt; **uno** ~ **di sole** a burst of sunlight.

squar'tare *vt* to quarter, cut up; (*cadavere*) to dismember.

squattri'nato, a *ag* penniless ♦ *sm/f* pauper.

squili'brare *vt* to unbalance.

squili'brato, a *ag* (*PSIC*) unbalanced ♦ *sm/f* deranged person.

squi'librio *sm* (*differenza, sbilancio*) imbalance; (*PSIC*) derangement.

squil'lante *ag* (*suono*) shrill, sharp; (*voce*) shrill.

squil'lare *vi* (*campanello, telefono*) to ring (out); (*tromba*) to blare.

'squillo *sm* ring, ringing *no pl*; blare ♦ *sf inv* (*anche*: **ragazza** ~) call girl.

squi'sito, a *ag* exquisite; (*cibo*) delicious; (*persona*) delightful.

squit'tire *vi* (*uccello*) to squawk; (*topo*) to squeak.

SR *sigla* = *Siracusa*.

sradi'care *vt* to uproot; (*fig*) to eradicate.

sragio'nare [zradʒo'nare] *vi* to talk nonsense, rave.

sregola'tezza [zregola'tettsa] *sf* (*nel mangiare, bere*) lack of moderation; (*di vita*) dissoluteness, dissipation.

srego'lato, a *ag* (*senza ordine: vita*) disorderly; (*smodato*) immoderate; (*dissoluto*) dissolute.

Sri 'Lanka [sri'lanka] *sm*: **lo** ~ Sri Lanka.

S.r.l. *abbr vedi* **società a responsabilità limitata**.

sroto'lare *vt*, ~**rsi** *vr* to unroll.

SS *sigla* = *Sassari*.

S.S. *abbr* (*REL*) = *Sua Santità; Santa Sede; santi, santissimo*; (*AUT*) = **strada statale**; *vedi* **statale**.

S.S.N. *abbr* (= *Servizio Sanitario Nazionale*) ≈

NHS.

sta etc vb vedi **stare.**

'stabbio sm (recinto) pen, fold; (di maiali) pigsty; (letame) manure.

'stabile ag stable, steady; (tempo: non variabile) settled; (TEAT: compagnia) resident ♦ sm (edificio) building; **teatro** ~ civic theatre.

stabili 'mento sm (edificio) establishment; (fabbrica) plant, factory; ~ **balneare** bathing establishment; ~ **tessile** textile mill.

stabi 'lire vt to establish; (fissare: prezzi, data) to fix; (decidere) to decide; ~**rsi** vr (prendere dimora) to settle; **resta stabilito che** ... it is agreed that ....

stabilità sf stability.

stabiliz 'zare [stabilid'dzare] vt to stabilize.

stabilizza 'tore [stabiliddza'tore] sm stabilizer; (fig) stabilizing force.

stabilizzazi 'one [stabiliddzat'tsjone] sf stabilization.

stacano 'vista, i, e sm/f (ironico) eager beaver.

stac 'care vt (levare) to detach, remove; (separare: anche fig) to separate, divide; (strappare) to tear off (o out); (scandire: parole) to pronounce clearly; (SPORT) to leave behind; ~**rsi** vr (bottone etc) to come off; (scostarsi): ~**rsi (da)** to move away (from); (fig: separarsi): ~**rsi da** to leave; **non** ~ **gli occhi da qn** not to take one's eyes off sb; ~ **la televisione/il telefono** to disconnect the television/the phone; ~ **un assegno** to write a cheque.

staccio 'nata [stattʃo'nata] sf (gen) fence; (IPPICA) hurdle.

'stacco, chi sm (intervallo) gap; (: tra due scene) break; (differenza) difference; (SPORT: nel salto) takeoff.

sta 'dera sf lever scales pl.

'stadio sm (SPORT) stadium; (periodo, fase) phase, stage.

'staffa sf (di sella, TECN) stirrup; **perdere le** ~**e** (fig) to fly off the handle.

staf 'fetta sf (messo) dispatch rider; (SPORT) relay race.

stagflazi 'one [stagflat'tsjone] sf (ECON) stagflation.

stagio 'nale [stadʒo'nale] ag seasonal ♦ sm/f seasonal worker.

stagio 'nare [stadʒo'nare] vt (legno) to season; (formaggi, vino) to mature.

stagio 'nato, a [stadʒo'nato] ag (vedi vb) seasoned; matured; (scherzoso: attempato) getting on in years.

stagi 'one [sta'dʒone] sf season; **alta/bassa** ~ high/low season.

stagli 'arsi [staʎ'ʎarsi] vr to stand out, be silhouetted.

sta 'gnante [staɲ'ɲante] ag stagnant.

sta 'gnare [staɲ'ɲare] vt (vaso, tegame) to tin-plate; (barca, botte) to make watertight; (sangue) to stop ♦ vi to stagnate.

sta 'gnino [staɲ'ɲino] sm tinsmith.

'stagno, a ['staɲɲo] ag (a tenuta d'acqua) watertight; (a tenuta d'aria) airtight ♦ sm (acquitrino) pond; (CHIM) tin.

sta 'gnola [staɲ'ɲɔla] sf tinfoil.

stalag 'mite sf stalagmite.

stalat 'tite sf stalactite.

stali 'nismo sm (POL) Stalinism.

'stalla sf (per bovini) cowshed; (per cavalli) stable.

stalli 'ere sm groom, stableboy.

'stallo sm stall, seat; (SCACCHI) stalemate; (AER) stall; **situazione di** ~ (fig) stalemate.

stal 'lone sm stallion.

sta 'mani, stamat 'tina av this morning.

stam 'becco, chi sm ibex.

stam 'berga, ghe sf hovel.

'stampa sf (TIP, FOT: tecnica) printing; (impressione, copia fotografica) print; (insieme di quotidiani, giornalisti etc): **la** ~ the press; **andare in** ~ to go to press; **mandare in** ~ to pass for press; **errore di** ~ printing error; **prova di** ~ print sample; **libertà di** ~ freedom of the press; **"~e"** "printed matter".

stam 'pante sf (INFORM) printer; ~ **seriale/termica** serial/thermal printer.

stam 'pare vt to print; (pubblicare) to publish; (coniare) to strike, coin; (imprimere: anche fig) to impress.

stampa 'tello sm block letters pl.

stam 'pato, a ag printed ♦ sm (opuscolo) leaflet; (modulo) form; ~**i** smpl printed matter sg.

stam 'pella sf crutch.

stampigli 'are [stampiʎ'ʎare] vt to stamp.

stampiglia 'tura [stampiʎʎa'tura] sf (atto) stamping; (marchio) stamp.

'stampo sm mould; (fig: indole) type, kind, sort.

sta 'nare vt to drive out.

stan 'care vt to tire, make tired; (annoiare) to bore; (infastidire) to annoy; ~**rsi** vr to get tired, tire o.s. out; ~**rsi (di)** (stufarsi) to grow weary (of), grow tired (of).

stan 'chezza [stan'kettsa] sf tiredness, fatigue.

'stanco, a, chi, che ag tired; ~ **di** tired of, fed up with.

stand [stand] sm inv (in fiera) stand.

'standard ['standərd] sm inv (livello)

standard.
standardiz'zare [standardid'dzare] *vt* to standardize.
stan'dista, i, e *sm/f* (*in una fiera etc*) person responsible for a stand.
'stanga, ghe *sm* bar; (*di carro*) shaft.
stan'gare *vt* (*fig*: *cliente*) to overcharge; (: *studente*) to fail.
stan'gata *sf* (*colpo*: *anche fig*) blow; (*cattivo risultato*) poor result; (*CALCIO*) shot.
stan'ghetta [stan'getta] *sf* (*di occhiali*) leg; (*MUS, di scrittura*) bar.
'stanno *vb vedi* **stare.**
sta'notte *av* tonight; (*notte passata*) last night.
'stante *prep* owing to, because of; **a sé ~** (*appartamento, casa*) independent, separate.
stan'tio, a, 'tii, 'tie *ag* stale; (*burro*) rancid; (*fig*) old.
stan'tuffo *sm* piston.
'stanza ['stantsa] *sf* room; (*POESIA*) stanza; **essere di ~ a** (*MIL*) to be stationed in; **~ da bagno** bathroom; **~ da letto** bedroom.
stanzia'mento [stantsja'mento] *sm* allocation.
stanzi'are [stan'tsjare] *vt* to allocate.
stan'zino [stan'tsino] *sm* (*ripostiglio*) storeroom; (*spogliatoio*) changing room (*BRIT*), locker room (*US*).
stap'pare *vt* to uncork; (*tappo a corona*) to uncap.
star [star] *sf* (*attore, attrice etc*) star.
'stare *vi* (*restare in un luogo*) to stay, remain; (*abitare*) to stay, live; (*essere situato*) to be, be situated; (*anche*: **~ in piedi**) to stand; (*essere, trovarsi*) to be; (*dipendere*): **se stesse in me** if it were up to me, if it depended on me; (*seguito da gerundio*): **sta studiando** he's studying; **~ per fare qc** to be about to do sth; **starci** (*esserci spazio*): **nel baule non ci sta più niente** there's no more room in the boot; (*accettare*): **ci stai?** is that okay with you?; **~ a** (*attenersi a*) to follow, stick to; (*seguito dall'infinito*): **~ a sentire** to listen; **staremo a vedere** let's wait and see; **stiamo a discutere** we're talking; (*toccare a*): **sta a te giocare** it's your turn to play; **sta a te decidere** it's up to you to decide; **~ a qn** (*abiti etc*) to fit sb; **queste scarpe mi stanno strette** these shoes are tight for me; **il rosso ti sta bene** red suits you; **come stai?** how are you?; **io sto bene/male** I'm very well/not very well; **~ fermo** to keep *o* stay still; **~ seduto** to sit, be sitting; **~ zitto** to keep quiet; **stando così le cose** given the situation; **stando a ciò**

che dice lui according to him *o* to his version.
starnaz'zare [starnat'tsare] *vi* to squawk.
starnu'tire *vi* to sneeze.
star'nuto *sm* sneeze.
sta'sera *av* this evening, tonight.
'stasi *sf* (*MED, fig*) stasis.
sta'tale *ag* state *cpd*, government *cpd* ♦ *sm/f* state employee; (*nell'amministrazione*) ≈ civil servant; **bilancio ~** national budget; **strada ~ ≈** trunk (*BRIT*) *o* main road.
stataliz'zare [statalid'dzare] *vt* to nationalize, put under state control.
'statico, a, ci, che *ag* (*ELETTR, fig*) static.
sta'tista, i *sm* statesman.
sta'tistico, a, ci, che *ag* statistical ♦ *sf* statistic; (*scienza*) statistics *sg*; **fare una ~a** to carry out a statistical examination.
'stato, a *pp di* **essere, stare** ♦ *sm* (*condizione*) state, condition; (*POL*) state; (*DIR*) status; **essere in ~ d'accusa** (*DIR*) to be committed for trial; **essere in ~ d'arresto** (*DIR*) to be under arrest; **essere in ~ interessante** to be pregnant; **~ d'assedio/ d'emergenza** state of siege/emergency; **~ civile** (*AMM*) marital status; **~ di famiglia** (*AMM*) *certificate giving details of a household and its dependents*; **~ maggiore** (*MIL*) general staff; **~ patrimoniale** (*COMM*) statement of assets and liabilities; **gli S~i Uniti (d'America)** the United States (of America).
'statua *sf* statue.
statuni'tense *ag* United States *cpd*, of the United States.
sta'tura *sf* (*ANAT*) height; (*fig*) stature; **essere alto/basso di ~** to be tall/short *o* small.
sta'tuto *sm* (*DIR*) statute; **regione a ~ speciale** *Italian region with political autonomy in certain matters*; **~ della società** (*COMM*) articles *pl* of association.
sta'volta *av* this time.
staziona'mento [stattsjona'mento] *sm* (*AUT*) parking; (: *sosta*) waiting; **freno di ~** handbrake.
stazio'nare [stattsjo'nare] *vi* (*veicoli*) to be parked.
stazio'nario, a [stattsjo'narjo] *ag* stationary; (*fig*) unchanged.
stazi'one [stat'tsjone] *sf* station; (*balneare, invernale etc*) resort; **~ degli autobus** bus station; **~ balneare** seaside resort; **~ climatica** health resort; **~ ferroviaria** railway (*BRIT*) *o* railroad (*US*) station; **~ invernale** winter sports resort; **~ di lavoro** work station; **~ di polizia** police station (*in small town*); **~ di servizio**

service *o* petrol (*BRIT*) *o* filling station; ~ termale spa.

'stazza ['stattsa] *sf* tonnage.

st. civ. *abbr* = stato civile.

'stecca, che *sf* stick; (*di ombrello*) rib; (*di sigarette*) carton; (*MED*) splint; (*stonatura*): fare una ~ to sing (*o* play) a wrong note.

stec'cato *sm* fence.

stec'chito, a [stek'kito] *ag* dried up; (*persona*) skinny; lasciar ~ qn (*fig*) to leave sb flabbergasted; morto ~ stone dead.

'stella *sf* star; ~ alpina (*BOT*) edelweiss; ~ cadente *o* filante shooting star; ~ di mare (*ZOOL*) starfish; ~ di Natale (*BOT*) poinsettia.

stel'lato, a *ag* (*cielo*, *notte*) starry.

'stelo *sm* stem; (*asta*) rod; lampada a ~ standard lamp (*BRIT*), floor lamp.

'stemma, i *sm* coat of arms.

'stemmo *vb vedi* stare.

stempe'rare *vt* (*calce*, *colore*) to dissolve.

stempi'ato, a *ag* with a receding hairline.

stempia'tura *sf* receding hairline.

sten'dardo *sm* standard.

'stendere *vt* (*braccia*, *gambe*) to stretch (out); (*tovaglia*) to spread (out); (*bucato*) to hang out; (*mettere a giacere*) to lay (down); (*spalmare*: *colore*) to spread; (*mettere per iscritto*) to draw up; ~rsi *vr* (*coricarsi*) to stretch out, lie down; (*estendersi*) to extend, stretch.

stendibianche'ria [stendibjanke'ria] *sm inv* clotheshorse.

stendi'toio *sm* (*locale*) drying room; (*stendibiancheria*) clotheshorse.

stenodattilogra'fia *sf* shorthand typing (*BRIT*), stenography (*US*).

stenodatti'lografo, a *sm/f* shorthand typist (*BRIT*), stenographer (*US*).

stenogra'fare *vt* to take down in shorthand.

stenogra'fia *sf* shorthand.

ste'nografo, a *sm/f* stenographer.

sten'tare *vi*: ~ a fare to find it hard to do, have difficulty doing.

sten'tato, a *ag* (*compito*, *stile*) laboured (*BRIT*), labored (*US*); (*sorriso*) forced.

'stento *sm* (*fatica*) difficulty; ~i *smpl* (*privazioni*) hardship *sg*, privation *sg*; a ~ *av* with difficulty, barely.

'steppa *sf* steppe.

'sterco *sm* dung.

stereofo'nia *sf* stereophony.

'stereo('fonico, a, ci, che) *ag* stereo(phonic).

stereoti'pato, a *ag* stereotyped.

stere'otipo *sm* stereotype; pensare per ~i to think in clichés.

'sterile *ag* sterile; (*terra*) barren; (*fig*) futile, fruitless.

sterilità *sf* sterility.

steriliz'zare [sterilid'dzare] *vt* to sterilize.

sterilizzazi'one [steriliddzat'tsjone] *sf* sterilization.

ster'lina *sf* pound (sterling).

stermi'nare *vt* to exterminate, wipe out.

stermi'nato, a *ag* immense, endless.

ster'minio *sm* extermination, destruction; campo di ~ death camp.

'sterno *sm* (*ANAT*) breastbone.

ster'paglia [ster'paʎʎa] *sf* brushwood.

'sterpo *sm* dry twig.

ster'rare *vt* to excavate.

ster'zare [ster'tsare] *vt*, *vi* (*AUT*) to steer.

'sterzo ['stertso] *sm* steering; (*volante*) steering wheel.

'steso, a *pp di* stendere.

'stessi *etc vb vedi* stare.

'stesso, a *ag* same; (*rafforzativo*: *in persona*, *proprio*): il re ~ the king himself *o* in person ♦ *pron*: lo(la) ~(a) the same (one); quello ~ giorno that very day; i suoi ~i avversari lo ammirano even his enemies admire him; fa lo ~ it doesn't matter; parto lo ~ I'm going all the same; per me è lo ~ it's all the same to me, it doesn't matter to me; *vedi* io, tu *etc*.

ste'sura *sf* (*azione*) drafting *no pl*, drawing up *no pl*; (*documento*) draft.

stetos'copio *sm* stethoscope.

'stetti *etc vb vedi* stare.

'stia *sf* hutch.

'stia *etc vb vedi* stare.

'stigma, i *sm* stigma.

'stigmate *sfpl* (*REL*) stigmata.

sti'lare *vt* to draw up, draft.

'stile *sm* style; (*classe*) style, class; (*SPORT*): ~ libero freestyle; mobili in ~ period furniture; in grande ~ in great style; è proprio nel suo ~ (*fig*) it's just like him.

sti'lismo *sm* concern for style.

sti'lista, i, e *sm/f* designer.

sti'listico, a, ci, che *ag* stylistic.

stiliz'zato, a [stilid'dzato] *ag* stylized.

stil'lare *vi* (*trasudare*) to ooze; (*gocciolare*) to drip.

stilli'cidio [stilli'tʃidjo] *sm* (*fig*) continual pestering (*o* moaning *etc*).

stilo'grafica, che *sf* (*anche*: penna ~) fountain pen.

Stim. *abbr* = stimata.

'stima *sf* esteem; valuation; assessment; estimate; avere ~ di qn to have respect for sb; godere della ~ di qn to enjoy sb's respect; fare la ~ di qc to estimate the value of sth.

sti'mare *vt* (*persona*) to esteem, hold in high regard; (*terreno, casa etc*) to value; (*stabilire in misura approssimativa*) to estimate, assess; (*ritenere*): ~ **che** to consider that; ~**rsi fortunato** to consider o.s. (to be) lucky.

Stim.ma *abbr* = *stimatissima.*

stimo'lante *ag* stimulating ♦ *sm* (*MED*) stimulant.

stimo'lare *vt* to stimulate; (*incitare*): ~ **qn (a fare)** to spur sb on (to do).

stimolazi'one [stimolat'tsjone] *sf* stimulation.

'stimolo *sm* (*anche fig*) stimulus.

'stinco, chi *sm* shin; shinbone.

'stingere ['stindʒere] *vt, vi* (*anche*: ~**rsi**) to fade.

'stinto, a *pp di* **stingere.**

sti'pare *vt* to cram, pack; ~**rsi** *vr* (*accalcarsi*) to crowd, throng.

stipendi'are *vt* (*pagare*) to pay (a salary to).

stipendi'ato, a *ag* salaried ♦ *sm/f* salaried worker.

sti'pendio *sm* salary.

'stipite *sm* (*di porta, finestra*) jamb.

stipu'lare *vt* (*redigere*) to draw up.

stipulazi'one [stipulat'tsjone] *sf* (*di contratto: stesura*) drafting; (: *firma*) signing.

stiracchi'are [stirak'kjare] *vt* (*fig: significato di una parola*) to stretch, force; ~**rsi** *vr* (*persona*) to stretch.

stira'mento *sm* (*MED*) sprain.

sti'rare *vt* (*abito*) to iron; (*distendere*) to stretch; (*strappare: muscolo*) to strain; ~**rsi** *vr* (*fam*) to stretch (o.s.).

stira'tura *sf* ironing.

'stirpe *sf* birth, stock; descendants *pl.*

stiti'chezza [stiti'kettsa] *sf* constipation.

'stitico, a, ci, che *ag* constipated.

'stiva *sf* (*di nave*) hold.

sti'vale *sm* boot.

stiva'letto *sm* ankle boot.

sti'vare *vt* to stow, load.

'stizza ['stittsa] *sf* anger, vexation.

stiz'zire [stit'tsire] *vt* to irritate ♦ *vi*, ~**rsi** *vr* to become irritated, become vexed.

stiz'zoso, a [stit'tsoso] *ag* (*persona*) quick-tempered, irascible; (*risposta*) angry.

stocca'fisso *sm* stockfish, dried cod.

Stoc'carda *sf* Stuttgart.

stoc'cata *sf* (*colpo*) stab, thrust; (*fig*) gibe, cutting remark.

Stoc'colma *sf* Stockholm.

stock [stɔk] *sm inv* (*COMM*) stock.

'stoffa *sf* material, fabric; (*fig*): **aver la** ~ **di**

to have the makings of; **avere della** ~ to have what it takes.

stoi'cismo [stoi'tʃizmo] *sm* stoicism.

'stoico, a, ci, che *ag* stoic(al).

sto'ino *sm* doormat.

'stola *sf* stole.

stol'tezza [stol'tettsa] *sf* stupidity; (*azione*) foolish action.

'stolto, a *ag* stupid, foolish.

'stomaco, chi *sm* stomach; **dare di** ~ to vomit, be sick.

sto'nare *vt* to sing (*o* play) out of tune ♦ *vi* to be out of tune, sing (*o* play) out of tune; (*fig*) to be out of place, jar; (: *colori*) to clash.

sto'nato, a *ag* (*persona*) off-key; (*strumento*) off-key, out of tune.

stona'tura *sf* (*suono*) false note.

stop *sm inv* (*TELEGRAFIA*) stop; (*AUT: cartello*) stop sign; (: *fanalino d'arresto*) brake-light (*BRIT*), stoplight.

'stoppa *sf* tow.

'stoppia *sf* (*AGR*) stubble.

stop'pino *sm* (*di candela*) wick; (*miccia*) fuse.

'storcere ['stɔrtʃere] *vt* to twist; ~**rsi** *vr* to writhe, twist; ~ **il naso** (*fig*) to turn up one's nose; ~**rsi la caviglia** to twist one's ankle.

stordi'mento *sm* (*gen*) dizziness; (*da droga*) stupefaction.

stor'dire *vt* (*intontire*) to stun, daze; ~**rsi** *vr*: ~**rsi col bere** to dull one's senses with drink.

stor'dito, a *ag* stunned; (*sventato*) scatterbrained, heedless.

'storia *sf* (*scienza, avvenimenti*) history; (*racconto, bugia*) story; (*faccenda, questione*) business *no pl*; (*pretesto*) excuse, pretext; ~**e** *sfpl* (*smancerie*) fuss *sg*; **passare alla** ~ to go down in history; **non ha fatto** ~**e** he didn't make a fuss.

storicità [storit'ʃi'ta] *sf* historical authenticity.

'storico, a, ci, che *ag* historic(al) ♦ *sm/f* historian.

storiogra'fia *sf* historiography.

stori'one *sm* (*ZOOL*) sturgeon.

stor'mire *vi* to rustle.

'stormo *sm* (*di uccelli*) flock.

stor'nare *vt* (*COMM*) to transfer.

stor'nello *sm* kind of folk song.

'storno *sm* starling.

storpi'are *vt* to cripple, maim; (*fig: parole*) to mangle; (: *significato*) to twist.

storpia'tura *sf* (*fig: di parola*) twisting, distortion.

'storpio, a *ag* crippled, maimed.

'storsi etc vb vedi **storcere**.

'storto, a pp di **storcere ♦** ag (chiodo) twisted, bent; (gamba, quadro) crooked; (fig: ragionamento) false, wrong **♦** sf (distorsione) sprain, twist; (recipiente) retort **♦** av: **guardare** ~ **qn** (fig) to look askance at sb; **andar** ~ to go wrong.

sto'viglie [sto'viʎʎe] sfpl dishes pl, crockery.

str. abbr (GEO) = **stretto**.

'strabico, a, ci, che ag squint-eyed; (occhi) squint.

strabili'ante ag astonishing, amazing.

strabili'are vi to astonish, amaze.

stra'bismo sm squinting.

strabuz'zare [strabud'dzare] vt: ~ **gli occhi** to open one's eyes wide.

stra'carico, a, chi, che ag overloaded.

strac'chino [strak'kino] sm type of soft cheese.

stracci'are [strat'tʃare] vt to tear.

'straccio, a, ci, ce ['strattʃo] ag: **carta** ~**a** waste paper **♦** sm rag; (per pulire) cloth, duster.

stracci'one, a [strat'tʃone] sm/f ragamuffin.

stracci'vendolo [strattʃi'vendolo] sm ragman.

'stracco, a, chi, che ag: ~ **(morto)** exhausted, dead tired.

stra'cotto, a ag overcooked **♦** sm (CUC) beef stew.

'strada sf road; (di città) street; (cammino, via, fig) way; ~ **facendo** on the way; **tre ore di** ~ **(a piedi)/(in macchina)** three hours' walk/drive; **essere sulla buona** ~ (nella vita) to be on the right road o path; (con indagine etc) to be on the right track; **essere fuori** ~ (fig) to be on the wrong track; **fare** ~ **a qn** to show sb the way; **fare** o **farsi** ~ (fig: persona) to get on in life; **portare qn sulla cattiva** ~ to lead sb astray; **donna di** ~ (fig peg) streetwalker; **ragazzo di** ~ (fig peg) street urchin; ~ **ferrata** railway (BRIT), railroad (US); ~ **principale** main road; ~ **senza uscita** dead end, cul-de-sac.

stra'dale ag road cpd; (polizia, regolamento) traffic cpd.

stra'dario sm street guide.

stra'dino sm road worker.

strafalci'one [strafal'tʃone] sm blunder, howler.

stra'fare vi to overdo it.

stra'fatto, a pp di **strafare**.

stra'foro : di ~ av (di nascosto) on the sly.

strafot'tente ag: **è** ~ he doesn't give a damn, he couldn't care less.

strafot'tenza [strafot'tentsa] sf arrogance.

'strage ['stradʒe] sf massacre, slaughter.

stra'grande ag: **la** ~ **maggioranza** the overwhelming majority.

stralci'are [stral'tʃare] vt to remove.

'stralcio ['straltʃo] sm (COMM): **vendere in** ~ to sell off (at bargain prices) **♦** ag inv: **legge** ~ abridged version of an act.

stralu'nato, a ag (occhi) rolling; (persona) beside o.s., very upset.

stramaz'zare [stramat'tsare] vi to fall heavily.

strambe'ria sf eccentricity.

'strambo, a ag strange, queer.

strampa'lato, a ag odd, eccentric.

strana'mente av oddly, strangely; **e lui,** ~, **ha accettato** and, surprisingly, he agreed.

stra'nezza [stra'nettsa] sf strangeness.

strango'lare vt to strangle; ~**rsi** vr to choke.

strani'ero, a ag foreign **♦** sm/f foreigner.

stra'nito, a ag dazed.

'strano, a ag strange, odd.

straordi'nario, a ag extraordinary; (treno etc) special **♦** sm (lavoro) overtime.

strapaz'zare [strapat'tsare] vt to ill-treat; ~**rsi** vr to tire o.s. out, overdo things.

strapaz'zato, a [strapat'tsato] ag: **uova** ~**e** scrambled eggs.

stra'pazzo [stra'pattso] sm strain, fatigue; **da** ~ (fig) third-rate.

strapi'eno, a ag full to overflowing.

strapi'ombo sm overhanging rock; **a** ~ overhanging.

strapo'tere sm excessive power.

strappa'lacrime ag inv (fam): **romanzo** (o **film** etc) ~ tear-jerker.

strap'pare vt (gen) to tear, rip; (pagina etc) to tear off, tear out; (sradicare) to pull up; (togliere): ~ **qc a qn** to snatch sth from sb; (fig) to wrest sth from sb; ~**rsi** vr (lacerarsi) to rip, tear; (rompersi) to break; ~**rsi un muscolo** to tear a muscle.

strap'pato, a ag torn, ripped.

'strappo sm (strattone) pull, tug; (lacerazione) tear, rip; (fig fam: passaggio) lift (BRIT), ride (US); **fare uno** ~ **alla regola** to make an exception to the rule; ~ **muscolare** torn muscle.

strapun'tino sm jump o foldaway seat.

strari'pare vi to overflow.

Stras'burgo sf Strasbourg.

strasci'care [straʃʃi'kare] vt to trail; (piedi) to drag; ~ **le parole** to drawl.

'strascico, chi ['straʃʃiko] sm (di abito) train; (conseguenza) after-effect.

strata'gemma, i [strata'dʒemma] sm stratagem.

stra'tega, ghi sm strategist.

strate'gia, 'gie [strate'dʒia] *sf* strategy.
stra'tegico, a, ci, che [stra'tɛdʒiko] *ag*
strategic.
'strato *sm* layer; (*rivestimento*) coat,
coating; (*GEO, fig*) stratum; (*METEOR*)
stratus.
stratos'fera *sf* stratosphere.
strat'tone *sm* tug, jerk; **dare uno ~ a qc** to
tug *o* jerk sth, give sth a tug *o* jerk.
stravac'cato, a *ag* sprawling.
strava'gante *ag* odd, eccentric.
strava'ganza [strava'gantsa] *sf*
eccentricity.
stra'vecchio, a [stra'vɛkkjo] *ag* very old.
strave'dere *vi*: **~ per qn** to dote on sb.
stra'visto, a *pp di* **stravedere.**
stra'vizio [stra'vittsjo] *sm* excess.
stra'volgere [stra'vɔldʒere] *vt* (*volto*) to
contort; (*fig: animo*) to trouble deeply;
(: *verità*) to twist, distort.
stra'volto, a *pp di* **stravolgere ♦** *ag* (*persona:
per stanchezza etc*) in a terrible state; (: *per
sofferenza*) distraught.
strazi'ante [strat'tsjante] *ag* (*scena*)
harrowing; (*urlo*) bloodcurdling; (*dolore*)
excruciating.
strazi'are [strat'tsjare] *vt* to torture,
torment.
'strazio ['strattsjo] *sm* torture; (*fig: cosa
fatta male*): **essere uno ~** to be appalling;
fare ~ di (*corpo, vittima*) to mutilate.
'strega, ghe *sf* witch.
stre'gare *vt* to bewitch.
stre'gone *sm* (*mago*) wizard; (*di tribù*)
witch doctor.
stregone'ria *sf* (*pratica*) witchcraft; **fare
una ~** to cast a spell.
'stregua *sf*: **alla ~ di** by the same standard
as.
stre'mare *vt* to exhaust.
'stremo *sm*: **essere allo ~** to be at the end
of one's tether.
'strenna *sf*: **~ natalizia** (*regalo*) Christmas
present; (*libro*) book published for the
Christmas market.
'strenuo, a *ag* brave, courageous.
strepi'tare *vi* to yell and shout.
'strepito *sm* (*di voci, folla*) clamour (*BRIT*),
clamor (*US*); (*di catene*) clanking, rattling.
strepi'toso, a *ag* clamorous, deafening;
(*fig: successo*) resounding.
stres'sante *ag* stressful.
stres'sare *vt* to put under stress.
stres'sato, a *ag* under stress.
'stretta *sf vedi* **stretto.**
stretta'mente *av* tightly; (*rigorosamente*)
strictly.
stret'tezza [stret'tettsa] *sf* narrowness; **~e**

sfpl (*povertà*) poverty *sg*, straitened
circumstances.
'stretto, a *pp di* **stringere ♦** *ag* (*corridoio,
limiti*) narrow; (*gonna, scarpe, nodo, curva*)
tight; (*intimo: parente, amico*) close;
(*rigoroso: osservanza*) strict; (*preciso:
significato*) precise, exact **♦** *sm* (*braccio di
mare*) strait **♦** *sf* (*di mano*) grasp;
(*finanziaria*) squeeze; (*fig: dolore,
turbamento*) pang; **a denti ~i** with
clenched teeth; **lo ~ necessario** the bare
minimum; **una ~a di mano** a handshake;
una ~a al cuore a sudden sadness; **essere
alle ~e** to have one's back to the wall.
stret'toia *sf* bottleneck; (*fig*) tricky
situation.
stri'ato, a *ag* streaked.
stria'tura *sf* (*atto*) streaking; (*effetto*)
streaks *pl*.
stric'nina *sf* strychnine.
'strida *sfpl* screaming *sg*.
stri'dente *ag* strident.
'stridere *vi* (*porta*) to squeak; (*animale*) to
screech, shriek; (*colori*) to clash.
'strido, *pl*(*f*) **strida** *sm* screech, shriek.
stri'dore *sm* screeching, shrieking.
'stridulo, a *ag* shrill.
'striglia ['striʎʎa] *sf* currycomb.
strigli'are [striʎ'ʎare] *vt* (*cavallo*) to curry.
strigli'ata [striʎ'ʎata] *sf* (*di cavallo*)
currying; (*fig*): **dare una ~ a qn** to give sb
a scolding.
stril'lare *vt, vi* to scream, shriek.
'strillo *sm* scream, shriek.
stril'lone *sm* newspaper seller.
strimin'zito, a [strimin'tsito] *ag* (*misero*)
shabby; (*molto magro*) skinny.
strimpel'lare *vt* (*MUS*) to strum.
'stringa, ghe *sf* lace; (*INFORM*) string.
strin'gare *vt* (*fig: discorso*) to condense.
strin'gato, a *ag* (*fig*) concise.
'stringere ['strindʒere] *vt* (*avvicinare due
cose*) to press (together), squeeze
(together); (*tenere stretto*) to hold tight,
clasp, clutch; (*pugno, mascella, denti*) to
clench; (*labbra*) to compress; (*avvitare*) to
tighten; (*abito*) to take in; (*sog: scarpe*) to
pinch, be tight for; (*fig: concludere: patto*)
to make; (: *accelerare: passo*) to quicken
♦ *vi* (*incalzare*) to be pressing; **~rsi** *vr*
(*accostarsi*): **~rsi a** to press o.s. up against;
~ la mano a qn to shake sb's hand; **~ gli
occhi** to screw up one's eyes; **~ amicizia
con qn** to make friends with sb; **stringi
stringi** in conclusion; **il tempo stringe**
time is short.
'strinsi *etc vb vedi* **stringere.**
'striscia, sce ['striʃʃa] *sf* (*di carta, tessuto*

etc) strip; (*riga*) stripe; ~**sce (pedonali)** zebra crossing *sg*; **a ~sce** striped.

strisci'ante [striʃ'ʃante] *ag* (*fig peg*) unctuous; (*ECON: inflazione*) creeping.

strisci'are [striʃ'ʃare] *vt* (*piedi*) to drag; (*muro, macchina*) to graze ♦ *vi* to crawl, creep.

'striscio ['striʃʃo] *sm* graze; (*MED*) smear; **colpire di** ~ to graze.

strisci'one [striʃ'ʃone] *sm* banner.

strito'lare *vt* to grind.

striz'zare [strit'tsare] *vt* (*arancia*) to squeeze; (*panni*) to wring (out); ~ **l'occhio** to wink.

striz'zata [strit'tsata] *sf*: **dare una** ~ **a qc** to give sth a wring; **una** ~ **d'occhio** a wink.

'strofa *sf*, **'strofe** *sf inv* strophe.

strofi'naccio [strofi'nattʃo] *sm* duster, cloth; (*per piatti*) dishcloth; (*per pavimenti*) floorcloth.

strofi'nare *vt* to rub.

stron'care *vt* to break off; (*fig: ribellione*) to suppress, put down; (*: film, libro*) to tear to pieces.

'stronzo ['strontso] *sm* (*sterco*) turd; (*fig fam!: persona*) shit (*!*).

stropicci'are [stropit'tʃare] *vt* to rub.

stroz'zare [strot'tsare] *vt* (*soffocare*) to choke, strangle; ~**rsi** *vr* to choke.

strozza'tura [strottsa'tura] *sf* (*restringimento*) narrowing; (*di strada etc*) bottleneck.

stroz'zino, a [strot'tsino] *sm/f* (*usuraio*) usurer; (*fig*) shark.

struc'care *vt* to remove make-up from; ~**rsi** *vr* to remove one's make-up.

'struggere ['struddʒere] *vt* (*fig*) to consume; ~**rsi** *vr* (*fig*): ~**rsi di** to be consumed with.

struggi'mento [struddʒi'mento] *sm* (*desiderio*) yearning.

strumen'tale *ag* (*MUS*) instrumental.

strumentaliz'zare [strumentalid'dzare] *vt* to exploit, use to one's own ends.

strumentalizzazi'one [strumentaliddzat'tsjone] *sf* exploitation.

strumentazi'one [strumentat'tsjone] *sf* (*MUS*) orchestration; (*TECN*) instrumentation.

stru'mento *sm* (*arnese, fig*) instrument, tool; (*MUS*) instrument; ~ **a corda o ad arco/a fiato** string(ed)/wind instrument.

'strussi *etc vb vedi* **struggere.**

'strutto *sm* lard.

strut'tura *sf* structure.

struttu'rare *vt* to structure.

'struzzo ['struttso] *sm* ostrich; **fare lo ~, fare la politica dello** ~ to bury one's head in the sand.

stuc'care *vt* (*muro*) to plaster; (*vetro*) to putty; (*decorare con stucchi*) to stucco.

stucca'tore, 'trice *sm/f* plasterer; (*artista*) stucco worker.

stuc'chevole [stuk'kevole] *ag* nauseating; (*fig*) tedious, boring.

'stucco, chi *sm* plaster; (*da vetri*) putty; (*ornamentale*) stucco; **rimanere di** ~ (*fig*) to be dumbfounded.

stu'dente, 'essa *sm/f* student; (*scolaro*) pupil, schoolboy/girl.

studen'tesco, a, schi, sche *ag* student . *cpd*.

studi'are *vt* to study; ~**rsi** *vr* (*sforzarsi*): ~**rsi di fare** to try *o* endeavour (*BRIT*) *o* endeavor (*US*) to do.

studi'ato, a *ag* (*modi, sorriso*) affected.

'studio *sm* studying; (*ricerca, saggio, stanza*) study; (*di professionista*) office; (*di artista, CINE, TV, RADIO*) studio; (*di medico*) surgery (*BRIT*), office (*US*); ~**i** *smpl* (*INS*) studies; **alla fine degli** ~**i** at the end of one's course (of studies); **secondo recenti** ~**i, appare che ...** recent research indicates that ...; **la proposta è allo** ~ the proposal is under consideration; ~ **legale** lawyer's office.

studi'oso, a *ag* studious, hardworking ♦ *sm/f* scholar.

'stufa *sf* stove; ~ **elettrica** electric fire *o* heater; ~ **a legna/carbone** wood-burning/coal stove.

stu'fare *vt* (*CUC*) to stew; (*fig fam*) to bore.

stu'fato *sm* (*CUC*) stew.

'stufo, a *ag* (*fam*): **essere** ~ **di** to be fed up with, be sick and tired of.

stu'oia *sf* mat.

stu'olo *sm* crowd, host.

stupefa'cente [stupefa'tʃɛnte] *ag* stunning, astounding ♦ *sm* drug, narcotic.

stupe'fare *vt* to stun, astound.

stupe'fatto, a *pp di* **stupefare.**

stupefazi'one [stupefat'tsjone] *sf* astonishment.

stu'pendo, a *ag* marvellous, wonderful.

stupi'daggine [stupi'daddʒine] *sf* stupid thing (to do *o* say).

stupidità *sf* stupidity.

'stupido, a *ag* stupid.

stu'pire *vt* to amaze, stun ♦ *vi* (*anche*: ~**rsi**): ~ **(di)** to be amazed (at), be stunned (by); **non c'è da** ~**rsi** that's not surprising.

stu'pore *sm* amazement, astonishment.

stu'prare *vt* to rape.

stupra'tore *sm* rapist.

'stupro *sm* rape.

stu'rare *vt* (*lavandino*) to clear.

stuzzica'denti [stuttsika'dɛnti] *sm*

toothpick.

stuzzi'cante [stuttsi'kante] *ag* (*gen*) stimulating; (*appetitoso*) appetizing.

stuzzi'care [stuttsi'kare] *vt* (*ferita etc*) to poke (at), prod (at); (*fig*) to tease; (: *appetito*) to whet; (: *curiosità*) to stimulate; ~ **i denti** to pick one's teeth.

═══════════ PAROLA CHIAVE

su (*su* + *il* = **sul**, *su* + *lo* = **sullo**, *su* + *l'* = **sull'**, *su* + *la* = **sulla**, *su* + *i* = **sui**, *su* + *gli* = **sugli**, *su* + *le* = **sulle**) *prep* **1** (*gen*) on; (*moto*) on(to); (*in cima a*) on (top of); **mettilo sul tavolo** put it on the table; **salire sul treno** to get on the train; **un paesino sul mare** a village by the sea; **è sulla destra** it's on the right; **cento metri sul livello del mare** a hundred metres above sea level; **fecero rotta** ~ **Palermo** they set out for Palermo; **sul vestito portava un golf rosso** she was wearing a red sweater over her dress

2 (*argomento*) about, on; **un libro** ~ **Cesare** a book on *o* about Caesar

3 (*circa*) about; **costerà sui 3 milioni** it will cost about 3 million; **una ragazza sui 17 anni** a girl of about 17 (years of age)

4: ~ **misura** made to measure; ~ **ordinazione** to order; ~ **richiesta** on request; **3 casi** ~ **dieci** 3 cases out of 10

♦ *av* **1** (*in alto, verso l'alto*) up; **vieni** ~ **come** on up; **guarda** ~ look up; **andare** ~ **e giù** to go up and down; ~ **le mani!** hands up!; **in** ~ (*verso l'alto*) up(wards); (*in poi*) onwards; **vieni** ~ **da me?** are you going to come up?; **dai 20 anni in** ~ from the age of 20 onwards

2 (*addosso*) on; **cos'hai** ~**?** what have you got on?

♦ *escl* **come on!**; ~ **avanti, muoviti!** come on, hurry up!; ~ **coraggio!** come on, cheer up!

'sua *vedi* **suo.**

sua'dente *ag* persuasive.

sub *sm/f inv* skin-diver.

su'bacqueo, a *ag* underwater ♦ *sm* skin-diver.

subaffit'tare *vt* to sublet.

subaf'fitto *sm* (*contratto*) sublet.

subal'terno, a *ag, sm* subordinate; (*MIL*) subaltern.

subappal'tare *vt* to subcontract.

subap'palto *sm* subcontract.

sub'buglio [sub'buʎʎo] *sm* confusion, turmoil; **essere/mettere in** ~ to be in/ throw into a turmoil.

sub'conscio, a [sub'kɔnʃo],

subcosci'ente [subkoʃ'ʃɛnte] *ag, sm* subconscious.

'subdolo, a *ag* underhand, sneaky.

suben'trare *vi*: ~ **a qn in qc** to take over sth from sb; **sono subentrati altri problemi** other problems arose.

su'bire *vt* to suffer, endure.

subis'sare *vt* (*fig*): ~ **di** to overwhelm with, load with.

subi'taneo, a *ag* sudden.

'subito *av* immediately, at once, straight away.

subli'mare *vt* (*PSIC*) to sublimate; (*CHIM*) to sublime.

su'blime *ag* sublime.

sublo'care *vt* to sublease.

sublocazi'one [sublokat'tsjone] *sf* sublease.

subnor'male *ag* subnormal ♦ *sm/f* mentally handicapped person.

subodo'rare *vt* (*insidia etc*) to smell, suspect.

subordi'nare *vt* to subordinate.

subordi'nato, a *ag* subordinate; (*dipendente*): ~ **a** dependent on, subject to.

subordinazi'one [subordinat'tsjone] *sf* subordination.

su'bordine *sm*: **in** ~ secondarily.

subur'bano, a *ag* suburban.

succe'daneo [suttʃe'daneo] *sm* substitute.

suc'cedere [sut'tʃedere] *vi* (*prendere il posto di qn*): ~ **a** to succeed; (*venire dopo*): ~ **a** to follow; (*accadere*) to happen; ~**rsi** *vr* to follow each other; ~ **al trono** to succeed to the throne; **sono cose che succedono** these things happen.

successi'one [suttʃes'sjone] *sf* succession; **tassa di** ~ death duty (*BRIT*), inheritance tax (*US*).

successiva'mente [suttʃessiva'mente] *av* subsequently.

succes'sivo, a [suttʃes'sivo] *ag* successive; **il giorno** ~ the following day; **in un momento** ~ subsequently.

suc'cesso, a [sut'tʃɛsso] *pp di* **succedere** ♦ *sm* (*esito*) outcome; (*buona riuscita*) success; **di** ~ (*libro, personaggio*) successful; **avere** ~ (*persona*) to be successful; (*idea*) to be well received.

succes'sore [suttʃes'sore] *sm* successor.

succhi'are [suk'kjare] *vt* to suck (up).

succhi'otto [suk'kjɔtto] *sm* dummy (*BRIT*), pacifier (*US*), comforter (*US*).

suc'cinto, a [sut'tʃinto] *ag* (*discorso*) succinct; (*abito*) brief.

'succo, chi *sm* juice; (*fig*) essence, gist; ~ **di frutta/pomodoro** fruit/tomato juice.

suc'coso, a *ag* juicy; (*fig*) pithy.

'succube sm/f victim; essere ~ di qn to be dominated by sb.

succur'sale sf branch (office).

sud sm south ♦ ag inv south; (regione) southern; verso ~ south, southwards; l'Italia del S~ Southern Italy; l'America del S~ South America.

Su'dafrica sm: il ~ South Africa.

sudafri'cano, a ag, sm/f South African.

Suda'merica sm: il ~ South America.

sudameri'cano, a ag, sm/f South American.

Su'dan sm: il ~ (the) Sudan.

suda'nese ag, sm/f Sudanese inv.

su'dare vi to perspire, sweat; ~ freddo to come out in a cold sweat.

su'dato, a ag (persona, mani) sweaty; (fig: denaro) hard-earned ♦ sf (anche fig) sweat; una vittoria ~a a hard-won victory; ho fatto una bella ~a per finirlo in tempo it was a real sweat to get it finished in time.

sud'detto, a ag above-mentioned.

suddi'tanza [suddi'tantsa] sf subjection; (cittadinanza) citizenship.

sud'dito, a sm/f subject.

suddi'videre vt to subdivide.

suddivisi'one sf subdivision.

suddi'viso, a pp di suddividere.

su'dest sm south-east; vento di ~ south-easterly wind; il ~ asiatico South-East Asia.

sudice'ria [suditʃe'ria] sf (qualità) filthiness, dirtiness; (cosa sporca) dirty thing.

'sudicio, a, ci, ce ['suditʃo] ag dirty, filthy.

sudici'ume [sudi'tʃume] sm dirt, filth.

su'dore sm perspiration, sweat.

su'dovest sm south-west; vento di ~ south-westerly wind.

'sue vedi suo.

'Suez ['suez] sm: il Canale di ~ the Suez Canal.

suffici'ente [suffi'tʃɛnte] ag enough, sufficient; (borioso) self-important; (INS) satisfactory.

sufficiente'mente [suffitʃɛnte'mente] av sufficiently, enough; (guadagnare, darsi da fare) enough.

suffici'enza [suffi'tʃɛntsa] sf (INS) pass mark; con un'aria di ~ (fig) with a condescending air; a ~ enough; ne ho avuto a ~! I've had enough of this!

suf'fisso sm (LING) suffix.

suffra'gare vt to support.

suf'fragio [suf'fradʒo] sm (voto) vote; ~ universale universal suffrage.

suggel'lare [suddʒel'lare] vt (fig) to seal.

suggeri'mento [suddʒeri'mento] sm suggestion; (consiglio) piece of advice, advice no pl; dietro suo ~ on his advice.

sugge'rire [suddʒe'rire] vt (risposta) to tell; (consigliare) to advise; (proporre) to suggest; (TEAT) to prompt; ~ a qn di fare qc to suggest to sb that he (o she) do sth.

suggeri'tore, 'trice [suddʒeri'tore] sm/f (TEAT) prompter.

suggestio'nare [suddʒestjo'nare] vt to influence.

suggesti'one [suddʒes'tjone] sf (PSIC) suggestion; (istigazione) instigation.

sugges'tivo, a [suddʒes'tivo] ag (paesaggio) evocative; (teoria) interesting, attractive.

'sughero ['sugero] sm cork.

'sugli ['suʎʎi] prep +det vedi su.

'sugo, ghi sm (succo) juice; (di carne) gravy; (condimento) sauce; (fig) gist, essence.

su'goso, a ag (frutto) juicy; (fig: articolo etc) pithy.

'sui prep +det vedi su.

sui'cida, i, e [sui'tʃida] ag suicidal ♦ sm/f suicide.

suici'darsi [suitʃi'darsi] vr to commit suicide.

sul'cidio [sui'tʃidjo] sm suicide.

su'ino, a ag: carne ~a pork ♦ sm pig; ~i smpl swine pl.

sul, sull', 'sulla, 'sulle, 'sullo prep + det vedi su.

sulfa'midico, a, ci, che ag, sm (MED) sulphonamide.

sulta'nina sf: (uva) ~ sultana.

sul'tano, a sm/f sultan/sultana.

Su'matra sf Sumatra.

'summit ['summit] sm inv summit.

S.U.N.I.A. sigla m (= sindacato unitario nazionale inquilini e assegnatari) national association of tenants.

sunnomi'nato, a ag aforesaid cpd.

'sunto ['sunto] sm summary.

'suo, 'sua, 'sue, su'oi det: il ~, la sua etc (di lui) his; (di lei) her; (di esso) its; (con valore indefinito) one's, his/her; (forma di cortesia: anche: S~) your ♦ pron: il ~, la sua etc his; hers; yours ♦ sm: ha speso del ~ he (o she etc) spent his (o her etc) own money ♦ sf: la ~a (opinione) his (o her etc) view; i suoi (parenti) his (o her etc) family; un ~ amico a friend of his (o hers etc); è dalla ~a he's on his (o her etc) side; anche lui ha avuto le ~e (disavventure) he's had his problems too; sta sulle ~e he keeps himself to himself.

su'ocero, a ['swɔtʃero] sm/f father/mother-in-law; i ~i smpl father- and mother-in-law.

su'oi vedi suo.

su'ola sf (di scarpa) sole.

su'olo *sm (terreno)* ground; *(terra)* soil.
suo'nare *vt (MUS)* to play; *(campana)* to ring; *(ore)* to strike; *(clacson, allarme)* to sound ♦ *vi* to play; *(telefono, campana)* to ring; *(ore)* to strike; *(clacson, fig: parole)* to sound.
suo'nato, a *ag (compiuto)*: **ha cinquant'anni** ~**i** he is well over fifty.
suona'tore, 'trice *sm/f* player; ~ **ambulante** street musician.
suone'ria *sf* alarm.
su'ono *sm* sound.
su'ora *sf (REL)* nun; **Suor Maria** Sister Maria.
'super *ag inv*: **(benzina)** ~ ≈ four-star (petrol) *(BRIT)*, premium *(US)*.
supera'mento *sm (di ostacolo)* overcoming; *(di montagna)* crossing.
supe'rare *vt (oltrepassare: limite)* to exceed, surpass; *(attraversare: fiume)* to cross; *(sorpassare: veicolo)* to overtake; *(fig: essere più bravo di)* to surpass, outdo; *(: difficoltà)* to overcome; *(: esame)* to get through; ~ **qn in altezza/peso** to be taller/heavier than sb; **ha superato la cinquantina** he's over fifty (years of age); ~ **i limiti di velocità** to exceed the speed limit; **stavolta ha superato se stesso** this time he has surpassed himself.
supe'rato, a *ag* outmoded.
supe'rattico, ci *sm* penthouse.
su'perbia *sf* pride.
su'perbo, a *ag* proud; *(fig)* magnificent, superb.
supercondut'tore *sm* superconductor.
superena'lotto *sm Italian national lottery.*
superfici'ale [superfi't∫ale] *ag* superficial.
superficialità [superfit∫ali'ta] *sf* superficiality.
super'ficie, ci [super'fit∫e] *sf* surface; **tornare in** ~ *(a galla)* to return to the surface; *(problemi)* to resurface; ~ **alare** *(AER)* wing area; ~ **velica** *(NAUT)* sail area.
su'perfluo, a *ag* superfluous.
superi'ora *sf (REL: anche:* **madre** ~*)* mother superior.
superi'ore *ag (piano, arto, classi)* upper; *(più elevato: temperatura, livello)*: ~ **(a)** higher (than); *(migliore)*: ~ **(a)** superior (to) ♦ *sf/pl*: **le** ~**i** *(INS) vedi* **scuola media superiore; il corso** ~ **di un fiume** the upper reaches of a river; **scuola media** ~ ≈ senior comprehensive school *(BRIT)*; ≈ senior high (school) *(US)*.
superiorità *sf* superiority.
superla'tivo, a *ag, sm* superlative.
superla'voro *sm* overwork.

super'market [super'market] *sm inv* = **supermercato.**
supermer'cato *sm* supermarket.
super'nova *sf* supernova.
superpo'tenza [superpo'tentsa] *sf (POL)* superpower.
super'sonico, a, ci, che *ag* supersonic.
su'perstite *ag* surviving ♦ *sm/f* survivor.
superstizi'one [superstit'tsjone] *sf* superstition.
superstizi'oso, a [superstit'tsjoso] *ag* superstitious.
super'strada *sf* ≈ expressway.
supervisi'one *sf* supervision.
supervi'sore *sm* supervisor.
su'pino, a *ag* supine; **accettazione** ~**a** *(fig)* blind acceptance.
suppel'lettile *sf* furnishings *pl.*
suppergiù [supper'dʒu] *av* more or less, roughly.
suppl. *abbr (= supplemento)* supp(l).
supplemen'tare *ag* extra; *(treno)* relief *cpd*; *(entrate)* additional.
supple'mento *sm* supplement.
sup'plente *ag* temporary; *(insegnante)* supply *cpd (BRIT)*, substitute *cpd (US)* ♦ *sm/f* temporary member of staff; supply *(o* substitute*)* teacher.
supp'lenza [sup'plɛntsa] *sf*: **fare** ~ to do supply *(BRIT) o* substitute *(US)* teaching.
supple'tivo, a *ag (gen)* supplementary; *(sessione d'esami)* extra.
'supplica, che *sf (preghiera)* plea; *(domanda scritta)* petition, request.
suppli'care *vt* to implore, beseech.
suppli'chevole [suppli'kevole] *ag* imploring.
sup'plire *vi*: ~ **a** to make up for.
sup'plizio [sup'plittsjo] *sm* torture.
sup'pongo, sup'poni *etc vb vedi* **supporre.**
sup'porre *vt* to suppose; **supponiamo che** ... let's *o* just suppose that ....
sup'porto *sm (sostegno)* support.
supposizi'one [suppozit'tsjone] *sf* supposition.
sup'posta *sf (MED)* suppository.
sup'posto, a *pp di* **supporre.**
suppu'rare *vi* to suppurate.
suprema'zia [supremat'tsia] *sf* supremacy.
su'premo, a *ag* supreme; **S**~**a Corte (di Cassazione)** Supreme Court.
surclas'sare *vt* to outclass.
surge'lare [surdʒe'lare] *vt* to (deep-)freeze.
surge'lato, a [surdʒe'lato] *ag* (deep-)frozen ♦ *smpl*: **i** ~**i** frozen food *sg.*
surme'nage [syrmə'naʒ] *sm (fisico)* overwork; *(mentale)* mental strain; *(SPORT)* overtraining.

sur'plus sm inv (ECON) surplus; ~ **di manodopera** overmanning.
surre'ale ag surrealistic.
surriscalda'mento sm (gen, TECN) overheating.
surriscal'dare vt to overheat.
surro'gato sm substitute.
suscet'tibile [suʃʃet'tibile] ag (sensibile) touchy, sensitive; (soggetto): ~ **di miglioramento** that can be improved, open to improvement.
suscettibilità [suʃʃettibili'ta] sf touchiness; **urtare la** ~ **di qn** to hurt sb's feelings.
susci'tare [suʃʃi'tare] vt to provoke, arouse.
su'sina sf plum.
su'sino sm plum (tree).
sussegu'ire vt to follow; ~**rsi** vr to follow one another.
sussidi'ario, a ag subsidiary; (treno) relief cpd; (fermata) extra.
sus'sidio sm subsidy; (aiuto) aid; ~**i didattici/audiovisivi** teaching/audiovisual aids; ~ **di disoccupazione** unemployment benefit (BRIT) o benefits (US); ~ **per malattia** sickness benefit.
sussi'ego sm haughtiness; **con aria di** ~ haughtily.
sussis'tenza [sussis'tɛntsa] sf subsistence.
sus'sistere vi to exist; (essere fondato) to be valid o sound.
sussul'tare vi to shudder.
sus'sulto sm start.
sussur'rare vt, vi to whisper, murmur; **si sussurra che ...** it's rumoured (BRIT) o rumored (US) that ....
sus'surro sm whisper, murmur.
su'tura sf (MED) suture.
sutu'rare vt to stitch up, suture.
suv'via escl come on!
SV sigla = Savona.
S.V. abbr vedi **Signoria Vostra**.
sva'gare vt (divertire) to amuse; (distrarre): ~ **qn** to take sb's mind off things; ~**rsi** vr to amuse o.s.; to take one's mind off things.
sva'gato, a ag (persona) absent-minded; (scolaro) inattentive.
'svago, ghi sm (riposo) relaxation; (ricreazione) amusement; (passatempo) pastime.
svaligi'are [zvali'dʒare] vt to rob, burgle (BRIT), burglarize (US).
svaligia'tore, 'trice [zvalidʒa'tore] sm/f (di banca) robber; (di casa) burglar.
svalu'tare vt (ECON) to devalue; (fig) to belittle; ~**rsi** vr (ECON) to be devalued.
svalutazi'one [zvalutat'tsjone] sf devaluation.

svam'pito, a ag absent-minded ♦ sm/f absent-minded person.
sva'nire vi to disappear, vanish.
sva'nito, a ag (fig: persona) absent-minded.
svantaggi'ato, a [zvantad'dʒato] ag at a disadvantage.
svan'taggio [zvan'taddʒo] sm disadvantage; (inconveniente) drawback, disadvantage; **tornerà a suo** ~ it will work against you.
svantaggi'oso, a [zvantad'dʒoso] ag disadvantageous; **è un'offerta** ~**a per me** it's not in my interest to accept this offer; **è un prezzo** ~ it is not an attractive price.
svapo'rare vi to evaporate.
svapo'rato, a ag (bibita) flat.
svari'ato, a ag (vario, diverso) varied; (numeroso) various.
'svastica, che sf swastika.
sve'dese ag Swedish ♦ sm/f Swede ♦ sm (LING) Swedish.
'sveglia ['zveʎʎa] sf waking up; (orologio) alarm (clock); **suonare la** ~ (MIL) to sound the reveille; ~ **telefonica** alarm call.
svegli'are [zveʎ'ʎare] vt to wake up; (fig) to awaken, arouse; ~**rsi** vr to wake up; (fig) to be revived, reawaken.
'sveglio, a ['zveʎʎo] ag awake; (fig) alert, quick-witted.
sve'lare vt to reveal.
svel'tezza [zvel'tettsa] sf (gen) speed; (mentale) quick-wittedness.
svel'tire vt (gen) to speed up; (procedura) to streamline.
'svelto, a ag (passo) quick; (mente) quick, alert; (linea) slim, slender; **alla** ~**a** quickly.
'svendere vt to sell off, clear.
'svendita sf (COMM) (clearance) sale.
sve'nevole ag mawkish.
'svengo etc vb vedi **svenire**.
sveni'mento sm fainting fit, faint.
sve'nire vi to faint.
sven'tare vt to foil, thwart.
sventa'tezza [zventa'tettsa] sf (distrazione) absent-mindedness; (mancanza di prudenza) rashness.
sven'tato, a ag (distratto) scatterbrained; (imprudente) rash.
'sventola sf (colpo) slap; **orecchie a** ~ sticking-out ears.
svento'lare vt, vi to wave, flutter.
sven'trare vt to disembowel.
sven'tura sf misfortune.
sventu'rato, a ag unlucky, unfortunate.
sve'nuto, a pp di **svenire**.
svergo'gnare [zvergoɲ'ɲare] vt to shame.

svergo'gnato, a [zvergoɲ'ɲato] *ag* shameless ♦ *sm/f* shameless person.

sver'nare *vi* to spend the winter.

sverrò *etc vb vedi* **svenire.**

sves'tire *vt* to undress; ~**rsi** *vr* to get undressed.

'Svezia ['zvɛttsja] *sf*: **la** ~ Sweden.

svez'zare [zvet'tsare] *vt* to wean.

svi'are *vt* to divert; (*fig*) to lead astray; ~**rsi** *vr* to go astray.

svico'lare *vi* to slip down an alley; (*fig*) to sneak off.

svi'gnarsela [zviɲ'ɲarsela] *vr* to slip away, sneak off.

svili'mento *sm* debasement.

svi'lire *vt* to debase.

svilup'pare *vt*, ~**rsi** *vr* to develop.

svi'luppo *sm* development; (*di industria*) expansion; **in via di** ~ in the process of development; **paesi in via di** ~ developing countries.

svinco'lare *vt* to free, release; (*merce*) to clear.

'svincolo *sm* (*COMM*) clearance; (*stradale*) motorway (*BRIT*) *o* expressway (*US*) intersection.

svisce'rare [zviʃʃe'rare] *vt* (*fig: argomento*) to examine in depth.

svisce'rato, a [zviʃʃe'rato] *ag* (*amore, odio*) passionate.

'svista *sf* oversight.

svi'tare *vt* to unscrew.

'Svizzera ['zvittsera] *sf*: **la** ~ Switzerland.

'svizzero, a ['zvittsero] *ag*, *sm/f* Swiss.

svoglia'tezza [zvoʎʎa'tettsa] *sf* listlessness; indolence.

svogli'ato, a [zvoʎ'ʎato] *ag* listless; (*pigro*) lazy, indolent.

svolaz'zare [zvolat'tsare] *vi* to flutter.

'svolgere ['zvɔldʒere] *vt* to unwind; (*srotolare*) to unroll; (*fig: argomento*) to develop; (: *piano, programma*) to carry out; ~**rsi** *vr* to unwind; to unroll; (*fig: aver luogo*) to take place; (: *procedere*) to go on; **tutto si è svolto secondo i piani** everything went according to plan.

svolgi'mento [zvoldʒi'mento] *sm* development; carrying out; (*andamento*) course.

'svolsi *etc vb vedi* **svolgere.**

'svolta *sf* (*atto*) turning *no pl*; (*curva*) turn, bend; (*fig*) turning-point; **essere ad una** ~ **nella propria vita** to be at a crossroads in one's life.

svol'tare *vi* to turn.

'svolto, a *pp di* **svolgere.**

svuo'tare *vt* to empty (out).

'Swaziland ['swadziland] *sm*: **lo** ~ Swaziland.

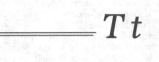

T, t [ti] *sf o m inv* (*lettera*) T, t; **T come Taranto** ≈ T for Tommy.

T *abbr* = **tabaccheria.**

t *abbr* = **tara; tonnellata.**

TA *sigla* = *Taranto.*

tabac'caio, a *sm/f* tobacconist.

tabacche'ria [tabakke'ria] *sf* tobacconist's (shop).

tabacchi'era [tabak'kjɛra] *sf* snuffbox.

ta'bacco, chi *sm* tobacco.

ta'bella *sf* (*tavola*) table; (*elenco*) list; ~ **di marcia** schedule; ~ **dei prezzi** price list.

tabel'lone *sm* (*per pubblicità*) billboard; (*per informazioni*) notice board (*BRIT*), bulletin board (*US*); (: *in stazione*) timetable board.

taber'nacolo *sm* tabernacle.

tabù *ag*, *sm inv* taboo.

'tabula 'rasa *sf* tabula rasa; **fare** ~ (*fig*) to make a clean sweep.

tabu'lare *vt* to tabulate.

tabu'lato *sm* (*INFORM*) printout.

tabula'tore *sm* tabulator.

TAC *sigla f* (*MED*: = *Tomografia Assiale Computerizzata*) CAT.

'tacca, che *sf* notch, nick; **di mezza** ~ (*fig*) mediocre.

taccagne'ria [takkaɲɲe'ria] *sf* meanness, stinginess.

tac'cagno, a [tak'kaɲɲo] *ag* mean, stingy.

tac'cheggio [tak'keddʒo] *sm* shoplifting.

tac'chino [tak'kino] *sm* turkey.

'taccia, ce ['tattʃa] *sf* bad reputation.

tacci'are [tat'tʃare] *vt*: ~ **qn di** (*vigliaccheria etc*) to accuse sb of.

'taccio *etc* ['tattʃo] *vb vedi* **tacere.**

'tacco, chi *sm* heel.

taccu'ino *sm* notebook.

ta'cere [ta'tʃere] *vi* to be silent *o* quiet; (*smettere di parlare*) to fall silent ♦ *vt* to keep to oneself, say nothing about; **far** ~ **qn** to make sb be quiet; (*fig*) to silence sb; **mettere a** ~ **qc** to hush sth up.

tachicar'dia [takikar'dia] *sf* (*MED*) tachycardia.

ta'chimetro [ta'kimetro] *sm* speedometer.

'tacito, a ['tatʃito] *ag* silent; (*sottinteso*) tacit, unspoken.

taci'turno, a [tatʃi'turno] *ag* taciturn.

taci'uto, a [ta'tʃuto] *pp di* **tacere.**
'tacqui *etc vb vedi* **tacere.**
ta'fano *sm* horsefly.
taffe'ruglio [taffe'ruʎʎo] *sm* brawl, scuffle.
taffettà *sm* taffeta.
'taglia ['taʎʎa] *sf* (*statura*) height; (*misura*) size; (*riscatto*) ransom; (*ricompensa*) reward; ~**e forti** (*ABBIGLIAMENTO*) outsize.
taglia'boschi [taʎʎa'bɔski] *sm inv* woodcutter.
taglia'carte [taʎʎa'karte] *sm inv* paperknife.
taglia'legna [taʎʎa'leɲɲa] *sm inv* woodcutter.
tagli'ando [taʎ'ʎando] *sm* coupon.
tagli'are [taʎ'ʎare] *vt* to cut; (*recidere, interrompere*) to cut off; (*intersecare*) to cut across, intersect; (*carne*) to carve; (*vini*) to blend ♦ *vi* to cut; (*prendere una scorciatoia*) to take a short-cut; ~ **la strada a qn** to cut across in front of sb; ~ **corto** (*fig*) to cut short.
taglia'telle [taʎʎa'tɛlle] *sfpl* tagliatelle *pl.*
tagli'ato, a [taʎ'ʎato] *ag:* **essere** ~ **per qc** (*fig*) to be cut out for sth.
taglia'unghie [taʎʎa'ungje] *sm inv* nail clippers *pl.*
tagli'ente [taʎ'ʎɛnte] *ag* sharp.
tagli'ere [taʎ'ʎɛrc] *sm* chopping board; (*per il pane*) bread board.
'taglio ['taʎʎo] *sm* (*anche fig*) cut; (*azione*) cutting *no pl*; (*di carne*) piece; (*di stoffa*) length; (*di vini*) blending; **di** ~ on edge, edgeways; **banconote di piccolo/grosso** ~ notes of small/large denomination; **un bel** ~ **di capelli** a nice haircut *o* hairstyle; **pizza al** ~ pizza by the slice.
tagli'one [taʎ'ʎone] *sm:* **la legge del** ~ the concept of an eye for an eye and a tooth for a tooth.
tagliuz'zare [taʎʎut'tsare] *vt* to cut into small pieces.
Ta'hiti [ta'iti] *sf* Tahiti.
tailan'dese *ag, sm/f, sm* Thai.
Tai'landia *sf:* **la** ~ Thailand.
tai'lleur [ta'jœr] *sm inv* lady's suit.
'talco *sm* talcum powder.

━━━━━━━━━━ *PAROLA CHIAVE* ━━━━━━━━━━

'tale *det* **1** (*simile, così grande*) such; **un(a)** ~ ... such (a) ...; **non accetto** ~**i discorsi** I won't allow such talk; **è di una** ~ **arroganza** he is so arrogant; **fa una** ~ **confusione!** he makes such a mess!
2 (*persona o cosa indeterminata*) such-and-such; **il giorno** ~ **all'ora** ~ on such-and-such a day at such-and-such a time; **la tal persona** that person; **ha telefonato una** ~ **Giovanna** somebody called

Giovanna phoned
3 (*nelle similitudini*): ~ ... ~ like ... like; ~ **padre** ~ **figlio** like father, like son; **hai il vestito** ~ **quale il mio** your dress is just *o* exactly like mine ♦ *pron* (*indefinito: persona*): **un(a)** ~ someone; **quel** (*o* **quella**) ~ that person, that man (*o* woman); **il tal dei** ~**i** what's-his-name.

━━━━━━━━━━━━━━━━━━━━━━━━━━━━

tale'bano *sm* Taliban.
ta'lento *sm* talent.
talis'mano *sm* talisman.
talk-'show [tɔlk'ʃo] *sm inv* talk *o* chat show.
tallo'nare *vt* to pursue; ~ **il pallone** (*CALCIO, RUGBY*) to heel the ball.
tallon'cino [tallon'tʃino] *sm* counterfoil (*BRIT*), stub; ~ **del prezzo** (*di medicinali*) tear-off tag.
tal'lone *sm* heel.
tal'mente *av* so.
ta'lora *av* = **talvolta.**
'talpa *sf* (*anche fig*) mole.
tal'volta *av* sometimes, at times.
tambu'rello *sm* tambourine.
tambu'rino *sm* drummer boy.
tam'buro *sm* drum; **freni a** ~ drum brakes; **a** ~ **battente** (*fig*) immediately, at once.
Ta'migi [ta'midʒi] *sm:* **il** ~ the Thames.
tampona'mento *sm* (*AUT*) collision; ~ **a catena** pile-up.
tampo'nare *vt* (*otturare*) to plug; (*urtare: macchina*) to crash *o* ram into.
tam'pone *sm* (*MED*) wad, pad; (*per timbri*) ink-pad; (*respingente*) buffer; ~ **assorbente** tampon.
'tamtam *sm inv* (*fig*) grapevine.
'tana *sf* lair, den; (*fig*) den, hideout.
'tanfo *sm* stench.
tan'gente [tan'dʒɛnte] *ag* (*MAT*): ~ **a** tangential to ♦ *sf* tangent; (*quota*) share; (*denaro estorto*) rake-off (*fam*), cut.
tangen'topoli [tandʒen'topoli] *sf* (*POL, MEDIA*) Bribesville; *vedi nota nel riquadro.*

━━━━━━━━━━━━━━━━━━━━━━━━━━━━
TANGENTOPOLI

Tangentopoli *refers to the corruption scandal of the early 1990s which involved a large number of politicians from all parties, including government ministers, as well as leading industrialists and business people. Subsequent investigations unearthed a complex series of illegal payments and bribes involving both public and private money. The scandal began in Milan, which came to be known as* **Tangentopoli,** *or "Bribesville".*

tangenzi'ale [tandʒen'tsjale] *sf* (*strada*) bypass.

'Tangeri ['tandʒeri] *sf* Tangiers.

tan'gibile [tan'dʒibile] *ag* tangible.

tangibil'mente [tandʒibil'mente] *av* tangibly.

'tango, ghi *sm* tango.

'tanica, che *sf* jerry can.

tan'nino *sm* tannin.

tan'tino: un ~ *av* (*un po'*); a little, a bit; (*alquanto*) rather.

====================== **PAROLA CHIAVE**

'tanto, a *det* **1** (*molto: quantità*) a lot of, much; (: *numero*) a lot of, many; ~ **pane/ latte** a lot of bread/milk; ~ **tempo** a lot of time, a long time; **~i auguri!** all the best!; **~e grazie** many thanks; ~ **persone** a lot of people, many people; **~e volte** many times, often; **ogni ~i chilometri** every so many kilometres

2: (*così* ~: *quantità*) so much, such a lot of; (: *numero*) so many, such a lot of; **~a fatica per niente!** a lot of trouble for nothing!; **ha** ~ **coraggio che** ... he's got so much courage that ..., he's so brave that ...; **ho aspettato per** ~ **tempo** I waited so long *o* for such a long time

3: ~ ... **quanto** (*quantità*) as much ... as; (*numero*) as many ... as; **ho ~a pazienza quanta ne hai tu** I have as much patience as you have *o* as you; **ha ~i amici quanti nemici** he has as many friends as he has enemies

♦ *pron* **1** (*molto*) much, a lot; (*così* ~) so much, such a lot; **~i, e** many, a lot; so many, such a lot; **credevo ce ne fosse** ~ I thought there was (such) a lot, I thought there was plenty; **una persona come ~e a** person just like any other; **è passato** ~ (*tempo*) it's been so long; **è** ~ **che aspetto** I've been waiting for a long time; ~ **di guadagnato!** so much the better!

2: ~ **quanto** (*denaro*) as much as; (*cioccolatini*) as many as; **ne ho** ~ **quanto basta** I have as much as I need; **due volte** ~ twice as much

3 (*indeterminato*) so much; ~ **per l'affitto,** ~ **per il gas** so much for the rent, so much for the gas; **costa un** ~ **al metro** it costs so much per metre; **di** ~ **in** ~, **ogni** ~ every so often; ~ **vale che** ... I (*o* we *etc*) may as well ...; ~ **meglio!** so much the better!; ~ **peggio per lui!** so much the worse for him!; **se** ~ **mi dà** ~ if that's how things are; **guardare qc con** ~ **d'occhi** to gaze wide-eyed at sth

♦ *av* **1** (*molto*) very; **vengo** ~ **volentieri** I'd

be very glad to come; **non ci vuole** ~ **a capirlo** it doesn't take much to understand it

2 (*così* ~: *con ag, av*) so; (: *con vb*) so much, such a lot; **è** ~ **bella!** she's so beautiful!; **non urlare** ~ **(forte)** don't shout so much; **sto** ~ **meglio adesso** I'm so much better now; **era** ~ **bella da non credere** she was incredibly beautiful; ~ ... **che** so ... (that); ~ ... **da** so ... as

3: ~ ... **quanto** as ... as; **conosco** ~ **Carlo quanto suo padre** I know both Carlo and his father; **non è poi** ~ **complicato quanto sembra** it's not as difficult as it seems; **è** ~ **bella quanto buona** she is as good as she is beautiful; ~ **più insisti,** ~ **più non mollerà** the more you insist, the more stubborn he'll be; **quanto più** ... ~ **meno** the more ... the less; **quanto più lo conosco** ~ **meno mi piace** the better I know him the less I like him

4 (*solamente*) just; ~ **per cambiare/ scherzare** just for a change/a joke; **una volta** ~ for once

5 (*a lungo*) (for) long

♦ *cong* after all; **non insistere,** ~ **è inutile** don't keep on, it's no use; **lascia stare,** ~ **è troppo tardi** forget it, it's too late.

Tanza'nia [tandza'nia] *sf*: **la** ~ Tanzania.

tapi'oca *sf* tapioca.

ta'piro *sm* (*ZOOL*) tapir.

'tappa *sf* (*luogo di sosta, fermata*) stop, halt; (*parte di un percorso*) stage, leg; (*SPORT*) lap; **a ~e** in stages; **bruciare le ~e** (*fig*) to be a whizz kid.

tappa'buchi [tappa'buki] *sm inv* stopgap; **fare da** ~ to act as a stopgap.

tap'pare *vt* to plug, stop up; (*bottiglia*) to cork; **~rsi il naso** to hold one's nose; **~rsi le orecchie** to turn a deaf ear; **~rsi gli occhi** to turn a blind eye.

tappa'rella *sf* rolling shutter.

tappe'tino *sm* (*per auto*) car mat; ~ **antiscivolo** (*da bagno*) non-slip mat.

tap'peto *sm* carpet; (*anche: tappetino*) rug; (*di tavolo*) cloth; (*SPORT*): **andare al** ~ to go down for the count; **mettere sul** ~ (*fig*) to bring up for discussion.

tappez'zare [tappet'tsare] *vt* (*con carta*) to paper; (*rivestire*): ~ **qc (di)** to cover sth (with).

tappezze'ria [tappettse'ria] *sf* (*arredamento*) soft furnishings *pl*; (*carta da parati*) wall covering; (*di automobile*) upholstery; **far da** ~ (*fig*) to be a wallflower.

tappezzi'ere [tappet'tsjɛre] *sm* upholsterer.

'**tappo** *sm* stopper; (*in sughero*) cork; ~ **a corona** bottle top; ~ **a vite** screw top.
TAR *sigla m* = *Tribunale Amministrativo Regionale.*
'**tara** *sf* (*peso*) tare; (*MED*) hereditary defect; (*difetto*) flaw.
taran'tella *sf* tarantella.
ta'rantola *sf* tarantula.
ta'rare *vt* (*COMM*) to tare; (*TECN*) to calibrate.
ta'rato, a *ag* (*COMM*) tared; (*MED*) with a hereditary defect.
tara'tura *sf* (*COMM*) taring; (*TECN*) calibration.
tarchi'ato, a [tar'kjato] *ag* stocky, thickset.
tar'dare *vi* to be late ♦ *vt* to delay; ~ **a fare** to delay doing.
'**tardi** *av* late; **più** ~ later (on); **al più** ~ at the latest; **sul** ~ (*verso sera*) late in the day; **far** ~ to be late; (*restare alzato*) to stay up late.
tar'divo, a *ag* (*primavera*) late; (*rimedio*) belated, tardy; (*fig: bambino*) retarded.
'**tardo, a** *ag* (*lento, fig: ottuso*) slow; (*tempo: avanzato*) late.
tar'dona *sf* (*peg*): **essere una** ~ to be mutton dressed as lamb.
'**targa, ghe** *sf* plate; (*AUT*) number (*BRIT*) *o* license (*US*) plate; *vedi anche* **circolazione.**
tar'gare *vt* (*AUT*) to register.
targ'hetta [tar'getta] *sf* (*con nome: su porta*) nameplate; (: *su bagaglio*) name tag.
ta'riffa *sf* (*gen*) rate, tariff; (*di trasporti*) fare; (*elenco*) price list; tariff; **la** ~ **in vigore** the going rate; ~ **normale/ridotta** standard/reduced rate; (*su mezzi di trasporto*) full/concessionary fare; ~ **salariale** wage rate; ~ **unica** flat rate; ~**e doganali** customs rates *o* tariff; ~**e postali/telefoniche** postal/telephone charges.
tarif'fario, ii *ag*: **aumento** ~ increase in charges *o* rates ♦ *sm* tariff, table of charges.
'**tarlo** *sm* woodworm.
'**tarma** *sf* moth.
tarmi'cida, i [tarmi'tʃida] *ag*, *sm* moth-killer.
ta'rocco, chi *sm* tarot card; ~**chi** *smpl* (*gioco*) tarot *sg.*
tar'pare *vt* (*fig*): ~ **le ali a qn** to clip sb's wings.
tartagli'are [tartaʎ'ʎare] *vi* to stutter, stammer.
'**tartaro, a** *ag*, *sm* (*in tutti i sensi*) tartar.
tarta'ruga, ghe *sf* tortoise; (*di mare*) turtle; (*materiale*) tortoiseshell.

tartas'sare *vt* (*fam*): ~ **qn** to give sb the works; ~ **qn a un esame** to give sb a grilling at an exam.
tar'tina *sf* canapé.
tar'tufo *sm* (*BOT*) truffle.
'**tasca, sche** *sf* pocket; **da** ~ pocket *cpd*; **fare i conti in** ~ **a qn** (*fig*) to meddle in sb's affairs.
tas'cabile *ag* (*libro*) pocket *cpd.*
tasca'pane *sm* haversack.
tas'chino [tas'kino] *sm* breast pocket.
Tas'mania *sf*: **la** ~ Tasmania.
'**tassa** *sf* (*imposta*) tax; (*doganale*) duty; (*per iscrizione: a scuola etc*) fee; ~ **di circolazione/di soggiorno** road/tourist tax.
tas'sametro *sm* taximeter.
tas'sare *vt* to tax; to levy a duty on.
tassa'tivo, a *ag* peremptory.
tassazi'one [tassat'tsjone] *sf* taxation; **soggetto a** ~ taxable.
tas'sello *sm* (*di legno, pietra*) plug; (*assaggio*) wedge.
tassì *sm inv* = **taxi.**
tas'sista, i, e *sm/f* taxi driver.
'**tasso** *sm* (*di natalità, d'interesse etc*) rate; (*BOT*) yew; (*ZOOL*) badger; ~ **di cambio/d'interesse** rate of exchange/interest; ~ **di crescita** growth rate.
tas'tare *vt* to feel; ~ **il terreno** (*fig*) to see how the land lies.
tasti'era *sf* keyboard.
tastie'rino *sm*: ~ **numerico** numeric keypad.
'**tasto** *sm* key; (*tatto*) touch, feel; **toccare un** ~ **delicato** (*fig*) to touch on a delicate subject; **toccare il** ~ **giusto** (*fig*) to strike the right note; ~ **funzione** (*INFORM*) function key; ~ **delle maiuscole** (*su macchina da scrivere etc*) shift key.
tas'toni *av*: **procedere (a)** ~ to grope one's way forward.
'**tata** *sf* (*linguaggio infantile*) nanny.
'**tattico, a, ci, che** *ag* tactical ♦ *sf* tactics *pl.*
'**tatto** *sm* (*senso*) touch; (*fig*) tact; **duro al** ~ hard to the touch; **aver** ~ to be tactful, have tact.
tatu'aggio [tatu'addʒo] *sm* tattooing; (*disegno*) tattoo.
tatu'are *vt* to tattoo.
tauma'turgico, a, ci, che [tauma'turdʒiko] *ag* (*fig*) miraculous.
ta'verna *sf* (*osteria*) tavern.
'**tavola** *sf* table; (*asse*) plank, board; (*lastra*) tablet; (*quadro*) panel (painting); (*illustrazione*) plate; ~ **calda** snack bar; ~ **pieghevole** folding table.
tavo'lata *sf* company at table.
tavo'lato *sm* boarding; (*pavimento*) wooden

floor.

tavo'letta *sf* tablet, bar; **a** ~ (*AUT*) flat out.

tavo'lino *sm* small table; (*scrivania*) desk; ~ **da tè/gioco** coffee/card table; **mettersi a** ~ to get down to work; **decidere qc a** ~ (*fig*) to decide sth on a theoretical level.

'tavolo *sm* table; ~ **da disegno** drawing board; ~ **da lavoro** desk; (*TECN*) workbench; ~ **operatorio** (*MED*) operating table.

tavo'lozza [tavo'lɔttsa] *sf* (*ARTE*) palette.

'taxi *sm inv* taxi.

'tazza ['tattsa] *sf* cup; ~ **da caffè/tè** coffee/tea cup; **una** ~ **di caffè/tè** a cup of coffee/tea.

taz'zina [tat'tsina] *sf* coffee cup.

TBC *abbr f* (= *tubercolosi*) TB.

TCI *sigla m* = *Touring Club Italiano*.

TE *sigla* = *Teramo*.

te *pron* (*soggetto: in forme comparative, oggetto*) you.

tè *sm inv* tea; (*trattenimento*) tea party.

tea'trale *ag* theatrical.

te'atro *sm* theatre; ~ **comico** comedy; ~ **di posa** film studio.

'tecnico, a, ci, che *ag* technical ♦ *sm/f* technician ♦ *sf* technique; (*tecnologia*) technology.

tecnolo'gia [teknolo'dʒia] *sf* technology; **alta** ~ high technology, hi-tech.

tecno'logico, a, ci, che [tekno'lɔdʒiko] *ag* technological.

te'desco, a, schi, sche *ag, sm/f, sm* German; ~ **orientale/occidentale** East/West German.

tedi'are *vt* (*infastidire*) to bother, annoy; (*annoiare*) to bore.

'tedio *sm* tedium, boredom.

tedi'oso, a *ag* tedious, boring.

te'game *sm* (*CUC*) pan; **al** ~ fried.

'teglia ['teʎʎa] *sf* (*CUC: per dolci*) (baking) tin (*BRIT*), cake pan (*US*); (: *per arrosti*) (roasting) tin.

'tegola *sf* tile.

Teh'ran *sf* Tehran.

tei'era *sf* teapot.

te'ina *sf* (*CHIM*) theine.

tel. *abbr* (= *telefono*) tel.

'tela *sf* (*tessuto*) cloth; (*per vele, quadri*) canvas; (*dipinto*) canvas, painting; **di** ~ (*calzoni*) (heavy) cotton *cpd*; (*scarpe, borsa*) canvas *cpd*; ~ **cerata** oilcloth; ~ **di ragno** spider's web.

te'laio *sm* (*apparecchio*) loom; (*struttura*) frame.

Tel A'viv *sf* Tel Aviv.

tele... *prefisso* tele....

teleabbo'nato *sm* television licence holder.

tele'camera *sf* television camera.

telecoman'dare *vt* to operate by remote control.

teleco'mando *sm* remote control; (*dispositivo*) remote-control device.

telecomunicazi'oni [telekomunikat'tsjoni] *sfpl* telecommunications.

teleconfe'renza *sf* teleconferencing.

tele'cronaca, che *sf* television report.

telecro'nista, i, e *sm/f* (television) commentator.

tele'ferica, che *sf* cableway.

tele'film *sm inv* television film.

telefo'nare *vi* to telephone, ring; (*fare una chiamata*) to make a phone call ♦ *vt* to telephone; ~ **a qn** to telephone sb, phone *o* ring *o* call sb (up).

telefo'nata *sf* (telephone) call; ~ **urbana/interurbana** local/long-distance call; ~ **a carico del destinatario** reverse-charge (*BRIT*) *o* collect (*US*) call; ~ **con preavviso** person-to-person call.

telefonica'mente *av* by (tele)phone.

tele'fonico, a, ci, che *ag* (tele)phone *cpd*.

telefo'nino *sm* (*cellulare*) mobile phone.

telefo'nista, i, e *sm/f* telephonist; (*d'impresa*) switchboard operator.

te'lefono *sm* telephone; **essere al** ~ to be on the (tele)phone; ~ **a gettoni** ≈ pay phone; ~ **azzurro** ≈ Childline; ~ **interno** internal phone; ~ **pubblico** public phone, call box (*BRIT*); ~ **rosa** ≈ rape crisis.

telegior'nale [teledʒor'nale] *sm* television news (programme).

telegra'fare *vt, vi* to telegraph, cable.

tele'grafico, a, ci, che *ag* telegraph *cpd*, telegraphic.

telegra'fista, i, e *sm/f* telegraphist.

te'legrafo *sm* telegraph; (*ufficio*) telegraph office.

tele'gramma, i *sm* telegram.

telela'voro *sm* teleworking.

tele'matica *sf* data transmission; telematics *sg*.

teleno'vela *sf* soap opera.

teleobiet'tivo *sm* telephoto lens *sg*.

telepa'tia *sf* telepathy.

tele'quiz [tele'kwits] *sm inv* (*TV*) game show.

teles'chermo [teles'kɛrmo] *sm* television screen.

teles'copio *sm* telescope.

telescri'vente *sf* teleprinter (*BRIT*), teletypewriter (*US*).

teleselet'tivo, a *ag*: **prefisso** ~ dialling code (*BRIT*), dial code (*US*).

teleselezi'one [teleselet'tsjone] *sf* direct dialling.

telespetta 'tore, 'trice *sm/f* (television) viewer.

tele 'text *sm inv* teletext.

tele 'vendita *sf* teleshopping.

tele 'video *sm videotext service.*

televisi 'one *sf* television; ~ **digitale** digital TV; *vedi nota nel riquadro.*

TELEVISIONE

Three state-owned channels, RAI 1, 2 and 3, and a large number of private companies broadcast television programmes in Italy. Some of the latter function at purely local level, while others are regional; some form part of a network, while others remain independent. As a public corporation, RAI reports to the Post and Telecommunications Ministry. Both RAI and the private-sector channels compete for advertising revenues.

---

televi 'sore *sm* television set.

'telex *sm inv* telex.

'telo *sm* length of cloth.

te 'lone *sm* (*per merci etc*) tarpaulin; (*sipario*) drop curtain.

'tema, i *sm* theme; (*INS*) essay.

te 'matica *sf* basic themes *pl.*

teme 'rario, a *ag* rash, reckless.

te 'mere *vt* to fear, be afraid of; (*essere sensibile a*: *freddo, calore*) to be sensitive to ♦ *vi* to be afraid; (*essere preoccupato*): ~ **per** to worry about, fear for; ~ **di/che** to be afraid of/that.

'tempera *sf* (*pittura*) tempera; (*dipinto*) painting in tempera.

temperama 'tite *sm inv* pencil sharpener.

tempera 'mento *sm* temperament.

tempe 'rante *ag* moderate.

tempe 'rare *vt* (*aguzzare*) to sharpen; (*fig*) to moderate, control, temper.

tempe 'rato, a *ag* moderate, temperate; (*clima*) temperate.

tempera 'tura *sf* temperature; ~ **ambiente** room temperature.

tempe 'rino *sm* penknife.

tem 'pesta *sf* storm; ~ **di sabbia/neve** sand/snowstorm.

tempes 'tare *vt* (*percuotere*): ~ **qn di colpi** to rain blows on sb; (*bombardare*): ~ **qn di domande** to bombard sb with questions; (*ornare*) to stud.

tempes 'tivo, a *ag* timely.

tempes 'toso, a *ag* stormy.

'tempia *sf* (*ANAT*) temple.

'tempio *sm* (*edificio*) temple.

tem 'pismo *sm* sense of timing.

tem 'pistiche [tem'pistike] *sfpl* (*COMM*) time and motion.

'tempo *sm* (*METEOR*) weather; (*cronologico*) time; (*epoca*) time, times *pl*; (*di film, gioco*: *parte*) part; (*MUS*) time; (: *battuta*) beat; (*LING*) tense; **un** ~ once; **da** ~ for a long time now; ~ **fa** some time ago; **poco** ~ **dopo** not long after; **a** ~ **e luogo** at the right time and place; **ogni cosa a suo** ~ we'll (*o* you'll *etc*) deal with it in due course; **al** ~ **stesso** *o* **a un** ~ at the same time; **per** ~ early; **per qualche** ~ for a while; **trovare il** ~ **di fare qc** to find the time to do sth; **aver fatto il proprio** ~ to have had its (*o* his *etc*) day; **primo/ secondo** ~ (*TEAT*) first/second part; (*SPORT*) first/second half; **rispettare i** ~**i** to keep to the timetable; **stringere i** ~**i** to speed things up; **con i** ~**i che corrono** these days; **in questi ultimi** ~**i** of late; **ai miei** ~**i** in my day; ~ **di cottura** cooking time; **in** ~ **utile** in due time *o* course; ~**i di esecuzione** (*COMM*) time scale *sg*; ~**i di lavorazione** (*COMM*) throughput time *sg*; ~**i morti** (*COMM*) downtime *sg*, idle time *sg*.

tempo 'rale *ag* temporal ♦ *sm* (*METEOR*) (thunder)storm.

tempora 'lesco, a, schi, sche *ag* stormy.

tempo 'raneo, a *ag* temporary.

temporeggi 'are [tempored'dʒare] *vi* to play for time, temporize.

'tempra *sf* (*TECN*: *atto*) tempering, hardening; (: *effetto*) temper; (*fig*: *costituzione fisica*) constitution; (: *intellettuale*) temperament.

tem 'prare *vt* to temper.

te 'nace [te'natʃe] *ag* strong, tough; (*fig*) tenacious.

te 'nacia [te'natʃa] *sf* tenacity.

te 'naglie [te'naʎʎe] *sfpl* pincers *pl.*

'tenda *sf* (*riparo*) awning; (*di finestra*) curtain; (*per campeggio etc*) tent.

ten 'daggio [ten'daddʒo] *sm* curtaining, curtains *pl*, drapes *pl* (*US*).

ten 'denza [ten'dentsa] *sf* tendency; (*orientamento*) trend; **avere** ~ **a** *o* **per qc** to have a bent for sth; ~ **al rialzo/ribasso** (*BORSA*) upward/downward trend.

tendenziosità [tendentsjosi'ta] *sf* tendentiousness.

tendenzi 'oso, a [tenden'tsjoso] *ag* tendentious, bias(s)ed.

'tendere *vt* (*allungare al massimo*) to stretch, draw tight; (*porgere*: *mano*) to hold out; (*fig*: *trappola*) to lay, set ♦ *vi*: ~ **a qc/a fare** to tend towards sth/to do; **tutti i nostri sforzi sono tesi a ...** all our efforts are geared towards ...; ~ **l'orecchio** to prick up one's ears; **il tempo tende al caldo** the weather is getting hot; **un blu che tende al verde** a greenish blue.

ten'dina *sf* curtain.

'tendine *sm* tendon, sinew.

ten'done *sm* (*da circo*) big top.

ten'dopoli *sf inv* (large) camp.

'tenebre *sfpl* darkness *sg*.

tene'broso, a *ag* dark, gloomy.

te'nente *sm* lieutenant.

te'nere *vt* to hold; (*conservare, mantenere*) to keep; (*ritenere, considerare*) to consider; (*spazio: occupare*) to take up, occupy; (*seguire: strada*) to keep to; (*dare: lezione, conferenza*) to give ♦ *vi* to hold; (*colori*) to be fast; (*dare importanza*): ~ **a** to care about; ~ **a fare** to want to do, be keen to do; ~**rsi** *vr* (*stare in una determinata posizione*) to stand; (*stimarsi*) to consider o.s.; (*aggrapparsi*): ~**rsi a** to hold on to; (*attenersi*): ~**rsi a** to stick to; ~ **in gran conto** *o* **considerazione qn** to have a high regard for sb, think highly of sb; ~ **conto di qc** to take sth into consideration; ~ **presente qc** to bear sth in mind; **non ci sono scuse che tengano** I'll take no excuses; ~**rsi per la mano** (*uso reciproco*) to hold hands; ~**rsi in piedi** to stay on one's feet.

tene'rezza [tene'rettsa] *sf* tenderness.

'tenero, a *ag* tender; (*pietra, cera, colore*) soft; (*fig*) tender, loving ♦ *sm*: **tra quei due c'è del** ~ there's a romance budding between those two.

'tengo *etc* *vb vedi* **tenere**.

'tenia *sf* tapeworm.

'tenni *etc* *vb vedi* **tenere**.

'tennis *sm* tennis; ~ **da tavolo** table tennis.

ten'nista, i, e *sm/f* tennis player.

te'nore *sm* (*tono*) tone; (*MUS*) tenor; ~ **di vita** way of life; (*livello*) standard of living.

tensi'one *sf* tension; **ad alta** ~ (*ELETTR*) high-voltage *cpd*, high-tension *cpd*.

tentaco'lare *ag* tentacular; (*fig: città*) magnet-like.

ten'tacolo *sm* tentacle.

ten'tare *vt* (*indurre*) to tempt; (*provare*): ~ **qc/di fare** to attempt *o* try sth/to do; ~ **la sorte** to try one's luck.

tenta'tivo *sm* attempt.

tentazi'one [tentat'tsjone] *sf* temptation; **aver la** ~ **di fare** to be tempted to do.

tentenna'mento *sm* (*fig*) hesitation, wavering; **dopo molti** ~**i** after much hesitation.

tenten'nare *vi* to shake, be unsteady; (*fig*)

to hesitate, waver ♦ *vt*: ~ **il capo** to shake one's head.

ten'toni *av*: **andare a** ~ (*anche fig*) to grope one's way.

'tenue *ag* (*sottile*) fine; (*colore*) soft; (*fig*) slender, slight.

te'nuta *sf* (*capacità*) capacity; (*divisa*) uniform; (*abito*) dress; (*AGR*) estate; **a** ~ **d'aria** airtight; ~ **di strada** roadholding power; **in** ~ **da lavoro** in one's working clothes; **in** ~ **da sci** in a skiing outfit.

teolo'gia [teolo'dʒia] *sf* theology.

teo'logico, a, ci, che [teo'lɔdʒiko] *ag* theological.

te'ologo, gi *sm* theologian.

teo'rema, i *sm* theorem.

teo'ria *sf* theory; **in** ~ in theory, theoretically.

te'orico, a, ci, che *ag* theoretic(al) ♦ *sm* theorist, theoretician; **a livello** ~, **in linea** ~**a** theoretically.

teoriz'zare [teorid'dzare] *vt* to theorize.

'tepido, a *ag* = **tiepido**.

te'pore *sm* warmth.

'teppa *sf* mob, hooligans *pl*.

tep'paglia [tep'paʎʎa] *sf* hooligans *pl*.

tep'pismo *sm* hooliganism.

tep'pista, i *sm* hooligan.

tera'peutico, a, ci, che *ag* therapeutic.

tera'pia *sf* therapy; ~ **di gruppo** group therapy.

tera'pista, i, e *sm/f* therapist.

tergicris'tallo [terdʒikris'tallo] *sm* windscreen (*BRIT*) *o* windshield (*US*) wiper.

tergiver'sare [terdʒiver'sare] *vi* to shilly-shally.

'tergo *sm*: **a** ~ behind; **vedi a** ~ please turn over.

'terital ® *sm inv* Terylene ®.

ter'male *ag* thermal.

'terme *sfpl* thermal baths.

'termico, a, ci, che *ag* thermal; **centrale** ~**a** thermal power station.

termi'nale *ag* (*fase, parte*) final; (*MED*) terminal ♦ *sm* terminal; **tratto** ~ (*di fiume*) lower reaches *pl*.

termi'nare *vt* to end; (*lavoro*) to finish ♦ *vi* to end.

terminazi'one [terminat'tsjone] *sf* (*fine*) end; (*LING*) ending; ~**i nervose** (*ANAT*) nerve endings.

'termine *sm* term; (*fine, estremità*) end; (*di territorio*) boundary, limit; **fissare un** ~ to set a deadline; **portare a** ~ **qc** to bring sth to a conclusion; **contratto a** ~ (*COMM*) forward contract; **a breve/lungo** ~ short-/long-term; **ai** ~**i di legge** by law; **in altri**

~i in other words; **parlare senza mezzi** ~i to talk frankly, not to mince one's words.
terminolo'gia [terminolo'dʒia] *sf* terminology.
'termite *sf* termite.
termoco'perta *sf* electric blanket.
ter'mometro *sm* thermometer.
termonucle'are *ag* thermonuclear.
'termos *sm inv* = **thermos.**
termosi'fone *sm* radiator; **(riscaldamento a)** ~ central heating.
ter'mostato *sm* thermostat.
'terna *sf* set of three; (*lista di tre nomi*) list of three candidates.
'terno *sm* (*al lotto etc*) (set of) three winning numbers; **vincere un** ~ **al lotto** (*fig*) to hit the jackpot.
'terra *sf* (*gen, ELETTR*) earth; (*sostanza*) soil, earth; (*opposto al mare*) land *no pl*; (*regione, paese*) land; (*argilla*) clay; ~**e** *sfpl* (*possedimento*) lands, land *sg*; **a o per** ~ (*stato*) on the ground (*o* floor); (*moto*) to the ground, down; **mettere a** ~ (*ELETTR*) to earth; **essere a** ~ (*fig: depresso*) to be at rock bottom; **via** ~ (*viaggiare*) by land, overland; **strada in** ~ **battuta** dirt track; ~ **di nessuno** no man's land; **la T**~ **Santa** the Holy Land; ~ **di Siena** sienna; ~ ~ (*fig: persona, argomento*) prosaic, pedestrian.
'terra-'aria *ag inv* (*MIL*) ground-to-air.
terra'cotta *sf* terracotta; **vasellame di** ~ earthenware.
terra'ferma *sf* dry land, terra firma; (*continente*) mainland.
ter'raglia [ter'raʎʎa] *sf* pottery; ~**e** *pl* (*oggetti*) crockery *sg*, earthenware *sg*.
Terra'nova *sf:* **la** ~ Newfoundland.
terrapi'eno *sm* embankment, bank.
'terra-'terra *ag inv* (*MIL*) surface-to-surface.
ter'razza [ter'rattsa] *sf,* **ter'razzo** [ter'rattso] *sm* terrace.
terremo'tato, a *ag* (*zona*) devastated by an earthquake ♦ *sm/f* earthquake victim.
terre'moto *sm* earthquake.
ter'reno, a *ag* (*vita, beni*) earthly ♦ *sm* (*suolo, fig*) ground; (*COMM*) land *no pl*, plot (of land); site; (*SPORT, MIL*) field; **perdere** ~ (*anche fig*) to lose ground; **un** ~ **montuoso** a mountainous terrain; ~ **alluvionale** (*GEO*) alluvial soil.
'terreo, a *ag* (*viso, colorito*) wan.
ter'restre *ag* (*superficie*) of the earth, earth's; (*di terra: battaglia, animale*) land *cpd*; (*REL*) earthly, worldly.
ter'ribile *ag* terrible, dreadful.
ter'riccio [ter'rittʃo] *sm* soil.
terri'ero, a *ag:* **proprietà** ~**a** landed

property; **proprietario** ~ landowner.
terrifi'cante *ag* terrifying.
ter'rina *sf* (*zuppiera*) tureen.
territori'ale *ag* territorial.
terri'torio *sm* territory.
ter'rone, a *sm/f derogatory term used by Northern Italians to describe Southern Italians.*
ter'rore *sm* terror; **avere il** ~ **di qc** to be terrified of sth.
terro'rismo *sm* terrorism.
terro'rista, i, e *sm/f* terrorist.
terroriz'zare [terrorid'dzare] *vt* to terrorize.
'terso, a *ag* clear.
ter'zetto [ter'tsetto] *sm* (*MUS*) trio, terzetto; (*di persone*) trio.
terzi'ario, a [ter'tsjarjo] *ag* (*GEO, ECON*) tertiary.
ter'zino [ter'tsino] *sm* (*CALCIO*) fullback, back.
'terzo, a ['tɛrtso] *ag* third ♦ *sm* (*frazione*) third; (*DIR*) third party ♦ *sf* (*gen*) third; (*AUT*) third (gear); (*di trasporti*) third class; (*SCOL: elementare*) third year at primary school; (*: media*) third year at secondary school; (*: superiore*) sixth year at secondary school; ~**i** *smpl* (*altri*) others, other people; **agire per conto di** ~**i** to act on behalf of a third party; **assicurazione contro** ~**i** third-party insurance (*BRIT*), liability insurance (*US*); **la** ~**a età** old age; **il** ~ **mondo** the Third World; **di terz'ordine** third rate; **la** ~**a pagina** (*STAMPA*) the Arts page.
'tesa *sf* brim; **a larghe** ~**e** wide-brimmed.
'teschio ['tɛskjo] *sm* skull.
'tesi *sf inv* thesis; ~ **di laurea** degree thesis.
'tesi *etc vb vedi* **tendere.**
'teso, a *pp di* **tendere** ♦ *ag* (*tirato*) taut, tight; (*fig*) tense.
tesore'ria *sf* treasury.
tesori'ere *sm* treasurer.
te'soro *sm* treasure; **il Ministero del T**~ the Treasury; **far** ~ **dei consigli di qn** to take sb's advice to heart.
'tessera *sf* (*documento*) card; (*di abbonato*) season ticket; (*di giornalista*) pass; **ha la** ~ **del partito** he's a party member.
tesse'rare *vt* (*iscrivere*) to give a membership card to.
tesse'rato, a *sm/f* (*di società sportiva etc*) (fully paid-up) member; (*POL*) (card-carrying) member.
'tessere *vt* to weave; ~ **le lodi di qn** (*fig*) to sing sb's praises.
'tessile *ag, sm* textile.
tessi'tore, 'trice *sm/f* weaver.
tessi'tura *sf* weaving.

tes'suto *sm* fabric, material; (*BIOL*) tissue; (*fig*) web.

'testa *sf* head; (*di cose: estremità, parte anteriore*) head, front; **5.000 euro a** ~ 5,000 euros apiece *o* a head *o* per person; **a** ~ **alta** with one's head held high; **a** ~ **bassa** (*correre*) headlong; (*con aria dimessa*) with head bowed; **di** ~ *ag* (*vettura etc*) front; **dare alla** ~ to go to one's head; **fare di** ~ **propria** to go one's own way; **in** ~ (*SPORT*) in the lead; **essere in** ~ **alla classifica** (*corridore*) to be number one; (*squadra*) to be at the top of the league table; (*disco*) to be top of the charts, be number one; **essere alla** ~ **di qc** (*società*) to be the head of; (*esercito*) to be at the head of; **tenere** ~ **a qn** (*nemico etc*) to stand up to sb; **una** ~ **d'aglio** a bulb of garlic; ~ **o croce?** heads or tails?; **avere la** ~ **dura** to be stubborn; ~ **di serie** (*TENNIS*) seed, seeded player.

'testa-'coda *sm inv* (*AUT*) spin.

testamen'tario, a *ag* (*DIR*) testamentary; **le sue disposizioni** ~**e** the provisions of his will.

testa'mento *sm* (*atto*) will, testament; **l'Antico/il Nuovo T**~ (*REL*) the Old/New Testament.

testar'daggine [testar'daddʒine] *sf* stubbornness, obstinacy.

tes'tardo, a *ag* stubborn, pig-headed.

tes'tare *vt* to test.

tes'tata *sf* (*parte anteriore*) head; (*intestazione*) heading; **missile a** ~ **nucleare** missile with a nuclear warhead.

'teste *sm/f* witness.

tes'ticolo *sm* testicle.

testi'era *sf* (*del letto*) headboard; (*di cavallo*) headpiece.

testi'mone *sm/f* (*DIR*) witness; **fare da** ~ **alle nozze di qn** to be a witness at sb's wedding; ~ **oculare** eye witness.

testimoni'anza [testimo'njantsa] *sf* (*atto*) deposition; (*effetto*) evidence; (*fig: prova*) proof; **accusare qn di falsa** ~ to accuse sb of perjury; **rilasciare una** ~ to give evidence.

testimoni'are *vt* to testify; (*fig*) to bear witness to, testify to ♦ *vi* to give evidence, testify; ~ **il vero** to tell the truth; ~ **il falso** to perjure o.s.

tes'tina *sf* (*di giradischi, registratore*) head.

'testo *sm* text; **fare** ~ (*opera, autore*) to be authoritative; (*fig: dichiarazione*) to carry weight.

testoste'rone *sm* testosterone.

testu'ale *ag* textual; **le sue parole** ~**i** his (*o* her) actual words.

tes'tuggine [tes'tuddʒine] *sf* tortoise; (*di mare*) turtle.

'tetano *sm* (*MED*) tetanus.

'tetro, a *ag* gloomy.

'tetta *sf* (*fam*) boob, tit.

tetta'rella *sf* teat.

'tetto *sm* roof; **abbandonare il** ~ **coniugale** to desert one's family; ~ **a cupola** dome.

tet'toia *sf* roofing; canopy.

'Tevere *sm*: **il** ~ the Tiber.

TG [tid'dʒi] *abbr m* (= *telegiornale*) TV news *sg*.

'thermos ® ['tɛrmos] *sm inv* vacuum *o* Thermos ® flask.

'thriller ['θrilə], 'thrilling ['θriliŋ] *sm inv* thriller.

ti *pron* (*dav lo, la, li, le, ne diventa* **te**) (*oggetto*) you; (*complemento di termine*) (to) you; (*riflessivo*) yourself; ~ **aiuto?** can I give you a hand?; **te lo ha dato?** did he give it to you?; ~ **sei lavato?** have you washed?

ti'ara *sf* (*REL*) tiara.

'Tibet *sm*: **il** ~ Tibet.

tibe'tano, a *ag, sm/f* Tibetan.

'tibia *sf* tibia, shinbone.

tic *sm inv* tic, (nervous) twitch; (*fig*) mannerism.

ticchet'tio [tikket'tio] *sm* (*di macchina da scrivere*) clatter; (*di orologio*) ticking; (*della pioggia*) patter.

'ticchio ['tikkjo] *sm* (*ghiribizzo*) whim; (*tic*) tic, (nervous) twitch.

'ticket *sm inv* (*MED*) prescription charge (*BRIT*).

ti'ene *etc vb vedi* **tenere**.

ti'epido, a *ag* lukewarm, tepid.

ti'fare *vi*: ~ **per** to be a fan of; (*parteggiare*) to side with.

'tifo *sm* (*MED*) typhus; (*fig*): **fare il** ~ **per** to be a fan of.

tifoi'dea *sf* typhoid.

ti'fone *sm* typhoon.

ti'foso, a *sm/f* (*SPORT etc*) fan.

tight ['tait] *sm inv* morning suit.

tigì [tid'dʒi] *sm inv* TV news.

'tiglio ['tiʎʎo] *sm* lime (tree), linden (tree).

'tigna ['tiɲɲa] *sf* (*MED*) ringworm.

ti'grato, a *ag* striped.

'tigre *sf* tiger.

tilt *sm*: **andare in** ~ (*fig*) to go haywire.

tim'ballo *sm* (*strumento*) kettledrum; (*CUC*) timbale.

tim'brare *vt* to stamp; (*annullare: francobolli*) to postmark; ~ **il cartellino** to clock in.

'timbro *sm* stamp; (*MUS*) timbre, tone.

timi'dezza [timi'dettsa] *sf* shyness, timidity.

'timido, a *ag* shy, timid.

'timo sm thyme.

ti'mone sm (NAUT) rudder.

timoni'ere sm helmsman.

timo'rato, a ag conscientious; ~ **di Dio** God-fearing.

ti'more sm (paura) fear; (rispetto) awe; **avere ~ di qc/qn** (paura) to be afraid of sth/sb.

timo'roso, a ag timid, timorous.

'timpano sm (ANAT) eardrum; (MUS): ~**i** kettledrums, timpani.

'tinca, che sf (ZOOL) tench.

ti'nello sm small dining room.

'tingere ['tindʒere] vt to dye.

'tino sm vat.

ti'nozza [ti'nɔttsa] sf tub.

'tinsi etc vb vedi **tingere**.

'tinta sf (materia colorante) dye; (colore) colour (BRIT), color (US), shade.

tinta'rella sf (fam) (sun)tan.

tintin'nare vi to tinkle.

tintin'nio sm tinkling.

'tinto, a pp di **tingere**.

tinto'ria sf (officina) dyeworks sg; (lavasecco) dry cleaner's (shop).

tin'tura sf (operazione) dyeing; (colorante) dye; ~ **di iodio** tincture of iodine.

'tipico, a, ci, che ag typical.

'tipo sm type; (genere) kind, type; (fam) chap, fellow; **vestiti di tutti i ~i** all kinds of clothes; **sul ~ di questo** of this sort; **sei un bel ~!** you're a fine one!

tipogra'fia sf typography.

tipo'grafico, a, ci, che ag typographic(al).

ti'pografo sm typographer.

tip 'tap [tip'tap] sm (ballo) tap dancing.

T.I.R. sigla m (= Transports Internationaux Routiers) International Heavy Goods Vehicle.

'tira e 'molla sm inv tug-of-war.

ti'raggio [ti'raddʒo] sm (di camino etc) draught (BRIT), draft (US).

Ti'rana sf Tirana.

tiranneggi'are [tiranned'dʒare] vt to tyrannize.

tiran'nia sf tyranny.

ti'ranno, a ag tyrannical ♦ sm tyrant.

ti'rante sm (NAUT, di tenda etc) guy; (EDIL) brace.

tirapi'edi sm/f inv hanger-on.

tira'pugni [tira'puɲɲi] sm inv knuckle-duster.

ti'rare vt (gen) to pull; (estrarre): ~ **qc da** to take o pull sth out of; to get sth out of; to extract sth from; (chiudere: tenda etc) to draw, pull; (tracciare, disegnare) to draw, trace; (lanciare: sasso, palla) to throw; (stampare) to print; (pistola, freccia) to fire

♦ vi (pipa, camino) to draw; (vento) to blow; (abito) to be tight; (fare fuoco) to fire; (fare del tiro, CALCIO) to shoot; ~ **qn da parte** to take o draw sb aside; ~ **un sospiro (di sollievo)** to heave a sigh (of relief); ~ **a indovinare** to take a guess; ~ **sul prezzo** to bargain; ~ **avanti** vi to struggle on ♦ vt (famiglia) to provide for; (ditta) to look after; ~ **fuori** to take out, pull out; ~ **giù** to pull down; ~ **su** to pull up; (capelli) to put up; (fig: bambino) to bring up; ~**rsi indietro** to move back; (fig) to back out; ~**rsi su** to pull o.s. up; (fig) to cheer o.s. up.

ti'rato, a ag (teso) taut; (fig: teso, stanco) drawn.

tira'tore sm gunman; **un buon ~** a good shot; ~ **scelto** marksman.

tira'tura sf (azione) printing; (di libro) (print) run; (di giornale) circulation.

tirchie'ria [tirkje'ria] sf meanness, stinginess.

'tirchio, a ['tirkjo] ag mean, stingy.

tiri'tera sf drivel, hot air.

'tiro sm shooting no pl, firing no pl; (colpo, sparo) shot; (di palla: lancio) throwing no pl; throw; (fig) trick; **essere a ~** to be in range; **giocare un brutto ~ o un ~ mancino a qn** to play a dirty trick on s.b.; **cavallo da ~** draught (BRIT) o draft (US) horse; ~ **a segno** target shooting; (luogo) shooting range.

tiroci'nante [tirotʃi'nante] ag, sm/f apprentice (cpd); trainee (cpd).

tiro'cinio [tiro'tʃinjo] sm apprenticeship; (professionale) training.

ti'roide sf thyroid (gland).

tiro'lese ag, sm/f Tyrolean, Tyrolese inv.

Ti'rolo sm: **il ~** the Tyrol.

tir'renico, a, ci, che ag Tyrrhenian.

Tir'reno sm: **il (mar) ~** the Tyrrhenian Sea.

ti'sana sf herb tea.

'tisi sf (MED) consumption.

'tisico, a, ci, che ag (MED) consumptive; (fig: gracile) frail ♦ sm/f consumptive (person).

ti'tanico, a, ci, che ag gigantic, enormous.

ti'tano sm (MITOLOGIA, fig) titan.

tito'lare ag appointed; (sovrano) titular ♦ sm/f incumbent; (proprietario) owner; (CALCIO) regular player.

tito'lato, a ag (persona) titled.

'titolo sm title; (di giornale) headline; (diploma) qualification; (COMM) security; (: azione) share; **a che ~?** for what reason?; **a ~ di amicizia** out of friendship; **a ~ di cronaca** for your information; **a ~ di premio** as a prize; ~ **di credito** share; ~

obbligazionario bond; ~ **al portatore** bearer bond; ~ **di proprietà** title deed; ~**i di stato** government securities; ~**i di testa** (*CINE*) credits.

titu'bante *ag* hesitant, irresolute.

tivù *sf inv* (*fam*) telly (*BRIT*), TV.

'tizio, a ['tittsjo] *sm/f* fellow, chap.

tiz'zone [tit'tsone] *sm* brand.

T.M.G. *abbr* (= *tempo medio di Greenwich*) GMT.

TN *sigla* = *Trento*.

TNT *sigla m* (= *trinitrotoluolo*) TNT.

TO *sigla* = *Torino*.

toast [toust] *sm inv* toasted sandwich.

toc'cante *ag* touching.

toc'care *vt* to touch; (*tastare*) to feel; (*fig: riguardare*) to concern; (: *commuovere*) to touch, move; (: *pungere*) to hurt, wound; (: *far cenno a: argomento*) to touch on, mention ♦ *vi*: ~ **a** (*accadere*) to happen to; (*spettare*) to be up to; **tocca a te difenderci** it's up to you to defend us; **a chi tocca?** whose turn is it?; **mi toccò pagare** I had to pay; ~ **il fondo** (*in acqua*) to touch the bottom; (*fig*) to touch rock bottom; ~ **con mano** (*fig*) to find out for o.s.; ~ **qn sul vivo** to cut sb to the quick.

tocca'sana *sm inv* cure-all, panacea.

toccherò *etc* [tokke'rɔ] *vb vedi* **toccare**.

'tocco, chi *sm* touch; (*ARTE*) stroke, touch.

toe'letta *sf* = **toilette**.

'toga, ghe *sf* toga; (*di magistrato, professore*) gown.

'togliere ['tɔʎʎere] *vt* (*rimuovere*) to take away (*o* off), remove; (*riprendere, non concedere più*) to take away, remove; (*MAT*) to take away, subtract; (*liberare*) to free; ~ **qc a qn** to take sth (away) from sb; **ciò non toglie che** ... nevertheless ..., be that as it may ...; ~**rsi il cappello** to take off one's hat.

'Togo *sm*: **il** ~ Togo.

toilette [twa'lɛt] *sf inv* (*gabinetto*) toilet; (*cosmesi*) make-up; (*abbigliamento*) gown, dress; (*mobile*) dressing table; **fare** ~ to get made up, make o.s. beautiful.

'Tokyo *sf* Tokyo.

to'letta *sf* = **toilette**.

'tolgo *etc vb vedi* **togliere**.

tolle'rante *ag* tolerant.

tolle'ranza [tolle'rantsa] *sf* tolerance; **casa di** ~ brothel.

tolle'rare *vt* to tolerate; **non tollero repliche** I won't stand for objections; **non sono tollerati i ritardi** lateness will not be tolerated.

To'losa *sf* Toulouse.

'tolsi *etc vb vedi* **togliere**.

'tolto, a *pp di* **togliere**.

to'maia *sf* (*di scarpa*) upper.

'tomba *sf* tomb.

tom'bale *ag*: **pietra** ~ tombstone, gravestone.

tom'bino *sm* manhole cover.

'tombola *sf* (*gioco*) tombola; (*ruzzolone*) tumble.

'tomo *sm* volume.

tomogra'fia *sf* (*MED*) tomography; ~ **assiale computerizzata** computerized axial tomography.

'tonaca, che *sf* (*REL*) habit.

to'nare *vi* = **tuonare**.

'tondo, a *ag* round.

'tonfo *sm* splash; (*rumore sordo*) thud; (*caduta*): **fare un** ~ to take a tumble.

'tonico, a, ci, che *ag* tonic ♦ *sm* tonic; (*cosmetico*) toner.

tonifi'cante *ag* invigorating, bracing.

tonifi'care *vt* (*muscoli, pelle*) to tone up; (*irrobustire*) to invigorate, brace.

ton'nara *sf* tuna-fishing nets *pl*.

ton'nato, a *ag* (*CUC*): **salsa** ~**a** tuna fish sauce; **vitello** ~ veal with tuna fish sauce.

tonnel'laggio [tonnel'laddʒo] *sm* (*NAUT*) tonnage.

tonnel'lata *sf* ton.

'tonno *sm* tuna (fish).

'tono *sm* (*gen, MUS*) tone; (*di colore*) shade, tone; **rispondere a** ~ (*a proposito*) to answer to the point; (*nello stesso modo*) to answer in kind; (*per le rime*) to answer back.

ton'silla *sf* tonsil.

tonsil'lite *sf* tonsillitis.

ton'sura *sf* tonsure.

'tonto, a *ag* dull, stupid ♦ *sm/f* blockhead, dunce; **fare il finto** ~ to play dumb.

top [tɔp] *sm inv* (*vertice, camicetta*) top.

to'paia *sf* (*di topo*) mousehole; (*di ratto*) rat's nest; (*fig: casa etc*) hovel, dump.

to'pazio [to'pattsjo] *sm* topaz.

topi'cida, i [topi'tʃida] *sm* rat poison.

'topless ['tɔplis] *sm inv* topless bathing costume.

'topo *sm* mouse; ~ **d'albergo** (*fig*) hotel thief; ~ **di biblioteca** (*fig*) bookworm.

topogra'fia *sf* topography.

topo'grafico, a, ci, che *ag* topographic, topographical.

to'ponimo *sm* place name.

'toppa *sf* (*serratura*) keyhole; (*pezza*) patch.

to'race [to'ratʃe] *sm* chest.

'torba *sf* peat.

'torbido, a *ag* (*liquido*) cloudy; (: *fiume*) muddy; (*fig*) dark; troubled ♦ *sm*: **pescare nel** ~ (*fig*) to fish in troubled waters.

'torcere ['tɔrtʃere] vt to twist; (biancheria) to wring (out); ~rsi vr to twist, writhe; dare del filo da ~ a qn to make life o things difficult for sb.

torchi'are [tor'kjare] vt to press.

'torchio ['tɔrkjo] sm press; mettere qn sotto il ~ (fig fam: interrogare) to grill sb; ~ tipografico printing press.

'torcia, ce ['tɔrtʃa] sf torch; ~ elettrica torch (BRIT), flashlight (US).

torci'collo [tortʃi'kɔllo] sm stiff neck.

'tordo sm thrush.

to'rero sm bullfighter, toreador.

tori'nese ag of (o from) Turin ♦ sm/f person from Turin.

To'rino sf Turin.

tor'menta sf snowstorm.

tormen'tare vt to torment; ~rsi vr to fret, worry o.s.

tor'mento sm torment.

torna'conto sm advantage, benefit.

tor'nado sm tornado.

tor'nante sm hairpin bend (BRIT) o curve (US).

tor'nare vi to return, go (o come) back; (ridiventare: anche fig) to become (again); (riuscire giusto, esatto: conto) to work out; (risultare) to turn out (to be), prove (to be); ~ al punto di partenza to start again; ~ a casa to go (o come) home; i conti tornano the accounts balance; ~ utile to prove o turn out (to be) useful.

torna'sole sm inv litmus.

tor'neo sm tournament.

'tornio sm lathe.

tor'nire vt (TECN) to turn (on a lathe); (fig) to shape, polish.

tor'nito, a ag (gambe, caviglie) well-shaped.

'toro sm bull; (dello zodiaco): T~ Taurus; essere del T~ to be Taurus.

tor'pedine sf torpedo.

torpedini'era sf torpedo boat.

tor'pore sm torpor.

'torre sf tower; (SCACCHI) rook, castle; ~ di controllo (AER) control tower.

torrefazi'one [torrefat'tsjone] sf roasting.

torreggi'are [torred'dʒare] vi: ~ (su) to tower (over).

tor'rente sm torrent.

torren'tizio, a [torren'tittsjo] ag torrential.

torrenzi'ale [torren'tsjale] ag torrential.

tor'retta sf turret.

'torrido, a ag torrid.

torri'one sm keep.

tor'rone sm nougat.

'torsi etc vb vedi torcere.

torsi'one sf twisting; (TECN) torsion.

'torso sm torso, trunk; (ARTE) torso; a ~

nudo bare-chested.

'torsolo sm (di cavolo etc) stump; (di frutta) core.

'torta sf cake.

tortel'lini smpl (CUC) tortellini.

torti'era sf cake tin (BRIT), cake pan (US).

'torto, a pp di torcere ♦ ag (ritorto) twisted; (storto) twisted, crooked ♦ sm (ingiustizia) wrong; (colpa) fault; a ~ wrongly; a ~ o a ragione rightly or wrongly; aver ~ to be wrong; fare un ~ a qn to wrong sb; essere/passare dalla parte del ~ to be/put o.s. in the wrong; lui non ha tutti i ~i there's something in what he says.

'tortora sf turtle dove.

tortu'oso, a ag (strada) twisting; (fig) tortuous.

tor'tura sf torture.

tortu'rare vt to torture.

'torvo, a ag menacing, grim.

tosa'erba sm o f inv (lawn)mower.

to'sare vt (pecora) to shear; (cane) to clip; (siepe) to clip, trim.

tosa'tura sf (di pecore) shearing; (di cani) clipping; (di siepi) trimming, clipping.

Tos'cana sf: la ~ Tuscany.

tos'cano, a ag, sm/f Tuscan ♦ sm (anche: sigaro ~) strong Italian cigar.

'tosse sf cough.

tossicità [tossitʃi'ta] sf toxicity.

'tossico, a, ci, che ag toxic.

tossicodipen'dente sm/f drug addict.

tossicodipen'denza [tossikodipen'dɛntsa] sf drug addiction.

tossi'comane sm/f drug addict.

tossicoma'nia sf drug addiction.

tos'sina sf toxin.

tos'sire vi to cough.

tosta'pane sm inv toaster.

tos'tare vt to toast; (caffè) to roast.

tosta'tura sf (di pane) toasting; (di caffè) roasting.

'tosto, a ag: faccia ~a cheek ♦ av at once, immediately; ~ che as soon as.

to'tale ag, sm total.

totalità sf: la ~ di all of, the total amount (o number) of; the whole + sg.

totali'tario, a ag totalitarian; (totale) complete, total; adesione ~a complete support.

totalita'rismo sm (POL) totalitarianism.

totaliz'zare [totalid'dzare] vt to total; (SPORT: punti) to score.

totalizza'tore [totaliddza'tore] sm (TECN) totalizator; (IPPICA) totalizator, tote (fam).

to'tip sm gambling pool betting on horse racing.

toto'calcio [toto'kaltʃo] sm gambling pool

betting on football results, ≈ (football) pools *pl* (*BRIT*).

tou'pet [tu'pɛ] *sm inv* toupee.

tour [tur] *sm inv* (*giro*) tour; (*CICLISMO*) tour de France.

tour de 'force ['tur də 'fɔrs] *sm inv* (*SPORT*: *anche fig*) tour de force.

tour'née [tur'ne] *sf* tour; **essere in** ~ to be on tour.

to'vaglia [to'vaʎʎa] *sf* tablecloth.

tovagli'olo [tovaʎ'ʎɔlo] *sm* napkin.

'tozzo, a ['tɔttso] *ag* squat ♦ *sm*: ~ **di pane** crust of bread.

TP *sigla* = *Trapani*.

TR *sigla* = *Terni*.

Tr *abbr* (*COMM*) = **tratta**.

tra *prep* (*di due persone, cose*) between; (*di più persone, cose*) among(st); (*tempo*: *entro*) within, in; **prendere qn** ~ **le braccia** to take sb in one's arms; **litigano** ~ (**di**) **loro** they're fighting amongst themselves; ~ **5 giorni** in 5 days' time; ~ **breve** *o* **poco** soon; ~ **sé e sé** (*parlare etc*) to oneself; **sia detto** ~ **noi** ... between you and me ...; ~ **una cosa e l'altra** what with one thing and another.

trabal'lante *ag* shaky.

trabal'lare *vi* to stagger, totter.

tra'biccolo *sm* (*peg*: *auto*) old banger (*BRIT*), jalopy.

traboc'care *vi* to overflow.

traboc'chetto [trabok'ketto] *sm* (*fig*) trap ♦ *ag inv* trap *cpd*; **domanda** ~ trick question.

traca'gnotto, a [trakaɲ'ɲɔtto] *ag* dumpy ♦ *sm/f* dumpy person.

tracan'nare *vt* to gulp down.

'traccia, ce ['trattʃa] *sf* (*segno, striscia*) trail, track; (*orma*) tracks *pl*; (*residuo, testimonianza*) trace, sign; (*abbozzo*) outline; **essere sulle** ~**ce di qn** to be on sb's trail.

tracci'are [trat'tʃare] *vt* to trace, mark (out); (*disegnare*) to draw; (*fig: abbozzare*) to outline; ~ **un quadro della situazione** to outline the situation.

tracci'ato [trat'tʃato] *sm* (*grafico*) layout, plan; ~ **di gara** (*SPORT*) race route.

tra'chea [tra'kɛa] *sf* windpipe, trachea.

tra'colla *sf* shoulder strap; **portare qc a** ~ to carry sth over one's shoulder; **borsa a** ~ shoulder bag.

tra'collo *sm* (*fig*) collapse, ruin; ~ **finanziario** crash; **avere un** ~ (*MED*) to have a setback; (*COMM*) to collapse.

traco'tante *ag* overbearing, arrogant.

traco'tanza [trako'tantsa] *sf* arrogance.

trad. *abbr* = **traduzione**.

tradi'mento *sm* betrayal; (*DIR, MIL*) treason; **a** ~ by surprise; **alto** ~ high treason.

tra'dire *vt* to betray; (*coniuge*) to be unfaithful to; (*doveri*: *mancare*) to fail in; (*rivelare*) to give away, reveal; **ha tradito le attese di tutti** he let everyone down.

tradi'tore, 'trice *sm/f* traitor.

tradizio'nale [tradittsjo'nale] *ag* traditional.

tradizi'one [tradit'tsjone] *sf* tradition.

tra'dotto, a *pp di* **tradurre** ♦ *sf* (*MIL*) troop train.

tra'durre *vt* to translate; (*spiegare*) to render, convey; (*DIR*): ~ **qn in carcere/ tribunale** to take sb to prison/court; ~ **in cifre** to put into figures; ~ **in atto** (*fig*) to put into effect.

tradut'tore, 'trice *sm/f* translator.

traduzi'one [tradut'tsjone] *sf* translation; (*DIR*) transfer.

'trae *vb vedi* **trarre**.

tra'ente *sm/f* (*ECON*) drawer.

trafe'lato, a *ag* out of breath.

traffi'cante *sm/f* dealer; (*peg*) trafficker.

traffi'care *vi* (*commerciare*): ~ (**in**) to trade (in), deal (in); (*affaccendarsi*) to busy o.s. ♦ *vt* (*peg*) to traffic in.

traffi'cato, a *ag* (*strada, zona*) busy.

'traffico, ci *sm* traffic; (*commercio*) trade, traffic; ~ **aereo/ferroviario** air/rail traffic; ~ **di droga** drug trafficking; ~ **stradale** traffic.

tra'figgere [tra'fiddʒere] *vt* to run through, stab; (*fig*) to pierce.

tra'fila *sf* procedure.

trafi'letto *sm* (*di giornale*) short article.

tra'fitto, a *pp di* **trafiggere**.

trafo'rare *vt* to bore, drill.

tra'foro *sm* (*azione*) boring, drilling; (*galleria*) tunnel.

trafu'gare *vt* to purloin.

tra'gedia [tra'dʒɛdja] *sf* tragedy.

'traggo *etc vb vedi* **trarre**.

traghet'tare [traget'tare] *vt* to ferry.

tra'ghetto [tra'getto] *sm* crossing; (*barca*) ferry(boat).

tragicità [tradʒitʃi'ta] *sf* tragedy.

'tragico, a, ci, che ['tradʒiko] *ag* tragic ♦ *sm* (*autore*) tragedian; **prendere tutto sul** ~ (*fig*) to take everything far too seriously.

tragi'comico, a, ci, che [tradʒi'kɔmiko] *ag* tragicomic.

tra'gitto [tra'dʒitto] *sm* (*passaggio*) crossing; (*viaggio*) journey.

tragu'ardo *sm* (*SPORT*) finishing line; (*fig*) goal, aim.

'trai *etc vb vedi* **trarre**.

traiet'toria *sf* trajectory.
trai'nante *ag* (*cavo, fune*) towing; (*fig*: *persona, settore*) driving.
trai'nare *vt* to drag, haul; (*rimorchiare*) to tow.
'training ['trεinin(g)] *sm inv* training.
'traino *sm* (*carro*) wagon; (*slitta*) sledge; (*carico*) load.
tralasci'are [trala∫'∫are] *vt* (*studi*) to neglect; (*dettagli*) to leave out, omit.
'tralcio ['tralt∫o] *sm* (*BOT*) shoot.
tra'liccio [tra'litt∫o] *sm* (*tela*) ticking; (*struttura*) trellis; (*ELETTR*) pylon.
tram *sm inv* tram (*BRIT*), streetcar (*US*).
'trama *sf* (*filo*) weft, woof; (*fig*: *argomento, maneggio*) plot.
traman'dare *vt* to pass on, hand down.
tra'mare *vt* (*fig*) to scheme, plot.
tram'busto *sm* turmoil.
trames'tio *sm* bustle.
tramez'zino [tramed'dzino] *sm* sandwich.
tra'mezzo [tra'mɛddzo] *sm* partition.
'tramite *prep* through ◆ *sm* means *pl*; **agire/fare da** ~ to act as/be a go-between.
tramon'tana *sf* (*METEOR*) north wind.
tramon'tare *vi* to set, go down.
tra'monto *sm* setting; (*del sole*) sunset.
tramor'tire *vi* to faint ◆ *vt* to stun.
trampo'lino *sm* (*per tuffi*) springboard, diving board; (*per lo sci*) ski-jump.
'trampolo *sm* stilt.
tramu'tare *vt*: ~ **in** to change into.
trance [trainns] *sf inv* (*di medium*) trance; **cadere in** ~ to fall into a trance.
'trancia, ce ['trant∫a] *sf* slice; (*cesoia*) shearing machine.
tranci'are [tran't∫are] *vt* (*TECN*) to shear.
'trancio ['trant∫o] *sm* slice.
tra'nello *sm* trap; **tendere un** ~ **a qn** to set a trap for sb.
trangugi'are [trangu'dʒare] *vt* to gulp down.
'tranne *prep* except (for), but (for); ~ **che** *cong* unless; **tutti i giorni** ~ **il venerdì** every day except *o* with the exception of Friday.
tranquil'lante *sm* (*MED*) tranquillizer.
tranquillità *sf* calm, stillness; quietness; peace of mind.
tranquilliz'zare [trankwillid'dzare] *vt* to reassure.
tran'quillo, a *ag* calm, quiet; (*bambino, scolaro*) quiet; (*sereno*) with one's mind at rest; **sta'** ~ don't worry.
transat'lantico, a, ci, che *ag* transatlantic ◆ *sm* transatlantic liner; (*POL*) corridor *used as a meeting place by members of the lower chamber of the Italian*

Parliament; vedi nota nel riquadro.

TRANSATLANTICO

The **transatlantico** *is a room in the Palazzo di Montecitorio which is used by "deputati" between parliamentary sessions for relaxation and conversation. It is also used for media interviews and press conferences.*

---

tran'satto, a *pp di* **transigere.**
transazi'one [transat'tsjone] *sf* (*DIR*) settlement; (*COMM*) transaction, deal.
tran'senna *sf* barrier.
tran'setto *sm* transept.
trans'genico, a, ci, che [trans'dʒεniko] *ag* genetically modified.
transiberi'ano, a *ag* trans-Siberian.
tran'sigere [tran'sidʒere] *vi* (*DIR*) to reach a settlement; (*venire a patti*) to compromise, come to an agreement.
tran'sistor *sm inv*, **transis'tore** *sm* transistor.
transi'tabile *ag* passable.
transi'tare *vi* to pass.
transi'tivo, a *ag* transitive.
'transito *sm* transit; **di** ~ (*merci*) in transit; (*stazione*) transit *cpd*; **"divieto di** ~**"** "no entry"; **"** ~ **interrotto"** "road closed".
transi'torio, a *ag* transitory, transient; (*provvisorio*) provisional.
transizi'one [transit'tsjone] *sf* transition.
tran 'tran *sm* routine; **il solito** ~ the same old routine.
tran'via *sf* tramway (*BRIT*), streetcar line (*US*).
tranvi'ario, a *ag* tram *cpd* (*BRIT*), streetcar *cpd* (*US*); **linea** ~**a** tramline, streetcar line.
tranvi'ere *sm* (*conducente*) tram driver (*BRIT*), streetcar driver (*US*); (*bigliettaio*) tram *o* streetcar conductor.
trapa'nare *vt* (*TECN*) to drill.
'trapano *sm* (*utensile*) drill; (: *MED*) trepan.
trapas'sare *vt* to pierce.
trapas'sato *sm* (*LING*) past perfect.
tra'passo *sm* passage; ~ **di proprietà** (*di case*) conveyancing; (*di auto etc*) legal transfer.
trape'lare *vi* to leak, drip; (*fig*) to leak out.
tra'pezio [tra'pεttsjo] *sm* (*MAT*) trapezium; (*attrezzo ginnico*) trapeze.
trape'zista, i, e [trapet'tsista] *sm/f* trapeze artist.
trapian'tare *vt* to transplant.
trapi'anto *sm* transplanting; (*MED*) transplant.
'trappola *sf* trap.
tra'punta *sf* quilt.

'**trarre** *vt* to draw, pull; (*prendere, tirare fuori*) to take (out), draw; (*derivare*) to obtain; ~ **beneficio** *o* **profitto da qc** to benefit from sth; ~ **le conclusioni** to draw one's own conclusions; ~ **esempio da qn** to follow sb's example; ~ **guadagno** to make a profit; ~ **qn d'impaccio** to get sb out of an awkward situation; ~ **origine da qc** to have its origins *o* originate in sth; ~ **in salvo** to rescue.

trasa'lire *vi* to start, jump.

trasan'dato, a *ag* shabby.

trasbor'dare *vt* to transfer; (*NAUT*) to tran(s)ship ♦ *vi* (*NAUT*) to change ship; (*AER*) to change plane; (*FERR*) to change (trains).

trascenden'tale [traʃʃenden'tale] *ag* transcendental.

tra'scendere [traʃ'ʃendere] *vt* (*FILOSOFIA, REL*) to transcend; (*fig: superare*) to surpass, go beyond.

tra'sceso, a [traʃ'ʃeso] *pp di* **trascendere**.

trasci'nare [traʃʃi'nare] *vt* to drag; ~**rsi** *vr* to drag o.s. along; (*fig*) to drag on.

tras'correre *vt* (*tempo*) to spend, pass ♦ *vi* to pass.

tras'corso, a *pp di* **trascorrere** ♦ *ag* past ♦ *sm* mistake.

tras'critto, a *pp di* **trascrivere**.

tras'crivere *vt* to transcribe.

trascrizi'one [traskrit'tsjone] *sf* transcription.

trascu'rare *vt* to neglect; (*non considerare*) to disregard.

trascura'tezza [traskura'tettsa] *sf* carelessness, negligence.

trascu'rato, a *ag* (*casa*) neglected; (*persona*) careless, negligent.

traseco'lato, a *ag* astounded, amazed.

trasferi'mento *sm* transfer; (*trasloco*) removal, move.

trasfe'rire *vt* to transfer; ~**rsi** *vr* to move.

tras'ferta *sf* transfer; (*indennità*) travelling expenses *pl*; (*SPORT*) away game.

trasfigu'rare *vt* to transfigure.

trasfor'mare *vt* to transform, change.

trasforma'tore *sm* transformer.

trasformazi'one [trasformat'tsjone] *sf* transformation.

trasfusi'one *sf* (*MED*) transfusion.

trasgre'dire *vt* to break, infringe; (*ordini*) to disobey.

trasgressi'one *sf* breaking, infringement; disobeying.

trasgres'sivo, a *ag* (*personaggio, atteggiamento*) rule-breaking.

trasgres'sore, trasgredi'trice [trazgredi'tritʃe] *sm/f* (*DIR*) transgressor.

tras'lato, a *ag* metaphorical, figurative.

traslo'care *vt* to move, transfer; ~**rsi** *vr* to move.

tras'loco, chi *sm* removal.

tras'messo, a *pp di* **trasmettere**.

tras'mettere *vt* (*passare*): ~ **qc a qn** to pass sth on to sb; (*mandare*) to send; (*TECN, TEL, MED*) to transmit; (*TV, RADIO*) to broadcast.

trasmetti'tore *sm* transmitter.

trasmissi'one *sf* (*gen, FISICA, TECN*) transmission; (*passaggio*) transmission, passing on; (*TV, RADIO*) broadcast.

trasmit'tente *sf* transmitting *o* broadcasting station.

traso'gnato, a [trasoɲ'ɲato] *ag* dreamy.

traspa'rente *ag* transparent.

traspa'renza [traspa'rentsa] *sf* transparency; **guardare qc in** ~ to look at sth against the light.

traspa'rire *vi* to show (through).

tras'parso, a *pp di* **trasparire**.

traspi'rare *vi* to perspire; (*fig*) to come to light, leak out.

traspirazi'one [traspirat'tsjone] *sf* perspiration.

tras'porre *vt* to transpose.

traspor'tare *vt* to carry, move; (*merce*) to transport, convey; **lasciarsi** ~ (**da qc**) (*fig*) to let o.s. be carried away (by sth).

tras'porto *sm* transport; (*fig*) rapture, passion; **con** ~ passionately; **compagnia di** ~ carriers *pl*; (*per strada*) hauliers *pl* (*BRIT*), haulers *pl* (*US*); **mezzi di** ~ means of transport; **nave/aereo da** ~ transport ship/aircraft *inv*; ~ **(funebre)** funeral procession; ~ **marittimo/aereo** sea/air transport; ~ **stradale** (road) haulage; **i** ~**i pubblici** public transport.

tras'posto, a *pp di* **trasporre**.

'**trassi** *etc vb vedi* **trarre**.

trastul'lare *vt* to amuse; ~**rsi** *vr* to amuse o.s.

tras'tullo *sm* game.

trasu'dare *vi* (*filtrare*) to ooze; (*sudare*) to sweat ♦ *vt* to ooze with.

trasver'sale *ag* (*taglio, sbarra*) cross(-); (*retta*) transverse; **via** ~ side street.

trasvo'lare *vt* to fly over.

'**tratta** *sf* (*ECON*) draft; (*di persone*): **la** ~ **delle bianche** the white slave trade; ~ **documentaria** documentary bill of exchange.

tratta'mento *sm* treatment; (*servizio*) service; **ricevere un buon** ~ (*cliente*) to get good service; ~ **di bellezza** beauty treatment; ~ **di fine rapporto** (*COMM*)

severance pay.
trat'tare *vt* (*gen*) to treat; (*commerciare*) to
deal in; (*svolgere: argomento*) to discuss,
deal with; (*negoziare*) to negotiate ♦ *vi:* ~
di to deal with; ~ **con** (*persona*) to deal
with; **si tratta di ...** it's about ...; **si
tratterebbe solo di poche ore** it would just
be a matter of a few hours.
tratta'tiva *sf* negotiation; ~**e** *sfpl* (*tra
governi, stati*) talks; **essere in** ~ **con** to be
in negotiation with.
trat'tato *sm* (*testo*) treatise; (*accordo*)
treaty; ~ **commerciale** trade agreement;
~ **di pace** peace treaty.
trattazi'one [trattat'tsjone] *sf* treatment.
tratteggi'are [tratted'dʒare] *vt* (*disegnare: a
tratti*) to sketch, outline; (: *col tratteggio*) to
hatch.
trat'teggio [trat'teddʒo] *sm* hatching.
tratte'nere *vt* (*far rimanere: persona*) to
detain; (*tenere, frenare, reprimere*) to hold
back, keep back; (*astenersi dal consegnare*)
to hold, keep; (*detrarre: somma*) to deduct;
~**rsi** *vr* (*astenersi*) to restrain o.s., stop o.s.;
(*soffermarsi*) to stay, remain; **sono stato
trattenuto in ufficio** I was delayed at the
office.
tratteni'mento *sm* entertainment; (*festa*)
party.
tratte'nuta *sf* deduction.
trat'tino *sm* dash; (*in parole composte*)
hyphen.
'tratto, a *pp di* **trarre** ♦ *sm* (*di penna, matita*)
stroke; (*parte*) part, piece; (*di strada*)
stretch; (*di mare, cielo*) expanse; (*di tempo*)
period (of time); ~**i** *smpl*
(*caratteristiche*) features; (*modo di
fare*) ways, manners; **a un** ~, **d'un** ~
suddenly.
trat'tore *sm* tractor.
tratto'ria *sf* (small) restaurant.
'trauma, i *sm* trauma; ~ **cranico**
concussion.
trau'matico, a, ci, che *ag* traumatic.
traumatiz'zare [traumatid'dzare] *vt* (*MED*)
to traumatize; (*fig: impressionare*) to
shock.
tra'vaglio [tra'vaʎʎo] *sm* (*angoscia*) pain,
suffering; (*MED*) pains *pl;* ~ **di parto**
labour pains.
trava'sare *vt* to pour; (*vino*) to decant.
tra'vaso *sm* pouring; decanting.
trava'tura *sf* beams *pl.*
'trave *sf* beam.
tra'veggole *sfpl:* **avere le** ~ to be seeing
things.
tra'versa *sf* (*trave*) crosspiece; (*via*)
sidestreet; (*FERR*) sleeper (*BRIT*),

(railroad) tie (*US*); (*CALCIO*) crossbar.
traver'sare *vt* to cross.
traver'sata *sf* crossing; (*AER*) flight, trip.
traver'sie *sfpl* mishaps, misfortunes.
traver'sina *sf* (*FERR*) sleeper (*BRIT*),
(railroad) tie (*US*).
tra'verso, a *ag* oblique; **di** ~ *ag* askew ♦ *av*
sideways; **andare di** ~ (*cibo*) to go down
the wrong way; **messo di** ~ sideways on;
guardare di ~ to look askance at; **via** ~**a**
side road; **ottenere qc per vie** ~**e** (*fig*) to
obtain sth in an underhand way.
travesti'mento *sm* disguise.
traves'tire *vt* to disguise; ~**rsi** *vr* to
disguise o.s.
traves'tito *sm* transvestite.
travi'are *vt* (*fig*) to lead astray.
travi'sare *vt* (*fig*) to distort, misrepresent.
travol'gente [travol'dʒɛnte] *ag*
overwhelming.
tra'volgere [tra'vɔldʒere] *vt* to sweep away,
carry away; (*fig*) to overwhelm.
tra'volto, a *pp di* **travolgere.**
trazi'one [trat'tsjone] *sf* traction; ~
anteriore/posteriore (*AUT*) front-wheel/
rear-wheel drive.
tre *num* three.
tre'alberi *sm inv* (*NAUT*) three-master.
'trebbia *sf* (*AGR: operazione*) threshing;
(: *stagione*) threshing season.
trebbi'are *vt* to thresh.
trebbia'trice [trebbja'tritʃe] *sf* threshing
machine.
trebbia'tura *sf* threshing.
'treccia, ce ['trettʃa] *sf* plait, braid;
lavorato a ~**ce** (*pullover etc*) cable-knit.
trecen'tesco, a, schi, sche [tretʃen'tesko]
ag fourteenth-century.
tre'cento [tre'tʃɛnto] *num* three hundred
♦ *sm:* **il T**~ the fourteenth century.
tredi'cenne [tredi'tʃɛnne] *ag, sm/f* thirteen-
year-old.
tredi'cesimo, a [tredi'tʃɛzimo] *num*
thirteenth ♦ *sf Christmas bonus of a
month's pay.*
'tredici ['treditʃi] *num* thirteen ♦ *sm inv:* **fare
** ~ (*TOTOCALCIO*) to win the pools (*BRIT*).
'tregua *sf* truce; (*fig*) respite; **senza** ~ non-
stop, without stopping, uninterruptedly.
tre'mante *ag* trembling, shaking.
tre'mare *vi* to tremble, shake; ~ **di** (*freddo
etc*) to shiver o tremble with; (*paura,
rabbia*) to shake o tremble with.
trema'rella *sf* shivers *pl.*
tremen'tina *sf* turpentine.
tre'mila *num* three thousand.
'tremito *sm* trembling *no pl;* shaking *no pl;*
shivering *no pl.*

tremo'lare *vi* to tremble; (*luce*) to flicker; (*foglie*) to quiver.

tremo'lio *sm* (*vedi vi*) tremble; flicker; quiver.

tre'more *sm* tremor.

'treno *sm* train; (*AUT*): ~ **di gomme** set of tyres; ~ **locale/diretto/espresso** local/ fast/express train; ~ **merci** goods (*BRIT*) *o* freight train; ~ **rapido** express (train) (*for which supplement must be paid*); ~ **straordinario** special train; ~ **viaggiatori** passenger train; *vedi nota nel riquadro.*

TRENI

There are several different types of train in Italy. "Regionali" and "interregionali" are local trains which stop at every small town and village; the former operate within regional boundaries, while the latter may cross them. "Diretti" are ordinary trains for which passengers do not pay a supplement; the main difference from "espressi" is that the latter are long-distance and mainly run at night. "Intercity" and "eurocity" are faster and entail a supplement. "Rapidi" only contain first-class seats, and the high-speed "pendolino", which offers both first- and second-class travel, runs between the major cities.

'trenta *num* thirty ♦ *sm inv* (*INS*): ~ **e lode** full marks plus distinction *o* cum laude.

tren'tenne *ag, sm/f* thirty-year-old.

tren'tennio *sm* period of thirty years.

tren'tesimo, a *num* thirtieth.

tren'tina *sf*: **una** ~ (**di**) thirty or so, about thirty.

tren'tino, a *ag* of (*o* from) Trento.

trepi'dante *ag* anxious.

trepi'dare *vi* to be anxious; ~ **per qn** to be anxious about sb.

'trepido, a *ag* anxious.

treppi'ede *sm* tripod; (*CUC*) trivet.

tre'quarti *sm inv* three-quarter-length coat.

'tresca, sche *sf* (*fig*) intrigue; (: *relazione amorosa*) affair.

'trespolo *sm* trestle.

trevigi'ano, a [trevi'dʒano] *ag* of (*o* from) Treviso.

triango'lare *ag* triangular.

tri'angolo *sm* triangle.

tribo'lare *vi* (*patire*) to suffer; (*fare fatica*) to have a lot of trouble.

tribolazi'one [tribolat'tsjone] *sf* suffering, tribulation.

tri'bordo *sm* (*NAUT*) starboard.

tribù *sf inv* tribe.

tri'buna *sf* (*podio*) platform; (*in aule etc*)

gallery; (*di stadio*) stand; ~ **della stampa/ riservata al pubblico** press/public gallery.

tribu'nale *sm* court; **presentarsi** *o* **comparire in** ~ to appear in court; ~ **militare** military tribunal; ~ **supremo** supreme court.

tribu'tare *vt* to bestow; ~ **gli onori dovuti a qn** to pay tribute to sb.

tribu'tario, a *ag* (*imposta*) fiscal, tax *cpd*; (*GEO*): **essere** ~ **di** to be a tributary of.

tri'buto *sm* tax; (*fig*) tribute.

tri'checo, chi [tri'kɛko] *sm* (*ZOOL*) walrus.

tri'ciclo [tri'tʃiklo] *sm* tricycle.

trico'lore *ag* three-coloured (*BRIT*), three-colored (*US*) ♦ *sm* tricolo(u)r; (*bandiera italiana*) Italian flag.

tri'dente *sm* trident.

trien'nale *ag* (*che dura 3 anni*) three-year *cpd*; (*che avviene ogni 3 anni*) three-yearly.

tri'ennio *sm* period of three years.

tries'tino, a *ag* of (*o* from) Trieste.

tri'fase *ag* (*ELETTR*) three-phase.

tri'foglio [tri'fɔʎʎo] *sm* clover.

trifo'lato, a *ag* (*CUC*) *cooked in oil, garlic and parsley.*

'triglia [ˈtriʎʎa] *sf* red mullet.

trigonome'tria *sf* trigonometry.

tril'lare *vi* (*MUS*) to trill.

'trillo *sm* trill.

tri'mestre *sm* period of three months; (*INS*) term, quarter (*US*); (*COMM*) quarter.

trimo'tore *sm* (*AER*) three-engined plane.

'trina *sf* lace.

trin'cea [trin'tʃɛa] *sf* trench.

trince'rare [trintʃe'rare] *vt* to entrench.

trinci'are [trin'tʃare] *vt* to cut up.

'Trinidad *sm*: ~ **e Tobago** Trinidad and Tobago.

Trinità *sf* (*REL*) Trinity.

'trio, pl 'trii *sm* trio.

trion'fale *ag* triumphal, triumphant.

trion'fante *ag* triumphant.

trion'fare *vi* to triumph, win; ~ **su** to triumph over, overcome.

tri'onfo *sm* triumph.

tripli'care *vt* to triple.

'triplice ['triplitʃe] *ag* triple; **in** ~ **copia** in triplicate.

'triplo, a *ag* triple, treble ♦ *sm*: **il** ~ (**di**) three times as much (as); **la spesa è** ~**a** it costs three times as much.

'tripode *sm* tripod.

'Tripoli *sf* Tripoli.

'trippa *sf* (*CUC*) tripe.

tri'pudio *sm* triumph, jubilation; (*fig: di colori*) galaxy.

tris *sm inv* (*CARTE*): ~ **d'assi/di re** *etc* three aces/kings *etc*.

'**triste** *ag* sad; (*luogo*) dreary, gloomy.
tris'tezza [tris'tettsa] *sf* sadness;
gloominess.
'**tristo, a** *ag* (*cattivo*) wicked, evil;
(*meschino*) sorry, poor.
trita'carne *sm inv* mincer, grinder (*US*).
trita'ghiaccio [trita'gjattʃo] *sm inv* ice
crusher.
tri'tare *vt* to mince, grind (*US*).
trita'tutto *sm inv* mincer, grinder (*US*).
'**trito, a** *ag* (*tritato*) minced, ground (*US*); ~
e ritrito (*idee, argomenti, frasi*) trite,
hackneyed.
tri'tolo *sm* trinitrotoluene.
tri'tone *sm* (*ZOOL*) newt.
'**trittico, ci** *sm* (*ARTE*) triptych.
tritu'rare *vt* to grind.
tri'vella *sf* drill.
trivel'lare *vt* to drill.
trivellazi'one [trivellat'tsjone] *sf* drilling;
torre di ~ derrick.
trivi'ale *ag* vulgar, low.
trivialità *sf inv* (*volgarità*) coarseness,
crudeness; (: *osservazione*) coarse *o* crude
remark.
tro'feo *sm* trophy.
'**trogolo** *sm* (*per maiali*) trough.
'**troia** *sf* (*ZOOL*) sow; (*fig peg*) whore.
'**tromba** *sf* (*MUS*) trumpet; (*AUT*) horn; ~
d'aria whirlwind; ~ **delle scale** stairwell.
trombet'tista, i, e *sm/f* trumpeter,
trumpet (player).
trom'bone *sm* trombone.
trom'bosi *sf* thrombosis.
tron'care *vt* to cut off; (*spezzare*) to break
off.
'**tronco, a, chi, che** *ag* cut off; broken off;
(*LING*) truncated ♦ *sm* (*BOT, ANAT*) trunk;
(*fig: tratto*) section; (: *pezzo: di lancia*)
stump; **licenziare qn in** ~ (*fig*) to fire sb on
the spot.
troneggi'are [troned'dʒare] *vi:* ~ (**su**) to
tower (over).
'**tronfio, a** *ag* conceited.
'**trono** *sm* throne.
tropi'cale *ag* tropical.
'**tropico, ci** *sm* tropic; ~ **del Cancro/
Capricorno** Tropic of Cancer/Capricorn; **i**
~**ci** the tropics.

========== *PAROLA CHIAVE* ==========

'**troppo, a** *det* (*in eccesso: quantità*) too
much; (: *numero*) too many; **ho messo** ~
zucchero I put too much sugar in; **c'era**
~**a gente** there were too many people
♦ *pron* (*in eccesso: quantità*) too much; (:
numero) too many; **ne hai messo** ~
you've put in too much; **meglio** ~**i che**

pochi better too many than too few
♦ *av* (*eccessivamente: con ag, av*) too; (: **con**
vb) too much; ~ **amaro/tardi** too bitter/
late; **lavora** ~ he works too much; ~
buono da parte tua! (*anche ironico*) you're
too kind!; **di** ~ too much; too many;
qualche tazza di ~ a few cups too many; **5
euro di** ~ 5 euros too much; **essere di** ~ to
be in the way.

'**trota** *sf* trout.
trot'tare *vi* to trot.
trotterel'lare *vi* to trot along; (*bambino*) to
toddle.
'**trotto** *sm* trot.
'**trottola** *sf* spinning top.
tro'vare *vt* to find; (*giudicare*): **trovo che** I
find *o* think that; ~**rsi** *vr* (*reciproco*:
incontrarsi) to meet; (*essere, stare*) to be;
(*arrivare, capitare*) to find o.s.; **andare a** ~
qn to go and see sb; ~ **qn colpevole** to find
sb guilty; **trovo giusto/sbagliato che ...** I
think/don't think it's right that ...; ~**rsi
bene/male** (*in un luogo, con qn*) to get on
well/badly; ~**rsi d'accordo con qn** to be in
agreement with sb.
tro'vata *sf* good idea; ~ **pubblicitaria**
advertising gimmick.
trova'tello, a *sm/f* foundling.
truc'care *vt* (*falsare*) to fake; (*attore etc*) to
make up; (*travestire*) to disguise; (*SPORT*)
to fix; (*AUT*) to soup up; ~**rsi** *vr* to make up
(one's face).
trucca'tore, 'trice *sm/f* (*CINE, TEAT*) make-
up artist.
'**trucco, chi** *sm* trick; (*cosmesi*) make-up; **i**
~**chi del mestiere** the tricks of the trade.
'**truce** ['trutʃe] *ag* fierce.
truci'dare [trutʃi'dare] *vt* to slaughter.
tru'ciolo ['trutʃolo] *sm* shaving.
'**truffa** *sf* fraud, swindle.
truf'fare *vt* to swindle, cheat.
truffa'tore, 'trice *sm/f* swindler, cheat.
'**truppa** *sf* troop.
TS *sigla* = Trieste.
tu *pron* you; ~ **stesso(a)** you yourself; **dare
del** ~ **a qn** to address sb as "tu"; **trovarsi
a** ~ **per** ~ **con qn** to find o.s. face to face
with sb.
'**tua** *vedi* **tuo**.
'**tuba** *sf* (*MUS*) tuba; (*cappello*) top hat.
tu'bare *vi* to coo.
tuba'tura *sf*, **tubazi'one** [tubat'tsjone] *sf*
piping *no pl*, pipes *pl*.
tuberco'losi *sf* tuberculosis.
'**tubero** *sm* (*BOT*) tuber.
tu'betto *sm* tube.
tu'bino *sm* (*cappello*) bowler (*BRIT*), derby

(*US*); (*abito da donna*) sheath dress.

'tubo *sm* tube; (*per conduttore*) pipe; ~ digerente (*ANAT*) alimentary canal, digestive tract; ~ di scappamento (*AUT*) exhaust pipe.

tubo'lare *ag* tubular ♦ *sm* tubeless tyre (*BRIT*) *o* tire (*US*).

'tue *vedi* tuo.

tuf'fare *vt* to plunge; (*intingere*) to dip; ~rsi *vr* to plunge, dive.

tuffa'tore, 'trice *sm/f* (*SPORT*) diver.

'tuffo *sm* dive; (*breve bagno*) dip.

tu'gurio *sm* hovel.

tuli'pano *sm* tulip.

'tulle *sm* (*tessuto*) tulle.

tume'fare *vt* to cause to swell; ~rsi *vr* to swell.

'tumido, a *ag* swollen.

tu'more *sm* (*MED*) tumour (*BRIT*), tumor (*US*).

tumulazi'one [tumulat'tsjone] *sf* burial.

tu'multo *sm* uproar, commotion; (*sommossa*) riot; (*fig*) turmoil.

tumultu'oso, a *ag* rowdy, unruly; (*fig*) turbulent, stormy.

tungs'teno *sm* tungsten.

'tunica, che *sf* tunic.

'Tunisi *sf* Tunis.

Tuni'sia *sf*: la ~ Tunisia.

tuni'sino, a *ag*, *sm/f* Tunisian.

'tunnel *sm inv* tunnel.

'tuo, 'tua, tu'oi, 'tue *det*: il ~, la tua *etc* your ♦ *pron*: il ~, la tua *etc* yours ♦ *sm*: hai speso del ~? did you spend your own money? ♦ *sf*: la ~a (*opinione*) your view; i tuoi (*genitori, famiglia*) your family; una ~a amica a friend of yours; è dalla ~a he is on your side; alla ~a! (*brindisi*) your health!; ne hai fatta una delle ~e! (*sciocchezze*) you've done it again!

tuo'nare *vi* to thunder; tuona it is thundering, there's some thunder.

tu'ono *sm* thunder.

tu'orlo *sm* yolk.

tu'racciolo [tu'rattʃolo] *sm* cap, top; (*di sughero*) cork.

tu'rare *vt* to stop, plug; (*con sughero*) to cork; ~rsi il naso to hold one's nose.

'turba *sf* (*folla*) crowd, throng; (: *peg*) mob; ~e *sfpl* disorder(s); soffrire di ~e psichiche to suffer from a mental disorder.

turba'mento *sm* disturbance; (*di animo*) anxiety, agitation.

tur'bante *sm* turban.

tur'bare *vt* to disturb, trouble; ~ la quiete pubblica (*DIR*) to disturb the peace.

tur'bato, a *ag* upset; (*preoccupato, ansioso*) anxious.

tur'bina *sf* turbine.

turbi'nare *vi* to whirl.

'turbine *sm* whirlwind; ~ di neve swirl of snow; ~ di polvere/sabbia dust/sandstorm.

turbi'noso, a *ag* (*vento, danza etc*) whirling.

turbo'lento, a *ag* turbulent; (*ragazzo*) boisterous, unruly.

turbo'lenza [turbo'lɛntsa] *sf* turbulence.

turboreat'tore *sm* turbojet engine.

tur'chese [tur'kese] *ag*, *sm*, *sf* turquoise.

Tur'chia [tur'kia] *sf*: la ~ Turkey.

tur'chino, a [tur'kino] *ag* deep blue.

'turco, a, chi, che *ag* Turkish ♦ *sm/f* Turk/Turkish woman ♦ *sm* (*LING*) Turkish; parlare ~ (*fig*) to talk double Dutch.

'turgido, a ['turdʒido] *ag* swollen.

tu'rismo *sm* tourism.

tu'rista, i, e *sm/f* tourist.

tu'ristico, a, ci, che *ag* tourist *cpd*.

tur'nista, i, e *sm/f* shift worker.

'turno *sm* turn; (*di lavoro*) shift; di ~ (*soldato, medico, custode*) on duty; a ~ (*rispondere*) in turn; (*lavorare*) in shifts; fare a ~ a fare qc to take turns to do sth; è il suo ~ it's your (*o* his *etc*) turn.

'turpe *ag* filthy, vile.

turpi'loquio *sm* obscene language.

'tuta *sf* overalls *pl*; (*SPORT*) tracksuit; ~ mimetica (*MIL*) camouflage clothing; ~ spaziale spacesuit; ~ subacquea wetsuit.

tu'tela *sf* (*DIR*: *di minore*) guardianship; (: *protezione*) protection; (*difesa*) defence (*BRIT*), defense (*US*); ~ dell'ambiente environmental protection; ~ del consumatore consumer protection.

tute'lare *vt* to protect, defend ♦ *ag* (*DIR*): giudice ~ *judge with responsibility for guardianship cases*.

tu'tore, 'trice *sm/f* (*DIR*) guardian.

tutta'via *cong* nevertheless, yet.

=================== PAROLA CHIAVE

'tutto, a *det* 1 (*intero*) all; ~ il latte all the milk; ~a la notte all night, the whole night; ~ il libro the whole book; ~a una bottiglia a whole bottle; in ~ il mondo all over the world

2 (*pl, collettivo*) all; every; ~i i libri all the books; ~e le notti every night; ~i i venerdì every Friday; ~i gli uomini all the men; (*collettivo*) all men; ~e le volte che every time (that); ~i e due both *o* each of us (*o* them *o* you); ~i e cinque all five of us (*o* them *o* you)

3 (*completamente*): era ~a sporca she was all dirty; tremava ~ he was trembling all over; è ~a sua madre she's just *o* exactly

like her mother
4: **a tutt'oggi** so far, up till now; **a ~a
velocità** at full *o* top speed
♦ **pron 1** (*ogni cosa*) everything, all;
(*qualsiasi cosa*) anything; **ha mangiato ~**
he's eaten everything; **dimmi ~** tell me
all about it; **~ compreso** all included, all-
in (*BRIT*); **~ considerato** all things
considered; **con ~ che** (*malgrado*)
although; **del ~** completely; **100 euro in ~**
100 euros in all; **in ~ eravamo 50** there
were 50 of us in all; **in ~ e per ~**
completely; **il che è ~ dire** and that's
saying a lot
2: **~i, e** (*ognuno*) all, everybody; **vengono
~i** they are all coming, everybody's
coming; **~i sanno che** everybody knows
that; **~i quanti** all and sundry
♦ *av* (*completamente*) entirely, quite; **è ~ il
contrario** it's quite the opposite; **tutt'al
più: saranno stati tutt'al più una cinquantina** there were about fifty of them at (the
very) most; **tutt'al più possiamo prendere
un treno** if the worst comes to the worst
we can take a train; **tutt'altro** on the
contrary; **è tutt'altro che felice** he's
anything but happy; **tutt'intorno** all
around; **tutt'a un tratto** suddenly
♦ *sm*: **il ~** the whole lot, all of it; **il ~ si è
svolto senza incidenti** it all went off
without incident; **il ~ le costerà due
milioni** the whole thing will cost you two
million.

tutto'fare *ag inv*: **domestica ~** general
maid; **ragazzo ~** office boy ♦ *sm/f inv*
handyman/woman.
tut'tora *av* still.
tutù *sm inv* tutu, ballet skirt.
TV [ti'vu] *sf inv* (= *televisione*) TV ♦ *sigla* =
Treviso.

U u

U, u [u] *sf o m inv* (*lettera*) U, u; **U come
Udine** ≈ U for Uncle; **inversione ad U**
U-turn.
ub'bia *sf* (*letterario*) irrational fear.
ubbidi'ente *ag* obedient.
ubbidi'enza [ubbi'djɛntsa] *sf* obedience.
ubbi'dire *vi* to obey; **~ a** to obey; (*sog*:

veicolo, macchina) to respond to.
ubicazi'one [ubikat'tsjone] *sf* site, location.
ubiquità *sf*: **non ho il dono dell'~** I can't be
everywhere at once.
ubria'care *vt*: **~ qn** to get sb drunk; (*sog:
alcool*) to make sb drunk; (*fig*) to make
sb's head spin *o* reel; **~rsi** *vr* to get drunk;
~rsi di (*fig*) to become intoxicated with.
ubria'chezza [ubria'kettsa] *sf* drunkenness.
ubri'aco, a, chi, che *ag, sm/f* drunk.
ubria'cone *sm* drunkard.
uccellagi'one [uttʃella'dʒone] *sf* bird
catching.
uccelli'era [uttʃel'ljɛra] *sf* aviary.
uccel'lino [uttʃel'lino] *sm* baby bird, chick.
uc'cello [ut'tʃɛllo] *sm* bird.
uc'cidere [ut'tʃidere] *vt* to kill; **~rsi** *vr*
(*suicidarsi*) to kill o.s.; (*perdere la vita*) to be
killed.
uccisi'one [uttʃi'zjone] *sf* killing.
uc'ciso, a [ut'tʃizo] *pp di* **uccidere**.
ucci'sore [uttʃi'zore] *sm* killer.
U'craina *sf* Ukraine.
u'craino, a *ag, sm/f* Ukrainian.
UD *sigla* = *Udine*.
U.D.C. *sigla f* (*POL*: = *Unione di Centro*)
centre party.
u'dente *sm/f*: **i non udenti** the hard of
hearing.
udi'enza [u'djɛntsa] *sf* audience; (*DIR*)
hearing; **dare ~ (a)** to grant an audience
(to); **~ a porte chiuse** hearing in camera.
u'dire *vt* to hear.
udi'tivo, a *ag* auditory.
u'dito *sm* (sense of) hearing.
udi'tore, 'trice *sm/f* listener; (*INS*)
unregistered student (*attending lectures*).
udi'torio *sm* (*persone*) audience.
UE *sigla f* (= *Unione Europea*) EU.
UEFA *sigla f* UEFA (= *Union of European
Football Associations*).
UEM *sigla f* (*Unione economica e monetaria*)
EMU.
'uffa *escl* tut!
uffici'ale [uffi'tʃale] *ag* official ♦ *sm* (*AMM*)
official, officer; (*MIL*) officer; **pubblico ~**
public official; **~ giudiziario** clerk of the
court; **~ di marina** naval officer; **~
sanitario** health inspector; **~ di stato
civile** registrar.
ufficializ'zare [uffitʃalid'dzare] *vt* to make
official.
uf'ficio [uf'fitʃo] *sm* (*gen*) office; (*dovere*)
duty; (*mansione*) task, function, job;
(*agenzia*) agency, bureau; (*REL*) service;
d'~ *ag* office *cpd*; official ♦ *av* officially;
provvedere d'~ to act officially;
convocare d'~ (*DIR*) to summons;

difensore *o* **avvocato d'**~ (*DIR*) court-appointed counsel for the defence; ~ **brevetti** patent office; ~ **di collocamento** employment office; ~ **informazioni** information bureau; ~ **oggetti smarriti** lost property office (*BRIT*), lost and found (*US*); ~ **postale** post office; ~ **vendite/del personale** sales/personnel department.
uffici'oso, a [uffi'tʃoso] *ag* unofficial.
'UFO *sm inv* (= *unidentified flying object*) UFO.
'ufo: a ~ *av* free, for nothing.
U'ganda *sf*: **l'**~ Uganda.
'uggia ['uddʒa] *sf* (*noia*) boredom; (*fastidio*) bore; **avere/prendere qn in** ~ to dislike/take a dislike to sb.
uggi'oso, a [ud'dʒoso] *ag* tiresome; (*tempo*) dull.
'ugola *sf* uvula.
uguagli'anza [ugwaʎ'ʎantsa] *sf* equality.
uguagli'are [ugwaʎ'ʎare] *vt* to make equal; (*essere uguale*) to equal, be equal to; (*livellare*) to level; ~**rsi** *vr*: ~**rsi a** *o* **con qn** (*paragonarsi*) to compare o.s. to sb.
ugu'ale *ag* equal; (*identico*) identical, the same; (*uniforme*) level, even ♦ *av*: **costano** ~ they cost the same; **sono bravi** ~ they're equally good.
ugual'mente *av* equally; (*lo stesso*) all the same.
U.I. *abbr* = *uso interno*.
UIL *sigla f* (= *Unione Italiana del Lavoro*) trade union federation.
'ulcera ['ultʃera] *sf* ulcer.
ulcerazi'one [ultʃerat'tsjone] *sf* ulceration.
u'liva *etc* = *oliva etc*.
U'livo *sm* (*POL*) centre-left coalition.
ulteri'ore *ag* further.
ultima'mente *av* lately, of late.
ulti'mare *vt* to finish, complete.
ulti'matum *sm inv* ultimatum.
ulti'missime *sfpl* latest news *sg*.
'ultimo, a *ag* (*finale*) last; (*estremo*) farthest, utmost; (*recente: notizia, moda*) latest; (*fig: sommo, fondamentale*) ultimate ♦ *smf* last (one); **fino all'**~ to the last, until the end; **da** ~, **in** ~ in the end; **per** ~ (*entrare, arrivare*) last; **abitare all'**~ **piano** to live on the top floor; **in** ~**a pagina** (*di giornale*) on the back page; **negli** ~**i tempi** recently; **all'**~ **momento** at the last minute; ... **la vostra lettera del 7 aprile** ~ **scorso** ... your letter of April 7th last; **in** ~**a analisi** in the final *o* last analysis; **in** ~ **luogo** finally.
ultrà *smf* ultra.
ultrasi'nistra *sf* (*POL*) extreme left.
ultrasu'ono *sm* ultrasound.

ultravio'letto, a *ag* ultraviolet.
ulu'lare *vi* to howl.
ulu'lato *sm* howling *no pl*; howl.
umana'mente *av* (*con umanità*) humanely; (*nei limiti delle capacità umane*) humanly.
uma'nesimo *sm* humanism.
umanità *sf* humanity.
umani'tario, a *ag* humanitarian.
umaniz'zare [umanid'dzare] *vt* to humanize.
u'mano, a *ag* human; (*comprensivo*) humane.
umbi'lico *sm* = **ombelico**.
'umbro, a *ag* of (*o* from) Umbria.
umet'tare *vt* to dampen, moisten.
umi'diccio, a, ci, ce [umi'dittʃo] *ag* (*terreno*) damp; (*mano*) moist, clammy.
umidifi'care *vt* to humidify.
umidifica'tore *sm* humidifier.
umidità *sf* dampness; moistness; humidity.
'umido, a *ag* damp; (*mano, occhi*) moist; (*clima*) humid ♦ *sm* dampness, damp; **carne in** ~ stew.
'umile *ag* humble.
umili'ante *ag* humiliating.
umili'are *vt* to humiliate; ~**rsi** *vr* to humble o.s.
umiliazi'one [umiljat'tsjone] *sf* humiliation.
umiltà *sf* humility, humbleness.
u'more *sm* (*disposizione d'animo*) mood; (*carattere*) temper; **di buon/cattivo** ~ in a good/bad mood.
umo'rismo *sm* humour (*BRIT*), humor (*US*); **avere il senso dell'**~ to have a sense of humo(u)r.
umo'rista, i, e *smf* humorist.
umo'ristico, a, ci, che *ag* humorous, funny.
un, un', una *vedi* **uno**.
u'nanime *ag* unanimous.
unanimità *sf* unanimity; **all'**~ unanimously.
'una 'tantum *ag* one-off *cpd* ♦ *sf* (*imposta*) one-off tax.
unci'nato, a [untʃi'nato] *ag* (*amo*) barbed; (*ferro*) hooked; **croce** ~**a** swastika.
un'cino [un'tʃino] *sm* hook.
undi'cenne [undi'tʃɛnne] *ag*, *smf* eleven-year-old.
undi'cesimo, a [undi'tʃɛzimo] *ag* eleventh.
'undici ['unditʃi] *num* eleven.
U'NESCO *sigla f* (= *United Nations Educational, Scientific and Cultural Organization*) UNESCO.
'ungere ['undʒere] *vt* to grease, oil; (*REL*) to anoint; (*fig*) to flatter, butter up; ~**rsi** *vr* (*sporcarsi*) to get covered in grease; ~**rsi con la crema** to put on cream.

unghe'rese [unge'rese] *ag, sm/f, sm* Hungarian.

Unghe'ria [unge'ria] *sf*: **l'~** Hungary.

'unghia ['ungja] *sf (ANAT)* nail; (*di animale*) claw; (*di rapace*) talon; (*di cavallo*) hoof; **pagare sull'~** (*fig*) to pay on the nail

unghi'ata [un'gjata] *sf (graffio)* scratch.

ungu'ento *sm* ointment.

unica'mente *av* only.

'UNICEF ['unitʃɛf] *sigla m* (= *United Nations International Children's Emergency Fund*) UNICEF.

'unico, a, ci, che *ag* (*solo*) only; (*ineguagliabile*) unique; (*singolo: binario*) single; **è figlio** ~ he's an only child; **atto** ~ (*TEAT*) one-act play; **agente** ~ (*COMM*) sole agent.

uni'corno *sm* unicorn.

unifi'care *vt* to unite, unify; (*sistemi*) to standardize.

unificazi'one [unifikat'tsjone] *sf* unification; standardization.

unifor'mare *vt* (*terreno, superficie*) to level; **~rsi** *vr*: **~rsi a** to conform to; ~ **qc a** to adjust *o* relate sth to.

uni'forme *ag* uniform; (*superficie*) even ♦ *sf* (*divisa*) uniform; **alta** ~ dress uniform.

uniformità *sf* uniformity; evenness.

unilate'rale *ag* one-sided; (*DIR, POL*) unilateral.

uninomi'nale *ag* (*POL: collegio, sistema*) single-candidate *cpd*.

uni'one *sf* union; (*fig: concordia*) unity, harmony; **U~ economica e monetaria** economic and monetary union; **U~ Europea** European Union; **l'U~ Sovietica** the Soviet Union.

u'nire *vt* to unite; (*congiungere*) to join, connect; (*: ingredienti, colori*) to combine; (*in matrimonio*) to unite, join together; **~rsi** *vr* to unite; (*in matrimonio*) to be joined together; ~ **qc a** to unite sth with; to join *o* connect sth with; to combine sth with; **~rsi a** (*gruppo, società*) to join.

u'nisono *sm*: **all'~** in unison.

unità *sf inv* (*unione, concordia*) unity; (*MAT, MIL, COMM, di misura*) unit; ~ **centrale (di elaborazione)** (*INFORM*) central processing unit; ~ **disco** (*INFORM*) disk drive; ~ **monetaria** monetary unit.

uni'tario, a *ag* unitary; **prezzo** ~ price per unit.

u'nito, a *ag* (*paese*) united; (*amici, famiglia*) close; **in tinta** ~**a** plain, self-coloured (*BRIT*), self-colored (*US*).

univer'sale *ag* universal; general.

universalità *sf* universality.

universal'mente *av* universally.

università *sf inv* university.

universi'tario, a *ag* university *cpd* ♦ *sm/f* (*studente*) university student; (*insegnante*) academic, university lecturer.

uni'verso *sm* universe.

u'nivoco, a, ci, che *ag* unambiguous.

═══════════════ *PAROLA CHIAVE*

'uno, a (*dav sm* **un** + *C, V,* **uno** + *s impura, gn, pn, ps, x, z; dav sf* **un'** + *V,* **una** + *C*) *det*
1 a; (*dav vocale*) an; **un bambino** a child; **~a strada** a street; ~ **zingaro** a gypsy
2 (*intensivo*): **ho avuto ~a paura!** I got such a fright!
♦ *pron* **1** one; **ce n'è** ~ **qui** there's one here; **prendine** ~ take one (of them); **l'~ o l'altro** either (of them); **l'~ e l'altro** both (of them); **aiutarsi l'un l'altro** to help one another; **sono entrati l'~ dopo l'altro** they came in one after the other; **a ~ a ~** one by one; **metà per** ~ half each
2 (*un tale*) someone, somebody; **ho incontrato** ~ **che ti conosce** I met somebody who knows you
3 (*con valore impersonale*) one, you; **se** ~ **vuole** if one wants, if you want; **cosa fa** ~ **in quella situazione?** what does one do in that situation?
♦ *num* one; **~a mela e due pere** one apple and two pears; ~ **più** ~ **fa due** one plus one equals two, one and one are two
♦ *sf*: **è l'~a** it's one (o'clock).

───────────────

'unsi *etc vb vedi* **ungere**.

'unto, a *pp di* **ungere** ♦ *ag* greasy, oily ♦ *sm* grease.

untu'oso, a *ag* greasy, oily.

unzi'one [un'tsjone] *sf*: **l'Estrema U~** (*REL*) Extreme Unction.

u'omini *pl* **u'omini** *sm* man; **da** ~ (*abito, scarpe*) men's, for men; **a memoria d'~** since the world began; **a passo d'~** at walking pace; ~ **d'affari** businessman; ~ **d'azione** man of action; ~ **di fiducia** right-hand man; ~ **di mondo** man of the world; ~ **di paglia** stooge; **l'~ della strada** the man in the street.

u'opo *sm*: **all'~** if necessary.

u'ovo *sm*, *pl(f)* **u'ova** *sm* egg; **cercare il pelo nell'~** (*fig*) to split hairs; ~ **affogato** *o* **in camicia** poached egg; ~ **bazzotto/sodo** soft-/hard-boiled egg; ~ **alla coque** boiled egg; ~ **di Pasqua** Easter egg; ~ **al tegame** *o* **all'occhio di bue** fried egg; **uova strapazzate** scrambled eggs.

ura'gano *sm* hurricane.

U'rali *smpl*: **gli ~, i Monti ~** the Urals, the Ural Mountains.

u'ranio *sm* uranium; ~ **impoverito** depleted uranium.

urba'nista, i, e *smf* town planner.

urba'nistica *sf* town planning.

urbanità *sf* urbanity.

ur'bano, a *ag* urban, city *cpd*, town *cpd*; (*TEL*: *chiamata*) local; (*fig*) urbane.

ur'gente [ur'dʒɛnte] *ag* urgent.

ur'genza [ur'dʒɛntsa] *sf* urgency; **in caso d'~** in (case of) an emergency; **d'~** *ag* emergency ♦ *av* urgently, as a matter of urgency; **non c'è** ~ there's no hurry; **questo lavoro va fatto con** ~ this work is urgent.

'urgere ['urdʒere] *vi* to be needed urgently.

u'rina *etc* = **orina** *etc*.

ur'lare *vi* (*persona*) to scream, yell; (*animale, vento*) to howl ♦ *vt* to scream, yell.

'urlo, *pl(m)* 'urli, *pl(f)* 'urla *sm* scream, yell; howl.

'urna *sf* urn; (*elettorale*) ballot box; **andare alle** ~**e** to go to the polls.

urrà *escl* hurrah!

U.R.S.S. *sigla f* (= *Unione delle Repubbliche Socialiste Sovietiche*): **l'~** the USSR.

ur'tare *vt* to bump into, knock against; (*fig*: *irritare*) to annoy ♦ *vi*: ~ **contro** *o* **in** to bump into, knock against; (*fig*: *imbattersi*) to come up against; ~**rsi** *vr* (*reciproco*: *scontrarsi*) to collide; (: *fig*) to clash; (*irritarsi*) to get annoyed.

'urto *sm* (*colpo*) knock, bump; (*scontro*) crash, collision; (*fig*) clash; **terapia d'~** (*MED*) shock treatment.

uruguai'ano, a *ag, smf* Uruguayan.

Urugu'ay *sm*: **l'~** Uruguay.

u.s. *abbr* = **ultimo scorso**.

'USA *smpl*: **gli** ~ the USA.

u'sanza [u'zantsa] *sf* custom; (*moda*) fashion.

u'sare *vt* to use, employ ♦ *vi* (*essere di moda*) to be fashionable; (*servirsi*): ~ **di** to use; (: *diritto*) to exercise; (*essere solito*): ~ **fare** to be in the habit of doing, be accustomed to doing ♦ *vb impers*: **qui usa così** it's the custom round here; ~ **la massima cura nel fare qc** to exercise great care when doing sth.

u'sato, a *ag* used; (*consumato*) worn; (*di seconda mano*) used, second-hand ♦ *sm* second-hand goods *pl*.

u'scente [uʃ'ʃɛnte] *ag* (*AMM*) outgoing.

usci'ere [uʃ'ʃɛre] *sm* usher.

'uscio ['uʃʃo] *sm* door.

u'scire [uʃ'ʃire] *vi* (*gen*) to come out; (*partire, andare a passeggio, a uno spettacolo etc*) to go out; (*essere sorteggiato: numero*) to come up; ~ **da** (*gen*) to leave; (*posto*) to go (*o* come) out of, leave; (*solco, vasca etc*) to come out of; (*muro*) to stick out of; (*competenza etc*) to be outside; (*infanzia, adolescenza*) to leave behind; (*famiglia nobile etc*) to come from; ~ **da** *o* **di casa** to go out; (*fig*) to leave home; ~ **in automobile** to go out in the car, go for a drive; ~ **di strada** (*AUT*) to go off *o* leave the road.

u'scita [uʃ'ʃita] *sf* (*passaggio, varco*) exit, way out; (*per divertimento*) outing; (*ECON*: *somma*) expenditure; (*fig*: *battuta*) witty remark; **"vietata l'~"** "no exit"; ~ **di sicurezza** emergency exit.

usi'gnolo [uziɲ'ɲɔlo] *sm* nightingale.

'uso *sm* (*utilizzazione*) use; (*esercizio*) practice (*BRIT*), practise (*US*); (*abitudine*) custom; **fare** ~ **di qc** to use sth; **con l'~** with practice; **a** ~ **di** for (the use of); **d'~** (*corrente*) in use; **fuori** ~ out of use; **essere in** ~ to be in common *o* current use.

ustio'nare *vt* to burn; ~**rsi** *vr* to burn o.s.

usti'one *sf* burn.

usu'ale *ag* common, everyday.

usufru'ire *vi*: ~ **di** (*giovarsi di*) to take advantage of, make use of.

usu'frutto *sm* (*DIR*) usufruct.

u'sura *sf* usury; (*logoramento*) wear (and tear).

usu'raio *sm* usurer.

usur'pare *vt* to usurp.

usurpa'tore, 'trice *smf* usurper.

uten'sile *sm* tool, implement ♦ *ag*: **macchina** ~ machine tool; ~**i da cucina** kitchen utensils.

utensile'ria *sf* (*utensili*) tools *pl*; (*reparto*) tool room.

u'tente *smf* user; (*di gas etc*) consumer; (*del telefono*) subscriber; ~ **finale** end user.

'utero *sm* uterus, womb; ~ **in affitto** host womb.

'utile *ag* useful ♦ *sm* (*vantaggio*) advantage, benefit; (*ECON*: *profitto*) profit; **rendersi** ~ to be helpful; **in tempo** ~ **per** in time for; **unire l'~ al dilettevole** to combine business with pleasure; **partecipare agli** ~**i** (*ECON*) to share in the profits.

utilità *sf* usefulness *no pl*; use; (*vantaggio*) benefit; **essere di grande** ~ to be very useful.

utili'tario, a *ag* utilitarian ♦ *sf* (*AUT*) economy car.

utiliz'zare [utilid'dzare] *vt* to use, make use of, utilize.

utilizzazi'one [utiliddzat'tsjone] *sf*

utilization, use.
uti'lizzo [uti'liddzo] sm (AMM) utilization;
(BANCA: di credito) availment.
util'mente av usefully, profitably.
uto'pia sf utopia; è pura ~ that's sheer
utopianism.
uto'pistico, a, ci, che ag utopian.
UVA abbr = ultravioletto prossimo.
'uva sf grapes pl; ~ passa raisins pl; ~
spina gooseberry.
UVB abbr = (ultravioletto lontano) UVB.

V v

V, v [vi, vu] sf o m inv (lettera) V, v; V come
Venezia ≈ V for Victor.
V abbr (= volt) V.
v. abbr (= vedi, verso, versetto) v.
VA sigla = Varese.
va, va' vb vedi andare.
va'cante ag vacant.
va'canza [va'kantsa] sf (l'essere vacante)
vacancy; (riposo, ferie) holiday(s pl) (BRIT),
vacation (US); (giorno di permesso) day
off, holiday; ~e sfpl (periodo di ferie)
holidays, vacation sg; essere/andare in ~
to be/go on holiday o vacation; far ~ to
have a holiday; ~e estive summer
holiday(s) o vacation.
'vacca, che sf cow.
vacci'nare [vattʃi'nare] vt to vaccinate; farsi
~ to have a vaccination, get
vaccinated.
vaccinazi'one [vattʃinat'tsjone] sf
vaccination.
vac'cino [vat'tʃino] sm (MED) vaccine.
vacil'lante [vatʃil'lante] ag (edificio, vecchio)
shaky, unsteady; (fiamma) flickering;
(salute, memoria) shaky, failing.
vacil'lare [vatʃil'lare] vi to sway; (fiamma)
to flicker; (fig: memoria, coraggio) to be
failing, falter.
'vacuo, a ag (fig) empty, vacuous ♦ sm
vacuum.
'vado etc vb vedi andare.
vagabon'daggio [vagabon'daddʒo] sm
wandering, roaming; (DIR) vagrancy.
vagabon'dare vi to roam, wander.
vaga'bondo, a sm/f tramp, vagrant;
(fannullone) idler, loafer.
va'gare vi to wander.

vagheggi'are [vaged'dʒare] vt to long for,
dream of.
vagherò etc [vage'rɔ] vb vedi vagare.
va'ghezza [va'gettsa] sf vagueness.
va'gina [va'dʒina] sf vagina.
va'gire [va'dʒire] vi to whimper.
va'gito [va'dʒito] sm cry, wailing.
'vaglia ['vaʎʎa] sm inv money order; ~
cambiario promissory note; ~ postale
postal order.
vagli'are [vaʎ'ʎare] vt to sift; (fig) to weigh
up.
'vaglio ['vaʎʎo] sm sieve; passare al ~ (fig)
to examine closely.
'vago, a, ghi, ghe ag vague.
va'gone sm (FERR: per passeggeri) carriage
(BRIT), car (US); (: per merci) truck, wagon;
~ letto sleeper, sleeping car; ~ ristorante
dining o restaurant car.
'vai vb vedi andare.
vai'olo sm smallpox.
val. abbr = valuta.
va'langa, ghe sf avalanche.
va'lente ag able, talented.
va'lenza [va'lɛntsa] sf (fig: significato)
content; (CHIM) valency.
va'lere vi (avere forza, potenza) to have
influence; (essere valido) to be valid;
(avere vigore, autorità) to hold, apply;
(essere capace: poeta, studente) to be good,
be able ♦ vt (prezzo, sforzo) to be worth;
(corrispondere) to correspond to;
(procurare): ~ qc a qn to earn sb sth; ~rsi
vr: ~rsi di to make use of, take advantage
of; far ~ (autorità etc) to assert; far ~ le
proprie ragioni to make o.s. heard; farsi ~
to make o.s. appreciated o respected;
vale a dire that is to say; ~ la pena to be
worth the effort o worth it; l'uno vale
l'altro the one is as good as the other,
they amount to the same thing; non vale
niente it's worthless; ~rsi dei consigli di
qn to take o act upon sb's advice.
valeri'ana sf (BOT, MED) valerian.
va'levole ag valid.
'valgo etc vb vedi valere.
vali'care vt to cross.
'valico, chi sm (passo) pass.
validità sf validity.
'valido, a ag valid; (rimedio) effective;
(persona) worthwhile; essere di ~ aiuto a
qn to be a great help to sb.
valige'ria [validʒe'ria] sf (assortimento)
leather goods pl; (fabbrica) leather goods
factory; (negozio) leather goods shop.
vali'getta [vali'dʒetta] sf: ~ ventiquattrore
overnight bag o case.
va'ligia, gie o ge [va'lidʒa] sf (suit)case;

fare le ~gie to pack (up); **~ diplomatica** diplomatic bag.
val 'lata *sf* valley.
'valle *sf* valley; **a ~** (*di fiume*) downstream; **scendere a ~** to go downhill.
val 'letto *sm* valet.
valligi 'ano, a [valli'dʒano] *sm/f* inhabitant of a valley.
va 'lore *sm* (*gen, COMM*) value; (*merito*) merit, worth; (*coraggio*) valour (*BRIT*), valor (*US*), courage; (*FINANZA*: *titolo*) security; **~i** *smpl* (*oggetti preziosi*) valuables; **crescere/diminuire di ~** to go up/down in value, gain/lose in value; **è di gran ~** it's worth a lot, it's very valuable; **privo di ~** worthless; **~ contabile** book value; **~ effettivo** real value; **~ nominale** *o* **facciale** nominal value; **~ di realizzo** break-up value; **~ di riscatto** surrender value; **~i bollati** (revenue) stamps.
valoriz 'zare [valorid'dzare] *vt* (*terreno*) to develop; (*fig*) to make the most of.
valo 'roso, a *ag* courageous.
'valso, a *pp di* **valere**.
va 'luta *sf* currency, money; (*BANCA*): **~ 15 gennaio** interest to run from January 15th; **~ estera** foreign currency.
valu 'tare *vt* (*casa, gioiello, fig*) to value; (*stabilire*: *peso, entrate, fig*) to estimate.
valu 'tario, a *ag* (*FINANZA*: *norme*) currency *cpd*.
valutazi 'one [valutat'tsjone] *sf* valuation; estimate.
'valva *sf* (*ZOOL, BOT*) valve.
'valvola *sf* (*TECN, ANAT*) valve; (*ELETTR*) fuse; **~ a farfalla del carburatore** (*AUT*) throttle; **~ di sicurezza** safety valve.
'valzer ['valtser] *sm inv* waltz.
vam 'pata *sf* (*di fiamma*) blaze; (*di calore*) blast; (: *al viso*) flush.
vam 'piro *sm* vampire.
vana 'gloria *sf* boastfulness.
van 'dalico, a, ci, che *ag* vandal *cpd*; **atto ~** act of vandalism.
vanda 'lismo *sm* vandalism.
'vandalo *sm* vandal.
vaneggia 'mento [vaneddʒa'mento] *sm* raving, delirium.
vaneggi 'are [vaned'dʒare] *vi* to rave.
va 'nesio, a *ag* vain, conceited.
'vanga, ghe *sf* spade.
van 'gare *vt* to dig.
van 'gelo [van'dʒɛlo] *sm* gospel.
vanifi 'care *vt* to nullify.
va 'niglia [va'niʎʎa] *sf* vanilla.
vanigli 'ato, a [vaniʎ'ʎato] *ag*: **zucchero ~** (*CUC*) vanilla sugar.
vanità *sf* vanity; (*di promessa*) emptiness;

(*di sforzo*) futility.
vani 'toso, a *ag* vain, conceited.
'vanno *vb vedi* **andare**.
'vano, a *ag* vain ♦ *sm* (*spazio*) space; (*apertura*) opening; (*stanza*) room; **il ~ della porta** the doorway; **il ~ portabagagli** (*AUT*) the boot (*BRIT*), the trunk (*US*).
van 'taggio [van'taddʒo] *sm* advantage; **trarre ~ da qc** to benefit from sth; **essere/portarsi in ~** (*SPORT*) to be in/take the lead.
vantaggi 'oso, a [vantad'dʒoso] *ag* advantageous, favourable (*BRIT*), favorable (*US*).
van 'tare *vt* to praise, speak highly of; **~rsi** *vr*: **~rsi (di/di aver fatto)** to boast *o* brag (about/about having done).
vante 'ria *sf* boasting.
'vanto *sm* boasting; (*merito*) virtue, merit; (*gloria*) pride.
'vanvera *sf*: **a ~** haphazardly; **parlare a ~** to talk nonsense.
va 'pore *sm* vapour (*BRIT*), vapor (*US*); (*anche*: **~ acqueo**) steam; (*nave*) steamer; **a ~** (*turbina etc*) steam *cpd*; **al ~** (*CUC*) steamed.
vapo 'retto *sm* steamer.
vapori 'era *sf* (*FERR*) steam engine.
vaporiz 'zare [vaporid'dzare] *vt* to vaporize.
vaporizza 'tore [vaporiddza'tore] *sm* spray.
vaporizzazi 'one [vaporiddzat'tsjone] *sf* vaporization.
vapo 'roso, a *ag* (*tessuto*) filmy; (*capelli*) soft and full.
va 'rare *vt* (*NAUT, fig*) to launch; (*DIR*) to pass.
var 'care *vt* to cross.
'varco, chi *sm* passage; **aprirsi un ~ tra la folla** to push one's way through the crowd.
vare 'china [vare'kina] *sf* bleach.
vari 'abile *ag* variable; (*tempo, umore*) changeable, variable ♦ *sf* (*MAT*) variable.
vari 'ante *sf* (*gen*) variation, change; (*di piano*) modification; (*LING*) variant; (*SPORT*) alternative route.
vari 'are *vt, vi* to vary; **~ di opinione** to change one's mind.
variazi 'one [varjat'tsjone] *sf* variation, change; (*MUS*) variation; **una ~ di programma** a change of plan.
va 'rice [va'ritʃe] *sf* varicose vein.
vari 'cella [vari'tʃɛlla] *sf* chickenpox.
vari 'coso, a *ag* varicose.
varie 'gato, a *ag* variegated.
varietà *sf inv* variety ♦ *sm inv* variety show.
'vario, a *ag* varied; (*parecchi*: **col sostantivo al pl**) various; (*mutevole*: *umore*)

changeable; ~e *sfpl*: ~e ed eventuali (*nell'ordine del giorno*) any other business.

vario'pinto, a *ag* multicoloured (*BRIT*), multicolored (*US*).

'varo *sm* (*NAUT, fig*) launch; (*di leggi*) passing.

varrò *etc vb vedi* valere.

Var'savia *sf* Warsaw.

va'saio *sm* potter.

'vasca, sche *sf* basin; (*anche:* ~ da bagno) bathtub, bath.

va'scello [vaʃ'ʃɛllo] *sm* (*NAUT*) vessel, ship.

vas'chetta [vas'ketta] *sf* (*per gelato*) tub; (*per sviluppare fotografie*) dish.

vase'lina *sf* vaseline.

vasel'lame *sm* (*stoviglie*) crockery; (: *di porcellana*) china; ~ d'oro/d'argento gold/silver plate.

'vaso *sm* (*recipiente*) pot; (: *barattolo*) jar; (: *decorativo*) vase; (*ANAT*) vessel; ~ da fiori vase; (*per piante*) flowerpot.

vas'sallo *sm* vassal.

vas'soio *sm* tray.

vastità *sf* vastness.

'vasto, a *ag* vast, immense; di ~e proporzioni (*incendio*) huge; (*fenomeno, rivolta*) widespread; su ~a scala on a vast o huge scale.

Vati'cano *sm*: il ~ the Vatican; la Città del ~ the Vatican City.

VB *sigla* = *Vibo Valenza.*

VC *sigla* = *Vercelli.*

VE *sigla* = *Venezia* ♦ *abbr* = *Vostra Eccellenza.*

ve *pron, av vedi* vi.

vecchi'aia [vek'kjaja] *sf* old age.

'vecchio, a ['vɛkkjo] *ag* old ♦ *sm/f* old man/woman; i ~i the old; è un mio ~ amico he's an old friend of mine; è un uomo ~ stile o stampo he's an old-fashioned man; è ~ del mestiere he's an old hand at the job.

'vece ['vetʃe] *sf*: in ~ di in the place of, for; fare le ~i di qn to take sb's place; firma del padre o di chi ne fa le ~i signature of the father or guardian.

ve'dere *vt, vi* to see; ~rsi *vr* to meet, see one another; ~ di fare qc to see (to it) that sth is done, make sure that sth is done; avere a che ~ con to have to do with; far ~ qc a qn to show sb sth; farsi ~ to show o.s.; (*farsi vivo*) to show one's face; farsi ~ da un medico to go and see a doctor; modo di ~ outlook, view of things; vedi pagina 8 (*rimando*) see page 8; è da ~ se ... it remains to be seen whether ...; non vedo la ragione di farlo I can't see any reason to do it; si era visto costretto a ... he found himself forced to ...; non (ci) si

vede (*è buio etc*) you can't see a thing; ci vediamo domani! see you tomorrow!; non lo posso ~ (*fig*) I can't stand him.

ve'detta *sf* (*sentinella, posto*) look-out; (*NAUT*) patrol boat.

ve'dette [və'dɛt] *sf inv* (*attrice*) star.

'vedovo, a *sm/f* widower/widow; rimaner ~ to be widowed.

vedrò *etc vb vedi* vedere.

ve'duta *sf* view; di larghe o ampie ~e broad-minded; di ~e limitate narrow-minded.

vee'mente *ag* (*discorso, azione*) vehement; (*assalto*) vigorous; (*passione*) overwhelming.

vee'menza [vee'mɛntsa] *sf* vehemence; con ~ vehemently.

vege'tale [vedʒe'tale] *ag, sm* vegetable.

vege'tare [vedʒe'tare] *vi* (*fig*) to vegetate.

vegetari'ano, a [vedʒeta'rjano] *ag, sm/f* vegetarian.

vegeta'tivo, a *ag* vegetative.

vegetazi'one [vedʒetat'tsjone] *sf* vegetation.

'vegeto, a ['vɛdʒcto] *ag* (*pianta*) thriving; (*persona*) strong, vigorous.

veg'gente [ved'dʒɛnte] *sm/f* (*indovino*) clairvoyant.

'veglia ['veʎʎa] *sf* (*sorveglianza*) watch; (*trattenimento*) evening gathering; tra la ~ e il sonno half awake; fare la ~ a un malato to watch over a sick person; ~ funebre wake.

vegli'ardo, a [veʎ'ʎardo] *sm/f* venerable old man/woman.

vegli'are [veʎ'ʎare] *vi* to stay o sit up; (*stare vigile*) to watch; to keep watch ♦ *vt* (*malato, morto*) to watch over, sit up with.

vegli'one [veʎ'ʎone] *sm* ball, dance.

ve'icolo *sm* vehicle; ~ spaziale spacecraft *inv*.

'vela *sf* (*NAUT: tela*) sail; (*sport*) sailing; tutto va a gonfie ~e (*fig*) everything is going perfectly.

ve'lare *vt* to veil; ~rsi *vr* (*occhi, luna*) to mist over; (*voce*) to become husky; ~rsi il viso to cover one's face (with a veil).

ve'lato, a *ag* veiled.

vela'tura *sf* (*NAUT*) sails *pl*.

veleggi'are [veled'dʒare] *vi* to sail; (*AER*) to glide.

ve'leno *sm* poison.

vele'noso, a *ag* poisonous.

ve'letta *sf* (*di cappello*) veil.

veli'ero *sm* sailing ship.

ve'lina *sf* (*anche:* carta ~: *per imballare*) tissue paper; (: *per copie*) flimsy paper; (*copia*) carbon copy.

ve'lista, i, e sm/f yachtsman/woman.
ve'livolo sm aircraft.
velleità sf inv vain ambition, vain desire.
vellei'tario, a ag unrealistic.
'vello sm fleece.
vellu'tato, a ag (stoffa, pesca, colore) velvety; (voce) mellow.
vel'luto sm velvet; ~ **a coste** cord.
'velo sm veil; (tessuto) voile.
ve'loce [ve'lotʃe] ag fast, quick ♦ av fast, quickly.
velo'cista, i, e [velo'tʃista] sm/f (SPORT) sprinter.
velocità [velotʃi'ta] sf speed; **a forte** ~ at high speed; ~ **di crociera** cruising speed.
ve'lodromo sm velodrome.
ven. abbr (= venerdì) Fri.
'vena sf (gen) vein; (filone) vein, seam; (fig: ispirazione) inspiration; (: umore) mood; **essere in** ~ **di qc** to be in the mood for sth.
ve'nale ag (prezzo, valore) market cpd; (fig) venal; mercenary.
venalità sf venality.
ve'nato, a ag (marmo) veined, streaked; (legno) grained.
vena'torio, a ag hunting; **la stagione** ~**a** the hunting season.
vena'tura sf (di marmo) vein, streak; (di legno) grain.
ven'demmia sf (raccolta) grape harvest; (quantità d'uva) grape crop, grapes pl; (vino ottenuto) vintage.
vendemmi'are vt to harvest ♦ vi to harvest the grapes.
'vendere vt to sell; ~ **all'ingrosso/al dettaglio** o **minuto** to sell wholesale/ retail; ~ **all'asta** to auction, sell by auction; "**vendesi**" "for sale".
ven'detta sf revenge.
vendi'care vt to avenge; ~**rsi** vr: ~**rsi (di)** to avenge o.s. (for); (per rancore) to take one's revenge (for); ~**rsi su qn** to revenge o.s. on sb.
vendica'tivo, a ag vindictive.
'vendita sf sale; **la** ~ (attività) selling; (smercio) sales pl; **in** ~ on sale; **mettere in** ~ to put on sale; **in** ~ **presso** on sale at; **contratto di** ~ sales agreement; **reparto** ~**e** sales department; ~ **all'asta** sale by auction; ~ **al dettaglio** o **minuto** retail; ~ **all'ingrosso** wholesale.
vendi'tore, 'trice sm/f seller, vendor; (gestore di negozio) trader, dealer.
ven'duto, a ag (merce) sold; (fig: corrotto) corrupt.
ve'nefico, a, ci, che ag poisonous.
vene'rabile ag, **vene'rando, a** ag

venerable.
vene'rare vt to venerate.
venerazi'one [venerat'tsjone] sf veneration.
venerdì sm inv Friday; **V~ Santo** Good Friday; per fraseologia vedi **martedì**.
'Venere sm, sf Venus.
ve'nereo, a ag venereal.
'veneto, a ag of (o from) the Veneto.
'veneto-giuli'ano, a ['vɛnetodʒu'ljano] ag of (o from) Venezia-Giulia.
Ve'nezia [ve'nɛttsja] sf Venice.
venezi'ano, a [venet'tsjano] ag, sm/f Venetian.
Venezu'ela [venettsu'ela] sm: **il** ~ Venezuela.
venezue'lano, a [venettsue'lano] ag, sm/f Venezuelan.
'vengo etc vb vedi **venire**.
veni'ale ag venial.
ve'nire vi to come; (riuscire: dolce, fotografia) to turn out; (come ausiliare: essere): **viene ammirato da tutti** he is admired by everyone; ~ **da** to come from; **quanto viene?** how much does it cost?; **far** ~ (mandare a chiamare) to send for; (medico) to call, send for; ~ **a capo di qc** to unravel sth, sort sth out; ~ **al dunque** o **nocciolo** o **fatto** to come to the point; ~ **fuori** to come out; ~ **giù** to come down; ~ **meno** (svenire) to faint; ~ **meno a qc** not to fulfil sth; ~ **su** to come up; ~ **via** to come away; ~ **a sapere qc** to learn sth; ~ **a trovare qn** to come and see sb; **negli anni a** ~ in the years to come, in future; **è venuto il momento di** ... the time has come to ....
'venni etc vb vedi **venire**.
ven'taglio [ven'taʎʎo] sm fan.
ven'tata sf gust (of wind).
venten'nale ag (che dura 20 anni) twenty-year cpd; (che ricorre ogni 20 anni) which takes place every twenty years.
ven'tenne ag, sm/f twenty-year-old.
ven'tennio sm period of twenty years; **il** ~ **fascista** the Fascist period.
ven'tesimo, a num twentieth.
'venti num twenty.
venti'lare vt (stanza) to air, ventilate; (fig: idea, proposta) to air.
venti'lato, a ag (camera, zona) airy; **poco** ~ airless.
ventila'tore sm fan; (su parete, finestra) ventilator, fan.
ventilazi'one [ventilat'tsjone] sf ventilation.
ven'tina sf: **una** ~ **(di)** around twenty, twenty or so.

ventiquat'tr'ore *sfpl* (*periodo*) twenty-four hours ♦ *sf inv* (*SPORT*) twenty-four-hour race; (*valigetta*) overnight case.

venti'sette *num* twenty-seven; **il** ~ (*giorno di paga*) (monthly) pay day.

ventitré *num* twenty-three ♦ *sfpl*: **portava il cappello sulle** ~ he wore his hat at a jaunty angle.

'vento *sm* wind; **c'è** ~ it's windy; **un colpo di** ~ a gust of wind; **contro** ~ against the wind; ~ **contrario** (*NAUT*) headwind.

'ventola *sf* (*AUT, TECN*) fan.

ven'tosa *sf* (*ZOOL*) sucker; (*di gomma*) suction pad.

ven'toso, a *ag* windy.

ven'totto *num* twenty-eight.

'ventre *sm* stomach.

ven'triloquo *sm* ventriloquist.

ven'tuno *num* twenty-one.

ven'tura *sf*: **andare alla** ~ to trust to luck; **soldato di** ~ mercenary.

ven'turo, a *ag* next, coming.

ve'nuto, a *pp di* **venire** ♦ *sm/f*: **il(la) primo(a)** ~(**a**) the first person who comes along ♦ *sf* coming, arrival.

ver. *abbr* = **versamento**.

'vera *sf* wedding ring.

ve'race [ve'ratʃe] *ag* (*testimone*) truthful; (*testimonianza*) accurate; (*cibi*) real, genuine.

vera'mente *av* really.

ve'randa *sf* veranda(h).

ver'bale *ag* verbal ♦ *sm* (*di riunione*) minutes *pl*; **accordo** ~ verbal agreement; **mettere a** ~ to place in the minutes *o* on record.

'verbo *sm* (*LING*) verb; (*parola*) word; (*REL*): **il V**~ the Word.

ver'boso, a *ag* verbose, wordy.

ver'dastro, a *ag* greenish.

'verde *ag, sm* green; ~ **bottiglia/oliva** *ag inv* bottle/olive green; **benzina** ~ lead-free *o* unleaded petrol; **i V**~**i** (*POL*) the Greens; **essere al** ~ (*fig*) to be broke.

verdeggi'ante [verded'dʒante] *ag* green, verdant.

verde'rame *sm* verdigris.

ver'detto *sm* verdict.

ver'dura *sf* vegetables *pl*.

vere'condia *sf* modesty.

vere'condo, a *ag* modest.

'verga, ghe *sf* rod.

ver'gato, a *ag* (*foglio*) ruled.

vergi'nale [verdʒi'nale] *ag* virginal.

'vergine ['verdʒine] *sf* virgin; (*dello zodiaco*): **V**~ Virgo ♦ *ag* virgin; (*ragazza*): **essere** ~ to be a virgin; **essere della V**~ (*dello zodiaco*) to be Virgo; **pura lana** ~ pure

new wool; **olio** ~ **d'oliva** unrefined olive oil.

verginità [verdʒini'ta] *sf* virginity.

ver'gogna [ver'goɲɲa] *sf* shame; (*timidezza*) shyness, embarrassment.

vergo'gnarsi [vergoɲ'ɲarsi] *vr*: ~ (**di**) to be *o* feel ashamed (of); to be shy (about), be embarrassed (about).

vergo'gnoso, a [vergoɲ'ɲoso] *ag* ashamed; (*timido*) shy, embarrassed; (*causa di vergogna*: *azione*) shameful.

veridicità [veriditʃi'ta] *sf* truthfulness.

ve'ridico, a, ci, che *ag* truthful.

ve'rifica, che *sf* checking *no pl*; check; **fare una** ~ **di** (*freni, testimonianza, firma*) to check; ~ **contabile** (*FINANZA*) audit.

verifi'care *vt* (*controllare*) to check; (*confermare*) to confirm, bear out; (*FINANZA*) to audit.

verità *sf inv* truth; **a dire la** ~, **per la** ~ truth to tell, actually.

veriti'ero, a *ag* (*che dice la verità*) truthful; (*conforme a verità*) true.

'verme *sm* worm.

vermi'celli [vermi'tʃelli] *smpl* vermicelli *sg*.

ver'miglio [ver'miʎʎo] *sm* vermilion, scarlet.

'vermut *sm inv* vermouth.

ver'nacolo *sm* vernacular.

ver'nice [ver'nitʃe] *sf* (*colorazione*) paint; (*trasparente*) varnish; (*pelle*) patent leather; "~ **fresca**" "wet paint".

vernici'are [verni'tʃare] *vt* to paint; to varnish.

vernicia'tura [vernitʃa'tura] *sf* painting; varnishing.

'vero, a *ag* (*veridico*: *fatti, testimonianza*) true; (*autentico*) real ♦ *sm* (*verità*) truth; (*realtà*) (real) life; **un** ~ **e proprio delinquente** a real criminal, an out and out criminal; **tant'è** ~ **che ...** so much so that ...; **a onor del** ~, **a dire il** ~ to tell the truth.

Ve'rona *sf* Verona.

vero'nese *ag* of (*o from*) Verona.

vero'simile *ag* likely, probable.

verrò *etc vb vedi* **venire**.

ver'ruca, che *sf* wart.

versa'mento *sm* (*pagamento*) payment; (*deposito di denaro*) deposit.

ver'sante *sm* slopes *pl*, side.

ver'sare *vt* (*fare uscire: vino, farina*) to pour (out); (*spargere: lacrime, sangue*) to shed; (*rovesciare*) to spill; (*ECON*) to pay; (*: depositare*) to deposit, pay in ♦ *vi*: ~ **in gravi difficoltà** to find o.s. with serious problems; ~**rsi** *vr* (*rovesciarsi*) to spill; (*fiume, folla*): ~**rsi (in)** to pour (into).

versa'tile *ag* versatile.
versatilità *sf* versatility.
ver'sato, a *ag*: ~ **in** to be (well-)versed in.
ver'setto *sm* (*REL*) verse.
versi'one *sf* version; (*traduzione*) translation.
'verso *sm* (*di poesia*) verse, line; (*di animale, uccello, venditore ambulante*) cry; (*direzione*) direction; (*modo*) way; (*di foglio di carta*) verso; (*di moneta*) reverse; ~**i** *smpl* (*poesia*) verse *sg*; **per un** ~ **o per l'altro** one way or another; **prendere qn/qc per il** ~ **giusto** to approach sb/sth the right way; **rifare il** ~ **a qn** (*imitare*) to mimic sb; **non c'è** ~ **di persuaderlo** there's no way of persuading him, he can't be persuaded ♦ *prep* (*in direzione di*) toward(s); (*nei pressi di*) near, around (about); (*in senso temporale*) about, around; (*nei confronti di*) for; ~ **di me** towards me; ~ **l'alto** upwards; ~ **il basso** downwards; ~ **sera** towards evening.
'vertebra *sf* vertebra.
verte'brale *ag* vertebral; **colonna** ~ spinal column, spine.
verte'brato, a *ag, sm* vertebrate.
ver'tenza [ver'tɛntsa] *sf* (*lite*) lawsuit, case; (*sindacale*) dispute.
'vertere *vi*: ~ **su** to deal with, be about.
verti'cale *ag, sf* vertical.
'vertice ['vɛrtitʃe] *sm* summit, top; (*MAT*) vertex; **conferenza al** ~ (*POL*) summit conference.
ver'tigine [ver'tidʒine] *sf* dizziness *no pl*; dizzy spell; (*MED*) vertigo; **avere le** ~**i** to feel dizzy.
vertigi'noso, a [vertidʒi'noso] *ag* (*altezza*) dizzy; (*fig*) breathtakingly high (*o* deep *etc*).
'verza ['verdza] *sf* Savoy cabbage.
ve'scica, che [veʃ'ʃika] *sf* (*ANAT*) bladder; (*MED*) blister.
vesco'vile *ag* episcopal.
'vescovo *sm* bishop.
'vespa *sf* wasp; (®: *veicolo*) (motor) scooter.
ves'paio *sm* wasps' nest; **suscitare un** ~ (*fig*) to stir up a hornets' nest.
vespasi'ano *sm* urinal.
'vespro *sm* (*REL*) vespers *pl*.
ves'sare *vt* to oppress.
vessazi'one [vessat'tsjone] *sf* oppression.
ves'sillo *sm* standard; (*bandiera*) flag.
ves'taglia [ves'taʎʎa] *sf* dressing gown, robe (*US*).
'veste *sf* garment; (*rivestimento*) covering; (*qualità, facoltà*) capacity; ~**i** *sfpl* clothes, clothing *sg*; **in** ~ **ufficiale** (*fig*) in an official

capacity; **in** ~ **di** in the guise of, as; ~ **da camera** dressing gown, robe (*US*); ~ **editoriale** layout.
vesti'ario *sm* wardrobe, clothes *pl*; **capo di** ~ article of clothing, garment.
ves'tibolo *sm* (entrance) hall.
ves'tigia [ves'tidʒa] *sfpl* (*tracce*) vestiges, traces; (*rovine*) ruins, remains.
ves'tire *vt* (*bambino, malato*) to dress; (*avere indosso*) to have on, wear; ~**rsi** *vr* to dress, get dressed; ~**rsi da** (*negozio, sarto*) to buy *o* get one's clothes at.
ves'tito, a *ag* dressed ♦ *sm* garment; (*da donna*) dress; (*da uomo*) suit; ~**i** *smpl* (*indumenti*) clothes; ~ **di bianco** dressed in white.
Ve'suvio *sm*: **il** ~ Vesuvius.
vete'rano, a *ag, sm/f* veteran.
veteri'nario, a *ag* veterinary ♦ *sm* veterinary surgeon (*BRIT*), veterinarian (*US*), vet ♦ *sf* veterinary medicine.
'veto *sm inv* veto; **porre il** ~ **a qc** to veto sth.
ve'traio *sm* glassmaker; (*per finestre*) glazier.
ve'trato, a *ag* (*porta, finestra*) glazed; (*che contiene vetro*) glass *cpd* ♦ *sf* glass door (*o* window); (*di chiesa*) stained glass window; **carta** ~**a** sandpaper.
vetre'ria *sf* (*stabilimento*) glassworks *sg*; (*oggetti di vetro*) glassware.
ve'trina *sf* (*di negozio*) (shop) window; (*armadio*) display cabinet.
vetri'nista, i, e *sm/f* window dresser.
ve'trino *sm* slide.
vetri'olo *sm* vitriol.
'vetro *sm* glass; (*per finestra, porta*) pane (of glass); ~ **blindato** bulletproof glass; ~ **infrangibile** shatterproof glass; ~ **di sicurezza** safety glass; **i** ~**i di Murano** Murano glassware *sg*.
ve'troso, a *ag* vitreous.
'vetta *sf* peak, summit, top.
vet'tore *sm* (*MAT, FISICA*) vector; (*chi trasporta*) carrier.
vetto'vaglie [vetto'vaʎʎe] *sfpl* supplies.
vet'tura *sf* (*carrozza*) carriage; (*FERR*) carriage (*BRIT*), car (*US*); (*auto*) car (*BRIT*), automobile (*US*); ~ **di piazza** hackney carriage.
vettu'rino *sm* coach driver, coachman.
vezzeggi'are [vettsed'dʒare] *vt* to fondle, caress.
vezzeggia'tivo [vettseddʒa'tivo] *sm* (*LING*) term of endearment.
'vezzo ['vettso] *sm* habit; ~**i** *smpl* (*smancerie*) affected ways; (*leggiadria*) charms.
vez'zoso, a [vet'tsoso] *ag* (*grazioso*)

charming, pretty; (*lezioso*) affected.

V.F. *abbr* = **vigili del fuoco.**

V.G. *abbr* = *Vostra Grazia.*

VI *sigla* = *Vicenza.*

vi (*dav lo, la, li, le, ne diventa* **ve**) *pron*
(*oggetto*) you; (*complemento di termine*)
(to) you; (*riflessivo*) yourselves; (*reciproco*)
each other ♦ *av* (*lì*) there; (*qui*) here; (*per
questo/quel luogo*) through here/there; ~
è/sono there is/are.

'via *sf* (*gen*) way; (*strada*) street; (*sentiero,
pista*) path, track; (*AMM: procedimento*)
channels *pl* ♦ *prep* (*passando per*) via, by
way of ♦ *av* away ♦ *escl* go away!; (*suvvia*)
come on!; (*SPORT*) go! ♦ *sm* (*SPORT*)
starting signal; **per** ~ **di** (*a causa di*)
because of, on account of; **in** *o* **per** ~ **on**
the way; **in** ~ **di guarigione** (*fig*) on the
road to recovery; **per** ~ **aerea** by air;
(*lettere*) by airmail; ~ **satellite** by
satellite; **andare/essere** ~ to go/be away;
~ ~ (*pian piano*) gradually; ~ ~ **che** (*a
mano a mano*) as; **e** ~ **dicendo, e** ~ **di
questo passo** and so on (and so forth);
dare il ~ (*SPORT*) to give the starting
signal; **dare il** ~ **a un progetto** to give the
green light to a project; **hanno dato il** ~
ai lavori they've begun *o* started work; **in**
~ **amichevole** in a friendly manner;
comporre una disputa in ~ **amichevole**
(*DIR*) to settle a dispute out of court; **in** ~
eccezionale as an exception; **in** ~ **privata**
o **confidenziale** (*dire etc*) in confidence; **in**
~ **provvisoria** provisionally; **V~ lattea**
(*ASTR*) Milky Way; ~ **di mezzo** middle
course; **non c'è** ~ **di scampo** *o* **d'uscita**
there's no way out; ~**e di comunicazione**
communication routes.

viabilità *sf* (*di strada*) practicability; (*rete
stradale*) roads *pl*, road network.

via'dotto *sm* viaduct.

viaggi'are [viad'dʒare] *vi* to travel; **le merci
viaggiano via mare** the goods go *o* are
sent by sea.

viaggia'tore, 'trice [viadd'ʒa'tore] *ag*
travelling (*BRIT*), traveling (*US*) ♦ *sm*
traveller (*BRIT*), traveler (*US*);
(*passeggero*) passenger.

vi'aggio [vi'addʒo] *sm* travel(ling); (*tragitto*)
journey, trip; **buon** ·· ! have a good trip!;
~ **d'affari** business trip; ~ **di nozze**
honeymoon; ~ **organizzato** package tour
o holiday.

vi'ale *sm* avenue.

vian'dante *sm/f* vagrant.

vi'atico, ci *sm* (*REL*) viaticum; (*fig*)
encouragement.

via'vai *sm* coming and going, bustle.

vi'brare *vi* to vibrate; (*agitarsi*): ~ (**di**) to
quiver (with).

vibra'tore *sm* vibrator.

vibrazi'one [vibrat'tsjone] *sf* vibration.

vi'cario *sm* (*apostolico etc*) vicar.

'vice ['vitʃe] *sm/f prefisso* vice.

vice'console [vitʃe'konsole] *sm* vice-consul.

vicediret'tore, 'trice [vitʃediret'tore] *sm/f*
assistant manager/manageress; (*di
giornale etc*) deputy editor.

vi'cenda [vi'tʃenda] *sf* event; ~**e** *sfpl* (*sorte*)
fortunes; **a** ~ in turn; **con alterne** ~**e** with
mixed fortunes.

vicen'devole [vitʃen'devole] *ag* mutual,
reciprocal.

vicen'tino, a [vitʃen'tino] *ag* of (*o* from)
Vicenza.

vicepresi'dente [vitʃepresi'dɛnte] *sm* vice-
president, vice-chairman.

vice'versa [vitʃe'vɛrsa] *av* vice versa; **da
Roma a Pisa e** ~ from Rome to Pisa and
back.

vi'chingo, a, ghi, ghe [vi'kingo] *ag, sm/f*
Viking.

vici'nanza [vitʃi'nantsa] *sf* nearness,
closeness; ~**e** *sfpl* (*paraggi*) neighbourhood
(*BRIT*), neighborhood (*US*), vicinity.

vici'nato [vitʃi'nato] *sm* neighbourhood
(*BRIT*), neighborhood (*US*); (*vicini*)
neighbo(u)rs *pl*.

vi'cino, a [vi'tʃino] *ag* (*gen*) near; (*nello
spazio*) near, nearby; (*accanto*) next; (*nel
tempo*) near, close at hand ♦ *sm/f*
neighbour (*BRIT*), neighbor (*US*) ♦ *av* near,
close; **da** ~ (*guardare*) close up;
(*esaminare, seguire*) closely; (*conoscere*)
well, intimately; ~ **a** *prep* near (to), close
to; (*accanto a*) beside; **mi sono stati molto**
~**i** (*fig*) they were very supportive
towards me; ~ **di casa** neighbo(u)r.

vicissi'tudini [vitʃissi'tudini] *sfpl* trials and
tribulations.

'vicolo *sm* alley; ~ **cieco** blind alley.

'video *sm inv* (*TV*: *schermo*) screen.

video'camera *sf* camcorder.

videocas'setta *sf* videocassette.

videodipen'dente *sm/f* telly addict ♦ *ag*: **un
pigrone** ~ a couch potato.

videofo'nino *sm* video mobile.

videogi'oco, chi [video'dʒɔko] *sm* video
game.

videono'leggio [videono'leddʒo] *sm* video
rental.

videoregistra'tore [videoredʒistra'tore] *sm*
(*apparecchio*) video (recorder).

video'teca, che *sf* video shop.

videote'lefono *sm* videophone.

videotermi'nale *sm* visual display unit.

'vidi etc vb vedi vedere.
vidi'mare vt (AMM) to authenticate.
vidimazi'one [vidimat'tsjone] sf (AMM) authentication.
Vi'enna sf Vienna.
vien'nese ag, smf Viennese inv.
vie'tare vt to forbid; (AMM) to prohibit; (libro) to ban; ~ a qn di fare to forbid sb to do; to prohibit sb from doing.
vie'tato, a ag (vedi vb) forbidden; prohibited; banned; "~ fumare/ l'ingresso" "no smoking/admittance"; ~ ai minori di 14/18 anni prohibited to children under 14/18; "senso ~" (AUT) "no entry"; "sosta ~a" (AUT) "no parking".
Viet'nam sm: il ~ Vietnam.
vietna'mita, i, e ag, smf, sm Vietnamese inv.
vi'gente [vi'dʒɛnte] ag in force.
'vigere ['vidʒere] vi (difettivo: si usa solo alla terza persona) to be in force; in casa mia vige l'abitudine di ... at home we are in the habit of ....
vigi'lante [vidʒi'lante] ag vigilant, watchful.
vigi'lanza [vidʒi'lantsa] sf vigilance; (sorveglianza: di operai, alunni) supervision; (: di sospetti, criminali) surveillance.
vigi'lare [vidʒi'lare] vt to watch over, keep an eye on; ~ che to make sure that, see to it that.
vigi'lato, a [vidʒi'lato] smf (DIR) person under police surveillance.
vigila'trice [vidʒila'tritʃe] sf: ~ d'infanzia nursery-school teacher; ~ scolastica school health officer.
'vigile ['vidʒile] ag watchful ♦ sm (anche: ~ urbano) policeman (in towns); ~ del fuoco fireman; vedi nota nel riquadro.

VIGILI URBANI

The vigili urbani are a municipal police force attached to the "Comune". Their duties involve everyday aspects of life such as traffic, public works and services, and commerce.

vigi'lessa [vidʒi'lessa] sf (traffic) policewoman.
vi'gilia [vi'dʒilja] sf (giorno antecedente) eve; la ~ di Natale Christmas Eve.
vigliacche'ria [viʎʎakke'ria] sf cowardice.
vigli'acco, a, chi, che [viʎ'ʎakko] ag cowardly ♦ smf coward.
'vigna ['viɲɲa] sf, vi'gneto [viɲ'ɲeto] sm vineyard.
vi'gnetta [viɲ'ɲetta] sf cartoon.
vi'gore sm vigour (BRIT), vigor (US); (DIR):

essere/entrare in ~ to be in/come into force; non è più in ~ it is no longer in force, it no longer applies.
vigo'roso, a ag vigorous.
'vile ag (spregevole) low, mean, base; (codardo) cowardly.
vili'pendere vt to despise, scorn.
vili'pendio sm contempt, scorn.
vili'peso, a pp di vilipendere.
'villa sf villa.
vil'laggio [vil'laddʒo] sm village; ~ turistico holiday village.
villa'nia sf rudeness, lack of manners; fare (o dire) una ~ a qn to be rude to sb.
vil'lano, a ag rude, ill-mannered ♦ smf boor.
villeggi'ante [villed'dʒante] smf holiday-maker (BRIT), vacationer (US).
villeggi'are [villed'dʒare] vi to holiday, spend one's holidays, vacation (US).
villeggia'tura [villeddʒa'tura] sf holiday(s pl) (BRIT), vacation (US); luogo di ~ (holiday) resort.
vil'letta sf, vil'lino sm small house (with a garden), cottage.
vil'loso, a ag hairy.
viltà sf cowardice no pl; (gesto) cowardly act.
Vimi'nale sm vedi nota nel riquadro.

VIMINALE

The Viminale, which takes its name from one of the famous Seven Hills of Rome on which it stands, is home to the Ministry of the Interior.

'vimine sm wicker; mobili di ~i wicker furniture sg.
vi'naio sm wine merchant.
'vincere ['vintʃere] vt (in guerra, al gioco, a una gara) to defeat, beat; (premio, guerra, partita) to win; (fig) to overcome, conquer ♦ vi to win; ~ qn in (abilità, bellezza) to surpass sb in.
'vincita ['vintʃita] sf win; (denaro vinto) winnings pl.
vinci'tore, 'trice [vintʃi'tore] smf winner; (MIL) victor.
vinco'lante ag binding.
vinco'lare vt to bind; (COMM: denaro) to tie up.
vinco'lato, a ag: deposito ~ (COMM) fixed deposit.
'vincolo sm (fig) bond, tie; (DIR) obligation.
vi'nicolo, a ag wine cpd; regione ~a wine-producing area.
vinificazi'one [vinifikat'tsjone] sf wine-

making.

'**vino** *sm* wine; ~ **bianco/rosso** white/red wine.

'**vinsi** *etc vb vedi* **vincere**.

'**vinto, a** *pp di* **vincere ♦** *ag*: **darla** ~**a a qn** to let sb have his (*o* her) way; **darsi per** ~ to give up, give in.

vi'ola *sf* (*BOT*) violet; (*MUS*) viola ♦ *ag, sm inv* (*colore*) purple.

vio'lare *vt* (*chiesa*) to desecrate, violate; (*giuramento, legge*) to violate.

violazi'one [violat'tsjone] *sf* desecration; violation; ~ **di domicilio** (*DIR*) breaking and entering.

violen'tare *vt* to use violence on; (*donna*) to rape.

vio'lento, a *ag* violent.

vio'lenza [vio'lɛntsa] *sf* violence; ~ **carnale** rape.

vio'letto, a *ag, sm* (*colore*) violet ♦ *sf* (*BOT*) violet.

violi'nista, i, e *sm/f* violinist.

vio'lino *sm* violin.

violoncel'lista, i, e [violontʃel'lista] *sm/f* cellist, cello player.

violon'cello [violon'tʃɛllo] *sm* cello.

vi'ottolo *sm* path, track.

VIP *sm/f inv* (= *Very Important Person*) VIP.

'**vipera** *sf* viper, adder.

vi'raggio [vi'raddʒo] *sm* (*NAUT, AER*) turn; (*FOT*) toning.

vi'rale *ag* viral.

vi'rare *vi* (*NAUT*) to come about; (*AER*) to turn; (*FOT*) to tone; ~ **di bordo** to change course.

vi'rata *sf* coming about; turning; change of course.

'**virgola** *sf* (*LING*) comma; (*MAT*) point.

virgo'lette *sfpl* inverted commas, quotation marks.

vi'rile *ag* (*proprio dell'uomo*) masculine; (*non puerile, da uomo*) manly, virile.

virilità *sf* masculinity; manliness; (*sessuale*) virility.

virtù *sf inv* virtue; **in** *o* **per** ~ **di** by virtue of, by.

virtu'ale *ag* virtual.

virtu'oso, a *ag* virtuous ♦ *sm/f* (*MUS etc*) virtuoso.

viru'lento, a *ag* virulent.

'**virus** *sm inv* virus.

visa'gista, i, e [viza'dʒista] *sm/f* beautician.

visce'rale [viʃʃe'rale] *ag* (*MED*) visceral; (*fig*) profound, deep-rooted.

'**viscere** ['viʃʃere] *sm* (*ANAT*) internal organ ♦ *sfpl* (*di animale*) entrails *pl*; (*fig*) depths *pl*, bowels *pl*.

'**vischio** ['viskjo] *sm* (*BOT*) mistletoe; (*pania*) birdlime.

vischi'oso, a [vis'kjoso] *ag* sticky.

viscidità [viʃʃidi'ta] *sf* sliminess.

'**viscido, a** ['viʃʃido] *ag* slimy.

vis'conte, 'essa *sm/f* viscount/viscountess.

viscosità *sf* viscosity.

vis'coso, a *ag* viscous.

vi'sibile *ag* visible.

visi'bilio *sm*: **andare in** ~ to go into raptures.

visibilità *sf* visibility.

visi'era *sf* (*di elmo*) visor; (*di berretto*) peak.

visio'nare *vt* (*gen*) to look at, examine; (*CINE*) to screen.

visio'nario, a *ag, sm/f* visionary.

visi'one *sf* vision; **prendere** ~ **di qc** to examine sth, look sth over; **prima/ seconda** ~ (*CINE*) first/second showing.

'**visita** *sf* visit; (*MED*) visit, call; (*: esame*) examination; **far** ~ **a qn, andare in** ~ **da qn** to visit sb, pay sb a visit; **in** ~ **ufficiale in Italia** on an official visit to Italy; **orario di** ~**e** (*ospedale*) visiting hours; ~ **di controllo** (*MED*) checkup; ~ **a domicilio** house call; ~ **guidata** guided tour; ~ **sanitaria** sanitary inspection.

visi'tare *vt* to visit; (*MED*) to visit, call on; (*: esaminare*) to examine.

visita'tore, 'trice *sm/f* visitor.

vi'sivo, a *ag* visual.

'**viso** *sm* face; **fare buon** ~ **a cattivo gioco** to make the best of things.

vi'sone *sm* mink.

'**visore** *sm* (*FOT*) viewer.

'**vispo, a** *ag* quick, lively.

'**vissi** *etc vb vedi* **vivere**.

vis'suto, a *pp di* **vivere ♦** *ag* (*aria, modo di fare*) experienced.

'**vista** *sf* (*facoltà*) (eye)sight; (*fatto di vedere*): **la** ~ **di** the sight of; (*veduta*) view; **con** ~ **sul lago** with a view over the lake; **sparare a** ~ to shoot on sight; **pagabile a** ~ payable on demand; **in** ~ in sight; **avere in** ~ **qc** to have sth in view; **mettersi in** ~ to draw attention to o.s.; (*peg*) to show off; **perdere qn di** ~ to lose sight of sb; (*fig*) to lose touch with sb; **far** ~ **di fare** to pretend to do; **a** ~ **d'occhio** as far as the eye can see; (*fig*) before one's very eyes.

vis'tare *vt* to approve; (*AMM: passaporto*) to visa.

'**visto, a** *pp di* **vedere ♦** *sm* visa; ~ **che** *cong* seeing (that); ~ **d'ingresso/di transito** entry/transit visa; ~ **permanente/di soggiorno** permanent/tourist visa.

vis'toso, a *ag* gaudy, garish; (*ingente*) considerable.

visu'ale *ag* visual.

visualiz'zare [vizualid'dzare] *vt* to visualize.

visualizza'tore [vizualiddza'tore] *sm* (*INFORM*) visual display unit, VDU.

visualizzazi'one [vizualiddzat'tsjone] *sf* (*INFORM*) display.

'vita *sf* life; (*ANAT*) waist; **essere in** ~ to be alive; **pieno di** ~ full of life; **a** ~ for life; **membro a** ~ life member.

vi'tale *ag* vital.

vitalità *sf* vitality.

vita'lizio, a [vita'littsjo] *ag* life *cpd* ♦ *sm* life annuity.

vita'mina *sf* vitamin.

'vite *sf* (*BOT*) vine; (*TECN*) screw; **giro di** ~ (*anche fig*) turn of the screw.

vi'tello *sm* (*ZOOL*) calf; (*carne*) veal; (*pelle*) calfskin.

vi'ticcio [vi'tittʃo] *sm* (*BOT*) tendril.

viticol'tore *sm* wine grower.

viticol'tura *sf* wine growing.

'vitreo, a *ag* vitreous; (*occhio, sguardo*) glassy.

'vittima *sf* victim.

vitti'mismo *sm* self-pity.

'vitto *sm* food; (*in un albergo etc*) board; ~ **e alloggio** board and lodging.

vit'toria *sf* victory.

vittori'ano, a *ag* Victorian.

vittori'oso, a *ag* victorious.

vitupe'rare *vt* to rail at *o* against.

vi'uzza [vi'uttsa] *sf* (*in città*) alley.

'viva *escl*: ~ **il re!** long live the king!

vivacchi'are [vivak'kjare] *vi* to scrape a living.

vi'vace [vi'vatʃe] *ag* (*vivo, animato*) lively; (*: mente*) lively, sharp; (*colore*) bright.

vivacità [vivatʃi'ta] *sf* liveliness; brightness.

vivaciz'zare [vivatʃid'dzare] *vt* to liven up.

vi'vaio *sm* (*di pesci*) hatchery; (*AGR*) nursery.

viva'mente *av* (*commuoversi*) deeply, profoundly; (*ringraziare etc*) sincerely, warmly.

vi'vanda *sf* food; (*piatto*) dish.

viva'voce [viva'votʃe] *sm inv* (*dispositivo*) loudspeaker ♦ *ag inv*: **telefono** ~ speakerphone; **mettere in** ~ to switch on the loudspeaker.

vi'vente *ag* living, alive; **i** ~**i** the living.

'vivere *vi* to live ♦ *vt* to live; (*passare: brutto momento*) to live through, go through; (*sentire: gioie, pene di qn*) to share ♦ *sm* life; (*anche*: **modo di** ~) way of life; ~**i** *smpl* food *sg*, provisions; ~ **di** to live on.

vi'veur [vi'vœr] *sm inv* pleasure-seeker.

'vivido, a *ag* (*colore*) vivid, bright.

vivifi'care *vt* to enliven, give life to; (*piante etc*) to revive.

vivisezi'one [viviset'tsjone] *sf* vivisection.

'vivo, a *ag* (*vivente*) alive, living; (*fig*) lively; (*: colore*) bright, brilliant ♦ *sm*: **entrare nel** ~ **di una questione** to get to the heart of a matter; **i** ~**i** the living; **esperimenti su animali** ~**i** experiments on live *o* living animals; ~ **e vegeto** hale and hearty; **farsi** ~ (*fig*) to show one's face; to keep in touch; **con** ~ **rammarico** with deep regret; **congratulazioni vivissime** heartiest congratulations; **con i più** ~**i ringraziamenti** with deepest *o* warmest thanks; **ritrarre dal** ~ to paint from life; **pungere qn nel** ~ (*fig*) to cut sb to the quick.

vivrò *etc vb vedi* **vivere**.

vizi'are [vit'tsjare] *vt* (*bambino*) to spoil; (*corrompere moralmente*) to corrupt; (*DIR*) to invalidate.

vizi'ato, a [vit'tsjato] *ag* spoilt; (*aria, acqua*) polluted; (*DIR*) invalid, invalidated.

'vizio ['vittsjo] *sm* (*morale*) vice; (*cattiva abitudine*) bad habit; (*imperfezione*) flaw, defect; (*errore*) fault, mistake; ~ **di forma** legal flaw *o* irregularity; ~ **procedurale** procedural error.

vizi'oso, a [vit'tsjoso] *ag* depraved; (*inesatto*) incorrect; **circolo** ~ vicious circle.

V.le *abbr* = **viale**.

vocabo'lario *sm* (*dizionario*) dictionary; (*lessico*) vocabulary.

vo'cabolo *sm* word.

vo'cale *ag* vocal ♦ *sf* vowel.

vocazi'one [vokat'tsjone] *sf* vocation; (*fig*) natural bent.

'voce ['votʃe] *sf* voice; (*diceria*) rumour (*BRIT*), rumor (*US*); (*di un elenco, in bilancio*) item; (*di dizionario*) entry; **parlare a alta/bassa** ~ to speak in a loud/low *o* soft voice; **fare la** ~ **grossa** to raise one's voice; **dar** ~ **a qc** to voice sth, give voice to sth; **a gran** ~ in a loud voice, loudly; **te lo dico a** ~ I'll tell you when I see you; **a una** ~ unanimously; **aver** ~ **in capitolo** (*fig*) to have a say in the matter; ~**i di corridoio** rumours.

voci'are [vo'tʃare] *vi* to shout, yell.

vocife'rante [votʃife'rante] *ag* noisy.

vo'cio [vo'tʃio] *sm* shouting.

'vodka *sf inv* vodka.

'voga *sf* (*NAUT*) rowing; (*usanza*): **essere in** ~ to be in fashion *o* in vogue.

vo'gare *vi* to row.

voga'tore, 'trice *sm/f* oarsman/woman ♦ *sm* rowing machine.

vogherò *etc* [voge'rɔ] *vb vedi* **vogare**.

'voglia ['vɔʎʎa] sf desire, wish; (macchia) birthmark; aver ~ di qc/di fare to feel like sth/like doing; (più forte) to want sth/to do; di buona ~ willingly.

'voglio etc ['vɔʎʎo] vb vedi volere.

vogli'oso, a [voʎ'ʎoso] ag (sguardo etc) longing; (più forte) full of desire.

'voi pron you; ~ stessi(e) you yourselves.

voi'altri pron you.

vol. abbr (= volume) vol.

vo'lano sm (SPORT) shuttlecock; (TECN) flywheel.

vo'lant [vɔ'lã] sm inv frill.

vo'lante ag flying ♦ sm (steering) wheel ♦ sf (POLIZIA: anche: squadra ~) flying squad.

volanti'naggio [volanti'naddʒo] sm leafleting.

volanti'nare vt (distribuire volantini) to leaflet, hand out leaflets.

volan'tino sm leaflet.

vo'lare vi (uccello, aereo, fig) to fly; (cappello) to blow away o off, fly away o off; ~ via to fly away o off.

vo'lata sf flight; (d'uccelli) flock, flight; (corsa) rush; (SPORT) final sprint; passare di ~ da qn to drop in on sb briefly.

vo'latile ag (CHIM) volatile ♦ sm (ZOOL) bird.

volatiliz'zarsi [volatilid'dzarsi] vr (CHIM) to volatilize; (fig) to vanish, disappear.

vo'lente ag: verrai ~ o nolente you'll come whether you like it or not.

volente'roso, a ag willing, keen.

volenti'eri av willingly; "~" "with pleasure", "I'd be glad to".

================= PAROLA CHIAVE

vo'lere sm will, wish(es); contro il ~ di against the wishes of; per ~ di qn in obedience to sb's will o wishes

♦ vt 1 (esigere, desiderare) to want; ~ fare qc to want to do sth; ~ che qn faccia qc to want sb to do sth; vorrei andarmene I'd like to go; vorrei che se ne andasse I'd like him to go; vorrei quello lì! I'd like that one; volevo parlartene I meant to talk to you about it; come vuoi as you like; ha voglia al telefono there's a call for you; che tu lo voglia o no whether you like it or not; vuoi un caffè? would you like a coffee?; senza ~ (inavvertitamente) without meaning to, unintentionally; te la sei voluta you asked for it; la tradizione vuole che ... custom requires that ...; la leggenda vuole che ... legend has it that ...

2 (consentire): vogliate attendere, per piacere please wait; vogliamo andare? shall we go?; vuole essere così gentile da

...? would you be so kind as to ...?; non ha voluto ricevermi he wouldn't see me

3: volerci (essere necessario: materiale, attenzione) to be needed; (: tempo) to take; quanta farina ci vuole per questa torta? how much flour do you need for this cake?; ci vuole un'ora per arrivare a Venezia it takes an hour to get to Venice; è quel che ci vuole it's just what is needed

4: voler bene a qn (amore) to love sb; (affetto) to be fond of sb, like sb very much; voler male a qn to dislike sb; volerne a qn to bear sb a grudge; voler dire to mean; voglio dire ... I mean ...; volevo ben dire! I thought as much!

vol'gare ag vulgar.

volgarità sf vulgarity.

volgariz'zare [volgarid'dzare] vt to popularize.

volgar'mente av (in modo volgare) vulgarly, coarsely; (del popolo) commonly, popularly.

'volgere ['vɔldʒere] vt to turn ♦ vi to turn; (tendere): ~ a: il tempo volge al brutto/al bello the weather is breaking/is setting fair; un rosso che volge al viola a red verging on purple; ~rsi vr to turn; ~ al peggio to take a turn for the worse; ~ al termine to draw to an end.

'volgo sm common people.

voli'era sf aviary.

voli'tivo, a ag strong-willed.

'volli etc vb vedi volere.

'volo sm flight; ci sono due ore di ~ da Londra a Milano it's a two-hour flight between London and Milan; al ~: colpire qc al ~ to hit sth as it flies past; prendere al ~ (autobus, treno) to catch at the last possible moment; (palla) to catch as it flies past; (occasione) to seize; capire al ~ to understand straight away; veduta a ~ d'uccello bird's-eye view; ~ di linea scheduled flight.

volontà sf inv will; a ~ (mangiare, bere) as much as one likes; buona/cattiva ~ goodwill/lack of goodwill; le sue ultime ~ (testamento) his last will and testament sg.

volontaria'mente av voluntarily.

volontari'ato sm (MIL) voluntary service; (lavoro) voluntary work.

volon'tario, a ag voluntary ♦ sm (MIL) volunteer.

'volpe sf fox.

vol'pino, a ag (pelo, coda) fox's; (aspetto, astuzia) fox-like ♦ sm (cane) Pomeranian.

vol'pone, a sm/f (fig) old fox.

'volsi etc vb vedi volgere.

volt *sm inv* (*ELETTR*) volt.

'volta *sf* (*momento, circostanza*) time; (*turno, giro*) turn; (*curva*) turn, bend; (*ARCHIT*) vault; (*direzione*): **partire alla** ~ **di** to set off for; **a mia** (*o* **tua** *etc*) ~ in turn; **una** ~ once; **una** ~ **sola** only once; **c'era una** ~ once upon a time there was; **le cose di una** ~ the things of the past; **due** ~**e** twice; **tre** ~**e** three times; **una cosa per** ~ one thing at a time; **una** ~ **o l'altra** one of these days; **una** ~ **per tutte** once and for all; **una** ~ **tanto** just for once; **lo facciamo un'altra** ~ we'll do it another time *o* some other time; **a** ~**e** at times, sometimes; **di** ~ **in** ~ from time to time; **una** ~ **che** (*temporale*) once; (*causale*) since; **3** ~**e 4 3 times 4; ti ha dato di** ~ **il cervello?** have you gone out of your mind?

volta'faccia [volta'fattʃa] *sm inv* (*fig*) volteface.

vol'taggio [vol'taddʒo] *sm* (*ELETTR*) voltage.

vol'tare *vt* to turn; (*girare: moneta*) to turn over; (*rigirare*) to turn round ♦ *vi* to turn; ~**rsi** *vr* to turn; to turn over; to turn round.

voltas'tomaco *sm* nausea; (*fig*) disgust.

volteggi'are [volted'dʒare] *vi* (*volare*) to circle; (*in equitazione*) to do trick riding; (*in ginnastica*) to vault.

'volto, a *pp di* **volgere** ♦ *ag* (*inteso a*): **il mio discorso è** ~ **a spiegare ...** in my speech I intend to explain ... ♦ *sm* face.

vo'lubile *ag* changeable, fickle.

vo'lume *sm* volume.

volumi'noso, a *ag* voluminous, bulky.

vo'luta *sf* (*gen*) spiral; (*ARCHIT*) volute.

voluttà *sf* sensual pleasure *o* delight.

voluttu'oso, a *ag* voluptuous.

vomi'tare *vt, vi* to vomit.

'vomito *sm* vomit; **ho il** ~ I feel sick.

'vongola *sf* clam.

vo'race [vo'ratʃe] *ag* voracious, greedy.

voracità [voratʃi'ta] *sf* voracity, voraciousness.

vo'ragine [vo'radʒine] *sf* abyss, chasm.

vorrò *etc vb vedi* **volere**.

'vortice ['vɔrtitʃe] *sm* whirl, vortex; (*fig*) whirl.

vorti'coso, a *ag* whirling.

'vostro, a *det*: **il(la)** ~**(a)** *etc* your ♦ *pron*: **il(la)** ~**(a)** *etc* yours ♦ *sm*: **avete speso del** ~? did you spend your own money? ♦ *sf*: **la** ~**a** (*opinione*) your view; **i** ~**i** (*famiglia*) your family; **un** ~ **amico** a friend of yours; **è dei** ~**i**, **è dalla** ~**a** he's on your side; **l'ultima** ~**a** (*COMM: lettera*) your most recent letter; **alla** ~**a!** (*brindisi*) here's to you!, your health!

vo'tante *sm/f* voter.

vo'tare *vi* to vote ♦ *vt* (*sottoporre a votazione*) to take a vote on; (*approvare*) to vote for; (*REL*): ~ **qc a** to dedicate sth to; ~**rsi** *vr* to devote o.s. to.

votazi'one [votat'tsjone] *sf* vote, voting; ~**i** *sfpl* (*POL*) votes; (*INS*) marks.

'voto *sm* (*POL*) vote; (*INS*) mark (*BRIT*), grade (*US*); (*REL*) vow; (*: offerta*) votive offering; **aver** ~**i belli/brutti** (*INS*) to get good/bad marks *o* grades; **prendere i** ~**i** to take one's vows; ~ **di fiducia** vote of confidence.

V.P. *abbr* (= *vicepresidente*) VP.

VR *sigla* = *Verona*.

v.r. *abbr* (= *vedi retro*) PTO.

vs. *abbr* (= *vostro*) yr.

v.s. *abbr* = *vedi sopra*.

VT *sigla* = *Viterbo*.

V.U. *abbr* = **vigile urbano**.

vul'canico, a, ci, che *ag* volcanic.

vulcanizzazi'one [vulkaniddzat'tsjone] *sf* vulcanization.

vul'cano *sm* volcano.

vulne'rabile *ag* vulnerable.

vulnerabilità *sf* vulnerability.

vu'oi, vu'ole *vb vedi* **volere**.

vuo'tare *vt*, ~**rsi** *vr* to empty.

vu'oto, a *ag* empty; (*fig: privo*): ~ **di** (*senso etc*) devoid of ♦ *sm* empty space, gap; (*spazio in bianco*) blank; (*FISICA*) vacuum; (*fig: mancanza*) gap, void; **a mani** ~**e** empty-handed; **assegno a** ~ dud cheque (*BRIT*), bad check (*US*); ~ **d'aria** air pocket; "~ **a perdere**" "no deposit"; "~ **a rendere**" "returnable bottle".

W w

W, w ['dɔppjovu] *sf o m inv* (*lettera*) W, w; **W come Washington** ≈ W for William.

W *abbr* = **viva, evviva**.

'wafer ['vafer] *sm inv* (*CUC, ELETTR*) wafer.

wagon-'lit [vagɔ̃'li] *sm inv* (*FERR*) sleeping car.

'walkman ® ['wɔːkmən] *sm inv* Walkman ®.

'water 'closet ['wɔːtə'klɔzɪt] *sm inv* toilet, lavatory.

watt [vat] *sm inv* (*ELETTR*) watt.

wat'tora [vat'tora] *sm inv* (*ELETTR*) watthour.

WC sm inv WC.
web [ueb] sm: **il** ~ the Web; **cercare nel** ~ **to**
search the Web ♦ ag inv: **pagina** ~
webpage.
'weekend ['wi:kend] sm inv weekend.
'western ['wɛstern] ag (CINE) cowboy cpd
♦ sm inv western, cowboy film; ~
all'italiana spaghetti western.
'whisky ['wiski] sm inv whisky.
'windsurf ['windsə:f] sm inv (tavola)
windsurfer, sailboard; (sport)
windsurfing.
'würstel ['vyrstəl] sm inv frankfurter.

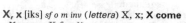

X x

X, x [iks] sf o m inv (lettera) X, x; **X come**
Xeres ≈ X for Xmas.
xenofo'bia [ksenofo'bia] sf xenophobia.
xe'nofobo, a [kse'nɔfobo] ag xenophobic
♦ sm/f xenophobe.
'xeres ['ksɛres] sm inv sherry.
xero'copia [ksero'kɔpja] sf xerox ®,
photocopy.
xerocopi'are [kseroko'pjare] vt to
photocopy.
xi'lofono [ksi'lɔfono] sm xylophone.

Y y

Y, y ['ipsilon] sf o m inv (lettera) Y, y; **Y come**
Yacht ≈ Y for Yellow (BRIT), Y for Yoke
(US).
yacht [jɔt] sm inv yacht.
'yankee ['jæŋki] sm/f inv Yank, Yankee.
Y.C.I. abbr = Yacht Club d'Italia.
'Yemen ['jemen] sm: **lo** ~ Yemen.
yen [jen] sm inv (moneta) yen.
'yiddish ['jidiʃ] ag inv, sm inv Yiddish.
'yoga ['jɔga] ag inv, sm yoga (cpd).
yogurt ['jɔgurt] sm inv yog(h)urt.

Z z

Z, z ['dzɛta] sf o m inv (lettera) Z, z; **Z come**
Zara ≈ Z for Zebra.
zabai'one [dzaba'jone] sm dessert made of
egg yolks, sugar and marsala.
zaf'fata [tsaf'fata] sf (tanfo) stench.
zaffe'rano [dzaffe'rano] sm saffron
zaf'firo [dzaf'firo] sm sapphire.
'zagara ['dzagara] sf orange blossom.
'zaino ['dzaino] sm rucksack.
Za'ire [dza'ire] sm: **lo** ~ Zaire.
'Zambia ['dzambja] sm: **lo** ~ Zambia.
'zampa ['tsampa] sf (di animale: gamba) leg;
(: piede) paw; **a quattro** ~**e** on all fours;
~**e di gallina** (calligrafia) scrawl; (rughe)
crow's feet.
zam'pata [tsam'pata] sf (di cane, gatto) blow
with a paw.
zampet'tare [tsampet'tare] vi to scamper.
zampil'lare [tsampil'lare] vi to gush, spurt.
zam'pillo [tsam'pillo] sm gush, spurt.
zam'pino [tsam'pino] sm paw; **qui c'è sotto**
il suo ~ (fig) he's had a hand in this.
zam'pogna [tsam'poɲɲa] sf instrument
similar to bagpipes.
'zanna ['tsanna] sf (di elefante) tusk; (di
carnivori) fang.
zan'zara [dzan'dzara] sf mosquito.
zanzari'era [dzandza'rjɛra] sf mosquito net.
'zappa ['tsappa] sf hoe.
zap'pare [tsap'pare] vt to hoe.
zappa'tura [tsappa'tura] sf (AGR) hoeing.
'zapping ['tsapɪŋ] sm (TV) channel-hopping.
zar, za'rina [tsar, tsa'rina] sm/f tsar/tsarina.
'zattera ['dzattera] sf raft.
za'vorra [dza'vɔrra] sf ballast.
'zazzera ['tsattsera] sf shock of hair.
'zebra ['dzɛbra] sf zebra; ~**e** sfpl (AUT) zebra
crossing sg (BRIT), crosswalk sg (US).
ze'brato, a [dze'brato] ag with black and
white stripes; **strisce** ~**e, attraversamento**
~ (AUT) zebra crossing (BRIT), crosswalk
(US).
'zecca, che ['tsekka] sf (ZOOL) tick; (officina
di monete) mint.
zec'chino [tsek'kino] sm gold coin; **oro** ~
pure gold.
ze'lante [dze'lante] ag zealous.
'zelo ['dzɛlo] sm zeal.

'zenit ['dzɛnit] sm zenith.
'zenzero ['dzendzero] sm ginger.
'zeppa ['tseppa] sf wedge.
'zeppo, a ['tseppo] ag: ~ di crammed o packed with.
zer'bino [dzer'bino] sm doormat.
'zero ['dzɛro] sm zero, nought; vincere per tre a ~ (SPORT) to win three-nil.
'zeta ['dzɛta] sm o f zed, (the letter) z.
'zia ['tsia] sf aunt.
zibel'lino [dzibel'lino] sm sable.
zi'gano, a [tsi'gano] ag, sm/f gypsy.
'zigomo ['dzigomo] sm cheekbone.
zigri'nare [dzigri'nare] vt (gen) to knurl; (pellame) to grain; (monete) to mill.
zig'zag [dzig'dzag] sm inv zigzag; andare a ~ to zigzag.
Zim'babwe [tsim'babwe] sm: lo ~ Zimbabwe.
zim'bello [dzim'bɛllo] sm (oggetto di burle) laughing-stock.
'zinco ['dzinko] sm zinc.
zinga'resco, a, schi, sche [dzinga'resko] ag gypsy cpd.
'zingaro, a ['dzingaro] sm/f gipsy.
'zio ['tsio], pl 'zii sm uncle; zii smpl (zio e zia) uncle and aunt.
zip'pare [dzip'pare] vt (INFORM) to zip.
zi'tella [dzi'tɛlla] sf spinster; (peg) old maid.
zit'tire [tsit'tire] vt to silence, hush o shut up ♦ vi to hiss.
'zitto, a ['tsitto] ag quiet, silent; sta' ~! be quiet!
ziz'zania [dzid'dzanja] sf (BOT) darnel; (fig) discord; gettare o seminare ~ to sow discord.
'zoccolo ['tsɔkkolo] sm (calzatura) clog; (di cavallo etc) hoof; (ARCHIT) plinth; (di parete) skirting (board); (di armadio) base.
zodia'cale [dzodia'kale] ag zodiac cpd; segno ~ sign of the zodiac.
zo'diaco [dzo'diako] sm zodiac.
zolfa'nello [tsolfa'nɛllo] sm (sulphur) match.
'zolfo ['tsolfo] sm sulphur (BRIT), sulfur (US).
'zolla ['dzolla] sf clod (of earth).
zol'letta [dzol'letta] sf sugar lump.
'zona ['dzɔna] sf zone, area; ~ di depressione (METEOR) trough of low pressure; ~ erogena erogenous zone; ~ pedonale pedestrian precinct; ~ verde (di abitato) green area.
'zonzo ['dzondzo]: a ~ av: andare a ~ to

wander about, stroll about.
'zoo ['dzɔo] sm inv zoo.
zoolo'gia [dzoolo'dʒia] sf zoology.
zoo'logico, a, ci, che [dzoo'lɔdʒiko] ag zoological.
zo'ologo, a, gi, ghe [dzo'ɔlogo] sm/f zoologist.
zoosa'fari [dzoosa'fari] sm inv safari park.
zoo'tecnico, a, ci, che [dzoo'tɛkniko] ag zootechnical; il patrimonio ~ di un paese a country's livestock resources.
zoppi'care [tsoppi'kare] vi to limp; (fig: mobile) to be shaky, rickety.
'zoppo, a ['tsɔppo] ag lame; (fig: mobile) shaky, rickety.
zoti'cone [dzoti'kone] sm lout.
ZTL [dzetati'ɛlle] sigla f (= Zona a Traffico Limitato) controlled traffic zone.
zu'ava [dzu'ava] sf: pantaloni mpl alla ~ knickerbockers.
'zucca, che ['tsukka] sf (BOT) marrow (BRIT), vegetable marrow (US); pumpkin; (scherzoso) head.
zucche'rare [tsukke'rare] vt to put sugar in.
zucche'rato, a [tsukke'rato] ag sweet, sweetened.
zuccheri'era [tsukke'rjɛra] sf sugar bowl.
zuccheri'ficio [tsukkeri'fitʃo] sm sugar refinery.
zucche'rino, a [tsukke'rino] ag sugary, sweet.
'zucchero ['tsukkero] sm sugar; ~ di canna cane sugar; ~ caramellato caramel; ~ filato candy floss, cotton candy (US); ~ a velo icing sugar (BRIT), confectioner's sugar (US).
zucche'roso, a [tsukke'roso] ag sugary.
zuc'china [tsuk'kina] sf, zuc'chino [tsuk'kino] sm courgette (BRIT), zucchini (US).
zuc'cotto [tsuk'kɔtto] sm ice-cream sponge.
'zuffa ['tsuffa] sf brawl.
zufo'lare [tsufo'lare] vt, vi to whistle.
'zufolo ['tsufolo] sm (MUS) flageolet.
'zuppa ['tsuppa] sf soup; (fig) mixture, muddle; ~ inglese (CUC) dessert made with sponge cake, custard and chocolate, ≈ trifle (BRIT).
zuppi'era [tsup'pjɛra] sf soup tureen.
'zuppo, a ['tsuppo] ag: ~ (di) drenched (with), soaked (with).
Zu'rigo [dzu'rigo] sf Zurich.

English-Italian
Inglese-Italiano

Aa

A, a [eɪ] n (letter) A, a for m inv; (SCOL: mark)
≈ 10 (ottimo); (MUS): **A** la m; **A for Andrew,**
(US) **A for Able** ≈ A come Ancona;
from A to Z dall'A alla Z; **A road** n (BRIT
AUT) ≈ strada statale; **A shares** npl (BRIT
STOCK EXCHANGE) azioni fpl senza diritto
di voto; **A to Z** ® n stradario.

=================================== KEYWORD

a [ə] (before vowel or silent h: **an**) indef art **1**
un (uno +s impure, gn, pn, ps, x, z), f una
(un' +vowel); ~ **book** un libro; ~ **mirror**
uno specchio; **an apple** una mela; **she's** ~
doctor è medico
2 (instead of the number "one") un(o), f
una; ~ **year ago** un anno fa; ~ **hundred/
thousand pounds** cento/mille sterline
3 (in expressing ratios, prices etc) a, per; **3**
~ **day/week** 3 al giorno/alla settimana; **10
km an hour** 10 km all'ora; **£5** ~ **person** 5
sterline a persona or per persona.

AA n abbr (BRIT: = Automobile Association)
≈ A.C.I. m (= Automobile Club d'Italia);
(US: = Associate in Art) titolo di studio;
(= Alcoholics Anonymous) A.A. f
(= Anonima Alcolisti); (MIL) = **anti-aircraft.**
AAA n abbr (= American Automobile
Association) ≈ A.C.I. m (= Automobile
Club d'Italia); (BRIT) = Amateur Athletics
Association.
AB abbr (BRIT) see **able-bodied seaman;**
(Canada) = Alberta.
aback [ə'bæk] adv: **to be taken** ~ essere
sbalordito(a).
abacus, pl **abaci** ['æbəkəs, -saɪ] n
pallottoliere m, abaco.
abandon [ə'bændən] vt abbandonare ♦ n

abbandono; **to** ~ **ship** abbandonare la
nave.
abandoned [ə'bændənd] adj (child, house
etc) abbandonato(a); (unrestrained:
manner) disinvolto(a).
abase [ə'beɪs] vt: **to** ~ **o.s. (so far as to do)**
umiliarsi or abbassarsi (al punto di fare).
abashed [ə'bæʃt] adj imbarazzato(a).
abate [ə'beɪt] vi calmarsi.
abatement [ə'beɪtmənt] n (of pollution,
noise) soppressione f, eliminazione f;
noise ~ **society** associazione f per la lotta
contro i rumori.
abattoir ['æbətwɑ:*] n (BRIT) mattatoio.
abbey ['æbɪ] n abbazia, badia.
abbot ['æbət] n abate m.
abbreviate [ə'bri:vɪeɪt] vt abbreviare.
abbreviation [əbri:vɪ'eɪʃən] n
abbreviazione f.
ABC n abbr (= American Broadcasting
Company) rete televisiva americana.
abdicate ['æbdɪkeɪt] vt abdicare a ♦ vi
abdicare.
abdication [æbdɪ'keɪʃən] n abdicazione f.
abdomen ['æbdəmən] n addome m.
abdominal [æb'dɒmɪnl] adj addominale.
abduct [æb'dʌkt] vt rapire.
abduction [æb'dʌkʃən] n rapimento.
Aberdonian [æbə'dəʊnɪən] adj di Aberdeen
♦ n abitante m/f di Aberdeen; originario/a
di Aberdeen.
aberration [æbə'reɪʃən] n aberrazione f.
abet [ə'bɛt] vt see **aid.**
abeyance [ə'beɪəns] n: **in** ~ in sospeso.
abhor [əb'hɔ:*] vt aborrire.
abhorrent [əb'hɒrənt] adj odioso(a).
abide [ə'baɪd] vt sopportare.
►**abide by** vt fus conformarsi a.

abiding [ə'baɪdɪŋ] *adj* (*memory etc*) persistente, duraturo(a).

ability [ə'bɪlɪtɪ] *n* abilità *f inv*; **to the best of my** ~ con il massimo impegno.

abject ['æbdʒɛkt] *adj* (*poverty*) abietto(a); (*apology*) umiliante; (*coward*) indegno(a), vile.

ablaze [ə'bleɪz] *adj* in fiamme; ~ **with light** risplendente di luce.

able ['eɪbl] *adj* capace; **to be** ~ **to do sth** essere capace di fare qc, poter fare qc.

able-bodied ['eɪbl'bɒdɪd] *adj* robusto(a).

able-bodied seaman (AB) *n* (*BRIT*) marinaio scelto.

ably ['eɪblɪ] *adv* abilmente.

ABM *n abbr* (= *anti-ballistic missile*) ABM *m*.

abnormal [æb'nɔːməl] *adj* anormale.

abnormality [æbnɔː'mælɪtɪ] *n* (*condition*) anormalità; (*instance*) anomalia.

aboard [ə'bɔːd] *adv* a bordo ♦ *prep* a bordo di; ~ **the train** in *or* sul treno.

abode [ə'bəud] *n* (*old*) dimora; (*LAW*) domicilio, dimora; **of no fixed** ~ senza fissa dimora.

abolish [ə'bɒlɪʃ] *vt* abolire.

abolition [æbəu'lɪʃən] *n* abolizione *f*.

abominable [ə'bɒmɪnəbl] *adj* abominevole.

aborigine [æbə'rɪdʒɪnɪ] *n* aborigeno/a.

abort [ə'bɔːt] *vt* (*MED*, *fig*) abortire; (*COMPUT*) interrompere l'esecuzione di.

abortion [ə'bɔːʃən] *n* aborto; **to have an** ~ avere un aborto, abortire.

abortionist [ə'bɔːʃənɪst] *n* abortista *m/f*.

abortive [ə'bɔːtɪv] *adj* abortivo(a).

abound [ə'baund] *vi* abbondare; **to** ~ **in** abbondare di.

================= *KEYWORD*

about [ə'baut] *adv* **1** (*approximately*) circa, quasi; ~ **a hundred/thousand** un centinaio/migliaio, circa cento/mille; **it takes** ~ **10 hours** ci vogliono circa 10 ore; **at** ~ **2 o'clock** verso le 2; **I've just** ~ **finished** ho quasi finito; **it's** ~ **here** è qui intorno, è qui vicino

2 (*referring to place*) qua e là, in giro; **to leave things lying** ~ lasciare delle cose in giro; **to run** ~ correre qua e là; **to walk** ~ camminare; **is Paul** ~? (*BRIT*) hai visto Paul in giro?; **it's the other way** ~ (*BRIT*) è il contrario

3: **to be** ~ **to do sth** stare per fare qc; **I'm not** ~ **to do all that for nothing** non ho intenzione di fare tutto questo per niente ♦ *prep* **1** (*relating to*) su, di; **a book** ~ **London** un libro su Londra; **what is it** ~? di che si tratta?; (*book, film etc*) di cosa tratta?; **we talked** ~ **it** ne abbiamo

parlato; **do something** ~ **it!** fai qualcosa!; **what** *or* **how** ~ **doing this?** che ne dici di fare questo?

2 (*referring to place*): **to walk** ~ **the town** camminare per la città; **her clothes were scattered** ~ **the room** i suoi vestiti erano sparsi *or* in giro per tutta la stanza.

about-face [ə'baut'feɪs] *n*, **about-turn** [ə'baut'tɔːn] *n* (*MIL*) dietro front *m inv*.

above [ə'bʌv] *adv*, *prep* sopra; **mentioned** ~ suddetto; **costing** ~ **£10** più caro di 10 sterline; **he's not** ~ **a bit of blackmail** non rifuggirebbe dal ricatto; ~ **all** soprattutto.

aboveboard [ə'bʌv'bɔːd] *adj* aperto(a); onesto(a).

abrasion [ə'breɪʒən] *n* abrasione *f*.

abrasive [ə'breɪzɪv] *adj* abrasivo(a).

abreast [ə'brɛst] *adv* di fianco; **3** ~ per 3 di fronte; **to keep** ~ **of** tenersi aggiornato su.

abridge [ə'brɪdʒ] *vt* ridurre.

abroad [ə'brɔːd] *adv* all'estero; **there is a rumour** ~ **that** … (*fig*) si sente dire in giro che …, circola la voce che ….

abrupt [ə'brʌpt] *adj* (*steep*) erto(a); (*sudden*) improvviso(a); (*gruff, blunt*) brusco(a).

abscess ['æbsɪs] *n* ascesso.

abscond [əb'skɒnd] *vi* scappare.

absence ['æbsəns] *n* assenza; **in the** ~ **of** (*person*) in assenza di; (*thing*) in mancanza di.

absent ['æbsənt] *adj* assente; **to be** ~ **without leave (AWOL)** (*MIL etc*) essere assente ingiustificato.

absentee [æbsən'tiː] *n* assente *m/f*.

absenteeism [æbsən'tiːɪzəm] *n* assenteismo.

absent-minded ['æbsənt'maɪndɪd] *adj* distratto(a).

absent-mindedness ['æbsənt'maɪndɪdnɪs] *n* distrazione *f*.

absolute ['æbsəluːt] *adj* assoluto(a).

absolutely [æbsə'luːtlɪ] *adv* assolutamente.

absolve [əb'zɒlv] *vt*: **to** ~ **sb (from)** (*sin etc*) assolvere qn (da); **to** ~ **sb from** (*oath*) sciogliere qn da.

absorb [əb'sɔːb] *vt* assorbire; **to be** ~**ed in a book** essere immerso(a) in un libro.

absorbent [əb'sɔːbənt] *adj* assorbente.

absorbent cotton *n* (*US*) cotone *m* idrofilo.

absorbing [əb'sɔːbɪŋ] *adj* avvincente, molto interessante.

absorption [əb'sɔːpʃən] *n* assorbimento.

abstain [əb'steɪn] *vi*: **to** ~ **(from)** astenersi (da).

abstemious [əb'stiːmɪəs] *adj* astemio(a).

abstention [əb'stɛnʃən] *n* astensione *f*.

abstinence ['æbstɪnəns] n astinenza.
abstract ['æbstrækt] adj astratto(a) ◊ n (summary) riassunto ◊ vt [æb'strækt] estrarre.
absurd [əb'səːd] adj assurdo(a).
absurdity [əb'səːdɪtɪ] n assurdità f inv.
ABTA ['æbtə] n abbr = Association of British Travel Agents.
Abu Dhabi ['æbuː'dɑːbɪ] n Abu Dhabi f.
abundance [ə'bʌndəns] n abbondanza.
abundant [ə'bʌndənt] adj abbondante.
abuse n [ə'bjuːs] abuso; (insults) ingiurie fpl ◊ vt [ə'bjuːz] abusare di; **open to** ~ che si presta ad abusi.
abusive [ə'bjuːsɪv] adj ingiurioso(a).
abysmal [ə'bɪzməl] adj spaventoso(a).
abyss [ə'bɪs] n abisso.
AC n abbr (US) = athletic club.
a/c abbr (BANKING etc: = account, current account) c.
academic [ækə'dɛmɪk] adj accademico(a); (pej: issue) puramente formale ◊ n universitario/a.
academic year n anno accademico.
academy [ə'kædəmɪ] n (learned body) accademia; (school) scuola privata; **military/naval** ~ scuola militare/navale; ~ **of music** conservatorio.
ACAS ['eɪkæs] n abbr (BRIT: = Advisory Conciliation and Arbitration Service) comitato governativo per il miglioramento della contrattazione collettiva.
accede [æk'siːd] vi: **to** ~ **to** (request) accedere a; (throne) ascendere a.
accelerate [æk'sɛləreɪt] vt, vi accelerare.
acceleration [æksɛlə'reɪʃən] n accelerazione f.
accelerator [æk'sɛləreɪtə*] n acceleratore m.
accent ['æksɛnt] n accento.
accentuate [æk'sɛntjueɪt] vt (syllable) accentuare; (need, difference etc) accentuare, mettere in risalto or in evidenza.
accept [ək'sɛpt] vt accettare.
acceptable [ək'sɛptəbl] adj accettabile.
acceptance [ək'sɛptəns] n accettazione f; **to meet with general** ~ incontrare il favore or il consenso generale.
access ['æksɛs] n accesso ◊ vt (COMPUT) accedere a; **to have** ~ **to** avere accesso a; **the burglars gained** ~ **through a window** i ladri sono riusciti a penetrare da or attraverso una finestra.
accessible [æk'sɛsəbl] adj accessibile.
accession [æk'sɛʃən] n (addition) aggiunta; (to library) accessione f, acquisto; (of king)

ascesa or salita al trono.
accessory [æk'sɛsərɪ] n accessorio; **toilet accessories** npl (BRIT) articoli mpl da toilette.
access road n strada d'accesso; (to motorway) raccordo di entrata.
access time n (COMPUT) tempo di accesso.
accident ['æksɪdənt] n incidente m; (chance) caso; **to meet with** or **to have an** ~ avere un incidente; ~**s at work** infortuni mpl sul lavoro; **by** ~ per caso.
accidental [æksɪ'dɛntl] adj accidentale.
accidentally [æksɪ'dɛntəlɪ] adv per caso.
accident insurance n assicurazione f contro gli infortuni.
accident-prone ['æksɪdənt'prəun] adj: **he's very** ~ è un vero passaguai.
acclaim [ə'kleɪm] vt acclamare ◊ n acclamazione f.
acclamation [æklə'meɪʃən] n (approval) acclamazione f; (applause) applauso.
acclimatize [ə'klaɪmətaɪz], (US) **acclimate** [ə'klaɪmeɪt] vt: **to become** ~d acclimatarsi.
accolade ['ækəleɪd] n encomio.
accommodate [ə'kɔmədeɪt] vt alloggiare; (oblige, help) favorire; **this car** ~**s 4 people comfortably** quest'auto può trasportare comodamente 4 persone.
accommodating [ə'kɔmədeɪtɪŋ] adj compiacente.
accommodation [əkɔmə'deɪʃən] n(pl) alloggio; (US) **accommodations** [əkɔmə'deɪʃən(z)] n(pl) alloggio; **seating** ~ (BRIT) posti a sedere; "~ **to let**" (BRIT) "camere in affitto"; **have you any** ~? avete posto?
accompaniment [ə'kʌmpənɪmənt] n accompagnamento.
accompanist [ə'kʌmpənɪst] n (MUS) accompagnatore/trice.
accompany [ə'kʌmpənɪ] vt accompagnare.
accomplice [ə'kʌmplɪs] n complice m/f.
accomplish [ə'kʌmplɪʃ] vt compiere; (achieve) ottenere.
accomplished [ə'kʌmplɪʃt] adj (person) esperto(a).
accomplishment [ə'kʌmplɪʃmənt] n compimento; (thing achieved) risultato; ~**s** npl (skills) doti fpl.
accord [ə'kɔːd] n accordo ◊ vt accordare; **of his own** ~ di propria iniziativa; **with one** ~ all'unanimità, di comune accordo.
accordance [ə'kɔːdəns] n: **in** ~ **with** in conformità con.
according [ə'kɔːdɪŋ]: ~ **to** prep secondo; **it went** ~ **to plan** è andata secondo il previsto.
accordingly [ə'kɔːdɪŋlɪ] adv in conformità.
accordion [ə'kɔːdɪən] n fisarmonica.

accost [əˈkɔst] vt avvicinare.

account [əˈkaunt] n (COMM) conto; (report) descrizione f; ~s npl (COMM) conti; "~ payee only" (BRIT) "assegno non trasferibile"; **to keep an** ~ **of** tenere nota di; **to bring sb to** ~ **for sth/for having done sth** chiedere a qn di render conto di qc/per aver fatto qc; **by all** ~s a quanto si dice; **of little** ~ di poca importanza; **on** ~ in acconto; **to buy sth on** ~ comprare qc a credito; **on no** ~ per nessun motivo; **on** ~ **of** a causa di; **to take into** ~, **take** ~ **of** tener conto di.
▸**account for** vt fus (explain) spiegare; giustificare; **all the children were** ~**ed for** nessun bambino mancava all'appello.

accountability [əˈkauntəˈbɪlɪtɪ] n responsabilità.

accountable [əˈkauntəbl] adj responsabile; **to be held** ~ **for sth** dover rispondere di qc.

accountancy [əˈkauntənsɪ] n ragioneria.

accountant [əˈkauntənt] n ragioniere/a.

accounting [əˈkauntɪŋ] n contabilità.

accounting period n esercizio finanziario, periodo contabile.

account number n numero di conto.

account payable n conto passivo.

account receivable n conto da esigere.

accredited [əˈkrɛdɪtɪd] adj accreditato(a).

accretion [əˈkriːʃən] n accrescimento.

accrue [əˈkruː] vi (mount up) aumentare; **to** ~ **to** derivare a; ~**d charges** ratei mpl passivi; ~**d interest** interesse m maturato.

accumulate [əˈkjuːmjuleɪt] vt accumulare ♦ vi accumularsi.

accumulation [əkjuːmjuˈleɪʃən] n accumulazione f.

accuracy [ˈækjurəsɪ] n precisione f.

accurate [ˈækjurɪt] adj preciso(a).

accurately [ˈækjurɪtlɪ] adv precisamente.

accusation [ækjuˈzeɪʃən] n accusa.

accusative [əˈkjuːzətɪv] n (LING) accusativo.

accuse [əˈkjuːz] vt accusare.

accused [əˈkjuːzd] n accusato/a.

accuser [əˈkjuːzə*] n accusatore/trice.

accustom [əˈkʌstəm] vt abituare; **to** ~ **o.s. to sth** abituarsi a qc.

accustomed [əˈkʌstəmd] adj (usual) abituale; ~ **to** abituato(a) a.

AC/DC abbr (= alternating current/direct current) c.a./c.c.

ACE [eɪs] n abbr = American Council on Education.

ace [eɪs] n asso; **within an** ~ **of** (BRIT) a un pelo da.

acerbic [əˈsɔːbɪk] adj (also fig) acido(a).

acetate [ˈæsɪteɪt] n acetato.

ache [eɪk] n male m, dolore m ♦ vi (be sore) far male, dolere; (yearn): **to** ~ **to do sth** morire dalla voglia di fare qc; **I've got stomach** ~ or (US) **a stomach** ~ ho mal di stomaco; **my head** ~**s** mi fa male la testa; **I'm aching all over** mi duole dappertutto.

achieve [əˈtʃiːv] vt (aim) raggiungere; (victory, success) ottenere; (task) compiere.

achievement [əˈtʃiːvmənt] n compimento; successo.

Achilles heel [əˈkɪliːz-] n tallone m d'Achille.

acid [ˈæsɪd] adj acido(a) ♦ n acido.

acidity [əˈsɪdɪtɪ] n acidità.

acid rain n pioggia acida.

acid test n (fig) prova del fuoco.

acknowledge [əkˈnɔlɪdʒ] vt riconoscere; (letter: also: ~ **receipt of**) accusare ricevuta di.

acknowledgement [əkˈnɔlɪdʒmənt] n riconoscimento; (of letter) conferma; ~s (in book) ringraziamenti mpl.

ACLU n abbr (= American Civil Liberties Union) unione americana per le libertà civili.

acme [ˈækmɪ] n culmine m, acme m.

acne [ˈæknɪ] n acne f.

acorn [ˈeɪkɔːn] n ghianda.

acoustic [əˈkuːstɪk] adj acustico(a); see also **acoustics**.

acoustic coupler [-ˈkʌplə*] n (COMPUT) accoppiatore m acustico.

acoustics [əˈkuːstɪks] n, npl acustica.

acquaint [əˈkweɪnt] vt: **to** ~ **sb with sth** far sapere qc a qn; **to be** ~**ed with** (person) conoscere.

acquaintance [əˈkweɪntəns] n conoscenza; (person) conoscente m/f; **to make sb's** ~ fare la conoscenza di qn.

acquiesce [ækwɪˈɛs] vi (agree): **to** ~ **(in)** acconsentire (a).

acquire [əˈkwaɪə*] vt acquistare.

acquired [əˈkwaɪəd] adj acquisito(a); **it's an** ~ **taste** è una cosa che si impara ad apprezzare.

acquisition [ækwɪˈzɪʃən] n acquisto.

acquisitive [əˈkwɪzɪtɪv] adj a cui piace accumulare le cose.

acquit [əˈkwɪt] vt assolvere; **to** ~ **o.s. well** comportarsi bene.

acquittal [əˈkwɪtl] n assoluzione f.

acre [ˈeɪkə*] n acro (= 4047 m²).

acreage [ˈeɪkərɪdʒ] n superficie f in acri.

acrid [ˈækrɪd] adj (smell) acre, pungente; (fig) pungente.

acrimonious [ækrɪ'məʊnɪəs] adj astioso(a).
acrobat ['ækrəbæt] n acrobata m/f.
acrobatic [ækrə'bætɪk] adj acrobatico(a).
acrobatics [ækrə'bætɪks] n acrobatica ♦ npl acrobazie fpl.
Acropolis [ə'krɔpəlɪs] n: the ~ l'Acropoli f.
across [ə'krɔs] prep (on the other side) dall'altra parte di; (crosswise) attraverso ♦ adv dall'altra parte; in larghezza; to walk ~ (the road) attraversare (la strada); to take sb ~ the road far attraversare la strada a qn; ~ from di fronte a; the lake is 12 km ~ il lago ha una larghezza di 12 km or è largo 12 km; to get sth ~ to sb (fig) far capire qc a qn.
acrylic [ə'krɪlɪk] adj acrilico(a) ♦ n acrilico.
ACT ® n abbr (= American College Test) esame di ammissione a college.
act [ækt] n atto; (in music-hall etc) numero; (LAW) decreto ♦ vi agire; (THEAT) recitare; (pretend) fingere ♦ vt (part) recitare; to catch sb in the ~ cogliere qn in flagrante or sul fatto; it's only an ~ è tutta scena, è solo una messinscena; ~ of God (LAW) calamità f inv naturale; to ~ Hamlet (BRIT) recitare la parte di Amleto; to ~ the fool (BRIT) fare lo stupido; to ~ as agire da; it ~s as a deterrent serve da deterrente; ~ing in my capacity as chairman, I … in qualità di presidente, io ….
▶act on vt: to ~ on sth agire in base a qc.
▶act out vt (event) ricostruire; (fantasies) dare forma concreta a.
acting ['æktɪŋ] adj che fa le funzioni di ♦ n (of actor) recitazione f; (activity): to do some ~ fare del teatro (or del cinema); he is the ~ manager fa le veci del direttore.
action ['ækʃən] n azione f; (MIL) combattimento; (LAW) processo; to take ~ agire; to put a plan into ~ realizzare un piano; out of ~ fuori combattimento; (machine etc) fuori servizio; killed in ~ (MIL) ucciso in combattimento; to bring an ~ against sb (LAW) intentare causa contro qn.
action replay n (BRIT TV) replay m inv.
activate ['æktɪveɪt] vt (mechanism) fare funzionare; (CHEM, PHYSICS) rendere attivo(a).
active ['æktɪv] adj attivo(a); to play an ~ part in partecipare attivamente a.
active duty (AD) n (US MIL) = active service.
actively ['æktɪvlɪ] adv attivamente.
active partner n (COMM) socio effettivo.
active service n (BRIT MIL): to be on ~ prestar servizio in zona di operazioni.

activist ['æktɪvɪst] n attivista m/f.
activity [æk'tɪvɪtɪ] n attività f inv.
activity holiday n vacanza attiva (in bici, a cavallo, in barca a vela ecc.).
actor ['æktə*] n attore m.
actress ['æktrɪs] n attrice f.
actual ['æktjʊəl] adj reale, vero(a).
actually ['æktjʊəlɪ] adv veramente; (even) addirittura.
actuary ['æktjʊərɪ] n attuario/a.
actuate ['æktjʊeɪt] vt attivare.
acuity [ə'kjuːɪtɪ] n acutezza.
acumen ['ækjʊmən] n acume m; business ~ fiuto negli affari.
acupuncture ['ækjʊpʌŋktʃə*] n agopuntura.
AD adv abbr (= Anno Domini) d. C. ♦ n abbr (US MIL) see active duty.
ad [æd] n abbr = advertisement.
adamant ['ædəmənt] adj irremovibile.
Adam's apple ['ædəmz-] n pomo di Adamo.
adapt [ə'dæpt] vt adattare ♦ vi: to ~ (to) adattarsi (a).
adaptability [ədæptə'bɪlɪtɪ] n adattabilità.
adaptable [ə'dæptəbl] adj (device) adattabile; (person) che sa adattarsi.
adaptation [ædæp'teɪʃən] n adattamento.
adapter, adaptor [ə'dæptə*] n (ELEC) adattatore m.
ADC n abbr (MIL) = aide-de-camp; (US: = Aid to Dependent Children) sussidio per figli a carico.
add [æd] vt aggiungere; (figures) addizionare ♦ vi: to ~ to (increase) aumentare.
▶add on vt aggiungere.
▶add up vt (figures) addizionare ♦ vi (fig): it doesn't ~ up non ha senso; it doesn't ~ up to much non è un granché.
adder ['ædə*] n vipera.
addict ['ædɪkt] n tossicomane m/f; (fig) fanatico/a; heroin ~ eroinomane m/f; drug ~ tossicodipendente m/f, tossicomane m/f.
addicted [ə'dɪktɪd] adj: to be ~ to (drink etc) essere dedito(a) a; (fig: football etc) essere tifoso(a) di.
addiction [ə'dɪkʃən] n (MED) tossicomania.
adding machine ['ædɪŋ-] n addizionatrice f.
addition [ə'dɪʃən] n addizione f; in ~ inoltre; in ~ to oltre.
additional [ə'dɪʃənl] adj supplementare.
additive ['ædɪtɪv] n additivo.
address [ə'drɛs] n (gen, COMPUT) indirizzo; (talk) discorso ♦ vt indirizzare; (speak to) fare un discorso a; form of ~ (gen) formula di cortesia; (in letters) formula d'indirizzo or di intestazione; to ~ o.s. to sth indirizzare le proprie energie verso

qc; **absolute/relative** ~ (*COMPUT*)
indirizzo assoluto/relativo.
address book *n* rubrica.
addressee [ædrɛ'siː] *n* destinatario/a.
Aden ['eɪdən] *n*: **the Gulf of** ~ il golfo di
Aden.
adenoids ['ædɪnɔɪdz] *npl* adenoidi *fpl.*
adept ['ædɛpt] *adj:* ~ **at** esperto(a) in.
adequate ['ædɪkwɪt] *adj* (*description,*
reward) adeguato(a); (*amount*) sufficiente;
to feel ~ **to a task** sentirsi all'altezza di
un compito.
adequately ['ædɪkwɪtlɪ] *adv*
adeguatamente; sufficientemente.
adhere [əd'hɪə*] *vi*: **to** ~ **to** aderire a; (*fig*:
rule, decision) seguire.
adhesion [əd'hiːʒən] *n* adesione *f.*
adhesive [əd'hiːzɪv] *adj* adesivo(a) ♦ *n*
adesivo; ~ **tape** (*BRIT*: *for parcels etc*)
nastro adesivo; (*US: MED*) cerotto
adesivo.
ad hoc [æd'hɔk] *adj* (*decision*) ad hoc *inv*;
(*committee*) apposito(a).
ad infinitum ['ædɪnfɪ'naɪtəm] *adv*
all'infinito.
adjacent [ə'dʒeɪsənt] *adj* adiacente; ~ **to**
accanto a.
adjective ['ædʒɛktɪv] *n* aggettivo.
adjoin [ə'dʒɔɪn] *vt* essere contiguo(a) *or*
attiguo(a) a.
adjoining [ə'dʒɔɪnɪŋ] *adj* accanto *inv*,
adiacente ♦ *prep* accanto a.
adjourn [ə'dʒɜːn] *vt* rimandare,
aggiornare; (*US: end*) sospendere ♦ *vi*
sospendere la seduta; (*PARLIAMENT*)
sospendere i lavori; (*go*) spostarsi; **to**
~ **a meeting till the following week**
aggiornare *or* rinviare un incontro alla
settimana seguente; **they** ~**ed to the pub**
(*col*) si sono trasferiti al pub.
adjournment [ə'dʒɜːnmənt] *n* rinvio,
aggiornamento; sospensione *f.*
Adjt *abbr* (*MIL*) = **adjutant.**
adjudicate [ə'dʒuːdɪkeɪt] *vt* (*contest*)
giudicare; (*claim*) decidere su.
adjudication [ədʒuːdɪ'keɪʃən] *n* decisione *f.*
adjust [ə'dʒʌst] *vt* aggiustare; (*COMM*)
rettificare ♦ *vi*: **to** ~ (**to**) adattarsi (a).
adjustable [ə'dʒʌstəbl] *adj* regolabile.
adjuster [ə'dʒʌstə*] *n see* **loss adjuster.**
adjustment [ə'dʒʌstmənt] *n* adattamento;
(*of prices, wages*) aggiustamento.
adjutant ['ædʒətənt] *n* aiutante *m.*
ad-lib [æd'lɪb] *vt*, *vi* improvvisare ♦ *n*
improvvisazione *f* ♦ *adv*: **ad lib a piacere, a**
volontà.
adman ['ædmæn] *n* (*col*) pubblicitario/a.
admin [æd'mɪn] *n abbr* (*col*)

= **administration.**
administer [əd'mɪnɪstə*] *vt* amministrare;
(*justice*) somministrare.
administration [ədmɪnɪs'treɪʃən] *n*
amministrazione *f*; **the A**~ (*US*) il
Governo.
administrative [əd'mɪnɪstrətɪv] *adj*
amministrativo(a).
administrator [əd'mɪnɪstreɪtə*] *n*
amministratore/trice.
admirable ['ædmərəbl] *adj* ammirevole.
admiral ['ædmərəl] *n* ammiraglio.
Admiralty ['ædmərəltɪ] *n* (*BRIT*: *also*: ~
Board) Ministero della Marina.
admiration [ædmə'reɪʃən] *n* ammirazione *f.*
admirer [əd'maɪərə*] *n* ammiratore/trice.
admiring [əd'maɪərɪŋ] *adj* (*glance etc*) di
ammirazione.
admissible [əd'mɪsəbl] *adj* ammissibile.
admission [əd'mɪʃən] *n* ammissione *f*; (*to*
exhibition, night club etc) ingresso;
(*confession*) confessione *f*; **by his own** ~
per sua ammissione; "~ **free**", "**free** ~"
"ingresso gratuito".
admit [əd'mɪt] *vt* ammettere; far entrare;
(*agree*) riconoscere; "**children not** ~**ted**"
"vietato l'ingresso ai bambini"; **this**
ticket ~**s two** questo biglietto è valido
per due persone; **I must** ~ **that** ... devo
ammettere *or* confessare che ....
► **admit of** *vt fus* lasciare adito a.
► **admit to** *vt fus* riconoscere.
admittance [əd'mɪtəns] *n* ingresso; "**no** ~"
"vietato l'ingresso".
admittedly [əd'mɪtɪdlɪ] *adv* bisogna pur
riconoscere (che).
admonish [əd'mɔnɪʃ] *vt* ammonire.
ad nauseam [æd'nɔːzɪæm] *adv* fino alla
nausea, a non finire.
ado [ə'duː] *n*: **without (any) more** ~ senza
più indugi.
adolescence [ædəu'lɛsns] *n* adolescenza.
adolescent [ædəu'lɛsnt] *adj, n* adolescente
(*m/f*).
adopt [ə'dɔpt] *vt* adottare.
adopted [ə'dɔptɪd] *adj* adottivo(a).
adoption [ə'dɔpʃən] *n* adozione *f.*
adore [ə'dɔː*] *vt* adorare.
adoring [ə'dɔːrɪŋ] *adj* adorante; **his** ~ **wife**
sua moglie che lo adora.
adoringly [ə'dɔːrɪŋlɪ] *adv* con adorazione.
adorn [ə'dɔːn] *vt* ornare.
adornment [ə'dɔːnmənt] *n* ornamento.
ADP *n abbr see* **automatic data processing.**
adrenalin [ə'drɛnəlɪn] *n* adrenalina; **it gets**
the ~ **going** ti dà una carica.
Adriatic (Sea) [eɪdrɪ'ætɪk-] *n* Adriatico.
adrift [ə'drɪft] *adv* alla deriva; **to come** ~

(*boat*) andare alla deriva; (*wire, rope etc*) essersi staccato(a) *or* sciolto(a).

adroit [ə'drɔɪt] *adj* abile, destro(a).

ADT *abbr* (*US*: = *Atlantic Daylight Time*) *ora legale di New York*.

adult ['ædʌlt] *n* adulto/a.

adult education *n* scuola per adulti.

adulterate [ə'dʌltəreɪt] *vt* adulterare.

adulterer [ə'dʌltərə*] *n* adultero.

adulteress [ə'dʌltərɪs] *n* adultera.

adultery [ə'dʌltərɪ] *n* adulterio.

adulthood ['ædʌlthud] *n* età adulta.

advance [əd'vɑːns] *n* avanzamento; (*money*) anticipo ♦ *vt* avanzare; (*date, money*) anticipare ♦ *vi* avanzare; **in** ~ **in** anticipo; **to make** ~**s to sb** (*gen*) fare degli approcci a qn; (*amorously*) fare delle avances a qn.

advanced [əd'vɑːnst] *adj* avanzato(a); (*SCOL: studies*) superiore; ~ **in years** avanti negli anni.

advancement [əd'vɑːnsmənt] *n* avanzamento.

advance notice *n* preavviso.

advantage [əd'vɑːntɪdʒ] *n* (*also TENNIS*) vantaggio; **to take** ~ **of** approfittarsi di; **it's to our** ~ è nel nostro interesse, torna a nostro vantaggio.

advantageous [ædvən'teɪdʒəs] *adj* vantaggioso(a).

advent ['ædvənt] *n* avvento; **A**~ (*REL*) Avvento.

Advent calendar *n* calendario dell'Avvento.

adventure [əd'ventʃə*] *n* avventura.

adventure playground *n* *area attrezzata di giochi per bambini con funi, strutture in legno etc*.

adventurous [əd'ventʃərəs] *adj* avventuroso(a).

adverb ['ædvəːb] *n* avverbio.

adversary ['ædvəsərɪ] *n* avversario/a.

adverse ['ædvəːs] *adj* avverso(a); **in** ~ **circumstances** nelle avversità; ~ **to** contrario(a) a.

adversity [əd'vəːsɪtɪ] *n* avversità.

advert ['ædvəːt] *n abbr* (*BRIT*) = **advertisement**.

advertise ['ædvətaɪz] *vi* (*vt*) fare pubblicità *or* réclame (a); fare un'inserzione (per vendere); **to** ~ **for** (*staff*) cercare tramite annuncio.

advertisement [əd'vəːtɪsmənt] *n* (*COMM*) réclame *f inv*, pubblicità *f inv*; (*in classified ads*) inserzione *f*.

advertiser ['ædvətaɪzə*] *n* azienda che reclamizza un prodotto; (*in newspaper*) inserzionista *m/f*.

advertising ['ædvətaɪzɪŋ] *n* pubblicità.

advertising agency *n* agenzia pubblicitaria *or* di pubblicità.

advertising campaign *n* campagna pubblicitaria.

advice [əd'vaɪs] *n* consigli *mpl*; (*notification*) avviso; **piece of** ~ consiglio; **to ask (sb) for** ~ chiedere il consiglio (di qn), chiedere un consiglio (a qn); **legal** ~ consulenza legale.

advice note *n* (*BRIT*) avviso di spedizione.

advisable [əd'vaɪzəbl] *adj* consigliabile.

advise [əd'vaɪz] *vt* consigliare; **to** ~ **sb of sth** informare qn di qc; **to** ~ **sb against sth/against doing sth** sconsigliare qc a qn/a qn di fare qc; **you will be well/ill** ~**d to go** fareste bene/male ad andare.

advisedly [əd'vaɪzɪdlɪ] *adv* (*deliberately*) deliberatamente.

adviser [əd'vaɪzə*] *n* consigliere/a; (*in business*) consulente *m/f*, consigliere/a.

advisory [əd'vaɪzərɪ] *adj* consultivo(a); **in an** ~ **capacity** in veste di consulente.

advocate *n* ['ædvɔkɪt] (*upholder*) sostenitore/trice ♦ *vt* ['ædvəkeɪt] propugnare; **to be an** ~ **of** essere a favore di.

advt. *abbr* = **advertisement**.

AEA *n abbr* (*BRIT*: = *Atomic Energy Authority*) *ente di controllo sulla ricerca e lo sviluppo dell'energia atomica*.

AEC *n abbr* (*US*: = *Atomic Energy Commission*) *ente di controllo sulla ricerca e lo sviluppo dell'energia atomica*.

Aegean (Sea) [iː'dʒiːən-] *n* (*mare m*) Egeo.

aegis ['iːdʒɪs] *n*: **under the** ~ **of** sotto gli auspici di.

aeon ['iːən] *n* eternità *f inv*.

aerial ['ɛərɪəl] *n* antenna ♦ *adj* aereo(a).

aerobatics ['ɛərəu'bætɪks] *npl* acrobazia aerea *sg*; (*stunts*) acrobazie *fpl* aeree.

aerobics [ɛə'rəubɪks] *n* aerobica.

aerodrome ['ɛərədrəum] *n* (*BRIT*) aerodromo.

aerodynamic ['ɛərəudaɪ'næmɪk] *adj* aerodinamico(a).

aeronautics [ɛərə'nɔːtɪks] *n* aeronautica.

aeroplane ['ɛərəpleɪn] *n* aeroplano.

aerosol ['ɛərəsɔl] *n* aerosol *m inv*.

aerospace industry ['ɛərəuspeɪs-] *n* industria aerospaziale.

aesthetic [ɪs'θetɪk] *adj* estetico(a).

afar [ə'fɑː*] *adv* lontano; **from** ~ da lontano.

AFB *n abbr* (*US*) = *Air Force Base*.

AFDC *n abbr* (*US*) = *Aid to Families with Dependent Children*.

affable ['æfəbl] *adj* affabile.

affair [ə'fɛə*] n affare m; (*also*: **love** ~) relazione f amorosa; ~s (*business*) affari; **the Watergate** ~ il caso Watergate.

affect [ə'fɛkt] vt toccare; (*feign*) fingere.

affectation [æfɛk'teɪʃən] n affettazione f.

affected [ə'fɛktɪd] adj affettato(a).

affection [ə'fɛkʃən] n affetto m.

affectionate [ə'fɛkʃənɪt] adj affettuoso(a).

affectionately [ə'fɛkʃənɪtlɪ] adv affettuosamente.

affidavit [æfɪ'deɪvɪt] n (*LAW*) affidavit m inv.

affiliated [ə'fɪlɪeɪtɪd] adj affiliato(a); ~ **company** filiale f.

affinity [ə'fɪnɪtɪ] n affinità f inv.

affirm [ə'fəːm] vt affermare, asserire.

affirmation [æfə'meɪʃən] n affermazione f.

affirmative [ə'fəːmətɪv] adj affermativo(a) ♦ n: **in the** ~ affermativamente.

affix [ə'fɪks] vt apporre; attaccare.

afflict [ə'flɪkt] vt affliggere.

affliction [ə'flɪkʃən] n afflizione f.

affluence ['æfluəns] n ricchezza.

affluent ['æfluənt] adj ricco(a); **the** ~ **society** la società del benessere.

afford [ə'fɔːd] vt permettersi; (*provide*) fornire; **I can't** ~ **the time** non ho veramente il tempo; **can we** ~ **a car?** possiamo permetterci un'automobile?

affordable [ə'fɔːdəbl] adj (che ha un prezzo) abbordabile.

affray [ə'freɪ] n (*BRIT LAW*) rissa.

affront [ə'frʌnt] n affronto.

affronted [ə'frʌntɪd] adj insultato(a).

Afghan ['æfgæn] adj, n afgano(a).

Afghanistan [æf'gænɪstɑːn] n Afganistan m.

afield [ə'fiːld] adv: **far** ~ lontano.

AFL-CIO n abbr (= *American Federation of Labor and Congress of Industrial Organizations*) confederazione sindacale.

afloat [ə'fləut] adj, adv a galla.

afoot [ə'fut] adv: **there is something** ~ si sta preparando qualcosa.

aforementioned [ə'fɔːmɛnʃənd] adj suddetto(a).

aforesaid [ə'fɔːsɛd] adj suddetto(a).

afraid [ə'freɪd] adj impaurito(a); **to be** ~ **of** aver paura di; **to be** ~ **of doing** or **to do** aver paura di fare; **I am** ~ **that I'll be late** mi dispiace, ma farò tardi; **I'm** ~ **so!** ho paura di sì!, temo proprio di sì!; **I'm** ~ **not** no, mi dispiace, purtroppo no.

afresh [ə'frɛʃ] adv di nuovo.

Africa ['æfrɪkə] n Africa.

African ['æfrɪkən] adj, n africano(a).

Afrikaans [æfrɪ'kɑːns] n afrikaans m.

Afrikaner [æfrɪ'kɑːnə*] n africander m inv.

Afro-American ['æfrəuə'mɛrɪkən] adj afroamericano(a).

Afro-Caribbean ['æfrəkæri'bɪːən] adj afrocaraibico(a).

AFT n abbr (= *American Federation of Teachers*) sindacato degli insegnanti.

aft [ɑːft] adv a poppa, verso poppa.

after ['ɑːftə*] prep, adv dopo; ~ **dinner** dopo cena; **the day** ~ **tomorrow** dopodomani; **what/who are you** ~? che/chi cerca?; **the police are** ~ **him** è ricercato dalla polizia; ~ **you!** dopo di lei!; ~ **all** dopo tutto.

afterbirth ['ɑːftəbəːθ] n placenta.

aftercare ['ɑːftəkɛə*] n (*BRIT MED*) assistenza medica post-degenza.

after-effects ['ɑːftərɪfɛkts] npl conseguenze fpl; (*of illness*) postumi mpl.

afterlife ['ɑːftəlaɪf] n vita dell'al di là.

aftermath ['ɑːftəmæθ] n conseguenze fpl; **in the** ~ **of** nel periodo dopo.

afternoon ['ɑːftə'nuːn] n pomeriggio; **good** ~! buon giorno!

afters ['ɑːftəz] n (*BRIT col*: *dessert*) dessert m inv.

after-sales service [ɑːftə'seɪlz-] n servizio assistenza clienti.

after-shave (lotion) ['ɑːftəʃeɪv-] n dopobarba m inv.

aftershock ['ɑːftəʃɔk] n scossa di assestamento.

aftersun ['ɑːftəsʌn] adj: ~ **(lotion/cream)** (lozione f/crema) doposole m inv.

aftertaste ['ɑːftəteɪst] n retrogusto.

afterthought ['ɑːftəθɔːt] n: **as an** ~ come aggiunta.

afterwards ['ɑːftəwədz] adv dopo.

again [ə'gɛn] adv di nuovo; **to begin/see** ~ ricominciare/rivedere; **he opened it** ~ l'ha aperto di nuovo, l'ha riaperto; **not** ... ~ non ... più; ~ **and** ~ ripetutamente; **now and** ~ di tanto in tanto, a volte.

against [ə'gɛnst] prep contro; ~ **a blue background** su uno sfondo azzurro; **leaning** ~ **the desk** appoggiato alla scrivania; **(as)** ~ (*BRIT*) in confronto a.

age [eɪdʒ] n età f inv ♦ vt, vi invecchiare; **what** ~ **is he?** quanti anni ha?; **he is 20 years of** ~ ha 20 anni; **under** ~ minorenne; **to come of** ~ diventare maggiorenne; **it's been** ~s **since** ... sono secoli che ....

aged ['eɪdʒd] adj: ~ **10** di 10 anni; **the** ~ ['eɪdʒɪd] npl (*elderly*) gli anziani.

age group n generazione f; **the 40 to 50** ~ le persone fra i 40 e i 50 anni.

ageing ['eɪdʒɪŋ] adj che diventa vecchio(a); **an** ~ **filmstar** una diva stagionata.

ageless ['eɪdʒlɪs] adj senza età.

age limit n limite m d'età.

agency ['eɪdʒənsɪ] n agenzia; **through** or **by the ~ of** grazie a.

agenda [ə'dʒendə] n ordine m del giorno; **on the ~** all'ordine del giorno.

agent ['eɪdʒənt] n agente m.

aggravate ['ægrəveɪt] vt aggravare, peggiorare; (annoy) esasperare.

aggravation [ægrə'veɪʃən] n peggioramento; esasperazione f.

aggregate ['ægrɪgeɪt] n aggregato; **on ~** (SPORT) con punteggio complessivo.

aggression [ə'greʃən] n aggressione f.

aggressive [ə'gresɪv] adj aggressivo(a).

aggressiveness [ə'gresɪvnɪs] n aggressività.

aggressor [ə'gresə*] n aggressore m.

aggrieved [ə'griːvd] adj addolorato(a).

aggro ['ægrəu] n (col: behaviour) aggressività f inv; (: hassle) rottura.

aghast [ə'gɑːst] adj sbigottito(a).

agile ['ædʒaɪl] adj agile.

agility [ə'dʒɪlɪtɪ] n agilità f inv.

agitate ['ædʒɪteɪt] vt turbare; agitare ♦ vi: **to ~ for** agitarsi per.

agitator ['ædʒɪteɪtə*] n agitatore/trice.

AGM n abbr see **annual general meeting**.

agnostic [æg'nɒstɪk] adj, n agnostico(a).

ago [ə'gəu] adv: **2 days ~** 2 giorni fa; **not long ~** poco tempo fa; **as long ~ as 1960** già nel 1960; **how long ~?** quanto tempo fa?

agog [ə'gɒg] adj: **(all) ~ (for)** ansioso(a) (di), impaziente (di).

agonize ['ægənaɪz] vi: **to ~ (over)** angosciarsi (per).

agonizing ['ægənaɪzɪŋ] adj straziante.

agony ['ægənɪ] n agonia; **I was in ~** avevo dei dolori atroci.

agony aunt n (BRIT col) chi tiene la rubrica della posta del cuore.

agony column n posta del cuore.

agree [ə'griː] vt (price) pattuire ♦ vi: **to ~ (with)** essere d'accordo (con); (LING) concordare (con); **to ~ to sth/to do sth** accettare qc/di fare qc; **to ~ that** (admit) ammettere che; **to ~ on sth** accordarsi su qc; **it was ~d that …** è stato deciso (di comune accordo) che …; **garlic doesn't ~ with me** l'aglio non mi va.

agreeable [ə'griːəbl] adj gradevole; (willing) disposto(a); **are you ~ to this?** è d'accordo con questo?

agreed [ə'griːd] adj (time, place) stabilito(a); **to be ~** essere d'accordo.

agreement [ə'griːmənt] n accordo; **in ~** d'accordo; **by mutual ~** di comune accordo.

agricultural [ægrɪ'kʌltʃərəl] adj agricolo(a).

agriculture ['ægrɪkʌltʃə*] n agricoltura.

aground [ə'graund] adv: **to run ~** arenarsi.

ahead [ə'hed] adv avanti; davanti; **~ of** davanti a; (fig: schedule etc) in anticipo su; **~ of time** in anticipo; **go ~!** avanti!; **go right** or **straight ~** tiri diritto; **they were (right) ~ of us** erano (proprio) davanti a noi.

AI n abbr = Amnesty International; (COMPUT) see **artificial intelligence**.

AID n abbr = artificial insemination by donor; (US: = Agency for International Development) A.I.D. f.

aid [eɪd] n aiuto ♦ vt aiutare; **with the ~ of** con l'aiuto di; **in ~ of** a favore di; **to ~ and abet** (LAW) essere complice di.

aide [eɪd] n (person) aiutante m.

aide-de-camp (ADC) ['eɪddə'kɒŋ] n (MIL) aiutante m di campo.

AIDS [eɪdz] n abbr (= acquired immune or immuno-deficiency syndrome) A.I.D.S. f.

AIH n abbr = artificial insemination by husband.

ailing ['eɪlɪŋ] adj sofferente; (fig: economy, industry etc) in difficoltà.

ailment ['eɪlmənt] n indisposizione f.

aim [eɪm] vt: **to ~ sth at** (gun) mirare qc a, puntare qc a; (camera, remark) rivolgere qc a; (missile) lanciare qc contro; (blow etc) tirare qc a ♦ vi (also: **to take ~**) prendere la mira ♦ n mira; **to ~ at** mirare; **to ~ to do** aver l'intenzione di fare.

aimless ['eɪmlɪs] adj, **aimlessly** ['eɪmlɪslɪ] adv senza scopo.

ain't [eɪnt] (col) = **am not; aren't; isn't**.

air [ɛə*] n aria ♦ vt (room, bed) arieggiare; (clothes) far prendere aria a; (idea, grievance) esprimere pubblicamente, manifestare; (views) far conoscere ♦ cpd (currents) d'aria; (attack) aereo(a); **by ~** (travel) in aereo; **to be on the ~** (RADIO, TV: station) trasmettere; (: programme) essere in onda.

air bag n airbag m inv.

air base n base f aerea.

airbed ['ɛəbɛd] n (BRIT) materassino.

airborne ['ɛəbɔːn] adj (plane) in volo; (troops) aerotrasportato(a); **as soon as the plane was ~** appena l'aereo ebbe decollato.

air cargo n carico trasportato per via aerea.

air-conditioned ['ɛəkən'dɪʃənd] adj con or ad aria condizionata.

air conditioning n condizionamento d'aria.

air-cooled ['ɛəkuːld] adj raffreddato(a) ad

aria.

aircraft ['ɛəkrɑːft] n (pl inv) apparecchio.

aircraft carrier n portaerei f inv.

air cushion n cuscino gonfiabile; (TECH) cuscino d'aria.

airfield ['ɛəfiːld] n campo d'aviazione.

Air Force n aviazione f militare.

air freight n spedizione f di merci per via aerea; (goods) carico spedito per via aerea.

airgun ['ɛəgʌn] n fucile m ad aria compressa.

air hostess n hostess f inv.

airily ['ɛərɪlɪ] adv con disinvoltura.

airing ['ɛərɪŋ] n: to give an ~ to (linen) far prendere aria a; (room) arieggiare; (fig: ideas etc) ventilare.

air letter n (BRIT) aerogramma m.

airlift ['ɛəlɪft] n ponte m aereo.

airline ['ɛəlaɪn] n linea aerea.

airliner ['ɛəlaɪnə*] n aereo di linea.

airlock ['ɛəlɔk] n cassa d'aria.

air mail n posta aerea; by ~ per via or posta aerea.

air mattress n materassino gonfiabile.

airplane ['ɛəpleɪn] n (US) aeroplano.

air pocket n vuoto d'aria.

airport ['ɛəpɔːt] n aeroporto.

air rage n comportamento aggressivo dei passeggeri di un aereo.

air raid n incursione f aerea.

air rifle n fucile m ad aria compressa.

airsick ['ɛəsɪk] adj: to be ~ soffrire di mal d'aereo.

airspace ['ɛəspeɪs] n spazio aereo.

airspeed ['ɛəspiːd] n velocità f inv di crociera (AER).

airstrip ['ɛəstrɪp] n pista d'atterraggio.

air terminal n air-terminal m inv.

airtight ['ɛətaɪt] adj ermetico(a).

air time n (RADIO) spazio radiofonico; (TV) spazio televisivo.

air traffic control n controllo del traffico aereo.

air traffic controller n controllore m del traffico aereo.

airway ['ɛəweɪ] n (AVIAT) rotte fpl aeree; (ANAT) vie fpl respiratorie.

airy ['ɛərɪ] adj arioso(a); (manners) noncurante.

aisle [aɪl] n (of church) navata laterale; navata centrale; (of plane) corridoio.

aisle seat n (on plane) posto sul corridoio.

ajar [ə'dʒɑː*] adj socchiuso(a).

AK abbr (US) = Alaska.

aka abbr (= also known as) alias.

akin [ə'kɪn] prep simile a.

AL abbr (US) = Alabama.

Ala. abbr (US) = Alabama.

à la carte [ɑːlɑː'kɑːt] adv alla carta.

alacrity [ə'lækrɪtɪ] n: with ~ con prontezza.

alarm [ə'lɑːm] n allarme m ♦ vt allarmare.

alarm clock n sveglia.

alarmed [ə'lɑːmd] adj (person) allarmato(a); (house, car etc) dotato(a) di allarme.

alarming [ə'lɑːmɪŋ] adj allarmante, preoccupante.

alarmingly [ə'lɑːmɪŋlɪ] adv in modo allarmante; ~ close pericolosamente vicino.

alarmist [ə'lɑːmɪst] n allarmista m/f.

alas [ə'læs] excl ohimè!, ahimè!

Alas. abbr (US) = Alaska.

Alaska [ə'læskə] n Alasca.

Albania [æl'beɪnɪə] n Albania.

Albanian [æl'beɪnɪən] adj albanese ♦ n albanese m/f; (LING) albanese m.

albatross ['ælbətrɔs] n albatros m inv.

albeit [ɔːl'biːɪt] conj sebbene + sub, benché + sub.

album ['ælbəm] n album m inv; (L.P.) 33 giri m inv, L.P. m inv.

albumen ['ælbjumɪn] n albume m.

alchemy ['ælkɪmɪ] n alchimia.

alcohol ['ælkəhɔl] n alcool m.

alcohol-free ['ælkəhɔl'friː] adj analcolico(a).

alcoholic [ælkə'hɔlɪk] adj alcolico(a) ♦ n alcolizzato/a.

alcoholism ['ælkəhɔlɪzəm] n alcolismo.

alcove ['ælkəuv] n alcova.

alderman ['ɔːldəmən] n consigliere m comunale.

ale [eɪl] n birra.

alert [ə'lɔːt] adj vivo(a); (watchful) vigile ♦ n allarme m ♦ vt: to ~ sb (to sth) avvisare qn (di qc), avvertire qn (di qc); to ~ sb to the dangers of sth mettere qn in guardia contro qc; on the ~ all'erta.

Aleutian Islands [ə'luːʃən-] npl isole fpl Aleutine.

A level n (BRIT) diploma di studi superiori.

Alexandria [ælɪg'zændrɪə] n Alessandria (d'Egitto).

alfresco [æl'freskəu] adj, adv all'aperto.

algebra ['ældʒɪbrə] n algebra.

Algeria [æl'dʒɪərɪə] n Algeria.

Algerian [æl'dʒɪərɪən] adj, n algerino(a).

Algiers [æl'dʒɪəz] n Algeri f.

algorithm ['ælgərɪðəm] n algoritmo.

alias ['eɪlɪəs] adv alias ♦ n pseudonimo, falso nome m.

alibi ['ælɪbaɪ] n alibi m inv.

alien ['eɪlɪən] n straniero/a ♦ adj: ~ (to) estraneo(a) (a).

alienate ['eɪlɪəneɪt] vt alienare.

alienation [eɪlɪə'neɪʃən] n alienazione f.

alight [ə'laɪt] *adj* acceso(a) ♦ *vi* scendere; (*bird*) posarsi.

align [ə'laɪn] *vt* allineare.

alignment [ə'laɪnmənt] *n* allineamento; **out of ~ (with)** non allineato (con).

alike [ə'laɪk] *adj* simile ♦ *adv* allo stesso modo; **to look ~** assomigliarsi; **winter and summer ~** sia d'estate che d'inverno.

alimony ['ælɪmənɪ] *n* (*payment*) alimenti *mpl*.

alive [ə'laɪv] *adj* vivo(a); (*active*) attivo(a); **~ with** pieno(a) di; **~ to** conscio(a) di.

alkali ['ælkəlaɪ] *n* alcali *m inv*.

============================ *KEYWORD*

all [ɔːl] *adj* tutto(a); **~ day** tutto il giorno; **~ night** tutta la notte; **~ men** tutti gli uomini; **~ five girls** tutt'e cinque le ragazze; **~ five came** sono venuti tutti e cinque; **~ the books** tutti i libri; **~ the food** tutto il cibo; **~ the time** tutto il tempo; (*always*) sempre; **~ his life** tutta la vita; **for ~ their efforts** nonostante tutti i loro sforzi

♦ *pron* **1** tutto(a); **is that ~?** non c'è altro?; (*in shop*) basta così?; **~ of them** tutti(e); **~ of it** tutto(a); **I ate it ~, I ate ~ of it** l'ho mangiato tutto; **~ of us went** tutti noi siamo andati; **~ of the boys went** tutti i ragazzi sono andati

2 (*in phrases*): **above ~** soprattutto; **after ~** dopotutto; **at ~: not at ~** (*in answer to question*) niente affatto; (*in answer to thanks*) prego!, di niente!, s'immagini!; **I'm not at ~ tired** non sono affatto stanco; **anything at ~ will do** andrà bene qualsiasi cosa; **~ in ~** tutto sommato

♦ *adv*: **~ alone** tutto(a) solo(a); **to be/feel ~ in** (*BRIT col*) essere/sentirsi sfinito(a) *or* distrutto(a); **~ out** *adv*: **to go ~ out** mettercela tutta; **it's not as hard as ~ that** non è poi così difficile; **~ the more/ the better** tanto più/meglio; **~ but** quasi; **the score is two ~** il punteggio è di due a due *or* è due pari.

allay [ə'leɪ] *vt* (*fears*) dissipare.

all clear *n* (*MIL*) cessato allarme *m inv*; (*fig*) okay *m*.

allegation [ælɪ'geɪʃən] *n* asserzione *f*.

allege [ə'lɛdʒ] *vt* asserire; **he is ~d to have said ...** avrebbe detto che ....

alleged [ə'lɛdʒd] *adj* presunto(a).

allegedly [ə'lɛdʒɪdlɪ] *adv* secondo quanto si asserisce.

allegiance [ə'liːdʒəns] *n* fedeltà.

allegory ['ælɪgərɪ] *n* allegoria.

all-embracing ['ɔːlɪm'breɪsɪŋ] *adj*

universale.

allergic [ə'lɜːdʒɪk] *adj*: **~ to** allergico(a) a.

allergy ['ælədʒɪ] *n* allergia.

alleviate [ə'liːvɪeɪt] *vt* alleviare.

alley ['ælɪ] *n* vicolo; (*in garden*) vialetto.

alleyway ['ælɪweɪ] *n* vicolo.

alliance [ə'laɪəns] *n* alleanza.

allied ['ælaɪd] *adj* alleato(a).

alligator ['ælɪgeɪtə*] *n* alligatore *m*.

all-important ['ɔːlɪm'pɔːtənt] *adj* importantissimo(a).

all-in ['ɔːlɪn] *adj* (*BRIT: also adv: charge*) tutto compreso.

all-in wrestling *n* (*BRIT*) lotta americana.

alliteration [əlɪtə'reɪʃən] *n* allitterazione *f*.

all-night ['ɔːl'naɪt] *adj* aperto(a) (*or che dura*) tutta la notte.

allocate ['æləkeɪt] *vt* (*share out*) distribuire; (*duties, sum, time*): **to ~ sth to** assegnare qc a; **to ~ sth for** stanziare qc per.

allocation [æləu'keɪʃən] *n*: **~ (of money)** stanziamento.

allot [ə'lɔt] *vt* (*share out*) spartire; **to ~ sth to** (*time*) dare qc a; (*duties*) assegnare qc a; **in the ~ted time** nel tempo fissato *or* prestabilito.

allotment [ə'lɔtmənt] *n* (*share*) spartizione *f*; (*garden*) lotto di terra.

all-out ['ɔːl'aut] *adj* (*effort etc*) totale ♦ *adv*: **to go all out for** mettercela tutta per.

allow [ə'lau] *vt* (*practice, behaviour*) permettere; (*sum to spend etc*) accordare; (*sum, time estimated*) dare; (*concede*): **to ~ that** ammettere che; **to ~ sb to do** permettere a qn di fare; **he is ~ed to (do it)** lo può fare; **smoking is not ~ed** è vietato fumare, non è permesso fumare; **we must ~ 3 days for the journey** dobbiamo calcolare 3 giorni per il viaggio.

▶**allow for** *vt fus* tener conto di.

allowance [ə'lauəns] *n* (*money received*) assegno; (*for travelling, accommodation*) indennità *f inv*; (*TAX*) detrazione *f* di imposta; **to make ~(s) for** tener conto di; (*person*) scusare.

alloy ['ælɔɪ] *n* lega.

all right *adv* (*feel, work*) bene; (*as answer*) va bene.

all-round ['ɔːl'raund] *adj* completo(a).

all-rounder [ɔːl'raundə*] *n* (*BRIT*): **to be a good ~** essere bravo(a) in tutto.

allspice ['ɔːlspaɪs] *n* pepe *m* della Giamaica.

all-time ['ɔːl'taɪm] *adj* (*record*) assoluto(a).

allude [ə'luːd] *vi*: **to ~ to** alludere a.

alluring [ə'ljuərɪŋ] *adj* seducente.

allusion [ə'luːʒən] *n* allusione *f*.

alluvium [ə'luːvɪəm] *n* materiale *m*

alluvionale.
ally n ['ælaɪ] alleato ♦ vt [ə'laɪ]: **to** ~ **o.s. with** allearsi con.
almighty [ɔːl'maɪtɪ] adj onnipotente.
almond ['ɑːmənd] n mandorla.
almost ['ɔːlməʊst] adv quasi; **he** ~ **fell** per poco non è caduto.
alms [ɑːmz] n elemosina.
aloft [ə'lɒft] adv in alto; (NAUT) sull'alberatura.
alone [ə'ləʊn] adj, adv solo(a); **to leave sb** ~ lasciare qn in pace; **to leave sth** ~ lasciare stare qc; **let** ~ ... figuriamoci poi ..., tanto meno ....
along [ə'lɒŋ] prep lungo ♦ adv: **is he coming** ~**?** viene con noi?; **he was limping** ~ veniva zoppicando; ~ **with** insieme con.
alongside [ə'lɒŋ'saɪd] prep accanto a; lungo ♦ adv accanto; (NAUT) sottobordo; **we brought our boat** ~ (of a pier/shore etc) abbiamo accostato la barca (al molo/alla riva etc).
aloof [ə'luːf] adj distaccato(a) ♦ adv a distanza, in disparte; **to stand** ~ tenersi a distanza or in disparte.
aloofness [ə'luːfnɪs] n distacco, riserbo.
aloud [ə'laud] adv ad alta voce.
alphabet ['ælfəbɛt] n alfabeto.
alphabetical [ælfə'bɛtɪkəl] adj alfabetico(a); **in** ~ **order** in ordine alfabetico.
alphanumeric [ælfənjuː'mɛrɪk] adj alfanumerico(a).
alpine ['ælpaɪn] adj alpino(a); ~ **hut** rifugio alpino; ~ **pasture** pascolo alpestre; ~ **skiing** sci alpino.
Alps [ælps] npl: **the** ~ le Alpi.
already [ɔːl'rɛdɪ] adv già.
alright ['ɔːl'raɪt] adv (BRIT) = **all right**.
Alsatian [æl'seɪʃən] n (BRIT: dog) pastore m tedesco, (cane m) lupo.
also ['ɔːlsəʊ] adv anche.
Alta. abbr (Canada) = Alberta.
altar ['ɔːltə*] n altare m.
alter ['ɔːltə*] vt, vi alterare.
alteration [ɔːltə'reɪʃən] n modificazione f, alterazione f; ~**s** (SEWING, ARCHIT) modifiche fpl; **timetable subject to** ~ orario soggetto a variazioni.
altercation [ɔːltə'keɪʃən] n alterco, litigio.
alternate adj [ɔl'tɜːnɪt] alterno(a) ♦ vi ['ɔltɜːneɪt] alternare; **on** ~ **days** ogni due giorni.
alternately [ɔl'tɜːnɪtlɪ] adv alternatamente.
alternating current ['ɔltəneɪtɪŋ-] n corrente f alternata.
alternative [ɔl'tɜːnətɪv] adj (solutions) alternativo(a); (solution) altro(a) ♦ n

(choice) alternativa; (other possibility) altra possibilità.
alternatively [ɔl'tɜːnətɪvlɪ] adv altrimenti, come alternativa.
alternative medicine n medicina alternativa.
alternator ['ɔltɜːneɪtə*] n (AUT) alternatore m.
although [ɔːl'ðəʊ] conj benché + sub, sebbene + sub.
altitude ['æltɪtjuːd] n altitudine f.
alto ['æltəʊ] n contralto.
altogether [ɔːltə'gɛðə*] adv del tutto, completamente; (on the whole) tutto considerato; (in all) in tutto; **how much is that** ~**?** quant'è in tutto?
altruism ['æltruɪzəm] n altruismo.
altruistic [æltru'ɪstɪk] adj altruistico(a).
aluminium [ælju'mɪnɪəm], (US) **aluminum** [ə'luːmɪnəm] n alluminio.
always ['ɔːlweɪz] adv sempre.
Alzheimer's ['æltshaɪməz] n (also: ~ **disease**) morbo di Alzheimer.
AM abbr (= amplitude modulation) AM ♦ n abbr (= Assembly Member) deputato gallese.
am [æm] vb see **be**.
a.m. adv abbr (= ante meridiem) della mattina.
AMA n abbr = American Medical Association.
amalgam [ə'mælgəm] n amalgama m.
amalgamate [ə'mælgəmeɪt] vt amalgamare ♦ vi amalgamarsi.
amalgamation [əmælgə'meɪʃən] n amalgamazione f; (COMM) fusione f.
amass [ə'mæs] vt ammassare.
amateur ['æmətə*] n dilettante m/f ♦ adj (SPORT) dilettante; ~ **dramatics** n filodrammatica.
amateurish ['æmətərɪʃ] adj (pej) da dilettante.
amaze [ə'meɪz] vt stupire; **to be** ~**d (at)** essere sbalordito(a) (da).
amazement [ə'meɪzmənt] n stupore m.
amazing [ə'meɪzɪŋ] adj sorprendente, sbalorditivo(a); (bargain, offer) sensazionale.
amazingly [ə'meɪzɪŋlɪ] adv incredibilmente, sbalorditivamente.
Amazon ['æməzən] n (MYTHOLOGY) Amazzone f; (river): **the** ~ il Rio delle Amazzoni ♦ cpd (basin, jungle) amazzonico(a).
Amazonian [æmə'zəunɪən] adj amazzonico(a).
ambassador [æm'bæsədə*] n ambasciatore/trice.
amber ['æmbə*] n ambra; **at** ~ (BRIT AUT) giallo.

ambidextrous [æmbɪ'dɛkstrəs] *adj* ambidestro(a).

ambience ['æmbɪəns] *n* ambiente *m*.

ambiguity [æmbɪ'gjuɪtɪ] *n* ambiguità *f inv*.

ambiguous [æm'bɪgjuəs] *adj* ambiguo(a).

ambition [æm'bɪʃən] *n* ambizione *f*; **to achieve one's ~** realizzare le proprie aspirazioni *or* ambizioni.

ambitious [æm'bɪʃəs] *adj* ambizioso(a).

ambivalent [æm'bɪvələnt] *adj* ambivalente.

amble ['æmbl] *vi* (*gen*: **to ~ along**) camminare tranquillamente.

ambulance ['æmbjuləns] *n* ambulanza.

ambush ['æmbuʃ] *n* imboscata ♦ *vt* fare un'imboscata a.

ameba [ə'miːbə] *n* (*US*) = **amoeba**.

ameliorate [ə'miːlɪəreɪt] *vt* migliorare.

amen ['ɑː'mɛn] *excl* così sia, amen.

amenable [ə'miːnəbl] *adj*: **~ to** (*advice etc*) ben disposto(a) a.

amend [ə'mɛnd] *vt* (*law*) emendare; (*text*) correggere ♦ *vi* emendarsi; **to make ~s** fare ammenda.

amendment [ə'mɛndmənt] *n* emendamento; correzione *f*.

amenities [ə'miːnɪtɪz] *npl* attrezzature *fpl* ricreative e culturali.

amenity [ə'miːnɪtɪ] *n* amenità *f inv*.

America [ə'mɛrɪkə] *n* America.

American [ə'mɛrɪkən] *adj*, *n* americano(a).

americanize [ə'mɛrɪkənaɪz] *vt* americanizzare.

amethyst ['æmɪθɪst] *n* ametista.

Amex ['æmɛks] *n abbr* – American Stock Exchange.

amiable ['eɪmɪəbl] *adj* amabile, gentile.

amicable ['æmɪkəbl] *adj* amichevole.

amicably ['æmɪkəblɪ] *adv*: **to part ~** lasciarsi senza rancori.

amid(st) [ə'mɪd(st)] *prep* fra, tra, in mezzo a.

amiss [ə'mɪs] *adj*, *adv*: **there's something ~** c'è qualcosa che non va bene; **don't take it ~** non avertene a male.

ammo ['æməu] *n abbr* (*col*) = **ammunition**.

ammonia [ə'məunɪə] *n* ammoniaca.

ammunition [æmju'nɪʃən] *n* munizioni *fpl*; (*fig*) arma.

ammunition dump *n* deposito di munizioni.

amnesia [æm'niːzɪə] *n* amnesia.

amnesty ['æmnɪstɪ] *n* amnistia; **to grant an ~ to** concedere l'amnistia a, amnistiare.

Amnesty International *n* Amnesty International *f*.

amoeba, (*US*) **ameba** [ə'miːbə] *n* ameba.

amok [ə'mɔk] *adv*: **to run ~** diventare pazzo(a) furioso(a).

among(st) [ə'mʌŋ(st)] *prep* fra, tra, in mezzo a.

amoral [eɪ'mɔrəl] *adj* amorale.

amorous ['æmərəs] *adj* amoroso(a).

amorphous [ə'mɔːfəs] *adj* amorfo(a).

amortization [əmɔːtaɪ'zeɪʃən] *n* (*COMM*) ammortamento.

amount [ə'maunt] *n* (*sum of money*) somma; (*of bill etc*) importo; (*quantity*) quantità *f inv* ♦ *vi*: **to ~ to** (*total*) ammontare a; (*be same as*) essere come; **this ~s to a refusal** questo equivale a un rifiuto.

amp(ère) ['æmp(ɛə*)] *n* ampere *m inv*; **a 13 ~ plug** una spina con fusibile da 13 ampere.

ampersand ['æmpəsænd] *n* e *f* commerciale.

amphetamine [æm'fɛtəmiːn] *n* anfetamina.

amphibian [æm'fɪbɪən] *n* anfibio.

amphibious [æm'fɪbɪəs] *adj* anfibio(a).

amphitheatre, (*US*) **amphitheater** ['æmfɪθɪətə*] *n* anfiteatro.

ample ['æmpl] *adj* ampio(a); spazioso(a); (*enough*): **this is ~** questo è più che sufficiente; **to have ~ time/room** avere assai tempo/posto.

amplifier ['æmplɪfaɪə*] *n* amplificatore *m*.

amplify ['æmplɪfaɪ] *vt* amplificare.

amply ['æmplɪ] *adv* ampiamente.

ampoule, (*US*) **ampule** ['æmpuːl] *n* (*MED*) fiala.

amputate ['æmpjuteɪt] *vt* amputare.

amputee [æmpju'tiː] *n* mutilato/a, chi ha subito un'amputazione.

Amsterdam [æmstə'dæm] *n* Amsterdam *f*.

amt *abbr* = **amount**.

amuck [ə'mʌk] *adv* = **amok**.

amuse [ə'mjuːz] *vt* divertire; **to ~ o.s. with sth/by doing sth** divertirsi con qc/a fare qc; **to be ~d at** essere divertito da; **he was not ~d** non l'ha trovato divertente.

amusement [ə'mjuːzmənt] *n* divertimento; **much to my ~** con mio grande spasso.

amusement arcade *n* sala giochi (*solo con macchinette a gettoni*).

amusement park *n* luna park *m inv*.

amusing [ə'mjuːzɪŋ] *adj* divertente.

an [æn, ən, n] *indef art see* **a**.

ANA *n abbr* = American Newspaper Association; American Nurses Association.

anachronism [ə'nækrənɪzəm] *n* anacronismo.

anaemia [ə'niːmɪə] *n* anemia.

anaemic [ə'niːmɪk] *adj* anemico(a).

anaesthetic [ænɪs'θɛtɪk] *adj* anestetico(a) ♦ *n* anestetico; **local/general ~** anestesia locale/totale; **under the ~** sotto anestesia.

anaesthetist [æ'niːsθɪtɪst] *n* anestesista *m/f*.

anagram ['ænəgræm] n anagramma m.
anal ['eɪnl] adj anale.
analgesic [ænæl'dʒiːsɪk] adj analgesico(a)
♦ n analgesico.
analogous [ə'næləgəs] adj: ~ to or with analogo(a) a.
analog(ue) ['ænələg] adj (watch, computer) analogico(a).
analogy [ə'nælədʒɪ] n analogia; to draw an ~ between fare un'analogia tra.
analyse ['ænəlaɪz] vt (BRIT) analizzare.
analysis, pl **analyses** [ə'næləsɪs, -siːz] n analisi f inv; in the last ~ in ultima analisi.
analyst ['ænəlɪst] n (political ~ etc) analista m/f; (US) (psic)analista m/f.
analytic(al) [ænə'lɪtɪk(l)] adj analitico(a).
analyze ['ænəlaɪz] vt (US) = analyse.
anarchic [æ'nɑːkɪk] adj anarchico(a).
anarchist ['ænəkɪst] adj, n anarchico(a).
anarchy ['ænəkɪ] n anarchia.
anathema [ə'næθɪmə] n: it is ~ to him non ne vuol neanche sentir parlare.
anatomical [ænə'tɔmɪkl] adj anatomico(a).
anatomy [ə'nætəmɪ] n anatomia.
ANC n abbr = African National Congress.
ancestor ['ænsɪstə*] n antenato/a.
ancestral [æn'sɛstrəl] adj avito(a).
ancestry ['ænsɪstrɪ] n antenati mpl; ascendenza.
anchor ['æŋkə*] n ancora ♦ vi (also: to drop ~) gettare l'ancora ♦ vt ancorare; to weigh ~ salpare or levare l'ancora.
anchorage ['æŋkərɪdʒ] n ancoraggio.
anchor man n (TV, RADIO) anchorman m inv.
anchor woman n (TV, RADIO) anchorwoman f inv.
anchovy ['æntʃəvɪ] n acciuga.
ancient ['eɪnʃənt] adj antico(a); (fig) anziano(a); ~ monument monumento storico.
ancillary [æn'sɪlərɪ] adj ausiliario(a).
and [ænd] conj e (often ed before vowel); ~ so on e così via; try ~ do it prova a farlo; come ~ sit here vieni a sedere qui; better ~ better sempre meglio; more ~ more sempre di più.
Andes ['ændiːz] npl: the ~ le Ande.
Andorra [æn'dɔːrə] n Andorra.
anecdote ['ænɪkdəut] n aneddoto.
anemia [ə'niːmɪə] etc = anaemia etc.
anemone [ə'nɛmənɪ] n (BOT) anemone m; (sea ~) anemone m di mare, attinia.
anesthetic [ænɪs'θɛtɪk] etc = anaesthetic etc.
anew [ə'njuː] adv di nuovo.
angel ['eɪndʒəl] n angelo.
angel dust n sedativo usato a scopo

allucinogeno.
anger ['æŋgə*] n rabbia ♦ vt arrabbiare.
angina [æn'dʒaɪnə] n angina pectoris.
angle ['æŋgl] n angolo ♦ vi: to ~ for (fig) cercare di avere; from their ~ dal loro punto di vista.
angler ['æŋglə*] n pescatore m con la lenza.
Anglican ['æŋglɪkən] adj, n anglicano(a).
anglicize ['æŋglɪsaɪz] vt anglicizzare.
angling ['æŋglɪŋ] n pesca con la lenza.
Anglo- ['æŋgləu] prefix anglo...; ~Italian adj, n italobritannico(a).
Anglo-Saxon ['æŋgləu'sæksən] adj, n anglosassone (m/f).
Angola [æŋ'gəulə] n Angola.
Angolan [æŋ'gəulən] adj, n angolano(a).
angrily ['æŋgrɪlɪ] adv con rabbia.
angry ['æŋgrɪ] adj arrabbiato(a), furioso(a); to be ~ with sb/at sth essere in collera con qn/per qc; to get ~ arrabbiarsi; to make sb ~ fare arrabbiare qn.
anguish ['æŋgwɪʃ] n angoscia.
anguished ['æŋgwɪʃt] adj angosciato(a), pieno(a) d'angoscia.
angular ['æŋgjulə*] adj angolare.
animal ['ænɪməl] adj, n animale (m).
animal rights npl diritti mpl degli animali.
animate vt ['ænɪmeɪt] animare ♦ adj ['ænɪmɪt] animato(a).
animated ['ænɪmeɪtɪd] adj animato(a).
animation [ænɪ'meɪʃən] n animazione f.
animosity [ænɪ'mɔsɪtɪ] n animosità.
aniseed ['ænɪsiːd] n semi mpl di anice.
Ankara ['æŋkərə] n Ankara.
ankle ['æŋkl] n caviglia.
ankle socks npl calzini mpl.
annex n ['ænɛks] (also: BRIT: annexe) edificio annesso ♦ vt [ə'nɛks] annettere.
annexation [ænɛk'seɪʃən] n annessione f.
annihilate [ə'naɪəleɪt] vt annientare.
annihilation [ənaɪə'leɪʃən] n annientamento.
anniversary [ænɪ'vɔːsərɪ] n anniversario.
anniversary dinner n cena commemorativa.
annotate ['ænəuteɪt] vt annotare.
announce [ə'nauns] vt annunciare; he ~d that he wasn't going ha dichiarato che non (ci) sarebbe andato.
announcement [ə'naunsmənt] n annuncio; (letter, card) partecipazione f; I'd like to make an ~ ho una comunicazione da fare.
announcer [ə'naunsə*] n (RADIO, TV: between programmes) annunciatore/trice; (: in a programme) presentatore/trice.
annoy [ə'nɔɪ] vt dare fastidio a; to be ~ed (at sth/with sb) essere seccato or irritato

(per qc/con qn); **don't get** ~**ed!** non
irritarti!
annoyance [əˈnɔɪəns] n fastidio; (*cause of*
~) noia.
annoying [əˈnɔɪɪŋ] *adj* irritante,
seccante.
annual [ˈænjuəl] *adj* annuale ♦ n (*BOT*)
pianta annua; (*book*) annuario.
annual general meeting (AGM) n (*BRIT*)
assemblea generale.
annually [ˈænjuəlɪ] *adv* annualmente.
annual report n relazione f annuale.
annuity [əˈnjuːɪtɪ] n annualità f inv; **life** ~
vitalizio.
annul [əˈnʌl] *vt* annullare; (*law*) rescindere.
annulment [əˈnʌlmənt] n annullamento;
rescissione f.
annum [ˈænəm] n see **per annum**.
Annunciation [ənʌnsɪˈeɪʃən] n
Annunciazione f.
anode [ˈænəud] n anodo.
anoint [əˈnɔɪnt] *vt* ungere.
anomalous [əˈnɔmələs] *adj* anomalo(a).
anomaly [əˈnɔməlɪ] n anomalia.
anon. [əˈnɔn] *abbr* = **anonymous.**
anonymity [ænəˈnɪmɪtɪ] n anonimato.
anonymous [əˈnɔnɪməs] *adj* anonimo(a); **to
remain** ~ mantenere l'anonimato.
anorak [ˈænəræk] n giacca a vento.
anorexia [ænəˈrɛksɪə] n (*also:* ~ **nervosa**)
anoressia.
anorexic [ænəˈrɛksɪk] *adj, n* anoressico(a).
another [əˈnʌðə*] *adj:* ~ **book** (*one more*)
un altro libro, ancora un libro; (*a
different one*) un altro libro ♦ *pron* un
altro(un'altra), ancora uno(a); ~ **drink?**
ancora qualcosa da bere?; **in** ~ **5 years**
fra altri 5 anni; *see also* **one.**
ANSI n *abbr* (= *American National Standards
Institute*) Istituto americano di
standardizzazione.
answer [ˈɑːnsə*] n risposta; soluzione f ♦ vi
rispondere ♦ *vt* (*reply to*) rispondere a;
(*problem*) risolvere; (*prayer*) esaudire; **in**
~ **to your letter** in risposta alla sua
lettera; **to** ~ **the phone** rispondere (al
telefono); **to** ~ **the bell** rispondere al
campanello; **to** ~ **the door** aprire la
porta.
▶**answer back** *vi* ribattere.
▶**answer for** *vt fus* essere responsabile di.
▶**answer to** *vt fus* (*description*)
corrispondere a.
answerable [ˈɑːnsərəbl] *adj:* ~ **(to sb/for
sth)** responsabile (verso qn/di qc); **I am** ~
to no one non devo rispondere a
nessuno.
answering machine [ˈɑːnsərɪŋ-] n

segreteria (telefonica) automatica.
ant [ænt] n formica.
antagonism [ænˈtægənɪzəm] n
antagonismo.
antagonist [ænˈtægənɪst] n antagonista m/f.
antagonistic [æntægəˈnɪstɪk] *adj*
antagonistico(a).
antagonize [ænˈtægənaɪz] *vt* provocare
l'ostilità di.
Antarctic [æntˈɑːktɪk] n: **the** ~ l'Antartide f
♦ *adj* antartico(a).
Antarctica [æntˈɑːktɪkə] n Antartide f.
Antarctic Circle n Circolo polare
antartico.
Antarctic Ocean n Oceano antartico.
ante [ˈæntɪ] n (*CARDS, fig*): **to up the** ~
alzare la posta in palio.
ante... [ˈæntɪ] *prefix* anti..., ante..., pre....
anteater [ˈæntiːtə*] n formichiere m.
antecedent [æntɪˈsiːdənt] n antecedente m,
precedente m.
antechamber [ˈæntɪtʃeɪmbə*] n
anticamera.
antelope [ˈæntɪləup] n antilope f.
antenatal [ˈæntɪˈneɪtl] *adj* prenatale.
antenatal clinic n assistenza medica
preparto.
antenna, pl antennae [ænˈtɛnə, -niː] n
antenna.
anthem [ˈænθəm] n antifona; **national** ~
inno nazionale.
ant-hill [ˈænthɪl] n formicaio.
anthology [ænˈθɔlədʒɪ] n antologia.
anthropologist [ænθrəˈpɔlədʒɪst] n
antropologo/a.
anthropology [ænθrəˈpɔlədʒɪ] n
antropologia.
anti- [ˈæntɪ] *prefix* anti....
anti-aircraft [ˈæntɪˈɛəkrɑːft] *adj*
antiaereo(a).
anti-aircraft defence n difesa antiaerea.
antiballistic [æntɪbəˈlɪstɪk] *adj*
antibalistico(a).
antibiotic [ˈæntɪbaɪˈɔtɪk] *adj* antibiotico(a)
♦ n antibiotico.
antibody [ˈæntɪbɔdɪ] n anticorpo.
anticipate [ænˈtɪsɪpeɪt] *vt* prevedere;
pregustare; (*wishes, request*) prevenire;
as ~**d** come previsto; **this is worse than I**
~**d** è peggio di quel che immaginavo *or*
pensavo.
anticipation [æntɪsɪˈpeɪʃən] n anticipazione
f; (*expectation*) aspettative fpl; **thanking
you in** ~ vi ringrazio in anticipo.
anticlimax [ˈæntɪˈklaɪmæks] n: **it was an** ~
fu una completa delusione.
anticlockwise [ˈæntɪˈklɔkwaɪz] *adj* in senso
antiorario.

antics ['æntɪks] npl buffonerie fpl.
anticyclone ['æntɪ'saɪkləun] n anticiclone m.
antidote ['æntɪdəut] n antidoto.
antifreeze ['æntɪfriːz] n anticongelante m.
anti-globalization ['æntɪgləubəlaɪ'zeɪʃən] adj antiglobalizzazione inv.
antihistamine [æntɪ'hɪstəmɪn] n antistaminico.
Antilles [æn'tɪliːz] npl: the ~ le Antille.
antipathy [æn'tɪpəθɪ] n antipatia.
antiperspirant ['æntɪ'pəːspərənt] adj antitraspirante.
Antipodean [æntɪpə'diːən] adj degli Antipodi.
Antipodes [æn'tɪpədiːz] npl: the ~ gli Antipodi.
antiquarian [æntɪ'kwɛərɪən] adj: ~ bookshop libreria antiquaria ♦ n antiquario/a.
antiquated ['æntɪkweɪtɪd] adj antiquato(a).
antique [æn'tiːk] n antichità f inv ♦ adj antico(a).
antique dealer n antiquario/a.
antique shop n negozio d'antichità.
antiquity [æn'tɪkwɪtɪ] n antichità f inv.
anti-semitic ['æntɪsɪ'mɪtɪk] adj antisemitico(a), antisemita.
anti-semitism ['æntɪ'sɛmɪtɪzəm] n antisemitismo.
antiseptic [æntɪ'sɛptɪk] adj antisettico(a) ♦ n antisettico.
antisocial ['æntɪ'səuʃəl] adj asociale; (against society) antisociale.
antitank [æntɪ'tæŋk] adj anticarro inv.
antithesis, pl antitheses [æn'tɪθɪsɪs, -siːz] n antitesi f inv; (contrast) carattere m antitetico.
anti-trust [æntɪ'trʌst] adj (COMM): ~ legislation legislazione f antitrust inv.
antlers ['æntləz] npl palchi mpl.
Antwerp ['æntwəːp] n Anversa.
anus ['eɪnəs] n ano.
anvil ['ænvɪl] n incudine f.
anxiety [æŋ'zaɪətɪ] n ansia; (keenness): ~ to do smania di fare.
anxious ['æŋkʃəs] adj ansioso(a), inquieto(a); (keen): ~ to do/that impaziente di fare/che + sub; I'm very ~ about you sono molto preoccupato or in pensiero per te.
anxiously ['æŋkʃəslɪ] adv ansiosamente, con ansia.

=================== KEYWORD

any ['ɛnɪ] adj 1 (in questions etc): have you ~ butter? hai del burro?, hai un po' di burro?; have you ~ children? hai

bambini?; if there are ~ tickets left se ci sono ancora (dei) biglietti, se c'è ancora qualche biglietto
2 (with negative): I haven't ~ money/books non ho soldi/libri; without ~ difficulty senza nessuna or alcuna difficoltà
3 (no matter which) qualsiasi, qualunque; choose ~ book you like scegli un libro qualsiasi
4 (in phrases): in ~ case in ogni caso; ~ day now da un giorno all'altro; at ~ moment in qualsiasi momento, da un momento all'altro; at ~ rate ad ogni modo
♦ pron 1 (in questions, with negative): have you got ~? ne hai?; can ~ of you sing? qualcuno di voi sa cantare?; I haven't ~ (of them) non ne ho
2 (no matter which one(s)): take ~ of those books (you like) prendi uno qualsiasi di quei libri
♦ adv 1 (in questions etc): do you want ~ more soup/sandwiches? vuoi ancora un po' di minestra/degli altri panini?; are you feeling ~ better? ti senti meglio?
2 (with negative): I can't hear him ~ more non lo sento più; don't wait ~ longer non aspettare più.

anybody ['ɛnɪbɔdɪ] pron qualsiasi persona; (in interrogative sentences) qualcuno; (in negative sentences): I don't see ~ non vedo nessuno.
anyhow ['ɛnɪhau] adv in qualsiasi modo; (haphazard) come capita; I shall go ~ ci andrò lo stesso or comunque.
anyone ['ɛnɪwʌn] pron = anybody.
anyplace ['ɛnɪpleɪs] pron (US col) = anywhere.
anything ['ɛnɪθɪŋ] pron qualsiasi cosa; (in interrogative sentences) qualcosa; (in negative sentences) non ... niente, non ... nulla; ~ else? (in shop) basta (così)?; it can cost ~ between £15 and £20 può costare qualcosa come 15 o 20 sterline.
anytime ['ɛnɪtaɪm] adv in qualunque momento; quando vuole.
anyway ['ɛnɪweɪ] adv in or ad ogni modo.
anywhere ['ɛnɪwɛə*] adv da qualsiasi parte; (in interrogative sentences) da qualche parte; I don't see him ~ non lo vedo da nessuna parte; ~ in the world dovunque nel mondo.
Anzac ['ænzæk] n abbr (= Australia-New Zealand Army Corps) A.N.Z.A.C. m.
Anzac Day n see boxed note.

ANZAC DAY

L'Anzac Day è una festa nazionale australiana e neozelandese che cade il 25 aprile e commemora il famoso sbarco delle forze armate congiunte dei due paesi a Gallipoli nel 1915, durante la prima guerra mondiale.

apart [ə'pɑːt] *adv* (*to one side*) a parte; (*separately*) separatamente; **with one's legs** ~ con le gambe divaricate; **10 miles/a long way** ~ a 10 miglia di distanza/molto lontani l'uno dall'altro; **they are living** ~ sono separati; ~ **from** *prep* a parte, eccetto.
apartheid [ə'pɑːteɪt] *n* apartheid *f*.
apartment [ə'pɑːtmənt] *n* (*US*) appartamento; ~**s** *npl* appartamento ammobiliato.
apartment building *n* (*US*) stabile *m*, caseggiato.
apathetic [æpə'θɛtɪk] *adj* apatico(a).
apathy ['æpəθɪ] *n* apatia.
APB *n abbr* (*US*: = *all points bulletin*: *police expression*) *espressione della polizia che significa "trovate e arrestate il sospetto"*.
ape [eɪp] *n* scimmia ♦ *vt* scimmiottare.
Apennines ['æpənaɪnz] *npl*: **the** ~ gli Apennini.
aperitif [ə'pɛrɪtiːf] *n* aperitivo.
aperture ['æpətʃjuə*] *n* apertura.
APEX ['eɪpɛks] *n abbr* (*AVIAT*: = *advance purchase excursion*) APEX *m inv*.
apex ['eɪpɛks] *n* apice *m*.
aphrodisiac [æfrəu'dɪzɪæk] *adj* afrodisiaco(a) ♦ *n* afrodisiaco.
apiece [ə'piːs] *adv* ciascuno(a).
aplomb [ə'plɔm] *n* disinvoltura.
APO *n abbr* (*US*: = *Army Post Office*) *ufficio postale dell'esercito*.
apocalypse [ə'pɔkəlɪps] *n* apocalisse *f*.
apolitical [eɪpə'lɪtɪkl] *adj* apolitico(a).
apologetic [əpɔlə'dʒɛtɪk] *adj* (*tone*, *letter*) di scusa; **to be very** ~ **about** scusarsi moltissimo di.
apologetically [əpɔlə'dʒɛtɪkəlɪ] *adv* per scusarsi.
apologize [ə'pɔlədʒaɪz] *vi*: **to** ~ (**for sth to sb**) scusarsi (di qc a qn), chiedere scusa (a qn per qc).
apology [ə'pɔlədʒɪ] *n* scuse *fpl*; **please accept my apologies** la prego di accettare le mie scuse.
apoplexy ['æpəplɛksɪ] *n* apoplessia.
apostle [ə'pɔsl] *n* apostolo.
apostrophe [ə'pɔstrəfɪ] *n* (*sign*) apostrofo.

appal [ə'pɔːl] *vt* atterrire; sgomentare.
Appalachian Mountains [æpə'leɪʃən-] *npl*: **the** ~ i Monti Appalachi.
appalling [ə'pɔːlɪŋ] *adj* spaventoso(a); **she's an** ~ **cook** è un disastro come cuoca.
apparatus [æpə'reɪtəs] *n* apparato.
apparel [ə'pærl] *n* (*US*) abbigliamento, confezioni *fpl*.
apparent [ə'pærənt] *adj* evidente.
apparently [ə'pærəntlɪ] *adv* evidentemente, a quanto pare.
apparition [æpə'rɪʃən] *n* apparizione *f*.
appeal [ə'piːl] *vi* (*LAW*) appellarsi alla legge ♦ *n* (*LAW*) appello; (*request*) richiesta; (*charm*) attrattiva; **to** ~ **for** chiedere (con insistenza); **to** ~ **to** (*subj*: *person*) appellarsi a; (: *thing*) piacere a; **to** ~ **to sb for mercy** chiedere pietà a qn; **it doesn't** ~ **to me** mi dice poco; **right of** ~ diritto d'appello.
appealing [ə'piːlɪŋ] *adj* (*moving*) commovente; (*attractive*) attraente.
appear [ə'pɪə*] *vi* apparire; (*LAW*) comparire; (*publication*) essere pubblicato(a); (*seem*) sembrare; **it would** ~ **that** sembra che; **to** ~ **in Hamlet** recitare nell'Amleto; **to** ~ **on TV** presentarsi in televisione.
appearance [ə'pɪərəns] *n* apparizione *f*; (*look*, *aspect*) aspetto; **to put in** *or* **make an** ~ fare atto di presenza; **by order of** ~ (*THEAT*) in ordine di apparizione; **to keep up** ~**s** salvare le apparenze; **to all** ~**s** a giudicar dalle apparenze.
appease [ə'piːz] *vt* calmare, appagare.
appeasement [ə'piːzmənt] *n* (*POL*) appeasement *m inv*.
append [ə'pɛnd] *vt* (*COMPUT*) aggiungere in coda.
appendage [ə'pɛndɪdʒ] *n* aggiunta.
appendicitis [əpɛndɪ'saɪtɪs] *n* appendicite *f*.
appendix, *pl* **appendices** [ə'pɛndɪks, -siːz] *n* appendice *f*; **to have one's** ~ **out** operarsi *or* farsi operare di appendicite.
appetite ['æpɪtaɪt] *n* appetito; **that walk has given me an** ~ la passeggiata mi ha messo appetito.
appetizer ['æpɪtaɪzə*] *n* (*food*) stuzzichino; (*drink*) aperitivo.
appetizing ['æpɪtaɪzɪŋ] *adj* appetitoso(a).
applaud [ə'plɔːd] *vt*, *vi* applaudire.
applause [ə'plɔːz] *n* applauso.
apple ['æpl] *n* mela; (*also*: ~ **tree**) melo; **the** ~ **of one's eye** la pupilla dei propri occhi.
apple turnover *n* sfogliatella alle mele.
appliance [ə'plaɪəns] *n* apparecchio; **electrical** ~**s** elettrodomestici *mpl*.
applicable [ə'plɪkəbl] *adj* applicabile; **to be**

~ **to** essere valido per; **the law is** ~ **from January** la legge entrerà in vigore in gennaio.

applicant ['æplɪkənt] n candidato/a; (ADMIN: for benefit etc) chi ha fatto domanda or richiesta.

application [æplɪ'keɪʃən] n applicazione f; (for a job, a grant etc) domanda; **on** ~ su richiesta.

application form n modulo di domanda.

application program n (COMPUT) programma applicativo.

applications package n (COMPUT) software m inv applicativo.

applied [ə'plaɪd] adj applicato(a); ~ **arts** arti fpl applicate.

apply [ə'plaɪ] vt: **to** ~ **(to)** (paint, ointment) dare (a); (theory, technique) applicare (a) ♦ vi: **to** ~ **to** (ask) rivolgersi a; (be suitable for, relevant to) riguardare, riferirsi a; **to** ~ **(for)** (permit, grant, job) fare domanda (per); **to** ~ **the brakes** frenare; **to** ~ **o.s. to** dedicarsi a.

appoint [ə'pɔɪnt] vt nominare.

appointee [əpɔɪn'tiː] n incaricato/a.

appointment [ə'pɔɪntmənt] n nomina; (arrangement to meet) appuntamento; **by** ~ su or per appuntamento; **to make an** ~ **with sb** prendere un appuntamento con qn; (PRESS): "~**s (vacant)**" "offerte fpl di impiego".

apportion [ə'pɔːʃən] vt attribuire.

appraisal [ə'preɪzl] n valutazione f.

appraise [ə'preɪz] vt (value) valutare, fare una stima di; (situation etc) fare il bilancio di.

appreciable [ə'priːʃəbl] adj apprezzabile.

appreciably [ə'priːʃəblɪ] adv notevolmente, sensibilmente.

appreciate [ə'priːʃɪeɪt] vt (like) apprezzare; (be grateful for) essere riconoscente di; (be aware of) rendersi conto di ♦ vi (COMM) aumentare; **I** ~**d your help** ti sono grato per l'aiuto.

appreciation [əpriːʃɪ'eɪʃən] n apprezzamento; (FINANCE) aumento del valore.

appreciative [ə'priːʃɪətɪv] adj (person) sensibile; (comment) elogiativo(a).

apprehend [æprɪ'hɛnd] vt (arrest) arrestare; (understand) comprendere.

apprehension [æprɪ'hɛnʃən] n (fear) inquietudine f.

apprehensive [æprɪ'hɛnsɪv] adj apprensivo(a).

apprentice [ə'prɛntɪs] n apprendista m/f ♦ vt: **to be** ~**d to** lavorare come apprendista presso.

apprenticeship [ə'prɛntɪsʃɪp] n apprendistato; **to serve one's** ~ fare il proprio apprendistato or tirocinio.

appro. ['æprəu] abbr (BRIT COMM: col) = **approval**.

approach [ə'prəutʃ] vi avvicinarsi ♦ vt (come near) avvicinarsi a; (ask, apply to) rivolgersi a; (subject, passer-by) avvicinare ♦ n approccio; accesso; (to problem) modo di affrontare; **to** ~ **sb about sth** rivolgersi a qn per qc.

approachable [ə'prəutʃəbl] adj accessibile.

approach road n strada d'accesso.

approbation [æprə'beɪʃən] n approvazione f, benestare m.

appropriate vt [ə'prəuprɪeɪt] (take) appropriarsi di ♦ adj [ə'prəuprɪt] appropriato(a); adatto(a); **it would not be** ~ **for me to comment** non sta a me fare dei commenti.

appropriately [ə'prəuprɪɪtlɪ] adv in modo appropriato.

appropriation [əprəuprɪ'eɪʃən] n stanziamento.

approval [ə'pruːvəl] n approvazione f; **on** ~ (COMM) in prova, in esame; **to meet with sb's** ~ soddisfare qn, essere di gradimento di qn.

approve [ə'pruːv] vt, vi approvare.

▶**approve of** vt fus approvare.

approved school n (BRIT: old) riformatorio.

approvingly [ə'pruːvɪŋlɪ] adv in approvazione.

approx. abbr = **approximately**.

approximate adj [ə'prɔksɪmɪt] approssimativo(a) ♦ vt [ə'prɔksɪmeɪt] essere un'approssimazione di, avvicinarsi a.

approximately [ə'prɔksɪmətlɪ] adv circa.

approximation [ə'prɔksɪ'meɪʃən] n approssimazione f.

APR n abbr (= annual percentage rate) tasso di percentuale annuo.

Apr. abbr (= April) apr.

apricot ['eɪprɪkɔt] n albicocca.

April ['eɪprəl] n aprile m; ~ **fool!** pesce d'aprile!; for phrases see also **July**.

April Fools' Day n see boxed note.

APRIL FOOLS' DAY

April Fools' Day è il primo aprile, il giorno degli scherzi e delle burle. Il nome deriva dal fatto che, se una persona cade nella trappola che gli è stata tesa, fa la figura del **fool**, cioè dello sciocco. Di recente gli scherzi stanno diventando sempre più elaborati, e persino i

*giornalisti a volte inventano vicende incredibili
per burlarsi dei lettori.*

apron ['eɪprən] *n* grembiule *m*; (*AVIAT*) area
di stazionamento.

apse [æps] *n* (*ARCHIT*) abside *f.*

APT *n abbr* (*BRIT*: = *advanced passenger train*)
treno ad altissima velocità.

apt [æpt] *adj* (*suitable*) adatto(a); (*able*)
capace; (*likely*): **to be** ~ **to do** avere
tendenza a fare.

Apt. *abbr* = **apartment.**

aptitude ['æptɪtjuːd] *n* abilità *f inv.*

aptitude test *n* test *m inv* attitudinale.

aptly ['æptlɪ] *adv* appropriatamente, in
modo adatto.

aqualung ['ækwəlʌŋ] *n* autorespiratore *m.*

aquarium [ə'kwɛərɪəm] *n* acquario.

Aquarius [ə'kwɛərɪəs] *n* Acquario; **to be** ~
essere dell'Acquario.

aquatic [ə'kwætɪk] *adj* acquatico(a).

aqueduct ['ækwɪdʌkt] *n* acquedotto.

AR *abbr* (*US*) = *Arkansas.*

ARA *n abbr* (*BRIT*) = *Associate of the Royal
Academy.*

Arab ['ærəb] *adj, n* arabo(a).

Arabia [ə'reɪbɪə] *n* Arabia.

Arabian [ə'reɪbɪən] *adj* arabo(a).

Arabian Desert *n* Deserto arabico.

Arabian Sea *n* mare *m* Arabico.

Arabic ['ærəbɪk] *adj* arabico(a) ♦ *n* arabo.

Arabic numerals *npl* numeri arabi *mpl*,
numerazione *f* araba.

arable ['ærəbl] *adj* arabile.

ARAM *n abbr* (*BRIT*) = *Associate of the Royal
Academy of Music.*

arbitrary ['ɑːbɪtrərɪ] *adj* arbitrario(a).

arbitrate ['ɑːbɪtreɪt] *vi* arbitrare.

arbitration [ɑːbɪ'treɪʃən] *n* (*LAW*) arbitrato;
(*INDUSTRY*) arbitraggio.

arbitrator ['ɑːbɪtreɪtə*] *n* arbitro.

ARC *n abbr* (= *American Red Cross*) C.R.I. *f*
(= *Croce Rossa Italiana*).

arc [ɑːk] *n* arco.

arcade [ɑː'keɪd] *n* portico; (*passage with
shops*) galleria.

arch [ɑːtʃ] *n* arco; (*of foot*) arco plantare
♦ *vt* inarcare ♦ *prefix*: ~(-) grande (*before
n*); per eccellenza.

archaeological [ɑːkɪə'lɔdʒɪkəl] *adj*
archeologico(a).

archaeologist [ɑːkɪ'ɔlədʒɪst] *n*
archeologo/a.

archaeology [ɑːkɪ'ɔlədʒɪ] *n* archeologia.

archaic [ɑː'keɪɪk] *adj* arcaico(a).

archangel ['ɑːkeɪndʒəl] *n* arcangelo.

archbishop [ɑːtʃ'bɪʃəp] *n* arcivescovo.

arched [ɑːtʃt] *adj* arcuato(a), ad arco.

arch-enemy ['ɑːtʃ'ɛnɪmɪ] *n* arcinemico/a.

archeology [ɑːkɪ'ɔlədʒɪ] *etc* = **archaeology**
etc.

archer ['ɑːtʃə*] *n* arciere *m.*

archery ['ɑːtʃərɪ] *n* tiro all'arco.

archetypal ['ɑːkɪtaɪpəl] *adj* tipico(a).

archipelago [ɑːkɪ'pɛlɪgəu] *n* arcipelago.

architect ['ɑːkɪtɛkt] *n* architetto.

architectural [ɑːkɪ'tɛktʃərəl] *adj*
architettonico(a).

architecture ['ɑːkɪtɛktʃə*] *n* architettura.

archive file *n* (*COMPUT*) file *m inv* di
archivio.

archives ['ɑːkaɪvz] *npl* archivi *mpl.*

archivist ['ɑːkɪvɪst] *n* archivista *m/f.*

archway ['ɑːtʃweɪ] *n* arco.

ARCM *n abbr* (*BRIT*) = *Associate of the Royal
College of Music.*

Arctic ['ɑːktɪk] *adj* artico(a) ♦ *n*: **the** ~
l'Artico.

Arctic Circle *n* Circolo polare artico.

Arctic Ocean *n* Oceano artico.

ARD *n abbr* (*US MED*) = *acute respiratory
disease.*

ardent ['ɑːdənt] *adj* ardente.

ardour, (*US*) **ardor** ['ɑːdə*] *n* ardore *m.*

arduous ['ɑːdjuəs] *adj* arduo(a).

are [ɑː*] *vb see* **be.**

area ['ɛərɪə] *n* (*GEOM*) area; (*zone*) zona;
(: *smaller*) settore *m*; **dining** ~ zona
pranzo; **the London** ~ la zona di Londra.

area code *n* (*US TEL*) prefisso.

arena [ə'riːnə] *n* arena.

aren't [ɑːnt] = **are not.**

Argentina [ɑːdʒən'tiːnə] *n* Argentina.

Argentinian [ɑːdʒən'tɪnɪən] *adj, n*
argentino(a).

arguable ['ɑːgjuəbl] *adj* discutibile; **it is** ~
whether ... è una cosa discutibile se ... +
sub.

arguably ['ɑːgjuəblɪ] *adv*: **it is** ~ ... si può
sostenere che sia ....

argue ['ɑːgjuː] *vi* (*quarrel*) litigare; (*reason*)
ragionare ♦ *vt* (*debate: case, matter*)
dibattere; **to** ~ **that** sostenere che; **to** ~
about sth (**with sb**) litigare per *or* a
proposito di qc (con qn).

argument ['ɑːgjumənt] *n* (*reasons*)
argomento; (*quarrel*) lite *f*; (*debate*)
discussione *f*; ~ **for/against** argomento a
or in favore di/contro.

argumentative [ɑːgju'mɛntətɪv] *adj*
litigioso(a).

aria ['ɑːrɪə] *n* aria.

ARIBA *n abbr* (*BRIT*) = *Associate of the Royal
Institute of British Architects.*

arid ['ærɪd] *adj* arido(a).

aridity [ə'rɪdɪtɪ] *n* aridità.

Aries ['ɛərɪz] n Ariete m; **to be ~** essere dell'Ariete.

arise, pt **arose**, pp **arisen** [ə'raɪz, ə'rəuz, ə'rɪzn] vi alzarsi; (opportunity, problem) presentarsi; **to ~ from** risultare da; **should the need ~** dovesse presentarsi la necessità, in caso di necessità.

aristocracy [ærɪs'tɔkrəsɪ] n aristocrazia.

aristocrat ['ærɪstəkræt] n aristocratico/a.

aristocratic [ærɪstə'krætɪk] adj aristocratico(a).

arithmetic [ə'rɪθmətɪk] n aritmetica.

arithmetical [ærɪθ'mɛtɪkəl] adj aritmetico(a).

Ariz. abbr (US) = Arizona.

ark [ɑːk] n: **Noah's A~** l'arca di Noè.

Ark. abbr (US) = Arkansas.

arm [ɑːm] n braccio; (MIL: branch) arma ♦ vt armare; **~ in ~** a braccetto; see also **arms.**

armaments ['ɑːməmənts] npl (weapons) armamenti mpl.

armband ['ɑːmbænd] n bracciale m.

armchair ['ɑːmtʃɛə*] n poltrona.

armed [ɑːmd] adj armato(a).

armed forces npl forze fpl armate.

armed robbery n rapina a mano armata.

Armenia [ɑː'miːnɪə] n Armenia.

Armenian [ɑː'miːnɪən] adj armeno(a) ♦ n armeno/a; (LING) armeno.

armful ['ɑːmful] n bracciata.

armistice ['ɑːmɪstɪs] n armistizio.

armour, (US) **armor** ['ɑːmə*] n armatura; (also: **~-plating**) corazza, blindatura; (MIL: tanks) mezzi mpl blindati.

armo(u)red car n autoblinda f inv.

armo(u)ry ['ɑːmərɪ] n arsenale m.

armpit ['ɑːmpɪt] n ascella.

armrest ['ɑːmrɛst] n bracciolo.

arms [ɑːmz] npl (weapons) armi fpl; (HERALDRY) stemma m.

arms control n controllo degli armamenti.

arms race n corsa agli armamenti.

army ['ɑːmɪ] n esercito.

aroma [ə'rəumə] n aroma.

aromatherapy [ərəumə'θɛrəpɪ] n aromaterapia.

aromatic [ærə'mætɪk] adj aromatico(a).

arose [ə'rəuz] pt of **arise.**

around [ə'raund] adv attorno, intorno ♦ prep intorno a; (fig: about): **~** £5/3 o'clock circa 5 sterline/le 3; **is he ~?** è in giro?

arousal [ə'rauzəl] n (sexual etc) eccitazione f; (awakening) risveglio.

arouse [ə'rauz] vt (sleeper) svegliare; (curiosity, passions) suscitare.

arrange [ə'reɪndʒ] vt sistemare; (programme) preparare ♦ vi: **we have ~d for a taxi to pick you up** la faremo venire

a prendere da un taxi; **it was ~d that ...** è stato deciso or stabilito che ...; **to ~ to do** sth mettersi d'accordo per fare qc.

arrangement [ə'reɪndʒmənt] n sistemazione f; (plans etc): **~s** progetti mpl, piani mpl; **by ~** su richiesta; **to come to an ~ (with sb)** venire ad un accordo (con qn), mettersi d'accordo or accordarsi (con qn); **I'll make ~s for you to be met** darò disposizioni or istruzioni perché ci sia qualcuno ad incontrarla.

arrant ['ærənt] adj: **~ nonsense** colossali sciocchezze fpl.

array [ə'reɪ] n fila; (COMPUT) array m inv, insiemi mpl.

arrears [ə'rɪəz] npl arretrati mpl; **to be in ~ with one's rent** essere in arretrato con l'affitto.

arrest [ə'rɛst] vt arrestare; (sb's attention) attirare ♦ n arresto; **under ~** in arresto.

arresting [ə'rɛstɪŋ] adj (fig) che colpisce.

arrival [ə'raɪvəl] n arrivo; (person) arrivato/a; **new ~** nuovo venuto.

arrive [ə'raɪv] vi arrivare.

▶**arrive at** vt fus arrivare a.

arrogance ['ærəgəns] n arroganza.

arrogant ['ærəgənt] adj arrogante.

arrow ['ærəu] n freccia.

arse [ɑːs] n (BRIT col!) culo(!).

arsenal ['ɑːsɪnl] n arsenale m.

arsenic ['ɑːsnɪk] n arsenico.

arson ['ɑːsn] n incendio doloso.

art [ɑːt] n arte f; (craft) mestiere m; **work of ~** opera d'arte; see also **arts.**

artefact, (US) **artifact** ['ɑːtɪfækt] n manufatto.

arterial [ɑː'tɪərɪəl] adj (ANAT) arterioso(a); (road etc) di grande comunicazione; **~ roads** le (grandi or principali) arterie.

artery ['ɑːtərɪ] n arteria.

artful ['ɑːtful] adj furbo(a).

art gallery n galleria d'arte.

arthritis [ɑː'θraɪtɪs] n artrite f.

artichoke ['ɑːtɪtʃəuk] n carciofo; **Jerusalem ~** topinambur m inv.

article ['ɑːtɪkl] n articolo; **~s** npl (BRIT LAW: training) contratto di tirocinio; **~s of clothing** indumenti mpl.

articles of association npl (COMM) statuto sociale.

articulate adj [ɑː'tɪkjulɪt] (person) che si esprime forbitamente; (speech) articolato(a) ♦ vi [ɑː'tɪkjuleɪt] articolare.

articulated lorry n (BRIT) autotreno.

artifact ['ɑːtɪfækt] n (US) = **artefact.**

artifice ['ɑːtɪfɪs] n (cunning) abilità, destrezza; (trick) artificio.

artificial [ɑːtɪ'fɪʃəl] adj artificiale.

artificial insemination [-ɪnsɛmɪ'neɪʃən] *n*
fecondazione *f* artificiale.
artificial intelligence (AI) *n* intelligenza
artificiale (IA).
artificial respiration *n* respirazione *f*
artificiale.
artillery [ɑː'tɪlərɪ] *n* artiglieria.
artisan ['ɑːtɪzæn] *n* artigiano/a.
artist ['ɑːtɪst] *n* artista *m/f*.
artistic [ɑː'tɪstɪk] *adj* artistico(a).
artistry ['ɑːtɪstrɪ] *n* arte *f*.
artless ['ɑːtlɪs] *adj* semplice, ingenuo(a).
arts [ɑːts] *npl* (*SCOL*) lettere *fpl*.
art school *n* scuola d'arte.
artwork ['ɑːtwɔːk] *n* materiale *m*
illustrativo.
ARV *n abbr* (= *American Revised Version*)
traduzione della Bibbia.
AS *n abbr* (*US SCOL*: = *Associate in Science*)
titolo di studio.

══════════════════════ KEYWORD

as [æz] *conj* **1** (*referring to time*) mentre; ~
the years went by col passare degli anni;
he came in ~ **I was leaving** arrivò mentre
stavo uscendo; ~ **from tomorrow** da
domani
2 (*in comparisons*): ~ **big** ~ grande come;
twice ~ **big** ~ due volte più grande di; ~
much/many ~ tanto quanto/tanti quanti;
~ **soon** ~ **possible** prima possibile
3 (*since, because*) dal momento che,
siccome
4 (*referring to manner, way*) come; **big** ~ **it**
is grande com'è; **much** ~ **I like them**, ...
per quanto mi siano simpatici, ...; **do** ~
you wish fa' come vuoi; ~ **she said** come
ha detto lei
5 (*concerning*): ~ **for** *or* **to that** per quanto
riguarda *or* quanto a quello
6: ~ **if** *or* **though come se; he looked** ~ **if**
he was ill sembrava stare male; *see also*
long; such; well
♦ *prep*: **he works** ~ **a driver** fa l'autista; ~
chairman of the company, he ... come
presidente della compagnia, lui ...; **he**
gave me it ~ **a present** me lo ha regalato.

ASA *n abbr* (= *American Standards*
Association) *associazione per la*
normalizzazione; (*BRIT*: = *Advertising*
Standards Association) ≈ Istituto di
Autodisciplina Pubblicitaria.
a.s.a.p. *abbr* (= *as soon as possible*) prima
possibile.
asbestos [æz'bɛstəs] *n* asbesto, amianto.
ascend [ə'sɛnd] *vt* salire.
ascendancy [ə'sɛndənsɪ] *n* ascendente *m*.

ascendant [ə'sɛndənt] *n*: **to be in the** ~
essere in auge.
ascension [ə'sɛnʃən] *n*: **the A**~ (*REL*)
l'Ascensione *f*.
Ascension Island *n* isola dell'Ascensione.
ascent [ə'sɛnt] *n* salita.
ascertain [æsə'teɪn] *vt* accertare.
ascetic [ə'sɛtɪk] *adj* ascetico(a).
asceticism [ə'sɛtɪsɪzəm] *n* ascetismo.
ASCII ['æskiː] *n abbr* (= *American Standard*
Code for Information Interchange) ASCII *m*.
ascribe [ə'skraɪb] *vt*: **to** ~ **sth to** attribuire
qc a.
ASCU *n abbr* (*US*) = *Association of State*
Colleges and Universities.
ASE *n abbr* = *American Stock Exchange*.
ASH [æʃ] *n abbr* (*BRIT*: = *Action on Smoking*
and Health) *iniziativa contro il fumo*.
ash [æʃ] *n* (*dust*) cenere *f*; ~ (**tree**) frassino.
ashamed [ə'ʃeɪmd] *adj* vergognoso(a); **to**
be ~ **of** vergognarsi di; **to be** ~ (**of o.s.**)
for having done vergognarsi di aver
fatto.
ashen ['æʃən] *adj* (*pale*) livido(a).
ashore [ə'ʃɔː*] *adv* a terra; **to go** ~
sbarcare.
ashtray ['æʃtreɪ] *n* portacenere *m*.
Ash Wednesday *n* Mercoledì *m inv* delle
Ceneri.
Asia Minor *n* Asia minore.
Asian ['eɪʃən] *adj*, *n* asiatico(a).
Asiatic [eɪsɪ'ætɪk] *adj* asiatico(a).
aside [ə'saɪd] *adv* da parte ♦ *n* a parte *m*; **to**
take sb ~ prendere qn da parte; ~ **from**
(*as well as*) oltre a; (*except for*) a parte.
ask [ɑːsk] *vt* (*request*) chiedere; (*question*)
domandare; (*invite*) invitare; **to** ~ **about**
sth informarsi su *or* di qc; **to** ~ **sb sth/sb**
to do sth chiedere qc a qn/a qn di fare
qc; **to** ~ **sb about sth** chiedere a qn di qc;
to ~ (**sb**) **a question** fare una domanda (a
qn); **to** ~ **sb the time** chiedere l'ora a qn;
to ~ **sb out to dinner** invitare qn a
mangiare fuori; **you should** ~ **at the**
information desk dovreste rivolgersi
all'ufficio informazioni.
▶**ask after** *vt fus* chiedere di.
▶**ask for** *vt fus* chiedere; **it's just** ~**ing for**
trouble *or* **for it** è proprio (come)
andarsele a cercare.
askance [ə'skɑːns] *adv*: **to look** ~ **at sb**
guardare qn di traverso.
askew [ə'skjuː] *adv* di traverso, storto.
asking price ['ɑːskɪŋ-] *n* prezzo di
partenza.
asleep [ə'sliːp] *adj* addormentato(a); **to be**
~ dormire; **to fall** ~ addormentarsi.
ASLEF ['æzlɛf] *n abbr* (*BRIT*: = *Associated*

Society of Locomotive Engineers and Firemen) sindacato dei conducenti dei treni e dei macchinisti.

asp [æsp] n cobra m inv egiziano.

asparagus [əs'pærəgəs] n asparagi mpl.

asparagus tips npl punte fpl d'asparagi.

ASPCA n abbr (= American Society for the Prevention of Cruelty to Animals) ≈ E.N.P.A. m (Ente Nazionale per la Protezione degli Animali).

aspect ['æspɛkt] n aspetto.

aspersions [əs'pəːʃənz] npl: **to cast ~ on** diffamare.

asphalt ['æsfælt] n asfalto.

asphyxiate [æs'fɪksɪeɪt] vt asfissiare.

asphyxiation [æsfɪksɪ'eɪʃən] n asfissia.

aspiration [æspə'reɪʃən] n aspirazione f.

aspire [əs'paɪə*] vi: **to ~ to** aspirare a.

aspirin ['æsprɪn] n aspirina.

aspiring [əs'paɪərɪŋ] adj aspirante.

ass [æs] n asino; (US col!) culo(!).

assail [ə'seɪl] vt assalire.

assailant [ə'seɪlənt] n assalitore m.

assassin [ə'sæsɪn] n assassino.

assassinate [ə'sæsɪneɪt] vt assassinare.

assassination [əsæsɪ'neɪʃən] n assassinio.

assault [ə'sɔːlt] n (MIL) assalto; (gen: attack) aggressione f; (LAW): **~ (and battery)** minacce e vie di fatto fpl ♦ vt assaltare; aggredire; (sexually) violentare.

assemble [ə'sɛmbl] vt riunire; (TECH) montare ♦ vi riunirsi.

assembly [ə'sɛmblɪ] n (meeting) assemblea; (construction) montaggio.

assembly language n (COMPUT) linguaggio assemblativo.

assembly line n catena di montaggio.

assent [ə'sɛnt] n assenso, consenso ♦ vi assentire; **to ~ (to sth)** approvare (qc).

assert [ə'səːt] vt asserire; (insist on) far valere; **to ~ o.s.** farsi valere.

assertion [ə'səːʃən] n asserzione f.

assertive [ə'səːtɪv] adj che sa imporsi.

assess [ə'sɛs] vt valutare.

assessment [ə'sɛsmənt] n valutazione f; (judgment): **~ (of)** giudizio (su).

assessor [ə'sɛsə*] n perito; funzionario del fisco.

asset ['æsɛt] n vantaggio; (person) elemento prezioso; **~s** npl (COMM) beni mpl; disponibilità fpl; attivo.

asset-stripping ['æsɛt'strɪpɪŋ] n (COMM) acquisto di una società in fallimento con lo scopo di rivenderne le attività.

assiduous [ə'sɪdjuəs] adj assiduo(a).

assign [ə'saɪn] vt: **to ~ (to)** (task) assegnare (a); (resources) riservare (a); (cause, meaning) attribuire (a); **to ~ a date to sth**

fissare la data di qc.

assignment [ə'saɪnmənt] n compito.

assimilate [ə'sɪmɪleɪt] vt assimilare.

assimilation [əsɪmɪ'leɪʃən] n assimilazione f.

assist [ə'sɪst] vt assistere, aiutare.

assistance [ə'sɪstəns] n assistenza, aiuto.

assistant [ə'sɪstənt] n assistente m/f; (BRIT: also: **shop ~**) commesso/a.

assistant manager n vicedirettore m.

assizes [ə'saɪzɪz] npl assise fpl.

associate [ə'səuʃɪɪt] adj associato(a); (member) aggiunto(a) ♦ n collega m/f; (in business) socio/a ♦ vb [ə'səuʃɪeɪt] vt associare ♦ vi: **to ~ with sb** frequentare qn.

associated company [ə'səusɪ'eɪtɪd-] n società collegata.

associate director n amministratore m aggiunto.

association [əsəusɪ'eɪʃən] n associazione f; **in ~ with** in collaborazione con.

association football n (BRIT) (gioco del) calcio.

assorted [ə'sɔːtɪd] adj assortito(a); **in ~ sizes** in diverse taglie.

assortment [ə'sɔːtmənt] n assortimento.

Asst. abbr = assistant.

assuage [ə'sweɪdʒ] vt alleviare.

assume [ə'sjuːm] vt supporre; (responsibilities etc) assumere; (attitude, name) prendere.

assumed name n nome m falso.

assumption [ə'sʌmpʃən] n supposizione f, ipotesi f inv; **on the ~ that ...** partendo dal presupposto che ....

assurance [ə'ʃuərəns] n assicurazione f; (self-confidence) fiducia in se stesso; **I can give you no ~s** non posso assicurarle or garantirle niente.

assure [ə'ʃuə*] vt assicurare.

assured [ə'ʃuəd] adj (confident) sicuro(a); (certain: promotion etc) assicurato(a).

AST abbr (US: = Atlantic Standard Time) ora invernale di New York.

asterisk ['æstərɪsk] n asterisco.

astern [ə'stəːn] adv a poppa.

asteroid ['æstərɔɪd] n asteroide m.

asthma ['æsmə] n asma.

asthmatic [æs'mætɪk] adj, n asmatico(a).

astigmatism [ə'stɪgmətɪzəm] n astigmatismo.

astir [ə'stəː*] adv in piedi; (excited) in fermento.

astonish [ə'stɔnɪʃ] vt stupire.

astonishing [ə'stɔnɪʃɪŋ] adj sorprendente, stupefacente; **I find it ~ that ...** mi stupisce che ....

astonishingly [ə'stɔnɪʃɪŋlɪ] adv straordinariamente, incredibilmente.

astonishment [ə'stɔnɪʃmənt] n stupore m; **to my** ~ con mia gran meraviglia, con mio grande stupore.

astound [ə'staund] vt sbalordire.

astray [ə'streɪ] adv: **to go** ~ smarrirsi; (fig) traviarsi; **to go** ~ **in one's calculations** sbagliare i calcoli.

astride [ə'straɪd] adv a cavalcioni ♦ prep a cavalcioni di.

astringent [əs'trɪndʒənt] adj, n astringente (m).

astrologer [əs'trɔlədʒə*] n astrologo/a.

astrology [əs'trɔlədʒɪ] n astrologia.

astronaut ['æstrənɔːt] n astronauta m/f.

astronomer [əs'trɔnəmə*] n astronomo/a.

astronomical [æstrə'nɔmɪkl] adj astronomico(a).

astronomy [əs'trɔnəmɪ] n astronomia.

astrophysics ['æstrəu'fɪzɪks] n astrofisica.

astute [əs'tjuːt] adj astuto(a).

asunder [ə'sʌndə*] adv: **to tear** ~ strappare.

ASV n abbr (= American Standard Version) traduzione della Bibbia.

asylum [ə'saɪləm] n asilo; (lunatic ~) manicomio; **to seek political** ~ chiedere asilo politico.

asymmetric(al) [eɪsɪ'mɛtrɪk(əl)] adj asimmetrico(a).

================= KEYWORD

at [æt] prep **1** (referring to position, direction) a; ~ **the top** in cima; ~ **the desk** al banco, alla scrivania; ~ **home/school** a casa/ scuola; ~ **Paolo's** da Paolo; ~ **the baker's** dal panettiere; **to look** ~ **sth** guardare qc; **to throw sth** ~ **sb** lanciare qc a qn
2 (referring to time) a; ~ **4 o'clock** alle 4; ~ **night** di notte; ~ **Christmas** a Natale; ~ **times** a volte
3 (referring to rates, speed etc) a; ~ **£1 a kilo** a 1 sterlina al chilo; **two** ~ **a time** due alla volta, due per volta; ~ **50 km/h** a 50 km/h; ~ **full speed** a tutta velocità
4 (referring to manner): ~ **a stroke** d'un solo colpo; ~ **peace** in pace
5 (referring to activity): **to be** ~ **work** essere al lavoro; **to play** ~ **cowboys** giocare ai cowboy; **to be good** ~ **sth/ doing sth** essere bravo in qc/a fare qc
6 (referring to cause): **shocked/surprised/ annoyed** ~ **sth** colpito da/sorpreso da/ arrabbiato per qc; **I went** ~ **his suggestion** ci sono andato dietro suo consiglio.

ate [eɪt] pt of **eat**.

atheism ['eɪθɪɪzəm] n ateismo.

atheist ['eɪθɪɪst] n ateo/a.

Athenian [ə'θiːnɪən] adj, n ateniese (m/f).

Athens ['æθɪnz] n Atene f.

athlete ['æθliːt] n atleta m/f.

athletic [æθ'lɛtɪk] adj atletico(a).

athletics [æθ'lɛtɪks] n atletica.

Atlantic [ət'læntɪk] adj atlantico(a) ♦ n: **the** ~ **(Ocean)** l'Atlantico, l'Oceano Atlantico.

atlas ['ætləs] n atlante m.

Atlas Mountains npl: **the** ~ i Monti dell'Atlante.

A.T.M. abbr (= automated teller machine) cassa automatica prelievi, sportello automatico.

atmosphere ['ætməsfɪə*] n atmosfera; (air) aria.

atmospheric [ætməs'fɛrɪk] adj atmosferico(a).

atmospherics [ætməs'fɛrɪks] npl (RADIO) scariche fpl.

atoll ['ætɔl] n atollo.

atom ['ætəm] n atomo.

atomic [ə'tɔmɪk] adj atomico(a).

atom(ic) bomb n bomba atomica.

atomizer ['ætəmaɪzə*] n atomizzatore m.

atone [ə'təun] vi: **to** ~ **for** espiare.

atonement [ə'təunmənt] n espiazione f.

ATP n abbr = Association of Tennis Professionals.

atrocious [ə'trəuʃəs] adj atroce, pessimo(a).

atrocity [ə'trɔsɪtɪ] n atrocità f inv.

atrophy ['ætrəfɪ] n atrofia ♦ vi atrofizzarsi.

attach [ə'tætʃ] vt attaccare; (document, letter) allegare; (MIL: troops) assegnare; **to be** ~**ed to sb/sth** (to like) essere affezionato(a) a qn/qc; **the** ~**ed letter** la lettera acclusa or allegata.

attaché [ə'tæʃeɪ] n addetto.

attaché case n valigetta per documenti.

attachment [ə'tætʃmənt] n (tool) accessorio; (love): ~ **(to)** affetto (per); (COMPUT) allegato.

attack [ə'tæk] vt attaccare; (task etc) iniziare; (problem) affrontare ♦ n attacco; (also: **heart** ~) infarto.

attacker [ə'tækə*] n aggressore m, assalitore/trice.

attain [ə'teɪn] vt (also: **to** ~ **to**) arrivare a, raggiungere.

attainments [ə'teɪnmənts] npl cognizioni fpl.

attempt [ə'tɛmpt] n tentativo ♦ vt tentare; ~**ed murder** (LAW) tentato omicidio; **to make an** ~ **on sb's life** attentare alla vita di qn; **he made no** ~ **to help** non ha (neanche) tentato or cercato di aiutare.

attend [ə'tɛnd] *vt* frequentare; (*meeting, talk*) andare a; (*patient*) assistere.
►**attend to** *vt fus* (*needs, affairs etc*) prendersi cura di; (*customer*) occuparsi di.
attendance [ə'tɛndəns] *n* (*being present*) presenza; (*people present*) gente *f* presente.
attendant [ə'tɛndənt] *n* custode *m/f*; persona di servizio ♦ *adj* concomitante.
attention [ə'tɛnʃən] *n* attenzione *f*; ~**s** premure *fpl*, attenzioni *fpl*; ~! (*MIL*) attenti!; **at** ~ (*MIL*) sull'attenti; **for the** ~ **of** (*ADMIN*) per l'attenzione di; **it has come to my** ~ **that** ... sono venuto a conoscenza (del fatto) che ....
attentive [ə'tɛntɪv] *adj* attento(a); (*kind*) premuroso(a).
attentively [ə'tɛntɪvlɪ] *adv* attentamente.
attenuate [ə'tɛnjueɪt] *vt* attenuare ♦ *vi* attenuarsi.
attest [ə'tɛst] *vi*: **to** ~ **to** attestare.
attic ['ætɪk] *n* soffitta.
attire [ə'taɪə*] *n* abbigliamento.
attitude ['ætɪtjuːd] *n* (*behaviour*) atteggiamento; (*posture*) posa; (*view*): ~ (**to**) punto di vista (nei confronti di).
attorney [ə'tɜːnɪ] *n* (*US: lawyer*) avvocato; (*having proxy*) mandatario; **power of** ~ procura.
Attorney General *n* (*BRIT*) Procuratore *m* Generale; (*US*) Ministro della Giustizia.
attract [ə'trækt] *vt* attirare.
attraction [ə'trækʃən] *n* (*gen pl: pleasant things*) attrattiva; (*PHYSICS, fig: towards sth*) attrazione *f*.
attractive [ə'træktɪv] *adj* attraente; (*idea, offer, price*) allettante, interessante.
attribute *n* ['ætrɪbjuːt] attributo ♦ *vt* [ə'trɪbjuːt]: **to** ~ **sth to** attribuire qc a.
attrition [ə'trɪʃən] *n*: **war of** ~ guerra di logoramento.
Atty. Gen. *abbr* = **Attorney General.**
atypical [eɪ'tɪpɪkl] *adj* atipico(a).
AU *n abbr* (= *African Union*) Unione Africana.
aubergine ['əubəʒiːn] *n* melanzana.
auburn ['ɔːbən] *adj* tizianesco(a).
auction ['ɔːkʃən] *n* (*also: sale by* ~) asta ♦ *vt* (*also: to sell by* ~) vendere all'asta; (*also: to put up for* ~) mettere all'asta.
auctioneer [ɔːkʃə'nɪə*] *n* banditore *m*.
auction room *n* sala dell'asta.
audacious [ɔː'deɪʃəs] *adj* (*bold*) audace; (*impudent*) sfrontato(a).
audacity [ɔː'dæsɪtɪ] *n* audacia.
audible ['ɔːdɪbl] *adj* udibile.
audience ['ɔːdɪəns] *n* (*people*) pubblico; spettatori *mpl*; ascoltatori *mpl*; (*interview*)

udienza.
audio-typist ['ɔːdɪəu'taɪpɪst] *n* dattilografo/a che trascrive da nastro.
audiovisual [ɔːdɪəu'vɪzjuəl] *adj* audiovisivo(a); ~ **aids** sussidi *mpl* audiovisivi.
audit ['ɔːdɪt] *n* revisione *f*, verifica ♦ *vt* rivedere, verificare.
audition [ɔː'dɪʃən] *n* (*THEAT*) audizione *f*; (*CINE*) provino ♦ *vi* fare un'audizione (*or* un provino).
auditor ['ɔːdɪtə*] *n* revisore *m*.
auditorium [ɔːdɪ'tɔːrɪəm] *n* sala, auditorio.
Aug. *abbr* (= *August*) ago., ag.
augment [ɔːg'mɛnt] *vt, vi* aumentare.
augur ['ɔːgə*] *vt* (*be a sign of*) predire ♦ *vi*: **it** ~**s well** promette bene.
August ['ɔːgəst] *n* agosto; *for phrases see also* **July.**
august [ɔː'gʌst] *adj* augusto(a).
aunt [ɑːnt] *n* zia.
auntie, aunty ['ɑːntɪ] *n* zietta.
au pair ['əu'pɛə*] *n* (*also:* ~ **girl**) (ragazza *f*) alla pari *inv*.
aura ['ɔːrə] *n* aura.
auspices ['ɔːspɪsɪz] *npl*: **under the** ~ **of** sotto gli auspici di.
auspicious [ɔːs'pɪʃəs] *adj* propizio(a).
austere [ɔs'tɪə*] *adj* austero(a).
austerity [ɔs'tɛrɪtɪ] *n* austerità *f inv*.
Australasia [ɔstrə'leɪzɪə] *n* Australasia.
Australia [ɔs'treɪlɪə] *n* Australia.
Australian [ɔs'treɪlɪən] *adj, n* australiano(a).
Austria ['ɔstrɪə] *n* Austria.
Austrian ['ɔstrɪən] *adj, n* austriaco(a).
AUT *n abbr* (*BRIT*: = *Association of University Teachers*) associazione dei docenti universitari.
authentic [ɔː'θɛntɪk] *adj* autentico(a).
authenticate [ɔː'θɛntɪkeɪt] *vt* autenticare.
authenticity [ɔːθɛn'tɪsɪtɪ] *n* autenticità.
author ['ɔːθə*] *n* autore/trice.
authoritarian [ɔːθɔrɪ'tɛərɪən] *adj* autoritario(a).
authoritative [ɔː'θɔrɪtətɪv] *adj* (*account etc*) autorevole; (*manner*) autoritario(a).
authority [ɔː'θɔrɪtɪ] *n* autorità *f inv*; (*permission*) autorizzazione *f*; **the authorities** *npl* le autorità; **to have** ~ **to do sth** avere l'autorizzazione a fare *or* il diritto di fare qc.
authorization [ɔːθəraɪ'zeɪʃən] *n* autorizzazione *f*.
authorize ['ɔːθəraɪz] *vt* autorizzare.
authorized capital *n* capitale *m* nominale.
authorship ['ɔːθəʃɪp] *n* paternità (*letteraria etc*).
autistic [ɔː'tɪstɪk] *adj* autistico(a).

auto ['ɔ:təu] n (US) auto f inv.
autobiography [ɔ:təbaɪ'ɔgrəfɪ] n autobiografia.
autocratic [ɔ:tə'krætɪk] adj autocratico(a).
Autocue ® ['ɔ:təukju:] n (BRIT) gobbo (TV).
autograph ['ɔ:təgrɑ:f] n autografo ♦ vt firmare.
autoimmune [ɔ:təuɪ'mju:n] adj autoimmune.
automat ['ɔ:təmæt] n (US) tavola calda fornita esclusivamente di distributori automatici.
automated ['ɔ:təmeɪtɪd] adj automatizzato(a).
automatic [ɔ:tə'mætɪk] adj automatico(a) ♦ n (gun) arma automatica; (car) automobile f con cambio automatico; (washing machine) lavatrice f automatica.
automatically [ɔ:tə'mætɪklɪ] adv automaticamente.
automatic data processing (ADP) n elaborazione f automatica dei dati (EAD).
automation [ɔ:tə'meɪʃən] n automazione f.
automaton, pl automata [ɔ:'tɔmətən, -tə] n automa m.
automobile ['ɔ:təməbi:l] n (US) automobile f.
autonomous [ɔ:'tɔnəməs] adj autonomo(a).
autopsy ['ɔ:tɔpsɪ] n autopsia.
autumn ['ɔ:təm] n autunno.
auxiliary [ɔ:g'zɪlɪərɪ] adj ausiliario(a) ♦ n ausiliare m/f.
AV n abbr (= Authorized Version) traduzione inglese della Bibbia ♦ abbr = **audiovisual**.
Av. abbr = **avenue**.
avail [ə'veɪl] vt: to ~ o.s. of servirsi di; approfittarsi di ♦ n: to no ~ inutilmente.
availability [əveɪlə'bɪlɪtɪ] n disponibilità.
available [ə'veɪləbl] adj disponibile; **every** ~ **means** tutti i mezzi disponibili; **to make sth** ~ **to sb** mettere qc a disposizione di qn; **is the manager** ~? è libero il direttore?
avalanche ['ævəlɑ:nʃ] n valanga.
avant-garde ['ævɑ̃'gɑ:d] adj d'avanguardia.
avarice ['ævərɪs] n avarizia.
avaricious [ævə'rɪʃəs] adj avaro(a).
avdp. abbr (= avoirdupois) sistema ponderale anglosassone basato su libbra, oncia e multipli.
Ave. abbr = **avenue**.
avenge [ə'vɛndʒ] vt vendicare.
avenue ['ævənju:] n viale m.
average ['ævərɪdʒ] n media ♦ adj medio(a) ♦ vt (also: ~ **out at**) aggirarsi in media su, essere in media di; **on** ~ in media; **above/below (the)** ~ sopra/sotto la media.

averse [ə'vɔ:s] adj: **to be** ~ **to sth/doing** essere contrario(a) a qc/a fare; **I wouldn't be** ~ **to a drink** non avrei nulla in contrario a bere qualcosa.
aversion [ə'vɔ:ʃən] n avversione f.
avert [ə'vɔ:t] vt evitare, prevenire; (one's eyes) distogliere.
avian flu ['eɪvɪən-] n influenza aviaria.
aviary ['eɪvɪərɪ] n voliera, uccelliera.
aviation [eɪvɪ'eɪʃən] n aviazione f.
avid ['ævɪd] adj avido(a).
avidly ['ævɪdlɪ] adv avidamente.
avocado [ævə'kɑ:dəu] n (also: BRIT: ~ **pear**) avocado m inv.
avoid [ə'vɔɪd] vt evitare.
avoidable [ə'vɔɪdəbl] adj evitabile.
avoidance [ə'vɔɪdəns] n l'evitare m.
avowed [ə'vaud] adj dichiarato(a).
AVP n abbr (US) = assistant vice-president.
AWACS ['eɪwæks] n abbr (= airborne warning and control system) sistema di allarme e controllo in volo.
await [ə'weɪt] vt aspettare; ~**ing attention** (COMM: letter) in attesa di risposta; (: order) in attesa di essere evaso; **long** ~**ed** tanto atteso(a).
awake [ə'weɪk] adj sveglio(a) ♦ vb (pt **awoke** [ə'wəuk], pp **awoken** [ə'wəukən] or **awaked**) vt svegliare ♦ vi svegliarsi; ~ **to** consapevole di.
awakening [ə'weɪknɪŋ] n risveglio.
award [ə'wɔ:d] n premio; (LAW) decreto ♦ vt assegnare; (LAW: damages) decretare.
aware [ə'wɛə*] adj: ~ **of** (conscious) conscio(a) di; (informed) informato(a) di; **to become** ~ **of** accorgersi di; **politically/socially** ~ politicamente/socialmente preparato; **I am fully** ~ **that** ... mi rendo perfettamente conto che ....
awareness [ə'wɛənɪs] n consapevolezza; coscienza; **to develop people's** ~ **(of)** sensibilizzare la gente (a).
awash [ə'wɔʃ] adj: ~ **(with)** inondato(a) (da).
away [ə'weɪ] adj, adv via; lontano(a); **two kilometres** ~ a due chilometri di distanza; **two hours** ~ **by car** a due ore di distanza in macchina; **the holiday was two weeks** ~ mancavano due settimane alle vacanze; ~ **from** lontano da; **he's** ~ **for a week** è andato via per una settimana; **he's** ~ **in Milan** è (andato) a Milano; **to take** ~ vt portare via; **he was working/pedalling** etc ~ la particella indica la continuità e l'energia dell'azione: **lavorava/pedalava** etc più che poteva; **to fade/wither** etc ~ la particella rinforza l'idea della

diminuzione.
away game n (*SPORT*) partita fuori casa.
awe [ɔː] n timore m.
awe-inspiring ['ɔːɪnspaɪərɪŋ], **awesome** ['ɔːsəm] *adj* imponente.
awestruck ['ɔːstrʌk] *adj* sgomento(a).
awful ['ɔːfəl] *adj* terribile; **an ~ lot of** (*people, cars, dogs*) un numero incredibile di; (*jam, flowers*) una quantità incredibile di.
awfully ['ɔːflɪ] *adv* (*very*) terribilmente.
awhile [ə'waɪl] *adv* (per) un po'.
awkward ['ɔːkwəd] *adj* (*clumsy*) goffo(a); (*inconvenient*) scomodo(a); (*embarrassing*) imbarazzante; (*difficult*) delicato(a), difficile.
awkwardness ['ɔːkwədnɪs] n goffaggine f; scomodità; imbarazzo; delicatezza, difficoltà.
awl ['ɔːl] n punteruolo.
awning ['ɔːnɪŋ] n (*of tent*) veranda; (*of shop, hotel etc*) tenda.
awoke [ə'wəuk] *pt of* awake.
awoken [ə'wəukən] *pp of* awake.
AWOL ['eɪwɔl] *abbr* (*MIL etc*) *see* absent without leave.
awry [ə'raɪ] *adv* di traverso ♦ *adj* storto(a); **to go ~** andare a monte.
axe, (US) ax [æks] n scure f ♦ *vt* (*project etc*) abolire; (*jobs*) sopprimere; **to have an ~ to grind** (*fig*) fare i propri interessi or il proprio tornaconto.
axiom ['æksɪəm] n assioma m.
axiomatic [æksɪəu'mætɪk] *adj* assiomatico(a).
axis, *pl* **axes** ['æksɪs, -siːz] n asse m.
axle ['æksl] n (*also:* ~**-tree**) asse m.
ay(e) [aɪ] *excl* (*yes*) sì.
AYH n *abbr* = American Youth Hostels.
AZ *abbr* (*US*) = Arizona.
azalea [ə'zeɪlɪə] n azalea.
Azerbaijan [æzəbaɪ'dʒɑːn] n Azerbaigian m.
Azerbaijani [æzəbaɪ'dʒɑːnɪ], **Azeri** [ə'zɛərɪ] *adj, n* azerbaigiano(a), azero(a).
Azores [ə'zɔːz] *npl:* **the ~** le Azzorre.
AZT n *abbr* (= azidothymidine) AZT m.
Aztec ['æztɛk] *adj, n* azteco(a).
azure ['eɪʒə*] *adj* azzurro(a).

Bb

B, b [biː] n (*letter*) B, b f *or* m *inv*; (*SCOL*: mark) ≈ 8 (*buono*); (*MUS*): **B** si m; **B for Benjamin,** (*US*) **B for Baker** ≈ B come Bologna; **B road** n (*BRIT AUT*) ≈ strada secondaria.
b. *abbr* = born.
BA n *abbr* = British Academy; (*SCOL*) *see* Bachelor of Arts.
babble ['bæbl] *vi* cianciare; mormorare ♦ n ciance *fpl*; mormorio.
babe [beɪb] n (*col*): **she's a real ~** è uno schianto di ragazza.
baboon [bə'buːn] n babbuino.
baby ['beɪbɪ] n bambino/a.
baby carriage n (*US*) carrozzina.
babyhood ['beɪbɪhud] n prima infanzia.
babyish ['beɪbɪɪʃ] *adj* infantile.
baby-minder ['beɪbɪ'maɪndə*] n (*BRIT*) bambinaia (*che tiene i bambini mentre la madre lavora*).
baby-sit ['beɪbɪsɪt] *vi* fare il (*or* la) babysitter.
baby-sitter ['beɪbɪsɪtə*] n baby-sitter *m/f inv*.
bachelor ['bætʃələ*] n scapolo; **B~ of Arts/Science (BA/BSc)** ≈ laureato/a in lettere/scienze; **B~ of Arts/Science degree (BA/BSc)** n ≈ laurea in lettere/scienze; *see boxed note.*

BACHELOR'S DEGREE

// **Bachelor's Degree** *è il riconoscimento che viene conferito a chi ha completato un corso di laurea di tre o quattro anni all'università. I Bachelor's degree più importanti sono il "BA" (Bachelor of Arts), il "BSc" (Bachelor of Science), il "BEd" (Bachelor of Education), e il "LLB" (Bachelor of Laws); vedi anche* **Master's degree, doctorate**.

---

bachelor party n (*US*) festa di addio al celibato.
back [bæk] n (*of person, horse*) dorso, schiena; (*of hand*) dorso; (*of house, car*) didietro; (*of train*) coda; (*of chair*) schienale m; (*of page*) rovescio; (*FOOTBALL*) difensore m; **~ to front**

all'incontrario; **to break the ~ of a job**
(*BRIT*) fare il grosso *or* il peggio di un
lavoro; **to have one's ~ to the wall** (*fig*)
essere *or* trovarsi con le spalle al muro
♦ *vt* (*financially*) finanziare; (*candidate*: *also*:
~ up) appoggiare; (*horse*: *at races*)
puntare su; (*car*) guidare a marcia
indietro ♦ *vi* indietreggiare; (*car etc*) fare
marcia indietro ♦ *adj* (*in compounds*)
posteriore, di dietro; arretrato(a); **~
seats/wheels** (*AUT*) sedili *mpl*/ruote *fpl*
posteriori; **~ payments/rent** arretrati
mpl; **~ garden/room** giardino/stanza sul
retro (della casa); **to take a ~ seat** (*fig*)
restare in secondo piano ♦ *adv* (*not
forward*) indietro; (*returned*): **he's ~ è**
tornato; **when will you be ~?** quando
torni?; **he ran ~** tornò indietro di corsa;
(*restitution*): **throw the ball ~** ritira la
palla; **can I have it ~?** posso riaverlo?;
(*again*): **he called ~** ha richiamato.
►**back down** *vi* (*fig*) fare marcia indietro.
►**back on to** *vt fus*: **the house ~s on to the
golf course** il retro della casa dà sul
campo da golf.
►**back out** *vi* (*of promise*) tirarsi indietro.
►**back up** *vt* (*support*) appoggiare,
sostenere; (*COMPUT*) fare una copia di
riserva di.
backache ['bækeɪk] *n* mal *m* di schiena.
back benches *npl* posti in Parlamento
occupati dai *backbencher; see boxed note.*

BACK BENCHES

*Nella "House of Commons", una delle camere
del Parlamento britannico, sono chiamati* **back
benches** *gli scanni dove siedono i
"backbencher", parlamentari che non hanno
incarichi né al governo né all'opposizione.
Nelle file davanti ad essi siedono i
"frontbencher"; vedi anche* **front bench.**

---

backbencher ['bæk'bɛntʃə*] *n* (*BRIT*)
parlamentare che non ha incarichi né al
governo né all'opposizione.
backbiting ['bækbaɪtɪŋ] *n* maldicenza.
backbone ['bækbəun] *n* spina dorsale; **the
~ of the organization** l'anima
dell'organizzazione.
backchat ['bæktʃæt] *n* (*BRIT col*)
impertinenza.
backcloth ['bækkləθ] *n* (*BRIT*) scena di
sfondo.
backcomb ['bækkəum] *vt* (*BRIT*) cotonare.
backdate [bæk'deɪt] *vt* (*letter*) retrodatare;
~d pay rise aumento retroattivo.
backdrop ['bækdrɔp] *n* = **backcloth.**

backer ['bækə*] *n* sostenitore/trice; (*COMM*)
fautore *m.*
backfire ['bæk'faɪə*] *vi* (*AUT*) dar ritorni di
fiamma; (*plans*) fallire.
backgammon ['bækgæmən] *n* tavola reale.
background ['bækgraund] *n* sfondo; (*of
events, COMPUT*) background *m inv*; (*basic
knowledge*) base *f*; (*experience*) esperienza
♦ *cpd* (*noise, music*) di fondo; **~ reading**
letture *fpl* sull'argomento; **family ~**
ambiente *m* familiare.
backhand ['bækhænd] *n* (*TENNIS*: *also*: **~
stroke**) rovescio.
backhanded [bæk'hændɪd] *adj* (*fig*)
ambiguo(a).
backhander ['bækhændə*] *n* (*BRIT*: *bribe*)
bustarella.
backing [bækɪŋ] *n* (*COMM*) finanziamento;
(*MUS*) accompagnamento; (*fig*) appoggio.
backlash ['bæklæʃ] *n* contraccolpo,
ripercussione *f.*
backlog ['bæklɔg] *n*: **~ of work** lavoro
arretrato.
back number *n* (*of magazine etc*) numero
arretrato.
backpack ['bækpæk] *n* zaino.
backpacker ['bækpækə*] *n chi viaggia con
zaino e sacco a pelo.*
back pay *n* arretrato di paga.
backpedal ['bækpɛdl] *vi* pedalare
all'indietro; (*fig*) far marcia indietro.
backseat driver ['bæksiːt-] *n passeggero
che dà consigli non richiesti al guidatore.*
backside [bæk'saɪd] *n* (*col*) sedere *m.*
backslash ['bækslæʃ] *n* backslash *m inv*,
barra obliqua inversa.
backslide ['bækslaɪd] *vi* ricadere.
backspace ['bækspeɪs] *vi* (*in typing*) battere
il tasto di ritorno.
backstage [bæk'steɪdʒ] *adv* nel retroscena.
back street *n* vicolo.
backstroke ['bækstrəuk] *n* nuoto sul dorso.
backtrack ['bæktræk] *vi* = **backpedal.**
backup ['bækʌp] *adj* (*train, plane*)
supplementare; (*COMPUT*) di riserva ♦ *n*
(*support*) appoggio, sostegno; (*COMPUT*:
also: **~ file**) file *m inv* di riserva.
backward ['bækwəd] *adj* (*movement*)
indietro *inv*; (*person*) tardivo(a); (*country*)
arretrato(a); **~ and forward movement**
movimento avanti e indietro.
backwards ['bækwədz] *adv* indietro; (*fall,
walk*) all'indietro; **to know sth ~** *or* (*US*) **~
and forwards** (*col*) sapere qc a menadito.
backwater ['bækwɔːtə*] *n* (*fig*) posto
morto.
back yard *n* cortile *m* sul retro.
bacon ['beɪkən] *n* pancetta.

bacteria [bæk'tɪərɪə] *npl* batteri *mpl*.
bacteriology [bæktɪərɪ'ɔlədʒɪ] *n*
batteriologia.
bad [bæd] *adj* cattivo(a); (*child*)
cattivello(a); (*meat, food*) andato(a) a
male; **his** ~ **leg** la sua gamba malata; **to
go** ~ (*meat, food*) andare a male; **to have
a** ~ **time of it** passarsela male; **I feel** ~
about it (*guilty*) mi sento un po' in colpa;
~ **debt** credito difficile da recuperare; ~
faith malafede *f*.
baddie, baddy ['bædɪ] *n* (*col*: *CINE etc*)
cattivo/a.
bade [bæd] *pt of* bid.
badge [bædʒ] *n* insegna; (*of policeman*)
stemma *m*; (*stick-on*) adesivo.
badger ['bædʒə*] *n* tasso ♦ *vt* tormentare.
badly ['bædlɪ] *adv* (*work, dress etc*) male;
things are going ~ le cose vanno male; ~
wounded gravemente ferito; **he needs it**
~ ne ha gran bisogno; ~ **off** *adj* povero(a).
bad-mannered [bæd'mænəd] *adj*
maleducato(a), sgarbato(a).
badminton ['bædmɪntən] *n* badminton *m*.
bad-tempered [bæd'tɛmpəd] *adj* irritabile;
(*in bad mood*) di malumore.
baffle ['bæfl] *vt* (*puzzle*) confondere.
baffling ['bæflɪŋ] *adj* sconcertante.
bag [bæg] *n* sacco; (*handbag etc*) borsa; (*of
hunter*) carniere *m*; bottino ♦ *vt* (*col*: *take*)
mettersi in tasca; prendersi; ~**s of** (*col*:
lots of) un sacco di; **to pack one's** ~**s** fare
le valigie; ~**s under the eyes** borse sotto
gli occhi.
bagful ['bægful] *n* sacco (pieno).
baggage ['bægɪdʒ] *n* bagagli *mpl*.
baggage allowance *n* peso bagaglio
consentito.
baggage car *n* (*US*) bagagliaio.
baggage claim *n* ritiro bagagli.
baggy ['bægɪ] *adj* largo(a), sformato(a).
Baghdad [bæg'dæd] *n* Bagdad *f*.
bag lady *n* (*col*) stracciona, barbona.
bagpipes ['bægpaɪps] *npl* cornamusa.
bag-snatcher ['bægsnætʃə*] *n* (*BRIT*)
scippatore/trice.
Bahamas [bə'hɑːməz] *npl*: **the** ~ le isole
Bahama.
Bahrain [bɑː'reɪn] *n* Bahrein *m*.
bail [beɪl] *n* cauzione *f* ♦ *vt* (*prisoner*: *gen*: **to
grant** ~ **to**) concedere la libertà
provvisoria su cauzione a; (*NAUT*: *also*: ~
out) *see* **bale out**; **to be released on** ~
essere rilasciato(a) su cauzione.
►**bail out** *vt* (*prisoner*) ottenere la libertà
provvisoria su cauzione di; (*fig*) tirare
fuori dai guai ♦ *vi see* **bale out**.
bailiff ['beɪlɪf] *n* usciere *m*; fattore *m*.

bait [beɪt] *n* esca ♦ *vt* (*hook*) innescare;
(*trap*) munire di esca; (*fig*) tormentare.
bake [beɪk] *vt* cuocere al forno ♦ *vi* cuocersi
al forno.
baked beans *npl* fagioli *mpl* all'uccelletto.
baked potato *n* patata (con la buccia)
cotta al forno.
baker ['beɪkə*] *n* fornaio/a, panettiere/a.
bakery ['beɪkərɪ] *n* panetteria.
baking ['beɪkɪŋ] *n* cottura (al forno).
baking powder *n* lievito in polvere.
baking tin *n* stampo, tortiera.
baking tray *n* teglia.
balaclava [bælə'klɑːvə] *n* (*also*: ~ **helmet**)
passamontagna *m inv*.
balance ['bæləns] *n* equilibrio; (*COMM*: *sum*)
bilancio; (*scales*) bilancia ♦ *vt* tenere in
equilibrio; (*pros and cons*) soppesare;
(*budget*) far quadrare; (*account*) pareggiare; (*compensate*) contrappesare; ~ **of
trade/payments** bilancia commerciale/
dei pagamenti; ~ **brought forward** saldo
riportato; ~ **carried forward** saldo da riportare; **to** ~ **the books** fare il bilancio.
balanced ['bælənst] *adj* (*personality, diet*)
equilibrato(a).
balance sheet *n* bilancio.
balcony ['bælkənɪ] *n* balcone *m*.
bald [bɔːld] *adj* calvo(a).
baldness ['bɔːldnɪs] *n* calvizie *f*.
bale [beɪl] *n* balla.
►**bale out** *vt* (*NAUT*: *water*) vuotare; (: *boat*)
aggottare ♦ *vi* (*of a plane*) gettarsi col
paracadute.
Balearic [bælɪ'ærɪk] *adj*: **the** ~ **Islands** le
(isole) Baleari.
baleful ['beɪlful] *adj* funesto(a).
balk [bɔːlk] *vi*: **to** ~ (**at**) tirarsi indietro (davanti a); (*horse*) recalcitrare (davanti a).
Balkan ['bɔːlkən] *adj* balcanico(a) ♦ *n*: **the**
~**s** i Balcani.
ball [bɔːl] *n* palla; (*football*) pallone *m*; (*for
golf*) pallina; (*dance*) ballo; **to play** ~ (**with
sb**) giocare a palla (con qn); (*fig*) stare al
gioco (di qn); **to be on the** ~ (*fig*:
competent) essere in gamba; (: *alert*) stare
all'erta; **to start the** ~ **rolling** (*fig*) fare la
prima mossa; **the** ~ **is in your court** (*fig*) a
lei la prossima mossa; *see also* **balls**.
ballad ['bæləd] *n* ballata.
ballast ['bæləst] *n* zavorra.
ball bearing *n* cuscinetto a sfere.
ball cock *n* galleggiante *m*.
ballerina [bælə'riːnə] *n* ballerina.
ballet ['bæleɪ] *n* balletto.
ballet dancer *n* ballerino/a.
ballistic [bə'lɪstɪk] *adj* balistico(a).
ballistics [bə'lɪstɪks] *n* balistica.

balloon [bə'lu:n] n pallone m; (in comic strip) fumetto ♦ vi gonfiarsi.
balloonist [bə'lu:nɪst] n aeronauta m/f.
ballot ['bælət] n scrutinio.
ballot box n urna (per le schede).
ballot paper n scheda.
ballpark ['bɔ:lpɑ:k] n (US) stadio di baseball.
ballpark figure n (col) cifra approssimativa.
ball-point pen ['bɔ:lpɔɪnt-] n penna a sfera.
ballroom ['bɔ:lrum] n sala da ballo.
balls [bɔ:lz] npl (col!) coglioni mpl (!).
balm [bɑ:m] n balsamo.
balmy ['bɑ:mɪ] adj (breeze, air) balsamico(a); (BRIT col) = **barmy**.
BALPA ['bælpə] n abbr (= British Airline Pilots' Association) sindacato dei piloti.
balsam ['bɔ:lsəm] n balsamo.
balsa (wood) ['bɔ:lsə-] n (legno di) balsa.
Baltic ['bɔ:ltɪk] adj, n: **the** ~ (**Sea**) il (mar) Baltico.
balustrade [bæləs'treɪd] n balaustrata.
bamboo [bæm'bu:] n bambù m.
bamboozle [bæm'bu:zl] vt (col) infinocchiare.
ban [bæn] n interdizione f ♦ vt interdire; **he was ~ned from driving** (BRIT) gli hanno ritirato la patente.
banal [bə'nɑ:l] adj banale.
banana [bə'nɑ:nə] n banana.
band [bænd] n banda; (at a dance) orchestra; (MIL) fanfara.
▶**band together** vi collegarsi.
bandage ['bændɪdʒ] n benda.
Band-Aid ® ['bændeɪd] n (US) cerotto.
bandit ['bændɪt] n bandito.
bandstand ['bændstænd] n palco dell'orchestra.
bandwagon ['bændwægən] n: **to jump on the** ~ (fig) seguire la corrente.
bandy ['bændɪ] vt (jokes, insults) scambiare.
▶**bandy about** vt far circolare.
bandy-legged ['bændɪ'lɛgɪd] adj dalle gambe storte.
bane [beɪn] n: **it** (or **he** etc) **is the** ~ **of my life** è la mia rovina.
bang [bæŋ] n botta; (of door) lo sbattere; (blow) colpo ♦ vt battere (violentemente); (door) sbattere ♦ vi scoppiare; sbattere; **to** ~ **at the door** picchiare alla porta; **to** ~ **into sth** sbattere contro qc ♦ adv: **to be** ~ **on time** (BRIT col) spaccare il secondo; see also **bangs**.
banger ['bæŋə*] n (BRIT: car: also: **old** ~) macinino; (BRIT col: sausage) salsiccia; (firework) mortaretto.
Bangkok ['bæŋkɔk] n Bangkok f.

Bangladesh [bɑ:ŋglə'dɛʃ] n Bangladesh m.
bangle ['bæŋgl] n braccialetto.
bangs [bæŋz] npl (US: fringe) frangia, frangetta.
banish ['bænɪʃ] vt bandire.
banister(s) ['bænɪstə(z)] n(pl) ringhiera.
banjo, ~**es** or ~**s** ['bændʒəu] n banjo m inv.
bank [bæŋk] n (for money) banca, banco; (of river, lake) riva, sponda; (of earth) banco.
▶**bank on** vt fus contare su.
bank account n conto in banca.
bank balance n saldo; **a healthy** ~ un solido conto in banca.
bank card n = **banker's card**.
bank charges npl (BRIT) spese fpl bancarie.
bank draft n assegno circolare or bancario.
banker ['bæŋkə*] n banchiere m; ~'**s card** (BRIT) carta f assegni inv; ~'**s order** (BRIT) ordine m di banca.
bank giro n bancogiro.
bank holiday n (BRIT) giorno di festa; see boxed note.

BANK HOLIDAY

Una **bank holiday**, *in Gran Bretagna, è una giornata in cui le banche e molti negozi sono chiusi. Generalmente le* **bank holidays** *cadono di lunedì e molti ne approfittano per fare una breve vacanza fuori città. Di conseguenza, durante questi fine settimana lunghi ("bank holiday weekends") si verifica un notevole aumento del traffico sulle strade, negli aeroporti e nelle stazioni e molte località turistiche registrano il tutto esaurito.*

banking ['bæŋkɪŋ] n attività bancaria; professione f di banchiere.
banking hours npl orario di sportello.
bank loan n prestito bancario.
bank manager n direttore m di banca.
banknote ['bæŋknəut] n banconota.
bank rate n tasso bancario.
bankrupt ['bæŋkrʌpt] adj, n fallito(a); **to go** ~ fallire.
bankruptcy ['bæŋkrʌptsɪ] n fallimento.
bank statement n estratto conto.
banned substance ['bænd-] n sostanza al bando (nello sport).
banner ['bænə*] n striscione m.
bannister(s) ['bænɪstə(z)] n(pl) = **banister(s)**.
banns [bænz] npl pubblicazioni fpl di matrimonio.
banquet ['bæŋkwɪt] n banchetto.
bantam-weight ['bæntəmweɪt] n peso gallo.
banter ['bæntə*] n scherzi mpl bonari.

baptism ['bæptɪzəm] n battesimo.
Baptist ['bæptɪst] adj, n battista (m/f).
baptize [bæp'taɪz] vt battezzare.
bar [bɑː*] n barra; (of window etc) sbarra; (of chocolate) tavoletta; (fig) ostacolo; restrizione f; (pub) bar m inv; (counter: in pub) banco; (MUS) battuta ♦ vt (road, window) sbarrare; (person) escludere; (activity) interdire; ~ of soap saponetta; the B~ (LAW) l'Ordine m degli avvocati; behind ~s (prisoner) dietro le sbarre; ~ none senza eccezione.
Barbados [bɑː'beɪdɔs] n Barbados fsg.
barbaric [bɑː'bærɪk], **barbarous** ['bɑːbərəs] adj barbaro(a); barbarico(a).
barbecue ['bɑːbɪkjuː] n barbecue m inv.
barbed wire ['bɑːbd-] n filo spinato.
barber ['bɑːbə*] n barbiere m.
barbiturate [bɑː'bɪtjurɪt] n barbiturico.
Barcelona [bɑːsɪ'ləunə] n Barcellona.
bar chart n diagramma m di frequenza.
bar code n codice m a barre.
bare [bɛə*] adj nudo(a) ♦ vt scoprire, denudare; (teeth) mostrare; the ~ essentials lo stretto necessario.
bareback ['bɛəbæk] adv senza sella.
barefaced ['bɛəfeɪst] adj sfacciato(a).
barefoot ['bɛəfut] adj, adv scalzo(a).
bareheaded [bɛə'hɛdɪd] adj, adv a capo scoperto.
barely ['bɛəlɪ] adv appena.
Barents Sea ['bærənts-] n: the ~ il mar di Barents.
bargain ['bɑːgɪn] n (transaction) contratto; (good buy) affare m ♦ vi (haggle) tirare sul prezzo; (trade) contrattare; into the ~ per giunta.
▶**bargain for** vt fus (col): to ~ for sth aspettarsi qc; he got more than he ~ed for gli è andata peggio di quel che si aspettasse.
bargaining ['bɑːgənɪŋ] n contrattazione f.
bargaining position n: to be in a weak/strong ~ non avere/avere potere contrattuale.
barge [bɑːdʒ] n chiatta.
▶**barge in** vi (walk in) piombare dentro; (interrupt talk) intromettersi a sproposito.
▶**barge into** vt fus urtare contro.
baritone ['bærɪtəun] n baritono.
barium meal ['bɛərɪəm-] n (pasto di) bario.
bark [bɑːk] n (of tree) corteccia; (of dog) abbaio ♦ vi abbaiare.
barley ['bɑːlɪ] n orzo.
barley sugar n zucchero d'orzo.
barmaid ['bɑːmeɪd] n cameriera al banco.
barman ['bɑːmən] n barista m.
barmy ['bɑːmɪ] adj (BRIT col) tocco(a).

barn [bɑːn] n granaio; (for animals) stalla.
barnacle ['bɑːnəkl] n cirripede m.
barn owl n barbagianni m inv.
barometer [bə'rɔmɪtə*] n barometro.
baron ['bærən] n barone m; (fig) magnate m; the oil ~s i magnati del petrolio; the press ~s i baroni della stampa.
baroness ['bærənɪs] n baronessa.
baronet ['bærənɪt] n baronetto.
barrack ['bærək] vt (BRIT): to ~ sb subissare qn di grida e fischi.
barracks ['bærəks] npl caserma.
barrage ['bærɑːʒ] n (MIL) sbarramento; a ~ of questions una raffica di or un fuoco di fila di domande.
barrel ['bærəl] n barile m; (of gun) canna.
barrel organ n organetto a cilindro.
barren ['bærən] adj sterile; (soil) arido(a).
barricade [bærɪ'keɪd] n barricata ♦ vt barricare.
barrier ['bærɪə*] n barriera; (BRIT: also: crash ~) guardrail m inv.
barrier cream n (BRIT) crema protettiva.
barring ['bɑːrɪŋ] prep salvo.
barrister ['bærɪstə*] n (BRIT) avvocato; see boxed note.

BARRISTER

Il **barrister** è un membro della più prestigiosa delle branche della professione legale (l'altra è quella dei "solicitors"); la sua funzione è quella di rappresentare i propri clienti in tutte le corti ("magistrates' court", "crown court" e "Court of Appeal"), generalmente seguendo le istruzioni del caso preparate dai "solicitors".

---

barrow ['bærəu] n (cart) carriola.
barstool ['bɑːstuːl] n sgabello.
Bart. abbr (BRIT) = baronet.
bartender ['bɑːtendə*] n (US) barista m.
barter ['bɑːtə*] n baratto ♦ vt: to ~ sth for barattare qc con.
base [beɪs] n base f ♦ adj vile ♦ vt: to ~ sth on basare qc su; to ~ at (troops) mettere di stanza a; coffee-~d a base di caffè; a Paris-~d firm una ditta con sede centrale a Parigi; I'm ~d in London sono di base or ho base a Londra.
baseball ['beɪsbɔːl] n baseball m.
baseboard ['beɪsbɔːd] n (US) zoccolo, battiscopa m inv.
base camp n campo m base inv.
Basel ['bɑːl] n = Basle.
baseline ['beɪslaɪn] n (TENNIS) linea di fondo.
basement ['beɪsmənt] n seminterrato; (of shop) sotterraneo.

base rate n tasso di base.
bases ['beisi:z] npl of **basis**; ['beisiz] npl of **base**.
bash [bæʃ] vt (col) picchiare ♦ n: **I'll have a ~ (at it)** (BRIT col) ci proverò; **~ed in** adj sfondato(a).
▶**bash up** vt (col: car) sfasciare; (: BRIT: person) riempire di or prendere a botte.
bashful ['bæʃful] adj timido(a).
bashing ['bæʃiŋ] n: **Paki-/queer-~** atti mpl di violenza contro i pachistani/gli omosessuali.
BASIC ['beisik] n (COMPUT) BASIC m.
basic ['beisik] adj (principles, precautions, rules) elementare; (salary) base inv (after n).
basically ['beisikli] adv fondamentalmente, sostanzialmente.
basic rate n (of tax) aliquota minima.
basil ['bæzl] n basilico.
basin ['beisn] n (vessel, also GEO) bacino; (also: **wash~**) lavabo; (BRIT: for food) terrina.
basis, pl **bases** ['beisis, -si:z] n base f; **on the ~ of what you've said** in base alle sue asserzioni.
bask [bɑ:sk] vi: **to ~ in the sun** crogiolarsi al sole.
basket ['bɑ:skit] n cesta; (smaller) cestino; (with handle) paniere m.
basketball ['bɑ:skitbɔ:l] n pallacanestro f.
basketball player n cestista m/f.
Basle [bɑ:l] n Basilea.
basmati rice [bɔz'mæti-] n riso basmati.
Basque [bæsk] adj, n basco(a).
bass [beis] n (MUS) basso.
bass clef n chiave f di basso.
bassoon [bə'su:n] n fagotto.
bastard ['bɑ:stəd] n bastardo/a; (col!) stronzo (!).
baste [beist] vt (CULIN) ungere con grasso; (SEWING) imbastire.
bastion ['bæstiən] n bastione m; (fig) baluardo.
bat [bæt] n pipistrello; (for baseball etc) mazza; (BRIT: for table tennis) racchetta; **off one's own ~** di propria iniziativa ♦ vt: **he didn't ~ an eyelid** non batté ciglio.
batch [bætʃ] n (of bread) infornata; (of papers) cumulo; (of applicants, letters) gruppo; (of work) sezione f; (of goods) partita, lotto.
batch processing n (COMPUT) elaborazione f a blocchi.
bated ['beitid] adj: **with ~ breath** col fiato sospeso.
bath [bɑ:θ, pl bɑ:ðz] n bagno; (bathtub) vasca da bagno ♦ vt far fare il bagno a; **to have a ~** fare un bagno; see also **baths**.
bathchair ['bɑ:θtʃɛə*] n (BRIT) poltrona a rotelle.
bathe [beið] vi fare il bagno ♦ vt bagnare; (wound etc) lavare.
bather ['beiðə*] n bagnante m/f.
bathing ['beiðiŋ] n bagni mpl.
bathing cap n cuffia da bagno.
bathing costume, (US) **bathing suit** n costume m da bagno.
bathmat ['bɑ:θmæt] n tappetino da bagno.
bathrobe ['bɑ:θrəub] n accappatoio.
bathroom ['bɑ:θrum] n stanza da bagno.
baths [bɑ:ðz] npl bagni mpl pubblici.
bath towel n asciugamano da bagno.
bathtub ['bɑ:θtʌb] n (vasca da) bagno.
batman ['bætmən] n (BRIT MIL) attendente m.
baton ['bætən] n bastone m; (MUS) bacchetta.
battalion [bə'tæliən] n battaglione m.
batten ['bætən] n (CARPENTRY) assicella, correntino; (for flooring) tavola per pavimenti; (NAUT) serretta; (: on sail) stecca.
▶**batten down** vt (NAUT): **to ~ down the hatches** chiudere i boccaporti.
batter ['bætə*] vt battere ♦ n pastetta.
battered ['bætəd] adj (hat) sformato(a); (pan) ammaccato(a); **~ wife/baby** consorte f/bambino(a) maltrattato(a).
battering ram ['bætəriŋ-] n ariete m.
battery ['bætəri] n batteria; (of torch) pila.
battery charger n caricabatterie m inv.
battle ['bætl] n battaglia ♦ vi battagliare, lottare; **to fight a losing ~** (fig) battersi per una causa persa; **that's half the ~** (col) è già una mezza vittoria.
battle dress n uniforme f da combattimento.
battlefield ['bætlfi:ld] n campo di battaglia.
battlements ['bætlmənts] npl bastioni mpl.
battleship ['bætlʃip] n nave f da guerra.
batty ['bæti] adj (col: person) svitato(a), strambo(a); (: behaviour, idea) strampalato(a).
bauble ['bɔ:bl] n ninnolo.
baud [bɔ:d] n (COMPUT) baud m inv.
baulk [bɔ:lk] vi = **balk**.
bauxite ['bɔ:ksait] n bauxite f.
Bavaria [bə'vɛəriə] n Bavaria.
Bavarian [bə'vɛəriən] adj, n bavarese (m/f).
bawdy ['bɔ:di] adj piccante.
bawl [bɔ:l] vi urlare.
bay [bei] n (of sea) baia; (BRIT: for parking) piazzola di sosta; (loading) piazzale m di (sosta e) carico; **to hold sb at ~** tenere qn a bada.

bay leaf *n* foglia d'alloro.
bayonet ['beɪənɪt] *n* baionetta.
bay tree *n* alloro.
bay window *n* bovindo.
bazaar [bə'zɑ:*] *n* bazar *m inv*; vendita di beneficenza.
bazooka [bə'zu:kə] *n* bazooka *m inv*.
BB *n abbr* (*BRIT*: = *Boys' Brigade*) *organizzazione giovanile a fine educativo*.
B & B *n abbr see* **bed and breakfast**.
BBB *n abbr* (*US*: = *Better Business Bureau*) *organismo per la difesa dei consumatori*.
BBC *n abbr* = *British Broadcasting Corporation*; *see boxed note*.

BBC

La BBC è l'azienda statale che fornisce il servizio radiofonico e televisivo in Gran Bretagna. Pur dovendo rispondere al Parlamento del proprio operato, la BBC non è soggetta al controllo dello stato per scelte e programmi, anche perché si autofinanzia con il ricavato dei canoni d'abbonamento. La BBC fornisce anche un servizio di informazione internazionale, il "BBC World Service", trasmesso in tutto il mondo.

BBE *n abbr* (*US*: = *Benevolent and Protective Order of Elks*) *organizzazione filantropica*.
BC *adv abbr* (= *before Christ*) a.C. ♦ *abbr* (*Canada*) = *British Columbia*.
BCG *n abbr* (= *Bacillus Calmette-Guérin*) *vaccino antitubercolare*.
BD *n abbr* (= *Bachelor of Divinity*) *titolo di studio*.
B/D *abbr* = **bank draft**.
BDS *n abbr* (= *Bachelor of Dental Surgery*) *titolo di studio*.

===================== KEYWORD

be [bi:] (*pt* **was, were**, *pp* **been**) *aux vb* **1** (*with present participle: forming continuous tenses*): **what are you doing?** che fai?, che stai facendo?; **they're coming tomorrow** vengono domani; **I've been waiting for her for hours** sono ore che l'aspetto
2 (*with pp: forming passives*) essere; **to ~ killed** essere *or* venire ucciso(a); **the box had been opened** la scatola era stata aperta; **the thief was nowhere to ~ seen** il ladro non si trovava da nessuna parte
3 (*in tag questions*): **it was fun, wasn't it?** è stato divertente, no?; **he's good-looking, isn't he?** è un bell'uomo, vero?; **she's back, is she?** così è tornata, eh?
4 (+ *to* + *infinitive*): **the house is to ~ sold**

abbiamo (*or* hanno *etc*) intenzione di vendere casa; **you're to ~ congratulated for all your work** dovremo farvi i complimenti per tutto il vostro lavoro; **am I to understand that ...?** devo dedurre che ...?; **he's not to open it** non deve aprirlo; **he was to have come yesterday** sarebbe dovuto venire ieri
♦ *vb* +*complement* **1** (*gen*) essere; **I'm English** sono inglese; **I'm tired** sono stanco(a); **I'm hot/cold** ho caldo/freddo; **he's a doctor** è medico; **2 and 2 are 4** 2 più 2 fa 4; **~ careful!** sta attento!; **~ good** sii buono; **if I were you ...** se fossi in te ...
2 (*of health*) stare; **how are you?** come sta?; **he's very ill** sta molto male
3 (*of age*): **how old are you?** quanti anni hai?; **I'm sixteen (years old)** ho sedici anni
4 (*cost*) costare; **how much was the meal?** quant'era *or* quanto costava il pranzo?; **that'll ~ £5, please** (sono) 5 sterline, per favore
♦ *vi* **1** (*exist, occur etc*) essere, esistere; **the best singer that ever was** il migliore cantante mai esistito *or* di tutti tempi; **~ that as it may** comunque sia, sia come sia; **so ~ it** sia pure, e sia
2 (*referring to place*) essere, trovarsi; **I won't ~ here tomorrow** non ci sarò domani; **Edinburgh is in Scotland** Edimburgo si trova in Scozia
3 (*referring to movement*): **where have you been?** dove sei stato?; **I've been to China** sono stato in Cina
♦ *impers vb* **1** (*referring to time, distance*) essere; **it's 5 o'clock** sono le 5; **it's the 28th of April** è il 28 aprile; **it's 10 km to the village** di qui al paese sono 10 km
2 (*referring to the weather*) fare; **it's too hot/cold** fa troppo caldo/freddo; **it's windy** c'è vento
3 (*emphatic*): **it's me** sono io; **it's only me** sono solo io; **it was Maria who paid the bill** è stata Maria che ha pagato il conto.

B/E *abbr* = **bill of exchange**.
beach [bi:tʃ] *n* spiaggia ♦ *vt* tirare in secco.
beach buggy *n* dune buggy *f inv*.
beachcomber ['bi:tʃkəumə*] *n* vagabondo (che s'aggira sulla spiaggia).
beachwear ['bi:tʃwɛə*] *n* articoli *mpl* da spiaggia.
beacon ['bi:kən] *n* (*lighthouse*) faro; (*marker*) segnale *m*; (*radio ~*) radiofaro.
bead [bi:d] *n* perlina; (*of dew, sweat*) goccia; **~s** (*necklace*) collana.
beady ['bi:dɪ] *adj*: **~ eyes** occhi *mpl* piccoli e

penetranti.
beagle ['bi:gl] n cane m da lepre.
beak [bi:k] n becco.
beaker ['bi:kə*] n coppa.
beam [bi:m] n trave f; (of light) raggio; (RADIO) fascio (d'onde) ♦ vi brillare; (smile): **to ~ at sb** rivolgere un radioso sorriso a qn; **to drive on full** or **main ~** or (US) **high ~** guidare con gli abbaglianti accesi.
beaming ['bi:mɪŋ] adj (sun, smile) raggiante.
bean [bi:n] n fagiolo; (of coffee) chicco.
beanpole ['bi:npəul] n (col) spilungone/a.
beansprouts ['bi:nsprauts] npl germogli mpl di soia.
bear [bɛə*] n orso; (STOCK EXCHANGE) ribassista m/f ♦ vb (pt **bore,** pp **borne** [bɔ:*, bɔ:n]) vt (gen) portare; (produce: fruit) produrre, dare; (: traces, signs) mostrare; (COMM: interest) fruttare; (endure) sopportare ♦ vi: **to ~ right/left** piegare a destra/sinistra; **to ~ the responsibility of** assumersi la responsabilità di; **to ~ comparison with** reggere al paragone con; **I can't ~ him** non lo posso soffrire or sopportare; **to bring pressure to ~ on sb** fare pressione su qn.
▶**bear out** vt (theory, suspicion) confermare, convalidare.
▶**bear up** vi farsi coraggio; **he bore up well under the strain** ha sopportato bene lo stress.
▶**bear with** vt fus (sb's moods, temper) sopportare (con pazienza); **~ with me a minute** solo un attimo, prego.
bearable ['bɛərəbl] adj sopportabile.
beard [bɪəd] n barba.
bearded ['bɪədɪd] adj barbuto(a).
bearer ['bɛərə*] n portatore m; (of passport) titolare m/f.
bearing ['bɛərɪŋ] n portamento; (connection) rapporto; **(ball) ~s** npl cuscinetti mpl a sfere; **to take a ~** fare un rilevamento; **to find one's ~s** orientarsi.
beast [bi:st] n bestia.
beastly ['bi:stlɪ] adj meschino(a); (weather) da cani.
beat [bi:t] n colpo; (of heart) battito; (MUS) tempo; battuta; (of policeman) giro ♦ vt (pt **beat,** pp **beaten**) battere; **off the ~en track** fuori mano; **to ~ about the bush** menare il cane per l'aia; **to ~ time** battere il tempo; **that ~s everything!** (col) questo è il colmo!
▶**beat down** vt (door) abbattere, buttare giù; (price) far abbassare; (seller) far scendere ♦ vi (rain) scrosciare; (sun)

picchiare.
▶**beat off** vt respingere.
▶**beat up** vt (col: person) picchiare.
beater ['bi:tə*] n (for eggs, cream) frullino.
beating ['bi:tɪŋ] n botte fpl; (defeat) batosta; **to take a ~** prendere una (bella) batosta.
beat-up [bi:t'ʌp] adj (col) scassato(a).
beautician [bju:'tɪʃən] n estetista m/f.
beautiful ['bju:tɪful] adj bello(a).
beautify ['bju:tɪfaɪ] vt abbellire.
beauty ['bju:tɪ] n bellezza; (concept) bello; **the ~ of it is that ...** il bello è che ....
beauty contest n concorso di bellezza.
beauty queen n miss f inv, reginetta di bellezza.
beauty salon n istituto di bellezza.
beauty sleep n: **to get one's ~** farsi un sonno ristoratore.
beauty spot n neo; (BRIT: TOURISM) luogo pittoresco.
beaver ['bi:və*] n castoro.
becalmed [bɪ'kɑ:md] adj in bonaccia.
became [bɪ'keɪm] pt of **become.**
because [bɪ'kɔz] conj perché; **~ of** prep a causa di.
beck [bɛk] n: **to be at sb's ~ and call** essere a completa disposizione di qn.
beckon ['bɛkən] vt (also: **~ to**) chiamare con un cenno.
become [bɪ'kʌm] vt (irreg: like **come**) diventare; **to ~ fat/thin** ingrassarsi/ dimagrire; **to ~ angry** arrabbiarsi; **it became known that ...** si è venuto a sapere che ...; **what has ~ of him?** che gli è successo?
becoming [bɪ'kʌmɪŋ] adj (behaviour) che si conviene; (clothes) grazioso(a).
BEd n abbr (= Bachelor of Education) laurea con abilitazione all'insegnamento.
bed [bɛd] n letto; (of flowers) aiuola; (of coal, clay) strato; (of sea, lake) fondo; **to go to ~** andare a letto.
▶**bed down** vi sistemarsi (per dormire).
bed and breakfast (B & B) n (terms) camera con colazione; (place) ≈ pensione f familiare; see boxed note.

BED AND BREAKFAST

I **bed and breakfasts,** *anche* **B & Bs,** *sono piccole pensioni a conduzione familiare, in case private o fattorie, dove si affittano camere e viene servita al mattino la tradizionale colazione all'inglese. Queste pensioni offrono un servizio di camera con prima colazione, appunto "bed and breakfast", a prezzi più contenuti rispetto agli alberghi.*

bedbug ['bɛdbʌg] n cimice f.
bedclothes ['bɛdkləʊðz] npl coperte e lenzuola fpl.
bedcover ['bɛdkʌvə*] n copriletto.
bedding ['bɛdɪŋ] n coperte e lenzuola fpl.
bedevil [bɪ'dɛvl] vt (person) tormentare; (plans) ostacolare continuamente.
bedfellow ['bɛdfɛləʊ] n: **they are strange ~s** (fig) fanno una coppia ben strana.
bedlam ['bɛdləm] n baraonda.
bedpan ['bɛdpæn] n padella.
bedpost ['bɛdpəʊst] n colonnina del letto.
bedraggled [bɪ'drægld] adj sbrindellato(a); (wet) fradicio(a).
bedridden ['bɛdrɪdən] adj costretto(a) a letto.
bedrock ['bɛdrɔk] n (GEO) basamento; (fig) fatti mpl di base.
bedroom ['bɛdrum] n camera da letto.
Beds abbr (BRIT) = Bedfordshire.
bed settee n divano m letto inv.
bedside ['bɛdsaɪd] n: **at sb's ~** al capezzale di qn.
bedside lamp n lampada da comodino.
bedsit(ter) ['bɛdsɪt(ə*)] n (BRIT) monolocale m.
bedspread ['bɛdsprɛd] n copriletto.
bedtime ['bɛdtaɪm] n: **it's ~** è ora di andare a letto.
bee [biː] n ape f; **to have a ~ in one's bonnet (about sth)** avere la fissazione (di qc).
beech [biːtʃ] n faggio.
beef [biːf] n manzo.
▶**beef up** vt (col) rinforzare.
beefburger ['biːfbɜːgə*] n hamburger m inv.
beefeater ['biːfiːtə*] n guardia della Torre di Londra.
beehive ['biːhaɪv] n alveare m.
bee-keeping ['biːkiːpɪŋ] n apicoltura.
beeline ['biːlaɪn] n: **to make a ~ for** buttarsi a capo fitto verso.
been [biːn] pp of be.
beep [biːp] n (of horn) colpo di clacson; (of phone etc) segnale m (acustico), bip m inv ♦ vi suonare.
beeper ['biːpə*] n (of doctor etc) cercapersone m inv.
beer [bɪə*] n birra.
beer belly n (col) stomaco da bevitore.
beer can n lattina di birra.
beetle ['biːtl] n scarafaggio; coleottero.
beetroot ['biːtruːt] n (BRIT) barbabietola.
befall [bɪ'fɔːl] vi(vt) (irreg: like fall) accadere (a).
befit [bɪ'fɪt] vt addirsi a.
before [bɪ'fɔː*] prep (in time) prima di; (in

space) davanti a ♦ conj prima che + sub; prima di ♦ adv prima; **~ going** prima di andare; **~ she goes** prima che vada; **the week ~** la settimana prima; **I've seen it ~** l'ho già visto; **I've never seen it ~** è la prima volta che lo vedo.
beforehand [bɪ'fɔːhænd] adv in anticipo.
befriend [bɪ'frɛnd] vt assistere; mostrarsi amico a.
befuddled [bɪ'fʌdld] adj confuso(a).
beg [bɛg] vi chiedere l'elemosina ♦ vt chiedere in elemosina; (favour) chiedere; (entreat) pregare; **I ~ your pardon** (apologising) mi scusi; (not hearing) scusi?; **this ~s the question of ...** questo presuppone che sia già risolto il problema di ....
began [bɪ'gæn] pt of begin.
beggar ['bɛgə*] n (also: ~man, ~woman) mendicante m/f.
begin, pt **began**, pp **begun** [bɪ'gɪn, bɪ'gæn, bɪ'gʌn] vt, vi cominciare; **to ~ doing** or **to do sth** incominciare or iniziare a fare qc; **I can't ~ to thank you** non so proprio come ringraziarla; **to ~ with, I'd like to know ...** tanto per cominciare vorrei sapere ...; **~ning from Monday** a partire da lunedì.
beginner [bɪ'gɪnə*] n principiante m/f.
beginning [bɪ'gɪnɪŋ] n inizio, principio; **right from the ~** fin dall'inizio.
begrudge [bɪ'grʌdʒ] vt: **to ~ sb sth** dare qc a qn a malincuore; invidiare qn per qc.
beguile [bɪ'gaɪl] vt (enchant) incantare.
beguiling [bɪ'gaɪlɪŋ] adj (charming) allettante; (deluding) ingannevole.
begun [bɪ'gʌn] pp of begin.
behalf [bɪ'hɑːf] n: **on ~ of**, (US) **in ~ of** per conto di; a nome di.
behave [bɪ'heɪv] vi comportarsi; (well: also: ~ o.s.) comportarsi bene.
behaviour, (US) behavior [bɪ'heɪvjə*] n comportamento, condotta.
behead [bɪ'hɛd] vt decapitare.
beheld [bɪ'hɛld] pt, pp of behold.
behind [bɪ'haɪnd] prep dietro; (followed by pronoun) dietro di; (time) in ritardo con ♦ adv dietro; in ritardo ♦ n didietro; **we're ~ them in technology** siamo più indietro or più arretrati di loro nella tecnica; **~ the scenes** dietro le quinte; **to be ~ (schedule) with sth** essere indietro con qc; (payments) essere in arretrato con qc; **to leave sth ~** dimenticare di prendere qc.
behold [bɪ'həʊld] vt (irreg: like hold) vedere, scorgere.

beige [beɪʒ] adj beige inv.
Beijing [beɪ'dʒɪŋ] n Pechino f.
being ['biːɪŋ] n essere m; **to come into** ~
cominciare ad esistere.
Beirut [beɪ'ruːt] n Beirut f.
Belarus ['bɛlærus] n Bielorussia.
Belarussian [bɛlə'rʌʃən] adj bielorusso(a)
♦ n bielorusso/a; (LING) bielorusso.
belated [bɪ'leɪtɪd] adj tardo(a).
belch [bɛltʃ] vi ruttare ♦ vt (gen: ~ **out**:
smoke etc) eruttare.
beleaguered [bɪ'liːgəd] adj (city)
assediato(a); (army) accerchiato(a); (fig)
assillato(a).
Belfast ['bɛlfɑːst] n Belfast f.
belfry ['bɛlfrɪ] n campanile m.
Belgian ['bɛldʒən] adj, n belga (m/f).
Belgium ['bɛldʒəm] n Belgio.
Belgrade [bɛl'greɪd] n Belgrado f.
belie [bɪ'laɪ] vt smentire; (give false
impression of) nascondere.
belief [bɪ'liːf] n (opinion) opinione f,
convinzione f; (trust, faith) fede f;
(acceptance as true) credenza; **in the** ~
that nella convinzione che; **it's beyond** ~
è incredibile.
believe [bɪ'liːv] vt, vi credere; **to** ~ **in** (God)
credere in; (ghosts) credere a; (method)
avere fiducia in; **I don't** ~ **in corporal
punishment** sono contrario alle punizioni
corporali; **he is** ~**d to be abroad** si pensa
(che) sia all'estero.
believer [bɪ'liːvə*] n (REL) credente m/f; (in
idea, activity): **to be a** ~ **in** credere in.
belittle [bɪ'lɪtl] vt sminuire.
Belize [bɛ'liːz] n Belize m.
bell [bɛl] n campana; (small, on door, electric)
campanello; **that rings a** ~ (fig) mi
ricorda qualcosa.
bell-bottoms ['bɛlbɔtəmz] npl calzoni mpl a
zampa d'elefante.
bellboy ['bɛlbɔɪ], (US) **bellhop** ['bɛlhɔp] n
ragazzo d'albergo, fattorino d'albergo.
belligerent [bɪ'lɪdʒərənt] adj (at war)
belligerante; (fig) bellicoso(a).
bellow ['bɛləu] vi muggire; (cry) urlare (a
squarciagola) ♦ vt (orders) urlare (a
squarciagola).
bellows ['bɛləuz] npl soffietto.
bell push n (BRIT) pulsante m del
campanello.
belly ['bɛlɪ] n pancia.
bellyache ['bɛlɪeɪk] n mal m di pancia ♦ vi
(col) mugugnare.
bellybutton ['bɛlɪbʌtn] n ombelico.
bellyful ['bɛlɪful] n (col): **to have had a** ~ **of**
(fig) averne piene le tasche (di).
belong [bɪ'lɔŋ] vi: **to** ~ **to** appartenere a;

(club etc) essere socio di; **this book** ~**s
here** questo libro va qui.
belongings [bɪ'lɔŋɪŋz] npl cose fpl, roba;
personal ~ effetti mpl personali.
Belorussia [bɛləu'rʌʃə] n Bielorussia.
Belorussian [bɛləu'rʌʃən] adj, n
= **Belarussian.**
beloved [bɪ'lʌvɪd] adj adorato(a).
below [bɪ'ləu] prep sotto, al di sotto di ♦ adv
sotto, di sotto; giù; **see** ~ vedi sotto or
oltre; **temperatures** ~ **normal**
temperature al di sotto del normale.
belt [bɛlt] n cintura; (TECH) cinghia ♦ vt
(thrash) picchiare ♦ vi (BRIT col) filarsela;
industrial ~ zona industriale.
►**belt out** vt (song) cantare a squarciagola.
►**belt up** vi (BRIT col) chiudere la
boccaccia.
beltway ['bɛltweɪ] n (US AUT)
circonvallazione f; (: motorway)
autostrada.
bemoan [bɪ'məun] vt lamentare.
bemused [bɪ'mjuːzd] adj perplesso(a),
stupito(a).
bench [bɛntʃ] n panca; (in workshop) banco;
the B~ (LAW) la Corte.
bench mark n banco di prova.
bend [bɛnd] vb (pt, pp **bent** [bɛnt]) vt
curvare; (leg, arm) piegare ♦ vi curvarsi;
piegarsi ♦ n (BRIT: in road) curva; (in pipe,
river) gomito.
►**bend down** vi chinarsi.
►**bend over** vi piegarsi.
bends [bɛndz] npl (MED) embolia.
beneath [bɪ'niːθ] prep sotto, al di sotto di;
(unworthy of) indegno(a) di ♦ adv sotto, di
sotto.
benefactor ['bɛnɪfæktə*] n benefattore m.
benefactress ['bɛnɪfæktrɪs] n benefattrice f.
beneficial [bɛnɪ'fɪʃəl] adj che fa bene;
vantaggioso(a); ~ **to** che giova a.
beneficiary [bɛnɪ'fɪʃərɪ] n (LAW)
beneficiario/a.
benefit ['bɛnɪfɪt] n beneficio, vantaggio;
(allowance of money) indennità f inv ♦ vt far
bene a ♦ vi: **he'll** ~ **from it** ne trarrà
beneficio or profitto.
benefit performance n spettacolo di
beneficenza.
Benelux ['bɛnɪlʌks] n Benelux m.
benevolent [bɪ'nɛvələnt] adj benevolo(a).
BEng n abbr (= Bachelor of Engineering)
laurea in ingegneria.
benign [bɪ'naɪn] adj benevolo(a); (MED)
benigno(a).
bent [bɛnt] pt, pp of **bend** ♦ n inclinazione f
♦ adj (wire, pipe) piegato(a), storto(a); (col:
dishonest) losco(a); **to be** ~ **on** essere

deciso(a) a.

bequeath [bɪ'kwiːð] vt lasciare in eredità.

bequest [bɪ'kwɛst] n lascito.

bereaved [bɪ'riːvd] adj in lutto ♦ npl: **the ~** i familiari in lutto.

bereavement [bɪ'riːvmənt] n lutto.

beret ['bɛreɪ] n berretto.

Bering Sea ['berɪŋ-] n: **the ~** il mar di Bering.

berk [bəːk] n (BRIT col) coglione/a (!).

Berks abbr (BRIT) = Berkshire.

Berlin [bəː'lɪn] n Berlino f; **East/West ~** Berlino est/ovest.

berm [bəːm] n (US AUT) corsia d'emergenza.

Bermuda [bəː'mjuːdə] n le Bermude.

Bermuda shorts npl bermuda mpl.

Bern [bəːn] n Berna f.

berry ['bɛrɪ] n bacca.

berserk [bə'səːk] adj: **to go ~** montare su tutte le furie.

berth [bəːθ] n (bed) cuccetta; (for ship) ormeggio ♦ vi (in harbour) entrare in porto; (at anchor) gettare l'ancora; **to give sb a wide ~** (fig) tenersi alla larga da qn.

beseech, pt, pp **besought** [bɪ'siːtʃ, bɪ'sɔːt] vt implorare.

beset, pt, pp **beset** [bɪ'sɛt] vt assalire ♦ adj: **a policy ~ with dangers** una politica irta or piena di pericoli.

besetting [bɪ'sɛtɪŋ] adj: **his ~ sin** il suo più grande difetto.

beside [bɪ'saɪd] prep accanto a; (compared with) rispetto a, in confronto a; **to be ~ o.s. (with anger)** essere fuori di sé; **that's ~ the point** non c'entra.

besides [bɪ'saɪdz] adv inoltre, per di più ♦ prep oltre a; (except) a parte.

besiege [bɪ'siːdʒ] vt (town) assediare; (fig) tempestare.

besotted [bɪ'sɔtɪd] adj (BRIT): **~ with** infatuato(a) di.

besought [bɪ'sɔːt] pt, pp of **beseech.**

bespectacled [bɪ'spɛktɪkld] adj occhialuto(a).

bespoke [bɪ'spəuk] adj (BRIT: garment) su misura; **~ tailor** sarto.

best [bɛst] adj migliore ♦ adv meglio; **the ~ thing to do is ...** la cosa migliore da fare or farsi è ...; **the ~ part of** (quantity) la maggior parte di; **at ~** tutt'al più; **to make the ~ of sth** cavare il meglio possibile da qc; **to do one's ~** fare del proprio meglio; **to the ~ of my knowledge** per quel che ne so; **to the ~ of my ability** al massimo delle mie capacità; **he's not exactly patient at the ~ of times**

non è mai molto paziente.

best-before date n (COMM) data limite d'utilizzò or di consumo.

best man n testimone m dello sposo.

bestow [bɪ'stəu] vt: **to ~ sth on sb** conferire qc a qn.

bestseller ['bɛst'sɛlə*] n bestseller m inv.

bet [bɛt] n scommessa ♦ vt, vi (pt, pp **bet** or **betted**) scommettere; **it's a safe ~** (fig) è molto probabile.

Bethlehem ['bɛθlɪhɛm] n Betlemme f.

betray [bɪ'treɪ] vt tradire.

betrayal [bɪ'treɪəl] n tradimento.

better ['bɛtə*] adj migliore ♦ adv meglio ♦ vt migliorare ♦ n: **to get the ~ of** avere la meglio su; **you had ~ do it** è meglio che lo faccia; **he thought ~ of it** cambiò idea; **to get ~** migliorare; **a change for the ~** un cambiamento in meglio; **that's ~!** così va meglio!; **I had ~ go** dovrei andare; **~ off** adj più ricco(a); (fig): **you'd be ~ off this way** starebbe meglio così.

betting ['bɛtɪŋ] n scommesse fpl.

betting shop n (BRIT) ufficio dell'allibratore.

between [bɪ'twiːn] prep tra ♦ adv in mezzo, nel mezzo; **the road ~ here and London** la strada da qui a Londra; **we only had £5 ~ us** fra tutti e due avevamo solo 5 sterline.

bevel ['bɛvl] n (also: **~(led) edge**) profilo smussato.

beverage ['bɛvərɪdʒ] n bevanda.

bevy ['bɛvɪ] n: **a ~ of** una banda di.

bewail [bɪ'weɪl] vt lamentare.

beware [bɪ'wɛə*] vt, vi: **to ~ (of)** stare attento(a) (a).

bewildered [bɪ'wɪldəd] adj sconcertato(a), confuso(a).

bewildering [bɪ'wɪldərɪŋ] adj sconcertante, sbalorditivo(a).

bewitching [bɪ'wɪtʃɪŋ] adj affascinante.

beyond [bɪ'jɔnd] prep (in space) oltre; (exceeding) al di sopra di ♦ adv di là; **~ doubt** senza dubbio; **~ repair** irreparabile.

b/f abbr see **brought forward.**

bhp n abbr (AUT: = brake horsepower) c.v. (= cavallo vapore).

bi... [baɪ] prefix bi....

biannual [baɪ'ænjuəl] adj semestrale.

bias ['baɪəs] n (prejudice) pregiudizio; (preference) preferenza.

bias(s)ed ['baɪəst] adj parziale; **to be ~ against** essere prevenuto(a) contro.

biathlon [baɪ'æθlən] n biathlon m.

bib [bɪb] n bavaglino.

Bible ['baɪbl] n Bibbia f.

bibliography [bɪblɪ'ɔgrəfɪ] n bibliografia.
bicarbonate of soda [baɪ'kɑːbənɪt-] n bicarbonato (di sodio).
bicentenary [baɪsɛn'tiːnərɪ], **bicentennial** [baɪsɛn'tɛnɪəl] n bicentenario.
biceps ['baɪsɛps] n bicipite m.
bicker ['bɪkə*] vi bisticciare.
bicycle ['baɪsɪkl] n bicicletta.
bicycle path n, **bicycle track** n sentiero ciclabile.
bicycle pump n pompa della bicicletta.
bid [bɪd] n offerta; (attempt) tentativo ♦ vb (pt **bade** [bæd] or **bid**, pp **bidden** ['bɪdn] or **bid**) vi fare un'offerta ♦ vt fare un'offerta di; to ~ **sb good day** dire buon giorno a qn.
bidder ['bɪdə*] n: **the highest** ~ il maggior offerente.
bidding ['bɪdɪŋ] n offerte fpl.
bide [baɪd] vt: to ~ **one's time** aspettare il momento giusto.
bidet ['biːdeɪ] n bidè m inv.
bidirectional ['baɪdɪ'rɛkʃənl] adj bidirezionale.
biennial [baɪ'ɛnɪəl] adj biennale ♦ n (pianta) biennale f.
bier [bɪə*] n bara.
bifocals [baɪ'fəuklz] npl occhiali mpl bifocali.
big [bɪg] adj grande; grosso(a); **my ~ brother** mio fratello maggiore; **to do things in a ~ way** fare le cose in grande.
bigamy ['bɪgəmɪ] n bigamia.
big dipper [-'dɪpə*] n montagne fpl russe, otto m inv volante.
big end n (AUT) testa di biella.
biggish ['bɪgɪʃ] adj (see big) piuttosto grande; piuttosto grosso(a); **a ~ rent** un affitto piuttosto alto.
bigheaded ['bɪg'hɛdɪd] adj presuntuoso(a).
big-hearted ['bɪg'hɑːtɪd] adj generoso(a).
bigot ['bɪgət] n persona gretta.
bigoted ['bɪgətɪd] adj gretto(a).
bigotry ['bɪgətrɪ] n grettezza.
big toe n alluce m.
big top n tendone m del circo.
big wheel n (at fair) ruota (panoramica).
bigwig ['bɪgwɪg] n (col) pezzo grosso.
bike [baɪk] n bici f inv.
bike lane n pista ciclabile.
bikini [bɪ'kiːnɪ] n bikini m inv.
bilateral [baɪ'lætərl] adj bilaterale.
bile [baɪl] n bile f.
bilingual [baɪ'lɪŋgwəl] adj bilingue.
bilious ['bɪlɪəs] adj biliare; (fig) bilioso(a).
bill [bɪl] n (in hotel, restaurant) conto; (COMM) fattura; (for gas, electricity) bolletta, conto; (POL) atto; (US: banknote) banconota; (notice) avviso; (THEAT): **on the** ~ in

cartellone; (of bird) becco ♦ vt mandare il conto a; **may I have the** ~ **please?** posso avere il conto per piacere?; "**stick** or **post no ~s**" "divieto di affissione"; **to fit** or **fill the** ~ (fig) fare al caso; ~ **of exchange** cambiale f, tratta; ~ **of lading** polizza di carico; ~ **of sale** atto di vendita.
billboard ['bɪlbɔːd] n tabellone m.
billet ['bɪlɪt] n alloggio ♦ vt (troops etc) alloggiare.
billfold ['bɪlfəuld] n (US) portafoglio.
billiards ['bɪljədz] n biliardo.
billion ['bɪljən] n (BRIT) bilione m; (US) miliardo.
billow ['bɪləu] n (of smoke) nuvola; (of sail) rigonfiamento ♦ vi (smoke) alzarsi in volute; (sail) gonfiarsi.
bills payable (B/P, b.p.) npl effetti mpl passivi.
bills receivable (B/R, b.r.) npl effetti mpl attivi.
billy goat ['bɪlɪgəut] n caprone m, becco.
bimbo ['bɪmbəu] n (col) pollastrella, svampitella.
bin [bɪn] n bidone m; (BRIT: also: **dust**~) pattumiera; (: also: **litter** ~) cestino.
binary ['baɪnərɪ] adj binario(a).
bind, pt, pp **bound** [baɪnd, baund] vt legare; (oblige) obbligare.
▶**bind over** vt (LAW) dare la condizionale a.
▶**bind up** vt (wound) fasciare, bendare; **to be bound up in** (work, research etc) essere completamente assorbito da; **to be bound up with** (person) dedicarsi completamente a.
binder ['baɪndə*] n (file) classificatore m.
binding ['baɪndɪŋ] n (of book) legatura ♦ adj (contract) vincolante.
binge [bɪndʒ] n (col): **to go on a** ~ fare baldoria.
bingo ['bɪŋgəu] n gioco simile alla tombola.
bin liner n sacchetto per l'immondizia.
binoculars [bɪ'nɔkjuləz] npl binocolo.
biochemistry [baɪəu'kɛmɪstrɪ] n biochimica.
biodegradable ['baɪəudɪ'greɪdəbl] adj biodegradabile.
biodiversity ['baɪəudaɪ'vɜːsɪtɪ] n biodiversità f inv.
biofuel ['baɪəufjuəl] n carburante m biologico.
biographer [baɪ'ɔgrəfə*] n biografo/a.
biographic(al) [baɪə'græfɪk(l)] adj biografico(a).
biography [baɪ'ɔgrəfɪ] n biografia.
biological [baɪə'lɔdʒɪkl] adj biologico(a).
biological clock n orologio biologico.

biologist [baɪ'ɔlədʒɪst] n biologo/a.
biology [baɪ'ɔlədʒɪ] n biologia.
biophysics [baɪəu'fɪzɪks] n biofisica.
biopic ['baɪəupɪk] n film m inv biografia inv.
biosphere ['baɪəusfɪə*] n biosfera.
biopsy ['baɪɔpsɪ] n biopsia.
biotechnology [baɪəutek'nɔlədʒɪ] n biotecnologia.
bioterrorism [baɪəu'tɛrərɪzəm] n bioterrorismo.
birch [bə:tʃ] n betulla.
bird [bə:d] n uccello; (BRIT col: girl) bambola.
bird flu n influenza aviaria.
bird of prey n (uccello) rapace m.
bird's-eye view ['bə:dzaɪ-] n vista panoramica.
bird watcher n ornitologo/a dilettante.
Biro ® ['baɪrəu] n biro ® f inv.
birth [bə:θ] n nascita; **to give** ~ **to** dare alla luce; (fig) dare inizio a.
birth certificate n certificato di nascita.
birth control n controllo delle nascite; contraccezione f.
birthday ['bə:θdeɪ] n compleanno.
birthmark ['bə:θmɑ:k] n voglia.
birthplace ['bə:θpleɪs] n luogo di nascita.
birth rate n indice m di natalità.
Biscay ['bɪskeɪ] n: **the Bay of** ~ il golfo di Biscaglia.
biscuit ['bɪskɪt] n (BRIT) biscotto; (US) panino al latte.
bisect [baɪ'sɛkt] vt tagliare in due (parti); (MATH) bisecare.
bisexual ['baɪ'sɛksjuəl] adj, n bisessual (m/f).
bishop ['bɪʃəp] n vescovo; (CHESS) alfiere m.
bistro ['bi:strəu] n bistrò m inv.
bit [bɪt] pt of **bite** ♦ n pezzo; (of tool) punta; (of horse) morso; (COMPUT) bit m inv; (US: coin) ottavo di dollaro; **a** ~ **of** un po' di; **a** ~ **mad/dangerous** un po' matto/ pericoloso; ~ **by** ~ a poco a poco; **to do one's** ~ fare la propria parte; **to come to** ~**s** (break) andare a pezzi; **bring all your** ~**s and pieces** porta tutte le tue cose.
bitch [bɪtʃ] n (dog) cagna; (col!) puttana (!).
bite [baɪt] vt, vi (pt **bit** [bɪt], pp **bitten** ['bɪtn]) mordere ♦ n morso; (insect ~) puntura; (mouthful) boccone m; **let's have a** ~ **(to eat)** mangiamo un boccone; **to** ~ **one's nails** mangiarsi le unghie.
biting ['baɪtɪŋ] adj pungente.
bit part n (THEAT) particina.
bitten ['bɪtn] pp of **bite**.
bitter ['bɪtə*] adj amaro(a); (wind, criticism) pungente; (icy: weather) gelido(a) ♦ n (BRIT: beer) birra amara; **to the** ~ **end** a oltranza.

bitterly ['bɪtəlɪ] adv (disappoint, complain, weep) amaramente; (oppose, criticise) aspramente; (jealous) profondamente; **it's** ~ **cold** fa un freddo gelido.
bitterness ['bɪtənɪs] n amarezza; gusto amaro.
bittersweet ['bɪtəswi:t] adj agrodolce.
bitty ['bɪtɪ] adj (BRIT col) frammentario(a).
bitumen ['bɪtjumɪn] n bitume m.
bivouac ['bɪvuæk] n bivacco.
bizarre [bɪ'zɑ:*] adj bizzarro(a).
bk abbr = **bank; book**.
BL n abbr (= Bachelor of Law(s), Bachelor of Letters) titolo di studio; (US: = Bachelor of Literature) titolo di studio.
B/L abbr = **bill of lading**.
blab [blæb] vi parlare troppo ♦ vt (also: ~ out) spifferare.
black [blæk] adj nero(a) ♦ n nero; (person): **B**~ negro/a ♦ vt (BRIT INDUSTRY) boicottare; ~ **coffee** caffè m inv nero; **to give sb a** ~ **eye** fare un occhio nero a qn; **in the** ~ (in credit) in attivo; **there it is in** ~ **and white** (fig) eccolo nero su bianco; ~ **and blue** adj tutto(a) pesto(a).
► **black out** vi (faint) svenire.
black belt n (SPORT) cintura nera; (US: area): **the** ~ zona abitata principalmente da negri.
blackberry ['blækbərɪ] n mora.
blackbird ['blækbə:d] n merlo.
blackboard ['blækbɔ:d] n lavagna.
black box n (AVIAT) scatola nera.
Black Country n (BRIT): **the** ~ zona carbonifera del centro dell'Inghilterra.
blackcurrant [blæk'kʌrənt] n ribes m inv.
black economy n (BRIT) economia sommersa.
blacken ['blækn] vt annerire.
Black Forest n: **the** ~ la Foresta Nera.
blackhead ['blækhɛd] n punto nero, comedone m.
black hole n (ASTRON) buco nero.
black ice n strato trasparente di ghiaccio.
blackjack ['blækdʒæk] n (CARDS) ventuno; (US: truncheon) manganello.
blackleg ['blæklɛg] n (BRIT) crumiro.
blacklist ['blæklɪst] n lista nera ♦ vt mettere sulla lista nera.
blackmail ['blækmeɪl] n ricatto ♦ vt ricattare/ **blackmailer** ['blækmeɪlə*] n ricattatore/ trice.
black market n mercato nero.
blackout ['blækaut] n oscuramento; (fainting) svenimento; (TV) interruzione f delle trasmissioni.
black pepper n pepe m nero.
Black Sea n: **the** ~ il mar Nero.

black sheep *n* pecora nera.
blacksmith ['blæksmɪθ] *n* fabbro ferraio.
black spot *n* (*AUT*) luogo famigerato per gli incidenti.
bladder ['blædə*] *n* vescica.
blade [bleɪd] *n* lama; (*of oar*) pala; ~ **of grass** filo d'erba.
blame [bleɪm] *n* colpa ♦ *vt*: **to** ~ **sb/sth for sth** dare la colpa di qc a qn/qc; **who's to** ~? chi è colpevole?; **I'm not to** ~ non è colpa mia.
blameless ['bleɪmlɪs] *adj* irreprensibile.
blanch [blɑːntʃ] *vi* (*person*) sbiancare in viso ♦ *vt* (*CULIN*) scottare.
bland [blænd] *adj* mite; (*taste*) blando(a).
blank [blæŋk] *adj* bianco(a); (*look*) distratto(a) ♦ *n* spazio vuoto; (*cartridge*) cartuccia a salve; **to draw a** ~ (*fig*) non aver nessun risultato.
blank cheque, (*US*) **blank check** *n* assegno in bianco; **to give sb a** ~ **to do** (*fig*) dare carta bianca a qn per fare.
blanket ['blæŋkɪt] *n* coperta ♦ *adj* (*statement, agreement*) globale.
blanket cover *n*: **to give** ~ (*subj: insurance policy*) coprire tutti i rischi.
blare [blɛə*] *vi* strombettare; (*radio*) suonare a tutto volume.
blasé ['blɑːzeɪ] *adj* blasé *inv*.
blasphemous ['blæsfɪməs] *adj* blasfemo(a).
blasphemy ['blæsfɪmɪ] *n* bestemmia.
blast [blɑːst] *n* (*of wind*) raffica; (*of air, steam*) getto; (*bomb* ~) esplosione *f* ♦ *vt* far saltare ♦ *excl* (*BRIT col*) mannaggia!; (**at**) **full** ~ a tutta forza.
▶**blast off** *vi* (*SPACE*) essere lanciato(a).
blast-off ['blɑːstɔf] *n* (*SPACE*) lancio.
blatant ['bleɪtənt] *adj* flagrante.
blatantly ['bleɪtəntlɪ] *adv*: **it's** ~ **obvious** è lampante.
blaze [bleɪz] *n* (*fire*) incendio; (*glow: of fire, sun etc*) bagliore *m*; (*fig*) vampata ♦ *vi* (*fire*) ardere, fiammeggiare; (*fig*) infiammarsi ♦ *vt*: **to** ~ **a trail** (*fig*) tracciare una via nuova; **in a** ~ **of publicity** circondato da grande pubblicità.
blazer ['bleɪzə*] *n* blazer *m inv*.
bleach [bliːtʃ] *n* (*also*: **household** ~) varechina ♦ *vt* (*material*) candeggiare.
bleached ['bliːtʃt] *adj* (*hair*) decolorato(a).
bleachers ['bliːtʃəz] *npl* (*US*) posti *mpl* di gradinata.
bleak [bliːk] *adj* (*prospect, future*) tetro(a); (*landscape*) desolato(a); (*weather*) gelido(a); (*smile*) pallido(a).
bleary-eyed ['blɪərɪ'aɪd] *adj* dagli occhi offuscati.
bleat [bliːt] *vi* belare.

bleed, *pt*, *pp* **bled** [bliːd, blɛd] *vt* dissanguare; (*brakes, radiator*) spurgare ♦ *vi* sanguinare; **my nose is** ~**ing** mi viene fuori sangue dal naso.
bleep [bliːp] *n* breve segnale *m* acustico, bip *m inv* ♦ *vi* suonare ♦ *vt* (*doctor*) chiamare con il cercapersone.
bleeper ['bliːpə*] *n* (*of doctor etc*) cercapersone *m inv*.
blemish ['blɛmɪʃ] *n* macchia.
blend [blɛnd] *n* miscela ♦ *vt* mescolare ♦ *vi* (*colours etc*) armonizzare.
blender ['blɛndə*] *n* (*CULIN*) frullatore *m*.
bless, *pt*, *pp* **blessed** *or* **blest** [blɛs, blɛst] *vt* benedire; ~ **you!** (*sneezing*) salute!; **to be** ~**ed with** godere di.
blessed ['blɛsɪd] *adj* (*REL: holy*) benedetto(a); (*happy*) beato(a); **every** ~ **day** tutti i santi giorni.
blessing ['blɛsɪŋ] *n* benedizione *f*; fortuna; **to count one's** ~**s** ringraziare Iddio, ritenersi fortunato; **it was a** ~ **in disguise** in fondo è stato un bene.
blest [blɛst] *pt*, *pp of* **bless**.
blew [bluː] *pt of* **blow**.
blight [blaɪt] *n* (*of plants*) golpe *f* ♦ *vt* (*hopes etc*) deludere; (*life*) rovinare.
blimey ['blaɪmɪ] *excl* (*BRIT col*) accidenti!
blind [blaɪnd] *adj* cieco(a) ♦ *n* (*for window*) avvolgibile *m*; (*Venetian* ~) veneziana ♦ *vt* accecare; **to turn a** ~ **eye** (**on** *or* **to**) chiudere un occhio (su).
blind alley *n* vicolo cieco.
blind corner *n* (*BRIT*) svolta cieca.
blind date *n* appuntamento combinato (*tra due persone che non si conoscono*).
blinders ['blaɪndəz] *npl* (*US*) = **blinkers**.
blindfold ['blaɪndfəuld] *n* benda ♦ *adj*, *adv* bendato(a) ♦ *vt* bendare gli occhi a.
blinding ['blaɪndɪŋ] *adj* (*flash, light*) accecante; (*pain*) atroce.
blindly ['blaɪndlɪ] *adv* ciecamente.
blindness ['blaɪndnɪs] *n* cecità.
blind spot *n* (*AUT etc*) punto cieco; (*fig*) punto debole.
blink [blɪŋk] *vi* battere gli occhi; (*light*) lampeggiare ♦ *n*: **to be on the** ~ (*col*) essere scassato(a).
blinkers ['blɪŋkəz] *npl* (*BRIT*) paraocchi *mpl*.
blinking ['blɪŋkɪŋ] *adj* (*BRIT col*): **this** ~ ... questo(a) maledetto(a) ....
blip [blɪp] *n* (*on radar etc*) segnale *m* intermittente; (*on graph*) piccola variazione *f*; (*fig*) momentanea battuta d'arresto.
bliss [blɪs] *n* estasi *f*.
blissful ['blɪsfəl] *adj* (*event, day*) stupendo(a), meraviglioso(a); (*smile*)

beato(a); in ~ **ignorance** nella (più) beata
ignoranza.
blissfully ['blɪsfəlɪ] adj (sigh, smile)
beatamente; ~ **happy** magnificamente
felice.
blister ['blɪstə*] n (on skin) vescica; (on
paintwork) bolla ♦ vi (paint) coprirsi di
bolle.
blithe [blaɪð] adj gioioso(a), allegro(a).
blithely ['blaɪðlɪ] adv allegramente.
blithering ['blɪðərɪŋ] adj (col): this ~ **idiot**
questa razza d'idiota.
BLit(t) n abbr (= Bachelor of Literature) titolo
di studio.
blitz [blɪts] n blitz m; to have a ~ on sth (fig)
prendere d'assalto qc.
blizzard ['blɪzəd] n bufera di neve.
bloated ['bləutɪd] adj gonfio(a).
blob [blɔb] n (drop) goccia; (stain, spot)
macchia.
bloc [blɔk] n (POL) blocco.
block [blɔk] n (gen, COMPUT) blocco; (in pipes)
ingombro; (toy) cubo; (of buildings) isolato
♦ vt (gen, COMPUT) bloccare; ~ **of flats**
caseggiato; **3 ~s from here** a 3 isolati di
distanza da qui; **mental** ~ blocco mentale.
▶**block up** vt bloccare; (pipe) ingorgare,
intasare.
blockade [blɔ'keɪd] n blocco ♦ vt assediare.
blockage ['blɔkɪdʒ] n ostacolo.
block and tackle n (TECH) paranco.
block booking n prenotazione f in blocco.
blockbuster ['blɔkbʌstə*] n libro or film
etc sensazionale.
block capitals npl stampatello.
blockhead ['blɔkhɛd] n testa di legno.
block letters npl stampatello.
block release n (BRIT) periodo pagato
concesso al tirocinante per effettuare
studi superiori.
block vote n (BRIT) voto per delega.
bloke [bləuk] n (BRIT col) tizio.
blond [blɔnd] n (man) biondo ♦ adj
biondo(a).
blonde [blɔnd] n (woman) bionda ♦ adj
biondo(a).
blood [blʌd] n sangue m; **new** ~ (fig) nuova
linfa.
blood bank n banca del sangue.
blood count n conteggio di globuli rossi e
bianchi.
bloodcurdling ['blʌdkɔːdlɪŋ] adj
raccapricciante, da far gelare il sangue.
blood donor n donatore/trice di sangue.
blood group n gruppo sanguigno.
bloodhound ['blʌdhaund] n segugio.
bloodless ['blʌdlɪs] adj (pale) smorto(a),
esangue; (coup) senza spargimento di

sangue.
bloodletting ['blʌdlɛtɪŋ] n (MED) salasso;
(fig) spargimento di sangue.
blood poisoning n setticemia.
blood pressure n pressione f sanguigna;
to have high/low ~ avere la pressione
alta/bassa.
bloodshed ['blʌdʃɛd] n spargimento di
sangue.
bloodshot ['blʌdʃɔt] adj: ~ **eyes** occhi
iniettati di sangue.
bloodstained ['blʌdsteɪnd] adj
macchiato(a) di sangue.
bloodstream ['blʌdstriːm] n flusso del
sangue.
blood test n analisi f inv del sangue.
bloodthirsty ['blʌdθɔːstɪ] adj assetato(a) di
sangue.
blood transfusion n trasfusione f di
sangue.
blood type n gruppo sanguigno.
blood vessel n vaso sanguigno.
bloody ['blʌdɪ] adj sanguinoso(a); (BRIT
col!): this ~ ... questo maledetto ...; a ~
awful day (col!) una giornata di merda
(!); ~ **good** (col!) maledettamente buono.
bloody-minded ['blʌdɪ'maɪndɪd] adj (BRIT
col) indisponente.
bloom [bluːm] n fiore m ♦ vi essere in fiore.
blooming ['bluːmɪŋ] adj (col): this ~ ...
questo(a) dannato(a) ....
blossom ['blɔsəm] n fiore m; (with pl sense)
fiori mpl ♦ vi essere in fiore; to ~ **into** (fig)
diventare.
blot [blɔt] n macchia ♦ vt macchiare; **to be**
a ~ **on the landscape** rovinare il
paesaggio; **to** ~ **one's copy book** (fig)
farla grossa.
▶**blot out** vt (memories) cancellare; (view)
nascondere; (nation, city) annientare.
blotchy ['blɔtʃɪ] adj (complexion) coperto(a)
di macchie.
blotter ['blɔtə*] n tampone m (di carta
assorbente).
blotting paper ['blɔtɪŋ-] n carta
assorbente.
blotto ['blɔtəu] adj (col) sbronzo(a).
blouse [blauz] n camicetta.
blow [bləu] n colpo ♦ vb (pt **blew,** pp **blown**
[bluː, bləun]) vi soffiare ♦ vt (fuse) far
saltare; **to come to** ~**s** venire alle mani;
to ~ **one's nose** soffiarsi il naso; **to** ~ **a**
whistle fischiare.
▶**blow away** vi volare via ♦ vt portare via.
▶**blow down** vt abbattere.
▶**blow off** vt far volare via; **to** ~ **off course**
far uscire di rotta.
▶**blow out** vi scoppiare.

▶**blow over** vi calmarsi.

▶**blow up** vi saltare in aria ♦ vt far saltare in aria; (tyre) gonfiare; (PHOT) ingrandire.

blow-dry ['bləudraɪ] n (hairstyle) messa in piega a föhn ♦ vt asciugare con il föhn.

blowlamp ['bləulæmp] n (BRIT) lampada a benzina per saldare.

blown [bləun] pp of **blow**.

blowout ['bləuaut] n (of tyre) scoppio; (col: big meal) abbuffata.

blowtorch ['bləutɔ:tʃ] n lampada a benzina per saldare.

blowzy ['blauzɪ] adj trasandato(a).

BLS n abbr (US) = Bureau of Labor Statistics.

blubber ['blʌbə*] n grasso di balena ♦ vi (pej) piangere forte.

bludgeon ['blʌdʒən] vt prendere a randellate.

blue [blu:] adj azzurro(a), celeste; (darker) blu inv; ~ **film/joke** film/barzelletta pornografico(a); (only) **once in a ~ moon** a ogni morte di papa; **out of the ~** (fig) all'improvviso; see also **blues**.

blue baby n neonato cianotico.

bluebell ['blu:bel] n giacinto di bosco.

bluebottle ['blu:bɔtl] n moscone m.

blue cheese n formaggio tipo gorgonzola.

blue-chip ['blu:tʃɪp] adj: ~ **investment** investimento sicuro.

blue-collar worker ['blu:kɔlə*-] n operaio/a.

blue jeans npl blue-jeans mpl.

blueprint ['blu:prɪnt] n cianografia; (fig): ~ **(for)** formula (di).

blues [blu:z] npl: **the ~** (MUS) il blues; **to have the ~** (col: feeling) essere a terra.

bluff [blʌf] vi bluffare ♦ n bluff m inv; (promontory) promontorio scosceso ♦ adj (person) brusco(a); **to call sb's ~** mettere alla prova il bluff di qn.

blunder ['blʌndə*] n abbaglio ♦ vi prendere un abbaglio; **to ~ into sb/sth** andare a sbattere contro qn/qc.

blunt [blʌnt] adj (edge) smussato(a); (point) spuntato(a); (knife) che non taglia; (person) brusco(a) ♦ vt smussare; spuntare; **this pencil is ~** questa matita non ha più la punta; **~ instrument** (LAW) corpo contundente.

bluntly ['blʌntlɪ] adv (speak) senza mezzi termini.

bluntness ['blʌntnɪs] n (of person) brutale franchezza.

blur [blə:*] n cosa offuscata ♦ vt offuscare.

blurb [blə:b] n trafiletto pubblicitario.

blurred [blə:d] adj (photo) mosso(a); (TV) sfuocato(a).

blurt out [blə:t-] vt lasciarsi sfuggire.

blush [blʌʃ] vi arrossire ♦ n rossore m.

blusher ['blʌʃə*] n fard m inv.

bluster ['blʌstə*] n spacconate fpl; (threats) vuote minacce fpl ♦ vi fare lo spaccone; minacciare a vuoto.

blustering ['blʌstərɪŋ] adj (tone etc) da spaccone.

blustery ['blʌstərɪ] adj (weather) burrascoso(a).

Blvd abbr = **boulevard**.

BM n abbr = British Museum; (SCOL) = Bachelor of Medicine) titolo di studio.

BMA n abbr = British Medical Association.

BMJ n abbr = British Medical Journal.

BMus n abbr (= Bachelor of Music) titolo di studio.

BMX n abbr (= bicycle motocross) BMX f inv; ~ **bike** mountain bike f inv per cross.

bn abbr = **billion**.

BO n abbr (col: = body odour) odori mpl sgradevoli (del corpo); = **box office**.

boar [bɔ:*] n cinghiale m.

board [bɔ:d] n tavola; (on wall) tabellone m; (for chess etc) scacchiera; (committee) consiglio, comitato; (in firm) consiglio d'amministrazione; (NAUT, AVIAT): **on ~ a** bordo ♦ vt (ship) salire a bordo di; (train) salire su; **full ~** (BRIT) pensione f completa; **half ~** (BRIT) mezza pensione; ~ **and lodging** vitto e alloggio; **above ~** (fig) regolare; **across the ~** (fig) adv per tutte le categorie ♦ adj generale; **to go by the ~** venir messo(a) da parte.

▶**board up** vt (door) chiudere con assi.

boarder ['bɔ:də*] n pensionante m/f; (SCOL) convittore/trice.

board game n gioco da tavolo.

boarding card ['bɔ:dɪŋ-] n (AVIAT, NAUT) carta d'imbarco.

boarding house n pensione f.

boarding party n squadra di ispezione (del carico di una nave).

boarding pass n (BRIT) = **boarding card**.

boarding school n collegio.

board meeting n riunione f di consiglio.

board room n sala del consiglio.

boardwalk ['bɔ:dwɔ:k] n (US) passeggiata a mare.

boast [bəust] vi: **to ~ (about or of)** vantarsi (di) ♦ vt vantare ♦ n vanteria; vanto.

boastful ['bəustful] adj vanaglorioso(a).

boastfulness ['bəustfulnɪs] n vanagloria.

boat [bəut] n nave f; (small) barca; **to go by ~** andare in barca or in nave; **we're all in the same ~** (fig) siamo tutti nella stessa barca.

boater ['bəutə*] n (hat) paglietta.

boating ['bəutɪŋ] n canottaggio.

boat people n boat people mpl.
boatswain ['bəusn] n nostromo.
bob [bɔb] vi (boat, cork on water: also: ~ **up**
and down) andare su e giù ♦ n (BRIT col)
= **shilling**.
▶**bob up** vi saltare fuori.
bobbin ['bɔbɪn] n bobina; (of sewing
machine) rocchetto.
bobby ['bɔbɪ] n (BRIT col) ≈ poliziotto.
bobsleigh ['bɔbsleɪ] n bob m inv.
bode [bəud] vi: **to ~ well/ill (for)** essere di
buon/cattivo auspicio (per).
bodice ['bɔdɪs] n corsetto.
bodily ['bɔdɪlɪ] adj (comfort, needs)
materiale; (pain) fisico(a) ♦ adv (carry) in
braccio; (lift) di peso.
body ['bɔdɪ] n corpo; (of car) carrozzeria;
(of plane) fusoliera; (organization)
associazione f, organizzazione f; (quantity)
quantità f inv; (of speech, document) parte f
principale; (also: ~ **stocking**) body m inv;
in a ~ in massa; **ruling ~** direttivo; **a wine**
with ~ un vino corposo.
body blow n (fig) duro colpo.
body-building ['bɔdɪ'bɪldɪŋ] n culturismo.
bodyguard ['bɔdɪgɑːd] n guardia del
corpo.
body language n linguaggio del corpo.
body repairs npl (AUT) lavori mpl di
carrozzeria.
body search n perquisizione f personale;
to submit to or **undergo a ~** essere
sottoposto(a) a perquisizione personale.
bodywork ['bɔdɪwɜːk] n carrozzeria.
boffin ['bɔfɪn] n scienziato.
bog [bɔg] n palude f ♦ vt: **to get ~ged down**
(fig) impantanarsi.
bogey ['bəugɪ] n (worry) spauracchio; (also:
~ **man**) babau m inv.
boggle ['bɔgl] vi: **the mind ~s** è incredibile.
Bogotá [bəugə'tɑː] n Bogotà f.
bogus ['bəugəs] adj falso(a); finto(a).
Bohemia [bəu'hiːmɪə] n Boemia f.
Bohemian [bəu'hiːmɪən] adj, n boemo(a).
boil [bɔɪl] vt, vi bollire ♦ n (MED) foruncolo;
to come to the or (US) **a ~** raggiungere
l'ebollizione; **to bring to the** or (US) **a ~**
portare a ebollizione; **~ed egg** uovo alla
coque; **~ed potatoes** patate fpl bollite or
lesse.
▶**boil down** vi (fig): **to ~ down to** ridursi
a.
▶**boil over** vi traboccare (bollendo).
boiler ['bɔɪlə*] n caldaia.
boiler suit n (BRIT) tuta.
boiling ['bɔɪlɪŋ] adj bollente; **I'm ~ (hot)**
(col) sto morendo di caldo.
boiling point n punto di ebollizione.

boil-in-the-bag [bɔɪlɪnðə'bæg] adj (rice etc)
da bollire nel sacchetto.
boisterous ['bɔɪstərəs] adj chiassoso(a).
bold [bəuld] adj audace; (child) impudente;
(outline) chiaro(a); (colour) deciso(a).
boldness ['bəuldnɪs] n audacia; impudenza.
bold type n (TYP) neretto, grassetto.
Bolivia [bə'lɪvɪə] n Bolivia.
Bolivian [bə'lɪvɪən] adj, n boliviano(a).
bollard ['bɔləd] n (NAUT) bitta; (BRIT AUT)
colonnina luminosa.
bolshy ['bɔlʃɪ] adj (BRIT col) piantagrane,
ribelle; **to be in a ~ mood** essere in vena
di piantar grane.
bolster ['bəulstə*] n capezzale m.
▶**bolster up** vt sostenere.
bolt [bəult] n chiavistello; (with nut) bullone
m ♦ adv: ~ **upright** diritto(a) come un fuso
♦ vt serrare; (food) mangiare in fretta ♦ vi
scappare via; **a ~ from the blue** (fig) un
fulmine a ciel sereno.
bomb [bɔm] n bomba ♦ vt bombardare.
bombard [bɔm'bɑːd] vt bombardare.
bombardment [bɔm'bɑːdmənt] n
bombardamento.
bombastic [bɔm'bæstɪk] adj ampolloso(a).
bomb disposal n: ~ **expert** artificiere m;
~ **unit** corpo degli artificieri.
bomber ['bɔmə*] n bombardiere m;
(terrorist) dinamitardo/a.
bombing ['bɔmɪŋ] n bombardamento.
bomb scare n stato di allarme (per
sospetta presenza di una bomba).
bombshell ['bɔmʃɛl] n (fig) notizia bomba.
bomb site n luogo bombardato.
bona fide ['bəunə'faɪdɪ] adj sincero(a);
(offer) onesto(a).
bonanza [bə'nænzə] n cuccagna.
bond [bɔnd] n legame m; (binding promise,
FINANCE) obbligazione f; **in ~** (of goods) in
attesa di sdoganamento.
bondage ['bɔndɪdʒ] n schiavitù f.
bonded warehouse ['bɔndɪd-] n
magazzino doganale.
bone [bəun] n osso; (of fish) spina, lisca ♦ vt
disossare; togliere le spine a.
bone china n porcellana fine.
bone-dry ['bəun'draɪ] adj asciuttissimo(a).
bone idle adj: **to be ~** essere un(a)
fannullone(a).
bone marrow n midollo osseo.
boner ['bəunə*] n (US) gaffe f inv.
bonfire ['bɔnfaɪə*] n falò m inv.
bonk [bɔŋk] vt, vi (hum, col) scopare (!).
bonkers ['bɔŋkəz] adj (BRIT col) suonato(a).
Bonn [bɔn] n Bonn f.
bonnet ['bɔnɪt] n cuffia; (BRIT: of car)
cofano.

bonny ['bɔnɪ] *adj* (*esp Scottish*) bello(a), carino(a).

bonus ['bəʊnəs] *n* premio; (*on wages*) gratifica.

bony ['bəʊnɪ] *adj* (*thin: person*) ossuto(a), angoloso(a); (*arm, face, MED: tissue*) osseo(a); (*meat*) pieno(a) di ossi; (*fish*) pieno(a) di spine.

boo [buː] *excl* ba! ♦ *vt* fischiare ♦ *n* fischio.

boob [buːb] *n* (*col: breast*) tetta; (: *BRIT: mistake*) gaffe *f inv*.

booby prize ['buːbɪ-] *n* premio per il peggior contendente.

booby trap ['buːbɪ-] *n* trabocchetto; (*bomb*) congegno che esplode al contatto.

booby-trapped ['buːbɪtræpt] *adj*: **a ~ car** una macchina con dell'esplosivo a bordo.

book [buk] *n* libro; (*of stamps etc*) blocchetto ♦ *vt* (*ticket, seat, room*) prenotare; (*driver*) multare; (*football player*) ammonire; **~s** *npl* (*COMM*) conti *mpl*; **to keep the ~s** (*COMM*) tenere la contabilità; **by the ~** secondo le regole; **to throw the ~ at sb** incriminare qn seriamente *or* con tutte le aggravanti.

▶**book in** *vi* (*BRIT: at hotel*) prendere una camera.

▶**book up** *vt* riservare, prenotare; **the hotel is ~ed up** l'albergo è al completo; **all seats are ~ed up** è tutto esaurito.

bookable ['bukəbl] *adj*: **seats are ~** si possono prenotare i posti.

bookcase ['bukkeɪs] *n* scaffale *m*.

book ends *npl* reggilibri *mpl*.

booking ['bukɪŋ] *n* (*BRIT*) prenotazione *f*.

booking office *n* (*BRIT*) biglietteria.

book-keeping ['buk'kiːpɪŋ] *n* contabilità.

booklet ['buklɪt] *n* opuscolo, libretto.

bookmaker ['bukmeɪkə*] *n* allibratore *m*.

bookmark ['bukmɑːk] *n* (*also COMPUT*) segnalibro ♦ *vt* (*COMPUT*) mettere un segnalibro a; (*Internet Explorer*) aggiungere a "Preferiti".

bookseller ['buksɛlə*] *n* libraio.

bookshelf ['bukʃɛlf] *n* mensola (per libri); **bookshelves** *npl* (*bookcase*) libreria.

bookshop ['bukʃɔp] *n* libreria.

bookstall ['bukstɔːl] *n* bancarella di libri.

bookstore ['bukstɔː*] *n* = **bookshop**.

book token *n* buono *m* libri *inv*.

book value *n* valore *m* contabile.

bookworm ['bukwəːm] *n* (*fig*) topo di biblioteca.

boom [buːm] *n* (*noise*) rimbombo; (*busy period*) boom *m inv* ♦ *vi* rimbombare; andare a gonfie vele.

boomerang ['buːməræŋ] *n* boomerang *m inv* ♦ *vi* (*fig*) avere effetto contrario; **to ~ on**

sb (*fig*) ritorcersi contro qn.

boom town *n* città *f inv* in rapidissima espansione.

boon [buːn] *n* vantaggio.

boorish ['buərɪʃ] *adj* maleducato(a).

boost [buːst] *n* spinta ♦ *vt* spingere; (*increase: sales, production*) incentivare; **to give a ~ to** (*morale*) tirar su; **it gave a ~ to his confidence** è stata per lui un'iniezione di fiducia.

booster ['buːstə*] *n* (*ELEC*) amplificatore *m*; (*TV*) amplificatore *m* di segnale; (*also: ~ rocket*) razzo vettore; (*MED*) richiamo.

booster seat *n* (*AUT: for children*) seggiolino di sicurezza.

boot [buːt] *n* stivale *m*; (*ankle ~*) stivaletto; (*for hiking*) scarpone *m* da montagna; (*for football etc*) scarpa; (*BRIT: of car*) portabagagli *m inv* ♦ *vt* (*COMPUT*) inizializzare; **to ~** (*in addition*) per giunta, in più; **to give sb the ~** (*col*) mettere qn alla porta.

booth [buːð] *n* (*at fair*) baraccone *m*; (*of cinema, telephone etc*) cabina; (*also: voting ~*) cabina (elettorale).

bootleg ['buːtlɛg] *adj* di contrabbando; **~ record** registrazione *f* pirata *inv*.

booty ['buːtɪ] *n* bottino.

booze [buːz] (*col*) *n* alcool *m* ♦ *vi* trincare.

boozer ['buːzə*] *n* (*col: person*) beone *m*; (*BRIT col: pub*) osteria.

border ['bɔːdə*] *n* orlo; margine *m*; (*of a country*) frontiera; **the B~** *la frontiera tra l'Inghilterra e la Scozia*; **the B~s** *la zona di confine tra l'Inghilterra e la Scozia*.

▶**border on** *vt fus* confinare con.

borderline ['bɔːdəlaɪn] *n* (*fig*) linea di demarcazione ♦ *adj*: **~ case** caso limite.

bore [bɔː*] *pt of* **bear** ♦ *vt* (*hole*) perforare; (*person*) annoiare ♦ *n* (*person*) seccatore/ trice; (*of gun*) calibro; **he's ~d to tears** *or* **~d to death** *or* **~d stiff** è annoiato a morte, si annoia da morire.

boredom ['bɔːdəm] *n* noia.

boring ['bɔːrɪŋ] *adj* noioso(a).

born [bɔːn] *adj*: **to be ~** nascere; **I was ~ in 1960** sono nato nel 1960; **~ blind** cieco dalla nascita; **a ~ comedian** un comico nato.

born-again [bɔːnə'gɛn] *adj*: **~ Christian** convertito(a) alla chiesa evangelica.

borne [bɔːn] *pp of* **bear**.

Borneo ['bɔːnɪəʊ] *n* Borneo.

borough ['bʌrə] *n* comune *m*.

borrow ['bɔrəʊ] *vt*: **to ~ sth (from sb)** prendere in prestito qc (da qn); **may I ~ your car?** può prestarmi la macchina?

borrower ['bɔrəʊə*] *n* (*gen*) chi prende a

prestito; (*ECON*) mutuatario/a.
borrowing ['bɔrəuɪŋ] *n* prestito.
borstal ['bɔːstl] *n* (*BRIT*) riformatorio.
Bosnia ['bɔznɪə] *n* Bosnia.
Bosnia-Herzegovina
['bɔznɪəhɜrzə'gəuviːnə] *n* (*also*: **Bosnia-Hercegovina**) Bosnia-Erzegovina.
Bosnian ['bɔznɪən] *adj*, *n* bosniaco(a).
bosom ['buzəm] *n* petto; (*fig*) seno.
bosom friend *n* amico/a del cuore.
boss [bɔs] *n* capo ♦ *vt* (*also*: ~ **about** *or* **around**) comandare a bacchetta; **stop** ~**ing everyone about!** smettila di dare ordini a tutti!
bossy ['bɔsɪ] *adj* prepotente.
bosun ['bəusn] *n* nostromo.
botanical [bə'tænɪkl] *adj* botanico(a).
botanist ['bɔtənɪst] *n* botanico/a.
botany ['bɔtənɪ] *n* botanica.
botch [bɔtʃ] *vt* fare un pasticcio di.
both [bəuθ] *adj* entrambi(e), tutt'e due
♦ *pron*: ~ (**of them**) entrambi(e) ♦ *adv*: **they sell** ~ **meat and poultry** vendono insieme la carne ed il pollame; ~ **of us went, we** ~ **went** ci siamo andati tutt'e due.
bother ['bɔðə*] *vt* (*worry*) preoccupare; (*annoy*) infastidire ♦ *vi* (*gen*: ~ **o.s.**) preoccuparsi ♦ *n*: **it is a** ~ **to have to do** è una seccatura dover fare ♦ *excl* uffa!, accidenti!; **to** ~ **doing sth** darsi la pena di fare qc; **I'm sorry to** ~ **you** mi dispiace disturbarla; **please don't** ~ non si scomodi; **it's no** ~ non c'è problema.
Botswana [bɔt'swɑːnə] *n* Botswana *m*.
bottle ['bɔtl] *n* bottiglia; (*of perfume, shampoo etc*) flacone *m*; (*baby's*) biberon *m inv* ♦ *vt* imbottigliare; ~ **of wine/milk** bottiglia di vino/latte; **wine/milk** ~ bottiglia da vino/del latte.
▶**bottle up** *vt* contenere.
bottle bank *n* contenitore *m* per la raccolta del vetro.
bottle-fed ['bɔtlfed] *adj* allattato(a) artificialmente.
bottleneck ['bɔtlnɛk] *n* ingorgo.
bottle-opener ['bɔtləupnə*] *n* apribottiglie *m inv*.
bottom ['bɔtəm] *n* fondo; (*of mountain, tree, hill*) piedi *mpl*; (*buttocks*) sedere *m* ♦ *adj* più basso(a); ultimo(a); **at the** ~ **of** in fondo a; **to get to the** ~ **of sth** (*fig*) andare al fondo di *or* in fondo a qc.
bottomless ['bɔtəmlɪs] *adj* senza fondo.
bottom line *n*: **the** ~ **is ...** in ultima analisi ....
botulism ['bɔtjulɪzəm] *n* botulismo.
bough [bau] *n* ramo.
bought [bɔːt] *pt*, *pp* *of* **buy.**

boulder ['bəuldə*] *n* masso (tondeggiante).
boulevard ['buːlvɑːd] *n* viale *m*.
bounce [bauns] *vi* (*ball*) rimbalzare; (*cheque*) essere restituito(a) ♦ *vt* far rimbalzare ♦ *n* (*rebound*) rimbalzo; **to** ~ **in** entrare di slancio *or* con foga; **he's got plenty of** ~ (*fig*) è molto esuberante.
bouncer ['baunsə*] *n* buttafuori *m inv*.
bouncy castle ® ['baunsɪ-] *n grande castello gonfiabile per giocare.*
bound [baund] *pt*, *pp* *of* **bind** ♦ *n* (*gen pl*) limite *m*; (*leap*) salto ♦ *vt* (*leap*) saltare ♦ *adj*: **to be** ~ **to do sth** (*obliged*) essere costretto(a) a fare qc; **he's** ~ **to fail** (*likely*) è certo di fallire; ~ **for** diretto(a) a; **out of** ~**s** il cui accesso è vietato.
boundary ['baundrɪ] *n* confine *m*.
boundless ['baundlɪs] *adj* illimitato(a).
bountiful ['bauntɪful] *adj* (*person*) munifico(a); (*God*) misericordioso(a); (*supply*) abbondante.
bounty ['bauntɪ] *n* (*generosity*) liberalità, munificenza; (*reward*) taglia.
bounty hunter *n* cacciatore *m* di taglie.
bouquet ['bukeɪ] *n* bouquet *m inv*.
bourbon ['buəbən] *n* (*US*: *also*: ~ **whiskey**) bourbon *m inv*.
bourgeois ['buəʒwɑː] *adj*, *n* borghese (*m/f*).
bout [baut] *n* periodo; (*of malaria etc*) attacco; (*BOXING etc*) incontro.
boutique [buː'tiːk] *n* boutique *f inv*.
bow¹ *n* [bəu] nodo; (*weapon*) arco; (*MUS*) archetto; (*NAUT*: *also*: ~**s**) prua.
bow² [bau] *n* (*with body*) inchino ♦ *vi* inchinarsi; (*yield*): **to** ~ **to** *or* **before** sottomettersi a; **to** ~ **to the inevitable** rassegnarsi all'inevitabile.
bowels [bauəlz] *npl* intestini *mpl*; (*fig*) viscere *fpl*.
bowl [bəul] *n* (*for eating*) scodella; (*for washing*) bacino; (*ball*) boccia; (*of pipe*) fornello; (*US*: *stadium*) stadio ♦ *vi* (*CRICKET*) servire (la palla); *see also* **bowls.**
▶**bowl over** *vt* (*fig*) sconcertare.
bow-legged ['bəu'lɛgɪd] *adj* dalle gambe storte.
bowler ['bəulə*] *n* giocatore *m* di bocce; (*CRICKET*) giocatore che serve la palla; (*BRIT*: *also*: ~ **hat**) bombetta.
bowling ['bəulɪŋ] *n* (*game*) gioco delle bocce; bowling *m*.
bowling alley *n* pista da bowling.
bowling green *n* campo di bocce.
bowls [bəulz] *n* gioco delle bocce.
bow tie *n* cravatta a farfalla.
box [bɔks] *n* scatola; (*also*: **cardboard** ~) (scatola di) cartone *m*; (*crate*; *also for*

money) cassetta; (*THEAT*) palco; (*BRIT AUT*) area d'incrocio ♦ *vi* fare pugilato ♦ *vt* mettere in (una) scatola; (*SPORT*) combattere contro.

boxer ['bɔksə*] *n* (*person*) pugile *m*; (*dog*) boxer *m inv*.

boxing ['bɔksɪŋ] *n* (*SPORT*) pugilato.

Boxing Day *n* (*BRIT*) ≈ Santo Stefano; *see boxed note*.

BOXING DAY

Il **Boxing Day** *è il primo giorno infrasettimanale dopo Natale e cade generalmente il 26 di dicembre. Prende il nome dall'usanza di donare pacchi regalo natalizi, un tempo chiamati "Christmas boxes", a fornitori e dipendenti, ed è un giorno di festa.*

---

boxing gloves *npl* guantoni *mpl* da pugile.

boxing ring *n* ring *m inv*.

box number *n* (*for advertisements*) casella.

box office *n* biglietteria.

box room *n* ripostiglio.

boy [bɔɪ] *n* ragazzo; (*small*) bambino; (*son*) figlio; (*servant*) servo.

boy band *n gruppo pop di soli ragazzi maschi creato per far presa su un pubblico giovane.*

boycott ['bɔɪkɔt] *n* boicottaggio ♦ *vt* boicottare.

boyfriend ['bɔɪfrɛnd] *n* ragazzo.

boyish ['bɔɪʃ] *adj* di *or* da ragazzo.

bp *abbr* = **bishop**.

bra [brɑ:] *n* reggipetto, reggiseno.

brace [breɪs] *n* sostegno; (*on teeth*) apparecchio correttore; (*tool*) trapano; (*TYP: also*: ~ **bracket**) graffa ♦ *vt* rinforzare, sostenere; **to** ~ **o.s.** (*fig*) farsi coraggio; *see also* **braces**.

bracelet ['breɪslɪt] *n* braccialetto.

braces ['breɪsɪz] *npl* (*BRIT*) bretelle *fpl*.

bracing ['breɪsɪŋ] *adj* invigorante.

bracken ['brækən] *n* felce *f*.

bracket ['brækɪt] *n* (*TECH*) mensola; (*group*) gruppo; (*TYP*) parentesi *f inv* ♦ *vt* mettere fra parentesi; (*fig: also*: ~ **together**) mettere insieme; **in** ~**s** tra parentesi; **round/square** ~**s** parentesi tonde/quadre; **income** ~ fascia di reddito.

brag [bræg] *vi* vantarsi.

braid [breɪd] *n* (*trimming*) passamano; (*of hair*) treccia.

Braille [breɪl] *n* braille *m*.

brain [breɪn] *n* cervello; ~**s** *npl* cervella *fpl*; **he's got** ~**s** è intelligente.

brainchild ['breɪntʃaɪld] *n* creatura, creazione *f*.

braindead ['breɪndɛd] *adj* (*MED*) che ha subito morte cerebrale.

brainless ['breɪnlɪs] *adj* deficiente, stupido(a).

brainstorm ['breɪnstɔːm] *n* (*fig*) attacco di pazzia; (*US*) = **brainwave**.

brainwash ['breɪnwɔʃ] *vt* fare un lavaggio di cervello a.

brainwave ['breɪnweɪv] *n* lampo di genio.

brainy ['breɪnɪ] *adj* intelligente.

braise [breɪz] *vt* brasare.

brake [breɪk] *n* (*on vehicle*) freno ♦ *vt, vi* frenare.

brake light *n* (fanalino dello) stop *m inv*.

brake pedal *n* pedale *m* del freno.

bramble ['bræmbl] *n* rovo; (*fruit*) mora.

bran [bræn] *n* crusca.

branch [brɑːntʃ] *n* ramo; (*COMM*) succursale *f*, filiale *f* ♦ *vi* diramarsi.

► **branch out** *vi*: **to** ~ **out into** intraprendere una nuova attività nel ramo di.

branch line *n* (*RAIL*) linea secondaria.

branch manager *n* direttore *m* di filiale.

brand [brænd] *n* marca ♦ *vt* (*cattle*) marcare (a ferro rovente); (*fig: pej*): **to** ~ **sb a communist** *etc* definire qn come comunista *etc*.

brandish ['brændɪʃ] *vt* brandire.

brand name *n* marca.

brand-new ['brænd'njuː] *adj* nuovo(a) di zecca.

brandy ['brændɪ] *n* brandy *m inv*.

brash [bræʃ] *adj* sfacciato(a).

brass [brɑːs] *n* ottone *m*; **the** ~ (*MUS*) gli ottoni.

brass band *n* fanfara.

brassière ['bræsɪə*] *n* reggipetto, reggiseno.

brass tacks *npl*: **to get down to** ~ (*col*) venire al sodo.

brat [bræt] *n* (*pej*) marmocchio, monello/a.

bravado [brə'vɑːdəʊ] *n* spavalderia.

brave [breɪv] *adj* coraggioso(a) ♦ *n* guerriero *m* pellerossa *inv* ♦ *vt* affrontare.

bravery ['breɪvərɪ] *n* coraggio.

bravo [brɑː'vəʊ] *excl* bravo!, bene!

brawl [brɔːl] *n* rissa ♦ *vi* azzuffarsi.

brawn [brɔːn] *n* muscolo; (*meat*) carne *f* di testa di maiale.

brawny ['brɔːnɪ] *adj* muscoloso(a).

bray [breɪ] *n* raglio ♦ *vi* ragliare.

brazen ['breɪzn] *adj* svergognato(a) ♦ *vt*: **to** ~ **it out** fare lo sfacciato.

brazier ['breɪzɪə*] *n* braciere *m*.

Brazil [brə'zɪl] *n* Brasile *m*.

Brazilian [brə'zɪljən] *adj, n* brasiliano(a).

Brazil nut *n* noce *f* del Brasile.

breach [briːtʃ] vt aprire una breccia in ♦ n (gap) breccia, varco; (estrangement) rottura; (of duty) abuso; (breaking): ~ **of contract** rottura di contratto; ~ **of the peace** violazione f dell'ordine pubblico; ~ **of trust** abuso di fiducia.

bread [brɛd] n pane m; (col: money) grana; **to earn one's daily** ~ guadagnarsi il pane; **to know which side one's** ~ **is buttered on** saper fare i propri interessi; ~ **and butter** n pane e burro; (fig) mezzi mpl di sussistenza.

breadbin ['brɛdbɪn] n (BRIT) cassetta f portapane inv.

breadboard ['brɛdbɔːd] n tagliere m (per il pane); (COMPUT) pannello per esperimenti.

breadbox ['brɛdbɔks] n (US) cassetta f portapane inv.

breadcrumbs ['brɛdkrʌmz] npl briciole fpl; (CULIN) pangrattato.

breadline ['brɛdlaɪn] n: **to be on the** ~ avere appena denaro per vivere.

breadth [brɛtθ] n larghezza.

breadwinner ['brɛdwɪnə*] n chi guadagna il pane per tutta la famiglia.

break [breɪk] vb (pt **broke** [brəuk], pp **broken** ['brəukən]) vt rompere; (law) violare; (promise) mancare a ♦ vi rompersi; (weather) cambiare ♦ n (gap) breccia; (fracture) rottura; (rest, also SCOL) intervallo; (: short) pausa; (chance) possibilità f inv; (holiday) vacanza; **to** ~ **one's leg** etc rompersi la gamba etc; **to** ~ **a record** battere un primato; **to** ~ **the news to sb** comunicare per primo la notizia a qn; **to** ~ **with sb** (fig) rompere con qn; **to** ~ **even** vi coprire le spese; **to** ~ **free** or **loose** liberarsi; **without a** ~ senza una pausa; **to have** or **take a** ~ (few minutes) fare una pausa; (holiday) prendere un po' di riposo; **a lucky** ~ un colpo di fortuna.

▶**break down** vt (figures, data) analizzare; (door etc) buttare giù, abbattere; (resistance) stroncare ♦ vi crollare; (MED) avere un esaurimento (nervoso); (AUT) guastarsi.

▶**break in** vt (horse etc) domare ♦ vi (burglar) fare irruzione.

▶**break into** vt fus (house) fare irruzione in.

▶**break off** vi (speaker) interrompersi; (branch) troncarsi ♦ vt (talks, engagement) rompere.

▶**break open** vt (door etc) sfondare.

▶**break out** vi evadere; **to** ~ **out in spots** coprirsi di macchie.

▶**break through** vi: **the sun broke through** il sole ha fatto capolino tra le nuvole ♦ vt (defences, barrier) sfondare, penetrare in; (crowd) aprirsi un varco in or tra, aprirsi un passaggio in or tra.

▶**break up** vi (partnership) sciogliersi; (friends) separarsi ♦ vt fare in pezzi, spaccare; (fight etc) interrompere, far cessare; (marriage) finire.

breakable ['breɪkəbl] adj fragile; ~**s** npl oggetti mpl fragili.

breakage ['breɪkɪdʒ] n rottura; **to pay for** ~**s** pagare i danni.

breakaway ['breɪkəweɪ] adj (group etc) scissionista, dissidente.

break-dancing ['breɪkdɑːnsɪŋ] n breakdance f.

breakdown ['breɪkdaun] n (AUT) guasto; (in communications) interruzione f; (MED: also: **nervous** ~) esaurimento nervoso; (of payments etc) resoconto.

breakdown service n (BRIT) servizio riparazioni.

breakdown van n carro m attrezzi inv.

breaker ['breɪkə*] n frangente m.

breakeven ['breɪk'iːvn] cpd: ~ **chart** diagramma m del punto di rottura or pareggio; ~ **point** punto di rottura or pareggio.

breakfast ['brɛkfəst] n colazione f.

breakfast cereal n fiocchi mpl d'avena or di mais etc.

break-in ['breɪkɪn] n irruzione f.

breaking point ['breɪkɪŋ-] n punto di rottura.

breakthrough ['breɪkθruː] n (MIL) breccia; (fig) passo avanti.

break-up ['breɪkʌp] n (of partnership, marriage) rottura.

break-up value n (COMM) valore m di realizzo.

breakwater ['breɪkwɔːtə*] n frangiflutti m inv.

breast [brɛst] n (of woman) seno; (chest) petto.

breast-feed ['brɛstfiːd] vt, vi (irreg: like **feed**) allattare (al seno).

breast pocket n taschino.

breast-stroke ['brɛststrəuk] n nuoto a rana.

breath [brɛθ] n fiato; **out of** ~ senza fiato; **to go out for a** ~ **of air** andare a prendere una boccata d'aria.

Breathalyser ® ['brɛθəlaɪzə*] n alcoltest m inv.

breathe [briːð] vt, vi respirare; **I won't** ~ **a word about it** non fiaterò.

▶**breathe in** vi inspirare ♦ vt respirare.

▶**breathe out** vt, vi espirare.

breather ['bri:ðə*] n attimo di respiro.
breathing ['bri:ðɪŋ] n respiro, respirazione f.
breathing space n (fig) attimo di respiro.
breathless ['brɛθlɪs] adj senza fiato; (with excitement) con il fiato sospeso.
breath-taking ['brɛθteɪkɪŋ] adj sbalorditivo(a).
breath test n ≈ prova del palloncino.
-bred [brɛd] suffix: **to be well/ill**~ essere ben educato(a)/maleducato(a).
breed [bri:d] vb (pt, pp **bred** [brɛd]) vt allevare; (fig: hate, suspicion) generare, provocare ♦ vi riprodursi ♦ n razza, varietà f inv.
breeder ['bri:də*] n (PHYSICS: also: ~ reactor) reattore m autofertilizzante.
breeding ['bri:dɪŋ] n riproduzione f; allevamento.
breeze [bri:z] n brezza.
breeze block n (BRIT) mattone composto di scorie di coke.
breezy ['bri:zɪ] adj arioso(a); allegro(a).
Breton ['brɛtən] adj, n brettone (m/f).
brevity ['brɛvɪtɪ] n brevità.
brew [bru:] vt (tea) fare un infuso di; (beer) fare; (plot) tramare ♦ vi (tea) essere in infusione; (beer) essere in fermentazione; (fig) bollire in pentola.
brewer ['bru:ə*] n birraio.
brewery ['bru:ərɪ] n fabbrica di birra.
briar ['braɪə*] n (thorny bush) rovo; (wild rose) rosa selvatica.
bribe [braɪb] n bustarella ♦ vt comprare; **to ~ sb to do sth** pagare qn sottobanco perché faccia qc.
bribery ['braɪbərɪ] n corruzione f.
bric-a-brac ['brɪkəbræk] n bric-a-brac m.
brick [brɪk] n mattone m.
bricklayer ['brɪkleɪə*] n muratore m.
brickwork ['brɪkwə:k] n muratura in mattoni.
brickworks ['brɪkwə:ks] n fabbrica di mattoni.
bridal ['braɪdl] adj nuziale; ~ **party** corteo nuziale.
bride [braɪd] n sposa.
bridegroom ['braɪdgru:m] n sposo.
bridesmaid ['braɪdzmeɪd] n damigella d'onore.
bridge [brɪdʒ] n ponte m; (NAUT) ponte di comando; (of nose) dorso; (CARDS, DENTISTRY) bridge m inv ♦ vt (river) fare un ponte sopra; (gap) colmare.
bridging loan ['brɪdʒɪŋ-] n (BRIT) anticipazione f sul mutuo.
bridle ['braɪdl] n briglia ♦ vt tenere a freno; (horse) mettere la briglia a ♦ vi (in anger

etc) adombrarsi, adontarsi.
bridle path n sentiero (per cavalli).
brief [bri:f] adj breve ♦ n (LAW) comparsa ♦ vt (MIL etc) dare istruzioni a; **in** ~ ... in breve ..., a farla breve ...; **to** ~ **sb (about sth)** mettere qn al corrente (di qc); see also **briefs**.
briefcase ['bri:fkeɪs] n cartella.
briefing ['bri:fɪŋ] n istruzioni fpl.
briefly ['bri:flɪ] adv (speak, visit) brevemente; (glimpse) di sfuggita.
briefness ['bri:fnɪs] n brevità.
briefs [bri:fs] npl mutande fpl.
Brig. abbr = **brigadier**.
brigade [brɪ'geɪd] n (MIL) brigata.
brigadier [brɪgə'dɪə*] n generale m di brigata.
bright [braɪt] adj luminoso(a); (person) sveglio(a); (colour) vivace; **to look on the** ~ **side** vedere il lato positivo delle cose.
brighten ['braɪtn] (also: ~ up) vt (room) rendere luminoso(a); rallegrare ♦ vi schiarirsi; (person) rallegrarsi.
brightly ['braɪtlɪ] adv (shine) vivamente, intensamente; (smile) radiosamente; (talk) con animazione.
brill [brɪl] excl (BRIT col) stupendo!, fantastico!
brilliance ['brɪljəns] n splendore m; (fig: of person) genialità, talento.
brilliant ['brɪljənt] adj brillante; (sunshine) sfolgorante.
brim [brɪm] n orlo.
brimful ['brɪm'ful] adj pieno(a) or colmo(a) fino all'orlo; (fig) pieno(a).
brine [braɪn] n acqua salmastra; (CULIN) salamoia.
bring, pt, pp **brought** [brɪŋ, brɔ:t] vt portare; **to ~ sth to an end** mettere fine a qc; **I can't ~ myself to sack him** non so risolvermi a licenziarlo.
►**bring about** vt causare.
►**bring back** vt riportare.
►**bring down** vt (lower) far scendere; (shoot down) abbattere; (government) far cadere.
►**bring forward** vt portare avanti; (in time) anticipare; (BOOK-KEEPING) riportare.
►**bring in** vt (person) fare entrare; (object) portare; (POL: bill) presentare; (: legislation) introdurre; (LAW: verdict) emettere; (produce: income) rendere.
►**bring off** vt (task, plan) portare a compimento; (deal) concludere.
►**bring out** vt (meaning) mettere in evidenza; (new product) lanciare; (book) pubblicare, fare uscire.
►**bring round** or **to** vt (unconscious person)

far rinvenire.
▶**bring up** vt allevare; (*question*)
introdurre.
brink [brɪŋk] n orlo; **on the ~ of doing sth**
sul punto di fare qc; **she was on the ~ of
tears** era lì lì per piangere.
brisk [brɪsk] adj (*person, tone*) spiccio(a),
sbrigativo(a); (: *abrupt*) brusco(a); (*wind*)
fresco(a); (*trade etc*) vivace, attivo(a); **to
go for a ~ walk** fare una camminata di
buon passo; **business is ~** gli affari
vanno bene.
bristle ['brɪsl] n setola ♦ vi rizzarsi; **bristling
with** irto(a) di.
bristly ['brɪslɪ] adj (*chin*) ispido(a); (*beard,
hair*) irsuto(a), setoloso(a).
Brit [brɪt] n abbr (*col*: = *British person*)
britannico/a.
Britain ['brɪtən] n Gran Bretagna.
British ['brɪtɪʃ] adj britannico(a); **the ~** npl i
Britannici; **the ~ Isles** npl le Isole
Britanniche.
British Summer Time n ora legale (*in
Gran Bretagna*).
Briton ['brɪtən] n britannico/a.
Brittany ['brɪtənɪ] n Bretagna.
brittle ['brɪtl] adj fragile.
Br(o) abbr (*REL*) = **brother**.
broach [brəʊtʃ] vt (*subject*) affrontare.
broad [brɔːd] adj largo(a); (*distinction*)
generale; (*accent*) spiccato(a) ♦ n (*US col*)
bellona; **~ hint** allusione f esplicita; **in ~
daylight** in pieno giorno; **the ~ outlines** le
grandi linee.
broadband ['brɔːdbænd] adj (*COMPUT*) a
banda larga ♦ n banda larga.
broad bean n fava.
broadcast ['brɔːdkɑːst] n trasmissione f
♦ vb (*pt, pp* **broadcast**) vt trasmettere per
radio (*or* per televisione) ♦ vi fare una
trasmissione.
broadcaster ['brɔːdkɑːstə*] n
annunciatore/trice radiotelevisivo(a) (*or*
radiofonico(a)).
broadcasting ['brɔːdkɑːstɪŋ] n
radiodiffusione f; televisione f.
broaden ['brɔːdn] vt allargare ♦ vi
allargarsi.
broadly ['brɔːdlɪ] adv (*fig*) in generale.
broad-minded ['brɔːd'maɪndɪd] adj di
mente aperta.
broadsheet ['brɔːdʃiːt] n (*BRIT*) giornale m
(*si contrappone al tabloid che è di formato
più piccolo*).
broccoli ['brɒkəlɪ] n (*BOT*) broccolo; (*CULIN*)
broccoli mpl.
brochure ['brəʊʃjʊə*] n dépliant m inv.
brogue [brəʊg] n (*shoe*) scarpa rozza in

cuoio; (*accent*) accento irlandese.
broil [brɔɪl] vt cuocere a fuoco vivo.
broke [brəʊk] pt of **break** ♦ adj (*col*)
squattrinato(a); **to go ~** fare fallimento.
broken ['brəʊkən] pp of **break** ♦ adj (*gen*)
rotto(a); (*stick, promise, vow*) spezzato(a);
(*marriage*) fallito(a); **he comes from a ~
home** i suoi sono divisi; **in ~ French/
English** in un francese/inglese stentato.
broken-down ['brəʊkən'daʊn] adj (*car*) in
panne, rotto(a); (*machine*) guasto(a),
fuori uso; (*house*) abbandonato(a), in
rovina.
broken-hearted ['brəʊkən'hɑːtɪd] adj: **to be
~** avere il cuore spezzato.
broker ['brəʊkə*] n agente m.
brokerage ['brəʊkərɪdʒ] n (*COMM*)
commissione f di intermediazione.
brolly ['brɒlɪ] n (*BRIT col*) ombrello.
bronchitis [brɒŋ'kaɪtɪs] n bronchite f.
bronze [brɒnz] n bronzo.
bronzed [brɒnzd] adj abbronzato(a).
brooch [brəʊtʃ] n spilla.
brood [bruːd] n covata ♦ vi (*hen*) covare;
(*person*) rimuginare.
broody ['bruːdɪ] adj (*fig*) cupo(a) e
taciturno(a).
brook [brʊk] n ruscello.
broom [brum] n scopa.
broomstick ['brumstɪk] n manico di scopa.
Bros. abbr (*COMM*: = *brothers*) F.lli
(= *Fratelli*).
broth [brɒθ] n brodo.
brothel ['brɒθl] n bordello.
brother ['brʌðə*] n fratello.
brotherhood ['brʌðəhud] n fratellanza;
confraternità f inv.
brother-in-law ['brʌðərɪnlɔː] n cognato.
brotherly ['brʌðəlɪ] adj fraterno(a).
brought [brɔːt] pt, pp of **bring**.
brought forward (b/f) adj (*COMM*)
riportato(a).
brow [braʊ] n fronte f; (*rare, gen*: **eye~**)
sopracciglio; (*of hill*) cima.
browbeat ['braʊbiːt] vt intimidire.
brown [braʊn] adj bruno(a), marrone; (*hair*)
castano(a) ♦ n (*colour*) color m bruno or
marrone ♦ vt (*CULIN*) rosolare; **to go ~**
(*person*) abbronzarsi; (*leaves*) ingiallire.
brown bread n pane m integrale, pane
nero.
brownie ['braʊnɪ] n giovane esploratrice f.
brown paper n carta da pacchi or da
imballaggio.
brown rice n riso greggio.
brown sugar n zucchero greggio.
browse [braʊz] vi (*animal*) brucare; (*in
bookshop etc*) curiosare; (*COMPUT*)

navigare (in Internet) ♦ *vt*: **to ~ the Web**
navigare in Internet ♦ *n*: **to have a ~**
(around) dare un'occhiata (in giro); **to ~**
through a book sfogliare un libro.
browser ['brauzə*] *n* (*COMPUT*) browser *sm*
inv.
bruise [bru:z] *n* ammaccatura; (*on person*)
livido ♦ *vt* ammaccare; (*leg etc*) farsi un
livido a; (*fig*: *feelings*) urtare ♦ *vi* (*fruit*)
ammaccarsi.
Brum [brʌm] *n abbr*, **Brummagem**
['brʌmədʒəm] *n* (*col*) = Birmingham.
Brummie ['brʌmɪ] *n* (*col*) abitante *m/f* di
Birmingham; originario/a di
Birmingham.
brunch [brʌntʃ] *n ricca colazione*
consumata in tarda mattinata.
brunette [bru:'net] *n* bruna.
brunt [brʌnt] *n*: **the ~ of** (*attack, criticism etc*)
il peso maggiore di.
brush [brʌʃ] *n* spazzola; (*quarrel*)
schermaglia ♦ *vt* spazzolare; (*gen*: ~ **past,**
~ **against**) sfiorare; **to have a ~ with sb**
(*verbally*) avere uno scontro con qn;
(*physically*) venire a diverbio *or* alle mani
con qn; **to have a ~ with the police** avere
delle noie con la polizia.
►**brush aside** *vt* scostare.
►**brush up** *vt* (*knowledge*) rinfrescare.
brushed [brʌʃt] *adj* (*TECH*: *steel, chrome etc*)
sabbiato(a); (*nylon, denim etc*)
pettinato(a).
brush-off ['brʌʃɔf] *n*: **to give sb the ~** dare
il ben servito a qn.
brushwood ['brʌʃwud] *n* macchia.
brusque [bru:sk] *adj* (*person, manner*)
brusco(a); (*tone*) secco(a).
Brussels ['brʌslz] *n* Bruxelles *f*.
Brussels sprout *n* cavolo di Bruxelles.
brutal ['bru:tl] *adj* brutale.
brutality [bru:'tælɪtɪ] *n* brutalità.
brutalize ['bru:təlaɪz] *vt* (*harden*) abbrutire;
(*ill-treat*) brutalizzare.
brute [bru:t] *n* bestia; **by ~ force** con la
forza, a viva forza.
brutish ['bru:tɪʃ] *adj* da bruto.
BS *n abbr* (*US*: = *Bachelor of Science*) *titolo di*
studio.
bs *abbr* = **bill of sale**.
BSA *n abbr* (*US*) = *Boy Scouts of America*.
BSc *n abbr see* **Bachelor of Science**.
BSE *n abbr* (= *bovine spongiform*
encephalopathy) encefalite *f* bovina
spongiforme.
BSI *n abbr* (= *British Standards Institution*)
associazione per la normalizzazione.
BST *abbr* (= *British Summer Time*) *ora*
legale.

Bt. *abbr* (*BRIT*) = **baronet**.
btu *n abbr* (= *British thermal unit*) Btu *m*
(= 1054.2 *joules*).
bubble ['bʌbl] *n* bolla ♦ *vi* ribollire; (*sparkle,*
fig) essere effervescente.
bubble bath *n* bagno *m* schiuma *inv*.
bubblejet printer ['bʌbldʒet-] *n* stampante
f a getto d'inchiostro.
bubbly ['bʌblɪ] *adj* (*also fig*) frizzante ♦ *n*
(*col*) (*champagne*) spumante *m*.
Bucharest [bu:kə'rest] *n* Bucarest *f*.
buck [bʌk] *n* maschio (*di camoscio, caprone,*
coniglio etc); (*US col*) dollaro ♦ *vi*
sgroppare; **to pass the ~ (to sb)**
scaricare (su di qn) la propria
responsabilità.
►**buck up** *vi* (*cheer up*) rianimarsi ♦ *vt*: **to ~**
one's ideas up mettere la testa a partito.
bucket ['bʌkɪt] *n* secchio ♦ *vi* (*BRIT col*): **the**
rain is ~ing (down) piove a catinelle.
Buckingham Palace ['bʌkɪŋəm-] *n see boxed*
note.

BUCKINGHAM PALACE

Buckingham Palace *è la residenza ufficiale a*
Londra del sovrano britannico. Costruita nel
1703 per il duca di Buckingham, fu acquistata
nel 1762 dal re Giorgio III e ricostruita tra il
1821 e il 1838 sotto la guida dell'architetto
John Nash. All'inizio del Novecento alcune sue
parti sono state ulteriormente modificate.

---

buckle ['bʌkl] *n* fibbia ♦ *vt* affibbiare; (*warp*)
deformare.
►**buckle down** *vi* mettersi sotto.
Bucks [bʌks] *abbr* (*BRIT*) = **Buckinghamshire**.
bud [bʌd] *n* gemma; (*of flower*) boccio ♦ *vi*
germogliare; (*flower*) sbocciare.
Budapest [bju:də'pest] *n* Budapest *f*.
Buddha ['budə] *n* Budda *m*.
Buddhism ['budɪzəm] *n* buddismo.
Buddhist ['budɪst] *adj*, *n* buddista (*m/f*).
budding ['bʌdɪŋ] *adj* (*flower*) in boccio;
(*poet etc*) in erba.
buddy ['bʌdɪ] *n* (*US*) compagno.
budge [bʌdʒ] *vt* scostare ♦ *vi* spostarsi.
budgerigar ['bʌdʒərɪgɑ:*] *n* pappagallino.
budget ['bʌdʒɪt] *n* bilancio preventivo ♦ *vi*:
to ~ for sth fare il bilancio per qc; **I'm on**
a tight ~ devo contare la lira; **she works**
out her ~ every month fa il preventivo
delle spese ogni mese.
budgie ['bʌdʒɪ] *n* = **budgerigar**.
Buenos Aires ['bweɪnɔs'aɪrɪz] *n* Buenos
Aires *f*.
buff [bʌf] *adj* color camoscio *inv* ♦ *n*
(*enthusiast*) appassionato/a.

buffalo, pl ~ or ~**es** ['bʌfələu] n bufalo; (US) bisonte m.
buffer ['bʌfə*] n respingente m; (COMPUT) memoria tampone, buffer m inv.
buffer state n stato cuscinetto.
buffer zone n zona f cuscinetto inv.
buffet n ['bufeɪ] (food, BRIT: bar) buffet m inv ♦ vt ['bʌfɪt] schiaffeggiare; scuotere; urtare.
buffet car n (BRIT RAIL) ≈ servizio ristoro.
buffet lunch n pranzo in piedi.
buffoon [bə'fuːn] n buffone m.
bug [bʌg] n (insect) cimice f; (: gen) insetto; (fig: germ) virus m inv; (spy device) microfono spia; (COMPUT) bug m inv, errore m nel programma ♦ vt mettere sotto controllo; (room) installare microfoni spia in; (annoy) scocciare; **I've got the travel ~** (fig) mi è presa la mania dei viaggi.
bugbear ['bʌgbɛə*] n spauracchio.
bugger ['bʌgə*] (col!) n bastardo (!) ♦ vb: ~ **off!** vaffanculo! (!); ~ **(it)!** merda! (!).
bugle ['bjuːgl] n tromba.
build [bɪld] n (of person) corporatura ♦ vt (pt, pp **built** [bɪlt]) costruire.
▶**build on** vt fus (fig) prendere il via da.
▶**build up** vt (establish: business) costruire; (: reputation) fare, consolidare; (increase: production) allargare, incrementare; **don't ~ your hopes up too soon** non sperarci troppo.
builder ['bɪldə*] n costruttore m.
building ['bɪldɪŋ] n costruzione f; edificio; (also: ~ **trade**) edilizia.
building contractor n costruttore m, imprenditore m (edile).
building industry n industria edilizia.
building site n cantiere m di costruzione.
building society n società immobiliare e finanziaria; see boxed note.

BUILDING SOCIETY

Le **building societies** sono società immobiliari e finanziarie che forniscono anche numerosi servizi bancari ai clienti che vi investono i risparmi. Chi ha bisogno di un prestito per l'acquisto di una casa si rivolge in genere a una **building society**.

---

building trade n = **building industry**.
build-up ['bɪldʌp] n (of gas etc) accumulo; (publicity): **to give sb/sth a good ~** fare buona pubblicità a qn/qc.
built [bɪlt] pt, pp of **build**; **well-~** robusto(a).
built-in ['bɪlt'ɪn] adj (cupboard) a muro; (device) incorporato(a).

built-up area ['bɪltʌp-] n abitato.
bulb [bʌlb] n (BOT) bulbo; (ELEC) lampadina.
Bulgaria [bʌl'gɛərɪə] n Bulgaria.
Bulgarian [bʌl'gɛərɪən] adj bulgaro(a) ♦ n bulgaro/a; (LING) bulgaro.
bulge [bʌldʒ] n rigonfiamento; (in birth rate, sales) punta ♦ vi essere protuberante or rigonfio(a); **to be bulging with** essere pieno(a) or zeppo(a) di.
bulimia [bə'lɪmɪə] n bulimia.
bulk [bʌlk] n massa, volume m; **the ~ of** il grosso di; **(to buy) in ~** (comprare) in grande quantità.
bulk buying n acquisto di merce in grande quantità.
bulk carrier n grossa nave f da carico.
bulkhead ['bʌlkhɛd] n paratia.
bulky ['bʌlkɪ] adj grosso(a); voluminoso(a).
bull [bul] n toro; (STOCK EXCHANGE) rialzista m/f; (REL) bolla (papale).
bulldog ['buldɔg] n bulldog m inv.
bulldoze ['buldəuz] vt aprire or spianare col bulldozer; **I was ~d into doing it** (fig col) mi ci hanno costretto con la prepotenza.
bulldozer ['buldəuzə*] n bulldozer m inv.
bullet ['bulɪt] n pallottola.
bulletin ['bulɪtɪn] n bollettino.
bulletin board n (COMPUT) bulletin board m inv.
bullet point n punto; ~**s** elenco sg puntato.
bullet-proof ['bulɪtpruːf] adj a prova di proiettile; ~ **vest** giubbotto antiproiettile.
bullfight ['bulfaɪt] n corrida.
bullfighter ['bulfaɪtə*] n torero.
bullfighting ['bulfaɪtɪŋ] n tauromachia.
bullion ['buljən] n oro in lingotti.
bullock ['bulək] n giovenco.
bullring ['bulrɪŋ] n arena (per corride).
bull's-eye ['bulzaɪ] n centro del bersaglio.
bullshit ['bulʃɪt] (col!) excl, n stronzate fpl (!) ♦ vi raccontare stronzate (!) ♦ vt raccontare stronzate a (!).
bully ['bulɪ] n prepotente m ♦ vt angariare; (frighten) intimidire.
bullying ['bulɪŋ] n prepotenze fpl.
bum [bʌm] n (col: backside) culo; (tramp) vagabondo/a; (US: idler) fannullone/a.
▶**bum around** vi (col) fare il vagabondo.
bumblebee ['bʌmblbiː] n (ZOOL) bombo.
bumf [bʌmf] n (col: forms etc) scartoffie fpl.
bump [bʌmp] n (blow) colpo; (jolt) scossa; (noise) botto; (on road etc) protuberanza; (on head) bernoccolo ♦ vt battere; (car) urtare, sbattere.
▶**bump along** vi procedere sobbalzando.
▶**bump into** vt fus scontrarsi con; (col:

meet) imbattersi in, incontrare per caso.
bumper ['bʌmpə*] n (BRIT) paraurti m inv
♦ adj: ~ **harvest** raccolto eccezionale.
bumper cars npl (US) autoscontri mpl.
bumph [bʌmf] n = **bumf**.
bumptious ['bʌmpʃəs] adj presuntuoso(a).
bumpy ['bʌmpɪ] adj (road) dissestato(a);
(journey, flight) movimentato(a).
bun [bʌn] n focaccia; (of hair) crocchia.
bunch [bʌntʃ] n (of flowers, keys) mazzo; (of
bananas) ciuffo; (of people) gruppo; ~ **of
grapes** grappolo d'uva.
bundle ['bʌndl] n fascio ♦ vt (also: ~ up)
legare in un fascio; (put): **to** ~ **sth/sb into**
spingere qc/qn in.
▶**bundle off** vt (person) mandare via in
gran fretta.
▶**bundle out** vt far uscire (senza tante
cerimonie).
bun fight n (BRIT: col) tè m inv (ricevimento).
bung [bʌŋ] n tappo ♦ vt (BRIT: throw: also: ~
into) buttare; (also: ~ **up:** pipe, hole)
tappare, otturare; **my nose is** ~**ed up**
(col) ho il naso otturato.
bungalow ['bʌŋgələu] n bungalow m inv.
bungee jumping ['bʌndʒi:'dʒʌmpɪŋ] n salto
nel vuoto da ponti, grattacieli etc con un
cavo fissato alla caviglia.
bungle ['bʌŋgl] vt abborracciare.
bunion ['bʌnjən] n callo (al piede).
bunk [bʌŋk] n cuccetta.
▶**bunk off** vi (BRIT col): **to** ~ **off school**
marinare la scuola; **I'll** ~ **off at 3 this
afternoon** oggi me la filo dal lavoro alle 3.
bunk beds npl letti mpl a castello.
bunker ['bʌŋkə*] n (coal store) ripostiglio
per il carbone; (MIL, GOLF) bunker m inv.
bunny ['bʌnɪ] n (also: ~ **rabbit**) coniglietto.
bunny hill n (US SKI) pista per principianti.
bunting ['bʌntɪŋ] n pavesi mpl, bandierine
fpl.
buoy [bɔɪ] n boa.
▶**buoy up** vt tenere a galla; (fig) sostenere.
buoyancy ['bɔɪənsɪ] n (of ship)
galleggiabilità.
buoyant ['bɔɪənt] adj galleggiante; (fig)
vivace; (COMM: market) sostenuto(a);
(prices, currency) stabile.
burden ['bə:dn] n carico, fardello ♦ vt
caricare; (oppress) opprimere; **to be a** ~
to sb essere di peso a qn.
bureau, pl ~**x** ['bjuərəu, -z] n (BRIT: writing
desk) scrivania; (US: chest of drawers)
cassettone m; (office) ufficio, agenzia.
bureaucracy [bjuə'rɔkrəsɪ] n burocrazia.
bureaucrat ['bjuərəkræt] n burocrate m/f.
bureaucratic [bjuərə'krætɪk] adj
burocratico(a).

burgeon ['bə:dʒən] vi svilupparsi
rapidamente.
burger ['bə:gə*] n hamburger m inv.
burglar ['bə:glə*] n scassinatore m.
burglar alarm n antifurto m inv.
burglarize ['bə:gləraɪz] vt (US) svaligiare.
burglary ['bə:glərɪ] n furto con scasso.
burgle ['bə:gl] vt svaligiare.
burial ['berɪəl] n sepoltura.
burial ground n cimitero.
burly ['bə:lɪ] adj robusto(a).
Burma ['bə:mə] n Birmania; see **Myanmar**.
Burmese [bə:'mi:z] adj birmano(a) ♦ n (pl
inv) birmano/a; (LING) birmano.
burn [bə:n] vt, vi (pt, pp **burned** or **burnt**
[bə:nt]) bruciare ♦ n bruciatura,
scottatura; (MED) ustione f; **I've** ~**t
myself!** mi sono bruciato!; **the cigarette**
~**t a hole in her dress** si è fatta un buco
nel vestito con la sigaretta.
▶**burn down** vt distruggere col fuoco.
▶**burn out** vt (subj: writer etc): **to** ~ **o.s. out**
esaurirsi.
burner ['bə:nə*] n fornello.
burning ['bə:nɪŋ] adj (building, forest) in
fiamme; (issue, question) scottante.
burnish ['bə:nɪʃ] vt brunire.
Burns Night n see boxed note.

BURNS NIGHT

Burns Night è la festa celebrata il 25
gennaio per commemorare il poeta scozzese
Robert Burns (1759-1796). Gli scozzesi
festeggiano questa data con una cena a base di
"haggis" e whisky, spesso al suono di una
cornamusa; durante la cena vengono recitate le
poesie di Robert Burns e vengono letti discorsi
alla sua memoria.

---

burnt [bə:nt] pt, pp of **burn**.
burp [bə:p] (col) n rutto ♦ vi ruttare.
burrow ['bʌrəu] n tana ♦ vt scavare.
bursar ['bə:sə*] n economo/a; (BRIT: student)
borsista m/f.
bursary ['bə:sərɪ] n (BRIT) borsa di studio.
burst [bə:st] vb (pt, pp **burst**) vt far
scoppiare or esplodere ♦ vi esplodere;
(tyre) scoppiare ♦ n scoppio; (also: ~ **pipe**)
rottura nel tubo, perdita; ~ **of energy/**
laughter scoppio d'energia/di risa; **a** ~ **of**
applause uno scroscio d'applausi; **a** ~ **of**
speed uno scatto (di velocità); ~ **blood**
vessel rottura di un vaso sanguigno; **the**
river has ~ **its banks** il fiume ha rotto gli
argini or ha straripato; **to** ~ **into flames/**
tears scoppiare in fiamme/lacrime; **to be**
~**ing with** essere pronto a scoppiare di;

to ~ **out laughing** scoppiare a ridere; **to ~ open** *vi* aprirsi improvvisamente; (*door*) spalancarsi.

▶**burst into** *vt fus* (*room etc*) irrompere in.

▶**burst out of** *vt fus* precipitarsi fuori da.

bury ['bɛrɪ] *vt* seppellire; **to ~ one's face in one's hands** nascondere la faccia tra le mani; **to ~ one's head in the sand** (*fig*) fare (la politica del)lo struzzo; **to ~ the hatchet** (*fig*) seppellire l'ascia di guerra.

bus, ~**es** [bʌs, 'bʌsɪz] *n* autobus *m inv*.

bus boy *n* (*US*) aiuto *inv* cameriere/a.

bush [buʃ] *n* cespuglio; (*scrub land*) macchia.

bushed [buʃt] *adj* (*col*) distrutto(a).

bushel ['buʃl] *n* staio.

bushfire ['buʃfaɪə*] *n grande incendio in aperta campagna*.

bushy ['buʃɪ] *adj* (*plant, tail, beard*) folto(a); (*eyebrows*) irsuto(a).

busily ['bɪzɪlɪ] *adv* con impegno, alacremente.

business ['bɪznɪs] *n* (*matter*) affare *m*; (*trading*) affari *mpl*; (*firm*) azienda; (*job, duty*) lavoro; **to be away on ~** essere andato via per affari; **I'm here on ~** sono qui per affari; **to do ~ with sb** fare affari con qn; **he's in the insurance ~** lavora nel campo delle assicurazioni; **it's none of my ~** questo non mi riguarda; **he means ~** non scherza.

business address *n* indirizzo di lavoro *or* d'ufficio.

business card *n* biglietto da visita della ditta.

businesslike ['bɪznɪslaɪk] *adj* serio(a); efficiente.

businessman ['bɪznɪsmən] *n* uomo d'affari.

business trip *n* viaggio d'affari.

businesswoman ['bɪznɪswumən] *n* donna d'affari.

busker ['bʌskə*] *n* (*BRIT*) suonatore/trice ambulante.

bus lane *n* (*BRIT*) corsia riservata agli autobus.

bus shelter *n* pensilina (*alla fermata dell'autobus*).

bus station *n* stazione *f* delle autolinee, autostazione *f*.

bus stop *n* fermata d'autobus.

bust [bʌst] *n* (*ART*) busto; (*bosom*) seno ♦ *adj* (*broken*) rotto(a) ♦ *vt* (*col: POLICE: arrest*) pizzicare, beccare; **to go ~** fallire.

bustle ['bʌsl] *n* movimento, attività ♦ *vi* darsi da fare.

bustling ['bʌslɪŋ] *adj* (*person*) indaffarato(a); (*town*) animato(a).

bust-up ['bʌstʌp] *n* (*BRIT col*) lite *f*.

busty ['bʌstɪ] *adj* (*col*) tettone(a).

busy ['bɪzɪ] *adj* occupato(a); (*shop, street*) molto frequentato(a) ♦ *vt*: **to ~ o.s.** darsi da fare; **he's a ~ man** (*normally*) è un uomo molto occupato; (*temporarily*) ha molto da fare, è molto occupato.

busybody ['bɪzɪbɔdɪ] *n* ficcanaso *m/f inv*.

busy signal *n* (*US*) segnale *m* di occupato.

━━━━━━━━━━ **KEYWORD**

but [bʌt] *conj* ma; **I'd love to come,** ~ **I'm busy** vorrei tanto venire, ma ho da fare ♦ *prep* (*apart from, except*) eccetto, tranne, meno; **nothing** ~ nient'altro che; **he was nothing** ~ **trouble** non dava altro che guai; **no-one** ~ **him** solo lui; **no-one** ~ **him can do it** nessuno può farlo tranne lui; **the last** ~ **one** (*BRIT*) il(la) penultimo(a); ~ **for you/your help** se non fosse per te/ per il tuo aiuto; **anything** ~ **that** tutto ma non questo; **anything** ~ **finished** tutt'altro che finito ♦ *adv* (*just, only*) solo, soltanto; **she's** ~ **a child** è solo una bambina; **had I** ~ **known** se lo avessi saputo; **I can** ~ **try** tentar non nuoce; **all** ~ **finished** quasi finito.

━━━━━━━━━━━━━━━━━━━━━━━

butane ['bjuːteɪn] *n* (*also:* ~ **gas**) butano.

butch [butʃ] *adj* (*woman: pej*) mascolino(a); (*man*) macho *inv*.

butcher ['butʃə*] *n* macellaio ♦ *vt* macellare; ~**'s (shop)** macelleria.

butler ['bʌtlə*] *n* maggiordomo.

butt [bʌt] *n* (*cask*) grossa botte *f*; (*thick end*) estremità *f inv* più grossa; (*of gun*) calcio; (*of cigarette*) mozzicone *m*; (*BRIT fig: target*) oggetto ♦ *vt* cozzare.

▶**butt in** *vi* (*interrupt*) interrompere.

butter ['bʌtə*] *n* burro ♦ *vt* imburrare.

buttercup ['bʌtəkʌp] *n* ranuncolo.

butter dish *n* burriera.

butterfingers ['bʌtəfɪŋgəz] *n* (*col*) mani *fpl* di ricotta.

butterfly ['bʌtəflaɪ] *n* farfalla; (*SWIMMING: also:* ~ **stroke**) (nuoto a) farfalla.

buttocks ['bʌtəks] *npl* natiche *fpl*.

button ['bʌtn] *n* bottone *m* ♦ *vt* (*also:* ~ **up**) abbottonare ♦ *vi* abbottonarsi.

buttonhole ['bʌtnhəul] *n* asola, occhiello ♦ *vt* (*person*) attaccar bottone a.

buttress ['bʌtrɪs] *n* contrafforte *m*.

buxom ['bʌksəm] *adj* formoso(a).

buy [baɪ] *vt* (*pt, pp* **bought** [bɔːt]) comprare, acquistare ♦ *n*: **a good/bad** ~ un buon/ cattivo acquisto *or* affare; **to ~ sb sth/ sth from sb** comprare qc per qn/qc da qn; **to ~ sb a drink** offrire da bere a qn.

▶**buy back** *vt* riprendersi, prendersi

indietro.
►**buy in** vt (BRIT: goods) far provvista di.
►**buy into** vt fus (BRIT COMM) acquistare delle azioni di.
►**buy off** vt (col: bribe) comprare.
►**buy out** vt (business) rilevare.
►**buy up** vt accaparrare.

buyer ['baɪə*] n compratore/trice; ~'s market mercato favorevole ai compratori.

buy-out ['baɪaut] n (COMM) acquisto di una società da parte dei suoi dipendenti.

buzz [bʌz] n ronzio; (col: phone call) colpo di telefono ♦ vi ronzare ♦ vt (call on intercom) chiamare al citofono; (: with buzzer) chiamare col cicalino; (AVIAT: plane, building) passare rasente; **my head is ~ing** mi gira la testa.
►**buzz off** vi (BRIT col) filare, levarsi di torno.

buzzard ['bʌzəd] n poiana.

buzzer ['bʌzə*] n cicalino.

buzz word n (col) termine m in voga.

═══════════ KEYWORD

by [baɪ] prep 1 (referring to cause, agent) da; **killed ~ lightning** ucciso da un fulmine; **surrounded ~ a fence** circondato da uno steccato; **a painting ~ Picasso** un quadro di Picasso

2 (referring to method, manner, means): ~ **bus/car/train** in autobus/macchina/treno, con l'autobus/la macchina/il treno; **to pay ~ cheque** pagare con (un) assegno; ~ **moonlight** al chiaro di luna; ~ **saving hard, he** ... risparmiando molto, lui ...

3 (via, through) per; **we came ~ Dover** siamo venuti via Dover

4 (close to, past) accanto a; **the house ~ the river** la casa sul fiume; **a holiday ~ the sea** una vacanza al mare; **she sat ~ his bed** si sedette accanto al suo letto; **she rushed ~ me** mi è passata accanto correndo; **I go ~ the post office every day** passo davanti all'ufficio postale ogni giorno

5 (not later than) per, entro; ~ **4 o'clock** per or entro le 4; ~ **this time tomorrow** domani a quest'ora; ~ **the time I got here it was too late** quando sono arrivato era ormai troppo tardi

6 (during): ~ **day/night** di giorno/notte

7 (amount) a; ~ **the kilo** a chili; **paid ~ the hour** pagato all'ora; **to increase ~ the hour** aumentare di ora in ora; **one ~ one** uno per uno; **little ~ little** a poco a poco

8 (MATH, measure): **to divide/multiply ~ 3** dividere/moltiplicare per 3; **a room 3**

metres ~ 4 una stanza di 3 metri per 4; **it's broader ~ a metre** è un metro più largo, è più largo di un metro

9 (according to) per; **to play ~ the rules** attenersi alle regole; **it's all right ~ me** per me va bene

10: **(all) ~ oneself** (tutto(a)) solo(a); **he did it (all) ~ himself** lo ha fatto (tutto) da solo

11: ~ **the way** a proposito; **this wasn't ~ my idea ~ the way** tra l'altro l'idea non è stata mia

♦ adv 1 see **go; pass** etc

2: ~ **and ~** (in past) poco dopo; (in future) fra breve; ~ **and large** nel complesso.

bye(-bye) ['baɪ('baɪ)] excl ciao!, arrivederci!

by(e)-law ['baɪlɔ:] n legge f locale.

by-election ['baɪɪlɛkʃən] n (BRIT) elezione f straordinaria; see boxed note.

┌─────────────────────┐
│ **BY-ELECTION**
└─────────────────────┘

Una **by-election** in Gran Bretagna e in alcuni paesi del Commonwealth è un'elezione che si tiene per coprire un posto in Parlamento resosi vacante, a governo ancora in carica. È importante in quanto serve a misurare il consenso degli elettori in vista delle successive elezioni politiche.

Byelorussia [bjɛləu'rʌʃə] n Bielorussia, Belorussia.

Byelorussian [bjɛləu'rʌʃən] adj, n – Belarussian.

bygone ['baɪgɔn] adj passato(a) ♦ n: **let ~s be ~s** mettiamoci una pietra sopra.

bypass ['baɪpɑ:s] n circonvallazione f; (MED) by-pass m inv ♦ vt fare una deviazione intorno a.

by-product ['baɪprɔdʌkt] n sottoprodotto; (fig) conseguenza secondaria.

byre ['baɪə*] n (BRIT) stalla.

bystander ['baɪstændə*] n spettatore/trice.

byte [baɪt] n (COMPUT) byte m inv.

byway ['baɪweɪ] n strada secondaria.

byword ['baɪwə:d] n: **to be a ~ for** essere sinonimo di.

by-your-leave ['baɪjɔ:'li:v] n: **without so much as a ~** senza nemmeno chiedere il permesso.

Cc

C, c [si:] n (letter) C, c f or m inv; (SCOL: mark)
≈ 6 (sufficiente); (MUS): **C** do; ~ **for Charlie**
≈ C come Como.
C abbr (= Celsius, centigrade) C.
c. abbr (= century) sec.; (= circa) c; (US etc)
= **cent(s)**.
CA abbr = **Central America;** (US) = California
♦ n abbr (BRIT) see **chartered accountant.**
ca. abbr (= circa) ca.
c/a abbr = **capital account; credit account;
current account.**
CAA n abbr (BRIT: = Civil Aviation Authority,
US: = Civil Aeronautics Authority)
organismo di controllo e di sviluppo
dell'aviazione civile.
CAB n abbr (BRIT: = Citizens' Advice Bureau)
organizzazione per la tutela del
consumatore.
cab [kæb] n taxi m inv; (of train, truck) cabina;
(horsedrawn) carrozza.
cabaret ['kæbəreɪ] n cabaret m inv.
cabbage ['kæbɪdʒ] n cavolo.
cabbie, cabby ['kæbɪ] n (col), **cab driver** n
tassista m/f.
cabin ['kæbɪn] n capanna; (on ship) cabina.
cabin cruiser n cabinato.
cabinet ['kæbɪnɪt] n (POL) consiglio dei
ministri; (furniture) armadietto; (also:
display ~) vetrinetta; **cocktail** ~ mobile m
bar inv.
cabinet-maker ['kæbɪnɪt'meɪkə*] n
stipettaio.
cabinet minister n ministro (membro del
Consiglio).
cable ['keɪbl] n cavo; fune f; (TEL)
cablogramma m ♦ vt telegrafare.
cable-car ['keɪblkɑː*] n funivia.
cablegram ['keɪblgræm] n cablogramma m.
cable railway n funicolare f.
cable television n televisione f via cavo.
cache [kæʃ] n nascondiglio; **a** ~ **of food** etc
un deposito segreto di viveri etc.
cackle ['kækl] vi schiamazzare.
cactus, pl cacti ['kæktəs, -taɪ] n cactus m inv.
CAD n abbr (= computer-aided design)
progettazione f con l'ausilio
dell'elaboratore.
caddie ['kædɪ] n caddie m inv.

cadet [kə'dɛt] n (MIL) cadetto; **police** ~
allievo poliziotto.
cadge [kædʒ] vt (col) scroccare; **to** ~ **a
meal (off sb)** scroccare un pranzo (a qn).
cadre ['kædrɪ] n quadro.
Caesarean, (US) **Cesarean** [si:'zɛərɪən] adj:
~ **(section)** (taglio) cesareo.
CAF abbr (BRIT: = cost and freight) Caf m.
café ['kæfeɪ] n caffè m inv.
cafeteria [kæfɪ'tɪərɪə] n self-service m inv.
caffein(e) ['kæfi:n] n caffeina.
cage [keɪdʒ] n gabbia ♦ vt mettere in
gabbia.
cagey ['keɪdʒɪ] adj (col) chiuso(a);
guardingo(a).
cagoule [kə'gu:l] n K-way ® m inv.
cahoots [kə'hu:ts] n: **to be in** ~ **(with sb)**
essere in combutta (con qn).
CAI n abbr (= computer-aided instruction)
istruzione f assistita dall'elaboratore.
Cairo ['kaɪərəu] n il Cairo.
cajole [kə'dʒəul] vt allettare.
cake [keɪk] n torta; ~ **of soap** saponetta; **it's
a piece of** ~ (col) è una cosa da nulla; **he
wants to have his** ~ **and eat it (too)** (fig)
vuole la botte piena e la moglie ubriaca.
caked [keɪkt] adj: ~ **with** incrostato(a) di.
cake shop n pasticceria.
Cal. abbr (US) = California.
calamitous [kə'læmɪtəs] adj disastroso(a).
calamity [kə'læmɪtɪ] n calamità f inv.
calcium ['kælsɪəm] n calcio.
calculate ['kælkjuleɪt] vt calcolare;
(estimate: chances, effect) valutare.
▶**calculate on** vt fus: **to** ~ **on sth/on doing
sth** contare su qc/di fare qc.
calculated ['kælkjuleɪtɪd] adj calcolato(a),
intenzionale; **a** ~ **risk** un rischio
calcolato.
calculating ['kælkjuleɪtɪŋ] adj
calcolatore(trice).
calculation [kælkju'leɪʃən] n calcolo.
calculator ['kælkjuleɪtə*] n calcolatrice f.
calculus ['kælkjuləs] n calcolo; **integral/
differential** ~ calcolo integrale/
differenziale.
calendar ['kæləndə*] n calendario.
calendar year n anno civile.
calf, pl calves [kɑːf, kɑːvz] n (of cow)
vitello; (of other animals) piccolo; (also:
~**skin**) (pelle f di) vitello; (ANAT)
polpaccio.
caliber ['kælɪbə*] n (US) = **calibre**.
calibrate ['kælɪbreɪt] vt (gun etc) calibrare;
(scale of measuring instrument) tarare.
calibre, (US) **caliber** ['kælɪbə*] n calibro.
calico ['kælɪkəu] n tela grezza, cotone m
grezzo; (US) cotonina stampata.

Calif. abbr (US) = California.

California [kælɪˈfɔːnɪə] n California.

calipers [ˈkælɪpəz] npl (US) = **callipers**.

call [kɔːl] vt (gen, also TEL) chiamare; (announce: flight) annunciare; (meeting, strike) indire, proclamare ♦ vi chiamare; (visit: also: ~ **in**, ~ **round**) passare ♦ n (shout) grido, urlo; visita; (summons: for flight etc) chiamata; (fig: lure) richiamo; (also: **telephone** ~) telefonata; **to be on** ~ essere a disposizione; **to make a** ~ telefonare, fare una telefonata; **please give me a** ~ **at 7** per piacere mi chiami alle 7; **to pay a** ~ **on sb** fare (una) visita a qn; **there's not much** ~ **for** these items non c'è molta richiesta di questi articoli; **she's** ~**ed Jane** si chiama Jane; **who is** ~**ing?** (TEL) chi parla?; **London** ~**ing** (RADIO) qui Londra.
► **call at** vt fus (subj: ship) fare scalo a; (: train) fermarsi a.
► **call back** vi (return) ritornare; (TEL) ritelefonare, richiamare ♦ vt (TEL) ritelefonare a, richiamare.
► **call for** vt fus (demand: action etc) richiedere; (collect: person) passare a prendere; (: goods) ritirare.
► **call in** vt (doctor, expert, police) chiamare, far venire.
► **call off** vt (meeting, race) disdire; (deal) cancellare; (dog) richiamare; **the strike was** ~**ed off** lo sciopero è stato revocato.
► **call on** vt fus (visit) passare da; (request): **to** ~ **on sb to do** chiedere a qn di fare.
► **call out** vi urlare ♦ vt (doctor, police, troops) chiamare.
► **call up** vt (MIL) richiamare.

Callanetics ® [kæləˈnɛtɪks] nsg tipo di ginnastica basata sulla ripetizione di piccoli movimenti.

callbox [ˈkɔːlbɒks] n (BRIT) cabina telefonica.

call centre n centre informazioni telefoniche.

caller [ˈkɔːlə*] n persona che chiama; visitatore/trice; **hold the line,** ~! (TEL) rimanga in linea, signore (or signora)!

call girl n ragazza f squillo inv.

call-in [ˈkɔːlɪn] n (US) = **phone-in**.

calling [ˈkɔːlɪŋ] n vocazione f.

calling card n (US) biglietto da visita.

callipers, (US) **calipers** [ˈkælɪpəz] npl (MED) gambale m; (MATH) calibro.

callous [ˈkæləs] adj indurito(a), insensibile.

callow [ˈkæləu] adj immaturo(a).

calm [kɑːm] adj calmo(a) ♦ n calma ♦ vt calmare.
► **calm down** vi calmarsi ♦ vt calmare.

calmly [ˈkɑːmlɪ] adv con calma.

calmness [ˈkɑːmnɪs] n calma.

Calor gas ® [ˈkælə*-] n (BRIT) butano.

calorie [ˈkælərɪ] n caloria; **low-**~ **product** prodotto a basso contenuto di calorie.

calve [kɑːv] vi figliare.

calves [kɑːvz] npl of **calf**.

CAM n abbr (= computer-aided manufacturing) fabbricazione f con l'ausilio dell'elaboratore.

camber [ˈkæmbə*] n (of road) bombatura.

Cambodia [kæmˈbəudjə] n Cambogia.

Cambodian [kæmˈbəudɪən] adj, n cambogiano(a).

Cambs abbr (BRIT) = Cambridgeshire.

camcorder [ˈkæmkɔːdə*] n videocamera.

came [keɪm] pt of **come**.

camel [ˈkæməl] n cammello.

cameo [ˈkæmɪəu] n cammeo.

camera [ˈkæmərə] n macchina fotografica; (CINE, TV) telecamera; (also: **cine**~, **movie** ~) cinepresa; **in** ~ a porte chiuse.

cameraman [ˈkæmərəmæn] n cameraman m inv.

camera phone n telefonino con fotocamera integrata.

Cameroon, Cameroun [kæməruːn] n Camerun m.

camouflage [ˈkæməflɑːʒ] n camuffamento; (MIL) mimetizzazione f ♦ vt camuffare; mimetizzare.

camp [kæmp] n campeggio; (MIL) campo ♦ vi campeggiare; accamparsi; **to go** ~**ing** andare in campeggio.

campaign [kæmˈpeɪn] n (MIL, POL etc) campagna ♦ vi: **to** ~ (**for/against**) (also fig) fare una campagna (per/contro).

campaigner [kæmˈpeɪnə*] n: ~ **for** fautore/trice di; ~ **against** oppositore/trice di.

campbed [ˈkæmpˈbɛd] n (BRIT) brandina.

camper [ˈkæmpə*] n campeggiatore/trice.

camping [ˈkæmpɪŋ] n campeggio.

camp(ing) site n campeggio.

campus [ˈkæmpəs] n campus m inv.

camshaft [ˈkæmʃɑːft] n albero a camme.

can [kæn] aux vb see next headword ♦ n (of milk) scatola; (of oil) bidone m; (of water) tanica; (tin) scatola ♦ vt mettere in scatola; **a** ~ **of beer** una lattina di birra; **to carry the** ~ (BRIT col) prendere la colpa.

━━━━━━━━━━━━━━━━━ KEYWORD

can [kæn] (negative **cannot, can't**; conditional and pt **could**) aux vb **1** (be able to) potere; **I** ~**'t go any further** non posso andare oltre; **you** ~ **do it if you try** sei in grado di farlo — basta provarci; **I'll help you all I** ~ ti aiuterò come potrò; **I** ~**'t see you** non ti vedo; ~ **you hear me?** mi senti?, riesci a sentirmi?

2 (know how to) sapere, essere capace di; **I ~ swim** so nuotare; **~ you speak French?** parla francese?

3 (may) potere; **could I have a word with you?** posso parlarle un momento?

4 (expressing disbelief, puzzlement etc): **it ~'t be true!** non può essere vero!; **what CAN he want?** cosa può mai volere?

5 (expressing possibility, suggestion etc): **he could be in the library** può darsi che sia in biblioteca; **they could have forgotten** potrebbero essersene dimenticati; **she could have been delayed** può aver avuto un contrattempo.

Canada ['kænədə] n Canada m.
Canadian [kə'neɪdɪən] adj, n canadese (m/f).
canal [kə'næl] n canale m.
canary [kə'nɛərɪ] n canarino.
Canary Islands, Canaries [kə'nɛərɪz] npl: **the ~** le (isole) Canarie.
Canberra ['kænbərə] n Camberra.
cancel ['kænsəl] vt annullare; (train) sopprimere; (cross out) cancellare.
▶**cancel out** vt (MATH) semplificare; (fig) annullare; **they ~ each other out** (also fig) si annullano a vicenda.
cancellation [kænsə'leɪʃən] n annullamento; soppressione f; cancellazione f; (TOURISM) prenotazione f annullata.
cancer ['kænsə*] n cancro; **C~** (sign) Cancro; **to be C~** essere del Cancro.
cancerous ['kænsərəs] adj canceroso(a).
cancer patient n malato/a di cancro.
cancer research n ricerca sul cancro.
C and F abbr (BRIT: = cost and freight) Caf m.
candid ['kændɪd] adj onesto(a).
candidacy ['kændɪdəsɪ] n candidatura.
candidate ['kændɪdeɪt] n candidato/a.
candidature ['kændɪdətʃə*] n (BRIT) = **candidacy.**
candied ['kændɪd] adj candito(a); **~ apple** (US) mela caramellata.
candle ['kændl] n candela.
candlelight ['kændl'laɪt] n: **by ~** a lume di candela.
candlestick ['kændlstɪk] n (also: **candle holder**) bugia; (bigger, ornate) candeliere m.
candour, (US) **candor** ['kændə*] n sincerità.
candy ['kændɪ] n zucchero candito; (US) caramella; caramelle fpl.
candy-floss ['kændɪflɔs] n (BRIT) zucchero filato.
candy store n (US) ≈ pasticceria.

cane [keɪn] n canna; (for baskets, chairs etc) bambù m; (SCOL) verga; (for walking) bastone m (da passeggio) ♦ vt (BRIT SCOL) punire a colpi di verga.
canine ['kænaɪn] adj canino(a).
canister ['kænɪstə*] n scatola metallica.
cannabis ['kænəbɪs] n canapa indiana.
canned ['kænd] adj (food) in scatola; (col: recorded: music) registrato(a); (BRIT col: drunk) sbronzo(a); (US col: worker) licenziato(a).
cannibal ['kænɪbəl] n cannibale m/f.
cannibalism ['kænɪbəlɪzəm] n cannibalismo.
cannon, pl **~** or **~s** ['kænən] n (gun) cannone m.
cannonball ['kænənbɔːl] n palla di cannone.
cannon fodder n carne f da macello.
cannot ['kænɔt] = **can not.**
canny ['kænɪ] adj furbo(a).
canoe [kə'nuː] n canoa; (SPORT) canotto.
canoeing [kə'nuːɪŋ] n (sport) canottaggio.
canoeist [kə'nuːɪst] n canottiere m.
canon ['kænən] n (clergyman) canonico; (standard) canone m.
canonize ['kænənaɪz] vt canonizzare.
can opener [-'əupnə*] n apriscatole m inv.
canopy ['kænəpɪ] n baldacchino.
cant [kænt] n gergo ♦ vt inclinare ♦ vi inclinarsi.
can't [kænt] = **can not.**
Cantab. abbr (BRIT: = cantabrigiensis) of Cambridge.
cantankerous [kæn'tæŋkərəs] adj stizzoso(a).
canteen [kæn'tiːn] n mensa; (BRIT: of cutlery) portaposate m inv.
canter ['kæntə*] n piccolo galoppo ♦ vi andare al piccolo galoppo.
cantilever ['kæntɪliːvə*] n trave f a sbalzo.
canvas ['kænvəs] n tela; **under ~** (camping) sotto la tenda; (NAUT) sotto la vela.
canvass ['kænvəs] vt (COMM: district) fare un'indagine di mercato in; (: citizens, opinions) fare un sondaggio di; (POL: district) fare un giro elettorale di; (: person) fare propaganda elettorale a.
canvasser ['kænvəsə*] n (COMM) agente m viaggiatore, piazzista m; (POL) propagandista m/f (elettorale).
canvassing ['kænvəsɪŋ] n sollecitazione f.
canyon ['kænjən] n canyon m inv.
CAP n abbr (= Common Agricultural Policy) PAC f.
cap [kæp] n (also FOOTBALL) berretto; (of pen) coperchio; (of bottle) tappo; (for swimming) cuffia; (BRIT: contraceptive: also: **Dutch ~**) diaframma m ♦ vt tappare;

(*outdo*) superare; ~**ped with** ricoperto(a) di; **and to** ~ **it all, he** ... (*BRIT*) e per completare l'opera, lui ....
capability [keɪpə'bɪlɪtɪ] *n* capacità *f inv*, abilità *f inv*.
capable ['keɪpəbl] *adj* capace; ~ **of** capace di; suscettibile di.
capacious [kə'peɪʃəs] *adj* capace.
capacity [kə'pæsɪtɪ] *n* capacità *f inv*; (*of lift etc*) capienza; **in his** ~ **as** nella sua qualità di; **to work at full** ~ lavorare al massimo delle proprie capacità; **filled to** ~ pieno zeppo; **in an advisory** ~ a titolo consultativo.
cape [keɪp] *n* (*garment*) cappa; (*GEO*) capo.
Cape of Good Hope *n* Capo di Buona Speranza.
caper ['keɪpə*] *n* (*CULIN*: *also*: ~**s**) cappero; (*leap*) saltello; (*escapade*) birichinata.
Cape Town *n* Città del Capo.
capita ['kæpɪtə] *see* **per capita**.
capital ['kæpɪtl] *n* (*also*: ~ **city**) capitale *f*; (*money*) capitale *m*; (*also*: ~ **letter**) (lettera) maiuscola.
capital account *n* conto capitale.
capital allowance *n* ammortamento fiscale.
capital assets *npl* capitale *m* fisso.
capital expenditure *n* spese *fpl* in capitale.
capital gains tax *n* imposta sulla plusvalenza.
capital goods *n* beni *mpl* d'investimento, beni *mpl* capitali.
capital-intensive ['kæpɪtlɪn'tɛnsɪv] *adj* ad alta intensità di capitale.
capitalism ['kæpɪtəlɪzəm] *n* capitalismo.
capitalist ['kæpɪtəlɪst] *adj, n* capitalista (*m/f*).
capitalize ['kæpɪtəlaɪz] *vt* (*provide with capital*) capitalizzare.
▶**capitalize on** *vt fus* (*fig*) trarre vantaggio da.
capital punishment *n* pena capitale.
capital transfer tax *n* (*BRIT*) imposta sui trasferimenti di capitali.
Capitol ['kæpɪtl] *n*: **the** ~ il Campidoglio; *see boxed note*.

CAPITOL

Il **Capitol** *è l'edificio che ospita le riunioni del Congresso degli Stati Uniti. È situato sull'omonimo colle, "Capitol Hill", a Washington DC. In molti stati americani il termine Capitol viene usato per indicare l'edificio dove si riuniscono i rappresentanti dello stato.*

---

capitulate [kə'pɪtjuleɪt] *vi* capitolare.
capitulation [kəpɪtju'leɪʃən] *n* capitolazione *f*.
capricious [kə'prɪʃəs] *adj* capriccioso(a).
Capricorn ['kæprɪkɔːn] *n* Capricorno; **to be** ~ essere del Capricorno.
caps [kæps] *abbr* = **capital letters**.
capsize [kæp'saɪz] *vt* capovolgere ♦ *vi* capovolgersi.
capstan ['kæpstən] *n* argano.
capsule ['kæpsjuːl] *n* capsula.
Capt. *abbr* (= *captain*) Cap.
captain ['kæptɪn] *n* capitano ♦ *vt* capitanare.
caption ['kæpʃən] *n* leggenda.
captivate ['kæptɪveɪt] *vt* avvincere.
captive ['kæptɪv] *adj, n* prigioniero(a).
captivity [kæp'tɪvɪtɪ] *n* prigionia; **in** ~ (*animal*) in cattività.
captor ['kæptə*] *n* (*lawful*) chi ha catturato; (*unlawful*) rapitore *m*.
capture ['kæptʃə*] *vt* catturare, prendere; (*attention*) attirare ♦ *n* cattura; (*data* ~) registrazione *f or* rilevazione *f* di dati.
car [kɑː*] *n* macchina, automobile *f*; (*US RAIL*) carrozza; **by** ~ in macchina.
carafe [kə'ræf] *n* caraffa.
carafe wine *n* (*in restaurant*) ≈ vino sfuso.
caramel ['kærəməl] *n* caramello.
carat ['kærət] *n* carato; **18** ~ **gold** oro a 18 carati.
caravan ['kærəvæn] *n* roulotte *f inv*.
caravan site *n* (*BRIT*) campeggio per roulotte.
caraway ['kærəweɪ] *n*: ~ **seed** seme *m* di cumino.
carbohydrates [kɑːbəu'haɪdreɪts] *npl* (*foods*) carboidrati *mpl*.
car bomb *n* ordigno esplosivo collocato in una macchina; **a** ~ **went off yesterday** ieri è esplosa un'autobomba.
carbon ['kɑːbən] *n* carbonio.
carbonated ['kɑːbəneɪtəd] *adj* (*drink*) gassato(a).
carbon copy *n* copia *f* carbone *inv*.
carbon dioxide [-daɪ'ɔksaɪd] *n* diossido di carbonio.
carbon paper *n* carta carbone.
carbon ribbon *n* nastro carbonato.
car boot sale *n* mercatino dell'usato dove la merce viene esposta nel bagagliaio delle macchine.
carburettor, (*US*) **carburetor** [kɑːbju'rɛtə*] *n* carburatore *m*.
carcass ['kɑːkəs] *n* carcassa.
carcinogenic [kɑːsɪnə'dʒɛnɪk] *adj*

cancerogeno(a).

card [kɑːd] *n* carta; (*thin cardboard*) cartoncino; (*visiting ~ etc*) biglietto; (*membership ~*) tessera; (*Christmas ~ etc*) cartolina; **to play ~s** giocare a carte.

cardamom ['kɑːdəməm] *n* cardamomo.

cardboard ['kɑːdbɔːd] *n* cartone *m*.

cardboard box *n* (scatola di) cartone *m*.

cardboard city *n luogo dove dormono in scatole di cartone emarginati senzatetto*.

card-carrying member ['kɑːd'kærɪɪŋ-] *n* tesserato/a.

card game *n* gioco di carte.

cardiac ['kɑːdɪæk] *adj* cardiaco(a).

cardigan ['kɑːdɪgən] *n* cardigan *m inv*.

cardinal ['kɑːdɪnl] *adj*, *n* cardinale (*m*).

card index *n* schedario.

cardphone ['kɑːdfəun] *n* telefono a scheda (magnetica).

cardsharp ['kɑːdʃɑːp] *n* baro.

card vote *n* (*BRIT*) voto (palese) per delega.

CARE [kɛə*] *n abbr* = *Cooperative for American Relief Everywhere*.

care [kɛə*] *n* cura, attenzione *f*; (*worry*) preoccupazione *f* ♦ *vi*: **to ~ about** interessarsi di; **would you ~ to/for ...?** le piacerebbe ...?; **I wouldn't ~ to do it** non lo vorrei fare; **in sb's ~** alle cure di qn; **to take ~** fare attenzione; **to take ~ of** curarsi di; (*details, arrangements*) occuparsi di; **I don't ~** non me ne importa; **I couldn't ~ less** non me ne importa un bel niente; **~ of (c/o)** (*on letter*) presso; **"with ~"** "fragile"; **the child has been taken into ~** il bambino è stato preso in custodia.

►**care for** *vt fus* aver cura di; (*like*) voler bene a.

careen [kə'riːn] *vi* (*ship*) sbandare ♦ *vt* carenare.

career [kə'rɪə*] *n* carriera; (*occupation*) professione *f* ♦ *vi* (*also*: *~ along*) andare di (gran) carriera.

career girl *n* donna dedita alla carriera.

careers officer *n* consulente *m/f* d'orientamento professionale.

carefree ['kɛəfriː] *adj* sgombro(a) di preoccupazioni.

careful ['kɛəful] *adj* attento(a); (*cautious*) cauto(a); (**be**) **~!** attenzione!; **he's very ~ with his money** bada molto alle spese.

carefully ['kɛəfəlɪ] *adv* con cura; cautamente.

careless ['kɛəlɪs] *adj* negligente; (*remark*) privo(a) di tatto.

carelessly ['kɛəlɪslɪ] *adv* negligentemente; senza tatto; (*without thinking*)

distrattamente.

carelessness ['kɛəlɪsnɪs] *n* negligenza; mancanza di tatto.

carer ['kɛərə*] *n chi si occupa di un familiare anziano o invalido*.

caress [kə'rɛs] *n* carezza ♦ *vt* accarezzare.

caretaker ['kɛəteɪkə*] *n* custode *m*.

caretaker government *n* (*BRIT*) governo *m* ponte *inv*.

car-ferry ['kɑːfɛrɪ] *n* traghetto.

cargo, ~es ['kɑːgəu] *n* carico.

cargo boat *n* cargo.

cargo plane *n* aereo di linea da carico.

car hire *n* (*BRIT*) autonoleggio.

Caribbean [kærɪ'biːən] *adj* caraibico(a); **the ~ (Sea)** il Mar dei Caraibi.

caricature ['kærɪkətjuə*] *n* caricatura.

caring ['kɛərɪŋ] *adj* (*person*) premuroso(a); (*society, organization*) umanitario(a).

carnage ['kɑːnɪdʒ] *n* carneficina.

carnal ['kɑːnl] *adj* carnale.

carnation [kɑː'neɪʃən] *n* garofano.

carnival ['kɑːnɪvəl] *n* (*public celebration*) carnevale *m*; (*US: funfair*) luna park *m inv*.

carnivorous [kɑː'nɪvərəs] *adj* carnivoro(a).

carol ['kærəl] *n*: (**Christmas**) **~** canto di Natale.

carouse [kə'rauz] *vi* far baldoria.

carousel [kærə'sɛl] *n* (*US*) giostra.

carp [kɑːp] *n* (*fish*) carpa.

►**carp at** *vt fus* trovare a ridire su.

car park *n* parcheggio.

carpenter ['kɑːpɪntə*] *n* carpentiere *m*.

carpentry ['kɑːpɪntrɪ] *n* carpenteria.

carpet ['kɑːpɪt] *n* tappeto; (*BRIT: fitted ~*) moquette *f inv* ♦ *vt* coprire con tappeto.

carpet bombing *n* bombardamento a tappeto.

carpet slippers *npl* pantofole *fpl*.

carpet sweeper *n* scopatappeti *m inv*.

car phone *n* telefonino per auto.

car rental *n* (*US*) autonoleggio.

carriage ['kærɪdʒ] *n* vettura; (*of goods*) trasporto; (*of typewriter*) carrello; (*bearing*) portamento; **~ forward** porto assegnato; **~ free** franco di porto; **~ paid** porto pagato.

carriage return *n* (*on typewriter etc*) leva (*or* tasto) del ritorno a capo.

carriageway ['kærɪdʒweɪ] *n* (*BRIT: part of road*) carreggiata.

carrier ['kærɪə*] *n* (*of disease*) portatore/trice; (*COMM*) impresa di trasporti; (*NAUT*) portaerei *f inv*.

carrier bag *n* (*BRIT*) sacchetto.

carrier pigeon *n* colombo viaggiatore.

carrion ['kærɪən] *n* carogna.

carrot ['kærət] *n* carota.

carry ['kærɪ] vt (subj: person) portare;
(: vehicle) trasportare; (a motion, bill) far
passare; (involve: responsibilities etc)
comportare; (COMM: goods) tenere;
(: interest) avere; (MATH: figure) riportare
♦ vi (sound) farsi sentire; **this loan carries
10% interest** questo prestito è sulla base
di un interesse del 10%; **to be carried
away** (fig) farsi trascinare.
►**carry forward** vt (MATH, COMM)
riportare.
►**carry on** vi: **to ~ on with sth/doing**
continuare qc/a fare ♦ vt mandare avanti.
►**carry out** vt (orders) eseguire;
(investigation) svolgere; (accomplish etc:
plan) realizzare; (perform, implement: idea,
threat) mettere in pratica.
carrycot ['kærɪkɔt] n (BRIT) culla portabile.
carry-on [kærɪ'ɔn] n (col: fuss) casino,
confusione f; (: annoying behaviour): **I've
had enough of your ~!** mi hai proprio
scocciato!
cart [kɑːt] n carro ♦ vt (col) trascinare,
scarrozzare.
carte blanche ['kɑːt'blɔŋʃ] n: **to give sb ~**
dare carta bianca a qn.
cartel [kɑː'tɛl] n (COMM) cartello.
cartilage ['kɑːtɪlɪdʒ] n cartilagine f.
cartographer [kɑː'tɔgrəfə*] n cartografo/a.
cartography [kɑː'tɔgrəfɪ] n cartografia.
carton ['kɑːtən] n (box) scatola di cartone;
(of yogurt) cartone m; (of cigarettes)
stecca.
cartoon [kɑː'tuːn] n (in newspaper etc)
vignetta; (CINE, TV) cartone m animato;
(ART) cartone.
cartoonist [kɑː'tuːnɪst] n vignettista m/f;
cartonista m/f.
cartridge ['kɑːtrɪdʒ] n (for gun, pen)
cartuccia; (for camera) caricatore m;
(music tape) cassetta; (of record player)
testina.
cartwheel ['kɑːtwiːl] n: **to turn a ~** (SPORT
etc) fare la ruota.
carve [kɑːv] vt (meat) trinciare; (wood,
stone) intagliare.
►**carve up** vt (meat) tagliare; (fig: country)
suddividere.
carving ['kɑːvɪŋ] n (in wood etc) scultura.
carving knife n trinciante m.
car wash n lavaggio auto.
Casablanca [kæsə'blæŋkə] n Casablanca.
cascade [kæs'keɪd] n cascata ♦ vi scendere
a cascata.
case [keɪs] n caso; (LAW) causa, processo;
(box) scatola; (also: **suit~**) valigia; (TYP):
lower/upper ~ (carattere m) minuscolo/
maiuscolo; **to have a good ~** avere

pretese legittime; **there's a strong ~ for
reform** ci sono validi argomenti a favore
della riforma; **in ~ of** in caso di; **in ~ he**
caso mai lui; **just in ~** in caso di bisogno.
case history n (MED) cartella clinica.
case-sensitive ['keɪs'sensɪtɪv] adj (COMPUT)
sensibile alle maiuscole o minuscole.
case study n studio di un caso.
cash [kæʃ] n (coins, notes) soldi mpl, denaro;
(col: money) quattrini mpl ♦ vt incassare;
to pay (in) ~ pagare in contanti; **to be
short of ~** essere a corto di soldi; **~ with
order/on delivery (COD)** (COMM)
pagamento all'ordinazione/alla consegna.
►**cash in** vt (insurance policy etc) riscuotere,
riconvertire.
►**cash in on** vt fus: **to ~ in on sth** sfruttare
qc.
cash account n conto m cassa inv.
cash-and-carry ['kæʃənd'kærɪ] n cash and
carry m inv.
cashbook ['kæʃbuk] n giornale m di cassa.
cash box n cassetta per il denaro
spicciolo.
cash card n carta per prelievi automatici.
cash desk n (BRIT) cassa.
cash discount n sconto per contanti.
cash dispenser n sportello automatico.
cashew [kæ'ʃuː] n (also: **~ nut**) anacardio.
cash flow n cash-flow m inv, liquidità f inv.
cashier [kæ'ʃɪə*] n cassiere/a ♦ vt (esp MIL)
destituire.
cashmere ['kæʃmɪə*] n cachemire m.
cash payment n pagamento in contanti.
cash price n prezzo per contanti.
cash register n registratore m di cassa.
cash sale n vendita per contanti.
casing ['keɪsɪŋ] n rivestimento.
casino [kə'siːnəu] n casinò m inv.
cask [kɑːsk] n botte f.
casket ['kɑːskɪt] n cofanetto; (US: coffin)
bara.
Caspian Sea ['kæspɪən-] n: **the ~** il mar
Caspio.
casserole ['kæsərəul] n casseruola; (food):
chicken ~ pollo in casseruola.
cassette [kæ'sɛt] n cassetta.
cassette deck n piastra di registrazione.
cassette player n riproduttore m a
cassette.
cassette recorder n registratore m a
cassette.
cast [kɑːst] vt (pt, pp **cast**) (throw) gettare;
(shed) perdere; spogliarsi di; (metal)
gettare, fondere ♦ n (THEAT) complesso di
attori; (mould) forma; (also: **plaster ~**)
ingessatura; (THEAT): **to ~ sb as Hamlet**
scegliere qn per la parte di Amleto; **to ~**

one's vote votare, dare il voto.
►**cast aside** vt (*reject*) mettere da parte.
►**cast off** vi (*NAUT*) salpare; (*KNITTING*) diminuire, calare ♦ vt (*NAUT*) disormeggiare; (*KNITTING*) diminuire, calare.
►**cast on** vt (*KNITTING*) avviare ♦ vi avviare (le maglie).
castanets [kæstə'nɛts] npl castagnette fpl.
castaway ['kɑːstəwɔɪ] n naufrago/a.
caste [kɑːst] n casta.
caster sugar ['kɑːstə-] n zucchero semolato.
casting vote ['kɑːstɪŋ-] n (*BRIT*) voto decisivo.
cast iron n ghisa ♦ adj: **cast-iron** (*fig*: *will*, *alibi*) di ferro, d'acciaio.
castle ['kɑːsl] n castello; (*fortified*) rocca.
castor ['kɑːstə*] n (*wheel*) rotella.
castor oil n olio di ricino.
castrate [kæs'treɪt] vt castrare.
casual ['kæʒjul] adj (*by chance*) casuale, fortuito(a); (*irregular: work etc*) avventizio(a); (*unconcerned*) noncurante, indifferente; ~ **wear** casual m.
casual labour n manodopera avventizia.
casually ['kæʒjulɪ] adv con disinvoltura; (*by chance*) casualmente.
casualty ['kæʒjultɪ] n ferito/a; (*dead*) morto/a, vittima; **heavy casualties** npl grosse perdite fpl.
casualty ward n (*BRIT*) pronto soccorso.
cat [kæt] n gatto.
catacombs ['kætəkuːmz] npl catacombe fpl.
catalogue, (*US*) **catalog** ['kætəlɔg] n catalogo ♦ vt catalogare.
catalyst ['kætəlɪst] n catalizzatore m.
catalytic converter [kætə'lɪtɪkkən'vəːtə*] n marmitta catalitica, catalizzatore m.
catapult ['kætəpʌlt] n catapulta; fionda.
cataract ['kætərækt] n (*also MED*) cateratta.
catarrh [kə'tɑː*] n catarro.
catastrophe [kə'tæstrəfɪ] n catastrofe f.
catastrophic [kætə'strɔfɪk] adj catastrofico(a).
catcall ['kætkɔːl] n (*at meeting etc*) fischio.
catch [kætʃ] vb (*pt, pp* **caught** [kɔːt]) vt (*train, thief, cold*) acchiappare; (*ball*) afferrare; (*person: by surprise*) sorprendere; (*understand*) comprendere; (*get entangled*) impigliare ♦ vi (*fire*) prendere ♦ n (*fish etc caught*) retata, presa; (*trick*) inganno; (*TECH*) gancio; **to** ~ **sb's attention** *or* **eye** attirare l'attenzione di qn; **to** ~ **fire** prendere fuoco; **to** ~ **sight of** scorgere.
►**catch on** vi (*become popular*) affermarsi, far presa; (*understand*): **to** ~ **on (to sth)** capire (qc).

►**catch out** vt (*BRIT fig*: *with trick question*) cogliere in fallo.
►**catch up** vi mettersi in pari ♦ vt (*also*: ~ **up with**) raggiungere.
catching ['kætʃɪŋ] adj (*MED*) contagioso(a).
catchment area ['kætʃmənt-] n (*BRIT SCOL*) circoscrizione f scolare; (*GEO*) bacino pluviale.
catch phrase n slogan m inv; frase f fatta.
catch-22 ['kætʃtwɛntɪ'tuː] n: **it's a** ~ **situation** non c'è via d'uscita.
catchy ['kætʃɪ] adj orecchiabile.
catechism ['kætɪkɪzəm] n catechismo.
categoric(al) [kætɪ'gɔrɪk(l)] adj categorico(a).
categorize ['kætɪgəraɪz] vt categorizzare.
category ['kætɪgərɪ] n categoria.
cater ['keɪtə*] vi (*gen*: ~ **for**) provvedere da mangiare (per).
►**cater for** vt fus (*BRIT: needs*) provvedere a; (: *consumers*) incontrare i gusti di.
caterer ['keɪtərə*] n fornitore m.
catering ['keɪtərɪŋ] n approvvigionamento.
catering trade n settore m ristoranti.
caterpillar ['kætəpɪlə*] n (*ZOOL*) bruco ♦ cpd (*vehicle*) cingolato(a); ~ **track** cingolo.
cat flap n gattaiola.
cathedral [kə'θiːdrəl] n cattedrale f, duomo.
cathode ['kæθəud] n catodo.
cathode ray tube n tubo a raggi catodici.
catholic ['kæθəlɪk] adj universale; aperto(a); eclettico(a); **C~** adj, n (*REL*) cattolico(a).
CAT scanner [kæt-] n (*MED*: = *computerized axial tomography scanner*) (rilevatore m per la) TAC f inv.
cat's-eye ['kæts'aɪ] n (*BRIT AUT*) catarifrangente m.
catsup ['kætsəp] n (*US*) ketchup m inv.
cattle ['kætl] npl bestiame m, bestie fpl.
catty ['kætɪ] adj maligno(a), dispettoso(a).
catwalk ['kætwɔːk] n passerella.
Caucasian [kɔː'keɪzɪən] adj, n caucasico(a).
caucus ['kɔːkəs] n (*US POL*) (riunione f del) comitato elettorale; (*BRIT POL: group*) comitato di dirigenti; *see boxed note.*

CAUCUS

Caucus è il termine usato, specialmente negli Stati Uniti, per indicare una riunione informale dei rappresentanti di spicco di un partito politico che precede una riunione ufficiale. Con uso estensivo, la parola indica il nucleo direttivo di un partito politico.

---

caught [kɔːt] pt, pp of **catch**.
cauliflower ['kɔlɪflauə*] n cavolfiore m.

cause [kɔːz] n causa ♦ vt causare; **there is no ~ for concern** non c'è ragione di preoccuparsi; **to ~ sb to do sth** far fare qc a qn; **to ~ sth to be done** far fare qc.
causeway ['kɔːzweɪ] n strada rialzata.
caustic ['kɔːstɪk] adj caustico(a).
caution ['kɔːʃən] n prudenza; (warning) avvertimento ♦ vt ammonire.
cautious ['kɔːʃəs] adj cauto(a), prudente.
cautiously ['kɔːʃəslɪ] adv prudentemente.
cautiousness ['kɔːʃəsnɪs] n cautela.
cavalier [kævə'lɪə*] n (knight) cavaliere m ♦ adj (pej: offhand) brusco(a).
cavalry ['kævəlrɪ] n cavalleria.
cave [keɪv] n caverna, grotta ♦ vi: **to go caving** fare speleologia.
▶**cave in** vi (roof etc) crollare.
caveman ['keɪvmæn] n uomo delle caverne.
cavern ['kævən] n caverna.
caviar(e) ['kævɪɑː*] n caviale m.
cavity ['kævɪtɪ] n cavità f inv.
cavity wall insulation n isolamento per pareti a intercapedine.
cavort [kə'vɔːt] vi far capriole.
cayenne (pepper) [keɪ'ɛn–] n pepe m di Caienna.
CB n abbr (BRIT: = Companion (of the Order) of the Bath) titolo; (= Citizens' Band (Radio)) C.B. m; **~ radio (set)** baracchino.
CBC n abbr = Canadian Broadcasting Corporation.
CBE n abbr (BRIT: = Companion (of the Order) of the British Empire) titolo.
CBI n abbr (= Confederation of British Industry) ≈ CONFINDUSTRIA (= Confederazione Generale dell'Industria Italiana).
CBS n abbr (US) = Columbia Broadcasting System.
CC abbr (BRIT) = county council.
cc abbr (= cubic centimetre) cc; (on letter etc) = carbon copy.
CCA n abbr (US: = Circuit Court of Appeals) corte f d'appello itinerante.
CCTV n abbr = closed-circuit television.
CCU n abbr (US: = coronary care unit) unità coronarica.
CD n abbr (= compact disk) compact disc m inv; **~ player** lettore m CD; (MIL) = Civil Defence (Corps) (BRIT), Civil Defense (US) ♦ abbr (BRIT: = Corps Diplomatique) C.D.
CD burner n masterizzatore m.
CDC n abbr (US) = center for disease control.
CD-I ®n CD-I m inv, compact disc m inv interattivo.
Cdr. abbr (= commander) Com.
CD-ROM ['siː'diː'rɔm] n abbr (= compact disc read-only memory) CD-ROM m inv.
CDT abbr (US: = Central Daylight Time) ora legale del centro; (BRIT SCOL: = Craft, Design and Technology) educazione tecnica.
CDW n abbr see collision damage waiver.
CD writer n masterizzatore m.
cease [siːs] vt, vi cessare.
ceasefire ['siːsfaɪə*] n cessate il fuoco m inv.
ceaseless ['siːslɪs] adj incessante.
CED n abbr (US) = Committee for Economic Development.
cedar ['siːdə*] n cedro.
cede [siːd] vt cedere.
CEEB n abbr (US: = College Entrance Examination Board) commissione f per l'esame di ammissione al college.
ceilidh ['keɪlɪ] n festa con musiche e danze popolari scozzesi o irlandesi.
ceiling ['siːlɪŋ] n soffitto; (fig: upper limit) tetto, limite m massimo.
celebrate ['sɛlɪbreɪt] vt, vi celebrare.
celebrated ['sɛlɪbreɪtɪd] adj celebre.
celebration [sɛlɪ'breɪʃən] n celebrazione f.
celebrity [sɪ'lɛbrɪtɪ] n celebrità f inv.
celeriac [sə'lɛrɪæk] n sedano m rapa inv.
celery ['sɛlərɪ] n sedano.
celestial [sɪ'lɛstɪəl] adj celeste.
celibacy ['sɛlɪbəsɪ] n celibato.
cell [sɛl] n cella; (BIOL) cellula; (ELEC) elemento (di batteria).
cellar ['sɛlə*] n sottosuolo, cantina.
cellist ['tʃɛlɪst] n violoncellista m/f.
cello ['tʃɛləu] n violoncello.
cellophane ®['sɛləfeɪn] n cellophane ® m.
cellphone ['sɛlfəun] n cellulare m.
cellular ['sɛljulə*] adj cellulare.
celluloid ['sɛljulɔɪd] n celluloide f.
cellulose ['sɛljuləus] n cellulosa.
Celsius ['sɛlsɪəs] adj Celsius inv.
Celt [kɛlt, sɛlt] n celta m/f.
Celtic ['kɛltɪk, 'sɛltɪk] adj celtico(a) ♦ n (LING) celtico.
cement [sə'mɛnt] n cemento ♦ vt cementare.
cement mixer n betoniera.
cemetery ['sɛmɪtrɪ] n cimitero.
cenotaph ['sɛnətɑːf] n cenotafio.
censor ['sɛnsə*] n censore m ♦ vt censurare.
censorship ['sɛnsəʃɪp] n censura.
censure ['sɛnʃə*] vt censurare.
census ['sɛnsəs] n censimento.
cent [sɛnt] n (of dollar, euro) centesimo; see also per cent.
centenary [sɛn'tiːnərɪ], **centennial** [sɛn'tɛnɪəl] n centenario.
center ['sɛntə*] n, vt (US) = centre.

centigrade ['sɛntɪgreɪd] *adj* centigrado(a).
centilitre, *(US)* **centiliter** ['sɛntɪliːtə*] *n* centilitro.
centimetre, *(US)* **centimeter** ['sɛntɪmiːtə*] *n* centimetro.
centipede ['sɛntɪpiːd] *n* centopiedi *m inv*.
central ['sɛntrəl] *adj* centrale.
Central African Republic *n* Repubblica centrafricana.
Central America *n* America centrale.
central heating *n* riscaldamento centrale.
centralize ['sɛntrəlaɪz] *vt* accentrare.
central processing unit (CPU) *n* *(COMPUT)* unità *f inv* centrale di elaborazione.
central reservation *n* *(BRIT AUT)* banchina *f* spartitraffico *inv*.
centre, *(US)* **center** ['sɛntə*] *n* centro ◆ *vt* *(concentrate)*: **to ~ (on)** concentrare (su).
centrefold, *(US)* **centerfold** ['sɛntəfəuld] *n* *(PRESS)* poster *m* (all'interno di rivista).
centre-forward ['sɛntə'fɔːwəd] *n* *(SPORT)* centroavanti *m inv*.
centre-half ['sɛntə'hɑːf] *n* *(SPORT)* centromediano.
centrepiece, *(US)* **centerpiece** ['sɛntəpiːs] *n* centrotavola *m*; *(fig)* punto centrale.
centre spread *n* *(BRIT)* pubblicità a doppia pagina.
centre-stage [sɛntə'steɪdʒ] *n*: **to take ~** porsi al centro dell'attenzione.
centrifugal [sɛn'trɪfjugəl] *adj* centrifugo(a).
centrifuge ['sɛntrɪfjuːʒ] *n* centrifuga.
century ['sɛntjurɪ] *n* secolo; **in the twentieth ~** nel ventesimo secolo.
CEO *n abbr see* **chief executive officer.**
ceramic [sɪ'ræmɪk] *adj* ceramico(a).
cereal ['siːrɪəl] *n* cereale *m*.
cerebral ['sɛrɪbrəl] *adj* cerebrale.
ceremonial [sɛrɪ'məunɪəl] *n* cerimoniale *m*; *(rite)* rito.
ceremony ['sɛrɪmənɪ] *n* cerimonia; **to stand on ~** fare complimenti.
cert [sɜːt] *n* *(BRIT col)*: **it's a dead ~** non c'è alcun dubbio.
certain ['sɜːtən] *adj* certo(a); **to make ~ of** assicurarsi di; **for ~** per certo, di sicuro.
certainly ['sɜːtənlɪ] *adv* certamente, certo.
certainty ['sɜːtəntɪ] *n* certezza.
certificate [sə'tɪfɪkɪt] *n* certificato; diploma *m*.
certified letter ['sɜːtɪfaɪd-] *n* *(US)* lettera raccomandata.
certified public accountant (CPA) ['sɜːtɪfaɪd-] *n* *(US)* ≈ commercialista *m/f*.
certify ['sɜːtɪfaɪ] *vt* certificare ◆ *vi*: **to ~ to** attestare a.
cervical ['sɜːvɪkl] *adj*: **~ cancer** cancro della

cervice, tumore *m* al collo dell'utero; **~ smear** Pap-test *m inv*.
cervix ['sɜːvɪks] *n* cervice *f*.
Cesarean [siː'zɛərɪən] *adj, n* *(US)* = **Caesarean.**
cessation [sə'seɪʃən] *n* cessazione *f*; arresto.
cesspit ['sɛspɪt] *n* pozzo nero.
CET *abbr* (= *Central European Time*) *fuso orario.*
Ceylon [sɪ'lɔn] *n* Ceylon *f*.
cf. *abbr* (= *compare*) cfr.
c/f *abbr* *(COMM)* = *carried forward.*
CFC *n abbr* (= *chlorofluorocarbon*) CFC *m inv*.
CG *n abbr* *(US)* = **coastguard.**
cg *abbr* (= *centigram*) cg.
CH *n abbr* *(BRIT*: = *Companion of Honour)* titolo.
ch. *abbr* (= *chapter*) cap.
Chad [tʃæd] *n* Chad *m*.
chafe [tʃeɪf] *vt* fregare, irritare ◆ *vi* *(fig)*: **to ~ against** scontrarsi con.
chaffinch ['tʃæfɪntʃ] *n* fringuello.
chagrin ['ʃægrɪn] *n* disappunto, dispiacere *m*.
chain [tʃeɪn] *n* catena ◆ *vt* *(also*: **~ up**) incatenare.
chain reaction *n* reazione *f* a catena.
chain-smoke ['tʃeɪnsməuk] *vi* fumare una sigaretta dopo l'altra.
chain store *n* negozio a catena.
chair [tʃɛə*] *n* sedia; *(armchair)* poltrona; *(of university)* cattedra ◆ *vt* *(meeting)* presiedere; **the ~** *(US*: *electric ~)* la sedia elettrica.
chairlift ['tʃɛəlɪft] *n* seggiovia.
chairman ['tʃɛəmən] *n* presidente *m*.
chairperson ['tʃɛəpəːsn] *n* presidente/essa.
chairwoman ['tʃɛəwumən] *n* presidentessa.
chalet ['ʃæleɪ] *n* chalet *m inv*.
chalice ['tʃælɪs] *n* calice *m*.
chalk [tʃɔːk] *n* gesso.
►**chalk up** *vt* scrivere col gesso; *(fig*: *success)* ottenere; *(: victory)* riportare.
challenge ['tʃælɪndʒ] *n* sfida ◆ *vt* sfidare; *(statement, right)* mettere in dubbio; **to ~ sb to a fight/game** sfidare qn a battersi/ad una partita; **to ~ sb to do** sfidare qn a fare.
challenger ['tʃælɪndʒə*] *n* *(SPORT)* sfidante *m/f*.
challenging ['tʃælɪndʒɪŋ] *adj* sfidante; *(remark, look)* provocatorio(a).
chamber ['tʃeɪmbə*] *n* camera; **~ of commerce** camera di commercio.
chambermaid ['tʃeɪmbəmeɪd] *n* cameriera.
chamber music *n* musica da camera.

chamberpot ['tʃeɪmbəpɔt] n vaso da notte.
chameleon [kə'miːlɪən] n camaleonte m.
chamois ['ʃæmwɑː] n camoscio.
chamois leather ['ʃæmɪ-] n pelle f di camoscio.
champagne [ʃæm'peɪn] n champagne m inv.
champers ['ʃæmpəz] nsg (col) sciampagna.
champion ['tʃæmpɪən] n campione/essa; (of cause) difensore m ♦ vt difendere.
championship ['tʃæmpɪənʃɪp] n campionato.
chance [tʃɑːns] n caso; (opportunity) occasione f; (likelihood) possibilità f inv ♦ vt: to ~ it rischiare, provarci ♦ adj fortuito(a); **there is little** ~ **of his coming** è molto improbabile che venga; **to take a** ~ rischiare; **by** ~ per caso; **it's the** ~ **of a lifetime** è un'occasione unica; **the ~s are that** ... probabilmente ..., è probabile che ... + sub; **to** ~ **to do sth** (formal: happen) fare per caso qc.
► **chance (up)on** vt fus (person) incontrare per caso, imbattersi in; (thing) trovare per caso.
chancel ['tʃɑːnsəl] n coro.
chancellor ['tʃɑːnsələ*] n cancelliere m; (of university) rettore m (onorario); **C~ of the Exchequer** (BRIT) Cancelliere m dello Scacchiere.
chandelier [ʃændə'lɪə*] n lampadario.
change [tʃeɪndʒ] vt cambiare; (transform): **to** ~ **sb into** trasformare qn in ♦ vi cambiarsi; (be transformed): **to** ~ **into** trasformarsi in ♦ n cambiamento; (money) resto; **to** ~ **one's mind** cambiare idea; **to** ~ **gear** (AUT) cambiare (marcia); **she ~d into an old skirt** si è cambiata e ha messo una vecchia gonna; **a** ~ **of clothes** un cambio (di vestiti); **for a** ~ tanto per cambiare; **small** ~ spiccioli mpl, moneta; **keep the** ~ tenga il resto; **can you give me** ~ **for £1?** mi può cambiare una sterlina?
changeable ['tʃeɪndʒəbl] adj (weather) variabile; (person) mutevole.
change machine n distributore m automatico di monete.
changeover ['tʃeɪndʒəʊvə*] n cambiamento, passaggio.
changing ['tʃeɪndʒɪŋ] adj che cambia; (colours) cangiante.
changing room n (BRIT: in shop) camerino; (: SPORT) spogliatoio.
channel ['tʃænl] n canale m; (of river, sea) alveo ♦ vt canalizzare; (fig: interest, energies): **to** ~ **into** concentrare su, indirizzare verso; **through the usual ~s** per le solite vie; **the (English) C~** la

Manica; **green/red** ~ (CUSTOMS) uscita "niente da dichiarare"/"merci da dichiarare".
channel-hopping ['tʃænl,hɔpɪŋ] n (TV) zapping m.
Channel Islands npl: **the** ~ le Isole Normanne.
Channel Tunnel n: **the** ~ il tunnel della Manica.
chant [tʃɑːnt] n canto; salmodia; (of crowd) slogan m inv ♦ vt cantare; salmodiare; **the demonstrators ~ed their disapproval** i dimostranti lanciavano slogan di protesta.
chaos ['keɪɔs] n caos m.
chaos theory n teoria del caos.
chaotic [keɪ'ɔtɪk] adj caotico(a).
chap [tʃæp] n (BRIT col: man) tipo ♦ vt (skin) screpolare; **old** ~ vecchio mio.
chapel ['tʃæpl] n cappella.
chaperone ['ʃæpərəʊn] n accompagnatore/ trice ♦ vt accompagnare.
chaplain ['tʃæplɪn] n cappellano.
chapped [tʃæpt] adj (skin, lips) screpolato(a).
chapter ['tʃæptə*] n capitolo.
char [tʃɑː*] vt (burn) carbonizzare ♦ vi (BRIT: cleaner) lavorare come domestica (a ore) ♦ n (BRIT) = **charlady**.
character ['kærɪktə*] n (gen, COMPUT) carattere m; (in novel, film) personaggio; (eccentric) originale m; **a person of good** ~ una persona a modo.
character code n (COMPUT) codice m di carattere.
characteristic ['kærɪktə'rɪstɪk] adj caratteristico(a) ♦ n caratteristica; ~ **of** tipico(a) di.
characterize ['kærɪktəraɪz] vt caratterizzare; (describe): **to** ~ **(as)** descrivere (come).
charade [ʃə'rɑːd] n sciarada.
charcoal ['tʃɑːkəʊl] n carbone m di legna.
charge [tʃɑːdʒ] n accusa; (cost) prezzo; (of gun, battery, MIL: attack) carica ♦ vt (gun, battery, MIL: enemy) caricare; (customer) fare pagare a; (sum) fare pagare; (LAW): **to** ~ **sb (with)** accusare qn (di) ♦ vi (gen with: up, along etc) lanciarsi; **~s** npl: **bank ~s** commissioni fpl bancarie; **labour ~s** costi mpl del lavoro; **to** ~ **in/out** precipitarsi dentro/fuori; **to** ~ **up/down** lanciarsi su/giù per; **is there a ~?** c'è da pagare?; **there's no** ~ non c'è niente da pagare; **extra** ~ supplemento; **to take** ~ **of** incaricarsi di; **to be in** ~ **of** essere responsabile per; **to have** ~ **of sb** aver cura di qn; **how much do you** ~ **for this**

repair? quanto chiede per la riparazione?; **to ~ an expense (up) to sb** addebitare una spesa a qn; **~ it to my account** lo metta *or* addebiti sul mio conto.
charge account *n* conto.
charge card *n* carta di credito commerciale.
chargé d'affaires ['ʃɑːʒeɪdæ'fɛə*] *n* incaricato d'affari.
chargehand ['tʃɑːdʒhænd] *n* (*BRIT*) caposquadra *m/f*.
charger ['tʃɑːdʒə*] *n* (*also:* **battery ~**) caricabatterie *m inv*; (*old:* warhorse) destriero.
chariot ['tʃærɪət] *n* carro.
charitable ['tʃærɪtəbl] *adj* caritatevole.
charity ['tʃærɪtɪ] *n* carità; (*organization*) opera pia.
charlady ['tʃɑːleɪdɪ] *n* (*BRIT*) domestica a ore.
charlatan ['ʃɑːlətən] *n* ciarlatano.
charm [tʃɑːm] *n* fascino; (*on bracelet*) ciondolo ♦ *vt* affascinare, incantare.
charm bracelet *n* braccialetto con ciondoli.
charming ['tʃɑːmɪŋ] *adj* affascinante.
chart [tʃɑːt] *n* tabella; grafico; (*map*) carta nautica; (*weather* ~) carta del tempo ♦ *vt* fare una carta nautica di; (*sales, progress*) tracciare il grafico di; **to be in the ~s** (*record, pop group*) essere in classifica.
charter ['tʃɑːtə*] *vt* (*plane*) noleggiare ♦ *n* (*document*) carta; **on** ~ a nolo.
chartered accountant (CA) ['tʃɑːtəd-] *n* (*BRIT*) ragioniere/a professionista.
charter flight *n* volo *m* charter *inv*.
charwoman ['tʃɑːwumən] *n* = **charlady**.
chase [tʃeɪs] *vt* inseguire; (*also:* ~ **away**) cacciare ♦ *n* caccia.
►**chase down** *vt* (*US*) = **chase up**.
►**chase up** *vt* (*BRIT: person*) scovare; (: *information*) scoprire, raccogliere.
chasm ['kæzəm] *n* abisso.
chassis ['ʃæsɪ] *n* telaio.
chastened ['tʃeɪsnd] *adj* abbattuto(a), provato(a).
chastening ['tʃeɪsnɪŋ] *adj* che fa riflettere.
chastise [tʃæs'taɪz] *vt* punire, castigare.
chastity ['tʃæstɪtɪ] *n* castità.
chat [tʃæt] *vi* (*also:* **have a ~**) chiacchierare ♦ *n* chiacchierata.
►**chat up** *vt* (*BRIT col: girl*) abbordare.
chatline ['tʃætlaɪn] *n* chat line *f inv*.
chat room *n* chat line *f inv*.
chat show *n* (*BRIT*) talk show *m inv*, conversazione *f* televisiva.
chattel ['tʃætl] *n see* **goods**.
chatter ['tʃætə*] *vi* (*person*) ciarlare ♦ *n*

ciarle *fpl*; **her teeth were ~ing** batteva i denti.
chatterbox ['tʃætəbɔks] *n* chiacchierone/a.
chattering classes ['tʃætərɪŋ-] *npl*: **the ~** (*col, pej*) ≈ gli intellettuali da salotto.
chatty ['tʃætɪ] *adj* (*style*) familiare; (*person*) chiacchierino(a).
chauffeur ['ʃəufə*] *n* autista *m*.
chauvinism ['ʃəuvɪnɪzəm] *n* (*also:* **male ~**) maschilismo; (*nationalism*) sciovinismo.
chauvinist ['ʃəuvɪnɪst] *n* (*also:* **male ~**) maschilista *m*; (*nationalist*) sciovinista *m/f*.
chauvinistic [ʃəuvɪ'nɪstɪk] *adj* sciovinistico(a).
ChE *abbr* = **chemical engineer**.
cheap [tʃiːp] *adj* a buon mercato; (*reduced: fare, ticket*) ridotto(a); (*joke*) grossolano(a); (*poor quality*) di cattiva qualità ♦ *adv* a buon mercato; **~er** meno caro; **~ day return** biglietto giornaliero ridotto di andata e ritorno; **~ money** denaro a basso tasso di interesse.
cheapen ['tʃiːpn] *vt* ribassare; (*fig*) avvilire.
cheaply ['tʃiːplɪ] *adv* a buon prezzo, a buon mercato.
cheat [tʃiːt] *vi* imbrogliare; (*at school*) copiare ♦ *vt* ingannare; (*rob*) defraudare ♦ *n* imbroglione *m*; copione *m*; (*trick*) inganno; **he's been ~ing on his wife** ha tradito sua moglie.
cheating ['tʃiːtɪŋ] *n* imbrogliare *m*; copiare *m*.
check [tʃɛk] *vt* verificare; (*passport, ticket*) controllare; (*halt*) fermare; (*restrain*) contenere ♦ *vi* (*official etc*) informarsi ♦ *n* verifica; controllo; (*curb*) freno; (*bill*) conto; (*pattern: gen pl*) quadretti *mpl*; (*US*) = **cheque** ♦ *adj*: **~ed:** (*pattern, cloth*) a scacchi, a quadretti; **to ~ with sb** chiedere a qn; **to keep a ~ on sb/sth** controllare qn/qc.
►**check in** *vi* (*in hotel*) registrare; (*at airport*) presentarsi all'accettazione ♦ *vt* (*luggage*) depositare.
►**check off** *vt* segnare.
►**check out** *vi* (*from hotel*) saldare il conto ♦ *vt* (*luggage*) ritirare; (*investigate: story*) controllare, verificare; (: *person*) prendere informazioni su.
►**check up** *vi*: **to ~ up (on sth)** investigare (qc); **to ~ up on sb** informarsi sul conto di qn.
checkbook ['tʃɛkbuk] *n* (*US*) = **chequebook**.
checkered ['tʃɛkəd] *adj* (*US*) = **chequered**.
checkers ['tʃɛkəz] *n* (*US*) dama.
check guarantee card *n* (*US*) carta *f*

assegni *inv.*
check-in ['tʃɛkɪn] *n* (*also:* ~ **desk**: *at airport*)
check-in *m inv*, accettazione *f* (*bagagli inv*).
checking account ['tʃɛkɪŋ-] *n* (*US*) conto
corrente.
checklist ['tʃɛklɪst] *n* lista di controllo.
checkmate ['tʃɛkmeɪt] *n* scaccomatto.
checkout ['tʃɛkaut] *n* (*in supermarket*)
cassa.
checkpoint ['tʃɛkpɔɪnt] *n* posto di blocco.
checkroom ['tʃɛkrum] *n* (*US*) deposito *m*
bagagli *inv.*
checkup ['tʃɛkʌp] *n* (*MED*) controllo
medico.
cheek [tʃiːk] *n* guancia; (*impudence*) faccia
tosta.
cheekbone ['tʃiːkbəun] *n* zigomo.
cheeky ['tʃiːkɪ] *adj* sfacciato(a).
cheep [tʃiːp] *n* (*of bird*) pigolio ♦ *vi* pigolare.
cheer [tʃɪə*] *vt* applaudire; (*gladden*)
rallegrare ♦ *vi* applaudire ♦ *n* (*gen pl*)
applausi *mpl*; evviva *mpl*; ~s! salute!
►**cheer on** *vt* (*person etc*) incitare.
►**cheer up** *vi* rallegrarsi, farsi animo ♦ *vt*
rallegrare.
cheerful ['tʃɪəful] *adj* allegro(a).
cheerfulness ['tʃɪəfulnɪs] *n* allegria.
cheerio ['tʃɪərɪ'əu] *excl* (*BRIT*) ciao!
cheerleader ['tʃɪəliːdə*] *n* cheerleader *f inv.*
cheerless ['tʃɪəlɪs] *adj* triste.
cheese [tʃiːz] *n* formaggio.
cheeseboard ['tʃiːzbɔːd] *n* piatto del (*or*
per il) formaggio.
cheeseburger ['tʃiːzbəːgə*] *n*
cheeseburger *m inv.*
cheesecake ['tʃiːzkeɪk] *n* specie di torta di
ricotta, a volte con frutta.
cheetah ['tʃiːtə] *n* ghepardo.
chef [ʃɛf] *n* capocuoco.
chemical ['kɛmɪkl] *adj* chimico(a) ♦ *n*
prodotto chimico.
chemical engineering *n* ingegneria
chimica.
chemist ['kɛmɪst] *n* (*BRIT*: *pharmacist*)
farmacista *m/f*; (*scientist*) chimico/a; ~'s
shop *n* (*BRIT*) farmacia.
chemistry ['kɛmɪstrɪ] *n* chimica.
chemo ['kiːməu] *n* chemio *f inv.*
chemotherapy [kiːməu'θɛrəpɪ] *n*
chemioterapia.
cheque, (*US*) **check** [tʃɛk] *n* assegno; **to**
pay by ~ pagare per assegno *or* con un
assegno.
chequebook, (*US*) **checkbook** ['tʃɛkbuk] *n*
libretto degli assegni.
cheque card *n* (*BRIT*) carta *f* assegni *inv.*
chequered, (*US*) **checkered** ['tʃɛkəd] *adj*
(*fig*) movimentato(a).

cherish ['tʃɛrɪʃ] *vt* aver caro; (*hope etc*)
nutrire.
cheroot [ʃə'ruːt] *n* sigaro spuntato.
cherry ['tʃɛrɪ] *n* ciliegia.
Ches *abbr* (*BRIT*) = Cheshire.
chess [tʃɛs] *n* scacchi *mpl.*
chessboard ['tʃɛsbɔːd] *n* scacchiera.
chessman ['tʃɛsmæn] *n* pezzo degli
scacchi.
chessplayer ['tʃɛspleɪə*] *n* scacchista *m/f.*
chest [tʃɛst] *n* petto; (*box*) cassa; **to get sth**
off one's ~ (*col*) sputare il rospo; ~ **of**
drawers cassettone *m.*
chest measurement *n* giro *m* torace *inv.*
chestnut ['tʃɛsnʌt] *n* castagna; (*also:* ~ *tree*)
castagno ♦ *adj* castano(a).
chesty ['tʃɛstɪ] *adj:* ~ **cough** tosse *f*
bronchiale.
chew [tʃuː] *vt* masticare.
chewing gum ['tʃuːɪŋ-] *n* chewing gum *m.*
chic [ʃiːk] *adj* elegante.
chick [tʃɪk] *n* pulcino; (*US col*) pollastrella.
chicken ['tʃɪkɪn] *n* pollo; (*col: coward*)
coniglio.
►**chicken out** *vi* (*col*) avere fifa; **to** ~ **out**
of sth tirarsi indietro da qc per fifa *or*
paura.
chicken feed *n* (*fig*) miseria.
chickenpox ['tʃɪkɪnpɔks] *n* varicella.
chick flick *n* (*col*) filmetto rosa.
chickpea ['tʃɪkpiː] *n* cece *m.*
chicory ['tʃɪkərɪ] *n* cicoria.
chide [tʃaɪd] *vt* rimproverare.
chief [tʃiːf] *n* capo ♦ *adj* principale; **C~ of**
Staff (*MIL*) Capo di Stato Maggiore.
chief constable *n* (*BRIT*) ≈ questore *m.*
chief executive, (*US*) **chief executive**
officer (CEO) *n* direttore *m* generale.
chiefly ['tʃiːflɪ] *adv* per lo più, soprattutto.
chiffon ['ʃɪfɔn] *n* chiffon *m inv.*
chilblain ['tʃɪlbleɪn] *n* gelone *m.*
child, *pl* ~**ren** [tʃaɪld, 'tʃɪldrən] *n*
bambino/a.
child abuse *n* molestie *fpl* a minori.
child abuser [-ə'bjuːzə*] *n* molestatore/
trice di bambini.
child benefit *n* (*BRIT*) ≈ assegni *mpl*
familiari.
childbirth ['tʃaɪldbəːθ] *n* parto.
childhood ['tʃaɪldhud] *n* infanzia.
childish ['tʃaɪldɪʃ] *adj* puerile.
childless ['tʃaɪldlɪs] *adj* senza figli.
childlike ['tʃaɪldlaɪk] *adj* fanciullesco(a).
child minder *n* (*BRIT*) bambinaia.
child prodigy *n* bambino *m* prodigio *inv.*
children ['tʃɪldrən] *npl of* **child.**
children's home *n* istituto per l'infanzia.
Chile ['tʃɪlɪ] *n* Cile *m.*

Chilean ['tʃɪlɪən] *adj, n* cileno(a).
chill [tʃɪl] *n* freddo; (*MED*) infreddatura ♦ *adj* freddo(a), gelido(a) ♦ *vt* raffreddare; (*CULIN*) mettere in fresco; **"serve ~ed"** "servire fresco".
▶**chill out** *vi* (*esp US*: *col*) darsi una calmata.
chilli, (*US*) **chili** ['tʃɪlɪ] *n* peperoncino.
chilling ['tʃɪlɪŋ] *adj* agghiacciante; (*wind*) gelido(a).
chilly ['tʃɪlɪ] *adj* freddo(a), fresco(a); (*sensitive to cold*) freddoloso(a); **to feel ~** sentirsi infreddolito(a).
chime [tʃaɪm] *n* carillon *m inv* ♦ *vi* suonare, scampanare.
chimney ['tʃɪmnɪ] *n* camino.
chimney sweep *n* spazzacamino.
chimpanzee [tʃɪmpæn'ziː] *n* scimpanzé *m inv*.
chin [tʃɪn] *n* mento.
China ['tʃaɪnə] *n* Cina.
china ['tʃaɪnə] *n* porcellana.
Chinese [tʃaɪ'niːz] *adj* cinese ♦ *n* (*pl inv*) cinese *m/f*; (*LING*) cinese *m*.
chink [tʃɪŋk] *n* (*opening*) fessura; (*noise*) tintinnio.
chip [tʃɪp] *n* (*gen pl*: *CULIN*) patatina fritta; (*: US*: *also*: **potato** ~) patatina; (*of wood, glass, stone*) scheggia; (*in gambling*) fiche *f inv*; (*COMPUT*: *micro*~) chip *m inv* ♦ *vt* (*cup, plate*) scheggiare; **when the ~s are down** (*fig*) al momento critico.
▶**chip in** *vi* (*col*: *contribute*) contribuire; (*: interrupt*) intromettersi.
chipboard ['tʃɪpbɔːd] *n* agglomerato.
chipmunk ['tʃɪpmʌŋk] *n* tamia *m* striato.
chippings ['tʃɪpɪŋz] *npl*: **loose ~** brecciame *m*.
chip shop *n* (*BRIT*) *see boxed note.*

CHIP SHOP

I **chip shops***, anche chiamati "fish-and-chip shops", sono friggitorie che vendono principalmente filetti di pesce impanati e patatine fritte che un tempo venivano serviti ai clienti avvolti in carta di giornale.*

---

chiropodist [kɪ'rɔpədɪst] *n* (*BRIT*) pedicure *m/f inv*.
chiropody [kɪ'rɔpədɪ] *n* (*BRIT*) mestiere *m* di callista.
chirp [tʃəːp] *n* cinguettio; (*of crickets*) cri cri *m* ♦ *vi* cinguettare.
chirpy ['tʃəːpɪ] *adj* (*col*) frizzante.
chisel ['tʃɪzl] *n* cesello.
chit [tʃɪt] *n* biglietto.
chitchat ['tʃɪttʃæt] *n* (*col*) chiacchiere *fpl*.

chivalrous ['ʃɪvəlrəs] *adj* cavalleresco(a).
chivalry ['ʃɪvəlrɪ] *n* cavalleria; cortesia.
chives [tʃaɪvz] *npl* erba cipollina.
chloride ['klɔːraɪd] *n* cloruro.
chlorinate ['klɔrɪneɪt] *vt* clorare.
chlorine ['klɔːriːn] *n* cloro.
chock-a-block ['tʃɔkə'blɔk], **chockfull** ['tʃɔk'ful] *adj* pieno(a) zeppo(a).
chocolate ['tʃɔklɪt] *n* (*substance*) cioccolato, cioccolata; (*drink*) cioccolata; (*a sweet*) cioccolatino.
choice [tʃɔɪs] *n* scelta ♦ *adj* scelto(a); **a wide ~** un'ampia scelta; **I did it by *or* from ~** l'ho fatto di mia volontà *or* per mia scelta.
choir ['kwaɪə*] *n* coro.
choirboy ['kwaɪəbɔɪ] *n* corista *m* fanciullo.
choke [tʃəuk] *vi* soffocare ♦ *vt* soffocare; (*block*) ingombrare ♦ *n* (*AUT*) valvola dell'aria.
cholera ['kɔlərə] *n* colera *m*.
cholesterol [kə'lɛstərɔl] *n* colesterolo.
choose, *pt* **chose,** *pp* **chosen** [tʃuːz, tʃəuz, 'tʃəuzn] *vt* scegliere; **to ~ to do** decidere di fare; **preferire fare; to ~ between** scegliere tra; **to ~ from** scegliere da *or* tra.
choosy ['tʃuːzɪ] *adj*: **(to be) ~** (fare lo(la)) schizzinoso(a).
chop [tʃɔp] *vt* (*wood*) spaccare; (*CULIN*: *also*: **~ up**) tritare ♦ *n* colpo netto; (*CULIN*) costoletta; **to get the ~** (*BRIT col*: *project*) essere bocciato(a); (*: person*: *be sacked*) essere licenziato(a); *see also* **chops**.
▶**chop down** *vt* (*tree*) abbattere.
choppy ['tʃɔpɪ] *adj* (*sea*) mosso(a).
chops [tʃɔps] *npl* (*jaws*) mascelle *fpl*.
chopsticks ['tʃɔpstɪks] *npl* bastoncini *mpl* cinesi.
choral ['kɔːrəl] *adj* corale.
chord [kɔːd] *n* (*MUS*) accordo.
chore [tʃɔː*] *n* faccenda; **household ~s** faccende *fpl* domestiche.
choreographer [kɔrɪ'ɔgrəfə*] *n* coreografo/a.
choreography [kɔrɪ'ɔgrəfɪ] *n* coreografia.
chorister ['kɔrɪstə*] *n* corista *m/f*.
chortle ['tʃɔːtl] *vi* ridacchiare.
chorus ['kɔːrəs] *n* coro; (*repeated part of song, also fig*) ritornello.
chose [tʃəuz] *pt of* **choose**.
chosen ['tʃəuzn] *pp of* **choose**.
chowder ['tʃaudə*] *n* zuppa di pesce.
Christ [kraɪst] *n* Cristo.
christen ['krɪsn] *vt* battezzare.
christening ['krɪsnɪŋ] *n* battesimo.
Christian ['krɪstɪən] *adj, n* cristiano(a).
Christianity [krɪstɪ'ænɪtɪ] *n* cristianesimo.

Christian name n nome m di battesimo.
Christmas ['krɪsməs] n Natale m; **happy** or **merry** ~! Buon Natale!
Christmas card n cartolina di Natale.
Christmas Day n il giorno di Natale.
Christmas Eve n la vigilia di Natale.
Christmas Island n isola di Christmas.
Christmas tree n albero di Natale.
chrome [krəum] n = **chromium**.
chromium ['krəumɪəm] n cromo; (also: ~ **plating**) cromatura.
chromosome ['krəuməsəum] n cromosoma m.
chronic ['krɒnɪk] adj cronico(a); (fig: liar, smoker) incallito(a).
chronicle ['krɒnɪkl] n cronaca.
chronological [krɒnə'lɒdʒɪkl] adj cronologico(a).
chrysanthemum [krɪ'sænθəməm] n crisantemo.
chubby ['tʃʌbɪ] adj paffuto(a).
chuck [tʃʌk] vt buttare, gettare; **to** ~ **(up** or **in)** (BRIT: job, person) piantare.
►**chuck out** vt buttar fuori.
chuckle ['tʃʌkl] vi ridere sommessamente.
chuffed [tʃʌft] adj (col): **to be** ~ **about sth** essere arcicontento(a) di qc.
chug [tʃʌg] vi (also: ~ **along**: train) muoversi sbuffando.
chum [tʃʌm] n compagno/a.
chump [tʃʌmp] n (col) idiota m/f.
chunk [tʃʌŋk] n pezzo; (of bread) tocco.
chunky [tʃʌŋkɪ] adj (furniture etc) basso(a) e largo(a); (person) ben piantato(a); (knitwear) di lana grossa.
Chunnel ['tʃʌnəl] n = **Channel Tunnel**.
church [tʃəːtʃ] n chiesa; **the C~ of England** la Chiesa anglicana.
churchyard ['tʃəːtʃjɑːd] n sagrato.
churlish ['tʃəːlɪʃ] adj rozzo(a), sgarbato(a).
churn [tʃəːn] n (for butter) zangola; (also: ~ **milk** ~) bidone m.
►**churn out** vt sfornare.
chute [ʃuːt] n cascata; (also: **rubbish** ~) canale m di scarico; (BRIT: children's slide) scivolo.
chutney ['tʃʌtnɪ] n salsa piccante (di frutta, zucchero e spezie).
CIA n abbr (US: = Central Intelligence Agency) C.I.A. f.
CID n abbr (BRIT) see **Criminal Investigation Department**.
cider ['saɪdə*] n sidro.
CIF abbr (= cost, insurance, and freight) C.I.F. m.
cigar [sɪ'gɑː*] n sigaro.
cigarette [sɪgə'rɛt] n sigaretta.
cigarette case n portasigarette m inv.

cigarette end n mozzicone m.
cigarette holder n bocchino.
C-in-C abbr see **commander-in-chief**.
cinch [sɪntʃ] n (col): **it's a** ~ è presto fatto; (sure thing) è una cosa sicura.
cinder ['sɪndə*] n cenere f.
Cinderella [sɪndə'rɛlə] n Cenerentola.
cine-camera ['sɪnɪ'kæmərə] n (BRIT) cinepresa.
cine-film ['sɪnɪfɪlm] n (BRIT) pellicola.
cinema ['sɪnəmə] n cinema m inv.
cine-projector ['sɪnɪprə'dʒɛktə*] n (BRIT) proiettore m.
cinnamon ['sɪnəmən] n cannella.
cipher ['saɪfə*] n cifra; (fig: faceless employee etc) persona di nessun conto; **in** ~ in codice.
circa ['səːkə] prep circa.
circle ['səːkl] n cerchio; (of friends etc) circolo; (in cinema) galleria ♦ vi girare in circolo ♦ vt (surround) circondare; (move round) girare intorno a.
circuit ['səːkɪt] n circuito.
circuit board n (COMPUT) tavola dei circuiti.
circuitous [səː'kjuɪtəs] adj indiretto(a).
circular ['səːkjulə*] adj circolare ♦ n (letter) circolare f, (as advertisement) volantino pubblicitario.
circulate ['səːkjuleɪt] vi circolare; (person: socially) girare e andare un po' da tutti ♦ vt far circolare.
circulating capital ['səːkjuleɪtɪŋ-] n (COMM) capitale m d'esercizio.
circulation [səːkju'leɪʃən] n circolazione f; (of newspaper) tiratura.
circumcise ['səːkəmsaɪz] vt circoncidere.
circumference [sə'kʌmfərəns] n circonferenza.
circumflex ['səːkəmflɛks] n (also: ~ **accent**) accento circonflesso.
circumscribe ['səːkəmskraɪb] vt circoscrivere; (fig: limit) limitare.
circumspect ['səːkəmspɛkt] adj circospetto(a).
circumstances ['səːkəmstənsɪz] npl circostanze fpl; (financial condition) condizioni fpl finanziarie; **in the** ~**s** date le circostanze; **under no** ~**s** per nessun motivo.
circumstantial ['səːkəm'stænʃəl] adj (report, statement) circostanziato(a), dettagliato(a); ~ **evidence** prova indiretta.
circumvent [səːkəm'vɛnt] vt (rule etc) aggirare.
circus ['səːkəs] n circo; (also: **C**~: in place names) piazza (di forma circolare).

cirrhosis [sɪ'rəusɪs] *n* (*also:* ~ **of the liver**) cirrosi *f inv* (epatica).

CIS *n abbr* (= *Commonwealth of Independent States*) CSI *f.*

cissy ['sɪsɪ] *n* = **sissy.**

cistern ['sɪstən] *n* cisterna; (*in toilet*) serbatoio d'acqua.

citation [saɪ'teɪʃən] *n* citazione *f.*

cite [saɪt] *vt* citare.

citizen ['sɪtɪzn] *n* (*POL*) cittadino/a; (*resident*): **the ~s of this town** gli abitanti di questa città.

Citizens' Advice Bureau *n* (*BRIT*) *organizzazione di volontari che offre gratuitamente assistenza legale e finanziaria.*

citizenship ['sɪtɪznʃɪp] *n* cittadinanza.

citric ['sɪtrɪk] *adj*: ~ **acid** acido citrico.

citrus fruit ['sɪtrəs-] *n* agrume *m.*

city ['sɪtɪ] *n* città *f inv*; **the C~** la Città di Londra (*centro commerciale*).

city centre *n* centro della città.

City Hall *n* (*US*) ≈ Comune *m.*

City Technology College *n* (*BRIT*) istituto tecnico superiore (*finanziato dall'industria*).

civic ['sɪvɪk] *adj* civico(a).

civic centre *n* (*BRIT*) centro civico.

civil ['sɪvɪl] *adj* civile; (*polite*) educato(a), gentile.

civil disobedience *n* disubbidienza civile.

civil engineer *n* ingegnere *m* civile.

civil engineering *n* ingegneria civile.

civilian [sɪ'vɪlɪən] *adj*, *n* borghese (*m/f*).

civilization [sɪvɪlaɪ'zeɪʃən] *n* civiltà *f inv.*

civilized ['sɪvɪlaɪzd] *adj* civilizzato(a); (*fig*) cortese.

civil law *n* codice *m* civile; (*study*) diritto civile.

civil liberties *npl* libertà *fpl* civili.

civil rights *npl* diritti *mpl* civili.

civil servant *n* impiegato/a statale.

Civil Service *n* amministrazione *f* statale.

civil war *n* guerra civile.

civvies ['sɪvɪz] *npl* (*col*): **in** ~ in borghese.

CJD *n abbr* (= *Creutzfeldt-Jakob disease*) malattia di Creutzfeldt-Jakob.

cl *abbr* (= *centilitre*) cl.

clad [klæd] *adj*: ~ (**in**) vestito(a) (di).

claim [kleɪm] *vt* (*rights etc*) rivendicare; (*damages*) richiedere; (*assert*) sostenere, pretendere ♦ *vi* (*for insurance*) fare una · domanda d'indennizzo ♦ *n* rivendicazione *f*; pretesa; (*right*) diritto; **to** ~ **that/to be** sostenere che/di essere; (*insurance*) ~ domanda d'indennizzo; **to put in a** ~ **for** **sth** fare una richiesta di qc.

claimant ['kleɪmənt] *n* (*ADMIN, LAW*)

richiedente *m/f.*

claim form *n* (*gen*) modulo di richiesta; (*for expenses*) modulo di rimborso spese.

clairvoyant [klɛə'vɔɪənt] *n* chiaroveggente *m/f.*

clam [klæm] *n* vongola.

▶**clam up** *vi* (*col*) azzittirsi.

clamber ['klæmbə*] *vi* arrampicarsi.

clammy ['klæmɪ] *adj* (*weather*) caldo(a) umido(a); (*hands*) viscido(a).

clamour, (*US*) **clamor** ['klæmə*] *n* (*noise*) clamore *m*; (*protest*) protesta ♦ *vi*: **to** ~ **for** **sth** chiedere a gran voce qc.

clamp [klæmp] *n* pinza; morsa ♦ *vt* ammorsare.

▶**clamp down** *vt fus* (*fig*): **to** ~ **down** (**on**) dare un giro di vite (a).

clampdown ['klæmpdaun] *n* stretta, giro di vite; **a** ~ **on sth/sb** un giro di vite a qc/ qn.

clan [klæn] *n* clan *m inv.*

clandestine [klæn'dɛstɪn] *adj* clandestino(a).

clang [klæŋ] *n* fragore *m*, suono metallico.

clanger ['klæŋə*] *n*: **to drop a** ~ (*BRIT col*) fare una gaffe.

clansman ['klænzmən] *n* membro di un clan.

clap [klæp] *vi* applaudire ♦ *vt*: **to** ~ **one's** **hands** battere le mani ♦ *n*: **a** ~ **of thunder** un tuono.

clapping ['klæpɪŋ] *n* applausi *mpl.*

claptrap ['klæptræp] *n* (*col*) stupidaggini *fpl.*

claret ['klærət] *n* vino di Bordeaux.

clarification [klærɪfɪ'keɪʃən] *n* (*fig*) chiarificazione *f*, chiarimento.

clarify ['klærɪfaɪ] *vt* chiarificare, chiarire.

clarinet [klærɪ'nɛt] *n* clarinetto.

clarity ['klærɪtɪ] *n* chiarezza.

clash [klæʃ] *n* frastuono; (*fig*) scontro ♦ *vi* (*MIL, fig*: *have an argument*) scontrarsi; (*colours*) stridere; (*dates, events*) coincidere.

clasp [klɑːsp] *n* fermaglio, fibbia ♦ *vt* stringere.

class [klɑːs] *n* classe *f*; (*group, category*) tipo, categoria ♦ *vt* classificare.

class-conscious ['klɑːskɔnʃəs] *adj* che ha coscienza di classe.

class consciousness *n* coscienza di classe.

classic ['klæsɪk] *adj* classico(a) ♦ *n* classico.

classical ['klæsɪkəl] *adj* classico(a).

classics ['klæsɪks] *npl* (*SCOL*) studi *mpl* umanistici.

classification [klæsɪfɪ'keɪʃən] *n* classificazione *f.*

classified ['klæsɪfaɪd] *adj* (*information*)

segreto(a), riservato(a); ~ ads annunci economici.

classify ['klæsɪfaɪ] vt classificare.

classless society ['klɑːslɪs-] n società f inv senza distinzioni di classe.

classmate ['klɑːsmeɪt] n compagno/a di classe.

classroom ['klɑːsrum] n aula.

classroom assistant n assistente m/f in classe dell'insegnante.

clatter ['klætə*] n acciottolio; scalpitio ♦ vi acciottolare; scalpitare.

clause [klɔːz] n clausola; (LING) proposizione f.

claustrophobia [klɔːstrə'fəubɪə] n claustrofobia.

claustrophobic [klɔːstrə'fəubɪk] adj claustrofobico(a).

claw [klɔː] n tenaglia; (of bird of prey) artiglio; (of lobster) pinza ♦ vt graffiare; afferrare.

clay [kleɪ] n argilla.

clean [kliːn] adj pulito(a); (clear, smooth) netto(a) ♦ vt pulire ♦ adv: he ~ forgot si è completamente dimenticato; **to come** ~ (col: admit guilt) confessare; **to have a** ~ **driving licence** or (US) **record** non aver mai preso contravvenzioni; **to** ~ **one's teeth** (BRIT) lavarsi i denti.

►**clean off** vt togliere.

►**clean out** vt ripulire.

►**clean up** vi far pulizia ♦ vt (also fig) ripulire; (fig: make profit): **to** ~ **up on** fare una barca di soldi con.

clean-cut ['kliːn'kʌt] adj (man) curato(a); (situation etc) ben definito(a).

cleaner ['kliːnə*] n (person) uomo/donna delle pulizie; (also: **dry** ~) tintore/a; (product) smacchiatore m.

cleaning ['kliːnɪŋ] n pulizia.

cleaning lady n donna delle pulizie.

cleanliness ['klɛnlɪnɪs] n pulizia.

cleanly ['kliːnlɪ] adv in modo netto.

cleanse [klɛnz] vt pulire; purificare.

cleanser ['klɛnzə*] n detergente m; (cosmetic) latte m detergente.

clean-shaven ['kliːn'ʃeɪvn] adj sbarbato(a).

cleansing department ['klɛnzɪŋ-] n (BRIT) nettezza urbana.

clean sweep n: **to make a** ~ **(of)** fare piazza pulita (di).

clean-up ['kliːnʌp] n pulizia.

clear [klɪə*] adj chiaro(a); (road, way) libero(a); (profit, majority) netto(a) ♦ vt sgombrare; liberare; (site, woodland) spianare; (COMM: goods) liquidare; (LAW: suspect) discolpare; (obstacle) superare; (cheque) fare la compensazione di ♦ vi

(weather) rasserenarsi; (fog) andarsene ♦ adv: ~ **of** distante da ♦ n: **to be in the** ~ (out of debt) essere in attivo; (out of suspicion) essere a posto; (out of danger) essere fuori pericolo; **to** ~ **the table** sparecchiare (la tavola); **to** ~ **one's throat** schiarirsi la gola; **to** ~ **a profit** avere un profitto netto; **to make o.s.** ~ spiegarsi bene; **to make it** ~ **to sb that ...** far capire a qn che ...; **I have a** ~ **day** tomorrow (BRIT) non ho impegni domani; **to keep** ~ **of sb/sth** tenersi lontano da qn/qc, stare alla larga da qn/qc.

►**clear off** vi (col: leave) svignarsela.

►**clear up** vi schiarirsi ♦ vt mettere in ordine; (mystery) risolvere.

clearance ['klɪərəns] n (removal) sgombro; (free space) spazio; (permission) autorizzazione f, permesso.

clearance sale n vendita di liquidazione.

clear-cut ['klɪə'kʌt] adj ben delineato(a), distinto(a).

clearing ['klɪərɪŋ] n radura; (BRIT BANKING) clearing m.

clearing bank n (BRIT) banca che fa uso della camera di compensazione.

clearing house n (COMM) camera di compensazione.

clearly ['klɪəlɪ] adv chiaramente.

clearway ['klɪəweɪ] n (BRIT) strada con divieto di sosta.

cleavage ['kliːvɪdʒ] n (of woman) scollatura.

cleaver ['kliːvə*] n mannaia.

clef [klɛf] n (MUS) chiave f.

cleft [klɛft] n (in rock) crepa, fenditura.

clemency ['klɛmənsɪ] n clemenza.

clement ['klɛmənt] adj (weather) mite, clemente.

clench [klɛntʃ] vt stringere.

clergy ['klɜːdʒɪ] n clero.

clergyman ['klɜːdʒɪmən] n ecclesiastico.

clerical ['klɛrɪkl] adj d'impiegato; (REL) clericale.

clerk [klɑːk, (US) klɜːrk] n impiegato/a; (US: salesman/woman) commesso/a; **C**~ **Court** (LAW) cancelliere m.

clever ['klɛvə*] adj (mentally) intelligente; (deft, skilful) abile; (device, arrangement) ingegnoso(a).

cleverly ['klɛvəlɪ] adv abilmente.

clew [kluː] n (US) = **clue**.

cliché ['kliːʃeɪ] n cliché m inv.

click [klɪk] vi scattare ♦ vt: **to** ~ **one's tongue** schioccare la lingua; **to** ~ **one's heels** battere i tacchi.

clickable ['klɪkəbl] adj cliccabile.

client ['klaɪənt] n cliente m/f.

clientele [kli:ã:n'tɛl] n clientela.
cliff [klɪf] n scogliera scoscesa, rupe f.
cliffhanger ['klɪfhæŋə*] n (TV, fig) episodio (or situazione etc) ricco(a) di suspense.
climactic [klaɪ'mæktɪk] adj culminante.
climate ['klaɪmɪt] n clima m.
climax ['klaɪmæks] n culmine m; (of play etc) momento più emozionante; (sexual ~) orgasmo.
climb [klaɪm] vi salire; (clamber) arrampicarsi; (plane) prendere quota ♦ vt salire; (CLIMBING) scalare ♦ n salita; arrampicata; scalata; **to ~ over a wall** scavalcare un muro.
▶**climb down** vi scendere; (BRIT fig) far marcia indietro.
climbdown ['klaɪmdaun] n (BRIT) ritirata.
climber ['klaɪmə*] n (also: **rock ~**) rocciatore/trice; alpinista m/f.
climbing ['klaɪmɪŋ] n (also: **rock ~**) alpinismo.
clinch [klɪntʃ] vt (deal) concludere.
clincher ['klɪntʃə*] n (col): **that was the ~** quello è stato il fattore decisivo.
cling, pt, pp clung [klɪŋ, klʌŋ] vi: **to ~ (to)** tenersi stretto(a) (a); (of clothes) aderire strettamente (a).
clingfilm ['klɪŋfɪlm] n pellicola trasparente (per alimenti).
clinic ['klɪnɪk] n clinica; (session) seduta; serie f di sedute.
clinical ['klɪnɪkəl] adj clinico(a); (fig) freddo(a), distaccato(a).
clink [klɪŋk] vi tintinnare.
clip [klɪp] n (for hair) forcina; (also: **paper ~**) graffetta; (BRIT: also: **bulldog ~**) fermafogli m inv; (holding hose etc) anello d'attacco ♦ vt (also: **~ together**: papers) attaccare insieme; (hair, nails) tagliare; (hedge) tosare.
clippers ['klɪpəz] npl macchinetta per capelli; (also: **nail ~**) forbicine fpl per le unghie.
clipping ['klɪpɪŋ] n (from newspaper) ritaglio.
clique [kli:k] n cricca.
cloak [kləuk] n mantello ♦ vt avvolgere.
cloakroom ['kləukrum] n (for coats etc) guardaroba m inv; (BRIT: W.C.) gabinetti mpl.
clock [klɔk] n orologio; (of taxi) tassametro; **around the ~** ventiquattr'ore su ventiquattro; **to sleep round the ~** or **the ~ round** dormire un giorno intero; **to work against the ~** lavorare in gara col tempo; **30,000 on the ~** (BRIT AUT) 30.000 sul contachilometri.
▶**clock in, clock on** vi (BRIT) timbrare il

cartellino (all'entrata).
▶**clock off, clock out** vi (BRIT) timbrare il cartellino (all'uscita).
▶**clock up** vt (miles, hours etc) fare.
clockwise ['klɔkwaɪz] adv in senso orario.
clockwork ['klɔkwə:k] n movimento or meccanismo a orologeria ♦ adj (toy, train) a molla.
clog [klɔg] n zoccolo ♦ vt intasare ♦ vi intasarsi, bloccarsi.
cloister ['klɔɪstə*] n chiostro.
clone [kləun] n clone m ♦ vt clonare.
close adj, adv and derivatives [kləus] adj vicino(a); (writing, texture) fitto(a); (watch) stretto(a); (examination) attento(a); (weather) afoso(a) ♦ adv vicino, dappresso; **~ to** prep vicino a; **~ by, ~ at hand** qui (or lì) vicino; **how ~ is Edinburgh to Glasgow?** quanto dista Edimburgo da Glasgow?; **a ~ friend** un amico intimo; **to have a ~ shave** (fig) scamparla bella; **at ~ quarters** da vicino ♦ vb, n and derivatives [kləuz] vt chiudere; (bargain, deal) concludere ♦ vi (shop etc) chiudere; (lid, door etc) chiudersi; (end) finire ♦ n (end) fine f; **to bring sth to a ~** terminare qc.
▶**close down** vt chiudere (definitivamente) ♦ vi cessare (definitivamente).
▶**close in** vi (hunters) stringersi attorno; (evening, night, fog) calare; **to ~ in on sb** accerchiare qn; **the days are closing in** le giornate si accorciano.
▶**close off** vt (area) chiudere.
closed [kləuzd] adj chiuso(a).
closed-circuit ['kləuzd'sə:kɪt] adj: **~ television** televisione f a circuito chiuso.
closed shop n azienda o fabbrica che impiega solo aderenti ai sindacati.
close-knit ['kləus'nɪt] adj (family, community) molto unito(a).
closely ['kləuslɪ] adv (examine, watch) da vicino; **we are ~ related** siamo parenti stretti; **a ~ guarded secret** un assoluto segreto.
close season ['kləuz-] n (FOOTBALL) periodo di vacanza del campionato; (HUNTING) stagione f di chiusura (di caccia, pesca etc).
closet ['klɔzɪt] n (cupboard) armadio.
close-up ['kləusʌp] n primo piano.
closing ['kləuzɪŋ] adj (stages, remarks) conclusivo(a), finale; **~ price** (STOCK EXCHANGE) prezzo di chiusura.
closing time n orario di chiusura.
closure ['kləuʒə*] n chiusura.
clot [klɔt] n (also: **blood ~**) coagulo; (col:

idiot) scemo/a ♦ *vi* coagularsi.

cloth [klɔθ] *n* (*material*) tessuto, stoffa; (*BRIT: also:* **tea**~) strofinaccio; (*also:* **table**~) tovaglia.

clothe [kləuð] *vt* vestire.

clothes ['kləuðz] *npl* abiti *mpl*, vestiti *mpl*; **to put one's** ~ **on** vestirsi; **to take one's** ~ **off** togliersi i vestiti, svestirsi.

clothes brush *n* spazzola per abiti.

clothes line *n* corda (per stendere il bucato).

clothes peg, (*US*) **clothes pin** *n* molletta.

clothing ['kləuðɪŋ] *n* = **clothes.**

clotted cream ['klɔtɪd-] *n* (*BRIT*) panna rappresa.

cloud [klaud] *n* nuvola; (*of dust, smoke, gas*) nube *f* ♦ *vt* (*liquid*) intorbidire; **to** ~ **the issue** distogliere dal problema; **every** ~ **has a silver lining** (*proverb*) non tutto il male vien per nuocere.

►**cloud over** *vi* rannuvolarsi; (*fig*) offuscarsi.

cloudburst ['klaudbɔ:st] *n* acquazzone *m*.

cloud-cuckoo-land ['klaud'kuku:'lænd] *n* (*BRIT*) mondo dei sogni.

cloudy ['klaudɪ] *adj* nuvoloso(a); (*liquid*) torbido(a).

clout [klaut] *n* (*blow*) colpo; (*fig*) influenza ♦ *vt* dare un colpo a.

clove [kləuv] *n* chiodo di garofano; ~ **of garlic** spicchio d'aglio.

clover ['kləuvə*] *n* trifoglio.

cloverleaf ['kləuvəli:f] *n* foglia di trifoglio; (*AUT*) raccordo (a quadrifoglio).

clown [klaun] *n* pagliaccio ♦ *vi* (*also:* ~ **about,** ~ **around**) fare il pagliaccio.

cloying ['klɔɪɪŋ] *adj* (*taste, smell*) nauseabondo(a).

club [klʌb] *n* (*society*) club *m inv*, circolo; (*weapon, GOLF*) mazza ♦ *vt* bastonare ♦ *vi:* **to** ~ **together** associarsi; ~**s** *npl* (*CARDS*) fiori *mpl*.

club car *n* (*US RAIL*) carrozza *or* vagone *m* ristorante.

club class *n* (*AVIAT*) classe *f* club.

clubhouse ['klʌbhaus] *n* sede *f* del circolo.

club soda *n* (*US*) = **soda.**

cluck [klʌk] *vi* chiocciare.

clue [klu:] *n* indizio; (*in crosswords*) definizione *f*; **I haven't a** ~ non ho la minima idea.

clued up, (*US*) **clued in** [klu:d-] *adj* (*col*) (ben) informato(a).

clump [klʌmp] *n:* ~ **of trees** folto d'alberi.

clumsy ['klʌmzɪ] *adj* (*person*) goffo(a), maldestro(a); (*object*) malfatto(a), mal costruito(a).

clung [klʌŋ] *pt, pp of* **cling.**

cluster ['klʌstə*] *n* gruppo ♦ *vi* raggrupparsi.

clutch [klʌtʃ] *n* (*grip, grasp*) presa, stretta; (*AUT*) frizione *f* ♦ *vt* afferrare, stringere forte; **to** ~ **at** aggrapparsi a.

clutter ['klʌtə*] *vt* (*also:* ~ **up**) ingombrare ♦ *n* confusione *f*, disordine *m*.

cm *abbr* (= *centimetre*) cm.

CNAA *n abbr* (*BRIT:* = *Council for National Academic Awards*) *organizzazione che conferisce premi accademici.*

CND *n abbr* (*BRIT*) = *Campaign for Nuclear Disarmament.*

CO *n abbr* (= *commanding officer*) Com.; (*BRIT*) = *Commonwealth Office* ♦ *abbr* (*US*) = Colorado.

Co. *abbr* = **county;** (= *company*) C., C.ia.

c/o *abbr* (= *care of*) c/o.

coach [kəutʃ] *n* (*bus*) pullman *m inv*; (*horse-drawn, of train*) carrozza; (*SPORT*) allenatore/trice ♦ *vt* allenare.

coach trip *n* viaggio in pullman.

coagulate [kəu'ægjuleɪt] *vt* coagulare ♦ *vi* coagularsi.

coal [kəul] *n* carbone *m*.

coalface ['kəulfeɪs] *n* fronte *f*.

coalfield ['kəulfi:ld] *n* bacino carbonifero.

coalition [kəuə'lɪʃən] *n* coalizione *f*.

coalman ['kəulmən] *n* negoziante *m* di carbone.

coalmine ['kəulmaɪn] *n* miniera di carbone.

coalminer ['kəulmaɪnə*] *n* minatore *m*.

coalmining ['kəulmaɪnɪŋ] *n* estrazione *f* del carbone.

coarse [kɔ:s] *adj* (*salt, sand etc*) grosso(a); (*cloth, person*) rozzo(a); (*vulgar: character, laugh*) volgare.

coast [kəust] *n* costa ♦ *vi* (*with cycle etc*) scendere a ruota libera.

coastal ['kəustəl] *adj* costiero(a).

coaster ['kəustə*] *n* (*NAUT*) nave *f* da cabotaggio; (*for glass*) sottobicchiere *m*.

coastguard ['kəustgɑ:d] *n* guardia costiera.

coastline ['kəustlaɪn] *n* linea costiera.

coat [kəut] *n* cappotto; (*of animal*) pelo; (*of paint*) mano *f* ♦ *vt* coprire; ~ **of arms** *n* stemma *m*.

coat hanger *n* attaccapanni *m inv*.

coating ['kəutɪŋ] *n* rivestimento.

co-author ['kəu'ɔ:θə*] *n* coautore/trice.

coax [kəuks] *vt* indurre (con moine).

cob [kɔb] *n see* **corn.**

cobbler ['kɔblə*] *n* calzolaio.

cobbles ['kɔblz], **cobblestones** ['kɔblstəunz] *npl* ciottoli *mpl*.

COBOL ['kəubɔl] *n* COBOL *m*.

cobra ['kəubrə] *n* cobra *m inv*.

cobweb ['kɔbwɛb] n ragnatela.
cocaine [kə'keɪn] n cocaina.
cock [kɔk] n (rooster) gallo; (male bird) maschio ♦ vt (gun) armare; to ~ one's ears (fig) drizzare le orecchie.
cock-a-hoop [kɔkə'huːp] adj euforico(a).
cockerel ['kɔkərəl] n galletto.
cock-eyed ['kɔkaɪd] adj (fig) storto(a); strampalato(a).
cockle ['kɔkl] n cardio.
cockney ['kɔknɪ] n cockney m/f inv (abitante dei quartieri popolari dell'East End di Londra).
cockpit ['kɔkpɪt] n abitacolo.
cockroach ['kɔkrəutʃ] n blatta.
cocktail ['kɔkteɪl] n cocktail m inv; prawn ~, (US) shrimp ~ cocktail m inv di gamberetti.
cocktail cabinet n mobile m bar inv.
cocktail party n cocktail m inv.
cocktail shaker n shaker m inv.
cocky ['kɔkɪ] adj spavaldo(a), arrogante.
cocoa ['kəukəu] n cacao.
coconut ['kəukənʌt] n noce f di cocco.
cocoon [kə'kuːn] n bozzolo.
COD abbr see cash on delivery, (US) see collect on delivery.
cod [kɔd] n merluzzo.
code [kəud] n codice m; ~ of behaviour regole fpl di condotta; ~ of practice codice professionale.
codeine ['kəudiːn] n codeina.
codger ['kɔdʒə*] n (BRIT col): an old ~ un simpatico nonnetto.
codicil ['kɔdɪsɪl] n codicillo.
codify ['kəudɪfaɪ] vt codificare.
cod-liver oil ['kɔdlɪvə*-] n olio di fegato di merluzzo.
co-driver ['kəu'draɪvə*] n (in race) copilota m; (of lorry) secondo autista m.
co-ed ['kəu'ɛd] adj abbr = coeducational ♦ n abbr (US: female student) studentessa presso un'università mista; (BRIT: school) scuola mista.
coeducational ['kəuɛdju'keɪʃənl] adj misto(a).
coerce [kəu'əːs] vt costringere.
coercion [kəu'əːʃən] n coercizione f.
coexistence ['kəuɪg'zɪstəns] n coesistenza.
C. of C. n abbr = chamber of commerce.
C of E abbr = Church of England.
coffee ['kɔfɪ] n caffè m inv; white ~, (US) ~ with cream caffellatte m.
coffee bar n (BRIT) caffè m inv.
coffee bean n grano or chicco di caffè.
coffee break n pausa per il caffè.
coffeecake ['kɔfɪkeɪk] n (US) panino dolce all'uva.

coffee cup n tazzina da caffè.
coffeepot ['kɔfɪpɔt] n caffettiera.
coffee table n tavolino da tè.
coffin ['kɔfɪn] n bara.
C of I abbr = Church of Ireland.
C of S abbr = Church of Scotland.
cog [kɔg] n dente m.
cogent ['kəudʒənt] adj convincente.
cognac ['kɔnjæk] n cognac m inv.
cogwheel ['kɔgwiːl] n ruota dentata.
cohabit [kəu'hæbɪt] vi (formal): to ~ (with sb) coabitare (con qn).
coherent [kəu'hɪərənt] adj coerente.
cohesion [kəu'hiːʒən] n coesione f.
cohesive [kəu'hiːsɪv] adj (fig) unificante, coesivo(a).
COI n abbr (BRIT) = Central Office of Information.
coil [kɔɪl] n rotolo; (one loop) anello; (AUT, ELEC) bobina; (contraceptive) spirale f; (of smoke) filo ♦ vt avvolgere.
coin [kɔɪn] n moneta ♦ vt (word) coniare.
coinage ['kɔɪnɪdʒ] n sistema m monetario.
coin-box ['kɔɪnbɔks] n (BRIT) cabina telefonica.
coincide [kəuɪn'saɪd] vi coincidere.
coincidence [kəu'ɪnsɪdəns] n combinazione f.
coin-operated ['kɔɪn'ɔpəreɪtɪd] adj (machine) (che funziona) a monete.
Coke ® [kəuk] n (Coca-Cola) coca f inv.
coke [kəuk] n coke m.
Col. abbr = colonel; (US) = Colorado.
COLA n abbr (US: = cost-of-living adjustment) ≈ scala mobile.
colander ['kɔləndə*] n colino.
cold [kəuld] adj freddo(a) ♦ n freddo; (MED) raffreddore m; it's ~ fa freddo; to be ~ aver freddo; to catch ~ prendere freddo; to catch a ~ prendere un raffreddore; in ~ blood a sangue freddo; to have ~ feet avere i piedi freddi; (fig) aver la fifa; to give sb the ~ shoulder ignorare qn.
cold-blooded [kəuld'blʌdɪd] adj (ZOOL) a sangue freddo.
cold call n chiamata pubblicitaria non richiesta.
cold cream n crema emolliente.
coldly ['kəuldlɪ] adv freddamente.
cold sore n erpete m.
cold sweat n: to be in a ~ (about sth) sudare freddo (per qc).
cold turkey n (col): to go ~ avere la scimmia (drogato).
Cold War n: the ~ la guerra fredda.
coleslaw ['kəulslɔː] n insalata di cavolo bianco.
colic ['kɔlɪk] n colica.

colicky ['kɒlɪkɪ] *adj* che soffre di coliche.
collaborate [kə'læbəreɪt] *vi* collaborare.
collaboration [kəlæbə'reɪʃən] *n*
    collaborazione *f*.
collaborator [kə'læbəreɪtə*] *n*
    collaboratore/trice.
collage [kɒ'lɑːʒ] *n* (*ART*) collage *m inv*.
collagen ['kɒlədʒən] *n* collageno.
collapse [kə'læps] *vi* (*gen*) crollare;
    (*government*) cadere; (*MED*) avere un
    collasso; (*plans*) fallire ♦ *n* crollo; caduta;
    collasso; fallimento.
collapsible [kə'læpsəbl] *adj* pieghevole.
collar ['kɒlə*] *n* (*of coat, shirt*) colletto; (*for
    dog*) collare *m*; (*TECH*) anello, fascetta ♦ *vt*
    (*col: person, object*) beccare.
collarbone ['kɒləbəun] *n* clavicola.
collate [kɒ'leɪt] *vt* collazionare.
collateral [kɒ'lætərəl] *n* garanzia.
collation [kɒ'leɪʃən] *n* collazione *f*.
colleague ['kɒliːg] *n* collega *m/f*.
collect [kə'lɛkt] *vt* (*gen*) raccogliere; (*as a
    hobby*) fare collezione di; (*BRIT: call for*)
    prendere; (*money owed, pension*)
    riscuotere; (*donations, subscriptions*) fare
    una colletta di ♦ *vi* (*people*) adunarsi,
    riunirsi; (*rubbish etc*) ammucchiarsi ♦ *adv*
    (*US TEL*): **to call** ~ fare una chiamata a
    carico del destinatario; **to** ~ **one's**
    thoughts raccogliere le idee; ~ **on**
    delivery (COD) (*US COMM*) pagamento alla
    consegna.
collected [kə'lɛktɪd] *adj*: ~ **works** opere *fpl*
    raccolte.
collection [kə'lɛkʃən] *n* collezione *f*;
    raccolta; (*for money*) colletta; (*POST*)
    levata.
collective [kə'lɛktɪv] *adj* collettivo(a) ♦ *n*
    collettivo.
collective bargaining *n* trattative *fpl*
    (sindacali) collettive.
collector [kə'lɛktə*] *n* collezionista *m/f*; (*of
    taxes*) esattore *m*; ~'**s item** *or* **piece** pezzo
    da collezionista.
college ['kɒlɪdʒ] *n* (*BRIT, US SCOL*) college *m
    inv*; (*of technology, agriculture etc*) istituto
    superiore; (*body*) collegio; ~ **of education**
    ≈ facoltà *f inv* di Magistero.
collide [kə'laɪd] *vi*: **to** ~ (**with**) scontrarsi
    (con).
collie ['kɒlɪ] *n* (*dog*) collie *m inv*.
colliery ['kɒlɪərɪ] *n* (*BRIT*) miniera di
    carbone.
collision [kə'lɪʒən] *n* collisione *f*, scontro; **to
    be on a** ~ **course** (*also fig*) essere in rotta
    di collisione.
collision damage waiver (CDW) *n*
    (*INSURANCE*) copertura per i danni alla

vettura.
colloquial [kə'ləukwɪəl] *adj* familiare.
collusion [kə'luːʒən] *n* collusione *f*; **in** ~
    with in accordo segreto con.
Colo. *abbr* (*US*) = *Colorado*.
Cologne [kə'ləun] *n* Colonia.
cologne [kə'ləun] *n* (*also*: **eau de** ~) acqua
    di colonia.
Colombia [kə'lɒmbɪə] *n* Colombia.
Colombian [kə'lɒmbɪən] *adj, n*
    colombiano(a).
colon ['kəulən] *n* (*sign*) due punti *mpl*; (*MED*)
    colon *m inv*.
colonel ['kəːnl] *n* colonnello.
colonial [kə'ləunɪəl] *adj* coloniale.
colonize ['kɒlənaɪz] *vt* colonizzare.
colony ['kɒlənɪ] *n* colonia.
color *etc* ['kʌlə*] (*US*) = **colour** *etc*.
Colorado beetle [kɒlə'rɑːdəu-] *n* dorifora.
colossal [kə'lɒsl] *adj* colossale.
colour, (US) color ['kʌlə*] *n* colore *m* ♦ *vt*
    colorare; (*tint, dye*) tingere; (*fig: affect*)
    influenzare ♦ *vi* arrossire ♦ *cpd* (*film,
    photograph, television*) a colori; ~**s** *npl* (*of
    party, club*) emblemi *mpl*.
colo(u)r bar *n* discriminazione *f* razziale
    (*in locali etc*).
colo(u)r-blind ['kʌləblaɪnd] *adj*
    daltonico(a).
colo(u)red ['kʌləd] *adj* colorato(a); (*photo*)
    a colori ♦ *n*: ~**s** gente *f* di colore.
colo(u)r film *n* (*for camera*) pellicola a
    colori.
colo(u)rful ['kʌləful] *adj* pieno(a) di colore,
    a vivaci colori; (*personality*) colorato(a).
colo(u)ring ['kʌlərɪŋ] *n* colorazione *f*;
    (*complexion*) colorito.
colo(u)r scheme combinazione *f* di colori.
colour supplement *n* (*BRIT PRESS*)
    supplemento a colori.
colo(u)r television *n* televisione *f* a colori.
colt [kəult] *n* puledro.
column ['kɒləm] *n* colonna; (*fashion* ~,
    sports ~ *etc*) rubrica; **the editorial** ~
    l'articolo di fondo.
columnist ['kɒləmnɪst] *n* articolista *m/f*.
coma ['kəumə] *n* coma *m inv*.
comb [kəum] *n* pettine *m* ♦ *vt* (*hair*)
    pettinare; (*area*) battere a tappeto.
combat ['kɒmbæt] *n* combattimento ♦ *vt*
    combattere, lottare contro.
combination [kɒmbɪ'neɪʃən] *n*
    combinazione *f*.
combination lock *n* serratura a
    combinazione.
combine *vb* [kəm'baɪn] *vt* combinare; (*one
    quality with another*): **to** ~ **sth with sth**
    unire qc a qc ♦ *vi* unirsi; (*CHEM*)

combinarsi ♦ n ['kɔmbaɪn] lega; (ECON)
associazione f; a ~d effort uno sforzo
collettivo.
combine (harvester) n mietitrebbia.
combo ['kɔmbəu] n (JAZZ etc) gruppo.
combustible [kəm'bʌstɪbl] adj
combustibile.
combustion [kəm'bʌstʃən] n combustione
f.
come, pt came, pp come [kʌm, keɪm] vi
venire; (arrive) venire, arrivare; ~ with
me vieni con me; we've just ~ from Paris
siamo appena arrivati da Parigi; nothing
came of it non è saltato fuori niente; to ~
into sight or view apparire; to ~ to
(decision etc) raggiungere; to ~ undone/
loose slacciarsi/allentarsi; coming!
vengo!; if it ~s to it nella peggiore delle
ipotesi.
►come about vi succedere.
►come across vt fus trovare per caso; to ~
across well/badly fare una buona/cattiva
impressione.
►come along vi (pupil, work) fare
progressi; ~ along! avanti!, andiamo!,
forza!
►come apart vi andare in pezzi; (become
detached) staccarsi.
►come away vi venire via; (become
detached) staccarsi.
►come back vi ritornare; (reply: col): can I
~ back to you on that one? possiamo
riparlarne più tardi?
►come by vt fus (acquire) ottenere;
procurarsi.
►come down vi scendere; (prices) calare;
(buildings) essere demolito(a).
►come forward vi farsi avanti;
presentarsi.
►come from vt fus venire da; provenire
da.
►come in vi entrare.
►come in for vt fus (criticism etc) ricevere.
►come into vt fus (money) ereditare.
►come off vi (button) staccarsi; (stain)
andar via; (attempt) riuscire.
►come on vi (lights, electricity) accendersi;
(pupil, undertaking) fare progressi; ~ on!
avanti!, andiamo!, forza!
►come out vi uscire; (strike) entrare in
sciopero.
►come over vt fus: I don't know what's ~
over him! non so cosa gli sia successo!
►come round vi (after faint, operation)
riprendere conoscenza, rinvenire.
►come through vi (survive) sopravvivere,
farcela; the call came through ci hanno
passato la telefonata.

►come to vi rinvenire ♦ vt (add up to:
amount): how much does it ~ to? quanto
costa?, quanto viene?
►come under vt fus (heading) trovarsi
sotto; (influence) cadere sotto, subire.
►come up vi venire su.
►come up against vt fus (resistance,
difficulties) urtare contro.
►come up to vt fus arrivare (fino) a; the
film didn't ~ up to our expectations il film
ci ha delusi.
►come up with vt fus: he came up with an
idea venne fuori con un'idea.
►come upon vt fus trovare per caso.
comeback ['kʌmbæk] n (THEAT etc) ritorno;
(reaction) reazione f; (response) risultato,
risposta.
comedian [kə'miːdiən] n comico.
comedienne [kəmiːdɪ'ɛn] n attrice f
comica.
comedown ['kʌmdaun] n rovescio.
comedy ['kɔmɪdɪ] n commedia.
comet ['kɔmɪt] n cometa.
comeuppance [kʌm'ʌpəns] n: to get one's
~ ricevere ciò che si merita.
comfort ['kʌmfət] n comodità f inv,
benessere m; (solace) consolazione f,
conforto ♦ vt consolare, confortare; see
also comforts.
comfortable ['kʌmfətəbl] adj comodo(a);
(income, majority) più che sufficiente; I
don't feel very ~ about it non mi sento
molto tranquillo.
comfortably ['kʌmfətəblɪ] adv (sit)
comodamente; (live) bene.
comforter ['kʌmfətə*] n (US) trapunta.
comforts ['kʌmfəts] npl comforts mpl,
comodità fpl.
comfort station n (US) gabinetti mpl.
comic ['kɔmɪk] adj comico(a) ♦ n comico;
(magazine) giornaletto.
comical ['kɔmɪkl] adj divertente, buffo(a).
comic strip n fumetto.
coming ['kʌmɪŋ] n arrivo ♦ adj (next)
prossimo(a); (future) futuro(a); in the ~
weeks nelle prossime settimane.
coming(s) and going(s) n(pl) andirivieni
m inv.
Comintern ['kɔmɪntəːn] n KOMINTERN m.
comma ['kɔmə] n virgola.
command [kə'mɑːnd] n ordine m, comando;
(MIL: authority) comando; (mastery)
padronanza; (COMPUT) command m inv,
comando ♦ vt comandare; to ~ sb to do
ordinare a qn di fare; to have/take ~ of
avere/prendere il comando di; to have at
one's ~ (money, resources etc) avere a
propria disposizione.

command economy n = **planned economy.**

commandeer [kɔmən'dɪə*] vt requisire.

commander [kə'mɑːndə*] n capo; (MIL) comandante m.

commander-in-chief (C-in-C) [kə'mɑːndər-ɪn'tʃiːf] n (MIL) comandante m in capo.

commanding [kə'mɑːndɪŋ] adj (appearance) imponente; (voice, tone) autorevole; (lead, position) dominante.

commanding officer n comandante m.

commandment [kə'mɑːndmənt] n (REL) comandamento.

command module n (SPACE) modulo di comando.

commando [kə'mɑːndəu] n commando m inv; membro di un commando.

commemorate [kə'mɛməreɪt] vt commemorare.

commemoration [kəmɛmə'reɪʃən] n commemorazione f.

commemorative [kə'mɛmərətɪv] adj commemorativo(a).

commence [kə'mɛns] vt, vi cominciare.

commend [kə'mɛnd] vt lodare; raccomandare.

commendable [kə'mɛndəbl] adj lodevole.

commendation [kɔmɛn'deɪʃən] n lode f; raccomandazione f; (for bravery etc) encomio.

commensurate [kə'mɛnʃərɪt] adj: ~ **with** proporzionato(a) a.

comment ['kɔment] n commento ♦ vi: **to** ~ **(on)** fare commenti (su); **to** ~ **that** osservare che; "**no** ~" "niente da dire".

commentary ['kɔməntərɪ] n commentario; (SPORT) radiocronaca; telecronaca.

commentator ['kɔməntɛɪtə*] n commentatore/trice; (SPORT) radiocronista m/f; telecronista m/f.

commerce ['kɔməːs] n commercio.

commercial [kə'məːʃəl] adj commerciale ♦ n (TV: also: ~ **break**) pubblicità f inv.

commercial bank n banca commerciale.

commercial college n ≈ istituto commerciale.

commercialism [kə'məːʃəlɪzəm] n affarismo.

commercial television n televisione f commerciale.

commercial traveller n commesso viaggiatore.

commercial vehicle n veicolo commerciale.

commiserate [kə'mɪzəreɪt] vi: **to** ~ **with** condolersi con.

commission [kə'mɪʃən] n commissione f;

(for salesman) commissione, provvigione f ♦ vt (MIL) nominare (al comando); (work of art) commissionare; **I get 10%** ~ ricevo il 10% sulle vendite; **out of** ~ (NAUT) in disarmo; (machine) fuori uso; **to** ~ **sb to do sth** incaricare qn di fare qc; **to** ~ **sth from sb** (painting etc) commissionare qc a qn; ~ **of inquiry** (BRIT) commissione f d'inchiesta.

commissionaire [kəmɪʃə'nɛə*] n (BRIT: at shop, cinema etc) portiere m in livrea.

commissioner [kə'mɪʃənə*] n commissionario; (POLICE) questore m.

commit [kə'mɪt] vt (act) commettere; (to sb's care) affidare; **to** ~ **o.s. (to do)** impegnarsi (a fare); **to** ~ **suicide** suicidarsi; **to** ~ **sb for trial** rinviare qn a giudizio.

commitment [kə'mɪtmənt] n impegno.

committed [kə'mɪtɪd] adj (writer) impegnato(a); (Christian) convinto(a).

committee [kə'mɪtɪ] n comitato; **to be on a** ~ far parte di un comitato or di una commissione.

committee meeting n riunione f di comitato or di commissione.

commodity [kə'mɔdɪtɪ] n prodotto, articolo; (food) derrata.

commodity exchange n borsa f merci inv.

common ['kɔmən] adj comune; (pej) volgare; (usual) normale ♦ n terreno comune; **in** ~ in comune; **in** ~ **use** di uso comune; **it's** ~ **knowledge that** è di dominio pubblico che; **to the** ~ **good** nell'interesse generale, per il bene comune; see also **Commons.**

common cold n: **the** ~ il raffreddore.

common denominator n denominatore m comune.

commoner ['kɔmənə*] n cittadino/a (non nobile).

common ground n (fig) terreno comune.

common land n terreno di uso pubblico.

common law n diritto consuetudinario.

common-law ['kɔmənlɔː] adj: ~ **wife** convivente f more uxorio.

commonly ['kɔmənlɪ] adv comunemente, usualmente.

Common Market n Mercato Comune.

commonplace ['kɔmənpleɪs] adj banale, ordinario(a).

commonroom ['kɔmənrum] n sala di riunione; (SCOL) sala dei professori.

Commons ['kɔmənz] npl (BRIT POL): **the (House of)** ~ la Camera dei Comuni.

common sense n buon senso.

Commonwealth ['kɔmənwɛlθ] n: **the** ~ il
Commonwealth; see boxed note.

> ### COMMONWEALTH
>
> Il **Commonwealth** è un'associazione di stati
> sovrani indipendenti e di alcuni territori
> annessi che facevano parte dell'antico Impero
> Britannico. Ancora oggi molti stati del
> Commonwealth riconoscono simbolicamente il
> sovrano britannico come capo di stato, e i loro
> rappresentanti si riuniscono per discutere
> questioni di comune interesse.

commotion [kə'məʊʃən] n confusione f,
tumulto.
communal ['kɔmjuːnl] adj (life) comunale;
(for common use) pubblico(a).
commune n ['kɔmjuːn] (group) comune f
♦ vi [kə'mjuːn]: **to** ~ **with** mettersi in
comunione con.
communicate [kə'mjuːnɪkeɪt] vt
comunicare, trasmettere ♦ vi: **to** ~ **(with)**
comunicare (con).
communication [kəmjuːnɪ'keɪʃən] n
comunicazione f.
communication cord n (BRIT) segnale m
d'allarme.
communications network n rete f delle
comunicazioni.
communications satellite n satellite m
per telecomunicazioni.
communicative [kə'mjuːnɪkətɪv] adj (gen)
loquace.
communion [kə'mjuːnɪən] n (also: **Holy C**~)
comunione f.
communiqué [kə'mjuːnɪkeɪ] n comunicato.
communism ['kɔmjunɪzəm] n comunismo.
communist ['kɔmjunɪst] adj, n comunista
(m/f).
community [kə'mjuːnɪtɪ] n comunità f inv.
community centre n circolo ricreativo.
community chest n (US) fondo di
beneficenza.
community health centre n centro
socio-sanitario.
community home n (BRIT) riformatorio.
community service n (BRIT) ≈ lavoro
sostitutivo.
community spirit n spirito civico.
commutation ticket [kɔmju'teɪʃən-] n (US)
biglietto di abbonamento.
commute [kə'mjuːt] vi fare il pendolare
♦ vt (LAW) commutare.
commuter [kə'mjuːtə*] n pendolare m/f.
compact adj [kəm'pækt] compatto(a) ♦ n
['kɔmpækt] (also: **powder** ~) portacipria m
inv.

compact disc n compact disc m inv; ~
player lettore m CD inv.
companion [kəm'pænjən] n compagno/a.
companionship [kəm'pænjənʃɪp] n
compagnia.
companionway [kəm'pænjənweɪ] n (NAUT)
scala.
company ['kʌmpənɪ] n (also COMM, MIL,
THEAT) compagnia; **he's good** ~ è di
buona compagnia; **we have** ~ abbiamo
ospiti; **to keep sb** ~ tenere compagnia a
qn; **to part** ~ **with** separarsi da; **Smith
and C**~ Smith e soci.
company car n macchina (di proprietà)
della ditta.
company director n amministratore m,
consigliere m di amministrazione.
company secretary n (BRIT COMM)
segretario/a generale.
comparable ['kɔmpərəbl] adj comparabile.
comparative [kəm'pærətɪv] adj (freedom,
cost) relativo(a); (adjective, adverb etc)
comparativo(a); (literature) comparato(a).
comparatively [kəm'pærətɪvlɪ] adv
relativamente.
compare [kəm'pɛə*] vt: **to** ~ **sth/sb with/to**
confrontare qc/qn con/a ♦ vi: **to** ~ **(with)**
reggere il confronto (con); ~**d with** or **to**
a paragone di, rispetto a; **how do the
prices** ~? che differenza di prezzo c'è?
comparison [kəm'pærɪsn] n confronto; **in** ~
(with) a confronto (di).
compartment [kəm'pɑːtmənt] n
compartimento; (RAIL) scompartimento.
compass ['kʌmpəs] n bussola; (**a pair of)
~es** (MATH) compasso; **within the** ~ **of**
entro i limiti di.
compassion [kəm'pæʃən] n compassione f.
compassionate [kəm'pæʃənɪt] adj
compassionevole; **on** ~ **grounds** per
motivi personali.
compassionate leave n congedo
straordinario (per gravi motivi di famiglia).
compatibility [kəmpætɪ'bɪlɪtɪ] n
compatibilità.
compatible [kəm'pætɪbl] adj compatibile.
compel [kəm'pɛl] vt costringere, obbligare.
compelling [kəm'pɛlɪŋ] adj (fig: argument)
irresistibile.
compendium [kəm'pɛndɪəm] n compendio.
compensate ['kɔmpənseɪt] vt risarcire ♦ vi:
to ~ **for** compensare.
compensation [kɔmpən'seɪʃən] n
compensazione f; (money) risarcimento.
compère ['kɔmpɛə*] n presentatore/trice.
compete [kəm'piːt] vi (take part)
concorrere; (vie): **to** ~ **(with)** fare
concorrenza (a).

competence ['kɔmpɪtəns] n competenza.

competent ['kɔmpɪtənt] adj competente.

competing [kəm'piːtɪŋ] adj (theories, ideas) opposto(a); (companies) in concorrenza; **three ~ explanations (of)** tre spiegazioni contrastanti tra di loro (di).

competition [kɔmpɪ'tɪʃən] n gara, concorso; (SPORT) gara; (ECON) concorrenza; **in ~ with** in concorrenza con.

competitive [kəm'pɛtɪtɪv] adj (sports) agonistico(a); (person) che ha spirito di competizione; (ECON) concorrenziale.

competitive examination n concorso.

competitor [kəm'pɛtɪtə*] n concorrente m/f.

compile [kəm'paɪl] vt compilare.

complacency [kəm'pleɪsnsɪ] n compiacenza di sé.

complacent [kəm'pleɪsnt] adj compiaciuto(a) di sé.

complain [kəm'pleɪn] vi: **to ~ (about)** lagnarsi (di); (in shop etc) reclamare (per).

▶**complain of** vt fus (MED) accusare.

complaint [kəm'pleɪnt] n lamento; reclamo; (MED) malattia.

complement n ['kɔmplɪmənt] complemento; (especially of ship's crew etc) effettivo ♦ vt ['kɔmplɪmɛnt] (enhance) accompagnarsi bene a.

complementary [kɔmplɪ'mɛntərɪ] adj complementare.

complete [kəm'pliːt] adj completo(a) ♦ vt completare; (a form) riempire; **it's a ~ disaster** è un vero disastro.

completely [kəm'pliːtlɪ] adv completamente.

completion [kəm'pliːʃən] n completamento; **to be nearing ~** essere in fase di completamento; **on ~ of contract** alla firma del contratto.

complex ['kɔmplɛks] adj complesso(a) ♦ n (PSYCH, buildings etc) complesso.

complexion [kəm'plɛkʃən] n (of face) carnagione f; (of event etc) aspetto.

complexity [kəm'plɛksɪtɪ] n complessità f inv.

compliance [kəm'plaɪəns] n acquiescenza; **in ~ with** (orders, wishes etc) in conformità con.

compliant [kəm'plaɪənt] adj acquiescente, arrendevole.

complicate ['kɔmplɪkeɪt] vt complicare.

complicated ['kɔmplɪkeɪtɪd] adj complicato(a).

complication [kɔmplɪ'keɪʃən] n complicazione f.

compliment n ['kɔmplɪmənt] complimento ♦ vt ['kɔmplɪmɛnt] fare un complimento a; **~s** npl complimenti mpl; rispetti mpl; **to pay sb a ~** fare un complimento a qn; **to ~ sb (on sth/on doing sth)** congratularsi or complimentarsi con qn (per qc/per aver fatto qc).

complimentary [kɔmplɪ'mɛntərɪ] adj complimentoso(a), elogiativo(a); (free) in omaggio.

complimentary ticket n biglietto d'omaggio.

compliments slip n cartoncino della società.

comply [kəm'plaɪ] vi: **to ~ with** assentire a; conformarsi a.

component [kəm'pəunənt] adj, n componente (m).

compose [kəm'pəuz] vt comporre; **to ~ o.s.** ricomporsi; **~d of** composto(a) di.

composed [kəm'pəuzd] adj calmo(a).

composer [kəm'pəuzə*] n (MUS) compositore/trice.

composite ['kɔmpəzɪt] adj composito(a); (MATH) composto(a).

composition [kɔmpə'zɪʃən] n composizione f.

compost ['kɔmpɔst] n composta, concime m.

composure [kəm'pəuʒə*] n calma.

compound ['kɔmpaund] n (CHEM, LING) composto; (enclosure) recinto ♦ adj composto(a) ♦ vt (fig: problem, difficulty) peggiorare.

compound fracture n frattura esposta.

compound interest n interesse m composto.

comprehend [kɔmprɪ'hɛnd] vt comprendere, capire.

comprehension [kɔmprɪ'hɛnʃən] n comprensione f.

comprehensive [kɔmprɪ'hɛnsɪv] adj comprensivo(a).

comprehensive insurance policy n polizza multi-rischio inv.

comprehensive (school) n (BRIT) scuola secondaria aperta a tutti.

compress vt [kəm'prɛs] comprimere ♦ n ['kɔmprɛs] (MED) compressa.

compression [kəm'prɛʃən] n compressione f.

comprise [kəm'praɪz] vt (also: **be ~d of**) comprendere.

compromise ['kɔmprəmaɪz] n compromesso ♦ vt compromettere ♦ vi venire a un compromesso ♦ cpd (decision, solution) di compromesso.

compulsion [kəm'pʌlʃən] n costrizione f; **under ~** sotto pressioni.

compulsive [kəm'pʌlsɪv] adj (PSYCH) incontrollabile; **he's a ~ smoker** non riesce a controllarsi nel fumare.

compulsory [kəm'pʌlsərɪ] adj obbligatorio(a).

compulsory purchase n espropriazione f.

compunction [kəm'pʌŋkʃən] n scrupolo; **to have no ~ about doing sth** non farsi scrupoli a fare qc.

computer [kəm'pjuːtə*] n computer m inv, elaboratore m elettronico.

computer game n computer game m inv.

computerization [kəmpjuːtəraɪ'zeɪʃən] n computerizzazione f.

computerize [kəm'pjuːtəraɪz] vt computerizzare.

computer language n linguaggio m macchina inv.

computer literate adj: **to be ~ essere in** grado di usare il computer.

computer peripheral n unità periferica.

computer program n programma m di computer.

computer programmer n programmatore/trice.

computer programming n programmazione f di computer.

computer science n informatica.

computer scientist n informatico/a.

computing [kəm'pjuːtɪŋ] n informatica.

comrade ['kɒmrɪd] n compagno/a.

comradeship ['kɒmrɪdʃɪp] n cameratismo.

Comsat ® ['kɒmsæt] n abbr = **communications satellite.**

con [kɒn] vt (col) truffare ♦ n truffa; **to ~ sb into doing sth** indurre qn a fare qc con raggiri.

concave ['kɒn'keɪv] adj concavo(a).

conceal [kən'siːl] vt nascondere.

concede [kən'siːd] vt concedere ♦ vi fare una concessione.

conceit [kən'siːt] n presunzione f, vanità.

conceited [kən'siːtɪd] adj presuntuoso(a), vanitoso(a).

conceivable [kən'siːvəbl] adj concepibile; **it is ~ that ...** può anche darsi che ....

conceivably [kən'siːvəblɪ] adv: **he may ~ be right** può anche darsi che abbia ragione.

conceive [kən'siːv] vt concepire ♦ vi concepire un bambino; **to ~ of sth/of doing sth** immaginare qc/di fare qc.

concentrate ['kɒnsəntreɪt] vi concentrarsi ♦ vt concentrare.

concentration [kɒnsən'treɪʃən] n concentrazione f.

concentration camp n campo di concentramento.

concentric [kɒn'sɛntrɪk] adj concentrico(a).

concept ['kɒnsɛpt] n concetto.

conception [kən'sɛpʃən] n concezione f; (idea) idea, concetto.

concern [kən'sɔːn] n affare m; (COMM) azienda, ditta; (anxiety) preoccupazione f ♦ vt riguardare; **to be ~ed (about)** preoccuparsi (di); **to be ~ed with** occuparsi di; **as far as I am ~ed** per quanto mi riguarda; **"to whom it may ~"** "a tutti gli interessati"; **the department ~ed** (under discussion) l'ufficio in questione; (relevant) l'ufficio competente.

concerning [kən'sɔːnɪŋ] prep riguardo a, circa.

concert ['kɒnsət] n concerto; **in ~ di** concerto.

concerted [kən'sɔːtɪd] adj concertato(a).

concert hall n sala da concerti.

concertina [kɒnsə'tiːnə] n piccola fisarmonica ♦ vi ridursi come una fisarmonica.

concerto [kən'tʃɔːtəu] n concerto.

concession [kən'sɛʃən] n concessione f.

concessionaire [kənsɛʃə'nɛə*] n concessionario.

concessionary [kən'sɛʃənərɪ] adj (ticket, fare) a prezzo ridotto.

conciliation [kənsɪlɪ'eɪʃən] n conciliazione f.

conciliatory [kən'sɪlɪətrɪ] adj conciliativo(a).

concise [kən'saɪs] adj conciso(a).

conclave ['kɒnkleɪv] n riunione f segreta; (REL) conclave m.

conclude [kən'kluːd] vt concludere ♦ vi (speaker) concludere; (events): **to ~ (with)** concludersi (con).

concluding [kən'kluːdɪŋ] adj (remarks etc) conclusivo(a), finale.

conclusion [kən'kluːʒən] n conclusione f; **to come to the ~ that ...** concludere che ..., arrivare alla conclusione che ....

conclusive [kən'kluːsɪv] adj conclusivo(a).

concoct [kən'kɒkt] vt inventare.

concoction [kən'kɒkʃən] n (food, drink) miscuglio.

concord ['kɒŋkɔːd] n (harmony) armonia, concordia; (treaty) accordo.

concourse ['kɒŋkɔːs] n (hall) atrio.

concrete ['kɒŋkriːt] n calcestruzzo ♦ adj concreto(a); (CONSTR) di calcestruzzo.

concrete mixer n betoniera.

concur [kən'kɔː*] vi concordare.

concurrently [kən'kʌrntlɪ] adv simultaneamente.

concussion [kən'kʌʃən] n (MED) commozione f cerebrale.

condemn [kən'dɛm] vt condannare.

condemnation [kɒndɛm'neɪʃən] n

condanna.
condensation [kɔnden'seɪʃən] *n* condensazione *f*.
condense [kən'dɛns] *vi* condensarsi ♦ *vt* condensare.
condensed milk *n* latte *m* condensato.
condescend [kɔndɪ'sɛnd] *vi* condiscendere; **to ~ to do sth** degnarsi di fare qc.
condescending [kɔndɪ'sɛndɪŋ] *adj* condiscendente.
condition [kən'dɪʃən] *n* condizione *f*; (*disease*) malattia ♦ *vt* condizionare, regolare; **in good/poor ~** in buone/cattive condizioni; **to have a heart ~** soffrire di (mal di) cuore; **weather ~s** condizioni meteorologiche; **on ~ that** a condizione che + *sub*, a condizione di.
conditional [kən'dɪʃənl] *adj* condizionale; **to be ~ upon** dipendere da.
conditioner [kən'dɪʃənə*] *n* (*for hair*) balsamo.
condo ['kɔndəu] *n abbr* (*US col*) = **condominium.**
condolences [kən'dəulənsɪz] *npl* condoglianze *fpl*.
condom ['kɔndəm] *n* preservativo.
condominium [kɔndə'mɪnɪəm] *n* (*US*) condominio.
condone [kən'dəun] *vt* condonare.
conducive [kən'djuːsɪv] *adj*: **~ to** favorevole a.
conduct *n* ['kɔndʌkt] condotta ♦ *vt* [kən'dʌkt] condurre; (*manage*) dirigere; amministrare; (*MUS*) dirigere; **to ~ o.s.** comportarsi.
conductor [kən'dʌktə*] *n* (*of orchestra*) direttore *m* d'orchestra; (*on bus*) bigliettaio; (*US RAIL*) controllore *m*; (*ELEC*) conduttore *m*.
conductress [kən'dʌktrɪs] *n* (*on bus*) bigliettaia.
conduit ['kɔndɪt] *n* condotto; tubo.
cone [kəun] *n* cono; (*BOT*) pigna.
confectioner [kən'fɛkʃənə*] *n*: **~'s (shop)** ≈ pasticceria.
confectionery [kən'fɛkʃənərɪ] *n* dolciumi *mpl*.
confederate [kən'fɛdərɪt] *adj* confederato(a) ♦ *n* (*pej*) complice *m/f*; (*US HISTORY*) confederato.
confederation [kənfɛdə'reɪʃən] *n* confederazione *f*.
confer [kən'fəː*] *vt*: **to ~ sth on** conferire qc a ♦ *vi* conferire; **to ~ (with sb about sth)** consultarsi (con qn su qc).
conference ['kɔnfərns] *n* congresso; **to be in ~** essere in riunione.
conference room *n* sala *f* conferenze *inv*.

confess [kən'fɛs] *vt* confessare, ammettere ♦ *vi* confessarsi.
confession [kən'fɛʃən] *n* confessione *f*.
confessional [kən'fɛʃənl] *n* confessionale *m*.
confessor [kən'fɛsə*] *n* confessore *m*.
confetti [kən'fɛtɪ] *n* coriandoli *mpl*.
confide [kən'faɪd] *vi*: **to ~ in** confidarsi con.
confidence ['kɔnfɪdns] *n* confidenza; (*trust*) fiducia; (*also*: **self-~**) sicurezza di sé; **to tell sb sth in strict ~** dire qc a qn in via strettamente confidenziale; **to have (every) ~ that ...** essere assolutamente certo(a) che ...; **motion of no ~** mozione *f* di sfiducia.
confidence trick *n* truffa.
confident ['kɔnfɪdənt] *adj* sicuro(a); (*also*: **self-~**) sicuro(a) di sé.
confidential [kɔnfɪ'dɛnʃəl] *adj* riservato(a); (*secretary*) particolare.
confidentiality ['kɔnfɪdɛnʃɪ'ælɪtɪ] *n* riservatezza, carattere *m* confidenziale.
configuration [kən'fɪgjuˈreɪʃən] *n* (*COMPUT*) configurazione *f*.
confine [kən'faɪn] *vt* limitare; (*shut up*) rinchiudere; **to ~ o.s. to doing sth** limitarsi a fare qc; *see also* **confines.**
confined [kən'faɪnd] *adj* (*space*) ristretto(a).
confinement [kən'faɪnmənt] *n* prigionia; (*MIL*) consegna; (*MED*) parto.
confines ['kɔnfaɪnz] *npl* confini *mpl*.
confirm [kən'fəːm] *vt* confermare; (*REL*) cresimare.
confirmation [kɔnfə'meɪʃən] *n* conferma; cresima.
confirmed [kən'fəːmd] *adj* inveterato(a).
confiscate ['kɔnfɪskeɪt] *vt* confiscare.
confiscation [kɔnfɪs'keɪʃən] *n* confisca.
conflagration [kɔnflə'greɪʃən] *n* conflagrazione *f*.
conflict *n* ['kɔnflɪkt] conflitto ♦ *vi* [kən'flɪkt] essere in conflitto.
conflicting [kən'flɪktɪŋ] *adj* contrastante; (*reports, evidence, opinions*) contraddittorio(a).
conform [kən'fɔːm] *vi*: **to ~ (to)** conformarsi (a).
conformist [kən'fɔːmɪst] *n* conformista *m/f*.
confound [kən'faund] *vt* confondere; (*amaze*) sconcertare.
confounded [kən'faundɪd] *adj* maledetto(a).
confront [kən'frʌnt] *vt* confrontare; (*enemy, danger*) affrontare.
confrontation [kɔnfrən'teɪʃən] *n* scontro.
confrontational [kɔnfrən'teɪʃənəl] *adj* polemico(a), aggressivo(a).
confuse [kən'fjuːz] *vt* imbrogliare; (*one*

thing with another) confondere.
confused [kən'fjuːzd] *adj* confuso(a); **to get**
~ confondersi.
confusing [kən'fjuːzɪŋ] *adj* che fa
confondere.
confusion [kən'fjuːʒən] *n* confusione *f*.
congeal [kən'dʒiːl] *vi (blood)* congelarsi.
congenial [kən'dʒiːnɪəl] *adj (person)*
simpatico(a); *(place, work, company)*
piacevole.
congenital [kən'dʒɛnɪtl] *adj* congenito(a).
conger eel ['kɔŋgər-] *n* grongo.
congested [kən'dʒɛstɪd] *adj*
congestionato(a); *(telephone lines)*
sovraccarico(a).
congestion [kən'dʒɛstʃən] *n* congestione *f*.
congestion charge *n pedaggio da pagare
per poter circolare in automobile nel
centro di alcune città, introdotto per la
prima volte a Londra nel 2002.*
conglomerate [kən'glɔmərɪt] *n (COMM)*
conglomerato.
conglomeration [kənglɔmə'reɪʃən] *n*
conglomerazione *f*.
Congo ['kɔŋgəu] *n* Congo.
congratulate [kən'grætjuleɪt] *vt*: **to** ~ **sb**
(on) congratularsi con qn (per *or* di).
congratulations [kəngrætju'leɪʃənz] *npl*: ~
(on) congratulazioni *fpl* (per) ♦ *excl*
congratulazioni!, rallegramenti!
congregate ['kɔŋgrɪgeɪt] *vi* congregarsi,
riunirsi.
congregation [kɔŋgrɪ'geɪʃən] *n*
congregazione *f*.
congress ['kɔŋgrɛs] *n* congresso; *(US POL)*:
C~ il Congresso; *see boxed note.*

CONGRESS

*Il **Congress** è l'assemblea statunitense che si
riunisce a Washington D.C. nel "Capitol" per
elaborare e discutere le leggi federali. È
costituita dalla "House of Representatives"
(435 membri, eletti nei vari stati in base al
numero degli abitanti) e dal "Senate" (100
senatori, due per ogni stato). Sia i membri della
"House of Representatives" che quelli del
"Senate" sono eletti direttamente dal popolo.*

---

congressman ['kɔŋgrɛsmən] *n (US)*
membro del Congresso.
congresswoman ['kɔŋgrɛswumən] *n (US)*
(donna) membro del Congresso.
conical ['kɔnɪkl] *adj* conico(a).
conifer ['kɔnɪfə*] *n* conifero.
coniferous [kə'nɪfərəs] *adj* di conifere.
conjecture [kən'dʒɛktʃə*] *n* congettura
♦ *vt, vi* congetturare.

conjoined twin [kən'dʒɔɪnd-] *n* fratello *(or*
sorella) siamese.
conjugal ['kɔndʒugl] *adj* coniugale.
conjugate ['kɔndʒugeɪt] *vt* coniugare.
conjugation [kɔndʒə'geɪʃən] *n*
coniugazione *f*.
conjunction [kən'dʒʌŋkʃən] *n* congiunzione
f; **in** ~ **with** in accordo con, insieme con.
conjunctivitis [kəndʒʌŋktɪ'vaɪtɪs] *n*
congiuntivite *f*.
conjure ['kʌndʒə*] *vi* fare giochi di
prestigio.
▶**conjure up** *vt (ghost, spirit)* evocare;
(memories) rievocare.
conjurer ['kʌndʒərə*] *n* prestigiatore/trice,
prestidigitatore/trice.
conjuring trick ['kʌndʒərɪŋ-] *n* gioco di
prestigio.
conker ['kɔŋkə*] *n (BRIT col)* castagna
(d'ippocastano).
conk out [kɔŋk-] *vi (col)* andare in panne.
conman ['kɔnmæn] *n* truffatore *m*.
Conn. *abbr (US)* = Connecticut.
connect [kə'nɛkt] *vt* connettere, collegare;
(ELEC) collegare; *(fig)* associare ♦ *vi*
(train): **to** ~ **with** essere in coincidenza
con; **to be** ~**ed with** aver rapporti con;
essere imparentato(a) con; **I am trying to**
~ **you** *(TEL)* sto cercando di darle la linea.
connection [kə'nɛkʃən] *n* relazione *f*,
rapporto; *(ELEC)* connessione *f*; *(TEL)*
collegamento; *(train etc)* coincidenza; **in** ~
with con riferimento a, a proposito di;
what is the ~ **between them?** in che
modo sono legati?; **business** ~**s** rapporti
d'affari; **to miss/get one's** ~ *(train etc)*
perdere/prendere la coincidenza.
connexion [kə'nɛkʃən] *n (BRIT)* =
connection.
conning tower ['kɔnɪŋ-] *n* torretta di
comando.
connive [kə'naɪv] *vi*: **to** ~ **at** essere
connivente in.
connoisseur [kɔnɪ'səː*] *n* conoscitore/
trice.
connotation [kɔnə'teɪʃən] *n* connotazione *f*.
connubial [kə'njuːbɪəl] *adj* coniugale.
conquer ['kɔŋkə*] *vt* conquistare; *(feelings)*
vincere.
conqueror ['kɔŋkərə*] *n* conquistatore *m*.
conquest ['kɔŋkwɛst] *n* conquista.
cons [kɔnz] *npl see* **pro; convenience.**
conscience ['kɔnʃəns] *n* coscienza; **in all** ~
onestamente, in coscienza.
conscientious [kɔnʃɪ'ɛnʃəs] *adj*
coscienzioso(a).
conscientious objector *n* obiettore *m* di
coscienza.

conscious ['kɔnʃəs] *adj* consapevole; (*MED*) conscio(a); (*deliberate*: *insult, error*) intenzionale, voluto(a); **to become ~ of sth/that** rendersi conto di qc/che.

consciousness ['kɔnʃəsnɪs] *n* consapevolezza; (*MED*) coscienza; **to lose/regain ~** perdere/riprendere coscienza.

conscript ['kɔnskrɪpt] *n* coscritto.

conscription [kən'skrɪpʃən] *n* coscrizione *f*.

consecrate ['kɔnsɪkreɪt] *vt* consacrare.

consecutive [kən'sɛkjutɪv] *adj* consecutivo(a); **on 3 ~ occasions** 3 volte di fila.

consensus [kən'sɛnsəs] *n* consenso; **the ~ of opinion** l'opinione *f* unanime *or* comune.

consent [kən'sɛnt] *n* consenso ♦ *vi*: **to ~ (to)** acconsentire (a); **age of ~**età legale (per avere rapporti sessuali); **by common ~** di comune accordo.

consenting adults [kən'sɛntɪŋ-] *npl* adulti *mpl* consenzienti.

consequence ['kɔnsɪkwəns] *n* conseguenza, risultato; importanza; **in ~** di conseguenza.

consequently ['kɔnsɪkwəntlɪ] *adv* di conseguenza, dunque.

conservation [kɔnsə'veɪʃən] *n* conservazione *f*; (*also*: **energy ~**) tutela dell'ambiente; **energy ~** risparmio energetico.

conservationist [kɔnsə'veɪʃənɪst] *n* fautore/trice della tutela dell'ambiente.

conservative [kən'sə:vətɪv] *adj* conservatore(trice); (*cautious*) cauto(a); **C~** *adj*, *n* (*BRIT POL*) conservatore(trice); **the C~ Party** il partito conservatore.

conservatory [kən'sə:vətrɪ] *n* (*greenhouse*) serra.

conserve [kən'sə:v] *vt* conservare ♦ *n* conserva.

consider [kən'sɪdə*] *vt* considerare; (*take into account*) tener conto di; **to ~ doing sth** considerare la possibilità di fare qc; **all things ~ed** tutto sommato *or* considerato; **~ yourself lucky** puoi dirti fortunato.

considerable [kən'sɪdərəbl] *adj* considerevole, notevole.

considerably [kən'sɪdərəblɪ] *adv* notevolmente, decisamente.

considerate [kən'sɪdərɪt] *adj* premuroso(a).

consideration [kənsɪdə'reɪʃən] *n* considerazione *f*; (*reward*) rimunerazione *f*; **out of ~ for** per riguardo a; **under ~ in** esame; **my first ~ is my family** il mio primo pensiero è per la mia famiglia.

considered [kən'sɪdəd] *adj*: **it is my ~ opinion that** ... dopo lunga riflessione il mio parere è che ....

considering [kən'sɪdərɪŋ] *prep* in considerazione di; **~ (that)** se si considera (che).

consign [kən'saɪn] *vt* consegnare; (*send*: *goods*) spedire.

consignee [kɔnsaɪ'ni:] *n* consegnatario/a, destinatario/a.

consignment [kən'saɪnmənt] *n* consegna; spedizione *f*.

consignment note *n* (*COMM*) nota di spedizione.

consist [kən'sɪst] *vi*: **to ~ of** constare di, essere composto(a) di.

consistency [kən'sɪstənsɪ] *n* consistenza; (*fig*) coerenza.

consistent [kən'sɪstənt] *adj* coerente; (*constant*) costante; **~ with** compatibile con.

consolation [kɔnsə'leɪʃən] *n* consolazione *f*.

console *vt* [kən'səul] consolare ♦ *n* ['kɔnsəul] quadro di comando.

consolidate [kən'sɔlɪdeɪt] *vt* consolidare.

consols ['kɔnsɔlz] *npl* (*STOCK EXCHANGE*) titoli *mpl* del debito consolidato.

consommé [kən'sɔmeɪ] *n* consommé *m inv*, brodo ristretto.

consonant ['kɔnsənənt] *n* consonante *f*.

consort ['kɔnsɔ:t] *n* consorte *m/f*; **prince ~** principe *m* consorte ♦ *vi* (*often pej*): **to ~ with sb** frequentare qn.

consortium [kən'sɔ:tɪəm] *n* consorzio.

conspicuous [kən'spɪkjuəs] *adj* cospicuo(a); **to make o.s. ~** farsi notare.

conspiracy [kən'spɪrəsɪ] *n* congiura, cospirazione *f*.

conspiratorial [kənspɪrə'tɔ:rɪəl] *adj* cospiratorio(a).

conspire [kən'spaɪə*] *vi* congiurare, cospirare.

constable ['kʌnstəbl] *n* (*BRIT*: *also*: **police ~**) ≈ poliziotto, agente *m* di polizia.

constabulary [kən'stæbjulərɪ] *n* forze *fpl* dell'ordine.

constant ['kɔnstənt] *adj* costante; continuo(a).

constantly ['kɔnstəntlɪ] *adv* costantemente; continuamente.

constellation [kɔnstə'leɪʃən] *n* costellazione *f*.

consternation [kɔnstə'neɪʃən] *n* costernazione *f*.

constipated ['kɔnstɪpeɪtɪd] *adj* stitico(a).

constipation [kɔnstɪ'peɪʃən] *n* stitichezza.

constituency [kən'stɪtjuənsɪ] *n* collegio elettorale; (*people*) elettori *mpl* (del collegio); *see boxed note.*

CONSTITUENCY

Con il termine **constituency** *viene indicato sia un collegio elettorale che i suoi elettori. In Gran Bretagna ogni collegio elegge un rappresentante che in seguito incontra regolarmente i propri elettori in riunioni chiamate "surgeries" per discutere questioni di interesse locale.*

---

constituency party *n* sezione *f* locale (del partito).
constituent [kən'stɪtjuənt] *n* elettore/trice; (*part*) elemento componente.
constitute ['kɔnstɪtjuːt] *vt* costituire.
constitution [kɔnstɪ'tjuːʃən] *n* costituzione *f*.
constitutional [kɔnstɪ'tjuːʃənl] *adj* costituzionale.
constitutional monarchy *n* monarchia costituzionale.
constrain [kən'streɪn] *vt* costringere.
constrained [kən'streɪnd] *adj* costretto(a).
constraint [kən'streɪnt] *n* (*restraint*) limitazione *f*, costrizione *f*; (*embarrassment*) imbarazzo, soggezione *f*.
constrict [kən'strɪkt] *vt* comprimere; opprimere.
construct [kən'strʌkt] *vt* costruire.
construction [kən'strʌkʃən] *n* costruzione *f*; (*fig: interpretation*) interpretazione *f*; **under** ~ in costruzione.
construction industry *n* edilizia, industria edile.
constructive [kən'strʌktɪv] *adj* costruttivo(a).
construe [kən'struː] *vt* interpretare.
consul ['kɔnsl] *n* console *m*.
consulate ['kɔnsjulɪt] *n* consolato.
consult [kən'sʌlt] *vt*: **to ~ sb (about sth)** consultare qn (su *or* riguardo a qc).
consultancy [kən'sʌltənsɪ] *n* consulenza.
consultancy fee *n* onorario di consulenza.
consultant [kən'sʌltənt] *n* (*MED*) consulente *m* medico; (*other specialist*) consulente ♦ *cpd*: ~ **engineer** *n* ingegnere *m* consulente; ~ **paediatrician** *n* specialista *m/f* in pediatria; **legal/ management** ~ consulente legale/ gestionale.
consultation [kɔnsəl'teɪʃən] *n* consultazione *f*; (*MED, LAW*) consulto; **in** ~ **with** consultandosi con.
consultative [kən'sʌltətɪv] *adj* di consulenza.
consulting room [kən'sʌltɪŋ-] *n* (*BRIT*) ambulatorio.

consume [kən'sjuːm] *vt* consumare.
consumer [kən'sjuːmə*] *n* consumatore/ trice; (*of electricity, gas etc*) utente *m/f*.
consumer credit *n* credito al consumatore.
consumer durables *npl* prodotti *mpl* di consumo durevole.
consumer goods *npl* beni *mpl* di consumo.
consumerism [kən'sjuːmərɪzəm] *n* (*consumer protection*) tutela del consumatore; (*ECON*) consumismo.
consumer society *n* società dei consumi.
consumer watchdog *n* comitato di difesa dei consumatori.
consummate ['kɔnsʌmeɪt] *vt* consumare.
consumption [kən'sʌmpʃən] *n* consumo; (*MED*) consunzione *f*; **not fit for human** ~ non commestibile.
cont. *abbr* (= *continued*) segue.
contact ['kɔntækt] *n* contatto; (*person*) conoscenza ♦ *vt* mettersi in contatto con; **to be in** ~ **with sb/sth** essere in contatto con qn/qc; **business** ~**s** contatti *mpl* d'affari.
contact lenses *npl* lenti *fpl* a contatto.
contagious [kən'teɪdʒəs] *adj* contagioso(a).
contain [kən'teɪn] *vt* contenere; **to ~ o.s.** contenersi.
container [kən'teɪnə*] *n* recipiente *m*; (*for shipping etc*) container *m*.
containerize [kən'teɪnəraɪz] *vt* mettere in container.
container ship *n* nave *f* container *inv*.
contaminate [kən'tæmɪneɪt] *vt* contaminare.
contamination [kəntæmɪ'neɪʃən] *n* contaminazione *f*.
cont'd *abbr* (= *continued*) segue.
contemplate ['kɔntəmpleɪt] *vt* contemplare; (*consider*) pensare a (*or* di).
contemplation [kɔntəm'pleɪʃən] *n* contemplazione *f*.
contemporary [kən'tɛmpərərɪ] *adj* contemporaneo(a); (*design*) moderno(a) ♦ *n* contemporaneo/a; (*of the same age*) coetaneo/a.
contempt [kən'tɛmpt] *n* disprezzo; ~ **of court** (*LAW*) oltraggio alla Corte.
contemptible [kən'tɛmptəbl] *adj* spregevole, vergognoso(a).
contemptuous [kən'tɛmptjuəs] *adj* sdegnoso(a).
contend [kən'tɛnd] *vt*: **to ~ that** sostenere che ♦ *vi*: **to ~ with** lottare contro; **he has a lot to ~ with** ha un sacco di guai.
contender [kən'tɛndə*] *n* contendente *m/f*; concorrente *m/f*.
content [kən'tɛnt] *adj* contento(a),

soddisfatto(a) ♦ vt contentare, soddisfare
♦ n ['kɔntɛnt] contenuto; ~s npl contenuto;
(of barrel etc: capacity) capacità f inv; (table
of) ~s indice m; to be ~ with essere
contento di; to ~ o.s. with sth/with doing
sth accontentarsi di qc/di fare qc.
contented [kən'tɛntɪd] adj contento(a),
soddisfatto(a).
contentedly [kən'tɛntɪdlɪ] adv con
soddisfazione.
contention [kən'tɛnʃən] n contesa;
(assertion) tesi f inv; **bone of** ~pomo della
discordia.
contentious [kən'tɛnʃəs] adj polemico(a).
contentment [kən'tɛntmənt] n
contentezza.
contest n ['kɔntɛst] lotta; (competition)
gara, concorso ♦ vt [kən'tɛst] contestare;
(LAW) impugnare; (compete for)
contendere.
contestant [kən'tɛstənt] n concorrente m/f;
(in fight) avversario/a.
context ['kɔntɛkst] n contesto; **in/out of** ~
nel/fuori dal contesto.
continent ['kɔntɪnənt] n continente m; the
C~ (BRIT) l'Europa continentale; **on the**
C~ in Europa.
continental [kɔntɪ'nɛntl] adj continentale
♦ n (BRIT) abitante m/f dell'Europa
continentale.
continental breakfast n colazione f
all'europea.
continental quilt n (BRIT) piumino.
contingency [kən'tɪndʒənsɪ] n eventualità f
inv.
contingency plan n misura d'emergenza.
contingent [kən'tɪndʒənt] n contingenza
♦ adj: **to be** ~ **upon** dipendere da.
continual [kən'tɪnjuəl] adj continuo(a).
continually [kən'tɪnjuəlɪ] adv di continuo.
continuation [kəntɪnju'eɪʃən] n
continuazione f; (after interruption)
ripresa; (of story) seguito.
continue [kən'tɪnju:] vi continuare ♦ vt
continuare; (start again) riprendere; **to be**
~**d** (story) continua; ~**d on page 10** segue
or continua a pagina 10.
continuing education [kən'tɪnjuɪŋ-] n
corsi mpl per adulti.
continuity [kɔntɪ'nju:ɪtɪ] n continuità;
(CINE) (ordine m della) sceneggiatura.
continuity girl n (CINE) segretaria di
edizione.
continuous [kən'tɪnjuəs] adj continuo(a),
ininterrotto(a); ~ **performance** (CINE)
spettacolo continuato; ~ **stationery**
(COMPUT) carta a moduli continui.
continuously [kən'tɪnjuəslɪ] adv (repeatedly)

continuamente; (uninterruptedly)
ininterrottamente.
contort [kən'tɔ:t] vt contorcere.
contortion [kən'tɔ:ʃən] n contorcimento;
(of acrobat) contorsione f.
contortionist [kən'tɔ:ʃənɪst] n
contorsionista m/f.
contour ['kɔntuə*] n contorno, profilo;
(also: ~ **line**) curva di livello.
contraband ['kɔntrəbænd] n contrabbando
♦ adj di contrabbando.
contraception [kɔntrə'sɛpʃən] n
contraccezione f.
contraceptive [kɔntrə'sɛptɪv] adj
contraccettivo(a) ♦ n contraccettivo.
contract n ['kɔntrækt] contratto ♦ cpd
['kɔntrækt] (price, date) del contratto;
(work) a contratto ♦ vi [kən'trækt] (COMM):
to ~ **to do sth** fare un contratto per fare
qc; (become smaller) contrarre; **to be**
under ~ **to do sth** aver stipulato un
contratto per fare qc; ~ **of employment**
contratto di lavoro.
►**contract in** vi impegnarsi (con un
contratto); (BRIT ADMIN) scegliere di
pagare i contributi per una pensione.
►**contract out** vi: **to** ~ **out (of)** ritirarsi
(da); (BRIT ADMIN) (scegliere di) non
pagare i contributi per una pensione.
contraction [kən'trækʃən] n contrazione f.
contractor [kən'træktə*] n imprenditore m.
contractual [kən'træktjuəl] adj
contrattuale.
contradict [kɔntrə'dɪkt] vt contraddire.
contradiction [kɔntrə'dɪkʃən] n
contraddizione f; **to be in** ~ **with**
discordare con.
contradictory [kɔntrə'dɪktərɪ] adj
contraddittorio(a).
contralto [kən'træltəu] n contralto.
contraption [kən'træpʃən] n (pej) aggeggio.
contrary ['kɔntrərɪ] adj contrario(a);
(unfavourable) avverso(a), contrario(a);
[kən'trɛərɪ] (perverse) bisbetico(a) ♦ n
contrario; **on the** ~ al contrario; **unless**
you hear to the ~ a meno che non si
disdica; ~ **to what we thought** a
differenza di or contrariamente a quanto
pensavamo.
contrast n ['kɔntrɑːst] contrasto ♦ vt
[kən'trɑːst] mettere in contrasto; **in** ~ **to**
or **with** a differenza di, contrariamente
a.
contrasting [kən'trɑːstɪŋ] adj contrastante,
di contrasto.
contravene [kɔntrə'vi:n] vt contravvenire.
contravention [kɔntrə'vɛnʃən] n: ~ **(of)**
contravvenzione f (a), infrazione f (di).

contribute [kən'trɪbjuːt] vi contribuire ♦ vt: **to ~ £10/an article to** dare 10 sterline/un articolo a; **to ~ to** contribuire a; (newspaper) scrivere per; (discussion) partecipare a.

contribution [kɔntrɪ'bjuːʃən] n contribuzione f.

contributor [kən'trɪbjutə*] n (to newspaper) collaboratore/trice.

contributory [kən'trɪbjutərɪ] adj (cause) che contribuisce; **it was a ~ factor in** ... quello ha contribuito a ....

contributory pension scheme n (BRIT) sistema di pensionamento finanziato congiuntamente dai contributi del lavoratore e del datore di lavoro.

contrite ['kɔntraɪt] adj contrito(a).

contrivance [kən'traɪvəns] n congegno; espediente m.

contrive [kən'traɪv] vt inventare; escogitare ♦ vi: **to ~ to do** fare in modo di fare.

control [kən'trəul] vt dominare; (firm, operation etc) dirigere; (check) controllare; (disease, fire) arginare, limitare ♦ n controllo; **~s** npl comandi mpl; **to take ~ of** assumere il controllo di; **to be in ~ of** aver autorità su; essere responsabile di; controllare; **to ~ o.s.** controllarsi; **everything is under ~** tutto è sotto controllo; **the car went out of ~** la macchina non rispondeva ai comandi; **circumstances beyond our ~** circostanze fpl che non dipendono da noi.

control key n (COMPUT) tasto di controllo.

controlled substance [kən'trəuld-] n sostanza stupefacente.

controller [kən'trəulə*] n controllore m.

controlling interest [kən'trəulɪŋ-] n (COMM) maggioranza delle azioni.

control panel n (on aircraft, ship, TV etc) quadro dei comandi.

control point n punto di controllo.

control room n (NAUT, MIL) sala di comando; (RADIO, TV) sala di regia.

control tower n (AVIAT) torre f di controllo.

control unit n (COMPUT) unità f inv di controllo.

controversial [kɔntrə'vəːʃl] adj controverso(a), polemico(a).

controversy ['kɔntrəvəːsɪ] n controversia, polemica.

conurbation [kɔnəː'beɪʃən] n conurbazione f.

convalesce [kɔnvə'lɛs] vi rimettersi in salute.

convalescence [kɔnvə'lɛsns] n

convalescenza.

convalescent [kɔnvə'lɛsnt] adj, n convalescente (m/f).

convector [kən'vɛktə*] n convettore m.

convene [kən'viːn] vt convocare; (meeting) organizzare ♦ vi convenire, adunarsi.

convenience [kən'viːnɪəns] n comodità f inv; **at your ~** a suo comodo; **at your earliest ~** (COMM) appena possibile; **all modern ~s**, (BRIT) **all mod cons** tutte le comodità moderne.

convenience foods npl cibi mpl precotti.

convenient [kən'viːnɪənt] adj conveniente, comodo(a); **if it is ~ to you** se per lei va bene, se non la incomoda.

conveniently [kən'viːnɪəntlɪ] adv (happen) a proposito; (situated) in un posto comodo.

convent ['kɔnvənt] n convento.

convention [kən'vɛnʃən] n convenzione f; (meeting) convegno.

conventional [kən'vɛnʃənl] adj convenzionale.

convent school n scuola retta da suore.

converge [kən'vəːdʒ] vi convergere.

conversant [kən'vəːsnt] adj: **to be ~ with** essere al corrente di; essere pratico(a) di.

conversation [kɔnvə'seɪʃən] n conversazione f.

conversational [kɔnvə'seɪʃənl] adj non formale; (COMPUT) conversazionale; **~ Italian** l'italiano parlato.

conversationalist [kɔnvə'seɪʃnəlɪst] n conversatore/trice.

converse n ['kɔnvəːs] contrario, opposto ♦ vi [kən'vəːs]: **to ~ (with sb about sth)** conversare (con qn su qc).

conversely [kɔn'vəːslɪ] adv al contrario

conversion [kən'vəːʃən] n conversione f; (BRIT: of house) trasformazione f, rimodernamento.

conversion table n tavola di equivalenze.

convert vt [kən'vəːt] (REL, COMM) convertire; (alter) trasformare ♦ n ['kɔnvəːt] convertito/a.

convertible [kən'vəːtəbl] n macchina decappottabile.

convex ['kɔnvɛks] adj convesso(a).

convey [kən'veɪ] vt trasportare; (thanks) comunicare; (idea) dare.

conveyance [kən'veɪəns] n (of goods) trasporto; (vehicle) mezzo di trasporto.

conveyancing [kən'veɪənsɪŋ] n (LAW) redazione f di transazioni di proprietà.

conveyor belt n nastro trasportatore.

convict vt [kən'vɪkt] dichiarare colpevole ♦ n ['kɔnvɪkt] carcerato/a.

conviction [kən'vɪkʃən] n condanna; (belief)

convinzione f.
convince [kən'vɪns] vt: to ~ sb (of sth/that) convincere qn (di qc/che).
convincing [kən'vɪnsɪŋ] adj convincente.
convincingly [kən'vɪnsɪŋlɪ] adv in modo convincente.
convivial [kən'vɪvɪəl] adj allegro(a).
convoluted ['kɔnvəluːtɪd] adj (shape) attorcigliato(a), avvolto(a); (argument) involuto(a).
convoy ['kɔnvɔɪ] n convoglio.
convulse [kən'vʌls] vt sconvolgere; to be ~d with laughter contorcersi dalle risa.
convulsion [kən'vʌlʃən] n convulsione f.
coo [kuː] vi tubare.
cook [kuk] vt cucinare, cuocere; (meal) preparare ♦ vi cuocere; (person) cucinare ♦ n cuoco/a.
►cook up vt (col: excuse, story) improvvisare, inventare.
cookbook ['kukbuk] n = cookery book.
cooker ['kukə*] n fornello, cucina.
cookery book n (BRIT) libro di cucina.
cookie ['kukɪ] n (US) biscotto; (COMPUT) cookie m inv.
cooking ['kukɪŋ] n cucina ♦ cpd (apples, chocolate) da cuocere; (utensils, salt, foil) da cucina.
cookout ['kukaut] n (US) pranzo (cucinato) all'aperto.
cool [kuːl] adj fresco(a); (not afraid) calmo(a); (unfriendly) freddo(a); (impertinent) sfacciato(a) ♦ vt raffreddare, rinfrescare ♦ vi raffreddarsi, rinfrescarsi; it's ~ (weather) fa fresco; to keep sth ~ or in a ~ place tenere qc in fresco.
►cool down vi raffreddarsi; (fig: person, situation) calmarsi.
coolant ['kuːlənt] n (liquido) refrigerante m.
cool box, (US) cooler ['kuːlə*] n borsa termica.
cooling ['kuːlɪŋ] adj (breeze) fresco(a).
cooling tower n torre f di raffreddamento.
coolly ['kuːlɪ] adv (calmly) con calma, tranquillamente; (audaciously) come se niente fosse; (unenthusiastically) freddamente.
coolness ['kuːlnɪs] n freschezza; sangue m freddo, calma.
coop [kuːp] n stia ♦ vt: to ~ up (fig) rinchiudere.
co-op ['kəuɔp] n abbr (= cooperative (society)) coop f.
cooperate [kəu'ɔpəreɪt] vi cooperare, collaborare.

cooperation [kəuɔpə'reɪʃən] n cooperazione f, collaborazione f.
cooperative [kəu'ɔpərətɪv] adj cooperativo(a) ♦ n cooperativa.
coopt [kəu'ɔpt] vt: to ~ sb into sth cooptare qn per qc.
coordinate vt [kəu'ɔːdɪneɪt] coordinare ♦ n [kəu'ɔːdɪnət] (MATH) coordinata; ~s npl (clothes) coordinati mpl.
coordination [kəuɔːdɪ'neɪʃən] n coordinazione f.
coot [kuːt] n folaga.
co-ownership [kəu'əunəʃɪp] n comproprietà.
cop [kɔp] n (col) sbirro.
cope [kəup] vi farcela; to ~ with (problems) far fronte a.
Copenhagen [kəupən'heɪgən] n Copenhagen f.
copier ['kɔpɪə*] n (also: photo~) (foto)copiatrice f.
co-pilot ['kəupaɪlət] n secondo pilota m.
copious ['kəupɪəs] adj copioso(a), abbondante.
copper ['kɔpə*] n rame m; (col: policeman) sbirro; ~s npl spiccioli mpl.
coppice ['kɔpɪs], copse [kɔps] n bosco ceduo.
copulate ['kɔpjuleɪt] vi accoppiarsi.
copy ['kɔpɪ] n copia; (book etc) esemplare m; (material: for printing) materiale m, testo ♦ vt (gen, COMPUT) copiare; (imitate) imitare; rough/fair ~ brutta/bella (copia); to make good ~ (fig) fare notizia.
►copy out vt ricopiare, trascrivere.
copycat ['kɔpɪkæt] n (pej) copione m.
copyright ['kɔpɪraɪt] n diritto d'autore; ~ reserved tutti i diritti riservati.
copy typist n dattilografo/a.
copywriter ['kɔpɪraɪtə*] n redattore m pubblicitario.
coral ['kɔrəl] n corallo.
coral reef n barriera corallina.
Coral Sea n: the ~ il mar dei Coralli.
cord [kɔːd] n corda; (ELEC) filo; (fabric) velluto a coste; ~s npl (trousers) calzoni mpl (di velluto) a coste.
cordial ['kɔːdɪəl] adj, n cordiale (m).
cordless ['kɔːdlɪs] adj senza cavo.
cordon ['kɔːdn] n cordone m.
►cordon off vt fare cordone intorno a.
corduroy ['kɔːdərɔɪ] n fustagno.
CORE [kɔː*] n abbr (US) = Congress of Racial Equality.
core [kɔː*] n (of fruit) torsolo; (TECH) centro; (of earth, nuclear reactor) nucleo; (of problem etc) cuore m, nocciolo ♦ vt estrarre il torsolo da; rotten to the ~

marcio fino al midollo.

Corfu [kɔː'fuː] *n* Corfù *f.*

coriander [kɔrɪ'ændə*] *n* coriandolo.

cork [kɔːk] *n* sughero; (*of bottle*) tappo.

corkage ['kɔːkɪdʒ] *n* somma da pagare se il cliente porta il proprio vino.

corked [kɔːkt], (*US*) **corky** ['kɔːkɪ] *adj* (*wine*) che sa di tappo.

corkscrew ['kɔːkskruː] *n* cavatappi *m inv.*

cormorant ['kɔːmərnt] *n* cormorano.

corn [kɔːn] *n* (*BRIT*: *wheat*) grano; (*US*: *maize*) granturco; (*on foot*) callo; ~ **on the cob** (*CULIN*) pannocchia cotta.

cornea ['kɔːnɪə] *n* cornea.

corned beef ['kɔːnd-] *n* carne *f* di manzo in scatola.

corner ['kɔːnə*] *n* angolo; (*AUT*) curva; (*FOOTBALL*: *also*: ~ **kick**) corner *m inv*, calcio d'angolo ♦ *vt* intrappolare; mettere con le spalle al muro; (*COMM*: *market*) accaparrare ♦ *vi* prendere una curva; **to cut** ~**s** (*fig*) prendere una scorciatoia.

corner flag *n* (*FOOTBALL*) bandierina d'angolo.

corner kick *n* (*FOOTBALL*) calcio d'angolo.

cornerstone ['kɔːnəstəun] *n* pietra angolare.

cornet ['kɔːnɪt] *n* (*MUS*) cornetta; (*BRIT*: *of ice-cream*) cono.

cornflakes ['kɔːnfleɪks] *npl* fiocchi *mpl* di granturco.

cornflour ['kɔːnflauə*] *n* (*BRIT*) ≈ fecola di patate.

cornice ['kɔːnɪs] *n* cornicione *m*; cornice *f.*

Cornish ['kɔːnɪʃ] *adj* della Cornovaglia.

corn oil *n* olio di mais.

cornstarch ['kɔːnstɑːtʃ] *n* (*US*) = **cornflour.**

cornucopia [kɔːnju'kəupɪə] *n* grande abbondanza.

Cornwall ['kɔːnwəl] *n* Cornovaglia.

corny ['kɔːnɪ] *adj* (*col*) trito(a).

corollary [kə'rɔlərɪ] *n* corollario.

coronary ['kɔrənərɪ] *n*: ~ **(thrombosis)** trombosi *f* coronaria.

coronation [kɔrə'neɪʃən] *n* incoronazione *f.*

coroner ['kɔrənə*] *n* magistrato incaricato di indagare la causa di morte in circostanze sospette.

coronet ['kɔrənɪt] *n* diadema *m.*

Corp. *abbr* = **corporation.**

corporal ['kɔːpərl] *n* caporalmaggiore *m* ♦ *adj*: ~ **punishment** pena corporale.

corporate ['kɔːpərɪt] *adj* comune; (*COMM*) costituito(a) (in corporazione).

corporate hospitality *n* omaggi *mpl* ai clienti (*come biglietti per spettacoli, cene etc*).

corporate identity, corporate image *n*

(*of organization*) immagine *f* di marca.

corporation [kɔːpə'reɪʃən] *n* (*of town*) consiglio comunale; (*COMM*) ente *m.*

corporation tax *n* ≈ imposta societaria.

corps [kɔː*], *pl* **corps** [kɔːz] *n* corpo; **press** ~ ufficio *m* stampa *inv.*

corpse [kɔːps] *n* cadavere *m.*

corpuscle ['kɔːpʌsl] *n* corpuscolo.

corral [kə'rɑːl] *n* recinto.

correct [kə'rɛkt] *adj* (*accurate*) corretto(a), esatto(a); (*proper*) corretto(a) ♦ *vt* correggere; **you are** ~ ha ragione.

correction [kə'rɛkʃən] *n* correzione *f.*

correlate ['kɔrɪleɪt] *vt* mettere in correlazione ♦ *vi*: **to** ~ **with** essere in rapporto con.

correlation [kɔrɪ'leɪʃən] *n* correlazione *f.*

correspond [kɔrɪs'pɔnd] *vi* corrispondere.

correspondence [kɔrɪs'pɔndəns] *n* corrispondenza.

correspondence course *n* corso per corrispondenza.

correspondent [kɔrɪs'pɔndənt] *n* corrispondente *m/f.*

corridor ['kɔrɪdɔː*] *n* corridoio.

corroborate [kə'rɔbəreɪt] *vt* corroborare, confermare.

corrode [kə'rəud] *vt* corrodere ♦ *vi* corrodersi.

corrosion [kə'rəuʒən] *n* corrosione *f.*

corrosive [kə'rəuzɪv] *adj* corrosivo(a).

corrugated ['kɔrəgeɪtɪd] *adj* increspato(a); ondulato(a).

corrugated iron *n* lamiera di ferro ondulata.

corrupt [kə'rʌpt] *adj* corrotto(a) ♦ *vt* corrompere; ~ **practices** (*dishonesty, bribery*) pratiche *fpl* illecite.

corruption [kə'rʌpʃən] *n* corruzione *f.*

corset ['kɔːsɪt] *n* busto.

Corsica ['kɔːsɪkə] *n* Corsica.

Corsican ['kɔːsɪkən] *adj*, *n* corso(a).

cortège [kɔː'teɪʒ] *n* corteo.

cortisone ['kɔːtɪzəun] *n* cortisone *m.*

coruscating ['kɔrəskeɪtɪŋ] *adj* scintillante.

cosh [kɔʃ] *n* (*BRIT*) randello (corto).

cosignatory [kəu'sɪgnətərɪ] *n* cofirmatario/a.

cosiness ['kəuzɪnɪs] *n* intimità.

cos lettuce ['kɔs-] *n* lattuga romana.

cosmetic [kɔz'mɛtɪk] *n* cosmetico ♦ *adj* (*preparation*) cosmetico(a); (*surgery*) estetico(a); (*fig*: *reforms*) ornamentale.

cosmic ['kɔzmɪk] *adj* cosmico(a).

cosmonaut ['kɔzmənɔːt] *n* cosmonauta *m/f.*

cosmopolitan [kɔzmə'pɔlɪtn] *adj* cosmopolita.

cosmos ['kɔzmɔs] *n* cosmo.

cosset ['kɔsɪt] vt vezzeggiare.

cost [kɔst] n costo ♦ vb (pt, pp **cost**) vi costare ♦ vt stabilire il prezzo di; ~**s** npl (LAW) spese fpl; **it** ~**s £5/too much** costa 5 sterline/troppo; **it** ~ **him his life/job** gli costò la vita/il suo lavoro; **how much does it** ~**?** quanto costa?, quanto viene?; **what will it** ~ **to have it repaired?** quanto costerà farlo riparare?; ~ **of living** costo della vita; **at all** ~**s** a ogni costo.

cost accountant n analizzatore m dei costi.

co-star ['kəustɑ:*] n attore/trice della stessa importanza del protagonista.

Costa Rica ['kɔstə'ri:kə] n Costa Rica.

cost centre n centro di costo.

cost control n controllo dei costi.

cost-effective ['kɔstɪ'fɛktɪv] adj (gen) conveniente, economico(a); (COMM) redditizio(a), conveniente.

cost-effectiveness ['kɔstɪ'fɛktɪvnɪs] n convenienza.

costing ['kɔstɪŋ] n (determinazione f dei) costi mpl.

costly ['kɔstlɪ] adj costoso(a), caro(a).

cost-of-living ['kɔstəv'lɪvɪŋ] adj: ~ **allowance** indennità f inv di contingenza; ~ **index** indice m della scala mobile.

cost price n (BRIT) prezzo all'ingrosso.

costume ['kɔstjuːm] n costume m; (lady's suit) tailleur m inv; (BRIT: also: **swimming** ~) costume da bagno.

costume jewellery n bigiotteria.

cosy, (US) **cozy** ['kəuzɪ] adj intimo(a); (room, atmosphere) accogliente.

cot [kɔt] n (BRIT: child's) lettino; (US: folding bed) brandina.

cot death n improvvisa e inspiegabile morte nel sonno di un neonato.

Cotswolds ['kɔtswəuldz] npl: **the** ~ zona collinare del Gloucestershire.

cottage ['kɔtɪdʒ] n cottage m inv.

cottage cheese n fiocchi mpl di latte magro.

cottage industry n industria artigianale basata sul lavoro a cottimo.

cottage pie n piatto a base di carne macinata in sugo e purè di patate.

cotton ['kɔtn] n cotone m; ~ **dress** etc vestito etc di cotone.

►**cotton on** vi (col): **to** ~ **on (to sth)** afferrare (qc).

cotton wool n (BRIT) cotone m idrofilo.

couch [kautʃ] n sofà m inv; (in doctor's surgery) lettino ♦ vt esprimere.

couchette [kuː'ʃɛt] n cuccetta.

couch potato n (col) pigrone/a teledipendente.

cough [kɔf] vi tossire ♦ n tosse f.

cough drop n pasticca per la tosse.

cough mixture, cough syrup n sciroppo per la tosse.

could [kud] pt of **can.**

couldn't ['kudnt] = **could not.**

council ['kaunsl] n consiglio; **city** or **town** ~ consiglio comunale; **C**~ **of Europe** Consiglio d'Europa.

council estate n (BRIT) quartiere m di case popolari.

council house n (BRIT) casa popolare.

council housing n alloggi mpl popolari.

councillor ['kaunsələ*] n consigliere/a.

council tax n (BRIT) tassa comunale sulla proprietà.

counsel ['kaunsl] n avvocato; consultazione f ♦ vt: **to** ~ **sth/sb to do sth** consigliare qc/a qn di fare qc; ~ **for the defence/the prosecution** avvocato difensore/di parte civile.

counsellor, (US) **counselor** ['kaunslə*] n consigliere/a; (US: lawyer) avvocato/essa.

count [kaunt] vt, vi contare ♦ n conto; (nobleman) conte m; **to** ~ **(up) to 10** contare fino a 10; **to** ~ **the cost of** calcolare il costo di; **not** ~**ing the children** senza contare i bambini; **10** ~**ing him** 10 compreso lui; ~ **yourself lucky** considerati fortunato; **it** ~**s for very little** non conta molto, non ha molta importanza; **to keep** ~ **of sth** tenere il conto di qc.

►**count on** vt fus contare su; **to** ~ **on doing sth** contare di fare qc.

►**count up** vt addizionare.

countdown ['kauntdaun] n conto alla rovescia.

countenance ['kauntɪnəns] n volto, aspetto ♦ vt approvare.

counter ['kauntə*] n banco; (position: in post office, bank) sportello; (in game) gettone m; (TECH) contatore m ♦ vt opporsi a; (blow) parare ♦ adv: ~ **to** contro; in opposizione a; **to buy under the** ~ (fig) comperare sottobanco; **to** ~ **sth with sth/by doing sth** rispondere a qc con qc/facendo qc.

counteract [kauntər'ækt] vt agire in opposizione a; (poison etc) annullare gli effetti di.

counterattack ['kauntərətæk] n contrattacco ♦ vi contrattaccare.

counterbalance ['kauntəbæləns] vt contrappesare.

counter-clockwise ['kauntə'klɔkwaɪz] adv in senso antiorario.

counter-espionage [kauntər'ɛspɪənɑːʒ] n

controspionaggio.
counterfeit ['kauntəfɪt] n contraffazione f, falso ♦ vt contraffare, falsificare ♦ adj falso(a).
counterfoil ['kauntəfɔɪl] n matrice f.
counterintelligence ['kauntərɪn'tɛlɪdʒəns] n = **counter-espionage**.
countermand ['kauntəmɑːnd] vt annullare.
countermeasure ['kauntəmɛʒə*] n contromisura.
counteroffensive ['kauntərə'fɛnsɪv] n controffensiva.
counterpane ['kauntəpeɪn] n copriletto m inv.
counterpart ['kauntəpɑːt] n (of document etc) copia; (of person) corrispondente m/f.
counterproductive ['kauntəprə'dʌktɪv] adj controproducente.
countersign ['kauntəsaɪn] vt controfirmare.
countersink ['kauntəsɪŋk] vt (hole) svasare.
countess ['kauntɪs] n contessa.
countless ['kauntlɪs] adj innumerevole.
countrified ['kʌntrɪfaɪd] adj rustico(a)
country ['kʌntrɪ] n paese m; (native land) patria; (as opposed to town) campagna; (region) regione f; **in the** ~ in campagna; **mountainous** ~ territorio montagnoso.
country and western (music) n musica country e western, country m.
country dancing n (BRIT) danza popolare.
country house n villa in campagna.
countryman ['kʌntrɪmən] n (national) compatriota m; (rural) contadino.
countryside ['kʌntrɪsaɪd] n campagna.
country-wide ['kʌntrɪ'waɪd] adj diffuso(a) in tutto il paese ♦ adv in tutto il paese.
county ['kauntɪ] n contea.
county council n (BRIT) consiglio di contea.
county town n (BRIT) capoluogo.
coup, ~s [kuː, -z] n (also: ~ **d'état**) colpo di Stato; (triumph) bel colpo.
coupé [kuː'peɪ] n coupé m inv.
couple ['kʌpl] n coppia ♦ vt (carriages) agganciare; (TECH) accoppiare; (ideas, names) associare; **a** ~ **of** un paio di.
couplet ['kʌplɪt] n distico.
coupling ['kʌplɪŋ] n (RAIL) agganciamento.
coupon ['kuːpɔn] n (voucher) buono; (COMM) coupon m inv.
courage ['kʌrɪdʒ] n coraggio.
courageous [kə'reɪdʒəs] adj coraggioso(a).
courgette [kuə'ʒɛt] n (BRIT) zucchina.
courier ['kurɪə*] n corriere m; (for tourists) guida.
course [kɔːs] n corso; (of ship) rotta; (for golf) campo; (part of meal) piatto; **first** ~ primo piatto; **of** ~ adv senz'altro,

naturalmente; **(no) of** ~ **not!** certo che no!, no di certo!; **in the** ~ **of the next few days** nel corso dei prossimi giorni; **in due** ~ a tempo debito; ~ **(of action)** modo d'agire; **the best** ~ **would be to** ... la cosa migliore sarebbe ...; **we have no other** ~ **but to** ... non possiamo far altro che ...; ~ **of lectures** corso di lezioni; **a** ~ **of treatment** (MED) una cura.
court [kɔːt] n corte f; (TENNIS) campo ♦ vt (woman) fare la corte a; (fig: favour, popularity) cercare di conquistare; (: death, disaster) sfiorare, rasentare; **out of** ~ (LAW: settle) in via amichevole; **to take to** ~ citare in tribunale; **C~ of Appeal** corte d'appello.
courteous ['kɜːtɪəs] adj cortese.
courtesan [kɔːtɪ'zæn] n cortigiana.
courtesy ['kɜːtəsɪ] n cortesia; **by** ~ **of** per gentile concessione di.
courtesy bus n navetta gratuita (di hotel, aeroporto).
courtesy car n vettura sostitutiva.
courtesy light n (AUT) luce f interna.
court-house ['kɔːthaus] n (US) palazzo di giustizia.
courtier ['kɔːtɪə*] n cortigiano/a.
courtmartial, pl courtsmartial ['kɔːt'mɑːʃəl] n corte f marziale.
courtroom ['kɔːtrum] n tribunale m.
court shoe n scarpa f décolleté inv.
courtyard ['kɔːtjɑːd] n cortile m.
cousin ['kʌzn] n cugino/a.
cove [kəuv] n piccola baia.
covenant ['kʌvənənt] n accordo ♦ vt: **to** ~ **to do sth** impegnarsi (per iscritto) a fare qc.
Coventry ['kɔvəntrɪ] n: **to send sb to** ~ (fig) dare l'ostracismo a qn.
cover ['kʌvə*] vt (gen) coprire; (distance) coprire, percorrere; (PRESS: report on) fare un servizio su ♦ n (of pan) coperchio; (over furniture) fodera; (of book) copertina; (shelter) riparo; (COMM, INSURANCE) copertura; **to take** ~ mettersi al coperto; **under** ~ al riparo; **under** ~ **of darkness** protetto dall'oscurità; **under separate** ~ (COMM) a parte, in plico separato; **£10 will** ~ **everything** 10 sterline saranno sufficienti.
▶**cover up** vt (child, object): **to** ~ **up (with)** coprire (di); (fig: hide: truth, facts) nascondere ♦ vi: **to** ~ **up for sb** (fig) coprire qn.
coverage ['kʌvərɪdʒ] n (PRESS, TV, RADIO): **to give full** ~ **to** fare un ampio servizio su.
coveralls ['kʌvərɔːlz] npl (US) tuta.

cover charge n coperto.

covering ['kʌvərɪŋ] n copertura.

covering letter, (US) cover letter n lettera d'accompagnamento.

cover note n (INSURANCE) polizza (di assicurazione) provvisoria.

cover price n prezzo di copertina.

covert ['kʌvət] adj nascosto(a); (glance) di sottecchi, furtivo(a).

cover-up ['kʌvərʌp] n occultamento (di informazioni).

covet ['kʌvɪt] vt bramare.

cow [kau] n vacca ♦ cpd femmina ♦ vt intimidire; ~ **elephant** n elefantessa.

cowardice ['kauədɪs] n vigliaccheria.

cowardly ['kauədlɪ] adj vigliacco(a).

cowboy ['kaubɔɪ] n cow-boy m inv.

cower ['kauə*] vi acquattarsi.

cowshed ['kauʃɛd] n stalla.

cowslip ['kauslɪp] n (BOT) primula (odorata).

coxswain ['kɔksn] n (abbr. cox) timoniere m.

coy [kɔɪ] adj falsamente timido(a).

coyote [kɔɪ'əutɪ] n coyote m inv.

cozy ['kəuzɪ] adj (US) = **cosy**.

CP n abbr (= Communist Party) P.C. m.

cp. abbr (= compare) cfr.

CPA n abbr (US) see **certified public accountant**.

CPI n abbr (US: = Consumer Price Index) indice dei prezzi al consumo.

Cpl. abbr = **corporal**.

CP/M n abbr (= Control Program for Microcomputers) CP/M m.

c.p.s. abbr (= characters per second) c.p.s.

CPSA n abbr (BRIT: = Civil and Public Services Association) sindacato dei servizi pubblici.

CPU n abbr see **central processing unit**.

cr. abbr = **credit; creditor**.

crab [kræb] n granchio.

crab apple n mela selvatica.

crack [kræk] n (split, slit) fessura, crepa; incrinatura; (noise) schiocco; (: of gun) scoppio; (joke) battuta; (col: attempt): **to have a ~ at sth** tentare qc; (DRUGS) crack m inv ♦ vt spaccare; incrinare; (whip) schioccare; (nut) schiacciare; (case, mystery: solve) risolvere; (code) decifrare ♦ cpd (athlete) di prim'ordine; **to ~ jokes** (col) dire battute, scherzare; **to get ~ing** (col) darsi una mossa.

►**crack down on** vt fus prendere serie misure contro, porre freno a.

►**crack up** vi crollare.

crackdown ['krækdaun] n repressione f.

cracked [krækt] adj (col) matto(a).

cracker ['krækə*] n cracker m inv; (firework) petardo; (Christmas ~) mortaretto natalizio (con sorpresa); **a ~ of a** ... (BRIT col) un(a) ... formidabile; **he's ~s** (BRIT col) è tocco.

crackle ['krækl] vi crepitare.

crackling ['kræklɪŋ] n crepitio; (on radio, telephone) disturbo; (of pork) cotenna croccante (del maiale).

crackpot ['krækpɔt] n (col) imbecille m/f con idee assurde, assurdo/a.

cradle ['kreɪdl] n culla ♦ vt (child) tenere fra le braccia; (object) reggere tra le braccia.

craft [krɑːft] n mestiere m; (cunning) astuzia; (boat) naviglio.

craftsman ['krɑːftsmən] n artigiano.

craftsmanship ['krɑːftsmənʃɪp] n abilità.

crafty ['krɑːftɪ] adj furbo(a), astuto(a).

crag [kræg] n roccia.

cram [kræm] vt (fill): **to ~ sth with** riempire qc di; (put): **to ~ sth into** stipare qc in.

cramming ['kræmɪŋ] n (fig: pej) sgobbare m.

cramp [kræmp] n crampo ♦ vt soffocare, impedire.

cramped [kræmpt] adj ristretto(a).

crampon ['kræmpən] n (CLIMBING) rampone m.

cranberry ['krænbərɪ] n mirtillo.

crane [kreɪn] n gru f inv ♦ vb, vi: **to ~ forward, to ~ one's neck** allungare il collo.

cranium, pl crania ['kreɪnɪəm, 'kreɪnɪə] n cranio.

crank [kræŋk] n manovella; (person) persona stramba.

crankshaft ['kræŋkʃɑːft] n albero a gomiti.

cranky ['kræŋkɪ] adj eccentrico(a); (bad-tempered): **to be ~** avere i nervi.

cranny ['krænɪ] n see **nook**.

crap [kræp] n (col!) fesserie fpl; **to have a ~** cacare (!).

crappy ['kræpɪ] adj (col) di merda (!).

crash [kræʃ] n fragore m; (of car) incidente m; (of plane) caduta; (of business) fallimento; (STOCK EXCHANGE) crollo ♦ vt fracassare ♦ vi (plane) fracassarsi; (car) avere un incidente; (two cars) scontrarsi; (fig) fallire, andare in rovina; **to ~ into** scontrarsi con; **he ~ed the car into a wall** andò a sbattere contro un muro con la macchina.

crash barrier n (BRIT AUT) guardrail m inv.

crash course n corso intensivo.

crash helmet n casco.

crash landing n atterraggio di fortuna.

crass [kræs] adj crasso(a).

crate [kreɪt] n gabbia.

crater ['kreɪtə*] n cratere m.

cravat(e) [krə'væt] n fazzoletto da collo.
crave [kreiv] vi: **to ~ for** desiderare ardentemente.
craving ['kreiviŋ] n: **~ (for)** (for food, cigarettes etc) (gran) voglia (di).
crawl [krɔːl] vi strisciare carponi; (child) andare a gattoni; (vehicle) avanzare lentamente ♦ n (SWIMMING) crawl m; **to ~ to sb** (col: suck up) arruffianarsi qn.
crawler lane ['krɔːlə*-] n (BRIT AUT) corsia riservata al traffico lento.
crayfish ['kreifiʃ] n (pl inv) gambero (d'acqua dolce).
crayon ['kreiən] n matita colorata.
craze [kreiz] n mania.
crazed [kreizd] adj (look, person) folle, pazzo(a); (pottery, glaze) incrinato(a).
crazy ['kreizi] adj matto(a); **to go ~** uscir di senno, impazzire; **to be ~ about sb** (col: keen) essere pazzo di qn; **to be ~ about sth** andare matto per qc.
crazy paving n (BRIT) lastricato a mosaico irregolare.
creak [kriːk] vi cigolare, scricchiolare.
cream [kriːm] n crema; (fresh) panna ♦ adj (colour) color crema inv; **whipped ~** panna montata.
▶**cream off** vt (best talents, part of profits) portarsi via.
cream cake n torta alla panna.
cream cheese n formaggio fresco.
creamery ['kriːməri] n (shop) latteria; (factory) caseificio.
creamy ['kriːmi] adj cremoso(a).
crease [kriːs] n grinza; (deliberate) piega ♦ vt sgualcire ♦ vi sgualcirsi.
crease-resistant ['kriːsrizistənt] adj ingualcibile.
create [kriː'eit] vt creare; (fuss, noise) fare.
creation [kriː'eiʃən] n creazione f.
creative [kriː'eitiv] adj creativo(a).
creativity [kriːei'tiviti] n creatività.
creator [kriː'eitə*] n creatore/trice.
creature ['kriːtʃə*] n creatura.
crèche, creche [krɛʃ] n asilo infantile.
credence ['kriːdns] n credenza, fede f.
credentials [kri'dɛnʃlz] npl (papers) credenziali fpl; (letters of reference) referenze fpl.
credibility [krɛdi'biliti] n credibilità.
credible ['krɛdibl] adj credibile; (witness, source) attendibile.
credit ['krɛdit] n credito; onore m; (SCOL: esp US) certificato del compimento di una parte del corso universitario ♦ vt (COMM) accreditare; (believe: also: **give ~ to**) credere, prestar fede a; **to ~ £5 to sb** accreditare 5 sterline a qn; **to ~ sb with**

sth (fig) attribuire qc a qn; **on ~ a** credito; **to one's ~ a** proprio onore; **to take the ~ for** farsi il merito di; **to be in ~** (person) essere creditore(trice); (bank account) essere coperto(a); **he's a ~ to his family** fa onore alla sua famiglia; see also **credits**.
creditable ['krɛditəbl] adj che fa onore, degno(a) di lode.
credit account n conto di credito.
credit agency n (BRIT) agenzia di analisi di credito.
credit balance n saldo attivo.
credit bureau n (US) agenzia di analisi di credito.
credit card n carta di credito.
credit control n controllo dei crediti.
credit facilities npl agevolazioni fpl creditizie.
credit limit n limite m di credito.
credit note n (BRIT) nota di credito.
creditor ['krɛditə*] n creditore/trice.
credits ['krɛdits] npl (CINE) titoli mpl.
credit transfer n bancogiro, postagiro.
creditworthy ['krɛditwɔːði] adj autorizzabile al credito.
credulity [kri'djuːliti] n credulità.
creed [kriːd] n credo; dottrina.
creek [kriːk] n insenatura; (US) piccolo fiume m.
creel ['kriːl] n cestino per il pesce; (also: **lobster ~**) nassa.
creep [kriːp] vi (pt, pp **crept** [krɛpt]) avanzare furtivamente (or pian piano); (plant) arrampicarsi ♦ n (col): **he's a ~** è un tipo viscido; **it gives me the ~s** (col) mi fa venire la pelle d'oca; **to ~ up on sb** avvicinarsi quatto quatto a qn; (fig: old age etc) cogliere qn alla sprovvista.
creeper ['kriːpə*] n pianta rampicante.
creepers ['kriːpəz] npl (US: rompers) tutina.
creepy ['kriːpi] adj (frightening) che fa accapponare la pelle.
creepy-crawly ['kriːpi'krɔːli] n (col) bestiolina, insetto.
cremate [kri'meit] vt cremare.
cremation [kri'meiʃən] n cremazione f.
crematorium, pl crematoria [krɛmə'tɔːriəm, -'tɔːriə] n forno crematorio.
creosote ['kriəsəut] n creosoto.
crêpe [kreip] n crespo.
crêpe bandage n (BRIT) fascia elastica.
crêpe paper n carta crespa.
crêpe sole n suola di para.
crept [krɛpt] pt, pp of **creep**.
crescendo [kri'ʃɛndəu] n crescendo.
crescent ['krɛsnt] n (shape) mezzaluna;

(*street*) strada semicircolare.
cress [kres] *n* crescione *m*.
crest [krest] *n* cresta; (*of helmet*) pennacchiera; (*of coat of arms*) cimiero.
crestfallen ['krestfɔːlən] *adj* mortificato(a).
Crete ['kriːt] *n* Creta.
crevasse [krɪ'væs] *n* crepaccio.
crevice ['krevɪs] *n* fessura, crepa.
crew [kruː] *n* equipaggio; (*CINE*) troupe *f inv*; (*gang*) banda, compagnia.
crew-cut ['kruːkʌt] *n*: **to have a** ~ avere i capelli a spazzola.
crew-neck ['kruːnek] *n* girocollo.
crib [krɪb] *n* culla; (*REL*) presepio ♦ *vt* (*col*) copiare.
cribbage ['krɪbɪdʒ] *n tipo di gioco di carte*.
crick [krɪk] *n* crampo; ~ **in the neck** torcicollo.
cricket ['krɪkɪt] *n* (*insect*) grillo; (*game*) cricket *m*.
cricketer ['krɪkɪtə*] *n* giocatore *m* di cricket.
crime [kraɪm] *n* (*in general*) criminalità; (*instance*) crimine *m*, delitto.
crime wave *n* ondata di criminalità.
criminal ['krɪmɪnl] *adj*, *n* criminale (*m/f*); **C~ Investigation Department (CID)** ≈ polizia giudiziaria
crimp [krɪmp] *vt* arricciare.
crimson ['krɪmzn] *adj* color cremisi *inv*.
cringe [krɪndʒ] *vi* acquattarsi; (*fig*) essere servile.
crinkle ['krɪŋkl] *vt* arricciare, increspare.
cripple ['krɪpl] *n* zoppo/a ♦ *vt* azzoppare; (*ship, plane*) avariare; (*production, exports*) rovinare; ~**d with arthritis** sciancato(a) per l'artrite.
crippling ['krɪplɪŋ] *adj* (*taxes, debts*) esorbitante; (*disease*) molto debilitante.
crisis, *pl* **crises** ['kraɪsɪs, -siːz] *n* crisi *f inv*.
crisp [krɪsp] *adj* croccante; (*fig*) frizzante; vivace; deciso(a).
crisps [krɪsps] *npl* (*BRIT*) patatine *fpl* fritte.
criss-cross ['krɪskrɔs] *adj* incrociato(a) ♦ *vt* incrociarsi.
criterion, *pl* **criteria** [kraɪ'tɪərɪən, -'tɪərɪə] *n* criterio.
critic ['krɪtɪk] *n* critico/a.
critical ['krɪtɪkl] *adj* critico(a); **to be** ~ **of sb/sth** criticare qn/qc, essere critico verso qn/qc.
critically ['krɪtɪklɪ] *adv* criticamente; ~ **ill** gravemente malato.
criticism ['krɪtɪsɪzəm] *n* critica.
criticize ['krɪtɪsaɪz] *vt* criticare.
critique [krɪ'tiːk] *n* critica, saggio critico.
croak [krəuk] *vi* gracchiare.
Croat ['krəuæt] *adj*, *n* = **Croatian**.

Croatia [krəu'eɪʃɪə] *n* Croazia.
Croatian [krəu'eɪʃɪən] *adj* croato(a) ♦ *n* croato/a; (*LING*) croato.
crochet ['krəuʃeɪ] *n* lavoro all'uncinetto.
crock [krɔk] *n* coccio; (*col*: *person*: *also*: **old** ~) rottame *m*; (: *car etc*) caffettiera, rottame *m*.
crockery ['krɔkərɪ] *n* vasellame *m*; (*plates, cups etc*) stoviglie *fpl*.
crocodile ['krɔkədaɪl] *n* coccodrillo.
crocus ['krəukəs] *n* croco.
croft [krɔft] *n* (*BRIT*) piccolo podere *m*.
crofter ['krɔftə*] *n* (*BRIT*) affittuario di un piccolo podere.
crone [krəun] *n* strega.
crony ['krəunɪ] *n* (*col*) amicone/a.
crook [kruk] *n* truffatore *m*; (*of shepherd*) bastone *m*.
crooked ['krukɪd] *adj* curvo(a), storto(a); (*person, action*) disonesto(a).
crop [krɔp] *n* raccolto; (*produce*) coltivazione *f*; (*of bird*) gozzo, ingluvie *f* ♦ *vt* (*cut*: *hair*) tagliare, rapare; (*subj*: *animals*: *grass*) brucare.
▶**crop up** *vi* presentarsi.
cropper ['krɔpə*] *n*: **to come a** ~ (*col*) fare fiasco.
crop spraying *n* spruzzatura di antiparassitari.
croquet ['krəukeɪ] *n* croquet *m*.
croquette [krə'ket] *n* crocchetta.
cross [krɔs] *n* croce *f*; (*BIOL*) incrocio ♦ *vt* (*street etc*) attraversare; (*arms, legs, BIOL*) incrociare; (*cheque*) sbarrare; (*thwart*: *person, plan*) contrastare, ostacolare ♦ *vi*: **the boat** ~**es from ... to ...** la barca fa la traversata da ... a ... ♦ *adj* di cattivo umore; **to** ~ **o.s.** fare il segno della croce, segnarsi; **we have a** ~**ed line** (*BRIT*: *on telephone*) c'è un'interferenza; **they've got their lines** ~**ed** (*fig*) si sono fraintesi; **to be/get** ~ **with sb (about sth)** essere arrabbiato(a)/arrabbiarsi con qn (per qc).
▶**cross out** *vt* cancellare.
▶**cross over** *vi* attraversare.
crossbar ['krɔsbɑː*] *n* traversa.
crossbow ['krɔsbəu] *n* balestra.
crossbreed ['krɔsbriːd] *n* incrocio.
cross-Channel ferry ['krɔs'tʃænl-] *n* traghetto che attraversa la Manica.
cross-check ['krɔstʃek] *n* controprova ♦ *vi* fare una controprova.
crosscountry (race) [krɔs'kʌntrɪ-] *n* cross-country *m inv*.
cross-dressing [krɔs'dresɪŋ] *n* travestitismo.
cross-examination ['krɔsɪgzæmɪ'neɪʃən] *n*

(*LAW*) controinterrogatorio.
cross-examine ['krɔsɪg'zæmɪn] *vt* (*LAW*)
sottoporre a controinterrogatorio.
cross-eyed ['krɔsaɪd] *adj* strabico(a).
crossfire ['krɔsfaɪə*] *n* fuoco incrociato.
crossing ['krɔsɪŋ] *n* incrocio; (*sea-passage*)
traversata; (*also*: **pedestrian** ~) passaggio
pedonale.
crossing point *n* valico di frontiera.
cross-purposes ['krɔs'pəːpəsɪz] *npl*: **to be
at ~ with sb** (*misunderstand*) fraintendere
qn; **to talk at ~** fraintendersi.
cross-question [krɔs'kwɛstʃən] *vt* (*LAW*) =
cross-examine; (*fig*) sottoporre ad un
interrogatorio.
cross-reference ['krɔs'rɛfərəns] *n* rinvio,
rimando.
crossroads ['krɔsrəudz] *n* incrocio.
cross section *n* (*BIOL*) sezione *f*
trasversale; (*in population*) settore *m*
rappresentativo.
crosswalk ['krɔswɔːk] *n* (*US*) strisce *fpl*
pedonali, passaggio pedonale.
crosswind ['krɔswɪnd] *n* vento di traverso.
crosswise ['krɔswaɪz] *adv* di traverso.
crossword ['krɔswəːd] *n* cruciverba *m inv*.
crotch [krɔtʃ] *n* (*ANAT*) inforcatura; (*of
garment*) pattina.
crotchet ['krɔtʃɪt] *n* (*MUS*) semiminima.
crotchety ['krɔtʃɪtɪ] *adj* (*person*)
burbero(a).
crouch [krautʃ] *vi* acquattarsi;
rannicchiarsi.
croup [kruːp] *n* (*MED*) crup *m*.
crouton ['kruːtɔn] *n* crostino.
crow [krəu] *n* (*bird*) cornacchia; (*of cock*)
canto del gallo ♦ *vi* (*cock*) cantare; (*fig*)
vantarsi; cantar vittoria.
crowbar ['krəubɑː*] *n* piede *m* di porco.
crowd [kraud] *n* folla ♦ *vt* affollare, stipare
♦ *vi* affollarsi; **~s of people** un sacco di
gente.
crowded ['kraudɪd] *adj* affollato(a); ~ **with**
stipato(a) di.
crowd scene *n* (*CINE, THEAT*) scena di
massa.
crown [kraun] *n* corona; (*of head*) calotta
cranica; (*of hat*) cocuzzolo; (*of hill*) cima
♦ *vt* incoronare; (*tooth*) incapsulare; **and
to ~ it all** ... (*fig*) e per giunta ..., e come
se non bastasse ...; *see boxed note.*

CROWN COURT

Nel sistema legale inglese, la **crown court** *è
un tribunale penale che si sposta da una città
all'altra. È formata da una giuria locale ed è
presieduta da un giudice che si sposta assieme*

---

*alla "court". Vi si discutono i reati più gravi,
mentre dei reati minori si occupano le
"magistrates' courts", presiedute da un giudice
di pace, ma senza giuria. È il giudice di pace
che decide se passare o meno un caso alla*
crown court.

---

crowning ['kraunɪŋ] *adj* (*achievement, glory*)
supremo(a).
crown jewels *npl* gioielli *mpl* della Corona.
crown prince *n* principe *m* ereditario.
crow's-feet ['krəuzfiːt] *npl* zampe *fpl* di
gallina.
crow's-nest ['krəuznɛst] *n* (*on sailing-ship*)
coffa.
crucial ['kruːʃl] *adj* cruciale, decisivo(a); ~
to essenziale per.
crucifix ['kruːsɪfɪks] *n* crocifisso.
crucifixion [kruːsɪ'fɪkʃən] *n* crocifissione *f*.
crucify ['kruːsɪfaɪ] *vt* crocifiggere, mettere
in croce; (*fig*) distruggere, fare a pezzi.
crude [kruːd] *adj* (*materials*) greggio(a); non
raffinato(a); (*fig: basic*) crudo(a);
primitivo(a); (*: vulgar*) rozzo(a),
grossolano(a).
crude (oil) *n* (*petrolio*) greggio.
cruel ['kruəl] *adj* crudele.
cruelty ['kruəltɪ] *n* crudeltà *f inv*.
cruet ['kruːɪt] *n* ampolla.
cruise [kruːz] *n* crociera ♦ *vi* andare a
velocità di crociera; (*taxi*) circolare.
cruise missile *n* missile *m* cruise *inv*.
cruiser ['kruːzə*] *n* incrociatore *m*.
cruising speed ['kruːzɪŋ-] *n* velocità *f inv* di
crociera.
crumb [krʌm] *n* briciola.
crumble ['krʌmbl] *vt* sbriciolare ♦ *vi*
sbriciolarsi; (*plaster etc*) sgretolarsi;
(*land, earth*) franare; (*building, fig*)
crollare.
crumbly ['krʌmblɪ] *adj* friabile.
crummy ['krʌmɪ] *adj* (*col: cheap*) di infima
categoria; (*: depressed*) giù *inv*.
crumpet ['krʌmpɪt] *n* specie di frittella.
crumple ['krʌmpl] *vt* raggrinzare,
spiegazzare.
crunch [krʌntʃ] *vt* sgranocchiare;
(*underfoot*) scricchiolare ♦ *n* (*fig*) punto *or*
momento cruciale.
crunchy ['krʌntʃɪ] *adj* croccante.
crusade [kruː'seɪd] *n* crociata ♦ *vi* (*fig*): **to ~
for/against** fare una crociata per/contro.
crusader [kruː'seɪdə*] *n* crociato; (*fig*): ~
(**for**) sostenitore/trice (di).
crush [krʌʃ] *n* folla; (*love*): **to have a ~ on
sb** avere una cotta per qn; (*drink*): **lemon
~** spremuta di limone ♦ *vt* schiacciare;
(*crumple*) sgualcire; (*grind, break up: garlic,*

ice) tritare; (*: grapes*) pigiare.
crushing ['krʌʃɪŋ] *adj* schiacciante.
crust [krʌst] *n* crosta.
crustacean [krʌs'teɪʃən] *n* crostaceo.
crusty ['krʌsti] *adj* (*bread*) croccante; (*person*) brontolone(a).
crutch [krʌtʃ] *n* (*MED*) gruccia; (*support*) sostegno; (*also:* **crotch**) pattina.
crux [krʌks] *n* nodo.
cry [kraɪ] *vi* piangere; (*shout: also:* ~ **out**) urlare ♦ *n* urlo, grido; (*of animal*) verso; **to** ~ **for help** gridare aiuto; **what are you** ~**ing about?** perché piangi?; **she had a good** ~ si è fatta un bel pianto; **it's a far** ~ **from** ... (*fig*) è tutt'un'altra cosa da ....
►**cry off** *vi* ritirarsi.
crying ['kraɪɪŋ] *adj* (*fig*) palese; urgente.
crypt [krɪpt] *n* cripta.
cryptic ['krɪptɪk] *adj* ermetico(a).
crystal ['krɪstl] *n* cristallo.
crystal-clear ['krɪstl'klɪə*] *adj* cristallino(a); (*fig*) chiaro(a) (come il sole).
crystallize ['krɪstəlaɪz] *vi* cristallizzarsi ♦ *vt* (*fig*) concretizzare, concretare; ~**d fruits** (*BRIT*) frutta candita.
CSA *n abbr* (*US*) = *Confederate States of America*; (*BRIT:* = *Child Support Agency*) *istituto a difesa dei figli di coppie separate, che si adopera affinché venga rispettato l'obbligo del mantenimento.*
CSC *n abbr* (= *Civil Service Commission*) *commissione per il reclutamento dei funzionari statali.*
CS gas *n* (*BRIT*) *tipo di gas lacrimogeno.*
CST *abbr* (*US:* = *central standard time*) *fuso orario.*
CT *abbr* (*US*) = *Connecticut.*
ct *abbr* = **cent, court.**
CTC *n abbr* (*BRIT:* = *city technology college*) *istituto tecnico superiore.*
cu. *abbr* = **cubic.**
cub [kʌb] *n* cucciolo; (*also:* ~ **scout**) lupetto.
Cuba ['kjuːbə] *n* Cuba.
Cuban ['kjuːbən] *adj, n* cubano(a).
cubbyhole ['kʌbɪhəul] *n* angolino.
cube [kjuːb] *n* cubo ♦ *vt* (*MATH*) elevare al cubo.
cube root *n* radice *f* cubica.
cubic ['kjuːbɪk] *adj* cubico(a); ~ **metre** *etc* metro *etc* cubo; ~ **capacity** (*AUT*) cilindrata.
cubicle ['kjuːbɪkl] *n* scompartimento separato; cabina.
cuckoo ['kuku:] *n* cucù *m inv.*
cuckoo clock *n* orologio a cucù.
cucumber ['kjuːkʌmbə*] *n* cetriolo.

cud [kʌd] *n:* **to chew the** ~ ruminare.
cuddle ['kʌdl] *vt* abbracciare, coccolare ♦ *vi* abbracciarsi.
cuddly ['kʌdlɪ] *adj* da coccolare.
cudgel ['kʌdʒl] *n* randello ♦ *vt:* **to** ~ **one's brains** scervellarsi, spremere le meningi.
cue [kjuː] *n* stecca; (*THEAT etc*) segnale *m.*
cuff [kʌf] *n* (*of shirt, coat etc*) polsino; (*US:* on *trousers*) = **turnup**; (*blow*) schiaffo ♦ *vt* dare uno schiaffo a; **off the** ~ *adv* improvvisando.
cufflink ['kʌflɪŋk] *n* gemello.
cu. ft. *abbr* = *cubic feet.*
cu. in. *abbr* = *cubic inches.*
cuisine [kwɪ'ziːn] *n* cucina.
cul-de-sac ['kʌldəsæk] *n* vicolo cieco.
cullnary ['kʌlɪnərɪ] *adj* culinario(a).
cull [kʌl] *vt* (*kill selectively:* animals) selezionare e abbattere.
culminate ['kʌlmɪneɪt] *vi:* **to** ~ **in** culminare con.
culmination [kʌlmɪ'neɪʃən] *n* culmine *m.*
culottes [kjuː'lɔts] *npl* gonna *f* pantalone *inv.*
culpable ['kʌlpəbl] *adj* colpevole.
culprit ['kʌlprɪt] *n* colpevole *m/f.*
cult [kʌlt] *n* culto.
cult figure *n* idolo.
cultivate ['kʌltɪveɪt] *vt* (*also fig*) coltivare.
cultivation [kʌltɪ'veɪʃən] *n* coltivazione *f.*
cultural ['kʌltʃərəl] *adj* culturale.
culture ['kʌltʃə*] *n* (*also fig*) cultura.
cultured ['kʌltʃəd] *adj* colto(a).
cumbersome ['kʌmbəsəm] *adj* ingombrante.
cumin ['kʌmɪn] *n* (*spice*) cumino.
cumulative ['kjuːmjulətɪv] *adj* cumulativo(a).
cunning ['kʌnɪŋ] *n* astuzia, furberia ♦ *adj* astuto(a), furbo(a); (*clever: device, idea*) ingegnoso(a).
cunt [kʌnt] (*col!*) *n* figa (*!*); (*insult*) stronzo/a (*!*).
cup [kʌp] *n* tazza; (*prize*) coppa; **a** ~ **of tea** una tazza di tè.
cupboard ['kʌbəd] *n* armadio.
cup final *n* (*BRIT FOOTBALL*) finale *f* di coppa.
Cupid ['kjuːpɪd] *n* Cupido; (*figurine*): **c**~ cupido.
cupidity [kjuː'pɪdɪtɪ] *n* cupidigia.
cupola ['kjuːpələ] *n* cupola.
cuppa ['kʌpə] *n* (*BRIT col*) tazza di tè.
cup-tie ['kʌptaɪ] *n* (*BRIT FOOTBALL*) partita di coppa.
curable ['kjuərəbl] *adj* curabile.
curate ['kjuərɪt] *n* cappellano.
curator [kjuə'reɪtə*] *n* direttore *m* (*di museo*

etc).

curb [kəːb] vt tenere a freno; (expenditure) limitare ◊ n freno; (US) = **kerb**.

curd cheese [kəːd-] n cagliata.

curdle ['kəːdl] vi cagliare.

curds [kəːdz] npl latte m cagliato.

cure [kjuə*] vt guarire; (CULIN) trattare; affumicare; essiccare ◊ n rimedio; **to be ~d of sth** essere guarito(a) da qc.

cure-all ['kjuərɔːl] n (also fig) panacea, toccasana m inv.

curfew ['kəːfjuː] n coprifuoco.

curio ['kjuərɪəu] n curiosità f inv.

curiosity [kjuərɪ'ɔsɪtɪ] n curiosità.

curious ['kjuərɪəs] adj curioso(a); **I'm ~ about him** m'incuriosisce.

curiously ['kjuərɪəslɪ] adv con curiosità; (strangely) stranamente; **~ enough, ...** per quanto possa sembrare strano, ...

curl [kəːl] n riccio; (of smoke etc) anello ◊ vt ondulare; (tightly) arricciare ◊ vi arricciarsi.

▶**curl up** vi avvolgersi a spirale; rannicchiarsi.

curler ['kəːlə*] n bigodino; (SPORT) giocatore/trice di curling.

curlew ['kəːluː] n chiurlo.

curling ['kəːlɪŋ] n (SPORT) curling m.

curling tongs, (US) curling irons npl (for hair) arricciacapelli m inv.

curly ['kəːlɪ] adj ricciuto(a).

currant ['kʌrnt] n uva passa.

currency ['kʌrnsɪ] n moneta; **foreign ~** divisa estera; **to gain ~** (fig) acquistare larga diffusione.

current ['kʌrnt] adj corrente; (tendency, price, event) attuale ◊ n corrente f; **in ~ use** in uso corrente, d'uso comune; **the ~ issue of a magazine** l'ultimo numero di una rivista; **direct/alternating ~** (ELEC) corrente continua/alternata.

current account n (BRIT) conto corrente.

current affairs npl attualità fpl.

current assets (COMM) attivo realizzabile e disponibile.

current liabilities npl (COMM) passività fpl correnti.

currently ['kʌrntlɪ] adv attualmente.

curriculum, pl **~s** or **curricula** [kə'rɪkjuləm, -lə] n curriculum m inv.

curriculum vitae (CV) [-'viːtaɪ] n curriculum vitae m inv.

curry ['kʌrɪ] n curry m inv ◊ vt: **to ~ favour with** cercare di attirarsi i favori di; **chicken ~** pollo al curry.

curry powder n curry m.

curse [kəːs] vt maledire ◊ vi bestemmiare ◊ n maledizione f; bestemmia.

cursor ['kəːsə*] n (COMPUT) cursore m.

cursory ['kəːsərɪ] adj superficiale.

curt [kəːt] adj secco(a).

curtail [kəː'teɪl] vt (visit etc) accorciare; (expenses etc) ridurre, decurtare.

curtain ['kəːtn] n tenda; (THEAT) sipario; **to draw the ~s** (together) chiudere or tirare le tende; (apart) aprire le tende.

curtain call n (THEAT) chinata alla ribalta.

curts(e)y ['kəːtsɪ] n inchino, riverenza ◊ vi fare un inchino or una riverenza.

curvature ['kəːvətʃə*] n curvatura.

curve [kəːv] n curva ◊ vt curvare ◊ vi curvarsi; (road) fare una curva.

curved [kəːvd] adj curvo(a).

cushion ['kuʃən] n cuscino ◊ vt (shock) fare da cuscinetto a.

cushy ['kuʃɪ] adj (col): **a ~ job** un lavoro di tutto riposo; **to have a ~ time** spassarsela.

custard ['kʌstəd] n (for pouring) crema.

custard powder n (BRIT) crema pasticcera in polvere.

custodial sentence [kʌs'təudɪəl-] n condanna a pena detentiva.

custodian [kʌs'təudɪən] n custode m/f; (of museum etc) soprintendente m/f.

custody ['kʌstədɪ] n (of child) custodia; (for offenders) arresto; **to take sb into ~** mettere qn in detenzione preventiva; **in the ~ of** alla custodia di.

custom ['kʌstəm] n costume m, usanza; (LAW) consuetudine f; (COMM) clientela; see also **customs**.

customary ['kʌstəmərɪ] adj consueto(a); **it is ~ to do** è consuetudine fare.

custom-built ['kʌstəm'bɪlt] adj see **custom-made**.

customer ['kʌstəmə*] n cliente m/f; **he's an awkward ~** (col) è un tipo incontentabile.

customer profile n profilo del cliente.

customized ['kʌstəmaɪzd] adj personalizzato(a); (car) fuoriserie inv.

custom-made ['kʌstəm'meɪd] adj (clothes) fatto(a) su misura; (other goods: also: **custom-built**) fatto(a) su ordinazione.

customs ['kʌstəmz] npl dogana; **to go through (the) ~** passare la dogana.

Customs and Excise n (BRIT) Ufficio Dazi e Dogana.

customs officer n doganiere m.

cut [kʌt] vb (pt, pp **cut**) vt tagliare; (shape, make) intagliare; (reduce) ridurre; (col: avoid: class, lecture, appointment) saltare ◊ vi tagliare; (intersect) tagliarsi ◊ n taglio; (in salary etc) riduzione f; **cold ~s** npl (US) affettati mpl; **power ~** mancanza di

corrente elettrica; **to ~ one's finger**
tagliarsi un dito; **to get one's hair ~** farsi
tagliare i capelli; **to ~ a tooth** mettere un
dente; **to ~ sb/sth short** interrompere
qn/qc; **to ~ sb dead** ignorare qn
completamente.
▶**cut back** *vt* (*plants*) tagliare; (*production,*
expenditure) ridurre.
▶**cut down** *vt* (*tree*) abbattere;
(*consumption, expenses*) ridurre; **to ~ sb**
down to size (*fig*) sgonfiare *or*
ridimensionare qn.
▶**cut down on** *vt fus* ridurre.
▶**cut in** *vi* (*interrupt conversation*): **to ~ in**
(on) intromettersi (in); (*AUT*) tagliare la
strada (a).
▶**cut off** *vt* tagliare; (*fig*) isolare; **we've**
been ~ off (*TEL*) è caduta la linea.
▶**cut out** *vt* tagliare; (*picture*) ritagliare.
▶**cut up** *vt* (*gen*) tagliare; (*chop: food*)
sminuzzare.
cut-and-dried ['kʌtən'draɪd] *adj* (*also*: **cut-**
and-dry) assodato(a).
cutback ['kʌtbæk] *n* riduzione *f*.
cute [kjuːt] *adj* grazioso(a); (*clever*)
astuto(a).
cut glass *n* cristallo.
cuticle ['kjuːtɪkl] *n* (*on nail*) pellicina,
cuticola.
cutlery ['kʌtlərɪ] *n* posate *fpl*.
cutlet ['kʌtlɪt] *n* costoletta.
cutoff ['kʌtɔf] *n* (*also*: **~ point**) limite *m*.
cutoff switch *n* interruttore *m*.
cutout ['kʌtaut] *n* (*switch*) interruttore *m*;
(*paper, cardboard figure*) ritaglio.
cut-price ['kʌt'praɪs], (*US*) **cut-rate**
['kʌt'reɪt] *adj* a prezzo ridotto.
cutthroat ['kʌtθrəut] *n* assassino ♦ *adj*: **~**
competition concorrenza spietata.
cutting ['kʌtɪŋ] *adj* tagliente; (*fig*) pungente
♦ *n* (*BRIT: PRESS*) ritaglio (di giornale);
(: *RAIL*) trincea; (*CINE*) montaggio.
cutting edge *n* (*of knife*) taglio, filo; **on** *or*
at the ~ of sth all'avanguardia di qc.
cut-up ['kʌtʌp] *adj* stravolto(a).
CV *n abbr see* **curriculum vitae.**
C & W *n abbr* = **country and western**
(music).
cwt. *abbr* = **hundredweight.**
cyanide ['saɪənaɪd] *n* cianuro.
cybercafé ['saɪbə,kæfeɪ] *n* cybercaffè *m inv*
cybernetics [saɪbə'nɛtɪks] *n* cibernetica.
cyberterrorism [saɪbə'tɛrərɪzəm] *n*
ciberterrorismo.
cyclamen ['sɪkləmən] *n* ciclamino.
cycle ['saɪkl] *n* ciclo; (*bicycle*) bicicletta ♦ *vi*
andare in bicicletta.
cycle path *n* percorso ciclabile.

cycle race *n* gara *or* corsa ciclistica.
cycle rack *n* portabiciclette *m inv*.
cycle track *n* percorso ciclabile; (*in*
velodrome) pista.
cycling ['saɪklɪŋ] *n* ciclismo; **to go on a ~**
holiday (*BRIT*) fare una vacanza in
bicicletta.
cyclist ['saɪklɪst] *n* ciclista *m/f*.
cyclone ['saɪkləun] *n* ciclone *m*.
cygnet ['sɪgnɪt] *n* cigno giovane.
cylinder ['sɪlɪndə*] *n* cilindro.
cylinder capacity *n* cilindrata.
cylinder head *n* testata.
cylinder head gasket *n* guarnizione *f*
della testata del cilindro.
cymbals ['sɪmblz] *npl* cembali *mpl*.
cynic ['sɪnɪk] *n* cinico/a.
cynical ['sɪnɪkl] *adj* cinico(a).
cynicism ['sɪnɪsɪzəm] *n* cinismo.
cypress ['saɪprɪs] *n* cipresso.
Cypriot ['sɪprɪət] *adj*, *n* cipriota (*m/f*).
Cyprus ['saɪprəs] *n* Cipro.
cyst [sɪst] *n* cisti *f inv*.
cystitis [sɪ'staɪtɪs] *n* cistite *f*.
CZ *n abbr* (*US*: = *Canal Zone*) *zona del*
Canale di Panama.
czar [zɑː*] *n* zar *m inv*.
Czech [tʃɛk] *adj* cceco(a) ♦ *n* ceco/a; (*LING*)
ceco; **the ~ Republic** la Repubblica Ceca.
Czechoslovak [tʃɛkə'sləuvæk] *adj*, *n* =
Czechoslovakian.
Czechoslovakia [tʃɛkəslə'vækɪə] *n*
Cecoslovacchia.
Czechoslovakian [tʃɛkəslə'vækɪən] *adj*, *n*
cecoslovacco(a).

D d

D, d [diː] *n* (*letter*) D, d *f or m inv*; (*MUS*): **D** re
m; **D for David**, (*US*) **D for Dog** ≈ D come
Domodossola.
D *abbr* (*US POL*) = **Democrat(ic).**
d *abbr* (*BRIT*: *old*) = **penny.**
d. *abbr* = **died.**
DA *n abbr* (*US*) *see* **district attorney.**
dab [dæb] *vt* (*eyes, wound*) tamponare;
(*paint, cream*) applicare (con leggeri
colpetti); **a ~ of paint** un colpetto di
vernice.
dabble ['dæbl] *vi*: **to ~ in** occuparsi (da
dilettante) di.

Dacca ['dækə] *n* Dacca *f*.
dachshund ['dækshund] *n* bassotto.
dad, daddy [dæd, 'dædɪ] *n* babbo, papà *m inv*.
daddy-long-legs [dædɪ'lɔŋlegz] *n* tipula, zanzarone *m*.
daffodil ['dæfədɪl] *n* trombone *m*, giunchiglia.
daft [dɑːft] *adj* sciocco(a); **to be ~ about sb** perdere la testa per qn; **to be ~ about sth** andare pazzo per qc.
dagger ['dægə*] *n* pugnale *m*.
dahlia ['deɪljə] *n* dalia.
daily ['deɪlɪ] *adj* quotidiano(a), giornaliero(a) ♦ *n* quotidiano; (*BRIT*: *servant*) donna di servizio ♦ *adv* tutti i giorni; **twice ~** due volte al giorno.
dainty ['deɪntɪ] *adj* delicato(a), grazioso(a).
dairy ['dɛərɪ] *n* (*shop*) latteria; (*on farm*) caseificio ♦ *cpd* caseario(a).
dairy cow *n* mucca da latte.
dairy farm *n* caseificio.
dairy produce *n* latticini *mpl*.
dais ['deɪɪs] *n* pedana, palco.
daisy ['deɪzɪ] *n* margherita.
daisy wheel *n* (*on printer*) margherita.
daisy-wheel printer ['deɪzɪwiːl-] *n* stampante *f* a margherita.
Dakar ['dækə*] *n* Dakar *f*.
dale [deɪl] *n* valle *f*.
dally ['dælɪ] *vi* trastullarsi.
dalmatian [dæl'meɪʃən] *n* (*dog*) dalmata *m*.
dam [dæm] *n* diga; (*reservoir*) bacino artificiale ♦ *vt* sbarrare; costruire dighe su.
damage ['dæmɪdʒ] *n* danno, danni *mpl*; (*fig*) danno ♦ *vt* danneggiare; (*fig*) recar danno a; **~ to property** danni materiali.
damages ['dæmɪdʒɪz] *npl* (*LAW*) danni *mpl*; **to pay £5000 in ~** pagare 5000 sterline di indennizzo.
damaging ['dæmɪdʒɪŋ] *adj*: **~ (to)** nocivo(a) (a).
Damascus [də'mɑːskəs] *n* Damasco *f*.
dame [deɪm] *n* (*title*, *US col*) donna; (*THEAT*) vecchia signora (*ruolo comico di donna recitato da un uomo*).
damn [dæm] *vt* condannare; (*curse*) maledire ♦ *n* (*col*): **I don't give a ~** non me ne importa un fico ♦ *adj* (*col*): **this ~...** questo maledetto ...; **~ (it)!** accidenti!
damnable ['dæmnəbl] *adj* (*col*: *behaviour*) vergognoso(a); (: *weather*) schifoso(a).
damnation [dæm'neɪʃən] *n* (*REL*) dannazione *f* ♦ *excl* (*col*) dannazione!, diavolo!
damning ['dæmɪŋ] *adj* (*evidence*) schiacciante.

damp [dæmp] *adj* umido(a) ♦ *n* umidità, umido ♦ *vt* (*also*: **~en**) (*cloth*, *rag*) inumidire, bagnare; (*enthusiasm etc*) spegnere.
dampcourse ['dæmpkɔːs] *n* strato *m* isolante antiumido *inv*.
damper ['dæmpə*] *n* (*MUS*) sordina; (*of fire*) valvola di tiraggio; **to put a ~ on sth** (*fig*: *atmosphere*) gelare; (: *enthusiasm*) far sbollire.
dampness ['dæmpnɪs] *n* umidità, umido.
damson ['dæmzən] *n* susina damaschina.
dance [dɑːns] *n* danza, ballo; (*ball*) ballo ♦ *vi* ballare; **to ~ about** saltellare.
dance hall *n* dancing *m inv*, sala da ballo.
dancer ['dɑːnsə*] *n* danzatore/trice; (*professional*) ballerino/a.
dancing ['dɑːnsɪŋ] *n* danza, ballo.
D and C *n abbr* (*MED*: = *dilation and curettage*) raschiamento.
dandelion ['dændɪlaɪən] *n* dente *m* di leone.
dandruff ['dændrəf] *n* forfora.
dandy ['dændɪ] *n* dandy *m inv*, elegantone *m* ♦ *adj* (*US col*) fantastico(a).
Dane [deɪn] *n* danese *m/f*.
danger ['deɪndʒə*] *n* pericolo; **there is a ~ of fire** c'è pericolo di incendio; **in ~** in pericolo; **out of ~** fuori pericolo; **he was in ~ of falling** rischiava di cadere.
danger list *n* (*MED*): **on the ~ list** in prognosi riservata.
dangerous ['deɪndʒrəs] *adj* pericoloso(a).
dangerously ['deɪndʒrəslɪ] *adv*: **~ ill** in pericolo di vita.
danger zone *n* area di pericolo.
dangle ['dæŋgl] *vt* dondolare; (*fig*) far balenare ♦ *vi* pendolare.
Danish ['deɪnɪʃ] *adj* danese ♦ *n* (*LING*) danese *m*.
Danish pastry *n* dolce *m* di pasta sfoglia.
dank [dæŋk] *adj* freddo(a) e umido(a).
Danube ['dænjuːb] *n*: **the ~** il Danubio.
dapper ['dæpə*] *adj* lindo(a).
Dardanelles [dɑːdə'nɛlz] *npl* Dardanelli *mpl*.
dare [dɛə*] *vt*: **to ~ sb to do** sfidare qn a fare ♦ *vi*: **to ~ (to) do sth** osare fare qc; **I ~n't tell him** (*BRIT*) non oso dirglielo; **I ~ say he'll turn up** immagino che spunterà.
daredevil ['dɛədɛvl] *n* scavezzacollo *m/f*.
Dar-es-Salaam [dɑːrɛssə'lɑːm] *n* Dar-es-Salaam *f*.
daring ['dɛərɪŋ] *adj* audace, ardito(a).
dark [dɑːk] *adj* (*night*, *room*) buio(a), scuro(a); (*colour*, *complexion*) scuro(a); (*fig*) cupo(a), tetro(a), nero(a) ♦ *n*: **in the ~** al buio; **it is/is getting ~** è/si sta facendo buio; **in the ~ about** (*fig*) all'oscuro di; **after ~** a notte fatta; **~**

chocolate cioccolata amara.
darken ['dɑːkən] *vt* (*room*) oscurare; (*photo*, *painting*) far scuro(a) ♦ *vi* oscurarsi; imbrunirsi.
dark glasses *npl* occhiali *mpl* scuri.
dark horse *n* (*fig*) incognita.
darkly ['dɑːklɪ] *adv* (*gloomily*) cupamente, con aria cupa; (*in a sinister way*) minacciosamente.
darkness ['dɑːknɪs] *n* oscurità, buio.
darkroom ['dɑːkruːm] *n* camera oscura.
darling ['dɑːlɪŋ] *adj* caro(a) ♦ *n* tesoro.
darn [dɑːn] *vt* rammendare.
dart [dɑːt] *n* freccetta ♦ *vi*: **to ~ towards** (*also*: **make a ~ towards**) precipitarsi verso; **to ~ along** passare come un razzo; **to ~ away** guizzare via; *see also* **darts**.
dartboard ['dɑːtbɔːd] *n* bersaglio (per freccette).
darts [dɑːts] *n* tiro al bersaglio (con freccette).
dash [dæʃ] *n* (*sign*) lineetta; (*small quantity*: *of liquid*) goccio, goccino; (: *of soda*) spruzzo ♦ *vt* (*missile*) gettare; (*hopes*) infrangere ♦ *vi*: **to ~ towards** (*also*: **make a ~ towards**) precipitarsi verso.
►**dash away** *vi* scappare via.
dashboard ['dæʃbɔːd] *n* cruscotto.
dashing ['dæʃɪŋ] *adj* ardito(a).
dastardly ['dæstədlɪ] *adj* vile.
DAT *n abbr* (= *digital audio tape*) cassetta *f* digitale audio *inv*.
data ['deɪtə] *npl* dati *mpl*.
database ['deɪtəbeɪs] *n* database *m*, base *f* di dati.
data capture *n* registrazione *f or* rilevazione *f* di dati.
data processing *n* elaborazione *f* (elettronica) dei dati.
data transmission *n* trasmissione *f* di dati.
date [deɪt] *n* data; (*appointment*) appuntamento; (*fruit*) dattero ♦ *vt* datare; (*col*: *girl etc*) uscire con; **what's the ~ today?** quanti ne abbiamo oggi?; **~ of birth** data di nascita; **closing ~** scadenza, termine *m*; **to ~** *adv* fino a oggi; **out of ~** scaduto(a); (*old-fashioned*) passato(a) di moda; **up to ~** moderno(a); aggiornato(a); **to bring up to ~** (*correspondence, information*) aggiornare; (*method*) modernizzare; (*person*) aggiornare, mettere al corrente; **~d the 13th** datato il 13; **thank you for your letter ~d 5th July** *or* (*US*) **July 5th** la ringrazio per la sua lettera in data 5 luglio.
dated ['deɪtɪd] *adj* passato(a) di moda.
dateline ['deɪtlaɪn] *n* linea del

cambiamento di data.
date rape *n* stupro perpetrato da persona conosciuta.
date stamp *n* timbro datario.
daub [dɔːb] *vt* imbrattare.
daughter ['dɔːtə*] *n* figlia.
daughter-in-law ['dɔːtərɪnlɔː] *n* nuora.
daunt [dɔːnt] *vt* intimidire.
daunting ['dɔːntɪŋ] *adj* non invidiabile.
dauntless ['dɔːntlɪs] *adj* intrepido(a).
dawdle ['dɔːdl] *vi* bighellonare; **to ~ over one's work** gingillarsi con il lavoro.
dawn [dɔːn] *n* alba ♦ *vi* (*day*) spuntare; (*fig*) venire in mente; **at ~** all'alba; **from ~ to dusk** dall'alba al tramonto; **it ~ed on him that ...** gli è venuto in mente che ....
dawn chorus *n* (*BRIT*) coro mattutino degli uccelli.
day [deɪ] *n* giorno; (*as duration*) giornata; (*period of time, age*) tempo, epoca; **the ~ before** il giorno avanti *or* prima; **the ~ after, the following ~** il giorno dopo, il giorno seguente; **the ~ before yesterday** l'altroieri; **the ~ after tomorrow** dopodomani; (**on**) **that ~** quel giorno; (**on**) **the ~ that ...** il giorno che *or* in cui ...; **to work an 8-hour ~** avere una giornata lavorativa di 8 ore; **by ~** di giorno; **~ by ~** giorno per giorno; **paid by the ~** pagato(a) a giornata; **these ~s, in the present ~** di questi tempi, oggigiorno.
daybook ['deɪbuk] *n* (*BRIT*) brogliaccio.
day boy *n* (*SCOL*) alunno esterno.
daybreak ['deɪbreɪk] *n* spuntar *m* del giorno.
day care centre *n* scuola materna.
daydream ['deɪdriːm] *n* sogno a occhi aperti ♦ *vi* sognare a occhi aperti.
day girl *n* (*SCOL*) alunna esterna.
daylight ['deɪlaɪt] *n* luce *f* del giorno.
daylight robbery *n*: **it's ~!** (*BRIT col*) è un vero furto!
Daylight Saving Time *n* (*US*) ora legale.
day release *n*: **to be on ~** *avere un giorno di congedo alla settimana per formazione professionale*.
day return (ticket) *n* (*BRIT*) biglietto giornaliero di andata e ritorno.
day shift *n* turno di giorno.
daytime ['deɪtaɪm] *n* giorno.
day-to-day ['deɪtə'deɪ] *adj* (*routine*) quotidiano(a); (*expenses*) giornaliero(a); **on a ~ basis** a giornata.
day trader *n* (*STOCK EXCHANGE*) day dealer *m/f inv*, *operatore che compra e vende titoli nel corso della stessa giornata*.
day trip *n* gita (di un giorno).
day tripper *n* gitante *m/f*.

daze [deɪz] vt (subj: drug) inebetire; (: blow) stordire ♦ n: in a ~ inebetito(a); stordito(a).

dazzle ['dæzl] vt abbagliare.

dazzling ['dæzlɪŋ] adj (light) abbagliante; (colour) violento(a); (smile) smagliante.

dB abbr (= decibel) db.

DC abbr (ELEC: = direct current) c.c.; (US) = District of Columbia.

DCC ® n abbr = digital compact cassette.

DD n abbr (= Doctor of Divinity) titolo di studio.

dd. abbr (COMM) = delivered.

DD abbr = direct debit.

D-day ['diːdeɪ] n giorno dello sbarco alleato in Normandia.

DDS n abbr (US: = Doctor of Dental Science; Doctor of Dental Surgery) titoli di studio.

DDT n abbr (= dichlorodiphenyl trichloroethane) D.D.T. m.

DE abbr (US) = Delaware.

deacon ['diːkən] n diacono.

dead [dɛd] adj morto(a); (numb) intirizzito(a) ♦ adv assolutamente, perfettamente; **the ~** npl i morti; **he was shot ~** fu colpito a morte; **~ on time** in perfetto orario; **~ tired** stanco(a) morto(a); **to stop ~** fermarsi in tronco; **the line has gone ~** (TEL) è caduta la linea.

dead beat adj (col) stanco(a) morto(a).

deaden ['dɛdn] vt (blow, sound) ammortire; (make numb) intirizzire.

dead end n vicolo cieco.

dead-end ['dɛdɛnd] adj: **a ~ job** un lavoro senza sbocchi.

dead heat n (SPORT): **to finish in a ~** finire alla pari.

dead-letter office [dɛd'lɛtə-] n ufficio della posta in giacenza.

deadline ['dɛdlaɪn] n scadenza; **to work to a ~** avere una scadenza.

deadlock ['dɛdlɔk] n punto morto.

dead loss n (col): **to be a ~** (person, thing) non valere niente.

deadly ['dɛdlɪ] adj mortale; (weapon, poison) micidiale ♦ adv: **~ dull** di una noia micidiale.

deadpan ['dɛdpæn] adj a faccia impassibile.

Dead Sea n: **the ~** il mar Morto.

deaf [dɛf] adj sordo(a); **to turn a ~ ear to sth** fare orecchi da mercante a qc.

deaf-aid ['dɛfeɪd] n apparecchio per la sordità.

deaf-and-dumb ['dɛfən'dʌm] adj (person) sordomuto(a); (alphabet) dei sordomuti.

deafen ['dɛfn] vt assordare.

deafening ['dɛfnɪŋ] adj fragoroso(a), assordante.

deaf-mute ['dɛfmjuːt] n sordomuto/a.

deafness ['dɛfnɪs] n sordità.

deal [diːl] n accordo; (business ~) affare m ♦ vt (pt, pp **dealt** [dɛlt]) (blow, cards) dare; **to strike a ~ with sb** fare un affare con qn; **it's a ~!** (col) affare fatto!; **he got a bad/fair ~ from them** l'hanno trattato male/bene; **a good ~ of, a great ~ of** molto(a).

▶ **deal in** vt fus (COMM) occuparsi di.

▶ **deal with** vt fus (COMM) fare affari con, trattare con; (handle) occuparsi di; (be about: book etc) trattare di.

dealer ['diːlə*] n commerciante m/f.

dealership ['diːləʃɪp] n rivenditore m.

dealings ['diːlɪŋz] npl rapporti mpl; (in goods, shares) transazioni fpl.

dealt [dɛlt] pt, pp of **deal**.

dean [diːn] n (REL) decano; (SCOL) preside m di facoltà (or di collegio).

dear [dɪə*] adj caro(a) ♦ n: **my ~** caro mio/cara mia; **~ me!** Dio mio!; **D~ Sir/Madam** (in letter) Egregio Signore/Egregia Signora; **D~ Mr/Mrs X** Gentile Signor/Signora X.

dearly ['dɪəlɪ] adv (love) moltissimo; (pay) a caro prezzo.

dear money n (COMM) denaro ad alto interesse.

dearth [dəːθ] n scarsità, carestia.

death [dɛθ] n morte f; (ADMIN) decesso.

deathbed ['dɛθbɛd] n letto di morte.

death certificate n atto di decesso.

death duty n (BRIT) imposta or tassa di successione.

deathly ['dɛθlɪ] adj di morte ♦ adv come un cadavere.

death penalty n pena di morte.

death rate n indice m di mortalità.

death row [-rəu] n (US): **to be on ~** essere nel braccio della morte.

death sentence n condanna a morte.

death squad n squadra della morte.

deathtrap ['dɛθtræp] n trappola mortale.

deb [dɛb] n abbr (col) = **debutante**.

debacle [deɪ'baːkl] n (defeat) disfatta; (collapse) sfacelo.

debar [dɪ'baː*] vt: **to ~ sb from a club** etc escludere qn da un club etc; **to ~ sb from doing** vietare a qn di fare.

debase [dɪ'beɪs] vt (currency) adulterare; (person) degradare.

debatable [dɪ'beɪtəbl] adj discutibile; **it is ~ whether ...** è in dubbio se ....

debate [dɪ'beɪt] n dibattito ♦ vt dibattere, discutere ♦ vi (consider): **to ~ whether** riflettere se.

debauchery [dɪ'bɔːtʃərɪ] *n* dissolutezza.
debenture [dɪ'bentʃə*] *n* (*COMM*) obbligazione *f*.
debilitate [dɪ'bɪlɪteɪt] *vt* debilitare.
debit ['dɛbɪt] *n* debito ♦ *vt*: **to** ~ **a sum to sb** *or* **to sb's account** addebitare una somma a qn.
debit balance *n* saldo debitore.
debit note *n* nota di addebito.
debonair [dɛbə'nɛə*] *adj* gioviale e disinvolto(a).
debrief [diː'briːf] *vt* chiamare a rapporto (a operazione ultimata).
debriefing [diː'briːfɪŋ] *n* rapporto.
debris ['dɛbriː] *n* detriti *mpl*.
debt [dɛt] *n* debito; **to be in** ~ essere indebitato(a); ~**s of £5000** debiti per 5000 sterline; **bad** ~ debito insoluto.
debt collector *n* agente *m* di recupero crediti.
debtor ['dɛtə*] *n* debitore/trice.
debug [diː'bʌg] *vt* (*COMPUT*) localizzare e rimuovere errori in.
debunk [diː'bʌŋk] *vt* (*col*: *theory*) demistificare; (: *claim*) smentire; (: *person, institution*) screditare.
debut ['deɪbjuː] *n* debutto.
debutante ['dɛbjutɑːnt] *n* debuttante *f*.
Dec. *abbr* (= *December*) dic.
decade ['dɛkeɪd] *n* decennio.
decadence ['dɛkədəns] *n* decadenza.
decadent ['dɛkədənt] *adj* decadente.
de-caff ['diːkæf] *n* (*col*) decaffeinato.
decaffeinated [dɪ'kæfɪneɪtɪd] *adj* decaffeinato(a).
decamp [dɪ'kæmp] *vi* (*col*) filarsela, levare le tende.
decant [dɪ'kænt] *vt* (*wine*) travasare.
decanter [dɪ'kæntə*] *n* caraffa.
decarbonize [diː'kɑːbənaɪz] *vt* (*AUT*) decarburare.
decathlon [dɪ'kæθlən] *n* decathlon *m*.
decay [dɪ'keɪ] *n* decadimento; imputridimento; (*fig*) rovina; (*also*: **tooth** ~) carie *f* ♦ *vi* (*rot*) imputridire; (*fig*) andare in rovina.
decease [dɪ'siːs] *n* decesso.
deceased [dɪ'siːst] *n*: **the** ~ il(la) defunto(a).
deceit [dɪ'siːt] *n* inganno.
deceitful [dɪ'siːtful] *adj* ingannevole, perfido(a).
deceive [dɪ'siːv] *vt* ingannare; **to** ~ **o.s.** illudersi, ingannarsi.
decelerate [diː'sɛləreɪt] *vt, vi* rallentare.
December [dɪ'sɛmbə*] *n* dicembre *m*; *for phrases see also* **July.**
decency ['diːsənsɪ] *n* decenza.

decent ['diːsənt] *adj* decente; **they were very** ~ **about it** si sono comportati da signori riguardo a ciò.
decently ['diːsəntlɪ] *adv* (*respectably*) decentemente, convenientemente; (*kindly*) gentilmente.
decentralization [diːsɛntrəlaɪ'zeɪʃən] *n* decentramento.
decentralize [diː'sɛntrəlaɪz] *vt* decentrare.
deception [dɪ'sɛpʃən] *n* inganno.
deceptive [dɪ'sɛptɪv] *adj* ingannevole.
decibel ['dɛsɪbɛl] *n* decibel *m inv*.
decide [dɪ'saɪd] *vt* (*person*) far prendere una decisione a; (*question, argument*) risolvere, decidere ♦ *vi* decidere, decidersi; **to** ~ **to do/that** decidere di fare/che; **to** ~ **on** decidere per; **to** ~ **against doing sth** decidere di non fare qc.
decided [dɪ'saɪdɪd] *adj* (*resolute*) deciso(a); (*clear, definite*) netto(a), chiaro(a).
decidedly [dɪ'saɪdɪdlɪ] *adv* indubbiamente, decisamente.
deciding [dɪ'saɪdɪŋ] *adj* decisivo(a).
deciduous [dɪ'sɪdjuəs] *adj* deciduo(a).
decimal ['dɛsɪməl] *adj*, *n* decimale (*m*); **to 3** ~ **places** al terzo decimale.
decimalize ['dɛsɪməlaɪz] *vt* (*BRIT*) convertire al sistema metrico decimale.
decimal point *n* ≈ virgola.
decimate ['dɛsɪmeɪt] *vt* decimare.
decipher [dɪ'saɪfə*] *vt* decifrare.
decision [dɪ'sɪʒən] *n* decisione *f*; **to make a** ~ prendere una decisione.
decisive [dɪ'saɪsɪv] *adj* (*victory, factor*) decisivo(a); (*influence*) determinante; (*manner, person*) risoluto(a), deciso(a); (*reply*) deciso(a), categorico(a).
deck [dɛk] *n* (*NAUT*) ponte *m*; (*of cards*) mazzo; (*of bus*): **top** ~ imperiale *m*; **to go up on** ~ salire in coperta; **below** ~ sotto coperta; **cassette** ~ piastra (di registrazione); **record** ~ piatto (giradischi).
deckchair ['dɛktʃɛə*] *n* sedia a sdraio.
deck hand *n* marinaio.
declaration [dɛklə'reɪʃən] *n* dichiarazione *f*.
declare [dɪ'klɛə*] *vt* dichiarare.
declassify [diː'klæsɪfaɪ] *vt* rendere accessibile al pubblico.
decline [dɪ'klaɪn] *n* (*decay*) declino; (*lessening*) ribasso ♦ *vt* declinare; rifiutare ♦ *vi* declinare; diminuire; ~ **in living standards** abbassamento del tenore di vita; **to** ~ **to do sth** rifiutar(si) di fare qc.
declutch [diː'klʌtʃ] *vi* (*BRIT*) premere la frizione.
decode [diː'kəud] *vt* decifrare.

decoder [di:'kəudə*] *n* (*COMPUT, TV*) decodificatore *m*.

decompose [di:kəm'pəuz] *vi* decomporre.

decomposition [di:kɔmpə'zɪʃən] *n* decomposizione *f*.

decompression [di:kəm'preʃən] *n* decompressione *f*.

decompression chamber *n* camera di decompressione.

decongestant [di:kən'dʒɛstənt] *n* decongestionante *m*.

decontaminate [di:kən'tæmɪneɪt] *vt* decontaminare.

decontrol [di:kən'trəul] *vt* (*trade*) liberalizzare; (*prices*) togliere il controllo governativo a.

decor ['deɪkɔ:*] *n* decorazione *f*.

decorate ['dɛkəreɪt] *vt* (*adorn, give a medal to*) decorare; (*paint and paper*) pitturare e tappezzare.

decoration [dɛkə'reɪʃən] *n* decorazione *f*.

decorative ['dɛkərətɪv] *adj* decorativo(a).

decorator ['dɛkəreɪtə*] *n* decoratore/trice.

decorum [dɪ'kɔ:rəm] *n* decoro.

decoy ['di:kɔɪ] *n* zimbello; **they used him as a ~ for the enemy** l'hanno usato come esca per il nemico.

decrease *n* ['di:kri:s] diminuzione *f* ♦ *vt, vi* [di:'kri:s] diminuire; **to be on the ~** essere in diminuzione.

decreasing [di:'kri:sɪŋ] *adj* sempre meno *inv*.

decree [dɪ'kri:] *n* decreto ♦ *vt*: **to ~ (that)** decretare (che + *sub*); **~ absolute** sentenza di divorzio definitiva; **~ nisi** [-'naɪsaɪ] sentenza provvisoria di divorzio.

decrepit [dɪ'krɛpɪt] *adj* decrepito(a); (*building*) cadente.

decry [dɪ'kraɪ] *vt* condannare, deplorare.

dedicate ['dɛdɪkeɪt] *vt* consacrare; (*book etc*) dedicare.

dedicated ['dɛdɪkeɪtɪd] *adj* coscienzioso(a); (*COMPUT*) specializzato(a), dedicato(a).

dedication [dɛdɪ'keɪʃən] *n* (*devotion*) dedizione *f*; (*in book*) dedica.

deduce [dɪ'dju:s] *vt* dedurre.

deduct [dɪ'dʌkt] *vt*: **to ~ sth (from)** dedurre qc (da); (*from wage etc*) trattenere qc (da).

deduction [dɪ'dʌkʃən] *n* (*deducting*) deduzione *f*; (*from wage etc*) trattenuta; (*deducing*) deduzione *f*, conclusione *f*.

deed [di:d] *n* azione *f*, atto; (*LAW*) atto; **~ of covenant** atto di donazione.

deem [di:m] *vt* (*formal*) giudicare, ritenere; **to ~ it wise to do** ritenere prudente fare.

deep [di:p] *adj* profondo(a) ♦ *adv*: **~ in snow** affondato(a) nella neve; **spectators stood**

20 ~ c'erano 20 file di spettatori; **knee-~ in water** in acqua fino alle ginocchia; **4 metres ~** profondo(a) 4 metri; **he took a ~ breath** fece un respiro profondo.

deepen ['di:pn] *vt* (*hole*) approfondire ♦ *vi* approfondirsi; (*darkness*) farsi più intenso(a).

deep-freeze [di:p'fri:z] *n* congelatore *m* ♦ *vt* congelare.

deep-fry ['di:p'fraɪ] *vt* friggere in olio abbondante.

deeply ['di:plɪ] *adv* profondamente; **to regret sth** ~ rammaricarsi sinceramente di qc.

deep-rooted ['di:p'ru:tɪd] *adj* (*prejudice*) profondamente radicato(a); (*affection*) profondo(a); (*habit*) inveterato(a).

deep-sea diver ['di:p'si:-] *n* palombaro.

deep-sea diving *n* immersione *f* in alto mare.

deep-sea fishing *n* pesca d'alto mare.

deep-seated ['di:p'si:tɪd] *adj* (*beliefs*) radicato(a).

deep-set ['di:psɛt] *adj* (*eyes*) infossato(a).

deep-vein thrombosis (DVT) *n* trombosi *f inv* venosa profonda.

deer [dɪə*] *n* (*pl inv*): **the** ~ i cervidi (*ZOOL*); **(red)** ~ cervo; **(fallow)** ~ daino; **(roe)** ~ capriolo.

deerskin ['dɪəskɪn] *n* pelle *f* di daino.

deerstalker ['dɪəstɔ:kə*] *n* berretto da cacciatore.

deface [dɪ'feɪs] *vt* imbrattare.

defamation [dɛfə'meɪʃən] *n* diffamazione *f*.

defamatory [dɪ'fæmətərɪ] *adj* diffamatorio(a).

default [dɪ'fɔ:lt] *vi* (*LAW*) essere contumace; (*gen*) essere inadempiente ♦ *n* (*COMPUT*: *also*: **~ value**) default *m inv*; **by ~** (*LAW*) in contumacia; (*SPORT*) per abbandono; **to ~ on a debt** non onorare un debito.

defaulter [dɪ'fɔ:ltə*] *n* (*on debt*) inadempiente *m/f*.

default option *n* (*COMPUT*) opzione *f* di default.

defeat [dɪ'fi:t] *n* sconfitta ♦ *vt* (*team, opponents*) sconfiggere; (*fig*: *plans, efforts*) frustrare.

defeatism [dɪ'fi:tɪzəm] *n* disfattismo.

defeatist [dɪ'fi:tɪst] *adj, n* disfattista (*m/f*).

defecate ['dɛfəkeɪt] *vi* defecare.

defect *n* ['di:fɛkt] difetto ♦ *vi* [dɪ'fɛkt]: **to ~ to the enemy/the West** passare al nemico/all'Ovest; **physical ~** difetto fisico; **mental ~** anomalia mentale.

defective [dɪ'fɛktɪv] *adj* difettoso(a).

defector [dɪ'fɛktə*] *n* rifugiato(a)

politico(a).

defence, (*US*) **defense** [dɪ'fɛns] *n* difesa; **in** ~ **of** in difesa di; **the Ministry of D**~, (*US*) **the Department of Defense** il Ministero della Difesa; **witness for the** ~ teste *m/f* a difesa.

defenceless [dɪ'fɛnslɪs] *adj* senza difesa.

defend [dɪ'fɛnd] *vt* difendere; (*decision, action*) giustificare; (*opinion*) sostenere.

defendant [dɪ'fɛndənt] *n* imputato/a.

defender [dɪ'fɛndə*] *n* difensore/a.

defending champion *n* (*SPORT*) campione/essa in carica.

defending counsel *n* (*LAW*) avvocato difensore.

defense [dɪ'fɛns] *n* (*US*) = **defence.**

defensive [dɪ'fɛnsɪv] *adj* **difensivo(a)** ♦ *n* difensiva; **on the** ~ sulla difensiva.

defer [dɪ'fə:*] *vt* (*postpone*) differire, rinviare ♦ *vi* (*submit*): **to** ~ **to sb/sth** rimettersi a qn/qc.

deference ['dɛfərəns] *n* deferenza; riguardo; **out of** *or* **in** ~ **to** per riguardo a.

defiance [dɪ'faɪəns] *n* sfida; **in** ~ **of** a dispetto di.

defiant [dɪ'faɪənt] *adj* (*attitude*) di sfida; (*person*) ribelle.

defiantly [dɪ'faɪəntlɪ] *adv* con aria di sfida.

deficiency [dɪ'fɪʃənsɪ] *n* deficienza; carenza; (*COMM*) ammanco.

deficiency disease *n* malattia da carenza.

deficient [dɪ'fɪʃənt] *adj* deficiente; insufficiente; **to be** ~ **in** mancare di.

deficit ['dɛfɪsɪt] *n* disavanzo.

defile *vb* [dɪ'faɪl] *vt* contaminare ♦ *vi* sfilare ♦ *n* ['di:faɪl] gola, stretta.

define [dɪ'faɪn] *vt* (*gen, COMPUT*) definire.

definite ['dɛfɪnɪt] *adj* (*fixed*) definito(a), preciso(a); (*clear, obvious*) ben definito(a), esatto(a); (*LING*) determinativo(a); **he was** ~ **about it** ne era sicuro.

definitely ['dɛfɪnɪtlɪ] *adv* indubbiamente.

definition [dɛfɪ'nɪʃən] *n* definizione *f.*

definitive [dɪ'fɪnɪtɪv] *adj* definitivo(a).

deflate [di:'fleɪt] *vt* sgonfiare; (*ECON*) deflazionare; (*pompous person*) fare abbassare la cresta a.

deflation [di:'fleɪʃən] *n* (*ECON*) deflazione *f.*

deflationary [di:'fleɪʃənrɪ] *adj* (*ECON*) deflazionistico(a).

deflect [dɪ'flɛkt] *vt* deflettere, deviare.

defog ['di:'fɔg] *vt* (*US AUT*) sbrinare.

defogger ['di:'fɔgə*] *n* (*US AUT*) sbrinatore *m.*

deform [dɪ'fɔ:m] *vt* deformare.

deformed [dɪ'fɔ:md] *adj* deforme.

deformity [dɪ'fɔ:mɪtɪ] *n* deformità *f inv.*

Defra *n abbr* (*BRIT*): = *Department for*

Environment, Food and Rural Affairs.

defraud [dɪ'frɔ:d] *vt*: **to** ~ **(of)** defraudare (di).

defray [dɪ'freɪ] *vt*: **to** ~ **sb's expenses** sostenere le spese di qn.

defrost [di:'frɔst] *vt* (*fridge*) disgelare; (*frozen food*) scongelare.

deft [dɛft] *adj* svelto(a), destro(a).

defunct [dɪ'fʌŋkt] *adj* defunto(a).

defuse [di:'fju:z] *vt* disinnescare; (*fig*) distendere.

defy [dɪ'faɪ] *vt* sfidare; (*efforts etc*) resistere a; (*refuse to obey: person*) rifiutare di obbedire a.

degenerate *vi* [dɪ'dʒɛnəreɪt] degenerare ♦ *adj* [dɪ'dʒɛnərɪt] degenere.

degradation [dɛgrə'deɪʃən] *n* degradazione *f.*

degrade [dɪ'greɪd] *vt* degradare.

degrading [dɪ'greɪdɪŋ] *adj* degradante.

degree [dɪ'gri:] *n* grado; (*SCOL*) laurea (universitaria); **10** ~**s below freezing** 10 gradi sotto zero; **a** (**first**) ~ **in maths** una laurea in matematica; **a considerable** ~ **of risk** una grossa percentuale di rischio; **by** ~**s** (*gradually*) gradualmente, a poco a poco; **to some** ~, **to a certain** ~ fino a un certo punto, in certa misura.

dehydrated [di:haɪ'dreɪtɪd] *adj* disidratato(a); (*milk, eggs*) in polvere.

dehydration [di:haɪ'dreɪʃən] *n* disidratazione *f.*

de-ice [di:'aɪs] *vt* (*windscreen*) disgelare.

de-icer ['di:aɪsə*] *n* sbrinatore *m.*

deign [deɪn] *vi*: **to** ~ **to do** degnarsi di fare.

deity ['di:ɪtɪ] *n* divinità *f inv*; dio/dea.

déjà vu [deɪʒɑ:'vu:] *n* déjà vu *m inv.*

dejected [dɪ'dʒɛktɪd] *adj* abbattuto(a), avvilito(a).

dejection [dɪ'dʒɛkʃən] *n* abbattimento, avvilimento.

Del. *abbr* (*US*) = *Delaware.*

delay [dɪ'leɪ] *vt* (*journey, operation*) ritardare, rinviare; (*travellers, trains*) ritardare; (*payment*) differire ♦ *n* ritardo; **without** ~ senza ritardo.

delayed-action [dɪ'leɪd'ækʃən] *adj* a azione ritardata.

delectable [dɪ'lɛktəbl] *adj* delizioso(a).

delegate *n* ['dɛlɪgɪt] delegato/a ♦ *vt* ['dɛlɪgeɪt] delegare; **to** ~ **sth to sb/sb to do sth** delegare qc a qn/qn a fare qc.

delegation [dɛlɪ'geɪʃən] *n* delegazione *f*; (*of work etc*) delega.

delete [dɪ'li:t] *vt* (*gen, COMPUT*) cancellare.

Delhi ['dɛlɪ] *n* Delhi *f.*

deli ['dɛlɪ] *n* = **delicatessen.**

deliberate *adj* [dɪ'lɪbərɪt] (*intentional*)

intenzionale; (*slow*) misurato(a) ♦ *vi*
[dɪ'lɪbəreɪt] deliberare, riflettere.
deliberately [dɪ'lɪbərɪtlɪ] *adv* (*on purpose*)
deliberatamente.
deliberation [dɪlɪbə'reɪʃən] *n* (*consideration*)
riflessione *f*; (*discussion*) discussione *f*,
deliberazione *f*.
delicacy ['dɛlɪkəsɪ] *n* delicatezza.
delicate ['dɛlɪkɪt] *adj* delicato(a).
delicately ['dɛlɪkɪtlɪ] *adv* (*gen*)
delicatamente; (*act, express*) con
delicatezza.
delicatessen [dɛlɪkə'tesn] *n* ≈ salumeria.
delicious [dɪ'lɪʃəs] *adj* delizioso(a),
squisito(a).
delight [dɪ'laɪt] *n* delizia, gran piacere *m*
♦ *vt* dilettare; **it is a ~ to the eyes** è un
piacere guardarlo; **to take ~ in** divertirsi
a; **to be the ~ of** essere la gioia di.
delighted [dɪ'laɪtɪd] *adj*: **~ (at** *or* **with sth)**
contentissimo(a) (di qc), felice (di qc); **to
be ~ to do sth/that** essere felice di fare
qc/che + *sub*; **I'd be ~** con grande piacere.
delightful [dɪ'laɪtful] *adj* (*person, place,
meal*) delizioso(a); (*smile, manner*)
incantevole.
delimit [diː'lɪmɪt] *vt* delimitare.
delineate [dɪ'lɪnɪeɪt] *vt* delineare.
delinquency [dɪ'lɪŋkwənsɪ] *n* delinquenza.
delinquent [dɪ'lɪŋkwənt] *adj, n* delinquente
(*m/f*).
delirious [dɪ'lɪrɪəs] *adj* (*MED, fig*) delirante,
in delirio; **to be ~** delirare; (*fig*)
farneticare.
delirium [dɪ'lɪrɪəm] *n* delirio.
deliver [dɪ'lɪvə*] *vt* (*mail*) distribuire;
(*goods*) consegnare; (*speech*)
pronunciare; (*free*) liberare; (*MED*) far
partorire; **to ~ a message** fare
un'ambasciata; **to ~ the goods** (*fig*)
partorire.
deliverance [dɪ'lɪvrəns] *n* liberazione *f*.
delivery [dɪ'lɪvərɪ] *n* distribuzione *f*;
consegna; (*of speaker*) dizione *f*; (*MED*)
parto; **to take ~ of** prendere in consegna.
delivery note *n* bolla di consegna.
delivery van, (*US*) **delivery truck** *n*
furgoncino (per le consegne).
delta ['dɛltə] *n* delta *m*.
delude [dɪ'luːd] *vt* deludere, illudere.
deluge ['dɛljuːdʒ] *n* diluvio ♦ *vt* (*fig*): **to ~
(with)** subissare (di), inondare (di).
delusion [dɪ'luːʒən] *n* illusione *f*.
de luxe [də'lʌks] *adj* di lusso.
delve [dɛlv] *vi*: **to ~ into** frugare in;
(*subject*) far ricerche in.
Dem. *abbr* (*US POL*) = **Democrat(ic)**.
demagogue ['dɛməgɔg] *n* demagogo.

demand [dɪ'mɑːnd] *vt* richiedere ♦ *n*
richiesta; (*ECON*) domanda; **to ~ sth (from**
or **of sb)** pretendere qc (da qn), esigere
qc (da qn); **in ~** ricercato(a), richiesto(a);
on ~ a richiesta.
demand draft *n* (*COMM*) tratta a vista.
demanding [dɪ'mɑːndɪŋ] *adj* (*boss*)
esigente; (*work*) impegnativo(a).
demarcation [diːmɑː'keɪʃən] *n*
demarcazione *f*.
demarcation dispute *n* (*INDUSTRY*)
controversia settoriale (*or* di categoria).
demean [dɪ'miːn] *vt*: **to ~ o.s.** umiliarsi.
demeanour, (*US*) **demeanor** [dɪ'miːnə*] *n*
comportamento; contegno.
demented [dɪ'mɛntɪd] *adj* demente,
impazzito(a).
demilitarized zone [diː'mɪlɪtəraɪzd-] *n* zona
smilitarizzata.
demise [dɪ'maɪz] *n* decesso.
demist [diː'mɪst] *vt* (*BRIT AUT*) sbrinare.
demister [diː'mɪstə*] *n* (*BRIT AUT*)
sbrinatore *m*.
demo ['dɛməu] *n abbr* (*col*) =
demonstration.
demobilize [diː'məubɪlaɪz] *vt* smobilitare.
democracy [dɪ'mɔkrəsɪ] *n* democrazia.
democrat ['dɛməkræt] *n* democratico/a.
democratic [dɛmə'krætɪk] *adj*
democratico(a); **the D~ Party** (*US*) il
partito democratico.
demography [dɪ'mɔgrəfɪ] *n* demografia.
demolish [dɪ'mɔlɪʃ] *vt* demolire.
demolition [dɛmə'lɪʃən] *n* demolizione *f*.
demon ['diːmən] *n* (*also fig*) demonio ♦ *cpd*:
a ~ squash player un mago dello squash;
a ~ driver un guidatore folle.
demonstrate ['dɛmənstreɪt] *vt* dimostrare,
provare ♦ *vi*: **to ~ (for/against)**
dimostrare (per/contro), manifestare
(per/contro).
demonstration [dɛmən'streɪʃən] *n*
dimostrazione *f*; (*POL*) manifestazione *f*,
dimostrazione; **to hold a ~** (*POL*) tenere
una manifestazione, fare una
dimostrazione.
demonstrative [dɪ'mɔnstrətɪv] *adj*
dimostrativo(a).
demonstrator ['dɛmənstreɪtə*] *n* (*POL*)
dimostrante *m/f*; (*COMM: sales person*)
dimostratore/trice; (: *car, computer etc*)
modello per dimostrazione.
demoralize [dɪ'mɔrəlaɪz] *vt* demoralizzare.
demote [dɪ'məut] *vt* far retrocedere.
demotion [dɪ'məuʃən] *n* retrocessione *f*,
degradazione *f*.
demur [dɪ'məː*] *vi* (*formal*): **to ~ (at)**
sollevare obiezioni (a *or* su) ♦ *n*: **without**

~ senza obiezioni.
demure [dɪ'mjuə*] *adj* contegnoso(a).
demurrage [dɪ'mʌrɪdʒ] *n* diritti *mpl* di immagazzinaggio; spese *fpl* di controstallia.
den [dɛn] *n* tana, covo.
denationalization ['diːnæʃnəlaɪ'zeɪʃən] *n* denazionalizzazione *f*.
denationalize [diː'næʃnəlaɪz] *vt* snazionalizzare.
denial [dɪ'naɪəl] *n* diniego; rifiuto.
denier ['dɛnɪə*] *n* denaro (*di filati, calze*).
denigrate ['dɛnɪgreɪt] *vt* denigrare.
denim ['dɛnɪm] *n* tessuto di cotone ritorto; *see also* **denims**.
denim jacket *n* giubbotto di jeans.
denims ['dɛnɪmz] *npl* blue jeans *mpl*.
denizen ['dɛnɪzən] *n* (*inhabitant*) abitante *m/f*; (*foreigner*) straniero(a) naturalizzato(a).
Denmark ['dɛnmaːk] *n* Danimarca.
denomination [dɪnɔmɪ'neɪʃən] *n* (*money*) valore *m*; (*REL*) confessione *f*.
denominator [dɪ'nɔmɪneɪtə*] *n* denominatore *m*.
denote [dɪ'nəut] *vt* denotare.
denounce [dɪ'nauns] *vt* denunciare.
dense [dɛns] *adj* fitto(a); (*stupid*) ottuso(a), duro(a).
densely ['dɛnslɪ] *adv*: ~ **wooded** fittamente boscoso(a); ~ **populated** densamente popolato(a).
density ['dɛnsɪtɪ] *n* densità *f inv*; **single/ double** ~ **disk** (*COMPUT*) disco a singola/ doppia densità di registrazione.
dent [dɛnt] *n* ammaccatura ♦ *vt* (*also*: **make a** ~ **in**) ammaccare; (*fig*) intaccare.
dental ['dɛntl] *adj* dentale.
dental floss [-flɔs] *n* filo interdentale.
dental surgeon *n* medico/a dentista.
dentist ['dɛntɪst] *n* dentista *m/f*; ~**'s surgery** (*BRIT*) gabinetto dentistico.
dentistry ['dɛntɪstrɪ] *n* odontoiatria.
denture(s) ['dɛntʃə(z)] *n(pl)* dentiera.
denunciation [dɪnʌnsɪ'eɪʃən] *n* denuncia.
deny [dɪ'naɪ] *vt* negare; (*refuse*) rifiutare; **he denies having said it** nega di averlo detto.
deodorant [diː'əudərənt] *n* deodorante *m*.
depart [dɪ'paːt] *vi* partire; **to** ~ **from** (*leave*) allontanarsi da, partire da; (*fig*) deviare da.
departed [dɪ'paːtɪd] *adj* estinto(a) ♦ *n*: **the** ~ il caro estinto/la cara estinta.
department [dɪ'paːtmənt] *n* (*COMM*) reparto; (*SCOL*) sezione *f*, dipartimento; (*POL*) ministero; **that's not my** ~ (*also fig*) questo non è di mia competenza; **D**~ **of State** (*US*) Dipartimento di Stato.

departmental [diːpaːt'mɛntl] *adj* (*dispute*) settoriale; (*meeting*) di sezione; ~ **manager** caporeparto *m/f*.
department store *n* grande magazzino.
departure [dɪ'paːtʃə*] *n* partenza; (*fig*): ~ **from** deviazione *f* da; **a new** ~ una novità.
departure lounge *n* sala d'attesa.
depend [dɪ'pɛnd] *vi*: **to** ~ (**up**)**on** dipendere da; (*rely on*) contare su; (*be dependent on*) dipendere (economicamente) da, essere a carico di; **it** ~**s** dipende; ~**ing on the result** ... a seconda del risultato ....
dependable [dɪ'pɛndəbl] *adj* fidato(a); (*car etc*) affidabile.
dependant [dɪ'pɛndənt] *n* persona a carico.
dependence [dɪ'pɛndəns] *n* dipendenza.
dependent [dɪ'pɛndənt] *adj*: **to be** ~ (**on**) (*gen*) dipendere (da); (*child, relative*) essere a carico (di) ♦ *n* = **dependant**.
depict [dɪ'pɪkt] *vt* (*in picture*) dipingere; (*in words*) descrivere.
depilatory [dɪ'pɪlətrɪ] *n* (*also*: ~ **cream**) crema depilatoria.
depleted [dɪ'pliːtɪd] *adj* diminuito(a).
deplorable [dɪ'plɔːrəbl] *adj* deplorevole, lamentevole.
deplore [dɪ'plɔː*] *vt* deplorare.
deploy [dɪ'plɔɪ] *vt* dispiegare.
depopulate [diː'pɔpjuleɪt] *vt* spopolare.
depopulation ['diːpɔpju'leɪʃən] *n* spopolamento.
deport [dɪ'pɔːt] *vt* deportare; espellere.
deportation [diːpɔː'teɪʃən] *n* deportazione *f*.
deportation order *n* foglio di via obbligatorio.
deportee [diːpɔː'tiː] *n* deportato/a.
deportment [dɪ'pɔːtmənt] *n* portamento.
depose [dɪ'pəuz] *vt* deporre.
deposit [dɪ'pɔzɪt] *n* (*COMM, GEO*) deposito; (*of ore, oil*) giacimento; (*CHEM*) sedimento; (*part payment*) acconto; (*for hired goods etc*) cauzione *f* ♦ *vt* depositare; dare in acconto; (*luggage etc*) mettere *or* lasciare in deposito; **to put down a** ~ **of £50** versare una caparra di 50 sterline.
deposit account *n* conto vincolato.
depositor [dɪ'pɔzɪtə*] *n* depositante *m/f*.
depository [dɪ'pɔzɪtərɪ] *n* (*person*) depositario/a; (*place*) deposito.
depot ['dɛpəu] *n* deposito.
depraved [dɪ'preɪvd] *adj* depravato(a).
depravity [dɪ'prævɪtɪ] *n* depravazione *f*.
deprecate ['dɛprɪkeɪt] *vt* deprecare.
deprecating ['dɛprɪkeɪtɪŋ] *adj* (*disapproving*) di biasimo; (*apologetic*): **a** ~ **smile** un sorriso di scusa.
depreciate [dɪ'priːʃɪeɪt] *vt* svalutare ♦ *vi*

svalutarsi.
depreciation [dɪpriːʃɪ'eɪʃən] *n* svalutazione *f.*
depress [dɪ'prɛs] *vt* deprimere; (*press down*) premere.
depressant [dɪ'prɛsnt] *n* (*MED*) sedativo.
depressed [dɪ'prɛst] *adj* (*person*) depresso(a), abbattuto(a); (*area*) depresso(a); (*COMM: market, trade*) stagnante, in ribasso; **to get ~** deprimersi.
depressing [dɪ'prɛsɪŋ] *adj* deprimente.
depression [dɪ'prɛʃən] *n* depressione *f.*
deprivation [dɛprɪ'veɪʃən] *n* privazione *f*; (*state*) indigenza; (*PSYCH*) carenza affettiva.
deprive [dɪ'praɪv] *vt*: **to ~ sb of** privare qn di.
deprived [dɪ'praɪvd] *adj* disgraziato(a).
dept. *abbr* = **department.**
depth [dɛpθ] *n* profondità *f inv*; **at a ~ of 3 metres** a una profondità di 3 metri, a 3 metri di profondità; **in the ~s of** nel profondo di; nel cuore di; **in the ~s of winter** in pieno inverno; **to study sth in ~** studiare qc in profondità; **to be out of one's ~** (*BRIT: swimmer*) essere dove non si tocca; (*fig*) non sentirsi all'altezza della situazione.
depth charge *n* carica di profondità.
deputation [dɛpju'teɪʃən] *n* deputazione *f*, delegazione *f.*
deputize ['dɛpjutaɪz] *vi*: **to ~ for** svolgere le funzioni di.
deputy ['dɛpjutɪ] *n* (*replacement*) supplente *m/f*; (*second in command*) vice *m/f* ♦ *cpd*: **~ chairman** vicepresidente *m*; **~ head** (*SCOL*) vicepreside *m/f*; **~ leader** (*BRIT POL*) sottosegretario.
derail [dɪ'reɪl] *vt* far deragliare; **to be ~ed** deragliare.
derailment [dɪ'reɪlmənt] *n* deragliamento.
deranged [dɪ'reɪndʒd] *adj*: **to be (mentally) ~** essere pazzo(a).
derby ['dəːbɪ] *n* (*US*) bombetta.
deregulate [diː'rɛgjuleɪt] *vt* eliminare la regolamentazione di.
deregulation ['diːrɛgju'leɪʃən] *n* eliminazione *f* della regolamentazione.
derelict ['dɛrɪlɪkt] *adj* abbandonato(a).
deride [dɪ'raɪd] *vt* deridere.
derision [dɪ'rɪʒən] *n* derisione *f.*
derisive [dɪ'raɪsɪv] *adj* di derisione.
derisory [dɪ'raɪsərɪ] *adj* (*sum*) irrisorio(a).
derivation [dɛrɪ'veɪʃən] *n* derivazione *f.*
derivative [dɪ'rɪvətɪv] *n* derivato ♦ *adj* derivato(a).
derive [dɪ'raɪv] *vt*: **to ~ sth from** derivare

qc da; trarre qc da ♦ *vi*: **to ~ from** derivare da.
dermatitis [dəːmə'taɪtɪs] *n* dermatite *f.*
dermatology [dəːmə'tɔlədʒɪ] *n* dermatologia.
derogatory [dɪ'rɔgətərɪ] *adj* denigratorio(a).
derrick ['dɛrɪk] *n* gru *f inv*; (*for oil*) derrick *m inv.*
derv [dəːv] *n* (*BRIT*) gasolio.
desalination [diːsælɪ'neɪʃən] *n* desalinizzazione *f*, dissalazione *f.*
descend [dɪ'sɛnd] *vt, vi* discendere, scendere; **to ~ from** discendere da; **in ~ing order of importance** in ordine decrescente d'importanza.
▶**descend on** *vt fus* (*subj: enemy, angry person*) assalire, piombare su; (: *misfortune*) arrivare addosso a; (: *fig: gloom, silence*) scendere su; **visitors ~ed (up)on us** ci sono arrivate visite tra capo e collo.
descendant [dɪ'sɛndənt] *n* discendente *m/f.*
descent [dɪ'sɛnt] *n* discesa; (*origin*) discendenza, famiglia.
describe [dɪs'kraɪb] *vt* descrivere.
description [dɪs'krɪpʃən] *n* descrizione *f*; (*sort*) genere *m*, specie *f*; **of every ~** di ogni genere e specie.
descriptive [dɪs'krɪptɪv] *adj* descrittivo(a).
desecrate ['dɛsɪkreɪt] *vt* profanare.
desert *n* ['dɛzət] deserto ♦ *vb* [dɪ'zəːt] *vt* lasciare, abbandonare ♦ *vi* (*MIL*) disertare; *see also* **deserts.**
deserter [dɪ'zəːtə*] *n* disertore *m.*
desertion [dɪ'zəːʃən] *n* diserzione *f.*
desert island *n* isola deserta.
deserts [dɪ'zəːts] *npl*: **to get one's just ~** avere ciò che si merita.
deserve [dɪ'zəːv] *vt* meritare.
deservedly [dɪ'zəːvɪdlɪ] *adv* meritatamente, giustamente.
deserving [dɪ'zəːvɪŋ] *adj* (*person*) meritevole, degno(a); (*cause*) meritorio(a).
desiccated ['dɛsɪkeɪtɪd] *adj* essiccato(a).
design [dɪ'zaɪn] *n* (*sketch*) disegno; (: *of dress, car*) modello; (*layout, shape*) linea; (*pattern*) fantasia; (*COMM*) disegno tecnico; (*intention*) intenzione *f* ♦ *vt* disegnare; progettare; **to have ~s on** aver mire su; **well-~ed** ben concepito(a); **industrial ~** disegno industriale.
designate *vt* ['dɛzɪgneɪt] designare ♦ *adj* ['dɛzɪgnɪt] designato(a).
designation [dɛzɪg'neɪʃən] *n* designazione *f.*
designer [dɪ'zaɪnə*] *n* (*TECH*) disegnatore/

trice, progettista *m/f;* (*of furniture*) **designer** *m/f inv;* (*fashion* ~) disegnatore/ trice di moda; (*of theatre sets*) scenografo/a.
designer baby *n* bambino progettato geneticamente prima della nascita.
desirability [dɪzaɪərə'bɪlɪtɪ] *n* desiderabilità; vantaggio.
desirable [dɪ'zaɪərəbl] *adj* desiderabile; **it is ~ that** è opportuno che + *sub.*
desire [dɪ'zaɪə*] *n* desiderio, voglia ♦ *vt* desiderare, volere; **to ~ sth/to do sth/ that** desiderare qc/di fare qc/che + *sub.*
desirous [dɪ'zaɪərəs] *adj:* ~ **of** desideroso(a) di.
desk [dɛsk] *n* (*in office*) scrivania; (*for pupil*) banco; (*BRIT: in shop, restaurant*) cassa; (*in hotel*) ricevimento; (*at airport*) accettazione *f.*
desk job *n* lavoro d'ufficio.
desktop computer ['dɛsktɔp-] *n* personal *m inv*, personal computer *m inv.*
desktop publishing *n* desktop publishing *m.*
desolate ['dɛsəlɪt] *adj* desolato(a).
desolation [dɛsə'leɪʃən] *n* desolazione *f.*
despair [dɪs'pɛə*] *n* disperazione *f* ♦ *vi:* **to ~ of** disperare di; **in ~** disperato(a).
despatch [dɪs'pætʃ] *n, vt* = **dispatch.**
desperate ['dɛspərɪt] *adj* disperato(a); (*measures*) estremo(a); (*fugitive*) capace di tutto; **we are getting ~** siamo sull'orlo della disperazione.
desperately ['dɛspərɪtlɪ] *adv* disperatamente; (*very*) terribilmente, estremamente; ~ **ill** in pericolo di vita.
desperation [dɛspə'reɪʃən] *n* disperazione *f;* **in ~** per disperazione.
despicable [dɪs'pɪkəbl] *adj* disprezzabile.
despise [dɪs'paɪz] *vt* disprezzare, sdegnare.
despite [dɪs'paɪt] *prep* malgrado, a dispetto di, nonostante.
despondent [dɪs'pɔndənt] *adj* abbattuto(a), scoraggiato(a).
despot ['dɛspɔt] *n* despota *m.*
dessert [dɪ'zɔːt] *n* dolce *m;* frutta.
dessertspoon [dɪ'zɔːtspuːn] *n* cucchiaio da dolci.
destabilize [diː'steɪbɪlaɪz] *vt* privare di stabilità; (*fig*) destabilizzare.
destination [dɛstɪ'neɪʃən] *n* destinazione *f.*
destine ['dɛstɪn] *vt* destinare.
destined ['dɛstɪnd] *adj:* **to be ~ to do sth** essere destinato(a) a fare qc; ~ **for London** diretto a Londra, con destinazione Londra.
destiny ['dɛstɪnɪ] *n* destino.
destitute ['dɛstɪtjuːt] *adj* indigente,

bisognoso(a); ~ **of** privo(a) di.
destroy [dɪs'trɔɪ] *vt* distruggere.
destroyer [dɪs'trɔɪə*] *n* (*NAUT*) cacciatorpediniere *m.*
destruction [dɪs'trʌkʃən] *n* distruzione *f.*
destructive [dɪs'trʌktɪv] *adj* distruttivo(a).
desultory ['dɛsəltərɪ] *adj* (*reading*) disordinato(a); (*conversation*) sconnesso(a); (*contact*) saltuario(a), irregolare.
detach [dɪ'tætʃ] *vt* staccare, distaccare.
detachable [dɪ'tætʃəbl] *adj* staccabile.
detached [dɪ'tætʃt] *adj* (*attitude*) distante.
detached house *n* villa.
detachment [dɪ'tætʃmənt] *n* (*MIL*) distaccamento; (*fig*) distacco.
detail ['diːteɪl] *n* particolare *m*, dettaglio; (*MIL*) piccolo distaccamento ♦ *vt* dettagliare, particolareggiare; (*MIL*): **to ~ sb (for)** assegnare qn (a); **in ~** nei particolari; **to go into ~(s)** scendere nei particolari.
detailed ['diːteɪld] *adj* particolareggiato(a).
detain [dɪ'teɪn] *vt* trattenere; (*in captivity*) detenere.
detainee [diːteɪ'niː] *n* detenuto/a.
detect [dɪ'tɛkt] *vt* scoprire, scorgere; (*MED, POLICE, RADAR etc*) individuare.
detection [dɪ'tɛkʃən] *n* scoperta; individuazione *f;* **crime** ~ indagini *fpl* criminali; **to escape** ~ (*criminal*) eludere le ricerche; (*mistake*) passare inosservato(a).
detective [dɪ'tɛktɪv] *n* investigatore/trice; **private** ~ investigatore *m* privato.
detective story *n* giallo.
detector [dɪ'tɛktə*] *n* rivelatore *m.*
détente [deɪ'tɑːnt] *n* distensione *f.*
detention [dɪ'tɛnʃən] *n* detenzione *f;* (*SCOL*) permanenza forzata per punizione.
deter [dɪ'tɔː*] *vt* dissuadere.
detergent [dɪ'tɔːdʒənt] *n* detersivo.
deteriorate [dɪ'tɪərɪəreɪt] *vi* deteriorarsi.
deterioration [dɪtɪərɪə'reɪʃən] *n* deterioramento.
determination [dɪtɔːmɪ'neɪʃən] *n* determinazione *f.*
determine [dɪ'tɔːmɪn] *vt* determinare; **to ~ to do sth** decidere di fare qc.
determined [dɪ'tɔːmɪnd] *adj* (*person*) risoluto(a), deciso(a); **to be ~ to do sth** essere determinato *or* deciso a fare qc; **a ~ effort** uno sforzo di volontà.
deterrence [dɪ'tɛrəns] *n* deterrenza.
deterrent [dɪ'tɛrənt] *n* deterrente *m;* **to act as a ~** fungere da deterrente.
detest [dɪ'tɛst] *vt* detestare.
detestable [dɪ'tɛstəbl] *adj* detestabile,

abominevole.
detonate ['dɛtəneɪt] *vi* detonare ♦ *vt* far
detonare.
detonator ['dɛtəneɪtə*] *n* detonatore *m*.
detour ['diːtuə*] *n* deviazione *f*.
detract [dɪ'trækt] *vt*: **to ~ from** detrarre da.
detractor [dɪ'træktə*] *n* detrattore/trice.
detriment ['dɛtrɪmənt] *n*: **to the ~ of** a
detrimento di; **without ~ to** senza danno
a.
detrimental [dɛtrɪ'mɛntl] *adj*: **~ to**
dannoso(a) a, nocivo(a) a.
deuce [djuːs] *n* (*TENNIS*) quaranta pari *m*
inv.
devaluation [diːvæljuˈeɪʃən] *n* svalutazione
f.
devalue ['diːˈvæljuː] *vt* svalutare.
devastate ['dɛvəsteɪt] *vt* devastare; **he was**
~d by the news la notizia fu per lui un
colpo terribile.
devastating ['dɛvəsteɪtɪŋ] *adj*
devastatore(trice).
devastation [dɛvəˈsteɪʃən] *n* devastazione
f.
develop [dɪ'vɛləp] *vt* sviluppare; (*habit*)
prendere (gradualmente) ♦ *vi*
svilupparsi; (*facts, symptoms: appear*)
manifestarsi, rivelarsi; **to ~ a taste for**
sth imparare a gustare qc; **to ~ into**
diventare.
developer [dɪ'vɛləpə*] *n* (*PHOT*)
sviluppatore *m*; **property ~** costruttore *m*
(edile).
developing country [dɪ'vɛləpɪŋ-] *n* paese
m in via di sviluppo.
development [dɪ'vɛləpmənt] *n* sviluppo.
development area *n* area di sviluppo
industriale.
deviant ['diːvɪənt] *adj* deviante.
deviate ['diːvɪeɪt] *vi*: **to ~ (from)** deviare
(da).
deviation [diːvɪ'eɪʃən] *n* deviazione *f*.
device [dɪ'vaɪs] *n* (*apparatus*) congegno;
(*explosive ~*) ordigno esplosivo.
devil ['dɛvl] *n* diavolo; demonio.
devilish ['dɛvlɪʃ] *adj* diabolico(a).
devil-may-care ['dɛvlmeɪ'kɛə*] *adj*
impudente.
devil's advocate *n*: **to play ~** fare
l'avvocato del diavolo.
devious ['diːvɪəs] *adj* (*means*) indiretto(a),
tortuoso(a); (*person*) subdolo(a).
devise [dɪ'vaɪz] *vt* escogitare, concepire.
devoid [dɪ'vɔɪd] *adj*: **~ of** privo(a) di.
devolution [diːvə'luːʃən] *n* (*POL*)
decentramento.
devolve [dɪ'vɔlv] *vi*: **to ~ (up)on** ricadere
su.

devote [dɪ'vəut] *vt*: **to ~ sth to** dedicare qc
a.
devoted [dɪ'vəutɪd] *adj* devoto(a); **to be ~**
to essere molto attaccato(a) a.
devotee [dɛvəu'tiː] *n* (*REL*) adepto/a; (*MUS,*
SPORT) appassionato/a.
devotion [dɪ'vəuʃən] *n* devozione *f*,
attaccamento; (*REL*) atto di devozione,
preghiera.
devour [dɪ'vauə*] *vt* divorare.
devout [dɪ'vaut] *adj* pio(a), devoto(a).
dew [djuː] *n* rugiada.
dexterity [dɛks'tɛrɪtɪ] *n* destrezza.
dext(e)rous ['dɛkstrəs] *adj* (*skilful*)
destro(a), abile; (*movement*) agile.
DfEE *n abbr* (*BRIT*: = *Department for Education*
and Employment) Ministero della pubblica
instruzione e dell'occupazione.
dg *abbr* (= *decigram*) dg.
diabetes [daɪə'biːtiːz] *n* diabete *m*.
diabetic [daɪə'bɛtɪk] *adj* diabetico(a);
(*chocolate, jam*) per diabetici ♦ *n*
diabetico/a.
diabolical [daɪə'bɔlɪkl] *adj* diabolico(a); (*col*:
dreadful) infernale, atroce.
diaeresis [daɪ'ɛrɪsɪs] *n* dieresi *f inv*.
diagnose [daɪəg'nəuz] *vt* diagnosticare.
diagnosis, *pl* **diagnoses** [daɪəg'nəusɪs,
-siːz] *n* diagnosi *f inv*.
diagonal [daɪ'ægənl] *adj, n* diagonale (*f*).
diagram ['daɪəgræm] *n* diagramma *m*.
dial ['daɪəl] *n* quadrante *m*; (*on telephone*)
disco combinatore ♦ *vt* (*number*) fare; **to**
~ a wrong number sbagliare numero;
can I ~ London direct? si può chiamare
Londra in teleselezione?
dial. *abbr* = **dialect.**
dialect ['daɪəlɛkt] *n* dialetto.
dialling code ['daɪəlɪŋ-], (*US*) **area code** *n*
prefisso.
dialling tone ['daɪəlɪŋ-], (*US*) **dial tone** *n*
segnale *m* di linea libera.
dialogue ['daɪəlɔg] *n* dialogo.
dialysis [daɪ'ælɪsɪs] *n* dialisi *f*.
diameter [daɪ'æmɪtə*] *n* diametro.
diametrically [daɪə'mɛtrɪklɪ] *adv*: **~**
opposed (to) diametralmente opposto(a)
(a).
diamond ['daɪəmənd] *n* diamante *m*; (*shape*)
rombo; **~s** *npl* (*CARDS*) quadri *mpl*.
diamond ring *n* anello di brillanti; (*with*
one diamond) anello con brillante.
diaper ['daɪəpə*] *n* (*US*) pannolino.
diaphragm ['daɪəfræm] *n* diaframma *m*.
diarrhoea, (*US*) **diarrhea** [daɪə'riːə] *n*
diarrea.
diary ['daɪərɪ] *n* (*daily account*) diario; (*book*)
agenda; **to keep a ~** tenere un diario.

diatribe ['daɪətraɪb] *n* diatriba.
dice [daɪs] *n* (*pl inv*) dado ♦ *vt* (*CULIN*) tagliare a dadini.
dicey ['daɪsɪ] *adj* (*col*): **it's a bit** ~ è un po' un rischio.
dichotomy [daɪ'kɔtəmɪ] *n* dicotomia.
dickhead ['dɪkhɛd] *n* (*BRIT col!*) testa *m* di cazzo(*!*).
Dictaphone ® ['dɪktəfəun] *n* dittafono.
dictate *vt* [dɪk'teɪt] dettare ♦ *vi*: **to** ~ **to** (*person*) dare ordini a, dettar legge a ♦ *n* ['dɪkteɪt] dettame *m*; **I won't be** ~**d to** non ricevo ordini.
dictation [dɪk'teɪʃən] *n* dettato; (*to secretary etc*) dettatura; **at** ~ **speed** a velocità di dettatura.
dictator [dɪk'teɪtə*] *n* dittatore *m*.
dictatorship [dɪk'teɪtəʃɪp] *n* dittatura.
diction ['dɪkʃən] *n* dizione *f*.
dictionary ['dɪkʃənrɪ] *n* dizionario.
did [dɪd] *pt of* **do**.
didactic [daɪ'dæktɪk] *adj* didattico(a).
didn't = **did not**.
die [daɪ] *n* (*pl*: **dies**) conio; matrice *f*; stampo ♦ *vi* morire; **to be dying** star morendo; **to be dying for sth/to do sth** morire dalla voglia di qc/di fare qc; **to** ~ (**of** *or* **from**) morire (di).
▶**die away** *vi* spegnersi a poco a poco.
▶**die down** *vi* abbassarsi.
▶**die out** *vi* estinguersi.
diehard ['daɪhɑːd] *n* reazionario/a.
diesel ['diːzl] *n* diesel *m*.
diesel engine *n* motore *m* diesel *inv*.
diesel fuel, diesel oil *n* gasolio (per motori diesel).
diet ['daɪət] *n* alimentazione *f*; (*restricted food*) dieta ♦ *vi* (*also*: **be on a** ~) stare a dieta; **to live on a** ~ **of** nutrirsi di.
dietician [daɪə'tɪʃən] *n* dietologo/a.
differ ['dɪfə*] *vi*: **to** ~ **from sth** differire da qc; essere diverso(a) da qc; **to** ~ **from sb over sth** essere in disaccordo con qn su qc.
difference ['dɪfrəns] *n* differenza; (*quarrel*) screzio; **it makes no** ~ **to me** per me è lo stesso; **to settle one's** ~**s** risolvere la situazione.
different ['dɪfrənt] *adj* diverso(a).
differential [dɪfə'renʃəl] *n* (*AUT, wages*) differenziale *m*.
differentiate [dɪfə'renʃɪeɪt] *vi* differenziarsi; **to** ~ **between** discriminare fra, fare differenza fra.
differently ['dɪfrəntlɪ] *adv* diversamente.
difficult ['dɪfɪkəlt] *adj* difficile; ~ **to understand** difficile da capire.
difficulty ['dɪfɪkəltɪ] *n* difficoltà *f inv*; **to**

have difficulties with (*police, landlord etc*) avere noie con; **to be in** ~ essere *or* trovarsi in difficoltà.
diffidence ['dɪfɪdəns] *n* mancanza di sicurezza.
diffident ['dɪfɪdənt] *adj* sfiduciato(a).
diffuse *adj* [dɪ'fjuːs] diffuso(a) ♦ *vt* [dɪ'fjuːz] diffondere, emanare.
dig [dɪg] *vb* (*pt, pp* **dug** [dʌg]) *vt* (*hole*) scavare; (*garden*) vangare ♦ *vi* scavare ♦ *n* (*prod*) gomitata; (*fig*) frecciata; (*ARCHAEOLOGY*) scavo, scavi *mpl*; **to** ~ **into** (*snow, soil*) scavare; **to** ~ **into one's pockets for sth** frugarsi le tasche cercando qc; **to** ~ **one's nails into** conficcare le unghie in; *see also* **digs**.
▶**dig in** *vi* (*col*: *eat*) attaccare a mangiare; (*also*: ~ **o.s. in**: *MIL*) trincerarsi; (: *fig*) insediarsi, installarsi ♦ *vt* (*compost*) interrare; (*knife, claw*) affondare; **to** ~ **in one's heels** (*fig*) impuntarsi.
▶**dig out** *vt* (*survivors, car from snow*) tirar fuori (scavando), estrarre (scavando).
▶**dig up** *vt* scavare; (*tree etc*) sradicare.
digest [daɪ'dʒɛst] *vt* digerire.
digestible [dɪ'dʒɛstəbl] *adj* digeribile.
digestion [dɪ'dʒɛstʃən] *n* digestione *f*.
digestive [dɪ'dʒɛstɪv] *adj* digestivo(a); ~ **system** apparato digerente.
digit ['dɪdʒɪt] *n* cifra; (*finger*) dito.
digital ['dɪdʒɪtəl] *adj* digitale.
digital camera *n* fotocamera digitale.
digital compact cassette *n* piastra digitale per CD.
digital radio *n* radio digitale.
digital TV *n* televisione *f* digitale.
dignified ['dɪgnɪfaɪd] *adj* dignitoso(a).
dignitary ['dɪgnɪtərɪ] *n* dignitario.
dignity ['dɪgnɪtɪ] *n* dignità.
digress [daɪ'grɛs] *vi*: **to** ~ **from** divagare da.
digression [daɪ'grɛʃən] *n* digressione *f*.
digs [dɪgz] *npl* (*BRIT col*) camera ammobiliata.
dilapidated [dɪ'læpɪdeɪtɪd] *adj* cadente.
dilate [daɪ'leɪt] *vt* dilatare ♦ *vi* dilatarsi.
dilatory ['dɪlətərɪ] *adj* dilatorio(a).
dilemma [daɪ'lɛmə] *n* dilemma *m*; **to be in a** ~ essere di fronte a un dilemma.
diligent ['dɪlɪdʒənt] *adj* diligente.
dill [dɪl] *n* aneto.
dilly-dally ['dɪlɪdælɪ] *vi* gingillarsi.
dilute [daɪ'luːt] *vt* diluire; (*with water*) annacquare ♦ *adj* diluito(a).
dim [dɪm] *adj* (*light, eyesight*) debole; (*memory, outline*) vago(a); (*stupid*) ottuso(a) ♦ *vt* (*light: also: US AUT*) abbassare; **to take a** ~ **view of sth** non vedere di buon occhio qc.

dime [daɪm] n (US) = 10 cents.
dimension [dɪ'mɛnʃən] n dimensione f.
-dimensional [dɪ'mɛnʃənl] adj suffix: **two**~
   bi-dimensionale.
diminish [dɪ'mɪnɪʃ] vt, vi diminuire.
diminished [dɪ'mɪnɪʃt] adj: ~ **responsibility**
   (LAW) incapacità d'intendere e di volere.
diminutive [dɪ'mɪnjutɪv] adj minuscolo(a)
   ♦ n (LING) diminutivo.
dimly ['dɪmlɪ] adv debolmente;
   indistintamente.
dimmer ['dɪmə*] n (also: ~ **switch**) dimmer
   m inv, interruttore m a reostato; ~**s** (US
   AUT) anabbaglianti mpl; (: parking lights)
   luci fpl di posizione.
dimple ['dɪmpl] n fossetta.
dim-witted ['dɪm'wɪtɪd] adj (col) sciocco(a).
din [dɪn] n chiasso, fracasso ♦ vt: **to** ~ **sth**
   into sb (col) ficcare qc in testa a qn.
dine [daɪn] vi pranzare.
diner ['daɪnə*] n (person: in restaurant)
   cliente m; (RAIL) carrozza or vagone m
   ristorante; (US: eating place) tavola calda.
dinghy ['dɪŋgɪ] n battello pneumatico;
   (also: **sailing** ~) dinghy m inv.
dingy ['dɪndʒɪ] adj grigio(a).
dining area ['daɪnɪŋ-] n zona pranzo inv.
dining car n vagone m ristorante.
dining room n sala da pranzo.
dinner ['dɪnə*] n pranzo; (evening meal)
   cena; (public) banchetto; ~**'s ready!** a
   tavola!
dinner jacket n smoking m inv.
dinner party n cena.
dinner service n servizio da tavola.
dinner time n ora di pranzo (or cena).
dinosaur ['daɪnəsɔ:*] n dinosauro.
dint [dɪnt] n: **by** ~ **of (doing) sth** a forza di
   (fare) qc.
diocese ['daɪəsɪs] n diocesi f inv.
dioxide [daɪ'ɔksaɪd] n biossido.
dip [dɪp] n (slope) discesa; (in sea) bagno
   ♦ vt immergere, bagnare; (BRIT AUT: lights)
   abbassare ♦ vi (road) essere in pendenza;
   (bird, plane) abbassarsi.
Dip. abbr (BRIT) = **diploma.**
diphtheria [dɪf'θɪərɪə] n difterite f.
diphthong ['dɪfθɒŋ] n dittongo.
diploma [dɪ'pləumə] n diploma m.
diplomacy [dɪ'pləuməsɪ] n diplomazia.
diplomat ['dɪpləmæt] n diplomatico.
diplomatic [dɪplə'mætɪk] adj
   diplomatico(a); **to break off** ~ **relations**
   rompere le relazioni diplomatiche.
diplomatic corps n corpo diplomatico.
diplomatic immunity n immunità f inv
   diplomatica.
dipstick ['dɪpstɪk] n (AUT) indicatore m di

livello dell'olio.
dipswitch ['dɪpswɪtʃ] n (BRIT AUT) levetta
   dei fari.
dire [daɪə*] adj terribile; estremo(a).
direct [daɪ'rɛkt] adj diretto(a); (manner,
   person) franco(a), esplicito(a) ♦ vt
   dirigere; **to** ~ **sb to do sth** dare direttive
   a qn di fare qc; **can you** ~ **me to ...?** mi
   può indicare la strada per ...?
direct cost n (COMM) costo diretto.
direct current n (ELEC) corrente f
   continua.
direct debit n (BANKING) addebito
   effettuato per ordine di un cliente di
   banca.
direct dialling n (TEL) ≈ teleselezione f.
direct hit n (MIL) colpo diretto.
direction [dɪ'rɛkʃən] n direzione f; (of play,
   film, programme) regia; ~**s** npl (advice)
   chiarimenti mpl; (instructions: to a place)
   indicazioni fpl; ~**s for use** istruzioni fpl; **to**
   ask for ~**s** chiedere la strada; **sense of** ~
   senso dell'orientamento; **in the** ~ **of** in
   direzione di.
directive [dɪ'rɛktɪv] n direttiva, ordine m; **a**
   government ~ una disposizione
   governativa.
direct labour n manodopera diretta.
directly [dɪ'rɛktlɪ] adv (in straight line)
   direttamente; (at once) subito.
direct mail n pubblicità diretta.
direct mailshot n (BRIT) materiale m
   pubblicitario ad approccio diretto.
directness [daɪ'rɛktnɪs] n (of person, speech)
   franchezza.
director [dɪ'rɛktə*] n direttore/trice;
   amministratore/trice; (THEAT, CINE, TV)
   regista m/f; **D**~ **of Public Prosecutions**
   (DPP) (BRIT) ≈ Procuratore m della
   Repubblica.
directory [dɪ'rɛktərɪ] n elenco; (street ~)
   stradario; (trade ~) repertorio del
   commercio; (COMPUT) directory m inv.
directory enquiries, (US) directory
   assistance n (TEL) servizio informazioni,
   informazioni fpl elenco abbonati.
dirt [dɜ:t] n sporcizia; immondizia; **to treat**
   sb like ~ trattare qn come uno straccio.
dirt-cheap ['dɜ:t'tʃi:p] adj da due soldi.
dirt road n strada non asfaltata.
dirty ['dɜ:tɪ] adj sporco(a) ♦ vt sporcare; ~
   bomb bomba convenzionale contenente
   materiale radioattivo; ~ **story** storia
   oscena; ~ **trick** brutto scherzo.
disability [dɪsə'bɪlɪtɪ] n invalidità f inv;
   (LAW) incapacità f inv.
disability allowance n pensione f
   d'invalidità.

disable [dɪs'eɪbl] vt (subj: illness, accident) rendere invalido(a); (tank, gun) mettere fuori uso.

disabled [dɪs'eɪbld] adj invalido(a); (maimed) mutilato(a); (through illness, old age) inabile.

disadvantage [dɪsəd'vɑːntɪdʒ] n svantaggio.

disadvantaged [dɪsəd'vɑːntɪdʒd] adj (person) svantaggiato(a).

disadvantageous [dɪsædvɑːn'teɪdʒəs] adj svantaggioso(a).

disaffected [dɪsə'fɛktɪd] adj: ~ (to or towards) scontento(a) di, insoddisfatto(a) di.

disaffection [dɪsə'fɛkʃən] n malcontento, insoddisfazione f.

disagree [dɪsə'griː] vi (differ) discordare; (be against, think otherwise): **to ~ (with)** essere in disaccordo (con), dissentire (da); **I ~ with you** non sono d'accordo con lei; **garlic ~s with me** l'aglio non mi va.

disagreeable [dɪsə'griːəbl] adj sgradevole; (person) antipatico(a).

disagreement [dɪsə'griːmənt] n disaccordo; (quarrel) dissapore m; **to have a ~ with sb** litigare con qn.

disallow ['dɪsə'lau] vt respingere; (BRIT FOOTBALL: goal) annullare.

disappear [dɪsə'pɪə*] vi scomparire.

disappearance [dɪsə'pɪərəns] n scomparsa.

disappoint [dɪsə'pɔɪnt] vt deludere.

disappointed [dɪsə'pɔɪntɪd] adj deluso(a).

disappointing [dɪsə'pɔɪntɪŋ] adj deludente.

disappointment [dɪsə'pɔɪntmənt] n delusione f.

disapproval [dɪsə'pruːvəl] n disapprovazione f.

disapprove [dɪsə'pruːv] vi: **to ~ of** disapprovare.

disapproving [dɪsə'pruːvɪŋ] adj di disapprovazione.

disarm [dɪs'ɑːm] vt disarmare.

disarmament [dɪs'ɑːməmənt] n disarmo.

disarming [dɪs'ɑːmɪŋ] adj (smile) disarmante.

disarray [dɪsə'reɪ] n: **in ~** (troops) in rotta; (thoughts) confuso(a); (clothes) in disordine; **to throw into ~** buttare all'aria.

disaster [dɪ'zɑːstə*] n disastro.

disaster area n zona disastrata.

disastrous [dɪ'zɑːstrəs] adj disastroso(a).

disband [dɪs'bænd] vt sbandare; (MIL) congedare ♦ vi sciogliersi.

disbelief ['dɪsbə'liːf] n incredulità; **in ~** incredulo(a).

disbelieve ['dɪsbə'liːv] vt (person, story) non

credere a, mettere in dubbio; **I don't ~ you** vorrei poterle credere.

disc [dɪsk] n disco.

disc. abbr (COMM) = **discount.**

discard [dɪs'kɑːd] vt (old things) scartare; (fig) abbandonare.

disc brake n freno a disco.

discern [dɪ'səːn] vt discernere, distinguere.

discernible [dɪ'səːnəbl] adj percepibile.

discerning [dɪ'səːnɪŋ] adj perspicace.

discharge vt [dɪs'tʃɑːdʒ] (duties) compiere; (settle: debt) pagare, estinguere; (ELEC, waste etc) scaricare; (MED) emettere; (patient) dimettere; (employee) licenziare; (soldier) congedare; (defendant) liberare ♦ n ['dɪstʃɑːdʒ] (FLEC) scarica; (MED, of gas, chemicals) emissione f; (vaginal ~) perdite fpl (bianche); (dismissal) licenziamento; congedo; liberazione f; **to ~ one's gun** fare fuoco.

discharged bankrupt [dɪs'tʃɑːdʒd-] n fallito cui il tribunale ha concesso la riabilitazione.

disciple [dɪ'saɪpl] n discepolo.

disciplinary ['dɪsɪplɪnərɪ] adj disciplinare; **to take ~ action against sb** prendere un provvedimento disciplinare contro qn.

discipline ['dɪsɪplɪn] n disciplina ♦ vt disciplinare; (punish) punire; **to ~ o.s. to do sth** imporsi di fare qc.

disc jockey (DJ) n disc jockey m inv.

disclaim [dɪs'kleɪm] vt negare, smentire.

disclaimer [dɪs'kleɪmə*] n smentita; **to issue a ~** pubblicare una smentita.

disclose [dɪs'kləuz] vt rivelare, svelare.

disclosure [dɪs'kləuʒə*] n rivelazione f.

disco ['dɪskəu] n abbr = **discothèque**.

discolour, (US) **discolor** [dɪs'kʌlə*] vt scolorire; (sth white) ingiallire ♦ vi sbiadire, scolorirsi; (sth white) ingiallire.

discolo(u)ration [dɪskʌlə'reɪʃən] n scolorimento.

discolo(u)red [dɪs'kʌləd] adj scolorito(a); ingiallito(a).

discomfort [dɪs'kʌmfət] n disagio; (lack of comfort) scomodità f inv.

disconcert [dɪskən'səːt] vt sconcertare.

disconnect [dɪskə'nɛkt] vt sconnettere, staccare; (ELEC, RADIO) staccare; (gas, water) chiudere.

disconnected [dɪskə'nɛktɪd] adj (speech, thought) sconnesso(a).

disconsolate [dɪs'kɔnsəlɪt] adj sconsolato(a).

discontent [dɪskən'tɛnt] n scontentezza.

discontented [dɪskən'tɛntɪd] adj scontento(a).

discontinue [dɪskən'tɪnjuː] vt smettere,

cessare; "~d" (COMM) "sospeso".
discord ['dɪskɔːd] n disaccordo; (MUS) dissonanza.
discordant [dɪs'kɔːdənt] adj discordante; dissonante.
discothèque ['dɪskəutɛk] n discoteca.
discount n ['dɪskaunt] sconto ♦ vt [dɪs'kaunt] scontare; (report etc) non badare a; at a ~ con uno sconto; to give sb a ~ on sth fare uno sconto a qn su qc; ~ for cash sconto m cassa inv.
discount house n (FINANCE) casa di sconto, discount house f inv; (COMM: also: discount store) discount m inv.
discount rate n tasso di sconto.
discourage [dɪs'kʌrɪdʒ] vt scoraggiare; (dissuade, deter) tentare di dissuadere.
discouragement [dɪs'kʌrɪdʒmənt] n (dissuasion) disapprovazione f; (depression) scoraggiamento; to act as a ~ to ostacolare.
discouraging [dɪs'kʌrɪdʒɪŋ] adj scoraggiante.
discourteous [dɪs'kəːtɪəs] adj scortese.
discover [dɪs'kʌvə*] vt scoprire.
discovery [dɪs'kʌvərɪ] n scoperta.
discredit [dɪs'krɛdɪt] vt screditare; mettere in dubbio ♦ n discredito.
discreet [dɪ'skriːt] adj discreto(a).
discreetly [dɪ'skriːtlɪ] adv con discrezione.
discrepancy [dɪ'skrɛpənsɪ] n discrepanza.
discretion [dɪ'skrɛʃən] n discrezione f; use your own ~ giudichi lei.
discretionary [dɪs'krɛʃənərɪ] adj (powers) discrezionale.
discriminate [dɪ'skrɪmɪneɪt] vi: to ~ between distinguere tra; to ~ against discriminare contro.
discriminating [dɪs'krɪmɪneɪtɪŋ] adj (ear, taste) fine, giudizioso(a); (person) esigente; (tax, duty) discriminante.
discrimination [dɪskrɪmɪ'neɪʃən] n discriminazione f; (judgement) discernimento; racial/sexual ~ discriminazione razziale/sessuale.
discus ['dɪskəs] n disco.
discuss [dɪ'skʌs] vt discutere; (debate) dibattere.
discussion [dɪ'skʌʃən] n discussione f; under ~ in discussione.
disdain [dɪs'deɪn] n disdegno.
disease [dɪ'ziːz] n malattia.
diseased [dɪ'ziːzd] adj malato(a).
disembark [dɪsɪm'baːk] vt, vi sbarcare.
disembarkation [dɪsɛmbaː'keɪʃən] n sbarco.
disembodied [dɪsɪm'bɔdɪd] adj disincarnato(a).

disembowel [dɪsɪm'bauəl] vt sbudellare, sventrare.
disenchanted [dɪsɪn'tʃaːntɪd] adj disincantato(a); ~ (with) deluso(a) (da).
disenfranchise [dɪsɪn'fræntʃaɪz] vt privare del diritto di voto; (COMM) revocare una condizione di privilegio commerciale a.
disengage [dɪsɪn'geɪdʒ] vt disimpegnare; (TECH) distaccare; (AUT) disinnestare.
disentangle [dɪsɪn'tæŋgl] vt sbrogliare.
disfavour, (US) disfavor [dɪs'feɪvə*] n sfavore m; disgrazia.
disfigure [dɪs'fɪgə*] vt sfigurare.
disgorge [dɪs'gɔːdʒ] vt (subj: river) riversare.
disgrace [dɪs'greɪs] n vergogna; (disfavour) disgrazia ♦ vt disonorare, far cadere in disgrazia.
disgraceful [dɪs'greɪsful] adj scandaloso(a), vergognoso(a).
disgruntled [dɪs'grʌntld] adj scontento(a), di cattivo umore.
disguise [dɪs'gaɪz] n travestimento ♦ vt travestire; (voice) contraffare; (feelings etc) mascherare; to ~ o.s. as travestirsi da; in ~ travestito(a); there's no disguising the fact that ... non si può nascondere (il fatto) che ....
disgust [dɪs'gʌst] n disgusto, nausea ♦ vt disgustare, far schifo a.
disgusting [dɪs'gʌstɪŋ] adj disgustoso(a).
dish [dɪʃ] n piatto; to do or wash the ~es fare i piatti.
▶dish out vt (food) servire; (advice) elargire; (money) tirare fuori; (exam papers) distribuire.
▶dish up vt (food) servire; (facts, statistics) presentare.
dishcloth ['dɪʃklɔθ] n strofinaccio dei piatti.
dishearten [dɪs'haːtn] vt scoraggiare.
dishevelled, (US) disheveled [dɪ'ʃɛvəld] adj arruffato(a); scapigliato(a).
dishonest [dɪs'ɔnɪst] adj disonesto(a).
dishonesty [dɪs'ɔnɪstɪ] n disonestà.
dishonour, (US) dishonor [dɪs'ɔnə*] n disonore m.
dishono(u)rable [dɪs'ɔnərəbl] adj disonorevole.
dish soap n (US) detersivo liquido (per stoviglie).
dishtowel ['dɪʃtauəl] n strofinaccio dei piatti.
dishwasher ['dɪʃwɔʃə*] n lavastoviglie f inv; (person) sguattero/a.
dishy ['dɪʃɪ] adj (BRIT col) figo(a).
disillusion [dɪsɪ'luːʒən] vt disilludere, disingannare ♦ n disillusione f; to become

~ed (with) perdere le illusioni (su).
disillusionment [dɪsɪ'luːʒənmənt] n
disillusione f.
disincentive [dɪsɪn'sɛntɪv] n: **to act as a ~**
(to) agire da freno (su); **to be a ~ to**
scoraggiare.
disinclined [dɪsɪn'klaɪnd] adj: **to be ~ to do**
sth essere poco propenso(a) a fare qc.
disinfect [dɪsɪn'fɛkt] vt disinfettare.
disinfectant [dɪsɪn'fɛktənt] n disinfettante
m.
disinflation [dɪsɪn'fleɪʃən] n disinflazione f.
disinformation [dɪsɪnfə'meɪʃən] n
disinformazione f.
disinherit [dɪsɪn'hɛrɪt] vt diseredare.
disintegrate [dɪs'ɪntɪgreɪt] vi disintegrarsi.
disinterested [dɪs'ɪntrəstɪd] adj
disinteressato(a).
disjointed [dɪs'dʒɔɪntɪd] adj sconnesso(a).
disk [dɪsk] n (COMPUT) disco; **single-/**
double-sided ~ disco m monofaccia inv/a
doppia faccia.
disk drive n disk drive m inv, unità f inv a
dischi magnetici.
disk operating system (DOS) n sistema
m operativo a disco.
diskette [dɪs'kɛt] n (COMPUT) dischetto.
dislike [dɪs'laɪk] n antipatia, avversione f
♦ vt: **he ~s it** non gli piace; **I ~ the idea**
l'idea non mi va; **to take a ~ to sb/sth**
prendere in antipatia qn/qc.
dislocate ['dɪsləkeɪt] vt (MED) slogare; (fig)
disorganizzare; **he ~d his shoulder** si è
lussato una spalla.
dislodge [dɪs'lɔdʒ] vt rimuovere, staccare;
(enemy) sloggiare.
disloyal [dɪs'lɔɪəl] adj sleale.
dismal ['dɪzml] adj triste, cupo(a).
dismantle [dɪs'mæntl] vt smantellare,
smontare; (fort, warship) disarmare.
dismast [dɪs'mɑːst] vt disalberare.
dismay [dɪs'meɪ] n costernazione f ♦ vt
sgomentare; **much to my ~** con mio gran
stupore.
dismiss [dɪs'mɪs] vt congedare; (employee)
licenziare; (idea) scacciare; (LAW)
respingere ♦ vi (MIL) rompere i ranghi.
dismissal [dɪs'mɪsəl] n congedo;
licenziamento.
dismount [dɪs'maʊnt] vi scendere ♦ vt
(rider) disarcionare.
disobedience [dɪsə'biːdɪəns] n
disubbidienza.
disobedient [dɪsə'biːdɪənt] adj
disubbidiente.
disobey [dɪsə'beɪ] vt disubbidire; (rule)
trasgredire.
disorder [dɪs'ɔːdə*] n disordine m; (rioting)

tumulto; (MED) disturbo; **civil ~** disordini
mpl interni.
disorderly [dɪs'ɔːdəlɪ] adj disordinato(a);
tumultuoso(a).
disorderly conduct n (LAW)
comportamento atto a turbare l'ordine
pubblico.
disorganize [dɪs'ɔːgənaɪz] vt
disorganizzare.
disorganized [dɪs'ɔːgənaɪzd] adj (person,
life) disorganizzato(a); (system, meeting)
male organizzato(a).
disorientated [dɪs'ɔːrɪɛnteɪtɪd] adj
disorientato(a).
disown [dɪs'əʊn] vt ripudiare.
disparaging [dɪs'pærɪdʒɪŋ] adj
spregiativo(a), sprezzante; **to be ~ about**
sb/sth denigrare qn/qc.
disparate ['dɪspərɪt] adj disparato(a).
disparity [dɪs'pærɪtɪ] n disparità f inv.
dispassionate [dɪs'pæʃənət] adj calmo(a),
freddo(a); imparziale.
dispatch [dɪs'pætʃ] vt spedire, inviare;
(deal with: business) sbrigare ♦ n
spedizione f, invio; (MIL, PRESS) dispaccio.
dispatch department n reparto
spedizioni.
dispatch rider n (MIL) corriere m,
portaordini m inv.
dispel [dɪs'pɛl] vt dissipare, scacciare.
dispensary [dɪs'pɛnsərɪ] n farmacia; (in
chemist's) dispensario.
dispense [dɪs'pɛns] vt distribuire,
amministrare; (medicine) preparare e
dare; **to ~ sb from** dispensare qn da.
▶**dispense with** vt fus fare a meno di;
(make unnecessary) rendere superfluo(a).
dispenser [dɪs'pɛnsə*] n (container)
distributore m.
dispensing chemist n (BRIT) farmacista
m/f.
dispersal [dɪs'pəːsl] n dispersione f.
disperse [dɪs'pəːs] vt disperdere;
(knowledge) disseminare ♦ vi disperdersi.
dispirited [dɪs'pɪrɪtɪd] adj scoraggiato(a),
abbattuto(a).
displace [dɪs'pleɪs] vt spostare.
displaced person n (POL) profugo/a.
displacement [dɪs'pleɪsmənt] n
spostamento.
display [dɪs'pleɪ] n mostra; esposizione f;
(of feeling etc) manifestazione f; (military
~) parata (militare); (computer ~) display
m inv; (pej) ostentazione f ♦ vt mostrare;
(goods) esporre; (results) ostentare;
(departure times) indicare; **on ~** (gen) in
mostra; (goods) in vetrina.
display advertising n pubblicità

tabellare.

displease [dıs'pliːz] *vt* dispiacere a, scontentare; ~**d with** scontento(a) di.

displeasure [dıs'plɛʒə*] *n* dispiacere *m*.

disposable [dıs'pəuzəbl] *adj* (*pack etc*) a perdere; (*income*) disponibile; ~ **nappy** (*BRIT*) pannolino di carta.

disposal [dıs'pəuzl] *n* (*of rubbish*) evacuazione *f*; distruzione *f*; (*of property etc*: *by selling*) vendita; (: *by giving away*) cessione *f*; **at one's** ~ alla sua disposizione; **to put sth at sb's** ~ mettere qc a disposizione di qn.

dispose [dıs'pəuz] *vt* disporre. ►**dispose of** *vt fus* (*time, money*) disporre di; (*COMM*: *sell*) vendere; (*unwanted goods*) sbarazzarsi di; (*problem*) eliminare.

disposed [dıs'pəuzd] *adj*: ~ **to do** disposto(a) a fare.

disposition [dıspə'zıʃən] *n* disposizione *f*; (*temperament*) carattere *m*.

dispossess ['dıspə'zɛs] *vt*: **to** ~ **sb (of)** spossessare qn (di).

disproportion [dısprə'pɔːʃən] *n* sproporzione *f*.

disproportionate [dısprə'pɔːʃənət] *adj* sproporzionato(a).

disprove [dıs'pruːv] *vt* confutare.

dispute [dıs'pjuːt] *n* disputa; (*also*: **industrial** ~) controversia (sindacale) ♦ *vt* contestare; (*matter*) discutere; (*victory*) disputare; **to be in** *or* **under** ~ (*matter*) essere in discussione; (*territory*) essere oggetto di contesa.

disqualification [dıskwɔlıfı'keıʃən] *n* squalifica; ~ **(from driving)** (*BRIT*) ritiro della patente.

disqualify [dıs'kwɔlıfaı] *vt* (*SPORT*) squalificare; **to** ~ **sb from sth/from doing** rendere qn incapace a qc/a fare; squalificare qn da qc/da fare; **to** ~ **sb from driving** (*BRIT*) ritirare la patente a qn.

disquiet [dıs'kwaıət] *n* inquietudine *f*.

disquieting [dıs'kwaıətıŋ] *adj* inquietante, allarmante.

disregard [dısrı'gaːd] *vt* non far caso a, non badare a ♦ *n* (*indifference*): ~ **(for)** (*feelings*) insensibilità (a), indifferenza (verso); (*danger*) noncuranza (di); (*money*) disprezzo (di).

disrepair [dısrı'pɛə*] *n* cattivo stato; **to fall into** ~ (*building*) andare in rovina; (*street*) deteriorarsi.

disreputable [dıs'rɛpjutəbl] *adj* (*person*) di cattiva fama; (*area*) malfamato(a), poco raccomandabile.

disrepute ['dısrı'pjuːt] *n* disonore *m*,

vergogna; **to bring into** ~ rovinare la reputazione di.

disrespectful [dısrı'spɛktful] *adj* che manca di rispetto.

disrupt [dıs'rʌpt] *vt* (*meeting, lesson*) disturbare, interrompere; (*public transport*) creare scompiglio in; (*plans*) scombussolare.

disruption [dıs'rʌpʃən] *n* disordine *m*; interruzione *f*.

disruptive [dıs'rʌptıv] *adj* (*influence*) negativo(a), deleterio(a); (*strike action*) paralizzante.

dissatisfaction [dıssætıs'fækʃən] *n* scontentezza, insoddisfazione *f*.

dissatisfied [dıs'sætısfaıd] *adj*: ~ **(with)** scontento(a) *or* insoddisfatto(a) (di).

dissect [dı'sɛkt] *vt* sezionare; (*fig*) sviscerare.

disseminate [dı'sɛmıneıt] *vt* disseminare.

dissent [dı'sɛnt] *n* dissenso.

dissenter [dı'sɛntə*] *n* (*REL, POL etc*) dissidente *m/f*.

dissertation [dısə'teıʃən] *n* (*SCOL*) tesi *f inv*, dissertazione *f*.

disservice [dıs'səːvıs] *n*: **to do sb a** ~ fare un cattivo servizio a qn.

dissident ['dısıdnt] *adj* dissidente; (*speech, voice*) di dissenso ♦ *n* dissidente *m/f*.

dissimilar [dı'sımılə*] *adj*: ~ **(to)** dissimile *or* diverso(a) (da).

dissipate ['dısıpeıt] *vt* dissipare.

dissipated ['dısıpeıtıd] *adj* dissipato(a).

dissociate [dı'səuʃıeıt] *vt* dissociare; **to** ~ **o.s. from** dichiarare di non avere niente a che fare con.

dissolute ['dısəluːt] *adj* dissoluto(a), licenzioso(a).

dissolve [dı'zɔlv] *vt* dissolvere, sciogliere; (*COMM, POL, marriage*) sciogliere ♦ *vi* dissolversi, sciogliersi; (*fig*) svanire.

dissuade [dı'sweıd] *vt*: **to** ~ **sb (from)** dissuadere qn (da).

distaff side ['dıstaːf-] *n ramo femminile di una famiglia.*

distance ['dıstns] *n* distanza; **in the** ~ in lontananza; **what's the** ~ **to London?** quanto dista Londra?; **it's within walking** ~ ci si arriva a piedi; **at a** ~ **of 2 metres** a 2 metri di distanza.

distant ['dıstnt] *adj* lontano(a), distante; (*manner*) riservato(a), freddo(a).

distaste [dıs'teıst] *n* ripugnanza.

distasteful [dıs'teıstful] *adj* ripugnante, sgradevole.

Dist. Atty. *abbr* (*US*) = **district attorney.**

distemper [dıs'tɛmpə*] *n* (*paint*) tempera; (*of dogs*) cimurro.

distend [dɪs'tɛnd] vt dilatare ♦ vi dilatarsi.
distended [dɪs'tɛndɪd] adj (stomach) dilatato(a).
distil, (US) **distill** [dɪs'tɪl] vt distillare.
distillery [dɪs'tɪlərɪ] n distilleria.
distinct [dɪs'tɪŋkt] adj distinto(a); (preference, progress) definito(a); **as ~ from** a differenza di.
distinction [dɪs'tɪŋkʃən] n distinzione f; (in exam) lode f; **to draw a ~ between** fare distinzione tra; **a writer of ~** uno scrittore di notevoli qualità.
distinctive [dɪs'tɪŋktɪv] adj distintivo(a).
distinctly [dɪs'tɪŋktlɪ] adv distintamente; (remember) chiaramente; (unhappy, better) decisamente.
distinguish [dɪs'tɪŋgwɪʃ] vt distinguere; discernere ♦ vi: **to ~ (between)** distinguere (tra); **to ~ o.s.** distinguersi.
distinguished [dɪs'tɪŋgwɪʃt] adj (eminent) eminente; (career) brillante; (refined) distinto(a), signorile.
distinguishing [dɪs'tɪŋgwɪʃɪŋ] adj (feature) distinto(a), caratteristico(a).
distort [dɪs'tɔːt] vt (also fig) distorcere; (account) falsare; (TECH) deformare.
distortion [dɪs'tɔːʃən] n (gen) distorsione f; (of truth etc) alterazione f; (of facts) travisamento; (TECH) deformazione f.
distract [dɪs'trækt] vt distrarre.
distracted [dɪs'træktɪd] adj distratto(a).
distraction [dɪs'trækʃən] n distrazione f; **to drive sb to ~** spingere qn alla pazzia.
distraught [dɪs'trɔːt] adj stravolto(a).
distress [dɪs'trɛs] n angoscia; (pain) dolore m ♦ vt affliggere; **in ~** (ship etc) in pericolo, in difficoltà; **~ed area** (BRIT) zona sinistrata.
distressing [dɪs'trɛsɪŋ] adj doloroso(a), penoso(a).
distress signal n segnale m di pericolo.
distribute [dɪs'trɪbjuːt] vt distribuire.
distribution [dɪstrɪ'bjuːʃən] n distribuzione f.
distribution cost n costo di distribuzione.
distributor [dɪs'trɪbjutə*] n distributore m; (COMM) concessionario.
district ['dɪstrɪkt] n (of country) regione f; (of town) quartiere m; (ADMIN) distretto.
district attorney (DA) n (US) ≈ sostituto procuratore m della Repubblica.
district council n organo di amministrazione locale; see boxed note.

DISTRICT COUNCIL

In Inghilterra e in Galles, il **district council** è l'organo responsabile dell'amministrazione dei

paesi più piccoli e dei distretti di campagna. È finanziato tramite una tassa locale e riceve un contributo da parte del governo. I **district councils** vengono eletti a livello locale ogni quattro anni. L'organo amministrativo nelle città è invece il "city council".

district nurse n (BRIT) infermiera di quartiere.
distrust [dɪs'trʌst] n diffidenza, sfiducia ♦ vt non aver fiducia in.
distrustful [dɪs'trʌstful] adj diffidente.
disturb [dɪs'təːb] vt disturbare; (inconvenience) scomodare; **sorry to ~ you** scusi se la disturbo.
disturbance [dɪs'təːbəns] n disturbo; (political etc) tumulto; (by drunks etc) disordini mpl; **~ of the peace** disturbo della quiete pubblica; **to cause a ~** provocare disordini.
disturbed [dɪs'təːbd] adj turbato(a); **to be emotionally ~** avere problemi emotivi; **to be mentally ~** essere malato(a) di mente.
disturbing [dɪs'təːbɪŋ] adj sconvolgente.
disuse [dɪs'juːs] n: **to fall into ~** cadere in disuso.
disused [dɪs'juːzd] adj abbandonato(a).
ditch [dɪtʃ] n fossa ♦ vt (col) piantare in asso.
dither ['dɪðə*] vi vacillare.
ditto ['dɪtəu] adv idem.
divan [dɪ'væn] n divano.
divan bed n divano letto inv.
dive [daɪv] n tuffo; (of submarine) immersione f; (AVIAT) picchiata; (pej) buco ♦ vi tuffarsi.
diver ['daɪvə*] n tuffatore/trice; (deep-sea ~) palombaro.
diverge [daɪ'vəːdʒ] vi divergere.
divergent [daɪ'vəːdʒənt] adj divergente.
diverse [daɪ'vəːs] adj vario(a).
diversification [daɪvəːsɪfɪ'keɪʃən] n diversificazione f.
diversify [daɪ'vəːsɪfaɪ] vt diversificare.
diversion [daɪ'vəːʃən] n (BRIT AUT) deviazione f; (distraction) divertimento.
diversionary tactics [daɪ'vəːʃənrɪ-] npl tattica fsg diversiva.
diversity [daɪ'vəːsɪtɪ] n diversità f inv, varietà f inv.
divert [daɪ'vəːt] vt (traffic, river) deviare; (train, plane) dirottare; (amuse) divertire.
divest [daɪ'vɛst] vt: **to ~ sb of** spogliare qn di.
divide [dɪ'vaɪd] vt dividere; (separate) separare ♦ vi dividersi; **to ~ (between or**

among) dividere (tra), ripartire (tra); **40 ~d by 5** 40 diviso 5.

►**divide out** *vt*: **to ~ out (between** or **among)** (*sweets etc*) distribuire (tra); (*tasks*) distribuire or ripartire (tra).

divided [dɪ'vaɪdɪd] *adj* (*country*) diviso(a); (*opinions*) discordi.

divided highway *n* (*US*) strada a doppia carreggiata.

divided skirt *n* gonna *f* pantalone *inv*.

dividend ['dɪvɪdɛnd] *n* dividendo.

dividend cover *n* rapporto dividendo profitti.

dividers [dɪ'vaɪdəz] *npl* compasso a punte fisse.

divine [dɪ'vaɪn] *adj* divino(a) ♦ *vt* (*future*) divinare, predire; (*truth*) indovinare; (*water, metal*) individuare tramite radioestesia.

diving ['daɪvɪŋ] *n* tuffo.

diving board *n* trampolino.

diving suit *n* scafandro.

divinity [dɪ'vɪnɪtɪ] *n* divinità *f inv*; teologia.

division [dɪ'vɪʒən] *n* divisione *f*; separazione *f*; (*BRIT FOOTBALL*) serie *f inv*; **~ of labour** divisione *f* del lavoro.

divisive [dɪ'vaɪsɪv] *adj* che è causa di discordia.

divorce [dɪ'vɔːs] *n* divorzio ♦ *vt* divorziare da.

divorced [dɪ'vɔːst] *adj* divorziato(a).

divorcee [dɪvɔː'siː] *n* divorziato/a.

divot ['dɪvət] *n* (*GOLF*) zolla di terra (*sollevata accidentalmente*).

divulge [daɪ'vʌldʒ] *vt* divulgare, rivelare.

D.I.Y. *adj, n abbr* (*BRIT*) *see* **do-it-yourself**.

dizziness ['dɪzɪnɪs] *n* vertigini *fpl*.

dizzy ['dɪzɪ] *adj* (*height*) vertiginoso(a); **to make sb ~** far girare la testa a qn; **to feel ~** avere il capogiro; **I feel ~** mi gira la testa, ho il capogiro.

DJ *n abbr see* **disc jockey**.

dj *n abbr* = **dinner jacket**.

Djakarta [dʒə'kɑːtə] *n* Giakarta.

DJIA *n abbr* (*US STOCK EXCHANGE*: = *Dow-Jones Industrial Average*) indice *m* Dow-Jones.

dl *abbr* (= *decilitre*) dl.

DLit(t) *n abbr* = *Doctor of Literature*; *Doctor of Letters*.

dm *abbr* (= *decimetre*) dm.

DMus *n abbr* = *Doctor of Music*.

DMZ *n abbr* (= *demilitarized zone*) zona smilitarizzata.

DNA *n abbr* (= *deoxyribonucleic acid*) DNA *m*; **~ test** test *m inv* del DNA.

═══════════════════ **KEYWORD**

do [duː] (*pt* **did**, *pp* **done**) *n* (*col*: *party etc*) festa; **it was rather a grand ~** è stato un ricevimento piuttosto importante

♦ *vb* **1** (*in negative constructions*) *non tradotto*; **I don't understand** non capisco **2** (*to form questions*) *non tradotto*; **didn't you know?** non lo sapevi?; **why didn't you come?** perché non sei venuto?

3 (*for emphasis, in polite expressions*): **she does seem rather late** sembra essere piuttosto in ritardo; **I DO wish I could ...** magari potessi ...; **but I DO like it!** sì che mi piace!; **~ sit down** si accomodi la prego, prego si sieda; **~ take care!** mi raccomando, stai attento!

4 (*used to avoid repeating vb*): **she swims better than I ~** lei nuota meglio di me; **~ you agree? — yes, I ~/no, I don't** sei d'accordo? — sì/no; **she lives in Glasgow — so ~ I** lei vive a Glasgow — anch'io; **he asked me to help him and I did** mi ha chiesto di aiutarlo ed io l'ho fatto; **they come here often — ~ they?** vengono qui spesso — ah sì?, davvero?

5 (*in question tags*): **you like him, don't you?** ti piace, vero?; **I don't know him, ~ I?** non lo conosco, vero?

♦ *vt* (*gen, carry out, perform etc*) fare; **what are you ~ing tonight?** che fai stasera?; **what can I ~ for you?** (*in shop*) desidera?; **I'll ~ all I can** farò tutto il possibile; **to ~ the cooking** cucinare; **to ~ the washing-up** fare i piatti; **to ~ one's teeth** lavarsi i denti; **to ~ one's hair/nails** farsi i capelli/ le unghie; **the car was ~ing 100** la macchina faceva i 100 all'ora; **how ~ you like your steak done?** come preferisce la bistecca?; **well done** ben cotto(a)

♦ *vi* **1** (*act, behave*) fare; **~ as I ~** faccia come me, faccia come faccio io; **what did he ~ with the cat?** che ne ha fatto del gatto?

2 (*get on, fare*) andare; **he's ~ing well/ badly at school** va bene/male a scuola; **how ~ you ~?** piacere!

3 (*suit*) andare bene; **this room will ~** questa stanza va bene

4 (*be sufficient*) bastare; **will £10 ~?** basteranno 10 sterline?; **that'll ~** basta così; **that'll ~!** (*in annoyance*) ora basta!; **to make ~ (with)** arrangiarsi (con)

►**do away with** *vt fus* (*kill*) far fuori; (*abolish*) abolire

►**do for** *vt fus* (*BRIT col*: *clean for*) fare i servizi per

►**do out of** *vt fus*: **to ~ sb out of sth**

fregare qc a qn
►**do up** *vt* (*laces*) allacciare; (*dress, buttons*) abbottonare; (*renovate: room, house*) rimettere a nuovo, rifare; **to** ~ **o.s. up** farsi bello(a)
►**do with** *vt fus* (*need*) aver bisogno di; **I could** ~ **with some help/a drink** un aiuto/ un bicchierino non guasterebbe; **it could** ~ **with a wash** una lavata non gli farebbe male; (*be connected*): **what has it got to** ~ **with you?** e tu che c'entri?; **I won't have anything to** ~ **with it** non voglio avere niente a che farci; **it has to** ~ **with money** si tratta di soldi
►**do without** *vi* fare senza ♦ *vt fus* fare a meno di.

do. *abbr* = **ditto.**
DOA *abbr* (= *dead on arrival*) morto(a) durante il trasporto.
d.o.b. *abbr* = **date of birth.**
doc [dɔk] *n* (*col*) dottore/essa.
docile ['dəusaɪl] *adj* docile.
dock [dɔk] *n* bacino; (*wharf*) molo; (*LAW*) banco degli imputati ♦ *vi* entrare in bacino ♦ *vt* (*pay etc*) decurtare.
dock dues *npl* diritti *mpl* di banchina.
docker ['dɔkə*] *n* scaricatore *m.*
docket ['dɔkɪt] *n* (*on parcel etc*) etichetta, cartellino.
dockyard ['dɔkjɑːd] *n* cantiere *m* navale.
doctor ['dɔktə*] *n* medico, dottore/essa; (*PhD etc*) dottore/essa ♦ *vt* (*interfere with*: *food, drink*) adulterare; (: *text, document*) alterare, manipolare; ~**'s office** (*US*) gabinetto medico, ambulatorio; **D~ of Philosophy (PhD)** dottorato di ricerca; (*person*) titolare *m/f* di un dottorato di ricerca.
doctorate ['dɔktərɪt] *n* dottorato di ricerca; *see boxed note.*

DOCTORATE

Il **doctorate** *è il riconoscimento accademico più prestigioso in tutti i campi del sapere e viene conferito in seguito alla presentazione di una tesi originale di fronte ad una commissione di esperti. Generalmente tale tesi è un compendio del lavoro svolto durante più anni di studi; vedi anche* **Bachelor's degree,** **Master's degree.**

---

doctrine ['dɔktrɪn] *n* dottrina.
docudrama [dɔkju'drɑːmə] *n* (*TV*) ricostruzione *f* filmata.
document *n* ['dɔkjumənt] documento ♦ *vt* ['dɔkjumɛnt] documentare.

documentary [dɔkju'mɛntərɪ] *adj* documentario(a); (*evidence*) documentato(a) ♦ *n* documentario.
documentation [dɔkjumən'teɪʃən] *n* documentazione *f.*
DOD *n abbr* (*US*) = **Department of Defense;** *see* **defence.**
doddering ['dɔdərɪŋ] *adj* traballante.
doddery ['dɔdərɪ] *adj* malfermo(a).
doddle ['dɔdl] *n*: **it's a** ~ (*col*) è un gioco da ragazzi.
dodge [dɔdʒ] *n* trucco; schivata ♦ *vt* schivare, eludere ♦ *vi* scansarsi; (*SPORT*) fare una schivata; **to** ~ **out of the way** scansarsi; **to** ~ **through the traffic** destreggiarsi nel traffico.
dodgems ['dɔdʒəmz] *npl* (*BRIT*) autoscontri *mpl.*
dodgy ['dɔdʒɪ] *adj* (*col: uncertain*) rischioso(a); (*untrustworthy*) sospetto(a).
DOE *n abbr* (*US*) = **Department of Energy;** *see* **energy.**
doe [dəu] *n* (*deer*) femmina di daino; (*rabbit*) coniglia.
does [dʌz] *see* **do.**
doesn't ['dʌznt] = **does not.**
dog [dɔg] *n* cane *m* ♦ *vt* (*follow closely*) pedinare; (*fig: memory etc*) perseguitare; **to go to the** ~**s** (*person*) ridursi male, lasciarsi andare; (*nation etc*) andare in malora.
dog biscuits *npl* biscotti *mpl* per cani.
dog collar *n* collare *m* di cane; (*fig*) collarino.
dog-eared ['dɔgɪəd] *adj* (*book*) con orecchie.
dog food *n* cibo per cani.
dogged ['dɔgɪd] *adj* ostinato(a), tenace.
doggie, doggy ['dɔgɪ] *n* (*col*) cane *m,* cagnolino.
doggy bag *n* sacchetto per gli avanzi (*da portare a casa*).
dogma ['dɔgmə] *n* dogma *m.*
dogmatic [dɔg'mætɪk] *adj* dogmatico(a).
do-gooder [duː'gudə*] *n* (*col pej*): **to be a** ~ fare il filantropo.
dogsbody ['dɔgzbɔdɪ] *n* (*BRIT*) factotum *m inv.*
doily ['dɔɪlɪ] *n* centrino di carta sottopiatto.
doing ['duːɪŋ] *n*: **this is your** ~ è opera tua, sei stato tu; ~**s** *npl* attività *fpl.*
do-it-yourself (DIY) ['duːɪtjɔː'sɛlf] *n* il far da sé.
doldrums ['dɔldrəmz] *npl* (*fig*): **to be in the** ~ essere giù; (*business*) attraversare un momento difficile.
dole [dəul] *n* (*BRIT*) sussidio di disoccupazione; **to be on the** ~ vivere del

sussidio.

▶**dole out** *vt* distribuire.

doleful ['dəulful] *adj* triste, doloroso(a).

doll [dɔl] *n* bambola.

▶**doll up** *vt*: **to ~ o.s. up** farsi bello(a).

dollar ['dɔlə*] *n* dollaro.

dollop ['dɔləp] *n* (*of food*) cucchiaiata.

dolly ['dɔlɪ] *n* bambola.

dolphin ['dɔlfɪn] *n* delfino.

domain [də'meɪn] *n* dominio; (*fig*) campo, sfera.

dome [dəum] *n* cupola.

domestic [də'mɛstɪk] *adj* (*duty, happiness, animal*) domestico(a); (*policy, affairs, flights*) nazionale; (*news*) dall'interno.

domesticated [də'mɛstɪkeɪtɪd] *adj* addomesticato(a); (*person*) casalingo(a).

domesticity [dəumɛs'tɪsɪtɪ] *n* vita di famiglia.

domestic servant *n* domestico/a.

domicile ['dɔmɪsaɪl] *n* domicilio.

dominant ['dɔmɪnənt] *adj* dominante.

dominate ['dɔmɪneɪt] *vt* dominare.

domination [dɔmɪ'neɪʃən] *n* dominazione *f*.

domineering [dɔmɪ'nɪərɪŋ] *adj* dispotico(a), autoritario(a).

Dominican Republic [də'mɪnɪkən-] *n* Repubblica Dominicana.

dominion [də'mɪnɪən] *n* dominio; sovranità; (*BRIT POL*) dominion *m inv*.

domino, ~es ['dɔmɪnəu] *n* domino; **~es** *n* (*game*) gioco del domino.

don [dɔn] *n* (*BRIT*) docente *m/f* universitario(a) ♦ *vt* indossare.

donate [də'neɪt] *vt* donare.

donation [də'neɪʃən] *n* donazione *f*.

done [dʌn] *pp* of **do**.

donkey ['dɔŋkɪ] *n* asino.

donkey-work ['dɔŋkɪwəːk] *n* (*BRIT col*) lavoro ingrato.

donor ['dəunə*] *n* donatore/trice.

donor card *n* tessera di donatore di organi.

don't [dəunt] *vb* = **do not**.

donut ['dəunʌt] *n* (*US*) = **doughnut**.

doodle ['duːdl] *n* scarabocchio ♦ *vi* scarabocchiare.

doom [duːm] *n* destino; rovina ♦ *vt*: **to be ~ed** (**to failure**) essere predestinato(a) (a fallire).

doomsday ['duːmzdeɪ] *n* il giorno del Giudizio.

door [dɔː*] *n* porta; (*of vehicle*) sportello, portiera; **from ~ to ~** di porta in porta.

doorbell ['dɔːbɛl] *n* campanello.

door handle *n* maniglia.

doorman ['dɔːmæn] *n* (*in hotel*) portiere *m* in livrea; (*in block of flats*) portinaio.

doormat ['dɔːmæt] *n* stuoia della porta.

doorstep ['dɔːstɛp] *n* gradino della porta.

door-to-door ['dɔːtə'dɔː*] *adj*: **~ selling** vendita porta a porta.

doorway ['dɔːweɪ] *n* porta; **in the ~** nel vano della porta.

dope [dəup] *n* (*col*: *drugs*) roba; (: *information*) dati *mpl* ♦ *vt* (*horse etc*) drogare.

dopey ['dəupɪ] *adj* (*col*) inebetito(a).

dormant ['dɔːmənt] *adj* inattivo(a); (*fig*) latente.

dormer ['dɔːmə*] *n* (*also*: **~ window**) abbaino.

dormice ['dɔːmaɪs] *npl* of **dormouse**.

dormitory ['dɔːmɪtrɪ] *n* dormitorio; (*US*: *hall of residence*) casa dello studente.

dormouse, *pl* **dormice** ['dɔːmaus, -maɪs] *n* ghiro.

DOS [dɔs] *n* *abbr see* **disk operating system**.

dosage ['dəusɪdʒ] *n* (*on medicine bottle*) posologia.

dose [dəus] *n* dose *f*; (*BRIT*: *bout*) attacco ♦ *vt*: **to ~ sb with sth** somministrare qc a qn; **a ~ of flu** una bella influenza.

dosser ['dɔsə*] *n* (*BRIT col*) barbone/a.

doss house ['dɔs-] *n* (*BRIT*) asilo notturno.

dossier ['dɔsɪeɪ] *n* dossier *m inv*.

DOT *n* *abbr* (*US*) = **Department of Transportation**; *see* **transportation**.

dot [dɔt] *n* punto; macchiolina ♦ *vt*: **~ted with** punteggiato(a) di; **on the ~** in punto.

dot command *n* (*COMPUT*) dot command *m inv*.

dote [dəut]: **to ~ on** *vt fus* essere infatuato(a) di.

dot-matrix printer [dɔt'meɪtrɪks-] *n* stampante *f* a matrice a punti.

dotted line ['dɔtɪd-] *n* linea punteggiata; **to sign on the ~** firmare (nell'apposito spazio); (*fig*) accettare.

dotty ['dɔtɪ] *adj* (*col*) strambo(a).

double ['dʌbl] *adj* doppio(a) ♦ *adv* (*fold*) in due, doppio; (*twice*): **to cost ~** (**sth**) costare il doppio (di qc) ♦ *n* sosia *m inv*; (*CINE*) controfigura ♦ *vt* raddoppiare; (*fold*) piegare doppio *or* in due ♦ *vi* raddoppiarsi; **spelt with a ~ "l"** scritto con due elle *or* con doppia elle; **~ five two six (5526)** (*BRIT TEL*) cinque due sei; **on the ~**, (*BRIT*) **at the ~** a passo di corsa; **to ~ as** (*have two uses etc*) funzionare *or* servire anche da; *see also* **doubles**.

▶**double back** *vi* (*person*) tornare sui propri passi.

▶**double up** *vi* (*bend over*) piegarsi in due; (*share room*) dividere la stanza.

double bass n contrabbasso.
double bed n letto matrimoniale.
double-breasted ['dʌbl'brestɪd] adj a doppio petto.
double-check ['dʌbl'tʃɛk] vt, vi ricontrollare.
double-clutch ['dʌbl'klʌtʃ] vi (US) fare la doppietta.
double cream n (BRIT) doppia panna.
doublecross ['dʌbl'krɔs] vt fare il doppio gioco con.
doubledecker ['dʌbl'dɛkə*] n autobus m inv a due piani.
double declutch vi (BRIT) fare la doppietta.
double exposure n (PHOT) sovrimpressione f.
double glazing n (BRIT) doppi vetri mpl.
double-page ['dʌblpeɪdʒ] adj: ~ **spread** pubblicità a doppia pagina.
double parking n parcheggio in doppia fila.
double room n camera per due.
doubles ['dʌblz] n (TENNIS) doppio.
double time n tariffa doppia per lavoro straordinario.
double whammy [-'wæmɪ] n doppia mazzata (fig).
doubly ['dʌblɪ] adv doppiamente.
doubt [daut] n dubbio ♦ vt dubitare di; **to ~ that** dubitare che + sub; **without (a) ~** senza dubbio; **beyond ~** fuor di dubbio; **I ~ it very much** ho i miei dubbi, nutro seri dubbi in proposito.
doubtful ['dautful] adj dubbioso(a), incerto(a); (person) equivoco(a); **to be ~ about sth** avere dei dubbi su qc, non essere convinto di qc; **I'm a bit ~** non ne sono sicuro.
doubtless ['dautlɪs] adv indubbiamente.
dough [dəu] n pasta, impasto; (col: money) grana.
doughnut, (US) donut ['dəunʌt] n bombolone m.
dour [duə*] adj arcigno(a).
douse [daus] vt (with water) infradiciare; (flames) spegnere.
dove [dʌv] n colombo/a.
Dover ['dəuvə*] n Dover f.
dovetail ['dʌvteɪl] n: ~ **joint** incastro a coda di rondine ♦ vi (fig) combaciare.
dowager ['dauədʒə*] n vedova titolata.
dowdy ['daudɪ] adj trasandato(a); malvestito(a).
Dow-Jones average ['dau'dʒəunz-] n (US) indice m Dow-Jones.
down [daun] n (fluff) piumino; (hill) collina, colle m ♦ adv giù, di sotto ♦ prep giù per

♦ vt (col: drink) scolarsi; ~ **there** laggiù, là in fondo; ~ **here** quaggiù; **I'll be ~ in a minute** scendo tra un minuto; **the price of meat is** ~ il prezzo della carne è sceso; **I've got it** ~ **in my diary** ce l'ho sulla mia agenda; **to pay £2** ~ dare 2 sterline in acconto or di anticipo; **I've been** ~ **with flu** sono stato a letto con l'influenza; **England is two goals** ~ l'Inghilterra sta perdendo per due goal; **to** ~ **tools** (BRIT) incrociare le braccia; ~ **with X!** abbasso X!
down-and-out ['daunəndaut] n (tramp) barbone m.
down-at-heel ['daunət'hiːl] adj scalcagnato(a); (fig) trasandato(a).
downbeat ['daunbiːt] n (MUS) tempo in battere ♦ adj (col) volutamente distaccato(a).
downcast ['daunkɑːst] adj abbattuto(a).
downer ['daunə*] n (col: drug) farmaco depressivo; **to be on a** ~ (depressed) essere giù.
downfall ['daunfɔːl] n caduta; rovina.
downgrade ['daungreɪd] vt (job, hotel) declassare; (employee) degradare.
downhearted [daun'hɑːtɪd] adj scoraggiato(a).
downhill ['daun'hɪl] adv verso il basso ♦ n (SKI: also: ~ **race**) discesa libera; **to go** ~ andare in discesa; (business) andare a rotoli.
Downing Street ['daunɪŋ-] n: **10** ~ residenza del primo ministro inglese; see boxed note.

download ['daunləud] vt (COMPUT) trasferire (per esempio da un grosso calcolatore ad un microcalcolatore).
down-market ['daun'mɑːkɪt] adj rivolto(a) ad una fascia di mercato inferiore.
down payment n acconto.
downplay ['daunpleɪ] vt (US) minimizzare.
downpour ['daunpɔ:*] n scroscio di pioggia.
downright ['daunraɪt] adj franco(a); (refusal) assoluto(a).

downsize ['daun'saız] *vt* (*workforce*) ridurre.

Down's syndrome *n* sindrome *f* di Down.

downstairs ['daun'stɛəz] *adv* di sotto; al piano inferiore; **to come ~, go ~** scendere giù.

downstream ['daun'striːm] *adv* a valle.

downtime ['dauntaım] *n* (*COMM*) tempi *mpl* morti.

down-to-earth ['dauntu'əːθ] *adj* pratico(a).

downtown ['daun'taun] *adv* in città ♦ *adj* (*US*): **~ Chicago** il centro di Chicago.

downtrodden ['dauntrɔdn] *adj* oppresso(a).

down under *adv* agli antipodi.

downward ['daunwəd] *adj* in giù, in discesa; **a ~ trend** una diminuzione progressiva.

downward(s) ['daunwəd(z)] *adv* in giù, in discesa.

dowry ['daurı] *n* dote *f*.

doz. *abbr* = **dozen**.

doze [dəuz] *vi* sonnecchiare.
▶**doze off** *vi* appisolarsi.

dozen ['dʌzn] *n* dozzina; **a ~ books** una dozzina di libri; **80p a ~** 80 pence la dozzina; **~s of times** centinaia *or* migliaia di volte.

DPh, DPhil *n abbr* (= *Doctor of Philosophy*) ≈ dottorato di ricerca.

DPP *n abbr* (*BRIT*) *see* **Director of Public Prosecutions**.

DPT *n abbr* (*MED*: = *diphtheria, pertussis, tetanus*) *vaccino*.

Dr, Dr. *abbr* (= *doctor*) Dr, Dott./Dott.ssa.

dr *abbr* (*COMM*) = **debtor**.

Dr. *abbr* (*in street names*) = **drive**.

drab [dræb] *adj* tetro(a), grigio(a).

draft [drɑːft] *n* abbozzo; (*COMM*) tratta; (*US MIL*) contingente *m*; (: *call-up*) leva ♦ *vt* abbozzare; (*document, report*) stendere (in versione preliminare); *see also* **draught**.

drag [dræg] *vt* trascinare; (*river*) dragare ♦ *vi* trascinarsi ♦ *n* (*AVIAT, NAUT*) resistenza (aerodinamica); (*col: person*) noioso/a; (: *task*) noia; (*women's clothing*): **in ~** travestito (da donna).
▶**drag away** *vt*: **to ~ away (from)** tirare via (da).
▶**drag on** *vi* tirar avanti lentamente.

dragnet ['drægnɛt] *n* giacchio; (*fig*) rastrellamento.

dragon ['drægən] *n* drago.

dragonfly ['drægənflaı] *n* libellula.

dragoon [drə'guːn] *n* (*cavalryman*) dragone *m* ♦ *vt*: **to ~ sb into doing sth** (*BRIT*) costringere qn a fare qc.

drain [dreın] *n* canale *m* di scolo; (*for sewage*) fogna; (*on resources*) salasso ♦ *vt*

(*land, marshes*) prosciugare; (*vegetables*) scolare; (*reservoir etc*) vuotare ♦ *vi* (*water*) defluire; **to feel ~ed** sentirsi svuotato(a), sentirsi sfinito(a).

drainage ['dreınıdʒ] *n* prosciugamento; fognatura.

draining board ['dreınıŋ-], **drainboard** (*US*) ['dreınbɔːd] *n* piano del lavello.

drainpipe ['dreınpaıp] *n* tubo di scarico.

drake [dreık] *n* maschio dell'anatra.

dram [dræm] *n* bicchierino (di whisky *etc*).

drama ['drɑːmə] *n* (*art*) dramma *m*, teatro; (*play*) commedia; (*event*) dramma.

dramatic [drə'mætık] *adj* drammatico(a).

dramatically [drə'mætıklı] *adv* in modo spettacolare.

dramatist ['dræmətıst] *n* drammaturgo/a.

dramatize ['dræmətaız] *vt* (*events etc*) drammatizzare; (*adapt: novel: for TV*) ridurre *or* adattare per la televisione; (: *for cinema*) ridurre *or* adattare per lo schermo.

drank [dræŋk] *pt of* **drink**.

drape [dreıp] *vt* drappeggiare; *see also* **drapes**.

draper ['dreıpə*] *n* (*BRIT*) negoziante *m/f* di stoffe.

drapes [dreıps] *npl* (*US*) tende *fpl*.

drastic ['dræstık] *adj* drastico(a).

drastically ['dræstıklı] *adv* drasticamente.

draught, (*US*) draft [drɑːft] *n* corrente *f* d'aria; (*NAUT*) pescaggio; **on ~** (*beer*) alla spina; *see also* **draughts**.

draught beer *n* birra alla spina.

draughtboard ['drɑːftbɔːd] *n* scacchiera.

draughts [drɑːfts] *n* (*BRIT*) (gioco della) dama.

draughtsman, (*US*) draftsman ['drɑːftsmən] *n* disegnatore *m*.

draughtsmanship, (*US*) draftsmanship ['drɑːftsmənʃıp] *n* disegno tecnico; (*skill*) arte *f* del disegno.

draw [drɔː] *vb* (*pt* **drew**, *pp* **drawn** [druː, drɔːn]) *vt* tirare; (*attract*) attirare; (*picture*) disegnare; (*line, circle*) tracciare; (*money*) ritirare; (*formulate: conclusion*) trarre, ricavare; (: *comparison, distinction*): **to ~ (between)** fare (tra) ♦ *vi* (*SPORT*) pareggiare ♦ *n* (*SPORT*) pareggio; (*in lottery*) estrazione *f*; (*attraction*) attrazione *f*; **to ~ to a close** avvicinarsi alla conclusione; **to ~ near** *vi* avvicinarsi.
▶**draw back** *vi*: **to ~ back (from)** indietreggiare (di fronte a), tirarsi indietro (di fronte a).
▶**draw in** *vi* (*BRIT: car*) accostarsi; (: *train*) entrare in stazione.
▶**draw on** *vt* (*resources*) attingere a;

(imagination, person) far ricorso a.
►**draw out** vi (lengthen) allungarsi ♦ vt
(money) ritirare.
►**draw up** vi (stop) arrestarsi, fermarsi
♦ vt (document) compilare; (plans)
formulare.
drawback ['drɔːbæk] n svantaggio,
inconveniente m.
drawbridge ['drɔːbrɪdʒ] n ponte m levatoio.
drawee [drɔː'iː] n trattario.
drawer [drɔː*] n cassetto; ['drɔːə*] (of
cheque) riscuotitore/trice.
drawing ['drɔːɪŋ] n disegno.
drawing board n tavola da disegno.
drawing pin n (BRIT) puntina da disegno.
drawing room n salotto.
drawl [drɔːl] n pronuncia strascicata.
drawn [drɔːn] pp of **draw** ♦ adj (haggard: with
tiredness) tirato(a); (: with pain)
contratto(a) (dal dolore).
drawstring ['drɔːstrɪŋ] n laccio (per
stringere maglie, sacche etc).
dread [drɛd] n terrore m ♦ vt tremare
all'idea di.
dreadful ['drɛdful] adj terribile; **I feel** ~! (ill)
mi sento uno straccio!; (ashamed) vorrei
scomparire (dalla vergogna)!
dream [driːm] n sogno ♦ vt, vi (pt, pp
dreamed or **dreamt** [drɛmt]) sognare; **to
have a** ~ **about sb/sth** fare un sogno su
qn/qc; **sweet** ~**s!** sogni d'oro!
►**dream up** vt (reason, excuse) inventare;
(plan, idea) escogitare.
dreamer ['driːmə*] n sognatore/trice.
dreamt [drɛmt] pt, pp of **dream**.
dreamy ['driːmɪ] adj (look, voice) sognante;
(person) distratto(a), sognatore(trice).
dreary ['drɪərɪ] adj tetro(a); monotono(a).
dredge [drɛdʒ] vt dragare.
►**dredge up** vt tirare alla superficie; (fig:
unpleasant facts) rivangare.
dredger ['drɛdʒə*] n draga; (BRIT: also:
sugar ~) spargizucchero m inv.
dregs [drɛgz] npl feccia.
drench [drɛntʃ] vt inzuppare; ~**ed to the
skin** bagnato(a) fino all'osso, bagnato(a)
fradicio(a).
dress [drɛs] n vestito; (clothing)
abbigliamento ♦ vt vestire; (wound)
fasciare; (food) condire; preparare; (shop
window) allestire ♦ vi vestirsi; **to** ~ **o.s.,
to get** ~**ed** vestirsi; **she** ~**es very well**
veste molto bene.
►**dress up** vi vestirsi a festa; (in fancy
dress) vestirsi in costume.
dress circle n prima galleria.
dress designer n disegnatore/trice di
moda.

dresser ['drɛsə*] n (THEAT) assistente m/f
del camerino; (also: **window** ~) vetrinista
m/f; (furniture) credenza.
dressing ['drɛsɪŋ] n (MED) benda; (CULIN)
condimento.
dressing gown n (BRIT) vestaglia.
dressing room n (THEAT) camerino;
(SPORT) spogliatoio.
dressing table n toilette f inv.
dressmaker ['drɛsmeɪkə*] n sarta.
dressmaking ['drɛsmeɪkɪŋ] n sartoria;
confezioni fpl per donna.
dress rehearsal n prova generale.
dress shirt n camicia da sera.
dressy ['drɛsɪ] adj (col) elegante.
drew [druː] pt of **draw**.
dribble ['drɪbl] vi gocciolare; (baby)
sbavare; (FOOTBALL) dribblare ♦ vt
dribblare.
dried [draɪd] adj (fruit, beans) secco(a);
(eggs, milk) in polvere.
drier ['draɪə*] n = **dryer.**
drift [drɪft] n (of current etc) direzione f;
forza; (of sand, snow) cumulo; (general
meaning) senso ♦ vi (boat) essere
trasportato(a) dalla corrente; (sand,
snow) ammucchiarsi; **to catch sb's** ~
capire dove qn vuole arrivare; **to let
things** ~ lasciare che le cose vadano
come vogliono; **to** ~ **apart** (friends)
perdersi di vista; (lovers) allontanarsi
l'uno dall'altro.
drifter ['drɪftə*] n persona che fa una vita
da zingaro.
driftwood ['drɪftwud] n resti mpl della
mareggiata.
drill [drɪl] n trapano; (MIL) esercitazione f
♦ vt trapanare; (soldiers) esercitare,
addestrare; (pupils: in grammar) fare
esercitare ♦ vi (for oil) fare trivellazioni.
drilling ['drɪlɪŋ] n (for oil) trivellazione f.
drilling rig n (on land) torre f di
perforazione; (at sea) piattaforma (per
trivellazioni subacquee).
drily ['draɪlɪ] adv = **dryly.**
drink [drɪŋk] n bevanda, bibita ♦ vt, vi (pt
drank, pp **drunk** [dræŋk, drʌŋk]) bere; **to
have a** ~ bere qualcosa; **a** ~ **of water** un
bicchier d'acqua; **would you like
something to** ~? vuole qualcosa da
bere?; **we had** ~**s before lunch** abbiamo
preso l'aperitivo.
►**drink in** vt (subj: person: fresh air)
aspirare; (: story) ascoltare avidamente;
(: sight) ammirare, bersi con gli occhi.
drinkable ['drɪŋkəbl] adj (not poisonous)
potabile; (palatable) bevibile.
drink-driving ['drɪŋk'draɪvɪŋ] n guida in

stato di ebbrezza.

drinker ['drɪŋkə*] n bevitore/trice.

drinking ['drɪŋkɪŋ] n (*drunkenness*) il bere, alcoolismo.

drinking fountain n fontanella.

drinking water n acqua potabile.

drip [drɪp] n goccia; (~*ping*) sgocciolio; (*MED*) fleboclisi *f inv*; (*col*: *spineless person*) lavativo ♦ *vi* gocciolare; (*washing*) sgocciolare; (*wall*) trasudare.

drip-dry ['drɪp'draɪ] *adj* (*shirt*) che non si stira.

drip-feed ['drɪpfiːd] *vt* alimentare mediante fleboclisi.

dripping ['drɪpɪŋ] n (*CULIN*) grasso d'arrosto ♦ *adj*: ~ **wet** fradicio(a).

drive [draɪv] n passeggiata *or* giro in macchina; (*also*: ~**way**) viale *m* d'accesso; (*energy*) energia; (*PSYCH*) impulso; bisogno; (*push*) sforzo eccezionale; campagna; (*SPORT*) drive *m inv*; (*TECH*) trasmissione *f*; (*COMPUT*: *also*: **disk** ~) disk drive *m inv*, unità *f inv* a dischi magnetici ♦ *vb* (*pt* **drove**, *pp* **driven** [drəuv, 'drɪvn]) *vt* (*vehicle*) guidare; (*nail*) piantare; (*push*) cacciare, spingere; (*TECH*: *motor*) azionare; far funzionare ♦ *vi* (*AUT*: *at controls*) guidare; (: *travel*) andare in macchina; **to go for a** ~ andare a fare un giro in macchina; **it's 3 hours'** ~ **from London** è a 3 ore di macchina da Londra; **left-/right-hand** ~ (*AUT*) guida a sinistra/ destra; **front-/rear-wheel** ~ (*AUT*) trazione *f* anteriore/posteriore; **to** ~ **sb to (do) sth** spingere qn a (fare) qc; **he** ~**s a taxi** fa il tassista; **to** ~ **at 50 km an hour** guidare *or* andare a 50 km all'ora.

▶**drive at** *vt fus* (*fig*: *intend*, *mean*) mirare a, voler dire.

▶**drive on** *vi* proseguire, andare (più) avanti ♦ *vt* (*incite*, *encourage*) sospingere, spingere.

drive-by ['draɪvbaɪ] n (*also*: ~ **shooting**) sparatoria dalla macchina; **he was killed in a** ~ **shooting** lo hanno ammazzato sparandogli da una macchina in corsa.

drive-in ['draɪvɪn] *adj*, n (*esp US*) drive-in (*m inv*).

drive-in window n (*US*) sportello di drive-in.

drivel ['drɪvl] n (*col*: *nonsense*) ciance *fpl*.

driven ['drɪvn] *pp of* **drive**.

driver ['draɪvə*] n conducente *m/f*; (*of taxi*) tassista *m*; (*of bus*) autista *m*; (*COMPUT*) driver *m inv*.

driver's license n (*US*) patente *f* di guida.

driveway ['draɪvweɪ] n viale *m* d'accesso.

driving ['draɪvɪŋ] *adj*: ~ **rain** pioggia

sferzante ♦ *n* guida.

driving force n forza trainante.

driving instructor n istruttore/trice di scuola guida.

driving lesson n lezione *f* di guida.

driving licence n (*BRIT*) patente *f* di guida.

driving school n scuola *f* guida *inv*.

driving test n esame *m* di guida.

drizzle ['drɪzl] n pioggerella ♦ *vi* piovigginare.

droll [drəul] *adj* buffo(a).

dromedary ['drɔmədərɪ] n dromedario.

drone [drəun] n ronzio; (*male bee*) fuco ♦ *vi* (*bee, aircraft, engine*) ronzare; (*also*: ~ **on**: *person*) continuare a parlare (in modo monotono); (: *voice*) continuare a ronzare.

drool [druːl] *vi* sbavare; **to** ~ **over sb/sth** (*fig*) andare in estasi per qn/qc.

droop [druːp] *vi* abbassarsi; languire.

drop [drɔp] n goccia; (*fall*: *in price*) calo, ribasso; (: *in salary*) riduzione *f*, taglio; (*also*: **parachute** ~) lancio; (*steep incline*) salto ♦ *vt* lasciar cadere; (*voice, eyes, price*) abbassare; (*set down from car*) far scendere ♦ *vi* cascare; (*decrease*: *wind, temperature, price, voice*) calare; (*numbers, attendance*) diminuire; ~**s** *npl* (*MED*) gocce *fpl*; **cough** ~**s** pastiglie *fpl* per la tosse; **a** ~ **of 10%** un calo del 10%; **to** ~ **sb a line** mandare due righe a qn; **to** ~ **anchor** gettare l'ancora.

▶**drop in** *vi* (*col*: *visit*): **to** ~ **in (on)** fare un salto (da), passare (da).

▶**drop off** *vi* (*sleep*) addormentarsi ♦ *vt*: **to** ~ **sb off** far scendere qn.

▶**drop out** *vi* (*withdraw*) ritirarsi; (*student etc*) smettere di studiare.

droplet ['drɔplɪt] n gocciolina.

dropout ['drɔpaut] n (*from society/university*) chi ha abbandonato (la società/gli studi).

dropper ['drɔpə*] n (*MED*) contagocce *m inv*.

droppings ['drɔpɪŋz] *npl* sterco.

dross [drɔs] n scoria; scarto.

drought [draut] n siccità *f inv*.

drove [drəuv] *pt of* **drive** ♦ *n*: ~**s of people** una moltitudine di persone.

drown [draun] *vt* affogare; (*also*: ~ **out**: *sound*) coprire ♦ *vi* affogare.

drowse [drauz] *vi* sonnecchiare.

drowsy ['drauzɪ] *adj* sonnolento(a), assonnato(a).

drudge [drʌdʒ] n (*person*) uomo/donna di fatica; (*job*) faticaccia.

drudgery ['drʌdʒərɪ] n fatica improba; **housework is sheer** ~ le faccende domestiche sono alienanti.

drug [drʌg] n farmaco; (*narcotic*) droga ♦ *vt* drogare; **he's on** ~**s** si droga; (*MED*) segue una cura.

drug abuser [-ə'bjuːzə*] n chi fa uso di droghe.

drug addict n tossicomane m/f.

druggist ['drʌgɪst] n (US) farmacista m/f.

drug peddler n spacciatore/trice di droga.

drugstore ['drʌgstɔː*] n (US) negozio di generi vari e di articoli di farmacia con un bar.

drum [drʌm] n tamburo; (for oil, petrol) fusto ♦ vt: **to ~ one's fingers on the table** tamburellare con le dita sulla tavola; **~s** npl (MUS) batteria.

▶**drum up** vt (enthusiasm, support) conquistarsi.

drummer ['drʌmə*] n batterista m/f.

drum roll n rullio di tamburi.

drumstick ['drʌmstɪk] n (MUS) bacchetta; (chicken leg) coscia di pollo.

drunk [drʌŋk] pp of **drink** ♦ adj ubriaco(a); ebbro(a) ♦ n ubriacone/a; **to get ~** ubriacarsi, prendere una sbornia.

drunkard ['drʌŋkəd] n ubriacone/a.

drunken ['drʌŋkən] adj ubriaco(a); da ubriaco; **~ driving** guida in stato di ebbrezza.

drunkenness ['drʌŋkənnɪs] n ubriachezza; ebbrezza.

dry [draɪ] adj secco(a); (day, clothes, fig: humour) asciutto(a); (uninteresting: lecture, subject) poco avvincente ♦ vt seccare; (clothes, hair, hands) asciugare ♦ vi asciugarsi; **on ~ land** sulla terraferma; **to ~ one's hands/hair/eyes** asciugarsi le mani/i capelli/gli occhi.

▶**dry up** vi seccarsi; (source of supply) esaurirsi; (fig: imagination etc) inaridirsi; (fall silent: speaker) azzittirsi.

dry-clean [draɪ'kliːn] vt pulire or lavare a secco.

dry-cleaner's [draɪ'kliːnəz] n lavasecco m inv.

dry-cleaning [draɪ'kliːnɪŋ] n pulitura a secco.

dry dock n (NAUT) bacino di carenaggio.

dryer ['draɪə*] n (for hair) föhn m inv, asciugacapelli m inv; (for clothes) asciugabiancheria m inv.

dry goods npl (COMM) tessuti mpl e mercerie fpl.

dry goods store n (US) negozio di stoffe.

dry ice n ghiaccio secco.

dryly ['draɪlɪ] adv con fare asciutto.

dryness ['draɪnɪs] n secchezza; (of ground) aridità.

dry rot n fungo del legno.

dry run n (fig) prova.

dry ski slope n pista artificiale.

DSc n abbr (= Doctor of Science) titolo di studio.

DSS n abbr (BRIT) = **Department of Social Security**; see **social security**.

DST abbr = **Daylight Saving Time**.

DTI n abbr (BRIT) = **Department of Trade and Industry**; see **trade**.

DTP n abbr = **desktop publishing**; (MED: = diphtheria, tetanus, pertussis) vaccino.

DT's n abbr (col) = **delirium tremens**.

dual ['djuəl] adj doppio(a).

dual carriageway n (BRIT) strada a doppia carreggiata.

dual-control ['djuəlkən'trəul] adj con doppi comandi.

dual nationality n doppia nazionalità.

dual-purpose ['djuəl'pəːpəs] adj a doppio uso.

dubbed [dʌbd] adj (CINE) doppiato(a); (nicknamed) soprannominato(a).

dubious ['djuːbɪəs] adj dubbio(a); (character, manner) ambiguo(a), equivoco(a); **I'm very ~ about it** ho i miei dubbi in proposito.

Dublin ['dʌblɪn] n Dublino f.

Dubliner ['dʌblɪnə*] n dublinese m/f.

duchess ['dʌtʃɪs] n duchessa.

duck [dʌk] n anatra ♦ vi abbassare la testa ♦ vt spingere sotto (acqua).

duckling ['dʌklɪŋ] n anatroccolo.

duct [dʌkt] n condotto; (ANAT) canale m.

dud [dʌd] n (shell) proiettile m che fa cilecca; (object, tool): **it's a ~** è inutile, non funziona ♦ adj (BRIT: cheque) a vuoto; (note, coin) falso(a).

due [djuː] adj dovuto(a); (expected) atteso(a); (fitting) giusto(a) ♦ n dovuto ♦ adv: **~ north** diritto verso nord; **~s** npl (for club, union) quota; (in harbour) diritti mpl di porto; **in ~ course** a tempo debito; finalmente; **~ to** dovuto a; a causa di; **the rent's ~ on the 30th** l'affitto scade il 30; **the train is ~ at 8** il treno è atteso per le 8; **she is ~ back tomorrow** dovrebbe essere di ritorno domani; **I am ~ 6 days' leave** mi spettano 6 giorni di ferie.

due date n data di scadenza.

duel ['djuəl] n duello.

duet [djuː'ɛt] n duetto.

duff [dʌf] adj (BRIT col) barboso(a).

duffelbag, duffle bag ['dʌflbæg] n sacca da viaggio di tela.

duffelcoat, duffle coat ['dʌflkəut] n montgomery m inv.

duffer ['dʌfə*] n (col) schiappa.

dug [dʌg] pt, pp of **dig**.

dugout ['dʌgaut] n (FOOTBALL) panchina.

duke [djuːk] n duca m.

dull [dʌl] adj (boring) noioso(a); (slow-witted) ottuso(a); (sound, pain) sordo(a); (weather, day) fosco(a), scuro(a); (blade) smussato(a) ♦ vt (pain, grief) attutire; (mind, senses) intorpidire.

duly ['djuːlɪ] adv (on time) a tempo debito; (as expected) debitamente.

dumb [dʌm] adj muto(a); (stupid) stupido(a); **to be struck ~** (fig) ammutolire, restare senza parole.

dumbbell ['dʌmbɛl] n (SPORT) manubrio, peso.

dumbfounded [dʌm'faundɪd] adj stupito(a), stordito(a).

dummy ['dʌmɪ] n (tailor's model) manichino; (SPORT) finto; (BRIT: for baby) tettarella ♦ adj falso(a), finto(a).

dummy run n giro di prova.

dump [dʌmp] n mucchio di rifiuti; (place) luogo di scarico; (MIL) deposito; (COMPUT) scaricamento, dump m inv ♦ vt (put down) scaricare; mettere giù; (get rid of) buttar via; (COMM: goods) svendere; (COMPUT) scaricare; **to be (down) in the ~s** (col) essere giù di corda.

dumping ['dʌmpɪŋ] n (ECON) dumping m; (of rubbish): **"no ~"** "vietato lo scarico".

dumpling ['dʌmplɪŋ] n specie di gnocco.

dumpy ['dʌmpɪ] adj tracagnotto(a).

dunce [dʌns] n asino.

dune [djuːn] n duna.

dung [dʌŋ] n concime m.

dungarees [dʌŋgə'riːz] npl tuta.

dungeon ['dʌndʒən] n prigione f sotterranea.

dunk [dʌŋk] vt inzuppare.

duo ['djuːəu] n (gen, MUS) duo m inv.

duodenal [djuːəu'diːnl] adj (ulcer) duodenale.

duodenum [djuːəu'diːnəm] n duodeno.

dupe [djuːp] vt gabbare, ingannare.

duplex ['djuːplɛks] n (US: also: ~ apartment) appartamento su due piani.

duplicate n ['djuːplɪkət] doppio; (copy of letter etc) duplicato ♦ vt ['djuːplɪkeɪt] raddoppiare; (on machine) ciclostilare ♦ adj (copy) conforme, esattamente uguale; **in ~** in duplice copia; **~ key** duplicato (della chiave).

duplicating machine ['djuːplɪkeɪtɪŋ-], **duplicator** ['djuːplɪkeɪtə*] n duplicatore m.

duplicity [djuː'plɪsɪtɪ] n doppiezza, duplicità.

Dur. abbr (BRIT) = Durham.

durability [djuərə'bɪlɪtɪ] n durevolezza; resistenza.

durable ['djuərəbl] adj durevole; (clothes,

metal) resistente.

duration [djuə'reɪʃən] n durata.

duress [djuə'rɛs] n: **under ~** sotto costrizione.

Durex ® ['djuərɛks] n (BRIT) preservativo.

during ['djuərɪŋ] prep durante, nel corso di.

dusk [dʌsk] n crepuscolo.

dusky ['dʌskɪ] adj scuro(a).

dust [dʌst] n polvere f ♦ vt (furniture) spolverare; (cake etc): **to ~ with** cospargere con.

▸**dust off** vt rispolverare.

dustbin ['dʌstbɪn] n (BRIT) pattumiera.

duster ['dʌstə*] n straccio per la polvere.

dust jacket n sopraccoperta.

dustman ['dʌstmən] n (BRIT) netturbino.

dustpan ['dʌstpæn] n pattumiera.

dusty ['dʌstɪ] adj polveroso(a).

Dutch [dʌtʃ] adj olandese ♦ n (LING) olandese m ♦ adv: **to go ~** or **d~** fare alla romana; **the ~** gli Olandesi.

Dutch auction n asta all'olandese.

Dutchman ['dʌtʃmən], **Dutchwoman** ['dʌtʃwumən] n olandese m/f.

dutiable ['djuːtɪəbl] adj soggetto(a) a dazio.

dutiful ['djuːtɪful] adj (child) rispettoso(a); (husband) premuroso(a); (employee) coscienzioso(a).

duty ['djuːtɪ] n dovere m; (tax) dazio, tassa; **duties** npl mansioni fpl; **on ~** di servizio; (MED: in hospital) di guardia; **off ~** libero(a), fuori servizio; **to make it one's ~ to do sth** assumersi l'obbligo di fare qc; **to pay ~ on sth** pagare il dazio su qc.

duty-free ['djuːtɪ'friː] adj esente da dazio; ~ **shop** duty free m inv.

duty officer n (MIL etc) ufficiale m di servizio.

duvet ['duːveɪ] n piumino, piumone m.

DV abbr (= Deo volente) D.V.

DVD n abbr (= digital versatile or video disc) DVD m inv.

DVD player n lettore m DVD.

DVLA n abbr (BRIT: = Driver and Vehicle Licensing Agency) ≈ I.M.C.T.C. m (= Ispettorato Generale della Motorizzazione Civile e dei Trasporti in Concessione).

DVM n abbr (US: = Doctor of Veterinary Medicine) titolo di studio.

DVT n abbr = **deep-vein thrombosis**.

dwarf [dwɔːf] n nano/a ♦ vt far apparire piccolo.

dwell [dwɛl], pt, pp **dwelt** [dwɛl, dwɛlt] vi dimorare.

▸**dwell on** vt fus indugiare su.

dweller ['dwɛlə*] n abitante m/f; **city ~** cittadino/a.

dwelling ['dwɛlɪŋ] n dimora.

dwelt [dwɛlt] *pt, pp of* **dwell.**

dwindle ['dwɪndl] *vi* diminuire, decrescere.

dwindling ['dwɪndlɪŋ] *adj* (*strength, interest*) che si affievolisce; (*resources, supplies*) in diminuzione.

dye [daɪ] *n* colore *m*; (*chemical*) colorante *m*, tintura ♦ *vt* tingere; **hair** ~ tinta per capelli.

dyestuffs ['daɪstʌfs] *npl* coloranti *mpl.*

dying ['daɪɪŋ] *adj* morente, moribondo(a).

dyke [daɪk] *n* diga; (*channel*) canale *m* di scolo; (*causeway*) sentiero rialzato.

dynamic [daɪ'næmɪk] *adj* dinamico(a).

dynamics [daɪ'næmɪks] *n or npl* dinamica.

dynamite ['daɪnəmaɪt] *n* dinamite *f* ♦ *vt* far saltare con la dinamite.

dynamo ['daɪnəməu] *n* dinamo *f inv.*

dynasty ['dɪnəstɪ] *n* dinastia.

dysentery ['dɪsntrɪ] *n* dissenteria.

dyslexia [dɪs'lɛksɪə] *n* dislessia.

dyslexic [dɪs'lɛksɪk] *adj, n* dislessico(a).

dyspepsia [dɪs'pɛpsɪə] *n* dispepsia.

dystrophy ['dɪstrəfɪ] *n* distrofia; **muscular** ~ distrofia muscolare.

E e

E, e [iː] *n* (*letter*) E, e *f or m inv*; (*MUS*): **E** mi *m*; **E for Edward,** (*US*) **E for Easy** ≈ E come Empoli.

E *abbr* (= *east*) E ♦ *n abbr* (= *Ecstasy*) ecstasy *f inv.*

e- ['iː] *prefix* e-.

E111 *n abbr* (*also:* **form** ~) E111 (*modulo UE per rimborso spese mediche*).

ea. *abbr* = **each.**

each [iːtʃ] *adj* ogni, ciascuno(a) ♦ *pron* ciascuno(a), ognuno(a); ~ **one** ognuno(a); ~ **other** si (*or* ci *etc*); **they hate** ~ **other** si odiano (l'un l'altro); **you are jealous of** ~ **other** siete gelosi l'uno dell'altro; ~ **day** ogni giorno; **they have 2 books** ~ hanno 2 libri ciascuno; **they cost £5** ~ costano 5 sterline l'uno; ~ **of us** ciascuno *or* ognuno di noi.

eager ['iːgə*] *adj* impaziente; desideroso(a); ardente; (*keen: pupil*) appassionato(a), attento(a); **to be** ~ **to do sth** non veder l'ora di fare qc; **to be** ~ **for** essere desideroso di fare qc; **to be** ~ **for** essere desideroso di, aver gran voglia di.

eagle ['iːgl] *n* aquila.

E & OE *abbr* (= *errors and omissions excepted*) S.E.O.

ear [ɪə*] *n* orecchio; (*of corn*) pannocchia; **up to the** ~**s in debt** nei debiti fino al collo.

earache ['ɪəreɪk] *n* mal *m* d'orecchi.

eardrum ['ɪədrʌm] *n* timpano.

earful ['ɪəful] *n*: **to give sb an** ~ fare una ramanzina a qn.

earl [əːl] *n* conte *m.*

earlier ['əːlɪə*] *adj* (*date etc*) anteriore; (*edition etc*) precedente, anteriore ♦ *adv* prima; **I can't come any** ~ non posso venire prima.

early ['əːlɪ] *adv* presto, di buon'ora; (*ahead of time*) in anticipo ♦ *adj* precoce; anticipato(a); che si fa vedere di buon'ora; (*man*) primitivo(a); (*Christians, settlers*) primo(a); ~ **in the morning/ afternoon** nelle prime ore del mattino/del pomeriggio; **you're** ~! sei in anticipo!; **have an** ~ **night/start** vada a letto/parta presto; **in the** ~ *or* ~ **in the spring/19th century** all'inizio della primavera/ dell'Ottocento; **she's in her** ~ **forties** ha appena passato la quarantina; **at your earliest convenience** (*COMM*) non appena possibile.

early retirement *n* ritiro anticipato.

early warning system *n* sistema *m* del preallarme.

earmark ['ɪəmɑːk] *vt*: **to** ~ **sth for** destinare qc a.

earn [əːn] *vt* guadagnare; (*rest, reward*) meritare; (*COMM: yield*) maturare; **to** ~ **one's living** guadagnarsi da vivere; **this** ~**ed him much praise, he** ~**ed much praise for this** si è attirato grandi lodi per questo.

earned income *n* reddito da lavoro.

earnest ['əːnɪst] *adj* serio(a) ♦ *n* (*also:* ~ **money**) caparra; **in** ~ *adv* sul serio.

earnings ['əːnɪŋz] *npl* guadagni *mpl*; (*of company etc*) proventi *mpl*; (*salary*) stipendio.

ear, nose and throat specialist *n* otorinolaringoiatra *m/f.*

earphones ['ɪəfəunz] *npl* cuffia.

earplugs ['ɪəplʌgz] *npl* tappi *mpl* per le orecchie.

earring ['ɪərɪŋ] *n* orecchino.

earshot ['ɪəʃɔt] *n*: **out of/within** ~ fuori portata/a portata d'orecchio.

earth [əːθ] *n* (*gen, also BRIT ELEC*) terra; (*of fox etc*) tana ♦ *vt* (*BRIT ELEC*) mettere a terra.

earthenware ['əːθənwɛə*] *n* terracotta;

stoviglie *fpl* di terracotta ♦ *adj* di terracotta.

earthly ['ɔ:θlɪ] *adj* terreno(a); ~ **paradise** paradiso terrestre; **there is no** ~ **reason to think** ... non vi è ragione di pensare ....

earthquake ['ɔ:θkweɪk] *n* terremoto.

earth-shattering ['ɔ:θʃætərɪŋ] *adj* stupefacente.

earth tremor *n* scossa sismica.

earthworks ['ɔ:θwɔ:ks] *npl* lavori *mpl* di sterro.

earthworm ['ɔ:θwɔ:m] *n* lombrico.

earthy ['ɔ:θɪ] *adj* (*fig*) grossolano(a).

earwax ['ɪəwæks] *n* cerume *m*.

earwig ['ɪəwɪg] *n* forbicina.

ease [i:z] *n* agio, comodo ♦ *vt* (*soothe*) calmare; (*loosen*) allentare ♦ *vi* (*situation*) allentarsi, distendersi; **life of** ~ vita comoda; **with** ~ senza difficoltà; **at** ~ a proprio agio; (*MIL*) a riposo; **to feel at** ~/ **ill at** ~ sentirsi a proprio agio/a disagio; **to** ~ **sth out/in** tirare fuori/infilare qc con delicatezza; facilitare l'uscita/ l'entrata di qc.

► **ease off, ease up** *vi* diminuire; (*slow down*) rallentarsi; (*fig*) rilassarsi.

easel ['i:zl] *n* cavalletto.

easily ['i:zɪlɪ] *adv* facilmente.

easiness ['i:zɪnɪs] *n* facilità, semplicità; (*of manners*) disinvoltura.

east [i:st] *n* est *m* ♦ *adj* dell'est ♦ *adv* a oriente; **the E~** l'Oriente *m*; (*POL*) i Paesi dell'Est.

Easter ['i:stə*] *n* Pasqua ♦ *adj* (*holidays*) pasquale, di Pasqua.

Easter egg *n* uovo di Pasqua.

Easter Island *n* isola di Pasqua.

easterly ['i:stəlɪ] *adj* dall'est, d'oriente.

Easter Monday *n* Pasquetta.

eastern ['i:stən] *adj* orientale, d'oriente; **E~ Europe** l'Europa orientale; **the E~ bloc** (*POL*) i Paesi dell'Est.

Easter Sunday *n* domenica di Pasqua.

East Germany *n* Germania dell'Est.

eastward(s) ['i:stwəd(z)] *adv* verso est, verso levante.

easy ['i:zɪ] *adj* facile; (*manner*) disinvolto(a); (*carefree*: *life*) agiato(a), tranquillo(a) ♦ *adv*: **to take it** *or* **things** ~ prendersela con calma; **I'm** ~ (*col*) non ho problemi; **easier said than done** tra il dire e il fare c'è di mezzo il mare; **payment on** ~ **terms** (*COMM*) facilitazioni *fpl* di pagamento.

easy chair *n* poltrona.

easy-going ['i:zɪ'gəʊɪŋ] *adj* accomodante.

eat, *pt* **ate**, *pp* **eaten** [i:t, eɪt, 'i:tn] *vt* mangiare.

► **eat away** *vt* (*subj*: *sea*) erodere; (: *acid*) corrodere.

► **eat away at, eat into** *vt fus* rodere.

► **eat out** *vi* mangiare fuori.

► **eat up** *vt* (*meal etc*) finire di mangiare; **it** ~**s up electricity** consuma un sacco di corrente.

eatable ['i:təbl] *adj* mangiabile; (*safe to eat*) commestibile.

eaten ['i:tn] *pp of* **eat**.

eau de Cologne ['əʊdəkə'ləʊn] *n* acqua di colonia.

eaves [i:vz] *npl* gronda.

eavesdrop ['i:vzdrɒp] *vi*: **to** ~ (**on a conversation**) origliare (una conversazione).

ebb [ɛb] *n* riflusso ♦ *vi* rifluire; (*fig*: *also*: ~ **away**) declinare; ~ **and flow** flusso e riflusso; **to be at a low** ~ (*fig*: *person*, *spirits*) avere il morale a terra; (: *business*) andar male.

ebony ['ɛbənɪ] *n* ebano.

ebullient [ɪ'bʌlɪənt] *adj* esuberante.

ECB *n abbr* (= *European Central Bank*) BCE *f*

eccentric [ɪk'sɛntrɪk] *adj*, *n* eccentrico(a).

ecclesiastic [ɪkli:zɪ'æstɪk] *n* ecclesiastico.

ecclesiastic(al) [ɪkli:zɪ'æstɪk(əl)] *adj* ecclesiastico(a).

ECG *n abbr see* **electrocardiogram**.

echo, ~ **es** ['ɛkəʊ] *n* eco *m or f* ♦ *vt* ripetere; fare eco a ♦ *vi* echeggiare; dare un eco.

éclair ['eɪkleə*] *n* ≈ bignè *m inv*.

eclipse [ɪ'klɪps] *n* eclissi *f inv* ♦ *vt* eclissare.

eco... ['i:kəʊ] *prefix* eco....

eco-friendly [i:kəʊ'frɛndlɪ] *adj* ecologico(a).

ecological [i:kə'lɒdʒɪkəl] *adj* ecologico(a).

ecologist [ɪ'kɒlədʒɪst] *n* ecologo/a.

ecology [ɪ'kɒlədʒɪ] *n* ecologia.

e-commerce ['i:kɒmɜ:s] *n* commercio elettronico, e-commerce *m inv*.

economic [i:kə'nɒmɪk] *adj* economico(a); (*profitable*: *price*) vantaggioso(a); (*business*) che rende.

economical [i:kə'nɒmɪkəl] *adj* economico(a); (*person*) economo(a).

economically [i:kə'nɒmɪklɪ] *adv* con economia; (*regarding economics*) dal punto di vista economico.

economics [i:kə'nɒmɪks] *n* economia ♦ *npl* aspetto *or* lato economico.

economist [ɪ'kɒnəmɪst] *n* economista *m/f*.

economize [ɪ'kɒnəmaɪz] *vi* risparmiare, fare economia.

economy [ɪ'kɒnəmɪ] *n* economia.

economies of scale (*COMM*) economie *fpl* di scala.

economy class *n* (*AVIAT etc*) classe *f* turistica.

economy size n confezione f economica.

ecosystem ['iːkəusıstəm] n ecosistema m.

eco-tourism [iːkəu'tuərızəm] n ecoturismo.

ECSC n abbr (= European Coal & Steel Community) C.E.C.A. f (= Comunità Europea del Carbone e dell'Acciaio).

ecstasy ['ɛkstəsı] n estasi f inv; **to go into ecstasies over** andare in estasi davanti a; **E~** (drug) ecstasy f inv.

ecstatic [ɛks'tætık] adj estatico(a), in estasi.

ECT n abbr see **electroconvulsive therapy**.

ECU, ecu ['eɪkjuː] n abbr (= European Currency Unit) ECU f inv, ecu f inv.

Ecuador ['ɛkwədɔː*] n Ecuador m.

ecumenical [iːkju'mɛnıkl] adj ecumenico(a).

eczema ['ɛksımə] n eczema m.

eddy ['ɛdı] n mulinello.

edge [ɛdʒ] n margine m; (of table, plate, cup) orlo; (of knife etc) taglio ♦ vt bordare ♦ vi: **to ~ away from** sgattaiolare da; **to ~ past** passar rasente; **to ~ forward** avanzare a poco a poco; **on ~** (fig) = **edgy**; **to have the ~ on** essere in vantaggio su.

edgeways ['ɛdʒweɪz] adv di fianco; **he couldn't get a word in ~** non riuscì a dire una parola.

edging ['ɛdʒıŋ] n bordo.

edgy ['ɛdʒı] adj nervoso(a).

edible ['ɛdıbl] adj commestibile; (meal) mangiabile.

edict ['iːdıkt] n editto.

edifice ['ɛdıfıs] n edificio.

edifying ['ɛdıfaıŋ] adj edificante.

Edinburgh ['ɛdınbərə] n Edimburgo f.

edit ['ɛdıt] vt curare; (newspaper, magazine) dirigere; (COMPUT) correggere e modificare, editare.

edition [ı'dıʃən] n edizione f.

editor ['ɛdıtə*] n (in newspaper) redattore/trice; redattore/trice capo; (of sb's work) curatore/trice; (film ~) responsabile m/f del montaggio.

editorial [ɛdı'tɔːrıəl] adj redazionale, editoriale ♦ n editoriale m; **the ~ staff** la redazione.

EDP n abbr see **electronic data processing**.

EDT abbr (US: = Eastern Daylight Time) ora legale di New York.

educate ['ɛdjukeıt] vt istruire; educare.

educated guess ['ɛdjukeıtıd-] n ipotesi f ben fondata.

education [ɛdju'keıʃən] n (teaching) insegnamento; istruzione f; (knowledge, culture) cultura; (SCOL: subject etc) pedagogia; **primary** or (US) **elementary/secondary ~** scuola primaria/secondaria.

educational [ɛdju'keıʃənl] adj pedagogico(a); scolastico(a); istruttivo(a); **~ technology** tecnologie fpl applicate alla didattica.

Edwardian [ɛd'wɔːdıən] adj edoardiano(a).

EE abbr = **electrical engineer**.

EEG n abbr see **electroencephalogram**.

eel [iːl] n anguilla.

EENT n abbr (US MED) = eye, ear, nose and throat.

EEOC n abbr (US) = **Equal Employment Opportunity Commission**.

eerie ['ıərı] adj che fa accapponare la pelle.

EET abbr (= Eastern European Time) fuso orario.

effect [ı'fɛkt] n effetto ♦ vt effettuare; **to take ~** (law) entrare in vigore; (drug) fare effetto; **to have an ~ on sb/sth** avere or produrre un effetto su qn/qc; **to put into ~** (plan) attuare; **in ~** effettivamente; **his letter is to the ~ that ...** il contenuto della sua lettera è che ...; see also **effects**.

effective [ı'fɛktıv] adj efficace; (striking) display, outfit) che fa colpo; **~ date** data d'entrata in vigore; **to become ~** (law) entrare in vigore.

effectively [ı'fɛktıvlı] adv (efficiently) efficacemente; (strikingly) ad effetto; (in reality) di fatto; (in effect) in effetti.

effectiveness [ı'fɛktıvnıs] n efficacia.

effects [ı'fɛkts] npl (THEAT) effetti mpl scenici; (property) effetti mpl.

effeminate [ı'fɛmınıt] adj effeminato(a).

effervescent [ɛfə'vɛsnt] adj effervescente.

efficacy ['ɛfıkəsı] n efficacia.

efficiency [ı'fıʃənsı] n efficienza; rendimento effettivo.

efficiency apartment n (US) miniappartamento.

efficient [ı'fıʃənt] adj efficiente; (remedy, product, system) efficace; (machine, car) che ha un buon rendimento.

efficiently [ı'fıʃəntlı] adv efficientemente; efficacemente.

effigy ['ɛfıdʒı] n effigie f.

effluent ['ɛfluənt] n effluente m.

effort ['ɛfət] n sforzo; **to make an ~ to do sth** sforzarsi di fare qc.

effortless ['ɛfətlıs] adj senza sforzo, facile.

effrontery [ı'frʌntərı] n sfrontatezza.

effusive [ı'fjuːsıv] adj (person) espansivo(a); (welcome, letter) caloroso(a); (thanks, apologies) interminabile.

EFL n abbr (SCOL) = English as a foreign language.

EFTA ['ɛftə] n abbr (= European Free Trade Association) E.F.T.A. f.

e.g. adv abbr (= exempli gratia: for example) p.es.

egalitarian [ɪgælɪ'tɛərɪən] adj egualitario(a).

egg [ɛg] n uovo.

▶**egg on** vt incitare.

eggcup ['ɛgkʌp] n portauovo m inv.

eggplant ['ɛgplɑːnt] n (esp US) melanzana.

eggshell ['ɛgʃɛl] n guscio d'uovo ♦ adj (colour) guscio d'uovo inv.

egg-timer ['ɛgtaɪmə*] n clessidra (per misurare il tempo di cottura delle uova).

egg white n albume m, bianco d'uovo.

egg yolk n tuorlo, rosso (d'uovo).

ego ['iːgəu] n ego m inv.

egoism ['ɛgəuɪzəm] n egoismo.

egoist ['ɛgəuɪst] n egoista m/f.

egotism ['ɛgəutɪzəm] n egotismo.

egotist ['ɛgəutɪst] n egotista m/f.

ego trip n: to be on an ~ gasarsi.

Egypt ['iːdʒɪpt] n Egitto.

Egyptian [ɪ'dʒɪpʃən] adj, n egiziano(a).

eiderdown ['aɪdədaun] n piumino.

eight [eɪt] num otto.

eighteen ['eɪ'tiːn] num diciotto.

eighth [eɪtθ] num ottavo(a).

eighty [eɪtɪ] num ottanta.

Eire ['ɛərə] n Repubblica d'Irlanda.

EIS n abbr (= Educational Institute of Scotland) principale sindacato degli insegnanti in Scozia.

either ['aɪðə*] adj l'uno(a) o l'altro(a); (both, each) ciascuno(a); **on** ~ **side** su ciascun lato ♦ pron: ~ **(of them)** (o) l'uno(a) o l'altro(a); **I don't like** ~ non mi piace né l'uno né l'altro ♦ adv neanche; **no, I don't** ~ no, neanch'io ♦ conj: ~ **good or bad** o buono o cattivo; **I haven't seen** ~ **one or the other** non ho visto né l'uno né l'altro.

ejaculation [ɪdʒækju'leɪʃən] n (PHYSIOL) eiaculazione f.

eject [ɪ'dʒɛkt] vt espellere; lanciare ♦ vi (pilot) catapultarsi.

ejector seat [ɪ'dʒɛktə-] n sedile m eiettabile.

eke [iːk]: **to** ~ **out** vt far durare; aumentare.

EKG n abbr (US) = **electrocardiogram.**

el [ɛl] n abbr (US col) see **elevated railroad.**

elaborate adj [ɪ'læbərɪt] elaborato(a), minuzioso(a) ♦ vb [ɪ'læbəreɪt] vt elaborare ♦ vi entrare in dettagli.

elapse [ɪ'læps] vi trascorrere, passare.

elastic [ɪ'læstɪk] adj elastico(a) ♦ n elastico.

elastic band n (BRIT) elastico.

elasticity [ɪlæs'tɪsɪtɪ] n elasticità.

elated [ɪ'leɪtɪd] adj pieno(a) di gioia.

elation [ɪ'leɪʃən] n gioia.

elbow ['ɛlbəu] n gomito ♦ vt: **to** ~ **one's way through the crowd** farsi largo tra la folla a gomitate.

elbow grease n: **to use a bit of** ~ usare un po' di olio di gomiti.

elbowroom ['ɛlbəurum] n spazio.

elder ['ɛldə*] adj maggiore, più vecchio(a) ♦ n (tree) sambuco; **one's** ~ s i più anziani.

elderly ['ɛldəlɪ] adj anziano(a) ♦ npl: **the** ~ gli anziani.

elder statesman n anziano uomo politico in pensione, ma ancora influente; (of company) anziano/a consigliere/a.

eldest ['ɛldɪst] adj, n: **the** ~ **(child)** il(la) maggiore (dei bambini).

elect [ɪ'lɛkt] vt eleggere; (choose): **to** ~ **to do** decidere di fare ♦ adj: **the president** ~ il presidente designato.

election [ɪ'lɛkʃən] n elezione f; **to hold an** ~ indire un'elezione.

election campaign n campagna elettorale.

electioneering [ɪlɛkʃə'nɪərɪŋ] n propaganda elettorale.

elector [ɪ'lɛktə*] n elettore/trice.

electoral [ɪ'lɛktərəl] adj elettorale.

electoral college n collegio elettorale.

electoral roll n (BRIT) registro elettorale.

electoral system n sistema m elettorale.

electorate [ɪ'lɛktərɪt] n elettorato.

electric [ɪ'lɛktrɪk] adj elettrico(a).

electrical [ɪ'lɛktrɪkəl] adj elettrico(a).

electrical engineer n ingegnere m elettrotecnico.

electrical failure n guasto all'impianto elettrico.

electric blanket n coperta elettrica.

electric chair n sedia elettrica.

electric cooker n cucina elettrica.

electric current n corrente f elettrica.

electric fire n (BRIT) stufa elettrica.

electrician [ɪlɛk'trɪʃən] n elettricista m.

electricity [ɪlɛk'trɪsɪtɪ] n elettricità; **to switch on/off the** ~ attaccare/staccare la corrente.

electricity board n (BRIT) ente m regionale per l'energia elettrica.

electric light n luce f elettrica.

electric shock n scossa (elettrica).

electrify [ɪ'lɛktrɪfaɪ] vt (RAIL) elettrificare; (audience) elettrizzare.

electro... [ɪ'lɛktrəu] prefix elettro....

electrocardiogram (ECG) [ɪ'lɛktrə-'kɑːdɪəgræm] n elettrocardiogramma m.

electro-convulsive therapy (ECT) [ɪ'lɛktrəkən'vʌlsɪv-] n elettroshockterapia.

electrocute [ɪ'lɛktrəkjuːt] vt fulminare.

electrode [ɪ'lɛktrəud] n elettrodo.

electroencephalogram (EEG)
[ɪ'lɛktrəuɛn'sɛfələgræm] n (MED)
elettroencefalogramma m (EEG).
electrolysis [ɪlɛk'trɔlɪsɪs] n elettrolisi f.
electromagnetic [ɪ'lɛktrəumæg'nɛtɪk] n
elettromagnetico(a).
electron [ɪ'lɛktrɔn] n elettrone m.
electronic [ɪlɛk'trɒnɪk] adj elettronico(a);
see also **electronics**.
electronic data processing (EDP) n
elaborazione f elettronica di dati.
electronic mail n posta elettronica.
electronics [ɪlɛk'trɒnɪks] n elettronica.
electron microscope n microscopio
elettronico.
electroplated [ɪ'lɛktrəu'pleɪtɪd] adj
galvanizzato(a).
electrotherapy [ɪ'lɛktrəu'θɛrəpɪ] n
elettroterapia.
elegance ['ɛlɪgəns] n eleganza.
elegant ['ɛlɪgənt] adj elegante.
element ['ɛlɪmənt] n elemento; (of heater,
kettle etc) resistenza.
elementary [ɛlɪ'mɛntərɪ] adj elementare.
elementary school n (US) see boxed note.

ELEMENTARY SCHOOL

Negli Stati Uniti e in Canada i bambini
frequentano la **elementary school** per
almeno sei anni, a volte anche per otto. Negli
Stati Uniti si chiama anche "grade school" o
"grammar school".

---

elephant ['ɛlɪfənt] n elefante/essa.
elevate ['ɛlɪveɪt] vt elevare.
elevated railroad (el) n (US) (ferrovia)
soprelevata.
elevation [ɛlɪ'veɪʃən] n elevazione f;
(height) altitudine f.
elevator ['ɛlɪveɪtə*] n elevatore m; (US: lift)
ascensore m.
eleven [ɪ'lɛvn] num undici.
elevenses [ɪ'lɛvnzɪz] npl (BRIT) caffè m a
metà mattina.
eleventh [ɪ'lɛvnθ] adj undicesimo(a); at the
~ hour (fig) all'ultimo minuto.
elf, pl elves [ɛlf, ɛlvz] n elfo.
elicit [ɪ'lɪsɪt] vt: to ~ (from) trarre (da),
cavare fuori (da); to ~ sth (from sb)
strappare qc (a qn).
eligible ['ɛlɪdʒəbl] adj eleggibile; (for
membership) che ha i requisiti; to be ~
for a pension essere pensionabile.
eliminate [ɪ'lɪmɪneɪt] vt eliminare.
elimination [ɪlɪmɪ'neɪʃən] n eliminazione f;
by process of ~ per eliminazione.
élite [eɪ'liːt] n élite f inv.

elitist [eɪ'liːtɪst] adj (pej) elitario(a).
elixir [ɪ'lɪksə*] n elisir m inv.
Elizabethan [ɪlɪzə'biːθən] n
elisabettiano(a).
ellipse [ɪ'lɪps] n ellisse f.
elliptical [ɪ'lɪptɪkl] adj ellittico(a).
elm [ɛlm] n olmo.
elocution [ɛlə'kjuːʃən] n elocuzione f.
elongated ['iːlɔŋgeɪtɪd] adj allungato(a).
elope [ɪ'ləup] vi (lovers) scappare.
eloquence ['ɛləkwəns] n eloquenza.
eloquent ['ɛləkwənt] adj eloquente.
else [ɛls] adv altro; **something** ~
qualcos'altro; **somewhere** ~ altrove;
everywhere ~ in qualsiasi altro luogo;
where ~? in quale altro luogo?; **little** ~
poco altro; **everyone** ~ tutti gli altri;
nothing ~ nient'altro; **or** ~ (otherwise)
altrimenti; **is there anything** ~ **I can do?**
posso fare qualcos'altro?
elsewhere [ɛls'wɛə*] adv altrove.
ELT n abbr (SCOL) = English Language
Teaching.
elucidate [ɪ'luːsɪdeɪt] vt delucidare.
elude [ɪ'luːd] vt eludere.
elusive [ɪ'luːsɪv] adj elusivo(a); (answer)
evasivo(a); **he is very** ~ è proprio
inafferrabile or irraggiungibile.
elves [ɛlvz] npl of **elf**.
emaciated [ɪ'meɪsɪeɪtɪd] adj emaciato(a).
E-mail, e-mail ['iːmeɪl] n abbr (= electronic
mail) posta elettronica ♦ vt: **to** ~ **sb**
comunicare con qn mediante posta
elettronica; ~ **address** indirizzo di posta
elettronica; ~ **account** account m inv di
posta elettronica.
emanate ['ɛməneɪt] vi: **to** ~ **from** emanare
da.
emancipate [ɪ'mænsɪpeɪt] vt emancipare.
emancipation [ɪmænsɪ'peɪʃən] n
emancipazione f.
emasculate [ɪ'mæskjuleɪt] vt (fig) rendere
impotente.
embalm [ɪm'bɑːm] vt imbalsamare.
embankment [ɪm'bæŋkmənt] n (of road,
railway) massicciata; (riverside) argine m;
(dyke) diga.
embargo [ɪm'bɑːgəu] n (pl ~es: COMM,
NAUT) embargo ♦ vt mettere l'embargo
su; **to put an** ~ **on sth** mettere l'embargo
su qc.
embark [ɪm'bɑːk] vi: **to** ~ **(on)** imbarcarsi
(su) ♦ vt imbarcare; **to** ~ **on** (fig)
imbarcarsi in; (journey) intraprendere.
embarkation [ɛmbɑː'keɪʃən] n imbarco.
embarkation card n carta d'imbarco.
embarrass [ɪm'bærəs] vt imbarazzare; **to
be** ~ed essere imbarazzato(a).

embarrassing [ɪmˈbærəsɪŋ] *adj* imbarazzante.
embarrassment [ɪmˈbærəsmənt] *n* imbarazzo.
embassy [ˈɛmbəsɪ] *n* ambasciata; **the** Italian E~ l'ambasciata d'Italia.
embed [ɪmˈbɛd] *vt* conficcare; incastrare.
embellish [ɪmˈbɛlɪʃ] *vt* abbellire; **to ~ (with)** (*fig*: *story, truth*) infiorare (con).
embers [ˈɛmbəz] *npl* braci *fpl*.
embezzle [ɪmˈbɛzl] *vt* appropriarsi indebitamente di.
embezzlement [ɪmˈbɛzlmənt] *n* appropriazione *f* indebita.
embezzler [ɪmˈbɛzlə*] *n* malversatore/trice.
embitter [ɪmˈbɪtə*] *vt* amareggiare; inasprire.
emblem [ˈɛmbləm] *n* emblema *m*.
embodiment [ɪmˈbɔdɪmənt] *n* personificazione *f*, incarnazione *f*.
embody [ɪmˈbɔdɪ] *vt* (*features*) racchiudere, comprendere; (*ideas*) dar forma concreta a, esprimere.
embolden [ɪmˈbəuldn] *vt* incitare.
embolism [ˈɛmbəlɪzəm] *n* embolia.
embossed [ɪmˈbɔst] *adj* in rilievo; goffrato(a); ~ **with** ... con in rilievo ....
embrace [ɪmˈbreɪs] *vt* abbracciare; (*include*) comprendere ♦ *vi* abbracciarsi ♦ *n* abbraccio.
embroider [ɪmˈbrɔɪdə*] *vt* ricamare; (*fig*: *story*) abbellire.
embroidery [ɪmˈbrɔɪdərɪ] *n* ricamo.
embroil [ɪmˈbrɔɪl] *vt*: **to become ~ed (in sth)** restare invischiato(a) (in qc).
embryo [ˈɛmbrɪəu] *n* (*also fig*) embrione *m*.
emcee [ɛmˈsiː] *n abbr* = **master of ceremonies**.
emend [ɪˈmɛnd] *vt* (*text*) correggere, emendare.
emerald [ˈɛmərəld] *n* smeraldo.
emerge [ɪˈməːdʒ] *vi* apparire, sorgere; **it ~s that** (*BRIT*) risulta che.
emergence [ɪˈməːdʒəns] *n* apparizione *f*; (*of nation*) nascita.
emergency [ɪˈməːdʒənsɪ] *n* emergenza; **in an ~** in caso di emergenza; **to declare a state of ~** dichiarare lo stato di emergenza.
emergency exit *n* uscita di sicurezza.
emergency landing *n* atterraggio forzato.
emergency lane *n* (*US AUT*) corsia d'emergenza.
emergency road service *n* (*US*) servizio riparazioni.

emergency service *n* servizio di pronto intervento.
emergency stop *n* (*BRIT AUT*) frenata improvvisa.
emergent [ɪˈməːdʒənt] *adj*: ~ **nation** paese *m* in via di sviluppo.
emery board [ˈɛmərɪ-] *n* limetta di carta smerigliata.
emery paper *n* carta smerigliata.
emetic [ɪˈmɛtɪk] *n* emetico.
emigrant [ˈɛmɪɡrənt] *n* emigrante *m/f*.
emigrate [ˈɛmɪɡreɪt] *vi* emigrare.
emigration [ɛmɪˈɡreɪʃən] *n* emigrazione *f*.
émigré [ˈɛmɪɡreɪ] *n* emigrato/a.
eminence [ˈɛmɪnəns] *n* eminenza.
eminent [ˈɛmɪnənt] *adj* eminente.
eminently [ˈɛmɪnəntlɪ] *adv* assolutamente, perfettamente.
emirate [ɛˈmɪərɪt] *n* emirato.
emission [ɪˈmɪʃən] *n* (*of gas, radiation*) emissione *f*.
emit [ɪˈmɪt] *vt* emettere.
emolument [ɪˈmɔljumənt] *n* (*often pl*: *formal*) emolumento.
emotion [ɪˈməuʃən] *n* emozione *f*; (*love, jealousy etc*) sentimento.
emotional [ɪˈməuʃənl] *adj* (*person*) emotivo(a); (*scene*) commovente; (*tone, speech*) carico(a) d'emozione.
emotionally [ɪˈməuʃnəlɪ] *adv* (*behave, be involved*) sentimentalmente; (*speak*) con emozione; ~ **disturbed** con turbe emotive.
emotive [ɪˈməutɪv] *adj* emotivo(a); ~ **power** capacità di commuovere.
empathy [ˈɛmpəθɪ] *n* immedesimazione *f*; **to feel ~ with sb** immedesimarsi con i sentimenti di qn.
emperor [ˈɛmpərə*] *n* imperatore *m*.
emphasis, *pl* **-ases** [ˈɛmfəsɪs, -siːz] *n* enfasi *f inv*; importanza; **to lay** *or* **place ~ on sth** (*fig*) mettere in risalto *or* in evidenza qc; **the ~ is on sport** si dà molta importanza allo sport.
emphasize [ˈɛmfəsaɪz] *vt* (*word, point*) sottolineare; (*feature*) mettere in evidenza.
emphatic [ɪmˈfætɪk] *adj* (*strong*) vigoroso(a); (*unambiguous, clear*) netto(a); categorico(a).
emphatically [ɪmˈfætɪkəlɪ] *adv* vigorosamente; nettamente.
emphysema [ɛmfɪˈsiːmə] *n* (*MED*) enfisema *m*.
empire [ˈɛmpaɪə*] *n* impero.
empirical [ɛmˈpɪrɪkl] *adj* empirico(a).
employ [ɪmˈplɔɪ] *vt* (*make use of*: *thing, method, person*) impiegare, servirsi di;

(*give job to*) dare lavoro a, impiegare; he's ~ed in a bank lavora in banca.
employee [ɪmplɔɪˈiː] *n* impiegato/a.
employer [ɪmˈplɔɪəʳ] *n* principale *m/f*, datore *m* di lavoro.
employment [ɪmˈplɔɪmənt] *n* impiego; **to find** ~ trovare impiego *or* lavoro; **without** ~ disoccupato(a); **place of** ~ posto di lavoro.
employment agency *n* agenzia di collocamento.
employment exchange *n* (*BRIT*) ufficio *m* collocamento *inv*.
empower [ɪmˈpauəʳ] *vt*: **to** ~ **sb to do** concedere autorità a qn di fare.
empress [ˈɛmprɪs] *n* imperatrice *f*.
emptiness [ˈɛmptɪnɪs] *n* vuoto.
empty [ˈɛmptɪ] *adj* vuoto(a); (*street, area*) deserto(a); (*threat, promise*) vano(a) ♦ *n* (*bottle*) vuoto ♦ *vt* vuotare ♦ *vi* vuotarsi; (*liquid*) scaricarsi; **on an** ~ **stomach** a stomaco vuoto
empty-handed [ɛmptɪˈhændɪd] *adj* a mani vuote.
empty-headed [ɛmptɪˈhɛdɪd] *adj* sciocco(a).
EMS *n abbr* (= *European Monetary System*) S.M.E. *m*.
EMT *n abbr* (*US*) = *emergency medical technician*.
EMU *n abbr* (= *European Monetary Union*) Unità *f* monetaria europea; (= *economic and monetary union*) UEM *f*.
emulate [ˈɛmjuleɪt] *vt* emulare.
emulsion [ɪˈmʌlʃən] *n* emulsione *f*; (*also:* ~ **paint**) colore *m* a tempera.
enable [ɪˈneɪbl] *vt*: **to** ~ **sb to do** permettere a qn di fare.
enact [ɪnˈækt] *vt* (*law*) emanare; (*play, scene*) rappresentare.
enamel [ɪˈnæməl] *n* smalto.
enamel paint *n* vernice *f* a smalto.
enamoured [ɪˈnæməd] *adj*: ~ **of** innamorato(a) di.
encampment [ɪnˈkæmpmənt] *n* accampamento.
encased [ɪnˈkeɪst] *adj*: ~ **in** racchiuso(a) in; rivestito(a) di.
enchant [ɪnˈtʃɑːnt] *vt* incantare; (*subj: magic spell*) catturare.
enchanting [ɪnˈtʃɑːntɪŋ] *adj* incantevole, affascinante.
encircle [ɪnˈsɜːkl] *vt* accerchiare.
enc(l). *abbr* (*on letters etc*: = *enclosed, enclosure*) all., alleg.
enclose [ɪnˈkləuz] *vt* (*land*) circondare, recingere; (*letter etc*): **to** ~ (**with**) allegare (con); **please find** ~**d** trovi qui accluso.

enclosure [ɪnˈkləuʒəʳ] *n* recinto; (*COMM*) allegato.
encoder [ɪnˈkəudəʳ] *n* (*COMPUT*) codificatore *m*.
encompass [ɪnˈkʌmpəs] *vt* comprendere.
encore [ɔŋˈkɔː] *excl, n* bis (*m inv*).
encounter [ɪnˈkauntəʳ] *n* incontro ♦ *vt* incontrare.
encourage [ɪnˈkʌrɪdʒ] *vt* incoraggiare; (*industry, growth etc*) favorire; **to** ~ **sb to do sth** incoraggiare qn a fare qc.
encouragement [ɪnˈkʌrɪdʒmənt] *n* incoraggiamento.
encouraging [ɪnˈkʌrɪdʒɪŋ] *adj* incoraggiante.
encroach [ɪnˈkrəutʃ] *vi*: **to** ~ (**up**)**on** (*rights*) usurpare; (*time*) abusare di; (*land*) oltrepassare i limiti di.
encrusted [ɪnˈkrʌstɪd] *adj*: ~ **with** incrostato(a) di.
encumbered [ɪnˈkʌmbəd] *adj*: **to be** ~ (**with**) essere carico(a) di.
encyclop(a)edia [ɛnsaɪkləuˈpiːdɪə] *n* enciclopedia.
end [ɛnd] *n* fine *f*; (*aim*) fine *m*; (*of table*) bordo estremo; (*of line, rope etc*) estremità *f inv*; (*of pointed object*) punta; (*of town*) parte *f* ♦ *vt* finire; (*also:* **bring to an** ~, **put an** ~ **to**) mettere fine a ♦ *vi* finire; **from** ~ **to** ~ da un'estremità all'altra; **to come to an** ~ arrivare alla fine, finire; **to be at an** ~ essere finito; **in the** ~ alla fine; **at the** ~ **of the street** in fondo alla strada; **at the** ~ **of the day** (*BRIT fig*) in fin dei conti; **on** ~ (*object*) ritto(a); **to stand on** ~ (*hair*) rizzarsi; **for 5 hours on** ~ per 5 ore di fila; **for hours on** ~ per ore e ore; **to this** ~, **with this** ~ **in view** a questo fine; **to** ~ (**with**) concludere (con).
► **end up** *vi*: **to** ~ **up in** finire in.
endanger [ɪnˈdeɪndʒəʳ] *vt* mettere in pericolo; **an** ~**ed species** una specie in via di estinzione.
endear [ɪnˈdɪəʳ] *vt*: **to** ~ **o.s. to sb** accattivarsi le simpatie di qn.
endearing [ɪnˈdɪərɪŋ] *adj* accattivante.
endearment [ɪnˈdɪəmənt] *n*: **to whisper** ~**s** sussurrare tenerezze; **term of** ~ vezzeggiativo, parola affettuosa.
endeavour, (*US*) **endeavor** [ɪnˈdɛvəʳ] *n* sforzo, tentativo ♦ *vi*: **to** ~ **to do** cercare *or* sforzarsi di fare.
endemic [ɛnˈdɛmɪk] *adj* endemico(a).
ending [ˈɛndɪŋ] *n* fine *f*, conclusione *f*; (*LING*) desinenza.
endive [ˈɛndaɪv] *n* (*curly*) indivia (riccia); (*smooth, flat*) indivia belga.

endless ['ɛndlɪs] *adj* senza fine; (*patience, resources*) infinito(a); (*possibilities*) illimitato(a).

endorse [ɪn'dɔːs] *vt* (*cheque*) girare; (*approve*) approvare, appoggiare.

endorsee [ɪndɔː'siː] *n* giratario/a.

endorsement [ɪn'dɔːsmənt] *n* (*approval*) approvazione *f*; (*signature*) firma; (*BRIT: on driving licence*) contravvenzione registrata sulla patente.

endorser [ɪn'dɔːsə*] *n* girante *m/f*.

endow [ɪn'dau] *vt* (*prize*) istituire; (*hospital*) fondare; (*provide with money*) devolvere denaro a; (*equip*): **to ~ with** fornire di, dotare di.

endowment [ɪn'daumənt] *n* istituzione *f*; fondazione *f*; (*amount*) donazione *f*.

endowment mortgage *n* mutuo che viene ripagato sotto forma di un'assicurazione a vita.

endowment policy *n* polizza-vita mista.

end product *n* (*INDUSTRY*) prodotto finito; (*fig*) risultato.

end result *n* risultato finale.

endurable [ɪn'djuərəbl] *adj* sopportabile.

endurance [ɪn'djuərəns] *n* resistenza; pazienza.

endurance test *n* prova di resistenza.

endure [ɪn'djuə*] *vt* sopportare, resistere a ♦ *vi* durare.

enduring [ɪn'djuərɪŋ] *adj* duraturo(a).

end user *n* (*COMPUT*) consumatore(trice) effettivo(a).

enema ['ɛnɪmə] *n* (*MED*) clistere *m*.

enemy ['ɛnəmɪ] *adj*, *n* nemico(a); **to make an ~ of sb** inimicarsi qn.

energetic [ɛnə'dʒɛtɪk] *adj* energico(a); attivo(a).

energy ['ɛnədʒɪ] *n* energia; **Department of E~** Ministero dell'Energia.

energy crisis *n* crisi *f* energetica.

energy-saving ['ɛnədʒɪ'seɪvɪŋ] *adj* (*policy*) del risparmio energetico; (*device*) che risparmia energia.

enervating ['ɛnəːveɪtɪŋ] *adj* debilitante.

enforce [ɪn'fɔːs] *vt* (*LAW*) applicare, far osservare.

enforced [ɪn'fɔːst] *adj* forzato(a).

enfranchise [ɪn'fræntʃaɪz] *vt* (*give vote to*) concedere il diritto di voto a; (*set free*) affrancare.

engage [ɪn'geɪdʒ] *vt* (*hire*) assumere; (*lawyer*) incaricare; (*attention, interest*) assorbire; (*MIL*) attaccare; (*TECH*): **to ~ gear/the clutch** innestare la marcia/la frizione ♦ *vi* (*TECH*) ingranare; **to ~ in** impegnarsi in; **he is ~d in research/a survey** si occupa di ricerca/di

un'inchiesta; **to ~ sb in conversation** attaccare conversazione con qn.

engaged [ɪn'geɪdʒd] *adj* (*BRIT: busy, in use*) occupato(a); (*betrothed*) fidanzato(a); **to get ~** fidanzarsi.

engaged tone *n* (*BRIT TEL*) segnale *m* di occupato.

engagement [ɪn'geɪdʒmənt] *n* impegno, obbligo; appuntamento; (*to marry*) fidanzamento; (*MIL*) combattimento; **I have a previous ~** ho già un impegno.

engagement ring *n* anello di fidanzamento.

engaging [ɪn'geɪdʒɪŋ] *adj* attraente.

engender [ɪn'dʒɛndə*] *vt* produrre, causare.

engine ['ɛndʒɪn] *n* (*AUT*) motore *m*; (*RAIL*) locomotiva.

engine driver *n* (*BRIT: of train*) macchinista *m*.

engineer [ɛndʒɪ'nɪə*] *n* ingegnere *m*; (*BRIT: for domestic appliances*) tecnico; (*US RAIL*) macchinista *m*; **civil/mechanical ~** ingegnere civile/meccanico.

engineering [ɛndʒɪ'nɪərɪŋ] *n* ingegneria ♦ *cpd* (*works, factory, worker etc*) metalmeccanico(a).

engine failure *n* guasto al motore.

engine trouble *n* panne *f*.

England ['ɪŋglənd] *n* Inghilterra.

English ['ɪŋglɪʃ] *adj* inglese ♦ *n* (*LING*) inglese *m*; **the ~** *npl* gli Inglesi; **to be an ~ speaker** essere anglofono(a).

English Channel *n*: **the ~** il Canale della Manica.

Englishman ['ɪŋglɪʃmən], **Englishwoman** ['ɪŋglɪʃwumən] *n* inglese *m/f*.

English-speaking ['ɪŋglɪʃspiːkɪŋ] *adj* di lingua inglese.

engrave [ɪn'greɪv] *vt* incidere.

engraving [ɪn'greɪvɪŋ] *n* incisione *f*.

engrossed [ɪn'grəust] *adj*: **~ in** assorbito(a) da, preso(a) da.

engulf [ɪn'gʌlf] *vt* inghiottire.

enhance [ɪn'hɑːns] *vt* accrescere; (*position, reputation*) migliorare.

enigma [ɪ'nɪgmə] *n* enigma *m*.

enigmatic [ɛnɪg'mætɪk] *adj* enigmatico(a).

enjoy [ɪn'dʒɔɪ] *vt* godere; (*have: success, fortune*) avere; (*have benefit of: health*) godere (di); **I ~ dancing** mi piace ballare; **to ~ o.s.** godersela, divertirsi.

enjoyable [ɪn'dʒɔɪəbl] *adj* piacevole.

enjoyment [ɪn'dʒɔɪmənt] *n* piacere *m*, godimento.

enlarge [ɪn'lɑːdʒ] *vt* ingrandire ♦ *vi*: **to ~ on** (*subject*) dilungarsi su.

enlarged [ɪn'lɑːdʒd] *adj* (*edition*)

ampliato(a); (*MED*: organ, gland) ingrossato(a).

enlargement [ɪn'lɑːdʒmənt] n (*PHOT*) ingrandimento.

enlighten [ɪn'laɪtn] vt illuminare; dare chiarimenti a.

enlightened [ɪn'laɪtnd] adj illuminato(a).

enlightening [ɪn'laɪtnɪŋ] adj istruttivo(a).

enlightenment [ɪn'laɪtnmənt] n progresso culturale; chiarimenti mpl; (*HISTORY*): the E~ l'Illuminismo.

enlist [ɪn'lɪst] vt arruolare; (*support*) procurare ♦ vi arruolarsi; ~ed man (*US MIL*) soldato semplice.

enliven [ɪn'laɪvn] vt (*people*) rallegrare; (*events*) ravvivare.

enmity ['ɛnmɪtɪ] n inimicizia.

ennoble [ɪ'nəubl] vt nobilitare; (*with title*) conferire un titolo nobiliare a.

enormity [ɪ'nɔːmɪtɪ] n enormità f inv.

enormous [ɪ'nɔːməs] adj enorme.

enormously [ɪ'nɔːməslɪ] adv enormemente.

enough [ɪ'nʌf] adj, n: ~ time/books assai tempo/libri; **have you got** ~? ne ha abbastanza or a sufficienza? ♦ adv: **big** ~ abbastanza grande; **he has not worked** ~ non ha lavorato abbastanza; ~! basta!; **it's hot** ~ (**as it is**)l fa abbastanza caldo così!; **will £5 be** ~? bastano 5 sterline?; **that's** ~ basta; **I've had** ~! non ne posso più!; **he was kind** ~ **to lend me the money** è stato così gentile da prestarmi i soldi; **... which, funnily** ~ ... che, strano a dirsi.

enquire [ɪn'kwaɪə*] vt, vi = **inquire**.

enrage [ɪn'reɪdʒ] vt fare arrabbiare.

enrich [ɪn'rɪtʃ] vt arricchire.

enrol, (*US***) enroll** [ɪn'rəul] vt iscrivere; (*at university*) immatricolare ♦ vi iscriversi.

enrol(l)ment [ɪn'rəulmənt] n iscrizione f.

en route [ɔn'ruːt] adv: ~ **for/from/to** in viaggio per/da/a.

ensconced [ɪn'skɔnst] adj: ~ **in** ben sistemato(a) in.

ensemble [ɑːn'sɑːmbl] n (*MUS*) ensemble m inv.

enshrine [ɪn'ʃraɪn] vt conservare come una reliquia.

ensign n (*NAUT*) ['ɛnsən] bandiera; (*MIL*) ['ɛnsaɪn] portabandiera m inv.

enslave [ɪn'sleɪv] vt fare schiavo.

ensue [ɪn'sjuː] vi seguire, risultare.

ensure [ɪn'ʃuə*] vt assicurare; garantire; **to** ~ **that** assicurarsi che.

ENT n abbr (*MED*: = ear, nose, and throat) O.R.L.

entail [ɪn'teɪl] vt comportare.

entangle [ɪn'tæŋgl] vt (*thread etc*) impigliare; **to become** ~d **in sth** (*fig*)

rimanere impegolato in qc.

enter ['ɛntə*] vt (*gen*) entrare in; (*club*) associarsi a; (*profession*) intraprendere; (*army*) arruolarsi in; (*competition*) partecipare a; (*sb for a competition*) iscrivere; (*write down*) registrare; (*COMPUT*: data) introdurre, inserire ♦ vi entrare.

►**enter for** vt fus iscriversi a.

►**enter into** vt fus (*explanation*) cominciare a dare; (*debate*) partecipare a; (*agreement*) concludere; (*negotiations*) prendere parte a.

►**enter (up)on** vt fus cominciare.

enteritis [ɛntə'raɪtɪs] n enterite f.

enterprise ['ɛntəpraɪz] n (*undertaking, company*) impresa; (*spirit*) iniziativa.

enterprising ['ɛntəpraɪzɪŋ] adj intraprendente.

entertain [ɛntə'teɪn] vt divertire; (*invite*) ricevere; (*idea, plan*) nutrire.

entertainer [ɛntə'teɪnə*] n comico/a.

entertaining [ɛntə'teɪnɪŋ] adj divertente ♦ n: **to do a lot of** ~ avere molti ospiti.

entertainment [ɛntə'teɪnmənt] n (*amusement*) divertimento; (*show*) spettacolo.

entertainment allowance n spese fpl di rappresentanza.

enthral [ɪn'θrɔːl] vt affascinare, avvincere.

enthralled [ɪn'θrɔːld] adj affascinato(a).

enthralling [ɪn'θrɔːlɪŋ] adj avvincente.

enthuse [ɪn'θuːz] vi: **to** ~ (**about** or **over**) entusiasmarsi (per).

enthusiasm [ɪn'θuːzɪæzəm] n entusiasmo.

enthusiast [ɪn'θuːzɪæst] n entusiasta m/f; **jazz** etc ~ un appassionato di jazz etc.

enthusiastic [ɪnθuːzɪ'æstɪk] adj entusiasta, entusiastico(a); **to be** ~ **about sth/sb** essere appassionato di qc/entusiasta di qn.

entice [ɪn'taɪs] vt allettare, sedurre.

enticing [ɪn'taɪsɪŋ] adj allettante.

entire [ɪn'taɪə*] adj intero(a).

entirely [ɪn'taɪəlɪ] adv completamente, interamente.

entirety [ɪn'taɪərətɪ] n: **in its** ~ nel suo complesso.

entitle [ɪn'taɪtl] vt (*give right*): **to** ~ **sb to sth/to do** dare diritto a qn a qc/a fare.

entitled [ɪn'taɪtld] adj (*book*) che si intitola; **to be** ~ **to sth/to do sth** avere diritto a qc/a fare qc.

entity ['ɛntɪtɪ] n entità f inv.

entrails ['ɛntreɪlz] npl interiora fpl.

entrance n ['ɛntrns] entrata, ingresso; (*of person*) entrata ♦ vt [ɪn'trɑːns] incantare, rapire; **to gain** ~ **to** (*university etc*) essere ammesso a.

entrance examination n (*to school*) esame m di ammissione.

entrance fee n tassa d'iscrizione; (*to museum etc*) prezzo d'ingresso.

entrance ramp n (*US AUT*) rampa di accesso.

entrancing [ɪn'trɑːnsɪŋ] *adj* incantevole.

entrant ['ɛntrnt] n partecipante *m/f*; concorrente *m/f*; (*BRIT: in exam*) candidato/a.

entreat [ɛn'triːt] *vt* supplicare.

entreaty [ɪn'triːtɪ] n supplica, preghiera.

entrée ['ɔntreɪ] n (*CULIN*) prima portata.

entrenched [ɛn'trɛntʃt] *adj* radicato(a).

entrepreneur ['ɔntrəprə'nɔː*] n imprenditore m.

entrepreneurial ['ɔntrəprə'nɔːrɪəl] *adj* imprenditoriale.

entrust [ɪn'trʌst] *vt*: **to ~ sth to** affidare qc a.

entry ['ɛntrɪ] n entrata; (*way in*) entrata, ingresso; (*in dictionary*) voce *f*; (*in diary, ship's log*) annotazione *f*; (*in account book, ledger, list*) registrazione *f*; **"no ~"** "vietato l'ingresso"; (*AUT*) "divieto di accesso"; **single/double ~ book-keeping** partita semplice/doppia.

entry form n modulo d'iscrizione.

entry phone n (*BRIT*) citofono.

entwine [ɪn'twaɪn] *vt* intrecciare.

E number n sigla di additivo alimentare.

enumerate [ɪ'njuːməreɪt] *vt* enumerare.

enunciate [ɪ'nʌnsɪeɪt] *vt* enunciare; pronunciare.

envelop [ɪn'vɛləp] *vt* avvolgere, avviluppare.

envelope ['ɛnvələup] n busta.

enviable ['ɛnvɪəbl] *adj* invidiabile.

envious ['ɛnvɪəs] *adj* invidioso(a).

environment [ɪn'vaɪərənmənt] n ambiente m; **Department of the E~** (*BRIT*) ≈ Ministero dell'Ambiente.

environmental [ɪnvaɪərən'mɛntl] *adj* ecologico(a); ambientale; **~ studies** (*in school etc*) ecologia.

environmentalist [ɪn'vaɪərən'mɛntəlɪst] n studioso/a della protezione dell'ambiente.

environmentally [ɪnvaɪərən'mɛntəlɪ] *adv*: **~ sound/friendly** che rispetta l'ambiente.

Environmental Protection Agency (EPA) n (*US*) ≈ Ministero dell'Ambiente.

envisage [ɪn'vɪzɪdʒ] *vt* immaginare; prevedere.

envision [ɪn'vɪʒən] *vt* concepire, prevedere.

envoy ['ɛnvɔɪ] n inviato/a.

envy ['ɛnvɪ] n invidia ♦ *vt* invidiare; **to ~ sb sth** invidiare qn per qc.

enzyme ['ɛnzaɪm] n enzima m.

EPA n *abbr* (*US*) *see* **Environmental Protection Agency**.

ephemeral [ɪ'fɛmərəl] *adj* effimero(a).

epic ['ɛpɪk] n poema m epico ♦ *adj* epico(a).

epicentre, (*US*) **epicenter** ['ɛpɪsɛntə*] n epicentro.

epidemic [ɛpɪ'dɛmɪk] n epidemia.

epilepsy ['ɛpɪlɛpsɪ] n epilessia.

epileptic [ɛpɪ'lɛptɪk] *adj, n* epilettico(a).

epilogue ['ɛpɪlɔg] n epilogo.

Epiphany [ɪ'pɪfənɪ] n Epifania.

episcopal [ɪ'pɪskəpəl] *adj* episcopale.

episode ['ɛpɪsəud] n episodio.

epistle [ɪ'pɪsl] n epistola.

epitaph ['ɛpɪtɑːf] n epitaffio.

epithet ['ɛpɪθɛt] n epiteto.

epitome [ɪ'pɪtəmɪ] n epitome *f*; quintessenza.

epitomize [ɪ'pɪtəmaɪz] *vt* (*fig*) incarnare.

epoch ['iːpɔk] n epoca.

epoch-making ['iːpɔkmeɪkɪŋ] *adj* che fa epoca.

eponymous [ɪ'pɔnɪməs] *adj* dello stesso nome.

equable ['ɛkwəbl] *adj* uniforme; (*climate*) costante; (*character*) equilibrato(a).

equal ['iːkwl] *adj, n* uguale (*m/f*) ♦ *vt* uguagliare; **~ to** (*task*) all'altezza di.

equality [iː'kwɔlɪtɪ] n uguaglianza.

equalize ['iːkwəlaɪz] *vt, vi* pareggiare.

equalizer ['iːkwəlaɪzə*] n punto del pareggio.

equally ['iːkwəlɪ] *adv* ugualmente; **they are ~ clever** sono intelligenti allo stesso modo.

Equal Opportunities Commission, (*US*) **Equal Employment Opportunity Commission** n commissione contro discriminazioni sessuali o razziali nel mondo del lavoro.

equal(s) sign n segno d'uguaglianza.

equanimity [ɛkwə'nɪmɪtɪ] n serenità.

equate [ɪ'kweɪt] *vt*: **to ~ sth with** considerare qc uguale a; (*compare*) paragonare qc con; **to ~ A to B** mettere in equazione A e B.

equation [ɪ'kweɪʒən] n (*MATH*) equazione *f*.

equator [ɪ'kweɪtə*] n equatore m.

Equatorial Guinea [ɛkwə'tɔːrɪəl-] n Guinea Equatoriale.

equestrian [ɪ'kwɛstrɪən] *adj* equestre ♦ *n* cavaliere/amazzone.

equilibrium [iːkwɪ'lɪbrɪəm] n equilibrio.

equinox ['iːkwɪnɔks] n equinozio.

equip [ɪ'kwɪp] *vt* equipaggiare, attrezzare;

to ~ sb/sth with fornire qn/qc di; **~ped with** (*machinery etc*) dotato(a) di; **he is well ~ped for the job** ha i requisiti necessari per quel lavoro.

equipment [ɪ'kwɪpmənt] *n* attrezzatura; (*electrical etc*) apparecchiatura.

equitable ['ɛkwɪtəbl] *adj* equo(a), giusto(a).

equities ['ɛkwɪtɪz] *npl* (*BRIT COMM*) azioni *fpl* ordinarie.

equity ['ɛkwɪtɪ] *n* equità.

equity capital *n* capitale *m* azionario.

equivalent [ɪ'kwɪvələnt] *adj*, *n* equivalente (*m*); **to be ~ to** equivalere a.

equivocal [ɪ'kwɪvəkl] *adj* equivoco(a); (*open to suspicion*) dubbio(a).

equivocate [ɪ'kwɪvəkeɪt] *vi* esprimersi in modo equivoco.

equivocation [ɪkwɪvə'keɪʃən] *n* parole *fpl* equivoche.

ER *abbr* (*BRIT*) = *Elizabeth Regina*.

ERA *n abbr* (*US POL*) = *Equal Rights Amendment*.

era ['ɪərə] *n* era, età *f inv*.

eradicate [ɪ'rædɪkeɪt] *vt* sradicare.

erase [ɪ'reɪz] *vt* cancellare.

eraser [ɪ'reɪzə*] *n* gomma.

erect [ɪ'rɛkt] *adj* eretto(a) ♦ *vt* costruire; (*monument, tent*) alzare.

erection [ɪ'rɛkʃən] *n* (*also PHYSIOL*) erezione *f*; (*of building*) costruzione *f*; (*of machinery*) montaggio.

ergonomics [əːgə'nɔmɪks] *n* ergonomia.

ERISA *n abbr* (*US*: = *Employee Retirement Income Security Act*) *legge relativa al pensionamento statale*.

Eritrea [ɛrɪ'treɪə] *n* Eritrea.

ERM *n abbr* (= *Exchange Rate Mechanism*) meccanismo dei tassi di cambio.

ermine ['əːmɪn] *n* ermellino.

ERNIE ['əːnɪ] *n abbr* (*BRIT*: = *Electronic Random Number Indicator Equipment*) *sistema che seleziona i numeri vincenti di buoni del Tesoro*.

erode [ɪ'rəud] *vt* erodere; (*metal*) corrodere.

erogenous zone [ɪ'rɔdʒənəs-] *n* zona erogena.

erosion [ɪ'rəuʒən] *n* erosione *f*.

erotic [ɪ'rɔtɪk] *adj* erotico(a).

eroticism [ɪ'rɔtɪsɪzəm] *n* erotismo.

err [əː*] *vi* errare; (*REL*) peccare.

errand ['ɛrənd] *n* commissione *f*; **to run ~s** fare commissioni; **~ of mercy** atto di carità.

errand boy *n* fattorino.

erratic [ɪ'rætɪk] *adj* imprevedibile; (*person, mood*) incostante.

erroneous [ɪ'rəunɪəs] *adj* erroneo(a).

error ['ɛrə*] *n* errore *m*; **typing/spelling ~** errore di battitura/di ortografia; **in ~** per errore; **~s and omissions excepted** salvo errori ed omissioni.

error message *n* (*COMPUT*) messaggio di errore.

erstwhile ['əːstwaɪl] *adv* allora, un tempo ♦ *adj* di allora.

erudite ['ɛrjudaɪt] *adj* erudito(a).

erupt [ɪ'rʌpt] *vi* erompere; (*volcano*) mettersi (*or* essere) in eruzione.

eruption [ɪ'rʌpʃən] *n* eruzione *f*; (*of anger, violence*) esplosione *f*.

ESA *n abbr* (= *European Space Agency*) ESA *f*.

escalate ['ɛskəleɪt] *vi* intensificarsi; (*costs*) salire.

escalation [ɛskə'leɪʃən] *n* escalation *f*; (*of prices*) aumento.

escalation clause *n* clausola di revisione.

escalator ['ɛskəleɪtə*] *n* scala mobile.

escapade [ɛskə'peɪd] *n* scappatella; avventura.

escape [ɪ'skeɪp] *n* evasione *f*; fuga; (*of gas etc*) fuga, fuoriuscita ♦ *vi* fuggire; (*from jail*) evadere, scappare; (*fig*) sfuggire; (*leak*) uscire ♦ *vt* sfuggire a; **to ~ from sb** sfuggire a qn; **to ~ to** (*another place*) fuggire in; (*freedom, safety*) fuggire verso; **to ~ notice** passare inosservato(a).

escape artist *n* mago della fuga.

escape clause *n* clausola scappatoia.

escapee [ɪskeɪ'piː] *n* evaso/a.

escape hatch *n* (*in submarine, space rocket*) portello di sicurezza.

escape key *n* (*COMPUT*) tasto di escape, tasto per cambio di codice.

escape route *n* percorso della fuga.

escapism [ɪs'keɪpɪzəm] *n* evasione *f* (dalla realtà).

escapist [ɪs'keɪpɪst] *adj* d'evasione ♦ *n* persona che cerca di evadere dalla realtà.

escapologist [ɛskə'pɔlədʒɪst] *n* (*BRIT*) = **escape artist**.

escarpment [ɪs'kɑːpmənt] *n* scarpata.

eschew [ɪs'tʃuː] *vt* evitare.

escort *n* ['ɛskɔːt] scorta; (*to dance etc*): **her ~** il suo cavaliere; **his ~** la sua dama ♦ *vt* [ɪ'skɔːt] scortare; accompagnare.

escort agency *n* agenzia di hostess.

Eskimo ['ɛskɪməu] *adj* eschimese ♦ *n* eschimese *m/f*; (*LING*) eschimese *m*.

ESL *n abbr* (*SCOL*) = *English as a Second Language*.

esophagus [iː'sɔfəgəs] *n* (*US*) = **oesophagus**.

esoteric [ɛsəu'tɛrɪk] *adj* esoterico(a).
ESP *n abbr see* **extrasensory perception**; (*SCOL*) = *English for Specific (or Special) Purposes.*
esp. *abbr* (= *especially*) spec.
especially [ɪ'spɛʃlɪ] *adv* specialmente; (*above all*) soprattutto; (*specifically*) espressamente; (*particularly*) particolarmente.
espionage ['ɛspɪənɑːʒ] *n* spionaggio.
esplanade [ɛsplə'neɪd] *n* lungomare *m*.
espouse [ɪ'spauz] *vt* abbracciare.
Esquire [ɪ'skwaɪə*] *n* (*BRIT: abbr* **Esq.**): **J. Brown,** ~ Signor J. Brown.
essay ['ɛseɪ] *n* (*SCOL*) composizione *f*; (*LITERATURE*) saggio.
essence ['ɛsns] *n* essenza; **in** ~ in sostanza; **speed is of the** ~ la velocità è di estrema importanza.
essential [ɪ'sɛnʃəl] *adj* essenziale; (*basic*) fondamentale ♦ *n* elemento essenziale; **it is** ~ **that** è essenziale che + *sub*.
essentially [ɪ'sɛnʃəlɪ] *adv* essenzialmente.
EST *abbr* (*US*: = *Eastern Standard Time*) *fuso orario.*
est. *abbr* = *established; estimate(d).*
establish [ɪ'stæblɪʃ] *vt* stabilire; (*business*) mettere su; (*one's power etc*) confermare; (*prove: fact, identity, sb's innocence*) dimostrare.
establishment [ɪs'tæblɪʃmənt] *n* stabilimento; (*business*) azienda; **the E**~ la classe dirigente; l'establishment *m*; **a teaching** ~ un istituto d'istruzione.
estate [ɪ'steɪt] *n* proprietà *f inv*; (*LAW*) beni *mpl*, patrimonio; (*BRIT: also:* **housing** ~) complesso edilizio.
estate agency *n* (*BRIT*) agenzia immobiliare.
estate agent *n* (*BRIT*) agente *m* immobiliare.
estate car *n* (*BRIT*) giardiniera.
esteem [ɪ'stiːm] *n* stima ♦ *vt* considerare; stimare; **I hold him in high** ~ gode di tutta la mia stima.
esthetic [ɪs'θɛtɪk] *adj* (*US*) = **aesthetic**.
estimate *n* ['ɛstɪmət] stima; (*COMM*) preventivo ♦ *vb* ['ɛstɪmeɪt] *vt* stimare, valutare ♦ *vi* (*BRIT COMM*): **to** ~ **for** fare il preventivo per; **to give sb an** ~ **of** fare a qn una valutazione approssimativa (*or* un preventivo) di; **at a rough** ~ approssimativamente.
estimation [ɛstɪ'meɪʃən] *n* stima; opinione *f*; **in my** ~ a mio giudizio, a mio avviso.
Estonia [ɛ'stəunɪə] *n* Estonia.
Estonian [ɛ'stəunɪən] *adj* estone *inv* ♦ *n* estone *m/f*; (*LING*) estone *m*.

estranged [ɪ'streɪndʒd] *adj* separato(a).
estrangement [ɪs'treɪndʒmənt] *n* alienazione *f*.
estrogen ['iːstrəudʒən] *n* (*US*) = **oestrogen**.
estuary ['ɛstjuərɪ] *n* estuario.
ET *abbr* (= *Eastern Time*) *fuso orario*
ETA *n abbr* (= *estimated time of arrival*) ora di arrivo prevista.
e-tailer ['iːteɪlə*] *n* venditore/trice *m* in Internet.
e-tailing ['iːteɪlɪŋ] *n* commercio in Internet.
et al. *abbr* (= *et alii: and others*) ed altri.
etc. *abbr* (= *et cetera*) ecc., etc.
etch [ɛtʃ] *vt* incidere all'acquaforte.
etching ['ɛtʃɪŋ] *n* acquaforte *f*.
ETD *n abbr* (= *estimated time of departure*) ora di partenza prevista.
eternal [ɪ'təːnl] *adj* eterno(a).
eternity [ɪ'təːnɪtɪ] *n* eternità.
ether ['iːθə*] *n* etere *m*.
ethereal [ɪ'θɪərɪəl] *adj* etereo(a).
ethical ['ɛθɪkl] *adj* etico(a), morale.
ethics ['ɛθɪks] *n* etica ♦ *npl* morale *f*.
Ethiopia [iːθɪ'əupɪə] *n* Etiopia.
Ethiopian [iːθɪ'əupɪən] *adj, n* etiope (*m/f*).
ethnic ['ɛθnɪk] *adj* etnico(a).
ethnic cleansing [-'klɛnzɪŋ] *n* pulizia etnica.
ethnic minority *n* minoranza etnica.
ethnology [ɛθ'nɔlədʒɪ] *n* etnologia.
ethos ['iːθɔs] *n* (*of culture, group*) norma di vita.
e-ticket ['iːtɪkɪt] *n* e-ticket *m inv*; biglietto elettronico.
etiquette ['ɛtɪkɛt] *n* etichetta.
ETV *n abbr* (*US*) = *Educational Television*.
etymology [ɛtɪ'mɔlədʒɪ] *n* etimologia.
EU *n abbr* (= *European Union*) UE *f*.
eucalyptus [juːkə'lɪptəs] *n* eucalipto.
eulogy ['juːlədʒɪ] *n* elogio.
euphemism ['juːfəmɪzəm] *n* eufemismo.
euphemistic [juːfə'mɪstɪk] *adj* eufemistico(a).
euphoria [juː'fɔːrɪə] *n* euforia.
Eurasia [juə'reɪʃə] *n* Eurasia.
Eurasian [juə'reɪʃən] *adj, n* eurasiano(a).
Euratom [juə'rætəm] *n abbr* (= *European Atomic Energy Community*) EURATOM *f*.
euro ['juərəu] *n* (*currency*) euro *m inv*.
Euro- ['juərəu] *prefix* euro-.
Eurocheque ['juərəutʃɛk] *n* eurochèque *m inv*.
Eurocrat ['juərəukræt] *n* eurocrate *m/f*.
Eurodollar ['juərəudɔlə*] *n* eurodollaro.
Euroland ['juərəu,lænd] *n* Eurolandia.
Europe ['juərəp] *n* Europa.
European [juərə'piːən] *adj, n* europeo(a).
European Court of Justice *n* Corte *f* di

Giustizia della Comunità Europea.
Europol ['juərəupɔl] *n* Europol *f*.
Euro-sceptic ['juərəuskɛptɪk] *n*
euroscettico/a.
Eurozone ['juərəuzəun] *n* zona euro.
euthanasia [ju:θə'neɪzɪə] *n* eutanasia.
evacuate [ɪ'vækjueɪt] *vt* evacuare.
evacuation [ɪvækju'eɪʃən] *n* evacuazione *f*.
evacuee [ɪvækju'i:] *n* sfollato/a.
evade [ɪ'veɪd] *vt* eludere; (*duties etc*)
sottrarsi a.
evaluate [ɪ'væljueɪt] *vt* valutare.
evangelist [ɪ'vændʒəlɪst] *n* evangelista *m*.
evangelize [ɪ'vændʒəlaɪz] *vt* evangelizzare.
evaporate [ɪ'væpəreɪt] *vi* evaporare ♦ *vt* far
evaporare.
evaporated milk *n* latte *m* concentrato.
evaporation [ɪvæpə'reɪʃən] *n* evaporazione
f.
evasion [ɪ'veɪʒən] *n* evasione *f*.
evasive [ɪ'veɪsɪv] *adj* evasivo(a).
eve [i:v] *n*: **on the** ~ **of** alla vigilia di.
even ['i:vn] *adj* regolare; (*number*) pari *inv*
♦ *adv* anche, perfino; ~ **if**, ~ **though** anche
se; ~ **more** ancora di più; **he loves her** ~
more la ama anche di più; ~ **faster**
ancora più veloce; ~ **so** ciò nonostante;
not ~ ... nemmeno ...; **to break** ~ finire in
pari *or* alla pari; **to get** ~ **with sb** dare la
pari a qn.
▶**even out** *vi* pareggiare.
even-handed ['i:vn'hændɪd] *adj* imparziale,
equo(a).
evening ['i:vnɪŋ] *n* sera; (*as duration, event*)
serata; **in the** ~ la sera; **this** ~ stasera,
questa sera; **tomorrow/yesterday** ~
domani/ieri sera.
evening class *n* corso serale.
evening dress *n* (*woman's*) abito da sera;
in ~ (*man*) in abito scuro; (*woman*) in
abito lungo.
evenly ['i:vənlɪ] *adv* (*distribute, space,
spread*) uniformemente; (*divide*) in parti
uguali.
evensong ['i:vnsɒŋ] *n* ≈ vespro.
event [ɪ'vɛnt] *n* avvenimento; (*SPORT*)
gara; **in the** ~ **of** in caso di; **at all** ~**s**
(*BRIT*), **in any** ~ in ogni caso; **in the** ~ in
realtà, di fatto; **in the course of** ~**s** nel
corso degli eventi.
eventful [ɪ'vɛntful] *adj* denso(a) di eventi.
eventing [ɪ'vɛntɪŋ] *n* (*HORSERIDING*)
concorso ippico.
eventual [ɪ'vɛntʃuəl] *adj* finale.
eventuality [ɪvɛntʃu'ælɪtɪ] *n* possibilità *f*
inv, eventualità *f inv*.
eventually [ɪ'vɛntʃuəlɪ] *adv* finalmente.
ever ['ɛvə*] *adv* mai; (*at all times*) sempre;

for ~ per sempre; **the best** ~ il migliore
che ci sia mai stato; **hardly** ~ **non** ... quasi
mai; **did you** ~ **meet him?** l'ha mai
incontrato?; **have you** ~ **been there?** c'è
mai stato?; ~ **so pretty** così bello(a);
thank you ~ **so much** grazie mille; **yours**
~ (*BRIT*: *in letters*) sempre tuo; ~ **since** *adv*
da allora ♦ *conj* sin da quando.
Everest ['ɛvərɪst] *n* (*also*: **Mount** ~) Everest
m.
evergreen ['ɛvəgri:n] *n* sempreverde *m*.
everlasting [ɛvə'lɑ:stɪŋ] *adj* eterno(a).
every ['ɛvrɪ] *adj* ogni; ~ **day** tutti i giorni,
ogni giorno; ~ **other/third day** ogni due/
tre giorni; ~ **other car** una macchina su
due; ~ **now and then** ogni tanto, di
quando in quando; **I have** ~ **confidence** in
him ho piena fiducia in lui.
everybody ['ɛvrɪbɔdɪ] *pron* ognuno, tutti *pl*;
~ **else** tutti gli altri; ~ **knows about it** lo
sanno tutti.
everyday ['ɛvrɪdeɪ] *adj* quotidiano(a); di
ogni giorno; (*use, occurrence, experience*)
comune; (*expression*) di uso corrente.
everyone ['ɛvrɪwʌn] = **everybody**.
everything ['ɛvrɪθɪŋ] *pron* tutto, ogni cosa;
~ **is ready** è tutto pronto; **he did** ~
possible ha fatto tutto il possibile.
everywhere ['ɛvrɪwɛə*] *adv* in ogni luogo,
dappertutto; (*wherever*) ovunque; ~ **you
go you meet** ... ovunque si vada si trova
....
evict [ɪ'vɪkt] *vt* sfrattare.
eviction [ɪ'vɪkʃən] *n* sfratto.
eviction notice *n* avviso di sfratto.
evidence ['ɛvɪdəns] *n* (*proof*) prova; (*of
witness*) testimonianza; (*sign*): **to show** ~
of dare segni di; **to give** ~ deporre; **in** ~
(*obvious*) in evidenza; in vista.
evident ['ɛvɪdənt] *adj* evidente.
evidently ['ɛvɪdəntlɪ] *adv* evidentemente.
evil ['i:vl] *adj* cattivo(a), maligno(a) ♦ *n*
male *m*.
evince [ɪ'vɪns] *vt* manifestare.
evocative [ɪ'vɔkətɪv] *adj* evocativo(a).
evoke [ɪ'vəuk] *vt* evocare; (*admiration*)
suscitare.
evolution [i:və'lu:ʃən] *n* evoluzione *f*.
evolve [ɪ'vɔlv] *vt* elaborare ♦ *vi* svilupparsi,
evolversi.
ewe [ju:] *n* pecora.
ex- [ɛks] *prefix* ex; (*out of*): **the price** ~ **works**
il prezzo franco fabbrica.
exacerbate [ɪk'sæsəbeɪt] *vt* (*pain*)
aggravare; (*fig: relations, situation*)
esacerbare, esasperare.
exact [ɪg'zækt] *adj* esatto(a) ♦ *vt*: **to** ~ **sth**
(**from**) estorcere qc (da); esigere qc (da).

exacting [ɪg'zæktɪŋ] _adj_ esigente; (_work_) faticoso(a).

exactitude [ɪg'zæktɪtjuːd] _n_ esattezza, precisione _f._

exactly [ɪg'zæktlɪ] _adv_ esattamente; ~! esatto!

exaggerate [ɪg'zædʒəreɪt] _vt, vi_ esagerare.

exaggeration [ɪgzædʒə'reɪʃən] _n_ esagerazione _f._

exalt [ɪg'zɔːlt] _vt_ esaltare; elevare.

exalted [ɪg'zɔːltɪd] _adj_ (_rank, person_) elevato(a); (_elated_) esaltato(a).

exam [ɪg'zæm] _n abbr_ (_SCOL_) = **examination.**

examination [ɪgzæmɪ'neɪʃən] _n_ (_SCOL_) esame _m_; (_MED_) controllo; **to take** _or_ (_BRIT_) **sit an** ~ sostenere _or_ dare un esame; **the matter is under** ~ la questione è all'esame.

examine [ɪg'zæmɪn] _vt_ esaminare; (_SCOL: orally, LAW: person_) interrogare; (_inspect: machine, premises_) ispezionare; (_luggage, passport_) controllare; (_MED_) visitare.

examiner [ɪg'zæmɪnə*] _n_ esaminatore/ trice.

example [ɪg'zɑːmpl] _n_ esempio; **for** ~ ad _or_ per esempio; **to set a good/bad** ~ dare il buon/cattivo esempio.

exasperate [ɪg'zɑːspəreɪt] _vt_ esasperare; ~**d by** (_or_ **at** _or_ **with**) esasperato da.

exasperating [ɪg'zɑːspəreɪtɪŋ] _adj_ esasperante.

exasperation [ɪgzɑːspə'reɪʃən] _n_ esasperazione _f._

excavate ['ɛkskəveɪt] _vt_ scavare.

excavation [ɛkskə'veɪʃən] _n_ escavazione _f._

excavator ['ɛkskəveɪtə*] _n_ scavatore _m_, scavatrice _f._

exceed [ɪk'siːd] _vt_ superare; (_one's powers, time limit_) oltrepassare.

exceedingly [ɪk'siːdɪŋlɪ] _adv_ eccessivamente.

excel [ɪk'sɛl] _vi_ eccellere ♦ _vt_ sorpassare; **to** ~ **o.s.** (_BRIT_) superare se stesso.

excellence ['ɛksələns] _n_ eccellenza.

Excellency ['ɛksələnsɪ] _n_: **His** ~ Sua Eccellenza.

excellent ['ɛksələnt] _adj_ eccellente.

except [ɪk'sɛpt] _prep_ (_also_: ~ **for**, ~**ing**) salvo, all'infuori di, eccetto ♦ _vt_ escludere; ~ **if/when** salvo se/quando; ~ **that** salvo che.

exception [ɪk'sɛpʃən] _n_ eccezione _f_; **to take** ~ **to** trovare a ridire su; **with the** ~ **of** ad eccezione di.

exceptional [ɪk'sɛpʃənl] _adj_ eccezionale.

excerpt ['ɛksəːpt] _n_ estratto.

excess [ɪk'sɛs] _n_ eccesso; **in** ~ **of** al di sopra di.

excess baggage _n_ bagaglio in eccedenza.

excess fare _n_ supplemento.

excessive [ɪk'sɛsɪv] _adj_ eccessivo(a).

excess supply _n_ eccesso di offerta.

exchange [ɪks'tʃeɪndʒ] _n_ scambio; (_also: telephone_ ~) centralino ♦ _vt_: **to** ~ (**for**) scambiare (con); **in** ~ **for** in cambio di; **foreign** ~ (_COMM_) cambio.

exchange control _n_ controllo sui cambi.

exchange market _n_ mercato dei cambi.

exchange rate _n_ tasso di cambio.

Exchequer [ɪks'tʃɛkə*] _n_: **the** ~ (_BRIT_) lo Scacchiere, ≈ il ministero delle Finanze.

excisable [ɪk'saɪzəbl] _adj_ soggetto(a) a dazio.

excise _n_ ['ɛksaɪz] imposta, dazio ♦ _vt_ [ɛk'saɪz] recidere.

excise duties _npl_ dazi _mpl._

excitable [ɪk'saɪtəbl] _adj_ eccitabile.

excite [ɪk'saɪt] _vt_ eccitare; **to get** ~**d** eccitarsi.

excitement [ɪk'saɪtmənt] _n_ eccitazione _f_; agitazione _f._

exciting [ɪk'saɪtɪŋ] _adj_ avventuroso(a); (_film, book_) appassionante.

excl. _abbr_ (= _excluding, exclusive (of)_) escl.

exclaim [ɪk'skleɪm] _vi_ esclamare.

exclamation [ɛksklə'meɪʃən] _n_ esclamazione _f._

exclamation mark _n_ punto esclamativo.

exclude [ɪk'skluːd] _vt_ escludere.

excluding [ɪk'skluːdɪŋ] _prep_: ~ **VAT** IVA esclusa.

exclusion [ɪk'skluːʒən] _n_ esclusione _f_; **to the** ~ **of** escludendo.

exclusion clause _n_ clausola di esclusione.

exclusion zone _n_ area interdetta.

exclusive [ɪk'skluːsɪv] _adj_ esclusivo(a); (_club_) selettivo(a); (_district_) snob _inv_ ♦ _adv_ (_COMM_) non compreso; ~ **of VAT** IVA esclusa; ~ **of postage** spese postali escluse; ~ **of service** servizio escluso; **from 1st to 15th March** ~ dal 1° al 15 marzo esclusi; ~ **rights** _npl_ (_COMM_) diritti _mpl_ esclusivi.

exclusively [ɪk'skluːsɪvlɪ] _adv_ esclusivamente.

excommunicate [ɛkskə'mjuːnɪkeɪt] _vt_ scomunicare.

excrement ['ɛkskrəmənt] _n_ escremento.

excruciating [ɪk'skruːʃɪeɪtɪŋ] _adj_ straziante, atroce.

excursion [ɪk'skəːʃən] _n_ escursione _f_, gita.

excursion ticket _n_ biglietto a tariffa escursionistica.

excusable [ɪk'skjuːzəbl] _adj_ scusabile.

excuse _n_ [ɪk'skjuːs] scusa ♦ _vt_ [ɪk'skjuːz] scusare; (_justify_) giustificare; **to make** ~**s**

for sb trovare giustificazioni per qn; **to ~ sb from** (*activity*) dispensare qn da; **~ me!** mi scusi!; **now if you will ~ me,** ... ora, mi scusi ma ...; **to ~ o.s.** (**for** (**doing**) **sth**) giustificarsi (per (aver fatto) qc).

ex-directory ['ɛksdɪ'rɛktərɪ] *adj* (*BRIT*): ~ (**phone**) **number** numero non compreso nell'elenco telefonico.

execrable ['ɛksɪkrəbl] *adj* (*gen*) pessimo(a); (*manners*) esecrabile.

execute ['ɛksɪkjuːt] *vt* (*prisoner*) giustiziare; (*plan etc*) eseguire.

execution [ɛksɪ'kjuːʃən] *n* esecuzione *f*.

executioner [ɛksɪ'kjuːʃnə*] *n* boia *m inv*.

executive [ɪg'zɛkjutɪv] *n* (*COMM*) dirigente *m*; (*POL*) esecutivo ♦ *adj* esecutivo(a); (*secretary*) di direzione; (*offices, suite*) della direzione; (*car, plane*) dirigenziale; (*position, job, duties*) direttivo(a).

executive director *n* amministratore/ trice.

executor [ɪg'zɛkjutə*] *n* esecutore(trice) testamentario(a).

exemplary [ɪg'zɛmplərɪ] *adj* esemplare.

exemplify [ɪg'zɛmplɪfaɪ] *vt* esemplificare.

exempt [ɪg'zɛmpt] *adj*: ~ (**from**) (*person*: *from tax*) esentato(a) (da); (: *from military service etc*) esonerato(a) (da); (*goods*) esente (da) ♦ *vt*: **to ~ sb from** esentare qn da.

exemption [ɪg'zɛmpʃən] *n* esenzione *f*.

exercise ['ɛksəsaɪz] *n* esercizio ♦ *vt* esercitare; (*dog*) portar fuori ♦ *vi* (*also*: **take ~**) fare del movimento *or* moto.

exercise bike *n* cyclette ℞ *f inv*.

exercise book *n* quaderno.

exert [ɪg'zəːt] *vt* esercitare; (*strength, force*) impiegare; **to ~ o.s.** sforzarsi.

exertion [ɪg'zəːʃən] *n* sforzo.

ex gratia ['ɛks'greɪʃə] *adj*: ~ **payment** gratifica.

exhale [ɛks'heɪl] *vt, vi* espirare.

exhaust [ɪg'zɔːst] *n* (*also*: ~ **fumes**) scappamento; (*also*: ~ **pipe**) tubo di scappamento ♦ *vt* esaurire; **to ~ o.s.** sfiancarsi.

exhausted [ɪg'zɔːstɪd] *adj* esaurito(a).

exhausting [ɪg'zɔːstɪŋ] *adj* estenuante.

exhaustion [ɪg'zɔːstʃən] *n* esaurimento; **nervous ~** sovraffaticamento mentale.

exhaustive [ɪg'zɔːstɪv] *adj* esauriente.

exhibit [ɪg'zɪbɪt] *n* (*ART*) oggetto esposto; (*LAW*) documento *or* oggetto esibito ♦ *vt* esporre; (*courage, skill*) dimostrare.

exhibition [ɛksɪ'bɪʃən] *n* mostra, esposizione *f*; (*of rudeness etc*) spettacolo; **to make an ~ of o.s.** dare spettacolo di sé.

exhibitionist [ɛksɪ'bɪʃənɪst] *n* esibizionista *m/f*.

exhibitor [ɪg'zɪbɪtə*] *n* espositore/trice.

exhilarating [ɪg'zɪləreɪtɪŋ] *adj* esilarante; stimolante.

exhilaration [ɪgzɪlə'reɪʃən] *n* esaltazione *f*, ebbrezza.

exhort [ɪg'zɔːt] *vt* esortare.

exile ['ɛksaɪl] *n* esilio; (*person*) esiliato/a ♦ *vt* esiliare; **in ~** in esilio.

exist [ɪg'zɪst] *vi* esistere.

existence [ɪg'zɪstəns] *n* esistenza; **to be in ~** esistere.

existentialism [ɛgzɪs'tɛnʃəlɪzəm] *n* esistenzialismo.

existing [ɪg'zɪstɪŋ] *adj* (*laws, regime*) attuale.

exit ['ɛksɪt] *n* uscita ♦ *vi* (*COMPUT, THEAT*) uscire.

exit poll *n* exit poll *m inv*, sondaggio all'uscita dei seggi.

exit ramp *n* (*US AUT*) rampa di uscita.

exit visa *n* visto d'uscita.

exodus ['ɛksədəs] *n* esodo.

ex officio ['ɛksə'fɪʃɪəu] *adj, adv* d'ufficio.

exonerate [ɪg'zɔnəreɪt] *vt*: **to ~ from** discolpare da.

exorbitant [ɪg'zɔːbɪtənt] *adj* (*price*) esorbitante; (*demands*) spropositato(a).

exorcize ['ɛksɔːsaɪz] *vt* esorcizzare.

exotic [ɪg'zɔtɪk] *adj* esotico(a).

expand [ɪk'spænd] *vt* (*chest, economy etc*) sviluppare; (*market, operations*) espandere; (*influence*) estendere; (*horizons*) allargare ♦ *vi* svilupparsi; (*also gas*) espandersi; (*metal*) dilatarsi; **to ~ on** (*notes, story etc*) ampliare.

expanse [ɪk'spæns] *n* distesa, estensione *f*.

expansion [ɪk'spænʃən] *n* (*gen*) espansione *f*; (*of town, economy*) sviluppo; (*of metal*) dilatazione *f*.

expansionism [ɪk'spænʃənɪzəm] *n* espansionismo.

expansionist [ɪk'spænʃənɪst] *adj* espansionistico(a).

expatriate *n* [ɛks'pætrɪət] espatriato/a ♦ *vt* [ɛks'pætrɪeɪt] espatriare.

expect [ɪk'spɛkt] *vt* (*anticipate*) prevedere, aspettarsi, prevedere *or* aspettarsi che + *sub*; (*count on*) contare su; (*hope for*) sperare; (*require*) richiedere, esigere; (*suppose*) supporre; (*await, also baby*) aspettare ♦ *vi*: **to be ~ing** essere in stato interessante; **to ~ sb to do** aspettarsi che qn faccia; **to ~ to do sth** pensare *or* contare di fare qc; **as ~ed** come previsto; **I ~ so** credo di sì.

expectancy [ɪk'spɛktənsɪ] *n* attesa; **life ~**

probabilità *fpl* di vita.
expectant [ɪk'spɛktənt] *adj* pieno(a) di
aspettative.
expectantly [ɪk'spɛktəntlɪ] *adv* (*look, listen*)
con un'aria d'attesa.
expectant mother *n* gestante *f*.
expectation [ɛkspɛk'teɪʃən] *n* aspettativa;
speranza; **in ~ of** in previsione di;
against *or* **contrary to all ~(s)** contro
ogni aspettativa; **to come** *or* **live up
to sb's ~s** rispondere alle attese
di qn.
expedience, expediency [ɪk'spiːdɪəns,
ɪk'spiːdɪənsɪ] *n* convenienza; **for the sake
of ~** per una questione di comodità.
expedient [ɪk'spiːdɪənt] *adj* conveniente;
vantaggioso(a) ♦ *n* espediente *m*.
expedite ['ɛkspədaɪt] *vt* sbrigare;
facilitare.
expedition [ɛkspə'dɪʃən] *n* spedizione *f*.
expeditionary force [ɛkspə'dɪʃənərɪ-] *n*
corpo di spedizione.
expeditious [ɛkspə'dɪʃəs] *adj* sollecito(a),
rapido(a).
expel [ɪk'spɛl] *vt* espellere.
expend [ɪk'spɛnd] *vt* spendere; (*use up*)
consumare.
expendable [ɪk'spɛndəbl] *adj* sacrificabile.
expenditure [ɪk'spɛndɪtʃə*] *n* spesa; (*of
time, effort*) dispendio.
expense [ɪk'spɛns] *n* spesa; (*high cost*)
costo; **~s** *npl* (*COMM*) spese *fpl*, indennità
fpl; **to go to the ~ of** sobbarcarsi la spesa
di; **at great ~** con grande impiego di
mezzi; **at the ~ of** a spese di.
expense account *n* conto *m* spese *inv*.
expensive [ɪk'spɛnsɪv] *adj* caro(a),
costoso(a); **she has ~ tastes** le piacciono
le cose costose.
experience [ɪk'spɪərɪəns] *n* esperienza ♦ *vt*
(*pleasure*) provare; (*hardship*) soffrire; **to
learn by ~** imparare per esperienza.
experienced [ɪk'spɪərɪənst] *adj* che ha
esperienza.
experiment *n* [ɪk'spɛrɪmənt] esperimento,
esperienza ♦ *vi* [ɪk'spɛrɪmɛnt] fare
esperimenti; **to perform** *or* **carry out an ~**
fare un esperimento; **as an ~** a titolo di
esperimento; **to ~ with a new vaccine**
sperimentare un nuovo vaccino.
experimental [ɪkspɛrɪ'mɛntl] *adj*
sperimentale; **at the ~ stage** in via di
sperimentazione.
expert ['ɛkspəːt] *adj, n* esperto(a); **~
witness** (*LAW*) esperto/a; **~ in** *or* **at doing
sth** esperto nel fare qc; **an ~ on sth** un
esperto di qc.
expertise [ɛkspəː'tiːz] *n* competenza.

expire [ɪk'spaɪə*] *vi* (*period of time, licence*)
scadere.
expiry [ɪk'spaɪərɪ] *n* scadenza.
explain [ɪk'spleɪn] *vt* spiegare.
► **explain away** *vt* dar ragione di.
explanation [ɛksplə'neɪʃən] *n* spiegazione *f*;
to find an ~ for sth trovare la
spiegazione di qc.
explanatory [ɪk'splænətrɪ] *adj*
esplicativo(a).
expletive [ɪk'spliːtɪv] *n* imprecazione *f*.
explicit [ɪk'splɪsɪt] *adj* esplicito(a); (*definite*)
netto(a).
explode [ɪk'spləud] *vi* esplodere ♦ *vt* (*fig:
theory*) demolire; **to ~ a myth**
distruggere un mito.
exploit *n* ['ɛksplɔɪt] impresa ♦ *vt* [ɪk'splɔɪt]
sfruttare.
exploitation [ɛksplɔɪ'teɪʃən] *n*
sfruttamento.
exploration [ɛksplə'reɪʃən] *n* esplorazione *f*.
exploratory [ɪk'splɔrətrɪ] *adj* (*fig: talks*)
esplorativo(a); **~ operation** (*MED*)
intervento d'esplorazione.
explore [ɪk'splɔː*] *vt* esplorare;
(*possibilities*) esaminare.
explorer [ɪk'splɔːrə*] *n* esploratore/trice.
explosion [ɪk'spləuʒən] *n* esplosione *f*.
explosive [ɪk'spləusɪv] *adj* esplosivo(a) ♦ *n*
esplosivo.
exponent [ɪk'spəunənt] *n* esponente *m/f*.
export *vt* [ɛk'spɔːt] esportare ♦ *n* ['ɛkspɔːt]
esportazione *f*; articolo di esportazione
♦ *cpd* d'esportazione.
exportation [ɛkspɔː'teɪʃən] *n* esportazione
f.
exporter [ɪk'spɔːtə*] *n* esportatore *m*.
export licence *n* licenza d'esportazione.
expose [ɪk'spəuz] *vt* esporre; (*unmask*)
smascherare; **to ~ o.s.** (*LAW*) oltraggiare
il pudore.
exposed [ɪk'spəuzd] *adj* (*land, house*)
esposto(a); (*ELEC: wire*) scoperto(a); (*pipe,
beam*) a vista.
exposition [ɛkspə'zɪʃən] *n* esposizione *f*.
exposure [ɪk'spəuʒə*] *n* esposizione *f*;
(*PHOT*) posa; (*MED*) assideramento; **to die
of ~** morire assiderato(a).
exposure meter *n* esposimetro.
expound [ɪk'spaund] *vt* esporre; (*theory,
text*) spiegare.
express [ɪk'sprɛs] *adj* (*definite*) chiaro(a),
espresso(a); (*BRIT: letter etc*) espresso *inv*
♦ *n* (*train*) espresso ♦ *adv*: **to send sth ~**
spedire qc per espresso ♦ *vt* esprimere;
to ~ o.s. esprimersi.
expression [ɪk'sprɛʃən] *n* espressione *f*.
expressionism [ɪk'sprɛʃənɪzəm] *n*

espressionismo.
expressive [ɪk'sprɛsɪv] *adj* espressivo(a).
expressly [ɪk'sprɛslɪ] *adv* espressamente.
expressway [ɪk'sprɛsweɪ] *n* (*US*)
autostrada che attraversa la città.
expropriate [ɛks'prəuprɪeɪt] *vt* espropriare.
expulsion [ɪk'spʌlʃən] *n* espulsione *f*.
exquisite [ɛk'skwɪzɪt] *adj* squisito(a).
ex-serviceman ['ɛks'sɔːvɪsmən] *n* ex
combattente *m*.
ext. *abbr* (*TEL*: = *extension*) int. (= *interno*).
extemporize [ɪk'stɛmpəraɪz] *vi*
improvvisare.
extend [ɪk'stɛnd] *vt* (*visit*) protrarre; (*road,
deadline*) prolungare; (*building*) ampliare;
(*offer*) offrire, porgere; (*COMM*: *credit*)
accordare ♦ *vi* (*land*) estendersi.
extension [ɪk'stɛnʃən] *n* (*of road, term*)
prolungamento; (*of contract, deadline*)
proroga; (*building*) annesso; (*to wire, table*)
prolunga; (*telephone*) interno; (: *in private
house*) apparecchio supplementare; ~
3718 (*TEL*) interno 3718.
extension cable *n* (*ELEC*) prolunga.
extensive [ɪk'stɛnsɪv] *adj* esteso(a),
ampio(a); (*damage*) su larga scala;
(*alterations*) notevole; (*inquiries*)
esauriente; (*use*) grande.
extensively [ɪk'stɛnsɪvlɪ] *adv* (*altered,
damaged etc*) radicalmente; **he's travelled
~** ha viaggiato molto.
extent [ɪk'stɛnt] *n* estensione *f*; (*of
knowledge, activities, power*) portata;
(*degree*: *of damage, loss*) proporzioni *fpl*; **to
some ~** fino a un certo punto; **to a
certain/large ~** in certa/larga misura; **to
what ~?** fino a che punto?; **to such an ~
that ...** a tal punto che ....
extenuating [ɪk'stɛnjueɪtɪŋ] *adj*: ~
circumstances attenuanti *fpl*.
exterior [ɛk'stɪərɪə*] *adj* esteriore,
esterno(a) ♦ *n* esteriore *m*, esterno;
aspetto (esteriore).
exterminate [ɪk'stɔːmɪneɪt] *vt* sterminare.
extermination [ɪkstɔːmɪ'neɪʃən] *n*
sterminio.
external [ɛk'stɔːnl] *adj* esterno(a), esteriore
♦ *n*: **the ~s** le apparenze; **for ~ use only**
(*MED*) solo per uso esterno; ~ **affairs** (*POL*)
affari *mpl* esteri.
externally [ɛk'stɔːnəlɪ] *adv* esternamente.
extinct [ɪk'stɪŋkt] *adj* estinto(a).
extinction [ɪk'stɪŋkʃən] *n* estinzione *f*.
extinguish [ɪk'stɪŋgwɪʃ] *vt* estinguere.
extinguisher [ɪk'stɪŋgwɪʃə*] *n* estintore *m*.
extol, (*US*) **extoll** [ɪk'stəul] *vt* (*merits,
virtues*) magnificare; (*person*) celebrare.
extort [ɪk'stɔːt] *vt*: **to ~ sth (from)**

estorcere qc (da).
extortion [ɪk'stɔːʃən] *n* estorsione *f*.
extortionate [ɪk'stɔːʃənɪt] *adj* esorbitante.
extra ['ɛkstrə] *adj* extra *inv*, supplementare
♦ *adv* (*in addition*) di più ♦ *n* supplemento;
(*THEAT*) comparso; **wine will cost ~** il
vino è extra; ~ **large sizes** taglie *fpl* forti.
extra... ['ɛkstrə] *prefix* extra....
extract *vt* [ɪk'strækt] estrarre; (*money,
promise*) strappare ♦ *n* ['ɛkstrækt]
estratto; (*passage*) brano.
extraction [ɪk'strækʃən] *n* estrazione *f*;
(*descent*) origine *f*.
extractor fan [ɪk'stræktə*-] *n* aspiratore *m*.
extracurricular [ɛkstrəkə'rɪkjulə*] *adj*
(*SCOL*) parascolastico(a).
extradite ['ɛkstrədaɪt] *vt* estradare.
extradition [ɛkstrə'dɪʃən] *n* estradizione *f*.
extramarital [ɛkstrə'mærɪtl] *adj*
extraconiugale.
extramural [ɛkstrə'mjuərl] *adj* fuori
dell'università.
extraneous [ɛk'streɪnɪəs] *adj*: ~ **to**
estraneo(a) a.
extraordinary [ɪk'strɔːdnrɪ] *adj*
straordinario(a); **the ~ thing is that ...** la
cosa strana è che ....
extraordinary general meeting *n*
assemblea straordinaria.
extrapolation [ɪkstræpə'leɪʃən] *n*
estrapolazione *f*.
extrasensory perception (ESP)
[ɛkstrə'sɛnsərɪ-] *n* percezione *f*
extrasensoriale.
extra time *n* (*FOOTBALL*) tempo
supplementare.
extravagance [ɪk'strævəgəns] *n* (*excessive
spending*) sperpero; (*thing bought*)
stravaganza.
extravagant [ɪk'strævəgənt] *adj*
stravagante; (*in spending*: *person*)
prodigo(a); (: *tastes*) dispendioso(a).
extreme [ɪk'striːm] *adj* estremo(a) ♦ *n*
estremo; **~s of temperature** eccessivi
sbalzi *mpl* di temperatura; **the ~ left/right**
(*POL*) l'estrema sinistra/destra.
extremely [ɪk'striːmlɪ] *adv* estremamente.
extremist [ɪk'striːmɪst] *adj, n* estremista
(*m/f*).
extremity [ɪk'strɛmɪtɪ] *n* estremità *f inv*.
extricate ['ɛkstrɪkeɪt] *vt*: **to ~ sth (from)**
districare qc (da).
extrovert ['ɛkstrəvɔːt] *n* estroverso/a.
exuberance [ɪg'zuːbərəns] *n* esuberanza.
exuberant [ɪg'zjuːbərənt] *adj* esuberante.
exude [ɪg'zjuːd] *vt* trasudare; (*fig*)
emanare.
exult [ɪg'zʌlt] *vi* esultare, gioire.

exultant [ɪg'zʌltənt] _adj_ (_person, smile_) esultante; (_shout, expression_) di giubilo.

exultation [ɛgzʌl'teɪʃən] _n_ giubilo; **in** ~ **per la gioia.**

eye [aɪ] _n_ occhio; (_of needle_) cruna ♦ _vt_ osservare; **to keep an** ~ **on** tenere d'occhio; **in the public** ~ esposto(a) al pubblico; **as far as the** ~ **can see** a perdita d'occhio; **with an** ~ **to doing sth** (_BRIT_) con l'idea di far qc; **to have an** ~ **for sth** avere occhio per qc; **there's more to this than meets the** ~ non è così semplice come sembra.

eyeball ['aɪbɔːl] _n_ globo dell'occhio.

eyebath ['aɪbɑːθ] _n_ occhino.

eyebrow ['aɪbrau] _n_ sopracciglio.

eyebrow pencil _n_ matita per le sopracciglia.

eye-catching ['aɪkætʃɪŋ] _adj_ che colpisce l'occhio.

eye cup _n_ (_US_) = **eyebath.**

eyedrops ['aɪdrɔps] _npl_ gocce _fpl_ oculari, collirio.

eyeful ['aɪful] _n_: **to get an** ~ (**of sth**) (_col_) avere l'occasione di dare una bella sbirciata (a qc).

eyeglass ['aɪglɑːs] _n_ monocolo.

eyelash ['aɪlæʃ] _n_ ciglio.

eyelet ['aɪlɪt] _n_ occhiello.

eye-level ['aɪlɛvl] _adj_ all'altezza degli occhi.

eyelid ['aɪlɪd] _n_ palpebra.

eyeliner ['aɪlaɪnə*] _n_ eye-liner _m inv._

eye-opener ['aɪəupnə*] _n_ rivelazione _f._

eyeshadow ['aɪʃædəu] _n_ ombretto.

eyesight ['aɪsaɪt] _n_ vista.

eyesore ['aɪsɔː*] _n_ pugno nell'occhio.

eyestrain ['aɪstreɪn] _n_: **to get** ~ stancarsi gli occhi.

eye-tooth, _pl_ **-teeth** ['aɪtuːθ, -tiːθ] _n_ canino superiore; **to give one's eye-teeth for sth/to do sth** (_fig_) dare non so che cosa per qc/per fare qc.

eyewash ['aɪwɔʃ] _n_ collirio; (_fig_) sciocchezze _fpl._

eye witness _n_ testimone _m/f_ oculare.

eyrie ['ɪərɪ] _n_ nido (d'aquila).

F, f [ɛf] _n_ (_letter_) F, f _f or m inv_; (_MUS_): F fa _m_; **F for Frederick,** (_US_) **F for Fox** ≈ F come Firenze.

F. _abbr_ (= _Fahrenheit_) F.

FA _n abbr_ (_BRIT_) = _Football Association._

FAA _n abbr_ (_US_) = _Federal Aviation Administration._

fable ['feɪbl] _n_ favola.

fabric ['fæbrɪk] _n_ stoffa, tessuto; (_ARCHIT_) struttura.

fabricate ['fæbrɪkeɪt] _vt_ fabbricare.

fabrication [fæbrɪ'keɪʃən] _n_ fabbricazione _f._

fabric ribbon _n_ (_for typewriter_) dattilonastro di tessuto.

fabulous ['fæbjuləs] _adj_ favoloso(a); (_col: super_) favoloso(a), fantastico(a).

façade [fə'sɑːd] _n_ facciata; (_fig_) apparenza.

face [feɪs] _n_ faccia, viso, volto; (_expression_) faccia; (_grimace_) smorfia; (_of clock_) quadrante _m_; (_of building_) facciata; (_side, surface_) faccia; (_of mountain, cliff_) parete _f_ ♦ _vt_ fronteggiare; (_fig_) affrontare; ~ **down** (_person_) bocconi; (_object_) a faccia in giù; **to lose/save** ~ perdere/salvare la faccia; **to pull a** ~ fare una smorfia; **in the** ~ **of** (_difficulties etc_) di fronte a; **on the** ~ **of it** a prima vista; **to** ~ **the fact that** ... riconoscere _or_ ammettere che ....

▶**face up to** _vt fus_ affrontare, far fronte a.

face cloth _n_ (_BRIT_) guanto di spugna.

face cream _n_ crema per il viso.

faceless ['feɪslɪs] _adj_ anonimo(a).

face lift _n_ lifting _m inv_; (_of façade etc_) ripulita.

face powder _n_ cipria.

face-saving ['feɪs'seɪvɪŋ] _adj_ che salva la faccia.

facet ['fæsɪt] _n_ faccetta, sfaccettatura; (_fig_) sfaccettatura.

facetious [fə'siːʃəs] _adj_ faceto(a).

face-to-face ['feɪstə'feɪs] _adv_ faccia a faccia.

face value ['feɪs'væljuː] _n_ (_of coin_) valore _m_ facciale _or_ nominale; **to take sth at** ~ (_fig_) giudicare qc dalle apparenze.

facia ['feɪʃə] _n_ = **fascia.**

facial ['feɪʃəl] _adj_ facciale ♦ _n_ trattamento del viso.

facile ['fæsaɪl] *adj* facile; superficiale.
facilitate [fə'sɪlɪteɪt] *vt* facilitare.
facility [fə'sɪlɪtɪ] *n* facilità; **facilities** *npl*
attrezzature *fpl*; **credit facilities**
facilitazioni *fpl* di credito.
facing ['feɪsɪŋ] *n* (*of wall etc*) rivestimento;
(*SEWING*) paramontura.
facsimile [fæk'sɪmɪlɪ] *n* facsimile *m inv.*
facsimile machine *n* telecopiatrice *f.*
fact [fækt] *n* fatto; **in** ~ infatti; **to know for**
a ~ **that** ... sapere per certo che ...; **the**
~ **(of the matter) is that** ... la verità è che
...; **the** ~**s of life** (*sex*) i fatti riguardanti
la vita sessuale; (*fig*) le realtà della vita.
fact-finding ['fæktfaɪndɪŋ] *adj*: **a** ~ **tour/**
mission un viaggio/una missione
d'inchiesta.
faction ['fækʃən] *n* fazione *f.*
factional ['fækʃənl] *adj*: ~ **fighting** scontri
mpl tra fazioni.
factor ['fæktə*] *n* fattore *m*; (*COMM*:
company) *organizzazione specializzata*
nell'incasso di crediti per conto terzi; (:
agent) agente *m* depositario ♦ *vi* incassare
crediti per conto terzi; **human** ~
elemento umano; **safety** ~ coefficiente *m*
di sicurezza.
factory ['fæktərɪ] *n* fabbrica, stabilimento.
factory farming *n* (*BRIT*) allevamento su
scala industriale.
factory floor *n*: **the** ~ (*workers*) gli operai;
(*area*) il reparto produzione; **on the** ~ nel
reparto produzione.
factory ship *n* nave *f* fattoria *inv.*
factual ['fæktjuəl] *adj* che si attiene ai fatti.
faculty ['fækəltɪ] *n* facoltà *f inv*; (*US*:
teaching staff) corpo insegnante.
fad [fæd] *n* mania; capriccio.
fade [feɪd] *vi* sbiadire, sbiadirsi; (*light,*
sound, hope) attenuarsi, affievolirsi;
(*flower*) appassire.
▶**fade in** *vt* (*picture*) aprire in dissolvenza;
(*sound*) aumentare gradualmente
d'intensità.
▶**fade out** *vt* (*picture*) chiudere in
dissolvenza; (*sound*) diminuire
gradualmente d'intensità.
faeces, (*US*) **feces** ['fiːsiːz] *npl* feci *fpl.*
fag [fæg] *n* (*BRIT col*: *cigarette*) cicca;
(: *chore*) sfacchinata; (*US col*: *homosexual*)
frocio.
fag end *n* (*BRIT col*) mozzicone *m.*
fagged out ['fægd-] *adj* (*BRIT col*) stanco(a)
morto(a).
fail [feɪl] *vt* (*exam*) non superare; (*candidate*)
bocciare; (*subj: courage, memory*)
mancare a ♦ *vi* fallire; (*student*) essere
respinto(a); (*supplies*) mancare; (*eyesight,*

health, light: also: **be** ~**ing**) venire a
mancare; (*brakes*) non funzionare; **to** ~ **to**
do sth (*neglect*) mancare di fare qc; (*be*
unable) non riuscire a fare qc; **without** ~
senza fallo; certamente.
failing ['feɪlɪŋ] *n* difetto ♦ *prep* in mancanza
di; ~ **that** se questo non è possibile.
failsafe ['feɪlseɪf] *adj* (*device etc*) di
sicurezza.
failure ['feɪljə*] *n* fallimento; (*person*)
fallito/a; (*mechanical etc*) guasto; (*in exam*)
insuccesso, bocciatura; (*of crops*) perdita;
his ~ **to come** il fatto che non sia venuto;
it was a complete ~ è stato un vero
fiasco.
faint [feɪnt] *adj* debole; (*recollection*)
vago(a); (*mark*) indistinto(a); (*smell,*
breeze, trace) leggero(a) ♦ *vi* svenire; **to**
feel ~ sentirsi svenire.
faintest ['feɪntɪst] *adj*: **I haven't the** ~ **idea**
non ho la più pallida idea.
faint-hearted [feɪnt'hɑːtɪd] *adj* pusillanime.
faintly ['feɪntlɪ] *adv* debolmente;
vagamente.
faintness ['feɪntnɪs] *n* debolezza.
fair [fɛə*] *adj* (*person, decision*) giusto(a),
equo(a); (*hair etc*) biondo(a); (*skin,*
complexion) bianco(a); (*weather*) bello(a),
clemente; (*good enough*) assai buono(a);
(*sizeable*) bello(a) ♦ *adv*: **to play** ~ giocare
correttamente ♦ *vi* svenire; (*BRIT: funfair*)
luna park *m inv*; (*also*: **trade** ~) fiera
campionaria; **it's not** ~! non è giusto!; **a**
~ **amount of** un bel po' di.
fair copy *n* bella copia.
fair game *n*: **to be** ~ (*person*) essere
bersaglio legittimo.
fairground ['fɛəgraʊnd] *n* luna park *m inv.*
fair-haired [fɛə'hɛəd] *adj* (*person*)
biondo(a).
fairly ['fɛəlɪ] *adv* equamente; (*quite*)
abbastanza.
fairness ['fɛənɪs] *n* equità, giustizia; **in all** ~
per essere giusti, a dire il vero.
fair play *n* correttezza.
fair trade *n* commercio equo e solidale.
fairy ['fɛərɪ] *n* fata.
fairy godmother *n* fata buona.
fairy lights *npl* (*BRIT*) lanternine *fpl*
colorate.
fairy tale *n* fiaba.
faith [feɪθ] *n* fede *f*; (*trust*) fiducia; (*sect*)
religione *f*, fede *f*; **to have** ~ **in sb/sth**
avere fiducia in qn/qc.
faithful ['feɪθful] *adj* fedele.
faithfully ['feɪθfəlɪ] *adv* fedelmente; **yours**
~ (*BRIT: in letters*) distinti saluti.
faith healer *n* guaritore/trice.

fake [feɪk] n imitazione f; (picture) falso; (person) impostore/a ♦ adj falso(a) ♦ vt (accounts) falsificare; (illness) fingere; (painting) contraffare; **his illness is a ~ fa** finta di essere malato.

falcon ['fɔːlkən] n falco, falcone m.

Falkland Islands ['fɔːlklənd-] npl: **the ~ le** isole Falkland.

fall [fɔːl] n caduta; (decrease) diminuzione f, calo; (in temperature) abbassamento; (in price) ribasso; (US: autumn) autunno ♦ vi (pt **fell**, pp **fallen** [fɛl, 'fɔːlən]) cadere; (temperature, price) abbassare; **a ~ of earth** uno smottamento; **a ~ of snow** (BRIT) una nevicata; **to ~ in love (with sb/sth)** innamorarsi (di qn/qc); **to ~ short of** (sb's expectations) non corrispondere a; **to ~ flat** vi (on one's face) cadere bocconi; (joke) fare cilecca; (plan) fallire; see also **falls.**

▶**fall apart** vi cadere a pezzi.

▶**fall back** vi indietreggiare; (MIL) ritirarsi.

▶**fall back on** vt fus ripiegare su; **to have sth to ~ back on** avere qc di riserva.

▶**fall behind** vi rimanere indietro; (fig: with payments) essere in arretrato.

▶**fall down** vi (person) cadere; (building, hopes) crollare.

▶**fall for** vt fus (person) prendere una cotta per; **to ~ for a trick** (or **a story** etc) cascarci.

▶**fall in** vi crollare; (MIL) mettersi in riga.

▶**fall in with** vt fus (sb's plans etc) trovarsi d'accordo con.

▶**fall off** vi cadere; (diminish) diminuire, abbassarsi.

▶**fall out** vi (friends etc) litigare.

▶**fall over** vi cadere.

▶**fall through** vi (plan, project) fallire.

fallacy ['fæləsɪ] n errore m.

fallback ['fɔːlbæk] adj: **~ position** posizione f di ripiego.

fallen ['fɔːlən] pp of **fall**.

fallible ['fælɪbl] adj fallibile.

falling ['fɔːlɪŋ] adj: **~ market** (COMM) mercato in ribasso.

falling-off ['fɔːlɪŋ'ɔf] n calo.

fallopian tube [fə'ləupɪən-] n (ANAT) tuba di Falloppio.

fallout ['fɔːlaut] n fall-out m.

fallout shelter n rifugio antiatomico.

fallow ['fæləu] adj incolto(a); a maggese.

falls [fɔːlz] npl (waterfall) cascate fpl.

false [fɔːls] adj falso(a); **under ~ pretences** con l'inganno.

false alarm n falso allarme m.

falsehood ['fɔːlshud] n menzogna.

falsely ['fɔːlslɪ] adv (accuse) a torto.

false teeth npl (BRIT) denti mpl finti.

falsify ['fɔːlsɪfaɪ] vt falsificare; (figures) alterare.

falter ['fɔːltə*] vi esitare, vacillare.

fame [feɪm] n fama, celebrità.

familiar [fə'mɪlɪə*] adj familiare; (common) comune; (close) intimo(a); **to be ~ with** (subject) conoscere; **to make o.s. ~ with** familiarizzarsi con; **to be on ~ terms with** essere in confidenza con.

familiarity [fəmɪlɪ'ærɪtɪ] n familiarità; intimità.

familiarize [fə'mɪlɪəraɪz] vt: **to ~ sb with sth** far conoscere qc a qn.

family ['fæmɪlɪ] n famiglia.

family allowance n (BRIT) assegni mpl familiari.

family business n impresa familiare.

family credit n (BRIT) ≈ assegni mpl familiari.

family doctor n medico di famiglia.

family life n vita familiare.

family man n padre m di famiglia.

family planning clinic n consultorio familiare.

family tree n albergo genealogico.

famine ['fæmɪn] n carestia.

famished ['fæmɪʃt] adj affamato(a); **I'm ~!** (col) ho una fame da lupo!

famous ['feɪməs] adj famoso(a).

famously ['feɪməslɪ] adv (get on) a meraviglia.

fan [fæn] n (folding) ventaglio; (machine) ventilatore m; (person) ammiratore/trice; (SPORT) tifoso/a ♦ vt far vento a; (fire, quarrel) alimentare.

▶**fan out** vi spargersi (a ventaglio).

fanatic [fə'nætɪk] n fanatico/a.

fanatical [fə'nætɪkl] adj fanatico(a).

fan belt n cinghia del ventilatore.

fancied ['fænsɪd] adj immaginario(a).

fanciful ['fænsɪful] adj fantasioso(a); (object) di fantasia.

fan club n fan club m inv.

fancy ['fænsɪ] n immaginazione f, fantasia; (whim) capriccio ♦ cpd (di) fantasia inv ♦ vt (feel like, want) aver voglia di; (imagine) immaginare, credere; **to take a ~ to** incapricciarsi di; **it took** or **caught my ~** mi è piaciuto; **when the ~ takes him** quando ne ha voglia; **to ~ that** immaginare che; **he fancies her** gli piace.

fancy dress n costume m (per maschera).

fancy-dress ball n ballo in maschera.

fancy goods npl articoli mpl di ogni genere.

fanfare ['fænfɛə*] n fanfara.

fanfold paper ['fænfəuld-] n carta a moduli

continui.

fang [fæŋ] n zanna; (of snake) dente m.

fan heater n (BRIT) stufa ad aria calda.

fanlight ['fænlaɪt] n lunetta.

fanny ['fænɪ] n (BRIT col!) figa(!); (US col) culo(!).

fantasize ['fæntəsaɪz] vi fantasticare, sognare.

fantastic [fæn'tæstɪk] adj fantastico(a).

fantasy ['fæntəsɪ] n fantasia, immaginazione f; fantasticheria; chimera.

fanzine ['fænziːn] n rivista specialistica (per appassionati).

FAO n abbr (= Food and Agriculture Organization) FAO f.

FAQ abbr (= tree alongside quay) franco lungo banchina; (COMPUT: = frequently asked question(s)) FAQ.

far [fɑː*] adj: the ~ side/end l'altra parte/ l'altro capo; the ~ left/right (POL) l'estrema sinistra/destra ♦ adv lontano; is it ~ to London? è lontana Londra?; it's not ~ (from here) non è lontano (da qui); ~ away, ~ off lontano, distante; ~ better assai migliore; ~ from lontano da; by ~ di gran lunga; as ~ back as the 13th century già nel duecento; go as ~ as the farm vada fino alla fattoria; as ~ as I know per quel che so; as ~ as possible nei limiti del possibile; how ~ have you got with your work? dov'è arrivato con il suo lavoro?

faraway ['fɑːrəweɪ] adj lontano(a); (voice, look) assente.

farce [fɑːs] n farsa.

farcical ['fɑːsɪkəl] adj farsesco(a).

fare [fɛə*] n (on trains, buses) tariffa; (in taxi) prezzo della corsa; (food) vitto, cibo ♦ vi passarsela.

Far East n: the ~ l'Estremo Oriente m.

farewell [fɛə'wɛl] excl, n addio ♦ cpd (party etc) d'addio.

far-fetched ['fɑː'fɛtʃt] adj (explanation) stiracchiato(a), forzato(a); (idea, scheme, story) inverosimile.

farm [fɑːm] n fattoria, podere m ♦ vt coltivare.

►**farm out** vt (work) dare in consegna.

farmer ['fɑːmə*] n coltivatore/trice; agricoltore/trice.

farmhand ['fɑːmhænd] n bracciante m agricolo.

farmhouse ['fɑːmhaus] n fattoria.

farming ['fɑːmɪŋ] n agricoltura; **intensive** ~ coltura intensiva; **sheep** ~ allevamento di pecore.

farm labourer n = **farmhand**.

farmland ['fɑːmlænd] n terreno da coltivare.

farm produce n prodotti mpl agricoli.

farm worker n = **farmhand**.

farmyard ['fɑːmjɑːd] n aia.

Faroe Islands ['fɛərəu-], **Faroes** ['fɛərəuz] npl: the ~ le isole Faeroer.

far-reaching ['fɑː'riːtʃɪŋ] adj di vasta portata.

far-sighted ['fɑː'saɪtɪd] adj presbite; (fig) lungimirante.

fart [fɑːt] (col!) n scoreggia(!) ♦ vi scoreggiare (!).

farther ['fɑːðə*] adv più lontano ♦ adj più lontano(a).

farthest ['fɑːðɪst] superlative of **far**.

FAS abbr (BRIT: = free alongside ship) franco banchina nave.

fascia ['feɪʃɪə] n (AUT) cruscotto; (of mobile phone) mascherina.

fascinate ['fæsɪneɪt] vt affascinare.

fascinating ['fæsɪneɪtɪŋ] adj affascinante.

fascination [fæsɪ'neɪʃən] n fascino.

fascism ['fæʃɪzəm] n fascismo.

fascist ['fæʃɪst] adj, n fascista (m/f).

fashion ['fæʃən] n moda; (manner) maniera, modo ♦ vt foggiare, formare; **in** ~ alla moda; **out of** ~ passato(a) di moda; **after a** ~ (finish, manage etc) così così; **in the Greek** ~ alla greca.

fashionable ['fæʃənəbl] adj alla moda, di moda; (writer) di grido.

fashion designer n disegnatore/trice di moda.

fashion show n sfilata di moda.

fast [fɑːst] adj rapido(a), svelto(a), veloce; (clock): **to be** ~ andare avanti; (dye, colour) solido(a) ♦ adv rapidamente; (stuck, held) saldamente ♦ n digiuno ♦ vi digiunare; ~ **asleep** profondamente addormentato; **as** ~ **as I can** più in fretta possibile; **my watch is 5 minutes** ~ il mio orologio va avanti di 5 minuti; **to make a boat** ~ (BRIT) ormeggiare una barca.

fasten ['fɑːsn] vt chiudere, fissare; (coat) abbottonare, allacciare ♦ vi chiudersi, fissarsi; abbottonarsi, allacciarsi.

►**fasten (up)on** vt fus (idea) cogliere al volo.

fastener ['fɑːsnə*], **fastening** ['fɑːsnɪŋ] n fermaglio, chiusura; (BRIT: zip ~) chiusura lampo.

fast food n fast food m inv.

fastidious [fæs'tɪdɪəs] adj esigente, difficile.

fast lane n (AUT) ≈ corsia di sorpasso.

fat [fæt] adj grasso(a) ♦ n grasso; **to live off the** ~ **of the land** vivere nel lusso, avere

ogni ben di Dio.
fatal ['feɪtl] *adj* fatale; mortale;
disastroso(a).
fatalism ['feɪtəlɪzəm] *n* fatalismo.
fatality [fə'tælɪtɪ] *n* (*road death etc*) morto/a,
vittima.
fatally ['feɪtəlɪ] *adv* a morte.
fate [feɪt] *n* destino; (*of person*) sorte *f*; **to
meet one's** ~ trovare la morte.
fated ['feɪtɪd] *adj* (*governed by fate*)
destinato(a); (*person, project etc*)
destinato(a) a finire male.
fateful ['feɪtful] *adj* fatidico(a).
fat-free ['fæt'friː] *adj* senza grassi.
father ['fɑːðə*] *n* padre *m*.
Father Christmas *n* Babbo Natale.
fatherhood ['fɑːðəhuːd] *n* paternità.
father-in-law ['fɑːðərɪnlɔː] *n* suocero.
fatherland ['fɑːðəlænd] *n* patria.
fatherly ['fɑːðəlɪ] *adj* paterno(a).
fathom ['fæðəm] *n* braccio (= *1828 mm*) ♦ *vt*
(*mystery*) penetrare, sondare.
fatigue [fə'tiːg] *n* stanchezza; (*MIL*) corvé *f*;
metal ~ fatica del metallo.
fatness ['fætnɪs] *n* grassezza.
fatten ['fætn] *vt*, *vi* ingrassare; **chocolate is**
~**ing** la cioccolata fa ingrassare.
fatty ['fætɪ] *adj* (*food*) grasso(a) ♦ *n* (*col*)
ciccione/a.
fatuous ['fætjuəs] *adj* fatuo(a).
faucet ['fɔːsɪt] *n* (*US*) rubinetto.
fault [fɔːlt] *n* colpa; (*TENNIS*) fallo; (*defect*)
difetto; (*GEO*) faglia ♦ *vt* criticare; **it's my**
~ è colpa mia; **to find** ~ **with** trovare da
ridire su; **at** ~ in fallo; **generous to a** ~
eccessivamente generoso.
faultless ['fɔːltlɪs] *adj* perfetto(a); senza
difetto; impeccabile.
faulty ['fɔːltɪ] *adj* difettoso(a).
fauna ['fɔːnə] *n* fauna.
faux pas [fəu'pɑː] *n* gaffe *f inv*.
favour, (*US***) favor** ['feɪvə*] *n* favore *m* ♦ *vt*
(*proposition*) favorire, essere favorevole
a; (*pupil etc*) favorire; (*team, horse*) dare
per vincente; **to do sb a** ~ fare un favore
or una cortesia a qn; **in** ~ **of** in favore di;
to be in ~ **of sth/of doing sth** essere
favorevole a qc/a fare qc; **to find** ~ **with**
sb (*subj: person*) entrare nelle buone
grazie di qn; (: *suggestion*) avere
l'approvazione di qn.
favo(u)rable ['feɪvərəbl] *adj* favorevole.
favo(u)rably ['feɪvərəblɪ] *adv*
favorevolmente.
favo(u)rite ['feɪvrɪt] *adj, n* favorito(a).
favo(u)ritism ['feɪvrɪtɪzəm] *n* favoritismo.
fawn [fɔːn] *n* daino ♦ *adj* (*also:* ~-**coloured**)
marrone chiaro *inv* ♦ *vi*: **to** ~ (**up**)**on**

adulare servilmente.
fax [fæks] *n* (*document, machine*) facsimile
m inv ♦ *vt* teletrasmettere, spedire in
facsimile.
FBI *n abbr* (*US*: = *Federal Bureau of
Investigation*) FBI *f*.
FCC *n abbr* (*US*) = *Federal Communications
Commission*.
FCO *n abbr* (*BRIT*: = *Foreign and
Commonwealth Office*) ≈ Ufficio affari
esteri.
FD *n abbr* (*US*) = **fire department**.
FDA *n abbr* (*US*) = *Food and Drug
Administration*.
FE *n abbr* = **further education**.
fear [fɪə*] *n* paura, timore *m* ♦ *vt* aver paura
di, temere ♦ *vi*: **to** ~ **for** temere per,
essere in ansia per; ~ **of heights**
vertigini *fpl*; **for** ~ **of** per paura di; **to** ~
that avere paura di (*or* che + *sub*), temere
di (*or* che + *sub*).
fearful ['fɪəful] *adj* pauroso(a); (*sight, noise*)
terribile, spaventoso(a); (*frightened*): **to
be** ~ **of** temere.
fearfully ['fɪəfəlɪ] *adv* (*timidly*)
timorosamente; (*col: very*) terribilmente,
spaventosamente.
fearless ['fɪəlɪs] *adj* intrepido(a), senza
paura.
fearsome ['fɪəsəm] *adj* (*opponent*)
formidabile, terribile; (*sight*) terrificante.
feasibility [fiːzə'bɪlɪtɪ] *n* praticabilità.
feasibility study *n* studio delle possibilità
di realizzazione.
feasible ['fiːzəbl] *adj* fattibile, realizzabile.
feast [fiːst] *n* festa, banchetto; (*REL: also:* ~
day) festa ♦ *vi* banchettare; **to** ~ **on**
godersi, gustare.
feat [fiːt] *n* impresa, fatto insigne.
feather ['fɛðə*] *n* penna ♦ *cpd* (*mattress, bed,
pillow*) di piume ♦ *vt*: **to** ~ **one's nest** (*fig*)
arricchirsi.
feather-weight ['fɛðəweɪt] *n* peso *m* piuma
inv.
feature ['fiːtʃə*] *n* caratteristica; (*article*)
articolo ♦ *vt* (*subj: film*) avere come
protagonista ♦ *vi* figurare; ~**s** *npl* (*of face*)
fisionomia; **a (special)** ~ **on sth/sb** un
servizio speciale su qc/qn; **it** ~**d
prominently in** ... ha avuto un posto di
prima importanza in ....
feature film *n* film *m inv* principale.
featureless ['fiːtʃəlɪs] *adj* anonimo(a),
senza caratteri distinti.
Feb. [fɛb] *abbr* (= *February*) feb.
February ['fɛbruərɪ] *n* febbraio; *for phrases
see also* **July**.
feces ['fiːsiːz] *npl* (*US*) = **faeces**.

feckless ['fɛklɪs] *adj* irresponsabile, incosciente.
Fed [fɛd] *abbr* (*US*) = **federal; federation**.
fed [fɛd] *pt, pp of* **feed; to be ~ up** essere stufo(a).
Fed. [fɛd] *n abbr* (*US col*) = **Federal Reserve Board**.
federal ['fɛdərəl] *adj* federale.
Federal Republic of Germany (FRG) *n* Repubblica Federale Tedesca (RFT).
Federal Reserve Board (Fed.) *n* (*US*) *organo di controllo del sistema bancario statunitense*.
Federal Trade Commission (FTC) *n* (*US*) *organismo di protezione contro le pratiche commerciali abusive*.
federation [fɛdə'reɪʃən] *n* federazione *f*.
fee [fiː] *n* pagamento; (*of doctor, lawyer*) onorario; (*for examination*) tassa d'esame; **school ~s** tasse *fpl* scolastiche; **entrance ~, membership ~** quota d'iscrizione; **for a small ~** per una somma modesta.
feeble ['fiːbl] *adj* debole.
feeble-minded [fiːbl'maɪndɪd] *adj* deficiente.
feed [fiːd] *n* (*of baby*) pappa ♦ *vt* (*pt, pp* **fed** [fɛd]) nutrire; (*horse etc*) dare da mangiare a; (*fire, machine*) alimentare ♦ *vi* (*baby, animal*) mangiare; **to ~ material into sth** introdurre materiale in qc; **to ~ data/information into sth** inserire dati/ informazioni in qc.
▶**feed back** *vt* (*results*) riferire.
▶**feed on** *vt fus* nutrirsi di.
feedback ['fiːdbæk] *n* feed-back *m*; (*from person*) reazioni *fpl*.
feeder ['fiːdə*] *n* (*bib*) bavaglino.
feeding bottle ['fiːdɪŋ-] *n* (*BRIT*) biberon *m inv*.
feel [fiːl] *n* sensazione *f*; (*sense of touch*) tatto; (*of substance*) consistenza ♦ *vt* (*pt, pp* **felt** [fɛlt]) toccare; palpare; tastare; (*cold, pain, anger*) sentire; (*grief*) provare; (*think, believe*): **to ~ (that)** pensare che; **I ~ that you ought to do it** penso che dovreste farlo; **to ~ hungry/cold** aver fame/ freddo; **to ~ lonely/better** sentirsi solo/ meglio; **I don't ~ well** non mi sento bene; **to ~ sorry for** dispiacersi per; **it ~s soft** è morbido al tatto; **it ~s colder out here** sembra più freddo qui fuori; **it ~s like velvet** sembra velluto (al tatto); **to ~ like** (*want*) aver voglia di; **to ~ about** *or* **around for** cercare a tastoni; **to ~ about** *or* **around in one's pocket for** frugarsi in tasca per cercare; **I'm still ~ing my way** (*fig*) sto ancora tastando il terreno; **to get the ~ of sth** (*fig*) abituarsi a qc.

feeler ['fiːlə*] *n* (*of insect*) antenna; **to put out ~s** (*fig*) fare un sondaggio.
feelgood ['fiːlgud] *adj* (*film, song*) allegro(a) e a lieto fine.
feeling ['fiːlɪŋ] *n* sensazione *f*; sentimento; (*impression*) senso, impressione *f*; **to hurt sb's ~s** offendere qn; **what are your ~s about the matter?** che cosa ne pensa?; **my ~ is that ...** ho l'impressione che ...; **I got the ~ that ...** ho avuto l'impressione che ...; **~s ran high about it** la cosa aveva provocato grande eccitazione.
fee-paying school ['fiːpeɪɪŋ-] *n* scuola privata.
feet [fiːt] *npl of* **foot**.
feign [feɪn] *vt* fingere, simulare.
felicitous [fɪ'lɪsɪtəs] *adj* felice.
fell [fɛl] *pt of* **fall** ♦ *vt* (*tree*) abbattere; (*person*) atterrare ♦ *adj*: **with one ~ blow** con un colpo terribile; **at one ~ swoop** in un colpo solo ♦ *n* (*BRIT: mountain*) monte *m*; (*: moorland*): **the ~s** la brughiera.
fellow ['fɛləu] *n* individuo, tipo; (*comrade*) compagno; (*of learned society*) membro; (*of university*) ≈ docente *m/f* ♦ *cpd*: **their ~ prisoners/students** i loro compagni di prigione/studio.
fellow citizen *n* concittadino/a.
fellow countryman *n* compatriota *m*.
fellow feeling *n* simpatia.
fellow men *npl* simili *mpl*.
fellowship ['fɛləuʃɪp] *n* associazione *f*; compagnia; (*SCOL*) specie di borsa di studio universitaria.
fellow traveller *n* compagno/a di viaggio; (*POL*) simpatizzante *m/f*.
fell-walking ['fɛlwɔːkɪŋ] *n* (*BRIT*) passeggiate *fpl* in montagna.
felon ['fɛlən] *n* (*LAW*) criminale *m/f*.
felony ['fɛlənɪ] *n* (*LAW*) reato, crimine *m*.
felt [fɛlt] *pt, pp of* **feel** ♦ *n* feltro.
felt-tip pen ['fɛlttɪp-] *n* pennarello.
female ['fiːmeɪl] *n* (*ZOOL*) femmina; (*pej: woman*) donna, femmina ♦ *adj* femminile; (*BIOL, ELEC*) femmina *inv*; **male and ~ students** studenti e studentesse.
female impersonator *n* (*THEAT*) attore comico che fa parti da donna.
feminine ['fɛmɪnɪn] *adj, n* femminile (*m*).
femininity [fɛmɪ'nɪnɪtɪ] *n* femminilità.
feminism ['fɛmɪnɪzəm] *n* femminismo.
feminist ['fɛmɪnɪst] *n* femminista *m/f*.
fen [fɛn] *n* (*BRIT*): **the F~s** la regione delle Fen.
fence [fɛns] *n* recinto; (*SPORT*) ostacolo; (*col: person*) ricettatore/trice ♦ *vt* (*also: ~ in*) recingere ♦ *vi* schermire; **to sit on the ~** (*fig*) rimanere neutrale.

fencing ['fɛnsɪŋ] n (SPORT) scherma.
fend [fɛnd] vi: **to ~ for o.s.** arrangiarsi.
▶**fend off** vt (attack, attacker) respingere, difendersi da; (blow) parare; (awkward question) eludere.
fender ['fɛndə*] n parafuoco; (US) parafango; paraurti m inv.
fennel ['fɛnl] n finocchio.
ferment vi [fə'mɛnt] fermentare ♦ n ['fɔːmɛnt] agitazione f, eccitazione f.
fermentation [fɔːmɛn'teɪʃən] n fermentazione f.
fern [fɔːn] n felce f.
ferocious [fə'rəuʃəs] adj feroce.
ferocity [fə'rɔsɪtɪ] n ferocità.
ferret ['fɛrɪt] n furetto.
▶**ferret about, ferret around** vi frugare.
▶**ferret out** vt (person) scovare, scoprire; (secret, truth) scoprire.
ferry ['fɛrɪ] n (small) traghetto; (large: also: ~**boat**) nave f traghetto inv ♦ vt traghettare; **to ~ sth/sb across** or **over** traghettare qc/qn da una parte all'altra.
ferryman ['fɛrɪmən] n traghettatore m.
fertile ['fɔːtaɪl] adj fertile; (BIOL) fecondo(a); ~ **period** periodo di fecondità.
fertility [fə'tɪlɪtɪ] n fertilità; fecondità.
fertility drug n farmaco fecondativo.
fertilize ['fɔːtɪlaɪz] vt fertilizzare; fecondare.
fertilizer ['fɔːtɪlaɪzə*] n fertilizzante m.
fervent ['fɔːvənt] adj ardente, fervente.
fervour, (US) **fervor** ['fɔːvə*] n fervore m, ardore m.
fester ['fɛstə*] vi suppurare.
festival ['fɛstɪvəl] n (REL) festa; (ART, MUS) festival m inv.
festive ['fɛstɪv] adj di festa; **the ~ season** (BRIT: Christmas) il periodo delle feste.
festivities [fɛs'tɪvɪtɪz] npl festeggiamenti mpl.
festoon [fɛ'stuːn] vt: **to ~ with** ornare di; decorare con.
fetch [fɛtʃ] vt andare a prendere; (sell for) essere venduto(a) per; **how much did it ~?** a or per quanto lo ha venduto?
▶**fetch up** vi (BRIT) andare a finire.
fetching ['fɛtʃɪŋ] adj attraente.
fête [feɪt] n festa.
fetid ['fɛtɪd] adj fetido(a).
fetish ['fɛtɪʃ] n feticcio.
fetter ['fɛtə*] vt (person) incatenare; (horse) legare; (fig) ostacolare.
fetters ['fɛtəz] npl catene fpl.
fettle ['fɛtl] n (BRIT): **in fine ~** in gran forma.
fetus ['fiːtəs] n (US) = **foetus.**

feud [fjuːd] n contesa, lotta ♦ vi essere in lotta; **a family ~** una lite in famiglia.
feudal ['fjuːdl] adj feudale.
feudalism ['fjuːdəlɪzəm] n feudalesimo.
fever ['fiːvə*] n febbre f; **he has a ~** ha la febbre.
feverish ['fiːvərɪʃ] adj (also fig) febbrile; (person) febbricitante.
few [fjuː] adj pochi(e) ♦ pron alcuni(e); ~ **succeed** pochi ci riescono; **they were ~** erano pochi; **a ~ ...** qualche ~**; I know a** ~ ne conosco alcuni; **a good ~, quite a ~** parecchi; **in the next ~ days** nei prossimi giorni; **in the past ~ days** negli ultimi giorni, in questi ultimi giorni; **every ~ days/months** ogni due o tre giorni/mesi; **a ~ more days** qualche altro giorno.
fewer ['fjuːə*] adj meno inv; meno numerosi(e) ♦ pron meno; **they are ~ now** adesso ce ne sono di meno.
fewest ['fjuːɪst] adj il minor numero di.
FFA n abbr = Future Farmers of America.
FH abbr (BRIT) = **fire hydrant.**
FHA n abbr (US) = Federal Housing Administration.
fiancé [fɪ'ɑːŋseɪ] n fidanzato.
fiancée [fɪ'ɑːŋseɪ] n fidanzata.
fiasco [fɪ'æskəu] n fiasco.
fib [fɪb] n piccola bugia.
fibre, (US) **fiber** ['faɪbə*] n fibra.
fibreboard, (US) **fiberboard** ['faɪbəbɔːd] n pannello di fibre.
fibre-glass, (US) **fiber-glass** ['faɪbəglɑːs] n fibra di vetro.
fibrositis [faɪbrə'saɪtɪs] n cellulite f.
FICA n abbr (US) = Federal Insurance Contributions Act.
fickle ['fɪkl] adj incostante, capriccioso(a).
fiction ['fɪkʃən] n narrativa; (sth made up) finzione f.
fictional ['fɪkʃənl] adj immaginario(a).
fictionalize ['fɪkʃənəlaɪz] vt romanzare.
fictitious [fɪk'tɪʃəs] adj fittizio(a).
fiddle ['fɪdl] n (MUS) violino; (cheating) imbroglio; truffa ♦ vt (BRIT: accounts) falsificare, falsare; **tax ~** frode f fiscale; **to work a ~** fare un imbroglio.
▶**fiddle with** vt fus gingillarsi con.
fiddler ['fɪdlə*] n violinista m/f.
fiddly ['fɪdlɪ] adj (task) da certosino; (object) complesso(a).
fidelity [fɪ'dɛlɪtɪ] n fedeltà; (accuracy) esattezza.
fidget ['fɪdʒɪt] vi agitarsi.
fidgety ['fɪdʒɪtɪ] adj agitato(a).
fiduciary [fɪ'djuːʃɪərɪ] n fiduciario.
field [fiːld] n (gen, COMPUT) campo; **to lead the ~** (SPORT, COMM) essere in testa,

essere al primo posto; **to have a ~ day**
(*fig*) divertirsi, spassarsela.
field glasses *npl* binocolo (da campagna).
field hospital *n* ospedale *m* da campo.
field marshal (FM) *n* feldmaresciallo.
fieldwork ['fi:ldwɔ:k] *n* ricerche *fpl* esterne;
(*ARCHEOLOGY, GEO*) lavoro sul campo.
fiend [fi:nd] *n* demonio.
fiendish ['fi:ndɪʃ] *adj* demoniaco(a).
fierce [fɪəs] *adj* (*look, fighting*) fiero(a);
(*wind*) furioso(a); (*attack*) feroce; (*enemy*)
acerrimo(a).
fiery ['faɪərɪ] *adj* ardente; infocato(a).
FIFA ['fi:fə] *n abbr* (= *Fédération
Internationale de Football Association*)
F.I.F.A. *f.*
fifteen [fɪf'ti:n] *num* quindici.
fifth [fɪfθ] *num* quinto(a).
fiftieth ['fɪftɪɪθ] *num* cinquantesimo(a).
fifty ['fɪftɪ] *num* cinquanta.
fifty-fifty ['fɪftɪ'fɪftɪ] *adj, adv*: **to go ~ with
sb** fare a metà con qn; **we have a ~
chance of success** abbiamo una
probabilità su due di successo.
fig [fɪg] *n* fico.
fight [faɪt] *n* zuffa, rissa; (*MIL*) battaglia,
combattimento; (*against cancer etc*) lotta
♦ *vb* (*pt, pp* **fought** [fɔ:t]) *vt* combattere;
(*cancer, alcoholism*) lottare contro,
combattere; (*LAW: case*) difendere ♦ *vi*
battersi, combattere; (*quarrel*): **to ~ (with
sb)** litigare (con qn); (*fig*): **to ~ (for/
against)** lottare (per/contro).
▶**fight back** *vi* difendersi; (*SPORT, after
illness*) riprendersi ♦ *vt* (*tears*) ricacciare.
▶**fight down** *vt* (*anger, anxiety*) vincere;
(*urge*) reprimere.
▶**fight off** *vt* (*attack, attacker*) respingere;
(*disease, sleep, urge*) lottare contro.
▶**fight out** *vt*: **to ~ it out** risolvere la
questione a pugni.
fighter ['faɪtə*] *n* combattente *m*; (*plane*)
aeroplano da caccia.
fighter-bomber ['faɪtəbɔmə*] *n*
cacciabombardiere *m.*
fighter pilot *n* pilota *m* di caccia.
fighting ['faɪtɪŋ] *n* combattimento; (*in
streets*) scontri *mpl.*
figment ['fɪgmənt] *n*: **a ~ of the
imagination** un parto della fantasia.
figurative ['fɪgjurətɪv] *adj* figurato(a).
figure ['fɪgə*] *n* (*DRAWING, GEOM, person*)
figura; (*number, cipher*) cifra; (*body,
outline*) forma ♦ *vi* (*appear*) figurare; (*US:
make sense*) spiegarsi; essere logico(a)
♦ *vt* (*US: think, calculate*) pensare,
immaginare; **public ~** personaggio
pubblico; **~ of speech** figura retorica.

▶**figure on** *vt fus* (*US*) contare su.
▶**figure out** *vt* riuscire a capire; calcolare.
figurehead ['fɪgəhɛd] *n* (*NAUT*) polena; (*pej*)
prestanome *m/f inv.*
figure skating *n* pattinaggio artistico.
Fiji (Islands) ['fi:dʒi:-] *n(pl)* le (isole) Figi.
filament ['fɪləmənt] *n* filamento.
filch [fɪltʃ] *vt* (*col: steal*) grattare.
file [faɪl] *n* (*tool*) lima; (*for nails*) limetta;
(*dossier*) incartamento; (*in cabinet*)
scheda; (*folder*) cartellina; (*for loose leaf*)
raccoglitore *m*; (*row*) fila; (*COMPUT*)
archivio, file *m inv* ♦ *vt* (*nails, wood*)
limare; (*papers*) archiviare; (*LAW: claim*)
presentare ♦ *vi*: **to ~ in/out** entrare/
uscire in fila; **to ~ past** marciare in fila
davanti a; **to ~ a suit against sb** intentare
causa contro qn.
file name *n* (*COMPUT*) nome *m* del file.
filibuster ['fɪlɪbʌstə*] (*esp US POL*) *n* (*also:
~er*) ostruzionista *m/f* ♦ *vi* fare
ostruzionismo.
filing ['faɪlɪŋ] *n* archiviare *m*; *see also* **filings.**
filing cabinet *n* casellario.
filing clerk *n* archivista *m/f.*
filings ['faɪlɪŋz] *npl* limatura.
Filipino [fɪlɪ'pi:nəu] *n* filippino/a; (*LING*)
tagal *m.*
fill [fɪl] *vt* riempire; (*tooth*) otturare; (*job*)
coprire; (*supply: order, requirements, need*)
soddisfare ♦ *n*: **to eat one's ~** mangiare a
sazietà; **we've already ~ed that vacancy**
abbiamo già assunto qualcuno per quel
posto.
▶**fill in** *vt* (*hole*) riempire; (*form*) compilare;
(*details, report*) completare ♦ *vi*: **to ~ in for
sb** sostituire qn; **to ~ sb in on sth** (*col*)
mettere qn al corrente di qc.
▶**fill out** *vt* (*form, receipt*) riempire.
▶**fill up** *vt* riempire ♦ *vi* (*AUT*) fare il pieno;
~ it up, please (*AUT*) mi faccia il pieno,
per piacere.
fillet ['fɪlɪt] *n* filetto.
fillet steak *n* bistecca di filetto.
filling ['fɪlɪŋ] *n* (*CULIN*) impasto, ripieno;
(*for tooth*) otturazione *f.*
filling station *n* stazione *f* di rifornimento.
fillip ['fɪlɪp] *n* incentivo, stimolo.
filly ['fɪlɪ] *n* puledra.
film [fɪlm] *n* (*CINE*) film *m inv*; (*PHOT*)
pellicola; (*thin layer*) velo ♦ *vt* (*scene*)
filmare.
film script *n* copione *m.*
film star *n* divo/a dello schermo.
filmstrip ['fɪlmstrɪp] *n* filmina.
film studio *n* studio cinematografico.
Filofax ® ['faɪləufæks] *n* agenda ad anelli.
filter ['fɪltə*] *n* filtro ♦ *vt* filtrare.

▶**filter in, filter through** vi (news) trapelare.

filter coffee n caffè m da passare al filtro.

filter lane n (BRIT AUT) corsia di svincolo.

filter tip n filtro.

filth [fɪlθ] n sporcizia; (fig) oscenità.

filthy ['fɪlθɪ] adj lordo(a), sozzo(a); (language) osceno(a).

fin [fɪn] n (of fish) pinna.

final ['faɪnl] adj finale, ultimo(a); definitivo(a) ♦ n (SPORT) finale f; ~s npl (SCOL) esami mpl finali; ~ **demand** ingiunzione f di pagamento.

finale [fɪ'nɑːlɪ] n finale m.

finalist ['faɪnəlɪst] n (SPORT) finalista m/f.

finality [faɪ'nælɪtɪ] n irrevocabilità; **with an air of** ~ con risolutezza.

finalize ['faɪnəlaɪz] vt mettere a punto.

finally ['faɪnəlɪ] adv (lastly) alla fine; (eventually) finalmente; (once and for all) definitivamente.

finance [faɪ'næns] n finanza; (funds) fondi mpl, capitale m ♦ vt finanziare; ~**s** npl finanze fpl.

financial [faɪ'nænʃəl] adj finanziario(a); ~ **statement** estratto conto finanziario.

financial adviser n consulente m/f finanziario(a).

financially [faɪ'nænʃəlɪ] adv finanziariamente.

financial year n anno finanziario, esercizio finanziario.

financier [faɪ'nænsɪə*] n finanziatore m.

find [faɪnd] vt (pt, pp **found** [faund]) trovare; (lost object) ritrovare ♦ n trovata, scoperta; **to** ~ (**some**) **difficulty in doing sth** trovare delle difficoltà nel fare qc; **to** ~ **sb guilty** (LAW) giudicare qn colpevole.

▶**find out** vt informarsi di; (truth, secret) scoprire; (person) cogliere in fallo ♦ vi: **to** ~ **out about** informarsi su; (by chance) venire a sapere.

findings ['faɪndɪŋz] npl (LAW) sentenza, conclusioni fpl; (of report) conclusioni.

fine [faɪn] adj bello(a); ottimo(a); (thin, subtle) fine ♦ adv (well) molto bene; (small) finemente ♦ n (LAW) multa ♦ vt (LAW) multare; **he's** ~ sta bene; **the weather is** ~ il tempo è bello; **you're doing** ~ te la cavi benissimo; **to cut it** ~ (of time, money) farcela per un pelo.

fine arts npl belle arti fpl.

finely ['faɪnlɪ] adv (splendidly) in modo stupendo; (chop) finemente; (adjust) con precisione.

fine print n: **the** ~ i caratteri minuti.

finery ['faɪnərɪ] n abiti mpl eleganti.

finesse [fɪ'nɛs] n finezza.

fine-tooth comb ['faɪntuːθ-] n: **to go through sth with a** ~ (fig) passare qc al setaccio.

finger ['fɪŋgə*] n dito ♦ vt toccare, tastare.

fingernail ['fɪŋgəneɪl] n unghia.

fingerprint ['fɪŋgəprɪnt] n impronta digitale ♦ vt (person) prendere le impronte digitali di.

fingerstall ['fɪŋgəstɔːl] n ditale m.

fingertip ['fɪŋgətɪp] n punta del dito; **to have sth at one's** ~**s** (fig) avere qc sulla punta delle dita.

finicky ['fɪnɪkɪ] adj esigente, pignolo(a); minuzioso(a).

finish ['fɪnɪʃ] n fine f; (SPORT: place) traguardo; (polish etc) finitura ♦ vt finire; (use up) esaurire ♦ vi finire; (session) terminare; **to** ~ **doing sth** finire di fare qc; **to** ~ **first/second** (SPORT) arrivare primo/secondo; **she's** ~**ed with him** ha chiuso con lui.

▶**finish off** vt compiere; (kill) uccidere.

▶**finish up** vi, vt finire.

finished ['fɪnɪʃt] adj (product) finito(a); (performance) perfetto(a); (col: tired) sfinito(a).

finishing line ['fɪnɪʃɪŋ-] n linea d'arrivo.

finishing school n scuola privata di perfezionamento (per signorine).

finishing touches npl ultimi ritocchi mpl.

finite ['faɪnaɪt] adj limitato(a); (verb) finito(a).

Finland ['fɪnlənd] n Finlandia.

Finn [fɪn] n finlandese m/f.

Finnish ['fɪnɪʃ] adj finlandese ♦ n (LING) finlandese m.

fiord [fjɔːd] n fiordo.

fir [fɜː*] n abete m.

fire [faɪə*] n fuoco; incendio ♦ vt (discharge): **to** ~ **a gun** scaricare un fucile; (fig) infiammare; (dismiss) licenziare ♦ vi sparare, far fuoco; **on** ~ in fiamme; **insured against** ~ assicurato contro gli incendi; **electric/gas** ~ stufa elettrica/a gas; **to set** ~ **to sth, set sth on** ~ dar fuoco a qc, incendiare qc; **to be/come under** ~ (**from**) essere/finire sotto il fuoco or il tiro (di).

fire alarm n allarme m d'incendio.

firearm ['faɪərɑːm] n arma da fuoco.

fire brigade n (BRIT) (corpo dei) pompieri mpl.

fire chief n (US) = **fire master**.

fire department n (US) = **fire brigade**.

fire door n porta f rompifuoco inv.

fire drill n esercitazione f antincendio.

fire engine n autopompa.

fire escape n scala di sicurezza.

fire extinguisher n estintore m.
fireguard ['faɪəgɑːd] n (BRIT) parafuoco.
fire hazard n: **that's a** ~ comporta rischi in caso d'incendio.
fire hydrant n idrante m.
fire insurance n assicurazione f contro gli incendi.
fireman ['faɪəmən] n pompiere m.
fire master n (BRIT) comandante m dei vigili del fuoco.
fireplace ['faɪəpleɪs] n focolare m.
fireplug ['faɪəplʌg] n (US) = **fire hydrant**.
fire practice n = **fire drill**.
fireproof ['faɪəpruːf] adj resistente al fuoco.
fire regulations npl norme fpl antincendio.
fire screen n parafuoco.
fireside ['faɪəsaɪd] n angolo del focolare.
fire station n caserma dei pompieri.
firewood ['faɪəwud] n legna.
firework ['faɪəwɜːk] n fuoco d'artificio.
firing ['faɪərɪŋ] n (MIL) spari mpl, tiro.
firing line n linea del fuoco; **to be in the** ~ (fig) essere sotto tiro.
firing squad n plotone m d'esecuzione.
firm [fɜːm] adj fermo(a); (offer, decision) definitivo(a) ♦ n ditta, azienda; **to be a** ~ **believer in sth** credere fermamente in qc.
firmly ['fɜːmlɪ] adv fermamente.
firmness ['fɜːmnɪs] n fermezza.
first [fɜːst] adj primo(a) ♦ adv (before others) il primo, la prima; (before other things) per primo; (for the first time) per la prima volta; (when listing reasons etc) per prima cosa ♦ n (person: in race) primo/a; (BRIT SCOL) laurea con lode; (AUT) prima; **at** ~ dapprima, all'inizio; ~ **of all** prima di tutto; **in the** ~ **instance** prima di tutto, in primo luogo; **I'll do it** ~ **thing tomorrow** lo farò per prima cosa domani; **from the (very)** ~ fin dall'inizio, fin dal primo momento; **the** ~ **of January** il primo (di) gennaio.
first aid n pronto soccorso.
first-aid kit ['fɜːst'eɪd-] n cassetta pronto soccorso.
first-class ['fɜːst'klɑːs] adj di prima classe.
first-class mail n ≈ espresso.
first-hand ['fɜːst'hænd] adj di prima mano; diretto(a).
first lady n (US) moglie f del presidente.
firstly ['fɜːstlɪ] adv in primo luogo.
first name n nome m di battesimo.
first night n (THEAT) prima.
first-rate ['fɜːst'reɪt] adj di prima qualità, ottimo(a).
first-time buyer ['fɜːsttaɪm-] n acquirente m/f di prima casa.
First World War n: **the** ~ la prima guerra mondiale.
fir tree n abete m.
fiscal ['fɪskəl] adj fiscale; ~ **year** anno fiscale.
fish [fɪʃ] n (pl inv) pesce m ♦ vt, vi pescare; **to** ~ **a river** pescare in un fiume; **to go** ~**ing** andare a pesca.
▶**fish out** vt (from water) ripescare; (from box etc) tirare fuori.
fish-and-chip shop [fɪʃən'tʃɪp-] n ≈ friggitoria; see **chip shop**.
fishbone ['fɪʃbəun] n lisca, spina.
fisherman ['fɪʃəmən] n pescatore m.
fishery ['fɪʃərɪ] n zona da pesca.
fish factory n (BRIT) fabbrica per la lavorazione del pesce.
fish farm n vivaio.
fish fingers npl (BRIT) bastoncini mpl di pesce (surgelati).
fish hook n amo.
fishing boat ['fɪʃɪŋ-] n barca da pesca.
fishing industry n industria della pesca.
fishing line n lenza.
fishing net n rete f da pesca.
fishing rod n canna da pesca.
fishing tackle n attrezzatura da pesca.
fish market n mercato del pesce.
fishmonger ['fɪʃmʌŋgə*] n pescivendolo; ~'**s (shop)** pescheria.
fish slice n (BRIT) posata per servire il pesce.
fish sticks npl (US) = **fish fingers**.
fishy ['fɪʃɪ] adj (fig) sospetto(a).
fission ['fɪʃən] n fissione f; **atomic/nuclear** ~ fissione atomica/nucleare.
fissure ['fɪʃə*] n fessura.
fist [fɪst] n pugno.
fistfight ['fɪstfaɪt] n scazzottata.
fit [fɪt] adj (MED, SPORT) in forma; (proper) adatto(a), appropriato(a); conveniente ♦ vt (subj: clothes) stare bene a; (match: facts etc) concordare con; (: description) corrispondere a; (adjust) aggiustare; (put in, attach) mettere; installare; (equip) fornire, equipaggiare ♦ vi (clothes) stare bene; (parts) andare bene, adattarsi; (in space, gap) entrare ♦ n (MED) attacco; ~ **to** in grado di; ~ **for** adatto(a) a; degno(a) di; **to keep** ~ tenersi in forma; ~ **for work** (after illness) in grado di riprendere il lavoro; **do as you think** or **see** ~ faccia come meglio crede; **this dress is a tight/good** ~ questo vestito è stretto/sta bene; ~ **of anger/enthusiasm** accesso d'ira/d'entusiasmo; **to have a** ~ (MED) avere un attacco di convulsioni; (col) andare su tutte le furie; **by** ~**s and starts** a sbalzi.
▶**fit in** vi accordarsi; adattarsi ♦ vt (object)

far entrare; (*fig*: *appointment, visitor*) trovare il tempo per; **to ~ in with sb's plans** adattarsi ai progetti di qn.
▶**fit out** *vt* (*BRIT*: *also*: ~ **up**) equipaggiare.
fitful ['fɪtful] *adj* saltuario(a).
fitment ['fɪtmənt] *n* componibile *m*.
fitness ['fɪtnɪs] *n* (*MED*) forma fisica; (*of remark*) appropriatezza.
fitted ['fɪtɪd] *adj*: ~ **carpet** moquette *f inv*; ~ **cupboards** armadi *mpl* a muro; ~ **kitchen** (*BRIT*) cucina componibile.
fitter ['fɪtə*] *n* aggiustatore *m or* montatore *m* meccanico; (*DRESSMAKING*) sarto/a.
fitting ['fɪtɪŋ] *adj* appropriato(a) ♦ *n* (*of dress*) prova; (*of piece of equipment*) montaggio, aggiustaggio; *see also* **fittings**.
fitting room *n* (*in shop*) camerino.
fittings ['fɪtɪŋz] *npl* impianti *mpl*.
five [faɪv] *num* cinque.
five-day week ['faɪvdeɪ-] *n* settimana di 5 giorni (lavorativi).
fiver ['faɪvə*] *n* (*col*: *BRIT*) biglietto da cinque sterline; (: *US*) biglietto da cinque dollari.
fix [fɪks] *vt* fissare; (*mend*) riparare; (*make ready*: *meal, drink*) preparare ♦ *n*: **to be in a** ~ essere nei guai; **the fight was a** ~ (*col*) l'incontro è stato truccato.
▶**fix up** *vt* (*arrange*: *date, meeting*) fissare, stabilire; **to ~ sb up with sth** procurare qc a qn.
fixation [fɪk'seɪʃən] *n* (*PSYCH*, *fig*) fissazione *f*, ossessione *f*.
fixed [fɪkst] *adj* (*prices etc*) fisso(a); **there's a** ~ **charge** c'è una quota fissa; **how are you** ~ **for money?** (*col*) a soldi come stai?
fixed assets *npl* beni *mpl* patrimoniali.
fixed penalty (fine) *n* contravvenzione *f* a importo fisso.
fixture ['fɪkstʃə*] *n* impianto (fisso); (*SPORT*) incontro (del calendario sportivo).
fizz [fɪz] *vi* frizzare.
fizzle ['fɪzl] *vi* frizzare; (*also*: ~ **out**: *enthusiasm, interest*) smorzarsi, svanire; (: *plan*) fallire.
fizzy ['fɪzi] *adj* frizzante; gassato(a).
fjord [fjɔːd] *n* = **fiord**.
FL, Fla. *abbr* (*US*) = *Florida*.
flabbergasted ['flæbəgɑːstɪd] *adj* sbalordito(a).
flabby ['flæbi] *adj* flaccido(a).
flag [flæg] *n* bandiera; (*also*: ~**stone**) pietra da lastricare ♦ *vi* stancarsi; affievolirsi; ~ **of convenience** bandiera di convenienza.
▶**flag down** *vt* fare segno (di fermarsi) a.
flagon ['flægən] *n* bottiglione *m*.
flagpole ['flægpəul] *n* albero.

flagrant ['fleɪgrənt] *adj* flagrante.
flag stop *n* (*US*: *for bus*) fermata facoltativa, fermata a richiesta.
flair [flɛə*] *n* (*for business etc*) fiuto; (*for languages etc*) facilità.
flak [flæk] *n* (*MIL*) fuoco d'artiglieria; (*col*: *criticism*) critiche *fpl*.
flake [fleɪk] *n* (*of rust, paint*) scaglia; (*of snow, soap powder*) fiocco ♦ *vi* (*also*: ~ **off**) sfaldarsi.
flaky ['fleɪkɪ] *adj* (*paintwork*) scrostato(a); (*skin*) squamoso(a); ~ **pastry** (*CULIN*) pasta sfoglia.
flamboyant [flæm'bɔɪənt] *adj* sgargiante.
flame [fleɪm] *n* fiamma; **old** ~ (*col*) vecchia fiamma.
flamingo [flə'mɪŋgəu] *n* fenicottero, fiammingo.
flammable ['flæməbl] *adj* infiammabile.
flan [flæn] *n* (*BRIT*) flan *m inv*.
Flanders ['flɑːndəz] *n* Fiandre *fpl*.
flange [flændʒ] *n* flangia; (*on wheel*) suola.
flank [flæŋk] *n* fianco.
flannel ['flænl] *n* (*BRIT*: *also*: **face** ~) guanto di spugna; (*fabric*) flanella; ~**s** *npl* pantaloni *mpl* di flanella.
flannelette [flænə'lɛt] *n* flanella di cotone.
flap [flæp] *n* (*of pocket*) patta; (*of envelope*) lembo; (*AVIAT*) flap *m inv* ♦ *vt* (*wings*) battere ♦ *vi* (*sail, flag*) sbattere; (*col*: *also*: **be in a** ~) essere in agitazione.
flapjack ['flæpdʒæk] *n* (*US*: *pancake*) frittella; (*BRIT*: *biscuit*) biscotto di avena.
flare [flɛə*] *n* razzo; (*in skirt etc*) svasatura.
▶**flare up** *vi* andare in fiamme; (*fig*: *person*) infiammarsi di rabbia; (: *revolt*) scoppiare.
flared ['flɛəd] *adj* (*trousers*) svasato(a).
flash [flæʃ] *n* vampata; (*also*: **news** ~) notizia *f* lampo *inv*; (*PHOT*) flash *m inv*; (*US*: *torch*) torcia elettrica, lampadina tascabile ♦ *vt* accendere e spegnere; (*send*: *message*) trasmettere; (*flaunt*) ostentare ♦ *vi* brillare; (*light on ambulance, eyes etc*) lampeggiare; **in a** ~ in un lampo; ~ **of inspiration** lampo di genio; **to ~ one's headlights** lampeggiare; **he** ~**ed by** *or* **past** ci passò davanti come un lampo.
flashback ['flæʃbæk] *n* flashback *m inv*.
flashbulb ['flæʃbʌlb] *n* cubo *m* flash *inv*.
flash card *n* (*SCOL*) scheda didattica.
flashcube ['flæʃkjuːb] *n* flash *m inv*.
flasher ['flæʃə*] *n* (*AUT*) lampeggiatore *m*.
flashlight ['flæʃlaɪt] *n* (*torch*) lampadina tascabile.
flashpoint ['flæʃpɔɪnt] *n* punto di infiammabilità; (*fig*) livello critico.
flashy ['flæʃɪ] *adj* (*pej*) vistoso(a).

flask [flɑːsk] n fiasco; (CHEM) beuta; (also: **vacuum ~**) thermos ® m inv.

flat [flæt] adj piatto(a); (tyre) sgonfio(a), a terra; (battery) scarico(a); (denial) netto(a); (MUS) bemolle inv; (: voice) stonato(a); (: instrument) scordato(a) ♦ n (BRIT: rooms) appartamento; (MUS) bemolle m; (AUT) pneumatico sgonfio ♦ adv: **(to work) ~ out** (lavorare) a più non posso; **~ rate of pay** tariffa unica di pagamento.

flat-footed ['flæt'futɪd] adj: **to be ~** avere i piedi piatti.

flatly ['flætlɪ] adv categoricamente, nettamente.

flatmate ['flætmeɪt] n (BRIT): **he's my ~** divide l'appartamento con me.

flatness ['flætnɪs] n (of land) assenza di rilievi.

flat-pack ['flætpæk] adj: **~ furniture** mobili mpl in kit ♦ n: **flat pack** kit m inv.

flat-screen ['flætskriːn] adj a schermo piatto.

flatten ['flætn] vt (also: **~ out**) appiattire; (house, city) abbattere, radere al suolo.

flatter ['flætə*] vt lusingare; (show to advantage) donare a.

flatterer ['flætərə*] n adulatore/trice.

flattering ['flætərɪŋ] adj lusinghiero(a); (clothes etc) che dona, che abbellisce.

flattery ['flætərɪ] n adulazione f.

flatulence ['flætjuləns] n flatulenza.

flaunt [flɔːnt] vt fare mostra di.

flavour, (US) **flavor** ['fleɪvə*] n gusto, sapore m ♦ vt insaporire, aggiungere sapore a; **vanilla-~ed** al gusto di vaniglia.

flavo(u)ring ['fleɪvərɪŋ] n essenza (artificiale).

flaw [flɔː] n difetto.

flawless ['flɔːlɪs] adj senza difetti.

flax [flæks] n lino.

flaxen ['flæksən] adj biondo(a).

flea [fliː] n pulce f.

flea market n mercato delle pulci.

fleck [flɛk] n (of mud, paint, colour) macchiolina; (of dust) granello ♦ vt (with blood, mud etc) macchiettare; **brown ~ed with white** marrone screziato di bianco.

fled [flɛd] pt, pp of **flee.**

fledg(e)ling ['flɛdʒlɪŋ] n uccellino.

flee, pt, pp **fled** [fliː, flɛd] vt fuggire da ♦ vi fuggire, scappare.

fleece [fliːs] n vello; (garment) pile sm inv ♦ vt (col) pelare.

fleecy ['fliːsɪ] adj (blanket) soffice; (cloud) come ovatta.

fleet [fliːt] n flotta; (of lorries etc) convoglio; (of cars) parco.

fleeting ['fliːtɪŋ] adj fugace; (visit) volante.

Flemish ['flɛmɪʃ] adj fiammingo(a) ♦ n (LING) fiammingo; **the ~** npl i Fiamminghi.

flesh [flɛʃ] n carne f; (of fruit) polpa.

flesh wound n ferita superficiale.

flew [fluː] pt of **fly.**

flex [flɛks] n filo (flessibile) ♦ vt flettere; (muscles) contrarre.

flexibility [flɛksɪ'bɪlɪtɪ] n flessibilità.

flexible ['flɛksəbl] adj flessibile.

flexitime ['flɛksɪtaɪm] n orario flessibile.

flick [flɪk] n colpetto; see also **flicks.**

▶**flick through** vt fus sfogliare.

flicker ['flɪkə*] vi tremolare ♦ n tremolio; **a ~ of light** un breve bagliore.

flick knife n (BRIT) coltello a serramanico.

flicks npl: **the ~** (col) il cine.

flier ['flaɪə*] n aviatore m.

flight [flaɪt] n volo; (escape) fuga; (also: **~ of steps**) scalinata; **to take ~** darsi alla fuga; **to put to ~** mettere in fuga.

flight attendant n (US) steward m, hostess f inv.

flight crew n equipaggio.

flight deck n (AVIAT) cabina di controllo; (NAUT) ponte m di comando.

flight path n (of aircraft) rotta di volo; (of rocket, projectile) traiettoria.

flight recorder n registratore m di volo.

flimsy ['flɪmzɪ] adj (fabric) inconsistente; (excuse) meschino(a).

flinch [flɪntʃ] vi ritirarsi; **to ~ from** tirarsi indietro di fronte a.

fling, pt, pp **flung** [flɪŋ, flʌŋ] vt lanciare, gettare ♦ n (love affair) avventura.

flint [flɪnt] n selce f; (in lighter) pietrina.

flip [flɪp] n colpetto ♦ vt dare un colpetto a; (US: pancake) far saltare (in aria) ♦ vi: **to ~ for sth** (US) fare a testa e croce per qc.

▶**flip through** vt fus (book, records) dare una scorsa a.

flippant ['flɪpənt] adj senza rispetto, irriverente.

flipper ['flɪpə*] n pinna.

flip side n (of record) retro.

flirt [flɜːt] vi flirtare ♦ n civetta.

flirtation [flɜː'teɪʃən] n flirt m inv.

flit [flɪt] vi svolazzare.

float [fləut] n galleggiante m; (in procession) carro; (sum of money) somma ♦ vi galleggiare; (bather) fare il morto; (COMM: currency) fluttuare ♦ vt far galleggiare; (loan, business) lanciare; **to ~ an idea** ventilare un'idea.

floating ['fləutɪŋ] adj a galla; **~ vote** voto oscillante; **~ voter** elettore m indeciso.

flock [flɔk] n gregge m; (of people) folla; (of birds) stormo.

floe [fləu] n (also: **ice** ~) banchisa.

flog [flɔg] vt flagellare.

flood [flʌd] n alluvione f; (of words, tears etc) diluvio ♦ vt inondare, allagare; (AUT: carburettor) ingolfare; **in** ~ in pieno; **to** ~ **the market** (COMM) inondare il mercato.

flooding ['flʌdɪŋ] n inondazione f.

floodlight ['flʌdlaɪt] n riflettore m ♦ vt illuminare a giorno.

floodlit ['flʌdlɪt] pt, pp of **floodlight** ♦ adj illuminato(a) a giorno.

flood tide n alta marea, marea crescente.

floodwater ['flʌdwɔːtə*] n acque fpl (di inondazione).

floor [flɔː*] n pavimento; (storey) piano; (of sea, valley) fondo; (fig: at meeting): **the** ~ il pubblico ♦ vt pavimentare; (knock down) atterrare; (baffle) confondere; (silence) far tacere; **on the** ~ sul pavimento, per terra; **ground** ~, (US) **first** ~ pianterreno; **first** ~, (US) **second** ~ primo piano; **top** ~ ultimo piano; **to have the** ~ (speaker) prendere la parola.

floorboard ['flɔːbɔːd] n tavellone m di legno.

flooring ['flɔːrɪŋ] n (floor) pavimento; (material) materiale m per pavimentazioni.

floor lamp n (US) lampada a stelo.

floor show n spettacolo di varietà.

floorwalker ['flɔːwɔːkə*] n (esp US) ispettore m di reparto.

flop [flɔp] n fiasco ♦ vi (fail) far fiasco.

floppy ['flɔpɪ] adj floscio(a), molle ♦ n (COMPUT) = **floppy disk**; ~ **hat** cappello floscio.

floppy disk n floppy disk m inv.

flora ['flɔːrə] n flora.

floral ['flɔːrl] adj floreale.

Florence ['flɔrəns] n Firenze f.

Florentine ['flɔrəntaɪn] adj fiorentino(a).

florid ['flɔrɪd] adj (complexion) florido(a); (style) fiorito(a).

florist ['flɔrɪst] n fioraio/a; **at the** ~'s **(shop)** dal fioraio.

flotation [fləu'teɪʃən] n (COMM) lancio.

flounce [flauns] n balzo.

▶**flounce out** vi uscire stizzito(a).

flounder ['flaundə*] vi annaspare ♦ n (ZOOL) passera di mare.

flour ['flauə*] n farina.

flourish ['flʌrɪʃ] vi fiorire ♦ vt brandire ♦ n abbellimento; svolazzo; (of trumpets) fanfara.

flourishing ['flʌrɪʃɪŋ] adj prosperoso(a), fiorente.

flout [flaut] vt (order) contravvenire a; (convention) sfidare.

flow [fləu] n flusso; circolazione f; (of river, also ELEC) corrente f ♦ vi fluire; (traffic, blood in veins) circolare; (hair) scendere.

flow chart n schema m di flusso.

flow diagram n organigramma m.

flower ['flauə*] n fiore m ♦ vi fiorire; **in** ~ in fiore.

flower bed n aiuola.

flowerpot ['flauəpɔt] n vaso da fiori.

flowery ['flauərɪ] adj fiorito(a).

flown [fləun] pp of **fly**.

flu [fluː] n influenza.

fluctuate ['flʌktjueɪt] vi fluttuare, oscillare.

fluctuation [flʌktjuˈeɪʃən] n fluttuazione f, oscillazione f.

flue [fluː] n canna fumaria.

fluency ['fluːənsɪ] n facilità, scioltezza; **his** ~ **in English** la sua scioltezza nel parlare l'inglese.

fluent ['fluːənt] adj (speech) facile, sciolto(a); **he's a** ~ **speaker/reader** si esprime/legge senza difficoltà; **he speaks** ~ **Italian, he's** ~ **in Italian** parla l'italiano correntemente.

fluently ['fluːəntlɪ] adv con facilità; correntemente.

fluff [flʌf] n lanugine f.

fluffy ['flʌfɪ] adj lanuginoso(a); (toy) di peluche.

fluid ['fluːɪd] adj fluido(a) ♦ n fluido; (in diet) liquido.

fluid ounce n (BRIT) = 0.028 l; 0.05 pints.

fluke [fluːk] n (col) colpo di fortuna.

flummox ['flʌməks] vt rendere perplesso(a).

flung [flʌŋ] pt, pp of **fling**.

flunky ['flʌŋkɪ] n tirapiedi m/f inv.

fluorescent [fluəˈrɛsnt] adj fluorescente.

fluoride ['fluəraɪd] n fluoruro.

fluorine ['fluəriːn] n fluoro.

flurry ['flʌrɪ] n (of snow) tempesta; **a** ~ **of activity/excitement** una febbre di attività/un'improvvisa agitazione.

flush [flʌʃ] n rossore m; (fig) ebbrezza ♦ vt ripulire con un getto d'acqua; (also: ~ **out**: birds) far alzare in volo; (: animals, fig: criminal) stanare ♦ vi arrossire ♦ adj: ~ **with** a livello di, pari a; ~ **against** aderente a; **hot** ~**es** (MED) vampate fpl di calore; **to** ~ **the toilet** tirare l'acqua.

flushed [flʌʃt] adj tutto(a) rosso(a).

fluster ['flʌstə*] n agitazione f.

flustered ['flʌstəd] adj sconvolto(a).

flute [fluːt] n flauto.

flutter ['flʌtə*] n agitazione f; (of wings) frullio ♦ vi (bird) battere le ali.

flux [flʌks] n: **in a state of** ~ in continuo mutamento.

fly [flaɪ] n (insect) mosca; (on trousers: also: **flies**) bracchetta ♦ vb (pt **flew**, pp **flown** [fluː, fləun]) vt pilotare; (passengers, cargo) trasportare (in aereo); (distances) percorrere ♦ vi volare; (passengers) andare in aereo; (escape) fuggire; (flag) sventolare; **to ~ open** spalancarsi all'improvviso; **to ~ off the handle** perdere le staffe, uscire dai gangheri.
►**fly away** vi volar via.
►**fly in** vi (plane) arrivare; (person) arrivare in aereo.
►**fly off** vi volare via.
►**fly out** vi (plane) partire; (person) partire in aereo.
fly-fishing ['flaɪfɪʃɪŋ] n pesca con la mosca.
flying ['flaɪɪŋ] n (activity) aviazione f; (action) volo ♦ adj: ~ **visit** visita volante; **with ~ colours** con risultati brillanti; **he doesn't like ~** non gli piace viaggiare in aereo.
flying buttress n arco rampante.
flying picket n picchetto (proveniente da fabbriche non direttamente coinvolte nello sciopero).
flying saucer n disco volante.
flying squad n (POLICE) (squadra) volante f.
flying start n: **to get off to a ~ start** partire come un razzo.
flyleaf ['flaɪliːf] n risguardo.
flyover ['flaɪəuvə*] n (BRIT: bridge) cavalcavia m inv.
flypast ['flaɪpɑːst] n esibizione f della pattuglia aerea.
flysheet ['flaɪʃiːt] n (for tent) sopratetto.
flyweight ['flaɪweɪt] n (SPORT) peso m mosca inv.
flywheel ['flaɪwiːl] n volano.
FM abbr see **frequency modulation**; (BRIT MIL) see **Field Marshal**.
FMB n abbr (US) = Federal Maritime Board.
FMCS n abbr (US: = Federal Mediation and Conciliation Service) organismo di conciliazione in caso di conflitti sul lavoro.
FO n abbr (BRIT) see **Foreign Office**.
foal [fəul] n puledro.
foam [fəum] n schiuma ♦ vi schiumare.
foam rubber n gommapiuma ®.
FOB abbr (= free on board) franco a bordo.
fob [fɔb] vt: **to ~ sb off with** appioppare qn con; sbarazzarsi di qn con ♦ n (also: **watch ~**: chain) catena per orologio; (: band of cloth) nastro per orologio.
foc abbr (BRIT) = **free of charge**.
focal ['fəukəl] adj focale.
focal point n punto focale.

focus ['fəukəs] n (pl ~**es**) fuoco; (of interest) centro ♦ vt (field glasses etc) mettere a fuoco; (light rays) far convergere ♦ vi: **to ~ on** (with camera) mettere a fuoco; (person) fissare lo sguardo su; **in ~** a fuoco; **out of ~** sfocato(a).
focus group n (POL) gruppo di discussione, focus group m inv.
fodder ['fɔdə*] n foraggio.
FOE n abbr (= Friends of the Earth) Amici mpl della Terra; (US: = Fraternal Order of Eagles) organizzazione filantropica.
foe [fəu] n nemico.
foetus, (US) **fetus** ['fiːtəs] n feto.
fog [fɔg] n nebbia.
fogbound ['fɔgbaund] adj fermo(a) a causa della nebbia.
foggy ['fɔgɪ] adj nebbioso(a); **it's ~** c'è nebbia.
fog lamp, (US) **fog light** n (AUT) faro m antinebbia inv.
foible ['fɔɪbl] n debolezza, punto debole.
foil [fɔɪl] vt confondere, frustrare ♦ n lamina di metallo; (also: **kitchen ~**) foglio di alluminio; (FENCING) fioretto; **to act as a ~ to** (fig) far risaltare.
foist [fɔɪst] vt: **to ~ sth on sb** rifilare qc a qn.
fold [fəuld] n (bend, crease) piega; (AGR) ovile m; (fig) gregge m ♦ vt piegare; **to ~ one's arms** incrociare le braccia.
►**fold up** vi (map etc) piegarsi; (business) crollare ♦ vt (map etc) piegare, ripiegare.
folder ['fəuldə*] n (for papers) cartella; cartellina; (binder) raccoglitore m.
folding ['fəuldɪŋ] adj (chair, bed) pieghevole.
foliage ['fəulɪdʒ] n fogliame m.
folk [fəuk] npl gente f ♦ cpd popolare; ~**s** npl famiglia.
folklore ['fəuklɔː*] n folclore m.
folk music n musica folk inv.
folk singer n cantante m/f folk inv.
folksong ['fəuksɔŋ] n canto popolare.
follow ['fɔləu] vt seguire ♦ vi seguire; (result) conseguire, risultare; **to ~ sb's advice** seguire il consiglio di qn; **I don't quite ~ you** non ti capisco or seguo affatto; **to ~ in sb's footsteps** seguire le orme di qn; **it ~s that ...** ne consegue che ...; **he ~ed suit** lui ha fatto lo stesso.
►**follow on** vi (continue): **to ~ on from** seguire.
►**follow out** vt (implement: idea, plan) eseguire, portare a termine.
►**follow through** vt = **follow out**.
►**follow up** vt (victory) sfruttare; (letter, offer) fare seguito a; (case) seguire.
follower ['fɔləuə*] n seguace m/f,

discepolo/a.

following ['fɔləʊɪŋ] adj seguente,
successivo(a) ♦ n seguito, discepoli mpl.
follow-up ['fɔləʊʌp] n seguito.
folly ['fɔlɪ] n pazzia, follia.
fond [fɔnd] adj (memory, look) tenero(a),
affettuoso(a); **to be ~ of** volere bene a;
she's ~ of swimming le piace nuotare.
fondle ['fɔndl] vt accarezzare.
fondly ['fɔndlɪ] adv (lovingly)
affettuosamente; (naïvely): **he ~ believed
that** ... ha avuto l'ingenuità di credere
che ....
fondness ['fɔndnɪs] n affetto; **~ (for sth)**
predilezione f (per qc).
font [fɔnt] n (REL) fonte m (battesimale);
(TYP) stile m di carattere.
food [fuːd] n cibo.
food chain n catena alimentare.
food mixer n frullatore m.
food poisoning n intossicazione f
alimentare.
food processor n tritatutto m inv elettrico.
food stamp n (US) buono alimentare dato
agli indigenti.
foodstuffs ['fuːdstʌfs] npl generi fpl
alimentari.
fool [fuːl] n sciocco/a; (HISTORY: of king)
buffone m; (CULIN) frullato ♦ vt ingannare
♦ vi (gen: ~ **around**) fare lo sciocco; **to
make a ~ of sb** prendere in giro qn; **to
make a ~ of o.s.** coprirsi di ridicolo; **you
can't ~ me** non mi inganna.
▶**fool about, fool around** vi (waste time)
perdere tempo.
foolhardy ['fuːlhɑːdɪ] adj avventato(a).
foolish ['fuːlɪʃ] adj scemo(a), stupido(a);
imprudente.
foolishly ['fuːlɪʃlɪ] adv stupidamente.
foolishness ['fuːlɪʃnɪs] n stupidità.
foolproof ['fuːlpruːf] adj (plan etc)
sicurissimo(a).
foolscap ['fuːlskæp] n carta protocollo.
foot [fʊt] n (pl **feet** [fiːt]) piede m; (measure)
piede (= 304 mm; 12 inches); (of animal)
zampa; (of page, stairs etc) fondo ♦ vt (bill)
pagare; **on ~** a piedi; **to put one's ~
down** (AUT) schiacciare l'acceleratore;
(say no) imporsi; **to find one's feet**
ambientarsi.
footage ['fʊtɪdʒ] n (CINE: length) ≈
metraggio; (: material) sequenza.
foot and mouth (disease) n afta
epizootica.
football ['fʊtbɔːl] n pallone m; (sport: BRIT)
calcio; (: US) football m americano.
footballer ['fʊtbɔːlə*] n (BRIT) = **football
player**.

football ground n campo di calcio.
football match n (BRIT) partita di calcio.
football player n (BRIT) calciatore m; (US)
giocatore m di football americano.
footbrake ['fʊtbreɪk] n freno a pedale.
footbridge ['fʊtbrɪdʒ] n passerella.
foothills ['fʊthɪlz] npl contrafforti fpl.
foothold ['fʊthəʊld] n punto d'appoggio.
footing ['fʊtɪŋ] n (fig) posizione f; **to lose
one's ~** mettere un piede in fallo; **on an
equal ~** in condizioni di parità.
footlights ['fʊtlaɪts] npl luci fpl della
ribalta.
footman ['fʊtmən] n lacchè m inv.
footnote ['fʊtnəʊt] n nota (a piè di pagina).
footpath ['fʊtpɑːθ] n sentiero; (in street)
marciapiede m.
footprint ['fʊtprɪnt] n orma, impronta.
footrest ['fʊtrɛst] n poggiapiedi m inv.
footsie ['fʊtsɪ] n (col): **to play ~ with sb**
fare piedino a qn.
Footsie (index) ['fʊtsɪ-] n (col) = Financial
Times Stock Exchange 100 Index.
footsore ['fʊtsɔː*] adj: **to be ~** avere mal di
piedi.
footstep ['fʊtstɛp] n passo.
footwear ['fʊtwɛə*] n calzatura.
FOR abbr (= free on rail) franco vagone.

================================ **KEYWORD**

for [fɔː*] prep **1** (indicating destination,
intention, purpose) per; **the train ~ London**
il treno per Londra; **he went ~ the paper**
è andato a prendere il giornale; **it's time
~ lunch** è ora di pranzo; **what's it ~?** a
che serve?; **what ~?** (why) perché?
2 (on behalf of, representing) per; **to work
~ sb/sth** lavorare per qn/qc; **I'll ask him
~ you** glielo chiederò a nome tuo; **G ~
George** G come George
3 (because of) per, a causa di; **~ this
reason** per questo motivo
4 (with regard to) per; **it's cold ~ July** è
freddo per luglio; **~ everyone who voted
yes, 50 voted no** per ogni voto a favore
ce n'erano 50 contro
5 (in exchange for) per; **I sold it ~ £5** l'ho
venduto per 5 sterline
6 (in favour of) per, a favore di; **are you ~
or against us?** sei con noi o contro di
noi?; **I'm all ~** it sono completamente a
favore
7 (referring to distance, time) per; **there are
roadworks ~ 5 km** ci sono lavori in corso
per 5 km; **he was away ~ 2 years** è stato
via per 2 anni; **she will be away ~ a
month** starà via un mese; **it hasn't rained
~ 3 weeks** non piove da 3 settimane; **can**

you do it ~ tomorrow? può farlo per
domani?
8 (*with infinitive clauses*): **it is not ~ me to
decide** non sta a me decidere; **it would be
best ~ you to leave** sarebbe meglio che
lei se ne andasse; **there is still time ~ you
to do it** ha ancora tempo per farlo; **~ this
to be possible** … perché ciò sia possibile
…
9 (*in spite of*) nonostante; **~ all his
complaints, he's very fond of her**
nonostante tutte le sue lamentele, le
vuole molto bene
♦ *conj* (*since, as*: *rather formal*) dal
momento che, poiché.

forage |ˈfɒrɪdʒ| *vi* foraggiare.
forage cap *n* bustina.
foray [ˈfɒreɪ] *n* incursione *f*.
forbad(e) [fəˈbæd] *pt of* **forbid**.
forbearing [fɔːˈbɛərɪŋ] *adj* paziente,
tollerante.
forbid, *pt* **forbad(e),** *pp* **forbidden** [fəˈbɪd,
-ˈbæd, -ˈbɪdn] *vt* vietare, interdire; **to ~ sb
to do sth** proibire a qn di fare qc.
forbidding [fəˈbɪdɪŋ] *adj* arcigno(a),
d'aspetto minaccioso.
force [fɔːs] *n* forza ♦ *vt* forzare; (*obtain by
~*: *smile, confession*) strappare; **the F~s**
npl (*BRIT*) le forze armate; **in ~** (*in large
numbers*) in gran numero; (*law*) in vigore;
to come into ~ entrare in vigore; **a ~ 5
wind** un vento forza 5; **to join ~s** unire le
forze; **the sales ~** (*COMM*) l'effettivo dei
rappresentanti; **to ~ sb to do sth**
costringere qn a fare qc.
►**force back** *vt* (*crowd, enemy*) respingere;
(*tears*) ingoiare.
►**force down** *vt* (*food*) sforzarsi di
mangiare.
forced [fɔːst] *adj* forzato(a).
force-feed [ˈfɔːsfiːd] *vt* sottoporre ad
alimentazione forzata.
forceful [ˈfɔːsful] *adj* forte, vigoroso(a).
forcemeat [ˈfɔːsmiːt] *n* (*BRIT CULIN*) ripieno.
forceps [ˈfɔːsɪps] *npl* forcipe *m*.
forcibly [ˈfɔːsəblɪ] *adv* con la forza;
(*vigorously*) vigorosamente.
ford [fɔːd] *n* guado ♦ *vt* guadare.
fore [fɔː*] *n*: **to the ~** in prima linea; **to
come to the ~** mettersi in evidenza.
forearm [ˈfɔːrɑːm] *n* avambraccio.
forebear [ˈfɔːbɛə*] *n* antenato.
foreboding [fɔːˈbəudɪŋ] *n* presagio di male.
forecast [ˈfɔːkɑːst] *n* previsione *f*; (*weather
~*) previsioni *fpl* del tempo ♦ *vt* (*irreg*: *like
cast*) prevedere.
foreclose [fɔːˈkləuz] *vt* (*LAW*: *also*: **~ on**)

sequestrare l'immobile ipotecato di.
foreclosure [fɔːˈkləuʒə*] *n* sequestro di
immobile ipotecato.
forecourt [ˈfɔːkɔːt] *n* (*of garage*) corte *f*
esterna.
forefathers [ˈfɔːfɑːðəz] *npl* antenati *mpl*, avi
mpl.
forefinger [ˈfɔːfɪŋgə*] *n* (dito) indice *m*.
forefront [ˈfɔːfrʌnt] *n*: **in the ~ of**
all'avanguardia di.
forego [fɔːˈgəu] *vt* = **forgo**.
foregoing [ˈfɔːgəuɪŋ] *adj* precedente.
foregone [ˈfɔːgɒn] *pp of* **forego** ♦ *adj*: **it's a ~
conclusion** è una conclusione scontata.
foreground [ˈfɔːgraund] *n* primo piano
♦ *cpd* (*COMPUT*) foreground *inv*, di primo
piano.
forehand [ˈfɔːhænd] *n* (*TENNIS*) diritto.
forehead [ˈfɒrɪd] *n* fronte *f*.
foreign [ˈfɒrən] *adj* straniero(a); (*trade*)
estero(a).
foreign body *n* corpo estraneo.
foreign currency *n* valuta estera.
foreigner [ˈfɒrənə*] *n* straniero/a.
foreign exchange *n* cambio di valuta;
(*currency*) valuta estera.
foreign exchange market *n* mercato
delle valute.
foreign exchange rate *n* cambio.
foreign investment *n* investimento
all'estero.
foreign minister *n* ministro degli Affari
esteri.
Foreign Office (FO) *n* (*BRIT*) Ministero
degli Esteri.
foreign secretary *n* (*BRIT*) ministro degli
Affari esteri.
foreleg [ˈfɔːlɛg] *n* zampa anteriore.
foreman [ˈfɔːmən] *n* caposquadra *m*; (*LAW*:
of jury) portavoce *m* della giuria.
foremost [ˈfɔːməust] *adj* principale; più in
vista ♦ *adv*: **first and ~** innanzitutto.
forename [ˈfɔːneɪm] *n* nome *m* di
battesimo.
forensic [fəˈrɛnsɪk] *adj*: **~ medicine**
medicina legale; **~ expert** esperto della
(polizia) scientifica.
foreplay [ˈfɔːpleɪ] *n* preliminari *mpl*.
forerunner [ˈfɔːrʌnə*] *n* precursore *m*.
foresee, *pt* **foresaw,** *pp* **foreseen** [fɔːˈsiː,
-ˈsɔː, -ˈsiːn] *vt* prevedere.
foreseeable [fɔːˈsiːəbl] *adj* prevedibile.
foreseen [fɔːˈsiːn] *pp of* **foresee**.
foreshadow [fɔːˈʃædəu] *vt* presagire, far
prevedere.
foreshorten [fɔːˈʃɔːtn] *vt* (*figure, scene*)
rappresentare in scorcio.
foresight [ˈfɔːsaɪt] *n* previdenza.

foreskin['fɔːskɪn] n (ANAT) prepuzio.
forest['fɔrɪst] n foresta.
forestall[fɔː'stɔːl] vt prevenire.
forestry['fɔrɪstrɪ] n silvicoltura.
foretaste['fɔːteɪst] n pregustazione f.
foretell,pt, pp **foretold** [fɔː'tɛl, -'təʊld] vt predire.
forethought['fɔːθɔːt] n previdenza.
foretold[fɔː'təʊld] pt, pp of **foretell**.
forever[fə'rɛvə*] adv per sempre; (fig) sempre, di continuo.
forewarn[fɔː'wɔːn] vt avvisare in precedenza.
forewent[fɔː'wɛnt] pt of **forego**.
foreword['fɔːwəːd] n prefazione f.
forfeit['fɔːfɪt] n ammenda, pena ♦ vt perdere; (one's happiness, health) giocarsi.
forgave[fə'geɪv] pt of **forgive**.
forge[fɔːdʒ] n fucina ♦ vt falsificare; (signature) contraffare, falsificare; (wrought iron) fucinare, foggiare.
▶**forge ahead**vi tirare avanti.
forger['fɔːdʒə*] n contraffattore m.
forgery['fɔːdʒərɪ] n falso; (activity) contraffazione f.
forget,pt **forgot**, pp **forgotten** [fə'gɛt, -'gɔt, -'gɔtn] vt, vi dimenticare.
forgetful[fə'gɛtful] adj di corta memoria; ~ **of** dimentico(a) di.
forgetfulness[fə'gɛtfulnɪs] n smemoratezza; (oblivion) oblio.
forget-me-not[fə'gɛtmɪnɔt] n nontiscordardimé m inv.
forgive,pt **forgave**, pp **forgiven** [fə'gɪv, -'geɪv, -'gɪvn] vt perdonare; **to ~ sb for sth/for doing sth** perdonare qc a qn/a qn di aver fatto qc.
forgiveness[fə'gɪvnɪs] n perdono.
forgiving[fə'gɪvɪŋ] adj indulgente.
forgo,pt **forwent**, pp **forgone** [fɔː'gəʊ, -'wɛnt, -'gɔn] vt rinunciare a.
forgot[fə'gɔt] pt of **forget**.
forgotten[fə'gɔtn] pp of **forget**.
fork[fɔːk] n (for eating) forchetta; (for gardening) forca; (of roads) bivio; (of railways) inforcazione f ♦ vi (road) biforcarsi.
▶**fork out**(col: pay) vt sborsare ♦ vi pagare.
forked[fɔːkt] adj (lightning) a zigzag.
fork-lift truck['fɔːklɪft-] n carrello elevatore.
forlorn[fə'lɔːn] adj (person) sconsolato(a); (deserted: cottage) abbandonato(a); (desperate: attempt) disperato(a).
form[fɔːm] n forma; (SCOL) classe f; (questionnaire) modulo ♦ vt formare; (circle, queue etc) fare; **in the ~ of** a forma di, sotto forma di; **to be in good ~**

(SPORT, fig) essere in forma; **in top ~** in gran forma; **to ~ part of sth** far parte di qc.
formal['fɔːməl] adj (offer, receipt) vero(a) e proprio(a); (person) cerimonioso(a); (occasion, dinner) formale, ufficiale; (ART, PHILOSOPHY) formale; ~ **dress** abito da cerimonia; (evening dress) abito da sera.
formality[fɔː'mælɪtɪ] n formalità f inv.
formalize['fɔːməlaɪz] vt rendere ufficiale.
formally['fɔːməlɪ] adv ufficialmente; formalmente; cerimoniosamente; **to be ~ invited** ricevere un invito ufficiale.
format['fɔːmæt] n formato ♦ vt (COMPUT) formattare.
formation[fɔː'meɪʃən] n formazione f.
formative['fɔːmətɪv] adj: ~ **years** anni mpl formativi.
former['fɔːmə*] adj vecchio(a) (before n), ex inv (before n); **the ~ president** l'ex presidente; **the ~ ... the latter** quello ... questo; **the ~ Yugoslavia/Soviet Union** l'ex Jugoslavia/Unione Sovietica.
formerly['fɔːməlɪ] adv in passato.
form feedn (on printer) alimentazione f modulo.
formidable['fɔːmɪdəbl] adj formidabile.
formula['fɔːmjʊlə] n formula; **F~ One** (AUT) formula uno.
formulate['fɔːmjʊleɪt] vt formulare.
fornicate['fɔːnɪkeɪt] vi fornicare.
forsake,pt **forsook**, pp **forsaken** [fə'seɪk, -'suk, -'seɪkən] vt abbandonare.
fort[fɔːt] n forte m; **to hold the ~** (fig) prendere le redini (della situazione).
forte['fɔːtɪ] n forte m.
forth[fɔːθ] adv in avanti; **to go back and ~** andare avanti e indietro; **and so ~** e così via.
forthcoming[fɔːθ'kʌmɪŋ] adj prossimo(a); (character) aperto(a), comunicativo(a).
forthright['fɔːθraɪt] adj franco(a), schietto(a).
forthwith[fɔːθ'wɪθ] adv immediatamente, subito.
fortieth['fɔːtɪɪθ] num quarantesimo(a).
fortification[fɔːtɪfɪ'keɪʃən] n fortificazione f.
fortified winen vino ad alta gradazione alcolica.
fortify['fɔːtɪfaɪ] vt fortificare.
fortitude['fɔːtɪtjuːd] n forza d'animo.
fortnight['fɔːtnaɪt] n (BRIT) quindici giorni mpl, due settimane fpl; **it's a ~ since ...** sono due settimane da quando ....
fortnightly['fɔːtnaɪtlɪ] adj bimensile ♦ adv ogni quindici giorni.
FORTRAN['fɔːtræn] n FORTRAN m.

fortress['fɔːtrɪs] n fortezza, rocca.

fortuitous[fɔː'tjuːɪtəs] adj fortuito(a).

fortunate['fɔːtʃənɪt] adj fortunato(a); **he is ~ to have …** ha la fortuna di avere …; **it is ~ that** è una fortuna che + sub.

fortunately['fɔːtʃənɪtlɪ] adv fortunatamente.

fortune['fɔːtʃən] n fortuna; **to make a ~** farsi una fortuna.

fortuneteller['fɔːtʃəntɛlə*] n indovino/a.

forty['fɔːtɪ] num quaranta.

forum['fɔːrəm] n foro; (fig) luogo di pubblica discussione.

forward['fɔːwəd] adj (movement, position) in avanti; (not shy) sfacciato(a); (COMM: delivery, sales, exchange) a termine ♦ n (SPORT) avanti m inv ♦ vt (letter) inoltrare; (parcel, goods) spedire; (fig) promuovere, appoggiare; **to move ~** avanzare; **"please ~"** "si prega di inoltrare"; **~ planning** programmazione f in anticipo.

forward(s)['fɔːwəd(z)] adv avanti.

forwent[fɔː'wɛnt] pt of **forgo**.

fossil['fɔsl] adj, n fossile (m); **~ fuel** combustibile m fossile.

foster['fɔstə*] vt incoraggiare, nutrire; (child) avere in affidamento.

foster brothern fratellastro.

foster childn bambino(a) preso(a) in affidamento.

foster mothern madre f affidataria.

fought[fɔːt] pt, pp of **fight**.

foul[faul] adj (smell, food) cattivo(a); (weather) brutto(a), orribile; (language) osceno(a); (deed) infame ♦ n (FOOTBALL) fallo ♦ vt sporcare; (football player) commettere un fallo su; (entangle: anchor, propeller) impigliarsi in.

foul playn (SPORT) gioco scorretto; **~ is not suspected** si è scartata l'ipotesi del delitto (or dell'attentato etc).

found[faund] pt, pp of **find** ♦ vt (establish) fondare.

foundation[faun'deɪʃən] n (act) fondazione f; (base) base f; (also: ~ **cream**) fondo tinta; **~s** npl (of building) fondamenta fpl; **to lay the ~s** gettare le fondamenta.

foundation stonen prima pietra.

founder['faundə*] n fondatore/trice ♦ vi affondare.

founding['faundɪŋ] adj: **~ fathers** (US) padri mpl fondatori; **~ member** socio fondatore.

foundry['faundrɪ] n fonderia.

fount[faunt] n fonte f; (TYP) stile m di carattere.

fountain['fauntɪn] n fontana.

fountain penn penna stilografica.

four[fɔː*] num quattro; **on all ~s** a carponi.

four-letter word['fɔːlɛtə-] n parolaccia.

four-poster['fɔː'pəustə*] n (also: ~ **bed**) letto a quattro colonne.

foursome['fɔːsəm] n partita a quattro; uscita in quattro.

fourteen['fɔːtiːn] num quattordici.

fourth[fɔːθ] num quarto(a) ♦ n (AUT: also: ~ **gear**) quarta.

four-wheel drive['fɔːwiːl-] n (AUT): **with ~** con quattro ruote motrici.

fowl[faul] n pollame m; volatile m.

fox[fɔks] n volpe f ♦ vt confondere.

fox furn volpe f, pelliccia di volpe.

foxglove['fɔksglʌv] n (BOT) digitale f.

fox-hunting['fɔkshʌntɪŋ] n caccia alla volpe.

foyer['fɔɪeɪ] n atrio; (THEAT) ridotto.

FPAn abbr (BRIT: = Family Planning Association) ≈ A.I.E.D. f (= Associazione Italiana Educazione Demografica).

Fr.abbr (REL) = **father; friar**.

fr.abbr (= franc) fr.

fracas['frækaː] n rissa, lite f.

fraction['frækʃən] n frazione f.

fractionally['frækʃnəlɪ] adv un tantino, minimamente.

fractious['frækʃəs] adj irritabile.

fracture['fræktʃə*] n frattura ♦ vt fratturare.

fragile['frædʒaɪl] adj fragile.

fragment['frægmənt] n frammento.

fragmentary['frægməntərɪ] adj frammentario(a).

fragrance['freɪgrəns] n fragranza, profumo.

fragrant['freɪgrənt] adj fragrante, profumato(a).

frail[freɪl] adj debole, delicato(a).

frame[freɪm] n (of building) armatura; (of human, animal) ossatura, corpo; (of picture) cornice f; (of door, window) telaio; (of spectacles: also: ~s) montatura ♦ vt (picture) incorniciare; **to ~ sb** (col) incastrare qn; **~ of mind** stato d'animo.

framework['freɪmwəːk] n struttura.

France[frɑːns] n Francia.

franchise['fræntʃaɪz] n (POL) diritto di voto; (COMM) concessione f.

franchisee[fræntʃaɪ'ziː] n concessionario.

franchiser['fræntʃaɪzə*] n concedente m.

frank[fræŋk] adj franco(a), aperto(a) ♦ vt (letter) affrancare.

Frankfurt['fræŋkfɔːt] n Francoforte f.

frankfurter['fræŋkfɔːtə*] n würstel m inv.

franking machine['fræŋkɪŋ-] n macchina affrancatrice.

frankly['fræŋklɪ] adv francamente,

sinceramente.

frankness ['fræŋknɪs] *n* franchezza.

frantic ['fræntɪk] *adj* (*activity, pace*)
frenetico(a); (*desperate: need, desire*)
pazzo(a), sfrenato(a); (: *search*)
affannoso(a); (*person*) fuori di sé.

frantically ['fræntɪklɪ] *adv* freneticamente;
affannosamente.

fraternal [frə'tɜ:nl] *adj* fraterno(a).

fraternity [frə'tɜ:nɪtɪ] *n* (*club*) associazione
f; (*spirit*) fratellanza.

fraternize ['frætənaɪz] *vi* fraternizzare.

fraud [frɔ:d] *n* truffa; (*LAW*) frode *f*;
(*person*) impostore/a.

fraudulent ['frɔ:djulənt] *adj* fraudolento(a).

fraught [frɔ:t] *adj* (*tense*) teso(a); ~ **with**
pieno(a) di, intriso(a) da.

fray [freɪ] *n* baruffa ♦ *vt* logorare ♦ *vi*
logorarsi; **to return to the** ~ tornare nella
mischia; **tempers were getting** ~**ed**
cominciavano ad innervosirsi; **her nerves
were** ~**ed** aveva i nervi a pezzi.

FRB *n abbr* (*US*) = **Federal Reserve Board**.

FRCM *n abbr* (*BRIT*) = *Fellow of the Royal
College of Music.*

FRCO *n abbr* (*BRIT*) = *Fellow of the Royal
College of Organists.*

FRCP *n abbr* (*BRIT*) = *Fellow of the Royal
College of Physicians.*

FRCS *n abbr* (*BRIT*) = *Fellow of the Royal
College of Surgeons.*

freak [fri:k] *n* fenomeno, mostro; (*col:
enthusiast*) fanatico/a ♦ *adj* (*storm,
conditions*) anormale; (*victory*) inatteso(a).

▶**freak out** *vi* (*col*) andare fuori di testa.

freakish ['fri:kɪʃ] *adj* (*result, appearance*)
strano(a), bizzarro(a); (*weather*)
anormale.

freckle ['frɛkl] *n* lentiggine *f*.

free [fri:] *adj* libero(a); (*gratis*) gratuito(a);
(*liberal*) generoso(a) ♦ *vt* (*prisoner, jammed
person*) liberare; (*jammed object*)
districare; ~ (**of charge**) gratuitamente;
admission ~ entrata libera; **to give sb a**
~ **hand** dare carta bianca a qn; ~ **and
easy** rilassato.

freebie ['fri:bɪ] *n* (*col*): **it's a** ~ è in
omaggio.

freedom ['fri:dəm] *n* libertà.

freedom fighter *n* combattente *m/f* per la
libertà.

free enterprise *n* liberalismo economico.

Freefone ® ['fri:fəun] *n* (*BRIT*) ≈ numero
verde.

free-for-all ['fri:fərɔ:l] *n* parapiglia *m*
generale.

free gift *n* regalo, omaggio.

freehold ['fri:həuld] *n* proprietà assoluta.

free kick *n* (*SPORT*) calcio libero.

freelance ['fri:lɑ:ns] *adj* indipendente; ~
work collaborazione *f* esterna.

freeloader ['fri:ləudə*] *n* (*pej*) scroccone/a.

freely ['fri:lɪ] *adv* liberamente; (*liberally*)
liberalmente.

free-market economy [fri:'mɑ:kɪt-] *n*
economia di libero mercato.

freemason ['fri:meɪsn] *n* massone *m*.

freemasonry ['fri:meɪsnrɪ] *n* massoneria.

freepost ['fri:pəust] *n* affrancatura a
carica del destinatario.

free-range ['fri:reɪndʒ] *adj* (*eggs*) di gallina
ruspante.

free sample *n* campione *m* gratuito.

free speech *n* libertà di parola.

freestyle ['fri:staɪl] *n* (*in swimming*) stile *m*
libero.

free trade *n* libero scambio.

freeway ['fri:weɪ] *n* (*US*) superstrada.

freewheel [fri:'wi:l] *vi* andare a ruota
libera.

freewheeling [fri:'wi:lɪŋ] *adj* a ruota libera.

free will *n* libero arbitrio; **of one's own** ~
di spontanea volontà.

freeze [fri:z] *vb* (*pt* **froze**, *pp* **frozen** [frəuz,
'frəuzn]) *vi* gelare ♦ *vt* gelare; (*food*)
congelare; (*prices, salaries*) bloccare ♦ *n*
gelo; blocco.

▶**freeze over** *vi* (*lake, river*) ghiacciarsi;
(*windows, windscreen*) coprirsi di
ghiaccio.

▶**freeze up** *vi* gelarsi.

freeze-dried ['fri:zdraɪd] *adj* liofilizzato(a).

freezer ['fri:zə*] *n* congelatore *m*.

freezing ['fri:zɪŋ] *adj*: **I'm** ~ mi sto
congelando ♦ *n* (*also*: ~ **point**) punto di
congelamento; **3 degrees below** ~ 3 gradi
sotto zero.

freight [freɪt] *n* (*goods*) merce *f*, merci *fpl*;
(*money charged*) spese *fpl* di trasporto; ~
forward spese a carico del destinatario;
~ **inward** spese di trasporto sulla merce
in entrata.

freight car *n* (*US*) carro *m* merci *inv*.

freighter ['freɪtə*] *n* (*NAUT*) nave *f* da
carico.

freight forwarder [-'fɔ:wədə*] *n*
spedizioniere *m*.

freight train *n* (*US*) treno *m* merci *inv*.

French [frɛntʃ] *adj* francese ♦ *n* (*LING*)
francese *m*; **the** ~ *npl* i Francesi.

French bean *n* fagiolino.

French Canadian *adj, n* franco-canadese
(*m/f*).

French dressing *n* (*CULIN*) condimento per
insalata.

French fried potatoes, (*US*) **French fries**

npl patate *fpl* fritte.
French Guiana [-gaɪ'ænə] *n* Guiana francese.
French loaf *n* ≈ filoncino.
Frenchman ['frɛntʃmən] *n* francese *m*.
French Riviera *n*: **the** ~ la Costa Azzurra.
French stick *n* baguette *f inv*.
French window *n* portafinestra.
Frenchwoman ['frɛntʃwumən] *n* francese *f*.
frenetic [frə'nɛtɪk] *adj* frenetico(a).
frenzy ['frɛnzɪ] *n* frenesia.
frequency ['friːkwənsɪ] *n* frequenza.
frequency modulation (FM) *n* modulazione *f* di frequenza (F.M.).
frequent *adj* ['friːkwənt] frequente ♦ *vt* [frɪ'kwɛnt] frequentare.
frequently ['friːkwəntlɪ] *adv* frequentemente, spesso.
fresco ['frɛskəu] *n* affresco.
fresh [frɛʃ] *adj* fresco(a); (*new*) nuovo(a); (*cheeky*) sfacciato(a); **to make a** ~ **start** cominciare da capo.
freshen ['frɛʃən] *vi* (*wind, air*) rinfrescare.
►**freshen up** *vi* rinfrescarsi.
freshener ['frɛʃnə*] *n*: **skin** ~ tonico rinfrescante; **air** ~ deodorante *m* per ambienti.
fresher ['frɛʃə*] *n* (*BRIT SCOL: col*) = **freshman**.
freshly ['frɛʃlɪ] *adv* di recente, di fresco.
freshman ['frɛʃmən] *n* (*SCOL*) matricola.
freshness ['frɛʃnɪs] *n* freschezza.
freshwater ['frɛʃwɔːtə*] *adj* (*fish*) d'acqua dolce.
fret [frɛt] *vi* agitarsi, affliggersi.
fretful ['frɛtful] *adj* (*child*) irritabile.
Freudian ['frɔɪdɪən] *adj* freudiano(a); ~ **slip** lapsus *m inv* freudiano.
FRG *n abbr see* **Federal Republic of Germany**.
Fri. *abbr* (= *Friday*) ven.
friar ['fraɪə*] *n* frate *m*.
friction ['frɪkʃən] *n* frizione *f*, attrito.
friction feed *n* (*on printer*) trascinamento ad attrito.
Friday ['fraɪdɪ] *n* venerdì *m inv*; *for phrases see also* **Tuesday**.
fridge [frɪdʒ] *n* (*BRIT*) frigo, frigorifero.
fridge-freezer ['frɪdʒ'friːzə*] *n* freezer *m inv*.
fried [fraɪd] *pt, pp of* **fry** ♦ *adj* fritto(a); ~ **egg** uovo fritto.
friend [frɛnd] *n* amico/a; **to make ~s with** fare amicizia con.
friendliness ['frɛndlɪnɪs] *n* amichevolezza.
friendly ['frɛndlɪ] *adj* amichevole ♦ *n* (*also*: ~ **match**) partita amichevole; **to be** ~ **with** essere amico di; **to be** ~ **to** essere cordiale con.

friendly fire *n* fuoco amico.
friendship ['frɛndʃɪp] *n* amicizia.
frieze [friːz] *n* fregio.
frigate ['frɪgɪt] *n* (*NAUT: modern*) fregata.
fright [fraɪt] *n* paura, spavento; **to take** ~ spaventarsi; **she looks a** ~! guarda com'è conciata!
frighten ['fraɪtn] *vt* spaventare, far paura a.
►**frighten away, frighten off** *vt* (*birds, children etc*) scacciare (facendogli paura).
frightened ['fraɪtnd] *adj*: **to be** ~ (**of**) avere paura (di).
frightening ['fraɪtnɪŋ] *adj* spaventoso(a), pauroso(a).
frightful ['fraɪtful] *adj* orribile.
frightfully ['fraɪtfulɪ] *adv* terribilmente; **I'm** ~ **sorry** mi dispiace moltissimo.
frigid ['frɪdʒɪd] *adj* (*woman*) frigido(a).
frigidity [frɪ'dʒɪdɪtɪ] *n* frigidità.
frill [frɪl] *n* balza; **without ~s** (*fig*) senza fronzoli.
frilly ['frɪlɪ] *adj* (*clothes, lampshade*) pieno(a) di fronzoli.
fringe [frɪndʒ] *n* frangia; (*edge: of forest etc*) margine *m*; (*fig*): **on the** ~ al margine.
fringe benefits *npl* vantaggi *mpl*.
fringe theatre *n* teatro d'avanguardia.
Frisbee ® ['frɪzbɪ] *n* frisbee ® *m inv*.
frisk [frɪsk] *vt* perquisire.
frisky ['frɪskɪ] *adj* vivace, vispo(a).
fritter ['frɪtə*] *n* frittella.
►**fritter away** *vt* sprecare.
frivolity [frɪ'vɔlɪtɪ] *n* frivolezza.
frivolous ['frɪvələs] *adj* frivolo(a).
frizzy ['frɪzɪ] *adj* crespo(a).
fro [frəu] *adv*: **to and** ~ avanti e indietro.
frock [frɔk] *n* vestito.
frog [frɔg] *n* rana; **to have a** ~ **in one's throat** avere la voce rauca.
frogman ['frɔgmən] *n* uomo *m* rana *inv*.
frogmarch ['frɔgmɑːtʃ] *vt* (*BRIT*): **to** ~ **sb in/out** portar qn dentro/fuori con la forza.
frolic ['frɔlɪk] *vi* sgambettare.

═══════════════ *KEYWORD*

from [frɔm] *prep* **1** (*indicating starting place, origin etc*) da; **where do you come ~?, where are you ~?** da dove viene?, di dov'è?; **where has he come ~?** da dove arriva?; ~ **London to Glasgow** da Londra a Glasgow; **a letter** ~ **my sister** una lettera da mia sorella; **tell him** ~ **me that** ... gli dica da parte mia che ...
2 (*indicating time*) da; ~ **one o'clock to** *or* **until** *or* **till two** dall'una alle due; **(as)** ~ **Friday** a partire da venerdì; ~ **January**

(on) da gennaio, a partire da gennaio
3 *(indicating distance)* da; **the hotel is 1 km
~ the beach** l'albergo è a 1 km dalla
spiaggia
4 *(indicating price, number etc)* da; ~ **a
pound** da una sterlina in su; **prices range
~ £10 to £50** i prezzi vanno dalle 10 alle
50 sterline
5 *(indicating difference)* da; **he can't tell
red ~ green** non sa distinguere il rosso
dal verde
6 *(because of, on the basis of)*: ~ **what he
says** da quanto dice lui; **weak ~ hunger**
debole per la fame.

frond [frɔnd] *n* fronda.

front [frʌnt] *n (of house, dress)* davanti *m
inv*; *(of train)* testa; *(of book)* copertina;
(promenade: also: **sea** ~) lungomare *m*;
(MIL, POL, METEOR) fronte *m*; *(fig:
appearances)* fronte *f* ♦ *adj* primo(a);
anteriore, davanti *inv* ♦ *vi*: **to ~ onto sth**
dare su qc, guardare verso qc; **in ~ (of)**
davanti (a).

frontage ['frʌntɪdʒ] *n* facciata.

frontal ['frʌntl] *adj* frontale.

front bench *n posti in Parlamento occupati dai frontbencher; see boxed note.*

FRONT BENCH

Nel Parlamento britannico, si chiamano **front
bench** *gli scanni della "House of Commons"
che si trovano alla sinistra e alla destra dello
"Speaker" davanti ai "back benches".* **I front
bench** *sono occupati dai "frontbenchers",
parlamentari che ricoprono una carica di
governo o che fanno parte dello "shadow
cabinet" dell'opposizione.*

---

frontbencher ['frʌnt'bentʃə*] *n (BRIT)
parlamentare con carica al governo o
all'opposizione.*

front desk *n (US: in hotel)* reception *f inv*; *(:
at doctor's)* accettazione *f*.

front door *n* porta d'entrata; *(of car)*
sportello anteriore.

frontier ['frʌntɪə*] *n* frontiera.

frontispiece ['frʌntɪspiːs] *n* frontespizio.

front page *n* prima pagina.

front room *n (BRIT)* salotto.

front runner *n (fig)* favorito/a.

front-wheel drive ['frʌntwiːl-] *n*
trasmissione *f* anteriore.

frost [frɔst] *n* gelo; *(also:* **hoar~)** brina.

frostbite ['frɔstbaɪt] *n* congelamento.

frosted ['frɔstɪd] *adj (glass)* smerigliato(a);
(US: cake) glassato(a).

frosting ['frɔstɪŋ] *n (US: on cake)* glassa.

frosty ['frɔstɪ] *adj (window)* coperto(a) di
ghiaccio; *(welcome)* gelido(a).

froth ['frɔθ] *n* spuma; schiuma.

frown [fraun] *n* cipiglio ♦ *vi* accigliarsi.
► **frown on** *vt fus (fig)* disapprovare.

froze [frəuz] *pt of* **freeze**.

frozen ['frəuzn] *pp of* **freeze** ♦ *adj (food)*
congelato(a); *(COMM: assets)* bloccato(a).

FRS *n abbr (BRIT)* = *Fellow of the Royal
Society*; *(US:* = *Federal Reserve System)
sistema bancario degli Stati Uniti.*

frugal ['fruːgəl] *adj* frugale; *(person)*
economo(a).

fruit [fruːt] *n (pl inv)* frutto; *(collectively)*
frutta.

fruiterer ['fruːtərə*] *n* fruttivendolo; **at the
~'s (shop)** dal fruttivendolo.

fruit fly *n* mosca della frutta.

fruitful ['fruːtful] *adj* fruttuoso(a); *(plant)*
fruttifero(a); *(soil)* fertile.

fruition [fruː'ɪʃən] *n*: **to come to ~**
realizzarsi.

fruit juice *n* succo di frutta.

fruitless ['fruːtlɪs] *adj (fig)* vano(a), inutile.

fruit machine *n (BRIT)* macchina *f*
mangiasoldi *inv*.

fruit salad *n* macedonia.

frump [frʌmp] *n*: **to feel a ~** sentirsi
infagottato(a).

frustrate [frʌs'treɪt] *vt* frustrare.

frustrated [frʌs'treɪtɪd] *adj* frustrato(a).

frustrating [frʌs'treɪtɪŋ] *adj (job)*
frustrante; *(day)* disastroso(a).

frustration [frʌs'treɪʃən] *n* frustrazione *f*.

fry, *pt, pp* **fried** [fraɪ, -d] *vt* friggere ♦ *npl*: **the
small ~** i pesci piccoli.

frying pan ['fraɪŋ-] *n* padella.

FT *n abbr (BRIT:* = *Financial Times)* giornale
finanziario; **the ~ index** l'indice FT.

ft. *abbr* = **foot, feet.**

FTC *n abbr (US) see* **Federal Trade
Commission.**

FT-SE 100 Index *n abbr* = *Financial Times
Stock Exchange 100 Index.*

fuchsia ['fjuːʃə] *n* fucsia.

fuck [fʌk] *vt, vi (col!)* fottere (*!*); ~ **off!**
vaffanculo! (*!*).

fuddled ['fʌdld] *adj (muddled)* confuso(a);
(col: tipsy) brillo(a).

fuddy-duddy ['fʌdɪdʌdɪ] *n (pej)* parruccone
m.

fudge [fʌdʒ] *n (CULIN)* specie di caramella
a base di latte, burro e zucchero ♦ *vt
(issue, problem)* evitare.

fuel [fjuəl] *n (for heating)* combustibile *m*;
(for propelling) carburante *m* ♦ *vt (furnace
etc)* alimentare; *(aircraft, ship etc)*

rifornire di carburante.
fuel oil n nafta.
fuel pump n (AUT) pompa del carburante.
fuel tank n deposito m nafta inv; (on vehicle)
serbatoio (della benzina).
fug [fʌg] n (BRIT) aria viziata.
fugitive ['fjuːdʒɪtɪv] n fuggitivo/a,
profugo/a; (from prison) evaso/a.
fulfil, (US) **fulfill** [ful'fɪl] vt (function)
compiere; (order) eseguire; (wish, desire)
soddisfare, appagare.
fulfilled [ful'fɪld] adj (person) realizzato(a),
soddisfatto(a).
fulfil(l)ment [ful'fɪlmənt] n (of wishes)
soddisfazione f, appagamento.
full [ful] adj pieno(a); (details, skirt)
ampio(a); (price) intero(a) ♦ adv: **to know**
~ **well that** sapere benissimo che; ~ **(up)**
(hotel etc) al completo; **I'm** ~ **(up)** sono
pieno; **a** ~ **two hours** due ore intere; **at** ~
speed a tutta velocità; **in** ~ per intero; **to**
pay in ~ pagare tutto; ~ **name** nome m e
cognome m; ~ **employment** piena
occupazione; ~ **fare** tariffa completa.
fullback ['fulbæk] n (RUGBY, FOOTBALL)
terzino.
full-blooded ['ful'blʌdɪd] adj (vigorous:
attack) energico(a); (virile: male) virile.
full-cream ['ful'kriːm] adj: ~ **milk** (BRIT)
latte m intero.
full-grown ['ful'grəun] adj maturo(a).
full-length ['ful'lɛŋθ] adj (portrait) in piedi;
(film) a lungometraggio.
full moon n luna piena.
full-scale ['fulskeɪl] adj (plan, model) in
grandezza naturale; (search, retreat) su
vasta scala.
full-sized ['ful'saɪzd] adj (portrait etc) a
grandezza naturale.
full stop n punto.
full-time ['ful'taɪm] adj, adv (work) a tempo
pieno ♦ n (SPORT) fine f partita.
fully ['fulɪ] adv interamente, pienamente,
completamente; (at least): ~ **as big**
almeno così grosso.
fully-fledged ['fulɪ'flɛdʒd] adj (bird)
adulto(a); (fig: teacher, member etc) a tutti
gli effetti.
fulsome ['fulsəm] adj (pej: praise)
esagerato(a), eccessivo(a); (: manner)
insincero.
fumble ['fʌmbl] vi brancolare, andare a
tentoni ♦ vt (ball) lasciarsi sfuggire.
▶**fumble with** vt fus trafficare.
fume [fjuːm] vi essere furioso(a); ~**s** npl
esalazioni fpl, vapori mpl.
fumigate ['fjuːmɪgeɪt] vt suffumicare.
fun [fʌn] n divertimento, spasso; **to have** ~

divertirsi; **for** ~ per scherzo; **it's not**
much ~ non è molto divertente; **to make**
~ **of** prendersi gioco di.
function ['fʌŋkʃən] n funzione f; cerimonia,
ricevimento ♦ vi funzionare; **to** ~ **as**
fungere da, funzionare da.
functional ['fʌŋkʃənl] adj funzionale.
function key n (COMPUT) tasto di funzioni.
fund [fʌnd] n fondo, cassa; (source) fondo;
(store) riserva; ~**s** npl (money) fondi mpl.
fundamental [fʌndə'mɛntl] adj
fondamentale; ~**s** npl basi fpl.
fundamentalism [fʌndə'mɛntəlɪzəm] n
fondamentalismo.
fundamentalist [fʌndə'mɛntəlɪst] n
fondamentalista m/f.
fundamentally [fʌndə'mɛntəlɪ] adv
essenzialmente, fondamentalmente.
funding ['fʌndɪŋ] n finanziamento.
fund-raising ['fʌndreɪzɪŋ] n raccolta di
fondi.
funeral ['fjuːnərəl] n funerale m.
funeral director n impresario di pompe
funebri.
funeral parlour n impresa di pompe
funebri.
funeral service n ufficio funebre.
funereal [fjuː'nɪərɪəl] adj funereo(a),
lugubre.
fun fair n luna park m inv.
fungus, pl **fungi** ['fʌŋgəs, -gaɪ] n fungo;
(mould) muffa.
funicular [fjuː'nɪkjulə*] adj (also: ~ **railway**)
funicolare f.
funky ['fʌŋkɪ] adj (music) funky inv; (col:
excellent) figo(a).
funnel ['fʌnl] n imbuto; (of ship) ciminiera.
funnily ['fʌnɪlɪ] adv in modo divertente;
(oddly) stranamente.
funny ['fʌnɪ] adj divertente, buffo(a);
(strange) strano(a), bizzarro(a).
funny bone n osso cubitale.
fun run n marcia non competitiva.
fur [fɔː*] n pelo; pelliccia; pelle f; (BRIT: in
kettle etc) deposito calcare.
fur coat n pelliccia.
furious ['fjuərɪəs] adj furioso(a); (effort)
accanito(a); (argument) violento(a).
furiously ['fjuərɪəslɪ] adv furiosamente;
accanitamente.
furl [fɔːl] vt (sail) piegare.
furlong ['fɔːlɔŋ] n = 201.17 m (termine
ippico).
furlough ['fɔːləu] n (US) congedo,
permesso.
furnace ['fɔːnɪs] n fornace f.
furnish ['fɔːnɪʃ] vt ammobiliare; (supply)
fornire; ~**ed flat** or (US) **apartment**

appartamento ammobiliato.
furnishings ['fɜːnɪʃɪŋz] *npl* mobili *mpl*, mobilia.
furniture ['fɜːnɪtʃə*] *n* mobili *mpl*; **piece of** ~ mobile *m*.
furore [fjuə'rɔːrɪ] *n (protests)* scalpore *m*; *(enthusiasm)* entusiasmo.
furrier ['fʌrɪə*] *n* pellicciaio/a.
furrow ['fʌrəu] *n* solco ♦ *vt (forehead)* segnare di rughe.
furry ['fɜːrɪ] *adj (animal)* peloso(a); *(toy)* di peluche.
further ['fɜːðə*] *adj* supplementare, altro(a); nuovo(a); più lontano(a) ♦ *adv* più lontano; *(more)* di più; *(moreover)* inoltre ♦ *vt* favorire, promuovere; **until** ~ **notice** fino a nuovo avviso; **how much** ~ **is it?** quanto manca *or* dista?; ~ **to your letter of ...** *(COMM)* con riferimento alla vostra lettera del ...; **to** ~ **one's interests** fare i propri interessi.
further education *n* ≈ corsi *mpl* di formazione.
furthermore [fɜːðə'mɔː*] *adv* inoltre, per di più.
furthermost ['fɜːðəməust] *adj* più lontano(a).
furthest ['fɜːðɪst] *superlative of* **far**.
furtive ['fɜːtɪv] *adj* furtivo(a).
fury ['fjuərɪ] *n* furore *m*.
fuse, *(US)* **fuze** [fjuːz] *n* fusibile *m*; *(for bomb etc)* miccia, spoletta ♦ *vt* fondere; *(ELEC):* **to** ~ **the lights** far saltare i fusibili ♦ *vi* fondersi; **a** ~ **has blown** è saltato un fusibile.
fuse box *n* cassetta dei fusibili.
fuselage ['fjuːzəlɑːʒ] *n* fusoliera.
fuse wire *n* filo (di fusibile).
fusillade [fjuːzɪ'leɪd] *n* scarica di fucileria; *(fig)* fuoco di fila, serie *f inv* incalzante.
fusion ['fjuːʒən] *n* fusione *f*.
fuss [fʌs] *n* chiasso, trambusto, confusione *f*; *(complaining)* storie *fpl* ♦ *vt (person)* infastidire, scocciare ♦ *vi* agitarsi; **to make a** ~ fare delle storie; **to make a** ~ **of sb** coprire qn di attenzioni.
▶**fuss over** *vt fus (person)* circondare di premure.
fusspot ['fʌspɔt] *n (col)*: **he's such a** ~ fa sempre tante storie.
fussy ['fʌsɪ] *adj (person)* puntiglioso(a), esigente; che fa le storie; *(dress)* carico(a) di fronzoli; *(style)* elaborato(a); **I'm not** ~ *(col)* per me è lo stesso.
fusty ['fʌstɪ] *adj (pej: archaic)* stantio(a); *(: smell)* che sa di stantio.
futile ['fjuːtaɪl] *adj* futile.
futility [fjuː'tɪlɪtɪ] *n* futilità.

futon ['fuːtɔn] *n* futon *m inv*, letto giapponese.
future ['fjuːtʃə*] *adj* futuro(a) ♦ *n* futuro, avvenire *m*; *(LING)* futuro; **in** ~ in futuro; **in the near** ~ in un prossimo futuro; **in the immediate** ~ nell'immediato futuro.
futures ['fjuːtʃəz] *npl (COMM)* operazioni *fpl* a termine.
futuristic [fjuːtʃə'rɪstɪk] *adj* futuristico(a).
fuze [fjuːz] *n*, *vt*, *vi (US)* = **fuse**.
fuzzy ['fʌzɪ] *adj (PHOT)* indistinto(a), sfocato(a); *(hair)* crespo(a).
fwd. *abbr* = **forward**.
fwy *abbr (US)* = **freeway**.
FY *abbr* = **fiscal year**.
FYI *abbr* = *for your information*.

G g

G, g [dʒiː] *n (letter)* G, g *f or m inv*; *(MUS):* **G** sol *m*; **G for George** ≈ G come Genova.
G *n abbr (BRIT SCOL: mark:* = *good)* ≈ buono; *(US CINE:* = *general audience)* per tutti.
g *abbr (*= *gram; gravity)* g.
G7 *n abbr (POL:* = *Group of Seven)* G7 *mpl*.
GA *abbr (US POST)* = *Georgia*.
gab [gæb] *n (col)*: **to have the gift of the** ~ avere parlantina.
gabble ['gæbl] *vi* borbottare; farfugliare.
gaberdine [gæbə'diːn] *n* gabardine *m inv*.
gable ['geɪbl] *n* frontone *m*.
Gabon [gə'bɔn] *n* Gabon *m*.
gad about [gæd-] *vi (col)* svolazzare (qua e là).
gadget ['gædʒɪt] *n* aggeggio.
Gaelic ['geɪlɪk] *adj* gaelico(a) ♦ *n (language)* gaelico.
gaffe [gæf] *n* gaffe *f inv*.
gaffer ['gæfə*] *n (BRIT col)* capo.
gag [gæg] *n* bavaglio; *(joke)* facezia, scherzo ♦ *vt (prisoner etc)* imbavagliare ♦ *vi (choke)* soffocare.
gaga ['gɑːgɑː] *adj*: **to go** ~ rimbambirsi.
gage [geɪdʒ] *n*, *vt (US)* = **gauge**.
gaiety ['geɪɪtɪ] *n* gaiezza.
gaily ['geɪlɪ] *adv* allegramente.
gain [geɪn] *n* guadagno, profitto ♦ *vt* guadagnare ♦ *vi (watch)* andare avanti; **to** ~ **in/by** aumentare di/con; **to** ~ **3lbs (in weight)** aumentare di 3 libbre; **to** ~ **ground** guadagnare terreno.

▶**gain (up)on** *vt fus* accorciare le distanze da, riprendere.

gainful ['geɪnful] *adj* profittevole, lucrativo(a).

gainfully ['geɪnfəlɪ] *adv*: **to be ~ employed** avere un lavoro retribuito.

gainsay [geɪn'seɪ] *vt irreg* (*like* **say**) contraddire; negare.

gait [geɪt] *n* andatura.

gal. *abbr* = **gallon.**

gala ['gɑːlə] *n* gala; **swimming ~** manifestazione *f* di nuoto.

Galapagos Islands [gə'læpəgəs-] *npl*: **the ~** le isole Galapagos.

galaxy ['gæləksɪ] *n* galassia.

gale [geɪl] *n* vento forte; burrasca; **~ force 10** vento forza 10.

gall [gɔːl] *n* (*ANAT*) bile *f*; (*fig*: *impudence*) fegato, faccia ♦ *vt* urtare (i nervi a).

gall. *abbr* = **gallon.**

gallant ['gælənt] *adj* valoroso(a); (*towards ladies*) galante, cortese.

gallantry ['gæləntrɪ] *n* valore *m* militare; galanteria, cortesia.

gall bladder ['gɔːl-] *n* cistifellea.

galleon ['gælɪən] *n* galeone *m*.

gallery ['gælərɪ] *n* galleria; loggia; (*for spectators*) tribuna; (*in theatre*) loggione *m*, balconata; (*also*: **art ~**: *state-owned*) museo; (: *private*) galleria.

galley ['gælɪ] *n* (*ship's kitchen*) cambusa; (*ship*) galea; (*also*: **~ proof**) bozza in colonna.

Gallic ['gælɪk] *adj* gallico(a); (*French*) francese.

galling ['gɔːlɪŋ] *adj* irritante.

gallon ['gælən] *n* gallone *m* (*BRIT*: = *4.543 l; 8 pints; US = 3.785 l*).

gallop ['gæləp] *n* galoppo ♦ *vi* galoppare; **~ing inflation** inflazione *f* galoppante.

gallows ['gæləuz] *n* forca.

gallstone ['gɔːlstəun] *n* calcolo biliare.

Gallup Poll ['gæləp-] *n* sondaggio a campione.

galore [gə'lɔː*] *adv* a iosa, a profusione.

galvanize ['gælvənaɪz] *vt* galvanizzare; **to ~ sb into action** (*fig*) galvanizzare qn, spronare qn all'azione.

Gambia ['gæmbɪə] *n* Gambia *m*.

gambit ['gæmbɪt] *n* (*fig*): (**opening**) **~** prima mossa.

gamble ['gæmbl] *n* azzardo, rischio calcolato ♦ *vt, vi* giocare; **to ~ on** (*fig*) giocare su; **to ~ on the Stock Exchange** giocare in Borsa.

gambler ['gæmblə*] *n* giocatore/trice d'azzardo.

gambling ['gæmblɪŋ] *n* gioco d'azzardo.

gambol ['gæmbəl] *vi* saltellare.

game [geɪm] *n* gioco; (*event*) partita; (*HUNTING*) selvaggina ♦ *adj* coraggioso(a); (*ready*): **to be ~ (for sth/to do)** essere pronto(a) (a qc/a fare); **~s** *npl* (*SCOL*) attività *fpl* sportive; **big ~** selvaggina grossa.

game bird *n* uccello selvatico.

gamekeeper ['geɪmkiːpə*] *n* guardacaccia *m inv*.

gamely ['geɪmlɪ] *adv* coraggiosamente.

game reserve *n* riserva di caccia.

games console *n* console *f inv* dei videogame.

gameshow ['geɪmʃəu] *n* gioco a premi.

gamesmanship ['geɪmzmənʃɪp] *n* abilità

gaming ['geɪmɪŋ] *n* gioco d'azzardo.

gammon ['gæmən] *n* (*bacon*) quarto di maiale; (*ham*) prosciutto affumicato.

gamut ['gæmət] *n* gamma.

gang [gæŋ] *n* banda, squadra ♦ *vi*: **to ~ up on sb** far combutta contro qn.

Ganges ['gændʒiːz] *n*: **the ~** il Gange.

gangland ['gæŋlænd] *adj* della malavita; **~ killer** sicario.

gangling ['gæŋglɪŋ] *adj* allampanato(a).

gangly ['gæŋglɪ] *adj* = **gangling.**

gangplank ['gæŋplæŋk] *n* passerella.

gangrene ['gæŋgriːn] *n* cancrena.

gangster ['gæŋstə*] *n* gangster *m inv*.

gangway ['gæŋweɪ] *n* passerella; (*BRIT*: *of bus*) passaggio.

gantry ['gæntrɪ] *n* (*for crane, railway signal*) cavalletto; (*for rocket*) torre *f* di lancio.

GAO *n abbr* (*US*: = *General Accounting Office*) ≈ Corte *f* dei Conti.

gaol [dʒeɪl] *n, vt* (*BRIT*) = **jail.**

gap [gæp] *n* buco; (*in time*) intervallo; (*fig*) lacuna; vuoto.

gape [geɪp] *vi* restare a bocca aperta.

gaping ['geɪpɪŋ] *adj* (*hole*) squarciato(a).

gap year *n* anno di pausa preso prima di iniziare l'università, per lavorare o viaggiare.

garage ['gærɑːʒ] *n* garage *m inv*.

garb [gɑːb] *n* abiti *mpl*, veste *f*.

garbage ['gɑːbɪdʒ] *n* immondizie *fpl*, rifiuti *mpl*; (*fig*: *film, book*) porcheria, robaccia; (: *nonsense*) fesserie *fpl*.

garbage can *n* (*US*) bidone *m* della spazzatura.

garbage collector *n* (*US*) spazzino/a.

garbage disposal unit *n* tritarifiuti *m inv*.

garbage truck *n* (*US*) camion *m inv* della spazzatura.

garbled ['gɑːbld] *adj* deformato(a); ingarbugliato(a).

garden ['gɑːdn] *n* giardino ♦ *vi* lavorare nel

giardino; ~s *npl* (*public*) giardini pubblici; (*private*) parco.

garden centren vivaio.

garden cityn (*BRIT*) città *f inv* giardino *inv*.

gardener['gɑːdnə*] *n* giardiniere/a.

gardening['gɑːdnɪŋ] *n* giardinaggio.

gargle['gɑːgl] *vi* fare gargarismi ♦ *n* gargarismo.

gargoyle['gɑːgɔɪl] *n* gargouille *f inv*.

garish['gɛərɪʃ] *adj* vistoso(a).

garland['gɑːlənd] *n* ghirlanda; corona.

garlic['gɑːlɪk] *n* aglio.

garment['gɑːmənt] *n* indumento.

garner['gɑːnə*] *vt* ammucchiare, raccogliere.

garnish['gɑːnɪʃ] *vt* guarnire.

garret['gærɪt] *n* soffitta.

garrison['gærɪsn] *n* guarnigione *f* ♦ *vt* guarnire.

garrulous['gærjuləs] *adj* ciarliero(a), loquace.

garter['gɑːtə*] *n* giarrettiera; (*US*: *suspender*) gancio (di reggicalze).

garter beltn (*US*) reggicalze *m inv*.

gas[gæs] *n* gas *m inv*; (*used as anaesthetic*) etere *m*; (*US*: *gasoline*) benzina ♦ *vt* asfissiare con il gas; (*MIL*) gasare.

gas cookern (*BRIT*) cucina a gas.

gas cylindern bombola del gas.

gaseous['gæsɪəs] *adj* gassoso(a).

gas firen (*BRIT*) radiatore *m* a gas.

gas-fired['gæsfaɪəd] *adj* (alimentato(a)) a gas.

gash[gæʃ] *n* sfregio ♦ *vt* sfregiare.

gasket['gæskɪt] *n* (*AUT*) guarnizione *f*.

gas maskn maschera *f* antigas *inv*.

gas metern contatore *m* del gas.

gasoline['gæsəliːn] *n* (*US*) benzina.

gasp[gɑːsp] *vi* ansare, boccheggiare; (*in surprise*) restare senza fiato.

▶**gasp out**vt dire affannosamente.

gas ringn fornello a gas.

gas stationn (*US*) distributore *m* di benzina.

gas stoven cucina a gas.

gassy['gæsɪ] *adj* gassoso(a).

gas tankn (*US AUT*) serbatoio (di benzina).

gas tapn (*on cooker*) manopola del gas; (*on pipe*) rubinetto del gas.

gastric['gæstrɪk] *adj* gastrico(a).

gastric ulcern ulcera gastrica.

gastroenteritis['gæstrəuentə'raɪtɪs] *n* gastroenterite *f*.

gastronomy[gæs'trɒnəmɪ] *n* gastronomia.

gasworks['gæswəːks] *n or npl* impianto di produzione del gas.

gate[geɪt] *n* cancello; (*of castle, town*) porta; (*at airport*) uscita; (*at level crossing*)

barriera.

gâteau,pl ~**x**['gætəu, -z] *n* torta.

gatecrash['geɪtkræʃ] *vt* partecipare senza invito a.

gatecrasher['geɪtkræʃə*] *n* intruso(a), ospite *m/f* non invitato(a).

gatehouse['geɪthaus] *n* casetta del custode (*all'entrata di un parco*).

gateway['geɪtweɪ] *n* porta.

gather['gæðə*] *vt* (*flowers, fruit*) cogliere; (*pick up*) raccogliere; (*assemble*) radunare; raccogliere; (*understand*) capire ♦ *vi* (*assemble*) radunarsi; (*dust*) accumularsi; (*clouds*) addensarsi; **to** ~ **speed** acquistare velocità; **to** ~ (**from/ that**) comprendere (da/che), dedurre (da/che); **as far as I can** ~ da quel che ho potuto capire.

gathering['gæðərɪŋ] *n* adunanza.

GATT[gæt] *n abbr* (= *General Agreement on Tariffs and Trade*) G.A.T.T. *m*.

gauche[gəuʃ] *adj* goffo(a), maldestro(a).

gaudy['gɔːdɪ] *adj* vistoso(a).

gauge[geɪdʒ] *n* (*standard measure*) calibro; (*RAIL*) scartamento; (*instrument*) indicatore *m* ♦ *vt* misurare; (*fig: sb's capabilities, character*) valutare, stimare; **to** ~ **the right moment** calcolare il momento giusto; **petrol** ~, (*US*) **gas** ~ indicatore *m or* spia della benzina.

gaunt[gɔːnt] *adj* scarno(a); (*grim, desolate*) desolato(a).

gauntlet['gɔːntlɪt] *n* (*fig*): **to run the** ~ **through an angry crowd** passare sotto il fuoco di una folla ostile; **to throw down the** ~ gettare il guanto.

gauze[gɔːz] *n* garza.

gave[geɪv] *pt of* **give**.

gawky['gɔːkɪ] *adj* goffo(a), sgraziato(a).

gawp[gɔːp] *vi*: **to** ~ **at** guardare a bocca aperta.

gay[geɪ] *adj* (*person*) gaio(a), allegro(a); (*colour*) vivace, vivo(a); (*col*) omosessuale.

gaze[geɪz] *n* sguardo fisso ♦ *vi*: **to** ~ **at** guardare fisso.

gazelle[gə'zɛl] *n* gazzella.

gazette[gə'zɛt] *n* (*newspaper*) gazzetta; (*official publication*) gazzetta ufficiale.

gazetteer[gæzə'tɪə*] *n* (*book*) dizionario dei nomi geografici; (*section of book*) indice *m* dei nomi geografici.

gazump[gə'zʌmp] *vt* (*BRIT*): **to** ~ **sb** *nella compravendita di immobili, venire meno all'impegno preso con un acquirente accettando un'offerta migliore fatta da altri*.

GBabbr (= *Great Britain*) GB.

GBHn abbr (BRIT LAW: col) see **grievous bodily harm.**

GCn abbr (BRIT: = George Cross) decorazione al valore.

GCEn abbr (BRIT: = General Certificate of Education) ≈ diploma m di maturità.

GCHQn abbr (BRIT: = Government Communications Headquarters) centro per l'intercettazione delle telecomunicazioni straniere.

GCSEn abbr (BRIT: = General Certificate of Secondary Education) diploma di istruzione secondaria conseguito a 16 anni in Inghilterra e Galles.

Gdns.abbr = gardens.

GDPn abbr = **gross domestic product.**

GDRn abbr (HIST) see **German Democratic Republic.**

gear[gɪə*] n attrezzi mpl, equipaggiamento; (belongings) roba; (TECH) ingranaggio; (AUT) marcia ♦ vt (fig: adapt) adattare; **top** or (US) **high/low/ bottom** ~ quarta (or quinta)/ seconda/ prima; **in** ~ in marcia; **out of** ~ in folle; **our service is** ~ **ed to meet the needs of the disabled** la nostra organizzazione risponde espressamente alle esigenze degli handicappati.

▶**gear up**vi: **to** ~ **up (to do)** prepararsi (a fare).

gear boxn scatola del cambio.

gear lever,(US) **gear shift**n leva del cambio.

GEDn abbr (US SCOL) = general educational development.

geese[giːs] npl of **goose.**

geezer['giːzə*] n (BRIT col) tizio.

Geiger counter['gaɪgə-] n geiger m inv.

gel[dʒɛl] n gel m inv.

gelatin(e)['dʒɛlətiːn] n gelatina.

gelignite['dʒɛlɪgnaɪt] n nitroglicerina.

gem[dʒɛm] n gemma.

Gemini['dʒɛmɪnaɪ] n Gemelli mpl; **to be** ~ essere dei Gemelli.

gen[dʒɛn] n (BRIT col): **to give sb the** ~ **on sth** mettere qn al corrente di qc.

Gen.abbr (MIL: = General) Gen.

gen.abbr (= general, generally) gen.

gender['dʒɛndə*] n genere m.

gene[dʒiːn] n (BIOL) gene m.

genealogy[dʒiːnɪ'ælədʒɪ] n genealogia.

general['dʒɛnərl] n generale m ♦ adj generale; **in** ~ in genere; **the** ~ **public** il grande pubblico.

general anaestheticn anestesia totale.

general deliveryn (US) fermo posta m.

general electionn elezioni fpl generali.

generalization['dʒɛnrəlaɪ'zeɪʃən] n

generalizzazione f.

generalize['dʒɛnrəlaɪz] vi generalizzare.

generally['dʒɛnrəlɪ] adv generalmente.

general managern direttore m generale.

general practitioner (GP)n medico generico; **who's your GP?** qual è il suo medico di fiducia?

general striken sciopero generale.

generate['dʒɛnəreɪt] vt generare.

generation[dʒɛnə'reɪʃən] n generazione f; (of electricity etc) produzione f.

generator['dʒɛnəreɪtə*] n generatore m.

generic[dʒɪ'nɛrɪk] adj generico(a).

generosity[dʒɛnə'rɔsɪtɪ] n generosità.

generous['dʒɛnərəs] adj generoso(a); (copious) abbondante.

genesis['dʒɛnɪsɪs] n genesi f.

genetic[dʒɪ'nɛtɪk] adj genetico(a); ~ **engineering** ingegneria genetica.

genetically modified[dʒɪ'nɛtɪklɪ 'mɔdɪfaɪd] adj geneticamente modificato(a), transgenico(a); ~ **organism** organismo geneticamente modificato.

genetic fingerprinting[-fɪŋgəprɪntɪŋ] n rilevamento delle impronte genetiche.

genetics[dʒɪ'nɛtɪks] n genetica.

Geneva[dʒɪ'niːvə] n Ginevra; **Lake** ~ il lago di Ginevra.

genial['dʒiːnɪəl] adj geniale, cordiale.

genitals['dʒɛnɪtlz] npl genitali mpl.

genitive['dʒɛnɪtɪv] n genitivo.

genius['dʒiːnɪəs] n genio.

Genoa['dʒɛnəuə] n Genova.

genocide[dʒɛnəusaɪd] n genocidio.

Genoese[dʒɛnəu'iːz] adj, n (pl inv) genovese (m/f).

gent[dʒɛnt] n abbr (BRIT col) = **gentleman.**

genteel[dʒɛn'tiːl] adj raffinato(a), distinto(a).

gentle['dʒɛntl] adj delicato(a); (person) dolce.

gentleman['dʒɛntlmən] n signore m; (well-bred man) gentiluomo; ~**'s agreement** impegno sulla parola.

gentlemanly['dʒɛntlmənlɪ] adj da gentiluomo.

gentleness['dʒɛntlnɪs] n delicatezza; dolcezza.

gently['dʒɛntlɪ] adv delicatamente.

gentry['dʒɛntrɪ] n nobiltà minore.

gents[dʒɛnts] n W.C. m (per signori).

genuine['dʒɛnjuɪn] adj autentico(a); sincero(a).

genuinely['dʒɛnjuɪnlɪ] adv genuinamente.

geographer[dʒɪ'ɔgrəfə*] n geografo/a.

geographic(al) [dʒɪə'græfɪk(l)] *adj* geografico(a).

geography [dʒɪ'ɔgrəfɪ] *n* geografia.

geological [dʒɪə'lɔdʒɪkl] *adj* geologico(a).

geologist [dʒɪ'ɔlədʒɪst] *n* geologo/a.

geology [dʒɪ'ɔlədʒɪ] *n* geologia.

geometric(al) [dʒɪə'mɛtrɪk(l)] *adj* geometrico(a).

geometry [dʒɪ'ɔmətrɪ] *n* geometria.

Geordie ['dʒɔːdɪ] *n (col)* abitante *m/f* del Tyneside; originario/a del Tyneside.

Georgia ['dʒɔːdʒə] *n* Georgia.

Georgian ['dʒɔːdʒən] *adj* georgiano(a) ♦ *n* georgiano/a; (*LING*) georgiano.

geranium [dʒɪ'reɪnɪəm] *n* geranio.

geriatric [dʒɛrɪ'ætrɪk] *adj* geriatrico(a).

germ [dʒəːm] *n (MED)* microbo; (*BIOL, fig*) germe *m*.

German ['dʒəːmən] *adj* tedesco(a) ♦ *n* tedesco/a; (*LING*) tedesco.

German Democratic Republic (GDR) *n* Repubblica Democratica Tedesca (R.D.T.).

germane [dʒəː'meɪn] *adj (formal)*: **to be ~ to sth** essere attinente a qc.

German measles *n* rosolia.

Germany ['dʒəːmənɪ] *n* Germania.

germination [dʒəːmɪ'neɪʃən] *n* germinazione *f*.

germ warfare *n* guerra batteriologica.

gerrymandering ['dʒɛrɪmændərɪŋ] *n* manipolazione *f* dei distretti elettorali.

gestation [dʒɛs'teɪʃən] *n* gestazione *f*.

gesticulate [dʒɛs'tɪkjuleɪt] *vi* gesticolare.

gesture ['dʒɛstjə*] *n* gesto; **as a ~ of friendship** in segno d'amicizia.

============== *KEYWORD*

get [gɛt] (*pt, pp* **got**, (*US*) *pp* **gotten**) *vi* **1** (*become, be*) diventare, farsi; **to ~ drunk** ubriacarsi; **to ~ killed** venire *or* rimanere ucciso(a); **it's ~ting late** si sta facendo tardi; **to ~ old** invecchiare; **to ~ paid** venire pagato(a); **to ~ ready** prepararsi; **to ~ shaved** farsi la barba; **to ~ tired** stancarsi; **to ~ washed** lavarsi

2 (*go*): **to ~ to/from** andare a/da; **to ~ home** arrivare *or* tornare a casa; **how did you ~ here?** come sei venuto?; **he got across the bridge** ha attraversato il ponte; **he got under the fence** è passato sotto il recinto

3 (*begin*) mettersi a, cominciare a; **to ~ to know sb** incominciare a conoscere qn; **let's ~ going** *or* **started** muoviamoci

4 (*modal aux vb*): **you've got to do it** devi farlo

♦ *vt* **1**: **to ~ sth done** (*do*) fare qc; (*have done*) far fare qc; **to ~ sth/sb ready** preparare qc/qn; **to ~ one's hair cut** tagliarsi *or* farsi tagliare i capelli; **to ~ sb to do sth** far fare qc a qn

2 (*obtain*: *money, permission, results*) ottenere; (*find*: *job, flat*) trovare; (*fetch*: *person, doctor*) chiamare; (: *object*) prendere; **to ~ sth for sb** prendere *or* procurare qc a qn; **~ me Mr Jones, please** (*TEL*) mi passi il signor Jones, per favore; **can I ~ you a drink?** le posso offrire da bere?

3 (*receive*: *present, letter, prize*) ricevere; (*acquire*: *reputation*) farsi; **how much did you ~ for the painting?** quanto le hanno dato per il quadro?

4 (*catch*) prendere; (*hit*: *target etc*) colpire; **to ~ sb by the arm/throat** afferrare qn per un braccio/alla gola; **~ him!** prendetelo!; **he really ~s me** (*fig*: *annoy*) mi dà proprio sui nervi

5 (*take, move*) portare; **to ~ sth to sb** far avere qc a qn; **do you think we'll ~ it through the door?** pensi che riusciremo a farlo passare per la porta?

6 (*catch, take*: *plane, bus etc*) prendere; **he got the last bus** ha preso l'ultimo autobus; **she got the morning flight to Milan** ha preso il volo per Milano del mattino

7 (*understand*) afferrare; (*hear*) sentire; **I've got it!** ci sono arrivato!, ci sono!; **I'm sorry, I didn't ~ your name** scusi, non ho capito (*or* sentito) come si chiama

8 (*have, possess*): **to have got** avere; **how many have you got?** quanti ne ha?

▶**get about** *vi* muoversi; (*news*) diffondersi

▶**get across** *vt*: **to ~ across (to)** (*message, meaning*) comunicare (a) ♦ *vi*: **to ~ across to** (*subj*: *speaker*) comunicare con

▶**get along** *vi* (*agree*) andare d'accordo; (*depart*) andarsene; (*manage*) = **get by**

▶**get at** *vt fus* (*attack*) prendersela con; (*reach*) raggiungere, arrivare a; **what are you ~ting at?** dove vuoi arrivare?

▶**get away** *vi* partire, andarsene; (*escape*) scappare

▶**get away with** *vt fus*: **he'll never ~ away with it!** non riuscirà a farla franca!

▶**get back** *vi* (*return*) ritornare, tornare ♦ *vt* riottenere, riavere; **to ~ back to** (*start again*) ritornare a; (*contact again*) rimettersi in contatto con

▶**get back at** *vt fus* (*col*): **to ~ back at sb (for sth)** rendere pan per focaccia a qn

(per qc)

▶ **get by** vi (pass) passare; (manage) farcela; **I can ~ by in Dutch** mi arrango in olandese

▶ **get down** vi, vt fus scendere ♦ vt far scendere; (depress) buttare giù

▶ **get down to** vt fus (work) mettersi a (fare); **to ~ down to business** venire al dunque

▶ **get in** vi entrare; (train) arrivare; (arrive home) ritornare, tornare ♦ vt (bring in: harvest) raccogliere; (: coal, shopping, supplies) fare provvista di; (insert) far entrare, infilare

▶ **get into** vt fus entrare in; **to ~ into a rage** incavolarsi; **to ~ into bed** mettersi a letto

▶ **get off** vi (from train etc) scendere; (depart: person, car) andare via; (escape) cavarsela ♦ vt (remove: clothes, stain) levare; (send off) spedire; (have as leave: days, time): **we got 2 days off** abbiamo avuto 2 giorni liberi ♦ vt fus (train, bus) scendere da; **to ~ off to a good start** (fig) cominciare bene

▶ **get on** vi: **how did you ~ on?** com'è andata?; **he got on quite well** ha fatto bene, (gli) è andata bene; **to ~ on (with sb)** andare d'accordo (con qn); **how are you ~ting on?** come va la vita? ♦ vt fus montare in; (horse) montare su

▶ **get on to** vt fus (BRIT col: contact: on phone etc) contattare, rintracciare; (: deal with) occuparsi di

▶ **get out** vi uscire; (of vehicle) scendere ♦ vt tirar fuori, far uscire; **to ~ out (of)** (money from bank etc) ritirare (da)

▶ **get out of** vt fus uscire da; (duty etc) evitare; **what will you ~ out of it?** cosa ci guadagni?

▶ **get over** vt fus (illness) riaversi da; (communicate: idea etc) comunicare, passare; **let's ~ it over (with)** togliamoci il pensiero

▶ **get round** vt fus aggirare; (fig: person) rigirare ♦ vi: **to ~ round to doing sth** trovare il tempo di fare qc

▶ **get through** vi (TEL) avere la linea ♦ vt fus (finish: work) sbrigare; (: book) finire

▶ **get through to** vt fus (TEL) parlare a

▶ **get together** vi riunirsi ♦ vt raccogliere; (people) adunare

▶ **get up** vi (rise) alzarsi ♦ vt fus salire su per

▶ **get up to** vt fus (reach) raggiungere; (prank etc) fare.

getaway ['gɛtəweɪ] n fuga.
getaway car n macchina per la fuga.

get-together ['gɛttəgɛðə*] n (piccola) riunione f; (party) festicciola.
get-up ['gɛtʌp] n (col: outfit) tenuta.
get-well card [gɛt'wɛl-] n cartolina di auguri di pronta guarigione.
geyser ['giːzə*] n scaldabagno; (GEO) geyser m inv.
Ghana ['gɑːnə] n Ghana m.
Ghanaian [gɑː'neɪən] adj, n ganaense (m/f).
ghastly ['gɑːstlɪ] adj orribile, orrendo(a).
gherkin ['gəːkɪn] n cetriolino.
ghetto ['gɛtəu] n ghetto.
ghetto blaster [-'blɑːstə*] n maxistereo portatile.
ghost [gəust] n fantasma m, spettro ♦ vt (book) fare lo scrittore ombra per.
ghostly ['gəustlɪ] adj spettrale.
ghostwriter ['gəustraɪtə*] n scrittore/trice ombra inv.
ghoul [guːl] n vampiro che si nutre di cadaveri.
ghoulish ['guːlɪʃ] adj (tastes etc) macabro(a).
GHQ n abbr (MIL: = general headquarters) ≈ comando di Stato maggiore.
GI n abbr (US col: = government issue) G.I. m, soldato americano.
giant ['dʒaɪənt] n gigante/essa ♦ adj gigante, enorme; **~ (size) packet** confezione f gigante.
giant killer n (SPORT) piccola squadra che riesce a batterne una importante.
gibber ['dʒɪbə*] vi (monkey) squittire confusamente; (idiot) farfugliare.
gibberish ['dʒɪbərɪʃ] n parole fpl senza senso.
gibe [dʒaɪb] n frecciata ♦ vi: **to ~ at** lanciare frecciate a.
giblets ['dʒɪblɪts] npl frattaglie fpl.
Gibraltar [dʒɪ'brɔːltə*] n Gibilterra.
giddiness ['gɪdɪnɪs] n vertigine f.
giddy ['gɪdɪ] adj (dizzy): **to be ~** aver le vertigini; (height) vertiginoso(a); **I feel ~** mi gira la testa.
gift [gɪft] n regalo, dono; (donation, ability) dono; (COMM: also: **free ~**) omaggio; **to have a ~ for sth** (talent) avere il dono di qc.
gifted ['gɪftɪd] adj dotato(a).
gift token, gift voucher n buono (acquisto).
gig [gɪg] n (col: of musician) serata.
gigabyte [giːgəbaɪt] n gigabyte m inv.
gigantic [dʒaɪ'gæntɪk] adj gigantesco(a).
giggle ['gɪgl] vi ridere scioccamente ♦ n risolino (sciocco).
GIGO ['gaɪgəu] abbr (COMPUT: col: = garbage in, garbage out) qualità di input = qualità di output.

gild [gɪld] vt dorare.
gill [dʒɪl] n (measure) = 0.25 pints (BRIT = 0.148 l; US = 0.118 l).
gills [gɪlz] npl (of fish) branchie fpl.
gilt [gɪlt] n doratura ♦ adj dorato(a).
gilt-edged ['gɪltɛdʒd] adj (stocks, securities) della massima sicurezza.
gimlet ['gɪmlɪt] n succhiello.
gimmick ['gɪmɪk] n trucco; sales ~ trovata commerciale.
gin [dʒɪn] n (liquor) gin m inv.
ginger ['dʒɪndʒə*] n zenzero.
►ginger up vt scuotere; animare.
ginger ale, ginger beer n bibita gassosa allo zenzero.
gingerbread ['dʒɪndʒəbrɛd] n pan m di zenzero.
ginger group n (BRIT) gruppo di pressione.
ginger-haired ['dʒɪndʒə'hɛəd] adj rossiccio(a).
gingerly ['dʒɪndʒəlɪ] adv cautamente.
gingham ['gɪŋəm] n percalle m a righe (or quadretti).
ginseng ['dʒɪnsɛŋ] n ginseng m.
gipsy ['dʒɪpsɪ] n zingaro/a ♦ adj degli zingari.
giraffe [dʒɪ'rɑːf] n giraffa.
girder ['gɜːdə*] n trave f.
girdle ['gɜːdl] n (corset) guaina.
girl [gɜːl] n ragazza; (young unmarried woman) signorina; (daughter) figlia, figliola; a little ~ una bambina.
girl band n gruppo pop di sole ragazze creato per far presa su un pubblico giovane.
girlfriend ['gɜːlfrɛnd] n (of girl) amica; (of boy) ragazza.
girlish ['gɜːlɪʃ] adj da ragazza.
Girl Scout n (US) Giovane Esploratrice f.
Giro ['dʒaɪrəu] n: the National ~ (BRIT) ≈ la or il Bancoposta.
giro ['dʒaɪrəu] n (bank ~) versamento bancario; (post office ~) postagiro.
girth [gɜːθ] n circonferenza; (of horse) cinghia.
gist [dʒɪst] n succo.
give [gɪv] n (of fabric) elasticità ♦ vb (pt gave, pp given [geɪv, 'gɪvn]) vt dare ♦ vi cedere; to ~ sb sth, to ~ sth to sb dare qc a qn; to ~ a cry/sigh emettere un grido/ sospiro; how much did you ~ for it? quanto (l')hai pagato?; 12 o'clock, ~ or take a few minutes mezzogiorno, minuto più minuto meno; to ~ way vi cedere; (BRIT AUT) dare la precedenza.
►give away vt dare via; (give free) fare dono di; (betray) tradire; (disclose)

rivelare; (bride) condurre all'altare.
►give back vt rendere.
►give in vi cedere ♦ vt consegnare.
►give off vt emettere.
►give out vt distribuire; annunciare ♦ vi (be exhausted: supplies) esaurirsi, venir meno; (fail: engine) fermarsi; (: strength) mancare.
►give up vi rinunciare ♦ vt rinunciare a; to ~ up smoking smettere di fumare; to ~ o.s. up arrendersi.
give-and-take [gɪvən'teɪk] n (col) elasticità (da ambo le parti), concessioni fpl reciproche.
giveaway ['gɪvəweɪ] n (col): her expression was a ~ le si leggeva tutto in volto; the exam was a ~! l'esame è stato uno scherzo! ♦ cpd: ~ prices prezzi stracciati.
given ['gɪvn] pp of give ♦ adj (fixed: time, amount) dato(a), determinato(a) ♦ conj: ~ (that) ... dato che ...; ~ the circumstances ... date le circostanze ....
glacial ['gleɪsɪəl] adj glaciale.
glacier ['glæsɪə*] n ghiacciaio.
glad [glæd] adj lieto(a), contento(a); to be ~ about sth/that essere contento or lieto di qc/che + sub; I was ~ of his help gli sono stato grato del suo aiuto.
gladden ['glædn] vt rallegrare, allietare.
glade [gleɪd] n radura.
gladioli [glædɪ'əulaɪ] npl gladioli mpl.
gladly ['glædlɪ] adv volentieri.
glamorous ['glæmərəs] adj (gen) favoloso(a); (person) affascinante, seducente; (occasion) brillante, elegante.
glamour ['glæmə*] n fascino.
glance [glɑːns] n occhiata, sguardo ♦ vi: to ~ at dare un'occhiata a.
►glance off vt fus (bullet) rimbalzare su.
glancing ['glɑːnsɪŋ] adj (blow) che colpisce di striscio.
gland [glænd] n ghiandola.
glandular ['glændjulə*] adj: ~ fever (BRIT) mononucleosi f.
glare [glɛə*] n riverbero, luce f abbagliante; (look) sguardo furioso ♦ vi abbagliare; to ~ at guardare male.
glaring ['glɛərɪŋ] adj (mistake) madornale.
glasnost ['glæznɔst] n glasnost f.
glass [glɑːs] n (substance) vetro; (tumbler) bicchiere m; (also: looking ~) specchio; see also glasses.
glass-blowing ['glɑːsbləuɪŋ] n soffiatura del vetro.
glass ceiling n (fig) barriera invisibile.
glasses ['glɑːsɪz] npl (spectacles) occhiali mpl.
glass fibre n fibra di vetro.

glasshouse ['glɑːshaus] n serra.
glassware ['glɑːswɛə*] n vetrame m.
glassy ['glɑːsɪ] adj (eyes) vitreo(a).
Glaswegian [glæs'wiːdʒən] adj di Glasgow ◊ n abitante m/f di Glasgow; originario/a di Glasgow.
glaze [gleɪz] vt (door) fornire di vetri; (pottery) smaltare; (CULIN) glassare ◊ n smalto; glassa.
glazed ['gleɪzd] adj (eye) vitreo(a); (tiles, pottery) smaltato(a).
glazier ['gleɪzɪə*] n vetraio.
gleam [gliːm] n barlume m; raggio ◊ vi luccicare; a ~ of hope un barlume di speranza.
gleaming ['gliːmɪŋ] adj lucente.
glean [gliːn] vt (information) racimolare.
glee [gliː] n allegrezza, gioia.
gleeful ['gliːful] adj allegro(a), gioioso(a).
glen [glɛn] n valletta.
glib [glɪb] adj dalla parola facile; facile.
glide [glaɪd] vi scivolare; (AVIAT, birds) planare ◊ n scivolata; planata.
glider ['glaɪdə*] n (AVIAT) aliante m.
gliding ['glaɪdɪŋ] n (AVIAT) volo a vela.
glimmer ['glɪmə*] vi luccicare ◊ n barlume m.
glimpse [glɪmps] n impressione f fugace ◊ vt vedere di sfuggita; to catch a ~ of vedere di sfuggita.
glint [glɪnt] n luccichio ◊ vi luccicare.
glisten ['glɪsn] vi luccicare.
glitter ['glɪtə*] vi scintillare ◊ n scintillio.
glitz [glɪts] n (col) vistosità, chiassosità.
gloat [gləʊt] vi: to ~ (over) gongolare di piacere (per).
global ['gləʊbl] adj globale; (world-wide) mondiale.
global warming n riscaldamento dell'atmosfera terrestre.
globe [gləʊb] n globo, sfera.
globetrotter ['gləʊbtrɔtə*] n giramondo m/f inv.
globule ['glɔbjuːl] n (ANAT) globulo; (of water etc) gocciolina.
gloom [gluːm] n oscurità, buio; (sadness) tristezza, malinconia.
gloomy ['gluːmɪ] adj fosco(a), triste; to feel ~ sentirsi giù or depresso.
glorification [glɔːrɪfɪ'keɪʃən] n glorificazione f.
glorify ['glɔːrɪfaɪ] vt glorificare; celebrare, esaltare.
glorious ['glɔːrɪəs] adj glorioso(a); magnifico(a).
glory ['glɔːrɪ] n gloria; splendore m ◊ vi: to ~ in gloriarsi di or in.
glory hole n (col) ripostiglio.

Glos abbr (BRIT) = Gloucestershire.
gloss [glɔs] n (shine) lucentezza; (also: ~ paint) vernice f a olio.
▶**gloss over** vt fus scivolare su.
glossary ['glɔsərɪ] n glossario.
glossy ['glɔsɪ] adj lucente ◊ n (also: ~ magazine) rivista di lusso.
glove [glʌv] n guanto.
glove compartment n (AUT) vano portaoggetti.
glow [gləʊ] vi ardere; (face) essere luminoso(a) ◊ n bagliore m; (of face) colorito acceso.
glower ['glauə*] vi: to ~ (at sb) guardare (qn) in cagnesco.
glowing ['gləʊɪŋ] adj (fire) ardente; (complexion) luminoso(a); (fig: report, description etc) entusiasta.
glow-worm ['gləʊwəːm] n lucciola.
glucose ['gluːkəʊs] n glucosio.
glue [gluː] n colla ◊ vt incollare.
glue-sniffing ['gluːsnɪfɪŋ] n sniffare m (colla).
glum [glʌm] adj abbattuto(a).
glut [glʌt] n eccesso ◊ vt saziare; (market) saturare.
glutinous ['gluːtɪnəs] adj colloso(a), appiccicoso(a).
glutton ['glʌtn] n ghiottone/a; a ~ for work un(a) patito(a) del lavoro.
gluttonous ['glʌtənəs] adj ghiotto(a), goloso(a).
gluttony ['glʌtənɪ] n ghiottoneria; (sin) gola.
glycerin(e) ['glɪsəriːn] n glicerina.
GM adj abbr = genetically modified.
gm abbr = gram.
GMAT n abbr (US: = Graduate Management Admissions Test) esame di ammissione all'ultimo biennio di scuola superiore.
GM-free [dʒiːɛm'friː] adj privo(a) di OGM.
GMO n abbr (= genetically modified organism) OGM m inv.
GMT abbr (= Greenwich Mean Time) T.M.G.
gnarled [nɑːld] adj nodoso(a).
gnash [næʃ] vt: to ~ one's teeth digrignare i denti.
gnat [næt] n moscerino.
gnaw [nɔː] vt rodere.
gnome [nəʊm] n gnomo.
GNP n abbr = gross national product.
go [gəʊ] vb (pt went, pp gone [wɛnt, gɔn]) vi andare; (depart) partire, andarsene; (work) funzionare; (break etc) cedere; (be sold): to ~ for £10 essere venduto per 10 sterline; (fit, suit): to ~ with andare bene con; (become): to ~ pale diventare pallido(a); to ~ mouldy ammuffire ◊ n (pl

~es): to have a ~ (at) provare; to be on the ~ essere in moto; whose ~ is it? a chi tocca?; to ~ by car/on foot andare in macchina/a piedi; he's ~ing to do sta per fare; to ~ for a walk andare a fare una passeggiata; to ~ dancing/shopping andare a ballare/fare la spesa; to ~ looking for sb/sth andare in cerca di qn/ qc; to ~ to sleep addormentarsi; to ~ and see sb, to ~ to see sb andare a trovare qn; how is it ~ing? come va (la vita)?; how did it ~? com'è andato?; to ~ round the back/by the shop passare da dietro/ davanti al negozio; my voice has gone m'è andata via la voce; the cake is all gone il dolce è finito tutto; I'll take whatever is ~ing (BRIT) prendo quello che c'è; ... to ~ (US: food) ... da portar via; the money will ~ towards our holiday questi soldi li mettiamo per la vacanza.

▶go about vi (also: ~ around) aggirarsi; (: rumour) correre, circolare ♦ vt fus: how do I ~ about this? qual è la prassi per questo?; to ~ about one's business occuparsi delle proprie faccende.

▶go after vt fus (pursue) correr dietro a, rincorrere; (job, record etc) mirare a.

▶go against vt fus (be unfavourable to) essere contro; (be contrary to) andare contro.

▶go ahead vi andare avanti; ~ ahead! faccia pure!

▶go along vi andare, avanzare ♦ vt fus percorrere; to ~ along with (accompany) andare con, accompagnare; (agree with: idea) sottoscrivere, appoggiare.

▶go away vi partire, andarsene.

▶go back vi tornare, ritornare; (go again) andare di nuovo.

▶go back on vt fus (promise) non mantenere.

▶go by vi (years, time) scorrere ♦ vt fus attenersi a, seguire (alla lettera); prestar fede a.

▶go down vi scendere; (ship) affondare; (sun) tramontare ♦ vt fus scendere; that should ~ down well with him dovrebbe incontrare la sua approvazione.

▶go for vt fus (fetch) andare a prendere; (like) andar matto(a) per; (attack) attaccare; saltare addosso a.

▶go in vi entrare.

▶go in for vt fus (competition) iscriversi a; (be interested in) interessarsi di.

▶go into vt fus entrare in; (investigate) indagare, esaminare; (embark on) lanciarsi in.

▶go off vi partire, andar via; (food)

guastarsi; (explode) esplodere, scoppiare; (lights etc) spegnersi; (event) passare ♦ vt fus: I've gone off chocolate la cioccolata non mi piace più; the gun went off il fucile si scaricò; the party went off well la festa è andata or è riuscita bene; to ~ off to sleep addormentarsi.

▶go on vi continuare; (happen) succedere; (lights) accendersi ♦ vt fus (be guided by: evidence etc) basarsi su, fondarsi su; to ~ on doing continuare a fare; what's ~ing on here? che succede or che sta succedendo qui?

▶go on at vt fus (nag) assillare.

▶go on with vt fus continuare, proseguire.

▶go out vi uscire; (fire, light) spegnersi; (ebb: tide) calare; to ~ out with sb uscire con qn.

▶go over vi (ship) ribaltarsi ♦ vt fus (check) esaminare; to ~ over sth in one's mind pensare bene a qc.

▶go round vi (circulate: news, rumour) circolare; (revolve) girare; (visit): to ~ round (to sb's) passare (da qn); (make a detour): to ~ round (by) passare (per); (suffice) bastare (per tutti).

▶go through vt fus (town etc) attraversare; (search through) frugare in; (examine: list, book) leggere da capo a fondo; (perform) fare.

▶go through with vt fus (plan, crime) mettere in atto, eseguire; I couldn't ~ through with it non sono riuscito ad andare fino in fondo.

▶go under vi (sink: ship) affondare, colare a picco; (: person) andare sotto; (fig: business, firm) fallire.

▶go up vi salire ♦ vt fus salire su per; to ~ up in flames andare in fiamme.

▶go without vt fus fare a meno di.

goad [gəud] vt spronare.

go-ahead ['gəuəhɛd] adj intraprendente ♦ n: to give sb/sth the ~ dare l'okay a qn/ qc.

goal [gəul] n (SPORT) gol m, rete f; (: place) porta; (fig: aim) fine m, scopo.

goal difference n differenza f reti inv.

goalie ['gəulɪ] n (col) portiere m.

goalkeeper ['gəulkiːpə*] n portiere m.

goalpost ['gəulpəust] n palo (della porta).

goat [gəut] n capra.

gobble ['gɔbl] vt (also: ~ down, ~ up) ingoiare.

go-between ['gəubɪtwiːn] n intermediario/ a.

Gobi Desert ['gəubɪ-] n: the ~ il Deserto dei Gobi.

goblet ['gɔblɪt] n calice m, coppa.

goblin ['gɔblɪn] n folletto.
go-cart ['gəʊkɑːt] n go-kart m inv ♦ cpd: ~ **racing** n kartismo.
god [gɔd] n dio; **G~** Dio.
god-awful [gɔd'ɔːfəl] adj (col) di merda (!).
godchild ['gɔdtʃaɪld] n figlioccio/a.
goddamn(ed) ['gɔddæm(d)] (esp US: col) excl: **goddamn!** porca miseria! ♦ adj fottuto(a) (!), maledetto(a) ♦ adv maledettamente.
goddaughter ['gɔddɔːtə*] n figlioccia.
goddess ['gɔdɪs] n dea.
godfather ['gɔdfɑːðə*] n padrino.
god-fearing ['gɔdfɪərɪŋ] adj timorato(a) di Dio.
god-forsaken ['gɔdfəseɪkən] adj desolato(a), sperduto(a).
godmother ['gɔdmʌðə*] n madrina.
godparents ['gɔdpɛərənts] npl: **the** ~ il padrino e la madrina.
godsend ['gɔdsɛnd] n dono del cielo.
godson ['gɔdsʌn] n figlioccio.
goes [gəʊz] vb see **go**.
gofer ['gəʊfə*] n (col) tuttofare m/f, tirapiedi m/f inv.
go-getter ['gəʊgɛtə*] n arrivista m/f.
goggle ['gɔgl] vi: **to** ~ **(at)** stare con gli occhi incollati or appiccicati (a or addosso a).
goggles ['gɔglz] npl occhiali mpl (di protezione).
going ['gəʊɪŋ] n (conditions) andare m, stato del terreno ♦ adj: **the** ~ **rate** la tariffa in vigore; a ~ **concern** un'azienda avviata; **it was slow** ~ si andava a rilento.
going-over [gəʊɪŋ'əʊvə*] n (col) controllata; (violent attack) pestaggio.
goings-on ['gəʊɪŋz'ɔn] npl (col) fatti mpl strani, cose fpl strane.
go-kart ['gəʊkɑːt] n = **go-cart**.
gold [gəʊld] n oro ♦ adj d'oro; (reserves) aureo(a).
golden ['gəʊldən] adj (made of gold) d'oro; (gold in colour) dorato(a).
golden age n età d'oro.
golden handshake n (BRIT) gratifica di fine servizio.
golden rule n regola principale.
goldfish ['gəʊldfɪʃ] n pesce m dorato or rosso.
gold leaf n lamina d'oro.
gold medal n (SPORT) medaglia d'oro.
goldmine ['gəʊldmaɪn] n miniera d'oro.
gold-plated ['gəʊld'pleɪtɪd] adj placcato(a) oro inv.
goldsmith ['gəʊldsmɪθ] n orefice m, orafo.
gold standard n tallone m aureo.
golf [gɔlf] n golf m.

golf ball n pallina da golf.
golf club n circolo di golf; (stick) bastone m or mazza da golf.
golf course n campo di golf.
golfer ['gɔlfə*] n giocatore/trice di golf.
golfing ['gɔlfɪŋ] n il giocare a golf.
gondola ['gɔndələ] n gondola.
gondolier [gɔndə'lɪə*] n gondoliere m.
gone [gɔn] pp of **go**.
goner ['gɔnə*] n (col): **I thought you were a** ~ pensavo che ormai fossi spacciato.
gong [gɔŋ] n gong m inv.
good [gud] adj buono(a); (kind) buono(a), gentile; (child) bravo(a) ♦ n bene m; ~! bene!, ottimo!; **to be** ~ **at** essere bravo(a) in; **it's** ~ **for you** fa bene; **it's a** ~ **thing you were there** meno male che c'era; **she is** ~ **with children/her hands** ci sa fare coi bambini/è abile nei lavori manuali; **to feel** ~ sentirsi bene; **it's** ~ **to see you** che piacere vederla; **he's up to no** ~ ne sta combinando qualcuna; **it's no** ~ **complaining** brontolare non serve a niente; **for the common** ~ nell'interesse generale, per il bene comune; **for** ~ (for ever) per sempre, definitivamente; **would you be** ~ **enough to ...?** avrebbe la gentilezza di ...?; **that's very** ~ **of you** è molto gentile da parte sua; **is this any** ~? (will it do?) va bene questo?; (what's it like?) com'è?; **a** ~ **deal (of)** molto(a), una buona quantità (di); **a** ~ **many** molti(e); ~ **morning!** buon giorno!; ~ **afternoon/evening!** buona sera!; ~ **night!** buona notte!; see also **goods**.
goodbye [gud'baɪ] excl arrivederci!; **to say** ~ **to** (person) salutare.
good faith n buona fede.
good-for-nothing ['gudfənʌθɪŋ] n buono/a a nulla, vagabondo/a.
Good Friday n Venerdì Santo.
good-humoured [gud'hjuːməd] adj (person) di buon umore; (remark, joke) bonario(a).
good-looking [gud'lukɪŋ] adj bello(a).
good-natured [gud'neɪtʃəd] adj (person) affabile; (discussion) amichevole, cordiale.
goodness ['gudnɪs] n (of person) bontà; **for** ~ **sake!** per amor di Dio!; ~ **gracious!** santo cielo!, mamma mia!
goods [gudz] npl (COMM etc) merci fpl, articoli mpl; ~ **and chattels** beni mpl e effetti mpl.
goods train n (BRIT) treno m merci inv.
goodwill [gud'wɪl] n amicizia, benevolenza; (COMM) avviamento.
goody-goody ['gudɪgudɪ] n (pej)

santarellino/a.
gooey ['guːɪ] *adj* (*BRIT col*: sticky) appiccicoso(a); (*cake, dessert*) troppo zuccherato(a).
goose, *pl* **geese** [guːs, giːs] *n* oca.
gooseberry ['guzbərɪ] *n* uva spina; **to play** ~ (*BRIT*) tenere la candela.
gooseflesh ['guːsflɛʃ] *n*, **goosepimples** ['guːspɪmplz] *npl* pelle *f* d'oca.
goose step *n* (*MIL*) passo dell'oca.
GOP *n abbr* (*US POL: col*: = Grand Old Party) partito repubblicano.
gopher ['gəufə*] *n* = **gofer**.
gore [gɔː*] *vt* incornare ♦ *n* sangue *m* (coagulato).
gorge [gɔːdʒ] *n* gola ♦ *vt*: **to** ~ **o.s. (on)** ingozzarsi (di).
gorgeous ['gɔːdʒəs] *adj* magnifico(a).
gorilla [gə'rɪlə] *n* gorilla *m inv*.
gormless ['gɔːmlɪs] *adj* (*BRIT col*) tonto(a); (: *stronger*) deficiente.
gorse [gɔːs] *n* ginestrone *m*.
gory ['gɔːrɪ] *adj* sanguinoso(a).
go-slow ['gəu'sləu] *n* (*BRIT*) rallentamento dei lavori (*per agitazione sindacale*).
gospel ['gɔspl] *n* vangelo.
gossamer ['gɔsəmə*] *n* (*cobweb*) fili *mpl* della Madonna *or* di ragnatela; (*light fabric*) stoffa sottilissima.
gossip ['gɔsɪp] *n* chiacchiere *fpl*; pettegolezzi *mpl*; (*person*) pettegolo/a ♦ *vi* chiacchierare; (*maliciously*) pettegolare; **a piece of** ~ un pettegolezzo.
gossip column *n* cronaca mondana.
got [gɔt] *pt, pp of* **get**.
Gothic ['gɔθɪk] *adj* gotico(a).
gotten ['gɔtn] (*US*) *pp of* **get**.
gouge [gaudʒ] *vt* (*also*: ~ **out**: *hole etc*) scavare; (: *initials*) scolpire; (: *sb's eyes*) cavare.
gourd [guəd] *n* zucca.
gourmet ['guəmeɪ] *n* buongustaio/a.
gout [gaut] *n* gotta.
govern ['gʌvən] *vt* governare; (*LING*) reggere.
governess ['gʌvənɪs] *n* governante *f*.
governing ['gʌvənɪŋ] *adj* (*POL*) al potere, al governo; ~ **body** consiglio di amministrazione.
government ['gʌvnmənt] *n* governo; (*BRIT: ministers*) ministero ♦ *cpd* statale; **local** ~ amministrazione *f* locale.
governmental [gʌvn'mɛntl] *adj* governativo(a).
government housing *n* (*US*) alloggi *mpl* popolari.
government stock *n* titoli *mpl* di stato.
governor ['gʌvənə*] *n* (*of state, bank*)

governatore *m*; (*of school, hospital*) amministratore *m*; (*BRIT: of prison*) direttore/trice.
Govt *abbr* = **government**.
gown [gaun] *n* vestito lungo; (*of teacher, judge*) toga.
GP *n abbr* (*MED*) *see* **general practitioner.**
GPMU *n abbr* (*BRIT*) = Graphical, Paper and Media Union.
GPO *n abbr* (*BRIT: old*) = General Post Office; (*US*: = Government Printing Office) ≈ Poligrafici dello Stato.
gr. *abbr* (*COMM*) = **gross.**
grab [græb] *vt* afferrare, arraffare; (*property, power*) impadronirsi di ♦ *vi*: **to** ~ **at** tentare disperatamente di afferrare.
grace [greɪs] *n* grazia; (*graciousness*) garbo, cortesia ♦ *vt* onorare; **5 days'** ~ dilazione *f* di 5 giorni; **to say** ~ dire il benedicite; **with a good/bad** ~ volentieri/ malvolentieri; **his sense of humour is his saving** ~ il suo senso dell'umorismo è quello che lo salva.
graceful ['greɪsful] *adj* elegante, aggraziato(a).
gracious ['greɪʃəs] *adj* grazioso(a); misericordioso(a) ♦ *excl*: (**good**) ~! madonna (mia)!
gradation [grə'deɪʃən] *n* gradazione *f*.
grade [greɪd] *n* (*COMM*) qualità *f inv*; classe *f*; categoria; (*in hierarchy*) grado; (*US SCOL*) voto; classe; (*gradient*) pendenza, gradiente *m* ♦ *vt* classificare; ordinare; graduare; **to make the** ~ (*fig*) farcela.
grade crossing *n* (*US*) passaggio a livello.
grade school *n* (*US*) scuola elementare *or* primaria.
gradient ['greɪdɪənt] *n* pendenza, gradiente *m*.
gradual ['grædjuəl] *adj* graduale.
gradually ['grædjuəlɪ] *adv* man mano, a poco a poco.
graduate *n* ['grædjuɪt] laureato/a; (*US SCOL*) diplomato/a, licenziato/a ♦ *vi* ['grædjueɪt] laurearsi.
graduated pension ['grædjueɪtɪd-] *n* pensione calcolata sugli ultimi stipendi.
graduation [grædju'eɪʃən] *n* cerimonia del conferimento della laurea; (*US SCOL*) consegna dei diplomi.
graffiti [grə'fiːtɪ] *npl* graffiti *mpl*.
graft [grɑːft] *n* (*AGR, MED*) innesto ♦ *vt* innestare; **hard** ~ (*col*) duro lavoro.
grain [greɪn] *n* (*no pl: cereals*) cereali *mpl*; (*US: corn*) grano; (*of sand*) granello; (*of wood*) venatura; **it goes against the** ~ (*fig*) va contro la mia (*or* la sua *etc*)

natura.
gram[græm] *n* grammo.
grammar['græmə*] *n* grammatica.
grammar school*n* (*BRIT*) ≈ liceo; (*US*) ≈ scuola elementare.
grammatical[grə'mætɪkl] *adj* grammaticale.
gramme[græm] *n* = **gram**.
gramophone['græməfəun] *n* (*BRIT*) grammofono.
granary['grænərɪ] *n* granaio.
grand[grænd] *adj* grande, magnifico(a); grandioso(a) ♦ *n* (*col*: *thousand*) mille dollari *mpl* (*or* sterline *fpl*).
grandchild,*pl* -**children**['græntʃaɪld, -tʃɪldrən] *n* nipote *m*.
granddad['grændæd] *n* (*col*) nonno.
granddaughter['grændɔːtə*] *n* nipote *f*.
grandeur['grændjə*] *n* (*of style, house*) splendore *m*; (*of occasion, scenery etc*) grandiosità, maestà.
grandfather['grændfɑːðə*] *n* nonno.
grandiose['grændɪəus] *adj* grandioso(a); (*pej*) pomposo(a).
grand jury*n* (*US*) giuria (*formata da 12 a 23 membri*).
grandma['grænmɑː] *n* (*col*) nonna.
grandmother['grænmʌðə*] *n* nonna.
grandpa['grænpɑː] *n* (*col*) = **granddad**.
grandparent['grænpɛərənt] *n* nonno/a.
grand piano*n* pianoforte *m* a coda.
Grand Prix['grɑː'priː] *n* (*AUT*) Gran Premio, Grand Prix *m inv*.
grandson['grænsʌn] *n* nipote *m*.
grandstand['grændstænd] *n* (*SPORT*) tribuna.
grand total*n* somma complessiva.
granite['grænɪt] *n* granito.
granny['grænɪ] *n* (*col*) nonna.
grant[grɑːnt] *vt* accordare; (*a request*) accogliere; (*admit*) ammettere, concedere ♦ *n* (*SCOL*) borsa; (*ADMIN*) sussidio, sovvenzione *f*; **to take sth for ~ed** dare qc per scontato.
granulated['grænjuleɪtɪd] *adj*: ~ **sugar** zucchero cristallizzato.
granule['grænjuːl] *n* granello.
grape[greɪp] *n* chicco d'uva, acino; **a bunch of ~s** un grappolo d'uva.
grapefruit['greɪpfruːt] *n* pompelmo.
grapevine['greɪpvaɪn] *n* vite *f*; **I heard it on the ~** (*fig*) me l'ha detto l'uccellino.
graph[grɑːf] *n* grafico.
graphic['græfɪk] *adj* grafico(a); (*vivid*) vivido(a); *see also* **graphics**.
graphic designer*n* grafico/a.
graphic equalizer*n* equalizzatore *m* grafico.

graphics['græfɪks] *n* (*art, process*) grafica; (*pl: drawings*) illustrazioni *fpl*.
graphite['græfaɪt] *n* grafite *f*.
graph paper*n* carta millimetrata.
grapple['græpl] *vi*: **to ~ with** essere alle prese con.
grappling iron['græplɪŋ-] *n* (*NAUT*) grappino.
grasp[grɑːsp] *vt* afferrare ♦ *n* (*grip*) presa; (*fig*) potere *m*; comprensione *f*; **to have sth within one's ~** avere qc a portata di mano; **to have a good ~ of** (*subject*) avere una buona padronanza di.
▶**grasp at***vt fus* (*rope etc*) afferrarsi a, aggrapparsi a; (*fig: opportunity*) non farsi sfuggire, approfittare di.
grasping['grɑːspɪŋ] *adj* avido(a).
grass[grɑːs] *n* erba; (*pasture*) pascolo, prato; (*BRIT col: informer*) informatore/ trice; (*ex-terrorist*) pentito/a.
grasshopper['grɑːshɔpə*] *n* cavalletta.
grassland['grɑːslænd] *n* prateria.
grass roots*npl* (*fig*) base *f*.
grass snake*n* natrice *f*.
grassy['grɑːsɪ] *adj* erboso(a).
grate[greɪt] *n* graticola (del focolare) ♦ *vi* cigolare, stridere ♦ *vt* (*CULIN*) grattugiare.
grateful['greɪtful] *adj* grato(a), riconoscente.
gratefully['greɪtfulɪ] *adv* con gratitudine.
grater['greɪtə*] *n* grattugia.
gratification[grætɪfɪ'keɪʃən] *n* soddisfazione *f*.
gratify['grætɪfaɪ] *vt* appagare; (*whim*) soddisfare.
gratifying['grætɪfaɪɪŋ] *adj* gradito(a); soddisfacente.
grating['greɪtɪŋ] *n* (*iron bars*) grata ♦ *adj* (*noise*) stridente, stridulo(a).
gratitude['grætɪtjuːd] *n* gratitudine *f*.
gratuitous[grə'tjuːɪtəs] *adj* gratuito(a).
gratuity[grə'tjuːɪtɪ] *n* mancia.
grave[greɪv] *n* tomba ♦ *adj* grave, serio(a).
gravedigger['greɪvdɪgə*] *n* becchino.
gravel['grævl] *n* ghiaia.
gravely['greɪvlɪ] *adv* gravemente, solennemente; ~ **ill** in pericolo di vita.
gravestone['greɪvstəun] *n* pietra tombale.
graveyard['greɪvjɑːd] *n* cimitero.
gravitate['grævɪteɪt] *vi* gravitare.
gravity['grævɪtɪ] *n* (*all senses*) gravità.
gravy['greɪvɪ] *n* intingolo della carne; salsa.
gravy boat*n* salsiera.
gravy train*n*: **the ~** (*col*) l'albero della cuccagna.
gray[greɪ] *adj* (*US*) = **grey**.

graze [greɪz] *vi* pascolare, pascere ♦ *vt* (*touch lightly*) sfiorare; (*scrape*) escoriare ♦ *n* (*MED*) escoriazione *f*.

grazing ['greɪzɪŋ] *n* pascolo.

grease [griːs] *n* (*fat*) grasso; (*lubricant*) lubrificante *m* ♦ *vt* ingrassare; lubrificare; to ~ the skids (*US*: *fig*) spianare la strada.

grease gun *n* ingrassatore *m*.

greasepaint ['griːspeɪnt] *n* cerone *m*.

greaseproof paper ['griːspruːf-] *n* (*BRIT*) carta oleata.

greasy ['griːsɪ] *adj* grasso(a); untuoso(a); (*BRIT*: *road*, *surface*) scivoloso(a); (*hands*, *clothes*) unto(a).

great [greɪt] *adj* grande; (*pain*, *heat*) forte, intenso(a); (*col*) magnifico(a), meraviglioso(a); they're ~ friends sono grandi amici; the ~ thing is that ... il bello è che ...; it was ~! è stato fantastico!; we had a ~ time ci siamo divertiti un mondo.

Great Barrier Reef *n*: the ~ la Grande Barriera Corallina.

Great Britain *n* Gran Bretagna.

great-grandchild, *pl* -children [greɪt'græntʃaɪld, -tʃɪldrən] *n* pronipote *m/f*.

great-grandfather [greɪt'grændfɑːðə*] *n* bisnonno.

great-grandmother [greɪt'grænmʌðə*] *n* bisnonna.

Great Lakes *npl*: the ~ i Grandi Laghi.

greatly ['greɪtlɪ] *adv* molto.

greatness ['greɪtnɪs] *n* grandezza.

Grecian ['griːʃən] *adj* greco(a).

Greece [griːs] *n* Grecia.

greed [griːd] *n* (*also*: ~iness) avarizia; (*for food*) golosità, ghiottoneria.

greedily ['griːdɪlɪ] *adv* avidamente; golosamente.

greedy ['griːdɪ] *adj* avido(a); goloso(a), ghiotto(a).

Greek [griːk] *adj* greco(a) ♦ *n* greco/a; (*LING*) greco; ancient/modern ~ greco antico/ moderno.

green [griːn] *adj* (*also POL*) verde; (*inexperienced*) inesperto(a), ingenuo(a) ♦ *n* verde *m*; (*stretch of grass*) prato; (*also*: village ~) ≈ piazza del paese; ~s *npl* (*vegetables*) verdura; (*of golf course*) green *m inv*; to have ~ fingers *or* (*US*) a ~ thumb (*fig*) avere il pollice verde; the G~ Party (*BRIT POL*) i Verdi.

green belt *n* (*round town*) cintura di verde.

green card *n* (*AUT*) carta verde.

greenery ['griːnərɪ] *n* verde *m*.

greenfly ['griːnflaɪ] *n* afide *f*.

greengage ['griːngeɪdʒ] *n* susina Regina Claudia.

greengrocer ['griːngrəusə*] *n* (*BRIT*) fruttivendolo/a, erbivendolo/a.

greenhouse ['griːnhaus] *n* serra.

greenhouse effect *n*: the ~ l'effetto serra.

greenhouse gas *n* gas *m inv* responsabile dell'effetto serra.

greenish ['griːnɪʃ] *adj* verdastro(a).

Greenland ['griːnlənd] *n* Groenlandia.

Greenlander ['griːnləndə*] *n* groenlandese *m/f*.

green light *n*: to give sb the ~ dare via libera a qn.

green pepper *n* peperone *m* verde.

greet [griːt] *vt* salutare.

greeting ['griːtɪŋ] *n* saluto; Christmas/ birthday ~s auguri *mpl* di Natale/di compleanno; Season's ~s Buone Feste.

greeting(s) card *n* cartolina d'auguri.

gregarious [grə'gɛərɪəs] *adj* gregario(a); socievole.

grenade [grə'neɪd] *n* (*also*: hand ~) granata.

grew [gruː] *pt of* grow.

grey [greɪ] *adj* grigio(a); to go ~ diventar grigio.

greyhound ['greɪhaund] *n* levriere *m*.

grid [grɪd] *n* grata; (*ELEC*) rete *f*; (*US AUT*) area d'incrocio.

griddle ['grɪdl] *n* piastra.

gridiron ['grɪdaɪən] *n* graticola.

gridlock ['grɪdlɔk] *n* (*traffic jam*) paralisi *f inv* del traffico.

grief [griːf] *n* dolore *m*; to come to ~ (*plan*) naufragare; (*person*) finire male.

grievance ['griːvəns] *n* doglianza, lagnanza; (*cause for complaint*) motivo di risentimento.

grieve [griːv] *vi* addolorarsi, soffrire ♦ *vt* addolorare; to ~ for sb compiangere qn; (*dead person*) piangere qn.

grievous bodily harm (GBH) ['griːvəs-] *n* (*LAW*) aggressione *f*.

grill [grɪl] *n* (*on cooker*) griglia ♦ *vt* (*BRIT*) cuocere ai ferri; (*question*) interrogare senza sosta; ~ed meat carne *f* ai ferri *or* alla griglia.

grille [grɪl] *n* grata; (*AUT*) griglia.

grill(room) ['grɪl(rum)] *n* rosticceria.

grim [grɪm] *adj* sinistro(a); brutto(a).

grimace [grɪ'meɪs] *n* smorfia ♦ *vi* fare smorfie.

grime [graɪm] *n* sudiciume *m*.

grimy ['graɪmɪ] *adj* sudicio(a).

grin [grɪn] *n* sorriso smagliante ♦ *vi*: to ~ (at) sorridere (a), fare un gran sorriso (a).

grind [graɪnd] *vb* (*pt*, *pp* ground [graund]) *vt*

macinare; (US: meat) tritare, macinare; (make sharp) arrotare; (polish: gem, lens) molare ♦ vi (car gears) grattare ♦ n (work) sgobbata; to ~ one's teeth digrignare i denti; to ~ to a halt (vehicle) arrestarsi con uno stridio di freni; (fig: talks, scheme) insabbiarsi; (: work, production) cessare del tutto; the daily ~ (col) il trantran quotidiano.

grinder ['graɪndə*] n (machine: for coffee) macinino.

grindstone ['graɪndstəun] n: to keep one's nose to the ~ darci sotto.

grip [grɪp] n presa; (holdall) borsa da viaggio ♦ vt afferrare; to come to ~s with affrontare; cercare di risolvere; to ~ the road (tyres) far presa sulla strada; (car) tenere bene la strada; to lose one's ~ perdere or allentare la presa; (fig) perdere la grinta.

gripe [graɪp] n (MED) colica; (col: complaint) lagna ♦ vi (col) brontolare.

gripping ['grɪpɪŋ] adj avvincente.

grisly ['grɪzlɪ] adj macabro(a), orrido(a).

grist [grɪst] n (fig): it's (all) ~ to the mill tutto aiuta.

gristle ['grɪsl] n cartilagine f.

grit [grɪt] n ghiaia; (courage) fegato ♦ vt (road) coprire di sabbia; to ~ one's teeth stringere i denti; I've got a piece of ~ in my eye ho un bruscolino nell'occhio.

grits [grɪts] npl (US) macinato grosso (di avena etc).

grizzle ['grɪzl] vi (BRIT) piagnucolare.

grizzly ['grɪzlɪ] n (also: ~ bear) orso grigio, grizzly m inv.

groan [grəun] n gemito ♦ vi gemere.

grocer ['grəusə*] n negoziante m di generi alimentari; ~'s (shop) negozio di alimentari.

groceries ['grəusərɪz] npl provviste fpl.

grocery ['grəusərɪ] n (shop) (negozio di) alimentari.

grog [grɒg] n grog m inv.

groggy ['grɒgɪ] adj barcollante.

groin [grɔɪn] n inguine m.

groom [gru:m] n palafreniere m; (also: bride~) sposo ♦ vt (horse) strigliare; (fig): to ~ sb for avviare qn a.

groove [gru:v] n scanalatura, solco.

grope [grəup] vi andare a tentoni; to ~ for sth cercare qc a tastoni.

gross [grəus] adj grossolano(a); (COMM) lordo(a) ♦ n (pl inv) (twelve dozen) grossa ♦ vt (COMM) incassare, avere un incasso lordo di.

gross domestic product (GDP) n prodotto interno lordo (P.I.L.).

grossly ['grəuslɪ] adv (greatly) molto.

gross national product (GNP) n prodotto nazionale lordo (P.N.L.).

grotesque [grəu'tɛsk] adj grottesco(a).

grotto ['grɒtəu] n grotta.

grotty ['grɒtɪ] adj (BRIT col) squallido(a).

grouch [grautʃ] (col) vi brontolare ♦ n (person) brontolone/a.

ground [graund] pt, pp of **grind** ♦ adj (coffee etc) macinato(a) ♦ n suolo, terra; (land) terreno; (SPORT) campo; (reason: gen pl) ragione f; (US: also: ~ wire) (presa a) terra ♦ vt (plane) tenere a terra a ♦ vi (ship) arenarsi; ~s npl (of coffee etc) fondi mpl; (gardens etc) terreno, giardini mpl; on/to the ~ per/a terra; below ~ sottoterra; common ~ terreno comune; to gain/lose ~ guadagnare/perdere terreno; he covered a lot of ~ in his lecture ha toccato molti argomenti nel corso della conferenza.

ground cloth n (US) = **groundsheet**.

ground control n (AVIAT, SPACE) base f di controllo.

ground floor n pianterreno.

grounding ['graundɪŋ] n (in education) basi fpl.

groundless ['graundlɪs] adj infondato(a).

groundnut ['graundnʌt] n arachide f.

ground rent n (BRIT) canone m di affitto di un terreno.

ground rules npl regole fpl fondamentali.

groundsheet ['graundʃi:t] n (BRIT) telone m impermeabile.

groundsman ['graundzmən], (US) **groundskeeper** ['graundzki:pə*] n (SPORT) custode m (di campo sportivo).

ground staff n personale m di terra.

groundswell ['graundswɛl] n maremoto; (fig) movimento.

ground-to-air ['graundtu'ɛə*] adj terra-aria inv.

ground-to-ground ['grauntə'graund] adj: ~ missile missile m terra-terra.

groundwork ['graundwə:k] n preparazione f.

group [gru:p] n gruppo; (MUS: pop ~) complesso, gruppo ♦ vt raggruppare ♦ vi raggrupparsi.

groupie ['gru:pɪ] n groupie m/f inv, fan m/f inv scatenato(a).

group therapy n terapia di gruppo.

grouse [graus] n (pl inv) (bird) tetraone m ♦ vi (complain) brontolare.

grove [grəuv] n boschetto.

grovel ['grɒvl] vi (fig): to ~ (before) strisciare (di fronte a).

grow, pt **grew,** pp **grown** [grəu, gruː, grəun] vi crescere; (increase) aumentare; (become): **to ~ rich/weak** arricchirsi/ indebolirsi ♦ vt coltivare, far crescere; **to ~ tired of waiting** stancarsi di aspettare.
► **grow apart** vi (fig) estraniarsi.
► **grow away from** vt fus (fig) allontanarsi da, staccarsi da.
► **grow on** vt fus: **that painting is ~ing on me** quel quadro più lo guardo più mi piace.
► **grow out of** vt fus (clothes) diventare troppo grande per indossare; (habit) perdere (col tempo); **he'll ~ out of it** gli passerà.
► **grow up** vi farsi grande, crescere.
grower ['grəuə*] n coltivatore/trice.
growing ['grəuɪŋ] adj (fear, amount) crescente; **~ pains** (also fig) problemi mpl di crescita.
growl [graul] vi ringhiare.
grown [grəun] pp of **grow** ♦ adj adulto(a), maturo(a).
grown-up [grəun'ʌp] n adulto/a, grande m/f.
growth [grəuθ] n crescita, sviluppo; (what has grown) crescita; (MED) escrescenza, tumore m.
growth rate n tasso di crescita.
grub [grʌb] n larva; (col: food) roba (da mangiare).
grubby ['grʌbɪ] adj sporco(a).
grudge [grʌdʒ] n rancore m ♦ vt: **to ~ sb sth** dare qc a qn di malavoglia; invidiare qc a qn; **to bear sb a ~ (for)** serbar rancore a qn (per).
grudgingly ['grʌdʒɪŋlɪ] adv di malavoglia, di malincuore.
gruelling, (US) **grueling** ['gruəlɪŋ] adj estenuante.
gruesome ['gruːsəm] adj orribile.
gruff [grʌf] adj rozzo(a).
grumble ['grʌmbl] vi brontolare, lagnarsi.
grumpy ['grʌmpɪ] adj stizzito(a).
grunge [grʌndʒ] n (MUS) grunge m inv; (style) moda f grunge inv.
grunt [grʌnt] vi grugnire ♦ n grugnito.
G-string ['dʒiːstrɪŋ] n (garment) tanga m inv.
GT abbr (AUT: = gran turismo) GT.
GU abbr (US POST) = Guam.
guarantee [gærən'tiː] n garanzia ♦ vt garantire; **he can't ~ (that) he'll come** non può garantire che verrà.
guarantor [gærən'tɔː*] n garante m/f.
guard [gɑːd] n guardia; (protection) riparo, protezione f; (BOXING) difesa; (one man) guardia, sentinella; (BRIT RAIL) capotreno; (safety device: on machine) schermo protettivo; (also: **fire ~**) parafuoco ♦ vt

fare la guardia a; **to ~ (against** or **from)** proteggere (da), salvaguardare (da); **to be on one's ~** (fig) stare in guardia.
► **guard against** vi: **to ~ against doing sth** guardarsi dal fare qc.
guard dog n cane m da guardia.
guarded ['gɑːdɪd] adj (fig) cauto(a), guardingo(a).
guardian ['gɑːdɪən] n custode m; (of minor) tutore/trice.
guard's van n (BRIT RAIL) vagone m di servizio.
Guatemala [gwɑːtə'mɑːlə] n Guatemala m.
Guernsey ['gəːnzɪ] n Guernesey f.
guerrilla [gə'rɪlə] n guerrigliero.
guerrilla warfare n guerriglia.
guess [gɛs] vi indovinare ♦ vt indovinare; (US) credere, pensare ♦ n congettura; **to take** or **have a ~** cercare di indovinare; **my ~ is that** ... suppongo che ...; **to keep sb ~ing** tenere qn in sospeso or sulla corda; **I ~ you're right** mi sa che hai ragione.
guesstimate ['gɛstɪmɪt] n (col) stima approssimativa.
guesswork ['gɛswəːk] n: **I got the answer by ~** ho azzeccato la risposta.
guest [gɛst] n ospite m/f; (in hotel) cliente m/f; **be my ~** (col) fai come (se fossi) a casa tua.
guest-house ['gɛsthaus] n pensione f.
guest room n camera degli ospiti.
guff [gʌf] n (col) stupidaggini fpl, assurdità fpl.
guffaw [gʌ'fɔː] n risata sonora ♦ vi scoppiare di una risata sonora.
guidance ['gaɪdəns] n guida, direzione f; **marriage/vocational ~** consulenza matrimoniale/per l'avviamento professionale.
guide [gaɪd] n (person, book etc) guida; (also: **girl ~**) giovane esploratrice f ♦ vt guidare; **to be ~d by sb/sth** farsi or lasciarsi guidare da qn/qc.
guidebook ['gaɪdbuk] n guida.
guided missile n missile m telecomandato.
guide dog n (BRIT) cane m guida inv.
guidelines ['gaɪdlaɪnz] npl (fig) indicazioni fpl, linee fpl direttive.
guild [gɪld] n arte f, corporazione f; associazione f.
guildhall ['gɪldhɔːl] n (BRIT) palazzo municipale.
guile [gaɪl] n astuzia.
guileless ['gaɪllɪs] adj candido(a).
guillotine ['gɪlətiːn] n ghigliottina.
guilt [gɪlt] n colpevolezza.

guilty ['gɪltɪ] *adj* colpevole; **to feel ~ (about)** sentirsi in colpa (per); **to plead ~/not ~** dichiararsi colpevole/innocente.

Guinea ['gɪnɪ] *n*: **Republic of ~** Repubblica di Guinea.

guinea ['gɪnɪ] *n* (*BRIT*) ghinea (= *21 shillings*: *valuta ora fuori uso*).

guinea pig *n* cavia.

guise [gaɪz] *n* maschera.

guitar [gɪ'tɑː*] *n* chitarra.

guitarist [gɪ'tɑːrɪst] *n* chitarrista *m/f*.

gulch [gʌltʃ] *n* (*US*) burrone *m*.

gulf [gʌlf] *n* golfo; (*abyss*) abisso; **the (Persian) G~** il Golfo Persico.

Gulf States *npl*: **the ~** i paesi del Golfo Persico.

Gulf Stream *n*: **the ~** la corrente del Golfo.

gull [gʌl] *n* gabbiano.

gullet ['gʌlɪt] *n* gola.

gullibility [gʌlɪ'bɪlɪtɪ] *n* semplicioneria.

gullible ['gʌlɪbl] *adj* credulo(a).

gully ['gʌlɪ] *n* burrone *m*; gola; canale *m*.

gulp [gʌlp] *vi* deglutire; (*from emotion*) avere il nodo in gola ♦ *vt* (*also*: ~ **down**) tracannare, inghiottire ♦ *n* (*of liquid*) sorso; (*of food*) boccone *m*; **in** *or* **at one ~** in un sorso, d'un fiato.

gum [gʌm] *n* (*ANAT*) gengiva; (*glue*) colla; (*sweet*) gelatina di frutta; (*also*: **chewing-~**) chewing-gum *m* ♦ *vt* incollare.

▶**gum up** *vt*: **to ~ up the works** (*col*) mettere il bastone tra le ruote.

gumboil ['gʌmbɔɪl] *n* ascesso (dentario).

gumboots ['gʌmbuːts] *npl* (*BRIT*) stivali *mpl* di gomma.

gumption ['gʌmpʃən] *n* buon senso, senso pratico.

gun [gʌn] *n* fucile *m*; (*small*) pistola, rivoltella; (*rifle*) carabina; (*shotgun*) fucile da caccia; (*cannon*) cannone *m* ♦ *vt* (*also*: ~ **down**) abbattere a colpi di pistola *or* fucile; **to stick to one's ~s** (*fig*) tener duro.

gunboat ['gʌnbəut] *n* cannoniera.

gun dog *n* cane *m* da caccia.

gunfire ['gʌnfaɪə*] *n* spari *mpl*.

gung-ho ['gʌŋ'həu] *adj* (*col*) stupidamente entusiasta.

gunk [gʌŋk] *n* porcherie *fpl*.

gunman ['gʌnmən] *n* bandito armato.

gunner ['gʌnə*] *n* artigliere *m*.

gunpoint ['gʌnpɔɪnt] *n*: **at ~** sotto minaccia di fucile.

gunpowder ['gʌnpaudə*] *n* polvere *f* da sparo.

gunrunning ['gʌnrʌnɪŋ] *n* contrabbando d'armi.

gunshot ['gʌnʃɔt] *n* sparo; **within ~** a portata di fucile.

gunsmith ['gʌnsmɪθ] *n* armaiolo.

gurgle ['gəːgl] *n* gorgoglio ♦ *vi* gorgogliare.

guru ['guruː] *n* guru *m inv*.

gush [gʌʃ] *n* fiotto, getto ♦ *vi* sgorgare; (*fig*) abbandonarsi ad effusioni.

gushing ['gʌʃɪŋ] *adj* che fa smancerie.

gusset ['gʌsɪt] *n* gherone *m*; (*in tights, pants*) rinforzo.

gust [gʌst] *n* (*of wind*) raffica.

gusto ['gʌstəu] *n* entusiasmo.

gusty ['gʌstɪ] *adj* (*wind*) a raffiche; (*day*) tempestoso(a).

gut [gʌt] *n* intestino, budello; (*MUS etc*) minugia; ~**s** *npl* (*col: innards*) budella *fpl*; (: *of animals*) interiora *fpl*; (*courage*) fegato ♦ *vt* (*poultry, fish*) levare le interiora a, sventrare; (*building*) svuotare; (: *subj: fire*) divorare l'interno di; **to hate sb's ~s** odiare qn a morte.

gut reaction *n* reazione *f* istintiva.

gutsy ['gʌtsɪ] *adj* (*col: style*) che ha mordente; (*plucky*) coraggioso(a).

gutted ['gʌtɪd] *adv* (*col: upset*) scioccato(a).

gutter ['gʌtə*] *n* (*of roof*) grondaia; (*in street*) cunetta.

gutter press *n*: **the ~** la stampa scandalistica.

guttural ['gʌtərl] *adj* gutturale.

guy [gaɪ] *n* (*also*: ~**rope**) cavo *or* corda di fissaggio; (*col: man*) tipo, elemento; (*figure*) effigie di Guy Fawkes.

Guyana [gaɪ'ænə] *n* Guayana *f*.

Guy Fawkes Night [-'fɔːks-] *n* (*BRIT*) *see boxed note*.

GUY FAWKES NIGHT

La sera del 5 novembre, in occasione della **Guy Fawkes Night**, *altrimenti chiamata* **Bonfire Night**, *viene commemorato con falò e fuochi d'artificio il fallimento della Congiura delle Polveri contro Giacomo I nel 1605. La festa prende il nome dal principale congiurato della cospirazione, Guy Fawkes, la cui effigie viene bruciata durante i festeggiamenti.*

---

guzzle ['gʌzl] *vi* gozzovigliare ♦ *vt* tranguiare.

gym [dʒɪm] *n* (*also*: **gymnasium**) palestra; (*also*: **gymnastics**) ginnastica.

gymkhana [dʒɪm'kɑːnə] *n* gimkana.

gymnasium [dʒɪm'neɪzɪəm] *n* palestra.

gymnast ['dʒɪmnæst] *n* ginnasta *m/f*.

gymnastics [dʒɪm'næstɪks] *n*, *npl* ginnastica.

gym shoes *npl* scarpe *fpl* da ginnastica.

gym slip n (BRIT) grembiule m da scuola (per ragazze).
gynaecologist, (US) **gynecologist** [gaɪnɪ'kɔlədʒɪst] n ginecologo/a.
gynaecology, (US) **gynecology** [gaɪnə'kɔlədʒɪ] n ginecologia.
gypsy ['dʒɪpsɪ] n = **gipsy**.
gyrate [dʒaɪ'reɪt] vi girare.
gyroscope ['dʒaɪərəskəup] n giroscopio.

H h

H, h [eɪtʃ] n (letter) H, h f or m inv; **H for Harry**, (US) **H for How** ≈ H come Hotel.
habeas corpus ['heɪbɪəs'kɔːpəs] n (LAW) habeas corpus m inv.
haberdashery ['hæbədæʃərɪ] n merceria.
habit ['hæbɪt] n abitudine f; (costume) abito; (REL) tonaca; **to get out of/into the ~ of doing sth** perdere/prendere l'abitudine di fare qc.
habitable ['hæbɪtəbl] adj abitabile.
habitat ['hæbɪtæt] n habitat m inv.
habitation [hæbɪ'teɪʃən] n abitazione f.
habitual [hə'bɪtjuəl] adj abituale; (drinker, liar) inveterato(a).
habitually [hə'bɪtjuəlɪ] adv abitualmente, di solito.
hack [hæk] vt tagliare, fare a pezzi ♦ n (cut) taglio; (blow) colpo; (old horse) ronzino; (pej: writer) negro.
hacker ['hækə*] n (COMPUT) pirata m informatico.
hackles ['hæklz] npl: **to make sb's ~ rise** (fig) rendere qn furioso.
hackney cab ['hæknɪ-] n carrozza a nolo.
hackneyed ['hæknɪd] adj comune, trito(a).
hacksaw ['hæksɔː] n seghetto (per metallo).
had [hæd] pt, pp of **have**.
haddock ['hædək] n eglefino.
hadn't ['hædnt] = **had not**.
haematology, (US) **hematology** [hiːmə'tɔlədʒɪ] n ematologia.
haemoglobin, (US) **hemoglobin** [hiːməu'ɡləubɪn] n emoglobina.
haemophilia, (US) **hemophilia** [hiːməu'fɪlɪə] n emofilia.
haemorrhage, (US) **hemorrhage** ['hɛmərɪdʒ] n emorragia.
haemorrhoids, (US) **hemorrhoids** ['hɛmərɔɪdz] npl emorroidi fpl.

hag [hæɡ] n (ugly) befana; (nasty) megera; (witch) strega.
haggard ['hæɡəd] adj smunto(a).
haggis ['hæɡɪs] n (Scottish) insaccato a base di frattaglie di pecora e avena.
haggle ['hæɡl] vi: **to ~ (over)** contrattare (su); (argue) discutere (su).
haggling ['hæɡlɪŋ] n contrattazioni fpl.
Hague [heɪɡ] n: **The ~** L'Aia.
hail [heɪl] n grandine f ♦ vt (call) chiamare; (greet) salutare ♦ vi grandinare; **to ~ (as)** acclamare (come); **he ~s from Scotland** viene dalla Scozia.
hailstone ['heɪlstəun] n chicco di grandine.
hailstorm ['heɪlstɔːm] n grandinata.
hair [hɛə*] n capelli mpl; (single hair: on head) capello; (: on body) pelo; **to do one's ~** pettinarsi.
hairbrush ['hɛəbrʌʃ] n spazzola per capelli.
haircut ['hɛəkʌt] n taglio di capelli; **I need a ~** devo tagliarmi i capelli.
hairdo ['hɛəduː] n acconciatura.
hairdresser ['hɛədrɛsə*] n parrucchiere/a.
hair-dryer ['hɛədraɪə*] n asciugacapelli m inv.
-haired [hɛəd] suffix: **fair/long~** dai capelli biondi/lunghi.
hairgrip ['hɛəɡrɪp] n forcina.
hairline ['hɛəlaɪn] n attaccatura dei capelli.
hairline fracture n incrinatura.
hair oil n brillantina.
hairpiece ['hɛəpiːs] n toupet m inv.
hairpin ['hɛəpɪn] n forcina.
hairpin bend, (US) **hairpin curve** n tornante m.
hair-raising ['hɛəreɪzɪŋ] adj orripilante.
hair remover n crema depilatoria.
hair spray n lacca per capelli.
hairstyle ['hɛəstaɪl] n pettinatura, acconciatura.
hairy ['hɛərɪ] adj irsuto(a); peloso(a); (col: frightening) spaventoso(a).
Haiti ['heɪtɪ] n Haiti f.
hake, pl ~ or ~s [heɪk] n nasello.
halal [haː'lɑːl] n: **~ meat** carne macellata secondo la legge mussulmana.
halcyon ['hælsɪən] adj sereno(a).
hale [heɪl] adj: **~ and hearty** che scoppia di salute.
half [hɑːf] n (pl **halves** [hɑːvz]) mezzo, metà f inv; (SPORT: of match) tempo; (: of ground) metà campo ♦ adj mezzo(a) ♦ adv a mezzo, a metà; **~ an hour** mezz'ora; **~ a dozen** mezza dozzina; **~ a pound** mezza libbra; **two and a ~** due e mezzo; **a week and a ~** una settimana e mezza; **~ (of it)** la metà; **~ (of)** la metà di; **~ the amount of** la metà

di; **to cut sth in** ~ tagliare qc in due; ~ **empty/closed** mezzo vuoto/chiuso, semivuoto/semichiuso; ~ **past 3** le 3 e mezza; **to go halves (with sb)** fare a metà (con qn).

half-back ['hɑːfbæk] *n* (*SPORT*) mediano.

half-baked [hɑːf'beɪkt] *adj* (*fig col: idea, scheme*) mal combinato(a), che non sta in piedi.

half-breed ['hɑːfbriːd] *n* = **half-caste**.

half-brother ['hɑːfbrʌðə*] *n* fratellastro.

half-caste ['hɑːfkɑːst] *n* meticcio/a.

half-hearted [hɑːf'hɑːtɪd] *adj* tiepido(a).

half-hour [hɑːf'auə*] *n* mezz'ora.

half-mast ['hɑːf'mɑːst] *n*: **at** ~ (*flag*) a mezz'asta.

halfpenny ['heɪpnɪ] *n* mezzo penny *m inv.*

half-price ['hɑːf'praɪs] *adj* a metà prezzo ♦ *adv* (*also*: **at** ~) a metà prezzo.

half term *n* (*BRIT SCOL*) vacanza a *or* di metà trimestre.

half-time [hɑːf'taɪm] *n* (*SPORT*) intervallo.

halfway [hɑːf'weɪ] *adv* a metà strada; **to meet sb** ~ (*fig*) arrivare a un compromesso con qn.

halfway house *n* (*hostel*) ostello dove possono alloggiare temporaneamente *ex detenuti*; (*fig*) via di mezzo.

half-wit ['hɑːfwɪt] *n* (*col*) idiota *m/f.*

half-yearly [hɑːf'jɪəlɪ] *adv* semestralmente, ogni sei mesi ♦ *adj* semestrale.

halibut ['hælɪbət] *n* (*pl inv*) ippoglosso.

halitosis [hælɪ'təusɪs] *n* alitosi *f.*

hall [hɔːl] *n* sala, salone *m*; (*entrance way*) entrata; (*corridor*) corridoio; (*mansion*) grande villa, maniero; ~ **of residence** *n* (*BRIT*) casa dello studente.

hallmark ['hɔːlmɑːk] *n* marchio di garanzia; (*fig*) caratteristica.

hallo [hə'ləu] *excl* = **hello**.

Halloween ['hæləu'iːn] *n* vigilia d'Ognissanti; *see boxed note.*

HALLOWEEN

Secondo la tradizione anglosassone, durante la notte di **Halloween***, il 31 di ottobre, è possibile vedere le streghe e i fantasmi. I bambini, travestiti da fantasmi, streghe, mostri o simili, vanno di porta in porta e raccolgono dolci e piccoli doni.*

---

hallucination [həluːsɪ'neɪʃən] *n* allucinazione *f.*

hallucinogenic [həluːsɪnəu'dʒɛnɪk] *adj* allucinogeno(a).

hallway ['hɔːlweɪ] *n* ingresso; corridoio.

halo ['heɪləu] *n* (*of saint etc*) aureola; (*of sun*)

alone *m.*

halt [hɔːlt] *n* fermata ♦ *vt* fermare ♦ *vi* fermarsi; **to call a** ~ (**to sth**) (*fig*) mettere *or* porre fine (a qc).

halter ['hɔːltə*] *n* (*for horse*) cavezza.

halterneck ['hɔːltənɛk] *adj* allacciato(a) dietro il collo.

halve [hɑːv] *vt* (*apple etc*) dividere a metà; (*expense*) ridurre di metà.

halves [hɑːvz] *npl of* **half.**

ham [hæm] *n* prosciutto; (*col: also:* **radio** ~) radioamatore/trice; (*also:* ~ **actor**) attore/trice senza talento.

Hamburg ['hæmbəːg] *n* Amburgo *f.*

hamburger ['hæmbəːgə*] *n* hamburger *m inv.*

ham-fisted ['hæm'fɪstɪd], (*US*) **ham-handed** ['hæm'hændɪd] *adj* maldestro(a).

hamlet ['hæmlɪt] *n* paesetto.

hammer ['hæmə*] *n* martello ♦ *vt* martellare; (*fig*) sconfiggere duramente ♦ *vi* (*at door*) picchiare; **to** ~ **a point home to sb** cacciare un'idea in testa a qn.

▶**hammer out** *vt* (*metal*) spianare (a martellate); (*fig: solution, agreement*) mettere a punto.

hammock ['hæmək] *n* amaca.

hamper ['hæmpə*] *vt* impedire ♦ *n* cesta.

hamster ['hæmstə*] *n* criceto.

hamstring ['hæmstrɪŋ] *n* (*ANAT*) tendine *m* del ginocchio.

hand [hænd] *n* mano *f*; (*of clock*) lancetta; (*handwriting*) scrittura; (*at cards*) mano; (*: game*) partita; (*worker*) operaio/a; (*measurement: of horse*) ≈ dieci centimetri ♦ *vt* dare, passare; **to give sb a** ~ dare una mano a qn; **at** ~ a portata di mano; **in** ~ a disposizione; (*work*) in corso; **we have the matter in** ~ ci stiamo occupando della cosa; **we have the situation in** ~ abbiamo la situazione sotto controllo; **to be on** ~ (*person*) essere disponibile; (*emergency services*) essere pronto(a) a intervenire; **to** ~ (*information etc*) a portata di mano; **to force sb's** ~ forzare la mano a qn; **to have a free** ~ avere carta bianca; **to have in one's** ~ (*also fig*) avere in mano *or* in pugno; **on the one** ~ **...**, **on the other** ~ da un lato ..., dall'altro.

▶**hand down** *vt* passare giù; (*tradition, heirloom*) tramandare; (*US: sentence, verdict*) emettere.

▶**hand in** *vt* consegnare.

▶**hand out** *vt* (*leaflets*) distribuire; (*advice*) elargire.

▶**hand over** *vt* passare; cedere.

▶**hand round** *vt* (*BRIT: information, papers*)

far passare; (*distribute*: *chocolates etc*) far
girare; (*subj*: *hostess*) offrire.
handbag ['hændbæg] *n* borsetta.
hand baggage *n* bagaglio a mano.
handball ['hændbɔːl] *n* pallamano *f*.
handbasin ['hændbeɪsn] *n* lavandino.
handbook ['hændbuk] *n* manuale *m*.
handbrake ['hændbreɪk] *n* freno a mano.
hand cream *n* crema per le mani.
handcuffs ['hændkʌfs] *npl* manette *fpl*.
handful ['hændful] *n* manciata, pugno.
hand-held ['hænd'held] *adj* portatile.
handicap ['hændɪkæp] *n* handicap *m inv* ♦ *vt*
handicappare; **to be mentally ~ped**
essere un handicappato mentale; **to be**
physically ~ped essere handicappato.
handicraft ['hændɪkrɑːft] *n* lavoro
d'artigiano.
handiwork ['hændɪwɔːk] *n* lavorazione *f* a
mano; **this looks like his ~** (*pej*) qui c'è il
suo zampino.
handkerchief ['hæŋkətʃɪf] *n* fazzoletto.
handle ['hændl] *n* (*of door etc*) maniglia; (*of*
cup etc) ansa; (*of knife etc*) impugnatura;
(*of saucepan*) manico; (*for winding*)
manovella ♦ *vt* toccare, maneggiare;
manovrare; (*deal with*) occuparsi di;
(*treat*: *people*) trattare; "~ **with care**"
"fragile".
handlebar(s) ['hændlbɑː(z)] *n*(*pl*) manubrio.
handling ['hændlɪŋ] *n* (*AUT*)
maneggevolezza; (*of issue*) modo di
affrontare.
handling charges *npl* commissione *f* per
la prestazione; (*for goods*) spese *fpl* di
trasporto; (*BANKING*) spese *fpl* bancarie.
hand-luggage ['hændlʌgɪdʒ] *n* bagagli *mpl*
a mano.
handmade [hænd'meɪd] *adj* fatto(a) a
mano; (*biscuits etc*) fatto(a) in casa.
handout ['hændaut] *n* (*leaflet*) volantino;
(*press ~*) comunicato stampa.
hand-picked [hænd'pɪkt] *adj* (*produce*)
scelto(a), selezionato(a); (*staff etc*)
scelto(a).
handrail ['hændreɪl] *n* (*on staircase etc*)
corrimano.
handset ['hændset] *n* (*TEL*) ricevitore *m*.
hands-free ['hændzfriː] *adj* (*telephone*) con
auricolare; (*microphone*) vivavoce.
handshake ['hændʃeɪk] *n* stretta di mano;
(*COMPUT*) colloquio.
handsome ['hænsəm] *adj* bello(a); (*reward*)
generoso(a); (*profit, fortune*)
considerevole.
hands-on ['hændz'ɒn] *adj*: **~ experience**
esperienza diretta *or* pratica.
handstand ['hændstænd] *n*: **to do a ~** fare

la verticale.
hand-to-mouth ['hændtə'mauθ] *adj*
(*existence*) precario(a).
handwriting ['hændraɪtɪŋ] *n* scrittura.
handwritten ['hændrɪtn] *adj* scritto(a) a
mano, manoscritto(a).
handy ['hændɪ] *adj* (*person*) bravo(a); (*close*
at hand) a portata di mano; (*convenient*)
comodo(a); (*useful*: *machine etc*)
pratico(a), utile; **to come in ~** servire.
handyman ['hændɪmæn] *n* tuttofare *m inv*;
tools for the ~ arnesi per il fatelo-da-voi.
hang, *pt*, *pp* **hung** [hæŋ, hʌŋ] *vt* appendere;
(*criminal*: *pt*, *pp* **hanged**) impiccare ♦ *vi*
pendere; (*hair*) scendere; (*drapery*)
cadere; **to get the ~ of (doing) sth** (*col*)
cominiciare a capire (come si fa) qc.
▶**hang about** *vi* bighellonare, ciondolare.
▶**hang back** *vi* (*hesitate*): **to ~ back (from**
doing) essere riluttante (a fare).
▶**hang on** *vi* (*wait*) aspettare ♦ *vt fus*
(*depend on*: *decision etc*) dipendere da; **to**
~ on to (*keep hold of*) aggrapparsi a,
attaccarsi a; (*keep*) tenere.
▶**hang out** *vt* (*washing*) stendere (fuori);
(*col*: *live*) stare ♦ *vi* penzolare, pendere.
▶**hang together** *vi* (*argument etc*) stare in
piedi.
▶**hang up** *vi* (*TEL*) riattaccare ♦ *vt*
appendere; **to ~ up on sb** (*TEL*) metter
giù il ricevitore a qn.
hangar ['hæŋə*] *n* hangar *m inv*.
hangdog ['hæŋdɒg] *adj* (*guilty*: *look,*
expression) da cane bastonato.
hanger ['hæŋə*] *n* gruccia.
hanger-on [hæŋər'ɒn] *n* parassita *m*.
hang-glider ['hæŋglaɪdə*] *n* deltaplano.
hang-gliding ['hæŋglaɪdɪŋ] *n* volo col
deltaplano.
hanging ['hæŋɪŋ] *n* (*execution*)
impiccagione *f*.
hangman ['hæŋmən] *n* boia *m*, carnefice *m*.
hangover ['hæŋəuvə*] *n* (*after drinking*)
postumi *mpl* di sbornia.
hang-up ['hæŋʌp] *n* complesso.
hank [hæŋk] *n* matassa.
hanker ['hæŋkə*] *vi*: **to ~ after** bramare.
hankering ['hæŋkərɪŋ] *n*: **to have a ~ for**
sth/to do sth avere una gran voglia di
qc/di fare qc.
hankie, hanky ['hæŋkɪ] *n abbr* =
handkerchief.
Hants *abbr* (*BRIT*) = **Hampshire**.
haphazard [hæp'hæzəd] *adj* a casaccio, alla
carlona.
hapless ['hæplɪs] *adj* disgraziato(a);
(*unfortunate*) sventurato(a).
happen ['hæpən] *vi* accadere, succedere;

she ~ed to be free per caso era libera; if anything ~ed to him se dovesse succedergli qualcosa; as it ~s guarda caso; what's ~ing? cosa succede?, cosa sta succedendo?
▸happen (up)on *vt fus* capitare su.
happening ['hæpnɪŋ] *n* avvenimento.
happily ['hæpɪlɪ] *adv* felicemente; fortunatamente.
happiness ['hæpɪnɪs] *n* felicità, contentezza.
happy ['hæpɪ] *adj* felice, contento(a); ~ with (*arrangements etc*) soddisfatto(a) di; yes, I'd be ~ to (certo,) con piacere, (ben) volentieri; ~ birthday! buon compleanno!; ~ Christmas/New Year! buon Natale/anno!
happy-go-lucky ['hæpɪgəu'lʌkɪ] *adj* spensierato(a).
happy hour *n orario in cui i pub hanno prezzi ridotti.*
harangue [hə'ræŋ] *vt* arringare.
harass ['hærəs] *vt* molestare.
harassed ['hærəst] *adj* assillato(a).
harassment ['hærəsmənt] *n* molestia.
harbour, (*US*) harbor ['hɑːbə*] *n* porto ♦ *vt* dare rifugio a; (*retain: grudge etc*) covare, nutrire.
harbo(u)r dues *npl* diritti *mpl* portuali.
harbo(u)r master *n* capitano di porto.
hard [hɑːd] *adj* duro(a) ♦ *adv* (*work*) sodo; (*think, try*) bene; to look ~ at guardare fissamente; esaminare attentamente; to drink ~ bere forte; ~ luck! peccato!; no ~ feelings! senza rancore!; to be ~ of hearing essere duro(a) d'orecchio; to be ~ on sb essere severo con qn; to be ~ done by essere trattato(a) ingiustamente; I find it ~ to believe that ... stento *or* faccio fatica a credere che ... + *sub.*
hard-and-fast ['hɑːdən'fɑːst] *adj* ferreo(a).
hardback ['hɑːdbæk] *n* libro rilegato.
hardboard ['hɑːdbɔːd] *n* legno precompresso.
hard-boiled egg ['hɑːd'bɔɪld-] *n* uovo sodo.
hard cash *n* denaro in contanti.
hard copy *n* (*COMPUT*) hard copy *f inv*, terminale *m* di stampa.
hard-core ['hɑːd'kɔː*] *adj* (*pornography*) hardcore *inv*; (*supporters*) irriducibile.
hard court *n* (*TENNIS*) campo in terra battuta.
hard disk *n* (*COMPUT*) hard disk *m inv*, disco rigido.
harden ['hɑːdn] *vt* indurire; (*steel*) temprare; (*fig: determination*) rafforzare ♦ *vi* (*substance*) indurirsi.

hardened ['hɑːdnd] *adj* (*criminal*) incallito(a); to be ~ to sth essere (diventato) insensibile a qc.
hard graft *n*: by sheer ~ lavorando da matti.
hard-headed ['hɑːd'hedɪd] *adj* pratico(a).
hard-hearted ['hɑːd'hɑːtɪd] *adj* che non si lascia commuovere, dal cuore duro.
hard-hitting ['hɑːd'hɪtɪŋ] *adj* molto duro(a); a ~ documentary un documentario *m* verità *inv.*
hard labour *n* lavori forzati *mpl.*
hardliner [hɑːd'laɪnə*] *n* fautore/trice della linea dura.
hard-luck story [hɑːd'lʌk-] *n* storia lacrimosa (*con un fine ben preciso*).
hardly ['hɑːdlɪ] *adv* (*scarcely*) appena, a mala pena; it's ~ the case non è proprio il caso; ~ anyone/anywhere quasi nessuno/da nessuna parte; I can ~ believe it stento a crederci.
hardness ['hɑːdnɪs] *n* durezza.
hard-nosed ['hɑːd'nəuzd] *adj* (*people*) con i piedi per terra.
hard-pressed ['hɑːd'prest] *adj* in difficoltà.
hard sell *n* (*COMM*) intensa campagna promozionale.
hardship ['hɑːdʃɪp] *n* avversità *f inv*; privazioni *fpl.*
hard shoulder *n* (*BRIT AUT*) corsia d'emergenza.
hard-up [hɑːd'ʌp] *adj* (*col*) al verde.
hardware ['hɑːdwɛə*] *n* ferramenta *fpl*; (*COMPUT*) hardware *m.*
hardware shop *n* (negozio di) ferramenta *fpl.*
hard-wearing [hɑːd'wɛərɪŋ] *adj* resistente, robusto(a).
hard-won ['hɑːd'wʌn] *adj* sudato(a).
hard-working [hɑːd'wəːkɪŋ] *adj* lavoratore(trice).
hardy ['hɑːdɪ] *adj* robusto(a); (*plant*) resistente al gelo.
hare [hɛə*] *n* lepre *f.*
hare-brained ['hɛəbreɪnd] *adj* folle; scervellato(a).
harelip ['hɛəlɪp] *n* (*MED*) labbro leporino.
harem [hɑː'riːm] *n* harem *m inv.*
hark back [hɑːk-] *vi*: to ~ back to (*former days*) rievocare; (*earlier occasion*) ritornare a *or* su.
harm [hɑːm] *n* male *m*; (*wrong*) danno ♦ *vt* (*person*) fare male a; (*thing*) danneggiare; to mean no ~ non avere l'intenzione d'offendere; out of ~'s way al sicuro; there's no ~ in trying tentar non nuoce.
harmful ['hɑːmful] *adj* dannoso(a).
harmless ['hɑːmlɪs] *adj* innocuo(a);

inoffensivo(a).

harmonic [hɑːˈmɒnɪk] *adj* armonico(a).

harmonica [hɑːˈmɒnɪkə] *n* armonica.

harmonics [hɑːˈmɒnɪks] *npl* armonia.

harmonious [hɑːˈməʊnɪəs] *adj* armonioso(a).

harmonium [hɑːˈməʊnɪəm] *n* armonium *m inv*.

harmonize [ˈhɑːmənaɪz] *vt, vi* armonizzare.

harmony [ˈhɑːmənɪ] *n* armonia.

harness [ˈhɑːnɪs] *n* bardatura, finimenti *mpl* ♦ *vt* (*horse*) bardare; (*resources*) sfruttare.

harp [hɑːp] *n* arpa ♦ *vi*: **to ~ on about** insistere tediosamente su.

harpist [ˈhɑːpɪst] *n* arpista *m/f*.

harpoon [hɑːˈpuːn] *n* arpione *m*.

harpsichord [ˈhɑːpsɪkɔːd] *n* clavicembalo.

harrow [ˈhærəʊ] *n* (*AGR*) erpice *m*.

harrowing [ˈhærəʊɪŋ] *adj* straziante.

harry [ˈhærɪ] *vt* (*MIL*) saccheggiare; (*person*) assillare.

harsh [hɑːʃ] *adj* (*hard*) duro(a); (*severe*) severo(a); (*unpleasant: sound*) rauco(a); (: *colour*) chiassoso(a); violento(a).

harshly [ˈhɑːʃlɪ] *adv* duramente; severamente.

harshness [ˈhɑːʃnɪs] *n* durezza; severità.

harvest [ˈhɑːvɪst] *n* raccolto; (*of grapes*) vendemmia ♦ *vt* fare il raccolto di, raccogliere; vendemmiare ♦ *vi* fare il raccolto; vendemmiare.

harvester [ˈhɑːvɪstə*] *n* (*machine*) mietitrice *f*; (*also*: **combine** ~) mietitrebbia; (*person*) mietitore/trice.

has [hæz] *see* **have**.

has-been [ˈhæzbiːn] *n* (*col: person*): **he's/she's a** ~ ha fatto il suo tempo.

hash [hæʃ] *n* (*CULIN*) *specie di spezzatino fatto con carne già cotta*; (*fig: mess*) pasticcio ♦ *n abbr* (*col*) = **hashish**.

hashish [ˈhæʃɪʃ] *n* hascisc *m*.

hasn't [ˈhæznt] = **has not**.

hassle [ˈhæsl] *n* (*col*) sacco di problemi.

haste [heɪst] *n* fretta.

hasten [ˈheɪsn] *vt* affrettare ♦ *vi* affrettarsi; **I ~ to add that** ... mi preme di aggiungere che ....

hastily [ˈheɪstɪlɪ] *adv* in fretta, precipitosamente.

hasty [ˈheɪstɪ] *adj* affrettato(a), precipitoso(a).

hat [hæt] *n* cappello.

hatbox [ˈhætbɒks] *n* cappelliera.

hatch [hætʃ] *n* (*NAUT: also*: ~**way**) boccaporto; (*BRIT: also*: **service** ~) portello di servizio ♦ *vi* schiudersi ♦ *vt* covare; (*fig: scheme, plot*) elaborare, mettere a punto.

hatchback [ˈhætʃbæk] *n* (*AUT*) tre (*or* cinque) porte *f inv*.

hatchet [ˈhætʃɪt] *n* accetta.

hatchet job *n* (*col*) attacco spietato; **to do a ~ on sb** fare a pezzi qn.

hatchet man *n* (*col*) tirapiedi *m inv*, scagnozzo.

hate [heɪt] *vt* odiare, detestare ♦ *n* odio; **to ~ to do** *or* **doing** detestare fare; **I ~ to trouble you, but** ... mi dispiace disturbarla, ma ....

hateful [ˈheɪtful] *adj* odioso(a), detestabile.

hatred [ˈheɪtrɪd] *n* odio.

hat trick *n* (*BRIT SPORT, also fig*): **to get a ~** segnare tre punti consecutivi (*or* vincere per tre volte consecutive).

haughty [ˈhɔːtɪ] *adj* altero(a), arrogante.

haul [hɔːl] *vt* trascinare, tirare ♦ *n* (*of fish*) pescata; (*of stolen goods etc*) bottino.

haulage [ˈhɔːlɪdʒ] *n* trasporto; autotrasporto.

haulage contractor *n* (*BRIT: firm*) impresa di trasporti; (: *person*) autotrasportatore *m*.

haulier [ˈhɔːlɪə*], (*US*) **hauler** [ˈhɔːlə*] *n* autotrasportatore *m*.

haunch [hɔːntʃ] *n* anca; **a ~ of venison** una coscia di cervo.

haunt [hɔːnt] *vt* (*subj: fear*) pervadere; (: *person*) frequentare ♦ *n* rifugio; **a ghost ~s this house** questa casa è abitata da un fantasma.

haunted [ˈhɔːntɪd] *adj* (*castle etc*) abitato(a) dai fantasmi *or* dagli spiriti; (*look*) ossessionato(a), tormentato(a).

haunting [ˈhɔːntɪŋ] *adj* (*sight, music*) ossessionante, che perseguita.

Havana [həˈvænə] *n* l'Avana.

═══════════════════════════ **KEYWORD**

have [hæv] (*pt, pp* **had**) *aux vb* **1** (*gen*) avere; essere; **to ~ arrived/gone** essere arrivato(a)/andato(a); **to ~ eaten/slept** avere mangiato/dormito; **he has been kind/promoted** è stato gentile/promosso; **having finished** *or* **when he had finished, he left** dopo aver finito, se n'è andato
2 (*in tag questions*): **you've done it, ~n't you?** l'hai fatto, (non è) vero?; **he hasn't done it, has he?** non l'ha fatto, vero?
3 (*in short answers and questions*): **you've made a mistake — no I ~n't/so I ~** ha fatto un errore — ma no, niente affatto/sì, è vero; **we ~n't paid — yes we ~!** non abbiamo pagato — ma sì che abbiamo pagato!; **I've been there before, ~ you?** ci sono già stato, e lei?
♦ *modal aux vb* (*be obliged*): **to ~ (got) to do sth** dover fare qc; **I ~n't got** *or* **I don't ~**

to **wear glasses** non ho bisogno di portare gli occhiali; **I had better leave** è meglio che io vada ♦ *vt* **1** (*possess, obtain*) avere; **he has (got) blue eyes/dark hair** ha gli occhi azzurri/i capelli scuri; ~ **you got** *or* **do you** ~ **a car/phone?** ha la macchina/il telefono?; **may I** ~ **your address?** potrebbe darmi il suo indirizzo?; **you can** ~ **it for £5** te lo do per 5 sterline **2** (+*noun: take, hold etc*): **to** ~ **a bath** fare un bagno; **to** ~ **breakfast** fare colazione; **to** ~ **a cigarette** fumare una sigaretta; **to** ~ **dinner** cenare; **to** ~ **a drink** bere qualcosa; **to** ~ **lunch** pranzare; **to** ~ **a party** dare *or* fare una festa; **to** ~ **an operation** avere *or* subire un'operazione; **to** ~ **a swim** fare una nuotata; **I'll** ~ **a coffee** prendo un caffè; **let me** ~ **a try** fammi *or* lasciami provare **3**: **to** ~ **sth done** far fare qc; **to** ~ **one's hair cut** tagliarsi *or* farsi tagliare i capelli; **he had a suit made** si fece fare un abito; **to** ~ **sb do sth** far fare qc a qn; **he had me phone his boss** mi ha fatto telefonare al suo capo **4** (*experience, suffer*) avere; **to** ~ **a cold/ flu** avere il raffreddore/l'influenza; **she had her bag stolen** le hanno rubato la borsa **5** (*phrases*): **you've been had!** ci sei cascato!; **I won't** ~ **it!** (*accept*) non mi sta affatto bene!; *see also* **haves**
▶**have in** *vt*: **to** ~ **it in for sb** (*col*) avercela con qn
▶**have on** *vt* (*garment*) avere addosso; (*be busy with*) avere da fare; **I don't** ~ **any money on me** non ho soldi con me; ~ **you anything on tomorrow?** (*BRIT*) ha qualcosa in programma per domani?; **to** ~ **sb on** (*BRIT col*) prendere in giro qn
▶**have out** *vt*: **to** ~ **it out with sb** (*settle a problem etc*) mettere le cose in chiaro con qn.

haven ['heɪvn] *n* porto; (*fig*) rifugio.
haversack ['hævəsæk] *n* zaino.
haves [hævz] *npl* (*col*): **the** ~ **and the have-nots** gli abbienti e i non abbienti.
havoc ['hævək] *n* confusione *f*, subbuglio; **to play** ~ **with sth** scombussolare qc; **to wreak** ~ **on sth** mettere in subbuglio qc.
Hawaii [hə'waiiː] *n* le Hawaii.
Hawaiian [hə'waɪjən] *adj* hawaiano(a) ♦ *n* hawaiano/a; (*LING*) lingua hawaiana.
hawk [hɔːk] *n* falco ♦ *vt* (*goods for sale*) vendere per strada.
hawker ['hɔːkə*] *n* venditore *m* ambulante.

hawkish ['hɔːkɪʃ] *adj* violento(a).
hawthorn ['hɔːθɔːn] *n* biancospino.
hay [heɪ] *n* fieno.
hay fever *n* febbre *f* da fieno.
haystack ['heɪstæk] *n* pagliaio.
haywire ['heɪwaɪə*] *adj* (*col*): **to go** ~ perdere la testa; impazzire.
hazard ['hæzəd] *n* (*chance*) azzardo; (*risk*) pericolo, rischio ♦ *vt* (*one's life*) rischiare, mettere a repentaglio; (*remark*) azzardare; **to be a health/fire** ~ essere pericoloso per la salute/in caso d'incendio; **to** ~ **a guess** tirare a indovinare.
hazardous ['hæzədəs] *adj* pericoloso(a), rischioso(a).
hazard pay *n* (*US*) indennità di rischio.
hazard warning lights *npl* (*AUT*) luci *fpl* di emergenza.
haze [heɪz] *n* foschia.
hazel ['heɪzl] *n* (*tree*) nocciolo ♦ *adj* (*eyes*) (*color*) nocciola *inv*.
hazelnut ['heɪzlnʌt] *n* nocciola.
hazy ['heɪzɪ] *adj* fosco(a); (*idea*) vago(a); (*photograph*) indistinto(a).
H-bomb ['eɪtʃbɔm] *n* bomba H.
h & c *abbr* (*BRIT*) = hot and cold (*water*).
HE *abbr* – high explosive; (*REL, DIPLOMACY*: = His (*or* Her) Excellency) S.E.
he [hiː] *pron* lui, egli; **it is** ~ **who** ... è lui che ...; **here** ~ **is** eccolo; ~**-bear** *etc* orso *etc* maschio.
head [hɛd] *n* testa, capo; (*leader*) capo; (*on tape recorder, computer etc*) testina ♦ *vt* (*list*) essere in testa a; (*group*) essere a capo di; ~**s** (**or tails**) testa (o croce), pari (o dispari); ~ **first** a capofitto; ~ **over heels in love** pazzamente innamorato(a); **£10 a** *or* **per** ~ 10 sterline a testa; **to sit at the** ~ **of the table** sedersi a capotavola; **to have a** ~ **for business** essere tagliato per gli affari; **to have no** ~ **for heights** soffrire di vertigini; **to lose/keep one's** ~ perdere/non perdere la testa; **to come to a** ~ (*fig: situation etc*) precipitare; **to** ~ **the ball** (*SPORT*) dare di testa alla palla.
▶**head for** *vt fus* dirigersi verso.
▶**head off** *vt* (*threat, danger*) sventare.
headache ['hɛdeɪk] *n* mal *m* di testa; **to have a** ~ aver mal di testa.
headband ['hɛdbænd] *n* fascia per i capelli.
headboard ['hɛdbɔːd] *n* testiera (del letto).
head cold *n* raffreddore *m* di testa.
headdress ['hɛddrɛs] *n* (*of Indian etc*) copricapo; (*of bride*) acconciatura.
headed notepaper ['hɛdɪd-] *n* carta intestata.
header ['hɛdə*] *n* (*BRIT col; FOOTBALL*) colpo

di testa; (: *fall*) caduta di testa.
head-first['hɛd'fə:st] *adv* a testa in giù;
(*fig*) senza pensare.
headhunt['hɛdhʌnt] *vt*: **to be ~ed** avere
un'offerta di lavoro da un cacciatore di
teste.
headhunter['hɛdhʌntə*] *n* cacciatore *m* di
teste.
heading['hɛdɪŋ] *n* titolo; intestazione *f*.
headlamp['hɛdlæmp] *n* (*BRIT*) = **headlight**.
headland['hɛdlənd] *n* promontorio.
headlight['hɛdlaɪt] *n* fanale *m*.
headline['hɛdlaɪn] *n* titolo.
headlong['hɛdlɔŋ] *adv* (*fall*) a capofitto;
(*rush*) precipitosamente.
headmaster[hɛd'mɑːstə*] *n* preside *m*.
headmistress[hɛd'mɪstrɪs] *n* preside *f*.
head officen sede *f* (centrale).
head-on[hɛd'ɔn] *adj* (*collision*) frontale.
headphones['hɛdfəunz] *npl* cuffia.
headquarters (HQ)[hɛd'kwɔːtəz] *npl*
ufficio centrale; (*MIL*) quartiere *m*
generale.
head-rest['hɛdrɛst] *n* poggiacapo.
headroom['hɛdrum] *n* (*in car*) altezza
dell'abitacolo; (*under bridge*) altezza
limite.
headscarf['hɛdskɑːf] *n* foulard *m inv*.
headset['hɛdsɛt] *n* = **headphones**.
headstone['hɛdstəun] *n* (*on grave*) lapide *f*,
pietra tombale.
headstrong['hɛdstrɔŋ] *adj* testardo(a).
head waitern capocameriere *m*.
headway['hɛdweɪ] *n*: **to make ~** fare
progressi *or* passi avanti.
headwind['hɛdwɪnd] *n* controvento.
heady['hɛdɪ] *adj* che dà alla testa;
inebriante.
heal[hiːl] *vt*, *vi* guarire.
health[hɛlθ] *n* salute *f*; **Department of H~**
≈ Ministero della Sanità.
health caren assistenza sanitaria.
health centren (*BRIT*) poliambulatorio.
health food(s)n(*pl*) alimenti *mpl* integrali.
health hazardn pericolo per la salute.
Health Servicen: **the ~** (*BRIT*) ≈ il
Servizio Sanitario Statale.
healthy['hɛlθɪ] *adj* (*person*) in buona salute;
(*climate*) salubre; (*food*) salutare; (*attitude
etc*) sano(a); (*economy*) florido(a); (*bank
balance*) solido(a).
heap[hiːp] *n* mucchio ♦ *vt* ammucchiare;
~s (of) (*col*: *lots*) un sacco (di), un
mucchio (di); **to ~ favours/praise/gifts**
etc **on sb** ricolmare qn di favori/lodi/
regali *etc*.
hear,*pt*, *pp* **heard** [hɪə*, hə:d] *vt* sentire;
(*news*) ascoltare; (*lecture*) assistere a;

(*LAW*: *case*) esaminare ♦ *vi* sentire; **to ~**
about sentire parlare di; (*have news of*)
avere notizie di; **did you ~ about the**
move? ha sentito del trasloco?; **to ~ from**
sb ricevere notizie da qn.
▶**hear out**vt ascoltare senza
interrompere.
hearing['hɪərɪŋ] *n* (*sense*) udito; (*of*
witnesses) audizione *f*; (*of a case*) udienza;
to give sb a ~ dare ascolto a qn.
hearing aidn apparecchio acustico.
hearsay['hɪəseɪ] *n* dicerie *fpl*, chiacchiere
fpl; **by ~** *adv* per sentito dire.
hearse[hə:s] *n* carro funebre.
heart[hɑːt] *n* cuore *m*; **~s** *npl* (*CARDS*) cuori
mpl; **at ~** in fondo; **by ~** (*learn*, *know*) a
memoria; **to take ~** farsi coraggio *or*
animo; **to lose ~** perdere coraggio,
scoraggiarsi; **to have a weak ~** avere il
cuore debole; **to set one's ~ on sth/on**
doing sth tenere molto a qc/a fare qc; **the**
~ of the matter il nocciolo della
questione.
heartache['hɑːteɪk] *n* pene *fpl*, dolori *mpl*.
heart attackn attacco di cuore.
heartbeat['hɑːtbiːt] *n* battito del cuore.
heartbreak['hɑːtbreɪk] *n* immenso dolore
m.
heartbreaking['hɑːtbreɪkɪŋ] *adj* straziante.
heartbroken['hɑːtbrəukən] *adj* affranto(a);
to be ~ avere il cuore spezzato.
heartburn['hɑːtbə:n] *n* bruciore *m* di
stomaco.
-hearted['hɑːtɪd] *suffix*: **a kind~ person** una
persona molto gentile.
heartening['hɑːtnɪŋ] *adj* incoraggiante.
heart failuren (*MED*) arresto cardiaco.
heartfelt['hɑːtfɛlt] *adj* sincero(a).
hearth[hɑːθ] *n* focolare *m*.
heartily['hɑːtɪlɪ] *adv* (*laugh*) di cuore; (*eat*)
di buon appetito; (*agree*) in pieno,
completamente; **to be ~ sick of** (*BRIT*)
essere veramente stufo di, essere
arcistufo di.
heartland['hɑːtlænd] *n* zona centrale;
Italy's industrial ~ il cuore dell'industria
italiana.
heartless['hɑːtlɪs] *adj* senza cuore,
insensibile; crudele.
heartstrings['hɑːtstrɪŋz] *npl*: **to tug at sb's**
~ toccare il cuore a qn, toccare qn nel
profondo.
heart-throb['hɑːtθrɔb] *n* rubacuori *m inv*.
heart-to-heart['hɑːttə'hɑːt] *adj*, *adv* a cuore
aperto.
heart transplantn trapianto del cuore.
heartwarming['hɑːtwɔːmɪŋ] *adj*
confortante, che scalda il cuore.

hearty['hɑːtɪ] adj caloroso(a); robusto(a), sano(a); vigoroso(a).

heat[hiːt] n calore m; (fig) ardore m; fuoco; (SPORT: also: **qualifying** ~) prova eliminatoria; (ZOOL): **in** or (BRIT) **on** ~ in calore ♦ vt scaldare.

►**heat up** vi (liquids) scaldarsi; (room) riscaldarsi ♦ vt riscaldare.

heated['hiːtɪd] adj riscaldato(a); (fig) appassionato(a); acceso(a), eccitato(a).

heater['hiːtə*] n stufa; radiatore m.

heath[hiːθ] n (BRIT) landa.

heathen['hiːðn] adj, n pagano(a).

heather['hɛðə*] n erica.

heating['hiːtɪŋ] n riscaldamento.

heat-resistant['hiːtrɪzɪstənt] adj termoresistente.

heat-seeking['hiːtsiːkɪŋ] adj che cerca fonti di calore.

heatstroke['hiːtstrəuk] n colpo di sole.

heatwave['hiːtweɪv] n ondata di caldo.

heave[hiːv] vt sollevare (con forza) ♦ vi sollevarsi ♦ n (push) grande spinta; **to** ~ **a sigh** emettere or mandare un sospiro.

►**heave to** (pt, pp **hove**) vi (NAUT) mettersi in cappa.

heaven['hɛvn] n paradiso, cielo; ~ **forbid!** Dio ce ne guardi!; **for** ~'s **sake!** (pleading) per amor del cielo!, per carità!; (protesting) santo cielo!, in nome del cielo!; **thank** ~! grazie al cielo!

heavenly['hɛvnlɪ] adj divino(a), celeste.

heavily['hɛvɪlɪ] adv pesantemente; (drink, smoke) molto.

heavy['hɛvɪ] adj pesante; (sea) grosso(a); (rain) forte; (drinker, smoker) gran (before noun); **it's** ~ **going** è una gran fatica; ~ **industry** industria pesante.

heavy cream n (US) doppia panna.

heavy-duty['hɛvɪ'djuːtɪ] adj molto resistente.

heavy goods vehicle (HGV) n (BRIT) veicolo per trasporti pesanti.

heavy-handed['hɛvɪ'hændɪd] adj (clumsy, tactless) pesante.

heavy metal n (MUS) heavy metal m.

heavy-set['hɛvɪ'sɛt] adj (esp US) tarchiato(a).

heavyweight['hɛvɪweɪt] n (SPORT) peso massimo.

Hebrew['hiːbruː] adj ebreo(a) ♦ n (LING) ebraico.

Hebrides['hɛbrɪdiːz] npl: **the** ~ le Ebridi.

heck[hɛk] (col) excl: **oh** ~! oh no! ♦ n: **a** ~ **of** **a lot of** un gran bel po' di.

heckle['hɛkl] vt interpellare e dare noia a (un oratore).

heckler['hɛklə*] n agitatore/trice.

hectare['hɛktɑː*] n (BRIT) ettaro.

hectic['hɛktɪk] adj movimentato(a); (busy) frenetico(a).

hector['hɛktə*] vt usare le maniere forti con.

he'd[hiːd] = **he would; he had.**

hedge[hɛdʒ] n siepe f ♦ vi essere elusivo(a); **as a** ~ **against inflation** per cautelarsi contro l'inflazione; **to** ~ **one's bets** (fig) coprirsi dai rischi.

►**hedge in** vt recintare con una siepe.

hedgehog['hɛdʒhɔg] n riccio.

hedgerow['hɛdʒrəu] n siepe f.

hedonism['hiːdənɪzəm] n edonismo.

heed[hiːd] vt (also: **take** ~ **of**) badare a, far conto di ♦ n: **to pay (no)** ~ **to, to take (no)** ~ **of** (non) ascoltare, (non) tener conto di.

heedless['hiːdlɪs] adj sbadato(a).

heel[hiːl] n (ANAT) calcagno; (of shoe) tacco ♦ vt (shoe) rifare i tacchi a; **to bring to** ~ addomesticare; **to take to one's** ~**s** (col) darsela a gambe, alzare i tacchi.

hefty['hɛftɪ] adj (person) solido(a); (parcel) pesante; (piece, price) grosso(a).

heifer['hɛfə*] n giovenca.

height[haɪt] n altezza; (high ground) altura; (fig: of glory) apice m; (: of stupidity) colmo; **what** ~ **are you?** quanto sei alto?; **of average** ~ di statura media; **to be afraid of** ~**s** soffrire di vertigini; **it's the** ~ **of fashion** è l'ultimo grido della moda.

heighten['haɪtn] vt innalzare; (fig) accrescere.

heinous['heɪnəs] adj nefando(a), atroce.

heir[ɛə*] n erede m.

heir apparent n erede m/f legittimo(a).

heiress['ɛərɛs] n erede f.

heirloom['ɛəluːm] n mobile m (or gioiello or quadro) di famiglia.

heist[haɪst] n (US col) rapina.

held[hɛld] pt, pp of **hold.**

helicopter['hɛlɪkɔptə*] n elicottero.

heliport['hɛlɪpɔːt] n eliporto.

helium['hiːlɪəm] n elio.

hell[hɛl] n inferno; **a** ~ **of a ...** (col) un(a) maledetto(a) ...; **oh** ~! (col) porca miseria!, accidenti!

he'll[hiːl] = **he will, he shall.**

hell-bent[hɛl'bɛnt] adj (col): **to be** ~ **on doing sth** voler fare qc a tutti i costi.

hellish['hɛlɪʃ] adj infernale.

hello[hə'ləu] excl buon giorno!; ciao! (to sb one addresses as "tu"); (surprise) ma guarda!

helm[hɛlm] n (NAUT) timone m.

helmet['hɛlmɪt] n casco.

helmsman['hɛlmzmən] n timoniere m.

help[hɛlp] n aiuto; (charwoman) donna di

servizio; (*assistant etc*) impiegato/a ♦ *vt*
aiutare; ~! aiuto!; **with the ~ of** con
l'aiuto di; **to be of ~ to sb** essere di aiuto
or essere utile a qn; **to ~ sb (to) do sth**
aiutare qn a far qc; **can I ~ you?** (*in shop*)
desidera?; ~ **yourself (to bread)** si serva
(del pane); **I can't ~ saying** non posso
evitare di dire; **he can't ~ it** non ci può
far niente.
helper ['hɛlpə*] *n* aiutante *m/f*, assistente
m/f.
helpful ['hɛlpful] *adj* di grande aiuto;
(*useful*) utile.
helping ['hɛlpɪŋ] *n* porzione *f*.
helping hand *n*: **to give sb a ~** dare una
mano a qn.
helpless ['hɛlplɪs] *adj* impotente; debole;
(*baby*) indifeso(a).
helplessly ['hɛlplɪslɪ] *adv* (*watch*) senza
poter fare nulla.
helpline ['hɛlplaɪn] *n* ≈ telefono amico;
(*COMM*) servizio *m* informazioni *inv* (*a
pagamento*).
Helsinki ['hɛlsɪŋkɪ] *n* Helsinki *f*.
helter-skelter ['hɛltə'skɛltə*] *n* (*BRIT: in
funfair*) scivolo (a spirale).
hem [hɛm] *n* orlo ♦ *vt* fare l'orlo a.
▶**hem in** *vt* cingere; **to feel ~med in** (*fig*)
sentirsi soffocare.
he-man ['hi:mæn] *n* (*col*) fusto.
hematology [hi:mə'tɔlədʒɪ] *n* (*US*) =
haematology.
hemisphere ['hɛmɪsfɪə*] *n* emisfero.
hemlock ['hɛmlɔk] *n* cicuta.
hemoglobin [hi:məu'gləubɪn] *n* (*US*) =
haemoglobin.
hemophilia [hi:məu'fɪlɪə] *n* (*US*) =
haemophilia.
hemorrhage *n* (*US*) = **haemorrhage**.
hemorrhoids ['hɛmərɔɪdz] *npl* (*US*) =
haemorrhoids.
hemp [hɛmp] *n* canapa.
hen [hɛn] *n* gallina; (*female bird*) femmina.
hence [hɛns] *adv* (*therefore*) dunque; **2 years
~** di qui a 2 anni.
henceforth [hɛns'fɔ:θ] *adv* d'ora in poi.
henchman ['hɛntʃmən] *n* (*pej*) caudatario.
henna ['hɛnə] *n* henna.
hen night *n* (*col*) addio al nubilato.
hen party *n* (*col*) festa di sole donne.
henpecked ['hɛnpɛkt] *adj* dominato dalla
moglie.
hepatitis [hɛpə'taɪtɪs] *n* epatite *f*.
her [hə:*] *pron* (*direct*) la, l' + *vowel*;
(*indirect*) le; (*stressed, after prep*) lei; *see
note at* **she** ♦ *adj* il(la) suo(a), i(le)
suoi(sue); **I see ~** la vedo; **give ~ a
book** le dia un libro; **after ~** dopo (di)
lei.
herald ['hɛrəld] *n* araldo ♦ *vt* annunciare.
heraldic [hɛ'rældɪk] *adj* araldico(a).
heraldry ['hɛrəldrɪ] *n* araldica.
herb [hə:b] *n* erba; **~s** *npl* (*CULIN*) erbette
fpl.
herbaceous [hə:'beɪʃəs] *adj* erbaceo(a).
herbal ['hə:bəl] *adj* di erbe; **~ tea** tisana.
herbicide ['hə:bɪsaɪd] *n* erbicida *m*.
herd [hə:d] *n* mandria; (*of wild animals,
swine*) branco ♦ *vt* (*drive, gather: animals*)
guidare; (: *people*) radunare; **~ed
together** ammassati (come bestie).
here [hɪə*] *adv* qui, qua ♦ *excl* ehi!; ~! (*at roll
call*) presente!; ~ **is**, ~ **are** ecco; ~**'s my
sister** ecco mia sorella; ~ **she is** eccola; ~
she comes eccola che viene; **come** ~!
vieni qui!; ~ **and there** qua e là.
hereabouts ['hɪərəbauts] *adv* da queste
parti.
hereafter [hɪər'ɑ:ftə*] *adv* in futuro; dopo
questo ♦ *n*: **the ~** l'al di là *m*.
hereby [hɪə'baɪ] *adv* (*in letter*) con la
presente.
hereditary [hɪ'rɛdɪtrɪ] *adj* ereditario(a).
heredity [hɪ'rɛdɪtɪ] *n* eredità.
heresy ['hɛrəsɪ] *n* eresia.
heretic ['hɛrətɪk] *n* eretico/a.
heretical [hɪ'rɛtɪkl] *adj* eretico(a).
herewith [hɪə'wɪð] *adv* qui accluso.
heritage ['hɛrɪtɪdʒ] *n* eredità; (*of country,
nation*) retaggio; **our national ~** il nostro
patrimonio nazionale.
hermetically [hə:'mɛtɪklɪ] *adv*
ermeticamente; ~ **sealed** ermeticamente
chiuso.
hermit ['hə:mɪt] *n* eremita *m*.
hernia ['hə:nɪə] *n* ernia.
hero, ~es ['hɪərəu] *n* eroe *m*.
heroic [hɪ'rəuɪk] *adj* eroico(a).
heroin ['hɛrəuɪn] *n* eroina (*droga*).
heroin addict *n* eroinomane *m/f*.
heroine ['hɛrəuɪn] *n* eroina (*donna*).
heroism ['hɛrəuɪzəm] *n* eroismo.
heron ['hɛrən] *n* airone *m*.
hero worship *n* divismo.
herring ['hɛrɪŋ] *n* aringa.
hers [hə:z] *pron* il(la) suo(a), i(le) suoi(sue);
a friend of ~ un suo amico; **this is ~**
questo è (il) suo.
herself [hə:'sɛlf] *pron* (*reflexive*) si;
(*emphatic*) lei stessa; (*after prep*) se stessa,
sé.
Herts *abbr* (*BRIT*) = Hertfordshire.
he's [hi:z] = **he is; he has**.
hesitant ['hɛzɪtənt] *adj* esitante,
indeciso(a); **to be ~ about doing sth**
esitare a fare qc.

hesitate ['hɛzɪteɪt] *vi*: **to** ~ **(about/to do)** esitare (su/a fare); **don't** ~ **to ask (me)** non aver timore *or* paura di chiedermelo.
hesitation [hɛzɪ'teɪʃən] *n* esitazione *f*; **I have no** ~ **in saying (that)** ... non esito a dire che ....
hessian ['hɛsɪən] *n* tela di canapa.
heterogeneous [hɛtərəu'dʒiːnɪəs] *adj* eterogeneo(a).
heterosexual [hɛtərəu'sɛksjuəl] *adj*, *n* eterosessuale *(m/f)*.
het up [hɛt'ʌp] *adj* agitato(a).
HEW *n abbr* (*US*: = *Department of Health, Education, and Welfare*) *ministero della sanità, della pubblica istruzione e della previdenza sociale*.
hew [hjuː] *vt* tagliare (con l'accetta).
hex [hɛks] (*US*) *n* stregoneria ♦ *vt* stregare.
hexagon ['hɛksəgən] *n* esagono.
hexagonal [hɛk'sægənl] *adj* esagonale.
hey [heɪ] *excl* ehi!
heyday ['heɪdeɪ] *n*: **the** ~ **of** i bei giorni di, l'età d'oro di.
HF *n abbr* (= *high frequency*) AF.
HGV *n abbr see* **heavy goods vehicle**.
HI *abbr* (*US*) = *Hawaii*.
hi [haɪ] *excl* ciao!
hiatus [haɪ'ɪtəs] *n* vuoto; (*LING*) iato.
hibernate ['haɪbəneɪt] *vi* ibernare.
hibernation [haɪbə'neɪʃən] *n* letargo, ibernazione *f*.
hiccough, hiccup ['hɪkʌp] *vi* singhiozzare ♦ *n* singhiozzo; **to have (the)** ~**s** avere il singhiozzo.
hick [hɪk] *n* (*US col*) buzzurro/a.
hid [hɪd] *pt of* **hide**.
hidden ['hɪdn] *pp of* **hide** ♦ *adj* nascosto(a); **there are no** ~ **extras** è veramente tutto compreso nel prezzo; ~ **agenda** programma *m* occulto.
hide [haɪd] *n* (*skin*) pelle *f* ♦ *vb* (*pt* **hid**, *pp* **hidden** [hɪd, 'hɪdn]) *vt*: **to** ~ **sth (from sb)** nascondere qc (a qn) ♦ *vi*: **to** ~ **(from sb)** nascondersi (da qn).
hide-and-seek ['haɪdən'siːk] *n* rimpiattino.
hideaway ['haɪdəweɪ] *n* nascondiglio.
hideous ['hɪdɪəs] *adj* laido(a); orribile.
hide-out ['haɪdaut] *n* nascondiglio.
hiding ['haɪdɪŋ] *n* (*beating*) bastonata; **to be in** ~ (*concealed*) tenersi nascosto(a).
hiding place *n* nascondiglio.
hierarchy ['haɪərɑːkɪ] *n* gerarchia.
hieroglyphic [haɪərə'glɪfɪk] *adj* geroglifico(a); ~**s** *npl* geroglifici *mpl*.
hi-fi ['haɪfaɪ] *adj*, *n abbr* (= *high fidelity*) hi-fi *(m) inv*.
higgledy-piggledy ['hɪgldɪ'pɪgldɪ] *adv* alla rinfusa.

high [haɪ] *adj* alto(a); (*speed, respect, number*) grande; (*wind*) forte; (*BRIT CULIN*: *meat, game*) frollato(a); (: *spoilt*) andato(a) a male; (*col*: *on drugs*) fatto(a); (: *on drink*) su di giri ♦ *adv* alto, in alto ♦ *n*: **exports have reached a new** ~ le esportazioni hanno toccato un nuovo record; **20m** ~ alto(a) 20m; **to pay a** ~ **price for sth** pagare (molto) caro qc.
highball ['haɪbɔːl] *n* (*US*: *drink*) whisky (*or* brandy) e soda con ghiaccio.
highboy ['haɪbɔɪ] *n* (*US*) cassettone *m*.
highbrow ['haɪbrau] *adj*, *n* intellettuale (*m/f*).
highchair ['haɪtʃeə*] *n* seggiolone *m*.
high-class ['haɪ'klɑːs] *adj* (*neighbourhood*) elegante; (*hotel*) di prim'ordine; (*person*) di gran classe; (*food*) raffinato(a).
High Court *n* alta corte *f*; *see boxed note*.

HIGH COURT

Nel sistema legale inglese e gallese, la **High Court** *e la "Court of Appeal" compongono la "Supreme Court of Judicature", e si occupa di casi più importanti e complessi. In Scozia, invece, la* **High Court** *è la corte che si occupa dei reati più gravi e corrisponde alla "crown court" inglese.*

---

higher ['haɪə*] *adj* (*form of life, study etc*) superiore ♦ *adv* più in alto, più in su.
higher education *n* istruzione *f* superiore, istruzione universitaria.
highfalutin [haɪfə'luːtɪn] *adj* (*col*) pretenzioso(a).
high finance *n* alta finanza.
high-flier, high-flyer [haɪ'flaɪə*] *n* (giovane) promessa (*fig*).
high-flying [haɪ'flaɪɪŋ] *adj* (*fig*) promettente.
high-handed [haɪ'hændɪd] *adj* prepotente.
high-heeled [haɪ'hiːld] *adj* a tacchi alti.
highjack ['haɪdʒæk] *vt*, *n* = **hijack**.
high jump *n* (*SPORT*) salto in alto.
highlands ['haɪləndz] *npl* zona montuosa; **the H**~ le Highlands scozzesi.
high-level ['haɪlɛvl] *adj* (*talks etc*, *COMPUT*) ad alto livello.
highlight ['haɪlaɪt] *n* (*fig*: *of event*) momento culminante ♦ *vt* mettere in evidenza; ~**s** *npl* (*in hair*) colpi *mpl* di sole.
highlighter ['haɪlaɪtə*] *n* (*pen*) evidenziatore *m*.
highly ['haɪlɪ] *adv* molto; ~ **paid** pagato molto bene; **to speak** ~ **of** parlare molto bene di.
highly-strung ['haɪlɪ'strʌŋ] *adj* teso(a) di nervi, eccitabile.

highness ['hamɪs] *n* altezza; **Her H~** Sua Altezza.
high-pitched [haɪ'pɪtʃt] *adj* acuto(a).
high point *n*: **the ~** il momento più importante.
high-powered ['haɪ'pauǝd] *adj* (*engine*) molto potente, ad alta potenza; (*fig*: *person*) di prestigio.
high-pressure ['haɪprɛʃǝ*] *adj* ad alta pressione; (*fig*) aggressivo(a).
high-rise block ['haɪraɪz-] *n* palazzone *m*.
high school *n* (*BRIT*) scuola secondaria; (*US*) istituto d'istruzione secondaria; *see boxed note.*

HIGH SCHOOL

Negli Stati Uniti la **high school** *è un istituto di istruzione secondaria. Si suddivide in "junior high school" (dal settimo al nono anno di corso) e "senior high school" (dal decimo al dodicesimo), dove vengono impartiti sia insegnamenti scolastici che di formazione professionale. In Gran Bretagna molte scuole secondarie si chiamano* **high school**.

---

high season *n* (*BRIT*) alta stagione.
high spirits *npl* buonumore *m*, euforia; **to be in ~** essere euforico(a).
high street *n* (*BRIT*) strada principale.
highway ['haɪweɪ] *n* strada maestra; **the information ~** l'autostrada telematica.
Highway Code *n* (*BRIT*) codice *m* della strada.
highwayman ['haɪweɪmǝn] *n* bandito.
hijack ['haɪdʒæk] *vt* dirottare ♦ *n* dirottamento; (*also*: **~ing**) pirateria aerea.
hijacker ['haɪdʒækǝ*] *n* dirottatore/trice.
hike [haɪk] *vi* fare un'escursione a piedi ♦ *n* escursione *f* a piedi; (*col*: *in prices etc*) aumento ♦ *vt* (*col*) aumentare.
hiker ['haɪkǝ*] *n* escursionista *m/f*.
hiking ['haɪkɪŋ] *n* escursioni *fpl* a piedi.
hilarious [hɪ'lɛǝrɪǝs] *adj* che fa schiantare dal ridere.
hilarity [hɪ'lærɪtɪ] *n* ilarità.
hill [hɪl] *n* collina, colle *m*; (*fairly high*) montagna; (*on road*) salita.
hillbilly ['hɪlbɪlɪ] *n* (*US*) montanaro/a dal sud degli Stati Uniti; (*pej*) zotico/a.
hillside ['hɪlsaɪd] *n* fianco della collina.
hill start *n* (*AUT*) partenza in salita.
hilly ['hɪlɪ] *adj* collinoso(a); montagnoso(a).
hilt [hɪlt] *n* (*fig*): **to the ~** fino in fondo.
him [hɪm] *pron* (*direct*) lo, l' + *vowel*; (*indirect*) gli; (*stressed, after prep*) lui; **I see ~** lo vedo; **give ~ a book** gli dia un libro; **after ~** dopo (di) lui.

Himalayas [hɪmǝ'leɪǝz] *npl*: **the ~** l'Himalaia *m*.
himself [hɪm'sɛlf] *pron* (*reflexive*) si; (*emphatic*) lui stesso; (*after prep*) se stesso, sé.
hind [haɪnd] *adj* posteriore ♦ *n* cerva.
hinder ['hɪndǝ*] *vt* ostacolare; (*delay*) tardare; (*prevent*): **to ~ sb from doing** impedire a qn di fare.
hindquarters ['haɪndkwɔ:tǝz] *npl* (*ZOOL*) posteriore *m*.
hindrance ['hɪndrǝns] *n* ostacolo, impedimento.
hindsight ['haɪndsaɪt] *n* senno di poi; **with the benefit of ~** con il senno di poi.
Hindu ['hɪndu:] *n* indù *m/f inv*.
hinge [hɪndʒ] *n* cardine *m* ♦ *vi* (*fig*): **to ~ on** dipendere da.
hint [hɪnt] *n* accenno, allusione *f*; (*advice*) consiglio ♦ *vt*: **to ~ that** lasciar capire che ♦ *vi*: **to ~ at** accennare a; **to drop a ~** lasciar capire; **give me a ~** (*clue*) dammi almeno un'idea, dammi un'indicazione.
hip [hɪp] *n* anca, fianco; (*BOT*) frutto della rosa canina.
hip flask *n* fiaschetta da liquore tascabile.
hip hop *n* hip-hop *m*.
hippie ['hɪpɪ] *n* hippy *m/f inv*.
hip pocket *n* tasca posteriore dei calzoni.
hippopotamus, *pl* **~es** *or* **hippopotami** [hɪpǝ'pɔtǝmǝs, -'pɔtǝmaɪ] *n* ippopotamo.
hippy ['hɪpɪ] *n* = **hippie**.
hire ['haɪǝ*] *vt* (*BRIT*: *car, equipment*) noleggiare; (*worker*) assumere, dare lavoro a ♦ *n* nolo, noleggio; **for ~** da nolo; (*taxi*) libero(a); **on ~** a nolo.
▶ **hire out** *vt* noleggiare, dare a nolo *or* noleggio, affittare.
hire(d) car *n* (*BRIT*) macchina a nolo.
hire purchase (HP) *n* (*BRIT*) acquisto (*or* vendita) rateale; **to buy sth on ~** comprare qc a rate.
his [hɪz] *adj*, *pron* il(la) suo(sua), i(le) suoi(sue); **this is ~** questo è (il) suo.
hiss [hɪs] *vi* fischiare; (*cat, snake*) sibilare ♦ *n* fischio; sibilo.
histogram ['hɪstǝgræm] *n* istogramma *m*.
historian [hɪ'stɔ:rɪǝn] *n* storico/a.
historic(al) [hɪ'stɔrɪk(l)] *adj* storico(a).
history ['hɪstǝrɪ] *n* storia; **there's a long ~ of that illness in his family** ci sono molti precedenti (della malattia) nella sua famiglia.
histrionics [hɪstrɪ'ɔnɪks] *n* istrionismo.
hit [hɪt] *vt* (*pt*, *pp* **hit**) colpire, picchiare; (*knock against*) battere; (*reach*: *target*) raggiungere; (*collide with*: *car*) urtare contro; (*fig*: *affect*) colpire; (*find*: *problem*)

incontrare ♦ n colpo; (*success, song*)
successo; **to ~ the headlines** far titolo; **to
~ the road** (*col*) mettersi in cammino; **to
~ it off with sb** andare molto d'accordo
con qn; **to get a ~/10,000 ~s** (*COMPUT*)
trovare una pagina Web/10.000 pagine
Web; **our web page had 10,000 hits last
month** lo scorso mese il nostro sito ha
avuto 10.000 visitori.
▶**hit back** *vi*: **to ~ back at sb** restituire il
colpo a qn.
▶**hit out at** *vt fus* sferrare dei colpi contro;
(*fig*) attaccare.
▶**hit (up)on** *vt fus* (*answer*) imbroccare,
azzeccare; (*solution*) trovare (per caso).
hit-and-run driver ['hɪtænd'rʌn-] *n* pirata *m*
della strada.
hitch [hɪtʃ] *vt* (*fasten*) attaccare; (*also:* ~
up) tirare su ♦ *n* (*difficulty*) intoppo,
difficoltà *f inv*; **technical** ~ difficoltà
tecnica; **to ~ a lift** fare l'autostop.
▶**hitch up** *vt* (*horse, cart*) attaccare.
hitch-hike ['hɪtʃhaɪk] *vi* fare l'autostop.
hitch-hiker ['hɪtʃhaɪkə*] *n* autostoppista
m/f.
hi-tech ['haɪ'tɛk] *adj* high-tech *inv*, a
tecnologia avanzata.
hitherto ['hɪðə'tuː] *adv* finora.
hit list *n* libro nero.
hitman ['hɪtmæn] *n* (*col*) sicario.
hit-or-miss ['hɪtə'mɪs] *adj* casuale; **it's ~
whether ...** è in dubbio se ...; **the service
in this hotel is very ~** il servizio
dell'albergo lascia a desiderare.
hit parade *n* hit-parade *f*.
HIV *n abbr* (= *human immunodeficiency virus*)
virus *m inv* di immunodeficienza; **~-
negative/-positive** sieronegativo(a)/
sieropositivo(a).
hive [haɪv] *n* alveare *m*; **the shop was a ~ of
activity** (*fig*) c'era una grande attività nel
negozio.
▶**hive off** *vt* (*col*) separare.
hl *abbr* (= *hectolitre*) hl.
HM *abbr* (= *His (or Her) Majesty*) S.M. (= *Sua
Maestà*).
HMG *abbr* (*BRIT*) = *His (or Her) Majesty's
Government*.
HMI *n abbr* (*BRIT SCOL*: = *His (or Her) Majesty's
Inspector*) ~ ispettore *m* scolastico.
HMO *n abbr* (*US*: = *Health Maintenance
Organization*) organo per la salvaguardia
della salute pubblica.
HMS *abbr* (*BRIT*) = *His (or Her) Majesty's
Ship*.
HNC *n abbr* (*BRIT*: = *Higher National
Certificate*) diploma di istituto tecnico o
professionale.

HND *n abbr* (*BRIT*: = *Higher National Diploma*)
diploma in materie tecniche equivalente
ad una laurea.
hoard [hɔːd] *n* (*of food*) provviste *fpl*; (*of
money*) gruzzolo ♦ *vt* ammassare.
hoarding ['hɔːdɪŋ] *n* (*BRIT*) tabellone *m* per
affissioni.
hoarfrost ['hɔːfrɔst] *n* brina.
hoarse [hɔːs] *adj* rauco(a).
hoax [həʊks] *n* scherzo; falso allarme.
hob [hɔb] *n* piastra (con fornelli).
hobble ['hɔbl] *vi* zoppicare.
hobby ['hɔbɪ] *n* hobby *m inv*, passatempo.
hobby-horse ['hɔbɪhɔːs] *n* cavallo a
dondolo; (*fig*) chiodo fisso.
hobnail(ed) boots ['hɔbneɪl(d)-] *n* scarponi
mpl chiodati.
hobnob ['hɔbnɔb] *vi*: **to ~ (with)** mescolarsi
(con).
hobo ['həʊbəʊ] *n* (*US*) vagabondo.
hock [hɔk] *n* (*BRIT*: *wine*) vino del Reno; (*of
animal, CULIN*) garretto; (*col*): **to be in ~**
avere debiti.
hockey ['hɔkɪ] *n* hockey *m*.
hocus-pocus ['həʊkəs'pəʊkəs] *n* (*trickery*)
trucco; (*words: of magician*) abracadabra
m inv; (: *jargon*) parolone *fpl*.
hod [hɔd] *n* (*TECH*) cassetta per portare i
mattoni.
hodgepodge ['hɔdʒpɔdʒ] *n* = **hotchpotch**.
hoe [həʊ] *n* zappa ♦ *vt* (*ground*) zappare.
hog [hɔg] *n* maiale *m* ♦ *vt* (*fig*) arraffare; **to
go the whole ~** farlo fino in fondo.
Hogmanay [hɔgmə'neɪ] *n* (*SCOTTISH*) ≈ San
Silvestro.
hogwash ['hɔgwɔʃ] *n* (*col*) stupidaggini *fpl*.
hoist [hɔɪst] *n* paranco ♦ *vt* issare.
hoity-toity [hɔɪtɪ'tɔɪtɪ] *adj* (*col*)
altezzoso(a).
hold [həʊld] *vb* (*pt, pp* **held** [hɛld]) *vt* tenere;
(*contain*) contenere; (*keep back*)
trattenere; (*believe*) mantenere;
considerare; (*possess*) avere, possedere;
detenere ♦ *vi* (*withstand pressure*) tenere;
(*be valid*) essere valido(a) ♦ *n* presa; (*fig*)
potere *m*; (*NAUT*) stiva; ~ **the line!** (*TEL*)
resti in linea!; **to ~ office** (*POL*) essere in
carica; **to ~ sb responsible for sth**
considerare *or* ritenere qn responsabile
di qc; **to ~ one's own** (*fig*) difendersi
bene; **he ~s the view that ...** è del parere
che ...; **to ~ firm** *or* **fast** resistere bene,
tenere; **to catch** *or* **get (a) ~ of** afferrare;
to get ~ of (*fig*) trovare; **to get ~ of o.s.**
trattenersi.
▶**hold back** *vt* trattenere; (*secret*) tenere
celato(a); **to ~ sb back from doing sth**
impedire a qn di fare qc.

▶**hold down** vt (person) tenere a terra; (job) tenere.

▶**hold forth** vi fare or tenere una concione.

▶**hold off** vt tener lontano ♦ vi (rain): **if the rain ~s off** se continua a non piovere.

▶**hold on** vi tener fermo; (wait) aspettare; **~ on!** (TEL) resti in linea!

▶**hold on to** vt fus tenersi stretto(a) a; (keep) conservare.

▶**hold out** vt offrire ♦ vi (resist): **to ~ out (against)** resistere (a).

▶**hold over** vt (meeting etc) rimandare, rinviare.

▶**hold up** vt (raise) alzare; (support) sostenere; (delay) ritardare; (traffic) rallentare; (rob: bank) assaltare.

holdall ['həʊldɔːl] n (BRIT) borsone m.

holder ['həʊldə*] n (of ticket, title) possessore/posseditrice; (of office etc) incaricato/a; (of passport, post) titolare; (of record) detentore/trice.

holding ['həʊldɪŋ] n (share) azioni fpl, titoli mpl; (farm) podere m, tenuta.

holding company n holding f inv.

holdup ['həʊldʌp] n (robbery) rapina a mano armata; (delay) ritardo; (BRIT: in traffic) blocco.

hole [həʊl] n buco, buca ♦ vt bucare; **~ in the heart** (MED) morbo blu; **to pick ~s in** (fig) trovare da ridire su.

▶**hole up** vi nascondersi, rifugiarsi.

holiday ['hɒlədɪ] n vacanza; (from work) ferie fpl; (day off) giorno di vacanza; (public) giorno festivo; **to be on ~** essere in vacanza; **tomorrow is a ~** domani è festa.

holiday camp n (BRIT: for children) colonia (di villeggiatura); (also: **holiday centre**) ≈ villaggio (di vacanze).

holiday-maker ['hɒlədɪmeɪkə*] n (BRIT) villeggiante m/f.

holiday pay n stipendio delle ferie.

holiday resort n luogo di villeggiatura.

holiday season n stagione f delle vacanze.

holiness ['həʊlɪnɪs] n santità.

holistic [həʊ'lɪstɪk] adj olistico(a).

Holland ['hɒlənd] n Olanda.

holler ['hɒlə*] vi gridare, urlare.

hollow ['hɒləʊ] adj cavo(a), vuoto(a); (fig) falso(a); vano(a) ♦ n cavità f inv; (in land) valletta, depressione f.

▶**hollow out** vt scavare.

holly ['hɒlɪ] n agrifoglio.

hollyhock ['hɒlɪhɒk] n malvone m.

holocaust ['hɒləkɔːst] n olocausto.

hologram ['hɒləgræm] n ologramma m.

hols [hɒlz] npl: **the ~** le vacanze.

holster ['həʊlstə*] n fondina (di pistola).

holy ['həʊlɪ] adj santo(a); (bread) benedetto(a); (ground) consacrato(a); **the H~ Father** il Santo Padre.

Holy Communion n la Santa Comunione.

Holy Ghost, Holy Spirit n Spirito Santo.

Holy Land n: **the ~** la Terra Santa.

holy orders npl ordini mpl (sacri).

homage ['hɒmɪdʒ] n omaggio; **to pay ~ to** rendere omaggio a.

home [həʊm] n casa; (country) patria; (institution) casa, ricovero ♦ cpd (life) familiare; (cooking etc) casalingo(a); (ECON, POL) nazionale, interno(a); (SPORT: team) di casa; (: match, win) in casa ♦ adv a casa; in patria; (right in: nail etc) fino in fondo; **at ~** a casa; **to go** (or **come**) **~** tornare a casa (or in patria); **it's near my ~** è vicino a casa mia; **make yourself at ~** si metta a suo agio.

▶**home in on** vt fus (missiles) dirigersi (automaticamente) verso.

home address n indirizzo di casa.

home-brew [həʊm'bruː] n birra or vino fatto(a) in casa.

homecoming ['həʊmkʌmɪŋ] n ritorno.

home computer n home computer m inv.

Home Counties npl contee fpl intorno a Londra.

home economics n economia domestica.

home ground n (fig): **to be on ~** essere sul proprio terreno.

home-grown [həʊm'grəʊn] adj nostrano(a), di produzione locale.

home help n (BRIT) collaboratore familiare per persone bisognose stipendiato dal comune.

homeland ['həʊmlænd] n patria.

homeless ['həʊmlɪs] adj senza tetto; spatriato(a); **the ~** npl i senzatetto.

home loan n prestito con garanzia immobiliare.

homely ['həʊmlɪ] adj semplice, alla buona; accogliente.

home-made [həʊm'meɪd] adj casalingo(a).

Home Office n (BRIT) ministero degli Interni.

homeopathy etc [həʊmɪ'ɒpəθɪ] (US) = **homoeopathy** etc.

home page n (COMPUT) home page f inv.

home rule n autogoverno.

Home Secretary n (BRIT) ministro degli Interni.

homesick ['həʊmsɪk] adj: **to be ~** avere la nostalgia.

homestead ['həʊmstɛd] n fattoria e terreni.

home town n città f inv natale.
home truth n: **to tell sb a few ~s** dire a qn qualche amara verità.
homeward ['həumwəd] adj (journey) di ritorno.
homeward(s) ['həumwəd(z)] adv verso casa.
homework ['həumwɔːk] n compiti mpl (per casa).
homicidal [hɔmɪ'saɪdl] adj omicida.
homicide ['hɔmɪsaɪd] n (US) omicidio.
homily ['hɔmɪlɪ] n omelia.
homing ['həumɪŋ] adj (device, missile) autocercante; **~ pigeon** piccione m viaggiatore.
homoeopath, (US) **homeopath** ['həumɪəupæθ] n omeopatico.
homoeopathic, (US) **homeopathic** ['həumɪəu'pæθɪk] adj omeopatico(a).
homoeopathy, (US) **homeopathy** [həumɪ'ɔpəθɪ] n omeopatia.
homogeneous [hɔməu'dʒiːnɪəs] adj omogeneo(a).
homogenize [hə'mɔdʒənaɪz] vt omogenizzare.
homosexual [hɔməu'sɛksjuəl] adj, n omosessuale (m/f).
Hon. abbr = **honourable; honorary.**
Honduras [hɔn'djuərəs] n Honduras m.
hone [həun] vt (sharpen) affilare; (fig) affinare.
honest ['ɔnɪst] adj onesto(a); sincero(a); **to be quite ~ with you** ... se devo dirle la verità ....
honestly ['ɔnɪstlɪ] adv onestamente; sinceramente.
honesty ['ɔnɪstɪ] n onestà.
honey ['hʌnɪ] n miele m; (US col) tesoro, amore m.
honeycomb ['hʌnɪkəum] n favo ♦ vt (fig): **~ed with tunnels** etc pieno(a) di gallerie etc.
honeymoon ['hʌnɪmuːn] n luna di miele, viaggio di nozze.
honeysuckle ['hʌnɪsʌkl] n caprifoglio.
Hong Kong ['hɔŋ'kɔŋ] n Hong Kong f.
honk [hɔŋk] n (AUT) colpo di clacson ♦ vi suonare il clacson.
Honolulu [hɔnə'luːluː] n Honolulu f.
honorary ['ɔnərərɪ] adj onorario(a); (duty, title) onorifico(a).
honour, (US) **honor** ['ɔnə*] vt onorare ♦ n onore m; **in ~ of** in onore di.
hono(u)rable ['ɔnərəbl] adj onorevole.
hono(u)r-bound ['ɔnə'baund] adj: **to be ~ to do** dover fare una questione di onore.
hono(u)rs degree n (SCOL) laurea (con

corso di studi di 4 o 5 anni); see boxed note.

honours list n (BRIT) elenco ufficiale dei destinati al conferimento di onorificenze; see boxed note.

Hons. [ɔnz] abbr (SCOL) = **hono(u)rs degree.**
hood [hud] n cappuccio; (BRIT AUT) capote f; (US AUT) cofano; (col) malvivente m/f.
hooded ['hudɪd] adj (robber) mascherato(a).
hoodlum ['huːdləm] n malvivente m/f.
hoodwink ['hudwɪŋk] vt infinocchiare.
hoof, pl **~s** or **hooves** [huːf, huːvz] n zoccolo.
hook [huk] n gancio; (for fishing) amo ♦ vt uncinare; (dress) agganciare; **to be ~ed on** (col) essere fanatico di; **~s and eyes** gancetti; **by ~ or by crook** in un modo o nell'altro.
▶**hook up** vt (RADIO, TV etc) allacciare, collegare.
hooligan ['huːlɪgən] n giovinastro, teppista m.
hooliganism ['huːlɪgənɪzəm] n teppismo.
hoop [huːp] n cerchio.
hoot [huːt] vi (AUT) suonare il clacson; (owl) gufare ♦ n colpo di clacson; **to ~ with laughter** farsi una gran risata.
hooter ['huːtə*] n (AUT) clacson m inv; (NAUT, at factory) sirena.
hoover ® ['huːvə*] n (BRIT) aspirapolvere m inv ♦ vt pulire con l'aspirapolvere.
hooves [huːvz] npl of **hoof.**
hop [hɔp] vi saltellare, saltare; (on one foot) saltare su una gamba ♦ n salto; **~s** npl luppoli mpl.
hope [həup] vt, vi sperare ♦ n speranza; **I ~**

so/not spero di sì/no.

hopeful['həupful] adj (person) pieno(a) di speranza; (situation) promettente; **I'm ~ that she'll manage to come** ho buone speranze che venga.

hopefully['həupfulɪ] adv con speranza; **~ he will recover** speriamo che si riprenda.

hopeless['həuplɪs] adj senza speranza, disperato(a); (useless) inutile.

hopelessly['həuplɪslɪ] adv (live etc) senza speranza; (involved, complicated) spaventosamente; (late) disperatamente, irrimediabilmente; **I'm ~ confused/lost** sono completamente confuso/perso.

hopper['hɔpə*] n (chute) tramoggia.

horde[hɔːd] n orda.

horizon[hə'raɪzn] n orizzonte m.

horizontal[hɔrɪ'zɔntl] adj orizzontale.

hormone['hɔːməun] n ormone m.

hormone replacement therapyn terapia ormonale (usata in menopausa).

horn[hɔːn] n corno; (AUT) clacson m inv.

horned[hɔːnd] adj (animal) cornuto(a).

hornet['hɔːnɪt] n calabrone m.

horny['hɔːnɪ] adj corneo(a); (hands) calloso(a).

horoscope['hɔrəskəup] n oroscopo.

horrendous[hɔ'rendəs] n orrendo(a).

horrible['hɔrɪbl] adj orribile, tremendo(a).

horrid['hɔrɪd] adj orrido(a); (person) antipatico(a).

horrific[hɔ'rɪfɪk] adj (accident) spaventoso(a); (film) orripilante.

horrify['hɔrɪfaɪ] vt lasciare inorridito(a).

horrifying['hɔrɪfaɪɪŋ] adj terrificante.

horror['hɔrə*] n orrore m.

horror filmn film m inv dell'orrore.

horror-struck['hɔrəstrʌk], **horror-stricken**['hɔrəstrɪkn] adj inorridito (a).

hors d'œuvre[ɔː'dəːvrə] n antipasto.

horse[hɔːs] n cavallo.

horseback['hɔːsbæk]: **on ~** adj, adv a cavallo.

horsebox['hɔːsbɔks] n carro or furgone m per il trasporto dei cavalli.

horse chestnutn ippocastano.

horse-drawn['hɔːsdrɔːn] adj tirato(a) da cavallo.

horsefly['hɔːsflaɪ] n tafano, mosca cavallina.

horseman['hɔːsmən] n cavaliere m.

horseplay['hɔːspleɪ] n giochi mpl scatenati.

horsepower (hp)['hɔːspauə*] n cavallo (vapore) (c/v).

horse-racing['hɔːsreɪsɪŋ] n ippica.

horseradish['hɔːsrædɪʃ] n rafano.

horseshoe['hɔːsʃuː] n ferro di cavallo.

horse shown concorso ippico, gare fpl ippiche.

horse-trading['hɔːstreɪdɪŋ] n mercanteggiamento.

horse trialsnpl = **horse show**.

horsewhip['hɔːswɪp] vt frustare.

horsewoman['hɔːswumən] n amazzone f.

horsey['hɔːsɪ] adj (col: person) che adora i cavalli; (appearance) cavallino(a), da cavallo.

horticulture['hɔːtɪkʌltʃə*] n orticoltura.

hose[həuz] n (also: **~pipe**) tubo; (also: **garden ~**) tubo per annaffiare.

► **hose down**vt lavare con un getto d'acqua.

hosepipe['həuzpaɪp] n see **hose**.

hosiery['həuzɪərɪ] n (in shop) (reparto di) calze fpl e calzini mpl.

hospice['hɔspɪs] n ricovero, ospizio.

hospitable[hɔ'spɪtəbl] adj ospitale.

hospital['hɔspɪtl] n ospedale m; **in ~**, (US) **in the ~** all'ospedale.

hospitality[hɔspɪ'tælɪtɪ] n ospitalità.

hospitalize['hɔspɪtəlaɪz] vt ricoverare (in or all'ospedale).

host[həust] n ospite m; (TV, RADIO) presentatore/trice; (REL) ostia; (large number): **a ~ of** una schiera di ♦ vt (TV programme, games) presentare.

hostage['hɔstɪdʒ] n ostaggio/a.

host countryn paese m ospite, paese che ospita.

hostel['hɔstl] n ostello; (for students, nurses etc) pensionato; (for homeless people) ospizio, ricovero; (also: **youth ~**) ostello della gioventù.

hostelling['hɔstəlɪŋ] n: **to go (youth) ~** passare le vacanze negli ostelli della gioventù.

hostess['həustɪs] n ospite f; (AVIAT) hostess f inv; (in nightclub) entraineuse f inv.

hostile['hɔstaɪl] adj ostile.

hostility[hɔ'stɪlɪtɪ] n ostilità f inv.

hot[hɔt] adj caldo(a); (as opposed to only warm) molto caldo(a); (spicy) piccante; (fig) accanito(a); ardente; violento(a), focoso(a); **to be ~** (person) aver caldo; (thing) essere caldo(a); (METEOR) far caldo.

► **hot up**(BRIT col) vi (situation) farsi più teso(a); (party) scaldarsi ♦ vt (pace) affrettare; (engine) truccare.

hot-air balloon[hɔt'ɛə-] n mongolfiera.

hotbed['hɔtbed] n (fig) focolaio.

hotchpotch['hɔtʃpɔtʃ] n (BRIT) pot-pourri m.

hot dogn hot dog m inv.

hotel[həu'tɛl] n albergo.

hotelier[həu'tɛljeɪ] n albergatore/trice.

hotel industryn industria alberghiera.
hotel roomn camera d'albergo.
hot flushn (BRIT) scalmana, caldana.
hotfoot['hɔtfut] adv di gran carriera.
hothead['hɔthɛd] n (fig) testa calda.
hotheaded[hɔt'hɛdɪd] adj focoso(a),
eccitabile.
hothouse['hɔthaus] n serra.
hot linen (POL) telefono rosso.
hotly['hɔtlɪ] adv violentemente.
hotplate['hɔtpleɪt] n fornello; piastra
riscaldante.
hotpot['hɔtpɔt] n (BRIT CULIN) stufato.
hot potaton (BRIT col) patata bollente; **to
drop sb/sth like a** ~ mollare subito qn/qc.
hot seatn (fig) posto che scotta.
hot spotn (fig) zona calda.
hot springn sorgente f termale.
hot-tempered[hɔt'tɛmpəd] adj irascibile.
hot-water bottle[hɔt'wɔːtə-] n borsa
dell'acqua calda.
hot-wire['hɔtwaɪə*] vt (col: car) avviare
mettendo in contatto i fili
dell'accensione.
hound[haund] vt perseguitare ♦ n segugio;
the ~s la muta.
hour['auə*] n ora; **at 30 miles an** ~ a 30
miglia all'ora; **lunch** ~ intervallo di
pranzo; **to pay sb by the** ~ pagare qn a
ore.
hourly['auəlɪ] adj (ad) ogni ora; (rate)
orario(a) ♦ adv ogni ora; ~ **paid** adj
pagato(a) a ore.
housen [haus] (pl ~s ['hauzɪz]) (also: firm)
casa; (POL) camera; (THEAT) sala;
pubblico; spettacolo ♦ vt [hauz] (person)
ospitare; **at (or to) my** ~ a casa mia; **the
H~ (of Commons/Lords)** (BRIT) la Camera
dei Comuni/Lords; **the H~ (of
Representatives)** (US) ≈ la Camera dei
Deputati; **on the** ~ (fig) offerto(a) dalla
casa.
house arrestn arresti mpl domiciliari.
houseboat['hausbəut] n house boat f inv.
housebound['hausbaund] adj confinato(a)
in casa.
housebreaking['hausbreɪkɪŋ] n furto con
scasso.
house-broken['hausbrəukn] adj (US) =
house-trained.
housecoat['hauskəut] n vestaglia.
household['haushəuld] n famiglia, casa.
householder['haushəuldə*] n padrone/a di
casa; (head of house) capofamiglia m/f.
household namen nome m che tutti
conoscono.
househunting['haushʌntɪŋ] n: **to go** ~
mettersi a cercar casa.

housekeeper['hauskiːpə*] n governante f.
housekeeping['hauskiːpɪŋ] n (work)
governo della casa; (also: ~ **money**) soldi
mpl per le spese di casa; (COMPUT) ausilio.
houseman['hausmən] n (BRIT MED) ≈
interno.
house-owner['hausəunə*] n possessore m/f
di casa.
house plantn pianta da appartamento.
house-proud['hauspraud] adj che è
maniaco(a) della pulizia.
house-to-house['haustə'haus] adj
(collection) di porta in porta; (search) casa
per casa.
house-train['haustreɪn] vt (pet animal)
addestrare a non sporcare in casa.
house-trained['haustreɪnd] adj (BRIT:
animal) che non sporca in casa.
house-warming party['hauswɔːmɪŋ-] n
festa per inaugurare la casa nuova.
housewife['hauswaɪf] n massaia,
casalinga.
housework['hauswɔːk] n faccende fpl
domestiche.
housing['hauzɪŋ] n alloggio ♦ cpd (problem,
shortage) degli alloggi.
housing associationn cooperativa
cdilizia.
housing benefitn (BRIT) contributo
abitativo (ad affittuari e a coloro che
comprano una casa).
housing conditionsnpl condizioni fpl di
abitazione.
housing development, (BRIT) **housing
estate**n zona residenziale con case
popolari e/o private.
hovel['hɔvl] n casupola.
hover['hɔvə*] vi (bird) librarsi; (helicopter)
volare a punto fisso; **to** ~ **round sb**
aggirarsi intorno a qn.
hovercraft['hɔvəkrɑːft] n hovercraft m inv.
hoverport['hɔvəpɔːt] n porto per
hovercraft.
how[hau] adv come; ~ **are you?** come sta?;
~ **do you do?** piacere!, molto lieto!; ~ **far
is it to ...?** quanto è lontano ...?; ~ **long
have you been here?** da quanto tempo sta
qui?; ~ **lovely!** che bello!; ~ **many?**
quanti(e)?; ~ **much?** quanto(a)?; ~ **many
people/much milk?** quante persone/
quanto latte?; ~ **old are you?** quanti anni
ha?; ~'**s life?** (col) come va (la vita)?; ~
about a drink? che ne diresti di andare a
bere qualcosa?; ~ **is it that ...?** com'è che
... + sub?
however[hau'ɛvə*] adv in qualsiasi modo
or maniera che; (+ adjective) per quanto
+ sub; (in questions) come ♦ conj

comunque, però.
howitzer ['hauɪtsə*] *n* (*MIL*) obice *m*.
howl [haul] *n* ululato ♦ *vi* ululare.
howler ['haulə*] *n* marronata.
howling ['haulɪŋ] *adj*: **a ~ wind** *or* **gale** un vento terribile.
HP *n abbr* (*BRIT*) *see* **hire purchase.**
hp *abbr* (*AUT*) *see* **horsepower.**
HQ *n abbr* (= *headquarters*) Q.G.
HR *n abbr* (*US*) = **House of Representatives;** (= *human resources*: *department*) ufficio personale; (: *staff*) risorse umane.
HRH *abbr* (= *His* (*or Her*) *Royal Highness*) S.A.R.
hr(s) *abbr* (= *hour(s)*) h.
HRT *n abbr* = **hormone replacement therapy.**
HS *abbr* (*US*) = **high school.**
HST *abbr* (= *Hawaiian Standard Time*) *fuso orario*.
HT *abbr* (= *high tension*) A.T.
HTML *n abbr* (= *hypertext markup language*) HTML *m*.
hub [hʌb] *n* (*of wheel*) mozzo; (*fig*) fulcro.
hubbub ['hʌbʌb] *n* baccano.
hubcap ['hʌbkæp] *n* (*AUT*) coprimozzo.
HUD *n abbr* (*US*) = *Department of Housing and Urban Development.*
huddle ['hʌdl] *vi*: **to ~ together** rannicchiarsi l'uno contro l'altro.
hue [hju:] *n* tinta; **~ and cry** *n* clamore *m*.
huff [hʌf] *n*: **in a ~** stizzito(a); **to take the ~** mettere il broncio.
huffy ['hʌfɪ] *adj* (*col*) stizzito(a), indispettito(a).
hug [hʌg] *vt* abbracciare; (*shore, kerb*) stringere ♦ *n* abbraccio, stretta; **to give sb a ~** abbracciare qn.
huge [hju:dʒ] *adj* enorme, immenso(a).
hulk [hʌlk] *n* carcassa.
hulking ['hʌlkɪŋ] *adj*: **~ (great)** grosso(a) e goffo(a).
hull [hʌl] *n* (*of ship*) scafo.
hullabaloo [hʌləbə'lu:] *n* (*col*: *noise*) fracasso.
hullo [hə'ləu] *excl* = **hello.**
hum [hʌm] *vt* (*tune*) canticchiare ♦ *vi* canticchiare; (*insect, plane*) ronzare ♦ *n* (*also ELEC*) ronzio; (*of traffic, machines*) rumore *m*; (*of voices etc*) mormorio, brusio.
human ['hju:mən] *adj* umano(a) ♦ *n* (*also*: **~ being**) essere *m* umano.
humane [hju:'meɪn] *adj* umanitario(a).
humanism ['hju:mənɪzəm] *n* umanesimo.
humanitarian [hju:mænɪ'tɛərɪən] *adj* umanitario(a).
humanity [hju:'mænɪtɪ] *n* umanità; **the humanities** gli studi umanistici.

humanly ['hju:mənlɪ] *adv* umanamente.
humanoid ['hju:mənɔɪd] *adj* che sembra umano(a) ♦ *n* umanoide *m/f*.
human rights *npl* diritti *mpl* dell'uomo.
humble ['hʌmbl] *adj* umile, modesto(a) ♦ *vt* umiliare.
humbly ['hʌmblɪ] *adv* umilmente, modestamente.
humbug ['hʌmbʌg] *n* inganno; sciocchezze *fpl*; (*BRIT*: *sweet*) caramella alla menta.
humdrum ['hʌmdrʌm] *adj* monotono(a), tedioso(a).
humid ['hju:mɪd] *adj* umido(a).
humidifier [hju:'mɪdɪfaɪə*] *n* umidificatore *m*.
humidity [hju:'mɪdɪtɪ] *n* umidità.
humiliate [hju:'mɪlɪeɪt] *vt* umiliare.
humiliation [hju:mɪlɪ'eɪʃən] *n* umiliazione *f*.
humility [hju:'mɪlɪtɪ] *n* umiltà.
humorist ['hju:mərɪst] *n* umorista *m/f*.
humorous ['hju:mərəs] *adj* umoristico(a); (*person*) buffo(a).
humour, (*US*) **humor** ['hju:mə*] *n* umore *m* ♦ *vt* (*person*) compiacere; (*sb's whims*) assecondare; **sense of ~** senso dell'umorismo; **to be in a good/bad ~** essere di buon/cattivo umore.
humo(u)rless ['hju:məlɪs] *adj* privo(a) di umorismo.
hump [hʌmp] *n* gobba.
humpback ['hʌmpbæk] *n* schiena d'asino; (*BRIT*: *also*: **~ bridge**) ponte *m* a schiena d'asino.
humus ['hju:məs] *n* humus *m*.
hunch [hʌntʃ] *n* gobba; (*premonition*) intuizione *f*; **I have a ~ that** ho la vaga impressione che.
hunchback ['hʌntʃbæk] *n* gobbo/a.
hunched [hʌntʃt] *adj* incurvato(a).
hundred ['hʌndrəd] *num* cento; **about a ~ people** un centinaio di persone; **~s of people** centinaia *fpl* di persone; **I'm a ~ per cent sure** sono sicuro al cento per cento.
hundredweight ['hʌndrɪdweɪt] *n* (*BRIT*) = 50.8 *kg*; 112 *lb*; (*US*) = 45.3 *kg*; 100 *lb*.
hung [hʌŋ] *pt, pp of* **hang.**
Hungarian [hʌŋ'gɛərɪən] *adj* ungherese ♦ *n* ungherese *m/f*; (*LING*) ungherese *m*.
Hungary ['hʌŋgərɪ] *n* Ungheria.
hunger ['hʌŋgə*] *n* fame *f* ♦ *vi*: **to ~ for** desiderare ardentemente.
hunger strike *n* sciopero della fame.
hungover [hʌŋ'əuvə*] *adj* (*col*): **to be ~** avere i postumi della sbornia.
hungrily ['hʌŋgrəlɪ] *adv* voracemente; (*fig*) avidamente.
hungry ['hʌŋgrɪ] *adj* affamato(a); **to be ~**

aver fame; ~ **for** (*fig*) assetato di.
hung up *adj* (*col*) complessato(a).
hunk [hʌŋk] *n* bel pezzo.
hunt [hʌnt] *vt* (*seek*) cercare; (*SPORT*)
   cacciare ♦ *vi* andare a caccia ♦ *n* caccia.
▶**hunt down** *vt* scovare.
hunter ['hʌntə*] *n* cacciatore *m*; (*BRIT*:
   horse) cavallo da caccia.
hunting ['hʌntɪŋ] *n* caccia.
hurdle ['hə:dl] *n* (*SPORT, fig*) ostacolo.
hurl [hə:l] *vt* lanciare con violenza.
hurling ['hə:lɪŋ] *n* (*SPORT*) hurling *m*.
hurly-burly ['hə:lɪ'bə:lɪ] *n* chiasso, baccano.
hurrah, hurray [hu'rɑ:, hu'reɪ] *excl* urra!,
   evviva!
hurricane ['hʌrɪkən] *n* uragano.
hurried ['hʌrɪd] *adj* affrettato(a); (*work*)
   fatto(a) in fretta.
hurriedly ['hʌrɪdlɪ] *adv* in fretta.
hurry ['hʌrɪ] *n* fretta ♦ *vi* affrettarsi ♦ *vt*
   (*person*) affrettare; (*work*) far in fretta; **to
   be in a** ~ aver fretta; **to do sth in a** ~
   fare qc in fretta; **to** ~ **in/out** entrare/
   uscire in fretta; **to** ~ **back/home**
   affrettarsi a tornare indietro/a casa.
▶**hurry along** *vi* camminare in fretta.
▶**hurry away, hurry off** *vi* andarsene in
   fretta.
▶**hurry up** *vi* sbrigarsi.
hurt [hə:t] *vb* (*pt, pp* **hurt**) *vt* (*cause pain to*)
   far male a; (*injure, fig*) ferire; (*business,
   interests etc*) colpire, danneggiare ♦ *vi* far
   male ♦ *adj* ferito(a); **I** ~ **my arm** mi sono
   fatto male al braccio; **where does it** ~?
   dove ti fa male?
hurtful ['hə:tful] *adj* (*remark*) che ferisce.
hurtle ['hə:tl] *vt* scagliare ♦ *vi*: **to** ~ **past/
   down** passare/scendere a razzo.
husband ['hʌzbənd] *n* marito.
hush [hʌʃ] *n* silenzio, calma ♦ *vt* zittire; ~!
   zitto(a)!
▶**hush up** *vt* (*fact*) cercare di far passare
   sotto silenzio.
hush-hush ['hʌʃ'hʌʃ] *adj* (*col*)
   segretissimo(a).
husk [hʌsk] *n* (*of wheat*) cartoccio; (*of rice,
   maize*) buccia.
husky ['hʌskɪ] *adj* roco(a) ♦ *n* cane *m*
   eschimese.
hustings ['hʌstɪŋz] *npl* (*BRIT POL*) comizi *mpl*
   elettorali.
hustle ['hʌsl] *vt* spingere, incalzare ♦ *n*
   pigia pigia *m inv*; ~ **and bustle** trambusto.
hut [hʌt] *n* rifugio; (*shed*) ripostiglio.
hutch [hʌtʃ] *n* gabbia.
hyacinth ['haɪəsɪnθ] *n* giacinto.
hybrid ['haɪbrɪd] *adj* ibrido(a) ♦ *n* ibrido.
hydrant ['haɪdrənt] *n* (*also*: **fire** ~) idrante

m.
hydraulic [haɪ'drɔlɪk] *adj* idraulico(a).
hydraulics [haɪ'drɔlɪks] *n* idraulica.
hydrochloric [haɪdrə'klɔrɪk] *adj*: ~ **acid**
   acido cloridrico.
hydroelectric [haɪdrəuɪ'lɛktrɪk] *adj*
   idroelettrico(a).
hydrofoil ['haɪdrəfɔɪl] *n* aliscafo.
hydrogen ['haɪdrədʒən] *n* idrogeno.
hydrogen bomb *n* bomba all'idrogeno.
hydrophobia [haɪdrə'fəubɪə] *n* idrofobia.
hydroplane ['haɪdrəupleɪn] *n* idrovolante *m*.
hyena [haɪ'i:nə] *n* iena.
hygiene ['haɪdʒi:n] *n* igiene *f*.
hygienic [haɪ'dʒi:nɪk] *adj* igienico(a).
hymn [hɪm] *n* inno; cantica.
hype [haɪp] *n* (*col*) clamorosa pubblicità.
hyperactive [haɪpər'æktɪv] *adj*
   iperattivo(a).
hypermarket ['haɪpəmɑ:kɪt] *n* (*BRIT*)
   ipermercato.
hypertension [haɪpə'tɛnʃən] *n* (*MED*)
   ipertensione *f*.
hypertext ['haɪpə,tɛkst] *n* (*COMPUT*)
   ipertesto.
hyphen ['haɪfn] *n* trattino.
hypnosis [hɪp'nəusɪs] *n* ipnosi *f*.
hypnotic [hɪp'nɔtɪk] *adj* ipnotico(a).
hypnotism ['hɪpnətɪzəm] *n* ipnotismo.
hypnotist ['hɪpnətɪst] *n* ipnotizzatore/trice.
hypnotize ['hɪpnətaɪz] *vt* ipnotizzare.
hypoallergenic [haɪpəuælə'dʒɛnɪk] *adj*
   ipoallergico(a).
hypochondriac [haɪpə'kɔndrɪæk] *n*
   ipocondriaco/a.
hypocrisy [hɪ'pɔkrɪsɪ] *n* ipocrisia.
hypocrite ['hɪpəkrɪt] *n* ipocrita *m/f*.
hypocritical [hɪpə'krɪtɪkl] *adj* ipocrita.
hypodermic [haɪpə'də:mɪk] *adj*
   ipodermico(a) ♦ *n* (*syringe*) siringa
   ipodermica.
hypotenuse [haɪ'pɔtɪnju:z] *n* ipotenusa.
hypothermia [haɪpəu'θə:mɪə] *n* ipotermia.
hypothesis, *pl* **hypotheses** [haɪ'pɔθɪsɪs,
   -si:z] *n* ipotesi *f inv*.
hypothetical [haɪpəu'θɛtɪkl] *adj*
   ipotetico(a).
hysterectomy [hɪstə'rɛktəmɪ] *n*
   isterectomia.
hysteria [hɪ'stɪərɪə] *n* isteria.
hysterical [hɪ'stɛrɪkl] *adj* isterico(a); **to
   become** ~ avere una crisi isterica.
hysterics [hɪ'stɛrɪks] *npl* accesso di isteria;
   (*laughter*) attacco di riso; **to have** ~ avere
   una crisi isterica.

I i

I, i[aɪ] n (*letter*) I, i *f or m inv*; **I for Isaac,** (*US*) **I for Item** ≈ I come Imola.

I[aɪ] *pron* io ♦ *abbr* (= *island, isle*) Is.

IA *abbr* (*US*) = *Iowa*.

IAEA n *abbr* = **International Atomic Energy Agency.**

IBA n *abbr* (*BRIT*: = *Independent Broadcasting Authority*) organo di controllo sulle reti televisive.

Iberian [aɪ'bɪərɪən] *adj* iberico(a).

Iberian Peninsula n: **the** ~ la Penisola iberica.

IBEW n *abbr* (*US*: = *International Brotherhood of Electrical Workers*) associazione internazionale degli elettrotecnici.

ib(**id**).['ɪb(ɪd)] *abbr* (= *ibidem*: *from the same source*) ibid.

i/c *abbr* (*BRIT*) = **in charge.**

ICBM n *abbr* (= *intercontinental ballistic missile*) ICBM *m inv.*

ICC n *abbr* (= *International Chamber of Commerce*) C.C.I. *f*; (*US*: = *Interstate Commerce Commission*) commissione per il commercio tra gli stati degli USA.

ice[aɪs] n ghiaccio; (*on road*) gelo ♦ vt (*cake*) glassare; (*drink*) mettere in fresco ♦ vi (*also*: ~ **over**) ghiacciare; (*also*: ~ **up**) gelare; **to keep sth on** ~ (*fig*: *plan, project*) mettere da parte (per il momento), accantonare.

Ice Age n era glaciale.

ice axe n piccozza da ghiaccio.

iceberg['aɪsbəːg] n iceberg *m inv*; **tip of the** ~ (*also fig*) punta dell'iceberg.

icebox['aɪsbɔks] n (*US*) frigorifero; (*BRIT*) reparto ghiaccio; (*insulated box*) frigo portatile.

icebreaker['aɪsbreɪkə*] n rompighiaccio *m inv.*

ice bucket n secchiello del ghiaccio.

ice-cap['aɪskæp] n calotta polare.

ice-cold[aɪs'kəuld] *adj* gelato(a).

ice cream n gelato.

ice-cream soda n (gelato) affogato al seltz.

ice cube n cubetto di ghiaccio.

iced[aɪst] *adj* (*drink*) ghiacciato(a); (*coffee, tea*) freddo(a); (*cake*) glassato(a).

ice hockey n hockey *m* su ghiaccio.

Iceland['aɪslənd] n Islanda.

Icelander['aɪsləndə*] n islandese *m/f.*

Icelandic[aɪs'lændɪk] *adj* islandese ♦ n (*LING*) islandese *m.*

ice lolly n (*BRIT*) ghiacciolo.

ice pick n piccone *m* per ghiaccio.

ice rink n pista di pattinaggio.

ice-skate['aɪsskeɪt] n pattino da ghiaccio ♦ vi pattinare sul ghiaccio.

ice-skating['aɪsskeɪtɪŋ] n pattinaggio sul ghiaccio.

icicle['aɪsɪkl] n ghiacciolo.

icing['aɪsɪŋ] n (*AVIAT etc*) patina di ghiaccio; (*CULIN*) glassa.

icing sugar n zucchero a velo.

ICJ n *abbr see* **International Court of Justice.**

icon['aɪkɔn] n icona; (*COMPUT*) immagine *f.*

ICR n *abbr* (*US*) = *Institute for Cancer Research.*

ICRC n *abbr* (= *International Committee of the Red Cross*) CICR *m.*

ICT n *abbr* (*BRIT SCOL*: = *Information and Communications Technology*) informatica.

ICU n *abbr see* **intensive care unit.**

icy['aɪsɪ] *adj* ghiacciato(a); (*weather, temperature*) gelido(a).

ID *abbr* (*US*) = *Idaho*; (= *identification document*) documento di identità.

I'd[aɪd] = **I would**; **I had.**

Ida. *abbr* (*US*) = *Idaho.*

ID card n = **identity card.**

IDD n *abbr* (*BRIT TEL*: = *International direct dialling*) teleselezione *f* internazionale.

idea[aɪ'dɪə] n idea; **good** ~! buon'idea!; **to have an** ~ **that ...** aver l'impressione che ...; **I haven't the least** ~ non ne ho la minima idea.

ideal[aɪ'dɪəl] *adj, n* ideale (*m*).

idealist[aɪ'dɪəlɪst] n idealista *m/f.*

ideally[aɪ'dɪəlɪ] *adv* perfettamente, assolutamente; ~ **the book should have** ... l'ideale sarebbe che il libro avesse ....

identical[aɪ'dɛntɪkl] *adj* identico(a).

identification[aɪdɛntɪfɪ'keɪʃən] n identificazione *f*; **means of** ~ carta d'identità.

identify[aɪ'dɛntɪfaɪ] vt identificare ♦ vi: **to** ~ **with** identificarsi con.

Identikit ®[aɪ'dɛntɪkɪt] n: ~ (**picture**) identikit *m inv.*

identity[aɪ'dɛntɪtɪ] n identità *f inv.*

identity card n carta d'identità.

identity parade n (*BRIT*) confronto all'americana.

ideological[aɪdɪə'lɔdʒɪkəl] *adj* ideologico(a).

ideology [aɪdɪ'ɔlədʒɪ] n ideologia.
idiocy ['ɪdɪəsɪ] n idiozia.
idiom ['ɪdɪəm] n idioma m; (phrase)
espressione f idiomatica.
idiomatic [ɪdɪə'mætɪk] adj idiomatico(a).
idiosyncrasy [ɪdɪəu'sɪŋkrəsɪ] n
idiosincrasia.
idiot ['ɪdɪət] n idiota m/f.
idiotic [ɪdɪ'ɔtɪk] adj idiota.
idle ['aɪdl] adj inattivo(a); (lazy) pigro(a),
ozioso(a); (unemployed) disoccupato(a);
(question, pleasures) ozioso(a) ♦ vi (engine)
girare al minimo; **to lie** ~ stare fermo,
non funzionare.
►**idle away** vt (time) sprecare, buttar via.
idleness ['aɪdlnɪs] n ozio; pigrizia.
idler ['aɪdlə*] n ozioso/a, fannullone/a.
idle time n tempi mpl morti.
idol ['aɪdl] n idolo.
idolize ['aɪdəlaɪz] vt idoleggiare.
idyllic [ɪ'dɪlɪk] adj idillico(a).
i.e. abbr (= id est: that is) cioè.
if [ɪf] conj se ♦ n: **there are a lot of** ~**s
and buts** ci sono molti se e ma; **I'd be
pleased** ~ **you could do it** sarei molto
contento se potesse farlo; ~ **necessary** se
(è) necessario; ~ **only he were here** se
solo fosse qui; ~ **only to show him my
gratitude** se non altro per esprimergli la
mia gratitudine.
iffy ['ɪfɪ] adj (col) incerto(a).
igloo ['ɪgluː] n igloo m inv.
ignite [ɪg'naɪt] vt accendere ♦ vi
accendersi.
ignition [ɪg'nɪʃən] n (AUT) accensione f; **to
switch on/off the** ~ accendere/spegnere
il motore.
ignition key n (AUT) chiave f
dell'accensione.
ignoble [ɪg'nəubl] adj ignobile.
ignominious [ɪgnə'mɪnɪəs] adj
vergognoso(a), ignominioso(a).
ignoramus [ɪgnə'reɪməs] n ignorante m/f.
ignorance ['ɪgnərəns] n ignoranza; **to keep
sb in** ~ **of sth** tenere qn all'oscuro di qc.
ignorant ['ɪgnərənt] adj ignorante; **to be** ~
of (subject) essere ignorante in; (events)
essere ignaro(a) di.
ignore [ɪg'nɔː*] vt non tener conto di;
(person, fact) ignorare.
ikon ['aɪkɔn] n = **icon**.
IL abbr (US) = Illinois.
ILA n abbr (US: = International
Longshoremen's Association) associazione
internazionale degli scaricatori di porto.
ill [ɪl] adj (sick) malato(a); (bad) cattivo(a)
♦ n male m; **to take** or **be taken** ~
ammalarsi; **to feel** ~ star male; **to**

speak/think ~ **of sb** parlar/pensar male
di qn.
I'll [aɪl] = **I will, I shall**.
Ill. abbr (US) = Illinois.
ill-advised [ɪləd'vaɪzd] adj (decision) poco
giudizioso(a); (person) mal consigliato(a).
ill-at-ease [ɪlət'iːz] adj a disagio.
ill-considered [ɪlkən'sɪdəd] adj (plan)
avventato(a).
ill-disposed [ɪldɪs'pəuzd] adj: **to be** ~
towards sb/sth essere maldisposto(a)
verso qn/qc or nei riguardi di qn/qc.
illegal [ɪ'liːgl] adj illegale.
illegally [ɪ'liːgəlɪ] adv illegalmente.
illegible [ɪ'lɛdʒɪbl] adj illeggibile.
illegitimate [ɪlɪ'dʒɪtɪmət] adj illegittimo(a).
ill-fated [ɪl'feɪtɪd] adj nefasto(a).
ill-favoured, (US) ill-favored [ɪl'feɪvəd] adj
sgraziato(a), brutto(a).
ill feeling n rancore m.
ill-gotten ['ɪlgɔtn] adj: ~ **gains** maltolto.
ill health n problemi mpl di salute.
illicit [ɪ'lɪsɪt] adj illecito(a).
ill-informed [ɪlɪn'fɔːmd] adj (judgement,
speech) pieno(a) di inesattezze; (person)
male informato(a).
illiterate [ɪ'lɪtərət] adj analfabeta,
illetterato(a); (letter) scorretto(a).
ill-mannered [ɪl'mænəd] adj maleducato(a),
sgarbato(a).
illness ['ɪlnɪs] n malattia.
illogical [ɪ'lɔdʒɪkl] adj illogico(a).
ill-suited [ɪl'suːtɪd] adj (couple) mal
assortito(a); **he is** ~ **to the job** è inadatto
a quel lavoro.
ill-timed [ɪl'taɪmd] adj intempestivo(a),
inopportuno(a).
ill-treat [ɪl'triːt] vt maltrattare.
ill-treatment [ɪl'triːtmənt] n
maltrattamenti mpl.
illuminate [ɪ'luːmɪneɪt] vt illuminare; ~**d
sign** insegna luminosa.
illuminating [ɪ'luːmɪneɪtɪŋ] adj
chiarificatore(trice).
illumination [ɪluːmɪ'neɪʃən] n illuminazione
f.
illusion [ɪ'luːʒən] n illusione f; **to be under
the** ~ **that** avere l'impressione che.
illusive [ɪ'luːsɪv], **illusory** [ɪ'luːsərɪ] adj
illusorio(a).
illustrate ['ɪləstreɪt] vt illustrare.
illustration [ɪlə'streɪʃən] n illustrazione f.
illustrator ['ɪləstreɪtə*] n illustratore/trice.
illustrious [ɪ'lʌstrɪəs] adj illustre.
ill will n cattiva volontà.
ILO n abbr (= International Labour
Organization) OIL f.
I'm [aɪm] = **I am.**

image ['ɪmɪdʒ] n immagine f; (public face) immagine (pubblica).

imagery ['ɪmɪdʒərɪ] n immagini fpl.

imaginable [ɪ'mædʒɪnəbl] adj immaginabile, che si possa immaginare.

imaginary [ɪ'mædʒɪnərɪ] adj immaginario(a).

imagination [ɪmædʒɪ'neɪʃən] n immaginazione f, fantasia.

imaginative [ɪ'mædʒɪnətɪv] adj immaginoso(a).

imagine [ɪ'mædʒɪn] vt immaginare.

imbalance [ɪm'bæləns] n squilibrio.

imbecile ['ɪmbəsi:l] n imbecille m/f.

imbue [ɪm'bju:] vt: to ~ sth with impregnare qc di.

IMF n abbr see International Monetary Fund.

imitate ['ɪmɪteɪt] vt imitare.

imitation [ɪmɪ'teɪʃən] n imitazione f.

imitator ['ɪmɪteɪtə*] n imitatore/trice.

immaculate [ɪ'mækjulət] adj immacolato(a); (dress, appearance) impeccabile.

immaterial [ɪmə'tɪərɪəl] adj immateriale, indifferente; it is ~ whether poco importa se or che + sub.

immature [ɪmə'tjuə*] adj immaturo(a).

immaturity [ɪmə'tjuərɪtɪ] n immaturità, mancanza di maturità.

immeasurable [ɪ'mɛʒərəbl] adj incommensurabile.

immediacy [ɪ'mi:dɪəsɪ] n immediatezza.

immediate [ɪ'mi:dɪət] adj immediato(a).

immediately [ɪ'mi:dɪətlɪ] adv (at once) subito, immediatamente; ~ next to proprio accanto a.

immense [ɪ'mɛns] adj immenso(a); enorme.

immensity [ɪ'mɛnsɪtɪ] n (of size, difference) enormità; (of problem etc) vastità.

immerse [ɪ'mə:s] vt immergere.

immersion heater [ɪ'mə:ʃən-] n (BRIT) scaldaacqua m inv a immersione.

immigrant ['ɪmɪgrənt] n immigrante m/f; (already established) immigrato/a.

immigration [ɪmɪ'greɪʃən] n immigrazione f.

immigration authorities npl ufficio stranieri.

immigration laws npl leggi fpl relative all'immigrazione.

imminent ['ɪmɪnənt] adj imminente.

immobile [ɪ'məubaɪl] adj immobile.

immobilize [ɪ'məubɪlaɪz] vt immobilizzare.

immoderate [ɪ'mɔdərɪt] adj (person) smodato(a), sregolato(a); (opinion, reaction, demand) eccessivo(a).

immodest [ɪ'mɔdɪst] adj (indecent) indecente, impudico(a); (boasting)

presuntuoso(a).

immoral [ɪ'mɔrl] adj immorale.

immorality [ɪmɔ'rælɪtɪ] n immoralità.

immortal [ɪ'mɔ:tl] adj, n immortale (m/f).

immortalize [ɪ'mɔ:təlaɪz] vt rendere immortale.

immovable [ɪ'mu:vəbl] adj (object) non movibile; (person) irremovibile.

immune [ɪ'mju:n] adj: ~ (to) immune (da).

immune system n sistema m immunitario.

immunity [ɪ'mju:nɪtɪ] n (also fig: of diplomat) immunità; diplomatic ~ immunità diplomatica.

immunization [ɪmjunaɪ'zeɪʃən] n immunizzazione f.

immunize ['ɪmjunaɪz] vt immunizzare.

imp [ɪmp] n folletto, diavoletto; (child) diavoletto.

impact ['ɪmpækt] n impatto.

impair [ɪm'pɛə*] vt danneggiare.

impaired [ɪm'pɛəd] adj indebolito(a).

-impaired [ɪm'pɛəd] suffix: visually~ videoleso(a).

impale [ɪm'peɪl] vt impalare.

impart [ɪm'pa:t] vt (make known) comunicare; (bestow) impartire.

impartial [ɪm'pa:ʃl] adj imparziale.

impartiality [ɪmpa:ʃɪ'ælɪtɪ] n imparzialità.

impassable [ɪm'pa:səbl] adj insuperabile; (road) impraticabile.

impasse [æm'pa:s] n impasse f inv.

impassioned [ɪm'pæʃənd] adj appassionato(a).

impassive [ɪm'pæsɪv] adj impassibile.

impatience [ɪm'peɪʃəns] n impazienza.

impatient [ɪm'peɪʃənt] adj impaziente; to get or grow ~ perdere la pazienza.

impeach [ɪm'pi:tʃ] vt accusare, attaccare; (public official) mettere sotto accusa.

impeachment [ɪm'pi:tʃmənt] n (LAW) imputazione f.

impeccable [ɪm'pɛkəbl] adj impeccabile.

impecunious [ɪmpɪ'kju:nɪəs] adj povero(a).

impede [ɪm'pi:d] vt impedire.

impediment [ɪm'pɛdɪmənt] n impedimento; (also: speech ~) difetto di pronuncia.

impel [ɪm'pɛl] vt (force): to ~ sb (to do sth) costringere or obbligare qn (a fare qc).

impending [ɪm'pɛndɪŋ] adj imminente.

impenetrable [ɪm'pɛnɪtrəbl] adj impenetrabile.

imperative [ɪm'pɛrətɪv] adj imperativo(a); necessario(a), urgente; (voice) imperioso(a) ♦ n (LING) imperativo.

imperceptible [ɪmpə'sɛptɪbl] adj impercettibile.

imperfect [ɪm'pə:fɪkt] adj imperfetto(a);

(*goods etc*) difettoso(a) ♦ *n* (*LING:* also: ~ **tense**) imperfetto.
imperfection [ɪmpə'fɛkʃən] *n* imperfezione *f*; (*flaw*) difetto.
imperial [ɪm'pɪərɪəl] *adj* imperiale; (*measure*) legale.
imperialism [ɪm'pɪərɪəlɪzəm] *n* imperialismo.
imperil [ɪm'pɛrɪl] *vt* mettere in pericolo.
imperious [ɪm'pɪərɪəs] *adj* imperioso(a).
impersonal [ɪm'pəːsənl] *adj* impersonale.
impersonate [ɪm'pəːsəneɪt] *vt* impersonare; (*THEAT*) imitare.
impersonation [ɪmpəːsə'neɪʃən] *n* (*LAW*) usurpazione *f* d'identità; (*THEAT*) imitazione *f*.
impersonator [ɪm'pəːsəneɪtə*] *n* (*gen, THEAT*) imitatore/trice.
impertinence [ɪm'pəːtɪnəns] *n* impertinenza.
impertinent [ɪm'pəːtɪnənt] *adj* impertinente.
imperturbable [ɪmpə'təːbəbl] *adj* imperturbabile.
impervious [ɪm'pəːvɪəs] *adj* impermeabile; (*fig*): ~ **to** insensibile a; impassibile di fronte a.
impetuous [ɪm'pɛtjuəs] *adj* impetuoso(a), precipitoso(a).
impetus ['ɪmpətəs] *n* impeto.
impinge [ɪm'pɪndʒ]: **to ~ on** *vt fus* (*person*) colpire; (*rights*) ledere.
impish ['ɪmpɪʃ] *adj* malizioso(a), birichino(a).
implacable [ɪm'plækəbl] *adj* implacabile.
implant [ɪm'plɑːnt] *vt* (*MED*) innestare; (*fig: idea, principle*) inculcare.
implausible [ɪm'plɔːzɪbl] *adj* non plausibile.
implement *n* ['ɪmplɪmənt] attrezzo; (*for cooking*) utensile *m* ♦ *vt* ['ɪmplɪment] effettuare.
implicate ['ɪmplɪkeɪt] *vt* implicare.
implication [ɪmplɪ'keɪʃən] *n* implicazione *f*; **by ~** implicitamente.
implicit [ɪm'plɪsɪt] *adj* implicito(a); (*complete*) completo(a).
implicitly [ɪm'plɪsɪtlɪ] *adv* implicitamente.
implore [ɪm'plɔː*] *vt* implorare.
imply [ɪm'plaɪ] *vt* insinuare; suggerire.
impolite [ɪmpə'laɪt] *adj* scortese.
imponderable [ɪm'pɔndərəbl] *adj* imponderabile.
import *vt* [ɪm'pɔːt] importare ♦ *n* ['ɪmpɔːt] (*COMM*) importazione *f*; (*meaning*) significato, senso ♦ *cpd* (*duty, licence etc*) d'importazione.
importance [ɪm'pɔːtns] *n* importanza; **to be of great/little ~** importare molto/poco,

essere molto/poco importante.
important [ɪm'pɔːtnt] *adj* importante; **it's not ~** non ha importanza; **it is ~ that** è importante che + *sub*.
importantly [ɪm'pɔːtəntlɪ] *adv* (*pej*) con (un'aria d')importanza; **but, more ~,** ... ma, quel che più conta *or* importa, ...
importation [ɪmpɔː'teɪʃən] *n* importazione *f*.
imported [ɪm'pɔːtɪd] *adj* importato(a).
importer [ɪm'pɔːtə*] *n* importatore/trice.
impose [ɪm'pəuz] *vt* imporre ♦ *vi*: **to ~ on sb** sfruttare la bontà di qn.
imposing [ɪm'pəuzɪŋ] *adj* imponente.
imposition [ɪmpə'zɪʃən] *n* imposizione *f*; **to be an ~ on** (*person*) abusare della gentilezza di.
impossibility [ɪmpɔsə'bɪlɪtɪ] *n* impossibilità.
impossible [ɪm'pɔsɪbl] *adj* impossibile; **it is ~ for me to leave now** mi è impossibile venir via adesso.
impostor [ɪm'pɔstə*] *n* impostore/a.
impotence ['ɪmpətns] *n* impotenza.
impotent ['ɪmpətnt] *adj* impotente.
impound [ɪm'paund] *vt* confiscare.
impoverished [ɪm'pɔvərɪʃt] *adj* impoverito(a).
impracticable [ɪm'præktɪkəbl] *adj* impraticabile.
impractical [ɪm'præktɪkl] *adj* non pratico(a).
imprecise [ɪmprɪ'saɪs] *adj* impreciso(a).
impregnable [ɪm'prɛgnəbl] *adj* (*fortress*) inespugnabile; (*fig*) inoppugnabile; irrefutabile.
impregnate ['ɪmprɛgneɪt] *vt* impregnare; (*fertilize*) fecondare.
impresario [ɪmprɪ'sɑːrɪəu] *n* impresario/a.
impress [ɪm'prɛs] *vt* impressionare; (*mark*) imprimere, stampare; **to ~ sth on sb** far capire qc a qn.
impression [ɪm'prɛʃən] *n* impressione *f*; **to be under the ~ that** avere l'impressione che; **to make a good/bad ~ on sb** fare una buona/cattiva impressione a *or* su qn.
impressionable [ɪm'prɛʃnəbl] *adj* impressionabile.
impressionist [ɪm'prɛʃənɪst] *n* impressionista *m/f*.
impressive [ɪm'prɛsɪv] *adj* impressionante.
imprint ['ɪmprɪnt] *n* (*PUBLISHING*) sigla editoriale.
imprinted [ɪm'prɪntɪd] *adj*: ~ **on** impresso(a) in.
imprison [ɪm'prɪzn] *vt* imprigionare.
imprisonment [ɪm'prɪznmənt] *n*

imprigionamento.

improbable [ɪm'prɔbəbl] *adj* improbabile; (*excuse*) inverosimile.

impromptu [ɪm'prɔmptjuː] *adj* improvvisato(a) ♦ *adv* improvvisando, così su due piedi.

improper [ɪm'prɔpə*] *adj* scorretto(a); (*unsuitable*) inadatto(a), improprio(a); sconveniente, indecente.

impropriety [ɪmprə'praɪətɪ] *n* sconvenienza; (*of expression*) improprietà.

improve [ɪm'pruːv] *vt* migliorare ♦ *vi* migliorare; (*pupil etc*) fare progressi.
► **improve (up)on** *vt fus* (*offer*) aumentare.

improvement [ɪm'pruːvmənt] *n* miglioramento; progresso; **to make ~s to** migliorare, apportare dei miglioramenti a.

improvisation [ɪmprəvaɪ'zeɪʃən] *n* improvvisazione *f*.

improvise ['ɪmprəvaɪz] *vt*, *vi* improvvisare.

imprudence [ɪm'pruːdns] *n* imprudenza.

imprudent [ɪm'pruːdnt] *adj* imprudente.

impudence ['ɪmpjudns] *n* impudenza.

impudent ['ɪmpjudnt] *adj* impudente, sfacciato(a).

impugn [ɪm'pjuːn] *vt* impugnare.

impulse ['ɪmpʌls] *n* impulso; **to act on ~** agire d'impulso *or* impulsivamente.

impulse buy *n* acquisto fatto d'impulso.

impulsive [ɪm'pʌlsɪv] *adj* impulsivo(a).

impunity [ɪm'pjuːnɪtɪ] *n*: **with ~** impunemente.

impure [ɪm'pjuə*] *adj* impuro(a).

impurity [ɪm'pjuərɪtɪ] *n* impurità *f inv*.

IN *abbr* (*US*) = Indiana.

════════════ KEYWORD

in [ɪn] *prep* **1** (*indicating place, position*) in; ~ **the house/garden** in casa/giardino; ~ **the box** nella scatola; ~ **the fridge** nel frigorifero; **I have it ~ my hand** ce l'ho in mano; ~ **town/the country** in città/campagna; ~ **school** a scuola; ~ **here/there** qui/lì dentro
2 (*with place names: of town, region, country*): ~ **London** a Londra; ~ **England** in Inghilterra; ~ **the United States** negli Stati Uniti; ~ **Yorkshire** nello Yorkshire
3 (*indicating time: during, in the space of*) in; ~ **spring/summer** in primavera/estate; ~ **1988** nel 1988; ~ **May** in *or* a maggio; **I'll see you ~ July** ci vediamo a luglio; ~ **the afternoon** nel pomeriggio; **at 4 o'clock ~ the afternoon** alle 4 del pomeriggio; **I did it ~ 3 hours/days** l'ho fatto in 3 ore/giorni; **I'll see you ~ 2**

weeks *or* ~ **2 weeks' time** ci vediamo tra 2 settimane; **once** ~ **a hundred years** una volta ogni cento anni
4 (*indicating manner etc*) a; ~ **a loud/soft voice** a voce alta/bassa; ~ **pencil** a matita; ~ **English/French** in inglese/francese; ~ **writing** per iscritto; **the boy** ~ **the blue shirt** il ragazzo con la camicia blu
5 (*indicating circumstances*): ~ **the sun** al sole; ~ **the shade** all'ombra; ~ **the rain** sotto la pioggia; **a rise** ~ **prices** un aumento dei prezzi
6 (*indicating mood, state*): ~ **tears** in lacrime; ~ **anger** per la rabbia; ~ **despair** disperato(a); ~ **good condition** in buono stato, in buone condizioni; **to live** ~ **luxury** vivere nel lusso
7 (*with ratios, numbers*): **1** ~ **10** 1 su 10; **20 pence** ~ **the pound** 20 pence per sterlina; **they lined up** ~ **twos** si misero in fila per due; ~ **hundreds** a centinaia
8 (*referring to people, works*) in; **the disease is common** ~ **children** la malattia è comune nei bambini; ~ **(the works of) Dickens** in Dickens, nelle opere di Dickens
9 (*indicating profession etc*) in; **to be** ~ **teaching** fare l'insegnante, insegnare; **to be** ~ **publishing** lavorare nell'editoria
10 (*after superlative*) di; **the best** ~ **the class** il migliore della classe
11 (*with present participle*): ~ **saying this** dicendo questo, nel dire questo
12: ~ **that** *conj* poiché
♦ *adv*: **to be** ~ (*person: at home, work*) esserci; (*train, ship, plane*) essere arrivato(a); (*in fashion*) essere di moda; **their party is** ~ il loro partito è al potere; **to ask sb** ~ invitare qn ad entrare; **to run/limp** *etc* ~ entrare di corsa/zoppicando *etc*
♦ *n*: **the ~s and outs of the problem** tutti gli aspetti del problema.

─────────────────────────

in., ins *abbr* = **inch(es)**.

inability [ɪnə'bɪlɪtɪ] *n* inabilità, incapacità; ~ **to pay** impossibilità di pagare.

inaccessible [ɪnək'sɛsɪbl] *adj* inaccessibile.

inaccuracy [ɪn'ækjurəsɪ] *n* inaccuratezza; inesattezza; imprecisione *f*.

inaccurate [ɪn'ækjurət] *adj* inaccurato(a); (*figures*) inesatto(a); (*translation*) impreciso(a).

inaction [ɪn'ækʃən] *n* inazione *f*.

inactivity [ɪnæk'tɪvɪtɪ] *n* inattività.

inadequacy [ɪn'ædɪkwəsɪ] *n* insufficienza.

inadequate [ɪn'ædɪkwət] *adj* insufficiente.

inadmissible [ɪnəd'mɪsəbl] *adj*

inammissibile.
inadvertent [ɪnəd'vɔːtənt] adj involontario(a).
inadvertently [ɪnəd'vɔːtntlɪ] adv senza volerlo.
inadvisable [ɪnəd'vaɪzəbl] adj sconsigliabile.
inane [ɪ'neɪn] adj vacuo(a), stupido(a).
inanimate [ɪn'ænɪmət] adj inanimato(a).
inapplicable [ɪn'æplɪkəbl] adj inapplicabile.
inappropriate [ɪnə'prəʊprɪət] adj disadatto(a); (word, expression) improprio(a).
inapt [ɪn'æpt] adj maldestro(a); fuori luogo.
inaptitude [ɪn'æptɪtjuːd] n improprietà.
inarticulate [ɪnɑː'tɪkjulət] adj (person) che si esprime male; (speech) inarticolato(a).
inasmuch as [ɪnəz'mʌtʃæz] adv in quanto che; (seeing that) poiché.
inattention [ɪnə'tɛnʃən] n mancanza di attenzione.
inattentive [ɪnə'tɛntɪv] adj disattento(a), distratto(a); negligente.
inaudible [ɪn'ɔːdɪbl] adj che non si riesce a sentire.
inaugural [ɪ'nɔːgjurəl] adj inaugurale.
inaugurate [ɪ'nɔːgjureɪt] vt inaugurare; (president, official) insediare.
inauguration [ɪnɔːgju'reɪʃən] n inaugurazione f; insediamento in carica.
inauspicious [ɪnɔːs'pɪʃəs] adj poco propizio(a).
in-between [ɪnbɪ'twiːn] adj fra i (or le) due.
inborn [ɪn'bɔːn] adj (feeling) innato(a); (defect) congenito(a).
inbred [ɪn'brɛd] adj innato(a); (family) connaturato(a).
inbreeding [ɪn'briːdɪŋ] n incrocio ripetuto di animali consanguinei; unioni fpl fra consanguinei.
Inc. abbr see **incorporated**.
Inca ['ɪŋkə] adj (also: ~n) inca inv ♦ n inca m/f inv.
incalculable [ɪn'kælkjuləbl] adj incalcolabile.
incapability [ɪnkeɪpə'bɪlɪtɪ] n incapacità.
incapable [ɪn'keɪpəbl] adj: ~ (of doing sth) incapace (di fare qc).
incapacitate [ɪnkə'pæsɪteɪt] vt: to ~ sb from doing rendere qn incapace di fare.
incapacitated [ɪnkə'pæsɪteɪtɪd] adj (LAW) inabilitato(a).
incapacity [ɪnkə'pæsɪtɪ] n incapacità.
incarcerate [ɪn'kɑːsəreɪt] vt imprigionare.
incarnate adj [ɪn'kɑːnɪt] incarnato(a) ♦ vt ['ɪnkɑːneɪt] incarnare.
incarnation [ɪnkɑː'neɪʃən] n incarnazione f.
incendiary [ɪn'sɛndɪərɪ] adj incendiario(a)

♦ n (bomb) bomba incendiaria.
incense n ['ɪnsɛns] incenso ♦ vt [ɪn'sɛns] (anger) infuriare.
incense burner n incensiere m.
incentive [ɪn'sɛntɪv] n incentivo.
incentive scheme n piano di incentivazione.
inception [ɪn'sɛpʃən] n inizio, principio.
incessant [ɪn'sɛsnt] adj incessante.
incessantly [ɪn'sɛsntlɪ] adv di continuo, senza sosta.
incest ['ɪnsɛst] n incesto.
inch [ɪntʃ] n pollice m (= 25 mm; 12 in a foot); **within an** ~ **of** a un pelo da; **he wouldn't give an** ~ (fig) non ha ceduto di un millimetro.
▶**inch forward** vi avanzare pian piano.
inch tape n (BRIT) metro a nastro (da sarto).
incidence ['ɪnsɪdns] n incidenza.
incident ['ɪnsɪdnt] n incidente m; (in book) episodio.
incidental [ɪnsɪ'dɛntl] adj accessorio(a), d'accompagnamento; (unplanned) incidentale; ~ **to** marginale a; ~ **expenses** npl spese fpl accessorie.
incidentally [ɪnsɪ'dɛntəlɪ] adv (by the way) a proposito.
incidental music n sottofondo (musicale), musica di sottofondo.
incident room n (POLICE) centrale f delle operazioni (per indagini).
incinerate [ɪn'sɪnəreɪt] vt incenerire.
incinerator [ɪn'sɪnəreɪtə*] n inceneritore m.
incipient [ɪn'sɪpɪənt] adj incipiente.
incision [ɪn'sɪʒən] n incisione f.
incisive [ɪn'saɪsɪv] adj incisivo(a); tagliante acuto(a).
incisor [ɪn'saɪzə*] n incisivo.
incite [ɪn'saɪt] vt incitare.
incl. abbr = **including, inclusive (of)**.
inclement [ɪn'klɛmənt] adj inclemente.
inclination [ɪnklɪ'neɪʃən] n inclinazione f.
incline n ['ɪnklaɪn] pendenza, pendío ♦ vb [ɪn'klaɪn] vt inclinare ♦ vi: to ~ to tendere a; to be ~d to do tendere a fare; essere propenso(a) a fare; to be well ~d towards sb essere ben disposto(a) verso qn.
include [ɪn'kluːd] vt includere, comprendere; the tip is/is not ~d la mancia è compresa/esclusa.
including [ɪn'kluːdɪŋ] prep compreso(a), incluso(a); ~ tip mancia compresa, compresa la mancia.
inclusion [ɪn'kluːʒən] n inclusione f.
inclusive [ɪn'kluːsɪv] adj incluso(a), compreso(a); £50, ~ of all surcharges 50

sterline, incluse tutte le soprattasse.
inclusive terms *npl* (*BRIT*) prezzo tutto compreso.
incognito [ɪnkɔg'niːtəu] *adv* in incognito.
incoherent [ɪnkəu'hɪərənt] *adj* incoerente.
income ['ɪnkʌm] *n* reddito; **gross/net** ~ reddito lordo/netto; ~ **and expenditure account** conto entrate ed uscite.
income support *n* (*BRIT*) sussidio di indigenza *or* povertà.
income tax *n* imposta sul reddito.
income tax inspector *n* ispettore *m* delle imposte dirette.
income tax return *n* dichiarazione *f* annuale dei redditi.
incoming ['ɪnkʌmɪŋ] *adj* (*passengers*) in arrivo; (*government, tenant*) subentrante; ~ **tide** marea montante.
incommunicado [ɪnkəmjunɪ'kaːdəu] *adj*: **to hold sb** ~ tenere qn in segregazione.
incomparable [ɪn'kɔmpərəbl] *adj* incomparabile.
incompatible [ɪnkəm'pætɪbl] *adj* incompatibile.
incompetence [ɪn'kɔmpɪtns] *n* incompetenza, incapacità.
incompetent [ɪn'kɔmpɪtnt] *adj* incompetente, incapace.
incomplete [ɪnkəm'pliːt] *adj* incompleto(a).
incomprehensible [ɪnkɔmprɪ'hɛnsɪbl] *adj* incomprensibile.
inconceivable [ɪnkən'siːvəbl] *adj* inimmaginabile.
inconclusive [ɪnkən'kluːsɪv] *adj* improduttivo(a); (*argument*) poco convincente.
incongruous [ɪn'kɔŋgruəs] *adj* poco appropriato(a); (*remark, act*) incongruo(a).
inconsequential [ɪnkɔnsɪ'kwɛnʃl] *adj* senza importanza.
inconsiderable [ɪnkən'sɪdərəbl] *adj*: **not** ~ non trascurabile.
inconsiderate [ɪnkən'sɪdərət] *adj* sconsiderato(a).
inconsistency [ɪnkən'sɪstənsɪ] *n* (*of actions etc*) incongruenza; (*of work*) irregolarità; (*of statement etc*) contraddizione *f*.
inconsistent [ɪnkən'sɪstnt] *adj* incoerente; poco logico(a); contraddittorio(a); ~ **with** in contraddizione con.
inconsolable [ɪnkən'səuləbl] *adj* inconsolabile.
inconspicuous [ɪnkən'spɪkjuəs] *adj* incospicuo(a); (*colour*) poco appariscente; (*dress*) dimesso(a); **to make o.s.** ~ cercare di passare inosservato(a).
inconstant [ɪn'kɔnstnt] *adj* incostante.

incontinence [ɪn'kɔntɪnəns] *n* incontinenza.
incontinent [ɪn'kɔntɪnənt] *adj* incontinente.
incontrovertible [ɪnkɔntrə'vəːtəbl] *adj* incontrovertibile.
inconvenience [ɪnkən'viːnjəns] *n* inconveniente *m*; (*trouble*) disturbo ♦ *vt* disturbare; **to put sb to great** ~ creare degli inconvenienti a qn.
inconvenient [ɪnkən'viːnjənt] *adj* scomodo(a); **that time is very** ~ **for me** quell'ora mi è molto scomoda, non è un'ora adatta per me.
incorporate [ɪn'kɔːpəreɪt] *vt* incorporare; (*contain*) contenere.
incorporated [ɪn'kɔːpəreɪtɪd] *adj*: ~ **company** (*US*: *abbr* **Inc.**) società *f inv* registrata.
incorrect [ɪnkə'rɛkt] *adj* scorretto(a); (*statement*) impreciso(a).
incorrigible [ɪn'kɔrɪdʒəbl] *adj* incorreggibile.
incorruptible [ɪnkə'rʌptɪbl] *adj* incorruttibile.
increase *n* ['ɪnkriːs] aumento ♦ *vi* [ɪn'kriːs] aumentare; **to be on the** ~ essere in aumento; **an** ~ **of £5/10%** un aumento di 5 sterline/del 10%.
increasing [ɪn'kriːsɪŋ] *adj* (*number*) crescente.
increasingly [ɪn'kriːsɪŋlɪ] *adv* sempre più.
incredible [ɪn'krɛdɪbl] *adj* incredibile.
incredulous [ɪn'krɛdjuləs] *adj* incredulo(a).
increment ['ɪnkrɪmənt] *n* aumento, incremento.
incriminate [ɪn'krɪmɪneɪt] *vt* compromettere.
incriminating [ɪn'krɪmɪneɪtɪŋ] *adj* incriminante.
incubate ['ɪnkjubeɪt] *vt* (*eggs*) covare ♦ *vi* (*egg*) essere in incubazione; (*disease*) avere un'incubazione.
incubation [ɪnkju'beɪʃən] *n* incubazione *f*.
incubation period *n* (periodo di) incubazione *f*.
incubator ['ɪnkjubeɪtə*] *n* incubatrice *f*.
inculcate ['ɪnkʌlkeɪt] *vt*: **to** ~ **sth in sb** inculcare qc a qn, instillare qc a qn.
incumbent [ɪn'kʌmbənt] *adj*: **it is** ~ **on him to do ...** è suo dovere fare ... ♦ *n* titolare *m/f*.
incur [ɪn'kəː*] *vt* (*expenses*) incorrere; (*debt*) contrarre; (*loss*) subire; (*anger, risk*) esporsi a.
incurable [ɪn'kjuərəbl] *adj* incurabile.
incursion [ɪn'kəːʃən] *n* incursione *f*.
Ind. *abbr* (*US*) = *Indiana*.
indebted [ɪn'dɛtɪd] *adj*: **to be** ~ **to sb** (**for**) essere obbligato(a) verso qn (per).

indecency [ɪn'diːsnsɪ] n indecenza.
indecent [ɪn'diːsnt] adj indecente.
indecent assault n (BRIT) aggressione f a scopo di violenza sessuale.
indecent exposure n atti mpl osceni in luogo pubblico.
indecipherable [ɪndɪ'saɪfərəbl] adj indecifrabile.
indecision [ɪndɪ'sɪʒən] n indecisione f.
indecisive [ɪndɪ'saɪsɪv] adj indeciso(a); (discussion) non decisivo(a).
indeed [ɪn'diːd] adv infatti; veramente; **yes ~!** certamente!
indefatigable [ɪndɪ'fætɪgəbl] adj infaticabile, instancabile.
indefensible [ɪndɪ'fɛnsəbl] adj (conduct) ingiustificabile.
indefinable [ɪndɪ'faɪnəbl] adj indefinibile.
indefinite [ɪn'dɛfɪnɪt] adj indefinito(a); (answer) vago(a); (period, number) indeterminato(a).
indefinitely [ɪn'dɛfɪnɪtlɪ] adv (wait) indefinitamente.
indelible [ɪn'dɛlɪbl] adj indelebile.
indelicate [ɪn'dɛlɪkɪt] adj (tactless) indelicato(a), privo(a) di tatto; (not polite) sconveniente.
Indemnify [ɪn'dɛmnɪfaɪ] vt indennizzare.
indemnity [ɪn'dɛmnɪtɪ] n (insurance) assicurazione f; (compensation) indennità, indennizzo.
indent [ɪn'dɛnt] vt (TYP: text) far rientrare dal margine.
indentation [ɪndɛn'teɪʃən] n dentellatura; (TYP) rientranza; (dent) tacca.
indented [ɪn'dɛntɪd] adj (TYP) rientrante.
indenture [ɪn'dɛntʃə*] n contratto m formazione inv.
independence [ɪndɪ'pɛndns] n indipendenza.
Independence Day n (US) see boxed note.

INDEPENDENCE DAY

Negli Stati Uniti il 4 luglio si festeggia l'**Independence Day**, il giorno in cui è stata firmata, nel 1776, la Dichiarazione di Indipendenza con la quale tredici colonie britanniche dichiaravano la propria autonomia dalla Gran Bretagna e la propria appartenenza agli Stati Uniti d'America.

---

independent [ɪndɪ'pɛndnt] adj indipendente.
independently [ɪndɪ'pɛndntlɪ] adv indipendentemente; separatamente; **~ of** indipendentemente da.
in-depth ['ɪn'dɛpθ] adj approfondito(a).

indescribable [ɪndɪ'skraɪbəbl] adj indescrivibile.
indestructible [ɪndɪ'strʌktəbl] adj indistruttibile.
indeterminate [ɪndɪ'təːmɪnɪt] adj indeterminato(a).
index ['ɪndɛks] n (pl ~es: in book) indice m; (: in library etc) catalogo; (pl **indices** ['ɪndɪsiːz]: ratio, sign) indice m.
index card n scheda.
index finger n (dito) indice m.
index-linked ['ɪndɛks'lɪŋkt], (US) **indexed** ['ɪndɛkst] adj legato(a) al costo della vita.
India ['ɪndɪə] n India.
Indian ['ɪndɪən] adj, n indiano(a).
Indian ink n inchiostro di china.
Indian Ocean n: **the ~** l'Oceano Indiano.
Indian Summer n (fig) estate f di San Martino.
India paper n carta d'India, carta bibbia.
India rubber n cacciù m.
indicate ['ɪndɪkeɪt] vt indicare ♦ vi (BRIT AUT): **to ~ left/right** mettere la freccia a sinistra/a destra.
indication [ɪndɪ'keɪʃən] n indicazione f, segno.
indicative [ɪn'dɪkətɪv] adj indicativo(a) ♦ n (LING) indicativo; **to be ~ of sth** essere indicativo(a) or un indice di qc.
indicator ['ɪndɪkeɪtə*] n (sign) segno; (AUT) indicatore m di direzione, freccia.
indices ['ɪndɪsiːz] npl of **index**.
indict [ɪn'daɪt] vt accusare.
indictable [ɪn'daɪtəbl] adj passibile di pena; **~ offence** atto che costituisce reato.
indictment [ɪn'daɪtmənt] n accusa.
indifference [ɪn'dɪfrəns] n indifferenza.
indifferent [ɪn'dɪfrənt] adj indifferente; (poor) mediocre.
indigenous [ɪn'dɪdʒɪnəs] adj indigeno(a).
indigestible [ɪndɪ'dʒɛstɪbl] adj indigeribile.
indigestion [ɪndɪ'dʒɛstʃən] n indigestione f.
indignant [ɪn'dɪgnənt] adj: **~ (at sth/with sb)** indignato(a) (per qc/contro qn).
indignation [ɪndɪg'neɪʃən] n indignazione f.
indignity [ɪn'dɪgnɪtɪ] n umiliazione f.
indigo ['ɪndɪgəu] adj, n indaco (inv).
indirect [ɪndɪ'rɛkt] adj indiretto(a).
indirectly [ɪndɪ'rɛktlɪ] adv indirettamente.
indiscreet [ɪndɪ'skriːt] adj indiscreto(a); (rash) imprudente.
indiscretion [ɪndɪ'skrɛʃən] n indiscrezione f; imprudenza.
indiscriminate [ɪndɪ'skrɪmɪnət] adj (person) che non sa discernere; (admiration) cieco(a); (killings) indiscriminato(a).
indispensable [ɪndɪ'spɛnsəbl] adj indispensabile.

indisposed[ɪndɪ'spəuzd] *adj* (*unwell*) indisposto(a).

indisposition[ɪndɪspə'zɪʃən] *n* (*illness*) indisposizione *f*.

indisputable[ɪndɪ'spjuːtəbl] *adj* incontestabile, indiscutibile.

indistinct[ɪndɪ'stɪŋkt] *adj* indistinto(a); (*memory, noise*) vago(a).

indistinguishable[ɪndɪ'stɪŋgwɪʃəbl] *adj* indistinguibile.

individual[ɪndɪ'vɪdjuəl] *n* individuo ♦ *adj* individuale; (*characteristic*) particolare, originale.

individualist[ɪndɪ'vɪdjuəlɪst] *n* individualista *m/f*.

individuality[ɪndɪvɪdju'ælɪtɪ] *n* individualità.

individually[ɪndɪ'vɪdjuəlɪ] *adv* singolarmente, uno(a) per uno(a).

indivisible[ɪndɪ'vɪzɪbl] *adj* indivisibile.

Indochina['ɪndəu'tʃaɪnə] *n* Indocina.

indoctrinate[ɪn'dɔktrɪneɪt] *vt* indottrinare.

indoctrination[ɪndɔktrɪ'neɪʃən] *n* indottrinamento.

indolent['ɪndələnt] *adj* indolente.

Indonesia[ɪndəu'niːzɪə] *n* Indonesia.

Indonesian[ɪndəu'niːzɪən] *adj, n* indonesiano(a); (*LING*) indonesiano.

indoor['ɪndɔː*] *adj* da interno; (*plant*) d'appartamento; (*swimming pool*) coperto(a); (*sport, games*) fatto(a) al coperto.

indoors[ɪn'dɔːz] *adv* all'interno; (*at home*) in casa.

indubitable[ɪn'djuːbɪtəbl] *adj* indubitabile.

induce[ɪn'djuːs] *vt* persuadere; (*bring about*) provocare; **to ~ sb to do sth** persuadere qn a fare qc.

inducement[ɪn'djuːsmənt] *n* incitamento; (*incentive*) stimolo, incentivo.

induct[ɪn'dʌkt] *vt* insediare; (*fig*) iniziare.

induction[ɪn'dʌkʃən] *n* (*MED: of birth*) parto indotto.

induction course*n* (*BRIT*) corso di avviamento.

indulge[ɪn'dʌldʒ] *vt* (*whim*) compiacere, soddisfare; (*child*) viziare ♦ *vi*: **to ~ in sth** concedersi qc; abbandonarsi a qc.

indulgence[ɪn'dʌldʒəns] *n* lusso (che uno si permette); (*leniency*) indulgenza.

indulgent[ɪn'dʌldʒənt] *adj* indulgente.

industrial[ɪn'dʌstrɪəl] *adj* industriale; (*injury*) sul lavoro; (*dispute*) di lavoro.

industrial action*n* azione *f* rivendicativa.

industrial estate*n* zona industriale.

industrialist[ɪn'dʌstrɪəlɪst] *n* industriale *m*.

industrialize[ɪn'dʌstrɪəlaɪz] *vt* industrializzare.

industrial park*n* (*US*) zona industriale.

industrial relations*npl* relazioni *fpl* industriali.

industrial tribunal*n* (*BRIT*) ≈ Tribunale *m* Amministrativo Regionale.

industrial unrest*n* (*BRIT*) agitazione *f* (sindacale).

industrious[ɪn'dʌstrɪəs] *adj* industrioso(a), assiduo(a).

industry['ɪndəstrɪ] *n* industria; (*diligence*) operosità.

inebriated[ɪ'niːbrɪeɪtɪd] *adj* ubriaco(a).

inedible[ɪn'ɛdɪbl] *adj* immangiabile; non commestibile.

ineffective[ɪnɪ'fɛktɪv] *adj* inefficace.

ineffectual[ɪnɪ'fɛktʃuəl] *adj* inefficace; incompetente.

inefficiency[ɪnɪ'fɪʃənsɪ] *n* inefficienza.

inefficient[ɪnɪ'fɪʃənt] *adj* inefficiente.

inelegant[ɪn'ɛlɪgənt] *adj* poco elegante.

ineligible[ɪn'ɛlɪdʒɪbl] *adj* (*candidate*) ineleggibile; **to be ~ for sth** non avere il diritto a qc.

inept[ɪ'nɛpt] *adj* inetto(a).

ineptitude[ɪ'nɛptɪtjuːd] *n* inettitudine *f*, stupidità.

inequality[ɪnɪ'kwɔlɪtɪ] *n* ineguaglianza.

inequitable[ɪn'ɛkwɪtəbl] *adj* iniquo(a).

ineradicable[ɪnɪ'rædɪkəbl] *adj* inestirpabile.

inert[ɪ'nəːt] *adj* inerte.

inertia[ɪ'nəːʃə] *n* inerzia.

inertia-reel seat belt[ɪ'nəːʃə'riːl-] *n* cintura di sicurezza con arrotolatore.

inescapable[ɪnɪ'skeɪpəbl] *adj* inevitabile.

inessential[ɪnɪ'sɛnʃl] *adj* non essenziale.

inestimable[ɪn'ɛstɪməbl] *adj* inestimabile, incalcolabile.

inevitable[ɪn'ɛvɪtəbl] *adj* inevitabile.

inevitably[ɪn'ɛvɪtəblɪ] *adv* inevitabilmente; **as ~ happens ...** come immancabilmente succede ....

inexact[ɪnɪg'zækt] *adj* inesatto(a).

inexcusable[ɪnɪks'kjuːzəbl] *adj* imperdonabile.

inexhaustible[ɪnɪg'zɔːstɪbl] *adj* inesauribile; (*person*) instancabile.

inexorable[ɪn'ɛksərəbl] *adj* inesorabile.

inexpensive[ɪnɪk'spɛnsɪv] *adj* poco costoso(a).

inexperience[ɪnɪk'spɪərɪəns] *n* inesperienza.

inexperienced[ɪnɪk'spɪərɪənst] *adj* inesperto(a), senza esperienza; **to be ~ in sth** essere poco pratico di qc.

inexplicable[ɪnɪk'splɪkəbl] *adj* inesplicabile.

inexpressible[ɪnɪk'sprɛsəbl] *adj*

inesprimibile.
inextricable[ɪnɪk'strɪkəbl] adj inestricabile.
infallibility[ɪnfælə'bɪlɪtɪ] n infallibilità.
infallible[ɪn'fælɪbl] adj infallibile.
infamous['ɪnfəməs] adj infame.
infamy['ɪnfəmɪ] n infamia.
infancy['ɪnfənsɪ] n infanzia.
infant['ɪnfənt] n bambino/a.
infantile['ɪnfəntaɪl] adj infantile.
infant mortalityn mortalità infantile.
infantry['ɪnfəntrɪ] n fanteria.
infantryman['ɪnfəntrɪmən] n fante m.
infant schooln (BRIT) scuola elementare
(per bambini dall'età di 5 a 7 anni).
infatuated[ɪn'fætjueɪtɪd] adj: ~ with
infatuato(a) di; to become ~ (with sb)
infatuarsi (di qn).
infatuation[ɪnfætju'eɪʃən] n infatuazione f.
infect[ɪn'fɛkt] vt infettare; ~ed with
(illness) affetto(a) da; to become ~ed
(wound) infettarsi.
infection[ɪn'fɛkʃən] n infezione f.
infectious[ɪn'fɛkʃəs] adj (disease)
infettivo(a), contagioso(a); (person,
laughter) contagioso(a).
infer[ɪn'fəː*] vt: to ~ (from) dedurre (da),
concludere (da).
inference['ɪnfərəns] n deduzione f,
conclusione f.
inferior[ɪn'fɪərɪə*] adj inferiore; (goods) di
qualità scadente ♦ n inferiore m/f; (in rank)
subalterno/a; to feel ~ sentirsi inferiore.
inferiority[ɪnfɪərɪ'ɔrɪtɪ] n inferiorità.
inferiority complexn complesso di
inferiorità.
infernal[ɪn'fəːnl] adj infernale.
inferno[ɪn'fəːnəu] n inferno.
infertile[ɪn'fəːtaɪl] adj sterile.
infertility[ɪnfəː'tɪlɪtɪ] n sterilità.
infested[ɪn'fɛstɪd] adj: ~ (with)
infestato(a) (di).
infidelity[ɪnfɪ'dɛlɪtɪ] n infedeltà.
in-fighting['ɪnfaɪtɪŋ] n lotte fpl intestine.
infiltrate['ɪnfɪltreɪt] vt (troops etc) far
penetrare; (enemy line etc) infiltrare ♦ vi
infiltrarsi.
infinite['ɪnfɪnɪt] adj infinito(a); an ~
amount of time/money un'illimitata
quantità di tempo/denaro.
infinitely['ɪnfɪnɪtlɪ] adv infinitamente.
infinitesimal[ɪnfɪnɪ'tɛsɪməl] adj
infinitesimale.
infinitive[ɪn'fɪnɪtɪv] n infinito.
infinity[ɪn'fɪnɪtɪ] n infinità; (also MATH)
infinito.
infirm[ɪn'fəːm] adj infermo(a).
infirmary[ɪn'fəːmərɪ] n ospedale m; (in
school, factory) infermeria.

infirmity[ɪn'fəːmɪtɪ] n infermità f inv.
inflamed[ɪn'fleɪmd] adj infiammato(a).
inflammable[ɪn'flæməbl] adj infiammabile.
inflammation[ɪnflə'meɪʃən] n
infiammazione f.
inflammatory[ɪn'flæmətərɪ] adj (speech)
incendiario(a).
inflatable[ɪn'fleɪtəbl] adj gonfiabile.
inflate[ɪn'fleɪt] vt (tyre, balloon) gonfiare;
(fig) esagerare; gonfiare; to ~ the
currency far ricorso all'inflazione.
inflated[ɪn'fleɪtɪd] adj (style) gonfio(a);
(value) esagerato(a).
inflation[ɪn'fleɪʃən] n (ECON) inflazione f.
inflationary[ɪn'fleɪʃənərɪ] adj
inflazionistico(a).
inflexible[ɪn'flɛksɪbl] adj inflessibile,
rigido(a).
inflict[ɪn'flɪkt] vt: to ~ on infliggere a.
infliction[ɪn'flɪkʃən] n inflizione f; afflizione
f.
in-flight['ɪnflaɪt] adj a bordo.
inflow['ɪnfləu] n afflusso.
influence['ɪnfluəns] n influenza ♦ vt
influenzare; under the ~ of sotto
l'influenza di; under the ~ of drink sotto
l'influenza or l'effetto dell'alcool.
influential[ɪnflu'ɛnʃl] adj influente.
influenza[ɪnflu'ɛnzə] n (MED) influenza.
influx['ɪnflʌks] n afflusso.
inform[ɪn'fɔːm] vt: to ~ sb (of) informare
qn (di) ♦ vi: to ~ on sb denunciare qn; to
~ sb about mettere qn al corrente di.
informal[ɪn'fɔːml] adj (person, manner) alla
buona, semplice; (visit, discussion)
informale; (invitation) non ufficiale;
"dress ~" "non è richiesto l'abito
scuro"; ~ language linguaggio
colloquiale.
informality[ɪnfɔː'mælɪtɪ] n semplicità,
informalità; carattere m non ufficiale.
informally[ɪn'fɔːməlɪ] adv senza cerimonie;
(invite) in modo non ufficiale.
informant[ɪn'fɔːmənt] n informatore/trice.
informatics[ɪnfə'mætɪks] n informatica.
information[ɪnfə'meɪʃən] n informazioni
fpl; particolari mpl; to get ~ on informarsi
su; a piece of ~ un'informazione; for your
~ a titolo d'informazione, per sua
informazione.
information bureaun ufficio m
informazioni inv.
information processingn elaborazione f
delle informazioni.
information retrievaln ricupero delle
informazioni.
information superhighwayn autostrada
informatica.

information technology (IT) *n*
informatica.
informative [ɪn'fɔːmətɪv] *adj* istruttivo(a).
informed [ɪn'fɔːmd] *adj (observer)* (ben)
informato(a); **an ~ guess** un'ipotesi
fondata.
informer [ɪn'fɔːmə*] *n* informatore/trice.
infra dig ['ɪnfrə'dɪg] *adj abbr (col:* = *infra
dignitatem:* beneath one's dignity)
indecoroso(a).
infra-red [ɪnfrə'rɛd] *adj* infrarosso(a).
infrastructure ['ɪnfrəstrʌktʃə*] *n*
infrastruttura.
infrequent [ɪn'friːkwənt] *adj* infrequente,
raro(a).
infringe [ɪn'frɪndʒ] *vt* infrangere ♦ *vi:* **to ~
on** calpestare.
infringement [ɪn'frɪndʒmənt] *n:* ~ **(of)**
infrazione *f* (di).
infuriate [ɪn'fjuərɪeɪt] *vt* rendere furioso(a).
infuriating [ɪn'fjuərɪeɪtɪŋ] *adj* molto
irritante.
infuse [ɪn'fjuːz] *vt (with courage,
enthusiasm):* **to ~ sb with sth** infondere
qc a qn, riempire qn di qc.
infusion [ɪn'fjuːʒən] *n (tea etc)* infuso,
infusione *f*.
ingenious [ɪn'dʒiːnjəs] *adj* ingegnoso(a).
ingenuity [ɪndʒɪ'njuːɪtɪ] *n* ingegnosità.
ingenuous [ɪn'dʒɛnjuəs] *adj* ingenuo(a).
ingot ['ɪŋgət] *n* lingotto.
ingrained [ɪn'greɪnd] *adj* radicato(a).
ingratiate [ɪn'greɪʃɪeɪt] *vt:* **to ~ o.s. with sb**
ingraziarsi qn.
ingratiating [ɪn'greɪʃɪeɪtɪŋ] *adj (smile,
speech)* suadente, cattivante; *(person)*
compiacente.
ingratitude [ɪn'grætɪtjuːd] *n* ingratitudine *f*.
ingredient [ɪn'griːdɪənt] *n* ingrediente *m*;
elemento.
ingrowing ['ɪngrəʊɪŋ], **ingrown** ['ɪngrəʊn]
adj: ~ **(toe)nail** unghia incarnita.
inhabit [ɪn'hæbɪt] *vt* abitare.
inhabitable [ɪn'hæbɪtəbl] *adj* abitabile.
inhabitant [ɪn'hæbɪtnt] *n* abitante *m/f*.
inhale [ɪn'heɪl] *vt* inalare ♦ *vi (in smoking)*
aspirare.
inhaler [ɪn'heɪlə*] *n* inalatore *m*.
inherent [ɪn'hɪərənt] *adj:* ~ **(in or to)**
inerente (a).
inherently [ɪn'hɪərəntlɪ] *adv (easy, difficult)*
di per sé; ~ **lazy** pigro di natura.
inherit [ɪn'hɛrɪt] *vt* ereditare.
inheritance [ɪn'hɛrɪtəns] *n* eredità.
inhibit [ɪn'hɪbɪt] *vt (PSYCH)* inibire; **to ~ sb
from doing** impedire a qn di fare.
inhibited [ɪn'hɪbɪtɪd] *adj (person)* inibito(a).
inhibiting [ɪn'hɪbɪtɪŋ] *adj* che inibisce.

inhibition [ɪnhɪ'bɪʃən] *n* inibizione *f*.
inhospitable [ɪnhɔs'pɪtəbl] *adj* inospitale.
in-house ['ɪn'haʊs] *adj* effettuato(a) da
personale interno, interno(a) ♦ *adv
(training)* all'interno dell'azienda.
inhuman [ɪn'hjuːmən] *adj* inumano(a),
disumano(a).
inhumane [ɪnhjuː'meɪn] *adj* inumano(a),
disumano(a).
inimitable [ɪ'nɪmɪtəbl] *adj* inimitabile.
iniquity [ɪ'nɪkwɪtɪ] *n* iniquità *f inv.*
initial [ɪ'nɪʃl] *adj* iniziale ♦ *n* iniziale *f* ♦ *vt*
siglare; ~**s** *npl* iniziali *fpl; (as signature)*
sigla.
initialize [ɪ'nɪʃəlaɪz] *vt (COMPUT)*
inizializzare.
initially [ɪ'nɪʃəlɪ] *adv* inizialmente, all'inizio.
initiate [ɪ'nɪʃɪeɪt] *vt (start)* avviare;
intraprendere; iniziare; *(person)* iniziare;
to ~ sb into sth iniziare qn a qc; **to ~
proceedings against sb** *(LAW)* intentare
causa a *or* contro qn.
initiation [ɪnɪʃɪ'eɪʃən] *n* iniziazione *f.*
initiative [ɪ'nɪʃətɪv] *n* iniziativa; **to take the
~** prendere l'iniziativa.
inject [ɪn'dʒɛkt] *vt (liquid)* iniettare; *(person)*
fare una puntura a; *(fig: money):* **to ~ into**
immettere in.
injection [ɪn'dʒɛkʃən] *n* iniezione *f*, puntura;
to have an ~ farsi fare un'iniezione *or*
una puntura.
injudicious [ɪndʒu'dɪʃəs] *adj* poco saggio(a).
injunction [ɪn'dʒʌŋkʃən] *n (LAW)*
ingiunzione *f*, intimazione *f*.
injure ['ɪndʒə*] *vt* ferire; *(wrong)* fare male
or torto a; *(damage: reputation etc)*
nuocere a; *(feelings)* offendere; **to ~ o.s.**
farsi male.
injured ['ɪndʒəd] *adj (person, leg etc)*
ferito(a); *(tone, feelings)* offeso(a); ~
party *(LAW)* parte *f* lesa.
injurious [ɪn'dʒuərɪəs] *adj:* ~ **(to)** nocivo(a)
(a), pregiudizievole (per).
injury ['ɪndʒərɪ] *n* ferita; *(wrong)* torto; **to
escape without** ~ rimanere illeso.
injury time *n (SPORT)* tempo di recupero.
injustice [ɪn'dʒʌstɪs] *n* ingiustizia; **you do
me an** ~ mi fa un torto, è ingiusto verso
di me.
ink [ɪŋk] *n* inchiostro.
ink-jet printer ['ɪŋkdʒɛt-] *n* stampante *f* a
getto d'inchiostro.
inkling ['ɪŋklɪŋ] *n* sentore *m*, vaga idea.
inkpad ['ɪŋkpæd] *n* tampone *m*, cuscinetto
per timbri.
inky ['ɪŋkɪ] *adj* macchiato(a) *or* sporco(a)
d'inchiostro.
inlaid ['ɪnleɪd] *adj* incrostato(a); *(table etc)*

intarsiato(a).

inland adj ['ɪnlənd] interno(a) ♦ adv [ɪn'lænd] all'interno; ~ **waterways** canali e fiumi mpl navigabili.

Inland Revenue n (BRIT) Fisco.

in-laws ['ɪnlɔːz] npl suoceri mpl; famiglia del marito (or della moglie).

inlet ['ɪnlɛt] n (GEO) insenatura, baia.

inlet pipe n (TECH) tubo d'immissione.

inmate ['ɪnmeɪt] n (in prison) carcerato/a; (in asylum) ricoverato/a.

inmost ['ɪnməust] adj più profondo(a), più intimo(a).

inn [ɪn] n locanda.

innards ['ɪnədz] npl (col) interiora fpl, budella fpl.

innate [ɪ'neɪt] adj innato(a).

inner ['ɪnə*] adj interno(a), interiore.

inner city n centro di una zona urbana.

innermost ['ɪnəməust] adj = **inmost**.

inner tube n camera d'aria.

innings ['ɪnɪŋz] n (CRICKET) turno di battuta; (BRIT fig): **he has had a good** ~ **ha** avuto molto dalla vita.

innocence ['ɪnəsns] n innocenza.

innocent ['ɪnəsnt] adj innocente.

innocuous [ɪ'nɔkjuəs] adj innocuo(a).

innovation [ɪnəu'veɪʃən] n innovazione f.

innuendo, ~ **es** [ɪnju'ɛndəu] n insinuazione f.

innumerable [ɪ'njuːmrəbl] adj innumerevole.

inoculate [ɪ'nɔkjuleɪt] vt: **to** ~ **sb with sth/ against sth** inoculare qc a qn/qn contro qc.

inoculation [ɪnɔkju'leɪʃən] n inoculazione f.

inoffensive [ɪnə'fɛnsɪv] adj inoffensivo(a), innocuo(a).

inopportune [ɪn'ɔpətjuːn] adj inopportuno(a).

inordinate [ɪ'nɔːdɪnɪt] adj eccessivo(a).

inordinately [ɪ'nɔːdɪnətlɪ] adv smoderatamente.

inorganic [ɪnɔː'gænɪk] adj inorganico(a).

in-patient ['ɪnpeɪʃənt] n ricoverato/a.

input ['ɪnput] n (ELEC) energia, potenza; (of machine) alimentazione f; (of computer) input m ♦ vt (COMPUT) inserire, introdurre.

inquest ['ɪnkwɛst] n inchiesta.

inquire [ɪn'kwaɪə*] vi informarsi ♦ vt domandare, informarsi di or su; **to** ~ **about** informarsi di or su, chiedere informazioni su; **to** ~ **when/where/ whether** informarsi di quando/su dove/ se.

▶**inquire after** vt fus (person) chiedere di; (sb's health) informarsi di.

▶**inquire into** vt fus indagare su, fare delle indagini or ricerche su.

inquiring [ɪn'kwaɪərɪŋ] adj (mind) inquisitivo(a).

inquiry [ɪn'kwaɪərɪ] n domanda; (LAW) indagine f, investigazione f; **to hold an** ~ **into sth** fare un'inchiesta su qc.

inquiry desk n (BRIT) banco delle informazioni.

inquiry office n (BRIT) ufficio m informazioni inv.

inquisition [ɪnkwɪ'zɪʃən] n inquisizione f, inchiesta; (REL): **the l**~ l'Inquisizione.

inquisitive [ɪn'kwɪzɪtɪv] adj curioso(a).

inroads ['ɪnrəudz] npl: **to make** ~ **into** (savings, supplies) intaccare (seriamente).

insane [ɪn'seɪn] adj matto(a), pazzo(a); (MED) alienato(a).

insanitary [ɪn'sænɪtərɪ] adj insalubre.

insanity [ɪn'sænɪtɪ] n follia; (MED) alienazione f mentale.

insatiable [ɪn'seɪʃəbl] adj insaziabile.

inscribe [ɪn'skraɪb] vt iscrivere; (book etc): **to** ~ **(to sb)** dedicare (a qn).

inscription [ɪn'skrɪpʃən] n iscrizione f; (in book) dedica.

inscrutable [ɪn'skruːtəbl] adj imperscrutabile.

inseam ['ɪnsiːm] n (US): ~ **measurement** lunghezza interna.

insect ['ɪnsɛkt] n insetto.

insect bite n puntura or morsicatura d'insetto.

insecticide [ɪn'sɛktɪsaɪd] n insetticida m.

insect repellent n insettifugo.

insecure [ɪnsɪ'kjuə*] adj malsicuro(a); (person) insicuro(a).

insecurity [ɪnsɪ'kjuərɪtɪ] n mancanza di sicurezza.

insensible [ɪn'sɛnsɪbl] adj insensibile; (unconscious) privo(a) di sensi.

insensitive [ɪn'sɛnsɪtɪv] adj insensibile.

insensitivity [ɪnsɛnsɪ'tɪvɪtɪ] n mancanza di sensibilità.

inseparable [ɪn'sɛprəbl] adj inseparabile.

insert vt [ɪn'səːt] inserire, introdurre ♦ n ['ɪnsəːt] inserto.

insertion [ɪn'səːʃən] n inserzione f.

in-service ['ɪn'səːvɪs] adj (course, training) dopo l'assunzione.

inshore [ɪn'ʃɔː*] adj costiero(a) ♦ adv presso la riva; verso la riva.

inside ['ɪn'saɪd] n interno, parte f interiore; (of road: BRIT) sinistra; (: US, in Europe etc) destra ♦ adj interno(a), interiore ♦ adv dentro, all'interno ♦ prep dentro, all'interno di; (of time): ~ **10 minutes** entro 10 minuti; ~**s** npl (col) ventre m; ~

out adv alla rovescia; **to turn sth ~ out** rivoltare qc; **to know sth ~ out** conoscere qc a fondo; **~ information** informazioni fpl riservate; **~ story** storia segreta.

inside forward n (SPORT) mezzala, interno.

inside lane n (AUT) corsia di marcia.

inside leg measurement n (BRIT) lunghezza interna.

insider [ɪn'saɪdə*] n uno(a) che ha le mani in pasta.

insider dealing, insider trading n (STOCK EXCHANGE) insider trading m inv.

insidious [ɪn'sɪdɪəs] adj insidioso(a).

insight ['ɪnsaɪt] n acume m, perspicacia; (glimpse, idea) percezione f; **to gain** or **get an ~ into sth** potersi render conto di qc.

insignia [ɪn'sɪɡnɪə] npl insegne fpl.

insignificant [ɪnsɪɡ'nɪfɪknt] adj insignificante.

insincere [ɪnsɪn'sɪə*] adj insincero(a).

insincerity [ɪnsɪn'sɛrɪtɪ] n falsità, insincerità.

insinuate [ɪn'sɪnjueɪt] vt insinuare.

insinuation [ɪnsɪnju'eɪʃən] n insinuazione f.

insipid [ɪn'sɪpɪd] adj insipido(a), insulso(a).

insist [ɪn'sɪst] vi insistere; **to ~ on doing** insistere per fare; **to ~ that** insistere perché + sub; (claim) sostenere che.

insistence [ɪn'sɪstəns] n insistenza.

insistent [ɪn'sɪstənt] adj insistente.

insofar [ɪnsəu'fɑ:*] conj: **~ as** in quanto.

insole ['ɪnsəul] n soletta; (fixed part of shoe) tramezza.

insolence ['ɪnsələns] n insolenza.

insolent ['ɪnsələnt] adj insolente.

insoluble [ɪn'sɔljubl] adj insolubile.

insolvency [ɪn'sɔlvənsɪ] n insolvenza.

insolvent [ɪn'sɔlvənt] adj insolvente.

insomnia [ɪn'sɔmnɪə] n insonnia.

insomniac [ɪn'sɔmnɪæk] n chi soffre di insonnia.

inspect [ɪn'spɛkt] vt ispezionare; (BRIT: ticket) controllare.

inspection [ɪn'spɛkʃən] n ispezione f; controllo.

inspector [ɪn'spɛktə*] n ispettore/trice; controllore m.

inspiration [ɪnspə'reɪʃən] n ispirazione f.

inspire [ɪn'spaɪə*] vt ispirare.

inspired [ɪn'spaɪəd] adj (writer, book etc) ispirato(a); **in an ~ moment** in un momento d'ispirazione.

inspiring [ɪn'spaɪərɪŋ] adj stimolante.

inst. [ɪnst] abbr (BRIT COMM: = instant) c.m. (=corrente mese).

instability [ɪnstə'bɪlɪtɪ] n instabilità.

install [ɪn'stɔ:l] vt installare.

installation [ɪnstə'leɪʃən] n installazione f.

installment plan n (US) acquisto a rate.

instalment, (US) **installment** [ɪn'stɔ:lmənt] n rata; (of TV serial etc) puntata; **to pay in ~s** pagare a rate.

instance ['ɪnstəns] n esempio, caso; **for ~** per or ad esempio; **in that ~** in quel caso; **in the first ~** in primo luogo.

instant ['ɪnstənt] n istante m, attimo ♦ adj immediato(a); urgente; (coffee, food) in polvere; **the 10th ~** il 10 corrente (mese).

instantaneous [ɪnstən'teɪnɪəs] adj istantaneo(a).

instantly ['ɪnstəntlɪ] adv immediatamente, subito.

instant replay n (US TV) replay m inv.

instead [ɪn'stɛd] adv invece; **~ of** invece di; **~ of sb** al posto di qn.

instep ['ɪnstɛp] n collo del piede; (of shoe) collo della scarpa.

instigate ['ɪnstɪɡeɪt] vt (rebellion, strike, crime) istigare a; (new ideas etc) promuovere.

instigation [ɪnstɪ'ɡeɪʃən] n istigazione f; **at sb's ~** per or in seguito al suggerimento di qn.

instil [ɪn'stɪl] vt: **to ~ (into)** inculcare (in).

instinct ['ɪnstɪŋkt] n istinto.

instinctive [ɪn'stɪŋktɪv] adj istintivo(a).

instinctively [ɪn'stɪŋktɪvlɪ] adv per istinto.

institute ['ɪnstɪtjuːt] n istituto ♦ vt istituire, stabilire; (inquiry) avviare; (proceedings) iniziare.

institution [ɪnstɪ'tjuːʃən] n istituzione f; istituto (d'istruzione); istituto (psichiatrico).

institutional [ɪnstɪ'tjuːʃnl] adj istituzionale; **~ care** assistenza presso un istituto.

instruct [ɪn'strʌkt] vt istruire; **to ~ sb in sth** insegnare qc a qn; **to ~ sb to do** dare ordini a qn di fare.

instruction [ɪn'strʌkʃən] n istruzione f; **~s (for use)** istruzioni per l'uso.

instruction book n libretto di istruzioni.

instructive [ɪn'strʌktɪv] adj istruttivo(a).

instructor [ɪn'strʌktə*] n istruttore/trice; (for skiing) maestro/a.

instrument ['ɪnstrumənt] n strumento.

instrumental [ɪnstru'mɛntl] adj (MUS) strumentale; **to be ~ in sth/in doing sth** avere un ruolo importante in qc/nel fare qc.

instrumentalist [ɪnstru'mɛntəlɪst] n strumentista m/f.

instrument panel n quadro m portastrumenti inv.

insubordinate [ɪnsə'bɔːdənɪt] *adj* insubordinato(a).

insubordination [ɪnsəbɔːdə'neɪʃən] *n* insubordinazione *f.*

insufferable [ɪn'sʌfrəbl] *adj* insopportabile.

insufficient [ɪnsə'fɪʃənt] *adj* insufficiente.

insufficiently [ɪnsə'fɪʃəntlɪ] *adv* in modo insufficiente.

insular ['ɪnsjulə*] *adj* insulare; (*person*) di mente ristretta.

insulate ['ɪnsjuleɪt] *vt* isolare.

insulating tape ['ɪnsjuleɪtɪŋ-] *n* nastro isolante.

insulation [ɪnsju'leɪʃən] *n* isolamento.

insulin ['ɪnsjulɪn] *n* insulina.

insult *n* ['ɪnsʌlt] insulto, affronto ♦ *vt* [ɪn'sʌlt] insultare.

insulting [ɪn'sʌltɪŋ] *adj* offensivo(a), ingiurioso(a).

insuperable [ɪn'sjuːprəbl] *adj* insormontabile, insuperabile.

insurance [ɪn'ʃuərəns] *n* assicurazione *f*; **fire/life** ~ assicurazione contro gli incendi/sulla vita; **to take out** ~ **(against)** fare un'assicurazione (contro), assicurarsi (contro).

insurance agent *n* agente *m* d'assicurazioni.

insurance broker *n* broker *m inv* d'assicurazioni.

insurance policy *n* polizza d'assicurazione.

insurance premium *n* premio assicurativo.

insure [ɪn'ʃuə*] *vt* assicurare; **to** ~ **sb or sb's life** assicurare qn sulla vita; **to be** ~**d for £5000** essere assicurato per 5000 sterline.

insured [ɪn'ʃuəd] *n*: **the** ~ l'assicurato/a.

insurer [ɪn'ʃuərə*] *n* assicuratore/trice.

insurgent [ɪn'sɔːdʒənt] *adj* ribelle ♦ *n* insorto/a, rivoltoso/a.

insurmountable [ɪnsə'mauntəbl] *adj* insormontabile.

insurrection [ɪnsə'rɛkʃən] *n* insurrezione *f.*

intact [ɪn'tækt] *adj* intatto(a).

intake ['ɪnteɪk] *n* (*TECH*) immissione *f*; (*of food*) consumo; (*of pupils etc*) afflusso.

intangible [ɪn'tændʒɪbl] *adj* intangibile.

integral ['ɪntɪgrəl] *adj* integrale; (*part*) integrante.

integrate ['ɪntɪgreɪt] *vt* integrare.

integrated circuit *n* (*COMPUT*) circuito integrato.

integration [ɪntɪ'greɪʃən] *n* integrazione *f*; **racial** ~ integrazione razziale.

integrity [ɪn'tɛgrɪtɪ] *n* integrità.

intellect ['ɪntəlɛkt] *n* intelletto.

intellectual [ɪntə'lɛktjuəl] *adj, n* intellettuale (*m/f*).

intelligence [ɪn'tɛlɪdʒəns] *n* intelligenza; (*MIL etc*) informazioni *fpl.*

intelligence quotient (IQ) *n* quoziente *m* d'intelligenza (Q.I.).

Intelligence Service *n* servizio segreto.

intelligence test *n* test *m inv* d'intelligenza.

intelligent [ɪn'tɛlɪdʒənt] *adj* intelligente.

intelligible [ɪn'tɛlɪdʒɪbl] *adj* intelligibile.

intemperate [ɪn'tɛmpərət] *adj* immoderato(a); (*drinking too much*) intemperante nel bere.

intend [ɪn'tɛnd] *vt* (*gift etc*): **to** ~ **sth for** destinare qc a; **to** ~ **to do** aver l'intenzione di fare.

intended [ɪn'tɛndɪd] *adj* (*insult*) intenzionale; (*effect*) voluto(a); (*journey, route*) progettato(a).

intense [ɪn'tɛns] *adj* intenso(a); (*person*) di forti sentimenti.

intensely [ɪn'tɛnslɪ] *adv* intensamente; profondamente.

intensify [ɪn'tɛnsɪfaɪ] *vt* intensificare.

intensity [ɪn'tɛnsɪtɪ] *n* intensità.

intensive [ɪn'tɛnsɪv] *adj* intensivo(a).

intensive care *n* terapia intensiva; ~ **unit (ICU)** *n* reparto terapia intensiva.

intent [ɪn'tɛnt] *n* intenzione *f* ♦ *adj*: ~ **(on)** intento(a) (a), immerso(a) (in); **to all** ~**s and purposes** a tutti gli effetti; **to be** ~ **on doing sth** essere deciso a fare qc.

intention [ɪn'tɛnʃən] *n* intenzione *f.*

intentional [ɪn'tɛnʃənl] *adj* intenzionale, deliberato(a).

intentionally [ɪn'tɛnʃənəlɪ] *adv* apposta.

intently [ɪn'tɛntlɪ] *adv* attentamente.

inter [ɪn'tɜː*] *vt* sotterrare.

interact [ɪntər'ækt] *vi* agire reciprocamente, interagire.

interaction [ɪntər'ækʃən] *n* azione *f* reciproca, interazione *f.*

interactive [ɪntər'æktɪv] *adj* interattivo(a).

intercede [ɪntə'siːd] *vi*: **to** ~ **(with sb/on behalf of sb)** intercedere (presso qn/a favore di qn).

intercept [ɪntə'sɛpt] *vt* intercettare; (*person*) fermare.

interception [ɪntə'sɛpʃən] *n* intercettamento.

interchange *n* ['ɪntətʃeɪndʒ] (*exchange*) scambio; (*on motorway*) incrocio pluridirezionale ♦ *vt* [ɪntə'tʃeɪndʒ] scambiare; sostituire l'uno(a) per l'altro(a).

interchangeable [ɪntə'tʃeɪndʒəbl] *adj* intercambiabile.

intercity [ɪntə'sɪtɪ] *adj*: ~ **(train)** ≈ (treno) rapido.
intercom ['ɪntəkɔm] *n* interfono.
interconnect [ɪntəkə'nɛkt] *vi* (*rooms*) essere in comunicazione.
intercontinental ['ɪntəkɔntɪ'nɛntl] *adj* intercontinentale.
intercourse ['ɪntəkɔːs] *n* rapporti *mpl*; (*sexual* ~) rapporti sessuali.
interdependent [ɪntədɪ'pendənt] *adj* interdipendente.
interest ['ɪntrɪst] *n* interesse *m*; (*COMM*: *stake, share*) interessi *mpl* ♦ *vt* interessare; **compound/simple** ~ interesse composto/semplice; **business** ~s attività *fpl* commerciali; **British** ~s **in the Middle East** gli interessi (commerciali) britannici nel Medio Oriente.
interested ['ɪntrɪstɪd] *adj* interessato(a); **to be** ~ **in** interessarsi di.
interest-free ['ɪntrɪst'friː] *adj* senza interesse.
interesting ['ɪntrɪstɪŋ] *adj* interessante.
interest rate *n* tasso di interesse.
interface ['ɪntəfeɪs] *n* (*COMPUT*) interfaccia.
interfere [ɪntə'fɪə*] *vi*: **to** ~ **(in)** (*quarrel, other people's business*) immischiarsi (in); **to** ~ **with** (*object*) toccare; (*plans*) ostacolare; (*duty*) interferire con.
interference [ɪntə'fɪərəns] *n* interferenza.
interfering [ɪntə'fɪərɪŋ] *adj* invadente.
interim ['ɪntərɪm] *adj* provvisorio(a) ♦ *n*: **in the** ~ nel frattempo; ~ **dividend** (*COMM*) acconto di dividendo.
interior [ɪn'tɪərɪə*] *n* interno; (*of country*) entroterra ♦ *adj* interiore, interno(a).
interior decorator, interior designer *n* decoratore/trice (d'interni).
interjection [ɪntə'dʒɛkʃən] *n* interiezione *f*.
interlock [ɪntə'lɔk] *vi* ingranarsi ♦ *vt* ingranare.
interloper ['ɪntələupə*] *n* intruso/a.
interlude ['ɪntəluːd] *n* intervallo; (*THEAT*) intermezzo.
intermarry [ɪntə'mærɪ] *vi* imparentarsi per mezzo di matrimonio; sposarsi tra parenti.
intermediary [ɪntə'miːdɪərɪ] *n* intermediario/a.
intermediate [ɪntə'miːdɪət] *adj* intermedio(a); (*SCOL*: *course, level*) medio(a).
interment [ɪn'təːmənt] *n* (*formal*) inumazione *f*.
interminable [ɪn'təːmɪnəbl] *adj* interminabile.
intermission [ɪntə'mɪʃən] *n* pausa; (*THEAT, CINE*) intermissione *f*, intervallo.

intermittent [ɪntə'mɪtnt] *adj* intermittente.
intermittently [ɪntə'mɪtntlɪ] *adv* a intermittenza.
intern *vt* [ɪn'təːn] internare ♦ *n* ['ɪntəːn] (*US*) medico interno.
internal [ɪn'təːnl] *adj* interno(a); ~ **injuries** lesioni *fpl* interne.
internally [ɪn'təːnəlɪ] *adv* all'interno; "**not to be taken** ~" "per uso esterno".
Internal Revenue (Service) (IRS) *n* (*US*) Fisco.
international [ɪntə'næʃənl] *adj* internazionale ♦ *n* (*BRIT SPORT*) partita internazionale.
International Atomic Energy Agency (IAEA) *n* Agenzia Internazionale per l'Energia Atomica (IAEA).
International Court of Justice (ICJ) *n* Corte *f* Internazionale di Giustizia.
international date line *n* linea del cambiamento di data.
internationally [ɪntə'næʃnəlɪ] *adv* a livello internazionale.
International Monetary Fund (IMF) *n* Fondo monetario internazionale (F.M.I.).
international relations *npl* rapporti *mpl* internazionali.
internecine [ɪntə'niːsaɪn] *adj* sanguinoso(a).
internee [ɪntəː'niː] *n* internato/a.
Internet ['ɪntə,nɛt] *n*: **the** ~ Internet *f*.
internment [ɪn'təːnmənt] *n* internamento.
interplay ['ɪntəpleɪ] *n* azione e reazione *f*.
Interpol ['ɪntəpɔl] *n* Interpol *f*.
interpret [ɪn'təːprɪt] *vt* interpretare ♦ *vi* fare da interprete.
interpretation [ɪntəːprɪ'teɪʃən] *n* interpretazione *f*.
interpreter [ɪn'təːprɪtə*] *n* interprete *m/f*.
interpreting [ɪn'təːprɪtɪŋ] *n* (*profession*) interpretariato.
interrelated [ɪntərɪ'leɪtɪd] *adj* correlato(a).
interrogate [ɪn'tɛrəugeɪt] *vt* interrogare.
interrogation [ɪntɛrəu'geɪʃən] *n* interrogazione *f*; (*of suspect etc*) interrogatorio.
interrogative [ɪntə'rɔgətɪv] *adj* interrogativo(a) ♦ *n* (*LING*) interrogativo.
interrogator [ɪn'tɛrəgeɪtə*] *n* interrogante *m/f*.
interrupt [ɪntə'rʌpt] *vt* interrompere.
interruption [ɪntə'rʌpʃən] *n* interruzione *f*.
intersect [ɪntə'sɛkt] *vt* intersecare ♦ *vi* (*roads*) intersecarsi.
intersection [ɪntə'sɛkʃən] *n* intersezione *f*; (*of roads*) incrocio.
intersperse [ɪntə'spəːs] *vt*: **to** ~ **with** costellare di.
intertwine [ɪntə'twaɪn] *vt* intrecciare ♦ *vi* intrecciarsi.

interval ['ɪntəvl] n intervallo; (BRIT SCOL) ricreazione f, intervallo; **bright ~s** (in weather) schiarite fpl; **at ~s** a intervalli.

intervene [ɪntə'viːn] vi (time) intercorrere; (event, person) intervenire.

intervention [ɪntə'vɛnʃən] n intervento.

interview ['ɪntəvjuː] n (RADIO, TV etc) intervista; (for job) colloquio ♦ vt intervistare; avere un colloquio con.

interviewee [ɪntəvju'iː] n (TV) intervistato/a; (for job) chi si presenta ad un colloquio di lavoro.

interviewer ['ɪntəvjuːə*] n intervistatore/trice.

intestate [ɪn'tɛsteɪt] adj intestato(a).

intestinal [ɪn'tɛstɪnl] adj intestinale.

intestine [ɪn'tɛstɪn] n intestino; **large/small** ~ intestino crasso/tenue.

intimacy ['ɪntɪməsɪ] n intimità.

intimate adj ['ɪntɪmət] intimo(a); (knowledge) profondo(a) ♦ vt ['ɪntɪmeɪt] lasciar capire.

intimately ['ɪntɪmɪtlɪ] adv intimamente.

intimation [ɪntɪ'meɪʃən] n annuncio.

intimidate [ɪn'tɪmɪdeɪt] vt intimidire, intimorire.

intimidation [ɪntɪmɪ'deɪʃən] n intimidazione f.

into ['ɪntu] prep dentro, in; **come ~ the house** vieni dentro la casa; **~ pieces** a pezzi; **~ Italian** in italiano; **to change pounds ~ dollars** cambiare delle sterline in dollari.

intolerable [ɪn'tɔlərəbl] adj intollerabile.

intolerance [ɪn'tɔlərns] n intolleranza.

intolerant [ɪn'tɔlərnt] adj: **~ (of)** intollerante (di).

intonation [ɪntəu'neɪʃən] n intonazione f.

intoxicate [ɪn'tɔksɪkeɪt] vt inebriare.

intoxicated [ɪn'tɔksɪkeɪtɪd] adj inebriato(a).

intoxication [ɪntɔksɪ'keɪʃən] n ebbrezza.

intractable [ɪn'træktəbl] adj intrattabile; (illness) difficile da curare; (problem) insolubile.

intranet ['ɪntrənɛt] n Intranet f.

intransigence [ɪn'trænsɪdʒəns] n intransigenza.

intransigent [ɪn'trænsɪdʒənt] adj intransigente.

intransitive [ɪn'trænsɪtɪv] adj intransitivo(a).

intra-uterine device (IUD) [ɪntrə'-juːtəraɪn-] n dispositivo intrauterino (IUD).

intravenous [ɪntrə'viːnəs] adj endovenoso(a).

in-tray ['ɪntreɪ] n raccoglitore m per le carte in arrivo.

intrepid [ɪn'trɛpɪd] adj intrepido(a).

intricacy ['ɪntrɪkəsɪ] n complessità f inv.

intricate ['ɪntrɪkət] adj intricato(a), complicato(a).

intrigue [ɪn'triːg] n intrigo ♦ vt affascinare ♦ vi complottare, tramare.

intriguing [ɪn'triːgɪŋ] adj affascinante.

intrinsic [ɪn'trɪnsɪk] adj intrinseco(a).

introduce [ɪntrə'djuːs] vt introdurre; **to ~ sb (to sb)** presentare qn (a qn); **to ~ sb to** (pastime, technique) iniziare qn a; **may I ~ ...?** permette che le presenti ...?

introduction [ɪntrə'dʌkʃən] n introduzione f; (of person) presentazione f; **a letter of ~** una lettera di presentazione.

introductory [ɪntrə'dʌktərɪ] adj introduttivo(a); **an ~ offer** un'offerta di lancio; **~ remarks** osservazioni fpl preliminari.

introspection [ɪntrəu'spɛkʃən] n introspezione f.

introspective [ɪntrəu'spɛktɪv] adj introspettivo(a).

introvert ['ɪntrəuvəːt] adj, n introverso(a).

intrude [ɪn'truːd] vi (person) intromettersi; **to ~ on** (person) importunare; **~ on** or **into** (conversation) intromettersi in; **am I intruding?** disturbo?

intruder [ɪn'truːdə*] n intruso/a.

intrusion [ɪn'truːʒən] n intrusione f.

intrusive [ɪn'truːsɪv] adj importuno(a).

intuition [ɪntju:'ɪʃən] n intuizione f.

intuitive [ɪn'tjuːɪtɪv] adj intuitivo(a); dotato(a) di intuito.

inundate ['ɪnʌndeɪt] vt: **to ~ with** inondare di.

inure [ɪn'juə*] vt: **to ~ (to)** assuefare (a).

invade [ɪn'veɪd] vt invadere.

invader [ɪn'veɪdə*] n invasore m.

invalid n ['ɪnvəlɪd] malato/a; (with disability) invalido/a ♦ adj [ɪn'vælɪd] (not valid) invalido(a), non valido(a).

invalidate [ɪn'vælɪdeɪt] vt invalidare.

invalid chair n (BRIT) sedia a rotelle.

invaluable [ɪn'væljuəbl] adj prezioso(a); inestimabile.

invariable [ɪn'vɛərɪəbl] adj costante, invariabile.

invariably [ɪn'vɛərɪəblɪ] adv invariabilmente; **she is ~ late** è immancabilmente in ritardo.

invasion [ɪn'veɪʒən] n invasione f.

invective [ɪn'vɛktɪv] n invettiva.

inveigle [ɪn'viːgl] vt: **to ~ sb into (doing) sth** circuire qn per (fargli fare) qc.

invent [ɪn'vɛnt] vt inventare.

invention [ɪn'vɛnʃən] n invenzione f.

inventive [ɪn'vɛntɪv] adj inventivo(a).

inventiveness [ɪn'vɛntɪvnɪs] n inventiva.

inventor [ɪn'vɛntə*] n inventore m.
inventory ['ɪnvəntrɪ] n inventario.
inventory control n (COMM) controllo delle giacenze.
inverse [ɪn'vɜːs] adj inverso(a) ♦ n inverso, contrario; **in ~ proportion (to)** in modo inversamente proporzionale (a).
inversely [ɪn'vɜːslɪ] adv inversamente.
invert [ɪn'vɜːt] vt invertire; (object) rovesciare.
invertebrate [ɪn'vɜːtɪbrɪt] n invertebrato.
inverted commas [ɪn'vɜːtɪd-] npl (BRIT) virgolette fpl.
invest [ɪn'vɛst] vt investire; (fig: time, effort) impiegare; (endow): **to ~ sb with sth** investire qn di qc ♦ vi fare investimenti; **to ~ in** investire in, fare (degli) investimenti in; (acquire) comprarsi.
investigate [ɪn'vɛstɪɡeɪt] vt investigare, indagare; (crime) fare indagini su.
investigation [ɪnvɛstɪ'ɡeɪʃən] n investigazione f; (of crime) indagine f.
investigative [ɪn'vɛstɪɡətɪv] adj: **~ journalism** giornalismo investigativo.
investigator [ɪn'vɛstɪɡeɪtə*] n investigatore/trice; **a private ~** un investigatore privato, un detective.
investiture [ɪn'vɛstɪtʃə*] n investitura.
investment [ɪn'vɛstmənt] n investimento.
investment income n reddito da investimenti.
investment trust n fondo comune di investimento.
investor [ɪn'vɛstə*] n investitore/trice; (shareholder) azionista m/f.
inveterate [ɪn'vɛtərət] adj inveterato(a).
invidious [ɪn'vɪdɪəs] adj odioso(a); (task) spiacevole.
invigilate [ɪn'vɪdʒɪleɪt] vt, vi (BRIT SCOL) sorvegliare.
invigilator [ɪn'vɪdʒɪleɪtə*] n (BRIT) chi sorveglia agli esami.
invigorating [ɪn'vɪɡəreɪtɪŋ] adj stimolante; vivificante.
invincible [ɪn'vɪnsɪbl] adj invincibile.
inviolate [ɪn'vaɪələt] adj inviolato(a).
invisible [ɪn'vɪzɪbl] adj invisibile.
invisible assets npl (BRIT) beni mpl immateriali.
invisible ink n inchiostro simpatico.
invisible mending n rammendo invisibile.
invitation [ɪnvɪ'teɪʃən] n invito; **by ~ only** esclusivamente su or per invito; **at sb's ~** dietro invito di qn.
invite [ɪn'vaɪt] vt invitare; (opinions etc) sollecitare; (trouble) provocare; **to ~ sb (to do)** invitare qn (a fare); **to ~ sb to**

dinner invitare qn a cena.
► **invite out** vt invitare fuori.
► **invite over** vt invitare (a casa).
inviting [ɪn'vaɪtɪŋ] adj invitante, attraente.
invoice ['ɪnvɔɪs] n fattura ♦ vt fatturare; **to ~ sb for goods** inviare a qn la fattura per le or delle merci.
invoke [ɪn'vəuk] vt invocare.
involuntary [ɪn'vɔləntrɪ] adj involontario(a).
involve [ɪn'vɔlv] vt (entail) richiedere, comportare; (associate): **to ~ sb (in)** implicare qn (in); coinvolgere qn (in); **to involve o.s. in sth** (politics etc) impegnarsi in qc.
involved [ɪn'vɔlvd] adj involuto(a), complesso(a); **to feel ~** sentirsi coinvolto(a); **to become ~ with sb** (socially) legarsi a qn; (emotionally) legarsi sentimentalmente a qn.
involvement [ɪn'vɔlvmənt] n implicazione f; coinvolgimento; impegno; partecipazione f.
invulnerable [ɪn'vʌlnərəbl] adj invulnerabile.
inward ['ɪnwəd] adj (movement) verso l'interno; (thought, feeling) interiore, intimo(a); see also **inward(s)**.
inwardly ['ɪnwədlɪ] adv (feel, think etc) nell'intimo, entro di sé.
inward(s) ['ɪnwəd(z)] adv verso l'interno.
I/O abbr (COMPUT: = input/output) I/O.
IOC n abbr (= International Olympic Committee) CIO m (= Comitato Internazionale Olimpico).
iodine ['aɪəudiːn] n iodio.
IOM abbr (BRIT) = Isle of Man.
ion ['aɪən] n ione m.
Ionian Sea [aɪ'əunɪən-] n: **the ~** il mare Ionio.
ioniser ['aɪənaɪzə*] n ionizzatore m.
iota [aɪ'əutə] n (fig) briciolo.
IOU n abbr (= I owe you) pagherò m inv.
IOW abbr (BRIT) = Isle of Wight.
IPA n abbr (= International Phonetic Alphabet) I.P.A. m.
IP address n (COMPUT) indirizzo IP.
IQ n abbr = **intelligence quotient.**
IRA n abbr (= Irish Republican Army) I.R.A. f; (US) = individual retirement account.
Iran [ɪ'rɑːn] n Iran m.
Iranian [ɪ'reɪnɪən] adj iraniano(a) ♦ n iraniano/a; (LING) iranico.
Iraq [ɪ'rɑːk] n Iraq m.
Iraqi [ɪ'rɑːkɪ] adj iracheno(a) ♦ n iracheno/a.
irascible [ɪ'ræsɪbl] adj irascibile.
irate [aɪ'reɪt] adj irato(a).

Ireland['aɪələnd] n Irlanda; **Republic of** ~ Repubblica d'Irlanda, Eire f.

iris, ~ **es**['aɪrɪs, -ɪz] n iride f; (BOT) giaggiolo, iride.

Irish['aɪrɪʃ] adj irlandese ♦ npl: **the** ~ **gli** Irlandesi.

Irishman['aɪrɪʃmən] n irlandese m.

Irish Sean: **the** ~ il mar d'Irlanda.

Irishwoman['aɪrɪʃwumən] n irlandese f.

irk[ə:k] vt seccare.

irksome['ə:ksəm] adj seccante.

IRNn abbr (= Independent Radio News) agenzia d'informazioni per la radio.

IROn abbr (= International Refugee Organization) O.I.R. f (= Organizzazione Internazionale per i Rifugiati).

iron['aɪən] n ferro; (for clothes) ferro da stiro ♦ adj di or in ferro ♦ vt (clothes) stirare; see also **irons**.

▶**iron out**vt (crease) appianare; (fig) spianare; far sparire.

Iron Curtainn (HIST): **the** ~ la cortina di ferro.

iron foundryn fonderia.

ironic(al)[aɪ'rɔnɪk(l)] adj ironico(a).

ironically[aɪ'rɔnɪklɪ] adv ironicamente.

ironing['aɪənɪŋ] n (act) stirare m; (clothes) roba da stirare.

ironing boardn asse f da stiro.

iron lungn (MED) polmone m d'acciaio.

ironmonger['aɪənmʌŋgə*] n (BRIT) negoziante m in ferramenta; ~ **'s (shop)** n negozio di ferramenta.

iron oren minerale m di ferro.

irons['aɪənz] npl (chains) catene fpl.

ironworks['aɪənwə:ks] n ferriera.

irony['aɪrənɪ] n ironia.

irrational[ɪ'ræʃənl] adj irrazionale; irragionevole; illogico(a).

irreconcilable[ɪrɛkən'saɪləbl] adj irreconciliabile; (opinion): ~ **with** inconciliabile con.

irredeemable[ɪrɪ'di:məbl] adj (COMM) irredimibile.

irrefutable[ɪrɪ'fju:təbl] adj irrefutabile.

irregular[ɪ'rɛgjulə*] adj irregolare.

irregularity[ɪrɛgju'lærɪtɪ] n irregolarità f inv.

irrelevance[ɪ'rɛləvəns] n inappropriatezza.

irrelevant[ɪ'rɛləvənt] adj non pertinente.

irreligious[ɪrɪ'lɪdʒəs] adj irreligioso(a).

irreparable[ɪ'rɛprəbl] adj irreparabile.

irreplaceable[ɪrɪ'pleɪsəbl] adj insostituibile.

irrepressible[ɪrɪ'prɛsəbl] adj irrefrenabile.

irreproachable[ɪrɪ'prəutʃəbl] adj irreprensibile.

irresistible[ɪrɪ'zɪstɪbl] adj irresistibile.

irresolute[ɪ'rɛzəlu:t] adj irresoluto(a), indeciso(a).

irrespective[ɪrɪ'spɛktɪv]: ~ **of** prep senza riguardo a.

irresponsible[ɪrɪ'spɔnsɪbl] adj irresponsabile.

irretrievable[ɪrɪ'tri:vəbl] adj (object) irrecuperabile; (loss) irreparabile.

irreverent[ɪ'rɛvərnt] adj irriverente.

irrevocable[ɪ'rɛvəkəbl] adj irrevocabile.

irrigate['ɪrɪgeɪt] vt irrigare.

irrigation[ɪrɪ'geɪʃən] n irrigazione f.

irritable['ɪrɪtəbl] adj irritabile.

irritant['ɪrɪtənt] n sostanza irritante.

irritate['ɪrɪteɪt] vt irritare.

irritation[ɪrɪ'teɪʃən] n irritazione f.

IRSn abbr (US) see **Internal Revenue Service**.

is[ɪz] vb see **be**.

ISA['aɪsə] n abbr (= individual savings account) forma di investimento detassata.

ISBNn abbr (= International Standard Book Number) I.S.B.N. m.

Islam['ɪzlɑ:m] n Islam m.

island['aɪlənd] n isola; (also: **traffic** ~) salvagente m.

islander['aɪləndə*] n isolano/a.

isle[aɪl] n isola.

isn't['ɪznt] = **is not**.

isolate['aɪsəleɪt] vt isolare.

isolated['aɪsəleɪtɪd] adj isolato(a).

isolation[aɪsə'leɪʃən] n isolamento.

isotope['aɪsəutəup] n isotopo.

ISPn abbr (COMPUT: = Internet service provider) ISP m inv.

Israel['ɪzreɪl] n Israele m.

Israeli[ɪz'reɪlɪ] adj, n israeliano(a).

issue['ɪʃju:] n questione f, problema m; (outcome) esito, risultato; (of banknotes etc) emissione f; (of newspaper etc) numero; (offspring) discendenza ♦ vt (rations, equipment) distribuire; (orders) dare; (book) pubblicare; (banknotes, cheques, stamps) emettere ♦ vi: **to** ~ **(from)** uscire (da), venir fuori (da); **at** ~ in gioco, in discussione; **to avoid the** ~ evitare la discussione; **to take** ~ **with sb (over sth)** prendere posizione contro qn (riguardo a qc); **to confuse** or **obscure the** ~ confondere le cose; **to make an** ~ **of sth** fare un problema di qc; **to** ~ **sth to sb, ~ sb with sth** consegnare qc a qn.

Istanbul[ɪstæn'bu:l] n Istanbul f.

isthmus['ɪsməs] n istmo.

ITn abbr see **information technology**.

================================ KEYWORD

it [ɪt] *pron* **1** (*specific: subject*) esso(a) (*mostly omitted in Italian*); (: *direct object*) lo(la), l'; (: *indirect object*) gli(le); **where's my book?** — ~'s **on the table** dov'è il mio libro? — è sulla tavola; **what is** ~? che cos'è?; (*what's the matter?*) cosa c'è?; **where is** ~? dov'è?; **I can't find** ~ non lo (*or* la) trovo; **give** ~ **to me** dammelo (*or* dammela); **about/from/of** ~ ne; **I spoke to him about** ~ gliene ho parlato; **what did you learn from** ~? quale insegnamento ne hai tratto?; **I'm proud of** ~ ne sono fiero; **in/ to/at** ~ ci; **did you go to** ~? ci sei andato?; **I wasn't at** ~ non c'ero; **above/ over** ~ sopra; **below/under** ~ sotto; **in front of/behind** ~ lì davanti/dietro **2** (*impers*): ~'s **raining** piove; ~'s **Friday tomorrow** domani è venerdì; ~'s **6 o'clock** sono le 6; ~'s **2 hours on the train** sono *or* ci vogliono 2 ore di treno; **who is** ~? — ~'s **me** chi è? — sono io.

Italian [ɪ'tæljən] *adj* italiano(a) ♦ *n* italiano/a; (*LING*) italiano; **the** ~**s** gli Italiani.

italic [ɪ'tælɪk] *adj* corsivo(a); ~**s** *npl* corsivo.

Italy ['ɪtəlɪ] *n* Italia.

ITC *n abbr* (*BRIT:* =*Independent Television Commission*) organo di controllo sulle reti televisive.

itch [ɪtʃ] *n* prurito ♦ *vi* (*person*) avere il prurito; (*part of body*) prudere; **to be** ~**ing to do** non veder l'ora di fare.

itchy ['ɪtʃɪ] *adj* che prude; **my back is** ~ ho prurito alla schiena.

it'd ['ɪtd] = **it would; it had**.

item ['aɪtəm] *n* articolo; (*on agenda*) punto; (*in programme*) numero; (*also:* **news** ~) notizia; ~**s of clothing** capi *mpl* di abbigliamento.

itemize ['aɪtəmaɪz] *vt* specificare.

itemized bill ['aɪtəmaɪzd-] *n* conto dettagliato.

itinerant [ɪ'tɪnərənt] *adj* ambulante.

itinerary [aɪ'tɪnərərɪ] *n* itinerario.

it'll ['ɪtl] = **it will, it shall**.

ITN *n abbr* (*BRIT:* = *Independent Television News*) agenzia d'informazioni per la televisione.

its [ɪts] *adj, pron* il(la) suo(a), i(le) suoi(sue).

it's [ɪts] = **it is; it has**.

itself [ɪt'sɛlf] *pron* (*emphatic*) esso(a) stesso(a); (*reflexive*) si.

ITV *n abbr* (*BRIT:* = *Independent Television*) rete televisiva indipendente; *see boxed note*.

ITV

La **ITV** *è un'azienda televisiva privata che comprende una serie di emittenti regionali, la prima delle quali è stata aperta nel 1955. Si autofinanzia tramite la pubblicità ed è sottoposta al controllo di un ente ufficiale, la* "*ITC*"; *vedi anche* **BBC**.

IUD *n abbr* = **intra-uterine device**.

I've [aɪv] = **I have**.

ivory ['aɪvərɪ] *n* avorio.

Ivory Coast *n* Costa d'Avorio.

ivory tower *n* torre *f* d'avorio.

ivy ['aɪvɪ] *n* edera.

Ivy League *n* (*US*) *see boxed note*.

IVY LEAGUE

Ivy League *è il termine usato per indicare le otto università più prestigiose degli Stati Uniti nordorientali (Brown, Columbia, Cornell, Dartmouth College, Harvard, Princeton, University of Pennsylvania e Yale).*

================================ *Jj*

J, j [dʒeɪ] *n* (*letter*) J, j *f or m inv*; **J for Jack,** (*US*) **J for Jig** ≈ J come Jersey.

JA *n abbr see* **judge advocate**.

J/A *abbr see* **joint account**.

jab [dʒæb] *vt*: **to** ~ **sth into** affondare *or* piantare qc dentro ♦ *vi*: **to** ~ **at** dare colpi a ♦ *n* colpo; (*MED: col*) puntura.

jabber ['dʒæbə*] *vt, vi* borbottare.

jack [dʒæk] *n* (*AUT*) cricco; (*BOWLS*) boccino, pallino; (*CARDS*) fante *m*.

▶**jack in** *vt* (*col*) mollare.

▶**jack up** *vt* sollevare sul cricco; (*raise: prices etc*) alzare.

jackal ['dʒækl] *n* sciacallo.

jackass ['dʒækæs] *n* (*also fig*) asino, somaro.

jackdaw ['dʒækdɔː] *n* taccola.

jacket ['dʒækɪt] *n* giacca; (*of book*) copertura; **potatoes in their** ~**s** (*BRIT*) patate *fpl* con la buccia.

jacket potato *n patata cotta al forno con la buccia.*

jack-in-the-box ['dʒækɪnðəbɔks] n scatola a
sorpresa (con pupazzo a molla).
jack-knife ['dʒæknaɪf] vi: **the lorry** ~**d**
l'autotreno si è piegato su se stesso.
jack-of-all-trades [dʒækəv'ɔːltreɪdz] n uno
che fa un po' di tutto.
jack plug n (BRIT) jack plug f inv.
jackpot ['dʒækpɔt] n primo premio (in
denaro).
Jacuzzi ® [dʒə'kuːzɪ] n vasca per
idromassaggio Jacuzzi ®.
jade [dʒeɪd] n (stone) giada.
jaded ['dʒeɪdɪd] adj sfinito(a), spossato(a).
jagged ['dʒægɪd] adj sbocconcellato(a);
(cliffs etc) frastagliato(a).
jaguar ['dʒægjuə*] n giaguaro.
jail [dʒeɪl] n prigione f ♦ vt mandare in
prigione.
jailbird ['dʒeɪlbəːd] n avanzo di galera.
jailbreak ['dʒeɪlbreɪk] n evasione f.
jailer ['dʒeɪlə*] n custode m del carcere.
jalopy [dʒə'lɔpɪ] n (col) macinino.
jam [dʒæm] n marmellata; (of shoppers etc)
ressa; (also: **traffic** ~) ingorgo ♦ vt
(passage etc) ingombrare, ostacolare;
(mechanism, drawer etc) bloccare; (RADIO)
disturbare con interferenze ♦ vi
(mechanism, sliding part) incepparsi,
bloccarsi; (gun) incepparsi; **to get sb out
of a** ~ tirare qn fuori dai pasticci; **to** ~
sth into forzare qc dentro; infilare qc a
forza dentro; **the telephone lines are**
~**med** le linee sono sovraccariche.
Jamaica [dʒə'meɪkə] n Giamaica.
Jamaican [dʒə'meɪkən] adj, n
giamaicano(a).
jamb [dʒæm] n stipite m.
jam-packed [dʒæm'pækt] adj: ~ (**with**)
pieno(a) zeppo(a) (di), strapieno(a)
(di).
jam session n improvvisazione f
jazzistica.
Jan. abbr (= January) gen., genn.
jangle ['dʒæŋgl] vi risuonare; (bracelet)
tintinnare.
janitor ['dʒænɪtə*] n (caretaker) portiere m;
(SCOL) bidello.
January ['dʒænjuərɪ] n gennaio; for phrases
see also **July**.
Japan [dʒə'pæn] n Giappone m.
Japanese [dʒæpə'niːz] adj giapponese ♦ n (pl
inv) giapponese m/f; (LING) giapponese m.
jar [dʒɑː*] n (container) barattolo, vasetto
♦ vi (sound) stridere; (colours etc)
stonare ♦ vt (shake) scuotere.
jargon ['dʒɑːgən] n gergo.
jarring ['dʒɑːrɪŋ] adj (sound, colour)
stonato(a).

Jas. abbr = James.
jasmin(e) ['dʒæzmɪn] n gelsomino.
jaundice ['dʒɔːndɪs] n itterizia.
jaundiced ['dʒɔːndɪst] adj (fig) invidioso(a)
e critico(a).
jaunt [dʒɔːnt] n gita.
jaunty ['dʒɔːntɪ] adj vivace; disinvolto(a),
spigliato(a).
Java ['dʒɑːvə] n Giava.
javelin ['dʒævlɪn] n giavellotto.
jaw [dʒɔː] n mascella; ~**s** (TECH: of vice etc)
morsa.
jawbone ['dʒɔːbəun] n mandibola.
jay [dʒeɪ] n ghiandaia.
jaywalker ['dʒeɪwɔːkə*] n pedone(a)
indisciplinato(a).
jazz [dʒæz] n jazz m.
▶**jazz up** vt rendere vivace.
jazz band n banda f jazz inv.
jazzy ['dʒæzɪ] adj vistoso(a), chiassoso(a).
JCB ® n scavatrice f.
JCS n abbr (US) = Joint Chiefs of Staff.
JD n abbr (US: = Doctor of Laws) titolo di
studio; (: = Justice Department) ministero
della Giustizia.
jealous ['dʒeləs] adj geloso(a).
jealously ['dʒeləslɪ] adv (enviously) con
gelosia; (watchfully) gelosamente.
jealousy ['dʒeləsɪ] n gelosia.
jeans [dʒiːnz] npl (blue-)jeans mpl.
Jeep ® [dʒiːp] n jeep m inv.
jeer [dʒɪə*] vi: **to** ~ (**at**) fischiare;
beffeggiare; see also **jeers**.
jeering ['dʒɪərɪŋ] adj (crowd) che urla e
fischia ♦ n fischi mpl; parole fpl di scherno.
jeers ['dʒɪəz] npl fischi mpl.
jelly ['dʒelɪ] n gelatina.
jellyfish ['dʒelɪfɪʃ] n medusa.
jeopardize ['dʒepədaɪz] vt mettere in
pericolo.
jeopardy ['dʒepədɪ] n: **in** ~ in pericolo.
jerk [dʒəːk] n sobbalzo, scossa; sussulto;
(col) povero scemo ♦ vt dare una scossa a
♦ vi (vehicles) sobbalzare.
jerkin ['dʒəːkɪn] n giubbotto.
jerky ['dʒəːkɪ] adj a scatti; a sobbalzi.
jerry-built ['dʒerɪbɪlt] adj fatto(a) di
cartapesta.
jerry can ['dʒerɪ-] n tanica.
Jersey ['dʒəːzɪ] n Jersey m.
jersey ['dʒəːzɪ] n maglia, jersey m.
Jerusalem [dʒə'ruːsələm] n Gerusalemme f.
jest [dʒest] n scherzo; **in** ~ per scherzo.
jester ['dʒestə*] n (HISTORY) buffone m.
Jesus ['dʒiːzəs] n Gesù m; ~ **Christ** Gesù
Cristo.
jet [dʒet] n (of gas, liquid) getto; (AUT)
spruzzatore m; (AVIAT) aviogetto.

jet-black ['dʒɛt'blæk] adj nero(a) come l'ebano, corvino(a).

jet engine n motore m a reazione.

jet lag n (problemi mpl dovuti allo) sbalzo dei fusi orari.

jetsam ['dʒɛtsəm] n relitti mpl di mare.

jet-setter ['dʒɛtsɛtə*] n membro del jet set.

jettison ['dʒɛtɪsn] vt gettare in mare.

jetty ['dʒɛtɪ] n molo.

Jew [dʒuː] n ebreo.

jewel ['dʒuːəl] n gioiello.

jeweller, (US) jeweler ['dʒuːələ*] n orefice m, gioielliere/a; ~'s (shop) n oreficeria, gioielleria.

jewellery, (US) jewelry ['dʒuːəlrɪ] n gioielli mpl.

Jewess ['dʒuːɪs] n ebrea.

Jewish ['dʒuːɪʃ] adj ebreo(a), ebraico(a).

JFK n abbr (US) = John Fitzgerald Kennedy International Airport.

jib [dʒɪb] n (NAUT) fiocco; (of crane) braccio ♦ vi (horse) impennarsi; to ~ at doing sth essere restio a fare qc.

jibe [dʒaɪb] n beffa.

jiffy ['dʒɪfɪ] n (col): in a ~ in un batter d'occhio.

jig [dʒɪg] n (dance, tune) giga.

jigsaw ['dʒɪgsɔː] n (tool) sega da traforo; (also: ~ puzzle) puzzle m inv.

jilt [dʒɪlt] vt piantare in asso.

jingle ['dʒɪŋgl] n (advert) sigla pubblicitaria ♦ vi tintinnare, scampanellare.

jingoism ['dʒɪŋgəʊɪzəm] n sciovinismo.

jinx [dʒɪŋks] n (col) iettatura; (person) iettatore/trice.

jitters ['dʒɪtəz] npl (col): to get the ~ aver fifa.

jittery ['dʒɪtərɪ] adj (col) teso(a), agitato(a); to be ~ aver fifa.

jiujitsu [dʒuː'dʒɪtsuː] n jujitsu m.

job [dʒɔb] n lavoro; (employment) impiego, posto; a part-time/full-time ~ un lavoro a mezza giornata/a tempo pieno; that's not my ~ non è compito mio; he's only doing his ~ non fa che il suo dovere; it's a good ~ that ... meno male che ...; just the ~! proprio quello che ci vuole!

jobber ['dʒɔbə*] n (BRIT STOCK EXCHANGE) intermediario tra agenti di cambio.

jobbing ['dʒɔbɪŋ] adj (BRIT: workman) a ore, a giornata.

Jobcentre ['dʒɔbsɛntə*] n ufficio di collocamento.

job creation scheme n progetto per la creazione di nuovi posti di lavoro.

job description n caratteristiche fpl (di un lavoro).

jobless ['dʒɔblɪs] adj senza lavoro,

disoccupato(a) ♦ npl: the ~ i senza lavoro.

job lot n partita di articoli disparati.

job satisfaction n soddisfazione f nel lavoro.

job security n sicurezza del posto di lavoro.

job share vi fare un lavoro ripartito ♦ n lavoro ripartito.

job specification n caratteristiche fpl (di un lavoro).

jockey ['dʒɔkɪ] n fantino, jockey m inv ♦ vi: to ~ for position manovrare per una posizione di vantaggio.

jockey box n (US AUT) vano portaoggetti.

jockstrap ['dʒɔkstræp] n conchiglia (per atleti).

jocular ['dʒɔkjulə*] adj gioviale; scherzoso(a).

jog [dʒɔg] vt urtare ♦ vi (SPORT) fare footing, fare jogging; to ~ along trottare; (fig) andare avanti pian piano; to ~ sb's memory stimolare la memoria di qn.

jogger ['dʒɔgə*] n persona che fa footing or jogging.

jogging ['dʒɔgɪŋ] n footing m, jogging m.

john [dʒɔn] n (US col): the ~ il gabinetto.

join [dʒɔɪn] vt unire, congiungere; (become member of) iscriversi a; (meet) raggiungere; riunirsi a ♦ vi (roads, rivers) confluire ♦ n giuntura; to ~ forces (with) allearsi (con or a); (fig) mettersi insieme (a); will you ~ us for dinner? viene a cena con noi?; I'll ~ you later vi raggiungo più tardi.

►join in vt fus unirsi a, prendere parte a, partecipare a ♦ vi partecipare.

►join up vi arruolarsi.

joiner ['dʒɔɪnə*] n falegname m.

joinery ['dʒɔɪnərɪ] n falegnameria.

joint [dʒɔɪnt] n (TECH) giuntura; giunto; (ANAT) articolazione f, giuntura; (BRIT CULIN) arrosto; (col: place) locale m ♦ adj comune; (responsibility) collettivo(a); (committee) misto(a).

joint account (J/A) n (at bank etc) conto in comune.

jointly ['dʒɔɪntlɪ] adv in comune, insieme.

joint ownership n comproprietà.

joint-stock company ['dʒɔɪntstɔk-] n società f inv per azioni.

joist [dʒɔɪst] n trave f.

joke [dʒəʊk] n scherzo; (funny story) barzelletta ♦ vi scherzare; to play a ~ on fare uno scherzo a.

joker ['dʒəʊkə*] n buffone/a, burlone/a; (CARDS) matta, jolly m inv.

joking ['dʒəʊkɪŋ] n scherzi mpl.

jollity ['dʒɔlɪtɪ] n allegria.

jolly ['dʒɒlɪ] *adj* allegro(a), gioioso(a) ♦ *adv* (*BRIT col*) veramente, proprio ♦ *vt* (*BRIT*): **to ~ sb along** cercare di tenere qn su (di morale); **~ good!** (*BRIT*) benissimo!

jolt [dʒəʊlt] *n* scossa, sobbalzo ♦ *vt* urtare.

Jordan ['dʒɔːdən] *n* (*country*) Giordania; (*river*) Giordano.

Jordanian [dʒɔː'deɪnɪən] *adj, n* giordano(a).

joss stick ['dʒɒs-] *n* bastoncino d'incenso.

jostle ['dʒɒsl] *vt* spingere coi gomiti ♦ *vi* farsi spazio coi gomiti.

jot [dʒɒt] *n*: **not one ~** nemmeno un po'.
▶**jot down** *vt* annotare in fretta, buttare giù.

jotter ['dʒɒtə*] *n* (*BRIT*) quaderno; blocco.

journal ['dʒɔːnl] *n* (*newspaper*) giornale *m*; (*periodical*) rivista; (*diary*) diario.

journalese [dʒɔːnə'liːz] *n* (*pej*) stile *m* giornalistico.

journalism ['dʒɔːnəlɪzəm] *n* giornalismo.

journalist ['dʒɔːnəlɪst] *n* giornalista *m/f*.

journey ['dʒɔːnɪ] *n* viaggio; (*distance covered*) tragitto; **a 5-hour ~** un viaggio *or* un tragitto di 5 ore.

jovial ['dʒəʊvɪəl] *adj* gioviale, allegro(a).

jowl [dʒaʊl] *n* mandibola; guancia.

joy [dʒɔɪ] *n* gioia.

joyful ['dʒɔɪful], **joyous** ['dʒɔɪəs] *adj* gioioso(a), allegro(a).

joyride ['dʒɔɪraɪd] *n*: **to go for a ~** rubare una macchina per farsi un giro.

joyrider ['dʒɔɪraɪdə*] *n* chi ruba una macchina per andare a farsi un giro.

joystick ['dʒɔɪstɪk] *n* (*AVIAT*) barra di comando; (*COMPUT*) joystick *m inv*.

JP *n abbr see* **Justice of the Peace.**

Jr. *abbr* = **junior.**

jubilant ['dʒuːbɪlnt] *adj* giubilante; trionfante.

jubilation [dʒuːbɪ'leɪʃən] *n* giubilo.

jubilee ['dʒuːbɪliː] *n* giubileo; **silver ~** venticinquesimo anniversario.

judge [dʒʌdʒ] *n* giudice *m/f* ♦ *vt* giudicare; (*consider*) ritenere; (*estimate: weight, size etc*) calcolare, valutare ♦ *vi*: **judging or to ~ by his expression** a giudicare dalla sua espressione; **as far as I can ~** a mio giudizio; **I ~d it necessary to inform him** ho ritenuto necessario informarlo.

judge advocate (JA) *n* (*MIL*) magistrato militare.

judg(e)ment ['dʒʌdʒmənt] *n* giudizio; (*punishment*) punizione *f*; **in my ~** a mio giudizio; **to pass ~ (on)** (*LAW*) pronunciare un giudizio (su); (*fig*) dare giudizi affrettati (su).

judicial [dʒuː'dɪʃl] *adj* giudiziale, giudiziario(a).

judiciary [dʒuː'dɪʃɪərɪ] *n* magistratura.

judicious [dʒuː'dɪʃəs] *adj* giudizioso(a).

judo ['dʒuːdəʊ] *n* judo.

jug [dʒʌg] *n* brocca, bricco.

jugged hare [dʒʌgd-] *n* (*BRIT*) lepre *f* in salmì.

juggernaut ['dʒʌgənɔːt] *n* (*BRIT: huge truck*) bestione *m*.

juggle ['dʒʌgl] *vi* fare giochi di destrezza.

juggler ['dʒʌglə*] *n* giocoliere/a.

Jugoslav ['juːgəʊslɑːv] *adj, n* = **Yugoslav.**

jugular ['dʒʌgjulə*] *adj*: **~ (vein)** vena giugulare.

juice [dʒuːs] *n* succo; (*of meat*) sugo; **we've run out of ~** (*col: petrol*) siamo rimasti a secco.

juicy ['dʒuːsɪ] *adj* succoso(a).

jukebox ['dʒuːkbɔks] *n* juke-box *m inv*.

Jul. *abbr* (= *July*) lug., lu.

July [dʒuː'laɪ] *n* luglio; **the first of ~** il primo luglio; **(on) the eleventh of ~** l'undici luglio; **in the month of ~** nel mese di luglio; **at the beginning/end of ~** all'inizio/alla fine di luglio; **in the middle of ~** a metà luglio; **during ~** durante (il mese di) luglio; **in ~ of next year** a luglio dell'anno prossimo; **each *or* every ~** ogni anno a luglio; **~ was wet this year** ha piovuto molto a luglio quest'anno.

jumble ['dʒʌmbl] *n* miscuglio ♦ *vt* (*also*: **~ up**, **~ together**) mischiare, mettere alla rinfusa.

jumble sale *n* ≈ vendita di beneficenza; *see boxed note.*

JUMBLE SALE

*La **jumble sale** è un mercatino dove vengono venduti vari oggetti, per lo più di seconda mano; viene organizzata in chiese, scuole o circoli ricreativi. I proventi delle vendite vengono devoluti in beneficenza o usati per una giusta causa.*

---

jumbo ['dʒʌmbəʊ] *adj*: **~ jet** jumbo-jet *m inv*; **~ size** formato gigante.

jump [dʒʌmp] *vi* saltare, balzare; (*start*) sobbalzare; (*increase*) rincarare ♦ *vt* saltare ♦ *n* salto, balzo; sobbalzo; (*SHOWJUMPING*) salto; (*fence*) ostacolo; **to ~ the queue** (*BRIT*) passare davanti agli altri (*in una coda*).
▶**jump about** *vi* fare salti, saltellare.
▶**jump at** *vt fus* (*fig*) cogliere *or* afferrare al volo; **he ~ed at the offer** si affrettò ad accettare l'offerta.
▶**jump down** *vi* saltare giù.
▶**jump up** *vi* saltare in piedi.

jumped-up ['dʒʌmptʌp] adj (BRIT pej) presuntuoso(a).

jumper ['dʒʌmpə*] n (BRIT: pullover) maglia; (US: pinafore dress) scamiciato; (SPORT) saltatore/trice.

jump leads, (US) **jumper cables** npl cavi mpl per batteria.

jump-start ['dʒʌmpstɑːt] vt (car) far partire spingendo; (fig) dare una spinta a, rimettere in moto.

jump suit n tuta.

jumpy ['dʒʌmpɪ] adj nervoso(a), agitato(a).

Jun. abbr (= June) giu.

Jun., Junr abbr = junior.

junction ['dʒʌŋkʃən] n (BRIT: of roads) incrocio; (of rails) nodo ferroviario.

juncture ['dʒʌŋktʃə*] n: **at this** ~ in questa congiuntura.

June [dʒuːn] n giugno; for phrases see also **July.**

jungle ['dʒʌŋgl] n giungla.

junior ['dʒuːnɪə*] adj, n: **he's** ~ **to me (by 2 years), he's my** ~ **(by 2 years)** è più giovane di me (di 2 anni); **he's** ~ **to me** (seniority) è al di sotto di me, ho più anzianità di lui.

junior high school n (US) scuola media (da 12 a 15 anni).

junior minister n (BRIT POL) ministro che non fa parte del Cabinet.

junior partner n socio meno anziano.

junior school n (BRIT) scuola elementare (da 8 a 11 anni).

juniper ['dʒuːnɪpə*] n: ~ **berry** bacca di ginepro.

junk [dʒʌŋk] n (rubbish) chincaglia; (ship) giunca ♦ vt disfarsi di.

junk bond n (COMM) titolo m spazzatura inv.

junk dealer n rigattiere m.

junket ['dʒʌŋkɪt] n (CULIN) giuncata; (BRIT col: also: ~ing): **to go on a** ~, **go** ~ing fare bisboccia.

junk food n porcherie fpl, cibo a scarso valore nutritivo.

junkie ['dʒʌŋkɪ] n (col) drogato/a.

junk mail n posta f spazzatura inv.

junk room n (US) ripostiglio.

junk shop n chincaglieria.

junta ['dʒʌntə] n giunta.

Jupiter ['dʒuːpɪtə*] n (planet) Giove m.

jurisdiction [dʒuərɪs'dɪkʃən] n giurisdizione f; **it falls** or **comes within/outside our** ~ è/ non è di nostra competenza.

jurisprudence [dʒuərɪs'pruːdəns] n giurisprudenza.

juror ['dʒuərə*] n giurato/a.

jury ['dʒuərɪ] n giuria.

jury box n banco della giuria.

juryman ['dʒuərɪmən] n = **juror.**

just [dʒʌst] adj giusto(a) ♦ adv: **he's** ~ **done it/left** lo ha appena fatto/è appena partito; ~ **as I expected** proprio come me lo aspettavo; ~ **right** proprio giusto; ~ **2 o'clock** le 2 precise; **we were** ~ **going** stavamo uscendo; **I was** ~ **about to phone** stavo proprio per telefonare; ~ **as he was leaving** proprio mentre se ne stava andando; **it was** ~ **before/enough/ here** era poco prima/appena assai/ proprio qui; **it's** ~ **me** sono solo io; **it's** ~ **a mistake** non è che uno sbaglio; ~ **missed/caught** appena perso/preso; ~ **listen to this!** senta un po' questo!; ~ **ask someone the way** basta che tu chieda la strada a qualcuno; **it's** ~ **as good** è altrettanto buono; **it's** ~ **as well you didn't go** per fortuna non ci sei andato; **not** ~ **now** non proprio adesso; ~ **a minute!,** ~ **one moment!** un attimo!

justice ['dʒʌstɪs] n giustizia; **Lord Chief J**~ (BRIT) presidente m della Corte d'Appello; **this photo doesn't do you** ~ questa foto non ti fa giustizia.

Justice of the Peace (JP) n giudice m conciliatore.

justifiable [dʒʌstɪ'faɪəbl] adj giustificabile.

justifiably [dʒʌstɪ'faɪəblɪ] adv legittimamente, con ragione.

justification [dʒʌstɪfɪ'keɪʃən] n giustificazione f; (TYP) giustezza.

justify ['dʒʌstɪfaɪ] vt giustificare; (TYP etc) allineare, giustificare; **to be justified in doing sth** avere ragione di fare qc.

justly ['dʒʌstlɪ] adv giustamente.

justness ['dʒʌstnɪs] n giustezza.

jut [dʒʌt] vi (also: ~ **out**) sporgersi.

jute [dʒuːt] n iuta.

juvenile ['dʒuːvənaɪl] adj giovane, giovanile; (court) dei minorenni; (books) per ragazzi ♦ n giovane m/f, minorenne m/f.

juvenile delinquency n delinquenza minorile.

juvenile delinquent n delinquente m/f minorenne.

juxtapose ['dʒʌkstəpəuz] vt giustapporre.

juxtaposition [dʒʌkstəpə'zɪʃən] n giustapposizione f.

K k

K, k [keɪ] n (*letter*) K, k *f or* m *inv*; **K for King** ≈ K come Kursaal.
K n *abbr* (= *one thousand*) mille ♦ *abbr* (*BRIT*: = *Knight*) titolo; (= *kilobyte*) K.
kaftan ['kæftæn] n caffettano.
Kalahari Desert [kælə'hɑːrɪ-] n Deserto di Calahari.
kale [keɪl] n cavolo verde.
kaleidoscope [kə'laɪdəskəup] n caleidoscopio.
kamikaze [kæmɪ'kɑːzɪ] adj da kamikaze.
Kampala [kæm'pɑːlə] n Kampala f.
Kampuchea [kæmpu'tʃɪə] n Kampuchea f.
kangaroo [kæŋgə'ruː] n canguro.
Kans. *abbr* (*US*) = Kansas.
kaput [kə'put] adj (*col*) kaputt inv.
karaoke [kɑːrə'əʊkɪ] n karaoke m inv.
karate [kə'rɑːtɪ] n karate m.
Kashmir [kæʃ'mɪə*] n Kashmir m.
Kazakhstan [kæzæk'stɑːn] n Kazakistan m.
KC n *abbr* (*BRIT LAW*: = King's Counsel) avvocato della Corona; *see also* **QC**.
kebab [kə'bæb] n spiedino.
keel [kiːl] n chiglia; **on an even ~** (*fig*) in uno stato normale.
►**keel over** vi (*NAUT*) capovolgersi; (*person*) crollare.
keen [kiːn] adj (*interest, desire*) vivo(a); (*eye, intelligence*) acuto(a); (*competition*) serrato(a); (*edge*) affilato(a); (*eager*) entusiasta; **to be ~ to do** *or* **on doing sth** avere una gran voglia di fare qc; **to be ~ on sth** essere appassionato(a) di qc; **to be ~ on sb** avere un debole per qn; **I'm not ~ on going** non mi va di andare.
keenly ['kiːnlɪ] adv (*enthusiastically*) con entusiasmo; (*acutely*) vivamente; in modo penetrante.
keenness ['kiːnnɪs] n (*eagerness*) entusiasmo.
keep [kiːp] vb (*pt, pp* **kept** [kɛpt]) vt tenere; (*hold back*) trattenere; (*feed: one's family etc*) mantenere, sostentare; (*a promise*) mantenere; (*chickens, bees, pigs etc*) allevare ♦ vi (*food*) mantenersi; (*remain: in a certain state or place*) restare ♦ n (*of castle*) maschio; (*food etc*): **enough for his**

~ abbastanza per vitto e alloggio; **to ~ doing sth** continuare a fare qc; fare qc di continuo; **to ~ sb from doing/sth happening** impedire a qn di fare/che qc succeda; **to ~ sb busy/a place tidy** tenere qn occupato(a)/un luogo in ordine; **to ~ sb waiting** far aspettare qn; **to ~ an appointment** andare ad un appuntamento; **to ~ a record** *or* **note of sth** prendere nota di qc; **to ~ sth to o.s.** tenere qc per sé; **to ~ sth (back) from sb** celare qc a qn; **to ~ time** (*clock*) andar bene; **~ the change** tenga il resto; *see also* **keeps**.
►**keep away** vt: **to ~ sth/sb away from sb** tenere qc/qn lontano da qn ♦ vi: **to ~ away (from)** stare lontano (da).
►**keep back** vt (*crowds, tears, money*) trattenere ♦ vi tenersi indietro.
►**keep down** vt (*control: prices, spending*) contenere, ridurre; (*retain: food*) trattenere, ritenere ♦ vi tenersi giù, stare giù.
►**keep in** vt (*invalid, child*) tenere a casa; (*SCOL*) trattenere a scuola ♦ vi (*col*): **to ~ in with sb** tenersi buono qn.
►**keep off** vt (*dog, person*) tenere lontano da ♦ vi stare alla larga; **~ your hands off!** non toccare!, giù le mani!; **"~ off the grass"** "non calpestare l'erba".
►**keep on** vi continuare a fare; **to ~ on doing** continuare a fare.
►**keep out** vt tener fuori ♦ vi restare fuori; **"~ out"** "vietato l'accesso".
►**keep up** vi mantenersi ♦ vt continuare, mantenere; **to ~ up with** tener dietro a, andare di pari passo con; (*work etc*) farcela a seguire; **to ~ up with sb** (*in race etc*) mantenersi al passo con qn.
keeper ['kiːpə*] n custode m/f, guardiano/a.
keep-fit [kiːp'fɪt] n ginnastica.
keeping ['kiːpɪŋ] n (*care*) custodia; **in ~ with** in armonia con; in accordo con.
keeps [kiːps] n: **for ~** (*col*) per sempre.
keepsake ['kiːpseɪk] n ricordo.
keg [kɛg] n barilotto.
Ken. *abbr* (*US*) = Kentucky.
kennel ['kɛnl] n canile m.
Kenya ['kɛnjə] n Kenia m.
Kenyan ['kɛnjən] adj, n Keniano(a), Keniota (m/f).
kept [kɛpt] pt, pp of **keep**.
kerb [kə:b] n (*BRIT*) orlo del marciapiede.
kerb crawler [-'krɔːlə*] n chi va in macchina in cerca di una prostituta.
kernel ['kə:nl] n nocciolo.
kerosene ['kɛrəsiːn] n cherosene m.
ketchup ['kɛtʃəp] n ketchup m inv.

kettle ['kɛtl] n bollitore m.

kettle drum n timpano.

key [kiː] n (gen, MUS) chiave f; (of piano, typewriter) tasto; (on map) leg(g)enda ♦ cpd (vital: position, industry etc) chiave inv.
► **key in** vt (text) introdurre da tastiera.

keyboard ['kiːbɔːd] n tastiera ♦ vt (text) comporre su tastiera.

keyboarder ['kiːbɔːdə*] n dattilografo(a).

keyed up [kiːd'ʌp] adj: **to be** ~ essere agitato(a).

keyhole ['kiːhəul] n buco della serratura.

keyhole surgery n chirurgia mininvasiva.

keynote ['kiːnəut] n (MUS) tonica; (fig) nota dominante.

keypad ['kiːpæd] n tastierino numerico.

key ring n portachiavi m inv.

keystroke ['kiːstrəuk] n battuta (di un tasto).

kg abbr (= kilogram) Kg.

KGB n abbr KGB m.

khaki ['kɑːkɪ] adj, n cachi (m).

kibbutz [kɪ'buts] n kibbutz m inv.

kick [kɪk] vt calciare, dare calci a ♦ vi (horse) tirar calci ♦ n calcio; (of rifle) contraccolpo; (thrill): **he does it for** ~**s** lo fa giusto per il piacere di farlo.
► **kick around** vi (col) essere in giro.
► **kick off** vi (SPORT) dare il primo calcio.

kick-off ['kɪkɔf] n (SPORT) calcio d'inizio.

kick-start ['kɪkstɑːt] n (also: ~**er**) pedale m d'avviamento.

kid [kɪd] n ragazzino/a; (animal, leather) capretto ♦ vi (col) scherzare ♦ vt (col) prendere in giro.

kid gloves npl: **to treat sb with** ~ trattare qn coi guanti.

kidnap ['kɪdnæp] vt rapire, sequestrare.

kidnapper ['kɪdnæpə*] n rapitore/trice.

kidnapping ['kɪdnæpɪŋ] n sequestro (di persona).

kidney ['kɪdnɪ] n (ANAT) rene m; (CULIN) rognone m.

kidney bean n fagiolo borlotto.

kidney machine n rene m artificiale.

Kilimanjaro [kɪlɪmən'dʒɑːrəu] n: **Mount** ~ il monte Kilimangiaro.

kill [kɪl] vt uccidere, ammazzare; (fig) sopprimere; sopraffare; ammazzare ♦ n uccisione f; **to** ~ **time** ammazzare il tempo.
► **kill off** vt sterminare; (fig) eliminare, soffocare.

killer ['kɪlə*] n uccisore m, killer m inv; assassino/a.

killer instinct n: **to have a/the** ~ essere spietato(a).

killing ['kɪlɪŋ] n assassinio; (massacre) strage f; (col): **to make a** ~ fare un bel colpo.

kill-joy ['kɪldʒɔɪ] n guastafeste m/f inv.

kiln [kɪln] n forno.

kilo ['kiːləu] n abbr (= kilogram) chilo.

kilobyte ['kɪləbaɪt] n kilobyte m inv.

kilogram(me) ['kɪləugræm] n chilogrammo.

kilometre, (US) **kilometer** ['kɪləmiːtə*] n chilometro.

kilowatt ['kɪləuwɔt] n chilowatt m inv.

kilt [kɪlt] n gonnellino scozzese.

kilter ['kɪltə*] n: **out of** ~ fuori fase.

kimono [kɪ'məunəu] n chimono.

kin [kɪn] n see **next of kin, kith**.

kind [kaɪnd] adj gentile, buono(a) ♦ n sorta, specie f; (species) genere m; **to be two of a** ~ essere molto simili; **would you be** ~ **enough to …?, would you be so** ~ **as to …?** sarebbe così gentile da …?; **it's very** ~ **of you (to do)** è molto gentile da parte sua (di fare); **in** ~ (COMM) in natura; (fig): **to repay sb in** ~ ripagare qn della stessa moneta.

kindergarten ['kɪndəgɑːtn] n giardino d'infanzia.

kind-hearted [kaɪnd'hɑːtɪd] adj di buon cuore.

kindle ['kɪndl] vt accendere, infiammare.

kindling ['kɪndlɪŋ] n frasche fpl, ramoscelli mpl.

kindly ['kaɪndlɪ] adj pieno(a) di bontà, benevolo(a) ♦ adv con bontà, gentilmente; **will you** ~ … vuole … per favore; **he didn't take it** ~ se l'è presa a male.

kindness ['kaɪndnɪs] n bontà, gentilezza.

kindred ['kɪndrɪd] adj imparentato(a); ~ **spirit** spirito affine.

kinetic [kɪ'nɛtɪk] adj cinetico(a).

king [kɪŋ] n re m inv.

kingdom ['kɪŋdəm] n regno, reame m.

kingfisher ['kɪŋfɪʃə*] n martin m inv pescatore.

kingpin ['kɪŋpɪn] n (TECH, fig) perno.

king-size(d) ['kɪŋsaɪz(d)] adj super inv; gigante; (cigarette) extra lungo(a).

kink [kɪŋk] n (of rope) attorcigliamento; (in hair) ondina; (fig) aberrazione f.

kinky ['kɪŋkɪ] adj (fig) eccentrico(a); dai gusti particolari.

kinship ['kɪnʃɪp] n parentela.

kinsman ['kɪnzmən] n parente m.

kinswoman ['kɪnzwumən] n parente f.

kiosk ['kiːɔsk] n edicola, chiosco; (BRIT: also: **telephone** ~) cabina (telefonica); (: also: **newspaper** ~) edicola.

kipper ['kɪpə*] n aringa affumicata.

Kirghizia [kəː'gɪzɪə] n Kirghizistan.

kiss[kɪs] n bacio ♦ vt baciare; **to ~ (each other)** baciarsi; **to ~ sb goodbye** congedarsi da qn con un bacio; **~ of life** (*BRIT*) respirazione *f* bocca a bocca.

kissagram['kɪsəgræm] n *servizio di recapito a domicilio di messaggi e baci augurali*.

kit[kɪt] n equipaggiamento, corredo; (*set of tools etc*) attrezzi *mpl*; (*for assembly*) scatola di montaggio; **tool ~** cassetta *or* borsa degli attrezzi.

►**kit out** *vt* (*BRIT*) attrezzare, equipaggiare.

kitbag['kɪtbæg] n zaino; sacco militare.

kitchen['kɪtʃɪn] n cucina.

kitchen garden n orto.

kitchen sink n acquaio.

kitchen unit n (*BRIT*) elemento da cucina.

kitchenware['kɪtʃɪnwɛə*] n stoviglie *fpl*; utensili *mpl* da cucina.

kite[kaɪt] n (*toy*) aquilone *m*; (*ZOOL*) nibbio.

kith[kɪθ] n: **~ and kin** amici e parenti *mpl*.

kitten['kɪtn] n gattino/a, micino/a.

kitty['kɪtɪ] n (*money*) fondo comune.

kiwi fruit['kiːwiː-] n kiwi *m inv*.

KKK n abbr (*US*) = *Ku Klux Klan*.

Kleenex ®['kliːnɛks] n fazzolettino di carta.

kleptomaniac[klɛptəu'meɪnɪæk] n cleptomane *m/f*.

km abbr (= *kilometre*) km.

km/h abbr (= *kilometres per hour*) km/h.

knack[næk] n: **to have a ~ (for doing)** avere una pratica (per fare); **to have the ~ of** avere l'abilità di; **there's a ~ to doing this** c'è un trucco per fare questo.

knackered['nækəd] adj (*col*) fuso(a).

knapsack['næpsæk] n zaino, sacco da montagna.

knave[neɪv] n (*CARDS*) fante *m*.

knead[niːd] vt impastare.

knee[niː] n ginocchio.

kneecap['niːkæp] n rotula ♦ vt gambizzare.

knee-deep['niː'diːp] adj: **the water was ~** l'acqua ci arrivava alle ginocchia.

kneel[niːl] vi (pt, pp **knelt** [nɛlt]) inginocchiarsi.

kneepad['niːpæd] n ginocchiera.

knell[nɛl] n rintocco.

knelt[nɛlt] pt, pp of **kneel**.

knew[njuː] pt of **know**.

knickers['nɪkəz] npl (*BRIT*) mutandine *fpl*.

knick-knack['nɪknæk] n ninnolo.

knife[naɪf] n (pl **knives**) coltello ♦ vt accoltellare, dare una coltellata a; **~, fork and spoon** coperto.

knife edge n: **to be on a ~** (*fig*) essere appeso(a) a un filo.

knight[naɪt] n cavaliere *m*; (*CHESS*) cavallo.

knighthood['naɪthud] n cavalleria; (*title*): **to get a ~** essere fatto cavaliere.

knit[nɪt] vt fare a maglia; (*fig*): **to ~ together** unire ♦ vi lavorare a maglia; (*broken bones*) saldarsi.

knitted['nɪtɪd] adj lavorato(a) a maglia.

knitting['nɪtɪŋ] n lavoro a maglia.

knitting machine n macchina per maglieria.

knitting needle n ferro (da calza).

knitting pattern n modello (per maglia).

knitwear['nɪtwɛə*] n maglieria.

knives[naɪvz] npl of **knife**.

knob[nɔb] n bottone *m*; manopola; (*BRIT*): **a ~ of butter** una noce di burro.

knobbly['nɔblɪ], (*US*) **knobby**['nɔbɪ] adj (*wood, surface*) nodoso(a); (*knee*) ossuto(a).

knock[nɔk] vt (*strike*) colpire; urtare; (*fig: col*) criticare ♦ vi (*engine*) battere; (*at door etc*): **to ~ at/on** bussare a ♦ n bussata; colpo, botta; **he ~ed at the door** ha bussato alla porta; **to ~ a nail into sth** conficcare un chiodo in qc.

►**knock down** vt abbattere; (*pedestrian*) investire; (*price*) abbassare.

►**knock off** vi (*col: finish*) smettere (di lavorare) ♦ vt (*strike off*) far cadere; (*col: steal*) sgraffignare, grattare; **to ~ off £10** fare uno sconto di 10 sterline.

►**knock out** vt stendere; (*BOXING*) mettere K.O., mettere fuori combattimento.

►**knock over** vt (*object*) far cadere; (*pedestrian*) investire.

knockdown['nɔkdaun] adj (*price*) fortemente scontato(a).

knocker['nɔkə*] n (*on door*) battente *m*.

knocking['nɔkɪŋ] n colpi *mpl*.

knock-kneed[nɔk'niːd] adj che ha le gambe ad x.

knockout['nɔkaut] n (*BOXING*) knock out *m inv*.

knockout competition n (*BRIT*) gara ad eliminazione.

knock-up['nɔkʌp] n (*TENNIS etc*) palleggio; **to have a ~** palleggiare.

knot[nɔt] n nodo ♦ vt annodare; **to tie a ~** fare un nodo.

knotty['nɔtɪ] adj (*fig*) spinoso(a).

know[nəu] vt (pt **knew**, pp **known** [njuː, nəun]) sapere; (*person, author, place*) conoscere ♦ vi sapere; **to ~ that** ... sapere che ...; **to ~ how to do** sapere fare; **to get to ~ sth** venire a sapere qc; **I ~ nothing about it** non ne so niente; **I don't ~ him** non lo conosco; **to ~ right from wrong** distinguere il bene dal male; **as far as I ~**

... che io sappia ..., per quanto io ne
sappia ...; **yes, I ~ sì**, lo so; **I don't ~ non**
lo so.
know-all ['nəuɔːl] *n* (*BRIT pej*) sapientone/a.
know-how ['nəuhau] *n* tecnica; pratica.
knowing ['nəuɪŋ] *adj* (*look etc*) d'intesa.
knowingly ['nəuɪŋlɪ] *adv* consapevolmente;
di complicità.
know-it-all ['nəuɪtɔːl] *n* (*US*) = **know-all**.
knowledge ['nɔlɪdʒ] *n* consapevolezza;
(*learning*) conoscenza, sapere *m*; **to have**
no ~ of ignorare, non sapere; **not to my**
~ che io sappia, no; **to have a working ~**
of Italian avere una conoscenza pratica
dell'italiano; **without my ~** a mia
insaputa; **it is common ~ that ...** è
risaputo che ...; **it has come to my ~ that**
... sono venuto a sapere che ....
knowledgeable ['nɔlɪdʒəbl] *adj* ben
informato(a).
known [nəun] *pp of* **know** ♦ *adj* (*thief, facts*)
noto(a); (*expert*) riconosciuto(a).
knuckle ['nʌkl] *n* nocca.
▶**knuckle down** *vi* (*col*): **to ~ down to**
some hard work mettersi sotto a
lavorare.
▶**knuckle under** *vi* (*col*) cedere.
knuckleduster ['nʌkldʌstə*] *n* tirapugni *m*
inv.
KO *abbr* (= *knock out*) *n* K.O. *m* ♦ *vt* mettere
K.O.
koala [kəu'ɑːlə] *n* (*also*: **~ bear**) koala *m inv.*
kook [kuːk] *n* (*US col*) svitato/a.
Koran [kɔ'rɑːn] *n* Corano.
Korea [kə'riːə] *n* Corea; **North/South ~**
Corea del Nord/Sud.
Korean [kə'riːən] *adj*, *n* coreano(a).
kosher ['kəuʃə*] *adj* kasher *inv.*
kowtow ['kau'tau] *vi*: **to ~ to sb** mostrarsi
ossequioso(a) verso qn.
Kremlin ['krɛmlɪn] *n*: **the ~** il Cremlino.
KS *abbr* (*US*) = *Kansas*.
Kt *abbr* (*BRIT*: = *Knight*) titolo.
Kuala Lumpur ['kwɑːlə'lumpuə*] *n* Kuala
Lumpur *f.*
kudos ['kjuːdɔs] *n* gloria, fama.
Kurd [kɔːd] *n* curdo/a.
Kuwait [ku'weɪt] *n* Kuwait *m.*
Kuwaiti [ku'weɪtɪ] *adj*, *n* kuwaitiano(a).
kW *abbr* (= *kilowatt*) kw.
KY, Ky. *abbr* (*US*) = *Kentucky*.

L, l [ɛl] *n* (*letter*) L, l *f or m inv*; **L for Lucy**, (*US*)
L for Love ≈ L come Livorno.
L *abbr* (= *lake*) l; (= *large*) taglia grande;
(= *left*) sin.; (*BRIT AUT*) = **learner**.
l *abbr* (= *litre*) l.
LA *n abbr* (*US*) = *Los Angeles* ♦ *abbr* (*US*)
= *Louisiana*.
La. *abbr* (*US*) = *Louisiana*.
lab [læb] *n abbr* (= *laboratory*) laboratorio.
Lab. *abbr* (*Canada*) = *Labrador*.
label ['leɪbl] *n* etichetta, cartellino; (*brand*:
of record) casa ♦ *vt* etichettare;
classificare.
labor *etc* ['leɪbə*] (*US*) = **labour** *etc*.
laboratory [lə'bɔrətərɪ] *n* laboratorio.
Labor Day *n* (*US*) festa del lavoro; *see boxed*
note.

LABOR DAY

Negli Stati Uniti e nel Canada il **Labor Day***, la*
festa del lavoro, cade il primo lunedì di
settembre, contrariamente a quanto accade
nella maggior parte dei paesi europei dove tale
celebrazione ha luogo il primo maggio.

laborious [lə'bɔːrɪəs] *adj* laborioso(a).
labor union *n* (*US*) sindacato.
Labour ['leɪbə*] *n* (*BRIT POL*: *also*: **the ~**
Party) il partito laburista, i laburisti.
labour, (*US*) **labor** ['leɪbə*] *n* (*task*) lavoro;
(*workmen*) manodopera; (*MED*) travaglio
del parto, doglie *fpl* ♦ *vi*: **to ~ (at)** lavorare
duro (a); **to be in ~** (*MED*) avere le doglie.
labo(u)r camp *n* campo dei lavori forzati.
labo(u)r cost *n* costo del lavoro.
labo(u)r dispute *n* conflitto tra lavoratori
e datori di lavoro.
labo(u)red ['leɪbəd] *adj* (*breathing*) affa-
ticato(a); (*style*) elaborato(a), pesante.
labo(u)rer ['leɪbərə*] *n* manovale *m*; (*on*
farm) lavoratore *m* agricolo.
labo(u)r force *n* manodopera.
labo(u)r-intensive [leɪbərɪn'tɛnsɪv] *adj* che
assorbe molta manodopera.
labo(u)r market *n* mercato del lavoro.
labo(u)r pains *npl* doglie *fpl.*
labo(u)r relations *npl* relazioni *fpl*

industriali.
labo(u)r-saving ['leɪbəseɪvɪŋ] adj che fa risparmiare fatica or lavoro.
labo(u)r unrest n agitazioni fpl degli operai.
labyrinth ['læbɪrɪnθ] n labirinto.
lace [leɪs] n merletto, pizzo; (of shoe etc) laccio ♦ vt (shoe) allacciare; (drink: fortify with spirits) correggere.
lacemaking ['leɪsmeɪkɪŋ] n fabbricazione f dei pizzi or dei merletti.
laceration [læsə'reɪʃən] n lacerazione f.
lace-up ['leɪsʌp] adj (shoes etc) con i lacci, con le stringhe.
lack [læk] n mancanza, scarsità ♦ vt mancare di; **through** or **for** ~ **of** per mancanza di; **to be** ~**ing (in)** mancare di.
lackadaisical [lækə'deɪzɪkl] adj disinteressato(a), noncurante.
lackey ['lækɪ] n (also fig) lacchè m inv.
lacklustre, (US) **lackluster** ['læklʌstə*] adj (surface) opaco(a); (style) scialbo(a); (eyes) spento(a).
laconic [lə'kɔnɪk] adj laconico(a).
lacquer ['lækə*] n lacca; **hair** ~ lacca per (i) capelli.
lacy ['leɪsɪ] adj (like lace) che sembra un pizzo.
lad [læd] n ragazzo, giovanotto; (BRIT: in stable etc) mozzo or garzone m di stalla.
ladder ['lædə*] n scala; (BRIT: in tights) smagliatura ♦ vt smagliare ♦ vi smagliarsi.
laden ['leɪdn] adj: ~ **(with)** carico(a) or caricato(a) (di); **fully** ~ (truck, ship) a pieno carico.
ladle ['leɪdl] n mestolo.
lady ['leɪdɪ] n signora; **L**~ **Smith** lady Smith; **the ladies' (toilets)** i gabinetti per signore; **a** ~ **doctor** una dottoressa.
ladybird ['leɪdɪbəːd], (US) **ladybug** ['leɪdɪbʌg] n coccinella.
lady-in-waiting ['leɪdɪɪn'weɪtɪŋ] n dama di compagnia.
ladykiller ['leɪdɪkɪlə*] n dongiovanni m inv.
ladylike ['leɪdɪlaɪk] adj da signora.
ladyship ['leɪdɪʃɪp] n: **your L**~ signora contessa etc.
lag [læg] n = **time** ~ ♦ vi (also: ~ **behind**) trascinarsi ♦ vt (pipes) rivestire di materiale isolante.
lager ['lɑːgə*] n lager m inv.
lager lout n (BRIT col) giovinastro ubriaco.
lagging ['lægɪŋ] n rivestimento di materiale isolante.
lagoon [lə'guːn] n laguna.
Lagos ['leɪgɔs] n Lagos f.
laid [leɪd] pt, pp of **lay**.

laid-back [leɪd'bæk] adj (col) rilassato(a).
lain [leɪn] pp of **lie**.
lair [lɛə*] n covo, tana.
laissez-faire [leseɪ'fɛə*] n liberismo.
laity ['leɪətɪ] n laici mpl.
lake [leɪk] n lago.
Lake District n: **the** ~ (BRIT) la regione dei laghi.
lamb [læm] n agnello.
lamb chop n cotoletta d'agnello.
lambskin ['læmskɪn] n (pelle f d')agnello.
lambswool ['læmzwul] n lamb's wool m.
lame [leɪm] adj zoppo(a); ~ **duck** (fig: person) persona inetta; (: firm) azienda traballante.
lamely ['leɪmlɪ] adv (fig) in modo poco convincente.
lament [lə'mɛnt] n lamento ♦ vt lamentare, piangere.
lamentable ['læməntəbl] adj doloroso(a); deplorevole.
laminated ['læmɪneɪtɪd] adj laminato(a).
lamp [læmp] n lampada.
lamplight ['læmplaɪt] n: **by** ~ a lume della lampada.
lampoon [læm'puːn] n satira.
lamppost ['læmppəust] n lampione m.
lampshade ['læmpʃeɪd] n paralume m.
lance [lɑːns] n lancia ♦ vt (MED) incidere.
lance corporal n (BRIT) caporale m.
lancet ['lɑːnsɪt] n (MED) bisturi m inv.
Lancs [læŋks] abbr (BRIT) = Lancashire.
land [lænd] n (as opposed to sea) terra (ferma); (country) paese m; (soil) terreno; (estate) terreni mpl, terre fpl ♦ vi (from ship) cadere ♦ vt (obtain) acchiappare; (passengers) sbarcare; (goods) scaricare; **to go/travel by** ~ andare/viaggiare per via di terra; **to own** ~ possedere dei terreni, avere delle proprietà (terriere); **to** ~ **on one's feet** cadere in piedi; (fig: to be lucky) cascar bene.
▶**land up** vi andare a finire.
landed gentry ['lændɪd-] n proprietari mpl terrieri.
landfill site ['lændfɪl-] n discarica dove i rifiuti vengono sepolti.
landing ['lændɪŋ] n (from ship) sbarco; (AVIAT) atterraggio; (of staircase) pianerottolo.
landing card n carta di sbarco.
landing craft n mezzo da sbarco.
landing gear n (AVIAT) carrello d'atterraggio.
landing stage n pontile m da sbarco.
landing strip n pista d'atterraggio.
landlady ['lændleɪdɪ] n padrona or

proprietaria di casa.
landlocked['lændlɔkt] *adj* senza sbocco sul mare.
landlord['lændlɔːd] *n* padrone *m* or proprietario di casa; (*of pub etc*) oste *m*.
landlubber['lændlʌbə*] *n* marinaio d'acqua dolce.
landmark['lændmɑːk] *n* punto di riferimento; (*fig*) pietra miliare.
landowner['lændəunə*] *n* proprietario(a) terriero(a).
landscape['lænskeɪp] *n* paesaggio.
landscape architect, landscape gardener*n* paesaggista *m/f*.
landscape painting*n* (*ART*) paesaggistica.
landslide['lændslaɪd] *n* (*GEO*) frana; (*fig*: *POL*) valanga.
lane[leɪn] *n* (*in country*) viottolo; (*in town*) stradetta; (*AUT*, *in race*) corsia; **shipping** ~ rotta (marittima).
language['læŋgwɪdʒ] *n* lingua; (*way one speaks*) linguaggio; **bad** ~ linguaggio volgare.
language laboratory*n* laboratorio linguistico.
language school*n* scuola di lingue.
languid['læŋgwɪd] *adj* languente; languido(a).
languish['læŋgwɪʃ] *vi* languire.
lank[læŋk] *adj* (*hair*) liscio(a) e opaco(a).
lanky['læŋkɪ] *adj* allampanato(a).
lanolin(e)['lænəlɪn] *n* lanolina.
lantern['læntn] *n* lanterna.
Laos[lauz] *n* Laos *m*.
lap[læp] *n* (*of track*) giro; (*of body*): **in** or **on one's** ~ in grembo ♦ *vt* (*also*: ~ **up**) papparsi, leccare ♦ *vi* (*waves*) sciabordare.
▶**lap up***vt* (*fig*: *compliments, attention*) bearsi di.
La Paz[læ'pæz] *n* La Paz *f*.
lapdog['læpdɔg] *n* cane *m* da grembo.
lapel[lə'pɛl] *n* risvolto.
Lapland['læplænd] *n* Lapponia.
Lapp[læp] *adj* lappone ♦ *n* lappone *m/f*; (*LING*) lappone *m*.
lapse[læps] *n* lapsus *m* *inv*; (*longer*) caduta; (*fault*) mancanza; (*in behaviour*) scorrettezza ♦ *vi* (*law, act*) cadere; (*ticket, passport*) scadere; **to** ~ **into bad habits** pigliare cattive abitudini; ~ **of time** spazio di tempo; **a** ~ **of memory** un vuoto di memoria.
laptop['læptɔp] *n* (*also*: ~ **computer**) laptop *m* *inv*.
larceny['lɑːsənɪ] *n* furto.
lard[lɑːd] *n* lardo.

larder['lɑːdə*] *n* dispensa.
large[lɑːdʒ] *adj* grande; (*person, animal*) grosso(a) ♦ *adv*: **by and** ~ generalmente; **at** ~ (*free*) in libertà; (*generally*) in generale; nell'insieme; **to make** ~**r** ingrandire; **a** ~ **number of people** molta gente; **on a** ~ **scale** su vasta scala.
largely['lɑːdʒlɪ] *adv* in gran parte.
large-scale['lɑːdʒ'skeɪl] *adj* (*map, drawing etc*) in grande scala; (*reforms, business activities*) su vasta scala.
lark[lɑːk] *n* (*bird*) allodola; (*joke*) scherzo, gioco.
▶**lark about***vi* fare lo stupido.
larva,*pl* **larvae**['lɑːvə, -iː] *n* larva.
laryngitis[lærɪn'dʒaɪtɪs] *n* laringite *f*.
larynx['lærɪŋks] *n* laringe *f*.
lasagne[lə'zænjə] *n* lasagne *fpl*.
lascivious[lə'sɪvɪəs] *adj* lascivo(a).
laser['leɪzə*] *n* laser *m*.
laser beam*n* raggio *m* laser *inv*.
laser printer*n* stampante *f* laser *inv*.
lash[læʃ] *n* frustata; (*also*: **eye**~) ciglio ♦ *vt* frustare; (*tie*) legare.
▶**lash down***vt* assicurare (con corde) ♦ *vi* (*rain*) scrosciare.
▶**lash out***vi*: **to** ~ **out** (**at** or **against sb/sth**) attaccare violentemente (qn/qc); **to** ~ **out** (**on sth**) (*col*: *spend*) spendere un sacco di soldi (per qc).
lashing['læʃɪŋ] *n* (*beating*) frustata, sferzata; ~**s of** (*BRIT col*) un mucchio di, una montagna di.
lass[læs] *n* ragazza.
lasso[læ'suː] *n* laccio ♦ *vt* acchiappare con il laccio.
last[lɑːst] *adj* ultimo(a); (*week, month, year*) scorso(a), passato(a) ♦ *adv* per ultimo ♦ *vi* durare; ~ **week** la settimana scorsa; ~ **night** ieri sera, la notte scorsa; **at** ~ finalmente, alla fine; ~ **but one** penultimo(a); **the** ~ **time** l'ultima volta; **it** ~**s (for) 2 hours** dura 2 ore.
last-ditch['lɑːst'dɪtʃ] *adj* ultimo(a) e disperato(a).
lasting['lɑːstɪŋ] *adj* durevole.
lastly['lɑːstlɪ] *adv* infine, per finire, per ultimo.
last-minute['lɑːstmɪnɪt] *adj* fatto(a) (or preso(a) *etc*) all'ultimo momento.
latch[lætʃ] *n* serratura a scatto.
▶**latch on to***vt fus* (*cling to*: *person*) attaccarsi a, appiccicarsi a; (: *idea*) afferrare, capire.
latchkey['lætʃkiː] *n* chiave *f* di casa.
late[leɪt] *adj* (*not on time*) in ritardo; (*far on in day etc*) tardi *inv*; tardo(a); (*recent*) recente, ultimo(a); (*former*) ex; (*dead*)

defunto(a) ♦ adv tardi; (behind time, schedule) in ritardo; to be (10 minutes) ~ essere in ritardo (di 10 minuti); to work ~ lavorare fino a tardi; ~ in life in età avanzata; of ~ di recente; in the ~ afternoon nel tardo pomeriggio; in ~ May verso la fine di maggio; the ~ Mr X il defunto Signor X.

latecomer ['leɪtkʌmə*] n ritardatario/a.

lately ['leɪtlɪ] adv recentemente.

lateness ['leɪtnɪs] n (of person) ritardo; (of event) tardezza, ora tarda.

latent ['leɪtnt] adj latente; ~ defect vizio occulto.

later ['leɪtə*] adj (date etc) posteriore; (version etc) successivo(a) ♦ adv più tardi; ~ on today oggi più tardi.

lateral ['lætərl] adj laterale.

latest ['leɪtɪst] adj ultimo(a), più recente; at the ~ al più tardi; the ~ news le ultime notizie.

latex ['leɪtɛks] n latice m.

lath, ~ s [læθ, læðz] n assicella.

lathe [leɪð] n tornio.

lather ['lɑːðə*] n schiuma di sapone ♦ vt insaponare ♦ vi far schiuma.

Latin ['lætɪn] n latino ♦ adj latino(a).

Latin America n America Latina.

Latin American adj sudamericano(a).

latitude ['lætɪtjuːd] n latitudine f; (fig: freedom) libertà d'azione.

latrine [lə'triːn] n latrina.

latter ['lætə*] adj secondo(a); più recente ♦ n: the ~ quest'ultimo, il secondo.

latterly ['lætəlɪ] adv recentemente, negli ultimi tempi.

lattice ['lætɪs] n traliccio; graticolato.

lattice window n finestra con vetrata a losanghe.

Latvia ['lætvɪə] n Lettonia.

Latvian ['lætvɪən] adj lettone inv ♦ n lettone m/f; (LING) lettone m.

laudable ['lɔːdəbl] adj lodevole.

laudatory ['lɔːdətrɪ] adj elogiativo(a).

laugh [lɑːf] n risata ♦ vi ridere.

▶laugh at vt fus (misfortune etc) ridere di; I ~ed at his joke la sua barzelletta mi fece ridere.

▶laugh off vt prendere alla leggera.

laughable ['lɑːfəbl] adj ridicolo(a).

laughing ['lɑːfɪŋ] adj (face) ridente; this is no ~ matter non è una cosa da ridere.

laughing gas n gas m esilarante.

laughing stock n: the ~ of lo zimbello di.

laughter ['lɑːftə*] n riso; risate fpl.

launch [lɔːntʃ] n (of rocket, product etc) lancio; (of new ship) varo; (boat) scialuppa; (also: motor ~) lancia ♦ vt

(rocket, product) lanciare; (ship, plan) varare.

▶launch out vi: to ~ out (into) lanciarsi (in).

launching ['lɔːntʃɪŋ] n lancio; varo.

launch(ing) pad n rampa di lancio.

launder ['lɔːndə*] vt lavare e stirare.

Launderette ® [lɔːn'drɛt], (US) Laundromat ® ['lɔːndrəmæt] n lavanderia (automatica).

laundry ['lɔːndrɪ] n lavanderia; (clothes) biancheria; to do the ~ fare il bucato.

laureate ['lɔːrɪət] adj see poet laureate.

laurel ['lɔrl] n lauro, alloro; to rest on one's ~s riposare or dormire sugli allori.

Lausanne [ləu'zæn] n Losanna.

lava ['lɑːvə] n lava.

lavatory ['lævətərɪ] n gabinetto.

lavatory paper n (BRIT) carta igienica.

lavender ['lævəndə*] n lavanda.

lavish ['lævɪʃ] adj abbondante; sontuoso(a); (giving freely): ~ with prodigo(a) di, largo(a) in ♦ vt: to ~ sth on sb/sth profondere qc a qn/qc.

lavishly ['lævɪʃlɪ] adv (give, spend) generosamente; (furnished) sontuosamente, lussuosamente.

law [lɔː] n legge f; against the ~ contro la legge; to study ~ studiare diritto; to go to ~ (BRIT) ricorrere alle vie legali; civil/ criminal ~ diritto civile/penale.

law-abiding ['lɔːəbaɪdɪŋ] adj ubbidiente alla legge.

law and order n l'ordine m pubblico.

lawbreaker ['lɔːbreɪkə*] n violatore/trice della legge.

law court n tribunale m, corte f di giustizia.

lawful ['lɔːful] adj legale.

lawfully ['lɔːfəlɪ] adv legalmente.

lawless ['lɔːlɪs] adj senza legge; illegale.

Law Lords npl ≈ Corte f Suprema.

lawmaker ['lɔːmeɪkə*] n legislatore m.

lawn [lɔːn] n tappeto erboso.

lawnmower ['lɔːnməuə*] n tosaerba m or f inv.

lawn tennis n tennis m su prato.

law school n facoltà f inv di legge.

law student n studente/essa di legge.

lawsuit ['lɔːsuːt] n processo, causa; to bring a ~ against intentare causa a.

lawyer ['lɔːjə*] n (consultant, with company) giurista m/f; (for sales, wills etc) ≈ notaio; (partner, in court) ≈ avvocato/essa.

lax [læks] adj (conduct) rilassato(a); (person: careless) negligente; (: on discipline) permissivo(a).

laxative ['læksətɪv] n lassativo.

laxity ['læksɪtɪ] n rilassatezza; negligenza.

lay [leɪ] pt of **lie** ♦ adj laico(a); secolare ♦ vt (pt, pp **laid** [leɪd]) posare, mettere; (eggs) fare; (trap) tendere; (plans) fare; elaborare; **to ~ the table** apparecchiare la tavola; **to ~ the facts/one's proposals before sb** presentare i fatti/delle proposte a qn; **to get laid** (col!) scopare (!); essere scopato(a) (!).

▸**lay aside, lay by** vt mettere da parte.

▸**lay down** vt mettere giù; **to ~ down the law** (fig) dettar legge.

▸**lay in** vt fare una scorta di.

▸**lay into** vt fus (col: attack, scold) aggredire.

▸**lay off** vt (workers) licenziare.

▸**lay on** vt (water, gas) installare, mettere; (provide: meal etc) fornire; (paint) applicare.

▸**lay out** vt (design) progettare; (display) presentare; (spend) sborsare.

▸**lay up** vt (to store) accumulare; (ship) mettere in disarmo; (subj: illness) costringere a letto.

layabout ['leɪəbaut] n sfaccendato/a, fannullone/a.

lay-by ['leɪbaɪ] n (BRIT) piazzola (di sosta).

lay days npl (NAUT) stallie fpl.

layer ['leɪə*] n strato.

layette [leɪ'ɛt] n corredino (per neonato).

layman ['leɪmən] n laico; profano.

lay-off ['leɪɔf] n sospensione f, licenziamento.

layout ['leɪaut] n lay-out m inv, disposizione f; (PRESS) impaginazione f.

laze [leɪz] vi oziare.

laziness ['leɪzɪnɪs] n pigrizia.

lazy ['leɪzɪ] adj pigro(a).

lb. abbr (= libra: pound) lb.

lbw abbr (CRICKET: = leg before wicket) fallo dovuto al fatto che il giocatore ha la gamba davanti alla porta.

LC n abbr (US) = Library of Congress.

lc abbr (TYP) = **lower case**.

L/C abbr = **letter of credit**.

LCD n abbr see **liquid crystal display**.

Ld abbr (BRIT: = lord) titolo.

LDS n abbr (BRIT: = Licentiate in Dental Surgery) specializzazione dopo la laurea; (= Latter-day Saints) Chiesa di Gesù Cristo dei Santi dell'Ultimo Giorno.

LEA n abbr (BRIT: = local education authority) ≈ Provveditorato degli Studi.

lead [liːd] n (front position) posizione f di testa; (distance, time ahead) vantaggio; (clue) indizio; (ELEC) filo (elettrico); (for dog) guinzaglio; (THEAT) parte f principale; [lɛd] (metal) piombo; (in pencil) mina ♦ vb (pt, pp **led** [lɛd]) vt menare,

guidare, condurre; (induce) indurre; (be leader of) essere a capo di; (: orchestra: BRIT) essere il primo violino di; (: US) dirigere; (SPORT) essere in testa a ♦ vi condurre, essere in testa; **to be in the ~** (SPORT) essere in testa; **to take the ~** (SPORT) passare in testa; (fig) prendere l'iniziativa; **to ~ to** menare a; condurre a; portare a; **to ~ astray** sviare; **to ~ sb to believe that ...** far credere a qn che ...; **to ~ sb to do sth** portare qn a fare qc.

▸**lead away** vt condurre via.

▸**lead back** vt riportare, ricondurre.

▸**lead off** vt portare ♦ vi partire da.

▸**lead on** vt (tease) tenere sulla corda.

▸**lead on to** vt (induce) portare a.

▸**lead up to** vt fus portare a; (fig) preparare la strada per.

leaded ['lɛdɪd] adj (petrol) con piombo; **~ windows** vetrate fpl (artistiche).

leaden ['lɛdn] adj di piombo.

leader ['liːdə*] n capo; leader m inv; (in newspaper) articolo di fondo; **they are ~s in their field** (fig) sono all'avanguardia nel loro campo; **the L~ of the House** (BRIT) il capo della maggioranza ministeriale.

leadership ['liːdəʃɪp] n direzione f; **under the ~ of ...** sotto la direzione or guida di ...; **qualities of ~** qualità fpl di un capo.

lead-free ['lɛdfriː] adj senza piombo.

leading ['liːdɪŋ] adj primo(a); principale; **a ~ question** una domanda tendenziosa; **~ role** ruolo principale.

leading lady n (THEAT) prima attrice.

leading light n (person) personaggio di primo piano.

leading man n (THEAT) primo attore.

lead pencil [lɛd-] n matita con la mina di grafite.

lead poisoning [lɛd-] n saturnismo.

lead time [liːd-] n (COMM) tempo di consegna.

lead weight [lɛd-] n piombino, piombo.

leaf [liːf] n (pl **leaves**) foglia; (of table) ribalta; **to turn over a new ~** (fig) cambiar vita; **to take a ~ out of sb's book** (fig) prendere esempio da qn.

▸**leaf through** vt (book) sfogliare.

leaflet ['liːflɪt] n dépliant m inv; (POL, REL) volantino.

leafy ['liːfɪ] adj ricco(a) di foglie.

league [liːg] n lega; (FOOTBALL) campionato; **to be in ~ with** essere in lega con.

league table n classifica.

leak [liːk] n (out) fuga; (in) infiltrazione f; (fig: of information) fuga di notizie ♦ vi (roof, bucket) perdere; (liquid) uscire; (shoes) lasciar passare l'acqua ♦ vt

(*liquid*) spandere; (*information*) divulgare.
►**leak out** *vi* uscire; (*information*)
trapelare.
leakage ['liːkɪdʒ] *n* (*of water, gas etc*) perdita.
leaky ['liːkɪ] *adj* (*pipe, bucket, roof*) che
perde; (*shoe*) che lascia passare l'acqua;
(*boat*) che fa acqua.
lean [liːn] *adj* magro(a) ♦ *n* (*of meat*) carne *f*
magra ♦ *vb* (*pt, pp* **leaned** *or* **leant** [lɛnt]) *vt*:
to ~ sth on appoggiare qc su ♦ *vi* (*slope*)
pendere; (*rest*): **to ~ against** appoggiarsi
contro; essere appoggiato(a) a; **to ~ on**
appoggiarsi a.
►**lean back** *vi* sporgersi indietro.
►**lean forward** *vi* sporgersi in avanti.
►**lean out** *vi*: **to ~ out (of)** sporgersi (da).
►**lean over** *vi* inclinarsi.
leaning ['liːnɪŋ] *n*: **~ (towards)** propensione
f (per) ♦ *adj* inclinato(a), pendente; **the L~
Tower of Pisa** la torre (pendente) di Pisa.
leant [lɛnt] *pt, pp of* **lean**.
lean-to ['liːntuː] *n* (*roof*) tettoia; (*building*)
*edificio con tetto appoggiato ad altro
edificio.*
leap [liːp] *n* salto, balzo ♦ *vi* (*pt, pp* **leaped** *or*
leapt [lɛpt]) saltare, balzare; **to ~ at an
offer** afferrare al volo una proposta.
►**leap up** *vi* (*person*) alzarsi d'un balzo,
balzare su.
leapfrog ['liːpfrɔg] *n* gioco della cavallina
♦ *vi*: **to ~ over sb/sth** saltare (alla
cavallina) qn/qc.
leapt [lɛpt] *pt, pp of* **leap**.
leap year *n* anno bisestile.
learn, *pt, pp* **learned** *or* **learnt** [lɔːn, -t] *vt, vi*
imparare; **to ~ how to do sth** imparare a
fare qc; **to ~ that** ... apprendere che ...;
to ~ about sth (*SCOL*) studiare qc; (*hear*)
apprendere qc; **we were sorry to ~ that It
was closing down** la notizia della
chiusura ci ha fatto dispiacere.
learned ['lɔːnɪd] *adj* erudito(a), dotto(a).
learner ['lɔːnə*] *n* principiante *m/f*;
apprendista *m/f*; **he's a ~ (driver)** (*BRIT*)
sta imparando a guidare.
learning ['lɔːnɪŋ] *n* erudizione *f*, sapienza.
learnt [lɔːnt] *pt, pp of* **learn**.
lease [liːs] *n* contratto d'affitto ♦ *vt*
affittare; **on ~** in affitto.
►**lease back** *vt* effettuare un lease-back
inv.
leaseback ['liːsbæk] *n* lease-back *m inv*.
leasehold ['liːshəuld] *n* (*contract*) contratto
di affitto (*a lungo termine con responsabilità
simili a quelle di un proprietario*) ♦ *adj* in
affitto.
leash [liːʃ] *n* guinzaglio.
least [liːst] *adj*: **the ~ +** *noun* il(la) più

piccolo(a), il(la) minimo(a); (*smallest
amount of*) il(la) meno ♦ *adv*: **the ~
+** *adjective*: **the ~ beautiful girl** la ragazza
meno bella; **the ~ expensive** il(la) meno
caro(a); **I have the ~ money** ho meno
denaro di tutti; **at ~** almeno; **not in the ~**
affatto, per nulla.
leather ['lɛðə*] *n* (*soft*) pelle *f*; (*hard*) cuoio
♦ *cpd* di *or* in pelle; di cuoio; **~ goods**
pelletteria, pelletterie *fpl*.
leave [liːv] *vb* (*pt, pp* **left** [lɛft]) *vt* lasciare;
(*go away from*) partire da ♦ *vi* partire,
andarsene ♦ *n* (*time off*) congedo; (*MIL,
also: consent*) licenza; **to be left** rimanere;
there's some milk left over c'è rimasto
del latte; **to take one's ~ of** congedarsi
di; **he's already left for the airport** è già
uscito per andare all'aeroporto; **to ~
school** finire la scuola; **~ it to me!** ci
penso io!, lascia fare a me!; **on ~** in
congedo; **on ~ of absence** in permesso;
(*public employee*) in congedo; (*MIL*) in
licenza.
►**leave behind** *vt* (*also fig*) lasciare
indietro; (*forget*) dimenticare.
►**leave off** *vt* non mettere; (*BRIT col: stop*):
to ~ off doing sth smetterla *or* piantarla
di fare qc.
►**leave on** *vt* lasciare su; (*light, fire, cooker*)
lasciare acceso(a).
►**leave out** *vt* omettere, tralasciare.
leaves [liːvz] *npl of* **leaf**.
leavetaking ['liːvteɪkɪŋ] *n* commiato, addio.
Lebanese [lɛbə'niːz] *adj*, *n* (*pl inv*) libanese
(*m/f*).
Lebanon ['lɛbənən] *n* Libano.
lecherous ['lɛtʃərəs] *adj* lascivo(a),
lubrico(a).
lectern ['lɛktəːn] *n* leggio.
lecture ['lɛktʃə*] *n* conferenza; (*SCOL*)
lezione *f* ♦ *vi* fare conferenze; fare
lezioni; (*reprove*) rimproverare, fare una
ramanzina a; **to ~ on** fare una
conferenza su; **to give a ~ (on)** (*BRIT*) fare
una conferenza (su); fare lezione (su).
lecture hall *n* aula magna.
lecturer ['lɛktʃərə*] *n* (*speaker*)
conferenziere/a; (*BRIT: at university*)
professore/essa, docente *m/f*; **assistant ~**
(*BRIT*) ≈ professore(essa) associato(a);
senior ~ (*BRIT*) ≈ professore(essa)
ordinario(a).
lecture theatre *n* = **lecture hall**.
LED *n abbr* (*ELEC.*: = *light-emitting diode*)
diodo a emissione luminosa.
led [lɛd] *pt, pp of* **lead**.
ledge [lɛdʒ] *n* (*of window*) davanzale *m*; (*on
wall etc*) sporgenza; (*of mountain*) cornice

f, cengia.

ledger ['lɛdʒə*] n libro maestro, registro.

lee [li:] n lato sottovento; **in the ~ of** a
ridosso di, al riparo di.

leech [li:tʃ] n sanguisuga.

leek [li:k] n porro.

leer [lɪə*] vi: **to ~ at sb** gettare uno sguardo
voglioso (or maligno) su qn.

leeward ['li:wəd] adj sottovento inv ♦ n lato
sottovento; **to ~** sottovento.

leeway ['li:weɪ] n (fig): **to have some ~**
avere una certa libertà di agire.

left [lɛft] pt, pp of **leave** ♦ adj sinistro(a) ♦ adv
a sinistra ♦ n sinistra; **on the ~, to the ~**
a sinistra; **the L~** (POL) la sinistra.

left-click ['lɛftklɪk] vi (COMPUT): **to ~ on**
fare clic con il pulsante sinistro del
mouse su.

left-hand drive ['lɛfthænd-] n (BRIT) guida a
sinistra.

left-handed [lɛft'hændɪd] adj mancino(a); **~
scissors** forbici fpl per mancini.

left-hand side ['lɛfthænd-] n lato or fianco
sinistro.

leftie ['lɛftɪ] n: **a ~** (col) uno/a di sinistra.

leftist ['lɛftɪst] adj (POL) di sinistra.

left-luggage (office) [lɛft'lʌgɪdʒ-] n
deposito m bagagli inv.

left-overs ['lɛftəuvəz] npl avanzi mpl, resti
mpl.

left wing n (MIL, SPORT) ala sinistra; (POL)
sinistra ♦ adj: **left-wing** (POL) di sinistra.

left-winger [lɛft'wɪŋə*] n (POL) uno/a di
sinistra; (SPORT) ala sinistra.

lefty ['lɛftɪ] n = **leftie**.

leg [lɛg] n gamba; (of animal) zampa; (of
furniture) piede m; (CULIN: of chicken)
coscia; (of journey) tappa; **1st/2nd ~**
(SPORT) partita di andata/ritorno; **~ of
lamb** (CULIN) cosciotto d'agnello; **to
stretch one's ~s** sgranchirsi le gambe.

legacy ['lɛgəsɪ] n eredità f inv; (fig) retaggio.

legal ['li:gl] adj legale; **to take ~ action** or
proceedings against sb intentare
un'azione legale contro qn, far causa a
qn.

legal adviser n consulente m/f legale.

legality [lɪ'gælɪtɪ] n legalità.

legalize ['li:gəlaɪz] vt legalizzare.

legally ['li:gəlɪ] adv legalmente; **~ binding**
legalmente vincolante.

legal tender n moneta legale.

legation [lɪ'geɪʃən] n legazione f.

legend ['lɛdʒənd] n leggenda.

legendary ['lɛdʒəndərɪ] adj leggendario(a).

-legged ['lɛgɪd] suffix: **two~** a due gambe
(or zampe), bipede.

leggings ['lɛgɪŋz] npl ghette fpl.

leggy ['lɛgɪ] adj dalle gambe lunghe.

legibility [lɛdʒɪ'bɪlɪtɪ] n leggibilità.

legible ['lɛdʒəbl] adj leggibile.

legibly ['lɛdʒəblɪ] adv in modo leggibile.

legion ['li:dʒən] n legione f.

legionnaire [li:dʒə'nɛə*] n legionario; **~'s
disease** morbo del legionario.

legislate ['lɛdʒɪsleɪt] vi legiferare.

legislation [lɛdʒɪs'leɪʃən] n legislazione f; **a
piece of ~** una legge.

legislative ['lɛdʒɪslətɪv] adj legislativo(a).

legislator ['lɛdʒɪsleɪtə*] n legislatore/trice.

legislature ['lɛdʒɪslətʃə*] n corpo
legislativo.

legitimacy [lɪ'dʒɪtɪməsɪ] n legittimità.

legitimate [lɪ'dʒɪtɪmət] adj legittimo(a).

legitimize [lɪ'dʒɪtɪmaɪz] vt (gen)
legalizzare, rendere legale; (child)
legittimare.

legless ['lɛglɪs] adj (BRIT col) sbronzo(a),
fatto(a).

leg-room ['lɛgru:m] n spazio per le gambe.

Leics abbr (BRIT) = Leicestershire.

leisure ['lɛʒə*] n agio, tempo libero;
ricreazioni fpl; **at ~** all'agio; **a proprio
comodo.

leisure centre n centro di ricreazione.

leisurely ['lɛʒəlɪ] adj tranquillo(a); fatto(a)
con comodo or senza fretta.

leisure suit n (BRIT) tuta (da ginnastica).

lemon ['lɛmən] n limone m.

lemonade [lɛmə'neɪd] n limonata.

lemon cheese, lemon curd n crema di
limone (che si spalma sul pane etc).

lemon juice n succo di limone.

lemon squeezer n spremiagrumi m inv.

lemon tea n tè m inv al limone.

lend, pt, pp **lent** [lɛnd, lɛnt] vt: **to ~ sth (to
sb)** prestare qc (a qn); **to ~ a hand** dare
una mano.

lender ['lɛndə*] n prestatore/trice.

lending library ['lɛndɪŋ-] n biblioteca
circolante.

length [lɛŋθ] n lunghezza; (section: of road,
pipe etc) pezzo, tratto; **~ of time** periodo
(di tempo); **what ~ is it?** quant'è lungo?;
it is 2 metres in ~ è lungo 2 metri; **to fall
full ~** cadere lungo disteso; **at ~** (at last)
finalmente, alla fine; (lengthily) a lungo; **to
go to any ~(s)** to do sth fare qualsiasi
cosa pur di or per fare qc.

lengthen ['lɛŋθən] vt allungare, prolungare
♦ vi allungarsi.

lengthways ['lɛŋθweɪz] adv per il lungo.

lengthy ['lɛŋθɪ] adj molto lungo(a).

leniency ['li:nɪənsɪ] n indulgenza,
clemenza.

lenient ['li:nɪənt] adj indulgente, clemente.

leniently ['li:nɪəntlɪ] adv con indulgenza.
lens [lɛnz] n lente f; (of camera) obiettivo.
Lent [lɛnt] n Quaresima.
lent [lɛnt] pt, pp of **lend**.
lentil ['lɛntl] n lenticchia.
Leo ['li:əu] n Leone m; **to be** ~ essere del Leone.
leopard ['lɛpəd] n leopardo.
leotard ['li:ətɑːd] n calzamaglia.
leper ['lɛpə*] n lebbroso/a.
leper colony n lebbrosario.
leprosy ['lɛprəsɪ] n lebbra.
lesbian ['lɛzbɪən] n lesbica ♦ adj lesbico(a).
lesion ['li:ʒən] n (MED) lesione f.
Lesotho [lɪ'su:tu] n Lesotho m.
less [lɛs] adj, pron, adv meno; ~ **than you/ ever** meno di lei/che mai; ~ **than half** meno della metà; ~ **and** ~ sempre meno; **the** ~ **he works** ... meno lavora ...; ~ **than £1/a kilo/3 metres** meno di una sterlina/ un chilo/3 metri; ~ **5%** meno il 5%.
lessee [lɛ'si:] n affittuario/a, locatario/a.
lessen ['lɛsn] vi diminuire, attenuarsi ♦ vt diminuire, ridurre.
lesser ['lɛsə*] adj minore, più piccolo(a); **to a** ~ **extent** or **degree** in grado or misura minore.
lesson ['lɛsn] n lezione f; **a maths** ~ una lezione di matematica; **to give** ~s **in** dare or impartire lezioni di; **it taught him a** ~ (fig) gli è servito di lezione.
lessor ['lɛsɔ:*, lɛ'sɔ:*] n locatore/trice.
lest [lɛst] conj per paura di + infinitive, per paura che + sub.
let, pt, pp **let** [lɛt] vt lasciare; (BRIT: lease) dare in affitto; **to** ~ **sb do sth** lasciar fare qc a qn, lasciare che qn faccia qc; **to** ~ **sb know sth** far sapere qc a qn; **to** ~ **sb have sth** dare qc a qn; **he** ~ **me go** mi ha lasciato andare; ~ **the water boil and** ... fate bollire l'acqua e ...; ~'s **go** andiamo; ~ **him come** lo lasci venire; "**to** ~" "affittasi".
▶**let down** vt (lower) abbassare; (dress) allungare; (hair) sciogliere; (disappoint) deludere; (BRIT: tyre) sgonfiare.
▶**let go** vi mollare ♦ vt mollare; (allow to go) lasciare andare.
▶**let in** vt lasciare entrare; (visitor etc) far entrare; **what have you** ~ **yourself in for?** in che guai or pasticci sei andato a cacciarti?
▶**let off** vt (allow to go) lasciare andare; (firework etc) far partire; (smell etc) emettere; (subj: taxi driver, bus driver) far scendere; **to** ~ **off steam** (fig col) sfogarsi, scaricarsi.
▶**let on** vi (col): **to** ~ **on that** ... lasciar

capire che ....
▶**let out** vt lasciare uscire; (dress) allargare; (scream) emettere; (rent out) affittare, dare in affitto.
▶**let up** vi diminuire.
let-down ['lɛtdaun] n (disappointment) delusione f.
lethal ['li:θl] adj letale, mortale.
lethargic [lɛ'θɑːdʒɪk] adj letargico(a).
lethargy ['lɛθədʒɪ] n letargia.
letter ['lɛtə*] n lettera; ~s npl (LITERATURE) lettere; **small/capital** ~ lettera minuscola/maiuscola; ~ **of credit** lettera di credito; **documentary** ~ **of credit** lettera di credito documentata.
letter bomb n lettera esplosiva.
letterbox ['lɛtəbɔks] n buca delle lettere.
letterhead ['lɛtəhɛd] n intestazione f.
lettering ['lɛtərɪŋ] n iscrizione f; caratteri mpl.
letter-opener ['lɛtərəupnə*] n tagliacarte m inv.
letterpress ['lɛtəprɛs] n (method) rilievografia.
letter quality n (of printer) qualità di stampa.
letters patent npl brevetto di invenzione.
lettuce ['lɛtɪs] n lattuga, insalata.
let-up ['lɛtʌp] n (col) interruzione f.
leukaemia, (US) **leukemia** [lu:'ki:mɪə] n leucemia.
level ['lɛvl] adj piatto(a), piano(a); orizzontale ♦ n livello; (also: **spirit** ~) livella (a bolla d'aria) ♦ vt livellare, spianare; (gun) puntare (verso); (accusation): **to** ~ (**against**) lanciare (a or contro) ♦ vi (col): **to** ~ **with sb** essere franco(a) con qn; **to be** ~ **with** essere alla pari di; **a** ~ **spoonful** (CULIN) un cucchiaio raso; **to draw** ~ **with** (team) mettersi alla pari di; (runner, car) affiancarsi a; **A** ~ **s** npl (BRIT) ≈ esami mpl di maturità; **O** ~ **s** npl (BRIT: formerly) diploma di istruzione secondaria conseguito a 16 anni in Inghilterra e Galles, ora sostituito dal GCSE; **on the** ~ piatto(a); (fig) onesto(a).
▶**level off, level out** vi (prices etc) stabilizzarsi; (ground) diventare pianeggiante; (aircraft) volare in quota.
level crossing n (BRIT) passaggio a livello.
level-headed [lɛvl'hɛdɪd] adj equilibrato(a).
levelling, (US) **leveling** ['lɛvlɪŋ] adj (process, effect) di livellamento.
level playing field n: **to compete on a** ~ (fig) competere ad armi pari.
lever ['li:və*] n leva ♦ vt: **to** ~ **up/out** sollevare/estrarre con una leva.

leverage ['li:vərɪdʒ] *n*: ~ **(on** *or* **with)** ascendente *m* (su).
levity ['lɛvɪtɪ] *n* leggerezza, frivolità.
levy ['lɛvɪ] *n* tassa, imposta ♦ *vt* imporre.
lewd [lu:d] *adj* osceno(a), lascivo(a).
lexicographer [lɛksɪ'kɔgrəfə*] *n* lessicografo/a.
lexicography [lɛksɪ'kɔgrəfɪ] *n* lessicografia.
LGV *n abbr* (*BRIT*: = *Large Goods Vehicle*) automezzo pesante.
LI *abbr* (*US*) = *Long Island*.
liabilities [laɪə'bɪlətɪz] *npl* debiti *mpl*; (*on balance sheet*) passivo.
liability [laɪə'bɪlətɪ] *n* responsabilità *f inv*; (*handicap*) peso.
liable ['laɪəbl] *adj* (*subject*): ~ **to** soggetto(a) a; passibile di; (*responsible*): ~ **(for)** responsabile (di); (*likely*): ~ **to do** propenso(a) a fare; **to be** ~ **to a fine** essere passibile di multa.
liaise [li:'eɪz] *vi*: **to** ~ **(with)** mantenere i contatti (con).
liaison [li:'eɪzɔn] *n* relazione *f*; (*MIL*) collegamento.
liar ['laɪə*] *n* bugiardo/a.
libel ['laɪbl] *n* libello, diffamazione *f* ♦ *vt* diffamare.
libellous, (*US*) **libelous** ['laɪbləs] *adj* diffamatorio(a).
liberal ['lɪbərl] *adj* liberale; (*generous*): **to be** ~ **with** distribuire liberalmente ♦ *n* (*POL*): **L~** liberale *m/f*.
Liberal Democrat *n* liberal-democratico(a).
liberality [lɪbə'rælɪtɪ] *n* (*generosity*) generosità, liberalità.
liberalize ['lɪbərəlaɪz] *vt* liberalizzare.
liberal-minded [lɪbərl'maɪndɪd] *adj* tollerante.
liberate ['lɪbəreɪt] *vt* liberare.
liberation [lɪbə'reɪʃən] *n* liberazione *f*.
liberation theology *n* teologia della liberazione.
Liberia [laɪ'bɪərɪə] *n* Liberia.
Liberian [laɪ'bɪərɪən] *adj*, *n* liberiano(a).
liberty ['lɪbətɪ] *n* libertà *f inv*; **at** ~ **to do** libero(a) di fare; **to take the** ~ **of** prendersi la libertà di, permettersi di.
libido [lɪ'bi:dəu] *n* libido *f*.
Libra ['li:brə] *n* Bilancia; **to be** ~ essere della Bilancia.
librarian [laɪ'brɛərɪən] *n* bibliotecario/a.
library ['laɪbrərɪ] *n* biblioteca.
library book *n* libro della biblioteca.
libretto [lɪ'brɛtəu] *n* libretto.
Libya ['lɪbɪə] *n* Libia.
Libyan ['lɪbɪən] *adj*, *n* libico(a).
lice [laɪs] *npl of* **louse**.

licence, (*US*) **license** ['laɪsns] *n* autorizzazione *f*, permesso; (*COMM*) licenza; (*RADIO*, *TV*) canone *m*, abbonamento; (*also*: **driving** ~, (*US*) **driver's** ~) patente *f* di guida; (*excessive freedom*) licenza; **import** ~ licenza di importazione; **produced under** ~ prodotto su licenza.
licence number *n* (*BRIT AUT*) numero di targa.
license ['laɪsns] *n* (*US*) = **licence** ♦ *vt* dare una licenza a; (*car*) pagare la tassa di circolazione *or* il bollo di.
licensed ['laɪsnst] *adj* (*for alcohol*) che ha la licenza di vendere bibite alcoliche.
licensed trade *n* commercio di bevande alcoliche con licenza speciale.
licensee [laɪsən'si:] *n* (*BRIT*: *of pub*) detentore/trice di autorizzazione alla vendita di bevande alcoliche.
license plate *n* (*esp US AUT*) targa (automobilistica).
licentious [laɪ'sɛnʃəs] *adj* licenzioso(a).
lichen ['laɪkən] *n* lichene *m*.
lick [lɪk] *vt* leccare; (*col*: *defeat*) suonarle a, stracciare ♦ *n* leccata; **a** ~ **of paint** una passata di vernice.
licorice ['lɪkərɪs] *n* = **liquorice**.
lid [lɪd] *n* coperchio; **to take the** ~ **off sth** (*fig*) smascherare qc.
lido ['laɪdəu] *n* piscina all'aperto; (*part of the beach*) lido, stabilimento balneare.
lie [laɪ] *n* bugia, menzogna ♦ *vi* mentire, dire bugie; (*pt* **lay**, *pp* **lain** [leɪ, leɪn]) (*rest*) giacere, star disteso(a); (*in grave*) giacere, riposare; (*of object*: *be situated*) trovarsi, essere; **to tell** ~**s** raccontare *or* dire bugie; **to** ~ **low** (*fig*) latitare.
► **lie about** *vi* (*things*) essere in giro; (*person*) bighellonare.
► **lie back** *vi* stendersi.
► **lie down** *vi* stendersi, sdraiarsi.
► **lie up** *vi* (*hide*) nascondersi.
Liechtenstein ['lɪktənstaɪn] *n* Liechtenstein *m*.
lie detector *n* macchina della verità.
lie-down ['laɪdaun] *n* (*BRIT*): **to have a** ~ sdraiarsi, riposarsi.
lie-in ['laɪɪn] *n* (*BRIT*): **to have a** ~ rimanere a letto.
lieu [lu:] *n*: **in** ~ **of** invece di, al posto di.
Lieut. *abbr* (= *lieutenant*) Ten.
lieutenant [lɛf'tɛnənt, (*US*) lu:'tɛnənt] *n* tenente *m*.
lieutenant-colonel [lɛf'tɛnənt'kə:nl, (*US*) lu:'tɛnənt'kə:nl] *n* tenente colonnello.
life [laɪf] *n* (*pl* **lives**) vita ♦ *cpd* di vita; della vita; **a** ~ a vita; **country/city** ~ vita di

campagna/di città; **to be sent to prison
for** ~ essere condannato all'ergastolo;
true to ~ fedele alla realtà; **to paint from**
~ dipingere dal vero.
life annuity n rendita vitalizia.
life assurance n (BRIT) = **life insurance**.
lifebelt ['laɪfbɛlt] n (BRIT) salvagente m.
lifeblood ['laɪfblʌd] n (fig) linfa vitale.
lifeboat ['laɪfbəut] n scialuppa di
salvataggio.
life expectancy n durata media della vita.
lifeguard ['laɪfgɑːd] n bagnino.
life imprisonment n ergastolo.
life insurance n assicurazione f sulla vita.
life jacket n giubbotto di salvataggio.
lifeless ['laɪflɪs] adj senza vita.
lifelike ['laɪflaɪk] adj che sembra vero(a);
rassomigliante.
lifeline ['laɪflaɪn] n cavo di salvataggio.
lifelong ['laɪflɔŋ] adj per tutta la vita.
life preserver n (US) salvagente m;
giubbotto di salvataggio; (BRIT)
sfollagente m inv.
lifer ['laɪfə*] n (col) ergastolano/a.
life-raft ['laɪfrɑːft] n zattera di salvataggio.
life-saver ['laɪfseɪvə*] n bagnino.
life sentence n (condanna all')ergastolo.
life-sized ['laɪfsaɪzd] adj a grandezza
naturale.
life span n (durata della) vita.
life style n stile m di vita.
life support system n (MED) respiratore
m automatico.
lifetime ['laɪftaɪm] n: **in his** ~ durante la
sua vita; **in a** ~ nell'arco della vita; in
tutta la vita; **the chance of a** ~
un'occasione unica.
lift [lɪft] vt sollevare, levare; (steal)
prendere, rubare ♦ vi (fog) alzarsi ♦ n
(BRIT: elevator) ascensore m; **to give sb a** ~
(BRIT) dare un passaggio a qn.
►**lift off** vt togliere ♦ vi (rocket) partire;
(helicopter) decollare.
►**lift out** vt tirar fuori; (troops, evacuees
etc) far evacuare per mezzo di elicotteri
(or aerei).
►**lift up** vt sollevare, alzare.
lift-off ['lɪftɔf] n decollo.
ligament ['lɪgəmənt] n legamento.
light [laɪt] n luce, lume m; (daylight) luce,
giorno; (lamp) lampada; (AUT: rear ~) luce
di posizione; (: headlamp) fanale m; (for
cigarette etc): **have you got a** ~? ha da
accendere? ♦ vt (pt, pp **lighted** or **lit** [lɪt])
(candle, cigarette, fire) accendere; (room)
illuminare ♦ adj (room, colour) chiaro(a);
(not heavy, also fig) leggero(a) ♦ adv
(travel) con poco bagaglio; ~**s** npl (AUT:

traffic ~s) semaforo; **in the** ~ **of** alla luce
di; **to turn the** ~ **on/off** accendere/
spegnere la luce; **to come to** ~ venire in
luce; **to cast** or **shed** or **throw** ~ **on**
gettare luce su; **to make** ~ **of sth** (fig)
prendere alla leggera qc, non dar peso a
qc.
►**light up** vi illuminarsi ♦ vt illuminare.
light bulb n lampadina.
lighten ['laɪtn] vi schiarirsi ♦ vt (give light
to) illuminare; (make lighter) schiarire;
(make less heavy) alleggerire.
lighter ['laɪtə*] n (also: **cigarette** ~)
accendino; (boat) chiatta.
light-fingered [laɪt'fɪŋgəd] adj lesto(a) di
mano.
light-headed ['laɪt'hɛdɪd] adj stordito(a).
light-hearted ['laɪt'hɑːtɪd] adj gioioso(a),
gaio(a).
lighthouse ['laɪthaus] n faro.
lighting ['laɪtɪŋ] n illuminazione f.
lighting-up time ['laɪtɪŋʌp-] n (BRIT) orario
per l'accensione delle luci.
lightly ['laɪtlɪ] adv leggermente; **to get off** ~
cavarsela a buon mercato.
light meter n (PHOT) esposimetro.
lightness ['laɪtnɪs] n chiarezza; (in weight)
leggerezza.
lightning ['laɪtnɪŋ] n lampo, fulmine m; **a
flash of** ~ un lampo, un fulmine.
lightning conductor, (US) **lightning rod**
n parafulmine m.
lightning strike n (BRIT) sciopero m lampo
inv.
light pen n penna luminosa.
lightship ['laɪtʃɪp] n battello m faro inv.
lightweight ['laɪtweɪt] adj (suit) leggero(a);
(boxer) peso leggero inv.
light year ['laɪtjɪə*] n anno m luce inv.
Ligurian [lɪ'gjuərɪən] adj, n ligure (m/f).
like [laɪk] vt (person) volere bene a; (activity,
object, food): **I** ~ **swimming/that book/
chocolate** mi piace nuotare/quel libro/il
cioccolato ♦ prep come ♦ adj simile, uguale
♦ n: **the** ~ uno(a) uguale; **I would** ~, **I'd** ~
mi piacerebbe, vorrei; **would you** ~ **a
coffee?** gradirebbe un caffè?; **if you** ~ se
vuoi; **to be/look** ~ **sb/sth** somigliare a qn/
qc; **what's he** ~? che tipo è?, com'è?;
what's the weather ~? che tempo fa?;
that's just ~ **him** è proprio da lui;
something ~ **that** qualcosa del genere; **I
feel** ~ **a drink** avrei voglia di bere
qualcosa; **there's nothing** ~ ... non c'è
niente di meglio di or niente come ...; **his**
~**s and dislikes** i suoi gusti.
likeable ['laɪkəbl] adj simpatico(a).
likelihood ['laɪklɪhud] n probabilità; **in all** ~

con ogni probabilità, molto
probabilmente.
likely['laɪklɪ] *adj* probabile; plausibile; **he's**
~ **to leave** probabilmente partirà, è
probabile che parta; **not** ~! (*col*) neanche
per sogno!
like-minded['laɪk'maɪndɪd] *adj* che pensa
allo stesso modo.
liken['laɪkən] *vt*: **to** ~ **sth to** paragonare qc
a.
likeness['laɪknɪs] *n* (*similarity*) somiglianza.
likewise['laɪkwaɪz] *adv* similmente, nello
stesso modo.
liking['laɪkɪŋ] *n*: ~ (**for**) simpatia (per);
debole *m* (per); **to be to sb's** ~ essere di
gusto *or* gradimento di qn; **to take a** ~ **to**
sb prendere qn in simpatia.
lilac['laɪlək] *n* lilla *m inv* ♦ *adj* lilla *inv.*
Lilo ®['laɪləu] *n* materassino gonfiabile.
lilt[lɪlt] *n* cadenza.
lilting['lɪltɪŋ] *adj* melodioso(a).
lily['lɪlɪ] *n* giglio; ~ **of the valley** mughetto.
Lima['li:mə] *n* Lima.
limb[lɪm] *n* membro; **to be out on a** ~ (*fig*)
sentirsi spaesato *or* tagliato fuori.
limber['lɪmbə*] : **to** ~ **up** *vi* riscaldarsi i
muscoli.
limbo['lɪmbəu] *n*: **to be in** ~ (*fig*) essere
lasciato(a) nel dimenticatoio.
lime[laɪm] *n* (*tree*) tiglio; (*fruit*) limetta;
(*GEO*) calce *f.*
lime juice*n* succo di limetta.
limelight['laɪmlaɪt] *n*: **in the** ~ (*fig*) alla
ribalta, in vista.
limerick['lɪmərɪk] *n poesiola umoristica di
cinque versi.*
limestone['laɪmstəun] *n* pietra calcarea;
(*GEO*) calcare *m.*
limit['lɪmɪt] *n* limite *m* ♦ *vt* limitare;
weight/speed ~ limite di peso/di
velocità; **within** ~**s** entro certi limiti.
limitation[lɪmɪ'teɪʃən] *n* limitazione *f,*
limite *m.*
limited['lɪmɪtɪd] *adj* limitato(a),
ristretto(a); ~ **edition** edizione *f* a bassa
tiratura.
limited (liability) company (Ltd)*n* (*BRIT*)
≈ società *f inv* a responsabilità limitata
(S.r.l.).
limitless['lɪmɪtlɪs] *adj* illimitato(a).
limousine['lɪməziːn] *n* limousine *f inv.*
limp[lɪmp] *n*: **to have a** ~ zoppicare ♦ *vi*
zoppicare ♦ *adj* floscio(a), flaccido(a).
limpet['lɪmpɪt] *n* patella.
limpid['lɪmpɪd] *adj* (*poet*) limpido(a).
linchpin['lɪntʃpɪn] *n* acciarino, bietta; (*fig*)
perno.
Lincs*abbr* (*BRIT*) = Lincolnshire.

line[laɪn] *n* (*gen*, *COMM*) linea; (*rope*) corda;
(*wire*) filo; (*of poem*) verso; (*row*, *series*)
fila, riga; coda ♦ *vt* (*clothes*): **to** ~ (**with**)
foderare (di); (*box*): **to** ~ (**with**) rivestire
or foderare (di); (*subj*: *trees*, *crowd*)
fiancheggiare; **to cut in** ~ (*US*) passare
avanti; **in his** ~ **of business** nel suo ramo
(di affari); **on the right** ~**s** sulla buona
strada; **a new** ~ **in cosmetics** una nuova
linea di cosmetici; **hold the** ~ **please** (*BRIT
TEL*) resti in linea per cortesia; **to be in** ~
for sth (*fig*) essere in lista per qc; **in** ~
with d'accordo con, in linea con; **to bring**
sth into ~ **with sth** mettere qc al passo
con qc; **to draw the** ~ **at (doing) sth** (*fig*)
rifiutarsi di fare qc; **to take the** ~ **that ...**
essere del parere che ....
▶**line up***vi* allinearsi, mettersi in fila ♦ *vt*
mettere in fila; **to have sth** ~**d up** avere
qc in programma; **to have sb** ~**d up**
avere qn in mente.
linear['lɪnɪə*] *adj* lineare.
lined[laɪnd] *adj* (*paper*) a righe, rigato(a);
(*face*) rugoso(a); (*clothes*) foderato(a).
line feed*n* (*COMPUT*) avanzamento di una
interlinea.
linen['lɪnɪn] *n* biancheria, panni *mpl*; (*cloth*)
tela di lino.
line printer*n* stampante *f* parallela.
liner['laɪnə*] *n* nave *f* di linea; **dustbin** ~
sacchetto per la pattumiera.
linesman['laɪnzmən] *n* guardalinee *m inv,*
segnalinee *m inv.*
line-up['laɪnʌp] *n* allineamento, fila; (*also*:
police ~) confronto all'americana;
(*SPORT*) formazione *f* di gioco.
linger['lɪŋgə*] *vi* attardarsi; indugiare;
(*smell*, *tradition*) persistere.
lingerie['lænʒəriː] *n* biancheria intima
(femminile).
lingering['lɪŋgərɪŋ] *adj* lungo(a);
persistente; (*death*) lento(a).
lingo, ~ **es**['lɪŋgəu] *n* (*pej*) gergo.
linguist['lɪŋgwɪst] *n* linguista *m/f*; poliglotta
m/f.
linguistic[lɪŋ'gwɪstɪk] *adj* linguistico(a).
linguistics[lɪŋ'gwɪstɪks] *n* linguistica.
lining['laɪnɪŋ] *n* fodera; (*TECH*)
rivestimento (interno); (*of brake*)
guarnizione *f.*
link[lɪŋk] *n* (*of a chain*) anello; (*connection*)
legame *m*, collegamento; (*COMPUT*) link,
collegamento ♦ *vt* collegare, unire,
congiungere; (*COMPUT*) creare un
collegamento con ♦ *vi* (*COMPUT*): **to** ~ **to a**
site creare un collegamento con un sitio;
rail ~ collegamento ferroviario; *see also*
links.

▶link up vt collegare, unire ♦ vi riunirsi; associarsi.
links [lɪŋks] npl pista or terreno da golf.
link-up ['lɪŋkʌp] n legame m; (of roads) nodo; (of spaceships) aggancio; (RADIO, TV) collegamento.
linoleum [lɪ'nəʊlɪəm] n linoleum m inv.
linseed oil ['lɪnsiːd-] n olio di semi di lino.
lint [lɪnt] n garza.
lintel ['lɪntl] n architrave f.
lion ['laɪən] n leone m.
lion cub n leoncino.
lioness ['laɪənɪs] n leonessa.
lip [lɪp] n labbro; (of cup etc) orlo; (insolence) sfacciataggine f.
liposuction ['lɪpəʊsʌkʃən] n liposuzione f.
lipread ['lɪpriːd] vi leggere sulle labbra.
lip salve n burro di cacao.
lip service n: to pay ~ to sth essere favorevole a qc solo a parole.
lipstick ['lɪpstɪk] n rossetto.
liquefy ['lɪkwɪfaɪ] vt liquefare ♦ vi liquefarsi.
liqueur [lɪ'kjʊə*] n liquore m.
liquid ['lɪkwɪd] n liquido ♦ adj liquido(a).
liquid assets npl attività fpl liquide, crediti mpl liquidi.
liquidate ['lɪkwɪdeɪt] vt liquidare.
liquidation [lɪkwɪ'deɪʃən] n liquidazione f; to go into ~ andare in liquidazione.
liquidator ['lɪkwɪdeɪtə*] n liquidatore m.
liquid crystal display (LCD) n visualizzazione f a cristalli liquidi.
liquidity [lɪ'kwɪdɪtɪ] n (COMM) liquidità.
liquidize ['lɪkwɪdaɪz] vt (BRIT CULIN) passare al frullatore.
liquidizer ['lɪkwɪdaɪzə*] n (BRIT CULIN) frullatore m (a brocca).
liquor ['lɪkə*] n alcool m.
liquorice ['lɪkərɪs] n liquirizia.
Lisbon ['lɪzbən] n Lisbona.
lisp [lɪsp] n difetto nel pronunciare le sibilanti.
lissom ['lɪsəm] adj leggiadro(a).
list [lɪst] n lista, elenco; (of ship) sbandamento ♦ vt (write down) mettere in lista; fare una lista di; (enumerate) elencare; (COMPUT) stampare (un prospetto di) ♦ vi (ship) sbandare; shopping ~ lista or nota della spesa.
listed building ['lɪstəd-] n (ARCHIT) edificio sotto la protezione delle Belle Arti.
listed company n società quotata in Borsa.
listen ['lɪsn] vi ascoltare; to ~ to ascoltare.
listener ['lɪsnə*] n ascoltatore/trice.
listeria [lɪs'tɪərɪə] n listeria.
listing ['lɪstɪŋ] n (COMPUT) lista stampata.

listless ['lɪstlɪs] adj svogliato(a); apatico(a).
listlessly ['lɪstlɪslɪ] adv svogliatamente; apaticamente.
list price n prezzo di listino.
lit [lɪt] pt, pp of light.
litany ['lɪtənɪ] n litania.
liter ['liːtə*] n (US) = litre.
literacy ['lɪtərəsɪ] n il sapere leggere e scrivere.
literacy campaign n lotta contro l'analfabetismo.
literal ['lɪtərl] adj letterale.
literally ['lɪtərəlɪ] adv alla lettera, letteralmente.
literary ['lɪtərərɪ] adj letterario(a).
literate ['lɪtərɪt] adj che sa leggere e scrivere.
literature ['lɪtərɪtʃə*] n letteratura; (brochures etc) materiale m.
lithe [laɪð] adj agile, snello(a).
lithography [lɪ'θɒgrəfɪ] n litografia.
Lithuania [lɪθju'eɪnɪə] n Lituania.
Lithuanian [lɪθju'eɪnɪən] adj lituano(a) ♦ n lituano/a; (LING) lituano.
litigate ['lɪtɪgeɪt] vt muovere causa a ♦ vi litigare.
litigation [lɪtɪ'geɪʃən] n causa.
litmus ['lɪtməs] n: ~ paper cartina di tornasole.
litre, (US) liter ['liːtə*] n litro.
litter ['lɪtə*] n (rubbish) rifiuti mpl; (young animals) figliata ♦ vt sparpagliare; lasciare rifiuti in; ~ed with coperto(a) di.
litter bin n (BRIT) cestino per rifiuti.
litter lout, (US) litterbug ['lɪtəbʌg] n persona che butta per terra le cartacce o i rifiuti.
little ['lɪtl] adj (small) piccolo(a); (not much) poco(a) ♦ adv poco; a ~ un po' (di); a ~ milk un po' di latte; with ~ difficulty senza fatica or difficoltà; ~ by ~ a poco a poco; as ~ as possible il meno possibile; for a ~ while per un po'; to make ~ of dare poca importanza a; ~ finger mignolo.
little-known ['lɪtl'nəʊn] adj poco noto(a).
liturgy ['lɪtədʒɪ] n liturgia.
live vi [lɪv] vivere; (reside) vivere, abitare ♦ adj [laɪv] (animal) vivo(a); (issue) scottante, d'attualità; (wire) sotto tensione; (broadcast) diretto(a); (ammunition: not blank) carico(a); (unexploded) inesploso(a); to ~ in London abitare a Londra; to ~ together vivere insieme, convivere.
▶live down vt far dimenticare (alla gente).
▶live in vi essere interno(a); avere vitto e

alloggio.

▶**live off** vi (land, fish etc) vivere di; (pej: parents etc) vivere alle spalle or a spese di.

▶**live on** vt fus (food) vivere di ♦ vi sopravvivere, continuare a vivere; **to** ~ **on £50 a week** vivere con 50 sterline la settimana.

▶**live out** vi (BRIT: students) essere esterno(a) ♦ vt: **to** ~ **out one's days** or **life** trascorrere gli ultimi anni.

▶**live up** vt: **to** ~ **it up** (col) fare la bella vita.

▶**live up to** vt fus tener fede a, non venir meno a.

live-in ['lɪvɪn] adj (col: partner) convivente; (servant) che vive in casa; **he has a** ~ **girlfriend** la sua ragazza vive con lui.

livelihood ['laɪvlɪhud] n mezzi mpl di sostentamento.

liveliness ['laɪvlɪnəs] n vivacità.

lively ['laɪvlɪ] adj vivace, vivo(a).

liven up ['laɪvn-] vt (room etc) ravvivare; (discussion, evening) animare.

liver ['lɪvə*] n fegato.

liverish ['lɪvərɪʃ] adj che soffre di mal di fegato; (fig) scontroso(a).

Liverpudlian [lɪvə'pʌdlɪən] adj di Liverpool ♦ n abitante m/f di Liverpool; originario/a di Liverpool.

livery ['lɪvərɪ] n livrea.

lives [laɪvz] npl of **life**.

livestock ['laɪvstɔk] n bestiame m.

live wire [laɪv-] n (col: fig): **to be a** ~ essere pieno(a) di vitalità.

livid ['lɪvɪd] adj livido(a); (furious) livido(a) di rabbia, furibondo(a).

living ['lɪvɪŋ] adj vivo(a), vivente ♦ n: **to earn** or **make a** ~ guadagnarsi la vita; **cost of** ~ costo della vita, carovita m; **within** ~ **memory** a memoria d'uomo.

living conditions npl condizioni fpl di vita.

living expenses npl spese fpl di mantenimento.

living room n soggiorno.

living standards npl tenore m di vita.

living wage n salario sufficiente per vivere.

lizard ['lɪzəd] n lucertola.

llama ['lɑːmə] n lama m inv.

LLB n abbr (= Bachelor of Laws) ≈ laurea in legge.

LLD n abbr (= Doctor of Laws) titolo di studio.

LMT abbr (US: = Local Mean Time) tempo medio locale.

load [ləud] n (weight) peso; (ELEC, TECH, thing carried) carico ♦ vt: **to** ~ **(with)** (lorry,

ship) caricare (di); (gun, camera) caricare (con); **a** ~ **of**, ~**s of** (fig) un sacco di; **to** ~ **a program** (COMPUT) caricare un programma.

loaded ['ləudɪd] adj (dice) falsato(a); (question, word) capzioso(a); (col: rich) pieno(a) di soldi.

loading bay ['ləudɪŋ-] n piazzola di carico.

loaf [ləuf] n (pl **loaves**) pane m, pagnotta ♦ vi (also: ~ **about**, ~ **around**) bighellonare.

loam [ləum] n terra di marna.

loan [ləun] n prestito ♦ vt dare in prestito; **on** ~ in prestito.

loan account n conto dei prestiti.

loan capital n capitale m di prestito.

loan shark n (col: pej) strozzino(a).

loath [ləuθ] adj: **to be** ~ **to do** essere restio(a) a fare.

loathe [ləuð] vt detestare, aborrire.

loathing ['ləuðɪŋ] n aborrimento, disgusto.

loathsome ['ləuðsəm] adj (gen) ripugnante; (person) detestabile, odioso(a).

loaves [ləuvz] npl of **loaf**.

lob [lɔb] vt (ball) lanciare.

lobby ['lɔbɪ] n atrio, vestibolo; (POL: pressure group) gruppo di pressione ♦ vt fare pressione su.

lobbyist ['lɔbɪɪst] n appartenente m/f ad un gruppo di pressione.

lobe [ləub] n lobo.

lobster ['lɔbstə*] n aragosta.

lobster pot n nassa per aragoste.

local ['ləukl] adj locale ♦ n (BRIT: pub) ≈ bar m inv all'angolo; **the** ~**s** npl la gente della zona.

local anaesthetic n anestesia locale.

local authority n autorità locale.

local call n (TEL) telefonata urbana.

local government n amministrazione f locale.

locality [ləu'kælɪtɪ] n località f inv; (position) posto, luogo.

localize ['ləukəlaɪz] vt localizzare.

locally ['ləukəlɪ] adv da queste parti; nel vicinato.

locate [ləu'keɪt] vt (find) trovare; (situate) collocare.

location [ləu'keɪʃən] n posizione f; **on** ~ (CINE) all'esterno.

loch [lɔx] n lago.

lock [lɔk] n (of door, box) serratura; (of canal) chiusa; (of hair) ciocca, riccio ♦ vt (with key) chiudere a chiave; (immobilize) bloccare ♦ vi (door etc) chiudersi; (wheels) bloccarsi, incepparsi; ~ **stock and barrel** (fig) in blocco; **on full** ~ (BRIT AUT) a tutto sterzo.

▶**lock away** vt (valuables) tenere

(rinchiuso(a)) al sicuro; (*criminal*) metter dentro.

▶**lock out** *vt* chiudere fuori; **to** ~ **workers out** fare una serrata.

▶**lock up** *vi* chiudere tutto (a chiave).

locker ['lɔkə*] *n* armadietto.

locket ['lɔkɪt] *n* medaglione *m*.

lockjaw ['lɔkdʒɔ:] *n* tetano.

lockout ['lɔkaut] *n* (*INDUSTRY*) serrata.

locksmith ['lɔksmɪθ] *n* magnano.

lock-up ['lɔkʌp] *n* (*prison*) prigione *f*; (*cell*) guardina; (*also*: ~ **garage**) box *m inv*.

locomotive [lɔukə'mɔutɪv] *n* locomotiva.

locum ['lɔukəm] *n* (*MED*) medico sostituto.

locust ['lɔukəst] *n* locusta.

lodge [lɔdʒ] *n* casetta, portineria; (*FREEMASONRY*) loggia ♦ *vi* (*person*): **to** ~ (**with**) essere a pensione (presso *or* da) ♦ *vt* (*appeal etc*) presentare, fare; **to** ~ **a complaint** presentare un reclamo; **to** ~ (**itself**) **in/between** piantarsi dentro/fra.

lodger ['lɔdʒə*] *n* affittuario/a; (*with room and meals*) pensionante *m/f*.

lodging ['lɔdʒɪŋ] *n* alloggio; *see also* **board**; **lodgings**.

lodging house *n* (*BRIT*) casa con camere in affitto.

lodgings ['lɔdʒɪŋz] *npl* camera d'affitto; camera ammobiliata.

loft [lɔft] *n* soffitta; (*AGR*) granaio; (*US*) appartamento ricavato da solaio (*or* granaio *etc*).

lofty ['lɔftɪ] *adj* alto(a); (*haughty*) altezzoso(a); (*sentiments, aims*) nobile.

log [lɔg] *n* (*of wood*) ceppo; (*book*) = **logbook** ♦ *n abbr* = **logarithm** ♦ *vt* registrare.

▶**log in, log on** *vi* (*COMPUT*) aprire una sessione (*con codice di riconoscimento*).

▶**log off, log out** *vi* (*COMPUT*) terminare una sessione.

logarithm ['lɔgərɪðm] *n* logaritmo.

logbook ['lɔgbuk] *n* (*NAUT, AVIAT*) diario di bordo; (*AUT*) libretto di circolazione; (*of lorry driver*) registro di viaggio; (*of events, movement of goods etc*) registro.

log cabin *n* capanna di tronchi.

log fire *n* fuoco di legna.

logger ['lɔgə*] *n* boscaiolo, taglialegna *m inv*.

loggerheads ['lɔgəhɛdz] *npl*: **at** ~ (**with**) ai ferri corti (con).

logic ['lɔdʒɪk] *n* logica.

logical ['lɔdʒɪkəl] *adj* logico(a).

logically ['lɔdʒɪkəlɪ] *adv* logicamente.

logistics [lɔ'dʒɪstɪks] *n* logistica.

logjam ['lɔgdʒæm] *n*: **to break the** ~ superare l'impasse.

logo ['lɔugəu] *n* logo *m inv*.

loin [lɔɪn] *n* (*CULIN*) lombata; ~**s** *npl* reni *fpl*.

loin cloth *n* perizoma *m*.

loiter ['lɔɪtə*] *vi* attardarsi; **to** ~ (**about**) indugiare, bighellonare.

loll [lɔl] *vi* (*also*: ~ **about**) essere stravaccato(a).

lollipop ['lɔlɪpɔp] *n* lecca lecca *m inv*.

lollipop man, lollipop lady *n* (*BRIT*) *see boxed note.*

LOLLIPOP MAN/LADY

In Gran Bretagna il **lollipop man** *e la* **lollipop lady** *sono persone incaricate di regolare il traffico in prossimità delle scuole e di aiutare i bambini ad attraversare la strada; usano una paletta la cui forma ricorda quella di un lecca lecca, in inglese, appunto, "lollipop".*

---

lollop ['lɔləp] *vi* (*BRIT*) camminare (*or* correre) goffamente.

lolly ['lɔlɪ] (*col*) *n* lecca lecca *m inv*; (*also*: **ice** ~) ghiacciolo; (*money*) grana.

Lombardy ['lɔmbədɪ] *n* Lombardia.

London ['lʌndən] *n* Londra.

Londoner ['lʌndənə*] *n* londinese *m/f*.

lone [lɔun] *adj* solitario(a).

loneliness ['lɔunlɪnɪs] *n* solitudine.

lonely ['lɔunlɪ] *adj* solitario(a); (*place*) isolato(a); **to feel** ~ sentirsi solo(a).

lonely hearts *adj*: ~ **ads**, ~ **column** messaggi *mpl* personali.

lone parent *n* (*unmarried*: *mother*) ragazza madre; (: *father*) ragazzo padre; (*divorced*) genitore *m* divorziato(a); (*widowed*) genitore rimasto vedovo.

loner ['lɔunə*] *n* solitario/a.

lonesome ['lɔunsəm] *adj* solo(a).

long [lɔŋ] *adj* lungo(a) ♦ *adv* a lungo, per molto tempo ♦ *n*: **the** ~ **and the short of it is that** ... (*fig*) a farla breve ... ♦ *vi*: **to** ~ **for sth/to do** desiderare qc/di fare; non veder l'ora di aver qc/di fare; **he had** ~ **understood that** ... aveva capito da molto tempo che ...; **how** ~ **is this river/course?** quanto è lungo questo fiume/corso?; **6 metres** ~ lungo 6 metri; **6 months** ~ che dura 6 mesi, di 6 mesi; **all night** ~ tutta la notte; **he no** ~**er comes** non viene più; ~ **before** molto tempo prima; **before** ~ (+ *future*) presto, fra poco; (+ *past*) poco tempo dopo; ~ **ago** molto tempo fa; **don't be** ~! faccia presto!; **I shan't be** ~ non ne avrò per molto; **at** ~ **last** finalmente; **in the** ~ **run** alla fin fine; **so** *or* **as** ~ **as** sempre che + *sub*.

long-distance [lɔŋ'dɪstəns] *adj* (*race*) di

fondo; (call) interurbano(a).
long-haired ['lɔŋ'hɛəd] adj (person) dai capelli lunghi; (animal) dal pelo lungo.
longhand ['lɔŋhænd] n scrittura normale.
longing ['lɔŋɪŋ] n desiderio, voglia, brama ♦ adj di desiderio; pieno(a) di nostalgia.
longingly ['lɔŋɪŋlɪ] adv con desiderio.
longitude ['lɔŋgɪtjuːd] n longitudine f.
long johns [-dʒɔnz] npl mutande fpl lunghe.
long jump n salto in lungo.
long-lost ['lɔŋlɔst] adj perduto(a) da tempo.
long-playing ['lɔŋpleɪɪŋ] adj: ~ **record (LP)** (disco) 33 giri m inv.
long-range [lɔŋ'reɪndʒ] adj a lunga portata; (weather forecast) a lungo termine.
longshoreman ['lɔŋʃɔːmən] n (US) scaricatore m (di porto), portuale m.
long-sighted [lɔŋ'saɪtɪd] adj (BRIT) presbite; (fig) lungimirante.
long-standing ['lɔŋstændɪŋ] adj di vecchia data.
long-suffering [lɔŋ'sʌfərɪŋ] adj estremamente paziente; infinitamente tollerante.
long-term ['lɔŋtəːm] adj a lungo termine.
long wave n (RADIO) onde fpl lunghe.
long-winded [lɔŋ'wɪndɪd] adj prolisso(a), interminabile.
loo [luː] n (BRIT col) W.C. m inv, cesso.
loofah ['luːfə] n luffa.
look [luk] vi guardare; (seem) sembrare, parere; (building etc): **to** ~ **south/on to the sea** dare a sud/sul mare ♦ n sguardo; (appearance) aspetto, aria; ~**s** npl aspetto; bellezza; **to** ~ **like** assomigliare a; **to** ~ **ahead** guardare avanti; **it** ~**s about 4 metres long** sarà lungo un 4 metri; **it** ~**s all right to me** a me pare che vada bene; **to have a** ~ **at sth** dare un'occhiata a qc; **to have a** ~ **for sth** cercare qc.
►**look after** vt fus occuparsi di, prendersi cura di; (keep an eye on) guardare, badare a.
►**look around** vi guardarsi intorno.
►**look at** vt fus guardare.
►**look back** vi: **to** ~ **back at sth/sb** voltarsi a guardare qc/qn; **to** ~ **back on** (event, period) ripensare a.
►**look down on** vt fus (fig) guardare dall'alto, disprezzare.
►**look for** vt fus cercare.
►**look forward to** vt fus non veder l'ora di; **I'm not** ~**ing forward to it** non ne ho nessuna voglia; ~**ing forward to hearing from you** (in letter) aspettando tue notizie.
►**look in** vi: **to** ~ **in on sb** (visit) fare un salto da qn.
►**look into** vt fus (matter, possibility)

esaminare.
►**look on** vi fare da spettatore.
►**look out** vi (beware): **to** ~ **out (for)** stare in guardia (per).
►**look out for** vt fus cercare; (watch out for): **to** ~ **out for sb/sth** guardare se arriva qn/qc.
►**look over** vt (essay) dare un'occhiata a, riguardare; (town, building) vedere; (person) esaminare.
►**look round** vi (turn) girarsi, voltarsi; (in shops) dare un'occhiata; **to** ~ **round for sth** guardarsi intorno cercando qc.
►**look through** vt fus (papers, book) scorrere; (telescope) guardare attraverso.
►**look to** vt fus stare attento(a) a; (rely on) contare su.
►**look up** vi alzare gli occhi; (improve) migliorare ♦ vt (word) cercare; (friend) andare a trovare.
►**look up to** vt fus avere rispetto per.
look-out ['lukaut] n posto d'osservazione; guardia; **to be on the** ~ **(for)** stare in guardia (per).
look-up table ['lukʌp-] n (COMPUT) tabella di consultazione.
loom [luːm] n telaio ♦ vi sorgere; (fig) minacciare.
loony ['luːnɪ] adj, n (col) pazzo(a).
loop [luːp] n cappio; (COMPUT) anello.
loophole ['luːphəul] n via d'uscita; scappatoia.
loose [luːs] adj (knot) sciolto(a); (screw) allentato(a); (stone) cadente; (clothes) ampio(a), largo(a); (animal) in libertà; (life, morals) dissoluto(a); (discipline) allentato(a); (thinking) poco rigoroso(a), vago(a) ♦ vt (untie) sciogliere; (slacken) allentare; (free) liberare; (BRIT: arrow) scoccare; ~ **connection** (ELEC) filo che fa contatto; **to be at a** ~ **end** or (US) **at** ~ **ends** (fig) non saper che fare; **to tie up** ~ **ends** (fig) avere ancora qualcosa da sistemare.
loose change n spiccioli mpl, moneta.
loose-fitting ['luːsfɪtɪŋ] adj ampio(a).
loose-leaf ['luːsliːf] adj: ~ **binder** or **folder** raccoglitore m.
loose-limbed [luːs'lɪmd] adj snodato(a), agile.
loosely ['luːslɪ] adv lentamente; approssimativamente.
loosely-knit ['luːslɪ'nɪt] adj non rigidamente strutturato(a).
loosen ['luːsn] vt sciogliere.
►**loosen up** vi (before game) sciogliere i muscoli, scaldarsi; (col: relax) rilassarsi.

loot [luːt] n bottino ♦ vt saccheggiare.
looter ['luːtə*] n saccheggiatore/trice.
looting ['luːtɪŋ] n saccheggio.
lop [lɔp] vt (also: ~ **off**) tagliare via, recidere.
lop-sided ['lɔp'saɪdɪd] adj non equilibrato(a), asimmetrico(a).
lord [lɔːd] n signore m; **L~ Smith** lord Smith; **the L~** (REL) il Signore; **the (House of) L~s** (BRIT) la Camera dei Lord.
lordly ['lɔːdlɪ] adj nobile, maestoso(a); (arrogant) altero(a).
lordship ['lɔːdʃɪp] n (BRIT): **your L~** Sua Eccellenza.
lore [lɔː*] n tradizioni fpl.
lorry ['lɔrɪ] n (BRIT) camion m inv.
lorry driver n (BRIT) camionista m.
lose, pt, pp **lost** [luːz, lɔst] vt perdere; (pursuers) distanziare ♦ vi perdere; **to ~ (time)** (clock) ritardare; **to ~ no time (in doing sth)** non perdere tempo (a fare qc); **to get lost** (person) perdersi, smarrirsi; (object) andare perso or perduto.
loser ['luːzə*] n perdente m/f; **to be a good/ bad ~** saper/non saper perdere.
loss [lɔs] n perdita; **to cut one's ~es** rimetterci il meno possibile; **to make a ~** subire una perdita; **to sell sth at a ~** vendere qc in perdita; **to be at a ~** essere perplesso(a); **to be at a ~ to explain sth** non saper come fare a spiegare qc.
loss adjuster n (INSURANCE) responsabile m/f della valutazione dei danni.
loss leader n (COMM) articolo a prezzo ridottissimo per attirare la clientela.
lost [lɔst] pt, pp of **lose** ♦ adj perduto(a); **~ in thought** immerso or perso nei propri pensieri; **~ and found property** n (US) oggetti mpl smarriti; **~ and found** n (US) ufficio oggetti smarriti.
lost property n (BRIT) oggetti mpl smarriti; **~ office** or **department** ufficio oggetti smarriti.
lot [lɔt] n (at auctions) lotto; (destiny) destino, sorte f; **the ~** tutto(a) quanto(a); tutti(e) quanti(e); **a ~** molto; **a ~ of** una gran quantità di, un sacco di; **~s of** molto(a); **to draw ~s (for sth)** tirare a sorte (per qc).
lotion ['ləʊʃən] n lozione f.
lottery ['lɔtərɪ] n lotteria.
loud [laud] adj forte, alto(a); (gaudy) vistoso(a), sgargiante ♦ adv (speak etc) forte; **out ~** ad alta voce.
loudhailer [laud'heɪlə*] n (BRIT) portavoce m inv.
loudly ['laudlɪ] adv fortemente, ad alta voce.

loudspeaker [laud'spiːkə*] n altoparlante m.
lounge [laundʒ] n salotto, soggiorno; (of hotel) salone m; (of airport) sala d'attesa ♦ vi oziare; starsene colle mani in mano.
lounge bar n bar m inv con servizio a tavolino.
lounge suit n (BRIT) completo da uomo.
louse [laus] n (pl **lice**) pidocchio.
►**louse up** vt (col) rovinare.
lousy ['lauzɪ] adj (fig) orrendo(a), schifoso(a).
lout [laut] n zoticone m.
louvre, (US) **louver** ['luːvə*] adj (door, window) con apertura a gelosia.
lovable ['lʌvəbl] adj simpatico(a), carino(a); amabile.
love [lʌv] n amore m ♦ vt amare; voler bene a; **to ~ to do: I ~ to do** mi piace fare; **I'd ~ to come** mi piacerebbe molto venire; **to be in ~ with** essere innamorato(a) di; **to fall in ~ with** innamorarsi di; **to make ~** fare l'amore; **~ at first sight** amore a prima vista, colpo di fulmine; **to send one's ~ to sb** mandare i propri saluti a qn; **~ from Anne, ~, Anne** con affetto, Anne; **"15 ~"** (TENNIS) "15 a zero".
love affair n relazione f.
love child n figlio/a dell'amore.
loved ones [lʌvd-] npl: **my ~** i miei cari.
love-hate relationship ['lʌv'heɪt-] n rapporto amore-odio inv.
love letter n lettera d'amore.
love life n vita sentimentale.
lovely ['lʌvlɪ] adj bello(a); (delicious: smell, meal) buono(a); **we had a ~ time** ci siamo divertiti molto.
lover ['lʌvə*] n amante m/f; (amateur): **a ~ of** un(un')amante di; un(un')appassionato(a) di.
lovesick ['lʌvsɪk] adj malato(a) d'amore.
lovesong ['lʌvsɔŋ] n canzone f d'amore.
loving ['lʌvɪŋ] adj affettuoso(a), amoroso(a), tenero(a).
low [ləʊ] adj basso(a) ♦ adv in basso ♦ n (METEOR) depressione f ♦ vi (cow) muggire; **to feel ~** sentirsi giù; **to reach a new** or **an all-time ~** toccare il livello più basso or il minimo; **to turn (down) ~** vt abbassare.
low-alcohol [ləʊ'ælkəhɔl] adj a basso contenuto alcolico.
lowbrow ['ləʊbrau] adj (person) senza pretese intellettuali.
low-calorie ['ləʊ'kælərɪ] adj a basso contenuto calorico.
low-cut ['ləʊkʌt] adj (dress) scollato(a).
low-down ['ləʊdaun] adj (mean) ignobile

◆ n (col): he gave me the ~ on it mi ha
messo al corrente dei fatti.
lower ['ləuə*] adj, adv comparative of **low** ◆ vt
(gen) calare; (reduce: price) abbassare,
ridurre; (resistance) indebolire.
lower case n minuscolo.
low-fat ['ləu'fæt] adj magro(a).
low-key ['ləu'ki:] adj moderato(a);
(operation) condotto(a) con discrezione.
lowland ['ləulənd] n bassopiano, pianura.
low-level ['ləulɛvl] adj a basso livello;
(flying) a bassa quota.
low-loader ['ləuləudə*] n camion m a
pianale basso.
lowly ['ləulɪ] adj umile, modesto(a).
low-lying [ləu'laɪɪŋ] adj a basso livello.
low-paid [ləu'peɪd] adj mal pagato(a).
low-rise ['ləuraɪz] adj di altezza contenuta.
low-tech ['ləu'tɛk] adj a basso contenuto
tecnologico.
loyal ['lɔɪəl] adj fedele, leale.
loyalist ['lɔɪəlɪst] n lealista m/f.
loyalty ['lɔɪəltɪ] n fedeltà, lealtà.
loyalty card n carta che offre sconti a
clienti abituali.
lozenge ['lɔzɪndʒ] n (MED) pastiglia;
(GEOM) losanga.
LP n abbr (= long-playing record) LP m.
LPG n abbr (= liquefied petroleum gas) GPL
(= gas di petrolio liquefatto).
L-plate n ≈ contrassegno P principiante;
see boxed note.

L-PLATE

Le **L-plates** sono delle tabelle bianche con una
L rossa che in Gran Bretagna i guidatori
principianti, "learners", in possesso di una
"provisional licence" che corrisponde al nostro
foglio rosa, devono applicare davanti e dietro
alla loro autovettura finché non ottengono la
patente.

LPN n abbr (US: = Licensed Practical Nurse)
≈ infermiera diplomata.
LRAM n abbr (BRIT: = Licentiate of the Royal
Academy of Music) specializzazione dopo
la laurea.
LSD n abbr (= lysergic acid diethylamide)
L.S.D. m; (BRIT: = pounds, shillings and
pence) sistema monetario in vigore in
Gran Bretagna fino al 1971.
LSE n abbr = London School of Economics.
LT abbr (ELEC: = low tension) B.T.
Lt. abbr (= lieutenant) Ten.
Ltd abbr (COMM) = **limited**.
lubricant ['lu:brɪkənt] n lubrificante m.
lubricate ['lu:brɪkeɪt] vt lubrificare.

lucid ['lu:sɪd] adj lucido(a).
lucidity [lu:'sɪdɪtɪ] n lucidità.
luck [lʌk] n fortuna, sorte f; **bad** ~ sfortuna,
mala sorte; **good** ~ (buona) fortuna; **to
be in** ~ essere fortunato(a); **to be out of**
~ essere sfortunato(a).
luckily ['lʌkɪlɪ] adv fortunatamente, per
fortuna.
luckless ['lʌklɪs] adj sventurato(a).
lucky ['lʌkɪ] adj fortunato(a); (number etc)
che porta fortuna.
lucrative ['lu:krətɪv] adj lucrativo(a),
lucroso(a), profittevole.
ludicrous ['lu:dɪkrəs] adj ridicolo(a),
assurdo(a).
ludo ['lu:dəu] n ≈ gioco dell'oca.
lug [lʌg] vt trascinare.
luggage ['lʌgɪdʒ] n bagagli mpl.
luggage rack n portabagagli m inv.
luggage van, (US) **luggage car** n (RAIL)
bagagliaio.
lugubrious [lu'gu:brɪəs] adj lugubre.
lukewarm ['lu:kwɔ:m] adj tiepido(a).
lull [lʌl] n intervallo di calma ◆ vt (child)
cullare; (person, fear) acquietare,
calmare.
lullaby ['lʌləbaɪ] n ninnananna.
lumbago [lʌm'beɪgəu] n lombaggine f.
lumber ['lʌmbə*] n roba vecchia ◆ vt (BRIT
col): **to** ~ **sb with sth/sb** affibbiare or
rifilare qc/qn a qn ◆ vi (also: ~ **about**, ~
along) muoversi pesantemente.
lumberjack ['lʌmbədʒæk] n boscaiolo.
lumber room n (BRIT) sgabuzzino.
lumber yard n segheria.
luminous ['lu:mɪnəs] adj luminoso(a).
lump [lʌmp] n pezzo; (in sauce) grumo;
(swelling) gonfiore m ◆ vt (also: ~ **together**)
riunire, mettere insieme.
lump sum n somma globale.
lumpy ['lʌmpɪ] adj (sauce) grumoso(a).
lunacy ['lu:nəsɪ] n demenza, follia, pazzia.
lunar ['lu:nə*] adj lunare.
lunatic ['lu:nətɪk] adj, n pazzo(a), matto(a).
lunatic asylum n manicomio.
lunch [lʌntʃ] n pranzo, colazione f; **to invite
sb to** or **for** ~ invitare qn a pranzo or a
colazione.
lunch break n intervallo del pranzo.
luncheon ['lʌntʃən] n pranzo.
luncheon meat n ≈ mortadella.
luncheon voucher n buono m pasto inv.
lunch hour n = **lunch break**.
lunchtime ['lʌntʃtaɪm] n ora di pranzo.
lung [lʌŋ] n polmone m.
lung cancer n cancro del polmone.
lunge [lʌndʒ] vi (also: ~ **forward**) fare un
balzo in avanti; **to** ~ **at sb** balzare su qn.

lupin ['lu:pɪn] n lupino.

lurch [lɜ:tʃ] vi vacillare, barcollare ♦ n scatto improvviso; **to leave sb in the** ~ piantare in asso qn.

lure [luə*] n richiamo; lusinga ♦ vt attirare (con l'inganno).

lurid ['luərɪd] adj sgargiante; (details etc) impressionante.

lurk [lɜ:k] vi stare in agguato.

luscious ['lʌʃəs] adj succulento(a); delizioso(a).

lush [lʌʃ] adj lussureggiante.

lust [lʌst] n lussuria; cupidigia; desiderio; (fig): ~ **for** sete f di.
► **lust after** vt fus bramare, desiderare.

luster ['lʌstə*] n (US) = **lustre**.

lustful ['lʌstful] adj lascivo(a), voglioso(a).

lustre, (US) **luster** ['lʌstə*] n lustro, splendore m.

lusty ['lʌstɪ] adj vigoroso(a), robusto(a).

lute [lu:t] n liuto.

Luxembourg ['lʌksəmbɜ:g] n (state) Lussemburgo m; (city) Lussemburgo f.

luxuriant [lʌg'zjuərɪənt] adj lussureggiante.

luxurious [lʌg'zjuərɪəs] adj sontuoso(a), di lusso.

luxury ['lʌkʃərɪ] n lusso ♦ cpd di lusso.

LV n abbr (BRIT) = **luncheon voucher**.

LW abbr (RADIO: = long wave) O.L.

Lycra ® ['laɪkrə] n lycra ® f inv.

lying ['laɪɪŋ] n bugie fpl, menzogne fpl ♦ adj (statement, story) falso(a); (person) bugiardo(a).

lynch [lɪntʃ] vt linciare.

lynx [lɪŋks] n lince f.

Lyons ['laɪənz] n Lione f.

lyre ['laɪə*] n lira.

lyric ['lɪrɪk] adj lirico(a); ~**s** npl (of song) parole fpl.

lyrical ['lɪrɪkl] adj lirico(a).

lyricism ['lɪrɪsɪzəm] n lirismo.

Mm

M, m [ɛm] n (letter) M, m f or m inv; **M for Mary,** (US) **M for Mike** ≈ M come Milano.

M n abbr (BRIT: = motorway): **the M8** ≈ l'A8 ♦ abbr (= medium) taglia media.

m abbr (= metre) m; = **mile; million**.

MA n abbr (SCOL) see **Master of Arts**; (US) = military academy ♦ (US) = **Massachusetts**.

mac [mæk] n (BRIT) impermeabile m.

macabre [mə'kɑ:brə] adj macabro(a).

macaroni [mækə'rəunɪ] n maccheroni mpl.

macaroon [mækə'ru:n] n amaretto (biscotto).

mace [meɪs] n mazza; (spice) macis m or f.

Macedonia [mæsɪ'dəunɪə] n Macedonia.

Macedonian [mæsɪ'dəunɪən] adj macedone ♦ n macedone m/f; (LING) macedone m.

machinations [mækɪ'neɪʃənz] npl macchinazioni fpl, intrighi mpl.

machine [mə'ʃi:n] n macchina ♦ vt (dress etc) cucire a macchina; (TECH) lavorare (a macchina).

machine code n (COMPUT) codice m di macchina, codice assoluto.

machine gun n mitragliatrice f.

machine language n (COMPUT) linguaggio m macchina inv.

machine-readable [mə'ʃi:nri:dəbl] adj (COMPUT) leggibile dalla macchina.

machinery [mə'ʃi:nərɪ] n macchinario, macchine fpl; (fig) macchina.

machine shop n officina meccanica.

machine tool n macchina utensile.

machine washable adj lavabile in lavatrice.

machinist [mə'ʃi:nɪst] n macchinista m/f.

macho ['mætʃəu] adj macho inv.

mackerel ['mækrəl] n (pl inv) sgombro.

mackintosh ['mækɪntɔʃ] n impermeabile m.

macro... ['mækrəu] prefix macro....

macroeconomics ['mækrəui:kə'nɔmɪks] n macroeconomia.

mad [mæd] adj matto(a), pazzo(a); (foolish) sciocco(a); (angry) furioso(a); **to go** ~ impazzire, diventar matto; ~ **(at or with sb)** furibondo(a) (con qn); **to be** ~ **(keen) about** or **on sth** (col) andar pazzo or matto per qc.

madam ['mædəm] n signora; **M**~ **Chairman** Signora Presidentessa.

madcap ['mædkæp] adj (col) senza senso, assurdo(a).

mad cow disease n encefalite f bovina spongiforme.

madden ['mædn] vt fare infuriare.

maddening ['mædnɪŋ] adj esasperante.

made [meɪd] pt, pp of **make**.

Madeira [mə'dɪərə] n (GEO) Madera; (wine) madera m.

made-to-measure ['meɪdtə'mɛʒə*] adj (BRIT) fatto(a) su misura.

madhouse ['mædhaus] n (also fig) manicomio.

madly ['mædlɪ] adv follemente; (love) alla follia.

madman ['mædmən] n pazzo, alienato.

madness['mædnɪs] n pazzia.
Madrid[mə'drɪd] n Madrid f.
Mafia['mæfɪə] n mafia f.
mag.[mæg] n abbr (BRIT col) = **magazine** (PRESS).
magazine[mægə'ziːn] n (PRESS) rivista; (MIL: store) magazzino, deposito; (of firearm) caricatore m.
maggot['mægət] n baco, verme m.
magic['mædʒɪk] n magia ♦ adj magico(a).
magical['mædʒɪkəl] adj magico(a).
magician[mə'dʒɪʃən] n mago/a.
magistrate['mædʒɪstreɪt] n magistrato; giudice m/f.
magistrates' courtn see **crown court**.
magnanimous[mæg'nænɪməs] adj magnanimo(a).
magnate['mægneɪt] n magnate m.
magnesium[mæg'niːzɪəm] n magnesio.
magnet['mægnɪt] n magnete m, calamita.
magnetic[mæg'nɛtɪk] adj magnetico(a).
magnetic diskn (COMPUT) disco magnetico.
magnetic tapen nastro magnetico.
magnetism['mægnɪtɪzəm] n magnetismo.
magnification[mægnɪfɪ'keɪʃən] n ingrandimento.
magnificence[mæg'nɪfɪsns] n magnificenza.
magnificent[mæg'nɪfɪsnt] adj magnifico(a).
magnify['mægnɪfaɪ] vt ingrandire.
magnifying glass['mægnɪfaɪɪŋ-] n lente f d'ingrandimento.
magnitude['mægnɪtjuːd] n grandezza; importanza.
magnolia[mæg'nəulɪə] n magnolia.
magpie['mægpaɪ] n gazza.
mahogany[mə'hɔgənɪ] n mogano ♦ cpd di or in mogano.
maid[meɪd] n domestica; (in hotel) cameriera; **old** ~ (pej) vecchia zitella.
maiden['meɪdn] n fanciulla ♦ adj (aunt etc) nubile; (speech, voyage) inaugurale.
maiden namen nome m nubile or da ragazza.
mail[meɪl] n posta ♦ vt spedire (per posta); **by** ~ per posta.
mailbox['meɪlbɔks] n (US) cassetta delle lettere; (COMPUT) mailbox f inv.
mailing list['meɪlɪŋ-] n elenco d'indirizzi.
mailman['meɪlmæn] n (US) portalettere m inv, postino.
mail-order['meɪlɔːdə*] n vendita (or acquisto) per corrispondenza ♦ cpd: ~ **firm** or **house** ditta di vendita per corrispondenza.
mailshot['meɪlʃɔt] n mailing m inv.
mail trainn treno postale.

mail truckn (US AUT) = **mail van**.
mail vann (BRIT: AUT) furgone m postale; (:RAIL) vagone m postale.
maim[meɪm] vt mutilare.
main[meɪn] adj principale ♦ n (pipe) conduttura principale; **the** ~**s** (ELEC) la linea principale; ~**s operated** adj che funziona a elettricità; **in the** ~ nel complesso, nell'insieme.
main coursen (CULIN) piatto principale, piatto forte.
mainframe['meɪnfreɪm] n (also: ~ **computer**) mainframe m inv.
mainland['meɪnlənd] n continente m.
mainline['meɪnlaɪn] adj (RAIL) della linea principale ♦ vb (drugs slang) vt bucarsi di ♦ vi bucarsi.
main linen (RAIL) linea principale.
mainly['meɪnlɪ] adv principalmente, soprattutto.
main roadn strada principale.
mainstay['meɪnsteɪ] n (fig) sostegno principale.
mainstream['meɪnstriːm] n (fig) corrente f principale.
maintain[meɪn'teɪn] vt mantenere; (affirm) sostenere; **to** ~ **that** ... sostenere che ....
maintenance['meɪntənəns] n manutenzione f; (alimony) alimenti mpl.
maintenance contractn contratto di manutenzione.
maintenance ordern (LAW) obbligo degli alimenti.
maisonette[meɪzə'nɛt] n (BRIT) appartamento a due piani.
maize[meɪz] n granturco, mais m.
Maj.abbr (MIL) = **major**.
majestic[mə'dʒɛstɪk] adj maestoso(a).
majesty['mædʒɪstɪ] n maestà f inv.
major['meɪdʒə*] n (MIL) maggiore m ♦ adj (greater, MUS) maggiore; (in importance) principale, importante ♦ vi (US SCOL): **to** ~ **(in)** specializzarsi (in); **a** ~ **operation** (MED) una grossa operazione.
Majorca[mə'jɔːkə] n Maiorca.
major generaln (MIL) generale m di divisione.
majority[mə'dʒɔrɪtɪ] n maggioranza ♦ cpd (verdict) maggioritario(a).
majority holdingn (COMM): **to have a** ~ essere maggiore azionista.
make[meɪk] vt (pt, pp made [meɪd]) fare; (manufacture) fare, fabbricare; (cause to be): **to** ~ **sb sad** etc rendere qn triste etc; (force): **to** ~ **sb do sth** costringere qn a fare qc, far fare qc a qn; (equal): **2 and 2** ~ **4** 2 più 2 fa 4 ♦ n fabbricazione f; (brand) marca; **to** ~ **it** (in time etc)

arrivare; (*succeed*) farcela; **what time do you** ~ **it?** che ora fai?; **to** ~ **good** *vi* (*succeed*) aver successo ♦ *vt* (*deficit*) colmare; (*losses*) compensare; **to** ~ **do with** arrangiarsi con.

▶make for *vt fus* (*place*) avviarsi verso.

▶make off *vi* svignarsela.

▶make out *vt* (*write out*) scrivere; (*understand*) capire; (*see*) distinguere; (: *numbers*) decifrare; (*claim, imply*): **to** ~ **out (that)** voler far credere (che); **to** ~ **out a case for sth** presentare delle valide ragioni in favore di qc.

▶make over *vt* (*assign*): **to** ~ **over (to)** passare (a), trasferire (a).

▶make up *vt* (*invent*) inventare; (*parcel*) fare ♦ *vi* conciliarsi; (*with cosmetics*) truccarsi; **to be made up of** essere composto di *or* formato da.

▶make up for *vt fus* compensare; ricuperare.

make-believe ['meɪkbɪliːv] *n*: **a world of** ~ un mondo di favole; **it's just** ~ è tutta un'invenzione.

maker ['meɪkə*] *n* fabbricante *m*; creatore/ trice, autore/trice.

makeshift ['meɪkʃɪft] *adj* improvvisato(a).

make-up ['meɪkʌp] *n* trucco.

make-up bag *n* borsa del trucco.

make-up remover *n* struccatore *m*.

making ['meɪkɪŋ] *n* (*fig*): **in the** ~ **in** formazione; **he has the** ~**s of an actor** ha la stoffa dell'attore.

maladjusted [mælə'dʒʌstɪd] *adj* disadattato(a).

maladroit [mælə'drɔɪt] *adj* maldestro(a).

malaise [mæ'leɪz] *n* malessere *m*.

malaria [mə'lɛərɪə] *n* malaria.

Malawi [mə'lɑːwɪ] *n* Malawi *m*.

Malay [mə'leɪ] *adj* malese ♦ *n* malese *m/f*; (*LING*) malese *m*.

Malaya [mə'leɪə] *n* Malesia.

Malayan [mə'leɪən] *adj, n* = **Malay**.

Malaysia [mə'leɪzɪə] *n* Malaysia.

Malaysian [mə'leɪzɪən] *adj, n* malaysiano(a).

Maldives ['mɔːldaɪvz] *npl*: **the** ~ **le** (isole) Maldive.

male [meɪl] *n* (*BIO, ELEC*) maschio ♦ *adj* (*gen, sex*) maschile; (*animal, child*) maschio(a); ~ **and female students** studenti e studentesse.

male chauvinist *n* maschilista *m*.

male nurse *n* infermiere *m*.

malevolence [mə'lɛvələns] *n* malevolenza.

malevolent [mə'lɛvələnt] *adj* malevolo(a).

malfunction [mæl'fʌŋkʃən] *n* funzione *f* difettosa.

malice ['mælɪs] *n* malevolenza.

malicious [mə'lɪʃəs] *adj* malevolo(a); (*LAW*) doloso(a).

malign [mə'laɪn] *vt* malignare su; calunniare.

malignant [mə'lɪgnənt] *adj* (*MED*) maligno(a).

malingerer [mə'lɪŋgərə*] *n* scansafatiche *m/f inv*.

mall [mɔːl] *n* (*also*: **shopping** ~) centro commerciale.

malleable ['mælɪəbl] *adj* malleabile.

mallet ['mælɪt] *n* maglio.

malnutrition [mælnjuː'trɪʃən] *n* denutrizione *f*.

malpractice [mæl'præktɪs] *n* prevaricazione *f*; negligenza.

malt [mɔːlt] *n* malto ♦ *cpd* (*whisky*) di malto.

Malta ['mɔːltə] *n* Malta.

Maltese [mɔːl'tiːz] *adj, n* (*pl inv*) maltese (*m/f*); (*LING*) maltese *m*.

maltreat [mæl'triːt] *vt* maltrattare.

mammal ['mæml] *n* mammifero.

mammoth ['mæməθ] *n* mammut *m inv* ♦ *adj* enorme, gigantesco(a).

man [mæn] *n* (*pl* **men**) uomo; (*CHESS*) pezzo; (*DRAUGHTS*) pedina ♦ *vt* fornire d'uomini; stare a; essere di servizio a.

Man. *abbr* (*Canada*) = Manitoba.

manacles ['mænəklz] *npl* manette *fpl*.

manage ['mænɪdʒ] *vi* farcela ♦ *vt* (*be in charge of*) occuparsi di; (*shop, restaurant*) gestire; **to** ~ **without sth/sb** fare a meno di qc/qn; **to** ~ **to do sth** riuscire a far qc.

manageable ['mænɪdʒəbl] *adj* maneggevole; (*task etc*) fattibile.

management ['mænɪdʒmənt] *n* amministrazione *f*, direzione *f*; gestione *f*; (*persons: of business, firm*) dirigenti *mpl*; (: *of hotel, shop, theatre*) direzione *f*; "**under new** ~" "sotto nuova gestione".

management accounting *n* contabilità di gestione.

management buyout *n* acquisto di una società da parte dei suoi dirigenti.

management consultant *n* consulente *m/f* aziendale.

manager ['mænɪdʒə*] *n* direttore *m*; (*of shop, restaurant*) gerente *m*; (*of artist*) manager *m inv*; **sales** ~ direttore *m* delle vendite.

manageress [mænɪdʒə'rɛs] *n* direttrice *f*; gerente *f*.

managerial [mænə'dʒɪərɪəl] *adj* dirigenziale.

managing director (MD) ['mænɪdʒɪŋ-] *n* amministratore *m* delegato.

Mancunian [mæŋ'kjuːnɪən] *adj* di Manchester ♦ *n* abitante *m/f* di

Manchester; originario/a di Manchester.
mandarin ['mændərɪn] n (person, fruit)
mandarino.
mandate ['mændeɪt] n mandato.
mandatory ['mændətərɪ] adj
obbligatorio(a); ingiuntivo(a).
mandolin(e) ['mændəlɪn] n mandolino.
mane [meɪn] n criniera.
maneuver [mə'nuːvə*] etc (US)
= **manoeuvre** etc.
manful ['mænful] adj coraggioso(a),
valoroso(a).
manfully ['mænfəlɪ] adv valorosamente.
manganese [mæŋgə'niːz] n manganese m.
mangetout ['mɔnʒ'tuː] n pisello dolce,
taccola.
mangle ['mæŋgl] vt straziare; mutilare ♦ n
strizzatoio.
mango, ~es ['mæŋgəu] n mango.
mangrove ['mæŋgrəuv] n mangrovia.
mangy ['meɪndʒɪ] adj rognoso(a).
manhandle ['mænhændl] vt (treat roughly)
malmenare; (move by hand: goods)
spostare a mano.
manhole ['mænhəul] n botola stradale.
manhood ['mænhud] n età virile; virilità.
man-hour ['mænauə*] n ora di lavoro.
manhunt ['mænhʌnt] n caccia all'uomo.
mania ['meɪnɪə] n mania.
maniac ['meɪnɪæk] n maniaco/a.
manic ['mænɪk] adj maniacale.
manic-depressive ['mænɪkdɪ'prɛsɪv] adj
maniaco-depressivo(a) ♦ n persona
affetta da mania depressiva.
manicure ['mænɪkjuə*] n manicure f inv.
manicure set n trousse f inv della
manicure.
manifest ['mænɪfɛst] vt manifestare ♦ adj
manifesto(a), palese ♦ n (AVIAT, NAUT)
manifesto.
manifestation [mænɪfɛs'teɪʃən] n
manifestazione f.
manifesto [mænɪ'fɛstəu] n manifesto.
manifold ['mænɪfəuld] adj molteplice ♦ n
(AUT etc): **exhaust** ~ collettore m di
scarico.
Manila [mə'nɪlə] n Manila.
manil(l)a [mə'nɪlə] adj (paper, envelope)
manilla inv.
manipulate [mə'nɪpjuleɪt] vt (tool)
maneggiare; (controls) azionare; (limb,
facts) manipolare.
manipulation [mənɪpju'leɪʃən] n
maneggiare m; capacità di azionare;
manipolazione f.
mankind [mæn'kaɪnd] n umanità, genere m
umano.
manliness ['mænlɪnɪs] n virilità.

manly ['mænlɪ] adj virile; coraggioso(a).
man-made ['mæn'meɪd] adj sintetico(a);
artificiale.
manna ['mænə] n manna.
mannequin ['mænɪkɪn] n (dummy)
manichino; (fashion model) indossatrice f.
manner ['mænə*] n maniera, modo; ~s npl
maniere fpl; (good) ~s buona educazione
f, buone maniere; **bad** ~s maleducazione
f; **all** ~ **of** ogni sorta di.
mannerism ['mænərɪzəm] n vezzo, tic m inv.
mannerly ['mænəlɪ] adj educato(a), civile.
manoeuvrable, (US) **maneuverable**
[mə'nuːvrəbl] adj facile da manovrare;
(car) maneggevole.
manoeuvre, (US) **maneuver** [mə'nuːvə*]
vt manovrare ♦ vi far manovre ♦ n
manovra; **to** ~ **sb into doing sth**
costringere abilmente qn a fare qc.
manor ['mænə*] n (also: ~ **house**) maniero.
manpower ['mænpauə*] n manodopera.
**Manpower Services Commission
(MSC)** n (BRIT) ente nazionale per
l'occupazione.
manservant, pl **menservants**
['mænsəːvənt, 'mɛn-] n domestico.
mansion ['mænʃən] n casa signorile.
manslaughter ['mænslɔːtə*] n omicidio
preterintenzionale.
mantelpiece ['mæntlpiːs] n mensola del
caminetto.
mantle ['mæntl] n mantello.
man-to-man ['mæntə'mæn] adj, adv da
uomo a uomo.
Mantua ['mæntjuə] n Mantova.
manual ['mænjuəl] adj, n manuale (m).
manual worker n manovale m.
manufacture [mænju'fæktʃə*] vt
fabbricare ♦ n fabbricazione f,
manifattura.
manufactured goods npl manufatti mpl.
manufacturer [mænju'fæktʃərə*] n
fabbricante m.
manufacturing industries
[mænju'fæktʃərɪŋ-] npl industrie fpl
manifatturiere.
manure [mə'njuə*] n concime m.
manuscript ['mænjuskrɪpt] n manoscritto.
many ['mɛnɪ] adj molti(e) ♦ pron molti(e),
un gran numero; **a great** ~ moltissimi(e),
un gran numero (di); ~ **a** ... molti(e) ...,
più di un(a) ...; **too** ~ **difficulties** troppe
difficoltà; **twice as** ~ due volte tanto;
how ~? quanti(e)?
Maori ['mauri] adj, n maori (m/f) inv.
map [mæp] n carta (geografica) ♦ vt fare
una carta di.
►**map out** vt tracciare un piano di; (fig:

career, holiday, essay) pianificare.
maple ['meɪpl] *n* acero.
mar [mɑ:*] *vt* sciupare.
Mar. *abbr* (= *March*) mar.
marathon ['mærəθən] *n* maratona ♦ *adj*: **a ~ session** una seduta fiume.
marathon runner *n* maratoneta *m/f*.
marauder [mə'rɔ:də*] *n* saccheggiatore *m*; predatore *m*.
marble ['mɑ:bl] *n* marmo; (*toy*) pallina, bilia; **~s** *n* (*game*) palline, bilie.
March [mɑ:tʃ] *n* marzo; *for phrases see also* **July**.
march [mɑ:tʃ] *vi* marciare; sfilare ♦ *n* marcia; (*demonstration*) dimostrazione *f*; **to ~ into a room** entrare a passo deciso in una stanza.
marcher ['mɑ:tʃə*] *n* dimostrante *m/f*.
marching ['mɑ:tʃɪŋ] *n*: **to give sb his ~ orders** (*fig*) dare il benservito a qn.
march-past ['mɑ:tʃpɑ:st] *n* sfilata.
mare [mɛə*] *n* giumenta.
marg [mɑ:dʒ] *n abbr* (*col*) = **margarine**.
margarine [mɑ:dʒə'ri:n] *n* margarina.
marge [mɑ:dʒ] *n abbr* (*col*) = **margarine**.
margin ['mɑ:dʒɪn] *n* margine *m*.
marginal ['mɑ:dʒɪnl] *adj* marginale; **~ seat** (*POL*) seggio elettorale ottenuto con una stretta maggioranza.
marginally ['mɑ:dʒɪnəlɪ] *adv* (*bigger, better*) lievemente, di poco; (*different*) un po'.
marigold ['mærɪɡəʊld] *n* calendola.
marijuana [mærɪ'wɑ:nə] *n* marijuana.
marina [mə'ri:nə] *n* marina.
marinade *n* [mærɪ'neɪd] marinata ♦ *vt* ['mærɪneɪd] = **marinate**.
marinate ['mærɪneɪt] *vt* marinare.
marine [mə'ri:n] *adj* (*animal, plant*) marino(a); (*forces, engineering*) marittimo(a) ♦ *n* fante *m* di marina; (*US*) marine *m inv*.
marine insurance *n* assicurazione *f* marittima.
marital ['mærɪtl] *adj* maritale, coniugale; **~ status** stato coniugale.
maritime ['mærɪtaɪm] *adj* marittimo(a).
maritime law *n* diritto marittimo.
marjoram ['mɑ:dʒərəm] *n* maggiorana.
mark [mɑ:k] *n* segno; (*stain*) macchia; (*of skid etc*) traccia; (*BRIT SCOL*) voto; (*SPORT*) bersaglio; (*currency*) marco; (*BRIT TECH*): **M~ 2/3** 1a/2a serie *f* ♦ *vt* segnare; (*stain*) macchiare; (*BRIT SCOL*) dare un voto a; correggere; (*SPORT: player*) marcare; **punctuation ~s** segni di punteggiatura; **to be quick off the ~ (in doing)** (*fig*) non perdere tempo (per fare); **up to the ~** (*in efficiency*) all'altezza; **to ~ time** segnare il passo.
▶**mark down** *vt* (*reduce*: *prices, goods*) ribassare, ridurre.
▶**mark off** *vt* (*tick off*) spuntare, cancellare.
▶**mark out** *vt* delimitare.
▶**mark up** *vt* (*price*) aumentare.
marked ['mɑ:kt] *adj* spiccato(a), chiaro(a).
markedly ['mɑ:kɪdlɪ] *adv* visibilmente, notevolmente.
marker ['mɑ:kə*] *n* (*sign*) segno; (*bookmark*) segnalibro.
market ['mɑ:kɪt] *n* mercato ♦ *vt* (*COMM*) mettere in vendita; (*promote*) lanciare sul mercato; **to play the ~** giocare *or* speculare in borsa; **to be on the ~** essere (messo) in vendita *or* in commercio; **open ~** mercato libero.
marketable ['mɑ:kɪtəbl] *adj* commercializzabile.
market analysis *n* analisi *f* di mercato.
market day *n* giorno di mercato.
market demand *n* domanda del mercato.
market economy *n* economia di mercato.
market forces *npl* forze *fpl* di mercato.
market garden *n* (*BRIT*) orto industriale.
marketing ['mɑ:kɪtɪŋ] *n* marketing *m*.
marketplace ['mɑ:kɪtpleɪs] *n* (piazza del) mercato; (*world of trade*) piazza, mercato.
market price *n* prezzo di mercato.
market research *n* indagine *f or* ricerca di mercato.
market value *n* valore *m* di mercato.
marking ['mɑ:kɪŋ] *n* (*on animal*) marcatura di colore; (*on road*) segnaletica orizzontale.
marksman ['mɑ:ksmən] *n* tiratore *m* scelto.
marksmanship ['mɑ:ksmənʃɪp] *n* abilità nel tiro.
mark-up ['mɑ:kʌp] *n* (*COMM*: *margin*) margine *m* di vendita; (: *increase*) aumento.
marmalade ['mɑ:məleɪd] *n* marmellata d'arance.
maroon [mə'ru:n] *vt* (*fig*): **to be ~ed (in** *or* **at)** essere abbandonato(a) (in) ♦ *adj* bordeaux *inv*.
marquee [mɑ:'ki:] *n* padiglione *m*.
marquess, marquis ['mɑ:kwɪs] *n* marchese *m*.
Marrakech, Marrakesh [mærə'kɛʃ] *n* Marrakesh *f*.
marriage ['mærɪdʒ] *n* matrimonio.
marriage bureau *n* agenzia matrimoniale.
marriage certificate *n* certificato di matrimonio.
marriage guidance, (*US***) marriage counseling** *n* consulenza matrimoniale.
marriage of convenience *n* matrimonio

di convenienza.
married ['mærɪd] *adj* sposato(a); (*life, love*) coniugale, matrimoniale.
marrow ['mærəu] *n* midollo; (*vegetable*) zucca.
marry ['mærɪ] *vt* sposare, sposarsi con; (*subj: father, priest etc*) dare in matrimonio ♦ *vi* (*also*: **get married**) sposarsi.
Mars [mɑːz] *n* (*planet*) Marte *m*.
Marseilles [mɑː'seɪlz] *n* Marsiglia.
marsh [mɑːʃ] *n* palude *f*.
marshal ['mɑːʃl] *n* maresciallo; (*US*: fire ~) capo; (: *police* ~) capitano; (*for demonstration, meeting*) membro del servizio d'ordine ♦ *vt* adunare.
marshalling yard ['mɑːʃlɪŋ-] *n* scalo smistamento.
marshmallow [mɑːʃ'mæləu] *n* (*BOT*) altea; (*sweet*) *caramella soffice e gommosa*.
marshy ['mɑːʃɪ] *adj* paludoso(a).
marsupial [mɑː'suːpɪəl] *adj, n* marsupiale (*m*).
martial ['mɑːʃl] *adj* marziale.
martial arts *npl* arti *fpl* marziali.
martial law *n* legge *f* marziale.
Martian ['mɑːʃən] *n* marziano/a.
martin ['mɑːtɪn] *n* (*also*: **house** ~) balestruccio.
martyr ['mɑːtə*] *n* martire *m/f* ♦ *vt* martirizzare.
martyrdom ['mɑːtədəm] *n* martirio.
marvel ['mɑːvl] *n* meraviglia ♦ *vi*: **to** ~ **(at)** meravigliarsi (di).
marvellous, (*US*) **marvelous** ['mɑːvələs] *adj* meraviglioso(a).
Marxism ['mɑːksɪzəm] *n* marxismo.
Marxist ['mɑːksɪst] *adj, n* marxista (*m/f*).
marzipan ['mɑːzɪpæn] *n* marzapane *m*.
mascara [mæs'kɑːrə] *n* mascara *m inv*.
mascot ['mæskət] *n* mascotte *f inv*.
masculine ['mæskjulɪn] *adj* maschile ♦ *n* genere *m* maschile.
masculinity [mæskju'lɪnɪtɪ] *n* mascolinità.
MASH [mæʃ] *n abbr* (*US MIL*: = *mobile army surgical hospital*) *ospedale di campo di unità mobile dell'esercito*.
mash [mæʃ] *vt* (*CULIN*) passare, schiacciare.
mashed [mæʃt] *adj*: ~ **potatoes** purè *m* di patate.
mask [mɑːsk] *n* (*gen, ELEC*) maschera ♦ *vt* mascherare.
masochism ['mæsəkɪzəm] *n* masochismo.
masochist ['mæsəkɪst] *n* masochista *m/f*.
mason ['meɪsn] *n* (*also*: **stone**~) scalpellino; (*also*: **free**~) massone *m*.
masonic [mə'sɔnɪk] *adj* massonico(a).
masonry ['meɪsnrɪ] *n* muratura.

masquerade [mæskə'reɪd] *n* ballo in maschera; (*fig*) mascherata ♦ *vi*: **to** ~ **as** farsi passare per.
mass [mæs] *n* moltitudine *f*, massa; (*PHYSICS*) massa; (*REL*) messa ♦ *vi* ammassarsi; **the** ~**es** le masse; **to go to** ~ andare a *or* alla messa.
Mass. *abbr* (*US*) = *Massachusetts*.
massacre ['mæsəkə*] *n* massacro ♦ *vt* massacrare.
massage ['mæsɑːʒ] *n* massaggio ♦ *vt* massaggiare.
masseur [mæ'sə:*] *n* massaggiatore *m*.
masseuse [mæ'sə:z] *n* massaggiatrice *f*.
massive ['mæsɪv] *adj* enorme, massiccio(a).
mass market *n* mercato di massa.
mass media *npl* mass media *mpl*.
mass meeting *n* riunione *f* generale; (*huge*) adunata popolare.
mass-produce ['mæsprə'djuːs] *vt* produrre in serie.
mass production *n* produzione *f* in serie.
mast [mɑːst] *n* albero; (*RADIO, TV*) pilone *m* (a traliccio).
mastectomy [mæs'tɛktəmɪ] *n* mastectomia.
master ['mɑːstə*] *n* padrone *m*; (*ART etc, teacher: in primary school*) maestro; (: *in secondary school*) professore *m*; (*title for boys*): **M~ X** Signorino X ♦ *vt* domare; (*learn*) imparare a fondo; (*understand*) conoscere a fondo; ~ **of ceremonies (MC)** *n* maestro di cerimonie; **M~'s degree** *n see boxed note*.

MASTER'S DEGREE

Il **Master's degree** *è il riconoscimento che viene conferito a chi segue un corso di specializzazione dopo aver conseguito un "Bachelor's degree". Vi sono diversi tipi di Master's Degree; i più comuni sono il "Master of Arts (MA)" e il "Master of Science (MSc)" che si ottengono dopo aver seguito un corso e aver presentato una tesi originale. Per il "Master of Letters (MLitt)" e il "Master of Philosophy (MPhil)" è invece sufficiente presentare la tesi; vedi anche* **doctorate**.

---

master disk *n* (*COMPUT*) disco *m* master *inv*, disco principale.
masterful ['mɑːstəful] *adj* autoritario(a), imperioso(a).
master key *n* chiave *f* maestra.
masterly ['mɑːstəlɪ] *adj* magistrale.
mastermind ['mɑːstəmaɪnd] *n* mente *f* superiore ♦ *vt* essere il cervello di.

masterpiece ['mɑːstəpiːs] n capolavoro.
master plan n piano generale.
master stroke n colpo maestro.
mastiff ['mæstɪf] n mastino inglese.
masturbate ['mæstəbeɪt] vi masturbare.
masturbation [mæstə'beɪʃən] n masturbazione f.
mat [mæt] n stuoia; (also: **door~**) stoino, zerbino ♦ adj = **matt**.
match [mætʃ] n fiammifero; (game) partita, incontro; (fig) uguale m/f; matrimonio; partito ♦ vt intonare; (go well with) andare benissimo con; (equal) uguagliare ♦ vi intonarsi; **to be a good** ~ andare bene.
►**match up** vt intonare.
matchbox ['mætʃbɔks] n scatola per fiammiferi.
matching ['mætʃɪŋ] adj ben assortito(a).
matchless ['mætʃlɪs] adj senza pari.
mate [meɪt] n compagno/a di lavoro; (col: friend) amico/a; (animal) compagno/a; (in merchant navy) secondo ♦ vi accoppiarsi ♦ vt accoppiare.
material [mə'tɪərɪəl] n (substance) materiale m, materia; (cloth) stoffa ♦ adj materiale; (important) essenziale; ~**s** npl (equipment etc) materiali mpl; occorrente m.
materialistic [mətɪərɪə'lɪstɪk] adj materialistico(a).
materialize [mə'tɪərɪəlaɪz] vi materializzarsi, realizzarsi.
materially [mə'tɪərɪəlɪ] adv dal punto di vista materiale; sostanzialmente.
maternal [mə'təɪnl] adj materno(a).
maternity [mə'təɪnɪtɪ] n maternità ♦ cpd di maternità; (clothes) pre-maman inv.
maternity benefit n sussidio di maternità.
maternity hospital n ≈ clinica ostetrica.
matey ['meɪtɪ] adj (BRIT col) amicone(a).
math [mæθ] n abbr (US) = **mathematics**.
mathematical [mæθə'mætɪkl] adj matematico(a).
mathematician [mæθəmə'tɪʃən] n matematico/a.
mathematics [mæθə'mætɪks] n matematica.
maths [mæθs] n abbr (BRIT) = **mathematics**.
matinée ['mætɪneɪ] n matinée f inv.
mating ['meɪtɪŋ] n accoppiamento.
mating call n chiamata all'accoppiamento.
mating season n stagione f degli amori.
matriarchal [meɪtrɪ'ɑːkl] adj matriarcale.
matrices ['meɪtrɪsiːz] npl of **matrix**.
matriculation [mətrɪkju'leɪʃən] n immatricolazione f.
matrimonial [mætrɪ'məunɪəl] adj matrimoniale, coniugale.

matrimony ['mætrɪmənɪ] n matrimonio.
matrix, pl matrices ['meɪtrɪks, 'meɪtrɪsiːz] n matrice f.
matron ['meɪtrən] n (in hospital) capoinfermiera; (in school) infermiera.
matronly ['meɪtrənlɪ] adj da matrona.
matt [mæt] adj opaco(a).
matted ['mætɪd] adj ingarbugliato(a).
matter ['mætə*] n questione f; (PHYSICS) materia, sostanza; (content) contenuto; (MED: pus) pus m ♦ vi importare; **it doesn't** ~ non importa; (I don't mind) non fa niente; **what's the** ~? che cosa c'è?; **no** ~ **what** qualsiasi cosa accada; **that's another** ~ quello è un altro affare; **as a** ~ **of course** come cosa naturale; **as a** ~ **of fact** in verità; **it's a** ~ **of habit** è una questione di abitudine; **printed** ~ stampe fpl; **reading** ~ (BRIT) qualcosa da leggere.
matter-of-fact [mætərəv'fækt] adj prosaico(a).
matting ['mætɪŋ] n stuoia.
mattress ['mætrɪs] n materasso.
mature [mə'tjuə*] adj maturo(a); (cheese) stagionato(a) ♦ vi maturare; stagionare; (COMM) scadere.
mature student n studente universitario che ha più di 25 anni.
maturity [mə'tjuərɪtɪ] n maturità.
maudlin ['mɔːdlɪn] adj lacrimoso(a).
maul [mɔːl] vt lacerare.
Mauritania [mɔrɪ'teɪnɪə] n Mauritania.
Mauritius [mə'rɪʃəs] n Maurizio.
mausoleum [mɔːsə'lɪəm] n mausoleo.
mauve [məuv] adj malva inv.
maverick ['mævərɪk] n (fig) chi sta fuori del branco.
mawkish ['mɔːkɪʃ] adj sdolcinato(a); insipido(a).
max. abbr = **maximum**.
maxim ['mæksɪm] n massima.
maxima ['mæksɪmə] npl of **maximum**.
maximize ['mæksɪmaɪz] vt (profits etc) massimizzare; (chances) aumentare al massimo.
maximum ['mæksɪməm] adj massimo(a) ♦ n (pl **maxima**) massimo.
May [meɪ] n maggio; for phrases see also **July**.
may [meɪ] vi (conditional: **might**) (indicating possibility): **he** ~ **come** può darsi che venga; (be allowed to): ~ **I smoke?** posso fumare?; ~ **I sit here?** le dispiace se mi siedo qua?; (wishes): ~ **God bless you!** Dio la benedica!; **he might be there** può darsi che ci sia; **he might come** potrebbe venire, può anche darsi che venga; **I might as well go** potrei anche andarmene; **you might like to try** forse le

piacerebbe provare.

maybe ['meɪbiː] adv forse, può darsi; ~ **he'll** ... può darsi che lui ... +sub, forse lui ...; ~ **not** forse no, può darsi di no.

mayday ['meɪdeɪ] n S.O.S. m, mayday m inv.

May Day n il primo maggio.

mayhem ['meɪhɛm] n cagnara.

mayonnaise [meɪə'neɪz] n maionese f.

mayor [mɛə*] n sindaco.

mayoress ['mɛərɛs] n sindaco (donna); moglie f del sindaco.

maypole ['meɪpəul] n palo ornato di fiori attorno a cui si danza durante la festa di maggio.

maze [meɪz] n labirinto, dedalo.

MB abbr (COMPUT) = megabyte; (Canada) = Manitoba.

MBA n abbr (= Master of Business Administration) titolo di studio.

MBE n abbr (BRIT: = Member of the Order of the British Empire) titolo.

MBO n abbr see **management buyout**.

MC n abbr see **master of ceremonies**; (US: = Member of Congress) membro del Congresso.

MCAT n abbr (US: = Medical College Admissions Test) esame di ammissione a studi superiori di medicina.

MD n abbr (= Doctor of Medicine) titolo di studio; (COMM) see **managing director** ♦ abbr (US) = Maryland.

Md. abbr (US) = Maryland.

MDT abbr (US: = Mountain Daylight Time) ora legale delle Montagne Rocciose.

ME abbr (US) = Maine ♦ n abbr (MED: = myalgic encephalomyelitis) sindrome f da affaticamento cronico; (US) see **medical examiner**.

me [miː] pron mi, m' + vowel; (stressed, after prep) me; **it's** ~ sono io; **it's for** ~ è per me.

meadow ['mɛdəu] n prato.

meagre, (US) **meager** ['miːgə*] adj magro(a).

meal [miːl] n pasto; (flour) farina; **to go out for a** ~ mangiare fuori.

meals on wheels n (BRIT) distribuzione f di pasti caldi a domicilio (per persone malate o anziane).

mealtime ['miːltaɪm] n l'ora di mangiare.

mealy-mouthed ['miːlɪmauðd] adj che parla attraverso eufemismi.

mean [miːn] adj (with money) avaro(a), gretto(a); (unkind) meschino(a), maligno(a); (US: vicious: animal) cattivo(a); (: person) perfido(a); (average) medio(a) ♦ vt (pt, pp **meant** [mɛnt]) (signify) significare, voler dire; (intend): **to** ~ **to do**

aver l'intenzione di fare ♦ n mezzo; (MATH) media; **to be meant for** essere destinato(a) a; **do you** ~ **it?** dice sul serio?; **what do you** ~**?** che cosa vuol dire?; see also **means**.

meander [mɪ'ændə*] vi far meandri; (fig) divagare.

meaning ['miːnɪŋ] n significato, senso.

meaningful ['miːnɪŋful] adj significativo(a); (relationship) valido(a).

meaningless ['miːnɪŋlɪs] adj senza senso.

meanness ['miːnnɪs] n avarizia; meschinità.

means [miːnz] npl mezzi mpl; **by** ~ **of** per mezzo di; (person) a mezzo di; **by all** ~ ma certo, prego.

means test n (ADMIN) accertamento dei redditi (per una persona che ha chiesto un aiuto finanziario).

meant [mɛnt] pt, pp of **mean**.

meantime ['miːntaɪm], **meanwhile** ['miːnwaɪl] adv (also: **in the** ~) nel frattempo.

measles ['miːzlz] n morbillo.

measly ['miːzlɪ] adj (col) miserabile.

measurable ['mɛʒərəbl] adj misurabile.

measure ['mɛʒə*] vt, vi misurare ♦ n misura; (ruler) metro; **a litre** ~ una misura da un litro; **some** ~ **of success** un certo successo; **to take** ~**s to do sth** prendere provvedimenti per fare qc.

►**measure up** vi: **to** ~ **up (to)** dimostrarsi or essere all'altezza (di).

measured ['mɛʒəd] adj misurato(a).

measurement ['mɛʒəmənt] n (act) misurazione f; (measure) misura; **chest/hip** ~ giro petto/fianchi; **to take sb's** ~**s** prendere le misure di qn.

meat [miːt] n carne f; **cold** ~**s** (BRIT) affettati mpl; **crab** ~ polpa di granchio.

meatball ['miːtbɔːl] n polpetta di carne.

meat pie n torta salata in pasta frolla con ripieno di carne.

meaty ['miːtɪ] adj che sa di carne; (fig) sostanzioso(a); (of person) corpulento(a); (of part of body) carnoso(a); ~ **meal** pasto a base di carne.

Mecca ['mɛkə] n La Mecca; (fig): **a** ~ **(for)** la Mecca (di).

mechanic [mɪ'kænɪk] n meccanico; see also **mechanics**.

mechanical [mɪ'kænɪkəl] adj meccanico(a).

mechanical engineering n (science) ingegneria meccanica; (industry) costruzioni fpl meccaniche.

mechanics [mə'kænɪks] n meccanica ♦ npl meccanismo.

mechanism ['mɛkənɪzəm] n meccanismo.

mechanization [mɛkənaɪˈzeɪʃən] *n* meccanizzazione *f*.

MEd *n abbr* (= *Master of Education*) titolo di studio.

medal [ˈmɛdl] *n* medaglia.

medallion [mɪˈdælɪən] *n* medaglione *m*.

medallist, (*US*) **medalist** [ˈmɛdəlɪst] *n* (*SPORT*) vincitore/trice di medaglia.

meddle [ˈmɛdl] *vi*: **to ~ in** immischiarsi in, mettere le mani in; **to ~ with** toccare.

meddlesome [ˈmɛdlsəm], **meddling** [ˈmɛdlɪŋ] *adj* (*interfering*) che mette il naso dappertutto; (*touching things*) che tocca tutto.

media [ˈmiːdɪə] *npl* (*PRESS, RADIO, TV*) media *mpl*; (*means*) *pl of* **medium**.

media circus *n* carrozzone *m* dell'informazione.

mediaeval [mɛdɪˈiːvl] *adj* = **medieval**.

median [ˈmiːdɪən] *n* (*US: also:* **~ strip**) banchina *f* spartitraffico *inv*.

media research *n* sondaggio tra gli utenti dei mass media.

mediate [ˈmiːdɪeɪt] *vi* interporsi; fare da mediatore/trice.

mediation [miːdɪˈeɪʃən] *n* mediazione *f*.

mediator [ˈmiːdɪeɪtə*] *n* mediatore/trice.

Medicaid [ˈmɛdɪkeɪd] *n* (*US*) *assistenza medica ai poveri*.

medical [ˈmɛdɪkl] *adj* medico(a); **~ (examination)** visita medica.

medical certificate *n* certificato medico.

medical examiner (ME) *n* (*US*) *medico incaricato di indagare la causa di morte in circostanze sospette*.

medical student *n* studente/essa di medicina.

Medicare [ˈmɛdɪkɛə*] *n* (*US*) *assistenza medica agli anziani*.

medicated [ˈmɛdɪkeɪtɪd] *adj* medicato(a).

medication [mɛdɪˈkeɪʃən] *n* (*drugs etc*) medicinali *mpl*, farmaci *mpl*.

medicinal [mɛˈdɪsɪnl] *adj* medicinale.

medicine [ˈmɛdsɪn] *n* medicina.

medicine chest *n* armadietto farmaceutico.

medicine man *n* stregone *m*.

medieval [mɛdɪˈiːvl] *adj* medievale.

mediocre [miːdɪˈəukə*] *adj* mediocre.

mediocrity [miːdɪˈɔkrɪtɪ] *n* mediocrità.

meditate [ˈmɛdɪteɪt] *vi*: **to ~ (on)** meditare (su).

meditation [mɛdɪˈteɪʃən] *n* meditazione *f*.

Mediterranean [mɛdɪtəˈreɪnɪən] *adj* mediterraneo(a); **the ~ (Sea)** il (mare) Mediterraneo.

medium [ˈmiːdɪəm] *adj* medio(a) ◆ *n* (*pl* **media**: *means*) mezzo; (*pl* **mediums**:

person) medium *m inv*; **the happy ~** una giusta via di mezzo; *see also* **media**.

medium-dry [ˈmiːdɪəmˈdraɪ] *adj* demisec *inv*.

medium-sized [ˈmiːdɪəmsaɪzd] *adj* (*tin etc*) di grandezza media; (*clothes*) di taglia media.

medium wave *n* (*RADIO*) onde *fpl* medie.

medley [ˈmɛdlɪ] *n* selezione *f*.

meek [miːk] *adj* dolce, umile.

meet, *pt, pp* **met** [miːt, mɛt] *vt* incontrare; (*for the first time*) fare la conoscenza di; (*fig*) affrontare; far fronte a; soddisfare; raggiungere ◆ *vi* incontrarsi; (*in session*) riunirsi; (*join: objects*) unirsi ◆ *n* (*BRIT HUNTING*) raduno (dei partecipanti alla caccia alla volpe); (*US SPORT*) raduno (sportivo); **I'll ~ you at the station** verrò a prenderla alla stazione; **pleased to ~ you!** lieto di conoscerla!, piacere!

▶**meet up** *vi*: **to ~ up with sb** incontrare qn.

▶**meet with** *vt fus* incontrare; **he met with an accident** ha avuto un incidente.

meeting [ˈmiːtɪŋ] *n* incontro; (*session: of club etc*) riunione *f*; (*interview*) intervista; (*formal*) colloquio; (*SPORT: rally*) raduno; **she's at a ~** (*COMM*) è in riunione; **to call a ~** convocare una riunione.

meeting place *n* luogo d'incontro.

megabyte [ˈmɛgəbaɪt] *n* megabyte *m inv*.

megalomaniac [mɛgələuˈmeɪnɪæk] *n* megalomane *m/f*.

megaphone [ˈmɛgəfəun] *n* megafono.

megawatt [ˈmɛgəwɔt] *n* megawatt *m inv*.

melancholy [ˈmɛlənkəlɪ] *n* malinconia ◆ *adj* malinconico(a).

mellow [ˈmɛləu] *adj* (*wine, sound*) ricco(a); (*person, light*) dolce; (*colour*) caldo(a); (*fruit*) maturo(a) ◆ *vi* (*person*) addolcirsi.

melodious [mɪˈləudɪəs] *adj* melodioso(a).

melodrama [ˈmɛləudrɑːmə] *n* melodramma *m*.

melodramatic [mɛlədrəˈmætɪk] *adj* melodrammatico(a).

melody [ˈmɛlədɪ] *n* melodia.

melon [ˈmɛlən] *n* melone *m*.

melt [mɛlt] *vi* (*gen*) sciogliersi, struggersi; (*metals*) fondersi; (*fig*) intenerirsi ◆ *vt* sciogliere, struggere; fondere; (*person*) commuovere; **~ed butter** burro fuso.

▶**melt away** *vi* sciogliersi completamente.

▶**melt down** *vt* fondere.

meltdown [ˈmɛltdaun] *n* melt-down *m inv*.

melting point [ˈmɛltɪŋ-] *n* punto di fusione.

melting pot [ˈmɛltɪŋ-] *n* (*fig*) crogiolo; **to be in the ~** essere ancora in discussione.

member [ˈmɛmbə*] *n* membro; (*of club*)

socio/a, iscritto/a; (of political party) iscritto/a; ~ country/state n paese m/stato membro; M~ of Parliament (MP) n (BRIT) deputato; M~ of the European Parliament (MEP) n eurodeputato; M~ of the House of Representatives (MHR) n (US) membro della Camera dei Rappresentanti.

membership ['membəʃɪp] n iscrizione f; (numero d')iscritti mpl, membri mpl.

membership card n tessera (di iscrizione).

membrane ['membreɪn] n membrana.

memento [mə'mentəu] n ricordo.

memo ['meməu] n appunto; (COMM etc) comunicazione f di servizio.

memoir ['memwɑː*] n memoria; ~s npl memorie fpl, ricordi mpl.

memo pad n blocchetto per appunti.

memorable ['memərəbl] adj memorabile.

memorandum, pl memoranda [memə'rændəm, -də] n appunto; (COMM etc) comunicazione f di servizio; (DIPLOMACY) memorandum m inv.

memorial [mɪ'mɔːrɪəl] n monumento commemorativo ♦ adj commemorativo(a).

Memorial Day n (US) see boxed note.

MEMORIAL DAY

Negli Stati Uniti il **Memorial Day** è una festa nazionale per la commemorazione di tutti i soldati americani caduti in guerra. Le celebrazioni sono tenute ogni anno l'ultimo lunedì di maggio.

---

memorize ['meməraɪz] vt imparare a memoria.

memory ['meməri] n (gen, COMPUT) memoria; (recollection) ricordo; in ~ of in memoria di; to have a good/bad ~ aver buona/ cattiva memoria; loss of ~ amnesia.

men [men] npl of man.

menace ['menɪs] n minaccia; (col: nuisance) peste f ♦ vt minacciare; a public ~ un pericolo pubblico.

menacing ['menɪsɪŋ] adj minaccioso(a).

menagerie [mɪ'nædʒəri] n serraglio.

mend [mend] vt aggiustare, riparare; (darn) rammendare ♦ n rammendo; on the ~ in via di guarigione.

mending ['mendɪŋ] n rammendo; (items to be mended) roba da rammendare.

menial ['miːnɪəl] adj da servo; umile.

meningitis [menɪn'dʒaɪtɪs] n meningite f.

menopause ['menəupɔːz] n menopausa.

menservants ['mensəːvənts] npl of manservant.

men's room n: the ~ (esp US) la toilette degli uomini.

menstruate ['menstrueɪt] vi mestruare.

menstruation [menstru'eɪʃən] n mestruazione f.

menswear ['menzweə*] n abbigliamento maschile.

mental ['mentl] adj mentale; ~ illness malattia mentale.

mental hospital n ospedale m psichiatrico.

mentality [men'tælɪtɪ] n mentalità f inv.

mentally ['mentlɪ] adv: to be ~ handicapped essere minorato psichico.

menthol ['menθɔl] n mentolo.

mention ['menʃən] n menzione f ♦ vt menzionare, far menzione di; don't ~ it! non c'è di che!, prego!; I need hardly ~ that ... inutile dire che ...; not to ~, without ~ing per non parlare di, senza contare.

mentor ['mentɔː*] n mentore m.

menu ['menjuː] n (set ~, COMPUT) menù m inv; (printed) carta.

menu-driven ['menjuːdrɪvn] adj (COMPUT) guidato(a) da menù.

MEP n abbr see Member of the European Parliament.

mercantile ['məːkəntaɪl] adj mercantile; (law) commerciale.

mercenary ['məːsɪnəri] adj venale ♦ n mercenario.

merchandise ['məːtʃəndaɪz] n merci fpl ♦ vt commercializzare.

merchandiser ['məːtʃəndaɪzə*] n merchandiser m inv.

merchant ['məːtʃənt] n (trader) commerciante m; (shopkeeper) negoziante m; timber/wine ~ negoziante di legno/ vino.

merchant bank n (BRIT) banca d'affari.

merchantman ['məːtʃəntmən] n mercantile m.

merchant navy, (US) merchant marine n marina mercantile.

merciful ['məːsɪful] adj pietoso(a), clemente.

mercifully ['məːsɪflɪ] adv con clemenza; (fortunately) per fortuna.

merciless ['məːsɪlɪs] adj spietato(a).

mercurial [məː'kjuərɪəl] adj (unpredictable) volubile.

mercury ['məːkjurɪ] n mercurio.

mercy ['məːsɪ] n pietà f; (REL) misericordia; to have ~ on sb aver pietà di qn; at the ~ of alla mercè di.

mercy killing n eutanasia.

mere [mɪə*] adj semplice; by a ~ chance

per mero caso.
merely ['mɪəlɪ] *adv* semplicemente, non ... che.
merge [mɜːdʒ] *vt* unire; (*COMPUT*: *files, text*) fondere ♦ *vi* fondersi, unirsi; (*COMM*) fondersi.
merger ['mɜːdʒə*] *n* (*COMM*) fusione *f*.
meridian [mə'rɪdɪən] *n* meridiano.
meringue [mə'ræŋ] *n* meringa.
merit ['merɪt] *n* merito, valore *m* ♦ *vt* meritare.
meritocracy [merɪ'tɔkrəsɪ] *n* meritocrazia.
mermaid ['mɜːmeɪd] *n* sirena.
merriment ['merɪmənt] *n* gaiezza, allegria.
merry ['merɪ] *adj* gaio(a), allegro(a); **M~ Christmas!** Buon Natale!
merry-go-round ['merɪɡəuraund] *n* carosello.
mesh [meʃ] *n* maglia; rete *f* ♦ *vi* (*gears*) ingranarsi; **wire ~** rete metallica.
mesmerize ['mezməraɪz] *vt* ipnotizzare; affascinare.
mess [mes] *n* confusione *f*, disordine *m*; (*fig*) pasticcio; (*MIL*) mensa; **to be (in) a ~** (*house, room*) essere in disordine (*or* molto sporco); (*fig: marriage, life*) essere un caos; **to be/get o.s. in a ~** (*fig*) essere/cacciarsi in un pasticcio.
▶ **mess about, mess around** *vi* (*col*) trastullarsi.
▶ **mess about** *or* **around with** *vt fus* (*col*) gingillarsi con; (*plans*) fare un pasticcio di.
▶ **mess up** *vt* sporcare; fare un pasticcio di; rovinare.
message ['mesɪdʒ] *n* messaggio; **to get the ~** (*fig col*) capire l'antifona.
message switching *n* (*COMPUT*) smistamento messaggi.
messenger ['mesɪndʒə*] *n* messaggero/a.
Messiah [mɪ'saɪə] *n* Messia *m*.
Messrs, Messrs. ['mesəz] *abbr* (*on letters:* = *messieurs*) Spett.
messy ['mesɪ] *adj* sporco(a); disordinato(a); (*confused: situation etc*) ingarbugliato(a).
Met [met] *n abbr* (*US*) = *Metropolitan Opera*.
met [met] *pt, pp of* **meet** ♦ *adj abbr* (= *meteorological*): **the M~ Office** l'Ufficio Meteorologico.
metabolism [me'tæbəlɪzəm] *n* metabolismo.
metal ['metl] *n* metallo ♦ *vt* massicciare.
metallic [me'tælɪk] *adj* metallico(a).
metallurgy [me'tælədʒɪ] *n* metallurgia.
metalwork ['metlwɜːk] *n* (*craft*) lavorazione *f* del metallo.
metamorphosis, *pl* **-phoses**

[metə'mɔːfəsɪs, -iːz] *n* metamorfosi *f inv.*
metaphor ['metəfə*] *n* metafora.
metaphysics [metə'fɪzɪks] *n* metafisica.
mete [miːt]: **to ~ out** *vt fus* infliggere.
meteor ['miːtɪə*] *n* meteora.
meteoric [miːtɪ'ɔrɪk] *adj* (*fig*) fulmineo(a).
meteorite ['miːtɪəraɪt] *n* meteorite *m*.
meteorological [miːtɪərə'lɔdʒɪkl] *adj* meteorologico(a).
meteorology [miːtɪə'rɔlədʒɪ] *n* meteorologia.
meter ['miːtə*] *n* (*instrument*) contatore *m*; (*parking ~*) parchimetro; (*US*) = **metre**.
methane ['miːθeɪn] *n* metano.
method ['meθəd] *n* metodo; **~ of payment** modo *or* modalità *f inv* di pagamento.
methodical [mɪ'θɔdɪkl] *adj* metodico(a).
Methodist ['meθədɪst] *adj, n* metodista (*m/f*).
methylated spirits ['meθɪleɪtɪd-] *n* (*BRIT: also:* **meths**) alcool *m* denaturato.
meticulous [me'tɪkjuləs] *adj* meticoloso(a).
metre, (*US*) **meter** ['miːtə*] *n* metro.
metric ['metrɪk] *adj* metrico(a); **to go ~** adottare il sistema metrico decimale.
metrical ['metrɪkl] *adj* metrico(a).
metrication [metrɪ'keɪʃən] *n* conversione *f* al sistema metrico.
metric system *n* sistema *m* metrico decimale.
metric ton *n* tonnellata.
metronome ['metrənəum] *n* metronomo.
metropolis [mɪ'trɔpəlɪs] *n* metropoli *f inv.*
metropolitan [metrə'pɔlɪtən] *adj* metropolitano(a).
Metropolitan Police *n* (*BRIT*): **the ~** la polizia di Londra.
mettle ['metl] *n* coraggio.
mew [mjuː] *vi* (*cat*) miagolare.
mews [mjuːz] *n* (*BRIT*): **~ flat** appartamentino ricavato da una vecchia scuderia.
Mexican ['meksɪkən] *adj, n* messicano(a).
Mexico ['meksɪkəu] *n* Messico.
Mexico City *n* Città del Messico.
mezzanine ['metsəniːn] *n* mezzanino.
MFA *n abbr* (*US*: = *Master of Fine Arts*) titolo di studio.
mfr *abbr* = **manufacture; manufacturer.**
mg *abbr* (= *milligram*) mg.
Mgr *abbr* (= *Monseigneur, Monsignor*) mons.; (*COMM*) = **manager.**
MHR *n abbr* (*US*) *see* **Member of the House of Representatives.**
MHz *abbr* (= *megahertz*) MHz.
MI *abbr* (*US*) = *Michigan.*
MI5 *n abbr* (*BRIT*: = *Military Intelligence, section five*) agenzia di controspionaggio.

MI6 n abbr (BRIT: = Military Intelligence, section 6) agenzia di spionaggio.
MIA abbr = **missing in action.**
miaow [miː'au] vi miagolare.
mice [maɪs] npl of **mouse.**
Mich. abbr (US) = Michigan.
microbe ['maɪkrəub] n microbio.
microbiology [maɪkrəubaɪ'ɔlədʒɪ] n microbiologia.
microchip ['maɪkrəutʃɪp] n microcircuito integrato, chip m inv.
microcomputer [maɪkrəukəm'pjuːtə*] n microcomputer m inv.
microcosm ['maɪkrəukɔzəm] n microcosmo.
microeconomics [maɪkrəuiːkə'nɔmɪks] n microeconomia.
microfiche ['maɪkrəufiːʃ] n microfiche f inv.
microfilm ['maɪkrəufɪlm] n microfilm m inv ♦ vt microfilmare.
microlight ['maɪkrəulaɪt] n aereo m biposto inv.
micrometer [maɪ'krɔmɪtə*] n micrometro, palmer m inv.
microphone ['maɪkrəfəun] n microfono.
microprocessor [maɪkrəu'prəusesə*] n microprocessore m.
micro-scooter ['maɪkrəuskuːtə*] n monopattino.
microscope ['maɪkrəskəup] n microscopio; **under the** ~ al microscopio.
microscopic [maɪkrə'skɔpɪk] adj microscopico(a).
microwavable, microwaveable ['maɪkrəuweɪvəbl] adj adatto(a) al forno a microonde.
microwave ['maɪkrəuweɪv] n (also: ~ **oven**) forno a microonde.
mid [mɪd] adj: ~ **May** metà maggio; ~ **afternoon** metà pomeriggio; **in** ~ **air** a mezz'aria; **he's in his** ~ **thirties** avrà circa trentacinque anni.
midday [mɪd'deɪ] n mezzogiorno.
middle ['mɪdl] n mezzo; centro; (waist) vita ♦ adj di mezzo; **I'm in the** ~ **of reading I** sto proprio leggendolo ora; **in the** ~ **of the night** nel mezzo della notte.
middle age n mezza età.
middle-aged [mɪdl'eɪdʒd] adj di mezza età.
Middle Ages npl: **the** ~ il Medioevo.
middle class adj (also: **middle-class**) ≈ borghese ♦ n: **the** ~(**es**) ≈ la borghesia.
Middle East n: **the** ~ il Medio Oriente.
middleman ['mɪdlmæn] n intermediario; agente m rivenditore.
middle management n quadri mpl intermedi.
middle name n secondo nome m.

middle-of-the-road ['mɪdləvðə'rəud] adj moderato(a).
middleweight ['mɪdlweɪt] n (BOXING) peso medio.
middling ['mɪdlɪŋ] adj medio(a).
midge [mɪdʒ] n moscerino.
midget ['mɪdʒɪt] n nano/a.
midi system ['mɪdɪ-] n (hi-fi) compatto.
Midlands ['mɪdləndz] npl contee del centro dell'Inghilterra.
midnight ['mɪdnaɪt] n mezzanotte f; **at** ~ a mezzanotte.
midriff ['mɪdrɪf] n diaframma m.
midst [mɪdst] n: **in the** ~ **of** in mezzo a.
midsummer [mɪd'sʌmə*] n mezza or piena estate f.
midway [mɪd'weɪ] adj, adv: ~ (**between**) a mezza strada (fra).
midweek [mɪd'wiːk] adv, adj a metà settimana.
midwife, pl **midwives** ['mɪdwaɪf, -vz] n levatrice f.
midwifery ['mɪdwɪfərɪ] n ostetrica.
midwinter [mɪd'wɪntə*] n pieno inverno.
miffed [mɪft] adj (col) seccato(a).
might [maɪt] vb see **may** ♦ n potere m, forza.
mighty ['maɪtɪ] adj forte, potente ♦ adv (col) molto.
migraine ['miːgreɪn] n emicrania.
migrant ['maɪgrənt] n (bird, animal) migratore m; (person) migrante m/f; nomade m/f ♦ adj migratore(trice); nomade; (worker) emigrato(a).
migrate [maɪ'greɪt] vi migrare.
migration [maɪ'greɪʃən] n migrazione f.
mike [maɪk] n abbr (= microphone) microfono.
Milan [mɪ'læn] n Milano f.
mild [maɪld] adj mite; (person, voice) dolce; (flavour) delicato(a); (illness) leggero(a) ♦ n birra leggera.
mildew ['mɪldjuː] n muffa.
mildly ['maɪldlɪ] adv mitemente; dolcemente; delicatamente; leggermente; **to put it** ~ a dire poco.
mildness ['maɪldnɪs] n mitezza; dolcezza; delicatezza; non gravità.
mile [maɪl] n miglio; **to do 20** ~**s per gallon** ≈ usare 14 litri per cento chilometri.
mileage ['maɪlɪdʒ] n distanza in miglia, ≈ chilometraggio.
mileage allowance n rimborso per miglio.
mileometer [maɪ'lɔmɪtə*] n (BRIT) = **milometer.**
milestone ['maɪlstəun] n pietra miliare.
milieu ['miːljəː] n ambiente m.
militant ['mɪlɪtnt] adj, n militante (m/f).

militarism ['mılıtərızəm] n militarismo.
militaristic [mılıtə'rıstık] adj
militaristico(a).
military ['mılıtərı] adj militare ♦ n: **the** ~ i
militari, l'esercito.
military service n servizio militare.
militate ['mılıteıt] vi: **to** ~ **against** essere
d'ostacolo a.
militia [mı'lıʃə] n milizia.
milk [mılk] n latte m ♦ vt (cow) mungere;
(fig) sfruttare.
milk chocolate n cioccolato al latte.
milk float n (BRIT) furgone m del lattaio.
milking ['mılkıŋ] n mungitura.
milkman ['mılkmən] n lattaio.
milk shake n frappé m inv.
milk tooth n dente m di latte.
milk truck n (US) = **milk float**.
milky ['mılkı] adj lattiginoso(a); (colour)
latteo(a).
Milky Way n Via Lattea.
mill [mıl] n mulino; (small: for coffee, pepper
etc) macinino; (factory) fabbrica; (spinning
~) filatura ♦ vt macinare ♦ vi (also: ~
about) formicolare.
millennium, pl ~s or **millennia**
[mı'lɛnɪəm, -'lɛnɪə] n millennio.
millennium bug n baco di fine
millennio.
miller ['mılə*] n mugnaio.
millet ['mılıt] n miglio.
milli... ['mılı] prefix milli....
milligram(me) ['mılıgræm] n milligrammo.
millilitre, (US) **milliliter** ['mılıliːtə*] n
millilitro.
millimetre, (US) **millimeter** ['mılımiːtə*] n
millimetro.
milliner ['mılınə*] n modista.
millinery ['mılınərı] n modisteria.
million ['mıljən] n milione m.
millionaire [mıljə'nɛə*] n milionario,
≈ miliardario.
millipede ['mılıpiːd] n millepiedi m inv.
millstone ['mılstəun] n macina.
millwheel ['mılwiːl] n ruota di mulino.
milometer [maı'lɔmıtə*] n
≈ contachilometri m inv.
mime [maım] n mimo ♦ vt, vi mimare.
mimic ['mımık] n imitatore/trice ♦ vt (subj:
comedian) imitare; (: animal, person)
scimmiottare.
mimicry ['mımıkrı] n imitazioni fpl; (ZOOL)
mimetismo.
Min. abbr (BRIT POL: = ministry) Min.
min. abbr (= minute, minimum) min.
minaret [mınə'rɛt] n minareto.
mince [mıns] vt tritare, macinare ♦ vi (in
walking) camminare a passettini ♦ n (BRIT

CULIN) carne f tritata; **he does not** ~ (his)
words parla chiaro e tondo.
mincemeat ['mınsmiːt] n frutta secca
tritata per uso in pasticceria.
mince pie n specie di torta con frutta
secca.
mincer ['mınsə*] n tritacarne m inv.
mincing ['mınsıŋ] adj lezioso(a).
mind [maınd] n mente f ♦ vt (attend to, look
after) badare a, occuparsi di; (be careful)
fare attenzione a, stare attento(a) a;
(object to): **I don't** ~ **the noise** il rumore
non mi dà alcun fastidio; **do you** ~ **if ...?**
le dispiace se ...?; **I don't** ~ non
m'importa; ~ **you,** ... sì, però va detto
che ...; **never** ~ non importa, non fa
niente; **it is on my** ~ mi preoccupa; **to**
change one's ~ cambiare idea; **to be in**
two ~**s about sth** essere incerto su qc; **to**
my ~ secondo me, a mio parere; **to be**
out of one's ~ essere uscito(a) di mente;
to keep sth in ~ non dimenticare qc; **to**
bear sth in ~ tener presente qc; **to have**
sb/sth in ~ avere in mente qn/qc; **to have**
in ~ **to do** aver l'intenzione di fare; **it**
went right out of my ~ mi è
completamente passato di mente, me ne
sono completamente dimenticato; **to**
bring or **call sth to** ~ riportare or
richiamare qc alla mente; **to make up**
one's ~ decidersi; "~ **the step**"
"attenzione allo scalino".
mind-boggling ['maındbɔglıŋ] adj (col)
sconcertante.
-minded ['maındıd] adj: **fair**~ imparziale;
an industrially~ **nation** una nazione
orientata verso l'industria.
minder ['maındə*] n (child ~) bambinaia;
(bodyguard) guardia del corpo.
mindful ['maındful] adj: ~ **of** attento(a) a;
memore di.
mindless ['maındlıs] adj idiota; (violence,
crime) insensato(a).
mine [maın] pron il(la) mio(a), pl i(le)
miei(mie); **this book is** ~ questo libro è
mio ♦ n miniera; (explosive) mina ♦ vt
(coal) estrarre; (ship, beach) minare.
mine detector n rivelatore m di mine.
minefield ['maınfiːld] n campo minato.
miner ['maınə*] n minatore m.
mineral ['mınərəl] adj minerale ♦ n
minerale m; ~**s** npl (BRIT: soft drinks)
bevande fpl gasate.
mineralogy [mınə'rælədʒı] n mineralogia.
mineral water n acqua minerale.
minesweeper ['maınswiːpə*] n dragamine
m inv.
mingle ['mıŋgl] vt mescolare, mischiare

♦ *vi:* to ~ with mescolarsi a, mischiarsi con.

mingy ['mɪndʒɪ] *adj (col: amount)* misero(a); (: *person*) spilorcio(a).

miniature ['mɪnətʃə*] *adj* in miniatura ♦ *n* miniatura.

minibus ['mɪnɪbʌs] *n* minibus *m inv.*

minicab ['mɪnɪkæb] *n (BRIT)* ≈ taxi *m inv.*

minicomputer ['mɪnɪkəm'pjuːtə*] *n* minicomputer *m inv.*

Minidisc ® ['mɪnɪdɪsk] *n* minidisc *m inv.*

minim ['mɪnɪm] *n (MUS)* minima.

minima ['mɪnɪmə] *npl of* **minimum.**

minimal ['mɪnɪml] *adj* minimo(a).

minimalist ['mɪnɪməlɪst] *adj, n* minimalista *(m/f).*

minimize ['mɪnɪmaɪz] *vt* minimizzare.

minimum ['mɪnɪməm] *n (pl* **minima)** minimo ♦ *adj* minimo(a); **to reduce to a** ~ ridurre al minimo; ~ **wage** salario minimo garantito.

minimum lending rate (MLR) *n (BRIT)* ≈ tasso ufficiale di sconto (T.U.S.).

mining ['maɪnɪŋ] *n* industria mineraria ♦ *adj* minerario(a); di minatori.

minion ['mɪnjən] *n (pej)* caudatario; favorito/a.

mini-series ['mɪnɪsɪəriːz] *n* miniserie *f inv.*

miniskirt ['mɪnɪskəːt] *n* minigonna.

minister ['mɪnɪstə*] *n (BRIT POL)* ministro; *(REL)* pastore *m* ♦ *vi:* to ~ to ~ sb assistere qn; to ~ to sb's needs provvedere ai bisogni di qn.

ministerial [mɪnɪs'tɪərɪəl] *adj (BRIT POL)* ministeriale.

ministry ['mɪnɪstrɪ] *n (BRIT POL)* ministero; *(REL):* to go into the ~ diventare pastore.

mink [mɪŋk] *n* visone *m.*

mink coat *n* pelliccia di visone.

Minn. *abbr (US)* = *Minnesota.*

minnow ['mɪnəu] *n* pesciolino d'acqua dolce.

minor ['maɪnə*] *adj* minore, di poca importanza; *(MUS)* minore ♦ *n (LAW)* minorenne *m/f.*

Minorca [mɪ'nɔːkə] *n* Minorca.

minority [maɪ'nɔrɪtɪ] *n* minoranza; to be in a ~ essere in minoranza.

minster ['mɪnstə*] *n* cattedrale *f (annessa a monastero).*

minstrel ['mɪnstrəl] *n* giullare *m,* menestrello.

mint [mɪnt] *n (plant)* menta; *(sweet)* pasticca di menta ♦ *vt (coins)* battere; **the (Royal) M~,** *(US)* **the (US) M~** la Zecca; **in** ~ **condition** come nuovo(a) di zecca.

mint sauce *n* salsa di menta.

minuet [mɪnju'ɛt] *n* minuetto.

minus ['maɪnəs] *n (also:* ~ **sign)** segno meno ♦ *prep* meno.

minuscule ['mɪnəskjuːl] *adj* minuscolo(a).

minute *adj* [maɪ'njuːt] minuscolo(a); *(detail)* minuzioso(a) ♦ *n* ['mɪnɪt] minuto; *(official record)* processo verbale, resoconto sommario; ~**s** *npl* verbale *m,* verbali *mpl;* **it is 5** ~**s past 3** sono le 3 e 5 (minuti); **wait a** ~! (aspetta) un momento!; **at the last** ~ all'ultimo momento; **up to the** ~ ultimissimo; modernissimo; **in** ~ **detail** minuziosamente.

minute book *n* libro dei verbali.

minute hand *n* lancetta dei minuti.

minutely [maɪ'njuːtlɪ] *adv (by a small amount)* di poco; *(in detail)* minuziosamente.

minutiae [mɪ'njuːʃiː] *npl* minuzie *fpl.*

miracle ['mɪrəkl] *n* miracolo.

miraculous [mɪ'rækjuləs] *adj* miracoloso(a).

mirage ['mɪrɑːʒ] *n* miraggio.

mire ['maɪə*] *n* pantano, melma.

mirror ['mɪrə*] *n* specchio ♦ *vt* rispecchiare, riflettere.

mirror image *n* immagine *f* speculare.

mirth [məːθ] *n* gaiezza.

misadventure [mɪsəd'vɛntʃə*] *n* disavventura; **death by** ~ *(BRIT)* morte *f* accidentale.

misanthropist [mɪ'zænθrəpɪst] *n* misantropo/a.

misapply [mɪsə'plaɪ] *vt* impiegare male.

misapprehension ['mɪsæprɪ'henʃən] *n* malinteso.

misappropriate [mɪsə'prəuprɪeɪt] *vt* appropriarsi indebitamente di.

misappropriation ['mɪsəprəuprɪ'eɪʃən] *n* appropriazione *f* indebita.

misbehave [mɪsbɪ'heɪv] *vi* comportarsi male.

misbehaviour, *(US)* **misbehavior** [mɪsbɪ'heɪvjə*] *n* comportamento scorretto.

misc. *abbr* = **miscellaneous.**

miscalculate [mɪs'kælkjuleɪt] *vt* calcolare male.

miscalculation ['mɪskælkju'leɪʃən] *n* errore *m* di calcolo.

miscarriage ['mɪskærɪdʒ] *n (MED)* aborto spontaneo; ~ **of justice** errore *m* giudiziario.

miscarry [mɪs'kærɪ] *vi (MED)* abortire; *(fail: plans)* andare a monte, fallire.

miscellaneous [mɪsɪ'leɪnɪəs] *adj (items)* vario(a); *(selection)* misto(a); ~ **expenses** spese varie.

miscellany [mɪ'sɛlənɪ] *n* raccolta.

mischance [mɪs'tʃɑːns] *n:* **by (some)** ~ per

sfortuna.

mischief['mɪstʃɪf] n (naughtiness) birichineria; (harm) male m, danno; (maliciousness) malizia.

mischievous['mɪstʃɪvəs] adj (naughty) birichino(a); (harmful) dannoso(a).

misconception[mɪskən'sɛpʃən] n idea sbagliata.

misconduct[mɪs'kɔndʌkt] n cattiva condotta; **professional** ~ reato professionale.

misconstrue[mɪskən'struː] vt interpretare male.

miscount[mɪs'kaunt] vt, vi contare male.

misdeed[mɪs'diːd] n (old) misfatto.

misdemeanour,(US) **misdemeanor** [mɪsdɪ'miːnə*] n misfatto; infrazione f.

misdirect[mɪsdɪ'rɛkt] vt mal indirizzare.

miser['maɪzə*] n avaro.

miserable['mɪzərəbl] adj infelice; (wretched) miserabile; (weather) deprimente; **to feel** ~ sentirsi avvilito or giù di morale.

miserably['mɪzərəblɪ] adv (fail, live, pay) miseramente; (smile, answer) tristemente.

miserly['maɪzəlɪ] adj avaro(a).

misery['mɪzərɪ] n (unhappiness) tristezza; (pain) sofferenza; (wretchedness) miseria.

misfire[mɪs'faɪə*] vi far cilecca; (car engine) perdere colpi.

misfit['mɪsfɪt] n (person) spostato/a.

misfortune[mɪs'fɔːtʃən] n sfortuna.

misgiving(s)[mɪs'ɡɪvɪŋ(z)] n(pl) dubbi mpl, sospetti mpl; **to have** ~**s about sth** essere diffidente or avere dei dubbi per quanto riguarda qc.

misguided[mɪs'ɡaɪdɪd] adj sbagliato(a); poco giudizioso(a).

mishandle[mɪs'hændl] vt (treat roughly) maltrattare; (mismanage) trattare male.

mishap['mɪshæp] n disgrazia.

mishear[mɪs'hɪə*] vt, vi irreg capire male.

mishmash['mɪʃmæʃ] n (col) minestrone m, guazzabuglio.

misinform[mɪsɪn'fɔːm] vt informare male.

misinterpret[mɪsɪn'təːprɪt] vt interpretare male.

misinterpretation['mɪsɪntəːprɪ'teɪʃən] n errata interpretazione f.

misjudge[mɪs'dʒʌdʒ] vt giudicare male.

mislay[mɪs'leɪ] vt irreg smarrire.

mislead[mɪs'liːd] vt irreg sviare.

misleading[mɪs'liːdɪŋ] adj ingannevole.

misled[mɪs'lɛd] pt, pp of **mislead**.

mismanage[mɪs'mænɪdʒ] vt gestire male; trattare male.

mismanagement[mɪs'mænɪdʒmənt] n

cattiva amministrazione f.

misnomer[mɪs'nəumə*] n termine m sbagliato or improprio.

misogynist[mɪ'sɔdʒɪnɪst] n misogino.

misplace[mɪs'pleɪs] vt smarrire; collocare fuori posto; **to be** ~**d** (trust etc) essere malriposto(a).

misprint['mɪsprɪnt] n errore m di stampa.

mispronounce[mɪsprə'nauns] vt pronunziare male.

misquote[mɪs'kwəut] vt citare erroneamente.

misread[mɪs'riːd] vt irreg leggere male.

misrepresent[mɪsrɛprɪ'zɛnt] vt travisare.

Miss[mɪs] n Signorina; **Dear** ~ **Smith** Cara Signorina; (more formal) Gentile Signorina.

miss[mɪs] vt (fail to get) perdere; (appointment, class) mancare a; (escape, avoid) evitare; (notice loss of: money etc) accorgersi di non avere più; (regret the absence of): **I** ~ **him/it** sento la sua mancanza, lui/esso mi manca ♦ vi mancare ♦ n (shot) colpo mancato; (fig): **that was a near** ~ c'è mancato poco; **the bus just** ~**ed the wall** l'autobus per un pelo non è andato a finire contro il muro; **you're** ~**ing the point** non capisce.

▶**miss out**vt (BRIT) omettere.

▶**miss out on**vt fus (fun, party) perdersi; (chance, bargain) lasciarsi sfuggire.

Miss.abbr (US) = Mississippi.

missal['mɪsl] n messale m.

misshapen[mɪs'ʃeɪpən] adj deforme.

missile['mɪsaɪl] n (AVIAT) missile m; (object thrown) proiettile m.

missile basen base f missilistica.

missile launchern lancia-missili m inv.

missing['mɪsɪŋ] adj perso(a), smarrito(a); **to go** ~ sparire; ~ **person** scomparso/a, disperso/a; ~ **in action** (MIL) disperso/a.

mission['mɪʃən] n missione f; **on a** ~ **to sb** in missione da qn.

missionary['mɪʃənrɪ] n missionario/a.

misspell[mɪs'spɛl] vt (irreg: like **spell**) sbagliare l'ortografia di.

misspent[mɪs'spɛnt] adj: **his** ~ **youth** la sua gioventù sciupata.

mist[mɪst] n nebbia, foschia ♦ vi (also: ~ **over**, ~ **up**) annebbiarsi; (BRIT: windows) appannarsi.

mistake[mɪs'teɪk] n sbaglio, errore m ♦ vt (irreg: like **take**) sbagliarsi di; fraintendere; **to** ~ **for** prendere per; **by** ~ per sbaglio; **to make a** ~ (in writing, calculating etc) fare uno sbaglio or un errore; **to make a** ~ **about sb/sth** sbagliarsi sul conto di qn/su qc.

mistaken [mɪs'teɪkən] pp of **mistake** ♦ adj (idea etc) sbagliato(a); **to be** ~ sbagliarsi.
mistaken identity n errore m di persona.
mistakenly [mɪs'teɪkənlɪ] adv per errore.
mister ['mɪstə*] n (col) signore m; see **Mr.**
mistletoe ['mɪsltəu] n vischio.
mistook [mɪs'tuk] pt of **mistake**.
mistranslation [mɪstræns'leɪʃən] n traduzione f errata.
mistreat [mɪs'triːt] vt maltrattare.
mistress ['mɪstrɪs] n padrona; (lover) amante f; (BRIT SCOL) insegnante f.
mistrust [mɪs'trʌst] vt diffidare di ♦ n: ~ (of) diffidenza (nei confronti di).
mistrustful [mɪs'trʌstful] adj: ~ (of) diffidente (nei confronti di).
misty ['mɪstɪ] adj nebbioso(a), brumoso(a).
misty-eyed ['mɪstɪ'aɪd] adj trasognato(a).
misunderstand [mɪsʌndə'stænd] vt, vi irreg capire male, fraintendere.
misunderstanding [mɪsʌndə'stændɪŋ] n malinteso, equivoco.
misunderstood [mɪsʌndə'stud] pt, pp of **misunderstand**.
misuse n [mɪs'juːs] cattivo uso; (of power) abuso ♦ vt [mɪs'juːz] far cattivo uso di; abusare di.
MIT n abbr (US) = Massachusetts Institute of Technology.
mite [maɪt] n (small quantity) briciolo; (BRIT: small child): **poor** ~! povera creaturina!
miter ['maɪtə*] n (US) = **miter**.
mitigate ['mɪtɪgeɪt] vt mitigare; (suffering) alleviare; **mitigating circumstances** circostanze fpl attenuanti.
mitigation [mɪtɪ'geɪʃən] n mitigazione f; alleviamento.
mitre, (US) **miter** ['maɪtə*] n mitra; (CARPENTRY) giunto ad angolo retto.
mitt(en) ['mɪt(n)] n mezzo guanto; manopola.
mix [mɪks] vt mescolare ♦ vi mescolarsi ♦ n mescolanza; preparato; **to** ~ **sth with sth** mischiare qc a qc; **to** ~ **business with pleasure** unire l'utile al dilettevole; **cake** ~ preparato per torta.
▶**mix in** vt (eggs etc) incorporare.
▶**mix up** vt mescolare; (confuse) confondere; **to be** ~**ed up in sth** essere coinvolto in qc.
mixed [mɪkst] adj misto(a).
mixed-ability ['mɪkstə'bɪlɪtɪ] adj (class etc) con alunni di capacità diverse.
mixed bag n miscuglio, accozzaglia; **it's a** ~ c'è un po' di tutto.
mixed blessing n: **it's a** ~ ha i suoi lati positivi e negativi.
mixed doubles npl (SPORT) doppio misto.

mixed economy n economia mista.
mixed grill n (BRIT) misto alla griglia.
mixed marriage n matrimonio misto.
mixed-up [mɪkst'ʌp] adj (confused) confuso(a).
mixer ['mɪksə*] n (for food: electric) frullatore m; (: hand) frullino; (person): **he is a good** ~ è molto socievole.
mixer tap n miscelatore m.
mixture ['mɪkstʃə*] n mescolanza; (blend: of tobacco etc) miscela; (MED) sciroppo.
mix-up ['mɪksʌp] n confusione f.
MK abbr (BRIT TECH) = **mark**.
mk abbr (HIST) = **mark** (currency).
mkt abbr = **market**.
MLitt n abbr (= Master of Literature, Master of Letters) titolo di studio.
MLR n abbr (BRIT) see **minimum lending rate**.
mm abbr (= millimetre) mm.
MN n abbr (BRIT) = **Merchant Navy**; (US) = Minnesota.
MO n abbr = medical officer; (US col: = modus operandi) modo d'agire ♦ abbr (US) = Missouri.
m.o. abbr = money order.
moan [məun] n gemito ♦ vi gemere; (col: complain): **to** ~ **(about)** lamentarsi (di).
moaner ['məunə*] n (col) uno/a che si lamenta sempre.
moaning ['məunɪŋ] n gemiti mpl.
moat [məut] n fossato.
mob [mɔb] n folla; (disorderly) calca; (pej): **the** ~ la plebaglia ♦ vt accalcarsi intorno a.
mobile ['məubaɪl] adj mobile ♦ n (ART) mobile m inv; **applicants must be** ~ (BRIT) i candidati devono essere disposti a viaggiare.
mobile home n grande roulotte f inv (utilizzata come domicilio).
mobile phone n telefonino.
mobile shop n (BRIT) negozio ambulante.
mobility [məu'bɪlɪtɪ] n mobilità; (of applicant) disponibilità a viaggiare.
mobilize ['məubɪlaɪz] vt mobilitare ♦ vi mobilitarsi.
moccasin ['mɔkəsɪn] n mocassino.
mock [mɔk] vt deridere, burlarsi di ♦ adj falso(a).
mockery ['mɔkərɪ] n derisione f; **to make a** ~ **of** rendere ridicolo.
mocking ['mɔkɪŋ] adj derisorio(a).
mockingbird ['mɔkɪŋbɔːd] n mimo (uccello).
mock-up ['mɔkʌp] n modello dimostrativo; abbozzo.
MOD n abbr (BRIT) = Ministry of Defence; see **defence**.

mod cons ['mɔd'kɔnz] *npl abbr* (*BRIT*) = **modern conveniences**.

mode [məud] *n* modo; (*of transport*) mezzo; (*COMPUT*) modalità *f inv*.

model ['mɔdl] *n* modello; (*person: for fashion*) indossatore/trice; (*: for artist*) modello/a ♦ *vt* modellare ♦ *vi* fare l'indossatore (*or* l'indossatrice) ♦ *adj* (*small-scale: railway etc*) in miniatura; (*child, factory*) modello *inv*; **to ~ clothes** presentare degli abiti; **to ~ sb/sth on** modellare qn/qc su.

modem ['məudɛm] *n* modem *m inv*.

moderate ['mɔdərɪt] *adj* moderato(a) ♦ *n* (*POL*) moderato/a ♦ *vb* ['mɔdəreɪt] *vi* moderarsi, placarsi ♦ *vt* moderare.

moderately ['mɔdərɪtlɪ] *adv* (*act*) con moderazione; (*expensive, difficult*) non troppo; (*pleased, happy*) abbastanza, discretamente; **~ priced** a prezzo modico.

moderation [mɔdə'reɪʃən] *n* moderazione *f*, misura; **in ~** in quantità moderata, con moderazione.

moderator ['mɔdəreɪtə*] *n* moderatore/ trice; (*REL*) moderatore *in importanti riunioni ecclesiastiche*.

modern ['mɔdən] *adj* moderno(a); **~ conveniences** comodità *fpl* moderne; **~ languages** lingue *fpl* moderne.

modernization [mɔdənaɪ'zeɪʃən] *n* rimodernamento, modernizzazione *f*.

modernize ['mɔdənaɪz] *vt* modernizzare.

modest ['mɔdɪst] *adj* modesto(a).

modesty ['mɔdɪstɪ] *n* modestia.

modicum ['mɔdɪkəm] *n*: **a ~ of** un minimo di.

modification [mɔdɪfɪ'keɪʃən] *n* modificazione *f*; **to make ~s** fare *or* apportare delle modifiche.

modify ['mɔdɪfaɪ] *vt* modificare.

modish ['məudɪʃ] *adj* (*liter*) à la page *inv*.

Mods [mɔdz] *n abbr* (*BRIT*: = *(Honour) Moderations*) *esame all'università di Oxford*.

modular ['mɔdjulə*] *adj* (*filing, unit*) modulare.

modulate ['mɔdjuleɪt] *vt* modulare.

modulation [mɔdju'leɪʃən] *n* modulazione *f*.

module ['mɔdju:l] *n* modulo.

Mogadishu [mɔgə'dɪʃu:] *n* Mogadiscio *f*.

mogul ['məugl] *n* (*fig*) magnate *m*, pezzo grosso; (*SKI*) cunetta.

MOH *n abbr* (*BRIT*: = *Medical Officer of Health*) ≈ ufficiale *m* sanitario.

mohair ['məuhɛə*] *n* mohair *m*.

Mohammed [məu'hæmɪd] *n* Maometto.

moist [mɔɪst] *adj* umido(a).

moisten ['mɔɪsn] *vt* inumidire.

moisture ['mɔɪstʃə*] *n* umidità; (*on glass*) goccioline *fpl* di vapore.

moisturize ['mɔɪstʃəraɪz] *vt* (*skin*) idratare.

moisturizer ['mɔɪstʃəraɪzə*] *n* idratante *f*.

molar ['məulə*] *n* molare *m*.

molasses [məu'læsɪz] *n* molassa.

mold [məuld] *etc* (*US*) = **mould** *etc*.

Moldavia [mɔl'deɪvɪə], **Moldova** [mɔl'dəuvə] *n* Moldavia.

Moldavian [mɔl'deɪvɪən], **Moldovan** [mɔl'dəuvən] *adj* moldavo(a).

mole [məul] *n* (*animal*) talpa; (*spot*) neo.

molecule ['mɔlɪkju:l] *n* molecola.

molehill ['məulhɪl] *n* cumulo di terra sulla tana di una talpa.

molest [məu'lɛst] *vt* molestare.

mollusc, (*US*) **mollusk** ['mɔləsk] *n* mollusco.

mollycoddle ['mɔlɪkɔdl] *vt* coccolare, vezzeggiare.

Molotov cocktail ['mɔlətɔf-] *n* (*bottiglia*) Molotov *f inv*.

molt [məult] *vi* (*US*) = **moult**.

molten ['məultən] *adj* fuso(a).

mom [mɔm] *n* (*US*) = **mum**.

moment ['məumənt] *n* momento, istante *m*; importanza; **at the ~** al momento, in questo momento; **for the ~** per il momento, per ora; **in a ~** tra un momento; **"one ~ please"** (*TEL*) "attenda, prego".

momentarily ['məuməntərɪlɪ] *adv* per un momento; (*US: very soon*) da un momento all'altro.

momentary ['məuməntərɪ] *adj* momentaneo(a), passeggero(a).

momentous [məu'mɛntəs] *adj* di grande importanza.

momentum [məu'mɛntəm] *n* velocità acquisita, slancio; (*PHYSICS*) momento; **to gather ~** aumentare di velocità; (*fig*) prendere *or* guadagnare terreno.

mommy ['mɔmɪ] *n* (*US*) mamma.

Mon. *abbr* (= *Monday*) lun.

Monaco ['mɔnəkəu] *n* Monaco *f*.

monarch ['mɔnək] *n* monarca *m*.

monarchist ['mɔnəkɪst] *n* monarchico/a.

monarchy ['mɔnəkɪ] *n* monarchia.

monastery ['mɔnəstərɪ] *n* monastero.

monastic [mə'næstɪk] *adj* monastico(a).

Monday ['mʌndɪ] *n* lunedì *m inv*; *for phrases see also* **Tuesday**.

Monegasque [mɔnə'gæsk] *adj*, *n* monegasco(a).

monetarist ['mʌnɪtərɪst] *n* monetarista *m/f*.

monetary ['mʌnɪtərɪ] *adj* monetario(a).

money ['mʌnɪ] *n* denaro, soldi *mpl*; **to make ~** (*person*) fare (i) soldi; (*business*) rendere; **danger** ~ (*BRIT*) indennità di rischio; **I've got no** ~ **left** non ho più neanche una lira.

moneyed ['mʌnɪd] *adj* ricco(a).

moneylender ['mʌnɪlɛndə*] *n* prestatore *m* di denaro.

moneymaker ['mʌnɪmeɪkə*] *n* (*BRIT col*: *business*) affare *m* d'oro.

moneymaking ['mʌnɪmeɪkɪŋ] *adj* che rende (bene *or* molto), lucrativo(a).

money market *n* mercato monetario.

money order *n* vaglia *m inv*.

money-spinner ['mʌnɪspɪnə*] *n* (*col*) miniera d'oro (*fig*).

money supply *n* liquidità monetaria.

Mongol ['mɔŋgəl] *n* mongolo/a; (*LING*) mongolo.

mongol ['mɔŋgəl] *adj*, *n* (*MED*) mongoloide (*m/f*).

Mongolia [mɔŋ'gəulɪə] *n* Mongolia.

Mongolian [mɔŋ'gəulɪən] *adj* mongolico(a) ♦ *n* mongolo/a; (*LING*) mongolo.

mongoose ['mɔŋguːs] *n* mangusta.

mongrel ['mʌŋgrəl] *n* (*dog*) cane *m* bastardo.

monitor ['mɔnɪtə*] *n* (*BRIT SCOL*) capoclasse *m/f*; (*US SCOL*) chi sorveglia agli esami; (*TV*, *COMPUT*) monitor *m inv* ♦ *vt* controllare; (*foreign station*) ascoltare le trasmissioni di.

monk [mʌŋk] *n* monaco.

monkey ['mʌŋkɪ] *n* scimmia.

monkey business *n* (*col*) scherzi *mpl*.

monkey nut *n* (*BRIT*) nocciolina americana.

monkey wrench *n* chiave *f* a rullino.

mono ['mɔnəu] *adj* mono *inv*; (*broadcast*) in mono.

mono... ['mɔnəu] *prefix* mono....

monochrome ['mɔnəkrəum] *adj* monocromo(a).

monocle ['mɔnəkl] *n* monocolo.

monogamous [mə'nɔgəməs] *adj* monogamo(a).

monogamy [mə'nɔgəmɪ] *n* monogamia.

monogram ['mɔnəgræm] *n* monogramma *m*.

monolith ['mɔnəlɪθ] *n* monolito.

monologue ['mɔnəlɔg] *n* monologo.

monoplane ['mɔnəupleɪn] *n* monoplano.

monopolize [mə'nɔpəlaɪz] *vt* monopolizzare.

monopoly [mə'nɔpəlɪ] *n* monopolio; **Monopolies and Mergers Commission** (*BRIT*) commissione *f* antimonopoli.

monorail ['mɔnəureɪl] *n* monorotaia.

monosodium glutamate (MSG) [mɔnə'səudɪəm'gluːtəmeɪt] *n* glutammato di sodio.

monosyllabic [mɔnəsɪ'læbɪk] *adj* monosillabico(a); (*person*) che parla a monosillabi.

monosyllable ['mɔnəsɪləbl] *n* monosillabo.

monotone ['mɔnətəun] *n* pronunzia (*or* voce *f*) monotona; **to speak in a** ~ parlare con voce monotona.

monotonous [mə'nɔtənəs] *adj* monotono(a).

monotony [mə'nɔtənɪ] *n* monotonia.

monoxide [mɔ'nɔksaɪd] *n*: **carbon** ~ ossido di carbonio.

monsoon [mɔn'suːn] *n* monsone *m*.

monster ['mɔnstə*] *n* mostro.

monstrosity [mɔn'strɔsɪtɪ] *n* mostruosità *f inv*.

monstrous ['mɔnstrəs] *adj* mostruoso(a).

Mont. *abbr* (*US*) = *Montana*.

montage [mɔn'tɑːʒ] *n* montaggio.

Mont Blanc [mɔblɑ̃] *n* Monte *m* Bianco.

month [mʌnθ] *n* mese *m*; **300 dollars a** ~ 300 dollari al mese; **every** ~ (*happen*) tutti i mesi; (*pay*) mensilmente, ogni mese.

monthly ['mʌnθlɪ] *adj* mensile ♦ *adv* al mese; ogni mese ♦ *n* (*magazine*) rivista mensile; **twice** ~ due volte al mese.

monument ['mɔnjumənt] *n* monumento.

monumental [mɔnju'mentl] *adj* monumentale; (*fig*) colossale.

monumental mason *n* lapidario.

moo [muː] *vi* muggire, mugghiare.

mood [muːd] *n* umore *m*; **to be in a good/bad** ~ essere di buon/cattivo umore; **to be in the** ~ **for** essere disposto(a) a, aver voglia di.

moody ['muːdɪ] *adj* (*variable*) capriccioso(a), lunatico(a); (*sullen*) imbronciato(a).

moon [muːn] *n* luna.

moonbeam ['muːnbiːm] *n* raggio di luna.

moon landing *n* allunaggio.

moonlight ['muːnlaɪt] *n* chiaro di luna ♦ *vi* fare del lavoro nero.

moonlighting ['muːnlaɪtɪŋ] *n* lavoro nero.

moonlit ['muːnlɪt] *adj* illuminato(a) dalla luna; **a** ~ **night** una notte rischiarata dalla luna.

moonshot ['muːnʃɔt] *n* lancio sulla luna.

moonstruck ['muːnstrʌk] *adj* lunatico(a).

moony ['muːnɪ] *adj* (*eyes*) sognante.

Moor [muə*] *n* moro/a.

moor [muə*] *n* brughiera ♦ *vt* (*ship*) ormeggiare ♦ *vi* ormeggiarsi.

moorings ['muərɪŋz] *npl* (*chains*) ormeggi *mpl*; (*place*) ormeggio.

Moorish ['muərɪʃ] *adj* moresco(a).
moorland ['muələnd] *n* brughiera.
moose [mu:s] *n* (*pl inv*) alce *m*.
moot [mu:t] *vt* sollevare ♦ *adj*: ~ **point**
punto discutibile.
mop [mɔp] *n* lavapavimenti *m inv*; (*also*: ~
of hair) zazzera ♦ *vt* lavare con lo
straccio; **to** ~ **one's brow** asciugarsi la
fronte.
►**mop up** *vt* asciugare con uno straccio.
mope [məup] *vi* fare il broncio.
►**mope about, mope around** *vi*
trascinarsi *or* aggirarsi con aria avvilita.
moped ['məupɛd] *n* (*BRIT*) ciclomotore *m*.
MOR *adj abbr* (*MUS*: = *middle-of-the-road*): ~
music musica leggera.
moral ['mɔrəl] *adj* morale ♦ *n* morale *f*; ~**s**
npl moralità.
morale [mɔ'rɑːl] *n* morale *m*.
morality [mə'rælɪtɪ] *n* moralità.
moralize ['mɔrəlaɪz] *vi*: **to** ~ (**about**) fare il
(*or* la) moralista (riguardo),
moraleggiare (riguardo).
morally ['mɔrəlɪ] *adv* moralmente.
moral victory *n* vittoria morale.
morass [mə'ræs] *n* palude *f*, pantano.
moratorium [mɔrə'tɔːrɪəm] *n* moratoria.
morbid ['mɔːbɪd] *adj* morboso(a).

=============================== KEYWORD

more [mɔː*] *adj* **1** (*greater in number etc*) più;
~ **people/letters than we expected** più
persone/lettere di quante ne
aspettavamo; **I have** ~ **wine/money than**
you ho più vino/soldi di te; **I have** ~ **wine**
than beer ho più vino che birra
2 (*additional*) altro(a), ancora; **do you**
want (some) ~ **tea?** vuole dell'altro tè?,
vuole ancora del tè?; **I have no** *or* **I don't**
have any ~ **money** non ho più soldi
♦ *pron* **1** (*greater amount*) più; ~ **than 10** più
di 10; **it cost** ~ **than we expected** è
costato più di quanto ci aspettassimo;
and what's ~ ... e per di più ...
2 (*further or additional amount*) ancora; **is**
there any ~**?** ce n'è ancora?; **there's no** ~
non ce n'è più; **a little** ~ ancora un po';
many/much ~ molti(e)/molto(a) di più
♦ *adv*: ~ **dangerous/easily (than)** più
pericoloso/facilmente (di); ~ **and** ~
sempre di più; ~ **and** ~ **difficult** sempre
più difficile; ~ **or less** più o meno; ~ **than**
ever più che mai; **once** ~ ancora (una
volta), un'altra volta; **no** ~, **not any** ~
non ... più; **I have no** ~ **money, I haven't**
any ~ **money** non ho più soldi.

moreover [mɔː'rəuvə*] *adv* inoltre, di più.

morgue [mɔːg] *n* obitorio.
MORI ['mɔːrɪ] *n abbr* (*BRIT*: = *Market &*
Opinion Research Institute) *istituto di*
sondaggio.
moribund ['mɔrɪbʌnd] *adj* moribondo(a).
morning ['mɔːnɪŋ] *n* mattina, mattino;
(*duration*) mattinata; **in the** ~ la mattina;
this ~ stamattina; **7 o'clock in the** ~ le 7
di *or* della mattina.
morning-after pill ['mɔːnɪŋ'ɑːftə-] *n* pillola
del giorno dopo.
morning sickness *n* nausee *fpl* mattutine.
Moroccan [mə'rɔkən] *adj*, *n* marocchino(a).
Morocco [mə'rɔkəu] *n* Marocco.
moron ['mɔːrɔn] *n* deficiente *m/f*.
moronic [mə'rɔnɪk] *adj* deficiente.
morose [mə'rəus] *adj* cupo(a), tetro(a).
morphine ['mɔːfiːn] *n* morfina.
morris dancing ['mɔrɪs-] *n* (*BRIT*) *antica*
danza tradizionale inglese.
Morse [mɔːs] *n* (*also*: ~ **code**) alfabeto
Morse.
morsel ['mɔːsl] *n* boccone *m*.
mortal ['mɔːtl] *adj*, *n* mortale (*m*).
mortality [mɔː'tælɪtɪ] *n* mortalità.
mortality rate *n* tasso di mortalità.
mortar ['mɔːtə*] *n* (*CONSTR*) malta; (*dish*)
mortaio.
mortgage ['mɔːgɪdʒ] *n* ipoteca; (*in house*
buying) mutuo ipotecario ♦ *vt* ipotecare;
to take out a ~ contrarre un mutuo (*or*
un'ipoteca).
mortgage company *n* (*US*) società *f inv*
immobiliare.
mortgagee [mɔːgɪ'dʒiː] *n* creditore *m*
ipotecario.
mortgagor ['mɔːgɪdʒə*] *n* debitore *m*
ipotecario.
mortician [mɔː'tɪʃən] *n* (*US*) impresario di
pompe funebri.
mortified ['mɔːtɪfaɪd] *adj* umiliato(a).
mortise lock ['mɔːtɪs-] *n* serratura
incastrata.
mortuary ['mɔːtjuərɪ] *n* camera mortuaria;
obitorio.
mosaic [məu'zeɪɪk] *n* mosaico.
Moscow ['mɔskəu] *n* Mosca.
Moslem ['mɔzləm] *adj*, *n* = **Muslim**.
mosque [mɔsk] *n* moschea.
mosquito, ~ **es** [mɔs'kiːtəu] *n* zanzara.
mosquito net *n* zanzariera.
moss [mɔs] *n* muschio.
mossy ['mɔsɪ] *adj* muscoso(a).
most [məust] *adj* la maggior parte di; il più
di ♦ *pron* la maggior parte ♦ *adv* più; (*work,*
sleep etc) di più; (*very*) molto,
estremamente; **the** ~ (*also*: + *adjective*)
il(la) più; ~ **fish** la maggior parte dei

pesci; ~ **of** la maggior parte di; ~ **of them** quasi tutti; **I saw** ~ ho visto più io; **at the (very)** ~ al massimo; **to make the** ~ **of** trarre il massimo vantaggio da.

mostly ['məustlɪ] *adv* per lo più.

MOT *n abbr* (*BRIT*: = *Ministry of Transport*): **the** ~ **(test)** *revisione obbligatoria degli autoveicoli.*

motel [məu'tɛl] *n* motel *m inv.*

moth [mɔθ] *n* farfalla notturna; tarma.

mothball ['mɔθbɔːl] *n* pallina di naftalina.

moth-eaten ['mɔθiːtn] *adj* tarmato(a).

mother ['mʌðə*] *n* madre *f* ♦ *vt* (*care for*) fare da madre a.

mother board *n* (*COMPUT*) scheda madre.

motherhood ['mʌðəhud] *n* maternità.

mother-in-law ['mʌðərɪnlɔː] *n* suocera.

mother-of-pearl [mʌðərəv'pɔːl] *n* madreperla.

mother's help *n* bambinaia.

mother-to-be [mʌðətə'biː] *n* futura mamma.

mother tongue *n* madrelingua.

mothproof ['mɔθpruːf] *adj* antitarmico(a).

motif [məu'tiːf] *n* motivo.

motion ['məuʃən] *n* movimento, moto; (*gesture*) gesto; (*at meeting*) mozione *f*; (*BRIT*: *also*: **bowel** ~) evacuazione *f* ♦ *vt*, *vi*: **to** ~ **(to) sb to do** fare cenno a qn di fare; **to be in** ~ (*vehicle*) essere in moto; **to set in** ~ avviare; **to go through the** ~**s of doing sth** (*fig*) fare qc pro forma.

motionless ['məuʃənlɪs] *adj* immobile.

motion picture *n* film *m inv.*

motivate ['məutɪveɪt] *vt* (*act, decision*) dare origine a, motivare; (*person*) spingere.

motivated ['məutɪveɪtɪd] *adj* motivato(a).

motivation [məutɪ'veɪʃən] *n* motivazione *f.*

motive ['məutɪv] *n* motivo ♦ *adj* motore(trice); **from the best** ~**s** con le migliori intenzioni.

motley ['mɔtlɪ] *adj* eterogeneo(a), molto vario(a).

motor ['məutə*] *n* motore *m*; (*BRIT col*: *vehicle*) macchina ♦ *adj* motore(trice).

motorbike ['məutəbaɪk] *n* moto *f inv.*

motorboat ['məutəbəut] *n* motoscafo.

motorcade ['məutəkeɪd] *n* corteo di macchine.

motorcar ['məutəkaː] *n* automobile *f.*

motorcoach ['məutəkəutʃ] *n* (*BRIT*) pullman *m inv.*

motorcycle ['məutəsaɪkl] *n* motocicletta.

motorcyclist ['məutəsaɪklɪst] *n* motociclista *m/f.*

motoring ['məutərɪŋ] *n* (*BRIT*) turismo automobilistico ♦ *adj* (*accident*) d'auto, automobilistico(a); (*offence*) di guida; ~

holiday vacanza in macchina.

motorist ['məutərɪst] *n* automobilista *m/f.*

motorize ['məutəraɪz] *vt* motorizzare.

motor oil *n* olio lubrificante.

motor racing *n* (*BRIT*) corse *fpl* automobilistiche.

motor scooter *n* motorscooter *m inv.*

motor vehicle *n* autoveicolo.

motorway ['məutəweɪ] *n* (*BRIT*) autostrada.

mottled ['mɔtld] *adj* chiazzato(a), marezzato(a).

motto, ~**es** ['mɔtəu] *n* motto.

mould, (US) mold [məuld] *n* forma, stampo; (*mildew*) muffa ♦ *vt* formare; (*fig*) foggiare.

mo(u)lder ['məuldə*] *vi* (*decay*) ammuffire.

mo(u)lding ['məuldɪŋ] *n* (*ARCHIT*) modanatura.

mo(u)ldy ['məuldɪ] *adj* ammuffito(a).

moult, (US) molt [məult] *vi* far la muta.

mound [maund] *n* rialzo, collinetta.

mount [maunt] *n* monte *m*, montagna; (*horse*) cavalcatura; (*for jewel etc*) montatura ♦ *vt* montare; (*horse*) montare a; (*exhibition*) organizzare; (*attack*) sferrare, condurre; (*picture, stamp*) sistemare ♦ *vi* salire; (*get on a horse*) montare a cavallo; (*also*: ~ **up**) aumentare.

mountain ['mauntɪn] *n* montagna ♦ *cpd* di montagna; **to make a** ~ **out of a molehill** fare di una mosca un elefante.

mountain bike *n* mountain bike *f inv.*

mountaineer [mauntɪ'nɪə*] *n* alpinista *m/f.*

mountaineering [mauntɪ'nɪərɪŋ] *n* alpinismo; **to go** ~ fare dell'alpinismo.

mountainous ['mauntɪnəs] *adj* montagnoso(a).

mountain range *n* catena montuosa.

mountain rescue team *n* ≈ squadra di soccorso alpino.

mountainside ['mauntɪnsaɪd] *n* fianco della montagna.

mounted ['mauntɪd] *adj* a cavallo.

mourn [mɔːn] *vt* piangere, lamentare ♦ *vi*: **to** ~ **(for sb)** piangere (la morte di qn).

mourner ['mɔːnə*] *n* parente *m/f* (*or* amico/a) del defunto.

mourning ['mɔːnɪŋ] *n* lutto ♦ *cpd* (*dress*) lutto; **in** ~ in lutto.

mouse, *pl* **mice** [maus, maɪs] *n* topo; (*COMPUT*) mouse *m inv.*

mousetrap ['maustræp] *n* trappola per i topi.

moussaka [mu'saːkə] *n* moussaka.

mousse [muːs] *n* mousse *f inv.*

moustache [məs'taːʃ] *n* baffi *mpl.*

mousy ['mausɪ] *adj* (*person*) timido(a); (*hair*)

né chiaro(a) né scuro(a).
mouth, ~**s** [mauθ, -ðz] *n* bocca; (*of river*) bocca, foce *f*; (*opening*) orifizio.
mouthful ['mauθful] *n* boccata.
mouth organ *n* armonica.
mouthpiece ['mauθpi:s] *n* (*MUS*) bocchino; (*TEL*) microfono; (*of breathing apparatus*) boccaglio; (*person*) portavoce *m/f*.
mouth-to-mouth ['mauθtə'mauθ] *adj*: ~ **resuscitation** respirazione *f* bocca a bocca.
mouthwash ['mauθwɔʃ] *n* collutorio.
mouth-watering ['mauθwɔ:tərɪŋ] *adj* che fa venire l'acquolina in bocca.
movable ['mu:vəbl] *adj* mobile.
move [mu:v] *n* (*movement*) movimento; (*in game*) mossa; (: *turn to play*) turno; (*change of house*) trasloco ♦ *vt* muovere, spostare; (*emotionally*) commuovere; (*POL: resolution etc*) proporre ♦ *vi* (*gen*) muoversi, spostarsi; (*traffic*) circolare; (*also:* ~ **house**) cambiar casa, traslocare; **to** ~ **towards** andare verso; **to** ~ **sb to do sth** indurre *or* spingere qn a fare qc; **to get a** ~ **on** affrettarsi, sbrigarsi; **to be** ~**d** (*emotionally*) essere commosso(a).
▶**move about, move around** *vi* (*fidget*) agitarsi; (*travel*) viaggiare.
▶**move along** *vi* muoversi avanti.
▶**move away** *vi* allontanarsi, andarsene.
▶**move back** *vi* indietreggiare; (*return*) ritornare.
▶**move forward** *vi* avanzare ♦ *vt* avanzare, spostare in avanti; (*people*) far avanzare.
▶**move in** *vi* (*to a house*) entrare (*in una nuova casa*).
▶**move off** *vi* partire.
▶**move on** *vi* riprendere la strada ♦ *vt* (*onlookers*) far circolare.
▶**move out** *vi* (*of house*) sgombrare.
▶**move over** *vi* spostarsi.
▶**move up** *vi* avanzare.
movement ['mu:vmənt] *n* (*gen*) movimento; (*gesture*) gesto; (*of stars, water, physical*) moto; ~ **(of the bowels)** (*MED*) evacuazione *f*.
mover ['mu:və*] *n* proponente *m/f*.
movie ['mu:vɪ] *n* film *m inv*; **the** ~**s** il cinema.
movie camera *n* cinepresa.
moviegoer ['mu:vɪɡəuə*] *n* (*US*) frequentatore/trice di cinema.
moving ['mu:vɪŋ] *adj* mobile; (*causing emotion*) commovente; (*instigating*) animatore(trice).
mow, *pt* **mowed,** *pp* **mowed** *or* **mown** [məu, -n] *vt* falciare; (*grass*) tagliare.
▶**mow down** *vt* falciare.

mower ['məuə*] *n* (*also:* **lawn** ~) tagliaerba *m inv*.
mown [məun] *pp of* **mow**.
Mozambique [məuzəm'bi:k] *n* Mozambico.
MP *n abbr* = *Military Police*; (*Canada*) = *Mounted Police*; (*BRIT*) *see* **Member of Parliament**.
MP3 *n* MP3 *m inv*.
MP3 player *n* lettore *m* MP3.
mpg *n abbr* = *miles per gallon* (*30 mpg* = *9.4 l. per 100 km*).
mph *n abbr* = *miles per hour* (*60 mph* = *96 km/h*).
MPhil *n abbr* (= *Master of Philosophy*) *titolo di studio*.
MPS *n abbr* (*BRIT*) = *Member of the Pharmaceutical Society*.
Mr, Mr. ['mɪstə*] *n*: ~ **X** Signor X, Sig. X.
MRC *n abbr* (*BRIT*: = *Medical Research Council*) *ufficio governativo per la ricerca medica in Gran Bretagna e nel Commonwealth*.
MRCP *n abbr* (*BRIT*) = *Member of the Royal College of Physicians*.
MRCS *n abbr* (*BRIT*) = *Member of the Royal College of Surgeons*.
MRCVS *n abbr* (*BRIT*) = *Member of the Royal College of Veterinary Surgeons*.
Mrs, Mrs. ['mɪsɪz] *n*: ~ **X** Signora X, Sig.ra X.
MS *n abbr* (*US*: = *Master of Science*) *titolo di studio*; (= *manuscript*) ms; (*MED*) = **multiple sclerosis** ♦ *abbr* (*US*) = *Mississippi*.
Ms, Ms. [mɪz] *n* (= *Miss or Mrs*): ~ **X** ≈ Signora X, Sig.ra X.
MSA *n abbr* (*US*: = *Master of Science in Agriculture*) *titolo di studio*.
MSc *n abbr see* **Master of Science**.
MSG *abbr see* **monosodium glutamate**.
MSP *n abbr* = *Member of the Scottish Parliament*.
MST *abbr* (*US*: = *Mountain Standard Time*) *ora invernale delle Montagne Rocciose*.
MSW *n abbr* (*US*: = *Master of Social Work*) *titolo di studio*.
MT *n abbr* = *machine translation* ♦ (*US*) = *Montana*.
Mt *abbr* (*GEO*: = *mount*) M.
mth *abbr* (= *month*) m.
MTV *n abbr* = *music television*.

=========================== KEYWORD

much [mʌtʃ] *adj, pron* molto(a); **he's done so** ~ **work** ha lavorato così tanto; **I have as** ~ **money as you** ho tanti soldi quanti ne hai tu; **how** ~ **is it?** quant'è?; **it's not** ~ non è tanto; **it costs too** ~ costa troppo; **as** ~ **as you want** quanto vuoi

♦ adv 1 (*greatly*) molto, tanto; **thank you very** ~ molte grazie; **I like it very/so** ~ mi piace moltissimo/così tanto; ~ **to my amazement** con mio enorme stupore; **he's very** ~ **the gentleman** è il vero gentiluomo; **I read as** ~ **as I can** leggo quanto posso; **as** ~ **as you** tanto quanto te **2** (*by far*) molto; **it's** ~ **the biggest company in Europe** è di gran lunga la più grossa società in Europa **3** (*almost*) grossomodo, praticamente; **they're** ~ **the same** sono praticamente uguali.

muck [mʌk] n (*mud*) fango; (*dirt*) sporcizia.
▶**muck about, muck around** vi (*col*) fare lo stupido; (: *waste time*) gingillarsi; (*tinker*) armeggiare.
▶**muck in** vi (*BRIT col*) mettersi insieme.
▶**muck out** vt (*stable*) pulire.
▶**muck up** vt (*col*: *dirty*) sporcare; (: *spoil*) rovinare.
muckraking ['mʌkreɪkɪŋ] n (*fig col*) caccia agli scandali ♦ adj scandalistico(a).
mucky ['mʌkɪ] adj (*dirty*) sporco(a), lordo(a).
mucus ['mju:kəs] n muco.
mud [mʌd] n fango.
muddle ['mʌdl] n confusione f, disordine m; pasticcio ♦ vt (*also*: ~ **up**) mettere sottosopra; confondere; **to be in a** ~ (*person*) non riuscire a raccapezzarsi; **to get in a** ~ (*while explaining*) imbrogliarsi.
▶**muddle along** vi andare avanti a casaccio.
▶**muddle through** vi cavarsela alla meno peggio.
muddle-headed [mʌdl'hɛdɪd] adj (*person*) confusionario(a).
muddy ['mʌdɪ] adj fangoso(a).
mud flats npl distesa fangosa.
mudguard ['mʌdgɑ:d] n parafango.
mudpack ['mʌdpæk] n maschera di fango.
mud-slinging ['mʌdslɪŋɪŋ] n (*fig*) infangamento.
muesli ['mju:zlɪ] n müsli m inv.
muff [mʌf] n manicotto ♦ vt (*shot, catch etc*) mancare, sbagliare; **to** ~ **it** sbagliare tutto.
muffin ['mʌfɪn] n specie di pasticcino soffice da tè.
muffle ['mʌfl] vt (*sound*) smorzare, attutire; (*against cold*) imbacuccare.
muffled ['mʌfld] adj smorzato(a), attutito(a).
muffler ['mʌflə*] n (*scarf*) sciarpa (pesante); (*US AUT*) marmitta; (*on motorbike*) silenziatore m.
mufti ['mʌftɪ] n: **in** ~ in borghese.

mug [mʌg] n (*cup*) tazzone m; (*for beer*) boccale m; (*col*: *face*) muso; (: *fool*) scemo/a ♦ vt (*assault*) assalire; **it's a** ~**'s game** (*BRIT*) è proprio (una cosa) da fessi.
▶**mug up** vt (*BRIT col*: *also*: ~ **up on**) studiare bene.
mugger ['mʌgə*] n aggressore m.
mugging ['mʌgɪŋ] n aggressione f (a scopo di rapina).
muggins ['mʌgɪnz] n (*col*) semplicione/a, sprovveduto/a.
muggy ['mʌgɪ] adj afoso(a).
mug shot n (*col*) foto f inv segnaletica.
mulatto, ~ **es** [mju:'lætəʊ] n mulatto/a.
mulberry ['mʌlbərɪ] n (*fruit*) mora (di gelso); (*tree*) gelso, moro.
mule [mju:l] n mulo.
mull [mʌl]: **to** ~ **over** vt rimuginare.
mulled [mʌld] adj: ~ **wine** vino caldo.
multi... ['mʌltɪ] prefix multi....
multi-access [mʌltɪ'æksɛs] adj (*COMPUT*) ad accesso multiplo.
multicoloured, (US) multicolored ['mʌltɪkʌləd] adj multicolore, variopinto(a).
multifarious [mʌltɪ'fɛərɪəs] adj molteplice, svariato(a).
multilateral [mʌltɪ'lætərəl] adj (*POL*) multilaterale.
multi-level ['mʌltɪlɛvl] adj (*US*) = multistorey.
multimillionaire [mʌltɪmɪljə'nɛə*] n multimiliardario/a.
multinational [mʌltɪ'næʃənl] adj, n multinazionale (f).
multiple ['mʌltɪpl] adj multiplo(a); molteplice ♦ n multiplo; (*BRIT*: *also*: ~ **store**) grande magazzino che fa parte di una catena.
multiple choice n esercizi mpl a scelta multipla.
multiple crash n serie f inv di incidenti a catena.
multiple sclerosis n sclerosi f a placche.
multiplex ['mʌltɪplɛks] n (*also*: ~ **cinema**) cinema m inv multisale inv.
multiplication [mʌltɪplɪ'keɪʃən] n moltiplicazione f.
multiplication table n tavola pitagorica.
multiplicity [mʌltɪ'plɪsɪtɪ] n molteplicità.
multiply ['mʌltɪplaɪ] vt moltiplicare ♦ vi moltiplicarsi.
multiracial [mʌltɪ'reɪʃəl] adj multirazziale.
multistorey [mʌltɪ'stɔ:rɪ] adj (*BRIT*: building, car park) a più piani.
multitude ['mʌltɪtju:d] n moltitudine f.
mum [mʌm] n (*BRIT*) mamma ♦ adj: **to keep** ~ non aprire bocca; ~**'s the word!** acqua

in bocca!

mumble['mʌmbl] vt, vi borbottare.

mumbo jumbo['mʌmbəu-] n (col) parole fpl incomprensibili.

mummify['mʌmɪfaɪ] vt mummificare.

mummy['mʌmɪ] n (BRIT: mother) mamma; (embalmed) mummia.

mumps[mʌmps] n orecchioni mpl.

munch[mʌntʃ] vt, vi sgranocchiare.

mundane[mʌn'deɪn] adj terra a terra inv.

Munich['mju:nɪk] n Monaco f (di Baviera).

municipal[mju:'nɪsɪpl] adj municipale.

municipality[mju:nɪsɪ'pælɪtɪ] n municipio.

munitions[mju:'nɪʃənz] npl munizioni fpl.

mural['mjuərəl] n dipinto murale.

murder['mɜ:də*] n assassinio, omicidio ♦ vt assassinare, to commit ~ commettere un omicidio.

murderer['mɜ:dərə*] n omicida m, assassino.

murderess['mɜ:dərɪs] n omicida f, assassina.

murderous['mɜ:dərəs] adj micidiale.

murk[mɜ:k] n oscurità, buio.

murky['mɜ:kɪ] adj tenebroso(a), buio(a).

murmur['mɜ:mə*] n mormorio ♦ vt, vi mormorare; **heart** ~ (MED) soffio al cuore.

MusB(ac)n abbr (= Bachelor of Music) titolo di studio.

muscle['mʌsl] n muscolo.
► **muscle in**vi immischiarsi.

muscular['mʌskjulə*] adj muscolare; (person, arm) muscoloso(a).

muscular dystrophyn distrofia muscolare.

MusD(oc)n abbr (= Doctor of Music) titolo di studio.

muse[mju:z] vi meditare, sognare ♦ n musa.

museum[mju:'zɪəm] n museo.

mush[mʌʃ] n pappa.

mushroom['mʌʃrum] n fungo ♦ vi (fig) svilupparsi rapidamente.

mushy['mʌʃɪ] adj (of food) spappolato(a); (sentimental) sdolcinato(a).

music['mju:zɪk] n musica.

musical['mju:zɪkəl] adj musicale ♦ n (show) commedia musicale.

music(al) boxn carillon m inv.

musical chairsn gioco delle sedie (in cui bisogna sedersi non appena cessa la musica); (fig) scambio delle poltrone.

musical instrumentn strumento musicale.

music centren impianto m stereo inv monoblocco inv.

music halln teatro di varietà.

musician[mju:'zɪʃən] n musicista m/f.

music standn leggio.

musk[mʌsk] n muschio.

musket['mʌskɪt] n moschetto.

muskrat['mʌskræt] n topo muschiato.

musk rosen (BOT) rosa muschiata.

Muslim['mʌzlɪm] adj, n musulmano(a).

muslin['mʌzlɪn] n mussola.

musquash['mʌskwɔʃ] n (fur) rat musqué m inv.

mussel['mʌsl] n cozza.

must[mʌst] aux vb (obligation): **I** ~ **do it** devo farlo; (probability): **he** ~ **be there by now** dovrebbe essere arrivato ormai; **I** ~ **have made a mistake** devo essermi sbagliato ♦ n: **this programme/trip is a** ~ è un programma/viaggio da non perdersi.

mustache['mʌstæʃ] n (US) = **moustache**.

mustard['mʌstəd] n senape f, mostarda.

mustard gasn iprite f.

muster['mʌstə*] vt radunare; (also: ~ **up**: strength, courage) fare appello a.

mustiness['mʌstɪnɪs] n odor di muffa or di stantio.

mustn't['mʌsnt] = **must not**.

musty['mʌstɪ] adj che sa di muffa or di rinchiuso.

mutant['mju:tənt] adj, n mutante (m).

mutate[mju:'teɪt] vi subire una mutazione.

mutation[mju:'teɪʃən] n mutazione f.

mute[mju:t] adj, n muto(a).

muted['mju:tɪd] adj (noise) attutito(a), smorzato(a); (criticism) attenuato(a); (MUS) in sordina; (: trumpet) con sordina.

mutilate['mju:tɪleɪt] vt mutilare.

mutilation[mju:tɪ'leɪʃən] n mutilazione f.

mutinous['mju:tɪnəs] adj (troops) ammutinato(a); (attitude) ribelle.

mutiny['mju:tɪnɪ] n ammutinamento ♦ vi ammutinarsi.

mutter['mʌtə*] vt, vi borbottare, brontolare.

mutton['mʌtn] n carne f di montone.

mutual['mju:tʃuəl] adj mutuo(a), reciproco(a).

mutually['mju:tʃuəlɪ] adv reciprocamente.

Muzak ®['mju:zæk] n (often pej) musica di sottofondo.

muzzle['mʌzl] n muso; (protective device) museruola; (of gun) bocca ♦ vt mettere la museruola a.

MVabbr (= motor vessel) M/N, m/n.

MVPn abbr (US SPORT: = most valuable player) titolo ottenuto da sportivo.

MWabbr (RADIO: = medium wave) O.M.; (= megawatt) megawatt m inv.

my[maɪ] adj il(la) mio(a), pl i(le) miei(mie).

Myanmar ['maɪænmɑ:*] *n* Myanma.
myopic [maɪ'ɔpɪk] *adj* miope.
myriad ['mɪrɪəd] *n* miriade *f.*
myself [maɪ'sɛlf] *pron (reflexive)* mi; *(emphatic)* io stesso(a); *(after prep)* me.
mysterious [mɪs'tɪərɪəs] *adj* misterioso(a).
mystery ['mɪstərɪ] *n* mistero.
mystery story *n* racconto del mistero.
mystic ['mɪstɪk] *adj, n* mistico(a).
mystical ['mɪstɪkəl] *adj* mistico(a).
mystify ['mɪstɪfaɪ] *vt* mistificare; *(puzzle)* confondere.
mystique [mɪs'ti:k] *n* fascino.
myth [mɪθ] *n* mito.
mythical ['mɪθɪkl] *adj* mitico(a).
mythological [mɪθə'lɔdʒɪkl] *adj* mitologico(a).
mythology [mɪ'θɔlədʒɪ] *n* mitologia.

N n

N, n [ɛn] *n (letter)* N, n *f or m inv;* **N for Nellie,** *(US)* **N for Nan** ≈ N come Napoli.
N *abbr (= north)* N.
NA *n abbr (US: = Narcotics Anonymous) associazione in aiuto dei tossicodipendenti;* (US) = *National Academy.*
n/a *abbr (= not applicable)* non pertinente.
NAACP *n abbr (US)* = *National Association for the Advancement of Colored People.*
NAAFI ['næfɪ] *n abbr (BRIT:* = *Navy, Army, & Air Force Institutes) organizzazione che gestisce negozi, mense ecc. per il personale militare.*
nab [næb] *vt (col)* beccare, acchiappare.
NACU *n abbr (US)* = *National Association of Colleges and Universities.*
nadir ['neɪdɪə*] *n (ASTRONOMY)* nadir *m;* *(fig)* punto più basso.
nag [næg] *n (pej: horse)* ronzino; *(person)* brontolone/a ♦ *vt* tormentare ♦ *vi* brontolare in continuazione.
nagging ['nægɪŋ] *adj (doubt, pain)* persistente ♦ *n* brontolii *mpl,* osservazioni *fpl* continue.
nail [neɪl] *n (human)* unghia; *(metal)* chiodo ♦ *vt* inchiodare; **to ~ sb down to a date/ price** costringere qn a un appuntamento/ ad accettare un prezzo; **to pay cash on the ~** (BRIT) pagare a tamburo battente.

nailbrush ['neɪlbrʌʃ] *n* spazzolino da *or* per unghie.
nailfile ['neɪlfaɪl] *n* lima da *or* per unghie.
nail polish *n* smalto da *or* per unghie.
nail polish remover *n* acetone *m,* solvente *m.*
nail scissors *npl* forbici *fpl* da *or* per unghie.
nail varnish *n (BRIT)* = **nail polish.**
Nairobi [naɪ'rəubɪ] *n* Nairobi *f.*
naive [naɪ'i:v] *adj* ingenuo(a).
naïveté [nɑ:i:v'teɪ], **naivety** [naɪ'i:vtɪ] *n* ingenuità *f inv.*
naked ['neɪkɪd] *adj* nudo(a); **with the ~ eye** a occhio nudo.
nakedness ['neɪkɪdnɪs] *n* nudità.
NAM *n abbr (US)* = *National Association of Manufacturers.*
name [neɪm] *n* nome *m;* *(reputation)* nome, reputazione *f* ♦ *vt (baby etc)* chiamare; *(person, object)* identificare; *(price, date)* fissare; **by ~** di nome; **she knows them all by ~** li conosce tutti per nome; **in the ~ of** in nome di; **what's your ~?** come si chiama?; **my ~ is Peter** mi chiamo Peter; **to take sb's ~ and address** prendere nome e indirizzo di qn; **to make a ~ for o.s.** farsi un nome; **to get (o.s.) a bad ~** farsi una cattiva fama *or* una brutta reputazione; **to call sb ~s** insultare qn.
name dropping *n* menzionare qualcuno per fare bella figura.
nameless ['neɪmlɪs] *adj* senza nome.
namely ['neɪmlɪ] *adv* cioè.
nameplate ['neɪmpleɪt] *n (on door etc)* targa.
namesake ['neɪmseɪk] *n* omonimo.
nan bread [nɑ:n-] *n tipo di pane indiano poco lievitato di forma allungata.*
nanny ['nænɪ] *n* bambinaia.
nanny goat *n* capra.
nap [næp] *n (sleep)* pisolino; *(of cloth)* peluria ♦ *vi:* **to be caught ~ping** essere preso alla sprovvista; **to have a ~** schiacciare un pisolino.
NAPA *n abbr (US:* = *National Association of Performing Artists) associazione nazionale degli artisti di palcoscenico.*
napalm ['neɪpɑ:m] *n* napalm *m.*
nape [neɪp] *n:* **~ of the neck** nuca.
napkin ['næpkɪn] *n* tovagliolo; *(BRIT: for baby)* pannolino.
Naples ['neɪplz] *n* Napoli *f.*
Napoleonic [nəpəulɪ'ɔnɪk] *adj* napoleonico(a).
nappy ['næpɪ] *n (BRIT)* pannolino.
nappy liner *n (BRIT)* fogliettino igienico.
narcissistic [nɑ:sɪ'sɪstɪk] *adj*

narcisistico(a).

narcissus, pl **narcissi** [nɑː'sɪsəs, -saɪ] n narciso.

narcotic [nɑː'kɔtɪk] n (MED) narcotico; ~s npl (drugs) narcotici, stupefacenti mpl.

nark [nɑːk] vt (BRIT col) scocciare.

narrate [nə'reɪt] vt raccontare, narrare.

narration [nə'reɪʃən] n narrazione f.

narrative ['nærətɪv] n narrativa ♦ adj narrativo(a).

narrator [nə'reɪtə*] n narratore/trice.

narrow ['nærəu] adj stretto(a); (resources, means) limitato(a), modesto(a); (fig): **to take a ~ view of** avere una visione limitata di ♦ vi restringersi; **to have a ~ escape** farcela per un pelo; **to ~ sth down to** ridurre qc a.

narrow gauge adj (RAIL) a scartamento ridotto.

narrowly ['nærəulɪ] adv: **Maria ~ escaped drowning** per un pelo Maria non è affogata; **he ~ missed hitting the cyclist** per poco non ha investito il ciclista.

narrow-minded [nærəu'maɪndɪd] adj meschino(a).

NAS n abbr (US) = National Academy of Sciences.

NASA ['næsə] n abbr (US: = National Aeronautics and Space Administration) N.A.S.A. f.

nasal ['neɪzl] adj nasale.

Nassau ['næsɔ:] n Nassau f.

nastily ['nɑːstɪlɪ] adv con cattiveria.

nastiness ['nɑːstɪnɪs] n (of person, remark) cattiveria; (: spitefulness) malignità.

nasturtium [nəs'tə:ʃəm] n cappuccina, nasturzio (indiano).

nasty ['nɑːstɪ] adj (person, remark) cattivo(a); (: spiteful) maligno(a); (smell, wound, situation) brutto(a); **to turn ~** (situation) mettersi male; (weather) guastarsi; (person) incattivirsi; **it's a ~ business** è una brutta faccenda, è un brutto affare.

NAS/UWT n abbr (BRIT: = National Association of Schoolmasters/Union of Women Teachers) sindacato di insegnanti in Inghilterra e Galles.

nation ['neɪʃən] n nazione f.

national ['næʃənl] adj nazionale ♦ n cittadino/a.

national anthem n inno nazionale.

National Curriculum n (BRIT) ≈ programma m scolastico ministeriale (in Inghilterra e Galles).

national debt n debito pubblico.

national dress n costume m nazionale.

National Guard n (US) milizia nazionale

(volontaria, in ogni stato).

National Health Service (NHS) n (BRIT) servizio nazionale di assistenza sanitaria, ≈ S.A.U.B. f.

National Insurance n (BRIT) ≈ Previdenza Sociale.

nationalism ['næʃnəlɪzəm] n nazionalismo.

nationalist ['næʃnəlɪst] adj, n nazionalista (m/f).

nationality [næʃə'nælɪtɪ] n nazionalità f inv.

nationalization [næʃnəlaɪ'zeɪʃən] n nazionalizzazione f.

nationalize ['næʃnəlaɪz] vt nazionalizzare.

nationally ['næʃnəlɪ] adv a livello nazionale.

national park n parco nazionale.

national press n stampa a diffusione nazionale.

National Security Council n (US) consiglio nazionale di sicurezza.

national service n (MIL) servizio militare.

National Trust n sovrintendenza ai beni culturali e ambientali; see boxed note.

NATIONAL TRUST

Fondato nel 1895, il **National Trust** è un'organizzazione che si occupa della tutela e salvaguardia di edifici e monumenti di interesse storico e di territori di interesse ambientale nel Regno Unito.

---

nation-wide ['neɪʃənwaɪd] adj diffuso(a) in tutto il paese ♦ adv in tutto il paese.

native ['neɪtɪv] n abitante m/f del paese; (in colonies) indigeno/a ♦ adj indigeno(a); (country) natio(a); (ability) innato(a); **a ~ speaker of French** una persona di madrelingua francese; **~ language** madrelingua.

Native American n discendente di tribù dell'America settentrionale.

Nativity [nə'tɪvɪtɪ] n (REL): **the ~** la Natività.

nativity play n recita sulla Natività.

NATO ['neɪtəu] n abbr (= North Atlantic Treaty Organization) N.A.T.O. f.

natter ['nætə*] (BRIT col) vi chiacchierare ♦ n chiacchierata.

natural ['nætʃrəl] adj naturale; (ability) innato(a); (manner) semplice; **death from ~ causes** (LAW) morte f per cause naturali.

natural childbirth n parto indolore.

natural gas n gas m metano.

natural history n storia naturale.

naturalist ['nætʃrəlɪst] n naturalista m/f.

naturalization [nætʃrəlaɪ'zeɪʃən] n

naturalizzazione f; acclimatazione f.
naturalize ['nætʃrəlaɪz] vt: to be ~d
(person) naturalizzarsi.
naturally ['nætʃrəlɪ] adv naturalmente; (by
nature: gifted) di natura.
naturalness ['nætʃrəlnɪs] n naturalezza.
natural resources npl risorse fpl naturali.
natural selection n selezione f naturale.
natural wastage n (INDUSTRY)
diminuzione f di manodopera (per
pensionamento, decesso etc).
nature ['neɪtʃə*] n natura; (character)
natura, indole f; by ~ di natura;
documents of a confidential ~ documenti
mpl di natura privata.
-natured ['neɪtʃəd] suffix: ill~
maldisposto(a).
nature reserve n (BRIT) parco naturale.
nature trail n percorso tracciato in parchi
nazionali ecc con scopi educativi.
naturist ['neɪtʃərɪst] n naturista m/f.
naught [nɔːt] n = nought.
naughtiness ['nɔːtɪnɪs] n cattiveria.
naughty ['nɔːtɪ] adj (child) birichino(a),
cattivello(a); (story, film) spinto(a).
nausea ['nɔːsɪə] n (MED) nausea; (fig:
disgust) schifo.
nauseate ['nɔːsɪeɪt] vt nauseare; far schifo
a.
nauseating ['nɔːsɪeɪtɪŋ] adj nauseante; (fig)
disgustoso(a).
nauseous ['nɔːsɪəs] adj nauseabondo(a);
(feeling sick): to be ~ avere la nausea.
nautical ['nɔːtɪkl] adj nautico(a).
nautical mile n miglio nautico or marino.
naval ['neɪvl] adj navale.
naval officer n ufficiale m di marina.
nave [neɪv] n navata centrale.
navel ['neɪvl] n ombelico.
navigable ['nævɪgəbl] adj navigabile.
navigate ['nævɪgeɪt] vt percorrere
navigando ♦ vi navigare; (AUT) fare da
navigatore.
navigation [nævɪ'geɪʃən] n navigazione f.
navigator ['nævɪgeɪtə*] n (NAUT, AVIAT)
ufficiale m di rotta; (explorer) navigatore
m; (AUT) copilota m/f.
navvy ['nævɪ] n manovale m.
navy ['neɪvɪ] n marina; Department of the
N~ (US) Ministero della Marina.
navy(-blue) ['neɪvɪ('bluː)] adj blu scuro inv.
Nazareth ['næzərɪθ] n Nazareth f.
Nazi ['nɑːtsɪ] adj, n nazista (m/f).
NB abbr (= nota bene) N.B.; (Canada) = New
Brunswick.
NBA n abbr (US: = National Basketball
Association) ≈ F.I.P. f (= Federazione
Italiana Pallacanestro); = National Boxing

Association.
NBC n abbr (US: = National Broadcasting
Company) compagnia nazionale di
radiodiffusione.
NBS n abbr (US: = National Bureau of
Standards) ufficio per la normalizzazione.
NC abbr (COMM etc: = no charge) gratis; (US)
= North Carolina.
NCC n abbr (US) = National Council of
Churches.
NCO n abbr see non-commissioned.
ND, N. Dak. abbr (US) = North Dakota.
NE abbr (US) = Nebraska; New England.
NEA n abbr (US) = National Education
Association.
neap [niːp] n (also: ~tide) marea di
quadratura.
Neapolitan [nɪə'pɒlɪtən] adj, n
napoletano(a).
near [nɪə*] adj vicino(a); (relation)
prossimo(a) ♦ adv vicino ♦ prep (also: ~ to)
vicino a, presso; (time) verso ♦ vt
avvicinarsi a; to come ~ avvicinarsi; ~
here/there qui/lì vicino; £25,000 or ~est
offer (BRIT) 25.000 sterline trattabili; in
the ~ future in un prossimo futuro; the
building is ~ing completion il palazzo è
quasi terminato or ultimato.
nearby [nɪə'baɪ] adj vicino(a) ♦ adv vicino.
Near East n: the ~ il Medio Oriente.
nearer ['nɪərə*] adj più vicino(a) ♦ adv più
vicino.
nearly ['nɪəlɪ] adv quasi; not ~ non ...
affatto; I ~ lost it per poco non lo
perdevo; she was ~ crying era lì lì per
piangere.
near miss n: that was a ~ c'è mancato
poco.
nearness ['nɪənɪs] n vicinanza.
nearside ['nɪəsaɪd] n (right-hand drive) lato
sinistro; (left-hand drive) lato destro ♦ adj
sinistro(a); destro(a).
near-sighted [nɪə'saɪtɪd] adj miope.
neat [niːt] adj (person, room) ordinato(a);
(work) pulito(a); (solution, plan) ben
indovinato(a), azzeccato(a); (spirits)
liscio(a).
neatly ['niːtlɪ] adv con ordine; (skilfully)
abilmente.
neatness ['niːtnɪs] n (tidiness) ordine m;
(skilfulness) abilità.
Nebr. abbr (US) = Nebraska.
nebulous ['nɛbjuləs] adj nebuloso(a); (fig)
vago(a).
necessarily ['nɛsɪsrɪlɪ] adv
necessariamente; not ~ non è detto, non
necessariamente.
necessary ['nɛsɪsrɪ] adj necessario(a); if ~

se necessario.
necessitate [nɪ'sɛsɪteɪt] *vt* rendere necessario(a).
necessity [nɪ'sɛsɪtɪ] *n* necessità *f inv;* **in case of** ~ in caso di necessità.
neck [nɛk] *n* collo; (*of garment*) colletto ♦ *vi* (*col*) pomiciare, sbaciucchiarsi; ~ **and** ~ testa a testa; **to stick one's** ~ **out** (*col*) rischiare (forte).
necklace ['nɛklɪs] *n* collana.
neckline ['nɛklaɪn] *n* scollatura.
necktie ['nɛktaɪ] *n* (*esp US*) cravatta.
nectar ['nɛktə*] *n* nettare *m.*
nectarine ['nɛktərɪn] *n* nocepesca.
née [neɪ] *adj:* ~ **Scott** nata Scott.
need [niːd] *n* bisogno ♦ *vt* aver bisogno di; **I** ~ **to do it** lo devo fare, bisogna che io lo faccia; **you don't** ~ **to go** non deve andare, non c'è bisogno che lei vada; **a signature is** ~**ed** occorre *or* ci vuole una firma; **to be in** ~ **of, have** ~ **of** aver bisogno di; **£10 will meet my immediate** ~**s** 10 sterline mi basteranno per le necessità più urgenti; **in case of** ~ in caso di bisogno *or* necessità; **there's no** ~ **for** ... non c'è bisogno *or* non occorre che ...; **there's no** ~ **to do** ... non occorre fare ...; **the** ~**s of industry** le esigenze dell'industria.
needle ['niːdl] *n* ago; (*on record player*) puntina ♦ *vt* punzecchiare.
needlecord ['niːdlkɔːd] *n* (*BRIT*) velluto a coste sottili.
needless ['niːdlɪs] *adj* inutile; ~ **to say,** ... inutile dire che ....
needlessly ['niːdlɪslɪ] *adv* inutilmente.
needlework ['niːdlwəːk] *n* cucito.
needn't ['niːdnt] = **need not.**
needy ['niːdɪ] *adj* bisognoso(a).
negation [nɪ'geɪʃən] *n* negazione *f.*
negative ['nɛgətɪv] *n* (*PHOT*) negativa, negativo; (*ELEC*) polo negativo; (*LING*) negazione *f* ♦ *adj* negativo(a); **to answer in the** ~ rispondere negativamente *or* di no.
negative equity *n* situazione in cui l'ammontare del mutuo su un immobile supera il suo valore sul mercato.
neglect [nɪ'glɛkt] *vt* trascurare ♦ *n* (*of person, duty*) negligenza; **state of** ~ stato di abbandono; **to** ~ **to do sth** trascurare *or* tralasciare di fare qc.
neglected [nɪ'glɛktɪd] *adj* trascurato(a).
neglectful [nɪ'glɛktful] *adj* (*gen*) negligente; **to be** ~ **of sb/sth** trascurare qn/qc.
negligee ['nɛglɪʒeɪ] *n* négligé *m inv.*
negligence ['nɛglɪdʒəns] *n* negligenza.
negligent ['nɛglɪdʒənt] *adj* negligente.
negligently ['nɛglɪdʒəntlɪ] *adv* con

negligenza.
negligible ['nɛglɪdʒɪbl] *adj* insignificante, trascurabile.
negotiable [nɪ'gəuʃɪəbl] *adj* negoziabile; (*cheque*) trasferibile; (*road*) transitabile.
negotiate [nɪ'gəuʃɪeɪt] *vi* negoziare ♦ *vt* (*COMM*) negoziare; (*obstacle*) superare; (*bend in road*) prendere; **to** ~ **with sb for sth** trattare con qn per ottenere qc.
negotiating table [nɪ'gəuʃɪeɪtɪŋ-] *n* tavolo delle trattative.
negotiation [nɪgəuʃɪ'eɪʃən] *n* trattativa; (*POL*) negoziato; **to enter into** ~**s with sb** entrare in trattative (*or* intavolare i negoziati) con qn.
negotiator [nɪ'gəuʃɪeɪtə*] *n* negoziatore/ trice.
Negress ['niːgrɪs] *n* negra.
Negro ['niːgrəu] *adj, n* (*pl* ~**es**) negro(a).
neigh [neɪ] *vi* nitrire.
neighbour, (*US*) **neighbor** ['neɪbə*] *n* vicino/a.
neighbo(u)rhood ['neɪbəhud] *n* vicinato.
neighbourhood watch *n* (*BRIT: also:* ~ **scheme**) sistema di vigilanza reciproca in un quartiere.
neighbo(u)ring ['neɪbərɪŋ] *adj* vicino(a).
neighbo(u)rly ['neɪbəlɪ] *adj:* **he is a** ~ **person** è un buon vicino.
neither ['naɪðə*] *adj, pron* né l'uno(a) né l'altro(a), nessuno(a) dei(delle) due ♦ *conj* neanche, nemmeno, neppure ♦ *adv:* ~ **good nor bad** né buono né cattivo; **I didn't move and** ~ **did Claude** io non mi mossi e nemmeno Claude; ... ~ **did I refuse** ..., ma non ho nemmeno rifiutato.
neo... ['niːəu] *prefix* neo....
neolithic [niːəu'lɪθɪk] *adj* neolitico(a).
neologism [nɪ'ɔlədʒɪzəm] *n* neologismo.
neon ['niːɔn] *n* neon *m.*
neon light *n* luce *f* al neon.
neon sign *n* insegna al neon.
Nepal [nɪ'pɔːl] *n* Nepal *m.*
nephew ['nɛvjuː] *n* nipote *m.*
nepotism ['nɛpətɪzəm] *n* nepotismo.
nerd [nəːd] *n* (*col*) sfigato/a, povero(a) fesso/a.
nerve [nəːv] *n* nervo; (*fig*) coraggio; (*impudence*) faccia tosta; **he gets on my** ~**s** mi dà ai nervi, mi fa venire i nervi; **a fit of** ~**s** una crisi di nervi; **to lose one's** ~ (*self-confidence*) perdere fiducia in se stesso; **I lost my** ~ (*courage*) mi è mancato il coraggio.
nerve centre *n* (*ANAT*) centro nervoso; (*fig*) cervello, centro vitale.
nerve gas *n* gas *m* nervino.
nerve-racking ['nəːvrækɪŋ] *adj* che spezza i

nervi.
nervous ['nɔːvəs] *adj* nervoso(a).
nervous breakdown *n* esaurimento
nervoso.
nervously ['nɔːvəslɪ] *adv* nervosamente.
nervousness ['nɔːvəsnɪs] *n* nervosismo.
nervous wreck *n*: **to be a** ~ (*col*) essere
nevrastenico(a).
nervy ['nɔːvɪ] *adj* agitato(a), nervoso(a).
nest [nɛst] *n* nido; ~ **of tables** tavolini *mpl*
cicogna *inv*.
nest egg *n* (*fig*) gruzzolo.
nestle ['nɛsl] *vi* accoccolarsi.
nestling ['nɛslɪŋ] *n* uccellino di nido.
net [nɛt] *n* rete *f*; (*fabric*) tulle *m*; **the N~**
(*Internet*) Internet *f* ♦ *adj* netto(a) ♦ *vt* (*subj*:
person) ricavare un utile netto di; (*deal*,
sale) dare un utile netto di; ~ **of tax** netto,
al netto di tasse; **he earns £10,000** ~ **per**
year guadagna 10.000 sterline nette
all'anno.
netball ['nɛtbɔːl] *n specie di pallacanestro*.
net curtains *npl* tende *fpl* di tulle.
Netherlands ['nɛðələndz] *npl*: **the** ~ **i** Paesi
Bassi.
net profit *n* utile *m* netto.
netsurfer ['nɛtsɔːfə*] *n* navigatore/trice in
Internet.
nett [nɛt] *adj* = **net**.
netting ['nɛtɪŋ] *n* (*for fence etc*) reticolato;
(*fabric*) tulle *m*.
nettle ['nɛtl] *n* ortica.
network ['nɛtwɔːk] *n* rete *f*.
neuralgia [njuə'rældʒə] *n* nevralgia.
neurological [njuərə'lɔdʒɪkl] *adj*
neurologico(a).
neurosis, *pl* **neuroses** [njuə'rəusɪs, -siːz] *n*
nevrosi *f inv*.
neurotic [njuə'rɔtɪk] *adj*, *n* nevrotico(a).
neuter ['njuːtə*] *adj* neutro(a)
♦ *n* neutro ♦ *vt* (*cat etc*) castrare.
neutral ['njuːtrəl] *adj* neutro(a); (*person*,
nation) neutrale ♦ *n* (*AUT*): **in** ~ in folle.
neutrality [njuː'trælɪtɪ] *n* neutralità.
neutralize ['njuːtrəlaɪz] *vt* neutralizzare.
Nev. *abbr* (*US*) = *Nevada*.
never ['nɛvə*] *adv* (non...) mai; ~ **again** mai
più; **I'll** ~ **go there again** non ci vado più;
~ **in my life** mai in vita mia; *see also*
mind.
never-ending [nɛvər'ɛndɪŋ] *adj*
interminabile.
nevertheless [nɛvəðə'lɛs] *adv* tuttavia, ciò
nonostante, ciò nondimeno.
new [njuː] *adj* nuovo(a); (*brand new*)
nuovo(a) di zecca; **as good as** ~ come
nuovo.
New Age *adj*, *n* New Age (*f*) *inv*.

newborn ['njuːbɔːn] *adj* neonato(a).
newcomer ['njuːkʌmə*] *n* nuovo(a)
venuto(a).
new-fangled ['njuːfæŋgld] *adj* (*pej*)
stramoderno(a).
new-found ['njuːfaund] *adj* nuovo(a).
Newfoundland ['njuːfənlənd] *n* Terranova.
New Guinea *n* Nuova Guinea.
newly ['njuːlɪ] *adv* di recente.
newly-weds ['njuːlɪwɛdz] *npl* sposini *mpl*,
sposi *mpl* novelli.
new moon *n* luna nuova.
newness ['njuːnɪs] *n* novità.
news [njuːz] *n* notizie *fpl*; (*RADIO*) giornale
m radio; (*TV*) telegiornale *m*; **a piece of** ~
una notizia; **good/bad** ~ buone/cattive
notizie; **financial** ~ (*PRESS*) pagina
economica e finanziaria; (*RADIO*, *TV*)
notiziario economico.
news agency *n* agenzia di stampa.
newsagent ['njuːzeɪdʒənt] *n* (*BRIT*)
giornalaio.
news bulletin *n* (*RADIO*, *TV*) notiziario.
newscaster ['njuːzkɑːstə*] *n* (*RADIO*, *TV*)
annunciatore/trice.
newsdealer ['njuːzdiːlə*] *n* (*US*)
= **newsagent**.
newsflash ['njuːzflæʃ] *n* notizia *f* lampo *inv*.
newsletter ['njuːzlɛtə*] *n* bollettino (*di*
ditta, *associazione*).
newspaper ['njuːzpeɪpə*] *n* giornale *m*;
daily ~ quotidiano; **weekly** ~ settimanale
m.
newsprint ['njuːzprɪnt] *n* carta da giornale.
newsreader ['njuːzriːdə*] *n* = **newscaster**.
newsreel ['njuːzriːl] *n* cinegiornale *m*.
newsroom ['njuːzrum] *n* (*PRESS*) redazione
f; (*RADIO*, *TV*) studio.
news stand *n* edicola.
newsworthy ['njuːzwɔːðɪ] *adj* degno(a) di
menzione (*per radio*, *TV ecc*); **to be** ~ fare
notizia.
newt [njuːt] *n* tritone *m*.
new town *n* (*BRIT*) nuovo centro urbano
creato con fondi pubblici.
New Year *n* Anno Nuovo; **Happy** ~! Buon
Anno!; **to wish sb a happy** ~ augurare
Buon Anno a qn.
New Year's Day *n* il Capodanno.
New Year's Eve *n* la vigilia di Capodanno.
New York [-'jɔːk] *n* New York *f*, Nuova
York *f*; (*also*: ~ **State**) stato di New York.
New Zealand [-'ziːlənd] *n* Nuova Zelanda
♦ *adj* neozelandese.
New Zealander [-'ziːləndə*] *n*
neozelandese *m/f*.
next [nɛkst] *adj* prossimo(a) ♦ *adv* accanto;
(*in time*) dopo; ~ **to** *prep* accanto a; ~ **to**

nothing quasi niente; ~ **time** adv la prossima volta; ~ **week** la settimana prossima; **the** ~ **week** la settimana dopo or seguente; **the week after** ~ fra due settimane; **the** ~ **day** il giorno dopo, l'indomani; ~ **year** l'anno prossimo or venturo; **"turn to the** ~ **page"** "vedi pagina seguente"; **who's** ~**?** a chi tocca?; **when do we meet** ~**?** quando ci rincontriamo?

next door adv accanto.

next of kin n parente m/f prossimo(a).

NF n abbr (BRIT POL: = National Front) partito di estrema destra ♦ abbr (Canada) = **Newfoundland**.

NFL n abbr (US) = National Football League.

Nfld. abbr (Canada) = **Newfoundland**.

NG abbr (US) = **National Guard**.

NGO n abbr = non-governmental organization.

NH abbr (US) = New Hampshire.

NHL n abbr (US: = National Hockey League) ≈ F.I.H.P. f (= Federazione Italiana Hockey e Pattinaggio).

NHS n abbr (BRIT) see **National Health Service**.

NI abbr = **Northern Ireland**; (BRIT) = **National Insurance**.

Niagara Falls [naɪ'ægərə-] npl: **the** ~ le cascate del Niagara.

nib [nɪb] n (of pen) pennino.

nibble ['nɪbl] vt mordicchiare.

Nicaragua [nɪkə'rægjuə] n Nicaragua m.

Nicaraguan [nɪkə'rægjuən] adj, n nicaraguense (m/f).

Nice [niːs] n Nizza.

nice [naɪs] adj (holiday, trip) piacevole; (flat, picture) bello(a); (person) simpatico(a), gentile; (taste, smell, meal) buono(a); (distinction, point) sottile.

nice-looking ['naɪslukɪŋ] adj bello(a).

nicely ['naɪslɪ] adv bene; **that will do** ~ andrà benissimo.

niceties ['naɪsɪtɪz] npl finezze fpl.

nick [nɪk] n tacca ♦ vt intaccare; tagliare; (col: steal) rubare; (: BRIT: arrest) beccare; **in the** ~ **of time** appena in tempo; **in good** ~ (BRIT col) decente, in buono stato; **to** ~ **o.s.** farsi un taglietto.

nickel ['nɪkl] n nichel m; (US) moneta da cinque centesimi di dollaro.

nickname ['nɪkneɪm] n soprannome m ♦ vt soprannominare.

Nicosia [nɪkə'siːə] n Nicosia.

nicotine ['nɪkətiːn] n nicotina.

nicotine patch n cerotto antifumo (a base di nicotina).

niece [niːs] n nipote f.

nifty ['nɪftɪ] adj (col: car, jacket) chic inv;

(: gadget, tool) ingegnoso(a).

Niger ['naɪdʒə*] n Niger m.

Nigeria [naɪ'dʒɪərɪə] n Nigeria.

Nigerian [naɪ'dʒɪərɪən] adj, n nigeriano(a).

niggardly ['nɪɡədlɪ] adj (person) tirchio(a), spilorcio(a); (allowance, amount) misero(a).

nigger ['nɪɡə*] n (col!: highly offensive) negro/a.

niggle ['nɪɡl] vt assillare ♦ vi fare il(la) pignolo(a).

niggling ['nɪɡlɪŋ] adj pignolo(a); (detail) insignificante; (doubt, pain) persistente.

night [naɪt] n notte f; (evening) sera; **at** ~ la notte; la sera; **by** ~ di notte; **in the** ~, **during the** ~ durante la notte; **the** ~ **before last** l'altro ieri notte; l'altro ieri sera.

night-bird ['naɪtbəːd] n uccello notturno; (fig) nottambulo/a.

nightcap ['naɪtkæp] n bicchierino prima di andare a letto.

night club n locale m notturno.

nightdress ['naɪtdrɛs] n camicia da notte.

nightfall ['naɪtfɔːl] n crepuscolo.

nightie ['naɪtɪ] n camicia da notte.

nightingale ['naɪtɪŋɡeɪl] n usignolo.

night life n vita notturna.

nightly ['naɪtlɪ] adj di ogni notte or sera; (by night) notturno(a) ♦ adv ogni notte or sera.

nightmare ['naɪtmɛə*] n incubo.

night porter n portiere m di notte.

night safe n cassa continua.

night school n scuola serale.

nightshade ['naɪtʃeɪd] n: **deadly** ~ (BOT) belladonna.

nightshift ['naɪtʃɪft] n turno di notte.

night-time ['naɪttaɪm] n notte f.

night watchman n guardiano notturno.

nihilism ['naɪɪlɪzəm] n nichilismo.

nil [nɪl] n nulla m; (SPORT) zero.

Nile [naɪl] n: **the** ~ il Nilo.

nimble ['nɪmbl] adj agile.

nine [naɪn] num nove.

9-11 n 11 settembre.

nineteen [naɪn'tiːn] num diciannove.

ninety ['naɪntɪ] num novanta.

ninth [naɪnθ] num nono(a).

nip [nɪp] vt pizzicare ♦ vi (BRIT col): **to** ~ **out/down/up** fare un salto fuori/giù/di sopra ♦ n (pinch) pizzico; (drink) goccio, bicchierino.

nipple ['nɪpl] n (ANAT) capezzolo.

nippy ['nɪpɪ] adj (weather) pungente; (BRIT: car, person) svelto(a).

nit [nɪt] n (of louse) lendine m; (col: idiot) cretino/a, scemo/a.

nit-pick ['nɪtpɪk] vi (col) cercare il pelo

nell'uovo.
nitrogen ['naɪtrədʒən] n azoto.
nitroglycerin(e) [naɪtrəu'glɪsəriːn] n nitroglicerina.
nitty-gritty ['nɪtɪ'grɪtɪ] n (col): to get down to the ~ venire al sodo.
nitwit ['nɪtwɪt] n (col) scemo/a.
NJ abbr (US) = New Jersey.
NLF n abbr (= National Liberation Front) ≈ F.L.N. m.
NLRB n abbr (US: = National Labor Relations Board) organismo per la tutela dei lavoratori.
NM, N. Mex. abbr (US) = New Mexico.

================================= KEYWORD

no [nəu] adv (opposite of "yes"): no; are you coming? — ~ (I'm not) viene? — no (non vengo); would you like some more? — ~ thank you ne vuole ancora un po'? — no, grazie; I have ~ more wine non ho più vino
♦ adj (not any) nessuno(a); I have ~ money/time/books non ho soldi/tempo/libri; ~ student would have done it nessuno studente lo avrebbe fatto; there is ~ reason to believe ... non c'è nessuna ragione per credere ...; "~ parking" "divieto di sosta"; "~ smoking" "vietato fumare"; "~ entry" "ingresso vietato"; "~ dogs" "vietato l'accesso ai cani"
♦ n (pl ~es) no m inv; I won't take ~ for an answer non accetterò un rifiuto.

no. abbr (= number) n.
nobble ['nɔbl] vt (BRIT col: bribe: person) comprare, corrompere; (: person to speak to, criminal) bloccare, beccare; (RACING: horse, dog) drogare.
Nobel prize [nəu'bɛl-] n premio Nobel.
nobility [nəu'bɪlɪtɪ] n nobiltà.
noble ['nəubl] adj, n nobile (m).
nobleman ['nəublmən] n nobile m, nobiluomo.
nobly ['nəublɪ] adv (selflessly) generosamente.
nobody ['nəubədɪ] pron nessuno.
no-claims bonus ['nəukleɪmz-] n bonus malus m inv.
nocturnal [nɔk'təːnl] adj notturno(a).
nod [nɔd] vi accennare col capo, fare un cenno; (sleep) sonnecchiare ♦ vt: to ~ one's head fare di sì col capo ♦ n cenno; they ~ded their agreement accennarono di sì (col capo).
► nod off vi assopirsi.
no-fly zone [nəu'flaɪ-] n zona di interdizione aerea.

noise [nɔɪz] n rumore m; (din, racket) chiasso.
noiseless ['nɔɪzlɪs] adj silenzioso(a).
noisily ['nɔɪzɪlɪ] adv rumorosamente.
noisy ['nɔɪzɪ] adj (street, car) rumoroso(a); (person) chiassoso(a).
nomad ['nəumæd] n nomade m/f.
nomadic [nəu'mædɪk] adj nomade.
no man's land n terra di nessuno.
nominal ['nɔmɪnl] adj nominale.
nominate ['nɔmɪneɪt] vt (propose) proporre come candidato; (elect) nominare.
nomination [nɔmɪ'neɪʃən] n nomina; candidatura.
nominee [nɔmɪ'niː] n persona nominata; candidato/a.
non... [nɔn] prefix non....
non-alcoholic ['nɔnælkə'hɔlɪk] adj analcolico(a).
non-breakable [nɔn'breɪkəbl] adj infrangibile.
nonce word ['nɔns-] n parola coniata per l'occasione.
nonchalant ['nɔnʃələnt] adj incurante, indifferente.
non-commissioned [nɔnkə'mɪʃnd] adj: ~ officer (NCO) sottufficiale m.
non-committal [nɔnkə'mɪtl] adj evasivo(a).
nonconformist [nɔnkən'fɔːmɪst] n anticonformista m/f; (BRIT REL) dissidente m/f ♦ adj anticonformista.
non-contributory [nɔnkən'trɪbjutərɪ] adj: ~ pension scheme or (US) plan sistema di pensionamento con i contributi interamente a carico del datore di lavoro.
non-cooperation ['nɔnkəuɔpə'reɪʃən] n non cooperazione f, non collaborazione f.
nondescript ['nɔndɪskrɪpt] adj qualunque inv.
none [nʌn] pron (not one thing) niente; (not one person) nessuno(a); ~ of you nessuno(a) di voi; I have ~ non ne ho nemmeno uno; I have ~ left non ne ho più; ~ at all proprio niente; (not one) nemmeno uno; he's ~ the worse for it non ne ha risentito.
nonentity [nɔ'nɛntɪtɪ] n persona insignificante.
non-essential [nɔnɪ'sɛnʃl] adj non essenziale ♦ n: ~s superfluo, cose fpl superflue.
nonetheless ['nʌnðə'lɛs] adv nondimeno.
non-event [nɔnɪ'vɛnt] n delusione f.
non-executive [nɔnɪg'zɛkjutɪv] adj: ~ director direttore m senza potere esecutivo.
non-existent [nɔnɪg'zɪstənt] adj

inesistente.
non-fiction[nɔn'fɪkʃən] n saggistica.
non-flammable[nɔn'flæməbl] adj
ininfiammabile.
non-intervention['nɔnɪntə'venʃən] n non
intervento.
no-no['nəunəu] n: **it's a** ~! (undesirable) è
inaccettabile!; (forbidden) non si può
fare!
non obst. abbr (= non obstante:
notwithstanding) nonostante.
no-nonsense[nəu'nɔnsəns] adj che va al
sodo.
non-payment[nɔn'peɪmənt] n mancato
pagamento.
nonplussed[nɔn'plʌst] adj sconcertato(a).
non-profit-making[nɔn'prɔfɪtmeɪkɪŋ] adj
senza scopo di lucro.
nonsense['nɔnsəns] n sciocchezze fpl; ~!
che sciocchezze!, che assurdità!; **it is** ~
to say that ... è un'assurdità or non ha
senso dire che ....
nonsensical[nɔn'sensɪkl] adj assurdo(a),
ridicolo(a).
non-shrink[nɔn'ʃrɪŋk] adj (BRIT)
irrestringibile.
non-skid[nɔn'skɪd] adj antisdrucciolo(a).
non-smoker['nɔn'sməukə*] n non
fumatore/trice.
non-starter[nɔn'stɑːtə*] n: **it's a** ~ è fallito
in partenza.
non-stick['nɔn'stɪk] adj antiaderente,
antiadesivo(a).
non-stop['nɔn'stɔp] adj continuo(a); (train,
bus) direttissimo(a) ♦ adv senza sosta.
non-taxable[nɔn'tæksəbl] adj: ~ **income**
reddito non imponibile.
non-U[nɔn'juː] adj abbr (BRIT col) = non-
upper class.
non-volatile[nɔn'vɔlətaɪl] adj: ~ **memory**
(COMPUT) memoria permanente.
non-voting[nɔn'vəutɪŋ] adj: ~ **shares**
azioni fpl senza diritto di voto.
non-white['nɔn'waɪt] adj di colore ♦ n
persona di colore.
noodles['nuːdlz] npl taglierini mpl.
nook[nuk] n: ~**s and crannies** angoli mpl.
noon[nuːn] n mezzogiorno.
no one['nəuwʌn] pron = **nobody**.
noose[nuːs] n nodo scorsoio, cappio;
(hangman's) cappio.
nor[nɔː*] conj = **neither** ♦ adv see **neither.**
norm[nɔːm] n norma.
normal['nɔːml] adj normale ♦ n: **to return
to** ~ tornare alla normalità.
normality[nɔː'mælɪtɪ] n normalità.
normally['nɔːməlɪ] adv normalmente.
Normandy['nɔːməndɪ] n Normandia.

north[nɔːθ] n nord m, settentrione m ♦ adj
nord inv, del nord, settentrionale ♦ adv
verso nord.
North African Africa del Nord.
North African adj, n nordafricano(a).
North American America del Nord.
North American adj, n nordamericano(a).
Northants[nɔː'θænts] abbr (BRIT)
= Northamptonshire.
northbound['nɔːθbaund] adj (traffic)
diretto(a) a nord; (carriageway) nord inv.
north-east[nɔːθ'iːst] n nord-est m.
northerly['nɔːðəlɪ] adj (wind) del nord;
(direction) verso nord.
northern['nɔːðən] adj del nord,
settentrionale.
Northern Irelandn Irlanda del Nord.
North Polen: **the** ~ il Polo Nord.
North Sean: **the** ~ il mare del Nord.
North Sea oiln petrolio del mare del
Nord.
northward(s)['nɔːθwəd(z)] adv verso nord.
north-west[nɔːθ'west] n nord-ovest m.
Norway['nɔːweɪ] n Norvegia.
Norwegian[nɔː'wiːdʒən] adj norvegese ♦ n
norvegese m/f; (LING) norvegese m.
nos. abbr (= numbers) nn.
nose[nəuz] n naso; (of animal) muso ♦ vi
(also: ~ **one's way**) avanzare cautamente;
to pay through the ~ (for sth) (col) pagare
(qc) un occhio della testa.
►**nose about, nose around**vi aggirarsi.
nosebleed['nəuzbliːd] n emorragia nasale.
nose-dive['nəuzdaɪv] n picchiata.
nose dropsnpl gocce fpl per il naso.
nosey['nəuzɪ] adj curioso(a).
nostalgia[nɔs'tældʒɪə] n nostalgia.
nostalgic[nɔs'tældʒɪk] adj nostalgico(a).
nostril['nɔstrɪl] n narice f; (of horse) frogia.
nosy['nəuzɪ] adj = **nosey.**
not[nɔt] adv non; ~ **at all** niente affatto;
(after thanks) prego, s'immagini; **you must**
~ **or mustn't do this** non deve fare
questo; **he isn't** ... egli non è ...; **I hope** ~
spero di no.
notable['nəutəbl] adj notevole.
notably['nəutəblɪ] adv notevolmente; (in
particular) in particolare.
notary['nəutərɪ] n (also: ~ **public**) notaio.
notation[nəu'teɪʃən] n notazione f.
notch[nɔtʃ] n tacca.
►**notch up**vt (score, victory) marcare,
segnare.
note[nəut] n nota; (letter, banknote)
biglietto ♦ vt prendere nota di; **to take** ~
of prendere nota di; **to take** ~s prendere
appunti; **to compare** ~s (fig) scambiarsi
le impressioni; **of** ~ eminente,

importante; **just a quick ~ to let you
know** ... ti scrivo solo due righe per
informarti ....
notebook ['nəutbuk] *n* taccuino; (*for
shorthand*) bloc-notes *m inv*.
note-case ['nəutkeɪs] *n* (*BRIT*) portafoglio.
noted ['nəutɪd] *adj* celebre.
notepad ['nəutpæd] *n* bloc-notes *m inv*,
blocchetto.
notepaper ['nəutpeɪpə*] *n* carta da lettere.
noteworthy ['nəutwɜːðɪ] *adj* degno(a) di
nota, importante.
nothing ['nʌθɪŋ] *n* nulla *m*, niente *m*; **he
does ~** non fa niente; **~ new** niente di
nuovo; **for ~** (*free*) per niente; **~ at all**
proprio niente.
notice ['nəutɪs] *n* avviso; (*of leaving*)
preavviso; (*BRIT: review: of play etc*)
critica, recensione *f* ♦ *vt* notare,
accorgersi di; **to take ~ of** fare
attenzione a; **to bring sth to sb's ~** far
notare qc a qn; **to give sb ~ of sth**
avvisare qn di qc; **to give ~, hand in
one's ~** (*subj: employee*) licenziarsi;
without ~ senza preavviso; **at short ~**
con un breve preavviso; **until further ~**
fino a nuovo avviso; **advance ~**
preavviso; **to escape** *or* **avoid ~** passare
inosservato; **it has come to my ~ that** ...
sono venuto a sapere che ....
noticeable ['nəutɪsəbl] *adj* evidente.
notice board *n* (*BRIT*) tabellone *m* per
affissi.
notification [nəutɪfɪ'keɪʃən] *n* annuncio;
notifica; denuncia.
notify ['nəutɪfaɪ] *vt*: **to ~ sth to sb** notificare
qc a qn; **to ~ sb of sth** avvisare qn di qc;
(*police*) denunciare qc a qn.
notion ['nəuʃən] *n* idea; (*concept*) nozione *f*.
notions ['nəuʃənz] *npl* (*US: haberdashery*)
merceria.
notoriety [nəutə'raɪətɪ] *n* notorietà.
notorious [nəu'tɔːrɪəs] *adj* famigerato(a).
notoriously [nəu'tɔːrɪəslɪ] *adv*
notoriamente.
Notts [nɔts] *abbr* (*BRIT*) = *Nottinghamshire*.
notwithstanding [nɔtwɪθ'stændɪŋ] *adv*
nondimeno ♦ *prep* nonostante, malgrado.
nougat ['nuːgɑː] *n* torrone *m*.
nought [nɔːt] *n* zero.
noun [naun] *n* nome *m*, sostantivo.
nourish ['nʌrɪʃ] *vt* nutrire.
nourishing ['nʌrɪʃɪŋ] *adj* nutriente.
nourishment ['nʌrɪʃmənt] *n* nutrimento.
Nov. *abbr* (= *November*) nov.
Nova Scotia ['nəuvə'skəuʃə] *n* Nuova
Scozia.
novel ['nɔvl] *n* romanzo ♦ *adj* nuovo(a).

novelist ['nɔvəlɪst] *n* romanziere/a.
novelty ['nɔvəltɪ] *n* novità *f inv*.
November [nəu'vɛmbə*] *n* novembre *m*; *for
phrases see also* **July**.
novice ['nɔvɪs] *n* principiante *m/f*; (*REL*)
novizio/a.
NOW [nau] *n abbr* (*US*: = *National
Organization for Women*) ≈ U.D.I. *f*
(= *Unione Donne Italiane*).
now [nau] *adv* ora, adesso ♦ *conj*: **~ (that)**
adesso che, ora che; **right ~** subito; **by ~**
ormai; **just ~**: **that's the fashion just ~** è
la moda del momento; **I saw her just ~**
l'ho vista proprio adesso; **I'll read it just ~**
lo leggo subito; **~ and then, ~ and again**
ogni tanto; **from ~ on** da ora in poi; **in 3
days from ~** fra 3 giorni; **between ~ and
Monday** da qui a lunedì, entro lunedì;
that's all for ~ per ora basta.
nowadays ['nauədeɪz] *adv* oggigiorno.
nowhere ['nəuwɛə*] *adv* in nessun luogo,
da nessuna parte; **~ else** in nessun altro
posto.
no-win situation [nəu'wɪn-] *n*: **to be in a ~**
aver perso in partenza.
noxious ['nɔkʃəs] *adj* nocivo(a).
nozzle ['nɔzl] *n* (*of hose etc*) boccaglio.
NP *n abbr* = **notary public**.
NS *abbr* (*Canada*) = **Nova Scotia**.
NSC *n abbr* (*US*) = **National Security
Council**.
NSF *n abbr* (*US*) = *National Science
Foundation*.
NSPCC *n abbr* (*BRIT*) = *National Society for
the Prevention of Cruelty to Children*.
NSW *abbr* (*Australia*) = *New South Wales*.
NT *n abbr* (= *New Testament*) N.T. ♦ *abbr*
(*Canada*) = *Northwest Territories*.
nth [ɛnθ] *adj*: **for the ~ time** (*col*) per
l'ennesima volta.
nuance ['njuːɑːns] *n* sfumatura.
nubile ['njuːbaɪl] *adj* nubile; (*attractive*)
giovane e desiderabile.
nuclear ['njuːklɪə*] *adj* nucleare; (*warfare*)
atomico(a).
nuclear disarmament *n* disarmo
nucleare.
nuclear family *n* famiglia nucleare.
nuclear-free zone ['njuːklɪə'friː-] *n* zona
denuclearizzata.
nucleus, *pl* **nuclei** ['njuːklɪəs, 'njuːklɪaɪ] *n*
nucleo.
NUCPS *n abbr* (*BRIT*) = *National Union of
Civil and Public Servants*.
nude [njuːd] *adj* nudo(a) ♦ *n* (*ART*) nudo; **in
the ~** tutto(a) nudo(a).
nudge [nʌdʒ] *vt* dare una gomitata a.
nudist ['njuːdɪst] *n* nudista *m/f*.

nudity ['njuːdɪtɪ] *n* nudità.
nugget ['nʌgɪt] *n* pepita.
nuisance ['njuːsns] *n*: **it's a** ~ **è** una seccatura; **he's a** ~ lui dà fastidio; **what a** ~! che seccatura!
NUJ *n abbr* (*BRIT*: = *National Union of Journalists*) *sindacato nazionale dei giornalisti.*
nuke [njuːk] *n* (*col*) bomba atomica.
null [nʌl] *adj*: ~ **and void** nullo(a).
nullify ['nʌlɪfaɪ] *vt* annullare.
NUM *n abbr* (*BRIT*: = *National Union of Mineworkers*) *sindacato nazionale dei dipendenti delle miniere.*
numb [nʌm] *adj* intorpidito(a) ♦ *vt* intorpidire; ~ **with** (*fear*) paralizzato(a) da; (*grief*) impietrito(a) da; ~ **with cold** intirizzito(a) (dal freddo).
number ['nʌmbə*] *n* numero ♦ *vt* numerare; (*include*) contare; **a** ~ **of** un certo numero di; **telephone** ~ numero di telefono; **wrong** ~ (*TEL*) numero sbagliato; **the staff** ~**s 20** gli impiegati sono in 20.
numbered account ['nʌmbəd-] *n* (*in bank*) conto numerato.
number plate *n* (*BRIT AUT*) targa.
Number Ten *n* (*BRIT*: = *10 Downing Street*) *residenza del Primo Ministro del Regno Unito.*
numbness ['nʌmnɪs] *n* intorpidimento; (*due to cold*) intirizzimento.
numbskull ['nʌmskʌl] *n* (*col*) imbecille *m/f*, idiota *m/f*.
numeral ['njuːmərəl] *n* numero, cifra.
numerate ['njuːmərɪt] *adj* (*BRIT*): **to be** ~ saper far di conto.
numerical [njuː'mɛrɪkl] *adj* numerico(a).
numerous ['njuːmərəs] *adj* numeroso(a).
nun [nʌn] *n* suora, monaca.
nunnery ['nʌnərɪ] *n* convento.
nuptial ['nʌpʃəl] *adj* nuziale.
nurse [nəːs] *n* infermiere/a; (*also*: ~**maid**) bambinaia ♦ *vt* (*patient, cold*) curare; (*baby*: *BRIT*) cullare; (: *US*) allattare, dare il latte a; (*hope*) nutrire.
nursery ['nəːsərɪ] *n* (*room*) camera dei bambini; (*institution*) asilo; (*for plants*) vivaio.
nursery rhyme *n* filastrocca.
nursery school *n* scuola materna.
nursery slope *n* (*BRIT SKI*) pista per principianti.
nursing ['nəːsɪŋ] *n* (*profession*) professione *f* di infermiere (*or* di infermiera) ♦ *adj* (*mother*) che allatta.
nursing home *n* casa di cura.
nurture ['nəːtʃə*] *vt* allevare; nutrire.
NUS *n abbr* (*BRIT*: = *National Union of Students*) *sindacato nazionale degli studenti.*
NUT *n abbr* (*BRIT*: = *National Union of Teachers*) *sindacato nazionale degli insegnanti.*
nut [nʌt] *n* (*of metal*) dado; (*fruit*) noce *f* (*or* nocciola *or* mandorla *etc*) ♦ *adj* (*chocolate etc*) alla nocciola *etc*; **he's** ~**s** (*col*) è matto.
nutcase ['nʌtkeɪs] *n* (*col*) mattarello/a.
nutcrackers ['nʌtkrækəz] *npl* schiaccianoci *m inv*.
nutmeg ['nʌtmɛg] *n* noce *f* moscata.
nutrient ['njuːtrɪənt] *adj* nutriente ♦ *n* sostanza nutritiva.
nutrition [njuː'trɪʃən] *n* nutrizione *f*.
nutritionist [njuː'trɪʃənɪst] *n* nutrizionista *m/f*.
nutritious [njuː'trɪʃəs] *adj* nutriente.
nutshell ['nʌtʃɛl] *n* guscio di noce; **in a** ~ **in** poche parole.
nutty ['nʌtɪ] *adj* di noce (*or* nocciola *or* mandorla *etc*); (*BRIT col*) tocco(a), matto(a).
nuzzle ['nʌzl] *vi*: **to** ~ **up to** strofinare il muso contro.
NV *abbr* (*US*) = *Nevada*.
NWT *abbr* (*Canada*) = *Northwest Territories*.
NY *abbr* (*US*) = **New York**.
NYC *abbr* (*US*) = *New York City*.
nylon ['naɪlɔn] *n* nailon *m*; ~**s** *npl* calze *fpl* di nailon.
nymph [nɪmf] *n* ninfa.
nymphomaniac [nɪmfəu'meɪnɪæk] *adj*, *n* ninfomane (*f*).
NYSE *abbr* (*US*) = *New York Stock Exchange*.

O o

O, o [əu] *n* (*letter*) O, o *f or m inv*; (*US SCOL*: = *outstanding*) ≈ ottimo; (*number*. *TEL etc*) zero; **O for Oliver**, (*US*) **O for Oboe** ≈ O come Otranto.
oaf [əuf] *n* zoticone *m*.
oak [əuk] *n* quercia ♦ *cpd* di quercia.
OAP *n abbr* (*BRIT*) *see* **old-age pensioner**.
oar [ɔː*] *n* remo; **to put** *or* **shove one's** ~ **in** (*fig col*) intromettersi.
oarsman ['ɔːzmən], **oarswoman** ['ɔːzwumən] *n* rematore/trice.
OAS *n abbr* (= *Organization of American*

States) O.S.A. f (= Organizzazione degli Stati Americani).

oasis, pl **oases** [əu'eɪsɪs, əu'eɪsiːz] n oasi f inv.

oath [əuθ] n giuramento; (swear word) bestemmia; **to take the** ~ giurare; **on** ~ (BRIT) or **under** ~ sotto giuramento.

oatmeal ['əutmiːl] n farina d'avena.

oats [əuts] npl avena.

obdurate ['ɔbdjurɪt] adj testardo(a); incallito(a); ostinato(a), irremovibile.

OBE n abbr (BRIT: = Order of the British Empire) titolo.

obedience [ə'biːdɪəns] n ubbidienza; **in** ~ **to** conformemente a.

obedient [ə'biːdɪənt] adj ubbidiente; **to be** ~ **to sb/sth** ubbidire a qn/qc.

obelisk ['ɔbɪlɪsk] n obelisco.

obese [əu'biːs] adj obeso(a).

obesity [əu'biːsɪtɪ] n obesità.

obey [ə'beɪ] vt ubbidire a; (instructions, regulations) osservare ♦ vi ubbidire.

obituary [ə'bɪtjuərɪ] n necrologia.

object n ['ɔbdʒɪkt] oggetto; (purpose) scopo, intento; (LING) complemento oggetto ♦ vi [əb'dʒɛkt]: **to** ~ **to** (attitude) disapprovare; (proposal) protestare contro, sollevare delle obiezioni contro; **I** ~! mi oppongo!; **he** ~ed that ... obiettò che ...; **do you** ~ **to my smoking?** la disturba se fumo?; **what's the** ~ **of doing that?** a che serve farlo?; **expense is no** ~ non si bada a spese.

objection [əb'dʒɛkʃən] n obiezione f; (drawback) inconveniente m; **if you have no** ~ se non ha obiezioni; **to make** or **raise an** ~ sollevare un'obiezione.

objectionable [əb'dʒɛkʃənəbl] adj antipatico(a); (smell) sgradevole; (language) scostumato(a).

objective [əb'dʒɛktɪv] n obiettivo ♦ adj obiettivo(a).

objectivity [ɔbdʒɪk'tɪvɪtɪ] n obiettività.

object lesson n: ~ **(in)** dimostrazione f (di).

objector [əb'dʒɛktə*] n oppositore/trice.

obligation [ɔblɪ'geɪʃən] n obbligo, dovere m; (debt) obbligo (di riconoscenza); **"without** ~**"** "senza impegno"; **to be under an** ~ **to sb/to do sth** essere in dovere verso qn/di fare qc.

obligatory [ə'blɪgətərɪ] adj obbligatorio(a).

oblige [ə'blaɪdʒ] vt (force): **to** ~ **sb to do** costringere qn a fare; (do a favour) fare una cortesia a; **to be** ~**d to sb for sth** essere grato a qn per qc; **anything to** ~! (col) questo e altro!

obliging [ə'blaɪdʒɪŋ] adj servizievole,

compiacente.

oblique [ə'bliːk] adj obliquo(a); (allusion) indiretto(a) ♦ n (BRIT TYP): ~ **(stroke)** barra.

obliterate [ə'blɪtəreɪt] vt cancellare.

oblivion [ə'blɪvɪən] n oblio.

oblivious [ə'blɪvɪəs] adj: ~ **of** incurante di; inconscio(a) di.

oblong ['ɔblɔŋ] adj oblungo(a) ♦ n rettangolo.

obnoxious [əb'nɔkʃəs] adj odioso(a); (smell) disgustoso(a), ripugnante.

oboe ['əubəu] n oboe m.

obscene [əb'siːn] adj osceno(a).

obscenity [əb'sɛnɪtɪ] n oscenità f inv.

obscure [əb'skjuə*] adj oscuro(a) ♦ vt oscurare; (hide: sun) nascondere.

obscurity [əb'skjuərɪtɪ] n oscurità; (obscure point) punto oscuro; (lack of fame) anonimato.

obsequious [əb'siːkwɪəs] adj ossequioso(a).

observable [əb'zɜːvəbl] adj osservabile; (appreciable) notevole.

observance [əb'zɜːvns] n osservanza; religious ~s pratiche fpl religiose.

observant [əb'zɜːvnt] adj attento(a).

observation [ɔbzə'veɪʃən] n osservazione f; (by police etc) sorveglianza.

observation post n (MIL) osservatorio.

observatory [əb'zɜːvətrɪ] n osservatorio.

observe [əb'zɜːv] vt osservare.

observer [əb'zɜːvə*] n osservatore/trice.

obsess [əb'sɛs] vt ossessionare; **to be** ~**ed by** or **with sb/sth** essere ossessionato da qn/qc.

obsession [əb'sɛʃən] n ossessione f.

obsessive [əb'sɛsɪv] adj ossessivo(a).

obsolescence [ɔbsə'lɛsns] n obsolescenza; **built-in** or **planned** ~ (COMM) obsolescenza programmata.

obsolescent [ɔbsə'lɛsnt] adj obsolescente.

obsolete ['ɔbsəliːt] adj obsoleto(a); (word) desueto(a).

obstacle ['ɔbstəkl] n ostacolo.

obstacle race n corsa agli ostacoli.

obstetrician [ɔbstə'trɪʃən] n ostetrico/a.

obstetrics [ɔb'stɛtrɪks] n ostetrica.

obstinacy ['ɔbstɪnəsɪ] n ostinatezza.

obstinate ['ɔbstɪnɪt] adj ostinato(a).

obstreperous [əb'strɛpərəs] adj turbolento(a).

obstruct [əb'strʌkt] vt (block) ostruire, ostacolare; (halt) fermare; (hinder) impedire.

obstruction [əb'strʌkʃən] n ostruzione f; ostacolo.

obstructive [əb'strʌktɪv] adj ostruttivo(a); che crea impedimenti.

obtain [əb'teɪn] vt ottenere ♦ vi essere in uso; **to ~ sth (for o.s.)** procurarsi qc.
obtainable [əb'teɪnəbl] adj ottenibile.
obtrusive [əb'truːsɪv] adj (person) importuno(a); (smell) invadente; (building etc) imponente e invadente.
obtuse [əb'tjuːs] adj ottuso(a).
obverse ['ɔbvəːs] n opposto, inverso.
obviate ['ɔbvɪeɪt] vt ovviare a, evitare.
obvious ['ɔbvɪəs] adj ovvio(a), evidente.
obviously ['ɔbvɪəslɪ] adv ovviamente; ~!
certo!; ~ **not!** certo che no!; **he was ~ not drunk** si vedeva che non era ubriaco; **he was not ~ drunk** non si vedeva che era ubriaco.
OCAS n abbr = Organization of Central American States.
occasion [ə'keɪʒən] n occasione f; (event) avvenimento ♦ vt cagionare; **on that ~** in quell'occasione, quella volta; **to rise to the ~** mostrarsi all'altezza della situazione.
occasional [ə'keɪʒənl] adj occasionale; **I smoke an ~ cigarette** ogni tanto fumo una sigaretta.
occasionally [ə'keɪʒənəlɪ] adv ogni tanto; **very ~** molto raramente.
occasional table n tavolino.
occult [ɔ'kʌlt] adj occulto(a) ♦ n: **the ~** l'occulto.
occupancy ['ɔkjupənsɪ] n occupazione f.
occupant ['ɔkjupənt] n occupante m/f; (of boat, car etc) persona a bordo.
occupation [ɔkju'peɪʃən] n occupazione f; (job) mestiere m, professione f; **unfit for ~** (house) inabitabile.
occupational [ɔkju'peɪʃənl] adj (disease) professionale; (hazard) del mestiere; ~ **accident** infortunio sul lavoro.
occupational guidance n (BRIT) orientamento professionale.
occupational pension scheme n sistema pensionistico programmato dal datore di lavoro.
occupational therapy n ergoterapia.
occupier ['ɔkjupaɪə*] n occupante m/f.
occupy ['ɔkjupaɪ] vt occupare; **to ~ o.s. by doing** occuparsi a fare; **to be occupied with sth/in doing sth** essere preso da qc/occupato a fare qc.
occur [ə'kəː*] vi accadere; (difficulty, opportunity) capitare; (phenomenon, error) trovarsi; **to ~ to sb** venire in mente a qn.
occurrence [ə'kʌrəns] n caso, fatto; presenza.
ocean ['əuʃən] n oceano; ~**s of** (col) un sacco di.
ocean bed n fondale m oceanico.

ocean-going ['əuʃəngəuɪŋ] adj d'alto mare.
Oceania [əuʃɪ'ɑːnɪə] n Oceania.
ocean liner n transatlantico.
ochre, (US) **ocher** ['əukə*] adj ocra inv.
o'clock [ə'klɔk] adv: **it is one ~** è l'una; **it is 5 ~** sono le 5.
OCR n abbr see **optical character reader; optical character recognition.**
Oct. abbr (= October) ott.
octagonal [ɔk'tægənl] adj ottagonale.
octane ['ɔkteɪn] n ottano; **high-~ petrol** or (US) **gas** benzina ad alto numero di ottani.
octave ['ɔktɪv] n ottavo.
October [ɔk'təubə*] n ottobre m; for phrases see also **July.**
octogenarian [ɔktəudʒɪ'nɛərɪən] n ottuagenario/a.
octopus ['ɔktəpəs] n polpo, piovra.
odd [ɔd] adj (strange) strano(a), bizzarro(a); (number) dispari inv; (left over) in più; (not of a set) spaiato(a); **60-~** 60 e oltre; **at ~ times** di tanto in tanto; **the ~ one out** l'eccezione f.
oddball ['ɔdbɔːl] n (col) eccentrico/a.
oddity ['ɔdɪtɪ] n bizzarria; (person) originale m/f.
odd-job man [ɔd'dʒɔb-] n tuttofare m inv.
odd jobs npl lavori mpl occasionali.
oddly ['ɔdlɪ] adv stranamente.
oddments ['ɔdmənts] npl (BRIT COMM) rimanenze fpl.
odds [ɔdz] npl (in betting) quota; **the ~ are against his coming** c'è poca probabilità che venga; **it makes no ~** non importa; **at ~** in contesa; **to succeed against all the ~** riuscire contro ogni aspettativa; **~ and ends** avanzi mpl.
odds-on [ɔdz'ɔn] adj (col) probabile; ~ **favourite** (RACING) favorito(a).
ode [əud] n ode f.
odious ['əudɪəs] adj odioso(a), ripugnante.
odometer [ɔ'dɔmɪtə*] n odometro.
odour, (US) **odor** ['əudə*] n odore m.
odo(u)rless ['əudəlɪs] adj inodoro(a).
OECD n abbr (= Organization for Economic Cooperation and Development) O.C.S.E. f (= Organizzazione per la Cooperazione e lo Sviluppo Economico).
oesophagus, (US) **esophagus** [iː'sɔfəgəs] n esofago.
oestrogen, (US) **estrogen** ['iːstraudʒən] n estrogeno.

═══════════════════ *KEYWORD*

of [ɔv, əv] prep **1** (gen) di; **a boy ~ 10** un ragazzo di 10 anni; **a friend ~ ours** un nostro amico; **that was kind ~ you** è stato

molto gentile da parte sua
2 (*expressing quantity, amount, dates etc*)
di; **a kilo ~ flour** un chilo di farina; **how
much ~ this do you need?** quanto gliene
serve?; **there were four ~ them** (*people*)
erano in quattro; (*objects*) ce n'erano
quattro; **three ~ us went** tre di noi sono
andati; **the 5th ~ July** il 5 luglio; **a quarter
~ 4** (*US*) le 4 meno un quarto
3 (*from, out of*) di, in; **made ~ wood**
(fatto) di *or* in legno.

Ofcom ['ɔfkɔm] *n abbr* (*BRIT*: = *Office of
Communications*) *organismo de
regolamentazione delle
telecomunicazioni.*

================= KEYWORD

off [ɔf] *adv* **1** (*distance, time*): **it's a long way
~ è** lontano; **the game is 3 days ~ la**
partita è tra 3 giorni
2 (*departure, removal*) via; **to go ~ to
Paris** andarsene a Parigi; **I must be ~**
devo andare via; **to take ~ one's coat**
togliersi il cappotto; **the button came ~ il**
bottone è venuto via *or* si è staccato; **10%
~** con lo sconto del 10%
3 (*not at work*): **to have a day ~** avere un
giorno libero; **to be ~ sick** essere assente
per malattia
♦ *adj* (*engine*) spento(a); (*tap*) chiuso(a);
(*cancelled*) sospeso(a); (*BRIT: food*)
andato(a) a male; **to be well/badly ~**
essere/non essere benestante; **the lid was
~** non c'era il coperchio; **I'm afraid the
chicken is ~** (*BRIT: not available*) purtroppo
il pollo è finito; **on the ~ chance** nel caso;
to have an ~ day non essere in forma;
that's a bit ~, isn't it? (*fig col*) non è molto
carino, vero?
♦ *prep* **1** (*motion, removal etc*) da; (*distant
from*) a poca distanza da; **a street ~ the
square** una strada che parte dalla piazza;
5km ~ the road a 5km dalla strada; **~ the
coast** al largo della costa; **a house ~ the
main road** una casa che non è sulla
strada principale
2: **to be ~ meat** non mangiare più la
carne.

offal ['ɔfl] *n* (*CULIN*) frattaglie *fpl.*
offbeat ['ɔfbiːt] *adj* eccentrico(a).
off-centre, (*US*) **off-center** [ɔf'sɛntə*] *adj*
storto(a), fuori centro.
off-colour ['ɔf'kʌlə*] *adj* (*BRIT: ill*) malato(a),
indisposto(a); **to feel ~** sentirsi poco
bene.
offence, (*US*) **offense** [ə'fɛns] *n* (*LAW*)

contravvenzione *f*; (: *more serious*) reato;
to give ~ to offendere; **to take ~ at**
offendersi per; **to commit an ~**
commettere un reato.
offend [ə'fɛnd] *vt* (*person*) offendere ♦ *vi*: **to
~ against** (*law, rule*) trasgredire.
offender [ə'fɛndə*] *n* delinquente *m/f*;
(*against regulations*) contravventore/trice.
offending [ə'fɛndɪŋ] *adj* (*often hum*): **the ~
word/object** la parola incriminata/
l'oggetto incriminato.
offense [ə'fɛns] *n* (*US*) = **offence.**
offensive [ə'fɛnsɪv] *adj* offensivo(a); (*smell
etc*) sgradevole, ripugnante ♦ *n* (*MIL*)
offensiva.
offer ['ɔfə*] *n* offerta, proposta ♦ *vt* offrire;
"on ~" (*COMM*) "in offerta speciale"; **to
make an ~ for sth** fare un'offerta per qc;
to ~ sth to sb, ~ sb sth offrire qc a qn; **to
~ to do sth** offrirsi di fare qc.
offering ['ɔfərɪŋ] *n* offerta.
offhand [ɔf'hænd] *adj* disinvolto(a),
noncurante ♦ *adv* all'impronto; **I can't tell
you ~** non posso dirglielo su due piedi.
office ['ɔfɪs] *n* (*place*) ufficio; (*position*)
carica; **doctor's ~** (*US*) ambulatorio; **to
take ~** entrare in carica; **through his
good ~s** con il suo prezioso aiuto; **O~ of
Fair Trading** (*BRIT*) *organismo di
protezione contro le pratiche
commerciali abusive.*
office automation *n* automazione *f*
d'ufficio, burotica.
office bearer *n* (*of club etc*) membro
dell'amministrazione.
office block, (*US*) **office building** *n*
complesso di uffici.
office boy *n* garzone *m.*
office hours *npl* orario d'ufficio; (*US MED*)
orario di visite.
office manager *n* capoufficio *m/f.*
officer ['ɔfɪsə*] *n* (*MIL etc*) ufficiale *m*; (*of
organization*) funzionario; (*also:* **police ~**)
agente *m* di polizia.
office work *n* lavoro d'ufficio.
office worker *n* impiegato/a d'ufficio.
official [ə'fɪʃl] *adj* (*authorized*) ufficiale ♦ *n*
ufficiale *m*; (*civil servant*) impiegato/a
statale; funzionario.
officialdom [ə'fɪʃəldəm] *n* burocrazia.
officially [ə'fɪʃəlɪ] *adv* ufficialmente.
official receiver *n* curatore *m*
fallimentare.
officiate [ə'fɪʃɪeɪt] *vi* (*REL*) ufficiare; **to ~ as
Mayor** esplicare le funzioni di sindaco; **to
~ at a marriage** celebrare un
matrimonio.
officious [ə'fɪʃəs] *adj* invadente.

offing ['ɔfɪŋ] n: **in the** ~ (fig) in vista.
off-key [ɔf'kiː] adj stonato(a) ♦ adv fuori tono.
off-licence ['ɔflaɪsns] n (BRIT) spaccio di bevande alcoliche; see boxed note.

OFF-LICENCE

In Gran Bretagna e in Irlanda, gli **off-licences** sono esercizi pubblici specializzati nella vendita strettamente regolamentata di bevande alcoliche, per la quale è necessario avere un'apposita licenza. In genere sono aperti fino a tarda sera.

---

off-limits [ɔf'lɪmɪts] adj (esp US) in cui vige il divieto d'accesso.
off line adj, adv (COMPUT) off line inv, fuori linea; (: switched off) spento(a).
off-load ['ɔfləud] vt scaricare.
off-peak ['ɔf'piːk] adj (ticket etc) a tariffa ridotta; (time) non di punta.
off-putting ['ɔfputɪŋ] adj (BRIT) un po' scostante.
off-season ['ɔfsiːzn] adj, adv fuori stagione.
offset ['ɔfset] vt irreg (counteract) controbilanciare ♦ n (also: ~ **printing**) offset m.
offshoot ['ɔffuːt] n (fig) diramazione f.
offshore [ɔf'fɔː*] adj (breeze) di terra; (island) vicino alla costa; (fishing) costiero(a); ~ **oilfield** giacimento petrolifero in mare aperto.
offside ['ɔf'saɪd] adj (SPORT) fuori gioco; (AUT: with right-hand drive) destro(a); (: with left-hand drive) sinistro(a) ♦ n destra; sinistra.
offspring ['ɔfsprɪŋ] n prole f, discendenza.
offstage [ɔf'steɪdʒ] adv dietro le quinte.
off-the-cuff [ɔfðə'kʌf] adv improvvisando.
off-the-job ['ɔfðə'dʒɔb] adj: ~ **training** addestramento fuori sede.
off-the-peg ['ɔfðə'peg], (US) **off-the-rack** ['ɔfðə'ræk] adv prêt-à-porter.
off-the-record ['ɔfðə'rekɔːd] adj ufficioso(a) ♦ adv in via ufficiosa.
off-white ['ɔfwaɪt] adj bianco sporco inv.
Ofgem ['ɔfdʒɛm] n abbr (BRIT: = Office of Gas and Electricity Markets) organo indipendente di controllo per la tutela dei consumatori.
often ['ɔfn] adv spesso; **how** ~ **do you go?** quanto spesso ci va?; **as** ~ **as not** quasi sempre.
Ofwat ['ɔfwɔt] n abbr (BRIT: = Office of Water Services) in Inghilterra e Galles, organo indipendente di controllo per la tutela dei consumatori.
ogle ['əugl] vt occhieggiare.

ogre ['əugə*] n orco.
OH abbr (US) = Ohio.
oh [əu] excl oh!
OHMS abbr (BRIT) = On His (or Her) Majesty's Service.
oil [ɔɪl] n olio; (petroleum) petrolio; (for central heating) nafta ♦ vt (machine) lubrificare.
oilcan ['ɔɪlkæn] n oliatore m a mano; (for storing) latta da olio.
oil change n cambio dell'olio.
oilfield ['ɔɪlfiːld] n giacimento petrolifero.
oil filter n (AUT) filtro dell'olio.
oil-fired ['ɔɪlfaɪəd] adj a nafta.
oil gauge n indicatore m del livello dell'olio.
oil industry n industria del petrolio.
oil level n livello dell'olio.
oil painting n quadro a olio.
oil refinery n raffineria di petrolio.
oil rig n derrick m inv; (at sea) piattaforma per trivellazioni subacquee.
oilskins ['ɔɪlskɪnz] npl indumenti mpl di tela cerata.
oil slick n chiazza d'olio.
oil tanker n petroliera.
oil well n pozzo petrolifero.
oily ['ɔɪlɪ] adj unto(a), oleoso(a); (food) untuoso(a).
ointment ['ɔɪntmənt] n unguento.
OK abbr (US) = Oklahoma.
O.K., okay [əu'keɪ] excl d'accordo! ♦ vt approvare ♦ n: **to give sth one's** ~ approvare qc ♦ adj: **is it** ~?, **are you** ~? tutto bene?; **it's** ~ **with** or **by me** per me va bene; **are you** ~ **for money?** sei a posto coi soldi?
Okla. abbr (US) = Oklahoma.
old [əuld] adj vecchio(a); (ancient) antico(a), vecchio(a); (person) vecchio(a), anziano(a); **how** ~ **are you?** quanti anni ha?; **he's 10 years** ~ ha 10 anni; ~**er brother/sister** fratello/sorella maggiore; **any** ~ **thing will do** va bene qualsiasi cosa.
old age n vecchiaia.
old-age pensioner (OAP) ['əuldeɪdʒ-] n (BRIT) pensionato/a.
old-fashioned ['əuld'fæʃnd] adj antiquato(a), fuori moda; (person) all'antica.
old maid n zitella.
old people's home n ricovero per anziani.
old-style ['əuldstaɪl] adj (di) vecchio stampo inv.
old-time ['əuldtaɪm] adj di una volta.

old-timer [ˈəuldˈtaɪmə*] *n* veterano/a.

old wives' tale *n* vecchia superstizione *f*.

O levels *npl* (*BRIT: formerly*) diploma di istruzione secondaria conseguito a 16 anni in Inghilterra e Galles, ora sostituito dal GCSE.

olive [ˈɔlɪv] *n* (*fruit*) oliva; (*tree*) olivo ♦ *adj* (*also*: ~**-green**) verde oliva *inv*.

olive oil *n* olio d'oliva.

Olympic [əuˈlɪmpɪk] *adj* olimpico(a); **the ~ Games, the ~s** i giochi olimpici, le Olimpiadi.

OM *n abbr* (*BRIT*: = *Order of Merit*) titolo.

Oman [əuˈmɑːn] *n* Oman *m*.

OMB *n abbr* (*US*: = *Office of Management and Budget*) servizio di consulenza al Presidente in materia di bilancio.

omelet(te) [ˈɔmlɪt] *n* omelette *f inv; ham/cheese ~* omelette al prosciutto/al formaggio.

omen [ˈəumən] *n* presagio, augurio.

ominous [ˈɔmɪnəs] *adj* minaccioso(a); (*event*) di malaugurio.

omission [əuˈmɪʃən] *n* omissione *f*.

omit [əuˈmɪt] *vt* omettere; **to ~ to do sth** tralasciare *or* trascurare di fare qc.

omnivorous [ɔmˈnɪvərəs] *adj* onnivoro(a).

ON *abbr* (*Canada*) = *Ontario*.

━━━━━━━━━━━━━━━━ *KEYWORD*

on [ɔn] *prep* **1** (*indicating position*) su; **~ the wall** sulla parete; **~ the left** a *or* sulla sinistra; **I haven't any money ~ me** non ho soldi con me

2 (*indicating means, method, condition etc*): **~ foot** a piedi; **~ the train/plane** in treno/aereo; **~ the telephone** al telefono; **~ the radio/television** alla radio/televisione; **to be ~ drugs** drogarsi; **~ holiday** in vacanza; **he's ~ £16,000 a year** guadagna 16.000 sterline all'anno; **this round's ~ me** questo giro lo offro io

3 (*referring to time*): **~ Friday** venerdì; **~ Fridays** il *or* di venerdì; **~ June 20th** il 20 giugno; **~ Friday, June 20th** venerdì, 20 giugno; **a week ~ Friday** venerdì a otto; **~ his arrival** al suo arrivo; **~ seeing this** vedendo ciò

4 (*about, concerning*) su, di; **information ~ train services** informazioni sui collegamenti ferroviari; **a book ~ Goldoni/physics** un libro su Goldoni/di *or* sulla fisica

♦ *adv* **1** (*referring to dress, covering*): **to have one's coat ~** avere indosso il cappotto; **to put one's coat ~** mettersi il cappotto; **what's she got ~?** cosa indossa?; **she put her boots/gloves/hat ~** si mise gli stivali/i guanti/il cappello; **screw the lid ~ tightly** avvita bene il coperchio

2 (*further, continuously*): **to walk ~, go ~** *etc* continuare, proseguire; **to read ~** continuare a leggere; **~ and off** ogni tanto; **from that day ~** da quel giorno in poi; **it was well ~ in the evening** era sera inoltrata

♦ *adj* **1** (*in operation: machine, TV, light*) acceso(a); (: *tap*) aperto(a); (: *brake*) inserito(a); **is the meeting still ~?** (*in progress*) la riunione è ancora in corso?; (*not cancelled*) è confermato l'incontro?; **there's a good film ~ at the cinema** danno un buon film al cinema; **when is the film ~?** quando c'è questo film?; **my father's always ~ at me to get a job** (*col*) mio padre mi tormenta sempre perché trovi un lavoro

2 (*col*): **that's not ~!** (*not acceptable*) non si fa così!; (*not possible*) non se ne parla neanche!

━━━━━━━━━━━━━━━━

once [wʌns] *adv* una volta ♦ *conj* non appena, quando; **~ he had left/it was done** dopo che se n'era andato/fu fatto; **at ~** subito; (*simultaneously*) a un tempo; **all at ~** (*tutto*) ad un tratto; **~ a week** una volta alla settimana; **~ more** ancora una volta; **I knew him ~** un tempo *or* in passato lo conoscevo; **~ and for all** una volta per sempre; **~ upon a time there was** ... c'era una volta ....

oncoming [ˈɔnkʌmɪŋ] *adj* (*traffic*) che viene in senso opposto.

━━━━━━━━━━━━━━━━ *KEYWORD*

one [wʌn] *num* uno(a); **~ hundred and fifty** centocinquanta; **~ day** un giorno; **it's ~ (o'clock)** è l'una; **to be ~ up on sb** essere avvantaggiato(a) rispetto a qn; **to be at ~ (with sb)** andare d'accordo (con qn)

♦ *adj* **1** (*sole*) unico(a); **the ~ book which** l'unico libro che; **the ~ man who** l'unico che

2 (*same*) stesso(a); **they came in the ~ car** sono venuti nella stessa macchina

♦ *pron* **1**: **this ~** questo(a); **that ~** quello(a); **which ~ do you want?** quale vuole?; **I've already got ~/a red ~** ne ho già uno/uno rosso; **~ by ~** uno per uno

2: **~ another** l'un l'altro; **to look at ~ another** guardarsi; **to help ~ another** aiutarsi l'un l'altro *or* a vicenda

3 (*impersonal*) si; **~ never knows** non si

sa mai; **to cut** ~'**s finger** tagliarsi un dito; **to express** ~'**s opinion** esprimere la propria opinione; ~ **needs to eat** bisogna mangiare.

one-armed bandit ['wɑːnɑːmd-] *n* slot-machine *f inv.*

one-day excursion ['wʌndeɪ-] *n* (*US*) biglietto giornaliero di andata e ritorno.

One-hundred share index ['wʌnhʌndrəd-] *n indice borsistico del Financial Times.*

one-man ['wʌn'mæn] *adj* (*business*) diretto(a) *etc* da un solo uomo.

one-man band *n suonatore ambulante con vari strumenti.*

one-off [wʌn'ɔf] (*BRIT col*) *n* fatto eccezionale ♦ *adj* eccezionale.

one-parent family ['wʌnpɛərənt-] *n* famiglia monogenitore.

one-piece ['wʌnpiːs] *adj* (*bathing suit*) intero(a).

onerous ['ɔnərəs] *adj* (*task, duty*) gravoso(a); (*responsibility*) pesante.

oneself [wʌn'sɛlf] *pron* si; (*after prep*) sé, se stesso(a); **to do sth (by)** ~ fare qc da sé.

one-shot [wʌn'ʃɔt] *n* (*US*) = **one-off.**

one-sided [wʌn'saɪdɪd] *adj* (*decision, view*) unilaterale; (*judgement, account*) parziale; (*game, contest*) impari *inv.*

one-time ['wʌntaɪm] *adj* ex *inv.*

one-to-one ['wʌntəwʌn] *adj* (*relationship*) univoco(a).

one-upmanship [wʌn'ʌpmənʃɪp] *n*: **the art of** ~ l'arte *f* di primeggiare.

one-way ['wʌnweɪ] *adj* (*street, traffic*) a senso unico.

ongoing ['ɔngəuɪŋ] *adj* in corso; in attuazione.

onion ['ʌnjən] *n* cipolla.

on line *adj* (*COMPUT*) on line *inv*, in linea; (: *switched on*) acceso(a).

onlooker ['ɔnlukə*] *n* spettatore/trice.

only ['əunlɪ] *adv* solo, soltanto ♦ *adj* solo(a), unico(a) ♦ *conj* solo che, ma; **an** ~ **child** un figlio unico; **not** ~ non solo; **I** ~ **took one** ne ho preso soltanto uno, non ne ho preso che uno; **I saw her** ~ **yesterday** l'ho vista appena ieri; **I'd be** ~ **too pleased to help** sarei proprio felice di essere d'aiuto; **I would come,** ~ **I'm very busy** verrei volentieri, solo che sono molto occupato.

ono *abbr* = **or nearest offer;** *see* **near.**

onset ['ɔnsɛt] *n* inizio; (*of winter*) arrivo.

onshore ['ɔnʃɔː*] *adj* (*wind*) di mare.

onslaught ['ɔnslɔːt] *n* attacco, assalto.

Ont. *abbr* (*Canada*) = Ontario.

on-the-job ['ɔnðə'dʒɔb] *adj*: ~ **training** addestramento in sede.

onto ['ɔntu] *prep* su, sopra.

onus ['əunəs] *n* onere *m*, peso; **the** ~ **is upon him to prove it** sta a lui dimostrarlo.

onward(s) ['ɔnwəd(z)] *adv* (*move*) in avanti; **from this time** ~ d'ora in poi.

onyx ['ɔnɪks] *n* onice *f.*

oops [ups] *excl* ops! (*esprime rincrescimento per un piccolo contrattempo*); ~-**a-daisy!** oplà!

ooze [uːz] *vi* stillare.

opacity [əu'pæsɪtɪ] *n* opacità.

opal ['əupl] *n* opale *m or f.*

opaque [əu'peɪk] *adj* opaco(a).

OPEC ['əupɛk] *n abbr* (= *Organization of Petroleum-Exporting Countries*) O.P.E.C. *f.*

open ['əupn] *adj* aperto(a); (*road*) libero(a); (*meeting*) pubblico(a); (*admiration*) evidente, franco(a); (*question*) insoluto(a); (*enemy*) dichiarato(a) ♦ *vt* aprire ♦ *vi* (*eyes, door, debate*) aprirsi; (*flower*) sbocciare; (*shop, bank, museum*) aprire; (*book etc*: *commence*) cominciare; **in the** ~ (**air**) all'aperto; **the** ~ **sea** il mare aperto, l'alto mare; ~ **ground** (*among trees*) radura; (*waste ground*) terreno non edificato; **to have an** ~ **mind (on sth)** non avere ancora deciso (su qc).

► **open on to** *vt fus* (*subj: room, door*) dare su.

► **open out** *vt* aprire ♦ *vi* aprirsi.

► **open up** *vt* aprire; (*blocked road*) sgombrare ♦ *vi* aprirsi.

open-air [əupn'ɛə*] *adj* all'aperto.

open-and-shut ['əupnən'ʃʌt] *adj*: ~ **case** caso indubbio.

open day *n* (*BRIT*) giornata di apertura al pubblico.

open-ended [əupn'ɛndɪd] *adj* (*fig*) aperto(a), senza limiti.

opener ['əupnə*] *n* (*also*: **can** ~, **tin** ~) apriscatole *m inv.*

open-heart [əupn'hɑːt] *adj*: ~ **surgery** chirurgia a cuore aperto.

opening ['əupnɪŋ] *n* apertura; (*opportunity*) occasione *f*, opportunità *f inv*; sbocco; (*job*) posto vacante.

opening night *n* (*THEAT*) prima.

open learning *n sistema educativo secondo il quale lo studente ha maggior controllo e gestione delle modalità di apprendimento.*

openly ['əupnlɪ] *adv* apertamente.

open-minded [əupn'maɪndɪd] *adj* che ha la mente aperta.

open-necked ['əupnnɛkt] *adj* col collo slacciato.

openness ['əupnnɪs] *n* (*frankness*) franchezza, sincerità.

open-plan ['əupn'plæn] adj senza pareti divisorie.

open prison n istituto di pena dove viene data maggiore libertà ai detenuti.

open sandwich n canapè m inv.

open shop n fabbrica o ditta dove sono accolti anche operai non iscritti ai sindacati.

Open University n (BRIT) see boxed note.

OPEN UNIVERSITY

La **Open University (OU)**, fondata in Gran Bretagna nel 1969, organizza corsi universitari per corrispondenza o via Internet, basati anche su lezioni che vengono trasmesse dalla BBC per radio e per televisione e su corsi estivi.

---

opera ['ɔpərə] n opera.

opera glasses npl binocolo da teatro.

opera house n opera.

opera singer n cantante m/f d'opera or lirico(a).

operate ['ɔpəreit] vt (machine) azionare, far funzionare; (system) usare ♦ vi funzionare; (drug, person) agire; **to ~ on sb (for)** (MED) operare qn (di).

operatic [ɔpə'rætik] adj dell'opera, lirico(a).

operating ['ɔpəreitiŋ] adj (COMM: costs etc) di gestione; (MED) operatorio(a).

operating room n (US) = **operating theatre.**

operating system n (COMPUT) sistema m operativo.

operating theatre n (MED) sala operatoria.

operation [ɔpə'reiʃən] n operazione f; **to be in ~** (machine) essere in azione or funzionamento; (system) essere in vigore; **to have an ~ (for)** (MED) essere operato(a) (di).

operational [ɔpə'reiʃənl] adj operativo(a); (COMM) di gestione, d'esercizio; (ready for use or action) in attività, in funzione.

operative ['ɔpərətiv] adj (measure) operativo(a) ♦ n (in factory) operaio/a; **the ~ word** la parola chiave.

operator ['ɔpəreitə*] n (of machine) operatore/trice; (TEL) centralinista m/f.

operetta [ɔpə'rɛtə] n operetta.

ophthalmologist [ɔfθæl'mɔlədʒist] n oftalmologo/a.

opinion [ə'pinjən] n opinione f, parere m; **in my ~** secondo me, a mio avviso; **to seek a second ~** (MED etc) consultarsi con un altro medico etc.

opinionated [ə'pinjəneitid] adj

dogmatico(a).

opinion poll n sondaggio di opinioni.

opium ['əupiəm] n oppio.

opponent [ə'pəunənt] n avversario/a.

opportune ['ɔpətjuːn] adj opportuno(a).

opportunist [ɔpə'tjuːnist] n opportunista m/f.

opportunity [ɔpə'tjuːniti] n opportunità f inv, occasione f; **to take the ~ to do or of doing** cogliere l'occasione per fare.

oppose [ə'pəuz] vt opporsi a; **~d to** contrario(a) a; **as ~d to** in contrasto con.

opposing [ə'pəuziŋ] adj opposto(a); (team) avversario(a).

opposite ['ɔpəzit] adj opposto(a); (house etc) di fronte ♦ adv di fronte, dirimpetto ♦ prep di fronte a ♦ n opposto, contrario; (of word) contrario; **"see ~ page"** "vedere pagina a fronte".

opposite number n controparte f, corrispondente m/f.

opposite sex n: **the ~** l'altro sesso.

opposition [ɔpə'ziʃən] n opposizione f.

oppress [ə'prɛs] vt opprimere.

oppression [ə'prɛʃən] n oppressione f.

oppressive [ə'prɛsiv] adj oppressivo(a).

opprobrium [ə'prəubriəm] n (formal) obbrobrio.

opt [ɔpt] vi: **to ~ for** optare per; **to ~ to do** scegliere di fare; **to ~ out of** (BRIT: of NHS) scegliere di non far più parte di; (of agreement, arrangement) scegliere di non partecipare a.

optical ['ɔptikl] adj ottico(a).

optical character reader/recognition (OCR) n lettore m ottico/lettura ottica di caratteri.

optical fibre n fibra ottica.

optician [ɔp'tiʃən] n ottico.

optics ['ɔptiks] n ottica.

optimism ['ɔptimizəm] n ottimismo.

optimist ['ɔptimist] n ottimista m/f.

optimistic [ɔpti'mistik] adj ottimistico(a).

optimum ['ɔptiməm] adj ottimale.

option ['ɔpʃən] n scelta; (SCOL) materia facoltativa; (COMM) opzione f; **to keep one's ~s open** (fig) non impegnarsi; **I have no ~** non ho scelta.

optional ['ɔpʃənl] adj facoltativo(a); (COMM) a scelta; **~ extra** optional m inv.

opulence ['ɔpjuləns] n opulenza.

opulent ['ɔpjulənt] adj opulento(a).

OR abbr (US) = Oregon.

or [ɔː*] conj o, oppure; (with negative): **he hasn't seen ~ heard anything** non ha visto né sentito niente; **~ else** se no, altrimenti; oppure.

oracle ['ɔrəkl] n oracolo.

oral ['ɔːrəl] adj orale ♦ n esame m orale.
orange ['ɔrɪndʒ] n (fruit) arancia ♦ adj arancione.
orangeade [ɔrɪndʒ'eɪd] n aranciata.
oration [ɔː'reɪʃən] n orazione f.
orator ['ɔrətə*] n oratore/trice.
oratorio [ɔrə'tɔːrɪəu] n oratorio.
orb [ɔːb] n orbe m.
orbit ['ɔːbɪt] n orbita ♦ vt orbitare intorno a; to be in/go into ~ (round) essere/entrare in orbita (attorno a).
orbital ['ɔːbɪtl] n (also: ~ motorway) raccordo anulare.
orchard ['ɔːtʃəd] n frutteto; apple ~ meleto.
orchestra ['ɔːkɪstrə] n orchestra; (US: seating) platea.
orchestral [ɔː'kestrəl] adj orchestrale; (concert) sinfonico(a).
orchestrate ['ɔːkɪstreɪt] vt (MUS, fig) orchestrare.
orchid ['ɔːkɪd] n orchidea.
ordain [ɔː'deɪn] vt (REL) ordinare; (decide) decretare.
ordeal [ɔː'diːl] n prova, travaglio.
order ['ɔːdə*] n ordine m; (COMM) ordinazione f ♦ vt ordinare; to ~ sb to do ordinare a qn di fare; in ~ in ordine; (of document) in regola; in ~ of size in ordine di grandezza; in ~ to do per fare; in ~ that affinché +sub; a machine in working ~ una macchina che funziona bene; to be out of ~ (machine, toilets) essere guasto(a); (telephone) essere fuori servizio; to place an ~ for sth with sb ordinare qc a qn; to the ~ of (BANKING) all'ordine di; to be under ~s to do sth avere l'ordine di fare qc; a point of ~ una questione di procedura; to be on ~ essere stato ordinato; made to ~ fatto su commissione; the lower ~s (pej) i ceti inferiori.
order book n copiacommissioni m inv.
order form n modulo d'ordinazione.
orderly ['ɔːdəlɪ] n (MIL) attendente m ♦ adj (room) in ordine; (mind) metodico(a); (person) ordinato(a), metodico(a).
order number n numero di ordinazione.
ordinal ['ɔːdɪnl] adj (number) ordinale.
ordinary ['ɔːdnrɪ] adj normale, comune; (pej) mediocre ♦ n: out of the ~ diverso dal solito, fuori dell'ordinario.
ordinary degree n laurea; see boxed note.

ORDINARY DEGREE

Il corso universitario di studi che porta al conferimento del "Bachelor's degree" può

avere una durata diversa, a seconda del profitto dello studente. Chi non è interessato a proseguire gli studi oltre tre anni di corso può optare per l'ordinary degree; vedi anche honours degree.

ordinary seaman (OS) n (BRIT) marinaio semplice.
ordinary shares npl azioni fpl ordinarie.
ordination [ɔːdɪ'neɪʃən] n ordinazione f.
ordnance ['ɔːdnəns] n (MIL: unit) (reparto di) sussistenza.
Ordnance Survey map n (BRIT) ≈ carta topografica dell'IGM.
ore [ɔː*] n minerale m grezzo.
Ore(g). abbr (US) = Oregon.
organ ['ɔːgən] n organo.
organic [ɔː'gænɪk] adj organico(a).
organism ['ɔːgənɪzəm] n organismo.
organist ['ɔːgənɪst] n organista m/f.
organization [ɔːgənaɪ'zeɪʃən] n organizzazione f.
organize ['ɔːgənaɪz] vt organizzare; to get ~d organizzarsi.
organized crime ['ɔːgənaɪzd-] n criminalità organizzata.
organized labour ['ɔːgənaɪzd-] n manodopera organizzata.
organizer ['ɔːgənaɪzə*] n organizzatore/trice.
orgasm ['ɔːgæzəm] n orgasmo.
orgy ['ɔːdʒɪ] n orgia.
Orient ['ɔːrɪənt] n: the ~ l'Oriente m.
oriental [ɔːrɪ'entl] adj, n orientale (m/f).
orientate ['ɔːrɪənteɪt] vt orientare.
orifice ['ɔrɪfɪs] n orifizio.
origin ['ɔrɪdʒɪn] n origine f; country of ~ paese m d'origine.
original [ə'rɪdʒɪnl] adj originale; (earliest) originario(a) ♦ n originale m.
originality [ərɪdʒɪ'nælɪtɪ] n originalità.
originally [ə'rɪdʒɪnəlɪ] adv (at first) all'inizio.
originate [ə'rɪdʒɪneɪt] vi: to ~ from venire da, essere originario(a) di; (suggestion) provenire da; to ~ in nascere in; (custom) avere origine in.
originator [ə'rɪdʒɪneɪtə*] n iniziatore/trice.
Orkneys ['ɔːknɪz] npl: the ~ (also: the Orkney Islands) le (isole) Orcadi.
ornament ['ɔːnəmənt] n ornamento; (trinket) ninnolo.
ornamental [ɔːnə'mentl] adj ornamentale.
ornamentation [ɔːnəmen'teɪʃən] n decorazione f, ornamento.
ornate [ɔː'neɪt] adj molto ornato(a).
ornithologist [ɔːnɪ'θɒlədʒɪst] n ornitologo/a.

ornithology[ɔːnɪ'θɒlədʒɪ] n ornitologia.
orphan['ɔːfn] n orfano/a ♦ vt: **to be ~ed**
diventare orfano.
orphanage['ɔːfənɪdʒ] n orfanotrofio.
orthodox['ɔːθədɔks] adj ortodosso(a).
orthopaedic,(US) **orthopedic**
[ɔːθə'piːdɪk] adj ortopedico(a).
OSabbr (BRIT: = Ordnance Survey) ≈ IGM m
(= Istituto Geografico Militare); (: NAUT) see
ordinary seaman; (: DRESS) = **outsize**.
O.S.abbr = **out of stock**.
oscillate['ɒsɪleɪt] vi oscillare.
OSHAn abbr (US: = Occupational Safety and
Health Administration) amministrazione
per la sicurezza e la salute sul lavoro.
Oslo['ɒzləu] n Oslo f.
ostensible[ɒs'tɛnsɪbl] adj preteso(a);
apparente.
ostensibly[ɒs'tɛnsɪblɪ] adv all'apparenza.
ostentation[ɒstɛn'teɪʃən] n ostentazione f.
ostentatious[ɒstɛn'teɪʃəs] adj
pretenzioso(a); ostentato(a).
osteopath['ɒstɪəpæθ] n specialista m/f di
osteopatia.
ostracize['ɒstrəsaɪz] vt dare l'ostracismo a.
ostrich['ɒstrɪtʃ] n struzzo.
OTabbr (= Old Testament) V.T.
OTBn abbr (US: = off-track betting) puntate
effettuate fuori dagli ippodromi.
OTEabbr (= on-target earnings) stipendio
compreso le commissioni.
other['ʌðə*] adj altro(a) ♦ pron: **the ~**
l'altro(a); **the ~s** gli altri; **the ~ day**
l'altro giorno; **some ~ people have still to
arrive** (alcuni) altri devono ancora
arrivare; **some actor or ~** un certo
attore; **somebody or ~** qualcuno; **~ than**
altro che; a parte; **the car was none ~
than Roberta's** la macchina era proprio
di Roberta.
otherwise['ʌðəwaɪz] adv, conj altrimenti;
an ~ good piece of work un lavoro
comunque buono.
OTTabbr (col) = **over the top**; see **top**.
otter['ɒtə*] n lontra.
OUn abbr (BRIT) see **Open University**.
ouch[autʃ] excl ohi!, ahi!
ought,pt **ought**[ɔːt] aux vb: **I ~ to do it**
dovrei farlo; **this ~ to have been
corrected** questo avrebbe dovuto essere
corretto; **he ~ to win** dovrebbe vincere;
you ~ to go and see it dovreste andare a
vederlo, fareste bene ad andarlo a
vedere.
ounce[auns] n oncia (= 28.35 g; 16 in a
pound).
our[auə*] adj il(la) nostro(a), pl i(le)
nostri(e).

ours[auəz] pron il(la) nostro(a), pl i(le)
nostri(e).
ourselves[auə'sɛlvz] pron pl (reflexive) ci;
(after preposition) noi; (emphatic) noi
stessi(e); **we did it (all) by ~** l'abbiamo
fatto (tutto) da soli.
oust[aust] vt cacciare, espellere.

===================================== KEYWORD

out[aut] adv (gen) fuori; **~ here/there** qui/
là fuori; **to speak ~ loud** parlare forte; **to
have a night ~** uscire una sera; **to be ~
and about** or (US) **around again** essere di
nuovo in piedi; **the boat was 10 km ~** la
barca era a 10 km dalla costa; **the
journey ~** l'andata; **3 days ~ from
Plymouth** a 3 giorni da Plymouth
♦ adj: **to be ~** (gen) essere fuori;
(unconscious) aver perso i sensi; (style,
singer) essere fuori moda; **before the
week was ~** prima che la settimana
fosse finita; **to be ~ to do sth** avere
intenzione di fare qc; **he's ~ for all he can
get** sta cercando di trarne il massimo
profitto; **to be ~ in one's calculations**
aver sbagliato i calcoli
♦ **out of**prep **1** (outside, beyond) fuori di;
to go ~ of the house uscire di casa; **to
look ~ of the window** guardare fuori
dalla finestra
2 (because of) per; **~ of pity** per pietà; **~
of boredom** per noia
3 (origin) da; **made ~ of wood** (fatto) di
or in legno; **to drink ~ of a cup** bere da
una tazza
4 (from among): **~ of 10** su 10
5 (without) senza; **~ of petrol** senza
benzina; **it's ~ of stock** (COMM) è
esaurito.

outage['autɪdʒ] n (esp US: power failure)
interruzione f or mancanza di corrente
elettrica.
out-and-out['autəndaut] adj vero(a) e
proprio(a).
outback['autbæk] n zona isolata; (in
Australia) interno, entroterra.
outbid,pt, pp **outbid**[aut'bɪd] vt fare
un'offerta più alta di.
outboard['autbɔːd] n: **~ (motor)** (motore
m) fuoribordo.
outbound['autbaund] adj: **~ (for or from)** in
partenza (per or da).
outbreak['autbreɪk] n scoppio; epidemia.
outbuilding['autbɪldɪŋ] n dipendenza.
outburst['autbəːst] n scoppio.
outcast['autkɑːst] n esule m/f; (socially)
paria m inv.

outclass [aut'klɑːs] vt surclassare.

outcome ['autkʌm] n esito, risultato.

outcrop ['autkrɔp] n affioramento.

outcry ['autkraɪ] n protesta, clamore m.

outdated [aut'deɪtɪd] adj (custom, clothes) fuori moda; (idea) sorpassato(a).

outdistance [aut'dɪstəns] vt distanziare.

outdo [aut'duː] vt irreg sorpassare.

outdoor [aut'dɔː*] adj all'aperto.

outdoors [aut'dɔːz] adv fuori; all'aria aperta.

outer ['autə*] adj esteriore; ~ suburbs estrema periferia.

outer space n spazio cosmico.

outfit ['autfɪt] n equipaggiamento; (clothes) abito; (col: organization) organizzazione f.

outfitter ['autfɪtə*] n (BRIT): "(gent's) ~s" "confezioni da uomo".

outgoing ['autgəuɪŋ] adj (president, tenant) uscente; (means of transport) in partenza; (character) socievole.

outgoings ['autgəuɪŋz] npl (BRIT: expenses) spese fpl.

outgrow [aut'grəu] vt irreg (clothes) diventare troppo grande per.

outhouse ['authaus] n costruzione f annessa.

outing ['autɪŋ] n gita; escursione f.

outlandish [aut'lændɪʃ] adj strano(a).

outlast [aut'lɑːst] vt sopravvivere a.

outlaw ['autlɔː] n fuorilegge m/f ♦ vt (person) mettere fuori della legge; (practice) proscrivere.

outlay ['autleɪ] n spesa.

outlet ['autlet] n (for liquid etc) sbocco, scarico; (for emotion) sfogo; (for goods) sbocco, mercato; (also: retail ~) punto di vendita; (US ELEC) presa di corrente.

outline ['autlaɪn] n contorno, profilo; (summary) abbozzo, grandi linee fpl.

outlive [aut'lɪv] vt sopravvivere a.

outlook ['autluk] n prospettiva, vista.

outlying ['autlaɪɪŋ] adj periferico(a).

outmanoeuvre, (US) outmaneuver [autmə'nuːvə*] vt (rival etc) superare in strategia.

outmoded [aut'məudɪd] adj passato(a) di moda; antiquato(a).

outnumber [aut'nʌmbə*] vt superare in numero.

out-of-court [autəv'kɔːt] adj extragiudiziale ♦ adv (settle) senza ricorrere al tribunale.

out-of-date [autəv'deɪt] adj (passport, ticket) scaduto(a); (theory, idea) sorpassato(a), superato(a); (custom) antiquato(a); (clothes) fuori moda.

out-of-the-way ['autəvðə'weɪ] adj (remote)

fuori mano; (unusual) originale, insolito(a).

outpatient ['autpeɪʃənt] n paziente m/f esterno(a).

outpost ['autpəust] n avamposto.

outpouring ['autpɔːrɪŋ] n (fig) torrente m.

output ['autput] n produzione f; (COMPUT) output m inv ♦ vt emettere.

outrage ['autreɪdʒ] n oltraggio; scandalo ♦ vt oltraggiare.

outrageous [aut'reɪdʒəs] adj oltraggioso(a).

outrider ['autraɪdə*] n (on motorcycle) battistrada m inv.

outright adv [aut'raɪt] completamente; schiettamente; apertamente; sul colpo ♦ adj ['autraɪt] completo(a); schietto(a) e netto(a).

outrun [aut'rʌn] vt irreg superare (nella corsa).

outset ['autset] n inizio.

outshine [aut'ʃaɪn] vt irreg (fig) eclissare.

outside [aut'saɪd] n esterno, esteriore m ♦ adj esterno(a), esteriore; (remote, unlikely): an ~ chance una vaga possibilità ♦ adv fuori, all'esterno ♦ prep fuori di, all'esterno di; at the ~ (fig) al massimo; ~ left/right n (FOOTBALL) ala sinistra/destra.

outside broadcast n (RADIO, TV) trasmissione f in esterno.

outside lane n (AUT) corsia di sorpasso.

outside line n (TEL) linea esterna.

outsider [aut'saɪdə*] n (in race etc) outsider m inv; (stranger) straniero/a.

outsize ['autsaɪz] adj enorme; (clothes) per taglie forti.

outskirts ['autskəːts] npl sobborghi mpl.

outsmart [aut'smɑːt] vt superare in astuzia.

outspoken [aut'spəukən] adj molto franco(a).

outspread ['autspred] adj (wings) aperto(a).

outstanding [aut'stændɪŋ] adj eccezionale, di rilievo; (unfinished) non completo(a); non evaso(a); non regolato(a); your account is still ~ deve ancora saldare il conto.

outstay [aut'steɪ] vt: to ~ one's welcome diventare un ospite sgradito.

outstretched [aut'stretʃt] adj (hand) teso(a); (body) disteso(a).

outstrip [aut'strip] vt (also fig) superare.

out-tray ['auttreɪ] n raccoglitore m per le carte da spedire.

outvote [aut'vəut] vt: to ~ sb (by) avere la maggioranza rispetto a qn (per); to ~ sth (by) respingere qc (per).

outward ['autwəd] adj (sign, appearances)

esteriore; (*journey*) d'andata.
outwardly ['autwǝdlɪ] *adv* esteriormente;
in apparenza.
outweigh [aut'weɪ] *vt* avere maggior peso
di.
outwit [aut'wɪt] *vt* superare in astuzia.
oval ['ǝuvl] *adj*, *n* ovale (*m*).
Oval Office *n* (*US*) *see boxed note.*

OVAL OFFICE

*L'***Oval Office** *è una grande stanza di forma
ovale nella "White House", la Casa Bianca,
dove ha sede l'ufficio del Presidente degli Stati
Uniti. Spesso il termine è usato per indicare la
stessa presidenza degli Stati Uniti.*

---

ovarian [ǝu'vɛǝrɪǝn] *adj* ovarico(a).
ovary ['ǝuvǝrɪ] *n* ovaia.
ovation [ǝu'veɪʃǝn] *n* ovazione *f*.
oven ['ʌvn] *n* forno.
ovenproof ['ʌvnpruːf] *adj* da forno.
oven-ready ['ʌvnrɛdɪ] *adj* pronto(a) da
infornare.
ovenware ['ʌvnwɛǝ*] *n* vasellame *m* da
mettere in forno.
over ['ǝuvǝ*] *adv* al di sopra; (*excessively*)
molto, troppo ♦ *adj* (*or adv*) (*finished*)
finito(a), terminato(a); (*too much*) troppo;
(*remaining*) che avanza ♦ *prep* su; sopra;
(*above*) al di sopra di; (*on the other side of*)
di là di; (*more than*) più di; (*during*)
durante; ~ **here** qui; ~ **there** là; **all** ~
(*everywhere*) dappertutto; (*finished*)
tutto(a) finito(a); ~ **and** ~ (**again**) più e
più volte; ~ **and above** oltre (a); **to ask**
sb ~ invitare qn (a passare); **now** ~ **to**
our Rome correspondent diamo ora la
linea al nostro corrispondente da Roma;
the world ~ in tutto il mondo; **she's not** ~
intelligent (*BRIT*) non è troppo
intelligente; **they fell out** ~ **money**
litigarono per una questione di denaro.
over... ['ǝuvǝ*] *prefix*: ~**abundant**
sovrabbondante.
overact [ǝuvǝr'ækt] *vi* (*THEAT*) esagerare *or*
strafare la propria parte.
overall *adj*, *n* ['ǝuvǝrɔːl] *adj* totale ♦ *n* (*BRIT*)
grembiule *m* ♦ *adv* [ǝuvǝr'ɔːl] nell'insieme,
complessivamente; ~**s** *npl* tuta (da
lavoro).
overall majority *n* maggioranza assoluta.
overanxious [ǝuvǝr'æŋkʃǝs] *adj* troppo
ansioso(a).
overawe [ǝuvǝr'ɔː] *vt* intimidire.
overbalance [ǝuvǝ'bælǝns] *vi* perdere
l'equilibrio.
overbearing [ǝuvǝ'bɛǝrɪŋ] *adj* imperioso(a),

prepotente.
overboard ['ǝuvǝbɔːd] *adv* (*NAUT*) fuori
bordo, in acqua; **to go** ~ **for sth** (*fig*)
impazzire per qc.
overbook [ǝuvǝ'buk] *vt* sovrapprenotare.
overcapitalize [ǝuvǝ'kæpɪtǝlaɪz] *vt*
sovraccapitalizzare.
overcast ['ǝuvǝkɑːst] *adj* coperto(a).
overcharge [ǝuvǝ'tʃɑːdʒ] *vt*: **to** ~ **sb for sth**
far pagare troppo caro a qn per qc.
overcoat ['ǝuvǝkǝut] *n* soprabito, cappotto.
overcome [ǝuvǝ'kʌm] *vt irreg* superare;
sopraffare; ~ **with grief** sopraffatto(a)
dal dolore.
overconfident [ǝuvǝ'kɔnfɪdǝnt] *adj* troppo
sicuro(a) (di sé), presuntuoso(a).
overcrowded [ǝuvǝ'kraudɪd] *adj*
sovraffollato(a).
overcrowding [ǝuvǝ'kraudɪŋ] *n*
sovraffollamento; (*in bus*) calca.
overdo [ǝuvǝ'duː] *vt irreg* esagerare;
(*overcook*) cuocere troppo; **to** ~ **it, to** ~
things (*work too hard*) lavorare troppo.
overdose ['ǝuvǝdǝus] *n* dose *f* eccessiva.
overdraft ['ǝuvǝdrɑːft] *n* scoperto (di
conto).
overdrawn [ǝuvǝ'drɔːn] *adj* (*account*)
scoperto(a).
overdrive ['ǝuvǝdraɪv] *n* (*AUT*) overdrive *m*
inv.
overdue [ǝuvǝ'djuː] *adj* in ritardo;
(*recognition*) tardivo(a); (*bill*) insoluto(a);
that change was long ~ quel
cambiamento ci voleva da tempo.
overemphasis [ǝuvǝr'ɛmfǝsɪs] *n*: ~ **on sth**
importanza eccessiva data a qc.
overemphasize [ǝuvǝr'ɛmfǝsaɪz] *vt* dare
un'importanza eccessiva a.
overestimate [ǝuvǝr'ɛstɪmeɪt] *vt*
sopravvalutare.
overexcited [ǝuvǝrɪk'saɪtɪd] *adj*
sovraeccitato(a).
overexertion [ǝuvǝrɪg'zǝːʃǝn] *n* logorio
(fisico).
overexpose [ǝuvǝrɪk'spǝuz] *vt* (*PHOT*)
sovraesporre.
overflow *vi* [ǝuvǝ'flǝu] traboccare ♦ *n*
['ǝuvǝflǝu] eccesso; (*also*: ~ **pipe**)
troppopieno.
overfly [ǝuvǝ'flaɪ] *vt irreg* sorvolare.
overgenerous [ǝuvǝ'dʒɛnǝrǝs] *adj* troppo
generoso(a).
overgrown [ǝuvǝ'grǝun] *adj* (*garden*)
ricoperto(a) di vegetazione; **he's just an**
~ **schoolboy** è proprio un bambinone.
overhang [ǝuvǝ'hæŋ] *irreg vt* sporgere da
♦ *vi* sporgere.
overhaul *vt* [ǝuvǝ'hɔːl] revisionare ♦ *n*

['əuvəhɔːl] revisione f.

overhead adv [əuvə'hɛd] di sopra ♦ adj ['əuvəhɛd] aereo(a); (lighting) verticale ♦ n (US) = **overheads**.

overheads ['əuvəhɛdz] npl (BRIT) spese fpl generali.

overhear [əuvə'hɪə*] vt irreg sentire (per caso).

overheat [əuvə'hiːt] vi surriscaldarsi.

overjoyed [əuvə'dʒɔɪd] adj pazzo(a) di gioia.

overkill ['əuvəkɪl] n (fig) strafare m.

overland ['əuvəlænd] adj, adv per via di terra.

overlap vi [əuvə'læp] sovrapporsi ♦ n ['əuvəlæp] sovrapposizione f.

overleaf [əuvə'liːf] adv a tergo.

overload [əuvə'ləud] vt sovraccaricare.

overlook [əuvə'luk] vt (have view of) dare su; (miss) trascurare; (forgive) passare sopra a.

overlord ['əuvəlɔːd] n capo supremo.

overmanning [əuvə'mænɪŋ] n eccedenza di manodopera.

overnight adv [əuvə'naɪt] (happen) durante la notte; (fig) tutto ad un tratto ♦ adj ['əuvənaɪt] di notte; fulmineo(a); **he stayed there** ~ ci ha passato la notte; **if you travel** ~ ... se viaggia di notte ...; **he'll be away** ~ passerà la notte fuori.

overpass ['əuvəpɑːs] n cavalcavia m inv.

overpay [əuvə'peɪ] vt: **to** ~ **sb by £50** pagare 50 sterline in più a qn.

overplay [əuvə'pleɪ] vt dare troppa importanza a; **to** ~ **one's hand** sopravvalutare la propria posizione.

overpower [əuvə'pauə*] vt sopraffare.

overpowering [əuvə'pauərɪŋ] adj irresistibile; (heat, stench) soffocante.

overproduction ['əuvəprə'dʌkʃən] n sovrapproduzione f.

overrate [əuvə'reɪt] vt sopravvalutare.

overreach [əuvə'riːtʃ] vt: **to** ~ **o.s.** volere strafare.

overreact [əuvəriː'ækt] vi reagire in modo esagerato.

override [əuvə'raɪd] vt (irreg: like **ride**) (order, objection) passar sopra a; (decision) annullare.

overriding [əuvə'raɪdɪŋ] adj preponderante.

overrule [əuvə'ruːl] vt (decision) annullare; (claim) respingere.

overrun [əuvə'rʌn] vt irreg (MIL: country etc) invadere; (time limit etc) superare, andare al di là di ♦ vi protrarsi; **the town is** ~ **with tourists** la città è invasa dai turisti.

overseas [əuvə'siːz] adv oltremare; (abroad) all'estero ♦ adj (trade) estero(a); (visitor)

straniero(a).

oversee [əuvə'siː] vt irreg sorvegliare.

overseer ['əuvəsɪə*] n (in factory) caposquadra m.

overshadow [əuvə'ʃædəu] vt (fig) eclissare.

overshoot [əuvə'ʃuːt] vt irreg superare.

oversight ['əuvəsaɪt] n omissione f, svista; **due to an** ~ per una svista.

oversimplify [əuvə'sɪmplɪfaɪ] vt rendere troppo semplice.

oversleep [əuvə'sliːp] vi irreg dormire troppo a lungo.

overspend [əuvə'spɛnd] vi irreg spendere troppo; **we have overspent by 5000 dollars** abbiamo speso 5000 dollari di troppo.

overspill ['əuvəspɪl] n eccedenza di popolazione.

overstaffed [əuvə'stɑːft] adj: **to be** ~ avere troppo personale.

overstate [əuvə'steɪt] vt esagerare.

overstatement [əuvə'steɪtmənt] n esagerazione f.

overstay [əuvə'steɪ] vt: **to** ~ **one's welcome** trattenersi troppo a lungo (come ospite).

overstep [əuvə'stɛp] vt: **to** ~ **the mark** superare ogni limite.

overstock [əuvə'stɔk] vt sovrapprovvigionare, sovraimmagazzinare.

overstretched [əuvə'strɛtʃt] adj sovraccarico(a); (budget) arrivato(a) al limite.

overstrike n ['əuvəstraɪk] (on printer) sovrapposizione f (di caratteri) ♦ vt irreg [əuvə'straɪk] sovrapporre.

overt [əu'vəːt] adj palese.

overtake [əuvə'teɪk] vt irreg sorpassare.

overtaking [əuvə'teɪkɪŋ] n (AUT) sorpasso.

overtax [əuvə'tæks] vt (ECON) imporre tasse eccessive a, tassare eccessivamente; (fig: strength, patience) mettere alla prova, abusare di; **to** ~ **o.s.** chiedere troppo alle proprie forze.

overthrow [əuvə'θrəu] vt irreg (government) rovesciare.

overtime ['əuvətaɪm] n (lavoro) straordinario; **to do** or **work** ~ fare lo straordinario.

overtime ban n rifiuto sindacale a fare gli straordinari.

overtone ['əuvətəun] n (also: ~s) sfumatura.

overture ['əuvətʃuə*] n (MUS) ouverture f inv; (fig) approccio.

overturn [əuvə'təːn] vt rovesciare ♦ vi rovesciarsi.

overview ['əuvəvjuː] n visione f d'insieme.

overweight [əuvə'weɪt] *adj* (*person*) troppo grasso(a); (*luggage*) troppo pesante.
overwhelm [əuvə'wɛlm] *vt* sopraffare; sommergere; schiacciare.
overwhelming [əuvə'wɛlmɪŋ] *adj* (*victory*) schiacciante; (*desire*) irresistibile; **one's ~ impression is of heat** l'impressione dominante è quella di caldo.
overwhelmingly [əuvə'wɛlmɪŋlɪ] *adv* in massa.
overwork [əuvə'wɔːk] *vt* far lavorare troppo ♦ *vi* lavorare troppo, strapazzarsi.
overwrite [əuvə'raɪt] *vt* (*COMPUT*) ricoprire.
overwrought [əuvə'rɔːt] *adj* molto agitato(a).
ovulation [ɔvju'leɪʃən] *n* ovulazione *f.*
owe [əu] *vt* dovere; **to ~ sb sth, to ~ sth to sb** dovere qc a qn.
owing to ['əuɪŋtuː] *prep* a causa di.
owl [aul] *n* gufo.
own [əun] *adj* proprio(a) ♦ *vt* possedere ♦ *vi* (*BRIT*): **to ~ to sth** ammettere qc; **to ~ to having done sth** ammettere di aver fatto qc; **a room of my ~** la mia propria camera; **to get one's ~ back** vendicarsi; **on one's ~** tutto(a) solo(a); **can I have it for my (very) ~?** posso averlo tutto per me?; **to come into one's ~** mostrare le proprie qualità.
▶**own up** *vi* confessare.
own brand *n* (*COMM*) etichetta propria.
owner ['əunə*] *n* proprietario/a.
owner-occupier ['əunər'ɔkjupaɪə*] *n* proprietario/a della casa in cui abita.
ownership ['əunəʃɪp] *n* possesso; **it's under new ~** ha un nuovo proprietario.
own goal *n* (*also fig*) autogol *m inv.*
ox, pl oxen [ɔks, 'ɔksn] *n* bue *m.*
Oxbridge ['ɔksbrɪdʒ] *n le università di Oxford e/o Cambridge*; *see boxed note.*

OXBRIDGE

La parola **Oxbridge** *deriva dalla fusione dei nomi Ox(ford) e (Cam)bridge e fa riferimento a queste due antiche università.*

Oxfam ['ɔksfæm] *n abbr* (*BRIT*: = *Oxford Committee for Famine Relief*) *organizzazione per aiuti al terzo mondo.*
oxide ['ɔksaɪd] *n* ossido.
Oxon. ['ɔksn] *abbr* (*BRIT*: = *Oxoniensis*) = *of Oxford.*
oxtail ['ɔksteɪl] *n*: **~ soup** minestra di coda di bue.
oxyacetylene ['ɔksɪə'sɛtɪliːn] *adj* ossiacetilenico(a); **~ burner, ~ lamp**

cannello ossiacetilenico.
oxygen ['ɔksɪdʒən] *n* ossigeno.
oxygen mask *n* maschera ad ossigeno.
oxygen tent *n* tenda ad ossigeno.
oyster ['ɔɪstə*] *n* ostrica.
oz. *abbr* = **ounce.**
ozone ['əuzəun] *n* ozono.
ozone-friendly ['əuzəun'frɛndlɪ] *adj* che non danneggia lo strato d'ozono.

Pp

P, p [piː] *n* (*letter*) P, p *f or m inv*; **P for Peter** ≈ P come Padova.
P *abbr* = **president; prince.**
p *abbr* (= *page*) p; (*BRIT*) = **penny, pence.**
PA *n abbr see* **personal assistant; public address system** ♦ *abbr* (*US*) = Pennsylvania.
pa [pɑː] *n* (*col*) papà *m inv*, babbo.
p.a. *abbr* = **per annum.**
PAC *n abbr* (*US*) = *political action committee.*
pace [peɪs] *n* passo; (*speed*) passo; velocità ♦ *vi*: **to ~ up and down** camminare su e giù; **to keep ~ with** camminare di pari passo a; (*events*) tenersi al corrente di; **to put sb through his ~s** (*fig*) mettere qn alla prova; **to set the ~** (*running*) fare l'andatura; (*fig*) dare il la or il tono.
pacemaker ['peɪsmeɪkə*] *n* (*MED*) pacemaker *m inv*, stimolatore *m* cardiaco; (*SPORT*) chi fa l'andatura.
pacific [pə'sɪfɪk] *adj* pacifico(a) ♦ *n*: **the P~ (Ocean)** il Pacifico, l'Oceano Pacifico.
pacification [pæsɪfɪ'keɪʃən] *n* pacificazione *f.*
pacifier ['pæsɪfaɪə*] *n* (*US*: *dummy*) succhiotto, ciuccio (*col*).
pacifist ['pæsɪfɪst] *n* pacifista *m/f.*
pacify ['pæsɪfaɪ] *vt* pacificare; (*soothe*) calmare.
pack [pæk] *n* (*packet*) pacco; (*COMM*) confezione *f*; (*US*: *of cigarettes*) pacchetto; (*of goods*) balla; (*of hounds*) muta; (*of wolves*) branco; (*of thieves etc*) banda; (*of cards*) mazzo ♦ *vt* (*goods*) impaccare, imballare; (*in suitcase etc*) mettere; (*box*) riempire; (*cram*) stipare, pigiare; (*press down*) tamponare; turare; (*COMPUT*) comprimere, impaccare ♦ *vi*: **to ~ (one's bags)** fare la valigia; **to send sb ~ing** (*col*) spedire via qn.

▶**pack in** (*BRIT col*) *vi* (*watch, car*) guastarsi
♦ *vt* mollare, piantare; ~ **it in!** piantala!
▶**pack off** *vt* (*person*) spedire.
▶**pack up** *vi* (*BRIT col*: *machine*) guastarsi;
(: *person*) far fagotto ♦ *vt* (*belongings,
clothes*) mettere in una valigia; (*goods,
presents*) imballare.
package ['pækɪdʒ] *n* pacco; balla; (*also*: ~
deal) pacchetto; forfait *m inv* ♦ *vt* (*goods*)
confezionare.
package holiday *n* (*BRIT*) vacanza
organizzata.
package tour *n* viaggio organizzato.
packaging ['pækɪdʒɪŋ] *n* confezione *f*,
imballo.
packed [pækt] *adj* (*crowded*) affollato(a); ~
lunch (*BRIT*) pranzo al sacco.
packer ['pækə*] *n* (*person*) imballatore/
trice.
packet ['pækɪt] *n* pacchetto.
packet switching [-swɪtʃɪŋ] *n* (*COMPUT*)
commutazione *f* di pacchetto.
pack ice ['pækaɪs] *n* banchisa.
packing ['pækɪŋ] *n* imballaggio.
packing case *n* cassa da imballaggio.
pact [pækt] *n* patto, accordo; trattato.
pad [pæd] *n* blocco; (*for inking*) tampone *m*;
(*col*: *flat*) appartamentino ♦ *vt* imbottire
♦ *vi*: **to** ~ **about/in** *etc* camminare/entrare
etc a passi felpati.
padded cell ['pædɪd-] *n* cella imbottita.
padding ['pædɪŋ] *n* imbottitura; (*fig*)
riempitivo.
paddle ['pædl] *n* (*oar*) pagaia ♦ *vi* sguazzare
♦ *vt* (*boat*) fare andare a colpi di pagaia.
paddle steamer *n* battello a ruote.
paddling pool ['pædlɪŋ-] *n* piscina per
bambini.
paddock ['pædək] *n* recinto; paddock *m inv*.
paddy ['pædɪ] *n* (*also*: ~ **field**) risaia.
padlock ['pædlɔk] *n* lucchetto ♦ *vt* chiudere
con il lucchetto.
padre ['pɑːdrɪ] *n* cappellano.
Padua ['pædʒuə] *n* Padova.
paediatrician, (*US*) **pediatrician**
[piːdɪə'trɪʃən] *n* pediatra *m/f*.
paediatrics, (*US*) **pediatrics** [piːdɪ'ætrɪks]
n pediatria.
paedophile, (*US*) **pedophile** ['piːdəufaɪl]
adj, n pedofilo(a).
pagan ['peɪgən] *adj, n* pagano(a).
page [peɪdʒ] *n* pagina; (*also*: ~ **boy**)
fattorino; (: *at wedding*) paggio ♦ *vt* (*in
hotel etc*) (far) chiamare.
pageant ['pædʒənt] *n* spettacolo storico;
grande cerimonia.
pageantry ['pædʒəntrɪ] *n* pompa.
page break *n* interruzione *f* di pagina.

pager ['peɪdʒə*] *n* cicalino, cercapersone
m.
paginate ['pædʒɪneɪt] *vt* impaginare.
pagination [pædʒɪ'neɪʃən] *n* impaginazione
f.
pagoda [pə'gəudə] *n* pagoda.
paid [peɪd] *pt, pp of* **pay** ♦ *adj* (*work, official*)
rimunerato(a); **to put** ~ **to** (*BRIT*) mettere
fine a.
paid-up ['peɪdʌp], (*US*) **paid in** ['peɪdɪn] *adj*
(*member*) che ha pagato la sua quota;
(*share*) interamente pagato(a); ~ **capital**
capitale *m* interamente versato.
pail [peɪl] *n* secchio.
pain [peɪn] *n* dolore *m*; **to be in** ~ soffrire,
aver male; **to have a** ~ **in** aver male *or* un
dolore a; **to take** ~**s to do** mettercela
tutta per fare; **on** ~ **of death** sotto pena
di morte.
pained [peɪnd] *adj* addolorato(a), afflitto(a).
painful ['peɪnful] *adj* doloroso(a), che fa
male; (*difficult*) difficile, penoso(a).
painfully ['peɪnfəlɪ] *adv* (*fig*: *very*) fin troppo.
painkiller ['peɪnkɪlə*] *n* antalgico,
antidolorifico.
painstaking ['peɪnzteɪkɪŋ] *adj* sollecito(a).
paint [peɪnt] *n* (*for house etc*) tinta, vernice
f; (*ART*) colore *m* ♦ *vt* (*ART, walls*)
dipingere; (*door etc*) verniciare; **a tin of** ~
un barattolo di tinta *or* vernice; **to** ~ **the
door blue** verniciare la porta di azzurro;
to ~ **in oils** dipingere a olio.
paintbox ['peɪntbɔks] *n* scatola di colori.
paintbrush ['peɪntbrʌʃ] *n* pennello.
painter ['peɪntə*] *n* (*artist*) pittore *m*;
(*decorator*) imbianchino.
painting ['peɪntɪŋ] *n* (*activity*: *of artist*)
pittura; (: *of decorator*) imbiancatura;
verniciatura; (*picture*) dipinto, quadro.
paint-stripper ['peɪntstrɪpə*] *n* prodotto
sverniciante.
paintwork ['peɪntwɜːk] *n* (*BRIT*) tinta; (: *of
car*) vernice *f*.
pair [pɛə*] *n* (*of shoes, gloves etc*) paio; (*of
people*) coppia; duo *m inv*; **a** ~ **of scissors/
trousers** un paio di forbici/pantaloni.
▶**pair off** *vi*: **to** ~ **off (with sb)** fare coppia
(con qn).
pajamas [pə'dʒɑːməz] *npl* (*US*) pigiama *m*.
Pakistan [pɑːkɪ'stɑːn] *n* Pakistan *m*.
Pakistani [pɑːkɪ'stɑːnɪ] *adj, n* pakistano(a).
PAL [pæl] *n abbr* (*TV*: = *phase alternation line*)
PAL *m*.
pal [pæl] *n* (*col*) amico/a, compagno/a.
palace ['pæləs] *n* palazzo.
palatable ['pælɪtəbl] *adj* gustoso(a).
palate ['pælɪt] *n* palato.
palatial [pə'leɪʃəl] *adj* sontuoso(a),

sfarzoso(a).

palaver [pə'lɑːvə*] n chiacchiere *fpl*; storie *fpl*.

pale [peɪl] *adj* pallido(a) ♦ *vi* impallidire ♦ *n*: **to be beyond the** ~ aver oltrepassato ogni limite; **to grow** *or* **turn** ~ (*person*) diventare pallido(a), impallidire; **to** ~ **into insignificance (beside)** perdere d'importanza (nei confronti di); ~ **blue** azzurro *or* blu pallido *inv*.

paleness ['peɪlnɪs] n pallore *m*.

Palestine ['pælɪstaɪn] n Palestina.

Palestinian [pælɪs'tɪnɪən] *adj*, n palestinese (*m/f*).

palette ['pælɪt] n tavolozza.

paling ['peɪlɪŋ] n (*stake*) palo; (*fence*) palizzata.

palisade [pælɪ'seɪd] n palizzata.

pall [pɔːl] n (*of smoke*) cappa ♦ *vi*: **to** ~ **(on)** diventare noioso(a) (a).

pallet ['pælɪt] n (*for goods*) paletta.

pallid ['pælɪd] *adj* pallido(a), smorto(a).

pallor ['pælə*] n pallore *m*.

pally ['pælɪ] *adj* (*col*) amichevole.

palm [pɑːm] n (*ANAT*) palma, palmo; (*also*: ~ **tree**) palma ♦ *vt*: **to** ~ **sth off on sb** (*col*) rifilare qc a qn.

palmist ['pɑːmɪst] n chiromante *m/f*.

Palm Sunday n Domenica delle Palme.

palpable ['pælpəbl] *adj* palpabile.

palpitation [pælpɪ'teɪʃən] n palpitazione *f*; **to have** ~**s** avere le palpitazioni.

paltry ['pɔːltrɪ] *adj* derisorio(a); insignificante.

pamper ['pæmpə*] *vt* viziare, accarezzare.

pamphlet ['pæmflət] n dépliant *m inv*; (*political etc*) volantino, manifestino.

pan [pæn] n (*also*: **sauce**~) casseruola; (*also*: **frying** ~) padella ♦ *vi* (*CINE*) fare una panoramica; **to** ~ **for gold** (lavare le sabbie aurifere per) cercare l'oro.

panacea [pænə'sɪə] n panacea.

panache [pə'næʃ] n stile *m*.

Panama ['pænəmɑː] n Panama *m*.

Panama Canal n canale *m* di Panama.

Panamanian [pænə'meɪnɪən] *adj*, n panamense (*m/f*).

pancake ['pænkeɪk] n frittella.

Pancake Day n (*BRIT*) martedì *m* grasso.

pancake roll n *crêpe ripiena di verdure alla cinese.*

pancreas ['pæŋkrɪəs] n pancreas *m inv*.

panda ['pændə] n panda *m inv*.

panda car n (*BRIT*) auto *f* della polizia.

pandemonium [pændɪ'məunɪəm] n pandemonio.

pander ['pændə*] *vi*: **to** ~ **to** lusingare; concedere tutto a.

p & h *abbr* (*US*: = *postage and handling*) affrancatura e trasporto.

P & L *abbr* (= *profit and loss*) P.P.

p & p *abbr* (*BRIT*: = *postage and packing*) affrancatura ed imballaggio.

pane [peɪn] n vetro.

panel ['pænl] n (*of wood, cloth etc*) pannello; (*RADIO, TV*) giuria.

panel game n (*BRIT*) quiz *m inv* a squadre.

panelling, (US) paneling ['pænəlɪŋ] n rivestimento a pannelli.

panellist, (US) panelist ['pænəlɪst] n partecipante *m/f* (al quiz, alla tavola rotonda *etc*).

pang [pæŋ] *n*: **to feel** ~**s of remorse** essere torturato(a) dal rimorso; ~**s of hunger** spasimi *mpl* della fame; ~**s of conscience** morsi *mpl* di coscienza.

panhandler ['pænhændlə*] n (*US col*) accattone/a.

panic ['pænɪk] n panico ♦ *vi* perdere il sangue freddo.

panic buying [-baɪɪŋ] n accaparramento.

panicky ['pænɪkɪ] *adj* (*person*) pauroso(a).

panic-stricken ['pænɪkstrɪkən] *adj* (*person*) in preda al panico; (*look*) terrorizzato(a).

pannier ['pænɪə*] n (*on bicycle*) borsa.

panorama [pænə'rɑːmə] n panorama *m*.

panoramic [pænə'ræmɪk] *adj* panoramico(a).

pansy ['pænzɪ] n (*BOT*) viola del pensiero.

pant [pænt] *vi* ansare.

panther ['pænθə*] n pantera.

panties ['pæntɪz] *npl* slip *m*, mutandine *fpl*.

pantihose ['pæntɪhəuz] n (*US*) collant *m inv*.

panto ['pæntəu] n (*BRIT col*) *see* **pantomime**.

pantomime ['pæntəmaɪm] n (*at Christmas*) spettacolo natalizio; (*tecnica*) pantomima; *see boxed note.*

PANTOMIME

In Gran Bretagna la **pantomime** *(abbreviata in* **panto**) *è una sorta di libera interpretazione delle favole più conosciute che vengono messe in scena nei teatri durante il periodo natalizio. Gli attori principali sono la dama, "dame", che è un uomo vestito da donna, il protagonista, "principal boy", che è una donna travestita da uomo, e il cattivo, "villain". È uno spettacolo per tutta la famiglia, che prevede la partecipazione del pubblico.*

---

pantry ['pæntrɪ] n dispensa.

pants [pænts] *npl* (*BRIT*) mutande *fpl*, slip *m*; (*US*: *trousers*) pantaloni *mpl*.

pantsuit ['pæntsuːt] n (*US*) completo *m* or tailleur *m inv* pantalone *inv*.

papacy ['peɪpəsɪ] n papato.
papal ['peɪpəl] adj papale, pontificio(a).
paparazzi [pæpə'rætsiː] npl paparazzi mpl.
paper ['peɪpə*] n carta; (also: **wall**~) carta da parati, tappezzeria; (also: **news**~) giornale m; (study, article) saggio; (exam) prova scritta ♦ adj di carta ♦ vt tappezzare; **a piece of** ~ (odd bit) un pezzo di carta; (sheet) un foglio (di carta); **to put sth down on** ~ mettere qc per iscritto; see also **papers**.
paper advance n (on printer) avanzamento della carta.
paperback ['peɪpəbæk] n tascabile m; edizione f economica ♦ adj: ~ **edition** edizione f tascabile.
paper bag n sacchetto di carta.
paperboy ['peɪpəbɔɪ] n (selling) strillone m; (delivering) ragazzo che recapita i giornali.
paper clip n graffetta, clip f inv.
paper handkerchief n fazzolettino di carta.
paper mill n cartiera.
paper money n cartamoneta, moneta cartacea.
paper profit n utile m teorico.
papers ['peɪpəz] npl (also: **identity** ~) carte fpl, documenti mpl.
paper shop n (BRIT) giornalaio (negozio).
paperweight ['peɪpəweɪt] n fermacarte m inv.
paperwork ['peɪpəwɜːk] n lavoro amministrativo.
papier-mâché ['pæpɪeɪ'mæʃeɪ] n cartapesta.
paprika ['pæprɪkə] n paprica.
Pap test, Pap smear ['pæp-] n (MED) pap-test m inv.
par [pɑː*] n parità, pari f; (GOLF) norma; **on a** ~ **with** alla pari con; **at/above/below** ~ (COMM) alla/sopra la/sotto la pari; **above/below** ~ (gen, GOLF) al di sopra/al di sotto della norma; **to feel below** or **under** or **not up to** ~ non sentirsi in forma.
parable ['pærəbl] n parabola (REL).
parabola [pə'ræbələ] n parabola (MATH).
parachute ['pærəʃuːt] n paracadute m inv ♦ vi scendere col paracadute.
parachute jump n lancio col paracadute.
parachutist ['pærəʃuːtɪst] n paracadutista m/f.
parade [pə'reɪd] n parata; (inspection) rivista, rassegna ♦ vt (fig) fare sfoggio di ♦ vi sfilare in parata; **a fashion** ~ (BRIT)

una sfilata di moda.
parade ground n piazza d'armi.
paradise ['pærədaɪs] n paradiso.
paradox ['pærədɔks] n paradosso.
paradoxical [pærə'dɔksɪkl] adj paradossale.
paradoxically [pærə'dɔksɪklɪ] adv paradossalmente.
paraffin ['pærəfɪn] n (BRIT): ~ **(oil)** paraffina; **liquid** ~ olio di paraffina.
paraffin heater n (BRIT) stufa al cherosene.
paraffin lamp n (BRIT) lampada al cherosene.
paragon ['pærəgən] n modello di perfezione or di virtù.
paragraph ['pærəgrɑːf] n paragrafo; **to begin a new** ~ andare a capo.
Paraguay ['pærəgwaɪ] n Paraguay m.
Paraguayan [pærə'gwaɪən] adj, n paraguaiano(a).
parallel ['pærəlɛl] adj (also COMPUT) parallelo(a); (fig) analogo(a) ♦ n (line) parallela; (fig, GEO) parallelo; ~ **(with** or **to)** parallelo(a) (a).
paralysis, pl **paralyses** [pə'rælɪsɪs, -siːz] n paralisi f inv.
paralytic [pærɪ'lɪtɪk] adj paralitico(a); (BRIT col: drunk) ubriaco(a) fradicio(a).
paralyze ['pærəlaɪz] vt paralizzare.
paramedic [pærə'mɛdɪk] n paramedico.
parameter [pə'ræmɪtə*] n parametro.
paramilitary [pærə'mɪlɪtərɪ] adj paramilitare.
paramount ['pærəmaunt] adj: **of** ~ **importance** di capitale importanza.
paranoia [pærə'nɔɪə] n paranoia.
paranoid ['pærənɔɪd] adj paranoico(a).
paranormal [pærə'nɔːml] adj paranormale.
paraphernalia [pærəfə'neɪlɪə] n attrezzi mpl, roba.
paraphrase ['pærəfreɪz] vt parafrasare.
paraplegic [pærə'pliːdʒɪk] n paraplegico(a).
parapsychology [pærəsaɪ'kɔlədʒɪ] n parapsicologia.
parasite ['pærəsaɪt] n parassita m.
parasol ['pærəsɔl] n parasole m inv.
paratrooper ['pærətruːpə*] n paracadutista m (soldato).
parcel ['pɑːsl] n pacco, pacchetto ♦ vt (also: ~ **up**) impaccare.
▶**parcel out** vt spartire.
parcel bomb n (BRIT) pacchetto esplosivo.
parcel post n servizio pacchi.
parch [pɑːtʃ] vt riardere.
parched ['pɑːtʃt] adj (person) assetato(a).

parchment['pɑːtʃmənt] n pergamena.
pardon['pɑːdn] n perdono; grazia ♦ vt
  perdonare; (*LAW*) graziare; ~! scusi!; ~
  me! mi scusi!; **I beg your** ~! scusi!; (**I beg
  your**) ~?, (*US*) ~ **me?** prego?
pare[pɛə*] vt (*BRIT*: *nails*) tagliarsi; (: *fruit
  etc*) sbucciare, pelare.
parent['pɛərənt] n padre m (*or* madre f); ~s
  npl genitori mpl.
parentage['pɛərəntɪdʒ] n natali mpl; **of
  unknown** ~ di genitori sconosciuti.
parental[pə'rɛntl] adj dei genitori.
parent company n società madre
  f inv.
parenthesis, pl **parentheses**[pə'rɛnθɪsɪs,
  -siːz] n parentesi f inv; **in parentheses** fra
  parentesi.
parenthood['pɛərənthud] n paternità or
  maternità.
parenting['pɛərəntɪŋ] n mestiere m di
  genitore.
Paris['pærɪs] n Parigi f.
parish['pærɪʃ] n parrocchia; (*civil*)
  ≈ municipio ♦ adj parrocchiale.
parish council n (*BRIT*) ≈ consiglio
  comunale.
parishioner[pə'rɪʃənə*] n parrocchia-
  no/a.
Parisian[pə'rɪzɪən] adj, n parigino(a).
parity['pærɪtɪ] n parità.
park[pɑːk] n parco; (*public*) giardino
  pubblico ♦ vt, vi parcheggiare.
parka['pɑːkə] n eskimo.
parking['pɑːkɪŋ] n parcheggio; "**no** ~"
  "sosta vietata".
parking lights npl luci fpl di posizione.
parking lot n (*US*) posteggio,
  parcheggio.
parking meter n parchimetro.
parking offence n (*BRIT*) infrazione f al
  divieto di sosta.
parking place n posto di parcheggio.
parking ticket n multa per sosta vietata.
parking violation n (*US*) = **parking
  offence**.
Parkinson's['pɑːkɪnsənz] n (*also*: ~
  disease) morbo di Parkinson.
parkway['pɑːkweɪ] n (*US*) viale m.
parlance['pɑːləns] n: **in common/modern**
  ~ nel gergo or linguaggio comune/
  moderno.
parliament['pɑːləmənt] n parlamento; *see
  boxed note*.

PARLIAMENT

*Nel Regno Unito il Parlamento, **Parliament**, è
formato da due camere: la "House of*

*Commons", e la "House of Lords". Nella
"House of Commons" siedono 650
parlamentari, chiamati "MPs", eletti per
votazione diretta del popolo nelle rispettive
circoscrizioni elettorali, le "constituencies". Le
sessioni del Parlamento sono presiedute e
moderate dal presidente della Camera, lo
"Speaker". Alla "House of Lords", i cui poteri
sono più limitati, in passato si accedeva per
nomina o per carica ereditaria mentre ora le
cariche ereditarie sono state ridotte e in futuro
verranno abolite.*

parliamentary[pɑːlə'mɛntərɪ] adj
  parlamentare.
parlour, (*US*) **parlor**['pɑːlə*] n salotto.
parlous['pɑːləs] adj periglioso(a).
Parmesan[pɑːmɪ'zæn] n parmigiano.
parochial[pə'rəukɪəl] adj parrocchiale;
  (*pej*) provinciale.
parody['pærədɪ] n parodia.
parole[pə'rəul] n: **on** ~ in libertà per buona
  condotta.
paroxysm['pærəksɪzəm] n (*MED*)
  parossismo; (*of anger, laughter, coughing*)
  convulso; (*of grief*) attacco.
parquet['pɑːkeɪ] n: ~ **floor(ing)** parquet m.
parrot['pærət] n pappagallo.
parrot fashion adv in modo pappagallesco.
parsimonious[pɑːsɪ'məunɪəs] adj
  parsimonioso(a).
parsley['pɑːslɪ] n prezzemolo.
parsnip['pɑːsnɪp] n pastinaca.
parson['pɑːsn] n prete m; (*Church of
  England*) parroco.
part[pɑːt] n parte f; (*of machine*) pezzo;
  (*THEAT etc*) parte, ruolo; (*MUS*) voce f;
  parte ♦ adj in parte ♦ adv = **partly** ♦ vt
  separare ♦ vi (*people*) separarsi; (*roads*)
  dividersi; **to take** ~ in prendere parte a;
  to take sb's ~ parteggiare per qn; **on his**
  ~ da parte sua; **for my** ~ per parte mia;
  for the most ~ in generale; nella maggior
  parte dei casi; **for the better** ~ **of the day**
  per la maggior parte della giornata; **to
  be** ~ **and parcel of** essere parte
  integrante di; **to take sth in good/bad** ~
  prendere bene/male qc; ~ **of speech**
  (*LING*) parte del discorso.
  ►**part with** vt fus separarsi da; rinunciare a.
partake[pɑː'teɪk] vi irreg (*formal*): **to** ~ **of
  sth** consumare qc, prendere qc.
part exchange n (*BRIT*): **in** ~ in pagamento
  parziale.
partial['pɑːʃl] adj parziale; **to be** ~ **to**
  avere un debole per.
partially['pɑːʃəlɪ] adv in parte.
participant[pɑː'tɪsɪpənt] n: ~ (**in**)

partecipante *m/f* (a).
participate[pɑː'tɪsɪpeɪt] *vi:* **to ~ (in)** prendere parte (a), partecipare (a).
participation[pɑːtɪsɪ'peɪʃən] *n* partecipazione *f.*
participle['pɑːtɪsɪpl] *n* participio.
particle['pɑːtɪkl] *n* particella.
particular[pə'tɪkjulə*] *adj* particolare; speciale; (*fussy*) difficile; meticoloso(a); **~ s**npl particolari *mpl,* dettagli *mpl*; (*information*) informazioni *fpl*; **in ~** in particolare, particolarmente; **to be very ~ about** essere molto pignolo(a) su; **I'm not ~** per me va bene tutto.
particularly[pə'tɪkjulǝlɪ] *adv* particolarmente; in particolare.
parting['pɑːtɪŋ] *n* separazione *f*; (*BRIT: in hair*) scriminatura ♦ *adj* d'addio; **~ shot** (*fig*) battuta finale.
partisan[pɑːtɪ'zæn] *n* partigiano/a ♦ *adj* partigiano(a); di parte.
partition[pɑː'tɪʃən] *n* (*POL*) partizione *f*; (*wall*) tramezzo.
partly['pɑːtlɪ] *adv* parzialmente; in parte.
partner['pɑːtnə*]*n*(*COMM*) socio/a;(*SPORT*) compagno/a;(*at dance*)cavaliere/dama.
partnership['pɑːtnəʃɪp] *n* associazione *f*; (*COMM*) società *f inv*; **to go into ~ (with)** mettersi in società (con), associarsi (a).
part paymentn acconto.
partridge['pɑːtrɪdʒ] *n* pernice *f.*
part-time['pɑːt'taɪm] *adj, adv* a orario ridotto, part-time (*inv*).
part-timer['pɑːt'taɪmə*] *n* (*also:* **part-time worker**) lavoratore/trice part-time.
party['pɑːtɪ] *n* (*POL*) partito; (*team*) squadra; gruppo; (*LAW*) parte *f*; (*celebration*) ricevimento; serata; festa; **dinner ~** cena; **to give** *or* **throw a ~** dare una festa *or* un party; **to be a ~ to a crime** essere coinvolto in un reato.
party linen (*POL*) linea del partito; (*TEL*) duplex *m inv.*
party piecen: **to do one's ~** (*BRIT col*) esibirsi nel proprio pezzo forte a una festa, cena etc.
party political broadcastn comunicato radiotelevisivo di propaganda.
pass[pɑːs] *vt* (*gen*) passare; (*place*) passare davanti a; (*exam*) passare, superare; (*candidate*) promuovere; (*overtake, surpass*) sorpassare, superare; (*approve*) approvare ♦ *vi* passare; (*SCOL*) essere promosso(a) ♦ *n* (*permit*) lasciapassare *m inv*; permesso; (*in mountains*) passo, gola; (*SPORT*) passaggio; (*SCOL: also:* **~ mark**): **to get a ~** prendere la sufficienza; **to ~ for** passare per; **could you ~ the**

vegetables round? potrebbe far passare i contorni?; **to make a ~ at sb** (*col*) fare delle proposte *or* delle avances a qn; **things have come to a pretty ~** (*BRIT*) ecco a cosa siamo arrivati.
▶**pass away**vi morire.
▶**pass by**vi passare ♦ *vt* trascurare.
▶**pass down**vt (*customs, inheritance*) tramandare, trasmettere.
▶**pass on**vi (*die*) spegnersi, mancare ♦ *vt* (*hand on*): **to ~ on (to)** (*news, information, object*) passare (a); (*cold, illness*) attaccare (a); (*benefits*) trasmettere (a); (*price rises*) riversare (su).
▶**pass out**vi svenire; (*BRIT MIL*) uscire dall'accademia.
▶**pass over**vi (*die*) spirare ♦ *vt* lasciare da parte.
▶**pass up**vt (*opportunity*) lasciarsi sfuggire, perdere.
passable['pɑːsəbl] *adj* (*road*) praticabile; (*work*) accettabile.
passage['pæsɪdʒ] *n* (*gen*) passaggio; (*also:* **~way**) corridoio; (*in book*) brano, passo; (*by boat*) traversata.
passenger[pæsɪndʒə*] *n* passeggero/a.
passer-by[pɑːsə'baɪ] *n* passante *m/f.*
passing['pɑːsɪŋ] *adj* (*fig*) fuggevole; **to mention sth in ~** accennare a qc di sfuggita.
passing placen (*AUT*) piazzola (di sosta).
passion['pæʃən] *n* passione *f*; amore *m*; **to have a ~ for sth** aver la passione di *or* per qc.
passionate['pæʃənɪt] *adj* appassionato(a).
passion fruitn frutto della passione.
passive['pæsɪv] *adj* (*also LING*) passivo(a).
passive smokingn fumo passivo.
passkey['pɑːskiː] *n* passe-partout *m inv.*
Passover['pɑːsəuvə*] *n* Pasqua ebraica.
passport['pɑːspɔːt] *n* passaporto.
passport controln controllo *m* passaporti *inv.*
passport officen ufficio *m* passaporti *inv.*
password['pɑːswəːd] *n* parola d'ordine.
past[pɑːst] *prep* (*further than*) oltre, di là di; dopo; (*later than*) dopo ♦ *adv*: **to run ~** passare di corsa; **to walk ~** passare ♦ *adj* passato(a); (*president etc*) ex *inv* ♦ *n* passato; **quarter/half ~ four** le quattro e un quarto/e mezzo; **ten/twenty ~ four** le quattro e dieci/venti; **he's ~ forty** ha più di quarant'anni; **it's ~ midnight** è mezzanotte passata; **for the ~ few days** da qualche giorno; in questi ultimi giorni; **for the ~ 3 days** negli ultimi 3 giorni; **in the ~** in *or* nel passato; (*LING*) al

passato; **I'm ~ caring** non me ne importa più nulla; **to be ~ it** (*BRIT col: person*) essere finito(a).

pasta ['pæstə] *n* pasta.

paste [peɪst] *n* (*glue*) colla; (*CULIN*) pâté *m inv*; pasta ♦ *vt* collare; **tomato ~** concentrato di pomodoro.

pastel ['pæstl] *adj* pastello *inv*.

pasteurized ['pæstəraɪzd] *adj* pastorizzato(a).

pastille ['pæstl] *n* pastiglia.

pastime ['pɑːstaɪm] *n* passatempo.

past master *n* (*BRIT*): **to be a ~ at** essere molto esperto(a) in.

pastor ['pɑːstə*] *n* pastore *m*.

pastoral ['pɑːstərl] *adj* pastorale.

pastry ['peɪstrɪ] *n* pasta.

pasture ['pɑːstʃə*] *n* pascolo.

pasty *n* ['pæstɪ] pasticcio di carne ♦ *adj* ['peɪstɪ] pastoso(a); (*complexion*) pallido(a).

pat [pæt] *vt* accarezzare, dare un colpetto (affettuoso) a ♦ *n*: **a ~ of butter** un panetto di burro; **to give sb/o.s. a ~ on the back** (*fig*) congratularsi *or* compiacersi con qn/se stesso; **he knows it (off) ~**, (*US*) **he has it down ~** lo conosce *or* sa a menadito.

patch [pætʃ] *n* (*of material*) toppa; (*spot*) macchia; (*of land*) pezzo ♦ *vt* (*clothes*) rattoppare; **a bad ~** (*BRIT*) un brutto periodo.

▶**patch up** *vt* rappezzare.

patchwork ['pætʃwəːk] *n* patchwork *m*.

patchy ['pætʃɪ] *adj* irregolare.

pate [peɪt] *n*: **a bald ~** una testa pelata.

pâté ['pæteɪ] *n* pâté *m inv*.

patent ['peɪtnt] *n* brevetto ♦ *vt* brevettare ♦ *adj* patente, manifesto(a).

patent leather *n* cuoio verniciato.

patently ['peɪtntlɪ] *adv* palesemente.

patent medicine *n* specialità *f inv* medicinale.

patent office *n* ufficio brevetti.

paternal [pə'təːnl] *adj* paterno(a).

paternity [pə'təːnɪtɪ] *n* paternità.

paternity suit *n* (*LAW*) causa di riconoscimento della paternità.

path [pɑːθ] *n* sentiero, viottolo; viale *m*; (*fig*) via, strada; (*of planet, missile*) traiettoria.

pathetic [pə'θɛtɪk] *adj* (*pitiful*) patetico(a); (*very bad*) penoso(a).

pathological [pæθə'lɔdʒɪkl] *adj* patologico(a).

pathologist [pə'θɔlədʒɪst] *n* patologo/a.

pathology [pə'θɔlədʒɪ] *n* patologia.

pathos ['peɪθɔs] *n* pathos *m*.

pathway ['pɑːθweɪ] *n* sentiero, viottolo.

patience ['peɪʃns] *n* pazienza; (*BRIT CARDS*) solitario; **to lose one's ~** spazientirsi.

patient ['peɪʃnt] *n* paziente *m/f*; malato/a ♦ *adj* paziente; **to be ~ with sb** essere paziente *or* aver pazienza con qn.

patiently ['peɪʃntlɪ] *adv* pazientemente.

patio ['pætɪəu] *n* terrazza.

patriot ['peɪtrɪət] *n* patriota *m/f*.

patriotic [pætrɪ'ɔtɪk] *adj* patriottico(a).

patriotism ['pætrɪətɪzəm] *n* patriottismo.

patrol [pə'trəul] *n* pattuglia ♦ *vt* pattugliare; **to be on ~** fare la ronda; essere in ricognizione; essere in perlustrazione.

patrol boat *n* guardacoste *m inv*.

patrol car *n* autoradio *f inv* (della polizia).

patrolman [pə'trəulmən] *n* (*US*) poliziotto.

patron ['peɪtrən] *n* (*in shop*) cliente *m/f*; (*of charity*) benefattore/trice; **~ of the arts** mecenate *m/f*.

patronage ['pætrənɪdʒ] *n* patronato.

patronize ['pætrənaɪz] *vt* essere cliente abituale di; (*fig*) trattare con condiscendenza.

patronizing ['pætrənaɪzɪŋ] *adj* condiscendente.

patron saint *n* patrono.

patter ['pætə*] *n* picchiettio; (*sales talk*) propaganda di vendita ♦ *vi* picchiettare.

pattern ['pætən] *n* modello; (*SEWING etc*) modello (di carta), cartamodello; (*design*) disegno, motivo; (*sample*) campione *m*; **behaviour ~s** tipi *mpl* di comportamento.

patterned ['pætənd] *adj* a disegni, a motivi; (*material*) fantasia *inv*.

paucity ['pɔːsɪtɪ] *n* scarsità.

paunch [pɔːntʃ] *n* pancione *m*.

pauper ['pɔːpə*] *n* indigente *m/f*; **~'s grave** fossa comune.

pause [pɔːz] *n* pausa ♦ *vi* fare una pausa, arrestarsi; **to ~ for breath** fermarsi un attimo per riprender fiato.

pave [peɪv] *vt* pavimentare; **to ~ the way for** aprire la via a.

pavement ['peɪvmənt] *n* (*BRIT*) marciapiede *m*; (*US*) pavimentazione *f* stradale.

pavilion [pə'vɪlɪən] *n* padiglione *m*; tendone *m*; (*SPORT*) edificio annesso ad un campo sportivo.

paving ['peɪvɪŋ] *n* pavimentazione *f*.

paving stone *n* lastra di pietra.

paw [pɔː] *n* zampa ♦ *vt* dare una zampata a; (*subj: person: pej*) palpare.

pawn [pɔːn] *n* pegno; (*CHESS*) pedone *m*; (*fig*) pedina ♦ *vt* dare in pegno.

pawnbroker ['pɔːnbrəukə*] *n* prestatore *m* su pegno.

pawnshop ['pɔːnʃɔp] *n* monte *m* di pietà.

pay [peɪ] n (gen) paga ♦ vb (pt, pp **paid** [peɪd])
vt pagare; (be profitable to: also fig)
convenire a ♦ vi pagare; (be profitable)
rendere; **to ~ attention (to)** fare
attenzione (a); **I paid £5 for that record**
quel disco l'ho pagato 5 sterline; **how**
much did you ~ for it? quanto l'ha
pagato?; **to ~ one's way** pagare la
propria parte; (company) coprire le
spese; **to ~ dividends** (fig) dare buoni
frutti.
►**pay back** vt rimborsare.
►**pay for** vt fus pagare.
►**pay in** vt versare.
►**pay off** vt (debts) saldare; (creditor)
pagare; (mortgage) estinguere; (workers)
licenziare ♦ vi (scheme) funzionare;
(patience) dare dei frutti; **to ~ sth off in**
instalments pagare qc a rate.
►**pay out** vt (money) sborsare, tirar fuori;
(rope) far allentare.
►**pay up** vt saldare.
payable ['peɪəbl] adj pagabile; **to make a**
cheque ~ to sb intestare un assegno a
(nome di) qn.
pay award n aumento salariale.
pay day n giorno di paga.
PAYE n abbr (BRIT: = pay as you earn)
pagamento di imposte tramite ritenute
alla fonte.
payee [peɪ'iː] n beneficiario/a.
pay envelope n (US) busta f paga inv.
paying ['peɪɪŋ] adj: **~ guest** ospite m/f
pagante, pensionante m/f.
payload ['peɪləud] n carico utile.
payment ['peɪmənt] n pagamento; **advance**
~ (part sum) anticipo, acconto; (total sum)
pagamento anticipato; **deferred ~, ~ by**
instalments pagamento dilazionato or a
rate; **in ~ for, in ~ of** in pagamento di; **on**
~ of £5 dietro pagamento di 5 sterline.
pay packet n (BRIT) busta f paga inv.
payphone ['peɪfəun] n cabina telefonica.
payroll ['peɪrəul] n ruolo (organico); **to be**
on a firm's ~ far parte del personale di
una ditta.
pay slip n (BRIT) foglio m paga inv.
pay station n (US) cabina telefonica.
PBS n abbr (US: = Public Broadcasting
Service) servizio che collabora alla
realizzazione di programmi per la rete
televisiva nazionale.
PBX abbr (= private branch exchange)
sistema telefonico con centralino.
PC n abbr see **personal computer**; (BRIT) see
police constable ♦ abbr (BRIT) = **Privy**
Councillor ♦ adj abbr = **politically correct**.
pc abbr = **per cent**; (= postcard) C.P.

p/c abbr = **petty cash**.
PCB n abbr see **printed circuit board**.
pcm abbr = per calendar month.
PD n abbr (US) = **police department**.
pd abbr = **paid**.
PDA n abbr (= personal digital assistant) PDA
m inv.
PDQ abbr (col) = pretty damn quick.
PDSA n abbr (BRIT: = People's Dispensary for
Sick Animals) assistenza veterinaria
gratuita.
PDT abbr (US: = Pacific Daylight Time) ora
legale del Pacifico.
PE n abbr (= physical education) ed. fisica
♦ abbr (Canada) = Prince Edward Island.
pea [piː] n pisello.
peace [piːs] n pace f; (calm) calma,
tranquillità; **to be at ~ with sb/sth** essere
in pace con qn/qc; **to keep the ~** (subj:
policeman) mantenere l'ordine pubblico;
(: citizen) rispettare l'ordine pubblico.
peaceable ['piːsəbl] adj pacifico(a).
peaceful ['piːsful] adj pacifico(a), calmo(a).
peacekeeping ['piːskiːpɪŋ] n mantenimento
della pace; **~ force** forza di pace.
peace offering n (fig) dono in segno di
riconciliazione.
peach [piːtʃ] n pesca.
peacock ['piːkɔk] n pavone m.
peak [piːk] n (of mountain) cima, vetta;
(mountain itself) picco; (fig) massimo; (: of
career) acme f.
peak-hour ['piːkauə*] adj (traffic etc) delle
ore di punta.
peak hours npl ore fpl di punta.
peak period n periodo di punta.
peak rate n tariffa massima.
peaky ['piːkɪ] adj (BRIT col) sbattuto(a).
peal [piːl] n (of bells) scampanio, carillon m
inv; **~s of laughter** scoppi mpl di risa.
peanut ['piːnʌt] n arachide f, nocciolina
americana.
peanut butter n burro di arachidi.
pear [pɛə*] n pera.
pearl [pɔːl] n perla.
peasant ['pɛznt] n contadino/a.
peat [piːt] n torba.
pebble ['pɛbl] n ciottolo.
peck [pɛk] vt (also: ~ at) beccare; (: food)
mangiucchiare ♦ n colpo di becco; (kiss)
bacetto.
pecking order ['pɛkɪŋ-] n (fig) ordine m
gerarchico.
peckish ['pɛkɪʃ] adj (BRIT col): **I feel ~** ho un
languorino.
peculiar [pɪ'kjuːlɪə*] adj strano(a),
bizzarro(a); (particular: importance,
qualities) particolare; **~ to** tipico(a) di,

caratteristico(a) di.
peculiarity [pɪkju:lɪˈærɪtɪ] *n* peculiarità *f inv*; (*oddity*) bizzarria.
pecuniary [pɪˈkju:nɪərɪ] *adj* pecuniario(a).
pedal [ˈpɛdl] *n* pedale *m* ♦ *vi* pedalare.
pedal bin *n* (*BRIT*) pattumiera a pedale.
pedantic [pɪˈdæntɪk] *adj* pedantesco(a).
peddle [ˈpɛdl] *vt* (*goods*) andare in giro a vendere; (*drugs*) spacciare; (*gossip*) mettere in giro.
peddler [ˈpɛdlə*] *n* venditore *m* ambulante.
pedestal [ˈpɛdəstl] *n* piedestallo.
pedestrian [pɪˈdɛstrɪən] *n* pedone/a ♦ *adj* pedonale; (*fig*) prosaico(a), pedestre.
pedestrian crossing *n* (*BRIT*) passaggio pedonale.
pedestrian mall *n* (*US*) zona pedonale.
pedestrian precinct *n* (*BRIT*) zona pedonale.
pediatrics [pi:dɪˈætrɪks] *n* (*US*) = **paediatrics**.
pedigree [ˈpɛdɪgri:] *n* stirpe *f*; (*of animal*) pedigree *m inv* ♦ *cpd* (*animal*) di razza.
pedlar [ˈpɛdlə*] *n* = **peddler**.
pee [pi:] *vi* (*col*) pisciare.
peek [pi:k] *vi* guardare furtivamente.
peel [pi:l] *n* buccia; (*of orange, lemon*) scorza ♦ *vt* sbucciare ♦ *vi* (*paint etc*) staccarsi.
▶**peel back** *vt* togliere, levare.
peeler [pi:lə*] *n*: **potato ~** sbucciapatate *m inv*.
peelings [ˈpi:lɪŋz] *npl* bucce *fpl*.
peep [pi:p] *n* (*BRIT*: *look*) sguardo furtivo, sbirciata; (*sound*) pigolio ♦ *vi* (*BRIT*) guardare furtivamente.
▶**peep out** *vi* (*BRIT*) mostrarsi furtivamente.
peephole [ˈpi:phəul] *n* spioncino.
peer [pɪə*] *vi*: **to ~ at** scrutare ♦ *n* (*noble*) pari *m inv*; (*equal*) pari *m/f inv*, uguale *m/f*.
peerage [ˈpɪərɪdʒ] *n* dignità di pari; pari *mpl*.
peerless [ˈpɪəlɪs] *adj* impareggiabile, senza pari.
peeved [pi:vd] *adj* stizzito(a).
peevish [ˈpi:vɪʃ] *adj* stizzoso(a).
peg [pɛg] *n* (*tent ~*) picchetto; (*for coat etc*) attaccapanni *m inv*; (*BRIT*: *also*: **clothes ~**) molletta ♦ *vt* (*clothes*) appendere con le mollette; (*BRIT*: *groundsheet*) fissare con i picchetti; (*fig*: *prices, wages*) fissare, stabilizzare; **off the ~** confezionato(a).
pejorative [pɪˈdʒɔrətɪv] *adj* peggiorativo(a).
Pekin [pi:ˈkɪn], **Peking** [pi:ˈkɪŋ] *n* Pechino *f*.
pekin(g)ese [pi:kɪˈni:z] *n* pechinese *m*.
pelican [ˈpɛlɪkən] *n* pellicano.
pelican crossing *n* (*BRIT AUT*)

attraversamento pedonale con semaforo a controllo manuale.
pellet [ˈpɛlɪt] *n* pallottola, pallina.
pell-mell [ˈpɛlˈmɛl] *adv* disordinatamente.
pelmet [ˈpɛlmɪt] *n* mantovana; cassonetto.
pelt [pɛlt] *vt*: **to ~ sb (with)** bombardare qn (con) ♦ *vi* (*rain*) piovere a dirotto ♦ *n* pelle *f*.
pelvis [ˈpɛlvɪs] *n* pelvi *f inv*, bacino.
pen [pɛn] *n* penna; (*for sheep*) recinto; (*US col*: *prison*) galera; **to put ~ to paper** prendere la penna in mano.
penal [ˈpi:nl] *adj* penale.
penalize [ˈpi:nəlaɪz] *vt* punire; (*SPORT*) penalizzare; (*fig*) svantaggiare.
penal servitude [-ˈsə:vɪtju:d] *n* lavori *mpl* forzati.
penalty [ˈpɛnltɪ] *n* penalità *f inv*; sanzione *f* penale; (*fine*) ammenda; (*SPORT*) penalizzazione *f*; (*FOOTBALL*: *also*: ~ **kick**) calcio di rigore.
penalty area *n* (*BRIT SPORT*) area di rigore.
penalty clause *n* penale *f*.
penalty kick *n* (*FOOTBALL*) calcio di rigore.
penalty shoot-out [-ˈʃu:taut] *n* (*FOOTBALL*) rigori *mpl*.
penance [ˈpɛnəns] *n* penitenza.
pence [pɛns] *npl* (*BRIT*) *of* **penny**.
penchant [ˈpɑ̃:ʃɑ̃:ŋ] *n* debole *m*.
pencil [ˈpɛnsl] *n* matita ♦ *vt* (*also*: ~ **in**) scrivere a matita.
pencil case *n* astuccio per matite.
pencil sharpener *n* temperamatite *m inv*.
pendant [ˈpɛndnt] *n* pendaglio.
pending [ˈpɛndɪŋ] *prep* in attesa di ♦ *adj* in sospeso.
pendulum [ˈpɛndjuləm] *n* pendolo.
penetrate [ˈpɛnɪtreɪt] *vt* penetrare.
penetrating [ˈpɛnɪtreɪtɪŋ] *adj* penetrante.
penetration [pɛnɪˈtreɪʃən] *n* penetrazione *f*.
penfriend [ˈpɛnfrɛnd] *n* (*BRIT*) corrispondente *m/f*.
penguin [ˈpɛŋgwɪn] *n* pinguino.
penicillin [pɛnɪˈsɪlɪn] *n* penicillina.
peninsula [pəˈnɪnsjulə] *n* penisola.
penis [ˈpi:nɪs] *n* pene *m*.
penitence [ˈpɛnɪtns] *n* penitenza.
penitent [ˈpɛnɪtnt] *adj* penitente.
penitentiary [pɛnɪˈtɛnʃərɪ] *n* (*US*) carcere *m*.
penknife [ˈpɛnnaɪf] *n* temperino.
Penn(a). *abbr* (*US*) = *Pennsylvania*.
pen name *n* pseudonimo.
pennant [ˈpɛnənt] *n* banderuola.
penniless [ˈpɛnɪlɪs] *adj* senza un soldo.
Pennines [ˈpɛnaɪnz] *npl*: **the ~** i Pennini.
penny, *pl* **pennies** *or* **pence** [ˈpɛnɪ, ˈpɛnɪz, pɛns] *n* penny *m* (*pl* pence); (*US*)

centesimo.

penpal ['pɛnpæl] n corrispondente m/f.

penpusher ['pɛnpuʃə*] n (pej) scribacchino/a.

pension ['pɛnʃən] n pensione f.

▶**pension off** vt mandare in pensione.

pensionable ['pɛnʃənəbl] adj (person) che ha diritto a una pensione, pensionabile; (age) pensionabile.

pensioner ['pɛnʃənə*] n (BRIT) pensionato/a.

pension fund n fondo pensioni.

pensive ['pɛnsɪv] adj pensoso(a).

pentagon ['pɛntəgən] n pentagono; **the P~** (US POL) il Pentagono; see boxed note.

> PENTAGON
>
> **Il Pentagon** è un edificio a pianta pentagonale che si trova ad Arlington, in Virginia, nel quale hanno sede gli uffici del Ministero della Difesa degli Stati Uniti. Il termine **Pentagon** è usato anche per indicare la dirigenza militare del paese.

Pentecost ['pɛntɪkɔst] n Pentecoste f.

penthouse ['pɛnthaus] n appartamento (di lusso) nell'attico.

pent-up ['pɛntʌp] adj (feelings) represso(a).

penultimate [pɪ'nʌltɪmət] adj penultimo(a).

penury ['pɛnjurɪ] n indigenza.

people ['piːpl] npl gente f; persone fpl; (citizens) popolo ♦ n (nation, race) popolo ♦ vt popolare; **old** ~ i vecchi; **young** ~ i giovani; ~ **at large** il grande pubblico; **a man of the** ~ un uomo del popolo; **4/several** ~ **came** 4/parecchie persone sono venute; **the room was full of** ~ la stanza era piena di gente; ~ **say that ...** si dice or la gente dice che ....

PEP [pɛp] n = personal equity plan.

pep [pɛp] n (col) dinamismo.

▶**pep up** vt vivacizzare; (food) rendere più gustoso(a).

pepper ['pɛpə*] n pepe m; (vegetable) peperone m ♦ vt pepare.

peppermint ['pɛpəmɪnt] n (plant) menta peperita; (sweet) pasticca di menta.

pepperoni [pɛpə'rəunɪ] n salsiccia piccante.

pepperpot ['pɛpəpɔt] n pepaiola.

peptalk ['pɛptɔːk] n (col) discorso di incoraggiamento.

per [pəː*] prep per; a; ~ **hour** all'ora; ~ **kilo** etc il chilo etc; ~ **day** al giorno; ~ **week** alla settimana; ~ **person** a testa, a or per persona; **as** ~ **your instructions** secondo le vostre istruzioni.

per annum adv all'anno.

per capita adj, adv pro capite.

perceive [pə'siːv] vt percepire; (notice) accorgersi di.

per cent adv per cento; **a 20** ~ **discount** uno sconto del 20 per cento.

percentage [pə'sɛntɪdʒ] n percentuale f; **on a** ~ **basis** a percentuale.

percentage point n punto percentuale.

perceptible [pə'sɛptɪbl] adj percettibile.

perception [pə'sɛpʃən] n percezione f; sensibilità; perspicacia.

perceptive [pə'sɛptɪv] adj percettivo(a); perspicace.

perch [pəːtʃ] n (fish) pesce m persico; (for bird) sostegno, ramo ♦ vi appollaiarsi.

percolate ['pəːkəleɪt] vt filtrare.

percolator ['pəːkəleɪtə*] n caffettiera a pressione; caffettiera elettrica.

percussion [pə'kʌʃən] n percussione f; (MUS) strumenti mpl a percussione.

peremptory [pə'rɛmptərɪ] adj perentorio(a).

perennial [pə'rɛnɪəl] adj perenne ♦ n pianta perenne.

perfect adj, n ['pəːfɪkt] adj perfetto(a) ♦ n (also: ~ **tense**) perfetto, passato prossimo ♦ vt [pə'fɛkt] perfezionare; mettere a punto; **he's a** ~ **stranger to me** mi è completamente sconosciuto.

perfection [pə'fɛkʃən] n perfezione f.

perfectionist [pə'fɛkʃənɪst] n perfezionista m/f.

perfectly ['pəːfɪktlɪ] adv perfettamente; **I'm** ~ **happy with the situation** sono completamente soddisfatta della situazione; **you know** ~ **well** sa benissimo.

perforate ['pəːfəreɪt] vt perforare.

perforated ulcer ['pəːfəreɪtɪd-] n (MED) ulcera perforata.

perforation [pəːfə'reɪʃən] n perforazione f; (line of holes) dentellatura.

perform [pə'fɔːm] vt (carry out) eseguire, fare; (symphony etc) suonare; (play, ballet) dare; (opera) fare ♦ vi suonare; recitare.

performance [pə'fɔːməns] n esecuzione f; (at theatre etc) rappresentazione f, spettacolo; (of an artist) interpretazione f; (of player etc) performance f; (of car, engine) prestazione f; **the team put up a good** ~ la squadra ha giocato una bella partita.

performer [pə'fɔːmə*] n artista m/f.

performing [pə'fɔːmɪŋ] adj (animal) ammaestrato(a).

performing arts npl: **the** ~ le arti dello spettacolo.

perfume ['pə:fju:m] *n* profumo ♦ *vt*
profumare.
perfunctory [pə'fʌŋktərɪ] *adj* superficiale,
per la forma.
perhaps [pə'hæps] *adv* forse; ~ **he'll come**
forse verrà, può darsi che venga; ~ **so/
not** forse sì/no, può darsi di sì/di no.
peril ['pɛrɪl] *n* pericolo.
perilous ['pɛrɪləs] *adj* pericoloso(a).
perilously ['pɛrɪləslɪ] *adv*: **they came ~
close to being caught** sono stati a un pelo
dall'esser presi.
perimeter [pə'rɪmɪtə*] *n* perimetro.
perimeter wall *n* muro di cinta.
period ['pɪərɪəd] *n* periodo; (*HISTORY*)
epoca; (*SCOL*) lezione *f*; (*full stop*) punto;
(*US FOOTBALL*) tempo; (*MED*) mestruazioni
fpl ♦ *adj* (*costume, furniture*) d'epoca; **for a**
~ **of three weeks** per un periodo di *or* per
la durata di tre settimane; **the holiday** ~
(*BRIT*) il periodo delle vacanze.
periodic [pɪərɪ'ɔdɪk] *adj* periodico(a).
periodical [pɪərɪ'ɔdɪkl] *adj* periodico(a) ♦ *n*
periodico.
periodically [pɪərɪ'ɔdɪklɪ] *adv*
periodicamente.
period pains *npl* (*BRIT*) dolori *mpl*
mestruali.
peripatetic [pɛrɪpə'tɛtɪk] *adj* (*salesman*)
ambulante; (*BRIT: teacher*) peripatetico(a).
peripheral [pə'rɪfərəl] *adj* periferico(a) ♦ *n*
(*COMPUT*) unità *f inv* periferica.
periphery [pə'rɪfərɪ] *n* periferia.
periscope ['pɛrɪskəup] *n* periscopio.
perish ['pɛrɪʃ] *vi* perire, morire; (*decay*)
deteriorarsi.
perishable ['pɛrɪʃəbl] *adj* deperibile.
perishables ['pɛrɪʃəblz] *npl* merci *fpl*
deperibili.
perishing ['pɛrɪʃɪŋ] *adj* (*BRIT col*): **it's ~
(cold)** fa un freddo da morire.
peritonitis [pɛrɪtə'naɪtɪs] *n* peritonite *f*.
perjure ['pə:dʒə*] *vt*: **to ~ o.s.** spergiurare.
perjury ['pə:dʒərɪ] *n* (*LAW: in court*) falso
giuramento; (*breach of oath*) spergiuro.
perk [pə:k] *n* vantaggio.
▶**perk up** *vi* (*cheer up*) rianimarsi.
perky ['pə:kɪ] *adj* (*cheerful*) vivace,
allegro(a).
perm [pə:m] *n* (*for hair*) permanente *f* ♦ *vt*:
to have one's hair ~ed farsi fare la
permanente.
permanence ['pə:mənəns] *n* permanenza.
permanent ['pə:mənənt] *adj* permanente;
(*job, position*) fisso(a); (*dye, ink*)
indelebile; ~ **address** residenza fissa; **I'm
not** ~ **here** non sono fisso qui.
permanently ['pə:mənəntlɪ] *adv*

definitivamente.
permeable ['pə:mɪəbl] *adj* permeabile.
permeate ['pə:mɪeɪt] *vi* penetrare ♦ *vt*
permeare.
permissible [pə'mɪsɪbl] *adj* permissibile,
ammissibile.
permission [pə'mɪʃən] *n* permesso; **to give
sb** ~ **to do sth** dare a qn il permesso di
fare qc.
permissive [pə'mɪsɪv] *adj* tollerante; **the** ~
society la società permissiva.
permit *n* ['pə:mɪt] permesso; (*entrance
pass*) lasciapassare *m* ♦ *vt*, *vi* [pə'mɪt]
permettere; **fishing** ~ licenza di pesca; **to**
~ **sb to do** permettere a qn di fare, dare
il permesso a qn di fare; **weather** ~**ting**
tempo permettendo.
permutation [pə:mju'teɪʃən] *n*
permutazione *f*.
pernicious [pə:'nɪʃəs] *adj* pernicioso(a),
nocivo(a).
pernickety [pə'nɪkɪtɪ] *adj* (*col: person*)
pignolo(a); (*: task*) da certosino.
perpendicular [pə:pən'dɪkjulə*] *adj*, *n*
perpendicolare (*f*).
perpetrate ['pə:pɪtreɪt] *vt* perpetrare,
commettere.
perpetual [pə'pɛtjuəl] *adj* perpetuo(a).
perpetuate [pə'pɛtjueɪt] *vt* perpetuare.
perpetuity [pə:pɪ'tju:ɪtɪ] *n*: **in** ~ **in**
perpetuo.
perplex [pə'plɛks] *vt* lasciare perplesso(a).
perplexing [pə'plɛksɪŋ] *adj* che lascia
perplesso(a).
perquisites ['pə:kwɪzɪts] *npl* (*also:* **perks**)
benefici *mpl* collaterali.
persecute ['pə:sɪkju:t] *vt* perseguitare.
persecution [pə:sɪ'kju:ʃən] *n* persecuzione
f.
perseverance [pə:sɪ'vɪərəns] *n*
perseveranza.
persevere [pə:sɪ'vɪə*] *vi* perseverare.
Persia ['pə:ʃə] *n* Persia.
Persian ['pə:ʃən] *adj* persiano(a) ♦ *n* (*LING*)
persiano; **the (~) Gulf** il Golfo Persico.
Persian cat *n* gatto persiano.
persist [pə'sɪst] *vi*: **to** ~ **(in doing)**
persistere (nel fare); ostinarsi (a
fare).
persistence [pə'sɪstəns] *n* persistenza;
ostinazione *f*.
persistent [pə'sɪstənt] *adj* persistente;
ostinato(a); (*lateness, rain*) continuo(a); ~
offender (*LAW*) delinquente *m/f* abituale.
persnickety [pə'snɪkɪtɪ] *adj* (*US col*)
= **pernickety**.
person ['pə:sn] *n* persona; **in** ~ di *or* in
persona, personalmente; **on** *or* **about**

one's ~ (weapon) su di sé; (money) con sé; **a** ~ **to** ~ **call** (TEL) una chiamata con preavviso.

personable ['pəːsnəbl] adj di bell'aspetto.

personal ['pəːsnl] adj personale; individuale; ~ **belongings**, ~ **effects** oggetti mpl d'uso personale; **a** ~ **interview** un incontro privato.

personal allowance n (TAX) quota del reddito non imponibile.

personal assistant (PA) n segretaria personale.

personal call n (TEL) chiamata con preavviso.

personal column n messaggi mpl personali.

personal computer (PC) n personal computer m inv.

personal details npl dati mpl personali.

personal equity plan n (FINANCE) fondo di investimento azionario con agevolazioni fiscali destinato al piccolo risparmiatore.

personal identification number (PIN) n (COMPUT, BANKING) numero di codice segreto.

personality [pəːsə'nælɪtɪ] n personalità f inv.

personally ['pəːsnəlɪ] adv personalmente.

personal organizer n agenda; (electronic) agenda elettronica.

personal property n beni mpl personali.

personal stereo n walkman ® m inv.

personify [pəː'sɒnɪfaɪ] vt personificare.

personnel [pəːsə'nɛl] n personale m.

personnel department n ufficio del personale.

personnel manager n direttore/trice del personale.

perspective [pə'spɛktɪv] n prospettiva; **to get sth into** ~ ridimensionare qc.

Perspex ® ['pəːspɛks] n (BRIT) tipo di resina termoplastica.

perspicacity [pəːspɪ'kæsɪtɪ] n perspicacia.

perspiration [pəːspɪ'reɪʃən] n traspirazione f, sudore m.

perspire [pə'spaɪə*] vi traspirare.

persuade [pə'sweɪd] vt: **to** ~ **sb to do sth** persuadere qn a fare qc; **to** ~ **sb of sth/ that** persuadere qn di qc/che.

persuasion [pə'sweɪʒən] n persuasione f; (creed) convinzione f, credo.

persuasive [pə'sweɪsɪv] adj persuasivo(a).

pert [pəːt] adj (bold) sfacciato(a), impertinente; (hat) spiritoso(a).

pertaining [pəː'teɪnɪŋ]: ~ **to** prep che riguarda.

pertinent ['pəːtɪnənt] adj pertinente.

perturb [pə'təːb] vt turbare.

perturbing [pə'təːbɪŋ] adj inquietante.

Peru [pə'ruː] n Perù m.

perusal [pə'ruːzl] n attenta lettura.

Peruvian [pə'ruːvjən] adj, n peruviano(a).

pervade [pə'veɪd] vt pervadere.

pervasive [pəː'veɪsɪv] adj (smell) penetrante; (influence) dilagante; (gloom, feelings) diffuso(a).

perverse [pə'vəːs] adj perverso(a).

perversion [pə'vəːʃən] n pervertimento, perversione f.

perversity [pə'vəːsɪtɪ] n perversità.

pervert n ['pəːvəːt] pervertito/a ◆ vt [pə'vəːt] pervertire.

pessimism ['pɛsɪmɪzəm] n pessimismo.

pessimist ['pɛsɪmɪst] n pessimista m/f.

pessimistic [pɛsɪ'mɪstɪk] adj pessimistico(a).

pest [pɛst] n animale m (or insetto) pestifero; (fig) peste f.

pest control n disinfestazione f.

pester ['pɛstə*] vt tormentare, molestare.

pesticide ['pɛstɪsaɪd] n pesticida m.

pestilence ['pɛstɪləns] n pestilenza.

pestle ['pɛsl] n pestello.

pet [pɛt] n animale m domestico; (favourite) favorito/a ◆ vt accarezzare ◆ vi (col) fare il petting; ~ **lion** etc leone m etc ammaestrato.

petal ['pɛtl] n petalo.

peter ['piːtə*]: **to** ~ **out** vi esaurirsi; estinguersi.

petite [pə'tiːt] adj piccolo(a) e aggraziato(a).

petition [pə'tɪʃən] n petizione f ◆ vi richiedere; **to** ~ **for divorce** presentare un'istanza di divorzio.

pet name n (BRIT) nomignolo.

petrified ['pɛtrɪfaɪd] adj (fig) morto(a) di paura.

petrify ['pɛtrɪfaɪ] vt pietrificare; (fig) terrorizzare.

petrochemical [pɛtrə'kɛmɪkl] adj petrolchimico(a).

petrodollars ['pɛtrəudɒləz] npl petrodollari mpl.

petrol ['pɛtrəl] n (BRIT) benzina.

petrol bomb n (BRIT) (bottiglia) molotov f inv.

petrol can n (BRIT) tanica per benzina.

petrol engine n (BRIT) motore m a benzina.

petroleum [pə'trəulɪəm] n petrolio.

petroleum jelly n vaselina.

petrol pump n (BRIT: in car, at garage) pompa di benzina.

petrol station n (BRIT) stazione f di rifornimento.

petrol tank n (BRIT) serbatoio della

benzina.
petticoat ['pɛtɪkəut] n sottana.
pettifogging ['pɛtɪfɔgɪŋ] adj cavilloso(a).
pettiness ['pɛtɪnɪs] n meschinità.
petty ['pɛtɪ] adj (mean) meschino(a); (unimportant) insignificante.
petty cash n piccola cassa.
petty officer n sottufficiale m di marina.
petulant ['pɛtjulənt] adj irritabile.
pew [pju:] n panca (di chiesa).
pewter ['pju:tə*] n peltro.
Pfc abbr (US MIL) = private first class.
PG n abbr (CINE: = parental guidance) consenso dei genitori richiesto.
PG13 abbr (US CINE: = Parental Guidance 13) vietato ai minori di 13 anni non accompagnati dai genitori.
PGA n abbr (= Professional Golfers Association) associazione dei giocatori di golf professionisti.
PH n abbr (US MIL: = Purple Heart) decorazione per ferite riportate in guerra.
PHA n abbr (US: = Public Housing Administration) amministrazione per l'edilizia pubblica.
phallic ['fælɪk] adj fallico(a).
phantom ['fæntəm] n fantasma m.
Pharaoh ['fɛərəu] n faraone m.
pharmaceutical [fɑːməˈsjuːtɪkl] adj farmaceutico(a) ♦ n: ~s prodotti mpl farmaceutici.
pharmacist ['fɑːməsɪst] n farmacista m/f.
pharmacy ['fɑːməsɪ] n farmacia.
phase [feɪz] n fase f, periodo ♦ vt: to ~ sth in/out introdurre/eliminare qc progressivamente.
PhD n abbr = Doctor of Philosophy.
pheasant ['fɛznt] n fagiano.
phenomenon, pl **phenomena** [fəˈnɔmɪnən, -nə] n fenomeno.
phew [fju:] excl uff!
phial ['faɪəl] n fiala.
philanderer [fɪˈlændərə*] n donnaiolo.
philanthropic [fɪlənˈθrɔpɪk] adj filantropico(a).
philanthropist [fɪˈlænθrəpɪst] n filantropo.
philatelist [fɪˈlætəlɪst] n filatelico/a.
philately [fɪˈlætəlɪ] n filatelia.
Philippines ['fɪlɪpiːnz] npl (also: **Philippine Islands**): the ~ le Filippine.
philosopher [fɪˈlɔsəfə*] n filosofo/a.
philosophical [fɪləˈsɔfɪkl] adj filosofico(a).
philosophy [fɪˈlɔsəfɪ] n filosofia.
phlegm [flɛm] n flemma.
phlegmatic [flɛgˈmætɪk] adj flemmatico(a).
phobia ['fəubjə] n fobia.
phone [fəun] n telefono ♦ vt telefonare a

♦ vi telefonare; **to be on the** ~ avere il telefono; (be calling) essere al telefono.
► **phone back** vt, vi richiamare.
phone book n guida del telefono, elenco telefonico.
phone box, **phone booth** n cabina telefonica.
phone call n telefonata.
phonecard ['fəunkɑːd] n scheda telefonica.
phone-in ['fəunɪn] n (BRIT RADIO, TV) trasmissione radiofonica o televisiva con intervento telefonico degli ascoltatori.
phone tapping [-tæpɪŋ] n intercettazioni fpl telefoniche.
phonetics [fəˈnɛtɪks] n fonetica.
phoney ['fəunɪ] adj falso(a), fasullo(a) ♦ n (person) ciarlatano.
phonograph ['fəunəgrɑːf] n (US) giradischi m inv.
phony ['fəunɪ] adj, n = **phoney**.
phosphate ['fɔsfeɪt] n fosfato.
phosphorus ['fɔsfərəs] n fosforo.
photo ['fəutəu] n foto f inv.
photo... ['fəutəu] prefix foto....
photocall ['fəutəukɔːl] n convocazione di fotoreporter a scopo pubblicitario.
photocopier ['fəutəukɔpɪə*] n fotocopiatrice f.
photocopy ['fəutəukɔpɪ] n fotocopia ♦ vt fotocopiare.
photoelectric [fəutəuɪˈlɛktrɪk] adj: ~ **cell** cellula fotoelettrica.
Photofit ® ['fəutəufɪt] n photofit m inv.
photogenic [fəutəuˈdʒɛnɪk] adj fotogenico(a).
photograph ['fəutəgræf] n fotografia ♦ vt fotografare; **to take a** ~ **of sb** fare una fotografia a or fotografare qn.
photographer [fəˈtɔgrəfə*] n fotografo.
photographic [fəutəˈgræfɪk] adj fotografico(a).
photography [fəˈtɔgrəfɪ] n fotografia.
photo opportunity n opportunità di scattare delle foto ad un personaggio importante.
Photostat ® ['fəutəustæt] n fotocopia.
photosynthesis [fəutəuˈsɪnθəsɪs] n fotosintesi f.
phrase [freɪz] n espressione f; (LING) locuzione f; (MUS) frase f ♦ vt esprimere; (letter) redigere.
phrasebook ['freɪzbuk] n vocabolarietto.
physical ['fɪzɪkl] adj fisico(a); ~ **examination** visita medica; ~ **education** educazione f fisica; ~ **exercises** ginnastica.
physically [fɪzɪklɪ] adv fisicamente.
physician [fɪˈzɪʃən] n medico.

physicist ['fɪzɪsɪst] n fisico.
physics ['fɪzɪks] n fisica.
physiological [fɪzɪə'lɒdʒɪkəl] adj fisiologico(a).
physiology [fɪzɪ'ɒlədʒɪ] n fisiologia.
physiotherapist [fɪzɪəu'θerəpɪst] n fisioterapista m/f.
physiotherapy [fɪzɪəu'θerəpɪ] n fisioterapia.
physique [fɪ'ziːk] n fisico.
pianist ['piːənɪst] n pianista m/f.
piano [pɪ'ænəu] n pianoforte m.
piano accordion n (BRIT) fisarmonica (a tastiera).
piccolo ['pɪkələu] n ottavino.
pick [pɪk] n (tool: also: ~-axe) piccone m ♦ vt scegliere; (gather) cogliere; (scab, spot) grattarsi ♦ vi: to ~ and choose scegliere con cura; take your ~ scelga; the ~ of il fior fiore di; to ~ one's nose mettersi le dita nel naso; to ~ one's teeth stuzzicarsi i denti; to ~ sb's brains farsi dare dei suggerimenti da qn; to ~ pockets borseggiare; to ~ a fight/quarrel with sb attaccar rissa/briga con qn; to ~ one's way through attraversare stando ben attento a dove mettere i piedi.
► **pick off** vt (kill) abbattere.
► **pick on** vt fus (person) avercela con.
► **pick out** vt scegliere; (distinguish) distinguere.
► **pick up** vi (improve) migliorarsi ♦ vt raccogliere; (collect) passare a prendere; (AUT: give lift to) far salire; (learn) imparare; (RADIO, TV, TEL) captare; to ~ o.s. up rialzarsi; to ~ up where one left off riprendere dal punto in cui ci si era fermati; to ~ up speed acquistare velocità.
pickaxe, (US) pickax ['pɪkæks] n piccone m.
picket ['pɪkɪt] n (in strike) scioperante m/f che fa parte di un picchetto; picchetto ♦ vt picchettare.
picket line n cordone m degli scioperanti.
pickings ['pɪkɪŋz] npl (pilferings): **there are good ~ to be had here** qui ci sono buone possibilità di intascare qualcosa sottobanco.
pickle ['pɪkl] n (also: ~s: as condiment) sottaceti mpl; (fig): **in a ~** nei pasticci ♦ vt mettere sottaceto; mettere in salamoia.
pick-me-up ['pɪkmiːʌp] n tiramisù m inv.
pickpocket ['pɪkpɒkɪt] n borsaiolo.
pickup ['pɪkʌp] n (BRIT: on record player) pick-up m inv; (small truck: also: ~ truck, ~ van) camioncino.
picnic ['pɪknɪk] n picnic m inv ♦ vi fare un picnic.
picnicker ['pɪknɪkə*] n chi partecipa a un picnic.
pictorial [pɪk'tɔːrɪəl] adj illustrato(a).
picture ['pɪktʃə*] n quadro; (painting) pittura; (photograph) foto(grafia); (drawing) disegno; (TV) immagine f; (film) film m inv ♦ vt raffigurarsi; **the ~s** (BRIT) il cinema; **to take a ~ of sb/sth** fare una foto a qn/di qc; **we get a good ~ here** (TV) la ricezione qui è buona; **the overall ~** il quadro generale; **to put sb in the ~** mettere qn al corrente.
picture book n libro illustrato.
picture messaging [-'mesɪdʒɪŋ] n picture messaging m, invio di messaggini con disegni.
picturesque [pɪktʃə'resk] adj pittoresco(a).
picture window n finestra panoramica.
piddling ['pɪdlɪŋ] adj (col) insignificante.
pidgin English ['pɪdʒɪn-] n inglese semplificato misto ad elementi indigeni.
pie [paɪ] n torta; (of meat) pasticcio.
piebald ['paɪbɔːld] adj pezzato(a).
piece [piːs] n pezzo; (of land) appezzamento; (DRAUGHTS etc) pedina; (item): **a ~ of furniture/advice** un mobile/consiglio ♦ vt: **to ~ together** mettere insieme; **in ~s** (broken) in pezzi; (not yet assembled) smontato(a); **to take to ~s** smontare; ~ **by** ~ poco alla volta; **a 10p ~** (BRIT) una moneta da 10 pence; **a six-~ band** un complesso di sei strumentisti; **in one ~** (object) intatto; **to get back all in one ~** (person) tornare a casa incolume or sano e salvo; **to say one's ~** dire la propria.
piecemeal ['piːsmiːl] adv pezzo a pezzo, a spizzico.
piece rate n tariffa a cottimo.
piecework ['piːswəːk] n (lavoro a) cottimo.
pie chart n grafico a torta.
Piedmont ['piːdmɒnt] n Piemonte m.
pier [pɪə*] n molo; (of bridge etc) pila.
pierce [pɪəs] vt forare; (with arrow etc) trafigere; **to have one's ears ~d** farsi fare i buchi per gli orecchini.
piercing ['pɪəsɪŋ] adj (cry) acuto(a).
piety ['paɪətɪ] n pietà, devozione f.
piffling ['pɪflɪŋ] adj insignificante.
pig [pɪg] n maiale m, porco.
pigeon ['pɪdʒən] n piccione m.
pigeonhole ['pɪdʒənhəul] n casella ♦ vt classificare.
pigeon-toed ['pɪdʒən'təud] adj che cammina con i piedi in dentro.
piggy bank ['pɪgɪ-] n salvadanaio.
pigheaded ['pɪg'hedɪd] adj caparbio(a),

cocciuto(a).

piglet ['pɪglɪt] n porcellino.

pigment ['pɪgmənt] n pigmento.

pigmentation [pɪgmən'teɪʃən] n pigmentazione f.

pigmy ['pɪgmɪ] n = **pygmy**.

pigskin ['pɪgskɪn] n cinghiale m.

pigsty ['pɪgstaɪ] n porcile m.

pigtail ['pɪgteɪl] n treccina.

pike [paɪk] n (spear) picca; (fish) luccio.

pilchard ['pɪltʃəd] n specie di sardina.

pile [paɪl] n (pillar, of books) pila; (heap) mucchio; (of carpet) pelo ♦ vb (also: ~ up) vt ammucchiare ♦ vi ammucchiarsi; **in a ~** ammucchiato; see also **piles**.

▶**pile on** vt: **to ~ it on** (col) esagerare, drammatizzare.

piles [paɪlz] npl (MED) emorroidi fpl.

pileup ['paɪlʌp] n (AUT) tamponamento a catena.

pilfer ['pɪlfə*] vt rubacchiare ♦ vi fare dei furtarelli.

pilfering ['pɪlfərɪŋ] n rubacchiare m.

pilgrim ['pɪlgrɪm] n pellegrino/a.

pilgrimage ['pɪlgrɪmɪdʒ] n pellegrinaggio.

pill [pɪl] n pillola; **to be on the ~** prendere la pillola.

pillage ['pɪlɪdʒ] vt saccheggiare.

pillar ['pɪlə*] n colonna.

pillar box n (BRIT) cassetta delle lettere (a colonnina).

pillion ['pɪljən] n (of motor cycle) sellino posteriore; **to ride ~** viaggiare dietro.

pillory ['pɪlərɪ] n berlina ♦ vt mettere alla berlina.

pillow ['pɪləu] n guanciale m.

pillowcase ['pɪləukeɪs], **pillowslip** ['pɪləuslɪp] n federa.

pilot ['paɪlət] n pilota m/f ♦ cpd (scheme etc) pilota inv ♦ vt pilotare.

pilot boat n pilotina.

pilot light n fiammella di sicurezza.

pimento [pɪ'mentəu] n peperoncino.

pimp [pɪmp] n mezzano.

pimple ['pɪmpl] n foruncolo.

pimply ['pɪmplɪ] adj foruncoloso(a).

PIN n abbr see **personal identification number**.

pin [pɪn] n spillo; (TECH) perno; (BRIT: drawing ~) puntina da disegno; (BRIT ELEC: of plug) spinotto ♦ vt attaccare con uno spillo; **~s and needles** formicolio; **to ~ sb against/to** inchiodare qn contro/a; **to ~ sth on sb** (fig) addossare la colpa di qc a qn.

▶**pin down** vt (fig): **to ~ sb down** obbligare qn a pronunziarsi; **there's something strange here but I can't quite**

~ it down c'è qualcosa di strano qua ma non riesco a capire cos'è.

pinafore ['pɪnəfɔ:*] n grembiule m (senza maniche).

pinafore dress n scamiciato.

pinball ['pɪnbɔ:l] n flipper m inv.

pincers ['pɪnsəz] npl pinzette fpl.

pinch [pɪntʃ] n pizzicotto, pizzico ♦ vt pizzicare; (col: steal) grattare ♦ vi (shoe) stringere; **at a ~** in caso di bisogno; **to feel the ~** (fig) trovarsi nelle ristrettezze.

pinched [pɪntʃt] adj (drawn) dai lineamenti tirati; (short): **~ for money/space** a corto di soldi/di spazio; **~ with cold** raggrinzito dal freddo.

pincushion ['pɪnkuʃən] n puntaspilli m inv.

pine [paɪn] n (also: ~ **tree**) pino ♦ vi: **to ~ for** struggersi dal desiderio di.

▶**pine away** vi languire.

pineapple ['paɪnæpl] n ananas m inv.

pine cone n pigna.

pine needles npl aghi mpl di pino.

ping [pɪŋ] n (noise) tintinnio.

Ping-Pong ® ['pɪŋpɔŋ] n ping-pong ® m.

pink [pɪŋk] adj rosa inv ♦ n (colour) rosa m inv; (BOT) garofano.

pinking shears ['pɪŋkɪŋ-] n forbici fpl a zigzag.

pin money n (BRIT) denaro per le piccole spese.

pinnacle ['pɪnəkl] n pinnacolo.

pinpoint ['pɪnpɔɪnt] vt indicare con precisione.

pinstripe ['pɪnstraɪp] n stoffa gessata; (also: ~ **suit**) gessato.

pint [paɪnt] n pinta (BRIT = 0.57 l; US = 0.47 l); (BRIT col: of beer) ≈ birra piccola.

pinup ['pɪnʌp] n pin-up girl f inv.

pioneer [paɪə'nɪə*] n pioniere/a ♦ vt essere un pioniere in.

pious ['paɪəs] adj pio(a).

pip [pɪp] n (seed) seme m; (time signal on radio) segnale m orario.

pipe [paɪp] n tubo; (for smoking) pipa; (MUS) piffero ♦ vt portare per mezzo di tubazione; **~s** npl (also: **bag~s**) cornamusa (scozzese).

▶**pipe down** vi (col) calmarsi.

pipe cleaner n scovolino.

piped music [paɪpt-] n musica di sottofondo.

pipe dream n vana speranza.

pipeline ['paɪplaɪn] n conduttura; (for oil) oleodotto; (for natural gas) metanodotto; **it is in the ~** (fig) è in arrivo.

piper ['paɪpə*] n piffero; suonatore/trice di cornamusa.

pipe tobacco n tabacco da pipa.

piping ['paɪpɪŋ] adv: ~ **hot** bollente.
piquant ['piːkənt] adj (sauce) piccante; (conversation) stimolante.
pique [piːk] n picca.
piracy ['paɪərəsɪ] n pirateria.
pirate ['paɪərət] n pirata m ♦ vt (record, video, book) riprodurre abusivamente.
pirate radio n (BRIT) radio pirata f inv.
pirouette [pɪruˈɛt] n piroetta ♦ vi piroettare.
Pisces ['paɪsiːz] n Pesci mpl; **to be** ~ essere dei Pesci.
piss [pɪs] vi (col!) pisciare; ~ **off!** vaffanculo! (!).
pissed [pɪst] adj (BRIT col: drunk) ubriaco(a) fradicio(a).
pistol ['pɪstl] n pistola.
piston ['pɪstən] n pistone m.
pit [pɪt] n buca, fossa; (also: **coal** ~) miniera; (also: **orchestra** ~) orchestra ♦ vt: **to** ~ **sb against sb** opporre qn a qn; ~**s** npl (AUT) box m; **to** ~ **o.s. against** opporsi a.
pitapat ['pɪtəˈpæt] adv (BRIT): **to go** ~ (heart) palpitare, battere forte; (rain) picchiettare.
pitch [pɪtʃ] n (throw) lancia; (MUS) tono; (of voice) altezza; (fig: degree) grado, punto; (also: **sales** ~) discorso di vendita, imbonimento; (BRIT SPORT) campo; (NAUT) beccheggio; (tar) pece f ♦ vt (throw) lanciare ♦ vi (fall) cascare; (NAUT) beccheggiare; **to** ~ **a tent** piantare una tenda; **at this** ~ a questo ritmo.
pitch-black [pɪtʃ'blæk] adj nero(a) come la pece.
pitched battle [pɪtʃt-] n battaglia campale.
pitcher ['pɪtʃə*] n brocca.
pitchfork ['pɪtʃfɔːk] n forcone m.
piteous ['pɪtɪəs] adj pietoso(a).
pitfall ['pɪtfɔːl] n trappola.
pith [pɪθ] n (of plant) midollo; (of orange) parte f interna della scorza; (fig) essenza, succo; vigore m.
pithead ['pɪthɛd] n (BRIT) imbocco della miniera.
pithy ['pɪθɪ] adj conciso(a); vigoroso(a).
pitiable ['pɪtɪəbl] adj pietoso(a).
pitiful ['pɪtɪful] adj (touching) pietoso(a); (contemptible) miserabile.
pitifully ['pɪtɪfəlɪ] adv pietosamente; **it's** ~ **obvious** è penosamente chiaro.
pitiless ['pɪtɪlɪs] adj spietato(a).
pittance ['pɪtns] n miseria, magro salario.
pitted ['pɪtɪd] adj: ~ **with** (potholes) pieno(a) di; (chickenpox) butterato(a) da.
pity ['pɪtɪ] n pietà ♦ vt aver pietà di, compatire, commiserare; **to have** or **take** ~ **on sb** aver pietà di qn; **it is a** ~ **that you can't come** è un peccato che non possa venire; **what a** ~! che peccato!
pitying ['pɪtɪɪŋ] adj compassionevole.
pivot ['pɪvət] n perno ♦ vi imperniarsi.
pixel ['pɪksl] n (COMPUT) pixel m inv.
pixie ['pɪksɪ] n folletto.
pizza ['piːtsə] n pizza.
placard ['plækɑːd] n affisso.
placate [plə'keɪt] vt placare, calmare.
placatory [plə'keɪtərɪ] adj conciliante.
place [pleɪs] n posto, luogo; (proper position, rank, seat) posto; (house) casa, alloggio; (home): **at/to his** ~ a casa sua; (in street names): **Laurel P**~ via dei Lauri ♦ vt (object) posare, mettere; (identify) riconoscere; individuare; (goods) piazzare; **to take** ~ aver luogo; **out of** ~ (not suitable) inopportuno(a); **I feel rather out of** ~ **here** qui mi sento un po' fuori posto; **in the first** ~ in primo luogo; **to change** ~**s with sb** scambiare il posto con qn; **to put sb in his** ~ (fig) mettere a posto qn, mettere qn al suo posto; **from** ~ **to** ~ da un posto all'altro; **all over the** ~ dappertutto; **he's going** ~**s** (fig col) si sta facendo strada; **it is not my** ~ **to do it** non sta a me farlo; **how are you** ~**d next week?** com'è messo la settimana prossima?; **to** ~ **an order with sb (for)** (COMM) fare un'ordinazione a qn (di).
placebo [plə'siːbəu] n placebo m inv.
place mat n sottopiatto; (in linen etc) tovaglietta.
placement ['pleɪsmənt] n collocamento; (job) lavoro.
place name n toponimo.
placenta [plə'sɛntə] n placenta.
placid ['plæsɪd] adj placido(a), calmo(a).
placidity [plə'sɪdɪtɪ] n placidità.
plagiarism ['pleɪdʒərɪzəm] n plagio.
plagiarist ['pleɪdʒjərɪst] n plagiario/a.
plagiarize ['pleɪdʒjəraɪz] vt plagiare.
plague [pleɪg] n peste f ♦ vt tormentare; **to** ~ **sb with questions** assillare qn di domande.
plaice [pleɪs] n (pl inv) pianuzza.
plaid [plæd] n plaid m inv.
plain [pleɪn] adj (clear) chiaro(a), palese; (simple) semplice; (frank) franco(a), aperto(a); (not handsome) bruttino(a); (without seasoning etc) scondito(a); naturale; (in one colour) tinta unita inv ♦ adv francamente, chiaramente ♦ n pianura; **to make sth** ~ **to sb** far capire chiaramente qc a qn; **in** ~ **clothes** (police) in borghese.

plain chocolate n cioccolato fondente.
plainly ['pleınlı] adv chiaramente; (frankly) francamente.
plainness ['pleınnıs] n semplicità.
plain speaking n: **there has been some ~ between the two leaders** i due leader si sono parlati chiaro.
plaintiff ['pleıntıf] n attore/trice.
plaintive ['pleıntıv] adj (voice, song) lamentoso(a); (look) struggente.
plait [plæt] n treccia ♦ vt intrecciare; **to ~ one's hair** farsi una treccia (or le trecce).
plan [plæn] n pianta; (scheme) progetto, piano ♦ vt (think in advance) progettare; (prepare) organizzare; (intend) avere in progetto ♦ vi: **to ~ (for)** far piani or progetti (per); **to ~ to do** progettare di fare, avere l'intenzione di fare; **how long do you ~ to stay?** quanto conta di restare?
plane [pleın] n (AVIAT) aereo; (tree) platano; (tool) pialla; (ART, MATH etc) piano ♦ adj piano(a), piatto(a) ♦ vt (with tool) piallare.
planet ['plænıt] n pianeta m.
planetarium [plænı'tɛərıəm] n planetario.
plank [plæŋk] n tavola, asse f.
plankton ['plæŋktən] n plancton m.
planned economy [plænd-] n economia pianificata.
planner ['plænə*] n pianificatore/trice; (chart) calendario; **town** or (US) **city ~** urbanista m/f.
planning ['plænıŋ] n progettazione f; (POL, ECON) pianificazione f; **family ~** pianificazione delle nascite.
planning permission n (BRIT) permesso di costruzione.
plant [plɑ:nt] n pianta; (machinery) impianto; (factory) fabbrica ♦ vt piantare; (bomb) mettere.
plantation [plæn'teıʃən] n piantagione f.
plant pot n (BRIT) vaso (di fiori).
plaque [plæk] n placca.
plasma ['plæzmə] n plasma m.
plaster ['plɑ:stə*] n intonaco; (also: **~ of Paris**) gesso; (BRIT: also: **sticking ~**) cerotto ♦ vt intonacare; ingessare; (cover): **to ~ with** coprire di; (col: mud etc) impiastricciare; **in ~** (BRIT: leg etc) ingessato(a).
plasterboard ['plɑ:stəbɔ:d] n lastra di cartone ingessato.
plaster cast n (MED) ingessatura, gesso; (model, statue) modello in gesso.
plastered ['plɑ:stəd] adj (col) ubriaco(a) fradicio(a).
plasterer ['plɑ:stərə*] n intonacatore m.
plastic ['plæstık] n plastica ♦ adj (made of

plastic) di or in plastica; (flexible) plastico(a), malleabile; (art) plastico(a).
plastic bag n sacchetto di plastica.
plastic bullet n pallottola di plastica.
plastic explosive n esplosivo al plastico.
plasticine ® ['plæstısi:n] n plastilina ®.
plastic surgery n chirurgia plastica.
plate [pleıt] n (dish) piatto; (sheet of metal) lamiera; (PHOT) lastra; (TYP) cliché m inv; (in book) tavola; (on door) targa, targhetta; (AUT: number ~) targa; (dishes): **gold ~** vasellame m d'oro; **silver ~** argenteria.
plateau ['plætəʊ, -z] n altipiano.
plateful ['pleıtful] n piatto.
plate glass n vetro piano.
platen ['plætən] n (on typewriter, printer) rullo.
plate rack n scolapiatti m inv.
platform ['plætfɔ:m] n (stage, at meeting) palco; (BRIT: on bus) piattaforma; (RAIL) marciapiede m; **the train leaves from ~ 7** il treno parte dal binario 7.
platform ticket n (BRIT) biglietto d'ingresso ai binari.
platinum ['plætınəm] n platino.
platitude ['plætıtju:d] n luogo comune.
platoon [plə'tu:n] n plotone m.
platter ['plætə*] n piatto.
plaudits ['plɔ:dıts] npl plauso.
plausible ['plɔ:zıbl] adj plausibile, credibile; (person) convincente.
play [pleı] n gioco; (THEAT) commedia ♦ vt (game) giocare a; (team, opponent) giocare contro; (instrument, piece of music) suonare; (play, part) interpretare ♦ vi giocare; suonare; recitare; **to bring** or **call into ~** (plan) mettere in azione; (emotions) esprimere; **~ on words** gioco di parole; **to ~ a trick on sb** fare uno scherzo a qn; **they're ~ing at soldiers** stanno giocando ai soldati; **to ~ for time** (fig) cercare di guadagnar tempo; **to ~ into sb's hands** (fig) fare il gioco di qn.
▶**play about, play around** vi (person) divertirsi; **to ~ about** or **around with** (fiddle with) giocherellare con; (idea) accarezzare.
▶**play along** vi: **to ~ along with** (fig: person) stare al gioco di; (: plan, idea) fingere di assecondare ♦ vt (fig): **to ~ sb along** tenere qn in sospeso.
▶**play back** vt riascoltare, risentire.
▶**play down** vt minimizzare.
▶**play on** vt fus (sb's feelings, credulity) giocare su; **to ~ on sb's nerves** dare sui nervi a qn.
▶**play up** vi (cause trouble) fare i capricci.

playact ['pleɪækt] vi fare la commedia.

playboy ['pleɪbɔɪ] n playboy m inv.

played-out ['pleɪd'aut] adj spossato(a).

player ['pleɪə*] n giocatore/trice; (THEAT) attore/trice; (MUS) musicista m/f.

playful ['pleɪful] adj giocoso(a).

playgoer ['pleɪɡəuə*] n assiduo(a) frequentatore(trice) di teatri.

playground ['pleɪɡraund] n (in school) cortile m per la ricreazione; (in park) parco m giochi inv.

playgroup ['pleɪɡruːp] n giardino d'infanzia.

playing card ['pleɪɪŋ-] n carta da gioco.

playing field ['pleɪɪŋ-] n campo sportivo.

playmaker ['pleɪmeɪkə*] n (SPORT) playmaker m inv.

playmate ['pleɪmeɪt] n compagno/a di gioco.

play-off ['pleɪɔf] n (SPORT) bella.

playpen ['pleɪpɛn] n box m inv.

playroom ['pleɪruːm] n stanza dei giochi.

plaything ['pleɪθɪŋ] n giocattolo.

playtime ['pleɪtaɪm] n (SCOL) ricreazione f.

playwright ['pleɪraɪt] n drammaturgo/a.

plc abbr (BRIT) see public limited company.

plea [pliː] n (request) preghiera, domanda; (excuse) scusa; (LAW) (argomento di) difesa.

plea bargaining n (LAW) patteggiamento.

plead [pliːd] vt patrocinare; (give as excuse) addurre a pretesto ♦ vi (LAW) perorare la causa; (beg): to ~ with sb implorare qn; to ~ for sth implorare qc; to ~ guilty/not guilty (defendant) dichiararsi colpevole/innocente.

pleasant ['plɛznt] adj piacevole, gradevole.

pleasantly ['plɛzntlɪ] adv piacevolmente.

pleasantry ['plɛzntrɪ] n (joke) scherzo; (polite remark): to exchange pleasantries scambiarsi i convenevoli.

please [pliːz] vt piacere a ♦ vi (think fit): do as you ~ faccia come le pare; ~! per piacere!; my bill, ~ il conto, per piacere; ~ yourself! come ti (or le) pare!; ~ don't cry! ti prego, non piangere!

pleased [pliːzd] adj (happy) felice, lieto(a); ~ (with) (satisfied) contento(a) (di); we are ~ to inform you that ... abbiamo il piacere di informarla che ...; ~ to meet you! piacere!

pleasing ['pliːzɪŋ] adj piacevole, che fa piacere.

pleasurable ['plɛʒərəbl] adj molto piacevole, molto gradevole.

pleasure ['plɛʒə*] n piacere m; with ~ con piacere, volentieri; "it's a ~" "prego"; is this trip for business or ~? è un viaggio

d'affari o di piacere?

pleasure cruise n crociera.

pleat [pliːt] n piega.

plebiscite ['plɛbɪsɪt] n plebiscito.

plebs [plɛbz] npl (pej) plebe f.

plectrum ['plɛktrəm] n plettro.

pledge [plɛdʒ] n pegno; (promise) promessa ♦ vt impegnare; promettere; to ~ support for sb impegnarsi a sostenere qn; to ~ sb to secrecy far promettere a qn di mantenere il segreto.

plenary ['pliːnərɪ] adj plenario(a); in ~ session in seduta plenaria.

plentiful ['plɛntɪful] adj abbondante, copioso(a).

plenty ['plɛntɪ] n abbondanza; ~ of tanto(a), molto(a); un'abbondanza di; we've got ~ of time to get there abbiamo un sacco di tempo per arrivarci.

pleurisy ['pluərɪsɪ] n pleurite f.

Plexiglas ® ['plɛksɪɡlɑːs] n (US) plexiglas ® m.

pliable ['plaɪəbl] adj flessibile; (person) malleabile.

pliers ['plaɪəz] npl pinza.

plight [plaɪt] n situazione f critica.

plimsolls ['plɪmsəlz] npl (BRIT) scarpe fpl da tennis.

plinth [plɪnθ] n plinto; piedistallo.

PLO n abbr (= Palestine Liberation Organization) O.L.P. f.

plod [plɒd] vi camminare a stento; (fig) sgobbare.

plodder ['plɒdə*] n sgobbone m.

plodding ['plɒdɪŋ] adj lento(a) e pesante.

plonk [plɒŋk] (col) n (BRIT: wine) vino da poco ♦ vt: to ~ sth down buttare giù qc bruscamente.

plot [plɒt] n congiura, cospirazione f; (of story, play) trama; (of land) lotto ♦ vt (mark out) fare la pianta di; rilevare; (: diagram etc) tracciare; (conspire) congiurare, cospirare ♦ vi congiurare; a vegetable ~ (BRIT) un orticello.

plotter ['plɒtə*] n cospiratore/trice; (COMPUT) plotter m inv, tracciatore m di curve.

plough, (US) plow [plau] n aratro ♦ vt (earth) arare.

►plough back vt (COMM) reinvestire.

►plough through vt fus (snow etc) procedere a fatica in.

ploughing, (US) plowing ['plauɪŋ] n aratura.

ploughman, (US) plowman ['plaumən] n aratore m; ~'s lunch (BRIT) semplice pasto a base di pane e formaggio.

ploy [plɔɪ] n stratagemma m.

pls *abbr* = **please.**

pluck [plʌk] *vt* (*fruit*) cogliere; (*musical instrument*) pizzicare; (*bird*) spennare ♦ *n* coraggio, fegato; **to ~ one's eyebrows** depilarsi le sopracciglia; **to ~ up courage** farsi coraggio.

plucky ['plʌkɪ] *adj* coraggioso(a).

plug [plʌg] *n* tappo; (*ELEC*) spina; (*AUT*: *also*: **spark(ing) ~**) candela ♦ *vt* (*hole*) tappare; (*col*: *advertise*) spingere; **to give sb/sth a ~** fare pubblicità a qn/qc.

▶**plug in** (*ELEC*) *vt* inserire la spina ♦ *vt* attaccare a una presa.

plughole ['plʌghəul] *n* (*BRIT*) scarico.

plum [plʌm] *n* (*fruit*) susina ♦ *cpd*: **~ job** (*col*) impiego ottimo *or* favoloso.

plumage ['pluːmɪdʒ] *n* piume *fpl*, piumaggio.

plumb [plʌm] *adj* verticale ♦ *n* piombo ♦ *adv* (*exactly*) esattamente ♦ *vt* sondare.

▶**plumb in** *vt* (*washing machine*) collegare all'impianto idraulico.

plumber ['plʌmə*] *n* idraulico.

plumbing ['plʌmɪŋ] *n* (*trade*) lavoro di idraulico; (*piping*) tubature *fpl*.

plumbline ['plʌmlaɪn] *n* filo a piombo.

plume [pluːm] *n* piuma, penna; (*decorative*) pennacchio.

plummet ['plʌmɪt] *vi* cadere a piombo.

plump [plʌmp] *adj* grassoccio(a) ♦ *vt*: **to ~ sth (down) on** lasciar cadere qc di peso su.

▶**plump for** *vt fus* (*col*) decidersi per.

▶**plump up** *vt* sprimacciare.

plunder ['plʌndə*] *n* saccheggio ♦ *vt* saccheggiare.

plunge [plʌndʒ] *n* tuffo ♦ *vt* immergere ♦ *vi* (*dive*) tuffarsi; (*fall*) cadere, precipitare; **to take the ~** (*fig*) saltare il fosso; **to ~ a room into darkness** far piombare una stanza nel buio.

plunger ['plʌndʒə*] *n* (*for blocked sink*) sturalavandini *m inv*.

plunging ['plʌndʒɪŋ] *adj* (*neckline*) profondo(a).

plural ['pluərl] *adj*, *n* plurale (*m*).

plus [plʌs] *n* (*also*: **~ sign**) segno più ♦ *prep* più ♦ *adj* (*MATH*, *ELEC*) positivo(a); **ten/ twenty ~** più di dieci/venti; **it's a ~** (*fig*) è un vantaggio.

plus fours *npl* calzoni *mpl* alla zuava.

plush [plʌʃ] *adj* lussuoso(a) ♦ *n* felpa.

plutonium [pluːˈtəunɪəm] *n* plutonio.

ply [plaɪ] *n* (*of wool*) capo; (*of wood*) strato ♦ *vt* (*tool*) maneggiare; (*a trade*) esercitare ♦ *vi* (*ship*) fare il servizio; **three ~** (**wool**) lana a tre capi; **to ~ sb with drink** dare da bere continuamente a qn.

plywood ['plaɪwud] *n* legno compensato.

PM *n abbr* (*BRIT*) *see* **prime minister.**

p.m. *adv abbr* (= *post meridiem*) del pomeriggio.

PMS *n abbr* (= *premenstrual syndrome*) sindrome *f* premestruale.

PMT *n abbr* (= *premenstrual tension*) sindrome *f* premestruale.

pneumatic [njuːˈmætɪk] *adj* pneumatico(a); **~ drill** martello pneumatico.

pneumonia [njuːˈməunɪə] *n* polmonite *f*.

PO *n abbr* (= *Post Office*) ≈ P.T. (= *Poste e Telegrafi*) ♦ *abbr* (*NAUT*) = **petty officer.**

po *abbr* = **postal order.**

POA *n abbr* (*BRIT*: = *Prison Officers' Association*) *sindacato delle guardie carcerarie.*

poach [pəutʃ] *vt* (*cook*) affogare; (*steal*) cacciare (*or* pescare) di frodo ♦ *vi* fare il bracconiere.

poached [pəutʃt] *adj* (*egg*) affogato(a).

poacher ['pəutʃə*] *n* bracconiere *m*.

poaching ['pəutʃɪŋ] *n* caccia (*or* pesca) di frodo.

PO box *n abbr see* **post office box.**

pocket ['pɔkɪt] *n* tasca ♦ *vt* intascare; **to be out of ~** rimetterci; **to be £5 in/out of ~** (*BRIT*) trovarsi con 5 sterline in più/in meno; **air ~** vuoto d'aria.

pocketbook ['pɔkɪtbuk] *n* (*wallet*) portafoglio; (*notebook*) taccuino; (*US*: *handbag*) busta.

pocket knife *n* temperino.

pocket money *n* paghetta, settimana.

pockmarked ['pɔkmɑːkt] *adj* (*face*) butterato(a).

pod [pɔd] *n* guscio ♦ *vt* sgusciare.

podgy ['pɔdʒɪ] *adj* grassoccio(a).

podiatrist [pɔˈdiːətrɪst] *n* (*US*) callista *m/f*.

podiatry [pɔˈdiːətrɪ] *n* (*US*) mestiere *m* di callista.

podium ['pəudɪəm] *n* podio.

POE *n abbr* = *port of embarkation*; *port of entry.*

poem ['pəuɪm] *n* poesia.

poet ['pəuɪt] *n* poeta/essa.

poetic [pəuˈetɪk] *adj* poetico(a).

poet laureate *n* (*BRIT*) poeta *m* laureato; *see boxed note.*

POET LAUREATE

In Gran Bretagna il **poet laureate** *è un poeta che riceve un vitalizio dalla casa reale britannica e che ha l'incarico di scrivere delle poesie commemorative in occasione delle festività ufficiali.*

poetry ['pəuɪtrɪ] *n* poesia.

poignant ['pɔɪnjənt] *adj* struggente.

point [pɔɪnt] *n* (*gen*) punto; (*tip*: *of needle etc*) punta; (*BRIT ELEC*: *also*: **power** ~) presa (di corrente); (*in time*) punto, momento; (*SCOL*) voto; (*main idea, important part*) nocciolo; (*also*: **decimal** ~): **2 ~ 3 (2.3)** 2 virgola 3 (2,3) ◊ *vt* (*show*) indicare; (*gun etc*): **to ~ sth at** puntare qc contro ◊ *vi* mostrare a dito; ~**s** *npl* (*AUT*) puntine *fpl*; (*RAIL*) scambio; **to ~ to** indicare; (*fig*) dimostrare; **to make a ~** fare un'osservazione; **to get the ~** capire; **to come to the ~** venire al fatto; **when it comes to the ~** quando si arriva al dunque; **to be on the ~ of doing sth** essere sul punto di *or* stare (proprio) per fare qc; **to be beside the ~** non entrarci; **to make a ~ of doing sth** non mancare di fare qc; **there's no ~ (in doing)** è inutile (fare); **in ~ of fact** a dire il vero; **that's the whole ~!** precisamente!, sta tutto lì!; **you've got a ~ there!** giusto!, ha ragione!; **the train stops at Carlisle and all ~s south** il treno ferma a Carlisle e in tutte le stazioni a sud di Carlisle; **good ~s** vantaggi *mpl*; (*of person*) qualità *fpl*; ~ **of departure** (*also fig*) punto di partenza; ~ **of order** mozione *f* d'ordine; ~ **of sale** (*COMM*) punto di vendita; ~ **of view** punto di vista.

▶**point out** *vt* far notare.

point-blank ['pɔɪnt'blæŋk] *adv* (*also*: **at ~ range**) a bruciapelo; (*fig*) categoricamente.

pointed ['pɔɪntɪd] *adj* (*shape*) aguzzo(a), appuntito(a); (*remark*) specifico(a).

pointedly ['pɔɪntɪdlɪ] *adv* in maniera inequivocabile.

pointer ['pɔɪntə*] *n* (*stick*) bacchetta; (*needle*) lancetta; (*clue*) indizio; (*advice*) consiglio; (*dog*) pointer *m*, cane *m* da punta.

pointless ['pɔɪntlɪs] *adj* inutile, vano(a).

poise [pɔɪz] *n* (*balance*) equilibrio; (*of head, body*) portamento; (*calmness*) calma ◊ *vt* tenere in equilibrio; **to be ~d for** (*fig*) essere pronto(a) a.

poison ['pɔɪzn] *n* veleno ◊ *vt* avvelenare.

poisoning ['pɔɪzniŋ] *n* avvelenamento.

poisonous ['pɔɪznəs] *adj* velenoso(a); (*fumes*) venefico(a), tossico(a); (*ideas, literature*) pernicioso(a); (*rumours, individual*) perfido(a).

poke [pəuk] *vt* (*fire*) attizzare; (*jab with finger, stick etc*) punzecchiare; (*put*): **to ~ sth in(to)** spingere qc dentro ◊ *n* (*jab*) colpetto; (*with elbow*) gomitata; **to ~**

one's head out of the window mettere la testa fuori dalla finestra; **to ~ fun at sb** prendere in giro qn.

▶**poke about** *vi* frugare.

poker ['pəukə*] *n* attizzatoio; (*CARDS*) poker *m*.

poker-faced ['pəukə'feɪst] *adj* dal viso impassibile.

poky ['pəukɪ] *adj* piccolo(a) e stretto(a).

Poland ['pəulənd] *n* Polonia.

polar ['pəulə*] *adj* polare.

polar bear *n* orso bianco.

polarize ['pəuləraɪz] *vt* polarizzare.

Pole [pəul] *n* polacco/a.

pole [pəul] *n* (*of wood*) palo; (*ELEC, GEO*) polo.

poleaxe, (US) poleax ['pəulæks] *vt* (*fig*) stendere.

pole bean *n* (*US*) fagiolino.

polecat ['pəulkæt] *n* puzzola; (*US*) moffetta.

Pol. Econ. ['pɔlɪkɔn] *n abbr* = *political economy*.

polemic [pɔ'lɛmɪk] *n* polemica.

pole star *n* stella polare.

pole vault *n* salto con l'asta.

police [pə'liːs] *n* polizia ◊ *vt* mantenere l'ordine in; (*streets, city, frontier*) presidiare; **a large number of ~ were hurt** molti poliziotti sono rimasti feriti.

police car *n* macchina della polizia.

police constable (PC) *n* (*BRIT*) agente *m* di polizia.

police department *n* (*US*) dipartimento di polizia.

police force *n* corpo di polizia, polizia.

policeman [pə'liːsmən] *n* poliziotto, agente *m* di polizia.

police officer *n* = **police constable**.

police record *n*: **to have a ~** avere precedenti penali.

police state *n* stato di polizia.

police station *n* posto di polizia.

policewoman [pə'liːswumən] *n* donna *f* poliziotto *inv*.

policy ['pɔlɪsɪ] *n* politica; (*of newspaper, company*) linea di condotta, prassi *f inv*; (*also*: **insurance** ~) polizza (d'assicurazione); **to take out a ~** (*INSURANCE*) stipulare una polizza di assicurazione.

policy holder *n* assicurato/a.

policy-making ['pɔlɪsɪmeɪkɪŋ] *n* messa a punto di programmi.

polio ['pəulɪəu] *n* polio *f*.

Polish ['pəulɪʃ] *adj* polacco(a) ◊ *n* (*LING*) polacco.

polish ['pɔlɪʃ] *n* (*for shoes*) lucido; (*for floor*)

cera; (for nails) smalto; (shine) lucentezza, lustro; (fig: refinement) raffinatezza ♦ vt lucidare; (fig: improve) raffinare.
▶polish off vt (work) sbrigare; (food) mangiarsi.
polished ['pɔlɪʃt] adj (fig) raffinato(a).
polite [pə'laɪt] adj cortese; it's not ~ to do that non è educato or buona educazione fare questo.
politely [pə'laɪtlɪ] adv cortesemente.
politeness [pə'laɪtnɪs] n cortesia.
politic ['pɔlɪtɪk] adj diplomatico(a).
political [pə'lɪtɪkl] adj politico(a).
political asylum n asilo politico.
politically [pə'lɪtɪklɪ] adv politicamente.
politically correct adj politicamente corretto(a).
politician [pɔlɪ'tɪʃən] n politico.
politics ['pɔlɪtɪks] n politica ♦ npl idee fpl politiche.
polka ['pɔlkə] n polca.
polka dot n pois m inv.
poll [pəul] n scrutinio; (votes cast) voti mpl; (also: opinion ~) sondaggio (d'opinioni) ♦ vt ottenere; to go to the ~s (voters) andare alle urne; (government) indire le elezioni.
pollen ['pɔlən] n polline m.
pollen count n tasso di polline nell'aria.
pollination [pɔlɪ'neɪʃən] n impollinazione f.
polling ['pəulɪŋ] n (BRIT POL) votazione f, votazioni fpl; (TEL) interrogazione f ciclica.
polling booth n (BRIT) cabina elettorale.
polling day n (BRIT) giorno delle elezioni.
polling station n (BRIT) sezione f elettorale.
pollster ['pəulstə*] n chi esegue sondaggi d'opinione.
poll tax n (BRIT) imposta locale sulla persona fisica (non più in vigore).
pollutant [pə'lu:tənt] n sostanza inquinante.
pollute [pə'lu:t] vt inquinare.
pollution [pə'lu:ʃən] n inquinamento.
polo ['pəuləu] n polo.
polo neck n collo alto; (also: ~ sweater) dolcevita ♦ adj a collo alto.
poly ['pɔlɪ] n abbr (BRIT) = polytechnic.
poly bag n (BRIT col) borsa di plastica.
polyester [pɔlɪ'ɛstə*] n poliestere m.
polygamy [pə'lɪgəmɪ] n poligamia.
polygraph ['pɔlɪgrɑ:f] n macchina della verità.
Polynesia [pɔlɪ'ni:zɪə] n Polinesia.
Polynesian [pɔlɪ'ni:zɪən] adj, n polinesiano(a).
polyp ['pɔlɪp] n (MED) polipo.

polystyrene [pɔlɪ'staɪri:n] n polistirolo.
polytechnic [pɔlɪ'tɛknɪk] n (college) istituto superiore ad indirizzo tecnologico.
polythene ['pɔlɪθi:n] n politene m.
polythene bag n borsa di plastica.
polyurethane ['pɔlɪ'juərɪθeɪn] n poliuretano.
pomegranate ['pɔmɪgrænɪt] n melagrana.
pommel ['pɔml] n pomo ♦ vt = pummel.
pomp [pɔmp] n pompa, fasto.
pompom ['pɔmpɔm] n pompon m inv.
pompous ['pɔmpəs] adj pomposo(a); (person) pieno(a) di boria.
pond [pɔnd] n stagno; (in park) laghetto.
ponder ['pɔndə*] vi riflettere, meditare ♦ vt ponderare, riflettere su.
ponderous ['pɔndərəs] adj ponderoso(a), pesante.
pong [pɔŋ] (BRIT col) n puzzo ♦ vi puzzare.
pontiff ['pɔntɪf] n pontefice m.
pontificate [pɔn'tɪfɪkeɪt] vi (fig): to ~ (about) pontificare (su).
pontoon [pɔn'tu:n] n pontone m; (BRIT CARDS) ventuno.
pony ['pəunɪ] n pony m inv.
ponytail ['pəunɪteɪl] n coda di cavallo.
pony trekking [-trɛkɪŋ] n (BRIT) escursione f a cavallo.
poodle ['pu:dl] n barboncino, barbone m.
pooh-pooh ['pu:'pu:] vt deridere.
pool [pu:l] n (of rain) pozza; (pond) stagno; (artificial) vasca; (also: swimming ~) piscina; (sth shared) fondo comune; (COMM: consortium) pool m inv; (US: monopoly trust) trust m inv; (billiards) specie di biliardo a buca ♦ vt mettere in comune; typing ~, (US) secretary ~ servizio comune di dattilografia; to do the (football) ~s ≈ fare la schedina, giocare al totocalcio.
poor [puə*] adj povero(a); (mediocre) mediocre, cattivo(a) ♦ npl: the ~ i poveri.
poorly ['puəlɪ] adv poveramente; (badly) male ♦ adj indisposto(a), malato(a).
pop [pɔp] n (noise) schiocco; (MUS) musica pop; (US col: father) babbo; (col: drink) bevanda gasata ♦ vt (put) mettere (in fretta) ♦ vi scoppiare; (cork) schioccare; she ~ped her head out (of the window) sporse fuori la testa.
▶pop in vi passare.
▶pop out vi fare un salto fuori.
▶pop up vi apparire, sorgere.
pop concert n concerto m pop inv.
popcorn ['pɔpkɔ:n] n pop-corn m.
pope [pəup] n papa m.
poplar ['pɔplə*] n pioppo.
poplin ['pɔplɪn] n popeline f.

popper ['pɔpə*] n (BRIT) bottone m automatico, bottone a pressione.

poppy ['pɔpɪ] n papavero.

poppycock ['pɔpɪkɔk] n (col) scempiaggini fpl.

Popsicle ® ['pɔpsɪkl] n (US) ghiacciolo.

populace ['pɔpjuləs] n popolo.

popular ['pɔpjulə*] adj popolare; (fashionable) in voga; **to be ~ (with)** (person) essere benvoluto(a) or ben visto(a) (da); (decision) essere gradito(a) (a); **a ~ song** una canzone di successo.

popularity [pɔpju'lærɪtɪ] n popolarità.

popularize ['pɔpjuləraɪz] vt divulgare; (science) volgarizzare.

populate ['pɔpjuleɪt] vt popolare.

population [pɔpju'leɪʃən] n popolazione f.

population explosion n forte espansione f demografica.

populous ['pɔpjuləs] adj popolato(a).

pop-up menu ['pɔpʌp-] n (COMPUT) menu m inv a comparsa.

porcelain ['pɔːslɪn] n porcellana.

porch [pɔːtʃ] n veranda.

porcupine ['pɔːkjupaɪn] n porcospino.

pore [pɔː*] n poro ♦ vi: **to ~ over** essere immerso(a) in.

pork [pɔːk] n carne f di maiale.

pork chop n braciola or costoletta di maiale.

porn [pɔːn] (col) n pornografia ♦ adj porno inv.

pornographic [pɔːnə'græfɪk] adj pornografico(a).

pornography [pɔː'nɔgrəfɪ] n pornografia.

porous ['pɔːrəs] adj poroso(a).

porpoise ['pɔːpəs] n focena.

porridge ['pɔrɪdʒ] n porridge m.

port¹ [pɔːt] n porto; (opening in ship) portello; (NAUT: left side) babordo; (COMPUT) porta; **to ~ (NAUT)** a babordo; **~ of call** (porto di) scalo.

port² [pɔːt] n (wine) porto.

portable ['pɔːtəbl] adj portatile.

portal ['pɔːtl] n portale m.

portcullis [pɔːt'kʌlɪs] n saracinesca.

portent ['pɔːtɛnt] n presagio.

porter ['pɔːtə*] n (for luggage) facchino, portabagagli m inv; (doorkeeper) portiere m, portinaio; (US RAIL) addetto ai vagoni letto.

portfolio [pɔːt'fəulɪəu] n (POL: office; ECON) portafoglio; (of artist) raccolta dei propri lavori.

porthole ['pɔːthəul] n oblò m inv.

portico ['pɔːtɪkəu] n portico.

portion ['pɔːʃən] n porzione f.

portly ['pɔːtlɪ] adj corpulento(a).

portrait ['pɔːtreɪt] n ritratto.

portray [pɔː'treɪ] vt fare il ritratto di; (character on stage) rappresentare; (in writing) ritrarre.

portrayal ['pɔːtreɪəl] n ritratto; rappresentazione f.

Portugal ['pɔːtjugl] n Portogallo.

Portuguese [pɔːtju'giːz] adj portoghese ♦ n (pl inv) portoghese m/f; (LING) portoghese m.

Portuguese man-of-war [-mænəv'wɔː*] n (jellyfish) medusa.

pose [pəuz] n posa ♦ vi posare; (pretend): **to ~ as** atteggiarsi a, posare a ♦ vt porre; **to strike a ~** mettersi in posa.

poser ['pəuzə*] n domanda difficile; (person) = **poseur**.

poseur [pəu'zɜː*] n (pej) persona affettata.

posh [pɔʃ] adj (col) elegante; (family) per bene ♦ adv (col): **to talk ~** parlare in modo snob.

position [pə'zɪʃən] n posizione f; (job) posto ♦ vt mettere in posizione, collocare; **to be in a ~ to do sth** essere nella posizione di fare qc.

positive ['pɔzɪtɪv] adj positivo(a); (certain) sicuro(a), certo(a); (definite) preciso(a); definitivo(a).

posse ['pɔsɪ] n (US) drappello.

possess [pə'zɛs] vt possedere; **like one ~ed** come un ossesso; **whatever can have ~ed you?** cosa ti ha preso?

possession [pə'zɛʃən] n possesso; (object) bene m; **to take ~ of sth** impossessarsi or impadronirsi di qc.

possessive [pə'zɛsɪv] adj possessivo(a).

possessiveness [pə'zɛsɪvnɪs] n possessività.

possessor [pə'zɛsə*] n possessore/posseditrice.

possibility [pɔsɪ'bɪlɪtɪ] n possibilità f inv; **he's a ~ for the part** è uno dei candidati per la parte.

possible ['pɔsɪbl] adj possibile; **it is ~ to do it** è possibile farlo; **if ~** se possibile; **as big as ~** il più grande possibile; **as far as ~** nei limiti del possibile.

possibly ['pɔsɪblɪ] adv (perhaps) forse; **if you ~ can** se le è possibile; **I cannot ~ come** proprio non posso venire.

post [pəust] n (BRIT: mail, letters, delivery) posta; (: collection) levata; (job, situation) posto; (pole) palo; (trading ~) stazione f commerciale ♦ vt (BRIT: send by post) impostare; (MIL) appostare; (notice) affiggere; (BRIT: appoint): **to ~ to** assegnare a; **by ~** (BRIT) per posta; **by return of ~** (BRIT) a giro di posta; **to keep sb ~ed** tenere qn al corrente.

post... [pəust] *prefix* post...; ~**-1990** dopo il 1990.
postage ['pəustɪdʒ] *n* affrancatura.
postage stamp *n* francobollo.
postal ['pəustəl] *adj* postale.
postal order *n* vaglia *m inv* postale.
postbag ['pəustbæg] *n* (*BRIT*) sacco postale, sacco della posta.
postbox ['pəustbɔks] *n* cassetta delle lettere.
postcard ['pəustkɑːd] *n* cartolina.
postcode ['pəustkəud] *n* (*BRIT*) codice *m* (di avviamento) postale.
postdate ['pəust'deɪt] *vt* (*cheque*) postdatare.
poster ['pəustə*] *n* manifesto, affisso.
poste restante [pəust'rɛstɑ̃ːnt] *n* (*BRIT*) fermo posta *m*.
posterior [pɔs'tɪərɪə*] *n* (*col*) deretano, didietro.
posterity [pɔs'tɛrɪtɪ] *n* posterità.
poster paint *n* tempera.
post exchange (PX) *n* (*US MIL*) spaccio militare.
post-free [pəust'friː] *adj, adv* (*BRIT*) franco di porto.
postgraduate ['pəust'grædjuət] *n* laureato/a che continua gli studi.
posthumous ['pɔstjuməs] *adj* postumo(a).
posthumously ['pɔstjuməslɪ] *adv* dopo la mia (*or* sua *etc*) morte.
posting ['pəustɪŋ] *n* (*BRIT*) incarico.
postman ['pəustmən] *n* postino.
postmark ['pəustmɑːk] *n* bollo *or* timbro postale.
postmaster ['pəustmɑːstə*] *n* direttore *m* di un ufficio postale.
Postmaster General *n* ≈ ministro delle Poste.
postmistress ['pəustmɪstrɪs] *n* direttrice *f* di un ufficio postale.
post-mortem [pəust'mɔːtəm] *n* autopsia; (*fig*) analisi *f inv* a posteriori.
postnatal ['pəust'neɪtl] *adj* post-parto *inv*.
post office *n* (*building*) ufficio postale; (*organization*) poste *fpl*.
post office box (PO box) *n* casella postale (C.P.).
post-paid ['pəust'peɪd] *adj* già affrancato(a).
postpone [pəust'pəun] *vt* rinviare.
postponement [pəust'pəunmənt] *n* rinvio.
postscript ['pəustskrɪpt] *n* poscritto.
postulate ['pɔstjuleɪt] *vt* postulare.
posture ['pɔstʃə*] *n* portamento; (*pose*) posa, atteggiamento ♦ *vi* posare.
postwar ['pəust'wɔː*] *adj* del dopoguerra.
posy ['pəuzɪ] *n* mazzetto di fiori.

pot [pɔt] *n* (*for cooking*) pentola; casseruola; (*for plants, jam*) vaso; (*piece of pottery*) ceramica; (*col: marijuana*) erba ♦ *vt* (*plant*) piantare in vaso; **to go to** ~ (*col*) andare in malora; ~**s of** (*BRIT col*) un sacco di.
potash ['pɔtæʃ] *n* potassa.
potassium [pə'tæsɪəm] *n* potassio.
potato, ~**es** [pə'teɪtəu] *n* patata.
potato crisps, (*US*) **potato chips** *npl* patatine *fpl*.
potato flour *n* fecola di patate.
potato peeler *n* sbucciapatate *m inv*.
potbellied ['pɔtbɛlɪd] *adj* (*from overeating*) panciuto(a); (*from malnutrition*) dal ventre gonfio.
potency ['pəutnsɪ] *n* potenza; (*of drink*) forza.
potent ['pəutnt] *adj* potente, forte.
potentate ['pəutnteɪt] *n* potentato.
potential [pə'tɛnʃl] *adj* potenziale ♦ *n* possibilità *fpl*; **to have** ~ essere promettente.
potentially [pə'tɛnʃəlɪ] *adv* potenzialmente.
pothole ['pɔthəul] *n* (*in road*) buca; (*BRIT: underground*) marmitta.
potholer ['pɔthəulə*] *n* (*BRIT*) speleologo/a.
potholing ['pɔthəulɪŋ] *n* (*BRIT*): **to go** ~ fare la speleologia.
potion ['pəuʃən] *n* pozione *f*.
potluck [pɔt'lʌk] *n*: **to take** ~ tentare la sorte.
potpourri [pəu'puriː] *n* (*dried petals etc*) miscuglio di petali essiccati profumati; (*fig*) pot-pourri *m inv*.
pot roast *n* brasato.
potshot ['pɔtʃɔt] *n*: **to take** ~**s at** tirare a casaccio contro.
potted ['pɔtɪd] *adj* (*food*) in conserva; (*plant*) in vaso; (*fig: shortened*) condensato(a).
potter ['pɔtə*] *n* vasaio ♦ *vi* (*BRIT*): **to** ~ **around,** ~ **about** lavoracchiare; **to** ~ **round the house** sbrigare con calma le faccende di casa; ~**'s wheel** tornio (da vasaio).
pottery ['pɔtərɪ] *n* ceramiche *fpl*; **a piece of** ~ una ceramica.
potty ['pɔtɪ] *adj* (*BRIT col: mad*) tocco(a) ♦ *n* (*child's*) vasino.
potty-trained ['pɔtɪtreɪnd] *adj* che ha imparato a farla nel vasino.
pouch [pautʃ] *n* borsa; (*ZOOL*) marsupio.
pouf(fe) [puːf] *n* (*stool*) pouf *m inv*.
poultice ['pəultɪs] *n* impiastro, cataplasma *m*.
poultry ['pəultrɪ] *n* pollame *m*.
poultry farm *n* azienda avicola.
poultry farmer *n* pollicoltore/trice.

pounce [pauns] vi: **to ~ (on)** balzare addosso (a), piombare (su) ♦ n balzo.

pound [paund] n (weight: = 453g, 16 ounces) libbra; (money: = 100 pence) (lira) sterlina; (for dogs) canile m municipale ♦ vt (beat) battere; (crush) pestare, polverizzare ♦ vi (beat) battere, martellare; **half a ~** mezza libbra; **a five-~ note** una banconota da cinque sterline.

pounding ['paundɪŋ] n: **to take a ~** (fig) prendere una batosta.

pound sterling n sterlina.

pour [pɔː*] vt versare ♦ vi riversarsi; (rain) piovere a dirotto.

▶**pour away, pour off** vt vuotare.

▶**pour in** vi (people) entrare in fiotto; **to come ~ing in** (water) entrare a fiotti; (letters) arrivare a valanghe; (cars, people) affluire in gran quantità.

▶**pour out** vi (people) riversarsi fuori ♦ vt vuotare; versare.

pouring ['pɔːrɪŋ] adj: **~ rain** pioggia torrenziale.

pout [paut] vi sporgere le labbra; fare il broncio.

poverty ['pɔvətɪ] n povertà, miseria.

poverty line n soglia di povertà.

poverty-stricken ['pɔvətɪstrɪkən] adj molto povero(a), misero(a).

poverty trap n (BRIT) circolo vizioso della povertà.

POW n abbr = **prisoner of war**.

powder ['paudə*] n polvere f ♦ vt spolverizzare; (face) incipriare; **~ed milk** latte m in polvere; **to ~ one's nose** incipriarsi il naso; (euphemism) andare alla toilette.

powder compact n portacipria m inv.

powder keg n (fig: area) polveriera; (: situation) situazione f esplosiva.

powder puff n piumino della cipria.

powder room n toilette f inv (per signore).

powdery ['paudərɪ] adj polveroso(a).

power ['pauə*] n (strength) potenza, forza; (ability, POL: of party, leader) potere m; (MATH) potenza; (ELEC) corrente f ♦ vt fornire di energia; azionare; **to be in ~** essere al potere; **to do all in one's ~ to help sb** fare tutto quello che si può per aiutare qn; **the world ~s** le grandi potenze; **mental ~s** capacità fpl mentali.

powerboat ['pauəbəut] n (BRIT) motobarca, imbarcazione f a motore.

power cut n (BRIT) interruzione f or mancanza di corrente.

powered ['pauəd] adj: **~ by** azionato(a) da; **nuclear-~ submarine** sottomarino a propulsione atomica.

power failure n guasto alla linea elettrica.

powerful ['pauəful] adj potente, forte.

powerhouse ['pauəhaus] n (fig: person) persona molto dinamica; **a ~ of ideas** una miniera di idee.

powerless ['pauəlɪs] adj impotente, senza potere.

power line n linea elettrica.

power of attorney n procura.

power point n (BRIT) presa di corrente.

power station n centrale f elettrica.

power steering n (AUT: also: **power-assisted steering**) servosterzo.

powwow ['pauwau] n riunione f.

pp abbr (= pages) pp.; (= per procurationem: by proxy): **~ J. Smith** per il Signor J. Smith.

PPE n abbr (BRIT SCOL: = philosophy, politics, and economics) corso di laurea.

PPS n abbr (BRIT: = parliamentary private secretary) parlamentare che assiste un ministro; = post postscriptum.

PQ abbr (Canada) = Province of Quebec.

PR n abbr see **proportional representation**; **public relations** ♦ abbr (US) = Puerto Rico.

Pr. abbr = **prince**.

practicability [præktɪkə'bɪlɪtɪ] n praticabilità.

practicable ['præktɪkəbl] adj (scheme) praticabile.

practical ['præktɪkl] adj pratico(a).

practicality [præktɪ'kælɪtɪ] n (of plan) fattibilità; (of person) senso pratico; **practicalities** dettagli mpl pratici.

practical joke n beffa.

practically ['præktɪklɪ] adv (almost) quasi, praticamente.

practice ['præktɪs] n pratica; (of profession) esercizio; (at football etc) allenamento; (business) gabinetto; clientela ♦ vt, vi (US) = **practise; in ~** (in reality) in pratica; **out of ~** fuori esercizio; **2 hours' piano ~** 2 ore di esercizio al pianoforte; **it's common ~** è d'uso; **to put sth into ~** mettere qc in pratica; **target ~** pratica di tiro.

practice match n partita di allenamento.

practise, (US) practice ['præktɪs] vt (work at: piano, one's backhand etc) esercitarsi a; (train for: skiing, running etc) allenarsi a; (a sport, religion) praticare; (method) usare; (profession) esercitare ♦ vi esercitarsi; (train) allenarsi; **to ~ for a match** allenarsi per una partita.

practised ['præktɪst] adj (BRIT: person) esperto(a); (: performance) da virtuoso(a); (: liar) matricolato(a); **with a ~ eye** con occhio esperto.

practising ['præktɪsɪŋ] adj (Christian etc)
praticante; (lawyer) che esercita la
professione; (homosexual) attivo(a).
practitioner [præk'tɪʃənə*] n professionista
m/f; (MED) medico.
pragmatic [præg'mætɪk] adj
prammatico(a).
Prague [prɑːg] n Praga.
prairie ['prɛərɪ] n prateria.
praise [preɪz] n elogio, lode f ♦ vt elogiare,
lodare.
praiseworthy ['preɪzwɔːðɪ] adj lodevole.
pram [præm] n (BRIT) carrozzina.
prance [prɑːns] vi (horse) impennarsi.
prank [præŋk] n burla.
prat [præt] n (BRIT col) cretino/a.
prattle ['prætl] vi cinguettare.
prawn [prɔːn] n gamberetto.
pray [preɪ] vi pregare.
prayer [prɛə*] n preghiera.
prayer book n libro di preghiere.
pre... [priː] prefix pre...; ~-1970 prima del
1970.
preach [priːtʃ] vt, vi predicare; **to ~ at sb**
fare la predica a qn.
preacher ['priːtʃə*] n predicatore/trice;
(US: minister) pastore m.
preamble [prɪ'æmbl] n preambolo.
prearranged [priːə'reɪndʒd] adj
organizzato(a) in anticipo.
precarious [prɪ'kɛərɪəs] adj precario(a).
precaution [prɪ'kɔːʃən] n precauzione f.
precautionary [prɪ'kɔːʃənərɪ] adj (measure)
precauzionale.
precede [prɪ'siːd] vt, vi precedere.
precedence ['presɪdəns] n precedenza; **to
take ~ over** avere la precedenza su.
precedent ['presɪdənt] n precedente m; **to
establish** or **set a ~** creare un
precedente.
preceding [prɪ'siːdɪŋ] adj precedente.
precept ['priːsept] n precetto.
precinct ['priːsɪŋkt] n (round cathedral)
recinto; (US: district) circoscrizione f; ~**s**
npl (neighbourhood) dintorni mpl, vicinanze
fpl; **pedestrian ~** zona pedonale; **shopping
~** (BRIT) centro commerciale.
precious ['preʃəs] adj prezioso(a) ♦ adv (col):
~ **little/few** ben poco/pochi; **your ~ dog**
(ironic) il suo amatissimo cane.
precipice ['presɪpɪs] n precipizio.
precipitate adj [prɪ'sɪpɪtɪt] (hasty)
precipitoso(a) ♦ vt [prɪ'sɪpɪteɪt]
accelerare.
precipitation [prɪsɪpɪ'teɪʃən] n
precipitazione f.
precipitous [prɪ'sɪpɪtəs] adj (steep) erto(a),
ripido(a).

précis, pl **précis** ['preɪsiː, -z] n riassunto.
precise [prɪ'saɪs] adj preciso(a).
precisely [prɪ'saɪslɪ] adv precisamente; ~!
appunto!
precision [prɪ'sɪʒən] n precisione f.
preclude [prɪ'kluːd] vt precludere,
impedire; **to ~ sb from doing** impedire a
qn di fare.
precocious [prɪ'kəuʃəs] adj precoce.
preconceived [priːkən'siːvd] adj (idea)
preconcetto(a).
preconception [priːkən'sepʃən] n
preconcetto.
precondition [priːkən'dɪʃən] n condizione f
necessaria.
precursor [priː'kəːsə*] n precursore m.
predate [priː'deɪt] vt (precede) precedere.
predator ['predətə*] n predatore m.
predatory ['predətərɪ] adj predatore(trice).
predecessor ['priːdɪsesə*] n predecessore/
a.
predestination [priːdestɪ'neɪʃən] n
predestinazione f.
predetermine [priːdɪ'təːmɪn] vt
predeterminare.
predicament [prɪ'dɪkəmənt] n situazione f
difficile.
predicate ['predɪkɪt] n (LING) predicativo.
predict [prɪ'dɪkt] vt predire.
predictable [prɪ'dɪktəbl] adj prevedibile.
predictably [prɪ'dɪktəblɪ] adv (behave,
react) in modo prevedibile; ~ **she didn't
arrive** come era da prevedere, non è
arrivata.
prediction [prɪ'dɪkʃən] n predizione f.
predispose [priːdɪs'pəuz] vt predisporre.
predominance [prɪ'dɒmɪnəns] n
predominanza.
predominant [prɪ'dɒmɪnənt] adj
predominante.
predominantly [prɪ'dɒmɪnəntlɪ] adv in
maggior parte; soprattutto.
predominate [prɪ'dɒmɪneɪt] vi
predominare.
pre-eminent [priː'emɪnənt] adj preminente.
pre-empt [prɪ'empt] vt acquistare per
diritto di prelazione; (fig) anticipare.
pre-emptive [prɪ'emptɪv] adj: ~ **strike**
azione f preventiva.
preen [priːn] vt: **to ~ itself** (bird) lisciarsi le
penne; **to ~ o.s.** agghindarsi.
prefab ['priːfæb] n casa prefabbricata.
prefabricated [priː'fæbrikeɪtɪd] adj
prefabbricato(a).
preface ['prefəs] n prefazione f.
prefect ['priːfekt] n (BRIT: in school)
studente/essa con funzioni disciplinari;
(in Italy) prefetto.

prefer [prɪˈfəː*] vt preferire; (LAW: charges, complaint) sporgere; (: action) intentare; **to ~ coffee to tea** preferire il caffè al tè.
preferable [ˈprɛfrəbl] adj preferibile.
preferably [ˈprɛfrəblɪ] adv preferibilmente.
preference [ˈprɛfrəns] n preferenza; **in ~ to sth** piuttosto che qc.
preference shares npl (BRIT) azioni fpl privilegiate.
preferential [prɛfəˈrɛnʃəl] adj preferenziale; **~ treatment** trattamento di favore.
preferred stock [prɪˈfəːd-] npl (US) = **preference shares**.
prefix [ˈpriːfɪks] n prefisso.
pregnancy [ˈprɛgnənsɪ] n gravidanza.
pregnancy test n test m inv di gravidanza.
pregnant [ˈprɛgnənt] adj incinta adj f; (animal) gravido(a); (fig: remark, pause) significativo(a); **3 months ~** incinta di 3 mesi.
prehistoric [ˈpriːhɪsˈtɔrɪk] adj preistorico(a).
prehistory [priːˈhɪstərɪ] n preistoria.
prejudge [priːˈdʒʌdʒ] vt pregiudicare.
prejudice [ˈprɛdʒudɪs] n pregiudizio; (harm) torto, danno ♦ vt pregiudicare, ledere; (bias): **to ~ sb in favour of/against** disporre bene/male qn verso.
prejudiced [ˈprɛdʒudɪst] adj (person) pieno(a) di pregiudizi; (view) prevenuto(a); **to be ~ against sb/sth** essere prevenuto contro qn/qc.
prelate [ˈprɛlət] n prelato.
preliminaries [prɪˈlɪmɪnərɪz] npl preliminari mpl.
preliminary [prɪˈlɪmɪnərɪ] adj preliminare.
prelude [ˈprɛljuːd] n preludio.
premarital [ˈpriːˈmærɪtl] adj prematrimoniale.
premature [ˈprɛmətʃuə*] adj prematuro(a); (arrival) (molto) anticipato(a); **you are being a little ~** è un po' troppo precipitoso.
premeditated [priːˈmɛdɪteɪtɪd] adj premeditato(a).
premeditation [priːmɛdɪˈteɪʃən] n premeditazione f.
premenstrual tension [priːˈmɛnstruəl-] n (MED) tensione f premestruale.
premier [ˈprɛmɪə*] adj primo(a) ♦ n (POL) primo ministro.
première [ˈprɛmɪɛə*] n prima.
premise [ˈprɛmɪs] n premessa.
premises [ˈprɛmɪsɪz] npl locale m; **on the ~** sul posto; **business ~** locali commerciali.

premium [ˈpriːmɪəm] n premio; **to be at a ~** (fig: housing etc) essere ricercatissimo; **to sell at a ~** (shares) vendere sopra la pari.
premium bond n (BRIT) obbligazione f a premio.
premium deal n (COMM) offerta speciale.
premium gasoline n (US) super f.
premonition [prɛməˈnɪʃən] n premonizione f.
preoccupation [priːɔkjuˈpeɪʃən] n preoccupazione f.
preoccupied [priːˈɔkjupaɪd] adj preoccupato(a).
prep [prɛp] n abbr (SCOL: = preparation) studio ♦ adj abbr: **~ school** = **preparatory school**.
prepackaged [priːˈpækɪdʒd] adj già impacchettato(a).
prepaid [priːˈpeɪd] adj pagato(a) in anticipo; (envelope) affrancato(a).
preparation [prɛpəˈreɪʃən] n preparazione f; **~s** npl (for trip, war) preparativi mpl; **in ~ for sth** in vista di qc.
preparatory [prɪˈpærətərɪ] adj preparatorio(a); **~ to sth/to doing sth** prima di qc/di fare qc.
preparatory school n (BRIT) scuola elementare privata; (US) scuola superiore privata; see boxed note.

PREPARATORY SCHOOL

In Gran Bretagna, la **prep(aratory) school** è una scuola privata frequentata da bambini dai 7 ai 13 anni in vista dell'iscrizione alla "public school". Negli Stati Uniti, invece, è una scuola superiore privata che prepara i ragazzi che si iscriveranno al "college".

---

prepare [prɪˈpɛə*] vt preparare ♦ vi: **to ~ for** prepararsi a.
prepared [prɪˈpɛəd] adj: **~ for** preparato(a) a; **~ to** pronto(a) a; **to be ~ to help sb** (willing) essere disposto or pronto ad aiutare qn.
preponderance [prɪˈpɔndərns] n preponderanza.
preposition [prɛpəˈzɪʃən] n preposizione f.
prepossessing [priːpəˈzɛsɪŋ] adj simpatico(a), attraente.
preposterous [prɪˈpɔstərəs] adj assurdo(a).
prerecord [ˈpriːrɪˈkɔːd] vt registrare in anticipo; **~ed broadcast** trasmissione f registrata; **~ed cassette** (musi)cassetta.
prerequisite [priːˈrɛkwɪzɪt] n requisito

indispensabile.

prerogative [prɪˈrɔɡətɪv] *n* prerogativa.

presbyterian [prɛzbɪˈtɪərɪən] *adj, n* presbiteriano(a).

presbytery [ˈprɛzbɪtərɪ] *n* presbiterio.

preschool [ˈpriːˈskuːl] *adj (age)* prescolastico(a); *(child)* in età prescolastica.

prescribe [prɪˈskraɪb] *vt* prescrivere; *(MED)* ordinare; ~**d books** *(BRIT SCOL)* testi *mpl* in programma.

prescription [prɪˈskrɪpʃən] *n* prescrizione *f*; *(MED)* ricetta; **to make up** *or (US)* **fill a** ~ preparare *or* fare una ricetta; *"only available on* ~*" "ottenibile solo dietro presentazione di ricetta medica".

prescription charges *npl (BRIT)* ticket *m inv.*

prescriptive [prɪˈskrɪptɪv] *adj* normativo(a).

presence [ˈprɛzns] *n* presenza; ~ **of mind** presenza di spirito.

present [ˈprɛznt] *adj* presente; *(wife, residence, job)* attuale ♦ *n* regalo; *(also:* ~ **tense)** tempo presente ♦ *vt* [prɪˈzɛnt] presentare; *(give)*: **to** ~ **sb with sth** offrire qc a qn; **to be** ~ **at** essere presente a; **those** ~ i presenti; **at** ~ al momento; **to make sb a** ~ **of sth** regalare qc a qn.

presentable [prɪˈzɛntəbl] *adj* presentabile.

presentation [prɛznˈteɪʃən] *n* presentazione *f*; *(gift)* regalo, dono; *(ceremony)* consegna ufficiale; **on** ~ **of the voucher** dietro presentazione del buono.

present-day [ˈprɛzntdeɪ] *adj* attuale.

presenter [prɪˈzɛntə*] *n (BRIT RADIO, TV)* presentatore/trice.

presently [ˈprɛzntlɪ] *adv (soon)* fra poco, presto; *(at present)* al momento; *(US: now)* adesso, ora.

preservation [prɛzəˈveɪʃən] *n* preservazione *f*, conservazione *f*.

preservative [prɪˈzəːvətɪv] *n* conservante *m*.

preserve [prɪˈzəːv] *vt (keep safe)* preservare, proteggere; *(maintain)* conservare; *(food)* mettere in conserva ♦ *n (for game, fish)* riserva; *(often pl: jam)* marmellata; *(: fruit)* frutta sciroppata.

preside [prɪˈzaɪd] *vi* presiedere.

presidency [ˈprɛzɪdənsɪ] *n* presidenza; *(US: of company)* direzione *f*.

president [ˈprɛzɪdənt] *n* presidente *m*; *(US: of company)* direttore/trice generale.

presidential [prɛzɪˈdɛnʃl] *adj* presidenziale.

press [prɛs] *n (tool, machine)* pressa; *(for wine)* torchio; *(newspapers)* stampa;

(crowd) folla ♦ *vt (push)* premere, pigiare; *(doorbell)* suonare; *(squeeze)* spremere; *(: hand)* stringere; *(clothes: iron)* stirare; *(pursue)* incalzare; *(insist)*: **to** ~ **sth on sb** far accettare qc da qn; *(urge, entreat)*: **to** ~ **sb to do** *or* **into doing sth** fare pressione su qn affinché faccia qc ♦ *vi* premere; accalcare; **to go to** ~ *(newspaper)* andare in macchina; **to be in the** ~ *(in the newspapers)* essere sui giornali; **we are** ~**ed for time** ci manca il tempo; **to** ~ **for sth** insistere per avere qc; **to** ~ **sb for an answer** insistere perché qn risponda; **to** ~ **charges against sb** *(LAW)* sporgere una denuncia contro qn.

▶**press ahead** *vi*: **to** ~ **ahead (with)** andare avanti (con).

▶**press on** *vi* continuare.

press agency *n* agenzia di stampa.

press clipping *n* ritaglio di giornale.

press conference *n* conferenza stampa.

press cutting *n* = **press clipping**.

press-gang [ˈprɛsɡæŋ] *vt*: **to** ~ **sb into doing sth** costringere qn a una viva forza a fare qc.

pressing [ˈprɛsɪŋ] *adj* urgente ♦ *n* stiratura.

press officer *n* addetto/a stampa *inv.*

press release *n* comunicato stampa.

press stud *n (BRIT)* bottone *m* a pressione.

press-up [ˈprɛsʌp] *n (BRIT)* flessione *f* sulle braccia.

pressure [ˈprɛʃə*] *n* pressione *f* ♦ *vt* = **to put** ~ **on; high/low** ~ alta/bassa pressione; **to put** ~ **on sb** fare pressione su qn.

pressure cooker *n* pentola a pressione.

pressure gauge *n* manometro.

pressure group *n* gruppo di pressione.

pressurize [ˈprɛʃəraɪz] *vt* pressurizzare; *(fig)*: **to** ~ **sb (into doing sth)** fare delle pressioni su qn (per costringerlo a fare qc).

pressurized [ˈprɛʃəraɪzd] *adj* pressurizzato(a).

Prestel ® [ˈprɛstɛl] *n* Videotel ® *m inv.*

prestige [prɛsˈtiːʒ] *n* prestigio.

prestigious [prɛsˈtɪdʒəs] *adj* prestigioso(a).

presumably [prɪˈzjuːməblɪ] *adv* presumibilmente; ~ **he did it** penso *or* presumo che l'abbia fatto.

presume [prɪˈzjuːm] *vt* supporre; **to** ~ **to do** *(dare)* permettersi di fare.

presumption [prɪˈzʌmpʃən] *n* presunzione *f*; *(boldness)* audacia.

presumptuous [prɪˈzʌmpʃəs] *adj* presuntuoso(a).

presuppose [priːsəˈpəuz] *vt* presupporre.

pre-tax [priːˈtæks] *adj* al lordo d'imposta.

pretence, (*US*) **pretense** [prɪˈtɛns] *n* (*claim*) pretesa; (*pretext*) pretesto, scusa; **to make a ~ of doing** far finta di fare; **on** *or* **under the ~ of doing sth** con il pretesto *or* la scusa di fare qc; **she is devoid of all ~** non si nasconde dietro false apparenze.

pretend [prɪˈtɛnd] *vt* (*feign*) fingere ♦ *vi* far finta; (*claim*): **to ~ to sth** pretendere a qc; **to ~ to do** far finta di fare.

pretense [prɪˈtɛns] *n* (*US*) = **pretence.**

pretension [prɪˈtɛnʃən] *n* (*claim*) pretesa; **to have no ~s to sth/to being sth** non avere la pretesa di avere qc/di essere qc.

pretentious [prɪˈtɛnʃəs] *adj* pretenzioso(a).

preterite [ˈprɛtərɪt] *n* preterito.

pretext [ˈpriːtɛkst] *n* pretesto; **on** *or* **under the ~ of doing sth** col pretesto di fare qc.

pretty [ˈprɪtɪ] *adj* grazioso(a), carino(a) ♦ *adv* abbastanza, assai.

prevail [prɪˈveɪl] *vi* (*win, be usual*) prevalere; (*persuade*): **to ~ (up)on sb to do** persuadere qn a fare.

prevailing [prɪˈveɪlɪŋ] *adj* dominante.

prevalent [ˈprɛvələnt] *adj* (*belief*) predominante; (*customs*) diffuso(a); (*fashion*) corrente; (*disease*) comune.

prevarication [prɪværɪˈkeɪʃən] *n* tergiversazione *f*.

prevent [prɪˈvɛnt] *vt* prevenire; **to ~ sb from doing** impedire a qn di fare.

preventable [prɪˈvɛntəbl] *adj* evitabile.

preventative [prɪˈvɛntətɪv] *adj* preventivo(a).

prevention [prɪˈvɛnʃən] *n* prevenzione *f*.

preventive [prɪˈvɛntɪv] *adj* preventivo(a).

preview [ˈpriːvjuː] *n* (*of film*) anteprima.

previous [ˈpriːvɪəs] *adj* precedente; anteriore; **I have a ~ engagement** ho già (preso) un impegno; **~ to doing** prima di fare.

previously [ˈpriːvɪəslɪ] *adv* prima.

prewar [ˈpriːˈwɔː*] *adj* anteguerra *inv*.

prey [preɪ] *n* preda ♦ *vi*: **to ~ on** far preda di; **it was ~ing on his mind** gli rodeva la mente.

price [praɪs] *n* prezzo; (*BETTING: odds*) quotazione *f* ♦ *vt* (*goods*) fissare il prezzo di; valutare; **what is the ~ of ...?** quanto costa ...?; **to go up** *or* **rise in ~** salire *or* aumentare di prezzo; **to put a ~ on sth** valutare *or* stimare qc; **he regained his freedom, but at a ~** ha riconquistato la sua libertà, ma a caro prezzo; **what ~ his promises now?** (*BRIT*) a che valgono ora

le sue promesse?; **to be ~d out of the market** (*article*) essere così caro da diventare invendibile; (*producer, nation*) non poter sostenere la concorrenza.

price control *n* controllo dei prezzi.

price-cutting [ˈpraɪskʌtɪŋ] *n* riduzione *f* dei prezzi.

priceless [ˈpraɪslɪs] *adj* di valore inestimabile; (*col: amusing*) impagabile, spassosissimo(a).

price list *n* listino (dei) prezzi.

price range *n* gamma di prezzi; **it's within my ~** rientra nelle mie possibilità.

price tag *n* cartellino del prezzo.

price war *n* guerra dei prezzi.

pricey [ˈpraɪsɪ] *adj* (*col*) caruccio(a).

prick [prɪk] *n* puntura ♦ *vt* pungere; **to ~ up one's ears** drizzare gli orecchi.

prickle [ˈprɪkl] *n* (*of plant*) spina; (*sensation*) pizzicore *m*.

prickly [ˈprɪklɪ] *adj* spinoso(a); (*fig: person*) permaloso(a); **~ heat** sudamina.

pride [praɪd] *n* orgoglio; superbia ♦ *vt*: **to ~ o.s. on** essere orgoglioso(a) di; vantarsi di; **to take (a) ~ in** tenere molto a; essere orgoglioso di; **to take a ~ in doing** andare orgoglioso di fare; **to have ~ of place** (*BRIT*) essere al primo posto.

priest [priːst] *n* prete *m*, sacerdote *m*.

priestess [ˈpriːstɪs] *n* sacerdotessa.

priesthood [ˈpriːsthud] *n* sacerdozio.

prig [prɪg] *n*: **he's a ~** è compiaciuto di se stesso.

prim [prɪm] *adj* pudico(a); contegnoso(a).

primacy [ˈpraɪməsɪ] *n* primato.

prima facie [ˈpraɪməˈfeɪʃɪ] *adj*: **to have a ~ case** (*LAW*) presentare una causa in apparenza fondata.

primal [ˈpraɪməl] *adj* primitivo(a).

primarily [ˈpraɪmərɪlɪ] *adv* principalmente.

primary [ˈpraɪmərɪ] *adj* primario(a); (*first in importance*) primo(a) ♦ *n* (*US: election*) primarie *fpl*; *see boxed note*.

PRIMARY

Negli Stati Uniti, attraverso le **primaries** *viene fatta una prima scrematura dei candidati dei partiti alle elezioni presidenziali. La scelta definitiva del candidato da presentare alla presidenza si basa sui risultati delle* **primaries** *e ha luogo durante le "Conventions" dei partiti, che si tengono in luglio e in agosto.*

---

primary colour *n* colore *m* fondamentale.

primary school *n* (*BRIT*) scuola elementare; *see boxed note*.

PRIMARY SCHOOL

In Gran Bretagna la primary school *è la scuola elementare, frequentata dai bambini dai 5 agli 11 anni di età. È suddivisa in "infant school" (5-7 anni) e "junior school" (7-11 anni); vedi anche* secondary school.

primate n (REL: ['praɪmɪt], ZOOL: ['praɪmeɪt]) primate m.

prime [praɪm] adj primario(a), fondamentale; (excellent) di prima qualità ♦ n: **in the ~ of life** nel fiore della vita ♦ vt (gun) innescare; (pump) adescare; (fig) mettere al corrente.

prime minister (PM) n primo ministro.

primer ['praɪmə*] n (book) testo elementare; (paint) vernice f base inv.

prime time n (RADIO, TV) fascia di massimo ascolto.

primeval [praɪ'miːvl] adj primitivo(a).

primitive ['prɪmɪtɪv] adj primitivo(a).

primrose ['prɪmrəuz] n primavera.

primus (stove) ® ['praɪməs-] n (BRIT) fornello a petrolio.

prince [prɪns] n principe m.

prince charming n principe m azzurro.

princess [prɪn'sɛs] n principessa.

principal ['prɪnsɪpl] adj principale ♦ n (of school, college etc) preside m/f; (money) capitale m; (in play) protagonista m/f.

principality [prɪnsɪ'pælɪtɪ] n principato.

principally ['prɪnsɪplɪ] adv principalmente.

principle ['prɪnsɪpl] n principio; **in ~** in linea di principio; **on ~** per principio.

print [prɪnt] n (mark) impronta; (letters) caratteri mpl; (fabric) tessuto stampato; (ART, PHOT) stampa ♦ vt imprimere; (publish) stampare, pubblicare; (write in capitals) scrivere in stampatello; **out of ~** esaurito(a).
▶**print out** vt (COMPUT) stampare.

printed circuit board (PCB) [prɪntɪd-] n circuito stampato.

printed matter [prɪntɪd-] n stampe fpl.

printer ['prɪntə*] n tipografo; (machine) stampante m.

printhead ['prɪnthɛd] n testa di stampa.

printing ['prɪntɪŋ] n stampa.

printing press n macchina tipografica.

print-out ['prɪntaut] n tabulato.

print wheel n margherita.

prior ['praɪə*] adj precedente ♦ n (REL) priore m; **~ to doing** prima di fare; **without ~ notice** senza preavviso; **to have a ~ claim to sth** avere un diritto di precedenza su qc.

priority [praɪ'ɔrɪtɪ] n priorità f inv; precedenza; **to have** or **take ~ over sth** avere la precedenza su qc.

priory ['praɪərɪ] n monastero.

prise [praɪz] vt: **to ~ open** forzare.

prism ['prɪzəm] n prisma m.

prison ['prɪzn] n prigione f.

prison camp n campo di prigionia.

prisoner ['prɪznə*] n prigioniero/a; **to take sb ~** far prigioniero qn; **the ~ at the bar** l'accusato, l'imputato; **~ of war** prigioniero/a di guerra.

prissy ['prɪsɪ] adj per benino.

pristine ['prɪstiːn] adj originario(a); intatto(a); puro(a).

privacy ['prɪvəsɪ] n solitudine f, intimità.

private ['praɪvɪt] adj privato(a); personale ♦ n soldato semplice; **"~"** (on envelope) "riservata"; **in ~** in privato; **in (his) ~ life** nella vita privata; **he is a very ~ person** è una persona molto riservata; **~ hearing** (LAW) udienza a porte chiuse; **to be in ~ practice** essere medico non convenzionato (con la mutua).

private enterprise n iniziativa privata.

private eye n investigatore m privato.

private limited company n (BRIT) società per azioni non quotata in Borsa.

privately ['praɪvɪtlɪ] adv in privato; (within o.s.) dentro di sé.

private parts npl (ANAT) parti fpl intime.

private property n proprietà privata.

private school n scuola privata.

privation [praɪ'veɪʃən] n (state) privazione f; (hardship) privazioni fpl, stenti mpl.

privatize ['praɪvɪtaɪz] vt privatizzare.

privet ['prɪvɪt] n ligustro.

privilege ['prɪvɪlɪdʒ] n privilegio.

privileged ['prɪvɪlɪdʒd] adj privilegiato(a); **to be ~ to do sth** avere il privilegio or l'onore di fare qc.

privy ['prɪvɪ] adj: **to be ~ to** essere al corrente di.

Privy Council n (BRIT) Consiglio della Corona; see boxed note.

PRIVY COUNCIL

Il **Privy Council**, *un gruppo di consiglieri del re, era il principale organo di governo durante il regno dei Tudor e degli Stuart. Col tempo ha perso la sua importanza e oggi è un organo senza potere effettivo formato da ministri e altre personalità politiche ed ecclesiastiche.*

Privy Councillor n (BRIT) Consigliere m della Corona.

prize [praɪz] n premio ♦ adj (example, idiot)

perfetto(a); (*bull, novel*) premiato(a) ♦ *vt*
apprezzare, pregiare.
prize-fighter ['praɪzfaɪtə*] *n* pugile *m* (*che si
batte per conquistare un premio*).
prize giving *n* premiazione *f*.
prize money *n* soldi *mpl* del premio.
prizewinner ['praɪzwɪnə*] *n* premiato/a.
prizewinning ['praɪzwɪnɪŋ] *adj* vincente;
(*novel, essay etc*) premiato(a).
PRO *n abbr* = **public relations officer**.
pro [prəu] *n* (*SPORT*) professionista *m/f*; **the
~s and cons** il pro e il contro.
pro- [prəu] *prefix* (*in favour of*) filo...; **~Soviet**
adj filosovietico(a).
pro-active [prəu'æktɪv] *adj*: **to be ~** agire
d'iniziativa.
probability [prɔbə'bɪlɪtɪ] *n* probabilità *f inv*;
in all ~ con ogni probabilità.
probable ['prɔbəbl] *adj* probabile; **it is ~/
hardly ~ that** ... è probabile/poco
probabile che ... + *sub*.
probably ['prɔbəblɪ] *adv* probabilmente.
probate ['prəubɪt] *n* (*LAW*) omologazione *f*
(*di un testamento*).
probation [prə'beɪʃən] *n* (*in employment*)
periodo di prova; (*LAW*) libertà vigilata;
(*REL*) probandato; **on ~** (*employee*) in
prova; (*LAW*) in libertà vigilata.
probationary [prəu'beɪʃənərɪ] *adj*: **~ period**
periodo di prova.
probe [prəub] *n* (*MED, SPACE*) sonda;
(*enquiry*) indagine *f*, investigazione *f* ♦ *vt*
sondare, esplorare; indagare.
probity ['prəubɪtɪ] *n* probità.
problem ['prɔbləm] *n* problema *m*; **to have
~s with the car** avere dei problemi con la
macchina; **what's the ~?** che cosa c'è?; **I
had no ~ in finding her** non mi è stato
difficile trovarla; **no ~!** ma certamente!,
non c'è problema!
problematic [prɔblə'mætɪk] *adj*
problematico(a).
problem-solving ['prɔbləmsɔlvɪŋ] *n*
risoluzione *f* di problemi.
procedure [prə'siːdʒə*] *n* (*ADMIN, LAW*)
procedura; (*method*) metodo.
proceed [prə'siːd] *vi* (*go forward*) avanzare,
andare avanti; (*go about it*) procedere;
(*continue*): **to ~ (with)** continuare; **to ~ to**
andare a; passare a; **to ~ to do** mettersi a
fare; **to ~ against sb** (*LAW*) procedere
contro qn; **I am not sure how to ~** non so
bene come fare.
proceedings [prə'siːdɪŋz] *npl* misure *fpl*;
(*LAW*) procedimento; (*meeting*) riunione *f*;
(*records*) rendiconti *mpl*; atti *mpl*.
proceeds ['prəusiːdz] *npl* profitto, incasso.
process ['prəuses] *n* processo; (*method*)

metodo, sistema *m* ♦ *vt* trattare;
(*information*) elaborare ♦ *vi* [prə'sɛs] (*BRIT
formal*: *go in procession*) sfilare, procedere
in corteo; **we are in the ~ of moving to** ...
stiamo per trasferirci a ....
processed cheese, (*US*) **process cheese**
n formaggio fuso.
processing ['prəusɛsɪŋ] *n* trattamento;
elaborazione *f*.
procession [prə'sɛʃən] *n* processione *f*,
corteo; **funeral ~** corteo funebre.
pro-choice [prəu'tʃɔɪs] *adj* per la libertà di
scelta di gravidanza.
proclaim [prə'kleɪm] *vt* proclamare,
dichiarare.
proclamation [prɔklə'meɪʃən] *n*
proclamazione *f*.
proclivity [prə'klɪvɪtɪ] *n* tendenza,
propensione *f*.
procrastination [prəukræstɪ'neɪʃən] *n*
procrastinazione *f*.
procreation [prəukrɪ'eɪʃən] *n* procreazione
f.
Procurator Fiscal ['prɔkjurɛɪtə-] *n*
(*Scottish*) procuratore *m*.
procure [prə'kjuə*] *vt* (*for o.s.*) procurarsi;
(*for sb*) procurare.
procurement [prə'kjuəmənt] *n*
approvvigionamento.
prod [prɔd] *vt* dare un colpetto a ♦ *n* (*push,
jab*) colpetto.
prodigal ['prɔdɪgl] *adj* prodigo(a).
prodigious [prə'dɪdʒəs] *adj* prodigioso(a).
prodigy ['prɔdɪdʒɪ] *n* prodigio.
produce *n* ['prɔdjuːs] (*AGR*) prodotto,
prodotti *mpl* ♦ *vt* [prə'djuːs] produrre; (*to
show*) esibire, mostrare; (*proof of identity*)
produrre, fornire; (*cause*) cagionare,
causare; (*THEAT*) mettere in scena.
producer [prə'djuːsə*] *n* (*THEAT*) direttore/
trice; (*AGR, CINE*) produttore *m*.
product ['prɔdʌkt] *n* prodotto.
production [prə'dʌkʃən] *n* produzione *f*;
(*THEAT*) messa in scena; **to put into ~**
mettere in produzione.
production agreement *n* (*US*) accordo
sui tempi di produzione.
production line *n* catena di lavorazione.
production manager *n* production
manager *m inv*, direttore *m* della
produzione.
productive [prə'dʌktɪv] *adj* produttivo(a).
productivity [prɔdʌk'tɪvɪtɪ] *n* produttività.
productivity agreement *n* (*BRIT*) accordo
sui tempi di produzione.
productivity bonus *n* premio di
produzione.
Prof. *abbr* (= *professor*) Prof.

profane [prə'feɪn] *adj* profano(a); (*language*) empio(a).

profess [prə'fɛs] *vt* professare; **I do not** ~ **to be an expert** non pretendo di essere un esperto.

professed [prə'fɛst] *adj* (*self-declared*) dichiarato(a).

profession [prə'fɛʃən] *n* professione *f*; **the** ~**s** le professioni liberali.

professional [prə'fɛʃənl] *n* (*SPORT*) professionista *m/f* ♦ *adj* professionale; (*work*) da professionista; **he's a** ~ **man** è un professionista; **to take** ~ **advice** consultare un esperto.

professionalism [prə'fɛʃnəlɪzəm] *n* professionismo.

professionally [prə'fɛʃnəlɪ] *adv* professionalmente, in modo professionale; (*SPORT*: *play*) come professionista; **I only know him** ~ con lui ho solo rapporti di lavoro.

professor [prə'fɛsə*] *n* professore *m* (*titolare di una cattedra*); (*US*: *teacher*) professore/essa.

professorship [prə'fɛsəʃɪp] *n* cattedra.

proffer ['prɒfə*] *vt* (*remark*) profferire; (*apologies*) porgere, presentare; (*one's hand*) porgere.

proficiency [prə'fɪʃənsɪ] *n* competenza, abilità.

proficient [prə'fɪʃənt] *adj* competente, abile.

profile ['prəufaɪl] *n* profilo; **to keep a low** ~ (*fig*) cercare di passare inosservato *or* di non farsi notare troppo; **to maintain a high** ~ mettersi in mostra.

profit ['prɒfɪt] *n* profitto; beneficio ♦ *vi*: **to** ~ (**by** *or* **from**) approfittare (di); ~ **and loss account** conto perdite e profitti; **to make a** ~ realizzare un profitto; **to sell sth at a** ~ vendere qc con un utile.

profitability [prɒfɪtə'bɪlɪtɪ] *n* redditività.

profitable ['prɒfɪtəbl] *adj* redditizio(a); (*fig*: *beneficial*) vantaggioso(a); (*: meeting, visit*) fruttuoso(a).

profit centre *n* centro di profitto.

profiteering [prɒfɪ'tɪərɪŋ] *n* (*pej*) affarismo.

profit-making ['prɒfɪtmeɪkɪŋ] *adj* a scopo di lucro.

profit margin *n* margine *m* di profitto.

profit-sharing ['prɒfɪtʃɛərɪŋ] *n* compartecipazione *f* agli utili.

profits tax *n* (*BRIT*) imposta sugli utili.

profligate ['prɒflɪgɪt] *adj* (*dissolute*: *behaviour*) dissipato(a); (*: person*) debosciato(a); (*extravagant*): **he's very** ~ **with his money** è uno che sperpera i suoi soldi.

pro forma ['prəu'fɔːmə] *adv*: ~ **invoice** fattura proforma.

profound [prə'faund] *adj* profondo(a).

profuse [prə'fjuːs] *adj* infinito(a), abbondante.

profusely [prə'fjuːslɪ] *adv* con grande effusione.

profusion [prə'fjuːʒən] *n* profusione *f*, abbondanza.

progeny ['prɒdʒɪnɪ] *n* progenie *f*; discendenti *mpl*.

programme, (*US*) **program** ['prəugræm] *n* programma *m* ♦ *vt* programmare.

program(m)er ['prəugræmə*] *n* programmatore/trice.

program(m)ing ['prəugræmɪŋ] *n* programmazione *f*.

program(m)ing language *n* linguaggio di programmazione.

progress *n* ['prəugrɛs] progresso ♦ *vi* [prə'grɛs] (*go forward*) avanzare, procedere; (*in time*) procedere; (*also*: **make** ~) far progressi; **in** ~ in corso.

progression [prə'grɛʃən] *n* progressione *f*.

progressive [prə'grɛsɪv] *adj* progressivo(a); (*person*) progressista.

progressively [prə'grɛsɪvlɪ] *adv* progressivamente.

progress report *n* (*MED*) bollettino medico; (*ADMIN*) rendiconto dei lavori.

prohibit [prə'hɪbɪt] *vt* proibire, vietare; **to** ~ **sb from doing sth** vietare *or* proibire a qn di fare qc; "**smoking** ~**ed**" "vietato fumare".

prohibition [prəuɪ'bɪʃən] *n* (*US*) proibizionismo.

prohibitive [prə'hɪbɪtɪv] *adj* (*price etc*) proibitivo(a).

project *n* ['prɒdʒɛkt] (*plan*) piano; (*venture*) progetto; (*SCOL*) studio, ricerca ♦ *vb* [prə'dʒɛkt] *vt* proiettare ♦ *vi* (*stick out*) sporgere.

projectile [prə'dʒɛktaɪl] *n* proiettile *m*.

projection [prə'dʒɛkʃən] *n* proiezione *f*; sporgenza.

projectionist [prə'dʒɛkʃənɪst] *n* (*CINE*) proiezionista *m/f*.

projection room *n* (*CINE*) cabina *or* sala di proiezione.

projector [prə'dʒɛktə*] *n* proiettore *m*.

proletarian [prəulɪ'tɛərɪən] *adj*, *n* proletario(a).

proletariat [prəulɪ'tɛərɪət] *n* proletariato.

pro-life [prəu'laɪf] *adj* per il diritto alla vita.

proliferate [prə'lɪfəreɪt] *vi* proliferare.

proliferation [prəlɪfə'reɪʃən] *n* proliferazione *f.*

prolific [prə'lɪfɪk] *adj* prolifico(a).

prologue, (*US*) **prolog** ['prəʊlɒg] *n* prologo.

prolong [prə'lɒŋ] *vt* prolungare.

prom [prɒm] *n abbr* = **promenade, promenade concert;** (*US*: *ball*) ballo studentesco; *see boxed note.*

PROM

In Gran Bretagna i **Proms** *(= promenade concerts) sono concerti di musica classica, i più noti dei quali sono quelli eseguiti nella Royal Albert Hall a Londra. Prendono il nome dal fatto che in origine il pubblico li ascoltava stando in piedi o passeggiando. Negli Stati Uniti, invece, con* **prom** *si intende il ballo studentesco di un'università o di un college.*

---

promenade [prɒmə'nɑːd] *n* (*by sea*) lungomare *m.*

promenade concert *n* concerto (*con posti in piedi*).

promenade deck *n* (*NAUT*) ponte *m* di passeggiata.

prominence ['prɒmɪnəns] *n* prominenza; importanza.

prominent ['prɒmɪnənt] *adj* (*standing out*) prominente; (*important*) importante; **he is ~ in the field of** ... è un'autorità nel campo di ....

prominently ['prɒmɪnəntlɪ] *adv* (*display, set*) ben in vista; **he figured ~ in the case** ha avuto una parte di primo piano nella faccenda.

promiscuity [prɒmɪs'kjuːɪtɪ] *n* (*sexual*) rapporti *mpl* multipli.

promiscuous [prə'mɪskjuəs] *adj* (*sexually*) di facili costumi.

promise ['prɒmɪs] *n* promessa ♦ *vt, vi* promettere; **to make sb a ~** fare una promessa a qn; **a young man of ~** un giovane promettente; **to ~ (sb) to do sth** promettere (a qn) di fare qc.

promising ['prɒmɪsɪŋ] *adj* promettente.

promissory note ['prɒmɪsərɪ-] *n* pagherò *m inv.*

promontory ['prɒməntrɪ] *n* promontorio.

promote [prə'məʊt] *vt* promuovere; (*venture, event*) organizzare; (*product*) lanciare, reclamizzare; **the team was ~d to the second division** (*BRIT FOOTBALL*) la squadra è stata promossa in serie B.

promoter [prə'məʊtə*] *n* (*of sporting event*) organizzatore/trice; (*of cause etc*) sostenitore/trice.

promotion [prə'məʊʃən] *n* promozione *f.*

prompt [prɒmpt] *adj* rapido(a), svelto(a); puntuale; (*reply*) sollecito(a) ♦ *adv* (*punctually*) in punto ♦ *n* (*COMPUT*) guida ♦ *vt* incitare; provocare; (*THEAT*) suggerire a; **at 8 o'clock ~** alle 8 in punto; **to ~ sb to do** spingere qn a fare.

prompter ['prɒmptə*] *n* (*THEAT*) suggeritore *m.*

promptly ['prɒmptlɪ] *adv* prontamente; puntualmente.

promptness ['prɒmptnɪs] *n* prontezza; puntualità.

prone [prəʊn] *adj* (*lying*) prono(a); **~ to** propenso(a) a, incline a; **to be ~ to illness** essere soggetto(a) a malattie; **she is ~ to burst into tears if** ... può facilmente scoppiare in lacrime se ....

prong [prɒŋ] *n* rebbio, punta.

pronoun ['prəʊnaun] *n* pronome *m.*

pronounce [prə'nauns] *vt* pronunziare ♦ *vi:* **to ~ (up)on** pronunziare su; **they ~d him unfit to drive** lo hanno dichiarato inabile alla guida.

pronounced [prə'naunst] *adj* (*marked*) spiccato(a).

pronouncement [prə'naunsmənt] *n* dichiarazione *f.*

pronunciation [prənʌnsɪ'eɪʃən] *n* pronunzia.

proof [pruːf] *n* prova; (*of book*) bozza; (*PHOT*) provino; (*of alcohol*): **70% ~** ≈ 40° in volume ♦ *vt* (*tent, anorak*) impermeabilizzare ♦ *adj:* **~ against** a prova di.

proofreader ['pruːfriːdə*] *n* correttore/trice di bozze.

prop [prɒp] *n* sostegno, appoggio ♦ *vt* (*also:* **~ up**) sostenere, appoggiare; (*lean*): **to ~ sth against** appoggiare qc contro *or* a.

Prop. *abbr* (*COMM*) = **proprietor.**

propaganda [prɒpə'gændə] *n* propaganda.

propagation [prɒpə'geɪʃən] *n* propagazione *f.*

propel [prə'pɛl] *vt* spingere (in avanti), muovere.

propeller [prə'pɛlə*] *n* elica.

propelling pencil [prə'pɛlɪŋ-] *n* (*BRIT*) matita a mina.

propensity [prə'pɛnsɪtɪ] *n* tendenza.

proper ['prɒpə*] *adj* (*suited, right*) adatto(a), appropriato(a); (*seemly*) decente; (*authentic*) vero(a); (*col: real*) *n* + vero(a) e proprio(a); **to go through the ~ channels** (*ADMIN*) seguire la regolare procedura.

properly ['prɒpəlɪ] *adv* decentemente; (*really, thoroughly*) veramente.

proper noun *n* nome *m* proprio.

property ['prɒpətɪ] *n* (*things owned*) beni *mpl;*

(land, building, CHEM etc) proprietà *f inv*.
property developer *n (BRIT)* costruttore *m* edile.
property owner *n* proprietario/a.
property tax *n* imposta patrimoniale.
prophecy ['prɔfɪsɪ] *n* profezia.
prophesy ['prɔfɪsaɪ] *vt* predire, profetizzare.
prophet ['prɔfɪt] *n* profeta *m*.
prophetic [prə'fɛtɪk] *adj* profetico(a).
proportion [prə'pɔːʃən] *n* proporzione *f*; *(share)* parte *f* ♦ *vt* proporzionare, commisurare; **to be in/out of** ~ **to** *or* **with sth** essere in proporzione/sproporzionato rispetto a qc; **to see sth in** ~*(fig)* dare il giusto peso a qc.
proportional [prə'pɔːʃənl] *adj* proporzionale.
proportional representation (PR) *n* rappresentanza proporzionale.
proportionate [prə'pɔːʃənɪt] *adj* proporzionato(a).
proposal [prə'pəuzl] *n* proposta; *(plan)* progetto; *(of marriage)* proposta di matrimonio.
propose [prə'pəuz] *vt* proporre, suggerire ♦ *vi* fare una proposta di matrimonio; **to** ~ **to do** proporsi di fare, aver l'intenzione di fare.
proposer [prə'pəuzə*] *n (BRIT: of motion)* proponente *m/f*.
proposition [prɔpə'zɪʃən] *n* proposizione *f*; *(proposal)* proposta; **to make sb a** ~ proporre qualcosa a qn.
propound [prə'paund] *vt* proporre, presentare.
proprietary [prə'praɪətərɪ] *adj:* ~ **article** prodotto con marchio depositato; ~ **brand** marchio di fabbrica.
proprietor [prə'praɪətə*] *n* proprietario/a.
propriety [prə'praɪətɪ] *n (seemliness)* decoro, rispetto delle convenienze sociali.
propulsion [prə'pʌlʃən] *n* propulsione *f*.
pro rata [prəu'rɑːtə] *adv* in proporzione.
prosaic [prəu'zeɪɪk] *adj* prosaico(a).
Pros. Atty. *abbr (US)* = **prosecuting attorney.**
proscribe [prə'skraɪb] *vt* proscrivere.
prose [prəuz] *n* prosa; *(SCOL: translation)* traduzione *f* dalla madrelingua.
prosecute ['prɔsɪkjuːt] *vt* intentare azione contro.
prosecuting attorney ['prɔsɪkjuːtɪŋ-] *n (US)* ≈ procuratore *m*.
prosecution [prɔsɪ'kjuːʃən] *n (LAW)* azione *f* giudiziaria; *(accusing side)* accusa.
prosecutor ['prɔsɪkjuːtə*] *n (also:* **public** ~)

≈ procuratore *m* della Repubblica.
prospect *n* ['prɔspɛkt] prospettiva; *(hope)* speranza ♦ *vb* [prə'spɛkt] *vt* esplorare ♦ *vi:* **to** ~ **for gold** cercare l'oro; **there is every** ~ **of an early victory** tutto lascia prevedere una rapida vittoria; *see also* **prospects.**
prospecting [prə'spɛktɪŋ] *n* prospezione *f*.
prospective [prə'spɛktɪv] *adj (buyer)* probabile; *(legislation, son-in-law)* futuro(a).
prospector [prə'spɛktə*] *n* prospettore *m*; **gold** ~ cercatore *m* d'oro.
prospects ['prɔspɛkts] *npl (for work etc)* prospettive *fpl*.
prospectus [prə'spɛktəs] *n* prospetto, programma *m*.
prosper ['prɔspə*] *vi* prosperare.
prosperity [prɔ'spɛrɪtɪ] *n* prosperità.
prosperous ['prɔspərəs] *adj* prospero(a).
prostate ['prɔsteɪt] *n (also:* ~ **gland)** prostata, ghiandola prostatica.
prostitute ['prɔstɪtjuːt] *n* prostituta; **male** ~ uomo che si prostituisce.
prostitution [prɔstɪ'tjuːʃən] *n* prostituzione *f*.
prostrate *adj* ['prɔstreɪt] prostrato(a) ♦ *vt* [prɔ'streɪt]: **to** ~ **o.s.** *(before sb)* prostrarsi.
protagonist [prə'tægənɪst] *n* protagonista *m/f*.
protect [prə'tɛkt] *vt* proteggere, salvaguardare.
protection [prə'tɛkʃən] *n* protezione *f*; **to be under sb's** ~ essere sotto la protezione di qn.
protectionism [prə'tɛkʃənɪzəm] *n* protezionismo.
protection racket *n* racket *m inv*.
protective [prə'tɛktɪv] *adj* protettivo(a); ~ **custody** *(LAW)* protezione *f*.
protector [prə'tɛktə*] *n* protettore/trice.
protégé ['prəutɪʒeɪ] *n* protetto.
protégée ['prəutɪʒeɪ] *n* protetta.
protein ['prəutiːn] *n* proteina.
pro tem [prəu'tɛm] *adv abbr (= pro tempore: for the time being)* pro tempore.
protest *n* ['prəutɛst] protesta ♦ *vt, vi* [prə'tɛst] protestare; **to do sth under** ~ fare qc protestando; **to** ~ **against/about** protestare contro/per.
Protestant ['prɔtɪstənt] *adj, n* protestante *(m/f)*.
protester, protestor [prə'tɛstə*] *n (in demonstration)* dimostrante *m/f*.
protest march *n* marcia di protesta.
protocol ['prəutəkɔl] *n* protocollo.
prototype ['prəutətaɪp] *n* prototipo.
protracted [prə'træktɪd] *adj* tirato(a) per le

lunghe.

protractor [prə'træktə*] n (GEOM) goniometro.

protrude [prə'tru:d] vi sporgere.

protuberance [prə'tju:bərəns] n sporgenza.

proud [praud] adj fiero(a), orgoglioso(a); (pej) superbo(a); **to be** ~ **to do sth** essere onorato(a) di fare qc; **to do sb** ~ non far mancare nulla a qn; **to do o.s.** ~ trattarsi bene.

proudly ['praudlɪ] adv con orgoglio, fieramente.

prove [pru:v] vt provare, dimostrare ♦ vi: **to** ~ **correct** etc risultare vero(a) etc; **to** ~ o.s. mostrare le proprie capacità; **to** ~ o.s./itself (to be) useful etc mostrarsi or rivelarsi utile etc; **he was** ~d right in the end alla fine i fatti gli hanno dato ragione.

Provence [prɔvɑ̃s] n Provenza.

proverb ['prɔvə:b] n proverbio.

proverbial [prə'və:bɪəl] adj proverbiale.

provide [prə'vaɪd] vt fornire, provvedere; **to** ~ **sb with sth** fornire or provvedere qn di qc; **to be** ~d **with** essere dotato or munito di.

▶**provide for** vt fus provvedere a.

provided [prə'vaɪdɪd] conj: ~ (that) purché + sub, a condizione che + sub.

Providence ['prɔvɪdəns] n Provvidenza.

providing [prə'vaɪdɪŋ] conj purché + sub, a condizione che + sub.

province ['prɔvɪns] n provincia.

provincial [prə'vɪnʃəl] adj provinciale.

provision [prə'vɪʒən] n (supply) riserva; (supplying) provvista; rifornimento; (stipulation) condizione f; ~s npl (food) provviste fpl; **to make** ~ **for** (one's family, future) pensare a; **there's no** ~ **for this in the contract** il contratto non lo prevede.

provisional [prə'vɪʒənl] adj provvisorio(a) ♦ n: **P**~ (Irish POL) provisional m inv.

provisional licence n (BRIT AUT) ≈ foglio m rosa inv.

provisionally [prə'vɪʒnəlɪ] adv provvisoriamente; (appoint) a titolo provvisorio.

proviso [prə'vaɪzəu] n condizione f; **with the** ~ **that** a condizione che + sub, a patto che + sub.

Provo ['prɔvəu] n abbr (col) = **Provisional**.

provocation [prɔvə'keɪʃən] n provocazione f.

provocative [prə'vɔkətɪv] adj (aggressive) provocatorio(a); (thought-provoking) stimolante; (seductive) provocante.

provoke [prə'vəuk] vt provocare; incitare; **to** ~ **sb to sth/to do** or **into doing sth**

spingere qn a qc/a fare qc.

provoking [prə'vəukɪŋ] adj irritante, esasperante.

provost ['prɔvəst] n (BRIT: of university) rettore m; (Scottish) sindaco.

prow [prau] n prua.

prowess ['prauɪs] n prodezza; **his** ~ **as a footballer** le sue capacità di calciatore.

prowl [praul] vi (also: ~ **about**, ~ **around**) aggirarsi furtivamente ♦ n: **on the** ~ **in** cerca di preda.

prowler ['praulə*] n tipo sospetto (che s'aggira con l'intenzione di rubare, aggredire etc).

proximity [prɔk'sɪmɪtɪ] n prossimità.

proxy ['prɔksɪ] n procura; **by** ~ per procura.

PRP n abbr (= performance related pay) retribuzione f commensurata al rendimento.

prude [pru:d] n puritano/a.

prudence ['pru:dns] n prudenza.

prudent ['pru:dnt] adj prudente.

prudish ['pru:dɪʃ] adj puritano(a).

prune [pru:n] n prugna secca ♦ vt potare.

pry [praɪ] vi: **to** ~ **into** ficcare il naso in.

PS n abbr (= postscript) P.S.

psalm [su:m] n salmo.

PSAT ® n abbr (US) = Preliminary Scholastic Aptitude Test.

PSBR n abbr (BRIT: = public sector borrowing requirement) fabbisogno di prestiti per il settore pubblico.

pseud ['sju:d] n (BRIT col: intellectually) intellettualoide m/f; (: socially) snob m/f inv.

pseudo- ['sju:dəu] prefix pseudo....

pseudonym ['sju:dənɪm] n pseudonimo.

PST abbr (US: = Pacific Standard Time) ora invernale del Pacifico.

psyche ['saɪkɪ] n psiche f.

psychedelic [saɪkɪ'dɛlɪk] adj psichedelico(a).

psychiatric [saɪkɪ'ætrɪk] adj psichiatrico(a).

psychiatrist [saɪ'kaɪətrɪst] n psichiatra m/f.

psychiatry [saɪ'kaɪətrɪ] n psichiatria.

psychic ['saɪkɪk] adj (also: ~al) psichico(a); (person) dotato(a) di qualità telepatiche.

psycho ['saɪkəu] n (col) folle m/f.

psychoanalyse [saɪkəu'ænəlaɪz] vt psicanalizzare.

psychoanalysis, pl -ses [saɪkəuə'nælɪsɪs, -si:z] n psicanalisi f inv.

psychoanalyst [saɪkəu'ænəlɪst] n psicanalista m/f.

psychological [saɪkə'lɔdʒɪkl] adj psicologico(a).

psychologist [saɪ'kɔlədʒɪst] n psicologo/a.

psychology [saɪ'kɔlədʒɪ] n psicologia.

psychopath ['saɪkəupæθ] n psicopatico/a.
psychosis, pl **psychoses** [saɪ'kəusɪs, -si:z] n psicosi f inv.
psychosomatic [saɪkəusə'mætɪk] adj psicosomatico(a).
psychotherapy [saɪkəu'θerəpɪ] n psicoterapia.
psychotic [saɪ'kɔtɪk] adj, n psicotico(a).
PT n abbr (BRIT: = physical training) ed. fisica.
pt abbr (= pint; point) pt.
Pt. abbr (in place names: = Point) Pt.
PTA n abbr (= Parent-Teacher Association) associazione genitori e insegnanti.
Pte. abbr (BRIT MIL) = **private.**
PTO abbr (= please turn over) v.r. (= vedi retro).
PTV n abbr (US) = pay television, public television.
pub [pʌb] n abbr (= public house) pub m inv; see boxed note.

PUB

In Gran Bretagna e in Irlanda i **pubs** sono locali dove vengono servite bibite alcoliche ed analcoliche e dove è anche possibile mangiare. Sono punti di ritrovo dove spesso si può giocare a biliardo, a freccette o guardare la televisione. Le leggi che regolano la vendita degli alcolici sono molto severe in Gran Bretagna e quindi gli orari di apertura e di chiusura vengono osservati scrupolosamente.

---

pub crawl n: **to go on a** ~ (BRIT col) fare il giro dei pub.
puberty ['pju:bətɪ] n pubertà.
pubic ['pju:bɪk] adj pubico(a), del pube.
public ['pʌblɪk] adj pubblico(a) ◆ n pubblico; **in** ~ in pubblico; **the general** ~ il pubblico; **to make sth** ~ render noto or di pubblico dominio qc; **to be** ~ **knowledge** essere di dominio pubblico; **to go** ~ (COMM) emettere le azioni sul mercato.
public address system (PA) n impianto di amplificazione.
publican ['pʌblɪkən] n (BRIT) gestore m (or proprietario) di un pub.
publication [pʌblɪ'keɪʃən] n pubblicazione f.
public company n ≈ società f inv per azioni (costituita tramite pubblica sottoscrizione).
public convenience n (BRIT) gabinetti mpl.
public holiday n (BRIT) giorno festivo, festa nazionale.
public house n (BRIT) pub m inv.
publicity [pʌb'lɪsɪtɪ] n pubblicità.
publicize ['pʌblɪsaɪz] vt fare (della)

pubblicità a, reclamizzare.
public limited company (plc) n ≈ società per azioni a responsabilità limitata (quotata in Borsa).
publicly ['pʌblɪklɪ] adv pubblicamente.
public opinion n opinione f pubblica.
public ownership n proprietà pubblica or sociale; **to be taken into** ~ essere statalizzato(a).
public prosecutor n pubblico ministero; **~'s office** ufficio del pubblico ministero.
public relations n pubbliche relazioni fpl.
public relations officer n addetto/a alle pubbliche relazioni.
public school n (BRIT) scuola privata; (US) scuola statale; see boxed note.

PUBLIC SCHOOL

In Inghilterra le **public schools** sono scuole o collegi privati di istruzione secondaria, spesso di un certo prestigio. In Scozia e negli Stati Uniti, invece, le **public schools** sono scuole pubbliche gratuite amministrate dallo stato.

---

public sector n settore m pubblico.
public service vehicle (PSV) n (BRIT) mezzo pubblico.
public-spirited [pʌblɪk'spɪrɪtɪd] adj che ha senso civico.
public transport, (US) **public transportation** n mezzi mpl pubblici.
public utility n servizio pubblico.
public works npl lavori mpl pubblici.
publish ['pʌblɪʃ] vt pubblicare.
publisher ['pʌblɪʃə*] n editore m; (firm) casa editrice.
publishing ['pʌblɪʃɪŋ] n (industry) editoria; (of a book) pubblicazione f.
publishing company n casa or società editrice.
puce [pju:s] adj color pulce inv.
puck [pʌk] n (ICE HOCKEY) disco.
pucker ['pʌkə*] vt corrugare.
pudding ['pudɪŋ] n budino; (dessert) dolce m; **black** ~, (US) **blood** ~ sanguinaccio; **rice** ~ budino di riso.
puddle ['pʌdl] n pozza, pozzanghera.
puerile ['pjuəraɪl] adj puerile.
Puerto Rico [ˈpwə:təuˈri:kəu] n Portorico.
puff [pʌf] n sbuffo; (also: **powder** ~) piumino ◆ vt (also: ~ **out**: sails, cheeks) gonfiare ◆ vi uscire a sbuffi; (pant) ansare; **to** ~ **out smoke** mandar fuori sbuffi di fumo.
puffed [pʌft] adj (col: out of breath) senza fiato.
puffin ['pʌfɪn] n puffino.

puff pastry, (US) **puff paste** n pasta sfoglia.
puffy ['pʌfɪ] adj gonfio(a).
pugnacious [pʌg'neɪʃəs] adj combattivo(a).
pull [pul] n (tug) strattone m, tirata; (of moon, magnet, the sea etc) attrazione f; (fig) influenza ♦ vt tirare; (muscle) strappare, farsi uno strappo a ♦ vi tirare; **to give sth a** ~ tirare su qc; **to** ~ **a face** fare una smorfia; **to** ~ **to pieces** fare a pezzi; **to** ~ **one's punches** (BOXING) risparmiare l'avversario; **not to** ~ **one's punches** (fig) non avere peli sulla lingua; **to** ~ **one's weight** dare il proprio contributo; **to** ~ **o.s. together** ricomporsi, riprendersi; **to** ~ **sb's leg** prendere in giro qn; **to** ~ **strings (for sb)** muovere qualche pedina (per qn).
▶**pull about** vt (BRIT: handle roughly: object) strapazzare; (: person) malmenare.
▶**pull apart** vt (break) fare a pezzi.
▶**pull down** vt (house) demolire; (tree) abbattere.
▶**pull in** vi (AUT: at the kerb) accostarsi; (RAIL) entrare in stazione.
▶**pull off** vt (deal etc) portare a compimento.
▶**pull out** vi partire; (withdraw) ritirarsi, (AUT: come out of line) spostarsi sulla mezzeria ♦ vt staccare; far uscire; (withdraw) ritirare.
▶**pull over** vi (AUT) accostare.
▶**pull round** vi (unconscious person) rinvenire; (sick person) ristabilirsi.
▶**pull through** vi farcela.
▶**pull up** vi (stop) fermarsi ♦ vt (uproot) sradicare; (stop) fermare.
pulley ['pulɪ] n puleggia, carrucola.
pull-out ['pulaut] n inserto ♦ cpd staccabile.
pullover ['puləuvə*] n pullover m inv.
pulp [pʌlp] n (of fruit) polpa; (for paper) pasta per carta; (magazines, books) stampa di qualità e di tono scadenti; **to reduce sth to** ~ spappolare qc.
pulpit ['pulpɪt] n pulpito.
pulsate [pʌl'seɪt] vi battere, palpitare.
pulse [pʌls] n polso; **to feel** or **take sb's** ~ sentire or tastare il polso a qn.
pulses ['pʌlsəz] npl (CULIN) legumi mpl.
pulverize ['pʌlvəraɪz] vt polverizzare.
puma ['pju:mə] n puma m inv.
pumice (stone) ['pʌmɪs-] n (pietra) pomice f.
pummel ['pʌml] vt dare pugni a.
pump [pʌmp] n pompa; (shoe) scarpetta ♦ vt pompare; (fig: col) far parlare; **to** ~ **sb for information** cercare di strappare delle informazioni a qn.

▶**pump up** vt gonfiare.
pumpkin ['pʌmpkɪn] n zucca.
pun [pʌn] n gioco di parole.
punch [pʌntʃ] n (blow) pugno; (fig: force) forza; (tool) punzone m; (drink) ponce m ♦ vt (hit): **to** ~ **sb/sth** dare un pugno a qn/qc; **to** ~ **a hole (in)** fare un buco (in).
▶**punch in** vi (US) timbrare il cartellino (all'entrata).
▶**punch out** vi (US) timbrare il cartellino (all'uscita).
punch-drunk ['pʌntʃdrʌŋk] adj (BRIT) stordito(a).
punch(ed) card ['pʌntʃ(t)-] n scheda perforata.
punch line n (of joke) battuta finale.
punch-up ['pʌntʃʌp] n (BRIT col) rissa.
punctual ['pʌŋktjuəl] adj puntuale.
punctuality [pʌŋktju'ælɪtɪ] n puntualità.
punctually ['pʌŋktjuəlɪ] adv puntualmente; **it will start** ~ **at 6** comincerà alle 6 precise or in punto.
punctuate ['pʌŋktjueɪt] vt punteggiare.
punctuation [pʌŋktju'eɪʃən] n interpunzione f, punteggiatura.
punctuation mark n segno d'interpunzione.
puncture ['pʌŋktʃə*] n (BRIT) foratura ♦ vt forare; **to have a** ~ (AUT) forare (una gomma).
pundit ['pʌndɪt] n sapientone/a.
pungent ['pʌndʒənt] adj piccante; (fig) mordace, caustico(a).
punish ['pʌnɪʃ] vt punire; **to** ~ **sb for sth/ for doing sth** punire qn per qc/per aver fatto qc.
punishable ['pʌnɪʃəbl] adj punibile.
punishing ['pʌnɪʃɪŋ] adj (fig: exhausting) sfiancante.
punishment ['pʌnɪʃmənt] n punizione f; (fig col): **to take a lot of** ~ (boxer) incassare parecchi colpi; (car) essere messo(a) a dura prova.
punk [pʌŋk] n (person: also: ~ **rocker**) punk m/f inv; (music: also: ~ **rock**) musica punk, punk rock m; (US col: hoodlum) teppista m.
punt [pʌnt] n (boat) barchino m; (FOOTBALL) colpo a volo; (Irish) sterlina irlandese ♦ vi (BRIT: bet) scommettere.
punter ['pʌntə*] n (BRIT: gambler) scommettitore/trice.
puny ['pju:nɪ] adj gracile.
pup [pʌp] n cucciolo/a.
pupil ['pju:pl] n allievo/a; (ANAT) pupilla.
puppet ['pʌpɪt] n burattino.
puppet government n governo fantoccio.
puppy ['pʌpɪ] n cucciolo/a, cagnolino/a.
purchase ['pə:tʃɪs] n acquisto, compera;

(*grip*) presa ♦ *vt* comprare; **to get a ~ on**
(*grip*) trovare un appoggio su.
purchase order *n* ordine *m* d'acquisto,
ordinazione *f*.
purchase price *n* prezzo d'acquisto.
purchaser ['pɔːtʃɪsə*] *n* compratore/trice.
purchase tax *n* (*BRIT*) tassa d'acquisto.
purchasing power ['pɔːtʃɪsɪŋ-] *n* potere *m*
d'acquisto.
pure [pjuə*] *adj* puro(a); **a ~ wool jumper**
un golf di pura lana; **it's laziness ~ and
simple** è pura pigrizia.
purebred ['pjuəbrɛd] *adj* di razza pura.
purée ['pjuəreɪ] *n* purè *m inv*.
purely ['pjuəlɪ] *adv* puramente.
purge [pɔːdʒ] *n* (*MED*) purga; (*POL*)
epurazione *f* ♦ *vt* purgare; (*fig*) epurare.
purification [pjuərɪfɪ'keɪʃən] *n*
purificazione *f*.
purify ['pjuərɪfaɪ] *vt* purificare.
purist ['pjuərɪst] *n* purista *m/f*.
puritan ['pjuərɪtən] *adj*, *n* puritano(a).
puritanical [pjuərɪ'tænɪkl] *adj* puritano(a).
purity ['pjuərɪtɪ] *n* purità.
purl [pɔːl] *n* punto rovescio ♦ *vt* lavorare a
rovescio.
purloin [pɔː'lɔɪn] *vt* rubare.
purple ['pɔːpl] *adj* di porpora; viola *inv*.
purport [pɔː'pɔːt] *vi*: **to ~ to be/do**
pretendere di essere/fare.
purpose ['pɔːpəs] *n* intenzione *f*, scopo; **on
~ apposta**, di proposito; **for illustrative ~s**
a titolo illustrativo; **for teaching ~s** per
l'insegnamento; **for the ~s of this
meeting** agli effetti di questa riunione; **to
no ~** senza nessun risultato, inutilmente.
purpose-built ['pɔːpəs'bɪlt] *adj* (*BRIT*)
costruito(a) allo scopo.
purposeful ['pɔːpəsful] *adj* deciso(a),
risoluto(a).
purposely ['pɔːpəslɪ] *adv* apposta.
purr [pɔː*] *n* fusa *fpl* ♦ *vi* fare le fusa.
purse [pɔːs] *n* borsellino; (*US: handbag*)
borsetta, borsa ♦ *vt* contrarre.
purser ['pɔːsə*] *n* (*NAUT*) commissario di
bordo.
purse snatcher [-'snætʃə*] *n* (*US*)
scippatore *m*.
pursue [pə'sjuː] *vt* inseguire; essere alla
ricerca di; (*inquiry, matter*) approfondire.
pursuer [pə'sjuːə*] *n* inseguitore/trice.
pursuit [pə'sjuːt] *n* inseguimento;
(*occupation*) occupazione *f*, attività *f inv*; **in
(the) ~ of sth** alla ricerca di qc; **scientific
~s** ricerche *fpl* scientifiche.
purveyor [pə'veɪə*] *n* fornitore/trice.
pus [pʌs] *n* pus *m*.
push [puʃ] *n* spinta; (*effort*) grande sforzo;

(*drive*) energia ♦ *vt* spingere; (*button*)
premere; (*thrust*): **to ~ sth (into)** ficcare
qc (in); (*fig*) fare pubblicità a ♦ *vi*
spingere; premere; **to ~ a door open/
shut** aprire/chiudere una porta con una
spinta *or* spingendola; **to be ~ed for
time/money** essere a corto di tempo/
soldi; **she is ~ing 50** (*col*) va per i 50; **to ~
for** (*better pay, conditions etc*) fare
pressione per ottenere; "**~**" (*on door*)
"spingere"; (*on bell*) "suonare"; **at a ~**
(*BRIT col*) in caso di necessità.
▶**push aside** *vt* scostare.
▶**push in** *vi* introdursi a forza.
▶**push off** *vi* (*col*) filare.
▶**push on** *vi* (*continue*) continuare.
▶**push over** *vt* far cadere.
▶**push through** *vt* (*measure*) far
approvare.
▶**push up** *vt* (*total, prices*) far salire.
push-bike ['puʃbaɪk] *n* (*BRIT*) bicicletta.
push-button ['puʃbʌtn] *adj* a pulsante.
pushchair ['puʃtʃeə*] *n* passeggino.
pusher ['puʃə*] *n* (*also:* **drug ~**)
spacciatore/trice (di droga).
pushover ['puʃəuvə*] *n* (*col*): **it's a ~** è un
lavoro da bambini.
push-up ['puʃʌp] *n* (*US*) flessione *f* sulle
braccia.
pushy ['puʃɪ] *adj* (*pej*) troppo
intraprendente.
puss, pussy(-cat) [pus, 'pusɪ(kæt)] *n* micio.
put, *pt, pp* **put** [put] *vt* mettere, porre; (*say*)
dire, esprimere; (*a question*) fare;
(*estimate*) stimare ♦ *adv*: **to stay ~** non
muoversi; **to ~ sb to bed** mettere qn a
letto; **to ~ sb in a good/bad mood**
mettere qn di buon/cattivo umore; **to ~
sb to a lot of trouble** scomodare qn; **to ~
a lot of time into sth** dedicare molto
tempo a qc; **to ~ money on a horse**
scommettere su un cavallo; **how shall I ~
it?** come dire?; **I ~ it to you that ...** (*BRIT*)
io sostengo che ....
▶**put about** *vi* (*NAUT*) virare di bordo ♦ *vt*
(*rumour*) diffondere.
▶**put across** *vt* (*ideas etc*) comunicare, far
capire.
▶**put aside** *vt* (*lay down: book etc*) mettere
da una parte, posare; (*save*) mettere da
parte; (*in shop*) tenere da parte.
▶**put away** *vt* (*clothes, toys etc*) mettere
via.
▶**put back** *vt* (*replace*) rimettere (a posto);
(*postpone*) rinviare; (*delay*) ritardare; (*set
back: watch, clock*) mettere indietro; **this
will ~ us back 10 years** questo ci farà
tornare indietro di 10 anni.

▶**put by** vt (money) mettere da parte.
▶**put down** vt (parcel etc) posare, mettere giù; (pay) versare; (in writing) mettere per iscritto; (suppress: revolt etc) reprimere, sopprimere; (attribute) attribuire.
▶**put forward** vt (ideas) avanzare, proporre; (date) anticipare.
▶**put in** vt (application, complaint) presentare.
▶**put in for** vt fus (job) far domanda per; (promotion) far domanda di.
▶**put off** vt (postpone) rimandare, rinviare; (discourage) dissuadere.
▶**put on** vt (clothes, lipstick etc) mettere; (light etc) accendere; (play etc) mettere in scena; (concert, exhibition etc) allestire, organizzare; (extra bus, train etc) mettere in servizio; (food, meal) servire; (brake) mettere; (assume: accent, manner) affettare; (col: tease) prendere in giro; (inform, indicate): **to ~ sb on to sb/sth** indicare qn/qc a qn; **to ~ on weight** ingrassare; **to ~ on airs** darsi delle arie.
▶**put out** vt mettere fuori; (one's hand) porgere; (light etc) spegnere; (person: inconvenience) scomodare; (dislocate: shoulder, knee) lussarsi; (: back) farsi uno strappo a ♦ vi (NAUT): **to ~ out to sea** prendere il largo; **to ~ out from Plymouth** partire da Plymouth.
▶**put through** vt (caller) mettere in comunicazione; (call) passare; **~ me through to Miss Blair** mi passi la signorina Blair.
▶**put together** vt mettere insieme, riunire; (assemble: furniture) montare; (: meal) improvvisare.
▶**put up** vt (raise) sollevare, alzare; (pin up) affiggere; (hang) appendere; (build) costruire, erigere; (increase) aumentare; (accommodate) alloggiare; (incite): **to ~ sb up to doing sth** istigare qn a fare qc; **to ~ sth up for sale** mettere in vendita qc.
▶**put upon** vt fus: **to be ~ upon** (imposed on) farsi mettere sotto i piedi.
▶**put up with** vt fus sopportare.
putrid ['pjuːtrɪd] adj putrido(a).
putt [pʌt] vt (ball) colpire leggermente ♦ n colpo leggero.
putter ['pʌtə*] n (GOLF) putter m inv ♦ vi (US) = **potter**.
putting green ['pʌtɪŋ-] n green m inv; campo da putting.
putty ['pʌtɪ] n stucco.
put-up ['putʌp] adj: **~ job** montatura.
puzzle ['pʌzl] n enigma m, mistero; (jigsaw) puzzle m ♦ vt confondere, rendere

perplesso(a) ♦ vi scervellarsi; **to be ~d about sth** domandarsi il perché di qc; **to ~ over** (sb's actions) cercare di capire; (mystery, problem) cercare di risolvere.
puzzling ['pʌzlɪŋ] adj (question) poco chiaro(a); (attitude, set of instructions) incomprensibile.
PVC n abbr (= polyvinyl chloride) P.V.C. m.
Pvt. abbr (US MIL) = **private**.
PW n abbr (US) = **prisoner of war**.
pw abbr = per week.
PX n abbr (US MIL) see **post exchange**.
pygmy ['pɪgmɪ] n pigmeo/a.
pyjamas, (US) **pajamas** [pə'dʒɑːməz] npl pigiama m; **a pair of ~** un pigiama.
pylon ['paɪlən] n pilone m.
pyramid ['pɪrəmɪd] n piramide f.
Pyrenees [pɪrə'niːz] npl: **the ~** i Pirenei.
Pyrex ® ['paɪrɛks] n Pirex ® m inv ♦ cpd: **~ dish** pirofila.
python ['paɪθən] n pitone m.

Q q

Q, q [kjuː] n (letter) Q, q f or m inv; **Q for Queen** ≈ Q come Quarto.
Qatar [kæ'tɑː*] n Qatar m.
QC n abbr (BRIT: = Queen's Counsel) avvocato della Corona.
QED abbr (= quod erat demonstrandum) qed.
QM n abbr see **quartermaster**.
q.t. n abbr (col: = quiet): **on the ~** di nascosto.
qty abbr = **quantity**.
quack [kwæk] n (of duck) qua qua m inv; (pej: doctor) ciarlatano/a.
quad [kwɔd] n abbr = **quadrangle**; **quadruple**; **quadruplet**.
quadrangle ['kwɔdræŋgl] n (MATH) quadrilatero; (courtyard) cortile m.
quadruped ['kwɔdrupɛd] n quadrupede m.
quadruple [kwɔ'druːpl] adj quadruplo(a) ♦ n quadruplo ♦ vt quadruplicare ♦ vi quadruplicarsi.
quadruplet [kwɔ'druːplɪt] n uno/a di quattro gemelli.
quagmire ['kwægmaɪə*] n pantano.
quail [kweɪl] n (ZOOL) quaglia ♦ vi: **to ~ at** or **before** perdersi d'animo davanti a.
quaint [kweɪnt] adj bizzarro(a); (old-

fashioned) antiquato(a) e pittoresco(a).
quake [kweɪk] *vi* tremare ♦ *n abbr*
= **earthquake**.
Quaker ['kweɪkə*] *n* quacchero/a.
qualification [kwɔlɪfɪ'keɪʃən] *n (degree etc)*
qualifica, titolo; *(ability)* competenza,
qualificazione *f*; *(limitation)* riserva,
restrizione *f*; **what are your ~s?** quali
sono le sue qualifiche?
qualified ['kwɔlɪfaɪd] *adj* qualificato(a);
(able) competente, qualificato(a); *(limited)*
condizionato(a); ~ **for/to do**
qualificato(a) per/per fare; **he's not ~ for**
the job non ha i requisiti necessari per
questo lavoro; **it was a ~ success** è stato
un successo parziale.
qualify ['kwɔlɪfaɪ] *vt* abilitare; *(limit:*
statement) modificare, precisare ♦ *vi:* **to ~**
(as) qualificarsi (come); **to ~ (for)**
acquistare i requisiti necessari (per);
(SPORT) qualificarsi (per *or* a); **to ~ as**
an èngineer diventare un perito
tecnico.
qualifying ['kwɔlɪfaɪɪŋ] *adj (exam)* di
ammissione; *(round)* eliminatorio(a).
qualitative ['kwɔlɪtətɪv] *adj* qualitativo(a).
quality ['kwɔlɪtɪ] *n* qualità *f inv* ♦ *cpd* di
qualità; **of good** ~ di buona qualità; **of**
poor ~ scadente; ~ **of life** qualità della
vita.
quality control *n* controllo di qualità.
quality papers *npl*, **quality press** *n (BRIT):*
the ~ la stampa d'informazione; *see boxed*
note.

QUALITY PRESS

Il termine **quality press** *si riferisce ai*
quotidiani o ai settimanali che offrono
un'informazione seria ed approfondita. Questi
giornali si differenziano da quelli popolari, i
"tabloid", per formato e contenuti. Questa
divisione tra tipi di giornali riflette il
tradizionale divario tra classi sociali nella
società britannica; vedi anche **tabloid press**.

---

qualm [kwɑːm] *n* dubbio; scrupolo; **to have**
~s about sth avere degli scrupoli per qc.
quandary ['kwɔndrɪ] *n:* **in a ~** in un
dilemma.
quango ['kwæŋgəu] *n abbr (BRIT:* = *quasi-*
autonomous non-governmental organization)
commissione consultiva di nomina
governativa.
quantifiable ['kwɔntɪfaɪəbl] *adj*
quantificabile.
quantitative ['kwɔntɪtətɪv] *adj*
quantitativo(a).

quantity ['kwɔntɪtɪ] *n* quantità *f inv;* **in ~** in
grande quantità.
quantity surveyor *n (BRIT)* geometra *m*
(specializzato nel calcolare la quantità e il
costo del materiale da costruzione).
quantum leap ['kwɔntəm-] *n (fig)* enorme
cambiamento.
quarantine ['kwɔrntiːn] *n* quarantena.
quark [kwɑːk] *n* quark *m inv.*
quarrel ['kwɔrl] *n* lite *f*, disputa ♦ *vi* litigare;
to have a ~ with sb litigare con qn; **I've**
no ~ with him non ho niente contro di
lui; **I can't ~ with that** non ho niente da
ridire su questo.
quarrelsome ['kwɔrəlsəm] *adj* litigioso(a).
quarry ['kwɔrɪ] *n (for stone)* cava; *(animal)*
preda ♦ *vt (marble etc)* estrarre.
quart [kwɔːt] *n* due pinte *fpl*, ≈ litro.
quarter ['kwɔːtə*] *n* quarto; *(of year)*
trimestre *m*; *(district)* quartiere *m*; *(US,*
Canada: 25 cents) quarto di dollaro, 25
centesimi ♦ *vt* dividere in quattro; *(MIL)*
alloggiare; **~s** *npl* alloggio; *(MIL)* alloggi
mpl, quadrato; **a ~ of an hour** un quarto
d'ora; **it's a ~ to 3,** *(US)* **it's a ~ of 3** sono
le 3 meno un quarto, manca un quarto
alle 3; **it's a ~ past 3,** *(US)* **it's a ~ after 3**
sono le 3 e un quarto; **from all ~s** da tutte
la parti *or* direzioni; **at close ~s** a
distanza ravvicinata.
quarterback ['kwɔːtəbæk] *n (US FOOTBALL)*
quarterback *m inv.*
quarter-deck ['kwɔːtədɛk] *n (NAUT)*
cassero.
quarter final *n* quarto di finale.
quarterly ['kwɔːtəlɪ] *adj* trimestrale ♦ *adv*
trimestralmente ♦ *n* periodico
trimestrale.
quartermaster (QM) ['kwɔːtəmɑːstə*] *n*
(MIL) furiere *m.*
quartet(te) [kwɔː'tɛt] *n* quartetto.
quarto ['kwɔːtəu] *adj*, *n* in quarto *(m) inv.*
quartz [kwɔːts] *n* quarzo ♦ *cpd* di quarzo;
(watch, clock) al quarzo.
quash [kwɔʃ] *vt (verdict)* annullare.
quasi- ['kweɪzaɪ] *prefix* quasi + *noun;* quasi,
pressoché + *adjective.*
quaver ['kweɪvə*] *n (BRIT MUS)* croma ♦ *vi*
tremolare.
quay [kiː] *n (also:* ~**side)** banchina.
Que. *abbr (Canada)* = **Quebec.**
queasy ['kwiːzɪ] *adj (stomach)* delicato(a);
to feel ~ aver la nausea.
Quebec [kwɪ'bɛk] *n* Quebec *m.*
queen [kwiːn] *n (gen)* regina; *(CARDS etc)*
regina, donna.
queen mother *n* regina madre.
Queen's speech *n (BRIT) see boxed note.*

QUEEN'S SPEECH

Durante la sessione di apertura del Parlamento britannico il sovrano legge un discorso redatto dal primo ministro, il **Queen's speech** *(se si tratta della regina), che contiene le linee generali del nuovo programma politico.*

---

queer [kwɪə*] *adj* strano(a), curioso(a); (*suspicious*) dubbio(a), sospetto(a); (*BRIT: sick*): **I feel ~ mi sento poco bene ♦** *n* (*col*) finocchio.

quell [kwɛl] *vt* domare.

quench [kwɛntʃ] *vt* (*flames*) spegnere; **to ~ one's thirst** dissetarsi.

querulous ['kwɛruləs] *adj* querulo(a).

query ['kwɪərɪ] *n* domanda, questione *f*; (*doubt*) dubbio ♦ *vt* mettere in questione; (*disagree with, dispute*) contestare.

quest [kwɛst] *n* cerca, ricerca.

question ['kwɛstʃən] *n* domanda, questione *f* ♦ *vt* (*person*) interrogare; (*plan, idea*) mettere in questione *or* in dubbio; **to ask sb a ~, put a ~ to sb** fare una domanda a qn; **to bring** *or* **call sth into ~** mettere in dubbio qc; **the ~ is ...** il problema è ...; **it's a ~ of doing** si tratta di fare; **there's some ~ of doing** c'è chi suggerisce di fare; **beyond ~** fuori di dubbio; **out of the ~** fuori discussione, impossibile.

questionable ['kwɛstʃənəbl] *adj* discutibile.

questioner['kwɛstʃənə*]*n* interrogante *m/f*.

questioning ['kwɛstʃənɪŋ] *adj* interrogativo(a) ♦ *n* interrogatorio.

question mark *n* punto interrogativo.

questionnaire [kwɛstʃə'nɛə*] *n* questionario.

queue [kjuː] *n* coda, fila ♦ *vi* fare la coda; **to jump the ~** passare davanti agli altri (in una coda).

quibble ['kwɪbl] *vi* cavillare.

quick [kwɪk] *adj* rapido(a), veloce; (*reply*) pronto(a); (*mind*) pronto(a), acuto(a) ♦ *adv* rapidamente, presto ♦ *n*: **cut to the ~** (*fig*) toccato(a) sul vivo; **be ~!** fa presto!; **to be ~ to act** agire prontamente; **she was ~ to see that ...** ha visto subito che ....

quicken ['kwɪkn] *vt* accelerare, affrettare; (*rouse*) animare, stimolare ♦ *vi* accelerare, affrettarsi.

quick fix *n* soluzione *f* tampone *inv*.

quicklime ['kwɪklaɪm] *n* calce *f* viva.

quickly ['kwɪklɪ] *adv* rapidamente, velocemente; **we must act ~** dobbiamo agire tempestivamente.

quickness ['kwɪknɪs] *n* rapidità; prontezza; acutezza.

quicksand ['kwɪksænd] *n* sabbie *fpl* mobili.

quickstep ['kwɪkstɛp] *n* tipo di ballo simile al *fox-trot*.

quick-tempered [kwɪk'tɛmpəd] *adj* che si arrabbia facilmente.

quick-witted [kwɪk'wɪtɪd] *adj* pronto(a) d'ingegno.

quid [kwɪd] *n* (*pl inv*: *BRIT col*) sterlina.

quid pro quo ['kwɪdprəu'kwəu] *n* contraccambio.

quiet ['kwaɪət] *adj* tranquillo(a), quieto(a); (*reserved*) quieto(a), taciturno(a); (*ceremony*) semplice; (*not noisy: engine*) silenzioso(a); (*not busy: day*) calmo(a), tranquillo(a); (*colour*) discreto(a) ♦ *n* tranquillità, calma ♦ *vt*, *vi* (*US*) = **quieten**; **keep ~!** sta zitto!; **on the ~** di nascosto; **I'll have a ~ word with him** gli dirò due parole in privato; **business is ~ at this time of year** questa è la stagione morta.

quieten ['kwaɪətn] (*BRIT: also*: **~ down**) *vi* calmarsi, chetarsi ♦ *vt* calmare, chetare.

quietly ['kwaɪətlɪ] *adv* tranquillamente, calmamente; silenziosamente.

quietness ['kwaɪətnɪs] *n* tranquillità, calma; silenzio.

quill [kwɪl] *n* penna d'oca.

quilt [kwɪlt] *n* trapunta; **continental ~** piumino.

quin [kwɪn] *n abbr* = **quintuplet**.

quince [kwɪns] *n* (mela) cotogna; (*tree*) cotogno.

quinine [kwɪ'niːn] *n* chinino.

quintet(te) [kwɪn'tɛt] *n* quintetto.

quintuplet [kwɪn'tjuːplɪt] *n* uno/a di cinque gemelli.

quip [kwɪp] *n* battuta di spirito.

quire ['kwaɪə*] *n* ventesima parte di una risma.

quirk [kwəːk] *n* ghiribizzo; **by some ~ of fate** per un capriccio della sorte.

quit, *pt*, *pp* **quit** *or* **quitted** [kwɪt] *vt* lasciare, partire da ♦ *vi* (*give up*) mollare; (*resign*) dimettersi; **to ~ doing** smettere di fare; **~ stalling!** (*US col*) non tirarla per le lunghe!; **notice to ~** (*BRIT*) preavviso (*dato all'inquilino*).

quite [kwaɪt] *adv* (*rather*) assai; (*entirely*) completamente, del tutto; **I ~ understand** capisco perfettamente; **~ a few of them** non pochi di loro; **~ (so)!** esatto!; **~ new** proprio nuovo; **that's not ~ right** non è proprio esatto; **she's ~ pretty** è piuttosto carina.

quits [kwɪts] *adj*: **~ (with)** pari (con); **let's call it ~** adesso siamo pari.

quiver ['kwɪvə*] *vi* tremare, fremere ♦ *n* (*for arrows*) faretra.

quiz [kwɪz] n (game) quiz m inv; indovinello
♦ vt interrogare.
quizzical ['kwɪzɪkəl] adj enigmatico(a).
quoits [kwɔɪts] npl gioco degli anelli.
quorum ['kwɔːrəm] n quorum m.
quota ['kwəutə] n quota.
quotation [kwəu'teɪʃən] n citazione f; (of
shares etc) quotazione f; (estimate)
preventivo.
quotation marks npl virgolette fpl.
quote [kwəut] n citazione f ♦ vt (sentence)
citare; (price) dare, indicare, fissare;
(shares) quotare ♦ vi: to ~ from citare; to
~ for a job dare un preventivo per un
lavoro; ~s npl (col) = quotation marks; in
~s tra virgolette; ~ ... unquote (in
dictation) aprire le virgolette ... chiudere
le virgolette.
quotient ['kwəuʃənt] n quoziente m.
qv abbr (= quod vide: which see) v.
qwerty keyboard ['kwəːtɪ-] n tastiera
qwerty inv.

R r

R, r [ɑː*] n (letter) R, r f or m inv; **R for Robert,**
(US) **R for Roger** ≈ R come Roma.
R abbr (= Réaumur (scale)) R; (= river) F;
(= right) D; (US CINE: = restricted)
≈ vietato; (US POL) = **Republican**; (BRIT)
= Rex, Regina.
RA n abbr (BRIT) = Royal Academy, Royal
Academician ♦ abbr = **rear admiral.**
RAAF n abbr = Royal Australian Air
Force.
Rabat [rə'bɑːt] n Rabat f.
rabbi ['ræbaɪ] n rabbino.
rabbit ['ræbɪt] n coniglio ♦ vi: to ~ (on)
(BRIT) blaterare.
rabbit hole n tana di coniglio.
rabbit hutch n conigliera.
rabble ['ræbl] n (pej) canaglia, plebaglia.
rabid ['ræbɪd] adj rabbioso(a); (fig)
fanatico(a).
rabies ['reɪbiːz] n rabbia.
RAC n abbr (BRIT: = Royal Automobile Club)
≈ A.C.I. m (= Automobile Club d'Italia).
raccoon [rə'kuːn] n procione m.
race [reɪs] n razza; (competition, rush) corsa
♦ vt (person) gareggiare (in corsa) con;
(horse) far correre; (engine) imballare

♦ vi correre; **the human** ~ la razza
umana; **he** ~**d across the road** ha
attraversato la strada di corsa; **to** ~ **in/
out** etc precipitarsi dentro/fuori etc.
race car n (US) = **racing car.**
race car driver n (US) = **racing driver.**
racecourse ['reɪskɔːs] n campo di corse,
ippodromo.
racehorse ['reɪshɔːs] n cavallo da corsa.
race relations npl rapporti razziali.
racetrack ['reɪstræk] n pista.
racial ['reɪʃl] adj razziale.
racial discrimination n discriminazione f
razziale.
racialism ['reɪʃəlɪzəm] n razzismo.
racialist ['reɪʃəlɪst] adj, n razzista (m/f).
racing ['reɪsɪŋ] n corsa.
racing car n (BRIT) macchina da corsa.
racing driver n (BRIT) corridore m
automobilista.
racism ['reɪsɪzəm] n razzismo.
racist ['reɪsɪst] adj, n (pej) razzista (m/f).
rack [ræk] n rastrelliera; (also: **luggage** ~)
rete f, portabagagli m inv; (also: **roof** ~)
portabagagli ♦ vt torturare, tormentare;
magazine ~ portariviste m inv; **shoe** ~
scarpiera; **toast** ~ portatoast m inv; **to go
to** ~ **and ruin** (building) andare in rovina;
(business) andare in malora or a
catafascio; **to** ~ **one's brains** scervellarsi.
▶**rack up** vt accumulare.
racket ['rækɪt] n (for tennis) racchetta;
(noise) fracasso, baccano; (swindle) racket
m inv.
racketeer [rækɪ'tɪə*] n (US) trafficante m/f.
racoon [rə'kuːn] n = **raccoon.**
racquet ['rækɪt] n racchetta.
racy ['reɪsɪ] adj brioso(a); piccante.
RADA ['rɑːdə] n abbr (BRIT) = Royal Academy
of Dramatic Art.
radar ['reɪdɑː*] n radar m ♦ cpd radar
inv.
radar trap n controllo della velocità con
radar.
radial ['reɪdɪəl] adj (also: ~-**ply**) radiale.
radiance ['reɪdɪəns] n splendore m,
radiosità.
radiant ['reɪdɪənt] adj raggiante; (PHYSICS)
radiante.
radiate ['reɪdɪeɪt] vt (heat) irraggiare,
irradiare ♦ vi (lines) irradiarsi.
radiation [reɪdɪ'eɪʃən] n irradiamento;
(radioactive) radiazione f.
radiation sickness n malattia da
radiazioni.
radiator ['reɪdɪeɪtə*] n radiatore m.
radiator cap n tappo del radiatore.

radiator grill n (AUT) mascherina, calandra.
radical ['rædɪkl] adj radicale.
radii ['reɪdɪaɪ] npl of **radius.**
radio ['reɪdɪəu] n radio f inv ♦ vt (information) trasmettere per radio; (one's position) comunicare via radio; (person) chiamare via radio ♦ vi: **to ~ to sb** comunicare via radio con qn; **on the ~** alla radio.
radio... ['reɪdɪəu] prefix radio....
radioactive ['reɪdɪəu'æktɪv] adj radioattivo(a).
radioactivity ['reɪdɪəuæk'tɪvɪtɪ] n radioattività.
radio announcer n annunciatore/trice della radio.
radio-controlled ['reɪdɪəukən'trəuld] adj radiocomandato(a), radioguidato(a).
radiographer [reɪdɪ'ɔgrəfə*] n radiologo/a (tecnico).
radiography [reɪdɪ'ɔgrəfɪ] n radiografia.
radiologist [reɪdɪ'ɔlədʒɪst] n radiologo/a (medico).
radiology [reɪdɪ'ɔlədʒɪ] n radiologia.
radio station n stazione f radio inv.
radio taxi n radiotaxi m inv.
radiotelephone ['reɪdɪəu'tɛlɪfəun] n radiotelefono.
radiotherapist ['reɪdɪəu'θɛrəpɪst] n radioterapista m/f.
radiotherapy ['reɪdɪəu'θɛrəpɪ] n radioterapia.
radish ['rædɪʃ] n ravanello.
radium ['reɪdɪəm] n radio.
radius, pl **radii** ['reɪdɪəs, -ɪaɪ] n raggio; (ANAT) radio; **within a ~ of 50 miles** in un raggio di 50 miglia.
RAF n abbr (BRIT) see **Royal Air Force.**
raffia ['ræfɪə] n rafia.
raffish ['ræfɪʃ] adj dal look trasandato.
raffle ['ræfl] n lotteria ♦ vt (object) mettere in palio.
raft [rɑːft] n zattera.
rafter ['rɑːftə*] n trave f.
rag [ræg] n straccio, cencio; (pej: newspaper) giornalaccio; (for charity) iniziativa studentesca a scopo benefico ♦ vt (BRIT) prendere in giro; **~s** npl stracci mpl, brandelli mpl; **in ~s** stracciato.
rag-and-bone man ['rægən'bəun-] n straccivendolo.
ragbag ['rægbæg] n (fig) guazzabuglio.
rag doll n bambola di pezza.
rage [reɪdʒ] n (fury) collera, furia ♦ vi (person) andare su tutte le furie; (storm) infuriare; **it's all the ~** fa furore; **to fly**

into a ~ andare or montare su tutte le furie.
ragged ['rægɪd] adj (edge) irregolare; (cuff) logoro(a); (appearance) pezzente.
raging ['reɪdʒɪŋ] adj (all senses) furioso(a); **in a ~ temper** su tutte le furie.
rag trade n (col): **the ~** l'abbigliamento.
rag week n (BRIT) see boxed note.

RAG WEEK

Durante il **rag week**, gli studenti universitari organizzano vari spettacoli e manifestazioni i cui proventi vengono devoluti in beneficenza.

---

raid [reɪd] n (MIL) incursione f; (criminal) rapina; (by police) irruzione f ♦ vt fare un'incursione in; rapinare; fare irruzione in.
raider ['reɪdə*] n rapinatore/trice; (plane) aeroplano da incursione.
rail [reɪl] n (on stair) ringhiera; (on bridge, balcony) parapetto; (of ship) battagliola; (for train) rotaia; **~s** npl binario, rotaie fpl; **by ~** per ferrovia, in treno.
railcard ['reɪlkɑːd] n (BRIT) tessera di riduzione ferroviaria.
railing(s) ['reɪlɪŋ(z)] n(pl) ringhiere fpl.
railway ['reɪlweɪ], (US) **railroad** ['reɪlrəud] n ferrovia.
railway engine n (BRIT) locomotiva.
railway line n (BRIT) linea ferroviaria.
railwayman ['reɪlweɪmən] n (BRIT) ferroviere m.
railway station n (BRIT) stazione f ferroviaria.
rain [reɪn] n pioggia ♦ vi piovere; **in the ~** sotto la pioggia; **it's ~ing** piove; **it's ~ing cats and dogs** piove a catinelle.
rainbow ['reɪnbəu] n arcobaleno.
raincoat ['reɪnkəut] n impermeabile m.
raindrop ['reɪndrɔp] n goccia di pioggia.
rainfall ['reɪnfɔːl] n pioggia; (measurement) piovosità.
rainforest ['reɪnfɔrɪst] n foresta pluviale or equatoriale.
rainproof ['reɪnpruːf] adj impermeabile.
rainstorm ['reɪnstɔːm] n pioggia torrenziale.
rainwater ['reɪnwɔːtə*] n acqua piovana.
rainy ['reɪnɪ] adj piovoso(a).
raise [reɪz] n aumento ♦ vt (lift) alzare, sollevare; (build) erigere; (increase) aumentare; (a protest, doubt, question) sollevare; (cattle, family) allevare; (crop) coltivare; (army, funds) raccogliere; (loan) ottenere; (end: siege, embargo) togliere; **to ~ one's voice** alzare la voce; **to ~ sb's**

hopes accendere le speranze di qn; **to ~ one's glass to sb/sth** brindare a qn/qc; **~ a laugh/a smile** far ridere/sorridere.

raisin ['reızn] n uva secca.

Raj [rɑːdʒ] n: **the ~** l'impero britannico (in India).

rajah ['rɑːdʒə] n ragià m inv.

rake [reɪk] n (tool) rastrello; (person) libertino ♦ vt (garden) rastrellare; (with machine gun) spazzare ♦ vi: **to ~ through** (fig: search) frugare tra.

rake-off ['reɪkɔf] n (col) parte f percentuale.

rakish ['reɪkɪʃ] adj dissoluto(a); disinvolto(a).

rally ['rælɪ] n (POL etc) riunione f; (AUT) rally m inv; (TENNIS) scambio ♦ vt riunire, radunare ♦ vi raccogliersi, radunarsi; (sick person, STOCK EXCHANGE) riprendersi.

▶**rally round** vt fus raggrupparsi intorno a; venire in aiuto di.

rallying point ['rælɪɪŋ-] n (POL, MIL) punto di riunione, punto di raduno.

RAM [ræm] n abbr (COMPUT: = random access memory) RAM f.

ram [ræm] n montone m, ariete m; (device) ariete ♦ vt conficcare; (crash into) cozzare, sbattere contro; percuotere; speronare.

ramble ['ræmbl] n escursione f ♦ vi (pej: also: **~ on**) divagare.

rambler ['ræmblə*] n escursionista m/f.

rambling ['ræmblɪŋ] adj (speech) sconnesso(a); (BOT) rampicante; (house) tutto(a) nicchie e corridoi.

rambunctious [ræm'bʌŋkʃəs] adj (US) = **rumbustious**.

RAMC n abbr (BRIT) = Royal Army Medical Corps.

ramification [ræmɪfɪ'keɪʃən] n ramificazione f.

ramp [ræmp] n rampa; (AUT) dosso artificiale.

rampage [ræm'peɪdʒ] n: **to go on the ~** scatenarsi in modo violento ♦ vi: **they went rampaging through the town** si sono scatenati in modo violento per la città.

rampant ['ræmpənt] adj (disease etc) che infierisce.

rampart ['ræmpɑːt] n bastione m.

ram raiding [-reɪdɪŋ] n il rapinare un negozio sfondandone la vetrina con un veicolo rubato.

ramshackle ['ræmʃækl] adj (house) cadente; (car etc) sgangherato(a).

ran [ræn] pt of **run**.

ranch [rɑːntʃ] n ranch m inv.

rancid ['rænsɪd] adj rancido(a).

rancour, (US) **rancor** ['ræŋkə*] n rancore

m.

R&B n abbr = rhythm and blues.

R&D n abbr see **research and development**.

random ['rændəm] adj fatto(a) or detto(a) per caso; (COMPUT, MATH) casuale ♦ n: **at ~ a** casaccio.

random access n (COMPUT) accesso casuale.

R & R n abbr (= rest and recreation) ricreazione f.

randy ['rændɪ] adj (col) arrapato(a); lascivo(a).

rang [ræŋ] pt of **ring**.

range [reɪndʒ] n (of mountains) catena; (of missile, voice) portata; (of products) gamma; (MIL: also: **shooting ~**) campo di tiro; (also: **kitchen ~**) fornello, cucina economica ♦ vt (place) disporre, allineare; (roam) vagare per ♦ vi: **to ~ over** coprire; **to ~ from ... to** andare da ... a; **price ~** gamma di prezzi; **do you have anything else in this price ~?** ha nient'altro su or di questo prezzo?; **within (firing) ~ a** portata di tiro; **~d left/right** (text) allineato(a) a destra/sinistra.

ranger ['reɪndʒə*] n guardia forestale.

Rangoon [ræŋ'guːn] n Rangun f.

rank [ræŋk] n fila; (MIL) grado; (BRIT: also: **taxi ~**) posteggio di taxi ♦ vi: **to ~ among** essere nel numero di ♦ adj (smell) puzzolente; (hypocrisy, injustice) vero(a) e proprio(a); **the ~s** (MIL) la truppa; **the ~ and file** (fig) la gran massa; **to close ~s** (MIL, fig) serrare i ranghi; **I ~ him sixth** gli do il sesto posto, lo metto al sesto posto.

rankle ['ræŋkl] vi: **to ~ (with sb)** bruciare (a qn).

rank outsider n outsider m/f inv.

ransack ['rænsæk] vt rovistare; (plunder) saccheggiare.

ransom ['rænsəm] n riscatto; **to hold sb to ~** (fig) esercitare pressione su qn.

rant [rænt] vi vociare.

ranting ['ræntɪŋ] n vociare m.

rap [ræp] n (noise) colpetti mpl; (at a door) bussata ♦ vt dare dei colpetti a; bussare a.

rape [reɪp] n violenza carnale, stupro ♦ vt violentare.

rape(seed) oil ['reɪp(siːd)-] n olio di ravizzone.

rapid ['ræpɪd] adj rapido(a).

rapidity [rə'pɪdɪtɪ] n rapidità.

rapidly ['ræpɪdlɪ] adv rapidamente.

rapids ['ræpɪdz] npl (GEO) rapida.

rapist ['reɪpɪst] n violentatore m.

rapport [ræ'pɔː*] n rapporto.

rapt [ræpt] adj (attention) rapito(a), profondo(a); **to be ~ in contemplation** essere in estatica contemplazione.

rapture ['ræptʃə*] n estasi f inv; **to go into ~s over** andare in solluchero per.

rapturous ['ræptʃərəs] adj estatico(a).

rare [rɛə*] adj raro(a); (CULIN: steak) al sangue; **it is ~ to find that ...** capita di rado or raramente che ... + sub.

rarebit ['rɛəbɪt] n see **Welsh rarebit**.

rarefied ['rɛərɪfaɪd] adj (air, atmosphere) rarefatto(a).

rarely ['rɛəlɪ] adv raramente.

raring ['rɛərɪŋ] adj: **to be ~ to go** (col) non veder l'ora di cominciare.

rarity ['rɛərɪtɪ] n rarità f inv.

rascal ['rɑːsklʲ] n mascalzone m.

rash [ræʃ] adj imprudente, sconsiderato(a) ♦ n (MED) eruzione f; **to come out in a ~** avere uno sfogo.

rasher ['ræʃə*] n fetta sottile (di lardo or prosciutto).

rasp [rɑːsp] n (tool) lima ♦ vt (speak: also: ~ out) gracchiare.

raspberry ['rɑːzbərɪ] n lampone m.

raspberry bush n lampone m (pianta).

rasping ['rɑːspɪŋ] adj stridulo(a).

Rastafarian [ræstəˈfɛərɪən] adj, n rastafariano(a).

rat [ræt] n ratto.

ratable ['reɪtəbl] adj = **rateable**.

ratchet ['rætʃɪt] n: **~ wheel** ruota dentata.

rate [reɪt] n (proportion) tasso, percentuale f; (speed) velocità f inv; (price) tariffa ♦ vt valutare; stimare; **to ~ sb/sth as** valutare qn/qc come; **to ~ sb/sth among** annoverare qn/qc tra; **to ~ sb/sth highly** stimare molto qn/qc; **at a ~ of 60 kph** alla velocità di 60 km all'ora; ~ **of exchange** tasso di cambio; ~ **of flow** flusso medio; ~ **of growth** tasso di crescita; ~ **of return** tasso di rendimento; **pulse** ~ frequenza delle pulsazioni; see also **rates**.

rateable value ['reɪtəbl-] n (BRIT) valore m imponibile (agli effetti delle imposte comunali).

ratepayer ['reɪtpeɪə*] n (BRIT) contribuente m/f (che paga le imposte comunali).

rates [reɪts] npl (BRIT) imposte fpl comunali.

rather ['rɑːðə*] adv piuttosto; (somewhat) abbastanza; (to some extent) un po'; **it's ~ expensive** è piuttosto caro; (too much) è un po' caro; **there's ~ a lot** ce n'è parecchio; **I would** or **I'd ~ go** preferirei andare; **I had ~ go** farei meglio ad andare; **I'd ~ not leave** preferirei non partire; **or ~** (more accurately) anzi, per essere (più) precisi; **I ~ think he won't**

come credo proprio che non verrà.

ratification [rætɪfɪˈkeɪʃən] n ratificazione f.

ratify ['rætɪfaɪ] vt ratificare.

rating ['reɪtɪŋ] n classificazione f; punteggio di merito; (NAUT: category) classe f; (: sailor: BRIT) marinaio semplice.

ratings ['reɪtɪŋz] npl (RADIO, TV) indice m di ascolto.

ratio ['reɪʃɪəu] n proporzione f; **in the ~ of 2 to 1** in rapporto di 2 a 1.

ration ['ræʃən] n razione f ♦ vt razionare.

rational ['ræʃənl] adj razionale, ragionevole; (solution, reasoning) logico(a).

rationale [ræʃə'nɑːl] n fondamento logico; giustificazione f.

reality TV n reality TV f.

rationalization [ræʃnəlaɪˈzeɪʃən] n razionalizzazione f.

rationalize ['ræʃnəlaɪz] vt razionalizzare.

rationally ['ræʃnəlɪ] adv razionalmente; logicamente.

rationing ['ræʃnɪŋ] n razionamento.

ratpack ['rætpæk] n (BRIT col) stampa scandalistica.

rat poison n veleno per topi.

rat race n carrierismo, corsa al successo.

rattan [ræ'tæn] n malacca.

rattle ['rætl] n tintinnio; (louder) rumore m di ferraglia; (object: of baby) sonaglino; (: of sports fan) raganella ♦ vi risuonare, tintinnare; fare un rumore di ferraglia ♦ vt agitare; far tintinnare; (col: disconcert) sconcertare.

rattlesnake ['rætlsneɪk] n serpente m a sonagli.

ratty ['rætɪ] adj (col) incavolato(a).

raucous ['rɔːkəs] adj sguaiato(a).

raucously ['rɔːkəslɪ] adv sguaiatamente.

raunchy ['rɔːntʃɪ] adj (col: person) allupato(a); (: voice, song) libidinoso(a).

ravage ['rævɪdʒ] vt devastare.

ravages ['rævɪdʒɪz] npl danni mpl.

rave [reɪv] vi (in anger) infuriarsi; (with enthusiasm) andare in estasi; (MED) delirare ♦ n: **a ~** (party) un rave ♦ adj (scene, culture, music) del fenomeno rave ♦ cpd: ~ **review** (col) critica entusiastica.

raven ['reɪvən] n corvo.

ravenous ['rævənəs] adj affamato(a).

ravine [rə'viːn] n burrone m.

raving ['reɪvɪŋ] adj: ~ **lunatic** pazzo(a) furioso(a).

ravings ['reɪvɪŋz] npl vaneggiamenti mpl.

ravioli [rævɪ'əulɪ] n ravioli mpl.

ravish ['rævɪʃ] vt (delight) estasiare.

ravishing ['rævɪʃɪŋ] adj incantevole.

raw [rɔː] adj (uncooked) crudo(a); (not

processed) greggio(a); *(sore)* vivo(a);
(inexperienced) inesperto(a); **to get a** ~
deal *(col: bad bargain)* prendere un
bidone; (: *harsh treatment)* venire trattato
ingiustamente.
Rawalpindi [rɔːlˈpɪndɪ] *n* Rawalpindi *f*.
raw material *n* materia prima.
ray [reɪ] *n* raggio.
rayon [ˈreɪɒn] *n* raion *m*.
raze [reɪz] *vt* radere, distruggere; *(also:* ~
to the ground) radere al suolo.
razor [ˈreɪzə*] *n* rasoio.
razor blade *n* lama di rasoio.
razzle(-dazzle) [ˈræzl(ˈdæzl)] *n* (*BRIT col*): **to
be/go on the** ~ darsi alla pazza gioia.
razzmatazz [ˈræzməˈtæz] *n* (*col*) clamore *m*.
RC *abbr* = **Roman Catholic**.
RCAF *n abbr* = *Royal Canadian Air Force*.
RCMP *n abbr* = *Royal Canadian Mounted
Police*.
RCN *n abbr* = *Royal Canadian Navy*.
RD *abbr* (*US POST*) = *rural delivery*.
Rd *abbr* = *road*.
RDC *n abbr* (*BRIT*) *see* **rural district council**.
RE *n abbr* (*BRIT MIL*: = *Royal Engineers*)
≈ G.M. (= *Genio Militare*); (*BRIT*) =
religious education.
re [riː] *prep* con riferimento a.
reach [riːtʃ] *n* portata; (*of river etc*) tratto
♦ *vt* raggiungere; arrivare a ♦ *vi*
stendersi; (*stretch out hand: also:* ~ **down**,
~ **over**, ~ **across** *etc*) allungare una
mano; **out of/within** ~ (*object*) fuori/a
portata di mano; **within easy** ~ (**of**) (*place*)
a breve distanza (di), vicino (a); **to** ~ **sb
by phone** contattare qn per telefono; **can
I** ~ **you at your hotel?** la posso contattare
al suo albergo?
▶**reach out** *vi*: **to** ~ **out for** stendere la
mano per prendere.
react [riːˈækt] *vi* reagire.
reaction [riːˈækʃən] *n* reazione *f*.
reactionary [riːˈækʃənrɪ] *adj, n*
reazionario(a).
reactor [riːˈæktə*] *n* reattore *m*.
read, *pt, pp* **read** [riːd, red] *vi* leggere ♦ *vt*
leggere; (*understand*) intendere,
interpretare; (*study*) studiare; **do you** ~
me? (*TEL*) mi ricevete?; **to take sth as
read** (*fig*) dare qc per scontato.
▶**read out** *vt* leggere ad alta voce.
▶**read over** *vt* rileggere attentamente.
▶**read through** *vt* (*quickly*) dare una
scorsa a; (*thoroughly*) leggere da cima a
fondo.
▶**read up** *vt*, **read up on** *vt fus* studiare
bene.
readable [ˈriːdəbl] *adj* leggibile; che si

legge volentieri.
reader [ˈriːdə*] *n* lettore/trice; (*book*) libro
di lettura; (*BRIT: at university*) professore
con funzioni preminenti di ricerca.
readership [ˈriːdəʃɪp] *n* (*of paper etc*)
numero di lettori.
readily [ˈrɛdɪlɪ] *adv* volentieri; (*easily*)
facilmente.
readiness [ˈrɛdɪnɪs] *n* prontezza; **in** ~
(*prepared*) pronto(a).
reading [ˈriːdɪŋ] *n* lettura; (*understanding*)
interpretazione *f*; (*on instrument*)
indicazione *f*.
reading lamp *n* lampada da studio.
reading room *n* sala di lettura.
readjust [riːəˈdʒʌst] *vt* raggiustare ♦ *vi*
(*person*): **to** ~ (**to**) riadattarsi (a).
ready [ˈrɛdɪ] *adj* pronto(a); (*willing*)
pronto(a), disposto(a); (*quick*) rapido(a);
(*available*) disponibile ♦ *n*: **at the** ~ (*MIL*)
pronto a sparare; (*fig*) tutto(a) pronto(a);
~ **for use** pronto per l'uso; **to be** ~ **to do
sth** essere pronto a fare qc; **to get** ~ *vi*
prepararsi ♦ *vt* preparare.
ready cash *n* denaro in contanti.
ready-cooked [rɛdɪˈkukt] *adj* già cotto(a).
ready-made [rɛdɪˈmeɪd] *adj*
prefabbricato(a); (*clothes*)
confezionato(a).
ready reckoner [-ˈrɛkənə*] *n* (*BRIT*)
prontuario di calcolo.
ready-to-wear [rɛdɪtəˈwɛə*] *adj* prêt-à-
porter *inv*.
reagent [riːˈeɪdʒənt] *n*: **chemical** ~ reagente
m chimico.
real [rɪəl] *adj* reale; vero(a) ♦ *adv* (*US col*:
very) veramente, proprio; **in** ~ **terms** in
realtà; **in** ~ **life** nella realtà.
real ale *n* birra ad effervescenza naturale.
real estate *n* beni *mpl* immobili.
realism [ˈrɪəlɪzəm] *n* (*also ART*) realismo.
realist [ˈrɪəlɪst] *n* realista *m/f*.
realistic [rɪəˈlɪstɪk] *adj* realistico(a).
reality [riːˈælɪtɪ] *n* realtà *f inv*; **in** ~ in
realtà, in effetti.
realization [rɪəlaɪˈzeɪʃən] *n* (*awareness*)
presa di coscienza; (*of hopes, project etc*)
realizzazione *f*.
realize [ˈrɪəlaɪz] *vt* (*understand*) rendersi
conto di; (*a project, COMM: asset*)
realizzare; **I** ~ **that** ... mi rendo conto *or*
capisco che ....
really [ˈrɪəlɪ] *adv* veramente, davvero.
realm [rɛlm] *n* reame *m*, regno.
real time *n* (*COMPUT*) tempo reale.
Realtor ® [ˈrɪəltɔː*] *n* (*US*) agente *m*
immobiliare.
ream [riːm] *n* risma; ~**s** (*fig col*) pagine e

pagine *fpl.*

reap [riːp] *vt* mietere; *(fig)* raccogliere.

reaper ['riːpə*] *n (machine)* mietitrice *f.*

reappear [riːə'pɪə*] *vi* ricomparire, riapparire.

reappearance [riːə'pɪərəns] *n* riapparizione *f.*

reapply [riːə'plaɪ] *vi:* to ~ for fare un'altra domanda per.

reappraisal [riːə'preɪzl] *n* riesame *m.*

rear [rɪə*] *adj* di dietro; *(AUT: wheel etc)* posteriore ♦ *n* didietro, parte *f* posteriore ♦ *vt (cattle, family)* allevare ♦ *vi (also:* ~ up: *animal)* impennarsi.

rear admiral *n* contrammiraglio.

rear-engined ['rɪər'ɛndʒɪnd] *adj (AUT)* con motore posteriore.

rearguard ['rɪəgɑːd] *n* retroguardia.

rearm [riː'ɑːm] *vt, vi* riarmare.

rearmament [riː'ɑːməmənt] *n* riarmo.

rearrange [riːə'reɪndʒ] *vt* riordinare.

rear-view mirror ['rɪəvjuː-] *n (AUT)* specchio retrovisivo.

reason ['riːzn] *n* ragione *f;* (cause, motive) ragione, motivo ♦ *vi:* to ~ with sb far ragionare qn; to have ~ to think avere motivi per pensare; it stands to ~ that è ovvio che; the ~ for/why la ragione *or* il motivo di/per cui; with good ~ a ragione; all the more ~ why you should not sell it ragione di più per non venderlo.

reasonable ['riːznəbl] *adj* ragionevole; *(not bad)* accettabile.

reasonably ['riːznəblɪ] *adv* ragionevolmente; one can ~ assume that ... uno può facilmente supporre che ....

reasoned ['riːznd] *adj (argument)* ponderato(a).

reasoning ['riːznɪŋ] *n* ragionamento.

reassemble [riːə'sɛmbl] *vt* riunire; *(machine)* rimontare.

reassert [riːə'səːt] *vt* riaffermare.

reassurance [riːə'ʃuərəns] *n* rassicurazione *f.*

reassure [riːə'ʃuə*] *vt* rassicurare; to ~ sb of rassicurare qn di *or* su.

reassuring [riːə'ʃuərɪŋ] *adj* rassicurante.

reawakening [riːə'weɪknɪŋ] *n* risveglio.

rebate ['riːbeɪt] *n* rimborso.

rebel *n* ['rɛbl] ribelle *m/f* ♦ *vi* [rɪ'bɛl] ribellarsi.

rebellion [rɪ'bɛljən] *n* ribellione *f.*

rebellious [rɪ'bɛljəs] *adj* ribelle.

rebirth [riː'bəːθ] *n* rinascita.

rebound *vi* [rɪ'baund] *(ball)* rimbalzare ♦ *n* ['riːbaund] rimbalzo.

rebuff [rɪ'bʌf] *n* secco rifiuto ♦ *vt* respingere.

rebuild [riː'bɪld] *vt irreg* ricostruire.

rebuke [rɪ'bjuːk] *n* rimprovero ♦ *vt* rimproverare.

rebut [rɪ'bʌt] *vt* rifiutare.

rebuttal [rɪ'bʌtl] *n* rifiuto.

recalcitrant [rɪ'kælsɪtrənt] *adj* recalcitrante.

recall [rɪ'kɔːl] *vt (gen, COMPUT)* richiamare; *(remember)* ricordare, richiamare alla mente ♦ *n* richiamo; beyond ~ irrevocabile.

recant [rɪ'kænt] *vi* ritrattarsi; *(REL)* fare abiura.

recap ['riːkæp] *n* ricapitolazione *f* ♦ *vt* ricapitolare ♦ *vi* riassumere.

recapture [riː'kæptʃə*] *vt* riprendere; *(atmosphere)* ricreare.

recd. *abbr = received.*

recede [rɪ'siːd] *vi* allontanarsi; ritirarsi; calare.

receding [rɪ'siːdɪŋ] *adj (forehead, chin)* sfuggente; he's got a ~ hairline è stempiato.

receipt [rɪ'siːt] *n (document)* ricevuta; *(act of receiving)* ricevimento; to acknowledge ~ of accusare ricevuta di; we are in ~ of ... abbiamo ricevuto ....

receipts [rɪ'siːts] *npl (COMM)* introiti *mpl.*

receivable [rɪ'siːvəbl] *adj (COMM)* esigibile; *(: owed)* dovuto(a).

receive [rɪ'siːv] *vt* ricevere; *(guest)* ricevere, accogliere; "~d with thanks" *(COMM)* "per quietanza".

Received Pronunciation (RP) *n (BRIT) see boxed note.*

RECEIVED PRONUNCIATION

Si chiama **Received Pronunciation (RP)** *l'accento dell'inglese parlato in alcune parti del sud-est dell'Inghilterra. In esso si identifica l'inglese "standard" delle classi colte, privo di inflessioni regionali e adottato tradizionalmente dagli annunciatori della BBC. È anche l'accento standard dell'inglese insegnato come lingua straniera.*

---

receiver [rɪ'siːvə*] *n (TEL)* ricevitore *m;* *(RADIO)* apparecchio ricevente; *(of stolen goods)* ricettatore/trice; *(LAW)* curatore *m* fallimentare.

receivership [rɪ'siːvəʃɪp] *n* curatela; to go into ~ andare in amministrazione controllata.

recent ['riːsnt] *adj* recente; in ~ years negli ultimi anni.

recently ['riːsntlɪ] *adv* recentemente; as ~ as ... soltanto ...; until ~ fino a poco tempo fa.

receptacle [rɪ'sɛptɪkl] *n* recipiente *m*.

reception [rɪ'sɛpʃən] *n* (*gen*) ricevimento; (*welcome*) accoglienza; (*TV*) ricezione *f*.

reception centre *n* (*BRIT*) centro di raccolta.

reception desk *n* (*in hotel*) reception *f inv*; (*in hospital, at doctor's*) accettazione *f*; (*in large building, offices*) portineria.

receptionist [rɪ'sɛpʃənɪst] *n* receptionist *m/f inv*.

receptive [rɪ'sɛptɪv] *adj* ricettivo(a).

recess [rɪ'sɛs] *n* (*in room*) alcova; (*POL etc*: *holiday*) vacanze *fpl*; (*US LAW*: *short break*) sospensione *f*; (*US SCOL*) intervallo.

recession [rɪ'sɛʃən] *n* (*ECON*) recessione *f*.

recharge [riː'tʃɑːdʒ] *vt* (*battery*) ricaricare.

rechargeable ['riː'tʃɑːdʒəbl] *adj* ricaricabile.

recipe ['rɛsɪpɪ] *n* ricetta.

recipient [rɪ'sɪpɪənt] *n* beneficiario/a; (*of letter*) destinatario/a.

reciprocal [rɪ'sɪprəkl] *adj* reciproco(a).

reciprocate [rɪ'sɪprəkeɪt] *vt* ricambiare.

recital [rɪ'saɪtl] *n* recital *m inv*; concerto (di solista).

recite [rɪ'saɪt] *vt* (*poem*) recitare.

reckless ['rɛkləs] *adj* (*driver etc*) spericolato(a); (*spender*) incosciente.

recklessly ['rɛkləslɪ] *adv* in modo spericolato; da incosciente.

reckon ['rɛkən] *vt* (*count*) calcolare; (*consider*) considerare, stimare; (*think*): **I ~ that ...** penso che ... ◆ *vi* contare, calcolare; **to ~ without sb/sth** non tener conto di qn/qc; **he is somebody to be ~ed with** è uno da non sottovalutare.

▶**reckon on** *vt fus* contare su.

reckoning ['rɛknɪŋ] *n* conto; stima; **the day of ~** il giorno del giudizio.

reclaim [rɪ'kleɪm] *vt* (*land*) bonificare; (*demand back*) richiedere, reclamare.

recline [rɪ'klaɪn] *vi* stare sdraiato(a).

reclining [rɪ'klaɪnɪŋ] *adj* (*seat*) ribaltabile.

recluse [rɪ'kluːs] *n* eremita *m*, recluso/a.

recognition [rɛkəg'nɪʃən] *n* riconoscimento; **to gain ~** essere riconosciuto(a); **in ~ of** in *or* come segno di riconoscimento per; **transformed beyond ~** irriconoscibile.

recognizable ['rɛkəgnaɪzəbl] *adj*: **~ (by)** riconoscibile (a *or* da).

recognize ['rɛkəgnaɪz] *vt*: **to ~ (by/as)** riconoscere (a *or* da/come).

recoil [rɪ'kɔɪl] *vi* (*gun*) rinculare; (*spring*): **to ~ (from)** balzare indietro; (*person*): **to ~ (from)** indietreggiare (davanti a) ◆ *n* (*of gun*) rinculo.

recollect [rɛkə'lɛkt] *vt* ricordare.

recollection [rɛkə'lɛkʃən] *n* ricordo; **to the best of my ~** per quello che mi ricordo.

recommend [rɛkə'mɛnd] *vt* raccomandare; (*advise*) consigliare; **she has a lot to ~ her** ha molti elementi a suo favore.

recommendation [rɛkəmɛn'deɪʃən] *n* raccomandazione *f*; consiglio.

recommended retail price (RRP) [rɛkə'mɛndɪd-] *n* (*BRIT*) prezzo raccomandato al dettaglio.

recompense ['rɛkəmpɛns] *vt* ricompensare; (*compensate*) risarcire ◆ *n* ricompensa; risarcimento.

reconcilable ['rɛkənsaɪləbl] *adj* conciliabile.

reconcile ['rɛkənsaɪl] *vt* (*two people*) riconciliare; (*two facts*) conciliare, quadrare; **to ~ o.s. to** rassegnarsi a.

reconciliation [rɛkənsɪlɪ'eɪʃən] *n* riconciliazione *f*; conciliazione *f*.

recondition [riːkən'dɪʃən] *vt* rimettere a nuovo; rifare.

reconnaissance [rɪ'kɔnɪsns] *n* (*MIL*) ricognizione *f*.

reconnoitre, (*US*) reconnoiter [rɛkə'nɔɪtə*] (*MIL*) *vt* fare una ricognizione di ◆ *vi* fare una ricognizione.

reconsider [riːkən'sɪdə*] *vt* riconsiderare.

reconstitute [riː'kɔnstɪtjuːt] *vt* ricostituire.

reconstruct [riːkən'strʌkt] *vt* ricostruire.

reconstruction [riːkən'strʌkʃən] *n* ricostruzione *f*.

reconvene [riːkən'viːn] *vt* riconvocare ◆ *vi* radunarsi.

record *n* ['rɛkɔːd] ricordo, documento; (*of meeting etc*) nota, verbale *m*; (*register*) registro; (*file*) pratica, dossier *m inv*; (*COMPUT*) record *m inv*, registrazione *f*; (*also*: **police ~**) fedina penale sporca; (*MUS*: *disc*) disco; (*SPORT*) record *m inv*, primato ◆ *vt* [rɪ'kɔːd] (*set down*) prendere nota di; (*relate*) raccontare; (*COMPUT, MUS*: *song etc*) registrare; **public ~s** archivi *mpl*; **Italy's excellent ~** i brillanti successi italiani; **in ~ time** a tempo di record; **to keep a ~ of** tener nota di; **to set the ~ straight** mettere le cose in chiaro; **off the ~** *adj* ufficioso(a) ◆ *adv* ufficiosamente; **he is on ~ as saying that** ... ha dichiarato pubblicamente che ....

record card *n* (*in file*) scheda.

recorded delivery letter [rɪ'kɔːdɪd-] *n* (*BRIT POST*) lettera raccomandata.

recorder [rɪ'kɔːdə*] *n* (*LAW*) avvocato che funge da giudice; (*MUS*) flauto diritto.

record holder *n* (*SPORT*) primatista *m/f*.

recording [rɪ'kɔːdɪŋ] *n* (*MUS*) registrazione *f*.

recording studio *n* studio di registrazione.
record player *n* giradischi *m inv.*
recount [rɪ'kaunt] *vt* raccontare, narrare.
re-count *n* ['riːkaunt] (*POL: of votes*) nuovo conteggio ♦ *vt* [riː'kaunt] ricontare.
recoup [rɪ'kuːp] *vt* ricuperare; **to ~ one's losses** ricuperare le perdite, rifarsi.
recourse [rɪ'kɔːs] *n*: **to have ~ to** ricorrere a.
recover [rɪ'kʌvə*] *vt* ricuperare ♦ *vi* (*from illness*) rimettersi (in salute), ristabilirsi; (*country, person: from shock*) riprendersi.
re-cover [riː'kʌvə*] *vt* (*chair etc*) ricoprire.
recovery [rɪ'kʌvərɪ] *n* ricupero; ristabilimento; ripresa.
recreate [riːkrɪ'eɪt] *vt* ricreare.
recreation [rɛkrɪ'eɪʃən] *n* ricreazione *f*; svago.
recreational [rɛkrɪ'eɪʃənəl] *adj* ricreativo(a).
recreational drug *n* droga usata saltuariamente.
recreational vehicle (RV) *n* (*US*) camper *m inv.*
recrimination [rɪkrɪmɪ'neɪʃən] *n* recriminazione *f.*
recruit [rɪ'kruːt] *n* recluta ♦ *vt* reclutare.
recruitment [rɪ'kruːtmənt] *n* reclutamento.
rectangle ['rɛktæŋgl] *n* rettangolo.
rectangular [rɛk'tæŋgjulə*] *adj* rettangolare.
rectify ['rɛktɪfaɪ] *vt* (*error*) rettificare; (*omission*) riparare.
rector ['rɛktə*] *n* (*REL*) parroco (*anglicano*); (*in Scottish universities*) personalità eletta dagli studenti per rappresentarli.
rectory ['rɛktərɪ] *n* presbiterio.
rectum ['rɛktəm] *n* (*ANAT*) retto.
recuperate [rɪ'kjuːpəreɪt] *vi* ristabilirsi.
recur [rɪ'kəː*] *vi* riaccadere; (*idea, opportunity*) riapparire; (*symptoms*) ripresentarsi.
recurrence [rɪ'kʌrəns] *n* ripresentarsi *m*; riapparizione *f.*
recurrent [rɪ'kʌrənt] *adj* ricorrente.
recurring [rɪ'kʌrɪŋ] *adj* (*MATH*) periodico(a).
recycle [riː'saɪkl] *vt* riciclare.
red [rɛd] *n* rosso, (*POL: pej*) rosso/a ♦ *adj* rosso(a); **in the ~** (*account*) scoperto; (*business*) in deficit.
red alert *n* allarme *m* rosso.
red-blooded ['rɛd'blʌdɪd] *adj* (*col*) gagliardo(a).
red-brick university ['rɛdbrɪk-] *n* (*BRIT*) *università di recente formazione; see boxed note.*

RED-BRICK UNIVERSITY

In Gran Bretagna, con **red-brick university** *(letteralmente, università di mattoni rossi) si indicano le università istituite tra la fine dell'Ottocento e i primi del Novecento, per contraddistinguerle dalle università più antiche, i cui edifici sono di pietra; vedi anche* **Oxbridge.**

red carpet treatment *n* cerimonia col gran pavese.
Red Cross *n* Croce *f* Rossa.
redcurrant ['rɛdkʌrənt] *n* ribes *m inv.*
redden ['rɛdn] *vt* arrossare ♦ *vi* arrossire.
reddish ['rɛdɪʃ] *adj* rossiccio(a).
redecorate [riː'dɛkəreɪt] *vt* tinteggiare (e tappezzare) di nuovo.
redeem [rɪ'diːm] *vt* (*debt*) riscattare; (*sth in pawn*) ritirare; (*fig, also REL*) redimere.
redeemable [rɪ'diːməbl] *adj* con diritto di riscatto; redimibile.
redeeming [rɪ'diːmɪŋ] *adj* (*feature*) che salva.
redefine [riːdɪ'faɪn] *vt* ridefinire.
redemption [rɪ'dɛmpʃən] *n* (*REL*) redenzione *f*; **past** *or* **beyond ~** irrecuperabile.
redeploy [riːdɪ'plɔɪ] *vt* (*MIL*) riorganizzare lo schieramento di; (*resources*) riorganizzare.
redeployment [riːdɪ'plɔɪmənt] *n* riorganizzazione *f.*
redevelop [riːdɪ'vɛləp] *vt* ristrutturare.
redevelopment [riːdɪ'vɛləpmənt] *n* ristrutturazione *f.*
red-handed [rɛd'hændɪd] *adj*: **to be caught ~** essere preso(a) in flagrante *or* con le mani nel sacco.
redhead ['rɛdhɛd] *n* rosso/a.
red herring *n* (*fig*) falsa pista.
red-hot [rɛd'hɔt] *adj* arroventato(a).
redirect [riːdaɪ'rɛkt] *vt* (*mail*) far seguire.
redistribute [riːdɪ'strɪbjuːt] *vt* ridistribuire.
red-letter day ['rɛdlɛtə-] *n* giorno memorabile.
red light *n*: **to go through a ~** (*AUT*) passare col rosso.
red-light district [rɛd'laɪt-] *n* quartiere *m* luce rossa *inv.*
red meat *n* carne *f* rossa.
redness ['rɛdnɪs] *n* rossore *m*; (*of hair*) rosso.
redo [riː'duː] *vt irreg* rifare.
redolent ['rɛdələnt] *adj*: **~ of** che sa di; (*fig*) che ricorda.

redouble [riː'dʌbl] *vt*: **to ~ one's efforts** raddoppiare gli sforzi.

redraft [riː'drɑːft] *vt* fare una nuova stesura di.

redress [rɪ'drɛs] *n* riparazione *f* ♦ *vt* riparare; **to ~ the balance** ristabilire l'equilibrio.

Red Sea *n*: **the ~** il mar Rosso.

redskin ['rɛdskɪn] *n* pellerossa *m/f*.

red tape *n* (*fig*) burocrazia.

reduce [rɪ'djuːs] *vt* ridurre; (*lower*) ridurre, abbassare; "**~ speed now**" (*AUT*) "rallentare"; **to ~ sth by/to** ridurre qc di/a; **to ~ sb to silence/despair/tears** ridurre qn al silenzio/alla disperazione/in lacrime.

reduced [rɪ'djuːst] *adj* (*decreased*) ridotto(a); **at a ~ price** a prezzo ribassato *or* ridotto; "**greatly ~ prices**" "grandi ribassi".

reduction [rɪ'dʌkʃən] *n* riduzione *f*; (*of price*) ribasso; (*discount*) sconto.

redundancy [rɪ'dʌndənsɪ] *n* licenziamento (per eccesso di personale); **compulsory ~** licenziamento; **voluntary ~** *forma di cassa integrazione volontaria*.

redundancy payment *n* (*BRIT*) indennità *f inv* di licenziamento.

redundant [rɪ'dʌndnt] *adj* (*BRIT*: *worker*) licenziato(a); (*detail, object*) superfluo(a); **to make ~** (*BRIT*) licenziare (per eccesso di personale).

reed [riːd] *n* (*BOT*) canna; (*MUS*: *of clarinet etc*) ancia.

re-educate [riː'edjukeɪt] *vt* rieducare.

reedy ['riːdɪ] *adj* (*voice, instrument*) acuto(a).

reef [riːf] *n* (*at sea*) scogliera; **coral ~** barriera corallina.

reek [riːk] *vi*: **to ~ (of)** puzzare (di).

reel [riːl] *n* bobina, rocchetto; (*TECH*) aspo; (*FISHING*) mulinello; (*CINE*) rotolo ♦ *vt* (*TECH*) annaspare; (*also*: **~ up**) avvolgere ♦ *vi* (*sway*) barcollare, vacillare; **my head is ~ing** mi gira la testa.

▸**reel off** *vt* snocciolare.

re-election [riːɪ'lekʃən] *n* rielezione *f*.

re-enter [riː'entə*] *vt* rientrare in.

re-entry [riː'entrɪ] *n* rientro.

re-export *vt* [riːɪk'spɔːt] riesportare ♦ *n* [riː'ekspɔːt] merce *f* riesportata, riesportazione *f*.

ref [rɛf] *n abbr* (*col*: = referee) arbitro.

ref. *abbr* (*COMM*: = with reference to) sogg.

refectory [rɪ'fɛktərɪ] *n* refettorio.

refer [rɪ'fə:*] *vt*: **to ~ sth to** (*dispute, decision*) deferire qc a; **to ~ sb to**

(*inquirer*: *for information*) indirizzare qn a; (*reader*: *to text*) rimandare qn a; **he ~red me to the manager** mi ha detto di rivolgermi al direttore.

▸**refer to** *vt fus* (*allude to*) accennare a; (*apply to*) riferire a; (*consult*) rivolgersi a; **~ring to your letter** (*COMM*) in riferimento alla Vostra lettera.

referee [rɛfə'riː] *n* arbitro; (*TENNIS*) giudice *m* di gara; (*BRIT*: *for job application*) referenza ♦ *vt* arbitrare.

reference ['rɛfrəns] *n* riferimento; (*mention*) menzione *f*, allusione *f*; (*for job application*: *letter*) referenza; lettera di raccomandazione; (: *person*) referenza; (*in book*) rimando; **with ~ to** riguardo a; (*COMM*: *in letter*) in *or* con riferimento a; "**please quote this ~**" (*COMM*) "si prega di far riferimento al numero di protocollo".

reference book *n* libro di consultazione.

reference library *n* biblioteca per la consultazione.

reference number *n* (*COMM*) numero di riferimento.

referendum, *pl* referenda [rɛfə'rɛndəm, -də] *n* referendum *m inv*.

referral [rɪ'fə:rəl] *n* deferimento; (*MED*) richiesta (di visita specialistica).

refill *vt* [riː'fɪl] riempire di nuovo; (*pen, lighter etc*) ricaricare ♦ *n* ['riːfɪl] (*for pen etc*) ricambio.

refine [rɪ'faɪn] *vt* raffinare.

refined [rɪ'faɪnd] *adj* raffinato(a).

refinement [rɪ'faɪnmənt] *n* (*of person*) raffinatezza.

refinery [rɪ'faɪnərɪ] *n* raffineria.

refit *n* ['riːfɪt] (*NAUT*) raddobbo ♦ *vt* [riː'fɪt] (*ship*) raddobbare.

reflate [riː'fleɪt] *vt* (*economy*) rilanciare.

reflation [riː'fleɪʃən] *n* rilancio.

reflationary [riː'fleɪʃənərɪ] *adj* nuovamente inflazionario(a).

reflect [rɪ'flɛkt] *vt* (*light, image*) riflettere; (*fig*) rispecchiare ♦ *vi* (*think*) riflettere, considerare.

▸**reflect on** *vt fus* (*discredit*) rispecchiarsi su.

reflection [rɪ'flɛkʃən] *n* riflessione *f*; (*image*) riflesso; (*criticism*): **~ on** giudizio su; attacco a; **on ~** pensandoci sopra.

reflector [rɪ'flɛktə*] *n* (*also AUT*) catarifrangente *m*.

reflex ['riːflɛks] *adj* riflesso(a) ♦ *n* riflesso.

reflexive [rɪ'flɛksɪv] *adj* (*LING*) riflessivo(a).

reform [rɪ'fɔːm] *n* riforma ♦ *vt* riformare.

reformat [rɪ'fɔːmæt] *vt* (*COMPUT*) riformattare.

Reformation [rɛfə'meɪʃən] n: **the ~** la Riforma.

reformatory [rɪ'fɔ:mətərɪ] n (US) riformatorio.

reformed [rɪ'fɔ:md] adj cambiato(a) (per il meglio).

reformer [rɪ'fɔ:mə*] n riformatore/trice.

refrain [rɪ'freɪn] vi: **to ~ from doing** trattenersi dal fare ♦ n ritornello.

refresh [rɪ'frɛʃ] vt rinfrescare; (subj: food, sleep) ristorare.

refresher course [rɪ'frɛʃə-] n (BRIT) corso di aggiornamento.

refreshing [rɪ'frɛʃɪŋ] adj (drink) rinfrescante; (sleep) riposante, ristoratore(trice); (change etc) piacevole; (idea, point of view) originale.

refreshment [rɪ'frɛʃmənt] n (eating, resting etc) ristoro; **~(s)** rinfreschi mpl.

refrigeration [rɪfrɪdʒə'reɪʃən] n refrigerazione f.

refrigerator [rɪ'frɪdʒəreɪtə*] n frigorifero.

refuel [ri:'fjuəl] vt rifornire (di carburante) ♦ vi far rifornimento (di carburante).

refuge ['rɛfju:dʒ] n rifugio; **to take ~ in** rifugiarsi in.

refugee [rɛfju'dʒi:] n rifugiato/a, profugo/a.

refugee camp n campo (di) profughi.

refund n ['ri:fʌnd] rimborso ♦ vt [rɪ'fʌnd] rimborsare.

refurbish [ri:'fə:bɪʃ] vt rimettere a nuovo.

refurnish [ri:'fə:nɪʃ] vt ammobiliare di nuovo.

refusal [rɪ'fju:zəl] n rifiuto; **to have first ~ on sth** avere il diritto d'opzione su qc.

refuse n ['rɛfju:s] rifiuti mpl ♦ vt, vi [rɪ'fju:z] rifiutare; **to ~ to do sth** rifiutare or rifiutarsi di fare qc.

refuse collection n raccolta di rifiuti.

refuse disposal n sistema m di scarico dei rifiuti.

refusenik [rɪ'fju:znɪk] n ebreo a cui il governo sovietico impediva di lasciare il paese.

refute [rɪ'fju:t] vt confutare.

regain [rɪ'geɪn] vt riguadagnare; riacquistare, ricuperare.

regal ['ri:gl] adj regale.

regale [rɪ'geɪl] vt: **to ~ sb with sth** intrattenere qn con qc.

regalia [rɪ'geɪlɪə] n insegne fpl reali.

regard [rɪ'gɑ:d] n riguardo, stima ♦ vt considerare, stimare; **to give my ~s to** porgere i suoi saluti a; **(kind) ~s** cordiali saluti; **as ~s, with ~ to** riguardo a.

regarding [rɪ'gɑ:dɪŋ] prep riguardo a, per quanto riguarda.

regardless [rɪ'gɑ:dlɪs] adv lo stesso; **~ of a**

dispetto di, nonostante.

regatta [rɪ'gætə] n regata.

regency ['ri:dʒənsɪ] n reggenza.

regenerate [rɪ'dʒɛnəreɪt] vt rigenerare; (feelings, enthusiasm) far rinascere ♦ vi rigenerarsi; rinascere.

regent ['ri:dʒənt] n reggente m.

reggae ['rɛgeɪ] n reggae m.

régime [reɪ'ʒi:m] n regime m.

regiment n ['rɛdʒɪmənt] reggimento ♦ vt ['rɛdʒɪment] irreggimentare.

regimental [rɛdʒɪ'mɛntl] adj reggimentale.

regimentation [rɛdʒɪmɛn'teɪʃən] n irreggimentazione f.

region ['ri:dʒən] n regione f; **in the ~ of (fig)** all'incirca di.

regional ['ri:dʒənl] adj regionale.

regional development n sviluppo regionale.

register ['rɛdʒɪstə*] n registro; (also: **electoral ~**) lista elettorale ♦ vt registrare; (vehicle) immatricolare; (luggage) spedire assicurato(a); (letter) assicurare; (subj: instrument) segnare ♦ vi iscriversi; (at hotel) firmare il registro; (make impression) entrare in testa; **to ~ a protest** fare un esposto; **to ~ for a course** iscriversi a un corso.

registered ['rɛdʒɪstəd] adj (design) depositato(a); (BRIT: letter) assicurato(a); (student, voter) iscritto(a).

registered company n società iscritta al registro.

registered nurse n (US) infermiere(a) diplomato(a).

registered office n sede f legale.

registered trademark n marchio depositato.

registrar ['rɛdʒɪstrɑ:*] n ufficiale m di stato civile; segretario.

registration [rɛdʒɪs'treɪʃən] n (act) registrazione f; iscrizione f; (AUT: also: **~ number**) numero di targa.

registry ['rɛdʒɪstrɪ] n ufficio del registro.

registry office n (BRIT) anagrafe f; **to get married in a ~ ≈** sposarsi in municipio.

regret [rɪ'grɛt] n rimpianto, rincrescimento ♦ vt rimpiangere; **I ~ that I/he cannot help** mi rincresce di non poter aiutare/ che lui non possa aiutare; **we ~ to inform you that ...** siamo spiacenti di informarla che ....

regretfully [rɪ'grɛtfəlɪ] adv con rincrescimento.

regrettable [rɪ'grɛtəbl] adj deplorevole.

regrettably [rɪ'grɛtəblɪ] adv purtroppo, sfortunatamente.

regroup [ri:'gru:p] vt raggruppare ♦ vi

raggrupparsi.

regt abbr (= regiment) Reg.

regular ['rɛgjulə*] adj regolare; (usual) abituale, normale; (listener, reader) fedele; (soldier) dell'esercito regolare; (COMM: size) normale ◊ n (client etc) cliente m/f abituale.

regularity [rɛgju'lærɪtɪ] n regolarità f inv.

regularly ['rɛgjuləlɪ] adv regolarmente.

regulate ['rɛgjuleɪt] vt regolare.

regulation [rɛgju'leɪʃən] n (rule) regola, regolamento; (adjustment) regolazione f ◊ cpd (MIL) di ordinanza.

rehabilitate [riːə'bɪlɪteɪt] vt (criminal, drug addict, invalid) ricuperare, reinserire.

rehabilitation ['riːəbɪlɪ'teɪʃən] n (see vb) ricupero, reinserimento.

rehash [riː'hæʃ] vt (col) rimaneggiare.

rehearsal [rɪ'hɔːsəl] n prova; **dress** ~ prova generale.

rehearse [rɪ'hɔːs] vt provare.

rehouse [riː'hauz] vt rialloggiare.

reign [reɪn] n regno ◊ vi regnare.

reigning ['reɪnɪŋ] adj (monarch) regnante; (champion) attuale.

reimburse [riːɪm'bɔːs] vt rimborsare.

rein [reɪn] n (for horse) briglia; **to give sb free** ~ (fig) lasciare completa libertà a qn.

reincarnation [riːɪnkɑː'neɪʃən] n reincarnazione f.

reindeer ['reɪndɪə*] n (pl inv) renna.

reinforce [riːɪn'fɔːs] vt rinforzare.

reinforced concrete [riːɪn'fɔːst-] n cemento armato.

reinforcement [riːɪn'fɔːsmənt] n (action) rinforzamento; ~**s** npl (MIL) rinforzi mpl.

reinstate [riːɪn'steɪt] vt reintegrare.

reinstatement [riːɪn'steɪtmənt] n reintegrazione f.

reissue [riː'ɪʃjuː] vt (book) ristampare, ripubblicare; (film) distribuire di nuovo.

reiterate [riː'ɪtəreɪt] vt reiterare, ripetere.

reject n ['riːdʒɛkt] (COMM) scarto ◊ vt [rɪ'dʒɛkt] rifiutare, respingere; (COMM: goods) scartare.

rejection [rɪ'dʒɛkʃən] n rifiuto.

rejoice [rɪ'dʒɔɪs] vi: **to** ~ (**at** or **over**) provare diletto (in).

rejoinder [rɪ'dʒɔɪndə*] n (retort) replica.

rejuvenate [rɪ'dʒuːvəneɪt] vt ringiovanire.

rekindle [riː'kɪndl] vt riaccendere.

relapse [rɪ'læps] n (MED) ricaduta.

relate [rɪ'leɪt] vt (tell) raccontare; (connect) collegare ◊ vi: **to** ~ **to** (refer to) riferirsi a; (get on with) stabilire un rapporto con.

related [rɪ'leɪtɪd] adj imparentato(a); collegato(a), connesso(a); ~ **to**

imparentato(a) con; collegato(a) or connesso(a) con.

relating [rɪ'leɪtɪŋ]: ~ **to** prep che riguarda, rispetto a.

relation [rɪ'leɪʃən] n (person) parente m/f; (link) rapporto, relazione f; **in** ~ **to** con riferimento a; **diplomatic/international** ~**s** rapporti diplomatici/internazionali; **to bear a** ~ **to** corrispondere a.

relationship [rɪ'leɪʃənʃɪp] n rapporto; (personal ties) rapporti mpl, relazioni fpl; (also: **family** ~) legami mpl di parentela; (affair) relazione f; **they have a good** ~ vanno molto d'accordo.

relative ['rɛlətɪv] n parente m/f ◊ adj relativo(a); (respective) rispettivo(a).

relatively ['rɛlətɪvlɪ] adv relativamente.

relax [rɪ'læks] vi rilasciarsi; (person: unwind) rilassarsi ◊ vt rilasciare; (mind, person) rilassare; ~! (calm down) calma!

relaxation [riːlæk'seɪʃən] n rilasciamento; rilassamento; (entertainment) ricreazione f, svago.

relaxed [rɪ'lækst] adj rilasciato(a); rilassato(a).

relaxing [rɪ'læksɪŋ] adj rilassante.

relay ['riːleɪ] n (SPORT) corsa a staffetta ◊ vt (message) trasmettere.

release [rɪ'liːs] n (from prison) rilascio; (from obligation) liberazione f; (of gas etc) emissione f; (of film etc) distribuzione f; (record) disco; (device) disinnesto ◊ vt (prisoner) rilasciare; (from obligation, wreckage etc) liberare; (book, film) fare uscire; (news) rendere pubblico(a); (gas etc) emettere; (TECH: catch, spring etc) disinnestare; (let go) rilasciare; lasciar andare; sciogliere; **to** ~ **one's grip** mollare la presa; **to** ~ **the clutch** (AUT) staccare la frizione.

relegate ['rɛləgeɪt] vt relegare; (SPORT): **to be** ~**d** essere retrocesso(a).

relent [rɪ'lɛnt] vi cedere.

relentless [rɪ'lɛntlɪs] adj implacabile.

relevance ['rɛləvəns] n pertinenza; ~ **of sth to sth** rapporto tra qc e qc.

relevant ['rɛləvənt] adj pertinente; (chapter) in questione; ~ **to** pertinente a.

reliability [rɪlaɪə'bɪlɪtɪ] n (of person) serietà f; (of machine) affidabilità.

reliable [rɪ'laɪəbl] adj (person, firm) fidato(a), che dà affidamento; (method) sicuro(a); (machine) affidabile.

reliably [rɪ'laɪəblɪ] adv: **to be** ~ **informed** sapere da fonti sicure.

reliance [rɪ'laɪəns] n: ~ (**on**) dipendenza (da).

reliant [rɪ'laɪənt] *adj*: **to be ~ on sth/sb** dipendere da qc/qn.

relic ['rɛlɪk] *n* (*REL*) reliquia; (*of the past*) resto.

relief [rɪ'liːf] *n* (*from pain, anxiety*) sollievo; (*help, supplies*) soccorsi *mpl*; (*of guard*) cambio; (*ART, GEO*) rilievo; **by way of light ~** come diversivo.

relief map *n* carta in rilievo.

relief road *n* (*BRIT*) circonvallazione *f*.

relieve [rɪ'liːv] *vt* (*pain, patient*) sollevare; (*bring help*) soccorrere; (*take over from*: *gen*) sostituire; (: *guard*) rilevare; **to ~ sb of sth** (*load*) alleggerire qn di qc; **to ~ sb of his command** (*MIL*) esonerare qn dal comando; **to ~ o.s.** (*euphemism*) fare i propri bisogni.

relieved [rɪ'liːvd] *adj* sollevato(a); **to be ~ that ...** essere sollevato(a) (dal fatto) che ...; **I'm ~ to hear it** mi hai tolto un peso con questa notizia.

religion [rɪ'lɪdʒən] *n* religione *f*.

religious [rɪ'lɪdʒəs] *adj* religioso(a).

religious education *n* religione *f*.

relinquish [rɪ'lɪŋkwɪʃ] *vt* abbandonare; (*plan, habit*) rinunziare a.

relish ['rɛlɪʃ] *n* (*CULIN*) condimento; (*enjoyment*) gran piacere *m* ♦ *vt* (*food etc*) godere; **to ~ doing** adorare fare.

relive [riː'lɪv] *vt* rivivere.

reload [riː'ləud] *vt* ricaricare.

relocate [riːləu'keɪt] *vt* (*business*) trasferire ♦ *vi*: **to ~ in** trasferire la propria sede a.

reluctance [rɪ'lʌktəns] *n* riluttanza.

reluctant [rɪ'lʌktənt] *adj* riluttante, mal disposto(a); **to be ~ to do sth** essere restio a fare qc.

reluctantly [rɪ'lʌktəntlɪ] *adv* di mala voglia, a malincuore.

rely [rɪ'laɪ]: **to ~ on** *vt fus* contare su; (*be dependent*) dipendere da.

remain [rɪ'meɪn] *vi* restare, rimanere; **to ~ silent** restare in silenzio; **I ~, yours faithfully** (*BRIT*: *in letters*) distinti saluti.

remainder [rɪ'meɪndə*] *n* resto; (*COMM*) rimanenza.

remaining [rɪ'meɪnɪŋ] *adj* che rimane.

remains [rɪ'meɪnz] *npl* resti *mpl*.

remand [rɪ'mɑːnd] *n*: **on ~** in detenzione preventiva ♦ *vt*: **to ~ in custody** rinviare in carcere; trattenere a disposizione della legge.

remand home *n* (*BRIT*) riformatorio, casa di correzione.

remark [rɪ'mɑːk] *n* osservazione *f* ♦ *vt* osservare, dire; (*notice*) notare ♦ *vi*: **to ~ on sth** fare dei commenti su qc.

remarkable [rɪ'mɑːkəbl] *adj* notevole;

eccezionale.

remarry [riː'mærɪ] *vi* risposarsi.

remedial [rɪ'miːdɪəl] *adj* (*tuition, classes*) di riparazione.

remedy ['rɛmədɪ] *n*: **~ (for)** rimedio (per) ♦ *vt* rimediare a.

remember [rɪ'mɛmbə*] *vt* ricordare, ricordarsi di; **I ~ seeing it, I ~ having seen it** (mi) ricordo di averlo visto; **she ~ed to do it** si è ricordata di farlo; **~ me to your wife and children!** saluti sua moglie e i bambini da parte mia!

remembrance [rɪ'mɛmbrəns] *n* memoria; ricordo.

Remembrance Sunday *n* (*BRIT*) *see boxed note.*

remind [rɪ'maɪnd] *vt*: **to ~ sb of sth** ricordare qc a qn; **to ~ sb to do** ricordare a qn di fare; **that ~s me!** a proposito!

reminder [rɪ'maɪndə*] *n* richiamo; (*note etc*) promemoria *m inv*.

reminisce [rɛmɪ'nɪs] *vi*: **to ~ (about)** abbandonarsi ai ricordi (di).

reminiscences [rɛmɪ'nɪsnsɪz] *npl* reminiscenze *fpl*, memorie *fpl*.

reminiscent [rɛmɪ'nɪsnt] *adj*: **~ of** che fa pensare a, che richiama.

remiss [rɪ'mɪs] *adj* negligente; **it was ~ of me** è stata una negligenza da parte mia.

remission [rɪ'mɪʃən] *n* remissione *f*; (*of fee*) esonero.

remit [rɪ'mɪt] *vt* rimettere.

remittance [rɪ'mɪtəns] *n* rimessa.

remnant ['rɛmnənt] *n* resto, avanzo; **~s** *npl* (*COMM*) scampoli *mpl*; fine *f* serie.

remonstrate ['rɛmənstreɪt] *vi* protestare; **to ~ with sb about sth** fare le proprie rimostranze a qn circa qc.

remorse [rɪ'mɔːs] *n* rimorso.

remorseful [rɪ'mɔːsful] *adj* pieno(a) di rimorsi.

remorseless [rɪ'mɔːslɪs] *adj* spietato(a).

remote [rɪ'məut] *adj* remoto(a), lontano(a); (*person*) distaccato(a); **there is a ~ possibility that ...** c'è una vaga possibilità che ... + *sub*.

remote control *n* telecomando.

remote-controlled [rɪ'məutkən'trəuld] *adj* telecomandato(a).

remotely [rɪ'məutlɪ] *adv* remotamente; (*slightly*) vagamente.

remould ['riːməuld] *n* (*BRIT: tyre*) gomma rivestita.

removable [rɪ'muːvəbl] *adj* (*detachable*) staccabile.

removal [rɪ'muːvəl] *n* (*taking away*) rimozione *f*; soppressione *f*; (*from house*) trasloco; (*from office: sacking*) destituzione *f*; (*MED*) ablazione *f*.

removal man *n* (*BRIT*) addetto ai traslochi.

removal van *n* (*BRIT*) furgone *m* per traslochi.

remove [rɪ'muːv] *vt* togliere, rimuovere; (*employee*) destituire; (*stain*) far sparire; (*doubt, abuse*) sopprimere, eliminare; **first cousin once ~d** cugino di secondo grado.

remover [rɪ'muːvə*] *n* (*for paint*) prodotto sverniciante; (*for varnish*) solvente *m*; **make-up ~** struccatore *m*.

remunerate [rɪ'mjuːnəreɪt] *vt* rimunerare.

remuneration [rɪmjuːnə'reɪʃən] *n* rimunerazione *f*.

Renaissance [rə'neɪsəns] *n*: **the ~** il Rinascimento.

rename [riː'neɪm] *vt* ribattezzare.

rend [rɛnd], *pt, pp* **rent** [rɛnd, rɛnt] *vt* lacerare.

render ['rɛndə*] *vt* rendere; (*CULIN: fat*) struggere.

rendering ['rɛndərɪŋ] *n* (*MUS etc*) interpretazione *f*.

rendez-vous ['rɒndɪvuː] *n* appuntamento; (*place*) luogo d'incontro; (*meeting*) incontro ♦ *vi* ritrovarsi; (*spaceship*) effettuare un rendez-vous.

rendition [rɛn'dɪʃən] *n* (*MUS*) interpretazione *f*.

renegade ['rɛnɪgeɪd] *n* rinnegato/a.

renew [rɪ'njuː] *vt* rinnovare; (*negotiations*) riprendere.

renewable [rɪ'njuːəbl] *adj* riutilizzabile; **~ energy, ~s** fonti *mpl* di energia rinnovabile.

renewal [rɪ'njuːəl] *n* rinnovamento; ripresa.

renounce [rɪ'nauns] *vt* rinunziare a; (*disown*) ripudiare.

renovate ['rɛnəveɪt] *vt* rinnovare; (*art work*) restaurare.

renovation [rɛnə'veɪʃən] *n* rinnovamento; restauro.

renown [rɪ'naun] *n* rinomanza.

renowned [rɪ'naund] *adj* rinomato(a).

rent [rɛnt] *pt, pp of* **rend** ♦ *n* affitto ♦ *vt* (*take for rent*) prendere in affitto; (*car, TV*)

noleggiare, prendere a noleggio; (*also: ~ out*) dare in affitto; (*car, TV*) noleggiare, dare a noleggio.

rental ['rɛntl] *n* (*cost: on TV, telephone*) abbonamento; (: *on car*) nolo, noleggio.

rent boy *n* (*BRIT col*) giovane prostituto.

renunciation [rɪnʌnsɪ'eɪʃən] *n* rinnegamento; (*self-denial*) rinunzia.

reopen [riː'əupən] *vt* riaprire.

reopening [riː'əupnɪŋ] *n* riapertura.

reorder [riː'ɔːdə*] *vt* ordinare di nuovo; (*rearrange*) riorganizzare.

reorganize [riː'ɔːgənaɪz] *vt* riorganizzare.

Rep *abbr* (*US POL*) = **representative**; **Republican.**

rep [rɛp] *n abbr* (*COMM*: = *representative*) rappresentante *m/f*; (*THEAT*: = *repertory*) teatro di repertorio.

repair [rɪ'pɛə*] *n* riparazione *f* ♦ *vt* riparare; **in good/bad ~** in buona/cattiva condizione; **under ~** in riparazione.

repair kit *n* corredo per riparazioni.

repair man *n* riparatore *m*.

repair shop *n* (*AUT etc*) officina.

repartee [rɛpaː'tiː] *n* risposta pronta.

repast [rɪ'paːst] *n* (*formal*) pranzo.

repatriate [riː'pætrɪeɪt] *vt* rimpatriare.

repay [riː'peɪ] *vt irreg* (*money, creditor*) rimborsare, ripagare; (*sb's efforts*) ricompensare.

repayment [riː'peɪmənt] *n* rimborsamento; ricompensa.

repeal [rɪ'piːl] *n* (*of law*) abrogazione *f*; (*of sentence*) annullamento ♦ *vt* abrogare; annullare.

repeat [rɪ'piːt] *n* (*RADIO, TV*) replica ♦ *vt* ripetere; (*pattern*) riprodurre; (*promise, attack, also COMM: order*) rinnovare ♦ *vi* ripetere.

repeatedly [rɪ'piːtɪdlɪ] *adv* ripetutamente, spesso.

repeat order *n* (*COMM*): **to place a ~ (for)** rinnovare l'ordinazione (di).

repel [rɪ'pɛl] *vt* respingere.

repellent [rɪ'pɛlənt] *adj* repellente ♦ *n*: **insect ~** prodotto *m* anti-insetti *inv*; **moth ~** anti-tarmico.

repent [rɪ'pɛnt] *vi*: **to ~ (of)** pentirsi (di).

repentance [rɪ'pɛntəns] *n* pentimento.

repercussion [riːpə'kʌʃən] *n* (*consequence*) ripercussione *f*.

repertoire ['rɛpətwaː*] *n* repertorio.

repertory ['rɛpətərɪ] *n* (*also:* **~ theatre**) teatro di repertorio.

repertory company *n* compagnia di repertorio.

repetition [rɛpɪ'tɪʃən] *n* ripetizione *f*; (*COMM: of order etc*) rinnovo.

repetitious [rɛpɪ'tɪʃəs] adj (speech) pieno(a) di ripetizioni.

repetitive [rɪ'pɛtɪtɪv] adj (movement) che si ripete; (work) monotono(a); (speech) pieno(a) di ripetizioni.

replace [rɪ'pleɪs] vt (put back) rimettere a posto; (take the place of) sostituire; (TEL): "~ **the receiver**" "riattaccare".

replacement [rɪ'pleɪsmənt] n rimessa; sostituzione f; (person) sostituto/a.

replacement part n pezzo di ricambio.

replay ['riːpleɪ] n (of match) partita ripetuta; (of tape, film) replay m inv.

replenish [rɪ'plɛnɪʃ] vt (glass) riempire; (stock etc) rifornire.

replete [rɪ'pliːt] adj: ~ **(with)** ripieno(a) (di); (well-fed) sazio(a) (di).

replica ['rɛplɪkə] n replica, copia.

reply [rɪ'plaɪ] n risposta ♦ vi rispondere; **in** ~ in risposta; **there's no** ~ (TEL) non risponde (nessuno).

reply coupon n buono di risposta.

report [rɪ'pɔːt] n rapporto; (PRESS etc) cronaca; (BRIT: also: **school** ~) pagella ♦ vt riportare; (PRESS etc) fare una cronaca su; (bring to notice: occurrence) segnalare; (: person) denunciare ♦ vi (make a report) fare un rapporto (or una cronaca); (present o.s.): **to** ~ **(to sb)** presentarsi (a qn); **to** ~ **(on)** fare un rapporto (su); **it is** ~**ed that** si dice che; **it is** ~**ed from Berlin that** ... ci è stato riferito da Berlino che ....

report card n (US, Scottish) pagella.

reportedly [rɪ'pɔːtɪdlɪ] adv: **she is** ~ **living in Spain** si dice che vive in Spagna.

reported speech [rɪ'pɔːtɪd-] n (LING) discorso indiretto.

reporter [rɪ'pɔːtə*] n (PRESS) cronista m/f, reporter m inv; (RADIO) radiocronista m/f; (TV) telecronista m/f.

repose [rɪ'pəuz] n: **in** ~ in riposo.

repossess [riːpə'zɛs] vt rientrare in possesso di.

repossession order [riːpə'zɛʃən-] n ordine m di espropriazione.

reprehensible [rɛprɪ'hɛnsɪbl] adj riprensibile.

represent [rɛprɪ'zɛnt] vt rappresentare.

representation [rɛprɪzɛn'teɪʃən] n rappresentazione f; ~**s** npl (protest) protesta.

representative [rɛprɪ'zɛntətɪv] n rappresentativo/a; (COMM) rappresentante m (di commercio); (US: POL) deputato/a ♦ adj: ~ **(of)** rappresentativo(a) (di).

repress [rɪ'prɛs] vt reprimere.

repression [rɪ'prɛʃən] n repressione f.

repressive [rɪ'prɛsɪv] adj repressivo(a).

reprieve [rɪ'priːv] n (LAW) sospensione f dell'esecuzione della condanna; (fig) dilazione f ♦ vt sospendere l'esecuzione della condanna a; accordare una dilazione a.

reprimand ['rɛprɪmɑːnd] n rimprovero ♦ vt rimproverare, redarguire.

reprint ['riːprɪnt] n ristampa ♦ vt ristampare.

reprisal [rɪ'praɪzl] n rappresaglia; **to take** ~**s** fare delle rappresaglie.

reproach [rɪ'prəutʃ] n rimprovero ♦ vt: **to** ~ **sb with sth** rimproverare qn di qc; **beyond** ~ irreprensibile.

reproachful [rɪ'prəutʃful] adj di rimprovero.

reproduce [riːprə'djuːs] vt riprodurre ♦ vi riprodursi.

reproduction [riːprə'dʌkʃən] n riproduzione f.

reproductive [riːprə'dʌktɪv] adj riproduttore(trice); riproduttivo(a).

reproof [rɪ'pruːf] n riprovazione f.

reprove [rɪ'pruːv] vt (action) disapprovare; (person): **to** ~ **(for)** biasimare (per).

reproving [rɪ'pruːvɪŋ] adj di disapprovazione.

reptile ['rɛptaɪl] n rettile m.

Repub. abbr (US POL) = Republican.

republic [rɪ'pʌblɪk] n repubblica.

republican [rɪ'pʌblɪkən] adj, n repubblicano(a).

repudiate [rɪ'pjuːdɪeɪt] vt ripudiare.

repugnant [rɪ'pʌgnənt] adj ripugnante.

repulse [rɪ'pʌls] vt respingere.

repulsion [rɪ'pʌlʃən] n ripulsione f.

repulsive [rɪ'pʌlsɪv] adj ripugnante, ripulsivo(a).

reputable ['rɛpjutəbl] adj di buona reputazione; (occupation) rispettabile.

reputation [rɛpju'teɪʃən] n reputazione f; **he has a** ~ **for being awkward** ha la fama di essere un tipo difficile.

repute [rɪ'pjuːt] n reputazione f.

reputed [rɪ'pjuːtɪd] adj reputato(a); **to be** ~ **to be rich/intelligent** etc essere ritenuto(a) ricco(a)/intelligente etc.

reputedly [rɪ'pjuːtɪdlɪ] adv secondo quanto si dice.

request [rɪ'kwɛst] n domanda; (formal) richiesta ♦ vt: **to** ~ **(of or from sb)** chiedere (a qn); **at the** ~ **of** su richiesta di; "**you are** ~**ed not to smoke**" "si prega di non fumare".

request stop n (BRIT: for bus) fermata facoltativa or a richiesta.

requiem ['rɛkwɪəm] *n* requiem *m or f inv.*

require [rɪ'kwaɪə*] *vt (need: subj: person)* aver bisogno di; (: *thing, situation*) richiedere; (*want*) volere; esigere; (*order*) obbligare; **to ~ sb to do sth/sth of sb** esigere che qn faccia qc/qc da qn; **what qualifications are ~d?** che requisiti ci vogliono?; **~d by law** prescritto dalla legge; **if ~d** in caso di bisogno.

required [rɪ'kwaɪəd] *adj* richiesto(a).

requirement [rɪ'kwaɪəmənt] *n (need)* esigenza; (*condition*) requisito; **to meet sb's ~s** soddisfare le esigenze di qn.

requisite ['rɛkwɪzɪt] *n* cosa necessaria ♦ *adj* necessario(a); **toilet ~s** articoli *mpl* da toletta.

requisition [rɛkwɪ'zɪʃən] *n*: **~ (for)** richiesta (di) ♦ *vt (MIL)* requisire.

reroute [riː'ruːt] *vt (train etc)* deviare.

resale ['riː'seɪl] *n* rivendita.

resale price maintenance (RPM) *n* prezzo minimo di vendita imposto.

rescind [rɪ'sɪnd] *vt* annullare; (*law*) abrogare; (*judgement*) rescindere.

rescue ['rɛskjuː] *n* salvataggio; (*help*) soccorso ♦ *vt* salvare; **to come/go to sb's ~** venire/andare in aiuto a *or* di qn.

rescue party *n* squadra di salvataggio.

rescuer ['rɛskjuə*] *n* salvatore/trice.

research [rɪ'səːtʃ] *n* ricerca, ricerche *fpl* ♦ *vt* fare ricerche su ♦ *vi*: **to ~ (into sth)** fare ricerca (su qc); **a piece of ~** un lavoro di ricerca; **~ and development (R&D)** ricerca e sviluppo.

researcher [rɪ'səːtʃə*] *n* ricercatore/trice.

research work *n* ricerche *fpl.*

resell [riː'sɛl] *vt irreg* rivendere.

resemblance [rɪ'zɛmbləns] *n* somiglianza; **to bear a strong ~ to** somigliare moltissimo a.

resemble [rɪ'zɛmbl] *vt* assomigliare a.

resent [rɪ'zɛnt] *vt* risentirsi di.

resentful [rɪ'zɛntful] *adj* pieno(a) di risentimento.

resentment [rɪ'zɛntmənt] *n* risentimento.

reservation [rɛzə'veɪʃən] *n (booking)* prenotazione *f*; (*doubt*) dubbio; (*protected area*) riserva; (*BRIT AUT: also*: **central ~**) spartitraffico *m inv*; **to make a ~** (in an hotel/a restaurant/on a plane) prenotare (una camera/una tavola/un posto); **with ~s** (*doubts*) con le dovute riserve.

reservation desk *n (US: in hotel)* reception *f inv.*

reserve [rɪ'zəːv] *n* riserva ♦ *vt (seats etc)* prenotare; **~s** *npl (MIL)* riserve *fpl*; **in ~** in serbo.

reserve currency *n* valuta di riserva.

reserved [rɪ'zəːvd] *adj (shy)* riservato(a); (*seat*) prenotato(a).

reserve price *n (BRIT)* prezzo di riserva, prezzo *m* base *inv.*

reserve team *n (BRIT SPORT)* seconda squadra.

reservist [rɪ'zəːvɪst] *n (MIL)* riservista *m.*

reservoir ['rɛzəvwɑː*] *n* serbatoio; (*artificial lake*) bacino idrico.

reset [riː'sɛt] *vt (COMPUT)* azzerare.

reshape [riː'ʃeɪp] *vt (policy)* ristrutturare.

reshuffle [riː'ʃʌfl] *n*: **Cabinet ~** (*POL*) rimpasto governativo.

reside [rɪ'zaɪd] *vi* risiedere.

residence ['rɛzɪdəns] *n* residenza; **to take up ~** prendere residenza; **in ~** (*queen etc*) in sede; (*doctor*) fisso.

residence permit *n (BRIT)* permesso di soggiorno.

resident ['rɛzɪdənt] *n (gen, COMPUT)* residente *m/f*; (*in hotel*) cliente *m/f* fisso(a) ♦ *adj* residente.

residential [rɛzɪ'dɛnʃəl] *adj* di residenza; (*area*) residenziale.

residue ['rɛzɪdjuː] *n* resto; (*CHEM, PHYSICS*) residuo.

resign [rɪ'zaɪn] *vt (one's post)* dimettersi da ♦ *vi*: **to ~ (from)** dimettersi (da), dare le dimissioni (da); **to ~ o.s. to** rassegnarsi a.

resignation [rɛzɪg'neɪʃən] *n* dimissioni *fpl*; rassegnazione *f*; **to tender one's ~** dare le dimissioni.

resilience [rɪ'zɪlɪəns] *n (of material)* elasticità, resilienza; (*of person*) capacità di recupero.

resilient [rɪ'zɪlɪənt] *adj* elastico(a); (*person*) che si riprende facilmente.

resin ['rɛzɪn] *n* resina.

resist [rɪ'zɪst] *vt* resistere a.

resistance [rɪ'zɪstəns] *n* resistenza.

resistant [rɪ'zɪstənt] *adj*: **~ (to)** resistente (a).

resolute ['rɛzəluːt] *adj* risoluto(a).

resolution [rɛzə'luːʃən] *n (resolve)* fermo proposito, risoluzione *f*; (*determination*) risolutezza; (*on screen*) risoluzione *f*; **to make a ~** fare un proposito.

resolve [rɪ'zɔlv] *n* risoluzione *f* ♦ *vi (decide)*: **to ~ to do** decidere di fare ♦ *vt (problem)* risolvere.

resolved [rɪ'zɔlvd] *adj* risoluto(a).

resonance ['rɛzənəns] *n* risonanza.

resonant ['rɛzənənt] *adj* risonante.

resort [rɪ'zɔːt] *n (town)* stazione *f*; (*place*) località *f inv*; (*recourse*) ricorso ♦ *vi*: **to ~ to** far ricorso a; **seaside/winter sports ~** stazione *f* balneare/di sport invernali; **as**

a last ~ come ultima risorsa.
resound [rɪ'zaund] *vi*: **to** ~ **(with)** risonare
(di).
resounding [rɪ'zaundɪŋ] *adj* risonante.
resource [rɪ'sɔːs] *n* risorsa; ~**s** *npl* risorse
fpl; **natural** ~**s** risorse naturali; **to leave**
sb to his (*or* **her**) **own** ~**s** (*fig*) lasciare
che qn si arrangi (per conto suo).
resourceful [rɪ'sɔːsful] *adj* pieno(a) di
risorse, intraprendente.
resourcefulness [rɪ'sɔːsfəlnɪs] *n*
intraprendenza.
respect [rɪs'pɛkt] *n* rispetto; (*point, detail*):
in some ~**s** sotto certi aspetti ♦ *vt*
rispettare; ~**s** *npl* ossequi *mpl*; **to have** *or*
show ~ **for** aver rispetto per; **out of** ~ **for**
per rispetto *or* riguardo a; **with** ~ **to**
rispetto a, riguardo a; **in** ~ **of** quanto a; **in**
this ~ per questo riguardo; **with (all) due**
~ **I** ... con rispetto parlando, io ....
respectability [rɪspɛktə'bɪlɪtɪ] *n*
rispettabilità.
respectable [rɪs'pɛktəbl] *adj* rispettabile;
(*quite big: amount etc*) considerevole;
(*quite good: player, result etc*) niente male
inv.
respectful [rɪs'pɛktful] *adj* rispettoso(a).
respective [rɪs'pɛktɪv] *adj* rispettivo(a).
respectively [rɪs'pɛktɪvlɪ] *adv*
rispettivamente.
respiration [rɛspɪ'reɪʃən] *n* respirazione *f*.
respirator ['rɛspɪreɪtə*] *n* respiratore *m*.
respiratory ['rɛspərətərɪ] *adj*
respiratorio(a).
respite ['rɛspaɪt] *n* respiro, tregua.
resplendent [rɪs'plɛndənt] *adj* risplendente.
respond [rɪs'pɔnd] *vi* rispondere.
respondent [rɪs'pɔndənt] *n* (*LAW*)
convenuto/a.
response [rɪs'pɔns] *n* risposta; **in** ~ **to** in
risposta a.
responsibility [rɪspɔnsɪ'bɪlɪtɪ] *n*
responsabilità *f inv*; **to take** ~ **for sth/sb**
assumersi *or* prendersi la responsabilità
di qc/per qn.
responsible [rɪs'pɔnsɪbl] *adj* (*liable*): ~ **(for)**
responsabile (di); (*trustworthy*) fidato(a);
(*job*) di (grande) responsabilità; **to be** ~
to sb (for sth) dover rispondere a qn (di
qc).
responsibly [rɪs'pɔnsəblɪ] *adv*
responsabilmente.
responsive [rɪs'pɔnsɪv] *adj* che reagisce.
rest [rɛst] *n* riposo; (*stop*) sosta, pausa;
(*MUS*) pausa; (*support*) appoggio,
sostegno; (*remainder*) resto, avanzi *mpl*
♦ *vi* riposarsi; (*remain*) rimanere, restare;
(*be supported*): **to** ~ **on** appoggiarsi su ♦ *vt*

(*lean*): **to** ~ **sth on/against** appoggiare qc
su/contro; **to set sb's mind at** ~
tranquillizzare qn; **the** ~ **of them** gli
altri; **to** ~ **one's eyes** *or* gaze on posare lo
sguardo su; ~ **assured that** ... stia
tranquillo che ...; **it** ~**s with him to decide**
sta a lui decidere.
restart [riː'staːt] *vt* (*engine*) rimettere in
marcia; (*work*) ricominciare.
restaurant ['rɛstərɔŋ] *n* ristorante *m*.
restaurant car *n* (*BRIT*) vagone *m*
ristorante.
rest cure *n* cura del riposo.
restful ['rɛstful] *adj* riposante.
rest home *n* casa di riposo.
restitution [rɛstɪ'tjuːʃən] *n* (*act*)
restituzione *f*; (*reparation*) riparazione *f*.
restive ['rɛstɪv] *adj* agitato(a), impaziente;
(*horse*) restio(a).
restless ['rɛstlɪs] *adj* agitato(a),
irrequieto(a); **to get** ~ spazientirsi.
restlessly ['rɛstlɪslɪ] *adv* in preda
all'agitazione.
restock [riː'stɔk] *vt* rifornire.
restoration [rɛstə'reɪʃən] *n* restauro;
restituzione *f*.
restorative [rɪ'stɔrətɪv] *adj* corroborante,
ristorativo(a) ♦ *n* ricostituente *m*.
restore [rɪ'stɔː*] *vt* (*building*) restaurare;
(*sth stolen*) restituire; (*peace, health*)
ristorare.
restorer [rɪ'stɔːrə*] *n* (*ART etc*)
restauratore/trice.
restrain [rɪs'treɪn] *vt* (*feeling*) contenere,
frenare; (*person*): **to** ~ **(from doing)**
trattenere (dal fare).
restrained [rɪs'treɪnd] *adj* (*style*)
contenuto(a), sobrio(a); (*manner*)
riservato(a).
restraint [rɪs'treɪnt] *n* (*restriction*)
limitazione *f*; (*moderation*) ritegno; **wage**
~ restrizioni *fpl* salariali.
restrict [rɪs'trɪkt] *vt* restringere, limitare.
restricted area [rɪs'trɪktɪd-] *n* (*AUT*) zona a
velocità limitata.
restriction [rɪs'trɪkʃən] *n* restrizione *f*,
limitazione *f*.
restrictive [rɪs'trɪktɪv] *adj* restrittivo(a).
restrictive practices *npl* (*INDUSTRY*)
pratiche restrittive di produzione.
rest room *n* (*US*) toletta.
restructure [riː'strʌktʃə*] *vt* ristrutturare.
result [rɪ'zʌlt] *n* risultato ♦ *vi*: **to** ~ **in** avere
per risultato; **as a** ~ **(of)** in *or* di
conseguenza (a), in seguito (a); **to** ~
(from) essere una conseguenza (di),
essere causato(a) (da).
resultant [rɪ'zʌltənt] *adj* risultante,

conseguente.
resume [rɪ'zjuːm] *vt, vi* (*work, journey*)
riprendere; (*sum up*) riassumere.
résumé ['reɪzjuːmeɪ] *n* riassunto; (*US*:
curriculum vitae) curriculum vitae *m inv*.
resumption [rɪ'zʌmpʃən] *n* ripresa.
resurgence [rɪ'səːdʒəns] *n* rinascita.
resurrection [rɛzə'rɛkʃən] *n* risurrezione *f*.
resuscitate [rɪ'sʌsɪteɪt] *vt* (*MED*)
risuscitare.
resuscitation [rɪsʌsɪ'teɪʃən] *n* rianimazione
f.
retail ['riːteɪl] *n* (vendita al) minuto ♦ *cpd* al
minuto ♦ *vt* vendere al minuto ♦ *vi*: **to ~ at**
essere in vendita al pubblico al prezzo
di.
retailer ['riːteɪlə*] *n* commerciante *m/f* al
minuto, dettagliante *m/f*.
retail outlet *n* punto di vendita al
dettaglio.
retail price *n* prezzo al minuto.
retail price index *n* indice *m* dei prezzi al
consumo.
retain [rɪ'teɪn] *vt* (*keep*) tenere, serbare.
retainer [rɪ'teɪnə*] *n* (*servant*) servitore *m*;
(*fee*) onorario.
retaliate [rɪ'tælɪeɪt] *vi*: **to ~ (against)**
vendicarsi (di); **to ~ on sb** fare una
rappresaglia contro qn.
retaliation [rɪtælɪ'eɪʃən] *n* rappresaglie *fpl*;
in ~ for per vendicarsi di.
retaliatory [rɪ'tælɪətərɪ] *adj* di rappresaglia,
di ritorsione.
retarded [rɪ'tɑːdɪd] *adj* ritardato(a); (*also*:
mentally ~) tardo(a) (di mente).
retch [rɛtʃ] *vi* aver conati di vomito.
retentive [rɪ'tɛntɪv] *adj* ritentivo(a).
rethink ['riː'θɪŋk] *vt* ripensare.
reticence ['rɛtɪsns] *n* reticenza.
reticent ['rɛtɪsnt] *adj* reticente.
retina ['rɛtɪnə] *n* retina.
retinue ['rɛtɪnjuː] *n* seguito, scorta.
retire [rɪ'taɪə*] *vi* (*give up work*) andare in
pensione; (*withdraw*) ritirarsi, andarsene;
(*go to bed*) andare a letto, ritirarsi.
retired [rɪ'taɪəd] *adj* (*person*) pensionato(a).
retirement [rɪ'taɪəmənt] *n* pensione *f*.
retirement age *n* età del pensionamento.
retiring [rɪ'taɪərɪŋ] *adj* (*person*) riservato(a);
(*departing*: *chairman*) uscente.
retort [rɪ'tɔːt] *n* (*reply*) rimbecco;
(*container*) storta ♦ *vi* rimbeccare.
retrace [riː'treɪs] *vt* ricostruire; **to ~ one's**
steps tornare sui propri passi.
retract [rɪ'trækt] *vt* (*statement*) ritrattare;
(*claws, undercarriage, aerial*) ritrarre,
ritirare ♦ *vi* ritrarsi.
retractable [rɪ'træktəbl] *adj* retrattile.

retrain [riː'treɪn] *vt* (*worker*) riaddestrare.
retraining [rɪ'treɪnɪŋ] *n* riaddestramento.
retread *vt* [riː'trɛd] (*AUT*: *tyre*) rigenerare
♦ *n* ['riːtrɛd] gomma rigenerata.
retreat [rɪ'triːt] *n* ritirata; (*place*) rifugio
♦ *vi* battere in ritirata; (*flood*) ritirarsi; **to**
beat a hasty ~ (*fig*) battersela.
retrial [riː'traɪəl] *n* nuovo processo.
retribution [rɛtrɪ'bjuːʃən] *n* castigo.
retrieval [rɪ'triːvəl] *n* ricupero.
retrieve [rɪ'triːv] *vt* (*sth lost*) ricuperare,
ritrovare; (*situation, honour*) salvare;
(*COMPUT*) ricuperare.
retriever [rɪ'triːvə*] *n* cane *m* da riporto.
retroactive [rɛtrəu'æktɪv] *adj*
retroattivo(a).
retrograde ['rɛtrəugreɪd] *adj* retrogrado(a).
retrospect ['rɛtrəspɛkt] *n*: **in ~** guardando
indietro.
retrospective [rɛtrə'spɛktɪv] *adj*
retrospettivo(a); (*law*) retroattivo(a) ♦ *n*
(*ART*) retrospettiva.
return [rɪ'təːn] *n* (*going or coming back*)
ritorno; (*of sth stolen etc*) restituzione *f*;
(*COMM*: *from land, shares*) profitto, reddito;
(: *of merchandise*) resa; (*report*) rapporto;
(*reward*): **in ~ (for)** in cambio (di) ♦ *cpd*
(*journey, match*) di ritorno; (*BRIT*: *ticket*) di
andata e ritorno ♦ *vi* tornare, ritornare
♦ *vt* rendere, restituire; (*bring back*)
riportare; (*send back*) mandare indietro;
(*put back*) rimettere; (*POL*: *candidate*)
eleggere; **~s** *npl* (*COMM*) incassi *mpl*;
profitti *mpl*; **by ~ of post** a stretto giro di
posta; **many happy ~s (of the day)!**
auguri!, buon compleanno!
returnable [rɪ'təːnəbl] *adj*: **~ bottle** vuoto a
rendere.
returner [rɪ'təːnə*] *n* donna che ritorna al
lavoro dopo la maternità.
returning officer [rɪ'təːnɪŋ-] *n* (*BRIT POL*)
funzionario addetto all'organizzazione
delle elezioni in un distretto.
return key *n* (*COMPUT*) tasto di ritorno.
reunion [riː'juːnɪən] *n* riunione *f*.
reunite [riːjuː'naɪt] *vt* riunire.
rev [rɛv] *n abbr* (= *revolution*: *AUT*) giro ♦ *vb*
(*also*: **~ up**) *vt* imballare ♦ *vi* imballarsi.
revaluation [riːvælju'eɪʃən] *n* rivalutazione
f.
revamp ['riː'væmp] *vt* rinnovare;
riorganizzare.
rev counter *n* contagiri *m inv*.
Rev(d). *abbr* = **reverend**.
reveal [rɪ'viːl] *vt* (*make known*) rivelare,
svelare; (*display*) rivelare, mostrare.
revealing [rɪ'viːlɪŋ] *adj* rivelatore(trice);
(*dress*) scollato(a).

reveille [rɪˈvælɪ] n (MIL) sveglia.
revel [ˈrɛvl] vi: **to ~ in sth/in doing** dilettarsi di qc/a fare.
revelation [rɛvəˈleɪʃən] n rivelazione f.
reveller [ˈrɛvlə*] n festaiolo/a.
revelry [ˈrɛvlrɪ] n baldoria.
revenge [rɪˈvɛndʒ] n vendetta; (in game etc) rivincita ♦ vt vendicare; **to take ~** vendicarsi; **to get one's ~ (for sth)** vendicarsi (di qc).
revengeful [rɪˈvɛndʒful] adj vendicatore(trice); vendicativo(a).
revenue [ˈrɛvənjuː] n reddito.
reverberate [rɪˈvəːbəreɪt] vi (sound) rimbombare; (light) riverberarsi.
reverberation [rɪvəːbəˈreɪʃən] n (of light, sound) riverberazione f.
revere [rɪˈvɪə*] vt venerare.
reverence [ˈrɛvərəns] n venerazione f, riverenza.
Reverend [ˈrɛvərənd] adj (in titles) reverendo(a).
reverent [ˈrɛvərənt] adj riverente.
reverie [ˈrɛvərɪ] n fantasticheria.
reversal [rɪˈvəːsl] n capovolgimento.
reverse [rɪˈvəːs] n contrario, opposto; (back) rovescio; (AUT: also: ~ **gear**) marcia indietro ♦ adj (order) inverso(a); (direction) opposto(a) ♦ vt (turn) invertire, rivoltare; (change) capovolgere, rovesciare; (LAW: judgement) cassare ♦ vi (BRIT AUT) fare marcia indietro; **in ~ order** in ordine inverso; **to go into ~** fare marcia indietro.
reverse-charge call n (BRIT TEL) telefonata con addebito al ricevente.
reverse video n reverse video m.
reversible [rɪˈvəːsəbl] adj (garment) double-face inv; (procedure) reversibile.
reversing lights [rɪˈvəːsɪŋ-] npl (BRIT AUT) luci fpl per la retromarcia.
reversion [rɪˈvəːʃən] n ritorno.
revert [rɪˈvəːt] vi: **to ~ to** tornare a.
review [rɪˈvjuː] n rivista; (of book, film) recensione f ♦ vt passare in rivista; fare la recensione di; **to come under ~** essere preso in esame.
reviewer [rɪˈvjuːə*] n recensore/a.
revile [rɪˈvaɪl] vt insultare.
revise [rɪˈvaɪz] vt (manuscript) rivedere, correggere; (opinion) emendare, modificare; (study: subject, notes) ripassare; **~d edition** edizione riveduta.
revision [rɪˈvɪʒən] n revisione f; ripasso; (revised version) versione f riveduta e corretta.
revitalize [riːˈvaɪtəlaɪz] vt ravvivare.
revival [rɪˈvaɪvəl] n ripresa; ristabilimento;

(of faith) risveglio.
revive [rɪˈvaɪv] vt (person) rianimare; (custom) far rivivere; (hope, courage) ravvivare; (play, fashion) riesumare ♦ vi (person) rianimarsi; (hope) ravvivarsi; (activity) riprendersi.
revoke [rɪˈvəuk] vt revocare; (promise, decision) rinvenire su.
revolt [rɪˈvəult] n rivolta, ribellione f ♦ vi rivoltarsi, ribellarsi; **to ~ (against sb/ sth)** ribellarsi (a qn/qc).
revolting [rɪˈvəultɪŋ] adj ripugnante.
revolution [rɛvəˈluːʃən] n rivoluzione f; (of wheel etc) rivoluzione, giro.
revolutionary [rɛvəˈluːʃənrɪ] adj, n rivoluzionario(a).
revolutionize [rɛvəˈluːʃənaɪz] vt rivoluzionare.
revolve [rɪˈvɔlv] vi girare.
revolver [rɪˈvɔlvə*] n rivoltella.
revolving [rɪˈvɔlvɪŋ] adj girevole.
revolving door n porta girevole.
revue [rɪˈvjuː] n (THEAT) rivista.
revulsion [rɪˈvʌlʃən] n ripugnanza.
reward [rɪˈwɔːd] n ricompensa, premio ♦ vt: **to ~ (for)** ricompensare (per).
rewarding [rɪˈwɔːdɪŋ] adj (fig) soddisfacente; **financially ~** conveniente dal punto di vista economico.
rewind [riːˈwaɪnd] vt irreg (watch) ricaricare; (ribbon etc) riavvolgere.
rewire [riːˈwaɪə*] vt (house) rifare l'impianto elettrico di.
reword [riːˈwəːd] vt formulare or esprimere con altre parole.
rewritable [riːˈraɪtəbl] adj riscrivibile.
rewrite [riːˈraɪt] vt irreg riscrivere.
Reykjavik [ˈreɪkjəviːk] n Reykjavik f.
RFD abbr (US POST) = rural free delivery.
RGN n abbr (BRIT: = Registered General Nurse) infermiera diplomata (dopo corso triennale).
Rh abbr (= rhesus) Rh.
rhapsody [ˈræpsədɪ] n (MUS) rapsodia; (fig) elogio stravagante.
rhesus negative [ˈriːsəs-] adj (MED) Rh-negativo(a).
rhesus positive adj (MED) Rh-positivo(a).
rhetoric [ˈrɛtərɪk] n retorica.
rhetorical [rɪˈtɔrɪkl] adj retorico(a).
rheumatic [ruːˈmætɪk] adj reumatico(a).
rheumatism [ˈruːmətɪzəm] n reumatismo.
rheumatoid arthritis [ˈruːmətɔɪd-] n artrite f reumatoide.
Rhine [raɪn] n: **the ~** il Reno.
rhinestone [ˈraɪnstəun] n diamante m falso.
rhinoceros [raɪˈnɔsərəs] n rinoceronte m.
Rhodes [rəudz] n Rodi f.

Rhodesia [rəu'diːʒə] n Rhodesia.
Rhodesian [rəu'diːʒən] adj, n Rhodesiano(a).
rhododendron [rəudə'dɛndrn] n rododendro.
Rhone [rəun] n: the ~ il Rodano.
rhubarb ['ruːbɑːb] n rabarbaro.
rhyme [raɪm] n rima; (verse) poesia ♦ vi: to ~ (with) fare rima (con); without ~ or reason senza capo né coda.
rhythm ['rɪðm] n ritmo.
rhythmic(al) ['rɪðmɪk(əl)] adj ritmico(a).
rhythmically ['rɪðmɪkəlɪ] adv con ritmo.
rhythm method n metodo Ogino-Knauss.
RI abbr (US POST) = Rhode Island ♦ n abbr (BRIT) = religious instruction.
rib [rɪb] n (ANAT) costola ♦ vt (tease) punzecchiare.
ribald ['rɪbəld] adj licenzioso(a), volgare.
ribbed [rɪbd] adj (knitting) a coste.
ribbon ['rɪbən] n nastro; in ~s (torn) a brandelli.
rice [raɪs] n riso.
ricefield ['raɪsfiːld] n risaia.
rice pudding n budino di riso.
rich [rɪtʃ] adj ricco(a); (clothes) sontuoso(a); the ~ npl i ricchi; ~es npl ricchezze fpl; to be ~ in sth essere ricco di qc.
richly ['rɪtʃlɪ] adv riccamente; (dressed) sontuosamente; (deserved) pienamente.
rickets ['rɪkɪts] n rachitismo.
rickety ['rɪkɪtɪ] adj zoppicante.
rickshaw ['rɪkʃɔː] n risciò m inv.
ricochet ['rɪkəʃeɪ] n rimbalzo ♦ vi rimbalzare.
rid, pt, pp rid [rɪd] vt: to ~ sb of sbarazzare or liberare qn di; to get ~ of sbarazzarsi di.
riddance ['rɪdns] n: good ~! che liberazione!
ridden ['rɪdn] pp of ride.
riddle ['rɪdl] n (puzzle) indovinello ♦ vt: to be ~d with essere crivellato(a) di.
ride [raɪd] n (on horse) cavalcata; (outing) passeggiata; (distance covered) cavalcata; corsa ♦ vb (pt rode, pp ridden [rəud, 'rɪdn]) vi (as sport) cavalcare; (go somewhere: on horse, bicycle) andare (a cavallo or in bicicletta etc); (journey: on bicycle, motorcycle, bus) andare, viaggiare ♦ vt (a horse) montare, cavalcare; to go for a ~ andare a fare una cavalcata; andare a fare un giro; can you ~ a bike? sai andare in bicicletta?; we rode all day/all the way abbiamo cavalcato tutto il giorno/per tutto il tragitto; to ~ a horse/bicycle/camel montare a cavallo/in bicicletta/in groppa a un cammello; to ~

at anchor (NAUT) essere alla fonda; horse ~ cavalcata; car ~ passeggiata in macchina; to take sb for a ~ (fig) prendere in giro qn; fregare qn.
►ride out vt: to ~ out the storm (fig) mantenersi a galla.
rider ['raɪdə*] n cavalcatore/trice; (jockey) fantino; (on bicycle) ciclista m/f; (on motorcycle) motociclista m/f; (in document) clausola addizionale, aggiunta.
ridge [rɪdʒ] n (of hill) cresta; (of roof) colmo; (of mountain) giogo; (on object) riga (in rilievo).
ridicule ['rɪdɪkjuːl] n ridicolo ♦ vt mettere in ridicolo; to hold sb/sth up to ~ mettere in ridicolo qn/qc.
ridiculous [rɪ'dɪkjuləs] adj ridicolo(a).
riding ['raɪdɪŋ] n equitazione f.
riding school n scuola d'equitazione.
rife [raɪf] adj diffuso(a); to be ~ with abbondare di.
riffraff ['rɪfræf] n canaglia, gentaglia.
rifle ['raɪfl] n carabina ♦ vt vuotare.
►rifle through vt fus frugare.
rifle range n campo di tiro; (at fair) tiro a segno.
rift [rɪft] n fessura, crepatura; (fig: disagreement) incrinatura.
rig [rɪg] n (also: oil ~: on land) derrick m inv; (: at sea) piattaforma di trivellazione ♦ vt (election etc) truccare.
►rig out vt (BRIT) attrezzare; (pej) abbigliare, agghindare.
►rig up vt allestire.
rigging ['rɪgɪŋ] n (NAUT) attrezzatura.
right [raɪt] adj giusto(a); (suitable) appropriato(a); (not left) destro(a) ♦ n (title, claim) diritto; (not left) destra ♦ adv (answer) correttamente; (not on the left) a destra ♦ vt raddrizzare; (fig) riparare ♦ excl bene!; the ~ time l'ora esatta; to be ~ (person) aver ragione; (answer) essere giusto(a) or corretto(a); to get sth ~ far giusto qc; you did the ~ thing ha fatto bene; let's get it ~ this time! cerchiamo di farlo bene stavolta!; to put a mistake ~ (BRIT) correggere un errore; ~ now proprio adesso; subito; ~ away subito; ~ before/after subito prima/dopo; to go ~ to the end of sth andare fino in fondo a qc; ~ against the wall proprio contro il muro; ~ ahead sempre diritto; proprio davanti; ~ in the middle proprio nel mezzo; by ~s di diritto; on the ~, to the ~ a destra; ~ and wrong il bene e il male; to have a ~ to sth aver diritto a qc; film ~s diritti di riproduzione cinematografica; ~ of way diritto di

passaggio; (*AUT*) precedenza.
right angle *n* angolo retto.
right-click ['raɪtklɪk] *vi* (*COMPUT*): **to ~ on**
fare clic con il pulsante destro del mouse
su.
righteous ['raɪtʃəs] *adj* retto(a),
virtuoso(a); (*anger*) giusto(a),
giustificato(a).
righteousness ['raɪtʃəsnɪs] *n* rettitudine *f*,
virtù *f*.
rightful ['raɪtful] *adj* (*heir*) legittimo(a).
rightfully ['raɪtfəlɪ] *adv* legittimamente.
right-handed [raɪt'hændɪd] *adj* (*person*) che
adopera la mano destra.
right-hand man ['raɪthænd-] *n* braccio
destro (*fig*).
right-hand side *n* lato destro.
rightly ['raɪtlɪ] *adv* bene, correttamente;
(*with reason*) a ragione; **if I remember ~** se
mi ricordo bene.
right-minded [raɪt'maɪndɪd] *adj* sensato(a).
rights issue *n* (*STOCK EXCHANGE*)
emissione *f* di azioni riservate agli
azionisti.
right wing *n* (*MIL*, *SPORT*) ala destra; (*POL*)
destra ♦ *adj*: **right-wing** (*POL*) di destra.
right-winger [raɪt'wɪŋə*] *n* (*POL*) uno/a di
destra; (*SPORT*) ala destra.
rigid ['rɪdʒɪd] *adj* rigido(a); (*principle*)
rigoroso(a).
rigidity [rɪ'dʒɪdɪtɪ] *n* rigidità.
rigidly ['rɪdʒɪdlɪ] *adv* rigidamente.
rigmarole ['rɪgmərəul] *n* tiritera;
commedia.
rigor ['rɪgə*] *n* (*US*) = **rigour**.
rigor mortis ['rɪgə'mɔːtɪs] *n* rigidità
cadaverica.
rigorous ['rɪgərəs] *adj* rigoroso(a).
rigorously ['rɪgərəslɪ] *adv* rigorosamente.
rigour, (*US*) **rigor** ['rɪgə*] *n* rigore *m*.
rig-out ['rɪgaut] *n* (*BRIT col*) tenuta.
rile [raɪl] *vt* irritare, seccare.
rim [rɪm] *n* orlo; (*of spectacles*) montatura;
(*of wheel*) cerchione *m*.
rimless ['rɪmlɪs] *adj* (*spectacles*) senza
montatura.
rimmed [rɪmd] *adj* bordato(a); cerchiato(a).
rind [raɪnd] *n* (*of bacon*) cotenna; (*of lemon
etc*) scorza.
ring [rɪŋ] *n* anello; (*also*: **wedding ~**) fede *f*;
(*of people, objects*) cerchio; (*of spies*) giro;
(*of smoke etc*) spirale *f*; (*arena*) pista,
arena; (*for boxing*) ring *m inv*; (*sound of
bell*) scampanio; (*telephone call*) colpo di
telefono ♦ *vb* (*pt* **rang**, *pp* **rung** [ræŋ, rʌŋ]) *vi*
(*person, bell, telephone*) suonare; (*also*: **~
out**: *voice, words*) risuonare; (*TEL*)
telefonare ♦ *vt* (*BRIT TEL*: *also*: **~ up**)

telefonare a; **to give sb a ~** (*TEL*) dare un
colpo di telefono a qn; **that has the ~ of
truth about it** questo ha l'aria d'essere
vero; **to ~ the bell** suonare il campanello;
the name doesn't ~ a bell (with me)
questo nome non mi dice niente.
▶**ring back** *vt*, *vi* (*BRIT TEL*) richiamare.
▶**ring off** *vi* (*BRIT TEL*) mettere giù,
riattaccare.
ring binder *n* classificatore *m* a anelli.
ring finger *n* anulare *m*.
ringing ['rɪŋɪŋ] *n* (*of bell*) scampanio;
(: *louder*) scampanellata; (*of telephone*)
squillo; (*in ears*) fischio, ronzio.
ringing tone *n* (*BRIT TEL*) segnale *m* di
libero.
ringleader ['rɪŋliːdə*] *n* (*of gang*)
capobanda *m*.
ringlets ['rɪŋlɪts] *npl* boccoli *mpl*.
ring road *n* (*BRIT*) raccordo anulare.
ring tone *n* (*TEL*) suoneria.
rink [rɪŋk] *n* (*also*: **ice ~**) pista di
pattinaggio; (*for roller-skating*) pista di
pattinaggio (a rotelle).
rinse [rɪns] *n* risciacquatura; (*hair tint*)
cachet *m inv* ♦ *vt* sciacquare.
Rio (de Janeiro) ['riːəu(dədʒə'nɪərəu)] *n* Rio
de Janeiro *f*.
riot ['raɪət] *n* sommossa, tumulto ♦ *vi*
tumultuare; **a ~ of colours** un'orgia di
colori; **to run ~** creare disordine.
rioter ['raɪətə*] *n* dimostrante *m/f* (*durante
dei disordini*).
riot gear *n*: **in ~** in assetto di guerra.
riotous ['raɪətəs] *adj* tumultuoso(a); che fa
crepare dal ridere.
riotously ['raɪətəslɪ] *adv*: **~ funny** che fa
crepare dal ridere.
riot police *n* ≈ la Celere.
RIP *abbr* (= *requiescat or requiescant in pace*)
R.I.P.
rip [rɪp] *n* strappo ♦ *vt* strappare ♦ *vi*
strapparsi.
▶**rip up** *vt* stracciare.
ripcord ['rɪpkɔːd] *n* cavo di spiegamento.
ripe [raɪp] *adj* (*fruit*) maturo(a); (*cheese*)
stagionato(a).
ripen ['raɪpən] *vt* maturare ♦ *vi* maturarsi;
stagionarsi.
ripeness ['raɪpnɪs] *n* maturità.
rip-off ['rɪpɔf] *n* (*col*): **it's a ~!** è un furto!
riposte [rɪ'pɔst] *n* risposta per le rime.
ripple ['rɪpl] *n* increspamento, ondulazione
f; mormorio ♦ *vi* incresparsi ♦ *vt*
increspare.
rise [raɪz] *n* (*slope*) salita, pendio; (*hill*)
altura; (*increase*: *in wages*) aumento; (: *in
prices, temperature*) rialzo, aumento; (*fig*:

to power etc) ascesa ♦ vi (pt rose, pp risen [rəuz, 'rɪzn]) alzarsi, levarsi; (prices) aumentare; (waters, river) crescere; (sun, wind) levarsi; (also: ~ up: rebel) insorgere; ribellarsi; to give ~ to provocare, dare origine a; to ~ to the occasion dimostrarsi all'altezza della situazione.

rising ['raɪzɪŋ] adj (increasing: number) sempre crescente; (prices) in aumento; (tide) montante; (sun, moon) nascente, che sorge ♦ n (uprising) sommossa.

rising damp n infiltrazioni fpl d'umidità.

rising star n (also fig) astro nascente.

risk [rɪsk] n rischio ♦ vt rischiare; to take or run the ~ of doing correre il rischio di fare; at ~ in pericolo; at one's own ~ a proprio rischio e pericolo; fire/health ~ rischio d'incendio/per la salute; I'll ~ it ci proverò lo stesso.

risk capital n capitale m di rischio.

risky ['rɪskɪ] adj rischioso(a).

risqué ['riːskeɪ] adj (joke) spinto(a).

rissole ['rɪsəul] n crocchetta.

rite [raɪt] n rito; last ~s l'estrema unzione.

ritual ['rɪtjuəl] adj, n rituale (m).

rival ['raɪvl] n rivale m/f; (in business) concorrente m/f ♦ adj rivale; che fa concorrenza ♦ vt essere in concorrenza con; to ~ sb/sth in competere con qn/qc in.

rivalry ['raɪvlrɪ] n rivalità; concorrenza.

river ['rɪvə*] n fiume m ♦ cpd (port, traffic) fluviale; up/down ~ a monte/valle.

riverbank ['rɪvəbæŋk] n argine m.

riverbed ['rɪvəbɛd] n alveo (fluviale).

riverside ['rɪvəsaɪd] n sponda del fiume.

rivet ['rɪvɪt] n ribattino, rivetto ♦ vt ribadire; (fig) concentrare, fissare.

riveting ['rɪvɪtɪŋ] adj (fig) avvincente.

Riviera [rɪvɪ'ɛərə] n: the (French) ~ la Costa Azzurra; the Italian ~ la Riviera.

Riyadh [rɪ'jɑːd] n Riad f.

RMT n abbr (= National Union of Rail, Maritime and Transport Workers) sindacato dei Ferrovieri, Marittimi e Trasportatori.

RN n abbr (BRIT) = Royal Navy; (US) = registered nurse.

RNA n abbr (= ribonucleic acid) R.N.A. m.

RNLI n abbr (BRIT: = Royal National Lifeboat Institution) associazione volontaria che organizza e dispone di scialuppe di salvataggio.

RNZAF n abbr = Royal New Zealand Air Force.

RNZN n abbr = Royal New Zealand Navy.

road [rəud] n strada; (small) cammino; (in town) via; main ~ strada principale; major/minor ~ strada con/senza diritto di precedenza; it takes 4 hours by ~ sono

4 ore di macchina (or in camion etc); on the ~ to success sulla via del successo; "~ up" (BRIT) "attenzione: lavori in corso".

road accident n incidente m stradale.

roadblock ['rəudblɔk] n blocco stradale.

road haulage n autotrasporti mpl.

roadhog ['rəudhɔg] n pirata m della strada.

road map n carta stradale.

road rage n aggressività al volante.

road safety n sicurezza sulle strade.

roadside ['rəudsaɪd] n margine m della strada; by the ~ a lato della strada.

roadsign ['rəudsaɪn] n cartello stradale.

roadsweeper ['rəudswiːpə*] n (BRIT: person) spazzino.

road user n utente m/f della strada.

roadway ['rəudweɪ] n carreggiata.

roadworks ['rəudwɔːks] npl lavori mpl stradali.

roadworthy ['rəudwɔːðɪ] adj in buono stato di marcia.

roam [rəum] vi errare, vagabondare ♦ vt vagare per.

roar [rɔː*] n ruggito; (of crowd) tumulto; (of thunder, storm) muggito ♦ vi ruggire; tumultuare; muggire; to ~ with laughter scoppiare dalle risa.

roaring ['rɔːrɪŋ] adj: a ~ fire un bel fuoco; to do a ~ trade fare affari d'oro; a ~ success un successo strepitoso.

roast [rəust] n arrosto ♦ vt (meat) arrostire.

roast beef n arrosto di manzo.

roasting ['rəustɪŋ] n (col): to give sb a ~ dare una lavata di capo a qn.

rob [rɔb] vt (person) rubare; (bank) svaligiare; to ~ sb of sth derubare qn di qc; (fig: deprive) privare qn di qc.

robber ['rɔbə*] n ladro; (armed) rapinatore m.

robbery ['rɔbərɪ] n furto; rapina.

robe [rəub] n (for ceremony etc) abito; (also: bath~) accappatoio ♦ vt vestire.

robin ['rɔbɪn] n pettirosso.

robot ['rəubɔt] n robot m inv.

robotics [rəubɔtɪks] n robotica.

robust [rəu'bʌst] adj robusto(a); (material) solido(a).

rock [rɔk] n (substance) roccia; (boulder) masso; roccia; (in sea) scoglio; (BRIT: sweet) zucchero candito ♦ vt (swing gently: cradle) dondolare; (: child) cullare; (shake) scrollare, far tremare ♦ vi dondolarsi; oscillare; on the ~s (drink) col ghiaccio; (ship) sugli scogli; (marriage etc) in crisi; to ~ the boat (fig) piantare grane.

rock and roll n rock and roll m.

rock-bottom ['rɔk'bɔtəm] n (fig) stremo; to reach or touch ~ (price) raggiungere il livello più basso; (person) toccare il fondo.

rock climber n rocciatore/trice, scalatore/trice.

rock climbing n roccia.

rockery ['rɔkərɪ] n giardino roccioso.

rocket ['rɔkɪt] n razzo; (MIL) razzo, missile m ♦ vi (prices) salire alle stelle.

rocket launcher [-lɔːntʃəˈ] n lanciarazzi m inv.

rock face n parete f della roccia.

rock fall n caduta di massi.

rocking chair ['rɔkɪŋ-] n sedia a dondolo.

rocking horse n cavallo a dondolo.

rocky ['rɔkɪ] adj (hill) roccioso(a); (path) sassoso(a); (unsteady: table) traballante.

Rocky Mountains npl: the ~ le Montagne Rocciose.

rod [rɔd] n (metallic, TECH) asta; (wooden) bacchetta; (also: fishing ~) canna da pesca.

rode [rəud] pt of **ride**.

rodent ['rəudnt] n roditore m.

rodeo ['rəudɪəu] n rodeo.

roe [rəu] n (species: also: ~ **deer**) capriolo; (of fish: also: **hard** ~) uova fpl di pesce; **soft** ~ latte m di pesce.

roe deer n (species) capriolo; (female deer: pl inv) capriolo femmina.

rogue [rəug] n mascalzone m.

roguish ['rəugɪʃ] adj birbantesco(a).

role [rəul] n ruolo.

role model n modello (di comportamento).

role-play ['rəulpleɪ], **role-playing** ['rəulpleɪŋ] n il recitare un ruolo, role-playing m inv.

roll [rəul] n rotolo; (of banknotes) mazzo; (also: **bread** ~) panino; (register) lista; (sound: of drums etc) rullo; (movement: of ship) rullìo ♦ vt rotolare; (also: ~ **up**: string) aggomitolare; (also: ~ **out**: pastry) stendere ♦ vi rotolare; (wheel) girare; **cheese** ~ panino al formaggio.

▶**roll about, roll around** vi rotolare qua e là; (person) rotolarsi.

▶**roll by** vi (time) passare.

▶**roll in** vi (mail, cash) arrivare a bizzeffe.

▶**roll over** vi rivoltarsi.

▶**roll up** vi (col: arrive) arrivare ♦ vt (carpet, cloth, map) arrotolare; (sleeves) rimboccare; **to** ~ o.s. **up into a ball** raggomitolarsi.

roll call n appello.

rolled gold [rəuld-] adj d'oro laminato.

roller ['rəuləˈ] n rullo; (wheel) rotella.

rollerblades ['rəuləbleɪdz] npl pattini mpl in linea.

roller blind n (BRIT) avvolgibile m.

roller coaster n montagne fpl russe.

roller skates npl pattini mpl a rotelle.

rollicking ['rɔlɪkɪŋ] adj allegro(a) e chiassoso(a).

rolling ['rəulɪŋ] adj (landscape) ondulato(a).

rolling pin n matterello.

rolling stock n (RAIL) materiale m rotabile.

roll-on-roll-off ['rəulɔn'rəulɔf] adj (BRIT: ferry) roll-on roll-off inv.

roly-poly ['rəulɪ'pəulɪ] n (BRIT CULIN) rotolo di pasta con ripieno di marmellata.

ROM [rɔm] n abbr (COMPUT: = read-only memory) ROM f.

Roman ['rəumən] adj, n romano(a).

Roman Catholic adj, n cattolico(a).

romance [rə'mæns] n storia (or avventura or film m inv) romantico(a); (charm) poesia; (love affair) idillio.

Romanesque [rəumə'nɛsk] adj romanico(a).

Romania [rəu'meɪnɪə] n Romania.

Romanian [rəu'meɪnɪən] adj romeno(a) ♦ n romeno/a; (LING) romeno.

Roman numeral n numero romano.

romantic [rə'mæntɪk] adj romantico(a); sentimentale.

romanticism [rə'mæntɪsɪzəm] n romanticismo.

Romany ['rɔmənɪ] adj zingaresco(a) ♦ n (person) zingaro/a; (LING) lingua degli zingari.

Rome [rəum] n Roma.

romp [rɔmp] n gioco chiassoso ♦ vi (also: ~ **about**) giocare chiassosamente; **to** ~ **home** (horse) vincere senza difficoltà, stravincere.

rompers ['rɔmpəz] npl pagliaccetto.

rondo ['rɔndəu] n (MUS) rondò m inv.

roof [ruːf] n tetto; (of tunnel, cave) volta ♦ vt coprire (con un tetto); ~ **of the mouth** palato.

roof garden n giardino pensile.

roofing ['ruːfɪŋ] n materiale m per copertura.

roof rack n (AUT) portabagagli m inv.

rook [ruk] n (bird) corvo nero; (CHESS) torre f ♦ vt (cheat) truffare, spennare.

rookie ['rukɪ] n (col: esp MIL) pivellino/a.

room [ruːm] n (in house) stanza, camera; (in school etc) sala; (space) posto, spazio; ~**s** npl (lodging) alloggio; "~**s to let**", (US) "~**s for rent**" "si affittano camere"; **is there** ~ **for this?** c'è spazio per questo?, ci sta anche questo?; **to make** ~ **for sb** far posto a qn; **there is** ~ **for improvement** si potrebbe migliorare.

rooming house ['ruːmɪŋ-] n (US) casa in

cui si affittano camere o appartamentini ammobiliati.

roommate ['ru:mmeɪt] *n* compagno/a di stanza.

room service *n* servizio da camera.

room temperature *n* temperatura ambiente.

roomy ['ru:mɪ] *adj* spazioso(a); (*garment*) ampio(a).

roost [ru:st] *n* appollaiato ♦ *vi* appollaiarsi.

rooster ['ru:stə*] *n* gallo.

root [ru:t] *n* radice *f* ♦ *vt* (*plant, belief*) far radicare; **to take** ~ (*plant*) attecchire, prendere; (*idea*) far presa; **the** ~ **of the problem is that** ... il problema deriva dal fatto che ....
► **root about** *vi* (*fig*) frugare.
► **root for** *vt fus* (*col*) fare il tifo per.
► **root out** *vt* estirpare.

root beer *n* (*US*) bibita dolce a base di estratti di erbe e radici.

rope [rəup] *n* corda, fune *f*; (*NAUT*) cavo ♦ *vt* (*box*) legare; (*climbers*) legare in cordata; **to** ~ **sb in** (*fig*) coinvolgere qn; **to know the** ~**s** (*fig*) conoscere i trucchi del mestiere.

rope ladder *n* scala di corda.

ropey ['rəupɪ] *adj* (*col*) scadente, da quattro soldi; **to feel** ~ (*ill*) sentirsi male.

rosary ['rəuzərɪ] *n* rosario; roseto.

rose [rəuz] *pt of* **rise** ♦ *n* rosa; (*also*: ~ **bush** rosaio; (*on watering can*) rosetta ♦ *adj* rosa *inv*.

rosé ['rəuzeɪ] *n* vino rosato.

rosebed ['rəuzbɛd] *n* roseto.

rosebud ['rəuzbʌd] *n* bocciolo di rosa.

rosebush ['rəuzbuʃ] *n* rosaio.

rosemary ['rəuzmərɪ] *n* rosmarino.

rosette [rəu'zɛt] *n* coccarda.

ROSPA ['rɔspə] *n abbr* (*BRIT*: = *Royal Society for the Prevention of Accidents*) ≈ E.N.P.I. *m* (= *Ente Nazionale Prevenzione Infortuni*).

roster ['rɔstə*] *n*: **duty** ~ ruolino di servizio.

rostrum ['rɔstrəm] *n* tribuna.

rosy ['rəuzɪ] *adj* roseo(a).

rot [rɔt] *n* (*decay*) putrefazione *f*; (*col*: *nonsense*) stupidaggini *fpl* ♦ *vt*, *vi* imputridire, marcire; **dry/wet** ~ *funghi parassiti del legno*; **to stop the** ~ (*BRIT fig*) salvare la situazione.

rota ['rəutə] *n* tabella dei turni; **on a** ~ **basis** a turno.

rotary ['rəutərɪ] *adj* rotante.

rotate [rəu'teɪt] *vt* (*revolve*) far girare; (*change round*: *crops*) avvicendare; (: *jobs*) fare a turno ♦ *vi* (*revolve*) girare.

rotating [rəu'teɪtɪŋ] *adj* (*movement*) rotante.

rotation [rəu'teɪʃən] *n* rotazione *f*; **in** ~ a turno, in rotazione.

rote [rəut] *n*: **to learn sth by** ~ imparare qc a memoria.

rotor ['rəutə*] *n* rotore *m*.

rotten ['rɔtn] *adj* (*decayed*) putrido(a), marcio(a); (: *teeth*) cariato(a); (*dishonest*) corrotto(a); (*col*: *bad*) brutto(a); (: *action*) vigliacco(a); **to feel** ~ (*ill*) sentirsi proprio male.

rotting ['rɔtɪŋ] *adj* in putrefazione.

rotund [rəu'tʌnd] *adj* grassoccio(a); tondo(a).

rouble, (*US*) **ruble** ['ru:bl] *n* rublo.

rouge [ru:ʒ] *n* belletto.

rough [rʌf] *adj* aspro(a); (*person, manner*: *coarse*) rozzo(a), aspro(a); (: *violent*) brutale; (*district*) malfamato(a); (*weather*) cattivo(a); (*plan*) abbozzato(a); (*guess*) approssimativo(a) ♦ *n* (*GOLF*) macchia; ~ **estimate** approssimazione *f*; **to** ~ **it far** vita dura; **to play** ~ far il gioco pesante; **to sleep** ~ (*BRIT*) dormire all'addiaccio; **to feel** ~ (*BRIT*) sentirsi male; **to have a** ~ **time (of it)** passare un periodaccio; **the sea is** ~ **today** c'è mare grosso oggi.
► **rough out** *vt* (*draft*) abbozzare.

roughage ['rʌfɪdʒ] *n* alimenti *mpl* ricchi di cellulosa.

rough-and-ready ['rʌfən'rɛdɪ] *adj* rudimentale.

rough-and-tumble ['rʌfən'tʌmbl] *n* zuffa.

roughcast ['rʌfkɑ:st] *n* intonaco grezzo.

rough copy, rough draft *n* brutta copia.

roughen ['rʌfn] *vt* (*a surface*) rendere ruvido(a).

rough justice *n* giustizia sommaria.

roughly ['rʌflɪ] *adv* (*handle*) rudemente, brutalmente; (*make*) grossolanamente; (*approximately*) approssimativamente; ~ **speaking** grosso modo, ad occhio e croce.

roughness ['rʌfnɪs] *n* asprezza; rozzezza; brutalità.

roughshod ['rʌfʃɔd] *adv*: **to ride** ~ **over** (*person*) mettere sotto i piedi; (*objection*) passare sopra a.

rough work *n* (*at school etc*) brutta copia.

roulette [ru:'lɛt] *n* roulette *f*.

Roumania *etc* [ru:'meɪnɪə] = **Romania** *etc*.

round [raund] *adj* rotondo(a) ♦ *n* tondo, cerchio; (*BRIT*: *of toast*) fetta; (*duty*: *of policeman, milkman etc*) giro; (: *of doctor*) visite *fpl*; (*game*: *of cards*, *in competition*) partita; (*BOXING*) round *m inv*; (*of talks*) serie *f inv* ♦ *vt* (*corner*) girare; (*bend*) prendere; (*cape*) doppiare ♦ *prep* intorno a ♦ *adv*: **right** ~, **all** ~ tutt'attorno; **the long way** ~ il giro più lungo; **all the year** ~

tutto l'anno; **in** ~ **figures** in cifra tonda; **it's just** ~ **the corner** (*also fig*) è dietro l'angolo; **to ask sb** ~ invitare qn (a casa propria); **I'll be** ~ **at 6 o'clock** ci sarò alle 6; **to go** ~ fare il giro; **to go** ~ **to sb's (house)** andare da qn; **to go** ~ **an obstacle** aggirare un ostacolo; **go** ~ **the back** passi da dietro; **to go** ~ **a house** visitare una casa; **enough to go** ~ abbastanza per tutti; **she arrived** ~ **(about) noon** è arrivata intorno a mezzogiorno; ~ **the clock** 24 ore su 24; **to go the** ~**s** (*illness*) diffondersi; (*story*) circolare, passare di bocca in bocca; **the daily** ~ (*fig*) la routine quotidiana; ~ **of ammunition** cartuccia; ~ **of applause** applausi *mpl*; ~ **of drinks** giro di bibite; ~ **of sandwiches** (*BRIT*) sandwich *m inv*.

▸**round off** *vt* (*speech etc*) finire.

▸**round up** *vt* radunare; (*criminals*) fare una retata di; (*prices*) arrotondare.

roundabout ['raundəbaut] *n* (*BRIT AUT*) rotatoria; (*at fair*) giostra ♦ *adj* (*route, means*) indiretto(a).

rounded ['raundɪd] *adj* arrotondato(a); (*style*) armonioso(a).

rounders ['raundəz] *npl* (*game*) gioco simile al baseball.

roundly ['raundlɪ] *adv* (*fig*) chiaro e tondo.

round robin *n* (*SPORT: also*: ~ **tournament**) ≈ torneo all'italiana.

round-shouldered [raund'ʃəuldəd] *adj* dalle spalle tonde.

round trip *n* (viaggio di) andata e ritorno.

roundup ['raundʌp] *n* raduno; (*of criminals*) retata; **a** ~ **of the latest news** un sommario *or* riepilogo delle ultime notizie.

rouse [rauz] *vt* (*wake up*) svegliare; (*stir up*) destare; provocare; risvegliare.

rousing ['rauzɪŋ] *adj* (*speech, applause*) entusiastico(a).

rout [raut] *n* (*MIL*) rotta ♦ *vt* mettere in rotta.

route [ru:t] *n* itinerario; (*of bus*) percorso; (*of trade, shipping*) rotta; **"all** ~**s"** (*AUT*) "tutte le direzioni"; **the best** ~ **to London** la strada migliore per andare a Londra; **en** ~ **for** in viaggio verso; **en** ~ **from** ... **to** viaggiando da ... a.

route map *n* (*BRIT: for journey*) cartina di itinerario; (*for trains etc*) pianta dei collegamenti.

routine [ru:'ti:n] *adj* (*work*) corrente, abituale; (*procedure*) solito(a) ♦ *n* (*pej*) routine *f*, tran tran *m*; (*THEAT*) numero; (*COMPUT*) sottoprogramma *m*; **daily** ~ orario quotidiano; ~ **procedure**

prassi *f*.

roving ['rəuvɪŋ] *adj* (*life*) itinerante.

roving reporter *n* reporter *m inv* volante.

row[1] [rəu] *n* (*line*) riga, fila; (*KNITTING*) ferro; (*behind one another: of cars, people*) fila ♦ *vi* (*in boat*) remare; (*as sport*) vogare ♦ *vt* (*boat*) manovrare a remi; **in a** ~ (*fig*) di fila.

row[2] [rau] *n* (*noise*) baccano, chiasso; (*dispute*) lite *f* ♦ *vi* litigare; **to make a** ~ far baccano; **to have a** ~ litigare.

rowboat ['rəubəut] *n* (*US*) barca a remi.

rowdiness ['raudɪnɪs] *n* baccano; (*fighting*) zuffa.

rowdy ['raudɪ] *adj* chiassoso(a); turbolento(a) ♦ *n* teppista *m/f*.

rowdyism ['raudɪɪzəm] *n* teppismo.

rowing ['rəuɪŋ] *n* canottaggio.

rowing boat *n* (*BRIT*) barca a remi.

royal ['rɔɪəl] *adj* reale.

Royal Academy *n* (*BRIT*) see boxed note.

Royal Air Force (RAF) *n* (*BRIT*) *aeronautica militare britannica.*

royal blue *adj* blu reale *inv*.

royalist ['rɔɪəlɪst] *adj, n* realista (*m/f*).

Royal Navy (RN) *n* (*BRIT*) *marina militare britannica.*

royalty ['rɔɪəltɪ] *n* (*royal persons*) (membri *mpl* della) famiglia reale; (*payment: to author*) diritti *mpl* d'autore; (: *to inventor*) diritti di brevetto.

RP *n abbr* (*BRIT*: = *received pronunciation*) pronuncia standard.

RPI *abbr* (*BRIT*: = *retail price index*) ≈ Indice dei prezzi al consumo.

rpm *abbr* (= *revolutions per minute*) giri/min.

RR *abbr* (*US* = *railroad*) Ferr.

R&R *n abbr* (*US MIL*: = *rest and recreation*) *permesso per militari.*

RRP *n abbr* (*BRIT*) see **recommended retail price.**

RSA *n abbr* (*BRIT*) = *Royal Society of Arts*; *Royal Scottish Academy.*

RSI *n abbr* (*MED*: = *repetitive strain injury*) *lesione al braccio tipica di violinisti e terminalisti.*

RSPB *n abbr* (*BRIT*: = *Royal Society for the Protection of Birds*) ≈ L.I.P.U. *f* (= Lega

RSPCA – rumple

Italiana Protezione Uccelli).
RSPCA *n abbr (BRIT:* = *Royal Society for the Prevention of Cruelty to Animals)*
≈ E.N.P.A. *m (= Ente Nazionale per la Protezione degli Animali).*
RSVP *abbr (= répondez s'il vous plaît)* R.S.V.P.
RTA *n abbr (= road traffic accident)* incidente *m* stradale.
Rt Hon. *abbr (BRIT:* = *Right Honourable)* ≈ On. *(= Onorevole).*
Rt Rev. *abbr (= Right Reverend)* Rev.
rub [rʌb] *n (with cloth)* fregata, strofinata; *(on person)* frizione *f*, massaggio ♦ *vt* fregare, strofinare; frizionare; **to ~ sb up** *or (US)* **~ sb the wrong way** lisciare qn contro pelo.
▶**rub down** *vt (body)* strofinare, frizionare; *(horse)* strigliare.
▶**rub in** *vt (ointment)* far penetrare (massaggiando *or* frizionando).
▶**rub off** *vi* andare via; **to ~ off on** lasciare una traccia su.
▶**rub out** *vt* cancellare ♦ *vi* cancellarsi.
rubber ['rʌbə*] *n* gomma.
rubber band *n* elastico.
rubber bullet *n* pallottola di gomma.
rubber plant *n* ficus *m inv.*
rubber ring *n (for swimming)* ciambella.
rubber stamp *n* timbro di gomma.
rubber-stamp [rʌbə'stæmp] *vt (fig)* approvare senza discussione.
rubbery ['rʌbərɪ] *adj* gommoso(a).
rubbish ['rʌbɪʃ] *n (from household)* immondizie *fpl*, rifiuti *mpl*; *(fig: pej)* cose *fpl* senza valore; robaccia; *(nonsense)* sciocchezze *fpl* ♦ *vt (col)* sputtanare.
rubbish bin *n (BRIT)* pattumiera.
rubbish dump *n* luogo di scarico.
rubbishy ['rʌbɪʃɪ] *adj (BRIT col)* scadente, che non vale niente.
rubble ['rʌbl] *n* macerie *fpl*; *(smaller)* pietrisco.
ruble ['ruːbl] *n (US)* = **rouble.**
ruby ['ruːbɪ] *n* rubino.
RUC *n abbr (BRIT:* = *Royal Ulster Constabulary)* forza di polizia dell'Irlanda del Nord.
rucksack ['rʌksæk] *n* zaino.
ructions ['rʌkʃənz] *npl* putiferio, finimondo.
rudder ['rʌdə*] *n* timone *m.*
ruddy ['rʌdɪ] *adj (face)* fresco(a); *(col: damned)* maledetto(a).
rude [ruːd] *adj (impolite: person)* scortese, rozzo(a); *(: word, manners)* grossolano(a), rozzo(a); *(shocking)* indecente; **to be ~ to sb** essere maleducato con qn.
rudely ['ruːdlɪ] *adv* scortesemente;

grossolanamente.
rudeness ['ruːdnɪs] *n* scortesia; grossolanità.
rudiment ['ruːdɪmənt] *n* rudimento.
rudimentary [ruːdɪ'mɛntərɪ] *adj* rudimentale.
rue [ruː] *vt* pentirsi amaramente di.
rueful ['ruːful] *adj* mesto(a), triste.
ruff [rʌf] *n* gorgiera.
ruffian ['rʌfɪən] *n* briccone *m*, furfante *m.*
ruffle ['rʌfl] *vt (hair)* scompigliare; *(clothes, water)* increspare; *(fig: person)* turbare.
rug [rʌg] *n* tappeto; *(BRIT: for knees)* coperta.
rugby ['rʌgbɪ] *n (also:* ~ **football)** rugby *m.*
rugged ['rʌgɪd] *adj (landscape)* aspro(a); *(features, determination)* duro(a); *(character)* brusco(a).
rugger ['rʌgə*] *n (col)* rugby *m.*
ruin ['ruːɪn] *n* rovina ♦ *vt* rovinare; *(spoil: clothes)* sciupare; **~s** *npl* rovine *fpl*, ruderi *mpl*; **in ~s** in rovina.
ruination [ruːɪ'neɪʃən] *n* rovina.
ruinous ['ruːɪnəs] *adj* rovinoso(a); *(expenditure)* inverosimile.
rule [ruːl] *n (gen)* regola; *(regulation)* regolamento, regola; *(government)* governo; *(dominion etc):* **under British ~** sotto la sovranità britannica ♦ *vt (country)* governare; *(person)* dominare; *(decide)* decidere ♦ *vi* regnare; decidere; *(LAW)* dichiarare; **to ~ against/in favour of/on** *(LAW)* pronunciarsi a sfavore di/in favore di/su; **it's against the ~s** è contro le regole *or* il regolamento; **by ~ of thumb** a lume di naso; **as a ~** normalmente, di regola.
▶**rule out** *vt* escludere; **murder cannot be ~d out** non si esclude che si tratti di omicidio.
ruled [ruːld] *adj (paper)* vergato(a).
ruler ['ruːlə*] *n (sovereign)* sovrano/a; *(leader)* capo (dello Stato); *(for measuring)* regolo, riga.
ruling ['ruːlɪŋ] *adj (party)* al potere; *(class)* dirigente ♦ *n (LAW)* decisione *f.*
rum [rʌm] *n* rum *m* ♦ *adj (BRIT col)* strano(a).
Rumania *etc* [ruː'meɪnɪə] = **Romania** *etc.*
rumble ['rʌmbl] *n* rimbombo; brontolio ♦ *vi* rimbombare; *(stomach, pipe)* brontolare.
rumbustious [rʌm'bʌstʃəs] *adj (person):* **to be ~** essere un terremoto.
rummage ['rʌmɪdʒ] *vi* frugare.
rumour, *(US)* **rumor** ['ruːmə*] *n* voce *f* ♦ *vt:* **it is ~ed that** corre voce che.
rump [rʌmp] *n (of animal)* groppa.
rumple ['rʌmpl] *vt (hair)* arruffare, scompigliare; *(clothes)* spiegazzare,

sgualcire.

rump steak *n* bistecca di girello.

rumpus ['rʌmpəs] *n* (*col*) baccano; (: *quarrel*) rissa; **to kick up a** ~ fare un putiferio.

run [rʌn] *n* corsa; (*outing*) gita (in macchina); (*distance travelled*) percorso, tragitto; (*series*) serie *f inv*; (*THEAT*) periodo di rappresentazione; (*SKI*) pista ♦ *vb* (*pt* **ran**, *pp* **run** [ræn, rʌn]) *vt* (*operate:* business) gestire, dirigere; (: *competition, course*) organizzare; (: *hotel*) gestire; (: *house*) governare; (*COMPUT*: *program*) eseguire; (*water, bath*) far scorrere; (*force through:* rope, pipe): **to** ~ **sth through** far passare qc attraverso; (*to pass:* hand, finger): **to** ~ **sth over** passare qc su ♦ *vi* correre; (*pass:* road etc) passare; (*work:* machine, factory) funzionare, andare; (*bus, train:* operate) far servizio; (: *travel*) circolare; (*continue:* play, contract) durare; (*slide:* drawer, flow: river, bath) scorrere; (*colours, washing*) stemperarsi; (*in election*) presentarsi come candidato; **to go for a** ~ andare a correre; (*in car*) fare un giro (in macchina); **to break into a** ~ mettersi a correre; **a** ~ **of luck** un periodo di fortuna; **to have the** ~ **of sb's house** essere libero di andare e venire in casa di qn; **there was a** ~ **on ...** c'era una corsa a ...; **in the long** ~ alla lunga; **in fin dei conti; in the short** ~ sulle prime; **on the** ~ in fuga; **to make a** ~ **for it** scappare, tagliare la corda; **I'll** ~ **you to the station** ti porto alla stazione; **to** ~ **a risk** correre un rischio; **to** ~ **errands** andare a fare commissioni; **the train** ~**s between Gatwick and Victoria** il treno collega Gatwick alla stazione Victoria; **the bus** ~**s every 20 minutes** c'è un autobus ogni 20 minuti; **it's very cheap to** ~ comporta poche spese; **to** ~ **on petrol** *or* (*US*) **gas/on diesel/off batteries** andare a benzina/a diesel/a batterie; **to** ~ **for the bus** fare una corsa per prendere l'autobus; **to** ~ **for president** presentarsi come candidato per la presidenza; **their losses ran into millions** le loro perdite hanno raggiunto i milioni; **to be** ~ **off one's feet** (*BRIT*) doversi fare in quattro.

►**run about** *vi* (*children*) correre qua e là.

►**run across** *vt fus* (*find*) trovare per caso.

►**run away** *vi* fuggire.

►**run down** *vi* (*clock*) scaricarsi ♦ *vt* (*AUT*) investire; (*criticize*) criticare; (*BRIT*: reduce: production) ridurre gradualmente; (: *factory, shop*) rallentare l'attività di; **to be** ~ **down** (*battery*) essere scarico(a);

(*person*) essere giù (di corda).

►**run in** *vt* (*BRIT*: car) rodare, fare il rodaggio di.

►**run into** *vt fus* (*meet:* person) incontrare per caso; (: *trouble*) incontrare, trovare; (*collide with*) andare a sbattere contro; **to** ~ **into debt** trovarsi nei debiti.

►**run off** *vi* fuggire ♦ *vt* (*water*) far defluire; (*copies*) fare.

►**run out** *vi* (*person*) uscire di corsa; (*liquid*) colare; (*lease*) scadere; (*money*) esaurirsi.

►**run out of** *vt fus* rimanere a corto di; **I've** ~ **out of petrol** *or* (*US*) **gas** sono rimasto senza benzina.

►**run over** *vt* (*AUT*) investire, mettere sotto ♦ *vt fus* (*revise*) rivedere.

►**run through** *vt fus* (*instructions*) dare una scorsa a.

►**run up** *vt* (*debt*) lasciar accumulare; **to** ~ **up against** (*difficulties*) incontrare.

runaround ['rʌnəraund] *n* (*col*): **to give sb the** ~ far girare a vuoto qn.

runaway ['rʌnəweɪ] *adj* (*person*) fuggiasco(a); (*horse*) in libertà; (*truck*) fuori controllo; (*inflation*) galoppante.

rundown ['rʌndaun] *n* (*BRIT*: of industry etc) riduzione *f* graduale dell'attività di.

rung [rʌŋ] *pp of* **ring** ♦ *n* (*of ladder*) piolo.

run-in ['rʌnɪn] *n* (*col*) scontro.

runner ['rʌnə*] *n* (*in race*) corridore *m*; (*on sledge*) pattino; (*for drawer etc, carpet*) guida.

runner bean *n* (*BRIT*) fagiolino.

runner-up [rʌnər'ʌp] *n* secondo(a) arrivato(a).

running ['rʌnɪŋ] *n* corsa; direzione *f*; organizzazione *f*; funzionamento ♦ *adj* (*water*) corrente; (*commentary*) simultaneo(a); **6 days** ~ 6 giorni di seguito; **to be in/out of the** ~ **for sth** essere/non essere più in lizza per qc.

running costs *npl* (*of business*) costi *mpl* d'esercizio; (*of car*) spese *fpl* di mantenimento.

running head *n* (*TYP, WORD PROCESSING*) testata, titolo corrente.

running mate *n* (*US POL*) candidato alla vicepresidenza.

runny ['rʌnɪ] *adj* che cola.

run-off ['rʌnɔf] *n* (*in contest, election*) confronto definitivo; (*extra race*) spareggio.

run-of-the-mill ['rʌnəvðə'mɪl] *adj* solito(a), banale.

runt [rʌnt] *n* (*also pej*) omuncolo; (*ZOOL*) animale *m* più piccolo del normale.

run-through ['rʌnθruː] *n* prova.

run-up ['rʌnʌp] n (BRIT): ~ to sth periodo che precede qc.

runway ['rʌnweɪ] n (AVIAT) pista (di decollo).

rupture ['rʌptʃə*] n (MED) ernia ♦ vt: to ~ o.s. farsi venire un'ernia.

rural ['ruərl] adj rurale.

rural district council (RDC) n (BRIT) consiglio (amministrativo) di distretto rurale.

ruse [ruːz] n trucco.

rush [rʌʃ] n corsa precipitosa; (of crowd) afflusso; (hurry) furia, fretta; (current) flusso; (BOT) giunco ♦ vt mandare or spedire velocemente; (attack: town etc) prendere d'assalto ♦ vi precipitarsi; is there any ~ for this? è urgente?; we've had a ~ of orders abbiamo avuto una valanga di ordinazioni; I'm in a ~ (to do) ho fretta or premura (di fare); gold ~ corsa all'oro; to ~ sth off spedire con urgenza qc; don't ~ me! non farmi fretta!

▶rush through vt (meal) mangiare in fretta; (book) dare una scorsa frettolosa a; (town) attraversare in fretta; (COMM: order) eseguire d'urgenza ♦ vt fus (work) sbrigare frettolosamente.

rush hour n ora di punta.

rush job n (urgent) lavoro urgente.

rush matting n stuoia.

rusk [rʌsk] n fetta biscottata.

Russia ['rʌʃə] n Russia.

Russian ['rʌʃən] adj russo(a) ♦ n russo/a; (LING) russo.

rust [rʌst] n ruggine f ♦ vi arrugginirsi.

rustic ['rʌstɪk] adj rustico(a) ♦ n (pej) cafone/a.

rustle ['rʌsl] vi frusciare ♦ vt (paper) far frusciare; (US: cattle) rubare.

rustproof ['rʌstpruːf] adj inossidabile.

rustproofing ['rʌstpruːfɪŋ] n trattamento antiruggine.

rusty ['rʌstɪ] adj arrugginito(a).

rut [rʌt] n solco; (ZOOL) fregola; to be in a ~ (fig) essersi fossilizzato(a).

rutabaga [ruːtə'beɪgə] n (US) rapa svedese.

ruthless ['ruːθlɪs] adj spietato(a).

ruthlessness ['ruːθlɪsnɪs] n spietatezza.

RV abbr (= revised version) versione riveduta della Bibbia ♦ n abbr (US) see recreational vehicle.

rye [raɪ] n segale f.

S, s [ɛs] n (letter) S, s f or m inv; (US SCOL: = satisfactory) ≈ sufficiente; S for Sugar ≈ S come Savona.

S abbr (= saint) S.; (= south) S; (on clothes) = small.

SA abbr = South Africa; South America.

Sabbath ['sæbəθ] n (Jewish) sabato; (Christian) domenica.

sabbatical [sə'bætɪkl] adj: ~ year anno sabbatico.

sabotage ['sæbətɑːʒ] n sabotaggio ♦ vt sabotare.

saccharin(e) ['sækərɪn] n saccarina.

sachet ['sæʃeɪ] n bustina.

sack [sæk] n (bag) sacco ♦ vt (dismiss) licenziare, mandare a spasso; (plunder) saccheggiare; to get the ~ essere mandato a spasso; to give sb the ~ licenziare qn, mandare qn a spasso.

sackful ['sækful] n: a ~ of un sacco di.

sacking ['sækɪŋ] n tela di sacco; (dismissal) licenziamento.

sacrament ['sækrəmənt] n sacramento.

sacred ['seɪkrɪd] adj sacro(a).

sacred cow n (fig: person) intoccabile m/f; (: institution) caposaldo; (: idea, belief) dogma m.

sacrifice ['sækrɪfaɪs] n sacrificio ♦ vt sacrificare; to make ~s (for sb) fare (dei) sacrifici (per qn).

sacrilege ['sækrɪlɪdʒ] n sacrilegio.

sacrosanct ['sækrəusæŋkt] adj sacrosanto(a).

sad [sæd] adj triste; (deplorable) deplorevole.

sadden ['sædn] vt rattristare.

saddle ['sædl] n sella ♦ vt (horse) sellare; to be ~d with sth (col) avere qc sulle spalle.

saddlebag ['sædlbæg] n bisaccia; (on bicycle) borsa.

sadism ['seɪdɪzəm] n sadismo.

sadist ['seɪdɪst] n sadico/a.

sadistic [sə'dɪstɪk] adj sadico(a).

sadly ['sædlɪ] adv tristemente; (regrettably) sfortunatamente; ~ lacking in penosamente privo di.

sadness ['sædnɪs] n tristezza.

sadomasochism [seɪdəu'mæsəkɪzəm] n

sadomasochismo.
sae *abbr* (*BRIT*) = **stamped addressed envelope**; *see* **stamp.**
safari [sə'fɑːrɪ] *n* safari *m inv.*
safari park *n* zoosafari *m inv.*
safe [seɪf] *adj* sicuro(a); (*out of danger*) salvo(a), al sicuro; (*cautious*) prudente ♦ *n* cassaforte *f*; ~ **from** al sicuro da; ~ **and sound** sano(a) e salvo(a); ~ **journey!** buon viaggio!; (**just**) **to be on the** ~ **side** per non correre rischi; **to play** ~ giocare sul sicuro; **it is** ~ **to say that** ... si può affermare con sicurezza che ....
safe bet *n*: **it's a** ~ è una cosa sicura.
safe-breaker ['seɪfbreɪkə*] *n* (*BRIT*) scassinatore *m.*
safe-conduct [seɪf'kɒndʌkt] *n* salvacondotto.
safe-cracker ['seɪfkrækə*] *n* = **safe-breaker.**
safe-deposit ['seɪfdɪpɒzɪt] *n* (*vault*) caveau *m inv*; (*box*) cassetta di sicurezza.
safeguard ['seɪfgɑːd] *n* salvaguardia ♦ *vt* salvaguardare.
safe haven *n* zona sicura *or* protetta.
safekeeping ['seɪf'kiːpɪŋ] *n* custodia.
safely ['seɪflɪ] *adv* sicuramente; sano(a) e salvo(a); prudentemente; **I can** ~ **say** ... posso tranquillamente asscrire ....
safe passage *n* passaggio sicuro.
safe sex *n* sesso sicuro.
safety ['seɪftɪ] *n* sicurezza; ~ **first!** la prudenza innanzitutto!
safety belt *n* cintura di sicurezza.
safety catch *n* sicura.
safety net *n* rete *f* di protezione.
safety pin *n* spilla di sicurezza.
safety valve *n* valvola di sicurezza.
saffron ['sæfrən] *n* zafferano.
sag [sæg] *vi* incurvarsi; afflosciarsi.
saga ['sɑːgə] *n* saga; (*fig*) odissea.
sage [seɪdʒ] *n* (*herb*) salvia; (*man*) saggio.
Sagittarius [sædʒɪ'tɛərɪəs] *n* Sagittario; **to be** ~ essere del Sagittario.
sago ['seɪgəu] *n* sagù *m.*
Sahara [sə'hɑːrə] *n*: **the** ~ **Desert** il Deserto del Sahara.
Sahel [sæ'hɛl] *n* Sahel *m.*
said [sɛd] *pt, pp of* **say.**
Saigon [saɪ'gɒn] *n* Saigon *f.*
sail [seɪl] *n* (*on boat*) vela; (*trip*): **to go for a** ~ fare un giro in barca a vela ♦ *vt* (*boat*) condurre, governare ♦ *vi* (*travel: ship*) navigare; (: *passenger*) viaggiare per mare; (*set off*) salpare; (*SPORT*) fare della vela; **they** ~**ed into Genoa** entrarono nel porto di Genova.
► **sail through** *vt fus* (*fig*) superare senza difficoltà ♦ *vi* farcela senza difficoltà.

sailboat ['seɪlbəut] *n* (*US*) barca a vela.
sailing ['seɪlɪŋ] *n* (*sport*) vela; **to go** ~ fare della vela.
sailing boat *n* barca a vela.
sailing ship *n* veliero.
sailor ['seɪlə*] *n* marinaio.
saint [seɪnt] *n* santo/a.
saintly ['seɪntlɪ] *adj* da santo(a); santo(a).
sake [seɪk] *n*: **for the** ~ **of** per, per amore di; **for pity's** ~ per pietà; **for the** ~ **of argument** tanto per fare un esempio; **art for art's** ~ l'arte per l'arte.
salad ['sæləd] *n* insalata; **tomato** ~ insalata di pomodori.
salad bowl *n* insalatiera.
salad cream *n* (*BRIT*) (tipo di) maionese *f.*
salad dressing *n* condimento per insalata.
salad oil *n* olio da tavola.
salami [sə'lɑːmɪ] *n* salame *m.*
salaried ['sælərɪd] *adj* stipendiato(a).
salary ['sælərɪ] *n* stipendio.
salary scale *n* scala dei salari.
sale [seɪl] *n* vendita; (*at reduced prices*) svendita, liquidazione *f*; **"for** ~**"** "in vendita"; **on** ~ in vendita; **on** ~ **or return** da vendere o rimandare; **a closing-down** *or* (*US*) **liquidation** ~ una liquidazione; ~ **and lease back** *n* lease back *m inv.*
saleroom ['seɪlrum] *n* sala delle aste.
sales assistant *n* (*BRIT*) commesso/a.
sales clerk *n* (*US*) commesso/a.
sales conference *n* riunione *f* marketing e vendite.
sales drive *n* campagna di vendita, sforzo promozionale.
sales force *n* personale *m* addetto alle vendite.
salesman ['seɪlzmən] *n* commesso; (*representative*) rappresentante *m.*
sales manager *n* direttore *m* commerciale.
salesmanship ['seɪlzmənʃɪp] *n* arte *f* del vendere.
sales tax *n* (*US*) imposta sulle vendite.
saleswoman ['seɪlzwumən] *n* commessa.
salient ['seɪlɪənt] *adj* saliente.
saline ['seɪlaɪn] *adj* salino(a).
saliva [sə'laɪvə] *n* saliva.
sallow ['sæləu] *adj* giallastro(a).
sally forth, sally out ['sælɪ-] *vi* uscire di gran carriera.
salmon ['sæmən] *n* (*pl inv*) salmone *m.*
salmon trout *n* trota (di mare).
saloon [sə'luːn] *n* (*US*) saloon *m inv*, bar *m inv*; (*BRIT AUT*) berlina; (*ship's lounge*) salone *m.*
SALT [sɔːlt] *n abbr* (= *Strategic Arms Limitation Talks/Treaty*) S.A.L.T. *m.*

salt [sɔːlt] n sale m ◆ vt salare ◆ cpd di sale; (CULIN) salato(a); **an old** ~ un lupo di mare.
▶**salt away** vt ammucchiare, mettere via.
salt cellar n saliera.
salt-free ['sɔːlt'friː] adj senza sale.
saltwater ['sɔːltwɔːtə*] adj (fish etc) di mare.
salty ['sɔːltɪ] adj salato(a).
salubrious [sə'luːbrɪəs] adj salubre; (fig: district etc) raccomandabile.
salutary ['sæljutərɪ] adj salutare.
salute [sə'luːt] n saluto ◆ vt salutare.
salvage ['sælvɪdʒ] n (saving) salvataggio; (things saved) beni mpl salvati or recuperati ◆ vt salvare, mettere in salvo.
salvage vessel n scialuppa di salvataggio.
salvation [sæl'veɪʃən] n salvezza.
Salvation Army n Esercito della Salvezza.
salver ['sælvə*] n vassoio.
salvo, ~**es** ['sælvəu] n salva.
Samaritan [sə'mærɪtən] n: **the** ~**s** (organization) ≈ telefono amico.
same [seɪm] adj stesso(a), medesimo(a) ◆ pron: **the** ~ lo(la) stesso(a), gli(le) stessi(e); **the** ~ **book as** lo stesso libro di (or che); **on the** ~ **day** lo stesso giorno; **at the** ~ **time** allo stesso tempo; **all** or **just the** ~ tuttavia; **to do the** ~ fare la stessa cosa; **to do the** ~ **as sb** fare come qn; **the** ~ **again** (in bar etc) un altro; **they're one and the** ~ (person/thing) sono la stessa persona/cosa; **and the** ~ **to you!** altrettanto a lei!; ~ **here!** anch'io!
sample ['sɑːmpl] n campione m ◆ vt (food) assaggiare; (wine) degustare; **to take a** ~ prelevare un campione; **free** ~ campione omaggio.
sanatorium, pl **sanatoria** [sænə'tɔːrɪəm, -rɪə] n sanatorio.
sanctify ['sæŋktɪfaɪ] vt santificare.
sanctimonious [sæŋktɪ'məunɪəs] adj bigotto(a), bacchettone(a).
sanction ['sæŋkʃən] n sanzione f ◆ vt sancire, sanzionare; **to impose economic** ~**s on** or **against** adottare sanzioni economiche contro.
sanctity ['sæŋktɪtɪ] n santità.
sanctuary ['sæŋktjuərɪ] n (holy place) santuario; (refuge) rifugio; (for wildlife) riserva.
sand [sænd] n sabbia ◆ vt cospargere di sabbia; (also: ~ **down**: wood etc) cartavetrare; see also **sands**.
sandal ['sændl] n sandalo.
sandbag ['sændbæg] n sacco di sabbia.
sandblast ['sændblɑːst] vt sabbiare.

sandbox ['sændbɔks] n (US: for children) buca di sabbia.
sandcastle ['sændkɑːsl] n castello di sabbia.
sand dune n duna di sabbia.
sander ['sændə*] n levigatrice f.
sandpaper ['sændpeɪpə*] n carta vetrata.
sandpit ['sændpɪt] n (BRIT: for children) buca di sabbia.
sands [sændz] npl spiaggia.
sandstone ['sændstəun] n arenaria.
sandstorm ['sændstɔːm] n tempesta di sabbia.
sandwich ['sændwɪtʃ] n tramezzino, panino, sandwich m inv ◆ vt (also: ~ **in**) infilare; **cheese/ham** ~ sandwich al formaggio/prosciutto; **to be** ~**ed between** essere incastrato(a) fra.
sandwich board n cartello pubblicitario (portato da un uomo sandwich).
sandwich course n (BRIT) corso di formazione professionale.
sandwich man n uomo m sandwich inv.
sandy ['sændɪ] adj sabbioso(a); (colour) color sabbia inv, biondo(a) rossiccio(a).
sane [seɪn] adj (person) sano(a) di mente; (outlook) sensato(a).
sang [sæŋ] pt of **sing**.
sanguine ['sæŋgwɪn] adj ottimista.
sanitarium, pl **sanitaria** [sænɪ'tɛərɪəm, -rɪə] n (US) = **sanatorium**.
sanitary ['sænɪtərɪ] adj (system, arrangements) sanitario(a); (clean) igienico(a).
sanitary towel, (US) **sanitary napkin** n assorbente m (igienico).
sanitation [sænɪ'teɪʃən] n (in house) impianti mpl sanitari; (in town) fognature fpl.
sanitation department n (US) nettezza urbana.
sanity ['sænɪtɪ] n sanità mentale; (common sense) buon senso.
sank [sæŋk] pt of **sink**.
San Marino [sænmə'riːnəu] n San Marino f.
Santa Claus [sæntə'klɔːz] n Babbo Natale.
Santiago [sæntɪ'ɑːgəu] n (also: ~ **de Chile**) Santiago (del Cile) f.
sap [sæp] n (of plants) linfa ◆ vt (strength) fiaccare.
sapling ['sæplɪŋ] n alberello.
sapphire ['sæfaɪə*] n zaffiro.
sarcasm ['sɑːkæzm] n sarcasmo.
sarcastic [sɑː'kæstɪk] adj sarcastico(a); **to be** ~ fare del sarcasmo.
sarcophagus, pl **sarcophagi** [sɑː'kɔfəgəs, -gaɪ] n sarcofago.
sardine [sɑː'diːn] n sardina.
Sardinia [sɑː'dɪnɪə] n Sardegna.

Sardinian [saː'dɪnɪən] adj, n sardo(a).
sardonic [saː'dɒnɪk] adj sardonico(a).
sari ['saːrɪ] n sari m inv.
SARS [saːz] n abbr (= severe acute respiratory syndrome) SARS f, polmonite atipica.
sartorial [saː'tɔːrɪəl] adj di sartoria.
SAS n abbr (BRIT MIL: = Special Air Service) reparto dell'esercito britannico specializzato in operazioni clandestine.
SASE n abbr (US: = self-addressed stamped envelope) busta affrancata e con indirizzo.
sash [sæʃ] n fascia.
sash window n finestra a ghigliottina.
SAT n abbr (US) = Scholastic Aptitude Test.
sat [sæt] pt, pp of **sit**.
Sat. abbr (= Saturday) sab.
Satan ['seɪtən] n Satana m.
satanic [sə'tænɪk] adj satanico(a).
satchel ['sætʃl] n cartella.
sated ['seɪtɪd] adj soddisfatto(a); sazio(a).
satellite ['sætəlaɪt] adj, n satellite (m).
satellite television n televisione f via satellite.
satiate ['seɪʃɪeɪt] vt saziare.
satin ['sætɪn] n satin m ♦ adj di or in satin; **with a ~ finish** satinato(a).
satire ['sætaɪə*] n satira.
satirical [sə'tɪrɪkl] adj satirico(a).
satirist ['sætərɪst] n (writer etc) scrittore(trice) etc satirico(a); (cartoonist) caricaturista m/f.
satirize ['sætɪraɪz] vt satireggiare.
satisfaction [sætɪs'fækʃən] n soddisfazione f; **has it been done to your ~?** ne è rimasto soddisfatto?
satisfactory [sætɪs'fæktərɪ] adj soddisfacente.
satisfied ['sætɪsfaɪd] adj (customer) soddisfatto(a); **to be ~ (with sth)** essere soddisfatto(a) (di qc).
satisfy ['sætɪsfaɪ] vt soddisfare; (convince) convincere; **to ~ the requirements** rispondere ai requisiti; **to ~ sb (that)** convincere qn (che), persuadere qn (che); **to ~ o.s. of sth** accertarsi di qc.
satisfying ['sætɪsfaɪɪŋ] adj soddisfacente.
SATs n abbr (BRIT: = standard assessment tasks or tests) esame di fine anno sostenuto dagli allievi delle scuole pubbliche inglesi a 7, 11 o 14 anni.
satsuma [sæt'suːmə] n agrume di provenienza giapponese.
saturate ['sætʃəreɪt] vt: **to ~ (with)** saturare (di).
saturated fat ['sætʃəreɪtɪd-] n grassi mpl saturi.
saturation [sætʃə'reɪʃən] n saturazione f.

Saturday ['sætədɪ] n sabato; for phrases see also **Tuesday**.
sauce [sɔːs] n salsa; (with meat, fish) sugo.
saucepan ['sɔːspən] n casseruola.
saucer ['sɔːsə*] n piattino.
saucy ['sɔːsɪ] adj impertinente.
Saudi Arabia ['saudɪ-] n Arabia Saudita.
Saudi (Arabian) adj, n saudita (m/f).
sauna ['sɔːnə] n sauna.
saunter ['sɔːntə*] vi andare a zonzo, bighellonare.
sausage ['sɒsɪdʒ] n salsiccia; (salami etc) salame m.
sausage roll n rotolo di pasta sfoglia ripieno di salsiccia.
sauté ['səuteɪ] adj (CULIN: potatoes) saltato(a); (: onions) soffritto(a) ♦ vt far saltare; far soffriggere.
savage ['sævɪdʒ] adj (cruel, fierce) selvaggio(a), feroce; (primitive) primitivo(a) ♦ n selvaggio/a ♦ vt attaccare selvaggiamente.
savagery ['sævɪdʒrɪ] n crudeltà, ferocia.
save [seɪv] vt (person, belongings, COMPUT) salvare; (money) risparmiare, mettere da parte; (time) risparmiare; (food) conservare; (avoid: trouble) evitare ♦ vi (also: ~ up) economizzare ♦ n (SPORT) parata ♦ prep salvo, a eccezione di; **it will ~ me an hour** mi farà risparmiare un'ora; **to ~ face** salvare la faccia; **God ~ the Queen!** Dio salvi la Regina!
saving ['seɪvɪŋ] n risparmio ♦ adj: **the ~ grace of** l'unica cosa buona di; **~s** npl risparmi mpl; **to make ~s** fare economia.
savings account n libretto di risparmio.
savings bank n cassa di risparmio.
saviour, (US) savior ['seɪvjə*] n salvatore m.
savour, (US) savor ['seɪvə*] n sapore m, gusto ♦ vt gustare.
savoury, (US) savory ['seɪvərɪ] adj saporito(a); (dish: not sweet) salato(a).
savvy ['sævɪ] n (col) arguzia.
saw [sɔː] pt of **see** ♦ n (tool) sega ♦ vt (pt sawed, pp sawed or sawn [sɔːn]) segare; **to ~ sth up** fare a pezzi qc con la sega.
sawdust ['sɔːdʌst] n segatura.
sawmill ['sɔːmɪl] n segheria.
sawn [sɔːn] pp of **saw**.
sawn-off ['sɔːnɒf], (US) **sawed-off** ['sɔːdɒf] adj: **~ shotgun** fucile m a canne mozze.
saxophone ['sæksəfəun] n sassofono.
say [seɪ] n: **to have one's ~** fare sentire il proprio parere; **to have a ~** avere voce in capitolo ♦ vt (pt, pp said [sɛd]) dire; **could you ~ that again?** potrebbe ripeterlo?; **to ~ yes/no** dire di

sì/di no; **she said (that) I was to give you this** ha detto di darle questo; **my watch ~s 3 o'clock** il mio orologio fa le 3; **shall we ~ Tuesday?** facciamo martedì?; **that doesn't ~ much for him** non torna a suo credito; **when all is said and done** a conti fatti; **there is something** *or* **a lot to be said for it** ha i suoi lati positivi; **that is to ~** cioè, vale a dire; **to ~ nothing of** per non parlare di; **~ that...** mettiamo *or* diciamo che...; **that goes without ~ing** va da sé.

saying ['seɪɪŋ] *n* proverbio, detto.

SBA *n abbr* (*US*: = *Small Business Administration*) *organismo ausiliario per piccole imprese.*

SC *n abbr* (*US*) = **supreme court** ♦ *abbr* (*US*) = *South Carolina.*

s/c *abbr* (= *self-contained*) indipendente.

scab [skæb] *n* crosta; (*pej*) crumiro/a.

scabby ['skæbɪ] *adj* crostoso(a).

scaffold ['skæfəuld] *n* impalcatura; (*gallows*) patibolo.

scaffolding ['skæfəldɪŋ] *n* impalcatura.

scald [skɔːld] *n* scottatura ♦ *vt* scottare.

scalding ['skɔːldɪŋ] *adj* (*also*: ~ **hot**) bollente.

scale [skeɪl] *n* scala; (*of fish*) squama ♦ *vt* (*mountain*) scalare; **pay ~** scala dei salari; **~ of charges** tariffa; **on a large ~** su vasta scala; **to draw sth to ~** disegnare qc in scala; **small-~ model** modello in scala ridotta; *see also* **scales.**

▶**scale down** *vt* ridurre (proporzionalmente).

scaled-down [skeɪld'daun] *adj* su scala ridotta.

scale drawing *n* disegno in scala.

scale model *n* modello in scala.

scales [skeɪlz] *npl* bilancia.

scallion ['skæljən] *n* cipolla; (*US*: *shallot*) scalogna; (: *leek*) porro.

scallop ['skɔləp] *n* pettine *m*.

scalp [skælp] *n* cuoio capelluto ♦ *vt* scotennare.

scalpel ['skælpl] *n* bisturi *m inv*.

scalper ['skælpə*] *n* (*US col*: *of tickets*) bagarino.

scam [skæm] *n* (*col*) truffa.

scamp [skæmp] *n* (*col*: *child*) peste *f.*

scamper ['skæmpə*] *vi*: **to ~ away, ~ off** darsela a gambe.

scampi ['skæmpɪ] *npl* scampi *mpl.*

scan [skæn] *vt* scrutare; (*glance at quickly*) scorrere, dare un'occhiata a; (*poetry*) scandire; (*TV*) analizzare; (*RADAR*) esplorare ♦ *n* (*MED*) ecografia.

scandal ['skændl] *n* scandalo; (*gossip*)

pettegolezzi *mpl.*

scandalize ['skændəlaɪz] *vt* scandalizzare.

scandalous ['skændələs] *adj* scandaloso(a).

Scandinavia [skændɪ'neɪvɪə] *n* Scandinavia.

Scandinavian [skændɪ'neɪvɪən] *adj, n* scandinavo(a).

scanner ['skænə*] *n* (*RADAR, MED*) scanner *m inv.*

scant [skænt] *adj* scarso(a).

scantily ['skæntɪlɪ] *adv*: **~ clad** *or* **dressed** succintamente vestito(a).

scanty ['skæntɪ] *adj* insufficiente; (*swimsuit*) ridotto(a).

scapegoat ['skeɪpgəut] *n* capro espiatorio.

scar [skɑː*] *n* cicatrice *f* ♦ *vt* sfregiare.

scarce [skɛəs] *adj* scarso(a); (*copy, edition*) raro(a).

scarcely ['skɛəslɪ] *adv* appena; **~ anybody** quasi nessuno; **I can ~ believe it** faccio fatica a crederci.

scarcity ['skɛəsɪtɪ] *n* scarsità, mancanza.

scarcity value *n* valore *m* di rarità.

scare [skɛə*] *n* spavento, paura ♦ *vt* spaventare, atterrire; **to ~ sb stiff** spaventare a morte qn; **bomb ~** evacuazione *f* per sospetta presenza di un ordigno esplosivo.

▶**scare away, scare off** *vt* mettere in fuga.

scarecrow ['skɛəkrəu] *n* spaventapasseri *m inv.*

scared [skɛəd] *adj*: **to be ~** aver paura.

scaremonger ['skɛəmʌŋgə*] *n* allarmista *m/f.*

scarf, *pl* **scarves** [skɑːf, skɑːvz] *n* (*long*) sciarpa; (*square*) fazzoletto da testa, foulard *m inv.*

scarlet ['skɑːlɪt] *adj* scarlatto(a).

scarlet fever *n* scarlattina.

scarper ['skɑːpə*] *vi* (*BRIT col*) darsela a gambe.

SCART socket ['skɑːt-] *n* presa *f* SCART *inv.*

scarves [skɑːvz] *npl of* **scarf.**

scary ['skɛərɪ] *adj* (*col*) che fa paura.

scathing ['skeɪðɪŋ] *adj* aspro(a); **to be ~ about sth** essere molto critico rispetto a qc.

scatter ['skætə*] *vt* spargere; (*crowd*) disperdere ♦ *vi* disperdersi.

scatterbrained ['skætəbreɪnd] *adj* scervellato(a), sbadato(a).

scattered ['skætəd] *adj* sparso(a).

scatty ['skætɪ] *adj* (*col*) scervellato(a), sbadato(a).

scavenge ['skævɪndʒ] *vi* (*person*): **to ~ (for)** frugare tra i rifiuti (alla ricerca di); (*hyenas etc*) nutrirsi di carogne.

scavenger ['skævəndʒə*] n spazzino.
SCE n abbr = Scottish Certificate of Education.
scenario [sɪ'nɑːrɪəu] n (THEAT, CINE) copione m; (fig) situazione f.
scene [siːn] n (THEAT, fig etc) scena; (of crime, accident) scena, luogo; (sight, view) vista, veduta; **behind the ~s** (also fig) dietro le quinte; **to appear** or **come on the ~** (also fig) entrare in scena; **the political ~ in Italy** il quadro politico in Italia; **to make a ~** (col: fuss) fare una scenata.
scenery ['siːnərɪ] n (THEAT) scenario; (landscape) panorama m.
scenic ['siːnɪk] adj scenico(a); panoramico(a).
scent [sɛnt] n odore m, profumo; (sense of smell) olfatto, odorato; (fig: track) pista; **to put** or **throw sb off the ~** (fig) far perdere le tracce a qn, sviare qn.
sceptic, (US) **skeptic** ['skɛptɪk] n scettico/a.
sceptical, (US) **skeptical** ['skɛptɪkl] adj scettico(a).
scepticism, (US) **skepticism** ['skɛptɪsɪzm] n scetticismo.
sceptre, (US) **scepter** ['sɛptə*] n scettro.
schedule ['ʃɛdjuːl, (US) 'skɛdjuːl] n programma m, piano; (of trains) orario; (of prices etc) lista, tabella ♦ vt fissare; **as ~d** come stabilito; **on ~** in orario; **to be ahead of/behind ~** essere in anticipo/ritardo sul previsto; **we are working to a very tight ~** il nostro programma di lavoro è molto intenso; **everything went according to ~** tutto è andato secondo i piani or secondo il previsto.
scheduled ['ʃɛdjuːld, (US) 'skɛdjuːld] adj (date, time) fissato(a); (visit, event) programmato(a); (train, bus, stop) previsto(a) (sull'orario); **~ flight** volo di linea.
schematic [skɪ'mætɪk] adj schematico(a).
scheme [skiːm] n piano, progetto; (method) sistema m; (dishonest plan, plot) intrigo, trama; (arrangement) disposizione f, sistemazione f ♦ vt progettare; (plot) ordire ♦ vi fare progetti; (intrigue) complottare; **colour ~** combinazione f di colori.
scheming ['skiːmɪŋ] adj intrigante ♦ n intrighi mpl, macchinazioni fpl.
schism ['skɪzəm] n scisma m.
schizophrenia [skɪtsə'friːnɪə] n schizofrenia.
schizophrenic [skɪtsə'frɛnɪk] adj, n schizofrenico(a).
scholar ['skɔlə*] n erudito/a.
scholarly ['skɔləlɪ] adj dotto(a), erudito(a).
scholarship ['skɔləʃɪp] n erudizione f;

(grant) borsa di studio.
school [skuːl] n scuola; (in university) scuola, facoltà f inv ♦ cpd scolare, scolastico(a) ♦ vt (animal) addestrare.
school age n età scolare.
schoolbook ['skuːlbuk] n libro scolastico.
schoolboy ['skuːlbɔɪ] n scolaro.
schoolchild, pl **-children** ['skuːltʃaɪld, -'tʃɪldrən] n scolaro/a.
schooldays ['skuːldeɪz] npl giorni mpl di scuola.
schoolgirl ['skuːlgəːl] n scolara.
schooling ['skuːlɪŋ] n istruzione f.
school-leaver ['skuːlliːvə*] n (BRIT) ≈ neodiplomato(a).
schoolmaster ['skuːlmɑːstə*] n (primary) maestro; (secondary) insegnante m.
schoolmistress ['skuːlmɪstrɪs] n (primary) maestra; (secondary) insegnante f.
school report n (BRIT) pagella.
schoolroom ['skuːlruːm] n classe f, aula.
schoolteacher ['skuːltiːtʃə*] n insegnante m/f, docente m/f; (primary) maestro/a.
schoolyard ['skuːljɑːd] n (US) cortile m della scuola.
schooner ['skuːnə*] n (ship) goletta, schooner m inv; (glass) bicchiere m alto da sherry.
sciatica [saɪ'ætɪkə] n sciatica.
science ['saɪəns] n scienza; **the ~s** le scienze; (SCOL) le materie scientifiche.
science fiction n fantascienza.
scientific [saɪən'tɪfɪk] adj scientifico(a).
scientist ['saɪəntɪst] n scienziato/a.
sci-fi ['saɪfaɪ] n abbr (col) = **science fiction**.
Scilly Isles ['sɪlɪ'aɪlz] npl, **Scillies** ['sɪlɪz] npl: **the ~** le isole Scilly.
scintillating ['sɪntɪleɪtɪŋ] adj scintillante; (wit, conversation, company) brillante.
scissors ['sɪzəz] npl forbici fpl; **a pair of ~** un paio di forbici.
sclerosis [sklɪ'rəusɪs] n sclerosi f.
scoff [skɔf] vt (BRIT col: eat) trangugiare, ingozzare ♦ vi: **to ~ (at)** (mock) farsi beffe (di).
scold [skəuld] vt rimproverare.
scolding ['skəuldɪŋ] n lavata di capo, sgridata.
scone [skɔn] n focaccina da tè.
scoop [skuːp] n mestolo; (for ice cream) cucchiaio dosatore; (PRESS) colpo giornalistico, notizia (in) esclusiva.
▶**scoop out** vt scavare.
▶**scoop up** vt tirare su, sollevare.
scooter ['skuːtə*] n (motor cycle) motoretta, scooter m inv; (toy) monopattino.
scope [skəup] n (capacity: of plan, undertaking) portata; (: of person) capacità

fpl; (*opportunity*) possibilità *fpl*; **to be within the ~ of** rientrare nei limiti di; **it's well within his ~ to** ... è perfettamente in grado di ...; **there is plenty of ~ for improvement** (*BRIT*) ci sono notevoli possibilità di miglioramento.

scorch [skɔːtʃ] *vt* (*clothes*) strinare, bruciacchiare; (*earth, grass*) seccare, bruciare.

scorched earth policy [skɔːtʃt-] *n* tattica della terra bruciata.

scorcher ['skɔːtʃə*] *n* (*col: hot day*) giornata torrida.

scorching ['skɔːtʃɪŋ] *adj* cocente, scottante.

score [skɔː*] *n* punti *mpl*, punteggio; (*MUS*) partitura, spartito; (*twenty*): **a ~ venti ♦** *vt* (*goal, point*) segnare, fare; (*success*) ottenere; (*cut: leather, wood, card*) incidere ♦ *vi* segnare; (*FOOTBALL*) fare un goal; (*keep score*) segnare i punti; **on that ~** a questo riguardo; **to have an old ~ to settle with sb** (*fig*) avere un vecchio conto da saldare con qn; **~s of people** (*fig*) un sacco di gente; **to ~ 6 out of 10** prendere 6 su 10.

▶**score out** *vt* cancellare con un segno.

scoreboard ['skɔːbɔːd] *n* tabellone *m* segnapunti.

scorecard ['skɔːkɑːd] *n* cartoncino segnapunti.

scoreline ['skɔːlaɪn] *n* (*SPORT*) risultato.

scorer ['skɔːrə*] *n* marcatore/trice; (*keeping score*) segnapunti *m inv*.

scorn [skɔːn] *n* disprezzo ♦ *vt* disprezzare.

scornful ['skɔːnful] *adj* sprezzante.

Scorpio ['skɔːpɪəu] *n* Scorpione *m*; **to be ~** essere dello Scorpione.

scorpion ['skɔːpɪən] *n* scorpione *m*.

Scot [skɔt] *n* scozzese *m/f*.

Scotch [skɔtʃ] *n* whisky *m* scozzese, scotch *m*.

scotch [skɔtʃ] *vt* (*rumour etc*) soffocare.

Scotch tape ® *n* scotch ® *m*.

scot-free ['skɔt'friː] *adj* impunito(a); **to get off ~** (*unpunished*) farla franca; (*unhurt*) uscire illeso(a).

Scotland ['skɔtlənd] *n* Scozia.

Scots [skɔts] *adj* scozzese.

Scotsman ['skɔtsmən] *n* scozzese *m*.

Scotswoman ['skɔtswumən] *n* scozzese *f*.

Scottish ['skɔtɪʃ] *adj* scozzese; **the ~ National Party** partito nazionalista scozzese; **the ~ Parliament** il Parlamento scozzese.

scoundrel ['skaundrl] *n* farabutto/a; (*child*) furfantello/a.

scour ['skauə*] *vt* (*clean*) pulire strofinando; raschiare via; ripulire; (*search*) battere,

perlustrare.

scourer ['skauərə*] *n* (*pad*) paglietta; (*powder*) (detersivo) abrasivo.

scourge [skəːdʒ] *n* flagello.

scout [skaut] *n* (*MIL*) esploratore *m*; (*also: boy ~*) giovane esploratore, scout *m inv*.

▶**scout around** *vi* cercare in giro.

scowl [skaul] *vi* accigliarsi, aggrottare le sopracciglia; **to ~ at** guardare torvo.

scrabble ['skræbl] *vi* (*claw*): **to ~ (at)** graffiare, grattare; **to ~ about** *or* **around for sth** cercare affannosamente qc ♦ *n*: **S~** ® Scarabeo ®.

scraggy ['skrægɪ] *adj* scarno(a).

scram [skræm] *vi* (*col*) filare via.

scramble ['skræmbl] *n* arrampicata ♦ *vi* inerpicarsi; **to ~ out** *etc* uscire *etc* in fretta; **to ~ for** azzuffarsi per; **to go scrambling** (*SPORT*) fare il motocross.

scrambled eggs *npl* uova *fpl* strapazzate.

scrap [skræp] *n* pezzo, pezzetto; (*fight*) zuffa; (*also: ~ iron*) rottami *mpl* di ferro, ferraglia ♦ *vt* demolire; (*fig*) scartare; **~s** *npl* (*waste*) scarti *mpl*; **to sell sth for ~** vendere qc come ferro vecchio.

scrapbook ['skræpbuk] *n* album *m inv* di ritagli.

scrap dealer *n* commerciante *m* di ferraglia.

scrape [skreɪp] *vt, vi* raschiare, grattare ♦ *n*: **to get into a ~** cacciarsi in un guaio.

▶**scrape through** *vi* (*succeed*) farcela per un pelo, cavarsela ♦ *vt fus* (*exam*) passare per miracolo, passare per il rotto della cuffia.

scraper ['skreɪpə*] *n* raschietto.

scrap heap *n* mucchio di rottami; **to throw sth on the ~** (*fig*) mettere qc nel dimenticatoio.

scrap merchant *n* (*BRIT*) commerciante *m* di ferraglia.

scrap metal *n* ferraglia.

scrap paper *n* cartaccia.

scrappy ['skræpɪ] *adj* frammentario(a), sconnesso(a).

scrap yard *n* deposito di rottami; (*for cars*) cimitero delle macchine.

scratch [skrætʃ] *n* graffio ♦ *cpd*: **~ team** squadra raccogliticcia ♦ *vt* graffiare, rigare; (*COMPUT*) cancellare ♦ *vi* grattare, graffiare; **to start from ~** cominciare *or* partire da zero; **to be up to ~** essere all'altezza.

scratch pad *n* (*US*) notes *m inv*, blocchetto.

scrawl [skrɔːl] *n* scarabocchio ♦ *vi* scarabocchiare.

scrawny ['skrɔːnɪ] *adj* scarno(a), pelle e ossa *inv*.

scream [skri:m] *n* grido, urlo ♦ *vi* urlare, gridare; **to ~ at sb (to do sth)** gridare a qn (di fare qc); **it was a ~** (*fig col*) era da crepar dal ridere; **he's a ~** (*fig col*) è una sagoma, è uno spasso.

scree [skri:] *n* ghiaione *m*.

screech [skri:tʃ] *n* strido; (*of tyres, brakes*) stridore *m* ♦ *vi* stridere.

screen [skri:n] *n* schermo; (*fig*) muro, cortina, velo ♦ *vt* schermare, fare schermo a; (*from the wind etc*) riparare; (*film*) proiettare; (*book*) adattare per lo schermo; (*candidates etc*) passare al vaglio; (*for illness*) sottoporre a controlli medici.

screen editing [-ɛdɪtɪŋ] *n* (*COMPUT*) correzione *f* e modifica su schermo.

screening ['skri:nɪŋ] *n* (*MED*) dépistage *m inv*; (*of film*) proiezione *f*; (*for security*) controlli *mpl* (di sicurezza).

screen memory *n* (*COMPUT*) memoria di schermo.

screenplay ['skri:npleɪ] *n* sceneggiatura.

screensaver *n* (*COMPUT*) screen saver *m inv*.

screen test *n* provino (cinematografico).

screw [skru:] *n* vite *f*; (*propeller*) elica ♦ *vt* avvitare; **to ~ sth to the wall** fissare qc al muro con viti.

▶**screw up** *vt* (*paper, material*) spiegazzare; (*col: ruin*) mandare a monte; **to ~ up one's face** fare una smorfia.

screwdriver ['skru:draɪvə*] *n* cacciavite *m*.

screwed-up ['skru:d'ʌp] *adj* (*col*): **she's totally ~** è nel pallone.

screwy ['skru:ɪ] *adj* (*col*) svitato(a).

scribble ['skrɪbl] *n* scarabocchio ♦ *vt* scribacchiare ♦ *vi* scarabocchiare; **to ~ sth down** scribacchiare qc.

scribe [skraɪb] *n* scriba *m*.

script [skrɪpt] *n* (*CINE etc*) copione *m*; (*in exam*) elaborato *or* compito d'esame; (*writing*) scrittura.

Scripture ['skrɪptʃə*] *n* Sacre Scritture *fpl*.

scriptwriter ['skrɪptraɪtə*] *n* soggettista *m/f*.

scroll [skrəʊl] *n* rotolo di carta ♦ *vt* (*COMPUT*) scorrere.

scroll bar *n* (*COMPUT*) barra di scorrimento.

scrotum ['skrəʊtəm] *n* scroto.

scrounge [skraʊndʒ] *vt* (*col*): **to ~ sth (off or from sb)** scroccare qc (a qn) ♦ *vi*: **to ~ on sb** vivere alle spalle di qn.

scrounger ['skraʊndʒə*] *n* scroccone/a.

scrub [skrʌb] *n* (*clean*) strofinata; (*land*) boscaglia ♦ *vt* pulire strofinando; (*reject*) annullare.

scrubbing brush ['skrʌbɪŋ-] *n* spazzolone *m*.

scruff [skrʌf] *n*: **by the ~ of the neck** per la collottola.

scruffy ['skrʌfɪ] *adj* sciatto(a).

scrum(mage) ['skrʌm(ɪdʒ)] *n* mischia.

scruple ['skru:pl] *n* scrupolo; **to have no ~s about doing sth** non avere scrupoli a fare qc.

scrupulous ['skru:pjuləs] *adj* scrupoloso(a).

scrupulously ['skru:pjuləslɪ] *adv* scrupolosamente; **he tries to be ~ fair/ honest** cerca di essere più imparziale/ onesto che può.

scrutinize ['skru:tɪnaɪz] *vt* scrutare, esaminare attentamente.

scrutiny ['skru:tɪnɪ] *n* esame *m* accurato; **under the ~ of sb** sotto la sorveglianza di qn.

scuba ['sku:bə] *n* autorespiratore *m*.

scuba diving *n* immersioni *fpl* subacquee.

scuff [skʌf] *vt* (*shoes*) consumare strascicando.

scuffle ['skʌfl] *n* baruffa, tafferuglio.

scullery ['skʌlərɪ] *n* retrocucina *m or f*.

sculptor ['skʌlptə*] *n* scultore *m*.

sculpture ['skʌlptʃə*] *n* scultura.

scum [skʌm] *n* schiuma; (*pej: people*) feccia.

scupper ['skʌpə*] *vt* (*BRIT*) autoaffondare; (*fig*) far naufragare.

scurrilous ['skʌrɪləs] *adj* scurrile, volgare.

scurry ['skʌrɪ] *vi* sgambare, affrettarsi.

scurvy ['skɜ:vɪ] *n* scorbuto.

scuttle ['skʌtl] *n* (*NAUT*) portellino; (*also*: **coal ~**) secchio del carbone ♦ *vt* (*ship*) autoaffondare ♦ *vi* (*scamper*): **to ~ away, ~ off** darsela a gambe, scappare.

scythe [saɪð] *n* falce *f*.

SD, S. Dak. *abbr* (*US*) = *South Dakota*.

SDI *n abbr* (= *Strategic Defense Initiative*) S.D.I. *f*.

SDLP *n abbr* (*BRIT POL*) = *Social Democratic and Labour Party*.

sea [si:] *n* mare *m* ♦ *cpd* marino(a), del mare; (*ship, port*) marittimo(a), di mare; **on the ~** (*boat*) in mare; (*town*) di mare; **to go by ~** andare per mare; **by** *or* **beside the ~** (*holiday*) al mare; (*village*) sul mare; **to look out to ~** guardare il mare; **(out) at ~** al largo; **heavy** *or* **rough ~(s)** mare grosso *or* agitato; **a ~ of faces** (*fig*) una marea di gente; **to be all at ~** (*fig*) non sapere che pesci pigliare.

sea bed *n* fondo marino.

sea bird *n* uccello di mare.

seaboard ['si:bɔ:d] *n* costa.

sea breeze *n* brezza di mare.

seafarer ['si:fɛərə*] *n* navigante *m*.

seafaring ['si:fɛərɪŋ] *adj* (*community*) marinaro(a); (*life*) da marinaio.

seafood ['si:fu:d] *n* frutti *mpl* di mare.

sea front *n* lungomare *m*.

seagoing ['si:gəʊɪŋ] *adj* (*ship*) d'alto mare.

seagull ['si:gʌl] *n* gabbiano.

seal [si:l] *n* (*animal*) foca; (*stamp*) sigillo; (*impression*) impronta del sigillo ♦ *vt* sigillare; (*decide*: *sb's fate*) segnare; (: *bargain*) concludere; ~ **of approval** beneplacito.

▶**seal off** *vt* (*close*) sigillare; (*forbid entry to*) bloccare l'accesso a.

sea level *n* livello del mare.

sealing wax ['si:lɪŋ-] *n* ceralacca.

sea lion *n* leone *m* marino.

sealskin ['si:lskɪn] *n* pelle *f* di foca.

seam [si:m] *n* cucitura; (*of coal*) filone *m*; **the hall was bursting at the ~s** l'aula era piena zeppa.

seaman ['si:mən] *n* marinaio.

seamanship ['si:mənʃɪp] *n* tecnica di navigazione.

seamless ['si:mlɪs] *adj* senza cucitura.

seamy ['si:mɪ] *adj* malfamato(a); squallido(a).

seance ['seɪɔns] *n* seduta spiritica.

seaplane ['si:pleɪn] *n* idrovolante *m*.

seaport ['si:pɔ:t] *n* porto di mare.

search [sɔ:tʃ] *n* (*for person, thing*) ricerca; (*of drawer, pockets*) esame *m* accurato; (*LAW*: *at sb's home*) perquisizione *f* ♦ *vt* perlustrare, frugare; (*scan, examine*) esaminare minuziosamente; (*COMPUT*) ricercare ♦ *vi*: **to ~ for** ricercare; **in ~ of** alla ricerca di; "~ **and replace**" (*COMPUT*) "ricercare e sostituire".

▶**search through** *vt fus* frugare.

search engine *n* (*COMPUT*) motore *m* di ricerca.

searcher ['sɔ:tʃə*] *n* chi cerca.

searching ['sɔ:tʃɪŋ] *adj* minuzioso(a); penetrante; (*question*) pressante.

searchlight ['sɔ:tʃlaɪt] *n* proiettore *m*.

search party *n* squadra di soccorso.

search warrant *n* mandato di perquisizione.

searing ['sɪərɪŋ] *adj* (*heat*) rovente; (*pain*) acuto(a).

seashore ['si:ʃɔ:*] *n* spiaggia; **on the ~** sulla riva del mare.

seasick ['si:sɪk] *adj* che soffre il mal di mare; **to be ~** avere il mal di mare.

seaside ['si:saɪd] *n* spiaggia; **to go to the ~** andare al mare.

seaside resort *n* stazione *f* balneare.

season ['si:zn] *n* stagione *f* ♦ *vt* condire, insaporire; **to be in/out of** ~ essere di/ fuori stagione; **the busy** ~ (*for shops*) il periodo di punta; (*for hotels etc*) l'alta stagione; **the open** ~ (*HUNTING*) la stagione della caccia.

seasonal ['si:zənl] *adj* stagionale.

seasoned ['si:znd] *adj* (*wood*) stagionato(a); (*fig*: *worker, actor, troops*) con esperienza; **a ~ campaigner** un veterano.

seasoning ['si:znɪŋ] *n* condimento.

season ticket *n* abbonamento.

seat [si:t] *n* sedile *m*; (*in bus, train*: *place*) posto; (*PARLIAMENT*) seggio; (*centre*: *of government etc, of infection*) sede *f*; (*buttocks*) didietro; (*of trousers*) fondo ♦ *vt* far sedere; (*have room for*) avere or essere fornito(a) di posti a sedere per; **are there any ~s left?** ci sono posti?; **to take one's** ~ prendere posto; **to be ~ed** essere seduto(a); **please be ~ed** accomodatevi per favore.

seat belt *n* cintura di sicurezza.

seating arrangements ['si:tɪŋ-] *npl* sistemazione *f* or disposizione *f* dei posti.

seating capacity *n* posti *mpl* a sedere.

SEATO ['si:təʊ] *n abbr* (= *Southeast Asia Treaty Organization*) SEATO *f*.

sea water *n* acqua di mare.

seaweed ['si:wi:d] *n* alghe *fpl*.

seaworthy ['si:wə:ðɪ] *adj* atto(a) alla navigazione.

SEC *n abbr* (*US*: = *Securities and Exchange Commission*) commissione di controllo sulle operazioni in Borsa.

sec. *abbr* = **second**.

secateurs [sɛkə'tə:z] *npl* forbici *fpl* per potare.

secede [sɪ'si:d] *vi*: **to ~ (from)** ritirarsi (da).

secluded [sɪ'klu:dɪd] *adj* isolato(a), appartato(a).

seclusion [sɪ'klu:ʒən] *n* isolamento.

second ['sɛkənd] *num* secondo(a) ♦ *adv* (*in race etc*) al secondo posto; (*RAIL*) in seconda ♦ *n* (*unit of time*) secondo; (*in series, position*) secondo/a; (*BRIT SCOL*) laurea con punteggio discreto; (*AUT*: *also*: ~ **gear**) seconda; (*COMM*: *imperfect*) scarto ♦ *vt* (*motion*) appoggiare; [sɪ'kɔnd] (*employee*) distaccare; **Charles the S~** Carlo Secondo; **just a ~!** un attimo!; ~ **floor** (*BRIT*) secondo piano; (*US*) primo piano; **to ask for a ~ opinion** (*MED*) chiedere un altro or ulteriore parere; **to have ~ thoughts (about doing sth)** avere dei ripensamenti (quanto a fare qc); **on ~ thoughts** or (*US*) **thought** a ripensarci, ripensandoci bene.

secondary ['sɛkəndərɪ] *adj* secondario(a).

secondary school *n* scuola secondaria; *see boxed note.*

second-best [sɛkənd'bɛst] *n* ripiego; **as a ~** in mancanza di meglio.

second-class [sɛkənd'klɑːs] *adj* di seconda classe ♦ *adv*: **to travel ~** viaggiare in seconda (classe); **to send sth ~** spedire qc per posta ordinaria; **~ citizen** cittadino di second'ordine.

second cousin *n* cugino di secondo grado.

seconder ['sɛkəndə*] *n* sostenitore/trice.

second-guess ['sɛkənd'gɛs] *vt (predict)* anticipare; *(after the event)* giudicare col senno di poi.

second hand *n (on clock)* lancetta dei secondi.

second-hand [sɛkənd'hænd] *adj* di seconda mano, usato(a) ♦ *adv (buy)* di seconda mano; **to hear sth ~** venire a sapere qc da terze persone.

second-in-command ['sɛkəndɪnkə'mɑːnd] *n (MIL)* comandante *m* in seconda; *(ADMIN)* aggiunto.

secondly ['sɛkəndlɪ] *adv* in secondo luogo.

secondment [sɪ'kɔndmənt] *n (BRIT)* distaccamento.

second-rate [sɛkənd'reɪt] *adj* scadente.

Second World War *n*: **the ~** la seconda guerra mondiale.

secrecy ['siːkrəsɪ] *n* segretezza.

secret ['siːkrɪt] *adj* segreto(a) ♦ *n* segreto; **in ~** in segreto, segretamente; **to keep sth ~ (from sb)** tenere qc segreto (a qn), tenere qc nascosto (a qn); **keep it ~** che rimanga un segreto; **to make no ~ of sth** non far mistero di qc.

secret agent *n* agente *m* segreto.

secretarial [sɛkrɪ'tɛərɪəl] *adj (work)* da segretario/a; *(college, course)* di segretariato.

secretariat [sɛkrɪ'tɛərɪət] *n* segretariato.

secretary ['sɛkrətrɪ] *n* segretario/a; **S~ of State** *(US POL)* ≈ Ministro degli Esteri; **S~ of State (for)** *(BRIT POL)* ministro (di).

secretary-general ['sɛkrətrɪ'dʒɛnərl] *n* segretario generale.

secrete [sɪ'kriːt] *vt (MED, ANAT, BIOL)* secernere; *(hide)* nascondere.

secretion [sɪ'kriːʃən] *n* secrezione *f*.

secretive ['siːkrətɪv] *adj* riservato(a).

secretly ['siːkrɪtlɪ] *adv* in segreto, segretamente.

secret police *n* polizia segreta.

secret service *n* servizi *mpl* segreti.

sect [sɛkt] *n* setta.

sectarian [sɛk'tɛərɪən] *adj* settario(a).

section ['sɛkʃən] *n* sezione *f*; *(of document)* articolo ♦ *vt* sezionare, dividere in sezioni; **the business ~** *(PRESS)* la pagina economica.

sector ['sɛktə*] *n* settore *m*.

secular ['sɛkjulə*] *adj* secolare.

secure [sɪ'kjuə*] *adj (free from anxiety)* sicuro(a); *(firmly fixed)* assicurato(a), ben fermato(a); *(in safe place)* al sicuro ♦ *vt (fix)* fissare, assicurare; *(get)* ottenere, assicurarsi; *(COMM: loan)* garantire; **to make sth ~** fissare bene qc; **to ~ sth for sb** procurare qc per *or* a qn.

security [sɪ'kjuərɪtɪ] *n* sicurezza; *(for loan)* garanzia; **securities** *npl (STOCK EXCHANGE)* titoli *mpl*; **to increase/tighten ~** aumentare/intensificare la sorveglianza; **~ of tenure** garanzia del posto di lavoro, garanzia di titolo *or* di godimento.

Security Council *n*: **the ~** il Consiglio di Sicurezza.

security forces *npl* forze *fpl* dell'ordine.

security guard *n* guardia giurata.

security risk *n* rischio per la sicurezza.

secy. *abbr* = **secretary.**

sedan [sə'dæn] *n (US AUT)* berlina.

sedate [sɪ'deɪt] *adj* posato(a); calmo(a) ♦ *vt* calmare.

sedation [sɪ'deɪʃən] *n (MED)*: **to be under ~** essere sotto l'azione di sedativi.

sedative ['sɛdɪtɪv] *n* sedativo, calmante *m*.

sedentary ['sɛdntrɪ] *adj* sedentario(a).

sediment ['sɛdɪmənt] *n* sedimento.

sedition [sɪ'dɪʃən] *n* sedizione *f*.

seduce [sɪ'djuːs] *vt* sedurre.

seduction [sɪ'dʌkʃən] *n* seduzione *f*.

seductive [sɪ'dʌktɪv] *adj* seducente.

see [siː] *vb (pt* **saw**, *pp* **seen** [sɔː, siːn]) *vt* vedere; *(accompany)*: **to ~ sb to the door** accompagnare qn alla porta ♦ *vi* vedere; *(understand)* capire ♦ *n* sede *f* vescovile; **to ~ that** *(ensure)* badare che + *sub*, fare in modo che + *sub*; **to go and ~ sb** andare a trovare qn; **~ you soon/later/tomorrow!** a presto/più tardi/domani!; **as far as I can ~** da quanto posso vedere; **there was nobody to be ~n** non c'era anima viva; **let me ~** *(show me)* fammi vedere; *(let me think)* vediamo (un po'); **~ for yourself** vai a vedere con i tuoi occhi; **I don't know what she ~s in him** non so

che cosa ci trovi in lui.
▶see about *vt fus* (*deal with*) occuparsi di.
▶see off *vt* salutare alla partenza.
▶see through *vt* portare a termine ♦ *vt fus* non lasciarsi ingannare da.
▶see to *vt fus* occuparsi di.
seed [si:d] *n* seme *m*; (*fig*) germe *m*; (*TENNIS*) testa di serie; to go to ~ fare seme; (*fig*) scadere.
seedless ['si:dlɪs] *adj* senza semi.
seedling ['si:dlɪŋ] *n* piantina di semenzaio.
seedy ['si:dɪ] *adj* (*shabby: person*) sciatto(a); (: *place*) cadente.
seeing ['si:ɪŋ] *conj*: ~ (that) visto che.
seek [si:k], *pt, pp* sought *vt* cercare; to ~ advice/help from sb chiedere consiglio/ aiuto a qn.
▶seek out *vt* (*person*) andare a cercare.
seem [si:m] *vi* sembrare, parere; there ~s to be ... sembra che ci sia ...; it ~s (that) ... sembra *or* pare che ... + *sub*; what ~s to be the trouble? cosa c'è che non va?
seemingly ['si:mɪŋlɪ] *adv* apparentemente.
seen [si:n] *pp of* see.
seep [si:p] *vi* filtrare, trapelare.
seer [sɪə*] *n* profeta/essa, veggente *m/f*.
seersucker ['sɪəsʌkə*] *n* cotone *m* indiano.
seesaw ['si:sɔ:] *n* altalena a bilico.
seethe [si:ð] *vi* ribollire; to ~ with anger fremere di rabbia.
see-through ['si:θru:] *adj* trasparente.
segment ['sɛgmənt] *n* segmento.
segregate ['sɛgrɪgeɪt] *vt* segregare, isolare.
segregation [sɛgrɪ'geɪʃən] *n* segregazione *f*.
Seine [seɪn] *n* Senna.
seismic ['saɪzmɪk] *adj* sismico(a).
seize [si:z] *vt* (*grasp*) afferrare; (*take possession of*) impadronirsi di; (*LAW*) sequestrare.
▶seize up *vi* (*TECH*) grippare.
▶seize (up)on *vt fus* ricorrere a.
seizure ['si:ʒə*] *n* (*MED*) attacco; (*LAW*) confisca, sequestro.
seldom ['sɛldəm] *adv* raramente.
select [sɪ'lɛkt] *adj* scelto(a); (*hotel, restaurant*) chic *inv*; (*club*) esclusivo(a) ♦ *vt* scegliere, selezionare; a ~ few pochi eletti *mpl*.
selection [sɪ'lɛkʃən] *n* selezione *f*, scelta.
selection committee *n* comitato di selezione.
selective [sɪ'lɛktɪv] *adj* selettivo(a).
selector [sɪ'lɛktə*] *n* (*person*) selezionatore/trice; (*TECH*) selettore *m*.
self [sɛlf] *n* (*pl* selves [sɛlvz]): the ~ l'io *m* ♦ *prefix* auto....

self-addressed ['sɛlfə'drɛst] *adj*: ~ envelope busta col proprio nome e indirizzo.
self-adhesive [sɛlfəd'hi:zɪv] *adj* autoadesivo(a).
self-assertive [sɛlfə'sə:tɪv] *adj* autoritario(a).
self-assurance [sɛlfə'ʃuərəns] *n* sicurezza di sé.
self-assured [sɛlfə'ʃuəd] *adj* sicuro(a) di sé.
self-catering [sɛlf'keɪtərɪŋ] *adj* (*BRIT*) in cui ci si cucina da sé; ~ apartment appartamento (per le vacanze).
self-centred, (*US*) self-centered [sɛlf'sɛntəd] *adj* egocentrico(a).
self-cleaning [sɛlf'kli:nɪŋ] *adj* autopulente.
self-confessed [sɛlfkən'fɛst] *adj* (*alcoholic etc*) dichiarato(a).
self-confidence [sɛlf'kɔnfɪdəns] *n* sicurezza di sé.
self-conscious [sɛlf'kɔnʃəs] *adj* timido(a).
self-contained [sɛlfkən'teɪnd] *adj* (*BRIT: flat*) indipendente.
self-control [sɛlfkən'trəul] *n* autocontrollo.
self-defeating [sɛlfdɪ'fi:tɪŋ] *adj* futile.
self-defence, (*US*) self-defense [sɛlfdɪ'fɛns] *n* autodifesa; (*LAW*) legittima difesa.
self-discipline [sɛlf'dɪsɪplɪn] *n* autodisciplina.
self-employed [sɛlfɪm'plɔɪd] *adj* che lavora in proprio.
self-esteem [sɛlfɪ'sti:m] *n* amor proprio *m*.
self-evident [sɛlf'ɛvɪdənt] *adj* evidente.
self-explanatory [sɛlfɪk'splænətərɪ] *adj* ovvio(a).
self-governing [sɛlf'gʌvənɪŋ] *adj* autonomo(a).
self-help ['sɛlf'hɛlp] *n* iniziativa individuale.
self-importance [sɛlfɪm'pɔ:tns] *n* sufficienza.
self-indulgent [sɛlfɪn'dʌldʒənt] *adj* indulgente verso se stesso(a).
self-inflicted [sɛlfɪn'flɪktɪd] *adj* autoinflitto(a).
self-interest [sɛlf'ɪntrɪst] *n* interesse *m* personale.
selfish ['sɛlfɪʃ] *adj* egoista.
selfishly ['sɛlfɪʃlɪ] *adv* egoisticamente.
selfishness ['sɛlfɪʃnɪs] *n* egoismo.
selfless ['sɛlflɪs] *adj* altruista.
selflessly ['sɛlflɪslɪ] *adv* altruisticamente.
selflessness ['sɛlflɪsnɪs] *n* altruismo.
self-made man ['sɛlfmeɪd-] *n* self-made man *m inv*, uomo che si è fatto da sé.
self-pity [sɛlf'pɪtɪ] *n* autocommiserazione *f*.
self-portrait [sɛlf'pɔ:trɪt] *n* autoritratto.

self-possessed [sɛlfpə'zɛst] *adj* controllato(a).

self-preservation ['sɛlfprɛzə'veɪʃən] *n* istinto di conservazione.

self-raising [sɛlf'reɪzɪŋ], (*US*) **self-rising** [sɛlf'raɪzɪŋ] *adj*: ~ **flour** miscela di farina e lievito.

self-reliant [sɛlfrɪ'laɪənt] *adj* indipendente.

self-respect [sɛlfrɪs'pɛkt] *n* rispetto di sé, amor proprio.

self-respecting [sɛlfrɪs'pɛktɪŋ] *adj* che ha rispetto di sé.

self-righteous [sɛlf'raɪtʃəs] *adj* soddisfatto(a) di sé.

self-rising [sɛlf'raɪzɪŋ] *adj* (*US*) = **self-raising**.

self-sacrifice [sɛlf'sækrɪfaɪs] *n* abnegazione *f*.

self-same ['sɛlfseɪm] *adj* stesso(a).

self-satisfied [sɛlf'sætɪsfaɪd] *adj* compiaciuto(a) di sé.

self-sealing [sɛlf'siːlɪŋ] *adj* autosigillante.

self-service [sɛlf'səːvɪs] *n* autoservizio, self-service *m*.

self-styled [sɛlf'staɪld] *adj* sedicente.

self-sufficient [sɛlfsə'fɪʃənt] *adj* autosufficiente.

self-supporting [sɛlfsə'pɔːtɪŋ] *adj* economicamente indipendente.

self-taught [sɛlf'tɔːt] *adj* autodidatta.

self-test ['sɛlftɛst] *n* (*COMPUT*) autoverifica.

sell, *pt*, *pp* **sold** [sɛl, səuld] *vt* vendere ♦ *vi* vendersi; **to** ~ **at** *or* **for 100 euros** essere in vendita a 100 euro; **to** ~ **sb an idea** (*fig*) far accettare un'idea a qn.

►**sell off** *vt* svendere, liquidare.

►**sell out** *vi*: **to** ~ **out (to sb/sth)** (*COMM*) vendere (tutto) (a qn/qc) ♦ *vt* esaurire; **the tickets are all sold out** i biglietti sono esauriti.

►**sell up** *vi* vendere (tutto).

sell-by date ['sɛlbaɪ-] *n* scadenza.

seller ['sɛlə*] *n* venditore/trice; ~'**s market** mercato favorevole ai venditori.

selling price ['sɛlɪŋ-] *n* prezzo di vendita.

Sellotape ®,['sɛləuteɪp] *n* (*BRIT*) nastro adesivo, scotch ® *m*.

sellout ['sɛlaut] *n* (*betrayal*) tradimento; (*of tickets*): **it was a** ~ registrò un tutto esaurito.

selves [sɛlvz] *npl of* **self**.

semantic [sɪ'mæntɪk] *adj* semantico(a).

semantics [sɪ'mæntɪks] *n* semantica.

semaphore ['sɛməfɔː*] *n* segnali *mpl* con bandiere; (*RAIL*) semaforo.

semblance ['sɛmbləns] *n* parvenza, apparenza.

semen ['siːmən] *n* sperma *m*.

semester [sɪ'mɛstə*] *n* (*US*) semestre *m*.

semi... ['sɛmɪ] *prefix* semi... ♦ *n*: **semi** = **semidetached (house)**.

semi-breve ['sɛmɪbriːv] *n* (*BRIT*) semibreve *f*.

semicircle ['sɛmɪsəːkl] *n* semicerchio.

semicircular ['sɛmɪ'səːkjulə*] *adj* semicircolare.

semicolon [sɛmɪ'kəulən] *n* punto e virgola.

semiconductor [sɛmɪkən'dʌktə*] *n* semiconduttore *m*.

semiconscious [sɛmɪ'kɔnʃəs] *adj* parzialmente cosciente.

semidetached (house) [sɛmɪdɪ'tætʃt-] *n* (*BRIT*) casa gemella.

semifinal [sɛmɪ'faɪnl] *n* semifinale *f*.

seminar ['sɛmɪnɑː*] *n* seminario.

seminary ['sɛmɪnərɪ] *n* (*REL*: *for priests*) seminario.

semiprecious [sɛmɪ'prɛʃəs] *adj* semiprezioso(a).

semiquaver ['sɛmɪkweɪvə*] *n* (*BRIT*) semicroma.

semiskilled ['sɛmɪ'skɪld] *adj*: ~ **worker** operaio(a) non specializzato(a).

semi-skimmed ['sɛmɪ'skɪmd] *adj* parzialmente scremato(a).

semitone ['sɛmɪtəun] *n* (*MUS*) semitono.

semolina [sɛmə'liːnə] *n* semolino.

Sen., sen. *abbr* = **senator; senior.**

senate ['sɛnɪt] *n* senato.

senator ['sɛnɪtə*] *n* senatore/trice.

send [sɛnd], *pt*, *pp* **sent** *vt* mandare; **to** ~ **by post** *or* (*US*) **mail** spedire per posta; **to** ~ **sb for sth** mandare qn a prendere qc; **to** ~ **word that ...** mandare a dire che ...; **she** ~**s (you) her love** ti saluta affettuosamente; **to** ~ **sb to Coventry** (*BRIT*) dare l'ostracismo a qn; **to** ~ **sb to sleep/into fits of laughter** far addormentare/scoppiare dal ridere qn; **to** ~ **sth flying** far volare via qc.

►**send away** *vt* (*letter, goods*) spedire; (*person*) mandare via.

►**send away for** *vt fus* richiedere per posta, farsi spedire.

►**send back** *vt* rimandare.

►**send for** *vt fus* mandare a chiamare, far venire; (*by post*) ordinare per posta.

►**send in** *vt* (*report, application, resignation*) presentare.

►**send off** *vt* (*goods*) spedire; (*BRIT SPORT*: *player*) espellere.

►**send on** *vt* (*BRIT*: *letter*) inoltrare; (*luggage etc*: *in advance*) spedire in anticipo.

►**send out** *vt* (*invitation*) diramare; (*emit*: *light, heat*) mandare, emanare; (: *signals*) emettere.

▶**send round** *vt* (*letter, document etc*) far circolare.

▶**send up** *vt* (*person, price*) far salire; (*BRIT: parody*) mettere in ridicolo.

sender ['sɛndə*] *n* mittente *m/f*.

send-off ['sɛndɔf] *n*: **to give sb a good ~** festeggiare la partenza di qn.

Senegal [sɛnɪ'gɔːl] *n* Senegal *m*.

Senegalese [sɛnɪgə'liːz] *adj, n* senegalese (*m/f*).

senile ['siːnaɪl] *adj* senile.

senility [sɪ'nɪlɪtɪ] *n* senilità *f*.

senior ['siːnɪə*] *adj* (*older*) più vecchio(a); (*of higher rank*) di grado più elevato ♦ *n* persona più anziana; (*in service*) persona con maggiore anzianità; **P. Jones ~ P. Jones senior, P. Jones padre.**

senior citizen *n* anziano/a.

senior high school *n* (*US*) ≈ liceo.

seniority [siːnɪ'ɔrɪtɪ] *n* anzianità; (*in rank*) superiorità.

sensation [sɛn'seɪʃən] *n* sensazione *f*; **to create a ~** fare scalpore.

sensational [sɛn'seɪʃənl] *adj* sensazionale; (*marvellous*) eccezionale.

sense [sɛns] *n* senso; (*feeling*) sensazione *f*, senso; (*meaning*) senso, significato; (*wisdom*) buonsenso ♦ *vt* sentire, percepire; **~s** *npl* (*sanity*) ragione *f*; **it makes ~** ha senso; **there is no ~ in (doing) that** non ha senso (farlo); **~ of humour** (senso dell')umorismo; **to come to one's ~s** (*regain consciousness*) riprendere i sensi; (*become reasonable*) tornare in sé; **to take leave of one's ~s** perdere il lume *or* l'uso della ragione.

senseless ['sɛnslɪs] *adj* sciocco(a); (*unconscious*) privo(a) di sensi.

sensibilities [sɛnsɪ'bɪlɪtɪz] *npl* sensibilità *fsg*.

sensible ['sɛnsɪbl] *adj* sensato(a), ragionevole.

sensitive ['sɛnsɪtɪv] *adj*: **~ (to)** sensibile (a); **he is very ~ about it** è un tasto che è meglio non toccare con lui.

sensitivity [sɛnsɪ'tɪvɪtɪ] *n* sensibilità.

sensual ['sɛnsjuəl] *adj* sensuale.

sensuous ['sɛnsjuəs] *adj* sensuale.

sent [sɛnt] *pt, pp of* **send.**

sentence ['sɛntns] *n* (*LING*) frase *f*; (*LAW: judgement*) sentenza; (: *punishment*) condanna ♦ *vt*: **to ~ sb to death/to 5 years** condannare qn a morte/a 5 anni; **to pass ~ on sb** condannare qn.

sentiment ['sɛntɪmənt] *n* sentimento; (*opinion*) opinione *f*.

sentimental [sɛntɪ'mɛntl] *adj* sentimentale.

sentimentality [sɛntɪmɛn'tælɪtɪ] *n*

sentimentalità, sentimentalismo.

sentry ['sɛntrɪ] *n* sentinella.

sentry duty *n*: **to be on ~** essere di sentinella.

Seoul [səul] *n* Seul *f*.

separable ['sɛprəbl] *adj* separabile.

separate *adj* ['sɛprɪt] separato(a) ♦ *vb* ['sɛpəreɪt] *vt* separare ♦ *vi* separarsi; **~ from** separato da; **under ~ cover** (*COMM*) in plico a parte; **to ~ into** dividere in; *see also* **separates.**

separately ['sɛprɪtlɪ] *adv* separatamente.

separates ['sɛprɪts] *npl* (*clothes*) coordinati *mpl*.

separation [sɛpə'reɪʃən] *n* separazione *f*.

Sept. *abbr* (= *September*) sett., set.

September [sɛp'tɛmbə*] *n* settembre *m*; *for phrases see also* **July.**

septic ['sɛptɪk] *adj* settico(a); (*wound*) infettato(a); **to go ~** infettarsi.

septicaemia, (*US*) **septicemia** [sɛptɪ'siːmɪə] *n* setticemia.

septic tank *n* fossa settica.

sequel ['siːkwl] *n* conseguenza; (*of story*) seguito.

sequence ['siːkwəns] *n* (*series*) serie *f inv*; (*order*) ordine *m*; **in ~** in ordine, di seguito; **~ of tenses** concordanza dei tempi.

sequential [sɪ'kwɛnʃəl] *adj*: **~ access** (*COMPUT*) accesso sequenziale.

sequin ['siːkwɪn] *n* lustrino, paillette *f inv*.

Serb [səːb] *adj, n* = **Serbian.**

Serbia ['səːbɪə] *n* Serbia.

Serbian ['səːbɪən] *adj* serbo(a) ♦ *n* serbo/a; (*LING*) serbo.

Serbo-Croat ['səːbəu'krəuæt] *n* (*LING*) serbocroato.

serenade [sɛrə'neɪd] *n* serenata ♦ *vt* fare la serenata a.

serene [sɪ'riːn] *adj* sereno(a), calmo(a).

serenity [sɪ'rɛnɪtɪ] *n* serenità, tranquillità.

sergeant ['sɑːdʒənt] *n* sergente *m*; (*POLICE*) brigadiere *m*.

sergeant major *n* maresciallo.

serial ['sɪərɪəl] *n* (*PRESS*) romanzo a puntate; (*RADIO, TV*) trasmissione *f* a puntate ♦ *cpd* (*number*) di serie; (*COMPUT*) seriale.

serialize ['sɪərɪəlaɪz] *vt* pubblicare a puntate; trasmettere a puntate.

serial killer *n* serial killer *m inv*.

serial number *n* numero di serie.

series ['sɪəriːz] *n* (*pl inv*) serie *f inv*; (*PUBLISHING*) collana.

serious ['sɪərɪəs] *adj* serio(a), grave; **are you ~ (about it)?** parla sul serio?

seriously ['sɪərɪəslɪ] *adv* seriamente; **he's ~**

rich (col: extremely) ha un casino di soldi; **to take sth/sb** ~ prendere qc/qn sul serio.

seriousness ['sɪərɪəsnɪs] n serietà, gravità.

sermon ['sɔːmən] n sermone m.

serrated [sɪ'reɪtɪd] adj seghettato(a).

serum ['sɪərəm] n siero.

servant ['sɔːvənt] n domestico/a.

serve [sɔːv] vt (employer etc) servire, essere a servizio di; (purpose) servire a; (customer, food, meal) servire; (apprenticeship) fare; (prison term) scontare ♦ vi (also TENNIS) servire; (soldier etc) prestare servizio; (be useful): **to** ~ **as/for/to do** servire da/per/per fare ♦ n (TENNIS) servizio; **are you being** ~**d?** la stanno servendo?; **to** ~ **on a committee/ jury** far parte di un comitato/una giuria; **it** ~**s him right** ben gli sta, se l'è meritata; **it** ~**s my purpose** fa al caso mio.

►**serve out, serve up** vt (food) servire.

server ['sɔːvə*] n (COMPUT) server sm inv.

service ['sɔːvɪs] n servizio; (AUT: maintenance) revisione f; (REL) funzione f ♦ vt (car, washing machine) revisionare; **the S**~**s** npl le forze armate; **to be of** ~ **to sb, to do sb a** ~ essere d'aiuto a qn; **to put one's car in for (a)** ~ portare la macchina in officina per una revisione; **dinner** ~ servizio da tavola.

serviceable ['sɔːvɪsəbl] adj pratico(a), utile; (usable, working) usabile.

service area n (on motorway) area di servizio.

service charge n (BRIT) servizio.

service industries npl settore m terziario.

serviceman ['sɔːvɪsmən] n militare m.

service provider n (COMPUT) provider sm inv.

service station n stazione f di servizio.

serviette [sɔːvɪ'ɛt] n (BRIT) tovagliolo.

servile ['sɔːvaɪl] adj servile.

session ['sɛʃən] n (sitting) seduta, sessione f; (SCOL) anno scolastico (or accademico); **to be in** ~ essere in seduta.

session musician n musicista m/f di studio.

set [sɛt] n serie f inv; (RADIO, TV) apparecchio; (TENNIS) set m inv; (group of people) mondo, ambiente m; (CINE) scenario; (THEA I: stage) scene fpl; (: scenery) scenario; (MATH) insieme m; (HAIRDRESSING) messa in piega ♦ adj (fixed) stabilito(a), determinato(a); (ready) pronto(a) ♦ vb (pt, pp set) (place) posare, mettere; (fix) fissare; (assign: task, homework) dare, assegnare; (adjust) regolare; (decide: rules etc) stabilire, fissare; (TYP) comporre ♦ vi (sun)

tramontare; (jam, jelly) rapprendersi; (concrete) fare presa; **to be** ~ **on doing** essere deciso a fare; **to be all** ~ **to do sth** essere pronto fare qc; **to be (dead)** ~ **against** essere completamente contrario a; ~ **in one's ways** abitudinario; **a novel** ~ **in Rome** un romanzo ambientato a Roma; **to** ~ **to music** mettere in musica; **to** ~ **on fire** dare fuoco a; **to** ~ **free** liberare; **to** ~ **sth going** mettere in moto qc; **to** ~ **sail** prendere il mare; **a** ~ **phrase** una frase fatta; **a** ~ **of false teeth** una dentiera; **a** ~ **of dining-room furniture** una camera da pranzo.

►**set about** vt fus (task) intraprendere, mettersi a; **to** ~ **about doing sth** mettersi a fare qc.

►**set aside** vt mettere da parte.

►**set back** vt (progress) ritardare; **to** ~ **back (by)** (in time) mettere indietro (di); **a house** ~ **back from the road** una casa a una certa distanza dalla strada.

►**set in** vi (infection) svilupparsi; (complications) intervenire; **the rain has** ~ **in for the day** ormai pioverà tutto il giorno.

►**set off** vi partire ♦ vt (bomb) far scoppiare; (cause to start) mettere in moto; (show up well) dare risalto a.

►**set out** vi partire; (aim): **to** ~ **out to do** proporsi di fare ♦ vt (arrange) disporre; (state) esporre, presentare.

►**set up** vt (organization) fondare, costituire; (record) stabilire; (monument) innalzare.

setback ['sɛtbæk] n (hitch) contrattempo, inconveniente m; (in health) ricaduta.

set menu n menù m inv fisso.

set square n squadra.

settee [sɛ'tiː] n divano, sofà m inv.

setting ['sɛtɪŋ] n ambiente m; (scenery) sfondo; (of jewel) montatura.

setting lotion n fissatore m.

settle ['sɛtl] vt (argument, matter) appianare; (problem) risolvere; (pay: bill, account) regolare, saldare; (MED: calm) calmare; (colonize: land) colonizzare ♦ vi (bird, dust etc) posarsi; (sediment) depositarsi; (also: ~ down) sistemarsi, stabilirsi; (become calmer) calmarsi; **to** ~ **to sth** applicarsi a qc; **to** ~ **for sth** accontentarsi di qc; **to** ~ **on sth** decidersi per qc; **that's** ~**d then** allora è deciso; **to** ~ **one's stomach** calmare il mal di stomaco.

►**settle in** vi sistemarsi.

►**settle up** vi: **to** ~ **up with sb** regolare i conti con qn.

settlement ['sɛtlmənt] n (payment)

pagamento, saldo; (*agreement*) accordo; (*colony*) colonia; (*village etc*) villaggio, comunità *f inv*; **in ~ of our account** (*COMM*) a saldo del nostro conto.
settler ['sɛtlə*] *n* colonizzatore/trice.
setup ['sɛtʌp] *n* (*arrangement*) sistemazione *f*; (*situation*) situazione; (*COMPUT*) setup *m inv*.
seven ['sɛvn] *num* sette.
seventeen [sɛvn'tiːn] *num* diciassette.
seventh ['sɛvnθ] *num* settimo(a).
seventy ['sɛvntɪ] *num* settanta.
sever ['sɛvə*] *vt* recidere, tagliare; (*relations*) troncare.
several ['sɛvərl] *adj, pron* alcuni(e), diversi(e); **~ of us** alcuni di noi; **~ times** diverse volte.
severance ['sɛvərəns] *n* (*of relations*) rottura.
severance pay *n* indennità di licenziamento.
severe [sɪ'vɪə*] *adj* severo(a); (*serious*) serio(a), grave; (*hard*) duro(a); (*plain*) semplice, sobrio(a).
severely [sɪ'vɪəlɪ] *adv* (*gen*) severamente; (*wounded, ill*) gravemente.
severity [sɪ'vɛrɪtɪ] *n* severità; gravità; (*of weather*) rigore *m*.
sew, pt sewed, pp sewn [səu, səud, səun] *vt, vi* cucire.
▶**sew up** *vt* ricucire; **it is all sewn up** (*fig*) è tutto apposto.
sewage ['suːɪdʒ] *n* acque *fpl* di scolo.
sewage works *n* stabilimento per la depurazione dei liquami.
sewer ['suːə*] *n* fogna.
sewing ['səuɪŋ] *n* cucito.
sewing machine *n* macchina da cucire.
sewn [səun] *pp of* **sew**.
sex [sɛks] *n* sesso; **to have ~ with** avere rapporti sessuali con.
sex act *n* atto sessuale.
sex appeal *n* sex appeal *m inv*.
sex education *n* educazione *f* sessuale.
sexism ['sɛksɪzəm] *n* sessismo.
sexist ['sɛksɪst] *adj* sessista.
sex life *n* vita sessuale.
sex object *n* oggetto sessuale; **to be treated like a ~** (*woman*) essere trattata da donna oggetto.
sextet [sɛks'tɛt] *n* sestetto.
sexual ['sɛksjuəl] *adj* sessuale; **~ assault** violenza carnale; **~ harassment** molestie *fpl* sessuali; **~ intercourse** rapporti *mpl* sessuali.
sexy ['sɛksɪ] *adj* provocante, sexy *inv*.
Seychelles [seɪ'ʃɛlz] *npl*: **the ~** le Seicelle.
SF *n abbr* = **science fiction**.

SG *n abbr* (*US*) = **Surgeon General**.
Sgt. *abbr* (= *sergeant*) serg.
shabbiness ['ʃæbɪnɪs] *n* trasandatezza; squallore *m*; meschinità.
shabby ['ʃæbɪ] *adj* trasandato(a); (*building*) squallido(a), malandato(a); (*behaviour*) meschino(a).
shack [ʃæk] *n* baracca, capanna.
shackles ['ʃæklz] *npl* ferri *mpl*, catene *fpl*.
shade [ʃeɪd] *n* ombra; (*for lamp*) paralume *m*; (*of colour*) tonalità *f inv*; (*US*: window ~) veneziana; (*small quantity*): **a ~ of** un po' *or* un'ombra di ♦ *vt* ombreggiare, fare ombra a; **~s** *npl* (*US*: sunglasses) occhiali *mpl* da sole; **in the ~** all'ombra; **a ~ smaller** un tantino più piccolo.
shadow ['ʃædəu] *n* ombra ♦ *vt* (*follow*) pedinare; **without** *or* **beyond a ~ of doubt** senz'ombra di dubbio.
shadow cabinet *n* (*BRIT POL*) governo *m* ombra *inv*.
shadowy ['ʃædəuɪ] *adj* ombreggiato(a), ombroso(a); (*dim*) vago(a), indistinto(a).
shady ['ʃeɪdɪ] *adj* ombroso(a); (*fig*: *dishonest*) losco(a), equivoco(a).
shaft [ʃɑːft] *n* (*of arrow, spear*) asta; (*AUT, TECH*) albero; (*of mine*) pozzo; (*of lift*) tromba; (*of light*) raggio; **ventilator ~** condotto di ventilazione.
shaggy ['ʃægɪ] *adj* ispido(a).
shake [ʃeɪk] *vb* (*pt* **shook**, *pp* **shaken** [ʃuk, 'ʃeɪkn]) *vt* scuotere; (*bottle, cocktail*) agitare ♦ *vi* tremare ♦ *n* scossa; **to ~ one's head** scuotere la testa; **to ~ hands with sb** stringere *or* dare la mano a qn.
▶**shake off** *vt* scrollare (via); (*fig*) sbarazzarsi di.
▶**shake up** *vt* scuotere.
shake-up ['ʃeɪkʌp] *n* riorganizzazione *f* drastica.
shakily ['ʃeɪkɪlɪ] *adv* (*reply*) con voce tremante; (*walk*) con passo malfermo; (*write*) con mano tremante.
shaky ['ʃeɪkɪ] *adj* (*hand, voice*) tremante; (*memory*) labile; (*knowledge*) incerto(a); (*building*) traballante.
shale [ʃeɪl] *n* roccia scistosa.
shall [ʃæl] *aux vb*: **I ~ go** andrò.
shallot [ʃə'lɔt] *n* (*BRIT*) scalogna.
shallow ['ʃæləu] *adj* poco profondo(a); (*fig*) superficiale.
sham [ʃæm] *n* finzione *f*, messinscena; (*jewellery, furniture*) imitazione *f* ♦ *adj* finto(a) ♦ *vt* fingere, simulare.
shambles ['ʃæmblz] *n* confusione *f*, baraonda, scompiglio; **the economy is (in) a complete ~** l'economia è nel caos più totale.

shambolic [ʃæm'bɔlɪk] *adj (col)* incasinato(a).

shame [ʃeɪm] *n* vergogna ♦ *vt* far vergognare; **it is a ~ (that/to do)** è un peccato (che + *sub*/fare); **what a ~!** che peccato!; **to put sb/sth to ~** *(fig)* far sfigurare qn/qc.

shamefaced ['ʃeɪmfeɪst] *adj* vergognoso(a).

shameful ['ʃeɪmful] *adj* vergognoso(a).

shameless ['ʃeɪmlɪs] *adj* sfrontato(a); *(immodest)* spudorato(a).

shampoo [ʃæm'puː] *n* shampoo *m inv* ♦ *vt* fare lo shampoo a; **~ and set** shampoo e messa in piega.

shamrock ['ʃæmrɔk] *n* trifoglio *(simbolo nazionale dell'Irlanda).*

shandy ['ʃændɪ] *n* birra con gassosa.

shan't [ʃaːnt] = **shall not.**

shanty town ['ʃæntɪ-] *n* bidonville *f inv.*

SHAPE [ʃeɪp] *n abbr (= Supreme Headquarters Allied Powers, Europe)* supremo quartier generale delle Potenze Alleate in Europa.

shape [ʃeɪp] *n* forma ♦ *vt (clay, stone)* dar forma a; *(fig: ideas, character)* formare; (: *course of events)* determinare; *(statement)* formulare; *(sb's ideas)* condizionare ♦ *vi (also: ~ up:* events) andare, mettersi; (: *person)* cavarsela; **to take ~** prendere forma; **in the ~ of a heart** a forma di cuore; **to get o.s. into ~** rimettersi in forma; **I can't bear gardening in any ~ or form** detesto il giardinaggio d'ogni genere e specie.

-shaped [ʃeɪpt] *suffix:* **heart-~** a forma di cuore.

shapeless ['ʃeɪplɪs] *adj* senza forma, informe.

shapely ['ʃeɪplɪ] *adj* ben proporzionato(a).

share [ʃɛə*] *n (thing received, contribution)* parte *f; (COMM)* azione *f* ♦ *vt* dividere; *(have in common)* condividere, avere in comune; **to ~ out (among** *or* **between)** dividere (tra); **to ~ in** partecipare a.

share capital *n* capitale *m* azionario.

share certificate *n* certificato azionario.

shareholder ['ʃɛəhəuldə*] *n* azionista *m/f.*

share index *n* listino di Borsa.

shark [ʃaːk] *n* squalo, pescecane *m.*

sharp [ʃaːp] *adj (razor, knife)* affilato(a); *(point)* acuto(a), acuminato(a); *(nose, chin)* aguzzo(a); *(outline)* netto(a); *(curve, bend)* stretto(a), accentuato(a); *(cold, pain)* pungente; *(voice)* stridulo(a); *(person: quick-witted)* sveglio(a); (: *unscrupulous)* disonesto(a); *(MUS):* **C ~ do** diesis ♦ *n (MUS)* diesis *m inv* ♦ *adv:* **at 2 o'clock ~** alle due in punto; **turn ~ left**

giri tutto a sinistra; **to be ~ with sb** rimproverare qn; **look ~!** sbrigati!

sharpen ['ʃaːpən] *vt* affilare; *(pencil)* fare la punta a; *(fig)* aguzzare.

sharpener ['ʃaːpnə*] *n (also:* **pencil ~**) temperamatite *m inv; (also:* **knife ~**) affilacoltelli *m inv.*

sharp-eyed [ʃaːp'aɪd] *adj* dalla vista acuta.

sharpish ['ʃaːpɪʃ] *adv (BRIT col:* quickly) subito.

sharply ['ʃaːplɪ] *adv (abruptly)* bruscamente; *(clearly)* nettamente; *(harshly)* duramente, aspramente.

sharp-tempered [ʃaːp'tɛmpəd] *adj* irascibile.

shatter ['ʃætə*] *vt* mandare in frantumi, frantumare; *(fig: upset)* distruggere; (: *ruin)* rovinare ♦ *vi* frantumarsi, andare in pezzi.

shattered ['ʃætəd] *adj (grief-stricken)* sconvolto(a); *(exhausted)* a pezzi, distrutto(a).

shatterproof ['ʃætəpruːf] *adj* infrangibile.

shave [ʃeɪv] *vt* radere, rasare ♦ *vi* radersi, farsi la barba ♦ *n:* **to have a ~** farsi la barba.

shaven ['ʃeɪvn] *adj (head)* rasato(a), tonsurato(a).

shaver ['ʃeɪvə*] *n (also:* **electric ~**) rasoio elettrico.

shaving ['ʃeɪvɪŋ] *n (action)* rasatura; **~s** *npl (of wood etc)* trucioli *mpl.*

shaving brush *n* pennello da barba.

shaving cream *n* crema da barba.

shaving soap *n* sapone *m* da barba.

shawl [ʃɔːl] *n* scialle *m.*

she [ʃiː] *pron* ella, lei; **there ~ is** eccola; **~-bear** orsa; **~-elephant** elefantessa; *NB: for ships, countries follow the gender of your translation.*

sheaf, *pl* **sheaves** [ʃiːf, ʃiːvz] *n* covone *m.*

shear [ʃɪə*] *vt (pt* **~ed,** *pp* **~ed** *or* **shorn** [ʃɔːn]) *(sheep)* tosare.

▶**shear off** *vi (break off)* spezzarsi.

shears ['ʃɪəz] *npl (for hedge)* cesoie *fpl.*

sheath [ʃiːθ] *n* fodero, guaina; *(contraceptive)* preservativo.

sheathe [ʃiːð] *vt* rivestire; *(sword)* rinfoderare.

sheath knife *n* coltello (con fodero).

sheaves [ʃiːvz] *npl of* **sheaf.**

shed [ʃɛd] *n* capannone *m* ♦ *vt (pt, pp* **shed**) *(leaves, fur etc)* perdere; *(tears)* versare; **to ~ light on** *(problem, mystery)* far luce su.

she'd [ʃiːd] = **she had; she would.**

sheen [ʃiːn] *n* lucentezza.

sheep [ʃiːp] *n (pl inv)* pecora.

sheepdog ['ʃiːpdɔg] n cane m da pastore.

sheep farmer n allevatore m di pecore.

sheepish ['ʃiːpɪʃ] adj vergognoso(a), timido(a).

sheepskin ['ʃiːpskɪn] n pelle f di pecora.

sheepskin jacket n (giacca di) montone m.

sheer [ʃɪə*] adj (utter) vero(a) (e proprio(a)); (steep) a picco, perpendicolare; (transparent) trasparente ♦ adv a picco; by ~ chance per puro caso.

sheet [ʃiːt] n (on bed) lenzuolo; (of paper) foglio; (of glass) lastra; (of metal) foglio, lamina.

sheet feed n (on printer) alimentazione f di fogli.

sheet lightning n lampo diffuso.

sheet metal n lamiera.

sheet music n fogli mpl di musica.

sheik(h) [ʃeɪk] n sceicco.

shelf, pl shelves [ʃɛlf, ʃɛlvz] n scaffale m, mensola.

shelf life n (COMM) durata di conservazione.

shell [ʃɛl] n (on beach) conchiglia; (of egg, nut etc) guscio; (explosive) granata; (of building) scheletro, struttura ♦ vt (peas) sgranare; (MIL) bombardare, cannoneggiare.

►shell out vi (col): to ~ out (for) sganciare soldi (per).

she'll [ʃiːl] = she will; she shall.

shellfish ['ʃɛlfɪʃ] n (pl inv) (crab etc) crostaceo; (scallop etc) mollusco; (pl: as food) crostacei; molluschi.

shellsuit ['ʃɛlsuːt] n tuta di acetato.

shelter ['ʃɛltə*] n riparo, rifugio ♦ vt riparare, proteggere; (give lodging to) dare rifugio or asilo a ♦ vi ripararsi, mettersi al riparo; to take ~ (from) mettersi al riparo (da).

sheltered ['ʃɛltəd] adj (life) ritirato(a); (spot) riparato(a), protetto(a).

shelve [ʃɛlv] vt (fig) accantonare, rimandare.

shelves [ʃɛlvz] npl of shelf.

shelving ['ʃɛlvɪŋ] n scaffalature fpl.

shepherd ['ʃɛpəd] n pastore m ♦ vt (guide) guidare.

shepherdess ['ʃɛpədɪs] n pastora.

shepherd's pie n timballo di carne macinata e purè di patate.

sherbet ['ʃɔːbət] n (BRIT: powder) polvere effervescente al gusto di frutta; (US: water ice) sorbetto.

sheriff ['ʃɛrɪf] n sceriffo.

sherry ['ʃɛrɪ] n sherry m inv.

she's [ʃiːz] = she is; she has.

Shetland ['ʃɛtlənd] n (also: the ~s, the ~

Isles) le (isole) Shetland.

Shetland pony n pony m inv delle Shetland.

shield [ʃiːld] n scudo ♦ vt: to ~ (from) riparare (da), proteggere (da or contro).

shift [ʃɪft] n (change) cambiamento; (of workers) turno ♦ vt spostare, muovere; (remove) rimuovere ♦ vi spostarsi, muoversi; ~ in demand (COMM) variazione f della domanda; the wind has ~ed to the south il vento si è girato e soffia da sud.

shift key n (on typewriter) tasto delle maiuscole.

shiftless ['ʃɪftlɪs] adj fannullone(a).

shift work n lavoro a squadre; to do ~ fare i turni.

shifty ['ʃɪftɪ] adj ambiguo(a); (eyes) sfuggente.

Shiite ['ʃiːaɪt] adj, n sciita (m/f).

shilling ['ʃɪlɪŋ] n (BRIT) scellino (= 12 old pence; 20 in a pound).

shilly-shally ['ʃɪlɪʃælɪ] vi tentennare, esitare.

shimmer ['ʃɪmə*] vi brillare, luccicare.

shimmering ['ʃɪmərɪŋ] adj (gen) luccicante, scintillante; (haze) tremolante; (satin etc) cangiante.

shin [ʃɪn] n tibia ♦ vi: to ~ up/down a tree arrampicarsi in cima a/scivolare giù da un albero.

shindig ['ʃɪndɪg] n (col) festa chiassosa.

shine [ʃaɪn] n splendore m, lucentezza ♦ vb (pt, pp shone [ʃɔn]) vi (ri)splendere, brillare ♦ vt far brillare, far risplendere; (torch): to ~ sth on puntare qc verso.

shingle ['ʃɪŋgl] n (on beach) ciottoli mpl; (on roof) assicella di copertura.

shingles ['ʃɪŋglz] n (MED) herpes zoster m.

shining ['ʃaɪnɪŋ] adj (surface, hair) lucente; (light) brillante.

shiny ['ʃaɪnɪ] adj lucente, lucido(a).

ship [ʃɪp] n nave f ♦ vt trasportare (via mare); (send) spedire (via mare); (load) imbarcare, caricare; on board ~ a bordo.

shipbuilder ['ʃɪpbɪldə*] n costruttore m navale.

shipbuilding ['ʃɪpbɪldɪŋ] n costruzione f navale.

ship chandler [-'tʃɑːndlə*] n fornitore m marittimo.

shipment ['ʃɪpmənt] n carico.

shipowner ['ʃɪpəunə*] n armatore m.

shipper ['ʃɪpə*] n spedizioniere m (marittimo).

shipping ['ʃɪpɪŋ] n (ships) naviglio; (traffic) navigazione f.

shipping agent n agente m marittimo.

shipping company n compagnia di navigazione.

shipping lane n rotta (di navigazione).

shipping line n = **shipping company.**

shipshape ['ʃɪpʃeɪp] adj in perfetto ordine.

shipwreck ['ʃɪprɛk] n relitto; (event) naufragio ♦ vt: **to be ~ed** naufragare, fare naufragio.

shipyard ['ʃɪpjɑːd] n cantiere m navale.

shire ['ʃaɪə*] n (BRIT) contea.

shirk [ʃəːk] vt sottrarsi a, evitare.

shirt [ʃəːt] n (man's) camicia; **in ~ sleeves** in maniche di camicia.

shirty ['ʃəːtɪ] adj (BRIT col) incavolato(a).

shit [ʃɪt] excl (col!) merda(!).

shiver ['ʃɪvə*] n brivido ♦ vi rabbrividire, tremare.

shoal [ʃəul] n (of fish) banco.

shock [ʃɔk] n (impact) urto, colpo; (ELEC) scossa; (emotional) colpo, shock m inv; (MED) shock ♦ vt colpire, scioccare; scandalizzare; **to give sb a ~** far venire un colpo a qn; **to be suffering from ~** essere in stato di shock; **it came as a ~ to hear that ...** è stata una grossa sorpresa sentire che ....

shock absorber n ammortizzatore m.

shocker ['ʃɔkə*] n: **it was a real ~** (col) è stata una vera bomba.

shocking ['ʃɔkɪŋ] adj scioccante, traumatizzante; (scandalous) scandaloso(a); (very bad: weather, handwriting) orribile; (: results) disastroso(a).

shockproof ['ʃɔkpruːf] adj antiurto inv.

shock therapy, shock treatment n (MED) shockterapia.

shock wave n onda d'urto; (fig: usually pl) impatto msg.

shod [ʃɔd] pt, pp of **shoe.**

shoddy ['ʃɔdɪ] adj scadente.

shoe [ʃuː] n scarpa; (also: **horse~**) ferro di cavallo; (brake ~) ganascia (del freno) ♦ vt (pt, pp **shod** [ʃɔd]) (horse) ferrare.

shoebrush ['ʃuːbrʌʃ] n spazzola per le scarpe.

shoehorn ['ʃuːhɔːn] n calzante m.

shoelace ['ʃuːleɪs] n stringa.

shoemaker ['ʃuːmeɪkə*] n calzolaio.

shoe polish n lucido per scarpe.

shoeshop ['ʃuːʃɔp] n calzoleria.

shoestring ['ʃuːstrɪŋ] n stringa (delle scarpe); **on a ~** (fig: do sth) con quattro soldi.

shoetree ['ʃuːtriː] n forma per scarpe.

shone [ʃɔn] pt, pp of **shine.**

shoo [ʃuː] excl sciò!, via! ♦ vt (also: ~ **away**, ~ **off**) cacciare (via).

shook [ʃuk] pt of **shake.**

shoot [ʃuːt] n (on branch, seedling) germoglio; (shooting party) partita di caccia; (competition) gara di tiro ♦ vb (pt, pp **shot** [ʃɔt]) vt (game: BRIT) cacciare, andare a caccia di; (person) sparare a; (execute) fucilare; (film) girare ♦ vi (with gun): **to ~ (at)** sparare (a), fare fuoco (su); (with bow): **to ~ (at)** tirare (su); (FOOTBALL) sparare, tirare (forte); **to ~ past sb** passare vicino a qn come un fulmine; **to ~ in/out** entrare/uscire come una freccia.

▶**shoot down** vt (plane) abbattere.

▶**shoot up** vi (fig) salire alle stelle.

shooting ['ʃuːtɪŋ] n (shots) sparatoria; (murder) uccisione f (a colpi d'arma da fuoco); (HUNTING) caccia; (CINE) riprese fpl.

shooting range n poligono (di tiro), tirassegno.

shooting star n stella cadente.

shop [ʃɔp] n negozio; (workshop) officina ♦ vi (also: **go ~ping**) fare spese; **repair ~** officina di riparazione; **to talk ~** (fig) parlare di lavoro.

▶**shop around** vi fare il giro dei negozi.

shopaholic ['ʃɔpə'hɔlɪk] n (col) maniaco/a dello shopping.

shop assistant n (BRIT) commesso/a.

shop floor n (BRIT: fig) operai mpl, maestranze fpl.

shopkeeper ['ʃɔpkiːpə*] n negoziante m/f, bottegaio/a.

shoplift ['ʃɔplɪft] vi taccheggiare.

shoplifter ['ʃɔplɪftə*] n taccheggiatore/trice.

shoplifting ['ʃɔplɪftɪŋ] n taccheggio.

shopper ['ʃɔpə*] n compratore/trice.

shopping ['ʃɔpɪŋ] n (goods) spesa, acquisti mpl.

shopping bag n borsa per la spesa.

shopping centre n centro commerciale.

shop-soiled ['ʃɔpsɔɪld] adj sciupato(a) a forza di stare in vetrina.

shop steward n (BRIT INDUSTRY) rappresentante m sindacale.

shop window n vetrina.

shore [ʃɔː*] n (of sea) riva, spiaggia; (of lake) riva ♦ vt: **to ~ (up)** puntellare; **on ~** a terra.

shore leave n (NAUT) franchigia.

shorn [ʃɔːn] pp of **shear.**

short [ʃɔːt] adj (not long) corto(a); (soon finished) breve; (person) basso(a); (curt) brusco(a), secco(a); (insufficient) insufficiente ♦ n (also: ~ **film**) cortometraggio; **it is ~ for** è l'abbreviazione or il diminutivo di; **a ~ time ago** poco tempo fa; **in the ~ term** nell'immediato futuro; **to be ~ of sth** essere a corto di or mancare di qc; **to run ~ of sth** rimanere senza qc; **to be in ~ supply** scarseggiare; **I'm 3 ~** me ne mancano 3; **in ~** in breve; **~ of doing a** meno che non si faccia; **everything ~ of** tutto fuorché; **to cut ~** (*speech, visit*) accorciare, abbreviare; (*person*) interrompere; **to fall ~ of** venire meno a; non soddisfare; **to stop ~** fermarsi di colpo; **to stop ~ of** non arrivare fino a; *see also* **shorts.**

shortage ['ʃɔːtɪdʒ] *n* scarsezza, carenza.

shortbread ['ʃɔːtbrɛd] *n* biscotto di pasta frolla.

short-change [ʃɔːt'tʃeɪndʒ] *vt*: **to ~ sb** imbrogliare qn sul resto.

short-circuit [ʃɔːt'sɜːkɪt] *n* cortocircuito ♦ *vt* cortocircuitare ♦ *vi* fare cortocircuito.

shortcoming ['ʃɔːtkʌmɪŋ] *n* difetto.

short(crust) pastry ['ʃɔːt(krʌst)-] *n* (*BRIT*) pasta frolla.

shortcut ['ʃɔːtkʌt] *n* scorciatoia.

shorten ['ʃɔːtn] *vt* accorciare, ridurre.

shortening ['ʃɔːtnɪŋ] *n* grasso per pasticceria.

shortfall ['ʃɔːtfɔːl] *n* deficienza.

shorthand ['ʃɔːthænd] *n* (*BRIT*) stenografia; **to take sth down in ~** stenografare qc.

shorthand notebook *n* (*BRIT*) bloc-notes *m inv* per stenografia.

shorthand typist *n* (*BRIT*) stenodattilografo/a.

short list *n* (*BRIT: for job*) rosa dei candidati.

short-lived ['ʃɔːt'lɪvd] *adj* effimero(a), di breve durata.

shortly ['ʃɔːtlɪ] *adv* fra poco.

shortness ['ʃɔːtnɪs] *n* brevità; insufficienza.

shorts [ʃɔːts] *npl* (*also*: **a pair of ~**) i calzoncini.

short-sighted [ʃɔːt'saɪtɪd] *adj* (*BRIT*) miope; (*fig*) poco avveduto(a).

short-staffed [ʃɔːt'stɑːft] *adj* a corto di personale.

short story *n* racconto, novella.

short-tempered [ʃɔːt'tɛmpəd] *adj* irascibile.

short-term ['ʃɔːtəːm] *adj* (*effect*) di or a breve durata.

short time *n* (*INDUSTRY*): **to work ~, be on ~** essere or lavorare a orario ridotto.

short wave *n* (*RADIO*) onde *fpl* corte.

shot [ʃɔt] *pt, pp of* **shoot** ♦ *n* sparo, colpo; (*shotgun pellets*) pallottole *fpl*; (*person*)

tiratore *m*; (*try*) prova; (*injection*) iniezione *f*; (*PHOT*) foto *f inv*; **like a ~** come un razzo; (*very readily*) immediatamente; **to fire a ~ at sb/sth** sparare un colpo a qn/qc; **to have a ~ at sth/doing sth** provarci con qc/a fare qc; **a big ~** (*col*) un pezzo grosso, un papavero; **to get ~ of sb/sth** (*col*) sbarazzarsi di qn/qc.

shotgun ['ʃɔtgʌn] *n* fucile *m* da caccia.

should [ʃud] *aux vb*: **I ~ go now** dovrei andare ora; **he ~ be there now** dovrebbe essere arrivato ora; **I ~ go if I were you** se fossi in lei andrei; **I ~ like to** mi piacerebbe; **~ he phone...** se telefonasse....

shoulder ['ʃəuldə*] *n* spalla; (*BRIT: of road*): **hard ~** corsia d'emergenza ♦ *vt* (*fig*) addossarsi, prendere sulle proprie spalle; **to look over one's ~** guardarsi alle spalle; **to rub ~s with sb** (*fig*) essere a contatto con qn; **to give sb the cold ~** (*fig*) trattare qn con freddezza.

shoulder bag *n* borsa a tracolla.

shoulder blade *n* scapola.

shoulder strap *n* bretella, spallina.

shouldn't ['ʃudnt] = **should not**.

shout [ʃaut] *n* urlo, grido ♦ *vt* gridare ♦ *vi* urlare, gridare; **to give sb a ~** chiamare qn gridando.

▶**shout down** *vt* zittire gridando.

shouting ['ʃautɪŋ] *n* urli *mpl*.

shouting match *n* (*col*) vivace scambio di opinioni.

shove [ʃʌv] *vt* spingere; (*col: put*): **to ~ sth in** ficcare qc in ♦ *n* spintone *m*; **he ~d me out of the way** mi ha spinto da parte.

▶**shove off** *vi* (*NAUT*) scostarsi.

shovel ['ʃʌvl] *n* pala ♦ *vt* spalare.

show [ʃəu] *n* (*of emotion*) dimostrazione *f*, manifestazione *f*; (*semblance*) apparenza; (*exhibition*) mostra, esposizione *f*; (*THEAT, CINE*) spettacolo; (*COMM, TECH*) salone *m*, fiera ♦ *vb* (*pt ~ed, pp* **shown** [ʃəun]) *vt* far vedere, mostrare; (*courage etc*) dimostrare, dar prova di; (*exhibit*) esporre ♦ *vi* vedersi, essere visibile; **to ~ sb to his seat/to the door** accompagnare qn al suo posto/alla porta; **to ~ a profit/loss** (*COMM*) registrare un utile/una perdita; **it just goes to ~ that ...** il che sta a dimostrare che ...; **to ask for a ~ of hands** chiedere che si voti per alzata di mano; **to be on ~** essere esposto; **it's just for ~** è solo per far scena; **who's running the ~ here?** (*col*) chi è il padrone qui?

▶**show in** *vt* far entrare.

▶**show off** *vi* (*pej*) esibirsi, mettersi in mostra ♦ *vt* (*display*) mettere in risalto;

(*pej*) mettere in mostra.

►**show out** *vt* accompagnare alla porta.

►**show up** *vi* (*stand out*) essere ben visibile; (*col: turn up*) farsi vedere ♦ *vt* mettere in risalto; (*unmask*) smascherare.

showbiz ['ʃəubɪz] *n* (*col*) = **show business**.

show business *n* industria dello spettacolo.

showcase ['ʃəukeɪs] *n* vetrina, bacheca.

showdown ['ʃəudaun] *n* prova di forza.

shower ['ʃauə*] *n* (*also*: ~ **bath**) doccia; (*rain*) acquazzone *m*; (*of stones etc*) pioggia; (*US: party*) festa (*di fidanzamento etc*) in cui si fanno regali alla persona festeggiata ♦ *vi* fare la doccia ♦ *vt*: **to ~ sb wіth** (*gifts, abuse etc*) coprire qn di; (*missiles*) lanciare contro qn una pioggia di; **to have** or **take a** ~ fare la doccia.

shower cap *n* cuffia da doccia.

showerproof ['ʃauəpru:f] *adj* impermeabile.

showery ['ʃauərɪ] *adj* (*weather*) con piogge intermittenti.

showground ['ʃəugraund] *n* terreno d'esposizione.

showing ['ʃəuɪŋ] *n* (*of film*) proiezione *f*.

show jumping *n* concorso ippico (di salto ad ostacoli).

showman ['ʃəumən] *n* (*at fair, circus*) impresario; (*fig*) attore *m*.

showmanship ['ʃəumənʃɪp] *n* abilità d'impresario.

shown [ʃəun] *pp of* **show**.

show-off ['ʃəuɔf] *n* (*col: person*) esibizionista *m/f*.

showpiece ['ʃəupi:s] *n* (*of exhibition*) pezzo forte; **that hospital is a** ~ è un ospedale modello.

showroom ['ʃəurum] *n* sala d'esposizione.

show trial *n* processo a scopo dimostrativo (*spesso ideologico*).

showy ['ʃəuɪ] *adj* vistoso(a), appariscente.

shrank [ʃræŋk] *pt of* **shrink**.

shrapnel ['ʃræpnl] *n* shrapnel *m*.

shred [ʃrɛd] *n* (*gen pl*) brandello; (*fig: of truth, evidence*) briciolo ♦ *vt* fare a brandelli; (*CULIN*) sminuzzare, tagliuzzare; (*documents*) distruggere, sminuzzare.

shredder ['ʃrɛdə*] *n* (*for documents, papers*) distruttore *m* di documenti, sminuzzatrice *f*.

shrew [ʃru:] *n* (*ZOOL*) toporagno; (*fig: pej: woman*) strega.

shrewd [ʃru:d] *adj* astuto(a), scaltro(a).

shrewdness ['ʃru:dnɪs] *n* astuzia.

shriek [ʃri:k] *n* strillo ♦ *vt*, *vi* strillare.

shrift [ʃrɪft] *n*: **to give sb short** ~ sbrigare qn.

shrill [ʃrɪl] *adj* acuto(a), stridulo(a), stridente.

shrimp [ʃrɪmp] *n* gamberetto.

shrine [ʃraɪn] *n* reliquario; (*place*) santuario.

shrink [ʃrɪŋk] *vb* (*pt* **shrank**, *pp* **shrunk** [ʃræŋk, ʃrʌŋk]) *vi* restringersi; (*fig*) ridursi ♦ *vt* (*wool*) far restringere ♦ *n* (*col: pej*) psicanalista *m/f*; **to ~ from doing sth** rifuggire dal fare qc.

shrinkage ['ʃrɪŋkɪdʒ] *n* restringimento.

shrink-wrap ['ʃrɪŋkræp] *vt* confezionare con plastica sottile.

shrivel ['ʃrɪvl] (*also*: ~ **up**) *vt* raggrinzare, avvizzire ♦ *vi* raggrinzirsi, avvizzire.

shroud [ʃraud] *n* lenzuolo funebre ♦ *vt*: ~**ed in mystery** avvolto(a) nel mistero.

Shrove Tuesday ['ʃrəuv-] *n* martedì *m* grasso.

shrub [ʃrʌb] *n* arbusto.

shrubbery ['ʃrʌbərɪ] *n* arbusti *mpl*.

shrug [ʃrʌg] *n* scrollata di spalle ♦ *vt*, *vi*: **to ~ (one's shoulders)** alzare le spalle, fare spallucce.

►**shrug off** *vt* passare sopra a; (*cold, illness*) sbarazzarsi di.

shrunk [ʃrʌŋk] *pp of* **shrink**.

shrunken ['ʃrʌŋkən] *adj* rattrappito(a).

shudder ['ʃʌdə*] *n* brivido ♦ *vi* rabbrividire.

shuffle ['ʃʌfl] *vt* (*cards*) mescolare; **to ~ (one's feet)** strascicare i piedi.

shun [ʃʌn] *vt* sfuggire, evitare.

shunt [ʃʌnt] *vt* (*RAIL: direct*) smistare; (: *divert*) deviare ♦ *vi*: **to ~ (to and fro)** fare la spola.

shunting yard *n* fascio di smistamento.

shush [ʃuʃ] *excl* zitto(a)!

shut, *pt*, *pp* **shut** [ʃʌt] *vt* chiudere ♦ *vi* chiudersi, chiudere.

►**shut down** *vt*, *vi* chiudere definitivamente.

►**shut off** *vt* (*stop: power*) staccare; (: *water*) chiudere; (: *engine*) spegnere; (*isolate*) isolare.

►**shut out** *vt* (*person, noise, cold*) non far entrare; (*block: view*) impedire, bloccare; (: *memory*) scacciare.

►**shut up** *vi* (*col: keep quiet*) stare zitto(a) ♦ *vt* (*close*) chiudere; (*silence*) far tacere.

shutdown ['ʃʌtdaun] *n* chiusura.

shutter ['ʃʌtə*] *n* imposta; (*PHOT*) otturatore *m*.

shuttle ['ʃʌtl] *n* spola, navetta; (*also*: ~ **service**) servizio *m* navetta *inv* ♦ *vi* (*subj: vehicle, person*) fare la spola ♦ *vt* (*to and* fro: *passengers*) portare (avanti e indietro).

shuttlecock ['ʃʌtlkɔk] *n* volano.

shuttle diplomacy *n* frequenti mediazioni *fpl* diplomatiche.

shy [ʃaɪ] *adj* timido(a) ♦ *vi*: **to ~ away from doing sth** (*fig*) rifuggire dal fare qc; **to fight ~ of** tenersi alla larga da; **to be ~ of doing sth** essere restio a fare qc.

shyness ['ʃaɪnɪs] *n* timidezza.

Siam [saɪ'æm] *n* Siam *m*.

Siamese [saɪə'miːz] *adj*: **~ cat** gatto siamese; **~ twins** fratelli *mpl* (*or* sorelle *fpl*) siamesi.

Siberia [saɪ'bɪərɪə] *n* Siberia.

sibling ['sɪblɪŋ] *n* (*formal*) fratello/sorella.

Sicilian [sɪ'sɪlɪən] *adj, n* siciliano(a).

Sicily ['sɪsɪlɪ] *n* Sicilia.

sick [sɪk] *adj* (*ill*) malato(a); (*vomiting*): **to be ~** vomitare; (*humour*) macabro(a); **to feel ~** avere la nausea; **to be ~ of** (*fig*) averne abbastanza di; **a ~ person** un malato; **to be (off) ~** essere assente perché malato; **to fall** *or* **take ~** ammalarsi.

sickbag ['sɪkbæg] *n* sacchetto (*da usarsi in caso di malessere*).

sick bay *n* infermeria.

sick building syndrome *n* malattia causata da mancanza di ventilazione e luce naturale.

sicken ['sɪkn] *vt* nauseare ♦ *vi*: **to be ~ing for sth** (*cold, flu etc*) covare qc.

sickening ['sɪknɪŋ] *adj* (*fig*) disgustoso(a), rivoltante.

sickle ['sɪkl] *n* falcetto.

sick leave *n* congedo per malattia.

sickle-cell anaemia ['sɪklsɛl-] *n* anemia drepanocitica.

sickly ['sɪklɪ] *adj* malaticcio(a); (*causing nausea*) nauseante.

sickness ['sɪknɪs] *n* malattia; (*vomiting*) vomito.

sickness benefit *n* indennità di malattia.

sick pay *n* sussidio per malattia.

sickroom ['sɪkruːm] *n* stanza di malato.

side [saɪd] *n* (*gen*) lato; (*of person, animal*) fianco; (*of lake*) riva; (*face, surface*: *gen*) faccia; (: *of paper*) facciata; (*fig*: *aspect*) aspetto, lato; (*team*: *SPORT*) squadra; (: *POL etc*) parte *f* ♦ *cpd* (*door, entrance*) laterale ♦ *vi*: **to ~ with sb** parteggiare per qn, prendere le parti di qn; **by the ~ of** a fianco di; (*road*) sul ciglio di; **~ by ~** fianco a fianco; **to take ~s (with)** schierarsi (con); **the right/wrong ~** il dritto/rovescio; **from ~ to ~** da una parte all'altra; **~ of beef** quarto di bue.

sideboard ['saɪdbɔːd] *n* credenza.

sideboards ['saɪdbɔːdz] (*BRIT*), **sideburns** ['saɪdbəːnz] *npl* (*whiskers*) basette *fpl*.

sidecar ['saɪdkɑː*] *n* sidecar *m inv*.

side dish *n* contorno.

side drum *n* (*MUS*) piccolo tamburo.

side effect *n* (*MED*) effetto collaterale.

sidekick ['saɪdkɪk] *n* (*col*) compagno/a.

sidelight ['saɪdlaɪt] *n* (*AUT*) luce *f* di posizione.

sideline ['saɪdlaɪn] *n* (*SPORT*) linea laterale; (*fig*) attività secondaria.

sidelong ['saɪdlɔŋ] *adj* obliquo(a); **to give a ~ glance at sth** guardare qc con la coda dell'occhio.

side plate *n* piattino.

side road *n* strada secondaria.

sidesaddle ['saɪdsædl] *adv* all'amazzone.

side show *n* attrazione *f*.

sidestep ['saɪdstɛp] *vt* (*question*) eludere; (*problem*) scavalcare ♦ *vi* (*BOXING etc*) spostarsi di lato.

side street *n* traversa.

sidetrack ['saɪdtræk] *vt* (*fig*) distrarre.

sidewalk ['saɪdwɔːk] *n* (*US*) marciapiede *m*.

sideways ['saɪdweɪz] *adv* (*move*) di lato, di fianco; (*look*) con la coda dell'occhio.

siding ['saɪdɪŋ] *n* (*RAIL*) binario di raccordo.

sidle ['saɪdl] *vi*: **to ~ up (to)** avvicinarsi furtivamente (a).

SIDS *n* (= *sudden infant death syndrome*) *see* **cot death.**

siege [siːdʒ] *n* assedio; **to lay ~ to** porre l'assedio a.

siege economy *n* economia da stato d'assedio.

Sierra Leone [sɪ'ɛrəlɪ'əun] *n* Sierra Leone *f*.

sieve [sɪv] *n* setaccio ♦ *vt* setacciare.

sift [sɪft] *vt* passare al crivello; (*fig*) vagliare ♦ *vi*: **to ~ through** esaminare minuziosamente.

sigh [saɪ] *n* sospiro ♦ *vi* sospirare.

sight [saɪt] *n* (*faculty*) vista; (*spectacle*) spettacolo; (*on gun*) mira ♦ *vt* avvistare; **in ~** in vista; **out of ~** non visibile; **at first ~** a prima vista; **to catch ~ of sth/sb** scorgere qc/qn; **to lose ~ of sb/sth** perdere di vista qn/qc; **to set one's ~s on sth/on doing sth** mirare a qc/a fare qc; **at ~** a vista; **I know her by ~** la conosco di vista.

sighted ['saɪtɪd] *adj* che ha il dono della vista; **partially ~** parzialmente cieco.

sightseeing ['saɪtsiːɪŋ] *n* turismo; **to go ~** visitare una località.

sightseer ['saɪtsiːə*] *n* turista *m/f*.

sign [saɪn] *n* segno; (*with hand etc*) segno, gesto; (*notice*) insegna, cartello; (*road ~*) segnale *m* ♦ *vt* firmare; **as a ~ of** in segno di; **it's a good/bad** ~ è buon/brutto segno; **to show** ~s/no ~ **of doing sth** accennare/non accennare a fare qc; **plus/minus** ~ segno del più/meno; **to** ~ **one's name** firmare, apporre la propria firma.

▶**sign away** *vt* (*rights etc*) cedere (con una firma).

▶**sign in** *vi* firmare il registro (all'arrivo).

▶**sign off** *vi* (*RADIO, TV*) chiudere le trasmissioni.

▶**sign on** *vi* (*MIL etc: enlist*) arruolarsi; (*as unemployed*) iscriversi sulla lista (dell'ufficio di collocamento); (*begin work*) prendere servizio; (*enrol*): **to** ~ **on for a course** iscriversi a un corso.

▶**sign out** *vi* firmare il registro (alla partenza).

▶**sign over** *vt*: **to** ~ **sth over to sb** cedere qc con scrittura legale a qn.

▶**sign up** (*MIL*) *vt* arruolare ♦ *vi* arruolarsi.

signal ['sɪgnl] *n* segnale *m* ♦ *vt* (*person*) fare segno a; (*message*) comunicare per mezzo di segnali ♦ *vi*: **to** ~ **to sb (to do sth)** far segno a qn (di fare qc); **to** ~ **a left/right turn** (*AUT*) segnalare un cambiamento di direzione a sinistra/destra.

signal box *n* (*RAIL*) cabina di manovra.

signalman ['sɪgnlmən] *n* (*RAIL*) deviatore *m*.

signatory ['sɪgnətərɪ] *n* firmatario/a.

signature ['sɪgnətʃə*] *n* firma.

signature tune *n* sigla musicale.

signet ring ['sɪgnət-] *n* anello con sigillo.

significance [sɪg'nɪfɪkəns] *n* (*of remark*) significato; (*of event*) importanza; **that is of no** ~ ciò non ha importanza.

significant [sɪg'nɪfɪkənt] *adj* (*improvement, amount*) notevole; (*discovery, event*) importante; (*evidence, smile*) significativo(a); **it is** ~ **that ... è** significativo che ....

significantly [sɪg'nɪfɪkəntlɪ] *adv* (*smile*) in modo eloquente; (*improve, increase*) considerevolmente, decisamente.

signify ['sɪgnɪfaɪ] *vt* significare.

sign language *n* linguaggio dei muti.

signpost ['saɪnpəust] *n* cartello indicatore.

silage ['saɪlɪdʒ] *n* insilato.

silence ['saɪlns] *n* silenzio ♦ *vt* far tacere, ridurre al silenzio.

silencer ['saɪlənsə*] *n* (*on gun, BRIT AUT*) silenziatore *m*.

silent ['saɪlnt] *adj* silenzioso(a); (*film*) muto(a); **to keep** *or* **remain** ~ tacere, stare zitto(a).

silently ['saɪlntlɪ] *adv* silenziosamente, in silenzio.

silent partner *n* (*COMM*) socio accomandante.

silhouette [sɪluː'ɛt] *n* silhouette *f inv* ♦ *vt*: **to be** ~**d against** stagliarsi contro.

silicon ['sɪlɪkən] *n* silicio.

silicon chip *n* chip *m inv* al silicio.

silicone ['sɪlɪkəun] *n* silicone *m*.

silk [sɪlk] *n* seta ♦ *cpd* di seta.

silky ['sɪlkɪ] *adj* di seta, come la seta.

sill [sɪl] *n* (*window*~) davanzale *m*; (*AUT*) predellino.

silly ['sɪlɪ] *adj* stupido(a), sciocco(a); **to do something** ~ fare una sciocchezza.

silo ['saɪləu] *n* silo.

silt [sɪlt] *n* limo.

silver ['sɪlvə*] *n* argento; (*money*) monete *da 5, 10, 20 o 50 pence*; (*also:* ~**ware**) argenteria ♦ *cpd* d'argento.

silver foil, (*BRIT*) **silver paper** *n* carta argentata, (*carta*) stagnola.

silver-plated [sɪlvə'pleɪtɪd] *adj* argentato(a).

silversmith ['sɪlvəsmɪθ] *n* argentiere *m*.

silverware ['sɪlvəwɛə*] *n* argenteria, argento.

silvery ['sɪlvərɪ] *adj* (*colour*) argenteo(a); (*sound*) argentino(a).

SIM card ['sɪm-] *n* (*TEL:* = *Subscriber Identity Module card*) SIM card *f inv*.

similar ['sɪmɪlə*] *adj*: ~ (**to**) simile (a).

similarity [sɪmɪ'lærɪtɪ] *n* somiglianza, rassomiglianza.

similarly ['sɪmɪləlɪ] *adv* (*in a similar way*) allo stesso modo; (*as is similar*) così pure.

simile ['sɪmɪlɪ] *n* similitudine *f*.

simmer ['sɪmə*] *vi* cuocere a fuoco lento.

▶**simmer down** *vi* (*fig col*) calmarsi.

simper ['sɪmpə*] *vi* fare lo(la) smorfioso(a).

simpering ['sɪmpərɪŋ] *adj* lezioso(a), smorfioso(a).

simple ['sɪmpl] *adj* semplice; **the** ~ **truth** la pura verità.

simple interest *n* (*MATH, COMM*) interesse *m* semplice.

simple-minded [sɪmpl'maɪndɪd] *adj* sempliciotto(a).

simpleton ['sɪmpltən] *n* semplicione/a, sempliciotto/a.

simplicity [sɪm'plɪsɪtɪ] *n* semplicità.

simplification [sɪmplɪfɪ'keɪʃən] *n* semplificazione *f*.

simplify ['sɪmplɪfaɪ] *vt* semplificare.

simply ['sɪmplɪ] *adv* semplicemente.

simulate ['sɪmjuleɪt] *vt* fingere, simulare.

simulation [sɪmju'leɪʃən] *n* simulazione *f*.

simultaneous [sɪməl'teɪnɪəs] *adj* simultaneo(a).

simultaneously [sɪməl'teɪnɪəslɪ] *adv*

simultaneamente, contemporaneamente.
sin [sɪn] n peccato ♦ vi peccare.
Sinai ['saɪnaɪ] n Sinai m.
since [sɪns] adv da allora ♦ prep da ♦ conj (time) da quando; (because) poiché, dato che; ~ **then** da allora; ~ **Monday** da lunedì; (**ever**) ~ **I arrived** (fin) da quando sono arrivato.
sincere [sɪn'sɪə*] adj sincero(a).
sincerely [sɪn'sɪəlɪ] adv sinceramente; **Yours** ~ (at end of letter) distinti saluti.
sincerity [sɪn'sɛrɪtɪ] n sincerità.
sine [saɪn] n (MATH) seno.
sinew ['sɪnjuː] n tendine m; ~**s** npl (muscles) muscoli mpl.
sinful ['sɪnful] adj peccaminoso(a).
sing, pt **sang**, pp **sung** [sɪŋ, sæŋ, sʌŋ] vt, vi cantare.
Singapore [sɪŋgə'pɔː*] n Singapore f.
singe [sɪndʒ] vt bruciacchiare.
singer ['sɪŋə*] n cantante m/f.
Singhalese [sɪŋə'liːz] adj = **Sinhalese**.
singing ['sɪŋɪŋ] n (of person, bird) canto; (of kettle, bullet, in ears) fischio.
single ['sɪŋgl] adj solo(a), unico(a); (unmarried: man) celibe; (: woman) nubile; (not double) semplice ♦ n (BRIT: also: ~ **ticket**) biglietto di (sola) andata; (record) 45 giri m inv; **not a** ~ **one was left** non ne è rimasto nemmeno uno; **every** ~ **day** tutti i santi giorni; see also **singles**.
►**single out** vt scegliere; (distinguish) distinguere.
single bed n letto a una piazza.
single-breasted ['sɪŋglbrɛstɪd] adj a un petto.
Single European Market n: **the** ~ il Mercato Unico.
single file n: **in** ~ in fila indiana.
single-handed [sɪŋgl'hændɪd] adv senza aiuto, da solo(a).
single-minded [sɪŋgl'maɪndɪd] adj tenace, risoluto(a).
single parent n ragazzo padre/ragazza madre; genitore m separato; ~ **family** famiglia monoparentale.
single room n camera singola.
singles ['sɪŋglz] npl (TENNIS) singolo; (US: single people) single m/f/pl.
singles bar n (esp US) bar m inv per single.
single-sex school ['sɪŋgl'sɛks-] n (for boys) scuola maschile; (for girls) scuola femminile.
singly ['sɪŋglɪ] adv separatamente.
singsong ['sɪŋsɔŋ] adj (tone) cantilenante ♦ n (songs): **to have a** ~ farsi una cantata.
singular ['sɪŋgjulə*] adj (LING) singolare; (unusual) strano(a), singolare ♦ n (LING)

singolare m; **in the feminine** ~ al femminile singolare.
singularly ['sɪŋgjuləlɪ] adv stranamente.
Sinhalese [sɪnhə'liːz] adj singalese.
sinister ['sɪnɪstə*] adj sinistro(a).
sink [sɪŋk] n lavandino, acquaio ♦ vb (pt **sank**, pp **sunk** [sæŋk, sʌŋk]) vt (ship) (fare) affondare, colare a picco; (foundations) scavare; (piles etc): **to** ~ **sth into** conficcare qc in ♦ vi affondare, andare a fondo; (ground etc) cedere, avvallarsi; **he sank into a chair/the mud** sprofondò in una poltrona/nel fango.
►**sink in** vi penetrare; **it took a long time to** ~ **in** ci ho (or ha etc) messo molto a capirlo.
sinking ['sɪŋkɪŋ] adj: **that** ~ **feeling** una stretta allo stomaco.
sinking fund n (COMM) fondo d'ammortamento.
sink unit n blocco lavello.
sinner ['sɪnə*] n peccatore/trice.
Sinn Féin [ʃɪn'feɪn] n movimento separatista irlandese.
sinuous ['sɪnjuəs] adj sinuoso(a).
sinus ['saɪnəs] n (ANAT) seno.
sip [sɪp] n sorso ♦ vt sorseggiare.
siphon ['saɪfən] n sifone m ♦ vt (funds) trasferire.
►**siphon off** vt travasare (con un sifone).
sir [sə*] n signore m; **S**~ **John Smith** Sir John Smith; **yes** ~ sì, signore; **Dear S**~ (in letter) Egregio signor (followed by name); **Dear S**~**s** Spettabile ditta.
siren ['saɪərn] n sirena.
sirloin ['səːlɔɪn] n controfiletto.
sirloin steak n bistecca di controfiletto.
sirocco [sɪ'rɔkəu] n scirocco.
sisal ['saɪsəl] n sisal f inv.
sissy ['sɪsɪ] n (col) femminuccia.
sister ['sɪstə*] n sorella; (nun) suora; (nurse) infermiera f caposala inv ♦ cpd: ~ **organization** organizzazione f affine; ~ **ship** nave f gemella.
sister-in-law ['sɪstərɪnlɔː] n cognata.
sit, pt, pp **sat** [sɪt, sæt] vi sedere, sedersi; (dress etc) cadere; (assembly) essere in seduta ♦ vt (exam) sostenere, dare; **to** ~ **on a committee** far parte di una commissione.
►**sit about, sit around** vi star seduto(a) (senza far nulla).
►**sit back** vi (in seat) appoggiarsi allo schienale.
►**sit down** vi sedersi; **to be** ~**ting down** essere seduto(a).
►**sit in** vi: **to** ~ **in on a discussion** assistere ad una discussione.

▶**sit up** vi tirarsi su a sedere; (not go to bed) stare alzato(a) fino a tardi.

sitcom ['sɪtkɔm] n abbr (TV: = situation comedy) sceneggiato a episodi (comico).

sit-down ['sɪtdaun] adj: ~ **strike** sciopero bianco (con occupazione della fabbrica); **a ~ meal** un pranzo.

site [saɪt] n posto; (also: **building** ~) cantiere m; (COMPUT) sito ♦ vt situare.

sit-in ['sɪtɪn] n (demonstration) sit-in m inv.

siting ['saɪtɪŋ] n ubicazione f.

sitter ['sɪtə*] n (for painter) modello/a; (also: **baby** ~) babysitter m/f inv.

sitting ['sɪtɪŋ] n (of assembly etc) seduta; (in canteen) turno.

sitting member n (POL) deputato/a in carica.

sitting room n soggiorno.

sitting tenant n (BRIT) attuale affittuario.

situate ['sɪtjueɪt] vt collocare.

situated ['sɪtjueɪtɪd] adj situato(a).

situation [sɪtju'eɪʃən] n situazione f; "~**s vacant/wanted**" (BRIT) "offerte/domande di impiego".

situation comedy n (THEAT) commedia di situazione.

six [sɪks] num sei.

six-pack ['sɪkspæk] n (esp US) confezione f da sei.

sixteen [sɪks'tiːn] num sedici.

sixth [sɪksθ] num sesto(a) ♦ n: **the upper/ lower** ~ (BRIT SCOL) l'ultimo/il penultimo anno di scuola superiore.

sixty ['sɪkstɪ] num sessanta.

size [saɪz] n dimensioni fpl; (of clothing) taglia, misura; (of shoes) numero; (glue) colla; **I take** ~ **14 in a dress** ≈ porto la 44 di vestiti; **I'd like the small/large** ~ (of soap powder etc) vorrei la confezione piccola/grande.

▶**size up** vt giudicare, farsi un'idea di.

sizeable ['saɪzəbl] adj considerevole.

sizzle ['sɪzl] vi sfrigolare.

SK abbr (Canada) = Saskatchewan.

skate [skeɪt] n pattino; (fish: pl inv) razza ♦ vi pattinare.

▶**skate over, skate around** vi (problem, issue) prendere alla leggera, prendere sottogamba.

skateboard ['skeɪtbɔːd] n skateboard m inv.

skater ['skeɪtə*] n pattinatore/trice.

skating ['skeɪtɪŋ] n pattinaggio.

skating rink n pista di pattinaggio.

skeleton ['skɛlɪtn] n scheletro.

skeleton key n passe-partout m inv.

skeleton staff n personale m ridotto.

skeptic etc ['skɛptɪk] (US) = **sceptic** etc.

sketch [skɛtʃ] n (drawing) schizzo, abbozzo; (THEAT etc) scenetta comica, sketch m inv ♦ vt abbozzare, schizzare.

sketch book n album m inv per schizzi.

sketch pad n blocco per schizzi.

sketchy ['skɛtʃɪ] adj incompleto(a), lacunoso(a).

skew [skjuː] n (BRIT): **on the** ~ di traverso.

skewer ['skjuːə*] n spiedo.

ski [skiː] n sci m inv ♦ vi sciare.

ski boot n scarpone m da sci.

skid [skɪd] n slittamento; (sideways slip) sbandamento ♦ vi slittare; sbandare; **to go into a** ~ slittare; sbandare.

skid mark n segno della frenata.

skier ['skiːə*] n sciatore/trice.

skiing ['skiːɪŋ] n sci m.

ski instructor n maestro/a di sci.

ski jump n (ramp) trampolino; (event) salto con gli sci.

skilful, (US) **skillful** ['skɪlful] adj abile.

ski lift n sciovia.

skill [skɪl] n abilità f inv, capacità f inv; (technique) tecnica.

skilled [skɪld] adj esperto(a); (worker) qualificato(a), specializzato(a).

skillet ['skɪlɪt] n padella.

skillful etc ['skɪlful] (US) = **skilful** etc.

skil(l)fully ['skɪlfəlɪ] adv abilmente.

skim [skɪm] vt (milk) scremare; (soup) schiumare; (glide over) sfiorare ♦ vi: **to ~ through** (fig) scorrere, dare una scorsa a.

skimmed milk n latte m scremato.

skimp [skɪmp] vi: **to ~ on**, vt (work) fare alla carlona; (cloth etc) lesinare.

skimpy ['skɪmpɪ] adj misero(a); striminzito(a); frugale.

skin [skɪn] n pelle f; (of fruit, vegetable) buccia; (on pudding, paint) crosta ♦ vt (fruit etc) sbucciare; (animal) scuoiare, spellare; **wet** or **soaked to the** ~ bagnato fino al midollo.

skin cancer n cancro alla pelle.

skin-deep [skɪn'diːp] adj superficiale.

skin diver n subacqueo.

skin diving n nuoto subacqueo.

skinflint ['skɪnflɪnt] n taccagno/a, tirchio/a.

skin graft n innesto epidermico.

skinhead ['skɪnhɛd] n skinhead m/f inv.

skinny ['skɪnɪ] adj molto magro(a).

skin test n prova di reazione cutanea.

skintight ['skɪntaɪt] adj aderente.

skip [skɪp] n saltello, balzo; (container) benna ♦ vi saltare; (with rope) saltare la corda ♦ vt (pass over) saltare; **to ~ school** (US) marinare la scuola.

ski pants npl pantaloni mpl da sci.

ski pass n ski pass m inv.

ski pole n racchetta (da sci).

skipper ['skɪpə*] n (NAUT, SPORT) capitano.
skipping rope ['skɪpɪŋ-] n (BRIT) corda per saltare.
ski resort n località f inv sciistica.
skirmish ['skə:mɪʃ] n scaramuccia.
skirt [skə:t] n gonna, sottana ♦ vt fiancheggiare, costeggiare.
skirting board ['skə:tɪŋ-] n (BRIT) zoccolo.
ski run n pista (da sci).
ski suit n tuta da sci.
skit [skɪt] n parodia; scenetta satirica.
ski tow n = **ski lift.**
skittle ['skɪtl] n birillo; ~s n (game) (gioco dei) birilli mpl.
skive [skaɪv] vi (BRIT col) fare il lavativo.
skulk [skʌlk] vi muoversi furtivamente.
skull [skʌl] n cranio, teschio.
skullcap ['skʌlkæp] n (worn by Jews) zucchetto; (worn by Pope) papalina.
skunk [skʌŋk] n moffetta.
sky [skaɪ] n cielo; **to praise sb to the skies** portare alle stelle qn.
sky-blue [skaɪ'blu:] adj azzurro(a), celeste.
sky-diving ['skaɪdaɪvɪŋ] n caduta libera, paracadutismo acrobatico.
sky-high [skaɪ'haɪ] adv (throw) molto in alto ♦ adj (col) esorbitante; **prices have gone ~** (col) i prezzi sono saliti alle stelle.
skylark ['skaɪlɑ:k] n allodola.
skylight ['skaɪlaɪt] n lucernario.
skyline ['skaɪlaɪn] n (horizon) orizzonte m; (of city) profilo.
sky marshal n agente m/f a bordo.
skyscraper ['skaɪskreɪpə*] n grattacielo.
slab [slæb] n lastra; (of wood) tavola; (of meat, cheese) pezzo.
slack [slæk] adj (loose) allentato(a); (slow) lento(a); (careless) negligente; (COMM: market) stagnante; (: demand) scarso(a); (period) morto(a) ♦ n (in rope etc) parte f non tesa; **business is ~** l'attività commerciale è scarsa; see also **slacks.**
slacken ['slækn] (also: ~ **off**) vi rallentare, diminuire ♦ vt allentare; (pressure) diminuire.
slacks [slæks] npl pantaloni mpl.
slag [slæg] n scorie fpl.
slag heap n ammasso di scorie.
slain [sleɪn] pp of **slay.**
slake [sleɪk] vt (one's thirst) spegnere.
slalom ['slɑ:ləm] n slalom m.
slam [slæm] vt (door) sbattere; (throw) scaraventare; (criticize) stroncare ♦ vi sbattere.
slammer ['slæmə*] n: **the ~** (col) la gattabuia.
slander ['slɑ:ndə*] n calunnia; (LAW) diffamazione f ♦ vt calunniare; diffamare.

slanderous ['slɑ:ndrəs] adj calunnioso(a); diffamatorio(a).
slang [slæŋ] n gergo, slang m.
slanging match ['slæŋɪŋ-] n (BRIT col) rissa verbale.
slant [slɑ:nt] n pendenza, inclinazione f; (fig) angolazione f, punto di vista.
slanted ['slɑ:ntɪd] adj tendenzioso(a).
slanting ['slɑ:ntɪŋ] adj in pendenza, inclinato(a).
slap [slæp] n manata, pacca; (on face) schiaffo ♦ vt dare una manata a; schiaffeggiare ♦ adv (directly) in pieno; **it fell ~ in the middle** cadde proprio nel mezzo.
slapdash ['slæpdæʃ] adj abborracciato(a).
slaphead ['slæphɛd] n (BRIT col) imbecille m/f.
slapstick ['slæpstɪk] n (comedy) farsa grossolana.
slap-up ['slæpʌp] adj (BRIT): **a ~ meal** un pranzo (or una cena) coi fiocchi.
slash [slæʃ] vt squarciare; (face) sfregiare; (fig: prices) ridurre drasticamente, tagliare.
slat [slæt] n (of wood) stecca.
slate [sleɪt] n ardesia ♦ vt (fig: criticize) stroncare, distruggere.
slaughter ['slɔ:tə*] n (of animals) macellazione f; (of people) strage f, massacro ♦ vt macellare; trucidare, massacrare.
slaughterhouse ['slɔ:təhaus] n macello, mattatoio.
Slav [slɑ:v] adj, n slavo(a).
slave [sleɪv] n schiavo/a ♦ vi (also: ~ **away**) lavorare come uno schiavo; **to ~ (away) at sth/at doing sth** ammazzarsi di fatica or sgobbare per qc/per fare qc.
slave driver n (col, pej) schiavista m/f.
slave labour n lavoro degli schiavi; (fig): **we're just ~ here** siamo solamente sfruttati qui dentro.
slaver ['slævə*] vi (dribble) sbavare.
slavery ['sleɪvərɪ] n schiavitù f.
Slavic ['slævɪk] adj slavo(a).
slavish ['sleɪvɪʃ] adj servile; pedissequo(a).
slavishly ['sleɪvɪʃlɪ] adv (copy) pedissequamente.
Slavonic [slə'vɔnɪk] adj slavo(a).
slay, pt **slew**, pp **slain** [sleɪ, slu:, sleɪn] vt (formal) uccidere.
sleazy ['sli:zɪ] adj trasandato(a).
sledge [slɛdʒ] n slitta.
sledgehammer ['slɛdʒhæmə*] n martello da fabbro.
sleek [sli:k] adj (hair, fur) lucido(a), lucente; (car, boat) slanciato(a), affusolato(a).

sleep [sli:p] n sonno ♦ vi (pt, pp **slept** [slɛpt]) dormire ♦ vt: **we can** ~ **4** abbiamo 4 posti letto, possiamo alloggiare 4 persone; **to have a good night's** ~ farsi una bella dormita; **to go to** ~ addormentarsi; **to** ~ **lightly** avere il sonno leggero; **to put to** ~ (patient) far addormentare; (animal: euphemistic: kill) abbattere; **to** ~ **with sb** (euphemistic: have sex) andare a letto con qn.
▶**sleep in** vi (lie late) alzarsi tardi; (oversleep) dormire fino a tardi.

sleeper ['sli:pə*] n (person) dormiente m/f; (BRIT RAIL: on track) traversina; (: train) treno di vagoni letto.

sleepily ['sli:pɪlɪ] adv con aria assonnata.

sleeping ['sli:pɪŋ] adj addormentato(a).

sleeping bag n sacco a pelo.

sleeping car n vagone m letto inv, carrozza f letto inv.

sleeping partner n (BRIT COMM) = **silent partner**.

sleeping pill n sonnifero.

sleeping sickness n malattia del sonno.

sleepless ['sli:plɪs] adj (person) insonne; **a** ~ **night** una notte in bianco.

sleeplessness ['sli:plɪsnɪs] n insonnia.

sleepover ['sli:pəuvə*] n il dormire a casa di amici, usato in riferimento a bambini.

sleepwalk ['sli:pwɔ:k] vi camminare nel sonno; (as a habit) essere sonnambulo(a).

sleepwalker ['sli:pwɔ:kə*] n sonnambulo/a.

sleepy ['sli:pɪ] adj assonnato(a), sonnolento(a); (fig) addormentato(a); **to be** or **feel** ~ avere sonno.

sleet [sli:t] n nevischio.

sleeve [sli:v] n manica; (of record) copertina.

sleeveless ['sli:vlɪs] adj (garment) senza maniche.

sleigh [sleɪ] n slitta.

sleight [slaɪt] n: ~ **of hand** gioco di destrezza.

slender ['slɛndə*] adj snello(a), sottile; (not enough) scarso(a), esiguo(a).

slept [slɛpt] pt, pp of **sleep**.

sleuth [slu:θ] n (col) segugio.

slew [slu:] vi (also: ~ **round**) girare ♦ pt of **slay**.

slice [slaɪs] n fetta ♦ vt affettare, tagliare a fette; ~**d bread** pane m a cassetta.

slick [slɪk] adj (clever) brillante; (insincere) untuoso(a), falso(a) ♦ n (also: **oil** ~) chiazza di petrolio.

slid [slɪd] pt, pp of **slide**.

slide [slaɪd] n (in playground) scivolo; (PHOT) diapositiva; (microscope ~) vetrino; (BRIT: also: **hair** ~) fermaglio (per capelli); (in

prices) caduta ♦ vb (pt, pp **slid** [slɪd]) vt far scivolare ♦ vi scivolare; **to let things** ~ (fig) lasciare andare tutto, trascurare tutto.

slide projector n proiettore m per diapositive.

slide rule n regolo calcolatore.

sliding ['slaɪdɪŋ] adj (door) scorrevole; ~ **roof** (AUT) capotte f inv.

sliding scale n scala mobile.

slight [slaɪt] adj (slim) snello(a), sottile; (frail) delicato(a), fragile; (trivial) insignificante; (small) piccolo(a) ♦ n offesa, affronto ♦ vt (offend) offendere, fare un affronto a; **the** ~**est** il minimo (or la minima); **not in the** ~**est** affatto, neppure per sogno.

slightly ['slaɪtlɪ] adv lievemente, un po'; ~ **built** esile.

slim [slɪm] adj magro(a), snello(a) ♦ vi dimagrire, fare (or seguire) una dieta dimagrante.

slime [slaɪm] n limo, melma; viscidume m.

slimming ['slɪmɪŋ] adj (diet, pills) dimagrante.

slimy ['slaɪmɪ] adj (also fig: person) viscido(a); (covered with mud) melmoso(a).

sling [slɪŋ] n (MED) benda al collo ♦ vt (pt, pp **slung** [slʌŋ]) lanciare, tirare; **to have one's arm in a** ~ avere un braccio al collo.

slink, pt, pp **slunk** [slɪŋk, slʌŋk] vi: **to** ~ **away**, ~ **off** svignarsela.

slinky ['slɪŋkɪ] adj (clothing) aderente, attillato(a).

slip [slɪp] n scivolata, scivolone m; (mistake) errore m, sbaglio; (underskirt) sottoveste f; (paper) bigliettino, talloncino ♦ vt (slide) far scivolare ♦ vi (slide) scivolare; (move smoothly): **to** ~ **into/out of** scivolare in/ via da; (decline) declinare; **to give sb the** ~ sfuggire qn; **a** ~ **of paper** un foglietto; **a** ~ **of the tongue** un lapsus linguae; **to** ~ **sth on/off** infilarsi/togliersi qc; **to let a chance** ~ **by** lasciarsi scappare un'occasione; **it** ~**ped from her hand** le sfuggì di mano.
▶**slip away** vi svignarsela.
▶**slip in** vt introdurre casualmente.
▶**slip out** vi uscire furtivamente.

slip-on ['slɪpɔn] adj (gen) comodo(a) da mettere; (shoes) senza allacciatura.

slipped disc ['slɪpt-] n spostamento delle vertebre.

slipper ['slɪpə*] n pantofola.

slippery ['slɪpərɪ] adj scivoloso(a); **it's** ~ si scivola.

slip road n (BRIT: to motorway) rampa di accesso.

slipshod ['slɪpʃɔd] adj sciatto(a), trasandato(a).

slip-up ['slɪpʌp] n granchio (fig).

slipway ['slɪpweɪ] n scalo di costruzione.

slit [slɪt] n fessura, fenditura; (cut) taglio; (tear) strappo ♦ vt (pt, pp slit) tagliare; **to ~ sb's throat** tagliare la gola a qn.

slither ['slɪðə*] vi scivolare, sdrucciolare.

sliver ['slɪvə*] n (of glass, wood) scheggia; (of cheese, sausage) fettina.

slob [slɔb] n (col) sciattone/a.

slog [slɔg] (BRIT) n faticata ♦ vi lavorare con accanimento, sgobbare.

slogan ['sləugən] n motto, slogan m inv.

slop [slɔp] vi (also: ~ **over**) traboccare; versarsi ♦ vt spandere; versare ♦ npl: ~**s** acqua sporca; sbobba.

slope [sləup] n pendio; (side of mountain) versante m; (of roof) pendenza; (of floor) inclinazione f ♦ vi: **to ~ down** declinare; **to ~ up** essere in salita.

sloping ['sləupɪŋ] adj inclinato(a).

sloppy ['slɔpɪ] adj (work) tirato(a) via; (appearance) sciatto(a); (film etc) sdolcinato(a).

slosh [slɔʃ] vi (col): **to ~ about** or **around** (person) sguazzare; (liquid) guazzare.

sloshed [slɔʃt] adj (col: drunk) sbronzo(a).

slot [slɔt] n fessura; (fig: in timetable, RADIO, TV) spazio ♦ vt: **to ~ into** introdurre in una fessura.

sloth [sləuθ] n (vice) pigrizia, accidia; (ZOOL) bradipo.

slot machine n (BRIT: vending machine) distributore m automatico; (for amusement) slot-machine f inv.

slot meter n contatore m a gettoni.

slouch [slautʃ] vi (when walking) camminare dinoccolato(a); **she was ~ed in a chair** era sprofondata in una poltrona.

►**slouch about, slouch around** vi (laze) oziare.

Slovak ['sləuvæk] adj slovacco(a) ♦ n slovacco/a; (LING) slovacco; **the ~ Republic** la Repubblica Slovacca.

Slovakia [sləu'vækɪə] n Slovacchia.

Slovakian [sləu'vækɪən] adj, n = **Slovak**.

Slovene ['sləuviːn] adj sloveno(a) ♦ n sloveno/a; (LING) sloveno.

Slovenia [sləu'viːnɪə] n Slovenia.

Slovenian [sləu'viːnɪən] adj, n = **Slovene**.

slovenly ['slʌvənlɪ] adj sciatto(a), trasandato(a).

slow [sləu] adj lento(a); (watch): **to be ~** essere indietro ♦ adv lentamente ♦ vt, vi (also: ~ **down**, ~ **up**) rallentare; "~" (road sign) "rallentare"; **at a ~ speed** a bassa velocità; **to be ~ to act/decide** essere lento ad agire/a decidere; **my watch is 20 minutes ~** il mio orologio è indietro di 20 minuti; **business is ~** (COMM) gli affari procedono a rilento; **to go ~** (driver) andare piano; (in industrial dispute) fare uno sciopero bianco.

slow-acting ['sləu'æktɪŋ] adj che agisce lentamente, ad azione lenta.

slowly ['sləulɪ] adv lentamente; **to drive ~** andare piano.

slow motion n: **in ~** al rallentatore.

slowness ['sləunɪs] n lentezza.

sludge [slʌdʒ] n fanghiglia.

slug [slʌg] n lumaca; (bullet) pallottola.

sluggish ['slʌgɪʃ] adj lento(a); (business, market, sales) stagnante, fiacco(a).

sluice [sluːs] n chiusa ♦ vt: **to ~ down** or **out** lavare (con abbondante acqua).

slum [slʌm] n catapecchia.

slumber ['slʌmbə*] n sonno.

slump [slʌmp] n crollo, caduta; (economic) depressione f, crisi f inv ♦ vi crollare; **he was ~ed over the wheel** era curvo sul volante.

slung [slʌŋ] pt, pp of **sling**.

slunk [slʌŋk] pt, pp of **slink**.

slur [sləː*] n pronuncia indistinta; (stigma) diffamazione f, calunnia; (MUS) legatura; (smear): ~ **(on)** macchia (su) ♦ vt pronunciare in modo indistinto; **to cast a ~ on sb** calunniare qn.

slurp [sləːp] vt, vi bere rumorosamente ♦ n rumore fatto bevendo.

slurred [sləːd] adj (pronunciation) inarticolato(a), disarticolato(a).

slush [slʌʃ] n neve f mista a fango.

slush fund n fondi mpl neri.

slushy ['slʌʃɪ] adj (snow) che si scioglie; (BRIT: fig) sdolcinato(a).

slut [slʌt] n donna trasandata, sciattona.

sly [slaɪ] adj furbo(a), scaltro(a); **on the ~** di soppiatto.

SM n abbr (= sadomasochism) sadomasochismo.

smack [smæk] n (slap) pacca; (on face) schiaffo ♦ vt schiaffeggiare; (child) picchiare ♦ vi: **to ~ of** puzzare di; **to ~ one's lips** fare uno schiocco con le labbra.

smacker ['smækə*] n (col: kiss) bacio; (: BRIT: pound note) sterlina; (: US: dollar bill) dollaro.

small [smɔːl] adj piccolo(a); (in height) basso(a); (letter) minuscolo(a) ♦ n: **the ~ of the back** le reni; **to get** or **grow ~er**

(*stain, town*) rimpicciolire; (*debt, organization, numbers*) ridursi; **to make ~er** (*amount, income*) ridurre; (*garden, object, garment*) rimpicciolire; **in the ~ hours** alle ore piccole; **a ~ shopkeeper** un piccolo negoziante.

small ads *npl* (*BRIT*) piccoli annunci *mpl*.

small arms *npl* armi *fpl* portatili *or* leggere.

small business *n* piccola impresa.

small change *n* moneta, spiccioli *mpl*.

smallholder ['smɔːlhəuldə*] *n* (*BRIT*) piccolo proprietario.

smallholding ['smɔːlhəuldɪŋ] *n* (*BRIT*) piccola tenuta.

smallish ['smɔːlɪʃ] *adj* piccolino(a).

small-minded [smɔːl'maɪndɪd] *adj* meschino(a).

smallpox ['smɔːlpɔks] *n* vaiolo.

small print *n* caratteri *mpl* piccoli; (*on document*) parte scritta in piccolo.

small-scale ['smɔːlskeɪl] *adj* (*map, model*) in scala ridotta; (*business, farming*) modesto(a).

small talk *n* chiacchiere *fpl*.

small-time ['smɔːltaɪm] *adj* (*col*) da poco; **a ~ thief** un ladro di polli.

small-town ['smɔːltaun] *adj* (*pej*) provinciale, di paese.

smarmy ['smɑːmɪ] *adj* (*BRIT pej*) untuoso(a), strisciante.

smart [smɑːt] *adj* elegante; (*also fig: clever*) intelligente; (*quick*) sveglio(a) ♦ *vi* bruciare; **the ~ set** il bel mondo; **to look ~** essere elegante; **my eyes are ~ing** mi bruciano gli occhi.

smartcard ['smɑːtkɑːd] *n* smartcard *f inv*, carta intelligente.

smarten up ['smɑːtn-] *vi* farsi bello(a) ♦ *vt* (*people*) fare bello(a); (*things*) abbellire.

smash [smæʃ] *n* (*also: ~-up*) scontro, collisione *f*; (*sound*) fracasso ♦ *vt* frantumare, fracassare; (*opponent*) annientare, schiacciare; (*hopes*) distruggere; (*SPORT: record*) battere ♦ *vi* frantumarsi, andare in pezzi.

▶**smash up** *vt* (*car*) sfasciare; (*room*) distruggere.

smash-hit [smæʃ'hɪt] *n* successone *m*.

smashing ['smæʃɪŋ] *adj* (*col*) favoloso(a), formidabile.

smattering ['smætərɪŋ] *n*: **a ~ of** un'infarinatura di.

smear [smɪə*] *n* macchia; (*MED*) striscio; (*insult*) calunnia ♦ *vt* ungere; (*fig*) denigrare, diffamare; **his hands were ~ed with oil/ink** aveva le mani sporche di olio/inchiostro.

smear campaign *n* campagna diffamatoria.

smear test *n* (*BRIT MED*) Pap-test *m inv*.

smell [smɛl] *n* odore *m*; (*sense*) olfatto, odorato ♦ *vb* (*pt, pp* **smelt** *or* **smelled** [smɛlt, smɛld]) *vt* sentire (l')odore di ♦ *vi* (*food etc*): **to ~** (*of*) avere odore (di); (*pej*) puzzare, avere un cattivo odore; **it ~s good** ha un buon odore.

smelly ['smɛlɪ] *adj* puzzolente.

smelt [smɛlt] *pt, pp of* **smell** ♦ *vt* (*ore*) fondere.

smile [smaɪl] *n* sorriso ♦ *vi* sorridere.

smiling ['smaɪlɪŋ] *adj* sorridente.

smirk [smɜːk] *n* sorriso furbo; sorriso compiaciuto.

smith [smɪθ] *n* fabbro.

smithy ['smɪðɪ] *n* fucina.

smitten ['smɪtn] *adj*: **~ with** colpito(a) da.

smock [smɔk] *n* grembiule *m*, camice *m*.

smog [smɔg] *n* smog *m*.

smoke [sməuk] *n* fumo ♦ *vt, vi* fumare; **to have a ~** fumarsi una sigaretta; **do you ~?** fumi?; **to go up in ~** (*house etc*) bruciare, andare distrutto dalle fiamme; (*fig*) andare in fumo.

smoked [sməukt] *adj* (*bacon, glass*) affumicato(a).

smokeless fuel ['sməuklɪs-] *n* carburante *m* che non dà fumo.

smokeless zone *n* (*BRIT*) zona dove sono vietati gli scarichi di fumo.

smoker ['sməukə*] *n* (*person*) fumatore/ trice; (*RAIL*) carrozza per fumatori.

smoke screen *n* cortina fumogena *or* di fumo; (*fig*) copertura.

smoke shop *n* (*US*) tabaccheria.

smoking ['sməukɪŋ] *n* fumo; **"no ~"** (*sign*) "vietato fumare"; **he's given up ~** ha smesso di fumare.

smoking compartment, (*US*) **smoking car** *n* carrozza (per) fumatori.

smoky ['sməukɪ] *adj* fumoso(a); (*surface*) affumicato(a).

smolder ['sməuldə*] *vi* (*US*) = **smoulder**.

smoochy ['smuːtʃɪ] *adj* (*col*) romantico(a).

smooth [smuːð] *adj* liscio(a); (*sauce*) omogeneo(a); (*flavour, whisky*) amabile; (*cigarette*) leggero(a); (*movement*) regolare; (*person*) mellifluo(a); (*landing, take-off, flight*) senza scosse ♦ *vt* lisciare, spianare; (*also: ~ out*): *difficulties*) appianare.

▶**smooth over** *vt*: **to ~ things over** (*fig*) sistemare le cose.

smoothly ['smuːðlɪ] *adv* (*easily*) liscio; **everything went ~** tutto andò liscio.

smother ['smʌðə*] *vt* soffocare.

smoulder, (*US*) **smolder** ['sməʊldə*] *vi* covare sotto la cenere.

SMS *n abbr* (= *short message service*) SMS *m* (*servizio*).

smudge [smʌdʒ] *n* macchia; sbavatura ♦ *vt* imbrattare, sporcare.

smug [smʌg] *adj* soddisfatto(a), compiaciuto(a).

smuggle ['smʌgl] *vt* contrabbandare; **to ~ in/out** (*goods etc*) far entrare/uscire di contrabbando.

smuggler ['smʌglə*] *n* contrabbandiere/a.

smuggling ['smʌglɪŋ] *n* contrabbando.

smut [smʌt] *n* (*grain of soot*) granello di fuliggine; (*mark*) segno nero; (*in conversation etc*) sconcezze *fpl.*

smutty ['smʌtɪ] *adj* (*fig*) osceno(a), indecente.

snack [snæk] *n* spuntino; **to have a ~** fare uno spuntino.

snack bar *n* tavola calda, snack bar *m inv.*

snag [snæg] *n* intoppo, ostacolo imprevisto.

snail [sneɪl] *n* chiocciola.

snake [sneɪk] *n* serpente *m.*

snap [snæp] *n* (*sound*) schianto, colpo secco; (*photograph*) istantanea; (*game*) rubamazzo ♦ *adj* improvviso(a) ♦ *vt* (far) schioccare; (*break*) spezzare di netto; (*photograph*) scattare un'istantanea di ♦ *vi* spezzarsi con un rumore secco; (*fig: person*) crollare; **to ~ at sb** rivolgersi a qn con tono brusco; (*subj: dog*) cercare di mordere qn; **to ~ open/shut** aprirsi/chiudersi di scatto; **to ~ one's fingers at** (*fig*) infischiarsi di; **a cold ~** (*of weather*) un'improvvisa ondata di freddo.

►**snap off** *vt* (*break*) schiantare.

►**snap up** *vt* afferrare.

snap fastener *n* bottone *m* automatico.

snappy ['snæpɪ] *adj* rapido(a); **make it ~!** (*col: hurry up*) sbrigati!, svelto!

snapshot ['snæpʃɔt] *n* istantanea.

snare [snɛə*] *n* trappola.

snarl [snɑːl] *vi* ringhiare ♦ *vt:* **to get ~ed up** (*wool, plans*) ingarbugliarsi; (*traffic*) intasarsi.

snatch [snætʃ] *n* (*fig*) furto; (*BRIT: small amount*): **~es** of frammenti *mpl* di ♦ *vt* strappare (con violenza); (*steal*) rubare ♦ *vi:* **don't ~!** non strappare le cose di mano!; **to ~ a sandwich** mangiarsi in fretta un panino; **to ~ some sleep** riuscire a dormire un po'.

►**snatch up** *vt* raccogliere in fretta.

snazzy ['snæzi] *adj* (*col: clothes*) sciccoso(a).

sneak [sniːk] *vi:* **to ~ in/out** entrare/uscire di nascosto ♦ *vt:* **to ~ a look at sth** guardare di sottecchi qc.

sneakers ['sniːkəz] *npl* scarpe *fpl* da ginnastica.

sneaking ['sniːkɪŋ] *adj:* **to have a ~ feeling/suspicion that ...** avere la vaga impressione/il vago sospetto che ....

sneaky ['sniːkɪ] *adj* falso(a), disonesto(a).

sneer [snɪə*] *n* ghigno, sogghigno ♦ *vi* ghignare, sogghignare; **to ~ at sb/sth** farsi beffe di qn/qc.

sneeze [sniːz] *n* starnuto ♦ *vi* starnutire.

snide [snaɪd] *adj* maligno(a).

sniff [snɪf] *n* fiutata, annusata ♦ *vi* fiutare, annusare; tirare su col naso; (*in contempt*) arricciare il naso ♦ *vt* fiutare, annusare; (*glue, drug*) sniffare.

►**sniff at** *vt fus:* **it's not to be ~ed at** non è da disprezzare.

sniffer dog ['snɪfə-] *n* cane *m* poliziotto (*per stupefacenti o esplosivi*).

snigger ['snɪgə*] *n* riso represso ♦ *vi* ridacchiare, ridere sotto i baffi.

snip [snɪp] *n* pezzetto; (*bargain*) (buon) affare *m*, occasione *f* ♦ *vt* tagliare.

sniper ['snaɪpə*] *n* franco tiratore *m*, cecchino.

snippet ['snɪpɪt] *n* frammento.

snivelling ['snɪvlɪŋ] *adj* piagnucoloso(a).

snob [snɔb] *n* snob *m/f inv.*

snobbery ['snɔbərɪ] *n* snobismo.

snobbish ['snɔbɪʃ] *adj* snob *inv.*

snog [snɔg] *vi* (*col*) pomiciare.

snooker ['snuːkə*] *n* tipo di gioco del biliardo.

snoop [snuːp] *vi:* **to ~ on sb** spiare qn; **to ~ about** curiosare.

snooper ['snuːpə*] *n* ficcanaso *m/f.*

snooty ['snuːtɪ] *adj* borioso(a), snob *inv.*

snooze [snuːz] *n* sonnellino, pisolino ♦ *vi* fare un sonnellino.

snore [snɔː*] *vi* russare.

snoring ['snɔːrɪŋ] *n* russare *m.*

snorkel ['snɔːkl] *n* (*of swimmer*) respiratore *m* a tubo.

snort [snɔːt] *n* sbuffo ♦ *vi* sbuffare ♦ *vt* (*drugs slang*) sniffare.

snotty ['snɔtɪ] *adj* moccioso(a).

snout [snaut] *n* muso.

snow [snəʊ] *n* neve *f* ♦ *vi* nevicare ♦ *vt:* **to be ~ed under with work** essere sommerso di lavoro.

snowball ['snəʊbɔːl] *n* palla di neve.

snowbound ['snəʊbaund] *adj* bloccato(a) dalla neve.

snow-capped ['snəʊkæpt] *adj* (*mountain*) con la cima coperta di neve; (*peak*) coperto(a) di neve.

snowdrift ['snəʊdrɪft] *n* cumulo di neve (*ammucchiato dal vento*).

snowdrop ['snəudrɔp] n bucaneve m inv.
snowfall ['snəufɔ:l] n nevicata.
snowflake ['snəufleɪk] n fiocco di neve.
snowman ['snəumæn] n pupazzo di neve.
snowplough, (US) **snowplow** ['snəuplau] n spazzaneve m inv.
snowshoe ['snəuʃu:] n racchetta da neve.
snowstorm ['snəustɔ:m] n tormenta.
snowy ['snəuɪ] adj nevoso(a).
SNP n abbr (BRIT POL) = Scottish National Party.
snub [snʌb] vt snobbare ♦ n offesa, affronto.
snub-nosed [snʌb'nəuzd] adj dal naso camuso.
snuff [snʌf] n tabacco da fiuto ♦ vt (also: ~ out: candle) spegnere.
snuff movie n (col) film porno dove una persona viene uccisa realmente.
snug [snʌg] adj comodo(a); (room, house), accogliente, comodo(a); **it's a ~ fit** è attillato.
snuggle ['snʌgl] vi: **to ~ down in bed** accovacciarsi a letto; **to ~ up to sb** stringersi a qn.
snugly ['snʌglɪ] adv comodamente; **it fits ~** (object in pocket etc) entra giusto giusto; (garment) sta ben attillato.
SO abbr (BANKING) = **standing order.**

=================== KEYWORD

so [səu] adv **1** (thus, likewise) così; **if ~ se** è così, quand'è così; **I didn't do it — you did ~!** non l'ho fatto io — sì che l'hai fatto!; **~ do I, ~ am I** anch'io; **it's 5 o'clock — ~ it is!** sono le 5 — davvero!; **I hope ~** lo spero; **I think ~** penso di sì; **quite ~!** esattamente!; **even ~** comunque; **~ far** finora, fin qui; (in past) fino ad allora
2 (in comparisons etc: to such a degree) così; **~ big (that)** così grande (che); **she's not ~ clever as her brother** lei non è (così) intelligente come suo fratello
3: **~ much** adj tanto(u) ♦ adv tanto; **I've got ~ much work/money** ho tanto lavoro/ tanti soldi; **I love you ~ much** ti amo tanto; **~ many** tanti(e)
4 (phrases): **10 or ~** circa 10; **~ long!** (col: goodbye) ciao!, ci vediamo!; **~ to speak** per così dire; **~ what?** (col) e allora?, e con questo?

♦ conj **1** (expressing purpose): **~ as to do in** modo or così da fare; **we hurried ~ as not to be late** ci affrettammo per non fare tardi; **~ (that)** affinché + sub, perché + sub
2 (expressing result): **he didn't arrive ~ I left** non è venuto così me ne sono andata; **~ you see, I could have gone** vedi, sarei potuto

andare; **~ that's the reason!** allora è questo il motivo!, ecco perché!

soak [səuk] vt inzuppare; (clothes) mettere a mollo ♦ vi inzupparsi; (clothes) essere a mollo; **to be ~ed through** essere fradicio.
►**soak in** vi penetrare.
►**soak up** vt assorbire.
soaking ['səukɪŋ] adj (also: ~ **wet**) fradicio(a).
so-and-so ['səuənsəu] n (somebody) un tale; **Mr/Mrs ~** signor/signora tal dei tali.
soap [səup] n sapone m.
soapbox ['səupbɔks] n palco improvvisato (per orazioni pubbliche).
soapflakes ['səupfleɪks] npl sapone m in scaglie.
soap opera n soap opera f inv.
soap powder n detersivo.
soapsuds ['səupsʌdz] npl saponata.
soapy ['səupɪ] adj insaponato(a).
soar [sɔ:*] vi volare in alto; (price, morale, spirits) salire alle stelle.
sob [sɔb] n singhiozzo ♦ vi singhiozzare.
s.o.b. n abbr (US col!: = son of a bitch) figlio di puttana (!).
sober ['səubə*] adj non ubriaco(a); (sedate) serio(a); (moderate) moderato(a); (colour, style) sobrio(a).
►**sober up** vt far passare la sbornia a ♦ vi farsi passare la sbornia.
sobriety [səu'braɪətɪ] n (not being drunk) sobrietà; (seriousness, sedateness) sobrietà, pacatezza.
sob story n (col, pej) storia lacrimosa.
Soc. abbr (= society) Soc.
so-called ['səu'kɔ:ld] adj cosiddetto(a).
soccer ['sɔkə*] n calcio.
soccer pitch n campo di calcio.
soccer player n calciatore m.
sociable ['səuʃəbl] adj socievole.
social ['səuʃl] adj sociale ♦ n festa, serata.
social climber n arrampicatore/trice sociale, arrivista m/f.
social club n club m inv sociale.
Social Democrat n socialdemocratico/a.
social insurance n (US) assicurazione f sociale.
socialism ['səuʃəlɪzəm] n socialismo.
socialist ['səuʃəlɪst] adj, n socialista (m/f).
socialite ['səuʃəlaɪt] n persona in vista nel bel mondo.
socialize ['səuʃəlaɪz] vi frequentare gente; farsi degli amici; **to ~ with** socializzare con.
social life n vita sociale.
socially ['səuʃəlɪ] adv socialmente, in società.

social science n scienze fpl sociali.
social security n previdenza sociale;
Department of S~ S~ (DSS) (BRIT) ≈
Istituto di Previdenza Sociale.
social services npl servizi mpl sociali.
social welfare n assistenza sociale.
social work n servizio sociale.
social worker n assistente m/f sociale.
society [sə'saɪətɪ] n società f inv; (club)
società, associazione f; (also: **high** ~) alta
società ♦ cpd (party, column) mondano(a).
socioeconomic ['səusɪəuiːkə'nɔmɪk] adj
socio-economico(a).
sociological [səusɪə'lɔdʒɪkl] adj
sociologico(a).
sociologist [səusɪ'ɔlədʒɪst] n sociologo/a.
sociology [səusɪ'ɔlədʒɪ] n sociologia.
sock [sɔk] n calzino ♦ vt (hit) dare un pugno
a; **to pull one's ~s up** (fig) darsi una
regolata.
socket ['sɔkɪt] n cavità f inv; (of eye) orbita;
(ELEC: also: **wall** ~) presa di corrente;
(: for light bulb) portalampada m inv.
sod [sɔd] n (of earth) zolla erbosa; (BRIT col!)
bastardo/a (!).
▶**sod off** vi: ~ **off!** (BRIT col!) levati dalle
palle! (!).
soda ['səudə] n (CHEM) soda; (also: ~ **water**)
acqua di seltz; (US: also: ~ **pop**) gassosa.
sodden ['sɔdn] adj fradicio(a).
sodium ['səudɪəm] n sodio.
sodium chloride n cloruro di sodio.
sofa ['səufə] n sofà m inv.
Sofia ['səufɪə] n Sofia.
soft [sɔft] adj (not rough) morbido(a); (not
hard) soffice; (not loud) sommesso(a);
(kind) gentile; (: look, smile) dolce; (not
strict) indulgente; (weak) debole; (stupid)
stupido(a).
soft-boiled ['sɔftbɔɪld] adj (egg) alla coque.
soft drink n analcolico.
soft drugs npl droghe fpl leggere.
soften ['sɔfn] vt ammorbidire; addolcire;
attenuare ♦ vi ammorbidirsi; addolcirsi;
attenuarsi.
softener ['sɔfnə*] n ammorbidente m.
soft fruit n (BRIT) ≈ frutti di bosco.
soft furnishings npl tessuti mpl d'arredo.
soft-hearted [sɔft'hɑːtɪd] adj sensibile.
softly ['sɔftlɪ] adv dolcemente;
morbidamente.
softness ['sɔftnɪs] n dolcezza; morbidezza.
soft option n soluzione f (più) facile.
soft sell n persuasione f all'acquisto.
soft target n obiettivo civile (e quindi facile
da colpire).
soft touch n (col): **to be a** ~ lasciarsi
spillare facilmente denaro.

soft toy n giocattolo di peluche.
software ['sɔftweə*] n software m.
software package n pacchetto di
software.
soft water n acqua non calcarea.
soggy ['sɔgɪ] adj inzuppato(a).
soil [sɔɪl] n (earth) terreno, suolo ♦ vt
sporcare; (fig) macchiare.
soiled [sɔɪld] adj sporco(a), sudicio(a).
sojourn ['sɔdʒəːn] n (formal) soggiorno.
solace ['sɔlɪs] n consolazione f.
solar ['səulə*] adj solare.
solarium, pl **solaria** [sə'lɛərɪəm, -rɪə] n
solarium m inv.
solar plexus [-'plɛksəs] n (ANAT) plesso
solare.
solar power n energia solare.
sold [səuld] pt, pp of **sell**.
solder ['səuldə*] vt saldare ♦ n saldatura.
soldier ['səuldʒə*] n soldato, militare m ♦ vi:
to ~ **on** perseverare; **toy** ~ soldatino.
sold out adj (COMM) esaurito(a).
sole [səul] n (of foot) pianta (del piede); (of
shoe) suola; (fish: pl inv) sogliola ♦ adj
solo(a), unico(a); (exclusive) esclusivo(a).
solely ['səullɪ] adv solamente, unicamente; **I
will hold you** ~ **responsible** la
considererò il solo responsabile.
solemn ['sɔləm] adj solenne; grave;
serio(a).
sole trader n (COMM) commerciante m in
proprio.
solicit [sə'lɪsɪt] vt (request) richiedere,
sollecitare ♦ vi (prostitute) adescare i
passanti.
solicitor [sə'lɪsɪtə*] n (BRIT: for wills etc) ≈
notaio; (in court) ≈ avvocato; see boxed note.

solid ['sɔlɪd] adj (not hollow) pieno(a);
(strong, reliable, not liquid) solido(a); (meal)
sostanzioso(a); (line) ininterrotto(a); (vote)
unanime ♦ n solido; **to be on** ~ **ground**
essere su terraferma; (fig) muoversi su
terreno sicuro; **we waited 2** ~ **hours**
abbiamo aspettato due ore buone.
solidarity [sɔlɪ'dærɪtɪ] n solidarietà.

solid fuel n combustibile m solido.
solidify [sə'lɪdɪfaɪ] vi solidificarsi ♦ vt solidificare.
solidity [sə'lɪdɪtɪ] n solidità.
solid-state ['sɒlɪdsteɪt] adj (ELEC) a transistor.
soliloquy [sə'lɪləkwɪ] n soliloquio.
solitaire [sɒlɪ'tɛə*] n (game, gem) solitario.
solitary ['sɒlɪtərɪ] adj solitario(a).
solitary confinement n (LAW): **to be in** ~ essere in cella d'isolamento.
solitude ['sɒlɪtjuːd] n solitudine f.
solo ['səʊləʊ] n (MUS) assolo.
soloist ['səʊləʊɪst] n solista m/f.
Solomon Islands ['sɒləmən-] n: **the** ~ le isole Salomone.
solstice ['sɒlstɪs] n solstizio.
soluble ['sɒljʊbl] adj solubile.
solution [sə'luːʃən] n soluzione f.
solve [sɒlv] vt risolvere.
solvency ['sɒlvənsɪ] n (COMM) solvenza, solvibilità.
solvent ['sɒlvənt] adj (COMM) solvibile ♦ n (CHEM) solvente m.
solvent abuse n abuso di colle e solventi.
Somali [sə'mɑːlɪ] adj somalo(a).
Somalia [sə'mɑːlɪə] n Somalia.
Somaliland [səʊ'mɑːlɪlænd] n paesi mpl del corno d'Africa.
sombre, (US) **somber** ['sɒmbə*] adj scuro(a); (mood, person) triste.

━━━━━━━━━━━━━ KEYWORD

some [sʌm] adj **1** (a certain amount or number of): ~ **tea/water/cream** del tè/dell'acqua/della panna; **there's** ~ **milk in the fridge** c'è (del) latte nel frigo; ~ **children/apples** dei bambini/delle mele; **after** ~ **time** dopo un po'; **at** ~ **length** a lungo
2 (certain: in contrasts) certo(a); ~ **people say that** ... alcuni dicono che ..., certa gente dice che ...
3 (unspecified) un(a) certo(a), qualche; ~ **woman was asking for you** una tale chiedeva di lei; ~ **day** un giorno; ~ **day next week** un giorno della prossima settimana; **in** ~ **form or other** in una forma o nell'altra
♦ pron **1** (a certain number) alcuni(e), certi(e); **I've got** ~ (books etc) ne ho alcuni; ~ (**of them**) **have been sold** alcuni sono stati venduti
2 (a certain amount) un po'; **I've got** ~ (money, milk) ne ho un po'; **I've read** ~ **of the book** ho letto parte del libro; ~ (**of it**)

was left ne è rimasto un po'; **could I have** ~ **of that cheese?** potrei avere un po' di quel formaggio?
♦ adv: ~ **10 people** circa 10 persone.

somebody ['sʌmbədɪ] pron qualcuno; ~ **or other** qualcuno.
someday ['sʌmdeɪ] adv uno di questi giorni, un giorno o l'altro.
somehow ['sʌmhaʊ] adv in un modo o nell'altro, in qualche modo; (for some reason) per qualche ragione.
someone ['sʌmwʌn] pron = **somebody**.
someplace ['sʌmpleɪs] adv (US) = **somewhere**.
somersault ['sʌməsɔːlt] n capriola; (in air) salto mortale ♦ vi fare una capriola (or un salto mortale); (car) cappottare.
something ['sʌmθɪŋ] pron qualcosa; ~ **interesting** qualcosa di interessante; ~ **to do** qualcosa da fare; **he's** ~ **like me** mi assomiglia un po'; **it's** ~ **of a problem** è un bel problema.
sometime ['sʌmtaɪm] adv (in future) una volta o l'altra; (in past): ~ **last month** durante il mese scorso; **I'll finish it** ~ lo finirò prima o poi.
sometimes ['sʌmtaɪmz] adv qualche volta.
somewhat ['sʌmwɒt] adv piuttosto.
somewhere ['sʌmwɛə*] adv in or da qualche parte; ~ **else** da qualche altra parte.
son [sʌn] n figlio.
sonar ['səʊnɑː*] n sonar m.
sonata [sə'nɑːtə] n sonata.
song [sɒŋ] n canzone f.
songbook ['sɒŋbʊk] n canzoniere m.
songwriter ['sɒŋraɪtə*] n compositore/trice di canzoni.
sonic ['sɒnɪk] adj (boom) sonico(a).
son-in-law ['sʌnɪnlɔː] n genero.
sonnet ['sɒnɪt] n sonetto.
sonny ['sʌnɪ] n (col) ragazzo mio.
soon [suːn] adv presto, fra poco; (early) presto; ~ **afterwards** poco dopo; **very/quite** ~ molto/abbastanza presto; **as** ~ **as possible** prima possibile; **I'll do it as** ~ **as I can** lo farò appena posso; **how** ~ **can you be ready?** fra quanto tempo sarà pronto?; **see you** ~! a presto!
sooner ['suːnə*] adv (time) prima; (preference): **I would** ~ **do** preferirei fare; ~ **or later** prima o poi; **no** ~ **said than done** detto fatto; **the** ~ **the better** prima è meglio è; **no** ~ **had we left than** ... eravamo appena partiti, quando ....
soot [sʊt] n fuliggine f.
soothe [suːð] vt calmare.

soothing ['su:ðɪŋ] adj (ointment etc) calmante; (tone, words etc) rassicurante.

SOP n abbr = standard operating procedure.

sop [sɔp] n: that's only a ~ è soltanto un contentino.

sophisticated [sə'fɪstɪkeɪtɪd] adj sofisticato(a); raffinato(a); (film, mind) sottile.

sophistication [səfɪstɪ'keɪʃən] n raffinatezza; (of machine) complessità; (of argument etc) sottigliezza.

sophomore ['sɔfəmɔ:*] n (US) studente/ essa del secondo anno.

soporific [sɔpə'rɪfɪk] adj soporifero(a).

sopping ['sɔpɪŋ] adj (also: ~ wet) bagnato(a) fradicio(a).

soppy ['sɔpɪ] adj (pej) sentimentale.

soprano [sə'prɑ:nəu] n (voice) soprano m; (singer) soprano m/f.

sorbet ['sɔ:beɪ] n sorbetto.

sorcerer ['sɔ:sərə*] n stregone m, mago.

sordid ['sɔ:dɪd] adj sordido(a).

sore [sɔ:*] adj (painful) dolorante; (col: offended) offeso(a) ♦ n piaga; my eyes are ~, I have ~ eyes mi fanno male gli occhi; ~ throat mal m di gola; it's a ~ point (fig) è un punto delicato.

sorely ['sɔ:lɪ] adv (tempted) fortemente.

sorrel ['sɔrəl] n acetosa.

sorrow ['sɔrəu] n dolore m.

sorrowful ['sɔrəuful] adj triste.

sorry ['sɔrɪ] adj spiacente; (condition, excuse) misero(a), pietoso(a); (sight, failure) triste; ~! scusa! (or scusi! or scusate!); to feel ~ for sb rincrescersi per qn; I'm ~ to hear that ... mi dispiace (sentire) che ...; to be ~ about sth essere dispiaciuto or spiacente di qc.

sort [sɔ:t] n specie f, genere m; (make: of coffee, car etc) tipo ♦ vt (also: ~ out: papers) classificare; ordinare; (: letters etc) smistare; (: problems) risolvere; (COMPUT) ordinare; what ~ of car? che tipo di macchina?; I shall do nothing of the ~! nemmeno per sogno!; it's ~ of awkward (col) è piuttosto difficile.

sortie ['sɔ:tɪ] n sortita.

sorting office ['sɔ:tɪŋ-] n ufficio m smistamento inv.

SOS n abbr S.O.S. m inv.

so-so ['səusəu] adv così così.

soufflé ['su:fleɪ] n soufflé m inv.

sought [sɔ:t] pt, pp of seek.

sought-after ['sɔ:tɑ:ftə*] adj richiesto(a).

soul [səul] n anima; the poor ~ had nowhere to sleep il poveraccio non aveva dove dormire; I didn't see a ~ non ho visto anima viva.

soul-destroying ['səuldɪ'strɔɪɪŋ] adj demoralizzante.

soulful ['səulful] adj pieno(a) di sentimento.

soulless ['səullɪs] adj senz'anima, inumano(a).

soul mate n anima gemella.

soul-searching ['səulsə:tʃɪŋ] n: after much ~ dopo un profondo esame di coscienza.

sound [saund] adj (healthy) sano(a); (safe, not damaged) solido(a), in buono stato; (reliable, not superficial) solido(a); (sensible) giudizioso(a), di buon senso; (valid: argument, policy, claim) valido(a) ♦ adv: ~ asleep profondamente addormentato ♦ n (noise) suono; rumore m; (GEO) stretto ♦ vt (alarm) suonare; (also: ~ out: opinions) sondare ♦ vi suonare; (fig: seem) sembrare; to be of ~ mind essere sano di mente; I don't like the ~ of it (fig: of film etc) non mi dice niente; (: of news) è preoccupante; it ~s as if ... ho l'impressione che ...; it ~s like French somiglia al francese; that ~s like them arriving mi sembra di sentirli arrivare.

▶**sound off** vi (col): to ~ off (about) (give one's opinions) fare dei grandi discorsi (su).

sound barrier n muro del suono.

soundbite ['saundbaɪt] n frase f incisiva.

sound effects npl effetti mpl sonori.

sound engineer n tecnico del suono.

sounding ['saundɪŋ] n (NAUT etc) scandagliamento.

sounding board n (MUS) cassa di risonanza; (fig): to use sb as a ~ for one's ideas provare le proprie idee su qn.

soundly ['saundlɪ] adv (sleep) profondamente; (beat) duramente.

soundproof ['saundpru:f] vt insonorizzare, isolare acusticamente ♦ adj insonorizzato(a), isolato(a) acusticamente.

sound system n impianto m audio inv.

soundtrack ['saundtræk] n (of film) colonna sonora.

soup [su:p] n minestra; (clear) brodo; (thick) zuppa; in the ~ (fig) nei guai.

soup course n minestra.

soup kitchen n mensa per i poveri.

soup plate n piatto fondo.

soupspoon ['su:pspu:n] n cucchiaio da minestra.

sour ['sauə*] adj aspro(a); (fruit) acerbo(a); (milk) acido(a), fermentato(a); (fig) acido(a); to go or turn ~ (milk, wine) inacidirsi; (fig: relationship, plans) guastarsi; it's ~ grapes (fig) è soltanto invidia.

source [sɔːs] n fonte f, sorgente f; (fig) fonte; **I have it from a reliable ~ that ... ho** saputo da fonte sicura che ....

south [sauθ] n sud m, meridione m, mezzogiorno ♦ adj del sud, sud inv, meridionale ♦ adv verso sud; **(to the)** ~ **of** a sud di; **the S~ of France** il sud della Francia; **to travel** ~ viaggiare verso sud.

South Africa n Sudafrica m.

South African adj, n sudafricano(a).

South America n Sudamerica m, America del sud.

South American adj, n sudamericano(a).

southbound ['sauθbaund] adj (gen) diretto(a) a sud; (carriageway) sud inv.

south-east [sauθ'iːst] n sud-est m.

South-East Asia n Asia sudorientale.

southerly ['sʌðəlɪ] adj del sud.

southern ['sʌðən] adj del sud, meridionale; (wall) esposto(a) a sud; **the** ~ **hemisphere** l'emisfero australe.

South Pole n Polo Sud.

South Sea Islands npl: **the** ~ le isole dei Mari del Sud.

South Seas npl: **the** ~ i Mari del Sud.

South Vietnam n Vietnam m del Sud.

southward(s) ['sauθwəd(z)] adv verso sud.

south-west [sauθ'west] n sud-ovest m.

souvenir [suːvə'nɪə*] n ricordo, souvenir m inv.

sovereign ['sɔvrɪn] adj, n sovrano(a).

sovereignty ['sɔvrəntɪ] n sovranità.

soviet ['səuvɪət] adj sovietico(a).

Soviet Union n: **the** ~ l'Unione f Sovietica.

sow n [sau] scrofa ♦ vt [səu] (pt ~ed, pp sown [səun]) seminare.

soya ['sɔɪə], (US) **soy** [sɔɪ] n: ~ **bean** seme m di soia; ~ **sauce** salsa di soia.

sozzled ['sɔzld] adj (BRIT col) sbronzo(a).

spa [spaː] n (resort) stazione f termale; (US: also: **health** ~) centro di cure estetiche.

space [speɪs] n spazio; (room) posto; spazio; (length of time) intervallo ♦ cpd spaziale ♦ vt (also: ~ **out**) distanziare; **in a confined** ~ in un luogo chiuso; **to clear a** ~ **for sth** fare posto per qc; **in a short** ~ **of time** in breve tempo; **(with)in the** ~ **of an hour/ three generations** nell'arco di un'ora/di tre generazioni.

space bar n (on typewriter) barra spaziatrice.

spacecraft ['speɪskraːft] n (pl inv) veicolo spaziale.

spaceman ['speɪsmæn] n astronauta m, cosmonauta m.

spaceship ['speɪsʃɪp] n astronave f, navicella spaziale.

space shuttle n shuttle m inv.

spacesuit ['speɪssuːt] n tuta spaziale.

spacewoman ['speɪswumən] n astronauta f, cosmonauta f.

spacing ['speɪsɪŋ] n spaziatura; **single/ double** ~ (TYP etc) spaziatura singola/ doppia.

spacious ['speɪʃəs] adj spazioso(a), ampio(a).

spade [speɪd] n (tool) vanga; pala; (child's) paletta; ~**s** npl (CARDS) picche fpl.

spadework ['speɪdwəːk] n (fig) duro lavoro preparatorio.

spaghetti [spə'ɡetɪ] n spaghetti mpl.

Spain [speɪn] n Spagna.

spam [spæm] n (COMPUT) spamming m ♦ vt: **to** ~ **sb** inviare a qn messaggi pubblicitari non richiesti via email.

span [spæn] n (of bird, plane) apertura alare; (of arch) campata; (in time) periodo; durata ♦ vt attraversare; (fig) abbracciare.

Spaniard ['spænjəd] n spagnolo/a.

spaniel ['spænjəl] n spaniel m inv.

Spanish ['spænɪʃ] adj spagnolo(a) ♦ n (LING) spagnolo; **the** ~ npl gli Spagnoli; ~ **omelette** frittata di cipolle, pomodori e peperoni.

spank [spæŋk] vt sculacciare.

spanner ['spænə*] n (BRIT) chiave f inglese.

spar [spaː*] n asta, palo ♦ vi (BOXING) allenarsi.

spare [spɛə*] adj di riserva, di scorta; (surplus) in più, d'avanzo ♦ n (part) pezzo di ricambio ♦ vt (do without) fare a meno di; (afford to give) concedere; (refrain from hurting, using) risparmiare; **to** ~ (surplus) d'avanzo; **there are 2 going** ~ (BRIT) ce ne sono 2 in più; **to** ~ **no expense** non badare a spese; **can you** ~ **the time?** ha tempo?; **I've a few minutes to** ~ ho un attimino di tempo; **there is no time to** ~ non c'è tempo da perdere; **can you** ~ **(me) £10?** puoi prestarmi 10 sterline?

spare part n pezzo di ricambio.

spare room n stanza degli ospiti.

spare time n tempo libero.

spare tyre n (AUT) gomma di scorta.

spare wheel n (AUT) ruota di scorta.

sparing ['spɛərɪŋ] adj (amount) scarso(a); (use) parsimonioso(a); **to be** ~ **with** essere avaro(a) di.

sparingly ['spɛərɪŋlɪ] adv moderatamente.

spark [spaːk] n scintilla.

spark(ing) plug ['spaːk(ɪŋ)-] n candela.

sparkle ['spaːkl] n scintillio, sfavillio ♦ vi scintillare, sfavillare; (bubble) spumeggiare, frizzare.

sparkler ['spaːklə*] n fuoco d'artificio.

sparkling ['spɑːklɪŋ] *adj* scintillante, sfavillante; (*wine*) spumante.

sparring partner ['spɑːrɪŋ-] *n* sparring partner *m inv*; (*fig*) interlocutore abituale in discussioni, dibattiti, tavole rotonde ecc.

sparrow ['spærəu] *n* passero.

sparse [spɑːs] *adj* sparso(a), rado(a).

spartan ['spɑːtən] *adj* (*fig*) spartano(a).

spasm ['spæzəm] *n* (*MED*) spasmo; (*fig*) accesso, attacco.

spasmodic [spæz'mɔdɪk] *adj* spasmodico(a); (*fig*) intermittente.

spastic ['spæstɪk] *n* spastico/a.

spat [spæt] *pt, pp of* **spit** ♦ *n* (*US*) battibecco.

spate [speɪt] *n* (*fig*): ~ **of** diluvio *or* fiume *m* di; **in** ~ (*river*) in piena.

spatial ['speɪʃəl] *adj* spaziale.

spatter ['spætə*] *vt, vi* schizzare.

spatula ['spætjulə] *n* spatola.

spawn [spɔːn] *vt* deporre; (*pej*) produrre ♦ *vi* deporre le uova ♦ *n* uova *fpl.*

SPCA *n abbr* (*US*: = *Society for the Prevention of Cruelty to Animals*) ≈ E.N.P.A. *m* (= *Ente Nazionale per la Protezione degli Animali*).

SPCC *n abbr* (*US*) = *Society for the Prevention of Cruelty to Children.*

speak, ** *pt* **spoke, ** *pp* **spoken [spiːk, spəuk, 'spəukn] *vt* (*language*) parlare; (*truth*) dire ♦ *vi* parlare; **to** ~ **to sb/of** *or* **about sth** parlare a qn/di qc; ~ **up!** parli più forte!; **to** ~ **at a conference/in a debate** partecipare ad una conferenza/ad un dibattito; ~**ing!** (*on telephone*) sono io!; **to** ~ **one's mind** dire quello che si pensa; **he has no money to** ~ **of** non si può proprio dire che sia ricco.

▶**speak for** *vt fus*: **to** ~ **for sb** parlare a nome di qn; **that picture is already spoken for** (*in shop*) quel quadro è già stato venduto.

speaker ['spiːkə*] *n* (*in public*) oratore/trice; (*also*: **loud**~) altoparlante *m*; (*POL*): **the S**~ *il presidente della Camera dei Comuni* (*BRIT*) *or dei Rappresentanti* (*US*); **are you a Welsh** ~? parla gallese?

speaking ['spiːkɪŋ] *adj* parlante; **Italian-**~ **people** persone che parlano italiano; **to be on** ~ **terms** parlarsi.

spear [spɪə*] *n* lancia.

spearhead ['spɪəhed] *n* punta di lancia; (*MIL*) reparto d'assalto ♦ *vt* (*attack etc*) condurre.

spearmint ['spɪəmɪnt] *n* (*BOT etc*) menta verde.

spec [spek] *n* (*BRIT col*): **on** ~ sperando bene; **to buy sth on** ~ comprare qc sperando di fare un affare.

special ['speʃl] *adj* speciale ♦ *n* (*train*) treno supplementare; **nothing** ~ niente di speciale; **take** ~ **care** siate particolarmente prudenti.

special agent *n* agente *m* segreto.

special correspondent *n* inviato speciale.

special delivery *n* (*POST*): **by** ~ per espresso.

special effects *npl* (*CINE*) effetti *mpl* speciali.

specialist ['speʃəlɪst] *n* specialista *m/f*; **a heart** ~ (*MED*) un cardiologo.

speciality [speʃɪ'ælɪtɪ], (*esp US*) **specialty** *n* specialità *f inv*.

specialize ['speʃəlaɪz] *vi*: **to** ~ (**in**) specializzarsi (in).

specially ['speʃəlɪ] *adv* specialmente, particolarmente.

special offer *n* (*COMM*) offerta speciale.

specialty ['speʃəltɪ] *n* (*esp US*) = **speciality.**

species ['spiːʃiːz] *n* (*pl inv*) specie *f inv.*

specific [spə'sɪfɪk] *adj* specifico(a); preciso(a); **to be** ~ **to** avere un legame specifico con.

specifically [spə'sɪfɪklɪ] *adv* (*explicitly: state, warn*) chiaramente, esplicitamente; (*especially: design, intend*) appositamente.

specification [spesɪfɪ'keɪʃən] *n* specificazione *f*; ~**s** *npl* (*of car, machine*) dati *mpl* caratteristici; (*for building*) dettagli *mpl.*

specify ['spesɪfaɪ] *vt* specificare, precisare; **unless otherwise specified** salvo indicazioni contrarie.

specimen ['spesɪmən] *n* esemplare *m*, modello; (*MED*) campione *m.*

specimen copy *n* campione *m.*

specimen signature *n* firma depositata.

speck [spek] *n* puntino, macchiolina; (*particle*) granello.

speckled ['spekld] *adj* macchiettato(a).

specs [speks] *npl* (*col*) occhiali *mpl.*

spectacle ['spektəkl] *n* spettacolo; *see also* **spectacles.**

spectacle case *n* (*BRIT*) fodero per gli occhiali.

spectacles ['spektəklz] *npl* (*BRIT*) occhiali *mpl.*

spectacular [spek'tækjulə*] *adj* spettacolare ♦ *n* (*CINE etc*) film *m inv etc* spettacolare.

spectator [spek'teɪtə*] *n* spettatore/trice.

spectator sport *n* sport *m inv* come spettacolo.

spectra ['spektrə] *npl of* **spectrum.**

spectre, ** (*US*) **specter ['spektə*] *n* spettro.

spectrum, ** *pl* **spectra ['spektrəm, -rə] *n* spettro; (*fig*) gamma.

speculate ['spɛkjuleɪt] vi speculare; (try to guess): **to** ~ **about** fare ipotesi su.

speculation [spɛkju'leɪʃən] n speculazione f; congetture fpl.

speculative ['spɛkjulətɪv] adj speculativo(a).

speculator ['spɛkjuleɪtə*] n speculatore/trice.

sped [spɛd] pt, pp of **speed**.

speech [spiːtʃ] n (faculty) parola; (talk) discorso; (manner of speaking) parlata; (language) linguaggio; (enunciation) elocuzione f.

speech day n (BRIT SCOL) giorno della premiazione.

speech impediment n difetto di pronuncia.

speechless ['spiːtʃlɪs] adj ammutolito(a), muto(a).

speech therapy n cura dei disturbi del linguaggio.

speed [spiːd] n velocità f inv; (promptness) prontezza; (AUT: gear) marcia ♦ vi (pt, pp **sped** [spɛd]): **to** ~ **along** procedere velocemente; **the years sped by** gli anni sono volati; (AUT: exceed ~ limit) andare a velocità eccessiva; **at** ~ (BRIT) velocemente, **at full** or **top** '~ a tutta velocità; **at a** ~ **of 70 km/h** a una velocità di 70 km l'ora; **shorthand/typing** ~**s** numero di parole al minuto in stenografia/dattilografia; **a five-~ gearbox** un cambio a cinque marce.

► **speed up**, pt, pp ~**ed up** vi, vt accelerare.

speedboat ['spiːdbəut] n motoscafo; fuoribordo m inv.

speed dating [-deɪtɪŋ] n sistema di appuntamenti grazie al quale si possono incontrare in pochissimo tempo diverse persone e scegliere eventualmente chi frequentare.

speedily ['spiːdɪlɪ] adv velocemente; prontamente.

speeding ['spiːdɪŋ] n (AUT) eccesso di velocità.

speed limit n limite m di velocità.

speedometer [spɪ'dɔmɪtə*] n tachimetro.

speed trap n (AUT) tratto di strada sul quale la polizia controlla la velocità dei veicoli.

speedway ['spiːdweɪ] n (SPORT) pista per motociclismo.

speedy ['spiːdɪ] adj veloce, rapido(a); (reply) pronto(a).

speleologist [spɛlɪ'ɔlədʒɪst] n speleologo/a.

spell [spɛl] n (also: **magic** ~) incantesimo; (period of time) (breve) periodo ♦ vt (pt, pp **spelt** or ~**ed** [spɛlt, spɛld]) (in writing) scrivere (lettera per lettera); (aloud) dire lettera per lettera; (fig) significare; **to cast a** ~ **on sb** fare un incantesimo a qn; **he can't** ~ fa errori di ortografia; **how do you** ~ **your name?** come si scrive il suo nome?; **can you** ~ **it for me?** me lo può dettare lettera per lettera?

spellbound ['spɛlbaund] adj incantato(a), affascinato(a).

spelling ['spɛlɪŋ] n ortografia.

spelt [spɛlt] pt, pp of **spell**.

spend, pt, pp **spent** [spɛnd, spɛnt] vt (money) spendere; (time, life) passare; **to** ~ **time/money/effort on sth** dedicare tempo/soldi/energie a qc.

spending ['spɛndɪŋ] n: **government** ~ spesa pubblica.

spending money n denaro per le piccole spese.

spending power n potere m d'acquisto.

spendthrift ['spɛndθrɪft] n spendaccione/a.

spent [spɛnt] pt, pp of **spend** ♦ adj (patience) esaurito(a); (cartridge, bullets, match) usato(a).

sperm [spəːm] n sperma m.

sperm bank n banca dello sperma.

sperm whale n capodoglio.

spew [spjuː] vt vomitare.

sphere [sfɪə*] n sfera.

spherical ['sfɛrɪkl] adj sferico(a).

sphinx [sfɪŋks] n sfinge f.

spice [spaɪs] n spezia ♦ vt aromatizzare.

spick-and-span ['spɪkən'spæn] adj impeccabile.

spicy ['spaɪsɪ] adj piccante.

spider ['spaɪdə*] n ragno; ~**'s web** ragnatela.

spiel [spiːl] n (col) tiritera.

spike [spaɪk] n punta; ~**s** npl (SPORT) scarpe fpl chiodate.

spike heel n (US) tacco a spillo.

spiky ['spaɪkɪ] adj (bush, branch) spinoso(a); (animal) ricoperto(a) di aculei.

spill, pt, pp **spilt** or ~**ed** [spɪl, -t, -d] vt versare, rovesciare ♦ vi versarsi, rovesciarsi; **to** ~ **the beans** (col) vuotare il sacco.

► **spill out** vi riversarsi fuori.

► **spill over** vi: **to** ~ **over** (into) (liquid) versarsi (in); (crowd) riversarsi (in).

spillage ['spɪlɪdʒ] n (event) fuoriuscita; (substance) sostanza fuoriuscita.

spin [spɪn] n (revolution of wheel) rotazione f; (AVIAT) avvitamento; (trip in car) giretto ♦ vb (pt, pp **spun** [spʌn]) vt (wool etc) filare; (wheel) far girare; (BRIT: clothes) mettere nella centrifuga ♦ vi girare; **to** ~ **a yarn** raccontare una storia; **to** ~ **a coin** (BRIT)

lanciare in aria una moneta.
► **spin out** *vt* far durare.
spina bifida ['spaɪnə'bɪfɪdə] *n* spina bifida.
spinach ['spɪnɪtʃ] *n* spinacio; (*as food*)
spinaci *mpl*.
spinal ['spaɪnl] *adj* spinale.
spinal column *n* colonna vertebrale,
spina dorsale.
spinal cord *n* midollo spinale.
spindly ['spɪndlɪ] *adj* lungo(a) e sottile,
filiforme.
spin doctor *n* (*col*) esperto di
comunicazioni responsabile
dell'immagine di un partito politico.
spin-dry ['spɪn'draɪ] *vt* asciugare con la
centrifuga.
spin-dryer [spɪn'draɪə*] *n* (*BRIT*) centrifuga.
spine [spaɪn] *n* spina dorsale; (*thorn*) spina.
spine-chilling ['spaɪntʃɪlɪŋ] *adj*
agghiacciante.
spineless ['spaɪnlɪs] *adj* invertebrato(a),
senza spina dorsale; (*fig*) smidollato(a).
spinner ['spɪnə*] *n* (*of thread*) tessitore/
trice.
spinning ['spɪnɪŋ] *n* filatura.
spinning top *n* trottola.
spinning wheel *n* filatoio.
spin-off ['spɪnɔf] *n* applicazione *f*
secondaria.
spinster ['spɪnstə*] *n* nubile *f*; zitella.
spiral ['spaɪərl] *n* spirale *f* ♦ *adj* a spirale ♦ *vi*
(*prices*) salire vertiginosamente; **the**
inflationary ~ la spirale dell'inflazione.
spiral staircase *n* scala a chiocciola.
spire ['spaɪə*] *n* guglia.
spirit ['spɪrɪt] *n* (*soul*) spirito, anima; (*ghost*)
spirito, fantasma *m*; (*mood*) stato
d'animo, umore *m*; (*courage*) coraggio; ~**s**
npl (*drink*) alcolici *mpl*; **in good** ~**s** di buon
umore; **in low** ~**s** triste, abbattuto(a);
community ~, **public** ~ senso civico.
spirit duplicator *n* duplicatore *m* a spirito.
spirited ['spɪrɪtɪd] *adj* vivace, vigoroso(a);
(*horse*) focoso(a).
spirit level *n* livella a bolla (d'aria).
spiritual ['spɪrɪtjuəl] *adj* spirituale ♦ *n* (*also*:
Negro ~) spiritual *m inv*.
spiritualism ['spɪrɪtjuəlɪzəm] *n* spiritismo.
spit [spɪt] *n* (*for roasting*) spiedo; (*spittle*)
sputo; (*saliva*) saliva ♦ *vi* (*pt, pp* **spat**
[spæt]) sputare; (*fire, fat*) scoppiettare.
spite [spaɪt] *n* dispetto ♦ *vt* contrariare, far
dispetto a; **in** ~ **of** nonostante, malgrado.
spiteful ['spaɪtful] *adj* dispettoso(a);
(*tongue, remark*) maligno(a), velenoso(a).
spitroast ['spɪt'rəust] *vt* cuocere allo
spiedo.
spitting ['spɪtɪŋ] *n*: "~ **prohibited**" "vietato

sputare" ♦ *adj*: **to be the** ~ **image of sb**
essere il ritratto vivente *or* sputato di qn.
spittle ['spɪtl] *n* saliva; sputo.
spiv [spɪv] *n* (*BRIT col*) imbroglione *m*.
splash [splæʃ] *n* spruzzo; (*sound*) tonfo; (*of*
colour) schizzo ♦ *vt* spruzzare ♦ *vi* (*also*: ~
about) sguazzare; **to** ~ **paint on the floor**
schizzare il pavimento di vernice.
splashdown ['splæʃdaun] *n* ammaraggio.
splay [spleɪ] *adj*: ~ **footed** che ha i piedi
piatti.
spleen [spli:n] *n* (*ANAT*) milza.
splendid ['splɛndɪd] *adj* splendido(a),
magnifico(a).
splendour, (*US*) **splendor** ['splɛndə*] *n*
splendore *m*.
splice [splaɪs] *vt* (*rope*) impiombare; (*wood*)
calettare.
splint [splɪnt] *n* (*MED*) stecca.
splinter ['splɪntə*] *n* scheggia ♦ *vi*
scheggiarsi.
splinter group *n* gruppo dissidente.
split [splɪt] *n* spaccatura; (*fig: division,*
quarrel) scissione *f* ♦ *vb* (*pt, pp* **split**) *vt*
spaccare; (*party*) dividere; (*work, profits*)
spartire, ripartire ♦ *vi* (*divide*) dividersi;
to do the ~**s** fare la spaccata; **to** ~ **the**
difference dividersi la differenza.
► **split up** *vi* (*couple*) separarsi, rompere;
(*meeting*) sciogliersi.
split-level ['splɪtlɛvl] *adj* (*house*) a piani
sfalsati.
split peas *npl* piselli *mpl* secchi spaccati.
split personality *n* doppia personalità.
split second *n* frazione *f* di secondo.
splitting ['splɪtɪŋ] *adj*: **a** ~ **headache** un mal
di testa da impazzire.
splutter ['splʌtə*] *vi* farfugliare;
sputacchiare.
spoil, *pt, pp* **spoilt** *or* ~**ed** [spɔɪl, -t, -d] *vt*
(*damage*) rovinare, guastare; (*mar*)
sciupare; (*child*) viziare; (*ballot paper*)
rendere nullo(a), invalidare; **to be** ~**ing**
for a fight morire dalla voglia di litigare.
spoils [spɔɪlz] *npl* bottino.
spoilsport ['spɔɪlspɔ:t] *n* guastafeste *m/f inv.*
spoilt [spɔɪlt] *pt, pp of* **spoil** ♦ *adj* (*child*)
viziato(a); (*ballot paper*) nullo(a).
spoke [spəuk] *pt of* **speak** ♦ *n* raggio.
spoken ['spəukn] *pp of* **speak**.
spokesman ['spəuksmən], **spokeswoman**
[-wumən] *n* portavoce *m/f inv.*
spokesperson ['spəukspə:sn] *n* portavoce
m/f.
sponge [spʌndʒ] *n* spugna; (*CULIN: also*:
~ **cake**) pan *m* di Spagna ♦ *vt* spugnare,
pulire con una spugna ♦ *vi*: **to** ~ **on** *or*
(*US*) **off of** scroccare a.

sponge bag n (BRIT) nécessaire m inv.

sponge cake n pan m di Spagna.

sponger ['spʌndʒə*] n (pej) parassita m/f, scroccone/a.

spongy ['spʌndʒɪ] adj spugnoso(a).

sponsor ['spɔnsə*] n (RADIO, TV, SPORT etc) sponsor m inv; (of enterprise, bill, for fund-raising) promotore/trice ♦ vt sponsorizzare; patrocinare; (POL: bill) presentare; I ~ed him at 3p a mile (in fund-raising race) ho offerto in beneficenza 3 penny per ogni miglio che fa.

sponsorship ['spɔnsəʃɪp] n sponsorizzazione f; patrocinio.

spontaneity [spɔntə'neɪtɪ] n spontaneità.

spontaneous [spɔn'teɪnɪəs] adj spontaneo(a).

spoof [spuːf] n presa in giro, parodia.

spooky ['spuːkɪ] adj che fa accapponare la pelle.

spool [spuːl] n bobina.

spoon [spuːn] n cucchiaio.

spoon-feed ['spuːnfiːd] vt nutrire con il cucchiaio; (fig) imboccare.

spoonful ['spuːnful] n cucchiaiata.

sporadic [spə'rædɪk] adj sporadico(a).

sport [spɔːt] n sport m inv; (person) persona di spirito; (amusement) divertimento ♦ vt sfoggiare; **indoor/outdoor** ~s sport mpl al chiuso/all'aria aperta; **to say sth in** ~ dire qc per scherzo.

sporting ['spɔːtɪŋ] adj sportivo(a); **to give sb a** ~ **chance** dare a qn una possibilità (di vincere).

sport jacket n (US) = **sports jacket**.

sports car n automobile f sportiva.

sports ground n campo sportivo.

sports jacket n giacca sportiva.

sportsman ['spɔːtsmən] n sportivo.

sportsmanship ['spɔːtsmənʃɪp] n spirito sportivo.

sports page n pagina sportiva.

sports utility vehicle (SUV) n (esp US) fuoristrada m inv.

sportswear ['spɔːtswɛə*] n abiti mpl sportivi.

sportswoman ['spɔːtswumən] n sportiva.

sporty ['spɔːtɪ] adj sportivo(a).

spot [spɔt] n punto; (mark) macchia; (dot: on pattern) pallino; (pimple) foruncolo; (place) posto; (also: ~ **advertisement**) spot m inv; (small amount): **a** ~ **of** un po' di ♦ vt (notice) individuare, distinguere; **on the** ~ sul posto; **to do sth on the** ~ fare qc immediatamente or lì per lì; **to put sb on the** ~ mettere qn in difficoltà; **to come out in** ~s coprirsi di foruncoli.

spot check n controllo senza preavviso.

spotless ['spɔtlɪs] adj immacolato(a).

spotlight ['spɔtlaɪt] n proiettore m; (AUT) faro ausiliario.

spot-on [spɔt'ɔn] adj (BRIT) esatto(a).

spot price n (COMM) prezzo del pronto.

spotted ['spɔtɪd] adj macchiato(a); a puntini, a pallini; ~ **with** punteggiato(a) di.

spotty ['spɔtɪ] adj (face) foruncoloso(a).

spouse [spauz] n sposo/a.

spout [spaut] n (of jug) beccuccio; (of liquid) zampillo, getto ♦ vi zampillare.

sprain [spreɪn] n storta, distorsione f ♦ vt: **to** ~ **one's ankle** storcersi una caviglia.

sprang [spræŋ] pt of **spring**.

sprawl [sprɔːl] vi sdraiarsi (in modo scomposto) ♦ n: **urban** ~ sviluppo urbanistico incontrollato; **to send sb** ~**ing** mandare qn a gambe all'aria.

spray [spreɪ] n spruzzo; (container) nebulizzatore m, spray m inv; (of flowers) mazzetto ♦ cpd (deodorant) spray inv ♦ vt spruzzare; (crops) irrorare.

spread [spred] n diffusione f; (distribution) distribuzione f; (PRESS, TYP: two pages) doppia pagina; (: across columns) articolo a più colonne; (CULIN) pasta (da spalmare) ♦ vb (pt, pp **spread**) vt (cloth) stendere, distendere; (butter etc) spalmare; (disease, knowledge) propagare, diffondere ♦ vi stendersi, distendersi; spalmarsi; propagarsi, diffondersi; **middle-age** ~ pancetta; **repayments will be** ~ **over 18 months** i versamenti saranno scaglionati lungo un periodo di 18 mesi.

spread-eagled ['spredi:gld] adj: **to be** or **lie** ~ essere disteso(a) a gambe e braccia aperte.

spreadsheet ['spredʃiːt] n (COMPUT) foglio elettronico.

spree [spriː] n: **to go on a** ~ fare baldoria.

sprig [sprɪg] n ramoscello.

sprightly ['spraɪtlɪ] adj vivace.

spring [sprɪŋ] n (leap) salto, balzo; (bounciness) elasticità; (coiled metal) molla; (season) primavera; (of water) sorgente f ♦ vi (pt **sprang**, pp **sprung** [spræŋ, sprʌŋ]) saltare, balzare ♦ vt: **to** ~ **a leak** (pipe etc) cominciare a perdere; **to walk with a** ~ **in one's step** camminare con passo elastico; **in** ~, **in the** ~ in primavera; **to** ~ **from** provenire da; **to** ~ **into action** entrare (rapidamente) in azione; **he sprang the news on me** mi ha sorpreso con quella notizia.

► **spring up** vi (problem) presentarsi.

springboard ['sprɪŋbɔːd] n trampolino.
spring-clean [sprɪŋ'kliːn] n (also: ~ing) grandi pulizie fpl di primavera.
spring onion n (BRIT) cipollina.
spring roll n involtino fritto di verdure o carne tipico della cucina cinese.
springtime ['sprɪŋtaɪm] n primavera.
springy ['sprɪŋɪ] adj elastico(a).
sprinkle ['sprɪŋkl] vt spruzzare; spargere; **to ~ water** etc **on, ~ with water** etc spruzzare dell'acqua etc su; **to ~ sugar** etc **on, ~ with sugar** etc spolverizzare di zucchero etc; **~d with** (fig) cosparso(a) di.
sprinkler ['sprɪŋklə*] n (for lawn etc) irrigatore m; (for fire-fighting) sprinkler m inv.
sprinkling ['sprɪŋklɪŋ] n (of water) qualche goccia; (of salt, sugar) pizzico.
sprint [sprɪnt] n scatto ♦ vi scattare; **the 200-metres ~** i 200 metri piani.
sprinter ['sprɪntə*] n velocista m/f.
sprite [spraɪt] n elfo, folletto.
spritzer ['sprɪtsə*] n spritz m inv.
sprocket ['sprɔkɪt] n (on printer etc) dente m, rocchetto.
sprout [spraut] vi germogliare.
sprouts [sprauts] npl (also: **Brussels ~**) cavolini mpl di Bruxelles.
spruce [spruːs] n abete m rosso ♦ adj lindo(a); azzimato(a).
▸**spruce up** vt (tidy) mettere in ordine; (smarten up: room etc) abbellire; **to ~ o.s.** up farsi bello(a).
sprung [sprʌŋ] pp of **spring**.
spry [spraɪ] adj arzillo(a), sveglio(a).
SPUC n abbr (= Society for the Protection of Unborn Children) associazione anti-abortista.
spun [spʌn] pt, pp of **spin**.
spur [spəː*] n sperone m; (fig) sprone m, incentivo ♦ vt (also: ~ **on**) spronare; **on the ~ of the moment** lì per lì.
spurious ['spjuərɪəs] adj falso(a).
spurn [spəːn] vt rifiutare con disprezzo, sdegnare.
spurt [spəːt] n getto; (of energy) esplosione f ♦ vi sgorgare; zampillare; **to put in** or **on a ~** (runner) fare uno scatto; (fig: in work etc) affrettarsi, sbrigarsi.
sputter ['spʌtə*] vi = **splutter**.
spy [spaɪ] n spia ♦ cpd (film, story) di spionaggio ♦ vi: **to ~ on** spiare ♦ vt (see) scorgere.
spying ['spaɪɪŋ] n spionaggio.
Sq. abbr (in address) = **square**.
sq. abbr (MATH etc) = **square**.
squabble ['skwɔbl] n battibecco ♦ vi

bisticciarsi.
squad [skwɔd] n (MIL) plotone m; (POLICE) squadra; **flying ~** (POLICE) volante f.
squad car n (BRIT POLICE) automobile f della polizia.
squaddie ['skwɔdɪ] n (MIL col) burba.
squadron ['skwɔdrn] n (MIL) squadrone m; (AVIAT, NAUT) squadriglia.
squalid ['skwɔlɪd] adj sordido(a).
squall [skwɔːl] n burrasca.
squalor ['skwɔlə*] n squallore m.
squander ['skwɔndə*] vt dissipare.
square [skwɛə*] n quadrato; (in town) piazza; (US: block of houses) blocco, isolato; (instrument) squadra ♦ adj quadrato(a); (honest) onesto(a); (col: ideas, person) di vecchio stampo ♦ vt (arrange) regolare; (MATH) elevare al quadrato ♦ vi (agree) accordarsi; **a ~ meal** un pasto abbondante; **2 metres ~** di 2 metri per 2; **1 ~ metre** 1 metro quadrato; **we're back to ~ one** (fig) siamo al punto di partenza; **all ~** pari; **to get one's accounts ~** mettere in ordine i propri conti; **I'll ~ it with him** (col) sistemo io le cose con lui; **can you ~ it with your conscience?** (reconcile) puoi conciliarlo con la tua coscienza?
▸**square up** vi (BRIT: settle) saldare, pagare; **to ~ up with sb** regolare i conti con qn.
square bracket n (TYP) parentesi f inv quadra.
squarely ['skwɛəlɪ] adv (directly) direttamente; (honestly, fairly) onestamente.
square root n radice f quadrata.
squash [skwɔʃ] n (BRIT: drink): **lemon/orange ~** sciroppo di limone/arancia; (vegetable) zucca; (SPORT) squash m ♦ vt schiacciare.
squat [skwɔt] adj tarchiato(a), tozzo(a) ♦ vi accovacciarsi; (on property) occupare abusivamente.
squatter ['skwɔtə*] n occupante m/f abusivo(a).
squawk [skwɔːk] vi emettere strida rauche.
squeak [skwiːk] vi squittire ♦ n (of hinge, wheel etc) cigolio; (of shoes) scricchiolio; (of mouse etc) squittio.
squeaky ['skwiːkɪ] adj (col) cigolante; **to be ~ clean** (fig) avere un'immagine pulita.
squeal [skwiːl] vi strillare.
squeamish ['skwiːmɪʃ] adj schizzinoso(a); disgustato(a).
squeeze [skwiːz] n pressione f; (also ECON) stretta; (credit ~) stretta creditizia ♦ vt

premere; (*hand, arm*) stringere ♦ *vi*: **to ~ in infilarsi**; **to ~ past/under sth** passare vicino/sotto a qc con difficoltà; **a ~ of lemon** una spruzzata di limone.
▶**squeeze out** *vt* spremere.
squelch [skwɛltʃ] *vi* fare ciac; sguazzare.
squib [skwɪb] *n* petardo.
squid [skwɪd] *n* calamaro.
squint [skwɪnt] *vi* essere strabico(a); (*in the sunlight*) strizzare gli occhi ♦ *n*: **he has a ~** è strabico; **to ~ at sth** guardare qc di traverso; (*quickly*) dare un'occhiata a qc.
squire ['skwaɪə*] *n* (*BRIT*) proprietario terriero.
squirm [skwəːm] *vi* contorcersi.
squirrel ['skwɪrəl] *n* scoiattolo.
squirt [skwəːt] *n* schizzo ♦ *vi* schizzare; zampillare.
Sr *abbr* = **senior; sister** (*REL*).
SRC *n abbr* (*BRIT*: = *Students' Representative Council*) *comitato di rappresentanza studenti*.
Sri Lanka [srɪ'læŋkə] *n* Sri Lanka *m*.
SRO *abbr* (*US*: = *standing room only*) solo posti in piedi.
SS *abbr* = **steamship**.
SSA *n abbr* (*US*: = *Social Security Administration*) ~ Previdenza Sociale.
SST *n abbr* (*US*) = *supersonic transport*.
ST *abbr* (*US*: = *Standard Time*) *ora ufficiale.*
St *abbr* = **saint; street**.
stab [stæb] *n* (*with knife etc*) pugnalata; (*col*: *try*): **to have a ~ at (doing) sth** provare a fare qc ♦ *vt* pugnalare; **to ~ sb to death** uccidere qn a coltellate.
stabbing ['stæbɪŋ] *n*: **there's been a ~** qualcuno è stato pugnalato ♦ *adj* (*pain, ache*) lancinante.
stability [stə'bɪlɪtɪ] *n* stabilità.
stabilization [steɪbəlaɪ'zeɪʃən] *n* stabilizzazione *f*.
stabilize ['steɪbəlaɪz] *vt* stabilizzare ♦ *vi* stabilizzarsi.
stabilizer ['steɪbəlaɪzə*] *n* (*AVIAT, NAUT*) stabilizzatore *m*.
stable ['steɪbl] *n* (*for horses*) scuderia; (*for cattle*) stalla ♦ *adj* stabile; **riding ~s** maneggio.
staccato [stə'kaːtəu] *adv* in modo staccato ♦ *adj* (*MUS*) staccato(a); (*sound*) scandito(a).
stack [stæk] *n* catasta, pila; (*col*) mucchio, sacco ♦ *vt* accatastare, ammucchiare; **there's ~s of time to finish it** (*BRIT col*) abbiamo un sacco di tempo per finirlo.
stadium ['steɪdɪəm] *n* stadio.
staff [staːf] *n* (*work force: gen*) personale *m*; (: *BRIT: SCOL*) personale insegnante; (:

servants) personale di servizio; (*MIL*) stato maggiore; (*stick*) bastone *m* ♦ *vt* fornire di personale.
staffroom ['staːfruːm] *n* sala dei professori.
Staffs *abbr* (*BRIT*) = *Staffordshire.*
stag [stæg] *n* cervo; (*BRIT STOCK EXCHANGE*) rialzista *m/f* su nuove emissioni.
stage [steɪdʒ] *n* (*platform*) palco; (*in theatre*) palcoscenico; (*profession*): **the ~** il teatro, la scena; (*point*) fase *f*, stadio ♦ *vt* (*play*) allestire, mettere in scena; (*demonstration*) organizzare; (*fig: perform*: *recovery etc*) effettuare; **in ~s** per gradi; a tappe; **in the early/final ~s** negli stadi iniziali/finali; **to go through a difficult ~** attraversare un periodo difficile.
stagecoach ['steɪdʒkəutʃ] *n* diligenza.
stage door *n* ingresso degli artisti.
stage fright *n* paura del pubblico.
stagehand ['steɪdʒhænd] *n* macchinista *m*.
stage-manage ['steɪdʒmænɪdʒ] *vt* allestire le scene per; montare.
stage manager *n* direttore *m* di scena.
stagger ['stægə*] *vi* barcollare ♦ *vt* (*person*) sbalordire; (*hours, holidays*) scaglionare.
staggering ['stægərɪŋ] *adj* (*amazing*) incredibile, sbalorditivo(a).
staging post ['steɪdʒɪŋ-] *n* passaggio obbligato.
stagnant ['stægnənt] *adj* stagnante.
stagnate [stæg'neɪt] *vi* (*also fig*) stagnare.
stagnation [stæg'neɪʃən] *n* stagnazione *f*, ristagno.
stag night, stag party *n* festa di addio al celibato.
staid [steɪd] *adj* posato(a), serio(a).
stain [steɪn] *n* macchia; (*colouring*) colorante *m* ♦ *vt* macchiare; (*wood*) tingere.
stained glass window ['steɪnd-] *n* vetrata.
stainless ['steɪnlɪs] *adj* (*steel*) inossidabile.
stain remover *n* smacchiatore *m*.
stair [stɛə*] *n* (*step*) gradino; **~s** *npl* (*flight of ~s*) scale *fpl*, scala.
staircase ['stɛəkeɪs], **stairway** ['stɛəweɪ] *n* scale *fpl*, scala.
stairwell ['stɛəwɛl] *n* tromba delle scale.
stake [steɪk] *n* palo, piolo; (*BETTING*) puntata, scommessa ♦ *vt* (*bet*) scommettere; (*risk*) rischiare; (*also*: **~ out**: *area*) delimitare con paletti; **to be at ~** essere in gioco; **to have a ~ in sth** avere un interesse in qc; **to ~ a claim (to sth)** rivendicare (qc).
stakeout ['steɪkaut] *n* sorveglianza.
stalactite ['stæləktaɪt] *n* stalattite *f*.

stalagmite ['stæləgmaɪt] n stalagmite f.

stale [steɪl] adj (bread) raffermo(a), stantio(a); (beer) svaporato(a); (smell) di chiuso.

stalemate ['steɪlmeɪt] n stallo; (fig) punto morto.

stalk [stɔːk] n gambo, stelo ♦ vt inseguire ♦ vi camminare impettito(a).

stall [stɔːl] n (BRIT: in street, market etc) bancarella; (in stable) box m inv di stalla ♦ vt (AUT) far spegnere ♦ vi (AUT) spegnersi, fermarsi; (fig) temporeggiare; ~s npl (BRIT: in cinema, theatre) platea; newspaper/flower ~ chiosco del giornalaio/del fioraio.

stallholder ['stɔːlhəʊldə*] n (BRIT) bancarellista m/f.

stallion ['stæljən] n stallone m.

stalwart ['stɔːlwət] n membro fidato.

stamen ['steɪmɛn] n stame m.

stamina ['stæmɪnə] n vigore m, resistenza.

stammer ['stæmə*] n balbuzie f ♦ vi balbettare.

stamp [stæmp] n (postage ~) francobollo; (implement) timbro; (mark, also fig) marchio, impronta; (on document) bollo; timbro ♦ vi (also: ~ one's foot) battere il piede ♦ vt battere; (letter) affrancare; (mark with a ~) timbrare; ~ed addressed envelope (sae) busta affrancata per la risposta.

►stamp out vt (fire) estinguere; (crime) eliminare; (opposition) soffocare.

stamp album n album m inv per francobolli.

stamp collecting n filatelia.

stamp duty n (BRIT) bollo.

stampede [stæm'piːd] n fuggi fuggi m inv; (of cattle) fuga precipitosa.

stamp machine n distributore m automatico di francobolli.

stance [stæns] n posizione f.

stand [stænd] n (position) posizione f; (MIL) resistenza; (structure) supporto, sostegno; (at exhibition) stand m inv; (at market) bancarella; (booth) chiosco; (SPORT) tribuna; (also: music ~) leggio m ♦ vb (pt, pp stood [stud]) vi stare in piedi; (rise) alzarsi in piedi; (be placed) trovarsi ♦ vt (place) mettere, porre; (tolerate, withstand) resistere, sopportare; to make a ~ prendere posizione; to take a ~ on an issue prendere posizione su un problema; to ~ for parliament (BRIT) presentarsi come candidato (per il parlamento); to ~ guard or watch (MIL) essere di guardia; it ~s to reason è logico; as things ~ stando così le cose; to

~ sb a drink/meal offrire da bere/un pranzo a qn; I can't ~ him non lo sopporto.

►stand aside vi farsi da parte, scostarsi.

►stand by vi (be ready) tenersi pronto(a) ♦ vt fus (opinion) sostenere.

►stand down vi (withdraw) ritirarsi; (LAW) lasciare il banco dei testimoni.

►stand for vt fus (signify) rappresentare, significare; (tolerate) sopportare, tollerare.

►stand in for vt fus sostituire.

►stand out vi (be prominent) spiccare.

►stand up vi (rise) alzarsi in piedi.

►stand up for vt fus difendere.

►stand up to vt fus tener testa a, resistere a.

stand-alone ['stændələʊn] adj (COMPUT) stand-alone inv.

standard ['stændəd] n modello, standard m inv; (level) livello; (flag) stendardo ♦ adj (size etc) normale, standard inv; (practice) normale; (model) di serie; ~s npl (morals) principi mpl, valori mpl; to be or come up to ~ rispondere ai requisiti; below or not up to ~ (work) mediocre; to apply a double ~ usare metri diversi (nel giudicare or fare etc); ~ of living livello di vita.

standardization [stændədaɪ'zeɪʃən] n standardizzazione f.

standardize ['stændədaɪz] vt normalizzare, standardizzare.

standard lamp n (BRIT) lampada a stelo.

standard time n ora ufficiale.

stand-by ['stændbaɪ] n riserva, sostituto; to be on ~ (gen) tenersi pronto(a); (doctor) essere di guardia; a ~ ticket un biglietto standby; to fly ~ essere in lista d'attesa per un volo.

stand-by generator n generatore m d'emergenza.

stand-by passenger n (AVIAT) passeggero/a in lista d'attesa.

stand-by ticket n (AVIAT) biglietto senza garanzia.

stand-in ['stændɪn] n sostituto/a; (CINE) controfigura.

standing ['stændɪŋ] adj diritto(a), in piedi; (permanent: committee) permanente; (: rule) fisso(a); (: army) regolare; (grievance) continuo(a); (duration): of 6 months' ~ che dura da 6 mesi ♦ n rango, condizione f, posizione f; it's a ~ joke è diventato proverbiale; he was given a ~ ovation tutti si alzarono per applaudirlo; a man of some ~ un uomo di una certa importanza.

standing committee n commissione f permanente.

standing order n (BRIT: at bank) ordine m di pagamento (permanente); ~s npl (MIL) regolamento.

standing room n posto all'impiedi.

stand-off ['stændɔf] n (esp US: stalemate) situazione f di stallo.

standoffish [stænd'ɔfiʃ] adj scostante, freddo(a).

standpat ['stændpæt] adj (US) irremovibile.

standpipe ['stændpaip] n fontanella.

standpoint ['stændpɔint] n punto di vista.

standstill ['stændstil] n: **at a** ~ fermo(a); (fig) a un punto morto; **to come to a** ~ fermarsi; giungere a un punto morto.

stank [stæŋk] pt of **stink**.

stanza ['stænzə] n stanza (poesia).

staple ['steipl] n (for papers) graffetta; (chief product) prodotto principale ♦ adj (food etc) di base; (crop, industry) principale ♦ vt cucire.

stapler ['steiplə*] n cucitrice f.

star [stɑ:*] n stella; (celebrity) divo/a; (principal actor) vedette f inv ♦ vi: **to** ~ **(in)** essere il (or la) protagonista (di) ♦ vt (CINE) essere interpretato(a) da; **four-**~ **hotel** ≈ albergo di prima categoria; **2-**~ **petrol** (BRIT) ≈ benzina normale; **4-**~ **petrol** (BRIT) ≈ super f.

star attraction n numero principale.

starboard ['stɑ:bəd] n dritta; **to** ~ a dritta.

starch [stɑ:tʃ] n amido.

starched ['stɑ:tʃt] adj (collar) inamidato(a).

starchy ['stɑ:tʃi] adj (food) ricco(a) di amido.

stardom ['stɑ:dəm] n celebrità.

stare [stɛə*] n sguardo fisso ♦ vi: **to** ~ **at** fissare.

starfish ['stɑ:fiʃ] n stella di mare.

stark [stɑ:k] adj (bleak) desolato(a); (simplicity, colour) austero(a); (reality, poverty, truth) crudo(a) ♦ adv: ~ **naked** completamente nudo(a).

starkers ['stɑ:kəz] adj: **to be** ~ (BRIT col) essere nudo(a) come un verme.

starlet ['stɑ:lit] n (CINE) stellina.

starlight ['stɑ:lait] n: **by** ~ alla luce delle stelle.

starling ['stɑ:liŋ] n storno.

starlit ['stɑ:lit] adj stellato(a).

starry ['stɑ:ri] adj stellato(a).

starry-eyed [stɑ:ri'aid] adj (idealistic, gullible) ingenuo(a); (from wonder) meravigliato(a).

Stars and Stripes npl: **the** ~ la bandiera a stelle e strisce.

star sign n segno zodiacale.

star-studded ['stɑ:stʌdid] adj: **a** ~ **cast** un cast di attori famosi.

start [stɑ:t] n inizio; (of race) partenza; (sudden movement) sobbalzo; (advantage) vantaggio ♦ vt cominciare, iniziare; (found: business, newspaper) fondare, creare ♦ vi cominciare; (on journey) partire, mettersi in viaggio; (jump) sobbalzare; **to** ~ **doing sth** (in)cominciare a fare qc; **at the** ~ all'inizio; **for a** ~ tanto per cominciare; **to make an early** ~ partire di buon'ora; **to** ~ **(off) with** ... (firstly) per prima cosa ...; (at the beginning) all'inizio; **to** ~ **a fire** provocare un incendio.

▸**start off** vi cominciare; (leave) partire.

▸**start over** vi (US) ricominciare.

▸**start up** vi cominciare; (car) avviarsi ♦ vt iniziare; (car) avviare.

starter ['stɑ:tə*] n (AUT) motorino d'avviamento; (SPORT: official) starter m inv; (: runner, horse) partente m/f; (BRIT CULIN) primo piatto.

starting handle ['stɑ:tiŋ-] n (BRIT) manovella d'avviamento.

starting point n punto di partenza.

starting price n prezzo m base inv.

startle ['stɑ:tl] vt far trasalire.

startling ['stɑ:tliŋ] adj sorprendente, sbalorditivo(a).

star turn n (BRIT) attrazione f principale.

starvation [stɑ:'veiʃən] n fame f, inedia; **to die of** ~ morire d'inedia.

starve [stɑ:v] vi morire di fame; soffrire la fame ♦ vt far morire di fame, affamare; **I'm starving** muoio di fame.

stash [stæʃ] vt: **to** ~ **sth away** (col) nascondere qc.

state [steit] n stato; (pomp): **in** ~ in pompa ♦ vt dichiarare, affermare; annunciare; **to be in a** ~ essere agitato(a); **the** ~ **of the art** il livello di tecnologia (or cultura etc); ~ **of emergency** stato di emergenza; ~ **of mind** stato d'animo.

state control n controllo statale.

stated ['steitid] adj fissato(a), stabilito(a).

State Department n (US) Dipartimento di Stato, ≈ Ministero degli Esteri.

state education n (BRIT) istruzione f pubblica or statale.

stateless ['steitlis] adj apolide.

stately ['steitli] adj maestoso(a), imponente.

stately home n residenza nobiliare (d'interesse storico o artistico spesso aperta al pubblico).

statement ['steitmənt] n dichiarazione f; (LAW) deposizione f; (FINANCE) rendiconto;

official ~ comunicato ufficiale; ~ **of account, bank** ~ estratto conto.

state-owned ['steɪt'əund] *adj* statalizzato(a).

States [steɪts] *npl:* **the** ~ *(USA)* gli Stati Uniti.

state school *n* scuola statale.

statesman ['steɪtsmən] *n* statista *m.*

static ['stætɪk] *n (RADIO)* scariche *fpl* ♦ *adj* statico(a); ~ **electricity** elettricità statica.

station ['steɪʃən] *n* stazione *f; (rank)* rango, condizione *f* ♦ *vt* collocare, disporre; **action** ~**s** posti *mpl* di combattimento; **to be** ~**ed in** *(MIL)* essere di stanza in.

stationary ['steɪʃənərɪ] *adj* fermo(a), immobile.

stationer ['steɪʃənə*] *n* cartolaio/a; ~**'s shop** cartoleria.

stationery ['steɪʃənərɪ] *n* articoli *mpl* di cancelleria; *(writing paper)* carta da lettere.

station master *n (RAIL)* capostazione *m.*

station wagon *n (US)* giardinetta.

statistic [stə'tɪstɪk] *n* statistica; *see also* **statistics.**

statistical [stə'tɪstɪkəl] *adj* statistico(a).

statistics [stə'tɪstɪks] *n (science)* statistica.

statue ['stætjuː] *n* statua.

statuesque [stætju'ɛsk] *adj* statuario(a).

statuette [stætju'ɛt] *n* statuetta.

stature ['stætʃə*] *n* statura.

status ['steɪtəs] *n* posizione *f,* condizione *f* sociale; *(prestige)* prestigio; *(legal, marital)* stato.

status quo [-'kwəu] *n:* **the** ~ lo statu quo.

status symbol *n* simbolo di prestigio.

statute ['stætjuːt] *n* legge *f;* ~**s** *npl (of club etc)* statuto.

statute book *n* codice *m.*

statutory ['stætjutərɪ] *adj* stabilito(a) dalla legge, statutario(a); ~ **meeting** *(COMM)* assemblea ordinaria.

staunch [stɔːntʃ] *adj* fidato(a), leale ♦ *vt (flow)* arrestare; *(blood)* arrestare il flusso di.

stave [steɪv] *n (MUS)* rigo ♦ *vt:* **to** ~ **off** *(attack)* respingere; *(threat)* evitare.

stay [steɪ] *n (period of time)* soggiorno, permanenza ♦ *vi* rimanere; *(reside)* alloggiare, stare; *(spend some time)* trattenersi, soggiornare; ~ **of execution** *(LAW)* sospensione *f* dell'esecuzione; **to** ~ **put** non muoversi; **to** ~ **with friends** stare presso amici; **to** ~ **the night** passare la notte.

▶**stay behind** *vi* restare indietro.

▶**stay in** *vi (at home)* stare in casa.

▶**stay on** *vi* restare, rimanere.

▶**stay out** *vi (of house)* rimanere fuori (di casa); *(strikers)* continuare lo sciopero.

▶**stay up** *vi (at night)* rimanere alzato(a).

staying power ['steɪɪŋ-] *n* capacità di resistenza.

STD *n abbr (BRIT:* = *subscriber trunk dialling)* teleselezione *f; (*= *sexually transmitted disease)* malattia venerea.

stead [stɛd] *n (BRIT):* **in sb's** ~ al posto di qn; **to stand sb in good** ~ essere utile a qn.

steadfast ['stɛdfɑːst] *adj* fermo(a), risoluto(a).

steadily ['stɛdɪlɪ] *adv* continuamente; *(walk)* con passo sicuro.

steady ['stɛdɪ] *adj* stabile, solido(a), fermo(a); *(regular)* costante; *(boyfriend etc)* fisso(a); *(person)* calmo(a), tranquillo(a) ♦ *vt* stabilizzare; calmare; **to** ~ **o.s.** ritrovare l'equilibrio.

steak [steɪk] *n (meat)* bistecca; *(fish)* trancia.

steakhouse ['steɪkhaus] *n ristorante specializzato in bistecche.*

steal, *pt* **stole,** *pp* **stolen** [stiːl, stəul, 'stəuln] *vt* rubare ♦ *vi (thieve)* rubare.

▶**steal away, steal off** *vi* svignarsela, andarsene alla chetichella.

stealth [stɛlθ] *n:* **by** ~ furtivamente.

stealthy ['stɛlθɪ] *adj* furtivo(a).

steam [stiːm] *n* vapore *m* ♦ *vt* trattare con vapore; *(CULIN)* cuocere a vapore ♦ *vi* fumare; *(ship):* **to** ~ **along** filare; **to let off** ~ *(fig)* sfogarsi; **under one's own** ~ *(fig)* da solo, con i propri mezzi; **to run out of** ~ *(fig: person)* non farcela più.

▶**steam up** *vi (window)* appannarsi; **to get** ~**ed up about sth** *(fig)* andare in bestia per qc.

steam engine *n* macchina a vapore; *(RAIL)* locomotiva a vapore.

steamer ['stiːmə*] *n* piroscafo, vapore *m;* *(CULIN)* pentola a vapore.

steam iron *n* ferro a vapore.

steamroller ['stiːmrəulə*] *n* rullo compressore.

steamship ['stiːmʃɪp] *n* piroscafo, vapore *m.*

steamy ['stiːmɪ] *adj* pieno(a) di vapore; *(window)* appannato(a).

steed [stiːd] *n (literary)* corsiero, destriero.

steel [stiːl] *n* acciaio ♦ *cpd* di acciaio.

steel band *n* banda di strumenti a percussione *(tipica dei Caribi).*

steel industry *n* industria dell'acciaio.

steel mill *n* acciaieria.

steelworks ['stiːlwəːks] *n* acciaieria.

steely ['sti:lı] adj (determination) inflessibile; (gaze) duro(a); (eyes) freddo(a); (gaze) come l'acciaio.

steep [sti:p] adj ripido(a), scosceso(a); (price) eccessivo(a) ♦ vt inzuppare; (washing) mettere a mollo.

steeple ['sti:pl] n campanile m.

steeplechase ['sti:pltʃeıs] n corsa a ostacoli, steeplechase m inv.

steeplejack ['sti:pldʒæk] n chi ripara campanili e ciminiere.

steer [stıə*] n manzo ♦ vt (ship) governare; (car) guidare ♦ vi (NAUT: person) governare; (: ship) rispondere al timone; (car) guidarsi; **to ~ clear of sb/sth** (fig) tenersi alla larga da qn/qc.

steering ['stıərıŋ] n (AUT) sterzo.

steering column n piantone m dello sterzo.

steering committee n comitato direttivo.

steering wheel n volante m.

stem [stɛm] n (of flower, plant) stelo; (of tree) fusto; (of glass) gambo; (of fruit, leaf) picciolo ♦ vt contenere, arginare.

▶**stem from** vt fus provenire da, derivare da.

stench [stɛntʃ] n puzzo, fetore m.

stencil ['stɛnsl] n (of metal, cardboard) stampino, mascherina; (in typing) matrice f.

stenographer [stɛ'nɔgrəfə*] n (US) stenografo/a.

stenography [stɛ'nɔgrəfı] n (US) stenografia.

step [stɛp] n passo; (stair) gradino, scalino; (action) mossa, azione f ♦ vi: **to ~ forward** fare un passo avanti; **~s** npl (BRIT) = **stepladder**; **~ by ~** un passo dietro l'altro; (fig) poco a poco; **to be in/out of ~ with** (also fig) stare/non stare al passo con.

▶**step down** vi (fig) ritirarsi.

▶**step in** vi fare il proprio ingresso.

▶**step off** vt fus scendere da.

▶**step over** vt fus scavalcare.

▶**step up** vt aumentare; intensificare.

step aerobics n step m inv.

stepbrother ['stɛpbrʌðə*] n fratellastro.

stepchild ['stɛptʃaıld] n figliastro/a.

stepdaughter ['stɛpdɔ:tə*] n figliastra.

stepfather ['stɛpfɑ:ðə*] n patrigno.

stepladder ['stɛplædə*] n scala a libretto.

stepmother ['stɛpmʌðə*] n matrigna.

stepping stone ['stɛpıŋ-] n pietra di un guado; (fig) trampolino.

step Reebok ® [-'ri:bɔk] n step m inv.

stepsister ['stɛpsıstə*] n sorellastra.

stepson ['stɛpsʌn] n figliastro.

stereo ['stɛrıəu] n (system) sistema m stereofonico; (record player) stereo m inv ♦ adj (also: ~phonic) stereofonico(a); **in ~** in stereofonia.

stereotype ['stıərıətaıp] n stereotipo.

sterile ['stɛraıl] adj sterile.

sterility [stɛ'rılıtı] n sterilità.

sterilization [stɛrılaı'zeıʃən] n sterilizzazione f.

sterilize ['stɛrılaız] vt sterilizzare.

sterling ['stə:lıŋ] adj (gold, silver) di buona lega; (fig) autentico(a), genuino(a) ♦ n (ECON) (lira) sterlina; **a pound ~** una lira sterlina.

sterling area n area della sterlina.

stern [stə:n] adj severo(a) ♦ n (NAUT) poppa.

sternum ['stə:nəm] n sterno.

steroid ['stɛrɔıd] n steroide m.

stethoscope ['stɛθəskəup] n stetoscopio.

stevedore ['sti:vıdɔ:*] n scaricatore m di porto.

stew [stju:] n stufato ♦ vt, vi cuocere in umido; **~ed tea** tè lasciato troppo in infusione; **~ed fruit** frutta cotta.

steward ['stju:əd] n (AVIAT, NAUT, RAIL) steward m inv; (in club etc) dispensiere m; (shop ~) rappresentante m/f sindacale.

stewardess ['stju:ədɛs] n assistente f di volo, hostess f inv.

stewardship ['stju:ədʃıp] n amministrazione f.

stewing steak ['stju:ıŋ-], (US) **stew meat** n carne f (di manzo) per stufato.

St. Ex. abbr = **stock exchange**.

stg abbr = **sterling**.

stick [stık] n bastone m; (of rhubarb, celery) gambo ♦ vb (pt, pp **stuck** [stʌk]) vt (glue) attaccare; (thrust): **to ~ sth into** conficcare or piantare or infiggere qc in; (col: put) ficcare; (: tolerate) sopportare ♦ vi conficcarsi; tenere; (remain) restare, rimanere; (get jammed: door, lift) bloccarsi; **to ~ to** (one's word, promise) mantenere; (principles) tener fede a; **to get hold of the wrong end of the ~** (fig) capire male; **it stuck in my mind** mi è rimasto in mente.

▶**stick around** vi (col) restare, fermarsi.

▶**stick out, stick up** vi sporgere, spuntare ♦ vt: **to ~ it out** (col) tener duro.

▶**stick up for** vt fus difendere.

sticker ['stıkə*] n cartellino adesivo.

sticking plaster ['stıkıŋ-] n cerotto adesivo.

sticking point n (fig) punto di stallo, impasse f inv.

stickleback ['stıklbæk] n spinarello.

stickler ['stıklə*] n: **to be a ~ for** essere

pignolo(a) su, tenere molto a.
stick-on ['stɪkɔn] *adj* (*label*) adesivo(a).
stick shift *n* (*US AUT*) cambio manuale.
stick-up ['stɪkʌp] *n* (*col*) rapina a mano armata.
sticky ['stɪkɪ] *adj* attaccaticcio(a), vischioso(a); (*label*) adesivo(a).
stiff [stɪf] *adj* rigido(a), duro(a); (*muscle*) legato(a), indolenzito(a); (*difficult*) difficile, arduo(a); (*cold*: *manner etc*) freddo(a), formale; (*strong*) forte; (*high*: *price*) molto alto(a); **to be** *or* **feel** ~ (*person*) essere *or* sentirsi indolenzito; **to have a** ~ **neck/back** avere il torcicollo/ mal di schiena; **to keep a** ~ **upper lip** (*BRIT fig*) conservare il sangue freddo.
stiffen ['stɪfn] *vt* irrigidire; rinforzare ♦ *vi* irrigidirsi; indurirsi.
stiffness ['stɪfnɪs] *n* rigidità; indolenzimento; difficoltà; freddezza.
stifle ['staɪfl] *vt* soffocare.
stifling ['staɪflɪŋ] *adj* (*heat*) soffocante.
stigma, *pl* (*BOT, MED*) ~**ta,** (*fig*) ~**s** ['stɪgmə, stɪg'mɑːtə] *n* stigma *m*.
stigmata [stig'mɑːtə] *npl* (*REL*) stigmate *fpl*.
stile [staɪl] *n* cavalcasiepe *m*; cavalcasteccato.
stiletto [stɪ'lɛtəu] *n* (*also*: ~ **heel**) tacco a spillo.
still [stɪl] *adj* fermo(a); (*quiet*) silenzioso(a); (*orange juice etc*) non gassato(a) ♦ *adv* (*up to this time, even*) ancora; (*nonetheless*) tuttavia, ciò nonostante ♦ *n* (*CINE*) fotogramma *m*; **keep** ~! stai fermo!; **he** ~ **hasn't arrived** non è ancora arrivato.
stillborn ['stɪlbɔːn] *adj* nato(a) morto(a).
still life *n* natura morta.
stilt [stɪlt] *n* trampolo; (*pile*) palo.
stilted ['stɪltɪd] *adj* freddo(a), formale; artificiale.
stimulant ['stɪmjulənt] *n* stimolante *m*.
stimulate ['stɪmjuleɪt] *vt* stimolare.
stimulating ['stɪmjuleɪtɪŋ] *adj* stimolante.
stimulation [stɪmju'leɪʃən] *n* stimolazione *f*.
stimulus, *pl* **stimuli** ['stɪmjuləs, 'stɪmjulaɪ] *n* stimolo.
sting [stɪŋ] *n* puntura; (*organ*) pungiglione *m*; (*col*) trucco ♦ *vt* (*pt, pp* **stung** [stʌŋ]) pungere ♦ *vi* bruciare; **my eyes are ~ing** mi bruciano gli occhi.
stingy ['stɪndʒɪ] *adj* spilorcio(a), tirchio(a).
stink [stɪŋk] *n* fetore *m*, puzzo ♦ *vi* (*pt* **stank**, *pp* **stunk** [stæŋk, stʌŋk]) puzzare.
stinker ['stɪŋkə*] *n* (*col*) porcheria; (*person*) fetente *m/f*.
stinking ['stɪŋkɪŋ] *adj* (*col*): **a** ~ ... uno schifo di ..., un(a) maledetto(a) ...; ~ **rich** ricco(a) da far paura.

stint [stɪnt] *n* lavoro, compito ♦ *vi*: **to** ~ **on** lesinare su.
stipend ['staɪpɛnd] *n* stipendio, congrua.
stipendiary [staɪ'pɛndɪərɪ] *adj*: ~ **magistrate** magistrato stipendiato.
stipulate ['stɪpjuleɪt] *vt* stipulare.
stipulation [stɪpju'leɪʃən] *n* stipulazione *f*.
stir [stəː*] *n* agitazione *f*, clamore *m* ♦ *vt* rimescolare; (*move*) smuovere, agitare ♦ *vi* muoversi; **to give sth a** ~ mescolare qc; **to cause a** ~ fare scalpore.
▶**stir up** *vt* provocare, suscitare.
stir-fry ['stəː'fraɪ] *vt* saltare in padella ♦ *n* pietanza al salto.
stirring ['stəːrɪŋ] *adj* eccitante; commovente.
stirrup ['stɪrəp] *n* staffa.
stitch [stɪtʃ] *n* (*SEWING*) punto; (*KNITTING*) maglia; (*MED*) punto (di sutura); (*pain*) fitta ♦ *vt* cucire, attaccare; suturare.
stoat [stəut] *n* ermellino.
stock [stɔk] *n* riserva, provvista; (*COMM*) giacenza, stock *m inv*; (*AGR*) bestiame *m*; (*CULIN*) brodo; (*FINANCE*) titoli *mpl*, azioni *fpl*; (*RAIL*: *also*: **rolling** ~) materiale *m* rotabile; (*descent, origin*) stirpe *f* ♦ *adj* (*fig*: *reply etc*) consueto(a); solito(a), classico(a); (*greeting*) usuale; (*COMM*: *goods, size*) standard *inv* ♦ *vt* (*have in stock*) avere, vendere; **well-~ed** ben fornito(a); **to have sth in** ~ avere qc in magazzino; **out of** ~ esaurito(a); **to take** ~ (*fig*) fare il punto; ~**s and shares** valori *mpl* di borsa; **government** ~ titoli di Stato.
▶**stock up** *vi*: **to** ~ **up (with)** fare provvista (di).
stockade [stɔ'keɪd] *n* palizzata.
stockbroker ['stɔkbrəukə*] *n* agente *m* di cambio.
stock control *n* gestione *f* magazzino.
stock cube *n* (*BRIT CULIN*) dado.
stock exchange *n* Borsa (valori).
stockholder ['stɔkhəuldə*] *n* (*FINANCE*) azionista *m/f*.
Stockholm ['stɔkhəum] *n* Stoccolma.
stocking ['stɔkɪŋ] *n* calza.
stock-in-trade ['stɔkɪn'treɪd] *n* (*fig*): **it's his** ~ è la sua specialità.
stockist ['stɔkɪst] *n* (*BRIT*) fornitore *m*.
stock market *n* (*BRIT*) Borsa, mercato finanziario.
stock phrase *n* cliché *m inv*.
stockpile ['stɔkpaɪl] *n* riserva ♦ *vt* accumulare riserve di.
stockroom ['stɔkrum] *n* magazzino.
stocktaking ['stɔkteɪkɪŋ] *n* (*BRIT COMM*) inventario.
stocky ['stɔkɪ] *adj* tarchiato(a), tozzo(a).

stodgy ['stɔdʒɪ] *adj* pesante, indigesto(a).
stoic ['stəʊɪk] *n* stoico/a.
stoical ['stəʊɪkəl] *adj* stoico(a).
stoke [stəʊk] *vt* alimentare.
stoker ['stəʊkə*] *n* fochista *m*.
stole [stəʊl] *pt of* **steal** ♦ *n* stola.
stolen ['stəʊln] *pp of* **steal**.
stolid ['stɔlɪd] *adj* impassibile.
stomach ['stʌmək] *n* stomaco; (*abdomen*) ventre *m* ♦ *vt* sopportare, digerire.
stomach ache *n* mal *m* di stomaco.
stomach pump *n* pompa gastrica.
stomach ulcer *n* ulcera allo stomaco.
stomp [stɔmp] *vi*: **to ~ in/out** *etc* entrare/ uscire *etc* con passo pesante.
stone [stəʊn] *n* pietra; (*pebble*) sasso, ciottolo; (*in fruit*) nocciolo; (*MED*) calcolo; (*BRIT: weight*) = *6.348 kg*.; *14 libbre* ♦ *cpd* di pietra ♦ *vt* lapidare; **within a ~'s throw of the station** a due passi dalla stazione.
Stone Age *n*: **the ~** l'età della pietra.
stone-cold [stəʊn'kəʊld] *adj* gelido(a).
stoned [stəʊnd] *adj* (*col: drunk*) sbronzo(a); (*on drugs*) fuori *inv*.
stone-deaf [stəʊn'dɛf] *adj* sordo(a) come una campana.
stonemason ['stəʊnmeɪsn] *n* scalpellino.
stonewall [stəʊn'wɔːl] *vi* fare ostruzionismo ♦ *vt* ostacolare.
stonework ['stəʊnwɔːk] *n* muratura.
stony ['stəʊnɪ] *adj* pietroso(a), sassoso(a).
stood [stʊd] *pt, pp of* **stand**.
stooge [stuːdʒ] *n* (*col*) tirapiedi *m/f inv*.
stool [stuːl] *n* sgabello.
stoop [stuːp] *vi* (*also*: **have a ~**) avere una curvatura; (*bend*) chinarsi, curvarsi; **to ~ to sth/doing sth** abbassarsi a qc/a fare qc.
stop [stɔp] *n* arresto; (*stopping place*) fermata; (*in punctuation*) punto ♦ *vt* arrestare, fermare; (*break off*) interrompere; (*also*: **put a ~ to**) porre fine a; (*prevent*) impedire ♦ *vi* fermarsi; (*rain, noise etc*) cessare, finire; **to ~ doing sth** cessare *or* finire di fare qc; **to ~ sb (from) doing sth** impedire a qn di fare qc; **to ~ dead** fermarsi di colpo; **~ it!** smettila!, basta!
▶**stop by** *vi* passare, fare un salto.
▶**stop off** *vi* sostare brevemente.
▶**stop up** *vt* (*hole*) chiudere, turare.
stopcock ['stɔpkɔk] *n* rubinetto di arresto.
stopgap ['stɔpgæp] *n* (*person*) tappabuchi *m/f inv*; (*measure*) ripiego ♦ *cpd* (*measure, solution*) di fortuna.
stoplights ['stɔplaɪts] *npl* (*AUT*) stop *mpl*.
stopover ['stɔpəʊvə*] *n* breve sosta; (*AVIAT*) scalo.

stoppage ['stɔpɪdʒ] *n* arresto, fermata; (*of pay*) trattenuta; (*strike*) interruzione *f* del lavoro.
stopper ['stɔpə*] *n* tappo.
stop press *n* ultimissime *fpl*.
stopwatch ['stɔpwɔtʃ] *n* cronometro.
storage ['stɔːrɪdʒ] *n* immagazzinamento; (*COMPUT*) memoria.
storage heater *n* (*BRIT*) radiatore *m* elettrico che accumula calore.
store [stɔː*] *n* provvista, riserva; (*depot*) deposito; (*BRIT: department* ~) grande magazzino; (*US: shop*) negozio ♦ *vt* mettere da parte; conservare; (*grain, goods*) immagazzinare; (*COMPUT*) registrare; **to set great/little ~ by sth** dare molta/poca importanza a qc; **who knows what is in ~ for us?** chissà cosa ci riserva il futuro?
▶**store up** *vt* mettere in serbo, conservare.
storehouse ['stɔːhaʊs] *n* magazzino, deposito.
storekeeper ['stɔːkiːpə*] *n* (*US*) negoziante *m/f*.
storeroom ['stɔːrum] *n* dispensa.
storey, (*US*) **story** ['stɔːrɪ] *n* piano.
stork [stɔːk] *n* cicogna.
storm [stɔːm] *n* tempesta; (*also*: **thunder~**) temporale *m* ♦ *vi* (*fig*) infuriarsi ♦ *vt* prendere d'assalto.
storm cloud *n* nube *f* temporalesca.
storm door *n* controporta.
stormy ['stɔːmɪ] *adj* tempestoso(a), burrascoso(a).
story ['stɔːrɪ] *n* storia; racconto; (*PRESS*) articolo; (*US*) = **storey**.
storybook ['stɔːrɪbuk] *n* libro di racconti.
storyteller ['stɔːrɪtelə*] *n* narratore/trice.
stout [staut] *adj* solido(a), robusto(a); (*brave*) coraggioso(a); (*fat*) corpulento(a), grasso(a) ♦ *n* birra scura.
stove [stəʊv] *n* (*for cooking*) fornello; (: *small*) fornelletto; (*for heating*) stufa; **gas/electric ~** cucina a gas/elettrica.
stow [stəʊ] *vt* mettere via.
stowaway ['stəʊəweɪ] *n* passeggero(a) clandestino(a).
straddle ['strædl] *vt* stare a cavalcioni di.
strafe [strɑːf] *vt* mitragliare.
straggle ['strægl] *vi* crescere (*or* estendersi) disordinatamente; trascinarsi; rimanere indietro; **~d along the coast** disseminat(e) lungo la costa.
straggler ['stræglə*] *n* sbandato/a.
straggling ['stræglɪŋ], **straggly** ['strægli] *adj* (*hair*) in disordine.
straight [streɪt] *adj* (*continuous, direct*)

dritto(a); (*frank*) onesto(a), franco(a);
(*plain, uncomplicated*) semplice; (*THEAT:
part, play*) serio(a); (*col: heterosexual*)
eterosessuale ♦ *adv* diritto; (*drink*) liscio
♦ *n*: **the** ~ la linea retta; (*RAIL*) il rettilineo;
(*SPORT*) la dirittura d'arrivo; **to put** *or*
get ~ mettere in ordine, mettere ordine
in; **to be (all)** ~ (*tidy*) essere a posto,
essere sistemato; (*clarified*) essere
chiaro; **ten** ~ **wins** dieci vittorie di fila;
~ **away,** ~ **off** (*at once*) immediatamente;
~ **off,** ~ **out** senza esitare; **I went** ~
home sono andato direttamente a casa.

straighten ['streɪtn] *vt* (*also:* ~ **out**)
raddrizzare; **to** ~ **things out** mettere le
cose a posto.

straight-faced [streɪt'feɪst] *adj* impassibile,
imperturbabile ♦ *adv* con il viso serio.

straightforward [streɪt'fɔːwəd] *adj*
semplice; (*frank*) onesto(a), franco(a).

strain [streɪn] *n* (*TECH*) sollecitazione *f*;
(*physical*) sforzo; (*mental*) tensione *f*;
(*MED*) strappo; (*streak, trace*) tendenza;
elemento; (*breed*) razza; (*of virus*) tipo ♦ *vt*
tendere; (*muscle*) slogare; (*ankle*)
storcere; (*friendship, marriage*) mettere a
dura prova; (*filter*) colare, filtrare ♦ *vi*
sforzarsi; ~**s** *npl* (*MUS*) note *fpl*; **she's
under a lot of** ~ è molto tesa, è sotto
pressione.

strained [streɪnd] *adj* (*laugh etc*) forzato(a);
(*relations*) teso(a).

strainer ['streɪnə*] *n* passino, colino.

strait [streɪt] *n* (*GEO*) stretto; **to be in dire**
~**s** (*fig*) essere nei guai.

straitjacket ['streɪtdʒækɪt] *n* camicia di
forza.

strait-laced [streɪt'leɪst] *adj* puritano(a).

strand [strænd] *n* (*of thread*) filo.

strange [streɪndʒ] *adj* (*not known*)
sconosciuto(a); (*odd*) strano(a),
bizzarro(a).

strangely ['streɪndʒlɪ] *adv* stranamente.

stranger ['streɪndʒə*] *n* (*unknown*)
sconosciuto/a; (*from another place*)
estraneo/a; **I'm a** ~ **here** non sono del
posto.

strangle ['stræŋgl] *vt* strangolare.

stranglehold ['stræŋglhəʊld] *n* (*fig*) stretta
(mortale).

strangulation [stræŋgju'leɪʃən] *n*
strangolamento.

strap [stræp] *n* cinghia; (*of slip, dress*)
spallina, bretella ♦ *vt* legare con una
cinghia; (*child etc*) punire (con una
cinghia).

straphanging ['stræphæŋɪŋ] *n* viaggiare *m*
in piedi (*su mezzi pubblici reggendosi a un*

sostegno).

strapless ['stræplɪs] *adj* (*bra, dress*) senza
spalline.

strapped [stræpt] *adj*: ~ **for cash** a corto di
soldi; **financially** ~ finanziariamente a
terra.

strapping ['stræpɪŋ] *adj* ben piantato(a).

Strasbourg ['stræzbɔːg] *n* Strasburgo *f*.

strata ['strɑːtə] *npl of* **stratum**.

stratagem ['strætɪdʒəm] *n* stratagemma *m*.

strategic [strə'tiːdʒɪk] *adj* strategico(a).

strategist ['strætɪdʒɪst] *n* stratega *m*.

strategy ['strætɪdʒɪ] *n* strategia.

stratosphere ['strætəsfɪə*] *n* stratosfera.

stratum, *pl* **strata** ['strɑːtəm, 'strɑːtə] *n*
strato.

straw [strɔː] *n* paglia; (*drinking* ~)
cannuccia; **that's the last** ~! è la goccia
che fa traboccare il vaso!

strawberry ['strɔːbərɪ] *n* fragola.

stray [streɪ] *adj* (*animal*) randagio(a) ♦ *vi*
perdersi; allontanarsi, staccarsi (dal
gruppo); ~ **bullet** proiettile *m* vagante.

streak [striːk] *n* striscia; (*fig: of madness
etc*): **a** ~ **of** una vena di ♦ *vt* striare,
screziare ♦ *vi*: **to** ~ **past** passare come un
fulmine; **to have** ~**s in one's hair** avere le
mèche nei capelli; **a winning/losing** ~ un
periodo fortunato/sfortunato.

streaker ['striːkə*] *n* streaker *m/f inv.*

streaky ['striːkɪ] *adj* screziato(a), striato(a).

streaky bacon *n* (*BRIT*) ≈ pancetta.

stream [striːm] *n* ruscello; corrente *f*; (*of
people*) fiume *m* ♦ *vt* (*SCOL*) dividere in
livelli di rendimento ♦ *vi* scorrere; **to** ~
in/out entrare/uscire a fiotti; **against the**
~ controcorrente; **on** ~ (*new power plant
etc*) in funzione, in produzione.

streamer ['striːmə*] *n* (*of paper*) stella
filante.

stream feed *n* (*on photocopier etc*)
alimentazione *f* continua.

streamline ['striːmlaɪn] *vt* dare una linea
aerodinamica a; (*fig*) razionalizzare.

streamlined ['striːmlaɪnd] *adj*
aerodinamico(a), affusolato(a); (*fig*)
razionalizzato(a).

street [striːt] *n* strada, via; **the back** ~**s** le
strade secondarie; **to be on the** ~**s**
(*homeless*) essere senza tetto; (*as
prostitute*) battere il marciapiede.

streetcar ['striːtkɑː*] *n* (*US*) tram *m inv.*

street cred [-krɛd] *n* (*col*) credibilità
presso i giovani.

street lamp *n* lampione *m.*

street lighting *n* illuminazione *f* stradale.

street map, street plan *n* pianta (di una
città).

street market n mercato all'aperto.
streetwise ['stri:twaɪz] adj (col) esperto(a) dei bassifondi.
strength [strɛŋθ] n forza; (of girder, knot etc) resistenza, solidità; (of chemical solution) concentrazione f; (of wine) gradazione f alcolica; **on the** ~ **of** sulla base di, in virtù di; **below/at full** ~ con gli effettivi ridotti/al completo.
strengthen ['strɛŋθən] vt rinforzare; (muscles) irrobustire; (economy, currency) consolidare.
strenuous ['strɛnjuəs] adj vigoroso(a), energico(a); (tiring) duro(a), pesante.
stress [strɛs] n (force, pressure) pressione f; (mental strain) tensione f; (accent) accento; (emphasis) enfasi f ♦ vt insistere su, sottolineare; **to be under** ~ essere sotto tensione; **to lay great** ~ **on sth** dare grande importanza a qc.
stressful ['strɛsful] adj (job) difficile, stressante.
stretch [strɛtʃ] n (of sand etc) distesa; (of time) periodo ♦ vi stirarsi; (extend): **to** ~ **to** or **as far as** estendersi fino a; (be enough: money, food): **to** ~ **(to)** bastare (per) ♦ vt tendere, allungare; (spread) distendere; (fig) spingere (al massimo); **at a** ~ ininterrottamente; **to** ~ **a muscle** tendere un muscolo; **to** ~ **one's legs** sgranchirsi le gambe.
►**stretch out** vi allungarsi, estendersi ♦ vt (arm etc) allungare, tendere; (to spread) distendere; **to** ~ **out for sth** allungare la mano per prendere qc.
stretcher ['strɛtʃə*] n barella, lettiga.
stretcher-bearer ['strɛtʃəbɛərə*] n barelliere m.
stretch marks npl smagliature fpl.
strewn [struːn] adj: ~ **with** cosparso(a) di.
stricken ['strɪkən] adj provato(a); affranto(a); ~ **with** colpito(a) da.
strict [strɪkt] adj (severe) rigido(a), severo(a); (: order, rule) rigoroso(a); (: supervision) stretto(a); (: precise) preciso(a), stretto(a); **in** ~ **confidence** in assoluta confidenza.
strictly ['strɪktlɪ] adv severamente; rigorosamente; strettamente; ~ **confidential** strettamente confidenziale; ~ **speaking** a rigor di termini; ~ **between ourselves** ... detto fra noi ....
stride [straɪd] n passo lungo ♦ vi (pt **strode**, pp **stridden** [strəud, 'strɪdn]) camminare a grandi passi; **to take in one's** ~ (fig: changes etc) prendere con tranquillità.
strident ['straɪdnt] adj stridente.
strife [straɪf] n conflitto; litigi mpl.

strike [straɪk] n sciopero; (of oil etc) scoperta; (attack) attacco ♦ vb (pt, pp **struck** [strʌk]) vt colpire; (oil etc) scoprire, trovare; (produce, make: coin, medal) coniare; (: agreement, deal) concludere ♦ vi far sciopero, scioperare; (attack) attaccare; (clock) suonare; **to go on** or **come out on** ~ mettersi in sciopero; **to** ~ **a match** accendere un fiammifero; **to** ~ **a balance** (fig) trovare il giusto mezzo.
►**strike back** vi (MIL) fare rappresaglie; (fig) reagire.
►**strike down** vt (fig) atterrare.
►**strike off** vt (from list) cancellare; (: doctor etc) radiare.
►**strike out** vt depennare.
►**strike up** vt (MUS) attaccare; **to** ~ **up a friendship** with fare amicizia con.
strikebreaker ['straɪkbreɪkə*] n crumiro/a.
striker ['straɪkə*] n scioperante m/f; (SPORT) attaccante m.
striking ['straɪkɪŋ] adj impressionante.
Strimmer ® ['strɪmə*] n tagliabordi m inv.
string [strɪŋ] n spago; (row) fila; sequenza; catena; (COMPUT) stringa, sequenza; (MUS) corda ♦ vt (pt, pp **strung** [strʌŋ]): **to** ~ **out** disporre di fianco; **to** ~ **together** mettere insieme; **the** ~**s** npl (MUS) gli archi; ~ **of pearls** filo di perle; **with no** ~**s attached** (fig) senza vincoli, senza obblighi; **to get a job by pulling** ~**s** ottenere un lavoro a forza di raccomandazioni.
string bean n fagiolino.
string(ed) instrument n (MUS) strumento a corda.
stringent ['strɪndʒənt] adj rigoroso(a); (reasons, arguments) stringente, impellente.
string quartet n quartetto d'archi.
strip [strɪp] n striscia; (SPORT): **wearing the Celtic** ~ con la divisa del Celtic ♦ vt spogliare; (also: ~ **down**: machine) smontare ♦ vi spogliarsi.
strip cartoon n fumetto.
stripe [straɪp] n striscia, riga.
striped ['straɪpt] adj a strisce or righe.
strip light n (BRIT) tubo al neon.
stripper ['strɪpə*] n spogliarellista.
strip-search ['strɪpsəːtʃ] vt: **to** ~ **sb** perquisire qn facendolo(a) spogliare ♦ n perquisizione f (facendo spogliare il perquisito).
striptease ['strɪptiːz] n spogliarello.
strive [straɪv], pt **strove**, pp **striven** [straɪv, strəuv, 'strɪvn] vi: **to** ~ **to do** sforzarsi di fare.
strobe [strəub] n (also: ~ **light**) luce f stroboscopica.

strode [strəud] *pt of* **stride**.
stroke [strəuk] *n* colpo; (*of piston*) corsa; (*MED*) colpo apoplettico; (*SWIMMING*: *style*) nuoto; (*caress*) carezza ♦ *vt* accarezzare; **at a** ~ in un attimo; **on the** ~ **of 5** alle 5 in punto, allo scoccare delle 5; **a** ~ **of luck** un colpo di fortuna; **two-**~ **engine** motore a due tempi.
stroll [strəul] *n* giretto, passeggiatina ♦ *vi* andare a spasso; **to go for a** ~, **have** *or* **take a** ~ andare a fare un giretto *or* due passi.
stroller ['strəulə*] *n* (*US*) passeggino.
strong [strɔŋ] *adj* (*gen*) forte; (*sturdy*: *table, fabric etc*) solido(a); (*concentrated, intense*: *bleach, acid*) concentrato(a); (*protest, letter, measures*) energico(a) ♦ *adv*: **to be going** ~ (*company*) andare a gonfie vele; (*person*) essere attivo(a); **they are 50** ~ sono in 50; ~ **language** (*swearing*) linguaggio volgare.
strong-arm ['strɔŋɑːm] *adj* (*tactics, methods*) energico(a).
strongbox ['strɔŋbɔks] *n* cassaforte *f*.
stronghold ['strɔŋhəuld] *n* fortezza, roccaforte *f*.
strongly ['strɔŋlɪ] *adv* fortemente, con forza; solidamente; energicamente; **to feel** ~ **about sth** avere molto a cuore qc.
strongman ['strɔŋmæn] *n* personaggio di spicco.
strongroom ['strɔŋrum] *n* camera di sicurezza.
stroppy ['strɔpɪ] *adj* (*BRIT col*) scontroso(a), indisponente.
strove [strəuv] *pt of* **strive**.
struck [strʌk] *pt, pp of* **strike**.
structural ['strʌktʃərəl] *adj* strutturale; (*CONSTR*) di costruzione; di struttura.
structurally ['strʌktʃrəlɪ] *adv* dal punto di vista della struttura.
structure ['strʌktʃə*] *n* struttura; (*building*) costruzione *f*, fabbricato.
struggle ['strʌgl] *n* lotta ♦ *vi* lottare; **to have a** ~ **to do sth** avere dei problemi per fare qc.
strum [strʌm] *vt* (*guitar*) strimpellare.
strung [strʌŋ] *pt, pp of* **string**.
strut [strʌt] *n* sostegno, supporto ♦ *vi* pavoneggiarsi.
strychnine ['strɪkniːn] *n* stricnina.
stub [stʌb] *n* mozzicone *m*; (*of ticket etc*) matrice *f*, talloncino ♦ *vt*: **to** ~ **one's toe (on sth)** urtare *or* sbattere il dito del piede (contro qc).
▶**stub out** *vt*: **to** ~ **out a cigarette** spegnere una sigaretta.
stubble ['stʌbl] *n* stoppia; (*on chin*) barba

ispida.
stubborn ['stʌbən] *adj* testardo(a), ostinato(a).
stubby ['stʌbɪ] *adj* tozzo(a).
stucco ['stʌkəu] *n* stucco.
stuck [stʌk] *pt, pp of* **stick** ♦ *adj* (*jammed*) bloccato(a); **to get** ~ bloccarsi.
stuck-up [stʌk'ʌp] *adj* presuntuoso(a).
stud [stʌd] *n* bottoncino; borchia; (*of horses*) scuderia, allevamento di cavalli; (*also*: ~ **horse**) stallone *m* ♦ *vt* (*fig*): ~**ded with** tempestato(a) di.
student ['stjuːdənt] *n* studente/essa ♦ *cpd* studentesco(a); universitario(a); degli studenti; **a law/medical** ~ uno studente di legge/di medicina.
student driver *n* (*US*) conducente *m/f* principiante.
students' union *n* (*BRIT*: *association*) circolo universitario; (: *building*) sede *f* del circolo universitario.
studied ['stʌdɪd] *adj* studiato(a), calcolato(a).
studio ['stjuːdɪəu] *n* studio.
studio flat, (*US*) **studio apartment** *n* appartamento monolocale.
studious ['stjuːdɪəs] *adj* studioso(a); (*studied*) studiato(a), voluto(a).
studiously ['stjuːdɪəslɪ] *adv* (*carefully*) deliberatamente, di proposito.
study ['stʌdɪ] *n* studio ♦ *vt* studiare; esaminare ♦ *vi* studiare; **to make a** ~ **of sth** fare uno studio su qc; **to** ~ **for an exam** prepararsi a un esame.
stuff [stʌf] *n* (*substance*) roba; (*belongings*) cose *fpl*, roba ♦ *vt* imbottire; (*animal*: *for exhibition*) impagliare; (*CULIN*) farcire; **my nose is** ~**ed up** ho il naso chiuso; **get** ~**ed!** (*col!*) va' a farti fottere! (*!*); ~**ed toy** giocattolo di peluche.
stuffing ['stʌfɪŋ] *n* imbottitura; (*CULIN*) ripieno.
stuffy ['stʌfɪ] *adj* (*room*) mal ventilato(a), senz'aria; (*ideas*) antiquato(a).
stumble ['stʌmbl] *vi* inciampare; **to** ~ **across** (*fig*) imbattersi in.
stumbling block ['stʌmblɪŋ-] *n* ostacolo, scoglio.
stump [stʌmp] *n* ceppo; (*of limb*) moncone *m* ♦ *vt*: **to be** ~**ed for an answer** essere incapace di rispondere.
stun [stʌn] *vt* stordire; (*amaze*) sbalordire.
stung [stʌŋ] *pt, pp of* **sting**.
stunk [stʌŋk] *pp of* **stink**.
stunning ['stʌnɪŋ] *adj* (*piece of news etc*) sbalorditivo(a); (*girl, dress*) favoloso(a), stupendo(a).
stunt [stʌnt] *n* bravata; trucco

pubblicitario; (*AVIAT*) acrobazia ♦ *vt* arrestare.
stunted ['stʌntɪd] *adj* stentato(a), rachitico(a).
stuntman ['stʌntmæn] *n* cascatore *m*.
stupefaction [stjuːpɪ'fækʃən] *n* stupefazione *f*, stupore *m*.
stupefy ['stjuːpɪfaɪ] *vt* stordire; intontire; (*fig*) stupire.
stupendous [stjuː'pɛndəs] *adj* stupendo(a), meraviglioso(a).
stupid ['stjuːpɪd] *adj* stupido(a).
stupidity [stjuː'pɪdɪtɪ] *n* stupidità.
stupidly ['stjuːpɪdlɪ] *adv* stupidamente.
stupor ['stjuːpə*] *n* torpore *m*.
sturdy ['stəːdɪ] *adj* robusto(a), vigoroso(a); solido(a).
sturgeon ['stəːdʒən] *n* storione *m*.
stutter ['stʌtə*] *n* balbuzie *f* ♦ *vi* balbettare.
Stuttgart ['ʃtutgart] *n* Stoccarda.
sty [staɪ] *n* (*of pigs*) porcile *m*.
stye [staɪ] *n* (*MED*) orzaiolo.
style [staɪl] *n* stile *m*; (*distinction*) eleganza, classe *f*; (*hair ~*) pettinatura; (*of dress etc*) modello, linea; **in the latest** ~ all'ultima moda.
styli ['staɪlaɪ] *npl of* **stylus**.
stylish ['staɪlɪʃ] *adj* elegante.
stylist ['staɪlɪst] *n*: **hair** ~ parrucchiere/a.
stylized ['staɪlaɪzd] *adj* stilizzato(a).
stylus, *pl* **styli** *or* **styluses** ['staɪləs, -laɪ] *n* (*of record player*) puntina.
Styrofoam ® ['staɪrəfəum] *n* (*US*) = **polystyrene** ♦ *adj* (*cup*) di polistirene.
suave [swɑːv] *adj* untuoso(a).
sub [sʌb] *n abbr* = **submarine; subscription**.
sub... [sʌb] *prefix* sub..., sotto....
subcommittee ['sʌbkəmɪtɪ] *n* sottocomitato.
subconscious [sʌb'kɔnʃəs] *adj, n* subcosciente (*m*).
subcontinent [sʌb'kɔntɪnənt] *n*: **the (Indian)** ~ il subcontinente (indiano).
subcontract *n* [sʌb'kɔntrækt] subappalto ♦ *vt* [sʌbkən'trækt] subappaltare.
subcontractor ['sʌbkən'træktə*] *n* subappaltatore/trice.
subdivide [sʌbdɪ'vaɪd] *vt* suddividere.
subdivision ['sʌbdɪvɪʒən] *n* suddivisione *f*.
subdue [səb'djuː] *vt* sottomettere, soggiogare.
subdued [səb'djuːd] *adj* pacato(a); (*light*) attenuato(a); (*person*) poco esuberante.
sub-editor ['sʌb'ɛdɪtə*] *n* (*BRIT*) redattore(trice) aggiunto(a).
subject ['sʌbdʒɪkt] *n* soggetto; (*citizen etc*) cittadino/a; (*SCOL*) materia ♦ *adj* (*liable*): ~ **to** soggetto(a) a ♦ *vt* [səb'dʒɛkt]: **to** ~ **to**

sottomettere a; esporre a; ~ **to confirmation in writing** a condizione di ricevere conferma scritta; **to change the** ~ cambiare discorso.
subjection [səb'dʒɛkʃən] *n* sottomissione *f*, soggezione *f*.
subjective [səb'dʒɛktɪv] *adj* soggettivo(a).
subject matter *n* argomento; contenuto.
sub judice [sʌb'dʒuːdɪsɪ] *adj* (*LAW*) sub iudice.
subjugate ['sʌbdʒugeɪt] *vt* sottomettere, soggiogare.
subjunctive [səb'dʒʌŋktɪv] *adj* congiuntivo(a) ♦ *n* congiuntivo.
sublet [sʌb'lɛt] *vt, vi irreg* subaffittare.
sublime [sə'blaɪm] *adj* sublime
subliminal [sʌb'lɪmɪnl] *adj* subliminale.
submachine gun ['sʌbmə'ʃiːn-] *n* mitra *m inv*.
submarine [sʌbmə'riːn] *n* sommergibile *m*.
submerge [səb'məːdʒ] *vt* sommergere; immergere ♦ *vi* immergersi.
submersion [səb'məːʃən] *n* sommersione *f*; immersione *f*.
submission [səb'mɪʃən] *n* sottomissione *f*; (*to committee etc*) richiesta, domanda.
submissive [səb'mɪsɪv] *adj* remissivo(a).
submit [səb'mɪt] *vt* sottomettere; (*proposal, claim*) presentare ♦ *vi* sottomettersi.
subnormal [sʌb'nɔːməl] *adj* subnormale.
subordinate [sə'bɔːdɪnət] *adj, n* subordinato(a).
subpoena [səb'piːnə] *n* (*LAW*) citazione *f*, mandato di comparizione ♦ *vt* (*LAW*) citare in giudizio.
subroutine [sʌbruː'tiːn] *n* (*COMPUT*) sottoprogramma *m*.
subscribe [səb'skraɪb] *vi* contribuire; **to** ~ **to** (*opinion*) approvare, condividere; (*fund*) sottoscrivere; (*newspaper*) abbonarsi a; essere abbonato(a) a.
subscriber [səb'skraɪbə*] *n* (*to periodical, telephone*) abbonato/a.
subscript ['sʌbskrɪpt] *n* deponente *m*.
subscription [səb'skrɪpʃən] *n* sottoscrizione *f*; abbonamento; **to take out a** ~ **to** abbonarsi a.
subsequent ['sʌbsɪkwənt] *adj* (*later*) successivo(a); (*further*) ulteriore; ~ **to** in seguito a.
subsequently ['sʌbsɪkwəntlɪ] *adv* in seguito, successivamente.
subservient [səb'səːvɪənt] *adj*: ~ **(to)** remissivo(a) (a), sottomesso(a) (a).
subside [səb'saɪd] *vi* cedere, abbassarsi; (*flood*) decrescere; (*wind*) calmarsi.
subsidence [səb'saɪdns] *n* cedimento, abbassamento.

subsidiarity [səbsɪdɪ'ærɪtɪ] n (POL)
principio del decentramento del potere.
subsidiary [səb'sɪdɪərɪ] adj sussidiario(a);
accessorio(a); (BRIT SCOL: subject)
complementare ♦ n filiale f.
subsidize ['sʌbsɪdaɪz] vt sovvenzionare.
subsidy ['sʌbsɪdɪ] n sovvenzione f.
subsist [səb'sɪst] vi: to ~ on sth vivere di
qc.
subsistence [səb'sɪstəns] n esistenza;
mezzi mpl di sostentamento.
subsistence allowance n indennità f inv di
trasferta.
subsistence level n livello minimo di vita.
substance ['sʌbstəns] n sostanza; (fig)
essenza; to lack ~ (argument) essere
debole.
substance abuse n abuso di sostanze
tossiche.
substandard [sʌb'stændəd] adj (goods,
housing) di qualità scadente.
substantial [səb'stænʃl] adj solido(a);
(amount, progress etc) notevole; (meal)
sostanzioso(a).
substantially [səb'stænʃəlɪ] adv
sostanzialmente; ~ bigger molto più
grande.
substantiate [səb'stænʃɪeɪt] vt
comprovare.
substitute ['sʌbstɪtjuːt] n (person)
sostituto/a; (thing) succedaneo, surrogato
♦ vt: to ~ sth/sb for sostituire qc/qn a.
substitute teacher n (US) supplente m/f.
substitution [sʌbstɪ'tjuːʃən] n sostituzione
f.
subterfuge ['sʌbtəfjuːdʒ] n sotterfugio.
subterranean [sʌbtə'reɪnɪən] adj
sotterraneo(a).
subtitle ['sʌbtaɪtl] n (CINE) sottotitolo.
subtle ['sʌtl] adj sottile; (flavour, perfume)
delicato(a).
subtlety ['sʌtltɪ] n sottigliezza.
subtly ['sʌtlɪ] adv sottilmente;
delicatamente.
subtotal [sʌb'təutl] n somma parziale.
subtract [səb'trækt] vt sottrarre.
subtraction [səb'trækʃən] n sottrazione f.
suburb ['sʌbəːb] n sobborgo; the ~s la
periferia.
suburban [sə'bəːbən] adj suburbano(a).
suburbia [sə'bəːbɪə] n periferia, sobborghi
mpl.
subversion [səb'vəːʃən] n sovversione f.
subversive [səb'vəːsɪv] adj sovversivo(a).
subway ['sʌbweɪ] n (US: underground)
metropolitana; (BRIT: underpass)
sottopassaggio.
subzero [sʌb'zɪərəu] adj: ~ temperatures

temperature fpl sotto zero.
succeed [sək'siːd] vi riuscire, avere
successo ♦ vt succedere a; to ~ in doing
riuscire a fare.
succeeding [sək'siːdɪŋ] adj (following)
successivo(a); ~ generations generazioni
fpl future.
success [sək'sɛs] n successo.
successful [sək'sɛsful] adj (venture)
coronato(a) da successo, riuscito(a); to
be ~ (in doing) riuscire (a fare).
successfully [sək'sɛsfəlɪ] adv con successo.
succession [sək'sɛʃən] n successione f; in ~
di seguito.
successive [sək'sɛsɪv] adj successivo(a);
consecutivo(a); on 3 ~ days per 3 giorni
consecutivi or di seguito.
successor [sək'sɛsə*] n successore m.
succinct [sək'sɪŋkt] adj succinto(a), breve.
succulent ['sʌkjulənt] adj succulento(a) ♦ n
(BOT): ~s piante fpl grasse.
succumb [sə'kʌm] vi soccombere.
such [sʌtʃ] adj tale; (of that kind): ~ a book
un tale libro, un libro del genere; ~
books tali libri, libri del genere; (so
much): ~ courage tanto coraggio ♦ adv: ~
a long trip un viaggio così lungo; ~ good
books libri così buoni; ~ a lot of talmente
or così tanto(a); making ~ a noise that
facendo un rumore tale che; ~ a long
time ago tanto tempo fa; ~ as (like) come;
a noise ~ as to un rumore tale da; ~
books as I have quei pochi libri che ho; as
~ come or in quanto tale; I said no ~
thing non ho detto niente del genere.
such-and-such ['sʌtʃənsʌtʃ] adj tale (after
noun).
suchlike ['sʌtʃlaɪk] pron (col): and ~ e così
via.
suck [sʌk] vt succhiare; (subj: baby)
poppare; (: pump, machine) aspirare.
sucker ['sʌkə*] n (ZOOL, TECH) ventosa;
(BOT) pollone m; (col) gonzo/a, babbeo/a.
suckle ['sʌkl] vt allattare.
sucrose ['suːkrəuz] n saccarosio.
suction ['sʌkʃən] n succhiamento; (TECH)
aspirazione f.
suction pump n pompa aspirante.
Sudan [suː'dɑːn] n Sudan m.
Sudanese [suːdə'niːz] adj, n sudanese (m/f).
sudden ['sʌdn] adj improvviso(a); all of a ~
improvvisamente, all'improvviso.
sudden-death [sʌdn'dɛθ] n (also: ~ playoff)
(SPORT) spareggio, bella.
suddenly ['sʌdnlɪ] adv bruscamente,
improvvisamente, di colpo.
suds [sʌdz] npl schiuma (di sapone).
sue [suː] vt citare in giudizio ♦ vi: to ~ (for)

intentare causa (per); **to ~ for divorce** intentare causa di divorzio; **to ~ sb for damages** citare qn per danni.

suede [sweɪd] n pelle f scamosciata ♦ cpd scamosciato(a).

suet ['suɪt] n grasso di rognone.

Suez ['suːɪz] n: **the ~ Canal** il Canale di Suez.

suffer ['sʌfə*] vt soffrire, patire; (bear) sopportare, tollerare; (undergo: loss, setback) subire ♦ vi soffrire; **to ~ from** soffrire di; **to ~ from the effects of alcohol/a fall** risentire degli effetti dell'alcool/di una caduta.

sufferance ['sʌfərəns] n: **he was only there on ~** era più che altro sopportato lì.

sufferer ['sʌfərə*] n (MED): **~ (from)** malato/a (di).

suffering ['sʌfərɪŋ] n sofferenza; (hardship, deprivation) privazione f.

suffice [sə'faɪs] vi essere sufficiente, bastare.

sufficient [sə'fɪʃənt] adj sufficiente; **~ money** abbastanza soldi.

sufficiently [sə'fɪʃəntlɪ] adv sufficientemente, abbastanza.

suffix ['sʌfɪks] n suffisso.

suffocate ['sʌfəkeɪt] vi (have difficulty breathing) soffocare; (die through lack of air) asfissiare.

suffocation [sʌfə'keɪʃən] n soffocamento; (MED) asfissia.

suffrage ['sʌfrɪdʒ] n suffragio.

suffuse [sə'fjuːz] vt: **to ~ (with)** (colour) tingere (di); (light) soffondere (di); **her face was ~d with joy** la gioia si dipingeva sul suo volto.

sugar ['ʃugə*] n zucchero ♦ vt zuccherare.

sugar beet n barbabietola da zucchero.

sugar bowl n zuccheriera.

sugar cane n canna da zucchero.

sugar-coated ['ʃugəkəutɪd] adj ricoperto(a) di zucchero.

sugar lump n zolletta di zucchero.

sugar refinery n raffineria di zucchero.

sugary ['ʃugərɪ] adj zuccherino(a), dolce; (fig) sdolcinato(a).

suggest [sə'dʒɛst] vt proporre, suggerire; (indicate) indicare; **what do you ~ I do?** cosa mi suggerisce di fare?

suggestion [sə'dʒɛstʃən] n suggerimento, proposta.

suggestive [sə'dʒɛstɪv] adj suggestivo(a); (indecent) spinto(a), indecente.

suicidal [suɪ'saɪdl] adj suicida inv; (fig) fatale, disastroso(a).

suicide ['suɪsaɪd] n (person) suicida m/f; (act) suicidio; **to commit ~** suicidarsi.

suicide attempt, suicide bid n tentato suicidio.

suicide bomber n attentatore/trice suicida.

suicide bombing n attentato suicida.

suit [suːt] n (man's) completo; (woman's) completo, tailleur m inv; (law~) causa; (CARDS) seme m, colore m ♦ vt andar bene a or per; essere adatto(a) a or per; (adapt): **to ~ sth to** adattare qc a; **to be ~ed to sth** (suitable for) essere adatto a qc; **well ~ed** (couple) fatti l'uno per l'altro; **to bring a ~ against sb** intentare causa a qn; **to follow ~** (fig) fare altrettanto.

suitable ['suːtəbl] adj adatto(a); appropriato(a); **would tomorrow be ~?** andrebbe bene domani?; **we found somebody ~** abbiamo trovato la persona adatta.

suitably ['suːtəblɪ] adv (dress) in modo adatto; (thank) adeguatamente.

suitcase ['suːtkeɪs] n valigia.

suite [swiːt] n (of rooms) appartamento; (MUS) suite f inv; (furniture): **bedroom/ dining room ~** arredo or mobilia per la camera da letto/sala da pranzo; **a three-piece ~** un salotto comprendente un divano e due poltrone.

suitor ['suːtə*] n corteggiatore m, spasimante m.

sulfate ['sʌlfeɪt] n (US) = **sulphate**.

sulfur etc ['sʌlfə*] (US) = **sulphur** etc.

sulk [sʌlk] vi fare il broncio.

sulky ['sʌlkɪ] adj imbronciato(a).

sullen ['sʌlən] adj scontroso(a); cupo(a).

sulphate, (US) **sulfate** ['sʌlfeɪt] n solfato; **copper ~** solfato di rame.

sulphur, (US) **sulfur** ['sʌlfə*] n zolfo.

sulphur dioxide n biossido di zolfo.

sulphuric, (US) **sulfuric** [sʌl'fjuərɪk] adj: **~ acid** acido solforico.

sultan ['sʌltən] n sultano.

sultana [sʌl'tɑːnə] n (fruit) uva (secca) sultanina.

sultry ['sʌltrɪ] adj afoso(a).

sum [sʌm] n somma; (SCOL etc) addizione f.

► **sum up** vt riassumere; (evaluate rapidly) valutare, giudicare ♦ vi riassumere.

Sumatra [su'mɑːtrə] n Sumatra.

summarize ['sʌmərraɪz] vt riassumere, riepilogare.

summary ['sʌmərɪ] n riassunto ♦ adj (justice) sommario(a).

summer ['sʌmə*] n estate f ♦ cpd d'estate, estivo(a); **in (the) ~** d'estate.

summer camp n (US) colonia (estiva).

summerhouse ['sʌməhaus] n (in garden)

padiglione m.
summertime ['sʌmətaɪm] n (*season*) estate
f.
summer time n (*by clock*) ora legale
(estiva).
summery ['sʌmərɪ] adj estivo(a).
summing-up [sʌmɪŋ'ʌp] n (*LAW*)
ricapitolazione f del processo.
summit ['sʌmɪt] n cima, sommità; (*POL*)
vertice m.
summit conference n conferenza al
vertice.
summon ['sʌmən] vt chiamare, convocare;
to ~ a witness citare un testimone.
▶**summon up** vt raccogliere, fare appello
a.
summons n ordine m di comparizione ♦ vt
citare; **to serve a ~ on sb** notificare una
citazione a qn.
sumo ['suːməu] n (*also:* **~ wrestling**) sumo.
sump [sʌmp] n (*AUT*) coppa dell'olio.
sumptuous ['sʌmptjuəs] adj sontuoso(a).
Sun. abbr (= *Sunday*) dom.
sun [sʌn] n sole m; **in the ~** al sole; **to catch
the ~** prendere sole; **they have
everything under the ~** hanno tutto ciò
che possono desiderare.
sunbathe ['sʌnbeɪð] vi prendere un bagno
di sole.
sunbeam ['sʌnbiːm] n raggio di sole.
sunbed ['sʌnbɛd] n lettino solare.
sunblock ['sʌnblɔk] n crema solare a
protezione totale.
sunburn ['sʌnbəːn] n (*tan*) abbronzatura;
(*painful*) scottatura.
sunburnt ['sʌnbəːnt], **sunburned**
['sʌnbəːnd] adj abbronzato(a); (*painfully*)
scottato(a) dal sole.
sun cream n crema solare.
sundae ['sʌndeɪ] n coppa di gelato
guarnita.
Sunday ['sʌndɪ] n domenica; *for phrases see
also* **Tuesday**.
Sunday paper n giornale m della
domenica; *see boxed note*.

SUNDAY PAPERS
l **Sunday papers** *sono i giornali che escono
di domenica. Sono generalmente corredati da
supplementi e riviste di argomento culturale,
sportivo e di attualità ed hanno un'alta tiratura.*

Sunday school n ≈ scuola di catechismo.
sundial ['sʌndaɪəl] n meridiana.
sundown ['sʌndaun] n tramonto.
sundries ['sʌndrɪz] npl articoli diversi.
sundry ['sʌndrɪ] adj vari(e), diversi(e); **all**

and ~ tutti quanti.
sunflower ['sʌnflauə*] n girasole m.
sung [sʌŋ] pp of **sing**.
sunglasses ['sʌnglɑːsɪz] npl occhiali mpl da
sole.
sunk [sʌŋk] pp of **sink**.
sunken ['sʌŋkən] adj sommerso(a); (*eyes*,
cheeks) infossato(a); (*bath*) incassato(a).
sunlamp ['sʌnlæmp] n lampada a raggi
ultravioletti.
sunlight ['sʌnlaɪt] n (luce f del) sole m.
sunlit ['sʌnlɪt] adj assolato(a),
soleggiato(a).
sunny ['sʌnɪ] adj assolato(a), soleggiato(a);
(*fig*) allegro(a), felice; **it is ~** c'è il sole.
sunrise ['sʌnraɪz] n levata del sole, alba.
sunroof ['sʌnruːf] n (*on building*) tetto a
terrazzo; (*AUT*) tetto apribile.
sunscreen ['sʌnskriːn] n crema solare
protettiva.
sunset ['sʌnsɛt] n tramonto.
sunshade ['sʌnʃeɪd] n parasole m.
sunshine ['sʌnʃaɪn] n (luce f del) sole m.
sunspot ['sʌnspɔt] n macchia solare.
sunstroke ['sʌnstrəuk] n insolazione f,
colpo di sole.
suntan ['sʌntæn] n abbronzatura.
suntanned ['sʌntænd] adj abbronzato(a).
suntan oil n olio solare.
suntrap ['sʌntræp*] n luogo molto assolato.
super ['suːpə*] adj (*col*) fantastico(a).
superannuation [suːpərænju'eɪʃən] n
contributi mpl pensionistici; pensione f.
superb [suː'pəːb] adj magnifico(a).
Super Bowl n (*US SPORT*) Super Bowl m
inv.
supercilious [suːpə'sɪlɪəs] adj sprezzante.
superconductor [suːpəkən'dʌktə*] n
superconduttore m.
superficial [suːpə'fɪʃəl] adj superficiale.
superficially [suːpə'fɪʃəlɪ] adv
superficialmente.
superfluous [su'pəːfluəs] adj superfluo(a).
superglue ['suːpəgluː] n colla a presa
rapida.
superhighway ['suːpəhaɪweɪ] n (*US*)
autostrada; **the information ~**
l'autostrada telematica.
superhuman [suːpə'hjuːmən] adj
sovrumano(a).
superimpose ['suːpərɪm'pəuz] vt
sovrapporre.
superintend [suːpərɪn'tɛnd] vt dirigere,
sovraintendere.
superintendent [suːpərɪn'tɛndənt] n
direttore/trice; (*POLICE*) ≈ commissario
(capo).
superior [su'pɪərɪə*] adj superiore; (*COMM*:

goods, quality) di prim'ordine, superiore;
(*smug: person*) che fa il superiore ♦ *n*
superiore *m/f*; **Mother S~** (*REL*) Madre *f*
Superiora, Superiora.
superiority [supɪərɪ'ɔrɪtɪ] *n* superiorità.
superlative [su'pə:lətɪv] *adj* superlativo(a),
supremo(a) ♦ *n* (*LING*) superlativo.
superman ['su:pəmæn] *n* superuomo.
supermarket ['su:pəmɑ:kɪt] *n*
supermercato.
supermodel ['su:pəmɔdl] *n* top model *m/f*
inv.
supernatural [su:pə'nætʃərəl] *adj*
soprannaturale.
supernova [su:pə'nəuvə] *n* supernova.
superpower ['su:pəpauə*] *n* (*POL*)
superpotenza.
superscript ['su:pəskrɪpt] *n* esponente *m*.
supersede [su:pə'si:d] *vt* sostituire,
soppiantare.
supersonic ['su:pə'sɔnɪk] *adj*
supersonico(a).
superstar ['su:pəstɑ:*] *adj, n* superstar (*f*)
inv.
superstition [su:pə'stɪʃən] *n* superstizione
f.
superstitious [su:pə'stɪʃəs] *adj*
superstizioso(a).
superstore ['su:pəstɔ:*] *n* (*BRIT*) grande
supermercato.
supertanker ['su:pətæŋkə*] *n*
superpetroliera.
supertax ['su:pətæks] *n* soprattassa.
supervise ['su:pəvaɪz] *vt* (*person etc*)
sorvegliare; (*organization*) soprintendere
a.
supervision [su:pə'vɪʒən] *n* sorveglianza,
supervisione *f*; **under medical ~** sotto
controllo medico.
supervisor ['su:pəvaɪzə*] *n* sorvegliante *m/
f*, soprintendente *m/f*; (*in shop*)
capocommesso/a; (*at university*) relatore/
trice.
supervisory ['su:pəvaɪzərɪ] *adj* di
sorveglianza.
supine ['su:paɪn] *adj* supino(a).
supper ['sʌpə*] *n* cena; **to have ~** cenare.
supplant [sə'plɑ:nt] *vt* soppiantare.
supple ['sʌpl] *adj* flessibile; agile.
supplement *n* ['sʌplɪmənt] supplemento
♦ *vt* [sʌplɪ'mɛnt] completare, integrare.
supplementary [sʌplɪ'mɛntərɪ] *adj*
supplementare.
supplementary benefit *n* (*BRIT*) *forma di*
indennità assistenziale.
supplier [sə'plaɪə*] *n* fornitore *m*.
supply [sə'plaɪ] *vt* (*goods*): **to ~ sth (to sb)**
fornire qc (a qn); (*people, organization*): **to**

~ sb (with sth) fornire a qn (qc); (*system,
machine*): **to ~ sth (with sth)** alimentare
qc (con qc); (*a need*) soddisfare ♦ *n*
riserva, provvista; (*supplying*)
approvvigionamento; (*TECH*)
alimentazione *f*; **supplies** *npl* (*food*) viveri
mpl; (*MIL*) sussistenza; **office supplies**
forniture *fpl* per ufficio; **to be in short ~**
scarseggiare, essere scarso(a); **the
electricity/water/gas ~** l'erogazione *f* di
corrente/d'acqua/di gas; **~ and demand**
la domanda e l'offerta; **the car comes
supplied with a radio** l'auto viene fornita
completa di radio.
supply teacher *n* (*BRIT*) supplente *m/f*.
support [sə'pɔ:t] *n* (*moral, financial etc*)
sostegno, appoggio; (*TECH*) supporto ♦ *vt*
sostenere; (*financially*) mantenere;
(*uphold*) sostenere, difendere; (*SPORT:
team*) fare il tifo per; **they stopped work
in ~ (of)** hanno smesso di lavorare per
solidarietà (con); **to ~ o.s.** (*financially*)
mantenersi.
supporter [sə'pɔ:tə*] *n* (*POL etc*)
sostenitore/trice, fautore/trice; (*SPORT*)
tifoso/a.
supporting [sə'pɔ:tɪŋ] *adj* (*wall*) di
sostegno.
supporting actor *n* attore *m* non
protagonista.
supporting actress *n* attrice *f* non
protagonista.
supporting role *n* ruolo non protagonista.
supportive [sə'pɔ:tɪv] *adj* d'appoggio; **I
have a ~ wife/family** mia moglie/la mia
famiglia mi appoggia.
suppose [sə'pəuz] *vt, vi* supporre;
immaginare; **to be ~d to do** essere
tenuto(a) a fare; **always supposing (that)
he comes** ammesso e non concesso che
venga; **I don't ~ she'll come** non credo
che venga; **he's ~d to be an expert**
dicono che sia un esperto, passa per un
esperto.
supposedly [sə'pəuzɪdlɪ] *adv*
presumibilmente; (*seemingly*)
apparentemente.
supposing [sə'pəuzɪŋ] *conj* se, ammesso
che + *sub*.
supposition [sʌpə'zɪʃən] *n* supposizione *f*,
ipotesi *f inv*.
suppository [sə'pɔzɪtərɪ] *n* supposta,
suppositorio.
suppress [sə'prɛs] *vt* reprimere;
sopprimere; tenere segreto(a).
suppression [sə'prɛʃən] *n* repressione *f*,
soppressione *f*.
suppressor [sə'prɛsə*] *n* (*ELEC etc*)

soppressore *m*.

supremacy [su'prɛməsɪ] *n* supremazia.

supreme [su'priːm] *adj* supremo(a).

Supreme Court *n* (*US*) Corte *f* suprema; ~ **of Judicature** *corte di giudizio suprema dell'Inghilterra e del Galles.*

supremo [su'priːməu] *n* autorità *f inv* massima.

Supt. *abbr* (*POLICE*) = **superintendent**.

surcharge ['səːtʃɑːdʒ] *n* supplemento; (*extra tax*) soprattassa.

sure [ʃuə*] *adj* sicuro(a); (*definite*, *convinced*) sicuro(a), certo(a) ♦ *adv* (*col*: *US*): **that ~ is pretty, that's ~ pretty** è veramente *or* davvero carino; ~! (*of course*) senz'altro!, certo!; ~ **enough** infatti; **to make ~ of** assicurarsi di; **to be** ~ **of sth** essere sicuro di qc; **to be** ~ **of o.s.** essere sicuro di sé; **I'm not ~ how/ why/when** non so bene come/perché/ quando + *sub*.

sure-fire ['ʃuəfaɪə*] *adj* (*col*) infallibile.

sure-footed [ʃuə'futɪd] *adj* dal passo sicuro.

surely ['ʃuəlɪ] *adv* sicuramente; certamente; ~ **you don't mean that!** non parlerà sul serio!

surety ['ʃuərətɪ] *n* garanzia; **to go** *or* **stand** ~ **for sb** farsi garante per qn.

surf [səːf] *n* (*waves*) cavalloni *mpl*; (*foam*) spuma ♦ *vt*: **to ~ the Net** navigare in Internet.

surface ['səːfɪs] *n* superficie *f* ♦ *vt* (*road*) asfaltare ♦ *vi* risalire alla superficie; (*fig*: *person*) venire a galla, farsi vivo(a); **on the ~ it seems that ...** (*fig*) superficialmente sembra che ....

surface area *n* superficie *f*.

surface mail *n* posta ordinaria.

surface-to-surface ['səːfɪstə'səːfɪs] *adj* (*MIL*) terra-terra *inv*.

surfboard ['səːfbɔːd] *n* tavola per surfing.

surfeit ['səːfɪt] *n*: **a ~ of** un eccesso di; un'indigestione di.

surfer ['səːfə*] *n* chi pratica il surfing.

surfing ['səːfɪŋ] *n* surfing *m*.

surge [səːdʒ] *n* (*strong movement*) ondata; (*of feeling*) impeto; (*ELEC*) sovracorrente *f* transitoria ♦ *vi* (*waves*) gonfiarsi; (*ELEC*: *power*) aumentare improvvisamente; **to ~ forward** buttarsi avanti.

surgeon ['səːdʒən] *n* chirurgo.

Surgeon General *n* (*US*) ≈ Ministro della Sanità.

surgery ['səːdʒərɪ] *n* chirurgia; (*BRIT MED*: *room*) studio *or* gabinetto medico, ambulatorio; (: *session*) visita ambulatoriale; (*BRIT*: *of MP etc*) incontri

mpl con gli elettori; **to undergo** ~ subire un intervento chirurgico.

surgery hours *npl* (*BRIT*) orario delle visite *or* di consultazione.

surgical ['səːdʒɪkl] *adj* chirurgico(a).

surgical spirit *n* (*BRIT*) alcool denaturato.

surly ['səːlɪ] *adj* scontroso(a), burbero(a).

surmise [səː'maɪz] *vt* supporre, congetturare.

surmount [səː'maunt] *vt* sormontare.

surname ['səːneɪm] *n* cognome *m*.

surpass [səː'pɑːs] *vt* superare.

surplus ['səːpləs] *n* eccedenza; (*ECON*) surplus *m inv* ♦ *adj* eccedente, d'avanzo; **it is ~ to our requirements** eccede i nostri bisogni; ~ **stock** merce *f* in sovrappiù.

surprise [sə'praɪz] *n* sorpresa; (*astonishment*) stupore *m* ♦ *vt* sorprendere; stupire; **to take by** ~ (*person*) cogliere di sorpresa; (*MIL*: *town*, *fort*) attaccare di sorpresa.

surprising [sə'praɪzɪŋ] *adj* sorprendente, stupefacente.

surprisingly [se'praɪzɪŋlɪ] *adv* sorprendentemente; (**somewhat**) ~, **he agreed** cosa (alquanto) sorprendente, ha accettato.

surrealism [sə'rɪəlɪzəm] *n* surrealismo.

surrealist [sə'rɪəlɪst] *adj*, *n* surrealista (*m/f*).

surrender [sə'rɛndə*] *n* resa, capitolazione *f* ♦ *vi* arrendersi ♦ *vt* (*claim*, *right*) rinunciare a.

surrender value *n* (*COMM*) valore *m* di riscatto.

surreptitious [sʌrəp'tɪʃəs] *adj* furtivo(a).

surrogate ['sʌrəgɪt] *n* (*BRIT*: *substitute*) surrogato ♦ *adj* surrogato(a).

surrogate mother *n* madre *f* sostitutiva.

surround [sə'raund] *vt* circondare; (*MIL etc*) accerchiare.

surrounding [sə'raundɪŋ] *adj* circostante.

surroundings [sə'raundɪŋz] *npl* dintorni *mpl*; (*fig*) ambiente *m*.

surtax ['səːtæks] *n* soprattassa.

surveillance [səː'veɪləns] *n* sorveglianza, controllo.

survey *n* ['səːveɪ] (*comprehensive view*: *of situation*, *development*) quadro generale; (*study*) indagine *f*, studio; (*in housebuying etc*) perizia; (*of land*) rilevamento, rilievo topografico ♦ *vt* [səː'veɪ] osservare; esaminare; (*SURVEYING*: *building*) fare una perizia di; (: *land*) fare il rilevamento di.

surveying [sə'veɪɪŋ] *n* (*of land*) agrimensura.

surveyor [sə'veɪə*] *n* perito; (*of land*) agrimensore *m*.

survival [sə'vaɪvl] *n* sopravvivenza; (*relic*)

reliquia, vestigio.
survival course n corso di sopravvivenza.
survival kit n equipaggiamento di prima
necessità.
survive [sə'vaɪv] vi sopravvivere ♦ vt
sopravvivere a.
survivor [sə'vaɪvə*] n superstite m/f,
sopravvissuto/a.
susceptible [sə'sɛptəbl] adj: ~ **(to)** sensibile
(a); (disease) predisposto(a) (a).
suspect adj, n ['sʌspɛkt] adj sospetto(a) ♦ n
persona sospetta ♦ vt [səs'pɛkt]
sospettare; (think likely) supporre; (doubt)
dubitare di.
suspected [səs'pɛktɪd] adj presunto(a); **to
have a** ~ **facture** avere una sospetta
frattura.
suspend [səs'pɛnd] vt sospendere.
suspended animation n: **in a state of** ~ in
stato comatoso.
suspended sentence n condanna con la
condizionale.
suspender belt [səs'pɛndə*-] n (BRIT)
reggicalze m inv.
suspenders [sə'spɛndəz] npl (BRIT)
giarrettiere fpl; (US) bretelle fpl.
suspense [səs'pɛns] n apprensione f; (in
film etc) suspense m.
suspension [səs'pɛnʃən] n (gen, AUT)
sospensione f; (of driving licence) ritiro
temporaneo.
suspension bridge n ponte m sospeso.
suspicion [səs'pɪʃən] n sospetto; **to be
under** ~ essere sospettato; **arrested on** ~
of murder arrestato come presunto
omicida.
suspicious [səs'pɪʃəs] adj (suspecting)
sospettoso(a); (causing suspicion)
sospetto(a); **to be** ~ **of** or **about sb/sth**
nutrire sospetti nei riguardi di qn/qc.
suss out vt (BRIT col): **I've** ~**ed it/him out**
ho capito come stanno le cose/che tipo è.
sustain [səs'teɪn] vt sostenere; sopportare;
(suffer) subire.
sustainable [səs'teɪnəbl] adj sostenibile.
sustained [sə'steɪnd] adj (effort)
prolungato(a).
sustenance ['sʌstɪnəns] n nutrimento;
mezzi mpl di sostentamento.
suture ['suːtʃə*] n sutura.
SUV n abbr see **sports utility vehicle**.
SW abbr (RADIO: = short wave) O.C.
swab [swɔb] n (MED) tampone m ♦ vt (NAUT:
also: ~ **down**) radazzare.
swagger ['swægə*] vi pavoneggiarsi.
swallow ['swɔləu] n (bird) rondine f; (of
food) boccone m; (of drink) sorso ♦ vt
inghiottire; (fig: story) bere.

►**swallow up** vt inghiottire.
swam [swæm] pt of **swim**.
swamp [swɔmp] n palude f ♦ vt
sommergere.
swampy ['swɔmpɪ] adj paludoso(a),
pantanoso(a).
swan [swɔn] n cigno.
swank [swæŋk] vi (col: talk boastfully) fare
lo spaccone; (: show off) mettersi in
mostra.
swan song n (fig) canto del cigno.
swap [swɔp] n scambio ♦ vt: **to** ~ **(for)**
scambiare (con).
SWAPO ['swɑːpəu] n abbr = South-West
Africa People's Organization.
swarm [swɔːm] n sciame m ♦ vi
formicolare; (bees) sciamare.
swarthy ['swɔːðɪ] adj di carnagione scura.
swashbuckling ['swɔʃbʌklɪŋ] adj (role,
hero) spericolato(a).
swastika ['swɔstɪkə] n croce f uncinata,
svastica.
SWAT [swɔt] n abbr (US: = Special Weapons
and Tactics) reparto speciale di polizia; **a**
~ **team** uno squadrone del reparto
speciale (di polizia).
swat [swɔt] vt schiacciare ♦ n (BRIT: also: **fly**
~) ammazzamosche m inv.
swathe [sweɪð] n fascio ♦ vt: **to** ~ **in**
(bandages, blankets) avvolgere in.
swatter ['swɔtə*] n (also: **fly** ~)
ammazzamosche m inv.
sway [sweɪ] vi (building) oscillare; (tree)
ondeggiare; (person) barcollare ♦ vt
(influence) influenzare ♦ n (rule, power): ~
(over) influenza (su); **to hold** ~ **over sb**
dominare qn.
Swaziland ['swɑːzɪlænd] n Swaziland m.
swear, pt **swore**, pp **sworn** [swɛə*, swɔː*,
swɔːn] vi (witness etc) giurare; (curse)
bestemmiare, imprecare ♦ vt: **to** ~ **an
oath** prestare giuramento; **to** ~ **to sth**
giurare qc.
►**swear in** vt prestare giuramento a.
swearword ['swɛəwɔːd] n parolaccia.
sweat [swɛt] n sudore m, traspirazione f
♦ vi sudare; **in a** ~ in un bagno di sudore.
sweatband ['swɛtbænd] n (SPORT) fascia
elastica (per assorbire il sudore).
sweater ['swɛtə*] n maglione m.
sweatshirt ['swɛtʃəːt] n maglione m in
cotone felpato.
sweatshop ['swɛtʃɔp] n azienda o fabbrica
dove i dipendenti sono sfruttati.
sweaty ['swɛtɪ] adj sudato(a); bagnato(a) di
sudore.
Swede [swiːd] n svedese m/f.
swede [swiːd] n (BRIT) rapa svedese.

Sweden ['swiːdn] *n* Svezia.
Swedish ['swiːdɪʃ] *adj* svedese ♦ *n* (*LING*)
svedese *m*.
sweep [swiːp] *n* spazzata; (*curve*) curva;
(*expanse*) distesa; (*range*) portata; (*also*:
chimney ~) spazzacamino ♦ *vb* (*pt, pp*
swept [swɛpt]) *vt* spazzare, scopare; (*subj*:
fashion, craze) invadere ♦ *vi* camminare
maestosamente; precipitarsi, lanciarsi;
(e)stendersi.
▶**sweep away** *vt* spazzare via; trascinare
via.
▶**sweep past** *vi* sfrecciare accanto;
passare accanto maestosamente.
▶**sweep up** *vt, vi* spazzare.
sweeper ['swiːpə*] *n* (*person*) spazzino/a;
(*machine*) spazzatrice *f*; (*FOOTBALL*)
libero.
sweeping ['swiːpɪŋ] *adj* (*gesture*) ampio(a);
(*changes, reforms*) ampio(a), radicale; **a ~
statement** un'affermazione generica.
sweepstake ['swiːpsteɪk] *n* lotteria (*spesso
abbinata alle corse dei cavalli*).
sweet [swiːt] *n* (*BRIT*) dolce *m*; (*candy*)
caramella ♦ *adj* dolce; (*fresh*) fresco(a);
(*kind*) gentile; (*cute*) carino(a) ♦ *adv*: **to
smell/taste ~** avere un odore/sapore
dolce; **~ and sour** *adj* agrodolce.
sweetbread ['swiːtbrɛd] *n* animella.
sweetcorn ['swiːtkɔːn] *n* granturco dolce.
sweeten ['swiːtn] *vt* addolcire; zuccherare.
sweetener ['swiːtnə*] *n* (*CULIN*)
dolcificante *m*.
sweetheart ['swiːthɑːt] *n* innamorato/a.
sweetly ['swiːtlɪ] *adv* dolcemente.
sweetness ['swiːtnɪs] *n* sapore *m* dolce;
dolcezza.
sweet pea *n* pisello odoroso.
sweet potato *n* patata americana, patata
dolce.
sweetshop ['swiːtʃɔp] *n* (*BRIT*) ≈
pasticceria.
sweet tooth *n*: **to have a ~** avere un
debole per i dolci.
swell [swɛl] *n* (*of sea*) mare *m* lungo ♦ *adj*
(*col: excellent*) favoloso(a) ♦ *vb* (*pt* **~ed**, *pp*
swollen, ~ed ['swəulən]) *vt* gonfiare,
ingrossare; (*numbers, sales etc*)
aumentare ♦ *vi* gonfiarsi, ingrossarsi;
(*sound*) crescere; (*MED*) gonfiarsi.
swelling ['swɛlɪŋ] *n* (*MED*) tumefazione *f*,
gonfiore *m*.
sweltering ['swɛltərɪŋ] *adj* soffocante.
swept [swɛpt] *pt, pp of* **sweep**.
swerve [swɔːv] *vi* deviare; (*driver*) sterzare;
(*boxer*) scartare.
swift [swɪft] *n* (*bird*) rondone *m* ♦ *adj*
rapido(a), veloce.

swiftly ['swɪftlɪ] *adv* rapidamente,
velocemente.
swiftness ['swɪftnɪs] *n* rapidità, velocità.
swig [swɪg] *n* (*col: drink*) sorsata.
swill [swɪl] *n* broda ♦ *vt* (*also*: **~ out, ~
down**) risciacquare.
swim [swɪm] *n*: **to go for a ~** andare a fare
una nuotata ♦ *vb* (*pt* **swam**, *pp* **swum**
[swæm, swʌm]) *vi* nuotare; (*SPORT*) fare
del nuoto; (*head, room*) girare ♦ *vt* (*river,
channel*) attraversare *or* percorrere a
nuoto; **to go ~ming** andare a nuotare; **to
~ a length** fare una vasca (a nuoto).
swimmer ['swɪmə*] *n* nuotatore/trice.
swimming ['swɪmɪŋ] *n* nuoto.
swimming baths *npl* (*BRIT*) piscina.
swimming cap *n* cuffia.
swimming costume *n* (*BRIT*) costume *m*
da bagno.
swimmingly ['swɪmɪŋlɪ] *adv*: **to go ~**
(*wonderfully*) andare a gonfie vele.
swimming pool *n* piscina.
swimming trunks *npl* costume *m* da
bagno (per uomo).
swimsuit ['swɪmsuːt] *n* costume *m* da
bagno.
swindle ['swɪndl] *n* truffa ♦ *vt* truffare.
swindler ['swɪndlə*] *n* truffatore/trice.
swine [swaɪn] *n* (*pl inv*) maiale *m*, porco;
(*col!*) porco (*!*).
swing [swɪŋ] *n* altalena; (*movement*)
oscillazione *f*; (*MUS*) ritmo; (*also*: ~
music) swing *m* ♦ *vb* (*pt, pp* **swung** [swʌŋ])
vt dondolare, far oscillare; (*also*: ~ **round**)
far girare ♦ *vi* oscillare, dondolare; (*also*: ~
round: *object*) roteare; (: *person*)
girarsi, voltarsi; **to be in full ~** (*activity*)
essere in piena attività; (*party etc*) essere
nel pieno; **a ~ to the left** (*POL*) una svolta
a sinistra; **to get into the ~ of things**
entrare nel pieno delle cose; **the road ~s
south** la strada prende la direzione sud.
swing bridge *n* ponte *m* girevole.
swing door *n* (*BRIT*) porta battente.
swingeing ['swɪndʒɪŋ] *adj* (*BRIT: defeat*)
violento(a); (: *price increase*) enorme.
swinging ['swɪŋɪŋ] *adj* (*step*) cadenzato(a),
ritmico(a); (*rhythm, music*) trascinante; ~
door (*US*) porta battente.
swipe [swaɪp] *n* forte colpo; schiaffo ♦ *vt*
(*hit*) colpire con forza; dare uno schiaffo
a; (*col: steal*) sgraffignare; (*credit card etc*)
far passare (nell'apposita macchinetta).
swirl [swɔːl] *n* turbine *m*, mulinello ♦ *vi*
turbinare, far mulinello.
swish [swɪʃ] *adj* (*col: smart*) all'ultimo
grido, alla moda ♦ *n* (*sound: of whip*)
sibilo; (: *of skirts, grass*) fruscio ♦ *vi*

sibilare.

Swiss [swɪs] *adj, n (pl inv)* svizzero(a).

Swiss French *adj* svizzero(a) francese.

Swiss German *adj* svizzero(a) tedesco(a).

switch [swɪtʃ] *n (for light, radio etc)* interruttore *m*; *(change)* cambiamento ♦ *vt (also:* ~ **round,** ~ **over)** cambiare; scambiare.

►**switch off** *vt* spegnere.

►**switch on** *vt* accendere; *(engine, machine)* mettere in moto, avviare; *(AUT: ignition)* inserire; *(BRIT: water supply)* aprire.

switchback ['swɪtʃbæk] *n (BRIT)* montagne *fpl* russe.

switchblade ['swɪtʃbleɪd] *n (also:* ~ **knife)** coltello a scatto.

switchboard ['swɪtʃbɔːd] *n* centralino.

switchboard operator *n* centralinista *m/f*.

Switzerland ['swɪtsələnd] *n* Svizzera.

swivel ['swɪvl] *vi (also:* ~ **round)** girare.

swollen ['swəulən] *pp of* **swell** ♦ *adj (ankle etc)* gonfio(a).

swoon [swuːn] *vi* svenire.

swoop [swuːp] *n (by police etc)* incursione *f*; *(of bird etc)* picchiata ♦ *vi (also:* ~ **down)** scendere in picchiata; *(police):* **to** ~ **(on)** fare un'incursione (in).

swop [swɔp] *n, vt* = **swap.**

sword [sɔːd] *n* spada.

swordfish ['sɔːdfɪʃ] *n* pesce *m* spada *inv*.

swore [swɔː*] *pt of* **swear.**

sworn [swɔːn] *pp of* **swear.**

swot [swɔt] *vt* sgobbare su ♦ *vi* sgobbare.

swum [swʌm] *pp of* **swim.**

swung [swʌŋ] *pt, pp of* **swing.**

sycamore ['sɪkəmɔː*] *n* sicomoro.

sycophant ['sɪkəfənt] *n* leccapiedi *m/f*.

sycophantic [sɪkə'fæntɪk] *adj* ossequioso(a), adulatore(trice).

Sydney ['sɪdnɪ] *n* Sydney *f*.

syllable ['sɪləbl] *n* sillaba.

syllabus ['sɪləbəs] *n* programma *m*; **on the** ~ in programma d'esame.

symbol ['sɪmbl] *n* simbolo.

symbolic(al) [sɪm'bɔlɪk(l)] *adj* simbolico(a); **to be** ~ **of sth** simboleggiare qc.

symbolism ['sɪmbəlɪzəm] *n* simbolismo.

symbolize ['sɪmbəlaɪz] *vt* simbolizzare.

symmetrical [sɪ'metrɪkl] *adj* simmetrico(a).

symmetry ['sɪmɪtrɪ] *n* simmetria.

sympathetic [sɪmpə'θetɪk] *adj (showing pity)* compassionevole; *(kind)* comprensivo(a); ~ **towards** ben disposto(a) verso; **to be** ~ **to a cause** *(well-disposed)* simpatizzare per una causa.

sympathetically [sɪmpə'θetɪklɪ] *adv* in

modo compassionevole; con comprensione.

sympathize ['sɪmpəθaɪz] *vi:* **to** ~ **with sb** compatire qn; partecipare al dolore di qn; *(understand)* capire qn.

sympathizer ['sɪmpəθaɪzə*] *n (POL)* simpatizzante *m/f*.

sympathy ['sɪmpəθɪ] *n* compassione *f*; **in** ~ **with** d'accordo con; *(strike)* per solidarietà con; **with our deepest** ~ con le nostre più sincere condoglianze.

symphonic [sɪm'fɔnɪk] *adj* sinfonico(a).

symphony ['sɪmfənɪ] *n* sinfonia.

symphony orchestra *n* orchestra sinfonica.

symposium [sɪm'pəuzɪəm] *n* simposio.

symptom ['sɪmptəm] *n* sintomo; indizio.

symptomatic [sɪmptə'mætɪk] *adj:* ~ **(of)** sintomatico(a) (di).

synagogue ['sɪnəgɔg] *n* sinagoga.

sync [sɪŋk] *n (col):* **in/out of** ~ in/fuori sincronia; *(fig: people)* **they are in** ~ sono in sintonia.

synchromesh [sɪŋkrəu'meʃ] *n* cambio sincronizzato.

synchronize ['sɪŋkrənaɪz] *vt* sincronizzare ♦ *vi:* **to** ~ **with** essere contemporaneo(a) a.

synchronized swimming *n* nuoto sincronizzato.

syncopated ['sɪŋkəpeɪtɪd] *adj* sincopato(a).

syndicate ['sɪndɪkɪt] *n* sindacato; *(PRESS)* agenzia di stampa.

syndrome ['sɪndrəum] *n* sindrome *f*.

synonym ['sɪnənɪm] *n* sinonimo.

synonymous [sɪ'nɔnɪməs] *adj:* ~ **(with)** sinonimo(a) (di).

synopsis, *pl* **synopses** [sɪ'nɔpsɪs, -siːz] *n* sommario, sinossi *f inv*.

syntax ['sɪntæks] *n* sintassi *f inv*.

synthesis, *pl* **syntheses** ['sɪnθəsɪs, -siːz] *n* sintesi *f inv*.

synthesizer ['sɪnθəsaɪzə*] *n (MUS)* sintetizzatore *m*.

synthetic [sɪn'θetɪk] *adj* sintetico(a) ♦ *n* prodotto sintetico; *(TEXTILES)* fibra sintetica.

syphilis ['sɪfɪlɪs] *n* sifilide *f*.

syphon ['saɪfən] *n, vb* = **siphon.**

Syria ['sɪrɪə] *n* Siria.

Syrian ['sɪrɪən] *adj, n* siriano(a).

syringe [sɪ'rɪndʒ] *n* siringa.

syrup ['sɪrəp] *n* sciroppo; *(also:* **golden** ~) melassa raffinata.

syrupy ['sɪrəpɪ] *adj* sciropposo(a).

system ['sɪstəm] *n* sistema *m*; *(network)* rete *f*; *(ANAT)* apparato; **it was a shock to his** ~ è stato uno shock per il suo

organismo.
systematic [sɪstə'mætɪk] *adj*
sistematico(a).
system disk *n* (*COMPUT*) disco del sistema.
systems analyst *n* analista *m/f* di sistemi.

T, t [tiː] *n* (*letter*) T, t *m or f inv*; **T for Tommy**
≈ T come Taranto.
TA *n abbr* (*BRIT*) = *Territorial Army*.
ta [tɑː] *excl* (*BRIT col*) grazie!
tab [tæb] *n abbr* = **tabulator** ♦ *n* (*loop on coat
etc*) laccetto; (*label*) etichetta; **to keep ~s
on** (*fig*) tenere d'occhio.
tabby ['tæbɪ] *n* (*also:* ~ **cat**) (gatto) soriano,
gatto tigrato.
tabernacle ['tæbənækl] *n* tabernacolo.
table ['teɪbl] *n* tavolo, tavola; (*chart*) tabella
♦ *vt* (*motion etc*) presentare; **to lay** *or* **set
the** ~ apparecchiare *or* preparare la
tavola; **to clear the** ~ sparecchiare;
league ~ (*FOOTBALL, RUGBY*) classifica; ~
of contents indice *m*.
tablecloth ['teɪblklɔθ] *n* tovaglia.
table d'hôte [tɑːblˈdəut] *adj* (*meal*) a prezzo
fisso.
table lamp *n* lampada da tavolo.
tablemat ['teɪblmæt] *n* sottopiatto.
table salt *n* sale *m* fino *or* da tavola.
tablespoon ['teɪblspuːn] *n* cucchiaio da
tavola; (*also:* ~**ful**) cucchiaiata.
tablet ['tæblɪt] *n* (*MED*) compressa; (: *for
sucking*) pastiglia; (*for writing*) blocco; (*of
stone*) targa; ~ **of soap** (*BRIT*) saponetta.
table tennis *n* tennis *m* da tavolo, ping-
pong ® *m*.
table wine *n* vino da tavola.
tabloid ['tæblɔɪd] *n* (*newspaper*) tabloid *m
inv*; **the ~s, the** ~ **press** i giornali
popolari; *see boxed note*.

TABLOID PRESS

Il termine **tabloid press** *si riferisce ai
quotidiani o ai settimanali popolari che,
rispetto ai "quality papers" hanno un formato
ridotto e presentano le notizie in modo più
sensazionalistico e meno approfondito; vedi
anche* **quality press**.

---

taboo [tə'buː] *adj, n* tabù (*m inv*).
tabulate ['tæbjuleɪt] *vt* (*data*) tabulare.
tabulator ['tæbjuleɪtə*] *n* tabulatore *m*.
tachograph ['tækəgrɑːf] *n* tachigrafo.
tachometer [tæ'kɔmɪtə*] *n* tachimetro.
tacit ['tæsɪt] *adj* tacito(a).
taciturn ['tæsɪtəːn] *adj* taciturno(a).
tack [tæk] *n* (*nail*) bulletta; (*stitch*) punto
d'imbastitura; (*NAUT*) bordo, bordata ♦ *vt*
imbullettare; imbastire ♦ *vi* bordeggiare;
to change ~ virare di bordo; **on the
wrong** ~ (*fig*) sulla strada sbagliata; **to** ~
sth on to (the end of) sth (*of letter, book*)
aggiungere qc alla fine di qc.
tackle ['tækl] *n* (*equipment*) attrezzatura,
equipaggiamento; (*for lifting*) paranco;
(*RUGBY*) placcaggio; (*FOOTBALL*)
contrasto ♦ *vt* (*difficulty*) affrontare;
(*RUGBY*) placcare; (*FOOTBALL*)
contrastare.
tacky ['tækɪ] *adj* colloso(a); ancora
bagnato(a); (*col: shabby*) scadente.
tact [tækt] *n* tatto.
tactful ['tæktful] *adj* delicato(a),
discreto(a); **to be** ~ avere tatto.
tactfully ['tæktfəlɪ] *adv* con tatto.
tactical ['tæktɪkl] *adj* tattico(a).
tactical voting *n* voto tattico.
tactician [tæk'tɪʃən] *n* tattico/a.
tactics ['tæktɪks] *n*, *npl* tattica.
tactless ['tæktlɪs] *adj* che manca di tatto.
tactlessly ['tæktlɪslɪ] *adv* senza tatto.
tadpole ['tædpəul] *n* girino.
taffy ['tæfɪ] *n* (*US*) caramella *f* mou *inv*.
tag [tæg] *n* etichetta; **price/name** ~
etichetta del prezzo/con il nome.
► **tag along** *vi* seguire.
Tahiti [tə'hiːti] *n* Tahiti *f*.
tail [teɪl] *n* coda; (*of shirt*) falda ♦ *vt* (*follow*)
seguire, pedinare; **to turn** ~ voltare la
schiena; *see also* **head**.
► **tail away, tail off** *vi* (*in size, quality etc*)
diminuire gradatamente.
tailback ['teɪlbæk] *n* (*BRIT*) ingorgo.
tail coat *n* marsina.
tail end *n* (*of train, procession etc*) coda; (*of
meeting etc*) fine *f*.
tailgate ['teɪlgeɪt] *n* (*AUT*) portellone *m*
posteriore.
tail light *n* (*AUT*) fanalino di coda.
tailor ['teɪlə*] *n* sarto ♦ *vt*: **to** ~ **sth (to)**
adattare qc (alle esigenze di); ~**'s (shop)**
sartoria (da uomo).
tailoring ['teɪlərɪŋ] *n* (*cut*) taglio.
tailor-made ['teɪlə'meɪd] *adj* (*also fig*)
fatto(a) su misura.
tailwind ['teɪlwɪnd] *n* vento di coda.
taint [teɪnt] *vt* (*meat, food*) far avariare;

(*fig: reputation*) infangare.
tainted ['teɪntɪd] *adj* (*food*) guasto(a);
(*water, air*) infetto(a); (*fig*) corrotto(a).
Taiwan [taɪ'wɑːn] *n* Taiwan *m*.
Tajikistan [tɑːdʒɪkɪ'stɑːn] *n* Tagikistan *m*.
take [teɪk] *vb* (*pt* **took**, *pp* **taken** [tuk, 'teɪkn])
vt prendere; (*gain: prize*) ottenere,
vincere; (*require: effort, courage*)
occorrere, volerci; (*tolerate*) accettare,
sopportare; (*hold: passengers etc*)
contenere; (*accompany*) accompagnare;
(*bring, carry*) portare; (*conduct: meeting*)
condurre; (*exam*) sostenere, presentarsi
a ♦ *vi* (*dye, fire etc*) prendere; (*injection*)
fare effetto; (*plant*) attecchire ♦ *n* (*CINE*)
ripresa; **I** ~ **it that** suppongo che; **to** ~ **for**
a walk (*child, dog*) portare a fare una
passeggiata; **to** ~ **sb's hand** prendere qn
per mano; **to** ~ **it upon o.s. to do sth**
prendersi la responsabilità di fare qc; **to**
be ~**n ill** avere un malore; **to be** ~**n with**
sb/sth (*attracted*) essere tutto preso da
qn/qc; **it won't** ~ **long** non ci vorrà molto
tempo; **it** ~**s a lot of time/courage**
occorre *or* ci vuole molto tempo/
coraggio; **it will** ~ **at least 5 litres**
contiene almeno 5 litri; ~ **the first on the**
left prenda la prima a sinistra; **to** ~
Russian at university fare russo
all'università; **I took him for a doctor** l'ho
preso per un dottore.
▶**take after** *vt fus* assomigliare a.
▶**take apart** *vt* smontare.
▶**take away** *vt* portare via; togliere; **to** ~
away (from) sottrarre (da).
▶**take back** *vt* (*return*) restituire; riportare;
(*one's words*) ritirare.
▶**take down** *vt* (*building*) demolire;
(*dismantle: scaffolding*) smontare; (*letter*
etc) scrivere.
▶**take in** *vt* (*lodger*) prendere, ospitare;
(*orphan*) accogliere; (*stray dog*)
raccogliere; (*SEWING*) stringere; (*deceive*)
imbrogliare, abbindolare; (*understand*)
capire; (*include*) comprendere, includere.
▶**take off** *vi* (*AVIAT*) decollare ♦ *vt* (*remove*)
togliere; (*imitate*) imitare.
▶**take on** *vt* (*work*) accettare,
intraprendere; (*employee*) assumere;
(*opponent*) sfidare, affrontare.
▶**take out** *vt* portare fuori; (*remove*)
togliere; (*licence*) prendere, ottenere; **to**
~ **sth out of** tirare qc fuori da; estrarre
qc da; **don't** ~ **it out on me!** non
prendertela con me!
▶**take over** *vt* (*business*) rilevare ♦ *vi*: **to** ~
over from sb prendere le consegne *or* il
controllo da qn.

▶**take to** *vt fus* (*person*) prendere in
simpatia; (*activity*) prendere gusto a;
(*form habit of*): **to** ~ **to doing sth** prendere
or cominciare a fare qc.
▶**take up** *vt* (*one's story*) riprendere;
(*dress*) accorciare; (*absorb: liquids*)
assorbire; (*accept: offer, challenge*)
accettare; (*occupy: time, space*) occupare;
(*engage in: hobby etc*) mettersi a; **to** ~ **up**
with sb fare amicizia con qn.
takeaway ['teɪkəweɪ] *adj* (*BRIT: food*) da
portar via.
take-home pay ['teɪkhəʊm-] *n* stipendio
netto.
taken ['teɪkn] *pp of* **take**.
takeoff ['teɪkɔf] *n* (*AVIAT*) decollo.
takeout ['teɪkaʊt] *adj* (*US*) = **takeaway**.
takeover ['teɪkəʊvə*] *n* (*COMM*)
assorbimento.
takeover bid *n* offerta di assorbimento.
takings ['teɪkɪŋz] *npl* (*COMM*) incasso.
talc [tælk] *n* (*also:* ~**um powder**) talco.
tale [teɪl] *n* racconto, storia; (*pej*) fandonia;
to tell ~**s** fare la spia.
talent ['tælənt] *n* talento.
talented ['tæləntɪd] *adj* di talento.
talent scout *n* talent scout *m/f inv*.
talisman ['tælɪzmən] *n* talismano.
talk [tɔːk] *n* discorso; (*gossip*) chiacchiere
fpl; (*conversation*) conversazione *f*;
(*interview*) discussione *f* ♦ *vi* parlare;
(*chatter*) chiacchierare; **to give a** ~ tenere
una conferenza; **to** ~ **about** parlare di;
(*converse*) discorrere *or* conversare su;
to ~ **sb out of/into doing** dissuadere qn
da/convincere qn a fare; **to** ~ **shop**
parlare del lavoro *or* degli affari; ~**ing of**
films, have you seen ...? a proposito di
film, ha visto ...?
▶**talk over** *vt* discutere.
talkative ['tɔːkətɪv] *adj* loquace,
ciarliero(a).
talking point ['tɔːkɪŋ-] *n* argomento di
conversazione.
talking-to ['tɔːkɪŋtuː] *n*: **to give sb a good**
~ fare una bella paternale a qn.
talk show *n* (*TV, RADIO*) intervista
(informale), talk show *m inv*.
tall [tɔːl] *adj* alto(a); **to be 6 feet** ~ ≈ essere
alto 1 metro e 80; **how** ~ **are you?** quanto
è alto?
tallboy ['tɔːlbɔɪ] *n* (*BRIT*) cassettone *m* alto.
tallness ['tɔːlnɪs] *n* altezza.
tall story *n* panzana, frottola.
tally ['tælɪ] *n* conto, conteggio ♦ *vi*: **to** ~
(with) corrispondere (a); **to keep a** ~ **of**
sth tener il conto di qc.
talon ['tælən] *n* artiglio.

tambourine [tæmbə'riːn] n tamburello.
tame [teɪm] adj addomesticato(a); (fig:
story, style) insipido(a), scialbo(a).
Tamil ['tæmɪl] adj tamil inv ♦ n tamil m/f inv;
(LING) tamil m.
tamper ['tæmpə*] vi: to ~ with
manomettere.
tampon ['tæmpɔn] n tampone m.
tan [tæn] n (also: sun~) abbronzatura ♦ vt
abbronzare ♦ vi abbronzarsi ♦ adj (colour)
marrone rossiccio inv; to get a ~
abbronzarsi.
tandem ['tændəm] n tandem m inv.
tandoori [tæn'duərɪ] adj nella cucina
indiana, detto di carni o verdure
cucinate allo spiedo in particolari forni.
tang [tæŋ] n odore m penetrante; sapore m
piccante.
tangent ['tændʒənt] n (MATH) tangente f; to
go off at a ~ (fig) partire per la tangente.
tangerine [tændʒə'riːn] n mandarino.
tangible ['tændʒəbl] adj tangibile; ~ assets
patrimonio reale.
Tangier [tæn'dʒɪə*] n Tangeri f.
tangle ['tæŋgl] n groviglio ♦ vt
aggrovigliare; to get in(to) a ~ finire in
un groviglio.
tango ['tæŋgəu] n tango.
tank [tæŋk] n serbatoio; (for processing)
vasca; (for fish) acquario; (MIL) carro
armato.
tankard ['tæŋkəd] n boccale m.
tanker ['tæŋkə*] n (ship) nave f cisterna inv;
(for oil) petroliera; (truck) autobotte f,
autocisterna.
tanned [tænd] adj abbronzato(a).
tannin ['tænɪn] n tannino.
tanning ['tænɪŋ] n (of leather) conciatura.
tannoy ® ['tænɔɪ] n (BRIT) altoparlante m;
over the ~ per altoparlante.
tantalizing ['tæntəlaɪzɪŋ] adj allettante.
tantamount ['tæntəmaunt] adj: ~ to
equivalente a.
tantrum ['tæntrəm] n accesso di collera; to
throw a ~ fare le bizze.
Tanzania [tænzə'nɪə] n Tanzania.
Tanzanian [tænzə'nɪən] adj, n
tanzaniano(a).
tap [tæp] n (on sink etc) rubinetto; (gentle
blow) colpetto ♦ vt dare un colpetto a;
(resources) sfruttare, utilizzare;
(telephone conversation) intercettare;
(telephone) mettere sotto controllo; on ~
(beer) alla spina; (fig: resources) a
disposizione.
tap-dancing ['tæpdɑːnsɪŋ] n tip tap m.
tape [teɪp] n nastro; (also: magnetic ~)
nastro (magnetico) ♦ vt (record)

registrare (su nastro); on ~ (song etc) su
nastro.
tape deck n piastra di registrazione.
tape measure n metro a nastro.
taper ['teɪpə*] n candelina ♦ vi
assottigliarsi.
tape-record ['teɪprɪkɔːd] vt registrare (su
nastro).
tape recorder n registratore m (a nastro).
tape recording n registrazione f.
tapered ['teɪpəd], **tapering** ['teɪpərɪŋ] adj
affusolato(a).
tapestry ['tæpɪstrɪ] n arazzo; tappezzeria.
tape-worm ['teɪpwəːm] n tenia, verme m
solitario.
tapioca [tæpɪ'əukə] n tapioca.
tappet ['tæpɪt] n punteria.
tar [tɑː*] n catrame m; low-/middle-~
cigarettes sigarette a basso/medio
contenuto di nicotina.
tarantula [tə'ræntjulə] n tarantola.
tardy ['tɑːdɪ] adj tardo(a); tardivo(a).
target ['tɑːgɪt] n bersaglio; (fig: objective)
obiettivo; to be on ~ (project) essere nei
tempi (di lavorazione).
target practice n tiro al bersaglio.
tariff ['tærɪf] n tariffa.
tarmac ['tɑːmæk] n (BRIT: on road)
macadam m al catrame; (AVIAT) pista di
decollo ♦ vt (BRIT) macadamizzare.
tarnish ['tɑːnɪʃ] vt offuscare, annerire; (fig)
macchiare.
tarot ['tærəu] n tarocco.
tarpaulin [tɑː'pɔːlɪn] n tela incatramata.
tarragon ['tærəgən] n dragoncello.
tart [tɑːt] n (CULIN) crostata; (BRIT col: pej:
woman) sgualdrina ♦ adj (flavour)
aspro(a), agro(a).
▶**tart up** vt (col): to ~ o.s. up farsi bello(a);
(pej) agghindarsi.
tartan ['tɑːtn] n tartan m inv.
tartar ['tɑːtə*] n (on teeth) tartaro.
tartar sauce n salsa tartara.
task [tɑːsk] n compito; to take to ~
rimproverare.
task force n (MIL, POLICE) unità operativa.
taskmaster ['tɑːskmɑːstə*] n: he's a hard ~
è un vero tiranno.
Tasmania [tæz'meɪnɪə] n Tasmania.
tassel ['tæsl] n fiocco.
taste [teɪst] n gusto; (flavour) sapore m,
gusto; (fig: glimpse, idea) idea ♦ vt gustare;
(sample) assaggiare ♦ vi: to ~ of (fish etc)
sapere di, avere sapore di; what does it
~ like? che sapore or gusto ha?; it ~s like
fish sa di pesce; you can ~ the garlic (in
it) (ci) si sente il sapore dell'aglio; can I
have a ~ of this wine? posso assaggiare

un po' di questo vino?; **to have a ~ of sth** assaggiare qc; **to have a ~ for sth** avere un'inclinazione per qc; **to be in bad** *or* **poor ~** essere di cattivo gusto.
taste bud *n* papilla gustativa.
tasteful ['teɪstful] *adj* di buon gusto.
tastefully ['teɪstfəlɪ] *adv* con gusto.
tasteless ['teɪstlɪs] *adj* (*food*) insipido(a); (*remark*) di cattivo gusto.
tasty ['teɪstɪ] *adj* saporito(a), gustoso(a).
tattered ['tætəd] *adj see* **tatters**.
tatters ['tætəz] *npl*: **in ~** (*also*: **tattered**) a brandelli, sbrindellato(a).
tattoo [tə'tuː] *n* tatuaggio; (*spectacle*) parata militare ♦ *vt* tatuare.
tatty ['tætɪ] *adj* (*BRIT col*) malandato(a).
taught [tɔːt] *pt, pp of* **teach**.
taunt [tɔːnt] *n* scherno ♦ *vt* schernire.
Taurus ['tɔːrəs] *n* Toro; **to be ~** essere del Toro.
taut [tɔːt] *adj* teso(a).
tavern ['tævən] *n* taverna.
tawdry ['tɔːdrɪ] *adj* pacchiano(a).
tawny ['tɔːnɪ] *adj* fulvo(a).
tax [tæks] *n* imposta, tassa; (*on income*) imposte *fpl*, tasse *fpl* ♦ *vt* tassare; (*fig*: *strain*: *patience etc*) mettere alla prova; **free of ~** esentasse *inv*, esente da imposte; **before/after ~** al lordo/netto delle tasse.
taxable ['tæksəbl] *adj* imponibile.
tax allowance *n* detrazione *f* d'imposta.
taxation [tæk'seɪʃən] *n* tassazione *f*; tasse *fpl*, imposte *fpl*; **system of ~** sistema *m* fiscale.
tax avoidance *n* l'evitare legalmente il pagamento di imposte.
tax collector *n* esattore *m* delle imposte.
tax disc *n* (*BRIT AUT*) ≈ bollo.
tax evasion *n* evasione *f* fiscale.
tax exemption *n* esenzione *f* fiscale.
tax exile *n* chi ripara all'estero per evadere le imposte.
tax-free [tæks'friː] *adj* esente da imposte.
tax haven *n* paradiso fiscale.
taxi ['tæksɪ] *n* taxi *m inv* ♦ *vi* (*AVIAT*) rullare.
taxidermist ['tæksɪdəːmɪst] *n* tassidermista *m/f*.
taxi driver *n* tassista *m/f*.
tax Inspector *n* (*BRIT*) ispettore *m* delle tasse.
taxi rank, (*US*) **taxi stand** *n* posteggio dei taxi.
tax payer *n* contribuente *m/f*.
tax rebate *n* rimborso fiscale.
tax relief *n* sgravio fiscale.
tax return *n* dichiarazione *f* dei redditi.
tax shelter *n* paradiso fiscale.

tax year *n* anno fiscale.
TB *n abbr* (= *tuberculosis*) TBC *f*.
tbc *abbr* (= *to be confirmed*) da confermarsi.
TD *n abbr* (*US*) = **Treasury Department**; (: *FOOTBALL*) = **touchdown**.
tea [tiː] *n* tè *m inv*; (*BRIT*: *snack*: *for children*) merenda; **high ~** (*BRIT*) cena leggera (*presa nel tardo pomeriggio*).
tea bag *n* bustina di tè.
tea break *n* (*BRIT*) intervallo per il tè.
teacake ['tiːkeɪk] *n* (*BRIT*) panino dolce all'uva.
teach, *pt, pp* taught [tiːtʃ, tɔːt] *vt*: **to ~ sb sth, ~ sth to sb** insegnare qc a qn ♦ *vi* insegnare; **it taught him a lesson** (*fig*) gli è servito da lezione.
teacher ['tiːtʃə*] *n* (*gen*) insegnante *m/f*; (*in secondary school*) professore/essa; (*in primary school*) maestro/a; **French ~** insegnante di francese.
teacher training college *n* (*for primary schools*) ≈ istituto magistrale; (*for secondary schools*) scuola universitaria per l'abilitazione all'insegnamento nelle medie superiori.
teaching ['tiːtʃɪŋ] *n* insegnamento.
teaching aids *npl* materiali *mpl* per l'insegnamento.
teaching hospital *n* (*BRIT*) clinica universitaria.
teaching staff *n* (*BRIT*) insegnanti *mpl*, personale *m* insegnante.
tea cosy *n* copriteiera *m inv*.
teacup ['tiːkʌp] *n* tazza da tè.
teak [tiːk] *n* teak *m*.
tea leaves *npl* foglie *fpl* di tè.
team [tiːm] *n* squadra; (*of animals*) tiro.
▶**team up** *vi*: **to ~ up (with)** mettersi insieme (a).
team games *npl* giochi *mpl* di squadra.
teamwork ['tiːmwəːk] *n* lavoro di squadra.
tea party *n* tè *m inv* (*ricevimento*).
teapot ['tiːpɔt] *n* teiera.
tear *n* [tɛə*] strappo; [tɪə*] lacrima ♦ *vb* [tɛə*] (*pt* tore, *pp* torn [tɔː*, tɔːn]) *vt* strappare ♦ *vi* strapparsi; **in ~s** in lacrime; **to burst into ~s** scoppiare in lacrime; **to ~ to pieces** *or* **to bits** *or* **to shreds** (*also fig*) fare a pezzi *or* a brandelli.
▶**tear along** *vi* (*rush*) correre all'impazzata.
▶**tear apart** *vt* (*also fig*) distruggere.
▶**tear away** *vt*: **to ~ o.s. away (from sth)** (*fig*) staccarsi (da qc).
▶**tear out** *vt* (*sheet of paper, cheque*) staccare.

▶**tear up** *vt* (*sheet of paper etc*) strappare.
tearaway ['tɛərəweɪ] *n* (*col*) monello/a.
teardrop ['tɪədrɒp] *n* lacrima.
tearful ['tɪəful] *adj* piangente, lacrimoso(a).
tear gas *n* gas *m* lacrimogeno.
tearoom ['tiːruːm] *n* sala da tè.
tease [tiːz] *vt* canzonare; (*unkindly*) tormentare.
tea set *n* servizio da tè.
teashop ['tiːʃɒp] *n* (*BRIT*) sala da tè.
Teasmaid ® ['tiːzmeɪd] *n* macchinetta per fare il tè.
teaspoon ['tiːspuːn] *n* cucchiaino da tè; (*also*: ~**ful**: *as measurement*) cucchiaino.
tea strainer *n* colino da tè.
teat [tiːt] *n* capezzolo; (*of bottle*) tettarella.
teatime ['tiːtaɪm] *n* ora del tè.
tea towel *n* (*BRIT*) strofinaccio (per i piatti).
tea urn *n* bollitore *m* per il tè.
tech [tɛk] *n abbr* (*col*) = **technical college**; **technology**.
technical ['tɛknɪkl] *adj* tecnico(a).
technical college *n* ≈ istituto tecnico.
technicality [tɛknɪ'kælɪtɪ] *n* tecnicità; (*detail*) dettaglio tecnico; **on a legal** ~ grazie a un cavillo legale.
technically ['tɛknɪklɪ] *adv* dal punto di vista tecnico.
technician [tɛk'nɪʃən] *n* tecnico/a.
technique [tɛk'niːk] *n* tecnica.
techno ['tɛknəu] *n* (*MUS*) techno *f inv*.
technocrat ['tɛknəkræt] *n* tecnocrate *m/f*.
technological [tɛknə'lɒdʒɪkl] *adj* tecnologico(a).
technologist [tɛk'nɒlədʒɪst] *n* tecnologo/a.
technology [tɛk'nɒlədʒɪ] *n* tecnologia.
teddy (bear) ['tɛdɪ-] *n* orsacchiotto.
tedious ['tiːdɪəs] *adj* noioso(a), tedioso(a).
tedium ['tiːdɪəm] *n* noia, tedio.
tee [tiː] *n* (*GOLF*) tee *m inv*.
teem [tiːm] *vi* abbondare, brulicare; **to** ~ **with** brulicare di; **it is** ~**ing (with rain)** piove a dirotto.
teenage ['tiːneɪdʒ] *adj* (*fashions etc*) per giovani, per adolescenti.
teenager ['tiːneɪdʒə*] *n* adolescente *m/f*.
teens [tiːnz] *npl*: **to be in one's** ~ essere adolescente.
tee-shirt ['tiːʃəːt] *n* = **T-shirt**.
teeter ['tiːtə*] *vi* barcollare, vacillare.
teeth [tiːθ] *npl of* **tooth**.
teethe [tiːð] *vi* mettere i denti.
teething ring ['tiːðɪŋ-] *n* dentaruolo.
teething troubles *npl* (*fig*) difficoltà *fpl* iniziali.
teetotal ['tiː'təutl] *adj* astemio(a).
teetotaller, (*US*) **teetotaler** ['tiː'təutlə*] *n*

astemio/a.
TEFL ['tɛfl] *n abbr* = Teaching of English as a Foreign Language.
Teflon ® ['tɛflɒn] *n* teflon ® *m*.
Tehran [tɛə'rɑːn] *n* Tehran *f*.
tel. *abbr* (= *telephone*) tel.
Tel Aviv ['tɛlə'viːv] *n* Tel Aviv *f*.
telecast ['tɛlɪkɑːst] *vt, vi* teletrasmettere.
telecommunications ['tɛlɪkəmjuːnɪ'keɪʃənz] *n* telecomunicazioni *fpl*.
teleconferencing ['tɛlɪkɒnfərənsɪŋ] *n* teleconferenza.
telegram ['tɛlɪgræm] *n* telegramma *m*.
telegraph ['tɛlɪgrɑːf] *n* telegrafo.
telegraphic [tɛlɪ'græfɪk] *adj* telegrafico(a).
telegraph pole *n* palo del telegrafo.
telegraph wire *n* filo del telegrafo.
telepathic [tɛlɪ'pæθɪk] *adj* telepatico(a).
telephone ['tɛlɪfəun] *n* telefono ♦ *vt* (*person*) telefonare a; (*message*) telefonare; **to have a** ~, (*BRIT*) **to be on the** ~ (*subscriber*) avere il telefono; **to be on the** ~ (*be speaking*) essere al telefono.
telephone booth, (*BRIT*) **telephone box** *n* cabina telefonica.
telephone call *n* telefonata.
telephone directory *n* elenco telefonico.
telephone number *n* numero di telefono.
telephone operator *n* centralinista *m/f*.
telephone tapping *n* intercettazione *f* telefonica.
telephonist [tə'lɛfənɪst] *n* (*BRIT*) telefonista *m/f*.
telephoto lens ['tɛlɪfəutəu-] *n* teleobiettivo.
teleprinter ['tɛlɪprɪntə*] *n* telescrivente *f*.
Teleprompter ® ['tɛlɪprɒmptə*] *n* (*US*) gobbo.
telesales ['tɛlɪseɪlz] *n* vendita per telefono.
telescope ['tɛlɪskəup] *n* telescopio ♦ *vi* chiudersi a telescopio; (*fig: vehicles*) accartocciarsi.
telescopic [tɛlɪs'kɒpɪk] *adj* telescopico(a); (*umbrella*) pieghevole.
Teletext ® ['tɛlɪtɛkst] *n* (*system*) teletext *m inv*; (*in Italy*) televideo.
telethon ['tɛlɪθɒn] *n* maratona televisiva.
televise ['tɛlɪvaɪz] *vt* teletrasmettere.
television ['tɛlɪvɪʒən] *n* televisione *f*; **on** ~ alla televisione.
television licence *n* (*BRIT*) abbonamento alla televisione.
television programme *n* programma *m* televisivo.
television set *n* televisore *m*.
teleworking ['tɛlɪwɜːkɪŋ] *n* telelavoro.
telex ['tɛlɛks] *n* telex *m inv* ♦ *vt* trasmettere

per telex ♦ *vi* mandare un telex; **to ~ sb
(about sth)** informare qn via telex (di
qc).

tell, *pt, pp* **told** [tɛl, təʊld] *vt* dire; (*relate*:
story) raccontare; (*distinguish*): **to ~ sth
from** distinguere qc da ♦ *vi* (*have effect*)
farsi sentire, avere effetto; **to ~ sb to do**
dire a qn di fare; **to ~ sb about sth** dire a
qn di qc; raccontare qc a qn; **to ~ the
time** leggere l'ora; **can you ~ me the
time?** può dirmi l'ora?; **(I) ~ you what ...**
so io che cosa fare ...; **I couldn't ~ them
apart** non riuscivo a distinguerli.
▶**tell off** *vt* rimproverare, sgridare.
▶**tell on** *vt fus* (*inform against*) denunciare.
teller ['tɛlə*] *n* (*in bank*) cassiere/a.
telling ['tɛlɪŋ] *adj* (*remark, detail*)
rivelatore(trice).
telltale ['tɛlteɪl] *adj* (*sign*) rivelatore(trice)
♦ *n* malalingua, pettegolo/a.
telly ['tɛlɪ] *n abbr* (*BRIT col*: = *television*) tivù *f
inv*.
temerity [tə'mɛrɪtɪ] *n* temerarietà.
temp [tɛmp] *abbr* (*BRIT col*: = *temporary*) *n*
impiegato(a) straordinario(a) ♦ *vi*
lavorare come impiegato(a)
straordinario(a).
temper ['tɛmpə*] *n* (*nature*) carattere *m*;
(*mood*) umore *m*; (*fit of anger*) collera ♦ *vt*
(*moderate*) temperare; **to be in a ~** essere
in collera; **to keep one's ~** restare calmo;
to lose one's ~ andare in collera.
temperament ['tɛmprəmənt] *n*
temperamento.
temperamental [tɛmprə'mɛntl] *adj*
capriccioso(a).
temperance ['tɛmpərns] *n* moderazione *f*,
(*in drinking*) temperanza nel bere.
temperate ['tɛmprət] *adj* moderato(a);
(*climate*) temperato(a).
temperature ['tɛmprətʃə*] *n* temperatura;
to have *or* **run a ~** avere la febbre.
tempered ['tɛmpəd] *adj* (*steel*) temprato(a).
tempest ['tɛmpɪst] *n* tempesta.
tempestuous [tɛm'pɛstjuəs] *adj*
(*relationship, meeting*) burrascoso(a).
tempi ['tɛmpiː] *npl of* **tempo**.
template, (*US*) **templet** ['tɛmplɪt] *n*
sagoma.
temple ['tɛmpl] *n* (*building*) tempio; (*ANAT*)
tempia.
templet ['tɛmplɪt] *n* (*US*) = **template**.
tempo, **~s** *or* **tempi** ['tɛmpəʊ, 'tɛmpiː] *n*
tempo; (*fig: of life etc*) ritmo.
temporal ['tɛmpərl] *adj* temporale.
temporarily ['tɛmpərərɪlɪ] *adv*
temporaneamente.
temporary ['tɛmpərərɪ] *adj* temporaneo(a);

(*job, worker*) avventizio(a),
temporaneo(a); **~ secretary** segretaria
temporanea; **~ teacher** supplente *m/f*.
temporize ['tɛmpəraɪz] *vi* temporeggiare.
tempt [tɛmpt] *vt* tentare; **to ~ sb into doing**
indurre qn a fare; **to be ~ed to do sth**
essere tentato di fare qc.
temptation [tɛmp'teɪʃən] *n* tentazione *f*.
tempting ['tɛmptɪŋ] *adj* allettante,
seducente.
ten [tɛn] *num* dieci ♦ *n* dieci; **~s of
thousands** decine di migliaia.
tenable ['tɛnəbl] *adj* sostenibile.
tenacious [tə'neɪʃəs] *adj* tenace.
tenacity [tə'næsɪtɪ] *n* tenacia.
tenancy ['tɛnənsɪ] *n* affitto; condizione *f* di
inquilino.
tenant ['tɛnənt] *n* inquilino/a.
tend [tɛnd] *vt* badare a, occuparsi di; (*sick
etc*) prendersi cura di ♦ *vi*: **to ~ to do**
tendere a fare; (*colour*): **to ~ to** tendere
a.
tendency ['tɛndənsɪ] *n* tendenza.
tender ['tɛndə*] *adj* tenero(a); (*sore*)
sensibile; (*fig: subject*) delicato(a) ♦ *n*
(*COMM: offer*) offerta; (*money*): **legal ~**
valuta (a corso legale) ♦ *vt* offrire; **to put
in a ~ (for)** fare un'offerta (per); **to put
work out to ~** (*BRIT*) dare lavoro in
appalto; **to ~ one's resignation**
presentare le proprie dimissioni.
tenderize ['tɛndəraɪz] *vt* (*CULIN*) far
intenerire.
tenderly ['tɛndəlɪ] *adv* teneramente.
tenderness ['tɛndənɪs] *n* tenerezza;
sensibilità.
tendon ['tɛndən] *n* tendine *m*.
tenement ['tɛnəmənt] *n* casamento.
Tenerife [tɛnə'riːf] *n* Tenerife *f*.
tenet ['tɛnət] *n* principio.
Tenn. *abbr* (*US*) = *Tennessee*.
tenner ['tɛnə*] *n* (*BRIT col*) (banconota da)
dieci sterline *fpl*.
tennis ['tɛnɪs] *n* tennis *m*.
tennis ball *n* palla da tennis.
tennis court *n* campo da tennis.
tennis elbow *n* (*MED*) gomito del tennista.
tennis match *n* partita di tennis.
tennis player *n* tennista *m/f*.
tennis racket *n* racchetta da tennis.
tennis shoes *npl* scarpe *fpl* da tennis.
tenor ['tɛnə*] *n* (*MUS, of speech etc*) tenore
m.
tenpin bowling ['tɛnpɪn] *n* (*BRIT*) bowling
m.
tense [tɛns] *adj* teso(a) ♦ *n* (*LING*) tempo ♦ *vt*
(*tighten: muscles*) tendere.
tenseness ['tɛnsnɪs] *n* tensione *f*.

tension ['tɛnʃən] n tensione f.
tent [tɛnt] n tenda.
tentacle ['tɛntəkl] n tentacolo.
tentative ['tɛntətɪv] adj esitante, incerto(a); (conclusion) provvisorio(a).
tenterhooks ['tɛntəhuks] npl: **on ~ sulle** spine.
tenth [tɛnθ] num decimo(a).
tent peg n picchetto da tenda.
tent pole n palo da tenda, montante m.
tenuous ['tɛnjuəs] adj tenue.
tenure ['tɛnjuə*] n (of property) possesso; (of job) incarico; (guaranteed employment): **to have ~** essere di ruolo.
tepid ['tɛpɪd] adj tiepido(a).
term [tə:m] n (limit) termine m; (word) vocabolo, termine; (SCOL) trimestre m; (LAW) sessione f ♦ vt chiamare, definire; **~s** npl (conditions) condizioni fpl; (COMM) prezzi mpl, tariffe fpl; **~ of imprisonment** periodo di prigionia; **during his ~ of office** durante il suo incarico; **in the short/long ~** a breve/lunga scadenza; **"easy ~s"** (COMM) "facilitazioni di pagamento"; **to be on good ~s with** essere in buoni rapporti con; **to come to ~s with** (person) arrivare a un accordo con; (problem) affrontare.
terminal ['tə:mɪnl] adj finale, terminale; (disease) nella fase terminale ♦ n (ELEC, COMPUT) terminale m; (AVIAT, for oil, ore etc) terminal m inv; (BRIT: also: **coach ~**) capolinea m.
terminate ['tə:mɪneɪt] vt mettere fine a ♦ vi: **to ~ in** finire in or con.
termination [tə:mɪ'neɪʃən] n fine f; (of contract) rescissione f; **~ of pregnancy** (MED) interruzione f della gravidanza.
termini ['tə:mɪnaɪ] npl of **terminus**.
terminology [tə:mɪ'nɔlədʒɪ] n terminologia.
terminus, pl **termini** ['tə:mɪnəs, 'tə:mɪnaɪ] n (for buses) capolinea m; (for trains) stazione f terminale.
termite ['tə:maɪt] n termite f.
term paper n (US UNIVERSITY) saggio scritto da consegnare a fine trimestre.
Ter(r). abbr = **terrace**.
terrace ['tɛrəs] n terrazza; (BRIT: row of houses) fila di case a schiera; **the ~s** npl (BRIT SPORT) le gradinate.
terraced ['tɛrɪst] adj (garden) a terrazze; (in a row: house, cottage etc) a schiera.
terrain [tɛ'reɪn] n terreno.
terrible ['tɛrɪbl] adj terribile; (weather) bruttissimo(a); (performance, report) pessimo(a).
terribly ['tɛrəblɪ] adv terribilmente; (very

badly) malissimo.
terrier ['tɛrɪə*] n terrier m inv.
terrific [tə'rɪfɪk] adj incredibile, fantastico(a); (wonderful) formidabile, eccezionale.
terrify ['tɛrɪfaɪ] vt terrorizzare; **to be terrified** essere atterrito(a).
territorial [tɛrɪ'tɔːrɪəl] adj territoriale.
territorial waters npl acque fpl territoriali.
territory ['tɛrɪtərɪ] n territorio.
terror ['tɛrə*] n terrore m.
terror attack n attentato terroristico.
terrorism ['tɛrərɪzəm] n terrorismo.
terrorist ['tɛrərɪst] n terrorista m/f.
terrorize ['tɛrəraɪz] vt terrorizzare.
terse [tə:s] adj (style) conciso(a); (reply) laconico(a).
tertiary ['tə:ʃərɪ] adj (gen) terziario(a); **~ education** (BRIT) educazione f superiore post-scolastica.
Terylene ® ['tɛrəli:n] n (BRIT) terital ® m, terilene ® m.
TESL ['tɛsl] n abbr = Teaching of English as a Second Language.
TESSA ['tɛsə] n abbr (BRIT: = Tax Exempt Special Savings Account) deposito a risparmio esente da tasse.
test [tɛst] n (trial, check) prova; (: of goods in factory) controllo, collaudo; (MED) esame m; (CHEM) analisi f inv; (exam: of intelligence etc) test m inv; (: in school) compito in classe; (also: **driving ~**) esame m di guida ♦ vt provare; controllare, collaudare; esaminare; analizzare; sottoporre ad esame; **to put sth to the ~** mettere qc alla prova; **to ~ sth for sth** analizzare qc alla ricerca di qc; **to ~ sb in history** esaminare qn in storia.
testament ['tɛstəmənt] n testamento; **the Old/New T~** il Vecchio/Nuovo testamento.
test ban n (also: **nuclear ~**) divieto di esperimenti nucleari.
test case n (LAW, fig) caso che farà testo.
testes ['tɛsti:z] npl testicoli mpl.
test flight n volo di prova.
testicle ['tɛstɪkl] n testicolo.
testify ['tɛstɪfaɪ] vi (LAW) testimoniare, deporre; **to ~ to sth** (LAW) testimoniare qc; (gen) comprovare or dimostrare qc; (be sign of) essere una prova di qc.
testimonial [tɛstɪ'məunɪəl] n (BRIT: reference) benservito; (gift) testimonianza di stima.
testimony ['tɛstɪmənɪ] n (LAW) testimonianza, deposizione f.
testing ['tɛstɪŋ] adj (difficult: time) duro(a).
test match n (CRICKET, RUGBY) partita

internazionale.
testosterone [tɛs'tɔstərəun] n testosterone m.
test paper n (SCOL) interrogazione f scritta.
test pilot n pilota m collaudatore.
test tube n provetta.
test-tube baby ['tɛsttjuːb-] n bambino(a) concepito(a) in provetta.
testy ['tɛstɪ] adj irritabile.
tetanus ['tɛtənəs] n tetano.
tetchy ['tɛtʃɪ] adj irritabile, irascibile.
tether ['tɛðə*] vt legare ♦ n: **at the end of one's** ~ al limite (della pazienza).
Tex. abbr (US) = Texas.
text [tɛkst] n testo; (TEL) messaggino, SMS m inv ♦ vt mandare un SMS a.
textbook ['tɛkstbuk] n libro di testo.
textile ['tɛkstaɪl] n tessile m; ~**s** npl tessuti mpl.
texting ['tɛkstɪŋ] n invio di SMS.
text message n (TEL) messaggino, SMS m inv.
textual ['tɛkstjuəl] adj testuale, del testo.
texture ['tɛkstʃə*] n tessitura; (of skin, paper etc) struttura.
TGIF abbr (col) = thank God it's Friday.
TGWU n abbr (BRIT: = Transport and General Workers' Union) sindacato degli operai dei trasporti e non specializzati.
Thai [taɪ] adj tailandese ♦ n tailandese m/f; (LING) tailandese m.
Thailand ['taɪlænd] n Tailandia.
thalidomide ® [θə'lɪdəmaɪd] n talidomide ® m.
Thames [tɛmz] n: **the** ~ il Tamigi.
than [ðæn, ðən] conj che; (with numerals, pronouns, proper names): **more** ~ **10/me/ Maria** più di 10/me/Maria; **you know her better** ~ **I do** la conosce meglio di me; **she has more apples** ~ **pears** ha più mele che pere; **it is better to phone** ~ **to write** è meglio telefonare che scrivere; **no sooner did he leave** ~ **the phone rang** non appena uscì il telefono suonò.
thank [θæŋk] vt ringraziare; ~ **you (very much)** grazie (tante); ~ **heavens/God!** grazie al cielo/a Dio!; see also **thanks.**
thankful ['θæŋkful] adj: ~ **(for)** riconoscente (per); ~ **for/that** (relieved) sollevato(a) da/dal fatto che.
thankfully ['θæŋkfəlɪ] adv con riconoscenza; con sollievo; ~ **there were few victims** grazie al cielo ci sono state poche vittime.
thankless ['θæŋklɪs] adj ingrato(a).
thanks [θæŋks] npl ringraziamenti mpl, grazie fpl ♦ excl grazie!; ~ **to** prep grazie a.

Thanksgiving (Day) ['θæŋksgɪvɪŋ-] n (US) giorno del ringraziamento; see boxed note.

> **THANKSGIVING**
>
> Negli Stati Uniti il quarto giovedì di novembre ricorre il **Thanksgiving (Day)**, festa nazionale in ricordo della celebrazione con cui i Padri Pellegrini, i puritani inglesi che fondarono la colonia di Plymouth nel Massachusetts, ringraziarono Dio del buon raccolto del 1621.

======================================= KEYWORD

that [ðæt](pl **those**) adj (demonstrative) quel(quell', quello) m; quella(quell') f; ~ **man/woman/book** quell'uomo/quella donna/quel libro; (not "this") quell'uomo/ quella donna/quel libro là; ~ **one** quello(a) là
♦ pron **1** (demonstrative) ciò; (not "this one") quello(a); **who's** ~? chi è quello là?; **what's** ~? cos'è quello?; **is** ~ **you?** sei tu?; **I prefer this to** ~ preferisco questo a quello; ~'**s what he said** questo è ciò che ha detto; **after** ~ dopo; **what happened after** ~? che è successo dopo?; ~ **is (to say)** cioè; **at or with** ~ **she ...** con ciò lei ...; **do it like** ~ fallo così
2 (relative: direct) che; (: indirect) cui; **the book** (~) **I read** il libro che ho letto; **the box** (~) **I put it in** la scatola in cui l'ho messo; **the people** (~) **I spoke to** le persone con cui or con le quali ho parlato; **not** ~ **I know of** non che io sappia
3 (relative: of time) in cui; **the day** (~) **came** il giorno in cui è venuto
♦ conj che; **he thought** ~ **I was ill** pensava che io fossi malato
♦ adv (demonstrative) così; **I can't work** ~ **much** non posso lavorare (così) tanto; ~ **high** così alto; **the wall's about** ~ **high and** ~ **thick** il muro è alto circa così e spesso circa così.

thatched [θætʃt] adj (roof) di paglia; ~ **cottage** cottage m inv col tetto di paglia.
Thatcherism ['θætʃərɪzəm] n thatcherismo m.
thaw [θɔː] n disgelo ♦ vi (ice) sciogliersi; (food) scongelarsi ♦ vt (food) (fare) scongelare; **it's** ~**ing** (weather) sta sgelando.

======================================= KEYWORD

the [ðiː, ðə] def art **1** (gen) il(lo, l') m; la(l') f; i(gli) mpl; le fpl; ~ **boy/girl/ink** il ragazzo/ la ragazza/l'inchiostro; ~ **books/pencils** i

libri/le matite; ~ **history of** ~ **world** la
storia del mondo; **give it to** ~ **postman** dallo
al postino; **I haven't** ~ **time/money** non ho
tempo/soldi; ~ **rich and** ~ **poor** i ricchi
e i poveri; **1.5 euros to** ~ **dollar** 1.5 euro
per un dollaro; **paid by** ~ **hour** pagato a ore
2 (*in titles*): **Elizabeth** ~ **First** Elisabetta
prima; **Peter** ~ **Great** Pietro il Grande
3 (*in comparisons*): ~ **more he works,** ~
more he earns più lavora più guadagna; ~
sooner ~ **better** prima è meglio è.

theatre, (*US*) **theater** ['θɪətə*] *n* teatro.
theatre-goer ['θɪətəgəʊə*] *n*
frequentatore/trice di teatri.
theatrical [θɪ'ætrɪkl] *adj* teatrale.
theft [θɛft] *n* furto.
their [ðɛə*] *adj* il(la) loro, *pl* i(le) loro.
theirs [ðɛəz] *pron* il(la) loro, *pl* i(le) loro; **it
is** ~ è loro; **a friend of** ~ un loro amico.
them [ðɛm, ðəm] *pron* (*direct*) li(le); (*indirect*)
gli, loro (*after vb*); (*stressed, after prep*:
people) loro; (: *people, things*) essi(e); **I see**
~ li vedo; **give** ~ **the book** dà loro *or*
dagli il libro; **give me a few of** ~
dammene un po' *or* qualcuno.
theme [θiːm] *n* tema *m*.
theme park *n* parco dei divertimenti a
soggetto.
theme song, theme tune *n* tema
musicale.
themselves [ðəm'sɛlvz] *pl pron* (*reflexive*) si;
(*emphatic*) loro stessi(e); (*after prep*) se
stessi(e); **between** ~ tra (di) loro.
then [ðɛn] *adv* (*at that time*) allora; (*next*)
poi, dopo; (*and also*) e poi ♦ *conj* (*therefore*)
perciò, dunque, quindi ♦ *adj*: **the** ~
president il presidente di allora; **from** ~
on da allora in poi; **until** ~ fino ad allora;
and ~ **what?** e poi?, e allora?; **what do
you want me to do** ~**?** allora cosa vuole
che faccia?
theologian [θɪə'ləʊdʒən] *n* teologo/a.
theological [θɪə'lɒdʒɪkl] *adj* teologico(a).
theology [θɪ'ɒlədʒɪ] *n* teologia.
theorem ['θɪərəm] *n* teorema *m*.
theoretical [θɪə'rɛtɪkl] *adj* teorico(a).
theorize ['θɪəraɪz] *vi* teorizzare.
theory ['θɪərɪ] *n* teoria; **in** ~ in teoria.
therapeutic(al) [θɛrə'pjuːtɪk(l)] *adj*
terapeutico(a).
therapist ['θɛrəpɪst] *n* terapista *m/f*.
therapy ['θɛrəpɪ] *n* terapia.

================== *KEYWORD*

there [ðɛə*] *adv* **1**: ~ **is,** ~ **are** c'è, ci sono; ~
are 3 of them (*people*) sono in 3; (*things*)
ce ne sono 3; ~ **is no-one here** non c'è

nessuno qui; ~ **has been an accident** c'è
stato un incidente
2 (*referring to place*) là, lì; **it's** ~ è là *or* lì;
up/in/down ~ lassù/là dentro/laggiù;
back ~ là dietro; **on** ~ lassù; **over** ~ là;
through ~ di là; **he went** ~ **on Friday** ci è
andato venerdì; **it takes two hours to go**
~ **and back** ci vogliono due ore per
andare e tornare; **I want that book** ~
voglio quel libro là *or* lì; ~ **he is!**
eccolo!
3: ~, ~ (*esp to child*) su, su.

thereabouts ['ðɛərəbaʊts] *adv* (*place*) nei
pressi, da quelle parti; (*amount*) giù di lì,
all'incirca.
thereafter [ðɛər'ɑːftə*] *adv* da allora in
poi.
thereby [ðɛə'baɪ] *adv* con ciò.
therefore ['ðɛəfɔː*] *adv* perciò,
quindi.
there's [ðɛəz] = **there is; there has.**
thereupon [ðɛərə'pɒn] *adv* (*at that point*) a
quel punto; (*formal*: *on that subject*) in
merito.
thermal ['θəːml] *adj* (*currents, spring*)
termale; (*underwear, printer*) termico(a);
(*paper*) termosensibile.
thermodynamics [θəːməʊdaɪ'næmɪks] *n*
termodinamica.
thermometer [θə'mɒmɪtə*] *n*
termometro.
thermonuclear ['θəːməʊ'njuːklɪə*] *adj*
termonucleare.
Thermos ® ['θəːməs] *n* (*also*: ~ **flask**)
thermos ® *m inv*.
thermostat ['θəːməstæt] *n* termostato.
thesaurus [θɪ'sɔːrəs] *n* dizionario dei
sinonimi.
these [ðiːz] *pl pron, adj* questi(e).
thesis, *pl* **theses** ['θiːsɪs, 'θiːsiːz] *n* tesi *f*
inv.
they [ðeɪ] *pl pron* essi(esse); (*people only*)
loro; ~ **say that** ... (*it is said that*) si dice
che ....
they'd [ðeɪd] = **they would; they had.**
they'll [ðeɪl] = **they will; they shall.**
they're [ðɛə*] = **they are.**
they've [ðeɪv] = **they have.**
thick [θɪk] *adj* spesso(a); (*crowd*)
compatto(a); (*stupid*) ottuso(a), lento(a)
♦ *n*: **in the** ~ **of** nel folto di; **it's 20 cm** ~ ha
uno spessore di 20 cm.
thicken ['θɪkən] *vi* ispessire ♦ *vt* (*sauce etc*)
ispessire, rendere più denso(a).
thicket ['θɪkɪt] *n* boscaglia.
thickly ['θɪklɪ] *adv* (*spread*) a strati spessi;
(*cut*) a fette grosse; (*populated*)

densamente.
thickness ['θɪknɪs] n spessore m.
thickset [θɪk'sɛt] adj tarchiato(a), tozzo(a).
thickskinned [θɪk'skɪnd] adj (fig)
  insensibile.
thief, pl **thieves** [θiːf, θiːvz] n ladro/a.
thieving ['θiːvɪŋ] n furti mpl.
thigh [θaɪ] n coscia.
thighbone ['θaɪbəʊn] n femore m.
thimble ['θɪmbl] n ditale m.
thin [θɪn] adj sottile; (person) magro(a);
  (soup) poco denso(a); (hair, crowd)
  rado(a); (fog) leggero(a) ♦ vt (hair) sfoltire
  ♦ vi (fog) diradarsi; (also: ~ **out**: crowd)
  disperdersi; **to** ~ (**down**) (sauce, paint)
  diluire; **his hair is** ~**ning** sta perdendo i
  capelli.
thing [θɪŋ] n cosa; (object) oggetto;
  (contraption) aggeggio; ~**s** npl (belongings)
  cose fpl; **for one** ~ tanto per cominciare;
  the best ~ **would be** to la cosa migliore
  sarebbe di; **the** ~ **is ...** il fatto è che ...;
  the main ~ **is to ...** la cosa più
  importante è di ...; **first** ~ (**in the
  morning**) come or per prima cosa (di
  mattina); **last** ~ (**at night**) come or per
  ultima cosa (di sera); **poor** ~ poveretto/a;
  she's got a ~ **about mice** è terrorizzata
  dai topi; **how are** ~**s?** come va?
think, pt, pp **thought** [θɪŋk, θɔːt] vi pensare,
  riflettere ♦ vt pensare, credere; (imagine)
  immaginare; **to** ~ **of** pensare a; **what did
  you** ~ **of them?** cosa ne ha pensato?; **to** ~
  about sth/sb pensare a qc/qn; **I'll** ~ **about
  it** ci penserò; **to** ~ **of doing** pensare di
  fare; **I** ~ **so** penso or credo di sì; **to** ~ **well
  of** avere una buona opinione di; **to** ~
  aloud pensare ad alta voce; ~ **again!**
  rifletti!, pensaci su!
►**think out** vt (plan) elaborare; (solution)
  trovare.
►**think over** vt riflettere su; **I'd like to** ~
  things over vorrei pensarci su.
►**think through** vt riflettere a fondo su.
►**think up** vt ideare.
thinking ['θɪŋkɪŋ] n: **to my (way of)** ~ a mio
  parere.
think tank n gruppo di esperti.
thinly ['θɪnlɪ] adv (cut) a fette sottili;
  (spread) in uno strato sottile.
thinness ['θɪnnɪs] n sottigliezza; magrezza.
third [θɜːd] n terzo(a) ♦ n terzo/a; (fraction)
  terzo, terza parte f; (BRIT SCOL: degree)
  laurea col minimo dei voti.
third-degree burns ['θɜːddɪ'griː-] npl
  ustioni fpl di terzo grado.
thirdly ['θɜːdlɪ] adv in terzo luogo.
third party insurance n (BRIT)

assicurazione f contro terzi.
third-rate [θɜːd'reɪt] adj di qualità
  scadente.
Third World n: **the** ~ il Terzo Mondo.
thirst [θɜːst] n sete f.
thirsty ['θɜːstɪ] adj (person) assetato(a), che
  ha sete; **to be** ~ aver sete.
thirteen [θɜː'tiːn] num tredici.
thirtieth ['θɜːtɪɪθ] num trentesimo(a).
thirty ['θɜːtɪ] num trenta.

============================ *KEYWORD*

this [ðɪs] (pl **these**) adj (demonstrative)
  questo(a); ~ **man/woman/book**
  quest'uomo/questa donna/questo libro;
  (not "that") quest'uomo/questa donna/
  questo libro qui; ~ **one** questo(a) qui; ~
  time questa volta; ~ **time last year** l'anno
  scorso in questo periodo; ~ **way** (in this
  direction) da questa parte; (in this fashion)
  così
  ♦ pron (demonstrative) questo(a); (not "that
  one") questo(a) qui; **who/what is** ~**?** chi
  è/che cos'è questo?; **I prefer** ~ **to that**
  preferisco questo a quello; ~ **is where I
  live** io abito qui; ~ **is what he said** questo
  è ciò che ha detto; **they were talking of** ~
  and that stavano parlando del più e del
  meno; ~ **is Mr Brown** (in introductions,
  photo) questo è il signor Brown; (on
  telephone) sono il signor Brown
  ♦ adv (demonstrative): ~ **high/long** etc
  alto/lungo etc così; **it's about** ~ **high** è
  alto circa così; **I didn't know things were**
  ~ **bad** non sapevo andasse così male.

thistle ['θɪsl] n cardo.
thong [θɒŋ] n cinghia.
thorn [θɔːn] n spina.
thorny ['θɔːnɪ] adj spinoso(a).
thorough ['θʌrə] adj (person) preciso(a),
  accurato(a); (search) minuzioso(a);
  (knowledge, research) approfondito(a),
  profondo(a); (cleaning) a fondo.
thoroughbred ['θʌrəbrɛd] n (horse)
  purosangue m/f inv.
thoroughfare ['θʌrəfɛə*] n strada
  transitabile; "**no** ~" (BRIT) "divieto di
  transito".
thoroughgoing ['θʌrəgəʊɪŋ] adj (analysis)
  approfondito(a); (reform) totale.
thoroughly ['θʌrəlɪ] adv accuratamente;
  minuziosamente; in profondità; a fondo;
  he ~ **agreed** fu completamente
  d'accordo.
thoroughness ['θʌrənɪs] n precisione f.
those [ðəʊz] pl pron quelli(e) ♦ pl adj
  quei(quegli) mpl; quelle fpl.

though [ðəu] *conj* benché, sebbene ♦ *adv* comunque, tuttavia; **even** ~ anche se; **it's not so easy,** ~ tuttavia non è così facile.

thought [θɔ:t] *pt, pp of* **think** ♦ *n* pensiero; (*opinion*) opinione *f;* (*intention*) intenzione *f;* **after much** ~ dopo molti ripensamenti; **I've just had a** ~ mi è appena venuta un'idea; **to give sth some** ~ prendere qc in considerazione, riflettere su qc.

thoughtful ['θɔ:tful] *adj* pensieroso(a), pensoso(a); ponderato(a); (*considerate*) premuroso(a).

thoughtfully ['θɔ:tfəlɪ] *adv* (*pensively*) con aria pensierosa.

thoughtless ['θɔ:tlɪs] *adj* sconsiderato(a); (*behaviour*) scortese.

thoughtlessly ['θɔ:tlɪslɪ] *adv* sconsideratamente; scortesemente.

thought-provoking ['θɔ:tprəvəukɪŋ] *adj* stimolante.

thousand ['θauzənd] *num* mille; **one** ~ mille; **~s of** migliaia di.

thousandth ['θauzəntθ] *num* millesimo(a).

thrash [θræʃ] *vt* picchiare; bastonare; (*defeat*) battere.
►**thrash about** *vi* dibattersi.
►**thrash out** *vt* dibattere, sviscerare.

thrashing ['θræʃɪŋ] *n*: **to give sb a** ~ = **to thrash sb**.

thread [θrɛd] *n* filo; (*of screw*) filetto ♦ *vt* (*needle*) infilare; **to** ~ **one's way between** infilarsi tra.

threadbare ['θrɛdbɛə*] *adj* consumato(a), logoro(a).

threat [θrɛt] *n* minaccia; **to be under** ~ **of** (*closure, extinction*) rischiare di; (*exposure*) essere minacciato(a) di.

threaten ['θrɛtn] *vi* (*storm*) minacciare ♦ *vt*: **to** ~ **sb with sth/to do** minacciare qn con qc/di fare.

threatening ['θrɛtnɪŋ] *adj* minaccioso(a).

three [θri:] *num* tre.

three-dimensional [θri:daɪ'mɛnʃənl] *adj* tridimensionale.

three-piece ['θri:pi:s]: ~ **suit** *n* completo (con gilè); ~ **suite** *n* salotto comprendente un divano e due poltrone.

three-ply [θri:'plaɪ] *adj* (*wood*) a tre strati; (*wool*) a tre fili.

three-quarters [θri:'kwɔ:təz] *npl* tre quarti *mpl;* ~ **full** pieno per tre quarti.

three-wheeler [θri:'wi:lə*] *n* (*car*) veicolo a tre ruote.

thresh [θrɛʃ] *vt* (*AGR*) trebbiare.

threshing machine ['θrɛʃɪŋ-] *n* trebbiatrice *f.*

threshold ['θrɛʃhəuld] *n* soglia; **to be on the** ~ **of** (*fig*) essere sulla soglia di.

threshold agreement *n* (*ECON*) ≈ scala mobile.

threw [θru:] *pt of* **throw**.

thrift [θrɪft] *n* parsimonia.

thrifty ['θrɪftɪ] *adj* economico(a), parsimonioso(a).

thrill [θrɪl] *n* brivido ♦ *vi* eccitarsi, tremare ♦ *vt* (*audience*) elettrizzare; **I was** ~**ed to get your letter** la tua lettera mi ha fatto veramente piacere.

thriller ['θrɪlə*] *n* film *m inv* (*or* dramma *m or* libro) del brivido.

thrilling ['θrɪlɪŋ] *adj* (*book, play etc*) pieno(a) di suspense; (*news, discovery*) entusiasmante.

thrive, *pt* **thrived, throve,** *pp* **thrived, thriven** [θraɪv, θrəuv, 'θrɪvn] *vi* crescere *or* svilupparsi bene; (*business*) prosperare; **he ~s on it** gli fa bene, ne gode.

thriving ['θraɪvɪŋ] *adj* (*industry etc*) fiorente.

throat [θrəut] *n* gola; **to have a sore** ~ avere (un *or* il) mal di gola.

throb [θrɔb] *n* (*of heart*) battito; (*of engine*) vibrazione *f;* (*of pain*) fitta ♦ *vi* (*heart*) palpitare; (*engine*) vibrare; (*with pain*) pulsare; **my head is ~bing** mi martellano le tempie.

throes [θrəuz] *npl*: **in the** ~ **of** alle prese con; in preda a; **in the** ~ **of death** in agonia.

thrombosis [θrɔm'bəusɪs] *n* trombosi *f.*

throne [θrəun] *n* trono.

throng [θrɔŋ] *n* moltitudine *f* ♦ *vt* affollare.

throttle ['θrɔtl] *n* (*AUT*) valvola a farfalla; (*on motorcycle*) (manopola del) gas ♦ *vt* strangolare.

through [θru:] *prep* attraverso; (*time*) per, durante; (*by means of*) per mezzo di; (*owing to*) a causa di ♦ *adj* (*ticket, train, passage*) diretto(a) ♦ *adv* attraverso; **(from) Monday** ~ **Friday** (*US*) da lunedì a venerdì; **I am halfway** ~ **the book** sono a metà libro; **to let sb** ~ lasciar passare qn; **to put sb** ~ **to sb** (*TEL*) passare qn a qn; **to be** ~ (*TEL*) ottenere la comunicazione; (*have finished*) avere finito; **"no** ~ **traffic"** (*US*) "divieto d'accesso"; **"no** ~ **road"** (*BRIT*) "strada senza sbocco".

throughout [θru:'aut] *prep* (*place*) dappertutto in; (*time*) per *or* durante tutto(a) ♦ *adv* dappertutto; sempre.

throughput ['θru:put] *n* (*of goods, materials*) materiale *m* in lavorazione; (*COMPUT*) volume *m* di dati immessi.

throve [θrəuv] *pt of* **thrive**.

throw [θrəu] *n* tiro, getto; (*SPORT*) lancio ♦ *vt* (*pt* **threw,** *pp* **thrown** [θru:, θrəun]) tirare, gettare; (*SPORT*) lanciare; (*rider*)

disarcionare; (fig) confondere; (pottery)
formare al tornio; **to ~ a party** dare una
festa; **to ~ open** (doors, windows)
spalancare; (house, gardens etc) aprire al
pubblico; (competition, race) aprire a tutti.
►**throw about, throw around** vt (litter
etc) spargere.
►**throw away** vt gettare or buttare via.
►**throw off** vt sbarazzarsi di.
►**throw out** vt buttare fuori; (reject)
respingere.
►**throw together** vt (clothes, meal etc)
mettere insieme; (essay) buttar giù.
►**throw up** vi vomitare.
throwaway ['θrəuəweı] adj da buttare.
throwback ['θrəubæk] n: **it's a ~ to** (fig) ciò
risale a.
throw-in ['θrəuın] n (SPORT) rimessa in
gioco.
thrown [θrəun] pp of **throw.**
thru [θruː] prep, adj, adv (US) = **through.**
thrush [θrʌʃ] n (ZOOL) tordo; (MED: esp in
children) mughetto; (: BRIT: in women)
candida.
thrust [θrʌst] n (TECH) spinta ♦ vt (pt, pp
thrust) spingere con forza; (push in)
conficcare.
thrusting ['θrʌstıŋ] adj (troppo)
intraprendente.
thud [θʌd] n tonfo.
thug [θʌg] n delinquente m.
thumb [θʌm] n (ANAT) pollice m ♦ vt (book)
sfogliare; **to ~ a lift** fare l'autostop; **to
give sb/sth the ~s up/down** approvare/
disapprovare qn/qc.
thumb index n indice m a rubrica.
thumbnail ['θʌmneıl] n unghia del pollice.
thumbnail sketch n descrizione f breve.
thumbtack ['θʌmtæk] n (US) puntina da
disegno.
thump [θʌmp] n colpo forte; (sound) tonfo
♦ vt battere su ♦ vi picchiare, battere.
thunder ['θʌndə*] n tuono ♦ vi tuonare;
(train etc): **to ~ past** passare con un
rombo.
thunderbolt ['θʌndəbəult] n fulmine m.
thunderclap ['θʌndəklæp] n rombo di
tuono.
thunderous ['θʌndərəs] adj fragoroso(a).
thunderstorm ['θʌndəstɔːm] n temporale
m.
thunderstruck ['θʌndəstrʌk] adj (fig)
sbigottito(a).
thundery ['θʌndərı] adj temporalesco(a)
Thur(s). abbr (= Thursday) gio.
Thursday ['θəːzdı] n giovedì m inv; for
phrases see also **Tuesday.**
thus [ðʌs] adv così.

thwart [θwɔːt] vt contrastare.
thyme [taım] n timo.
thyroid ['θaırɔıd] n tiroide f.
tiara [tı'ɑːrə] n (woman's) diadema m.
Tiber ['taıbə*] n: **the ~** il Tevere.
Tibet [tı'bɛt] n Tibet m.
Tibetan [tı'bɛtən] adj tibetano(a) ♦ n
(person) tibetano/a; (LING) tibetano.
tibia ['tıbıə] n tibia.
tic [tık] n tic m inv.
tick [tık] n (sound: of clock) tic tac m inv;
(mark) segno; spunta; (ZOOL) zecca; (BRIT
col): **in a ~** in un attimo; (BRIT col: credit):
to buy sth on ~ comprare qc a credito
♦ vi fare tic tac ♦ vt spuntare; **to put a ~
against sth** fare un segno di fianco a qc.
►**tick off** vt spuntare; (person) sgridare.
►**tick over** vi (BRIT: engine) andare al
minimo.
ticker tape ['tıkə-] n nastro di
telescrivente; (US: in celebrations) stelle
fpl filanti.
ticket ['tıkıt] n biglietto; (in shop: on goods)
etichetta; (: from cash register) scontrino;
(for library) scheda; (US POL) lista dei
candidati; **to get a (parking) ~** (AUT)
prendere una multa (per sosta vietata).
ticket agency n (THEAT) agenzia di vendita
di biglietti.
ticket collector n bigliettaio.
ticket holder n persona munita di
biglietto.
ticket inspector n controllore m.
ticket office n biglietteria.
tickle ['tıkl] n solletico ♦ vt fare il solletico
a, solleticare; (fig) stuzzicare; piacere a;
far ridere.
ticklish ['tıklıʃ] adj che soffre il solletico;
(which tickles: blanket, cough) che provoca
prurito.
tidal ['taıdl] adj di marea.
tidal wave n onda anomala.
tidbit ['tıdbıt] n (US) = **titbit.**
tiddlywinks ['tıdlıwıŋks] n gioco della
pulce.
tide [taıd] n marea; (fig: of events) corso
♦ vt: **will £20 ~ you over till Monday?** ti
basteranno 20 sterline fino a lunedì?;
high/low ~ alta/bassa marea; **the ~ of
public opinion** l'orientamento
dell'opinione pubblica.
tidily ['taıdılı] adv in modo ordinato; **to
arrange ~** sistemare; **to dress ~** vestirsi
per benino.
tidiness ['taıdınıs] n ordine m.
tidy ['taıdı] adj (room) ordinato(a), lindo(a);
(dress, work) curato(a), in ordine; (person)
ordinato(a); (mind) organizzato(a) ♦ vt

(*also*: ~ **up**) riordinare, mettere in ordine; **to** ~ **o.s. up** rassettarsi.

tie [taɪ] *n* (*string etc*) legaccio; (*BRIT*: *also*: **neck~**) cravatta; (*fig*: *link*) legame *m*; (*SPORT*: *draw*) pareggio (: *match*) incontro; (*US RAIL*) traversina ♦ *vt* (*parcel*) legare; (*ribbon*) annodare ♦ *vi* (*SPORT*) pareggiare; **"black/white** ~**"** "smoking/abito di rigore"; **family** ~**s** legami familiari; **to** ~ **sth in a bow** annodare qc; **to** ~ **a knot in sth** fare un nodo a qc.

▶**tie down** *vt* fissare con una corda; (*fig*): **to** ~ **sb down to** costringere qn ad accettare.

▶**tie in** *vi*: **to** ~ **in (with)** (*correspond*) corrispondere (a).

▶**tie on** *vt* (*BRIT*: *label etc*) attaccare.

▶**tie up** *vt* (*parcel, dog*) legare; (*boat*) ormeggiare; (*arrangements*) concludere; **to be** ~**d up** (*busy*) essere occupato *or* preso.

tie-break(er) ['taɪbreɪk(ə*)] *n* (*TENNIS*) tie-break *m inv*; (*in quiz*) spareggio.

tie-on ['taɪɔn] *adj* (*BRIT*: *label*) volante.

tie-pin ['taɪpɪn] *n* (*BRIT*) fermacravatta *m inv*.

tier [tɪə*] *n* fila; (*of cake*) piano, strato.

Tierra del Fuego [tɪ'ɛrədɛl'fweɪgəu] *n* Terra del Fuoco.

tie tack *n* (*US*) fermacravatta *m inv*.

tiff [tɪf] *n* battibecco.

tiger ['taɪgə*] *n* tigre *f*.

tight [taɪt] *adj* (*rope*) teso(a), tirato(a); (*clothes*) stretto(a); (*budget, programme, bend*) stretto(a); (*control*) severo(a), fermo(a); (*col*: *drunk*) sbronzo(a) ♦ *adv* (*squeeze*) fortemente; (*shut*) ermeticamente; **to be packed** ~ (*suitcase*) essere pieno zeppo; (*people*) essere pigiati; **everybody hold** ~**!** tenetevi stretti!; *see also* **tights**.

tighten ['taɪtn] *vt* (*rope*) tendere; (*screw*) stringere; (*control*) rinforzare ♦ *vi* tendersi; stringersi.

tight-fisted [taɪt'fɪstɪd] *adj* avaro(a).

tight-lipped ['taɪt'lɪpt] *adj*: **to be** ~ essere reticente; (*angry*) tenere le labbra serrate.

tightly ['taɪtlɪ] *adv* (*grasp*) bene, saldamente.

tightrope ['taɪtrəup] *n* corda (da acrobata).

tightrope walker *n* funambolo/a.

tights [taɪts] *npl* (*BRIT*) collant *m inv*.

tigress ['taɪgrɪs] *n* tigre *f* (femmina).

tilde ['tɪldə] *n* tilde *f*.

tile [taɪl] *n* (*on roof*) tegola; (*on floor*) mattonella; (*on wall*) piastrella ♦ *vt* (*floor, bathroom etc*) piastrellare.

tiled [taɪld] *adj* rivestito(a) di tegole; a mattonelle; a piastrelle.

till [tɪl] *n* registratore *m* di cassa ♦ *vt* (*land*) coltivare ♦ *prep, conj* = **until**.

tiller ['tɪlə*] *n* (*NAUT*) barra del timone.

tilt [tɪlt] *vt* inclinare, far pendere ♦ *vi* inclinarsi, pendere ♦ *n* (*slope*) pendio; **to wear one's hat at a** ~ portare il cappello sulle ventitrè; **(at) full** ~ a tutta velocità.

timber ['tɪmbə*] *n* (*material*) legname *m*; (*trees*) alberi *mpl* da legname.

time [taɪm] *n* tempo; (*epoch*: *often pl*) epoca, tempo; (*by clock*) ora; (*moment*) momento; (*occasion, also MATH*) volta; (*MUS*) tempo ♦ *vt* (*race*) cronometrare; (*programme*) calcolare la durata di; (*remark etc*): **to** ~ **sth well/badly** scegliere il momento più/ meno opportuno per qc; **a long** ~ molto tempo; **for the** ~ **being** per il momento; **from** ~ **to** ~ ogni tanto; ~ **after** ~, ~ **and again** mille volte; **in** ~ (*soon enough*) in tempo; (*after some time*) col tempo; (*MUS*) a tempo; **at** ~**s** a volte; **to take one's** ~ prenderla con calma; **in a week's** ~ fra una settimana; **in no** ~ in un attimo; **on** ~ puntualmente; **to be 30 minutes behind/ ahead of** ~ avere 30 minuti di ritardo/ anticipo; **by the** ~ **he arrived** quando è arrivato; **5** ~**s 5** 5 volte 5, 5 per 5; **what** ~ **is it?** che ora è?, che ore sono?; **what** ~ **do you make it?** che ora fa?; **to have a good** ~ divertirsi; **they had a hard** ~ **of it** è stato duro per loro; ~**'s up!** è (l')ora!; **to be behind the** ~**s** vivere nel passato; **I've no** ~ **for it** (*fig*) non ho tempo da perdere con cose del genere; **he'll do it in his own** (**good**) ~ (*without being hurried*) lo farà quando avrà (un minuto di) tempo; **he'll do it in** *or* (*US*) **on his own** ~ (*out of working hours*) lo farà nel suo tempo libero; **the bomb was** ~**d to explode 5 minutes later** la bomba era stata regolata in modo da esplodere 5 minuti più tardi.

time-and-motion study ['taɪmənd 'məuʃən-] *n* analisi *f inv* dei tempi e dei movimenti.

time bomb *n* bomba a orologeria.

time card *n* cartellino (da timbrare).

time clock *n* orologio *m* marcatempo *inv*.

time-consuming ['taɪmkənsjuːmɪŋ] *adj* che richiede molto tempo.

time difference *n* differenza di fuso orario.

time frame *n* tempi *mpl*.

time-honoured, (*US*) **time-honored** ['taɪmɔnəd] *adj* consacrato(a) dal tempo.

timekeeper ['taɪmkiːpə*] *n* (*SPORT*) cronometrista *m/f*.

time lag n intervallo, ritardo; (in travel) differenza di fuso orario.

timeless ['taɪmlɪs] adj eterno(a).

time limit n limite m di tempo.

timely ['taɪmlɪ] adj opportuno(a).

time off n tempo libero.

timer ['taɪmə*] n (in kitchen) contaminuti m inv; (TECH) timer m inv, temporizzatore m.

time-saving ['taɪmseɪvɪŋ] adj che fa risparmiare tempo.

time scale n tempi mpl d'esecuzione.

time-sharing ['taɪmʃɛərɪŋ] n (COMPUT) divisione f di tempo.

time sheet n = **time card**.

time signal n segnale m orario.

tIme switch n interruttore m a tempo.

timetable ['taɪmteɪbl] n orario; (programme of events etc) programma m.

time zone n fuso orario.

timid ['tɪmɪd] adj timido(a); (easily scared) pauroso(a).

timidity [tɪ'mɪdɪtɪ] n timidezza.

timing ['taɪmɪŋ] n sincronizzazione f; (fig) scelta del momento opportuno, tempismo; (SPORT) cronometraggio.

timing device n (on bomb) timer m inv.

timpani ['tɪmpənɪ] npl timpani mpl.

tin [tɪn] n stagno; (also: ~ **plate**) latta; (BRIT: can) barattolo (di latta), lattina, scatola; (for baking) teglia; **a** ~ **of paint** un barattolo di tinta or vernice.

tin foil n stagnola.

tinge [tɪndʒ] n sfumatura ♦ vt: ~**d with** tinto(a) di.

tingle ['tɪŋgl] vi (cheeks, skin: from cold) pungere, pizzicare; (: from bad circulation) formicolare.

tinker ['tɪŋkə*] n stagnino ambulante; (gipsy) zingaro/a.

▶**tinker with** vt fus armeggiare intorno a; cercare di riparare.

tinkle ['tɪŋkl] vi tintinnare ♦ n (col): **to give sb a** ~ dare un colpo di telefono a qn.

tin mine n miniera di stagno.

tinned [tɪnd] adj (BRIT: food) in scatola.

tinnitus [tɪ'naɪtəs] n (MED) ronzio auricolare.

tinny ['tɪnɪ] adj metallico(a).

tin-opener ['tɪnəupnə*] n (BRIT) apriscatole m inv.

tinsel ['tɪnsl] n decorazioni fpl natalizie (argentate).

tint [tɪnt] n tinta; (for hair) shampoo m inv colorante ♦ vt (hair) fare uno shampoo colorante a.

tinted ['tɪntɪd] adj (hair) tinto(a); (spectacles, glass) colorato(a).

tiny ['taɪnɪ] adj minuscolo(a).

tip [tɪp] n (end) punta; (protective: on umbrella etc) puntale m; (gratuity) mancia; (for coal) discarica; (for rubbish) immondezzaio; (advice) suggerimento ♦ vt (waiter) dare la mancia a; (tilt) inclinare; (overturn: also: ~ **over**) capovolgere; (empty: also: ~ **out**) scaricare; (predict: winner) pronosticare; (: horse) dare vincente; **he** ~**ped out the contents of the box** ha rovesciato il contenuto della scatola.

▶**tip off** vt fare una soffiata a.

tip-off ['tɪpɔf] n (hint) soffiata.

tipped ['tɪpt] adj (BRIT: cigarette) col filtro; **steel-**~ con la punta d'acciaio.

Tipp-Ex ® ['tɪpɛks] n (BRIT) liquido correttore.

tipple ['tɪpl] (BRIT) vi sbevazzare ♦ n: **to have a** ~ prendere un bicchierino.

tipster ['tɪpstə*] n (RACING) chi vende informazioni sulle corse e altre manifestazioni oggetto di scommesse.

tipsy ['tɪpsɪ] adj brillo(a).

tiptoe ['tɪptəu] n: **on** ~ in punta di piedi.

tiptop ['tɪptɔp] adj: **in** ~ **condition** in ottime condizioni.

tirade [taɪ'reɪd] n filippica.

tire ['taɪə*] vt stancare ♦ vi stancarsi ♦ n (US) = **tyre**.

▶**tire out** vt sfinire, spossare.

tired ['taɪəd] adj stanco(a); **to be/feel/look** ~ essere/sentirsi/sembrare stanco; **to be** ~ **of** essere stanco or stufo di.

tiredness ['taɪədnɪs] n stanchezza.

tireless ['taɪəlɪs] adj instancabile.

tiresome ['taɪəsəm] adj noioso(a).

tiring ['taɪərɪŋ] adj faticoso(a).

tissue ['tɪʃuː] n tessuto; (paper handkerchief) fazzolettino di carta.

tissue paper n carta velina.

tit [tɪt] n (bird) cinciallegra; (col: breast) tetta; **to give** ~ **for tat** rendere pan per focaccia.

titanium [tɪ'teɪnɪəm] n titanio.

titbit ['tɪtbɪt], (US) **tidbit** ['tɪdbɪt] n (food) leccornia; (news) notizia ghiotta.

titillate ['tɪtɪleɪt] vt titillare.

titivate ['tɪtɪveɪt] vt agghindare.

title ['taɪtl] n titolo; (LAW: right): ~ **(to)** diritto (a).

title deed n (LAW) titolo di proprietà.

title page n frontespizio.

title role n ruolo or parte f principale.

titter ['tɪtə*] vi ridere scioccamente.

tittle-tattle ['tɪtltætl] n chiacchiere fpl,

pettegolezzi *mpl.*

titular ['tɪtjulə*] *adj* (*in name only*) nominale.

tizzy ['tɪzɪ] *n* (*col*): **to be in a ~** essere in agitazione.

T-junction ['tiː'dʒʌŋkʃən] *n* incrocio a T.

TM *n abbr* (= *transcendental meditation*) M.T.

f; (*COMM*) = **trademark.**

TN *abbr* (*US*) = Tennessee.

TNT *n abbr* (= *trinitrotoluene*) T.N.T. *m.*

======================= **KEYWORD**

to [tuː, tə] *prep* **1** (*direction*) a; **to go ~ France/London/school** andare in Francia/a Londra/a scuola; **to go ~ town** andare in città; **to go ~ Paul's/the doctor's** andare da Paul/dal dottore; **the road ~ Edinburgh** la strada per Edimburgo; **~ the left/right** a sinistra/ destra

2 (*as far as*) (fino) a; **from here ~ London** da qui a Londra; **to count ~ 10** contare fino a 10; **from 40 ~ 50 people** da 40 a 50 persone

3 (*with expressions of time*): **a quarter ~ 5** le 5 meno un quarto; **it's twenty ~ 3** sono le 3 meno venti

4 (*for, of*): **the key ~ the front door** la chiave della porta d'ingresso; **a letter ~ his wife** una lettera per la moglie

5 (*expressing indirect object*) a; **to give sth ~ sb** dare qc a qn; **give it ~ me** dammelo; **to talk ~ sb** parlare a qn; **it belongs ~ him** gli appartiene, è suo; **to be a danger ~ sb/sth** rappresentare un pericolo per qn/qc

6 (*in relation to*) a; **3 goals ~ 2** 3 goal a 2; **30 miles ~ the gallon** ≈ 11 chilometri con un litro; **4 apples ~ the kilo** 4 mele in un chilo

7 (*purpose, result*): **to come ~ sb's aid** venire in aiuto a qn; **to sentence sb ~ death** condannare a morte qn; **~ my surprise** con mia sorpresa

♦ *with vb* **1** (*simple infinitive*): **~ go/eat** *etc* andare/mangiare *etc*

2 (*following another vb*): **to want/try/start ~ do** volere/cercare di/cominciare a fare

3 (*with vb omitted*): **I don't want ~** non voglio (farlo); **you ought ~** devi (farlo)

4 (*purpose, result*) per; **I did it ~ help you** l'ho fatto per aiutarti

5 (*equivalent to relative clause*): **I have things ~ do** ho da fare; **the main thing is ~ try** la cosa più importante è provare

6 (*after adjective etc*): **ready ~ go** pronto(a) a partire; **too old/young ~ ...**

troppo vecchio(a)/giovane per ...

♦ *adv*: **to push the door ~** accostare la porta; **to go ~ and fro** andare e tornare.

toad [təud] *n* rospo.

toadstool ['təudstuːl] *n* fungo (velenoso).

toady ['təudɪ] *vi* adulare.

toast [təust] *n* (*CULIN*) toast *m*, pane *m* abbrustolito; (*drink, speech*) brindisi *m inv* ♦ *vt* (*CULIN*) abbrustolire; (*drink to*) brindare a; **a piece** *or* **slice of ~** una fetta di pane abbrustolito.

toaster ['təustə*] *n* tostapane *m inv*.

toastmaster ['təustmɑːstə*] *n* direttore *m* dei brindisi.

toast rack *n* portatoast *m inv*.

tobacco [tə'bækəu] *n* tabacco; **pipe ~** tabacco da pipa.

tobacconist [tə'bækənɪst] *n* tabaccaio/a; **~ (shop)** tabaccheria.

Tobago [tə'beɪgəu] *n see* **Trinidad and Tobago.**

toboggan [tə'bɔgən] *n* toboga *m inv*; (*child's*) slitta.

today [tə'deɪ] *adv*, *n* (*also fig*) oggi (*m inv*); **what day is it ~?** che giorno è oggi?; **what date is it ~?** quanti ne abbiamo oggi?; **~ is the 4th of March** (oggi) è il 4 di marzo; **~'s paper** il giornale di oggi; **a fortnight ~** quindici giorni a oggi.

toddler ['tɔdlə*] *n* bambino/a che impara a camminare.

toddy ['tɔdɪ] *n* grog *m inv*.

to-do [tə'duː] *n* (*fuss*) storie *fpl*.

toe [təu] *n* dito del piede; (*of shoe*) punta ♦ *vt*: **to ~ the line** (*fig*) stare in riga, conformarsi; **big ~** alluce *m*; **little ~** mignolino.

TOEFL ['təufl] *n abbr* = *Test(ing) of English as a Foreign Language*.

toehold ['təuhəuld] *n* punto d'appoggio.

toenail ['təuneɪl] *n* unghia del piede.

toffee ['tɔfɪ] *n* caramella.

toffee apple *n* (*BRIT*) mela caramellata.

tofu ['təufuː] *n* tofu *m* (*latte di soia non fermentato*).

toga ['təugə] *n* toga.

together [tə'gɛðə*] *adv* insieme; (*at same time*) allo stesso tempo; **~ with** insieme a.

togetherness [tə'gɛðənɪs] *n* solidarietà; intimità.

toggle switch ['tɔgl-] *n* (*COMPUT*) tasto bistabile.

Togo ['təugəu] *n* Togo.

togs [tɔgz] *npl* (*col: clothes*) vestiti *mpl*.

toil [tɔɪl] *n* travaglio, fatica ♦ *vi* affannarsi, sgobbare.

toilet ['tɔɪlət] *n* (*BRIT: lavatory*) gabinetto

♦ cpd (soap etc) da toletta; **to go to the** ~ andare al gabinetto or al bagno.

toilet bag n (BRIT) nécessaire m inv da toilette.

toilet bowl n vaso or tazza del gabinetto.

toilet paper n carta igienica.

toiletries ['tɔɪlɪtrɪz] npl articoli mpl da toletta.

toilet roll n rotolo di carta igienica.

toilet water n acqua di colonia.

to-ing and fro-ing ['tuːɪŋən'frəʊɪŋ] n (BRIT) andirivieni m inv.

token ['təʊkən] n (sign) segno; (voucher) buono ♦ cpd (fee, strike) simbolico(a); **book/record** ~ (BRIT) buono-libro/-disco; **by the same** ~ (fig) per lo stesso motivo.

tokenism ['təʊkənɪzəm] n (POL) concessione f pro forma inv.

Tokyo ['təʊkjəʊ] n Tokyo f.

told [təʊld] pt, pp of **tell**.

tolerable ['tɔlərəbl] adj (bearable) tollerabile; (fairly good) passabile.

tolerably ['tɔlərəblɪ] adv (good, comfortable) abbastanza.

tolerance ['tɔlərns] n (also TECH) tolleranza.

tolerant ['tɔlərnt] adj: ~ (of) tollerante (nei confronti di).

tolerate ['tɔləreɪt] vt sopportare; (MED, TECH) tollerare.

toleration [tɔlə'reɪʃən] n tolleranza.

toll [təʊl] n (tax, charge) pedaggio ♦ vi (bell) suonare; **the accident** ~ **on the roads** il numero delle vittime della strada.

tollbridge ['təʊlbrɪdʒ] n ponte m a pedaggio.

toll call n (US TEL) (telefonata) interurbana.

toll-free ['təʊl'friː] (US) adj senza addebito, gratuito(a) ♦ adv gratuitamente; ~ **number** ≈ numero verde.

tomato, ~es [tə'mɑːtəʊ] n pomodoro.

tomb [tuːm] n tomba.

tombola [tɔm'bəʊlə] n tombola.

tomboy ['tɔmbɔɪ] n maschiaccio.

tombstone ['tuːmstəʊn] n pietra tombale.

tomcat ['tɔmkæt] n gatto.

tomorrow [tə'mɔrəʊ] adv, n (also fig) domani (m inv); **the day after** ~ dopodomani; **a week** ~ domani a otto; ~ **morning** domani mattina.

ton [tʌn] n tonnellata (BRIT: = 1016 kg; 20 cwt; US = 907 kg; metric = 1000 kg); (NAUT: also: **register** ~) tonnellata di stazza (= 2.83 cu.m; 100 cu.ft); ~**s of** (col) un mucchio or sacco di.

tonal ['təʊnl] adj tonale.

tone [təʊn] n tono; (of musical instrument) timbro ♦ vi intonarsi.

▶**tone down** vt (colour, criticism, sound) attenuare.

▶**tone up** vt (muscles) tonificare.

tone-deaf [təʊn'dɛf] adj che non ha orecchio (musicale).

toner ['təʊnə*] n (for photocopier) colorante m organico, toner m.

Tonga ['tɔŋgə] n isole fpl Tonga.

tongs [tɔŋz] npl tenaglie fpl; (for coal) molle fpl; (for hair) arricciacapelli m inv.

tongue [tʌŋ] n lingua; ~ **in cheek** (fig) ironicamente.

tongue-tied ['tʌŋtaɪd] adj (fig) muto(a).

tongue-twister ['tʌŋtwɪstə*] n scioglilingua m inv.

tonic ['tɔnɪk] n (MED) ricostituente m; (skin ~) tonico; (MUS) nota tonica; (also: ~ **water**) acqua tonica.

tonight [tə'naɪt] adv stanotte; (this evening) stasera ♦ n questa notte; questa sera; **I'll see you** ~ ci vediamo stasera.

tonnage ['tʌnɪdʒ] n (NAUT) tonnellaggio, stazza.

tonne [tʌn] n (BRIT: metric ton) tonnellata.

tonsil ['tɔnsl] n tonsilla; **to have one's** ~**s out** farsi operare di tonsille.

tonsillitis [tɔnsɪ'laɪtɪs] n tonsillite f; **to have** ~ avere la tonsillite.

too [tuː] adv (excessively) troppo; (also) anche; **it's** ~ **sweet** è troppo dolce; **I went** ~ ci sono andato anch'io; ~ **much** adv troppo ♦ adj troppo(a); ~ **many** adj troppi(e); ~ **bad!** tanto peggio!; peggio così!

took [tuk] pt of **take**.

tool [tuːl] n utensile m, attrezzo; (fig: person) strumento ♦ vt lavorare con un attrezzo.

tool box n cassetta f portautensili inv.

tool kit n cassetta di attrezzi.

toot [tuːt] vi suonare; (with car horn) suonare il clacson.

tooth, pl teeth [tuːθ, tiːθ] n (ANAT, TECH) dente m; **to clean one's teeth** lavarsi i denti; **to have a** ~ **out** or (US) **pulled** farsi togliere un dente; **by the skin of one's teeth** per il rotto della cuffia.

toothache ['tuːθeɪk] n mal m di denti; **to have** ~ avere il mal di denti.

tooth fairy n fatina che porta soldini in regalo a un bimbo quando perde un dentino di latte, ≈ topolino.

toothpaste ['tuːθpeɪst] n dentifricio.

toothpick ['tuːθpɪk] n stuzzicadenti m inv.

tooth powder n dentifricio in polvere.

top [tɔp] n (of mountain, page, ladder) cima; (of box, cupboard, table) sopra m inv, parte f superiore; (lid: of box, jar) coperchio; (: of *bottle*) tappo; (*toy*) trottola; (*DRESS: blouse etc*) camicia (*or* maglietta *etc*); (*of pyjamas*) giacca ♦ *adj* più alto(a); (*in rank*) primo(a); (*best*) migliore ♦ *vt* (*exceed*) superare; (*be first in*) essere in testa a; **on ~ of** sopra, in cima a; (*in addition to*) oltre a; **from ~ to toe** (*BRIT*) dalla testa ai piedi; **at the ~ of the stairs/page/street** in cima alle scale/alla pagina/alla strada; **the ~ of the milk** (*BRIT*) la panna; **at ~ speed** a tutta velocità; **at the ~ of one's voice** (*fig*) a squarciagola; **over the ~** (*col: behaviour etc*) eccessivo(a); **to go over the ~** esagerare.

▶**top up,** (*US*) **top off** *vt* riempire.

topaz ['təupæz] *n* topazio.

top-class ['tɔp'klɑːs] *adj* di prim'ordine.

topcoat ['tɔpkəut] *n* soprabito.

topflight ['tɔpflait] *adj* di primaria importanza.

top floor *n* ultimo piano.

top hat *n* cilindro.

top-heavy [tɔp'hɛvɪ] *adj* (*object*) con la parte superiore troppo pesante.

topic ['tɔpɪk] *n* argomento.

topical ['tɔpɪkəl] *adj* d'attualità.

topless ['tɔplɪs] *adj* (*bather etc*) col seno scoperto; **~ swimsuit** topless *m inv*.

top-level ['tɔplɛvl] *adj* (*talks*) ad alto livello.

topmost ['tɔpməust] *adj* il(la) più alto(a).

top-notch ['tɔp'nɔtʃ] *adj* (*col: player, performer*) di razza; (: *school, car*) eccellente.

topography [tə'pɔgrəfɪ] *n* topografia.

topping ['tɔpɪŋ] *n* (*CULIN*) guarnizione *f*.

topple ['tɔpl] *vt* rovesciare, far cadere ♦ *vi* cadere; traballare.

top-ranking ['tɔp'ræŋkɪŋ] *adj* di massimo grado.

top-secret ['tɔp'siːkrɪt] *adj* segretissimo(a).

top-security ['tɔpsɪ'kjuərɪtɪ] *adj* (*BRIT*) di massima sicurezza.

topsy-turvy ['tɔpsɪ'təːvɪ] *adj, adv* sottosopra (*inv*).

top-up ['tɔpʌp] *n:* **would you like a ~?** vuole che le riempia il bicchiere (*or* la tazza *etc*)?

top-up loan *n* (*BRIT*) prestito integrativo.

torch [tɔːtʃ] *n* torcia; (*BRIT: electric*) lampadina tascabile.

tore [tɔː*] *pt of* **tear**.

torment *n* ['tɔːmɛnt] tormento ♦ *vt* [tɔː'mɛnt] tormentare; (*fig: annoy*) infastidire.

torn [tɔːn] *pp of* **tear** ♦ *adj:* **~ between** (*fig*) combattuto(a) tra.

tornado, ~es [tɔː'neɪdəu] *n* tornado.

torpedo, ~es [tɔː'piːdəu] *n* siluro.

torpedo boat *n* motosilurante *f*.

torpor ['tɔːpə*] *n* torpore *m*.

torrent ['tɔrnt] *n* torrente *m*.

torrential [tɔ'rɛnʃl] *adj* torrenziale.

torrid ['tɔrɪd] *adj* torrido(a); (*fig*) denso(a) di passione.

torso ['tɔːsəu] *n* torso.

tortoise ['tɔːtəs] *n* tartaruga.

tortoiseshell ['tɔːtəʃɛl] *adj* di tartaruga.

tortuous ['tɔːtjuəs] *adj* tortuoso(a).

torture ['tɔːtʃə*] *n* tortura ♦ *vt* torturare.

torturer ['tɔːtʃərə*] *n* torturatore/trice.

Tory ['tɔːrɪ] *adj* tory *inv*, conservatore(trice) ♦ *n* tory *m/f inv*, conservatore/trice.

toss [tɔs] *vt* gettare, lanciare; (*BRIT: pancake*) far saltare; (*head*) scuotere ♦ *n* (*movement: of head etc*) movimento brusco; (*of coin*) lancio; **to win/lose the ~** vincere/perdere a testa o croce; (*SPORT*) vincere/perdere il sorteggio; **to ~ a coin** fare a testa o croce; **to ~ up for sth** fare a testa o croce per qc; **to ~ and turn** (*in bed*) girarsi e rigirarsi.

tot [tɔt] *n* (*BRIT: drink*) bicchierino; (*child*) bimbo/a.

▶**tot up** *vt* (*BRIT: figures*) sommare.

total ['təutl] *adj* totale ♦ *n* totale *m* ♦ *vt* (*add up*) sommare; (*amount to*) ammontare a; **in ~** in tutto.

totalitarian [təutælɪ'tɛərɪən] *adj* totalitario(a).

totality [təu'tælɪtɪ] *n* totalità.

totally ['təutəlɪ] *adv* completamente.

tote bag ['təut-] *n* sporta.

totem pole ['təutəm-] *n* totem *m inv*.

totter ['tɔtə*] *vi* barcollare; (*object, government*) vacillare.

touch [tʌtʃ] *n* tocco; (*sense*) tatto; (*contact*) contatto; (*FOOTBALL*) fuori gioco *m* ♦ *vt* toccare; **a ~ of** (*fig*) un tocco di; un pizzico di; **to get in ~ with** mettersi in contatto con; **to lose ~** (*friends*) perdersi di vista; **I'll be in ~** mi farò sentire; **to be out of ~ with events** essere tagliato fuori; **the personal ~** una nota personale; **to put the finishing ~es to sth** dare gli ultimi ritocchi a qc.

▶**touch on** *vt fus* (*topic*) sfiorare, accennare a.

▶**touch up** *vt* (*improve*) ritoccare.

touch-and-go ['tʌtʃən'gəu] *adj* incerto(a); **it was ~ with the sick man** il malato era tra la vita e la morte.

touchdown ['tʌtʃdaun] *n* atterraggio; (*on sea*) ammaraggio; (*US FOOTBALL*) meta.

touched [tʌtʃt] *adj* commosso(a); (*col*) tocco(a), toccato(a).

touching ['tʌtʃɪŋ] adj commovente.
touchline ['tʌtʃlaɪn] n (SPORT) linea laterale.
touch-screen ['tʌtʃskriːn] n (COMPUT) touch-screen m inv, schermo sensibile.
touch-sensitive ['tʌtʃ'sɛnsɪtɪv] adj sensibile al tatto.
touch-type ['tʌtʃtaɪp] vi dattilografare (senza guardare i tasti).
touchy ['tʌtʃɪ] adj (person) suscettibile.
tough [tʌf] adj duro(a); (resistant) resistente; (meat) duro(a), tiglioso(a); (journey) faticoso(a), duro(a); (person: rough) violento(a), brutale ♦ n (gangster etc) delinquente m/f; ~ **luck!** che sfortuna!
toughen ['tʌfn] vt indurire, rendere più resistente.
toughness ['tʌfnɪs] n durezza; resistenza.
toupee ['tuːpeɪ] n parrucchino.
tour [tuə*] n viaggio; (also: **package** ~) viaggio organizzato; (of town, museum) visita; (by artist) tournée f inv ♦ vt visitare; **to go on a** ~ **of** (region, country) fare il giro di; (museum, castle) visitare; **to go on** ~ andare in tournée.
tour guide n accompagnatore/trice turistico(a).
touring ['tuərɪŋ] n turismo.
tourism ['tuərɪzəm] n turismo.
tourist ['tuərɪst] n turista m/f ♦ adv (travel) in classe turistica ♦ cpd turistico(a); **the** ~ **trade** il turismo.
tourist class n (AVIAT) classe f turistica.
tourist office n pro loco f inv.
tournament ['tuənəmənt] n torneo.
tourniquet ['tuənɪkeɪ] n (MED) laccio emostatico, pinza emostatica.
tour operator n (BRIT) operatore m turistico.
tousled ['tauzld] adj (hair) arruffato(a).
tout [taut] vi: **to** ~ **for** procacciare, raccogliere; cercare clienti per ♦ n (BRIT: also: **ticket** ~) bagarino; **to** ~ **sth (around)** (BRIT) cercare di (ri)vendere qc.
tow [təu] vt rimorchiare ♦ n rimorchio; **"on** ~**"**, (US) **"in** ~**"** (AUT) "veicolo rimorchiato"; **to give sb a** ~ rimorchiare qn.
toward(s) [tə'wɔːd(z)] prep verso; (of attitude) nei confronti di; (of purpose) per; ~ **noon/the end of the year** verso mezzogiorno/la fine dell'anno; **to feel friendly** ~ **sb** provare un sentimento d'amicizia per qn.
towel ['tauəl] n asciugamano; (also: **tea** ~) strofinaccio; **to throw in the** ~ (fig) gettare la spugna.
towelling ['tauəlɪŋ] n (fabric) spugna.
towel rail, (US) **towel rack** n

portasciugamano.
tower [tauə*] n torre f ♦ vi (building, mountain) innalzarsi; **to** ~ **above** or **over sb/sth** sovrastare qn/qc.
tower block n (BRIT) palazzone m.
towering ['tauərɪŋ] adj altissimo(a), imponente.
towline ['təulaɪn] n (cavo da) rimorchio.
town [taun] n città f inv; **to go to** ~ andare in città; (fig) mettercela tutta; **in (the)** ~ in città; **to be out of** ~ essere fuori città.
town centre n centro (città).
town clerk n segretario comunale.
town council n consiglio comunale.
town crier [-'kraɪə*] n (BRIT) banditore/trice.
town hall n ≈ municipio.
townie ['taunɪ] n (BRIT col) uno/a di città.
town plan n pianta della città.
town planner n urbanista m/f.
town planning n urbanistica.
township ['taunʃɪp] n township f inv.
townspeople ['taunzpiːpl] npl cittadinanza, cittadini mpl.
towpath ['təupɑːθ] n alzaia.
towrope ['təurəup] n (cavo da) rimorchio.
tow truck n (US) carro m attrezzi inv.
toxic ['tɒksɪk] adj tossico(a).
toxin ['tɒksɪn] n tossina.
toy [tɔɪ] n giocattolo.
►**toy with** vt fus giocare con; (idea) accarezzare, trastullarsi con.
toyshop ['tɔɪʃɒp] n negozio di giocattoli.
trace [treɪs] n traccia ♦ vt (draw) tracciare; (follow) seguire; (locate) rintracciare; **without** ~ (disappear) senza lasciare traccia; **there was no** ~ **of it** non ne restava traccia.
trace element n oligoelemento.
trachea [trə'kɪə] n (ANAT) trachea.
tracing paper ['treɪsɪŋ-] n carta da ricalco.
track [træk] n (mark: of person, animal) traccia; (on tape, SPORT; path: gen) pista; (: of bullet etc) traiettoria; (: of suspect, animal) pista, tracce fpl; (RAIL) binario, rotaie fpl; (COMPUT) traccia, pista ♦ vt seguire le tracce di; **to keep** ~ **of** seguire; **to be on the right** ~ (fig) essere sulla buona strada.
►**track down** vt (prey) scovare; snidare; (sth lost) rintracciare.
tracker dog ['trækə-] n (BRIT) cane m poliziotto inv.
track events npl (SPORT) prove fpl su pista.
tracking station ['trækɪŋ-] n (SPACE) osservatorio spaziale.
track meet n (US) meeting m inv di atletica.
track record n: **to have a good** ~ (fig)

avere un buon curriculum.

tracksuit ['trӕksuːt] n tuta sportiva.

tract [trӕkt] n (GEO) tratto, estensione f; (pamphlet) opuscolo, libretto; **respiratory** ~ (ANAT) apparato respiratorio.

traction ['trӕkʃən] n trazione f.

tractor ['trӕktə*] n trattore m.

trade [treɪd] n commercio; (skill, job) mestiere m; (industry) industria, settore m ♦ vi commerciare; **to** ~ **with/in** commerciare con/in; **foreign** ~ commercio estero; **Department of T**~ **and Industry (DTI)** (BRIT) ≈ Ministero del Commercio.
▶**trade in** vt (old car etc) dare come pagamento parziale.

trade barrier n barriera commerciale.

trade deficit n bilancio commerciale in deficit.

Trade Descriptions Act n (BRIT) legge f a tutela del consumatore.

trade discount n sconto sul listino.

trade fair n fiera campionaria.

trade-in ['treɪdɪn] n: **to take as a** ~ accettare in permuta.

trade-in price n prezzo di permuta.

trademark ['treɪdmɑːk] n marchio di fabbrica.

trade mission n missione f commerciale.

trade name n marca, nome m depositato.

trade-off ['treɪdɔf] n compromesso, accomodamento.

trader ['treɪdə*] n commerciante m/f.

trade secret n segreto di fabbricazione.

tradesman ['treɪdzmən] n fornitore m; (shopkeeper) negoziante m.

trade union n sindacato.

trade unionist [-'juːnjənɪst] n sindacalista m/f.

trade wind n aliseo.

trading ['treɪdɪŋ] n commercio.

trading estate n (BRIT) zona industriale.

trading stamp n bollo premio.

tradition [trə'dɪʃən] n tradizione f; ~**s** npl tradizioni, usanze fpl.

traditional [trə'dɪʃənl] adj tradizionale.

traffic ['trӕfɪk] n traffico ♦ vi: **to** ~ **in** (pej: liquor, drugs) trafficare in.

traffic calming [-'kɑːmɪŋ] n uso di accorgimenti per rallentare il traffico in zone abitate.

traffic circle n (US) isola rotatoria.

traffic island n salvagente m, isola f spartitraffico inv.

traffic jam n ingorgo (del traffico).

trafficker ['trӕfɪkə*] n trafficante m/f.

traffic lights npl semaforo.

traffic offence n (BRIT) infrazione f al codice stradale.

traffic sign n cartello stradale.

traffic violation n (US) = **traffic offence**.

traffic warden n addetto/a al controllo del traffico e del parcheggio.

tragedy ['trӕdʒədɪ] n tragedia.

tragic ['trӕdʒɪk] adj tragico(a).

trail [treɪl] n (tracks) tracce fpl, pista; (path) sentiero; (of smoke etc) scia ♦ vt trascinare, strascicare; (follow) seguire ♦ vi essere al traino; (dress etc) strusciare; (plant) arrampicarsi; strisciare; **to be on sb's** ~ essere sulle orme di qn.
▶**trail away, trail off** vi (sound) affievolirsi; (interest, voice) spegnersi a poco a poco.
▶**trail behind** vi essere al traino.

trailer ['treɪlə*] n (AUT) rimorchio; (US) roulotte f inv; (CINE) prossimamente m inv.

trailer truck n (US) autoarticolato.

train [treɪn] n treno; (of dress) coda, strascico; (BRIT: series): ~ **of events** serie f di avvenimenti a catena ♦ vt (apprentice, doctor etc) formare; (sportsman) allenare; (dog) addestrare; (memory) esercitare; (point: gun etc): **to** ~ **sth on** puntare qc contro ♦ vi formarsi; allenarsi; (learn a skill) fare pratica, fare tirocinio; **to go by** ~ andare in or col treno; **one's** ~ **of thought** il filo dei propri pensieri; **to** ~ **sb to do sth** preparare qn a fare qc.

train attendant n (US) addetto/a ai vagoni letto.

trained [treɪnd] adj qualificato(a); allenato(a); addestrato(a).

trainee [treɪ'niː] n allievo/a; (in trade) apprendista m/f; **he's a** ~ **teacher** sta facendo tirocinio come insegnante.

trainer ['treɪnə*] n (SPORT) allenatore/trice; (of dogs etc) addestratore/trice; ~**s** npl (shoes) scarpe fpl da ginnastica.

training ['treɪnɪŋ] n formazione f; allenamento; addestramento; **in** ~ (SPORT) in allenamento; (fit) in forma.

training college n istituto professionale.

training course n corso di formazione professionale.

traipse [treɪps] vi: **to** ~ **in/out** etc entrare/uscire etc trascinandosi.

trait [treɪt] n tratto.

traitor ['treɪtə*] n traditore/trice.

trajectory [trə'dʒɛktərɪ] n traiettoria.

tram [trӕm] n (BRIT: also: ~**car**) tram m inv.

tramline ['trӕmlaɪn] n linea tranviaria.

tramp [trӕmp] n (person) vagabondo/a; (col: pej: woman) sgualdrina ♦ vi camminare con passo pesante ♦ vt (walk through: town, streets) percorrere a piedi.

trample ['træmpl] vt: **to ~ (underfoot)** calpestare.

trampoline ['træmpəli:n] n trampolino.

trance [trɑːns] n trance f inv; (MED) catalessi f inv; **to go into a ~** cadere in trance.

tranquil ['træŋkwɪl] adj tranquillo(a).

tranquillity, (US) **tranquility** [træŋ'kwɪlɪtɪ] n tranquillità.

tranquillizer, (US) **tranquilizer** ['træŋkwɪlaɪzə*] n (MED) tranquillante m.

transact [træn'zækt] vt (business) trattare.

transaction [træn'zækʃən] n transazione f; **~s** npl (minutes) atti mpl; **cash ~** operazione f in contanti.

transatlantic ['trænzət'læntɪk] adj transatlantico(a).

transcend [træn'sɛnd] vt trascendere; (excel over) superare.

transcendental [trænsɛn'dɛntl] adj: **~ meditation** meditazione f trascendentale.

transcribe [træn'skraɪb] vt trascrivere.

transcript ['trænskrɪpt] n trascrizione f.

transcription [træn'skrɪpʃən] n trascrizione f.

transept ['trænsɛpt] n transetto.

transfer n ['trænsfə*] (gen, also SPORT) trasferimento; (POL: of power) passaggio; (picture, design) decalcomania, (. stick-un) autoadesivo ♦ vt [træns'fə:*] trasferire; passare; decalcare; **by bank ~** tramite trasferimento bancario; **to ~ the charges** (BRIT TEL) telefonare con addebito al ricevente.

transferable [træns'fɔːrəbl] adj trasferibile; **not ~** non cedibile, personale.

transfix [træns'fɪks] vt trafiggere; (fig): **~ed with fear** paralizzato dalla paura.

transform [træns'fɔːm] vt trasformare.

transformation [trænsfə'meɪʃən] n trasformazione f.

transformer [træns'fɔːmə*] n (ELEC) trasformatore m.

transfusion [træns'fjuːʒən] n trasfusione f.

transgress [træns'grɛs] vt (go beyond) infrangere; (violate) trasgredire, infrangere.

tranship [træn'ʃɪp] vt trasbordare.

transient ['trænzɪənt] adj transitorio(a), fugace.

transistor [træn'zɪstə*] n (ELEC) transistor m inv; (also: **~ radio**) radio f inv a transistor.

transit ['trænzɪt] n: **in ~** in transito.

transit camp n campo (di raccolta) profughi.

transition [træn'zɪʃən] n passaggio, transizione f.

transitional [træn'zɪʃənl] adj di transizione.

transitive ['trænzɪtɪv] adj (LING) transitivo(a).

transit lounge n (AVIAT) sala di transito.

transitory ['trænzɪtərɪ] adj transitorio(a).

translate [trænz'leɪt] vt tradurre; **to ~ (from/into)** tradurre (da/in).

translation [trænz'leɪʃən] n traduzione f; (SCOL: as opposed to prose) versione f.

translator [trænz'leɪtə*] n traduttore/trice.

translucent [trænz'luːsnt] adj traslucido(a).

transmission [trænz'mɪʃən] n trasmissione f.

transmit [trænz'mɪt] vt trasmettere.

transmitter [trænz'mɪtə*] n trasmettitore m.

transparency [træns'pɛərnsɪ] n (PHOT) diapositiva.

transparent [træns'pærnt] adj trasparente.

transpire [træns'paɪə*] vi (happen) succedere; **it finally ~d that** ... alla fine si è venuto a sapere che ....

transplant vt [træns'plɑːnt] trapiantare ♦ n ['trænsplɑːnt] trapianto; **to have a heart ~** subire un trapianto cardiaco.

transport n ['trænspɔːt] trasporto ♦ vt [træns'pɔːt] trasportare; **public ~** mezzi mpl pubblici; **Department of T~** (BRIT) Ministero dei Trasporti.

transportation ['trænspɔː'teɪʃən] n (mezzo di) trasporto; (of prisoners) deportazione f; **Department of T~** (US) Ministero dei Trasporti.

transport café n (BRIT) trattoria per camionisti.

transpose [træns'pəuz] vt trasporre.

transsexual [trænz'sɛksjuəl] adj, n transessuale (m/f).

transverse ['trænzvɔːs] adj trasversale.

transvestite [trænz'vɛstaɪt] n travestito/a.

trap [træp] n (snare, trick) trappola; (carriage) calesse m ♦ vt prendere in trappola, intrappolare; (immobilize) bloccare; (jam) chiudere, schiacciare; **to set** or **lay a ~ (for sb)** tendere una trappola (a qn); **to ~ one's finger in the door** chiudersi il dito nella porta; **shut your ~!** (col) chiudi quella boccaccia!

trap door n botola.

trapeze [trə'piːz] n trapezio.

trapper ['træpə*] n cacciatore m di animali da pelliccia.

trappings ['træpɪŋz] npl ornamenti mpl; indoratura, sfarzo.

trash [træʃ] n (pej: goods) ciarpame m; (: nonsense) sciocchezze fpl; (US: rubbish) rifiuti mpl, spazzatura.

trash can n (US) secchio della spazzatura.

trashy ['træʃɪ] adj (col) scadente.

trauma ['trɔːmə] n trauma m.

traumatic [trɔː'mætɪk] adj (PSYCH, fig) traumatico(a), traumatizzante.

travel ['trævl] n viaggio; viaggi mpl ♦ vi viaggiare; (move) andare, spostarsi ♦ vt (distance) percorrere; **this wine doesn't ~ well** questo vino non resiste agli spostamenti.

travel agency n agenzia (di) viaggi.

travel agent n agente m di viaggio.

travel brochure n dépliant m di viaggi.

traveller, (US) **traveler** ['trævlə*] n viaggiatore/trice; (COMM) commesso viaggiatore.

traveller's cheque, (US) **traveler's check** n assegno turistico.

travelling, (US) **traveling** ['trævlɪŋ] n viaggi mpl ♦ adj (circus, exhibition) itinerante ♦ cpd (bag, clock) da viaggio; (expenses) di viaggio.

travel(l)ing salesman n commesso viaggiatore.

travelogue ['trævəlɔg] n (book, film) diario or documentario di viaggio; (talk) conferenza sui viaggi.

travel sickness n mal m d'auto (or di mare or d'aria).

traverse ['trævəs] vt traversare, attraversare.

travesty ['trævəstɪ] n parodia.

trawler ['trɔːlə*] n peschereccio (a strascico).

tray [treɪ] n (for carrying) vassoio; (on desk) vaschetta.

treacherous ['tretʃərəs] adj traditore(trice); **road conditions today are ~** oggi il fondo stradale è pericoloso.

treachery ['tretʃərɪ] n tradimento.

treacle ['triːkl] n melassa.

tread [tred] n passo; (sound) rumore m di passi; (of tyre) battistrada m inv ♦ vi (pt trod, pp **trodden** [trɔd, 'trɔdn]) camminare.

▶**tread on** vt fus calpestare.

treadle ['tredl] n pedale m.

treas. abbr = treasurer.

treason ['triːzn] n tradimento.

treasure ['treʒə*] n tesoro ♦ vt (value) tenere in gran conto, apprezzare molto; (store) custodire gelosamente.

treasure hunt n caccia al tesoro.

treasurer [treʒərə*] n tesoriere/a.

treasury ['treʒərɪ] n tesoreria; (POL): **the T~,** (US) **the T~ Department** ≈ il Ministero del Tesoro.

treasury bill n buono del tesoro.

treat [triːt] n regalo ♦ vt trattare; (MED) curare; (consider) considerare; **it was a ~** mi (or ci etc) ha fatto veramente piacere;

to ~ sb to sth offrire qc a qn; **to ~ sth as** a joke considerare qc uno scherzo.

treatise ['triːtɪz] n trattato.

treatment ['triːtmənt] n trattamento; **to have ~ for sth** (MED) farsi curare qc.

treaty ['triːtɪ] n patto, trattato.

treble [trebl] adj triplo(a), triplice ♦ n (MUS) soprano m/f ♦ vt triplicare ♦ vi triplicarsi.

treble clef n chiave f di violino.

tree [triː] n albero.

tree-lined ['triːlaɪnd] adj fiancheggiato(a) da alberi.

treetop ['triːtɔp] n cima di un albero.

tree trunk n tronco d'albero.

trek [trek] n (hike) spedizione f; (tiring walk) camminata sfiancante ♦ vi (as holiday) fare dell'escursionismo.

trellis ['trelɪs] n graticcio, pergola.

tremble ['trembl] vi tremare; (machine) vibrare.

trembling ['tremblɪŋ] n tremito ♦ adj tremante.

tremendous [trɪ'mendəs] adj (enormous) enorme; (excellent) meraviglioso(a), formidabile.

tremendously [trɪ'mendəslɪ] adv incredibilmente; **he enjoyed it ~** gli è piaciuto da morire.

tremor [tremə*] n tremore m, tremito; (also: **earth ~**) scossa sismica.

trench [trentʃ] n trincea.

trench coat n trench m inv.

trench warfare n guerra di trincea.

trend [trend] n (tendency) tendenza; (of events) corso; (fashion) moda; **~ towards/ away from** tendenza a/ad allontanarsi da; **to set the ~** essere all'avanguardia; **to set a ~** lanciare una moda.

trendy ['trendɪ] adj (idea) di moda; (clothes) all'ultima moda.

trepidation [trepɪ'deɪʃən] n trepidazione f, agitazione f.

trespass ['trespəs] vi: **to ~ on** entrare abusivamente in; (fig) abusare di; **"no ~ing"** "proprietà privata", "vietato l'accesso".

trespasser ['trespəsə*] n trasgressore m; **"~s will be prosecuted"** "i trasgressori saranno puniti secondo i termini di legge".

trestle ['tresl] n cavalletto.

trestle table n tavola su cavalletti.

trial ['traɪəl] n (LAW) processo; (test: of machine etc) collaudo; (hardship) prova, difficoltà f inv; (worry) cruccio; **~s** npl (ATHLETICS) prove fpl di qualificazione; **horse ~s** concorso ippico; **to be on ~** essere sotto processo; **~ by jury** processo penale con giuria; **to be sent for** ~ essere rinviato a giudizio; **to bring sb to** ~ **(for a crime)** portare qn in giudizio (per un reato); **by** ~ **and error** a tentoni.

trial balance n (COMM) bilancio di verifica.

trial basis n: **on a** ~ in prova.

trial run n periodo di prova.

triangle ['traɪæŋgl] n (MATH, MUS) triangolo.

triangular [traɪ'æŋgjulə*] adj triangolare.

triathlon [traɪ'æθlən] n triathlon m inv.

tribal ['traɪbəl] adj tribale.

tribe [traɪb] n tribù f inv.

tribesman ['traɪbzmən] n membro della tribù.

tribulation [trɪbju'leɪʃən] n tribolazione f.

tribunal [traɪ'bjuːnl] n tribunale m.

tributary ['trɪbjuːtərɪ] n (river) tributario, affluente m.

tribute ['trɪbjuːt] n tributo, omaggio; **to pay** ~ **to** rendere omaggio a.

trice [traɪs] n: **in a** ~ in un attimo.

trick [trɪk] n trucco; (clever act) stratagemma m; (joke) tiro; (CARDS) presa ♦ vt imbrogliare, ingannare; **to play a** ~ **on sb** giocare un tiro a qn; **it's a** ~ **of the light** è un effetto ottico; **that should do the** ~ (col) vedrai che funziona; **to** ~ **sb into doing sth** convincere qn a fare qc con l'inganno; **to** ~ **sb out of sth** fregare qc a qn.

trickery ['trɪkərɪ] n inganno.

trickle ['trɪkl] n (of water etc) rivolo; gocciolio ♦ vi gocciolare; **to** ~ **in/out** (people) entrare/uscire alla spicciolata.

trick question n domanda f trabocchetto inv.

trickster ['trɪkstə*] n imbroglione/a.

tricky ['trɪkɪ] adj difficile, delicato(a).

tricycle ['traɪsɪkl] n triciclo.

trifle ['traɪfl] n sciocchezza; (BRIT CULIN) ≈ zuppa inglese ♦ adv: **a** ~ **long** un po' lungo ♦ vi: **to** ~ **with** prendere alla leggera.

trifling ['traɪflɪŋ] adj insignificante.

trigger ['trɪgə*] n (of gun) grilletto.

▶**trigger off** vt dare l'avvio a.

trigonometry [trɪgə'nɔmətrɪ] n trigonometria.

trilby ['trɪlbɪ] n (BRIT: also: ~ **hat**) cappello floscio di feltro.

trill [trɪl] n (of bird, MUS) trillo.

trilogy ['trɪlədʒɪ] n trilogia.

trim [trɪm] adj ordinato(a); (house, garden) ben tenuto(a); (figure) snello(a) ♦ n (haircut etc) spuntata, regolata; (embellishment) finiture fpl; (on car) guarnizioni fpl ♦ vt spuntare; (decorate): **to** ~ **(with)** decorare (con); (NAUT: a sail)

orientare; **to keep in (good)** ~ mantenersi in forma.

trimmings ['trɪmɪŋz] npl decorazioni fpl; (extras: gen CULIN) guarnizione f.

Trinidad and Tobago ['trɪnɪdæd-] n Trinidad e Tobago m.

Trinity ['trɪnɪtɪ] n: **the** ~ la Trinità.

trinket ['trɪŋkɪt] n gingillo; (piece of jewellery) ciondolo.

trio ['triːəu] n trio.

trip [trɪp] n viaggio; (excursion) gita, escursione f; (stumble) passo falso ♦ vi inciampare; (go lightly) camminare con passo leggero; **on a** ~ in viaggio.

▶**trip up** vi inciampare ♦ vt fare lo sgambetto a.

tripartite [traɪ'pɑːtaɪt] adj (agreement) tripartito(a); (talks) a tre.

tripe [traɪp] n (CULIN) trippa; (pej: rubbish) sciocchezze fpl, fesserie fpl.

triple ['trɪpl] adj triplo(a) ♦ adv: **the distance/the speed** tre volte più lontano/ più veloce.

triple jump n triplo salto.

triplets ['trɪplɪts] npl bambini(e) trigemini(e).

triplicate ['trɪplɪkət] n: **in** ~ in triplice copia.

tripod ['traɪpɔd] n treppiede m.

Tripoli ['trɪpəlɪ] n Tripoli f.

tripper ['trɪpə*] n (BRIT) gitante m/f.

tripwire ['trɪpwaɪə*] n filo in tensione che fa scattare una trappola, allarme etc.

trite [traɪt] adj banale, trito(a).

triumph ['traɪʌmf] n trionfo ♦ vi: **to** ~ **(over)** trionfare (su).

triumphal [traɪ'ʌmfl] adj trionfale.

triumphant [traɪ'ʌmfənt] adj trionfante.

trivia ['trɪvɪə] npl banalità fpl.

trivial ['trɪvɪəl] adj (matter) futile; (excuse, comment) banale; (amount) irrisorio(a); (mistake) di poco conto.

triviality [trɪvɪ'ælɪtɪ] n frivolezza; (trivial detail) futilità.

trivialize ['trɪvɪəlaɪz] vt sminuire.

trod [trɔd] pt of **tread**.

trodden ['trɔdn] pp of **tread**.

trolley ['trɔlɪ] n carrello; (in hospital) lettiga.

trolley bus n filobus m inv.

trollop ['trɔləp] n prostituta.

trombone [trɔm'bəun] n trombone m.

troop [truːp] n gruppo; (MIL) squadrone m; ~**s** npl (MIL) truppe fpl; ~**ing the colour** (BRIT: ceremony) sfilata della bandiera.

▶**troop in** vi entrare a frotte.

▶**troop out** vi uscire a frotte.

troop carrier n (plane) aereo per il

trasporto (di) truppe; (NAUT: also: troopship) nave f per il trasporto (di) truppe.

trooper ['tru:pə*] n (MIL) soldato di cavalleria; (US: policeman) poliziotto (della polizia di stato).

troopship ['tru:pʃɪp] n nave f per il trasporto (di) truppe.

trophy ['trəufɪ] n trofeo.

tropic ['trɔpɪk] n tropico; in the ~s ai tropici; T~ of Cancer/Capricorn tropico del Cancro/Capricorno.

tropical ['trɔpɪkəl] adj tropicale.

trot [trɔt] n trotto ♦ vi trottare; on the ~ (BRIT fig) di fila, uno(a) dopo l'altro(a).

▶trot out vt (excuse, reason) tirar fuori; (names, facts) recitare di fila.

trouble ['trʌbl] n (problems) difficoltà fpl, problemi mpl; (worry) preoccupazione f; (bother, effort) sforzo; (with sth mechanical) noie fpl; (POL) conflitti mpl, disordine m; (MED): stomach etc ~ disturbi mpl gastrici etc ♦ vt disturbare; (worry) preoccupare ♦ vi: to ~ to do disturbarsi a fare; ~s npl (POL etc) disordini mpl; to be in ~ avere dei problemi; (for doing wrong) essere nei guai; to go to the ~ of doing darsi la pena di fare; it's no ~! di niente!; what's the ~? cosa c'è che non va?; the ~ is…c'è che…, il guaio è che…; to have ~ doing sth avere delle difficoltà a fare qc; please don't ~ yourself non si disturbi.

troubled ['trʌbld] adj (person) preoccupato(a), inquieto(a); (epoch, life) agitato(a), difficile.

trouble-free ['trʌblfri:] adj senza problemi.

troublemaker ['trʌblmeɪkə*] n elemento disturbatore, agitatore/trice.

troubleshooter ['trʌblʃu:tə*] n (in conflict) conciliatore m.

troublesome ['trʌblsəm] adj fastidioso(a), seccante.

trouble spot n zona calda.

troubling ['trʌblɪŋ] adj (thought) preoccupante; these are ~ times questi sono tempi difficili.

trough [trɔf] n (also: drinking ~) abbeveratoio; (also: feeding ~) trogolo, mangiatoia; (channel) canale m; ~ of low pressure (METEOROLOGY) depressione f.

trounce [trauns] vt (defeat) sgominare.

troupe [tru:p] n troupe f inv.

trouser press n stirapantaloni m inv.

trousers ['trauzəz] npl pantaloni mpl, calzoni mpl; short ~ (BRIT) calzoncini mpl.

trouser suit n (BRIT) completo m or tailleur m inv pantalone inv.

trousseau, pl ~x or ~s ['tru:səu, -z] n corredo da sposa.

trout [traut] n (pl inv) trota.

trowel ['trauəl] n cazzuola.

truant ['truənt] n: to play ~ (BRIT) marinare la scuola.

truce [tru:s] n tregua.

truck [trʌk] n autocarro, camion m inv; (RAIL) carro merci aperto; (for luggage) carrello m portabagagli inv.

truck driver, (US) trucker ['trʌkə*] n camionista m/f.

truck farm n (US) orto industriale.

trucking ['trʌkɪŋ] n (esp US) autotrasporto.

trucking company n (esp US) impresa di trasporti.

truculent ['trʌkjulənt] adj aggressivo(a), brutale.

trudge [trʌdʒ] vi trascinarsi pesantemente.

true [tru:] adj vero(a); (accurate) accurato(a), esatto(a); (genuine) reale; (faithful) fedele; (wall, beam) a piombo; (wheel) centrato(a); to come ~ avverarsi; ~ to life verosimile.

truffle ['trʌfl] n tartufo.

truly ['tru:lɪ] adv veramente; (truthfully) sinceramente; (faithfully) fedelmente; yours ~ (in letter-writing) distinti saluti.

trump [trʌmp] n (CARDS) atout m inv; to turn up ~s (fig) fare miracoli.

trump card n atout m inv; (fig) asso nella manica.

trumped-up [trʌmpt'ʌp] adj inventato(a).

trumpet ['trʌmpɪt] n tromba.

truncated [trʌŋ'keɪtɪd] adj tronco(a).

truncheon ['trʌntʃən] n sfollagente m inv.

trundle ['trʌndl] vt, vi: to ~ along rotolare rumorosamente.

trunk [trʌŋk] n (of tree, person) tronco; (of elephant) proboscide f; (case) baule m; (US AUT) bagagliaio.

trunk call n (BRIT TEL) (telefonata) interurbana.

trunk road n (BRIT) strada principale.

trunks [trʌŋks] npl (also: swimming ~) calzoncini mpl da bagno.

truss [trʌs] n (MED) cinto erniario ♦ vt: to ~ (up) (CULIN) legare.

trust [trʌst] n fiducia; (LAW) amministrazione f fiduciaria; (COMM) trust m inv ♦ vt (have confidence in) fidarsi di; (rely on) contare su; (entrust): to ~ sth to sb affidare qc a qn; (hope): to ~ (that) sperare (che); you'll have to take it on ~ deve credermi sulla parola; in ~ (LAW) amministrazione fiduciaria.

trust company n trust m inv.

trusted ['trʌstɪd] adj fidato(a).

trustee [trʌs'ti:] n (LAW)

amministratore(trice) fiduciario(a); (of school etc) amministratore/trice.

trustful ['trʌstful] adj fiducioso(a).

trust fund n fondo fiduciario.

trusting ['trʌstɪŋ] adj = **trustful**.

trustworthy ['trʌstwəːðɪ] adj fidato(a), degno(a) di fiducia.

trusty ['trʌstɪ] adj fidato(a).

truth, ~**s** [truːθ, truːðz] n verità f inv.

truthful ['truːθful] adj (person) sincero(a); (description) veritiero(a), esatto(a).

truthfully ['truːθfəlɪ] adv sinceramente.

truthfulness ['truːθfəlnɪs] n veracità.

try [traɪ] n prova, tentativo; (RUGBY) meta ♦ vt (LAW) giudicare; (test: sth new) provare; (strain: patience, person) mettere alla prova ♦ vi provare; **to** ~ **to do** provare a fare; (seek) cercare di fare; **to give sth a** ~ provare qc; **to** ~ **one's (very) best** or **one's (very) hardest** mettercela tutta.

▶**try on** vt (clothes) provare, mettere alla prova; **to** ~ **it on** (fig) cercare di farla.

▶**try out** vt provare, mettere alla prova.

trying ['traɪɪŋ] adj (day, experience) logorante, pesante; (child) difficile, insopportabile.

tsar [zɑː*] n zar m inv.

T-shirt ['tiːʃəːt] n maglietta.

TSO n abbr (BRIT: = The Stationery Office) ≈ Poligrafici mpl dello Stato.

T-square ['tiːskwɛə*] n riga a T.

TT adj abbr (BRIT col) = **teetotal** ♦ abbr (US) = Trust Territory.

tub [tʌb] n tinozza; mastello; (bath) bagno.

tuba ['tjuːbə] n tuba.

tubby ['tʌbɪ] adj grassoccio(a).

tube [tjuːb] n tubo; (BRIT: underground) metropolitana; (for tyre) camera d'aria; (col: television): **the** ~ la tele.

tubeless ['tjuːblɪs] adj (tyre) senza camera d'aria.

tuber ['tjuːbə*] n (BOT) tubero.

tuberculosis (TB) [tjubəːkjuˈləusɪs] n tubercolosi f.

tube station n (BRIT) stazione f del metrò.

tubing ['tjuːbɪŋ] n tubazione f; **a piece of** ~ un tubo.

tubular ['tjuːbjulə*] adj tubolare.

TUC n abbr (BRIT: = Trades Union Congress) confederazione f dei sindacati britannici.

tuck [tʌk] n (SEWING) piega ♦ vt (put) mettere.

▶**tuck away** vt riporre.

▶**tuck in** vt mettere dentro; (child) rimboccare ♦ vi (eat) mangiare di buon appetito; abbuffarsi.

▶**tuck up** vt (child) rimboccare.

tuck shop n negozio di pasticceria (in una

scuola).

Tue(s). abbr (= Tuesday) mar.

Tuesday ['tjuːzdɪ] n martedì m inv; (the date) today is ~ 23rd March oggi è martedì 23 marzo; **on** ~ martedì; **on** ~**s** di martedì; **every** ~ tutti i martedì; **every other** ~ ogni due martedì; **last/next** ~ martedì scorso/prossimo; ~ **next** martedì prossimo; **the following** ~ (in past) il martedì successivo; (in future) il martedì dopo; **a week/fortnight on** ~, ~ **week/ fortnight** martedì fra una settimana/ quindici giorni; **the** ~ **before last** martedì di due settimane fa; **the** ~ **after next** non questo martedì ma il prossimo; ~ **morning/lunchtime/afternoon/evening** martedì mattina/all'ora di pranzo/ pomeriggio/sera; ~ **night** martedì sera; (overnight) martedì notte; ~**'s newspaper** il giornale di martedì.

tuft [tʌft] n ciuffo.

tug [tʌg] n (ship) rimorchiatore m ♦ vt tirare con forza.

tug-of-love [tʌgəvˈlʌv] n contesa per la custodia dei figli; ~ **children** bambini mpl coinvolti nella contesa per la custodia.

tug-of-war [tʌgəvˈwɔː*] n tiro alla fune.

tuition [tjuːˈɪʃən] n (BRIT: lessons) lezioni fpl; (US: fees) tasse fpl scolastiche (or universitarie).

tulip ['tjuːlɪp] n tulipano.

tumble ['tʌmbl] n (fall) capitombolo ♦ vi capitombolare, ruzzolare; (somersault) fare capriole ♦ vt far cadere; **to** ~ **to sth** (col) realizzare qc.

tumbledown ['tʌmbldaun] n cadente, diroccato(a).

tumble dryer n (BRIT) asciugatrice f.

tumbler ['tʌmblə*] n bicchiere m (senza stelo).

tummy ['tʌmɪ] n (col) pancia.

tumour, (US) **tumor** ['tjuːmə*] n tumore m.

tumult ['tjuːmʌlt] n tumulto.

tumultuous [tjuːˈmʌltjuəs] adj tumultuoso(a).

tuna ['tjuːnə] n (pl inv) (also: ~ **fish**) tonno.

tune [tjuːn] n (melody) melodia, aria ♦ vt (MUS) accordare; (RADIO, TV, AUT) regolare, mettere a punto; **to be in/out of** ~ (instrument) essere accordato(a)/ scordato(a); (singer) essere intonato(a)/ stonato(a); **to the** ~ **of** (fig: amount) per la modesta somma di; **in** ~ **with** (fig) in accordo con.

▶**tune in** vi (RADIO, TV): **to** ~ **in (to)** sintonizzarsi (su).

▶**tune up** vi (musician) accordare lo strumento.

tuneful ['tju:nful] *adj* melodioso(a).
tuner ['tju:nə*] *n* (*radio set*) sintonizzatore *m*; **piano** ~ accordatore/trice di pianoforte.
tuner amplifier *n* amplificatore *m* di sintonia.
tungsten ['tʌŋstn] *n* tungsteno.
tunic ['tju:nɪk] *n* tunica.
tuning ['tju:nɪŋ] *n* messa a punto.
tuning fork *n* diapason *m inv*.
Tunis ['tju:nɪs] *n* Tunisi *f*.
Tunisia [tju:'nɪzɪə] *n* Tunisia.
Tunisian [tju:'nɪzɪən] *adj, n* tunisino(a).
tunnel ['tʌnl] *n* galleria ♦ *vi* scavare una galleria.
tunnel vision *n* (*MED*) riduzione *f* del campo visivo; (*fig*) visuale *f* ristretta.
tunny ['tʌnɪ] *n* tonno.
turban ['tə:bən] *n* turbante *m*.
turbid ['tə:bɪd] *adj* torbido(a).
turbine ['tə:baɪn] *n* turbina.
turbo ['tə:bəu] *n* turbo *m inv*.
turbojet ['tə:bəu'dʒɛt] *n* turboreattore *m*.
turboprop ['tə:bəu'prɔp] *n* turboelica *m inv*.
turbot ['tə:bət] *n* (*pl inv*) rombo gigante.
turbulence ['tə:bjuləns] *n* turbolenza.
turbulent ['tə:bjulənt] *adj* turbolento(a); (*sea*) agitato(a).
tureen [tə'ri:n] *n* zuppiera.
turf [tə:f] *n* terreno erboso; (*clod*) zolla ♦ *vt* coprire di zolle erbose; **the T~** l'ippodromo.
▶**turf out** *vt* (*col*) buttar fuori.
turf accountant *n* (*BRIT*) allibratore *m*.
turgid ['tə:dʒɪd] *adj* (*speech*) ampolloso(a), pomposo(a).
Turin [tjuə'rɪn] *n* Torino *f*.
Turk [tə:k] *n* turco/a.
Turkey ['tə:kɪ] *n* Turchia.
turkey ['tə:kɪ] *n* tacchino.
Turkish ['tə:kɪʃ] *adj* turco(a) ♦ *n* (*LING*) turco.
Turkish bath *n* bagno turco.
Turkish delight *n* gelatine ricoperte di zucchero a velo.
turmeric ['tə:mərɪk] *n* curcuma.
turmoil ['tə:mɔɪl] *n* confusione *f*, tumulto.
turn [tə:n] *n* giro; (*in road*) curva; (*tendency: of mind, events*) tendenza; (*performance*) numero; (*MED*) crisi *f inv*, attacco ♦ *vt* girare, voltare; (*milk*) far andare a male; (*shape: wood, metal*) tornire; (*change*): **to ~ sth into** trasformare qc in ♦ *vi* girare; (*person: look back*) girarsi, voltarsi; (*reverse direction*) girarsi indietro; (*change*) cambiare; (*become*) diventare; **to ~ into** trasformarsi in; **a good ~** un buon servizio; **a bad ~** un brutto tiro; **it**

gave me quite a ~ mi ha fatto prendere un bello spavento; **"no left** ~**"** (*AUT*) "divieto di svolta a sinistra"; **it's your** ~ tocca a lei; **in** ~ a sua volta; **a turno**; **to take** ~**s (at sth)** fare (qc) a turno; **at the** ~ **of the year/century** alla fine dell'anno/del secolo; **to take a** ~ **for the worse** (*situation, events*) volgere al peggio; (*patient, health*) peggiorare; **to** ~ **left/right** girare a sinistra/destra.
▶**turn about** *vi* girarsi indietro.
▶**turn away** *vi* girarsi (dall'altra parte) ♦ *vt* (*reject: person*) mandar via; (: *business*) rifiutare.
▶**turn back** *vi* ritornare, tornare indietro.
▶**turn down** *vt* (*refuse*) rifiutare; (*reduce*) abbassare; (*fold*) ripiegare.
▶**turn in** (*col: go to bed*) andare a letto ♦ *vt* (*fold*) voltare in dentro.
▶**turn off** *vi* (*from road*) girare, voltare ♦ *vt* (*light, radio, engine etc*) spegnere.
▶**turn on** *vt* (*light, radio etc*) accendere; (*engine*) avviare.
▶**turn out** *vt* (*light, gas*) chiudere, spegnere; (*produce: goods*) produrre; (: *novel, good pupils*) creare ♦ *vi* (*appear, attend: troops, doctor etc*) presentarsi; **to out to be** ... rivelarsi ..., risultare ....
▶**turn over** *vi* (*person*) girarsi; (*car etc*) capovolgersi ♦ *vt* girare.
▶**turn round** *vi* girare; (*person*) girarsi.
▶**turn up** *vi* (*person*) arrivare, presentarsi; (*lost object*) saltar fuori ♦ *vt* (*collar, sound, gas etc*) alzare.
turnabout ['tə:nəbaut], **turnaround** ['tə:nəraund] *n* (*fig*) dietrofront *m inv*.
turncoat ['tə:nkəut] *n* voltagabbana *m/f inv*.
turned-up ['tə:ndʌp] *adj* (*nose*) all'insù.
turning ['tə:nɪŋ] *n* (*in road*) curva; (*side road*) strada laterale; **the first** ~ **on the right** la prima a destra.
turning circle *n* (*BRIT*) diametro di sterzata.
turning point *n* (*fig*) svolta decisiva.
turning radius *n* (*US*) = **turning circle**.
turnip ['tə:nɪp] *n* rapa.
turnout ['tə:naut] *n* presenza, affluenza.
turnover ['tə:nəuvə*] *n* (*COMM: amount of money*) giro di affari; (: *of goods*) smercio; (*CULIN*): **apple** *etc* ~ sfogliatella alle mele *etc*; **there is a rapid** ~ **in staff** c'è un ricambio molto rapido di personale.
turnpike ['tə:npaɪk] *n* (*US*) autostrada a pedaggio.
turnstile ['tə:nstaɪl] *n* tornella.
turntable ['tə:nteɪbl] *n* (*on record player*) piatto.

turn-up ['tə:nʌp] n (*BRIT: on trousers*) risvolto.

turpentine ['tə:pəntaɪn] n (*also*: **turps**) acqua ragia.

turquoise [tə:kwɔɪz] n (*stone*) turchese m ♦ *adj* color turchese; di turchese.

turret ['tʌrɪt] n torretta.

turtle ['tə:tl] n testuggine f.

turtleneck (sweater) ['tə:tlnɛk-] n maglione m con il collo alto.

Tuscan ['tʌskən] *adj*, n toscano(a).

Tuscany ['tʌskənɪ] n Toscana.

tusk [tʌsk] n zanna.

tussle ['tʌsl] n baruffa, mischia.

tutor ['tju:tə*] n (*in college*) docente m/f (*responsabile di un gruppo di studenti*); (*private teacher*) precettore m.

tutorial [tju:'tɔ:rɪəl] n (*SCOL*) lezione f con discussione (*a un gruppo limitato*).

tuxedo [tʌk'si:dəu] n (*US*) smoking m inv.

TV [ti:'vi:] n abbr (= *television*) tivù f inv.

TV dinner n pasto surgelato pronto in due minuti.

twaddle ['twɔdl] n scemenze fpl.

twang [twæŋ] n (*of instrument*) suono vibrante; (*of voice*) accento nasale ♦ vi vibrare ♦ vt (*guitar*) pizzicare le corde di.

tweak [twi:k] vt (*nose*) pizzicare; (*ear, hair*) tirare.

tweed [twi:d] n tweed m inv.

tweezers ['twi:zəz] npl pinzette fpl.

twelfth [twelfθ] num dodicesimo(a).

Twelfth Night n la notte dell'Epifania.

twelve [twelv] num dodici; **at** ~ alle dodici, a mezzogiorno; (*midnight*) a mezzanotte.

twentieth ['twentɪɪθ] num ventesimo(a).

twenty ['twentɪ] num venti.

twerp [twə:p] n (*col*) idiota m/f.

twice [twaɪs] *adv* due volte; ~ **as much** due volte tanto; ~ **a week** due volte alla settimana; **she is** ~ **your age** ha il doppio dei suoi anni.

twiddle ['twɪdl] vt, vi: **to** ~ **(with) sth** giocherellare con qc; **to** ~ **one's thumbs** (*fig*) girarsi i pollici.

twig [twɪg] n ramoscello ♦ vt, vi (*col*) capire.

twilight ['twaɪlaɪt] n (*evening*) crepuscolo; (*morning*) alba; **in the** ~ nella penombra.

twill [twɪl] n spigato.

twin [twɪn] *adj*, n gemello(a).

twin(-bedded) room ['twɪn('bɛdɪd)-] n stanza con letti gemelli.

twin beds npl letti mpl gemelli.

twin-carburettor ['twɪnkɑ:bju'rɛtə*] adj a doppio carburatore.

twine [twaɪn] n spago, cordicella ♦ vi (*plant*) attorcigliarsi; (*road*) serpeggiare.

twin-engined ['twɪn'ɛndʒɪnd] *adj* a due

motori; ~ **aircraft** bimotore m.

twinge [twɪndʒ] n (*of pain*) fitta; **a** ~ **of conscience/regret** un rimorso/rimpianto.

twinkle ['twɪŋkl] n scintillio ♦ vi scintillare; (*eyes*) brillare.

twin town n città f inv gemella.

twirl [twə:l] n piroetta ♦ vt far roteare ♦ vi roteare.

twist [twɪst] n torsione f; (*in wire, flex*) storta; (*in story*) colpo di scena; (*bend*) svolta, piega ♦ vt attorcigliare; (*weave*) intrecciare; (*roll around*) arrotolare; (*fig*) deformare ♦ vi attorcigliarsi; arrotolarsi; (*road*) serpeggiare; **to** ~ **one's ankle/wrist** (*MED*) slogarsi la caviglia/il polso.

twisted ['twɪstɪd] *adj* (*wire, rope*) attorcigliato(a); (*ankle, wrist*) slogato(a); (*fig: logic, mind*) contorto(a).

twit [twɪt] n (*col*) minchione/a.

twitch [twɪtʃ] n tiratina; (*nervous*) tic m inv ♦ vi contrarsi; avere un tic.

two [tu:] num due; ~ **by** ~, **in** ~**s** a due a due; **to put** ~ **and** ~ **together** (*fig*) trarre le conclusioni.

two-bit [tu:'bɪt] *adj* (*esp US: col, pej*) da quattro soldi.

two-door [tu:'dɔ:*] *adj* (*AUT*) a due porte.

two-faced ['tu:'feɪst] *adj* (*pej: person*) falso(a).

twofold ['tu:fəuld] *adv*: **to increase** ~ aumentare del doppio ♦ *adj* (*increase*) doppio(a); (*reply*) in due punti.

two-piece [tu:'pi:s] n (*also*: ~ **suit**) due pezzi m inv; (*also*: ~ **swimsuit**) (costume m da bagno a) due pezzi m inv.

two-seater ['tu:'si:tə*] n (*plane*) biposto; (*car*) macchina a due posti.

twosome ['tu:səm] n (*people*) coppia.

two-stroke ['tu:strəuk] n (*engine*) due tempi m inv ♦ *adj* a due tempi.

two-tone ['tu:təun] *adj* (*colour*) bicolore.

two-way ['tu:weɪ] *adj* (*traffic*) a due sensi; ~ **radio** radio f inv ricetrasmittente.

TX *abbr* (*US*) = *Texas*.

tycoon [taɪ'ku:n] n: (**business**) ~ magnate m.

type [taɪp] n (*category*) genere m; (*model*) modello; (*example*) tipo; (*TYP*) tipo, carattere m ♦ vt (*letter etc*) battere (a macchina), dattilografare; **what** ~ **do you want?** che tipo vuole?; **in bold/italic** ~ in grassetto/corsivo.

type-cast ['taɪpkɑ:st] *adj* (*actor*) a ruolo fisso.

typeface ['taɪpfeɪs] n carattere m tipografico.

typescript ['taɪpskrɪpt] *n* dattiloscritto.
typeset ['taɪpsɛt] *vt* comporre.
typesetter ['taɪpsɛtə*] *n* compositore *m*.
typewriter ['taɪpraɪtə*] *n* macchina da
scrivere.
typewritten ['taɪprɪtn] *adj* dattiloscritto(a),
battuto(a) a macchina.
typhoid ['taɪfɔɪd] *n* tifoidea.
typhoon [taɪ'fuːn] *n* tifone *m*.
typhus ['taɪfəs] *n* tifo.
typical ['tɪpɪkl] *adj* tipico(a).
typify ['tɪpɪfaɪ] *vt* essere tipico(a) di.
typing ['taɪpɪŋ] *n* dattilografia.
typing error *n* errore *m* di battitura.
typing pool *n* ufficio *m* dattilografia *inv*.
typist ['taɪpɪst] *n* dattilografo/a.
typo ['taɪpəu] *n* *abbr* (*col*: = *typographical
error*) refuso.
typography [taɪ'pɔgrəfɪ] *n* tipografia.
tyranny ['tɪrənɪ] *n* tirannia.
tyrant ['taɪərnt] *n* tiranno.
tyre, (*US*) **tire** ['taɪə*] *n* pneumatico,
gomma.
tyre pressure *n* pressione *f* (delle
gomme).
Tyrol [tɪ'rəul] *n* Tirolo.
Tyrolean [tɪrə'liːən], **Tyrolese** [tɪrə'liːz] *adj*,
n tirolese (*m/f*).
Tyrrhenian Sea [tɪ'riːnɪən-] *n*: **the** ~ il mar
Tirreno.

U u

U, u [juː] *n* (*letter*) U, u *m or f inv*; **U for Uncle**
≈ U come Udine.
U *n abbr* (*BRIT CINE*: = *universal*) per tutti.
UAW *n abbr* (*US*: = *United Automobile
Workers*) *sindacato degli operai
automobilistici*.
UB40 *n abbr* (*BRIT*: = *unemployment benefit
form 40*) *modulo per la richiesta del
sussidio di disoccupazione*.
U-bend ['juːbɛnd] *n* (*in pipe*) sifone *m*.
ubiquitous [juː'bɪkwɪtəs] *adj* onnipresente.
UCAS ['juːkæs] *n abbr* (*BRIT*) = *Universities
and Colleges Admissions Service*.
UDA *n abbr* (*BRIT*: = *Ulster Defence
Association*) *organizzazione paramilitare
protestante*.
UDC *n abbr* (*BRIT*) = *Urban District Council*.
udder ['ʌdə*] *n* mammella.

UDI *abbr* (*BRIT POL*) = *unilateral declaration of
independence*.
UDR *n abbr* (*BRIT*: = *Ulster Defence Regiment*)
*reggimento dell'esercito britannico in
Irlanda del Nord*.
UEFA [juː'eɪfə] *n abbr* (= *Union of European
Football Associations*) U.E.F.A. *f*.
UFO ['juːfəu] *n abbr* (= *unidentified flying
object*) UFO *m inv*.
Uganda [juː'gændə] *n* Uganda.
Ugandan [juː'gændən] *adj*, *n* ugandese (*m/f*).
UGC *n abbr* (*BRIT*: = *University Grants
Committee*) *organo che autorizza
sovvenzioni alle università*.
ugh [əːh] *excl* puah!
ugliness ['ʌglɪnɪs] *n* bruttezza.
ugly ['ʌglɪ] *adj* brutto(a).
UHF *abbr* = *ultra-high frequency*.
UHT *adj abbr* (= *ultra heat treated*): ~ **milk** *n*
latte *m* UHT.
UK *n abbr see* **United Kingdom**.
Ukraine [juː'kreɪn] *n* Ucraina.
Ukrainian [juː'kreɪnɪən] *adj* ucraino(a) ♦ *n*
(*person*) ucraino/a; (*LING*) ucraino.
ulcer ['ʌlsə*] *n* ulcera; **mouth** ~ afta.
Ulster ['ʌlstə*] *n* Ulster *m*.
ulterior [ʌl'tɪərɪə*] *adj* ulteriore; ~ **motive**
secondo fine *m*.
ultimata [ʌltɪ'meɪtə] *npl of* **ultimatum**.
ultimate ['ʌltɪmɪt] *adj* ultimo(a), finale;
(*authority*) massimo(a), supremo(a) ♦ *n*:
the ~ **in luxury** il non plus ultra del lusso.
ultimately ['ʌltɪmɪtlɪ] *adv* alla fine; in
definitiva, in fin dei conti.
ultimatum, *pl* ~**s** *or* **ultimata**
[ʌltɪ'meɪtəm, -tə] *n* ultimatum *m inv*.
ultrasonic [ʌltrə'sɔnɪk] *adj* ultrasonico(a).
ultrasound [ʌltrə'saund] *n* (*MED*) ecografia.
ultraviolet ['ʌltrə'vaɪəlɪt] *adj*
ultravioletto(a).
umbilical [ʌm'bɪlɪkl] *adj*: ~ **cord** cordone *m*
ombelicale.
umbrage ['ʌmbrɪdʒ] *n*: **to take** ~
offendersi, impermalirsi.
umbrella [ʌm'brɛlə] *n* ombrello; **under the**
~ **of** (*fig*) sotto l'egida di.
umlaut ['umlaut] *n* Umlaut *m inv*.
umpire ['ʌmpaɪə*] *n* arbitro.
umpteen [ʌmp'tiːn] *adj* non so quanti(e);
for the ~**th time** per l'ennesima volta.
UMW *n abbr* (= *United Mineworkers of
America*) *unione dei minatori d'America*.
UN *n abbr see* **United Nations**.
unabashed [ʌnə'bæʃt] *adj* imperturbato(a).
unabated [ʌnə'beɪtɪd] *adj* non diminuito(a).
unable [ʌn'eɪbl] *adj*: **to be** ~ **to** non potere,
essere nell'impossibilità di; (*not to know
how to*) essere incapace di, non sapere.

unabridged [ʌnə'brɪdʒd] *adj* integrale.
unacceptable [ʌnək'sɛptəbl] *adj* (*proposal, behaviour*) inaccettabile; (*price*) impossibile.
unaccompanied [ʌnə'kʌmpənɪd] *adj* (*child, lady*) non accompagnato(a); (*singing, song*) senza accompagnamento.
unaccountably [ʌnə'kauntəblɪ] *adv* inesplicabilmente.
unaccounted [ʌnə'kauntɪd] *adj*: **two passengers are ~ for** due passeggeri mancano all'appello.
unaccustomed [ʌnə'kʌstəmd] *adj* insolito(a); **to be ~ to sth** non essere abituato(a) a qc.
unacquainted [ʌnə'kweɪntɪd] *adj*: **to be ~ with** (*facts*) ignorare, non essere al corrente di.
unadulterated [ʌnə'dʌltəreɪtɪd] *adj* (*gen*) puro(a); (*wine*) non sofisticato(a).
unaffected [ʌnə'fɛktɪd] *adj* (*person, behaviour*) naturale, spontaneo(a); (*emotionally*): **to be ~ by** non essere toccato(a) da.
unafraid [ʌnə'freɪd] *adj*: **to be ~** non aver paura.
unaided [ʌn'eɪdɪd] *adv* senza aiuto.
unanimity [juːnə'nɪmɪtɪ] *n* unanimità.
unanimous [juː'nænɪməs] *adj* unanime.
unanimously [juː'nænɪməslɪ] *adv* all'unanimità.
unanswered [ʌn'ɑːnsəd] *adj* (*question, letter*) senza risposta; (*criticism*) non confutato(a).
unappetizing [ʌn'æpɪtaɪzɪŋ] *adj* poco appetitoso(a).
unappreciative [ʌnə'priːʃɪətɪv] *adj* che non apprezza.
unarmed [ʌn'ɑːmd] *adj* (*person*) disarmato(a); (*combat*) senz'armi.
unashamed [ʌnə'ʃeɪmd] *adj* sfacciato(a); senza vergogna.
unassisted [ʌnə'sɪstɪd] *adj, adv* senza nessun aiuto.
unassuming [ʌnə'sjuːmɪŋ] *adj* modesto(a), senza pretese.
unattached [ʌnə'tætʃt] *adj* senza legami, libero(a).
unattended [ʌnə'tɛndɪd] *adj* (*car, child, luggage*) incustodito(a).
unattractive [ʌnə'træktɪv] *adj* privo(a) di attrattiva, poco attraente.
unauthorized [ʌn'ɔːθəraɪzd] *adj* non autorizzato(a).
unavailable [ʌnə'veɪləbl] *adj* (*article, room, book*) non disponibile; (*person*) impegnato(a).
unavoidable [ʌnə'vɔɪdəbl] *adj* inevitabile.

unavoidably [ʌnə'vɔɪdəblɪ] *adv* (*detained*) per cause di forza maggiore.
unaware [ʌnə'wɛə*] *adj*: **to be ~ of** non sapere, ignorare.
unawares [ʌnə'wɛəz] *adv* di sorpresa, alla sprovvista.
unbalanced [ʌn'bælənst] *adj* squilibrato(a).
unbearable [ʌn'bɛərəbl] *adj* insopportabile.
unbeatable [ʌn'biːtəbl] *adj* imbattibile.
unbeaten [ʌn'biːtn] *adj* (*team, army*) imbattuto(a); (*record*) insuperato(a).
unbecoming [ʌnbɪ'kʌmɪŋ] *adj* (*unseemly*: *language, behaviour*) sconveniente; (*unflattering*: *garment*) che non dona.
unbeknown(st) [ʌnbɪ'nəun(st)] *adv*: **~ to** all'insaputa di.
unbelief [ʌnbɪ'liːf] *n* incredulità.
unbelievable [ʌnbɪ'liːvəbl] *adj* incredibile.
unbelievingly [ʌnbɪ'liːvɪŋlɪ] *adv* con aria incredula.
unbend [ʌn'bɛnd] *vb* (*irreg*) *vi* distendersi ♦ *vt* (*wire*) raddrizzare.
unbending [ʌn'bɛndɪŋ] *adj* (*fig*) inflessibile, rigido(a).
unbias(s)ed [ʌn'baɪəst] *adj* obiettivo(a), imparziale.
unblemished [ʌn'blɛmɪʃt] *adj* senza macchia.
unblock [ʌn'blɔk] *vt* (*pipe, road*) sbloccare.
unborn [ʌn'bɔːn] *adj* non ancora nato(a).
unbounded [ʌn'baundɪd] *adj* sconfinato(a), senza limite.
unbreakable [ʌn'breɪkəbl] *adj* infrangibile.
unbridled [ʌn'braɪdld] *adj* sbrigliato(a).
unbroken [ʌn'brəukən] *adj* (*intact*) intero(a); (*continuous*) continuo(a); (*record*) insuperato(a).
unbuckle [ʌn'bʌkl] *vt* slacciare.
unburden [ʌn'bəːdn] *vt*: **to ~ o.s.** sfogarsi.
unbutton [ʌn'bʌtn] *vt* sbottonare.
uncalled-for [ʌn'kɔːldfɔː*] *adj* (*remark*) fuori luogo *inv*; (*action*) ingiustificato(a).
uncanny [ʌn'kænɪ] *adj* misterioso(a), strano(a).
unceasing [ʌn'siːsɪŋ] *adj* incessante.
unceremonious [ʌnsɛrɪ'məunɪəs] *adj* (*abrupt, rude*) senza tante cerimonie.
uncertain [ʌn'səːtn] *adj* incerto(a); **it's ~ whether ...** non è sicuro se ...; **in no terms** chiaro e tondo, senza mezzi termini.
uncertainty [ʌn'səːtntɪ] *n* incertezza.
unchallenged [ʌn'tʃælɪndʒd] *adj* incontestato(a); **to go ~** non venire contestato, non trovare opposizione.
unchanged [ʌn'tʃeɪndʒd] *adj* immutato(a).
uncharitable [ʌn'tʃærɪtəbl] *adj* duro(a), severo(a).

uncharted [ʌn'tʃɑːtɪd] *adj* inesplorato(a).
unchecked [ʌn'tʃekt] *adj* incontrollato(a).
uncivilized [ʌn'sɪvɪlaɪzd] *adj* (*gen*) selvaggio(a); (*fig*) incivile, barbaro(a).
uncle ['ʌŋkl] *n* zio.
unclear [ʌn'klɪə*] *adj* non chiaro(a); **I'm still** ~ **about what I'm supposed to do** non ho ancora ben capito cosa dovrei fare.
uncoil [ʌn'kɔɪl] *vt* srotolare ♦ *vi* srotolarsi, svolgersi.
uncomfortable [ʌn'kʌmfətəbl] *adj* scomodo(a); (*uneasy*) a disagio, agitato(a); (*situation*) sgradevole.
uncomfortably [ʌn'kʌmfətəblɪ] *adv* scomodamente; (*uneasily:* say) con voce inquieta; (: *think*) con inquietudine.
uncommitted [ʌnkə'mɪtɪd] *adj* (*attitude, country*) neutrale.
uncommon [ʌn'kɔmən] *adj* raro(a), insolito(a), non comune.
uncommunicative [ʌnkə'mjuːnɪkətɪv] *adj* poco comunicativo(a), chiuso(a).
uncomplicated [ʌn'kɔmplɪkeɪtɪd] *adj* semplice, poco complicato(a).
uncompromising [ʌn'kɔmprəmaɪzɪŋ] *adj* intransigente, inflessibile.
unconcerned [ʌnkən'səːnd] *adj* (*unworried*) tranquillo(a); **to be** ~ **about** non darsi pensiero di, non preoccuparsi di *or* per.
unconditional [ʌn'kən'dɪʃənl] *adj* incondizionato(a), senza condizioni.
uncongenial [ʌnkən'dʒiːnɪəl] *adj* (*work, surroundings*) poco piacevole.
unconnected [ʌnkə'nɛktɪd] *adj* (*unrelated*) senza connessione, senza rapporto; **to be** ~ **with** essere estraneo(a) a.
unconscious [ʌn'kɔnʃəs] *adj* privo(a) di sensi, svenuto(a); (*unaware*) inconsapevole, inconscio(a) ♦ *n:* **the** ~ l'inconscio; **to knock sb** ~ far perdere i sensi a qn con un pugno.
unconsciously [ʌn'kɔnʃəslɪ] *adv* inconsciamente.
unconstitutional [ʌnkɔnstɪ'tjuːʃənl] *adj* incostituzionale.
uncontested [ʌnkən'tɛstɪd] *adj* (*champion*) incontestato(a); (*POL: seat*) non disputato(a).
uncontrollable [ʌnkən'trəuləbl] *adj* incontrollabile, indisciplinato(a).
uncontrolled [ʌnkən'trəuld] *adj* (*child, dog, emotion*) sfrenato(a); (*inflation, price rises*) che sfugge al controllo.
unconventional [ʌnkən'vɛnʃənl] *adj* poco convenzionale.
unconvinced [ʌnkən'vɪnst] *adj:* **to be** *or* **remain** ~ non essere convinto(a).
unconvincing [ʌnkən'vɪnsɪŋ] *adj* non

convincente, poco persuasivo(a).
uncork [ʌn'kɔːk] *vt* stappare.
uncorroborated [ʌnkə'rɔbəreɪtɪd] *adj* non convalidato(a).
uncouth [ʌn'kuːθ] *adj* maleducato(a), grossolano(a).
uncover [ʌn'kʌvə*] *vt* scoprire.
unctuous ['ʌŋktjuəs] *adj* untuoso(a).
undamaged [ʌn'dæmɪdʒd] *adj* (*goods*) in buono stato; (*fig: reputation*) intatto(a).
undaunted [ʌn'dɔːntɪd] *adj* intrepido(a).
undecided [ʌndɪ'saɪdɪd] *adj* indeciso(a).
undelivered [ʌndɪ'lɪvəd] *adj* non recapitato(a); **if** ~ **return to sender** in caso di mancato recapito rispedire al mittente.
undeniable [ʌndɪ'naɪəbl] *adj* innegabile, indiscutibile.
under ['ʌndə*] *prep* sotto; (*less than*) meno di; al disotto di; (*according to*) secondo, in conformità a ♦ *adv* (al) disotto; **from** ~ **sth** da sotto a *or* dal disotto di qc; ~ **there** là sotto; **in** ~ **2 hours** in meno di 2 ore; ~ **anaesthetic** sotto anestesia; ~ **discussion** in discussione; ~ **repair** in riparazione; ~ **the circumstances** date le circostanze.
under... ['ʌndə*] *prefix* sotto..., sub....
under-age [ʌndər'eɪdʒ] *adj* minorenne.
underarm ['ʌndərɑːm] *n* ascella ♦ *adj* ascellare ♦ *adv* da sotto in su.
undercapitalized [ʌndə'kæpɪtəlaɪzd] *adj* carente di capitali.
undercarriage ['ʌndəkærɪdʒ] *n* (*BRIT AVIAT*) carrello (d'atterraggio).
undercharge [ʌndə'tʃɑːdʒ] *vt* far pagare di meno a.
underclass ['ʌndəklɑːs] *n* sottoproletariato.
underclothes ['ʌndəkləuðz] *npl* biancheria (intima).
undercover ['ʌndəkʌvə*] *adj* segreto(a), clandestino(a).
undercurrent ['ʌndəkʌrənt] *n* corrente *f* sottomarina.
undercut [ʌndə'kʌt] *vt irreg* vendere a prezzo minore di.
underdeveloped ['ʌndədɪ'vɛləpt] *adj* sottosviluppato(a).
underdog ['ʌndədɔg] *n* oppresso/a.
underdone [ʌndə'dʌn] *adj* (*CULIN*) poco cotto(a).
under-employment [ʌndərɪm'plɔɪmənt] *n* sottoccupazione *f*.
underestimate [ʌndər'ɛstɪmeɪt] *vt* sottovalutare.
underexposed [ʌndərɪks'pəuzd] *adj* (*PHOT*) sottoesposto(a).
underfed [ʌndə'fɛd] *adj* denutrito(a).
underfoot [ʌndə'fut] *adv* sotto i piedi.

under-funded ['ʌndə'fʌndɪd] adj insufficientemente sovvenzionato(a).

undergo [ʌndə'gəu] vt irreg subire; (treatment) sottoporsi a; **the car is ~ing repairs** la macchina è in riparazione.

undergraduate [ʌndə'grædjuɪt] n studente(essa) universitario(a) ♦ cpd: ~ **courses** corsi mpl di laurea.

underground ['ʌndəgraund] n metropolitana; (POL) movimento clandestino ♦ adj sotterraneo(a); (fig) clandestino(a); (ART, CINE) underground inv ♦ adv sottoterra; clandestinamente.

undergrowth ['ʌndəgrəuθ] n sottobosco.

underhand(ed) [ʌndə'hænd(ɪd)] adj (fig) furtivo(a), subdolo(a).

underinsured [ʌndərɪn'ʃuəd] adj non sufficientemente assicurato(a).

underlie [ʌndə'laɪ] vt irreg essere alla base di; **the underlying cause** il motivo di fondo.

underline [ʌndə'laɪn] vt sottolineare.

underling ['ʌndəlɪŋ] n (pej) subalterno/a, tirapiedi m/f inv.

undermanning [ʌndə'mænɪŋ] n carenza di personale.

undermentioned [ʌndə'mɛnʃənd] adj (riportato(a)) qui sotto or qui di seguito.

undermine [ʌndə'maɪn] vt minare.

underneath [ʌndə'niːθ] adv sotto, disotto ♦ prep sotto, al di sotto di.

undernourished [ʌndə'nʌrɪʃt] adj denutrito(a).

underpaid [ʌndə'peɪd] adj mal pagato(a).

underpants ['ʌndəpænts] npl (BRIT) mutande fpl, slip m inv.

underpass ['ʌndəpɑːs] n (BRIT) sottopassaggio.

underpin [ʌndə'pɪn] vt puntellare; (argument, case) corroborare.

underplay [ʌndə'pleɪ] vt minimizzare.

underpopulated [ʌndə'pɔpjuleɪtɪd] adj scarsamente popolato(a), sottopopolato(a).

underprice [ʌndə'praɪs] vt vendere a un prezzo inferiore al dovuto.

underprivileged [ʌndə'prɪvɪlɪdʒd] adj svantaggiato(a).

underrate [ʌndə'reɪt] vt sottovalutare.

underscore [ʌndə'skɔː*] vt sottolineare.

underseal ['ʌndəsiːl] vt rendere stagno il fondo di.

undersecretary [ʌndə'sɛkrətrɪ] n sottosegretario.

undersell [ʌndə'sɛl] vt irreg (competitors) vendere a prezzi più bassi di.

undershirt ['ʌndəʃɜːt] n (US) maglietta.

undershorts ['ʌndəʃɔːts] npl (US) mutande

fpl, slip m inv.

underside ['ʌndəsaɪd] n disotto.

undersigned ['ʌndəsaɪnd] adj, n sottoscritto(a).

underskirt ['ʌndəskɜːt] n sottoveste f.

understaffed [ʌndə'stɑːft] adj a corto di personale.

understand [ʌndə'stænd] vb (irreg: like stand) vt, vi capire, comprendere; **I ~ that** ... sento che ...; credo di capire che ...; **to make o.s. understood** farsi capire.

understandable [ʌndə'stændəbl] adj comprensibile.

understanding [ʌndə'stændɪŋ] adj comprensivo(a) ♦ n comprensione f; (agreement) accordo; **on the ~ that** ... a patto che or a condizione che ...; **to come to an ~ with sb** giungere ad un accordo con qn.

understate [ʌndə'steɪt] vt minimizzare, sminuire.

understatement [ʌndə'steɪtmənt] n: **that's an ~!** a dire poco!

understood [ʌndə'stud] pt, pp of **understand** ♦ adj inteso(a); (implied) sottinteso(a).

understudy ['ʌndəstʌdɪ] n sostituto/a, attore/trice supplente.

undertake [ʌndə'teɪk] vt irreg intraprendere; **to ~ to do sth** impegnarsi a fare qc.

undertaker ['ʌndəteɪkə*] n impresario di pompe funebri.

undertaking [ʌndə'teɪkɪŋ] n impresa; (promise) promessa.

undertone ['ʌndətəun] n (low voice) tono sommesso; (of criticism etc) vena, sottofondo; **in an ~** sottovoce.

undervalue [ʌndə'væljuː] vt svalutare, sottovalutare.

underwater [ʌndə'wɔːtə*] adv sott'acqua ♦ adj subacqueo(a).

underwear ['ʌndəwɛə*] n biancheria (intima).

underweight [ʌndə'weɪt] adj al di sotto del giusto peso; (person) sottopeso inv.

underworld ['ʌndəwɜːld] n (of crime) malavita.

underwrite ['ʌndəraɪt] vt (FINANCE) sottoscrivere; (INSURANCE) assicurare.

underwriter ['ʌndəraɪtə*] n sottoscrittore/trice; assicuratore/trice.

undeserving [ʌndɪ'zɜːvɪŋ] adj: **to be ~ of** non meritare, non essere degno di.

undesirable [ʌndɪ'zaɪərəbl] adj indesiderabile, sgradito(a).

undeveloped [ʌndɪ'vɛləpt] adj (land, resources) non sfruttato(a).

undies ['ʌndɪz] npl (col) robina, biancheria

intima da donna.
undiluted [ˌʌndaɪˈluːtɪd] *adj* non diluito(a).
undiplomatic [ˌʌndɪpləˈmætɪk] *adj* poco
diplomatico(a).
undischarged [ˈʌndɪsˈtʃɑːdʒd] *adj*: ~
bankrupt fallito non riabilitato.
undisciplined [ʌnˈdɪsɪplɪnd] *adj*
indisciplinato(a).
undisguised [ˌʌndɪsˈɡaɪzd] *adj* (*dislike*,
amusement etc) palese.
undisputed [ˌʌndɪsˈpjuːtɪd] *adj*
indiscusso(a).
undistinguished [ˌʌndɪsˈtɪŋɡwɪʃt] *adj*
mediocre, qualunque.
undisturbed [ˌʌndɪsˈtɜːbd] *adj* tranquillo(a);
to leave sth ~ lasciare qc così com'è.
undivided [ˌʌndɪˈvaɪdɪd] *adj*: I want your ~
attention esigo tutta la sua attenzione.
undo [ʌnˈduː] *vt irreg* disfare.
undoing [ʌnˈduːɪŋ] *n* rovina, perdita.
undone [ʌnˈdʌn] *pp of* undo; to come ~
slacciarsi.
undoubted [ʌnˈdautɪd] *adj* sicuro(a),
certo(a).
undoubtedly [ʌnˈdautɪdlɪ] *adv* senza alcun
dubbio.
undress [ʌnˈdrɛs] *vi* spogliarsi.
undrinkable [ʌnˈdrɪŋkəbl] *adj* (*unpalatable*)
imbevibile; (*poisonous*) non potabile.
undue [ʌnˈdjuː] *adj* eccessivo(a).
undulating [ˈʌndjuleɪtɪŋ] *adj* ondeggiante;
ondulato(a).
unduly [ʌnˈdjuːlɪ] *adv* eccessivamente.
undying [ʌnˈdaɪɪŋ] *adj* imperituro(a).
unearned [ʌnˈɜːnd] *adj* (*praise*, *respect*)
immeritato(a); ~ income rendita.
unearth [ʌnˈɜːθ] *vt* dissotterrare; (*fig*)
scoprire.
unearthly [ʌnˈɜːθlɪ] *adj* soprannaturale;
(*hour*) impossibile.
uneasy [ʌnˈiːzɪ] *adj* a disagio; (*worried*)
preoccupato(a); **to feel** ~ **about doing sth**
non sentirsela di fare qc.
uneconomic(al) [ˈʌniːkəˈnɒmɪk(l)] *adj* non
economico(a), antieconomico(a).
uneducated [ʌnˈɛdjukeɪtɪd] *adj* senza
istruzione, incolto(a).
unemployed [ʌnɪmˈplɔɪd] *adj*
disoccupato(a) ♦ *npl*: the ~ i disoccupati.
unemployment [ʌnɪmˈplɔɪmənt] *n*
disoccupazione *f*.
unemployment benefit, (*US*)
unemployment compensation *n*
sussidio di disoccupazione.
unending [ʌnˈɛndɪŋ] *adj* senza fine.
unenviable [ʌnˈɛnvɪəbl] *adj* poco
invidiabile.
unequal [ʌnˈiːkwəl] *adj* (*length*, *objects*)

disuguale; (*amounts*) diverso(a); (*division*
of labour) ineguale.
unequalled, (*US*) **unequaled** [ʌnˈiːkwəld]
adj senza pari, insuperato(a).
unequivocal [ʌnɪˈkwɪvəkəl] *adj* (*answer*)
inequivocabile; (*person*) esplicito(a),
chiaro(a).
unerring [ʌnˈɜːrɪŋ] *adj* infallibile.
UNESCO [juːˈnɛskəu] *n abbr* (= *United
Nations Educational, Scientific and Cultural
Organization*) U.N.E.S.C.O. *f*.
unethical [ʌnˈɛθɪkəl] *adj* (*methods*) poco
ortodosso(a), non moralmente
accettabile; (*doctor's behaviour*)
contrario(a) all'etica professionale.
uneven [ʌnˈiːvn] *adj* ineguale; (*ground*)
disuguale, accidentato(a); (*heartbeat*)
irregolare.
uneventful [ʌnɪˈvɛntful] *adj* senza
sorprese, tranquillo(a).
unexceptional [ʌnɪkˈsɛpʃənl] *adj* che non
ha niente d'eccezionale.
unexciting [ʌnɪkˈsaɪtɪŋ] *adj* (*news*) poco
emozionante; (*film*, *evening*) poco
interessante.
unexpected [ʌnɪkˈspɛktɪd] *adj* inatteso(a),
imprevisto(a).
unexpectedly [ʌnɪkˈspɛktɪdlɪ] *adv*
inaspettatamente.
unexplained [ʌnɪkˈspleɪnd] *adj*
inspiegato(a).
unexploded [ʌnɪkˈspləudɪd] *adj*
inesploso(a).
unfailing [ʌnˈfeɪlɪŋ] *adj* (*supply*, *energy*)
inesauribile; (*remedy*) infallibile.
unfair [ʌnˈfɛə*] *adj*: ~ (**to**) ingiusto(a) (nei
confronti di); **it's** ~ **that** ... non è giusto
che ... + *sub*.
unfair dismissal *n* licenziamento
ingiustificato.
unfairly [ʌnˈfɛəlɪ] *adv* ingiustamente.
unfaithful [ʌnˈfeɪθful] *adj* infedele.
unfamiliar [ʌnfəˈmɪlɪə*] *adj* sconosciuto(a),
strano(a); **to be** ~ **with sth** non essere
pratico di qc, non avere familiarità con
qc.
unfashionable [ʌnˈfæʃnəbl] *adj* (*clothes*)
fuori moda *inv*; (*district*) non alla moda.
unfasten [ʌnˈfɑːsn] *vt* slacciare; sciogliere.
unfathomable [ʌnˈfæðəməbl] *adj*
insondabile.
unfavourable, (*US*) **unfavorable**
[ʌnˈfeɪvərəbl] *adj* sfavorevole.
unfavo(u)rably [ʌnˈfeɪvərəblɪ] *adv*: **to look**
~ **upon** vedere di malocchio.
unfeeling [ʌnˈfiːlɪŋ] *adj* insensibile,
duro(a).
unfinished [ʌnˈfɪnɪʃt] *adj* incompiuto(a).

unfit [ʌn'fɪt] *adj* inadatto(a); (*ill*) non in forma; (*incompetent*): ~ **(for)** incompetente (in); (: *work, MIL*) inabile (a); ~ **for habitation** inabitabile.

unflagging [ʌn'flægɪŋ] *adj* instancabile.

unflappable [ʌn'flæpəbl] *adj* calmo(a), composto(a).

unflattering [ʌn'flætərɪŋ] *adj* (*dress, hairstyle*) che non dona.

unflinching [ʌn'flɪntʃɪŋ] *adj* che non indietreggia, risoluto(a).

unfold [ʌn'fəuld] *vt* spiegare; (*fig*) rivelare ♦ *vi* (*view*) distendersi; (*story*) svelarsi.

unforeseeable ['ʌnfɔː'siːəbl] *adj* imprevedibile.

unforeseen [ʌnfɔː'siːn] *adj* imprevisto(a).

unforgettable [ʌnfə'gɛtəbl] *adj* indimenticabile.

unforgivable [ʌnfə'gɪvəbl] *adj* imperdonabile.

unformatted [ʌn'fɔːmætɪd] *adj* (*disk, text*) non formattato(a).

unfortunate [ʌn'fɔːtʃnɪt] *adj* sfortunato(a); (*event, remark*) infelice.

unfortunately [ʌn'fɔːtʃnɪtlɪ] *adv* sfortunatamente, purtroppo.

unfounded [ʌn'faundɪd] *adj* infondato(a).

unfriendly [ʌn'frɛndlɪ] *adj* poco amichevole, freddo(a).

unfulfilled [ʌnful'fɪld] *adj* (*ambition*) non realizzato(a); (*prophecy*) che non si è avverato(a); (*desire*) insoddisfatto(a); (*promise*) non mantenuto(a); (*terms of contract*) non rispettato(a); (*person*) frustrato(a).

unfurl [ʌn'fəːl] *vt* spiegare.

unfurnished [ʌn'fəːnɪʃt] *adj* non ammobiliato(a).

ungainly [ʌn'geɪnlɪ] *adj* goffo(a), impacciato(a).

ungodly [ʌn'gɔdlɪ] *adj* empio(a); **at an** ~ **hour** a un'ora impossibile.

ungrateful [ʌn'greɪtful] *adj* ingrato(a).

unguarded [ʌn'gɑːdɪd] *adj*: **in an** ~ **moment** in un momento di distrazione.

unhappily [ʌn'hæpɪlɪ] *adv* (*unfortunately*) purtroppo, sfortunatamente.

unhappiness [ʌn'hæpɪnɪs] *n* infelicità.

unhappy [ʌn'hæpɪ] *adj* infelice; ~ **with** (*arrangements etc*) insoddisfatto(a) di.

unharmed [ʌn'hɑːmd] *adj* incolume, sano(a) e salvo(a).

UNHCR *n abbr* (= *United Nations High Commission for Refugees*) Alto Commissariato delle Nazioni Unite per Rifugiati.

unhealthy [ʌn'hɛlθɪ] *adj* (*gen*) malsano(a); (*person*) malaticcio(a).

unheard-of [ʌn'həːdɔv] *adj* inaudito(a), senza precedenti.

unhelpful [ʌn'hɛlpful] *adj* poco disponibile.

unhesitating [ʌn'hɛzɪteɪtɪŋ] *adj* (*loyalty*) che non vacilla; (*reply, offer*) pronto(a), immediato(a).

unholy [ʌn'həulɪ] *adj*: **an** ~ **alliance** un'alleanza nefasta; **he returned at an** ~ **hour** è tornato ad un'ora indecente.

unhook [ʌn'huk] *vt* sganciare; sfibbiare.

unhurt [ʌn'həːt] *adj* incolume, sano(a) e salvo(a).

unhygienic [ʌnhaɪ'dʒiːnɪk] *adj* non igienico(a).

UNICEF ['juːnɪsɛf] *n abbr* (= *United Nations International Children's Emergency Fund*) U.N.I.C.E.F. *m*.

unicorn ['juːnɪkɔːn] *n* unicorno.

unidentified [ʌnaɪ'dɛntɪfaɪd] *adj* non identificato(a).

uniform ['juːnɪfɔːm] *n* uniforme *f*, divisa ♦ *adj* uniforme.

uniformity [juːnɪ'fɔːmɪtɪ] *n* uniformità.

unify ['juːnɪfaɪ] *vt* unificare.

unilateral [juːnɪ'lætərəl] *adj* unilaterale.

unimaginable [ʌnɪ'mædʒɪnəbl] *adj* inimmaginabile, inconcepibile.

unimaginative [ʌnɪ'mædʒɪnətɪv] *adj* privo(a) di fantasia, a corto di idee.

unimpaired [ʌnɪm'pɛəd] *adj* intatto(a), non danneggiato(a).

unimportant [ʌnɪm'pɔːtənt] *adj* senza importanza, di scarsa importanza.

unimpressed [ʌnɪm'prɛst] *adj* niente affatto impressionato(a).

uninhabited [ʌnɪn'hæbɪtɪd] *adj* disabitato(a).

uninhibited [ʌnɪn'hɪbɪtɪd] *adj* senza inibizioni; senza ritegno.

uninjured [ʌn'ɪndʒəd] *adj* incolume.

uninspiring [ʌnɪn'spaɪərɪŋ] *adj* banale.

uninstall [ʌnɪn'stɔːl] *vt* (*COMPUT*) disinstallare.

unintelligent [ʌnɪn'tɛlɪdʒənt] *adj* poco intelligente.

unintentional [ʌnɪn'tɛnʃənəl] *adj* involontario(a).

unintentionally [ʌnɪn'tɛnʃnəlɪ] *adv* senza volerlo, involontariamente.

uninvited [ʌnɪn'vaɪtɪd] *adj* non invitato(a).

uninviting [ʌnɪn'vaɪtɪŋ] *adj* (*place, food*) non invitante, poco invitante; (*offer*) poco allettante.

union ['juːnjən] *n* unione *f*; (*also*: **trade** ~) sindacato ♦ *cpd* sindacale; **the U**~ (*US*) gli stati dell'Unione.

unionize ['juːnjənaɪz] *vt* sindacalizzare, organizzare in sindacato.

Union Jack n bandiera nazionale britannica.
Union of Soviet Socialist Republics (USSR) n (HIST) Unione f delle Repubbliche Socialiste Sovietiche (U.R.S.S.).
union shop n stabilimento in cui tutti gli operai sono tenuti ad aderire ad un sindacato.
unique [juːˈniːk] adj unico(a).
unisex [ˈjuːnɪsɛks] adj unisex inv.
Unison [ˈjuːnɪsn] n (trade union) sindacato generale dei funzionari.
unison [ˈjuːnɪsn] n: **in** ~ all'unisono.
unit [ˈjuːnɪt] n unità f inv; (section: of furniture etc) elemento; (team, squad) reparto, squadra; **production** ~ reparto m produzione inv; **sink** ~ blocco m lavello inv.
unit cost n costo unitario.
unite [juːˈnaɪt] vt unire ♦ vi unirsi.
united [juːˈnaɪtɪd] adj unito(a); (efforts) congiunto(a).
United Arab Emirates npl Emirati mpl Arabi Uniti.
United Kingdom (UK) n Regno Unito.
United Nations (Organization) (UN, UNO) n (Organizzazione f delle) Nazioni Unite (O.N.U.).
United States (of America) (US, USA) n Stati mpl Uniti (d'America) (USA).
unit price n prezzo unitario.
unit trust n (BRIT COMM) fondo d'investimento.
unity [ˈjuːnɪtɪ] n unità.
Univ. abbr = **university**.
universal [juːnɪˈvɜːsl] adj universale.
universe [ˈjuːnɪvɜːs] n universo.
university [juːnɪˈvɜːsɪtɪ] n università f inv ♦ cpd (student, professor, education) universitario(a); (year) accademico(a).
university degree n laurea.
unjust [ʌnˈdʒʌst] adj ingiusto(a).
unjustifiable [ˈʌndʒʌstɪˈfaɪəbl] adj ingiustificabile.
unjustified [ʌnˈdʒʌstɪfaɪd] adj ingiustificato(a); (TYP) non allineato(a).
unkempt [ʌnˈkɛmpt] adj trasandato(a); spettinato(a).
unkind [ʌnˈkaɪnd] adj poco gentile, villano(a).
unkindly [ʌnˈkaɪndlɪ] adv (speak) in modo sgarbato; (treat) male.
unknown [ʌnˈnəun] adj sconosciuto(a); ~ **to me** ... a mia insaputa ...; ~ **quantity** (MATH, fig) incognita.
unladen [ʌnˈleɪdn] adj (ship, weight) a vuoto.
unlawful [ʌnˈlɔːful] adj illecito(a), illegale.

unleaded [ʌnˈlɛdɪd] adj senza piombo; ~ **petrol** benzina verde or senza piombo.
unleash [ʌnˈliːʃ] vt sguinzagliare; (fig) scatenare.
unleavened [ʌnˈlɛvnd] adj non lievitato(a), azzimo(a).
unless [ʌnˈlɛs] conj a meno che (non) + sub; ~ **otherwise stated** salvo indicazione contraria; ~ **I am mistaken** se non mi sbaglio.
unlicensed [ʌnˈlaɪsənst] adj (BRIT) senza licenza per la vendita di alcolici.
unlike [ʌnˈlaɪk] adj diverso(a) ♦ prep a differenza di, contrariamente a.
unlikelihood [ʌnˈlaɪklɪhud] adj improbabilità.
unlikely [ʌnˈlaɪklɪ] adj improbabile; (explanation) inverosimile.
unlimited [ʌnˈlɪmɪtɪd] adj illimitato(a).
unlisted [ʌnˈlɪstɪd] adj (US TEL): **to be** ~ non essere sull'elenco; (STOCK EXCHANGE) non quotato(a).
unlit [ʌnˈlɪt] adj (room) senza luce; (road) non illuminato(a).
unload [ʌnˈləud] vt scaricare.
unlock [ʌnˈlɔk] vt aprire.
unlucky [ʌnˈlʌkɪ] adj sfortunato(a); (object, number) che porta sfortuna, di malaugurio; **to be** ~ (person) essere sfortunato, non avere fortuna.
unmanageable [ʌnˈmænɪdʒəbl] adj (tool, vehicle) poco maneggevole; (situation) impossibile.
unmanned [ʌnˈmænd] adj (spacecraft) senza equipaggio.
unmannerly [ʌnˈmænəlɪ] adj maleducato(a).
unmarked [ʌnˈmɑːkt] adj (unstained) pulito(a), senza macchie; ~ **police car** civetta della polizia.
unmarried [ʌnˈmærɪd] adj non sposato(a); (man only) scapolo, celibe; (woman only) nubile.
unmarried mother n ragazza f madre inv.
unmask [ʌnˈmɑːsk] vt smascherare.
unmatched [ʌnˈmætʃt] adj senza uguali.
unmentionable [ʌnˈmɛnʃnəbl] adj (vice, topic) innominabile; (word) irripetibile.
unmerciful [ʌnˈmɜːsɪful] adj spietato(a).
unmistakable [ʌnmɪsˈteɪkəbl] adj indubbio(a); facilmente riconoscibile.
unmitigated [ʌnˈmɪtɪgeɪtɪd] adj (disaster etc) totale, assoluto(a).
unnamed [ʌnˈneɪmd] adj (nameless) senza nome; (anonymous) anonimo(a).
unnatural [ʌnˈnætʃrəl] adj innaturale; contro natura.
unnecessary [ʌnˈnɛsəsərɪ] adj inutile,

superfluo(a).

unnerve [ʌn'nəːv] vt (subj: accident) sgomentare; (: hostile attitude) bloccare; (: long wait, interview) snervare.

unnoticed [ʌn'nəutɪst] adj: **to go** or **pass** ~ passare inosservato(a).

UNO ['juːnəu] n abbr see **United Nations Organization**.

unobservant [ʌnəb'zəːvənt] adj: **to be** ~ non avere spirito di osservazione.

unobtainable [ʌnəb'teɪnəbl] adj (TEL) non ottenibile.

unobtrusive [ʌnəb'truːsɪv] adj discreto(a).

unoccupied [ʌn'ɔkjupaɪd] adj (house) vuoto(a); (seat, MIL: zone) libero(a), non occupato(a).

unofficial [ʌnə'fɪʃl] adj non ufficiale; (strike) non dichiarato(a) dal sindacato.

unopened [ʌn'əupənd] adj (letter) non aperto(a); (present) ancora incartato(a).

unopposed [ʌnə'pəuzd] adj senza incontrare opposizione.

unorthodox [ʌn'ɔːθədɔks] adj non ortodosso(a).

unpack [ʌn'pæk] vi disfare la valigia (or le valigie).

unpaid [ʌn'peɪd] adj (holiday) non pagato(a); (work) non retribuito(a); (bill, debt) da pagare.

unpalatable [ʌn'pælətəbl] adj (food) immangiabile; (drink) imbevibile; (truth) sgradevole.

unparalleled [ʌn'pærəlɛld] adj incomparabile, impareggiabile.

unpatriotic ['ʌnpætrɪ'ɔtɪk] adj (person) poco patriottico(a); (speech, attitude) antipatriottico(a).

unplanned [ʌn'plænd] adj (visit) imprevisto(a); (baby) non previsto(a).

unpleasant [ʌn'plɛznt] adj spiacevole; (person, remark) antipatico(a); (day, experience) brutto(a).

unplug [ʌn'plʌg] vt staccare.

unpolluted [ʌnpə'luːtɪd] adj non inquinato(a).

unpopular [ʌn'pɔpjulə*] adj impopolare; **to make o.s.** ~ **(with)** rendersi antipatico (a); (subj: politician etc) alienarsi le simpatie (di).

unprecedented [ʌn'prɛsɪdəntɪd] adj senza precedenti.

unpredictable [ʌnprɪ'dɪktəbl] adj imprevedibile.

unprejudiced [ʌn'prɛdʒudɪst] adj (not biased) obiettivo(a), imparziale; (having no prejudices) senza pregiudizi.

unprepared [ʌnprɪ'pɛəd] adj (person) impreparato(a); (speech)

improvvisato(a).

unprepossessing [ʌnpriːpə'zɛsɪŋ] adj insulso(a).

unpretentious [ʌnprɪ'tɛnʃəs] adj senza pretese.

unprincipled [ʌn'prɪnsɪpld] adj senza scrupoli.

unproductive [ʌnprə'dʌktɪv] adj improduttivo(a); (discussion) sterile.

unprofessional ['ʌnprə'fɛʃənl] adj: ~ **conduct** scorrettezza professionale.

unprofitable [ʌn'prɔfɪtəbl] adj (financially) non redditizio(a); (job, deal) poco lucrativo(a).

UNPROFOR ['ʌnprəfɔː*] n abbr (= United Nations Protection Force) reparto di protezione dell'ONU.

unprotected ['ʌnprə'tɛktɪd] adj (sex) non protetto(a).

unprovoked [ʌnprə'vəukt] adj non provocato(a).

unpunished [ʌn'pʌnɪʃt] adj: **to go** ~ restare impunito(a).

unqualified [ʌn'kwɔlɪfaɪd] adj (worker) non qualificato(a); (in professions) non abilitato(a); (success) assoluto(a), senza riserve.

unquestionably [ʌn'kwɛstʃənəblɪ] adv indiscutibilmente.

unquestioning [ʌn'kwɛstʃənɪŋ] adj (obedience, acceptance) cieco(a).

unravel [ʌn'rævl] vt dipanare, districare.

unreal [ʌn'rɪəl] adj irreale.

unrealistic [ʌnrɪə'lɪstɪk] adj (idea) illusorio(a); (estimate) non realistico(a).

unreasonable [ʌn'riːznəbl] adj irragionevole; **to make** ~ **demands on sb** voler troppo da qn.

unrecognizable [ʌn'rɛkəgnaɪzəbl] adj irriconoscibile.

unrecognized [ʌn'rɛkəgnaɪzd] adj (talent, genius) misconosciuto(a); (POL: regime) non ufficialmente riconosciuto(a).

unrecorded [ʌnrɪ'kɔːdɪd] adj non documentato(a), non registrato(a).

unrefined [ʌnrɪ'faɪnd] adj (sugar, petroleum) greggio(a); (person) rozzo(a).

unrehearsed [ʌnrɪ'həːst] adj (THEAT etc) improvvisato(a); (spontaneous) imprevisto(a).

unrelated [ʌnrɪ'leɪtɪd] adj: ~ **(to)** senza rapporto (con); (by family) non imparentato(a) (con).

unrelenting [ʌnrɪ'lɛntɪŋ] adj implacabile; accanito(a).

unreliable [ʌnrɪ'laɪəbl] adj (person, machine) che non dà affidamento; (news, source of information) inattendibile.

unrelieved [ʌnrɪ'liːvd] *adj* (*monotony*) uniforme.

unremitting [ʌnrɪ'mɪtɪŋ] *adj* incessante, infaticabile.

unrepeatable [ʌnrɪ'piːtəbl] *adj* (*offer*) unico(a).

unrepentant [ʌnrɪ'pɛntənt] *adj* impenitente.

unrepresentative [ʌnrɛprɪ'zɛntətɪv] *adj* atipico(a), poco rappresentativo(a).

unreserved [ʌnrɪ'zɔːvd] *adj* (*seat*) non prenotato(a), non riservato(a); (*approval, admiration*) senza riserve.

unresponsive [ʌnrɪs'pɔnsɪv] *adj* che non reagisce.

unrest [ʌn'rɛst] *n* agitazione *f*.

unrestricted [ʌnrɪ'strɪktɪd] *adj* (*power, time*) illimitato(a); (*access*) libero(a).

unrewarded [ʌnrɪ'wɔːdɪd] *adj* non ricompensato(a).

unripe [ʌn'raɪp] *adj* acerbo(a).

unrivalled, (*US*) **unrivaled** [ʌn'raɪvəld] *adj* senza pari.

unroll [ʌn'rəul] *vt* srotolare.

unruffled [ʌn'rʌfld] *adj* (*person*) calmo(a) e tranquillo(a), imperturbato(a); (*hair*) a posto.

unruly [ʌn'ruːlɪ] *adj* indisciplinato(a).

unsafe [ʌn'seɪf] *adj* pericoloso(a), rischioso(a); ~ **to drink** non potabile; ~ **to eat** non commestibile.

unsaid [ʌn'sɛd] *adj*: **to leave sth** ~ passare qc sotto silenzio.

unsaleable, (*US*) **unsalable** [ʌn'seɪləbl] *adj* invendibile.

unsatisfactory ['ʌnsætɪs'fæktərɪ] *adj* che lascia a desiderare, insufficiente.

unsavoury, (*US*) **unsavory** [ʌn'seɪvərɪ] *adj* (*fig: person*) losco(a); (: *reputation, subject*) disgustoso(a), ripugnante.

unscathed [ʌn'skeɪðd] *adj* incolume.

unscientific ['ʌnsaɪən'tɪfɪk] *adj* poco scientifico(a).

unscrew [ʌn'skruː] *vt* svitare.

unscrupulous [ʌn'skruːpjuləs] *adj* senza scrupoli.

unseat [ʌn'siːt] *vt* (*rider*) disarcionare; (*fig: an official*) spodestare.

unsecured [ʌnsɪ'kjuəd] *adj*: ~ **creditor** creditore *m* chirografario.

unseeded [ʌn'siːdɪd] *adj* (*SPORT*) che non è una testa di serie.

unseemly [ʌn'siːmlɪ] *adj* sconveniente.

unseen [ʌn'siːn] *adj* (*person*) inosservato(a); (*danger*) nascosto(a).

unselfish [ʌn'sɛlfɪʃ] *adj* (*person*) altruista; (*act*) disinteressato(a).

unsettled [ʌn'sɛtld] *adj* (*person, future*)

incerto(a); (*question*) non risolto(a); (*weather, market*) instabile; **to feel** ~ sentirsi disorientato(a).

unsettling [ʌn'sɛtlɪŋ] *adj* inquietante.

unshak(e)able [ʌn'ʃeɪkəbl] *adj* irremovibile.

unshaven [ʌn'ʃeɪvn] *adj* non rasato(a).

unsightly [ʌn'saɪtlɪ] *adj* brutto(a), sgradevole a vedersi.

unskilled [ʌn'skɪld] *adj*: ~ **worker** manovale *m*.

unsociable [ʌn'səuʃəbl] *adj* (*person*) poco socievole; (*behaviour*) antipatico(a).

unsocial [ʌn'səuʃəl] *adj*: ~ **hours** orario sconveniente.

unsold [ʌn'səuld] *adj* invenduto(a).

unsolicited [ʌnsə'lɪsɪtɪd] *adj* non richiesto(a).

unsophisticated [ʌnsə'fɪstɪkeɪtɪd] *adj* semplice, naturale.

unsound [ʌn'saund] *adj* (*health*) debole, cagionevole; (*in construction: floor, foundations*) debole, malsicuro(a); (*policy, advice*) poco sensato(a); (*judgment, investment*) poco sicuro(a).

unspeakable [ʌn'spiːkəbl] *adj* (*bad*) abominevole.

unspoken [ʌn'spəukən] *adj* (*words*) non detto(a); (*agreement, approval*) tacito(a).

unsteady [ʌn'stɛdɪ] *adj* instabile, malsicuro(a).

unstinting [ʌn'stɪntɪŋ] *adj* (*support*) incondizionato(a); (*generosity*) illimitato(a); (*praise*) senza riserve.

unstuck [ʌn'stʌk] *adj*: **to come** ~ scollarsi; (*fig*) fare fiasco.

unsubscribe [ʌnsʌb'scraɪb] *vi* (*COMPUT*) disdire l'abbonamento.

unsubstantiated [ʌnsəb'stænʃɪeɪtɪd] *adj* (*rumour, accusation*) infondato(a).

unsuccessful [ʌnsək'sɛsful] *adj* (*writer, proposal*) che non ha successo; (*marriage, attempt*) mal riuscito(a), fallito(a); **to be** ~ (*in attempting sth*) non riuscire; non avere successo; (*application*) non essere considerato(a).

unsuccessfully [ʌnsək'sɛsfəlɪ] *adv* senza successo.

unsuitable [ʌn'suːtəbl] *adj* inadatto(a); (*moment*) inopportuno(a).

unsuited [ʌn'suːtɪd] *adj*: **to be** ~ **for** *or* **to** non essere fatto(a) per.

unsung ['ʌn'sʌŋ] *adj*: **an** ~ **hero** un eroe misconosciuto.

unsupported [ʌnsə'pɔːtɪd] *adj* (*claim*) senza fondamento; (*theory*) non dimostrato(a).

unsure [ʌn'ʃuə*] *adj*: ~ (**of** *or* **about**) incerto(a) (su); **to be** ~ **of o.s.** essere

insicuro(a).
unsuspecting [ʌnsə'spɛktɪŋ] adj che non sospetta niente.
unsweetened [ʌn'swiːtnd] adj senza zucchero.
unswerving [ʌn'swəːvɪŋ] adj fermo(a).
unsympathetic ['ʌnsɪmpə'θɛtɪk] adj (attitude) poco incoraggiante; (person) antipatico(a); ~ (to) non solidale (verso).
untangle [ʌn'tæŋgl] vt sbrogliare.
untapped [ʌn'tæpt] adj (resources) non sfruttato(a).
untaxed [ʌn'tækst] adj (goods) esente da imposte; (income) non imponibile.
unthinkable [ʌn'θɪŋkəbl] adj impensabile, inconcepibile.
unthinkingly ['ʌn'θɪŋkɪŋlɪ] adv senza pensare.
untidy [ʌn'taɪdɪ] adj (room) in disordine; (appearance, work) trascurato(a); (person, writing) disordinato(a).
untie [ʌn'taɪ] vt (knot, parcel) disfare; (prisoner, dog) slegare.
until [ʌn'tɪl] prep fino a; (after negative) prima di ♦ conj finché, fino a quando; (in past, after negative) prima che + sub, prima di + infinitive; ~ now finora; ~ then fino ad allora; **from morning ~ night** dalla mattina alla sera.
untimely [ʌn'taɪmlɪ] adj intempestivo(a), inopportuno(a); (death) prematuro(a).
untold [ʌn'təʊld] adj incalcolabile; indescrivibile.
untouched [ʌn'tʌtʃt] adj (not used etc) non toccato(a), intatto(a); (safe: person) incolume; (unaffected): ~ **by** insensibile a.
untoward [ʌntə'wɔːd] adj sfortunato(a), sconveniente.
untrained ['ʌn'treɪnd] adj (worker) privo(a) di formazione professionale; (troops) privo(a) di addestramento; **to the ~ eye** ad un occhio inesperto.
untrammelled [ʌn'træmld] adj illimitato(a).
untranslatable [ʌntrænz'leɪtəbl] adj intraducibile.
untrue [ʌn'truː] adj (statement) falso(a), non vero(a).
untrustworthy [ʌn'trʌstwəːðɪ] adj di cui non ci si può fidare.
unusable [ʌn'juːzəbl] adj inservibile, inutilizzabile.
unused [ʌn'juːzd] adj (new) nuovo(a); (not made use of) non usato(a), non utilizzato(a); **to be ~ to sth/to doing sth** non essere abituato(a) a qc/a fare qc.
unusual [ʌn'juːʒʊəl] adj insolito(a), eccezionale, raro(a).

unusually [ʌn'juːʒʊəlɪ] adv insolitamente.
unveil [ʌn'veɪl] vt scoprire, svelare.
unwanted [ʌn'wɒntɪd] adj non desiderato(a).
unwarranted [ʌn'wɒrəntɪd] adj ingiustificato(a).
unwary [ʌn'wɛərɪ] adj incauto(a).
unwavering [ʌn'weɪvərɪŋ] adj fermo(a), incrollabile.
unwelcome [ʌn'wɛlkəm] adj (gen) non gradito(a); **to feel ~** sentire che la propria presenza non è gradita.
unwell [ʌn'wɛl] adj indisposto(a); **to feel ~** non sentirsi bene.
unwieldy [ʌn'wiːldɪ] adj poco maneggevole.
unwilling [ʌn'wɪlɪŋ] adj: **to be ~ to do** non voler fare.
unwillingly [ʌn'wɪlɪŋlɪ] adv malvolentieri.
unwind [ʌn'waɪnd] vb (irreg) vt svolgere, srotolare ♦ vi (relax) rilassarsi.
unwise [ʌn'waɪz] adj (decision, act) avventato(a).
unwitting [ʌn'wɪtɪŋ] adj involontario(a).
unworkable [ʌn'wəːkəbl] adj (plan etc) inattuabile.
unworthy [ʌn'wəːðɪ] adj indegno(a); **to be ~ of sth/to do sth** non essere degno di qc/di fare qc.
unwrap [ʌn'ræp] vt disfare; (present) aprire.
unwritten [ʌn'rɪtn] adj (agreement) tacito(a).
unzip [ʌn'zɪp] vt aprire (la chiusura lampo di); (COMPUT) dezippare.

===================================== KEYWORD

up [ʌp] prep su; **he went ~ the stairs/the hill** è salito su per le scale/sulla collina; **the cat was ~ a tree** il gatto era su un albero; **they live further ~ the street** vivono un po' più su nella stessa strada
♦ adv **1** (upwards, higher) su, in alto; ~ **in the sky/the mountains** su nel cielo/in montagna; ~ **there** lassù; ~ **above** su in alto; ~ **with Leeds United!** viva il Leeds United!
2: **to be ~** (out of bed) essere alzato(a); (prices, level) essere salito(a); (building) essere terminato(a); (tent) essere piantato(a); (curtains, shutters, wallpaper) essere su; **"this side ~"** "alto"; **to be ~ (by)** (in price, value) essere salito(a) or aumentato(a) (di); **when the year was ~** (finished) finito l'anno; **time's ~** il tempo è scaduto; **he's well ~ in or on politics** (BRIT) è molto informato di or sulla politica
3: ~ **to** (as far as) fino a; ~ **to now** finora

4: to be ~ to (*depending on*): **it's ~ to you** sta a lei, dipende da lei; (*equal to*): **he's not ~ to it** (*job, task etc*) non ne è all'altezza; (*col: be doing*): **what is he ~ to?** cosa sta combinando?; **what's ~?** (*col: wrong*) che c'è?; **what's ~ with him?** che ha?, che gli prende? ♦ *n:* **~s and downs** alti e bassi *mpl* ♦ *vi* (*col*): **she ~ped and left** improvvisamente se ne andò.

up-and-coming ['ʌpənd'kʌmɪŋ] *adj* pieno(a) di promesse, promettente.

upbeat ['ʌpbiːt] *n* (*MUS*) tempo in levare; (*in economy, prosperity*) incremento ♦ *adj* (*col*) ottimistico(a).

upbraid [ʌp'breɪd] *vt* rimproverare.

upbringing ['ʌpbrɪŋɪŋ] *n* educazione *f.*

upcoming ['ʌpkʌmɪŋ] *adj* imminente, prossimo(a).

update [ʌp'deɪt] *vt* aggiornare.

upend [ʌp'end] *vt* rovesciare.

upfront [ʌp'frʌnt] *adj* (*col*) franco(a), aperto(a) ♦ *adv* (*pay*) subito.

upgrade [ʌp'greɪd] *vt* promuovere; (*job*) rivalutare; (*COMPUT*) far passare a potenza superiore.

upheaval [ʌp'hiːvl] *n* sconvolgimento; tumulto.

uphill [ʌp'hɪl] *adj* in salita; (*fig: task*) difficile ♦ *adv:* **to go ~** andare in salita, salire.

uphold [ʌp'həuld] *vt irreg* approvare; sostenere.

upholstery [ʌp'həulstərɪ] *n* tappezzeria.

upkeep ['ʌpkiːp] *n* manutenzione *f.*

up-market [ʌp'mɑːkɪt] *adj* (*product*) che si rivolge ad una fascia di mercato superiore.

upon [ə'pɔn] *prep* su.

upper ['ʌpə*] *adj* superiore ♦ *n* (*of shoe*) tomaia; **the ~ class** ≈ l'alta borghesia.

upper case *n* maiuscolo.

upper-class [ʌpə'klɑːs] *adj* dell'alta borghesia; (*district*) signorile; (*accent*) aristocratico(a); (*attitude*) snob *inv.*

uppercut ['ʌpəkʌt] *n* uppercut *m inv,* montante *m.*

upper hand *n:* **to have the ~** avere il coltello dalla parte del manico.

Upper House *n:* **the ~** (*in Britain*) la Camera Alta, la Camera dei Lords; (*in US etc*) il Senato.

uppermost ['ʌpəməust] *adj* il(la) più alto(a); predominante; **it was ~ in my mind** è stata la mia prima preoccupazione.

Upper Volta [-'vɔltə] *n* Alto Volta *m.*

upright ['ʌpraɪt] *adj* diritto(a); verticale;

(*fig*) diritto(a), onesto(a) ♦ *n* montante *m.*

uprising ['ʌpraɪzɪŋ] *n* insurrezione *f,* rivolta.

uproar ['ʌprɔ:*] *n* tumulto, clamore *m.*

uproarious [ʌp'rɔːrɪəs] *adj* clamoroso(a); (*hilarious*) esilarante; **~ laughter** risata sonora.

uproot [ʌp'ruːt] *vt* sradicare.

upset *n* ['ʌpset] turbamento ♦ *vt* [ʌp'set] (*irreg: like* set) (*glass etc*) rovesciare; (*plan, stomach*) scombussolare; (*person: offend*) contrariare; (*: grieve*) addolorare; sconvolgere ♦ *adj* [ʌp'set] contrariato(a); addolorato(a); (*stomach*) scombussolato(a), disturbato(a); **to have a stomach ~** (*BRIT*) avere lo stomaco in disordine or scombussolato; **to get ~** contrariarsi; addolorarsi.

upset price *n* (*US, Scottish*) prezzo di riserva.

upsetting [ʌp'setɪŋ] *adj* (*saddening*) sconvolgente; (*offending*) offensivo(a); (*annoying*) fastidioso(a).

upshot ['ʌpʃɔt] *n* risultato; **the ~ of it all was that ...** la conclusione è stata che ....

upside down ['ʌpsaɪd-] *adv* sottosopra; **to turn ~** capovolgere; (*fig*) mettere sottosopra.

upstage ['ʌp'steɪdʒ] *vt:* **to ~ sb** rubare la scena a qn.

upstairs [ʌp'steəz] *adv, adj* di sopra, al piano superiore ♦ *n* piano di sopra.

upstart ['ʌpstɑːt] *n* parvenu *m inv.*

upstream [ʌp'striːm] *adv* a monte.

upsurge ['ʌpsɜːdʒ] *n* (*of enthusiasm etc*) ondata.

uptake ['ʌpteɪk] *n:* **he is quick/slow on the ~** è pronto/lento di comprendonio.

uptight [ʌp'taɪt] *adj* (*col*) teso(a).

up-to-date ['ʌptə'deɪt] *adj* moderno(a); aggiornato(a).

upturn ['ʌptɜːn] *n* (*in luck*) svolta favorevole; (*in value of currency*) rialzo.

upturned ['ʌptɜːnd] *adj* (*nose*) all'insù.

upward ['ʌpwəd] *adj* ascendente; verso l'alto.

upwardly-mobile ['ʌpwədlɪ'məubaɪl] *n:* **to be ~** salire nella scala sociale.

upward(s) ['ʌpwəd(z)] *adv* in su, verso l'alto.

URA *n abbr* (*US:* = *Urban Renewal Administration*) *amministrazione per il rinnovamento urbano.*

Ural Mountains ['juərəl-] *npl:* **the ~** (*also:* **the Urals**) gli Urali, i Monti Urali.

uranium [juə'reɪnɪəm] *n* uranio.

Uranus [juə'reɪnəs] *n* (*planet*) Urano.

urban ['ɜːbən] *adj* urbano(a).

urbane [əːˈbeɪn] *adj* civile, urbano(a), educato(a).

urbanization [əːbənaɪˈzeɪʃən] *n* urbanizzazione *f*.

urchin [ˈəːtʃɪn] *n* monello; **sea** ~ riccio di mare.

Urdu [ˈuəduː] *n* urdu *m inv*.

urge [əːdʒ] *n* impulso, stimolo ♦ *vt* (*caution etc*) raccomandare vivamente; **to** ~ **sb to do** esortare qn a fare, spingere qn a fare; raccomandare a qn di fare.
► **urge on** *vt* spronare.

urgency [ˈəːdʒənsɪ] *n* urgenza; (*of tone*) insistenza.

urgent [ˈəːdʒənt] *adj* urgente; (*earnest, persistent: plea*) pressante; (*: tone*) insistente, incalzante.

urgently [ˈəːdʒəntlɪ] *adv* d'urgenza, urgentemente; con insistenza.

urinal [ˈjuərɪnl] *n* (*BRIT: building*) vespasiano; (*: vessel*) orinale *m*, pappagallo.

urinate [ˈjuərɪneɪt] *vi* orinare.

urine [ˈjuərɪn] *n* orina.

urn [əːn] *n* urna; (*also: tea* ~) bollitore *m* per il tè.

Uruguay [ˈjuərəgwaɪ] *n* Uruguay *m*.

Uruguayan [juərəˈgwaɪən] *adj, n* uruguaiano(a).

US *n abbr see* **United States**.

us [ʌs] *pron* ci; (*stressed, after prep*) noi.

USA *n abbr* (*GEO*) *see* **United States** (*of America*); (*MIL*) = *United States Army*.

usable [ˈjuːzəbl] *adj* utilizzabile, usabile.

USAF *n abbr* = *United States Air Force*.

usage [ˈjuːzɪdʒ] *n* uso.

USCG *n abbr* = *United States Coast Guard*.

USDA *n abbr* = *Union of Shop, Distributive, and Allied Workers*.

USDAW [ˈʌzdɔː] *n abbr* (*BRIT*: = *Union of Shop, Distributive and Allied Workers*) sindacato dei dipendenti di negozi, reti di distribuzione e simili.

USDI *n abbr* = *United States Department of the Interior*.

use *n* [juːs] uso; impiego, utilizzazione *f* ♦ *vt* [juːz] usare, utilizzare, servirsi di; **she** ~**d to do it** lo faceva (una volta), era solita farlo; **in** ~ in uso; **out of** ~ fuori uso; **to be of** ~ essere utile, servire; **to make** ~ **of sth** far uso di qc, utilizzare qc; **ready for** ~ pronto per l'uso; **it's no** ~ non serve, è inutile; **to have the** ~ **of** poter usare; **what's this** ~**d for?** a che serve?; **to be** ~**d to** avere l'abitudine di; **to get** ~**d to** abituarsi a, fare l'abitudine a.
► **use up** *vt* finire; (*supplies*) dare fondo a; (*left-overs*) utilizzare.

used [juːzd] *adj* (*car*) d'occasione.

useful [ˈjuːsful] *adj* utile; **to come in** ~ fare comodo, tornare utile.

usefulness [ˈjuːsfəlnɪs] *n* utilità.

useless [ˈjuːslɪs] *adj* inutile; (*unusable: object*) inservibile.

user [ˈjuːzə*] *n* utente *m/f*; (*of petrol, gas etc*) consumatore/trice.

user-friendly [ˈjuːzəˈfrɛndlɪ] *adj* orientato(a) all'utente.

USES *n abbr* = *United States Employment Service*.

usher [ˈʌʃə*] *n* usciere *m*; (*in cinema*) maschera ♦ *vt*: **to** ~ **sb in** far entrare qn.

usherette [ʌʃəˈrɛt] *n* (*in cinema*) maschera.

USIA *n abbr* = *United States Information Agency*.

USM *n abbr* = *United States Mint; United States Mail*.

USN *n abbr* = *United States Navy*.

USP *n abbr* = *unique selling point or proposition*.

USPHS *n abbr* = *United States Public Health Service*.

USPO *n abbr* = *United States Post Office*.

USS *abbr* = *United States Ship* (*or Steamer*).

USSR *n abbr* (*HIST*) *see* **Union of Soviet Socialist Republics**.

usu. *abbr* = **usually**.

usual [ˈjuːʒuəl] *adj* solito(a); **as** ~ come al solito, come d'abitudine.

usually [ˈjuːʒuəlɪ] *adv* di solito.

usurer [ˈjuːʒərə*] *adj* usuraio/a.

usurp [juːˈzəːp] *vt* usurpare.

UT *abbr* (*US*) = *Utah*.

utensil [juːˈtɛnsl] *n* utensile *m*.

uterus [ˈjuːtərəs] *n* utero.

utilitarian [juːtɪlɪˈtɛərɪən] *adj* utilitario(a).

utility [juːˈtɪlɪtɪ] *n* utilità; (*also: public* ~) servizio pubblico.

utility room *n* locale adibito alla stiratura dei panni etc.

utilization [juːtɪlaɪˈzeɪʃən] *n* utilizzazione *f*.

utilize [ˈjuːtɪlaɪz] *vt* utilizzare; sfruttare.

utmost [ˈʌtməust] *adj* estremo(a) ♦ *n*: **to do one's** ~ fare il possibile *or* di tutto; **of the** ~ **importance** della massima importanza; **it is of the** ~ **importance that ...** è estremamente importante che ... + *sub*.

utter [ˈʌtə*] *adj* assoluto(a), totale ♦ *vt* pronunciare, proferire; emettere.

utterance [ˈʌtərəns] *n* espressione *f*; parole *fpl*.

utterly [ˈʌtəlɪ] *adv* completamente, del tutto.

U-turn [ˈjuːtəːn] *n* inversione *f* a U; (*fig*) voltafaccia *m inv*.

Uzbekistan [ʌzbɛkɪˈstɑːn] *n* Uzbekistan.

V v

V, v [vi:] n (letter) V, v m or f inv; **V for Victor**
≈ V come Venezia.
v abbr (= verse; = vide: see) v.; (= volt) V.;
(= versus) contro.
VA, Va. abbr (US) = Virginia.
vac [væk] n abbr (BRIT col) = **vacation.**
vacancy ['veɪkənsɪ] n (job) posto libero;
(room) stanza libera; **"no vacancies"**
"completo"; **have you any vacancies?**
(office) avete bisogno di personale?;
(hotel) avete una stanza?
vacant ['veɪkənt] adj (job, seat etc) libero(a);
(expression) assente.
vacant lot n terreno non occupato; (for
sale) terreno in vendita.
vacate [və'keɪt] vt lasciare libero(a).
vacation [və'keɪʃən] n (esp US) vacanze fpl;
to take a ~ prendere una vacanza,
prendere le ferie; **on** ~ in vacanza, in
ferie.
vacation course n corso estivo.
vaccinate ['væksɪneɪt] vt vaccinare.
vaccination [væksɪ'neɪʃən] n vaccinazione
f.
vaccine ['væksiːn] n vaccino.
vacuum ['vækjum] n vuoto.
vacuum bottle n (US) = **vacuum flask.**
vacuum cleaner n aspirapolvere m inv.
vacuum flask n (BRIT) thermos ® m inv.
vacuum-packed ['vækjum'pækt] adj
confezionato(a) sottovuoto.
vagabond ['vægəbɔnd] n vagabondo/a.
vagary ['veɪgərɪ] n capriccio.
vagina [və'dʒaɪnə] n vagina.
vagrancy ['veɪgrənsɪ] n vagabondaggio.
vagrant ['veɪgrənt] n vagabondo/a.
vague [veɪg] adj vago(a); (blurred: photo,
memory) sfocato(a); **I haven't the** ~**st idea**
non ho la minima or più pallida idea.
vaguely ['veɪglɪ] adv vagamente.
vain [veɪn] adj (useless) inutile, vano(a);
(conceited) vanitoso(a); **in** ~ inutilmente,
invano.
valance ['væləns] n volant m inv, balza.
valedictory [vælɪ'dɪktərɪ] adj di commiato.
valentine ['væləntaɪn] n (also: ~ **card**)
cartolina or biglietto di San Valentino.
valet ['vælɪt] n cameriere m personale.

valet parking n parcheggio effettuato da
un dipendente (dell'albergo etc).
valet service n (for clothes) servizio di
lavanderia; (for car) servizio completo di
lavaggio.
valiant ['vælɪənt] adj valoroso(a),
coraggioso(a).
valid ['vælɪd] adj valido(a), valevole;
(excuse) valido(a).
validate ['vælɪdeɪt] vt (contract, document)
convalidare; (argument, claim)
comprovare.
validity [və'lɪdɪtɪ] n validità.
valise [və'liːz] n borsa da viaggio.
valley ['vælɪ] n valle f.
valour, (US) valor ['vælə*] n valore m.
valuable ['væljuəbl] adj (jewel) di (grande)
valore; (time) prezioso(a); ~**s** npl oggetti
mpl di valore.
valuation [vælju'eɪʃən] n valutazione f,
stima.
value ['væljuː] n valore m ♦ vt (fix price)
valutare, dare un prezzo a; (cherish)
apprezzare, tenere a; **to be of great** ~ **to
sb** avere molta importanza per qn; **to
lose (in)** ~ (currency) svalutarsi; (property)
perdere (di) valore; **to gain (in)** ~
(currency) guadagnare; (property)
aumentare di valore; **you get good** ~ **(for
money) in that shop** si compra bene in
quel negozio.
value added tax (VAT) n (BRIT) imposta
sul valore aggiunto (I.V.A.).
valued ['væluːd] adj (appreciated)
stimato(a), apprezzato(a).
valuer ['væljuə*] n stimatore/trice.
valve [vælv] n valvola.
vampire ['væmpaɪə*] n vampiro.
van [væn] n (AUT) furgone m; (BRIT RAIL)
vagone m.
V and A n abbr (BRIT) = Victoria and Albert
Museum.
vandal ['vændl] n vandalo/a.
vandalism ['vændəlɪzəm] n vandalismo.
vandalize ['vændəlaɪz] vt vandalizzare.
vanguard ['vængɑːd] n avanguardia.
vanilla [və'nɪlə] n vaniglia ♦ cpd (ice cream)
alla vaniglia.
vanish ['vænɪʃ] vi svanire, scomparire.
vanity ['vænɪtɪ] n vanità.
vanity case n valigetta per cosmetici.
vantage ['vɑːntɪdʒ] n: ~ **point** posizione f or
punto di osservazione; (fig) posizione
vantaggiosa.
vaporize ['veɪpəraɪz] vt vaporizzare ♦ vi
vaporizzarsi.
vapour, (US) vapor ['veɪpə*] n vapore m.
variable ['vɛərɪəbl] adj variabile; (mood)

mutevole ♦ n fattore m variabile, variabile f.

variance ['vɛərɪəns] n: **to be at ~ (with)** essere in disaccordo (con); (facts) essere in contraddizione (con).

variant ['vɛərɪənt] n variante f.

variation [vɛərɪ'eɪʃən] n variazione f; (in opinion) cambiamento.

varicose ['værɪkəus] adj: **~ veins** varici fpl.

varied ['vɛərɪd] adj vario(a), diverso(a).

variety [və'raɪətɪ] n varietà f inv; (quantity): **a wide ~ of** ... una vasta gamma di ...; **for a ~ of reasons** per una serie di motivi.

variety show n spettacolo di varietà.

various ['vɛərɪəs] adj vario(a), diverso(a); (several) parecchi(e), molti(e); **at ~ times** in momenti diversi; (several) diverse volte.

varnish ['vɑːnɪʃ] n vernice f; (for nails) smalto ♦ vt verniciare; **to ~ one's nails** mettersi lo smalto sulle unghie.

vary ['vɛərɪ] vt, vi variare, mutare; **to ~ (with or according to)** variare (con or a seconda di).

varying ['vɛərɪɪŋ] adj variabile.

vase [vɑːz] n vaso.

vasectomy [væ'sɛktəmɪ] n vasectomia.

Vaseline ® ['væsɪliːn] n vaselina.

vast [vɑːst] adj vasto(a); (amount, success) enorme.

vastly ['vɑːstlɪ] adv enormemente.

vastness ['vɑːstnɪs] n vastità.

VAT [væt] n abbr (BRIT) see **value added tax**.

vat [væt] n tino.

Vatican ['vætɪkən] n: **the ~** il Vaticano.

vatman ['vætmæn] n (BRIT col): **the ~** ≈ l'ispettore m dell'IVA; (Inland Revenue) (il) fisco.

vault [vɔːlt] n (of roof) volta; (tomb) tomba; (in bank) camera blindata; (jump) salto ♦ vt (also: ~ **over**) saltare (d'un balzo).

vaunted ['vɔːntɪd] adj: **much-~** tanto celebrato(a).

VC n abbr (BRIT: = Victoria Cross) medaglia al coraggio; = **vice-chairman**.

VCR n abbr see **video cassette recorder**.

VD n abbr see **venereal disease**.

VDU n abbr see **visual display unit**.

veal [viːl] n vitello.

veer [vɪə*] vi girare; virare.

veg. [vɛdʒ] n abbr (BRIT col: = vegetable(s)) ≈ contorno.

vegan ['viːgən] n (BRIT) vegetaliano/a.

vegeburger, veggieburger ['vɛdʒɪbəːgə*] n hamburger m inv vegetariano.

vegetable ['vɛdʒtəbl] n verdura, ortaggio ♦ adj vegetale.

vegetable garden n orto.

vegetarian [vɛdʒɪ'tɛərɪən] adj, n vegetariano(a).

vegetate ['vɛdʒɪteɪt] vi vegetare.

vegetation [vɛdʒɪ'teɪʃən] n vegetazione f.

vegetative ['vɛdʒɪtətɪv] adj (also BOT) vegetativo(a).

vehemence ['viːɪməns] n veemenza, violenza.

vehement ['viːɪmənt] adj veemente, violento(a); profondo(a).

vehicle ['viːɪkl] n veicolo; (fig) mezzo.

vehicular [vɪ'hɪkjulə*] adj: **"no ~ traffic"** "chiuso al traffico di veicoli".

veil [veɪl] n velo ♦ vt velare; **under a ~ of secrecy** (fig) protetto da una cortina di segretezza.

veiled [veɪld] adj (also fig) velato(a).

vein [veɪn] n vena; (on leaf) nervatura; (fig: mood) vena, umore m.

Velcro ® ['vɛlkrəu] n velcro ® m inv.

vellum ['vɛləm] n (writing paper) carta patinata.

velocity [vɪ'lɒsɪtɪ] n velocità f inv.

velour [və'luə*] n velours m inv.

velvet ['vɛlvɪt] n velluto.

vending machine ['vɛndɪŋ-] n distributore m automatico.

vendor ['vɛndə*] n venditore/trice; **street ~** venditore ambulante.

veneer [və'nɪə*] n impiallacciatura; (fig) vernice f.

venerable ['vɛnərəbl] adj venerabile.

venereal disease (VD) [vɪ'nɪərɪəl-] n malattia venerea.

Venetian [vɪ'niːʃən] adj, n veneziano(a).

Venetian blind n (tenda alla) veneziana.

Venezuela [vɛnɪ'zweɪlə] n Venezuela m.

Venezuelan [vɛnɪ'zweɪlən] adj, n venezuelano(a).

vengeance ['vɛndʒəns] n vendetta; **with a ~** (fig) davvero; furiosamente.

vengeful ['vɛndʒful] adj vendicativo(a).

Venice ['vɛnɪs] n Venezia.

venison ['vɛnɪsn] n carne f di cervo.

venom ['vɛnəm] n veleno.

venomous ['vɛnəməs] adj velenoso(a).

vent [vɛnt] n foro, apertura; (in dress, jacket) spacco ♦ vt (fig: one's feelings) sfogare, dare sfogo a.

ventilate ['vɛntɪleɪt] vt (room) dare aria a, arieggiare.

ventilation [vɛntɪ'leɪʃən] n ventilazione f.

ventilation shaft n condotto di aerazione.

ventilator ['vɛntɪleɪtə*] n ventilatore m.

ventriloquist [vɛn'trɪləkwɪst] n ventriloquo/a.

venture ['vɛntʃə*] n impresa (rischiosa) ♦ vt rischiare, azzardare ♦ vi arrischiarsi, venture capital – un'iniziativa commerciale; to ~ to do sth azzardarsi a fare qc.

venture capital n capitale m di rischio.

venue ['vɛnjuː] n luogo di incontro; (SPORT) luogo (designato) per l'incontro.

Venus ['viːnəs] n (planet) Venere m.

veracity [və'ræsɪtɪ] n veridicità.

veranda(h) [və'rændə] n veranda.

verb [vəːb] n verbo.

verbal ['vəːbəl] adj verbale; (translation) letterale.

verbally ['vəːbəlɪ] adv a voce.

verbatim [vəː'beɪtɪm] adv, adj parola per parola.

verbose [vəː'bəus] adj verboso(a).

verdict ['vəːdɪkt] n verdetto; (opinion) giudizio, parere m; ~ of guilty/not guilty verdetto di colpevolezza/non colpevolezza.

verge [vəːdʒ] n bordo, orlo; "soft ~s" (BRIT) "banchina cedevole"; on the ~ of doing sul punto di fare.
► verge on vt fus rasentare.

verger ['vəːdʒə*] n (REL) sagrestano.

verification [vɛrɪfɪ'keɪʃən] n verifica.

verify ['vɛrɪfaɪ] vt verificare; (prove the truth of) confermare.

veritable ['vɛrɪtəbl] adj vero(a).

vermin ['vəːmɪn] npl animali mpl nocivi; (insects) insetti mpl parassiti.

vermouth ['vəːməθ] n vermut m inv.

vernacular [və'nækjulə*] n vernacolo.

versatile ['vəːsətaɪl] adj (person) versatile; (machine, tool etc) (che si presta) a molti usi.

verse [vəːs] n (of poem) verso; (stanza) stanza, strofa; (in bible) versetto; (no pl: poetry) versi mpl; in ~ in versi.

versed [vəːst] adj: (well-)~ in versato(a) in.

version ['vəːʃən] n versione f.

versus ['vəːsəs] prep contro.

vertebra, pl ~ e ['vəːtɪbrə, -briː] n vertebra.

vertebrate ['vəːtɪbrɪt] n vertebrato.

vertebrae ['vəːtɪbriː] npl of vertebra.

vertical ['vəːtɪkl] adj, n verticale (m).

vertically ['vəːtɪklɪ] adv verticalmente.

vertigo ['vəːtɪgəu] n vertigine f; to suffer from ~ soffrire di vertigini.

verve [vəːv] n brio; entusiasmo.

very ['vɛrɪ] adv molto ♦ adj: the ~ book which proprio il libro che; ~ much moltissimo; ~ well molto bene; ~ little molto poco; at the ~ end proprio alla fine; the ~ last proprio l'ultimo; at the ~ least almeno; the ~ thought (of it) alarms me il solo pensiero mi spaventa, sono spaventato solo al pensiero.

vespers ['vɛspəz] npl vespro.

vessel ['vɛsl] n (ANAT) vaso; (NAUT) nave f; (container) recipiente m.

vest [vɛst] n (BRIT) maglia; (: sleeveless) canottiera; (US: waistcoat) gilè m inv ♦ vt: to ~ sb with sth, to ~ sth in sb conferire qc a qn.

vested interest n: to have a ~ in doing avere tutto l'interesse a fare; ~s npl (COMM) diritti mpl acquisiti.

vestibule ['vɛstɪbjuːl] n vestibolo.

vestige ['vɛstɪdʒ] n vestigio.

vestment ['vɛstmənt] n (REL) paramento liturgico.

vestry ['vɛstrɪ] n sagrestia.

Vesuvius [vɪ'suːvɪəs] n Vesuvio.

vet [vɛt] n abbr (= veterinary surgeon) veterinario; (US: col) = veteran ♦ vt esaminare minuziosamente; (text) rivedere; to ~ sb for a job raccogliere delle informazioni dettagliate su qn prima di offrirgli un posto.

veteran ['vɛtərn] n veterano; (also: war ~) reduce m ♦ adj: she's a ~ campaigner for ... lotta da sempre per ....

veteran car n auto f inv d'epoca (anteriore al 1919).

veterinarian [vɛtrɪ'nɛərɪən] n (US) = veterinary surgeon.

veterinary ['vɛtrɪnərɪ] adj veterinario(a).

veterinary surgeon n (BRIT) veterinario.

veto ['viːtəu] n (pl ~es) veto ♦ vt opporre il veto a; to put a ~ on opporre il veto a.

vetting ['vɛtɪŋ] n: positive ~ indagine per accertare l'idoneità di un aspirante ad una carica ufficiale.

vex [vɛks] vt irritare, contrariare.

vexed [vɛkst] adj (question) controverso(a), dibattuto(a).

VFD n abbr (US) = voluntary fire department.

VG abbr (BRIT: SCOL etc: = very good) ottimo.

VHF abbr (= very high frequency) VHF.

VI abbr (US) = Virgin Islands.

via ['vaɪə] prep (by way of) via; (by means of) tramite.

viability [vaɪə'bɪlɪtɪ] n attuabilità.

viable ['vaɪəbl] adj attuabile; vitale.

viaduct ['vaɪədʌkt] n viadotto.

vial ['vaɪəl] n fiala.

vibes [vaɪbz] npl (col): I got good/bad ~ ho trovato simpatica/antipatica l'atmosfera.

vibrant ['vaɪbrənt] adj (sound) vibrante; (colour) vivace, vivo(a).

vibraphone ['vaɪbrəfəun] n vibrafono.

vibrate [vaɪ'breɪt] vi: to ~ (with) vibrare (di); (resound) risonare (di).

vibration [vaɪ'breɪʃən] n vibrazione f.

vibrator [vaɪ'breɪtə*] n vibratore m.

vicar ['vɪkə*] n pastore m.
vicarage ['vɪkərɪdʒ] n presbiterio.
vicarious [vɪ'kɛərɪəs] adj sofferto(a) al posto di un altro; **to get ~ pleasure out of sth** trarre piacere indirettamente da qc.
vice [vaɪs] n (evil) vizio; (TECH) morsa.
vice- [vaɪs] prefix vice ....
vice-chairman [vaɪs'tʃɛəmən] n vicepresidente m.
vice-chancellor [vaɪs'tʃɑːnsələ*] n (BRIT SCOL) rettore m (per elezione).
vice-president [vaɪs'prɛzɪdənt] n vicepresidente m.
viceroy ['vaɪsrɔɪ] n viceré m inv.
vice squad n (squadra del) buon costume f.
vice versa ['vaɪsɪ'vəːsə] adv viceversa.
vicinity [vɪ'sɪnɪtɪ] n vicinanze fpl.
vicious ['vɪʃəs] adj (remark) maligno(a), cattivo(a); (blow) violento(a); **a ~ circle** un circolo vizioso.
viciousness ['vɪʃəsnɪs] n malignità, cattiveria; ferocia.
vicissitudes [vɪ'sɪsɪtjuːdz] npl vicissitudini fpl.
victim ['vɪktɪm] n vittima; **to be the ~ of** essere vittima di.
victimization [vɪktɪmaɪ'zeɪʃən] n persecuzione f; rappresaglie fpl.
victimize ['vɪktɪmaɪz] vt perseguitare; compiere delle rappresaglie contro.
victor ['vɪktə*] n vincitore m.
Victorian [vɪk'tɔːrɪən] adj vittoriano(a).
victorious [vɪk'tɔːrɪəs] adj vittorioso(a).
victory ['vɪktərɪ] n vittoria; **to win a ~ over sb** riportare una vittoria su qn.
video ['vɪdɪəu] cpd video... ♦ n (~ film) video m inv; (also: ~ cassette) videocassetta; (also: ~ cassette recorder) videoregistratore m.
video camera n videocamera.
video cassette n videocassetta.
video (cassette) recorder n videoregistratore m.
videodisc ['vɪdɪəudɪsk] n disco ottico.
video game n videogioco.
video nasty n video estremamente violento o porno.
videophone ['vɪdɪəufəun] n videotelefono.
video recording n registrazione f su video.
video tape n videotape m inv.
vie [vaɪ] vi: **to ~ with** competere con, rivaleggiare con.
Vienna [vɪ'ɛnə] n Vienna.
Vietnam, Viet Nam [vjɛt'næm] n Vietnam m.
Vietnamese [vjɛtnə'miːz] adj vietnamita

♦ n vietnamita m/f; (LING) vietnamita m.
view [vjuː] n vista, veduta; (opinion) opinione f ♦ vt (situation) considerare; (house) visitare; **on ~** (in museum etc) esposto(a); **to be in** or **within ~ (of sth)** essere in vista (di qc); **in full ~ of sb** sotto gli occhi di qn; **an overall ~ of the situation** una visione globale della situazione; **in my ~** a mio avviso, secondo me; **in ~ of the fact that** considerato che; **to take** or **hold the ~ that ...** essere dell'opinione che ...; **with a ~ to doing sth** con l'intenzione di fare qc.
viewdata ['vjuːdeɪtə] n (BRIT) sistema di televideo.
viewer ['vjuːə*] n (viewfinder) mirino; (small projector) visore m; (TV) telespettatore/trice.
viewfinder ['vjuːfaɪndə*] n mirino.
viewpoint ['vjuːpɔɪnt] n punto di vista.
vigil ['vɪdʒɪl] n veglia; **to keep ~** vegliare.
vigilance ['vɪdʒɪləns] n vigilanza.
vigilant ['vɪdʒɪlənt] adj vigile.
vigilante [vɪdʒɪ'læntɪ] n cittadino che si fa giustizia da solo.
vigorous ['vɪgərəs] adj vigoroso(a).
vigour, (US) vigor ['vɪgə*] n vigore m.
vile [vaɪl] adj (action) vile; (smell) disgustoso(a), nauseante; (temper) pessimo(a).
vilify ['vɪlɪfaɪ] vt diffamare.
villa ['vɪlə] n villa.
village ['vɪlɪdʒ] n villaggio.
villager ['vɪlɪdʒə*] n abitante m/f di villaggio.
villain ['vɪlən] n (scoundrel) canaglia; (criminal) criminale m; (in novel etc) cattivo.
VIN n abbr (US) = vehicle identification number.
vinaigrette [vɪneɪ'grɛt] n vinaigrette f inv.
vindicate ['vɪndɪkeɪt] vt comprovare; giustificare.
vindication [vɪndɪ'keɪʃən] n: **in ~ of** per giustificare; a discolpa di.
vindictive [vɪn'dɪktɪv] adj vendicativo(a).
vine [vaɪn] n vite f; (climbing plant) rampicante m.
vinegar ['vɪnɪgə*] n aceto.
vine grower n viticoltore m.
vine-growing ['vaɪngrəuɪŋ] adj viticolo(a) ♦ n viticoltura.
vineyard ['vɪnjɑːd] n vigna, vigneto.
vintage ['vɪntɪdʒ] n (year) annata, produzione f; **the 1970 ~** il vino del 1970.
vintage car n auto f inv d'epoca.
vintage wine n vino d'annata.
vinyl ['vaɪnl] n vinile m.

viola [vɪ'əulə] *n* viola.
violate ['vaɪəleɪt] *vt* violare.
violation [vaɪə'leɪʃən] *n* violazione *f*; ~ **of** sth violando qc.
violence ['vaɪələns] *n* violenza; (*POL etc*) incidenti *mpl* violenti.
violent [vaɪələnt] *adj* violento(a); **a** ~ **dislike of sb/sth** una violenta avversione per qn/qc.
violently ['vaɪələntlɪ] *adv* violentemente; (*ill, angry*) terribilmente.
violet ['vaɪələt] *adj* (*colour*) viola *inv*, violetto(a) ♦ *n* (*plant*) violetta.
violin [vaɪə'lɪn] *n* violino.
violinist [vaɪə'lɪnɪst] *n* violinista *m/f*.
VIP *n abbr* (= *very important person*) V.I.P. *m/f inv*.
viper ['vaɪpə*] *n* vipera.
viral ['vaɪərəl] *adj* virale.
virgin ['vəːdʒɪn] *n* vergine *f* ♦ *adj* vergine *inv*; **she is a** ~ lei è vergine; **the Blessed V**~ la Beatissima Vergine.
virginity [vəː'dʒɪnɪtɪ] *n* verginità.
Virgo ['vəːgəu] *n* (*sign*) Vergine *f*; **to be** ~ essere della Vergine.
virile ['vɪraɪl] *adj* virile.
virility [vɪ'rɪlɪtɪ] *n* virilità.
virtual ['vəːtjuəl] *adj* effettivo(a), vero(a); (*COMPUT, PHYSICS*) virtuale; (*in effect*): **it's a** ~ **impossibility** è praticamente impossibile; **the** ~ **leader** il capo all'atto pratico.
virtually ['vəːtjuəlɪ] *adv* (*almost*) praticamente; **it is** ~ **impossible** è praticamente impossibile.
virtual reality *n* realtà *f inv* virtuale.
virtue ['vəːtjuː] *n* virtù *f inv*; (*advantage*) pregio, vantaggio; **by** ~ **of** grazie a.
virtuosity [vəːtju'ɔsɪtɪ] *n* virtuosismo.
virtuoso [vəːtju'əuzəu] *n* virtuoso.
virtuous ['vəːtjuəs] *adj* virtuoso(a).
virulent ['vɪrulənt] *adj* virulento(a).
virus ['vaɪərəs] *n* virus *m inv*.
visa ['viːzə] *n* visto.
vis-à-vis [viːzə'viː] *prep* rispetto a, nei riguardi di.
viscount ['vaɪkaunt] *n* visconte *m*.
viscous ['vɪskəs] *adj* viscoso(a).
vise [vaɪs] *n* (*US TECH*) = **vice**.
visibility [vɪzɪ'bɪlɪtɪ] *n* visibilità.
visible ['vɪzəbl] *adj* visibile; ~ **exports/imports** esportazioni *fpl*/importazioni *fpl* visibili.
visibly ['vɪzəblɪ] *adv* visibilmente.
vision ['vɪʒən] *n* (*sight*) vista; (*foresight, in dream*) visione *f*.
visionary ['vɪʒənərɪ] *n* visionario/a.
visit ['vɪzɪt] *n* visita; (*stay*) soggiorno ♦ *vt*

(*person*) andare a trovare; (*place*) visitare; **to pay a** ~ **to** (*person*) fare una visita a; (*place*) andare a visitare; **on a private/official** ~ in visita privata/ ufficiale.
visiting ['vɪzɪtɪŋ] *adj* (*speaker, professor, team*) ospite.
visiting card *n* biglietto da visita.
visiting hours *npl* orario delle visite.
visitor ['vɪzɪtə*] *n* visitatore/trice; (*guest*) ospite *m/f*.
visitors' book *n* libro d'oro; (*in hotel*) registro.
visor ['vaɪzə*] *n* visiera.
VISTA ['vɪstə] *n abbr* (= *Volunteers In Service To America*) volontariato in zone depresse degli Stati Uniti.
vista ['vɪstə] *n* vista, prospettiva.
visual ['vɪzjuəl] *adj* visivo(a); visuale; ottico(a).
visual aid *n* sussidio visivo.
visual arts *npl* arti *fpl* figurative.
visual display unit (VDU) *n* unità *f inv* di visualizzazione.
visualize ['vɪzjuəlaɪz] *vt* immaginare, figurarsi; (*foresee*) prevedere.
visually ['vɪzjuəlɪ] *adv*: ~ **appealing** piacevole a vedersi; ~ **handicapped** con una menomazione della vista.
vital ['vaɪtl] *adj* vitale; **of** ~ **importance (to sb/sth)** di vitale importanza (per qn/qc).
vitality [vaɪ'tælɪtɪ] *n* vitalità.
vitally ['vaɪtəlɪ] *adv* estremamente.
vital statistics *npl* (*of population*) statistica demografica; (*col: woman's*) misure *fpl*.
vitamin ['vɪtəmɪn] *n* vitamina.
vitiate ['vɪʃɪeɪt] *vt* viziare.
vitreous ['vɪtrɪəs] *adj* (*rock*) vetroso(a); (*china, enamel*) vetrificato(a).
vitriolic [vɪtrɪ'ɔlɪk] *adj* (*fig*) caustico(a).
viva ['vaɪvə] *n* (*also:* ~ **voce**) (*esame m*) orale.
vivacious [vɪ'veɪʃəs] *adj* vivace.
vivacity [vɪ'væsɪtɪ] *n* vivacità.
vivid ['vɪvɪd] *adj* vivido(a).
vividly ['vɪvɪdlɪ] *adv* (*describe*) vividamente; (*remember*) con precisione.
vivisection [vɪvɪ'sekʃən] *n* vivisezione *f*.
vixen ['vɪksn] *n* volpe *f* femmina; (*pej: woman*) bisbetica.
viz *abbr* (= *vide licet: namely*) cioè.
VLF *abbr* (= *very low frequency*) bassissima frequenza.
V-neck ['viːnɛk] *n* maglione *m* con lo scollo a V.
VOA *n abbr* (= *Voice of America*) voce *f* dell'America (*alla radio*).
vocabulary [vəu'kæbjulərɪ] *n* vocabolario.

vocal ['vəukl] *adj* (*MUS*) vocale; (*communication*) verbale; (*noisy*) rumoroso(a).

vocal cords *npl* corde *fpl* vocali.

vocalist ['vəukəlɪst] *n* cantante *m/f* (*in un gruppo*).

vocation [vəu'keɪʃən] *n* vocazione *f*.

vocational [vəu'keɪʃənl] *adj* professionale; ~ **guidance** orientamento professionale; ~ **training** formazione *f* professionale.

vociferous [və'sɪfərəs] *adj* rumoroso(a).

vodka ['vɔdkə] *n* vodka *f inv*.

vogue [vəug] *n* moda; (*popularity*) popolarità, voga; **to be in** ~, **be the** ~ essere di moda.

voice [vɔɪs] *n* voce *f* ♦ *vt* (*opinion*) esprimere; **in a loud/soft** ~ a voce alta/bassa; **to give** ~ **to** esprimere.

voice mail *n* servizio di segreteria telefonica.

voice-over ['vɔɪsəuvə*] *n* voce *f* fuori campo *inv*.

void [vɔɪd] *n* vuoto ♦ *adj*: ~ **of** privo(a) di.

voile [vɔɪl] *n* voile *m*.

vol. *abbr* (= *volume*) vol.

volatile ['vɔlətaɪl] *adj* volatile; (*fig*) volubile.

volcanic [vɔl'kænɪk] *adj* vulcanico(a).

volcano, ~**es** [vɔl'keɪnəu] *n* vulcano.

volition [və'lɪʃən] *n*: **of one's own** ~ di propria volontà.

volley ['vɔlɪ] *n* (*of gunfire*) salva; (*of stones etc*) raffica, gragnola; (*TENNIS etc*) volata.

volleyball ['vɔlɪbɔːl] *n* pallavolo *f*.

volt [vəult] *n* volt *m inv*.

voltage ['vəultɪdʒ] *n* tensione *f*, voltaggio; **high/low** ~ alta/bassa tensione.

voluble ['vɔljubl] *adj* loquace, ciarliero(a).

volume ['vɔljuːm] *n* volume *m*; (*of tank*) capacità *f inv*; ~ **one/two** (*of book*) volume primo/secondo; **his expression spoke** ~**s** la sua espressione lasciava capire tutto.

volume control *n* (*RADIO, TV*) regolatore *m or* manopola del volume.

voluminous [və'luːmɪnəs] *adj* voluminoso(a); (*notes etc*) abbondante.

voluntarily ['vɔləntrɪlɪ] *adv* volontariamente; gratuitamente.

voluntary ['vɔləntərɪ] *adj* volontario(a); (*unpaid*) gratuito(a), non retribuito(a).

voluntary liquidation *n* (*COMM*) liquidazione *f* volontaria.

volunteer [vɔlən'tɪə*] *n* volontario/a ♦ *vi* (*MIL*) arruolarsi volontario; **to** ~ **to do** (*offrire* (*volontariamente*) *di* fare.

voluptuous [və'lʌptjuəs] *adj* voluttuoso(a).

vomit ['vɔmɪt] *n* vomito ♦ *vt, vi* vomitare.

voracious [və'reɪʃəs] *adj* (*appetite*) smisurato(a); (*reader*) avido(a).

vote [vəut] *n* voto, suffragio; (*cast*) voto; (*franchise*) diritto di voto ♦ *vi* votare ♦ *vt* (*gen*) votare; (*sum of money etc*) votare a favore di; **to** ~ **to do sth** votare a favore di fare qc; **he was** ~**d secretary** è stato eletto segretario; **to put sth to the** ~, **to take a** ~ **on sth** mettere qc ai voti; ~ **for/ against** voto a favore/contrario; **to pass a** ~ **of confidence/no confidence** dare il voto di fiducia/sfiducia; ~ **of thanks** discorso di ringraziamento.

voter ['vəutə*] *n* elettore/trice.

voting ['vəutɪŋ] *n* scrutinio.

voting paper *n* (*BRIT*) scheda elettorale.

voting right *n* diritto di voto.

vouch [vautʃ]: **to** ~ **for** *vt fus* farsi garante di.

voucher ['vautʃə*] *n* (*for meal, petrol*) buono; (*receipt*) ricevuta; **travel** ~ voucher *m inv*, tagliando.

vow [vau] *n* voto, promessa solenne ♦ *vi* giurare; **to take** *or* **make a** ~ **to do sth** fare voto di fare qc.

vowel ['vauəl] *n* vocale *f*.

voyage ['vɔɪɪdʒ] *n* viaggio per mare, traversata.

voyeur [vwɑː'jəː*] *n* guardone/a.

VP *n abbr* (= *vice-president*) V.P.

vs *abbr* (= *versus*) contro.

VSO *n abbr* (*BRIT*: = *Voluntary Service Overseas*) *servizio volontario in paesi sottosviluppati.*

VT, Vt. *abbr* (*US*) = *Vermont.*

vulgar ['vʌlgə*] *adj* volgare.

vulgarity [vʌl'gærɪtɪ] *n* volgarità.

vulnerability [vʌlnərə'bɪlɪtɪ] *n* vulnerabilità.

vulnerable ['vʌlnərəbl] *adj* vulnerabile.

vulture ['vʌltʃə*] *n* avvoltoio.

W w

W, w ['dʌbljuː] *n* (*letter*) W, w *m or f inv*; **W for William** ≈ W come Washington.

W *abbr* (= *west*) O; (*ELEC*: = *watt*) w.

WA *abbr* (*US*) = *Washington.*

wad [wɔd] *n* (*of cotton wool, paper*) tampone *m*; (*of banknotes etc*) fascio.

wadding ['wɔdɪŋ] *n* imbottitura.

waddle ['wɔdl] *vi* camminare come una papera.

wade [weɪd] *vi:* **to ~ through** camminare a stento in ♦ *vt* guadare.

wafer ['weɪfə*] *n (CULIN)* cialda; *(REL)* ostia; *(COMPUT)* wafer *m inv.*

wafer-thin ['weɪfə'θɪn] *adj* molto sottile.

waffle ['wɔfl] *n (CULIN)* cialda; *(col)* ciance *fpl;* riempitivo ♦ *vi* cianciare; parlare a vuoto.

waffle iron *n* stampo per cialde.

waft [wɔft] *vt* portare ♦ *vi* diffondersi.

wag [wæg] *vt* agitare, muovere ♦ *vi* agitarsi; **the dog ~ged its tail** il cane scodinzolò.

wage [weɪdʒ] *n (also:* **~s**) salario, paga ♦ *vt:* **to ~ war** fare la guerra; **a day's ~s** un giorno di paga.

wage claim *n* rivendicazione *f* salariale.

wage differential *n* differenza di salario.

wage earner *n* salariato/a.

wage freeze *n* blocco dei salari.

wage packet *n (BRIT)* busta *f* paga *inv.*

wager ['weɪdʒə*] *n* scommessa.

waggle ['wægl] *vt* dimenare, agitare ♦ *vi* dimenarsi, agitarsi.

wag(g)on ['wægən] *n (horse-drawn)* carro; *(truck)* furgone *m;* (*BRIT RAIL*) vagone *m* (merci).

wail [weɪl] *n* gemito; *(of siren)* urlo ♦ *vi* gemere; urlare.

waist [weɪst] *n* vita, cintola.

waistcoat ['weɪskəut] *n* panciotto, gilè *m inv.*

waistline ['weɪstlaɪn] *n* (giro di) vita.

wait [weɪt] *n* attesa ♦ *vi* aspettare, attendere; **to ~ for** aspettare; **to keep sb ~ing** far aspettare qn; **~ a moment!** (aspetti) un momento!; **"repairs while you ~"** "riparazioni lampo"; **I can't ~ to** ... (*fig*) non vedo l'ora di ...; **to lie in ~ for** stare in agguato a.

▶**wait behind** *vi* rimanere (ad aspettare).

▶**wait on** *vt fus* servire.

▶**wait up** *vi* restare alzato(a) (ad aspettare); **don't ~ up for me** non rimanere alzato per me.

waiter ['weɪtə*] *n* cameriere *m.*

waiting ['weɪtɪŋ] *n: "no ~"* (*BRIT AUT*) "divieto di sosta".

waiting list *n* lista d'attesa.

waiting room *n* sala d'aspetto *or* d'attesa.

waitress ['weɪtrɪs] *n* cameriera.

waive [weɪv] *vt* rinunciare a, abbandonare.

waiver ['weɪvə*] *n* rinuncia.

wake [weɪk] *vb (pt* **woke, ~d,** *pp* **woken, ~d** [wəuk, 'wəukn]) *vt (also:* **~ up**) svegliare ♦ *vi (also:* **~ up**) svegliarsi ♦ *n (for dead person)* veglia funebre; (*NAUT*) scia; **to ~ up to sth** (*fig*) rendersi conto di qc; **in the**

~ of sulla scia di; **to follow in sb's ~** (*fig*) seguire le tracce di qn.

waken ['weɪkn] *vt, vi* = **wake.**

Wales [weɪlz] *n* Galles *m.*

walk [wɔ:k] *n* passeggiata; *(short)* giretto; *(gait)* passo, andatura; *(path)* sentiero; *(in park etc)* sentiero, vialetto ♦ *vi* camminare; *(for pleasure, exercise)* passeggiare ♦ *vt (distance)* fare *or* percorrere a piedi; *(dog)* accompagnare, portare a passeggiare; **10 minutes' ~ from** 10 minuti di cammino *or* a piedi da; **to go for a ~** andare a fare quattro passi; andare a fare una passeggiata; **from all ~s of life** di tutte le condizioni sociali; **to ~ in one's sleep** essere sonnambulo(a); **I'll ~ you home** ti accompagno a casa.

▶**walk out** *vi (go out)* uscire; *(as protest)* uscire (in segno di protesta); *(strike)* scendere in sciopero; **to ~ out on sb** piantare in asso qn.

walkabout ['wɔ:kəbaut] *n:* **to go (on a) ~** avere incontri informali col pubblico *(durante una visita ufficiale).*

walker ['wɔ:kə*] *n (person)* camminatore/ trice.

walkie-talkie ['wɔ:kɪ'tɔ:kɪ] *n* walkie-talkie *m inv.*

walking ['wɔ:kɪŋ] *n* camminare *m;* **it's within ~ distance** ci si arriva a piedi.

walking holiday *n* vacanza fatta di lunghe camminate.

walking shoes *npl* scarpe *fpl* da passeggio.

walking stick *n* bastone *m* da passeggio.

Walkman ® ['wɔ:kmən] *n* walkman ® *m inv.*

walk-on ['wɔ:kɔn] *adj (THEAT: part)* da comparsa.

walkout ['wɔ:kaut] *n (of workers)* sciopero senza preavviso *or* a sorpresa.

walkover ['wɔ:kəuvə*] *n (col)* vittoria facile, gioco da ragazzi.

walkway ['wɔ:kweɪ] *n* passaggio pedonale.

wall [wɔ:l] *n* muro; *(internal, of tunnel, cave)* parete *f;* **to go to the ~** (*fig: firm etc*) fallire.

▶**wall in** *vt (garden etc)* circondare con un muro.

wall cupboard *n* pensile *m.*

walled [wɔ:ld] *adj (city)* fortificato(a).

wallet ['wɔlɪt] *n* portafoglio.

wallflower ['wɔ:lflauə*] *n* violacciocca; **to be a ~** (*fig*) fare da tappezzeria.

wall hanging *n* tappezzeria.

wallop ['wɔləp] *vt (col)* pestare.

wallow ['wɔləu] *vi* sguazzare, rotolarsi; **to ~ in one's grief** crogiolarsi nel proprio dolore.

wallpaper ['wɔ:lpeɪpə*] *n* carta da parati;

(*COMPUT*) sfondo.
wall-to-wall ['wɔːltə'wɔːl] *adj*: ~ **carpeting** moquette *f*.
walnut ['wɔːlnʌt] *n* noce *f*; (*tree*) noce *m*.
walrus, *pl* ~ *or* ~**es** ['wɔːlrəs] *n* tricheco.
waltz [wɔːlts] *n* valzer *m inv* ♦ *vi* ballare il valzer.
wan [wɔn] *adj* pallido(a), smorto(a); triste.
wand [wɔnd] *n* (*also*: **magic** ~) bacchetta (magica).
wander ['wɔndə*] *vi* (*person*) girare senza meta, girovagare; (*thoughts*) vagare; (*river*) serpeggiare.
wanderer ['wɔndərə*] *n* vagabondo/a.
wandering ['wɔndrɪŋ] *adj* (*tribe*) nomade; (*minstrel, actor*) girovago(a); (*path, river*) tortuoso(a); (*glance, mind*) distratto(a).
wane [weɪn] *vi* (*moon*) calare; (*reputation*) declinare.
wangle ['wæŋgl] (*BRIT col*) *vt* procurare (con l'astuzia) ♦ *n* astuzia.
wanker ['wæŋkə*] *n* (*col!*) segaiolo (*!*); (*as insult*) coglione (*!*) *m*.
want [wɔnt] *vt* volere; (*need*) aver bisogno di; (*lack*) mancare di ♦ *n* (*poverty*) miseria, povertà; ~**s** *npl* (*needs*) bisogni *mpl*; **for** ~ **of** per mancanza di; **to** ~ **to do** volere fare; **to** ~ **sb to do** volere che qn faccia; **you're** ~**ed on the phone** la vogliono al telefono; "**cook** ~**ed**" "cercasi cuoco".
want ads *npl* (*US*) piccoli annunci *mpl*.
wanting ['wɔntɪŋ] *adj*: **to be** ~ (**in**) mancare (di); **to be found** ~ non risultare all'altezza.
wanton ['wɔntn] *adj* sfrenato(a); senza motivo.
war [wɔː*] *n* guerra; **to go to** ~ entrare in guerra.
warble ['wɔːbl] *n* (*of bird*) trillo ♦ *vi* trillare.
war cry *n* grido di guerra.
ward [wɔːd] *n* (*in hospital*: *room*) corsia; (: *section*) reparto; (*POL*) circoscrizione *f*; (*LAW*: *child*) pupillo/a.
►**ward off** *vt* parare, schivare.
warden ['wɔːdn] *n* (*of institution*) direttore/ trice; (*of park, game reserve*) guardiano/a; (*BRIT*: *also*: **traffic** ~) addetto/a al controllo del traffico e del parcheggio.
warder ['wɔːdə*] *n* (*BRIT*) guardia carceraria.
wardrobe ['wɔːdrəub] *n* (*cupboard*) guardaroba *m inv*, armadio; (*clothes*) guardaroba; (*THEAT*) costumi *mpl*.
warehouse ['wɛəhaus] *n* magazzino.
wares [wɛəz] *npl* merci *fpl*.
warfare ['wɔːfɛə*] *n* guerra.
war game *n* war game *m inv*.
warhead ['wɔːhɛd] *n* (*MIL*) testata, ogiva.

warily ['wɛərɪlɪ] *adv* cautamente, con prudenza.
warlike ['wɔːlaɪk] *adj* guerriero(a).
warm [wɔːm] *adj* caldo(a); (*welcome, applause*) caloroso(a); (*person, greeting*) cordiale; (*heart*) d'oro; (*supporter*) convinto(a); **it's** ~ fa caldo; **I'm** ~ ho caldo; **to keep sth** ~ tenere qc al caldo; **with my** ~**est thanks** con i miei più sentiti ringraziamenti.
►**warm up** *vi* scaldarsi, riscaldarsi; (*athlete, discussion*) riscaldarsi ♦ *vt* scaldare, riscaldare; (*engine*) far scaldare.
warm-blooded ['wɔːm'blʌdɪd] *adj* a sangue caldo.
war memorial *n* monumento ai caduti.
warm-hearted [wɔːm'hɑːtɪd] *adj* affettuoso(a).
warmly ['wɔːmlɪ] *adv* caldamente; calorosamente; vivamente.
warmonger ['wɔːmʌŋgə*] *n* guerrafondaio.
warmongering ['wɔːmʌŋgrɪŋ] *n* bellicismo.
warmth [wɔːmθ] *n* calore *m*.
warm-up ['wɔːmʌp] *n* (*SPORT*) riscaldamento.
warn [wɔːn] *vt* avvertire, avvisare; **to** ~ **sb not to do sth** *or* **against doing sth** avvertire qn di non fare qc.
warning ['wɔːnɪŋ] *n* avvertimento; (*notice*) avviso; **without** (**any**) ~ senza preavviso; **gale** ~ avviso di burrasca.
warning light *n* spia luminosa.
warning triangle *n* (*AUT*) triangolo.
warp [wɔːp] *n* (*TEXTILES*) ordito ♦ *vi* deformarsi ♦ *vt* deformare; (*fig*) corrompere.
warpath ['wɔːpɑːθ] *n*: **to be on the** ~ (*fig*) essere sul sentiero di guerra.
warped [wɔːpt] *adj* (*wood*) curvo(a); (*fig*: *character, sense of humour etc*) contorto(a).
warrant ['wɔrnt] *n* (*LAW*: *to arrest*) mandato di cattura; (: *to search*) mandato di perquisizione ♦ *vt* (*justify, merit*) giustificare.
warrant officer (**WO**) *n* sottufficiale *m*.
warranty ['wɔrəntɪ] *n* garanzia; **under** ~ (*COMM*) in garanzia.
warren ['wɔrən] *n* (*of rabbits*) tana.
warring ['wɔːrɪŋ] *adj* (*interests etc*) opposto(a), in lotta; (*nations*) in guerra.
warrior ['wɔrɪə*] *n* guerriero/a.
Warsaw ['wɔːsɔː] *n* Varsavia.
warship ['wɔːʃɪp] *n* nave *f* da guerra.
wart [wɔːt] *n* verruca.
wartime ['wɔːtaɪm] *n*: **in** ~ in tempo di guerra.

wary ['wεərɪ] *adj* prudente; **to be ~ about** *or* **of doing sth** andare cauto nel fare qc.

was [wɔz] *pt of* **be.**

wash [wɔʃ] *vt* lavare; (*sweep, carry: sea etc*) portare, trascinare ♦ *vi* lavarsi ♦ *n*: **to give sth a ~** lavare qc, dare una lavata a qc; **to have a ~** lavarsi; **he was ~ed overboard** fu trascinato in mare (dalle onde).

▶**wash away** *vt* (*stain*) togliere lavando; (*subj: river etc*) trascinare via.

▶**wash down** *vt* lavare.

▶**wash off** *vi* andare via con il lavaggio.

▶**wash up** *vi* lavare i piatti; (*US: have a wash*) lavarsi.

Wash. *abbr* (*US*) = *Washington.*

washable ['wɔʃəbl] *adj* lavabile.

washbasin ['wɔʃbeɪsn] *n* lavabo.

washcloth ['wɔʃklɔθ] *n* (*US*) pezzuola (per lavarsi).

washer ['wɔʃə*] *n* (*TECH*) rondella.

washing ['wɔʃɪŋ] *n* (*BRIT: linen etc*) bucato; **dirty ~** biancheria da lavare.

washing line *n* (*BRIT*) corda del bucato.

washing machine *n* lavatrice *f.*

washing powder *n* (*BRIT*) detersivo (in polvere).

Washington ['wɔʃɪŋtən] *n* Washington *f.*

washing-up [wɔʃɪŋ'ʌp] *n* (*dishes*) piatti *mpl* sporchi; **to do the ~** lavare i piatti, rigovernare.

washing-up liquid *n* (*BRIT*) detersivo liquido (per stoviglie).

wash-out ['wɔʃaut] *n* (*col*) disastro.

washroom ['wɔʃrum] *n* gabinetto.

wasn't ['wɔznt] = **was not.**

Wasp, WASP [wɔsp] *n abbr* (*US*: = *White Anglo-Saxon Protestant*) W.A.S.P. *m* (*protestante bianco anglosassone*).

wasp [wɔsp] *n* vespa.

waspish ['wɔspɪʃ] *adj* litigioso(a).

wastage ['weɪstɪdʒ] *n* spreco; (*in manufacturing*) scarti *mpl.*

waste [weɪst] *n* spreco; (*of time*) perdita; (*rubbish*) rifiuti *mpl* ♦ *adj* (*material*) di scarto; (*food*) avanzato(a); (*energy, heat*) sprecato(a); (*land, ground: in city*) abbandonato(a); (: *in country*) incolto(a) ♦ *vt* sprecare; (*time, opportunity*) perdere; **~s** *npl* distesa desolata; **it's a ~ of money** sono soldi sprecati; **to go to ~** andare sprecato; **to lay ~** devastare.

▶**waste away** *vi* deperire.

wastebasket ['weɪstbɑːskɪt] *n* = **wastepaper basket.**

waste disposal (unit) *n* (*BRIT*) eliminatore *m* di rifiuti.

wasteful ['weɪstful] *adj* sprecone(a);

(*process*) dispendioso(a).

waste ground *n* (*BRIT*) terreno incolto *or* abbandonato.

wasteland ['weɪstlænd] *n* terra desolata.

wastepaper basket ['weɪstpeɪpə-] *n* cestino per la carta straccia.

waste pipe *n* tubo di scarico.

waste products *npl* (*INDUSTRY*) materiali *mpl* di scarto.

waster ['weɪstə*] *n* (*col*) buono/a a nulla.

watch [wɔtʃ] *n* (*wrist~*) orologio; (*act of watching*) sorveglianza; (*guard: MIL, NAUT*) guardia; (*NAUT: spell of duty*) quarto ♦ *vt* (*look at*) osservare; (: *match, programme*) guardare; (*spy on, guard*) sorvegliare, tenere d'occhio; (*be careful of*) fare attenzione a ♦ *vi* osservare, guardare; (*keep guard*) fare *or* montare la guardia; **to keep a close ~ on sb/sth** tener bene d'occhio qn/qc; **~ how you drive/what you're doing** attento a come guidi/quel che fai.

▶**watch out** *vi* fare attenzione.

watchband ['wɔtʃbænd] *n* (*US*) cinturino da orologio.

watchdog ['wɔtʃdɔg] *n* cane *m* da guardia; (*fig*) sorvegliante *m/f.*

watchful ['wɔtʃful] *adj* attento(a), vigile.

watchmaker ['wɔtʃmeɪkə*] *n* orologiaio/a.

watchman ['wɔtʃmən] *n* guardiano; (*also: night ~*) guardiano notturno.

watch stem *n* (*US*) corona di carica.

watch strap *n* cinturino da orologio.

watchword ['wɔtʃwɔːd] *n* parola d'ordine.

water [wɔːtə*] *n* acqua ♦ *vt* (*plant*) annaffiare ♦ *vi* (*eyes*) piangere; **in British ~s** nelle acque territoriali britanniche; **I'd like a drink of ~** vorrei un bicchier d'acqua; **to pass ~** orinare; **to make sb's mouth ~** far venire l'acquolina in bocca a qn.

▶**water down** *vt* (*milk*) diluire; (*fig: story*) edulcorare.

water closet *n* (*BRIT*) W.C. *m inv*, gabinetto.

watercolour, (*US***) watercolor** ['wɔːtəkʌlə*] *n* (*picture*) acquerello; **~s** *npl* colori *mpl* per acquerelli.

water-cooled ['wɔːtəkuːld] *adj* raffreddato(a) ad acqua.

watercress ['wɔːtəkrεs] *n* crescione *m.*

waterfall ['wɔːtəfɔːl] *n* cascata.

waterfront ['wɔːtəfrʌnt] *n* (*seafront*) lungomare *m*; (*at docks*) banchina.

water heater *n* scaldabagno.

water hole *n* pozza d'acqua.

water ice *n* (*BRIT*) sorbetto.

watering can ['wɔːtərɪŋ-] *n* annaffiatoio.

water level *n* livello dell'acqua; (*of flood*)

livello delle acque.
water lily n ninfea.
waterline ['wɔ:təlaɪn] n (NAUT) linea di
galleggiamento.
waterlogged ['wɔ:tələgd] adj saturo(a)
d'acqua; imbevuto(a) d'acqua; (football
pitch etc) allagato(a).
watermark ['wɔ:təmɑ:k] n (on paper)
filigrana.
watermelon ['wɔ:təmɛlən] n anguria,
cocomero.
water polo n pallanuoto f.
waterproof ['wɔ:təpru:f] adj impermeabile.
water-repellent ['wɔ:tərɪ'pɛlənt] adj
idrorepellente.
watershed ['wɔ:təʃɛd] n (GEO, fig)
spartiacque m.
water-skiing ['wɔ:təski:ɪŋ] n sci m
acquatico.
water softener n addolcitore m;
(substance) anti-calcare m.
water tank n serbatoio d'acqua.
watertight ['wɔ:tətaɪt] adj stagno(a).
water vapour n vapore m acqueo.
waterway ['wɔ:təweɪ] n corso d'acqua
navigabile.
waterworks ['wɔ:təwə:ks] npl impianto
idrico.
watery ['wɔ:tərɪ] adj (colour) slavato(a);
(coffee) acquoso(a).
watt [wɔt] n watt m inv.
wattage ['wɔtɪdʒ] n wattaggio.
wattle ['wɔtl] n graticcio.
wave [weɪv] n onda; (of hand) gesto, segno;
(in hair) ondulazione f; (fig: of enthusiasm,
strikes etc) ondata ♦ vi fare un cenno con
la mano; (flag) sventolare ♦ vt
(handkerchief) sventolare; (stick) brandire;
(hair) ondulare; **short/medium/long** ~
(RADIO) onde corte/medie/lunghe; **the
new** ~ (CINE, MUS) la new wave; **to** ~ **sb
goodbye, to** ~ **goodbye to sb** fare un
cenno d'addio a qn; **he** ~**d us over to his
table** ci invitò con un cenno al suo tavolo.
▶**wave aside, wave away** vt (person): **to**
~ **sb aside** fare cenno a qn di spostarsi;
(fig: suggestion, objection) respingere,
rifiutare; (: doubts) scacciare.
waveband ['weɪvbænd] n gamma di
lunghezze d'onda.
wavelength ['weɪvlɛŋθ] n lunghezza
d'onda.
waver ['weɪvə*] vi vacillare; (voice)
tremolare.
wavy ['weɪvɪ] adj ondulato(a); ondeggiante.
wax [wæks] n cera ♦ vt dare la cera a; (car)
lucidare ♦ vi (moon) crescere.
waxworks ['wækswə:ks] npl cere fpl; museo

delle cere.
way [weɪ] n via, strada; (path, access)
passaggio; (distance) distanza; (direction)
parte f, direzione f; (manner) modo, stile
m; (habit) abitudine f; (condition)
condizione f; **which** ~? — **this** ~ da che
parte or in quale direzione? — da questa
parte or per di qua; **to crawl one's** ~ **to** ...
raggiungere ... strisciando; **he lied his** ~
out of it se l'è cavata mentendo; **to lose
one's** ~ perdere la strada; **on the** ~ (en
route) per strada; (expected) in arrivo;
you pass it on your ~ **home** ci passi
davanti andando a casa; **to be on one's** ~
essere in cammino or sulla strada; **to be
in the** ~ bloccare il passaggio; (fig)
essere tra i piedi or d'impiccio; **to keep
out of sb's** ~ evitare qn; **it's a long** ~
away è molto lontano da qui; **the village
is rather out of the** ~ il villaggio è
abbastanza fuori mano; **to go out of one's
** ~ **to do** (fig) mettercela tutta or fare di
tutto per fare; **to be under** ~ (work,
project) essere in corso; **to make** ~ (for
sb/sth) far strada (a qn/qc); (fig) lasciare
il posto or far largo (a qn/qc); **to get
one's own** ~ fare come si vuole; **put it
the right** ~ **up** (BRIT) mettilo in piedi dalla
parte giusta; **to be the wrong** ~ **round**
essere al contrario; **he's in a bad** ~ è
ridotto male; **in a** ~ in un certo senso; **in
some** ~s sotto certi aspetti; **in the** ~ of
come; **by** ~ of (through) attraverso; (as a
sort of) come; "~ **in**" "entrata",
"ingresso"; "~ **out**" "uscita"; **the** ~ **back**
la via del ritorno; **this** ~ **and that** di qua e
di là; "**give** ~" (BRIT AUT) "dare la
precedenza"; **no** ~! (col) assolutamente
no!
waybill ['weɪbɪl] n (COMM) bolla di
accompagnamento.
waylay [weɪ'leɪ] vt irreg tendere un agguato
a; attendere al passaggio; (fig): **I got
waylaid** ho avuto un contrattempo.
wayside ['weɪsaɪd] n bordo della strada; **to
fall by the** ~ (fig) perdersi lungo la
strada.
way station n (US RAIL) stazione f
secondaria; (fig) tappa.
wayward ['weɪwəd] adj capriccioso(a);
testardo(a).
WC n abbr (BRIT: = water closet) W.C. m inv,
gabinetto.
WCC n abbr (= World Council of Churches)
Consiglio Ecumenico delle Chiese.
we [wi:] pl pron noi; **here** ~ are eccoci.
weak [wi:k] adj debole; (health) precario(a);
(beam etc) fragile; (tea, coffee) leggero(a);

to grow ~(er) indebolirsi.
weaken['wi:kən] *vi* indebolirsi ♦ *vt* indebolire.
weak-kneed['wi:k'ni:d] *adj* (*fig*) debole, codardo(a).
weakling['wi:klɪŋ] *n* smidollato/a; debole *m/f*.
weakly['wi:klɪ] *adj* deboluccio(a), gracile ♦ *adv* debolmente.
weakness['wi:knɪs] *n* debolezza; (*fault*) punto debole, difetto.
wealth[wɛlθ] *n* (*money, resources*) ricchezza, ricchezze *fpl*; (*of details*) abbondanza, profusione *f*.
wealthy['wɛlθɪ] *adj* ricco(a).
wean[wi:n] *vt* svezzare.
weapon['wɛpən] *n* arma; **~s of mass destruction** armi di distruzione di massa.
wear[wɛə*] *n* (*use*) uso; (*deterioration through use*) logorio, usura; (*clothing*): **sports/baby ~** abbigliamento sportivo/ per neonati ♦ *vb* (*pt* **wore,** *pp* **worn** [wɔ:*, wɔ:n]) *vt* (*clothes*) portare; mettersi; (*look, smile, beard etc*) avere; (*damage: through use*) consumare ♦ *vi* (*last*) durare; (*rub etc through*) consumarsi; **~ and tear** usura, consumo; **town/evening ~** abiti *mpl or* tenuta da città/sera; **to ~ a hole in sth** bucare qc a furia di usarlo.
▶**wear away** *vt* consumare; erodere ♦ *vi* consumarsi; essere eroso(a).
▶**wear down** *vt* consumare; (*strength*) esaurire.
▶**wear off** *vi* sparire lentamente.
▶**wear on** *vi* passare.
▶**wear out** *vt* consumare; (*person, strength*) esaurire.
wearable['wɛərəbl] *adj* indossabile.
wearily['wɪərɪlɪ] *adv* stancamente.
weariness['wɪərɪnɪs] *n* stanchezza.
wearisome['wɪərɪsəm] *adj* (*tiring*) estenuante; (*boring*) noioso(a).
weary['wɪərɪ] *adj* stanco(a); (*tiring*) faticoso(a) ♦ *vt* stancare ♦ *vi*: **to ~ of** stancarsi di.
weasel['wi:zl] *n* (*ZOOL*) donnola.
weather['wɛðə*] *n* tempo ♦ *vt* (*wood*) stagionare; (*storm, crisis*) superare; **what's the ~ like?** che tempo fa?; **under the ~** (*fig: ill*) poco bene.
weather-beaten['wɛðəbi:tn] *adj* (*person*) segnato(a) dalle intemperie; (*building*) logorato(a) dalle intemperie.
weather forecast *n* previsioni *fpl* del tempo, bollettino meteorologico.
weatherman['wɛðəmæn] *n* meteorologo.
weatherproof['wɛðəpru:f] *adj* (*garment*) impermeabile.

weather report *n* bollettino meteorologico.
weather vane *n* = **weather cock.**
weave, *pt* **wove,** *pp* **woven** [wi:v, wəuv, 'wəuvn] *vt* (*cloth*) tessere; (*basket*) intrecciare ♦ *vi* (*fig: pt, pp* **~d:** *move in and out*) zigzagare.
weaver['wi:və*] *n* tessitore/trice.
weaving['wi:vɪŋ] *n* tessitura.
web[wɛb] *n* (*of spider*) ragnatela; (*on foot*) palma; (*fabric, also fig*) tessuto; **the (World Wide) W~** la Rete.
webbed[wɛbd] *adj* (*foot*) palmato(a).
webbing['wɛbɪŋ] *n* (*on chair*) cinghie *fpl*.
web page *n* (*COMPUT*) pagina *f* web *inv*.
website['wɛbsaɪt] *n* (*COMPUT*) sito.
wed[wɛd] *vt* (*pt, pp* **wedded**) sposare ♦ *n*: **the newly-~s** gli sposi novelli.
Wed. *abbr* (= *Wednesday*) mer.
we'd[wi:d] = **we had; we would.**
wedded['wɛdɪd] *pt, pp of* **wed.**
wedding['wɛdɪŋ] *n* matrimonio; **silver/ golden ~** nozze *fpl* d'argento/d'oro.
wedding anniversary *n* anniversario di matrimonio.
wedding day *n* giorno delle nozze *or* del matrimonio.
wedding dress *n* abito nuziale.
wedding present *n* regalo di nozze.
wedding ring *n* fede *f*.
wedge[wɛdʒ] *n* (*of wood etc*) cuneo; (*under door etc*) zeppa; (*of cake*) spicchio, fetta ♦ *vt* mettere una zeppa sotto (*or* in); **to ~ a door open** tenere aperta una porta con un fermo.
wedge-heeled shoes['wɛdʒhi:ld-] *npl* scarpe *fpl* con tacco a zeppa.
wedlock['wɛdlɔk] *n* vincolo matrimoniale.
Wednesday['wɛdnzdɪ] *n* mercoledì *m inv*; *for phrases see also* **Tuesday.**
wee[wi:] *adj* (*Scottish*) piccolo(a).
weed[wi:d] *n* erbaccia ♦ *vt* diserbare.
▶**weed out** *vt* fare lo spoglio di.
weed-killer['wi:dkɪlə*] *n* diserbante *m*.
weedy['wi:dɪ] *adj* (*man*) allampanato.
week[wi:k] *n* settimana; **once/twice a ~** una volta/due volte alla settimana; **in 2 ~s' time** fra 2 settimane, fra 15 giorni; **Tuesday ~, a ~ on Tuesday** martedì a otto.
weekday['wi:kdeɪ] *n* giorno feriale; (*COMM*) giornata lavorativa; **on ~s** durante la settimana.
weekend[wi:k'ɛnd] *n* fine settimana *m or f inv*, weekend *m inv*.
weekly['wi:klɪ] *adv* ogni settimana, settimanalmente ♦ *adj, n* settimanale (*m*).
weep, *pt, pp* **wept** [wi:p, wɛpt] *vi* (*person*)

piangere; (*MED*: *wound etc*) essudare.
weeping willow ['wi:pɪŋ-] *n* salice *m*
piangente.
weepy ['wi:pɪ] *n* (*col*) film *m* *inv* or storia
strappalacrime.
weigh [weɪ] *vt*, *vi* pesare; **to ~ anchor**
salpare *or* levare l'ancora; **to ~ the pros
and cons** valutare i pro e i contro.
►**weigh down** *vt* (*branch*) piegare; (*fig*:
with worry) opprimere, caricare.
►**weigh out** *vt* (*goods*) pesare.
►**weigh up** *vt* valutare.
weighbridge ['weɪbrɪdʒ] *n* bascula.
weighing machine ['weɪŋ-] *n* pesa.
weight [weɪt] *n* peso; **sold by ~** venduto(a)
a peso; **~s and measures** pesi e misure;
to put on/lose ~ ingrassare/dimagrire.
weighting ['weɪtɪŋ] *n*: **~ allowance**
indennità *f inv* speciale (*per carovita etc*).
weightlessness ['weɪtlɪsnɪs] *n* mancanza
di peso.
weightlifter ['weɪtlɪftə*] *n* pesista *m*.
weight training *n*: **to do ~** allenarsi con i
pesi.
weighty ['weɪtɪ] *adj* pesante; (*fig*)
importante, grave.
weir [wɪə*] *n* diga.
weird [wɪəd] *adj* strano(a), bizzarro(a);
(*eerie*) soprannaturale.
weirdo ['wɪədəu] *n* (*col*) tipo/a allucinante.
welcome ['welkəm] *adj* benvenuto(a) ♦ *n*
accoglienza, benvenuto ♦ *vt* accogliere
cordialmente; (*also*: **bid ~**) dare il
benvenuto a; (*be glad of*) rallegrarsi di; **to
be ~** essere il(la) benvenuto(a); **to make
sb ~** accogliere bene qn; **you're ~** (*after
thanks*) prego; **you're ~ to try** provi pure.
welcoming ['welkəmɪŋ] *adj* accogliente.
weld [weld] *n* saldatura ♦ *vt* saldare.
welder ['weldə*] *n* (*person*) saldatore *m*.
welding ['weldɪŋ] *n* saldatura (autogena).
welfare ['welfɛə*] *n* benessere *m*.
welfare state *n* stato sociale.
welfare work *n* assistenza sociale.
well [wel] *n* pozzo ♦ *adv* bene ♦ *adj*: **to be ~**
(*person*) stare bene ♦ *excl* allora!; ma!;
ebbene!; **~ done!** bravo(a)!; **get ~ soon!**
guarisci presto!; **to do ~ in sth** riuscire
in qc; **to be doing ~** stare bene; **to think
~ of sb** avere una buona opinione di qn; **I
don't feel ~** non mi sento bene; **as ~** (*in
addition*) anche; **X as ~ as Y** sia X che Y;
he did as ~ as he could ha fatto come
meglio poteva; **you might as ~ tell me**
potresti anche dirmelo; **it would be as ~
to ask** sarebbe bene chiedere; **~, as I was
saying** ... dunque, come stavo dicendo ....
►**well up** *vi* (*tears, emotions*) sgorgare.

we'll [wi:l] = **we will**; **we shall.**
well-behaved ['welbɪ'heɪvd] *adj* ubbidiente.
well-being ['wel'bi:ɪŋ] *n* benessere *m*.
well-bred ['wel'bred] *adj* educato(a),
beneducato(a).
well-built ['wel'bɪlt] *adj* (*person*) ben
fatto(a).
well-chosen ['wel'tʃəuzn] *adj* (*remarks,
words*) ben scelto(a), appropriato(a).
well-developed ['weldɪ'veləpt] *adj*
sviluppato(a).
well-disposed ['weldɪs'pəuzd] *adj*: **~
to(wards)** bendisposto(a) verso.
well-dressed ['wel'drest] *adj* ben vestito(a),
vestito(a) bene.
well-earned ['wel'ɜ:nd] *adj* (*rest*)
meritato(a).
well-groomed ['wel'gru:md] *adj* curato(a),
azzimato(a).
well-heeled ['wel'hi:ld] *adj* (*col*: *wealthy*)
agiato(a), facoltoso(a).
well-informed ['welɪn'fɔ:md] *adj* ben
informato(a).
Wellington ['welɪŋtən] *n* Wellington *f*.
wellingtons ['welɪŋtənz] *npl* (*also*:
wellington boots) stivali *mpl* di gomma.
well-kept ['wel'kept] *adj* (*house, grounds,
secret*) ben tenuto(a); (*hair, hands*) ben
curato(a).
well-known ['wel'nəun] *adj* noto(a),
famoso(a).
well-mannered ['wel'mænəd] *adj* ben
educato(a).
well-meaning ['wel'mi:nɪŋ] *adj* ben
intenzionato(a).
well-nigh ['wel'naɪ] *adv*: **~ impossible** quasi
impossibile.
well-off ['wel'ɔf] *adj* benestante,
danaroso(a).
well-read ['wel'red] *adj* colto(a).
well-spoken ['wel'spəukn] *adj* che parla
bene.
well-stocked ['wel'stɔkt] *adj* (*shop, larder*)
ben fornito(a).
well-timed ['wel'taɪmd] *adj* opportuno(a).
well-to-do ['weltə'du:] *adj* abbiente,
benestante.
well-wisher ['welwɪʃə*] *n* ammiratore/
trice; **letters from ~s** lettere *fpl* di
incoraggiamento.
well-woman clinic ['welwumən-] *n* ≈
consultorio (familiare).
Welsh [welʃ] *adj* gallese ♦ *n* (*LING*) gallese
m; **the ~** *npl* i gallesi; **the ~ National
Assembly** il Parlamento gallese.
Welshman, Welshwoman ['welʃmən,
-wumən] *n* gallese *m/f*.
Welsh rarebit *n* crostino al formaggio.

welter ['wɛltə*] *n* massa, mucchio.
went [wɛnt] *pt of* **go.**
wept [wɛpt] *pt, pp of* **weep.**
were [wəː*] *pt of* **be.**
we're [wɪə*] = **we are.**
weren't [wəːnt] = **were not.**
werewolf, *pl* **-wolves** ['wɪəwulf, -wulvz] *n* licantropo, lupo mannaro (*col*).
west [wɛst] *n* ovest *m*, occidente *m*, ponente *m* ♦ *adj* (a) ovest *inv*, occidentale ♦ *adv* verso ovest; **the W~** l'Occidente.
westbound ['wɛstbaund] *adj* (*traffic*) diretto(a) a ovest; (*carriageway*) ovest *inv*.
West Country *n*: **the ~** il sud-ovest dell'Inghilterra.
westerly ['wɛstəlɪ] *adj* (*wind*) occidentale, da ovest.
western ['wɛstən] *adj* occidentale, dell'ovest ♦ *n* (*CINE*) western *m inv*.
westerner ['wɛstənə*] *n* occidentale *m/f*.
westernized ['wɛstənaɪzd] *adj* occidentalizzato(a).
West German *adj, n* tedesco(a) occidentale.
West Germany *n* Germania Occidentale.
West Indian *adj* delle Indie Occidentali ♦ *n* abitante *m/f* (*or* originario/a) delle Indie Occidentali.
West Indies [-'ɪndɪz] *npl*: **the ~** le Indie Occidentali.
Westminster ['wɛstmɪnstə*] *n* il parlamento (britannico).
westward(s) ['wɛstwəd(z)] *adv* verso ovest.
wet [wɛt] *adj* umido(a), bagnato(a); (*soaked*) fradicio(a); (*rainy*) piovoso(a) ♦ *vt*: **to ~ one's pants** *or* **o.s.** farsi la pipì addosso; **to get ~** bagnarsi; **"~ paint"** "vernice fresca".
wet blanket *n* (*fig*) guastafeste *m/f inv*.
wetness ['wɛtnɪs] *n* umidità.
wet suit *n* tuta da sub.
we've [wiːv] = **we have.**
whack [wæk] *vt* picchiare, battere.
whacked [wækt] *adj* (*col*: *tired*) sfinito(a), a pezzi.
whale [weɪl] *n* (*ZOOL*) balena.
whaler ['weɪlə*] *n* (*ship*) baleniera.
whaling ['weɪlɪŋ] *n* caccia alla balena.
wharf, *pl* **wharves** [wɔːf, wɔːvz] *n* banchina.

KEYWORD

what [wɔt] *adj* **1** (*in direct/indirect questions*) che; quale; **~ size is it?** che taglia è?; **~ colour is it?** di che colore è?; **~ books do you want?** quali *or* che libri vuole?; **for ~ reason?** per quale motivo?
2 (*in exclamations*) che; **~ a mess!** che disordine!
♦ *pron* **1** (*interrogative*) che cosa, cosa, che; **~'s in there?** cosa c'è lì dentro?; **~ is his address?** qual è il suo indirizzo?; **~ will it cost?** quanto costerà?; **~ are you doing?** che *or* (che) cosa fai?; **~ are you talking about?** di che cosa parli?; **~'s happening?** che *or* (che) cosa succede?; **~ is it called?** come si chiama?; **~ about me?** e io?; **~ about doing ...?** e se facessimo ...?
2 (*relative*) ciò che, quello che; **I saw ~ you did** ho visto quello che hai fatto; **I saw ~ was on the table** ho visto cosa c'era sul tavolo; **~ I want is a cup of tea** ciò che voglio adesso è una tazza di tè
3 (*indirect use*) (che) cosa; **he asked me ~ she had said** mi ha chiesto che cosa avesse detto; **tell me ~ you're thinking about** dimmi a cosa stai pensando; **I don't know ~ to do** non so cosa fare
♦ *excl* (*disbelieving*) cosa!, come!

whatever [wɔt'ɛvə*] *adj*: **~ book** qualunque *or* qualsiasi libro + *sub* ♦ *pron*: **do ~ is necessary/you want** faccia qualunque *or* qualsiasi cosa sia necessaria/lei voglia; **~ happens** qualunque cosa accada; **no reason ~** *or* **whatsoever** nessuna ragione affatto *or* al mondo; **~ it costs** costi quello che costi.
whatsoever [wɔtsəu'ɛvə*] *adj, pron* = **whatever.**
wheat [wiːt] *n* grano, frumento.
wheatgerm ['wiːtdʒəːm] *n* germe *m* di grano.
wheatmeal ['wiːtmiːl] *n* farina integrale di frumento.
wheedle ['wiːdl] *vt*: **to ~ sb into doing sth** convincere qn a fare qc (con lusinghe); **to ~ sth out of sb** ottenere qc da qn (con lusinghe).
wheel [wiːl] *n* ruota; (*AUT*: *also*: **steering ~**) volante *m*; (*NAUT*) (ruota del) timone *m* ♦ *vt* spingere ♦ *vi* (*also*: **~ round**) girare.
wheelbarrow ['wiːlbærəu] *n* carriola.
wheelbase ['wiːlbeɪs] *n* interasse *m*.
wheelchair ['wiːltʃɛə*] *n* sedia a rotelle.
wheel clamp *n* (*AUT*) morsetto *m* bloccaruota *inv*.
wheeler-dealer ['wiːlə'diːlə*] *n* trafficone *m*, maneggione *m*.
wheelie-bin ['wiːlɪbɪn] *n* (*BRIT*) bidone *m* (della spazzatura) a rotelle.
wheeling ['wiːlɪŋ] *n*: **~ and dealing** maneggi *mpl*.
wheeze [wiːz] *n* respiro affannoso ♦ *vi*

ansimare.
wheezy ['wi:zɪ] adj (person) che respira
con affanno; (breath) sibilante.

========================= KEYWORD

when [wɛn] adv quando; ~ **did it happen?**
quando è successo?

♦ conj **1** (at, during, after the time that)
quando; **she was reading** ~ **I came in**
quando sono entrato lei leggeva; **that
was** ~ **I needed you** era allora che avevo
bisogno di te
2 (on, at which): **on the day** ~ **I met him** il
giorno in cui l'ho incontrato; **one day** ~ **it
was raining** un giorno che pioveva
3 (whereas) quando, mentre; **you said I
was wrong** ~ **in fact I was right** mi hai
detto che avevo torto, quando in realtà
avevo ragione.

whenever [wɛn'ɛvə*] adv quando mai ♦ conj
quando; (every time that) ogni volta che; **I
go** ~ **I can** ci vado ogni volta che posso.
where [wɛə*] adv, conj dove; **this is** ~ è qui
che; ~ **are you from?** di dov'è?; ~
possible quando è possibile, se possibile.
whereabouts ['wɛərəbauts] adv dove ♦ n:
sb's ~ luogo dove qn si trova.
whereas [wɛər'æz] conj mentre.
whereby [wɛə'baɪ] adv (formal) per cui.
whereupon [wɛərə'pɒn] adv al che.
wherever [wɛər'ɛvə*] adv dove mai ♦ conj
dovunque + sub; **sit** ~ **you like** si sieda
dove vuole.
wherewithal ['wɛəwɪðɔːl] n: **the** ~ **(to do
sth)** i mezzi (per fare qc).
whet [wɛt] vt (appetite etc) stimolare.
whether ['wɛðə*] conj se; **I don't know** ~ **to
accept or not** non so se accettare o no;
it's doubtful ~ è poco probabile che; ~
you go or not che lei vada o no.
whey [weɪ] n siero.

========================= KEYWORD

which [wɪtʃ] adj **1** (interrogative: direct,
indirect) quale; ~ **picture do you want?**
quale quadro vuole?; ~ **one?** quale?; ~
one of you did it? chi di voi lo ha fatto?
2: **in** ~ **case** nel qual caso; **by** ~ **time** e a
quel punto
♦ pron **1** (interrogative) quale; ~ **(of these)
are yours?** quali di questi sono suoi?; ~ **of
you are coming?** chi di voi viene?
2 (relative) che; (: indirect) cui, il (la)
quale; **the apple** ~ **you ate/**~ **is on the
table** la mela che hai mangiato/che è sul
tavolo; **the chair on** ~ **you are sitting** la
sedia sulla quale or su cui sei seduto; **the

book of ~ **we were speaking** il libro del
quale stavamo parlando; **he said he
knew,** ~ **is true** ha detto che lo sapeva, il
che è vero; **I don't mind** ~ non mi
importa quale; **after** ~ dopo di che.

whichever [wɪtʃ'ɛvə*] adj: **take** ~ **book you
prefer** prenda qualsiasi libro che
preferisce; ~ **book you take** qualsiasi
libro prenda; ~ **way you** ... in qualunque
modo lei ... + sub.
whiff [wɪf] n odore m; **to catch a** ~ **of sth**
sentire l'odore di qc.
while [waɪl] n momento ♦ conj mentre; (as
long as) finché; (although) sebbene + sub;
for a ~ per un po'; **in a** ~ tra poco, all the
~ tutto il tempo; **we'll make it worth your
~** faremo in modo che le valga la pena.
►**while away** vt (time) far passare.
whilst [waɪlst] conj = **while**.
whim [wɪm] n capriccio.
whimper ['wɪmpə*] n piagnucolìo ♦ vi
piagnucolare.
whimsical ['wɪmzɪkl] adj (person)
capriccioso(a); (look) strano(a).
whine [waɪn] n gemito ♦ vi gemere;
uggiolare; piagnucolare.
whip [wɪp] n frusta; (for riding) frustino;
(POL: person) capogruppo ♦ vt frustare;
(CULIN: cream etc) sbattere; (snatch)
sollevare (or estrarre) bruscamente; see
boxed note.
►**whip up** vt (cream) montare, sbattere;
(col: meal) improvvisare; (: stir up: support,
feeling) suscitare, stimolare.

┌─────────────────────────────────────┐
│ **WHIP**   │
│   │
│ Nel Parlamento britannico i **whips** sono │
│ parlamentari incaricati di mantenere la │
│ disciplina tra i deputati del loro partito durante │
│ le votazioni e di verificare la loro presenza in │
│ aula.   │
└─────────────────────────────────────┘

whiplash ['wɪplæʃ] n (MED: also: ~ **injury**)
colpo di frusta.
whipped cream ['wɪpt-] n panna montata.
whipping boy ['wɪpɪŋ-] n (fig) capro
espiatorio.
whip-round ['wɪpraund] n (BRIT) colletta.
whirl [wəːl] n turbine m ♦ vt (far) girare
rapidamente; (far) turbinare ♦ vi
turbinare; (dancers) volteggiare; (leaves,
dust) sollevarsi in un vortice.
whirlpool ['wəːlpuːl] n mulinello.
whirlwind ['wəːlwɪnd] n turbine m.
whirr [wəː*] vi ronzare.
whisk [wɪsk] n (CULIN) frusta; frullino ♦ vt

sbattere, frullare; **to ~ sb away** *or* **off** portar via qn a tutta velocità.
whiskers ['wɪskəz] *npl* (*of animal*) baffi *mpl*; (*of man*) favoriti *mpl*.
whisky, (*Irish, US*) **whiskey** ['wɪskɪ] *n* whisky *m inv*.
whisper ['wɪspə*] *n* bisbiglio, sussurro; (*rumour*) voce *f* ♦ *vt, vi* bisbigliare, sussurrare; **to ~ sth to sb** bisbigliare qc a qn.
whispering ['wɪspərɪŋ] *n* bisbiglio.
whist [wɪst] *n* (*BRIT*) whist *m*.
whistle ['wɪsl] *n* (*sound*) fischio; (*object*) fischietto ♦ *vi, vt* fischiare; **to ~ a tune** fischiettare un motivetto.
whistle-stop ['wɪslstɔp] *adj*: **~ tour** (*POL, fig*) rapido giro.
Whit [wɪt] *n* Pentecoste *f*.
white [waɪt] *adj* bianco(a); (*with fear*) pallido(a) ♦ *n* bianco; (*person*) bianco/a; **to turn** *or* **go ~** (*person*) sbiancare; (*hair*) diventare bianco; **the ~s** (*washing*) i capi bianchi; **tennis ~s** completo da tennis.
whitebait ['waɪtbeɪt] *n* bianchetti *mpl*.
white-collar worker ['waɪtkɔlə-] *n* impiegato/a.
white elephant *n* (*fig*) oggetto (*or* progetto) costoso ma inutile.
white goods *npl* (*appliances*) elettrodomestici *mpl*; (*linens*) biancheria per la casa.
white-hot [waɪt'hɔt] *adj* (*metal*) incandescente.
White House *n*: **the ~** la Casa Bianca; *see boxed note*.

WHITE HOUSE

La **White House** *è la residenza ufficiale del presidente degli Stati Uniti e ha sede a Washington DC. Spesso il termine viene usato per indicare l'esecutivo del governo statunitense.*

---

white lie *n* bugia pietosa.
whiteness ['waɪtnɪs] *n* bianchezza.
white noise *n* rumore *m* bianco.
white paper *n* (*POL*) libro bianco.
whitewash ['waɪtwɔʃ] *n* (*paint*) bianco di calce ♦ *vt* imbiancare; (*fig*) coprire.
whiting ['waɪtɪŋ] *n* (*pl inv*) merlango.
Whit Monday *n* lunedì *m inv* di Pentecoste.
Whitsun ['wɪtsn] *n* Pentecoste *f*.
whittle ['wɪtl] *vt*: **to ~ away, ~ down** ridurre, tagliare.
whizz [wɪz] *vi* passare sfrecciando.
whizz kid *n* (*col*) prodigio.

WHO *n abbr* (= *World Health Organization*) O.M.S. *f* (= *Organizzazione mondiale della sanità*).

═══════════════════ *KEYWORD*

who [huː] *pron* **1** (*interrogative*) chi; **~ is it?, ~'s there?** chi è?
2 (*relative*) che; **the man ~ spoke to me** l'uomo che ha parlato con me; **those ~ can swim** quelli che sanno nuotare.
---

whodunit [huː'dʌnɪt] *n* (*col*) giallo.
whoever [huː'ɛvə*] *pron*: **~ finds it** chiunque lo trovi; **ask ~ you like** lo chieda a chiunque vuole; **~ told you that?** chi mai gliel'ha detto?
whole [həul] *adj* (*complete*) tutto(a), completo(a); (*not broken*) intero(a), intatto(a) ♦ *n* (*total*) totale *m*; (*sth not broken*) tutto; **the ~ lot** (**of it**) tutto; **the ~ lot** (**of them**) tutti; **the ~ of the time** tutto il tempo; **the ~ of the town** la città intera; **on the ~, as a ~** nel complesso, nell'insieme; **~ villages were destroyed** interi paesi furono distrutti.
wholehearted [həul'hɑːtɪd] *adj* sincero(a).
wholemeal ['həulmiːl] *adj* (*BRIT*: *flour, bread*) integrale.
whole note *n* (*US*) semibreve *f*.
wholesale ['həulseɪl] *n* commercio *or* vendita all'ingrosso ♦ *adj* all'ingrosso; (*destruction*) totale.
wholesaler ['həulseɪlə*] *n* grossista *m/f*.
wholesome ['həulsəm] *adj* sano(a); (*climate*) salubre.
wholewheat ['həulwiːt] *adj* = **wholemeal**.
wholly ['həulɪ] *adv* completamente, del tutto.

═══════════════════ *KEYWORD*

whom [huːm] *pron* **1** (*interrogative*) chi; **~ did you see?** chi hai visto?; **to ~ did you give it?** a chi lo hai dato?
2 (*relative*) che, *prep* + il (la) quale; **the man ~ I saw** l'uomo che ho visto; **the man to ~ I spoke** l'uomo al *or* con il quale ho parlato; **those to ~ I spoke** le persone alle *or* con le quali ho parlato.
---

whooping cough ['huːpɪŋ-] *n* pertosse *f*.
whoops [wuːps] *excl*: **~-a-daisy!** ops!
whoosh [wuːʃ] *n*: **it came out with a ~** (*sauce etc*) è uscito di getto; (*air*) è uscito con un sibilo.
whopper ['wɔpə*] *n* (*col*: *lie*) balla; (: *large*

thing) cosa enorme.
whopping ['wɔpɪŋ] *adj* (*col*: *big*) enorme.
whore [hɔː*] *n* (*pej*) puttana.

============= KEYWORD

whose [huːz] *adj* **1** (*possessive: interrogative*)
di chi; ~ **book is this?**, ~ **is this book?** di
chi è questo libro?; ~ **daughter are you?**
di chi sei figlia?; ~ **pencil have you
taken?** di chi è la matita che hai preso?
  2 (*possessive: relative*): **the man** ~ **son you
rescued** l'uomo il cui figlio hai salvato *or*
a cui hai salvato il figlio; **the girl** ~ **sister
you were speaking to** la ragazza alla cui
sorella stavi parlando
  ♦ *pron* di chi; ~ **is this?** di chi è questo?; **I
know** ~ **it is** so di chi è.

Who's Who ['huːz'huː] *n elenco di
personalità*.
why [waɪ] *adv*, *conj* perché ♦ *excl* (*surprise*)
ma guarda un po'!; (*remonstrating*) ma
(via)!; (*explaining*) ebbene!; ~ **not?**
perché no?; ~ **not do it now?** perché non
farlo adesso?; **the reason** ~ il motivo per
cui.
whyever [waɪ'ɛvə*] *adv* perché mai.
WI *n abbr* (*BRIT*: = *Women's Institute*) circolo
femminile ♦ *abbr* (*GEO*) = **West Indies;**
(*US*) = *Wisconsin.*
wick [wɪk] *n* lucignolo, stoppino.
wicked ['wɪkɪd] *adj* cattivo(a), malvagio(a);
(*mischievous*) malizioso(a); (*terrible*: *prices,
weather*) terribile.
wicker ['wɪkə*] *n* vimine *m*; (*also*: ~**work**)
articoli *mpl* di vimini.
wicket ['wɪkɪt] *n* (*CRICKET*) porta; area tra
le due porte.
wicket keeper *n* (*CRICKET*) ≈ portiere *m*.
wide [waɪd] *adj* largo(a); (*region, knowledge*)
vasto(a); (*choice*) ampio(a) ♦ *adv*: **to open**
~ spalancare; **to shoot** ~ tirare a vuoto
or fuori bersaglio; **it is 3 metres** ~ è largo
3 metri.
wide-angle lens ['waɪdæŋgl-] *n*
grandangolare *m*.
wide-awake [waɪdə'weɪk] *adj*
completamente sveglio(a).
wide-eyed [waɪd'aɪd] *adj* con gli occhi
spalancati.
widely ['waɪdlɪ] *adv* (*different*) molto,
completamente; (*believed*) generalmente;
~ **spaced** molto distanziati(e); **to be** ~
read (*author*) essere molto letto, (*reader*)
essere molto colto.
widen ['waɪdn] *vt* allargare, ampliare.
wideness ['waɪdnɪs] *n* larghezza; vastità;
ampiezza.

wide open *adj* spalancato(a).
wide-ranging [waɪd'reɪndʒɪŋ] *adj* (*survey,
report*) vasto(a); (*interests*) svariato(a).
widescreen ['waɪdskriːn] *adj* (*television*) a
schermo panoramico.
widespread ['waɪdsprɛd] *adj* (*belief etc*)
molto *or* assai diffuso(a).
widow ['wɪdəu] *n* vedova.
widowed ['wɪdəud] *adj* (che è rimasto(a))
vedovo(a).
widower ['wɪdəuə*] *n* vedovo.
width [wɪdθ] *n* larghezza; **it's 7 metres in** ~
è largo 7 metri.
widthways ['wɪdθweɪz] *adv*
trasversalmente.
wield [wiːld] *vt* (*sword*) maneggiare;
(*power*) esercitare.
wife, *pl* **wives** [waɪf, waɪvz] *n* moglie *f*.
wig [wɪg] *n* parrucca.
wigging ['wɪgɪŋ] *n* (*BRIT col*) lavata di capo.
wiggle ['wɪgl] *vt* dimenare, agitare ♦ *vi*
(*loose screw etc*) traballare; (*worm*)
torcersi.
wiggly ['wɪglɪ] *adj* (*line*) ondulato(a),
sinuoso(a).
wild [waɪld] *adj* (*animal, plant*) selvatico(a);
(*countryside, appearance*) selvaggio(a);
(*sea*) tempestoso(a); (*idea, life*) folle; (*col:
angry*) arrabbiato(a), furibondo(a);
(*enthusiastic*): **to be** ~ **about** andar
pazzo(a) per ♦ *n*: **the** ~ la natura; ~**s** *npl*
regione *f* selvaggia.
wild card *n* (*COMPUT*) carattere *m* jolly *inv*.
wildcat ['waɪldkæt] *n* gatto(a) selvatico(a).
wildcat strike *n* ≈ sciopero selvaggio.
wilderness ['wɪldənɪs] *n* deserto.
wildfire ['waɪldfaɪə*] *n*: **to spread like** ~
propagarsi rapidamente.
wild-goose chase [waɪld'guːs-] *n* (*fig*) pista
falsa.
wildlife ['waɪldlaɪf] *n* natura.
wildly ['waɪldlɪ] *adv* (*applaud*)
freneticamente; (*hit, guess*) a casaccio;
(*happy*) follemente.
wiles [waɪlz] *npl* astuzie *fpl*.
wilful, (*US*) **willful** ['wɪlful] *adj* (*person*)
testardo(a); ostinato(a); (*action*)
intenzionale; (*crime*) premeditato(a).

============= KEYWORD

will [wɪl] *aux vb* **1** (*forming future tense*): **I** ~
finish it tomorrow lo finirò domani; **I** ~
have finished it by tomorrow lo finirò
entro domani, ~ **you do it?** – **yes I** ~/**no I
won't** lo farai? – sì (lo farò)/no (non lo
farò); **the car won't start** la macchina non
parte
  2 (*in conjectures, predictions*): **he** ~ *or* **he'll**

be there by now dovrebbe essere
arrivato a quest'ora; **that** ~ **be the
postman** sarà il postino
3 (*in commands, requests, offers*): ~ **you be
quiet!** vuoi stare zitto?; ~ **you sit down?**
(*politely*) prego, si accomodi; (*angrily*)
vuoi metterti seduto?; ~ **you come?** vieni
anche tu?; ~ **you help me?** mi aiuti?, mi
puoi aiutare?; **you won't lose it,** ~ **you?**
non lo perderai, vero?; ~ **you have a cup
of tea?** vorrebbe una tazza di tè?; **I won't
put up with it!** non lo accetterò!

♦ *vt* (*pt, pp* ~**ed**): **to** ~ **sb to do** pregare tra
sé perché qn faccia; **he** ~**ed himself to go
on** continuò grazie a un grande sforzo di
volontà
♦ *n* **1** (*desire*) volontà; **against sb's** ~
contro la volontà *or* il volere di qn; **to do
sth of one's own free** ~ fare qc di propria
volontà
2 (*LAW*) testamento; **to make a/one's** ~
fare testamento.

willful ['wɪlful] *adj* (*US*) = **wilful.**
willing ['wɪlɪŋ] *adj* volonteroso(a) ♦ *n*: **to
show** ~ dare prova di buona volontà; ~
to do disposto(a) a fare.
willingly ['wɪlɪŋlɪ] *adv* volentieri.
willingness ['wɪlɪŋnɪs] *n* buona volontà.
will-o'-the-wisp [wɪləðə'wɪsp] *n* (*also fig*)
fuoco fatuo.
willow ['wɪləu] *n* salice *m*.
will power *n* forza di volontà.
willy-nilly ['wɪlɪ'nɪlɪ] *adv* volente o nolente.
wilt [wɪlt] *vi* appassire.
Wilts [wɪlts] *abbr* (*BRIT*) = *Wiltshire.*
wily ['waɪlɪ] *adj* furbo(a).
wimp [wɪmp] *n* (*col*) mezza calzetta.
win [wɪn] *n* (*in sports etc*) vittoria ♦ *vb* (*pt, pp*
won [wʌn]) *vt* (*battle, prize*) vincere;
(*money*) guadagnare; (*popularity*)
conquistare; (*contract*) aggiudicarsi ♦ *vi*
vincere.
►**win over,** (*BRIT*) **win round** *vt*
convincere.
wince [wɪns] *n* trasalimento, sussulto ♦ *vi*
trasalire.
winch [wɪntʃ] *n* verricello, argano.
Winchester disk ['wɪntʃɪstə-] *n* (*COMPUT*)
disco Winchester.
wind *n* [wɪnd] vento; (*MED*) flatulenza,
ventosità ♦ *vb* [waɪnd] (*pt, pp* **wound**
[waund]) *vt* attorcigliare; (*wrap*)
avvolgere; (*clock, toy*) caricare; (*take
breath away*: [wɪnd]) far restare senza
fiato ♦ *vi* (*road, river*) serpeggiare; **the** ~**(s)**
(*MUS*) i fiati; **into** *or* **against the** ~
controvento; **to get** ~ **of sth** venire a

sapere qc; **to break** ~ scoreggiare (*col*).
►**wind down** *vt* (*car window*) abbassare;
(*fig*: *production, business*) diminuire.
►**wind up** *vt* (*clock*) caricare; (*debate*)
concludere.
windbreak ['wɪndbreɪk] *n* frangivento.
windcheater ['wɪndtʃiːtə*], (*US*)
windbreaker ['wɪndbreɪkə*] *n* giacca a
vento.
winder ['waɪndə*] *n* (*BRIT*: *on watch*) corona
di carica.
windfall ['wɪndfɔːl] *n* colpo di fortuna.
winding ['waɪndɪŋ] *adj* (*road*) serpeggiante;
(*staircase*) a chiocciola.
wind instrument *n* (*MUS*) strumento a
fiato.
windmill ['wɪndmɪl] *n* mulino a vento.
window ['wɪndəu] *n* (*gen*, *COMPUT*) finestra;
(*in car, train*) finestrino; (*in shop etc*)
vetrina; (*also*: ~ **pane**) vetro.
window box *n* cassetta da fiori.
window cleaner *n* (*person*) pulitore *m* di
finestre.
window dressing *n* allestimento della
vetrina.
window envelope *n* busta a finestra.
window frame *n* telaio di finestra.
window ledge *n* davanzale *m*.
window pane *n* vetro.
window-shopping ['wɪndəuʃɔpɪŋ] *n*: **to go**
~ andare a vedere le vetrine.
windowsill ['wɪndəusɪl] *n* davanzale *m*.
windpipe ['wɪndpaɪp] *n* trachea.
wind power *n* energia eolica.
windscreen ['wɪndskriːn], (*US*)
windshield ['wɪndʃiːld] *n* parabrezza *m*
inv.
windscreen washer *n* lavacristallo.
windscreen wiper *n* tergicristallo.
windshield ['wɪndʃiːld] *n* (*US*) =
windscreen.
windsurfing ['wɪndsəːfɪŋ] *n* windsurf *m inv*.
windswept ['wɪndswɛpt] *adj* spazzato(a)
dal vento.
wind tunnel *n* galleria aerodinamica *or*
del vento.
windy ['wɪndɪ] *adj* ventoso(a); **it's** ~ c'è
vento.
wine [waɪn] *n* vino ♦ *vt*: **to** ~ **and dine sb**
offrire un ottimo pranzo a qn.
wine bar *n* enoteca.
wine cellar *n* cantina.
wine glass *n* bicchiere *m* da vino.
wine list *n* lista dei vini.
wine merchant *n* commerciante *m* di
vino.
wine tasting *n* degustazione *f* dei vini.
wine waiter *n* sommelier *m inv*.

wing [wɪŋ] n ala; ~s npl (THEAT) quinte fpl.
winger ['wɪŋə*] n (SPORT) ala.
wing mirror n (BRIT) specchietto retrovisore esterno.
wing nut n galletto.
wingspan ['wɪŋspæn], **wingspread** ['wɪŋsprɛd] n apertura alare, apertura d'ali.
wink [wɪŋk] n occhiolino, strizzatina d'occhi ♦ vi ammiccare, fare l'occhiolino.
winkle ['wɪŋkl] n litorina.
winner ['wɪnə*] n vincitore/trice.
winning ['wɪnɪŋ] adj (team) vincente; (goal) decisivo(a); (charming) affascinante; see also **winnings**.
winning post n traguardo.
winnings ['wɪnɪŋz] npl vincite fpl.
winsome ['wɪnsəm] adj accattivante.
winter ['wɪntə*] n inverno; **in** ~ d'inverno, in inverno.
winter sports npl sport mpl invernali.
wintry ['wɪntrɪ] adj invernale.
wipe [waɪp] n pulita, passata ♦ vt pulire (strofinando); (dishes) asciugare; **to give sth a** ~ dare una pulita or una passata a qc; **to** ~ **one's nose** soffiarsi il naso.
▶**wipe off** vt cancellare; (stains) togliere strofinando.
▶**wipe out** vt (debt) pagare, liquidare; (memory) cancellare; (destroy) annientare.
▶**wipe up** vt asciugare.
wire ['waɪə*] n filo; (ELEC) filo elettrico; (TEL) telegramma m ♦ vt (ELEC: house) fare l'impianto elettrico di; (: circuit) installare; (also: ~ **up**) collegare, allacciare.
wire brush n spazzola metallica.
wire cutters [-kʌtəz] npl tronchese m or f.
wireless ['waɪəlɪs] n (BRIT) telegrafia senza fili; (set) (apparecchio m) radio f inv ♦ adj (technology) wireless inv, senza fili.
wire netting n rete f metallica.
wire service n (US) = **news agency**.
wire-tapping ['waɪə'tæpɪŋ] n intercettazione f telefonica.
wiring ['waɪərɪŋ] n (ELEC) impianto elettrico.
wiry ['waɪərɪ] adj magro(a) e nerboruto(a).
Wis(c). abbr (US) = Wisconsin.
wisdom ['wɪzdəm] n saggezza; (of action) prudenza.
wisdom tooth n dente m del giudizio.
wise [waɪz] adj saggio(a); (advice, remark) prudente; **I'm none the** ~r ne so come prima.
▶**wise up** vi (col): **to** ~ **up to** divenire più consapevole di.

... **wise** [waɪz] suffix: **time**~ per quanto riguarda il tempo, in termini di tempo.
wisecrack ['waɪzkræk] n battuta spiritosa.
wish [wɪʃ] n (desire) desiderio; (specific desire) richiesta ♦ vt desiderare, volere; **best** ~**es** (on birthday etc) i migliori auguri; **with best** ~**es** (in letter) cordiali saluti, con i migliori saluti; **give her my best** ~**es** le faccia i migliori auguri da parte mia; **to** ~ **sb goodbye** dire arrivederci a qn; **he** ~**ed me well** mi augurò di riuscire; **to** ~ **to do/sb to do** desiderare or volere fare/che qn faccia; **to** ~ **for** desiderare; **to** ~ **sth on sb** rifilare qc a qn.
wishbone ['wɪʃbəun] n forcella.
wishful ['wɪʃful] adj: **it's** ~ **thinking** è prendere i desideri per realtà.
wishy-washy ['wɪʃɪ'wɔʃɪ] adj insulso(a).
wisp [wɪsp] n ciuffo, ciocca; (of smoke, straw) filo.
wistful ['wɪstful] adj malinconico(a); (nostalgic) nostalgico(a).
wit [wɪt] n (gen pl) intelligenza; presenza di spirito; (wittiness) spirito, arguzia; (person) bello spirito; **to be at one's** ~**s'** **end** (fig) non sapere più cosa fare; **to have** or **keep one's** ~**s about one** avere presenza di spirito; **to** ~ adv cioè.
witch [wɪtʃ] n strega.
witchcraft ['wɪtʃkrɑːft] n stregoneria.
witch doctor n stregone m.
witch-hunt ['wɪtʃhʌnt] n (fig) caccia alle streghe.

=============================== KEYWORD

with [wɪð, wɪθ] prep **1** (in the company of) con; **I was** ~ **him** ero con lui; **we stayed** ~ **friends** siamo stati da amici; **I'll be** ~ **you in a minute** vengo subito
2 (descriptive) con; **a room** ~ **a view** una camera con vista (sul mare or sulle montagne etc); **the man** ~ **the grey hat/blue eyes** l'uomo con il cappello grigio/gli occhi blu
3 (indicating manner, means, cause): ~ **tears in her eyes** con le lacrime agli occhi; **red** ~ **anger** rosso(a) dalla rabbia; **to shake** ~ **fear** tremare di paura; **covered** ~ **snow** coperto(a) di neve
4: I'm ~ **you** (I understand) la seguo; **I'm not really** ~ **it today** (col) oggi sono un po' fuori.

withdraw [wɪθ'drɔː] vb (irreg) vt ritirare; (money from bank) ritirare, prelevare ♦ vi ritirarsi; **to** ~ **into o.s.** chiudersi in se stesso.

withdrawal [wɪθ'drɔːəl] *n* ritiro; prelievo; (*of army*) ritirata; (*MED*) stato di privazione.

withdrawal symptoms *npl* crisi *f* di astinenza.

withdrawn [wɪθ'drɔːn] *pp of* **withdraw** ♦ *adj* distaccato(a).

wither ['wɪðə*] *vi* appassire.

withered ['wɪðəd] *adj* appassito(a); (*limb*) atrofizzato(a).

withhold [wɪθ'həuld] *vt irreg* (*money*) trattenere; (*permission*): **to** ~ **(from)** rifiutare (a); (*information*): **to** ~ **(from)** nascondere (a).

within [wɪð'ɪn] *prep* all'interno di; (*in time, distances*) entro ♦ *adv* all'interno, dentro; ~ **sight of** in vista di; ~ **a mile of** entro un miglio da; ~ **the week** prima della fine della settimana; ~ **an hour from now** da qui a un'ora; **to be** ~ **the law** restare nei limiti della legge.

without [wɪð'aut] *prep* senza; **to go** *or* **do** ~ **sth** fare a meno di qc; ~ **anybody knowing** senza che nessuno lo sappia.

withstand [wɪθ'stænd] *vt irreg* resistere a.

witness ['wɪtnɪs] *n* (*person*) testimone *m/f* ♦ *vt* (*event*) essere testimone di; (*document*) attestare l'autenticità di ♦ *vi*: **to** ~ **to sth/having seen sth** testimoniare qc/di aver visto qc; **to bear** ~ **to sth** testimoniare qc; ~ **for the prosecution/ defence** testimone a carico/discarico.

witness box, (*US*) **witness stand** *n* banco dei testimoni.

witticism ['wɪtɪsɪzəm] *n* spiritosaggine *f*.

witty ['wɪtɪ] *adj* spiritoso(a).

wives [waɪvz] *npl of* **wife**.

wizard ['wɪzəd] *n* mago.

wizened ['wɪznd] *adj* raggrinzito(a).

wk *abbr* = **week**.

Wm. *abbr* = *William*.

WMD *n abbr see* **weapons of mass destruction**.

WO *n abbr see* **warrant officer**.

wobble ['wɔbl] *vi* tremare; (*chair*) traballare.

wobbly ['wɔblɪ] *adj* (*hand, voice*) tremante; (*table, chair*) traballante; (*object about to fall*) che oscilla pericolosamente.

woe [wəu] *n* dolore *m*; disgrazia.

woeful ['wəuful] *adj* (*sad*) triste; (*deplorable*) deplorevole.

wok [wɔk] *n* wok *m inv* (*padella concava usata nella cucina cinese*).

woke [wəuk] *pt of* **wake**.

woken ['wəukn] *pp of* **wake**.

wolf, *pl* **wolves** [wulf, wulvz] *n* lupo.

woman, *pl* **women** ['wumən, 'wɪmɪn] *n*

donna ♦ *cpd*: ~ **doctor** *n* dottoressa; ~ **friend** *n* amica; ~ **teacher** *n* insegnante *f*; **women's page** *n* (*PRESS*) rubrica femminile.

womanize ['wumənaɪz] *vi* essere un donnaiolo.

womanly ['wumənlɪ] *adj* femminile.

womb [wuːm] *n* (*ANAT*) utero.

women ['wɪmɪn] *npl of* **woman**.

Women's (Liberation) Movement *n* (*also*: **Women's Lib**) Movimento per la Liberazione della Donna.

won [wʌn] *pt, pp of* **win**.

wonder ['wʌndə*] *n* meraviglia ♦ *vi*: **to** ~ **whether** domandarsi se; **to** ~ **at** essere sorpreso(a) di; meravigliarsi di; **to** ~ **about** domandarsi di; pensare a; **it's no** ~ **that** c'è poco *or* non c'è da meravigliarsi che + *sub*.

wonderful ['wʌndəful] *adj* meraviglioso(a).

wonderfully ['wʌndəfəlɪ] *adv* (+ *adjective*) meravigliosamente; (+ *verb*) a meraviglia.

wonky ['wɔŋkɪ] *adj* (*BRIT col*) traballante.

wont [wəunt] *n*: **as is his/her** ~ com'è solito/a fare.

won't [wəunt] = **will not**.

woo [wuː] *vt* (*woman*) fare la corte a.

wood [wud] *n* legno; (*timber*) legname *m*; (*forest*) bosco ♦ *cpd* di bosco, silvestre.

wood carving *n* scultura in legno, intaglio.

wooded ['wudɪd] *adj* boschivo(a); boscoso(a).

wooden ['wudn] *adj* di legno; (*fig*) rigido(a); inespressivo(a).

woodland ['wudlənd] *n* zona boscosa.

woodpecker ['wudpɛkə*] *n* picchio.

wood pigeon *n* colombaccio, palomba.

woodwind ['wudwɪnd] *npl* (*MUS*): **the** ~ i legni.

woodwork ['wudwəːk] *n* parti *fpl* in legno; (*craft, subject*) falegnameria.

woodworm ['wudwəːm] *n* tarlo del legno.

woof [wuf] *n* (*of dog*) bau bau *m* ♦ *vi* abbaiare; ~, ~! bau bau!

wool [wul] *n* lana; **to pull the** ~ **over sb's eyes** (*fig*) fargliela a qn.

woollen, (*US*) **woolen** ['wulən] *adj* di lana ♦ *n*: ~**s** indumenti *mpl* di lana.

woolly, (*US*) **wooly** ['wulɪ] *adj* lanoso(a); (*fig: ideas*) confuso(a).

woozy ['wuːzɪ] *adj* (*col*) stordito(a).

word [wəːd] *n* parola; (*news*) notizie *fpl* ♦ *vt* esprimere, formulare; ~ **for** ~ parola per parola, testualmente; **what's the** ~ **for "pen" in Italian?** come si dice "pen" in italiano?; **to put sth into** ~**s** esprimere qc a parole; **in other** ~**s** in altre parole; **to**

have a ~ with sb scambiare due parole con qn; **to have ~s with sb** (*quarrel with*) avere un diverbio con qn; **to break/keep one's ~** non mantenere/mantenere la propria parola; **I'll take your ~ for it** la crederò sulla parola; **to send ~ of** avvisare di; **to leave ~ (with** *or* **for sb) that** ... lasciare detto (a qn) che ....
wording ['wəːdɪŋ] *n* formulazione *f*.
word of mouth *n* passaparola *m*; **I learned it by** *or* **through ~** lo so per sentito dire.
word-perfect ['wəːd'pəfɪkt] *adj* (*speech etc*) imparato(a) a memoria.
word processing *n* word processing *m*, elaborazione *f* testi.
word processor *n* word processor *m* *inv*.
wordwrap ['wəːdræp] *n* (*COMPUT*) ritorno carrello automatico.
wordy ['wəːdɪ] *adj* verboso(a), prolisso(a).
wore [wɔː*] *pt of* **wear**.
work [wəːk] *n* lavoro; (*ART, LITERATURE*) opera ♦ *vi* lavorare; (*mechanism, plan etc*) funzionare; (*medicine*) essere efficace ♦ *vt* (*clay, wood etc*) lavorare; (*mine etc*) sfruttare; (*machine*) far funzionare; **to be at ~ (on sth)** lavorare (a qc); **to set to ~**, **to start ~** mettersi all'opera; **to go to ~** andare al lavoro; **to be out of ~** essere disoccupato(a); **to ~ one's way through a book** riuscire a leggersi tutto un libro; **to ~ one's way through college** lavorare per pagarsi gli studi; **to ~ hard** lavorare sodo; **to ~ loose** allentarsi; *see also* **works**.
►**work on** *vt fus* lavorare a; (*principle*) basarsi su; **he's ~ing on the car** sta facendo dei lavori alla macchina.
►**work out** *vi* (*plans etc*) riuscire, andare bene; (*SPORT*) allenarsi ♦ *vt* (*problem*) risolvere; (*plan*) elaborare; **it ~s out at £100** fa 100 sterline.
workable ['wəːkəbl] *adj* (*solution*) realizzabile.
workaholic [wəːkə'hɔlɪk] *n* stacanovista *m/f*.
workbench ['wəːkbɛntʃ] *n* banco (da lavoro).
worked up *adj*: **to get ~** andare su tutte le furie; eccitarsi.
worker ['wəːkə*] *n* lavoratore/trice; (*esp AGR, INDUSTRY*) operaio/a; **office ~** impiegato/a.
work force *n* forza lavoro.
work-in ['wəːkɪn] *n* (*BRIT*) sciopero alla rovescia.
working ['wəːkɪŋ] *adj* (*day*) feriale; (*tools, conditions*) di lavoro; (*clothes*) da lavoro; (*wife*) che lavora; (*partner*) attivo(a); **in ~ order** funzionante; **~ knowledge**

conoscenza pratica.
working capital *n* (*COMM*) capitale *m* d'esercizio.
working class *n* classe *f* operaia *or* lavoratrice ♦ *adj*: **working-class** operaio(a).
working man *n* lavoratore *m*.
working party *n* (*BRIT*) commissione *f*.
working week *n* settimana lavorativa.
work-in-progress ['wəːkɪn'prəugrɛs] *n* (*products*) lavoro in corso; (*value*) valore *m* del manufatto in lavorazione.
workload ['wəːkləud] *n* carico di lavoro.
workman ['wəːkmən] *n* operaio.
workmanship ['wəːkmənʃɪp] *n* (*of worker*) abilità; (*of thing*) fattura.
workmate ['wəːkmeɪt] *n* collega *m/f*.
workout ['wəːkaut] *n* (*SPORT*) allenamento.
work permit *n* permesso di lavoro.
works [wəːks] *n* (*BRIT: factory*) fabbrica ♦ *npl* (*of clock, machine*) meccanismo; **road ~** opere stradali.
works council *n* consiglio aziendale.
work sheet *n* (*COMPUT*) foglio col programma di lavoro.
workshop ['wəːkʃɔp] *n* officina.
work station *n* stazione *f* di lavoro.
work study *n* studio di organizzazione del lavoro.
worktop ['wəːktɔp] *n* piano di lavoro.
work-to-rule ['wəːktə'ruːl] *n* (*BRIT*) sciopero bianco.
world [wəːld] *n* mondo ♦ *cpd* (*tour*) del mondo; (*record, power, war*) mondiale; **all over the ~** in tutto il mondo; **to think the ~ of sb** pensare un gran bene di qn; **out of this ~** (*fig*) formidabile; **what in the ~ is he doing?** che cavolo sta facendo?; **to do sb a ~ of good** fare un gran bene a qn; **W~ War One/Two** la prima/seconda guerra mondiale.
world champion *n* campione/essa mondiale.
World Cup *n* (*FOOTBALL*) Coppa del Mondo.
world-famous [wəːld'feɪməs] *adj* di fama mondiale.
worldly ['wəːldlɪ] *adj* di questo mondo.
world music *n* musica etnica.
World Series *n*: **the ~** (*US BASEBALL*) la finalissima di baseball.
world-wide ['wəːld'waɪd] *adj* universale.
worm [wəːm] *n* verme *m*.
worn [wɔːn] *pp of* **wear** ♦ *adj* usato(a).
worn-out ['wɔːnaut] *adj* (*object*) consumato(a), logoro(a); (*person*) sfinito(a).
worried ['wʌrɪd] *adj* preoccupato(a); **to be**

~ **about sth** essere preoccupato per qc.
worrier ['wʌriə*] n ansioso/a.
worrisome ['wʌrisəm] adj preoccupante.
worry ['wʌri] n preoccupazione f ♦ vt preoccupare ♦ vi preoccuparsi; **to** ~ **about** or **over sth/sb** preoccuparsi di qc/ per qn.
worrying ['wʌriɪŋ] adj preoccupante.
worse [wəːs] adj peggiore ♦ adv, n peggio; **a change for the** ~ un peggioramento; **to get** ~, **to grow** ~ peggiorare; **he is none the** ~ **for it** non ha avuto brutte conseguenze; **so much the** ~ **for you!** tanto peggio per te!
worsen ['wəːsn] vt, vi peggiorare.
worse off adj in condizioni (economiche) peggiori; (fig): **you'll be** ~ **this way** così sarà peggio per lei; **he is now** ~ **than before** ora è in condizioni peggiori di prima.
worship ['wəːʃip] n culto ♦ vt (God) adorare, venerare; (person) adorare; **Your W**~ (to mayor) signor sindaco; (to judge) signor giudice.
worshipper ['wəːʃipə*] n adoratore/trice; (in church) fedele m/f, devoto/a.
worst [wəːst] adj peggiore ♦ adv, n peggio; **at** ~ al peggio, per male che vada; **to come off** ~ avere la peggio; **if the** ~ **comes to the** ~ nel peggior dei casi.
worst-case ['wəːst'keɪs] adj: **the** ~ **scenario** la peggiore delle ipotesi.
worsted ['wustɪd] n: **(wool)** ~ lana pettinata.
worth [wəːθ] n valore m ♦ adj: **to be** ~ valere; **how much is it** ~? quanto vale?; **it's** ~ **it** ne vale la pena; **it's not** ~ **the trouble** non ne vale la pena; **50 pence** ~ **of apples** 50 pence di mele.
worthless ['wəːθlis] adj di nessun valore.
worthwhile ['wəːθ'waɪl] adj (activity) utile; (cause) lodevole; **a** ~ **book** un libro che vale la pena leggere.
worthy ['wəːðɪ] adj (person) degno(a); (motive) lodevole; ~ **of** degno di.

=========================== **KEYWORD**

would [wud] aux vb **1** (conditional tense): **if you asked him he** ~ **do it** se glielo chiedesse lo farebbe; **if you had asked him he** ~ **have done it** se glielo avesse chiesto lo avrebbe fatto
2 (in offers, invitations, requests): ~ **you like a biscuit?** vorrebbe or vuole un biscotto?; ~ **you ask him to come in?** lo faccia entrare, per cortesia; ~ **you open the window please?** apra la finestra, per

favore
3 (in indirect speech): **I said I** ~ **do it** ho detto che l'avrei fatto
4 (emphatic): **it WOULD have to snow today!** doveva proprio nevicare oggi!
5 (insistence): **she** ~**n't do it** non ha voluto farlo
6 (conjecture): **it** ~ **have been midnight** sarà stata mezzanotte; **it** ~ **seem so** sembrerebbe proprio di sì
7 (indicating habit): **he** ~ **go there on Mondays** andava lì ogni lunedì.

would-be ['wudbiː] adj (pej) sedicente.
wound vb [waund] pt, pp of **wind** ♦ n, vt [wuːnd] n ferita ♦ vt ferire; ~**ed in the leg** ferito(a) alla gamba.
wove [wəuv] pt of **weave**.
WP abbr (BRIT col: = weather permitting) tempo permettendo ♦ n abbr = **word processing; word processor.**
WPC n abbr (BRIT: = woman police constable) donna poliziotto.
wpm abbr (= words per minute) p.p.m.
WRAC n abbr (BRIT: = Women's Royal Army Corps) ausiliarie dell'esercito.
WRAF n abbr (BRIT: = Women's Royal Air Force) ausiliarie dell'aeronautica militare.
wrangle ['ræŋgl] n litigio ♦ vi litigare.
wrap [ræp] n (stole) scialle m; (cape) mantellina ♦ vt (also: ~ **up**) avvolgere; (parcel) incartare; **under** ~**s** segreto.
wrapper ['ræpə*] n (of book) copertina; (on chocolate) carta.
wrapping paper ['ræpɪŋ-] n carta da pacchi; (for gift) carta da regali.
wrath [rɔθ] n collera, ira.
wreak [riːk] vt (destruction) portare, causare; **to** ~ **vengeance on** vendicarsi su; **to** ~ **havoc on** portare scompiglio in.
wreath [riːθ], ~**s** [riːθ, riːðz] n corona.
wreck [rɛk] n (sea disaster) naufragio; (ship) relitto; (pej: person) rottame m ♦ vt demolire; (ship) far naufragare; (fig) rovinare.
wreckage ['rɛkɪdʒ] n rottami mpl; (of building) macerie fpl; (of ship) relitti mpl.
wrecker ['rɛkə*] n (US: breakdown van) carro m attrezzi inv.
WREN [rɛn] n abbr (BRIT) membro del WRNS.
wren [rɛn] n (ZOOL) scricciolo.
wrench [rɛntʃ] n (TECH) chiave f; (tug) torsione f brusca; (fig) strazio ♦ vt strappare; storcere; **to** ~ **sth from sb** strappare qc a or da.
wrest [rɛst] vt: **to** ~ **sth from sb** strappare

qc a qn.

wrestle ['rɛsl] *vi*: **to** ~ **(with sb)** lottare (con qn); **to** ~ **with** (*fig*) combattere *or* lottare contro.

wrestler ['rɛslə*] *n* lottatore/trice.

wrestling ['rɛslɪŋ] *n* lotta; (*also*: **all-in** ~: *BRIT*) catch *m*, lotta libera.

wrestling match *n* incontro di lotta (*or* lotta libera).

wretch [rɛtʃ] *n* disgraziato/a, sciagurato/a; **little** ~! (*often humorous*) birbante!

wretched ['rɛtʃɪd] *adj* disgraziato(a); (*col*: *weather, holiday*) orrendo(a), orribile; (: *child, dog*) pestifero(a).

wriggle ['rɪgl] *n* contorsione *f* ♦ *vi* dimenarsi; (*snake, worm*) serpeggiare, muoversi serpeggiando.

wring *pt, pp* **wrung** [rɪŋ, rʌŋ] *vt* torcere; (*wet clothes*) strizzare; (*fig*): **to** ~ **sth out of** strappare qc a.

wringer ['rɪŋə*] *n* strizzatoio (manuale).

wringing ['rɪŋɪŋ] *adj* (*also*: ~ **wet**) bagnato(a) fradicio(a).

wrinkle ['rɪŋkl] *n* (*on skin*) ruga; (*on paper etc*) grinza ♦ *vt* corrugare; raggrinzire ♦ *vi* corrugarsi; raggrinzirsi.

wrinkled ['rɪŋkld], **wrinkly** ['rɪŋklɪ] *adj* (*fabric, paper*) stropicciato(a); (*surface*) corrugato(a), increspato(a); (*skin*) rugoso(a).

wrist [rɪst] *n* polso.

wristband ['rɪstbænd] *n* (*of shirt*) polsino; (*of watch*) cinturino.

wrist watch *n* orologio da polso.

writ [rɪt] *n* ordine *m*; mandato; **to issue a** ~ **against sb, serve a** ~ **on sb** notificare un mandato di comparizione a qn.

write, *pt* **wrote,** *pp* **written** [raɪt, rəut, 'rɪtn] *vt, vi* scrivere; **to** ~ **sb a letter** scrivere una lettera a qn.

▶**write away** *vi*: **to** ~ **away for** (*information*) richiedere per posta; (*goods*) ordinare per posta.

▶**write down** *vt* annotare; (*put in writing*) mettere per iscritto.

▶**write off** *vt* (*debt*) cancellare; (*depreciate*) deprezzare; (*smash up*: *car*) distruggere.

▶**write out** *vt* scrivere; (*copy*) ricopiare.

▶**write up** *vt* redigere.

write-off ['raɪtɔf] *n* perdita completa; **the car is a** ~ la macchina va bene per il demolitore.

write-protect ['raɪtprə'tɛkt] *vt* (*COMPUT*) proteggere contro scrittura.

writer ['raɪtə*] *n* autore/trice, scrittore/trice.

write-up ['raɪtʌp] *n* (*review*) recensione *f*.

writhe [raɪð] *vi* contorcersi.

writing ['raɪtɪŋ] *n* scrittura; (*of author*) scritto, opera; **in** ~ per iscritto; **in my own** ~ scritto di mio pugno.

writing desk *n* scrivania, scrittoio.

writing paper *n* carta da scrivere.

written ['rɪtn] *pp of* **write**.

WRNS *n abbr* (*BRIT*: = *Women's Royal Naval Service*) ausiliarie della marina militare.

wrong [rɒŋ] *adj* sbagliato(a); (*not suitable*) inadatto(a); (*wicked*) cattivo(a); (*unfair*) ingiusto(a) ♦ *adv* in modo sbagliato, erroneamente ♦ *n* (*evil*) male *m*; (*injustice*) torto ♦ *vt* fare torto a; **to be** ~ (*answer*) essere sbagliato; (*in doing, saying*) avere torto; **you are** ~ **to do it** ha torto a farlo; **you are** ~ **about that, you've got it** ~ si sbaglia; **to be in the** ~ avere torto; **what's** ~? cosa c'è che non va?; **there's nothing** ~ va tutto bene; **what's** ~ **with the car?** cos'ha la macchina che non va?; **to go** ~ (*person*) sbagliarsi; (*plan*) fallire, non riuscire; (*machine*) guastarsi; **it's** ~ **to steal, stealing is** ~ è male rubare.

wrongdoer ['rɒŋduːə*] *n* malfattore/trice.

wrong-foot [rɒŋ'fut] *vt* (*SPORT*; *also fig*) prendere in contropiede.

wrongful ['rɒŋful] *adj* illegittimo(a); ingiusto(a); ~ **dismissal** licenziamento ingiustificato.

wrongly ['rɒŋlɪ] *adv* (*accuse, dismiss*) a torto; (*answer, do, count*) erroneamente; (*treat*) ingiustamente.

wrong number *n*: **you have the** ~ (*TEL*) ha sbagliato numero.

wrong side *n* (*of cloth*) rovescio.

wrote [rəut] *pt of* **write**.

wrought [rɔ:t] *adj*: ~ **iron** ferro battuto.

wrung [rʌŋ] *pt, pp of* **wring**.

WRVS *n abbr* (*BRIT*) = *Women's Royal Voluntary Service*.

wry [raɪ] *adj* storto(a).

wt. *abbr* = **weight**.

WV, W. Va. *abbr* (*US*) = *West Virginia*.

WWW *n abbr* (= *World Wide Web*): **the** ~ la Rete.

WY, Wyo. *abbr* (*US*) = *Wyoming*.

WYSIWYG ['wɪzɪwɪg] *abbr* (*COMPUT*) = *what you see is what you get*.

X, x [ɛks] n (letter) X, x f or m inv; (BRIT CINE: old) ≈ film vietato ai minori di 18 anni; **X for Xmas** ≈ X come Xeres.

Xerox ® ['zɪərɔks] n (also: ~ **machine**) fotocopiatrice f; (photocopy) fotocopia ♦ vt fotocopiare.

XL abbr = extra large.

Xmas ['ɛksməs] n abbr = **Christmas**.

X-rated ['ɛks'reɪtɪd] adj (US: film) ≈ vietato ai minori di 18 anni.

X-ray ['ɛks'reɪ] n raggio X; (photograph) radiografia ♦ vt radiografare; **to have an** ~ farsi fare una radiografia.

xylophone ['zaɪləfəun] n xilofono.

Y, y [waɪ] n (letter) Y, y f or m inv; **Y for Yellow,** (US) **Y for Yoke** ≈ Y come Yacht.

yacht [jɔt] n panfilo, yacht m inv.

yachting ['jɔtɪŋ] n yachting m, sport m della vela.

yachtsman ['jɔtsmən] n yachtsman m inv.

yam [jæm] n igname m; (sweet potato) patata dolce.

Yank [jæŋk], **Yankee** ['jæŋkɪ] n (pej) yankee m/f inv, nordamericano/a.

yank [jæŋk] n strattone m ♦ vt tirare, dare uno strattone a.

yap [jæp] vi (dog) guaire.

yard [jɑːd] n (of house etc) cortile m; (US: garden) giardino; (measure) iarda (= 914 mm; 3 feet); **builder's** ~ deposito di materiale da costruzione.

yardstick ['jɑːdstɪk] n (fig) misura, criterio.

yarn [jɑːn] n filato; (tale) lunga storia.

yawn [jɔːn] n sbadiglio ♦ vi sbadigliare.

yawning ['jɔːnɪŋ] adj (gap) spalancato(a).

yd. abbr = yard.

yeah [jɛə] adv (col) sì.

year [jɪə*] n (gen, SCOL) anno; (referring to

harvest, wine etc) annata; **every** ~ ogni anno, tutti gli anni; **this** ~ quest'anno; ~ **in,** ~ **out** anno dopo anno; **she's three** ~**s old** ha tre anni; **a** or **per** ~ all'anno.

yearbook ['jɪəbuk] n annuario.

yearly ['jɪəlɪ] adj annuale ♦ adv annualmente; **twice-**~ semestrale.

yearn [jəːn] vi: **to** ~ **for sth/to do** desiderare ardentemente qc/di fare.

yearning ['jəːnɪŋ] n desiderio intenso.

yeast [jiːst] n lievito.

yell [jɛl] n urlo ♦ vi urlare.

yellow ['jɛləu] adj giallo(a).

yellow fever n febbre f gialla.

yellowish ['jɛləuɪʃ] adj giallastro(a), giallognolo(a).

Yellow Pages ® npl pagine fpl gialle.

Yellow Sea n: **the** ~ il mar Giallo.

yelp [jɛlp] n guaito, uggiolio ♦ vi guaire, uggiolare.

Yemen ['jɛmən] n Yemen m.

yen [jɛn] n (currency) yen m inv; (craving): ~ **for/to do** gran voglia di/di fare.

yeoman ['jəumən] n: **Y**~ **of the Guard** guardiano della Torre di Londra.

yes [jɛs] adv, n sì (m inv); **to say** ~ **(to)** dire di sì (a), acconsentire (a).

yesterday ['jɛstədɪ] adv, n ieri (m inv); ~ **morning/evening** ieri mattina/sera; **the day before** ~ l'altro ieri; **all day** ~ ieri tutto il giorno.

yet [jɛt] adv ancora; già ♦ conj ma, tuttavia; **it is not finished** ~ non è ancora finito; **the best** ~ il migliore finora; **as** ~ finora; ~ **again** di nuovo; **must you go just** ~? deve andarsene di già?; **a few days** ~ ancora qualche giorno.

yew [juː] n tasso (albero).

Y-fronts ® ['waɪfrʌnts] npl (BRIT) slip m inv da uomo.

YHA n abbr (BRIT: = Youth Hostels Association) Y.H.A. f.

Yiddish ['jɪdɪʃ] n yiddish m.

yield [jiːld] n resa; (of crops etc) raccolto ♦ vt produrre, rendere; (surrender) cedere ♦ vi cedere; (US AUT) dare la precedenza; **a** ~ **of 5%** un profitto or un interesse del 5%.

YMCA n abbr (= Young Men's Christian Association) Y.M.C.A. m.

yob(bo) ['jɔb(əu)] n (BRIT col) bullo.

yodel ['jəudl] vi cantare lo jodel or alla tirolese.

yoga ['jəugə] n yoga m.

yog(h)ourt, yog(h)urt ['jəugət] n iogurt m inv.

yoke [jəuk] n giogo ♦ vt (also: ~ **together:** oxen) aggiogare.

yolk [jəuk] *n* tuorlo, rosso d'uovo.
yonder ['jɔndə*] *adv* là.
yonks [jɔŋks] *npl*: **for** ~ (*col*) da una vita.
Yorks [jɔːks] *abbr* (*BRIT*) = *Yorkshire*.

═══════════════════════ KEYWORD

you [juː] *pron* **1** (*subject*) tu; (*: polite form*)
lei; (*: pl*) voi; (*: very formal*) loro; ~ **Italians
enjoy your food** a voi italiani piace
mangiare bene; ~ **and I will go** andiamo
io e te (*or* lei ed io); **if I was** *or* **were** ~ se
fossi in te (*or* lei *etc*)
2 (*object: direct*) ti; la; vi; loro (*after vb*);
(*: indirect*) ti; le; vi; loro (*after vb*); **I know**
~ ti (*or* la *or* vi) conosco; **I'll see** ~
tomorrow ci vediamo domani; **I gave it to**
~ te l'ho dato; gliel'ho dato; ve l'ho dato;
l'ho dato loro
3 (*stressed, after prep, in comparisons*) te;
lei; voi; loro; **I told YOU to do it** ho detto a
TE (*or* a LEI *etc*) di farlo; **she's younger
than** ~ è più giovane di te (*or* lei *etc*)
4 (*impers: one*) si; **fresh air does** ~ **good**
l'aria fresca fa bene; ~ **never know** non
si sa mai.

you'd [juːd] = **you had; you would.**
you'll [juːl] = **you will; you shall.**
young [jʌŋ] *adj* giovane ♦ *npl* (*of animal*)
piccoli *mpl*; (*people*): **the** ~ i giovani, la
gioventù; **a** ~ **man** un giovanotto; **a** ~
lady una signorina; **a** ~ **woman** una
giovane donna; **the** ~**er generation** la
nuova generazione; **my** ~**er brother** il
mio fratello minore.
youngish ['jʌŋɪʃ] *adj* abbastanza giovane.
youngster ['jʌŋstə*] *n* giovanotto/a; (*child*)
bambino/a.
your [jɔː*] *adj* il(la) tuo(a), *pl* i(le) tuoi(tue);
(*polite form*) il(la) suo(a), *pl* i(le) suoi(sue);
(*pl*) il(la) vostro(a), *pl* i(le) vostri(e);
(*: very formal*) il(la) loro, *pl* i(le) loro.
you're [juə*] = **you are.**
yours [jɔːz] *pron* il(la) tuo(a), *pl* i(le)
tuoi(tue); (*polite form*) il(la) suo(a), *pl* i(le)
suoi(sue); (*pl*) il(la) vostro(a), *pl* i(le)
vostri(e); (*: very formal*) il(la) loro, *pl* i(le)
loro; ~ **sincerely/faithfully** (*in letter*)
cordiali/distinti saluti; **a friend of** ~ un
tuo (*or* suo *etc*) amico; **is it** ~**?** è tuo (*or*
suo *etc*)?
yourself [jɔː'sɛlf] *pron* (*reflexive*) ti; (*: polite
form*) si; (*after prep*) te; se; (*emphatic*) tu
stesso(a); lei stesso(a); **you** ~ **told me** me
l'hai detto proprio tu, tu stesso me l'hai
detto.
yourselves [jɔː'sɛlvz] *pl pron* (*reflexive*) vi; (*:
polite form*) si; (*after prep*) voi; loro;

(*emphatic*) voi stessi(e); loro stessi(e).
youth [juːθ] *n* gioventù *f*; (*young man*: *pl* ~**s**
[juːðz]) giovane *m*, ragazzo; **in my** ~ da
giovane, quando ero giovane.
youth club *n* centro giovanile.
youthful ['juːθful] *adj* giovane; da giovane;
giovanile.
youthfulness ['juːθfəlnɪs] *n* giovinezza.
youth hostel *n* ostello della gioventù.
youth movement *n* movimento giovanile.
you've [juːv] = **you have.**
yowl [jaul] *n* (*of dog, person*) urlo; (*of cat*)
miagolio ♦ *vi* urlare; miagolare.
yr *abbr* = **year.**
YT *abbr* (*Canada*) = *Yukon Territory*.
Yugoslav ['juːgəuslɑːv] *adj, n* jugoslavo(a).
Yugoslavia [juːgəu'slɑːvɪə] *n* Jugoslavia.
Yugoslavian [juːgəu'slɑːvɪən] *adj, n*
jugoslavo(a).
Yule log [juːl-] *n* ceppo nel caminetto a
Natale.
yuppie ['jʌpɪ] *adj, n* (*col*) yuppie (*m/f*) *inv*.
YWCA *n abbr* (= *Young Women's Christian
Association*) Y.W.C.A. *m*.

═══════════════ Z z

Z, z [zɛd, (*US*) ziː] *n* (*letter*) Z, z *f or m inv*; **Z
for Zebra** ≈ Z come Zara.
Zaire [zɑː'ɪə*] *n* Zaire *m*.
Zambia ['zæmbɪə] *n* Zambia *m*.
Zambian ['zæmbɪən] *adj, n* zambiano(a).
zany ['zeɪnɪ] *adj* un po' pazzo(a).
zap [zæp] *vt* (*COMPUT*) cancellare.
zeal [ziːl] *n* zelo; entusiasmo.
zealot ['zɛlət] *n* zelota *m/f*.
zealous ['zɛləs] *adj* zelante; premuroso(a).
zebra ['ziːbrə] *n* zebra.
zebra crossing *n* (*BRIT*) (passaggio
pedonale a) strisce *fpl*, zebre *fpl*.
zenith ['zɛnɪθ] *n* zenit *m inv*; (*fig*) culmine *m*.
zero ['zɪərəu] *n* zero; **5° below** ~ 5° sotto
zero.
zero hour *n* l'ora zero.
zero option *n* (*POL*) opzione *f* zero.
zero-rated ['zɪərəu'reɪtɪd] *adj* (*BRIT*) ad
aliquota zero.
zest [zɛst] *n* gusto; (*CULIN*) buccia.
zigzag ['zɪgzæg] *n* zigzag *m inv* ♦ *vi*
zigzagare.
Zimbabwe [zɪm'bɑːbwɪ] *n* Zimbabwe *m*.

Zimbabwean [zɪm'bɑːbwɪən] *adj* dello
Zimbabwe.

Zimmer ® ['zɪmə*] *n* (*also*: ~ **frame**)
deambulatore *m*.

zinc [zɪŋk] *n* zinco.

Zionism ['zaɪənɪzəm] *n* sionismo.

Zionist ['zaɪənɪst] *adj* sionistico(a) ♦ *n*
sionista *m/f*.

zip [zɪp] *n* (*also*: ~ **fastener,** (*US*) ~**per**)
chiusura *f or* cerniera *f* lampo *inv*; (*energy*)
energia, forza ♦ *vt* (*also*: ~ **up**) chiudere
con una cerniera lampo; (*COMPUT*)
zippare.

zip code *n* (*US*) codice *m* di avviamento
postale.

zither ['zɪðə*] *n* cetra.

zodiac ['zəudɪæk] *n* zodiaco.

zombie ['zɔmbɪ] *n* (*fig*): **like a** ~ come un
morto che cammina.

zone [zəun] *n* zona.

zoo [zuː] *n* zoo *m inv*.

zoological [zuə'lɔdʒɪkl] *adj* zoologico(a).

zoologist [zuː'ɔlədʒɪst] *n* zoologo/a.

zoology [zuː'ɔlədʒɪ] *n* zoologia.

zoom [zuːm] *vi*: **to** ~ **past** sfrecciare; **to** ~
in (on sb/sth) (*PHOT, CINE*) zumare (su qn/
qc).

zoom lens *n* zoom *m inv*, obiettivo a focale
variabile.

zucchini [zuː'kiːnɪ] *n* (*pl inv*) (*US*) zucchina.

Zulu ['zuːluː] *adj*, *n* zulù (*m/f*) *inv*.

Zürich ['zjuərɪk] *n* Zurigo *f*.

ITALIAN IN ACTION

INGLESE ATTIVO

Contributors/Collaboratori

Loredana Riu   Daphne Day   Gabriella Bacchelli

Coordination/Coordinamento

Isobel Gordon

INTRODUZIONE

Il supplemento INGLESE ATTIVO vi aiuterà ad esprimervi in modo semplice e corretto, usando espressioni tipiche della lingua realmente parlata.

La sezione LOCUZIONI DI BASE contiene centinaia di frasi seguite dalla traduzione degli elementi chiave, utilizzabili nella costruzione di moltissime altre frasi.

Nella sezione sulla corrispondenza troverete diversi modelli di lettere in inglese, sia personali che commerciali, le formule più comuni usate per iniziare e concludere una lettera, indicazioni su dove e come scrivere indirizzo e mittente sulla busta e così via. Troverete anche un esempio di curriculum vitae, una domanda di assunzione e utili consigli su come adattare questi modelli alle vostre particolari esigenze.

C'è inoltre una sezione a parte sull'invio di fax e di messaggi di posta elettronica e sui diversi tipi di conversazioni telefoniche.

Siamo sicuri che, assieme al dizionario, il supplemento INGLESE ATTIVO, sarà uno strumento prezioso per aiutarvi a scrivere e a comunicare in inglese nel modo più corretto, naturale e adatto ad ogni situazione.

INDICE

INTRODUCTION

The aim of ITALIAN IN ACTION is to help you express yourself simply but correctly in fluent, natural Italian.

The SENTENCE BUILDER section provides hundreds of phrases in which the key elements have been translated, providing an invaluable point of reference when you then construct your own sentences.

The section on correspondence provides practical models of personal and business letters, job applications and CVs, together with examples of standard opening and closing formulae and information on how to address an envelope. This section also offers guidance notes to help the user adapt these models to his/her needs.

A separate section covers fax and e-mail correspondence as well as all the expressions you might need to make different types of phone calls.

We hope you will find ITALIAN IN ACTION both relevant and useful and that, used in conjunction with the dictionary, it will improve your understanding and enjoyment of Italian.

CONTENTS

❏ *Gusti e preferenze*

Per dire ciò che ci piace

I **like** cakes.	Mi piacciono ...
I **like** things to be in their proper place.	Mi piace che ...
I **really liked** the film.	... mi è piaciuto molto.
I **love** going to clubs.	Adoro ...
What I **like best** about Matthew are his eyes.	Quello che mi piace di più ...
What I **enjoy most is** an evening with friends.	La cosa che mi piace di più è ...
I **very much enjoyed** the trip to the vineyards.	... mi è piaciuta molto.
I've never tasted **anything better than** this chicken.	... niente di meglio di ...
I've **got a weakness for** chocolate cakes.	Ho un debole per ...
You **can't beat** a good cup of tea.	Non c'è niente come ...
There's **nothing quite like** a nice hot bath!	Non c'è niente di meglio di ...
My **favourite** dish is risotto.	Il mio ... preferito ...
Reading is **one of my favourite** pastimes.	... uno dei miei ... preferiti.
I **don't mind** being alone.	Non mi dispiace ...

Per dire ció che non ci piace

I **don't like** fish.	Non mi piace ...
I **don't like** him **at all**.	... non mi piace per niente.
I'm **not very keen on** speaking in public.	Non mi piace molto ...
I'm **not particularly keen on** the idea.	Non è che ... mi faccia impazzire.
I **hate** chemistry.	Odio ...
I **loathe** sport.	Detesto ...
I **can't stand** being lied to.	Non sopporto ...
If there's one thing I hate it's ironing.	Se c'è una cosa che odio è ...

Per esprimere una preferenza

I **prefer** pop **to** classical music.	Preferisco ... alla ...
I **would rather** live in Rome.	Preferirei ...
I'**d rather** starve **than** ask him a favour.	Preferirei ... piuttosto che ...

Per esprimere indifferenza

It's all the same to me.	*Per me fa lo stesso.*
I have no particular preference.	*Non ho preferenze.*
As you like.	*Come vuoi.*
It doesn't matter in the least.	*Non ha nessuna importanza.*
I don't mind.	*È indifferente.*

Rivolgendosi ad altri

Do you like chocolate?	*Ti piace ...*
Do you like cooking?	*Ti piace ...*
Which do you like better: football or cricket?	*Cosa preferisci ...*
Which would you rather have: the red one or the black one?	*Quale preferisci ...*
Do you prefer living in the town or in the country?	*Preferisci ...*
What do you like best on television?	*Cosa ti piace di più ...*

❏ *Opinioni*

Per chiedere l'opinione di qualcuno

What do you think about it?	*Cosa ne pensa?*
What do you think about divorce?	*Cosa pensa del ...*
What do you think of his behaviour?	*Come ti sembra ...*
I'd like to know what you think of his work.	*Vorrei sapere cosa pensi del ...*
I would like to know your views on this.	*Mi piacerebbe sapere il suo parere o la sua opinione su ...*
What is your opinion on the team's chances of success?	*Qual è la sua opinione sulle ...*
Could you give me your opinion on this proposal?	*Potrebbe dirmi cosa pensa di ...*
In your opinion, are men and women equal?	*A suo parere o avviso ...*
In your opinion, is this the best solution?	*Secondo lei ...*

Per esprimere un'opinione

You are right.	Hai ragione.
He is wrong.	Ha torto.
He was wrong to resign.	Ha sbagliato a ...
I think it ought to be possible.	Penso che ...
I think it's a bit premature.	Credo che sia ...
I think it's quite natural.	Mi sembra che sia ...
Personally, I think that it's a waste of money.	Personalmente, ritengo che sia ...
I have the impression that her parents don't understand her.	Ho l'impressione che ...
I'm sure he is completely sincere.	Sono sicuro che ...
I'm convinced that there are other possibilities.	Sono convinto che ...
In my opinion, he hasn't changed.	A mio parere o avviso ...
In my view, he's their best player.	Secondo me ...

Per rispondere senza dare un'opinione

It depends.	Dipende.
It all depends on what you mean by patriotism.	Dipende da cosa intendi per ...
I'd rather not express an opinion.	Preferisco non pronunciarmi.
Actually, I've never thought about it.	A dire il vero, non ci ho mai pensato.

❏ Approvazione e accordo

I think it's an excellent idea.	Mi sembra una magnifica idea.
What a good idea!	Ottima idea!
I was very impressed by his speech.	Ho apprezzato moltissimo ...
It's a very good thing.	È un'ottima cosa.
I think you're right to be wary.	Secondo me hai ragione a ...
Newspapers are right to publish these stories.	... fanno bene a ...

You were **right to** leave your bags in left-luggage.

Hai fatto bene a ...

Third World countries **rightly believe that** most pollution comes from developed countries.

... ritengono giustamente che ...

You're quite justified in complaining.

Non hai torto a ...

I share this view.

Condivido l'opinione.

I fully share your concern.

Condivido pienamente la sua ...

We support the creation of jobs.

Siamo favorevoli alla ...

We are in favour of a united Europe.

Siamo a favore dell' ...

It is true that mistakes were made.

È vero che ...

I agree with you.

Sono d'accordo con lei.

I entirely agree with you.

Sono assolutamente d'accordo con lei.

❏ *Disapprovazione e dissenso*

I think he was wrong to borrow so much money.

Trovo che abbia sbagliato a ...

It's a pity that you didn't tell me.

È un peccato che ...

It is regrettable that they allowed this to happen.

C'è da rammaricarsi che ...

I dislike the idea **intensely.**

... non mi piace per niente.

I can't stand lies.

Non sopporto ...

We are against hunting.

Siamo contro ...

We do not condone violence.

Crediamo che ... sia ingiustificabile o non abbia scusanti.

I am opposed to compulsory screening.

Sono contrario al ...

I don't share this point of view.

Non condivido questo punto di vista.

I am disappointed by his attitude.

Sono deluso del ...

I am deeply disappointed.

Sono profondamente deluso.

You shouldn't have said that.

Non avresti dovuto ...

What gives him the right to act like this?

Che diritto ha di ...

I disagree.

Non sono d'accordo.

We don't agree with them.

Non siamo d'accordo con ...

I totally disagree with what he said.

Non sono affatto d'accordo con ...

It is not true to say that the disaster was inevitable.
You are wrong!

Non è vero che ...
Ti sbagli!

❏ *Scuse*

Per chiedere scusa

Sorry.
Oh, sorry! I've got the wrong number.
Sorry to bother you.
I'm sorry I woke you.
I'm terribly sorry about the misunderstanding.

I do apologize.
We hope our readers will excuse this oversight.

Scusa.
Oh, scusi!
Scusi se la disturbo.
Scusa se ...
Sono terribilmente
   spiacente per ...
La prego di scusarmi.
Preghiamo ... di ...

... ammettendo responsabilità

It's my fault; I should have left earlier.

I shouldn't have laughed at her.
We were wrong not to check this information.

I take full responsibility for what I did.

If only I had done my homework!

È colpa mia, sarei
   dovuto ...
Non avrei dovuto ...
Abbiamo sbagliato a
   non ...
Mi assumo la piena
   responsabilità delle ...
Se solo avessi ...

... declinando responsabilità

It's not my fault.
It isn't my fault if we're late.
I didn't do it on purpose.
I had no option.

But I thought that it was okay to park here.
I thought I was doing the right thing in warning him.

Non è colpa mia.
Non è colpa mia se ...
Non l'ho fatto apposta.
Non ho potuto fare
   altrimenti.
Pensavo che ...
Credevo di fare bene ad ...

Per esprimere rammarico

I'm sorry, but it's impossible.	Mi dispiace, ma ...
I'm afraid we're fully booked.	Purtroppo ...
Unfortunately we are unable to meet your request.	Purtroppo non siamo in grado di ...

❏ *Spiegazioni*

Cause

I didn't buy anything **because** I had no money.	... perché ...
I arrived late **because of** the traffic.	... a causa del ...
Since you insist, I'll come again tomorrow.	Visto o dato che ...
As I lived near the library, I used it a lot.	Siccome ...
I got through it **thanks to** the support of my friends.	... grazie all'...
Given the present situation, finding a job will be difficult.	Vista o Data ...
Given that there is an economic crisis, it is difficult to find work.	Dato che ...
Considering how many problems we had, we did well.	Considerando ...
It was a broken axle **that caused** the derailment.	È stata ... che ha causato ...
He resigned **for** health **reasons.**	... per motivi di ...
The theatre is closing, **due to** lack of funds.	... per ...
The project was abandoned **owing to** legal problems.	... a causa di ...
Many cancers **are linked to** smoking.	... sono legati al ...
The problem is that people are afraid of computers.	Il problema è che ...
The drop in sales **is the result of** high interest rates.	... è il risultato dei ...
The quarrel **resulted from** a misunderstanding.	... ha avuto origine da ...

Per spiegare le conseguenze di una situazione

I have to leave tonight; **so** I can't come with you.	... quindi ...
Distribution has been improved **so that** readers now get their newspaper earlier.	... cosicché ...
This cider is fermented for a very short time and is **consequently** low in alcohol.	... di conseguenza ...

Our lack of consultation **has resulted in** a duplication of effort.	*... ha avuto come consequenza ...*
That's why they are easy to remember.	*Ecco perché ...*

❏ *Paragoni*

Gambling **can be compared to** a drug.	*Si può paragonare ... a ...*
The gas has a smell **that can be compared to** rotten eggs.	*... paragonabile a ...*
The shape of Italy **is often compared to** a boot.	*... è spesso paragonata a ...*
The noise **was comparable to** that of a large motorbike.	*... era paragonabile a ...*
Africa is still underpopulated **compared with** Asia.	*Paragonata all'...*
In the UK, the rate of inflation increased slightly **compared to** the previous year.	*... rispetto all'...*
What is so special about a holiday in Florida **as compared to** one in Spain?	*... a paragone di ...*
This story **is like** a fairy tale.	*... sembra ...*
He loved this countryside, which **reminded him of** Ireland.	*... gli ricordava ...*
Frightening levels of unemployment, **reminiscent of those** of the 30s.	*... che ricordano ...*
The snowboard **is the equivalent** on snow **of** the skateboard.	*... è l'equivalente dello ...*
This sum **corresponds to** six months' salary.	*... corrisponde a ...*
A 'bap'? **It's the same thing as** a bread roll.	*È esattamente come ...*
It comes to the same thing in terms of calories.	*... è perfettamente equivalente.*
This record **is no better and no worse than** the others.	*... non è né meglio né peggio degli ...*

Sottolineando le differenze ...

No catastrophe **can compare with** Chernobyl.	*... non ha uguali.*
Modern factories **cannot be compared with** those our grandparents worked in.	*... non si possono paragonare con ...*
The actions of this group **are in no way comparable to** those of terrorists.	*... non hanno niente in comune con ...*
The newspaper reports **differ** on this point.	*... si differenziano ...*

The history of the United States **in no way resembles** our own.	... non assomiglia affatto alla ...
There are worse things than losing a European cup final.	C'è di peggio che ...
This film **is less** interesting **than** his first one.	... è meno ... del ...
Women's life expectancy is 81 years, **while** men's is 72.	... mentre ...
While the consumption of wine and beer is decreasing, the consumption of bottled water is increasing.	Mentre ...

❑ *Richieste e offerte*

Richieste

I'd like another beer.	Vorrei ...
I'd like to know the times of trains to Edinburgh.	Vorrei ...
Could you give us a hand?	Potresti ...
Can you tell Eleanor the good news?	Puoi ...
Could you please show me the way out?	Potrebbe per cortesia ...
Could I ask you for a few minutes of your time?	Può concedermi ...
Be an angel, pop to the baker's for me.	Sii gentile ...
If you wouldn't mind waiting for a moment.	Se non le dispiace ...
Would you mind opening the window?	Le spiacerebbe ...
Would you be very kind and save my seat for me?	Potrebbe farmi la cortesia di ...
I would be grateful if you could reply as soon as possible.	Le sarei grato se ...

Offerte

I can come and pick you up **if** you like.	Posso ... se ...
I could go with you.	Potrei ...
Do you fancy a bit of Stilton?	Ti va ...
How about a pear tart?	Che ne dici di ...
Would you like to see my photos?	Vi piacerebbe ...

| Would you like to have dinner with me one evening? | Ti andrebbe di ... |
| Do you want me to go and get your car? | Vuoi che ... |

❏ Consigli e suggerimenti

Per chiedere un consiglio

What would you do, if you were me?	Cosa faresti, al posto mio?
Would you accept, **if you were me?**	Se fossi in me ...
What's your opinion on this?	Cosa ne pensi?
What, in your opinion, should be done to reduce pollution?	Cosa bisognerebbe fare, secondo voi, per ...
What would you advise?	Cosa consigli?
What would you advise me to do?	Cosa mi consigli di fare?
Which would you recommend, Majorca or Ibiza?	Quale ci consiglia ...
If we were to sponsor a player, **who would you recommend?**	... chi raccomanderesti?
What strategy **do you suggest?**	Che ... proponi?
How would you deal with unemployment?	Come affrontereste ...

Per dare un suggerimento

If I were you, I'd be a bit wary.	Se fossi in te ...
If I were you I wouldn't say anything.	Al posto tuo ...
Take my advice, buy your tickets in advance.	Se posso darle un consiglio ...
A word of advice: read the instructions.	Un consiglio ...
A useful tip: always have some pasta in your cupboard.	Un consiglio ...
As you like languages, **you ought to** train as a translator.	... dovresti ...
You should see a specialist.	Dovresti ...
You would do well to see a solicitor.	Faresti bene a ...
You would do better to spend the money on a new car.	Faresti meglio a ...

You could perhaps ask someone to go with you.	Forse potresti ...
You could try being a little more understanding.	Potresti ...
Perhaps you should speak to a plumber about it.	Forse dovresti ...
Perhaps we ought to try a different approach.	Forse dovremmo ...
Why don't you phone him?	Perché non ...
How about renting a video?	E se ...
How about 3 March at 10.30am?	Io proporrei ...
It might be better to give her money rather than jewellery.	Forse sarebbe meglio ...
It would be better to wait a bit.	Sarebbe meglio ...

Avvertimenti

I warn you, I intend to get my own back.	Ti avverto ...
I'd better warn you that he knows you did it.	Ti avverto che ...
Don't forget to keep a copy of your income tax return.	Ricordati di ...
Remember: appearances can be deceptive.	Non fidarti: l'apparenza inganna.
Beware of buying tickets from touts.	Diffidate dei ...
Whatever you do, don't leave your camera in the car.	Soprattutto, non ... mai ...
If you don't book early you risk being disappointed.	... rischi di ...

❏ *Intenzioni e desideri*

Per chiedere a qualcuno cosa intenda fare

What are you going to do?	Cosa pensi di fare?
What will you do if you fail your exams?	Cosa farai se ...
What are you going to do when you get back? Do you have anything planned?	Cosa conti di fare ... Hai dei progetti?
Can we expect you next Sunday?	Vi aspettiamo ...
Are you planning to spend all of the holiday here?	Conti di ...
Are you planning on staying long?	Conti di ...

What are you planning to do with your collection?	*Cosa conti di fare della ...*
What are you thinking of doing?	*Cosa pensi di fare?*
Do you intend to go into teaching?	*Hai intenzione di ...*
Are you thinking of making another film in Europe?	*Conta di ...*

Per esprimere le proprie intenzioni

I was planning to go to New York on 8 July.	*Pensavo di ...*
She plans to go to India for a year.	*Prevede di ...*
There are plans to build a new stadium.	*È prevista ...*
The bank intends to close a hundred branches.	*... ha intenzione di ...*
I am thinking of giving up politics.	*Sto pensando di ...*
I have decided to get a divorce.	*Ho deciso di ...*
I have made up my mind to stop smoking.	*Ho deciso di ...*
We never had any intention of talking to the press.	*Non è mai stata nostra intenzione ...*
That's settled, we'll go to Florida in May.	*È deciso ...*
For me, living abroad is out of the question.	*... è fuori discussione.*

Desideri

I'd like to be able to play as well as him.	*Vorrei ...*
I'd like to go hang-gliding.	*Mi piacerebbe ...*
I would like my photos to be published.	*Vorrei che ...*
I would like to have had a brother.	*Mi sarebbe piaciuto avere ...*
I want to act in films.	*Voglio ...*
Ian wanted at all costs to prevent his boss finding out.	*... voleva a tutti i costi ...*
We wish to preserve our independence.	*È nostro desiderio ...*
I hope to have children.	*Spero di ...*
We hope that children will watch this programme with their parents.	*Ci auguriamo che ...*
Do you dream of winning the lottery?	*Sogni di ...*
I dream of having a big house.	*Il mio sogno sarebbe di ...*

❏ *Obbligo*

I **must** find somewhere to live.	*Devo ...*
We **really must** see each other more often!	*Dobbiamo assolutamente ...*
If you're going to Poland, **you must** learn Polish.	*... devi ...*
He **made** his secretary answer all his calls.	*Esigeva che ...*
My mother **makes me** eat spinach.	*... mi costringe a ...*
The hijackers **demanded that** the plane fly to New York.	*... hanno preteso che ...*
A serious illness **forced me to** cancel my holiday.	*... mi ha costretto a ...*
He **was obliged to** borrow more and more money.	*Ha dovuto ...*
Mary **had no choice but to** invite him.	*... non poteva fare altro che ...*
The **only thing you can do is** say no.	*Non puoi fare altro che ...*
Many mothers **have to** work; **they have no other option.**	*... devono ... non hanno scelta.*
She had the baby adopted because **she had no other option.**	*... non poteva fare altrimenti.*
School **is compulsory** until the age of sixteen.	*... è obbligatoria ...*
It is essential to know some history, if we are to understand the situation.	*È indispensabile ...*

❏ *Permesso*

Per chiedere il permesso

Can I use the phone?	*Posso ...*
Can I ask you something?	*Posso ...*
Is it okay if I come now, or is it too early?	*Va bene se ...*
Do you mind if I smoke?	*Le dà fastidio se ...*
Do you mind if I open the window?	*Le spiace se ...*
Would you mind if I had a look in your briefcase, madam?	*Permette che ...*
Could I have permission to leave early?	*Posso ...*

Per concedere il permesso

Do as you please.	*Fate come volete.*
Go ahead!	*Faccia pure!*
No, of course I don't mind.	*No, non ci sono problemi.*
I have nothing against it.	*Non ho niente in contrario.*
Pupils **are allowed to** wear what they like.	*... possono ...*

Per negare il permesso

I **forbid you to** go out!	*Ti proibisco di ...*
It's **forbidden**.	*È vietato.*
Smoking in the toilet **is forbidden**.	*È vietato ...*
Child labour is **strictly forbidden by** a UN convention.	*... assolutamente proibito da ...*
No entry.	*Vietato l'ingresso.*
No parking.	*Sosta vietata.*
It's **not allowed**.	*Non è permesso.*
You **are not allowed to** swim in the lake.	*È vietato ...*
We **weren't allowed to** eat or drink while on duty.	*Non potevamo ...*
That's **out of the question**.	*È fuori discussione.*

❏ Certezza, probabilità e possibilità

Certezza

Undoubtedly, there will be problems.	*... senz'altro ...*
There is no doubt that the country's image has suffered.	*Non c'è alcun dubbio che ...*
It's bound to cause trouble.	*Sicuramente ...*
Clearly the company is in difficulties.	*È evidente che ...*
A foreign tourist is **quite obviously** a rare sight here.	*... ovviamente ...*
It is undeniable that she was partly to blame.	*È innegabile che ...*
I am sure you will like my brother.	*Sono sicuro che ...*
I am sure that I will win.	*Sono sicuro di ...*
I'm sure that I won't get bored working with him.	*Sono sicuro che ...*

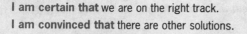

I am **certain that** we are on the right track.

I am **convinced that** there are other solutions.

Sono sicuro che ...

Sono convinto che ...

Probabilità

The price of petrol will **probably** rise.

Inflation will **very probably** exceed 10%.

It is highly probable that they will abandon the project.

The trend **is likely** to continue.

80% of skin problems **undoubtedly** have psychological origins.

They were **no doubt** right.

The construction work **should** start in April.

He **must have** forgotten to open the windows.

È probabile che ...

Molto probabilmente ...

È molto probabile che ...

È probabile che ...

... senza dubbio ...

... senza dubbio ...

... dovrebbero ...

Deve avere ...

Possibilità

It's possible.

It is possible that they got your name from the electoral register.

It is not impossible that he has gone to Manchester.

That might be more expensive.

He may have misunderstood.

This virus **may** be extremely infectious.

It may be that it will take time to achieve peace.

In a few months everything **could** change.

Perhaps I am mistaken.

È possibile.

È possibile che ...

Non è da escludersi che ...

Potrebbe essere ...

Potrebbe avere ...

... potrebbe ...

Potrebbe darsi che ...

... potrebbe ...

Puo darsi che ...

❑ Dubbio, improbabilità e impossibilità

Dubbio

I'm not sure it's useful.

I'm not sure I'll manage.

I'm not sure that it's a good idea.

Non sono sicuro che sia ...

Non sono sicuro di ...

Non sono sicuro che ...

We cannot be sure that the problem will be solved.	Non sappiamo con certezza se ...
I very much doubt he'll adapt to not working.	Dubito fortemente che ...
Is it wise? I doubt it.	Ne dubito.
He began to have doubts about his doctor's competence.	... dubitare della ...
I wonder if we've made much progress in this area.	Mi domando se ...
There is no guarantee that a vaccine can be developed.	Non è sicuro che ...
Nobody knows exactly what happened.	Non si sa esattamente ...

Improbabilità

He probably won't change his mind.	Probabilmente non ...
It is unlikely that there'll be any tickets left.	È poco probabile che ...
I'd be surprised if they had your size.	Mi sorprenderebbe se ...
They are not likely to get the Nobel prize for Economics!	È improbabile che ...
There is not much chance the growth rate will exceed 1.5%.	Ci sono poche probabilità che ...
There's no danger we'll get bored.	Non c'è pericolo di ...
It would be amazing if everything went according to plan.	Sarebbe sorprendente che ...

Impossibilità

It's impossible.	È impossibile.
It is not possible for the government to introduce this bill before the recess.	Non è possibile per ...
This information cannot be wrong.	È impossibile che ...
There is no chance of their helping us.	Non c'è alcuna possibilità che ...

❏ *Saluti*

Hello!	Ciao! o Salve!
Hi!	Ciao!
Good morning!	Buongiorno!

Good afternoon!	Buonasera!
Good evening!	Buonasera!
How's it going?	Come va?
How's things?	Come vanno le cose?
How's life?	Come va la vita?
How are you?	Come sta?

Come rispondere

Very well, and you?	Molto bene grazie, e lei?
Fine, thanks.	Bene, grazie.
So-so.	Così così.
Could be worse.	Potrebbe andare peggio.

Per fare le presentazioni

This is Charles.	Questo è ...
Let me introduce you to my girlfriend.	Le presento ...
I'd like you to meet my husband.	Ti voglio far conoscere ...
I don't believe you know one another.	Non credo che vi conosciate.

Cosa dire durante le presentazioni

Pleased to meet you.	Piacere.
How do you do?	Molto piacere.
Hi, I'm Jane.	Ciao, sono ...

Accomiatarsi

Bye!	Ciao!
Goodbye!	Arrivederci!
Good night!	Buonanotte!
See you!	Ci vediamo!
See you later!	A più tardi!

See you soon!	A presto!
See you tomorrow!	A domani!
See you next week!	Alla settimana prossima!
See you Thursday!	A giovedì!

Auguri

Happy Birthday!	Buon compleanno!
Many happy returns!	Cento di questi giorni!
Happy Christmas!	Buon Natale!
Happy New Year!	Buon Anno!
Happy Anniversary!	Buon anniversario!
Congratulations!	Congratulazioni! o Complimenti!
Welcome!	Benvenuti!
Good luck!	Buona fortuna!
Safe journey!	Buon viaggio!
Get well soon!	Guarisci presto!
Take care!	Stammi bene!
Have fun!	Divertiti!
Cheers!	Cin cin! o Salute!
Enjoy your meal!	Buon appetito!

❏ *Corrispondenza*

Come intestare una lettera in Gran Bretagna

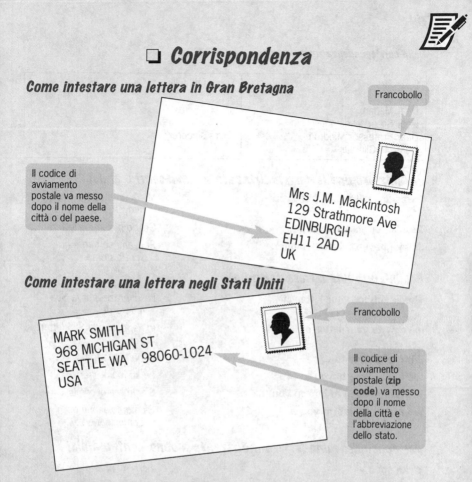

Francobollo

Il codice di avviamento postale va messo dopo il nome della città o del paese.

Mrs J.M. Mackintosh
129 Strathmore Ave
EDINBURGH
EH11 2AD
UK

Come intestare una lettera negli Stati Uniti

Francobollo

MARK SMITH
968 MICHIGAN ST
SEATTLE WA   98060-1024
USA

Il codice di avviamento postale (**zip code**) va messo dopo il nome della città e l'abbreviazione dello stato.

Abbreviazioni usate comunemente negli indirizzi

Ave = avenue	Dr = drive	Pl = place	Sq = square
Cres = crescent	Gdns = gardens	Rd = road	St = street

Formule di apertura e chiusura standard

Per scrivere a conoscenti o amici

Dear Mr and Mrs Roberts	Yours (*abbastanza formale*)
Dear Kate and Jeremy	With best wishes
Dear Aunt Jane and Uncle Alan	Love from
Dear Granny	Lots of love from (*informale*)

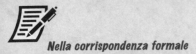

Nella corrispondenza formale

Dear Sirs Dear Sir Dear Madam Dear Sir or Madam Dear Professor Meldrum Dear Ms Gilmour	Yours faithfully Yours sincerely

Per iniziare una lettera indirizzata a conoscenti o amici

It was lovely to hear from you.	Mi ha fatto molto piacere ricevere tue notizie.
Thanks for your letter ...	Grazie per la tua lettera ...
Sorry I haven't written sooner.	Scusami se non ti ho scritto prima.

Per iniziare una lettera formale

Thank you for your letter of ...	La ringrazio per la Sua lettera del ...
In reply to your letter of ...	In risposta alla Sua lettera del ...
With reference to ...	In riferimento a ...
We are writing to you to ...	Le scriviamo per ...
We are pleased to inform you ...	Siamo lieti di comunicarle ...
We regret to inform you ...	Siamo spiacenti di comunicarle ...

Per concludere una lettera indirizzata a conoscenti o amici

Write soon.	Scrivimi presto.
Give my regards to ...	Salutami ...
... sends his/her best wishes.	Saluti da ...
Give my love to ...	Dà un bacio da parte mia a ...

Per chiudere una lettera formale

I look forward to hearing from you.	Resto in attesa di una Sua cortese risposta.
Thanking you in advance for your help.	RingraziandoLa anticipatamente del Suo aiuto.
If you require any further information please do not hesitate to contact me.	Resto a Sua disposizione per eventuali ulteriori informazioni.

❏ *Lettera di ringraziamento*

Indirizzo del mittente.

18 Slateford Ave
Leeds
LS24 3PR

9th May 2004

Data.

Dear Gran and Grandpa,

Thank you both very much for the CDs which you sent me for my birthday. They are two of my favourite groups and I'll really enjoy listening to them.

There's not much news here. I seem to be spending most of my time studying for my exams which start in two weeks. I'm hoping to pass all of them but I'm not looking forward to the Maths exam as that's my worst subject.

Mum says that you're off to Crete on holiday next week, so I hope that you have a great time and come back with a good tan.

Tony sends his love.

With love from

Per le alternative, vedi pag.21.

Prenotazione alberghiera

109 Bellview Road
Cumbernauld
CA7 4TX

14th June 2004

Data.

Mrs Elaine Crawford
Manager
Poppywell Cottage
Westleigh
Devon
DV3 8SP

Nome e indirizzo del destinatario della lettera.

Dear Mrs Crawford,

My sister stayed with you last year and has highly recommended your guest house.

I would like to reserve a family room for one week from 18th to 24th August of this year. I would be obliged if you would let me know how much this would be for two adults and two children, and whether you have a room available on those dates.

I hope to hear from you soon.

Yours sincerely,

Andrew Naismith

Questa formula va usata quando si conosce il nome della persona a cui si scrive.

❑ *Lettera di reclamo*

Per le alternative, vedi pag.22.

85 Rush Lane
Triptown
Lancs
LC4 2DT

20th February 2004

Woodpecker Restaurant
145 Main Street
Triptown
Lancs
LC4 3EF

Dear Sir/Madam

I was to have dined in your restaurant last Thursday by way of celebrating my wedding anniversary with my wife and young son but am writing to let you know of our great dissatisfaction.

I had reserved a corner table for two with a view of the lake. However, when we arrived we had to wait for more than 20 minutes for a table and even then, not in the area which I had chosen. There was no highchair for my son as was promised and your staff made no effort whatsoever to accommodate our needs. In fact, they were downright discourteous. Naturally we went elsewhere, and not only have you lost any future custom from me, but I will be sure to advise my friends and colleagues against your establishment.

Yours faithfully

T. Greengage

Questa formula va usata quando non si conosce il nome della persona a cui si scrive.

❏ *Curriculum Vitae*

CURRICULUM VITAE

Name:	Rosalind A. Williamson
Address:	11 North Street, Barnton NE6 2BT
Telephone:	01294 476230
E-mail:	rosalindw@metalcomp.co.uk
Date of Birth:	18/4/1980
Nationality:	British
Marital Status:	Single

CAREER

2/97 to date: Sales and Marketing Executive,
Metal Company plc, Barnton

11/95-1/97:   Marketing Assistant,
Metal Company plc

QUALIFICATIONS

1991-1995:   University of Newby
BA (Hons) Italian with French – 2:1

1984-1991:   Barnton Comprehensive School
A-levels: English Literature (D), French (B), Italian (A)
GCSEs: Art, Chemistry, English Language, English Literature, French, German, Italian, Maths

OTHER SKILLS

Computer literate (Word for Windows, Excel, QuarkXPress), good keyboarding skills, full, clean driving licence.

INTERESTS

Travel (have travelled extensively throughout Europe and North America), riding and sailing.

REFEREES

Ms Alice Bluegown
Sales and Marketing Manager
Metal Company plc
Barnton
NE4 3KL

Dr I.O. Sono
Department of Italian
University of Newby
Newby
S13 2RR

11 North Street
Barnton
NE6 2BT

18 August 2004

The Personnel Director
Clifton Manufacturing Ltd
Firebrick House
Clifton
MK45 6RB

> Questa formula va utilizzata se non si conosce il sesso della persona a cui si sta scrivendo. Se invece si conosce il nome della persona a cui si sta scrivendo, per esempio:
> **Mrs Lynn Kerr**
> **Personnel Director**
> **Clifton Manufacturing Ltd** ecc.
> la lettera va iniziata con la seguente formula:
> **Dear Mrs Kerr**

Dear Sir or Madam

With reference to your advertisement in the Guardian of 15 August, I wish to apply for the position of Marketing Manager in your company.

I am currently employed as a Sales and Marketing Executive for the Metal Company in Barnton where my main role is maintaining and developing links with our customers within the UK and producing material for marketing purposes.

I am interested in this position as it offers an opportunity to apply my sales and marketing skills in a new and challenging direction. I enclose my Curriculum Vitae for your consideration. Please do not hesitate to contact me if you require any further details.

Yours faithfully

Rosalind Williamson

Enc.

> Questa formula va usata quando non si conosce il nome della persona a cui si scrive.

> = **enclosures.** Da aggiungere se si allegano alla lettera ulteriori informazioni, p. es. un curriculum vitae.

Convocazione ad un colloquio di lavoro

Le aziende spesso inseriscono un numero di riferimento nella corrispondenza per facilitarne l'archiviazione.

CLIFTON MANUFACTURING LTD.

Firebrick House • Clifton MK45 6RB
Tel: (01367) 345 900 • Fax: (01367) 345 901
E-mail: personnel@cliftman.co.uk

Ref: RW/LK

27 August 2004

Ms Rosalind Williamson
11 North Street
Barnton
NE6 2BT

Dear Ms Williamson

Following your recent application for the position of Marketing Manager, I would like to invite you to attend an interview at the above office on Friday 3 September at 11am.

The interview will be conducted by the Sales and Marketing Director and myself and should last approximately one hour.

If this date does not suit please notify Jane Simpson on extension 3287 to arrange an alternative date.

We look forward to meeting you.

Yours sincerely

Lynn Kerr

Lynn Kerr (Mrs)
Personnel Director

Questa formula va usata se la lettera comincia con **Dear Ms Williamson** ecc.

❑ *Fax*

Brown & Sons

Northport Enterprise Park
Birmingham B45 6JH
Tel: 0121 346 3287
Fax: 0121 346 3288
E-mail: orders@brownandsons.co.uk

FAX

To: Emma Scott, Westcott Hotel

Date: 6 November 2004

From: Malcolm Marshall

No. of pages to follow: 1

Re your order of 23 October for 100 tablecloths (Catalogue number 435789), I regret to inform you that these items are currently out of stock.

The next delivery will be in approximately four weeks' time. However, if this delay is unacceptable to you, please can you let me know so that I can cancel the order.

I am sorry for any inconvenience this may cause.

Regards

Malcolm Marshall

**IF THERE ARE ANY PROBLEMS WITH THIS MESSAGE, PLEASE CONTACT
CLAIRE NEWPORT ON 0121 346 3287**

❏ *Posta elettronica*

Mandare un messaggio

New Message							⊠
File	**Edit**	**View**	**Tools**	**Compose**	**Help**	**Send**	

To: andrew@pmdesigns.co.uk	**New**	
Cc:	**Reply to Sender**	
Bcc:	**Reply to All**	
Subject: Meeting	**Forward**	
	Attachment	

Re our conversation this morning, would next Monday morning
10am be convenient for a meeting about the project's progress?
If this doesn't suit, I'm also free Wednesday morning.

Mark

New Message	Componi messaggio
File	File
Edit	Modifica
View	Visualizza
Tools	Strumenti
Compose	Componi
Help	Help
Send	Invia
New	Componi messaggio
Reply to Sender	Rispondi all'autore

❏ *Posta elettronica*

Ricevere un messaggio

Meeting					
File	**Edit**	**View**	**Tools**	**Compose**	**Help**

From: Andrew Collins (andrew@pmdesigns.co.uk)

Sent: 30 November 2004 08.30

To: mark.gordon@typo.co.uk

Subject: Meeting

> In inglese per comunicare a qualcuno il proprio indirizzo di posta elettronica si dice: **"andrew at pmdesigns dot co dot uk"**.

Mark,

Unfortunately I'm away on business all next week. Would it be possible to arrange a working lunch, Thursday or Friday of this week?

Sorry about this!

Andrew

Reply to All	Rispondi a tutti
Forward	Inoltra
Attachment	Inserisci file
To	A
Cc (carbon copy)	Cc
Bcc (blind carbon copy)	Ccn
Subject	Oggetto
From	Da
Sent	Data

❏ *Telefono*

Diversi tipi di telefonate

Local/national call.	Comunicazione urbana/interurbana.
I want to make an international call.	Vorrei chiamare all'estero.
I want to make a reverse-charge call *(Brit)* to a Paris number *o* I want to call a Paris number collect *(US)*.	Vorrei fare una chiamata a ... con addebito al destinatario.
How do I get an outside line?	Cosa devo fare per ottenere una linea esterna?

Come chiedere informazioni

What is the number for directory enquiries *(Brit)* o directory assistance *(US)*?	Qual è il numero del servizio informazioni?
Can you give me the number of Europost, 20 Cumberland Street, Newquay?	Vorrei il numero di ...
What is the code for Martinique?	Qual è il prefisso del ...
What is the number for the speaking clock?	Qual è il numero dell'ora esatta?

Come ricevere informazioni

The number you require is 0181-613 3297. *(o-one-eight-one six-one-three three-two-nine-seven)*	Il numero da lei richiesto è ...
I'm sorry, there's no listing under that name.	Spiacente, non c'è nessun abbonato con questo nome.
The number you require is ex-directory *(Brit)* o unlisted *(US)*.	Il numero da lei richiesto è fuori elenco.

Quando l'abbonato risponde

Could I speak to Mr Sanderson, please?	Vorrei o Potrei parlare con ...
Could you put me through to Dr Evans, please?	Può passarmi ...
Can I have extension 6578, please?	Può passarmi l'interno ...
I'll call back in half an hour.	Richiamo tra ...
Would you ask him to ring me when he gets back?	Può chiedergli di richiamarmi appena rientra?

Risponde il centralino

Who shall I say is calling?	Chi devo dire?
I'm putting you through.	Glielo passo.

I have a call from Tokyo for Mrs Thomson.	C'è una chiamata da ... per ...
I've got Miss Martin on the line.	Ho in linea ...
Dr Roberts is on another line. Do you want to wait?	... è occupato sull'altra linea, attende?
Please hold.	Attenda, prego.
There's no reply.	Non risponde.
Would you like to leave a message?	Desidera lasciare un messaggio?

Messaggi registrati

The number you have dialled has not been recognized. Please hang up.	Il numero selezionato è inesistente. Si prega di riattaccare.
The number you have dialled has been changed to 0171-789 0044.	L'abbonato ha cambiato numero. Il nuovo numero è ...
All the lines are busy right now. Please try again later.	A causa dell'ingente traffico, non ci è possibile dar seguito alla sua chiamata. La preghiamo di richiamare più tardi.
Hello, you have reached Sunspot Insurance. Please wait, your call will be answered shortly.	Buongiorno, siete in linea con ... Vi preghiamo di attendere: un operatore risponderà appena possibile.
Hello, you are through to Emma and Matthew Hargreaves. Please leave a message after the tone and we'll get back to you. Thanks.	Buongiorno, risponde la segreteria telefonica di ... Lasciate un messaggio dopo il bip, sarete richiamati al più presto.

Per rispondere al telefono

Hello, it's Anne speaking.	Pronto, sono ...
Speaking.	Sono io.
Who's speaking?	Chi parla?

In caso di difficoltà

I can't get through.	Non riesco a prendere la linea.
Their phone is out of order.	Il loro telefono è guasto.
We have been cut off.	È caduta la linea.
I must have dialled the wrong number.	Credo di aver sbagliato numero.
We've got a crossed line.	C'è un'interferenza sulla linea.
This is a very bad line.	La linea è molto disturbata.

❏ *Likes, dislikes and preferences*

Saying what you like

Mi piacciono i dolci.	*I like ...*
Mi piace che le cose siano al loro posto.	*I like ...*
Il film **mi è piaciuto**.	*I liked ...*
La visita ai vigneti **mi è piaciuta molto**.	*I very much enjoyed ...*
Adoro andare in discoteca.	*I love ...*
La cosa che mi piace di più è passare una serata con amici.	*What I like most is ...*
Il mio piatto **preferito** è il risotto.	*My favourite ...*
Leggere è **uno dei miei** passatempi **preferiti**.	*... one of my favourite ...*
Ho un debole per i dolci al cioccolato.	*I've got a weakness for ...*
Vado matto per la musica jazz.	*I'm crazy about ...*
Non c'è niente di meglio di un bel bagno caldo!	*There's nothing better than ...*
Non mi dispiace stare da solo.	*I don't mind ...*

Saying what you dislike

Non mi piace il pesce.	*I don't like ...*
Non mi piace molto parlare in pubblico.	*I'm not very keen on ...*
La birra **non mi piace per niente**.	*I don't like ... at all.*
Il suo comportamento **non mi piace per niente**.	*I don't like ... at all.*
Odio la chimica.	*I hate ...*
Detesto lo sport.	*I loathe ...*
Non sopporto che mi si dicano bugie.	*I can't stand ...*
Se c'è una cosa che odio è aspettare sotto la pioggia.	*What I hate most is ...*
Non è che l'idea **mi faccia impazzire**.	*I'm not madly keen on ...*

Saying what you prefer

Preferisco il rock **alla** musica classica.	*I prefer ... to ...*
Preferirei vivere a Parigi.	*I would rather ...*
Preferirei morire di fame **piuttosto che** chiedergli un favore.	*I'd rather ... than ...*
Mi piacerebbe di più lavorare a casa.	*I'd rather ...*

Expressing indifference

Per me fa lo stesso.	It's all the same to me.
Non ho preferenze.	I have no particular preference.
Come vuole _or_ preferisce.	As you like.
Non ha nessuna importanza.	It doesn't matter in the least.
È indifferente.	I don't mind.
Fai come credi, **per me è uguale.**	... it's all the same to me.

Asking what someone likes

Ti piacciono le patate fritte?	Do you like ...
Ti piace cucinare?	Do you like ...
Le piace vivere in città?	Do you like ...
Cosa preferisci: il mare o la montagna?	Which do you like better ...
Quale preferisci: il rosso o il nero?	Which do you prefer ...
Preferisci vivere in città o in campagna?	Do you prefer ...
Cosa ti piace di più in un uomo?	What do you like best ...

☐ *Opinions*

Asking for opinions

Cosa pensa del divorzio?	What do you think about ...
Cosa ne pensa?	What do you think about it?
Potrebbe dirmi la sua opinione su questo programma?	Could you tell me your opinion of ...
Vorrei sapere cosa pensi del suo lavoro.	I'd like to know what you think of ...
Qual è la sua opinione sulle probabilità di successo?	What is your opinion on ...
Mi piacerebbe sentire il suo parere su questo problema.	I'd like to hear your views on ...
Come ti sembra il suo modo di fare?	What do you think of ...
A suo parere, c'è parità tra uomini e donne?	In your opinion ...
A suo avviso, lui c'entra?	In your view ...
Secondo te, bisognerebbe ripensarci?	In your opinion ...

Expressing opinions

Hai ragione.	*You are right.*
Ha torto.	*He is wrong.*
Ha sbagliato a dimettersi.	*He was wrong to ...*
Sono sicuro che sia in buonafede.	*I'm sure he's ...*
Sono convinto che esistano altre soluzioni.	*I'm convinced that ...*
Sono convinto che sia la soluzione migliore.	*I'm sure that it's ...*
Penso che sarà possibile.	*I think ...*
Penso che tu sbagli.	*I think ...*
Credo che sia un po' prematuro.	*I think it's ...*
Credo che sia in ritardo.	*I think he's ...*
Mi sembra che sia normale.	*I think it's ...*
A mio parere, non è cambiato.	*In my opinion ...*
A mio avviso, è il caso di intervenire.	*In my opinion ...*
Per me, ha sbagliato.	*In my view ...*
Secondo me, è stato un grave errore.	*In my view ...*
Personalmente, ritengo che sia denaro sprecato.	*Personally, I think that it's ...*
Ho l'impressione che i suoi non la capiscano.	*I have the impression that ...*

Being noncommittal

Non ho un'opinione precisa al riguardo.	*I have no particular opinion on this.*
A dire il vero, non ci ho mai pensato.	*Actually, I have never thought about it.*
Dipende da cosa intendi per patriottismo.	*It all depends what you mean by ...*
Dipende.	*It depends.*
Preferisco non pronunciarmi.	*I'd rather not express an opinion.*

❏ *Approval and agreement*

Mi sembra una magnifica idea.	*I think it's an excellent idea.*
Ottima idea!	*What a good idea!*

Hai fatto bene a lasciare le valigie al deposito bagagli.	*You were right to ...*
Ho apprezzato moltissimo il suo articolo sul razzismo.	*I was very impressed by ...*
I giornali **fanno bene a** pubblicare queste notizie.	*... are right to ...*
Secondo me lei **ha ragione a** diffidarne.	*I think you're right to ...*
È un'ottima cosa.	*It's a very good thing.*
Non hai torto a lamentarti.	*You're quite justified in ...*
Condivido la sua opinione.	*I share your view.*
Condivido pienamente la sua apprensione.	*I fully share your ...*
Siamo favorevoli alla creazione di posti di lavoro.	*We are in favour of ...*
Siamo a favore dell'Europa unita.	*We are in favour of ...*
Ritengono giustamente che l'inquinamento provenga dalla fabbrica.	*They rightly believe that ...*
Sono d'accordo con lei.	*I agree with you.*
Sono pienamente d'accordo con te.	*I entirely agree with you.*
È vero che ci sono meno matrimoni oggi.	*It is true that ...*

❑ *Disapproval and disagreement*

Non sono d'accordo.	*I disagree.*
Non siamo d'accordo con loro.	*We don't agree with ...*
Non sono affatto d'accordo con quello che ha detto.	*I totally disagree with ...*
Non è vero che il risultato era inevitabile.	*It is not true to say that ...*
Ti sbagli!	*You are wrong!*
Non condivido il punto di vista degli euroscettici.	*I don't share the ... point of view.*
Siamo contro la caccia.	*We are against ...*
L'idea **non mi piace per niente.**	*I dislike ... intensely.*
Non sopporto le bugie.	*I can't stand ...*
La violenza è **ingiustificabile.**	*... cannot be justified.*
Sono contrario al test obbligatorio per l'AIDS.	*I am opposed to ...*
Trovo che abbia sbagliato a chiedere un prestito così grosso.	*I think he was wrong to ...*
Non avresti dovuto parlargli così.	*You shouldn't have ...*
Sono deluso del suo atteggiamento.	*I am disappointed by ...*

Sono profondamente deluso.	I am deeply disappointed.
È un peccato che costi così caro.	It's a pity that ...
È deplorevole che non siano in grado di trovare una soluzione.	It is highly regrettable that ...
Non possiamo permettere che la situazione peggiori.	We must not allow ...
Che diritto ha di agire così?	What gives him the right to ...

❏ *Apologies*

How to say sorry

Scusi.	Sorry.
Oh, scusi! Devo aver sbagliato piano.	Oh, sorry!
Scusi se la disturbo.	Sorry to bother you.
Scusa se ti ho svegliato.	I am sorry I ...
Mi dispiace per tutto quello che è successo.	I am sorry about ...
La prego di scusarmi.	I do apologize.
Preghiamo i lettori di scusare questa omissione.	We hope our readers will ...

Admitting responsibility

È colpa mia, sarei dovuto partire prima.	It's my fault, I should have ...
Non avrei dovuto ridere di lei.	I shouldn't have ...
Abbiamo sbagliato a non verificare questa informazione.	We were wrong not to ...
Mi assumo la piena responsabilità delle mie azioni.	I take full responsibility for ...
Purtroppo abbiamo commesso un errore nel conteggio.	We unfortunately made a mistake ...

Disclaiming responsibility

Non è colpa mia.	It's not my fault.
Non è colpa mia se siamo in ritardo.	It isn't my fault if ...
Non l'ho fatto apposta.	I didn't do it on purpose.
Non ho potuto fare altrimenti.	I had no option.

Mi era sembrato di capire che si potesse parcheggiare qui.

I thought that ...

Credevo di far bene a dirglielo.

I thought I was doing the right thing in ...

Apologizing for being unable to do something

Mi dispiace, ma è impossibile.

I'm sorry, but ...

Non posso fare altrimenti.

I have no other option.

Sono spiacente, ma purtroppo siamo al completo.

I'm sorry, but unfortunately ...

Siamo desolati di non poter soddisfare la sua richiesta.

We are very sorry we ...

❏ Explanations

Causes

Sono arrivato in ritardo **a causa del** traffico.

... because of ...

Il programma è stato abbandonato **a causa di** problemi legali.

.... owing to ...

Ha detto che è qui **per via del** fratello.

... because of ...

Sono riuscito a cavarmela **grazie all'**aiuto dei miei amici.

... thanks to ...

Non ho comprato niente **perché** non ho soldi.

... because ...

Visto or **dato che** insisti, tornerò domani.

Since ...

Siccome abitavo vicino alla biblioteca ci andavo spesso.

As ...

Vista la situazione attuale, non si può sperare in un miglioramento immediato.

Given ...

Dato che c'è una crisi economica, è difficile trovare lavoro.

Given that ...

Dati i problemi che abbiamo avuto, non ce la siamo cavata male.

Considering ...

È stata la rottura di un asse **che ha causato** il deragliamento.

It was ... that caused ...

Si è dimesso **per motivi di** salute.

... for ... reasons.

Il teatro chiude **per** mancanza di fondi.

... due to ...

Molte forme di tumore **sono legate al** fumo.

... are linked to ...

Il problema è che la gente è intimorita dai computer.

The problem is that ...

Il calo delle vendite **è il risultato dei** tassi d'interesse alti.

... is the result of ...

Consequences

Devo partire stasera, **quindi** non potrò venire con te.	... so ...
I contadini ora possono coltivare più terra, **col risultato che** la produzione di riso è aumentata.	... with the result that ...
La distribuzione è stata migliorata, **e dunque** i lettori riceveranno prima il loro giornale.	... and so ...
Il nuovo sidro viene fermentato molto poco e **di conseguenza** ha un basso contenuto alcolico.	... consequently ...
La mancanza di fondi **ha portato ad** un rallentamento del progetto.	... has resulted in ...
Sono tutti uguali **e perciò** è facile confondersi.	... and so ...

❏ Comparisons

Questo trattamento costa poco **se lo si paragona ad** altri.	... if one compares it to ...
Si può paragonare il gioco d'azzardo **a** una droga.	... can be compared to ...
Il gas di scarico ha un odore **simile a** quello delle uova marce.	... similar to ...
Il Vittoriale di d'Annunzio è **spesso paragonato a** una nave.	... is often compared to ...
Il rumore **era paragonabile a** quello di una grossa moto.	... was comparable to ...
L'Africa è ancora un continente sottopopolato **paragonato all'**Asia.	... compared with ...
L'Irlanda, **a paragone dell'**Islanda, ha un clima tropicale.	Compared to ...
In Francia, gli investimenti pubblicitari sono aumentati leggermente **rispetto all'**anno precedente.	... compared to ...
Questa storia **sembra** una favola.	... is like ...
Amava questa campagna che **gli ricordava** l'Irlanda.	... reminded him of ...
Livelli di disoccupazione **che ricordano** quelli degli anni '30.	... reminiscent of ...
La televisione è **l'equivalente** moderno **dei** circhi romani.	... is the ... equivalent of ...
Questa cifra **corrisponde a** sei mesi di stipendio.	... amounts to ...
'La schiacciata'? **È la stessa cosa che** la focaccia.	It's the same thing as ...
In termini di calorie è **equivalente**.	It comes to the same thing ...

Questo disco **non è né migliore né peggiore** dell'ultimo.

... is no better and no worse than ...

Stressing differences

Nessuna catastrofe **può essere paragonata a** quella di Černobyl.

No ... can compare with ...

Le fabbriche moderne **non si possono paragonare a** quelle in cui lavoravano i nostri nonni.

... cannot be compared with ...

Le azioni di questo gruppo **non hanno niente in comune con** le attività terroristiche.

... are in no way comparable to ...

I due personaggi **si differenziano** anche nei loro rapporti con le donne.

... differ ...

La storia degli Stati Uniti **non assomiglia affatto alla** nostra.

... in no way resembles ...

C'è di peggio che perdere la finale di Coppa Europa.

There are worse things than ...

Questo film **è meno** interessante **del** suo film d'esordio.

... is less ... than ...

Questo programma è **più** interessante **rispetto a** quello che ho visto ieri.

... is more ... than ...

La durata media della vita delle donne è di 81 anni, **mentre** quella degli uomini è di 72.

... while ...

❏ *Requests and offers*

Requests

Vorrei un'altra birra.

I'd like ...

Vorrei sapere gli orari dei treni per Padova.

I'd like to ...

Potrebbe darci una mano?

Could you ...

Può dare lei la buona notizia a Cinzia?

Can you ...

Sii gentile, fai un salto in panetteria.

Be an angel ...

Se non le dispiace attendere un attimo ...

If you wouldn't mind ...

Sarebbe così gentile da darci la ricetta?

Would you be so kind as to ...

Potrebbe farmi la cortesia di tenermi il posto?

Would you be very kind and ...

Potrebbe per cortesia indicarmi l'uscita?	*Could you please ...*
Può concedermi qualche minuto?	*Could you spare me ...*
Le spiacerebbe aprire la finestra?	*Would you mind ...*
Gradirei che mi comunicaste la decisione entro venerdì.	*I would be grateful if ...*
Le sarei grato se provvedesse affinché questo non si ripeta più.	*I would be grateful if ...*

Offers

Posso passare a prenderti, **se** vuoi.	*I can ... if ...*
Potrei accompagnarti io.	*I could ...*
Ti va un po' di gelato?	*Do you fancy ...*
Vi piacerebbe vedere le mie foto?	*Would you like to ...*
Che ne diresti di una crostata alle pere?	*Do you fancy ...*
Vuoi che vada a prendere la macchina?	*Do you want me to ...*
Le andrebbe di venire a cena con me una di queste sere?	*Would you like to ...*

❏ *Advice and suggestions*

Asking for advice or suggestions

Cosa faresti, al posto mio?	*What would you do, if you were me?*
È una questione complicata. **Tu cosa ne pensi?**	*What's your opinion?*
Quale ci consiglia, Majorca o Ibiza?	*Which would you recommend ...*
Cosa mi consiglia?	*What would you advise?*
Cosa mi consiglia di fare?	*What would you advise me to do?*
Se volessimo sponsorizzare un corridore, **chi raccomanderebbe?**	*... who would you recommend?*
Che strategia **proponi?**	*What ... do you suggest?*
Cosa bisognerebbe fare, secondo voi, per ridurre l'inquinamento?	*What, in your opinion, should be done to ...*
Come affrontereste la disoccupazione?	*How would you deal with ...*

Offering advice or suggestions

Se posso darle un consiglio, tenga le negative.	*If I may give you a bit of advice ...*
Un consiglio: leggete le istruzioni.	*A word of advice ...*
Se fossi in lei non mi fiderei.	*If I were you ...*
Al posto tuo non ne farei parola.	*If I were you ...*
Perché non gli telefoni?	*Why don't you ...*
Lei dovrebbe andare da uno specialista.	*You should ...*
Forse dovresti parlarne con un idraulico.	*Perhaps you should ...*
Farebbe bene a consultare un avvocato.	*You would do well to ...*
Faresti meglio a spendere quei soldi per comprare una macchina nuova.	*You would do better to ...*
Forse potrebbe chiedere a qualcuno di tradurglielo.	*You could perhaps ...*
Potresti essere un po' più comprensivo.	*You could ...*
Dato che hai senso del ritmo **dovresti** imparare a ballare.	*... you ought to ...*
Forse dovremmo tentare un approccio diverso.	*Perhaps we ought to ...*
E se noleggiassimo un video?	*How about ...*
Io proporrei il 3 marzo alle 10 e 30.	*How about ...*
Sarebbe bello rivedersi a Parigi.	*It would be nice to ...*
Forse sarebbe meglio regalarle dei soldi anziché dei gioielli.	*It might be better to ...*
Sarebbe meglio attendere i risultati del referendum.	*It would be better to ...*

Warnings

Soprattutto, non lasciare **mai** la macchina fotografica in auto.	*Whatever you do, don't ...*
Diffidate dei bagarini.	*Beware of ...*
Non fidarti: l'apparenza inganna.	*Remember: appearances can be deceptive.*
Se non prenoti per tempo **rischi** di non trovare posto.	*... you risk ...*
Ti avverto, mi vendicherò.	*I warn you ...*
Si ricordi di tenere una copia della dichiarazione dei redditi.	*Don't forget to ...*

❑ *Intentions and desires*

Asking what someone intends to do

Che progetti avete?	*What are your plans?*
Cosa conti di fare quando torni? **Hai dei progetti?**	*What are you going to do ... Do you have anything planned?*
Cosa conta di fare della sua collezione?	*What are you planning to do with ...*
Conta di restare molto tempo?	*Are you planning on ...*
Conta di girare un altro film in Europa?	*Are you thinking of ...*
Come pensi di fare?	*What are you thinking of doing?*
Cosa pensi di fare dopo la laurea?	*What are you thinking of doing ...*
Cosa farai se non passi agli esami?	*What will you do if ...*
Vi aspettiamo domenica prossima, d'accordo?	*We'll expect you ...*
Hai intenzione di seguire questa carriera?	*Do you intend to ...*

Talking about intentions

Pensavo di andare ad Ajaccio l'8 luglio.	*I was planning to ...*
Contiamo di vendere oltre centomila dischi.	*We reckon to ...*
Sto pensando di ritirarmi dalla politica.	*I am thinking of ...*
Prevede di trascorrere un anno in India.	*She plans to ...*
È prevista la costruzione di un nuovo stadio.	*There are plans to ...*
Ho deciso di divorziare.	*I have decided to ...*
È deciso, andiamo in Florida.	*That's settled ...*
È mia intenzione dirglielo prima possibile.	*I intend to ...*
La banca **ha intenzione di** chiudere oltre un centinaio di succursali.	*... intends to ...*
Non è mai stata nostra intenzione parlare male della stampa.	*We never had any intention of ...*
Per me vivere all'estero **è fuori discussione**.	*... is out of the question.*

Wishes

Voglio fare del cinema.	I want to ...
Vorrei suonare come Louis Armstrong.	I'd like to ...
Vorrei che le mie foto venissero pubblicate.	I would like ...
Mi piacerebbe fare qualche sport.	I'd like to ...
Mi sarebbe piaciuto avere un fratello.	I would have liked to ...
Spero di potermi sposare e avere dei bambini.	I hope to ...
Ci auguriamo che i bambini guardino questo programma con i genitori.	We hope that ...
Carlos **voleva a tutti i costi** impedire al capo di scoprirlo.	... wanted at all costs to ...
Sogni di vincere alla lotteria?	Do you dream of ...
Il mio sogno è quello di avere una casa grande.	I dream of ...
È nostro desiderio mantenere buoni rapporti.	We wish to ...

❏ Obligation

Devo trovare un alloggio.	I must ...
Dobbiamo assolutamente rivederci prima del 23!	We really must ...
Se vieni in Polonia **devi** imparare il polacco.	... you must ...
La scuola **è obbligatoria** come il servizio militare.	... is compulsory ...
Esigeva che la sua guardia del corpo dormisse nel corridoio.	He made ...
Mia madre **mi costringe a** mangiare spinaci.	... makes me ...
I dirottatori **hanno chiesto che** l'aereo ripartisse alla volta di New York.	... demanded that ...
Un attacco d'asma **mi ha costretto a** interrompere il viaggio.	... forced me to ...
Ha dovuto chiedere in prestito sempre più soldi.	... was obliged to ...
Non puoi fare altro che rifiutare.	You have no choice but to ...
Ha dato il bambino in adozione perché **non poteva fare altrimenti**.	... she had no other option.
Molte madri **sono obbligate a** lavorare, **non hanno scelta**.	... have to ...; they have no other option.
È indispensabile conoscere un po' la storia per comprendere la situazione.	It is essential to ...

❏ *Permission*

Asking for permission

Posso usare il telefono?	*Could I ...*
Posso chiederle qualcosa?	*Can I ...*
Va bene se vengo ora, o è troppo presto?	*Is it alright if ...*
Le spiace se apro la finestra?	*Do you mind if ...*
Le dà fastidio se fumo?	*Do you mind if ...*
Permette che guardi nella sua valigetta, signora?	*Would you mind if ...*
Posso avere il permesso di andare via prima?	*May I have permission to ...*

Giving permission

Fate come volete.	*Do as you please.*
Vai pure!	*Of course you can go!*
Non ho niente in contrario.	*I have nothing against it.*
Alle 8 **mi hanno detto che potevo** andarmene.	*... they told me I could ...*
I ragazzi **possono** uscire due volte alla settimana.	*... are allowed to ...*
Ti permetto di andarci se mi prometti di telefonare quando arrivi.	*I'll let you ...*

Saying something is not allowed

Ti proibisco di uscire!	*I forbid you to ...*
È proibito.	*It's forbidden.*
È vietato fumare nella toilette.	*... is forbidden.*
Vietato l'ingresso.	*No entry.*
Sosta vietata.	*No parking.*
Divieto di sosta.	*No parking.*
Non è permesso.	*It's not allowed.*
Proibisce ai bambini **di** vedere i nonni.	*She forbids ... to ...*
Il lavoro infantile è **formalmente proibito da** una convenzione dell'ONU.	*... is strictly forbidden by ...*
Non potevamo né mangiare né bere, in servizio.	*We weren't allowed to ...*
È fuori discussione.	*That's out of the question.*
Non se ne parla nemmeno.	*It's out of the question.*

❏ Certainty, probability and possibility

Certainty

Ci saranno **senz'altro** dei problemi.	*Undoubtedly ...*
È evidente che l'azienda è in difficoltà.	*Clearly ...*
È innegabile che fosse in parte colpa sua.	*It is undeniable that ...*
Non c'è alcun dubbio che l'immagine del paese ne abbia risentito.	*There is no doubt that ...*
Vedere un turista è **ovviamente** una cosa rarissima.	*... quite obviously ...*
Sono sicuro che mio fratello ti piacerà.	*I am sure that ...*
Sono sicuro che siamo sulla pista giusta.	*I am certain that ...*
Sono sicuro di vincere.	*I am sure that I ...*
Ho la certezza di non annoiarmi, lavorando con lui.	*I am sure that ...*
Sono convinto che esistano altre soluzioni.	*I am convinced that ...*

Probability

L'80% dei problemi dermatologici è **senza dubbio** di origine psicologica.	*... undoubtedly ...*
È probabile che il costo della benzina aumenti.	*... probably ...*
Bisogna **probabilmente** rivedere i dati.	*... probably ...*
L'inflazione supererà **molto probabilmente** il 100%.	*... very probably ...*
Deve avere dimenticato di aprire la finestra.	*He must have ...*
I lavori di costruzione **dovrebbero** iniziare ad aprile.	*... should ...*
Potrebbe darsi che stiano osservando le nostre reazioni.	*It is quite possible that ...*

Possibility

È possibile.	*It is possible.*
È possibile che l'America sia stata scoperta dai cinesi.	*It is possible that ...*
Potrebbe essere più costoso.	*That might be ...*
Tra qualche mese **potrebbe** cambiare tutto.	*... could ...*
Questo virus **potrebbe** essere estremamente contagioso.	*... may ...*
Non è da escludersi che sia andato a Parigi.	*It is not impossible that ...*

Può darsi che ci voglia del tempo per concludere la pace. *It may be that ...*

Magari sbaglio. *Perhaps ...*

❏ *Doubt, improbability and impossibility*

Doubt

Non sono sicuro che sia utile.	*I'm not sure it's ...*
Non sono sicuro di aver ragione.	*I'm not sure ...*
Non sono certo che sia una buona idea.	*I'm not sure that it's ...*
Mi domando se abbiamo fatto molti progressi in questo campo.	*I wonder if ...*
È saggio? **Ne dubito.**	*I doubt it.*
Cominciò a **dubitare della** competenza del proprio medico.	*... have doubts about ...*
Dubito fortemente che possa adattarsi alla situazione.	*I very much doubt ...*
Non è sicuro che riesca ad arrivare in tempo.	*There is no certainty that ...*
Non sappiamo con certezza se è stato lui.	*We don't know for sure that ...*
Non si sa esattamente cosa sia successo.	*Nobody knows exactly ...*

Improbability

Probabilmente non cambierà idea.	*... probably won't ...*
È poco probabile che siano rimasti dei biglietti.	*It is unlikely that ...*
Mi sorprenderebbe se avessero il tuo numero.	*I'd be surprised if ...*
Non rischiamo di annoiarci.	*There's no danger of ...*
Ci sono poche probabilità che il tasso di crescita superi l'1,5%.	*It is unlikely that ...*
Sarebbe da stupirsi se tutto andasse liscio.	*It would be amazing if ...*

Impossibility

È impossibile.	*It's impossible.*
Non è possibile per l'80% dei giovani continuare gli studi superiori.	*It is not possible for ...*

È impossibile che quest'informazione sia falsa.

Non c'è alcuna possibilità che ci aiutino.

... cannot be ...

There is no chance of ...

❏ *Greetings*

Ciao!	Hello! or Hi!
Salve! *(more formal)*	Hello!
Come sta?	How are you?
Come va?	How's it going?
Come vanno le cose?	How's things?
Come va la vita?	How's life?
Buongiorno!	Good morning!
Buonasera!	Good afternoon! or Good evening!

What to say in reply

Molto bene grazie, e lei?	Fine thanks, and you?
Benone!	Great!
Così così.	So-so.
Non c'è male.	Not so bad.

Introductions

Questo è Charles.	This is ...
Le presento la mia ragazza.	May I introduce ...
Le voglio far conoscere mio marito.	I'd like you to meet ...

Replying to an introduction

Piacere.	Pleased to meet you.
Molto lieto.	How do you do

Leavetaking

Arrivederci!	Goodbye!
Buonanotte!	Good night!

Ciao!	Bye!
Ci vediamo!	See you!
A più tardi!	See you later!
A presto!	See you soon!
A domani!	See you tomorrow!
Alla settimana prossima!	See you next week!
A giovedì!	See you Thursday!

Best wishes

Buon compleanno!	Happy Birthday!
Cento di questi giorni!	Many happy returns!
Buon anniversario!	Happy Anniversary!
Buon Natale!	Merry Christmas!
Buon Anno!	Happy New Year!
Congratulazioni!	Congratulations!
Buon viaggio!	Safe journey!
Buon appetito!	Enjoy your meal!
Buona fortuna!	Good luck!
Divertiti!	Have fun!
Cin cin!	Cheers!
Buon riposo!	Sleep well!
Benvenuti!	Welcome!
Guarisci presto!	Get well soon!
Stammi bene!	Take care!

❏ *Correspondence*

How to address an envelope

Stamp

Gent. Sig.ra Bellini
Via dei Cairoli, 24
50131 FIRENZE

The postcode
precedes the name
of the town or area.

Common abbreviations used in addresses

Egr.	= Egregio	P.zza	= Piazza	Spett.	= Spettabile
Gent.	= Gentile	Sig.	= Signor	V.	= Via
P.le	= Piazzale	Sig.ra	= Signora	V.le	= Viale

Standard opening and closing formulae

In personal correspondence

Caro Signor Bianchi	Cari saluti *(quite informal)*
Cara Giovanna	A presto
Carissimo Pietro	Ti abbraccio affettuosamente
Cari Anna e Marco	Un abbraccio
Cara zia Bruna	Baci *(very informal)*

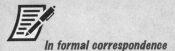

In formal correspondence

Egregio Sig. Millo Egr. Dott. Marsi Gent. Sig.ra Coretti Gent. Dott. Milesi Spett. Ditta	Distinti saluti Cordiali saluti

Starting a personal letter

Ti ringrazio per la tua lettera.

Mi ha fatto molto piacere ricevere vostre notizie.

Scusami se rispondo alla tua lettera solo ora, ma purtroppo ...

Thank you for your letter.

It was lovely to have your news.

Sorry for not replying sooner but unfortunately ...

Starting a formal letter

In riferimento alla Sua lettera del ...

Le scrivo in seguito alla nostra conversazione telefonica avvenuta il ...

Desidero innanzitutto ringraziarLa per la Sua lettera.

Le scrivo a proposito di ...

Abbiamo il piacere d'informarLa che ...

... ci dispiace doverLa informare che ...

Further to your letter of ...

Further to our telephone conversation of ...

Thank you very much for your letter.

I am writing to you about ...

We are pleased to inform you that ...

... we regret to inform you that ...

Ending a personal letter

Tanti saluti anche a ...

Dà un bacione da parte mia anche a ...

Mi raccomando, scrivimi presto!

Non vedo l'ora di avere vostre notizie.

Best wishes to ...

Give my love to ...

Write soon!

I look forward to hearing from you.

Ending a formal letter

RingraziandoLa anticipatamente, Le porgo i miei più cordiali saluti.

In attesa di una Vostra gentile risposta, invio distinti saluti.

Thanking you in advance. Yours sincerely ...

I look forward to hearing from you. Yours sincerely ...

☐ *Thank you letter*

Livorno, 7 gennaio 2004

Date.

Cari Simona e Gianluca,

grazie ancora per la stupenda festa di Capodanno. È stato un piacere immenso rivedere tanti vecchi amici che avevamo un po' perso di vista.

Non vediamo l'ora di incontrarvi di nuovo per fare una chiacchierata e per mostrarvi le foto che Stefano ha scattato durante la festa. Che ne dite di venire da noi a prendere un aperitivo e vedere le foto? Vi telefoneremo la settimana prossima per accordarci sulla data.

Una caro abbraccio

For alternatives see p51.

Annamaria e Stefano

❏ *Hotel booking*

Massimo Lupini
Via G. Murat, 12
00190 Roma

Name and address of sender.

Roma, 9 maggio 2004

Date.

Name and address of letter's recipient.

Spett. Direzione
Hotel Roma
Piazza Garibaldi, 4
38100 Trento

Spett. Direzione,

in seguito alla nostra conversazione telefonica del 28 aprile, vi scrivo per prenotare una camera singola per le notti del 16, 17 e 18 c.m. presso il vostro albergo. Arriverò a Trento mercoledì 16 verso le 23 e ripartirò sabato 19 in tarda mattinata.

Vi sarei grato se poteste confermarmi le tariffe e la prenotazione via fax al numero 06-6389836.

In attesa di un vostro gentile riscontro, invio cordiali saluti.

Massimo Lupini

❏ *Letter of complaint*

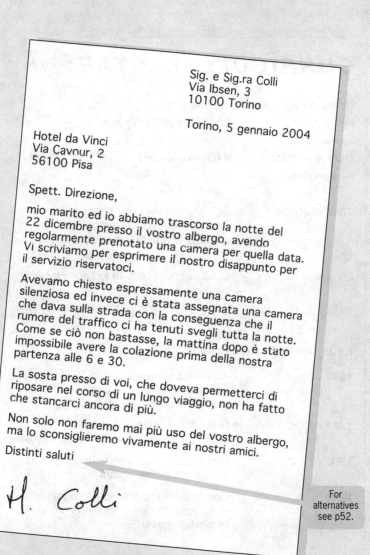

Sig. e Sig.ra Colli
Via Ibsen, 3
10100 Torino

Torino, 5 gennaio 2004

Hotel da Vinci
Via Cavour, 2
56100 Pisa

Spett. Direzione,

mio marito ed io abbiamo trascorso la notte del
22 dicembre presso il vostro albergo, avendo
regolarmente prenotato una camera per quella data.
Vi scriviamo per esprimere il nostro disappunto per
il servizio riservatoci.

Avevamo chiesto espressamente una camera
silenziosa ed invece ci è stata assegnata una camera
che dava sulla strada con la conseguenza che il
rumore del traffico ci ha tenuti svegli tutta la notte.
Come se ciò non bastasse, la mattina dopo è stato
impossibile avere la colazione prima della nostra
partenza alle 6 e 30.

La sosta presso di voi, che doveva permetterci di
riposare nel corso di un lungo viaggio, non ha fatto
che stancarci ancora di più.

Non solo non faremo mai più uso del vostro albergo,
ma lo sconsiglieremo vivamente ai nostri amici.

Distinti saluti

H. Colli

For
alternatives
see p52.

❏ Curriculum Vitae

CURRICULUM VITAE

If you have British or American qualifications you should give them, followed by a brief description in Italian.

Nome e cognome	Michela Grini
Indirizzo	Piazza Annali 23, Varese
Telefono	0332 45 67 89
Data di nascita	7 novembre 1981
Nazionalità	italiana

Titoli di studio	Diploma di ragioneria conseguito presso l'Istituto Fermi di Varese nel 1989 Diploma di dattilografia conseguito presso l'Istituto Manzoni di Varese.
Lingue	Ottima conoscenza della lingua inglese parlata e scritta Buona conoscenza della lingua francese parlata e scritta

Esperienze Professionali

1995 a oggi	Asole Costruzioni S.p.A. di Varese, con mansioni di segretaria personale dell'Amministratore unico
1993 - 1995	Presti S.p.A. di Varese, con mansioni di segretaria personale dell'Amministratore
1990 - 1992	Impresa Lanic di Varese, con mansioni di segretaria dattilografa
Varie	Conoscenza dei principali programmi di videoscrittura e di gestione ufficio Patente di guida

Michela Grini
Piazza Annali, 23
21100 Varese

Varese, 21 ottobre 2004

> INFOCOMP Sistemi Informatici
> Ufficio Assunzioni
> Via del Fiore, 9
> 25100 Brescia

Spett. INFOCOMP,

ho letto con molto interesse il Vostro annuncio
pubblicato su "La Gazzetta di Brescia" di oggi
e vorrei propormi per l'incarico di segretaria
bilingue. Come risulta dalla copia del
curriculum che allego, ho maturato una vasta
esperienza come segretaria, ho un'ottima
conoscenza delle lingue e possiedo buone
conoscenze informatiche.

Resto in attesa di una Vostra cortese risposta
e colgo l'occasione per inviarVi i miei più
cordiali saluti.

For alternatives see p52.

Michela Grini

❏ *Invitation to interview*

It is becoming very common to include an e-mail address in correspondence.

INFOCOMP SISTEMI INFORMATICI
Via del Fiore, 9 • 25100 BRESCIA
Tel.: 030-4829847 • e-mail: infocomp@com.it

Sig.ra Michela Grini
Piazza Annali, 23
21100 VARESE

Brescia, 29 ottobre 2004

Rif: am6

This is used to aid filing of correspondence.

Gent. Sig.ra Grini,

in risposta alla Sua recente candidatura al posto di segretaria bilingue, sono lieto di invitarLa ad un colloquio con il nostro direttore generale, Dott. Carlo Robini, lunedì 7 novembre alle ore 10 presso i nostri uffici di Brescia.

Qualora fosse impossibilitata a presentarsi al colloquio in tale data, La prego di contattare la nostra segretaria, Sig.ra Maria Ponzi (tel. 030-4829850), per concordare un altro appuntamento.

Cordiali saluti

Giancarlo Marchesini

Dott. Giancarlo Marchesini
Capo Ufficio Personale

The forms of address **Dott.** and **Dott.ssa** precede the names of all graduates.

❏ *Fax*

Studio legale Dott. Bini

Via Ghiberti, 25
33105 FIRENZE
Tel: 055–3453821
Fax: 055–3453822

FAX

Per: Sig. Carlo Salesi

Da: Maria Nelli

Oggetto: richiesta listini

Data: 19 novembre, 2004

Pagine: 1, inclusa questa

Gent. Sig. Salesi,

dovendo acquistare urgentemente 2 stampanti laser per il nostro studio,
Le scrivo per avere qualche informazione sulle stampanti fornite dalla
Sua ditta. Avremmo bisogno di un modello adatto alla stampa della
modulistica per le dichiarazioni dei redditi che possa servire anche per
le normali operazioni d'ufficio (invio lettere, ecc.).

Le sarei estremamente grata se potesse inviarmi al più presto via fax un
elenco completo delle stampanti attualmente disponibili specificando le
caratteristiche tecniche di ciascun esemplare e il prezzo.

Distinti saluti

Maria Nelli

**PER PROBLEMI DI RICEZIONE DEL FAX CONTATTARE IL NUMERO
055–3453821**

❏ E-mail

Sending messages

Componi messaggio				
File Modifica Visualizza Strumenti	**Componi**	?	Invia ✉	

A: francesca@abc.it	**Componi messaggio**
Cc:	**Rispondi all'autore**
Ccn:	**Rispondi a tutti**
Oggetto: Sono tornata!	**Inoltra**
	Inserisci file

Cara Francesca,

ho ricevuto il tuo messaggio solo oggi dato che sono appena ritornata
da una settimana di vacanza a Rimini. Ti manderò prima possibile
l'indirizzo che mi hai chiesto.

Un bacione,

Cristina

File	File
Modifica	Edit
Visualizza	View
Strumenti	Tools
Componi	Compose
Invia	Send
Componi messaggio	New
Rispondi all'autore	Reply to sender
Rispondi a tutti	Reply to all

❏ E-mail

Receiving messages

☐		**Re: Sono tornata!**			⊡

File	Modifica	Visualizza	Strumenti	Componi	?

Da: Francesca Maggi (francesca@abc.it)

Data: 28 giugno, 2004

A: cristina_benelli@abc.it

Oggetto: Re: Sono tornata!

> In Italian, when telling someone your e-mail address you say: **"francesca chiocciolina abc punto it"**.

Cara Cristina,

adesso capisco dov'eri finita per tutto questo tempo! Ti sei divertita a Rimini? Scrivimi presto e raccontami tutto.

Ciao,

Francesca

PS. Non preoccuparti per quell'indirizzo: l'ho già trovato.

Inoltra	Forward
Inserisci file	Attachment
A	To
Cc (copia carbone)	Cc
Ccn (copia carbone nascosta)	Bcc
Oggetto	Subject
Da	From
Data	Sent

❏ *Telephone*

Different types of call

Chiamata urbana/interurbana/internazionale.	Local/national/international call.
Vorrei fare una telefonata internazionale.	I want to make an international call.
Vorrei fare una telefonata a carico del destinatario	I want to make a reverse-charge call (Brit) or I want to call collect (US).

Asking for information

Vorrei il numero della ditta Decapex di Vercelli.	I'd like the number of ...
Qual è il prefisso di Livorno?	What is the code for ...
Posso telefonare in Colombia direttamente?	Can I dial direct to ...
Qual è il prefisso per telefonare in Francia?	What is the code for calling ...

Receiving information

Il numero da lei richiesto è: 0432 37 49 95. (zero quattro tre due tre sette quattro nove nove cinque)	The number you require is ...
Mi dispiace, ma non c'è nessun abbonato con questo nome.	I'm sorry, but there's no listing under that name.
Mi dispiace, il numero da lei richiesto è fuori elenco.	... the number you have asked for is ex-directory (Brit) or unlisted (US).

When your number answers

Vorrei parlare con il signor Matta, per favore.	Could I speak to ...
Mia può passare l'interno 516, per cortesia?	Could I have extension ...
Richiamerò più tardi.	I'll try again later.
Potrei lasciare un messaggio?	Can I leave a message?
Potrebbe chiedergli di chiamarmi quando rientra?	Would you ask him to call me when he gets back?

The switchboard operator speaks

Pronto, Hotel Rex, desidera?	Hello ... can I help you?
Chi parla, per cortesia?	Who's calling ...
Glielo passo subito.	I'm putting you through now.
C'è una telefonata in linea da Tokyo per la signora Marelli.	I have a call from ... for ...

C'è la signorina Martini **in linea.** ..... *is on the line.*

Non risponde nessuno. *There's no reply.*

Attenda in linea, prego or **Rimanga in linea,** *Hold the line ...*
per favore.

Vuole lasciare un messaggio? *Would you like to leave a*
messsage?

Recorded messages

Telecom Italia: **informazione gratuita. Il numero** *You have not been charged*
da lei selezionato è inesistente. *for this call. The number*
you have dialled has not
been recognised

Telecom Italia: **servizio gratuito. L'utente da lei** *You have not been charged*
chiamato ha cambiato numero. Attenda in *for this call. This number*
linea senza riagganciare poiché stiamo *has been changed. Please*
inoltrando automaticamente la sua chiamata *hold while we transfer your*
al nuovo numero 040–45 63 02. Per le *call. The new number is ...*
prossime comunicazioni la preghiamo di
utilizzare la nuova numerazione. Grazie.

Benvenuti al servizio assistenza della ditta *Welcome to ... customer*
Se.Ge.Co. *services.*

Tutte le linee sono momentaneamente occupate. *All the lines are busy right*
La preghiamo di attendere. La sua chiamata *now. Please hold the line*
sarà inoltrata prima possibile. *and we will deal with your*
call as soon as possible.

Risponde la segreteria telefonica della famiglia *You have reached ... Please*
Boni. Lasciate un messaggio dopo il segnale *leave a message after the*
acustico. Grazie. *tone.*

Answering the telephone

Pronto, sono Anna. *Hello, this is ...*

Sì, sono io. *Speaking.*

Chi parla? *Who's calling?*

When in trouble

Non riesco a prendere la linea. *I can't get through.*

L'apparecchio è fuori servizio. *The phone is out of order.*

È caduta la linea. *We've been cut off.*

Ho sbagliato numero. *I must have dialled the wrong*
number.

C'è un'interferenza sulla linea. *We've got a crossed line.*

La linea è molto disturbata. *This is a very bad line.*